Eight
American Writers

Edgar Allan Poe · STOVALL

Ralph Waldo Emerson · WHICHER

Henry David Thoreau · HARDING

Nathaniel Hawthorne · FOGLE

Herman Melville · HOWARD

Walt Whitman · MILLER

Samuel L. Clemens · BELLAMY

Henry James · FALK

Eight

American Writers

AN ANTHOLOGY OF
AMERICAN LITERATURE

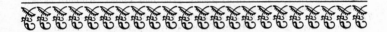

Norman Foerster & Robert P. Falk

GENERAL EDITORS

Floyd Stovall
University of Virginia

Stephen E. Whicher
Late of Cornell University

Walter Harding
State University of New York, College of Education at Geneseo

Richard H. Fogle
Tulane University

Leon Howard
University of California at Los Angeles

James E. Miller, Jr.
University of Chicago

Gladys C. Bellamy
Southwestern State Teachers College

Robert P. Falk
University of California at Los Angeles

W · W · NORTON & COMPANY · INC · *New York*

Contents

RALPH WALDO EMERSON   173

Contents · *vii*

HENRY DAVID THOREAU

HENRY JAMES   1383

HENRY JAMES

Preface

In the consensus of our time eight writers—Poe, Emerson, Thoreau, Hawthorne, Melville, Whitman, Mark Twain, and Henry James—constitute our "American Classics." In the general course in American literature, nearly every teacher in the land feels called upon to present to his students these eight writers. They are the core of our literary heritage—so varied and so interesting in their points of view, their forms, their styles that, even taken alone, they offer an impressive subject for a semester or year course.

By concentrating upon these masters—unquestioned major writers—we have been able to allot to them *double* the space available in anthologies which, ostensibly devoted to the greatest, include many lesser writers from Edward Taylor to our contemporaries. Such a compromise between the multi-author survey and the selection of accepted masters seems to lack any rationale, whereas a full presentation of a few masters, like a survey anthology, serves a clear, definite purpose. Of course it would be tempting to give some space to the contemporary field, but if there are "classics" among the writers since James it would seem to us premature to name and include them now, without perspective, without any general agreement, and without adequate selection. In this situation teachers who desire to add recent writers will wish to be left free to choose them.

How the current consensus became manifest is intriguing enough to be reviewed. At the beginning of our century, the foremost writer (judging not quite fairly by space given in literary histories) was, in Barrett Wendell's eyes, Oliver Wendell Holmes; in W. P. Trent's, James Russell Lowell. After the first World War a revolution in taste and opinion brought about a revaluation of the American past. The Boston-Cambridge group—Longfellow, Lowell, Holmes—and Whittier as well lost their high place. On the other hand Hawthorne, Emerson, and Whitman gained in reputation, while Melville rose from obscurity to enthusiastic acceptance. During the decade of the Depression a great advance in interest and admiration came to Thoreau. After the second World War, Mark Twain and Henry James were recognized more fully than ever before, and the revised list of conceded masters was well established.

In 1949 the American Literature Group of the Modern Language Association conducted a poll of twenty-seven leading scholars and critics, in response to a request from UNESCO for the twenty "best representatives of the literary art of our country." The first eight authors, precisely those included in the present volume, seemed obvious, while the rest of the list showed great uncertainty. Two years after the poll, Randall Stewart, then chairman of the Group, proposed a book of bibliographical essays on the major authors—the same eight. This very useful work was published in 1956 by the Modern Language Association with the title *Eight American Authors*, recently reissued with a supplement in a paperback Norton Library edition. In the preface Floyd Stovall reported: "After I became editor, only the names of Howells and Dickinson were presented as candidates for inclusion, and only the latter was seriously considered. No one proposed that we could omit any of the eight originally selected."

The same agreement, evident in emphasis on these authors in anthologies for broad surveys, has apparently dominated the choice of paperback editions for intensive study of a few authors. The time would seem to have come for a collection like the present one: a single inexpensive volume (cloth or paperback) avoiding the fluctuating tides of taste and generously representing the eight indispensable authors. Such a book can readily avoid the uneven quality and inconsistent editing involved in the use of mass-produced paperbacks. Furthermore, unlike one-author collections, it enables instructor and student to compare one author with another for parallels and contrasts.

The introductions are substantial essays bearing on the author's life, personality, and literary achievement, directed especially toward a critical reading of the selections included. The notes are intended to be full enough for the average student while not superfluous for the superior student. The bibliographies are both descriptive and critical, designed to facilitate finding the kind of reference desired.

This scholarly equipment, together with the choice of selections, is the work of eight contributing editors whose special competence is well known through their publications. It seemed inappropriate to impose a too rigid pattern of editing upon a group of scholars with reputations for research on the writers and periods they here represent. The panel of editors was, however, held to a sufficiently common purpose and method by an exchange of ideas among themselves and with the general editors.

N. F.
R. F.

Eight
American Writers

Edgar Allan Poe

Like many another genius, Poe presents the paradox of the artist trapped in an uncongenial environment and at war with himself. Endowed by nature with the sensibility of a poet, he was introduced as a child into a social situation which fostered this sensibility and encouraged him to hope for the means and leisure to cultivate it. This hope was soon dashed, however, and he was left at eighteen to survive or perish by such talents as he possessed, chiefly creative and analytical.

It was inevitable that these talents should find an outlet in the magazine, which was already beginning to dominate the literary scene in the 1830's, and that his developing critical powers should carry him eventually into the editor's chair. With prudence and reasonable luck he might have acquired the material comforts he needed and the popular acclaim he craved. But he was driven by his temperament into excesses that made lasting enemies, and he was beset by misfortunes for which he was in no way accountable.

Even in death the "imp of the perverse" pursued him. The Rev. R. W. Griswold, whom he had chosen to be his literary executor, betrayed him by publishing immediately after Poe's death a slanderous account of his life that has persisted to this day. A few conscientious biographers have tried with little success to supplant Griswold's falsehoods and distortions with the authentic record, but others, less conscientious and with an eye to boosting sales, have added to the original injustice by emphasizing his faults and insinuating all kinds of abnormalities, supporting their conclusions by arguments which treat his imaginative creations as if they were autobiographical documents. As a consequence, Poe is known, not for his best qualities, but for his worst.

I

The facts of Edgar Poe's life are soon told. He was born in Boston on January 19, 1809, the son of itinerant actors, both of whom were dead before he was three years old. A pretty child, he was adopted (though not legally) by John Allan, a prosperous merchant of Richmond, Virginia, and was cherished and probably spoiled by Mrs. Allan. He attended good English schools from 1815 to 1820 while the Allans were living in London, studied subsequently in the best academies of Richmond, and entered the newly established University of Virginia on February 14, 1826. Here Edgar's romantic temperament and the expensive tastes he had been allowed to develop led him to incur debts which so displeased the dour and parsimonious John Allan that he refused to send him back to the

University after his first year. Poe did well in his studies, and there is no evidence that he misbehaved except to gamble and contract debts in an effort to live like the sons of other rich men on the pittance allowed him by his foster father.

At home, he was very unhappy, and his unhappiness was sharpened by the discovery that Sarah Elmira Royster, the girl who had pledged him her love before he went to the University, was now engaged to marry another man. After a violent quarrel with Mr. Allan, Poe got money somehow, perhaps through Mrs. Allan, and left Richmond in bitterness of spirit for the city of his birth. In Boston he arranged for the printing of his first volume, *Tamerlane and Other Poems* (1827), and presently joined the army under the name of Edgar A. Perry. He remained in the army nearly two years and rose to the rank of Sergeant Major, but was discharged in April, 1829, through the intervention of Mr. Allan, so that he might apply for an appointment at West Point. While awaiting this appointment he published in Baltimore his second volume of poems, *Al Aaraaf, Tamerlane, and Minor Poems*, some of which he must have written while in the army.

Admitted to the Academy near the end of June, 1830, Poe was soon asking Mr. Allan again for money, complaining that he was sent to West Point, as he had been sent to the University of Virginia, with inadequate funds. When he was convinced that Mr. Allan would not assist him further, Poe deliberately absented himself from his duties and was court-martialed and dismissed from the Academy. He departed for New York on February 19, 1831, first having circulated a subscription list for a new volume of poetry, which was published by Elam Bliss in New York in April. Once the book was out, Poe returned to Baltimore, where he lived for the next four years in extreme poverty with his aunt Maria Clemm. John Allan died in March, 1834, leaving Poe nothing.

Poe now turned from poetry, by which he could earn nothing, to the short story, for which there was a market. During the next three or four years he wrote about a dozen short stories, one of which, "MS Found in a Bottle," won a fifty-dollar prize. John P. Kennedy, a judge in the contest, became Poe's friend and recommended him to Thomas W. White in 1835 for an editorial position on the *Southern Literary Messenger.* Mrs. Clemm and her daughter Virginia joined him in Richmond and in May, 1836, Edgar and Virginia were married, she being then not quite fourteen years old. Although he proved to be a successful editor, he resigned in January, 1837, and went to New York, where he tried free-lance writing for more than a year.

Moving with his family to Philadelphia in the summer of 1838, he entered upon the most prosperous period of his life. During his six years in Philadelphia, he published some of his greatest short stories, including "Ligeia," "The Fall of the House of Usher," and "Eleonora," and, in 1840, his first collection of short stories, in two volumes, under the title *Tales of the Grotesque and Arabesque.* He was editor of *Burton's Gentleman's Magazine* for a year (1839–40) and of *Graham's* from early in 1841 to midsummer of 1842. About this time he had great hopes of establishing a literary review of his own, but he failed then, as he was always to fail in this aim thereafter.

In April, 1844, he left Philadelphia to try his fortunes again in New York. For a while he was on the editorial staff of the *Evening Mirror*, where "The Raven" was first published on January 29, 1845. Later he bought an interest in the *Broadway Journal*, a weekly, and eventually became its sole proprietor. But it was far from the journal he had dreamed of owning, and after a few precarious months, during which he tried to boost its circulation by printing in its columns his ill-considered attacks on Longfellow, it expired. He was often ill at this period and sometimes half-distracted, suspecting enemies on all hands. His very efforts to defend himself only made more enemies and alienated some who would have been his friends. Yet he was not without success of a kind. "The Raven" was widely reprinted and quoted, and during 1845 he had published a new edition of his *Tales* and a new volume of poems entitled *The Raven and Other Poems*. It is one of the ironies of Poe's life that now, at the beginning of 1846, though famous at home and beginning to be favorably known abroad, he was penniless and desperately trying to borrow fifty dollars to purchase the sheer necessities while he struggled to produce more salable manuscripts. In the summer of 1846 he moved with his family to a cottage at Fordham, New York, where he found moments of peace in the beauty of woodland scenes. But there his beloved Virginia, who had more than once been at death's door since her first illness in 1842, rapidly declined and died of tuberculosis in January, 1847.

During the remainder of his life Poe was subject to protracted periods of illness, mental perhaps as well as physical, and more than ever bedeviled by his weakness for drink. His frantic courtships were part of a persistent effort to fill the void in his emotional life created by the death of Virginia. His published writing showed no loss of power, and some of it was more than usually lucid. *Eureka* (1848), whatever may be said about its philosophical soundness, is well written and an integral part of his intellectual system. One of his best critical essays, "The Poetic Principle," was written at this time. Mrs. Clemm, devoted though not always wise, looked after his interests as well as she could, and he loved her as if she had been his own mother. Visiting in Richmond in the summer of 1849, he signed a temperance pledge, renewed old acquaintances, and revived his youthful romance with Sarah Elmira Royster, now Mrs. Shelton and a widow. He proposed marriage and was apparently accepted. Mrs. Clemm was to live with them after their wedding, and so he left Richmond hopefully to fetch her from New York. Stopping in Baltimore on the way, however, he became intoxicated, was taken to a hospital, and died there a few days afterwards, on October 7, 1849.

II

Since Poe was a poet before he became a writer of prose fiction or a critic, the discussion of his literary work may properly begin with his early poems. In the poems of 1827 the hero is a proud and passionate youth whose worldly hopes have been thwarted, and the two dominant moods are resentment against the agents of this hero's defeat, as in "Spirits of the Dead," and the renunciation of the real world, as in "Dreams." Most of these poems were either dropped from later editions or extensively revised. "Tamerlane" is a long Byronic narrative of an ambitious youth who has left the girl he loved to conquer the world and lay it at her feet, only to return victorious and find her dead. In the next edition it was cut almost in half and intensified by the deletion of many specific details. "Stanzas," one of the poems never reprinted, contains the germ of his poetic theory in a Wordsworthian passage describing a moment of illumination in which familiar objects are endowed with unsuspected beauty and meaning. This transformation of the commonplace is a symbol, the poem affirms,

> Of what in other worlds shall be—and giv'n
> In beauty by our God, to those alone
> Who otherwise would fall from life and Heav'n,
> Drawn by their heart's passion * * *

Only "The Lake: To ———" was retained, with minor changes, in all later editions. Its association of love and death with beauty that may be terrible or fair sets the tone of all Poe's later poems and of some of his best tales.

The new poems of his second edition indicate that after two years in the army Poe had learned to accept his fate calmly and to strike a positive note now and then above the dominant tone of renunciation. This change is recorded in the poem "Preface," later entitled "Romance," in which he turns from imitative romanticism, pictured as a "painted paroquet," to embrace genuine romanticism, pictured as a singing bird among green leaves, unseen except as it is mirrored in the shadowy waters below. The poem suggests that the poet is concerned with truth, but only as it is perceived in the image of beauty. His poetry will be sincere, from the heart, but without the "heart's passion." So the idea first presented in "Stanzas" is here somewhat further developed.

This idea is still further elaborated and clarified in "Al Aaraaf," the major poem of the 1829 edition. A short poem without title, later called "Sonnet—To Science," prefaces "Al Aaraaf" and asserts that science has altered the unity of man's world by separating the "real" from the "ideal" so that only the former is accepted by the finite intellect as true, thus driving all forms of ideal beauty away from earth to "some happier star." This happier star, named Al Aaraaf apparently because, like the Mohammedan *al áraf* ("the wall"), it was placed between the heaven of pure truth and the hell of evil passions, is the dwelling place of beauty; its native spirit, Nesace, is the personification of beauty, and its resident spirits may include none except lovers of the beautiful. Nesace receives God's truth as a ray of pure light that is refracted in passing through the diamond pane in the dome of her palace so that it falls upon her in the colors of the spectrum. Nesace then conveys God's messages in forms of beauty to her attendant spirits, who pass them on in the same way to all God's creatures. Thus, for the artist, beauty is identical with truth in a manner analogous to the way in which the colored light of the spectrum is identical with the white light of the unrefracted ray. The poet's truth imaged in forms of beauty is nearer God's truth than the scientist's "dull realities."

The 1831 edition contained "Al Aaraaf" with some revisions, later removed, and its prefatory sonnet; "Tamerlane" with parts of two earlier poems embedded in it, also removed later; "Romance" and "Fairy-Land" reprinted from the 1829 edition with lengthy additions later deleted; and six new poems besides a prose "Letter to Mr. ———— ————," later entitled "Letter to B———," which was intended as a critical introduction. Of the new poems, four were among the best he ever wrote and were not drastically revised afterwards: these were "To Helen," "Israfel," "The Doomed City" (later "The City in the Sea"), and "Irene" (later "The Sleeper"). The other two new poems were "A Pæan" and "The Valley Nis." The former was completely rewritten before 1845 as "Lenore" and the latter cut from 46 to 27 lines, with many revisions in the lines retained.

The title of "Romance" is changed in this edition from "Preface" to "Introduction" and the poem expanded from 21 to 66 lines. The additions explain in some detail how he turned from passion first to melancholy and then to dreams. The additions to "Fairy-Land" altered its tone and transformed it into something like a dramatic love poem. In both cases he had allowed himself to slip back into a manner resembling the 1827 version of "Tamerlane." In subsequent publications of these two poems Poe restored the text of 1829.

The quality of Poe's genius is demonstrated for the first time unmistakably in "To Helen," "Israfel," "The Doomed City," and "Irene." "To Helen" is both a statement and an exemplification of Poe's theory of beauty as the sole concern of the poet. As a boat carries the wanderer home from stormy seas, the beauty of Helen has brought the poet to the realization that the proper subject of poetry is not passion but beauty. The classical world of glory and grandeur is, like Al Aaraaf, the home of the lover of beauty, the poet. In the third stanza, Helen is identified with Psyche, the soul, to suggest that, for the poet, beauty is spiritual, not sensual. The realm of beauty is the home of the soul of the artist and hence for him holy land. In the 1831 edition Helen holds a folded scroll in her hand, the symbol of knowledge, but in later revised versions she holds an agate lamp. The light of the lamp is evidently the symbol of truth (as distinguished from knowledge), and the agate base with its varied colors must be the symbol of beauty. Thus the agate lamp becomes the symbol of truth revealed through beauty. The poem may be read, then, as an imaginative record of Poe's discovery of the poet's true function.

In "Israfel" Poe describes the poet as he might be if he were free of earth's limitations. The angel Israfel can properly make truth and passion his themes because he dwells in Heaven, where deep thoughts are a duty and where love is spiritual. The poet of earth, subject to the imperfections of finite existence, must shun the passions and approach truth only through the veil of beautiful forms.

Although Poe had not yet formulated his theory that the proper tone of poetry is melancholy and that the most poetical topic is the death of a beautiful woman, all four of the remaining new poems in this volume are melancholy in tone and two of them concern the death of a beautiful woman. Of these, "Irene" and "The Doomed City" require particular notice. In "Irene" (or "The Sleeper") the lady is obviously dead, yet the poet describes her as though she were partially conscious and might be frightened by the moving shadows made by the wind-blown canopy in the moonlight, portending a spiritual restlessness yet to come. The symbols intensify the mood of strangeness and fear—the opiate vapor from

the moon, the rosemary that nods upon the grave foreboding oblivion,
the lake that looks like Lethe, the strangely long hair. A key to the literal
meaning of the poem is to be found in the following lines in the 1831
text which Poe characteristically omitted from later texts as perhaps too
specific:

> The lady sleeps: the *dead* all sleep—
> At least as long as Love doth weep:
> Entranc'd, the spirit loves to lie
> As long as—tears on Memory's eye:
> But when a week or two go by,
> And the light laughter chokes the sigh,
> Indignant from the tomb doth take
> Its way to some remember'd lake,
> Where oft—in life—with friends—it went
> To bathe in the pure element,
> And there, from the untrodden grass,
> Wreathing for its transparent brow
> Those flowers that say (ah hear them now!)
> "Ai! ai! alas!—alas!"
> Pores for a moment, ere it go,
> On the clear waters there that flow,
> Then sinks within (weigh'd down by wo)
> Th' uncertain, shadowy heaven below.

These omitted lines tell us what the poet means by the symbolic pictures
of the poem, but they do not change its meaning or its mood, which
is one of melancholy mingled with terror at the waste of beauty through
death and the annihilation of the spirit through the callous forgetfulness
of surviving friends.

A similar mood is evoked by the description of "The Doomed City"
(or "The City in the Sea"). It is a mistake to seek the archetype of Poe's
city among the sunken cities of antiquity or to associate it, as some have
done, with the final dwelling place of the wicked dead. It is not a real
place at all but a state of mind, the melancholy mood of all forgotten
spirits who, like Irene, pore mournfully on the still surface of memory
before they sink forever into the waters of oblivion. Death reigns and
no stars look down. The structures there, though suggestive of some
ancient ruined city, are the monuments of the dead in all the cemeteries
of the world imagined as existing at one time and in one place. The hell
that rises to meet the sinking city is not the place to which Christian
theology condemns the unredeemed, but the universal oblivion into which,
sooner or later, every living thing must sink.

Poe did not lose interest in poetry after 1831, as his continued revision
of his early verses bears eloquent testimony, but thereafter the necessity
of earning his living drove him to the writing of prose almost exclusively.
Though already at the age of 22 he had published almost as many lines
of poetry as he was to produce throughout the remaining eighteen years
of his life, he suffered no irrecoverable loss of poetic power; he came,
however, to depend too much on artfulness instead of art and on novel
effects instead of the values inherent in his themes. All of the short poems
written between 1831 and 1844 preserve the earlier manner except "The
Haunted Palace" and "The Conqueror Worm." These two are allegories.

The former, describing the deranged mind of a poet, is later appropriately introduced into "The Fall of the House of Usher" as one of Roderick's poems; the latter, melodramatically and cynically representing the futility of human existence, is eventually included, less appropriately, in "Ligeia" as one of the heroine's compositions. "Dream-Land" (1844), the best of Poe's poems of the middle period, is closer to his characteristic manner. It has sometimes been interpreted as if the eidolon Night were symbolic of death and as if the region described as out of space and time were the afterworld to which wicked spirits are condemned; in fact, however, Night is merely night and the region described is out of space and time because it is the land of dreams. The landscape, surely unlike anything in waking experience, is the objective correlative by which the poet hopes to evoke in the reader a mood similar to his own. In this it resembles some early poems, like "The Lake: To ———" and "The City in the Sea." Its moderate use of repetition and parallelism, first cautiously employed in "Bridal Ballad" (1837), is in Poe's late style, in which his language grows more artificial, his rhythm more spasmodic, and his mood closer to hysteria. Critics have been disposed to attribute this change to mental deterioration, but it is probably the result of Poe's increasing preoccupation with the details of his poetic theory and his journalist's appeal to the popular taste for the bizarre.

"The Raven" has been Poe's most popular poem and will doubtless continue to be, though Poe thought it inferior to "The Sleeper." "The Raven" cannot be dismissed, however, as a mere tour de force. Though not written as deliberately as Poe claims in "The Philosophy of Composition," it is nevertheless best understood in the light of what he says there. The poem describes the experience of a bereaved lover who rejects all rational comfort in order to suffer the utmost of hopeless grief. Its tone ranges from serious to comic, from stately to grotesque, with the varying moods of the lover. The movement halts and recovers but tends inevitably to the climax of the lover's last fatal question. The most original element of the poem, as Poe pointed out, is the intricate and varied stanza, where rhyme and metrical pattern and shifting caesura are combined with skillfully manipulated parallelism and refrain to produce subtle effects easily overlooked by the casual reader. The stanza structure of "Ulalume" is equally complex, and the novelties of language, rhyme, and parallel structure are more striking. Only two rhymes are employed in each stanza, and each line has three stresses, though the number of syllables in the line varies from seven to eleven. The rhythmic and tonal effects are mournful and monotonous like those of a funeral march. The symbolism is less obvious than in "The Raven," but the central theme is the same: the conflict in a bereaved lover between the desire for comfort and the unconscious but compulsive desire to suffer.

Only two other late poems require special comment. "For Annie" is composed in lines of two stresses arranged in stanzas of six to ten lines, the number depending on the extent to which parallelism is used. Only one rhyme occurs in each stanza; it is at the end of even-numbered lines, and except for its first occurrence it is an identical rhyme. The effect is strange but in keeping with the theme of the poem. Here a man speaks from the grave to say that he is happy at last to have escaped from the fever of life, and now rests composedly in dreams of the beauty and truth of his Annie, whose caresses express love without passion. The theme of spiritual versus sensual love associates this poem with "Al Aaraaf" and with "To Helen" and "Israfel" of the 1831 volume. "The Bells" is an exercise in onomatopoeia, the sounds of the four types of bells evoking moods of merriment, happiness, alarm, and melancholy. Each stanza is longer, more complex, and more intense than the preceding one; the effect is climactic and even tragic. The poem is also a quaternion: the four bells symbolize the four stages in man's life: childhood, marriage, maturity, and old age culminating in death.

Poe was too much the individualist to be categorized, but one may say in general that he began writing poetry in the manner of Byron and Thomas Moore and developed quickly through the influence of Coleridge, Shelley, and Keats a richly romantic style of his own. In the 1840's he adopted some of the studied arts of the lesser Victorians, but not their moralism. His greatest strength was in the mastery of language which enabled him to evoke in an imaginative reader the sense of the beautiful which he himself felt; his greatest weakness the tendency in his later poems to mistake mere novelty for originality. His range was narrow—he was not moved to poetic expression by the human comedy and he completed no work of magnitude—but within his proper range and judged solely as an artist he was superb.

III

Poe's poems may have been written solely to please himself, but his tales were carefully composed to please the popular taste. In a letter to the proprietor of the *Southern Literary Messenger* (April 30, 1835), he described the qualities that make for success in magazine fiction as "the ludicrous heightened into the grotesque: the fearful coloured into the horrible: the witty exaggerated into the burlesque: the singular wrought out into the strange and mystical." One or more of these qualities can be seen in each of Poe's early stories and in many of his later ones. He also very soon discovered that he could make literary capital out of current events and interests such as the cholera epidemic of 1832, Antarctic expeditions, balloon flights, mesmerism, and German metaphysical speculation. The tale as he conceived it, may, unlike the poem, be used to produce various effects, such as humor, terror, horror, and even the truth of the intellect. He invented the ratiocinative technique, which utilizes analysis and logical reasoning, to produce effects of truth—a method widely used since his time in the detective story. His attempts at humor, from the witty burlesque to the ludicrous grotesque, were mostly failures, but he apparently never realized that his sense of humor was seriously defective. He is at his best in that kind of story, described in his review of Hawthorne's *Twice-Told Tales*, in which the artist deliberately chooses the effect he wishes to produce and then sets to work constructing a tale which will produce it, maintaining strict unity of tone and admitting no single word which does not contribute to the preconceived effect.

With few exceptions, the tales are related in the first person, and in most of them the narrator is the principal character. Typically he is rich, learned, the scion of an aristocratic family; he is frequently addicted to alcohol, opiates, and gambling, and sometimes he is or has been insane. In the tales of ratiocination and a few others the narrator is not the main character but participates in the action. These tales, with their emphasis on rational thought, and others which undertake to make incredible events credible are narrated in a simple and direct style appropriate to matters of fact. Stories of atmosphere, however, involving the strange and the marvelous, are sometimes related in the heightened and rhythmic language suited to poetry. Poe does not often use dialogue skillfully and rarely attempts it in his serious stories. His characters, always subordinated to plot or theme, are at best idealizations and at worst caricatures of real people. Yet as works of art these stories may be said to have a life of their own in the world of pure form and to be useful as a discipline of the mind. His nearest approach to the novel, *The Narrative of A. Gordon Pym* (1838), which some recent critics, following the French, have admired as unconscious autobiography, has some of the elements of an excellent adventure story, but the interest is not sustained and the work as a whole lacks the controlled artistry of the tales. Whether Poe's fiction unconsciously reflects his life is debatable. It is a fact that he did his best writing when he was well and enjoying some degree of worldly success. He produced perhaps a dozen tales that are acknowledged masterpieces, all but one of which were written during his residence in Philadelphia from 1838 to 1844. The first of these was "Ligeia" (1838), and the last was "The Cask of Amontillado" (1946), written while he lived in New York.

Poe once said that "Ligeia" was the best of his tales because it was the work of highest imagination. Since it is a work of high imagination, the perceptive reader is not content to accept it for what on the surface it appears to be—a supernatural tale in which the surviving spirit of the dead Ligeia attempts by an act of the will to possess the body of Rowena. If this were the only meaning of the story it would be entitled to small consideration as a work of art. But it is also one of the best of Poe's many studies of abnormal states of mind, a genre in which he was a pioneer and for which he has not been given the credit he deserves. Rightly understood, "Ligeia" is the story of the narrator's insane attempt to recall the spirit of the dead Ligeia by the power of his own will and to reincarnate it in the body of Rowena, whom, it appears, he destroys for this purpose. The image of Ligeia that rises before him from the deathbed of Rowena is a hallucination, of course. Ligeia, one may infer, never existed except in the mind of the narrator, where she was originally conceived as truth and beauty personified. Later this idea becomes an obsession, and in the narrator's disordered imagination Ligeia is a real woman who has died and for love of him has possessed the body of Rowena to live again. Poe thus provides two levels of meaning, the supernatural for casual readers and the psychological for readers of more discernment.

Two other masterful studies of abnormal states of mind were written within a year after "Ligeia." They were "The Fall of the House of Usher," which is also a metaphysical speculation on the identity of matter and spirit, and "William Wilson," a study of conscience. In the former, Roderick Usher has come to believe that his family and the ancient mansion they occupy have through long association acquired a common identity. From remote times the Ushers had descended in a direct line from father to son until the present generation, which consists of a brother and a sister who are twins. The spiritual element of the family identity seems to have been concentrated in Roderick and the material element in Madeline. Consequently he develops a preternatural acuteness of the senses which threatens to destroy his reason, whereas she is apathetic and physically diseased. Roderick realizes that if his theory proves true, he and his sister must die together and their house fall with them. Hence his growing fear until she apparently dies, and hence his refusal to give her permanent burial; he hears her movements in the coffin, and his terror mounts until it destroys him in the end.

"William Wilson" describes the struggle of the will to overcome the conscience, here represented as a second William Wilson. Some critics think that the second William Wilson really exists throughout the story, whereas others think he has no real existence at all. The fact is that the second William Wilson really exists as a child in the school which he attended with the first William Wilson, the narrator, but after the narrator leaves the academy to go to Eton he never again sees the second William Wilson except as an apparition of his disordered mind. During his last months at school, the narrator, by some strange fatality or perversity, becomes obsessed with the idea that his namesake is assuming the role of guardian and spokesman of his conscience, and from time to time thereafter when he does something he knows is wrong he sees the apparition of the other Wilson. In the end, believing he has destroyed his tormentor, he turns to a life of unrestrained crime. Now, as he is about to die, his life in retrospect seems a dream.

Two other stories involving madness in some degree must be considered here. One of these, "Eleanora," a richly colored prose poem published in 1842, is an allegory representing the evolution of the artist's mind in three phases. The story tells how the youthful artist's innate sense of unity with truth and beauty is lost through the passions of maturity but eventually recovered by the power of imagination. The theme is not unlike that of Wordsworth's "Ode: Intimations of Immortality," but it almost certainly had its origin in Poe's own experience. The other story involving madness is "The Cask of Amontillado," a story of revenge and ironic humor, in which there is no evidence of the narrator's insanity except the enormity of his crime.

These stories are superior because they achieve their effects by processes which, though they are the acts of madmen, are psychologically consistent and believable. Other stories of madness, both earlier and later ones, are defective in one way or another. "Berenice" is not subtle, "Morella" is not believable, "The Tell-Tale Heart" offers no rational motive for the narrator's crime, and "The Imp of the Perverse" is merely an anecdote to illustrate the narrator's theory of human perversity. "The Black Cat" is more substantial because it tells how a normally kind man deteriorates to meanness and crime through intemperate drinking, and then perversely exposes his guilt through overconfidence.

In all the stories discussed thus far the action develops out of character or situation and in most of them—"Eleanora" being a notable exception—this action is calculated to produce the effect of horror or terror. There is a large group of stories, however, in which the action does not so develop, but is designed to illustrate some fact or theory of science or pseudoscience. "A Descent into the Maelström" is made believable by an explanation of the movements of cylindrical bodies in a vortex, "The Gold-Bug" offers the author an opportunity to explain a method of cryptography, "The

Facts in the Case of M. Valdemar" demonstrates the power of mesmer- ism, and "Mesmeric Revelation" is essentially a metaphysical essay. Of the three stories in which Dupin is the hero, "The Murders in the Rue Morgue" and "The Mystery of Marie Rogêt" emphasize the horror of the action above the theory by which the mysteries are solved, but "The Purloined Letter," the best of them, places the emphasis where it belongs, on the hero's exercise of the related faculties of analysis and imagination. Even some of the humorous tales carry the weight of ideas, such as "Premature Burial" and "Some Words with a Mummy." Only two of Poe's great stories are concerned with an effect virtually independent of an idea. They are "The Masque of the Red Death," a story of atmosphere, and "The Pit and the Pendulum," a story of action and suspense. Another on a somewhat lower level, "Hop Frog," is a grimly humorous story of revenge.

Poe's tales are of uneven quality, ranging from the incredibly weak to the superlatively fine. His strength lies in his original conceptions, his mastery of the principle of unity of tone and effect, his narrative skill, and his pioneer work in the two fields of the psychological story and the story of ratio- cination. His weakness derives from occasional poor taste and defective humor, the haste of journalistic composition, and a lack of sympathetic interest in the ordinary virtues and frailties of human nature. The aesthetic qualities of the tales are the same as those of the poems. They express not so much the truth of life as the truth of art.

IV

Poe was known to his contemporaries as an important critic long before he had established himself as a successful poet or writer of fiction. His critical writing falls into two distinct but closely related categories, the the- oretical and the practical. The selections chosen for this volume are more theoretical than practical, but they exemplify the interdependence of the two categories. In "The Philosophy of Composition" he purports to explain how the composition of "The Raven" developed from his theory. Poe's ideas are well summarized in these five essays, but to comprehend them fully one must also know "Eureka," "Marginalia," "The Rationale of Verse," and perhaps a dozen of his most important reviews, including the reviews of the poems of Joseph Drake and Fitz-Greene Halleck (1836), Longfellow's *Ballads and Other Poems* (1842), R. H. Horne's *Orion* (1844), and the American drama (1845).

The basic principles of Poe's theory of poetry may be briefly stated as follows: beauty is the sole province of the poem, especially beauty that has the quality of strangeness; melancholy is its proper tone, and music is an essential element in it; since pleasure is its immediate object, it is not di- rectly concerned with truth or the passions; and since it must have unity of effect or interest, it must be brief. All of these principles had been il- lustrated in his poems by 1831, though in the "Letter to B——," the prose introduction to the edition of that year, he mentions only two: that the immediate object of poetry is pleasure, not truth, and that music is essen- tial to it. As has been seen, Poe had committed himself as early as "Al Aaraaf" to the theory that beauty is the sole province of the poem, which therefore must avoid the passions, and that melancholy is its proper tone. The theory defining the proper length of the poem he had not then con- ceived, but he himself attempted no long poems after 1829. In a review of

Mrs. Sigourney's poems in January, 1836, he first mentions "unity or totality of interest" (crediting "Schlegel," presumably A. W.) as a requirement of the short poem, and asserts that a long poem can give a reader pleasure only in its separate parts. These ideas are repeated and developed in numerous reviews and essays during the following years.

Poe attempted for the first time to formulate his general theory of poetry in the *Messenger* for April, 1836, in a review of the poems of Drake and Halleck. Using terms borrowed from phrenology, he defined the sentiment of poetry as the faculty of ideality, which he identified with imagination and related to veneration, the sentiment of religion, and added that it is innate in all men, though more intensely felt by poets than by others. The poem itself is the means by which the poetic sentiment may be excited in the reader; and though the poem originates in the poetic sentiment, it requires for its completion the faculty of causality, or metaphysical acumen, and the faculty of comparison, or fancy. In this review he accepted Coleridge's dictum that the imagination creates whereas the fancy merely combines, but in a review of Moore's *Alciphron* in *Burton's* four years later he tried, not very successfully, to prove that his own theory was different. In a review of Longfellow's *Ballads and Other Poems* in *Graham's* in 1842 he first referred to the irreconcilable oils and waters of poetry and truth, distinguished taste from the pure intellect and the moral sense as that part of the mind which informs us of beauty, and formulated his famous definition of poetry as the "rhythmical creation of beauty." His theory of poetry was then virtually complete and was not materially altered in later publications.

The basic principles of Poe's theory of the tale or short story are very similar to the basic principles, above outlined, of his theory of the poem. The tale, like the poem, must have unity or totality of effect or interest, but since it involves narrative it puts special emphasis on plot and it also makes a broader allowance of effects, which may include the truths of the intellect and the passions of the heart. The best and fullest statement of these principles, mentioned earlier in this essay, was made in the review of Hawthorne's *Twice-Told Tales* in the issue of *Graham's Magazine* for May, 1842, and repeated in the review of Hawthorne's work in November, 1847.

A brief comment is appropriate at this point on Poe's speculative thought, since it is pertinent to his aesthetic principles. His interest in science and in the truths that lie beyond the limits of rational knowledge developed early and was manifested even in "Al Aaraaf," but more definitely in his tales from 1839 on. In 1848 he brought these ideas together in *Eureka*, which he subtitled *A Prose Poem* but which is a carefully reasoned essay on cosmology. He argues that God created the material universe out of His own spirit in a condition of absolute unity, that is, without particles. Then working from within this aboriginal particle, through His own volition He created the particled and expanded world and continued inseparable from it. Hence Poe's general proposition is: "In the Original Unity of the First Thing lies the Secondary Cause of All Things, with the Germ of their Inevitable Annihilation." The annihilation is to begin when the volition of God is withdrawn at the moment of maximum expansion, thence by contraction to restore eventually the original particle. Poe specifically compares God's creation to a plotted work of fiction, saying the universe is a plot of God. Its end is predetermined in its beginning, and it is so constructed that no part of it can be displaced without ruin to the whole. In the artist's creative process, the intuition or poetic sentiment is the primary cause, from which is derived the secondary cause, the artist's constructive skill. Hence, as Coleridge had declared, the creation of a work of art is a repetition in the finite of God's original creation.

Poe's contemporaries were not impressed by his aesthetics or his metaphysics, but they were bound to take account of his practical criticism. From the beginning of his editorial responsibility on the *Southern Literary Messenger* his acute and sometimes caustic reviews of books attracted nation-wide attention. Sometimes, as in his review of Theodore S. Fay's *Norman Leslie*, in December, 1835, he was savage and perhaps unfair. When accused of emphasizing faults and leaving virtues unnoticed he justified himself on the ground that excellence is self-evident and that it is the critic's responsibility to protect readers against mediocrity posing as excellence. His principles of practical criticism are summarized in "Exordium," a statement in *Graham's* for January, 1842. He deplored the American habit of deferring to British critics in matters of literary judgment, but he ridiculed those who tended to praise everything American merely because it was American. He regretted to see American reviewers aping the reviewers of the British quarterlies by writing general essays instead of careful analyses of the books reviewed. He would limit criticism to the book itself as a work of art. His judgments of individual writers of his own time were usually sound, though he sometimes overpraised the works of literary ladies and was too severe with writers who had offended him. He attacked some New England transcendentalists, but he respected transcendentalism itself, and he eventually developed his own type of transcendentalism, which was closely akin to Emerson's. He rated Bulwer and R. H. Horne too high, but he was right in his estimate of William Cullen Bryant, Hawthorne, Shelley, and Coleridge. He was a little extravagant in calling Tennyson "the noblest poet that ever lived," but it must be remembered that in this opinion he was referring to Tennyson's poetic art. He admired Longfellow in spite of his frenzied attempts to prove him a plagiarist. His greatest weakness as a critic was his habit of judging all writers, even those of established fame, by the theories which he had developed from his own creative experience.

v

After Poe's death many friends rushed to his defense against Griswold's calumnies, including George Graham, his former publisher, N. P. Willis, a colleague for a while in the editorial offices of the *Mirror*, and Mrs. Helen Whitman, who loved him and for a time was engaged to marry him. A few others, though not personal friends, did justice to his literary achievement. But ill opinion proved more persuasive than good, and Poe's enemies were not silenced. There have been numerous biographies of Poe, some of them by conscientious writers such as J. H. Ingram and George E. Woodberry in the late 19th century and Hervey Allen in the 20th, but until the publication of A. H. Quinn's biography in 1941, no account of Poe's life has been both full and trustworthy. Critical opinion has been varied. Early in this century W. C. Brownell declared that Poe's imaginative works were without substance and his critical theories without force, yet he included him among his six American prose masters and devoted a long essay to his work. Since then much scholarship has been spent in source hunting, but most of the serious critical writing on Poe has been unfavorable.

In France Poe was extravagantly admired by the Symbolist poets Charles Baudelaire, Stéphane Mallarmé, Paul Valéry, and their friends. Baudelaire found in him a kindred spirit, translated his prose, and set out to make him a great writer in France. Mallarmé, a little later, translated his poems and called him master. At the end of the century Valéry praised Poe as a critic and as an impeccable writer. Léon Lemmonnier, perhaps the best historian of Poe's influence in France, said that "Poe has haunted all the poets who followed Baudelaire, even those who resembled him in nothing." But he also said that Baudelaire created a hybrid person, half Poe and half Baudelaire, whom he induced the French to accept as the real Poe.

In our time some American critics of note have rediscovered Poe through the French writers whose work they admire. They appear to be somewhat puzzled, for though they cannot perceive in Poe the greatness the French have proclaimed they are not comfortable in denying it. T. S. Eliot, who rates Poe as a gifted adolescent, supposes the French admired his work only because they did not understand the English language well enough to detect his defects of style. Allen Tate assumes that Poe is worth understanding and professes to feel in him a kindred spirit, yet he concludes that Poe's sensibility was impoverished and that his perceptual powers remained undeveloped. An American reader moving toward an understanding of Poe should be wary in making the detour by way of France. The French praised in Poe the qualities which they sought to justify in themselves, and this bias sometimes distorted their judgment. They failed to see much that was characteristically American in Poe's writing because they conceived of him as a displaced European whose genius was stifled in an unfriendly environment. Besides, they knew only a portion of his work. We shall understand Poe best by a direct and earnest analysis of his total work.

Of this total work a considerable portion, no doubt, is journalistic chaff; another portion can be appreciated only by those who will take the trouble to become acquainted with the contemporary events and taste which called it forth; a third portion, the only one which will seriously affect Poe's permanent reputation, consists of hardly more than a dozen poems and an equal number of tales and works of literary criticism. These are masterpieces whether measured by strictly American or by universal standards. Like every other artist, Poe is entitled to be judged by positive, not negative, evidence, and the weakness of the man ought not to be charged against the strength of the artist. So judged he must be accepted as one of the most finished artists of his time in the three fields of poetry, the short story, and literary criticism. Though any final estimate of his importance must take into account his total achievement in all these fields, his greatest single achievement was the creation of a few specimens of strange and unforgettable poetry.

Spirits of the Dead[1]

I

Thy soul shall itself alone
'Mid dark thoughts of the gray tombstone—
Not one, of all the crowd, to pry
Into thine hour of secrecy.

II

Be silent in that solitude,
　　Which is not loneliness—for then　　　　　5
The spirits of the dead who stood
　　In life before thee are again
In death around thee—and their will
Shall overshadow thee: be still.　　　　　　10

III

The night, tho' clear, shall frown—
And the stars shall look not down,
From their high thrones in the heaven,
With light like Hope to mortals given—
But their red orbs, without beam,
To thy weariness shall seem　　　　　　　　15
As a burning and a fever
Which would cling to thee for ever.

IV

Now are thoughts thou shalt not banish—
Now are visions ne'er to vanish—
From thy spirit shall they pass　　　　　　20
No more—like dew-drop from the grass.

V

The breeze—the breath of God—is still—
And the mist upon the hill,
Shadowy—shadowy—yet unbroken,
Is a symbol and a token—　　　　　　　　　25
How it hangs upon the trees,
A mystery of mysteries!

1827, 1839

1. The text is that of *Burton's Gentle-man's Magazine* for July, 1839. It is difficult to see why Poe omitted this poem from his final (1845) collection, *The Raven and Other Poems,* since it is surely one of the best in the 1827 edition. The poem seems to foretell a dark hour in which the person ad-dressed shall be dominated by mem-ories of those who, while they lived, were subject to his will. Some critics have conjectured that Poe was think-ing of John Allan or Sarah Elmira Royster, but there is no evidence that he had any particular person in mind.

The Lake: To ———[2]

In spring of youth it was my lot
To haunt of the wide world a spot
The which I could not love the less—
So lovely was the loneliness
Of a wild lake, with black rock bound,   5
And the tall pines that towered around.

But when the Night had thrown her pall
Upon that spot, as upon all,
And the mystic wind went by
Murmuring in melody—   10
Then—ah then I would awake
To the terror of the lone lake.

Yet the terror was not fright,
But a tremulous delight—
A feeling not the jewelled mine   15
Could teach or bribe me to define—
Nor Love—although the Love were thine.

Death was in that poisonous wave,
And in its gulf a fitting grave
For him who thence could solace bring   20
To his lone imagining—
Whose solitary soul could make
An Eden of that dim lake.

1827, 1845

Song from Al Aaraaf[3]

" 'Neath blue-bell or streamer—
   Or tufted wild spray
That keeps, from the dreamer,
   The moonbeam away—
Bright beings! that ponder,[4]   5
   With half closing eyes,
On the stars which your wonder
   Hath drawn from the skies,
Till they glance thro' the shade, and
   Come down to your brow   10

2. The text is that of 1845. Poe's early mastery of the technique of versification is demonstrated in this poem, where much of the tonal effect is produced by the skillful manipulation of stresses, vowels, and liquid consonants.
3. Nesace's song, in Part II; the text is that of 1845. Nesace, the personification of beauty, is a native spirit and queen of Al Aaraaf. Ligeia, also a native spirit, is her lieutenant and the personification of harmony.
4. The "bright beings" are the spirits of former inhabitants of earth and other worlds that have been transported to Al Aaraaf at death because of their love of beauty. See the discussion in the introduction to Poe.

Like—eyes of the maiden[5]
   Who calls on you now—
Arise! from your dreaming
   In violet bowers,
To duty beseeming   15
   These star-litten hours—
And shake from your tresses
   Encumber'd with dew
The breath of those kisses
   That cumber them too—   20
(O! how, without you, Love![6]
   Could angels be blest?)
Those kisses of true love
   That lull'd ye to rest!
Up!—shake from your wing   25
   Each hindering thing:
The dew of the night—
   It would weigh down your flight;
And true love caresses—
   O! leave them apart!   30
They are light on the tresses,
   But lead on the heart.

Ligeia! Ligeia!
   My beautiful one!
Whose harshest idea
   Will to melody run,   35
O! is it thy will
   On the breezes to toss?
Or, capriciously still,
   Like the lone Albatross,
Incumbent on night   40
   (As she on the air)
To keep watch with delight
   On the harmony there?

"Ligeia! wherever   45
   Thy image may be,
No magic shall sever
   Thy music from thee.
Thou hast bound many eyes
   In a dreamy sleep—   50
But the strains still arise
   Which *thy* vigilance keep—
The sound of the rain
   Which leaps down to the flower,
And dances again   55
   In the rhythm of the shower—
The murmur that springs

5. Nesace.
6. Spiritual love is proper among spirits of Al Aaraaf; passionate love is forbidden.

From the growing of grass
  Are the music of things—
    But are modell'd, alas!⁷—   60
Away, then my dearest,
  O! hie thee away
To springs that lie clearest
  Beneath the moon-ray—
To lone lake that smiles,   65
  In its dream of deep rest,
At the many star-isles
  That enjewel its breast—
Where wild flowers, creeping,
  Have mingled their shade,   70
On its margin is sleeping
  Full many a maid—
Some have left the cool glade, and
  Have slept with the bee—
Arouse them my maiden,   75
  On moorland and lea—
Go! breathe on their slumber,
  All softly in ear,
The musical number
  They slumber'd to hear—   80
For what can awaken
  An angel so soon
Whose sleep hath been taken
  Beneath the cold moon,
As the spell which no slumber   85
  Of witchery may test,
The rhythmical number
  Which lull'd him to rest?"

1829, 1845

Sonnet—To Science⁸

Science! true daughter of Old Time thou art!
  Who alterest all things with thy peering eyes.
Why preyest thou thus upon the poet's heart,
  Vulture, whose wings are dull realities?
How should he love thee? or how deem thee wise?   5
  Who wouldst not leave him in his wandering
To seek for treasure in the jewelled skies,
  Albeit he soared with an undaunted wing?
Hast thou not dragged Diana⁹ from her car?

7. The sense of lines 45–60 is that the music of "things"—of earthly sounds, for example—is the "image" of the music of the spirit world—of Al Aaraaf, in this case. The general idea is Platonic. Cf. "Israfel."
8. The text is that of 1845. In the editions of 1829 and 1831 this poem appeared without title as a prelude to "Al Aaraaf."
9. In classical mythology, goddess of the moon. Science is the daughter of Time because it also changes all things; in this case it is accused of destroying

And driven the Hamadryad from the wood   10
To seek a shelter in some happier star?
    Hast thou not torn the Naiad from her flood,
The Elfin from the green grass, and from me
The summer dream beneath the tamarind tree?

1829, 1845

Romance[1]

Romance, who loves to nod and sing,
With drowsy head and folded wing,
Among the green leaves as they shake
Far down within some shadowy lake,
To me a painted paroquet   5
Hath been—a most familiar bird—
Taught me my alphabet to say—
To lisp my very earliest word
While in the wild wood I did lie,
A child—with a most knowing eye.   10

Of late, eternal Condor[2] years
So shake the very Heaven on high
With tumult as they thunder by,
I have no time for idle cares
Through gazing on the unquiet sky.   15
And when an hour with calmer wings
Its down upon my spirit flings—
That little time with lyre and rhyme
To while away—forbidden things!
My heart would feel to be a crime   20
Unless it trembled with the strings.

1829, 1845

To Helen[3]

Helen, thy beauty is to me
  Like those Nicéan barks[4] of yore,

the poetry of nature by revealing its dull realities. The hamadryad (line 10) is a tree nymph, the naiad (line 12) a water nymph.

1. The text is that of the 1845 edition. Except for two or three verbal changes, this is the version first printed as "Preface" in the 1829 edition. It was expanded to 66 lines, retitled "Introduction," and given first place in the 1831 edition. The 45 new lines were added, apparently, to apologize for the original publication of his early poems of passion and to explain their omission in this edition. These added lines were omitted from subsequent texts of the poem.

2. A very large vulture, native to South America. Cf. "The Conqueror Worm" (the poem in "Ligeia"), line 15. The word "vulture" appears in a similar context in "Sonnet—To Science," line 4.
3. The text is that of 1845. In so far as it has a personal reference, the poem is a tribute to Mrs. Jane Stith Stanard of Richmond, whose beauty and whose tragic death in 1824 touched Poe deeply. In the context of the poem the name "Helen" refers to the Helen of Greek legend, the idealization of beauty in woman.
4. A summary of interpretations of "Nicéan barks" may be found in Ed-

That gently, o'er a perfumed sea,
 The weary, way-worn wanderer bore
 To his own native shore.   5

On desperate seas long wont to roam,
 Thy hyacinth hair, thy classic face,
Thy Naiad airs have brought me home
 To the glory that was Greece
And the grandeur that was Rome.   10

Lo! in yon brilliant window-niche
 How statue-like I see thee stand!
 The agate lamp within thy hand,
Ah, Psyche, from the regions which
 Are Holy-Land!   15

                                    1831, 1845

Israfel[5]

In Heaven a spirit doth dwell
"Whose heart-strings are a lute";[6]
None sing so wildly well
As the angel Israfel,
And the giddy stars (so legends tell)   5
Ceasing their hymns, attend the spell
 Of his voice, all mute.

Tottering above
 In her highest noon,
 The enamoured moon   10
Blushes with love,
 While, to listen, the red levin
 (With the rapid Pleiads, even,
 Which were seven,)[7]
Pauses in Heaven.   15

And they say (the starry choir
 And the other listening things)
That Israfeli's fire
Is owing to that lyre
By which he sits and sings—   20

ward Snyder's "Poe's Nicéan Barks,"
Classical Journal, XLVIII (February,
1953), 159–69. The meaning of the
poem depends very little on the source
of the term. See the discussion in the
introduction to Poe.
5. "And the angel Israfel, whose heart-
strings are a lute, and who has the
sweetest voice of all God's creatures.
—Koran" [Poe's note]. The text of the
poem is that of 1845.

6. Adapted from "Le Refus," by
Pierre Jean de Béranger; cf. the epigraph to "The Fall of the House of
Usher."
7. The Pleiades are a group of stars in
the constellation Taurus; they are
named after the seven daughters of
Atlas, one of whom concealed herself
from shame for having loved a mortal.
"Levin" is lightning.

The trembling living wire
  Of those unusual strings.

But the skies that angel trod,
  Where deep thoughts are a duty—
Where Love's a grown up God—
  Where the Houri[8] glances are
Imbued with all the beauty
  Which we worship in a star.

Therefore, thou art not wrong,
  Israfeli, who despisest
An unimpassioned song;
To thee the laurels belong,
  Best bard, because the wisest!
Merrily live, and long!

The ecstasies above
  With thy burning measures suit—
Thy grief, thy joy, thy hate, thy love,
  With the fervour of thy lute—
Well may the stars be mute!

Yes, Heaven is thine; but this
  Is a world of sweets and sours;
  Our flowers are merely—flowers,
And the shadow of thy perfect bliss
  Is the sunshine of ours.

If I could dwell
Where Israfel
  Hath dwelt, and he where I,
He might not sing so wildly well
  A mortal melody,
While a bolder note than this might swell
  From my lyre within the sky.

1831, 1845

The Sleeper[9]

At midnight, in the month of June,
I stand beneath the mystic moon.
An opiate vapour, dewy, dim,
Exhales from out her golden rim,
And, softly dripping, drop by drop,
Upon the quiet mountain top,
Steals drowsily and musically
Into the universal valley.

8. A nymph of the Mohammedan paradise.
9. This poem, entitled "Irene" in the 1831 volume, was much revised in four subsequent reprintings before 1845. The text here followed is that of 1845.

The rosemary[1] nods upon the grave;
The lily lolls upon the wave;   10
Wrapping the fog about its breast,
The ruin moulders into rest;
Looking like Lethe,[2] see! the lake
A conscious slumber seems to take,
And would not, for the world, awake.   15
All Beauty sleeps!—and lo! where lies
(Her casement open to the skies)
Irene, with her Destinies!

Oh, lady bright! can it be right—
This window open to the night?   20
The wanton airs, from the tree-top,
Laughingly through the lattice drop—
The bodiless airs, a wizard rout,
Flit through thy chamber in and out,
And wave the curtain canopy   25
So fitfully—so fearfully—
Above the closed and fringed lid
'Neath which thy slumb'ring soul lies hid,
That, o'er the floor and down the wall,
Like ghosts the shadows rise and fall!   30
Oh, lady dear, hast thou no fear?
Why and what art thou dreaming here?
Sure thou art come o'er far-off seas,
A wonder to these garden trees!
Strange is thy pallor! strange thy dress!   35
Strange, above all, thy length of tress,[3]
And this all solemn silentness!

The lady sleeps! Oh, may her sleep,
Which is enduring, so be deep!
Heaven have her in its sacred keep!   40
This chamber changed for one more holy,
This bed for one more melancholy,
I pray to God that she may lie
Forever with unopened eye,
While the dim sheeted ghosts go by!   45

My love, she sleeps! Oh, may her sleep,
As it is lasting, so be deep!
Soft may the worms about her creep!
Far in the forest, dim and old,
For her may some tall vault unfold—   50
Some vault that oft hath flung its black
And winged pannels fluttering back,
Triumphant, o'er the crested palls,

1. The symbol of remembrance.
2. A river in Hades whose water induced forgetfulness in those who drank
it.

3. According to an old superstition,
human hair continues to grow after
death.

Of her grand family funerals—
Some sepulchre, remote, alone,   55
Against whose portal she hath thrown,
In childhood, many an idle stone—
Some tomb from out whose sounding door
She ne'er shall force an echo more,
Thrilling to think, poor child of sin!   60
It was the dead who groaned within.

1831, 1845

The City in the Sea[4]

Lo! Death has reared himself a throne
In a strange city lying alone
Far down within the dim West,
Where the good and the bad and the worst and the best
Have gone to their eternal rest.   5
There shrines and palaces and towers
(Time-eaten towers that tremble not!)
Resemble nothing that is ours.
Around, by lifting winds forgot,
Resignedly beneath the sky   10
The melancholy waters lie.

No rays from the holy heaven come down
On the long night-time of that town;
But light from out the lurid sea
Streams up the turrets silently—   15
Gleams up the pinnacles far and free—
Up domes—up spires—up kingly halls—
Up fanes—up Babylon-like walls—
Up shadowy long-forgotten bowers
Of sculptured ivy and stone flowers—   20
Up many and many a marvellous shrine
Whose wreathèd friezes intertwine
The viol, the violet, and the vine.

Resignedly beneath the sky
The melancholy waters lie.
So blend the turrets and shadows there   25
That all seem pendulous in air,
While from a proud tower in the town
Death looks gigantically down.

There open fanes and gaping graves
Yawn level with the luminous waves;   30
But not the riches there that lie

4. The text is that of 1845. The earlier titles of this poem, "The Doomed City" (1831) and "The City of Sin" (1836), have led some inter- preters to identify Poe's city as the dwelling place of the wicked exclusively after death, but line 4 clearly contra- dicts such an interpretation.

In each idol's diamond eye—
Not the gaily-jewelled dead
Tempt the waters from their bed;   35
For no ripples curl, alas!
Along that wilderness of glass—
No swellings tell that winds may be
Upon some far-off happier sea—
No heavings hint that winds have been   40
On seas less hideously serene.

But lo, a stir is in the air!
The wave—there is a movement there!
As if the towers had thrust aside,
In slightly sinking, the dull tide—   45
As if their tops had feebly given
A void within the filmy Heaven.
The waves have now a redder glow—
The hours are breathing faint and low—
And when, amid no earthly moans,   50
Down, down that town shall settle hence,
Hell, rising from a thousand thrones,
Shall do it reverence.

                                    1831, 1845

The Valley of Unrest[5]

Once it smiled a silent dell
Where the people did not dwell;
They had gone unto the wars,
Trusting to the mild-eyed stars,
Nightly, from their azure towers,   5
To keep watch above the flowers,
In the midst of which all day
The red sun-light lazily lay.
Now each visiter shall confess
The sad valley's restlessness.   10
Nothing there is motionless—
Nothing save the airs that brood
Over the magic solitude.
Ah, by no wind are stirred those trees
That palpitate like the chill seas   15
Around the misty Hebrides!
Ah, by no wind those clouds are driven
That rustle through the unquiet Heaven
Uneasily, from morn till even,
Over the violets there that lie   20

5. The text is that of 1845. Early
versions of this poem, under the title
"The Valley Nis," ran to 46 lines and
are very inferior to the final version
given here. The poem is best understood as a companion piece to "The
Sleeper" and "The City in the Sea."

In myriad types of the human eye—
Over the lilies there that wave
And weep above a nameless grave!
They wave:—from out their fragrant tops
Eternal dews come down in drops.   25
They weep:—from off their delicate stems
Perennial tears descend in gems.

1831, 1845

Lenore[6]

Ah, broken is the golden bowl![7] the spirit flown forever!
Let the bell toll!—a saintly soul floats on the Stygian river;
And, Guy De Vere, hast *thou* no tear?—weep now or never more!
See! on yon drear and rigid bier low lies thy love, Lenore!
Come! let the burial rite be read—the funeral song be sung!—   5
An anthem for the queenliest dead that ever died so young—
A dirge for her the doubly dead in that she died so young.

"Wretches! ye loved her for her wealth and hated her for her pride,
And when she fell in feeble health, ye blessed her—that she died!
How *shall* the ritual, then, be read?—the requiem how be sung   10
By you—by yours, the evil eye,—by yours, the slanderous tongue
That did to death the innocence that died, and died so young?"

Peccavimus;[8] but rave not thus! and let a Sabbath song
Go up to God so solemnly the dead may feel no wrong!
The sweet Lenore hath "gone before," with Hope, that flew beside,   15
Leaving thee wild for the dear child that should have been thy
    bride—
For her, the fair and *debonair*, that now so lowly lies,
The life upon her yellow hair but not within her eyes—
The life still there, upon her hair—the death upon her eyes.

"Avaunt!—avaunt! from fiends below, the indignant ghost is
    riven—   20
From Hell unto a high estate far up within the Heaven—
From grief and groan, to a golden throne, beside the King of
    Heaven!—
Let no bell toll, then!—lest her soul, amid its hallowed mirth,
Should catch the note as it doth float up from the damnèd Earth!—
And I!—to-night my heart is light!—No dirge will I upraise   25
But waft the angel on her flight with a Pæan of old days!"

1831, 1845

6. The text is that of 1845. In the 1831 edition this poem was called "A Pæan" and consisted of ten stanzas of four lines each. It was completely re-written in 1843 for Lowell's *Pioneer*, where it was given an odelike form and retitled "Lenore." The present long line and stanza form were first used in the version in *Graham's Magazine* (1845).
7. See Ecclesiastes xii. 6.
8. "We have sinned."

The Coliseum[9]

Type of the antique Rome! Rich reliquary
Of lofty contemplation left to Time
By buried centuries of pomp and power!
At length—at length—after so many days
Of weary pilgrimage and burning thirst,   5
(Thirst for the springs of lore that in thee lie,)
I kneel, an altered and an humble man,
Amid thy shadows, and so drink within
My very soul thy grandeur, gloom, and glory!

Vastness! and Age! and Memories of Eld!   10
Silence! and Desolation! and dim Night!
I feel ye now—I feel ye in your strength—
O spells more sure than e'er Judæan king[1]
Taught in the gardens of Gethsemane!
O charms more potent than the rapt Chaldee[2]   15
Ever drew down from out the quiet stars!

Here, where a hero fell, a column falls!
Here, where the mimic eagle glared in gold,
A midnight vigil holds the swarthy bat!
Here, where the dames of Rome their gilded hair   20
Waved to the wind, now wave the reed and thistle!
Here, where on golden throne the monarch lolled,
Glides, spectre-like, unto his marble home,
Lit by the wan light of the hornéd moon,
The swift and silent lizard of the stones!   25

But stay! these walls—these ivy-clad arcades—
These mouldering plinths—these sad and blackened shafts—
These vague entablatures—this crumbling frieze—
These shattered cornices—this wreck—this ruin—
These stones—alas! these gray stones—are they all—   30
All of the famed, and the colossal left
By the corrosive Hours to Fate and me?

"Not all"—the Echoes answer me—"not all!
Prophetic sounds and loud, arise forever
From us, and from all Ruin, unto the wise,   35
As melody from Memnon[3] to the Sun.
We rule the hearts of mightiest men—we rule
With a despotic sway all giant minds.
We are not impotent—we pallid stones.
Not all our power is gone—not all our fame—   40

9. The text is that of 1845.
1. The reference is presumably to
Jesus Christ. Gethsemane is the garden
outside the walls of Jerusalem where
Jesus was arrested.
2. Chaldean. The Chaldeans were a
Semitic people related to the ancient
Babylonians, and were fabled masters
of astrology.
3. A gigantic statue at Thebes of the
Egyptian king whom the Greeks called
"Memnon" (ca. 1400 b.c.); according
to legend, the statue emitted a musical
sound at sunrise.

Not all the magic of our high renown—
Not all the wonder that encircles us—
Not all the mysteries that in us lie—
Not all the memories that hang upon
And cling around about us as a garment,
Clothing us in a robe of more than glory."   45

1833, 1845

To One in Paradise[4]

Thou wast all that to me, love,
   For which my soul did pine—
A green isle in the sea, love,
   A fountain and a shrine,
All wreathed with fairy fruits and flowers,   5
   And all the flowers were mine.

Ah, dream too bright to last!
   Ah, starry Hope! that didst arise
But to be overcast!
   A voice from out the Future cries,   10
"On! on!"—but o'er the Past
   (Dim gulf!) my spirit hovering lies
Mute, motionless, aghast!

For, alas! alas! with me
   The light of Life is o'er!
No more—no more—no more—   15
   (Such language holds the solemn sea
   To the sands upon the shore)
Shall bloom the thunder-blasted tree,
   Or the stricken eagle soar!   20

And all my days are trances,
   And all my nightly dreams
Are where thy dark eye glances,
   And where thy footstep gleams—
In what ethereal dances,
   By what eternal streams.

1834, 1845

4. The text is that of 1845. Originally published without title in *Godey's Lady's Book* for January, 1834, as part of "The Visionary" (later "The Assignation"), where it is attributed to the hero of that tale. It was first published separately in *Burton's Gentleman's Magazine* for July, 1839, where it was given the title "To Ianthe in Heaven." The theory, often repeated, that the poem refers to Sarah Elmira Royster (Mrs. Shelton at the time it was written) is purely conjectural.

Bridal Ballad[5]

The ring is on my hand,
  And the wreath is on my brow;
Satins and jewels grand
Are all at my command,
  And I am happy now.   5

And my lord he loves me well;
  But, when first he breathed his vow,
I felt my bosom swell—
For the words rang as a knell,
And the voice seemed *his* who fell   10
In the battle down the dell,
  And who is happy now.

But he spoke to re-assure me,
  And he kissed my pallid brow,
While a reverie came o'er me,   15
And to the church-yard bore me,
And I sighed to him before me,
Thinking him dead D'Elormie,
  "Oh, I am happy now!"

And thus the words were spoken,   20
  And this the plighted vow,
And, though my faith be broken,
And, though my heart be broken,
Behold the golden token
  That *proves* me happy now!   25

Would God I could awaken!
  For I dream I know not how,
And my soul is sorely shaken
Lest an evil step be taken,—
Lest the dead who is forsaken   30
  May not be happy now.

                                        1837, 1845

Sonnet—Silence[6]

There are some qualities—some incorporate things,
  That have a double life, which thus is made

5. The text is that of 1845. The theory that this poem refers to the marriage of Miss Royster to Mr. Shelton, though plausible, is based chiefly on internal evidence. The poetic devices of parallelism, repetition, and refrain, used extensively for the first time in this poem, are characteristic of Poe's later verse.

6. The text is that of 1845. Of the four sonnets known to have been written by Poe, only this one violates the conventional limit of fourteen lines, but all have minor irregularities except "To My Mother" (1849), which adheres closely to the Shakespearean pattern.

A type of that twin entity which springs
  From matter and light, evinced in solid and shade.
There is a two-fold *Silence*—sea and shore—   5
  Body and soul. One dwells in lonely places,
  Newly with grass o'ergrown; some solemn graces,
Some human memories and tearful lore,
Render him terrorless: his name's "No More."
He is the corporate Silence: dread him not!   10
  No power hath he of evil in himself;
But should some urgent fate (untimely lot!)
  Bring thee to meet his shadow (nameless elf,
That haunteth the lone regions where hath trod
No foot of man,) commend thyself to God!   15

1840, 1845

Dream-Land[7]

By a route obscure and lonely,
Haunted by ill angels only,
Where an Eidolon,[8] named NIGHT,
On a black throne reigns upright,
I have reached these lands but newly   5
From an ultimate dim Thule[9]
From a wild weird clime that lieth, sublime,
    Out of SPACE—out of TIME.

Bottomless vales and boundless floods,
And chasms, and caves, and Titan woods,   10
With forms that no man can discover
For the dews that drip all over;
Mountains toppling evermore
Into seas without a shore;
Seas that restlessly aspire,   15
Surging, unto skies of fire;
Lakes that endlessly outspread
Their lone waters—lone and dead,—
Their still waters—still and chilly
With the snows of the lolling lily.   20

By the lakes that thus outspread
Their lone waters, lone and dead,—
Their sad waters, sad and chilly
With the snows of the lolling lily,—
By the mountains—near the river   25
Murmuring lowly, murmuring ever,—
By the grey woods,—by the swamp

7. The text is that of 1845.
8. An image; here, the personified image of the power that rules the night, the realm of dreams.

9. The strangest and most remote region imaginable (in ancient geography, the northernmost region of the world).

Where the toad and the newt encamp,—
By the dismal tarns and pools
    Where dwell the Ghouls,[1]—   30
By each spot the most unholy—
In each nook most melancholy,—
There the traveller meets aghast
Sheeted Memories of the Past—   35
Shrouded forms that start and sigh
As they pass the wanderer by—
White-robed forms of friends long given,
In agony, to the Earth—and Heaven.

For the heart whose woes are legion
'Tis a peaceful, soothing region—   40
For the spirit that walks in shadow
'Tis—oh 'tis an Eldorado!
But the traveller, travelling through it,
May not—dare not openly view it;
Never its mysteries are exposed   45
To the weak human eye unclosed;
So wills its King, who hath forbid
The uplifting of the fringéd lid;
And thus the sad Soul that here passes
Beholds it but through darkened glasses.   50

By a route obscure and lonely,
Haunted by ill angels only,
Where an Eidolon, named NIGHT,
On a black throne reigns upright,
I have wandered home but newly   55
From this ultimate dim Thule.

                        1844, 1845

The Raven[2]

Once upon a midnight dreary, while I pondered, weak and weary,
Over many a quaint and curious volume of forgotten lore,
While I nodded, nearly napping, suddenly there came a tapping,
As of some one gently rapping, rapping at my chamber door.
" 'Tis some visitor," I muttered, "tapping at my chamber door—   5
            Only this, and nothing more."

Ah, distinctly I remember it was in the bleak December,
And each separate dying ember wrought its ghost upon the floor.
Eagerly I wished the morrow;—vainly I had sought to borrow

1. In folklore, demons who feed on the flesh of the dead; here they are part of the dismal setting in which memories rise in the mind of the dreamer as phantoms from the grave.
2. The text is that of 1845. Poe's account in "The Philosophy of Composition" of the genesis and composition of "The Raven" may not be accurate in every detail, but it is an illuminating commentary on his theory of the creative process. The novelty of the poem inheres more in its structure than in its theme.

From my books surcease of sorrow—sorrow for the lost Lenore— 10
For the rare and radiant maiden whom the angels name Lenore—
       Nameless here for evermore.

And the silken sad uncertain rustling of each purple curtain
Thrilled me—filled me with fantastic terrors never felt before;
So that now, to still the beating of my heart, I stood repeating 15
" 'Tis some visitor entreating entrance at my chamber door—
Some late visitor entreating entrance at my chamber door;—
       This it is, and nothing more."

Presently my soul grew stronger; hesitating then no longer,
"Sir," said I, "or Madam, truly your forgiveness I implore; 20
But the fact is I was napping, and so gently you came rapping,
And so faintly you came tapping, tapping at my chamber door,
That I scarce was sure I heard you"—here I opened wide the door;—
       Darkness there, and nothing more.

Deep into that darkness peering, long I stood there wondering, fear-
   ing,
Doubting, dreaming dreams no mortal ever dared to dream before; 25
But the silence was unbroken, and the darkness gave no token,
And the only word there spoken was the whispered word, "Lenore!"
This I whispered, and an echo murmured back the word, "Lenore!"—
       Merely this, and nothing more. 30

Back into the chamber turning, all my soul within me burning,
Soon I heard again a tapping somewhat louder than before.
"Surely," said I, "surely that is something at my window lattice;
Let me see, then, what thereat is, and this mystery explore—
Let my heart be still a moment and this mystery explore;— 35
       'Tis the wind and nothing more!"

Open here I flung the shutter, when, with many a flirt and flutter,
In there stepped a stately raven of the saintly days of yore;
Not the least obeisance made he; not an instant stopped or stayed
   he;
But, with mien of lord or lady, perched above my chamber door— 40
Perched upon a bust of Pallas[3] just above my chamber door—
       Perched, and sat, and nothing more.

Then this ebony bird beguiling my sad fancy into smiling,
By the grave and stern decorum of the countenance it wore,
"Though thy crest be shorn and shaven, thou," I said, "art sure no
   craven,
Ghastly grim and ancient raven wandering from the Nightly shore— 45
Tell me what thy lordly name is on the Night's Plutonian shore!"
       Quoth the raven, "Nevermore."

Much I marvelled this ungainly fowl to hear discourse so plainly,
Though its answer little meaning—little relevancy bore; 50

3. Athena, the Greek goddess of wisdom—an appropriate decoration for the room of the narrator, who is a student.

For we cannot help agreeing that no living human being
Ever yet was blessed with seeing bird above his chamber door—
Bird or beast upon the sculptured bust above his chamber door,
                With such name as "Nevermore."

But the raven, sitting lonely on the placid bust, spoke only   55
That one word, as if his soul in that one word he did outpour.
Nothing farther then he uttered—not a feather then he fluttered—
Till I scarcely more than muttered "Other friends have flown be-
    fore—
On the morrow *he* will leave me, as my hopes have flown before."
              Then the bird said "Nevermore."   60

Startled at the stillness broken by reply so aptly spoken,
"Doubtless," said I, "what it utters is its only stock and store
Caught from some unhappy master whom unmerciful Disaster
Followed fast and followed faster till his songs one burden bore—
Till the dirges of his Hope that melancholy burden bore   65
            Of 'Never—nevermore.' "

But the raven still beguiling all my sad soul into smiling,
Straight I wheeled a cushioned seat in front of bird and bust and
    door;
Then, upon the velvet sinking, I betook myself to linking
Fancy unto fancy, thinking what this ominous bird of yore—   70
What this grim, ungainly, ghastly, gaunt, and ominous bird of yore
          Meant in croaking "Nevermore."

This I sat engaged in guessing, but no syllable expressing
To the fowl whose fiery eyes now burned into my bosom's core;
This and more I sat divining, with my head at ease reclining   75
On the cushion's velvet lining that the lamplight gloated[4] o'er,
But whose velvet violet lining with the lamplight gloating o'er,
         She shall press, ah, nevermore!

Then, methought, the air grew denser, perfumed from an unseen
    censer
Swung by angels whose faint foot-falls tinkled on the tufted floor. 80
"Wretch," I cried, "thy God hath lent thee—by these angels he
    hath sent thee
Respite—respite and nepenthe[5] from thy memories of Lenore!
Quaff, oh quaff this kind nepenthe and forget this lost Lenore!"
         Quoth the raven, "Nevermore."

"Prophet!" said I, "thing of evil!—prophet still, if bird or devil!—
Whether Tempter sent, or whether tempest tossed thee here ashore,
Desolate, yet all undaunted, on this desert land enchanted— 87
On this home by Horror haunted—tell me truly, I implore—

---

4. The Century Dictionary gives as one definition of "gloat": "to cast a sidelong glance or ray." The lamp was presumably on the wall above the door and above the bust of Pallas, and so its light slanted downward.
5. A drug reputed by the Greeks to cause forgetfulness of sorrow.

Is there—*is* there balm in Gilead?[6]—tell me—tell me, I implore!"
       Quoth the raven, "Nevermore."   90

"Prophet!" said I, "thing of evil—prophet still, if bird or devil!
By that Heaven that bends above us—by that God we both adore—
Tell this soul with sorrow laden if, within the distant Aidenn,
It shall clasp a sainted maiden whom the angels name Lenore—
Clasp a rare and radiant maiden whom the angels name Lenore."   95
       Quoth the raven, "Nevermore."

"Be that word our sign of parting, bird or fiend!" I shrieked, up-
    starting—
"Get thee back into the tempest and the Night's Plutonian shore!
Leave no black plume as a token of that lie thy soul hath spoken!
Leave my loneliness unbroken!—quit the bust above my door!   100
Take thy beak from out my heart, and take thy form from off
    my door!"
       Quoth the raven, "Nevermore."

And the raven, never flitting, still is sitting, still is sitting
On the palid bust of Pallas just above my chamber door;
And his eyes have all the seeming of a demon's that is dreaming,   105
And the lamp-light o'er him streaming throws his shadow on the
    floor;
And my soul from out that shadow that lies floating on the floor
       Shall be lifted—nevermore!

                            1845

Ulalume[7]

  The skies they were ashen and sober;
    The leaves they were crispéd and sere—
    The leaves they were withering and sere:
  It was night, in the lonesome October
    Of my most immemorial year;
  It was hard by the dim lake of Auber,   5
    In the misty mid region of Weir[8]—
  It was down by the dank tarn of Auber,
    In the ghoul-haunted woodland of Weir.

  Here once, through an alley Titanic,   10
    Of cypress, I roamed with my Soul—
    Of cypress, with Psyche, my Soul.
  These were days when my heart was volcanic

6. Cf. Jeremiah viii. 22: "Is there no
balm in Gilead?" (Gilead was a region in Palestine).
7. The text is that of Griswold's 1850
edition of Poe's *Works*, except for the
restoration of the last stanza, which
was there omitted. Killis Campbell
(*The Poems of Edgar Allan Poe*, p.
273) suggests that Poe may have derived the title from the Latin *ululare*,
"to wail." The word obviously connotes gloom.
8. The place names "Auber," "Weir,"
and "Yaanek" (line 16) are probably
invented.

As the scoriac rivers that roll—
  As the lavas that restlessly roll   15
Their sulphurous currents down Yaanek
  In the ultimate climes of the pole—
That groan as they roll down Mount Yaanek
  In the realms of the boreal pole.

Our talk had been serious and sober,   20
  But our thoughts they were palsied and sere—
  Our memories were treacherous and sere—
For we knew not the month was October,
And we marked not the night of the year
  (Ah, night of all nights in the year!)—   25
We noted not the dim lake of Auber—
  (Though once we had journeyed down here)—
Remembered not the dank tarn of Auber,
  Nor the ghoul-haunted woodland of Weir.

And now, as the night was senescent   30
  And star-dials pointed to morn—
  As the star-dials hinted of morn—
At the end of our path a liquescent
  And nebulous lustre was born,
Out of which a miraculous crescent   35
  Arose with a duplicate horn—
Astarte's bediamonded crescent
  Distinct with its duplicate horn.

And I said—"She is warmer than Dian;
  She rolls through an ether of sighs—   40
  She revels in a region of sighs—
She has seen that the tears are not dry on
  These cheeks, where the worm never dies,
And has come past the stars of the Lion,
  To point us the path to the skies—   45
  To the Lethean⁹ peace of the skies—
Come up, in despite of the Lion,
  To shine on us with her bright eyes—
Come up through the lair of the Lion,
  With love in her luminous eyes."¹   50

9. I.e., inducing forgetfulness.
1. The symbolism of this stanza is difficult. Astarte (line 37) was worshipped by the ancients both as the moon goddess and the goddess of fertility; in Egypt she was sometimes identified with the lewd Babylonian mother goddess Ishtar and represented as standing on the back of a lion. Poe would have known that because of the precession of the equinoxes the constellation Leo ("the Lion," line 44) lies in the zodiacal sign of Virgo, thirty degrees in advance of its original position. The rational mind of the narrator accepts the rising of the planet Venus (Astarte) as beneficent because he mistakenly supposes her to be in the sign of Virgo, "the Virgin" (August 23–September 23), whereas in fact she is in Libra (September 23–October 24) or more probably in Scorpio (October 24–November 22), and hence neutral or even malign. The intuitive soul of the narrator recognizes the planet as a harbinger of evil.

But Psyche, uplifting her finger,
 Said—"Sadly this star I mistrust—
 Her pallor I strangely mistrust:—
Oh, hasten!—oh, let us not linger!
 Oh, fly!—let us fly!—for we must."
In terror she spoke, letting sink her   55
 Wings till they trailed in the dust—
In agony sobbed, letting sink her
 Plumes till they trailed in the dust—
 Till they sorrowfully trailed in the dust.   60

I replied: "This is nothing but dreaming:
 Let us on by this tremulous light!
 Let us bathe in this crystalline light!
Its Sibylic[2] splendor is beaming
 With Hope and in Beauty to-night:—   65
 See!—it flickers up the sky through the night!
Ah, we safely may trust to its gleaming,
 And be sure it will lead us aright—
We safely may trust to a gleaming,
 That cannot but guide us aright,
 Since it flickers up to Heaven through the night." 70

Thus I pacified Psyche and kissed her,
 And tempted her out of her gloom—
 And conquered her scruples and gloom;
And we passed to the end of the vista,
 But were stopped by the door of a tomb— 75
 By the door of a legended tomb;
And I said—"What is written, sweet sister,
 On the door of this legended tomb?"
She replied: "Ulalume—Ulalume—
 'Tis the vault of thy lost Ulalume!"   80

Then my heart it grew ashen and sober
 As the leaves that were crispéd and sere—
 As the leaves that were withering and sere,
And I cried—"It was surely October
 On *this* very night of last year   85
 That I journeyed—I journeyed down here—
 That I brought a dread burden down here—
 On this night of all nights in the year,
 Ah, what demon has tempted me here?
Well I know, now, this dim lake of Auber— 90
 This misty mid region of Weir—
Well I know, now, this dank tarn of Auber,
 This ghoul-haunted woodland of Weir."

2. Prophetic.

Said we, then—the two, then: "Ah, can it   95
    Have been that the woodlandish ghouls—
    The pitiful, the merciful ghouls—
To bar up our way and to ban it
    From the secret that lies in these wolds—
    From the thing that lies hidden in these wolds—   100
Have drawn up the spectre of a planet
    From the limbo of lunary souls—
This sinfully scintillant planet
    From the Hell of the planetary souls?"

                                        1847, 1850

The Bells[3]

I

Hear the sledges with the bells—
        Silver bells!
What a world of merriment their melody foretells!
    How they tinkle, tinkle, tinkle,
        In the icy air of night!   5
    While the stars that oversprinkle
    All the heavens, seem to twinkle
        With a crystalline delight;
        Keeping time, time, time,
        In a sort of Runic[4] rhyme,   10
To the tintinnabulation that so musically wells
        From the bells, bells, bells, bells,
            Bells, bells, bells—
From the jingling and the tinkling of the bells.

II

Hear the mellow wedding bells—   15
        Golden bells!
What a world of happiness their harmony foretells!
    Through the balmy air of night
    How they ring out their delight!—
        From the molten-golden notes,   20
            And all in tune,
        What a liquid ditty floats
To the turtle-dove that listens, while she gloats
            On the moon!

3. The text is that of the version printed in *Sartain's Union Magazine* for November, 1849. There were several versions of the poem, the earliest, written in the summer of 1848, consisting of only seventeen lines. Another early version, though printed in *Sartain's Union Magazine* for December, 1849, has eighteen lines. The poem grew by accretion. It is a quaternion, the four types of bells representing four stages in human life.

Emphasis is obtained through repetition, thus lengthening the stanza. For example, the word "bells" is repeated ten times in the first stanza, thirteen in the second, fifteen in the third, and 24 in the fourth.
4. The apparent movement of the twinkling stars keeps time with the rhythm of the tinkling bells. Runes were characters of an ancient Teutonic alphabet, used as symbols of mysterious import.

Oh, from out the sounding cells,   25
What a gush of euphony voluminously wells!
How it swells!
How it dwells
On the Future!—how it tells
Of the rapture that impels   30
To the swinging and the ringing
Of the bells, bells, bells—
Of the bells, bells, bells, bells,
Bells, bells, bells—
To the rhyming and the chiming of the bells!   35

III

Hear the loud alarum bells—
Brazen bells!
What a tale of terror, now, their turbulency tells!
In the startled ear of night
How they scream out their affright!
Too much horrified to speak,   40
They can only shriek, shriek,
Out of tune,
In a clamorous appealing to the mercy of the fire,
In a mad expostulation with the deaf and frantic fire,
Leaping higher, higher, higher,   45
With a desperate desire,
And a resolute endeavor
Now—now to sit, or never,
By the side of the pale-faced moon.
Oh, the bells, bells, bells!   50
What a tale their terror tells
Of Despair!
How they clang, and clash, and roar!
What a horror they outpour
On the bosom of the palpitating air!   55
Yet the ear, it fully knows,
By the twanging
And the clanging,
How the danger ebbs and flows;
Yet the ear distinctly tells,   60
In the jangling
And the wrangling,
How the danger sinks and swells,
By the sinking or the swelling in the anger of the bells—   65
Of the bells—
Of the bells, bells, bells, bells,
Bells, bells, bells—
In the clamor and the clangor of the bells!

IV

Hear the tolling of the bells—   70
Iron bells!
What a world of solemn thought their monody compels!

In the silence of the night,
How we shiver with affright
At the melancholy menace of their tone!   75
For every sound that floats
From the rust within their throats
    Is a groan.
    And the people—ah, the people—
    They that dwell up in the steeple,   80
      All alone,
And who tolling, tolling, tolling,
    In that muffled monotone,
Feel a glory in so rolling
    On the human heart a stone—   85
They are neither man nor woman—
They are neither brute nor human—
    They are Ghouls:—
And their king it is who tolls:—
And he rolls, rolls, rolls,   90
    Rolls
    A pæan from the bells!
And his merry bosom swells
    With the pæan of the bells!
And he dances, and he yells;   95
Keeping time, time, time,
In a sort of Runic rhyme,
    To the pæan of the bells—
    Of the bells:—
Keeping time, time, time,   100
In a sort of Runic rhyme,
    To the throbbing of the bells—
Of the bells, bells, bells—
    To the sobbing of the bells:—
Keeping time, time, time,   105
    As he knells, knells, knells,
In a happy Runic rhyme,
    To the rolling of the bells—
Of the bells, bells, bells:—
    To the tolling of the bells—   110
Of the bells, bells, bells, bells,
    Bells, bells, bells—
To the moaning and the groaning of the bells.

1849

Eldorado[5]

Gaily bedight,
A gallant knight,
In sunshine and in shadow,
Had journeyed long,
Singing a song,
In search of Eldorado.   5

But he grew old—
This knight so bold—
And o'er his heart a shadow
Fell as he found
No spot of ground   10
That looked like Eldorado.

And, as his strength
Failed him at length,
He met a pilgrim shadow—
"Shadow," said he,   15
"Where can it be—
This land of Eldorado?"

"Over the Mountains
Of the Moon,
Down the Valley of the Shadow,   20
Ride, boldly ride,"
The shade replied,—
"If you seek for Eldorado!"

1849, 1850

For Annie[6]

Thank Heaven! the crisis—
The danger is past,

5. The text is that of Griswold's edition (1850). The words "El Dorado" are Spanish and mean literally "the gilded," or "the gilded one." Poe may have had in mind the 16th-century legend of a king or chief in South America who was so rich in gold that at annual festivals he covered his body with gold dust. The term "Eldorado" came to be applied to his city or country, and eventually to any place of fabulous wealth; during the gold rush of 1849, the newspapers often used it in reference to California. The poem, however, is universal in its meaning. The clue is in the changing meanings of the word "shadow," which in the first stanza is purely physical, in the second a symbol of sadness, in the third a synonym of "spirit," and in the fourth the symbol of death.

6. The text is that of Griswold's edition (1850). "Annie" was Mrs. Annie Richmond, of Lowell, Massachusetts, to whom Poe wrote glowing letters of affection during the last year of his life. He sent her a copy of this poem in March, 1849, and in the accompanying letter wrote: "I think the lines 'For Annie' * * * much the *best* I have ever written." A few critics have agreed with this judgment, but most have not. The poet imagines himself dead and buried but still strangely conscious and comforted by the memory of the pure love of Annie, which affects him as the odor of rosemary mingled with those of rue and pansies.

And the lingering illness
  Is over at last—
And the fever called "Living"   5
  Is conquered at last.

Sadly, I know
  I am shorn of my strength,
And no muscle I move
  As I lie at full length—   10
But no matter!—I feel
  I am better at length.

And I rest so composedly,
  Now, in my bed,
That any beholder   15
  Might fancy me dead—
Might start at beholding me,
  Thinking me dead.

The moaning and groaning,
  The sighing and sobbing,   20
Are quieted now,
  With that horrible throbbing
At heart:—ah, that horrible,
  Horrible throbbing!

The sickness—the nausea—   25
  The pitiless pain—
Have ceased, with the fever
  That maddened my brain—
With the fever called "Living"
  That burned in my brain.   30

And oh! of all tortures
  That torture the worst
Has abated—the terrible
  Torture of thirst
For the napthaline[7] river   35
  Of Passion accurst:—
I have drank of a water
  That quenches all thirst:—

Of a water that flows,
  With a lullaby sound,   40
From a spring but a very few
  Feet under ground—
From a cavern not very far
  Down under ground.

And ah, let it never   45
  Be foolishly said

---

7. An adjective form which Poe derives from "naphtha," an inflammable liquid which comes from petroleum.

That my room it is gloomy
 And narrow my bed;
For man never slept
 In a different bed—
And, to *sleep*, you must slumber   50
 In just such a bed.

My tantalized spirit
 Here blandly reposes,
Forgetting, or never
 Regretting its roses—   55
Its old agitations
 Of myrtles and roses:

For now, while so quietly
 Lying, it fancies
A holier odor   60
 About it, of pansies—
A rosemary odor,
 Commingled with pansies—
With rue and the beautiful
 Puritan pansies.   65

And so it lies happily,
 Bathing in many
A dream of the truth
 And the beauty of Annie—
Drowned in a bath   70
 Of the tresses of Annie.

She tenderly kissed me,
 She fondly caressed,
And then I fell gently
 To sleep on her breast—   75
Deeply to sleep
 From the heaven of her breast.

When the light was extinguished,
 She covered me warm,
And she prayed to the angels   80
 To keep me from harm—
To the queen of the angels
 To shield me from harm.

And I lie so composedly,
 Now, in my bed,   85
(Knowing her love)
 That you fancy me dead—
And I rest so contentedly,
 Now, in my bed,
(With her love at my breast)   90
 That you fancy me dead—

That you shudder to look at me,
Thinking me dead:—

But my heart it is brighter   95
Than all of the many
Stars of the sky,
For it sparkles with Annie—
It glows with the light
Of the love of my Annie—   100
With the thought of the light
Of the eyes of my Annie.

1849, 1850

To My Mother[8]

Because I feel that, in the Heavens above,
The angels, whispering to one another,
Can find, among their burning terms of love,
None so devotional as that of "Mother,"
Therefore by that dear name I long have called you—   5
You who are more than mother unto me,
And fill my heart of hearts, where Death installed you
In setting my Virginia's spirit free.
My mother—my own mother, who died early,
Was but the mother of myself; but you   10
Are mother to the one I loved so dearly,
And thus are dearer than the mother I knew
By that infinity with which my wife
Was dearer to my soul than its soul-life.

1849, 1850

Annabel Lee[9]

It was many and many a year ago,
In a kingdom by the sea,
That a maiden there lived whom you may know
By the name of Annabel Lee;—
And this maiden she lived with no other thought   5
Than to love and be loved by me.

She was a child and *I* was a child,
In this kingdom by the sea,
But we loved with a love that was more than love—
I and my Annabel Lee—   10

8. The text is that of Griswold's edition (1850). The poem is a tribute to Poe's aunt and mother-in-law, Mrs. Maria Clemm.
9. The text is that of the *Southern Literary Messenger*, November, 1849. This was probably the last poem Poe wrote. It is often said to refer to his wife Virginia, but it is surely a story of ideal love; a ballad, he called it.

With a love that the wingèd seraphs of Heaven
    Coveted her and me.

And this was the reason that, long ago,
    In this kingdom by the sea,
A wind blew out of a cloud by night
    Chilling my Annabel Lee;   15
So that her high-born kinsman came
    And bore her away from me,
To shut her up in a sepulchre
    In this kingdom by the sea.
     20

The angels, not half so happy in Heaven,
    Went envying her and me;
Yes! that was the reason (as all men know,
    In this kingdom by the sea)
That the wind came out of the cloud, chilling   25
    And killing my Annabel Lee.

But our love it was stronger by far than the love
    Of those who were older than we—
    Of many far wiser than we—
And neither the angels in Heaven above
    Nor the demons down under the sea   30
Can ever dissever my soul from the soul
    Of the beautiful Annabel Lee:—

For the moon never beams without bringing me dreams
    Of the beautiful Annabel Lee;
And the stars never rise but I see the bright eyes   35
    Of the beautiful Annabel Lee;
And so, all the night-tide, I lie down by the side
Of my darling, my darling, my life and my bride
    In her sepulchre there by the sea—
    In her tomb by the side of the sea.   40

1849

Ligeia[1]

And the will therein lieth, which dieth not. Who knoweth the mysteries of the will, with its vigor? For God is but a great will pervading all things by nature of its intentness. Man doth not yield himself to the angels, nor unto death utterly, save only through the weakness of his feeble will.

—JOSEPH GLANVILL[2]

I cannot, for my soul, remember how, when, or even precisely where, I first became acquainted with the lady Ligeia. Long years have since elapsed, and my memory is feeble through much suffering. Or, perhaps, I cannot *now* bring these points to mind, be-

1. The text is that of the *Broadway Journal*, September 27, 1845.
2. Joseph Glanvill (1636–80) was associated with the Cambridge Platonists. This quotation has not, however, been found in his published works.

cause, in truth, the character of my beloved, her rare learning, her singular yet placid cast of beauty, and the thrilling and enthralling eloquence of her low musical language, made their way into my heart by paces so steadily and stealthily progressive that they have been unnoticed and unknown. Yet I believe that I met her first and most frequently in some large, old, decaying city near the Rhine. Of her family—I have surely heard her speak. That it is of a remotely ancient date cannot be doubted. Ligeia! Ligeia! Buried in studies of a nature more than all else adapted to deaden impressions of the outward world, it is by that sweet word alone—by Ligeia—that I bring before mine eyes in fancy the image of her who is no more. And now, while I write, a recollection flashes upon me that I have *never known* the paternal name of her who was my friend and my betrothed, and who became the partner of my studies, and finally the wife of my bosom. Was it a playful charge on the part of my Ligeia? or was it a test of my strength of affection, that I should institute no inquiries upon this point? or was it rather a caprice of my own—a wildly romantic offering on the shrine of the most passionate devotion? I but indistinctly recall the fact itself—what wonder that I have utterly forgotten the circumstances which originated or attended it. And, indeed, if ever that spirit which is entitled *Romance*—if ever she, the wan and the misty-winged *Ashtophet*[3] of idolatrous Egypt, presided, as they tell, over marriages ill-omened, then most surely she presided over mine.

There is one dear topic, however, on which my memory fails me not. It is the *person* of Ligeia. In stature she was tall, somewhat slender, and, in her latter days, even emaciated. I would in vain attempt to portray the majesty, the quiet ease, of her demeanor, or the incomprehensible lightness and elasticity of her footfall. She came and departed as a shadow. I was never made aware of her entrance into my closed study save by the dear music of her low sweet voice, as she placed her marble hand upon my shoulder. In beauty of face no maiden ever equalled her. It was the radiance of an opium dream—an airy and spirit-lifting vision more wildly divine than the phantasies which hovered about the slumbering souls of the daughters of Delos.[4] Yet her features were not of that regular mould which we have been falsely taught to worship in the classical labors of the heathen. "There is no exquisite beauty," says Bacon, Lord Verulam, speaking truly of all the forms and *genera* of beauty, "without some *strangeness* in the proportion." Yet, although I saw

3. Poe apparently invented this goddess by combining "Ashtoreth," the ancient Phoenician goddess of love and fertility, with the Biblical "Tophet," where human sacrifices by fire were made to the god Moloch.
4. An island in the Aegean Sea, legendary birthplace of the goddess Artemis and her twin brother Apollo, and site of an ancient temple of Apollo.

that the features of Ligeia were not of a classic regularity—although I perceived that her loveliness was indeed "exquisite," and felt that there was much of "strangeness" pervading it, yet I have tried in vain to detect the irregularity and to trace home my own perception of "the strange." I examined the contour of the lofty and pale forehead—it was faultless—how cold indeed that word when applied to a majesty so divine!—the skin rivalling the purest ivory, the commanding extent and repose, the gentle prominence of the regions above the temples; and then the raven-black, the glossy, the luxuriant and naturally-curling tresses, setting forth the full force of the Homeric epithet, "hyacinthine!" I looked at the delicate outlines of the nose—and nowhere but in the graceful medallions of the Hebrews had I beheld a similar perfection. There were the same luxurious smoothness of surface, the same scarcely perceptible tendency to the aquiline, the same harmoniously curved nostrils speaking the free spirit. I regarded the sweet mouth. Here was indeed the triumph of all things heavenly—the magnificent turn of the short upper lip—the soft, voluptuous slumber of the under—the dimples which sported, and the color which spoke— the teeth glancing back, with a brilliancy almost startling, every ray of the holy light which fell upon them in her serene and placid, yet most exultingly radiant of all smiles. I scrutinized the formation of the chin—and here, too, I found the gentleness of breadth, the softness and the majesty, the fullness and the spirituality, of the Greek—the contour which the god Apollo revealed but in a dream, to Cleomenes,[5] the son of the Athenian. And then I peered into the large eyes of Ligeia.

For eyes we have no models in the remotely antique. It might have been, too, that in these eyes of my beloved lay the secret to which Lord Verulam alludes. They were, I must believe, far larger than the ordinary eyes of our own race. They were even fuller than the fullest of the gazelle eyes of the tribe of the valley of Nourjahad.[6] Yet it was only at intervals—in moments of intense excitement—that this peculiarity became more than slightly noticeable in Ligeia. And at such moments was her beauty—in my heated fancy thus it appeared perhaps—the beauty of beings either above or apart from the earth—the beauty of the fabulous Houri[7] of the Turk. The hue of the orbs was the most brilliant of black, and, far over them, hung jetty lashes of great length. The brows, slightly irregular in outline, had the same tint. The "strangeness," however, which I found in the eyes, was of a nature distinct from the formation, or the color, or the brilliancy of the features, and

5. A Greek sculptor (ca. 200 or 300 B.C.), mentioned by Pliny.
6. A reference to the Oriental romance *The History of the Nourjahad* (1767)
by Mrs. Frances Sheridan.
7. A nymph of the Moslem paradise. Cf. "Israfel," lines 26–28.

must, after all, be referred to the *expression*. Ah, word of no meaning! behind whose vast latitude of mere sound we intrench our ignorance of so much of the spiritual. The expression of the eyes of Ligeia! How for long hours have I pondered upon it! How have I, through the whole of a midsummer night, struggled to fathom it! What was it—that something more profound than the well of Democritus[8]—which lay far within the pupils of my beloved? What *was* it? I was possessed with a passion to discover. Those eyes! those large, those shining, those divine orbs! they became to me twin stars of Leda,[9] and I to them devoutest of astrologers.

There is no point, among the many incomprehensible anomalies of the science of mind, more thrillingly exciting than the fact—never, I believe, noticed in the schools—that, in our endeavors to recall to memory something long forgotten, we often find ourselves *upon the very verge* of remembrance, without being able, in the end, to remember. And thus how frequently, in my intense scrutiny of Ligeia's eyes, have I felt approaching the full knowledge of their expression—felt it approaching—yet not quite be mine—and so at length entirely depart! And (strange, oh strangest mystery of all!) I found, in the commonest objects of the universe, a circle of analogies to that expression. I mean to say that, subsequently to the period when Ligeia's beauty passed into my spirit, there dwelling as in a shrine, I derived, from many existences in the material world, a sentiment such as I felt always aroused within me by her large and luminous orbs. Yet not the more could I define that sentiment, or analyze, or even steadily view it. I recognized it, let me repeat, sometimes in the survey of a rapidly-growing vine—in the contemplation of a moth, a butterfly, a chrysalis, a stream of running water. I have felt it in the ocean; in the falling of a meteor. I have felt it in the glances of unusually aged people. And there are one or two stars in heaven (one especially, a star of the sixth magnitude, double and changeable, to be found near the large star in Lyra[1]) in a telescopic scrutiny of which I have been made aware of the feeling. I have been filled with it by certain sounds from stringed instruments, and not unfrequently by passages from books. Among innumerable other instances, I well remember something in a volume of Joseph Glanvill, which (perhaps merely from its quaintness—who shall say?) never failed to inspire me with the sentiment;—"And the will therein lieth, which dieth not. Who knoweth the mysteries of the will, with its vigor? For God is but

8. A Greek philosopher of the 5th century B.C., from whom is derived the proverb, "Truth lies at the bottom of a well."
9. Castor and Pollux, twin sons of Leda, a Spartan queen, and Zeus, who visited her in the form of a swan.
1. A northern constellation between Hercules and Cygnus, said to resemble the harp of Orpheus. Vega is the largest star in it.

a great will pervading all things by nature of its intentness. Man doth not yield him to the angels, nor unto death utterly, save only through the weakness of his feeble will."

Length of years, and subsequent reflection, have enabled me to trace, indeed, some remote connection between this passage in the English moralist and a portion of the character of Ligeia. An *intensity* in thought, action, or speech, was possibly, in her, a result, or at least an index, of that gigantic volition which, during our long intercourse, failed to give other and more immediate evidence of its existence. Of all the women whom I have ever known, she, the outwardly calm, the ever-placid Ligeia, was the most violently a prey to the tumultuous vultures of stern passion. And of such passion I could form no estimate, save by the miraculous expansion of those eyes which at once so delighted and appalled me—by the almost magical melody, modulation, distinctness and placidity of her very low voice—and by the fierce energy (rendered doubly effective by contrast with her manner of utterance) of the wild words which she habitually uttered.

I have spoken of the learning of Ligeia: it was immense—such as I have never known in woman. In the classical tongues was she deeply proficient, and as far as my own acquaintance extended in regard to the modern dialects of Europe, I have never known her at fault. Indeed upon any theme of the most admired, because simply the most abstruse of the boasted erudition of the academy, have I *ever* found Ligeia at fault? How singularly—how thrillingly, this one point in the nature of my wife has forced itself, at this late period only, upon my attention! I said her knowledge was such as I have never known in woman—but where breathes the man who has traversed, and successfully, *all* the wide areas of moral, physical, and mathematical science? I saw not then what I now clearly perceive, that the acquisitions of Ligeia were gigantic, were astounding; yet I was sufficiently aware of her infinite supremacy to resign myself, with a child-like confidence, to her guidance through the chaotic world of metaphysical investigation at which I was most busily occupied during the earlier years of our marriage. With how vast a triumph—with how vivid a delight—with how much of all that is ethereal in hope—did I *feel*, as she bent over me in studies but little sought—but less known—that delicious vista by slow degrees expanding before me, down whose long, gorgeous, and all untrodden path, I might at length pass onward to the goal of a wisdom too divinely precious not to be forbidden!

How poignant, then, must have been the grief with which, after some years, I beheld my well-grounded expectations take wings to themselves and fly away! Without Ligeia I was but as a child groping benighted. Her presence, her readings alone, rendered vividly luminous the many mysteries of the transcendentalism in which we were immersed. Wanting the radiant lustre of her eyes, letters, lambent and golden, grew duller than Saturnian lead. And now those eyes shone less and less frequently upon the pages over which I pored. Ligeia grew ill. The wild eyes blazed with a too—too glorious effulgence; the pale fingers became of the transparent waxen hue of the grave, and the blue veins upon the lofty forehead swelled and sank impetuously with the tides of the most gentle emotion. I saw that she must die—and I struggled desperately in spirit with the grim Azrael.[2] And the struggles of the passionate wife were, to my astonishment, even more energetic than my own. There had been much in her stern nature to impress me with the belief that, to her, death would have come without its terrors;—but not so. Words are impotent to convey any just idea of the fierceness of resistance with which she wrestled with the Shadow. I groaned in anguish at the pitiable spectacle. I would have soothed—I would have reasoned; but, in the intensity of her wild desire for life,—for life—*but* for life—solace and reason were alike the uttermost of folly. Yet not until the last instance, amid the most convulsive writhings of her fierce spirit, was shaken the external placidity of her demeanor. Her voice grew more gentle—grew more low—yet I would not wish to dwell upon the wild meaning of the quietly uttered words. My brain reeled as I hearkened entranced, to a melody more than mortal—to assumptions and aspirations which mortality had never before known.

That she loved me I should not have doubted; and I might have been easily aware that, in a bosom such as hers, love would have reigned no ordinary passion. But in death only, was I fully impressed with the strength of her affection. For long hours, detaining my hand, would she pour out before me the overflowing of a heart whose more than passionate devotion amounted to idolatry. How had I deserved to be so blessed by such confessions?—how had I deserved to be so cursed with the removal of my beloved in the hour of her making them? But upon this subject I cannot bear to dilate. Let me say only, that in Ligeia's more than womanly abandonment to a love, alas! all unmerited, all unworthily bestowed, I at length recognized the principle of her longing with so wildly earnest a desire for the life which was now fleeing so rapidly away. It is this wild longing—it is this eager vehemence of desire for life—*but* for life—that I have no power to portray—no utterance capable of expressing.

At high noon of the night in which she departed, beckoning me,

2. The angel of death.

peremptorily, to her side, she bade me repeat certain verses composed by herself not many days before. I obeyed her.—They were these:[3]

> Lo! 'tis a gala night
>   Within the lonesome latter years!
> An angel throng, bewinged, bedight
>   In veils, and drowned in tears,
> Sit in a theatre, to see
>   A play of hopes and fears,
> While the orchestra breathes fitfully
>   The music of the spheres.
>
> Mimes, in the form of God on high,
>   Mutter and mumble low,
> And hither and thither fly—
>   Mere puppets they, who come and go
> At bidding of vast formless things
>   That shift the scenery to and fro,
> Flapping from out their Condor wings
>   Invisible Wo!
>
> That motley drama!—oh, be sure
>   It shall not be forgot!
> With its Phantom chased forevermore,
>   By a crowd that seize it not,
> Through a circle that ever returneth in
>   To the self-same spot,
> And much of Madness and more of Sin,
>   And Horror the soul of the plot.
>
> But see, amid the mimic rout,
>   A crawling shape intrude!
> A blood-red thing that writhes from out
>   The scenic solitude!
> It writhes!—it writhes! with mortal pangs
>   The mimes become its food,
> And the seraphs sob at vermin fangs
>   In human gore imbued.
>
> Out—out are the lights—out all!
>   And over reach quivering form,
> The curtain, a funeral pall,
>   Comes down with the rush of a storm,
> And the angels, all pallid and wan,
>   Uprising, unveiling, affirm
> That the play is the tragedy, "Man,"
>   And its hero the Conqueror Worm.

3. This poem was published separately as "The Conqueror Worm" in *Graham's Magazine* for January, 1843; it was first incorporated in "Ligeia" when that story was printed in the *Broadway Journal* for September 27, 1845.

"O God!" half shrieked Ligeia, leaping to her feet and extending her arms aloft with a spasmodic movement, as I made an end of these lines—"O God! O Divine Father!—shall these things be un-deviatingly so?—shall this Conqueror be not once conquered? Are we not part and parcel in Thee? Who—who knoweth the mysteries of the will with its vigor? Man doth not yield him to the angels, *nor unto death utterly*, save only through the weakness of his feeble will."

And now, as if exhausted with emotion, she suffered her white arms to fall, and returned solemnly to her bed of Death. And as she breathed her last sighs, there came mingled with them a low mur-mur from her lips. I bent to them my ear and distinguished, again, the concluding words of the passage in Glanvill—"*Man doth not yield him to the angels, nor unto death utterly, save only through the weakness of his feeble will.*"

She died;—and I, crushed into the very dust with sorrow, could no longer endure the lonely desolation of my dwelling in the dim and decaying city by the Rhine. I had no lack of what the world calls wealth. Ligeia had brought me far more, very far more than or-dinarily falls to the lot of mortals. After a few months, therefore, of weary and aimless wandering, I purchased, and put in some re-pair, an abbey, which I shall not name, in one of the wildest and least frequented portions of fair England. The gloomy and dreary grandeur of the building, the almost savage aspect of the domain, the many melancholy and time-honored memories connected with both, had much in unison with the feelings of utter abandonment which had driven me into that remote and unsocial region of the country. Yet although the external abbey, with its verdant decay hanging about it, suffered but little alteration, I gave way, with a child-like perversity, and perchance with a faint hope of alleviating my sorrows, to a display of more than regal magnificence within.— For such follies, even in childhood, I had imbibed a taste and now they came back to me as if in the dotage of grief. Alas, I feel how much even of incipient madness might have been discovered in the gorgeous and fantastic draperies, in the solemn carvings of Egypt, in the wild cornices and furniture, in the Bedlam patterns of the carpets of tufted gold! I had become a bounden slave in the tram-mels of opium, and my labors and my orders had taken a coloring from my dreams. But these absurdities I must not pause to detail. Let me speak only of that one chamber, ever accursed, whither in a moment of mental alienation, I led from the altar as my bride— as the successor of the unforgotten Ligeia—the fair-haired and blue-eyed Lady Rowena Trevanion, of Tremaine.

There is no individual portion of the architecture and decoration of that bridal chamber which is not now visibly before me. Where were the souls of the haughty family of the bride, when, through thirst of gold, they permitted to pass the threshold of an apartment so bedecked, a maiden and a daughter so beloved? I have said that I minutely remember the details of the chamber—yet I am sadly forgetful on topics of deep moment—and here there was no system, no keeping, in the fantastic display, to take hold upon the memory. The room lay in a high turret of the castellated abbey, was pentagonal in shape, and of capacious size. Occupying the whole southern face of the pentagon was the sole window—an immense sheet of unbroken glass from Venice—a single pane, and tinted of a leaden hue, so that the rays of either the sun or moon, passing through it, fell with a ghastly lustre on the objects within. Over the upper portion of this huge window, extended the trellice-work of an aged vine, which clambered up the massy walls of the turret. The ceiling, of gloomy-looking oak, was excessively lofty, vaulted, and elaborately fretted with the wildest and most grotesque specimens of a semi-Gothic, semi-Druidical device. From out the most central recess of this melancholy vaulting, depended, by a single chain of gold with long links, a huge censer of the same metal, Saracenic in pattern, and with many perforations so contrived that there writhed in and out of them, as if endued with a serpent vitality, a continual succession of parti-colored fires.

Some few ottomans and golden candelabra, of Eastern figure, were in various stations about—and there was the couch, too—the bridal couch—of an Indian model, and low, and sculptured of solid ebony, with a pall-like canopy above. In each of the angles of the chamber stood on end a gigantic sarcophagus of black granite, from the tombs of the kings over against Luxor,[4] with their aged lids full of immemorial sculpture. But in the draping of the apartment lay, alas! the chief phantasy of all. The lofty walls, gigantic in height—even unproportionably so—were hung from summit to foot, in vast folds, with a heavy and massive-looking tapestry—tapestry of a material which was found alike as a carpet on the floor, as a covering for the ottomans and the ebony bed, as a canopy for the bed, and as the gorgeous volutes of the curtains which partially shaded the window. The material was the richest cloth of gold. It was spotted all over, at irregular intervals, with arabesque figures, about a foot in diameter, and wrought upon the cloth in patterns of the most jetty black. But these figures partook of the true character of the arabesque only when regarded from a single point of view. By a contrivance now common, and indeed traceable to a very remote period of antiquity, they were made changeable in aspect. To one entering the room, they bore the appearance of simple monstrosities; but upon a farther advance, this appearance gradually departed; and step

4. An Egyptian town on the Nile near the site of the ancient Thebes.

by step, as the visitor moved his station in the chamber, he saw himself surrounded by an endless succession of the ghastly forms which belong to the superstition of the Norman, or arise in the guilty slumbers of the monk. The phantasmagoric effect was vastly heightened by the artificial introduction of a strong continual current of wind behind the draperies—giving a hideous and uneasy animation to the whole.

In halls such as these—in a bridal chamber such as this—I passed, with the Lady of Tremaine, the unhallowed hours of the first month of our marriage—passed them with but little disquietude. That my wife dreaded the fierce moodiness of my temper—that she shunned me and loved me but little—I could not help perceiving; but it gave me rather pleasure than otherwise. I loathed her with a hatred belonging more to demon than to man. My memory flew back (oh, with what intensity of regret!) to Ligeia, the beloved, the august, the beautiful, the entombed. I revelled in recollections of her purity, of her wisdom, of her lofty, her ethereal nature, of her passionate, her idolatrous love. Now, then, did my spirit fully and freely burn with more than all the fires of her own. In the excitement of my opium dreams (for I was habitually fettered in the shackles of the drug) I would call aloud upon her name, during the silence of the night, or among the sheltered recesses of the glens by day, as if, through the wild eagerness, the solemn passion, the consuming ardor of my longing for the departed, I could restore her to the pathway she had abandoned—ah, *could* it be forever?—upon the earth.

About the commencement of the second month of the marriage, the Lady Rowena was attacked with sudden illness, from which her recovery was slow. The fever which consumed her rendered her nights uneasy; and in her perturbed state of half-slumber, she spoke of sounds, and of motions, in and about the chamber of the turret, which I concluded had no origin save in the distemper of her fancy, or perhaps in the phantasmagoric influence of the chamber itself. She became at length convalescent—finally well. Yet but a brief period elapsed, ere a second more violent disorder again threw her upon a bed of suffering; and from this attack her frame, at all times feeble, never altogether recovered. Her illnesses were, after this epoch, of alarming character, and of more alarming recurrence, defying alike the knowledge and the great exertions of her physicians. With the increase of the chronic disease which had thus, apparently, taken too sure hold upon her constitution to be eradicated by human means, I could not fail to observe a similar increase in the nervous irritation of her temperament, and in her excitability by trivial causes of fear. She spoke again, and now more frequently and pertinaciously, of the sounds—of the slight sounds—

and of the unusual motions among the tapestries, to which she had formerly alluded.

One night, near the closing in of September, she pressed this distressing subject with more than usual emphasis upon my attention. She had just awakened from an unquiet slumber, and I had been watching, with feelings half of anxiety, half of a vague terror, the workings of her emaciated countenance. I sat by the side of her ebony bed, upon one of the ottomans of India. She partly arose, and spoke, in an earnest low whisper, of sounds which she *then* heard, but which I could not hear—of motions which she *then* saw, but which I could not perceive. The wind was rushing hurriedly behind the tapestries, and I wished to show her (what, let me confess it, I could not *all* believe) that those almost inarticulate breathings, of those very gentle variations of the figures upon the wall, were but the natural effects of that customary rushing of the wind. But a deadly pallor, overspreading her face, had proved to me that my exertions to reassure her would be fruitless. She appeared to be fainting, and no attendants were within call. I remembered where was deposited a decanter of light wine which had been ordered by her physicians, and hastened across the chamber to procure it. But, as I stepped beneath the light of the censer, two circumstances of a startling nature attracted my attention. I had felt that some palpable although invisible object had passed lightly by my person; and I saw that there lay upon the golden carpet, in the very middle of the rich lustre thrown from the censer, a shadow—a faint, indefinite shadow of angelic aspect—such as might be fancied for the shadow of a shade. But I was wild with the excitement of an immoderate dose of opium, and heeded these things but little, nor spoke of them to Rowena. Having found the wine, I recrossed the chamber, and poured out a goblet-ful, which I held to the lips of the fainting lady. She had now partially recovered, however, and took the vessel herself, while I sank upon an ottoman near me, with my eyes fastened upon her person. It was then that I became distinctly aware of a gentle foot-fall upon the carpet, and near the couch; and in a second thereafter, as Rowena was in the act of raising the wine to her lips, I saw, or may have dreamed that I saw, fall within the goblet, as if from some invisible spring in the atmosphere of the room, three or four large drops of a brilliant and ruby colored fluid. If this I saw—not so Rowena. She swallowed the wine unhesitatingly, and I forbore to speak to her of a circumstance which must, after all, I considered, have been but the suggestion of a vivid imagination, rendered morbidly active by the terror of the lady, by the opium, and by the hour.

Yet I cannot conceal it from my own perception that, immediately subsequent to the fall of the ruby-drops, a rapid change for

the worse took place in the disorder of my wife; so that, on the third
subsequent night, the hands of her menials prepared her for the
tomb, and on the fourth, I sat alone, with her shrouded body, in
that fantastic chamber which had received her as my bride.—Wild
visions, opium-engendered, flitted, shadow-like, before me. I gazed
with unquiet eye upon the sarcophagi in the angles of the room,
upon the varying figures of the drapery, and upon the writhing of
the parti-colored fires in the censer overhead. My eyes then fell, as
I called to mind the circumstances of a former night, to the spot
beneath the glare of the censer where I had seen the faint traces
of the shadow. It was there, however, no longer; and breathing with
greater freedom, I turned my glances to the pallid and rigid figure
upon the bed. Then rushed upon me a thousand memories of Ligeia
—and then came back upon my heart, with the turbulent violence
of a flood, the whole of that unutterable wo with which I had regarded *her* thus enshrouded. The night waned; and still, with a
bosom full of bitter thoughts of the one only and supremely beloved, I remained gazing upon the body of Rowena.

It might have been midnight, or perhaps earlier, or later, for I
had taken no note of time, when a sob, low, gentle, but very distinct, startled me from my revery.—I *felt* that it came from the bed
of ebony—the bed of death. I listened in an agony of superstitious
terror—but there was no repetition of the sound. I strained my
vision to detect any motion in the corpse—but there was not the
slightest perceptible. Yet I could not have been deceived. I *had*
heard the noise, however faint, and my soul was awakened within
me. I resolutely and perseveringly kept my attention riveted upon
the body. Many minutes elapsed before any circumstance occurred
tending to throw light upon the mystery. At length it became evident that a slight, a very feeble, and barely noticeable tinge of color
had flushed up within the cheeks, and along the sunken small veins
of the eyelids. Through a species of unutterable horror and awe, for
which the language of mortality has no sufficiently energetic expression, I felt my heart cease to beat, my limbs grow rigid where I sat.
Yet a sense of duty finally operated to restore my self-possession. I
could no longer doubt that we had been precipitate in our preparations—that Rowena still lived. It was necessary that some immediate exertion be made; yet the turret was altogether apart from the
portion of the abbey tenanted by the servants—there were none
within call—I had no means of summoning them to my aid without leaving the room for many minutes—and this I could not venture to do. I therefore struggled alone in my endeavors to call back
the spirit still hovering. In a short period it was certain, however,
that a relapse had taken place; the color disappeared from both
eyelid and cheek, leaving a wanness even more than that of marble;

the lips became doubly shrivelled and pinched up in the ghastly expression of death; a repulsive clamminess and coldness overspread rapidly the surface of the body; and all the usual rigorous stiffness immediately supervened. I fell back with a shudder upon the couch from which I had been so startlingly aroused, and again gave myself up to passionate waking visions of Ligeia.

An hour thus elapsed when (could it be possible?) I was a second time aware of some vague sound issuing from the region of the bed. I listened—in extremity of horror. The sound came again—it was a sigh. Rushing to the corpse, I saw—distinctly saw—a tremor upon the lips. In a minute afterward they relaxed, disclosing a bright line of the pearly teeth. Amazement now struggled in my bosom with the profound awe which had hitherto reigned there alone. I felt that my vision grew dim, that my reason wandered; and it was only by a violent effort that I at length succeeded in nerving myself to the task which duty thus once more had pointed out. There was now a partial glow upon the forehead and upon the cheek and throat; a perceptible warmth pervaded the whole frame; there was even a slight pulsation at the heart. The lady *lived*; and with redoubled ardor I betook myself to the task of restoration. I chafed and bathed the temples and the hands, and used every exertion which experience, and no little medical reading, could suggest. But in vain. Suddenly, the color fled, the pulsation ceased, the lips resumed the expression of the dead, and, in an instant afterward, the whole body took upon itself the icy chilliness, the livid hue, the intense rigidity, the sunken outline, and all the loathsome peculiarities of that which has been, for many days, a tenant of the tomb.

And again I sunk into visions of Ligeia—and again (what marvel that I shudder while I write?) *again* there reached my ears a low sob from the region of the ebony bed. But why shall I minutely detail the unspeakable horrors of that night? Why shall I pause to relate how, time after time, until near the period of the gray dawn, this hideous drama of revivification was repeated; how each terrific relapse was only into a sterner and apparently more irredeemable death; how each agony wore the aspect of a struggle with some invisible foe; and how each struggle was succeeded by I know not what of wild change in the personal appearance of the corpse? Let me hurry to a conclusion.

The greater part of the fearful night had worn away, and she who had been dead, once again stirred—and now more vigorously than hitherto, although arousing from a dissolution more appalling in its utter hopelessness than any. I had long ceased to struggle or to move, and remained sitting rigidly upon the ottoman, a helpless prey to a whirl of violent emotions, of which extreme awe was perhaps the least terrible, the least consuming. The corpse, I repeat, stirred, and now more vigorously than before. The hues of life flushed up with unwonted energy into the countenance—the limbs relaxed—and, save that the eyelids were yet pressed heavily together, and that the bandages and draperies of the grave still imparted their charnel character to the figure, I might have dreamed that Rowena had indeed shaken off, utterly, the fetters of Death. But if this idea was not, even then, altogether adopted, I could at least doubt no longer, when, arising from the bed, tottering, with feeble steps, with closed eyes, and with the manner of one bewildered in a dream, the thing that was enshrouded advanced boldly and palpably into the middle of the apartment.

I trembled not—I stirred not—for a crowd of unutterable fancies connected with the air, the stature, the demeanor of the figure, rushing hurriedly through my brain, had paralyzed—had chilled me into stone. I stirred not—but gazed upon the apparition. There was a mad disorder in my thoughts—a tumult unappeasable. Could it, indeed, be the *living* Rowena who confronted me? Could it indeed be Rowena *at all*—the fair-haired, the blue-eyed Lady Rowena Trevanion of Tremaine? Why, *why* should I doubt it? The bandage lay heavily about the mouth—but then might it not be the mouth of the breathing Lady of Tremaine? And the cheeks—there were the roses as in her noon of life—yes, these might indeed be the fair cheeks of the living Lady of Tremaine. And the chin, with its dimples, as in health, might it not be hers?—but *had she then grown taller since her malady?* What inexpressible madness seized me with that thought? One bound, and I had reached her feet! Shrinking from my touch, she let fall from her head, unloosened, the ghastly cerements which had confined it, and there streamed forth, into the rushing atmosphere of the chamber, huge masses of long and dishevelled hair; *it was blacker than the raven wings of the midnight!* And now slowly opened *the eyes* of the figure which stood before me. "Here then, at least," I shrieked aloud, "can I never—can I never be mistaken—these are the full, and the black, and the wild eyes—of my lost love—of the lady—of the LADY LIGEIA!"

1838, 1845

The Fall of the House of Usher[5]

Son cœur est un luth suspendu;
Sitôt qu'on le touche il résonne.
—DE BÉRANGER[6]

During the whole of a dull, dark, and soundless day in the autumn of the year, when the clouds hung oppressively low in the heavens, I had been passing alone, on horseback, through a singularly dreary tract of country; and at length found myself, as the shades of the evening drew on, within view of the melancholy House of Usher. I know not how it was—but, with the first glimpse of the building, a sense of insufferable gloom pervaded my spirit. I say insufferable; for the feeling was unrelieved by any of that half-pleasurable, because poetic, sentiment, with which the mind usually receives even the sternest natural images of the desolate or terrible. I looked upon the scene before me—upon the mere house, and the simple landscape features of the domain—upon the bleak walls—upon the vacant eye-like windows—upon a few rank sedges —and upon a few white trunks of decayed trees—with an utter depression of soul which I can compare to no earthly sensation more properly than to the after-dream of the reveller upon opium —the bitter lapse into every-day life—the hideous dropping off of the veil. There was an iciness, a sinking, a sickening of the heart —an unredeemed dreariness of thought which no goading of the imagination could torture into aught of the sublime. What was it —I paused to think—what was it that so unnerved me in the contemplation of the House of Usher? It was a mystery all insoluble; nor could I grapple with the shadowy fancies that crowded upon me as I pondered. I was forced to fall back upon the unsatisfactory conclusion, that while, beyond doubt, there *are* combinations of very simple natural objects which have the power of thus affecting us, still the analysis of this power lies among considerations beyond our depth. It was possible, I reflected, that a mere different arrangement of the particulars of the scene, of the details of the picture, would be sufficient to modify, or perhaps to annihilate its capacity for sorrowful impression; and, acting upon this idea, I reined my horse to the precipitous brink of a black and lurid tarn that lay in unruffled lustre by the dwelling, and gazed down—but with a shudder even more thrilling than before—upon the remodelled and inverted images of the gray sedge, and the ghastly tree-stems, and the vacant and eye-like windows.

Nevertheless, in this mansion of gloom I now proposed to myself

5. The text is that of *Tales* (1845).
6. Pierre Jean de Béranger (1780–1857). The lines, adapted slightly from "Le Refus" (1830–31), may be translated: "His heart is a suspended lute; when one touches it, it resounds" (Poe changed "Mon cœur" to "Son cœur"). Cf. "Israfel," line 2.

a sojourn of some weeks. Its proprietor, Roderick Usher, had been one of my boon companions in boyhood; but many years had elapsed since our last meeting. A letter, however, had lately reached me in a distant part of the country—a letter from him—which, in its wildly importunate nature, had admitted of no other than a personal reply. The MS. gave evidence of nervous agitation. The writer spoke of acute bodily illness—of a mental disorder which oppressed him—and of an earnest desire to see me, as his best, and indeed his only personal friend, with a view of attempting, by the cheerfulness of my society, some alleviation of his malady. It was the manner in which all this, and much more, was said—it was the apparent *heart* that went with his request—which allowed me no room for hesitation; and I accordingly obeyed forthwith what I still considered a very singular summons.

Although, as boys, we had been even intimate associates, yet I really knew little of my friend. His reserve had been always excessive and habitual. I was aware, however, that his very ancient family had been noted, time out of mind, for a peculiar sensibility of temperament, displaying itself, through long ages, in many works of exalted art, and manifested, of late, in repeated deeds of munificent yet unobtrusive charity, as well as in a passionate devotion to the intricacies, perhaps even more than to the orthodox and easily recognizable beauties, of musical science. I had learned, too, the very remarkable fact, that the stem of the Usher race, all time-honored as it was, had put forth, at no period, any enduring branch; in other words, that the entire family lay in the direct line of descent, and had always, with very trifling and very temporary variation, so lain. It was this deficiency, I considered, while running over in thought the perfect keeping of the character of the premises with the accredited character of the people, and while speculating upon the possible influence which the one, in the long lapse of centuries, might have exercised upon the other—it was this deficiency, perhaps, of collateral issue, and the consequent undeviating transmission, from sire to son, of the patrimony with the name, which had, at length, so identified the two as to merge the original title of the estate in the quaint and equivocal appellation of the "House of Usher"—an appellation which seemed to include, in the minds of the peasantry who used it, both the family and the family mansion.

I have said that the sole effect of my somewhat childish experiment—that of looking down within the tarn—had been to deepen the first singular impression. There can be no doubt that the consciousness of the rapid increase of my superstition—for why should I not so term it?—served mainly to accelerate the increase itself. Such, I have long known, is the paradoxical law of all sentiments having terror as a basis. And it might have been for this reason only, that, when I again uplifted my eyes to the house itself, from its image in the pool, there grew in my mind a strange fancy—a fancy so ridiculous, indeed, that I but mention it to show the vivid force of the sensations which oppressed me. I had so worked upon my imagination as really to believe that about the whole mansion and domain there hung an atmosphere peculiar to themselves and their immediate vicinity—an atmosphere which had no affinity with the air of heaven, but which had reeked up from the decayed trees, and the gray wall, and the silent tarn—a pestilent and mystic vapor, dull, sluggish, faintly discernible, and leaden-hued.

Shaking off from my spirit what *must* have been a dream, I scanned more narrowly the real aspect of the building. Its principal feature seemed to be that of an excessive antiquity. The discoloration of ages had been great. Minute fungi overspread the whole exterior, hanging in a fine tangled web-work from the eaves. Yet all this was apart from any extraordinary dilapidation. No portion of the masonry had fallen; and there appeared to be a wild inconsistency between its still perfect adaptation of parts, and the crumbling condition of the individual stones. In this there was much that reminded me of the specious totality of old wood-work which has rotted for long years in some neglected vault, with no disturbance from the breath of the external air. Beyond this indication of extensive decay, however, the fabric gave little token of instability. Perhaps the eye of a scrutinizing observer might have discovered a barely perceptible fissure, which, extending from the roof of the building in front, made its way down the wall in a zigzag direction, until it became lost in the sullen waters of the tarn.

Noticing these things, I rode over a short causeway to the house. A servant in waiting took my horse, and I entered the Gothic archway of the hall. A valet, of stealthy step, thence conducted me, in silence, through many dark and intricate passages in my progress to the *studio* of his master. Much that I encountered on the way contributed, I know not how, to heighten the vague sentiments of which I have already spoken. While the objects around me—while the carvings of the ceilings, the sombre tapestries of the walls, the ebon blackness of the floors, and the phantasmagoric armorial trophies which rattled as I strode, were but matters to which, or to such as which, I had been accustomed from my infancy—while I hesitated not to acknowledge how familiar was all this—I still wondered to find how unfamiliar were the fancies which ordinary images were stirring up. On one of the staircases, I met the physician of the family. His countenance, I thought, wore a mingled expression of low cunning and perplexity. He accosted me with trepidation and passed on. The valet now threw open a door and ushered me into the presence of his master.

The room in which I found myself was very large and lofty. The windows were long, narrow, and pointed, and at so vast a distance from the black oaken floor as to be altogether inaccessible from within. Feeble gleams of encrimsoned light made their way through the trellised panes, and served to render sufficiently distinct the more prominent objects around; the eye, however, struggled in vain to reach the remoter angles of the chamber, or the recesses of the vaulted and fretted ceiling. Dark draperies hung upon the walls. The general furniture was profuse, comfortless, antique, and tattered. Many books and musical instruments lay scattered about, but failed to give any vitality to the scene. I felt that I breathed an atmosphere of sorrow. An air of stern, deep, and irredeemable gloom hung over and pervaded all.

Upon my entrance, Usher arose from a sofa on which he had been lying at full length, and greeted me with a vivacious warmth which had much in it, I at first thought, of an overdone cordiality—of the constrained effort of the *ennuyé* man of the world. A glance, however, at his countenance convinced me of his perfect sincerity. We sat down; and for some moments, while he spoke not, I gazed upon him with a feeling half of pity, half of awe. Surely, man had never before so terribly altered, in so brief a period, as had Roderick Usher! It was with difficulty that I could bring myself to admit the identity of the wan being before me with the companion of my early boyhood. Yet the character of his face had been at all times remarkable. A cadaverousness of complexion; an eye large, liquid, and luminous beyond comparison; lips somewhat thin and very pallid, but of a surpassingly beautiful curve; a nose of a delicate Hebrew model, but with a breadth of nostril unusual in similar formations; a finely moulded chin, speaking, in its want of prominence, of a want of moral energy; hair of a more than web-like softness and tenuity; these features, with an inordinate expansion above the regions of the temple, made up altogether a countenance not easily to be forgotten. And now in the mere exaggeration of the prevailing character of these features, and of the expression they were wont to convey, lay so much of change that I doubted to whom I spoke. The now ghastly pallor of the skin, and the now miraculous lustre of the eye, above all things startled and even awed me. The silken hair, too, had been suffered to grow all unheeded, and as, in its wild gossamer texture, it floated rather than fell about the face, I could not, even with effort, connect its Arabesque expression with any idea of simple humanity.

In the manner of my friend I was at once struck with an incoherence—an inconsistency; and I soon found this to arise from a series

of feeble and futile struggles to overcome an habitual trepidancy—
an excessive nervous agitation. For something of this nature I had
indeed been prepared, no less by his letter, than by reminiscences of
certain boyish traits, and by conclusions deduced from his peculiar
physical conformation and temperament. His action was alternately vivacious and sullen. His voice varied rapidly from a tremulous indecision (when the animal spirits seemed utterly in abeyance)
to that species of energetic concision—that abrupt, weighty, unhurried, and hollow-sounding enunciation—that leaden, self-balanced and perfectly modulated guttural utterance, which may be
observed in the lost drunkard, or the irreclaimable eater of opium,
during the periods of his most intense excitement.

It was thus that he spoke of the object of my visit, of his earnest
desire to see me, and of the solace he expected me to afford him.
He entered, at some length, into what he conceived to be the nature of his malady. It was, he said, a constitutional and a family
evil, and one for which he despaired to find a remedy—a mere nervous affection, he immediately added, which would undoubtedly
soon pass off. It displayed itself in a host of unnatural sensations.
Some of these, as he detailed them, interested and bewildered me;
although, perhaps, the terms and the general manner of their narration had their weight. He suffered much from a morbid acuteness
of the senses; the most insipid food was alone endurable; he could
wear only garments of certain texture; the odors of all flowers were
oppressive; his eyes were tortured by even a faint light; and there
were but peculiar sounds, and these from stringed instruments,
which did not inspire him with horror.

To an anomalous species of terror I found him a bounden slave.
"I shall perish," said he, "I *must* perish in this deplorable folly.
Thus, thus, and not otherwise, shall I be lost. I dread the events
of the future, not in themselves, but in their results. I shudder at
the thought of any, even the most trivial, incident, which may
operate upon this intolerable agitation of soul. I have, indeed, no
abhorrence of danger, except in its absolute effect—in terror. In
this unnerved—in this pitiable, condition—I feel that the period
will sooner or later arrive when I must abandon life and reason
together, in some struggle with the grim phantasm, Fear."

I learned, moreover, at intervals, and through broken and equivocal hints, another singular feature of his mental condition. He was
enchained by certain superstitious impressions in regard to the
dwelling which he tenanted, and whence, for many years, he had
never ventured forth—in regard to an influence whose supposititious force was conveyed in terms too shadowy here to be re-stated—
an influence which some peculiarities in the mere form and substance of his family mansion had, by dint of long sufferance, he said,

obtained over his spirit—an effect which the *physique* of the gray walls and turrets, and of the dim tarn into which they all looked down, had, at length, brought about upon the *morale* of his existence.

He admitted, however, although with hesitation, that much of the peculiar gloom which thus afflicted him could be traced to a more natural and far more palpable origin—to the severe and long-continued illness—indeed to the evidently approaching dissolution—of a tenderly beloved sister—his sole companion for long years—his last and only relative on earth. "Her decease," he said, with a bitterness which I can never forget, "would leave him (him the hopeless and the frail) the last of the ancient race of the Ushers." While he spoke, the lady Madeline (for so was she called) passed through a remote portion of the apartment, and, without having noticed my presence, disappeared. I regarded her with an utter astonishment not unmingled with dread—and yet I found it impossible to account for such feelings. A sensation of stupor oppressed me, as my eyes followed her retreating steps. When a door, at length, closed upon her, my glance sought instinctively and eagerly the countenance of the brother—but he had buried his face in his hands, and I could only perceive that a far more than ordinary wanness had overspread the emaciated fingers through which trickled many passionate tears.

The disease of the lady Madeline had long baffled the skill of her physicians. A settled apathy, a gradual wasting away of the person, and frequent although transient affections of a partially cataleptical character were the unusual diagnosis. Hitherto she had steadily borne up against the pressure of her malady, and had not betaken herself finally to bed; but on the closing in of the evening of my arrival at the house, she succumbed (as her brother told me at night with inexpressible agitation) to the prostrating power of the destroyer; and I learned that the glimpse I had obtained of her person would thus probably be the last I should obtain—that the lady, at least while living, would be seen by me no more.

For several days ensuing, her name was unmentioned by either Usher or myself; and during this period I was busied in earnest endeavors to alleviate the melancholy of my friend. We painted and read together, or I listened, as if in a dream, to the wild improvisations of his speaking guitar. And thus, as a closer and still closer intimacy admitted me more unreservedly into the recesses of his spirit, the more bitterly did I perceive the futility of all attempt at cheering a mind from which darkness, as if an inherent positive quality, poured forth upon all objects of the moral and physical universe, in one unceasing radiation of gloom.

I shall ever bear about me a memory of the many solemn hours

I thus spent alone with the master of the House of Usher. Yet I should fail in any attempt to convey an idea of the exact character of the studies, or of the occupations, in which he involved me, or led me the way. An excited and highly distempered ideality threw a sulphureous lustre over all. His long improvised dirges will ring forever in my ears. Among other things, I hold painfully in mind a certain singular perversion and amplification of the wild air of the last waltz of Von Weber.[7] From the paintings over which his elaborate fancy brooded, and which grew, touch by touch, into vaguenesses at which I shuddered the more thrillingly, because I shuddered knowing not why;—from these paintings (vivid as their images now are before me) I would in vain endeavor to educe more than a small portion which should lie within the compass of merely written words. By the utter simplicity, by the nakedness of his designs, he arrested and overawed attention. If ever mortal painted an idea, that mortal was Roderick Usher. For me at least, in the circumstances then surrounding me, there arose out of the pure abstractions which the hypochondriac contrived to throw upon his canvas, an intensity of intolerable awe, no shadow of which felt I ever yet in the contemplation of the certainly glowing yet too concrete reveries of Fuseli.[8]

One of the phantasmagoric conceptions of my friend, partaking not so rigidly of the spirit of abstraction, may be shadowed forth, although feebly, in words. A small picture presented the interior of an immensely long and rectangular vault or tunnel, with low walls, smooth, white, and without interruption or device. Certain accessory points of the design served well to convey the idea that this excavation lay at an exceeding depth below the surface of the earth. No outlet was observed in any portion of its vast extent, and no torch or other artificial source of light was discernible; yet a flood of intense rays rolled throughout, and bathed the whole in a ghastly and inappropriate splendor.

I have just spoken of that morbid condition of the auditory nerve which rendered all music intolerable to the sufferer, with the exception of certain effects of stringed instruments. It was, perhaps, the narrow limits to which he thus confined himself upon the guitar which gave birth, in great measure, to the fantastic character of his performances. But the fervid *facility* of his *impromptus* could not be so accounted for. They must have been, and were, in the notes, as well as in the words of his wild fantasias (for he not unfrequently accompanied himself with rhymed verbal improvisa-

7. Poe probably refers to No. 5 of *Danses brillantes pour le pianoforte,* by Karl Gottlieb Reissiger (1798–1859), which is called "Weber's Last Waltz."
8. Henry Fuseli, born Johann Heinrich Füssli (1742–1825), was a Swiss painter and a friend of William Blake; he lived the latter half of his life in London. Some of his paintings attempt to suggest the sublime through terror. His most famous painting (1781) was called "The Nightmare."

tions), the result of that intense mental collectedness and concentration to which I have previously alluded as observable only in particular moments of the highest artificial excitement. The words of one of these rhapsodies I have easily remembered. I was, perhaps, the more forcibly impressed with it as he gave it, because, in the under or mystic current of its meaning, I fancied that I perceived, and for the first time, a full consciousness on the part of Usher of the tottering of his lofty reason upon her throne. The verses, which were entitled "The Haunted Palace,"[9] ran very nearly, if not accurately, thus:—

I.

In the greenest of our valleys,
    By good angels tenanted,
Once a fair and stately palace—
    Radiant palace—reared its head.
In the monarch Thought's dominion—
    It stood there!
Never seraph spread a pinion
    Over fabric half so fair.

II.

Banners yellow, glorious, golden,
    On its roof did float and flow
(This—all this—was in the olden
    Time long ago);
And every gentle air that dallied,
    In that sweet day,
Along the ramparts plumed and pallid,
    A winged odor went away.

III.

Wanderers in that happy valley
    Through two luminous windows saw
Spirits moving musically
    To a lute's well-tunèd law;
Round about a throne, were sitting
    (Porphyrogene![1])
In state his glory well befitting,
    The ruler of the realm was seen.

IV.

And all with pearl and ruby glowing
    Was the fair palace door,
Through which came flowing, flowing, flowing
    And sparkling evermore,
A troop of Echoes whose sweet duty
    Was but to sing,
In voices of surpassing beauty,
    The wit and wisdom of their king.

9. This poem was incorporated in the first publication of the present story, but it had been published separately in the *Baltimore Museum* for April, 1839.
1. "Born to the purple."

v.

But evil things, in robes of sorrow,
    Assailed the monarch's high estate;
(Ah, let us mourn, for never morrow
    Shall dawn upon him, desolate!)
And, round about his home, the glory
    That blushed and bloomed
Is but a dim-remembered story
    Of the old time entombed.

vi.

And travellers now within that valley,
    Through the red-litten windows, see
Vast forms that move fantastically
    To a discordant melody;
While, like a rapid ghastly river,
    Through the pale door,
A hideous throng rush out forever,
    And laugh—but smile no more.

I well remember that suggestions arising from this ballad led us into a train of thought wherein there became manifest an opinion of Usher's which I mention not so much on account of its novelty (for other men[2] have thought thus), as on account of the pertinacity with which he maintained it. This opinion, in its general form, was that of the sentience of all vegetable things. But, in his disordered fancy, the idea had assumed a more daring character, and trespassed, under certain conditions, upon the kingdom of inorganization. I lack words to express the full extent, or the earnest *abandon* of his persuasion. The belief, however, was connected (as I have previously hinted) with the gray stones of the home of his forefathers. The conditions of the sentience had been here, he imagined, fulfilled in the method of collocation of these stones—in the order of their arrangement, as well as in that of the many *fungi* which overspread them, and of the decayed trees which stood around—above all, in the long undisturbed endurance of this arrangement, and in its reduplication in the still waters of the tarn. Its evidence—the evidence of the sentience—was to be seen, he said (and I here started as he spoke) in the gradual yet certain condensation of an atmosphere of their own about the waters and the walls. The result was discoverable, he added, in that silent, yet importunate and terrible influence which for centuries had moulded the destinies of his family, and which made *him* what I now saw him—what he was. Such opinions need no comment, and I will make none.

Our books—the books which, for years, had formed no small

2. "Watson, Dr. Percival, Spallanzani, and especially the Bishop of Llandaff. —See 'Chemical Essays,' vol. v" [Poe's note].

portion of the mental existence of the invalid—were, as might be supposed, in strict keeping with this character of phantasm. We pored together over such works as the Ververt et Chartreuse of Gresset; the Belphegor of Machiavelli; the Heaven and Hell of Swedenborg; the Subterranean Voyage of Nicholas Klimm of Holberg; the Chiromancy of Robert Flud, of Jean D'Indaginé, and of De la Chambre; the Journey into the Blue Distance of Tieck; and the City of the Sun of Campanella. One favorite volume was a small octavo edition of the *Directorium Inquisitorium*, by the Dominican Eymeric de Gironne; and there were passages in Pomponius Mela, about the old African Satyrs and Ægipans, over which Usher would sit dreaming for hours. His chief delight, however, was found in the perusal of an exceedingly rare and curious book in quarto Gothic—the manual of a forgotten church—the *Vigiliæ Mortuorum secundum Chorum Ecclesiæ Maguntinæ*.[3]

I could not help thinking of the wild ritual of this work, and of its probable influence upon the hypochondriac, when, one evening, having informed me abruptly that the lady Madeline was no more, he stated his intention of preserving her corpse for a fortnight (previously to its final interment), in one of the numerous vaults within the main walls of the building. The worldly reason, however, assigned for this singular proceeding, was one which I did not feel at liberty to dispute. The brother had been led to his resolution (so he told me) by consideration of the unusual character of the malady of the deceased, of certain obtrusive and eager inquiries on the part of her medical men,[4] and of the remote and exposed situation of the burial-ground of the family. I will not deny that when I called to mind the sinister countenance of the person whom I met upon the staircase, on the day of my arrival at the house, I had no desire to oppose what I regarded as at best but a harmless, and by no means an unnatural, precaution.

At the request of Usher, I personally aided him in the arrangements for the temporary entombment. The body having been encoffined, we two alone bore it to its rest. The vault in which we placed it (and which had been so long unopened that our torches, half smothered in its oppressive atmosphere, gave us little opportunity for investigation) was small, damp, and entirely without

3. Most, but not all, of the books mentioned here reflect Usher's strange and esoteric taste. Gresset's *Vert Vert* and *Chartreuse* are rather frivolous 18th-century anticlerical satires, and Machiavelli's little novel is a satire on marriage. The other works mentioned are concerned with various types of mysticism, romantic marvels, strange worlds, pseudoscience, and medieval terrors. The *Vigiliae Mortuorum secundum Chorum Ecclesiae Maguntinae*

("Watches of the Dead According to the Ritual of the Church at Maguntina") has not hitherto been identified: apparently a 16th-century book, it is listed by J. G. T. Graesse in *Trésor de Livres Rare et Précieux* (Berlin, 1922), VII, 490.

4. Usher feared Madeline's body would be exhumed by physicians for an autopsy in the interests of medical science if she were buried in an open cemetery.

means of admission for light; lying, at great depth, immediately beneath that portion of the building in which was my own sleeping apartment. It had been used, apparently, in remote feudal times, for the worst purposes of a donjon-keep, and, in later days, as a place of deposit for powder, or some other highly combustible substance, as a portion of its floor, and the whole interior of a long archway through which we reached it, were carefully sheathed with copper. The door, of massive iron, had been, also, similarly protected. Its immense weight caused an unusually sharp, grating sound, as it moved upon its hinges.

Having deposited our mournful burden upon tressels within this region of horror, we partially turned aside the yet unscrewed lid of the coffin, and looked upon the face of the tenant. A striking similitude between the brother and sister now first arrested my attention; and Usher, divining, perhaps, my thoughts, murmured out some few words from which I learned that the deceased and himself had been twins, and that sympathies of a scarcely intelligible nature had always existed between them. Our glances, however, rested not long upon the dead—for we could not regard her unawed. The disease which had thus entombed the lady in the maturity of youth, had left, as usual in all maladies of a strictly cataleptical character, the mockery of a faint blush upon the bosom and the face, and that suspiciously lingering smile upon the lip which is so terrible in death. We replaced and screwed down the lid, and, having secured the door of iron, made our way, with toil, into the scarcely less gloomy apartments of the upper portion of the house.

And now, some days of bitter grief having elapsed, an observable change came over the features of the mental disorder of my friend. His ordinary manner had vanished. His ordinary occupations were neglected or forgotten. He roamed from chamber to chamber with hurried, unequal, and objectless step. The pallor of his countenance had assumed, if possible, a more ghastly hue—but the luminousness of his eye had utterly gone out. The once occasional huskiness of his tone was heard no more; and a tremulous quaver, as if of extreme terror, habitually characterized his utterance. There were times, indeed, when I thought his unceasingly agitated mind was laboring with some oppressive secret, to divulge which he struggled for the necessary courage. At times, again, I was obliged to resolve all into the mere inexplicable vagaries of madness, for I beheld him gazing upon vacancy for long hours, in an attitude of the profoundest attention, as if listening to some imaginary sound. It was no wonder that his condition terrified—that it infected me. I felt creeping upon me, by slow yet certain degrees, the wild influences of his own fantastic yet impressive superstitions.

It was, especially, upon retiring to bed late in the night of the seventh or eighth day after the placing of the lady Madeline within the donjon, that I experienced the full power of such feelings. Sleep came not near my couch—while the hours waned and waned away. I struggled to reason off the nervousness which had dominion over me. I endeavored to believe that much, if not all of what I felt, was due to the bewildering influence of the gloomy furniture of the room—of the dark and tattered draperies, which, tortured into motion by the breath of a rising tempest, swayed fitfully to and fro upon the walls, and rustled uneasily about the decorations of the bed. But my efforts were fruitless. An irrepressible tremor gradually pervaded my frame; and, at length, there sat upon my very heart an incubus of utterly causeless alarm. Shaking this off with a gasp and a struggle, I uplifted myself upon the pillows, and, peering earnestly within the intense darkness of the chamber, hearkened—I know not why, except that an instinctive spirit prompted me—to certain low and indefinite sounds which came, through the pauses of the storm, at long intervals, I knew not whence. Overpowered by an intense sentiment of horror, unaccountable yet unendurable, I threw on my clothes with haste (for I felt that I should sleep no more during the night), and endeavored to arouse myself from the pitiable condition into which I had fallen, by pacing rapidly to and fro through the apartment.

I had taken but few turns in this manner, when a light step on an adjoining staircase arrested my attention. I presently recognized it as that of Usher. In an instant afterward he rapped, with a gentle touch, at my door, and entered, bearing a lamp. His countenance was, as usual, cadaverously wan—but, moreover, there was a species of mad hilarity in his eyes—an evidently restrained *hysteria* in his whole demeanor. His air appalled me—but any thing was preferable to the solitude which I had so long endured, and I even welcomed his presence as a relief.

"And you have not seen it?" he said abruptly, after having stared about him for some moments in silence—"you have not then seen it?—but, stay! you shall." Thus speaking, and having carefully shaded his lamp, he hurried to one of the casements, and threw it freely open to the storm.

The impetuous fury of the entering gust nearly lifted us from our feet. It was, indeed, a tempestuous yet sternly beautiful night, and one wildly singular in its terror and its beauty. A whirlwind had apparently collected its force in our vicinity; for there were frequent and violent alterations in the direction of the wind; and the exceeding density of the clouds (which hung so low as to press upon the turrets of the house) did not prevent our perceiving the life-like velocity with which they flew careering from all points against each other, without passing away into the distance. I say that even their exceeding density did not prevent our perceiving this—yet we had no glimpse of the moon or stars—nor was there any flashing forth of the lightning. But the under surfaces of the huge masses of agitated vapor, as well as all terrestrial objects immediately around us, were glowing in the unnatural light of a faintly luminous and distinctly visible gaseous exhalation which hung about and enshrouded the mansion.

"You must not—you shall not behold this!" said I, shudderingly, to Usher, as I led him, with a gentle violence, from the window to a seat. "These appearances, which bewilder you, are merely electrical phenomena not uncommon—or it may be that they have their ghastly origin in the rank miasma of the tarn. Let us close this casement;—the air is chilling and dangerous to your frame. Here is one of your favorite romances. I will read, and you shall listen;—and so we will pass away this terrible night together."

The antique volume which I had taken up was the "Mad Trist" of Sir Launcelot Canning;[5] but I had called it a favorite of Usher's more in sad jest than in earnest; for, in truth, there is little in its uncouth and unimaginative prolixity which could have had interest for the lofty and spiritual ideality of my friend. It was, however, the only book immediately at hand; and I indulged a vague hope that the excitement which now agitated the hypochondriac, might find relief (for the history of mental disorder is full of similar anomalies) even in the extremeness of the folly which I should read. Could I have judged, indeed, by the wild overstrained air of vivacity with which he hearkened, or apparently hearkened, to the words of the tale, I might well have congratulated myself upon the success of my design.

I had arrived at that well-known portion of the story where Ethelred, the hero of the Trist, having sought in vain for peaceable admission into the dwelling of the hermit, proceeds to make good an entrance by force. Here, it will be remembered, the words of the narrative run thus:

"And Ethelred, who was by nature of a doughty heart, and who was now mighty withal, on account of the powerfulness of the wine which he had drunken, waited no longer to hold parley with the hermit, who, in sooth, was of an obstinate and maliceful turn, but, feeling the rain upon his shoulders, and fearing the rising of the tempest, uplifted his mace outright, and, with blows, made quickly room in the plankings of the door for his gauntleted hand; and now pulling therewith sturdily, he so cracked, and ripped, and tore all asunder, that the noise of the dry and hollow-sounding wood

5. This author and book have not been identified; they were probably invented by Poe for this story.

alarummed and reverberated throughout the forest."

At the termination of this sentence I started and, for a moment, paused; for it appeared to me (although I at once concluded that my excited fancy had deceived me)—it appeared to me that, from some very remote portion of the mansion, there came, indistinctly, to my ears, what might have been, in its exact similarity of character, the echo (but a stifled and dull one certainly) of the very cracking and ripping sound which Sir Launcelot had so particularly described. It was, beyond doubt, the coincidence alone which had arrested my attention; for, amid the rattling of the sashes of the casements, and the ordinary commingled noises of the still increasing storm, the sound, in itself, had nothing, surely, which should have interested or disturbed me. I continued the story:

"But the good champion Ethelred, now entering within the door, was sore enraged and amazed to perceive no signal of the maliceful hermit; but, in the stead thereof, a dragon of a scaly and prodigious demeanor, and of a fiery tongue, which sate in guard before a palace of gold, with a floor of silver; and upon the wall there hung a shield of shining brass with this legend enwritten—

> Who entereth herein, a conqueror hath bin;
> Who slayeth the dragon, the shield he shall win;

And Ethelred uplifted his mace, and struck upon the head of the dragon, which fell before him, and gave up his pesty breath, with a shriek so horrid and harsh, and withal so piercing, that Ethelred had fain to close his ears with his hands against the dreadful noise of it, the like whereof was never before heard."

Here again I paused abruptly, and now with a feeling of wild amazement—for there could be no doubt whatever that, in this instance, I did actually hear (although from what direction it proceeded I found it impossible to say) a low and apparently distant, but harsh, protracted, and most unusual screaming or grating sound—the exact counterpart of what my fancy had already conjured up for the dragon's unnatural shriek as described by the romancer.

Oppressed, as I certainly was, upon the occurrence of this second and most extraordinary coincidence, by a thousand conflicting sensations, in which wonder and extreme terror were predominant, I still retained sufficient presence of mind to avoid exciting, by any observation, the sensitive nervousness of my companion. I was by no means certain that he had noticed the sounds in question; although, assuredly, a strange alteration had, during the last few minutes, taken place in his demeanor. From a position fronting my own, he had gradually brought round his chair, so as to sit with his face to the door of the chamber; and thus I could but partially perceive his features, although I saw that his lips trembled as if he were murmuring inaudibly. His head had dropped upon his breast —yet I knew that he was not asleep, from the wide and rigid opening of the eye as I caught a glance of it in profile. The motion of his body, too, was at variance with this idea—for he rocked from side to side with a gentle yet constant and uniform sway. Having rapidly taken notice of all this, I resumed the narrative of Sir Launcelot, which thus proceeded:

"And now, the champion, having escaped from the terrible fury of the dragon, bethinking himself of the brazen shield, and of the breaking up of the enchantment which was upon it, removed the carcass from out of the way before him, and approached valorously over the silver pavement of the castle to where the shield was upon the wall; which in sooth tarried not for his full coming, but fell down at his feet upon the silver floor, with a mighty great and terrible ringing sound."

No sooner had these syllables passed my lips, than—as if a shield of brass had indeed, at the moment, fallen heavily upon a floor of silver—I became aware of a distinct, hollow, metallic, and clangorous, yet apparently muffled, reverberation. Completely unnerved, I leaped to my feet; but the measured rocking movement of Usher was undisturbed. I rushed to the chair in which he sat. His eyes were bent fixedly before him, and throughout his whole countenance there reigned a stony rigidity. But, as I placed my hand upon his shoulder, there came a strong shudder over his whole person; a sickly smile quivered about his lips; and I saw that he spoke in a low, hurried, and gibbering murmur, as if unconscious of my presence. Bending closely over him, I at length drank in the hideous import of his words.

"Now hear it?—yes, I hear it, and *have* heard it. Long—long— long—many minutes, many hours, many days, have I heard it—yet I dared not—oh, pity me, miserable wretch that I am!—I dared not—I *dared* not speak! *We have put her living in the tomb!* Said I not that my senses were acute? I *now* tell you that I heard her feeble first movements in the hollow coffin. I heard them—many, many days ago—yet I dared not—*I dared not speak!* And now— to-night—Ethelred—ha! ha!—the breaking of the hermit's door, and the death-cry of the dragon, and the clangor of the shield— say, rather, the rending of her coffin, and the grating of the iron hinges of her prison, and her struggles within the coppered archway of the vault! Oh! whither shall I fly? Will she not be here anon? Is she not hurrying to upbraid me for my haste? Have I not heard her footstep on the stair? Do I not distinguish that heavy and horrible beating of her heart? Madman!"—here he sprang furiously to his feet, and shrieked out his syllables, as if in the effort he were giving up his soul—"MADMAN! I TELL YOU THAT SHE NOW STANDS WITHOUT THE DOOR!"

As if in the superhuman energy of his utterance there had been found the potency of a spell, the huge antique pannels to which the speaker pointed threw slowly back, upon the instant, their ponderous and ebony jaws. It was the work of the rushing gust—but then without those doors there *did* stand the lofty and enshrouded figure of the lady Madeline of Usher. There was blood upon her white robes, and the evidence of some bitter struggle upon every portion of her emaciated frame. For a moment she remained trembling and reeling to and fro upon the threshold—then, with a low moaning cry, fell heavily inward upon the person of her brother, and in her violent and now final death-agonies, bore him to the floor a corpse, and a victim to the terrors he had anticipated.

From that chamber, and from that mansion, I fled aghast. The storm was still abroad in all its wrath as I found myself crossing the old causeway. Suddenly there shot along the path a wild light, and I turned to see whence a gleam so unusual could have issued; for the vast house and its shadows were alone behind me. The radiance was that of the full, setting, and blood-red moon, which now shone vividly through that once barely discernible fissure, of which I have before spoken as extending from the roof of the building, in a zigzag direction, to the base. While I gazed, this fissure rapidly widened—there came a fierce breath of the whirlwind—the entire orb of the satellite burst at once upon my sight—my brain reeled as I saw the mighty walls rushing asunder—there was a long tumultuous shouting sound like the voice of a thousand waters—and the deep and dank tarn at my feet closed sullenly and silently over the fragments of the "*House of Usher*."

1839, 1845

William Wilson[6]

What say of it? what say [of] CONSCIENCE grim,
That spectre in my path?
CHAMBERLAYNE'S *Pharronida*.[7]

Let me call myself, for the present, William Wilson. The fair page now lying before me need not be sullied with my real appellation. This has been already too much an object for the scorn—for the horror—for the detestation of my race. To the uttermost regions of the globe have not the indignant winds bruited its unparalleled infamy? Oh, outcast of all outcasts most abandoned!—

6. The text is that of the *Broadway Journal*, August 30, 1845.
7. Poe's epigraph is from a source not yet identified; it is not in the *Pharronida*, an epic poem by William Chamberlayne (1619–89).

to the earth art thou not forever dead? to its honors, to its flowers, to its golden aspirations?—and a cloud, dense, dismal, and limitless, does it not hang eternally between thy hopes and heaven?

I would not, if I could, here or to-day, embody a record of my later years of unspeakable misery, and unpardonable crime. This epoch—these later years—took unto themselves a sudden elevation in turpitude, whose origin alone it is my present purpose to assign. Men usually grow base by degrees. From me, in an instant, all virtue dropped bodily as a mantle. From comparatively trivial wickedness I passed, with the stride of a giant, into more than the enormities of an Elah-Gabalus.[8] What chance—what one event brought this evil thing to pass, bear with me while I relate. Death approaches; and the shadow which foreruns him has thrown a softening influence over my spirit. I long, in passing through the dim valley, for the sympathy—I had nearly said for the pity—of my fellow men. I would fain have them believe that I have been, in some measure, the slave of circumstances beyond human control. I would wish them to seek out for me, in the details I am about to give, some little oasis of *fatality* amid a wilderness of error. I would have them allow—what they cannot refrain from allowing—that, although temptation may have erewhile existed as great, man was never *thus*, at least, tempted before—certainly, never *thus* fell. And is it therefore that he has never thus suffered? Have I not indeed been living in a dream? And am I not now dying a victim to the horror and the mystery of the wildest of all sublunary visions?

I am the descendant of a race whose imaginative and easily excitable temperament has at all times rendered them remarkable; and, in my earliest infancy, I gave evidence of having fully inherited the family character. As I advanced in years it was more strongly developed; becoming, for many reasons, a cause of serious disquietude to my friends, and of positive injury to myself. I grew self-willed, addicted to the wildest caprices, and a prey to the most ungovernable passions. Weak-minded, and beset with constitutional infirmities akin to my own, my parents could do but little to check the evil propensities which distinguished me. Some feeble and ill-directed efforts resulted in complete failure on their part, and, of course, in total triumph on mine. Thenceforward my voice was a household law; and at an age when few children have abandoned their leading-strings, I was left to the guidance of my own will, and became, in all but name, the master of my own actions.

My earliest recollections of a school-life, are connected with a large, rambling, Elizabethan house, in a misty-looking village of England, where were a vast number of gigantic and gnarled trees, and where all the houses were excessively ancient. In truth, it was

8. Elagabalus or Heliogabalus, Emperor of Rome (reigned A.D. 218–22).

a dream-like and spirit-soothing place, that venerable old town. At this moment, in fancy, I feel the refreshing chilliness of its deeply-shadowed avenues, inhale the fragrance of its thousand shrubberies, and thrill anew with undefinable delight, at the deep hollow note of the church-bell, breaking, each hour, with sullen and sudden roar, upon the stillness of the dusky atmosphere in which the fretted Gothic steeple lay imbedded and asleep.

It gives me, perhaps, as much of pleasure as I can now in any manner experience, to dwell upon minute recollections of the school and its concerns. Steeped in misery as I am—misery, alas! only too real—I shall be pardoned for seeking relief, however slight and temporary, in the weakness of a few rambling details. These, moreover, utterly trivial, and even ridiculous in themselves, assume, to my fancy, adventitious importance, as connected with a period and a locality when and where I recognise the first ambiguous monitions of the destiny which afterwards so fully overshadowed me. Let me then remember.

The house, I have said, was old and irregular. The grounds were extensive, and a high and solid brick wall, topped with a bed of mortar and broken glass, encompassed the whole. This prison-like rampart formed the limit of our domain; beyond it we saw but thrice a week—once every Saturday afternoon, when, attended by two ushers, we were permitted to take brief walks in a body through some of the neighbouring fields—and twice during Sunday, when we were paraded in the same formal manner to the morning and evening service in the one church of the village. Of this church the principal of our school was pastor. With how deep a spirit of wonder and perplexity was I wont to regard him from our remote pew in the gallery, as, with step solemn and slow, he ascended the pulpit! This reverend man, with countenance so demurely benign, with robes so glossy and so clerically flowing, with wig so minutely powdered, so rigid and so vast,—could this be he who, of late, with sour visage, and in snuffy habiliments, administered, ferule in hand, the Draconian[9] laws of the academy? Oh, gigantic paradox, too utterly monstrous for solution!

At an angle of the ponderous wall frowned a more ponderous gate. It was riveted and studded with iron bolts, and surmounted with jagged iron spikes. What impressions of deep awe did it inspire! It was never opened save for the three periodical egressions and ingressions already mentioned; then, in every creak of its mighty hinges, we found a plenitude of mystery—a world of matter for solemn remark, or for more solemn meditation.

The extensive enclosure was irregular in form, having many ca-

9. Harsh. Draco was an Athenian statesman who drew up a rigorous code of laws ca. 621 B.C.

pacious recesses. Of these, three or four of the largest constituted the play-ground. It was level, and covered with fine hard gravel. I well remember it had no trees, nor benches, nor anything similar within it. Of course it was in the rear of the house. In front lay a small parterre, planted with box and other shrubs; but through this sacred division we passed only upon rare occasions indeed—such as a first advent to school or final departure thence, or perhaps, when a parent or friend having called for us, we joyfully took our way home for the Christmas or Midsummer holy-days.

But the house!—how quaint an old building was this!—to me how veritably a palace of enchantment! There was really no end to its windings—to its incomprehensible subdivisions. It was diffi-cult, at any given time, to say with certainty upon which of its two stories one happened to be. From each room to every other there were sure to be found three or four steps either in ascent or descent. Then the lateral branches were innumerable—inconceivable—and so returning in upon themselves, that our most exact ideas in regard to the whole mansion were not very far different from those with which we pondered upon infinity. During the five years of my residence here, I was never able to ascertain with precision, in what remote locality lay the little sleeping apartment assigned to myself and some eighteen or twenty other scholars.

The school-room was the largest in the house—I could not help thinking, in the world. It was very long, narrow, and dismally low, with pointed Gothic windows and a ceiling of oak. In a remote and terror-inspiring angle was a square enclosure of eight or ten feet, comprising the *sanctum*, "during hours," of our principal, the Reverend Dr. Bransby.[1] It was a solid structure, with massy door, sooner than open which in the absence of the "Dominie," we would all have willingly perished by the *peine forte et dure*.[2] In other angles were two other similar boxes, far less reverenced, indeed, but still greatly matters of awe. One of these was the pulpit of the "classical" usher,[3] one of the "English and mathematical." Inter-spersed about the room, crossing and recrossing in endless irregu-larity, were innumerable benches and desks, black, ancient, and time-worn, piled desperately with much-bethumbed books, and so beseamed with initial letters, names at full length, grotesque fig-ures, and other multiplied efforts of the knife, as to have entirely lost what little of original form might have been their portion in days long departed. A huge bucket with water stood at one ex-tremity of the room, and a clock of stupendous dimensions at the other.

1. As a boy of eight or nine to eleven Poe attended a school in an English village very much like the one described in this story, and the principal of Poe's school was the Rev. John Bransby, M.A.
2. "A punishment strong and harsh."
3. In England an assistant instructor is called an "usher."

Encompassed by the massy walls of this venerable academy, I passed, yet not in tedium or disgust, the years of the third lustrum of my life. The teeming brain of childhood requires no external world of incident to occupy or amuse it; and the apparently dismal monotony of a school was replete with more intense excitement than my riper youth has derived from luxury, or my full manhood from crime. Yet I must believe that my first mental development had in it much of the uncommon—even much of the *outré*. Upon mankind at large the events of very early existence rarely leave in mature age any definite impression. All is gray shadow—a weak and irregular remembrance—an indistinct regathering of feeble pleasures and phantasmagoric pains. With me this is not so. In childhood I must have felt with the energy of a man what I now find stamped upon memory in lines as vivid, as deep, and as durable as the *exergues*[4] of the Carthaginian medals.

Yet in fact—in the fact of the world's view—how little was there to remember! The morning's awakening, the nightly summons to bed; the connings, the recitations; the periodical half-holidays, and perambulations; the play-ground, with its broils, its pastimes, its intrigues;—these, by a mental sorcery long forgotten, were made to involve a wilderness of sensation, a world of rich incident, an universe of varied emotion, of excitement the most passionate and spirit-stirring. "*Oh, le bon temps, que ce siècle de fer!*"[5]

In truth, the ardor, the enthusiasm, and the imperiousness of my disposition, soon rendered me a marked character among my schoolmates, and by slow, but natural gradations, gave me an ascendancy over all not greatly older than myself;—over all with a single exception. This exception was found in the person of a scholar, who, although no relation, bore the same Christian and surname as myself;—a circumstance, in fact, little remarkable; for, notwithstanding a noble descent, mine was one of those every-day appellations which seem, by prescriptive right, to have been, time out of mind, the common property of the mob. In this narrative I have therefore designated myself as William Wilson,—a fictitious title not very dissimilar to the real. My namesake alone, of those who in school phraseology constituted "our set," presumed to compete with me in the studies of the class—in the sports and broils of the play-ground—to refuse implicit belief in my assertions, and submission to my will—indeed, to interfere with my arbitrary dictation in any respect whatsoever. If there is on earth a supreme and unqualified despotism, it is the despotism of a master mind in boyhood over the less energetic spirits of its companions.

4. Inscriptions between the rim and the pictures or designs on the medals. Carthage was an ancient city in northern Africa, destroyed by Rome in 146 B.C.
5. "Oh, the good time, that iron century!"

Wilson's rebellion was to me a source of the greatest embarrassment;—the more so as, in spite of the bravado with which in public I made a point of treating him and his pretensions, I secretly felt that I feared him, and could not help thinking the equality which he maintained so easily with myself, a proof of his true superiority; since not to be overcome cost me a perpetual struggle. Yet this superiority—even this equality—was in truth acknowledged by no one but myself; our associates, by some unaccountable blindness, seemed not even to suspect it. Indeed, his competition, his resistance, and especially his impertinent and dogged interference with my purposes, were not more pointed than private. He appeared to be destitute alike of the ambition which urged, and of the passionate energy of mind which enabled me to excel. In his rivalry he might have been supposed actuated solely by a whimsical desire to thwart, astonish, or mortify myself; although there were times when I could not help observing, with a feeling made up of wonder, abasement, and pique, that he mingled with his injuries, his insults, or his contradictions, a certain most inappropriate, and assuredly most unwelcome *affectionateness* of manner. I could only conceive this singular behavior to arise from a consummate self-conceit assuming the vulgar airs of patronage and protection.

Perhaps it was this latter trait in Wilson's conduct, conjoined with our identity of name, and the mere accident of our having entered the school upon the same day, which set afloat the notion that we were brothers, among the senior classes in the academy. These do not usually inquire with much strictness into the affairs of their juniors. I have before said, or should have said, that Wilson was not, in the most remote degree, connected with my family. But assuredly if we *had* been brothers we must have been twins; for, after leaving Dr. Bransby's, I casually learned that my namesake was born on the nineteenth of January, 1813—and this is a somewhat remarkable coincidence; for the day is precisely that of my own nativity.[6]

It may seem strange that in spite of the continual anxiety occasioned me by the rivalry of Wilson, and his intolerable spirit of contradiction, I could not bring myself to hate him altogether. We had, to be sure, nearly every day a quarrel in which, yielding me publicly the palm of victory, he, in some manner, contrived to make me feel that it was he who had deserved it; yet a sense of pride on my part, and a veritable dignity on his own, kept us always upon what are called "speaking terms," while there were many points of strong congeniality in our tempers, operating to awake in me a sentiment which our position alone, perhaps, prevented from ripening into friendship. It is difficult, indeed, to define, or even to de-

6. Poe sometimes gave 1813 as the year of his birth.

scribe, my real feelings towards him. They formed a motley and heterogeneous admixture;—some petulant animosity, which was not yet hatred, some esteem, more respect, much fear, with a world of uneasy curiosity. To the moralist it will be unnecessary to say, in addition, that Wilson and myself were the most inseparable of companions.

It was no doubt the anomalous state of affairs existing between us, which turned all my attacks upon him, (and they were many, either open or covert) into the channel of banter or practical joke (giving pain while assuming the aspect of mere fun) rather than into a more serious and determined hostility. But my endeavours on this head were by no means uniformly successful, even when my plans were the most wittily concocted; for my namesake had much about him, in character, of that unassuming and quiet austerity which, while enjoying the poignancy of its own jokes, has no heel of Achilles in itself, and absolutely refuses to be laughed at. I could find, indeed, but one vulnerable point, and that, lying in a personal peculiarity, arising, perhaps, from constitutional disease, would have been spared by any antagonist less at his wit's end than myself;—my rival had a weakness in the faucial or guttural organs, which precluded him from raising his voice at any time *above a very low whisper*. Of this defect I did not fail to take what poor advantage lay in my power.

Wilson's retaliations in kind were many; and there was one form of his practical wit that disturbed me beyond measure. How his sagacity first discovered at all that so petty a thing would vex me, is a question I never could solve; but, having discovered, he habitually practised the annoyance. I had always felt aversion to my uncourtly patronymic, and its very common, if not plebeian prænomen. The words were venom in my ears; and when, upon the day of my arrival, a second William Wilson came also to the academy, I felt angry with him for bearing the name, and doubly disgusted with the name because a stranger bore it, who would be the cause of its twofold repetition, who would be constantly in my presence, and whose concerns, in the ordinary routine of the school business, must inevitably, on account of the detestable coincidence, be often confounded with my own.

The feeling of vexation thus engendered grew stronger with every circumstance tending to show resemblance, moral or physical, between my rival and myself. I had not then discovered the remarkable fact that we were of the same age; but I saw that we were of the same height, and I perceived that we were even singularly alike in general contour of person and outline of feature. I was galled, too, by the rumor touching a relationship, which had grown current in the upper forms. In a word, nothing could more seriously disturb me, (although I scrupulously concealed such disturbance,) than any allusion to a similarity of mind, person, or condition existing between us. But, in truth, I had no reason to believe that (with the exception of the matter of relationship, and in the case of Wilson himself,) this similarity had ever been made a subject of comment, or even observed at all by our schoolfellows. That *he* observed it in all its bearings, and as fixedly as I, was apparent; but that he could discover in such circumstances so fruitful a field of annoyance, can only be attributed, as I said before, to his more than ordinary penetration.

His cue, which was to perfect an imitation of myself, lay both in words and in actions; and most admirably did he play his part. My dress it was an easy matter to copy; my gait and general manner were, without difficulty, appropriated; in spite of his constitutional defect, even my voice did not escape him. My louder tones were, of course, unattempted, but then the key, it was identical; *and his singular whisper, it grew the very echo of my own.*

How greatly this most exquisite portraiture harassed me, (for it could not justly be termed a caricature,) I will not now venture to describe. I had but one consolation—in the fact that the imitation, apparently, was noticed by myself alone, and that I had to endure only the knowing and strangely sarcastic smiles of my namesake himself. Satisfied with having produced in my bosom the intended effect, he seemed to chuckle in secret over the sting he had inflicted, and was characteristically disregardful of the public applause which the success of his witty endeavours might have so easily elicited. That the school, indeed, did not feel his design, perceive its accomplishment, and participate in his sneer, was, for many anxious months, a riddle I could not resolve. Perhaps the *gradation* of his copy rendered it not so readily perceptible; or, more possibly, I owed my security to the masterly air of the copyist, who, disdaining the letter, (which in a painting is all the obtuse can see,) gave but the full spirit of his original for my individual contemplation and chagrin.

I have already more than once spoken of the disgusting air of patronage which he assumed toward me, and of his frequent officious interference with my will. This interference often took the ungracious character of advice; advice not openly given, but hinted or insinuated. I received it with a repugnance which gained strength as I grew in years. Yet, at this distant day, let me do him the simple justice to acknowledge that I can recall no occasion when the suggestions of my rival were on the side of those errors or follies so usual to his immature age and seeming inexperience; that his moral sense, at least, if not his general talents and worldly wisdom, was far keener than my own; and that I might, to-day, have been a better, and thus a happier man, had I less frequently rejected the counsels embodied in those meaning whispers which I then but too cordially hated and too bitterly despised.

As it was, I at length grew restive in the extreme under his distasteful supervision, and daily resented more and more openly what I considered his intolerable arrogance. I have said that, in the first years of our connexion as schoolmates, my feelings in regard to him might have been easily ripened into friendship: but, in the latter months of my residence at the academy, although the intrusion of his ordinary manner had, beyond doubt, in some measure, abated, my sentiments, in nearly similar proportion, partook very much of positive hatred. Upon one occasion he saw this, I think, and afterwards avoided, or made a show of avoiding me.

It was about the same period, if I remember aright, that, in an altercation of violence with him, in which he was more than usually thrown off his guard, and spoke and acted with an openness of demeanor rather foreign to his nature, I discovered, or fancied I discovered, in his accent, his air, and general appearance, a something which first startled, and then deeply interested me, by bringing to mind dim visions of my earliest infancy—wild, confused and thronging memories of a time when memory herself was yet unborn. I cannot better describe the sensation which oppressed me than by saying that I could with difficulty shake off the belief of my having been acquainted with the being who stood before me, at some epoch very long ago—some point of the past even infinitely remote. The delusion, however, faded rapidly as it came; and I mention it at all but to define the day of the last conversation I there held with my singular namesake.

The huge old house, with its countless subdivisions, had several large chambers communicating with each other, where slept the greater number of the students. There were, however, (as must necessarily happen in a building so awkwardly planned,) many little nooks or recesses, the odds and ends of the structure; and these the economic ingenuity of Dr. Bransby had also fitted up as dormitories; although, being the merest closets, they were capable of accommodating but a single individual. One of these small apartments was occupied by Wilson.

One night, about the close of my fifth year at the school, and immediately after the altercation just mentioned, finding every one wrapped in sleep, I arose from bed, and, lamp in hand, stole through a wilderness of narrow passages from my own bedroom to that of my rival. I had long been plotting one of those ill-natured pieces of practical wit at his expense in which I had hitherto been so uniformly unsuccessful. It was my intention, now, to put my scheme in operation, and I resolved to make him feel the whole extent of the malice with which I was imbued. Having reached his closet, I noiselessly entered, leaving the lamp, with a shade over it, on the outside. I advanced a step, and listened to the sound of his tranquil breathing. Assured of his being asleep, I returned, took the light, and with it again approached the bed. Close curtains were around it, which, in the prosecution of my plan, I slowly and quietly withdrew, when the bright rays fell vividly upon the sleeper, and my eyes, at the same moment, upon his countenance. I looked; —and a numbness, an iciness of feeling instantly pervaded my frame. My breast heaved, my knees tottered, my whole spirit became possessed with an objectless yet intolerable horror. Gasping for breath, I lowered the lamp in still nearer proximity to the face. Were these —*these* the lineaments of William Wilson? I saw, indeed, that they were his, but I shook as if with a fit of the ague in fancying they were not. What *was* there about them to confound me in this manner? I gazed;—while my brain reeled with a multitude of incoherent thoughts. Not thus he appeared—assuredly not *thus*—in the vivacity of his waking hours. The same name! the same contour of person! the same day of arrival at the academy! And then his dogged and meaningless imitation of my gait, my voice, my habits, and my manner! Was it, in truth, within the bounds of human possibility, that *what I now saw* was the result, merely, of the habitual practice of this sarcastic imitation? Awe-stricken, and with a creeping shudder, I extinguished the lamp, passed silently from the chamber, and left, at once, the halls of that old academy, never to enter them again.

After a lapse of some months, spent at home in mere idleness, I found myself a student at Eton. The brief interval had been sufficient to enfeeble my remembrance of the events at Dr. Bransby's, or at least to effect a material change in the nature of the feelings with which I remembered them. The truth—the tragedy—of the drama was no more. I could now find room to doubt the evidence of my senses; and seldom called up the subject at all but with wonder at the extent of human credulity, and a smile at the vivid force of the imagination which I hereditarily possessed. Neither was this species of scepticism likely to be diminished by the character of the life I led at Eton. The vortex of thoughtless folly into which I there so immediately and so recklessly plunged, washed away all but the froth of my past hours, engulfed at once every solid or serious impression, and left to memory only the veriest levities of a former existence.

I do not wish, however, to trace the course of my miserable profligacy here—a profligacy which set at defiance the laws, while it eluded the vigilance of the institution. Three years of folly, passed without profit, had but given me rooted habits of vice, and added, in a somewhat unusual degree, to my bodily stature, when, after a week of soulless dissipation, I invited a small party of the most dissolute students to a secret carousal in my chambers. We met at a late hour of the night; for our debaucheries were to be faithfully protracted until morning. The wine flowed freely, and there were not wanting other and perhaps more dangerous seductions; so that the grey dawn had already faintly appeared in the east, while our delirious extravagance was at its height. Madly flushed with cards and intoxication, I was in the act of insisting upon a toast of more than wonted profanity, when my attention was suddenly diverted by the violent, although partial unclosing of the door of the apartment, and by the eager voice of a servant from without. He said that some person, apparently in great haste, demanded to speak with me in the hall.

Wildly excited with wine, the unexpected interruption rather delighted than surprised me. I staggered forward at once, and a few steps brought me to the vestibule of the building. In this low and small room there hung no lamp; and now no light at all was admitted, save that of the exceedingly feeble dawn which made its way through the semi-circular window. As I put my foot over the threshold, I became aware of the figure of a youth about my own height, and habited in a white kerseymere morning frock, cut in the novel fashion of the one I myself wore at the moment. This the faint light enabled me to perceive; but the features of his face I could not distinguish. Upon my entering he strode hurriedly up to me, and, seizing me by the arm with a gesture of petulant impatience, whispered the words "William Wilson!" in my ear.

I grew perfectly sober in an instant.

There was that in the manner of the stranger, and in the tremulous shake of his uplifted finger, as he held it between my eyes and the light, which filled me with unqualified amazement; but it was not this which had so violently moved me. It was the pregnancy of solemn admonition in the singular, low, hissing utterance; and, above all, it was the character, the tone, *the key*, of those few, simple, and familiar, yet *whispered* syllables, which came with a thousand thronging memories of bygone days, and struck upon my soul with the shock of a galvanic battery. Ere I could recover the use of my senses he was gone.

Although this event failed not of a vivid effect upon my disordered imagination, yet was it evanescent as vivid. For some weeks, indeed, I busied myself in earnest inquiry, or was wrapped in a cloud of morbid speculation. I did not pretend to disguise from my perception the identity of the singular individual who thus perseveringly interfered with my affairs, and harassed me with his insinuated counsel. But who and what was this Wilson?—and whence came he?—and what were his purposes? Upon neither of these points could I be satisfied; merely ascertaining, in regard to him, that a sudden accident in his family had caused his removal from Dr. Bransby's academy on the afternoon of the day in which I myself had eloped. But in a brief period I ceased to think upon the subject; my attention being all absorbed in a contemplated departure for Oxford. Thither I soon went; the uncalculating vanity of my parents furnishing me with an outfit and annual establishment, which would enable me to indulge at will in the luxury already so dear to my heart,—to vie in profuseness of expenditure with the haughtiest heirs of the wealthiest earldoms in Great Britain.

Excited by such appliances to vice, my constitutional temperament broke forth with redoubled ardor, and I spurned even the common restraints of decency in the mad infatuation of my revels. But it were absurd to pause in the detail of my extravagance. Let it suffice, that among spendthrifts I out-Heroded Herod,[7] and that, giving name to a multitude of novel follies, I added no brief appendix to the long catalogue of vices then usual in the most dissolute university of Europe.

It could hardly be credited, however, that I had, even here, so utterly fallen from the gentlemanly estate, as to seek acquaintance with the vilest arts of the gambler by profession, and, having become an adept in his despicable science, to practise it habitually as a means of increasing my already enormous income at the expense of the weak-minded among my fellow-collegians. Such, nevertheless, was the fact. And the very enormity of this offence against all manly and honourable sentiment proved, beyond doubt, the main if not the sole reason of the impunity with which it was committed. Who, indeed, among my most abandoned associates, would not rather have disputed the clearest evidence of his senses, than have suspected of such courses, the gay, the frank, the generous William Wilson—the noblest and most liberal commoner at Oxford—him whose follies (said his parasites) were but the follies of youth and unbridled fancy—whose errors but inimitable whim—whose darkest vice but a careless and dashing extravagance?

I had been now two years successfully busied in this way, when there came to the university a young *parvenu* nobleman, Glendinning—rich, said report, as Herodes Atticus[8]—his riches, too, as easily acquired. I soon found him of weak intellect, and, of course,

7. I.e., he was a greater spendthrift than the most notorious spendthrift. The phrase "out-Herod Herod," from *Hamlet* (III.ii.15), alludes to the violent way in which Herod the king was acted in medieval mystery plays.

8. Ca. 101–77 A.D.; a Greek tutor to Marcus Aurelius, he was given lucrative public offices under the Emperors Antonius Pius and Marcus Aurelius, and secured the erection of many public buildings in Grecian cities.

marked him as a fitting subject for my skill. I frequently engaged him in play, and contrived, with the gambler's usual art, to let him win considerable sums, the more effectually to entangle him in my snares. At length, my schemes being ripe, I met him (with the full intention that this meeting should be final and decisive) at the chambers of a fellow-commoner, (Mr. Preston,) equally intimate with both, but who, to do him justice, entertained not even a remote suspicion of my design. To give to this a better coloring, I had contrived to have assembled a party of some eight or ten, and was solicitously careful that the introduction of cards should appear accidental, and originate in the proposal of my contemplated dupe himself. To be brief upon a vile topic, none of the low finesse was omitted, so customary upon similar occasions that it is a just matter for wonder how any are still found so besotted as to fall its victim.

We had protracted our sitting far into the night, and I had at length effected the manœuvre of getting Glendinning as my sole antagonist. The game, too, was my favorite *écarté*. The rest of the company, interested in the extent of our play, had abandoned their own cards, and were standing around us as spectators. The *parvenu*, who had been induced by my artifices in the early part of the evening, to drink deeply, now shuffled, dealt, or played, with a wild nervousness of manner for which his intoxication, I thought, might partially, but could not altogether account. In a very short period he had become my debtor to a large amount, when, having taken a long draught of port, he did precisely what I had been coolly anticipating—he proposed to double our already extravagant stakes. With a well-feigned show of reluctance, and not until after my repeated refusal had seduced him into some angry words which gave a color of *pique* to my compliance, did I finally comply. The result, of course, did but prove how entirely the prey was in my toils; in less than an hour he had quadrupled his debt. For some time his countenance had been losing the florid tinge lent it by the wine; but now, to my astonishment, I perceived that it had grown to a pallor truly fearful. I say to my astonishment. Glendinning had been represented to my eager inquiries as immeasurably wealthy; and the sums which he had as yet lost, although in themselves vast, could not, I supposed, very seriously annoy, much less so violently affect him. That he was overcome by the wine just swallowed, was the idea which most readily presented itself; and, rather with a view to the preservation of my own character in the eyes of my associates, than from any less interested motive, I was about to insist, peremptorily, upon a discontinuance of the play, when some expressions at my elbow from among the company, and an ejaculation evincing utter despair on the part of

Glendinning, gave me to understand that I had effected his total ruin under circumstances which, rendering him an object for the pity of all, should have protected him from the ill offices even of a fiend.

What now might have been my conduct it is difficult to say. The pitiable condition of my dupe had thrown an air of embarrassed gloom over all; and, for some moments, a profound silence was maintained, during which I could not help feeling my cheeks tingle with the many burning glances of scorn or reproach cast upon me by the less abandoned of the party. I will even own that an intolerable weight of anxiety was for a brief instant lifted from my bosom by the sudden and extraordinary interruption which ensued. The wide, heavy folding doors of the apartment were all at once thrown open, to their full extent, with a vigorous and rushing impetuosity that extinguished, as if by magic, every candle in the room. Their light, in dying, enabled us just to perceive that a stranger had entered, about my own height, and closely muffled in a cloak. The darkness, however, was now total; and we could only *feel* that he was standing in our midst. Before any one of us could recover from the extreme astonishment into which this rudeness had thrown all, we heard the voice of the intruder.

"Gentlemen," he said, in a low, distinct, and never-to-be-forgotten *whisper* which thrilled to the very marrow of my bones, "Gentlemen, I make no apology for this behaviour, because in thus behaving, I am but fulfilling a duty. You are, beyond doubt, uninformed of the true character of the person who has to-night won at *écarté* a large sum of money from Lord Glendinning. I will therefore put you upon an expeditious and decisive plan of obtaining this very necessary information. Please to examine, at your leisure, the inner linings of the cuff of his left sleeve, and the several little packages which may be found in the somewhat capacious pockets of his embroidered morning wrapper."

While he spoke, so profound was the stillness that one might have heard a pin drop upon the floor. In ceasing, he departed at once, and as abruptly as he had entered. Can I—shall I describe my sensations?—must I say that I felt all the horrors of the damned? Most assuredly I had little time given for reflection. Many hands roughly seized me upon the spot, and lights were immediately reprocured. A search ensued. In the lining of my sleeve were found all the court cards essential in *écarté*, and, in the pockets of my wrapper, a number of packs, fac-similes of those used at our sittings, with the single exception that mine were of the species called, technically, *arrondées*; the honours being slightly convex at the ends, the lower cards slightly convex at the sides. In this disposition, the dupe who cuts, as custom-

ary, at the length of the pack, will invariably find that he cuts
his antagonist an honor; while the gambler, cutting at the breadth,
will, as certainly, cut nothing for his victim which may count in
the records of the game.

Any burst of indignation upon this discovery would have affected me less than the silent contempt, or the sarcastic composure, with which it was received.

"Mr. Wilson," said our host, stooping to remove from beneath
his feet an exceedingly luxurious cloak of rare furs, "Mr. Wilson,
this is your property." (The weather was cold; and, upon quitting
my own room, I had thrown a cloak over my dressing wrapper,
putting it off upon reaching the scene of play.) "I presume it is
supererogatory to seek here (eyeing the folds of the garment with
a bitter smile) for any farther evidence of your skill. Indeed, we
have had enough. You will see the necessity, I hope, of quitting
Oxford—at all events, of quitting instantly my chambers."

Abased, humbled to the dust as I then was, it is probable that
I should have resented this galling language by immediate personal
violence, had not my whole attention been at the moment arrested
by a fact of the most startling character. The cloak which I had
worn was of a rare description of fur; how rare, how extravagantly
costly, I shall not venture to say. Its fashion, too, was of my own
fantastic invention; for I was fastidious to an absurd degree of
coxcombry, in matters of this frivolous nature. When, therefore,
Mr. Preston reached me that which he had picked up upon the
floor, and near the folding doors of the apartment, it was with an
astonishment nearly bordering upon terror, that I perceived my
own already hanging on my arm, (where I had no doubt unwittingly
placed it,) and that the one presented me was but its exact counterpart in every, in even the minutest possible particular. The singular being who had so disastrously exposed me, had been muffled,
I remembered, in a cloak; and none had been worn at all by any
of the members of our party with the exception of myself. Retaining some presence of mind, I took the one offered me by Preston;
placed it, unnoticed, over my own; left the apartment with a resolute scowl of defiance; and, next morning ere dawn of day, commenced a hurried journey from Oxford to the continent, in a perfect agony of horror and of shame.

I fled in vain. My evil destiny pursued me as if in exultation,
and proved, indeed, that the exercise of its mysterious dominion
had as yet only begun. Scarcely had I set foot in Paris ere I had
fresh evidence of the detestable interest taken by this Wilson in
my concerns. Years flew, while I experienced no relief. Villain!
—at Rome, with how untimely, yet with how spectral an officiousness, stepped he in between me and my ambition! At Vienna,

too—at Berlin—and at Moscow! Where, in truth, had I *not* bitter cause to curse him within my heart? From his inscrutable tyranny did I at length flee, panic-stricken, as from a pestilence; and to the very ends of the earth I *fled in vain.*

And again, and again, in secret communion with my own spirit, would I demand the questions "Who is he?—whence came he? —and what are his objects?" But no answer was there found. And then I scrutinized, with a minute scrutiny, the forms, and the methods, and the leading traits of his impertinent supervision. But even here there was very little upon which to base a conjecture. It was noticeable, indeed, that, in no one of the multiplied instances in which he had of late crossed my path, had he so crossed it except to frustrate those schemes, or to disturb those actions, which, if fully carried out, might have resulted in bitter mischief. Poor justification this, in truth, for an authority so imperiously assumed! Poor indemnity for natural rights of self-agency so pertinaciously, so insultingly denied!

I had also been forced to notice that my tormentor, for a very long period of time, (while scrupulously and with miraculous dexterity maintaining his whim of an identity of apparel with myself,) had so contrived it, in the execution of his varied interference with my will, that I saw not, at any moment, the features of his face. Be Wilson what he might, *this*, at least, was but the veriest of affectation, or of folly. Could he, for an instant, have supposed that, in my admonisher at Eton—in the destroyer of my honor at Oxford,—in him who thwarted my ambition at Rome, my revenge at Paris, my passionate love at Naples, or what he falsely termed my avarice in Egypt,—that in this, my arch-enemy and evil genius, I could fail to recognise the William Wilson of my school-boy days, —the namesake, the companion, the rival,—the hated and dreaded rival at Dr. Bransby's? Impossible!—But let me hasten to the last eventful scene of the drama.

Thus far I had succumbed supinely to this imperious domination. The sentiment of deep awe with which I habitually regarded the elevated character, the majestic wisdom, the apparent omnipresence and omnipotence of Wilson, added to a feeling of even terror, with which certain other traits in his nature and assumptions inspired me, had operated, hitherto, to impress me with an idea of my own utter weakness and helplessness, and to suggest an implicit, although bitterly reluctant submission to his arbitrary will. But, of late days, I had given myself up entirely to wine; and its maddening influence upon my hereditary temper rendered me more and more impatient of control. I began to murmur,—to hesitate,—to resist. And was it only fancy which induced me to believe that, with the increase of my own firmness, that of my tormentor underwent a proportional diminution? Be this as it may, I now began to feel the inspiration of a burning hope, and at length nurtured in my secret thoughts a stern and desperate resolution that I would submit no longer to be enslaved.

It was at Rome, during the Carnival of 18—, that I attended a masquerade in the palazzo of the Neapolitan Duke Di Broglio. I had indulged more freely than usual in the excesses of the wine-table; and now the suffocating atmosphere of the crowded rooms irritated me beyond endurance. The difficulty, too, of forcing my way through the mazes of the company contributed not a little to the ruffling of my temper; for I was anxiously seeking, (let me not say with what unworthy motive) the young, the gay, the beautiful wife of the aged and doting Di Broglio. With a too unscrupulous confidence she had previously communicated to me the secret of the costume in which she would be habited, and now, having caught a glimpse of her person, I was hurrying to make my way into her presence.—At this moment I felt a light hand placed upon my shoulder, and that ever-remembered, low, damnable *whisper* within my ear.

In an absolute phrenzy of wrath, I turned at once upon him who had thus interrupted me, and seized him violently by the collar. He was attired, as I had expected, in a costume altogether similar to my own; wearing a Spanish cloak of blue velvet, begirt about the waist with a crimson belt sustaining a rapier. A mask of black silk entirely covered his face.

"Scoundrel!" I said, in a voice husky with rage, while every syllable I uttered seemed as new fuel to my fury, "scoundrel! impostor! accursed villain! you shall not—you *shall not* dog me unto death! Follow me, or I stab you where you stand!"—and I broke my way from the ball-room into a small ante-chamber adjoining —dragging him unresistingly with me as I went.

Upon entering, I thrust him furiously from me. He staggered against the wall, while I closed the door with an oath, and commanded him to draw. He hesitated but for an instant; then, with a slight sigh, drew in silence, and put himself upon his defence.

The contest was brief indeed. I was frantic with every species of wild excitement, and felt within my single arm the energy and power of a multitude. In a few seconds I forced him by sheer strength against the wainscoting, and thus, getting him at mercy, plunged my sword, with brute ferocity, repeatedly through and through his bosom.

At that instant some person tried the latch of the door. I hastened to prevent an intrusion, and then immediately returned to my dying antagonist. But what human language can adequately portray *that* astonishment, *that* horror which possessed me at the spectacle then presented to view? The brief moment in which I averted my eyes had been sufficient to produce, apparently, a material change in the arrangements at the upper or farther end of the room. A large mirror,—so at first it seemed to me in my confusion —now stood where none had been perceptible before; and, as I stepped up to it in extremity of terror, mine own image, but with features all pale and dabbled in blood, advanced to meet me with a feeble and tottering gait.

Thus it appeared, I say, but was not. It was my antagonist— it was Wilson, who then stood before me in the agonies of his dissolution. His mask and cloak lay, where he had thrown them, upon the floor. Not a thread in all his raiment—not a line in all the marked and singular lineaments of his face which was not, even in the most absolute identity, *mine own!*

It was Wilson; but he spoke no longer in a whisper, and I could have fancied that I myself was speaking while he said:

"*You have conquered, and I yield. Yet, henceforward art thou also dead—dead to the World, to Heaven and to Hope! In me didst thou exist—and, in my death, see by this image, which is thine own, how utterly thou hast murdered thyself.*"

1839, 1845

Eleonora[9]

Sub conservatione formæ specificæ salva anima.—RAYMOND LULLY.[1]

I am come of a race noted for vigor of fancy and ardor of passion. Men have called me mad; but the question is not yet settled, whether madness is or is not the loftiest intelligence—whether much that is glorious—whether all that is profound—does not spring from disease of thought—from *moods* of mind exalted at the expense of the general intellect. They who dream by day are cognizant of many things which escape those who dream only by night. In their grey visions they obtain glimpses of eternity, and thrill, in awaking, to find that they have been upon the verge of the great secret. In snatches, they learn something of the wisdom which is of good, and more of the mere knowledge which is of evil. They penetrate, however rudderless or compassless, into the vast ocean of the "light ineffable" and again, like the adventurers of the Nubian geographer, "*agressi sunt mare tenebrarum, quid in eo esset exploraturi.*"[2]

9. The text is that of the *Broadway Journal*, May 24, 1845.
1. Lully was a 13th-century scholastic philosopher. The epigraph may be translated: "While preserved in a specific form, the soul is safe."
2. "They entered the sea of darkness that they might investigate what was therein."

We will say, then, that I am mad. I grant, at least, that there are two distinct conditions of my mental existence—the condition of a lucid reason, not to be disputed, and belonging to the memory of events forming the first epoch of my life—and a condition of shadow and doubt, appertaining to the present, and to the recollection of what constitutes the second great era of my being. Therefore, what I shall tell of the earlier period, believe; and to what I may relate of the later time, give only such credit as may seem due; or doubt it altogether; or, if doubt it ye cannot, then play unto its riddle the Oedipus.[3]

She whom I loved in youth, and of whom I now pen calmly and distinctly these remembrances, was the sole daughter of the only sister of my mother long departed. Eleonora was the name of my cousin. We had always dwelled together, beneath a tropical sun, in the Valley of the Many-Colored Grass. No unguided footstep ever came upon that vale; for it lay far away up among a range of giant hills that hung beetling around about it, shutting out the sunlight from its sweetest recesses. No path was trodden in its vicinity; and, to reach our happy home, there was need of putting back, with force, the foliage of many thousands of forest trees, and of crushing to death the glories of many millions of fragrant flowers. Thus it was that we lived all alone, knowing nothing of the world without the valley,—I, and my cousin, and her mother.

From the dim regions beyond the mountains at the upper end of our encircled domain, there crept out a narrow and deep river, brighter than all save the eyes of Eleonora; and, winding stealthily about in mazy courses, it passed away, at length, through a shadowy gorge, among hills still dimmer than those whence it had issued. We called it the "River of Silence," for there seemed to be a hushing influence in its flow. No murmur arose from its bed, and so gently it wandered along, that the pearly pebbles upon which we loved to gaze, far down within its bosom, stirred not at all, but lay in a motionless content, each in its own old station, shining on gloriously forever.

The margin of the river, and of the many dazzling rivulets that glided, through devious ways, into its channel, as well as the spaces that extended from the margins away down into the depths of the streams until they reached the bed of pebbles at the bottom,—

3. Oedipus answered the riddle of the Sphinx, who sat at the gate of Thebes. She asked, "What animal is that which in the morning goes on four feet, at noon on two, and in the evening upon three?" Oedipus replied, "Man, who in childhood creeps, in manhood walks, and in old age goes with a staff." The solution of the riddle is a key to the meaning of the story, for the narrator finds in Ermengarde a substitute for Eleonora; hence love is preserved, as the soul in the epigraph, through a specific form.

these spots, not less than the whole surface of the valley, from the river to the mountains that girdled it in, were carpeted all by a soft green grass, thick, short, perfectly even, and vanilla-perfumed, but so besprinkled throughout with the yellow buttercup, the white daisy, the purple violet, and the ruby-red asphodel, that its exceeding beauty spoke to our hearts, in loud tones, of the love and of the glory of God.

And, here and there, in groves about this grass, like wildernesses of dreams, sprang up fantastic trees, whose tall slender stems stood not upright, but slanted gracefully towards the light that peered at noon-day into the centre of the valley. Their bark was speckled with the vivid alternate splendor of ebony and silver, and was smoother than all save the cheeks of Eleonora; so that but for the brilliant green of the huge leaves that spread from their summits in long tremulous lines, dallying with the Zephyrs, one might have fancied them giant serpents of Syria doing homage to their Sovereign the Sun.

Hand in hand about this valley, for fifteen years, roamed I with Eleonora before Love entered within our hearts. It was one evening at the close of the third lustrum of her life, and of the fourth of my own, that we sat, locked in each other's embrace, beneath the serpent-like trees, and looked down within the waters of the River of Silence at our images therein. We spoke no words during the rest of that sweet day; and our words even upon the morrow were tremulous and few. We had drawn the god Eros from that wave, and now we felt that he had enkindled within us the fiery souls of our forefathers. The passions which had for centuries distinguished our race, came thronging with the fancies for which they had been equally noted, and together breathed a delirious bliss over the Valley of the Many-Colored Grass. A change fell upon all things. Strange brilliant flowers, star-shaped, burst out upon the trees where no flowers had been known before. The tints of the green carpet deepened; and when, one by one, the white daisies shrank away, there sprang up, in place of them, ten by ten of the ruby-red asphodel. And life arose in our paths; for the tall flamingo, hitherto unseen, with all gay glowing birds, flaunted his scarlet plumage before us. The golden and silver fish haunted the river, out of the bosom of which issued, little by little, a murmur that swelled, at length, into a lulling melody more divine than that of the harp of Æolus[4]—sweeter than all save the voice of Eleonora. And now, too, a voluminous cloud, which we had long watched in the regions of Hesper,[5] floated out thence, all gorgeous in crimson and gold, and settling in peace above us, sank, day by day, lower and lower, until

---

4. In Greek mythology, Aeolus was god of the winds; hence "wind harp."

5. Hesperus, the evening star. In this case Poe may have had Venus in mind.

its edges rested upon the tops of the mountains, turning all their dimness into magnificence, and shutting us up, as if forever, within a magic prison-house of grandeur and of glory.

The loveliness of Eleonora was that of the Seraphim; but she was a maiden artless and innocent as the brief life she had led among the flowers. No guile disguised the fervor of love which animated her heart, and she examined with me its inmost recesses as we walked together in the Valley of the Many-Colored Grass, and discoursed of the mighty changes which had lately taken place therein.

At length, having spoken one day, in tears, of the last sad change which must befall Humanity, she thenceforward dwelt only upon this one sorrowful theme, interweaving it into all our converse, as, in the songs of the bard of Schiraz,[6] the same images are found occurring, again and again, in every impressive variation of phrase.

She had seen that the finger of Death was upon her bosom—that, like the ephemeron, she had been made perfect in loveliness only to die; but the terrors of the grave, to her, lay solely in a consideration which she revealed to me, one evening at twilight, by the banks of the River of Silence. She grieved to think that, having entombed her in the Valley of the Many-Colored Grass, I would quit forever its happy recesses, transferring the love which now was so passionately her own to some maiden of the outer and every-day world. And, then and there, I threw myself hurriedly at the feet of Eleonora, and offered up a vow, to herself and to Heaven, that I would never bind myself in marriage to any daughter of Earth—that I would in no manner prove recreant to her dear memory, or to the memory of the devout affection with which she had blessed me. And I called the Mighty Ruler of the Universe to witness the pious solemnity of my vow. And the curse which I invoked of *Him* and of her, a saint in Helusion, should I prove traitorous to that promise, involved a penalty the exceeding great horror of which will not permit me to make record of it here. And the bright eyes of Eleonora grew brighter at my words; and she sighed as if a deadly burthen had been taken from her breast; and she trembled and very bitterly wept; but she made acceptance of the vow, (for what was she but a child?) and it made easy to her the bed of her death. And she said to me, not many days afterwards, tranquilly dying, that, because of what I had done for the comfort of her spirit, she would watch over me in that spirit when departed, and, if so it were permitted her, return to me visibly in the watches of the night; but, if this thing were, indeed, beyond the power of the souls in Paradise, that she would, at least, give me

---

6. A variant spelling of "Shiraz," a city in Persia, the birthplace of the 14th-century poet Hafiz.

frequent indications of her presence; sighing upon me in the evening winds, or filling the air which I breathed with perfume from the censers of the angels. And, with these words upon her lips, she yielded up her innocent life, putting an end to the first epoch of my own.

Thus far I have faithfully said. But as I pass the barrier in Time's path formed by the death of my beloved, and proceed with the second era of my existence, I feel that a shadow gathers over my brain, and I mistrust the perfect sanity of the record. But let me on.—Years dragged themselves along heavily, and still I dwelled within the Valley of the Many-Colored Grass;—but a second change had come upon all things. The star-shaped flowers shrank into the stems of the trees, and appeared no more. The tints of the green carpet faded; and, one by one, the ruby-red asphodels withered away; and there sprang up, in place of them, ten by ten, dark eye-like violets that writhed uneasily and were ever encumbered with dew. And Life departed from our paths; for the tall flamingo flaunted no longer his scarlet plumage before us, but flew sadly from the vale into the hills, with all the gay glowing birds that had arrived in his company. And the golden and silver fish swam down through the gorge at the lower end of our domain and bedecked the sweet river never again. And the lulling melody that had been softer than the wind-harp of Æolus and more divine than all save the voice of Eleonora, it died little by little away, in murmurs growing lower and lower, until the stream returned, at length, utterly, into the solemnity of its original silence. And then, lastly the voluminous cloud uprose, and, abandoning the tops of the mountains to the dimness of old, fell back into the regions of Hesper, and took away all its manifold golden and gorgeous glories from the Valley of the Many-Colored Grass.

Yet the promises of Eleonora were not forgotten; for I heard the sounds of the swinging of the censers of the angels; and streams of a holy perfume floated ever and ever about the valley; and at lone hours, when my heart beat heavily, the winds that bathed my brow came unto me laden with soft sighs; and indistinct murmurs filled often the night air; and once—oh, but once only! I was awakened from a slumber like the slumber of death by the pressing of spiritual lips upon my own.

But the void within my heart refused, even thus, to be filled. I longed for the love which had before filled it to overflowing. At length the valley *pained* me through its memories of Eleonora, and I left it forever for the vanities and the turbulent triumphs of the world.

I found myself within a strange city, where all things might have served to blot from recollection the sweet dreams I had dreamed so long in the Valley of the Many-Colored Grass. The pomps and pageantries of a stately court, and the mad clangor of arms, and the radiant loveliness of woman, bewildered and intoxicated my brain. But as yet my soul had proved true to its vows, and the indications of the presence of Eleonora were still given me in the silent hours of the night. Suddenly, these manifestations they ceased; and the world grew dark before mine eyes; and I stood aghast at the burning thoughts which possessed—at the terrible temptations which beset me; for there came from some far, far distant and unknown land, into the gay court of the king I served, a maiden to whose beauty my whole recreant heart yielded at once—at whose footstool I bowed down without a struggle, in the most ardent, in the most abject worship of love. What indeed was my passion for the young girl of the valley in comparison with the fervor, and the delirium, and the spirit-lifting ecstasy of adoration with which I poured out my whole soul in tears at the feet of the ethereal Ermengarde?—Oh bright was the seraph Ermengarde! and in that knowledge I had room for none other.—Oh divine was the angel Ermengarde! and as I looked down into the depths of her memorial eyes I thought only of them—and *of her*.

I wedded;—nor dreaded the curse I had invoked; and its bitterness was not visited upon me. And once—but once again in the silence of the night, there came through my lattice the soft sighs which had forsaken me; and they modelled themselves into familiar and sweet voice, saying:

"Sleep in peace!—for the Spirit of Love reigneth and ruleth, and, in taking to thy passionate heart her who is Ermengarde, thou art absolved, for reasons which shall be made known to thee in Heaven, of thy vows unto Eleonora."

1842, 1845

The Masque of the Red Death[7]

The "Red Death" had long devastated the country. No pestilence had ever been so fatal, or so hideous. Blood was its Avatar[8] and its seal—the redness and the horror of blood. There were sharp pains, and sudden dizziness, and then profuse bleeding at the pores, with dissolution. The scarlet stains upon the body and especially upon the face of the victim, were the pest ban which shut him out from the aid and from the sympathy of his fellow-men. And the

---

7. The text is that of the *Broadway Journal*, July 19, 1845.
8. Bodily manifestation. In the Hindu religion the Avatar was a god incarnated.

whole seizure, progress and termination of the disease, were the incidents of half an hour.

But the Prince Prospero was happy and dauntless and sagacious. When his dominions were half depopulated, he summoned to his presence a thousand hale and light-hearted friends from among the knights and dames of his court, and with these retired to the deep seclusion of one of his castellated abbeys. This was an extensive and magnificent structure, the creation of the prince's own eccentric yet august taste. A strong and lofty wall girdled it in. This wall had gates of iron. The courtiers, having entered, brought furnaces and massy hammers and welded the bolts. They resolved to leave means neither of ingress or egress to the sudden impulses of despair or of frenzy from within. The abbey was amply provisioned. With such precautions the courtiers might bid defiance to contagion. The external world could take care of itself. In the meantime it was folly to grieve, or to think. The prince had provided all the appliances of pleasure. There were buffoons, there were improvisatori, there were ballet-dancers, there were musicians, there was Beauty, there was wine. All these and security were within. Without was the "Red Death."

It was toward the close of the fifth or sixth month of his seclusion, and while the pestilence raged most furiously abroad, that the Prince Prospero entertained his thousand friends at a masked ball of the most unusual magnificence.

It was a voluptuous scene, that masquerade. But first let me tell of the rooms in which it was held. There were seven—an imperial suite. In many palaces, however, such suites form a long and straight vista, while the folding doors slide back nearly to the walls on either hand, so that the view of the whole extent is scarcely impeded. Here the case was very different; as might have been expected from the duke's love of the *bizarre*. The apartments were so irregularly disposed that the vision embraced but little more than one at a time. There was a sharp turn at every twenty or thirty yards, and at each turn a novel effect. To the right and left, in the middle of each wall, a tall and narrow Gothic window looked out upon a closed corridor which pursued the windings of the suite. These windows were of stained glass whose color varied in accordance with the prevailing hue of the decorations of the chamber into which it opened. That at the eastern extremity was hung, for example, in blue—and vividly blue were its windows. The second chamber was purple in its ornaments and tapestries, and here the panes were purple. The third was green throughout, and so were the casements. The fourth was furnished and lighted with orange—the fifth with white—the sixth with violet. The seventh apartment was closely shrouded in black velvet tapestries that hung all over the ceiling and down the walls, falling in heavy folds upon a carpet of the same material and hue. But in this chamber only, the color of the windows failed to correspond with the decorations. The panes here were scarlet—a deep blood color. Now in no one of the seven apartments was there any lamp or candelabrum, amid the profusion of golden ornaments that lay scattered to and fro or depended from the roof. There was no light of any kind emanating from lamp or candle within the suite of chambers. But in the corridors that followed the suite, there stood, opposite to each window, a heavy tripod, bearing a brazier of fire that projected its rays through the tinted glass and so glaringly illumined the room. And thus were produced a multitude of gaudy and fantastic appearances. But in the western or black chamber the effect of the fire-light that streamed upon the dark hangings through the blood-tinted panes, was ghastly in the extreme, and produced so wild a look upon the countenances of those who entered, that there were few of the company bold enough to set foot within its precincts at all.

It was in this apartment, also, that there stood against the western wall, a gigantic clock of ebony. Its pendulum swung to and fro with a dull, heavy, monotonous clang; and when the minute-hand made the circuit of the face, and the hour was to be stricken, there came from the brazen lungs of the clock a sound which was clear and loud and deep and exceedingly musical, but of so peculiar a note and emphasis that, at each lapse of an hour, the musicians of the orchestra were constrained to pause, momentarily, in their performance, to hearken to the sound; and thus the waltzers perforce ceased their evolutions; and there was a brief disconcert of the whole gay company; and, while the chimes of the clock yet rang, it was observed that the giddiest grew pale, and the more aged and sedate passed their hands over their brows as if in confused reverie or meditation. But when the echoes had fully ceased, a light laughter at once pervaded the assembly; the musicians looked at each other and smiled as if at their own nervousness and folly, and made whispering vows, each to the other, that the next chiming of the clock should produce in them no similar emotion; and then, after the lapse of sixty minutes, (which embrace three thousand and six hundred seconds of the Time that flies,) there came yet another chiming of the clock, and then were the same disconcert and tremulousness and meditation as before.

But, in spite of these things, it was a gay and magnificent revel. The tastes of the duke were peculiar. He had a fine eye for colors and effects. He disregarded the *decora*[9] of mere fashion. His plans were bold and fiery, and his conceptions glowed with barbaric lustre.

9. Modesties.

There are some who would have thought him mad. His followers felt that he was not. It was necessary to hear and see and touch him to be *sure* that he was not.

He had directed, in great part, the moveable embellishments of the seven chambers, upon occasion of this great *fête*; and it was his own guiding taste which had given character to the masqueraders. Be sure they were grotesque. There were much glare and glitter and piquancy and phantasm—much of what has been since seen in "Hernani." There were arabesque figures with unsuited limbs and appointments. There were delirious fancies such as the madman fashions. There was much of the beautiful, much of the wanton, much of the *bizarre*, something of the terrible, and not a little of that which might have excited disgust. To and fro in the seven chambers there stalked, in fact, a multitude of dreams. And these—the dreams—writhed in and about, taking hue from the rooms, and causing the wild music of the orchestra to seem as the echo of their steps. And, anon, there strikes the ebony clock which stands in the hall of the velvet. And then, for a moment, all is still, and all is silent save the voice of the clock. The dreams are stiff-frozen as they stand. But the echoes of the chime die away —they have endured but an instant—and a light, half-subdued laughter floats after them as they depart. And now again the music swells, and the dreams live, and writhe to and fro more merrily than ever, taking hue from the many-tinted windows through which stream the rays from the tripods. But to the chamber which lies most westwardly of the seven, there are now none of the maskers who venture; for the night is waning away; and there flows a ruddier light through the blood-colored panes; and the blackness of the sable drapery appals; and to him whose foot falls upon the sable carpet, there comes from the near clock of ebony a muffled peal more solemnly emphatic than any which reaches *their* ears who indulge in the more remote gaieties of the other apartments.

But these other apartments were densely crowded, and in them beat feverishly the heart of life. And the revel went whirlingly on, until at length there commenced the sounding of midnight upon the clock. And then the music ceased, as I have told; and the evolutions of the waltzers were quieted; and there was an uneasy cessation of all things as before. But now there were twelve strokes to be sounded by the bell of the clock; and thus it happened, perhaps, that more of thought crept, with more of time, into the meditations of the thoughtful among those who revelled. And thus, too, it happened, perhaps, that before the last echoes of the last chimes had utterly sunk into silence, there were many individuals in the crowd who had found leisure to become aware of the presence of a masked figure which had arrested the attention of no single individual before. And the rumor of this new presence having spread itself whisperingly around, there arose at length from the whole company a buzz, or murmur, expressive of disapprobation and surprise—then, finally, of terror, of horror, and of disgust.

In an assembly of phantasms such as I have painted, it may well be supposed that no ordinary appearance could have excited such sensation. In truth the masquerade license of the night was nearly unlimited; but the figure in question had out-Heroded Herod, and gone beyond the bounds of even the prince's indefinite decorum. There are chords in the hearts of the most reckless which cannot be touched without emotion. Even with the utterly lost, to whom life and death are equally jests, there are matters of which no jest can be made. The whole company, indeed, seemed now deeply to feel that in the costume and bearing of the stranger neither wit nor propriety existed. The figure was tall and gaunt, and shrouded from head to foot in the habiliments of the grave. The mask which concealed the visage was made so nearly to resemble the countenance of a stiffened corpse that the closest scrutiny must have had difficulty in detecting the cheat. And yet all this might have been endured, if not approved, by the mad revellers around. But the mummer had gone so far as to assume the type of the Red Death. His vesture was dabbled in *blood*—and his broad brow, with all the features of the face, was besprinkled with the scarlet horror.

When the eyes of Prince Prospero fell upon this spectral image (which with a slow and solemn movement, as if more fully to sustain its *rôle*, stalked to and fro among the waltzers) he was seen to be convulsed, in the first moment with a strong shudder either of terror or distaste; but, in the next, his brow reddened with rage.

"Who dares?" he demanded hoarsely of the courtiers who stood near him—"who dares insult us with this blasphemous mockery? Seize him and unmask him—that we may know whom we have to hang at sunrise, from the battlements!"

It was in the eastern or blue chamber in which stood the Prince Prospero as he uttered these words. They rang throughout the seven rooms loudly and clearly—for the prince was a bold and robust man, and the music had become hushed at the waving of his hand.

It was in the blue room where stood the prince, with a group of pale courtiers by his side. At first, as he spoke, there was a slight rushing movement of this group in the direction of the intruder, who at the moment was also near at hand, and now, with deliberate and stately step, made closer approach to the speaker. But from a certain nameless awe with which the mad assumptions of the mummer had inspired the whole party, there were found none who put forth hand to seize him; so that, unimpeded, he passed within a yard of the prince's person; and, while the vast assembly, as if with one impulse, shrank from the centres of the rooms to the walls, he made his way uninterruptedly, but with the same solemn and measured step which had distinguished him from the first, through the blue chamber to the purple—through the purple to the green—through the green to the orange—through this again to the white—and even thence to the violet, ere a decided movement had been made to arrest him. It was then, however, that the Prince Prospero, maddening with rage and the shame of his own momentary cowardice, rushed hurriedly through the six chambers, while none followed him on account of a deadly terror that had seized upon all. He bore aloft a drawn dagger, and had approached, in rapid impetuosity, to within three or four feet of the retreating figure, when the latter, having attained the extremity of the velvet apartment, turned suddenly and confronted his pursuer. There was a sharp cry—and the dagger dropped gleaming upon the sable carpet, upon which, instantly afterwards, fell prostrate in death the Prince Prospero. Then, summoning the wild courage of despair, a throng of the revellers at once threw themselves into the black apartment, and, seizing the mummer, whose tall figure stood erect and motionless within the shadow of the ebony clock, gasped in unutterable horror at finding the grave-cerements and corpse-like mask which they handled with so violent a rudeness, untenanted by any tangible form.

And now was acknowledged the presence of the Red Death. He had come like a thief in the night. And one by one dropped the revellers in the blood-bedewed halls of their revel, and died each in the despairing posture of his fall. And the life of the ebony clock went out with that of the last of the gay. And the flames of the tripods expired. And Darkness and Decay and the Red Death held illimitable dominion over all.

1842, 1845

The Pit and the Pendulum[1]

Impia tortorum longos hic turba furores
Sanguinis innocui, non satiata, aluit.
Sospite nunc patriâ, fracto nunc funeris antro,
Mors ubi dira fuit vita salusque patent.[2]

[QUATRAIN COMPOSED FOR THE GATES OF A MARKET TO BE
ERECTED UPON THE SITE OF THE JACOBIN CLUB HOUSE AT PARIS.]

I was sick—sick unto death with that long agony; and when they at length unbound me, and I was permitted to sit, I felt that

1. The text is that of the *Broadway Journal*, May 17, 1845.
2. The epigraph may be freely translated: "The ungodly torturers long maintained here their mad and insatiable lust for the blood of innocent people. Now our country saved, the dungeons of death destroyed, there is life and health where death once prevailed."

my senses were leaving me. The sentence—the dread sentence of death—was the last of distinct accentuation which reached my ears. After that, the sound of the inquisitorial voices seemed merged in one dreamy indeterminate hum. It conveyed to my soul the idea of *revolution*—perhaps from its association in fancy with the burr of a mill-wheel. This only for a brief period; for presently I heard no more. Yet, for a while, I saw; but with how terrible an exaggeration! I saw the lips of the black-robed judges. They appeared to me white—whiter than the sheet upon which I trace these words—and thin even to grotesqueness; thin with the intensity of their expression of firmness—of immoveable resolution—of stern contempt of human torture. I saw that the decrees of what to me was Fate, were still issuing from those lips. I saw them writhe with a deadly locution. I saw them fashion the syllables of my name; and I shuddered because no sound succeeded. I saw, too, for a few moments of delirious horror, the soft and nearly imperceptible waving of the sable draperies which enwrapped the walls of the apartment. And then my vision fell upon the seven tall candles upon the table. At first they wore the aspect of charity, and seemed white slender angels who would save me; but then, all at once, there came a most deadly nausea over my spirit, and I felt every fibre in my frame thrill as if I had touched the wire of a galvanic battery, while the angel forms became meaningless spectres, with heads of flame, and I saw that from them there would be no help. And then there stole into my fancy, like a rich musical note, the thought of what sweet rest there must be in the grave. The thought came gently and stealthily, and it seemed long before it attained full appreciation; but just as my spirit came at length properly to feel and entertain it, the figures of the judges vanished, as if magically, from before me; the tall candles sank into nothingness; their flames went out utterly; the blackness of darkness supervened; all sensations appeared swallowed up in a mad rushing descent as of the soul into Hades. Then silence, and stillness, and night were the universe.

I had swooned; but still will not say that all of consciousness was lost. What of it there remained I will not attempt to define, or even to describe; yet all was not lost. In the deepest slumber —no! In delirium—no! In a swoon—no! In death—no! even in the grave all *is not* lost. Else there is no immortality for man. Arousing from the most profound of slumbers, we break the gossamer web of *some* dream. Yet in a second afterward, (so frail may that web have been) we remember not that we have dreamed. In the return to life from the swoon there are two stages; first, that of the sense of mental or spiritual; secondly, that of the sense of physical, existence. It seems probable that if, upon reaching the second stage, we could recall the impressions of the first, we should find these impressions eloquent in memories of the gulf beyond. And that gulf is—what? How at least shall we distinguish its shadows from those of the tomb? But if the impressions of what I have termed the first stage, are not, at will, recalled, yet, after long interval, do they not come unbidden, while we marvel whence they come? He who has never swooned, is not he who finds strange palaces and wildly familiar faces in coals that glow; is not he who beholds floating in mid-air the sad visions that the many may not view; is not he who ponders over the perfume of some novel flower—is not he whose brain grows bewildered with the meaning of some musical cadence which has never before arrested his attention.

Amid frequent and thoughtful endeavors to remember; amid earnest struggles to regather some token of the state of seeming nothingness into which my soul had lapsed, there have been moments when I have dreamed of success; there have been brief, very brief periods when I have conjured up remembrances which the lucid reason of a later epoch assures me could have had reference only to that condition of seeming unconsciousness. These shadows of memory tell, indistinctly, of tall figures that lifted and bore me in silence down—down—still down—till a hideous dizziness oppressed me at the mere idea of the interminableness of the descent. They tell also of a vague horror at my heart, on account of that heart's unnatural stillness. Then comes a sense of sudden motionlessness throughout all things; as if those who bore me (a ghastly train!) had outrun, in their descent, the limits of the limitless, and paused from the wearisomeness of their toil. After this I call to mind flatness and dampness; and then all is *madness*—the madness of a memory which busies itself among forbidden things.

Very suddenly there came back to my soul motion and sound—the tumultuous motion of the heart, and, in my ears, the sound of its beating. Then a pause in which all is blank. Then again sound, and motion, and touch—a tingling sensation pervading my frame. Then the mere consciousness of existence, without thought—a condition which lasted long. Then, very suddenly, *thought*, and shuddering terror, and earnest endeavor to comprehend my true state. Then a strong desire to lapse into insensibility. Then a rushing revival of soul and a successful effort to move. And now a full memory of the trial, of the judges, of the sable draperies, of the sentence, of the sickness, of the swoon. Then entire forgetfulness of all that followed; of all that a later day and much earnestness of endeavor have enabled me vaguely to recall.

So far, I had not opened my eyes. I felt that I lay upon my back, unbound. I reached out my hand, and it fell heavily upon something damp and hard. There I suffered it to remain for many minutes, while I strove to imagine where and *what* I could be. I longed, yet dared not to employ my vision. I dreaded the first glance at objects around me. It was not that I feared to look upon things horrible, but that I grew aghast lest there should be *nothing* to see. At length, with a wild desperation at heart, I quickly unclosed my eyes. My worst thoughts, then, were confirmed. The blackness of eternal night encompassed me. I struggled for breath. The intensity of the darkness seemed to oppress and stifle me. The atmosphere was intolerably close. I still lay quietly, and made effort to exercise my reason. I brought to mind the inquisitorial proceedings, and attempted from that point to deduce my real condition. The sentence had passed; and it appeared to me that a very long interval of time had since elapsed. Yet not for a moment did I suppose myself actually dead. Such a supposition, notwithstanding what we read in fiction, is altogether inconsistent with real existence;—but where and in what state was I? The condemned to death, I knew, perished usually at the *autos-da-fé*,[3] and one of these had been held on the very night of the day of my trial. Had I been remanded to my dungeon, to await the next sacrifice, which would not take place for many months? This I at once saw could not be. Victims had been in immediate demand. Moreover, my dungeon, as well as all the condemned cells at Toledo,[4] had stone floors, and light was not altogether excluded.

A fearful idea now suddenly drove the blood in torrents upon my heart, and for a brief period, I once more relapsed into insensibility. Upon recovering, I at once started to my feet, trembling convulsively in every fibre. I thrust my arms wildly above and around me in all directions. I felt nothing; yet dreaded to move a step, lest I should be impeded by the walls of a *tomb*. Perspiration burst from every pore, and stood in cold big beads upon my forehead. The agony of suspense grew at length intolerable, and I cautiously moved forward, with my arms extended, and my eyes straining from their sockets, in the hope of catching some faint ray of light. I proceeded for many paces; but still all was blackness and vacancy. I breathed more freely. It seemed evident that mine was not, at least, the most hideous of fates.

And now, as I still continued to step cautiously onward, there came thronging upon my recollection a thousand vague rumors of the horrors of Toledo. Of the dungeons there had been strange things narrated—fables I had always deemed them—but yet strange, and too ghastly to repeat, save in a whisper. Was I left to perish

3. The phrase *auto-da-fé* is Portuguese and means, literally, "act of faith." It is properly applied to the ceremonies by which the Spanish Inquisition tried and sentenced a heretic. It came to be used, as Poe uses it here, to refer to the execution of the sentence by the secular authorities, in extreme cases by public burning.
4. A city in central Spain.

of starvation in this subterranean world of darkness; or what fate, perhaps even more fearful, awaited me? That the result would be death, and a death of more than customary bitterness, I knew too well the character of my judges to doubt. The mode and the hour were all that occupied or distracted me.

My outstretched hands at length encountered some solid obstruction. It was a wall, seemingly of stone masonry—very smooth, slimy, and cold. I followed it up; stepping with all the careful distrust with which certain antique narratives had inspired me. This process, however, afforded me no means of ascertaining the dimensions of my dungeon; as I might make its circuit, and return to the point whence I set out, without being aware of the fact; so perfectly uniform seemed the wall. I therefore sought the knife which had been in my pocket, when led into the inquisitorial chamber; but it was gone; my clothes had been exchanged for a wrapper of coarse serge. I had thought of forcing the blade in some minute crevice of the masonry, so as to identify my point of departure. The difficulty, nevertheless, was but trivial; although, in the disorder of my fancy, it seemed at first insuperable. I tore a part of the hem from the robe and placed the fragment at full length, and at right angles to the wall. In groping my way around the prison, I could not fail to encounter this rag upon completing the circuit. So, at least I thought: but I had not counted upon the extent of the dungeon, or upon my own weakness. The ground was moist and slippery. I staggered onward for some time, when I stumbled and fell. My excessive fatigue induced me to remain prostrate; and sleep soon overtook me as I lay.

Upon awaking, and stretching forth an arm, I found beside me a loaf and a pitcher with water. I was too much exhausted to reflect upon this circumstance, but ate and drank with avidity. Shortly afterward, I resumed my tour around the prison, and with much toil, came at last upon the fragment of the serge. Up to the period when I fell I had counted fifty-two paces, and upon resuming my walk, I had counted forty-eight more;—when I arrived at the rag. There were in all, then, a hundred paces; and, admitting two paces to the yard, I presumed the dungeon to be fifty yards in circuit. I had met, however, with many angles in the wall, and thus I could form no guess at the shape of the vault; for vault I could not help supposing it to be.

I had little object—certainly no hope—in these researches; but a vague curiosity prompted me to continue them. Quitting the wall, I resolved to cross the area of the enclosure. At first I proceeded with extreme caution, for the floor, although seemingly of solid material, was treacherous with slime. At length, however, I took courage, and did not hesitate to step firmly; endeavoring to cross in as direct a line as possible. I had advanced some ten or twelve paces in this manner, when the remnant of the torn hem of my robe became entangled between my legs. I stepped on it, and fell violently on my face.

In the confusion attending my fall, I did not immediately apprehend a somewhat startling circumstance, which yet, in a few seconds afterward, and while I still lay prostrate, arrested my attention. It was this—my chin rested upon the floor of the prison, but my lips and the upper portion of my head, although seemingly at a less elevation than the chin, touched nothing. At the same time my forehead seemed bathed in a clammy vapor, and the peculiar smell of decayed fungus arose to my nostrils. I put forward my arm, and shuddered to find that I had fallen at the very brink of a circular pit, whose extent, of course, I had no means of ascertaining at the moment. Groping about the masonry just below the margin, I succeeded in dislodging a small fragment, and let it fall into the abyss. For many seconds I hearkened to its reverberations as it dashed against the sides of the chasm in its descent; at length there was a sullen plunge into water, succeeded by loud echoes. At the same moment there came a sound resembling the quick opening, and as rapid closing of a door overhead, while a faint gleam of light flashed suddenly through the gloom, and as suddenly faded away.

I saw clearly the doom which had been prepared for me, and congratulated myself upon the timely accident by which I had escaped. Another step before my fall, and the world had seen me no more. And the death just avoided, was of that very character which I had regarded as fabulous and frivolous in the tales respecting the Inquisition. To the victims of its tyranny, there was the choice of death with its direst physical agonies, or death with its most hideous moral horrors. I had been reserved for the latter. By long suffering my nerves had been unstrung, until I trembled at the sound of my own voice, and had become in every respect a fitting subject for the species of torture which awaited me.

Shaking in every limb, I groped my way back to the wall; resolving there to perish rather than risk the terrors of the wells, of which my imagination now pictured many in various positions about the dungeon. In other conditions of mind I might have had courage to end my misery at once by a plunge into one of these abysses; but now I was the veriest of cowards. Neither could I forget what I had read of these pits—that the *sudden* extinction of life formed no part of their most horrible plan.

Agitation of spirit kept me awake for many long hours; but at length I again slumbered. Upon arousing, I found by my side, as before, a loaf and a pitcher of water. A burning thirst consumed me, and I emptied the vessel at a draught. It must have been drugged; for scarcely had I drunk, before I became irresistibly drowsy. A deep sleep fell upon me—a sleep like that of death. How long it lasted of course, I know not; but when, once again, I unclosed my eyes, the objects around me were visible. By a wild sulphurous lustre, the origin of which I could not at first determine, I was enabled to see the extent and aspect of the prison.

In its size I had been greatly mistaken. The whole circuit of its walls did not exceed twenty-five yards. For some minutes this fact occasioned me a world of vain trouble; vain indeed! for what could be of less importance, under the terrible circumstances which environed me, than the mere dimensions of my dungeon? But my soul took a wild interest in trifles, and I busied myself in endeavors to account for the error I had committed in my measurement. The truth at length flashed upon me. In my first attempt at exploration I had counted fifty-two paces, up to the period when I fell; I must then have been within a pace or two of the fragment of serge; in fact, I had nearly performed the circuit of the vault. I then slept, and upon awaking, I must have returned upon my steps—thus supposing the circuit nearly double what it actually was. My confusion of mind prevented me from observing that I began my tour with the wall to the left, and ended it with the wall to the right.

I had been deceived, too, in respect to the shape of the enclosure. In feeling my way I had found many angles, and thus deduced an idea of great irregularity; so potent is the effect of total darkness upon one arousing from lethargy or sleep! The angles were simply those of a few slight depressions, or niches, at odd intervals. The general shape of the prison was square. What I had taken for masonry seemed now to be iron, or some other metal, in huge plates, whose sutures or joints occasioned the depression. The entire surface of this metallic enclosure was rudely daubed in all the hideous and repulsive devices to which the charnel superstition of the monks has given rise. The figures of fiends in aspects of menace, with skeleton forms, and other more really fearful images, overspread and disfigured the walls. I observed that the outlines of these monstrosities were sufficiently distinct, but that the colors seemed faded and blurred, as if from the effects of a damp atmosphere. I now noticed the floor, too, which was of stone. In the centre yawned the circular pit from whose jaws I had escaped; but it was the only one in the dungeon.

All this I saw indistinctly and by much effort: for my personal condition had been greatly changed during slumber. I now lay upon my back, and at full length, on a species of low framework of wood. To this I was securely bound by a long strap resembling a surcingle. It passed in many convolutions about my limbs and body, leaving at liberty only my head, and my left arm to such extent that I could, by dint of much exertion, supply myself with food from an earthen dish which lay by my side on the floor. I saw, to my horror, that the pitcher had been removed. I say to my horror; for I was consumed with intolerable thirst. This thirst it appeared to be the design of my persecutors to stimulate: for the food in the dish was meat pungently seasoned.

Looking upward, I surveyed the ceiling of my prison. It was some thirty or forty feet overhead, and constructed much as the side walls. In one of its panels a very singular figure riveted my whole attention. It was the painted figure of Time as he is commonly represented, save that, in lieu of a scythe, he held what, at a casual glance, I supposed to be the pictured image of a huge pendulum such as we see on antique clocks. There was something, however, in the appearance of this machine which caused me to regard it more attentively. While I gazed directly upward at it (for its position was immediately over my own) I fancied that I saw it in motion. In an instant afterward the fancy was confirmed. Its sweep was brief, and of course slow. I watched it for some minutes, somewhat in fear, but more in wonder. Wearied at length with observing its dull movement, I turned my eyes upon the other objects in the cell.

A slight noise attracted my notice, and, looking to the floor, I saw several enormous rats traversing it. They had issued from the well, which lay just within view to my right. Even then, while I gazed, they came up in troops, hurriedly, with ravenous eyes, allured by the scent of the meat. From this it required much effort and attention to scare them away.

It might have been half an hour, perhaps even an hour, (for I could take but imperfect note of time) before I again cast my eyes upward. What I then saw confounded and amazed me. The sweep of the pendulum had increased in extent by nearly a yard. As a natural consequence, its velocity was also much greater. But what mainly disturbed me was the idea that it had perceptibly *descended*. I now observed—with what horror it is needless to say—that its nether extremity was formed of a crescent of glittering steel, about a foot in length from horn to horn; the horns upward, and the under edge evidently as keen as that of a razor. Like a razor also, it seemed massy and heavy, tapering from the edge into a solid and broad structure above. It was appended to a weighty rod of brass, and the whole *hissed* as it swung through the air.

I could no longer doubt the doom prepared for me by monkish ingenuity in torture. My cognizance of the pit had become known to the inquisitorial agents—*the pit* whose horrors had been destined for so bold a recusant as myself—*the pit,* typical of hell, and regarded by rumor as the Ultima Thule[5] of all their punishments. The plunge into this pit I had avoided by the merest of accidents, and I knew that surprise, or entrapment into torment, formed an important portion of all the grotesquerie of these dungeon deaths. Having failed to fall, it was no part of the demon plan to hurl me into the abyss; and thus (there being no alternative) a different and a milder destruction awaited me. Milder! I half smiled in my agony as I thought of such application of such a term.

What boots it to tell of the long, long hours of horror more than mortal, during which I counted the rushing vibrations of the steel! Inch by inch—line by line—with a descent only appreciable at intervals that seemed ages—down and still down it came! Days passed—it might have been that many days passed —ere it swept so closely over me as to fan me with its acrid breath. The odor of the sharp steel forced itself into my nostrils. I prayed— I wearied heaven with my prayer for its more speedy descent. I grew frantically mad, and struggled to force myself upward against the sweep of the fearful scimitar. And then I fell suddenly calm, and lay smiling at the glittering death, as a child at some rare bauble.

There was another interval of utter insensibility; it was brief; for, upon again lapsing into life there had been no perceptible descent in the pendulum. But it might have been long; for I knew there were demons who took note of my swoon, and who could have arrested the vibration at pleasure. Upon my recovery, too, I felt very—oh, inexpressibly sick and weak, as if through long inanition. Even amid the agonies of that period, the human nature craved food. With painful effort I outstretched my left arm as far as my bonds permitted, and took possession of the small remnant which had been spared me by the rats. As I put a portion of it within my lips, there rushed to my mind a half formed thought of joy—of hope. Yet what business had *I* with hope? It was, as I say, a half formed thought—man has many such which are never completed. I felt that it was of joy—of hope; but I felt also that it had perished in its formation. In vain I struggled to perfect—to regain it. Long suffering had nearly annihilated all my ordinary powers of mind. I was an imbecile—an idiot.

The vibration of the pendulum was at right angles to my length. I saw that the crescent was designed to cross the region of the heart. It would fray the serge of my robe—it would return and repeat its operations—again—and again. Notwithstanding its terrifically wide sweep (some thirty feet or more) and the hissing

5. The utmost.

vigor of its descent, sufficient to sunder these very walls of iron, still the fraying of my robe would be all that, for several minutes, it would accomplish. And at this thought I paused. I dared not go farther than this reflection. I dwelt upon it with a pertinacity of attention—as if, in so dwelling, I could arrest *here* the descent of the steel. I forced myself to ponder upon the sound of the crescent as it should pass across the garment—upon the peculiar thrilling sensation which the friction of cloth produces on the nerves. I pondered upon all this frivolity until my teeth were on edge.

Down—steadily down it crept. I took a frenzied pleasure in contrasting its downward with its lateral velocity. To the right— to the left—far and wide—with the shriek of a damned spirit; to my heart with the stealthy pace of the tiger! I alternately laughed and howled as the one or the other idea grew predominant.

Down—certainly, relentlessly down! It vibrated within three inches of my bosom! I struggled violently, furiously, to free my left arm. This was free only from the elbow to the hand. I could reach the latter, from the platter beside me, to my mouth, with great effort, but no farther. Could I have broken the fastenings above the elbow, I would have seized and attempted to arrest the pendulum. I might as well have attempted to arrest an avalanche!

Down—still unceasingly—still inevitably down! I gasped and struggled at each vibration. I shrunk convulsively at its every sweep. My eyes followed its outward or upward whirls with the eagerness of the most unmeaning despair; they closed themselves spasmodically at the descent, although death would have been a relief, oh! how unspeakable! Still I quivered in every nerve to think how slight a sinking of the machinery would precipitate that keen, glistening axe upon my bosom. It was *hope* that prompted the nerve to quiver—the frame to shrink. It was *hope* —the hope that triumphs on the rack—that whispers to the death-condemned even in the dungeons of the Inquisition.

I saw that some ten or twelve vibrations would bring the steel in actual contact with my robe, and with this observation there suddenly came over my spirit all the keen, collected calmness of despair. For the first time during many hours—or perhaps days—I *thought*. It now occurred to me that the bandage, or surcingle, which enveloped me, was *unique*. I was tied by no separate cord. The first stroke of the razor-like crescent athwart any portion of the band, would so detach it that it might be un-wound from my person by means of my left hand. But how fear-ful, in that case, the proximity of the steel! The result of the slightest struggle how deadly! Was it likely, moreover, that the minions of the torturer had not foreseen and provided for this possibility? Was it probable that the bandage crossed my bosom in the track of the pendulum? Dreading to find my faint, and, as it seemed, my last hope frustrated, I so far elevated my head as to obtain a distinct view of my breast. The surcingle enveloped my limbs and body close in all directions—*save in the path of the destroying crescent.*

Scarcely had I dropped my head back into its original position, when there flashed upon my mind what I cannot better describe than as the unformed half of that idea of deliverance to which I have previously alluded, and of which a moiety only floated indeterminately through my brain when I raised food to my burning lips. The whole thought was now present—feeble, scarcely sane, scarcely definite,—but still entire. I proceeded at once, with the nervous energy of despair, to attempt its execution.

For many hours the immediate vicinity of the low framework upon which I lay, had been literally swarming with rats. They were wild, bold, ravenous; their red eyes glaring upon me as if they waited but for motionlessness on my part to make me their prey. "To what food," I thought, "have they been accustomed in the well?"

They had devoured, in spite of all my efforts to prevent them, all but a small remnant of the contents of the dish. I had fallen into an habitual see-saw, or wave of the hand about the platter: and, at length, the unconscious uniformity of the movement deprived it of effect. In their voracity the vermin frequently fastened their sharp fangs in my fingers. With the particles of the oily and spicy viand which now remained, I thoroughly rubbed the bandage wherever I could reach it; then, raising my hand from the floor, I lay breathlessly still.

At first the ravenous animals were startled and terrified at the change—at the cessation of movement. They shrank alarmedly back; many sought the well. But this was only for a moment. I had not counted in vain upon their voracity. Observing that I remained without motion, one or two of the boldest leaped upon the frame-work, and smelt at the surcingle. This seemed the signal for a general rush. Forth from the well they hurried in fresh troops. They clung to the wood—they overran it, and leaped in hundreds upon my person. The measured movement of the pendulum disturbed them not at all. Avoiding its strokes they busied themselves with the anointed bandage. They pressed —they swarmed upon me in ever accumulating heaps. They writhed upon my throat; their cold lips sought my own; I was half stifled by their thronging pressure; disgust, for which the world has no name, swelled my bosom, and chilled, with a heavy clamminess, my heart. Yet one minute, and I felt that the struggle would be over. Plainly I perceived the loosening of the bandage. I knew that in more than one place it must be already severed. With a more than human resolution I lay *still*.

Nor had I erred in my calculations—nor had I endured in vain. I at length felt that I was *free*. The surcingle hung in ribands from my body. But the stroke of the pendulum already pressed upon my bosom. It had divided the serge of the robe. It had cut through the linen beneath. Twice again it swung, and a sharp sense of pain shot through every nerve. But the moment of escape had arrived. At a wave of my hand my deliverers hurried tumultuously away. With a steady movement—cautious, sidelong, shrinking, and slow—I slid from the embrace of the bandage and beyond the reach of the scimitar. For the moment, at least, *I was free.*

Free!—and in the grasp of the Inquisition! I had scarcely stepped from my wooden bed of horror upon the stone floor of the prison, when the motion of the hellish machine ceased and I beheld it drawn up, by some invisible force, through the ceiling. This was a lesson which I took desperately to heart. My every motion was undoubtedly watched. Free!—I had but escaped death in one form of agony, to be delivered unto worse than death in some other. With that thought I rolled my eyes nervously around on the barriers of iron that hemmed me in. Something unusual—some change which, at first, I could not appreciate distinctly—it was obvious, had taken place in the apartment. For many minutes of a dreamy and trembling abstraction, I busied myself in vain, unconnected conjecture. During this period, I became aware, for the first time, of the origin of the sulphurous light which illumined the cell. It proceeded from a fissure, about half an inch in width, extending entirely around the prison at the base of the walls, which thus appeared, and were, completely separated from the floor. I endeavored, but of course in vain, to look through the aperture.

As I arose from the attempt, the mystery of the alteration in the chamber broke at once upon my understanding. I have observed that, although the outlines of the figures upon the walls were sufficiently distinct, yet the colors seemed blurred and indefinite. These colors had now assumed, and were momentarily assuming, a startling and most intense brilliancy, that gave to the spectral and fiendish portraitures an aspect that might have thrilled even firmer nerves than my own. Demon eyes, of a wild and ghastly vivacity, glared upon me in a thousand directions, where none had been visible before, and gleamed with the lurid lustre of a fire that I could not force my imagination to regard as unreal.

Unreal!—Even while I breathed there came to my nostrils

the breath of the vapor of heated iron! A suffocating odor pervaded the prison! A deeper glow settled each moment in the eyes that glared at my agonies! A richer tint of crimson diffused itself over the pictured horrors of blood. I panted! I gasped for breath! There could be no doubt of the design of my tormentors —oh! most unrelenting! oh! most demoniac of men! I shrank from the glowing metal to the centre of the cell. Amid the thought of the fiery destruction that impended, the idea of the coolness of the well came over my soul like balm. I rushed to its deadly brink. I threw my straining vision below. The glare from the enkindled roof illumined its inmost recesses. Yet, for a wild moment, did my spirit refuse to comprehend the meaning of what I saw. At length it forced—it wrestled its way into my soul—it burned itself in upon my shuddering reason.—Oh! for a voice to speak!—oh! horror!—oh! any horror but this! With a shriek, I rushed from the margin, and buried my face in my hands —weeping bitterly.

The heat rapidly increased, and once again I looked up, shuddering as with a fit of the ague. There had been a second change in the cell—and now the change was obviously in the *form*. As before, it was in vain that I, at first, endeavoured to appreciate or understand what was taking place. But not long was I left in doubt. The Inquisitorial vengeance had been hurried by my two-fold escape, and there was to be no more dallying with the King of Terrors. The room had been square. I saw that two of its iron angles were now acute—two, consequently, obtuse. The fearful difference quickly increased with a low rumbling or moaning sound. In an instant the apartment had shifted its form into that of a lozenge. But the alterations stopped not here— I neither hoped nor desired it to stop. I could have clasped the red walls to my bosom as a garment of eternal peace. "Death," I said, "any death but that of the pit!" Fool! might I have not known that *into the pit* it was the object of the burning iron to urge me? Could I resist its glow? or, if even that, could I withstand its pressure? And now, flatter and flatter grew the lozenge, with a rapidity that left me no time for contemplation. Its centre, and of course, its greatest width, came just over the yawning gulf. I shrank back —but the closing walls pressed me resistlessly onward. At length for my seared and writhing body there was no longer an inch of foothold on the firm floor of the prison. I struggled no more, but the agony of my soul found vent in one loud, long, and final scream of despair. I felt that I tottered upon the brink—I averted my eyes—

There was a discordant hum of human voices! There was a loud blast as of many trumpets! There was a harsh grating as of a thousand thunders! The fiery walls rushed back! An out-stretched arm caught my own as I fell, fainting, into the abyss. It was that of General Lasalle. The French army had entered Toledo.[6] The Inquisition was in the hands of its enemies.

1843, 1845

The Purloined Letter[7]

Nil sapientiae odiosius acumine nimio.[8]
SENECA.

At Paris, just after dark one gusty evening in the autumn of 18—, I was enjoying the twofold luxury of meditation and a meerschaum, in company with my friend C. Auguste Dupin, in his little back library, or book-closet, *au troisième, No. 33, Rue Dunôt, Faubourg St. Germain.* For one hour at least we had maintained a profound silence; while each, to any casual observer, might have seemed intently and exclusively occupied with the curling eddies of smoke that oppressed the atmosphere of the chamber. For myself, however, I was mentally discussing certain topics which had formed matter for conversation between us at an earlier period of the evening; I mean the affair of the Rue Morgue, and the mystery attending the murder of Marie Rogêt. I looked upon it, therefore, as something of a coincidence, when the door of our apartment was thrown open and admitted our old acquaintance, Monsieur G——, the Prefect of the Parisian police.

We gave him a hearty welcome; for there was nearly half as much of the entertaining as of the contemptible about the man, and we had not seen him for several years. We had been sitting in the dark, and Dupin now arose for the purpose of lighting a lamp, but sat down again, without doing so, upon G.'s saying that he had called to consult us, or rather to ask the opinion of my friend, about some official business which had occasioned a great deal of trouble.

"If it is any point requiring reflection," observed Dupin, as he forbore to enkindle the wick, "we shall examine it to better purpose in the dark."

"That is another of your odd notions," said the Prefect, who had a fashion of calling every thing "odd" that was beyond his comprehension, and thus lived amid an absolute legion of "oddities."

"Very true," said Dupin, as he supplied his visiter with a pipe,

6. This occurred in 1808.
7. The text is that of *Tales* (1845).
8. "Nothing is more offensive to good sense than too much cunning." The epigraph has not been found in Seneca.

and rolled towards him a comfortable chair.

"And what is the difficulty now?" I asked. "Nothing more in the assassination way, I hope?"

"Oh no; nothing of that nature. The fact is, the business is *very* simple indeed, and I make no doubt that we can manage it sufficiently well ourselves; but then I thought Dupin would like to hear the details of it, because it is so excessively *odd*."

"Simple and odd," said Dupin.

"Why, yes; and not exactly that, either. The fact is, we have all been a good deal puzzled because the affair *is* so simple, and yet baffles us altogether."

"Perhaps it is the very simplicity of the thing which puts you at fault," said my friend.

"What nonsense you *do* talk!" replied the Prefect, laughing heartily.

"Perhaps the mystery is a little *too* plain," said Dupin.

"Oh, good heavens! who ever heard of such an idea?"

"A little *too* self-evident."

"Ha! ha! ha!—ha! ha! ha!—ho! ho! ho!"—roared our visiter, profoundly amused, "oh, Dupin, you will be the death of me yet!"

"And what, after all, *is* the matter on hand?" I asked.

"Why, I will tell you," replied the Prefect, as he gave a long, steady, and contemplative puff, and settled himself in his chair. "I will tell you in a few words; but, before I begin, let me caution you that this is an affair demanding the greatest secrecy, and that I should most probably lose the position I now hold, were it known that I confided it to any one."

"Proceed," said I.

"Or not," said Dupin.

"Well, then; I have received personal information, from a very high quarter, that a certain document of the last importance, has been purloined from the royal apartments. The individual who purloined it is known; this beyond a doubt; he was seen to take it. It is known, also, that it still remains in his possession."

"How is this known?" asked Dupin.

"It is clearly inferred," replied the Prefect, "from the nature of the document, and from the non-appearance of certain results which would at once arise from its passing *out* of the robber's possession;—that is to say, from his employing it as he must design in the end to employ it."

"Be a little more explicit," I said.

"Well, I may venture so far as to say that the paper gives its holder a certain power in a certain quarter where such power is immensely valuable." The Prefect was fond of the cant of diplomacy.

"Still I do not quite understand," said Dupin.

"No? Well; the disclosure of the document to a third person, who shall be nameless, would bring in question the honor of a personage of most exalted station; and this fact gives the holder of the document an ascendancy over the illustrious personage whose honor and peace are so jeopardized."

"But this ascendancy," I interposed, "would depend upon the robber's knowledge of the loser's knowledge of the robber. Who would dare—"

"The thief," said G., "is the Minister D——, who dares all things, those unbecoming as well as those becoming a man. The method of the theft was not less ingenious than bold. The document in question—a letter, to be frank—had been received by the personage robbed while alone in the royal *boudoir*. During its perusal she was suddenly interrupted by the entrance of the other exalted personage from whom especially it was her wish to conceal it. After a hurried and vain endeavor to thrust it in a drawer, she was forced to place it, open as it was, upon a table. The address, however, was uppermost, and, the contents thus unexposed, the letter escaped notice. At this juncture enters the Minister D——. His lynx eye immediately perceives the paper, recognises the handwriting of the address, observes the confusion of the personage addressed, and fathoms her secret. After some business transactions, hurried through in his ordinary manner, he produces a letter somewhat similar to the one in question, opens it, pretends to read it, and then places it in close juxtaposition to the other. Again he converses, for some fifteen minutes, upon the public affairs. At length, in taking leave, he takes also from the table the letter to which he had no claim. Its rightful owner saw, but, of course, dared not call attention to the act, in the presence of the third personage who stood at her elbow. The minister decamped; leaving his own letter—one of no importance—upon the table."

"Here, then," said Dupin to me, "you have precisely what you demand to make the ascendancy complete—the robber's knowledge of the loser's knowledge of the robber."

"Yes," replied the Prefect; "and the power thus attained has, for some months past, been wielded, for political purposes, to a very dangerous extent. The personage robbed is more thoroughly convinced, every day, of the necessity of reclaiming her letter. But this, of course, cannot be done openly. In fine, driven to despair, she has committed the matter to me."

"Then whom," said Dupin, amid a perfect whirlwind of smoke, "no more sagacious agent could, I suppose, be desired, or even imagined."

"You flatter me," replied the Prefect; "but it is possible that some such opinion may have been entertained."

"It is clear," said I, "as you observe, that the letter is still in possession of the minister; since it is this possession, and not any employment of the letter, which bestows the power. With the employment the power departs."

"True," said G.; "and upon this conviction I proceeded. My first care was to make thorough search of the minister's hotel; and here my chief embarrassment lay in the necessity of searching without his knowledge. Beyond all things, I have been warned of the danger which would result from giving him reason to suspect our design."

"But," said I, "you are quite *au fait* in these investigations. The Parisian police have done this thing often before."

"O yes; and for this reason I did not despair. The habits of the minister gave me, too, a great advantage. He is frequently absent from home all night. His servants are by no means numerous. They sleep at a distance from their master's apartment, and, being chiefly Neapolitans, are readily made drunk. I have keys, as you know, with which I can open any chamber or cabinet in Paris. For three months a night has not passed, during the greater part of which I have not been engaged, personally, in ransacking the D—— Hôtel. My honor is interested, and, to mention a great secret, the reward is enormous. So I did not abandon the search until I had become fully satisfied that the thief is a more astute man than myself. I fancy that I have investigated every nook and corner of the premises in which it is possible that the paper can be concealed."

"But is it not possible," I suggested, "that although the letter may be in possession of the minister, as it unquestionably is, he may have concealed it elsewhere than upon his own premises?"

"This is barely possible," said Dupin. "The present peculiar condition of affairs at court, and especially of those intrigues in which D—— is known to be involved, would render the instant availability of the document—its susceptibility of being produced at a moment's notice—a point of nearly equal importance with its possession."

"Its susceptibility of being produced?" said I.

"That is to say, of being *destroyed*," said Dupin.

"True," I observed; "the paper is clearly then upon the premises. As for its being upon the person of the minister, we may consider that as out of the question."

"Entirely," said the Prefect. "He has been twice waylaid, as if by footpads, and his person rigorously searched under my own inspection."

"You might have spared yourself this trouble," said Dupin. "D——, I presume, is not altogether a fool, and, if not, must have anticipated these waylayings, as a matter of course."

"Not *altogether* a fool," said G., "but then he's a poet, which I take to be only one remove from a fool."

"True," said Dupin, after a long and thoughtful whiff from his meerschaum, "although I have been guilty of certain doggerel myself."

"Suppose you detail," said I, "the particulars of your search."

"Why the fact is, we took our time, and we searched *every where*. I have had long experience in these affairs. I took the entire building, room by room; devoting the nights of a whole week to each. We examined, first, the furniture of each apartment. We opened every possible drawer; and I presume you know that, to a properly trained police agent, such a thing as a *secret* drawer is impossible. Any man is a dolt who permits a 'secret' drawer to escape him in a search of this kind. The thing is *so* plain. There is a certain amount of bulk—of space—to be accounted for in every cabinet. Then we have accurate rules. The fiftieth part of a line could not escape us. After the cabinets we took the chairs. The cushions we probed with the fine long needles you have seen me employ. From the tables we removed the tops."

"Why so?"

"Sometimes the top of a table, or other similarly arranged piece of furniture, is removed by the person wishing to conceal an article; then the leg is excavated, the article deposited within the cavity, and the top replaced. The bottoms and tops of bedposts are employed in the same way."

"But could not the cavity be detected by sounding?" I asked.

"By no means, if, when the article is deposited, a sufficient wadding of cotton be placed around it. Besides, in our case, we were obliged to proceed without noise."

"But you could not have removed—you could not have taken to pieces *all* articles of furniture in which it would have been possible to make a deposit in the manner you mention. A letter may be compressed into a thin spiral roll, not differing much in shape or bulk from a large knitting-needle, and in this form it might be inserted into the rung of a chair, for example. You did not take to pieces all the chairs?"

"Certainly not; but we did better—we examined the rungs of every chair in the hotel, and, indeed, the jointings of every description of furniture, by the aid of a most powerful microscope. Had there been any traces of recent disturbance we should not have failed to detect it instantly. A single grain of gimlet-dust, for example, would have been as obvious as an apple. Any disorder in the glueing—any unusual gaping in the joints—would have sufficed to insure detection."

"I presume you looked to the mirrors, between the boards and the plates, and you probed the beds and the bed-clothes, as well as the curtains and carpets."

"That of course; and when we had absolutely completed every particle of the furniture in this way, then we examined the house itself. We divided its entire surface into compartments, which we numbered, so that none might be missed; then we scrutinized each individual square inch throughout the premises, including the two houses immediately adjoining, with the microscope, as before."

"The two houses adjoining!" I exclaimed; "you must have had a great deal of trouble."

"We had; but the reward offered is prodigious."

"You include the *grounds* about the houses?"

"All the grounds are paved with brick. They gave us comparatively little trouble. We examined the moss between the bricks, and found it undisturbed."

"You looked among D——'s papers, of course, and into the books of the library?"

"Certainly; we opened every package and parcel; we not only opened every book, but we turned over every leaf in each volume, not contenting ourselves with a mere shake, according to the fashion of some of our police officers. We also measured the thickness of every book-*cover*, with the most accurate admeasurement, and applied to each the most jealous scrutiny of the microscope. Had any of the bindings been recently meddled with, it would have been utterly impossible that the fact should have escaped observation. Some five or six volumes, just from the hands of the binder, we carefully probed, longitudinally, with the needles."

"You explored the floors beneath the carpets?"

"Beyond doubt. We removed every carpet, and examined the boards with the microscope."

"And the paper on the walls?"

"Yes."

"You looked into the cellars?"

"We did."

"Then," I said, "you have been making a miscalculation, and the letter is *not* upon the premises, as you suppose."

"I fear you are right there," said the Prefect. "And now, Dupin, what would you advise me to do?"

"To make a thorough re-search of the premises."

"That is absolutely needless," replied G——. "I am not more sure that I breathe than I am that the letter is not at the Hôtel."

"I have no better advice to give you," said Dupin. "You have, of course, an accurate description of the letter?"

"Oh yes!"—And here the Prefect, producing a memorandum-book, proceeded to read aloud a minute account of the internal, and especially of the external appearance of the missing document. Soon after finishing the perusal of this description, he took his departure, more entirely depressed in spirits than I had ever known the good gentleman before.

In about a month afterwards he paid us another visit, and found us occupied very nearly as before. He took a pipe and a chair and entered into some ordinary conversation. At length I said,—

"Well, but G——, what of the purloined letter? I presume you have at last made up your mind that there is no such thing as overreaching the Minister?"

"Confound him, say I—yes; I made the re-examination, however, as Dupin suggested—but it was all labor lost, as I knew it would be."

"How much was the reward offered, did you say?" asked Dupin.

"Why, a very great deal—a *very* liberal reward—I don't like to say how much, precisely; but one thing I *will* say, that I wouldn't mind giving my individual check for fifty thousand francs to any one who could obtain me that letter. The fact is, it is becoming of more and more importance every day; and the reward has been lately doubled. If it were trebled, however, I could do no more than I have done."

"Why, yes," said Dupin, drawlingly, between the whiffs of his meerschaum, "I really—think, G——, you have not exerted yourself—to the utmost in this matter. You might—do a little more, I think, eh?"

"How?—in what way?"

"Why—puff, puff—you might—puff, puff—employ counsel in the matter, eh?—puff, puff, puff. Do you remember the story they tell of Abernethy?"

"No; hang Abernethy!"

"To be sure! hang him and welcome. But, once upon a time, a certain rich miser conceived the design of spunging upon this Abernethy for a medical opinion. Getting up, for this purpose, an ordinary conversation in a private company, he insinuated his case to the physician, as that of an imaginary individual.

" 'We will suppose,' said the miser, 'that his symptoms are such and such; now, doctor, what would *you* have directed him to take?'

" 'Take!' said Abernethy, 'why, take *advice*, to be sure.' "

"But," said the Prefect, a little discomposed, "I am *perfectly* willing to take advice, and to pay for it. I would *really* give fifty thousand francs to any one who would aid me in the matter."

"In that case," replied Dupin, opening a drawer, and producing a check-book, "you may as well fill me up a check for the amount mentioned. When you have signed it, I will hand you the letter."

I was astounded. The Prefect appeared absolutely thunderstricken. For some minutes he remained speechless and motionless, looking incredulously at my friend with open mouth, and eyes that seemed starting from their sockets; then, apparently recovering himself in some measure, he seized a pen, and after several pauses and vacant stares, finally filled up and signed a check for fifty thousand francs, and handed it across the table to Dupin. The latter examined it carefully and deposited it in his pocket-book; then, unlocking an *escritoire*, took thence a letter and gave it to the Prefect. This functionary grasped it in a perfect agony of joy, opened it with a trembling hand, cast a rapid glance at its contents, and then, scrambling and struggling to the door, rushed at length unceremoniously from the room and from the house, without having uttered a syllable since Dupin had requested him to fill up the check.

When he had gone, my friend entered into some explanations.

"The Parisian police," he said, "are exceedingly able in their way. They are persevering, ingenious, cunning, and thoroughly versed in the knowledge which their duties seem chiefly to demand. Thus, when G—— detailed to us his mode of searching the premises at the Hôtel D——, I felt entire confidence in his having made a satisfactory investigation—so far as his labors extended."

"So far as his labors extended?" said I.

"Yes," said Dupin. "The measures adopted were not only the best of their kind, but carried out to absolute perfection. Had the letter been deposited within the range of their search, these fellows would, beyond a question, have found it."

I merely laughed—but he seemed quite serious in all that he said.

"The measures, then," he continued, "were good in their kind, and well executed; their defect lay in their being inapplicable to the case, and to the man. A certain set of highly ingenious resources are, with the Prefect, a sort of Procrustean bed,[9] to which he forcibly adapts his designs. But he perpetually errs by being too deep or too shallow, for the matter in hand; and many a schoolboy is a better reasoner than he. I knew one about eight years of age, whose success at guessing in the game of 'even and odd' attracted universal admiration. This game is simple, and is played with marbles. One player holds in his hand a number of

9. In Greek mythology Procrustes was a giant who cut travelers' legs off or stretched them to fit his iron bed.

these toys, and demands of another whether that number is even or odd. If the guess is right, the guesser wins one; if wrong, he loses one. The boy to whom I allude won all the marbles of the school. Of course he had some principle of guessing; and this lay in mere observation and admeasurement of the astuteness of his opponents. For example, an arrant simpleton is his opponent, and, holding up his closed hand, asks, 'are they even or odd?' Our schoolboy replies, 'odd,' and loses; but upon the second trial he wins, for he then says to himself, 'the simpleton had them even upon the first trial, and his amount of cunning is just sufficient to make him have them odd upon the second; I will therefore guess odd;'—he guesses odd, and wins. Now, with a simpleton a degree above the first, he would have reasoned thus: 'This fellow finds that in the first instance I guessed odd, and, in the second, he will propose to himself upon the first impulse, a simple variation from even to odd, as did the first simpleton; but then a second thought will suggest that this is too simple a variation, and finally he will decide upon putting it even as before. I will therefore guess even;'—he guesses even, and wins. Now this mode of reasoning in the schoolboy, whom his fellows termed 'lucky,'—what, in its last analysis, is it?"

"It is merely," I said, "an identification of the reasoner's intellect with that of his opponent."

"It is," said Dupin; "and, upon inquiring of the boy by what means he effected the *thorough* identification in which his success consisted, I received answer as follows: 'When I wish to find out how wise, or how stupid, or how good, or how wicked is any one, or what are his thoughts at the moment, I fashion the expression of my face, as accurately as possible, in accordance with the expression of his, and then wait to see what thoughts or sentiments arise in my mind or heart, as if to match or correspond with the expression.' This response of the schoolboy lies at the bottom of all the spurious profundity which has been attributed to Rochefoucauld, to La Bougive, to Machiavelli, and to Campanella."[1]

"And the identification," I said, "of the reasoner's intellect with that of his opponent, depends, if I understand you aright, upon the accuracy with which the opponent's intellect is admeasured."

"For its practical value it depends upon this," replied Dupin; "and the Prefect and his cohort fail so frequently, first, by default of this identification, and, secondly, by ill-admeasurement, or rather through non-admeasurement, of the intellect with which

1. François, Duc de La Rochefoucauld (1613–80), French, author of *Maxims;* Niccolò Machiavelli (1469–1527), Italian, statesman and advocate of craft in politics; Tommaso Campanella (1568–1639), Italian, advocate of the experimental method in science; La Bougive cannot be identified.

they are engaged. They consider only their *own* ideas of ingenuity; and, in searching for anything hidden, advert only to the
modes in which *they* would have hidden it. They are right in this
much—that their own ingenuity is a faithful representative of
that of *the mass*; but when the cunning of the individual felon is
diverse in character from their own, the felon foils them, of
course. This always happens when it is above their own, and very
usually when it is below. They have no variation of principle in
their investigations; at best, when urged by some unusual emergency—by some extraordinary reward—they extend or exaggerate their old modes of *practice*, without touching their principles. What, for example, in this case of D——, has been done to
vary the principle of action? What is all this boring, and probing, and sounding, and scrutinizing with the microscope, and dividing the surface of the building into registered square inches—
what is it all but an exaggeration *of the application* of the one
principle or set of principles of search, which are based upon the
one set of notions regarding human ingenuity, to which the Prefect, in the long routine of his duty, has been accustomed? Do
you not see he has taken it for granted that *all* men proceed to
conceal a letter,—not exactly in a gimlet-hole bored in a chair-
leg—but, at least, in *some* out-of-the-way hole or corner suggested by the same tenor of thought which would urge a man to
secrete a letter in a gimlet-hole bored in a chair-leg? And do you
not see also, that such *recherchés* nooks for concealment are
adapted only for ordinary occasions, and would be adopted only
by ordinary intellects; for, in all cases of concealment, a disposal
of the article concealed—a disposal of it in this *recherché* manner,—is, in the very first instance, presumable and presumed; and
thus its discovery depends, not at all upon the acumen, but altogether upon the mere care, patience, and determination of the
seekers; and where the case is of importance—or, what amounts
to the same thing in the policial eyes, when the reward is of
magnitude,—the qualities in question have *never* been known to
fail. You will now understand what I meant in suggesting that,
had the purloined letter been hidden any where within the limits
of the Prefect's examination—in other words, had the principle
of its concealment been comprehended within the principles of
the Prefect—its discovery would have been a matter altogether
beyond question. This functionary, however, has been thoroughly
mystified; and the remote source of his defeat lies in the supposition that the Minister is a fool, because he has acquired renown
as a poet. All fools are poets; this the Prefect *feels*; and he is
merely guilty of a *non distributio medii*[2] in thence inferring that

2. "Undistributed middle," a fallacy in logic.

all poets are fools."

"But is this really the poet?" I asked. "There are two brothers, I know; and both have attained reputation in letters. The Minister I believe has written learnedly on the Differential Calculus. He is a mathematician, and no poet."

"You are mistaken; I know him well; he is both. As poet *and* mathematician, he would reason well; as mere mathematician, he could not have reasoned at all, and thus would have been at the mercy of the Prefect."

"You surprise me," I said, "by these opinions, which have been contradicted by the voice of the world. You do not mean to set at naught the well-digested idea of centuries. The mathematical reason has long been regarded as *the* reason *par excellence*."

" '*Il y a à parier*,' " replied Dupin, quoting from Chamfort, " '*que toute idée publique, toute convention reçue, est une sottise, car elle a convenu au plus grand nombre*.' ³ The mathematicians, I grant you, have done their best to promulgate the popular error to which you allude, and which is none the less an error for its promulgation as truth. With an art worthy a better cause, for example, they have insinuated the term 'analysis' into application to algebra. The French are the originators of this particular deception; but if a term is of any importance—if words derive any value from applicability—then 'analysis' conveys 'algebra' about as much as, in Latin, '*ambitus*' implies 'ambition,' '*religio*' 'religion,' or '*homines honesti*,' a set of *honorable* men."

"You have a quarrel on hand, I see," said I, "with some of the algebraists of Paris; but proceed."

"I dispute the availability, and thus the value, of that reason which is cultivated in any especial form other than the abstractly logical. I dispute, in particular, the reason educed by mathematical study. The mathematics are the science of form and quantity; mathematical reasoning is merely logic applied to observation upon form and quantity. The great error lies in supposing that even the truths of what is called *pure* algebra, are abstract or general truths. And this error is so egregious that I am confounded at the universality with which it has been received. Mathematical axioms are *not* axioms of general truth. What is true of *relation*—of form and quantity—is often grossly false in regard to morals, for example. In this latter science it is very usually *un*true that the aggregated parts are equal to the whole. In chemistry also the axiom fails. In the consideration of motive it fails; for two motives, each of a given value, have not, necessarily, a value when united, equal to the sum of their values

---

3. "The odds are that every public idea, every received convention, is stupid because it is agreeable to the majority."

apart. There are numerous other mathematical truths which are only truths within the limits of *relation*. But the mathematician argues, from his *finite truths*, through habit, as if they were of an absolutely general applicability—as the world indeed imagines them to be. Bryant, in his very learned 'Mythology,'[4] mentions an analogous source of error, when he says that 'although the Pagan fables are not believed, yet we forget ourselves continually, and make inferences from them as existing realities.' With the algebraists, however, who are Pagans themselves, the 'Pagan fables' *are* believed, and the inferences are made, not so much through lapse of memory, as through an unaccountable addling of the brains. In short, I never yet encountered the mere mathematician who could be trusted out of equal roots, or one who did not clandestinely hold it as a point of his faith that $x^2 + px$ was absolutely and unconditionally equal to q. Say to one of these gentlemen, by way of experiment, if you please, that you believe occasions may occur where $x^2 + px$ is *not* altogether equal to q, and, having made him understand what you mean, get out of his reach as speedily as convenient, for, beyond doubt, he will endeavor to knock you down.

"I mean to say," continued Dupin, while I merely laughed at his last observations, "that if the Minister had been no more than a mathematician, the Prefect would have been under no necessity of giving me this check. I knew him, however, as both mathematician and poet, and my measures were adapted to his capacity, with reference to the circumstances by which he was surrounded. I knew him as a courtier, too, and as a bold *intriguant*. Such a man, I considered, could not fail to be aware of the ordinary policial modes of action. He could not have failed to anticipate—and events have proved that he did not fail to anticipate—the waylayings to which he was subjected. He must have foreseen, I reflected, the secret investigations of his premises. His frequent absences from home at night, which were hailed by the Prefect as certain aids to his success, I regarded only as ruses, to afford opportunity for thorough search to the police, and thus the sooner to impress them with the conviction to which G——, in fact, did finally arrive—the conviction that the letter was not upon the premises. I felt, also, that the whole train of thought, which I was at some pains in detailing to you just now, concerning the invariable principle of policial action in searches for articles concealed—I felt that this whole train of thought would necessarily pass through the mind of the Minister. It would imperatively lead him to despise all the ordinary *nooks* of conceal-

4. Presumably Jacob Bryant's *A New System, or, An Analysis of Ancient Mythology* (1774–76).

ment. He could not, I reflected, be so weak as not to see that the most intricate and remote recess of his hotel would be as open as his commonest closets to the eyes, to the probes, to the gimlets, and to the microscopes of the Prefect. I saw, in fine, that he would be driven, as a matter of course, to *simplicity*, if not deliberately induced to it as a matter of choice. You will remember, perhaps, how desperately the Prefect laughed when I suggested, upon our first interview, that it was just possible this mystery troubled him so much on account of its being so *very* self-evident."

"Yes," said I, "I remember his merriment well. I really thought he would have fallen into convulsions."

"The material world," continued Dupin, "abounds with very strict analogies to the immaterial; and thus some color of truth has been given to the rhetorical dogma, that metaphor, or simile, may be made to strengthen an argument, as well as to embellish a description. The principle of the *vis inertiæ*,[5] for example, seems to be identical in physics and metaphysics. It is not more true in the former, that a large body is with more difficulty set in motion than a smaller one, and that its subsequent *momentum* is commensurate with this difficulty, than it is, in the latter, that intellects of the vaster capacity, while more forcible, more constant, and more eventful in their movements than those of inferior grade, are yet the less readily moved, and more embarrassed and full of hesitation in the first few steps of their progress. Again: have you ever noticed which of the street signs, over the shop doors, are the most attractive of attention?"

"I have never given the matter a thought," I said.

"There is a game of puzzles," he resumed, "which is played upon a map. One party playing requires another to find a given word—the name of town, river, state or empire—any word, in short, upon the motley and perplexed surface of the chart. A novice in the game generally seeks to embarrass his opponents by giving them the most minutely lettered names; but the adept selects such words as stretch, in large characters, from one end of the chart to the other. These, like the over-largely lettered signs and placards of the street, escape observation by dint of being excessively obvious; and here the physical oversight is precisely analogous with the moral inapprehension by which the intellect suffers to pass unnoticed those considerations which are too obtrusively and too palpably self-evident. But this is a point, it appears, somewhat above or beneath the understanding of the Prefect. He never once thought it probable, or possible, that the Minister had deposited the letter immediately beneath the nose of the whole world, by way of best preventing any portion of that

5. "The force of inertia."

world from perceiving it.

"But the more I reflected upon the daring, dashing, and discriminating ingenuity of D——; upon the fact that the document must always have been *at hand*, if he intended to use it to good purpose; and upon the decisive evidence, obtained by the Prefect, that it was not hidden within the limits of that dignitary's ordinary search—the more satisfied I became that, to conceal this letter, the Minister had resorted to the comprehensive and sagacious expedient of not attempting to conceal it at all.

"Full of these ideas, I prepared myself with a pair of green spectacles, and called one fine morning, quite by accident, at the Ministerial hotel. I found D—— at home, yawning, lounging, and dawdling, as usual, and pretending to be in the last extremity of *ennui*. He is, perhaps, the most really energetic human being now alive—but that is only when nobody sees him.

"To be even with him, I complained of my weak eyes, and lamented the necessity of the spectacles, under cover of which I cautiously and thoroughly surveyed the apartment, while seemingly intent only upon the conversation of my host.

"I paid special attention to a large writing-table near which he sat, and upon which lay confusedly, some miscellaneous letters and other papers, with one or two musical instruments and a few books. Here, however, after a long and very deliberate scrutiny, I saw nothing to excite particular suspicion.

"At length my eyes, in going the circuit of the room, fell upon a trumpery fillagree card-rack of paste-board, that hung dangling by a dirty blue ribbon, from a little brass knob just beneath the middle of the mantel-piece. In this rack, which had three or four compartments, were five or six visiting cards and a solitary letter. This last was much soiled and crumpled. It was torn nearly in two, across the middle—as if a design, in the first instance, to tear it entirely up as worthless, had been altered, or stayed, in the second. It had a large black seal, bearing the D—— cipher *very* conspicuously, and was addressed, in a diminutive female hand, to D——, the minister, himself. It was thrust carelessly, and even, as it seemed, contemptuously, into one of the upper divisions of the rack.

"No sooner had I glanced at this letter, than I concluded it to be that of which I was in search. To be sure, it was, to all appearance, radically different from the one of which the Prefect had read us so minute a description. Here the seal was large and black, with the D—— cipher; there it was small and red, with the ducal arms of the S—— family. Here, the address, to the Minister, was diminutive and feminine; there the superscription, to a certain royal personage, was markedly bold and decided; the size alone formed a point of correspondence. But, then, the *radicalness* of these differences, which was excessive; the dirt; the soiled and torn condition of the paper, so inconsistent with the *true* methodical habits of D——, and so suggestive of a design to delude the beholder into an idea of the worthlessness of the document; these things, together with the hyperobtrusive situation of this document, full in the view of every visiter, and thus exactly in accordance with the conclusions to which I had previously arrived; these things, I say, were strongly corroborative of suspicion, in one who came with the intention to suspect.

"I protracted my visit as long as possible, and, while I maintained a most animated discussion with the Minister, on a topic which I knew well had never failed to interest and excite him, I kept my attention really riveted upon the letter. In this examination, I committed to memory its external appearance and arrangement in the rack; and also fell, at length, upon a discovery which set at rest whatever trivial doubt I might have entertained. In scrutinizing the edges of the paper, I observed them to be more *chafed* than seemed necessary. They presented the *broken* appearance which is manifested when a stiff paper, having been once folded and pressed with a folder, is refolded in a reversed direction, in the same creases or edges which had formed the original fold. This discovery was sufficient. It was clear to me that the letter had been turned, as a glove, inside out, re-directed, and re-sealed. I bade the Minister good morning, and took my departure at once, leaving a gold snuff-box upon the table.

"The next morning I called for the snuff-box, when we resumed, quite eagerly, the conversation of the preceding day. While thus engaged, however, a loud report, as if of a pistol, was heard immediately beneath the windows of the hotel, and was succeeded by a series of fearful screams, and the shoutings of a mob. D—— rushed to a casement, threw it open, and looked out. In the meantime, I stepped to the card-rack, took the letter, put it in my pocket, and replaced it by a *fac-simile*, (so far as regards externals,) which I had carefully prepared at my lodgings; imitating the D—— cipher, very readily, by means of a seal formed of bread.

"The disturbance in the street had been occasioned by the frantic behavior of a man with a musket. He had fired it among a crowd of women and children. It proved, however, to have been without ball, and the fellow was suffered to go his way as a lunatic or a drunkard. When he had gone, D—— came from the window, whither I had followed him immediately upon securing the object in view. Soon afterwards I bade him farewell. The pretended lunatic was a man in my own pay."

"But what purpose had you," I asked, "in replacing the letter by a *fac-simile?* Would it not have been better, at the first visit, to have seized it openly, and departed?"

"D——," replied Dupin, "is a desperate man, and a man of nerve. His hotel, too, is not without attendants devoted to his interests. Had I made the wild attempt you suggest, I might never have left the Ministerial presence alive. The good people of Paris might have heard of me no more. But I had an object apart from these considerations. You know my political prepossessions. In this matter, I act as a partisan of the lady concerned. For eighteen months the Minister has had her in his power. She has now him in hers—since, being unaware that the letter is not in his possession, he will proceed with his exactions as if it was. Thus will he inevitably commit himself, at once, to his political destruction. His downfall, too, will not be more precipitate than awkward. It is all very well to talk about the *facilis descensus Averni;*[6] but in all kinds of climbing, as Catalani said of singing, it is far more easy to get up than to come down. In the present instance I have no sympathy—at least no pity—for him who descends. He is that *monstrum horrendum,* an unprincipled man of genius. I confess, however, that I should like very well to know the precise character of his thoughts, when, being defied by her whom the Prefect terms 'a certain personage,' he is reduced to opening the letter which I left for him in the card-rack."

"How? did you put any thing particular in it?"

"Why—it did not seem altogether right to leave the interior blank—that would have been insulting. D——, at Vienna once, did me an evil turn, which I told him, quite good-humoredly, that I should remember. So, as I knew he would feel some curiosity in regard to the identity of the person who had outwitted him, I thought it a pity not to give him a clue. He is well acquainted with my MS., and I just copied into the middle of the blank sheet the words—

——Un dessein si funeste,
S'il n'est digne d'Atrée, est digne de Thyeste.[7]

They are to be found in Crébillon's 'Atrée.' "

1845

6. "Easy descent to Avernus [Hell]" (*Aeneid* VI. 126). Catalani is probably Angelica Catalani (1780–1849), a noted Italian singer.
7. "Such a deadly plot is worthy of Thyestes, if not of Atreus." In Greek legend, Thyestes seduced the wife of his brother Atreus and plotted his death, but in revenge Atreus killed the three sons of Thyestes and served them to him at a banquet. The quotation is from Crébillon's play *Atrée et Thyeste* (1707), V.iv.13–14.

The Cask of Amontillado[8]

The thousand injuries of Fortunato I had borne as I best could; but when he ventured upon insult, I vowed revenge. You, who so well know the nature of my soul, will not suppose, however, that I gave utterance to a threat. *At length* I would be avenged; this was a point definitely settled—but the very definitiveness with which it was resolved precluded the idea of risk. I must not only punish, but punish with impunity. A wrong is unredressed when retribution overtakes its redresser. It is equally unredressed when the avenger fails to make himself felt as such to him who has done the wrong.

It must be understood, that neither by word nor deed had I given Fortunato cause to doubt my good will. I continued, as was my wont, to smile in his face, and he did not perceive that my smile *now* was at the thought of his immolation.

He had a weak point—this Fortunato—although in other regards he was a man to be respected and even feared. He prided himself on his connoisseurship in wine. Few Italians have the true virtuoso spirit. For the most part their enthusiasm is adopted to suit the time and opportunity—to practise imposture upon the British and Austrian *millionnaires*. In painting and gemmary Fortunato, like his countrymen, was a quack—but in the matter of old wines he was sincere. In this respect I did not differ from him materially: I was skilful in the Italian vintages myself, and bought largely whenever I could.

It was about dusk, one evening during the supreme madness of the carnival season, that I encountered my friend. He accosted me with excessive warmth, for he had been drinking much. The man wore motley. He had on a tight-fitting parti-striped dress, and his head was surmounted by the conical cap and bells. I was so pleased to see him, that I thought I should never have done wringing his hand.

I said to him—"My dear Fortunato, you are luckily met. How remarkably well you are looking to-day! But I have received a pipe of what passes for Amontillado, and I have my doubts."

"How?" said he. "Amontillado? A pipe? Impossible! And in the middle of the carnival!"

"I have my doubts," I replied; "and I was silly enough to pay the full Amontillado price without consulting you in the matter. You were not to be found, and I was fearful of losing a bargain."

"Amontillado!"

"I have my doubts."

"Amontillado!"

8. The text is that of Griswold's edition (1850).

"And I must satisfy them."

"Amontillado!"

"As you are engaged, I am on my way to Luchesi. If any one has a critical turn, it is he. He will tell me——"

"Luchesi cannot tell Amontillado from Sherry."

"And yet some fools will have it that his taste is a match for your own."

"Come, let us go."

"Whither?"

"To your vaults."

"My friend, no; I will not impose upon your good nature. I perceive you have an engagement. Luchesi——"

"I have no engagement;—come."

"My friend, no. It is not the engagement, but the severe cold with which I perceive you are afflicted. The vaults are insufferably damp. They are encrusted with nitre."

"Let us go, nevertheless. The cold is merely nothing. Amontillado! You have been imposed upon. And as for Luchesi, he cannot distinguish Sherry from Amontillado."

Thus speaking, Fortunato possessed himself of my arm. Putting on a mask of black silk, and drawing a *roquelaire* closely about my person, I suffered him to hurry me to my palazzo.

There were no attendants at home; they had absconded to make merry in honor of the time. I had told them that I should not return until the morning, and had given them explicit orders not to stir from the house. These orders were sufficient, I well knew, to insure their immediate disappearance, one and all, as soon as my back was turned.

I took from their sconces two flambeaux, and giving one to Fortunato, bowed him through several suites of rooms to the archway that led into the vaults. I passed down a long and winding staircase, requesting him to be cautious as he followed. We came at length to the foot of the descent, and stood together on the damp ground of the catacombs of the Montresors.

The gait of my friend was unsteady, and the bells upon his cap jingled as he strode.

"The pipe," said he.

"It is farther on," said I; "but observe the white web-work which gleams from these cavern walls."

He turned toward me, and looked into my eyes with two filmy orbs that distilled the rheum of intoxication.

"Nitre?" he asked, at length.

"Nitre," I replied. "How long have you had that cough?"

"Ugh! ugh! ugh!—ugh! ugh! ugh!—ugh! ugh! ugh!—ugh! ugh! ugh!—ugh! ugh! ugh!"

My poor friend found it impossible to reply for many minutes. "It is nothing," he said, at last.

"Come," I said, with decision, "we will go back; your health is precious. You are rich, respected, admired, beloved; you are happy, as once I was. You are a man to be missed. For me it is no matter. We will go back; you will be ill, and I cannot be responsible. Besides, there is Luchesi——"

"Enough," he said; "the cough is a mere nothing; it will not kill me. I shall not die of a cough."

"True—true," I replied; "and, indeed, I had no intention of alarming you unnecessarily; but you should use all proper caution. A draught of this Medoc will defend us from the damps."

Here I knocked off the neck of a bottle which I drew from a long row of its fellows that lay upon the mould.

"Drink," I said, presenting him the wine.

He raised it to his lips with a leer. He paused and nodded to me familiarly, while his bells jingled.

"I drink," he said, "to the buried that repose around us."

"And I to your long life."

He again took my arm, and we proceeded.

"These vaults," he said, "are extensive."

"The Montresors," I replied, "were a great and numerous family."

"I forget your arms."

"A huge human foot d'or, in a field azure; the foot crushes a serpent rampant whose fangs are imbedded in the heel."

"And the motto?"

"*Nemo me impune lacessit.*"[9]

"Good!" he said.

The wine sparkled in his eyes and the bells jingled. My own fancy grew warm with the Medoc. We had passed through walls of piled bones, with casks and puncheons intermingling, into the inmost recesses of the catacombs. I paused again, and this time I made bold to seize Fortunato by an arm above the elbow.

"The nitre!" I said; "see, it increases. It hangs like moss upon the vaults. We are below the river's bed. The drops of moisture trickle among the bones. Come, we will go back ere it is too late. Your cough——"

"It is nothing," he said; "let us go on. But first, another draught of the Medoc."

I broke and reached him a flagon of De Grâve. He emptied it at a breath. His eyes flashed with a fierce light. He laughed and threw the bottle upward with a gesticulation I did not understand.

I looked at him in surprise. He repeated the movement—a gro-

9. "No man provokes me with impunity."

tesque one.

"You do not comprehend?" he said.

"Not I," I replied.

"Then you are not of the brotherhood."

"How?"

"You are not of the masons."[1]

"Yes, yes," I said; "yes, yes."

"You? Impossible! A mason?"

"A mason," I replied.

"A sign," he said.

"It is this," I answered, producing a trowel from beneath the folds of my *roquelaire*.

"You jest," he exclaimed, recoiling a few paces. "But let us proceed to the Amontillado."

"Be it so," I said, replacing the tool beneath the cloak, and again offering him my arm. He leaned upon it heavily. We continued our route in search of the Amontillado. We passed through a range of low arches, descended, passed on, and descending again, arrived at a deep crypt, in which the foulness of the air caused our flambeaux rather to glow than flame.

At the most remote end of the crypt there appeared another less spacious. Its walls had been lined with human remains, piled to the vault overhead, in the fashion of the great catacombs of Paris. Three sides of this interior crypt were still ornamented in this manner. From the fourth the bones had been thrown down, and lay promiscuously upon the earth, forming at one point a mound of some size. Within the wall thus exposed by the displacing of the bones, we perceived a still interior recess, in depth about four feet, in width three, in height six or seven. It seemed to have been constructed for no especial use within itself, but formed merely the interval between two of the colossal supports of the roof of the catacombs, and was backed by one of their circumscribing walls of solid granite.

It was in vain that Fortunato, uplifting his dull torch, endeavored to pry into the depth of the recess. Its termination the feeble light did not enable us to see.

"Proceed," I said; "herein is the Amontillado. As for Luchesi——"

"He is an ignoramus," interrupted my friend, as he stepped unsteadily forward, while I followed immediately at his heels. In an instant he had reached the extremity of the niche, and finding his progress arrested by the rock, stood stupidly bewildered. A moment more and I had fettered him to the granite. In its surface were two iron staples, distant from each other about two feet, horizontally.

1. Fortunato refers to the secret society of Freemasons.

From one of these depended a short chain, from the other a pad-lock. Throwing the links about his waist, it was but the work of a few seconds to secure it. He was too much astounded to resist. Withdrawing the key I stepped back from the recess.

"Pass your hand," I said, "over the wall; you cannot help feeling the nitre. Indeed it is *very* damp. Once more let me *implore* you to return. No? Then I must positively leave you. But I must first render you all the little attentions in my power."

"The Amontillado!" ejaculated my friend, not yet recovered from his astonishment.

"True," I replied; "the Amontillado."

As I said these words I busied myself among the pile of bones of which I have before spoken. Throwing them aside, I soon uncovered a quantity of building stone and mortar. With these materials and with the aid of my trowel, I began vigorously to wall up the entrance of the niche.

I had scarcely laid the first tier of the masonry when I discovered that the intoxication of Fortunato had in a great measure worn off. The earliest indication I had of this was a low moaning cry from the depth of the recess. It was *not* the cry of a drunken man. There was then a long and obstinate silence. I laid the second tier, and the third, and the fourth; and then I heard the furious vibrations of the chain. The noise lasted for several minutes, during which, that I might hearken to it with the more satisfaction, I ceased my labors and sat down upon the bones. When at last the clanking subsided, I resumed the trowel, and finished without interruption the fifth, the sixth, and the seventh tier. The wall was now nearly upon a level with my breast. I again paused, and holding the flambeaux over the mason-work, threw a few feeble rays upon the figure within.

A succession of loud and shrill screams, bursting suddenly from the throat of the chained form, seemed to thrust me violently back. For a brief moment I hesitated—I trembled. Unsheathing my rapier, I began to grope with it about the recess; but the thought of an instant reassured me. I placed my hand upon the solid fabric of the catacombs, and felt satisfied. I reapproached the wall. I replied to the yells of him who clamored. I re-echoed—I aided—I surpassed them in volume and in strength. I did this, and the clamorer grew still.

It was now midnight, and my task was drawing to a close. I had completed the eighth, the ninth, and the tenth tier. I had finished a portion of the last and the eleventh; there remained but a single stone to be fitted and plastered in. I struggled with its weight; I placed it partially in its destined position. But now there came from out the niche a low laugh that erected the hairs upon my head. It

was succeeded by a sad voice, which I had difficulty in recognizing
as that of the noble Fortunato. The voice said—

"Ha! ha! ha!—he! he!—a very good joke indeed—an excellent
jest. We will have many a rich laugh about it at the palazzo—he!
he! he!—over our wine—he! he! he!"

"The Amontillado!" I said.

"He! he! he!—he! he! he!—yes, the Amontillado. But is it not
getting late? Will not they be awaiting us at the palazzo, the Lady
Fortunato and the rest? Let us be gone."

"Yes," I said, "let us be gone."

"For the love of God, Montresor!"

"Yes," I said, "for the love of God!"

But to these words I hearkened in vain for a reply. I grew impatient. I called aloud—

"Fortunato!"

No answer. I called again—

"Fortunato!"

No answer still. I thrust a torch through the remaining aperture
and let it fall within. There came forth in return only a jingling of
the bells. My heart grew sick—on account of the dampness of the
catacombs. I hastened to make an end of my labor. I forced the
last stone into its position; I plastered it up. Against the new
masonry I re-erected the old rampart of bones. For the half of a
century no mortal has disturbed them. *In pace requiescat!*[2]

1846, 1850

Letter to B——[3]

It has been said that a good critique on a poem may be written
by one who is no poet himself. This, according to *your* idea and
mine of poetry, I feel to be false—the less poetical the critic, the
less just the critique, and the converse. On this account, and because there are but few B——s in the world, I would be as much
ashamed of the world's good opinion as proud of your own. Another
than yourself might here observe, "Shakspeare is in possession of
the world's good opinion, and yet Shakspeare is the greatest of
poets. It appears then that the world judge correctly, why should
you be ashamed of their favorable judgment?" The difficulty lies
in the interpretation of the word "judgment" or "opinion." The
opinion is the world's, truly, but it may be called theirs as a man
would call a book his, having bought it; he did not write the book,

2. "May he rest in peace."
3. The text is that of the *Southern Literary Messenger,* July, 1836. In the 1831 edition of Poe's poems the article opened as a letter addressed to "Dear B——," who is generally assumed to have been Elam Bliss, Poe's publisher. The asterisks appear in both versions and do not signify omissions.

but it is his; they did not originate the opinion, but it is theirs.
A fool, for example, thinks Shakspeare a great poet—yet the fool
has never read Shakspeare. But the fool's neighbor, who is a step
higher on the Andes of the mind, whose head (that is to say his
more exalted thought) is too far above the fool to be seen or understood, but whose feet (by which I mean his every-day actions)
are sufficiently near to be discerned, and by means of which that
superiority is ascertained, which *but* for them would never have
been discovered—this neighbor asserts that Shakspeare is a great
poet—the fool believes him, and it is henceforward his *opinion*.
This neighbor's own opinion has, in like manner, been adopted
from one above *him*, and so, ascendingly, to a few gifted individuals, who kneel around the summit, beholding, face to face, the
master spirit who stands upon the pinnacle.   *   *

You are aware of the great barrier in the path of an American
writer. He is read, if at all, in preference to the combined and
established wit of the world. I say established; for it is with
literature as with law or empire—an established name is an estate
in tenure, or a throne in possession. Besides, one might suppose
that books, like their authors, improve by travel—their having
crossed the sea is, with us, so great a distinction. Our antiquaries
abandon time for distance; our very fops glance from the binding to
the bottom of the title-page, where the mystic characters which
spell London, Paris, or Genoa, are precisely so many letters of
recommendation.

                *   *   *   *   *

I mentioned just now a vulgar error as regards criticism. I think
the notion that no poet can form a correct estimate of his own
writings is another. I remarked before, that in proportion to the
poetical talent, would be the justice of a critique upon poetry.
Therefore, a bad poet would, I grant, make a false critique, and his
self-love would infallibly bias his little judgment in his favor; but
a poet, who is indeed a poet, could not, I think, fail of making a
just critique. Whatever should be deducted on the score of self-
love, might be replaced on account of his intimate acquaintance
with the subject; in short, we have more instances of false criticism
than of just, where one's own writings are the test, simply because
we have more bad poets than good. There are of course many objections to what I say: Milton is a great example of the contrary;
but his opinion with respect to the Paradise Regained, is by no
means fairly ascertained. By what trivial circumstances men are
often led to assert what they do not really believe! Perhaps an
inadvertent word has descended to posterity. But, in fact, the

Paradise Regained is little, if at all, inferior to the Paradise Lost, and is only supposed so to be, because men do not like epics, whatever they may say to the contrary, and reading those of Milton in their natural order, are too much wearied with the first to derive any pleasure from the second.

I dare say Milton preferred Comus to either—if so—justly.

*   *   *   *   *

As I am speaking of poetry, it will not be amiss to touch slightly upon the most singular heresy in its modern history—the heresy of what is called very foolishly, the Lake School. Some years ago I might have been induced, by an occasion like the present, to attempt a formal refutation of their doctrine; at present it would be a work of supererogation. The wise must bow to the wisdom of such men as Coleridge and Southey, but being wise, have laughed at poetical theories so prosaically exemplified.

Aristotle, with singular assurance, has declared poetry the most philosophical of all writing[4]—but it required a Wordsworth to pronounce it the most metaphysical. He seems to think that the end of poetry is, or should be, instruction—yet it is a truism that the end of our existence is happiness; if so, the end of every separate part of our existence—every thing connected with our existence should be still happiness. Therefore the end of instruction should be happiness; and happiness is another name for pleasure;—therefore the end of instruction should be pleasure: yet we see the above mentioned opinion implies precisely the reverse.

To proceed: *ceteris paribus,*[5] he who pleases, is of more importance to his fellow men than he who instructs, since utility is happiness, and pleasure is the end already obtained which instruction is merely the means of obtaining.

I see no reason, then, why our metaphysical poets should plume themselves so much on the utility of their works, unless indeed they refer to instruction with eternity in view; in which case, sincere respect for their piety would not allow me to express my contempt for their judgment; contempt which it would be difficult to conceal, since their writings are professedly to be understood by the few, and it is the many who stand in need of salvation. In such case I should no doubt be tempted to think of the devil in Melmoth,[6] who labors indefatigably through three octavo volumes, to ac-

4. "Spoudiotaton kaí philosophikotaton genos" [Poe's note]. What Aristotle says in the passage from which the quotation is taken (*Poetics* ix.3) is that poetry is more philosophical than history because it expresses the universal, whereas history expresses the particular.
5. "Other things being equal."
6. *Melmoth the Wanderer* (1820), by Charles Maturin.

complish the destruction of one or two souls, while any common
devil would have demolished one or two thousand.

*   *   *   *   *

Against the subtleties which would make poetry a study—not
a passion—it becomes the metaphysician to reason—but the poet
to protest. Yet Wordsworth and Coleridge are men in years; the
one imbued in contemplation from his childhood, the other a giant
in intellect and learning. The diffidence, then, with which I venture to dispute their authority would be overwhelming, did I not
feel, from the bottom of my heart, that learning has little to do
with the imagination—intellect with the passions—or age with
poetry.   *   *   *

"Trifles, like straws, upon the surface flow,
He who would search for pearls must dive below," [7]

are lines which have done much mischief. As regards the greater
truths, men oftener err by seeking them at the bottom than at the
top; the depth lies in the huge abysses where wisdom is sought—
not in the palpable palaces where she is found. The ancients were
not always right in hiding the goddess in a well: witness the light
which Bacon has thrown upon philosophy; witness the principles
of our divine faith—that moral mechanism by which the simplicity
of a child may overbalance the wisdom of a man.

We see an instance of Coleridge's liability to err in his Biographia Literaria—professedly his literary life and opinions, but,
in fact, a treatise *de omni scibili et quibusdam aliis*. [8] He goes
wrong by reason of his very profundity, and of his error we have
a natural type in the contemplation of a star. He who regards it
directly and intensely sees, it is true, the star, but it is the star without a ray—while he who surveys it less inquisitively is conscious
of all for which the star is useful to us below—its brilliancy and its
beauty.

*   *   *   *   *

As to Wordsworth, I have no faith in him. That he had, in
youth, the feelings of a poet I believe—for there are glimpses of
extreme delicacy in his writings—(and delicacy is the poet's own
kingdom—his *El Dorado*)—but they have the appearance of a better day recollected; and glimpses, at best, are little evidence of
present poetic fire—we know that a few straggling flowers spring
up daily in the crevices of the glacier.

He was to blame in wearing away his youth in contemplation

7. From the Prologue to John Dryden's
All for Love, lines 25–26. Poe substituted "trifles" for Dryden's "errors."
8. "Of everything knowable and certain
other things." Coleridge's *Biographia
Literaria* (1817) became a major influence in the development of Poe's
critical theory.

with the end of poetizing in his manhood. With the increase of his judgment the light which should make it apparent has faded away. His judgment consequently is too correct. This may not be understood, but the old Goths of Germany would have understood it, who used to debate matters of importance to their State twice, once when drunk, and once when sober—sober that they might not be deficient in formality—drunk lest they should be destitute of vigor.

The long wordy discussions by which he tries to reason us into admiration of his poetry, speak very little in his favor: they are full of such assertions as this—(I have opened one of his volumes at random) "Of genius the only proof is the act of doing well what is worthy to be done, and what was never done before"—indeed! then it follows that in doing what is *un*worthy to be done, or what *has* been done before, no genius can be evinced: yet the picking of pockets is an unworthy act, pockets have been picked time immemorial, and Barrington, the pick-pocket, in point of genius, would have thought hard of a comparison with William Wordsworth, the poet.

Again—in estimating the merit of certain poems, whether they be Ossian's or M'Pherson's, can surely be of little consequence, yet, in order to prove their worthlessness, Mr. W. has expended many pages in the controversy. *Tantœne animis?*[9] Can great minds descend to such absurdity? But worse still: that he may bear down every argument in favor of these poems, he triumphantly drags forward a passage, in his abomination of which he expects the reader to sympathize. It is the beginning of the epic poem *"Temora."*[1] "The blue waves of Ullin roll in light; the green hills are covered with day; trees shake their dusky heads in the breeze." And this—this gorgeous, yet simple imagery—where all is alive and panting with immortality—this—William Wordsworth, the author of Peter Bell, has *selected* for his contempt. We shall see what better he, in his own person, has to offer.[2] Imprimis:

> "And now she's at the pony's head,
> And now she's at the pony's tail,
> On that side now, and now on this,
> And almost stifled her with bliss—
> A few sad tears does Betty shed,
> She pats the pony where or when

9. "Why so much feeling?"
1. This was one of the poems published by James Macpherson (1736–96) as translations from the Gaelic of the legendary Celtic bard Ossian. (Samuel Johnson, a contemporary of Macpherson, called them forgeries; the question of their authenticity has been widely debated.)
2. Poe's first example is from "The Idiot Boy" and the second from "The Pet Lamb," slightly altered.

> She knows not: happy Betty Foy!
> O Johnny! never mind the Doctor!"

Secondly:

> "The dew was falling fast, the—stars began to blink,
> I heard a voice, it said—drink, pretty creature, drink;
> And looking o'er the hedge, be—fore me I espied
> A snow-white mountain lamb with a—maiden at its side.
> No other sheep were near, the lamb was all alone,
> And by a slender cord was—tether'd to a stone."

Now we have no doubt this is all true; we *will* believe it, indeed we will, Mr. W. Is it sympathy for the sheep you wish to excite? I love a sheep from the bottom of my heart.

*   *   *   *   *

But there *are* occasions, dear B———, there are occasions when even Wordsworth is reasonable. Even Stamboul, it is said, shall have an end, and the most unlucky blunders must come to a conclusion. Here is an extract from his preface—

"Those who have been accustomed to the phraseology of modern writers, if they persist in reading this book to a conclusion (*impossible!*) will, no doubt, have to struggle with feelings of awkwardness; (ha! ha! ha!) they will look round for poetry (ha! ha! ha! ha!) and will be induced to inquire by what species of courtesy these attempts have been permitted to assume that title." Ha! ha! ha! ha! ha!

Yet let not Mr. W. despair; he has given immortality to a wagon, and the bee Sophocles has transmitted to eternity a sore toe, and dignified a tragedy with a chorus of turkeys.

*   *   *   *   *

Of Coleridge I cannot speak but with reverence. His towering intellect! his gigantic power! He is one more evidence of the fact "que la plupart des sectes ont raison dans une bonne partie de ce qu'elles avancent, mais non pas en ce qu'elles nient." [3] He has imprisoned his own conceptions by the barrier he has erected against those of others. It is lamentable to think that such a mind should be buried in metaphysics, and, like the Nyctanthes,[4] waste its perfume upon the night alone. In reading his poetry I tremble—like one who stands upon a volcano, conscious, from the very dark-

---

3. "That most sects are right in much of what they advocate, but not in what they deny."

4. A genus of shrubs native to East India, of which the only surviving example is the hursinghar, a small tree bearing fragrant white flowers that open only at night.

ness bursting from the crater, of the fire and the light that are weltering below.

*   *   *   *   *

What is Poetry? Poetry! that Proteus-like idea, with as many appellations as the nine-titled Corcyra![5] Give me, I demanded of a scholar some time ago, give me a definition of poetry. "Tres volontiers,"—and he proceeded to his library, brought me a Dr. Johnson, and overwhelmed me with a definition. Shade of the immortal Shakspeare! I imagined to myself the scowl of your spiritual eye upon the profanity of that scurrilous Ursa Major. Think of poetry, dear B——, think of poetry, and then think of—Dr. Samuel Johnson! Think of all that is airy and fairy-like, and then of all that is hideous and unwieldy; think of his huge bulk, the Elephant! and then—and then think of the Tempest—the Midsummer Night's Dream—Prospero—Oberon—and Titania!

*   *   *   *   *

A poem, in my opinion, is opposed to a work of science by having, for its *immediate* object, pleasure, not truth; to romance, by having for its object an *indefinite* instead of a *definite* pleasure, being a poem only so far as this object is attained: romance presenting perceptible images with definite, poetry with *in*definite sensations, to which end music is an *essential*, since the comprehension of sweet sound is our most indefinite conception. Music, when combined with a pleasurable idea, is poetry; music without the idea is simply music; the idea without the music is prose from its very definitiveness.

What was meant by the invective against him who had no music in his soul?

*   *   *   *   *

To sum up this long rigmarole, I have, dear B——, what you no doubt perceive, for the metaphysical poets, *as* poets, the most sovereign contempt. That they have followers proves nothing—

> No Indian prince has to his palace
> More followers than a thief to the gallows.[6]

Exordium

In commencing, with the New Year, a New Volume,[7] we shall be permitted to say a very few words by way of *exordium* to our

5. Modern Corfu, a Greek island which has had several names.
6. From Samuel Butler's *Hudibras* II.

i. 272–73 (1664).
7. Of *Graham's Magazine*, January, 1842. The text is that of *Graham's*.

usual chapter of Reviews, or, as we should prefer calling them, of Critical Notices. Yet we speak *not* for the sake of *exordium*, but because we have really something to say, and know not when or where better to say it.

That the public attention, in America, has, of late days, been more than usually directed to the matter of literary criticism, is plainly apparent. Our periodicals are beginning to acknowledge the importance of the science (shall we so term it?) and to disdain the flippant *opinion* which so long has been made its substitute.

Time was when we imported our critical decisions from the mother country. For many years we enacted a perfect farce of subserviency to the *dicta* of Great Britain. At last a revulsion of feeling, with self-disgust, necessarily ensued. Urged by these, we plunged into the opposite extreme. In throwing *totally* off that "authority," whose voice had so long been so sacred, we even surpassed, and by much, our original folly. But the watchword now was, "A national literature!"—as if any true literature *could be* "national"—as if the world at large were not the only proper stage for the literary *histrio*.[8] We became, suddenly, the merest and maddest *partizans* in letters. Our papers spoke of "tariffs" and "protection." Our Magazines had habitual passages about that "truly native novelist, Mr. Cooper," or that "staunch American genius, Mr. Paulding."[9] Unmindful of the spirit of the axioms that "a prophet has no honor in his own land" and that "a hero is never a hero to his *valet-de-chambre*"—axioms founded in reason and in truth—our reviews urged the propriety—our booksellers the necessity, of strictly "American" themes. A foreign subject, at this epoch, was a weight more than enough to drag down into the very depths of critical damnation the finest writer owning nativity in the States; while, on the reverse, we found ourselves daily in the paradoxical dilemma of liking, or pretending to like, a stupid book the better because (sure enough) its stupidity was of our own growth, and discussed our own affairs.

It is, in fact, but very lately that this anomalous state of feeling has shown any signs of subsidence. Still it *is* subsiding. Our views of literature in general having expanded, we begin to demand the use—to inquire into the offices and provinces of criticism—to regard it more as an art based immoveably in nature, less as a mere system of fluctuating and conventional dogmas. And, with the prevalence of these ideas, has arrived a distaste even to the home-dictation of the bookseller-*coteries*. If our editors are not as yet *all* independent of the will of a publisher, a majority of them scruple, at least, *to confess* a subservience, and enter into no positive

8. Actor.
9. James Kirke Paulding (1778–1860), a well-known literary man in Poe's time;

author of *The Dutchman's Fireside* (1831) and other novels.

combinations against the minority who despise and discard it. And this is a *very* great improvement of exceedingly late date.

Escaping these quicksands, our criticism is nevertheless in some danger—some very little danger—of falling into the pit of a most detestable species of cant—the cant of *generality*. This tendency has been given it, in the first instance, by the onward and tumultuous spirit of the age. With the increase of the thinking-material comes the desire, if not the necessity, of abandoning particulars for masses. Yet in our individual case, as a nation, we seem merely to have adopted this bias from the British Quarterly Reviews, upon which our own Quarterlies have been slavishly and pertinaciously modelled. In the foreign journal, the review or criticism properly so termed has gradually yet steadily degenerated into what we see it at present—that is to say, into anything but criticism. Originally a "review" was not so called as *lucus a non lucendo*.[1] Its name conveyed a just idea of its design. It reviewed, or surveyed the book whose title formed its text, and, giving an analysis of its contents, passed judgment upon its merits or defects. But, through the system of anonymous contribution, this natural process lost ground from day to day. The name of a writer being known only to a few, it became to him an object not so much to write well, as to write fluently, at so many guineas per sheet. The analysis of a book is a matter of time and of mental exertion. For many classes of composition there is required a deliberate perusal, with notes, and subsequent generalization. An easy substitute for this labor was found in a digest or compendium of the work noticed, with copious extracts —or a still easier, in random comments upon such passages as accidentally met the eye of the critic, with the passages themselves copied at full length. The mode of reviewing most in favor, however, because carrying with it the greatest *semblance* of care, was that of diffuse essay upon the subject matter of the publication, the reviewer (?) using the facts alone which the publication supplied, and using them as material for some theory, the sole concern, bearing, and intention of which, was mere difference of opinion with the author. These came at length to be understood and habitually practised as the customary or conventional *fashions* of review; and although the nobler order of intellects did not fall into the full heresy of these fashions—we may still assert that even Macaulay's nearest approach to criticism in its legitimate sense, is to be found in his article upon Ranke's "History of the Popes"—an article in which the whole strength of the reviewer is put forth *to account* for a single fact—the

---

1. Literally, "a grove from not being light." Here it means something etymologically absurd and illogical.

progress of Romanism—which the book under discussion has established.

Now, while we do not mean to deny that a good essay is a good thing, we yet assert that these papers on general topics have nothing whatever to do with that *criticism* which their evil example has nevertheless infected *in se*.[2] Because these dogmatising pamphlets, which *were once* "Reviews," have lapsed from their original faith, it does not follow that the faith itself is extinct— that "there shall be no more cakes and ale"—that criticism, in its old acceptation, does not exist. But we complain of a growing inclination on the part of our lighter journals to believe, on such grounds, that such is the fact—that because the British Quarterlies, through supineness, and our own, through a degrading imitation, have come to merge all varieties of vague generalization in the one title of "Review," it therefore results that criticism, being everything in the universe, is, consequently, nothing whatever in fact. For to this end, and to none other conceivable, is the tendency of such propositions, for example, as we find in a late number of that very clever monthly magazine, Arcturus.

"But *now*" (the emphasis on the *now* is our own)—"But *now*," says Mr. Mathews,[3] in the preface to the first volume of his journal, "criticism has a wider scope and a universal interest. It dismisses errors of grammar, and hands over an imperfect rhyme or a false quantity to the proof-reader; it looks *now* to the heart of the subject and the author's design. It is a test of opinion. Its acuteness is not pedantic, but philosophical; it unravels the web of the author's mystery to interpret his meaning to others; it detects his sophistry, because sophistry is injurious to the heart and life; it promulgates his beauties with liberal, generous praise, because this is its true duty as the servant of truth. Good criticism may be well asked for, since it is the type of literature of the day. It gives method to the universal inquisitiveness on every topic relating to life or action. A criticism, *now*, includes every form of literature except perhaps the imaginative and the strictly dramatic. It is an essay, a sermon, an oration, a chapter in history, a philosophical speculation, a prose-poem, an art-novel, a dialogue; it admits of humor, pathos, the personal feelings of auto-biography, the broadest views of statesmanship. As the ballad and the epic were the productions of the days of Homer, the review is the native characteristic growth of the nineteenth century."

We respect the talent of Mr. Mathews, but must dissent from nearly all that he here says. The species of "review" which he designates as the "characteristic growth of the nineteenth cen-

2. "In itself." 3. Cornelius Mathews (1817–89), editor of *Arcturus*.

tury" is only the growth of the last twenty or thirty years *in Great Britain.* The French Reviews, for example, which are *not* anonymous, are very different things, and preserve the *unique* spirit of true criticism. And what need we say of the Germans? —what of Winckelmann, of Novalis, of Schelling, of Goethe, of Augustus William, and of Frederick Schlegel?—that their magnificent *critiques raisonnées* differ from those of Kames, of Johnson, and of Blair, in principle not at all, (for the principles of these artists will not fail until Nature herself expires,) but solely in their more careful elaboration, their greater thoroughness, the more profound analysis and application of the principles themselves. That a criticism *"now"* should be different in spirit, as Mr. Mathews supposes, from a criticism at any previous period, is to insinuate a charge of variability in laws that cannot vary—the laws of man's heart and intellect—for these are the sole basis upon which the true critical art is established. And this art *"now"* no more than in the days of the "Dunciad," can, without neglect of its duty, "dismiss errors of grammar," or "hand over an imperfect rhyme or a false quantity to the proofreader." What is meant by a "test of opinion" in the connexion here given the words by Mr. M., we do not comprehend as clearly as we could desire. By this phrase we are as completely enveloped in doubt as was Mirabeau in the castle of *If.* To our imperfect appreciation it seems to form a portion of that general vagueness which is the *tone* of the whole philosophy at this point:—but all that which our journalist describes a criticism to be, is all that which we sturdily maintain it *is not.* Criticism is *not,* we think, an essay, nor a sermon, nor an oration, nor a chapter in history, nor a philosophical speculation, nor a prose-poem, nor an art novel, nor a dialogue. In fact, it *can be* nothing in the world but—a criticism. But if it were all that Arcturus imagines, it is not very clear why it might not be equally "imaginative" or "dramatic"—a romance or a melo-drama, or both. That it would be a farce cannot be doubted.

It is against this frantic spirit of *generalization* that we protest. We have a word, "criticism," whose import is sufficiently distinct, through long usage, at least; and we have an art of high importance and clearly-ascertained limit, which this word is quite well enough understood to represent. Of that conglomerate science to which Mr. Mathews so eloquently alludes, and of which we are instructed that it is anything and everything at once— of this science we know nothing, and really wish to know less; but we object to our contemporary's appropriation in its behalf, of a term to which we, in common with a large majority of mankind, have been accustomed to attach a certain and very definite idea. Is there no word but "criticism" which may be made to serve the purposes of "Arcturus"? Has it any objection to Orphicism, or Dialism, or Emersonism, or any other pregnant compound indicative of confusion worse confounded?[4]

Still, we must not pretend a total misapprehension of the idea of Mr. Mathews, and we should be sorry that he misunderstood *us*. It may be granted that we differ only in terms—although the difference will yet be found not unimportant in effect. Following the highest authority, we would wish, in a word, to limit literary criticism to comment upon *Art*. A book is written—and it is only *as the book* that we subject it to review. With the opinions of the work, considered otherwise than in their relation to the work itself, the critic has really nothing to do. It is his part simply to decide upon *the mode* in which these opinions are brought to bear. Criticism is thus no "test of opinion." For this test, the work, divested of its pretensions as an *art-product*, is turned over for discussion to the world at large—and first, to that class which it especially addresses—if a history, to the historian—if a metaphysical treatise, to the moralist. In this, the only true and intelligible sense, it will be seen that criticism, the test or analysis of *Art*, (*not* of opinion,) is only properly employed upon productions which have their basis in art itself, and although the journalist (whose duties and objects are multiform) may turn aside, at pleasure, from the *mode* or vehicle of opinion to discussion of the opinion conveyed—it is still clear that he is "*critical*" only in so much as he deviates from his true province not at all.

And of the critic himself what shall we say?—for as yet we have spoken only the *proem* to the true *epopea*.[5] What *can* we better say of him than, with Bulwer, that "he must have courage to blame boldly, magnanimity to eschew envy, genius to appreciate, learning to compare, an eye for beauty, an ear for music, and a heart for feeling." Let us add, a talent for analysis and a solemn indifference to abuse.

1842

Hawthorne's *Twice-Told Tales*[6]

We said a few hurried words about Mr. Hawthorne in our last number, with the design of speaking more fully in the present. We

4. "Orphicism" here means "mysticism," "occultism." A. B. Alcott was sometimes called the "Orphic Poet." The *Dial* was a magazine (1840–44) devoted to transcendental ideas and edited by Margaret Fuller and Emerson.

5. Epic.

6. The text is that of *Graham's Magazine*, May, 1842. Poe reprinted this review, with considerable revision, in *Godey's Lady's Book* for November, 1847.

are still, however, pressed for room, and must necessarily discuss his volumes more briefly and more at random than their high merits deserve.

The book professes to be a collection of *tales*, yet is, in two respects, misnamed. These pieces are now in their third republication, and, of course, are thrice-told. Moreover, they are by no means *all* tales, either in the ordinary or in the legitimate understanding of the term. Many of them are pure essays; for example, "Sights from a Steeple," "Sunday at Home," "Little Annie's Ramble," "A Rill from the Town Pump," "The Toll-Gatherer's Day," "The Haunted Mind," "The Sister Years," "Snow-Flakes," "Night Sketches," and "Foot-Prints on the Sea-Shore." We mention these matters chiefly on account of their discrepancy with that marked precision and finish by which the body of the work is distinguished.

Of the Essays just named, we must be content to speak in brief. They are each and all beautiful, without being characterized by the polish and adaptation so visible in the tales proper. A painter would at once note their leading or predominant feature, and style it *repose.* There is no attempt at effect. All is quiet, thoughtful, subdued. Yet this repose may exist simultaneously with high originality of thought; and Mr. Hawthorne has demonstrated the fact. At every turn we meet with novel combinations; yet these combinations never surpass the limits of the quiet. We are soothed as we read; and withal is a calm astonishment that ideas so apparently obvious have never occurred or been presented to us before. Herein our author differs materially from Lamb or Hunt or Hazlitt—who, with vivid originality of manner and expression, have less of the true novelty of thought than is generally supposed, and whose originality, at best, has an uneasy and meretricious quaintness, replete with startling effects unfounded in nature, and inducing trains of reflection which lead to no satisfactory result. The Essays of Hawthorne have much of the character of Irving, with more of originality, and less of finish; while, compared with the Spectator, they have a vast superiority at all points. The Spectator, Mr. Irving, and Mr. Hawthorne have in common that tranquil and subdued manner which we have chosen to denominate *repose*; but, in the case of the two former, this repose is attained rather by the absence of novel combination, or of originality, than otherwise, and consists chiefly in the calm, quiet, unostentatious expression of commonplace thoughts, in an unambitious, unadulterated Saxon. In them, by strong effort, we are made to conceive the absence of all. In the essays before us the absence of effort is too obvious to be mistaken, and a strong under-current of *suggestion* runs continuously beneath the upper stream of the tranquil thesis. In short, these effusions of Mr. Hawthorne are the product of a truly imaginative intellect, restrained, and in some

notes

measure repressed, by fastidiousness of taste, by constitutional melancholy and by indolence.

But it is of his tales that we desire principally to speak. The tale proper, in our opinion, affords unquestionably the fairest field for the exercise of the loftiest talent, which can be afforded by the wide domains of mere prose. Were we bidden to say how the highest genius could be most advantageously employed for the best display of its own powers, we should answer, without hesitation—in the composition of a rhymed poem, not to exceed in length what might be perused in an hour. Within this limit alone can the highest order of true poetry exist. We need only here say, upon this topic, that, in almost all classes of composition, the unity of effect or impression is a point of the greatest importance. It is clear, moreover, that this unity cannot be thoroughly preserved in productions whose perusal cannot be completed at one sitting. We may continue the reading of a prose composition, from the very nature of prose itself, much longer than we can persevere, to any good purpose, in the perusal of a poem. This latter, if truly fulfilling the demands of the poetic sentiment, induces an exaltation of the soul which cannot be long sustained. All high excitements are necessarily transient. Thus a long poem is a paradox. And, without unity of impression, the deepest effects cannot be brought about. Epics were the offspring of an imperfect sense of Art, and their reign is no more. A poem *too* brief may produce a vivid, but never an intense or enduring impression. Without a certain continuity of effort—without a certain duration or repetition of purpose—the soul is never deeply moved. There must be the dropping of the water upon the rock. De Béranger[7] has wrought brilliant things—pungent and spirit-stirring —but, like all immassive bodies, they lack *momentum*, and thus fail to satisfy the Poetic Sentiment. They sparkle and excite, but, from want of continuity, fail deeply to impress. Extreme brevity will degenerate into epigrammatism; but the sin of extreme length is even more unpardonable. *In medio tutissimus ibis.*[8]

Were we called upon, however, to designate that class of composition which, next to such a poem as we have suggested, should best fulfil the demands of high genius—should offer it the most advantageous field of exertion—we should unhesitatingly speak of the prose tale, as Mr. Hawthorne has here exemplified it. We allude to the short prose narrative, requiring from a half-hour to one or two hours in its perusal. The ordinary novel is objectionable, from its length, for reasons already stated in substance. As it cannot be read at one sitting, it deprives itself, of course, of the immense force derivable from *totality*. Worldly interests intervening during the pauses

7. French lyric poet, quoted or referred to also in "Israfel," "The Fall of the House of Usher," and "The Poetic Principle."

8. "You will go most safely in the middle way." From Ovid's *Metamorphoses.*

of perusal, modify, annul, or counteract, in a greater or less degree, the impressions of the book. But simple cessation in reading would, of itself, be sufficient to destroy the true unity. In the brief tale, however, the author is enabled to carry out the fulness of his intention, be it what it may. During the hour of perusal the soul of the reader is at the writer's control. There are no external or extrinsic influences—resulting from weariness or interruption.

A skilful literary artist has constructed a tale. If wise, he has not fashioned his thoughts to accommodate his incidents; but having conceived, with deliberate care, a certain unique or single *effect* to be wrought out, he then invents such incidents—he then combines such events as may best aid him in establishing this preconceived effect. If his very initial sentence tend not to the outbringing of this effect, then he has failed in his first step. In the whole composition there should be no word written, of which the tendency, direct or indirect, is not to the one pre-established design. And by such means, with such care and skill, a picture is at length painted which leaves in the mind of him who contemplates it with a kindred art, a sense of the fullest satisfaction. The idea of the tale has been presented unblemished, because undisturbed; and this is an end unattainable by the novel. Undue brevity is just as exceptionable here as in the poem; but undue length is yet more to be avoided.

We have said that the tale has a point of superiority even over the poem. In fact, while the *rhythm* of this latter is an essential aid in the development of the poem's highest idea—the idea of the Beautiful—the artificialities of this rhythm are an inseparable bar to the development of all points of thought or expression which have their basis in *Truth*. But Truth is often, and in very great degree, the aim of the tale. Some of the finest tales are tales of ratiocination. Thus the field of this species of composition, if not in so elevated a region on the mountain of Mind, is a table-land of far vaster extent than the domain of the mere poem. Its products are never so rich, but infinitely more numerous, and more appreciable by the mass of mankind. The writer of the prose tale, in short, may bring to his theme a vast variety of modes or inflections of thought and expression— (the ratiocinative, for example, the sarcastic, or the humorous) which are not only antagonistical to the nature of the poem, but absolutely forbidden by one of its most peculiar and indispensable adjuncts; we allude, of course, to rhythm. It may be added here, *par parenthèse*, that the author who aims at the purely beautiful in a prose tale is laboring at a great disadvantage. For Beauty can be better treated in the poem. Not so with terror, or passion, or horror, or a multitude of such other points. And here it will be seen how full of prejudice are the usual animadversions against those *tales of effect*, many fine examples of which were found in the earlier numbers of Blackwood. The impressions produced were wrought in a legitimate sphere of action, and constituted a legitimate although sometimes an exaggerated interest. They were relished by every man of genius: although there were found many men of genius who condemned them without just ground. The true critic will but demand that the design intended be accomplished, to the fullest extent, by the means most advantageously applicable.

We have very few American tales of real merit—we may say, indeed, none, with the exception of "The Tales of a Traveller" of Washington Irving, and these "Twice-Told Tales" of Mr. Hawthorne. Some of the pieces of Mr. John Neal[9] abound in vigor and originality; but, in general, his compositions of this class are excessively diffuse, extravagant, and indicative of an imperfect sentiment of Art. Articles at random are, now and then, met with in our periodicals which might be advantageously compared with the best effusions of the British Magazines; but, upon the whole, we are far behind our progenitors in this department of literature.

Of Mr. Hawthorne's Tales we should say, emphatically, that they belong to the highest region of Art—an Art subservient to genius of a very lofty order. We had supposed, with good reason for so supposing, that he had been thrust into his present position by one of the impudent *cliques* which beset our literature, and whose pretensions it is our full purpose to expose at the earliest opportunity; but we have been most agreeably mistaken. We know of few compositions which the critic can more honestly commend than these "Twice-Told Tales." As Americans, we feel proud of the book.

Mr. Hawthorne's distinctive trait is invention, creation, imagination, originality—a trait which, in the literature of fiction, is positively worth all the rest. But the nature of the originality, so far as regards its manifestation in letters, is but imperfectly understood. The inventive or original mind as frequently displays itself in novelty of *tone* as in novelty of matter. Mr. Hawthorne is original at *all* points.

It would be a matter of some difficulty to designate the best of these tales; we repeat that, without exception, they are beautiful. "Wakefield" is remarkable for the skill with which an old idea—a well-known incident—is worked up or discussed. A man of whims conceives the purpose of quitting his wife and residing *incognito*, for twenty years, in her immediate neighborhood. Something of this kind actually happened in London. The force of Mr. Hawthorne's tale lies in the analysis of the motives which must or might have impelled the husband to such folly, in the first instance, with the possible causes of his perseverance. Upon this thesis a sketch of singular power has been constructed.

"The Wedding Knell" is full of the boldest imagination—an im-

9. John Neal (1793–1876), poet, journalist, and novelist; the first literary man of note to recognize the worth of Poe's poems.

agination fully controlled by taste. The most captious critic could find no flaw in this production.

"The Minister's Black Veil" is a masterly composition, of which the sole defect is that to the rabble its exquisite skill will be *caviare*.[1] The *obvious* meaning of this article will be found to smother its insinuated one. The *moral* put into the mouth of the dying minister will be supposed to convey the *true* import of the narrative; and that a crime of dark dye, (having reference to the "young lady") has been committed, is a point which only minds congenial with that of the author will perceive.

"Mr. Higginbotham's Catastrophe" is vividly original, and managed most dexterously.

"Dr. Heidegger's Experiment" is exceedingly well imagined, and executed with surpassing ability. The artist breathes in every line of it.

"The White Old Maid" is objectionable, even more than the "Minister's Black Veil," on the score of its mysticism. Even with the thoughtful and analytic, there will be much trouble in penetrating its entire import.

"The Hollow of the Three Hills" we would quote in full had we space;—not as evincing higher talent than any of the other pieces, but as affording an excellent example of the author's peculiar ability. The subject is commonplace. A witch subjects the Distant and the Past to the view of a mourner. It has been the fashion to describe, in such cases, a mirror in which the images of the absent appear; or a cloud of smoke is made to arise, and thence the figures are gradually unfolded. Mr. Hawthorne has wonderfully heightened his effect by making the ear, in place of the eye, the medium by which the fantasy is conveyed. The head of the mourner is enveloped in the cloak of the witch, and within its magic folds there arise sounds which have an all-sufficient intelligence. Throughout this article also, the artist is conspicuous—not more in positive than in negative merits. Not only is all done that should be done, but (what perhaps is an end with more difficulty attained) there is nothing done which should not be. Every word *tells*, and there is not a word which does *not* tell.

In "Howe's Masquerade" we observe something which resembles plagiarism[2]—but which *may be* a very flattering coincidence of thought. We quote the passage in question.

> "*With a dark flush of wrath* upon his brow they saw the general *draw his sword* and *advance to meet* the figure *in the cloak* before the latter had stepped one pace upon the floor.

1. That is, unappreciated by those of uncultivated taste.
2. One of the least admirable features of Poe's criticism was his penchant for accusing his contemporaries of plagiar-ism on insufficient evidence. The unprejudiced reader will see only a casual resemblance between the passage quoted from "Howe's Masquerade" and the two paragraphs from "William Wilson."

" 'Villain, *unmuffle* yourself,' cried he, 'you pass no farther!'

"The figure, without blanching a hair's breadth from the sword which was pointed at his breast, made a solemn pause, and lowered the cape of the cloak from his face, yet not sufficiently for the spectators to catch a glimpse of it. But Sir William Howe had evidently seen enough. The sternness of his countenance gave place to a look of wild amazement, if not horror, while he recoiled several steps from the figure, *and let fall his sword* upon the floor."

The idea here is, that the figure in the cloak is the phantom or reduplication of Sir William Howe; but in an article called "William Wilson," one of the *Tales of the Grotesque and Arabesque,* we have not only the same idea, but the same idea similarly presented in several respects. We quote two paragraphs, which our readers may compare with what has been already given. We have italicized, above, the immediate particulars of resemblance.

"The brief moment in which I averted my eyes had been sufficient to produce, apparently, a material change in the arrangement at the upper or farther end of the room. A large mirror, it appeared to me, now stood where none had been perceptible before: and as I stepped up to it in extremity of terror, mine own image, but with features pale and dabbled in blood, *advanced* with a feeble and tottering gait to meet me.

"Thus it appeared I say, but was not. It was Wilson, who then stood before me in the agonies of dissolution. Not a line in all the marked and singular lineaments of that face which was not even identically mine own. *His mask and cloak lay where he had thrown them, upon the floor.*"

Here it will be observed that, not only are the two general conceptions identical, but there are various *points* of similarity. In each case the figure seen is the wraith or duplication of the beholder. In each case the scene is a masquerade. In each case the figure is cloaked. In each, there is a quarrel—that is to say, angry words pass between the parties. In each the beholder is enraged. In each the cloak and sword fall upon the floor. The "villain, unmuffle yourself," of Mr. H. is precisely paralleled by a passage at page 56 of "William Wilson."

In the way of objection we have scarcely a word to say of these tales. There is, perhaps, a somewhat too general or prevalent *tone* —a tone of melancholy and mysticism. The subjects are insufficiently varied. There is not so much of *versatility* evinced as we might well be warranted in expecting from the high powers of Mr. Hawthorne. But beyond these trivial exceptions we have really none to make. The style is purity itself. Force abounds. High imagination gleams from every page. Mr. Hawthorne is a man of the truest genius. We only regret that the limits of our Magazine will not permit us to pay him that full tribute of commendation, which, under other circumstances, we should be so eager to pay.

1842

The Philosophy of Composition[3]

Charles Dickens, in a note now lying before me, alluding to an examination I once made of the mechanism of "Barnaby Rudge,"[4] says—"By the way, are you aware that Godwin wrote his 'Caleb Williams' backwards? He first involved his hero in a web of difficulties, forming the second volume, and then, for the first, cast about him for some mode of accounting for what had been done."

I cannot think this the *precise* mode of procedure on the part of Godwin—and indeed what he himself acknowledges, is not altogether in accordance with Mr. Dickens's idea—but the author of "Caleb Williams" was too good an artist not to perceive the advantage derivable from at least a somewhat similar process. Nothing is more clear than that every plot, worth the name, must be elaborated to its *dénouement* before anything be attempted with the pen. It is only with the *dénouement* constantly in view that we can give a plot its indispensable air of consequence, or causation, by making the incidents, and especially the tone at all points, tend to the development of the intention.

There is a radical error, I think, in the usual mode of constructing a story. Either history affords a thesis—or one is suggested by an incident of the day—or, at best, the author sets himself to work in the combination of striking events to form merely the basis of his narrative—designing, generally, to fill in with description, dialogue, or autorial comment, whatever crevices of fact, or action, may, from page to page, render themselves apparent.

I prefer commencing with the consideration of an *effect*. Keeping originality *always* in view—for he is false to himself who ventures to dispense with so obvious and so easily attainable a source of interest—I say to myself, in the first place, "Of the innumerable effects, or impressions, of which the heart, the intellect, or (more generally) the soul is susceptible, what one shall I, on the present occasion, select?" Having chosen a novel, first, and secondly a vivid effect, I consider whether it can be best wrought by incident or tone—whether by ordinary incidents and peculiar tone, or the converse, or by peculiarity both of incident and tone—afterward

3. The text is that of Griswold's edition of 1850.
4. Poe wrote a brief review of *Barnaby Rudge* for the Philadelphia *Saturday Evening Post* of May 1, 1841, while the novel was being published serially, in which he deduced the solution of the murder of the gardener long before it was revealed by the author.

looking about me (or rather within) for such combinations of event, or tone, as shall best aid me in the construction of the effect.

I have often thought how interesting a magazine paper might be written by any author who would—that is to say who could—detail, step by step, the processes by which any one of his compositions attained its ultimate point of completion. Why such a paper has never been given to the world, I am much at a loss to say—but, perhaps, the autorial vanity has had more to do with the omission than any one other cause. Most writers—poets in especial—prefer having it understood that they compose by a species of fine frenzy—an ecstatic intuition—and would positively shudder at letting the public take a peep behind the scenes, at the elaborate and vacillating crudities of thought—at the true purposes seized only at the last moment—at the innumerable glimpses of idea that arrived not at the maturity of full view—at the fully matured fancies discarded in despair as unmanageable—at the cautious selections and rejections—at the painful erasures and interpolations—in a word, at the wheels and pinions—the tackle for scene-shifting—the step-ladders and demon-traps—the cock's feathers, the red paint, and the black patches, which, in ninety-nine cases out of the hundred, constitute the properties of the literary *histrio*.

I am aware, on the other hand, that the case is by no means common, in which an author is at all in condition to retrace the steps by which his conclusions have been attained. In general, suggestions, having arisen pell-mell, are pursued and forgotten in a similar manner.

For my own part, I have neither sympathy with the repugnance alluded to, nor, at any time, the least difficulty in recalling to mind the progressive steps of any of my compositions; and, since the interest of an analysis, or reconstruction, such as I have considered a *desideratum*, is quite independent of any real or fancied interest in the thing analyzed, it will not be regarded as a breach of decorum on my part to show the *modus operandi* by which some one of my own works was put together. I select "The Raven" as most generally known. It is my design to render it manifest that no one point in its composition is referrible either to accident or intuition—that the work proceeded, step by step, to its completion with the precision and rigid consequence of a mathematical problem.

Let us dismiss, as irrelevant to the poem, *per se*, the circumstance —or say the necessity—which, in the first place, gave rise to the intention of composing *a* poem that should suit at once the popular and the critical taste.

We commence, then, with this intention.

The initial consideration was that of extent. If any literary work is too long to be read at one sitting, we must be content to dispense with the immensely important effect derivable from unity of impression—for, if two sittings be required, the affairs of the world interfere, and every thing like totality is at once destroyed. But since, *ceteris paribus*,[5] no poet can afford to dispense with *any thing* that may advance his design, it but remains to be seen whether there is, in extent, any advantage to counterbalance the loss of unity which attends it. Here I say no, at once. What we term a long poem is, in fact, merely a succession of brief ones—that is to say, of brief poetical effects. It is needless to demonstrate that a poem is such, only inasmuch as it intensely excites, by elevating, the soul; and all intense excitements are, through a psychal necessity, brief. For this reason, at least one half of the "Paradise Lost" is essentially prose —a succession of poetical excitements interpersed, *inevitably*, with corresponding depressions—the whole being deprived, through the extremeness of its length, of the vastly important artistic element, totality, or unity, of effect.

It appears evident, then, that there is a distinct limit, as regards length, to all works of literary art—the limit of a single sitting— and that, although in certain classes of prose composition, such as "Robinson Crusoe" (demanding no unity,) this limit may be advantageously overpassed, it can never properly be overpassed in a poem. Within this limit, the extent of a poem may be made to bear mathematical relation to its merit—in other words, to the excitement or elevation—again, in other words, to the degree of the true poetical effect which it is capable of inducing; for it is clear that the brevity must be in direct ratio of the intensity of the intended effect:—this, with one proviso—that a certain degree of duration is absolutely requisite for the production of any effect at all.

Holding in view these considerations, as well as that degree of excitement which I deemed not above the popular, while not below the critical, taste, I reached at once what I conceived the proper *length* for my intended poem—a length of about one hundred lines. It is, in fact, a hundred and eight.

My next thought concerned the choice of an impression, or effect, to be conveyed; and here I may as well observe that, throughout the construction, I kept steadily in view the design of rendering the work *universally* appreciable. I should be carried too far out of my immediate topic were I to demonstrate a point upon which I have repeatedly insisted, and which, with the poetical, stands not in the slightest need of demonstration—the point, I mean, that Beauty is the sole legitimate province of the poem. A few words, however, in elucidation of my real meaning, which some of my friends have evinced a disposition to misrepresent. That pleasure which is at once

5. "Other things being equal."

the most intense, the most elevating, and the most pure, is, I believe, found in the contemplation of the beautiful. When, indeed, men speak of Beauty, they mean, precisely, not a quality, as is supposed, but an effect—they refer, in short, just to that intense and pure elevation of *soul*—*not* of intellect, or of heart—upon which I have commented, and which is experienced in consequence of contemplating "the beautiful." Now I designate Beauty as the province of the poem, merely because it is an obvious rule of Art that effects should be made to spring from direct causes—that objects should be attained through means best adapted for their attainment—no one as yet having been weak enough to deny that the peculiar elevation alluded to is *most readily* attained in the poem. Now the object, Truth, or the satisfaction of the intellect, and the object Passion, or the excitement of the heart, are, although attainable, to a certain extent, in poetry, far more readily attainable in prose. Truth, in fact, demands a precision, and Passion a *homeliness* (the truly passionate will comprehend me) which are absolutely antagonistic to that Beauty which, I maintain, is the excitement, or pleasurable elevation, of the soul. It by no means follows from any thing here said, that passion, or even truth, may not be introduced, and even profitably introduced, into a poem—for they may serve in elucidation, or aid the general effect, as do discords in music, by contrast —but the true artist will always contrive, first, to tone them into proper subservience to the predominant aim, and, secondly, to enveil them, as far as possible, in that Beauty which is the atmosphere and the essence of the poem.

Regarding, then, Beauty as my province, my next question referred to the *tone* of its highest manifestation—and all experience has shown that this tone is one of *sadness*. Beauty of whatever kind, in its supreme development, invariably excites the sensitive soul to tears. Melancholy is thus the most legitimate of all the poetical tones.

The length, the province, and the tone, being thus determined, I betook myself to ordinary induction, with the view of obtaining some artistic piquancy which might serve me as a key-note in the construction of the poem—some pivot upon which the whole structure might turn. In carefully thinking over all the usual artistic effects—or more properly *points*, in the theatrical sense—I did not fail to perceive immediately that no one had been so universally employed as that of the *refrain*. The universality of its employment sufficed to assure me of its intrinsic value, and spared me the necessity of submitting it to analysis. I considered it, however, with regard to its susceptibility of improvement, and soon saw it to be in a primitive condition. As commonly used, the *refrain*, or burden, not only is limited to lyric verse, but depends for its impression upon the force of monotone—both in sound and thought. The pleasure is deduced solely from the sense of identity—of repetition. I resolved to diversify, and so heighten, the effect, by adhering, in general, to the monotone of sound, while I continually varied that of thought: that is to say, I determined to produce continuously novel effects, by the variation *of the application* of the *refrain*—the *refrain* itself remaining, for the most part, unvaried.

These points being settled, I next bethought me of the *nature* of my *refrain*. Since its application was to be repeatedly varied, it was clear that the *refrain* itself must be brief, for there would have been an insurmountable difficulty in frequent variations of application in any sentence of length. In proportion to the brevity of the sentence, would, of course, be the facility of the variation. This led me at once to a single word as the best *refrain*.

The question now arose as to the *character* of the word. Having made up my mind to a *refrain*, the division of the poem into stanzas was, of course, a corollary: the *refrain* forming the close to each stanza. That such a close, to have force, must be sonorous and susceptible of protracted emphasis, admitted no doubt: and these considerations inevitably led me to the long *o* as the most sonorous vowel, in connection with *r* as the most producible consonant.

The sound of the *refrain* being thus determined, it became necessary to select a word embodying this sound, and at the same time in the fullest possible keeping with that melancholy which I had predetermined as the tone of the poem. In such a search it would have been absolutely impossible to overlook the word "Nevermore." In fact, it was the very first which presented itself.

The next *desideratum* was a pretext for the continuous use of the one word "nevermore." In observing the difficulty which I at once found in inventing a sufficiently plausible reason for its continuous repetition, I did not fail to perceive that this difficulty arose solely from the pre-assumption that the word was to be so continuously or monotonously spoken by a *human* being—I did not fail to perceive, in short, that the difficulty lay in the reconciliation of this monotony with the exercise of reason on the part of the creature repeating the word. Here, then, immediately arose the idea of a *non*-reasoning creature capable of speech; and, very naturally, a parrot, in the first instance, suggested itself, but was superseded forthwith by a Raven, as equally capable of speech, and infinitely more in keeping with the intended *tone*.

I had now gone so far as the conception of a Raven—the bird of ill omen—monotonously repeating the one word, "Nevermore," at the conclusion of each stanza, in a poem of melancholy tone, and in length about one hundred lines. Now, never losing sight of the object *supremeness*, or perfection, at all points, I asked myself—"Of all melancholy topics, what, according to the *universal* understanding of mankind, is the *most* melancholy?" Death—was the obvious reply. "And when," I said, "is this most melancholy of topics most poetical?" From what I have already explained at some length, the answer, here also, is obvious—"When it most closely allies itself to *Beauty*: the death, then, of a beautiful woman is, unquestionably, the most poetical topic in the world—and equally is it beyond doubt that the lips best suited for such topic are those of a bereaved lover."

I had now to combine the two ideas, of a lover lamenting his deceased mistress and a Raven continuously repeating the word "Nevermore."—I had to combine these, bearing in mind my design of varying, at every turn, the *application* of the word repeated; but the only intelligible mode of such combination is that of imagining the Raven employing the word in answer to the queries of the lover. And here it was that I saw at once the opportunity afforded for the effect on which I had been depending—that is to say, the effect of the *variation of application*. I saw that I could make the first query propounded by the lover—the first query to which the Raven should reply "Nevermore"—that I could make this first query a commonplace one—the second less so—the third still less, and so on—until at length the lover, startled from his original *nonchalance* by the melancholy character of the word itself —by its frequent repetition—and by a consideration of the ominous reputation of the fowl that uttered it—is at length excited to superstition, and wildly propounds queries of a far different character—queries whose solution he has passionately at heart—propounds them half in superstition and half in that species of despair which delights in self-torture—propounds them not altogether because he believes in the prophetic or demoniac character of the bird (which, reason assures him, is merely repeating a lesson learned by rote) but because he experiences a frenzied pleasure in so modeling his questions as to receive from the *expected* "Nevermore" the most delicious because the most intolerable of sorrow. Perceiving the opportunity thus afforded me—or, more strictly, thus forced upon me in the progress of the construction—I first established in mind the climax, or concluding query—that query to which "Nevermore" should be in the last place an answer—that query in reply to which this word "Nevermore" should involve the utmost conceivable amount of sorrow and despair.

Here then the poem may be said to have its beginning—at the end, where all works of art should begin—for it was here, at this point of my preconsiderations, that I first put pen to paper in the composition of the stanza:

"Prophet," said I, "thing of evil! prophet still if bird or devil!
By that heaven that bends above us—by that God we both adore,

Tell this soul with sorrow laden, if within the distant Aidenn,
It shall clasp a sainted maiden whom the angels name Lenore—
Clasp a rare and radiant maiden whom the angels name Lenore."
                    Quoth the Raven, "Nevermore."

I composed this stanza, at this point, first that, by establishing
the climax, I might the better vary and graduate, as regards seriousness and importance, the preceding queries of the lover and—secondly, that I might definitely settle the rhythm, the metre, and the
length and general arrangement of the stanza,—as well as graduate
the stanzas which were to precede, so that none of them might
surpass this in rhythmical effect. Had I been able, in the subsequent
composition, to construct more vigorous stanzas, I should, without
scruple, have purposely enfeebled them, so as not to interfere with
the climacteric effect.

And here I may as well say a few words of the versification. My
first object (as usual) was originality. The extent to which this has
been neglected, in versification, is one of the most unaccountable
things in the world. Admitting that there is little possibility of
variety in mere *rhythm*, it is still clear that the possible varieties of
metre and stanza are absolutely infinite—and yet, *for centuries, no
man, in verse, has ever done, or ever seemed to think of doing, an
original thing*. The fact is, that originality (unless in minds of very
unusual force) is by no means a matter, as some suppose, of impulse or intuition. In general, to be found, it must be elaborately
sought, and although a positive merit of the highest class, demands
in its attainment less of invention than negation.

Of course, I pretend to no originality in either the rhythm or
metre of the "Raven." The former is trochaic—the latter is octa-
meter acatalectic, alternating with heptameter catalectic repeated in
the *refrain* of the fifth verse, and terminating with tetrameter
catalectic. Less pedantically—the feet employed throughout (tro-
chees) consist of a long syllable followed by a short: the first line
of the stanza consists of eight of these feet—the second of seven
and a half (in effect two-thirds)—the third of eight—the fourth of
seven and a half—the fifth the same—the sixth three and a half.
Now, each of these lines, taken individually, has been employed before, and what originality the "Raven" has, is in their *combination
into stanza*; nothing even remotely approaching this combination
has ever been attempted. The effect of this originality of combination is aided by other unusual, and some altogether novel effects,
arising from an extension of the application of the principles of
rhyme and alliteration.

The next point to be considered was the mode of bringing together the lover and the Raven—and the first branch of this consideration was the *locale*. For this the most natural suggestion

might seem to be a forest, or the fields—but it has always appeared to me that a close *circumscription of space* is absolutely necessary to the effect of insulated incident:—it has the force of a frame to a picture. It has an indisputable moral power in keeping concentrated the attention, and, of course, must not be confounded with mere unity of place.

I determined, then, to place the lover in his chamber—in a chamber rendered sacred to him by memories of her who had frequented it. The room is represented as richly furnished—this in mere pursuance of the ideas I have already explained on the subject of Beauty, as the sole true poetical thesis.

The *locale* being thus determined, I had now to introduce the bird—and the thought of introducing him through the window, was inevitable. The idea of making the lover suppose, in the first instance, that the flapping of the wings of the bird against the shutter, is a "tapping" at the door, originated in a wish to increase, by prolonging, the reader's curiosity, and in a desire to admit the incidental effect arising from the lover's throwing open the door, finding all dark, and thence adopting the half-fancy that it was the spirit of his mistress that knocked.

I made the night tempestuous, first, to account for the Raven's seeking admission, and secondly, for the effect of contrast with the (physical) serenity within the chamber.

I made the bird alight on the bust of Pallas, also for the effect of contrast between the marble and the plumage—it being understood that the bust was absolutely *suggested* by the bird—the bust of *Pallas* being chosen, first, as most in keeping with the scholarship of the lover, and secondly, for the sonorousness of the word, Pallas, itself.

About the middle of the poem, also, I have availed myself of the force of contrast, with a view of deepening the ultimate impression. For example, an air of the fantastic—approaching as nearly to the ludicrous as was admissible—is given to the Raven's entrance. He comes in "with many a flirt and flutter."

Not the *least obeisance made he*—not a moment stopped or stayed he,
But *with mien of lord or lady*, perched above my chamber door.

In the two stanzas which follow, the design is more obviously carried out:—

Then this ebony bird beguiling my sad fancy into smiling
By the *grave and stern decorum of the countenance it wore*,
"Though thy *crest be shorn and shaven* thou," I said, "art sure no craven,

Ghastly grim and ancient Raven wandering from the nightly shore—
Tell me what thy lordly name is on the Night's Plutonian shore?"
Quoth the Raven, "Nevermore."
Much I marvelled *this ungainly fowl* to hear discourse so plainly,
Though its answer little meaning—little relevancy bore;
For we cannot help agreeing that no living human being
Ever yet was blessed with seeing bird above his chamber door—
Bird or beast upon the sculptured bust above his chamber door,
With such name as "Nevermore."

The effect of the *dénouement* being thus provided for, I immediately drop the fantastic for a tone of the most profound seriousness:—this tone commencing in the stanza directly following the
one last quoted, with the line,

But the Raven, sitting lonely on that placid bust, spoke only, etc.

From this epoch the lover no longer jests—no longer sees any
thing even of the fantastic in the Raven's demeanor. He speaks of
him as a "grim, ungainly, ghastly, gaunt, and ominous bird of yore,"
and feels the "fiery eyes" burning into his "bosom's core." This
revolution of thought, or fancy, on the lover's part, is intended to
induce a similar one on the part of the reader—to bring the mind
into a proper frame for the *dénouement*—which is now brought
about as rapidly and as *directly* as possible.

With the *dénouement* proper—with the Raven's reply, "Nevermore," to the lover's final demand if he shall meet his mistress in
another world—the poem, in its obvious phase, that of a simple
narrative, may be said to have its completion. So far, every thing is
within the limits of the accountable—of the real. A raven, having
learned by rote the single word "Nevermore," and having escaped
from the custody of its owner, is driven at midnight, through the
violence of a storm, to seek admission at a window from which a
light still gleams—the chamber-window of a student, occupied half
in poring over a volume, half in dreaming of a beloved mistress deceased. The casement being thrown open at the fluttering of the
bird's wings, the bird itself perches on the most convenient seat out
of the immediate reach of the student, who, amused by the incident and the oddity of the visitor's demeanor, demands of it, in jest
and without looking for a reply, its name. The raven addressed, answers with its customary word, "Nevermore"—a word which finds
immediate echo in the melancholy heart of the student, who, giving
utterance aloud to certain thoughts suggested by the occasion, is
again startled by the fowl's repetition of "Nevermore." The student
now guesses the state of the case, but is impelled, as I have before
explained, by the human thirst for self-torture, and in part by super-

stition, to propound such queries to the bird as will bring him, the lover, the most of the luxury of sorrow, through the anticipated answer "Nevermore." With the indulgence, to the extreme, of this self-torture, the narration, in what I have termed its first or obvious phase, has a natural termination, and so far there has been no overstepping of the limits of the real.

But in subjects so handled, however skilfully, or with however vivid an array of incident, there is always a certain hardness or nakedness, which repels the artistical eye. Two things are invariably required—first, some amount of complexity, or more properly, adaptation; and, secondly, some amount of suggestiveness—some under-current, however indefinite, of meaning. It is this latter, in especial, which imparts to a work of art so much of that *richness* (to borrow from colloquy a forcible term) which we are too fond of confounding with *the ideal*. It is the *excess* of the suggested meaning—it is the rendering this the upper instead of the under current of the theme—which turns into prose (and that of the very flattest kind) the so-called poetry of the so-called transcendentalists.

Holding these opinions, I added the two concluding stanzas of the poem—their suggestiveness being thus made to pervade all the narrative which has preceded them. The under-current of meaning is rendered first apparent in the lines—

"Take thy beak from out *my heart*, and take thy form from off my
    door!"
                        Quoth the Raven, "Nevermore!"

It will be observed that the words, "from out my heart," involve the first metaphorical expression in the poem. They, with the answer, "Nevermore," dispose the mind to seek a moral in all that has been previously narrated. The reader begins now to regard the Raven as emblematical—but it is not until the very last line of the very last stanza, that the intention of making him emblematical of *Mournful and Never-ending Remembrance* is permitted distinctly to be seen:

And the Raven, never flitting, still is sitting, still is sitting,
On the pallid bust of Pallas, just above my chamber door;
And his eyes have all the seeming of a demon's that is dreaming,
And the lamplight o'er him streaming throws his shadow on the
    floor;
And my soul *from out that shadow* that lies floating on the floor
                        Shall be lifted—nevermore.

                                                    1846, 1850

From The Poetic Principle[6]

In speaking of the Poetic Principle, I have no design to be either thorough or profound. While discussing, very much at random, the essentiality of what we call Poetry, my principal purpose will be to cite for consideration some few of those minor English or American poems which best suit my own taste, or which, upon my own fancy, have left the most definite impression. By "minor poems" I mean, of course, poems of little length. And here, in the beginning, permit me to say a few words in regard to a somewhat peculiar principle, which, whether rightfully or wrongfully, has always had its influence in my own critical estimate of the poem. I hold that a long poem does not exist. I maintain that the phrase, "a long poem," is simply a flat contradiction in terms.

I need scarcely observe that a poem deserves its title only inasmuch as it excites, by elevating the soul. The value of the poem is in the ratio of this elevating excitement. But all excitements are, through a psychal necessity, transient. That degree of excitement which would entitle a poem to be so called at all, cannot be sustained throughout a composition of any great length. After the lapse of half an hour, at the very utmost, it flags—fails—a revulsion ensues—and then the poem is, in effect, and in fact, no longer such.

There are, no doubt, many who have found difficulty in reconciling the critical dictum that the "Paradise Lost" is to be devoutly admired throughout, with the absolute impossibility of maintaining for it, during perusal, the amount of enthusiasm which that critical dictum would demand. This great work, in fact, is to be regarded as poetical only when, losing sight of that vital requisite in all works of Art, Unity, we view it merely as a series of minor poems. If, to preserve its Unity—its totality of effect or impression—we read it (as would be necessary) at a single sitting, the result is but a constant alternation of excitement and depression. After a passage of what we feel to be true poetry, there follows, inevitably, a passage of platitude which no critical pre-judgment can force us to admire; but if, upon completing the work, we read it again, omitting the first book—that is to say, commencing with the second—we shall be surprised at now finding that admirable which we before condemned—that damnable which we had previously so much admired. It follows from all this that the ultimate, aggregate, or absolute effect of even the best epic under the sun, is a nullity:—and this is precisely the fact.

In regard to the Iliad, we have, if not positive proof, at least very good reason for believing it intended as a series of lyrics; but, grant-

6. This essay was delivered several times as a lecture before it was published. The text is that of Sartain's *Union Magazine* for October, 1850.

ing the epic intention, I can say only that the work is based in an imperfect sense of art. The modern epic is, of the supposititious ancient model, but an inconsiderate and blindfold imitation. But the day of these artistic anomalies is over. If, at any time, any very long poem *were* popular in reality, which I doubt, it is at least clear that no very long poem will ever be popular again.

That the extent of a poetical work is, *ceteris paribus*,[7] the measure of its merit, seems undoubtedly, when we thus state it, a proposition sufficiently absurd—yet we are indebted for it to the Quarterly Reviews. Surely there can be nothing in mere *size*, abstractly considered—there can be nothing in mere *bulk*, so far as a volume is concerned, which has so continuously elicited admiration from these saturnine pamphlets! A mountain, to be sure, by the mere sentiment of physical magnitude which it conveys, *does* impress us with a sense of the sublime—but no man is impressed after *this* fashion by the material grandeur of even "The Columbiad."[8] Even the Quarterlies have not instructed us to be so impressed by it. As *yet*, they have not *insisted* on our estimating Lamartine by the cubic foot, or Pollok by the pound—but what else are we to *infer* from their continued prating about "sustained effort"? If, by "sustained effort," any little gentleman has accomplished an epic, let us frankly commend him for the effort—if this indeed be a thing commendable—but let us forbear praising the epic on the effort's account. It is to be hoped that common sense, in the time to come, will prefer deciding upon a work of art, rather by the impression it makes, by the effect it produces, than by the time it took to impress the effect, or by the amount of "sustained effort" which had been found necessary in effecting the impression. The fact is, that perseverance is one thing, and genius quite another; nor can all the Quarterlies in Christendom confound them. By and by, this proposition, with many which I have been just urging, will be received as self-evident. In the meantime, by being generally condemned as falsities, they will not be essentially damaged as truths.

On the other hand, it is clear that a poem may be improperly brief. Undue brevity degenerates into mere epigrammatism. A *very* short poem, while now and then producing a brilliant or vivid, never produces a profound or enduring effect. There must be the steady pressing down of the stamp upon the wax. De Béranger[9] has wrought innumerable things, pungent and spirit-stirring; but, in general, they have been too imponderous to stamp themselves deeply into the public attention; and thus, as so many feathers of fancy, have been blown aloft only to be whistled down the wind.

7. "Other things being equal."
8. The revised title of Joel Barlow's epic (1807), originally published as "The Vision of Columbus" in 1787.
9. French lyric poet. Cf. Poe's review of *Twice-Told Tales*, note 2.

A remarkable instance of the effect of undue brevity in depressing a poem—in keeping it out of the popular view—is afforded by the following exquisite little Serenade.

> I arise from dreams of thee
>   In the first sweet sleep of night,
> When the winds are breathing low,
>   And the stars are shining bright;
> I arise from dreams of thee,
>   And a spirit in my feet
> Has led me—who knows how?—
>   To thy chamber-window, sweet!
>
> The wandering airs, they faint
>   On the dark, the silent stream—
> The champak odors fail
>   Like sweet thoughts in a dream;
> The nightingale's complaint,
>   It dies upon her heart,
> As I must die on thine,
>   O, beloved as thou art!
>
> O, lift me from the grass!
>   I die, I faint, I fail!
> Let thy love in kisses rain
>   On my lips and eyelids pale.
> My cheek is cold and white, alas!
>   My heart beats loud and fast:
> Oh! press it close to thine again,
>   Where it will break at last!

Very few perhaps are familiar with these lines—yet no less a poet than Shelley is their author. Their warm, yet delicate and ethereal imagination will be appreciated by all—but by none so thoroughly as by him who has himself arisen from sweet dreams of one beloved, to bathe in the aromatic air of a southern midsummer night.

One of the finest poems by Willis[1]—the very best, in my opinion, which he has ever written—has, no doubt, through this same defect of undue brevity, been kept back from its proper position, not less in the critical than in the popular view.

> The shadows lay along Broadway,
>   'Twas near the twilight-tide—
> And slowly there a lady fair
>   Was walking in her pride.
> Alone walk'd she; but, viewlessly,
>   Walk'd spirits at her side.
>
> Peace charm'd the street beneath her feet,
>   And Honour charm'd the air;

---

1. "Unseen Spirits," by Nathaniel Parker Willis, a friend of Poe.

And all astir looked kind on her,
    And call'd her good and fair—
For all God ever gave to her
    She kept with chary care.

She kept with care her beauties rare
    From lovers warm and true—
For her heart was cold to all but gold,
    And the rich came not to woo—
But honour'd well are charms to sell,
    If priests the selling do.

Now walking there was one more fair—
    A slight girl, lily-pale;
And she had unseen company
    To make the spirit quail—
'Twixt Want and Scorn she walk'd forlorn,
    And nothing could avail.

No mercy now can clear her brow
    For this world's peace to pray;
For, as love's wild prayer dissolved in air,
    Her woman's heart gave way!—
But the sin forgiven by Christ in Heaven
    By man is cursed alway!

In this composition we find it difficult to recognize the Willis who has written so many mere "verses of society." The lines are not only richly ideal, but full of energy; while they breathe an earnestness—an evident sincerity of sentiment—for which we look in vain throughout all the other works of this author.

While the epic mania—while the idea that, to merit in poetry, prolixity is indispensable—has, for some years past, been gradually dying out of the public mind by mere dint of its own absurdity—we find it succeeded by a heresy too palpably false to be long tolerated, but one which, in the brief period it has already endured, may be said to have accomplished more in the corruption of our Poetical Literature than all its other enemies combined. I allude to the heresy of *The Didactic*. It has been assumed, tacitly and avowedly, directly and indirectly, that the ultimate object of all Poetry is Truth. Every poem, it is said, should inculcate a moral; and by this moral is the poetical merit of the work to be adjudged. We Americans, especially, have patronized this happy idea; and we Bostonians, very especially, have developed it in full. We have taken it into our heads that to write a poem simply for the poem's sake, and to acknowledge such to have been our design, would be to confess ourselves radically wanting in the true Poetic dignity and force:—but the simple fact is, that, would we but permit ourselves to look into our own souls, we should immediately there discover that under the sun there neither exists nor *can* exist any work more thoroughly dignified—more supremely noble than this very poem—this poem *per se*—this poem which is a poem and nothing more—this poem written solely for the poem's sake.

With as deep a reverence for the True as ever inspired the bosom of man, I would, nevertheless, limit, in some measure, its modes of inculcation. I would limit to enforce them. I would not enfeeble them by dissipation. The demands of Truth are severe. She has no sympathy with the myrtles. All *that* which is so indispensable in Song, is precisely all *that* with which *she* has nothing whatever to do. It is but making her a flaunting paradox, to wreathe her in gems and flowers. In enforcing a truth, we need severity rather than efflorescence of language. We must be simple, precise, terse. We must be cool, calm, unimpassioned. In a word, we must be in that mood which, as nearly as possible, is the exact converse of the poetical. *He* must be blind indeed who does not perceive the radical and chasmal differences between the truthful and the poetical modes of inculcation. He must be theory-mad beyond redemption who, in spite of these differences, shall still persist in attempting to reconcile the obstinate oils and waters of Poetry and Truth.

Dividing the world of mind into its three most immediately obvious distinctions, we have the Pure Intellect, Taste, and the Moral Sense. I place Taste in the middle, because it is just this position which, in the mind, it occupies. It holds intimate relations with either extreme; but from the Moral Sense is separated by so faint a difference that Aristotle has not hesitated to place some of its operations among the virtues themselves. Nevertheless, we find the *offices* of the trio marked with a sufficient distinction. Just as the Intellect concerns itself with Truth, so Taste informs us of the Beautiful while the Moral Sense is regardful of Duty. Of this latter, while Conscience teaches the obligation, and Reason the expediency, Taste contents herself with displaying the charms:— waging war upon Vice solely on the ground of her deformity— her disproportion—her animosity to the fitting, to the appropriate, to the harmonious—in a word, to Beauty.

An immortal instinct, deep within the spirit of man, is thus, plainly, a sense of the Beautiful. This it is which administers to his delight in the manifold forms, and sounds, and odours, and sentiments amid which he exists. And just as the lily is repeated in the lake, or the eyes of Amaryllis in the mirror, so is the mere oral or written repetition of these forms, and sounds, and colours, and odours, and sentiments, a duplicate source of delight. But this mere repetition is not poetry. He who shall simply sing, with however glowing enthusiasm, or with however vivid a truth of description, of the sights, and sounds, and odours, and colours, and sentiments, which greet *him* in common with all mankind—he, I say, has yet failed to prove his divine title. There is still a something in the distance which he has been unable to attain. We have still a thirst unquenchable, to allay which he has not shown us the crystal springs. This thirst belongs to the immortality of Man. It is at once a consequence and an indication of his perennial existence. It is the desire of the moth for the star. It is no mere appreciation of the Beauty before us—but a wild effort to reach the Beauty above. Inspired by an ecstatic prescience of the glories beyond the grave, we struggle, by multiform combinations among the things and thoughts of Time, to attain a portion of that Loveliness whose very elements, perhaps, appertain to eternity alone. And thus when by Poetry—or when by Music, the most entrancing of the Poetic moods—we find ourselves melted into tears—we weep then—not as the Abbate Gravina[2] supposes—through excess of pleasure, but through a certain, petulant, impatient sorrow at our inability to grasp *now*, wholly, here on earth, at once and for ever, those divine and rapturous joys, of which *through* the poem or *through* the music, we attain to but brief and indeterminate glimpses.

The struggle to apprehend the supernal Loveliness—this struggle, on the part of souls fittingly constituted—has given to the world all *that* which it (the world) has ever been enabled at once to understand and to *feel* as poetic.

The Poetic Sentiment, of course, may develope itself in various modes—in Painting, in Sculpture, in Architecture, in the Dance—very especially in Music—and very peculiarly, and with a wide field, in the composition of the Landscape Garden. Our present theme, however, has regard only to its manifestation in words. And here let me speak briefly on the topic of rhythm. Contenting myself with the certainty that Music, in its various modes of metre, rhythm, and rhyme, is of so vast a moment in Poetry as never to be wisely rejected—is so vitally important an adjunct, that he is simply silly who declines its assistance, I will not now pause to maintain its absolute essentiality. It is in Music, perhaps, that the soul most nearly attains the great end for which, when inspired by the Poetic Sentiment, it struggles—the creation of supernal Beauty. It *may* be, indeed, that here this sublime end is, now and then, attained *in fact*. We are often made to feel, with a shivering delight, that from an earthly harp are stricken notes which cannot have been unfamiliar to the angels. And thus there can be little doubt that in the union of Poetry with Music in its popular sense, we shall find the widest field for the Poetic development. The old Bards and Minnesingers had advantages which we do not possess—and

2. Giovanni Vincenzo Gravina (1664–1718), Italian poet and critic.

Thomas Moore,[3] singing his own songs, was, in the most legitimate manner, perfecting them as poems.

To recapitulate, then:—I would define, in brief, the Poetry of Words as *The Rhythmical Creation of Beauty*. Its sole arbiter is Taste. With the Intellect or with the Conscience, it has only collateral relations. Unless incidentally, it has no concern whatever either with Duty or with Truth.

A few words, however, in explanation. *That* pleasure which is at once the most pure, the most elevating, and the most intense, is derived, I maintain, from the contemplation of the Beautiful. In the contemplation of Beauty we alone find it possible to attain that pleasurable elevation, or excitement, *of the soul*, which we recognize as the Poetic Sentiment, and which is so easily distinguished from Truth, which is the satisfaction of the Reason, or from Passion, which is the excitement of the heart. I make Beauty, therefore— using the word as inclusive of the sublime—I make Beauty the province of the poem, simply because it is an obvious rule of Art that effects should be made to spring as directly as possible from their causes:—no one as yet having been weak enough to deny that the peculiar elevation in question is at least *most readily* attainable in the poem. It by no means follows, however, that the incitements of Passion, or the precepts of Duty, or even the lessons of Truth, may not be introduced into a poem, and with advantage; for they may subserve, incidentally, in various ways, the general purposes of the work:—but the true artist will always contrive to tone them down in proper subjection to that *Beauty* which is the atmosphere and the real essence of the poem.

I cannot better introduce the few poems which I shall present for your consideration, than by the citation of the Proem to Mr. Longfellow's "Waif":[4]

> The day is done, and the darkness
>   Falls from the wings of Night,
> As a feather is wafted downward
>   From an Eagle in his flight.
>
> I see the lights of the village
>   Gleam through the rain and the mist,
> And a feeling of sadness comes o'er me,
>   That my soul cannot resist;
>
> A feeling of sadness and longing,
>   That is not akin to pain,

3. Irish poet (1779–1852) who influenced Poe's early verse.
4. Title of an anthology of poetry edited by Longfellow in 1844. Longfellow's poem is "The Day Is Done."

And resembles sorrow only
    As the mist resembles the rain.

Come, read to me some poem,
    Some simple and heartfelt lay,
That shall soothe this restless feeling,
    And banish the thoughts of day.

Not from the grand old masters,
    Not from the bards sublime,
Whose distant footsteps echo
    Through the corridors of Time.

For, like strains of martial music,
    Their mighty thoughts suggest
Life's endless toil and endeavor;
    And to-night I long for rest.

Read from some humbler poet,
    Whose songs gushed from his heart,
As showers from the clouds of summer,
    Or tears from the eyelids start;

Who through long days of labour,
    And nights devoid of ease,
Still heard in his soul the music
    Of wonderful melodies.

Such songs have power to quiet
    The restless pulse of care,
And come like the benediction
    That follows after prayer.

Then read from the treasured volume
    The poem of thy choice,
And lend to the rhyme of the poet
    The beauty of thy voice.

And the night shall be filled with music,
    And the cares, that infest the day,
Shall fold their tents, like the Arabs,
    And as silently steal away.

With no great range of imagination, these lines have been justly admired for their delicacy of expression. Some of the images are very effective. Nothing can be better than

——The bards sublime,
    Whose distant footsteps echo
    Down the corridors of Time.

The idea of the last quatrain is also very effective. The poem, on the whole, however, is chiefly to be admired for the graceful *insou-*

ciance of its metre, so well in accordance with the character of the sentiments, and especially for the *ease* of the general manner. This "ease," or naturalness, in a literary style, it has long been the fashion to regard as ease in appearance alone—as a point of really difficult attainment. But not so:—a natural manner is difficult only to him who should never meddle with it—to the unnatural. It is but the result of writing with the understanding, or with the instinct, that the *tone*, in composition, should always be that which the mass of mankind would adopt—and must perpetually vary, of course, with the occasion. The author who, after the fashion of "The North American Review," should be, upon all occasions, merely "quiet," must necessarily upon *many* occasions be simply silly, or stupid; and has no more right to be considered "easy," or "natural," than the Cockney exquisite, or than the sleeping Beauty in the wax-works.

Among the minor poems of Bryant, none has so much impressed me as the one which he entitles "June." I quote only a portion of it:

> There, through the long, long summer hours,
>   The golden light should lie,
> And thick young herbs and groups of flowers
>   Stand in their beauty by.
> The oriole should build and tell
> His love-tale, close beside my cell;
>   The idle butterfly
> Should rest him there, and there be heard
> The housewife-bee and humming bird.
>
> And what, if cheerful shouts, at noon,
>   Come, from the village sent,
> Or songs of maids, beneath the moon,
>   With fairy laughter blent?
> And what, if in the evening light,
> Betrothed lovers walk in sight
>   Of my low monument?
> I would the lovely scene around
> Might know no sadder sight nor sound.
>
> I know, I know I should not see
>   The season's glorious show,
> Nor would its brightness shine for me,
>   Nor its wild music flow;
> But if, around my place of sleep,
> The friends I love should come to weep,
>   They might not haste to go.
> Soft airs, and song, and light, and bloom
> Should keep them lingering by my tomb.

These to their softened hearts should bear
　　The thought of what has been,
And speak of one who cannot share
　　The gladness of the scene;
Whose part in all the pomp that fills
The circuit of the summer hills,
　　Is—that his grave is green;
And deeply would their hearts rejoice
To hear again his living voice.

The rhythmical flow, here, is even voluptuous—nothing could be more melodious. The poem has always affected me in a remarkable manner. The intense melancholy which seems to well up, perforce, to the surface of all the poet's cheerful sayings about his grave, we find thrilling us to the soul—while there is the truest poetic elevation in the thrill. The impression left is one of a pleasurable sadness.

And if, in the remaining compositions which I shall introduce to you, there be more or less of a similar tone always apparent, let me remind you that (how or why we know not) this certain taint of sadness is inseparably connected with all the higher manifestations of true Beauty.[5] * * *

From Alfred Tennyson—although in perfect sincerity I regard him as the noblest poet that ever lived—I have left myself time to cite only a very brief specimen. I call him, and *think* him the noblest of poets—*not* because the impressions he produces are, at *all* times, the most profound—*not* because the poetical excitement which he induces is, at *all* times, the most intense—but because it *is*, at all times, the most ethereal—in other words, the most elevating and most pure. No poet is so little of the earth, earthy. What I am about to read is from his last long poem, "The Princess":

　　Tears, idle tears, I know not what they mean,
　　Tears from the depth of some divine despair
　　Rise in the heart, and gather to the eyes,
　　In looking on the happy Autumn-fields,
　　And thinking of the days that are no more.

　　Fresh as the first beam glittering on a sail,
　　That brings our friends up from the underworld,
　　Sad as the last which reddens over one
　　That sinks with all we love below the verge;
　　So sad, so fresh, the days that are no more.

　　Ah, sad and strange as in dark summer dawns
　　The earliest pipe of half-awaken'd birds

---

5. Omitted at this point are minor poems by Edward Coate Pinckney, Thomas Hood, Moore, and Byron, with Poe's brief comments, which contribute but slightly to the subject under discussion.

To dying ears, when unto dying eyes
The casement slowly grows a glimmering square;
So sad, so strange, the days that are no more.

Dear as remember'd kisses after death,
And sweet as those by hopeless fancy feign'd
On lips that are for others; deep as love,
Deep as first love, and wild with all regret;
O Death in Life, the days that are no more.

Thus, although in a very cursory and imperfect manner, I have endeavoured to convey to you my conception of the Poetic Principle. It has been my purpose to suggest that, while this Principle itself is, strictly and simply, the Human Aspiration for Supernal Beauty, the manifestation of the Principle is always found in *an elevating excitement of the Soul*—quite independent of that passion which is the intoxication of the Heart—or of that Truth which is the satisfaction of the Reason. For, in regard to Passion, alas! its tendency is to degrade, rather than to elevate the Soul. Love, on the contrary—Love—the true, the divine Eros—the Uranian, as distinguished from the Dionaean Venus[6]—is unquestionably the purest and truest of all poetical themes. And in regard to Truth— if, to be sure, through the attainment of a truth, we are led to perceive a harmony where none was apparent before, we experience, at once, the true poetical effect—but this effect is referable to the harmony alone, and not in the least degree to the truth which merely served to render the harmony manifest.

We shall reach, however, more immediately a distinct conception of what the true Poetry is, by mere reference to a few of the simple elements which induce in the Poet himself the true poetical effect. He recognizes the ambrosia which nourishes his soul, in the bright orbs that shine in Heaven—in the volutes of the flower— in the clustering of low shrubberies—in the waving of the grain-fields—in the slanting of tall, Eastern trees—in the blue distance of mountains—in the grouping of clouds—in the twinkling of half-hidden brooks—in the gleaming of silver rivers—in the repose of sequestered lakes—in the star-mirroring depths of lonely wells. He perceives it in the songs of birds—in the harp of Æolus[7]—in the sighing of the night-wind—in the repining voice of the forest— in the surf that complains to the shore—in the fresh breath of the woods—in the scent of the violet—in the voluptuous perfume of the hyacinth—in the suggestive odour that comes to him, at eventide, from far-distant, undiscovered islands, over dim oceans, illimitable and unexplored. He owns it in all noble thoughts—in all unworldly

6. The "Uranian" is heavenly (spiritual) love, distinguished from the "Dionaean," earthly (passionate) love.

7. The aeolian harp, a stringed instrument which gives off musical sounds when the wind blows across it.

motives—in all holy impulses—in all chivalrous, generous, and self-sacrificing deeds. He feels it in the beauty of woman—in the grace of her step—in the lustre of her eye—in the melody of her voice—in her soft laughter—in her sigh—in the harmony of the rustling of her robes. He deeply feels it in her winning endearments—in her burning enthusiasms—in her gentle charities—in her meek and devotional endurances—but above all—ah, far above all—he kneels to it—he worships it in the faith, in the purity, in the strength, in the altogether divine majesty—of her love.[8]   * * *

1850

8. Omitted is Poe's concluding paragraph, which includes a poem by the Scottish romantic, William Motherwell, with a few introductory remarks.

Ralph Waldo Emerson

Something will really have to be done about Emerson. This benign apostle of self-sufficiency, this self-appointed exception to the human race, ambiguously smiling from his island fastness with a calm like a reproof, making us small with his talk of greatness, instructing us with his air of omniscience that if we are very good we will be happy, that all our hurts are really benefits, that there is nothing we cannot do if we really want to, that everything is for the best—surely we have had enough of this. Growing up, as individuals or as a nation, means to put away such things. The man is a schoolmaster—"that is," as Henry Adams said, "a man employed to tell lies to little boys." If he were a great artist we might endure him, but not a single piece of his, in prose or verse, is indisputably a masterpiece. Like Melville, he could have said, in fact, did say, "all my books are botches," but without Melville's excuse. Why not lay him decently away with all the other unread authors whom once every schoolboy knew?

Anyone who has not at one time or another felt this way about Emerson is simply not an honest reader. Emerson created a public role for himself—the scholar, as he called it, the preacher and teacher—which his times welcomed and our times detest. The only difficulty with our natural impulse to be rid of this "encumbrance" (Eliot's term) is that he won't stay dead. Do we wish to set him aside for Melville? We find that "if we feel Melville as one of ours, we must take Emerson into the bargain, whether we like it or not." Are we impressed with Poe's uncanny anticipation of the direction of modern literature? Then we must reckon with the fact that what he thought his greatest work announces a philosophy which can only be called Emersonian. Do we want to get to the heart of Hawthorne's solitary darkness? We soon come to see that he and the prophet of Self-Reliance are two halves of a whole, neither of which can be fully understood without the other. Have we discovered Whitman's "buried masterpiece," the first edition of *Leaves of Grass*? Then we must know our Emerson, for the book is an exuberant fantasia on themes by him. Are we exploring the meanings of *Walden*? We must use Emerson's *Nature* as our guide. A sound approach to later writers such as Emily Dickinson, Edwin Arlington Robinson, or Robert Frost is impossible except through him. An account of the consequences of Puritanism, the impact of the Enlightenment, or the origins of Pragmatism, a history of either the conservative or the liberal tradition in American political thought, a treatment of American aesthetics—all demand a close attention to Emerson. The most resolute modernist, as soon as he turns to acknowledge the remarkable modernity of the major American authors, their anticipations of Symbolism, Existentialism, Formalism, promptly confronts the inevitable Emerson. Emerson's mark is plowed too deep into American literary history for us to remove it if we would. We either enter American literature through this door or stay outside.

The juxtaposition of Emerson's unacceptability with his extraordinary centrality should warn us that in him we have to do with something quite special about which snap judgments are useless. He is a baffling and therefore absorbing phenomenon that can only be discussed and understood from the inside. The reward of the effort to do this is to discover a mind that is not essentially alien or unacceptable after all, that still speaks to some aspects of our condition as it did to that of our predecessors. If in some ways Emerson dates, in other and more important ways he is ahead of our day, as he was of his own.

The purpose of the present essay is to lay bare the living Emerson and so help to recover an indispensable part of our heritage. This is a large order, possibly more than ought to be crammed into an anthology. In the present state of Emerson studies, however, the attempt must be made, or our introduction will not be able to shake the hard-set stereotypes that now threaten to cut him off from us. We pass by, then, a formal exposition of the comparatively less important and easily accessible facts of his outer life and ask the modern student of literature to plunge with us at once to the heart of the matter, the inner life. What can be more human, after all, than the life of a mind, if the mind is a good one?

I

The first fact to record about Emerson is his piety—not in the sense of religious reverence, though he had that too, but *pietas*, "faithfulness to natural ties" of family, region, and country. Not only were his family ties so deep and strong that he was scarcely capable of any other close relation to persons, but his course in life was controlled at every point by local loyalties. Born in 1803, the son of a Boston minister who died when Ralph was eight, he grew up in Boston but for the first thirty years or so of his life knew no one permanent home. In 1834, however, he returned to "the quiet fields of my fathers" in Concord, Massachusetts, a town his ancestors had helped to found and a number of them, including his grandfather, had served as ministers; he established there his lares and penates and settled down to the life of a country gentleman and man of letters. Thereafter he was as good a neighbor and citizen as his townsmen would permit him to be, serving faithfully in all the offices to which they called him, from hogreeve to a member of the school board. His literary activities, outside of his early preaching, also began with his service as lecturer in the local "lyceums" for adult education that were then springing up throughout the region. Lecturing first on subjects proposed to him—natural science, the lives of great men, English literature—he soon instituted in Boston a yearly series of his own on such omnibus topics as "Human Culture," "Human Life," or "The Times," to which he brought his crop of reflections for the year, and in the same period (1836–41) also delivered a number of memorable occasional addresses at Harvard and other New England colleges.

All this speaking had a humble practical motive, since half of his income depended on it, but its larger purpose was to help meet the needs of a community just emerging from its provincial cocoon. His lonely year in Europe in 1832–33 and his pilgrimage to the great men of English literature—Wordsworth, Coleridge, Landor, Carlyle—had confirmed him in his decision not to court the "great literary and fashionable army" for whom they wrote but to accept instead "the dignities and duties of country lyceums" at home. His choice sprang partly from modesty but more from an instinctive consent to the sphere of activity to which providence had called him. When later, after the publication of his *Essays* (*First Series*, 1841; *Second Series*, 1844), his sphere enlarged to national and even, with his second trip to England in 1847–48, to international size, his attitude remained the same, though his loyalty enlarged correspondingly from New England to the nation, and beyond that, as its uttermost reach, to a more tenuous solidarity with "Saxondom" (as expressed in *English Traits*, 1856). With this last loyalty of race he stopped, as some of his remarks on the Irish, the Negroes, or the French make plain. The abstract humanitarianism that led Tom Paine to say "My country is the world" was not in his scope. He spoke of Man but his loyalty was to men. Nothing really is stranger than that he should ever have seemed in any way the spokesman for an atomistic individualism, for he was a *member* in every fiber of his nature.

Yet if Emerson was a conservative he was also the revolutionary who boasted, "I unsettle all things." Since his revolutionary side, however, is more conspicuous and better known, it is important to begin with his conservative one, which he himself insisted on less, not because it was less important to him, but because it was so instinctive as not to call for much explicit justification. From this point of view two traditional roles emerge into prominence, the preacher and the gentleman.

In old-time New England the minister was a commanding figure, a member of what Oliver Wendell Holmes called the Brahmin class. Emerson delighted in tales of the "godly lives and godly deaths" of his own "sainted kindred," such as Father Samuel Moody: "When the offended parishioners would rise to go out of the church he cried, 'Come back, you graceless sinner, come back!' And when his parishioners ventured into the ale-house on a Saturday night, the valiant pastor went in, collared them, and dragged them forth and sent them home." That Emerson burned to serve the Lord with the same commanding authority is written between the lines of every page of his early *Journals*. Beneath what he called the "lounging" which his health then required lay an unrelenting sense of heroic vocation. One reason for this dedication was his aunt Mary Moody Emerson, who intermittently helped his mother with her hard task of feeding her boarders and raising her boys. A keen, impatient, waspish little woman, she took the place of a father to the boys and stung them with her own high-minded zeal. "Scorn trifles"; "lift your aims"; "do what you are afraid to do" were among her favorite maxims. Her hope, her nephew wrote, was that her boys "should be richly and holily qualified and bred to purify the old faith of what narrowness and error adhered to it, and import all its fire into the new age." This hope was also his when, alone among his brothers, he dedicated himself to the church. "My trust," he wrote at the age of 21, "is that my profession shall be my regeneration of mind, manners, inward and outward estate; or rather my starting-point, for I have hoped to put on eloquence as a robe, and by goodness and zeal and the awfulness of Virtue to press and prevail over the false judgments, the rebel passions and corrupt habits of men."

This trust proved premature. After serving from 1829 to 1832 as pastor of the Second Church (Unitarian) of Boston he broke with his congregation and never thereafter accepted a regular charge; he dropped the title "Reverend" and after 1838 discontinued preaching almost entirely. He abandoned his profession, however, the better to serve his vocation. His apostasy had roots in tradition hardly less deep than the organized church it rejected. Puritans had taught the worthlessness of the "natural man," who was born fallen and deserving of damnation, but they had also taught the infinity of Christ's love and mercy extended to all those who should believe in Him. One symptom of the powerful emotional pressures which these teachings brought to bear on Puritan society was the repeated emergence from within it of the kind of heresy it labeled Antinomianism, the unconditional claim of regeneration *now* that asserted, like Shaw's St. Joan, a private faith based on the immediate voice of God in the heart. Antinomian groups of this sort, universalists, perfectionists, millennialists, come-outers, were conspicuous in the New England of Emerson's day.

His apostasy is an "enlightened" version of the same enthusiasm. Taught by the rationalism of the Harvard Unitarianism to which he was bred to reject the Calvinist doctrine of "total depravity" and affirm the moral worth of the natural man, yet impelled by his deep Calvinist heritage to reject the "mere morality" of the Unitarians and press like his Puritan ancestors toward an assurance of salvation by faith, he went the antinomians one better and affirmed the salvation now of *every* man, by nature. As a student of Jonathan Edwards, the great New England Calvinist, has pointed out, Emerson's "voice of God in the intuition of the heart is merely Edwards' 'divine and supernatural light, immediately imparted to the soul by the spirit of God,' extended from the elect minority to the human race as a whole." It had dawned on Emerson, to his joy and amazement, that the perfection which Adam was supposed to have lost had never been lost at all. The Fall of Man was a fiction. In some men God is "agent," in others latent, but for all, "the whole *is* now potentially in the bottom of his heart."

His discovery of God, not at the transcendent distance from man where Puritanism had placed Him, but immanent in his own soul, so that there was "no bar or wall in the soul, where man, the effect, ceases, and God, the cause, begins," transformed a pleasant but unexciting Unitarian preacher into a leader of thought who would eventually be hailed, in the famous words of Matthew Arnold, as "the friend and aider of all who would live in the spirit." All the doubts that had oppressed him evaporated in the sun of his vision and he set out to bear witness to the one true light. But if his message became the discovery of the "native immortal air" of every man, the obligation to *testify* to it remained the special vocation of the New England Brahmin. This was the vocation of the "Scholar" he described in 1837, to find and expound the Truth and convert the world. The didactic tone of much of Emerson's writing throughout his life becomes more understandable and perhaps more excusable when we see that, for all the changed circumstances, he is still attempting to fulfill the ancestral calling "to press and prevail over the false judgments * * * of men."

Closely connected with the role of the preacher and scholar was that of the gentleman, the responsible leader of the community. The New England minister had belonged to this class, along with the men of substance and education among the laymen. Though in a democratic society such a class was a loose one, both as fact and as idea it was real and powerful in the New England of Emerson's time. Without question Emerson saw himself as a member and even a spokesman of this class; with characteristic loyalty he accepted his position and set out to perpetuate and renovate the gentlemanly ideal. As Alfred Kloeckner has shown, even Emerson's most idealized reflections on human nature, though expressed in universal language, carry a certain class reservation: while all men are potentially capable of self-reliance and a life in obedience to the "moral sentiment," only the "well-born" can be expected actually to achieve such ends. Emerson's thought remains stoutly democratic in that he envisages an aristocracy of virtue and talent, not of inherited wealth or social position. But he is much more of a hard-headed realist in these matters than he is sometimes given the credit or discredit for being. The class of "best people," the fact of wealth and aristocracy, is founded on the inescapable natural fact that some men are superior to others, and that the *doers*, the men of superior force and executive capacity, will in a free society inevitably rise to the top.

His objection to superior men was not that they existed but that they were not superior enough. Some of his fiercest scorn was directed at "fine gentlemen," members of the privileged group who in their selfishness and irresponsibility gave nothing in return for what they received. Instead he drew from observation and tradition a code for the true gentleman of which Edwin Cady has said, "There is nothing so thorough, candid, or exalted among either American or British gentlemanly credos." It was not for nothing that his favorite passage from Chaucer was the discussion in the Wife of Bath's Tale of "gentilesse," for his gentlemanly ideal was essentially an adaptation to the needs of a modern democratic society of the medieval code of "gentle blood and knighthood." Its purpose was the same, to identify the socially "best" with the intrinsically best and so draw the whole society together in a common loyalty not merely to its "institutions and orders" but to its highest ethical and cultural traditions.

II

But it is time to leave Emerson's loyalty and treat his disloyalty, since a representative American, if he is to be true to the best traditions of Americanism, should have both. Emerson delighted in subversion. If one image for him is the Man of Character, the enlightened conservative, another is the Reformer, of whom he wrote, "Beware when the great God lets loose a thinker on this planet. Then all things are at risk. It is as when a conflagration has broken out in a great city, and no man knows what is safe, or where it will end. * * * The very hopes of man, the thoughts of his heart, the religion of nations, the manners and morals of mankind are all at the mercy of a new generalization." For all the pretense of alarm in this passage, no one can miss what he himself calls the "thrill" of delight that inspires it.

If this introduction has a thesis, it is the principle of polarity that controls Emerson's thought. Invariably it falls into opposites which he did not attempt to reconcile so much as to exploit. Truthful thinking, he believed, could not come from the vain quest for consistency ("Damn consistency!" he wrote in his journal), but only from respect for the integrity of the individual insight. He understood what John Stuart Mill meant when he pointed out that we do not come into "real contact" with an idea unless we hear it from "persons who actually believe" it. Thinking has no vitality unless it has not just clarity but conviction. To capture the life as well as the sense of a thought it must be given its head, pushed to its limit, until every drop of its truth has been extracted from it; then, when the rhythm of the mind reverses to "resume the overstaid fraction," as Whitman put it, that also must be ridden as far as it will carry us. Emerson hoped, it is true, that his various fractions of truth sketched "arcs" which at some indefinite future time he might bring together into one Great Circle. Actually, however, he knew very well that if he was sketching arcs at all they were arcs of an ellipse, not a circle. So in the present and central case, Emerson's pendulum swung freely between the opposite "walls" of conservatism and revolt without adhering to either. To follow him we must swing freely too.

His radical instincts were awakened at the time of his break with his church in 1832. If one influence that helped him take this step was the antinomian tradition in New England, another was certain explosive currents of thought in his time which we include under the name of romanticism, though Emerson's contemporaries chose the clumsy label "transcendentalism." This kind of romanticism had sprung up as the proper and inevitable protest against a rationalism which had reached a point of self-destruction. Applied to the external world, 18th-century reason had painted a world picture that seemed to make mind superfluous and to reduce man to one link in an iron chain of mechanical cause and effect. Turned on the mind itself, on the other hand, it had created the "problem of knowledge" and left man, in Emerson's words, "in the splendid labyrinth of [his] perceptions, to wander without end." In either case, "reason" had threatened to eliminate the human mind as an original force in nature.

The typical romantic strategy in this crisis had been an envelopment. Beyond ordinary reason—rechristened by Coleridge "the understanding"—drawing its inferences from sense experience, lay a higher Reason, the romantics had held, that brought immediate insight into truths beyond sense experience. Where the understanding, looking outward, saw a system of atoms in motion, or else a labyrinth of perceptions, the Reason, looking inward, found God and freedom in the heart of the self. This "Copernican revolution," unintentionally initiated by Immanuel Kant, and carried to completion by J. G. Fichte and other German thinkers after him, by the early 19th century had affected some seminal minds in France and England, notably Coleridge, and by the 1830's had begun to penetrate even the unspeculative atmosphere of the United States.

Emerson was one of those timely men, like Tom Paine, who have the prescience to sense the need of the moment and the strength to force it to its crisis. In his first book, *Nature* (1836), in the historic addresses "The American Scholar" (1837) and the "Divinity School Address" (1838), and in essays like "Self-Reliance" (1841) he spoke as with the voice of their own souls to the young dissenters of his time. What he stirred in them, and still can stir, was a new self-respect. We begin to live, he taught, only as we learn to trust our inner force, the "me of me," as our sole and sufficient resource. What we call human nature is merely an outer shell, a crust of habit that holds in unnatural sleep a man's true powers. In the might of his nature-beyond-nature, once awakened, he can transcend the fear of life from which habit draws its strength and reach the completely "inner-directed" life that is at once his highest achievement and his natural condition. The "Concord Hymn" is really a celebration of this natural-supernatural spirit in man that bids him rise above the time and nature that must sweep him away and dare even to die for an idea: that is why it is the greatest occasional poem in our literature.

In thus speaking for the supremacy of mind Emerson was certainly not alone among romantics. Blake, Shelley, Wordsworth, to name only three, had made the power of mind their theme, and had done so in far richer language than Emerson's. His peculiar realm was that of moral decision; his imagination was not primarily verbal or sensuous or mythological, but ethical. His power was a unique fusion of the romantic vision of possibility and the Puritan pressure of obligation. The barrier familiar in romantic thought between the truth of insight and the facts of experience, between the Ideal and the Actual, became under the spell of his words something transparent and evanescent, something we are not merely to see beyond in prophetic vision but by some exertion of force are to surmount and destroy here and now. His distinctive note among romantic "seers" is his urgency: his words are a "kind of action"; they strike the mind at just the point where imagination and will unite.

Plainly, one who thus calls for "the conversion of the world" has declared war on experience—and experience soon fights back. Emerson's vision of man's self-sufficiency encountered two major limits—the barriers he named Illusion and Fate. By Illusion he meant a sense of dream that swallowed up not only the world of fact but his vision too, and left him, as it seemed, cut off from all reality. A faith like Emerson's was vulnerable to this threat because it was based on immediate intuition, a "certain brief experience" of the God in the heart. The inevitable dwindling of such experiences as he grew older threw a severe strain on his confidence. In his "skeptical" essays "Experience" (1844) and "Montaigne" (1850) he even experimented with a philosophy of experience that would leave out altogether the frustrating gleams on which his faith had been based. Though in those same essays he rejected the result, the very experiment is a revealing demonstration of the inroads Illusion was making on his intuitive faith.

As for Fate, that was his name for all that large part of his experience which, originating outside of his own will, threatened his initiative and even his identity as a self-sufficient person. It was thus hardly more than a dramatic name for the 18th-century system of Necessity that he had set the Self against and that remained throughout his life the great opponent the Self must dominate. The experience of Illusion also was simply the cause or result of a failure to do so: Illusion named the inner loss of power, Fate the sense of subjection to an outer force that then moved in to take possession of his spirit. The story of Emerson's thought is thus as simple as it is basic—a revolt against the 18th-century world of mechanical necessity, the assertion of the sovereignty of the Self as a counter to it, and a battle thereafter to maintain this "true romance" against all the aspects of experience that united to suggest that such a way of escape was vain and Necessity master after all.

In this battle Emerson showed himself resourceful, maintaining his trust in the soul through all the assaults of the "Not-Me." In time, moreover, the war of Self and Necessity found a measure of resolution. At first he had argued that, since "the All is within you," the world is an "other me" and will fall into step with the will of the self-reliant man. But a more reasonable and traditional position was to reverse the thought: since "self-reliance is God-reliance," the self-reliant man will always fall into step with the ordained course of things. As the Puritans had argued long before, the enlightened will merges with the will of God. To the older man the world came to seem a huge cosmic drama in which he was no longer, as Self, a central figure, though he might still at moments make one with the Will it obeyed. As this way of looking at things began to sink in, he took up the idea of natural evolution as it came to him from a number of pre-Darwinian sources, at the same time that he responded with ever deepening sympathy to the vast scale and vaster acquiescence of Oriental thought.

With this resolution of his private drama his whole concern with Self and Necessity shifted somewhat into the background, while the foreground became occupied with practical ethics, especially with the compelling moral questions of the developing antislavery crisis and the civil war which followed. In "The Conduct of Life" (1860), for example, his stress falls on self-improvement rather than on self-sufficiency, on refining the raw egotism of the natural man through culture and manners rather than on pursuing greatness through freedom. Such a stress, of course, implies a considerable measure of human freedom and responsibility, for all the "Beautiful Necessity" in the background, but now simply as a relative practical fact rather than the total claim of his transcendental years. On this all-but-serene note of theoretical optimism and practical meliorism Emerson's adventure in thought came to a close.

The dialectical movement within Emerson's thought is paralleled in his relations to the work of others. He played a central part in the Great Conversation which, R. W. B. Lewis suggests, is now emerging as the true subject of the concentrated study that has been given the major American authors in recent times. The main lines of this implicit dialogue have yet to be fixed, so that it is still possible for the student of American literature, starting with no more than the materials provided in this anthology, to work out some part of it for himself without having to feel that the answers to the questions he raises are all filed somewhere in a final synopticon of which his professor holds the key. To do so, however, he must start and end with Emerson, for a peculiarity of this imaginary conversation is that to a considerable degree it has gone on among authors largely unresponsive to each other except as they all responded to him. A main issue was the one Emerson himself raised, the adequacy of the individual to cope with the world in which he finds himself. Emerson called on his contemporaries in everything he said or wrote to reject the alternative that pressed on them as it does on us, the flight from freedom into some collective anonymity, and to trust the sufficiency of the independent mind before all the terrors of the "huge world."

All important American authors without exception responded in some way to this vision (though it did not always come to them from Emerson) and shared his contempt for the "dead alive" who could not do so, but their responses ran the gamut from enthusiasm to despair. The chief challenge to his challenge came independently from a number of writers whose most profound spokesman looks at the moment like Hawthorne, but who included such figures as Melville, Poe, Emily Dickinson, and even Whitman, to say nothing of later writers, all of whom pointed out, each in his own way, that the mastery of mind over fate, if it was possible at all, was no such assured matter as Emerson suggested. Melville's Ahab and Pierre, both heroes of self-reliance, immolate themselves on the bitter knowledge that the huge world will *not* "come round" to them; Hawthorne's Goodman Brown, a guileless 17th-century Thoreau, trusts himself to step aside for one night from the village into the forest, only to enter a lifelong nightmare. "Over Descartian vortices you hover," warned Melville—or as Gerard Manley Hopkins wrote,

> O the mind, mind has mountains; cliffs of fall
> Frightful, sheer, no-man-fathomed. Hold them cheap
> May who ne'er hung there.

Poe and Emily Dickinson would have agreed. Yet still came Emerson's "voice of cherub scorn"—"let the soul be erect, and all things will go well." The great question he raised, which is not settled yet, is whether this preternatural confidence contained in some way an answer in turn to the challenge it evoked from those who could not share it, or whether before their acid appeal to experience it "all slid to confusion." Must we, with them, "dwell in the House of Pain," or can we, with Emerson, rise above it? What is certain is that if his security had been, as some maintain, merely a shallow obliviousness, it could never have aroused the deep and lasting response it has had. Somehow Emerson touched a nerve of the American imagination and contributed more than any other single force to give it direction and impetus. He was, in short, a poet. Since he was an unusual sort of poet, and mostly in prose at that, a look at his literary theory and practice may help bring him to definition.

III

No one has said better things *about* prose style than Emerson. "The sincerity and marrow of the man," he writes of Montaigne, "reaches to his sentences. I know not anywhere the book that seems less written. It is the language of conversation transferred to a book. Cut these words, and they would bleed; they are vascular and alive. One has the same pleasure in it that he feels in listening to the necessary speech of men about their work, when any unusual circumstance gives momentary importance to the dialogue. For blacksmiths and teamsters do not trip in their speech; it is a shower of bullets. It is Cambridge men who correct themselves and begin again at every half sentence, and moreover, will pun, and refine too much, and swerve from the matter to the expression." As an ideal of good prose, this famous statement is singularly modern, or rather timeless. The best prose writers of our speech—Swift, Dryden, Shaw, Mark Twain, Hemingway—have simply practiced what it preaches, and all our rhetorics teach little else. The only trouble with it as a statement is that it is a poor description of Emerson's own prose, either in its purpose or its achievements. Unintentionally it reminds us that Emerson too was a Cambridge man. A major stumbling-block to the appreciation of Emerson is the undeniable gap between the ideal of a natural, organic style like speech which he found realized in favorite authors such as Montaigne and Plutarch and his own practice, which often seems all too *written*.

For an example, we need go no further than this statement. "Cut these words, and they would bleed." Surely this is not "necessary speech" but the heightened language of a literary man seeking "color." "It is a shower of bullets" has a similarly self-conscious ring. Even "marrow," while a brilliant choice, is an idiosyncratic usage which hardly suggests conversation. All this is very good writing of a kind: it has force, precision, vividness, individuality, compactness, coherence, rhythmic mastery; but it is not of the kind it describes, nor is it of a kind the modern reader at least finds half so congenial.

One reason for this curious gap between the principles and the practice of so adept a writer is a conflict of principles. We get a hint of this in the same paragraph about Montaigne, when after speaking of his lack of enthusiasms, Emerson adds, "There is but one exception,—in his love for Socrates. In speaking of him, for once his cheek flushes and his style rises to passion." The remark suggests that writing which did rise to passion would be better than that which held the level of conversation, and in so doing it reflects a central principle in Emerson's literary theory. In praising a natural and organic style he conceals, as so often, a "higher" meaning beyond the plain one. The best writing, he believes, is the necessary speech of a man's *best moments*, the spontaneous overflow of a powerful passion. The true writer should be the organ of an "irresistible persuasion" which lifts his readers to a responding release of their own imaginative energy. The ideal of ideals is not the informal ease which his praise of Montaigne suggests but an enraptured or vatic utterance, the "screams" (Emerson's word) of the visionary, which can "alter in a pair of hours * * * the convictions and habits of years." The naturalness of Montaigne is the vestibule of the temple, but the inspiration of the Poet is the inner sanctum.

Here we touch one source of Emerson's difficulties as a prose artist, for such an exalted ideal is beyond ordinary human powers. By this standard all but a few peaks of achievement sink below the sea level of mere talk. Consequently a man whose temperament, after all, was so little inclined to the fury of the possessed as Emerson's would tend to simulate what he could not reach, and a note of strain would enter his work to mar its ease. Melville ran into a similar dilemma with Ahab. Typically, as in the passage just discussed, if we stop to scrutinize something in Emerson that seems displeasing, we are likely to find, as O. W. Firkins has shown, that in one way or another he has sacrificed naturalness for an excess of force. Another source of Emerson's difficulties emerges when we contrast the stress on naturalness in his theory with his own painstaking habits of composition. Somehow his theory did not mesh with his practice, but seems intended if anything to offer a visionary release from the exacting labor which he accepted in fact. Once more we touch on one of those polarities by which he lived. Emerson really had two standards of good writing: the ideal freedom described in "The Poet" and the actual discipline by which he got his work done. Emerson the writer, like Emerson the man, has two faces: the Poet and the "Cambridge man."

If we ask how the Cambridge man saw the task of writing, as distinct from the Poet, the answer has the irrelevance to the vision that is the hallmark of these Emersonian dualities. What this Emerson really worked for was not the unbuttoned ease of Montaigne, still less the visionary's inspired power, but a deliberate platform effect. The tradition that shapes his purpose is neither that of the familiar essay nor that of the Platonic poet but that of classical oratory. His image of himself is the image he actually did present in the lecture hall—the calm, restrained, almost dry speaker quietly reading without gesture from a manuscript, holding his hearers by the simple authority of his "low tones that decide." Now that the taste for eloquence which Emerson took for granted has evaporated it is obvious that the principles that controlled his practice in composition ran directly counter to the principles of inspiration he himself proclaimed. No one has ever urged abandon with more self-possession.

Yet we must give his practice its due. It has in distinguished measure the virtues appropriate to its kind, conspicuous among which is firm organization. An ancient libel, encouraged by Emerson himself, has it that he could not organize larger units—"paragraphs incompressible, each sentence an infinitely repellent particle." Readers who cannot follow Emerson must be deprived of this refuge: whatever he wrote to Carlyle, in humorous self-deprecation, knowing that a fellow writer would understand him, he is in fact always coherent. If anything, he is over-organized; one trouble with *Nature*, for example, is excessive organization. Often he will carefully number his points—a practice, as has been pointed out, that "is thought to be the acme, almost the pedantry, of order." Or he adopts the structure of the classical oration, the clear and explicit division of an argument into its logical parts. Still another structure is the ascending scale, where the writer begins with the most obvious view of his topic and then gradually raises his readers to more and more ideal views until he has brought them as far as he believes they can go. A variation on this is the rondo form, in which the writer returns repeatedly to the same point, each time revealing more of his whole meaning. A fourth kind of structure is the dialectical. In this, the writer presents conflicting views, giving each its head and permitting the irresistible statement of one to balance the irrefutable statement of the other. Often, though not always, such a structure will fall into tripartite form, a statement, a counterstatement, and some kind of resolution.

These structure types are paradigms which Emerson modified or combined in many ways, but if we look for something like them as we read we will at least recognize what is invariably the case—that *some* structure is present. "Experience," for example, deliberately written to seem tentative and merely enumerative, has actually a dialectical organization which turns out to be an ascending scale also, though in places, as in *Nature*, Emerson impatiently leaps to the top at a bound before returning to lead us up the gradual ascent he has prepared for us. In "Experience" Emerson perhaps comes closest to the organic form he dreamed of, in which the thought finds the unique organization that belongs to it alone. Generally his form does not "grow from within" in this sense so much as it is an appropriate shape imposed on his thoughts from the outside. The kind of subtly intuitive symbolic or musical form such as Whitman reached at his best is not in Emerson's range, either in prose or poetry. His form, while not absent, is inert. He remains in this respect a descendant of the rational traditions of the 18th century.

Here we touch on the deepest ground of Emerson's difficulties with organization, for he was not writing speeches in the 18th-century sense. As Roland Lee has convincingly shown, the most adequate statement of what he was trying to do is to be found not in his own theory but in the writings of his Danish contemporary, Søren Kierkegaard. He also, like Kierkegaard, was uninterested in "results," the transfer of propositions from intellect to intellect. "If truth is spirit, it is an inward transformation, a realization of inwardness," Kierkegaard wrote. " * * * The communication of results is an unnatural form of intercourse between man and man, in so far as every man is a spiritual being, for whom the truth consists in nothing else than the self-activity of personal appropriation, which the communication of a result tends to prevent." Emerson also aimed to bring about an "inward transformation": "There is no teaching until the pupil is brought into the same state or principle in which you are; a transfusion takes place; he is you and you are he; then is a teaching, and by no unfriendly chance or bad company can he ever quite lose the benefit. But your propositions run out of one ear as they ran in at the other."

To accomplish this "transfusion," to stir the "self-activity of personal appropriation," mere exposition was useless; it had to be "indirect," as Kierkegaard (and Whitman) put it, had to speak to the imagination as well as to the intellect; had, in short, to be literature. What both Kierkegaard and Emerson, in effect, were working toward was a kind of dramatic monologue, a form which of course has its own dramatic principles of organization. Emerson's root difficulty is that he has not gone far enough in this direction: the single part of a given essay is a dramatic performance, the voice of a speaker who is, in Sherwood Anderson's phrase, a "slip-off section" of the author, but the structure of the whole remains bound to the methods of direct exposition. A consequence is his most typical failing, to build the part with too little regard for the effect of the whole. Like a bad actor, he goes all out everywhere.

A good illustration of this trouble is "Self-Reliance," which opens quietly enough, but at once begins a rapid crescendo until by the third paragraph the whole orchestra is playing *forte*. This premature climax is quite deliberate. In the lecture from which this paragraph came, the last sentence read, "And we are now men and must accept in the highest mind the same transcendent destiny and not pinched in a corner not cowards fleeing before revolution but pious aspirants to be noble clay plastic in the Almighty effort, we must advance and advance into Chaos and the Dark." The corresponding sentence in the essay is noticeably more strident. At each stage of the essay he tries for the same knockout punch; the result is powerful but exhausting. This is an extreme case, paralleled only by certain other essays of 1841, like "The Over-Soul," which are also partly anthologies of climaxes from the lectures of the 1830's. Yet the tendency to heighten the part until it clogs instead of furthering the movement of the whole is a mark of all Emerson's formal writing and a major reason for the illusion of disorganization it creates.

The other side of this coin, of course, is Emerson's memorable success with individual passages, as in "Self-Reliance." His literary reputation must always rest on the power with which he expresses the single thought. The adventure of reading him is the unpredictable explosion with which a given passage, one we have perhaps read before without attention, suddenly captures our whole mind and cannot thereafter be dislodged. John Jay Chapman's famous description of this peculiar power in Emerson deserves to be quoted:

> Your attention is arrested by the reality of this gentleman in his garden, by the firsthand quality of his mind. It matters not on what subject he talks. While you are musing, still pleased and patronizing, he has picked up the bow of Ulysses, bent it with the ease of Ulysses, and sent a shaft clear through the twelve axes, nor missed one of them. But this, it seems, was mere byplay and marksmanship; for before you have done wondering, Ulysses rises to his feet in anger, and pours flight after flight, arrow after arrow, from the great bow. The shafts sing and strike; the suitors fall in heaps. The brow of Ulysses shines with unearthly splendor. The air is filled with lightning. After a little, without shock or transition, without apparent change of tone, Mr. Emerson is offering you a biscuit before you leave, and bidding you mind the last step at the garden end. If the man who can do these things be not an artist, then must we have a new vocabulary and rename the professions.

As with the essays, so with the poems. Their practice also is half controlled by traditional forms and purposes, half struggling toward new principles which we can now recognize as much like the symbolist forms which Whitman was shortly to innovate and which are dominant in modern verse. Many of Emerson's strongest poems, as we might expect, are short pieces in which, unhampered by large problems of organization, he can capture the distilled essence of one thought. His longer poems are not usually so successful, either because he has trouble managing the verse forms he has chosen, or because he has not been able to solve his problem of fitting the parts to the whole. Again, they are usually not without form: the "Ode to Channing," Andrew Schiller has shown, is organized like an oration; "The Sphinx" has a dialectical structure—challenge, counterchallenge, and resolution; "Uriel" is mythological narrative; and so on. But his forms are often simple rational containers rather than the organic unity, growing from within, which he called for in his theory of poetry.

One reason he could not achieve this aim, aside from its lofty ideal character, was a conflict in his own purposes. On the one hand he was groping toward the large bardic manner which he recognized and welcomed in Whitman's 1855 *Leaves of Grass*; on the other he was aiming at what has well been called "gnomic structure," a verse built on short,

pithy, epigrammatic utterances. To a degree these aims canceled each
other out. The result is a verse of great power and much unevenness. The
long poems, for all their diffuseness, have an undeniable cumulative effect.
And again and again, as with the essays but with even greater impact, a
line or two in any poem will flash out and grip the mind, or a passage of
packed and cryptic thought will challenge it; then some false note or other
will scatter our attention. In general the verdict must be recorded that the
form from which he hoped most was the least congenial to him, making
possible some work which will stand to be compared with the work of any
poet, but also in its concentration betraying him into much that was
simply inept. As he said of Thoreau, his genius was greater than his talent.

The advantage of the *Journals* is that they are nothing *but* parts, so that
in them Emerson's skill at shooting a thought on the wing has free play.
In addition, as working notebooks intended for private use their expression
is relatively easy, nervous, free-flowing, unimpeded by the more self-conscious rhetoric that for a modern reader mars the essays. Nor do they lack
a kind of unity, one that is in some ways more organic than any he imposed
on his formal work, that imparted by a single, vigorously personal point
of view. They do not have the intimacy of other famous journals, revealing
rather, as his friends discovered, that Emerson had no other life than the
life of the mind harvested in his public works. But they make plain, as
Alfred Kazin and Daniel Aaron have recently said, that Emerson "is, above
all else, an observer and recorder, a genius at catching life's quickness, a
man who knows how to seize whatever occurs to him as a reflection of
the circumambient reality in which man is placed." For him, they add,
"life *is* thought"; "everything starts not merely from the record of inner
experience, from the 'I' faithfully and even doggedly capturing every spiritual adventure, but from his response to those 'moments,' to those mystical
flights, even to those special passages and 'lustres' of light in other people's books, which for him were the height of all being and the reason
for it." This is what he meant in that sentence which might stand as a
motto for his whole achievement, "The one thing in the world, of value,
is the active soul."

The greatness of the *Journals* is partly in the record they provide of fifty
years of a continuously "active soul," always freshly responsive to the "moment"; partly also in the fine tact with which he recognizes that the moment has passed and cheerfully reels in his line to cast again. From time
to time, to continue the metaphor, he hooks something, plays it for a
while, then nets it and throws it back, or keeps it to stuff and mount in
an essay—complaining sometimes of the tedium of doing so. To para-
phrase Eliot on James, he had a mind so fine that no idea could capture it.
From the *Journals* we can move outward to see his whole work in a fresh
perspective. If the *Journals* recorded, as has been said, "the original leap
and grasp of the mind," the essays were a kind of Indian rope trick in
which the mind climbed steadily, *toward* finality, until the thought

could bear no more,
But dipped its top and set [it] down again.

His work in its totality provides one of the finest demonstrations in our literature of something greater than any of his single works, the life of intelligence.

IV

It is in this direction we can look for Emerson's present relevance. To find it we need mentally to take a step back from his own emphases. The final truth, for him, was the "Beautiful Necessity," the Law that guaranteed the rule of good. His courage to live rested on a trust in the impossibility of radical mischief. Somehow, "let the victory fall where it will, we are on that side." Such agnostic optimism is basically a matter of temperament and is therefore untransferable. Since Emerson's day its acceptability has been steadily reduced, until now for many it has virtually ceased to be a "live option."

Yet to strip Emerson of his assurance that "all things go well" is not to destroy his relevance, though he himself might have thought so. Rather it brings out all the more clearly the other side of his teaching, the creative resources of the mind. The center of life for him was the moment when, as he put it, fact flowered into truth, when the *words* came to order perception and illumine the will. His work is one long celebration of the miracle of language. Properly, it has its toughness as well as its promise. The flash of "genius" (original insight) must be destructive as well as creative, shattering dead forms and formulas with new life as the life in a seed cracks and bursts a pavement. Beneath his gentlemanly decorum was a militant zeal, like that of the Puritan "saints" from whom he was descended, that left him no leisure "to come into the dark and lament."

Emerson is finally to be judged, not for what he lacked, but for what he had. His single devotion was to an urgent truth beyond grief or love, the power of the free mind. His challenge has reverberated throughout American literature; like one of the "archetypal poems" called for in Whitman's *Democratic Vistas*, it has spoken not just for one man but for a society. "We dress our garden, eat our dinners, discuss the household with our wives, and these things make no impression, are forgotten next week; but, in the solitude to which every man is always returning, he has a sanity and revelations which in his passage into new worlds he will carry with him. Never mind the ridicule, never mind the defeat; up again, old heart!—it seems to say,—there is victory yet for all justice; and the true romance which the world exists to realize will be the transformation of genius into practical power." Passages like this, and there are many of them, have lost and can lose little of their relevance as long as free men have minds of their own at all. To the degree that we recover from our present immersion in self-pity we will recover them too.

Nature[1]

A subtle chain of countless rings
The next unto the farthest brings;
The eye reads omens where it goes,
And speaks all languages the rose;
And, striving to be man, the worm
Mounts through all the spires of form.

Introduction

Our age is retrospective. It builds the sepulchres of the fathers.
It writes biographies, histories, and criticism. The fore-going generations beheld God and nature face to face; we, through their eyes.
Why should not we also enjoy an original relation to the universe?
Why should not we have a poetry and philosophy of insight and not
of tradition, and a religion by revelation to us, and not the history
of theirs? Embosomed for a season in nature, whose floods of life
stream around and through us, and invite us, by the powers they
supply, to action proportioned to nature, why should we grope
among the dry bones of the past, or put the living generation into
masquerade out of its faded wardrobe? The sun shines to-day also.
There is more wool and flax in the fields. There are new lands, new
men, new thoughts. Let us demand our own works and laws and
worship.

Undoubtedly we have no questions to ask which are unanswerable.
We must trust the perfection of the creation so far as to believe that
whatever curiosity the order of things has awakened in our minds,

1. On shipboard, returning from Europe
in 1833, Emerson said in his *Journals*,
"I like my book about Nature," though
presumably not a line of it had yet been
written. Some part of it took shape in
the lectures on "natural history" which
he proceeded to give in the next year,
and more in the lectures on "English
Literature" in 1835. The bulk of *Nature*
(his first book), however, was written
in the spring and summer of 1836, immediately before publication in September. Its starting point is the problem
later formulated by Matthew Arnold:
"There is not a creed which is not
shaken, not an accredited dogma which
is not shown to be questionable, not a
received tradition which does not
threaten to dissolve. Our religion has
materialized itself in the fact, in the
supposed fact; it has attached its emotion to the fact, and now the fact is failing it." With the failure of "the fact,"
Emerson begins, we must turn from received tradition to nature. "To what end
is nature?" he asks, meaning, how can
nature help to restore our confidence
and release our powers, as the fact of
historical religion once did? *Nature* consists of a series of answers to this question. It is an audacious attempt to rescue nature from the natural scientists

and to sketch instead a human or poetic science. Though it takes ideas and
"lustres" from a wide range of reading
—Plato, the Bible, Shakespeare, Berkeley, Swedenborg, Coleridge, Carlyle,
Goethe, even Alcott—they all unite on
the one point of moment, the power of
imagination to elicit a human truth
from nature. The thought toward which
all its rapid cross-play of eclectic echoes
steadily moves was summarized in the
Journals for March, 1836, when Emerson was in the heat of composition (see
Journals, passage 98). For all its quaint
scholastic air, *Nature* has, like Whitman's *Song of Myself*, a special force
the author never quite reached again.
The reason is the same in both cases:
the discovery of a well of life where
there had seemed only desert. The wave
of millennial hope in the "unsearched
might of man" that lifted Thoreau and
Whitman began with Emerson's *Nature*.

When the first edition of *Nature* was
published (anonymously, in 1836) the
epigraph was taken from Plotinus: "Nature is but an image or imitation of
wisdom, the last thing of the soul; Nature being a thing which doth only do,
but not know." When *Nature* was reprinted in 1849, the present epigraph
was substituted.

the order of things can satisfy. Every man's condition is a solution in hieroglyphic to those inquiries he would put. He acts it as life, before he apprehends it as truth. In like manner, nature is already, in its forms and tendencies, describing its own design. Let us interrogate the great apparition that shines so peacefully around us. Let us inquire, to what end is nature?

All science has one aim, namely, to find a theory of nature. We have theories of races and of functions, but scarcely yet a remote approach to an idea of creation. We are now so far from the road to truth, that religious teachers dispute and hate each other, and speculative men are esteemed unsound and frivolous. But to a sound judgment, the most abstract truth is the most practical. Whenever a true theory appears, it will be its own evidence. Its test is, that it will explain all phenomena. Now many are thought not only unexplained but inexplicable; as language, sleep, madness, dreams, beasts, sex.

Philosophically considered, the universe is composed of Nature and the Soul. Strictly speaking, therefore, all that is separate from us, all which Philosophy distinguishes as the NOT ME,[2] that is, both nature and art, all other men and my own body, must be ranked under this name, NATURE. In enumerating the values of nature and casting up their sum, I shall use the word in both senses;—in its common and in its philosophical import. In inquiries so general as our present one, the inaccuracy is not material; no confusion of thought will occur. *Nature*, in the common sense, refers to essences unchanged by man; space, the air, the river, the leaf. *Art* is applied to the mixture of his will with the same things, as in a house, a canal, a statue, a picture. But his operations taken together are so insignificant, a little chipping, baking, patching, and washing, that in an impression so grand as that of the world on the human mind, they do not vary the result.

I. Nature

To go into solitude, a man needs to retire as much from his chamber as from society. I am not solitary whilst I read and write, though nobody is with me. But if a man would be alone, let him look at the stars. The rays that come from those heavenly worlds will separate between him and what he touches. One might think the atmosphere was made transparent with this design, to give man, in the heavenly bodies, the perpetual presence of the sublime. Seen in the streets of cities, how great they are! If the stars should appear one night in a

2. Term borrowed from Thomas Carlyle's *Sartor Resartus* (1833–34). A vernacular translation of the *Nicht-Ich* (Not-Self) or Non-Ego of German post-Kantian philosophy. Its opposite, the "ME," is the Self of "Self-Reliance." "How many changes men ring on these two words *in* and *out*. It is all our philosophy" (*Journals*, 1831).

thousand years, how would men believe and adore; and preserve for many generations the remembrance of the city of God which had been shown! But every night come out these envoys of beauty, and light the universe with their admonishing smile.

The stars awaken a certain reverence, because though always present, they are inaccessible; but all natural objects make a kindred impression, when the mind is open to their influence. Nature never wears a mean appearance. Neither does the wisest man extort her secret, and lose his curiosity by finding out all her perfection. Nature never became a toy to a wise spirit. The flowers, the animals, the mountains, reflected the wisdom of his best hour, as much as they had delighted the simplicity of his childhood.

When we speak of nature in this manner, we have a distinct but most poetical sense in the mind. We mean the integrity of impression made by manifold natural objects. It is this which distinguishes the stick of timber of the wood-cutter from the tree of the poet. The charming landscape which I saw this morning is indubitably made up of some twenty or thirty farms. Miller owns this field, Locke that, and Manning the woodland beyond. But none of them owns the landscape. There is a property in the horizon which no man has but he whose eye can integrate all the parts, that is, the poet. This is the best part of these men's farms, yet to this their warranty-deeds give no title.[3]

To speak truly, few adult persons can see nature. Most persons do not see the sun. At least they have a very superficial seeing. The sun illuminates only the eye of the man, but shines into the eye and the heart of the child. The lover of nature is he whose inward and outward senses are still truly adjusted to each other; who has retained the spirit of infancy even into the era of manhood.[4] His intercourse with heaven and earth becomes part of his daily food. In the presence of nature a wild delight runs through the man, in spite of real sorrows. Nature says,—he is my creature, and maugre[5] all his impertinent griefs, he shall be glad with me. Not the sun or the summer alone, but every hour and season yields its tribute of delight; for every hour and change corresponds to and authorizes a different state of the mind, from breathless noon to grimmest midnight. Nature is a setting that fits equally well a comic or a mourning piece. In good health, the air is a cordial of incredible virtue. Crossing a bare common, in snow puddles, at twilight, under a clouded sky, without having in my thoughts any occurrence of special good fortune, I have enjoyed a perfect exhilaration. I am glad to the brink of fear. In the woods, too, a man casts off his years, as the snake his

3. Cf. "Each and All" and *Walden* (beginning of Chapter II).
4. "To carry on the feelings of childhood into the powers of manhood;

* * * this is the character and privilege of genius" (Coleridge, *Biographia Literaria*, Chapter IV).
5. In spite of.

slough, and at what period soever of life, is always a child. In the woods is perpetual youth. Within these plantations of God, a decorum and sanctity reign, a perennial festival is dressed, and the guest sees not how he should tire of them in a thousand years. In the woods, we return to reason and faith. There I feel that nothing can befall me in life,—no disgrace, no calamity (leaving me my eyes), which nature cannot repair. Standing on the bare ground,—my head bathed by the blithe air, and uplifted into infinite space,—all mean egotism vanishes. I become a transparent eyeball; I am nothing; I see all; the currents of the Universal Being circulate through me; I am part or parcel[6] of God. The name of the nearest friend sounds then foreign and accidental: to be brothers, to be acquaintances,— master or servant, is then a trifle and a disturbance.[7] I am the lover of uncontained and immortal beauty. In the wilderness, I find something more dear and connate[8] than in streets or villages. In the tranquil landscape, and especially in the distant line of the horizon, man beholds somewhat as beautiful as his own nature.

The greatest delight which the fields and woods minister is the suggestion of an occult relation[9] between man and the vegetable. I am not alone and unacknowledged. They nod to me, and I to them. The waving of the boughs in the storm is new to me and old. It takes me by surprise, and yet is not unknown. Its effect is like that of a higher thought or a better emotion coming over me, when I deemed I was thinking justly or doing right.

Yet it is certain that the power to produce this delight does not reside in nature, but in man, or in a harmony of both. It is necessary to use these pleasures with great temperance. For nature is not always tricked in holiday attire, but the same scene which yesterday breathed perfume and glittered as for the frolic of nymphs, is overspread with melancholy to-day. Nature always wears the colors of the spirit.[1] To a man laboring under calamity, the heat of his own fire hath sadness in it. Then there is a kind of contempt of the landscape felt by him who has just lost by death a dear friend.[2] The sky is less grand as it shuts down over less worth in the population.

II. Commodity[3]

Whoever considers the final cause[4] of the world will discern a multitude of uses that enter as parts into that result. They all admit of being thrown into one of the following classes: Commodity; Beauty; Language; and Discipline.

6. The editions before 1903 read "particle."
7. Cf. *Journals* (passage 97).
8. Cognate, related.
9. Cf. *Journals* (passage 96).
1. Cf. Coleridge, "Dejection: An Ode."

2. Emerson had just lost his brother Charles. Cf. the end of Chapter V, "Discipline."
3. Usefulness, serviceability.
4. Purpose (Aristotelian term).

Under the general name of commodity, I rank all those advantages which our senses owe to nature. This, of course, is a benefit which is temporary and mediate, not ultimate, like its service to the soul. Yet although low, it is perfect in its kind, and is the only use of nature which all men apprehend. The misery of man appears like childish petulance, when we explore the steady and prodigal provision that has been made for his support and delight on this green ball which floats him through the heavens. What angels invented these splendid ornaments, these rich conveniences, this ocean of air above, this ocean of water beneath, this firmament of earth between? this zodiac of lights, this tent of dropping clouds, this striped coat of climates, this fourfold year? Beasts, fire, water, stones, and corn serve him. The field is at once his floor, his work-yard, his playground, his garden, and his bed.

> "More servants wait on man
> Than he'll take notice of."[5]

Nature, in its ministry to man, is not only the material, but is also the process and the result. All the parts incessantly work into each other's hands for the profit of man. The wind sows the seed; the sun evaporates the sea; the wind blows the vapor to the field; the ice, on the other side of the planet, condenses rain on this; the rain feeds the plant; the plant feeds the animal; and thus the endless circulations of the divine charity nourish man.

The useful arts are reproductions or new combinations by the wit of man, of the same natural benefactors. He no longer waits for favoring gales, but by means of steam, he realizes the fable of Æolus's bag,[6] and carries the two and thirty winds in the boiler of his boat. To diminish friction, he paves the road with iron bars, and, mounting a coach with a ship-load of men, animals, and merchandise behind him, he darts through the country, from town to town, like an eagle or a swallow through the air. By the aggregate of these aids, how is the face of the world changed, from the era of Noah to that of Napoleon! The private poor man hath cities, ships, canals, bridges, built for him. He goes to the post-office, and the human race run on his errands; to the book-shop, and the human race read and write of all that happens, for him; to the court-house, and nations repair his wrongs. He sets his house upon the road, and the human race go forth every morning, and shovel out the snow, and cut a path for him.

But there is no need of specifying particulars in this class of uses. The catalogue is endless, and the examples so obvious, that I shall

5. From George Herbert's poem "Man," most of which Emerson quotes in Chapter VIII, "Prospects."
6. A reference to *Odyssey* X: Aeolus, Greek god of the winds, gave Odysseus a bag containing favorable winds—which Odysseus' sailors released all at once, producing a storm.

leave them to the reader's reflection, with the general remark, that this mercenary benefit is one which has respect to a farther good. A man is fed, not that he may be fed, but that he may work.

III. Beauty

A nobler want of man is served by nature, namely, the love of Beauty.

The ancient Greeks called the world κόσμος,[7] beauty. Such is the constitution of all things, or such the plastic[8] power of the human eye, that the primary forms, as the sky, the mountain, the tree, the animal, give us a delight *in and for themselves*; a pleasure arising from outline, color, motion, and grouping. This seems partly owing to the eye itself. The eye is the best of artists. By the mutual action of its structure and of the laws of light, perspective is produced, which integrates every mass of objects, of what character soever, into a well colored and shaded globe, so that where the particular objects are mean and unaffecting, the landscape which they compose is round and symmetrical. And as the eye is the best composer, so light is the first of painters. There is no object so foul that intense light will not make beautiful. And the stimulus it affords to the sense, and a sort of infinitude which it hath, like space and time, make all matter gay. Even the corpse has its own beauty. But besides this general grace diffused over nature, almost all the individual forms are agreeable to the eye, as is proved by our endless imitations of some of them, as the acorn, the grape, the pine-cone, the wheat-ear, the egg, the wings and forms of most birds, the lion's claw, the serpent, the butterfly, sea-shells, flames, clouds, buds, leaves, and the forms of many trees, as the palm.

For better consideration, we may distribute the aspects of Beauty in a threefold manner.

1. First, the simple perception of natural forms is a delight. The influence of the forms and actions in nature is so needful to man, that, in its lowest functions, it seems to lie on the confines of commodity and beauty. To the body and mind which have been cramped by noxious work or company, nature is medicinal and restores their tone. The tradesman, the attorney comes out of the din and craft of the street and sees the sky and the woods, and is a man again. In their eternal calm, he finds himself. The health of the eye seems to demand a horizon. We are never tired, so long as we can see far enough.

But in other hours, Nature satisfies by its loveliness, and without any mixture of corporeal benefit. I see the spectacle of morning from the hilltop over against my house, from daybreak to sunrise, with emotions which an angel might share. The long slender bars of cloud

---

7. Kosmos (order). 8. Creative.

float like fishes in the sea of crimson light. From the earth, as a shore, I look out into that silent sea. I seem to partake its rapid transformations; the active enchantment reaches my dust, and I dilate and conspire with[9] the morning wind. How does Nature deify us with a few and cheap elements! Give me health and a day, and I will make the pomp of emperors ridiculous. The dawn is my Assyria; the sunset and moonrise my Paphos,[1] and unimaginable realms of faerie; broad noon shall be my England of the senses and the understanding; the night shall be my Germany[2] of mystic philosophy and dreams.

Not less excellent, except for our less susceptibility in the afternoon, was the charm, last evening, of a January sunset. The western clouds divided and subdivided themselves into pink flakes modulated with tints of unspeakable softness, and the air had so much life and sweetness that it was a pain to come within doors. What was it that nature would say? Was there no meaning in the live repose of the valley behind the mill, and which Homer or Shakespeare could not re-form for me in words? The leafless trees become spires of flame in the sunset, with the blue east for their background, and the stars of the dead calices of flowers, and every withered stem and stubble rimed with frost, contribute something to the mute music.

The inhabitants of cities suppose that the country landscape is pleasant only half the year. I please myself with the graces of the winter scenery, and believe that we are as much touched by it as by the genial[3] influences of summer. To the attentive eye, each moment of the year has its own beauty, and in the same field, it beholds, every hour, a picture which was never seen before, and which shall never be seen again. The heavens change every moment, and reflect their glory or gloom on the plains beneath. The state of the crop in the surrounding farms alters the expression of the earth from week to week. The succession of native plants in the pastures and roadsides, which make the silent clock by which time tells the summer hours, will make even the divisions of the day sensible to a keen observer. The tribes of birds and insects, like the plants punctual to their time, follow each other, and the year has room for all. By watercourses, the variety is greater. In July, the blue pontederia or pickerel-weed blooms in large beds in the shallow parts of our pleasant river,[4] and swarms with yellow butterflies in continual motion. Art cannot rival this pomp of purple and gold. Indeed the river is a perpetual gala, and boasts each month a new ornament.

But this beauty of Nature which is seen and felt as beauty, is the least part. The shows of day, the dewy morning, the rainbow, moun-

---

9. Breathe with.
1. Place names from ancient history. Assyria connotes empire, Paphos (a city in Cyprus, noted for its worship of Venus) love.

2. British "commonsense" philosophy is contrasted with the newer Idealism of the post-Kantians.
3. Generative.
4. The Concord.

tains, orchards in blossom, stars, moonlight, shadows in still water, and the like, if too eagerly hunted, become shows merely, and mock us with their unreality. Go out of the house to see the moon, and 'tis mere tinsel; it will not please as when its light shines upon your necessary journey. The beauty that shimmers in the yellow afternoons of October, who ever could clutch it? Go forth to find it, and it is gone; 'tis only a mirage as you look from the windows of diligence.

2. The presence of a higher, namely, of the spiritual element is essential to its perfection. The high and divine beauty which can be loved without effeminacy, is that which is found in combination with the human will. Beauty is the mark God sets upon virtue. Every natural action is graceful. Every heroic act is also decent,[5] and causes the place and the bystanders to shine. We are taught by great actions that the universe is the property of every individual in it. Every rational creature has all nature for his dowry and estate. It is his, if he will. He may divest himself of it; he may creep into a corner, and abdicate his kingdom, as most men do, but he is entitled to the world by his constitution. In proportion to the energy of his thought and will, he takes up the world into himself. "All those things for which men plough, build, or sail, obey virtue;" said Sallust. "The winds and waves," said Gibbon, "are always on the side of the ablest navigators."[6] So are the sun and moon and all the stars of heaven. When a noble act is done,—perchance in a scene of great natural beauty; when Leonidas and his three hundred martyrs consume one day in dying, and the sun and moon come each and look at them once in the steep defile of Thermopylæ; when Arnold Winkelried, in the high Alps, under the shadow of the avalanche, gathers in his side a sheaf of Austrian spears to break the line for his comrades; are not these heroes entitled to add the beauty of the scene to the beauty of the deed?[7] When the bark of Columbus nears the shore of America;—before it, the beach lined with savages, fleeing out of all their huts of cane; the sea behind; and the purple mountains of the Indian Archipelago around, can we separate the man from the living picture? Does not the New World clothe his form with her palm-groves and savannahs as fit drapery? Ever does natural beauty steal in like air, and envelope great actions. When Sir Harry Vane[8] was dragged up the Tower-hill, sitting on a sled, to

5. Comely.
6. Sallust, a Roman historian (1st century B.C.); Edmund Gibbon, 18th-century British historian, author of *The Decline and Fall of the Roman Empire*.
7. The pass at Thermopylae was the site of the defense—and death—of King Leonidas and his small group of three hundred Spartans against the entire Persian army. Winkelried was a traditional hero of Swiss independence; in the battle of Sempach (1386), he provided a breach in the Austrian ranks through which the Swiss rushed to victory by drawing to himself the entire volley of Austrian spears.
8. Vane was a Puritan; he had once been colonial governor of Massachusetts. He opposed the restoration of Charles II, and was executed for treason.

suffer death as the champion of the English laws, one of the multitude cried out to him, "You never sate on so glorious a seat!" Charles
II., to intimidate the citizens of London, caused the patriot Lord
Russell[9] to be drawn in an open coach through the principal streets
of the city on his way to the scaffold. "But," his biographer says,
"the multitude imagined they saw liberty and virtue sitting by his
side." In private places, among sordid objects, an act of truth or
heroism seems at once to draw to itself the sky as its temple, the sun
as its candle. Nature stretches out her arms to embrace man, only
let his thoughts be of equal greatness. Willingly does she follow his
steps with the rose and the violet, and bend her lines of grandeur
and grace to the decoration of her darling child. Only let his thoughts
be of equal scope, and the frame will suit the picture. A virtuous man
is in unison with her works, and makes the central figure of the
visible sphere. Homer, Pindar, Socrates, Phocion,[1] associate themselves fitly in our memory with the geography and climate of Greece.
The visible heavens and earth sympathize with Jesus. And in common life whosoever has seen a person of powerful character and
happy genius, will have remarked how easily he took all things along
with him,—the persons, the opinions, and the day, and nature
became ancillary to a man.

3. There is still another aspect under which the beauty of the
world may be viewed, namely, as it becomes an object of the intellect. Beside the relation of things to virtue, they have a relation to
thought. The intellect searches out the absolute order of things as
they stand in the mind of God, and without the colors of affection.
The intellectual and the active powers seem to succeed each other,
and the exclusive activity of the one generates the exclusive activity
of the other. There is something unfriendly in each to the other, but
they are like the alternate periods of feeding and working in animals;
each prepares and will be followed by the other. Therefore does
beauty, which, in relation to actions, as we have seen, comes unsought, and comes because it is unsought, remain for the apprehension and pursuit of the intellect; and then again, in its turn, of
the active power. Nothing divine dies. All good is eternally reproduc-
tive. The beauty of nature re-forms itself in the mind, and not for
barren contemplation, but for new creation.

All men are in some degree impressed by the face of the world;
some men even to delight. This love of beauty is Taste. Others have
the same love in such excess, that, not content with admiring, they
seek to embody it in new forms. The creation of beauty is Art.

---

9. William, Lord Russell (1639–83),
was executed for treason on perjured
testimony connecting him with the Rye
House plot.
1. Phocion was an Athenian statesman
(4th century B.C.) whose *Life* by
Plutarch was a favorite of Emerson's;
Pindar was the great lyric poet, composer of heroic odes (5th century B.C.).

The production of a work of art throws a light upon the mystery of humanity. A work of art is an abstract or epitome of the world. It is the result or expression of nature, in miniature. For although the works of nature are innumerable and all different, the result or the expression of them all is similar and single. Nature is a sea of forms radically alike and even unique.[2] A leaf, a sunbeam, a landscape, the ocean, make an analogous impression on the mind. What is common to them all,—that perfectness and harmony, is beauty. The standard of beauty is the entire circuit of natural forms,—the totality of nature; which the Italians expressed by defining beauty "il più nell' uno."[3] Nothing is quite beautiful alone; nothing but is beautiful in the whole. A single object is only so far beautiful as it suggests this universal grace. The poet, the painter, the sculptor, the musician, the architect, seek each to concentrate this radiance of the world on one point, and each in his several work to satisfy the love of beauty which stimulates him to produce. Thus is Art a nature passed through the alembic[4] of man. Thus in art does Nature work through the will of a man filled with the beauty of her first works.

The world thus exists to the soul to satisfy the desire of beauty. This element I call an ultimate end. No reason can be asked or given why the soul seeks beauty. Beauty, in its largest and profoundest sense, is one expression for the universe. God is the all-fair. Truth, and goodness, and beauty, are but different faces of the same All. But beauty in nature is not ultimate. It is the herald of inward and eternal beauty, and is not alone a solid and satisfactory good. It must stand as a part, and not as yet the last or highest expression of the final cause of Nature.

IV. *Language*

Language is a third use which Nature subserves to man. Nature is the vehicle of thought, and in a simple, double, and threefold degree.

1. Words are signs of natural facts.
2. Particular natural facts are symbols of particular spiritual facts.
3. Nature is the symbol of spirit.

1. Words are signs of natural facts. The use of natural history is to give us aid in supernatural history: the use of the outer creation, to give us language for the beings and changes of the inward creation. Every word which is used to express a moral or intellectual fact, if traced to its root, is found to be borrowed from some material appearance. *Right* means *straight*; *wrong* means *twisted*. *Spirit* primarily means *wind*; *transgression*, the *crossing of a line*; *supercilious*,

2. I.e., at bottom alike and even one.
3. "The many in one" (a phrase Emerson picked up from Coleridge).
4. An instrument for distillation.

the *raising of the eyebrow*. We say the *heart* to express emotion, the *head* to denote thought; and *thought* and *emotion* are words borrowed from sensible things, and now appropriated to spiritual nature. Most of the process by which this transformation is made, is hidden from us in the remote time when language was framed; but the same tendency may be daily observed in children. Children and savages use only nouns or names of things, which they convert into verbs, and apply to analogous mental acts.

2. But this origin of all words that convey a spiritual import,—so conspicuous a fact in the history of language,—is our least debt to nature. It is not words only that are emblematic; it is things which are emblematic. Every natural fact is a symbol of some spiritual fact. Every appearance in nature coresponds to some state of the mind, and that state of the mind can only be described by presenting that natural appearance as its picture. An enraged man is a lion, a cunning man is a fox, a firm man is a rock, a learned man is a torch. A lamb is innocence; a snake is subtle spite; flowers express to us the delicate affections. Light and darkness are our familiar expression for knowledge and ignorance; and heat for love. Visible distance behind and before us, is respectively our image of memory and hope.

Who looks upon a river in a meditative hour and is not reminded of the flux of all things? Throw a stone into the stream, and the circles that propagate themselves are the beautiful type of all influence. Man is conscious of a universal soul within or behind his individual life, wherein, as in a firmament, the natures of Justice, Truth, Love, Freedom, arise and shine. This universal soul, he calls Reason: it is not mine, or thine, or his, but we are its; we are its property and men. And the blue sky in which the private earth is buried, the sky with its eternal calm, and full of everlasting orbs, is the type of Reason. That which, intellectually considered, we call Reason, considered in relation to nature, we call Spirit. Spirit is the Creator. Spirit hath life in itself. And man in all ages and countries, embodies it in his language, as the FATHER.

It is easily seen that there is nothing lucky or capricious in these analogies, but that they are constant, and pervade nature. These are not the dreams of a few poets, here and there, but man is an analogist, and studies relations in all objects. He is placed in the centre of beings, and a ray of relation passes from every other being to him. And neither can man be understood without these objects, nor these objects without man. All the facts in natural history taken by themselves, have no value, but are barren, like a single sex. But marry it to human history, and it is full of life. Whole Floras, all Linnaeus' and Buffon's[5] volumes, are dry catalogues of facts; but the most trivial

5. Linnaeus (Carl von Linné, 1707–78), Swedish founder of modern plant-classification system; Comte de Buffon (George Louis Le Clerc, 1707–88), French initiator of and important collaborator on 44-volume *Histoire Naturelle* (finished 1804), comprehensive formulation of botanical science.

of these facts, the habit of a plant, the organs, or work, or noise of an insect, applied to the illustration of a fact in intellectual philosophy, or, in any way associated to human nature, affects us in the most lively and agreeable manner. The seed of a plant,—to what affecting analogies in the nature of man, is that little fruit made use of, in all discourse, up to the voice of Paul, who calls the human corpse a seed,—"It is sown a natural body; it is raised a spiritual body."[6] The motion of the earth round its axis, and round the sun, makes the day, and the year. These are certain amounts of brute light and heat. But is there no intent of an analogy between man's life and the seasons? And do the seasons gain no grandeur or pathos from that analogy? The instincts of the ant are very unimportant, considered as the ant's; but the moment a ray of relation is seen to extend from it to man, and the little drudge is seen to be a monitor, a little body with a mighty heart, then all its habits, even that said to be recently observed, that it never sleeps, become sublime.

Because of this radical correspondence between visible things and human thoughts, savages, who have only what is necessary, converse in figures. As we go back in history, language becomes more picturesque, until its infancy, when it is all poetry; or all spiritual facts are represented by natural symbols. The same symbols are found to make the original elements of all languages. It has moreover been observed, that the idioms of all languages approach each other in passages of the greatest eloquence and power. And as this is the first language, so is it the last. This immediate dependence of language upon nature, this conversion of an outward phenomenon into a type of somewhat in human life, never loses its power to affect us. It is this which gives that piquancy to the conversation of a strong-natured farmer or back-woodsman, which all men relish.

A man's power to connect his thought with its proper symbol, and so to utter it, depends on the simplicity of his character, that is, upon his love of truth, and his desire to communicate it without loss. The corruption of man is followed by the corruption of language. When simplicity of character and the sovereignty of ideas is broken up by the prevalence of secondary desires, the desires of riches, of pleasure, of power, and of praise,—and duplicity and falsehood take place of simplicity and truth, the power over nature as an interpreter of the will, is in a degree lost; new imagery ceases to be created, and old words are perverted to stand for things which are not; a paper currency is employed, when there is no bullion in the vaults. In due time, the fraud is manifest, and words lose all power to stimulate the understanding or the affections. Hundreds of writers may be found in every long-civilized nation, who for a short time believe, and make others believe, that they see and utter truths, who do not of themselves clothe one thought in its natural garment, but who feed un-

6. I Corinthians xv.44.

consciously on the language created by the primary writers[7] of the country, those, namely, who hold primarily on nature.

But wise men pierce this rotten diction and fasten words again to visible things; so that picturesque language is at once a commanding certificate that he who employs it, is a man in alliance with truth and God. The moment our discourse rises above the ground line of familiar facts, and is inflamed with passion or exalted by thought, it clothes itself in images. A man conversing in earnest, if he watch his intellectual processes, will find that a material image, more or less luminous, arises in his mind, contemporaneous with every thought, which furnishes the vestment of the thought. Hence, good writing and brilliant discourse are perpetual allegories. This imagery is spontaneous. It is the blending of experience with the present action of the mind. It is proper creation. It is the working of the Original Cause through the instruments he has already made.

These facts may suggest the advantage which the country-life possesses for a powerful mind, over the artificial and curtailed life of cities. We know more from nature than we can at will communicate. Its light flows into the mind evermore, and we forget its presence. The poet, the orator, bred in the woods, whose senses have been nourished by their fair and appeasing changes, year after year, without design and without heed,—shall not lose their lesson altogether, in the roar of cities or the broil of politics. Long hereafter, amidst agitation and terror in national councils,—in the hour of revolution,—these solemn images shall reappear in their morning lustre, as fit symbols and words of the thoughts which the passing events shall awaken. At the call of a noble sentiment, again the woods wave, the pines murmur, the river rolls and shines, and the cattle low upon the mountains, as he saw and heard them in his infancy. And with these forms, the spells of persuasion, the keys of power are put into his hands.

3. We are thus assisted by natural objects in the expression of particular meanings. But how great a language to convey such peppercorn informations! Did it need such noble races of creatures, this profusion of forms, this host of orbs in heaven, to furnish man with the dictionary and grammar of his municipal[8] speech? Whilst we use this grand cipher to expedite the affairs of our pot and kettle, we feel that we have not yet put it to its use, neither are able. We are like travellers using the cinders of a volcano to roast their eggs. Whilst we see that it always stands ready to clothe what we would say, we cannot avoid the question whether the characters are not significant of themselves. Have mountains, and waves, and skies, no significance but what we consciously give them, when we employ them as emblems of our thoughts? The world is emblematic. Parts

7. Cf. *Journals* (passage 25). 8. Local.

of speech are metaphors, because the whole of nature is a metaphor of the human mind. The laws of moral nature answer to those of matter as face to face in a glass. "The visible world and the relation of its parts, is the dial plate of the invisible."[9] The axioms of physics translate the laws of ethics. Thus, "the whole is greater than its part;" "reaction is equal to action;" "the smallest weight may be made to lift the greatest, the difference of weight being compensated by time;" and many the like propositions, which have an ethical as well as physical sense. These propositions have a much more extensive and universal sense when applied to human life, than when confined to technical use.

In like manner, the memorable words of history, and the proverbs of nations, consists usually of a natural fact, selected as a picture or parable of a moral truth. Thus; A rolling stone gathers no moss; A bird in the hand is worth two in the bush; A cripple in the right way, will beat a racer in the wrong; Make hay while the sun shines; 'Tis hard to carry a full cup even; Vinegar is the son of wine; The last ounce broke the camel's back; Long-lived trees make roots first;—and the like. In their primary sense these are trivial facts, but we repeat them for the value of their analogical import. What is true of proverbs, is true of all fables, parables, and allegories.

This relation between the mind and matter is not fancied by some poet, but stands in the will of God, and so is free to be known by all men. It appears to men, or it does not appear. When in fortunate hours we ponder this miracle, the wise man doubts, if, at all other times, he is not blind and deaf;

———'Can such things be,
And overcome us like a summer's cloud,
Without our special wonder?"[1]

for the universe becomes transparent, and the light of higher laws than its own shines through it. It is the standing problem which has exercised the wonder and the study of every fine genius since the world began; from the era of the Egyptians and the Brahmins to that of Pythagoras, of Plato, of Bacon, of Leibnitz, of Swedenborg.[2] There sits the Sphinx at the road-side, and from age to age, as each prophet comes by, he tries his fortune at reading her riddle.[3] There seems to be a necessity in spirit to manifest itself in material forms;

9. Quoted from a Swedenborgian source (see note 2, immediately below).
1. *Macbeth* III.iv.110–12.
2. Pythagoras was a Greek philosopher (6th century B.C.) who was supposed to have taught the transmigration of souls (see also *Journals*, passage 122). Wilhelm von Leibnitz (1646–1716), German philosopher, taught the "preestablished harmony" of the mental and the physical. Emanuel Swedenborg (1688–1772) at the age of 54 experienced "the opening of physical sight," whereby he could interpret the threefold sense of Scripture, converse with angels, and see and describe the spiritual world. See also note 4, p. 236, "The American Scholar."
3. Cf. "The Sphinx."

and day and night, river and storm, beast and bird, acid and alkali, preëxist in necessary Ideas in the mind of God, and are what they are by virtue of preceding affections[4] in the world of spirit. A Fact is the end or last issue of spirit. The visible creation is the terminus or the circumference of the invisible world. "Material objects," said a French philosopher, "are necessarily kinds of *scoriae*[5] of the substantial thoughts of the Creator, which must always preserve an exact relation to their first origin; in other words, visible nature must have a spiritual and moral side."[6]

This doctrine is abstruse, and though the images of "garment," "scoriae," "mirror," &c., may stimulate the fancy, we must summon the aid of subtler and more vital expositors to make it plain. "Every scripture is to be interpreted by the same spirit which gave it forth,"[7] —is the fundamental law of criticism. A life in harmony with nature, the love of truth and of virtue, will purge the eyes to understand her text. By degrees we may come to know the primitive sense of the permanent objects of nature, so that the world shall be to us an open book, and every form significant of its hidden life and final cause.

A new interest surprises us, whilst, under the view now suggested, we contemplate the fearful extent and multitude of objects; since "every object rightly seen, unlocks a new faculty of the soul." That which was unconscious truth, becomes, when interpreted and defined in an object, a part of the domain of knowledge,—a new weapon in the magazine of power.

V. *Discipline*

In view of the significance of nature, we arrive at once at a new fact, that nature is a discipline.[8] This use of the world includes the preceding uses, as parts of itself.

Space, time, society, labor, climate, food, locomotion, the animals, the mechanical forces, give us sincerest lessons, day by day, whose meaning is unlimited. They educate both the Understanding and the Reason. Every property of matter is a school for the understanding,—its solidity or resistance, its inertia, its extension, its figure, its divisibility. The understanding adds, divides, combines, measures, and finds nutriment and room for its activity in this worthy scene. Meantime, Reason transfers all these lessons into its own world of thought, by perceiving the analogy that marries Matter and Mind.

1. Nature is a discipline of the understanding in intellectual truths. Our dealing with sensible objects is a constant exercise in the necessary lessons of difference, of likeness, of order, of being

---

4. Modifications.
5. Slag.
6. From a Swedenborgian source.
7. A maxim of George Fox, the founder of the Society of Friends (Quakers).
8. "A trained ecclesiastic, Emerson utilizes the dualism of this word, signifying at once a controlled obedience to the absolute, and, secondly, the ecclesiastical discipline of practical rules affecting conduct" (Bradley, Beatty, and Long).

and seeming, of progressive arrangement; of ascent from particular to general; of combination to one end of manifold forces. Proportioned to the importance of the organ to be formed, is the extreme care with which its tuition[9] is provided,—a care pretermitted in no single case. What tedious training, day after day, year after year, never ending, to form the common sense; what continual reproduction of annoyances, inconveniences, dilemmas; what rejoicing over us of little men; what disputing of prices, what reckonings of interest,—and all to form the Hand of the mind;—to instruct us that "good thoughts are no better than good dreams, unless they be executed!"

The same good office is performed by Property and its filial systems of debt and credit. Debt, grinding debt, whose iron face the widow, the orphan, and the sons of genius fear and hate;—debt, which consumes so much time, which so cripples and disheartens a great spirit with cares that seem so base, is a preceptor whose lessons cannot be forgone, and is needed most by those who suffer from it most. Moreover, property, which has been well compared to snow,—"if it fall level to-day, it will be blown into drifts to-morrow,"—is the surface action of internal machinery, like the index on the face of a clock. Whilst now it is the gymnastics of the understanding, it is hiving, in the foresight of the spirit, experience in profounder laws.

The whole character and fortune of the individual are affected by the least inequalities in the culture of the understanding; for example, in the perception of differences. Therefore is Space, and therefore Time, that man may know that things are not huddled and lumped, but sundered and individual. A bell and a plough have each their use, and neither can do the office of the other. Water is good to drink, coal to burn, wool to wear; but wool cannot be drunk, nor water spun, nor coal eaten. The wise man shows his wisdom in separation, in gradation, and his scale of creatures and of merits is as wide as nature. The foolish have no range in their scale, but suppose every man is as every other man. What is not good they call the worst, and what is not hateful, they call the best.

In like manner, what good heed nature forms in us! She pardons no mistakes. Her yea is yea, and her nay, nay.

The first steps in Agriculture, Astronomy, Zoölogy, (those first steps which the farmer, the hunter, and the sailor take,) teach that nature's dice are always loaded;[1] that in her heaps and rubbish are concealed sure and useful results.

How calmly and genially the mind apprehends one after another the laws of physics! What noble emotions dilate the mortal as he enters into the counsels of the creation, and feels by knowledge the privilege to BE! His insight refines him. The beauty of nature shines

---

9. Guardianship.

1. "The dice of Zeus ever fall aright" (Sophoclean Fragment 763).

in his own breast. Man is greater that he can see this, and the universe less, because Time and Space relations vanish as laws are known.

Here again we are impressed and even daunted by the immense Universe to be explored. "What we know, is a point to what we do not know."[2] Open any recent journal of science, and weigh the problems suggested concerning Light, Heat, Electricity, Magnetism, Physiology, Geology, and judge whether the interest of natural science is likely to be soon exhausted.

Passing by many particulars of the discipline of nature, we must not omit to specify two.

The exercise of the Will or the lesson of power is taught in every event. From the child's successive possession of his several senses up to the hour when he saith, "Thy will be done!" he is learning the secret, that he can reduce under his will, not only particular events, but great classes, nay the whole series of events, and so conform all facts to his character. Nature is thoroughly mediate. It is made to serve. It receives the dominion of man as meekly as the ass on which the Savior rode. It offers all its kingdoms to man as the raw material which he may mould into what is useful. Man is never weary of working it up. He forges the subtile and delicate air into wise and melodious words, and gives them wing as angels of persuasion and command. One after another, his victorious thought comes up with and reduces all things, until the world becomes at last only a realized will,—the double of the man.

2. Sensible objects conform to the premonitions of Reason and reflect the conscience. All things are moral; and in their boundless changes have an unceasing reference to spiritual nature. Therefore is nature glorious with form, color, and motion, that every globe in the remotest heaven; every chemical change from the rudest crystal up to the laws of life; every change of vegetation from the first principle of growth in the eye of a leaf, to the tropical forest and antediluvian coal-mine; every animal function from the sponge up to Hercules, shall hint or thunder to man the laws of right and wrong, and echo the Ten Commandments. Therefore is nature ever the ally of Religion: lends all her pomp and riches to the religious sentiment. Prophet and priest, David, Isaiah, Jesus, have drawn deeply from this source. This ethical character so penetrates the bone and marrow of nature, as to seem the end for which it was made. Whatever private purpose is answered by any member or part, this is its public and universal function, and is never omitted. Nothing in nature is exhausted in its first use. When a thing has served an end to the uttermost, it is wholly new for an ulterior service. In God, every end is converted into a new means. Thus

2. A saying of Sir Isaac Newton's.

the use of commodity, regarded by itself, is mean and squalid. But it is to the mind an education in the doctrine of Use, namely, that a thing is good only so far as it serves; that a conspiring of parts and efforts to the production of an end is essential to any being. The first and gross manifestations of this truth is our inevitable and hated training in values and wants, in corn and meat.

It has already been illustrated, that every natural process is a version of a moral sentence. The moral law lies at the centre of nature and radiates to the circumference. It is the pith and marrow of every substance, every relation, and every process. All things with which we deal, preach to us. What is a farm but a mute gospel? The chaff and the wheat, weeds and plants, blight, rain, insects, sun,—it is a sacred emblem from the first furrow of spring to the last stack which the snow of winter overtakes in the fields. But the sailor, the shepherd, the miner, the merchant, in their several resorts, have each an experience precisely parallel, and leading to the same conclusion: because all organizations are radically alike. Nor can it be doubted that this moral sentiment which thus scents the air, grows in the grain, and impregnates the waters of the world, is caught by man and sinks into his soul. The moral influence of nature upon every individual is that amount of truth which it illustrates to him. Who can estimate this? Who can guess how much firmness the sea-beaten rock has taught the fisherman? how much tranquillity has been reflected to man from the azure sky, over whose unspotted deeps the winds forevermore drive flocks of stormy clouds, and leave no wrinkle or stain? how much industry and providence and affection we have caught from the pantomime of brutes? What a searching preacher of self-command is the varying phenomenon of Health!

Herein is especially apprehended the unity of Nature,—the unity in variety,—which meets us everywhere. All the endless variety of things make an identical impression. Xenophanes[3] complained in his old age, that, look where he would, all things hastened back to Unity. He was weary of seeing the same entity in the tedious variety of forms. The fable of Proteus has a cordial truth.[4] A leaf, a drop, a crystal, a moment of time, is related to the whole, and partakes of the perfection of the whole. Each particle is a microcosm, and faithfully renders the likeness of the world.

Not only resemblances exist in things whose analogy is obvious, as when we detect the type of the human hand in the flipper of the fossil saurus,[5] but also in objects wherein there is great superficial unlikeness. Thus architecture is called "frozen music," by De

3. Greek philosopher (pre-Socratic, 6th century B.C.) who taught "All is one" —the unity of existence.
4. Proteus, in Greek fable, was able continually to change his form. "Cordial" means "vital, of the heart."
5. Dinosaur.

Stael and Goethe. Vitruvius thought an architect should be a musician. "A Gothic church," said Coleridge, "is a petrified religion."[6] Michael Angelo maintained, that, to an architect, a knowledge of anatomy is essential. In Haydn's oratorios, the notes present to the imagination not only motions, as, of the snake, the stag, and the elephant, but colors also; as the green grass. The law of harmonic sounds reappears in the harmonic colors. The granite is differenced in its laws only by the more or less of heat from the river that wears it away. The river, as it flows, resembles the air that flows over it; the air resembles the light which traverses it with more subtile currents; the light resembles the heat which rides with it through Space. Each creature is only a modification of the other; the likeness in them is more than the difference, and their radical law is one and the same. A rule of one art, or a law of one organization, holds true throughout nature. So intimate is this Unity, that, it is easily seen, it lies under the undermost garment of nature, and betrays its source in Universal Spirit. For it pervades Thought also. Every universal truth which we express in words, implies or supposes every other truth. *Omne verum vero consonat.*[7] It is like a great circle on a sphere, comprising all possible circles; which, however, may be drawn and comprise it in like manner. Every such truth is the absolute Ens[8] seen from one side. But it has innumerable sides.

The central Unity is still more conspicuous in actions. Words are finite organs of the infinite mind. They cannot cover the dimensions of what is in truth. They break, chop, and impoverish it. An action is the perfection and publication of thought. A right action seems to fill the eye, and to be related to all nature. "The wise man, in doing one thing, does all; or, in the one thing he does rightly, he sees the likeness of all which is done rightly."

Words and actions are not the attributes of brute nature. They introduce us to the human form, of which all other organizations appear to be degradations. When this appears among so many that surround it, the spirit prefers it to all others. It says, "From such as this, have I drawn joy and knowledge; in such as this, have I found and beheld myself; I will speak to it; it can speak again; it can yield me thought already formed and alive." In fact, the eye,—the mind, —is always accompanied by these forms, male and female; and these are incomparably the richest informations[9] of the power and order that lie at the heart of things. Unfortunately every one of them bears the marks as of some injury; is marred and superficially

6. See Coleridge's "A Lecture on the General Characteristics of the Gothic Mind in the Middle Ages" (1836). Vitruvius was a Roman architect (1st century B.C.). Madame de Staël (1766–1817) was a French "bluestocking" and early publicist of German thought.
7. "Every truth agrees with every other."
8. Being.
9. Products of a form-giving power. Cf. Chapter VI, "Idealism," section 3.

defective. Nevertheless, far different from the deaf and dumb nature around them, these all rest like fountain-pipes on the unfathomed sea of thought and virtue whereto they alone, of all organizations, are the entrances.

It were a pleasant inquiry to follow into detail their ministry to our education, but where would it stop? We are associated in adolescent and adult life with some friends, who, like skies and waters, are co-extensive with our idea; who, answering each to a certain affection of the soul, satisfy our desire on that side; whom we lack power to put at such focal distance from us, that we can mend or even analyze them. We cannot choose but love them. When much intercourse with a friend has supplied us with a standard of excellence, and has increased our respect for the resources of God who thus sends a real person to outgo our ideal; when he has, moreover, become an object of thought, and, whilst his character retains all its unconscious effect, is converted in the mind into solid and sweet wisdom,—it is a sign to us that his office is closing, and he is commonly withdrawn from our sight in a short time.[1]

VI. *Idealism*

Thus is the unspeakable but intelligible and practicable meaning of the world conveyed to man, the immortal pupil, in every object of sense. To this one end of Discipline, all parts of nature conspire.

A noble doubt perpetually suggests itself,—whether this end be not the Final Cause of the Universe; and whether nature outwardly exists. It is a sufficient account of that Appearance we call the World, that God will teach a human mind, and so makes it the receiver of a certain number of congruent sensations, which we call sun and moon, man and woman, house and trade. In my utter impotence to test the authenticity of the report of my senses, to know whether the impressions they make on me correspond with outlying objects, what difference does it make, whether Orion is up there in heaven, or some god paints the image in the firmament of the soul? The relations of parts and the end of the whole remaining the same, what is the difference, whether land and sea interact, and worlds revolve and intermingle without number or end, —deep yawning under deep,[2] and galaxy balancing galaxy, throughout absolute space,—or whether, without relations of time and space, the same appearances are inscribed in the constant faith of man? Whether nature enjoy a substantial existence without, or is only in the apocalypse[3] of the mind, it is alike useful and alike venerable to me. Be it what it may, it is ideal to me so long as I

1. Emerson is again thinking of Charles (cf. p. 191); the passage is a kind of brief elegy for him, ending, as is the way of elegies, with an effort at consola- tion. It concludes the first half of Emerson's book.
2. Cf. Psalms xlii.7.
3. Prophetic revelation.

cannot try the accuracy of my senses.

The frivolous make themselves merry with the Ideal theory,[4] as if its consequences were burlesque; as if it affected the stability of nature. It surely does not. God never jests with us, and will not compromise the end of nature by permitting any inconsequence in its procession. Any distrust of the permanence of laws would paralyze the faculties of man. Their permanence is sacredly respected, and his faith therein is perfect. The wheels and springs of man are all set to the hypothesis of the permanence of nature. We are not built like a ship to be tossed, but like a house to stand. It is a natural consequence of this structure, that so long as the active powers predominate over the reflective, we resist with indignation any hint that nature is more short-lived or mutable than spirit. The broker, the wheelwright, the carpenter, the tollman, are much displeased at the intimation.

But whilst we acquiesce entirely in the permanence of natural laws, the question of the absolute existence of nature still remains open. It is the uniform effect of culture on the human mind, not to shake our faith in the stability of particular phenomena, as of heat, water, azote;[5] but to lead us to regard nature as phenomenon, not a substance; to attribute necessary existence to spirit; to esteem nature as an accident and an effect.

To the senses and the unrenewed understanding, belongs a sort of instinctive belief in the absolute existence of nature. In their view man and nature are indissolubly joined. Things are ultimates, and they never look beyond their sphere. The presence of Reason mars this faith. The first effort of thought tends to relax this despotism of the senses which binds us to nature as if we were a part of it, and shows us nature aloof, and, as it were, afloat. Until this higher agency intervened, the animal eye sees, with wonderful accuracy, sharp outlines and colored surfaces. When the eye of Reason opens, to outline and surface are at once added grace and expression. These proceed from imagination and affection, and abate somewhat of the angular distinctness of objects. If the Reason be stimulated to more earnest vision, outlines and surfaces become transparent, and are no longer seen; causes and spirits are seen through them. The best moments of life are these delicious awakenings of the higher powers, and the reverential withdrawing of nature before its God.

Let us proceed to indicate the effects of culture.[6]

4. Term applied by the "Realistic" philosophy, in which Emerson was trained, to theories like those of Bishop George Berkeley (1685–1753) and David Hume (1711–76) that we can know only "ideas" or "impressions" in the mind and not material things in themselves. These four paragraphs expound the essential position of Berkeley. Cf. "Experience."

5. Nitrogen.

6. Awakening of thought.

1. Our first institution[7] in the Ideal philosophy is a hint from Nature herself.

Nature is made to conspire with spirit to emancipate us. Certain mechanical changes, a small alteration in our local position, apprises us of a dualism. We are strangely affected by seeing the shore from a moving ship, from a balloon, or through the tints of an unusual sky. The least change in our point of view gives the whole world a pictorial air. A man who seldom rides, needs only to get into a coach and traverse his own town, to turn the street into a puppet-show. The men, the women,—talking, running, bartering, fighting, —the earnest mechanic, the lounger, the beggar, the boys, the dogs, are unrealized[8] at once, or, at least, wholly detached from all relation to the observer, and seen as apparent, not substantial beings. What new thoughts are suggested by seeing a face of country quite familiar, in the rapid movement of the railroad car! Nay, the most wonted objects, (make a very slight change in the point of vision,) please us most. In a camera obscura,[9] the butcher's cart, and the figure of one of our own family amuse us. So a portrait of a well-known face gratifies us. Turn the eyes upside down, by looking at the landscape through your legs, and how agreeable is the picture, though you have seen it any time these twenty years!

In these cases, by mechanical means, is suggested the difference between the observer and the spectacle—between man and nature. Hence arises a pleasure mixed with awe; I may say, a low degree of the sublime is felt, from the fact, probably, that man is hereby apprised that whilst the world is a spectacle, something in himself is stable.

2. In a higher manner the poet communicates the same pleasure. By a few strokes he delineates, as on air, the sun, the mountain, the camp, the city, the hero, the maiden, not different from what we know them, but only lifted from the ground and afloat before the eye. He unfixes the land and the sea, makes them revolve around the axis of his primary thought, and disposes them anew. Possessed himself by a heroic passion, he uses matter as symbols of it. The sensual man conforms thoughts to things; the poet conforms things to his thoughts.[1] The one esteems nature as rooted and fast; the other, as fluid, and impresses his being thereon. To him, the refractory world is ductile and flexible; he invests dust and stones

7. Instruction.
8. Made unreal. Cf. Josiah Royce, American Idealist, when he bumped into the tree: "I saw it but I did not realize it."
9. Ancestor of the present-day camera.
1. Cf. a favorite quotation of Emerson's from Bacon: "[Poesy] was ever thought to have some participation of divineness, because it doth raise and erect the mind, by submitting the shows of things to the desires of the mind; whereas reason doth buckle and bow the mind unto the nature of things" (*The Advancement of Learning* II.iv.2).

with humanity, and makes them the words of the Reason. The
Imagination may be defined to be the use which the Reason makes
of the material world. Shakespeare possesses the power of subordinating nature for the purposes of expression, beyond all poets. His
imperial muse tosses the creation like a bauble from hand to hand,
and uses it to embody any caprice of thought that is uppermost in
his mind. The remotest spaces of nature are visited, and the farthest
sundered things are brought together, by a subtile spiritual connection. We are made aware that magnitude of material things is
relative, and all objects shrink and expand to serve the passion of
the poet. Thus in his sonnets, the lays of birds, the scents and dyes
of flowers he finds to be the *shadow* of his beloved; time, which
keeps her from him, is his *chest;*[2] the suspicion she has awakened,
is her *ornament;*

> The ornament of beauty is Suspect,
> A crow which flies in heaven's sweetest air.[3]

His passion is not the fruit of chance; it swells, as he speaks, to a
city, or a state,

> No, it was builded far from accident;
> It suffers not in smiling pomp, nor falls
> Under the brow of thralling discontent;
> It fears not policy, that heretic,
> That works on leases of short numbered hours,
> But all alone stands hugely politic.

In the strength of his constancy, the Pyramids[4] seem to him
recent and transitory. The freshness of youth and love dazzles him
with its resemblance to morning;

> Take those lips away
> Which so sweetly were forsworn;
> And those eyes,—the break of day,
> Lights that do mislead the morn.

The wild beauty of this hyperbole, I may say in passing, it would
not be easy to match in literature.

This transfiguration which all material objects undergo through
the passion of the poet,—this power which he exerts to dwarf the
great, to magnify the small,—might be illustrated by a thousand
examples from his Plays. I have before me the Tempest, and will
cite only these few lines.

> PROSPERO. The strong based promontory
> Have I made shake, and by the spurs plucked up
> The pine and cedar.

2. Emerson refers to *Sonnets* 98 and
65, respectively.
3. *Sonnet* 70, lines 3–4; the next quotation is from *Sonnet* 124.

4. Cf. *Sonnet* 123, line 2. The quotation
following is from a song in *Measure
for Measure* IV.i.

Prospero calls for music to soothe the frantic Alonzo, and his companions;

> A solemn air, and the best comforter
> To an unsettled fancy, cure my brains
> Now useless, boiled within thy skull.

Again;

> The charm dissolves apace,
> And, as the morning steals upon the night,
> Melting the darkness, so their rising senses
> Begin to chase the ignorant fumes that mantle
> Their clearer reason.
>   Their understanding
> Begins to swell: and the approaching tide
> Will shortly fill the reasonable shores
> That now lie foul and muddy.[5]

The perception of real affinities between events (that is to say, of *ideal* affinities, for those only are real), enables the poet thus to make free with the most imposing forms and phenomena of the world, and to assert the predominance of the soul.

3. Whilst thus the poet animates[6] nature with his own thoughts, he differs from the philosopher only herein, that the one proposes Beauty as his main end; the other Truth. But the philosopher, not less than the poet, postpones the apparent order and relations of things to the empire of thought. "The problem of philosophy," according to Plato, "is, for all that exists conditionally, to find a ground unconditioned and absolute."[7] It proceeds on the faith that a law determines all phenomena, which being known, the phenomena can be predicted. That law, when in the mind, is an idea. Its beauty is infinite. The true philosopher and the true poet are one, and a beauty, which is truth, and a truth, which is beauty, is the aim of both. Is not the charm of one of Plato's or Aristotle's definitions strictly like that of the Antigone of Sophocles? It is, in both cases, that a spiritual life has been imparted to nature; that the solid seeming block of matter has been pervaded and dissolved by a thought; that this feeble human being has penetrated the vast masses of nature with an informing soul, and recognized itself in their harmony, that is, seized their law. In physics, when this is attained, the memory disburthens itself of its cumbrous catalogues of particulars, and carries centuries of observation in a single formula.

Thus even in physics, the material is degraded before the spiritual. The astronomer, the geometer, rely on their irrefragable analysis,

5. *The Tempest* V.i.
6. Gives a soul to.

7. Kant, not Plato; quoted from Coleridge.

and disdain the results of observation. The sublime remark of Euler[8] on his law of arches, "This will be found contrary to all experience, yet is true," had already transferred nature into the mind, and left matter like an outcast corpse.

4. Intellectual science has been observed to beget invariably a doubt of the existence of matter. Turgot[9] said, "He that has never doubted the existence of matter, may be assured he has no aptitude for metaphysical inquiries." It fastens the attention upon immortal necessary uncreated natures, that is, upon Ideas; and in their presence we feel that the outward circumstance is a dream and a shade. Whilst we wait in this Olympus of gods, we think of nature as an appendix to the soul. We ascend into their region, and know that these are the thoughts of the Supreme Being. "These are they who were set up from everlasting, from the beginning, or even the earth was. When he prepared the heavens, they were there; when he established the clouds above, when he strengthened the fountains of the deep. Then they were by him, as one brought up with him. Of them took he counsel."[1]

Their influence is proportionate. As objects of science they are accessible to few men. Yet all men are capable of being raised by piety or by passion, into their region. And no man touches these divine natures, without becoming, in some degree, himself divine. Like a new soul, they renew the body. We become physically nimble and lightsome; we tread on air; life is no longer irksome, and we think it will never be so. No man fears age or misfortune or death in their serene company, for he is transported out of the district of change. Whilst we behold unveiled the nature of Justice and Truth, we learn the difference between the absolute and the conditional or relative. We apprehend the absolute. As it were, for the first time, *we exist*. We become immortal, for we learn that time and space are relations of matter; that with a perception of truth or a virtuous will they have no affinity.[2]

5. Finally, religion and ethics, which may be fitly called the practice of ideas, or the introduction of ideas into life, have an analogous effect with all lower culture, in degrading nature and suggesting its dependence on spirit. Ethics and religion differ herein; that the one is the system of human duties commencing from man; the other, from God. Religion includes the personality of God; Ethics does not. They are one to our present design. They both put nature under foot. The first and last lesson of religion is, "The things that are seen, are temporal; the things that are unseen, are eternal."[3] It

8. Leonhard Euler, 18th-century Swiss mathematician. Quoted from Coleridge.
9. Anne Robert Jacques Turgot, 18th-century French statesman and economist.

1. Cf. Proverbs viii.23–30.
2. Cf. Socrates' speech in the *Symposium*.
3. II Corinthians iv.18.

puts an affront upon nature. It does that for the unschooled, which philosophy does for Berkeley and Viasa.[4] The uniform language that may be heard in the churches of the most ignorant sects is,— "Contemn the unsubstantial shows of the world; they are vanities, dreams, shadows, unrealities; seek the realities of religion." The devotee flouts nature. Some theosophists[5] have arrived at a certain hostility and indignation towards nature, as the Manichean and Plotinus.[6] They distrusted in themselves any looking back to these flesh-pots of Egypt. Plotinus was ashamed of his body. In short, they might all say of matter, what Michael Angelo said of external beauty, "It is the frail and weary weed, in which God dresses the soul which he has called into time."[7]

It appears that motion, poetry, physical and intellectual science, and religion, all tend to affect our convictions of the reality of the external world. But I own there is something ungrateful in expanding too curiously the particulars of the general proposition, that all culture tends to imbue us with idealism. I have no hostility to nature, but a child's love to it. I expand and live in the warm day like corn and melons. Let us speak her fair. I do not wish to fling stones at my beautiful mother, nor soil my gentle nest. I only wish to indicate the true position of nature in regard to man, wherein to establish man all right education tends; as the ground which to attain is the object of human life, that is, of man's connection with nature. Culture inverts the vulgar views of nature, and brings the mind to call that apparent which it uses to call real, and that real which it uses to call visionary. Children, it is true, believe in the external world. The belief that it appears only, is an after-thought, but with culture this faith will as surely arise on the mind as did the first.

The advantage of the ideal theory over the popular faith is this, that it presents the world in precisely that view which is most desirable to the mind. It is, in fact, the view which Reason, both speculative and practical, that is, philosophy and virtue, take. For seen in the light of thought, the world always is phenomenal;[8] and virtue subordinates it to the mind. Idealism sees the world in God. It beholds the whole circle of persons and things, of actions and events, of country and religion, not as painfully accumulated, atom after atom, act after act, in an aged creeping Past, but as one vast picture which God paints on the instant eternity for the con-

4. Viasa is the legendary author of the *Vedas* (the Hindu scriptures).
5. Emerson here uses the broadest possible application of "theosophists": all theologians who claim direct knowledge of God from mystic revelation.
6. Plotinus was a 3rd-century Neo-Platonist. The followers of the Persian Mani (3rd century) believed in a war between the principle of darkness and the principle of light. For the "flesh-pots of Egypt," see Exodus xvi.3.
7. Emerson had lectured on Michel-angelo in 1835.
8. I.e., an appearance, not knowable as an independent substance.

templation of the soul. Therefore the soul holds itself off from a too trivial and microscopic study of the universal tablet. It respects the end too much to immerse itself in the means. It sees something more important in Christianity than the scandals of ecclesiastical history or the niceties of criticism; and, very incurious concerning persons or miracles, and not at all disturbed by chasms of historical evidence, it accepts from God the phenomenon, as it finds it, as the pure and awful form of religion in the world. It is not hot and passionate at the appearance of what it calls its own good or bad fortune, at the union or opposition of other persons. No man is its enemy. It accepts whatsoever befalls, as part of its lesson. It is a watcher more than a doer, and it is a doer, only that it may the better watch.

VII. *Spirit*

It is essential to a true theory of nature and of man, that it should contain somewhat progressive. Uses that are exhausted or that may be, and facts that end in the statement, cannot be all that is true of this brave lodging wherein man is harbored, and wherein all his faculties find appropriate and endless exercise. And all the uses of nature admit of being summed in one, which yields the activity of man an infinite scope. Through all its kingdoms, to the suburbs and outskirts of things, it is faithful to the cause whence it had its origin. It always speaks of Spirit. It suggests the absolute. It is a perpetual effect. It is a great shadow pointing always to the sun behind us.

The aspect of Nature is devout. Like the figure of Jesus, she stands with bended head, and hands folded upon the breast. The happiest man is he who learns from nature the lesson of worship.

Of that ineffable essence which we call Spirit, he that thinks most, will say least. We can foresee God in the coarse, and, as it were, distant phenomena of matter; but when we try to define and describe himself, both language and thought desert us, and we are as helpless as fools and savages. That essence refuses to be recorded in propositions, but when man has worshipped him intellectually, the noblest ministry of nature is to stand as the apparition[9] of God. It is the organ through which the universal spirit speaks to the individual, and strives to lead back the individual to it.

When we consider Spirit, we see that the views already presented do not include the whole circumference of man. We must add some related thoughts.

Three problems are put by nature to the mind: What is matter? Whence is it? and Whereto? The first of these questions only, the ideal theory answers. Idealism saith: matter is a phenomenon, not a

9. Visible state.

substance. Idealism acquaints us with the total disparity between the evidence of our own being and the evidence of the world's being. The one is perfect; the other, incapable of any assurance; the mind is a part of the nature of things; the world is a divine dream, from which we may presently awake to the glories and certainties of day. Idealism is a hypothesis to account for nature by other principles than those of carpentry and chemistry. Yet, if it only deny the existence of matter, it does not satisfy the demands of the spirit. It leaves God out of me. It leaves me in the splendid labyrinth of my perceptions, to wander without end. Then the heart resists it, because it balks the affections in denying substantive being to men and women. Nature is so pervaded with human life that there is something of humanity in all and in every particular. But this theory makes nature foreign to me, and does not account for that consanguinity which we acknowledge to it.

Let it stand then, in the present state of our knowledge, merely as a useful introductory hypothesis, serving to apprise us of the eternal distinction between the soul and the world.

But when, following the invisible steps of thought, we come to inquire, Whence is matter? and Whereto? many truths arise to us out of the recesses of consciousness. We learn that the highest is present to the soul of man; that the dread universal essence, which is not wisdom, or love, or beauty, or power, but all in one, and each entirely, is that for which all things exist, and that by which they are; that spirit creates; that behind nature, throughout nature, spirit is present; one and not compound it does not act upon us from without, that is, in space and time, but spiritually, or through ourselves: therefore, that spirit, that is, the Supreme Being, does not build up nature around us, but puts it forth through us, as the life of the tree puts forth new branches and leaves through the pores of the old.[1] As a plant upon the earth, so a man rests upon the bosom of God; he is nourished by unfailing fountains, and draws at his need inexhaustible power. Who can set bounds to the possibilities of man? Once inhale the upper air, being admitted to behold the absolute natures of justice and truth, and we learn that man has access to the entire mind of the Creator, is himself the creator in the finite. This view, which admonishes me where the sources of wisdom and power lie, and points to virtue as to

"The golden key
Which opes the palace of eternity,"[2]

---

1. Cf. "The Transcendentalist" (1841): "His experience inclines him to behold the procession of facts you call the world, as flowing perpetually outward from an invisible, unsounded center in himself, center alike of him and of them, and necessitating him to regard all things as having a subjective or relative existence, relative to that aforesaid Unknown Center of him."

2. Milton, "Comus," lines 13–14.

carries upon its face the highest certificate of truth, because it animates me to create my own world through the purification of my soul.

The world proceeds from the same spirit as the body of man. It is a remoter and inferior incarnation of God, a projection of God in the unconscious. But it differs from the body in one important respect. It is not, like that, now subjected to the human will. Its serene order is inviolable by us. It is, therefore, to us, the present expositor of the divine mind. It is a fixed point whereby we may measure our departure. As we degenerate, the contrast between us and our house is more evident. We are as much strangers in nature as we are aliens from God. We do not understand the notes of birds. The fox and the deer run away from us; the bear and tiger rend us. We do not know the uses of more than a few plants, as corn and the apple, the potato and the vine. Is not the landscape, every glimpse of which hath a grandeur, a face of him? Yet this may show us what discord is between man and nature, for you cannot freely admire a noble landscape if laborers are digging in the field hard by. The poet finds something ridiculous in his delight until he is out of the sight of men.

VIII. *Prospects*

In inquiries respecting the laws of the world and the frame of things, the highest reason is always the truest. That which seems faintly possible—it is so refined, is often faint and dim because it is deepest seated in the mind among the eternal verities. Empirical science is apt to cloud the sight, and by the very knowledge of functions and processes, to bereave the student of the manly contemplation of the whole. The savant[3] becomes unpoetic. But the best read naturalist who lends an entire and devout attention to truth, will see that there remains much to learn of his relation to the world, and that it is not to be learned by any addition or subtraction or other comparison of known quantities, but is arrived at by untaught sallies of the spirit, by a continual self-recovery, and by entire humility. He will perceive that there are far more excellent qualities in the student than preciseness and infallibility; that a guess is often more fruitful than an indisputable affirmation, and that a dream may let us deeper into the secret of nature than a hundred concerted experiments.

For the problems to be solved are precisely those which the physiologist and the naturalist omit to state. It is not so pertinent to man to know all the individuals of the animal kingdom, as it is to know whence and whereto is this tyrannizing unity in his constitution, which evermore separates and classifies things, endeavor-

3. Man of knowledge.

ing to reduce the most diverse to one form. When I behold a rich landscape, it is less to my purpose to recite correctly the order and superposition of the strata, than to know why all thought of multitude is lost in a tranquil sense of unity. I cannot greatly honor minuteness in details, so long as there is no hint to explain the relation between things and thoughts; no ray upon the *metaphysics* of conchology, of botany, of the arts, to show the relation of the forms of flowers, shells, animals, architecture, to the mind, and build science upon ideas. In a cabinet of natural history, we become sensible of a certain occult recognition and sympathy in regard to the most unwieldy and eccentric forms of beast, fish, and insect. The American who has been confined, in his own country, to the sight of buildings designed after foreign models, is surprised on entering York Minster or St. Peter's at Rome, by the feeling that these structures are imitations also,—faint copies of an invisible archetype.[4] Nor has science sufficient humanity, so long as the naturalist overlooks that wonderful congruity which subsists between man and the world; of which he is lord, not because he is the most subtile inhabitant, but because he is its head and heart, and finds something of himself in every great and small thing, in every mountain stratum, in every new law of color, fact of astronomy, or atmospheric influence which observation or analysis lays open. A perception of this mystery inspires the muse of George Herbert, the beautiful psalmist of the seventeenth century. The following lines are part of his little poem on Man.

> "Man is all symmetry,
> Full of proportions, one limb to another,
>   And to all the world besides.
>   Each part may call the farthest, brother;
> For head with foot hath private amity,
>   And both with moons and tides.

> "Nothing hath got so far
> But man hath caught and kept it as his prey;
>   His eyes dismount the highest star:
>   He is in little all the sphere.
> Herbs gladly cure our flesh, because that they
>   Find their acquaintance there.

> "For us, the winds do blow,
> The earth doth rest, heaven move, and fountains flow;
>   Nothing we see, but means our good,
>   As our delight, or as our treasure;
> The whole is either our cupboard of food,
>   Or cabinet of pleasure.

4. Cf. "The Problem."

"The stars have us to bed:
Night draws the curtain; which the sun withdraws.
Music and light attend our head.
All things unto our flesh are kind,
In their descent and being; to our mind,
In their ascent and cause.

"More servants wait on man
Than he'll take notice of. In every path,
He treads down that which doth befriend him
When sickness makes him pale and wan.
Oh mighty love! Man is one world, and hath
Another to attend him."

The perception of this class of truths makes the attraction which draws men to science, but the end is lost sight of in attention to the means. In view of this half-sight of science, we accept the sentence of Plato, that "poetry comes nearer to vital truth than history."[5] Every surmise and vaticination[6] of the mind is entitled to a certain respect, and we learn to prefer imperfect theories, and sentences which contain glimpses of truth, to digested systems which have no one valuable suggestion. A wise writer will feel that the ends of study and composition are best answered by announcing undiscovered regions of thought, and so communicating, through hope, new activity to the torpid spirit.

I shall therefore conclude this essay with some traditions of man and nature, which a certain poet[7] sang to me; and which, as they have always been in the world, and perhaps reappear to every bard, may be both history and prophecy.

"The foundations of man are not in matter, but in spirit. But the element of spirit is eternity. To it, therefore, the longest series of events, the oldest chronologies are young and recent. In the cycle of the universal man, from whom the known individuals proceed, centuries are points, and all history is but the epoch of one degradation.

"We distrust and deny inwardly our sympathy with nature. We own and disown our relation to it, by turns. We are, like Nebuchadnezzar,[8] dethroned, bereft of reason, and eating grass like an ox. But who can set limits to the remedial force of spirit?

"A man is a god in ruins. When men are innocent, life shall be longer, and shall pass into the immortal, as gently as we awake from

5. Actually Aristotle, not Plato: "Poetry is something more philosophic and of graver import than history * * * " (*Poetics* IX).
6. Prophetic insight.
7. An imaginary persona of Emerson's own, perhaps in part suggested by the conversation of Emerson's arch-Idealist friend, Bronson Alcott, who had just been visiting Emerson when these passages were written. See *Journals* (passages 74–77).
8. Cf. Daniel iv.31–33.

dreams. Now, the world would be insane and rabid, if these disorganizations should last for hundreds of years. It is kept in check by death and infancy. Infancy is the perpetual Messiah, which comes into the arms of fallen men, and pleads with them to return to paradise.

"Man is the dwarf of himself. Once he was permeated and dissolved by spirit. He filled nature with his overflowing currents. Out from him sprang the sun and moon; from man the sun; from woman, the moon. The laws of his mind, the periods of his actions externized themselves into day and night, into the year and the seasons. But, having made for himself this huge shell, his waters retired; he no longer fills the veins and veinless; he is shrunk to a drop. He sees, that the structure still fits him, but fits him colossally. Say, rather, once it fitted him, now it corresponds to him from far and on high. He adores timidly his own work. Now is man the follower of the sun, and woman the follower of the moon. Yet sometimes he starts in his slumber, and wonders at himself and his house, and muses strangely at the resemblance betwixt him and it. He perceives that if his law is still paramount, if still he have elemental power, if his word is sterling yet in nature, it is not conscious power, it is not inferior but superior to his will. It is instinct." Thus my Orphic poet[9] sang.

At present, man applies to nature but half his force. He works on the world with his understanding alone. He lives in it, and masters it by a penny-wisdom; and he that works most in it, is but a half-man and whilst his arms are strong and his digestion good, his mind is imbruted, and he is a selfish savage. His relation to nature, his power over it, is through the understanding; as by manure; the economic use of fire, wind, water, and the mariner's needle; steam, coal, chemical agriculture; the repairs of the human body by the dentist and the surgeon. This is such a resumption of power, as if a banished king should buy his territories inch by inch, instead of vaulting at once into his throne. Meantime, in the thick darkness, there are not wanting gleams of a better light,—occasional examples of the action of man upon nature with his entire force,— with reason as well as understanding. Such examples are the traditions of miracles in the earliest antiquity of all nations; the history of Jesus Christ; the achievements of a principle, as in religious and political revolutions, and in the abolition of the Slave-trade; the miracles of enthusiasm,[1] as those reported of Swedenborg, Hohen-

9. Orpheus was a legendary Greek poet whose song swayed all nature, thus the type of the poet-prophet.
1. Religious possession. Alexander Leopold, Prince of Hohenlohe, a German priest of Emerson's day, had stirred up controversy with his miraculous cures. The Shakers were an "enthusiastic" sect who founded a number of religious communities, one of them within walking distance of Concord.

lohe, and the Shakers; many obscure and yet contested facts, now arranged under the name of Animal Magnetism;[2] prayer; eloquence; self-healing; and the wisdom of children. These are examples of Reason's momentary grasp of the sceptre; the exertions of a power which exists not in time or space, but an instantaneous instreaming causing power. The difference between the actual and the ideal force of man is happily figured by the schoolmen,[3] in saying that the knowledge of man is an evening knowledge, *vespertina cognitio*, but that of God is a morning knowledge, *matutina cognitio*.

The problem of restoring to the world original and eternal beauty, is solved by the redemption of the soul. The ruin or the blank that we see when we look at nature, is in our own eye. The axis of vision is not coincident with the axis of things, and so they appear not transparent but opaque. The reason why the world lacks unity, and lies broken, and in heaps, is, because man is disunited with himself. He cannot be a naturalist, until he satisfies all the demands of the spirit. Love is as much its demand as perception. Indeed, neither can be perfect without the other. In the uttermost meaning of the words, thought is devout, and devotion is thought. Deep calls unto deep.[4] But in actual life, the marriage is not celebrated. There are innocent men who worship God after the tradition of their fathers, but their sense of duty has not yet extended to the use of all their faculties. And there are patient naturalists, but they freeze their subject under the wintry light of the understanding. Is not prayer also a study of truth,—a sally of the soul into the unfound infinite? No man ever prayed heartily without learning something. But when a faithful thinker, resolute to detach every object from personal relations and see it in the light of thought, shall, at the same time, kindle science with the fire of the holiest affections, then will God go forth anew into the creation.

It will not need, when the mind is prepared for study, to search for objects. The invariable mark of wisdom is to see the miraculous in the common. What is a day? What is a year? What is summer? What is woman? What is a child? What is sleep? To our blindness, these things seem unaffecting. We make fables to hide the baldness of the fact and conform it, as we say, to the higher law of the mind. But when the fact is seen under the light of an idea, the gaudy fable fades and shrivels. We behold the real higher law. To the wise, therefore, a fact is true poetry, and the most beautiful of fables. These wonders are brought to our own door. You also are a man. Man and woman and their social life, poverty, labor, sleep, fear, fortune, are known to you. Learn that none of these things is superficial, but that each phenomenon has its roots in the faculties

2. The name given to hypnotism by followers of Franz Anton Mesmer (1734–1815), an early practitioner.

3. Scholastic philosophers of the Middle Ages.

4. Cf. Psalms xlii.7.

and affections of the mind. Whilst the abstract question occupies your intellect, nature brings it in the concrete to be solved by your hands. It were a wise inquiry for the closet,[5] to compare, point by point, especially at remarkable crises in life, our daily history with the rise and progress of ideas in the mind.

So shall we come to look at the world with new eyes. It shall answer the endless inquiry of the intellect,—What is truth? and of the affections,—What is good? by yielding itself passive to the educated Will. Then shall come to pass what my poet said; "Nature is not fixed but fluid. Spirit alters, moulds, makes it. The immobility or bruteness of nature, is the absence of spirit; to pure spirit, it is fluid, it is volatile, it is obedient. Every spirit builds itself a house; and beyond its house a world; and beyond its world, a heaven. Know then, that the world exists for you. For you is the phenomenon perfect. What we are, that only can we see. All that Adam had, all that Caesar could, you have and can do. Adam called his house, heaven and earth; Caesar called his house, Rome; you perhaps call yours, a cobler's trade; a hundred acres of ploughed land; or a scholar's garret. Yet line for line and point for point, your dominion is as great as theirs, though without fine names. Build, therefore, your own world. As fast as you conform your life to the pure idea in your mind, that will unfold its great proportions. A correspondent revolution in things will attend the influx of the spirit. So fast will disagreeable appearances, swine, spiders, snakes, pests, mad-houses, prisons, enemies, vanish; they are temporary and shall be no more seen. The sordor and filths of nature, the sun shall dry up, and the wind exhale. As when the summer comes from the south the snow-banks melt, and the face of the earth becomes green before it, so shall the advancing spirit create its ornaments along its path, and carry with it the beauty it visits and the song which enchants it; it shall draw beautiful faces, warm hearts, wise discourse, and heroic acts, around its way, until evil is no more seen. The kingdom of man over nature, which cometh not with observation,[6]—a dominion such as now is beyond his dream of God,—he shall enter without more wonder than the blind man feels who is gradually restored to perfect sight."

1833–36   1836

The American Scholar[7]

Mr. President and Gentlemen,

I greet you on the re-commencement of our literary year. Our anniversary is one of hope, and, perhaps, not enough of labor. We do

5. Private study.
6. Luke xvii.20.

7. Emerson's "most famous speech," as Bliss Perry called it (*The Praise of*

not meet for games of strength or skill, for the recitation of histories, tragedies, and odes, like the ancient Greeks; for parliaments of love and poesy, like the Troubadours; nor for the advancement of science, like our contemporaries in the British and European capitals. Thus far, our holiday has been simply a friendly sign of the survival of the love of letters amongst a people too busy to give to letters any more. As such, it is precious as the sign of an indestructible instinct. Perhaps the time is already come, when it ought to be, and will be, something else; when the sluggard intellect of this continent will look from under its iron lids, and fill the postponed expectation of the world with something better than the exertions of mechanical skill. Our day of dependence, our long apprenticeship to the learning of other lands, draws to a close. The millions, that around us are rushing into life, cannot always be fed on the sere remains of foreign harvests. Events, actions arise, that must be sung, that will sing themselves. Who can doubt, that poetry will revive and lead in a new age, as the star[8] in the constellation Harp, which now flames in our zenith, astronomers announce, shall one day be the pole-star for a thousand years?

In this hope I accept the topic which not only usage, but the nature of our association, seem to prescribe to this day,—the AMERICAN SCHOLAR.[9] Year by year, we come up hither to read one more chapter of his biography. Let us inquire what light new days and events have thrown on his character and his hopes.

It is one of those fables which, out of an unknown antiquity, convey an unlooked-for wisdom, that the gods, in the beginning, divided Man into men, that he might be more helpful to himself;[1] just as the hand was divided into fingers, the better to answer its end.

The old fable covers a doctrine ever new and sublime; that there

Folly, 1923), delivered on August 31, 1837, at the annual meeting of the Harvard Chapter of the Phi Beta Kappa Society, was on a topic both "prescribed" and self-chosen. The "theory of the scholar's office" had been in his thoughts for at least two years, long before the invitation to speak. The reason, Henry Nash Smith has shown (*New England Quarterly,* XII, 1939, 52–67), is that he was attempting to define a new vocation for himself to replace the one he had abandoned. The result is heroic. The "Address" (as it was first modestly called), for all its decorum of tone, speaks more clearly than anything else Emerson wrote for the millennial enthusiasm then at his heart, "the presentiment of a faith proper to man in his integrity" which he afterwards defined as "the Saturnalia or excess of Faith." The American scholar as Emerson conceives him is not merely to throw off his dependence on Europe but on Church, State, society,

the past, all the ligatures that bind the body politic, until he is free "even to the definition of freedom, 'without any hindrance that does not arise out of his own constitution.'" No wonder the speech, in Lowell's words, "was an event without any former parallel in our literary annals. * * * What crowded and breathless aisles, what windows clustering with eager heads, what enthusiasm of approval, what grim silence of foregone dissent!" "The young men," Holmes adds, "went out from it as if a prophet had been proclaiming to them 'Thus saith the Lord.'"

8. Vega, in Lyra (Harp).
9. It was conventional on such occasions to call for an independent national literary culture. Emerson has poured his new wine into an old bottle.
1. Cf. the speech of Aristophanes in Plato's *Symposium;* also "Of Brotherly Love" in Plutarch's *Morals.*

is One Man,—present to all particular men only partially, or through one faculty; and that you must take the whole society to find the whole man. Man is not a farmer, or a professor, or an engineer, but he is all. Man is priest, and scholar, and statesman, and producer, and soldier. In the *divided* or social state, these functions are parcelled out to individuals, each of whom aims to do his stint of the joint work, whilst each other performs his. The fable implies, that the individual, to possess himself, must sometimes return from his own labor to embrace all the other laborers. But unfortunately, this original unit, this fountain of power, has been so distributed to multitudes, has been so minutely subdivided and peddled out, that it is spilled into drops, and cannot be gathered. The state of society is one in which the members have suffered amputation from the trunk, and strut about so many walking monsters,—a good finger, a neck, a stomach, an elbow, but never a man.

Man is thus metamorphosed into a thing, into many things. The planter, who is Man sent out into the field to gather food, is seldom cheered by any idea of the true dignity of his ministry. He sees his bushel and his cart, and nothing beyond, and sinks into the farmer, instead of Man on the farm. The tradesman scarcely ever gives an ideal worth to his work, but is ridden by the routine of his craft, and the soul is subject to dollars. The priest becomes a form; the attorney, a statute-book; the mechanic, a machine; the sailor, a rope of a ship.

In this distribution of functions, the scholar is the delegated intellect. In the right state, he is *Man Thinking*. In the degenerate state, when the victim of society, he tends to become a mere thinker, or, still worse, the parrot of other men's thinking.[2]

In this view of him, as Man Thinking, the theory of his office is contained. Him nature solicits with all her placid, all her monitory pictures; him the past instructs; him the future invites. Is not, indeed, every man a student, and do not all things exist for the student's behoof? And, finally, is not the true scholar the only true master? But the old oracle said, "All things have two handles: beware of the wrong one." In life, too often, the scholar errs with mankind and forfeits his privilege. Let us see him in his school, and consider him in reference to the main influences he receives.

I. The first in time and the first in importance of the influences upon the mind is that of nature. Every day, the sun; and, after sunset, night and her stars. Ever the winds blow; ever the grass grows. Every day, men and women, conversing, beholding and beholden. The scholar is he of all men whom this spectacle most engages. He must settle its value in his mind. What is nature to

2. Note that this paragraph makes a *threefold* distinction: a class and two subclasses.

him? There is never a beginning, there is never an end, to the inexplicable continuity of this web of God, but always circular power returning into itself.[3] Therein it resembles his own spirit, whose beginning, whose ending, he never can find,—so entire, so boundless. Far, too, as her splendors shine, system on system shooting like rays, upward, downward, without centre, without circumference,—in the mass and in the particle, nature hastens to render account of herself to the mind. Classification begins. To the young mind, every thing is individual, stands by itself. By and by, it finds how to join two things, and see in them one nature; then three, then three thousand; and so, tyrannized over by its own unifying instinct, it goes on tying things together, diminishing anomalies, discovering roots running under ground, whereby contrary and remote things cohere, and flower out from one stem. It presently learns, that since the dawn of history, there has been a constant accumulation and classifying of facts. But what is classification but the perceiving that these objects are not chaotic, and are not foreign, but have a law which is also a law of the human mind? The astronomer discovers that geometry, a pure abstraction of the human mind, is the measure of planetary motion. The chemist finds proportions and intelligible method throughout matter; and science is nothing but the finding of analogy, identity, in the most remote parts. The ambitious soul sits down before each refractory fact; one after another, reduces all strange constitutions, all new powers, to their class and their law, and goes on for ever to animate[4] the last fibre of organization, the outskirts of nature, by insight.

Thus to him, to this school-boy under the bending dome of day, is suggested, that he and it proceed from one root; one is leaf and one is flower; relation, sympathy, stirring in every vein. And what is that Root? Is not that the soul of his soul?—A thought too bold,—a dream too wild. Yet when this spiritual light shall have revealed the law of more earthly natures,—when he has learned to worship the soul, and to see that the natural philosophy that now is, is only the first gropings of its gigantic hand, he shall look forward to an ever expanding knowledge as to a becoming creator.[5] He shall see, that nature is the opposite of the soul, answering to it part for part. One is seal, and one is print. Its beauty is the beauty of his own mind. Its laws are the laws of his own mind. Nature then becomes to him the measure of his attainments. So much of nature as he is ignorant of, so much of his own mind does he not yet possess. And, in fine, the ancient precept, "Know thyself," and the modern precept, "Study nature," become at last one maxim.

3. Cf. "Uriel."
4. Carry mind into.

5. To a creator that is becoming ("progressive")? Or, to becoming a creator?

II. The next great influence[6] into the spirit of the scholar, is, the mind of the Past,—in whatever form, whether of literature, of art, of institutions, that mind is inscribed. Books are the best type of the influence of the past, and perhaps we shall get at the truth,— learn the amount of this influence more conveniently,—by considering their value alone.

The theory of books is noble. The scholar of the first age received into him the world around; brooded thereon; gave it the new arrangement of his own mind, and uttered it again. It came into him, life; it went out from him, truth. It came to him, short-lived actions; it went out from him, immortal thoughts. It came to him, business;[7] it went from him, poetry. It was dead fact; now, it is quick thought. It can stand, and it can go. It now endures, it now flies, it now inspires.[8] Precisely in proportion to the depth of mind from which it issued, so high does it soar, so long does it sing.

Or, I might say, it depends on how far the process had gone, of transmuting life into truth. In proportion to the completeness of the distillation, so will the purity and imperishableness of the product be. But none is quite perfect. As no air-pump can by any means make a perfect vacuum, so neither can any artist entirely exclude the conventional, the local, the perishable from his book, or write a book of pure thought, that shall be as efficient, in all respects, to a remote posterity, as to contemporaries, or rather to the second age. Each age, it is found, must write its own books; or rather, each generation for the next succeeding. The books of an older period will not fit this.

Yet hence arises a grave mischief. The sacredness which attaches to the act of creation,—the act of thought,—is transferred to the record. The poet chanting, was felt to be a divine man: henceforth the chant is divine also. The writer was a just and wise spirit: henceforward it is settled, the book is perfect; as love of the hero corrupts into worship of his statue. Instantly, the book becomes noxious: the guide is a tyrant. The sluggish and perverted mind of the multitude, slow to open to the incursions of Reason, having once so opened, having once received this book, stands upon it, and makes an outcry, if it is disparaged. Colleges are built on it. Books are written on it by thinkers, not by Man Thinking; by men of talent, that is, who start wrong, who set out from accepted dogmas, not from their own sight of principles. Meek young men grow up in libraries, believing it their duty to accept the views which Cicero, which Locke, which Bacon, have given, forgetful that Cicero, Locke, and Bacon were only young men in libraries, when they wrote

6. Inflowing.
7. Activity.

8. Breathes.

these books.

Hence, instead of Man Thinking, we have the bookworm. Hence, the book-learned class, who value books, as such; not as related to nature and the human constitution, but as making a sort of Third Estate[9] with the world and the soul. Hence, the restorers of readings, the emendators, the bibliomaniacs of all degrees.

Books are the best of things, well used; abused, among the worst. What is the right use? What is the one end which all means go to effect? They are for nothing but to inspire. I had better never see a book, than to be warped by its attraction clean out of my own orbit, and made a satellite instead of a system. The one thing in the world, of value, is the active soul. This every man is entitled to; this every man contains within him, although, in almost all men, obstructed, and as yet unborn. The soul active sees absolute truth; and utters truth, or creates. In this action, it is genius; not the privilege of here and there a favorite, but the sound estate of every man. In its essence, it is progressive. The book, the college, the school of art, the institution of any kind, stop with some past utterance of genius. This is good, say they,—let us hold by this. They pin me down. They look backward and not forward. But genius looks forward: the eyes of man are set in his forehead, not in his hind-head: man hopes: genius creates. Whatever talents may be, if the man create not, the pure efflux of the Deity is not his;—cinders and smoke there may be, but not yet flame. There are creative manners, there are creative actions, and creative words; manners, actions, words, that is, indicative of no custom or authority, but springing spontaneous from the mind's own sense of good and fair.

On the other part, instead of being its own seer, let it receive from another mind its truth, though it were in torrents of light, without periods of solitude, inquest, and self-recovery, and a fatal disservice is done. Genius is always sufficiently the enemy of genius by over-influence. The literature of every nation bears me witness. The English dramatic poets have Shakspearized now for two hundred years.

Undoubtedly there is a right way of reading, so it be sternly subordinated. Man Thinking must not be subdued by his instruments. Books are for the scholar's idle times. When he can read God directly, the hour is too precious to be wasted in other men's transcripts of their readings. But when the intervals of darkness come, as come they must,—when the sun is hid and the stars withdraw their shining,—we repair to the lamps which were kindled by their ray, to guide our steps to the East again, where the dawn is. We

9. A medieval division of the population for legislative purposes was into the three "estates" of nobility, clergy, and common people, the "third estate" being therefore the lowliest.

hear, that we may speak. The Arabian proverb says, "A fig tree, looking on a fig tree, becometh fruitful."

It is remarkable, the character of the pleasure we derive from the best books. They impress us with the conviction, that one nature wrote and the same reads. We read the verses of one of the great English poets, of Chaucer, of Marvell, of Dryden, with the most modern joy,—with a pleasure, I mean, which is in great part caused by the abstraction of all *time* from their verses. There is some awe mixed with the joy of our surprise, when this poet, who lived in some past world, two or three hundred years ago, says that which lies close to my own soul, that which I also had well nigh thought and said. But for the evidence thence afforded to the philosophical doctrine of the identity of all minds, we should suppose some pre-established harmony, some foresight of souls that were to be, and some preparation of stores for their future wants, like the fact observed in insects, who lay up food before death for the young grub they shall never see.

I would not be hurried by any love of system, by any exaggeration of instincts, to underrate the Book. We all know, that, as the human body can be nourished on any food, though it were boiled grass and the broth of shoes, so the human mind can be fed by any knowledge. And great and heroic men have existed, who had almost no other information than by the printed page. I only would say that it needs a strong head to bear that diet. One must be an inventor to read well. As the proverb says, "He that would bring home the wealth of the Indies, must carry out the wealth of the Indies." There is then creative reading as well as creative writing. When the mind is braced by labor and invention, the page of whatever book we read becomes luminous with manifold allusion. Every sentence is doubly significant, and the sense of our author is as broad as the world. We then see, what is always true, that, as the seer's hour of vision is short and rare among heavy days and months, so is its record, perchance, the least part of his volume. The discerning will read, in his Plato or Shakespeare, only that least part,— only the authentic utterances of the oracle;—all the rest he rejects, were it never so many times Plato's and Shakespeare's.

Of course, there is a portion of reading quite indispensable to a wise man. History and exact science he must learn by laborious reading. Colleges, in like manner, have their indispensable office,—to teach elements. But they can only highly serve us, when they aim not to drill, but to create; when they gather from far every ray of various genius to their hospitable halls, and by the concentrated fires, set the hearts of their youth on flame. Thought and knowledge are natures in which apparatus and pretension avail nothing. Gowns, and pecuniary foundations, though of towns of gold, can never countervail the least sentence or syllable of wit.[1] Forget this, and our American colleges will recede in their public importance, whilst they grow richer every year.

III. There goes in the world a notion, that the scholar should be a recluse, a valetudinarian,—as unfit for any handiwork or public labor as a penknife for an axe. The so-called "practical men" sneer at speculative men, as if, because they speculate or *see*, they could do nothing. I have heard it said that the clergy,—who are always, more universally than any other class, the scholars of their day,—are addressed as women; that the rough, spontaneous conversation of men they do not hear, but only a mincing and diluted speech. They are often virtually disfranchised; and, indeed, there are advocates for their celibacy. As far as this is true of the studious classes, it is not just and wise. Action is with the scholar subordinate, but it is essential. Without it, he is not yet man. Without it, thought can never ripen into truth. Whilst the world hangs before the eye as a cloud of beauty, we cannot even see its beauty. Inaction is cowardice, but there can be no scholar without the heroic mind. The preamble of thought, the transition through which it passes from the unconscious to the conscious, is action. Only so much do I know, as I have lived. Instantly we know whose words are loaded with life, and whose not.

The world,—this shadow of the soul, or *other me*, lies wide around. Its attractions are the keys which unlock my thoughts and make me acquainted with myself. I run eagerly into this resounding tumult. I grasp the hands of those next me, and take my place in the ring to suffer and to work, taught by an instinct, that so shall the dumb abyss be vocal with speech. I pierce its order; I dissipate its fear; I dispose of it within the circuit of my expanding life. So much only of life as I know by experience, so much of the wilderness have I vanquished and planted, or so far have I extended my being, my dominion. I do not see how any man can afford, for the sake of his nerves and his nap, to spare any action in which he can partake.[2] It is pearls and rubies to his discourse. Drudgery, calamity, exasperation, want, are instructors in eloquence and wisdom. The true scholar grudges every opportunity of action past by, as a loss of power. It is the raw material out of which the intellect moulds her splendid products. A strange process too, this, by which experience is converted into thought, as a mulberry leaf is converted into satin. The manufacture goes forward at all hours.

1. Intellect.
2. When Emerson wrote an open letter to President Van Buren protesting the expropriation of the Cherokees in 1838 he wrote a friend, "I hate myself when I go out of my sphere, but a man must have bowels sometimes." Cf. *Journals* (passages 57, 58, 60).

The actions and events of our childhood and youth, are now matters of calmest observation. They lie like fair pictures in the air. Not so with our recent actions,—with the business which we now have in hand. On this we are quite unable to speculate. Our affections as yet circulate through it. We no more feel or know it, than we feel the feet, or the hand, or the brain of our body. The new deed is yet a part of life,—remains for a time immersed in our unconscious life. In some contemplative hour, it detaches itself from the life like a ripe fruit, to become a thought of the mind. Instantly it is raised, transfigured; the corruptible has put on incorruption.[3] Henceforth it is an object of beauty, however base its origin and neighborhood. Observe, too, the impossibility of antedating this act. In its grub state, it cannot fly, it cannot shine, it is a dull grub. But suddenly, without observation, the selfsame thing unfurls beautiful wings, and is an angel of wisdom. So is there no fact, no event, in our private history, which shall not, sooner or later, lose its adhesive, inert form, and astonish us by soaring from our body into the empyrean. Cradle and infancy, school and playground, the fear of boys, and dogs, and ferules, the love of little maids and berries, and many another fact that once filled the whole sky, are gone already; friend and relative, profession and party, town and country, nation and world, must also soar and sing.

Of course, he who has put forth his total strength in fit actions, has the richest return of wisdom. I will not shut myself out of this globe of action, and transplant an oak into a flower-pot, there to hunger and pine; nor trust the revenue of some single faculty, and exhaust one vein of thought, much like those Savoyards, who, getting their livelihood by carving shepherds, shepherdesses, and smoking Dutchmen, for all Europe, went out one day to the mountain to find stock, and discovered that they had whittled up the last of their pine-trees. Authors we have, in numbers, who have written out their vein, and who, moved by a commendable prudence, sail for Greece or Palestine, follow the trapper into the prairie, or ramble round Algiers, to replenish their merchantable stock.

If it were only for a vocabulary, the scholar would be covetous of action. Life is our dictionary. Years are well spent in country labors; in town,—in the insight into trades and manufactures; in frank intercourse with many men and women; in science; in art; to the one end of mastering in all their facts a language by which to illustrate and embody our perceptions. I learn immediately from any speaker how much he has already lived, through the poverty or the splendor of his speech. Life lies behind us as the quarry from whence we get tiles and copestones for the masonry of to-day. This

3. I Corinthians xv.54.

is the way to learn grammar. Colleges and books only copy the language which the field and the work-yard made.

But the final value of action, like that of books, and better than books, is, that it is a resource. That great principle of Undulation in nature, that shows itself in the inspiring and expiring of the breath; in desire and satiety; in the ebb and flow of the sea; in day and night; in heat and cold; and, as yet more deeply ingrained in every atom and every fluid, is known to us under the name of Polarity,— these "fits of easy transmission and reflection," as Newton called them,[4] are the law of nature because they are the law of spirit.

The mind now thinks; now acts; and each fit reproduces the other. When the artist has exhausted his materials, when the fancy no longer paints, when thoughts are no longer apprehended and books are a weariness,—he has always the resource to *live*. Character is higher than intellect. Thinking is the function. Living is the functionary. The stream retreats to its source. A great soul will be strong to live, as well as strong to think. Does he lack organ or medium to impart his truths? He can still fall back on this elemental force of living them. This is a total act. Thinking is a partial act. Let the grandeur of justice shine in his affairs. Let the beauty of affection cheer his lowly roof. Those "far from fame," who dwell and act with him, will feel the force of his constitution in the doings and passages of the day better than it can be measured by any public and designed display. Time shall teach him, that the scholar loses no hour which the man lives. Herein he unfolds the sacred germ of his instinct, screened from influence. What is lost in seemliness is gained in strength. Not out of those, on whom systems of education have exhausted their culture, comes the helpful giant to destroy the old or to build the new, but out of unhandselled [5] savage nature, out of terrible Druids and Berserkers come at last Alfred and Shakspeare.[6]

I hear therefore with joy whatever is beginning to be said of the dignity and necessity of labor to every citizen. There is virtue yet in the hoe and the spade, for learned as well as for unlearned hands. And labor is everywhere welcome; always we are invited to work; only be this limitation observed, that a man shall not for the sake of wider activity sacrifice any opinion to the popular judgments and modes of action.

I have now spoken of the education of the scholar by nature, by books, and by action. It remains to say somewhat of his duties.

4. In his *Optics* (1704), a treatise on light. The concept was much stressed by Coleridge.
5. Unused, undomesticated. ("To handsel" is to try or use a new article for the first time.) Cf. *Journals* (passage 114).
6. King Alfred the Great (849–99), Saxon lawgiver and writer. Berserkers (whence the word "berserk") were frenziedly savage Norse warriors. Cf. "Terminus," line 28.

They are such as become Man Thinking. They may all be comprised in self-trust. The office of the scholar is to cheer, to raise, and to guide men by showing them facts amidst appearances. He plies the slow, unhonored, and unpaid task of observation. Flamsteed and Herschel, in their glazed observatories, may catalogue the stars with the praise of all men, and, the results being splendid and useful, honor is sure. But he, in his private observatory, cataloguing obscure and nebulous stars of the human mind, which as yet no man has thought of as such,—watching days and months, sometimes, for a few facts; correcting still his old records;—must relinquish display and immediate fame. In the long period of his preparation, he must betray often an ignorance and shiftlessness in popular arts, incurring the disdain of the able who shoulder him aside. Long he must stammer in his speech; often forego the living for the dead. Worse yet, he must accept,—how often! poverty and solitude. For the ease and pleasure of treading the old road, accepting the fashions, the education, the religion of society, he takes the cross of making his own, and, of course, the self-accusation, the faint heart, the frequent uncertainty and loss of time, which are the nettles and tangling vines in the way of the self-relying and self-directed; and the state of virtual hostility in which he seems to stand to society, and especially to educated society.[7] For all this loss and scorn, what offset? He is to find consolation in exercising the highest functions of human nature. He is one, who raises himself from private considerations, and breathes and lives on public and illustrious thoughts. He is the world's eye. He is the world's heart. He is to resist the vulgar prosperity that retrogrades ever to barbarism, by preserving and communicating heroic sentiments, noble biographies, melodious verse, and the conclusions of history. Whatsoever oracles the human heart, in all emergencies, in all solemn hours, has uttered as its commentary on the world of actions,—these he shall receive and impart. And whatsoever new verdict Reason from her inviolable seat pronounces on the passing men and events of to-day,—this he shall hear and promulgate.

These being the functions, it becomes him to feel all confidence in himself, and to defer never to the popular cry. He and he only knows the world. The world of any moment is the merest appearance. Some great decorum,[8] some fetish of a government, some ephemeral trade, or war, or man, is cried up by half mankind and cried down by the other half, as if all depended on this particular up or down. The odds are that the whole question is not worth the poorest thought which the scholar has lost in listening to the controversy. Let him not quit his belief that a popgun is a popgun,

7. This disguised self-portrait helps to explain the heroic self-exhortation here and in "Self-Reliance."
8. Code of propriety.

though the ancient and honorable of the earth affirm it to be the crack of doom. In silence, in steadiness, in severe abstraction, let him hold by himself; add observation to observation, patient of neglect, patient of reproach, and bide his own time,—happy enough, if he can satisfy himself alone, that this day he has seen something truly. Success treads on every right step. For the instinct is sure, that prompts him to tell his brother what he thinks. He then learns, that in going down into the secrets of his own mind, he has descended into the secrets of all minds. He learns that he who has mastered any law in his private thoughts, is master to that extent of all men whose language he speaks, and of all into whose language his own can be translated. The poet, in utter solitude remembering his spontaneous thoughts and recording them, is found to have recorded that, which men in crowded cities find true for them also. The orator distrusts at first the fitness of his frank confessions,—his want of knowledge of the persons he addresses,—until he finds that he is the complement of his hearers;—that they drink his words because he fulfils for them their own nature; the deeper he dives into his privatest, secretest presentiment, to his wonder he finds, this is the most acceptable, most public, and universally true. The people delight in it; the better part of every man feels, This is my music; this is myself.

In self-trust, all the virtues are comprehended. Free should the scholar be,—free and brave. Free even to the definition of freedom,[9] "without any hindrance that does not arise out of his own constitution." Brave; for fear is a thing, which a scholar by his very function puts behind him. Fear always springs from ignorance. It is a shame to him if his tranquillity, amid dangerous times, arise from the presumption that, like children and women, his is a protected class; or if he seek a temporary peace by the diversion of his thoughts from politics or vexed questions, hiding his head like an ostrich in the flowering bushes, peeping into microscopes, and turning rhymes, as a boy whistles to keep his courage up. So is the danger a danger still; so is the fear worse. Manlike let him turn and face it. Let him look into its eye and search its nature, inspect its origin,—see the whelping of this lion,—which lies no great way back; he will then find in himself a perfect comprehension of its nature and extent; he will have made his hands meet on the other side, and can henceforth defy it, and pass on superior. The world is his, who can see through its pretension. What deafness, what stone-blind custom, what overgrown error you behold, is there only by sufferance,—by your sufferance. See it to be a lie, and you have already dealt it its mortal blow.

Yes, we are the cowed,—we the trustless. It is a mischievous no-

9. Immanuel Kant's definition.

tion that we are come late into nature; that the world was finished
a long time ago. As the world was plastic and fluid in the hands of
God, so it is ever to so much of his attributes as we bring to it. To
ignorance and sin, it is flint. They adapt themselves to it as they
may; but in proportion as a man has any thing in him divine, the
firmament flows before him and takes his signet and form. Not he
is great who can alter matter, but he who can alter my state of
mind. They are the kings of the world who give the color of their
present thought to all nature and all art, and persuade men by the
cheerful serenity of their carrying the matter, that this thing which
they do, is the apple which the ages have desired to pluck, now at
last ripe, and inviting nations to the harvest. The great man makes
the great thing. Wherever Macdonald sits, there is the head of the
table.[1] Linnaeus makes botany the most alluring of studies, and
wins it from the farmer and the herb-woman; Davy, chemistry; and
Cuvier, fossils.[2] The day is always his who works in it with serenity
and great aims. The unstable estimates of men crowd to him whose
mind is filled with a truth, as the heaped waves of the Atlantic follow the moon.

For this self-trust, the reason is deeper than can be fathomed,—
darker than can be enlightened. I might not carry with me the feeling of my audience in stating my own belief. But I have already
shown the ground of my hope, in adverting to the doctrine that
man is one. I believe man has been wronged; he has wronged himself. He has almost lost the light that can lead him back to his
prerogatives. Men are become of no account. Men in history, men
in the world of today, are bugs, are spawn, and are called "the
mass" and "the herd." In a century, in a millennium, one or two
men; that is to say,—one or two approximations to the right
state of every man. All the rest behold in the hero or the poet
their own green and crude being,—ripened; yes, and are content
to be less, so *that* may attain to its full stature. What a testimony,
—full of grandeur, full of pity, is borne to the demands of his own
nature, by the poor clansman, the poor partisan, who rejoices in the
glory of his chief. The poor and the low find some amends to
their immense moral capacity, for their acquiescence in a political
and social inferiority. They are content to be brushed like flies from
the path of a great person, so that justice shall be done by him
to that common nature which it is the dearest desire of all to see
enlarged and glorified. They sun themselves in the great man's
light, and feel it to be their own element. They cast the dignity
of man from their downtrod selves upon the shoulders of a hero,

1. Source obscure. "Macdonald" is presumably the head of the clan.
2. Sir Humphry Davy (1778–1829),
English chemist, pioneer in electrolysis;
Baron Georges Cuvier (1769–1832),
French naturalist, founder of sciences
of comparative anatomy and paleon-
tology.

and will perish to add one drop of blood to make that great heart bleat, those giant sinews combat and conquer. He lives for us, and we live in him.

Men such as they are, very naturally seek money or power; and power because it is as good as money,—the "spoils," so called, "of office." And why not? For they aspire to the highest, and this, in their sleep-walking, they dream is highest. Wake them, and they shall quit the false good, and leap to the true, and leave governments to clerks and desks. This revolution is to be wrought by the gradual domestication of the idea of Culture.[3] The main enterprise of the world for splendor, for extent, is the upbuilding of a man. Here are the materials strown along the ground. The private life of one man shall be a more illustrious monarchy,—more formidable to its enemy, more sweet and serene in its influence to its friend, than any kingdom in history. For a man, rightly viewed, comprehendeth the particular natures of all men. Each philosopher, each bard, each actor has only done for me, as by a delegate, what one day I can do for myself. The books which once we valued more than the apple of the eye, we have quite exhausted. What is that but saying, that we have come up with the point of view which the universal mind took through the eyes of one scribe; we have been that man, and have passed on. First, one; then, another; we drain all cisterns, and, waxing greater by all these supplies, we crave a better and more abundant food. The man has never lived that can feed us ever. The human mind cannot be enshrined in a person, who shall set a barrier on any one side to this unbounded, unboundable empire. It is one central fire, which, flaming now out of the lips of Etna, lightens the capes of Sicily; and, now out of the throat of Vesuvius, illuminates the towers and vineyards of Naples. It is one light which beams out of a thousand stars. It is one soul which animates all men.

But I have dwelt perhaps tediously upon this abstraction of the Scholar. I ought not to delay longer to add what I have to say, of nearer reference to the time and to this country.

Historically, there is thought to be a difference in the ideas which predominate over successive epochs, and there are data for marking the genius of the Classic, of the Romantic, and now of the Reflective or Philosophical age. With the views I have intimated of

3. A "magic" word in Emerson's day, since to the traditional English sense of "tillage," or "plant-breeding" had been grafted a deeper if vaguer sense from the Germanic term, *Kultur*. Eventually it came to mean to Emerson much what it meant to Matthew Arnold: "an acquaintance with the best that has been thought and said." At this time, however, it rather meant the awakening of a man's hitherto unsuspected possibilities: "Culture, in the high sense, does not consist in polishing or varnishing, but in so presenting the attractions of nature that the slumbering attributes of man may burst their iron sleep and rush, full-grown, into day" (*Journals*, 1837).

the oneness or the identity of the mind through all individuals, I do not much dwell on these differences. In fact, I believe each individual passes through all three. The boy is a Greek; the youth, romantic; the adult, reflective. I deny not, however, that a revolution in the leading idea may be distinctly enough traced.

Our age is bewailed as the age of Introversion. Must that needs be evil? We, it seems, are critical; we are embarrassed with second thoughts; we cannot enjoy any thing for hankering to know whereof the pleasure consists; we are lined with eyes; we see with our feet; the time is infected with Hamlet's unhappiness,—

"Sicklied o'er with the pale cast of thought."

It is so bad then? Sight is the last thing to be pitied. Would we be blind? Do we fear lest we should outsee nature and God, and drink truth dry? I look upon the discontent of the literary class, as a mere announcement of the fact, that they find themselves not in the state of mind of their fathers, and regret the coming state as untried; as a boy dreads the water before he has learned that he can swim. If there is any period one would desire to be born in,—is it not the age of Revolution; when the old and the new stand side by side, and admit of being compared; when the energies of all men are searched by fear and by hope; when the historic glories of the old can be compensated by the rich possibilities of the new era? This time, like all times, is a very good one, if we but know what to do with it.

I read with some joy of the auspicious signs of the coming days, as they glimmer already through poetry and art, through philosophy and science, through church and state.

One of these signs is the fact, that the same movement which effected the elevation of what was called the lowest class in the state, assumed in literature a very marked and as benign an aspect. Instead of the sublime and beautiful, the near, the low, the common was explored and poetized. That, which had been negligently trodden under foot by those who were harnessing and provisioning themselves for long journeys into far countries, is suddenly found to be richer than all foreign parts. The literature of the poor, the feelings of the child, the philosophy of the street, the meaning of household life, are the topics of the time. It is a great stride. It is a sign—is it not? of new vigor when the extremities are made active, when currents of warm life run into the hands and the feet. I ask not for the great, the remote, the romantic; what is doing in Italy or Arabia; what is Greek art, or Provençal minstrelsy; I embrace the common, I explore and sit at the feet of the familiar, the low. Give me insight into to-day, and you may have the antique and future worlds. What would we really know the meaning of? The meal in the firkin; the milk in the pan; the ballad in the street; the news of the boat; the glance of the eye; the form and the gait of the body;—show me the ultimate reason of these matters; show me the sublime presence of the highest spiritual cause lurking, as always it does lurk, in these suburbs and extremities of nature; let me see every trifle bristling with the polarity that ranges it instantly on an eternal law; and the shop, the plough, and the ledger, referred to the like cause by which light undulates and poets sing;—and the world lies no longer a dull miscellany and lumber-room, but has form and order; there is no trifle; there is no puzzle; but one design unites and animates the farthest pinnacle and the lowest trench.

This idea has inspired the genius of Goldsmith, Burns, Cowper, and, in a newer time, of Goethe, Wordsworth, and Carlyle. This idea they have differently followed and with various success. In contrast with their writing, the style of Pope, of Johnson, of Gibbon, looks cold and pedantic. This writing is bloodwarm. Man is surprised to find that things near are not less beautiful and wondrous than things remote. The near explains the far. The drop is a small ocean. A man is related to all nature. This perception of the worth of the vulgar is fruitful in discoveries. Goethe, in this very thing the most modern of the moderns, has shown us, as none ever did, the genius of the ancients.

There is one man of genius, who has done much for this philosophy of life, whose literary value has never yet been rightly estimated;—I mean Emanuel Swedenborg.[4] The most imaginative of men, yet writing with the precision of a mathematician, he endeavored to engraft a purely philosophical Ethics on the popular Christianity of his time. Such an attempt, of course, must have difficulty, which no genius could surmount. But he saw and showed the connection between nature and the affections of the soul. He pierced the emblematic or spiritual character of the visible, audible, tangible world. Especially did his shade-loving muse hover over and interpret the lower parts of nature; he showed the mysterious bond that allies moral evil to the foul material forms, and has given in epical parables a theory of insanity, of beasts,

4. Swedish scientist and administrator (1688–1772), who at the age of 54 experienced "the opening of his spiritual sight" whereby he could interpret the threefold sense of Scripture, converse with angels, and see and describe the spiritual world. A group of his New England followers, in particular a young man Emerson once called his "early oracle," Sampson Reed, early attracted Emerson's attention to Swedenborg, especially through their publication, the *New Jerusalem Magazine*. For a while, especially when he was writing *Nature* and "The American Scholar," he was fascinated with Swedenborg's elaborate development of the idea of an emblematic "language of nature." Later, when he wrote his chapter on Swedenborg for *Representative Men*, he had become much more critical of Swedenborg's literalism. But the man's unprecedentedly thorough demonstration of the poet's power to see natural facts as the symbols of spiritual facts always held his respect. Cf. "The Poet," p. 280.

of unclean and fearful things.

Another sign of our times, also marked by an analogous political movement, is the new importance given to the single person. Every thing that tends to insulate the individual,—to surround him with barriers of natural respect, so that each man shall feel the world is his, and man shall treat with man as a sovereign state with a sovereign state;—tends to true union as well as greatness. "I learned," said the melancholy Pestalozzi,[5] "that no man in God's wide earth is either willing or able to help any other man." Help must come from the bosom alone. The scholar is that man who must take up into himself all the ability of the time, all the contributions of the past, all the hopes of the future. He must be an university of knowledges. If there be one lesson more than another, which should pierce his ear, it is, The world is nothing, the man is all; in yourself is the law of all nature, and you know not yet how a globule of sap ascends; in yourself slumbers the whole of Reason; it is for you to know all; it is for you to dare all. Mr. President and Gentlemen, this confidence in the unsearched might of man belongs, by all motives, by all prophecy, by all preparation, to the American Scholar. We have listened too long to the courtly muses of Europe. The spirit of the American freeman is already suspected to be timid, imitative, tame. Public and private avarice make the air we breathe thick and fat. The scholar is decent, indolent, complaisant. See already the tragic consequence. The mind of this country, taught to aim at low objects, eats upon itself. There is no work for any but the decorous and the complaisat. Young men of the fairest promise, who begin life upon our shores, inflated by the mountain winds, shined upon by all the stars of God, find the earth below not in unison with these,—but are hindered from action by the disgust which the principles on which business is managed inspire, and turn drudges, or die of disgust,—some of them suicides. What is the remedy? They did not yet see, and thousands of young men as hopeful now crowding to the barriers for the career, do not yet see, that, if the single man plant himself indomitably on his instincts, and there abide, the huge world will come round to him. Patience,—patience;—with the shades of all the good and great for company; and for solace, the perspective of your own infinite life; and for work, the study and the communication of principles, the making those instincts prevalent,[6] the conversion of the world. Is it not the chief disgrace in the world, not to be an unit;—not to be reckoned one character;—not to

---

5. Johann Heinrich Pestalozzi (1746–1827), "progressive" Swiss educator, came to Emerson's attention through Bronson Alcott's attempt to use his methods, which had had little acceptance in his own day—hence his "melancholy."

6. I.e., making them prevail.

yield that peculiar fruit which each man was created to bear, but to be reckoned in the gross, in the hundred, or the thousand, of the party, the section, to which we belong; and our opinion predicted geographically, as the north, or the south? Not so, brothers and friends,—please God, ours shall not be so. We will walk on our own feet; we will work with our own hands; we will speak our own minds. The study of letters shall be no longer a name for pity, for doubt, and for sensual indulgence. The dread of man and the love of man shall be a wall of defence and a wreath of joy around all. A nation of men will for the first time exist, because each believes himself inspired by the Divine Soul which also inspires all men.

1837

Self-Reliance[7]

"Ne te quæsiveris extra."[8]

"Man is his own star; and the soul that can
Render an honest and a perfect man
Commands all light, all influence, all fate;
Nothing to him falls early or too late.
Our acts our angels are, or good or ill,
Our fatal shadows that walk by us still."
—EPILOGUE TO BEAUMONT AND
    FLETCHER'S HONEST MAN'S FORTUNE

Cast the bantling on the rocks,
Suckle him with the she-wolf's teat,
Wintered with the hawk and fox,
Power and speed be hands and feet.

I read the other day some verses written by an eminent painter which were original and not conventional. The soul always hears an admonition in such lines, let the subject be what it way. The senti-

7. Emerson's stress on self-reliance has been attacked as a merely initiatory teaching, as a lesson for adolescents, or else as an encouragement to irresponsible predatory behavior where 19th-century America needed no encouragement. To understand its meaning to Emerson we must remember what it replaced: two centuries of emphasis on man's "total depravity." Though Boston had been working loose from this old doctrine for over a hundred years, Emerson proclaims its overthrow as if its whole burden were still resting on his own shoulders. Partly this was because it still did so in the form of a "New England conscience," partly because he was not merely rejecting an old pattern of feeling but completing a new one. The answer to the Fall had always been Grace. Emerson hails the "absolutely trustworthy" seated at the heart with the astonished joy of a "saint" newly saved. Anyone who has assessed the continuing power of the same "terrific thought" of Original Sin over Emerson's contemporary and fellow townsman, Hawthorne, should be able to grasp the urgency and daring of the Emersonian gamble: "I am *not* fallen, for God is within me; 'of whom shall I be afraid'?" The essay is largely an anthology of passages on this crucial article of faith from the lectures and *Journals* of the 1830's, all carefully revised for this first appearance in print, and further revised in later editions. Not only are some of them among the most memorable in Emerson, but the structure of the whole is a strong and workmanlike job.
8. "Do not seek outside yourself," "do not imitate." From the *Satires* of Persius. All three of these mottoes date from the first edition of 1841. The last quatrain—Emerson's own—was dropped from the second edition of 1847, even as he added original mottoes to ten other essays. The *Honest Man's Fortune* was a play of 1613.

ment they instil is of more value than any thought they may contain. To believe your own thought, to believe that what is true for you in your private heart is true for all men,—that is genius. Speak your latent conviction, and it shall be the universal sense; for the inmost in due time becomes the outmost,—and our first thought is rendered back to us by the trumpets of the Last Judgment. Familiar as the voice of the mind is to each, the highest merit we ascribe to Moses, Plato, and Milton is that they set at naught books and traditions, and spoke not what men, but what they thought. A man should learn to detect and watch that gleam of light which flashes across his mind from within, more than the lustre of the firmament of bards and sages. Yet he dismisses without notice his thought, because it is his. In every work of genius we recognize our own rejected thoughts: they come back to us with a certain alienated majesty. Great works of art have no more affecting lesson for us than this. They teach us to abide by our spontaneous impression with good-humored inflexibility then most when the whole cry of voices is on the other side. Else, to-morrow a stranger will say with masterly good sense precisely what we have thought and felt all the time, and we shall be forced to take with shame our own opinion from another.

There is a time in every man's education when he arrives at the conviction that envy is ignorance; that imitation is suicide; that he must take himself for better for worse as his portion; that though the wide universe is full of good, no kernel of nourishing corn can come to him but through his toil bestowed on that plot of ground which is given to him to till. The power which resides in him is new in nature, and none but he knows what that is which he can do, nor does he know until he has tried. Not for nothing one face, one character, one fact, makes much impression on him, and another none. This sculpture in the memory is not without preëstablished harmony. The eye was placed where one ray should fall, that it might testify of that particular ray. We but half express ourselves, and are ashamed of that divine idea which each of us represents. It may be safely trusted as proportionate and of good issues, so it be faithfully imparted, but God will not have his work made manifest by cowards. A man is relieved and gay when he has put his heart into his work and done his best; but what he has said or done otherwise shall give him no peace. It is a deliverance which does not deliver. In the attempt his genius deserts him; no muse befriends; no invention, no hope.

Trust thyself: every heart vibrates to that iron string. Accept the place the divine providence has found for you, the society of your contemporaries, the connection of events. Great men have always done so, and confided themselves childlike to the genius of their age, betraying their perception that the absolutely trustworthy was seated at their heart, working through their hands, predominating in all their being. And we are now men, and must accept in the highest mind the same transcendent destiny; and not minors and invalids in a protected corner, not cowards fleeing before a revolution, but guides, redeemers, and benefactors, obeying the Almighty effort, and advancing on Chaos and the Dark.

What pretty oracles nature yields us on this text, in the face and behaviour of children, babes, and even brutes! That divided and rebel mind, that distrust of a sentiment because our arithmetic has computed the strength and means opposed to our purpose, these have not. Their mind being whole, their eye is as yet unconquered, and when we look in their faces, we are disconcerted. Infancy conforms to nobody: all conform to it, so that one babe commonly makes four or five out of the adults who prattle and play to it. So God has armed youth and puberty and manhood no less with its own piquancy and charm, and made it enviable and gracious and its claims not to be put by, if it will stand by itself. Do not think the youth has no force, because he cannot speak to you and me. Hark! in the next room his voice is sufficiently clear and emphatic. It seems he knows how to speak to his contemporaries. Bashful or bold, then, he will know how to make us seniors very unnecessary.

The nonchalance of boys who are sure of a dinner, and would disdain as much as a lord to do or say aught to conciliate one, is the healthy attitude of human nature. A boy is in the parlour what the pit is in the playhouse; independent, irresponsible, looking out from his corner on such people and facts as pass by, he tries and sentences them on their merits, in the swift, summary ways of boys, as good, bad, interesting, silly, eloquent, troublesome. He cumbers himself never about consequences, about interests: he gives an independent, genuine verdict. You must court him: he does not court you. But the man is, as it were, clapped into jail by his consciousness. As soon as he has once acted or spoken with éclat, he is a committed person, watched by the sympathy or the hatred of hundreds, whose affections must now enter into his account. There is no Lethe[9] for this. Ah, that he could pass again into his neutrality! Who can thus avoid all pledges, and having observed, observe again from the same unaffected, unbiased, unbribable, unaffrighted innocence, must always be formidable. He would utter opinions on all passing affairs, which being seen to be not private, but necessary, would sink like darts into the ear of men, and put them in fear.

These are the voices which we hear in solitude, but they grow faint and inaudible as we enter into the world. Society everywhere

9. River of forgetfulness in the Greek Hades or underworld.

is in conspiracy against the manhood of every one of its members. Society is a joint-stock company, in which the members agree, for the better securing of his bread to each shareholder, to surrender the liberty and culture of the eater. The virtue in most request is conformity. Self-reliance is its aversion. It loves not realities and creators, but names and customs.

Whoso would be a man, must be a nonconformist. He who would gather immortal palms must not be hindered by the name of goodness, but must explore if it be goodness. Nothing is at last sacred but the integrity of your own mind. Absolve you to yourself, and you shall have the suffrage of the world. I remember an answer which when quite young I was prompted to make to a valued adviser,[1] who was wont to importune me with the dear old doctrines of the church. On my saying, What have I to do with the sacredness of traditions, if I live wholly from within? my friend suggested,—"But these impulses may be from below, not from above." I replied, "They do not seem to me to be such; but if I am the Devil's child, I will live then from the Devil." No law can be sacred to me but that of my nature. Good and bad are but names very readily transferable to that or this; the only right is what is after my constitution, the only wrong what is against it. A man is to carry himself in the presence of all opposition as if everything were titular[2] and ephemeral but he. I am ashamed to think how easily we capitulate to badges and names, to large societies and dead institutions. Every decent and well-spoken individual affects and sways me more than is right. I ought to go upright and vital, and speak the rude truth in all ways. If malice and vanity wear the coat of philanthropy, shall that pass? If an angry bigot assumes this bountiful cause of Abolition, and comes to me with his last news from Barbadoes,[3] why should I not say to him, "Go love thy infant; love thy wood-chopper; be good-natured and modest: have that grace; and never varnish your hard, uncharitable ambition with this incredible tenderness for black folk a thousand miles off. Thy love afar is spite at home." Rough and graceless would be such greeting, but truth is handsomer than the affectation of love. Your goodness must have some edge to it,—else it is none. The doctrine of hatred must be preached as the counteraction of the doctrine of love when that pules and whines. I shun father and mother and wife and brother, when my genius calls me. I would

1. Probably his aunt Mary Moody Emerson, who sharply disapproved of Emerson's break with the established church.
2. Possessed of a title only, without real substance.
3. Britain had abolished slavery in the West Indies in 1833. The lecture on "Slavery" (1835) of Emerson's brother Charles shows him to have been a zealous collector of such information. The Emerson home early became a stopping place for antislavery visitors. While Emerson sympathized, this passage is not the only evidence of his private revulsion from their "angry" politics.

write on the lintels of the door-post, *Whim*.[4] I hope it is somewhat better than whim at last, but we cannot spend the day in explanation. Expect me not to show cause why I seek or why I exclude company. Then, again, do not tell me, as a good man did to-day, of my obligation to put all poor men in good situations. Are they *my* poor? I tell thee, thou foolish philanthropist, that I grudge the dollar, the dime, the cent I give to such men as do not belong to me and to whom I do not belong. There is a class of persons to whom by all spiritual affinity I am bought and sold; for them I will go to prison, if need be; but your miscellaneous popular charities; the education at college of fools; the building of meeting-houses to the vain end to which many now stand; alms to sots; and the thousandfold Relief Societies;—though I confess with shame I sometimes succumb and give the dollar, it is a wicked dollar, which by and by I shall have the manhood to withhold.

Virtues are, in the popular estimate, rather the exception than the rule. There is the man *and* his virtues. Men do what is called a good action, as some piece of courage or charity, much as they would pay a fine in expiation of daily nonappearance on parade. Their works are done as an apology or extenuation of their living in the world,—as invalids and the insane pay a high board. Their virtues are penances. I do not wish to expiate, but to live. My life is for itself and not for a spectacle. I much prefer that it should be of a lower strain, so it be genuine and equal, than that it should be glittering and unsteady. I wish it to be sound and sweet, and not to need diet and bleeding. I ask primary evidence that you are a man, and refuse this appeal from the man to his actions. I know that for myself it makes no difference whether I do or forbear those actions which are reckoned excellent. I cannot consent to pay for a privilege where I have intrinsic right. Few and mean as my gifts may be, I actually am, and do not need for my own assurance or the assurance of my fellows any secondary testimony.

What I must do is all that concerns me, not what the people think. This rule, equally arduous in actual and in intellectual life, may serve for the whole distinction between greatness and meanness. It is the harder, because you will always find those who think they know what is your duty better than you know it. It is easy in the world to live after the world's opinion; it is easy in solitude to live after our own; but the great man is he who in the midst of the crowd keeps with perfect sweetness the independence of solitude.

The objection to conforming to usages that have become dead to you is, that it scatters your force. It loses your time and blurs the impression of your character. If you maintain a dead church, contribute to a dead Bible-society, vote with a great party either for the

4. Cf. Matthew x.34–77; Exodus xii.17.

government or against it, spread your table like base housekeepers,
—under all these screens I have difficulty to detect the precise
man you are. And, of course, so much force is withdrawn from all
your proper life. But do your work, and I shall know you. Do your
work, and you shall reinforce yourself. A man must consider what
a blind man's-buff is this game of conformity. If I know your sect,
I anticipate your argument. I hear a preacher announce for his text
and topic the expediency of one of the institutions of his church.
Do I not know beforehand that not possibly can he say a new and
spontaneous word? Do I not know that, with all this ostentation of
examining the grounds of the institution, he will do no such thing?
Do I not know that he is pledged to himself not to look but at one
side,—the permitted side, not as a man, but as a parish minister?
He is a retained attorney, and these airs of the bench are the emp-
tiest affectation. Well, most men have bound their eyes with one or
another handkerchief, and attached themselves to some one of
these communities of opinion. This conformity makes them not
false in a few particulars, authors of a few lies, but false in all
particulars. Their every truth is not quite true. Their two is not
the real two, their four not the real four; so that every word they
say chagrins us, and we know not where to begin to set them right.
Meantime nature is not slow to equip us in the prison-uniform of
the party to which we adhere. We come to wear one cut of face
and figure, and acquire by degrees the gentlest asinine expression.
There is a mortifying experience in particular, which does not fail
to wreak itself also in the general history; I mean "the foolish face
of praise,"[5] the forced smile which we put on in company where
we do not feel at ease in answer to conversation which does not
interest us. The muscles, not spontaneously moved, but moved by
a low usurping wilfulness, grow tight about the outline of the face,
with the most disagreeable sensation.

For nonconformity the world whips you with its displeasure. And
therefore a man must know how to estimate a sour face. The bystanders look askance on him in the public street or in the friend's
parlour. If this aversion had its origin in contempt and resistance
like his own, he might well go home with a sad countenance; but
the sour faces of the multitude, like their sweet faces, have no deep
cause, but are put on and off as the wind blows and a newspaper
directs. Yet is the discontent of the multitude more formidable than
that of the senate and the college. It is easy enough for a firm man
who knows the world to brook the rage of the cultivated classes.
Their rage is decorous and prudent, for they are timid as being
very vulnerable themselves. But when to their feminine rage the
indignation of the people is added, when the ignorant and the poor

5. Alexander Pope, "Epistle to Dr. Arbuthnot," line 212.

are aroused, when the unintelligent brute force that lies at the bottom of society is made to growl and mow,[6] it needs the habit of magnanimity and religion to treat it godlike as a trifle of no concernment.

The other terror that scares us from self-trust is our consistency; a reverence for our past act or word, because the eyes of others have no other data for computing our orbit than our past acts, and we are loth to disappoint them.

But why should you keep your head over your shoulder? Why drag about this corpse of your memory, lest you contradict somewhat you have stated in this or that public place? Suppose you should contradict yourself; what then? It seems to be a rule of wisdom never to rely on your memory alone, scarcely even in acts of pure memory, but to bring the past for judgment into the thousand-eyed present, and live ever in a new day. In your metaphysics you have denied personality to the Deity: yet when the devout motions of the soul come, yield to them heart and life, though they should clothe God with shape and color.[7] Leave your theory, as Joseph his coat in the hand of the harlot,[8] and flee.

A foolish consistency is the hobgoblin of little minds, adored by little statesmen and philosophers and divines. With consistency a great soul has simply nothing to do. He may as well concern himself with his shadow on the wall. Speak what you think now in hard words, and to-morrow speak what to-morrow thinks in hard words again, though it contradict every thing you said to-day.—"Ah, so you shall be sure to be misunderstood."—Is it so bad, then, to be misunderstood? Pythagoras was misunderstood, and Socrates, and Jesus, and Luther, and Copernicus, and Galileo, and Newton, and every pure and wise spirit that ever took flesh. To be great is to be misunderstood.

I suppose no man can violate his nature. All the sallies of his will are rounded in by the law of his being, as the inequalities of Andes and Himmaleh are insignificant in the curve of the sphere. Nor does it matter how you gauge and try him. A character is like an acrostic or Alexandrian stanza;—read it forward, backward, or across, it still spells the same thing. In this pleasing, contrite wood-life which God allows me, let me record day by day my honest thought without prospect or retrospect, and, I cannot doubt, it will be found symmetrical, though I mean it not, and see it not. My book should smell of pines and resound with the hum of insects. The swallow over my window should interweave that thread or straw he carries in his bill into my web also. We pass for what we are. Character teaches above our wills. Men imagine that they

6. Make threatening faces.   8. Cf. Genesis xii.
7. Cf. *Journals* (passage 19).

communicate their virtue or vice only by overt actions, and do not see that virtue or vice emit a breath every moment.

There will be an agreement in whatever variety of actions, so they be each honest and natural in their hour. For of one will, the actions will be harmonious, however unlike they seem. These varieties are lost sight of at a little distance, at a little height of thought. One tendency unites them all. The voyage of the best ship is a zigzag line of a hundred tacks. See the line from a sufficient distance, and it straightens itself to the average tendency. Your genuine action will explain itself, and will explain your other genuine actions. Your conformity explains nothing. Act singly, and what you have already done singly will justify you now. Greatness appeals to the future. If I can be firm enough to-day to do right, and scorn eyes, I must have done so much right before as to defend me now. Be it how it will, do right now. Always scorn appearances, and you always may. The force of character is cumulative. All the foregone days of virtue work their health into this. What makes the majesty of the heroes of the senate and the field, which so fills the imagination? The consciousness of a train of great days and victories behind. They shed a united light on the advancing actor. He is attended as by a visible escort of angels. That is it which throws thunder into Chatham's[9] voice, and dignity into Washington's port, and America into Adams's[1] eye. Honor is venerable to us because it is no ephemera. It is always ancient virtue. We worship it to-day because it is not of to-day. We love it and pay it homage, because it is not a trap for our love and homage, but is self-dependent, self-derived, and therefore of an old immaculate pedigree, even if shown in a young person.

I hope in these days we have heard the last of conformity and consistency. Let the words be gazetted[2] and ridiculous henceforward. Instead of the gong for dinner, let us hear a whistle from the Spartan fife.[3] Let us never bow and apologize more. A great man is coming to eat at my house. I do not wish to please him; I wish that he should wish to please me. I will stand here for humanity, and though I would make it kind, I would make it true. Let us affront and reprimand the smooth mediocrity and squalid contentment of the times, and hurl in the face of custom, and trade, and office, the fact which is the upshot of all history, that there is a great responsible Thinker and Actor working wherever

9. William Pitt, Earl of Chatham (1708–78), great English orator, who supported the American colonists in Parliament.
1. Probably John Quincy Adams, sixth President of the United States, whose eloquence Emerson praises in "Eloquence" (*Letters and Social Aims*,

1876), and who at the time of this writing was fighting the slave interests as a United States Congressman.
2. Announced as dismissed. An allusion to the official British "gazettes," which announced dismissals as well as honors.
3. An allusion to the strict discipline of the Spartans.

a man works; that a true man belongs to no other time or place, but is the centre of things. Where he is, there is nature. He measures you, and all men, and all events. Ordinarily, every body in society reminds us of somewhat else, or of some other person. Character, reality, reminds you of nothing else; it takes place of the whole creation. The man must be so much, that he must make all circumstances indifferent. Every true man is a cause, a country, and an age; requires infinite spaces and numbers and time fully to accomplish his design;—and posterity seem to follow his steps as a train of clients. A man Caesar is born, and for ages after we have a Roman Empire. Christ is born, and millions of minds so grow and cleave to his genius that he is confounded with virtue and the possible of man. An institution is the lengthened shadow of one man; as, Monachism, of the Hermit Antony;[4] the Reformation, of Luther; Quakerism, of Fox; Methodism, of Wesley; Abolition, of Clarkson. Scipio, Milton called "the height of Rome;"[5] and all history resolves itself very easily into the biography of a few stout and earnest persons.

Let a man then know his worth, and keep things under his feet. Let him not peep or steal, or skulk up and down with the air of a charity-boy, a bastard, or an interloper, in the world which exists for him. But the man in the street, finding no worth in himself which corresponds to the force which built a tower or sculptured a marble god, feels poor when he looks on these. To him a palace, a statue, or a costly book have an alien and forbidding air, much like a gay equipage, and seem to say like that, "Who are you, Sir?" Yet they all are his, suitors for his notice, petitioners to his faculties that they will come out and take possession. The picture waits for my verdict: it is not to command me, but I am to settle its claims to praise. That popular fable of the sot who was picked up dead drunk in the street, carried to the duke's house, washed and dressed and laid in the duke's bed, and, on his waking, treated with all obsequious ceremony like the duke, and assured that he had been insane,[6] owes its popularity to the fact, that it symbolizes so well the state of man, who is in the world a sort of sot, but now and then wakes up, exercises his reason and finds himself a true prince.

Our reading is mendicant and sycophantic. In history, our imagination plays us false. Kingdom and lordship, power and estate, are a gaudier vocabulary than private John and Edward in a small house and common day's work; but the things of life are the same to both;

4. Christian monasticism may be said to have begun with the hermitages of St. Anthony (ca. 250–350).
5. Scipio Africanus (237–183 B.C.) was the conqueror of Hannibal. Thomas Clarkson was a leader of the British antislavery movement.

6. Emerson is thinking of the "Induction" to The Taming of the Shrew. An ancient story: Kåre Foss has traced it to the 16th-century Spaniard Vives, thence to Hans Sachs and Calderon as well as Shakespeare, and thereafter to many other European authors.

the sum total of both is the same. Why all this deference to Alfred, and Scanderbeg, and Gustavus?[7] Suppose they were virtuous; did they wear out virtue? As great a stake depends on your private act to-day, as followed their public and renowned steps. When private men shall act with original views, the lustre will be transferred from the actions of kings to those of gentlemen.

The world has been instructed by its kings, who have so magnetized the eyes of nations. It has been taught by this colossal symbol the mutual reverence that is due from man to man. The joyful loyalty with which men have everywhere suffered the king, the noble, or the great proprietor to walk among them by a law of his own, make his own scale of men and things, and reverse theirs, pay for benefits not with money but with honor, and represent the law in his person, was the hieroglyphic by which they obscurely signified their consciousness of their own right and comeliness,[8] the right of every man.

The magnetism which all original action exerts is explained when we inquire the reason of self-trust. Who is the Trustee? What is the aboriginal Self, on which a universal reliance may be grounded? What is the nature and power of that science-baffling star, without parallax,[9] without calculable elements, which shoots a ray of beauty even into trivial and impure actions, if the least mark of independence appear? The inquiry leads us to that source, at once the essence of genius, of virtue, and of life, which we call Spontaneity or Instinct. We denote this primary wisdom as Intuition, whilst all later teachings are tuitions. In that deep force, the last fact behind which analysis cannot go, all things find their common origin. For the sense of being which in calm hours rises, we know not how, in the soul, is not diverse from things, from space, from light, from time, from man, but one with them, and proceeds obviously from the same source whence their life and being also proceed. We first share the life by which things exist, and afterwards see them as appearances in nature, and forget that we have shared their cause. Here is the fountain of action and of thought. Here are the lungs of that inspiration which giveth man wisdom, and which cannot be denied without impiety and atheism. We lie in the lap of immense intelligence, which makes us receivers of its truth and organs of its activity. When we discern justice, when we discern truth, we do nothing of ourselves, but allow a passage to its beams. If we ask whence this comes, if we seek to pry into the soul that causes, all philosophy is at fault. Its presence or its absence is all we can affirm. Every man discriminates between the voluntary acts of his mind, and his involuntary perceptions, and knows that to his involuntary

7. Saxon, Albanian, Swedish national heroes, respectively.
8. Fitness. "He hath no form nor come-liness" (Isaiah liii.2).
9. I.e., that cannot be measured.

perceptions a perfect faith is due. He may err in the expression of them, but he knows that these things are so, like day and night, not to be disputed. My wilful actions and acquisitions are but roving;—the idlest reverie, the faintest native emotion, command my curiosity and respect. Thoughtless people contradict as readily the statement of perceptions as of opinions, or rather much more readily; for they do not distinguish between perception and notion. They fancy that I choose to see this or that thing. But perception is not whimsical, but fatal. If I see a trait, my children will see it after me, and in course of time, all mankind,—although it may chance that no one has seen it before me. For my perception of it is as much a fact as the sun.[1]

The relations of the soul to the divine spirit are so pure, that it is profane to seek to interpose helps. It must be that when God speaketh he should communicate, not one thing, but all things; should fill the world with his voice; should scatter forth light, nature, time, souls, from the centre of the present thought; and new date and new create the whole. Whenever a mind is simple, and receives a divine wisdom, old things pass away,—means, teachers, texts, temples fall; it lives now, and absorbs past and future in to the present hour. All things are made sacred by relation to it,—one as much as another. All things are dissolved to their centre by their cause, and, in the universal miracle, petty and particular miracles disappear. If, therefore, a man claims to know and speak of God, and carries you backward to the phraseology of some old mouldered nation in another country, in another world, believe him not. Is the acorn better than the oak which is its fulness and completion? Is the parent better than the child into whom he has cast his ripened being? Whence, then, this worship of the past? The centuries are conspirators against the sanity and authority of the soul. Time and space are but physiological colors which the eye makes,[2] but the soul is light; where it is, is day; where it was, is night; and history is an impertinence and an injury, if it be anything more than a cheerful apologue or parable of my

1. This passage alludes to a distinction of Coleridge's that is a key to the entire essay: "For what is enthusiasm but the oblivion and swallowing up of self in an object dearer than self, or in an idea more vivid? * * * In the genuine enthusiasm of morals, religion, and patriotism, this enlargement and elevation of the soul above its mere self attest the presence, and accompany the intuition, of ultimate principles alone. These alone can interest the undegraded human spirit deeply and enduringly, because these alone belong to its essence, and will remain with it permanently.

"Notions, the depthless abstractions of fleeting *phenomena*, the shadows of sailing vapors, the colorless repetitions of rainbows, have effected their utmost when they have added to the distinctness of our knowledge. * * * But every principle is actualized by an idea; and every idea is living, productive, partaketh of infinity, and (as Bacon has sublimely observed) containeth an endless power of semination" (*The Statesman's Manual*).
2. Kant had taught that space and time were "forms" or conditions of "sensible intuition" and not realities independent of sense experience. In Carlyle's *Sartor Resartus*, they became the last "clothes" of the spirit.

being and becoming.

Man is timid and apologetic; he is no longer upright; he dares not say "I think," "I am," but quotes some saint or sage. He is ashamed before the blade of grass or the blowing rose. These roses under my window make no reference to former roses or to better ones; they are for what they are; they exist with God to-day. There is no time to them. There is simply the rose; it is perfect in every moment of its existence. Before a leaf-bud has burst, its whole life acts; in the full-blown flower there is no more; in the leafless root there is no less. Its nature is satisfied, and it satisfies nature, in all moments alike. But man postpones or remembers; he does not live in the present, but with reverted eye laments the past, or, heedless of the riches that surround him, stands on tiptoe to foresee the future. He cannot be happy and strong until he too lives with nature in the present, above time.

This should be plain enough. Yet see what strong intellects dare not yet hear God himself, unless he speaks the phraseology of I know not what David, or Jeremiah, or Paul. We shall not always set so great a price on a few texts, on a few lives. We are like children who repeat by rote the sentences of grandames and tutors, and, as they grow older, of the men of talents and character they chance to see,—painfully recollecting the exact words they spoke; afterwards, when they come into the point of view which those had who uttered these sayings, they understand them, and are willing to let the words go; for, at any time, they can use words as good when occasion comes. If we live truly, we shall see truly. It is as easy for the strong man to be strong, as it is for the weak to be weak. When we have new perception, we shall gladly disburden the memory of its hoarded treasures as old rubbish. When a man lives with God, his voice shall be as sweet as the murmur of the brook and the rustle of the corn.

And now at last the highest truth on this subject remains unsaid; probably cannot be said; for all that we say is the far-off remembering of the intuition. That thought, by what I can now nearest approach to say it, is thus. When good is near you, when you have life in yourself, it is not by any known or accustomed way; you shall not discern the foot-prints of any other; you shall not see the face of man; you shall not hear any name;—the way, the thought, the good, shall be wholly strange and new. It shall exclude example and experience. You take the way from man, not to man. All persons that ever existed are its forgotten ministers. Fear and hope are alike beneath it. There is somewhat low even in hope. In the hour of vision, there is nothing that can be called gratitude, nor properly joy. The soul raised over passion beholds identity and eternal causation, perceives the self-existence of Truth and Right, and calms itself with knowing that all things go well. Vast spaces of nature, the Atlantic Ocean, the South Sea,—long intervals of time, years, centuries,—are of no account. This which I think and feel underlay every former state of life and circumstances, as it does underlie my present, and what is called life, and what is called death.[3]

Life only avails, not the having lived. Power ceases in the instant of repose; it resides in the moment of transition from a past to a new state, in the shooting of the gulf, in the darting to an aim. This one fact the world hates, that the soul *becomes*; for that forever degrades the past, turns all riches to poverty, all reputation to a shame, confounds the saint with the rogue, shoves Jesus and Judas equally aside. Why, then, do we prate of self-reliance? Inasmuch as the soul is present, there will be power not confident but agent. To talk of reliance is a poor external way of speaking. Speak rather of that which relies, because it works and is. Who has more obedience than I masters me, though he should not raise his finger. Round him I must revolve by the gravitation of spirits. We fancy it rhetoric, when we speak of eminent virtue. We do not yet see that virtue is Height, and that a man or a company of men, plastic and permeable to principles, by the law of nature must overpower and ride all cities, nations, kings, rich men, poets, who are not.

This is the ultimate fact which we so quickly reach on this, as on every topic, the resolution of all into the ever-blessed ONE. Self-existence is the attribute of the Supreme Cause, and it constitutes the measure of good by the degree in which it enters into all lower forms. All things real are so by so much virtue as they contain. Commerce, husbandry, hunting, whaling, war, eloquence, personal weight, are somewhat, and engage my respect as examples of its presence and impure action. I see the same law working in nature for conservation and growth. Power is in nature the essential measure of right. Nature suffers nothing to remain in her kingdoms which cannot help itself. The genesis and maturation of a planet, its poise and orbit, the bended tree recovering itself from the strong wind, the vital resources of every animal and vegetable, are demonstrations of the self-sufficing, and therefore self-relying soul.

Thus all concentrates: let us not rove; let us sit at home with the cause. Let us stun and astonish the intruding rabble of men and books and institutions, by a simple declaration of the divine fact. Bid the invaders take the shoes from off their feet, for God is here within.[4] Let our simplicity judge them, and our docility to our own

3. This and the previous paragraph, together with the paragraph but one before that ("The relations"), largely derive, by way of a lecture of 1839, from a long *Journal* entry for November, 1838, that is plainly one of the private repercussions to the outcry over the "Divinity School Address." Cf. *Journals* (passage 7) and "Uriel."

4. Cf. Joshua v.15 and Exodus iii.5.

law demonstrate the poverty of nature and fortune beside our native riches.

But now we are a mob. Man does not stand in awe of man, nor is his genius admonished to stay at home, to put itself in communication with the internal ocean, but it goes abroad to beg a cup of water of the urns of other men. We must go alone. I like the silent church before the service begins, better than any preaching. How far off, how cool, how chaste the persons look, begirt each one with a precinct or sanctuary![5] So let us always sit. Why should we assume the faults of our friends, or wife, or father, or child, because they sit around our hearth, or are said to have the same blood? All men have my blood, and I all men's. Not for that will I adopt their petulance or folly, even to the extent of being ashamed of it. But your isolation must not be mechanical, but spiritual, that is, must be elevation. At times the whole world seems to be in conspiracy to importune you with emphatic trifles. Friend, client, child, sickness, fear, want, charity, all knock at once at thy closet door, and say,— "Come out unto us." But keep thy state; come not into their confusion. The power men possess to annoy me, I give them by a weak curiosity. No man can come near me but through my act. "What we love that we have, but by desire we bereave ourselves of the love."

If we cannot at once rise to the sanctities of obedience and faith, let us at least resist our temptations; let us enter into the state of war, and wake Thor and Woden,[6] courage and constancy, in our Saxon breasts. This is to be done in our smooth times by speaking the truth. Check this lying hospitality and lying affection. Live no longer to the expectation of these deceived and deceiving people with whom we converse. Say to them, "O father, O mother, O wife, O brother, O friend, I have lived with you after appearances hitherto. Henceforward I am the truth's. Be it known unto you that henceforward I obey no law less than the eternal law. I will have no covenants but proximities. I shall endeavor to nourish my parents, to support my family, to be the chaste husband of one wife,—but these relations I must fill after a new and unprecedented way. I appeal from your customs. I must be myself. I cannot break myself any longer for you, or you. If you can love me for what I am, we shall be the happier. If you cannot, I will still seek to deserve that you should. I will not hide my tastes or aversions. I will so trust that what is deep is holy, that I will do strongly before the sun and moon whatever inly rejoices me, and the heart appoints. If you are noble, I will love you; if you are not, I will not hurt you and myself by hypocritical attentions. If you are true, but not in the same

5. One of many evidences of the attractions of Quakerism to Emerson. Cf. Whittier, *First-Day Thoughts.*
6. Norse, Teutonic gods of war.

truth with me, cleave to your companions; I will seek my own. I do this not selfishly but humbly and truly. It is alike your interest, and mine, and all men's, however long we have dwelt in lies, to live in truth. Does this sound harsh to-day? You will soon love what is dictated by your nature as well as mine, and if we follow the truth, it will bring us out safe at last."—But so you may give these friends pain. Yes, but I cannot sell my liberty and my power, to save their sensibility. Besides, all persons have their moments of reason, when they look out into the region of absolute truth; then will they justify me, and do the same thing.

The populace think that your rejection of popular standards is a rejection of all standard, and mere antinomianism;[7] and the bold sensualist will use the name of philosophy to gild his crimes. But the law of consciousness abides. There are two confessionals, in one or the other of which we must be shriven. You may fulfil your round of duties by clearing yourself in the *direct,* or in the *reflex* way. Consider whether you have satisfied your relations to father, mother, cousin, neighbour, town, cat and dog; whether any of these can upbraid you. But I may also neglect this reflex standard, and absolve me to myself. I have my own stern claims and perfect circle. It denies the name of duty to many offices that are called duties. But if I can discharge its debts, it enables me to dispense with the popular code. If any one imagines that this law is lax, let him keep its commandment one day.

And truly it demands something godlike in him who has cast off the common motives of humanity, and has ventured to trust himself for a taskmaster. High be his heart, faithful his will, clear his sight, that he may in good earnest be doctrine, society, law, to himself, that a simple purpose may be to him as strong as iron necessity is to others![8]

If any man consider the present aspects of what is called by distinction *society,* he will see the need of these ethics. The sinew and heart of man seem to be drawn out, and we are become timorous, desponding whimperers. We are afraid of truth, afraid of fortune, afraid of death, and afraid of each other. Our age yields no great and perfect persons. We want men and women who shall renovate life and our social state, but we see that most natures are insolvent, cannot satisfy their own wants, have an ambition out of all proportion to their practical force and do lean and beg day and night continually. Our housekeeping is mendicant, our arts, our occupations, our marriages, our religion, we have not chosen, but society has

---

7. Emerson's position *is* antinomian, as his answer to his "valued adviser" (p. 241) makes explicit; he is repudiating the popular notion of antinomianism as the mere rejection of all religion and

morality. Modern critics of Emerson have repeated the charge.
8. A paragraph dating from 1834 and expressing an early resolve.

chosen for us. We are parlour soldiers. We shun the rugged battle of fate, where strength is born.

If our young men miscarry in their first enterprises, they lose all heart. If the young merchant fails, men say he is *ruined*. If the finest genius studies at one of our colleges, and is not installed in an office within one year afterwards in the cities or suburbs of Boston or New York, it seems to his friends and to himself that he is right in being disheartened, and in complaining the rest of his life. A sturdy lad from New Hampshire or Vermont, who in turn tries all the professions, who *teams it, farms it, peddles*, keeps a school, preaches, edits a newspaper, goes to Congress, buys a township, and so forth, in successive years, and always, like a cat, falls on his feet, is worth a hundred of these city dolls. He walks abreast with his days, and feels no shame in not "studying a profession," for he does not postpone his life, but lives already. He has not one chance, but a hundred chances.[9] Let a Stoic open the resources of man, and tell men they are not leaning willows, but can and must detach themselves; that with the exercise of self-trust, new powers shall appear; that a man is the word made flesh,[1] born to shed healing to the nations, that he should be ashamed of our compassion, and that the moment he acts from himself, tossing the laws, the books, idolatries, and customs out of the window, we pity him no more, but thank and revere him,—and that teacher shall restore the life of man to splendor, and make his name dear to all history.

It is easy to see that a greater self-reliance must work a revolution in all the offices and relations of men; in their religion; in their education; in their pursuits; their modes of living; their association; in their property; in their speculative views.

1. In what prayers do men allow themselves! That which they call a holy office is not so much as brave and manly. Prayer looks abroad and asks for some foreign addition to come through some foreign virtue, and loses itself in endless mazes of natural and supernatural, and mediatorial and miraculous. Prayer that craves a particular commodity,—anything less than all good,—is vicious. Prayer is the contemplation of the facts of life from the highest point of view. It is the soliloquy of a beholding and jubilant soul. It is the spirit of God pronouncing his works good.[2] But prayer as a means to effect a private end is meanness and theft. It supposes dualism and not unity in nature and consciousness. As soon as the

9. The original *Journal* entry (May 27, 1839) read at this point: "My brave Henry [Thoreau] here who is content to live now, and feels no shame in not studying any profession, for he does not postpone his life, but lives already, —pours contempt on these cry-babies of routine and Boston. He has not one chance but a hundred chances. Now let a stern preacher arise * * * " These two paragraphs relate closely to the first two chapters of *Walden*.
1. Cf. John i.14.
2. Cf. Genesis i.25. Emerson is setting the living language of Scripture against the dead language of doctrinal orthodoxy echoed a few sentences above.

man is at one with God, he will not beg. He will then see prayer in all action. The prayer of the farmer kneeling in his field to weed it, the prayer of the rower kneeling with the stroke of his oar, are true prayers heard throughout nature, though for cheap ends. Caratach, in Fletcher's Bonduca,[3] when admonished to inquire the mind of the god Audate, replies,—

> "His hidden meaning lies in our endeavours;
> Our valors are our best gods."

Another sort of false prayers are our regrets. Discontent is the want of self-reliance: it is infirmity of will. Regret calamities, if you can thereby help the sufferer; if not, attend your own work, and already the evil begins to be repaired. Our sympathy is just as base. We come to them who weep foolishly, and sit down and cry for company, instead of imparting to them truth and health in rough electric shocks, putting them once more in communication with their own reason. The secret of fortune is joy in our hands. Welcome evermore to gods and men is the self-helping man. For him all doors are flung wide: him all tongues greet, all honors crown, all eyes follow with desire. Our love goes out to him and embraces him, because he did not need it. We solicitously and apologetically caress and celebrate him, because he held on his way and scorned our disapprobation. The gods love him because men hated him. "To the persevering mortal," said Zoroaster, "the blessed Immortals are swift."[4]

As men's prayers are a disease of the will, so are their creeds a disease of the intellect. They say with those foolish Israelites, "Let not God speak to us, lest we die. Speak thou, speak any man with us, and we will obey."[5] Everywhere I am hindered of meeting God in my brother, because he has shut his own temple doors, and recites fables merely of his brother's, or his brother's brother's God. Every new mind is a new classification.[6] If it prove a mind of uncommon activity and power, a Locke, a Lavoisier, a Hutton, a Bentham, a Fourier, it imposes its classification on other men, and lo! a new system. In proportion to the depth of the thought, and so to the number of the objects it touches and brings within reach of the pupil, is his complacency. But chiefly is this apparent in creeds and churches, which are also classifications of some power-

3. English play of about 1614.
4. The "Chaldaean oracles" were attributed to Zoroaster, founder (6th century B.C.) of ancient Persian religion. Emerson printed a number of them, including this one, in *The Dial* (1844).
5. Cf. Exodus xx.19.
6. Each of the following was a pioneer of some "classification": John Locke (1632–1704), of theories of knowledge and government; Antoine Laurent Lavoisier (1743–94), of chemistry, and James Hutton (1726–97), of geology; Jeremy Bentham (1748–1832) of utilitarian concepts of law and government; François Marie Charles Fourier (1772–1837), of plans for the co-operative organization of society.

ful mind acting on the elemental thought of duty, and man's relation to the Highest. Such is Calvinism, Quakerism, Swedenborgism. The pupil takes the same delight in subordinating every thing to the new terminology, as a girl who has just learned botany in seeing a new earth and new seasons thereby. It will happen for a time, that the pupil will find his intellectual power has grown by the study of his master's mind. But in all unbalanced minds, the classification is idolized, passes for the end, and not for a speedily exhaustible means, so that the walls of the system blend to their eye in the remote horizon with the walls of the universe; the luminaries of heaven seem to them hung on the arch their master built. They cannot imagine how you aliens have any right to see, —how you can see; "It must be somehow that you stole the light from us." They do not yet perceive that light, unsystematic, indomitable, will break into any cabin, even into theirs. Let them chirp awhile and call it their own. If they are honest and do well, presently their neat new pinfold[7] will be too strait and low, will crack, will lean, will rot and vanish, and the immortal light, all young, and joyful, million-orbed, million-colored, will beam over the universe as on the first morning.

2. It is for want of self-culture that the superstition of Travelling, whose idols are Italy, England, Egypt, retains its fascination for all educated Americans. They who made England, Italy, or Greece venerable in the imagination did so by sticking fast where they were, like an axis of the earth. In manly hours, we feel that duty is our place. The soul is no traveller; the wise man stays at home, and when his necessities, his duties, on any occasion call him from his house, or into foreign lands, he is at home still, and shall make men sensible by the expression of his countenance, that he goes the missionary of wisdom and virtue, and visits cities and men like a sovereign, and not like an interloper or a valet.

I have no churlish objection to the circumnavigation of the globe, for the purposes of art, of study, and benevolence, so that the man is first domesticated, or does not go abroad with the hope of finding somewhat greater than he knows. He who travels to be amused, or to get somewhat which he does not carry, travels away from himself, and grows old even in youth among old things. In Thebes, in Palmyra, his will and mind have become old and dilapidated as they. He carries ruins to ruins.

Travelling is a fool's paradise. Our first journeys discover to us the indifference of places. At home I dream that at Naples, at Rome, I can be intoxicated with beauty, and lose my sadness. I pack my trunk, embrace my friends, embark on the sea and at last wake up in Naples, and there beside me is the stern fact, the sad

7. Pen for animals.

self, unrelenting, identical, that I fled from. I seek the Vatican, and the palaces. I affect to be intoxicated with sights and suggestions, but I am not intoxicated. My giant goes with me wherever I go.[8]

3. But the rage of travelling is a symptom of a deeper unsoundness affecting the whole intellectual action. The intellect is vagabond, and our system of education fosters restlessness. Our minds travel when our bodies are forced to stay at home. We imitate; and what is imitation but the travelling of the mind? Our houses are built with foreign taste; our shelves are garnished with foreign ornaments; our opinions, our tastes, our faculties, lean, and follow the Past and the Distant. The soul created the arts wherever they have flourished.[9] It was in his own mind that the artist sought his model. It was an application of his own thought to the thing to be done and the conditions to be observed. And why need we copy the Doric or the Gothic model? Beauty, convenience, grandeur of thought, and quaint expression are as near to us as to any, and if the American artist will study with hope and love the precise thing to be done by him, considering the climate, the soil, the length of the day, the wants of the people, the habit and form of the government, he will create a house in which all these will find themselves fitted, and taste and sentiment will be satisfied also.

Insist on yourself; never imitate. Your own gift you can present every moment with the cumulative force of a whole life's cultivation; but of the adopted talent of another, you have only an extemporaneous half possession. That which each can do best, none but his Maker can teach him. No man yet knows what it is, nor can, till that person has exhibited it. Where is the master who could have taught Shakspeare? Where is the master who could have instructed Franklin, or Washington, or Bacon, or Newton? Every great man is a unique. The Scipionism of Scipio is precisely that part he could not borrow.[1] Shakspeare will never be made by the study of Shakspeare. Do that which is assigned you, and you cannot hope too much or dare too much. There is at this moment for you an utterance brave and grand as that of the colossal chisel of Phidias, or trowel of the Egyptians, or the pen of Moses, or Dante, but different from all these. Not possibly with the soul, all rich, all eloquent, with thousand-cloven tongue, deign to repeat itself but if you can hear what these patriarchs say, surely you can reply to them in the same pitch of voice; for the ear and the tongue are two organs of one nature. Abide in the simple and noble regions of thy life, obey thy heart, and thou shall reproduce

8. Emerson is remembering the mood of his own year in Europe (1832–33).
9. Cf. "The Problem."
1. The paragraph to this point is based on a *Journal* entry of 1832, the earliest

material in the essay. The theme, however, appears much earlier and was used in a number of sermons. Cf. *Journals* (passage 1).

the Foreworld again.

4. As our Religion, our Education, our Art look abroad, so does our spirit of society. All men plume themselves on the improvement of society, and no man improves.

Society never advances.[2] It recedes as fast on one side as it gains on the other. It undergoes continual changes; it is barbarous, it is civilized, it is christianized, it is rich, it is scientific; but this change is not amelioration. For every thing that is given, something is taken. Society acquires new arts, and loses old instincts. What a contrast between the well-clad, reading, writing, thinking American, with a watch, a pencil, and a bill of exchange in his pocket, and the naked New Zealander, whose property is a club, a spear, a mat, and an undivided twentieth of a shed to sleep under! But compare the health of the two men, and you shall see that the white man has lost his aboriginal strength. If the traveller tell us truly, strike the savage with a broad-axe and in a day or two the flesh shall unite and heal as if you struck the blow into soft pitch, and the same blow shall send the white to his grave.

The civilized man has built a coach, but has lost the use of his feet. He is supported on crutches, but lacks so much support of muscle. He has a fine Geneva watch, but he fails of the skill to tell the hour by the sun. A Greenwich nautical almanac he has, and so being sure of the information when he wants it, the man in the street does not know a star in the sky. The solstice he does not observe; the equinox he knows as little; and the whole bright calendar of the year is without a dial in his mind. His note-books impair his memory; his libraries overload his wit; the insurance-office increases the number of accidents; and it may be a question whether machinery does not encumber; whether we have not lost by refinement some energy, by a Christianity, entrenched in establishments and forms, some vigor of wild virtue. For every Stoic was a Stoic; but in Christendom where is the Christian?

There is no more deviation in the moral standard than in the standard of height or bulk. No greater men are now than ever were. A singular equality may be observed between the great men of the first and of the last ages; nor can all the science, art, religion, and philosophy of the nineteenth century avail to educate greater men than Plutarch's heroes, three or four and twenty centuries ago. Not in time is the race progressive. Phocion, Socrates, Anaxagoras, Diogenes, are great men, but they leave no class. He who is really of their class will not be called by their name, but will be his own man, and in his turn the founder of a sect. The arts and inventions of each period are only its costume, and do not invigorate men. The harm of the improved machinery may

2. Much of this section comes from a lecture of 1837. The theme was initiated in the lecture "Naturalist" of 1834.

compensate its good. Hudson and Behring accomplished so much in their fishing-boats, as to astonish Parry and Franklin,[3] whose equipment exhausted the resources of science and art. Galileo, with an opera-glass, discovered a more splendid series of celestial phenomena than any one since. Columbus found the New World in an undecked boat. It is curious to see the periodical disuse and perishing of means and machinery, which were introduced with loud laudation a few years or centuries before. The great genius returns to essential man. We reckoned the improvements of the art of war among the triumphs of science, and yet Napoleon conquered Europe by the bivouac, which consisted of falling back on naked valor, and disencumbering it of all aids. The Emperor held it impossible to make a perfect army, says Las Casas, "without abolishing our arms, magazines, commissaries, and carriages, until, in imitation of the Roman custom, the soldier should receive his supply of corn, grind it in his hand-mill, and bake his bread himself."

Society is a wave. The wave moves onward, but the water of which it is composed does not. The same particle does not rise from the valley to the ridge. Its unity is only phenomenal. The persons who make up a nation to-day, next year die, and their experience dies with them.

And so the reliance on Property, including the reliance on governments which protect it, is the want of self-reliance. Men have looked away from themselves and at things so long, that they have come to esteem the religious, learned, and civil institutions as guards of property, and they deprecate assaults on these, because they feel them to be assaults on property. They measure their esteem of each other by what each has, and not by what each is. But a cultivated man becomes ashamed of his property, out of new respect for his nature. Especially he hates what he has, if he sees that it is accidental,—came to him by inheritance, or gift, or crime; then he feels that it is not having, it does not belong to him, has no root in him, and merely lies there, because no revolution or no robber takes it away. But that which a man is, does always by necessity acquire, and what the man acquires is living property, which does not wait the beck of rulers, or mobs, or revolutions, or fire, or storm, or bankruptcies, but perpetually renews itself wherever the man breathes. "Thy lot or portion of life," said the Caliph Ali,[4] "is seeking after thee; therefore be at rest from seeking after it." Our dependence on these foreign goods leads

3. Henry Hudson (d. 1611) and Vitus Bering (or Behring) (1680–1741) were early explorers (cf. the Hudson River and the Bering Straits); Sir William E. Parry and Sir John Franklin were English explorers of the Arctic in Emerson's time.

4. Ali ibn-abu-Talib (600?–661), the fourth Moslem Caliph and son-in-law of Mohammed; a translation of his reputed sayings, surviving as proverbs, had appeared in 1832.

us to our slavish respect for numbers. The political parties meet in numerous conventions; the greater the concourse, and with each new uproar of announcement. The delegation from Essex! The Democrats from New Hampshire! The Whigs of Maine! the young patriot feels himself stronger than before by a new thousand of eyes and arms. In like manner the reformers summon conventions, and vote and resolve in multitude. Not so, O friends! will the God deign to enter and inhabit you, but by a method precisely the reverse. It is only as a man puts off all foreign support, and stands alone, that I see him to be strong and to prevail. He is weaker by every recruit to his banner. Is not a man better than a town? Ask nothing of men, and, in the endless mutation, thou only firm column must presently appear the upholder of all that surrounds thee. He who knows that power is inborn, that he is weak because he has looked for good out of him and elsewhere, and so perceiving, throws himself unhesitatingly on his thought, instantly rights himself, stands in the erect position, commands his limbs, works miracles; just as a man who stands on his feet is stronger than a man who stands on his head.

So use all that is called Fortune. Most men gamble with her, and gain all, and lose all, as her wheel rolls. But do thou leave as unlawful these winnings, and deal with Cause and Effect, the chancellors of God. In the Will work and acquire, and thou hast chained the wheel of Chance, and shalt sit hereafter out of fear from her rotations. A political victory, a rise of rents, the recovery of your sick, or the return of your absent friend, or some other favorable event, raise your spirits, and you think good days are preparing for you. Do not believe it. Nothing can bring you peace but yourself. Nothing can bring you peace but the triumph of principles.[5]

1832–40   1841

5. See the quotation from Coleridge's *Statesman's Manual* in note 1, p. 248.

Experience[6]

The lords of life, the lords of life,—
I saw them pass,
In their own guise,
Like and unlike,
Portly and grim,
Use and Surprise,
Surface and Dream,
Succession swift, and spectral Wrong,
Temperament without a tongue,
And the inventor of the game
Omnipresent without name;—
Some to see, some to be guessed.
They marched from east to west:
Little man, least of all,
Among the legs of his guardians tall,
Walked about with puzzled look:—
Him by the hand dear Nature took;
Dearest Nature, strong and kind,
Whispered, "Darling, never mind!
To-morrow they will wear another face,
The founder thou! these are thy race!"[7]

Where do we find ourselves? In a series of which we do not know the extremes, and believe that it has none. We wake and find ourselves on a stair; there are stairs below us, which we seem to have ascended; there are stairs above us, many a one, which go upward and out of sight. But the Genius which according to the old belief stands at the door by which we enter, and gives us the lethe[8] to drink, that we may tell no tales, mixed the cup too strongly, and we cannot shake off the lethargy now at noonday. Sleep lingers all our lifetime about our eyes, as night hovers all

6. Written out consecutively for *Essays, Second Series* (1844) and never used as a lecture, "Experience" differs in tone and organization from nearly everything Emerson had previously published. It balances, probably deliberately, the other new essay beside which Emerson set it, that on "The Poet." The poet, he wrote, "stands among partial men for the complete man." He is "representative of man" as he might be and "traverses the whole scale of experience." But there is another kind of experience than this "whole scale," namely that portion of it open to the great majority of men as they are, who are not poets. "Experience" is almost the first of Emerson's writings to accept that kind of experience as permanent and to treat it with entire respect. Together with "The Poet," it sums up his growing sense of life as forever suspended between two equal antagonists, irreconcilable, yet each including and implying the other—the principles he variously named Power and Form, Thought and Fact, Reality and Illusion, Freedom and Fate, Idea and Experience. The poet was a "liberating god" because he made the Idea real: "in a moment * * * the dream displaces the working day and working world and they are now the dream and this the reality." "Experience" speaks for the honesty that balanced and ballasted this "dream," the steady confrontation of the working day and working world. In so doing it starts from and remains colored by a number of darker moods which, if they do not call up the "whole scale" of Emerson's thought, are nevertheless a valuable confession of the ever present challenge of hard fact that underlies all his work. Like Melville's Bulkington, he had turned from the easy optimisms of the conventional shore to launch into "an original relation to the universe." Though the venture was successful, "the sea," as Melville drily remarked, "is the sea," and "Experience" is the chief evidence we have that Emerson did not forget it.
7. Cf. the "lords of life" paragraph (p. 278).
8. Water of the river of forgetfulness in the Greek Hades. "Genius": personal guardian spirit. Emerson plays with this term throughout the essay.

day in the boughs of the fir-tree. All things swim and glitter. Our life is not so much threatened as our perception. Ghostlike we glide through nature, and should not know our place again. Did our birth fall in some fit of indigence and frugality in nature, that she was so sparing of her fire and so liberal of her earth that it appears to us that we lack the affirmative principle, and though we have health and reason, yet we have no superfluity of spirit for new creation? We have enough to live and bring the year about, but not an ounce to impart or to invest. Ah that our Genius were a little more of a genius! We are like millers on the lower levels of a stream, when the factories above them have exhausted the water. We too fancy that the upper people must have raised their dams.

If any of us knew what we were doing, or where we are going, then when we think we best know! We do not know to-day whether we are busy or idle. In times when we thought ourselves indolent, we have afterwards discovered that much was accomplished and much was begun in us. All our days are so unprofitable while they pass, that 'tis wonderful where or when we ever got anything of this which we call wisdom, poetry, virtue. We never got it on any dated calendar day. Some heavenly days must have been intercalated somewhere, like those that Hermes won with dice of the Moon, that Osiris might be born.[9] It is said all martyrdoms looked mean when they were suffered. Every ship is a romantic object, except that we sail in. Embark, and the romance quits our vessel and hangs on every other sail in the horizon. Our life looks trivial, and we shun to record it. Men seem to have learned of the horizon the art of perpetual retreating and reference. "Yonder uplands are rich pasturage, and my neighbor has fertile meadow, but my field," says the querulous farmer, "only holds the world together." I quote another man's saying; unluckily that other withdraws himself in the same way, and quotes me. 'Tis the trick of nature thus to degrade to-day; a good deal of buzz, and somewhat a result slipped magically in. Every roof is agreeable to the eye until it is lifted; then we find tragedy and moaning women and hard-eyed husbands and deluges of lethe, and the men ask, "What's the news?" as if the old were so bad. How many individuals can we count in society? how many actions? how many opinions? So much of our time is preparation, so much is routine, and so much retrospect, that the pith of each man's genius contracts itself to a very few hours. The history of

9. Kronos, father of the Greek gods, had decreed that Rhea, his wife, should not give birth to her lover's child on any day; but Hermes defeated the Moon at dice and won five extra days for the calendar, on the first of which Rhea bore Osiris, the greatest Egyptian god. See Plutarch's *Morals,* "Of Isis and Osiris."

literature—take the net result of Tiraboschi, Warton, or Schlegel[1] —is a sum of very few ideas and of very few original tales; all the rest being variation of these. So in this great society wide lying around us, a critical analysis would find very few spontaneous actions. It is almost all custom and gross sense. There are even few opinions, and these seem organic in the speakers, and do not disturb the universal necessity.

What opium is instilled into all disaster! It shows formidable as we approach it, but there is at last no rough rasping friction, but the most slippery sliding surfaces; we fall soft on a thought; *Ate Dea*[2] is gentle,—

> "Over men's heads walking aloft,
> With tender feet treading so soft."

People grieve and bemoan themselves, but it is not half so bad with them as they say. There are moods in which we court suffering, in the hope that here at least we shall find reality, sharp peaks and edges of truth. But it turns out to be scene-painting and counterfeit. The only thing grief has taught me is to know how shallow it is. That, like all the rest, plays about the surface, and never introduces me into the reality, for contact with which we would even pay the costly price of sons and lovers. Was it Boscovich who found out that bodies never come in contact?[3] Well, souls never touch their objects. An innavigable sea washes with silent waves between us and the things we aim at and converse with. Grief too will make us idealists. In the death of my son, now more than two years ago, I seem to have lost a beautiful estate,—no more. I cannot get it nearer to me. If to-morrow I should be informed of the bankruptcy of my principal debtors, the loss of my property would be a great inconvenience to me, perhaps, for many years; but it would leave me as it found me,— neither better nor worse. So is it with this calamity; it does not touch me; something which I fancied was a part of me, which could not be torn away without tearing me nor enlarged without enriching me, falls off from me and leaves no scar. It was caducous. I grieve that grief can teach me nothing, nor carry me one step into real nature. The Indian who was laid under a curse that the wind should not blow on him, nor water flow to him, nor fire burn him,[4] is a type of us all. The dearest events are summer-rain, and we the Para[5] coats that shed every drop. Nothing is left us now but

1. Historians of Italian, British, European literature, respectively.
2. Ate was the Greek goddess of mischief. The following lines translate the *Iliad* XIX.91.
3. Ruggiero Guiseppe Boscovich (1711– 87) elaborated a molecular theory of matter.
4. In *The Curse of Kehama* (1810) by Robert Southey, English poet. Emerson's remarks are a strong expression of grief, not a repudiation of it. Cf. *Journals* (passage 90).
5. Para rubber.

death. We look to that with a grim satisfaction, saying, There at least is reality that will not dodge us.[6]

I take this evanescence and lubricity of all objects, which lets them slip through our fingers then when we clutch hardest, to be the most unhandsome part of our condition. Nature does not like to be observed, and likes that we should be her fools and playmates. We may have the sphere for our cricket-ball, but not a berry for our philosophy. Direct strokes she never gave us power to make; all our blows glance, all our hits are accidents. Our relations to each other are oblique and casual.

Dream delivers us to dream, and there is no end to illusion. Life is a train of moods like a string of beads, and as we pass through them they prove to be many-colored lenses which paint the world their own hue, and each shows only what lies in its focus. From the mountain you see the mountain. We animate what we can, and we see only what we animate. Nature and books belong to the eyes that see them. It depends on the mood of the man whether he shall see the sunset or the fine poem. There are always sunsets, and there is always genius; but only a few hours so serene that we can relish nature or criticism. The more or less depends on structure or temperament. Temperament is the iron wire on which the beads are strung. Of what use is fortune or talent to a cold and defective nature? Who cares what sensibility or discrimination a man has at some time shown, if he falls asleep in his chair? or if he laugh and giggle? or if he apologize? or is infected with egotism? or thinks of his dollar? or cannot go by food? or has gotten a child in his boyhood? Of what use is genius, if the organ is too convex or too concave and cannot find a focal distance within the actual horizon of human life? Of what use, if the brain is too cold or too hot, and the man does not care enough for results to stimulate him to experiment, and hold him up in it? or if the web is too finely woven, too irritable by pleasure and pain, so that life stagnates from too much reception without due outlet? Of what use to make heroic vows of amendment, if the same old law-breaker is to keep them? What cheer can the religious sentiment yield, when that is suspected to be secretly dependent on the seasons of the year and the state of the blood? I knew a witty physician who found the creed in the biliary duct, and used to affirm that if there was disease in the liver, the man became a Calvinist, and if that organ was sound, he became a Unitarian. Very mortifying is the reluctant experience that some unfriendly excess or imbecility neutralizes the promise of genius. We see young men who owe us a new world, so readily

6. Cf. *Walden,* Chapter II: "Be it life or death, we crave only reality."

and lavishly they promise, but they never acquit the debt;[7] they die young and dodge the account; or if they live they lose themselves in the crowd.

Temperament also enters fully into the system of illusions and shuts us in a prison of glass which we cannot see. There is an optical illusion about every person we meet. In truth they are all creatures of given temperament, which will appear in a given character, whose boundaries they will never pass; but we look at them, they seem alive, and we presume there is impulse in them. In the moment it seems impulse; in the year, in the lifetime, it turns out to be a certain uniform tune which the revolving barrel of the music-box must play. Men resist the conclusion in the morning, but adopt it as the evening wears on, that temper prevails over everything of time, place and condition, and is inconsumable in the flames of religion. Some modifications the moral sentiment avails to impose, but the individual texture holds its dominion, if not to bias the moral judgments, yet to fix the measure of activity and of enjoyment.

I thus express the law as it is read from the platform of ordinary life, but must not leave it without noticing the capital exception. For temperament is a power which no man willingly hears any one praise but himself. On the platform of physics we cannot resist the contracting influences of so-called science. Temperament puts all divinity to rout. I know the mental proclivity of physicians. I hear the chuckle of the phrenologists.[8] Theoretic kidnappers and slave-drivers, they esteem each man the victim of another, who winds him round his finger by knowing the law of his being; and, by such cheap signboards as the color of his beard or the slope of his occiput, reads the inventory of his fortunes and character. The grossest ignorance does not disgust like this impudent knowingness. The physicians say they are not materialists; but they are:—Spirit is matter reduced to an extreme thinness: O *so* thin!—But the definition of *spiritual* should be, *that which is its own evidence.*[9] What notions do they attach to love! what to religion! One would not willingly pronounce these words in their hearing, and give them the occasion to profane them. I saw a gracious gentleman who adapts his conversation to the form of the head of the man he talks with! I had fancied that the value of life lay in its inscrutable possibilities; in the fact that I never know, in addressing myself to a new individual, what may befall me. I carry the keys of my castle in my hand, ready to throw them at the feet of my lord, whenever and in what disguise soever he shall

7. In the *Journals,* this is said of Thoreau. In the next clause, it has been suggested, Emerson is thinking again of his lost brothers Charles and Edward.
8. Phrenology is the "science" of de-
ducing a man's character from the conformation of his cranium.
9. Cf. Coleridge: "The idea [of God] is its own evidence" (*The Statesman's Manual*).

appear. I know he is in the neighborhood, hidden among vagabonds. Shall I preclude my future by taking a high seat and kindly adapting my conversation to the shape of heads? When I come to that, the doctors shall buy me for a cent.—"But, sir, medical history; the report to the Institute; the proven facts!"—I distrust the facts and the inferences. Temperament is the veto or limitation-power in the constitution, very justly applied to restrain an opposite excess in the constitution, but absurdly offered as a bar to original equity. When virtue is in presence, all subordinate powers sleep. On its own level, or in view of nature, temperament is final. I see not, if one be once caught in this trap of so-called sciences, any escape for the man from the links of the chain of physical necessity. Given such an embryo, such a history must follow. On this platform one lives in a sty of sensualism, and would soon come to suicide. But it is impossible that the creative power should exclude itself. Into every intelligence there is a door which is never closed, through which the creator passes. The intellect, seeker of absolute truth, or the heart, lover of absolute good, intervenes for our succor, and at one whisper of these high powers we awake from ineffectual struggles with this nightmare. We hurl it into its own hell, and cannot again contract ourselves to so base a state.

The secret of the illusoriness is in the necessity of a succession of moods or objects. Gladly we would anchor, but the anchorage is quicksand. This onward trick of nature is too strong for us: *Pero si muove.*[1] When at night I look at the moon and stars, I seem stationary, and they to hurry. Our love of the real draws us to permanence, but health of body consists in circulation, and sanity of mind in variety or facility of association. We need change of objects. Dedication to one thought is quickly odious. We house with the insane, and must humor them; then conversation dies out. Once I took such delight in Montaigne that I thought I should not need any other book; before that, in Shakespeare; then in Plutarch; then in Plotinus; at one time in Bacon; afterwards in Goethe; even in Bettine;[2] but now I turn the pages of either of them languidly, whilst I still cherish their genius. So with pictures; each will bear an emphasis of attention once, which it cannot retain, though we fain would continue to be pleased in that manner. How strongly I have felt of pictures that when you have seen one well, you must take your leave of it; you shall never see it again. I have had good lessons from pictures which I have since seen without emotion or remark. A deduction

---

1. "Just the same, it moves." Words uttered by Galileo after he had obeyed the command of the Inquisition and retracted his heresy that the earth revolved around the sun.

2. Elizabeth (Brentano) von Arnim (1785–1859), whose alleged correspondence with Goethe, published as *Letters to a Child* in 1835, was much discussed in Emerson's circle in 1839.

must be made from the opinion which even the wise express on a new book or occurrence. Their opinion gives me tidings of their mood, and some vague guess at the new fact, but is nowise to be trusted as the lasting relation between that intellect and that thing. The child asks, "Mamma, why don't I like the story as well as when you told it me yesterday?" Alas! child, it is even so with the oldest cherubim of knowledge. But will it answer thy question to say, Because thou wert born to a whole and this story is a particular? The reason of the pain this discovery causes us (and we make it late in respect to works of art and intellect) is the plaint of tragedy which murmurs from it in regard to persons, to friendship and love.[3]

That immobility and absence of elasticity which we find in the arts, we find with more pain in the artist. There is no power of expansion in men. Our friends early appear to us as representatives of certain ideas which they never pass or exceed. They stand on the brink of the ocean of thought and power, but they never take the single step that would bring them there.[4] A man is like a bit of Labrador spar, which has no lustre as you turn it in your hand until you come to a particular angle; then it shows deep and beautiful colors. There is no adaptation or universal applicability in men, but each has his special talent, and the mastery of successful men consists in adroitly keeping themselves where and when that turn shall be oftenest to be practised. We do what we must, and call it by the best names we can, and would fain have the praise of having intended the result which ensues. I cannot recall any form of man who is not superfluous sometimes. But is not this pitiful? Life is not worth the taking, to do tricks in.

Of course it needs the whole society to give the symmetry we seek. The party-colored wheel must revolve very fast to appear white. Something is earned too by conversing with so much folly and defect. In fine, whoever loses, we are always of the gaining party. Divinity is behind our failures and follies also. The plays of children are nonsense, but very educative nonsense. So it is with the largest and solemnest things, with commerce, government, church, marriage, and so with the history of every man's bread, and the ways by which he is to come by it. Like a bird which alights nowhere, but hops perpetually from bough to bough, is the Power which abides in no man and in no woman, but for a moment speaks from this one, and for another moment from that one.

But what help from these fineries or pedantries? What help from thought? Life is not dialectics. We, I think, in these times, have had

---

3. Cf. "Give All to Love."
4. "I call it self-distrust," Emerson wrote in 1837—"a fear to launch away into the deep, which they might freely and safely do. It is as if the dolphins should float on rafts, or creep and squirm along the shore in fear to trust themselves to the element which is really native to them" (*Journals*). "Labrador spar" is labradorite, a crystalline rock.

lessons enough of the futility of criticism. Our young people have thought and written much on labor and reform, and for all that they have written, neither the world nor themselves have got on a step. Intellectual tasting of life will not supersede muscular activity. If a man should consider the nicety of the passage of a piece of bread down his throat, he would starve. At Education Farm[5] the noblest theory of life sat on the noblest figures of young men and maidens, quite powerless and melancholy. It would not rake or pitch a ton of hay; it would not rub down a horse; and the men and maidens it left pale and hungry. A political orator wittily compared our party promises to western roads, which opened stately enough, with planted trees on either side to tempt the traveller, but soon became narrow and narrower and ended in a squirrel-track and ran up a tree. So does culture with us; it ends in headache. Unspeakably sad and barren does life look to those who a few months ago were dazzled with the splendor of the promise of the times. "There is now no longer any right course of action nor any self-devotion left among the Iranis."[6] Objections and criticism we have had our fill of. There are objections to every course of life and action, and the practical wisdom infers an indifferency, from the omnipresence of objection. The whole frame of things preaches indifferency. Do not craze yourself with thinking, but go about your business anywhere. Life is not intellectual or critical, but sturdy. Its chief good is for well-mixed people who can enjoy what they find, without question. Nature hates peeping, and our mothers speak her very sense when they say, "Children, eat your victuals, and say no more of it." To fill the hour,— that is happiness; to fill the hour and leave no crevice for a repentance or an approval. We live amid surfaces, and the true art of life is to skate well on them. Under the oldest mouldiest conventions a man of native force prospers just as well as in the newest world, and that by skill of handling and treatment. He can take hold anywhere. Life itself is a mixture of power and form,[7] and will not bear the least excess of either. To finish the moment, to find the journey's end in every step of the road, to live the greatest number of good hours, is wisdom. It is not the part of men, but of fanatics, or of mathematicians if you will, to say that, the shortness of life considered, it is not worth caring whether for so short a duration we were sprawling in want or sitting high. Since our office is with moments, let us husband them. Five minutes of to-day are worth as much to me as five minutes in the next millennium. Let us be poised, and wise, and our own, to-day. Let us treat the men and women

5. An allusion to Brook Farm. Cf. *Journals* (passages 74–75).
6. Ascribed to Zoroaster (6th century B.C.?), founder of the Persian religion.
7. I.e., creative innovation and settled custom. Cf. the distinction by Captain Vere in Melville's *Billy Budd* of "nature" and "forms, measured forms." Note how this part of this essay contradicts such other passages as the conclusion of "The American Scholar," with its proclamation of the infinitude of power, and how it is in turn contradicted elsewhere in this essay.

well; treat them as if they were real; perhaps they are. Men live in their fancy, like drunkards whose hands are too soft and tremulous for successful labor. It is a tempest of fancies, and the only ballast I know is a respect to the present hour. Without any shadow of doubt, amidst this vertigo of shows and politics, I settle myself ever the firmer in the creed that we should not postpone and refer and wish, but do broad justice where we are, by whomsoever we deal with, accepting our actual companions and circumstances, however humble or odious, as the mystic officials to whom the universe has delegated its whole pleasure for us. If these are mean and malignant, their contentment, which is the last victory of justice, is a more satisfying echo to the heart than the voice of poets and the casual sympathy of admirable persons. I think that however a thoughtful man may suffer from the defects and absurdities of his company, he cannot without affectation deny to any set of men and women a sensibility to extraordinary merit. The coarse and frivolous have an instinct of superiority, if they have not a sympathy, and honor it in their blind capricious way with sincere homage.

The fine young people despise life, but in me, and in such as with me are free from dyspepsia, and to whom a day is a sound and solid good, it is a great excess of politeness to look scornful and to cry for company. I am grown by sympathy a little eager and sentimental, but leave me alone and I should relish every hour and what it brought me, the potluck of the day, as heartily as the oldest gossip in the bar-room. I am thankful for small mercies. I compared notes with one of my friends who expects everything of the universe and is disappointed when anything is less than the best, and I found that I begin at the other extreme, expecting nothing, and am always full of thanks for moderate goods. I accept the clangor and jangle of contrary tendencies. I find my account in sots and bores also. They give a reality to the circumjacent picture which such a vanishing meteorous appearance can ill spare. In the morning I awake and find the old world, wife, babes and mother, Concord and Boston, the dear old spiritual world and even the dear old devil not far off. If we will take the good we find, asking no questions, we shall have heaping measures. The great gifts are not got by analysis. Everything good is on the highway. The middle region of our being is the temperate zone. We may climb into the thin and cold realm of pure geometry and lifeless science, or sink into that of sensation. Between these extremes is the equator of life, of thought, of spirit, of poetry,—a narrow belt. Moreover, in popular experience everything good is on the highway. A collector peeps into all the picture-shops of Europe for a landscape of Poussin, a crayon-sketch of Salvator; but the Transfiguration, the Last Judgment, the Communion of Saint Jerome,[8] and what are as transcendent as these, are on the walls of the Vatican, the Uffizi, or the Louvre, where every footman may see them; to say nothing of Nature's pictures in every street, of sunsets and sunrises every day, and the sculpture of the human body never absent. A collector recently bought at public auction, in London, for one hundred and fifty-seven guineas, an autograph of Shakspeare; but for nothing a school-boy can read Hamlet and can detect secrets of highest concernment yet unpublished therein. I think I will never read any but the commonest books,—the Bible, Homer, Dante, Shakspeare and Milton. Then we are impatient of so public a life and planet, and run hither and thither for nooks and secrets. The imagination delights in the woodcraft of Indians, trappers and bee-hunters. We fancy that we are strangers, and not so intimately domesticated in the planet as the wild man and the wild beast and bird. But the exclusion reaches them also; reaches the climbing, flying, gliding, feathered and four-footed man. Fox and woodchuck, hawk and snipe and bittern, when nearly seen, have no more root in the deep world than man, and are just such superficial tenants of the globe. Then the new molecular philosophy[9] shows astronomical interspaces betwixt atom and atom, shows that the world is all outside; it has no inside.

The mid-world is best. Nature, as we know her, is no saint. The lights of the church, the ascetics, Gentoos[1] and corn-eaters, she does not distinguish by any favor. She comes eating and drinking and sinning. Her darlings, the great, the strong, the beautiful, are not children of our law; do not come out of the Sunday School, nor weigh their food, nor punctually keep the commandments. If we will be strong with her strength we must not harbor such disconsolate consciences, borrowed too from the consciences of other nations. We must set up the strong present tense against all the rumors of wrath, past or to come. So many things are unsettled which it is of the first importance to settle;—and, pending their settlement, we will do as we do. Whilst the debate goes forward on the equity of commerce, and will not be closed for a century or two, New and Old England may keep shop. Law of copyright and international copyright is to be discussed, and in the interim we will sell our books for the most we can.[2] Expediency of literature, reason of literature, lawfulness of writing down a thought, is

8. By Raphael, Michelangelo, and Domenichino respectively; all in the Vatican; all old favorites of Emerson's. The artists mentioned above are Nicholas Poussin and Salvator Rosa (both 17th century).
9. A reference either to Boscovich's molecular theory or to Dalton's atomic theory.
1. A Hindu sect, the Telugu.
2. The failure of the United States to adhere to an international copyright law before 1891 hurt American authors by throwing them into competition with pirated British authors; hence it was often "to be discussed" by them.

questioned; much is to say on both sides, and, while the fight waxes hot, thou, dearest scholar, stick to thy foolish task, add a line every hour, and between whiles add a line. Right to hold land, right of property, is disputed, and the conventions convene, and before the vote is taken, dig away in your garden, and spend your earnings as a waif or godsend[3] to all serene and beautiful purposes. Life itself is a bubble and a scepticism, and a sleep within a sleep. Grant it, and as much more as they will,—but thou, God's darling! heed thy private dream; thou wilt not be missed in the scorning and scepticism; there are enough of them; stay there in thy closet and toil until the rest are agreed what to do about it. Thy sickness, they say, and thy puny habit require that thou do this or avoid that, but know that thy life is a flitting state, a tent for a night, and do thou, sick or well, finish that stint. Thou art sick, but shalt not be worse, and the universe, which holds thee dear, shall be the better.

Human life is made up of the two elements, power and form, and the proportion must be invariably kept if we would have it sweet and sound. Each of these elements in excess makes a mischief as hurtful as its defect. Everything runs to excess; every good quality is noxious if unmixed, and, to carry the danger to the edge of ruin, nature causes each man's peculiarity to superabound. Here, among the farms, we adduce the scholars as examples of this treachery. They are nature's victims of expression. You who see the artist, the orator, the poet, too near, and find their life no more excellent than that of mechanics or farmers, and themselves victims of partiality, very hollow and haggard, and pronounce them failures, not heroes, but quacks,—conclude very reasonably that these arts are not for man, but are disease. Yet nature will not bear you out. Irresistible nature made men such, and makes legions more of such, every day. You love the boy reading in a book, gazing at a drawing or a cast; yet what are these millions who read and behold, but incipient writers and sculptors? Add a little more of that quality which now reads and sees, and they will seize the pen and chisel. And if one remembers how innocently he began to be an artist, he perceives that nature joined with his enemy. A man is a golden impossibility.[4] The line he must walk is a hair's breadth. The wise through excess of wisdom is made a fool.

How easily, if fate would suffer it, we might keep forever these beautiful limits, and adjust ourselves, once for all, to the perfect calculation of the kingdom of known cause and effect. In the street and in the newspapers, life appears so plain a business that manly

---

3. I.e., as a "find" or piece of good fortune.
4. Cf. the ideal of Aristotelian ethics, the "perfect calculation" of a golden mean. Also Confucius' *Doctrine of the Mean*, which Emerson read in 1843.

resolution and adherence to the multiplication-table through all weathers will insure success. But ah! presently comes a day, or is it only a half-hour, with its angel-whispering,—which discomfits the conclusions of nations and of years! To-morrow again every thing looks real and angular, the habitual standards are reinstated, common-sense is as rare as genius,—is the basis of genius, and experience is hands and feet to every enterprise;—and yet, he who should do his business on this understanding would be quickly bankrupt. Power keeps quite another road than the turnpikes of choice and will; namely the subterranean and invisible tunnels and channels of life. It is ridiculous that we are diplomatists, and doctors, and considerate people; there are no dupes like these. Life is a series of surprises, and would not be worth taking or keeping if it were not. God delights to isolate us every day, and hide from us the past and the future. We would look about us, but with grand politeness he draws down before us an impenetrable screen of purest sky, and another behind us of purest sky. "You will not remember," he seems to say, "and you will not expect." All good conversation, manners and action come from a spontaneity which forgets usages and makes the moment great. Nature hates calculators; her methods are saltatory and impulsive. Man lives by pulses; our organic movements are such; and the chemical and ethereal agents are undulatory and alternate; and the mind goes antagonizing on, and never prospers but by fits. We thrive by casualties.[5] Our chief experiences have been casual. The most attractive class of people are those who are powerful obliquely and not by the direct stroke; men of genius, but not yet accredited; one gets the cheer of their light without paying too great a tax. Theirs is the beauty of the bird or the morning light, and not of art. In the thought of genius there is always a surprise; and the moral sentiment is well called "the newness," for it is never other; as new to the oldest intelligence as to the young child;—"the kingdom that cometh without observation."[6] In like manner, for practical success, there must not be too much design. A man will not be observed in doing that which he can do best. There is a certain magic about his properest action which stupefies your powers of observation, so that though it is done before you, you wist not of it. The art of life has a pudency, and will not be exposed. Every man is an impossibility until he is born; every thing impossible until we see a success. The ardors of piety agree at last with the coldest scepticism,—that nothing is of us or our works,—that all is of God. Nature will not spare us the smallest leaf of laurel. All writing comes by the grace

5. Chance occurrences. With this passage, cf. "The American Scholar," p. 230.

6. Cf. the conclusion to *Nature* and Luke xvii.20.

of God, and all doing and having. I would gladly be moral and keep due metes and bounds, which I dearly love, and allow the most to the will of man; but I have set my heart on honesty in this chapter, and I can see nothing at last, in success or failure, than more or less of vital force supplied from the Eternal. The results of life are uncalculated and uncalculable. The years teach much which the days never know. The persons who compose our company converse, and come and go, and design and execute many things, and somewhat comes of it all, but an unlooked-for result. The individual is always mistaken. He designed many things, and drew in other persons as coadjutors, quarrelled with some or all, blundered much, and something is done; all are a little advanced, but the individual is always mistaken. It turns out somewhat new and very unlike what he promised himself.

The ancients, struck with this irreducibleness of the elements of human life to calculation, exalted Chance into a divinity; but that is to stay too long at the spark, which glitters truly at one point, but the universe is warm with the latency of the same fire. The miracle of life which will not be expounded but will remain a miracle, introduces a new element. In the growth of the embryo, Sir Everard Home I think noticed that the evolution was not from one central point, but coactive from three or more points. Life has no memory. That which proceeds in succession might be remembered, but that which is coexistent, or ejaculated from a deeper cause, as yet far from being conscious, knows not its own tendency. So is it with us, now sceptical or without unity, because immersed in forms and effects all seeming to be of equal yet hostile value, and now religious, whilst in the reception of spiritual law. Bear with these distractions, with this coetaneous growth of the parts; they will one day be *members*, and obey one will. On that one will, on that secret cause, they nail our attention and hope. Life is hereby melted into an expectation or a religion. Underneath the inharmonious and trivial particulars, is a musical perfection; the Ideal journeying always with us, the heaven without rent or seam. Do but observe the mode of our illumination. When I converse with a profound mind, or if at any time being alone I have good thoughts, I do not at once arrive at satisfactions, as when, being thirsty, I drink water; or go to the fire, being cold; no! but I am at first apprised of my vicinity to a new and excellent region of life. By persisting to read or to think, this region gives further sign of itself, as it were in flashes of light, in sudden discoveries of its profound beauty and repose, as if the clouds that covered it parted at intervals and showed the approaching traveller the inland mountains, with the tranquil eternal meadows spread at their base, whereon flocks graze and shepherds pipe and dance.[7] But every insight from this realm of thought is felt as initial, and promises a sequel. I do not make it; I arrive there, and behold what was there already. I make! O no! I clap my hands in infantine joy and amazement before the first opening to me of this august magnificence, old with the love and homage of innumerable ages, young with the life of life, the sunbright Mecca of the desert. And what a future it opens! I feel a new heart beating with the love of the new beauty. I am ready to die out of nature and be born again into this new yet unapproachable America I have found in the West:—

> "Since neither now nor yesterday began
> These thoughts, which have been ever, nor yet can
> A man be found who their first entrance knew."[8]

If I have described life as a flux of moods, I must now add that there is that in us which changes not and which ranks all sensations and states of mind. The consciousness in each man is a sliding scale, which identifies him now with the First Cause, and now with the flesh of his body; life above life, in infinite degrees. The sentiment from which it sprung determines the dignity of any deed, and the question ever is, not what you have done or forborne, but at whose command you have done or forborne it.

Fortune, Minerva, Muse, Holy Ghost,—these are quaint names, too narrow to cover this unbounded substance. The baffled intellect must still kneel before this cause, which refuses to be named,—ineffable cause, which every fine genius has essayed to represent by some emphatic symbol, as, Thales by water, Anaximenes by air, Anaxagoras by (Noûs) thought, Zoroaster by fire, Jesus and the moderns by love; and the metaphor of each has become a national religion. The Chinese Mencius[9] has not been the least successful in his generalization. "I fully understand language," he said, "and nourish well my vast-flowing vigor."—"I beg to ask what you call vast-flowing vigor?" said his companion. "The explanation," replied Mencius, "is difficult. This vigor is supremely great, and in the highest degree unbending. Nourish it correctly and do it no injury, and it will fill up the vacancy between heaven and earth. This vigor accords with and assists justice and reason, and leaves no hunger." —In our more correct writing we give to this generalization the name of Being, and thereby confess that we have arrived as far as we can go. Suffice it for the joy of the universe that we have not arrived at a wall, but at interminable oceans. Our life seems not present so much as prospective; not for the affairs on which it is

7. Cf. the conclusion of "Illusions."
8. From Sophocles' *Antigone.*
9. Meng-tse, 3rd century B.C., compiled the earliest classic of Chinese Confucianism. Emerson first read him in 1843.

wasted, but as a hint of this vast-flowing vigor. Most of life seems to be mere advertisement of faculty; information is given us not to sell ourselves cheap; that we are very great. So, in particulars, our greatness is always in a tendency or direction, not in an action. It is for us to believe in the rule, not in the exception. The noble are thus known from the ignoble. So in accepting the leading of the sentiments, it is not what we believe concerning the immortality of the soul or the like, but *the universal impulse to believe,*[1] that is the material circumstance and is the principal fact in the history of the globe. Shall we describe this cause as that which works directly? The spirit is not helpless or needful of mediate organs. It has plentiful powers and direct effects. I am explained without explaining, I am felt without acting, and where I am not. Therefore all just persons are satisfied with their own praise. They refuse to explain themselves, and are content that new actions should do them that office. They believe that we communicate without speech and above speech, and that no right action of ours is quite unaffecting to our friends, at whatever distance; for the influence of action is not to be measured by miles. Why should I fret myself because a circumstance has occurred which hinders my presence where I was expected? If I am not at the meeting, my presence where I am should be as useful to the commonwealth of friendship and wisdom, as would be my presence in that place. I exert the same quality of power in all places. Thus journeys the mighty Ideal before us; it never was known to fall into the rear. No man ever came to an experience which was satiating, but his good is tidings of a better. Onward and onward! In liberated moments we know that a new picture of life and duty is already possible; the elements already exist in many minds around you of a doctrine of life which shall transcend any written record we have. The new statement will comprise the scepticisms as well as the faiths of society, and out of unbeliefs a creed shall be formed. For scepticisms are not gratuitous or lawless, but are limitations of the affirmative statement, and the new philosophy must take them in and make affirmations outside of them, just as much as it must include the oldest beliefs.

It is very unhappy, but too late to be helped, the discovery we have made that we exist.[2] That discovery is called the Fall of Man. Ever afterwards we suspect our instruments. We have learned that we do not see directly, but mediately, and that we have no means of correcting these colored and distorting lenses which we are, or of computing the amount of their errors. Perhaps these subject-

1. Cf. p. 264 and its note 9.
2. Cf. the chapters "Idealism" and "Spirit" in *Nature* with the following passage.

lenses have a creative power; perhaps there are no objects. Once we lived in what we saw; now, the rapaciousness of this new power, which threatens to absorb all things, engages us. Nature, art, persons, letters, religions, objects, successively tumble in, and God is but one of its ideas. Nature and literature are subjective phenomena; every evil and every good thing is a shadow which we cast. The street is full of humiliations to the proud. As the fop contrived to dress his bailiffs in his livery and make them wait on his guests at table, so the chagrins which the bad heart gives off as bubbles, at once take form as ladies and gentlemen in the street, shopmen or bar-keepers in hotels, and threaten or insult whatever is threatenable and insultable in us. 'Tis the same with our idolatries. People forget that it is the eye which makes the horizon, and the rounding mind's eye which makes this or that man a type or representative of humanity, with the name of hero or saint. Jesus, the "providential man," is a good man on whom many people are agreed that these optical laws shall take effect. By love on one part and by forbearance to press objection on the other part, it is for a time settled that we will look at him in the center of the horizon, and ascribe to him the properties that will attach to any man so seen. But the longest love or aversion has a speedy term. The great and crescive self, rooted in absolute nature, supplants all relative existence and ruins the kingdom of mortal friendship and love. Marriage (in what is called the spiritual world) is impossible, because of the inequality between every subject and every object. The subject is the receiver of Godhead, and at every comparison must feel his being exhanced by that cryptic might. Though not in energy, yet by presence, this magazine of substance cannot be otherwise than felt; nor can any force of intellect attribute to the object the proper deity which sleeps or wakes forever in every subject. Never can love make consciousness and ascription[3] equal in force. There will be the same gulf between every me and thee as between the original and the picture. The universe is the bride of the soul. All private sympathy is partial. Two human beings are like globes, which can touch only in a point, and whilst they remain in contact all other points of each of the spheres are inert; their turn must also come, and the longer a particular union lasts the more energy of appetency the parts not in union acquire.

Life will be imagined, but cannot be divided nor doubled. Any invasion of its unity would be chaos. The soul is not twin-born but the only begotten, and though revealing itself as child in time, child in appearance, is of a fatal and universal power, admitting no co-life. Every day, every act betrays the ill-concealed deity. We believe in ourselves as we do not believe in others. We permit all things to

3. Ascription, that is, of consciousness to another.

ourselves, and that which we call sin in others is experiment for us. It is an instance of our faith in ourselves that men never speak of crime as lightly as they think; or every man thinks a latitude safe for himself which is nowise to be indulged to another. The act looks very differently on the inside and on the outside; in its quality and in its consequences. Murder in the murderer is no such ruinous thought as poets and romancers will have it; it does not unsettle him or fright him from his ordinary notice of trifles; it is an act quite easy to be contemplated; but in its sequel it turns out to be a horrible jangle and confounding of all relations. Especially the crimes that spring from love seem right and fair from the actor's point of view, but when acted are found destructive of society. No man at last believes that he can be lost, or that the crime in him is as black as in the felon. Because the intellect qualifies in our own case the moral judgments. For there is no crime to the intellect. That is antinomian or hypernomian,[4] and judges law as well as fact. "It is worse than a crime, it is a blunder," said Napoleon, speaking the language of the intellect. To it, the world is a problem in mathematics or the science of quantity, and it leaves out praise and blame and all weak emotions. All stealing is comparative. If you come to absolutes, pray who does not steal? Saints are sad, because they behold sin (even when they speculate) from the point of view of the conscience, and not of the intellect; a confusion of thought. Sin, seen from the thought, is a diminution, or *less*; seen from the conscience or will, it is pravity or *bad*. The intellect names it shade, absence of light, and no essence. The conscience must feel it as essence, essential evil. This it is not; it has an objective existence, but no subjective.

Thus inevitably does the universe wear our color, and every object fall successively into the subject itself. The subject exists, the subject enlarges; all things sooner or later fall into place. As I am, so I see; use what language we will, we can never say anything but what we are; Hermes, Cadmus, Columbus, Newton, Bonaparte,[5] are the mind's ministers. Instead of feeling a poverty when we encounter a great man, let us treat the newcomer like a travelling geologist who passes through our estate and shows us good slate, or limestone, or anthracite, in our brush pasture. The partial action of each strong mind in one direction is a telescope for the objects on which it is pointed. But every other part of knowledge is to be pushed to the same extravagance, ere the soul attains her due sphericity. Do you see that kitten chasing so prettily her own tail? If you could look with her eyes you might see her surrounded

4. Outside or above the law.
5. All inventors, innovators (Hermes, messenger of the gods, was god of invention; Cadmus introduced the alphabet and, by sowing dragon's teeth, created the Thebans).

with hundreds of figures performing complex dramas, with tragic and comic issues, long conversations, many characters, many ups and downs of fate,—and meantime it is only puss and her tail. How long before our masquerade will end its noise of tambourines, laughter and shouting, and we shall find it was a solitary performance? A subject and an object,—it takes so much to make the galvanic circuit complete, but magnitude adds nothing. What imports it whether it is Kepler[6] and the sphere, Columbus and America, a reader and his book, or puss with her tail?

It is true that all the muses and love and religion hate these developments, and will find a way to punish the chemist who publishes in the parlor the secrets of the laboratory. And we cannot say too little of our constitutional necessity of seeing things under private aspects, or saturated with our humors. And yet is the God the native of these bleak rocks. That need makes in morals the capital virtue of self-trust. We must hold hard to this poverty, however scandalous, and by more vigorous self-recoveries, after the sallies of action, possess our axis more firmly. The life of truth is cold and so far mournful; but it is not the slave of tears, contritions and perturbations. It does not attempt another's work, nor adopt another's facts. It is a main lesson of wisdom to know your own from another's. I have learned that I cannot dispose of other people's facts; but I possess such a key to my own as persuades me, against all their denials, that they also have a key to theirs. A sympathetic person is placed in the dilemma of a swimmer among drowning men, who all catch at him, and if he give so much as a leg or a finger they will drown him. They wish to be saved from the mischiefs of their vices, but not from their vices. Charity would be wasted on this poor waiting on the symptoms. A wise and hardy physician will say, *Come out of that*,[7] as the first condition of advice.

In this our talking America we are ruined by our good nature and listening on all sides. This compliance takes away the power of being greatly useful. A man should not be able to look other than directly and forthright. A preoccupied attention is the only answer to the importunate frivolity of other people; an attention, and to an aim which makes their wants frivolous. This is a divine answer, and leaves no appeal and no hard thoughts. In Flaxman's[8] drawing of the Eumenides of Æschylus, Orestes supplicates Apollo, whilst the Furies sleep on the threshold. The face of the god expresses a shade of regret and compassion, but is calm with the conviction of the

6. Johannes Kepler, the 16th-century German physicist who discovered the fundamental laws of planetary motion.
7. Cf. II Corinthians vi.17.
8. John Flaxman (1755–1826), well-known English illustrator. The scene referred to is near the beginning of the last play of Aeschylus' Orestes trilogy; Orestes is supplicating to be released from the blood-guilt of having killed his mother, while the Furies wait to avenge it.

278 · *Ralph Waldo Emerson*

irreconcilableness of the two spheres. He is born into other politics, into the eternal and beautiful. The man at his feet asks for his interest in turmoils of the earth, into which his nature cannot enter. And the Eumenides there lying express pictorially this disparity. The god is surcharged with his divine destiny.

Illusion, Temperament, Succession, Surface, Surprise, Reality, Subjectiveness,—these are threads on the loom of time, these are the lords of life. I dare not assume to give their order, but I name them as I find them in my way. I know better than to claim any completeness for my picture. I am a fragment, and this is a fragment of me. I can very confidently announce one or another law, which throws itself into relief and form, but I am too young yet by some ages to compile a code. I gossip for my hour concerning the eternal politics. I have seen many fair pictures not in vain. A wonderful time I have lived in. I am not the novice I was fourteen, nor yet seven years ago.[9] Let who will ask, Where is the fruit? I find a private fruit sufficient. This is a fruit,—that I should not ask for a rash effect from meditations, counsels and the hiving of truths. I should feel it pitiful to demand a result on this town and county, an overt effect on the instant month and year. The effect is deep and secular[1] as the cause. It works on periods in which mortal lifetime is lost. All I know is reception; I am and I have: but I do not get, and when I have fancied I had gotten anything, found I did not. I worship with wonder the great Fortune. My reception has been so large, that I am not annoyed by receiving this or that superabundantly. I say to the Genius, if he will pardon the proverb, *In for a mill, in for a million.* When I receive a new gift, I do not macerate my body to make the account square, for if I should die I could not make the account square. The benefit overran the merit the first day, and has overrun the merit ever since. The merit itself, so-called, I reckon part of the receiving.

Also that hankering after an overt or practical effect seems to me an apostasy. In good earnest I am willing to spare this most unnecessary deal of doing. Life wears to me a visionary face. Hardest roughest action is visionary also. It is but a choice between soft and turbulent dreams. People disparage knowing and the intellectual life, and urge doing. I am very content with knowing, if only I could know. That is an august entertainment, and would suffice me a great while. To know a little would be worth the expense of this world. I hear always the law of Adrastia,[2] "that every soul which had acquired any truth, should be safe from harm until another

9. Perhaps arbitrary numbers; but seven years before Emerson had delivered "The American Scholar" address, while fourteen years before he was just discovering the new truths that would drive him from his Unitarian pastorate.
1. Pertaining to a long period of time.
2. Nemesis. The reference is to Plato's *Phaedrus* (248C).

period."

I know that the world I converse with in the city and in the farms, is not the world I *think.* I observe that difference, and shall observe it. One day I shall know the value and law of this discrepance. But I have not found that much was gained by manipular attempts to realize the world of thought. Many eager persons successively make an experiment in this way, and make themselves ridiculous. They acquire democratic manners, they foam at the mouth, they hate and deny. Worse, I observe that in the history of mankind there is never a solitary example of success,—taking their own tests of success. I say this polemically, or in reply to the inquiry, Why not realize[3] your world? But far be from me the despair which prejudges the law by a paltry empiricism;—since there never was a right endeavor but it succeeded. Patience and patience, we shall win at the last. We must be very suspicious of the deceptions of the element of time. It takes a good deal of time to eat or to sleep, or to earn a hundred dollars, and a very little time to entertain a hope and an insight which becomes the light of our life. We dress our garden, eat our dinners, discuss the household with our wives, and these things make no impression, are forgotten next week; but, in the solitude to which every man is always returning, he has a sanity and revelations which in his passage into new worlds he will carry with him. Never mind the ridicule, never mind the defeat; up again, old heart!—it seems to say, —there is victory yet for all justice; and the true romance which the world exists to realize will be the transformation of genius[4] into practical power.

1843   1844

The Poet[5]

A moody child and wildly wise
Pursued the game with joyful eyes,
Which chose, like meteors, their way,
And rived the dark with private ray:
They overleapt the horizon's edge,
Searched with Apollo's privilege;
Through man, and woman, and sea, and star
Saw the dance of nature forward far;
Through worlds, and races, and terms, and times
Saw musical order, and pairing rhymes.

Olympian bards who sung
Divine ideas below,
Which always find us young,
And always keep us so.[6]

Those who are esteemed umpires of taste are often persons who have acquired some knowledge of admired pictures or sculptures,

3. Make real.
4. Creative insight; power of thought.
5. In his course of lectures on "The Times" (1841–42) Emerson included

one on "The Poet" which still survives in manuscript. The present essay, however, is almost entirely new and was never used as a lecture. While in

and have an inclination for whatever is elegant; but if you inquire whether they are beautiful souls, and whether their own acts are like fair pictures, you learn that they are selfish and sensual. Their cultivation is local, as if you should rub a log of dry wood in one spot to produce fire, all the rest remaining cold. Their knowledge of the fine arts is some study of rules and particulars, or some limited judgment of color or form, which is exercised for amusement or for show. It is a proof of the shallowness of the doctrine of beauty as it lies in the minds of our amateurs, that men seem to have lost the perception of the instant dependence of form upon soul. There is no doctrine of forms in our philosophy. We were put into our bodies, as fire is put into a pan to be carried about; but there is no accurate adjustment between the spirit and the organ, much less is the latter the germination of the former. So in regard to other forms, the intellectual men do not believe in any essential dependence of the material world on thought and volition. Theologians think it a pretty air-castle to talk of the spiritual meaning of a ship or a cloud, of a city or a contract, but they prefer to come again to the solid ground of historical evidence; and even the poets are contented with a civil and conformed manner of living, and to write poems from the fancy, at a safe distance from their own experience. But the highest minds of the world have never ceased to explore the double meaning, or shall I say the quadruple or the centuple or of much more manifold meaning, of every sensuous fact; Orpheus, Empedocles, Heraclitus, Plato, Plutarch, Dante, Swedenborg,[7] and the masters of sculpture, picture and poetry. For we are not pans and barrows, nor ever porters of the fire and torch-bearers, but children of the fire, made of it, and only the same divinity transmuted and at two or three removes, when we know least about it. And this hidden truth, that the fountains whence all this

coloration much of it is Platonic, echoing particularly the myth in the *Phaedrus,* its central stress, as in the treatment of the poet in *Nature,* is modern, on the power of creative imagination by which the inert facts of "common sense" come to life as symbols of an inner truth. The poet's "*dream*-power" restores to us our own meaning-making power and so "keeps us young" by releasing us, for the moment at least, from what Paul Tillich calls "spiritual non-being." With the single substitution of "truths" for "fictions" Wallace Stevens was summarizing this essay when he wrote, "What makes the poet the potent figure that he is, or was, or ought to be is that he creates the world to which we turn incessantly and without knowing it and that he gives to life the supreme fictions without which we are unable to conceive of it." Although by "poet"

Emerson obviously means much more than writer, the essay has become a classic American "Defence of Poetry." Its impact on Whitman should be obvious to any reader of the Preface to the 1855 *Leaves of Grass.*
6. Part of "Ode to Beauty." The first motto is part of a never-completed poem on "The Poet" that is printed in the Appendix to Volume IX (*Poems*) of the Centenary Edition.
7. All these figures in different ways subordinated the material world to "thought and volition": Orpheus was a legendary type of the poet-prophet; Empedocles was a Greek philosopher who professed miraculous and prophetic powers; Heraclitus was another Greek (known as the "weeping philosopher"); Swedenborg was a Swedish mystic (cf. Emerson's discussion of him in the concluding paragraphs of "The American Scholar").

river of Time and its creatures floweth are intrinsically ideal and
beautiful, draws us to the consideration of the nature and functions of the Poet, or the man of Beauty; to the means and materials
he uses, and to the general aspect of the art in the present time.[8]

The breadth of the problem is great, for the poet is representative. He stands among partial men for the complete man, and
apprises us not of his wealth, but of the common wealth. The
young man reveres men of genius, because, to speak truly, they are
more himself than he is. They receive of the soul as he also receives, but they more. Nature enhances her beauty, to the eye of
loving men, from their belief that the poet is beholding her shows
at the same time. He is isolated among his contemporaries by truth
and by his art, but with this consolation in his pursuits, that they
will draw all men sooner or later. For all men live by truth and
stand in need of expression. In love, in art, in avarice, in politics, in
labor, in games, we study to utter our painful secret. The man is
only half himself, the other half is his expression.

Notwithstanding this necessity to be published, adequate expression is rare. I know not how it is that we need an interpreter,
but the great majority of men seem to be minors, who have not yet
come into possession of their own, or mutes, who cannot report
the conversation they have had with nature. There is no man who
does not anticipate a supersensual utility in the sun and stars, earth
and water. These stand and wait to render him a peculiar service.
But there is some obstruction or some excess of phlegm in our constitution, which does not suffer them to yield the due effect. Too
feeble fall the impressions of nature on us to make us artists.
Every touch should thrill. Every man should be so much an artist
that he could report in conversation what had befallen him. Yet,
in our experience, the rays or appulses have sufficient force to arrive at the senses, but not enough to reach the quick and compel
the reproduction of themselves in speech. The poet is the person
in whom these powers are in balance, the man without impedi-
ment, who sees and handles that which others dream of, traverses
the whole scale of experience, and is representative of man, in virtue of being the largest power to receive and to impart.

For the universe has three children, born at one time, which re-
appear under different names in every system of thought, whether
they be called cause, operation and effect; or, more poetically, Jove,
Pluto, Neptune; or, theologically, the Father, the Spirit and the
Son; but which we will call here the Knower, the Doer and the
Sayer. These stand respectively for the love of truth, for the love

8. A brief outline of what is to follow. In this essay, it has been argued, Emerson reverses his frequent method of ascending a scale from lower to higher, and instead starts with the ideal and general and works down to the immediate and concrete.

of good, and for the love of beauty. These three are equal. Each is that which he is, essentially, so that he cannot be surmounted or analyzed, and each of these three has the power of the others latent in him and his own, patent.

The poet is the sayer, the namer, and represents beauty. He is a sovereign, and stands on the center. For the world is not painted or adorned, but is from the beginning beautiful; and God has not made some beautiful things, but Beauty is the creator of the universe. Therefore the poet is not any permissive potentate, but is emperor in his own right. Criticism is infested with a cant of materialism, which assumes that manual skill and activity is the first merit of all men, and disparages such as say and do not, over-looking the fact that some men, namely poets, are natural sayers, sent into the world to the end of expression, and confounds them with those whose province is action but who quit it to imitate the sayers. But Homer's words are as costly and admirable to Homer as Agamemnon's victories are to Agamemnon. The poet does not wait for the hero or the sage, but, as they act and think primarily, so he writes primarily what will and must be spoken, reckoning the others, though primaries also, yet, in respect to him, secondaries and servants; as sitters or models in the studio of a painter, or as assistants who bring building-materials to an architect.

For poetry was all written before time was, and whenever we are so finely organized that we can penetrate into that region where the air is music, we hear those primal warblings and attempt to write them down, but we lose ever and anon a word or a verse and substitute something of our own, and thus miswrite the poem. The men of more delicate ear write down these cadences more faithfully, and these transcripts, though imperfect, become the songs of the nations.[9] For nature is as truly beautiful as it is good, or as it is reasonable, and must as much appear as it must be done, or be known. Words and deeds are quite indifferent modes of the divine energy. Words are also actions, and actions are a kind of words.

The sign and credentials of the poet are that he announces that which no man foretold. He is the true and only doctor;[1] he knows and tells; he is the only teller of news, for he was present and privy to the appearance which he describes. He is a beholder of ideas and an utterer of the necessary and causal. For we do not speak now of men of poetical talents, or of industry and skill in meter, but of the true poet. I took part in a conversation the other day concerning a recent writer of lyrics, a man of subtle mind,

9. The first of many Platonic reminis- *Phaedrus.*
cences in this essay. Cf. especially the   1. Teacher.

whose head appeared to be a music-box of delicate tunes and rhythms, and whose skill and command of language we could not sufficiently praise. But when the question arose whether he was not only a lyrist but a poet, we were obliged to confess that he is plainly a contemporary, not an eternal man. He does not stand out of our low limitations, like a Chimborazo[2] under the line, running up from a torrid base through all the climates of the globe, with belts of the herbage of every latitude on its high and mottled sides; but this genius is the landscape-garden of a modern house, adorned with fountains and statues, with well-bred men and women standing and sitting in the walks and terraces. We hear, through all the varied music, the ground-tone of conventional life. Our poets are men of talents who sing, and not the children of music. The argument is secondary, the finish of the verses is primary.

For it is not meters, but a meter-making argument that makes a poem,—a thought so passionate and alive that like the spirit of a plant or an animal it has an architecture of its own, and adorns nature with a new thing. The thought and the form are equal in the order of time, but in the order of genesis the thought is prior to the form. The poet has a new thought; he has a whole new experience to unfold; he will tell us how it was with him, and all men will be the richer in his fortune. For the experience of each new age requires a new confession, and the world seems always waiting for its poet. I remember when I was young how much I was moved one morning by tidings that genius had appeared in a youth who sat near me at table. He had left his work and gone rambling none knew whither, and had written hundreds of lines, but could not tell whether that which was in him was therein told; he could tell nothing but that all was changed,—man, beast, heaven, earth and sea. How gladly we listened! how credulous! Society seemed to be compromised. We sat in the aurora of a sunrise which was to put out all the stars. Boston seemed to be at twice the distance it had the night before, or was much farther than that. Rome,—what was Rome? Plutarch and Shakespeare were in the yellow leaf, and Homer no more should be heard of. It is much to know that poetry has been written this very day, under this very roof, by your side. What! that wonderful spirit has not expired! These stony moments are still sparkling and animated! I had fancied that the oracles were all silent, and nature had spent her fires; and behold! all night, from every pore, these fine auroras[3] have been streaming. Every one has some interest in the advent of the poet, and no one knows how much it may concern him. We know that the secret of the world is profound, but who or what shall be our interpreter,

2. Mountain in Ecuador.   3. Northern lights.

we know not. A mountain ramble, a new style of face, a new person, may put the key into our hands. Of course the value of genius to us is in the veracity of its report. Talent may frolic and juggle; genius realizes[4] and adds. Mankind in good earnest have availed so far in understanding themselves and their work, that the foremost watchman on the peak announces his news. It is the truest word ever spoken, and the phrase will be the fittest, most musical, and the unerring voice of the world for that time.

All that we call sacred history attests that the birth of a poet is the principal event in chronology. Man, never so often deceived, still watches for the arrival of a brother who can hold him steady to a truth until he has made it his own. With what joy I begin to read a poem which I confide in as an inspiration! And now my chains are to be broken; I shall mount above these clouds and opaque airs in which I live,—opaque, though they seem transparent,—and from the heaven of truth I shall see and comprehend my relations. That will reconcile me to life and renovate nature, to see trifles animated by a tendency, and to know what I am doing. Life will no more be a noise; now I shall see men and women, and know the signs by which they may be discerned from fools and satans. This day shall be better than my birthday: then I became an animal; now I am invited into the science of the real. Such is the hope, but the fruition is postponed. Oftener it falls that this winged man, who will carry me into the heaven, whirls me into mists, then leaps and frisks about with me as it were from cloud to cloud, still affirming that he is bound heavenward; and I, being myself a novice, am slow in perceiving that he does not know the way into the heavens, and is merely bent that I should admire his skill to rise like a fowl or a flying fish, a little way from the ground or the water; but the all-piercing, all-feeding and ocular air of heaven that man shall never inhabit. I tumble down again soon into my old nooks, and lead the life of exaggerations as before, and have lost my faith in the possibility of any guide who can lead me thither where I would be.

But, leaving these victims of vanity, let us, with new hope, observe how nature, by worthier impulses, has insured the poet's fidelity to his office of announcement and affirming, namely by the beauty of things, which becomes a new and higher beauty when expressed. Nature offers all her creatures to him as a picture-language. Being used as a type, a second wonderful value appears in the object, far better than its old value; as the carpenter's stretched cord, if you hold your ear close enough, is musical in the breeze. "Things more excellent than every image," says Jamblichus, "are

---

4. As usual with Emerson: "makes real."

expressed through images."[5] Things admit of being used as symbols because nature is a symbol, in the whole, and in every part. Every line we can draw in the sand has expression; and there is no body without its spirit or genius. All form is an effect of character; all condition, of the quality of the life; all harmony, of health; and for this reason a perception of beauty should be sympathetic, or proper only to the good. The beautiful rests on the foundations of the necessary. The soul makes the body, as the wise Spenser teaches:—

> "So every spirit, as it is more pure,
> And hath in it the more of heavenly light,
> So it the fairer body doth procure
> To habit in, and it more fairly dight,
> With cheerful grace and amiable sight.
> For, of the soul, the body form doth take,
> For soul is form, and doth the body make."[6]

Here we find ourselves suddenly not in a critical speculation but in a holy place, and should go very warily and reverently. We stand before the secret of the world, there where Being passes into Appearance and Unity into Variety.

The Universe is the externization of the soul. Wherever the life is, that bursts into appearance around it. Our science is sensual,[7] and therefore superficial. The earth and the heavenly bodies, physics and chemistry, we sensually treat, as if they were self-existent; but these are the retinue of that Being we have. "The mighty heaven," said Proclus,[8] "exhibits, in its transfigurations, clear images of the splendor of intellectual perceptions; being moved in conjunction with the unapparent periods of intellectual natures." Therefore science always goes abreast with the just elevation of the man, keeping step with religion and metaphysics; or the state of science is an index of our self-knowledge. Since every thing in nature answers to a moral power, if any phenomenon remains brute and dark it is because the corresponding faculty in the observer is not yet active.

No wonder then, if these waters be so deep, that we hover over them with a religious regard. The beauty of the fable proves the importance of the sense; to the poet, and to all others; or, if you please, every man is so far a poet as to be susceptible of these enchantments of nature; for all men have the thoughts whereof the universe is the celebration. I find that the fascination resides in the

5. Greek philosopher (4th century A.D.), leading representative of Syrian Neo-Platonism. Cf. *Journals* (passage 20).
6. *An Hymne in Honour of Beautie* (1596).
7. Materialistic.
8. Neo-Platonist (5th century A.D.), a pupil of Plotinus.

symbol. Who loves nature? Who does not? Is it only poets, and men of leisure and cultivation, who live with her? No; but also hunters, farmers, grooms and butchers, though they express their affection in their choice of life and not in their choice of words. The writer wonders what the coachman or the hunter values in riding, in horses and dogs. It is not superficial qualities. When you talk with him he holds these at as slight a rate as you. His worship is sympathetic; he has no definitions, but he is commanded in nature by the living power which he feels to be there present. No imitation or playing of these things would content him; he loves the earnest of the north wind, of rain, of stone and wood and iron. A beauty not explicable is dearer than a beauty which we can see to the end of. It is nature the symbol, nature certifying the supernatural, body overflowed by life which he worships with coarse but sincere rites.

The inwardness and mystery of this attachment drive men of every class to the use of emblems. The schools of poets and philosophers are not more intoxicated with their symbols than the populace with theirs. In our political parties, compute the power of badges and emblems. See the great ball which they roll from Baltimore to Bunker Hill! In the political processions, Lowell goes in a loom, and Lynn in a shoe, and Salem in a ship. Witness the cider-barrel, the log-cabin, the hickory-stick, the palmetto, and all the cognizances of party. See the power of national emblems. Some stars, lilies, leopards, a crescent, a lion, an eagle, or other figure which came into credit God knows how, on an old rag of bunting, blowing in the wind on a fort at the ends of the earth, shall make the blood tingle under the rudest or the most conventional exterior. The people fancy they hate poetry, and they are all poets and mystics![9]

Beyond this universality of the symbolic language, we are apprised of the divineness of this superior use of things, whereby the world is a temple whose walls are covered with emblems, pictures and commandments of the Deity,—in this, that there is no fact in nature which does not carry the whole sense of nature; and the distinctions which we make in events and in affairs, of low and high, honest and base, disappear when nature is used as a symbol. Thought makes everything fit for use. The vocabulary of an omniscient man would embrace words and images excluded from polite conversation. What would be base, or even obscene, to the obscene, becomes illustrious, spoken in a new connection of thought. The piety of the Hebrew prophets purges their grossness. The circumcision is an example of the power of poetry to raise the

9. Most of this paragraph is from the other (unpublished) lecture on "The Poet" which Emerson delivered in 1841. The "great ball" was rolled by the Whigs in the campaign of 1840 to symbolize the gathering majority.

low and offensive. Small and mean things serve as well as great symbols. The meaner the type by which a law is expressed, the more pungent it is, and the more lasting in the memories of men; just as we choose the smallest box or case in which any needful utensil can be carried. Bare lists of words are found suggestive to an imaginative and excited mind, as it is related of Lord Chatham[1] that he was accustomed to read in Bailey's Dictionary when he was preparing to speak in Parliament. The poorest experience is rich enough for all the purposes of expressing thought. Why covet a knowledge of new facts? Day and night, house and garden, a few books, a few actions, serve us as well as would all trades and all spectacles. We are far from having exhausted the significance of the few symbols we use. We can come to use them yet with a terrible simplicity. It does not need that a poem should be long. Every word was once a poem. Every new relation is a new word. Also we use defects and deformities to a sacred purpose, so expressing our sense that the evils of the world are such only to the evil eye. In the old mythology, mythologists observe, defects are ascribed to divine natures, as lameness to Vulcan, blindness to Cupid, and the like,—to signify exuberances.[2]

For as it is dislocation and detachment from the life of God that makes things ugly, the poet, who re-attaches things to nature and the Whole,—re-attaching even artificial things and violation of nature, to nature, by a deeper insight,—disposes very easily of the most disagreeable facts. Readers of poetry see the factory-village and the railway, and fancy that the poetry of the landscape is broken up by these; for these works of art are not yet consecrated in their reading; but the poet sees them fall within the great Order not less than the beehive or the spider's geometrical web. Nature adopts them very fast into her vital circles, and the gliding train of cars she loves like her own. Besides, in a centered mind, it signifies nothing how many mechanical inventions you exhibit. Though you add millions, and never so surprising, the fact of mechanics has not gained a grain's weight. The spiritual fact remains unalterable, by many or by few particulars; as no mountain is of any appreciable height to break the curve of the sphere. A shrewd country-boy goes to the city for the first time, and the complacent citizen is not satisfied with his little wonder. It is not that he does not see all the fine houses and know that he never saw such before, but he disposes of them as easily as the poet finds place for the railway. The chief value of the new fact is to enhance the great and constant fact of Life, which can dwarf any and every circumstance, and to which the belt of wampum and the commerce of

1. William Pitt, Earl of Chatham, greatest 18th-century English orator.   2. Superabundance.

America are alike.

The world being thus put under the mind for verb and noun, the poet is he who can articulate it. For though life is great, and fascinates and absorbs; and though all men are intelligent of the symbols through which it is named; yet they cannot originally use them. We are symbols and inhabit symbols; workmen, work, and tools, words and things, birth and death, all are emblems; but we sympathize with the symbols, and being infatuated with the economical uses of things, we do not know that they are thoughts. The poet, by an ulterior intellectual perception, gives them a power which makes their old use forgotten, and puts eyes and a tongue into every dumb and inanimate object. He perceives the independence of the thought on the symbol, the stability of the thought, the accidency and fugacity of the symbol. As the eyes of Lyncaeus[3] were said to see through the earth, so the poet turns the world to glass, and shows us all things in their right series and procession. For through that better perception he stands one step nearer to things, and sees the flowing or metamorphosis; perceives that thought is multiform; that within the form of every creature is a force compelling it to ascend into a higher form;[4] and following with his eyes the life, uses the forms which express that life, and so his speech flows with the flowing of nature. All the facts of the animal economy, sex, nutriment, gestation, birth, growth, are symbols of the passage of the world into the soul of man, to suffer there a change and reappear a new and higher fact. He uses forms according to the life, and not according to the form. This is true science. The poet alone knows astronomy, chemistry, vegetation and animation, for he does not stop at these facts, but employs them as signs. He knows why the plain or meadow of space was strown with these flowers we call suns and moons and stars; why the great deep is adorned with animals, with men, and gods; for in every word he speaks he rides on them as the horses of thought.

By virtue of this science the poet is the Namer or Language-maker, naming things sometimes after their appearance, sometimes after their essence, and giving to every one its own name and not another's, thereby rejoicing the intellect, which delights in detachment or boundary. The poets made all the words, and therefore language is the archives of history, and, if we must say it, a sort of tomb of the muses. For though the origin of most of our words is forgotten, each word was at first a stroke of genius, and obtained currency because for the moment it symbolized the world to the first speaker and to the hearer. The etymologist finds the deadest word to have been once a brilliant picture. Language is fossil

3. The keenest-sighted of the Argonauts (the band of fifty heroes who, in Greek legend, accompanied Jason in his quest for the Golden Fleece).
4. Cf. the 1849 motto to *Nature*.

poetry. As the limestone of the continent consists of infinite masses of the shells of animalcules, so language is made up of images or tropes, which now, in their secondary use, have long ceased to remind us of their poetic origin. But the poet names the thing because he sees it, or comes one step nearer to it than any other. This expression or naming is not art, but a second nature, grown out of the first, as a leaf out of a tree. What we call nature is a certain self-regulated motion or change; and nature does all things by her own hands, and does not leave another to baptize her but baptizes herself; and this through the metamorphosis again. I remember that a certain poet described it to me thus:[5]—

Genius is the activity which repairs the decays of things, whether wholly or partly of a material and finite kind. Nature, through all her kingdoms, insures herself. Nobody cares for planting the poor fungus; so she shakes down from the gills of one agaric countless spores, any one of which, being preserved, transmits new billions of spores tomorrow or next day. The new agaric of this hour has a chance which the old one had not. This atom of seed is thrown into a new place, not subject to the accidents which destroyed its parent two rods off. She makes a man; and having brought him to ripe age, she will no longer run the risk of losing this wonder at a blow, but she detaches from him a new self, that the kind may be safe from accidents to which the individual is exposed. So when the soul of the poet has come to ripeness of thought, she detaches and sends away from it its poems or songs,—a fearless, sleepless, deathless progeny, which is not exposed to the accidents of the weary kingdom of time; a fearless, vivacious offspring, clad with wings (such was the virtue of the soul out of which they came) which carry them fast and far, and infix them irrecoverably into the hearts of men. These wings are the beauty of the poet's soul. The songs, thus flying immortal from their mortal parent, are pursued by clamorous flights of censures, which swarm in far greater numbers and threaten to devour them; but these last are not winged. At the end of a very short leap they fall plump down and rot, having received from the souls out of which they came no beautiful wings. But the melodies of the poet ascend and leap and pierce into the deeps of infinite time.

So far the bard taught me, using his freer speech. But nature has a higher end, in the production of new individuals, than security, namely *ascension*, or the passage of the soul into higher forms. I knew in my younger days the sculptor who made the statue of the youth which stands in the public garden. He was, as

5. Another Platonic reminiscence. The "certain poet" is Emerson's fiction.

I remember, unable to tell directly what made him happy or unhappy, but by wonderful indirections he could tell. He rose one
day, according to his habit, before the dawn, and saw the morning
break, grand as the eternity out of which it came, and for many
days after, he strove to express this tranquillity, and lo! his chisel
had fashioned out of marble the form of a beautiful youth, Phos-
phorus,[6] whose aspect is such that it is said all persons who look on
it become silent. The poet also resigns himself to his mood, and
that thought which agitated him is expressed, but *alter idem*,[7] in
a manner totally new. The expression is organic, or the new type
which things themselves take when liberated. As, in the sun, objects paint their images on the retina of the eye, so they, sharing
the aspiration of the whole universe, tend to paint a far more delicate copy of their essence in his mind. Like the metamorphosis
of things into higher organic forms is their change into melodies.
Over everything stands its daemon or soul, and, as the form of the
thing is reflected by the eye, so the soul of the thing is reflected
by a melody. The sea, the mountain-ridge, Niagara, and every
flower-bed, pre-exist, or super-exist, in pre-cantations, which sail
like odors in the air, and when any man goes by with an ear sufficiently fine, he overhears them and endeavors to write down the
notes without diluting or depraving them. And herein is the
legitimation of criticism, in the mind's faith that the poems are
a corrupt version of some text in nature with which they ought to
be made to tally. A rhyme in one of our sonnets should not be less
pleasing than the iterated nodes of a seashell, or the resembling
difference of a group of flowers. The pairing of the birds is an
idyl, not tedious as our idyls are; a tempest is a rough ode, without
falsehood or rant; a summer, with its harvest sown, reaped and
stored, is an epic song, subordinating how many admirably executed parts. Why should not the symmetry and truth that mod-
ulate these, glide into our spirits, and we participate the invention
of nature?

This insight, which expresses itself by what is called Imagination, is a very high sort of seeing, which does not come by study,
but by the intellect being where and what it sees; by sharing the
path or circuit of things through forms, and so making them trans-
lucid to others. The path of things is silent. Will they suffer a
speaker to go with them? A spy they will not suffer; a lover, a poet,
is the transcendency of their own nature,—him they will suffer.
The condition of true naming, on the poet's part, is his resigning
himself to the divine *aura*[8] which breathes through forms, and ac-

6. The morning star (Greek).
7. The same yet different.
8. In mesmeric "science," the impalpable substance supposed to emanate
from each living thing, constituting the
individual's essence. Cf. *Journals* (passage 25).

companying that.

It is a secret which every intellectual man quickly learns, that beyond the energy of his possessed and conscious intellect he is capable of a new energy (as of an intellect doubled on itself), by abandonment to the nature of things; that beside his privacy of power as an individual man, there is a great public power on which he can draw, by unlocking, at all risks, his human doors, and suffering the ethereal tides to roll and circulate through him; then he is caught up into the life of the Universe, his speech is thunder, his thought is law, and his words are universally intelligible as the plants and animals. The poet knows that he speaks adequately then only when he speaks somewhat wildly, or "with the flower of the mind"; not with the intellect used as an organ, but with the intellect released from all service and suffered to take its direction from its celestial life; or as the ancients were wont to express themselves, not with intellect alone but with the intellect inebriated by nectar. As the traveler who has lost his way throws his reins on his horse's neck and trusts to the instinct of the animal to find his road, so must we do with the divine animal who carries us through this world. For if in any manner we can stimulate this instinct, new passages are opened for us into nature; the mind flows into and through things hardest and highest, and the metamorphosis is possible.

This is the reason why bards love wine, mead, narcotics, coffee, tea, opium, the fumes of sandalwood and tobacco, or whatever other procurers of animal exhilaration. All men avail themselves of such means as they can, to add this extraordinary power to their normal powers; and to this end they prize conversation, music, pictures, sculpture, dancing, theaters, traveling, war, mobs, fires, gaming, politics, or love, or science, or animal intoxication,—which are several coarser or finer *quasi*-mechanical substitutes for the true nectar, which is the ravishment of the intellect by coming nearer to the fact. These are auxiliaries to the centrifugal tendency of a man, to his passage out into free space, and they help him to escape the custody of that body in which he is pent up, and of that jail-yard of individual relations in which he is enclosed. Hence a great number of such as were professionally expressers of Beauty, as painters, poets, musicians and actors, have been more than others wont to lead a life of pleasure and indulgence; all but the few who received the true nectar; and, as it was a spurious mode of attaining freedom, as it was an emancipation not into the heavens but into the freedom of baser places, they were punished for that advantage they won, by a dissipation and deterioration. But never can any advantage be taken of nature by a trick. The spirit of the world, the great calm presence of the Creator, comes not forth to the sorceries of opium or of wine. The sublime vision comes to the pure and simple soul in a clean and chaste body. That is not an inspiration, which we owe to narcotics, but some counterfeit excitement and fury. Milton says that the lyric poet may drink wine and live generously, but the epic poet, he who shall sing of the gods and their descent unto men, must drink water out of a wooden bowl.[9] For poetry is not "Devil's wine," but God's wine. It is with this as it is with toys. We fill the hands and nurseries of our children with all manner of dolls, drums and horses; withdrawing their eyes from the plain face and sufficing objects of nature, the sun and moon, the animals, the water and stones, which should be their toys. So the poet's habit of living should be set on a key so low that the common influences should delight him. His cheerfulness should be the gift of the sunlight; the air should suffice for his inspiration, and he should be tipsy with water. That spirit which suffices quiet hearts, which seems to come forth to such from every dry knoll of sere grass, from every pine stump and half-imbedded stone on which the dull March sun shines, comes forth to the poor and hungry, and such as are of simple taste. If thou fill thy brain with Boston and New York, with fashion and covetousness, and wilt stimulate thy jaded senses with wine and French coffee, thou shalt find no radiance of wisdom in the lonely waste of the pine woods.

If the imagination intoxicates the poet, it is not inactive in other men. The metamorphosis excites in the beholder an emotion of joy. The use of symbols has a certain power of emancipation and exhilaration for all men. We seem to be touched by a wand which makes us dance and run about happily, like children. We are like persons who come out of a cave or cellar into the open air. This is the effect on us of tropes, fables, oracles and all poetic forms. Poets are thus liberating gods. Men have really got a new sense, and found within their world another world, or nest of worlds; for, the metamorphosis once seen, we divine that it does not stop. I will not now consider how much this makes the charm of algebra and the mathematics, which also have their tropes, but it is felt in every definition; as when Aristotle defines *space* to be an immovable vessel in which things are contained;—or when Plato defines a *line* to be a flowing point; or *figure* to be a bound of solid; and many the like. What a joyful sense of freedom we have when Vitruvius announces the old opinion of artists that no architect can build any house well who does not know something of anatomy. When Socrates, in Charmides, tells us that the soul is cured of its maladies by certain incantations, and that these in-

9. In a Latin poem, *Elegia VI*. Emerson had cited this passage in a lecture of 1835.

cantations are beautiful reasons, from which temperance is generated in souls; when Plato calls the world an animal, and Timaeus affirms that the plants also are animals; or affirms a man to be a heavenly tree, growing with his root, which is his head, upward; and, as George Chapman, following him, writes,

> "So in our tree of man, whose nervie root
> Springs in his top;"—

when Orpheus speaks of hoariness as "that white flower which marks extreme old age"; when Proclus calls the universe the statue of the intellect; when Chaucer, in his praise of "Gentilesse," compares good blood in mean condition to fire, which, though carried to the darkest house betwixt this and the mount of Caucasus, will yet hold its natural office and burn as bright as if twenty thousand men did it behold; when John saw, in the Apocalypse, the ruin of the world through evil, and the stars fall from heaven as the fig tree casteth her untimely fruit; when Aesop reports the whole catalogue of common daily relations through the masquerade of birds and beasts;[1]—we take the cheerful hint of the immortality of our essence and its versatile habit and escapes, as when the gypsies say of themselves "it is in vain to hang them, they cannot die."

The poets are thus liberating gods. The ancient British bards had for the title of their order, "Those who are free throughout the world." They are free, and they make free. An imaginative book renders us much more service at first, by stimulating us through its tropes, than afterward when we arrive at the precise sense of the author. I think nothing is of any value in books excepting the transcendental and extraordinary. If a man is inflamed and carried away by his thought, to that degree that he forgets the authors and the public and heeds only this one dream which holds him like an insanity, let me read his paper, and you may have all the arguments and histories and criticism. All the value which attaches to Pythagoras, Paracelsus, Cornelius Agrippa, Cardan, Kepler, Swedenborg, Schelling, Oken,[2] or any other who introduces

1. This passage demonstrates the powerful memory that made Emerson one of the most skillful quoters in modern literature: Vitruvius, a Roman architect, was author of *De Architectura*; *Charmides* and *Timaeus* are both by Plato (the echo of *Timaeus* 90 by George Chapman, 16th-century poet, is from the Dedication to Chapman's Homer). Orpheus was a legendary Greek poet-prophet; Proclus a 5th-century Neo-Platonist. Chaucer's praise of "Gentilesse" is in the Wife of Bath's Tale (Emerson quoted it extensively in a lecture of 1835). For John see Revelation vi.13.

2. These are the names, respectively, of an ancient Greek mathematician and mystical teacher; two 16th-century alchemists; a 16th-century mathematician and astrologer; an early 17th-century astronomer; an 18th-century religious visionary; two late 18th-century German "transcendental" or *a priori* naturalists. The precision and range of this list testifies to the extent of Emerson's interest in the twilight zones of imaginative speculation. A "cosmogony" is an account of the origin of the universe.

questionable facts into his cosmogony, as angels, devils, magic, astrology, palmistry, mesmerism, and so on, is the certificate we have of departure from routine, and that here is a new witness. That also is the best success in conversation, the magic of liberty, which puts the world like a ball in our hands. How cheap even the liberty then seems; how mean to study, when an emotion communicates to the intellect the power to sap and upheave nature; how great the perspective! nations, times, systems, enter and disappear like threads in tapestry of large figure and many colors; dream delivers us to dream, and while the drunkenness lasts we will sell our bed, our philosophy, our religion, in our opulence.

There is good reason why we should prize this liberation. The fate of the poor shepherd, who, blinded and lost in the snow-storm, perishes in a drift within a few feet of his cottage door, is an emblem of the state of man. On the brink of the waters of life and truth, we are miserably dying. The inaccessibleness of every thought but that we are in, is wonderful. What if you come near to it; you are as remote when you are nearest as when you are farthest. Every thought is also a prison; every heaven is also a prison. Therefore we love the poet, the inventor, who in any form, whether in an ode or in an action or in looks and behavior, has yielded us a new thought. He unlocks our chains and admits us to a new scene.

This emancipation is dear to all men, and the power to impart it, as it must come from greater depth and scope of thought, is a measure of intellect. Therefore all books of the imagination endure, all which ascend to that truth that the writer sees nature beneath him, and uses it as his exponent.[3] Every verse or sentence possessing this virtue will take care of its own immortality. The religions of the world are the ejaculations[4] of a few imaginative men.

But the quality of the imagination is to flow, and not to freeze. The poet did not stop at the color or the form, but read their meaning; neither may he rest in this meaning, but he makes the same objects exponents of his new thought. Here is the difference betwixt the poet and the mystic, that the last nails a symbol to one sense, which was a true sense for a moment, but soon becomes old and false.[5] For all symbols are fluxional; all language is vehicular and transitive, and is good, as ferries and horses are, for conveyance, not as farms and houses are, for homestead. Mysticism consists in the mistake of an accidental and individual symbol for an universal one. The morning-redness happens to be the favorite meteor to

3. Means of expounding his thought.
4. Throwings out.

5. Emerson's chief criticism of Swedenborg.

the eyes of Jacob Behmen,[6] and comes to stand to him for truth and faith; and, he believes, should stand for the same realities to every reader. But the first reader prefers as naturally the symbol of a mother and child, or a gardener and his bulb, or a jeweler polishing a gem. Either of these, or of a myriad more, are equally good to the person to whom they are significant. Only they must be held lightly, and be very willingly translated into the equivalent terms which others use. And the mystic must be steadily told,—All that you say is just as true without the tedious use of that symbol as with it. Let us have a little algebra, instead of this trite rhetoric, —universal signs, instead of these village symbols,—and we shall both be gainers. The history of hierarchies seems to show that all religious error consisted in making the symbol too stark[7] and solid, and was at last nothing but an excess of the organ of language.

Swedenborg,[8] of all men in the recent ages, stands eminently for the translator of nature into thought. I do not know the man in history to whom things stood so uniformly for words. Before him the metamorphosis continually plays. Everything on which his eye rests, obeys the impulses of moral nature. The figs become grapes whilst he eats them. When some of his angels affirmed a truth, the laurel twig which they held blossomed in their hands. The noise which at a distance appeared like gnashing and thumping, on coming nearer was found to be the voice of disputants. The men in one of his visions, seen in heavenly light, appeared like dragons, and seemed in darkness; but to each other they appeared as men, and when the light from heaven shone into their cabin, they complained of the darkness, and were compelled to shut the window that they might see.

There was this perception in him which makes the poet or seer an object of awe and terror, namely that the same man or society of men may wear one aspect to themselves and their companions, and a different aspect to higher intelligences. Certain priests, whom he describes as conversing very learnedly together, appeared to the children who were at some distance, like dead horses; and many the like misappearances. And instantly the mind inquires whether these fishes under the bridge, yonder oxen in the pasture, those dogs in the yard, are immutably fishes, oxen and dogs, or only so appear to me, and perchance to themselves appear upright men; and whether I appear as a man to all eyes. The Brahmins and Pythagoras propounded the same question, and if any poet has witnessed the transformation he doubtless found it in harmony

6. 17th-century German mystic, who anticipated a number of Emerson's central ideas.
7. Strong. Cf. "Terminus," line 27.

8. Cf. Emerson's discussion of this 18th-century Swedish mystic in the concluding paragraphs of "The American Scholar."

with various experiences. We have all seen changes as considerable in wheat and caterpillars. He is the poet and shall draw us with love and terror, who sees through the flowing vest the firm nature, and can declare it.

I look in vain for the poet whom I describe. We do not with sufficient plainness or sufficient profoundness address ourselves to life, nor dare we chaunt our own times and social circumstance. If we filled the day with bravery, we should not shrink from celebrating it. Time and nature yield us many gifts, but not yet the timely man, the new religion, the reconciler, whom all things await. Dante's praise is that he dared to write his autobiography in colossal cipher, or into universality. We have had no genius in America, with tyrannous eye, which knew the value of our incomparable materials, and saw, in the barbarism and materialism of the times, another carnival of the same gods whose picture he so much admires in Homer; then in the Middle Age; then in Calvinism. Banks and tariffs, the newspaper and caucus, Methodism and Unitarianism, are flat and dull to dull people, but rest on the same foundations of wonder as the town of Troy and the temple of Delphi, and are as swiftly passing away. Our log-rolling, our stumps and their politics, our fisheries, our Negroes and Indians, our boats[9] and our repudiations, the wrath of rogues and the pusillanimity of honest men, the northern trade, the southern planting, the western clearing, Oregon and Texas, are yet unsung. Yet America is a poem in our eyes; its ample geography dazzles the imagination, and it will not wait long for meters. If I have not found that excellent combination of gifts in my countrymen which I seek, neither could I aid myself to fix the idea of the poet by reading now and then in Chalmers's collection of five centuries of English poets. These are wits[1] more than poets, though there have been poets among them. But when we adhere to the ideal of the poet, we have our difficulties even with Milton and Homer. Milton is too literary, and Homer too literal and historical.

But I am not wise enough for a national criticism, and must use the old largeness a little longer, to discharge my errand from the muse to the poet concerning his art.

Art is the path of the creator to his work. The paths or methods are ideal and eternal, though few men ever see them; not the artist himself for years, or for a lifetime, unless he come into the conditions. The painter, the sculptor, the composer, the epic rhapsodist, the orator, all partake one desire, namely to express themselves symmetrically and abundantly, not dwarfishly and fragmentarily.

---

9. Early editions have a comma here. If Emerson had written "boasts" (no comma), that might easily, in his hand-writing, have been misread "boats" (comma); it surely makes better sense.
1. Intellectuals.

They found or put themselves in certain conditions, as, the painter and sculptor before some impressive human figures; the orator into the assembly of the people; and the others in such scenes as each has found exciting to his intellect; and each presently feels the new desire. He hears a voice, he sees a beckoning. Then he is apprised, with wonder, what herds of daemons hem him in. He can no more rest; he says, with the old painter, "By God it is in me and must go forth of me." He pursues a beauty, half seen, which flies before him. The poet pours out verses in every solitude. Most of the things he says are conventional, no doubt; but by and by he says something which is original and beautiful. That charms him. He would say nothing else but such things. In our way of talking we say "That is yours, this is mine"; but the poet knows well that it is not his; that it is as strange and beautiful to him as to you; he would fain hear the like eloquence at length. Once having tasted this immortal ichor,[2] he cannot have enough of it, and as an admirable creative power exists in these intellections, it is of the last importance that these things get spoken. What a little of all we know is said! What drops of all the sea of our science are baled up! and by what accident it is that these are exposed, when so many secrets sleep in nature! Hence the necessity of speech and song; hence these throbs and heart-beatings in the orator, at the door of the assembly, to the end namely that thought may be ejaculated as Logos, or Word.

Doubt not, O poet, but persist. Say "It is in me, and shall out." Stand there, balked and dumb, stuttering and stammering, hissed and hooted, stand and strive, until at last rage draw out of thee that *dream*-power which every night shows thee is thine own; a power transcending all limit and privacy, and by virtue of which a man is the conductor of the whole river of electricity. Nothing walks, or creeps, or grows, or exists, which must not in turn arise and walk before him as exponent of his meaning. Comes he to that power, his genius is no longer exhaustible. All the creatures by pairs and by tribes pour into his mind as into a Noah's ark, to come forth again to people to a new world. This is like the stock of air for our respiration or for the combustion of our fireplace; not a measure of gallons, but the entire atmosphere if wanted. And therefore the rich poets, as Homer, Chaucer, Shakespeare, and Raphael, have obviously no limits to their works except the limits of their lifetime, and resemble a mirror carried through the street, ready to render an image of every created thing.

O poet! a new nobility is conferred in groves and pastures, and

2. Blood of the gods (Greek). Perhaps Emerson means nectar, the drink of the gods; or perhaps he is alluding to the Greek belief that the shades of the dead in the realm of Hades had to drink blood before they could speak.

not in castles or by the sword-blade any longer. The conditions are hard, but equal. Thou shalt leave the world, and know the muse only. Thou shalt not know any longer the times, customs, graces, politics, or opinions of men, but shall take all from the muse. For the time of towns is tolled from the world by funereal chimes, but in nature the universal hours are counted by succeeding tribes of animals and plants, and by growth of joy on joy. God wills also that thou abdicate a manifold and duplex life, and that thou be content that others speak for thee. Others shall be thy gentlemen and shall represent all courtesy and worldly life for thee; others shall do the great and resounding actions also. Thou shalt lie close hid with nature, and canst not be afforded to the Capitol or the Exchange. The world is full of renunciations and apprenticeships, and this is thine; thou must pass for a fool and a churl for a long season. This is the screen and sheath in which Pan has protected his well-beloved flower, and thou shalt be known only to thine own, and they shall console thee with tenderest love. And thou shalt not be able to rehearse the names of thy friends in thy verse, for an old shame before the holy ideal. And this is the reward; that the ideal shall be real to thee, and the impressions of the actual world shall fall like summer rain, copious, but not troublesome to thy invulnerable essence. Thou shalt have the whole land for thy park and manor, the sea for thy bath and navigation, without tax and without envy; the woods and the rivers thou shalt own, and thou shalt possess that wherein others are only tenants and boarders. Thou true land-lord! sea-lord! air-lord! Wherever snow falls or water flows or birds fly, wherever day and night meet in twilight, wherever the blue heaven is hung by clouds or sown with stars, wherever are forms with transparent boundaries, wherever are outlets into celestial space, wherever is danger, and awe, and love,—there is Beauty, plenteous as rain, shed for thee, and though thou shouldst walk the world over, thou shalt not be able to find a condition inopportune or ignoble.

1844

Illusions[3]

Flow, flow the waves hated,
Accursed, adored.
The waves of mutation;
No anchorage is.
Sleep is not, death is not;
Who seem to die live.
House you were born in,
Friends of your spring-time,
Old man and young maid,
Day's toil and its guerdon,
They are all vanishing,
Fleeing to fables,
Cannot be moored.
See the stars through them,
Through treacherous marbles.
Know the stars yonder,
The stars everlasting,
Are fugitive also,
And emulate, vaulted,
The lambent heat-lightning,
And fire-fly's flight.

When thou dost return
On the wave's circulation,
Beholding the shimmer,
The wild dissipation;
And, out of endeavor
To change and to flow,
The gas become solid,
And phantoms and nothings
Return to be things,
And endless imbroglio
Is law and the world,—
Then first shalt thou know,
That in the wild turmoil,
Horsed on the Proteus,
Thou ridest to power,
And to endurance.

Some years ago, in company with an agreeable party, I spent a long summer day in exploring the Mammoth Cave in Kentucky. We traversed, through spacious galleries affording a solid masonry foundation for the town and county overhead, the six or eight black miles from the mouth of the cavern to the innermost

3. At the end of his last major book of essays, *The Conduct of Life* (1860), Emerson returned to the central theme of "Experience," the problem of Illusion. Shorter and simpler, more austere and more assured, less troubled but less hopeful, the later essay has now reduced the baffling "lords of life" to two: illusion and "the essential identity." This shift in scale and spirit reflects above all the cumulative effect of his years of Oriental reading (cf. "Brahma"). "In the history of intellect," he jotted in a notebook, "no more important fact than the Hindoo theology, teaching that the beatitudes or Supreme Good is to be obtained through science; namely, by perception of the real and unreal, setting aside matter, and qualities and affections, or emotions and persons and actions as

Maias or illusions, and thus arriving at the contemplation of the one Eternal Life and Cause * * * [and so] to recover that unity which had been clouded and obscured by the magical illusions of reality." Of the majestic version of this recovery with which Emerson concluded his essay and his book Carlyle wrote him, "The finale of all, * * * —what a *Fiat Lux* [let there be light] is there, into the deeps of a philosophy, which the vulgar has not, which hardly three men living *have*, yet dreamt of!" The dark that is the shadow of this "light" emerges openly in a late *Journal* entry. "There may be two or three or four steps, according to the genius of each, but for every seeing soul there are two absorbing facts,—*I and the Abyss.*"

recess which tourists visit,—a niche or grotto made of one seam-
less stalactite, and called, I believe, Serena's Bower. I lost the light
of one day. I saw high domes and bottomless pits; heard the voice
of unseen waterfalls; paddled three quarters of a mile in the deep
Echo River, whose waters are peopled with the blind fish; crossed
the streams "Lethe" and "Styx;" plied with music and guns the
echoes in these alarming galleries; saw every form of stalagmite
and stalactite in the sculptured and fretted chambers;—icicle,
orange-flower, acanthus, grapes and snowball. We shot Bengal
lights[4] into the vaults and groins of the sparry cathedrals and examined all the masterpieces which the four combined engineers,
water, limestone, gravitation and time, could make in the dark.

The mysteries and scenery of the cave had the same dignity
that belongs to all natural objects, and which shames the fine things
to which we foppishly compare them. I remarked especially the
mimetic habit with which nature, on new instruments, hums her
old tunes, making night to mimic day, and chemistry to ape vegetation. But I then took notice and still chiefly remember that the
best thing which the cave had to offer was an illusion. On arriving
at what is called the "Star-Chamber," our lamps were taken from
us by the guide and extinguished or put aside, and, on looking upwards, I saw or seemed to see the night heaven thick with stars
glimmering more or less brightly over our heads, and even what
seemed a comet flaming among them. All the party were touched
with astonishment and pleasure. Our musical friends sung with
much feeling a pretty song, "The stars are in the quiet sky," etc.,
and I sat down on the rocky floor to enjoy the serene picture. Some
crystal specks in the black ceiling high overhead, reflecting the light
of a half-hid lamp, yielded this magnificent effect.

I own I did not like the cave so well for eking out its sublimities
with this theatrical trick. But I have had many experiences like it,
before and since; and we must be content to be pleased without too
curiously analyzing the occasions. Our conversation with nature is
not just what it seems. The cloud-rack, the sunrise and sunset glories,
rainbows and Northern Lights are not quite so spheral as our childhood thought them, and the part our organization plays in them is
too large. The senses interfere everywhere and mix their own structure with all they report of.[5] Once we fancied the earth a plane,
and stationary. In admiring the sunset we do not yet deduct the
rounding, coördinating, pictorial powers of the eye.

The same interference from our organization creates the most of
our pleasure and pain. Our first mistake is the belief that the circumstance gives the joy which we give to the circumstance. Life is

4. Colored lights or flares used for
signaling.

5. Cf. "Experience," p. 263.

an ecstasy. Life is sweet as nitrous oxide;[6] and the fisherman dipping all day over a cold pond, the switchman at the railway intersection, the farmer in the field, the negro in the rice-swamp, the fop in the street, the hunter in the woods, the barrister with the jury, the belle at the ball, all ascribe a certain pleasure to their employment, which they themselves give it. Health and appetite impart the sweetness to sugar, bread and meat. We fancy that our civilization has got on far, but we still come back to our primers.

We live by our imaginations, by our admirations, by our sentiments. The child walks amid heaps of illusions, which he does not like to have disturbed. The boy, how sweet to him is his fancy! how dear the story of barons and battles! What a hero he is, whilst he feeds on his heroes! What a debt is his to imaginative books! He has no better friend or influence than Scott, Shakspeare, Plutarch and Homer. The man lives to other objects, but who dare affirm that they are more real? Even the prose of the streets is full of refractions. In the life of the dreariest alderman, fancy enters into all details and colors them with rosy hue. He imitates the air and actions of people whom he admires, and is raised in his own eyes. He pays a debt quicker to a rich man than to a poor man. He wishes the bow and compliment of some leader in the state or in society; weighs what he says; perhaps he never comes nearer to him for that, but dies at last better contented for this amusement of his eyes and his fancy.

The world rolls, the din of life is never hushed. In London, in Paris, in Boston, in San Francisco, the carnival, the masquerade is at its height. Nobody drops his domino. The unities, the fictions of the piece it would be an impertinence to break. The chapter of fascinations is very long. Great is paint; nay, God is the painter; and we rightly accuse the critic who destroys too many illusions. Society does not love its unmaskers. It was wittily if somewhat bitterly said by D'Alembert, *"qu'un état de vapeur était un état très fâcheux, parcequ'il nous faisait voir les choses comme elles sont."*[7] I find men victims of illusion in all parts of life. Children, youths, adults and old men, all are led by one bawble or another. Yoganidra, the goddess of illusion, Proteus, or Mormus, or Gylfi's Mocking,[8]—for the Power has many names,—is stronger than the Titans, stronger than Apollo. Few have overheard the gods or sur

---

6. "Laughing gas," still occasionally used as an anesthetic.
7. "That a mist was very annoying because it showed us things as they really are"—i.e., as nothing. Jean Le Rond D'Alembert (1717–1783), scientist, writer, skeptic, wrote the Preliminary Discourse to the French *Encyclopaedia*.
8. Told in the *Younger Edda* of the Icelander Snorri Sturluson (1178–1241): Gylfi, a king, was received at Asgard, the home of the gods, with illusions and riddles. Yoganidra, or Maya, was the Hindu principle of variety or "illusion." Proteus, Greek sea god, was able to change his shape continually. Momus, the Greek god of laughter, was often represented holding a mask.

prised their secret. Life is a succession of lessons which must be lived to be understood. All is riddle, and the key to a riddle is another riddle.[9] There are as many pillows of illusion as flakes in a snow-storm. We wake from one dream into another dream. The toys to be sure are various, and are graduated in refinement to the quality of the dupe. The intellectual man requires a fine bait; the sots are easily amused. But everybody is drugged with his own frenzy, and the pageant marches at all hours, with music and banner and badge.

Amid the joyous troop who give in to the charivari, comes now and then a sad-eyed boy whose eyes lack the requisite refractions to clothe the show in due glory, and who is afflicted with a tendency to trace home the glittering miscellany of fruits and flowers to one root. Science is a search after identity, and the scientific whim is lurking in all corners. At the State Fair a friend of mine complained that all the varieties of fancy pears in our orchards seem to have been selected by somebody who had a whim for a particular kind of pear, and only cultivated such as had that perfume; they were all alike. And I remember the quarrel of another youth with the confectioners, that when he racked his wit to choose the best comfits in the shop, in all the endless varieties of sweetmeat he could find only three flavors, or two. What then? Pears and cakes are good for something; and because you unluckily have an eye or nose too keen, why need you spoil the comfort which the rest of us find in them? I knew a humorist who in a good deal of rattle had a grain or two of sense. He shocked the company by maintaining that the attributes of God were two,—power and risibility, and that it was the duty of every pious man to keep up the comedy. And I have known gentlemen of great stake in the community, but whose sympathies were cold,—presidents of colleges and governors and senators,—who held themselves bound to sign every temperance pledge, and act with Bible societies and missions and peace-makers, and cry *Hist-a-boy!* to every good dog. We must not carry comity[1] too far, but we all have kind impulses in this direction. When the boys come into my yard for leave to gather horse-chestnuts, I own I enter into nature's game, and affect to grant the permission reluctantly, fearing that any moment they will find out the imposture of that showy chaff.[2] But this tenderness is quite unnecessary; the enchantments are laid on very thick. Their young life is thatched with them. Bare and grim to tears is the lot of the children in the hovel I saw yesterday; yet not the less they hung it round with frippery romance, like the children of the happiest fortune, and talked of "the dear cottage where so many

9. Cf. "The Sphinx."
1. Civility.
2. The East Primary Schoolhouse of Concord was across the road from Emerson's house.

joyful hours had flown." Well, this thatching of hovels is the custom of the country. Women, more than all, are the element and kingdom of illusion. Being fascinated, they fascinate. They see through Claude-Lorraines.[3] And how dare any one, if he could, pluck away the *coulisses*,[4] stage effects and ceremonies, by which they live? Too pathetic, too pitiable, is the region of affection, and its atmosphere always liable to *mirage*.

We are not very much to blame for our bad marriages. We live amid hallucinations; and this especial trap is laid to trip up our feet with, and all are tripped up first or last. But the mighty Mother who had been so sly with us, as if she felt that she owed us some indemnity, insinuates into the Pandora-box[5] of marriage some deep and serious benefits and some great joys. We find a delight in the beauty and happiness of children that makes the heart too big for the body. In the worst-assorted connections there is ever some mixture of true marriage. Teague and his jade[6] get some just relations of mutual respect, kindly observation, and fostering of each other; learn something, and would carry themselves wiselier if they were now to begin.

'Tis fine for us to point at one or another fine madman, as if there were any exempts. The scholar in his library is none. I, who have all my life heard any number of orations and debates, read poems and miscellaneous books, conversed with many geniuses, am still the victim of any new page; and if Marmaduke, or Hugh, or Moosehead,[7] or any other, invent a new style or mythology, I fancy that the world will be all brave and right if dressed in these colors, which I had not thought of. Then at once I will daub with this new paint; but it will not stick. 'Tis like the cement which the peddler sells at the door; he makes broken crockery hold with it, but you can never buy of him a bit of the cement which will make it hold when he is gone.

Men who make themselves felt in the world avail themselves of a certain fate in their constitution which they know how to use. But they never deeply interest us unless they lift a corner of the curtain, or betray, never so slightly, their penetration of what is behind it. 'Tis the charm of practical men that outside of their

3. Claude Lorrain was an idealized-landscape painter of the 17th-century. The point appears to be that women are fascinated by the arts of illusion, and thus on the one hand think them important, while on the other hand they are quick to see through the illusions of another.
4. Wings (stage term).
5. Pandora (All-gifts), in Greek legend, was sent by the gods, as punishment for Prometheus's theft of fire, with a box full of all the plagues and evils of mankind. After they had been released, however, Hope remained trapped in the box. In another version Pandora herself, the original woman, was the evil.
6. I.e., the most illiterate and brutish couple (a "jade" is a wench). Emerson, in common with most Yankees of the day, held strong opinions of the Irish laborers then coming into New England.
7. Invented names. Moosehead is a lake in Maine.

practicality are a certain poetry and play, as if they led the good horse Power by the bridle, and preferred to walk, though they can ride so fiercely. Bonaparte is intellectual, as well as Cæsar; and the best soldiers, sea-captains and railway men have a gentleness when off duty, a good-natured admission that there are illusions, and who shall say that he is not their sport? We stigmatize the cast-iron fellows who cannot so detach themselves, as "dragon-ridden," "thun-der-stricken," and fools of fate, with whatever powers endowed.

Since our tuition is through emblems and indirections, it is well to know that there is method in it, a fixed scale and rank above rank in the phantasms. We begin low with coarse masks and rise to the most subtle and beautiful. The red men told Columbus "they had an herb which took away fatigue," but he found the illusion of "arriving from the east at the Indies" more composing to his lofty spirit than any tobacco. Is not our faith in the im-penetrability of matter more sedative than narcotics? You play with jackstraws, balls, bowls, horse and gun, estates and politics; but there are finer games before you. Is not time a pretty toy? Life will show you masks that are worth all your carnivals. Yonder moun-tain must migrate into your mind. The fine star-dust and nebulous blur in Orion, "the portentous year of Mizar and Alcor,"[8] must come down and be dealt with in your household thought. What if you shall come to discern that the play and playground of all this pompous history are radiations from yourself, and that the sun borrows his beams? What terrible questions we are learning to ask! The former men believed in magic, by which temples, cities and men were swallowed up, and all trace of them gone. We are coming on the secret of a magic which sweeps out of men's minds all vestige of theism and beliefs which they and their fathers held and were framed upon.

There are deceptions of the senses, deceptions of the passions, and the structural, beneficent illusions of sentiment and of the intellect. There is the illusion of love, which attributes to the be-loved person all which that person shares with his or her family, sex, age or condition, nay, with the human mind itself. 'Tis these which the lover loves, and Anna Matilda gets the credit of them. As if one shut up always in a tower, with one window through which the face of heaven and earth could be seen, should fancy that all the marvels he beheld belonged to that window. There is the illusion of time, which is very deep; who has disposed of it? —or come to the conviction that what seems the *succession* of thought is only the distribution of wholes into causal series? The intellect sees that every atom carries the whole of nature; that the

8. Stars. Emerson had read that Mizar revolved once around Alcor every 190,000 terrestrial years.

mind opens to omnipotence; that, in the endless striving and ascents, the metamorphosis is entire, so that the soul doth not know itself in its own act when that act is perfected. There is illusion that shall deceive even the elect. There is illusion that shall deceive even the performer of the miracle. Though he make his body, he denies that he makes it. Though the world exist from thought, thought is daunted in presence of the world. One after the other we accept the mental laws, still resisting those which follow, which however must be accepted. But all our concessions only compel us to new profusion. And what avails it that science has come to treat space and time as simply forms of thought, and the material world as hypothetical,⁹ and withal our pretension of *property* and even of self-hood are fading with the rest,¹ if, at last, even our thoughts are not finalities, but the incessant flowing and ascension reach these also, and each thought which yesterday was a finality, to-day is yielding to a larger generalization?

With such volatile elements to work in, 'tis no wonder if our estimates are loose and floating. We must work and affirm, but we have no guess of the value of what we say or do. The cloud is now as big as your hand, and now it covers a county. That story of Thor, who was set to drain the drinking-horn of Asgard and to wrestle with the old woman and to run with the runner Lok, and presently found that he had been drinking up the sea, and wrestling with Time, and racing with Thought,—describes us, who are contending, amid these seeming trifles, with the supreme energies of nature. We fancy we have fallen into bad company and squalid condition, low debts, shoe-bills, broken glass to pay for, pots to buy, butcher's meat, sugar, milk and coal. 'Set me some great task, ye gods! and I will show my spirit.' 'Not so,' says the good Heaven; 'plod and plough, vamp your old coats and hats, weave a shoe-string; great affairs and the best wine by and by.' Well, 'tis all phantasm; and if we weave a yard of tape in all humility and as well as we can, long hereafter we shall see it was no cotton tape at all but some galaxy which we braided, and that the threads were Time and Nature.

We cannot write the order of the variable winds. How can we penetrate the law of our shifting moods and susceptibility? Yet they differ as all and nothing. Instead of the firmament of yesterday, which our eyes require, it is to-day an egg-shell which coops us in; we cannot even see what or where our stars of destiny are. From day to day the capital facts of human life are hidden from our eyes. Suddenly the mist rolls up and reveals them, and we think how much good time is gone that might have been saved had any hint

9. Cf. "Self-Reliance," p. 248, and   1. Cf. "Hamatreya."
"Nature," p. 208.

of these things been shown. A sudden rise in the road shows us the system of mountains, and all the summits, which have been just as near us all the year, but quite out of mind. But these alternations are not without their order, and we are parties to our various fortune. If life seem a succession of dreams, yet poetic justice is done in dreams also. The visions of good men are good; it is the undisciplined will that is whipped with bad thoughts and bad fortunes. When we break the laws, we lose our hold on the central reality. Like sick men in hospitals, we change only from bed to bed, from one folly to another; and it cannot signify much what becomes of such castaways, wailing, stupid, comatose creatures, lifted from bed to bed, from the nothing of life to the nothing of death.

In this kingdom of illusions we grope eagerly for stays and foundations. There is none but a strict and faithful dealing at home and a severe barring out of all duplicity or illusion there. Whatever games are played with us, we must play no games with ourselves, but deal in our privacy with the last honesty and truth. I look upon the simple and childish virtues of veracity and honesty as the root of all that is sublime in character. Speak as you think, be what you are, pay your debts of all kinds. I prefer to be owned as sound and solvent, and my word as good as my bond, and to be what cannot be skipped, or dissipated, or undermined, to all the *éclat* in the universe. This reality is the foundation of friendship, religion, poetry and art. At the top or at the bottom of all illusions, I set the cheat which still leads us to work and live for appearances; in spite of our conviction, in all sane hours, that it is what we really are that avails with friends, with strangers, and with fate or fortune.

One would think from the talk of men that riches and poverty were a great matter; and our civilization mainly respects it. But the Indians say that they do not think the white man, with his brow of care, always toiling, afraid of heat and cold, and keeping within doors, has any advantage of them. The permanent interest of every man is never to be in a false position, but to have the weight of nature to back him in all that he does. Riches and poverty are a thick or thin costume; and our life—the life of all of us—identical. For we transcend the circumstance continually and taste the real quality of existence; as in our employments, which only differ in the manifestations but express the same laws; or in our thoughts, which wear no silks and taste no ice-creams. We see God face to face every hour, and know the savor of nature.

The early Greek philosophers Heraclitus and Xenophanes measured their force on this problem of identity.[2] Diogenes of Apollonia

2. Heraclitus held that all bodies were transformations of fire. Xenophanes, pre-Socratic Greek philosopher, taught the unity of existence.

said that unless the atoms were made of one stuff, they could never blend and act with one another. But the Hindoos, in their sacred writings, express the liveliest feeling, both of the essential identity and of that illusion which they conceive variety to be. "The notions, 'I am,' and 'This is mine,' which influence mankind, are but delusions of the mother of the world. Dispel, O Lord of all creatures! the conceit of knowledge which proceeds from ignorance." And the beatitude of man they hold to lie in being freed from fascination.

The intellect is stimulated by the statement of truth in a trope, and the will by clothing the laws of life in illusions. But the unities of Truth and of Right are not broken by the disguise. There need never be any confusion in these. In a crowded life of many parts and performers, on a stage of nations, or in the obscurest hamlet in Maine or California, the same elements offer the same choices to each new comer, and, according to his election, he fixes his fortune in absolute Nature. It would be hard to put more mental and moral philosophy than the Persians have thrown into a sentence,—

> "Fooled thou must be, though wisest of the wise:
> Then be the fool of virtue, not of vice."

There is no chance and no anarchy in the universe. All is system and gradation. Every god is there sitting in his sphere. The young mortal enters the hall of the firmament; there is he alone with them alone, they pouring on him benedictions and gifts, and beckoning him up to their thrones. On the instant, and incessantly, fall snow-storms of illusions. He fancies himself in a vast crowd which sways this way and that and whose movement and doings he must obey: he fancies himself poor, orphaned, insignificant. The mad crowd drives hither and thither, now furiously commanding this thing to be done, now that. What is he that he should resist their will, and think or act for himself? Every moment new changes and new showers of deceptions to baffle and distract him. And when, by and by, for an instant, the air clears and the cloud lifts a little, there are the gods still sitting around him on their thrones,—they alone with him alone.

1860

Thoreau[3]

Henry David Thoreau was the last male descendant of a French ancestor who came to this country from the Isle of Guernsey.

3. This portrait is Emerson's revision of the obituary address he read at Thoreau's funeral, May 9, 1862. Having discovered Henry Thoreau, encouraged him, befriended him, employed him, housed him, printed him, recom-

His character exhibited occasional traits drawn from this blood, in singular combination with a very strong Saxon genius.

He was born in Concord, Massachusetts, on the 12th of July, 1817. He was graduated at Harvard College in 1837, but without any literary distinction. An iconoclast in literature, he seldom thanked colleges for their service to him, holding them in small esteem, whilst yet his debt to them was important. After leaving the University, he joined his brother in teaching a private school, which he soon renounced. His father was a manufacturer of lead-pencils, and Henry applied himself for a time to this craft, believing he could make a better pencil than was then in use. After completing his experiments, he exhibited his work to chemists and artists in Boston, and having obtained their certificates to its excellence and to its equality with the best London manufacture, he returned home contented. His friends congratulated him that he had now opened his way to fortune. But he replied that he should never make another pencil. "Why should I? I would not do again what I have done once." He resumed his endless walks and miscellaneous studies, making every day some new acquaintance with Nature, though as yet never speaking of zoölogy or botany, since, though very studious of natural facts, he was incurious of technical and textual science.

At this time, a strong, healthy youth, fresh from college, whilst all his companions were choosing their profession, or eager to begin some lucrative employment, it was inevitable that his thoughts should be exercised on the same question, and it required rare decision to refuse all the accustomed paths and keep his solitary freedom at the cost of disappointing the natural expectations of his family and friends: all the more difficult that he had a perfect probity, was exact in securing his own independence, and in holding every man to the like duty. But Thoreau never faltered. He was a born protestant.[4] He declined to give up his large ambition of knowledge and action for any narrow craft or profession, aiming at a much more comprehensive calling, the art of living well. If he slighted and defied the opinions of others, it was only that he was more intent to reconcile his practice with his own belief. Never idle or self-indulgent, he preferred, when

mended him, and endured him (cf. *Journals*, passages 68–73), no doubt Emerson assumed that he was fitted to memorialize him. The assumption has been questioned. Emerson's essay clearly underrates Thoreau's achievement as a writer and probably overstates his aloofness and Stoicism. A reason for this, as Edmund Berry shows in his *Emerson's Plutarch*, is that Emerson is not writing a merely factual memoir but a "Life" on the model of the *Lives* of Plutarch, who also used biographical fact to support and illustrate a firmly conceived type of character. As a "character" in this classical sense the piece is a skillful and worthy performance. Like a good portrait, it is a recognizable likeness, and reveals much of Thoreau's essential quality, especially his "heroic" aspect.

4. In its original meaning, of course: "one who protests."

he wanted money, earning it by some piece of manual labor agreeable to him, as building a boat or a fence, planting, grafting, surveying or other short work, to any long engagements. With his hardy habits and few wants, his skill in wood-craft, and his powerful arithmetic, he was very competent to live in any part of the world. It would cost him less time to supply his wants than another. He was therefore secure of his leisure.

A natural skill for mensuration, growing out of his mathematical knowledge and his habit of ascertaining the measures and distances of objects which interested him, the size of trees, the depth and extent of ponds and rivers, the height of mountains and the air-line distance of his favorite summits,—this, and his intimate knowledge of the territory about Concord, made him drift into the profession of land-surveyor. It had the advantage for him that it led him continually into new and secluded grounds, and helped his studies of Nature. His accuracy and skill in this work were readily appreciated, and he found all the employment he wanted.

He could easily solve the problems of the surveyor, but he was daily beset with graver questions, which he manfully confronted. He interrogated every custom, and wished to settle all his practice on an ideal foundation. He was a protestant *à outrance*,[5] and few lives contain so many renunciations. He was bred to no profession; he never married; he lived alone; he never went to church; he never voted; he refused to pay a tax to the State; he ate no flesh, he drank no wine, he never knew the use of tobacco; and, though a naturalist, he used neither trap nor gun. He chose, wisely no doubt for himself, to be the bachelor of thought and Nature. He had no talent for wealth, and knew how to be poor without the least hint of squalor or inelegance. Perhaps he fell into his way of living without forecasting it much, but approved it with later wisdom. "I am often reminded," he wrote in his journal, "that if I had bestowed on me the wealth of Croesus, my aims must be still the same, and my means essentially the same." He had no temptations to fight against—no appetites, no passions, no taste for elegant trifles. A fine house, dress, the manners and talk of highly cultivated people were all thrown away on him. He much preferred a good Indian, and considered these refinements as impediments to conversation, wishing to meet his companion on the simplest terms. He declined invitations to dinner-parties, because there each was in every one's way, and he could not meet the individuals to any purpose. "They make their pride," he said, "in making their dinner cost much; I make my pride in making my dinner cost little." When asked at table what dish he preferred, he answered, "The nearest." He did not like the taste of wine, and

5. To the limit.

never had a vice in his life. He said,—"I have a faint recollection of pleasure derived from smoking dried lily-stems, before I was a man. I had commonly a supply of these. I have never smoked anything more noxious."

He chose to be rich by making his wants few, and supplying them himself. In his travels, he used the railroad only to get over so much country as was unimportant to the present purpose, walking hundreds of miles, avoiding taverns, buying a lodging in farmers' and fishermen's houses, as cheaper, and more agreeable to him, and because there he could better find the men and the information he wanted.

There was somewhat military in his nature, not to be subdued, always manly and able, but rarely tender, as if he did not feel himself except in opposition. He wanted a fallacy to expose, a blunder to pillory, I may say required a little sense of victory, a roll of the drum, to call his powers into full exercise. It cost him nothing to say No; indeed he found it much easier than to say Yes. It seemed as if his first instinct on hearing a proposition was to controvert it, so impatient was he of the limitations of our daily thought. This habit, of course, is a little chilling to the social affections; and though the companion would in the end acquit him of any malice or untruth, yet it mars conversation. Hence, no equal companion stood in affectionate relations with one so pure and guileless. "I love Henry," said one of his friends,[6] "but I cannot like him; and as for taking his arm, I should as soon think of taking the arm of an elm-tree."

Yet, hermit and stoic as he was, he was really fond of sympathy, and threw himself heartily and childlike into the company of young people whom he loved, and whom he delighted to entertain, as he only could, with the varied and endless anecdotes of his experiences by field and river: and he was always ready to lead a huckleberry-party or a search for chestnuts or grapes. Talking, one day, of a public discourse, Henry remarked that whatever succeeded with the audience was bad. I said, "Who would not like to write something which all can read, like Robinson Crusoe? and who does not see with regret that his page is not solid with a right materialistic treatment, which delights everybody?" Henry objected, of course, and vaunted the better lectures which reached only a few persons. But, at supper, a young girl, understanding that he was to lecture at the Lyceum, sharply asked him, "Whether his lecture would be a nice, interesting story, such as she wished to hear, or whether it was one of those old philosophical things that she did not care about." Henry turned to her, and bethought himself, and, I saw, was trying to believe that he had matter that

6. Emerson himself.

might fit her and her brother, who were to sit up and go to the lecture, if it was a good one for them.

He was a speaker and actor of the truth, born such, and was ever running into dramatic situations from this cause. In any circumstance it interested all bystanders to know what part Henry would take, and what he would say; and he did not disappoint expectation, but used an original judgment on each emergency. In 1845 he built himself a small framed house on the shores of Walden Pond, and lived there two years alone, a life of labor and study. This action was quite native and fit for him. No one who knew him would tax him with affectation. He was more unlike his neighbors in his thought than in his action. As soon as he had exhausted the advantages of that solitude, he abandoned it. In 1847,[7] not approving some uses to which the public expenditure was applied, he refused to pay his town tax, and was put in jail. A friend paid the tax for him, and he was released. The like annoyance was threatened the next year. But as his friends paid the tax, notwithstanding his protest, I believe he ceased to resist. No opposition or ridicule had any weight with him. He coldly and fully stated his opinion without affecting to believe that it was the opinion of the company. It was of no consequence if every one present held the opposite opinion. On one occasion he went to the University Library to procure some books. The librarian refused to lend them. Mr. Thoreau repaired to the President, who stated to him the rules and usages, which permitted the loan of books to resident graduates, to clergymen who were alumni, and to some others resident within a circle of ten miles' radius from the College. Mr. Thoreau explained to the President that the railroad had destroyed the old scale of distances,—that the library was useless, yes, and President and College useless, on the terms of his rules,—that the one benefit he owed to the College was its library,—that, at this moment, not only his want of books was imperative, but he wanted a large number of books, and assured him that he, Thoreau, and not the librarian, was the proper custodian of these. In short, the President found the petitioner so formidable, and the rules getting to look so ridiculous, that he ended by giving him a privilege which in his hands proved unlimited thereafter.

No truer American existed than Thoreau. His preference of his country and condition was genuine, and his aversation from English and European manners and tastes almost reached contempt. He listened impatiently to news or *bonmots* gleaned from London circles; and though he tried to be civil, these anecdotes fatigued him. The men were all imitating each other, and on a small mold. Why can they not live as far apart as possible, and each be

7. Actually 1846. Cf. *Journals* (passage 41).

a man by himself? What he sought was the most energetic nature; and he wished to go to Oregon, not to London. "In every part of Great Britain," he wrote in his diary, "are discovered traces of the Romans, their funeral urns, their camps, their roads, their dwellings. But New England, at least, is not based on any Roman ruins. We have not to lay the foundations of our houses on the ashes of a former civilization."

But idealist as he was, standing for abolition of slavery, abolition of tariffs, almost for abolition of government, it is needless to say he found himself not only unrepresented in actual politics, but almost equally opposed to every class of reformers. Yet he paid the tribute of his uniform respect to the Anti-Slavery party. One man, whose personal acquaintance he had formed, he honored with exceptional regard. Before the first friendly word had been spoken for Captain John Brown, he sent notices to most houses in Concord that he would speak in a public hall on the condition and character of John Brown, on Sunday evening, and invited all people to come. The Republican Committee, the Abolitionist Committee, sent him word that it was premature and not advisable. He replied,—"I did not send to you for advice, but to announce that I am to speak." The hall was filled at an early hour by people of all parties, and his earnest eulogy of the hero was heard by all respectfully, by many with a sympathy that surprised themselves.

It was said of Plotinus[8] that he was ashamed of his body, and 'tis very likely he had good reason for it,—that his body was a bad servant, and he had not skill in dealing with the material world, as happens often to men of abstract intellect. But Mr. Thoreau was equipped with a most adapted and serviceable body. He was of short stature, firmly built, of light complexion, with strong, serious blue eyes, and a grave aspect,—his face covered in the late years with a becoming beard. His senses were acute, his frame well-knit and hardy, his hands strong and skilful in the use of tools. And there was a wonderful fitness of body and mind. He could pace sixteen rods more accurately than another man could measure them with rod and chain. He could find his path in the woods at night, he said, better by his feet than his eyes. He could estimate the measure of a tree very well by his eyes; he could estimate the weight of a calf or a pig, like a dealer. From a box containing a bushel or more of loose pencils, he could take up with his hands fast enough just a dozen pencils at every grasp. He was a good swimmer, runner, skater, boatman, and would probably outwalk most countrymen in a day's journey. And the relation of body to mind was still finer than we have indicated. He said he wanted every stride his legs made. The length of his walk uniformly made

8. Greek mystic, founder of Neo-Platonism.

the length of his writing. If shut up in the house he did not write at all.

He had a strong common sense, like that which Rose Flammock, the weaver's daughter in Scott's romance,[9] commends in her father, as resembling a yardstick, which, whilst it measures dowlas and diaper, can equally well measure tapestry and cloth of gold. He had always a new resource. When I was planting forest trees, and had procured half a peck of acorns, he said that only a small portion of them would be sound, and proceeded to examine them and select the sound ones. But finding this took time, he said, "I think if you put them all into water the good ones will sink"; which experiment we tried with success. He could plan a garden or a house or a barn; would have been competent to lead a "Pacific Exploring Expedition"; could give judicious counsel in the gravest private or public affairs.

He lived for the day, not cumbered and mortified by his memory. If he brought you yesterday a new proposition, he would bring you today another not less revolutionary. A very industrious man, and setting, like all highly organized men, a high value on his time, he seemed the only man of leisure in town, always ready for any excursion that promised well, or for conversation prolonged into late hours. His trenchant sense was never stopped by his rules of daily prudence, but was always up to the new occasion. He liked and used the simplest food, yet, when some one urged a vegetable diet, Thoreau thought all diets a very small matter, saying that "the man who shoots the buffalo lives better than the man who boards at the Graham House."[1] He said,—"You can sleep near the railroad, and never be disturbed: Nature knows very well what sounds are worth attending to, and has made up her mind not to hear the railroad-whistle. But things respect the devout mind, and a mental ecstasy was never interrupted." He noted what repeatedly befell him, that, after receiving from a distance a rare plant, he would presently find the same in his own haunts. And those pieces of luck which happen only to good players happened to him. One day, walking with a stranger, who inquired where Indian arrow-heads could be found, he replied, "Everywhere," and, stooping forward, picked one on the instant from the ground. At Mount Washington, in Tuckerman's Ravine, Thoreau had a bad fall, and sprained his foot. As he was in the act of getting up from his fall, he saw for the first time the leaves of the *Arnica mollis*.[2]

His robust common sense, armed with stout hands, keen perceptions and strong will, cannot yet account for the superiority

9. *The Betrothed* (1825).
1. Boardinghouse run on the severe principles of Sylvester Graham, dietary reformer.
2. Plant medicinal for sprains.

which shone in his simple and hidden life. I must add the cardinal fact, that there was an excellent wisdom in him, proper to a rare class of men, which showed him the material world as a means and symbol. This discovery, which sometimes yields to poets a certain casual and interrupted light, serving for the ornament of their writing, was in him an unsleeping insight; and whatever faults or obstructions of temperament might cloud it, he was not disobedient to the heavenly vision. In his youth, he said, one day, "The other world is all my art; my pencils will draw no other; my jack-knife will cut nothing else; I do not use it as a means." This was the muse and genius that ruled his opinions, conversation, studies, work and course of life. This made him a searching judge of men. At first glance he measured his companion, and, though insensible to some fine traits of culture, could very well report his weight and calibre. And this made the impression of genius which his conversation sometimes gave.

He understood the matter in hand at a glance, and saw the limitations and poverty of those he talked with, so that nothing seemed concealed from such terrible eyes. I have repeatedly known young men of sensibility converted in a moment to the belief that this was the man they were in search of, the man of men, who could tell them all they should do. His own dealing with them was never affectionate, but superior, didactic, scorning their petty ways, —very slowly conceding, or not conceding at all, the promise of his society at their houses, or even at his own. "Would he not walk with them?" "He did not know. There was nothing so important to him as his walk; he had no walks to throw away on company." Visits were offered him from respectful parties, but he declined them. Admiring friends offered to carry him at their own cost to the Yellowstone River,—to the West Indies,—to South America. But though nothing could be more grave or considered than his refusals, they remind one, in quite new relations, of that fop Brummel's reply to the gentleman who offered him his carriage in a shower, "But where will *you* ride, then?"—and what accusing silences, and what searching and irresistible speeches, battering down all defenses, his companions can remember!

Mr. Thoreau dedicated his genius with such entire love to the fields, hills and waters of his native town, that he made them known and interesting to all reading Americans, and to people over the sea. The river on whose banks he was born and died he knew from its springs to its confluence with the Merrimack. He had made summer and winter observations on it for many years, and at every hour of the day and night. The result of the recent survey of the Water Commissioners appointed by the State of Massachusetts he had reached by his private experiments, several years earlier. Every fact which occurs in the bed, on the banks or in the air over it; the fishes, and their spawning and nests, their manners, their food; the shad-flies which fill the air on a certain evening once a year, and which are snapped at by the fishes so ravenously that many of these die of repletion; the conical heaps of small stones on the river-shallows, the huge nests of small fishes, one of which will sometimes overfill a cart; the birds which frequent the stream, heron, duck, sheldrake, loon, osprey; the snake, muskrat, otter, wood-chuck and fox, on the banks; the turtle, frog, hyla and cricket, which make the banks vocal—were all known to him, and, as it were, townsmen and fellow creatures; so that he felt an absurdity or violence in any narrative of one of these by itself apart, and still more of its dimensions on an inch-rule, or in the exhibition of its skeleton, or the specimen of a squirrel or a bird in brandy. He liked to speak of the manners of the river, as itself a lawful creature, yet with exactness, and always to an observed fact. As he knew the river, so the ponds in this region.

One of the weapons he used, more important to him than micro-scope or alcohol-receiver to other investigators, was a whim which grew on him by indulgence, yet appeared in gravest statement, namely, of extolling his own town and neighborhood as the most favored center for natural observation. He remarked that the Flora of Massachusetts embraced almost all the important plants in America,—most of the oaks, most of the willows, the best pines, the ash, the maple, the beech, the nuts. He returned Kane's Arctic Voyage to a friend of whom he had borrowed it, with the remark, that "Most of the phenomena noted might be observed in Concord." He seemed a little envious of the Pole, for the coincident sunrise and sunset, or five minutes' day after six months: a splendid fact, which Annursnuc[3] had never afforded him. He found red snow in one of his walks, and told me that he expected to find yet the *Victoria regia*[4] in Concord. He was the attorney of the indigenous plants, and owned to a preference of the weeds to the imported plants, as of the Indian to the civilized man, and noticed, with pleasure, that the willow bean-poles of his neighbor had grown more than his beans. "See these weeds," he said, "which have been hoed at by a million farmers all spring and summer, and yet have prevailed, and just now come out triumphant over all lanes, pas-tures, fields and gardens, such is their vigor. We have insulted them with low names, too,—as Pigweed, Wormwood, Chickweed, Shad-blossom." He says, "They have brave names, too,—Am-brosia, Stellaria, Amelanchier, Amaranth, etc."

I think his fancy for referring everything to the meridian of

3. Annursnack, a local hill.
4. South American water lily, or "water platter"; the first to blossom in cultiva-

tion in Northern latitudes was pre-sented in 1849 to Queen Victoria, after whom it was named.

Concord did not grow out of any ignorance or depreciation of other longitudes or latitudes, but was rather a playful expression of his conviction of the indifferency of all places, and that the best place for each is where he stands. He expressed it once in this wise: "I think nothing is to be hoped from you, if this bit of mold under your feet is not sweeter to you to eat than any other in this world, or in any world."

The other weapon with which he conquered all obstacles in science was patience. He knew how to sit immovable, a part of the rock he rested on, until the bird, the reptile, the fish, which had retired from him, should come back and resume its habits, nay, moved by curiosity, should come to him and watch him.

It was a pleasure and a privilege to walk with him. He knew the country like a fox or a bird, and passed through it as freely by paths of his own. He knew every track in the snow or on the ground, and what creature had taken this path before him. One must submit abjectly to such a guide, and the reward was great. Under his arm he carried an old music-book to press plants; in his pocket, his diary and pencil, a spy-glass for birds, microscope, jack-knife and twine. He wore a straw hat, stout shoes, strong gray trousers, to brave scrub-oaks and smilax, and to climb a tree for a hawk's or a squirrel's nest. He waded into the pool for the water-plants, and his strong legs were no insignificant part of his armor. On the day I speak of he looked for the Menyanthes,[5] detected it across the wide pool, and, on examination of the florets, decided that it had been in flower five days. He drew out of his breast-pocket his diary, and read the names of all the plants that should bloom on this day, whereof he kept account as a banker when his notes fall due. The Cypripedium[6] not due till tomorrow. He thought that, if waked up from a trance, in this swamp, he could tell by the plants what time of the year it was within two days. The redstart was flying about, and presently the fine grosbeaks, whose brilliant scarlet "makes the rash gazer wipe his eye," [7] and whose fine clear note Thoreau compared to that of a tanager which has got rid of its hoarseness. Presently he heard a note which he called that of the night-warbler, a bird he had never identified, had been in search of twelve years, which always, when he saw it, was in the act of diving down into a tree or bush, and which it was vain to seek; the only bird which sings indifferently by night and by day. I told him he must beware of finding and booking it, lest life should have nothing more to show him. He said, "What you seek in vain for, half your life, one day you come full upon, all the family at dinner. You seek it like a dream, and as soon as you find it

5. Bogbean.
6. Lady's-slipper.

7. George Herbert, "Virtue" (1633).

you become its prey."

His interest in the flower or the bird lay very deep in his mind, was connected with Nature,—and the meaning of Nature was never attempted to be defined by him. He would not offer a memoir of his observations to the Natural History Society. "Why should I? To detach the description from its connections in my mind would make it no longer true or valuable to me: and they do not wish what belongs to it." His power of observation seemed to indicate additional senses. He saw as with microscope, heard as with ear-trumpet, and his memory was a photographic register of all he saw and heard. And yet none knew better than he that it is not the fact that imports, but the impression or effect of the fact on your mind. Every fact lay in glory in his mind, a type of the order and beauty of the whole.

His determination on[8] Natural History was organic. He confessed that he sometimes felt like a hound or a panther, and, if borne among Indians, would have been a fell hunter. But, restrained by his Massachusetts culture, he played out the game in his mild form of botany and ichthyology. His intimacy with animals suggested what Thomas Fuller records of Butler the apiologist, that "either he had told the bees things or the bees had told him." Snakes coiled round his legs; the fishes swam into his hand, and he took them out of the water; he pulled the woodchuck out of its hole by the tail, and took the foxes under his protection from the hunters. Our naturalist had perfect magnanimity; he had no secrets: he would carry you to the heron's haunt, or even to his most prized botanical swamp,—possibly knowing that you could never find it again, yet willing to take his risks.

No college ever offered him a diploma, or a professor's chair; no academy made him its corresponding secretary, its discoverer or even its member. Perhaps these learned bodies feared the satire of his presence. Yet so much knowledge of Nature's secret and genius few others possessed; none in a more large and religious synthesis. For not a particle of respect had he to the opinions of any man or body of men, but homage solely to the truth itself; and as he discovered everywhere among doctors[9] some learning of courtesy, it discredited them. He grew to be revered and admired by his townsmen, who had at first known him only as an oddity. The farmers who employed him as a surveyor soon discovered his rare accuracy and skill, his knowledge of their lands, of trees, of birds, of Indian remains and the like, which enabled him to tell every farmer more than he knew before of his own farm; so that he began to feel a little as if Mr. Thoreau had better rights in his land than he. They felt, too, the superiority of character which

---

8. Inclination toward.   9. Learned men.

addressed all men with a native authority.

Indian relics abound in Concord,—arrow-heads, stone chisels, pestles and fragments of pottery; and on the river-bank, large heaps of clam-shells and ashes mark spots which the savages frequented. These, and every circumstance touching the Indian, were important in his eyes. His visits to Maine were chiefly for love of the Indian. He had the satisfaction of seeing the manufacture of the bark canoe, as well as of trying his hand in its management on the rapids. He was inquisitive about the making of the stone arrow-head, and in his last days charged a youth setting out for the Rocky Mountains to find an Indian who could tell him that: "It was well worth a visit to California to learn it." Occasionally, a small party of Penobscot Indians would visit Concord, and pitch their tents for a few weeks in summer on the river-bank. He failed not to make acquaintance with the best of them; though he well knew that asking questions of Indians is like catechizing beavers and rabbits. In his last visit to Maine he had great satisfaction from Joseph Polis, an intelligent Indian of Oldtown, who was his guide for some weeks.

He was equally interested in every natural fact. The depth of his perception found likeness of law throughout Nature, and I know not any genius who so swiftly inferred universal law from the single fact. He was no pedant of a department. His eye was open to beauty, and his ear to music. He found these, not in rare conditions, but wheresoever he went. He thought the best of music was in single strains; and he found poetic suggestion in the humming of the telegraph-wire.

His poetry might be bad or good; he no doubt wanted a lyric facility and technical skill, but he had the source of poetry in his spiritual perception. He was a good reader and critic, and his judgment on poetry was to the ground of it. He could not be deceived as to the presence or absence of the poetic element in any composition, and his thirst for this made him negligent and perhaps scornful of superficial graces. He would pass by many delicate rhythms, but he would have detected every live stanza or line in a volume and knew very well where to find an equal poetic charm in prose. He was so enamoured of the spiritual beauty that he held all actual written poems in very light esteem in the comparison. He admired Aeschylus and Pindar; but when some one was commending them, he said that Aeschylus and the Greeks, in describing Apollo and Orpheus, had given no song, or no good one. "They ought not to have moved trees, but to have chanted to the gods such a hymn as would have sung all their old ideas out of their heads, and new ones in." His own verses are often rude and defective. The gold does not yet run pure, is drossy and crude.

The thyme and marjoram are not yet honey. But if he want lyric fineness and technical merits, if he have not the poetic temperament, he never lacks the causal thought, showing that his genius was better than his talent. He knew the worth of the Imagination for the uplifting and consolation of human life, and liked to throw every thought into a symbol. The fact you tell is of no value, but only the impression. For this reason his presence was poetic, always piqued the curiosity to know more deeply the secrets of his mind. He had many reserves, an unwillingness to exhibit to profane eyes what was still sacred in his own, and knew well how to throw a poetic veil over his experience. All readers of Walden will remember his mythical record of his disappointments:—

"I long ago lost a hound, a bay horse and a turtle-dove, and am still on their trail. Many are the travelers I have spoken concerning them, describing their tracks, and what calls they answered to. I have met one or two who have heard the hound, and the tramp of the horse, and even seen the dove disappear behind a cloud; and they seemed as anxious to recover them as if they had lost them themselves."

His riddles were worth the reading, and I confide that if at any time I do not understand the expression, it is yet just. Such was the wealth of his truth that it was not worth his while to use words in vain. His poem entitled "Sympathy" reveals the tenderness under that triple steel of stoicism, and the intellectual subtility it could animate. His classic poem on "Smoke" suggests Simonides,[1] but is better than any poem of Simonides. His biography is in his verses. His habitual thought makes all his poetry a hymn to the Cause of causes, the Spirit which vivifies and controls his own:—

> "I hearing get, who had but ears,
> And sight, who had but eyes before;
> I moments live, who lived but years,
> And truth discern, who knew but learning's lore."

And still more in these religious lines:—

> "Now chiefly is my natal hour,
> And only now my prime of life;
> I will not doubt the love untold,
> Which not my worth nor want have bought,
> Which wooed me young, and wooes me old,
> And to this evening hath me brought."[2]

Whilst he used in his writings a certain petulance of remark in reference to churches or churchmen, he was a person of a rare,

1. Greek lyrist of the 6th century B.C.
2. Both from "Inspiration," as quoted
in Thoreau's *Week on the Concord and Merrimack Rivers.*

tender and absolute religion, a person incapable of any profanation, by act or by thought. Of course, the same isolation which belonged to his original thinking and living detached him from the social religious forms. This is neither to be censured nor regretted. Aristotle long ago explained it, when he said, "One who surpasses his fellow citizens in virtue is no longer a part of the city. Their law is not for him, since he is a law to himself."

Thoreau was sincerity itself, and might fortify the convictions of prophets in the ethical laws by his holy living. It was an affirmative experience which refused to be set aside. A truth-speaker he, capable of the most deep and strict conversation; a physician to the wounds of any soul; a friend, knowing not only the secret of friendship, but almost worshipped by those few persons who resorted to him as their confessor and prophet, and knew the deep value of his mind and great heart. He thought that without religion or devotion of some kind nothing great was ever accomplished: and he thought that the bigoted sectarian had better bear this in mind.

His virtues, of course, sometimes ran into extremes. It was easy to trace to the inexorable demand on all for exact truth that austerity which made this willing hermit more solitary even than he wished. Himself of a perfect probity, he required not less of others. He had a disgust at crime, and no worldly success would cover it. He detected paltering as readily in dignified and prosperous persons as in beggars, and with equal scorn. Such dangerous frankness was in his dealing that his admirers called him "that terrible Thoreau," as if he spoke when silent, and was still present when he had departed. I think the severity of his ideal interfered to deprive him of a healthy sufficiency of human society.

The habit of a realist to find things the reverse of their appearance inclined him to put every statement in a paradox. A certain habit of antagonism defaced his earlier writings,—a trick of rhetoric not quite outgrown in his later, of substituting for the obvious word and thought its diametrical opposite. He praised wild mountains and winter forests for their domestic air, in snow and ice he would find sultriness, and commended the wilderness for resembling Rome and Paris. "It was so dry, that you might call it wet."

The tendency to magnify the moment, to read all the laws of Nature in the one object or one combination under your eye, is of course comic to those who do not share the philosopher's perception of identity. To him there was no such thing as size. The pond was a small ocean; the Atlantic, a large Walden Pond. He referred every minute fact to cosmical laws. Though he meant to be just, he seemed haunted by a certain chronic assumption that the

science of the day pretended completeness, and he had just found
out that the *savans*[3] had neglected to discriminate a particular
botanical variety, had failed to describe the seeds or count the
sepals. "That is to say," we replied, "the blockheads were not born
in Concord; but who said they were? It was their unspeakable
misfortune to be born in London, or Paris, or Rome; but, poor fellows, they did what they could, considering that they never saw
Bateman's Pond, or Nine-Acre Corner, or Becky Stow's Swamp;
besides, what were you sent into the world for, but to add this
observation?"

Had his genius been only contemplative, he had been fitted to
his life, but with his energy and practical ability he seemed born
for great enterprise and for command; and I so much regret the
loss of his rare powers of action, that I cannot help counting it a
fault in him that he had no ambition. Wanting this, instead of
engineering for all America, he was the captain of a huckleberry-
party. Pounding beans is good to the end of pounding empires
one of these days; but if, at the end of years, it is still only beans![4]

But these foibles, real or apparent, were fast vanishing in the incessant growth of a spirit so robust and wise, and which effaced
its defeats with new triumphs. His study of Nature was a perpetual ornament to him, and inspired his friends with curiosity to
see the world through his eyes, and to hear his adventures. They
possessed every kind of interest.

He had many elegancies of his own, whilst he scoffed at conventional elegance. Thus, he could not bear to hear the sound of
his own steps, the grit of gravel; and therefore never willingly
walked in the road, but in the grass, on mountains and in woods.
His senses were acute, and he remarked that by night every dwelling-house gives out bad air, like a slaughter-house. He liked the
pure fragrance of melilot.[5] He honored certain plants with special
regard, and, over all, the pond-lily,—then, the gentian, and the
Mikania scandens,[6] and "life-everlasting," and a bass-tree which he
visited every year when it bloomed, in the middle of July. He
thought the scent a more oracular inquisition than the sight,—
more oracular and trustworthy. The scent, of course, reveals what
is concealed from the other senses. By it he detected earthiness.
He delighted in echoes, and said they were almost the only kind
of kindred voices that he heard. He loved Nature so well, was so
happy in her solitude, that he became very jealous of cities and the
sad work which their refinements and artifices made with man and

3. Men of knowledge.
4. Emerson's son suggests that this passage, written before Thoreau's death,
was the expression of a mood only. Its
apparent lack of sympathy with Thoreau's proper heroism is belied by much
of the rest of the essay.
5. Sweet clover.
6. Climbing hempweed.

his dwelling. The axe was always destroying his forest. "Thank God," he said, "they cannot cut down the clouds!" "All kinds of figures are drawn on the blue ground with this fibrous white paint."

I subjoin a few sentences taken from his unpublished manuscripts, not only as records of his thought and feeling, but for their power of description and literary excellence:—

> "Some circumstantial evidence is very strong, as when you find a trout in the milk."

> "The chub is a soft fish, and tastes like boiled brown paper salted."

> "The youth gets together his materials to build a bridge to the moon, or, perchance, a palace or temple on the earth, and, at length the middle-aged man concludes to build a wood-shed with them."

> "The locust z-ing."

> "Devil's-needles zigzagging along the Nut-Meadow brook."

> "Sugar is not so sweet to the palate as sound to the healthy ear."

> "I put on some hemlock-boughs, and the rich salt crackling of their leaves was like mustard to the ear, the crackling of uncountable regiments. Dead trees love the fire."

> "The bluebird carries the sky on his back."

> "The tanager flies through the green foliage as if it would ignite the leaves."

> "If I wish for a horse-hair for my compass-sight I must go to the stable; but the hair-bird, with her sharp eyes, goes to the road."

> "Immortal water, alive even to the superficies."

> "Fire is the most tolerable third party."

> "Nature made ferns for pure leaves, to show what she could do in that line."

> "No tree has so fair a bole and so handsome an instep as the beech."

> "How did these beautiful rainbow-tints get into the shell of the fresh-water clam, buried in the mud at the bottom of our dark river?"

> "Hard are the times when the infant's shoes are second-foot."

> "We are strictly confined to our men to whom we give liberty."

> "Nothing is so much to be feared as fear. Atheism may comparatively be popular with God himself."

> "Of what significance the things you can forget? A little thought is sexton to all the world."

> "How can we expect a harvest of thought who have not had a seed-time of character?"

> "Only he can be trusted with gifts who can present a face of bronze to expectations."

> "I ask to be melted. You can only ask of the metals that they be tender to the fire that melts them. To nought else can they be tender."

There is a flower known to botanists, one of the same genus with our summer plant called "Life-Everlasting," a *Gnaphalium* like that, which grows on the most inaccessible cliffs of the Tyrolese mountains, where the chamois dare hardly venture, and which the hunter, tempted by its beauty, and by his love (for it is immensely valued by the Swiss maidens), climbs the cliffs to gather, and is sometimes found dead at the foot, with the flower in his hand. It is called by botanists the *Gnaphalium leontopodium,* but by the Swiss *Edelweisse,* which signifies *Noble Purity.* Thoreau seemed to me living in the hope to gather this plant, which belonged to him of right. The scale on which his studies proceeded was so large as to require longevity, and we were the less prepared for his sudden disappearance. The country knows not yet, or in the least part, how great a son it has lost. It seems an injury that he should leave in the midst his broken task which none else can finish, a kind of indignity to so noble a soul that he should depart out of Nature before yet he has been really shown to his peers for what he is. But he, at least, is content. His soul was made for the noblest society; he had in a short life exhausted the capabilities of this world; wherever there is knowledge, wherever there is virtue, wherever there is beauty, he will find a home.

1862

From Journals *and* Letters[7]
["*The Message Committed to Me*"]

[1]

Suicidal is this distrust of reason; this fear to think; this doctrine that 'tis pious to believe on other's words, impious to trust entirely to yourself. To think is to receive. Is a man afraid that the faculties which God made can outsee God, can find more than he made, or different, can bring any report hostile to himself? To reflect is to receive truth immediately from God without any medium. That is living faith. To take on trust certain facts is a dead faith, inoperative. A trust in yourself is the height, not of pride, but of piety, an unwillingness to learn of any but God him-

7. Emerson's *Journals* contain (in addition to collections of quotations from his reading, trial compositions, drafts of poems, etc.) an almost daily record of his thoughts and experiences for sixty years. The following selections give some idea of the range of this mass of writing. To permit them to comment on each other they are arranged in a series of loose cycles, each with a title supplied by the editor. The order within each cycle is usually chronological. In a few cases, a passage is not the version in the *Journals* but that in the essay in which it was eventually used; the source of each of these is given in a note. The date is in all cases that of the original journal passage; the present editor has inserted these, after each passage, within angle brackets. Parts of a few letters are also included, where they bear on a theme important to the *Journals.* For ease of reference, the passages have been numbered.

self. It will come only to one who feels that he is nothing. It is by yourself without ambassador that God speaks to you. * * * ⟨July 29, 1831⟩

[2]

* * * Is it not all in us, how strangely! Look at this congregation of men;—the words might be spoken,—though now here be none here to speak them,—but the words might be said that would make them stagger and reel like a drunken man. Who doubts it? Were you ever instructed by a wise and eloquent man? Remember then, were not the words that made your blood run cold, that brought the blood to your cheeks, that made you tremble or delighted you,—did they not sound to you as old as yourself? Was it not truth that you knew before, or do you ever expect to be moved from the pulpit or from man by anything but plain truth? Never. It is God in you that responds to God without, or affirms his own words trembling on the lips of another. ⟨October 27, 1831⟩

[3]

I have sometimes thought that, in order to be a good minister, it was necessary to leave the ministry.[8] The profession is antiquated. In an altered age, we worship in the dead forms of our forefathers. Were not a Socratic paganism better than an effete, superannuated Christianity? ⟨June 2, 1832⟩

[4]

Has the doctrine ever been fairly preached of man's moral nature? The whole world holds on to formal Christianity, and nobody teaches the essential truth, the heart of Christianity, for fear of shocking, etc. Every teacher, when once he finds himself insisting with all his might upon a great truth, turns up the ends of it at last with a cautious showing *how* it is agreeable to the life and teaching of Jesus, as if that was any recommendation, as if the blessedness of Jesus' life and teaching were not because they were agreeable to the truth. Well, this cripples his teaching. It bereaves the truth he inculcates of more than half its force, by representing it as something secondary that can't stand alone. The truth of truth consists in this, that it is self-evident, self-subsistent. It is light. You don't get a candle to see the sun rise.

Instead of making Christianity a vehicle of truth, you make truth only a horse for Christianity. It is a very operose[9] way of making people good. You must be humble because Christ says, "Be humble." "But why must I obey Christ?" "Because God sent him." But how do I know God sent him? Because your own heart teaches

8. Emerson broke with his Boston parish in the autumn of 1832, but in his thoughts he had begun to do so long before.
9. Laborious.

the same thing he taught. Why then shall I not go to my own heart at first? ⟨*October 1, 1832*⟩

[5]

> Henceforth, please God, forever I forego
> The yoke of men's opinions. I will be
> Light-hearted as a bird and live with God.

* * *

> Who says the heart's a blind guide? It is not.
> My heart did never counsel me to sin.

* * *

> I never taught it what it teaches me,
> I only follow when I act aright.
> Whence then did this omniscient spirit come?
> From God it came. It is the Deity. ⟨*October, 1832*⟩

[6]

To the music of the surly storm[1] that thickens the darkness of the night abroad, and rocks the walls and fans my cheek through the chinks and cracks, I would sing my strain, though hoarse and small. Yet, please God, it shall be lowly, affectionate and true. It were worth trial whether the distinction between a spiritual and traditional religion could not be made apparent to an ordinary congregation.[2] There are parts of faith so great, so self-evident, that when the mind rests in them the pretensions of the most illuminated, most pretending sect pass for nothing. * * *

But to show men the nullity of church-going compared with a real exaltation of their being, I think might even promote parish objects and draw them to church. To show the reality and infinite depth of spiritual laws, that all the maxims of Christ are true to the core of the world; that there is not, can't be, any cheating of nature, might be apprehended.

Every spiritual law, I suppose, would be a contradiction to common sense. Thus I should begin with my old saws, that nothing can be given; everything is sold; love compels love; hatred, hatred; action and reaction always are equal; no evil in society but has its check which coexists; the moral, the physical, the social world is a *plenum*,[3] and any flood in one place produces equal ebb in another; nothing is free but the will of man, and that only to procure his own virtue: on every other side but that one he beats the air with his pompous action; that punishment not follows but accom-

---

1. Carl Strauch conjectures that the same storm occasioned "The Snow-Storm."
2. By the end of 1834 Emerson had moved to Concord and was living temporarily in the Old Manse, where Hawthorne was soon to succeed him. His new freedom only increased his "conviction that men are convertible" and his hope to be the means of their awakening.
3. Filled space.

panies crime.[4]

They have said in churches in this age, "Mere Morality."[5] O God, they know thee not who speak contemptuously of all that is grand. It is the distinction of Christianity, that it is moral. All that is personal in it is nought. When anyone comes who speaks with better insight into moral nature, he will be the new gospel; miracle or not, inspired or uninspired, he will be the Christ; persons are nothing. If I could tell you what you know not; could, by my knowledge of the divine being, put that within your grasp which now you dimly apprehend, and make you feel the moral sublime, you would never think of denying my inspiration. The whole power of Christianity resides in this fact, that it is more agreeable to the constitution of man than any other teaching. But from the constitution of man may be got better teaching still.

Morality requires purity, but purity is not it; requires justice, but justice is not that; requires beneficence, but is something better. Indeed there is a kind of descent and accommodation felt when we leave speaking of Moral Nature to urge a virtue it enjoins. For to the soul in her pure action all the virtues are natural, and not painfully acquired. Excite the soul, and it becomes suddenly virtuous. Touch the deep heart, and all these listless, stingy, beef-eating bystanders will see the dignity of a sentiment; will say, This is good, and all I have I will give for that. Excite the soul, and the weather and the town and your condition in the world all disappear; the world itself loses its solidity, nothing remains but the soul and the Divine Presence in which it lives. Youth and age are indifferent in this presence. ⟨December 29, 1834⟩

[7]

There is no terror like that of being known.[6] The world lies in night of sin. It bears not the cock crowing: it sees not the grey streak in the East. At the first entering ray of light, society is shaken with fear and anger from side to side. Who opened that shutter? they cry, Wo to him! They belie it, they call it darkness that comes in, affirming that they were in light before.[7] Before the man who has spoken to them the dread word, they tremble and flee. They flee to new topics, to their learning, to the solid institutions about them, to their great men, to their windows, and look-out on the road and passengers, to their very furniture, and

<hr>

4. This paragraph is a compact statement of one of Emerson's earliest articles of faith, the doctrine he called Compensation.

5. A phrase in condemnation of the tendency of rationalists to belittle or deny the supernatural authority of a special Christian Revelation.

6. In 1838 Emerson attempted to make "the distinction between a spiritual and a traditional religion" apparent in his "Address" to the graduating class of the Harvard Divinity School. The publication of this address in August drew on him the attacks of many conservative Unitarians, including certain professors at the Divinity School.

7. Cf. the discussion of Swedenborg in "The Poet," p. 295.

meats, and drinks,—anywhere, anyhow to escape the apparition. The wild horse has heard the whisper of the Tamer: the maniac has caught the glance of the Keeper. They try to forget the memory of the speaker, to put him down into the same obscure place he occupied in their minds before he spake to them. It is all in vain. They even flatter themselves that they have killed and buried the enemy, when they have magisterially denied and denounced him. But vain, vain, all vain. It was but the first mutter of the distant storm they heard,—it was the first cry of the Revolution,—it was the touch, the palpitation that goes before the Earthquake. Even now society is shaken because a thought or two have been thrown into the midst. The sects, the colleges, the church, the statesmen all have forebodings. It now works only in a handful. What does State Street and Wall Street and the Royal Exchange and the Bourse at Paris care for these few thoughts and these few men? Very little; truly; most truly. But the doom of State Street, and Wall Street, of London, and France, of the whole world, is advertised by those thoughts; is in the procession[8] of the Soul which comes after those few thoughts. ⟨*October 30, 1838*⟩

[8]

When I look at life, and see the snatches of thought, the gleams of goodness here and there amid the wide and wild madness, I seem to be a god dreaming; and when shall I awake and dissipate these fumes and phantoms?[9] ⟨*October 31, 1838*⟩

[9]

I lament that I find in me no enthusiasm, no resources for the instruction and guidance of the people, when they shall discover that their present guides are blind.[1] * * * I hate preaching, whether in pulpits or in teachers' meetings. Preaching is a pledge, and I wish to say what I think and feel today, with the proviso that tomorrow perhaps I shall contradict it all. Freedom boundless I wish. I will not pledge myself not to drink wine, not to drink ink, not to lie, and not to commit adultery, lest I hanker tomorrow to do these very things by reason of my having tied my hands. Besides, man is so poor he cannot afford to part with any advantages, or bereave himself of the functions even of one hair. I do not like to speak to the Peace Society,[2] if so I am to restrain me in so extreme a privilege as the use of the sword and bullet. For the

8. Advance, issuing forth. Cf. "Love": "In the procession of the soul from within outward, it enlarges its circles ever, like the pebble thrown into the pond, or the light proceeding from an orb."
9. The poem "Uriel" is a further comment in allegory on the "Divinity School Address" and its reception.

1. After the episode of the "Divinity School Address," Emerson lost some of his hope for "the conversion of the world" to his truth, but continued resolutely and cheerfully to pursue his "distinct vocation."
2. Emerson had done so on March 12, 1838.

peace of the man who has forsworn the use of the bullet seems to me not quite peace, but a canting impotence: but with knife and pistol in my hands, if I, from greater bravery and honor, cast them aside, then I know the glory of peace. ⟨*September 14, 1839*⟩

[10]

Lectures.—In these golden days it behooves me once more to make my annual inventory of the world. For the five last years I have read each winter a new course of lectures in Boston, and each was my creed and confession of faith. Each told all I thought of the past, the present and the future. Once more I must renew my work, and I think only once in the same form, though I see that he who thinks he does something for the last time ought not to do it at all. Yet my objection is not to the thing, but with the form: and the concatenation of errors called *society* to which I still consent, until my plumes be grown, makes even a duty of this concession also. So I submit to sell tickets again.

But the form is neither here nor there. What shall be the substance of my shrift? Adam in the garden, I am to new name all the beasts in the field and all the gods in the sky. I am to invite men drenched in Time to recover themselves and come out of time, and taste their native immortal air. I am to fire with what skill I can the artillery of sympathy and emotion. I am to indicate constantly, though all unworthy, the Ideal and Holy Life, the life within life, the Forgotten Good, the Unknown Cause in which we sprawl and sin. I am to try the magic of sincerity, that luxury permitted only to kings and poets. I am to celebrate the spiritual powers in their infinite contrast to the mechanical powers and the mechanical philosophy of this time. I am to console the brave sufferers under evils whose end they cannot see by appeals to the great optimism, self-affirmed in all bosoms. ⟨*October 18, 1839*⟩

[11]

In all my lectures, I have taught one doctrine, namely, the infinitude of the private man. This the people accept readily enough, and even with loud commendation, as long as I call the lecture Art, or Politics, or Literature, or the Household; but the moment I call it Religion, they are shocked, though it be only the application of the same truth which they receive everywhere else, to a new class of facts. ⟨*April, 1840*⟩

[12]

People came, it seems, to my lectures with expectation that I was to realize the Republic I described, and ceased to come when they found this reality no nearer. They mistook me. I am and always was a painter. I paint still with might and main, and choose the best subjects I can. Many have I seen come and go with false hopes and fears, and dubiously affected by my pictures. But I paint on. I count this distinct vocation which never leaves me in doubt what to do, but in all times, places, and fortunes gives me an open future, to be the great felicity of my lot. * * * ⟨1843⟩

[*Poetry and Inspiration*]

[13] LETTER TO LYDIA JACKSON[3]

February 1, 1835

* * * Under this morning's severe but beautiful light I thought, dear friend, that hardly should I get away from Concord. I must win you to love it. I am born a poet, of a low class without doubt, yet a poet. That is my nature and vocation. My singing, be sure, is very "husky," and is for the most part in prose. Still am I a poet in the sense of a perceiver and dear lover of the harmonies that are in the soul and in matter, and specially of the correspondences between these and those. A sunset, a forest, a snow-storm, a certain river-view, are more to me than many friends and do ordinarily divide my day with my books. Wherever I go therefore I guard and study my rambling propensities with a care that is ridiculous to people, but to me is the care of my high calling. * * *

[14]

Looked over S. G. Ward's portfolio of drawings and prints.[4] In landscapes it ought to be that the painter should give us not surely the enjoyment of a real landscape,—for air, light, motion, life, dampness, heat, and actual infinite space he cannot give us, —but the suggestion of a better, fairer creation than we know; he should crowd a greater number of beautiful effects into his picture than coexist in any real landscape. All the details, all the prose of nature, he should omit, and give us only the spirit and splendor. So that we should find his landscape more exalting to the inner man than is Walden Pond or the Pays de Vaud.[5] All spiritual activity is abridgment, selection. ⟨*September 1, 1838*⟩

[15]

Education.— * * * An education in things is not. We all are involved in the condemnation of words, an age of words. We are shut up in schools and college recitation rooms for ten or fifteen years, and come out at last with a bellyful of words and do not know a thing. We cannot use our hands, or our legs, or our eyes, or our arms. We do not know an edible root in the woods. We cannot tell our course by the stars, nor the hour of the day by the sun. It is well if we can swim and skate. We are afraid of a horse,

---

3. His fiancée and second wife. After they were married (in 1835), he called her "Lidian."
4. Samuel Gray Ward, a young transcendentalist who contributed several pieces on art to the journal of transcendentalism, *The Dial*. He remained a lifelong friend of Emerson.
5. A scenic Swiss canton.

of a cow, of a dog, of a cat, of a spider. Far better was the Roman rule to teach a boy nothing that he could not learn standing. Now here are my wise young neighbors[6] who, instead of getting, like the woodmen, into a railroad-car, where they have not even the activity of holding the reins, have got into a boat which they have built with their own hands, with sails which they have contrived to serve as a tent by night, and gone up the Merrimack to live by their wits on the fish of the stream and the berries of the wood. My worthy neighbor Dr. Bartlett expressed a true parental instinct when he desired to send his boy with them to learn something. The farm, the farm, is the right school. The reason of my deep respect for the farmer is that he is a realist, and not a dictionary. The farm is a piece of the world, the school-house is not. The farm, by training the physical, rectifies and invigorates the meta-physical and moral nature.

Now so bad we are that the world is stripped of love and of terror. Here came the other night an Aurora[7] so wonderful, a curtain of red and blue and silver glory, that in any other age or nation it would have moved the awe and wonder of men and mingled with the profoundest sentiments of religion and love, and we all saw it with cold, arithmetical eyes, we knew how many colors shone, how many degrees it extended, how many hours it lasted, and of this heavenly flower we beheld nothing more: a primrose by the brim of the river of time.

Shall we not wish back again the Seven Whistlers, the Flying Dutchman,[8] the lucky and unlucky days, and the terrors of the Day of Doom? ⟨*September 14, 1839*⟩

[16]

Treat Things Poetically.—Everything should be treated poeti-cally,—law, politics, housekeeping, money. A judge and a banker must drive their craft poetically as well as a dancer or a scribe. That is, they must exert that higher vision which causes the ob-ject to become fluid and plastic. Then they are inventive, they detect its capabilities. If they do not this, they have nothing that can be called success, but the work and the workman become blockish and near the point of everlasting congelation. All human affairs need the perpetual intervention of this elastic principle to preserve them supple and alive, as the earth needs the presence of caloric through its pores to resist the tendency to absolute solidity. If you would write a code, or logarithms, or a cookbook, you can-not spare the poetic impulse. We must not only have hydrogen in balloons, and steel springs under coaches, but we must have

6. John and Henry Thoreau.
7. Aurora borealis, the northern lights.
8. The most famous of the "ghost ships." The "Seven Whistlers" were the souls of the Jews who crucified Christ.

fire under the Andes at the core of the world. * * * ⟨*December,* 1839⟩

[17]

Rhyme.—Rhyme; not tinkling rhyme, but grand Pindaric[9] strokes, as firm as the tread of a horse. Rhyme that vindicates itself as an art, the stroke of the bell of a cathedral. Rhyme which knocks at prose and dullness with the stroke of a cannon ball. Rhyme which builds out into Chaos and old night[1] a splendid architecture to bridge the impassable, and call aloud on all the children of morning that the Creation is recommencing. I wish to write such rhymes as shall not suggest a restraint, but contrariwise the wildest freedom. ⟨*June 27, 1839*⟩

[18]

* * * I love spring water and wild air, and not the manufacture of the chemist's shop. I see in a moment, on looking into our new *Dial*,[2] which is the wild poetry, and which the tame, and see that one wild line out of a private heart saves the whole book. ⟨*October 17, 1840*⟩

[19]

The Bible.— * * * The most original book in the world is the Bible. This old collection of the ejaculations of love and dread, of the supreme desires and contritions of men, proceeding out of the region of the grand and eternal, by whatsoever different mouths spoken, and through a wide extent of times and countries, seems the alphabet of the nations, and all posterior literature either the chronicle of facts under very inferior Ideas, or, when it rises to sentiment, the combinations, analogies or degradations of this.

It is in the nature of things that the highest originality must be moral. The only person who can be entirely independent of this fountain of literature and equal to it, must be a prophet in his own proper person. Shakespeare, the first literary genius of the world, leans on the Bible: his poetry supposes it. If we examine this brilliant influence, Shakespeare, as it lies in our minds, we shall find it reverent, deeply indebted to the traditional morality,—in short, compared with the tone of the prophets, *Secondary.* On the other hand, the Prophets do not imply the existence of Shakespeare or Homer,—advert to no books or arts,—only to dread Ideas and emotions. People imagine that the place which the Bible holds in the world, it owes to miracles. It owes it simply to the fact that it came out of a profounder depth of thought than any other book,

---

9. Pindar, an early Greek poet (5th century B.C.), author of odes in honor of victors in the Olympic games.
1. Cf. Milton, *Paradise Lost* I.543: the kingdom of darkness and disorder between Heaven and Hell.
2. The journal of transcendentalism (1840–44); edited by Emerson from 1842.

and the effect must be precisely proportionate. * * *

I have used in the above remarks the Bible for the Ethical Revelation considered generally, including, that is, the Vedas,[3] the Sacred Writings of every nation, and not of the Hebrews alone; although these last, for the very reason I have given, precede all similar writings so far as to be commonly called *The Book*, or Bible, alone. ⟨*November 17, 1839*⟩

[20]

I am for preserving all those religious writings which were in their origin poetic, ecstatic expressions which the first user of did not know what he said, but they were spoken through him and from above, not from his level; things which seemed a happy casualty, but which were no more random than the human race are a random formation. "It is necessary," says Iamblichus,[4] "that ancient prayers, like sacred *asyla*, should be preserved invariably the same, neither taking anything from them nor adding anything to them which is elsewhere derived."

This is the reason, doubtless, why Homer declares that Jove loved the Ethiopians. And Iamblichus in answer to the query, "Why of significant names we prefer such as are barbaric[5] to our own?" says, among other reasons: "Barbarous names have much emphasis, great conciseness, and less ambiguity, variety, and multitude"; and then afterwards: "But the Barbarians are stable in their manners, and firmly continue to employ the same words. Hence they are dear to the gods, and proffer words which are grateful to them." And the ancients spoke of the Egyptians and Chaldaeans as "sacred nations."

Now the words "God," "Grace," "Prayer," "Heaven," "Hell," are these barbarous and sacred words, to which we must still return, whenever we would speak an ecstatic and universal sense. There are objections to them, no doubt, for academical use, but when the professor's gown is taken off, Man will come back to them. ⟨*November, 1841*⟩

[21]

The Bible will not be ended until the creation is. ⟨*1856*⟩

[22]

The metamorphosis of Nature shows itself in nothing more than this, that there is no word in our language that cannot become typical to us of Nature by giving it emphasis. The world is a Dancer; it is a Rosary; it is a Torrent; it is a Boat; a Mist; a Spider's Snare; it is what you will; and the metaphor will hold, and it will give the imagination keen pleasure. Swifter than light the world converts itself into that thing you name, and all things find their

3. Hindu scriptures.
4. Neo-Platonist (4th century A.D.), author of a *Life of Pythagoras*. "*Asyla*" are sanctuaries.
5. Foreign.

right place under this new and capricious classification. There is nothing small or mean to the soul. It derives as grand a joy from symbolizing the Godhead or his universe under the form of a moth or a gnat as of a Lord of Hosts. Must I call the heaven and the earth a maypole and country fair with booths, or an anthill, or an old coat, in order to give you the shock of pleasure which the imagination loves and the sense of spiritual greatness? Call it a blossom, a rod, a wreath of parsley, an tamarisk-crown, a cock, a sparrow, the ear instantly hears and the spirit leaps to the trope.[6] * * * ⟨1841⟩

[23]

Every gardener can change his flowers and leaves into fruit and so is the genius that today can upheave and balance and toss every object in Nature for his metaphor, capable in his next manifestation of playing such a game with his hands instead of his brain. An instinctive suspicion that this may befal, seems to have crept into the mind of men. What would happen to us who live on the surface, if this fellow in some new transmigration should have acquired power to do what he now delights to say? He must be watched. ⟨September, 1841⟩

[24]

All writing is by the grace of God. People do not deserve to have good writing, they are so pleased with bad. In these sentences that you show me, I can find no beauty, for I see death in every clause and every word. There is a fossil or a mummy character which pervades this book. The best sepulchres, the vastest catacombs, Thebes and Cairo Pyramids are sepulchres to me. I like gardens and nurseries. Give me initiative, spermatic, prophesying, man-making words. ⟨1841⟩

[25]

Now and then, rarely, comes a stout man like Luther, Montaigne, Pascal, Herbert,[7] who utters a thought or feeling in a virile manner, and it is unforgettable. Then follow any number of spiritual eunuchs and women, who talk about that thought, imply it, in pages and volumes. * * * Great bands of female souls who only receive the spermatic *aura*[8] and brood on the same but add nothing.

Do not spend one moment on the last; they are mere publishers and diluters and critics. ⟨1859⟩

6. Metaphor.
7. Michel de Montaigne (1533–95), French author of *Essays;* Blaise Pascal (1623–62), French author of *Thoughts;* George Herbert (1593–1633), English metaphysical poet. Emerson had lectured on Luther and Herbert; the subject of one of the chapters of *Representative Men* (1850) was Montaigne.
8. A term from mesmeric "science." An impalpable substance supposed to emanate from each living thing, constituting the essence of the individual.

[26] LETTER TO THOMAS CARLYLE

Concord, December 31, 1844

* * * Thanks to you for the kind thought of a "Notice,"[9] and for its friendly wit. You shall not do this thing again, if I should send you any more books. A Preface from you is a sort of banner or oriflamme,[1] a little too splendid for my occasion, and misleads. I fancy my readers to be a very quiet, plain, even obscure class,— men and women of some religious culture and aspirations, young, or else mystical, and by no means including the great literary and fashionable army, which no man can count, who now read your books. If you introduce me, your readers and the literary papers try to read me, and with false expectations. I had rather have fewer readers and only such as belong to me.

I doubt not your stricture[2] on the book as sometimes unconnected and inconsecutive is just. Your words are very gentle. I should describe it much more harshly. My knowledge of the defects of these things I write is all but sufficient to hinder me from writing at all. I am only a sort of lieutenant here in the deplorable absence of captains, and write the laws ill as thinking it a better homage than universal silence. You Londoners know little of the dignities and duties of country lyceums. But of what you say now and heretofore respecting the remoteness of my writing and thinking from real life, though I hear substantially the same criticism made by my countrymen, I do not know what it means. If I can at any time express the law and the ideal right, that should satisfy me without measuring the divergence from it of the last act of Congress. And though I sometimes accept a popular call, and preach on Temperance or the Abolition of Slavery, as lately on the 1st of August,[3] I am sure to feel, before I have done with it, what an intrusion it is into another sphere, and so much loss of virtue in my own. * * *

[27]

I like man, but not men. Instincts, tendencies,—they do no wrong: they are beautiful, and may be confided in and obeyed. Though they slay us, let us trust them.[4] Why should eggs and tadpoles talk? All is mere sketch, symptomatic, possible, or probable, for us,—we dwellers in tents, we outlines in chalk, we jokes and buffooneries, why should we be talking? Let us have the grace to be abstemious. The etiquette of society should guard and consecrate a poet; he should not be visited, nor be shown at dinner-tables: too costly to be seen except on high holidays. He should be

9. Carlyle's preface to the English edition of *Essays, Second Series*.
1. A special ensign of the King of France.
2. In a private letter.

3. Emerson's "Address Delivered in Concord on the Anniversary of the Emancipation of the Negroes in the British West Indies, August 1, 1844."
4. Cf. Job xiii.15.

relieved of visits and trivial correspondence. His time is the time of his nation.

Yes, we want a poet, the genuine poet of our time, no parrot, and no child. The poets that we praise, or try to, the Brownings, Barretts,[5] Bryants, Tennysons,—are all abortive Homers; they at least show tendency, the direction of Nature to the star in Lyra.[6] Boys still whistle, and every newspaper and girl's album attest the ineradicable appetite for melody. Oh, no, we have not done with music, nor must console ourselves with prose poets. We wish the undrawn line of tendency to be drawn for us. Where is the Euclid who can sum up these million errors, and compute the beautiful mean? We do not wish to make believe be instructed; we wish to be ravished, inspired, and taught. ⟨April, 1846⟩

[28]

Classic and Romantic.—The classic art was the art of necessity: modern romantic art bears the stamp of caprice and chance. One is the product of inclination, of caprice, of haphazard; the other carries its law and necessity within itself.

The politics of monarchy, when all hangs on the accidents of life and temper of a single person, may be called romantic politics. The democratic, when the power proceeds organically from the people and is responsible to them, are classic politics.

Republics run into romance when they lose sight of the inner necessity and organism that must be in their laws, and act from whim. * * *

Madame George Sand,[7] though she writes fast and miscellaneously, is yet fundamentally classic and necessitated: and I, who tack things strangely enough together, and consult my ease rather than my strength, and often write *on the other side*, am yet an adorer of the *One*.

To be classic, then, *de rigueur*, is the prerogative of a vigorous mind who is able to execute what he conceives.

The classic unfolds: the romantic adds.[8] * * * ⟨1856⟩

[29]

Naïveté.—Uses of Nature, to be sure!—Why, this is foremost. What we value, all we value, is the *naturel*, or peculiar quality of each man; and, in a large, healthy individual, this is the antagonist of gravitation, vegetation, chemistry, nay, of matter itself, and as good at least as they. This is the saliency, the principle of levity, the *sal volatile*,[9] which is the balance, or offset, to the mountains and masses. This is forever a surprise, and engaging, and a man

5. I.e., Elizabeth Barrett Browning, popular Victorian poetess.
6. The star toward which the motion of the sun is directed.
7. Pseudonym of Amandine Aurore Dupin, 19th-century French novelist.
8. Part of the passage is printed here as it appeared in "Art and Criticism" (1893).
9. Ammonium carbonate, used in smelling salts. "Saliency": leaping quality.

is therefore and thus wonderful and lovely. Now Homer, Shakespeare, Burns, Scott, Voltaire, Rabelais, Montaigne, Hafiz,[1] have these spirits or intuitions, and are magnetic, or interesting to all men. We are curious about them, can't be satisfied with watching the primal springs, and their movements, wish to know their law, if we could. Well, every man has the like potency in him, more or less. This wit is related to the secret of the world, to the primitive power, the incessant creation. It is in harmony with gravity, and the orbit of stars, and the growth of grass, and the angles of crystals. There is no luck or choice about it, but law in it, from first to last. It is the next finer ascent or metamorphosis of gravity, chemistry, vegetation, animal life, the same thing, on the next higher plane; as the *morale*[2] is a still higher ascent or metamorphosis, and kindred to it. But the essence of it is, that it be native and intuitive. * * * ⟨1857⟩

[30]

I am a natural reader, and only a writer in the absence of natural writers. In a true time, I should never have written. ⟨April, 1859⟩

[31]

Beatitudes of Intellect.—Am I not, one of these days, to write consecutively of the beatitude of intellect? It is too great for feeble souls, and they are over-excited. The wineglass shakes, and the wine is spilled. What then? The joy which will not let me sit in my chair, which brings me bolt upright to my feet, and sends me striding around my room, like a tiger in his cage, and I cannot have composure and concentration enough even to set down in English words the thought which thrills me—is not that joy a certificate of the elevation? What if I never write a book or a line? for a moment, the eyes of my eyes were opened, the affirmative experience remains, and consoles through all suffering. ⟨August, 1859⟩

[32]

* * * The fancy carries out all the sentiments into form, and makes angels in the sky, and organizes remorse into a Judgment Day, and the universe at court; and so we have painted out our heaven and hell.

But I do not know but the sad realist has an equal or better content in keeping his hard nut. He sees the eternal symmetry, the world persisting to be itself, the unstooping morals of Nature, and says, "I can trust it." There is no fancy in my innate, uniform essential perception of Right, unique though million-formed or -faced. Through all processes, through all enemies, the result is Benefit, Beauty, the aim is the Best. I can well omit this parish

---

1. Hafiz was a great Persian poet (14th century A.D.). His themes were similar to those of Omar Khayyám.
2. Moral.

propensity of casting it in small, in creeds, in *Punch*[3] pictures, as the popular religions do, into Westminster Catechisms; Athanasian creeds;[4] Egyptian, Christian, Mahometan or Hindu paradises and hells. I will not be the fool of fancy, nor a child with toys.

The positive degree is manly, and suits me better: the truth is stranger and grander than the gayest fable. I cling to astronomy, botany, zoölogy, as read by the severe Intellect, and will live and die assured that I cannot go out of the Power and Deity which rule in all my experience, whether sensuous or spiritual. ⟨1866⟩

[*Reform*]

[33]

I see a good in such emphatic and universal calamity as the times bring,[5] that they dissatisfy me with society. Under common burdens we say there is much virtue in the world, and what evil co-exists is inevitable. I am not aroused to say, "I have sinned; I am in the gall of bitterness, and bond of iniquity";[6] but when these full measures come, it then stands confessed,—society has played out its last stake; it is check-mated. Young men have no hope. Adults stand like day-laborers idle in the streets. None calleth us to labor. The old wear no crown of warm life on their gray hairs. The present generation is bankrupt of principles and hope, as of property. I see man is not what man should be. He is the treadle of a wheel. He is a tassel at the apron-string of society. He is a money-chest. He is the servant of his belly.[7] This is the causal bankruptcy, this the cruel oppression, that the ideal should serve the actual; that the head should serve the feet. Then first, I am forced to inquire if the Ideal might not also be tried. Is it to be taken for granted that it is impracticable? Behold the boasted world has come to nothing. Prudence itself is at her wits' end. Pride, and Thrift, and Expediency, who jeered and chirped and were so well pleased with themselves, and made merry with the dream, as they termed it, of Philosophy and Love,—behold they are all flat, and here is the Soul erect and unconquered still. What answer is it now to say, It has always been so? I acknowledge that, as far back as I can see the widening procession of humanity, the marchers are lame and blind and deaf; but to the soul that whole past is but one finite series in its infinite scope. Deteriorating ever and now desperate. Let me begin anew. Let me teach the finite to know its master. Let me ascend above my fate and work down upon my world. ⟨May 21, 1837⟩

---

3. English comic magazine.
4. The Westminster Catechism is a creed for Puritans; the Athanasian Creed, for Catholics.
5. 1837 was a year of severe depression, in which the banks in many cities suspended specie payments.
6. Acts viii.23.
7. Cf. Romans xvi.18.

[34]

Reform.—The past has baked my loaf, and in the strength of its bread I break up the old oven. ⟨*July, 1839*⟩

[35]

People hold to you as long as you please yourself with the Ideal life only as a pretty dream and concede a resistless force to the limitations of the same, to structure, or organization, and to society. But as quickly as you profess your unlimited allegiance to the first, so far as to be no longer contented with doing the best you can in the circumstances, but demand that these mountain circumstance should skip like rams and the little hills like lambs[8] before the presence of the Soul, then they distrust your wisdom and defy your resolutions. And yet Nature is in earnest. * * * The moral nature is not a patch of light here, whilst the social world is a lump of darkness there, but tends incessantly to rectify and ennoble the whole circumference of facts.

Never was anything gained by admitting the omnipotence of limitations, but all immortal action is an overstepping of these busy rules. * * * ⟨*November 6, 1839*⟩

[30]

Yesterday George and Sophia Ripley, Margaret Fuller and Alcott discussed here the new Social Plans.[9] I wished to be convinced, to be thawed, to be made nobly mad by the kindlings before my eye of a new dawn of human piety. But this scheme was arithmetic and comfort: this was a hint borrowed from the Tremont House and United States Hotel; a rage in our poverty and politics to live rich and gentleman-like, an anchor to leeward against a change of weather; a prudent forecast on the probable issue of the great questions of Pauperism and Poverty. And not once could I be inflamed, but sat aloof and thoughtless; my voice faltered and fell. It was not the cave of persecution which is the palace of spiritual power, but only a room in the Astor House hired for the Transcendentalists. I do not wish to remove from my present prison to a prison a little larger. I wish to break all prisons. I have not yet conquered my own house. It irks and repents me. Shall I raise the siege of this hencoop, and march baffled away to a pretended siege of Babylon? It seems to me that so to do were to dodge the problem I am set to solve, and to hide my impotency in the thick of a crowd. I can see too, afar,—that I should not find myself more than now,—no, not so much, in that select, but not by me selected, fraternity. Moreover, to join this body would be to

---

8. Psalms cxiv.4.
9. For Brook Farm, a co-operative community intended "to insure a more natural union between intellectual and manual labor than now exists," and to "permit a more wholesome and simple life than can be led amidst the pressure of our competitive institutions." It was founded this same year and lasted eight years.

traverse all my long trumpeted theory, and the instinct which spoke from it, that one man is a counterpoise to a city,—that a man is stronger than a city, that his solitude is more prevalent and beneficent than the concert of crowds. ⟨*October 17, 1840*⟩

[37]

I told Garrison[1] that I thought he must be a very young man, or his time hang very heavy on his hands, who can afford to think much and talk much about the foibles of his neighbors, or "*denounce*," and play "the son of thunder" as he called it. I am one who believe all times to be pretty much alike, and yet I sympathize so keenly with this. We want to be expressed, yet you take from us War, that great opportunity which allowed the accumulations of electricity to stream off from both poles, the positive and the negative,—well, now you take from us our cup of alcohol, as before you took our cup of wrath. We had become canting moths of peace, our helm was a skillet, and now we must become temperance water-sops. You take away, but what do you give me? * * * Good vent or bad we must have for our nature, somewhere we must let out all the length of all the reins. Make love a crime, and we shall have lust. If you cannot contrive to raise us up to the love of science and make brute matter our antagonist which we shall have joy in handling, mastering, penetrating, condensing to adamant, dissolving to light, then we must brawl, carouse, gamble, or go to bull-fights. If we can get no full demonstration of our heart and mind, we feel wronged and incarcerated: the philosophers and divines we shall hate most, as the upper turnkeys. We wish to take the gas which allows us to break through your wearisome proprieties, to plant the foot, to set the teeth, to fling abroad the arms, and dance and sing. ⟨*October, 1841*⟩

[38]

Do not gloze[2] and prate and mystify. Here is our dear, grand Alcott[3] says, You shall dig in my field for a day and I will give you a dollar when it is done, and it shall not be a business transaction! It makes me sick. Whilst money is the measure *really* adopted by us all as the most convenient measure of all material values, let us not affectedly disuse the name, and mystify ourselves and others; let us not "say no, and take it." We may very well and honestly have theoretical and practical objections to it; if they are fatal to the use of money and barter, let us disuse them;[4] if they are less grave than the inconvenience of abolishing traffic, let us not pretend to have done with it, whilst we eat and drink and wear and breathe it. ⟨*November, 1842*⟩

1. William Lloyd Garrison, militant abolitionist and reformer.
2. Talk speciously.
3. Bronson Alcott, writer and teacher.

Cf. passages 74–78.
4. As was done by Edward Palmer, who visited Emerson and won his respect.

[39]

Belief and Unbelief.— * * * The two parties in life are the believers and unbelievers, variously named. The believer is poet, saint, democrat, theocrat, free-trade, no church, no capital punishment, idealist. The unbeliever supports the church, education, the fine arts, etc., as *amusements.* * * *

But the unbelief is very profound: Who can escape it? I am nominally a believer: yet I hold on to property: I eat my bread with unbelief. I approve every wild action of the experimenters. I say what they say concerning celibacy, or money, or community of goods, and my only apology for not doing their work is preoccupation of mind. I have a work of my own which I know I can do with some success. It would leave that undone if I should undertake with them, and I do not see in myself any vigor equal to such an enterprise. My genius loudly calls me to stay where I am, even with the degradation of owning bank-stock and seeing poor men suffer, whilst the Universal Genius apprises me of this disgrace and beckons me to the martyr's and redeemer's office.

This is belief, too, this debility of practice, this staying by our work. For the obedience to a man's genius is the *particular* of Faith: by and by, shall come the *universal* of Faith. ⟨*December 31, 1843*⟩

[40]

Conservatism has in the present society every advantage. All are on its side. Of those who pretend to ideas, all are really and in practice on the side of the state. They know that, if they should persist in actualizing their theories, it would be all convulsion and plunging. Their talk is the mere brag of liberalism. Yet, yet, they like to feel their wings. The soul, with Plato in *Phaedrus*, likes to feel its wings;[5] and they indulge themselves with this religious luxury, assured that, though the lion is as yet only half disengaged from the soil,[6] the dream of today is prophetic of the experience of tomorrow. ⟨1845⟩

[41]

The State is a poor, good beast who means the best: it means friendly. A poor cow who does well by you,—do not grudge it its hay.[7] It cannot eat bread, as you can; let it have without grudge a little grass for its four stomachs. It will not stint to yield you milk from its teat. You, who are a man walking cleanly on two feet, will not pick a quarrel with a poor cow. Take this handful of clover and welcome. But if you go to hook me when I walk in the fields, then, poor cow, I will cut your throat.

---

5. I.e., the wings of its aspiration to see truth and become immortal. See Plato's *Phaedrus* 246 ff.

6. As in some pictures of the Creation.

7. Thoreau had just refused to pay his poll tax, as had Alcott some years before. Cf. Thoreau's *Civil Disobedience.*

Don't run amuck against the world. Have a good case to try the question on. It is the part of a fanatic to fight out a revolution on the shape of a hat or surplice, on paedo-baptism, or altar-rails, or fish on Friday.[8] As long as the state means you well, do not refuse your pistareen.[9] You have a tottering cause: ninety parts of the pistareen it will spend for what you think also good: ten parts for mischief. You cannot fight heartily for a fraction. But wait until you have a good difference to join issue upon. Thus Socrates was told he should not teach. "Please God, but I will." And he could die well for that. And Jesus had a cause. You will get one by and by. But now I have no sympathy. * * *

Alcott thought he could find as good a ground for quarrel in the state tax as Socrates did in the edict of the Judges. Then I say, Be consistent, and never more put an apple or a kernel of corn into your mouth. Would you feed the devil? Say boldly, "There is a sword sharp enough to cut sheer between flesh and spirit, and I will use it, and not any longer belong to this double-faced, equivocating, mixed, Jesuitical universe."

The Abolitionists should resist, because they are literalists; they know exactly what they object to, and there is a government possible which will content them. Remove a few specified grievances, and this present commonwealth will suit them. They are the new Puritans, and as easily satisfied. But you, nothing will content. No government short of a monarchy consisting of one king and one subject, will appease you. Your objection, then, to the State of Massachusetts is deceptive. Your true quarrel is with the state of Man. * * * ⟨*July, 1846*⟩

[42]

People here[1] expect a revolution. There will be no revolution, none that deserves to be called so. There may be a scramble for money. But as all the people we see want the things we now have, and not better things, it is very certain that they will, under whatever change of forms, keep the old system. When I see changed men, I shall look for a changed world. Whoever is skilful in heaping money now will be skilful in heaping money again. * * *

There must be a relation between power and probity. We seem already to have more [power] than we can be trusted with. And this preparation for a superior race is a higher omen of revolution than any other I have seen. Except to better men, the augmented science is a mere chemic experiment of the quickest poison. * * * ⟨*April, 1848*⟩

8. Issues raised by various Protestant sects. Pedobaptism is the baptism of infants. "The Anabaptists laugh at pedobaptism" (Jeremy Taylor).

9. Peseta; very small coin.
1. Written in London at the time of the 1848 revolution in France and the Chartist demonstrations in England.

[*Aristocracy, Wealth*]

[43]

Van Burenism.—I passed by the shop and saw my spruce neighbor, the dictator of our rural Jacobins,[2] teaching his little circle of villagers their political lessons. And here, thought I, is one who loves what I hate; here is one wholly reversing my code. I hate persons who are nothing but persons. I hate numbers. He cares for nothing but numbers and persons. All the qualities of man, all his accomplishments, affections, enterprises, except solely the ticket he votes for, are nothing to this philosopher. Numbers of majorities are all he sees in the newspaper. All of North or South, all in Georgia, Alabama, Pennsylvania or New England that this man considers is, What is the relation of Mr. Clay, or of Mr. Van Buren, to those mighty mountain chains, those vast, fruitful champaigns, those expanding nations of men. What an existence is this, to have no home, no heart, but to feed on the very refuse and old straw and chaff of men, the numbers and names of voters!

One thing deserves the thought of the modern Jacobin. It seems the relations of society, the position of classes, irk and sting him, and he lends himself to each malignant party that assails what is eminent. He will one day know that this is not removable, but a distinction in the nature of things; that neither the caucus, nor the newspaper, nor the Congress, nor the mob, nor the guillotine, nor fire, nor all together, can avail to outlaw, cut out, burn or destroy the offence of superiority in persons. The manners, the pretension, which annoy me so much, are not superficial, but built on a real distinction in the nature of my companion. The superiority in him is inferiority in me, and if this particular companion were wiped by a sponge out of Nature, my inferiority would still be made evident to me by other persons everywhere and every day.[3] ⟨*October 9, 1838*⟩

[44]

Wealth.—Conversation, character, were the avowed ends; wealth was good as it appeased the animal cravings, cured the smoky chimney, silenced the creaking door, brought friends together in a warm and quiet room, and kept the children and the dinner-table in a different apartment. Thought, virtue, beauty, were the ends; but it was known that men of thought and virtue sometimes had the headache, or wet feet, or could lose good time whilst the room was getting warm in winter days. Unluckily, in the exertions necessary to remove these inconveniences, the main at-

2. Martin Van Buren, President of the U.S. (1837–41), attempted to continue the policies of Andrew Jackson. "Jacobin" was a pejorative term used by conservatives for political opponents, roughly equivalent to "Socialist" today. 3. Part of this passage is printed here as it appeared in "Aristocracy" (1884).

tention has been diverted to this object; the old aims have been lost sight of, and to remove friction has come to be the end. That is the ridicule of rich men; and Boston, London, Vienna, and now the governments generally of the world, are cities and governments of the rich; and the masses are not men, but *poor men*, that is, men who would be rich; this is the ridicule of the class, that they arrive with pains and sweat and fury nowhere; when all is done, it is for nothing. They are like one who has interrupted the conversation of a company to make his speech, and now has forgotten what he went to say. * * * Hence the appearance which everywhere strikes the eye of an aimless society, an aimless nation, an aimless world.[4] * * * ⟨*October, 1841*⟩

[45]

Not the phrenologist but the philosopher may well say, Let me see his brain, and I will tell you if he shall be poet, king, founder of cities, rich, magnetic, of a secure hand, of a scientific memory, a right classifier; or whether he shall be a bungler, driveler, unlucky, heavy and tedious.

It were to dispute against the sun, to deny this difference of brain. I see well enough that when I bring one man into an estate, he sees vague capabilities, what others might, could, would or should do with it. If I bring another, he sees what *he* should do with it. He appreciates the water-privilege, land fit for orchard, tillage, pasturage, wood-lot, cranberry-meadow; but just as easily he foresees all the means, all the steps of the process, and could lay his hand as readily on one as on another point in that series which opens the capability to the last point. The poet sees wishfully enough the result; the well-built head supplies all the steps, one as perfect as the other, in the series. Seeing this working head in him, it becomes to me as certain that he will have the direction of estates, as that there are estates. If we see tools in a magazine, as a file, an anchor, a plough, a pump, a paint-brush, a cider-press, a diving-bell, we can predict well enough their destination; and the man's associations, fortunes, love, hatred, residence, rank, the books he will buy, the roads he will traverse are predetermined in his organism. Men will need him, and he is rich and eminent by nature. That man cannot be too late or too early. Let him not hurry or hesitate. Though millions are already arrived, his seat is reserved. Though millions attend, they only multiply his friends and agents. It never troubles the Senator what multitudes crack the benches and bend the galleries to hear. He who understands the art of war, reckons the hostile battalions and cities, opportunities and spoils.

An aristocracy could not exist unless it were organic. Men are

4. Part of this passage appeared in "Nature" (1844) in the form given here.

born to command, and—it is even so—"come into the world booted and spurred to ride." The blood royal never pays, we say. It obtains service, gifts, supplies, furtherance of all kinds from the love and joy of those who feel themselves honored by the service they render.

Dull people think it Fortune that makes one rich and another poor. Is it? Yes, but the fortune was earlier than they think, namely, in the balance or adjustment between devotion to what is agreeable today and the forecast of what will be valuable tomorrow.[5] ⟨*September, 1847*⟩

[46]

Natural Aristocracy.—It is a vulgar error to suppose that a gentleman must be ready to fight. The utmost that can be demanded of the gentleman is that he be incapable of a lie. There is a man who has good sense, is well informed, well read, obliging, cultivated, capable, and has an absolute devotion to truth. He always means what he says, and says what he means, however courteously. You may spit upon him;—nothing could induce him to spit upon you,—no praises, and no possessions, no compulsion of public opinion. You may kick him;—he will think it the kick of a brute: but he is not a brute, and will not kick you in return. But neither your knife and pistol, nor your gifts and courting will ever make the smallest impression on his vote or word; for he is the truth's man, and will speak and act the truth until he dies. He is the truth's Thug, and goes willingly to ruin for his Thugee.[6] Is not he a gentleman? ⟨*December, 1849*⟩

[47]

Wealth.—The world is babyish, and the use of wealth is: it is made a toy. Men of sense esteem wealth to be the assimilation of Nature to themselves, the converting the sap and juices of the planet to the nutriment and incarnation of their design. Power is what they want, not candy, and they will pay any prices. Power for what? Power to execute their idea,—which, in any well-constituted man, of course, appears the end to which the universe exists and all its resources might be well applied. Each of the elm trees that you see over the land sends its roots far and wide; every great one to some river or watercourse; its roots will run a mile; and the education of each vascular [7] man goes on well in proportion as his masculine roots draw from all the natures around him their tribute. ⟨*1851*⟩

---

5. Part of this passage is printed here as it appeared in "Aristocracy" (1884).
6. A Thug was a member of a society of religious fanatics in India who worshiped the goddess Kali by the practice of thuggee, or assassination by strangling. The British had been taking vigorous measures for their suppression.
7. With a good circulatory system; well provided with sap.

[*Politics*]

[48]

* * * It is said that the people can look after their own interests; that "common sense, though no science, is fairly worth the seven"; that a plain, practical man is better to the state than a scholar, etc.

He were a benefactor to his countrymen who would expose and pillory this stale sophism. * * * There is imparted to every man the Divine light of reason, sufficient not only to plant corn and grind wheat by, but also to illuminate all his life, his social, political, religious actions. * * * But does it mean that because a farmer, acting on deep conviction, shall give a reason as good as Bacon could have given, that therefore the ordinary arguments of farmers are to be preferred to those of statesmen? that whatever crude remarks a circle of people talking in a bar-room throw out, are entitled to equal weight with the sifted and chosen conclusions of experienced public men? And because God has made you capable of Reason, therefore must I hear and accept all your selfish railing, your proven falsehoods, your unconsidered guesses as truth? No; I appeal from you to your Reason, which, with me, condemns you. * * * Democracy, Freedom, has its root in the sacred truth that every man hath in him the divine Reason, or that, though few men since the creation of the world live according to the dictates of Reason, yet all men are created capable of so doing. That is the equality and the only equality of all men. To this truth we look when we say, Reverence thyself; Be true to thyself. Because every man has within him somewhat really divine, therefore is slavery the unpardonable outrage it is. ⟨*December 9, 1834*⟩

[49]

In the republic must always happen what happened here,[8] that the steamboats and stages and hotels vote one way and the nation votes the other: and it seems to every meeting of readers and writers as if it were intolerable that Broad Street Paddies and bar-room politicians, the sots and loafers and all manner of ragged and unclean and foul-mouthed persons without a dollar in their pocket should control the property of the country and make the lawgiver and the law. But is that any more than their share whilst you hold property selfishly? They are opposed to you: yes, but first you are opposed to them: they, to be sure, malevolently, menacingly, with songs and rowdies and mobs; you cunningly, plausibly, and well-bred; you cheat and they strike; you sleep and eat at their expense; they vote and threaten and sometimes throw stones, at yours. ⟨*October, 1841*⟩

8. Emerson alludes to the demagogic campaign of 1840.

[50]

Every reform is only a mask under cover of which a more terrible reform, which dares not yet name itself, advances. Slavery and anti-slavery is the question of property and no property, rent and anti-rent; and anti-slavery dare not yet say that every man must do his own work, or, at least, receive no interest for money. Yet that is at last the upshot. ⟨1846⟩

[51]

The puny race of Scholars in this country have no counsel to give, and are not felt. Every wretched partisan, every village brawler, every man with talents for contention, every clamorous place-hunter makes known what he calls his opinion, all over the country, that is, as loud as he can scream. Really, no opinions are given; only the wishes of each side are expressed, of the spoils party, that is, and of the malcontents. But the voice of the intelligent and the honest, of the unconnected and independent, the voice of truth and equity, is suppressed. In England, it is not so. You can always find in their journals and newspapers a better and a best sense, as well as the low, coarse party cries. ⟨1845⟩

[52]

Alas for America, as I must so often say, the ungirt, the diffuse, the profuse, procumbent,—one wide ground juniper, out of which no cedar, no oak will rear up a mast to the clouds! It all runs to leaves, to suckers, to tendrils, to miscellany. The air is loaded with poppy,[9] with imbecility, with dispersion and sloth.

Eager, solicitous, hungry, rabid, busy-bodied America attempting many things, vain, ambitious to feel thy own existence, and convince others of thy talent, by attempting and hastily accomplishing much; yes, catch thy breath and correct thyself, and failing here, prosper out there; speed and fever are never greatness; but reliance and serenity and waiting and perseverance, heed of the work, and negligence of the effect.

Great country, diminutive minds.

America is formless, has no terrible and no beautiful condensation. Genius, always anthropomorphist, runs every idea into a fable, constructs, finishes, as the plastic[1] Italian cannot build a post or a pump-handle but it terminates in a human head. ⟨1847⟩

[53]

An American in this ardent climate gets up early some morning and buys a river; and advertises for twelve or fifteen hundred Irishmen; digs a new channel for it, brings it to his mills, and has a head of twenty-four feet of water; then, to give him an appetite for his breakfast, he raises a house; then carves out, within doors, a

9. I.e., is sleep-inducing.   1. Creative.

quarter township into streets and building lots, tavern, school, and Methodist meeting-house—sends up an engineer into New Hampshire, to see where his water comes from, and, after advising with him, sends a trusty man of business to buy of all the farmers such mill-privileges as will serve him among their waste hill and pasture lots, and comes home with great glee announcing that he is now owner of the great Lake Winnipisogee, as reservoir for his Lowell mills at midsummer.

They are an ardent race, and are as fully possessed with that hatred of labor, which is the principle of progress in the human race, as any other people. They must and will have the enjoyment without the sweat. So they buy slaves, where the women will permit it; where they will not, they make the wind, the tide, the waterfall, the steam, the cloud, the lightning, do the work, by every art and device their cunningest brain can achieve. ⟨1847⟩

[54]

We go to Europe to see aristocratic society with as few abatements as possible. We go to be Americanized, to import what we can. This country has its proper glory, though now shrouded and unknown. We will let it shine. Patriotism is balderdash. Our side, our state, our town, is boyish enough. But it is true that every foot of soil has its proper quality, that the grape on either side of the same fence has its own flavor, and so every acre on the globe, every group of people, every point of climate, has its own moral meaning whereof it is the symbol. For such a patriotism let us stand. * * * ⟨1847⟩

[55]

On further consideration of this practical quality, by which our people are proud to be marked, I concede its excellence; but practice or practicalness consists in the consequent or logical following out of a good theory. Here are they practical, i.e., they confound the means with the ends, and lose the ends thereby out of sight— freedom, worth, and beauty of life. ⟨1856⟩

[56]

Because our education is defective, because we are superficial and ill-read, we were forced to make the most of that position, of ignorance; to idealize ignorance. Hence America is a vast know-nothing party,[2] and we disparage books, and cry up intuition. With a few clever men we have made a reputable thing of that, and denouncing libraries and severe culture and magnifying the mother-wit swagger of bright boys from the country colleges, we

2. The name applied to various nativist organizations which agitated against alleged German and Irish political domination. In 1854 they formed the American Party, which in 1856 chose Millard Fillmore as a presidential candidate (he was defeated).

have even come so far as to deceive everybody, except ourselves, into an admiration of un-learning and inspiration, forsooth. ⟨1857⟩

[57]

The badness of the times is making death attractive.[3] ⟨April, 1850⟩

[58]

I waked at night, and bemoaned myself, because I had not thrown myself into this deplorable question of Slavery, which seems to want nothing so much as a few assured voices. But then, in hours of sanity, I recover myself, and say, "God must govern his own world, and knows his way out of this pit, without my desertion of my post, which has none to guard it but me. I have quite other slaves to free than those negroes, to wit, imprisoned spirits, imprisoned thoughts, far back in the brain of man,—far retired in the heaven of invention, and which, important to the republic of Man, have no watchman, or lover, or defender, but I." ⟨August, 1852⟩

[59]

The head of Washington hangs in my dining-room for a few days past, and I cannot keep my eyes off of it. It has a certain Appalachian strength, as if it were truly the first-fruits of America, and expressed the country. The heavy, leaden eyes turn on you, as the eyes of an ox in a pasture. And the mouth has a gravity and depth of quiet, as if this MAN had absorbed all the serenity of America, and left none for his restless, rickety, hysterical countrymen. Noble, aristocratic head, with all kinds of elevation in it, that come out by turns. Such majestical ironies, as he hears the day's politics, at table. We imagine him hearing the letter of General Cass, the letter of General Scott, the letter of Mr. Pierce,[4] the effronteries of Mr. Webster recited. This man listens like a god to these low conspirators. ⟨July 6, 1852⟩

[60]

Philip Randolph[5] was surprised to find me speaking to the politics of anti-slavery, in Philadelphia. I suppose, because he thought me a believer in general laws, and that it was a kind of distrust of my own general teachings to appear in active sympathy with these temporary heats.

He is right so far as that it is becoming in the scholar to insist on central soundness, rather than on superficial applications. I

3. Webster's "Seventh of March" speech in 1850, widely interpreted as a betrayal of the cause of the North, and the passage of the Fugitive Slave Law in 1851 deeply shook Emerson's conviction that the "scholar" could hold aloof from practical politics, and thereafter he spoke out vigorously on the antislavery side.
4. A Democratic politician, the Whig candidate for President, the Democratic candidate, respectively.
5. A young friend of Emerson's in Philadelphia.

am to give a wise and just ballot, though no man else in the republic doth. I am not to compromise or mix or accommodate. I
am to demand the absolute right, affirm that, and do that; but not
push Boston into a false, showy, and theatrical attitude, endeavoring to persuade her she is more virtuous than she is. Thereby I
am robbing myself, more than I am enriching the public. After
twenty, fifty, a hundred years, it will be quite easy to discriminate
who stood for the right, and who for the expedient.

The vulgar, comprising ranks on ranks of fine gentlemen, clergymen, college presidents and professors, and great Democratic
statesmen bellowing for Liberty, will of course go for safe degrees
of liberty,—that is, will side with property against the Spirit,
subtle and absolute, which keeps no terms. ⟨*February, 1855*⟩

[61]

Opposition is our belt and tonic. No opinion will pass, but must
stand the tug of war.

Men wish to pay homage to courage and perseverance, to a man
whose steps have no choice, but are planted, each one. We know
the austere law of liberty,—that it must be reconquered day by
day, that it subsists in a state of war, that it is always slipping away
from those who boast it, to those who fight for it. ⟨1855⟩

[62]

Very little reliance must be put on the common stories that circulate of Mr. Webster's or Mr. Choate's[6] learning, their Greek,
or their varied literature. That ice won't bear. Reading!—do
you mean that this senator or this lawyer, who stood by and allowed the passage of infamous laws, was a reader of Greek books?
That is not the question; but to what purpose did they read? I
allow them the merit of that reading which appears in their opinions, tastes, beliefs and practice. They read that they might know,
did they not? Well, these men did not know. They blundered;
they were utterly ignorant of that which every boy or girl of fifteen
knows perfectly,—the rights of men and women. And this big-
mouthed talker, among his dictionaries and Leipzig editions of
Lysias, had lost his knowledge. But the President of the Bank
nods to the President of the Insurance Office, and relates that at
Virginia Springs this idol of the forum exhausted a trunkful of
classic authors. There is always the previous question, How came
you on that side? You are a very elegant writer, but you can't write
up what gravitates down.[7] ⟨1859⟩

[63]

Courage charms us, because it indicates that a man loves an idea
better than all things in the world, that he is thinking neither of

6. Rufus Choate, lawyer and orator.
7. Part of this passage is printed here
as it appeared in "The Man of Letters"
(1884).

his bed, nor his dinner, nor his money, but will venture all to put in act the invisible thought of his mind.[8] ⟨*October, 1859*⟩

[64]

Liberty, like religion, is a short and hasty fruit of rare and happy conditions. ⟨*February, 1861*⟩

[65]

[The English] write better, but we read more out of their books than they do. They have better blowpipe; we have not yet narrowed our heat to a focus,—a continent full of coal. England possesses drastic skill, always better artists than we: Carlyle a better writer, Gladstone or Bright[9] a better debater, I suppose, than any of ours. Tennyson a better poet; but is the scope as high? Is the material of Tennyson better, or does not our dumb muse see stars and horizons they do not? In England, in France, in Germany, is the popular sentiment as illuminated as here? As I wrote the other day,—our native politics are ideal.[1] These women, old wives sitting by the chimneyside here, shrill their exclamations of impatience and indignation, shame on Mr. Seward,[2] shame on the Senate, etc., for their want of humanity, of mere morality; they stand on the ground of simple morality, and not on the class feeling which narrows the perception of English, French, German people, at home. We are affirmative; they live under obstructions and negations. England's six points of Chartism[3] are still postponed. They have all been granted here to begin with. England has taken in more partners, stands better on its legs than once, but still has huge load to carry. See how this moderates the ferocity incident elsewhere to political changes. We, in the midst of a great Revolution, still enacting the sentiment of the Puritans, and the dreams of young people thirty years ago; we, passing out of the old remainders of barbarism into pure Christianity and humanity, into freedom of thought, of religion, of speech, of the press, and of trade, and of suffrage, or political right; and working through this tremendous ordeal, which elsewhere went by beheadings, and massacre, and reigns of terror,—passing through all this and through states and territories, like a sleep, and drinking our tea the while. 'Tis like a brick house moved from its old foundations and place, and passing through our streets, whilst all the family are pursuing their domestic work inside.

I hate to have the egotism thrust in with such effrontery. This

---

8. Written shortly after John Brown's raid on Harpers Ferry.
9. British statesmen.
1. The coming of the war, for all its "madness," restored Emerson's confidence in the conscience and destiny of his country. He never questioned the justice of the Northern cause.

2. The Secretary of State.
3. Universal male suffrage, equal electoral districts, secret ballot, annual general elections, payment of and no property qualifications for members of Parliament were urged in the People's Charter, May 8, 1838.

revolution is the work of no man, but the effervescence of Nature. It never did not work. But nothing that has occurred but has been a surprise, and as much to the leaders as to the hindmost. And not an Abolitionist, not an idealist, can say without effrontery, I did it. It is the fly on the coach, again. Go boost the globe, or scotch the globe, to accelerate or retard it in its orb! It is elemental, it is the old eternal gravitations: beware of the swing and of the recoil! Who knows, or has computed, the periods? A little earlier, and you would have been burned or crazed; a little later, you are unnecessary. * * * ⟨*November, 1863*⟩

[People and Places]

[66]

One has patience with every kind of living thing, but not with the dead alive. I, at least, hate to see persons of that lumpish class who are here they know not why, and ask not whereto, but live as the larva of the ant or the bee, to be lugged into the sun, and then lugged back into the cell, and then fed. The end of nature for such, is that they should be fatted. If mankind should pass a vote on the subject, I think they would throw them in sacks into the sea. ⟨*January 29, 1837*⟩

[67]

I hate goodies. I hate goodness that preaches. Goodness that preaches undoes itself. A little electricity of virtue lurks here and there in kitchens and among the obscure, chiefly women, that flashes out occasional light and makes the existence of the thing still credible. But one had as lief curse and swear as be guilty of this odious religion that watches the beef and watches the cider in the pitcher at table, that shuts the mouth hard at any remark it cannot twist nor wrench into a sermon, and preaches as long as itself and its hearer is awake. Goodies make us very bad. * * * We will almost sin to spite them. Better indulge yourself, feed fat, drink liquors, than go straitlaced for such cattle as these. ⟨*June 23, 1838*⟩

[68]

A man avails much to us, like a point of departure to the seaman, or his stake and stones to the surveyor. I am my own man more than most men, yet the loss of a few persons would be most impoverishing;—a few persons who give flesh to what were, else, mere thoughts, and which now I am not at liberty to slight, or in any manner treat as fictions.[4] It were too much to say that the Platonic world I might have learned to treat as cloud-land, had I

---

4. For all Emerson's scorn of the many-too-many, he was deeply indebted to a few "affirmative men," two in chief being his fellow townsmen Bronson Alcott and Thoreau. Though both Thoreau and Emerson complained of each other in their private journals, their relationship was of deep importance to both men.

not known Alcott, who is a native of that country, yet I will say that he makes it as solid as Massachusetts to me; and Thoreau gives me, in flesh and blood and pertinacious Saxon belief, my own ethics. He is far more real, and daily practically obeying them, than I; and fortifies my memory at all times with an affirmative experience which refuses to be set aside. ⟨*July, 1852*⟩

[69]

* * * I told Henry Thoreau that his freedom is in the form, but he does not disclose new matter. I am very familiar with all his thoughts,—they are my own quite originally drest. But if the question be, what new ideas has he thrown into circulation, he has not yet told what that is which he was created to say. I said to him what I often feel, I only know three persons who seem to me fully to see this law of reciprocity or compensation,—himself, Alcott, and myself: and 'tis odd that we should all be neighbors, for in the wide land or the wide earth I do not know another who seems to have it as deeply and originally as these three Gothamites.[5] ⟨*October, 1841*⟩

[70]

Henry Thoreau's conversation consisted of a continual coining of the present moment into a sentence and offering it to me. I compared it to a boy, who, from the universal snow lying on the earth, gathers up a little in his hand, rolls it into a ball, and flings it at me. ⟨*1844*⟩

[71]

Henry said that the other world was all his art; that his pencils would draw no other; that his jackknife would cut nothing else. He does not use it as a means. Henry is a good substantial Childe,[6] not encumbered with himself. He has no troublesome memory, no wake, but lives *ex tempore*, and brings to-day a new proposition as radical and revolutionary as that of yesterday, but different. The only man of leisure in the town. He is a good Abbot Samson;[7] and carries counsel in his breast. If I cannot show his performance much more manifest than that of the other grand promisers, at least I can see that, with his practical faculty, he has declined all the kingdoms of this world. Satan has no bribe for him.[8] ⟨*1847*⟩

[72]

If I knew only Thoreau, I should think cooperation of good men impossible. Must we always talk for victory, and never once for truth, for comfort, and joy? Centrality he has, and penetration, strong understanding, and the higher gifts—the insight of the real, or from the real, and the moral rectitude that belongs to it;

5. The three wise men of Gotham were legendary fools.
6. A noble youth, a knight.
7. Abbot of St. Edmundsbury in Carlyle's *Past and Present*.
8. Cf. Matthew iv.8–10.

but all this and all his resources of wit and invention are lost to me, in every experiment, year after year, that I make, to hold intercourse with his mind. Always some weary cautious paradox to fight you with, and the time and temper wasted. ⟨1856⟩

[73]

In reading Henry Thoreau's journal, I am very sensible of the vigor of his constitution. That oaken strength which I noted whenever he walked, or worked, or surveyed wood-lots, the same unhesitating hand with which a field-laborer accosts a piece of work, which I should shun as a waste of strength, Henry shows in his literary task. He has muscle, and ventures on and performs feats which I am forced to decline. In reading him, I find the same thought, the same spirit that is in me, but he takes a step beyond, and illustrates by excellent images that which I should have conveyed in a sleepy generality. 'Tis as if I went into a gymnasium, and saw youths leap, climb, and swing with a force unapproachable,—though their feats are only continuations of my initial grapplings and jumps. ⟨June, 1863⟩

[74]

* * * I begged Alcott to paint out his project,[9] and he proceeded to say that there should be found a farm of a hundred acres in excellent condition, with good buildings, a good orchard, and grounds which admitted of being laid out with great beauty; and this should be purchased and given to them, in the first place. I replied, You ask too much. This is not solving the problem; there are hundreds of innocent young persons, whom, if you will thus stablish and endow and protect, will find it no hard matter to keep their innocency. And to see their tranquil household, after all this has been done for them, will in no wise instruct or strengthen me. But he will instruct and strengthen me, who, there where he is, unaided, in the midst of poverty, toil, and traffic, extricates himself from the corruptions of the same and builds on his land a house of peace and benefit, good customs, and free thoughts. But, replied Alcott, how is this to be done? How can I do it who have a wife and family to maintain? I answered that he was not the person to do it, or he would not ask the question. When he that shall come is born, he will not only see the thing to be done, but invent the life, invent the ways and means of doing it. * * *

This fatal fault in the logic of our friends still appears: Their

9. Amos Bronson Alcott (1799–1888) was an inspired teacher, an uninspired writer, an incessant talker, and a fervent idealist. In 1843, in company with the English reformer Charles Lane and his own long-suffering family, he started the Utopian community of Fruitlands, which broke up that same winter. At its collapse, Edward Emerson writes, "Mr. Alcott was so grieved that he was in despair and refused food, and was restored to normal life and cheer with difficulty."

whole doctrine is spiritual, but they always end with saying,
Give us much land and money. If I should give them anything,
it would be facility and not beneficence. Unless one should say
after the maxims of the world, Let them drink their own error
to saturation, and this will be the best hellebore.[1] * * * ⟨No-
vember 19, 1842⟩

[75]

The sun and the evening sky do not look calmer than Alcott
and his family at Fruitlands. They seemed to have arrived at the
fact, to have got rid of the show, and so to be serene. Their
manners and behavior in the house and in the field were those
of superior men, of men at rest. What had they to conceal?
What had they to exhibit? And it seemed so high an attainment
that I thought, as often before, so now more, because they had a
fit home or the picture was fitly framed, that these men ought
to be maintained in their place by the country for its culture.
Young men and young maidens, old men and women, should
visit them and be inspired. I think there is as much merit in
beautiful manners as in hard work. I will not prejudge them
successful. They look well in July. We will see them in December. I know they are better for themselves than as partners. One
can easily see that they have yet to settle several things. Their
saying that things are clear, and they sane, does not make them
so. If they will in very deed be lovers and not selfish; if they will
serve the town of Harvard, and make their neighbors feel them
as benefactors wherever they touch them, they are as safe as the
sun. ⟨July 8, 1843⟩

[76]

Very sad, indeed, it was to see this half-god driven to the wall,
reproaching men, and hesitating whether he should not reproach
the gods. The world was not, on trial, a possible element for him
to live in. A lover of law had tried whether law could be kept in
this world, and all things answered, No. He had entertained the
thought of leaving it, and going where freedom and an element
could be found. And if he should be found tomorrow at the road-
side, it would be the act of the world. We pleaded guilty to perceiving the inconvenience and the inequality of property, and he
said, "I will not be a convict." Very tedious and prosing and
egotistical and narrow he is, but a profound insight, a Power, a
majestical man, looking easily along the centuries to explore *his
contemporaries*, with a painful sense of being an orphan and a
hermit here. I feel his statement to be partial and to have fatal
omissions, but I think I shall never attempt to set him right any

1. A drastic cathartic.

more. It is not for me to answer him: though I feel the limitations and exaggeration of his picture, and the wearisome personalities. His statement proves too much: it is a *reductio ad absurdum*. But I was quite ashamed to have just revised and printed last week the old paper denying the existence of tragedy, when this modern Prometheus was in the heat of his quarrel with the gods. * * * ⟨*April, 1844*⟩

[77]

* * * For every opinion or sentence of Alcott, a reason may be sought and found, not in his will or fancy, but in the necessity of nature itself, which has daguerred[2] that fatal impression on his susceptible soul. He is as good as a lens or a mirror, a beautiful susceptibility, every impression on which is not to be reasoned against, or derided, but to be accounted for, and until accounted for, registered as an addition to our catalogue of natural facts. There are defects in the lens, and errors of refraction and position, etc., to be allowed for, and it needs one acquainted with the lens by frequent use, to make these allowances; but 'tis the best instrument I have ever met with. ⟨*1856*⟩

[78]

Society an imperfect union.—Is it not pathetic that the action of men on men is so partial? We never touch but at points. The most that I can have or be to my fellow man, is it the reading of his book, or the hearing of his project in conversation? I approach some Carlyle with desire and joy. I am led on from month to month with an expectation of some total embrace and oneness with a noble mind, and learn at last that it is only so feeble and remote and hiant[3] action as reading a Mirabeau or a Diderot paper, and a few the like. This is all that can be looked for. More we shall not be to each other. Baulked soul! It is not that the sea and poverty and pursuit separate us. Here is Alcott by my door, yet is the union more profound? No, the Sea, vocation, poverty, are seeming fences, but man is insular and cannot be touched. Every man is an infinitely repellent orb, and holds his individual being on that condition. ⟨*May 19, 1837*⟩

[79]

Nathaniel Hawthorne's reputation as a writer is a very pleasing fact, because his writing is not good for anything, and this is a tribute to the man.[4] ⟨*September, 1842*⟩

2. Imprinted as by photography.
3. Gaping. Honoré Riqueti, Comte de Mirabeau, was a writer and the most important figure in the first two years of the French Revolution; Denis Diderot, 18th-century French writer, edited the *Encyclopédie*.

4. For many years Nathaniel Hawthorne was also a neighbor. He and Emerson were benevolently aware of each other, but each kept his distance, Emerson illustrating the problem of optimism to Hawthorne, Hawthorne that of solitude to Emerson.

[80]

Yesterday, May 23, we buried Hawthorne in Sleepy Hollow, in a pomp of sunshine and verdure, and gentle winds. James Freeman Clarke read the service in the church and at the grave. Longfellow, Lowell, Holmes, Agassiz, Hoar, Dwight, Whipple, Norton, Alcott, Hillard, Fields, Judge Thomas, and I attended the hearse as pallbearers. Franklin Pierce[5] was with the family. The church was copiously decorated with white flowers delicately arranged. The corpse was unwillingly shown,—only a few moments to this company of his friends. But it was noble and serene in its aspect, —nothing amiss,—a calm and powerful head. A large company filled the church and the grounds of the cemetery. All was so bright and quiet that pain or mourning was hardly suggested, and Holmes said to me that it looked like a happy meeting.

Clarke in the church said that Hawthorne had done more justice than any other to the shades of life, shown a sympathy with the crime in our nature, and, like Jesus, was the friend of sinners.

I thought there was a tragic element in the event, that might be more fully rendered,—in the painful solitude of the man, which, I suppose, could not longer be endured, and he died of it.

I have found in his death a surprise and disappointment. I thought him a greater man than any of his works betray, that there was still a great deal of work in him, and that he might one day show a purer power. Moreover, I have felt sure of him in his neighborhood, and in his necessities of sympathy and intelligence, —that I could well wait his time,—his unwillingness and caprice, —and might one day conquer a friendship. It would have been a happiness, doubtless to both of us, to have come into habits of unreserved intercourse. It was easy to talk with him,—there were no barriers,—only, he said so little, that I talked too much, and stopped only because, as he gave no indications, I feared to exceed. He showed no egotism or self-assertion, rather a humility, and, at one time, a fear that he had written himself out. One day, when I found him on the top of his hill, in the woods, he paced back the path to his house, and said, "This path is the only remembrance of me that will remain." Now it appears that I waited too long.

Lately he had removed himself the more by the indignation his perverse politics and unfortunate friendship for that paltry Franklin Pierce awakened, though it rather moved pity for Hawthorne, and the assured belief that he would outlive it, and come right at last. ⟨*May 24, 1864*⟩

5. President of the U.S. (1852–56), Bowdoin classmate and lifelong friend of Hawthorne.

[81] LETTER TO WALT WHITMAN

Concord, July 21, 1855

I am not blind to the worth of the wonderful gift of *Leaves of Grass*. I find it the most extraordinary piece of wit and wisdom that America has yet contributed. I am very happy in reading it, as great power makes us happy. It meets the demand I am always making of what seemed the sterile and stingy Nature, as if too much handiwork, or too much lymph in the temperament, were making our Western wits fat and mean.[6]

I give you joy of your free and brave thought. I have great joy in it. I find incomparable things said incomparably well, as they must be. I find the courage of treatment which so delights us, and which large perception only can inspire.

I greet you at the beginning of a great career, which yet must have had a long foreground somewhere, for such a start. I rubbed my eyes a little, to see if this sunbeam were no illusion; but the solid sense of the book is a sober certainty. It has the best merits, namely, of fortifying and encouraging. * * *

[82] LETTER TO THOMAS CARLYLE

Concord, May 6, 1856

* * * One book, last summer, came out in New York, a non-descript monster which yet had terrible eyes and buffalo strength, and was indisputably American,—which I thought to send you; but the book throve so badly with the few to whom I showed it, and wanted good morals so much, that I never did. Yet I believe now again, I shall. It is called *Leaves of Grass*,—was written and printed by a journeyman printer in Brooklyn, New York, named Walter Whitman; and after you have looked into it, if you think, as you may, that it is only an auctioneer's inventory of a warehouse, you can light your pipe with it. * * *

[83]

At Washington, January 31, February 1, 2, and 3, saw Sumner,[7] who, on the 2d, carried me to Mr. Chase, Mr. Bates, Mr. Stanton, Mr. Welles, Mr. Seward, Lord Lyons,[8] and President Lincoln. The President impressed me more favorably than I had hoped. A frank, sincere, well-meaning man, with a lawyer's habit of mind, good clear statement of his fact; correct enough, not vulgar, as described, but with a sort of boyish cheerfulness, or that kind of sincerity and jolly good meaning that our class meetings on Commencement

6. The disapproval of Emerson's friends and family, together with Whitman's brash publication of his letter of congratulation, soon modified his enthusiasm. Cf. "The Poet" and the *Journals* section on "[Poetry and Inspiration]," above.
7. Charles Sumner, Senator from Massachusetts.
8. Members of the Cabinet, except for Lord Lyons, the British ambassador.

Days show, in telling our old stories over. When he has made his remark, he looks up at you with great satisfaction, and shows all his white teeth, and laughs. He argued to Sumner the whole case of Gordon, the slave-trader, point by point, and added that he was not quite satisfied yet, and meant to refresh his memory by looking again at the evidence. All this showed a fidelity and conscientiousness very honorable to him.

When I was introduced to him, he said, "Oh, Mr. Emerson, I once heard you say in a lecture, that a Kentuckian seems to say by his air and manners, 'Here am I; if you don't like me, the worse for you.'" ⟨*January 31, 1862*⟩

[84]

Lincoln.—We must accept the results of universal suffrage, and not try to make it appear that we can elect fine gentlemen. We shall have coarse men, with a fair chance of worth and manly ability, but not men to please the English or French.

You cannot refine Mr. Lincoln's taste, or extend his horizon; he will not walk dignifiedly through the tradition part of the President of America, but will pop out his head at each railroad station and make a little speech, and get into an argument with Squire A. and Judge B. He will write letters to Horace Greeley,[9] and any editor or reporter or saucy party committee that writes to him, and cheapen himself.

But this we must be ready for, and let the clown appear, and hug ourselves that we are well off, if we have got good nature, honest meaning, and fidelity to public interest, with bad manners,—instead of an elegant *roué* and malignant self-seeker. ⟨1863⟩

[85] LETTER TO LIDIAN EMERSON[1]

St. Louis, June 16, 1850

* * * Cairo, you know, is a tongue of low land which separates the Ohio and Mississippi. Many years ago it was seized upon by speculators as a point that must necessarily be a depot of immense importance. The land for ten miles from the point was bought and lots were laid out and the biggest city of the world was to be here. The Rothschilds[2] are or have been owners or mortgagees of the property. But the river during a large part of the year keeps the whole of it under water, and the houses that were built by the Companies are now wide open to every pedlar and boatman to enter and take possession, if he will. The only habitable place seemed to be (what is often seen in these rivers) an old steamboat

9. Founder and editor of the *New-York Tribune*. The allusion is to Lincoln's letter to Greeley of August 22, 1862, in which he reiterated that his purpose was to save the Union, with or without slavery.
1. His wife Lydia.
2. Wealthy international banking house.

whose engine has been taken out and the boat moored and fitted up into the dirtiest of Ann-street boarding-houses. Here we took in wood, and tinkered at our engine—an operation, this last, almost as frequent in my recent experience as the first. The boats are very cheaply and poorly built, no "palaces" at all, just made to keep above water from port to port, and generally disabled of one wheel. Well, we got away from Cairo, its sailor-shops, tenpin-alleys, and faro-tables, still on the green and almost transparent Ohio, which now seemed so broad that the yellow line in front for which we were steering, looked hopelessly narrow; but [the] yellow line widened as we drew nigh, and at last we reached and crossed the perfectly-marked line of green on one side, and mud-hue on the other, and entered the Mississippi. It is one of the great river landscapes of the world—wide, wide eddying waters, low shores. The great river takes in the Ohio which had grown so large, turns it all to its own mud color, and does not become perceptibly larger.

The great sweeps of the Mississippi, the number of its large islands made and unmade in short periods, your distance from either shore, and the unvarying character of the green wilderness on either side from hour to hour, from day to day,—the loneliest river—no towns, no houses, no dents in the forest, no boats almost,—we met I believe but one steam-boat in the first hundred miles;—now and then we notice a flat wood-boat lying under the shore, blow our whistle, ring our bell, and near the land; then out of some log-shed appear black or white men, and hastily put out their boat, a large mud-scow, loaded with corded wood. "How do you sell your wood?" cries the captain. "A dollar and a half." "Well, uncle, you'll help the men." So the scow is made fast to the boat, which immediately puts on steam again, and both go up the river amicably, till the negroes and sailors have got all the wood on board; then the scow is let go, and floats down stream home again. * * * Then there were planters traveling, one with his family of slaves (6 blacks); peaceable-looking, farmer-like men who, when they stretch themselves in the pauses of conversation, disclose the butts of their pistols in their breast-pockets. Then a knot of gamblers playing quite ostentatiously on the cabin-tables, and large sums changing owners rapidly, and, as we Yankees fancied, with some glances of hope aimed at us that we should sit down with these amiable gentlemen who professed to be entire strangers to each other, and, if asked any question respecting the river, "had never been on these waters before." * * *

[86]

Went to Yarmouth Sunday, 3d; to Orleans Monday, 4th; to Nauset Light on the back side of Cape Cod. Collins, the keeper, told us he found obstinate resistance on Cape Cod to the project of building a lighthouse on this coast, as it would injure the wrecking business. He had to go to Boston, and obtain the strong recommendation of the Port Society. From the high hill in the rear of Higgins's, in Orleans, I had a good view of the whole Cape and the sea on both sides. The Cape looks like one of the Newfoundland Banks just emerged, a huge tract of sand half-covered with poverty grass and beach grass, and for trees, abele and locust and plantations of pitch pine. Some good oak, and in Dennis and Brewster were lately good trees for ship lumber, and [they] still are well wooded on the east side. But the view I speak of looked like emaciated Orkneys,[3]—Mull, Islay, and so forth,—made of salt dust, gravel, and fish bones. They say the wind makes the roads, and, as at Nantucket, a large part of the real estate was freely moving back and forth in the air. I heard much of the coming railroad which is about to reach Yarmouth and Hyannis, and they hope will come to Provincetown. I fancied the people were only waiting for the railroad to reach them in order to evacuate the country. For the stark nakedness of the country could not be exaggerated. But no; nothing was less true. They are all attached to what they call *the soil*. Mr. Collins had been as far as Indiana; but, he said, hill on hill,—he felt stifled, and "longed for the Cape, where he could see out." And whilst I was fancying that they would gladly give away land to anybody that would come and live there, and be a neighbor: no, they said, all real estate had risen, all over the Cape, and you could not buy land at less than fifty dollars per acre. And, in Provincetown, a lot on the Front Street of forty feet square would cost five or six hundred dollars.

Still, I saw at the Cape, as at Nantucket, they are a little tender about your good opinion: for if a gentleman at breakfast says he don't like Yarmouth, all real estate seems to them at once depreciated two or three per cent.

They are very careful to give you directions what road you shall take from town to town; but, as the country has the shape of a piece of tape, it is not easy to lose your way. For the same reason it behooves everybody who goes on to the Cape to behave well, as he must stop on his return at all the same houses, unless he takes the packet at Provincetown for Boston, six hours in good weather, and a week in bad. ⟨September 5, 1853⟩

[*Emerson Himself*]

[87]

Last night a remembering and remembering talk with Lidian. I went back to the first smile of Ellen on the door-stone at Con-

---

3. Islands to the north of Scotland.

cord. I went back to all that delicious relation to feel, as ever, how many shades, how much reproach. Strange is it that I can go back to no part of youth, no past relation, without shrinking and shrinking. Not Ellen, not Edward, not Charles.[4] Infinite compunctions embitter each of those dear names, and all who surrounded them. Ah! could I have felt in the presence of the first, as now I feel, my own power and hope, and so have offered her in every word and look the heart of a man humble and wise, but resolved to be true and perfect with God, and not, as I fear it seemed, the uneasy, uncentered joy of one who received in her a good—a lovely good—out of all proportion to his deserts, I might haply have made her days longer and certainly sweeter, and at least have recalled her seraph smile without a pang. I console myself with the thought that if Ellen, if Edward, if Charles, could have read my entire heart, they should have seen nothing but rectitude of purpose and generosity conquering the superficial coldness and prudence. But I ask now, Why was not I made like all these beatified mates of mine, *superficially* generous and noble, as well as *internally* so? They never needed to shrink at any remembrance;—and I at so many sad passages that look to me now as if I [had] been blind and mad. Well, O God, I will try and learn from this sad memory to be brave and circumspect and true henceforth and weave now a web that will not shrink. This is the thorn in the flesh. ⟨*March 4, 1838*⟩

[88]

Last night E. H.[5] described the apathy from which she suffers. I own I was at a loss to prescribe, as I did not sufficiently understand the state of mind she paints. * * *

I complain in my own experience of the feeble influence of thought on life, a ray as pale and ineffectual as that of the sun in our cold and bleak spring. They seem to lie—the actual life and the intellectual intervals—in parallel lines and never meet. Yet we doubt not they act and react ever, that one is even cause of the other; that one is causal and one servile, a mere vesture. Yet it takes a great deal of elevation of thought to produce a very little elevation of life. How slowly the highest raptures of the intellect break through the trivial forms of habit. Yet imperceptibly they do. Gradually, in long years, we bend our living toward our idea, but we serve seven years and twice seven for Rachel.[6] If Mr. G., that old gander (I owned) should now stop at my gate, I should duck to him as to an angel, and waste all my time for him, etc., etc., instead of telling him, as truth

4. Ellen Tucker, his first wife, died of tuberculosis in 1832 after less than two years of marriage. Edward and Charles were two brothers who died, also of tuberculosis (from which Emerson himself suffered), in the 1830's.
5. Elizabeth Hoar(?).
6. Genesis xxix.

seems to require, that his visit and his babble was an impertinence, and bidding him Begone. Just so, when Miss W. and Mrs.
G. and Miss M. come, I straightway sit glued to my chair, all
thought, all action, all play, departed and paralyzed, and acquiesce, and become less than they are, instead of nodding slightly
to them and treating them like shadows, and persisting in the
whim of pathos, or the whim of fun, or the whim of poetry in
which they found me, and constraining them to accept the law
of this higher thought (also theirs) instead of kneeling to their
triviality.

*I'll tell you what to do; try to make humanity lovely unto
them.*[7] ⟨May 5, 1838⟩

[89]

I finish this morning transcribing my old essay on Love, but I
see well its inadequateness. I, cold because I am hot,—cold at
the surface only as a sort of guard and compensation for the fluid
tenderness of the core,—have much more experience than I have
written there, more than I will, more than I can write. In silence
we must wrap much of our life, because it is too fine for speech,
because also we cannot explain it to others, and because somewhat
we cannot yet understand. We do not live as angels, eager to introduce each other to new perfections in our brothers and sisters,
and frankly avowing our delight in each new trait of character, in
the magic of each new eyebeam, but that which passes for love in
the world gets official, and instead of embracing, hates all the divine
traits that dare to appear in other persons. A better and holier
society will mend this selfish cowardice, and we shall have brave
ties of affection, not petrified by law, not dated or ordained by law
to last for one year, for five years, or for life; but drawing their date,
like all friendship, from itself only; brave as I said, because innocent, and religiously abstinent from the connubial endearments,
being a higher league on a purely spiritual basis. This nobody believes possible who is not good. The good know it is possible.
* * * ⟨June 11, 1840⟩

[90] LETTER TO CAROLINE STURGIS[8]

Concord, February 4, 1842

The days of our mourning ought, no doubt, to be accomplished
ere this, and the innocent and beautiful should not be sourly and
gloomily lamented, but with music and fragrant thoughts and

---

7. Edward Emerson writes: "This sentence is faintly pencilled underneath,
and very possibly was written by Mrs.
Emerson." The thought, however, was
a favorite one of Emerson's.

8. Later Mrs. Tappan. She and her sister Ellen were friends of Margaret
Fuller (see passage 93) and contributed
poems to *The Dial*.

sportive recollections.[9] Alas! I chiefly grieve that I cannot grieve; that this fact takes no more deep hold than other facts, is as dream-like as they; a lambent flame that will not burn playing on the surface of my river. Must every experience—those that promised to be dearest and most penetrative,—only kiss my cheek like the wind and pass away? I think of Ixion and Tantalus and Kehama.[1] Dear Boy, too precious and unique a creation to be huddled aside into the waste and prodigality of things! * * * Calm and wise, calmly and wisely happy, the beautiful Creative power looked out from him and spoke of anything but chaos and interruption; signi-fied strength and unity—and gladdening, all-uniting life. * * *

[91]

I comprehend nothing of this fact but its bitterness. Explana-tion I have none, consolation none that rises out of the fact itself; only diversion; only oblivion of this and pursuit of new objects. ⟨*March*, 1842⟩

[92]

Man sheds grief as his skin sheds rain. A preoccupied mind an immense protection. There is a great concession on all hands to the ideal decorum in grief, as well as joy, but few hearts are broken. ⟨*May*, 1843⟩

[93] LETTER TO MARGARET FULLER[2]

Concord, June 7, 1843

* * * I love life—never little,—and now, I think, more and more, entertained and puzzled though I be by this lubricity of it, and inaccessibleness of its pith and heart. The variety of our vital game delights me. I seem in the bosom of all possibility and have never tried but one or two trivial experiments. In happy hours it seems as if one could not lie too lightly on it and like a cloud it would buoy him up and convey him anywhither. But by infirm faith we lose our delicate balance, flounder about and come into the realms and under the laws of mud and stones. The depth of the notes which we accidentally sound on the strings of nature are out of all proportion to our taught and ascertained power and teach us what strangers and novices we are in nature, vagabond in this universe of pure power to which we have not the smallest key. I will at least be glad of my days—I who have so many of them—

9. On January 27, 1842, Emerson's eldest son, Waldo, died at the age of five of scarlet fever. Emerson never got over this loss, recalling it even on his own deathbed. For a while after the blow, he felt under a curse of "dead-heartedness"; then a measure of "effi-cient faith" returned.
1. An allusion to Southey's *Curse of*
Kehama (1810). Ixion and Tantalus were punished in Hades: Ixion was bound to an ever turning wheel, while Tantalus, standing in water near the branches of fruit trees, found that both eluded him forever.
2. Writer, lecturer, feminist, and friend of the transcendentalists; she edited *The Dial* for its first two years.

and having been informed by God though in the casualest manner that my funds are inexhaustible I will believe it with all my heart. * * *

[94] LETTERS TO LIDIAN EMERSON

London, March 8, 1848

* * * Ah, you still ask me for that unwritten letter always due, it seems, always unwritten, from year to year, by me to you, dear Lidian,—I fear too more widely true than you mean,—always due and unwritten by me to every sister and brother of the human race. I have only to say that I also bemoan myself daily for the same cause, that I cannot write this letter, that I have not stamina and constitution enough to mind the two functions of seraph and cherub—oh no, let me not use such great words, rather say that a photometer cannot be a stove. It must content you for the time, that I truly acknowledge a poverty of nature, and have really no proud defence at all to set up, but ill-health, puniness, and Stygian limitation. * * *

London, April 20, 1848

* * * You wrote me the kindest and best account of your reading in the precious file of letters. Your feeling was just and noble. And they deserved all you have said. For they came out of a heart which nature and destiny conspired to keep as inviolate, as are still those three children of whom you send me such happy accounts. But I am deeply gratified by your pleasure and sympathy in them. Ah, how we wander from goal to goal of our life, and often it seems as if one thread of consciousness did not tie the far parts together. Who am I that roam these desarts, and knew this and that in old years? But you should have seen Ellen. When she left this world, I valued everybody who had seen her, and disliked to meet those who had not. * * *

[95]

What came over me with delight as I sat on the ledge in the warm light of last Sunday was the memory of young days at College, the delicious sensibility of youth, how the air rings to it! how all light is festal to it! how it at any moment extemporizes a holiday! I remember how boys riding out together on a fine day looked to me! ah, there was a romance! How sufficing was mere melody! The thought, the meaning, was insignificant; the whole joy was in the melody. For that I read poetry, and wrote it; and in the light of that memory I ought to understand the doctrine of musicians, that the words are nothing, the air is all. What a joy I found, and still can find, in the Aeolian harp![3] What a youth find

3. Wind harp. An instrument with tuned strings and sounding board placed in a window for the wind to play. Cf. Coleridge, "The Æolian Harp."

I still in Collins's "Ode to Evening," and in Gray's "Eton College"! What delight I owed to Moore's insignificant but melodious poetry.[4]

That is the merit of Clough's "Bothie," that the joy of youth is in it. Ah the power of the spring! and, ah, the voice of the bluebird! And the witchcraft of the Mount Auburn dell, in those days! I shall be a Squire Slender[5] for a week. ⟨*February, 1861*⟩

[Nature]

[96]

Here[6] we are impressed with the inexhaustible riches of nature. The universe is a more amazing puzzle than ever, as you glance along this bewildering series of animated forms,—the hazy butterflies, the carved shells, the birds, beasts, fishes, insects, snakes, and the upheaving principle of life everywhere incipient, in the very rock aping organized forms. Not a form so grotesque, so savage, nor so beautiful but is an expression of some property inherent in man the observer,—an occult relation between the very scorpions and man. I feel the centipede in me,—cayman, carp, eagle, and fox. I am moved by strange sympathies; I say continually, "I will be a naturalist." ⟨*1833*⟩

[97]

As I walked in the woods I felt what I often feel, that nothing can befal me in life, no calamity, no disgrace, (leaving me my eyes) to which Nature will not offer a sweet consolation. Standing on the bare ground with my head bathed by the blithe air, and uplifted into the infinite space, I become happy in my universal relations. The name of the nearest friend sounds then foreign and accidental. I am the heir of uncontained beauty and power. And if then I walk with a companion, he should speak from his Reason to my Reason; that is, both from God. To be brothers, to be acquaintances, master or servant, is then a trifle too insignificant for remembrance. O, keep this humor, (which in your lifetime may not come to you twice,) as the apple of your eye. Set a lamp before it in your memory which shall never be extinguished.[7] ⟨*March 19, 1835*⟩

[98]

Man is an analogist. He cannot help seeing everything under its relations to all other things and to himself. * * * The delight

4. William Collins (1721–59); Thomas Gray (1716–71), author of "Ode on a Distant Prospect of Eton College" (1742); Thomas Moore (1779–1852), author of *Irish Melodies* (1807–35); Arthur Hugh Clough (1819–61), author of *The Bothie of Tober-na-Vuolich* (1848), a story of young love (a "bothie" is a hut or cottage).

5. Emerson means Justice Shallow, who (*2 Henry IV*) is always recollecting his bygone youth.
6. Written after a visit to the Jardin des Plantes in Paris, a famous botanical and zoological garden.
7. Cf. the revised version in *Nature*, pp. 190–91.

that man finds in classification[8] is the first index of his Destiny. He is to put nature under his feet by a knowledge of Laws. * * * Science [is] to apprehend Nature in Ideas. The moment an idea is introduced among facts the God takes possession. Until then, facts conquer us. The beast rules man. Thus through nature is there a striving upward. Commodity points to a greater good. Beauty is naught until the spiritual element. Language refers to that which is to be said. Finally, Nature is a discipline, and points to the pupil and exists for the pupil. Her being is subordinate; his is superior. Man underlies Ideas. Nature receives them as her God. ⟨1836⟩

[99]

"Miracles have ceased." Have they indeed? When? They had not ceased this afternoon when I walked into the wood and got into bright, miraculous sunshine, in shelter from the roaring wind. Who sees a pine-cone, or the turpentine exuding from the tree, or a leaf, the unit of vegetation, fall from its bough, as if it said, "the year is finished," or hears in the quiet, piny glen the titmouse chirping his cheerful note, or walks along the lofty promontory-like ridges which, like natural causeways, traverse the morass, or gazes upward at the rushing clouds, or downward at a moss or a stone and says to himself, "Miracles have ceased"? Tell me, good friend, when this hillock on which your foot stands swelled from the level of the sphere by volcanic force; pick up that pebble at your feet; look at its gray sides, its sharp crystal, and tell me what fiery inundation of the world melted the minerals like wax, and, as if the globe were one glowing crucible, gave this stone its shape. There is the truth-speaking pebble itself, to affirm to endless ages the thing was so. Tell me where is the manufactory of this air, so thin, so blue, so restless, which eddies around you, in which your life floats, of which your lungs are but an organ, and which you coin into musical words. I am agitated with curiosity to know the secret of nature. Why cannot geology, why cannot botany speak and tell me what has been, what is, as I run along the forest promontory, and ask when it rose like a blister on heated steel? Then I looked up and saw the sun shining in the vast sky, and heard the wind bellow above and the water glistened in the vale. These were the forces that wrought then and work now. Yes, there they grandly speak to all plainly, in proportion as we are quick to apprehend. ⟨November, 1837⟩

[100]

The moon and Jupiter side by side last night stemmed the sea of clouds and plied their voyage in convoy through the sublime

8. Note that Emerson has "captured" this term: it signifies here not separation into classes but unification into organic wholes. With this whole passage, cf. *Nature*, including the 1836 motto.

Deep as I walked the old and dusty road. The snow and the enchantment of the moonlight make all landscapes alike, and the
road that is so tedious and homely that I never take it by day,
—by night is Italy or Palmyra.[9] In these divine pleasures permitted to me of walks in the June night under moon and stars,
I can put my life as a fact before me and stand aloof from its
honor and shame. ⟨*June 28, 1838*⟩

[101]

Nature.—I think I must do these eyes of mine the justice to
write a new chapter on Nature.[1] This delight we all take in every
show of night or day, of field or forest or sea or city, down to the
lowest particulars, is not without sequel, though we be as yet only
wishers and gazers, not at all knowing what we want. We are pre-
dominated herein, as elsewhere, by an upper wisdom, and resemble
those great discoverers who are haunted for years, sometimes from
infancy, with a passion for the fact or class of facts in which the
secret lies which they are destined to unlock, and they let it not
go until the blessing is won. So these sunsets and starlights, these
swamps and rocks, these birdnotes and animal forms off which we
cannot get our eyes and ears, but hover still, as moths, round a
lamp, are no doubt a Sanscrit cipher covering the whole religious
history of the universe, and presently we shall read it off into action
and character. The pastures are full of ghosts for me, the morning
woods full of angels. Now and then they give me a broad hint.
Every natural fact is trivial until it becomes symbolical or moral.
⟨*June, 1840*⟩

[102]

That bread which we ask of Nature is that she should entrance
us, but amidst her beautiful or her grandest pictures I cannot escape the *second thought.* I walked this P.M. in the woods, but
there too the snowbanks were sprinkled with tobacco-juice. We
have the wish to forget night and day, father and mother, food
and ambition, but we never lose our dualism. Blessed, wonderful
Nature, nevertheless! without depth, but with immeasurable lateral
spaces. If we look before us, if we compute our path, it is very
short. Nature has only the thickness of a shingle or a slate: we
come straight to the extremes; but sidewise, and at unawares,
the present moment opens into other moods and moments, rich,
prolific, leading onward without end. * * * ⟨1844⟩

9. Ancient ruined city in Syria.   *Second Series* (1844; not the book of
1. Emerson did so in "Nature," *Essays,*   1836).

[Evolution]

[103]

There are always two histories of man in literature contending for our faith.[2] One is the scientific or skeptical, and derives his origin from the gradual composition, subsidence, and refining,—from the Negro, from the ape, progressive from the animalcule savages of the waterdrop, from *volvox globator*,[3] up to the wise man of the nineteenth century. The other is the believer's, the poet's, the faithful history, always testified by the mystic and the devout, the history of the Fall, of a descent from a superior and pure race, attested in actual history by the grand remains of elder ages, of a science in the East unintelligible to the existing population; Cyclopean architecture[4] in all quarters of the world. * * * The faithful dogma assumes that the other is an optical show, but that the universe was long already complete through law; and that the tiger and the midge are only penal forms, the Auburn and Sing-Sing of nature; men, men, all and everywhere. ⟨August, 1845⟩

[104]

* * * Metamorphosis is the law of the universe. All forms are fluent, and as the bird alights on the bough and pauses for rest, then plunges into the air again on its way, so the thoughts of God pause but for a moment in any form, but pass into a new form, as if by touching the earth again in burial, to acquire new energy. A wise man is not deceived by the pause: he knows that it is momentary: he already foresees the new departure, and departure after departure, in long series. Dull people think they have traced the matter far enough if they have reached the history of one of these temporary forms, which they describe as fixed and final. ⟨1845⟩

[105]

The melioration in pears, or in sheep and horses, is the only hint we have that suggests the creation of man. Everything has a family likeness to him. All natural history from the first fossil points at him. The resemblances approach very near in the satyr, to the Negro, or lowest man, and food, climate, and concurrence of happy stars, a guided fortune, will have at last piloted the poor quadrumanous[5] over the awful bar that separates the fixed beast from the versatile man. In no other direction have we any hint of the *modus* in which the infant man could be preserved. The fixity

2. As the 1836 motto to *Nature* suggests, Emerson at first inclined to the traditional Neo-Platonist view of nature as an emanation, "the last thing of the soul." Notions of evolution, however, soon filtered into his thought from many pre-Darwinian sources; their influence can be seen in the motto to *Na-* *ture* which he substituted in 1849.

3. A species of algae.

4. Certain huge ancient constructions were traditionally ascribed to the Cyclopes (a race of giants that figure in the *Odyssey*).

5. Four-handed.

or unpassableness or inconvertibility of races, as we see them, is a feeble argument, since all the historical period is but a point to the duration in which Nature was wrought. Any the least and solitariest fact in our natural history has the worth of a power in the opportunity of geologic periods. All our apples came from the little crab. ⟨1855⟩

[106]

Seek things in their purity. Well, we try, on each subject we accost, to ascend to principles; to dip our pen in the blackest of the pot; and to be sure, find the cause of the trait in some organ, as spleen, or bone, or blood. We are not nearer; we are still outside. Nature itself is nothing but a skin, and all these but coarser cuticles. A god or genius sits regent over every plant and animal, and causes this, and knits this to that, after an order or plan which is intellectual. The botanist, the physicist, is not then the man deepest immersed in nature, as if he were ready to bear apples or to shoot out four legs, but one filled with the lightest and purest air, who sympathizes with the creative spirit, anticipates the tendency, and where the bird will next alight; being himself full of the same tendency. ⟨1856⟩

[Fate and Possibility]

[107]

It is the largest part of a man that is not inventoried. He has many enumerable parts: he is social, professional, political, sectarian, literary, and is this or that set and corporation. But after the most exhausting census has been made, there remains as much more which no tongue can tell. And this remainder is that which interests. This is that which the preacher and the poet and the musician speak to. This is that which the strong genius works upon; the region of destiny, of aspiration, of the unknown. Ah, they have a secret persuasion that as little as they pass for in the world, they are immensely rich in expectancy and power. Nobody has ever yet dispossessed this adhesive self to arrive at any glimpse or guess of the awful Life that lurks under it.

Far the best part, I repeat, of every mind is not that which he knows, but that which hovers in gleams, suggestions, tantalizing, unpossessed, before him. His firm recorded knowledge soon loses all interest for him. But this dancing chorus of thoughts and hopes is the quarry of his future, is his possibility, and teaches him that his man's life is of a ridiculous brevity and meanness, but that it is his first age and trial only of his young wings, [and] that vast revolutions, migrations, and gyres on gyres in the celestial societies invite him. ⟨1845⟩

[108]

Day creeps after day, each full of facts, dull, strange, despised things that we cannot enough despise,—call heavy, prosaic, and desart. And presently the aroused intellect finds gold and gems in one of these scorned facts, then finds that the day of facts is a rock of diamonds, that a fact is an Epiphany of God, that on every fact of his life he should rear a temple of wonder, joy, and praise; that in going to eat meat, to buy, or sell, to meet a friend, or thwart an adversary, to communicate a piece of news, or buy a book, he celebrates the arrival of an inconceivably remote purpose and law at last on the shores of Being, and into the ripeness and term of nature. And because nothing chances, but all is locked and wheeled and chained in Law, in these motes and dust he can read the writing of the True Life and of a startling sublimity.[6] ⟨June 21, 1838⟩

[109]

Conjure with the great name. Who forbade you to create? Fear. And who made fear? Sin; Inaction; Ignorance. What is this astounding greatness of other men that they should be as god to you? Why, it is two things: First, your littleness, which makes them seem so large; and, second, your identity with them, which makes them delightful to you as the colossal portrait of yourself. If society sleeps and snores, if there is no art, no poetry, no genius, no virtue, do not say that such things cannot be, but remember in your own sorrowful life the sin that is also in theirs, namely, the surrender of hope, the voluntary abdication that somewhere was, covered up now in the bushes and wilderness of so many years. When you said,—"As others do, so will I; I renounce—I am sorry for it—my early visions. I must eat the good of the land, and let learning and romantic expectations go until a more convenient season,"—then died the man in you; then perished the buds of art and poetry and genius. Had you stood firm, had many stood firm, Oh God! had all,—we should no longer speak of society with cold disapproval, warning you against it, but we should see in it the half-gods, whose traces are not yet quite obliterated, careering in contest or in love, in the still grand remains of Greek art. ⟨June 22, 1838⟩

[110]

Circumstances are dreams, which, springing unawares from ourselves, amuse us whilst we doze and sleep, but when we wake, nothing but causes can content us. The life of man is the true romance which, when it is valiantly conducted and all the stops of the instrument opened, will go nigh to craze the reader with anxiety, wonder and love. I am losing all relish for books and for feats of

6. With this and the following passage, cf. the poem "Days."

skill in my delight in this Power. Do not accuse me of sloth. Do not ask me to your philanthropics, charities, and duties, as you term them;—mere circumstances;—flakes of the snow-cloud, leaves of the trees;—I sit at home with the cause, grim or glad. I think I may never do anything that you shall call a deed again. I have been writing with some pains Essays on various matters as a sort of apology to my country for my apparent idleness. But the poor work has looked poorer daily, as I strove to end it. My genius seemed to quit me in such a mechanical work, a seeming wise— a cold exhibition of dead thoughts. When I write a letter to any- one whom I love, I have no lack of words or thoughts. I am wiser than myself and read my paper with the pleasure of one who re- ceives a letter, but what I write to fill up the gaps of a chapter is hard and cold, is grammar and logic; there is no magic in it; I do not wish to see it again. Settle with yourself your accusations of me. If I do not please you, ask me not to please you, but please yourself. What you call my indolence, Nature does not accuse; the twinkling leaves, the sailing fleets of water-flies, the deep sky, like me well enough and know me for their own. With them I have no embarrassments, diffidences or compunctions; with them I mean to stay. You think it is because I have an income which exempts me from your day-labor, that I waste (as you call it) my time in sun-gazing and star-gazing. You do not know me. If my debts, as they threaten, should consume what money I have, I should live just as I do now: I should eat worse food, and wear a coarser coat, and should wonder in a potato patch instead of in the wood,—but it is I, and not my twelve hundred dollars a year, that love God. ⟨*October 7, 1840*⟩

[111] LETTER TO SAMUEL GRAY WARD

Concord, July 18, 1840

* * * In the sleep of the great heats there was nothing for me but to read the Vedas,[7] the bible of the tropics, which I find I come back upon every three or four years. It is sublime as heat and night and a breathless ocean. It contains every religious sentiment, all the grand ethics which visit in turn each noble and poetic mind, and nothing is easier than to separate what must have been the primeval inspiration from the endless ceremonial nonsense which caricatures and contradicts it through every chapter. It is of no use to put away the book: if I trust myself in the woods or in a boat upon the pond, nature makes a Brahmin of me presently: eternal necessity, eternal compensation, unfathomable power, unbroken silence,—this is her creed. Peace, she saith to me, and purity and

7. Hindu scriptures.

absolute abandonment—these penances expiate all sin and bring you to the beatitude of the "Eight Gods." * * *

Nantasket Beach, July, 1841

* * * But is it the picture of the unbounded sea, or is it the lassitude of this Syrian summer, that more and more draws the cords of Will out of my thought and leaves me nothing but perpetual observation, perpetual acquiescence and perpetual thankfulness? Shall I not be Turk and fatalist before today's sun shall set? and in this thriving New England too, full of din and snappish activity and invention and wilfulness. Can you not save me, dip me into ice water, find me some girding belt, that I glide not away into a stream or a gas, and decease in infinite diffusion? Reinforce me, I entreat you, with showing me some man, work, aim or fact under the *angle of practice*, that I may see you as an elector and rejector, an agent, an antagonist and a commander. I have seen enough of the obedient sea wave forever lashing the obedient shore. I find no emblems here that speak any other language than the sleep and abandonment of my woods and blueberry pastures at home. If you know the ciphers of rudder and direction, communicate them to me without delay. Noah's flood and the striae which the good geologist finds on every mountain and rock seem to me the records of a calamity less universal than this metaphysical flux which threatens every enterprise, every thought and every thinker. How high will this Nile, this Mississippi, this Ocean, rise, and will ever the waters be stayed? * * *

[113]

Do not cast about for reasons among their shop of reasons, but adduce yourself as the only reason. We forget daily our high call to be discoverers—we forget that we are embarked on a holy, unknown sea in whose blue recesses we have a secret warrant that we shall yet arrive at the Fortunate Isles[8] hid from men; and at each saucy wood-craft or revenue cutter or rum-boat that hails us, we are astonished, and put off from our purpose, and ready to return to the rotten towns we have left, and quit our seeking of the Virgin Shore.

No great man ever complains of want of opportunity,—no, nor of any want except of being wanting to himself. All that he lays to the charge of his fortune accuses himself only. Want of opportunity! Why, did not divine necessity create him? Did he not come into being because something must there be, and be done, which thing he and none other is and does? If *I see*, the world is visible enough, clothed in brightness and prismatic hues. If again I see

8. Where heroes went after death (Greek). Cf. Tennyson's *Ulysses*.

from a deeper energy,—I pierce the gay surface on all sides, and every mountain and rock and man and operation grows transparent before me. * * *

When I wish, it is permitted me to say, These hands, this body, this history of Waldo Emerson are profane and wearisome, but I, I descend not to mix myself with that, or with any man. Above his life, above all creatures, I flow down forever, a sea of benefit into races of individuals. Nor can the stream ever roll backward, or the sin or death of a man taint the immutable energy which distributes itself into men, as the sun into rays, or the sea into drops. ⟨April 23, 1841⟩

[114]

The history of Christ is the best document of the power of Character which we have. A youth who owed nothing to fortune and who was "hanged at Tyburn,"[9]—by the pure quality of his nature has shed this epic splendor around the facts of his death which has transfigured every particular into a grand universal symbol for the eyes of all mankind ever since.

He did well. This great Defeat is hitherto the highest fact we have. But he that shall come[1] shall do better. The mind requires a far higher exhibition of character, one which shall make itself good to the senses as well as to the soul; a success to the senses as well as to the soul. This was a great Defeat; we demand Victory. More character will convert judge and jury, soldier and king; will rule human and animal and mineral nature; will command irresistibly and blend with the course of Universal Nature.

In short, there ought to be no such thing as Fate. As long as we use this word, it is a sign of our impotence and that we are not yet ourselves. There is now a sublime revelation in each of us which makes us so strangely aware and certain of our riches that although I have never since I was born for so much as one moment expressed the truth, and although I have never heard the expression of it from any other, I know that the whole is here,— the wealth of the Universe is for me, everything is explicable and practicable for me. And yet whilst I adore this ineffable life which is at my heart, it will not condescend to gossip with me, it will not announce to me any particulars of science, it will not enter into the details of my biography, and say to me why I have a son and daughters born to me, or why my son dies in his sixth year of joy. Herein, then, I have this latent omniscience coexistent with omni-ignorance. Moreover, whilst this Deity glows at the heart, and by his unlimited presentiments gives me all Power, I know that to-morrow will be as this day, I am a dwarf, and I remain a dwarf.

9. The most notorious place of execution in London.
1. Emerson often speaks as a Seeker, one looking for a Second Coming and a new Relevation.

That is to say, I believe in Fate. As long as I am weak, I shall talk of Fate; wherever the God fills me with his fulness, I shall see the disappearance of Fate.

I am *Defeated* all the time; yet to Victory I am born. ⟨*April,* 1842⟩

[115]

If I should write an honest diary, what should I say? Alas, that life has halfness, shallowness. I have almost completed thirty-nine years, and I have not yet adjusted my relation to my fellows on the planet, or to my own work. Always too young or too old, I do not satisfy myself; how can I satisfy others? ⟨*April 14, 1842*⟩

[116]

Q. Why not great and good?

Ans. Because I am not what I ought to be.

Q. But why not what you ought?

Ans. The Deity still solicits me, but this self, this individuality, this will resists.

Q. Well for you that it does: if it did yield, you would die, as it is called. But why does it resist?

Ans. I can only reply, God is great: it is the will of God. When he wills, he enters: when he does not will, he enters not.[2] ⟨*April 28, 1842*⟩

[117]

Fate.—The Indian system[3] is full of fate, the Greek not. The Greek uses the word, indeed, but in his mind the Fates are three respectable old women who spin and shear a symbolic thread,— so narrow, so limitary is the sphere allowed them, and it is with music. We are only at a more beautiful opera, or at private theatricals. But in India, it is the dread reality, it is the cropping-out in our planted gardens of the core of the world: it is the abysmal Force, untameable and immense. They who wrestle with Hari see their doom in his eye before the fight begins. ⟨*October, 1845*⟩

[118]

There must be the Abyss, Nox[4] and Chaos, out of which all come, and they must never be far off. Cut off the connection between any of our works and this dread origin, and the work is shallow and unsatisfying. That is the strength and excellence of the people, that they lean on this, and the mob is not quite so bad an argument as we are apt to represent it, for it has this divine side.

There is a moment in the history of every nation when, proceed-

2. Cf. "Experience," p. 271.
3. By the 1840's Emerson was reading habitually in the great classics of Hindu scripture, notably the *Vishnu Purana* and the *Bhagavad-Gita.*

4. Night. The term "Abyss" was used by the German mystic, Jakob Boehme, for the Nothingness in which Creation began.

ing out of this brute youth, the perceptive powers reach with delight their greatest strength and have not yet become microscopic, so that the man at that instant extends across the entire scale, and, with his feet still planted on the immense forces of Night, converses by his eyes and brain with solar and stellar creation. That is the moment of perfect health, the culmination of their star of Empire.

Ah, let the twilight linger! We love the morning spread abroad among the mountains, but too fast comes on the broad noon blaze, only exposing the poverty and barrenness of our globe, the listlessness and meanness of its inhabitants. ⟨1845⟩

[119]

* * * It seems as if this Plato's[5] power of grading or ranking all that offers itself at sight was as good as a duration of a thousand years. The reason why life is short is, because we are confounded by the dazzle of new things, and by the seeming equality which custom sheds on great and small, and we are obliged to spend a large part of life in corrections which we should save, if our judgment was sure when we first beheld things. Plato is like those tamers who have charmed down the ferocity of vicious animals, or who by some virulence or ferocity in their own nature have terrified frantic madmen. He looks through things at a glance, and they fly into place, and he walks in life with the security of a god. It seems as if the winds of ages swept through this universal thinking, so wide, so just, yet so minute, that it is impossible that an air of such calmness and long maturity can belong to the hasty, crude, experimental blotting of one lifetime. ⟨1849⟩

[120]

Today, carpets; yesterday, the aunts; the day before, the funeral of poor S.; and every day, the remembrance in the library of the rope of work which I must spin;—in this way life is dragged down and confuted. We try to listen to the hymn of gods, and must needs hear this perpetual *cock-a-doodle-doo*, and *ke-tar-kut* right under the library windows. They, the gods, ought to respect a life, you say, whose objects are their own. But steadily they throw mud and eggs at us, roll us in the dirt, and jump on us. ⟨1849⟩

[121]

For the skeptic, yes, we may give ourselves what allowance we will, for once admitted to the heaven of thought, we see no relapse into night, but infinite invitation on the other side. Heaven is within heaven, and sky over sky, and we are encompassed with divinities. To what purpose dark ages and barbarous Irish, if I

5. Always a favorite author, Plato was the subject of a lecture in 1845, to which Emerson added "New Readings" when he published it in *Representative Men* (1850).

know, as I know, five or six men, without hardly going out of my village, to whom and with whom all is possible, who restore to me Plato, Shakespeare, Montaigne, Hindu cosmology, yea, Buddh himself, with their audacious intellectual adventure? We are as elastic as the gas of gunpowder, and small and tame as we walk here with our hands in our pockets, an imaginative book sets free our fancy, and in a moment our head is bathed in the galaxy, and our feet tread on the hells. Our indeterminate size is the delicious secret which books of imagination reveal to us.

O endless ends, O living child! how can you fail! To you I open the ill-kept secret that you are Hari, divine and invincible,— cousin to the four elements and the four hundred gods. * * * It is time you should show yourself. Fate is in your eye. You will yet be a horse, a lizard, a dragonfly, and a swamp full of alligators, but time and space are cheap to you, Hari; you can afford to be multiplied and divided, to bite and to be bitten, to be a bankrupt tradesman, or an acre of sand; divided you will reunite, and you thrive by dying; do not care, O Hari, for the speech of men, do not care for a shabby appearance![6] ⟨1849⟩

[122]

The ancients most truly and poetically represented the incarnation or descent into Nature of Pythagoras,[7] his condescension to be born, as his first virtue.

It is indeed a perilous adventure, this serious act of venturing into mortality, swimming in a sea strewn with wrecks, where none indeed go undamaged. It is as bad as going to Congress; none comes back innocent.

Those who conquer,—the victory was born with them. They may well be serene. They seem to fight, but their lives are insured and their victories. You like better to hear what they say. Well you may, for they announce this success in every syllable.

As Vishnu in the Vedas pursues Maya in all forms, * * * so our metaphysics should be able to follow the flying force through all transformations, and name the new pair, identical through all variety. For Memory, Imagination, Reason, Sense are only masks of one power, as physical and spiritual laws are only new phases of limitation. The poet is the lover loving; the critic is the lover advised.

For the rest of man remains only the stoic resignation. They bridge up by their dying bodies the path of their successors. They are the corallines[8] who make the new world, theater of new Re-

6. This passage concludes one of the manuscript journals.
7. Greek philosopher (6th century B.C.) who was supposed to have taught the transmigration of souls and to have recollected previous existences of his own.
8. Coral insects.

demption, and find their wages in an immense faith. * * *
⟨1851⟩

[123] LETTER TO CAROLINE STURGIS TAPPAN

Concord, July 22, 1853

* * * Friends are few, thoughts are few, facts few—only one;
one only fact, now tragically, now tenderly, now exultingly illustrated in sky, in earth, in men and women, Fate, Fate. The universe
is all chemistry, with a certain hint of a magnificent *Whence* or
Whereto gilding or opalizing every angle of the old salt-acid acid-
salt, endlessly reiterated and masqueraded through all time and
space and form. The addition of that hint everywhere, saves
things. Heavy and loathsome is the bounded world, bounded
everywhere. An immense Boston or Hanover Street with mountains of ordinary women, trains and trains of mean, leathern men
all immoveably bounded, no liquidity of hope or genius. But
they are made chemically good, like oxen. In the absence of religion, they are polarized to decorum, which is its blockhead;[9]
—thrown mechanically into parallelism with the high *Whence*
and *Whither*, which makes mountains of rubbish reflect the
morning sun and the evening star. And we all are privy counsellors
to that Hint which homeopathically[1] doses the system, and can co-
operate with the slow and secular escape of these oxen and semi-
oxen from their quadruped estate, and invite them to be men and
hail them such. I do not know—now that Stoicism and Christianity have for two millenniums preached liberty, somewhat fulsomely—but it is the turn of Fatalism. And it has great conveniences for a public creed. Fatalism, foolish and flippant, is as bad
as Unitarianism or Mormonism. But Fatalism held by an intelligent soul who knows how to humor and obey the infinitesimal
pulses of spontaneity, is by much the truest theory in use. All the
great would call their thought fatalism, or concede that ninety-
nine parts are nature and one part power, though that hundredth
is elastic, miraculous, and, whenever it is in energy, dissolving all
the rest.

[124]

Our doctrine must begin with the necessary and eternal, and
discriminate Fate from the necessary. There is no limitation
about the Eternal. Thought, Will, is co-eternal with the world;
and, as soon as intellect is awaked in any man, it shares so far
of the eternity,—is of the maker, not of the made. But Fate

9. The wooden head on which a hat was shaped.
1. Homeopathy: the treatment of a disease by the administration of small amounts of those drugs which produce in a healthy person symptoms like those of the disease.

is the name we give to the action of that one eternal, all-various necessity on the brute myriads, whether in things, animals, or in men in whom the intellect pure is not yet opened. To such it is only a burning wall which hurts those who run against it.

The great day in the man is the birth of perception, which instantly throws him on the party of the Eternal. He sees what must be, and that it is not more that which must be, than it is that which should be, or what is best. To be then becomes the infinite good, and breath is jubilation. A breath of Will blows through the universe eternally in the direction of the right or necessary; it is the air which all intellects inhale and exhale, and all things are blown or moved by it in order and orbit. * * * ⟨May, 1859⟩

[Death]

[125]

The event of death is always astounding; our philosophy never reaches, never possesses it; we are always at the beginning of our catechism; always the definition is yet to be made. What is death?

I see nothing to help beyond observing what the mind's habit is in regard to that crisis. Simply I have nothing to do with it. It is nothing to me. After I have made my will and set my house in order, I shall do in the immediate expectation of death the same things I should do without it.

But more difficult is it to know the death of another. * * * In us there ought to be remedy. There ought to be, there can be nothing to which the soul is called, to which the soul is not equal. And I suppose that the roots of my relation to every individual are in my own constitution, and not less the causes of his disappearance from me.

Why should we lie so? A question is asked of the Understanding which lies in the province of the Reason, and we foolishly try to make an answer. Our constructiveness overpowers our love of truth. How noble is it when the mourner looks for comfort in your face to give only sympathy and confession; confession that it is a great grief, and the greater because the apprehension of its nature still loiters.

Who set you up for Professor of omniscience and *cicerone*[2] to the Universe? Why teach? Learn rather. ⟨October 28, 1837⟩

[126]

The belief of some of our friends in their duration suggests one of those musty householders who keep every broomstick and old grate, put in a box every old tooth that falls out of their heads,

2. Guide.

preserve [the] ancient frippery of their juvenile wardrobe, and they think God saves all the old souls which he has used up. What does he save them for? ⟨*June 1, 1852*⟩

[127]

* * * There is such an obvious accumulation of dexterity in the use of tools in the old scholar and thinker that it is not to be believed Nature will be such a spendthrift as to sponge all this out, like figures from a slate. * * * ⟨*June, 1852*⟩

[128]

A man of thought is willing to die, willing to live; I suppose because he has seen the thread on which the beads are strung, and perceived that it reaches up and down, existing quite independently of the present illusions. A man of affairs is afraid to die, is pestered with terrors, because he has not this vision. Yet the first cannot explain it to the second. ⟨*1855*⟩

[129]

Within, I do not find wrinkles and used heart, but unspent youth. ⟨*1864*⟩

[130]

Immortality.—The path of spirits is in silence and hidden from sense. Who knows where or how the soul has existed, before it was incarnated in mortal body? Who knows where or how it thinks and works when it drops its fleshly frame? Like those asteroids, which we call shooting stars, which revolve forever in space, but sweeping for a moment through some arc of our atmosphere and heated by the friction, give out a dazzling gleam, then pass out of it again on their endless orbit invisible. ⟨*1865*⟩

Each and All

Little thinks, in the field, yon red-cloaked clown[3]
Of thee from the hill-top looking down;
The heifer that lows in the upland farm,
Far-heard, lows not thine ear to charm;
The sexton, tolling his bell at noon,   5
Deems not that great Napoleon
Stops his horse, and lists with delight,
Whilst his files sweep round yon Alpine height;
Nor knowest thou what argument
Thy life to thy neighbor's creed has lent.   10
All are needed by each one;
Nothing is fair or good alone.
I thought the sparrow's note from heaven,

3. A reminiscence of northern Italy. On the theme of this poem, see the several similar passages in *Nature,* notably p. 190.

Singing at dawn on the alder bough;
I brought him home, in his nest, at even; 15
He sings the song, but it cheers not now,
For I did not bring home the river and sky;—
He sang to my ear,—they sang to my eye.
The delicate shells lay on the shore;
The bubbles of the latest wave 20
Fresh pearls to their enamel gave,
And the bellowing of the savage sea
Greeted their safe escape to me.
I wiped away the weeds and foam,
I fetched my sea-born treasures home; 25
But the poor, unsightly, noisome things
Had left their beauty on the shore
With the sun and the sand and the wild uproar.
The lover watched his graceful maid,
As 'mid the virgin train she strayed, 30
Nor knew her beauty's best attire
Was woven still by the snow-white choir.
At last she came to his hermitage,
Like the bird from the woodlands to the cage;—
The gay enchantment was undone, 35
A gentle wife, but fairy none.
Then I said, "I covet truth;
Beauty is unripe childhood's cheat;
I leave it behind with the games of youth:"—
As I spoke, beneath my feet 40
The ground-pine curled its pretty wreath,
Running over the club-moss burrs;
I inhaled the violet's breath;
Around me stood the oaks and firs;
Pine-cones and acorns lay on the ground; 45
Over me soared the eternal sky,
Full of light and of deity;
Again I saw, again I heard,
The rolling river, the morning bird;—
Beauty through my senses stole; 50
I yielded myself to the perfect whole.

1834   1839

The Snow-Storm[4]

Announced by all the trumpets of the sky,
Arrives the snow, and, driving o'er the fields,
Seems nowhere to alight: the whited air

4. Perhaps prompted by the great snow-storm of December, 1834; cf. *Journals* (passage 6). The poem inspired Whittier's "Snowbound," which quotes the first nine lines as a motto; also Emily Dickinson's "It sifts from leaden sieves."

Hides hills and woods, the river, and the heaven,
And veils the farm-house at the garden's end.   5
The sled and traveler stopped, the courier's feet
Delayed, all friends shut out, the housemates sit
Around the radiant fireplace, enclosed
In a tumultuous privacy of storm.

Come see the north wind's masonry.   10
Out of an unseen quarry evermore
Furnished with tile, the fierce artificer
Curves his white bastions with projected roof
Round every windward stake, or tree, or door.
Speeding, the myriad-handed, his wild work   15
So fanciful, so savage, nought cares he
For number or proportion. Mockingly,
On coop or kennel he hangs Parian[5] wreaths;
A swan-like form invests the hidden thorn;
Fills up the farmer's lane from wall to wall,   20
Maugre[6] the farmer's sighs; and at the gate
A tapering turret overtops the work.
And when his hours are numbered, and the world
Is all his own, retiring, as he were not,
Leaves, when the sun appears, astonished Art   25
To mimic in slow structures, stone by stone,
Built in an age, the mad wind's night-work,
The frolic architecture of the snow.

1835   1841

Concord Hymn

SUNG AT THE COMPLETION OF THE BATTLE MONUMENT,[7]
JULY 4, 1837

By the rude bridge that arched the flood,
 Their flag to April's breeze unfurled,
Here once the embattled farmers stood
 And fired the shot heard round the world.

The foe long since in silence slept;   5
 Alike the conqueror silent sleeps;
And Time the ruined bridge has swept
 Down the dark stream which seaward creeps.

On this green bank, by this soft stream,
 We set to-day a votive stone;   10
That memory may their deed redeem,
 When, like our sires, our sons are gone.

Spirit, that made those heroes dare
 To die, and leave their children free,

5. Marble.
6. In spite of.   7. The battle, of course, was that of
                                      April 19, 1775.

Bid Time and Nature gently spare   15
   The shaft we raise to them and thee.

1837

The Humble-Bee[8]

Burly, dozing humble-bee,
Where thou art is clime for me.
Let them sail for Porto Rique,[9]
Far-off heats through seas to seek;
I will follow thee alone,   5
Thou animated torrid-zone!
Zigzag steerer, desert cheerer,
Let me chase thy waving lines;
Keep me nearer, me thy hearer,
Singing over shrubs and vines.   10

Insect lover of the sun,
Joy of thy dominion!
Sailor of the atmosphere;
Swimmer through the waves of air;
Voyager of light and noon;   15
Epicurean[1] of June;
Wait, I prithee, till I come
Within earshot of thy hum,—
All without is martyrdom.

When the south wind, in May days,   20
With a net of shining haze
Silvers the horizon wall,
And with softness touching all,
Tints the human countenance
With a color of romance,   25
And infusing subtle heats,
Turns the sod to violets,
Thou, in sunny solitudes,
Rover of the underwoods,
The green silence dost displace   30
With thy mellow, breezy bass.

Hot midsummer's petted crone,
Sweet to me thy drowsy tone
Tells of countless sunny hours,
Long days, and solid banks of flowers;   35
Of gulfs of sweetness without bound
In Indian wildernesses found;

8. The poem was apparently a response
to the depression of 1837. With this
poem, cf. the conclusion of *Nature*.
9. Emerson's brother Edward had sailed
for Puerto Rico in 1830 in a vain search
for health.
1. One who believes a rational pleasure
to be the chief end of life.

Of Syrian peace, immortal leisure,
Firmest cheer, and bird-like pleasure.
Aught unsavory or unclean   40
Hath my insect never seen;
But violets and bilberry bells,
Maple-sap and daffodels,
Grass with green flag half-mast high,
Succory to match the sky,   45
Columbine with horn of honey,
Scented fern, and agrimony,
Clover, catchfly, adder's-tongue
And brier-roses, dwelt among;
All beside was unknown waste,   50
All was picture as he passed.

Wiser far than human seer,
Yellow-breeched philosopher!
Seeing only what is fair,
Sipping only what is sweet,   55
Thou dost mock at fate and care,
Leave the chaff, and take the wheat.
When the fierce northwestern blast
Cools sea and land so far and fast,
Thou already slumberest deep;   60
Woe and want thou canst outsleep;
Want and woe, which torture us,
Thy sleep makes ridiculous.

1837   1846

Berrying

'May be true what I had heard,—
Earth's a howling wilderness,
Truculent with fraud and force,'
Said I, strolling through the pastures,
And along the river-side.   5
Caught among the blackberry vines,
Feeding on the Ethiops sweet,
Pleasant fancies overtook me.
I said, 'What influence me preferred,
Elect, to dreams thus beautiful?'   10
The vines replied, 'And didst thou deem
No wisdom from our berries went?'

1846

The Problem[2]

I like a church; I like a cowl;
I love a prophet of the soul;
And on my heart monastic aisles
Fall like sweet strains, or pensive smiles;
Yet not for all his faith can see   5
Would I that cowléd churchman be.

Why should the vest on him allure,
Which I could not on me endure?

Not from a vain or shallow thought
His awful Jove young Phidias[3] brought;   10
Never from lips of cunning fell
The thrilling Delphic oracle;
Out from the heart of nature rolled
The burdens of the Bible old;
The litanies of nations came,   15
Like the volcano's tongue of flame,
Up from the burning core below,—
The canticles of love and woe:
The hand that rounded Peter's dome
And groined the aisles of Christian Rome   20
Wrought in a sad sincerity;
Himself from God he could not free;
He builded better than he knew;—
The conscious stone to beauty grew.

Know'st thou what wove yon woodbird's nest   25
Of leaves, and feathers from her breast?
Or how the fish outbuilt her shell,
Painting with morn each annual cell?
Or how the sacred pine-tree adds
To her old leaves new myriads?   30
Such and so grew these holy piles,
Whilst love and terror laid the tiles.
Earth proudly wears the Parthenon,
As the best gem upon her zone,
And Morning opes with haste her lids   35
To gaze upon the Pyramids;

2. The prose thought from which this poem sprang is found in the *Journals* for 1838: "It is very grateful to my feelings to go into a Roman Cathedral, yet I look as my countrymen do at the Roman priesthood. It is very grateful to me to go into an English Church and hear the liturgy read. Yet nothing would induce me to be the English priest. I find an unpleasant dilemma in this, nearer home. I dislike to be a clergyman and refuse to be one. Yet how rich a music would be to me a holy clergyman in my town. It seems to me he cannot be a man, quite and whole; yet how plain is the need of one, and how high, yes, highest, is the function. Here is division of labor that I like not. A man must sacrifice his manhood for the social good. Something is wrong, I see not what."
3. Sculptor of the Parthenon and of a colossal Zeus at Elis.

O'er England's abbeys bends the sky,
As on its friends, with kindred eye;
For out of Thought's interior sphere
These wonders rose to upper air;   40
And Nature gladly gave them place,
Adopted them into her race,
And granted them an equal date
With Andes and with Ararat.

These temples grew as grows the grass;   45
Art might obey, but not surpass.
The passive Master lent his hand
To the vast soul that o'er him planned;
And the same power that reared the shrine
Bestrode the tribes that knelt within.   50
Ever the fiery Pentecost[4]
Girds with one flame the countless host,
Trances the heart through chanting choirs,
And through the priest the mind inspires.
The word unto the prophet spoken   55
Was writ on tables yet unbroken;
The word by seers or sibyls told,
In groves of oak, or fanes of gold,
Still floats upon the morning wind,
Still whispers to the willing mind.   60
One accent of the Holy Ghost
The heedless world hath never lost.
I know what say the fathers wise,—
The Book itself before me lies,
Old *Chrysostom*,[5] best Augustine,   65
And he who blent both in his line,
The younger *Golden Lips* or mines,
Taylor,[6] the Shakespeare of divines.
His words are music in my ear,
I see his cowlèd portrait dear;   70
And yet, for all his faith could see,
I would not the good bishop be.

1839   1840

The Sphinx[7]

The Sphinx is drowsy,
    Her wings are furled:

4. The day of the descent of the Holy Spirit on the Apostles (Acts ii).
5. "Golden Lips," St. John of Antioch (307?–407), bishop of Constantinople.
6. Jeremy Taylor (1613–67) wrote *Holy Living* and *Holy Dying*.
7. Emerson wrote in 1859: "I have often been asked the meaning of 'The Sphinx.' It is this,—The perception of identity unites all things and explains one by another, and the most rare and strange is equally facile as the most common. But if the mind live only in particulars, and see only differences (wanting the power to see the whole— all in each), then the world addresses

Her ear is heavy,
   She broods on the world.
"Who'll tell me my secret,   5
   The ages have kept?—
I awaited the seer
   While they slumbered and slept:—

"The fate of the man-child,
   The meaning of man;   10
Known fruit of the unknown;
   Daedalian[8] plan;
Out of sleeping a waking,
   Out of waking a sleep;
Life death overtaking;   15
   Deep underneath deep?

"Erect as a sunbeam,
   Upspringeth the palm;
The elephant browses,
   Undaunted and calm;   20
In beautiful motion
   The thrush plies his wings;
Kind leaves of his covert,
   Your silence he sings.

"The waves, unashaméd,   25
   In difference sweet,
Play glad with the breezes,
   Old playfellows meet;
The journeying atoms,
   Primordial wholes,   30
Firmly draw, firmly drive,
   By their animate poles.

"Sea, earth, air, sound, silence,
   Plant, quadruped, bird,
By one music enchanted,   35
   One deity stirred,—
Each the other adorning,
   Accompany still;
Night veileth the morning,
   The vapor the hill.   40

"The babe by its mother
   Lies bathéd in joy;
Glide its hours uncounted,—
   The sun is its toy;

---

to this mind a question it cannot answer, and each new fact tears it to
pieces, and it is vanquished by the distracting variety." Cf. also *Nature*,
pp. 201–2.
8. Daedalus built the Cretan labyrinth.

Shines the peace of all being,   45
  Without cloud, in its eyes;
And the sum of the world
  In soft miniature lies.

"But man crouches and blushes,
  Absconds and conceals;   50
He creepeth and peepeth,
  He palters and steals;
Infirm, melancholy,
  Jealous glancing around,
An oaf, an accomplice,   55
  He poisons the ground.

"Out spoke the great mother,
  Beholding his fear;—
At the sound of her accents
  Cold shuddered the sphere:—   60
'Who has drugged my boy's cup?
  Who has mixed my boy's bread?
Who, with sadness and madness,
  Has turned my child's head?' "

I heard a poet answer   65
  Aloud and cheerfully,
"Say on, sweet Sphinx! thy dirges
  Are pleasant songs to me.
Deep love lieth under
  These pictures of time;   70
They fade in the light of
  Their meaning sublime.

"The fiend that man harries
  Is love of the Best;
Yawns the pit of the Dragon,   75
  Lit by rays from the Blest.
The Lethe of Nature
  Can't trance him again,
Whose soul sees the perfect,
  Which his eyes seek in vain.   80

"To vision profounder,
  Man's spirit must dive;
His aye-rolling orb
  At no goal will arrive;
The heavens that now draw him   85
  With sweetness untold,
Once found,—for new heavens
  He spurneth the old.

"Pride ruined the angels,
   Their shame them restores; 90
Lurks the joy that is sweetest
   In stings of remorse.
Have I a lover
   Who is noble and free?—
I would he were nobler 95
   Than to love me.

"Eterne alternation
   Now follows, now flies;
And under pain, pleasure,—
   Under pleasure, pain lies. 100
Love works at the center,
   Heart-heaving alway;
Forth speed the strong pulses
   To the borders of day.

"Dull Sphinx, Jove keep thy five wits;[9] 105
   Thy sight is growing blear;
Rue, myrrh and cummin[1] for the Sphinx,
   Her muddy eyes to clear!"
The old Sphinx bit her thick lip,—
   Said, "Who taught thee me to name? 110
I am thy spirit, yoke-fellow;
   Of thine eye I am eyebeam.

"Thou art the unanswered question;
   Couldst see thy proper eye,
Alway it asketh, asketh; 115
   And each answer is a lie.
So take thy quest through nature,
   It through thousand natures ply;
Ask on, thou clothed eternity;
   Time is the false reply." 120

Uprose the merry Sphinx,
   And crouched no more in stone;
She melted into purple cloud,
   She silvered in the moon;
She spired into a yellow flame; 125
   She flowered in blossoms red;
She flowed into a foaming wave:
   She stood Monadnoc's[2] head.

Through a thousand voices
   Spoke the universal dame; 130

9. The five senses.   2. Monadnock is a peak in southern
1. Aromatic (and healing?) plants.   New Hampshire.

"Who telleth one of my meanings
Is master of all I am."

1841

Merops[3]

What care I, so they stand the same,—
  Things of the heavenly mind,—
How long the power to give them name
  Tarries yet behind?

Thus far today your favors reach,   5
  O fair, appeasing presences!
Ye taught my lips a single speech,
  And a thousand silences.

Space grants beyond his fated road
  No inch to the god of day;   10
And copious language still bestowed
  One word, no more, to say.

1846

Uriel[4]

It fell in the ancient periods
  Which the brooding soul surveys,
Or ever the wild Time coined itself
  Into calendar months and days.

This was the lapse of Uriel,   5
Which in Paradise befell.
Once, among the Pleiads walking,
Seyd[5] overheard the young gods talking;
And the treason, too long pent,
To his ears was evident.   10
The young deities discussed
Laws of form, and meter just,
Orb, quintessence, and sunbeams,
What subsisteth, and what seems.
One, with low tones that decide,   15
And doubt and reverend use defied,
With a look that solved the sphere,
And stirred the devils everywhere,
Gave his sentiment divine

3. A Greek name, meaning "Articulate."
4. An ironic allegory of the reception of the "Divinity School Address." For its germ, see *Journals* (passage 7). The name Uriel, from the Apocrypha, was given by Milton in *Paradise Lost* to the archangel of the sun.
5. The Poet. Emerson took the name from Saadi, a Persian poet, whom he read in 1843.

Against the being of a line.   20
"Line in nature is not found;
Unit and universe are round;
In vain produced, all rays return;
Evil will bless, and ice will burn."
As Uriel spoke with piercing eye,   25
A shudder ran around the sky;
The stern old war-gods shook their heads,
The seraphs frowned from myrtle-beds;
Seemed to the holy festival
The rash word boded ill to all;   30
The balance-beam of Fate was bent;
The bounds of good and ill were rent;
Strong Hades could not keep his own,
But all slid to confusion.

A sad self-knowledge, withering, fell   35
On the beauty of Uriel;
In heaven once eminent, the god
Withdrew, that hour, into his cloud;
Whether doomed to long gyration
In the sea of generation,[6]   40
Or by knowledge grown too bright
To hit the nerve of feebler sight.
Straightway, a forgetting wind
Stole over the celestial kind,
And their lips the secret kept,   45
If in ashes the fire-seed slept.
But now and then, truth-speaking things
Shamed the angels' veiling wings;
And, shrilling from the solar course,
Or from fruit of chemic force,   50
Procession of a soul in matter,
Or the speeding change of water,
Or out of the good of evil born,
Came Uriel's voice of cherub scorn,
And a blush tinged the upper sky,   55
And the gods shook, they knew not why.

                                                    1846

Give All to Love[7]

Give all to love;
Obey thy heart;

---

6. Cf. the Neo-Platonist Proclus: "Every partial soul must make periods of ascent from and descent into generation, and this forever and ever."
7. Cf. "Compensation": "We cannot let our angels go. We do not see that they only go out that archangels may come in." Cf. also *Nature*, p. 206. The poem is more an expression of Puritanic "cosmic optimism" than of Platonic idealism.

Friends, kindred, days,
Estate, good-fame,
Plans, credit and the Muse,— 5
Nothing refuse.

'Tis a brave master;
Let it have scope:
Follow it utterly,
Hope beyond hope: 10
High and more high
It dives into noon,
With wing unspent,
Untold intent;
But it is a god, 15
Knows its own path
And the outlets of the sky.

It was never for the mean;
It requireth courage stout.
Souls above doubt, 20
Valor unbending,
It will reward,—
They shall return
More than they were,
And ever ascending. 25

Leave all for love;
Yet, hear me, yet,
One word more thy heart behoved,
One pulse more of firm endeavor,—
Keep thee to-day, 30
To-morrow, forever,
Free as an Arab
Of thy beloved.

Cling with life to the maid;
But when the surprise, 35
First vague shadow of surmise
Flits across her bosom young,
Of a joy apart from thee,
Free be she, fancy-free;
Nor thou detain her vesture's hem, 40
Nor the palest rose she flung
From her summer diadem.

Though thou loved her as thyself,
As a self of purer clay,
Though her parting dims the day, 45
Stealing grace from all alive;
Heartily know,

When half-gods go,
The gods arrive.

1846

Ode to Beauty[8]

Who gave thee, O Beauty,
The keys of this breast,—
Too credulous lover
Of blest and unblest?
Say, when in lapsed ages   5
Thee knew I of old?
Or what was the service
For which I was sold?
When first my eyes saw thee,
I found me thy thrall,   10
By magical drawings,
Sweet tyrant of all!
I drank at thy fountain
False waters of thirst;
Thou intimate stranger,   15
Thou latest and first!
Thy dangerous glances
Make women of men;
New-born, we are melting
Into nature again.   20

Lavish, lavish promiser,
Nigh persuading gods to err!
Guest of million painted forms,
Which in turn thy glory warms!
The frailest leaf, the mossy bark,   25
The acorn's cup, the rain-drop's arc,
The swinging spider's silver line,
The ruby of the drop of wine,
The shining pebble of the pond,
Thou inscribest with a bond,   30
In thy momentary play,
Would bankrupt nature to repay.

Ah, what avails it
To hide or to shun
Whom the Infinite One   35
Hath granted his throne?
The heaven high over
Is the deep's lover;

8. Cf. *Nature*, Chapter III, "Beauty," and the motto to "Art."

The sun and sea,
Informed by thee,   40
Before me run
And draw me on,
Yet fly me still,
As Fate refuses
To me the heart Fate for me chooses.   45
Is it that my opulent soul
Was mingled from the generous whole;
Sea-valleys and the deep of skies
Furnished several supplies;
And the sands whereof I'm made   50
Draw me to them, self-betrayed?
I turn the proud portfolio
Which holds the grand designs
Of Salvator, of Guercino,
And Piranesi's lines.[9]   55
I hear the lofty paeans
Of the masters of the shell,[1]
Who heard the starry music
And recount the numbers well;
Olympian bards who sung   60
Divine Ideas below,
Which always find us young
And always keep us so.
Oft, in streets or humblest places,
I detect far-wandered graces,   65
Which, from Eden wide astray,
In lowly homes have lost their way.

Thee gliding through the sea of form,
Like the lightning through the storm,
Somewhat not to be possessed,   70
Somewhat not to be caressed,
No feet so fleet could ever find,
No perfect form could ever bind.
Thou eternal fugitive,
Hovering over all that live,   75
Quick and skilful to inspire
Sweet, extravagant desire,
Starry space and lily-bell
Filling with thy roseate smell,
Wilt not give the lips to taste   80
Of the nectar which thou hast.

9. Salvator, Guercino, Piranesi were Italian painters of the 17th and 18th centuries. Emerson was lent portfolios of etchings of such painters by friends like Margaret Fuller or Samuel Gray Ward; cf. *Journals* (passage 14).
1. Apollo formed the lyre of a turtle shell; hence poets are "masters of the shell."

All that's good and great with thee
Works in close conspiracy;
Thou hast bribed the dark and lonely
To report thy features only,   85
And the cold and purple morning
Itself with thoughts of thee adorning;
The leafy dell, the city mart,
Equal trophies of thine art;
E'en the flowing azure air   90
Thou hast touched for my despair;
And, if I languish into dreams,
Again I meet the ardent beams.
Queen of things! I dare not die
In Being's deeps past ear and eye;   95
Lest there I find the same deceiver
And be the sport of Fate forever.
Dread Power, but dear! if God thou be,
Unmake me quite, or give thyself to me!

1843

Blight[2]

Give me truths;
For I am weary of the surfaces,
And die of inanition. If I knew
Only the herbs and simples of the wood,
Rue, cinquefoil, gill, vervain and agrimony,   5
Blue-vetch and trillium, hawkweed, sassafras,
Milkweeds and murky brakes, quaint pipes and sun-dew,
And rare and virtuous roots, which in these woods
Draw untold juices from the common earth,
Untold, unknown, and I could surely spell   10
Their fragrance, and their chemistry apply
By sweet affinities to human flesh,
Driving the foe and stablishing the friend,—
O, that were much, and I could be a part
Of the round day, related to the sun   15
And planted world, and full executor
Of their imperfect functions.
But these young scholars, who invade our hills,
Bold as the engineer who fells the wood,
And travelling often in the cut he makes,   20
Love not the flower they pluck, and know it not,
And all their botany is Latin names.
The old men studied magic in the flowers,
And human fortunes in astronomy,

2. Cf. "Experience" and "Illusions." For this less rhapsodic poem Emerson chose, not the "ode" form, but a "Shakespearian" blank verse.

And an omnipotence in chemistry,   25
Preferring things to names, for these were men,
Were unitarians of the united world,
And, wheresoever their clear eye-beams fell,
They caught the footsteps of the SAME. Our eyes
Are armed, but we are strangers to the stars,   30
And strangers to the mystic beast and bird,
And strangers to the plant and to the mine.
The injured elements say, 'Not in us;'
And night and day, ocean and continent,
Fire, plant and mineral say, 'Not in us;'   35
And haughtily return us stare for stare.
For we invade them impiously for gain;
We devastate them unreligiously,
And coldly ask their pottage, not their love.
Therefore they shove us from them, yield to us   40
Only what to our griping toil is due;
But the sweet affluence of love and song,
The rich results of the divine consents
Of man and earth, of world beloved and lover,
The nectar and ambrosia, are withheld;   45
And in the midst of spoils and slaves, we thieves
And pirates of the universe, shut out
Daily to a more thin and outward rind,
Turn pale and starve. Therefore, to our sick eyes,
The stunted trees look sick, the summer short,   50
Clouds shade the sun, which will not tan our hay,
And nothing thrives to reach its natural term;
And life, shorn of its venerable length,
Even at its greatest space is a defeat,
And dies in anger that it was a dupe;   55
And, in its highest noon and wantonness,
Is early frugal, like a beggar's child;
Even in the hot pursuit of the best aims
And prizes of ambition, checks its hand,
Like Alpine cataracts frozen as they leaped,   60
Chilled with a miserly comparison
Of the toy's purchase with the length of life.

1843   1846

Hamatreya[3]

Bulkeley, Hunt, Willard, Hosmer, Meriam, Flint,
Possessed the land which rendered to their toil

3. Apparently a variant on Maitreya, the personage who is addressed in the passage this poem is based on from the Hindu *Vishnu Purana*, the theme of which is "The words 'I and mine' constitute ignorance." Emerson also echoes local names and other phrases from his address ten years earlier at the second centennial of Concord's founding, his purpose being to give local immediacy to the wisdom of the Orient.

Hay, corn, roots, hemp, flax, apples, wool and wood.
Each of these landlords walked amidst his farm,
Saying, " 'Tis mine, my children's and my name's.   5
How sweet the west wind sounds in my own trees!
How graceful climb those shadows on my hill!
I fancy these pure waters and the flags
Know me, as does my dog: we sympathize;
And, I affirm, my actions smack of the soil."   10

Where are these men? Asleep beneath their grounds:
And strangers, fond as they, their furrows plough.
Earth laughs in flowers, to see her boastful boys
Earth-proud, proud of the earth which is not theirs;
Who steer the plough, but cannot steer their feet   15
Clear of the grave.
They added ridge to valley, brook to pond,
And sighed for all that bounded their domain;
"This suits me for a pasture; that's my park;
We must have clay, lime, gravel, granite-ledge,   20
And misty lowland, where to go for peat.
The land is well,—lies fairly to the south.
'Tis good, when you have crossed the sea and back,
To find the sitfast acres where you left them."
Ah! the hot owner sees not Death, who adds   25
Him to his land, a lump of mold the more.
Hear what the Earth says:

Earth-Song

"Mine and yours;
Mine, not yours.
Earth endures;
Stars abide—   30
Shine down in the old sea;
Old are the shores;
But where are old men?
I who have seen much,   35
Such have I never seen.

"The lawyer's deed
Ran sure,
In tail,[4]
To them, and to their heirs   40
Who shall succeed,
Without fail,
Forevermore.

"Here is the land,
Shaggy with wood,   45

4. A pun ("to entail" is to settle property inalienably on a person and his descendants).

With its old valley,
Mound and flood.
But the heritors?—
Fled like the flood's foam.
The lawyer, and the laws,   50
And the kingdom,
Clean swept herefrom.

"They called me theirs,
Who so controlled me;
Yet every one   55
Wished to stay, and is gone,
How am I theirs,
If they cannot hold me,
But I hold them?"

When I heard the Earth-song   60
I was no longer brave;
My avarice cooled
Like lust in the chill of the grave.

1846

Ode

INSCRIBED TO W. H. CHANNING[5]

Though loath to grieve
The evil time's sole patriot,
I cannot leave
My honied thought
For the priest's cant,   5
Or statesman's rant.

If I refuse
My study for their politique,
Which at the best is trick,
The angry Muse   10
Puts confusion in my brain.

But who is he that prates
Of the culture of mankind,
Of better arts and life?
Go, blindworm, go,   15
Behold the famous States
Harrying Mexico
With rifle and with knife![6]

5 Channing was an earnest transcendentalist, reformer, and abolitionist,
who had visited Concord at about the
time this poem was written.
6. A reference to the Mexican War
(1846–48), which Emerson opposed.

Or who, with accent bolder,
Dare praise the freedom-loving mountaineer?   20
I found by thee, O rushing Contoocook!
And in thy valleys, Agiochook![7]
The jackals of the negro-holder.

The God who made New Hampshire
Taunted the lofty land   25
With little men;—
Small bat and wren
House in the oak:—
If earth-fire cleave
The upheaved land, and bury the folk,   30
The southern crocodile would grieve.[8]
Virtue palters; Right is hence;
Freedom praised, but hid;
Funeral eloquence
Rattles the coffin-lid.   35

What boots thy zeal,
O glowing friend,
That would indignant rend
The northland from the south?
Wherefore? to what good end?   40
Boston Bay and Bunker Hill
Would serve things still;
Things are of the snake.

The horseman serves the horse,
The neatherd serves the neat,[9]   45
The merchant serves the purse,
The eater serves his meat;
'Tis the day of the chattel,
Web to weave, and corn to grind;
Things are in the saddle,   50
And ride mankind.

There are two laws discrete,
Not reconciled,—
Law for man, and law for thing;
The last builds town and fleet,   55
But it runs wild,
And doth the man unking.

'Tis fit the forest fall,
The steep be graded,

7. Contoocook is a river in southern New Hampshire; Agiochook, the Indian name for the White Mountains of New Hampshire.

8. I.e., the South would weep "crocodile tears."

9. Ox.

The mountain tunneled,   60
The sand shaded,
The orchard planted,
The glebe tilled,
The prairie granted,
The steamer built.   65

Let man serve law for man;
Live for friendship, live for love,
For truth's and harmony's behoof;
The state may follow how it can,
As Olympus follows Jove.   70

    Yet do not I implore
The wrinkled shopman to my sounding woods,
Nor bid the unwilling senator
Ask votes of thrushes in the solitudes.
Every one to his chosen work;—   75
Foolish hands may mix and mar;
Wise and sure the issues are.
Round they roll till dark is light,
Sex to sex, and even to odd;—
The over-god   80
Who marries Right to Might,
Who peoples, unpeoples,—
He who exterminates
Races by stronger races,
Black by white faces,—   85
Knows to bring honey
Out of the lion;
Grafts gentlest scion
On pirate and Turk.

The Cossack eats Poland,[1]   90
Like stolen fruit;
Her last noble is ruined,
Her last poet mute:
Straight, into double band
The victors divide;   95
Half for freedom strike and stand;—
The astonished Muse finds thousands at her side.

                                    1846

1. Russia annexed much of Poland in 1796; an unsuccessful insurrection occurred in 1830–31.

Merlin[2]

I

Thy trivial harp will never please
Or fill my craving ear;
Its chords should ring as blows the breeze,
Free, peremptory, clear.
No jingling serenader's art,   5
Nor tinkle of piano strings,
Can make the wild blood start
In its mystic springs.
The kingly bard
Must smite the chords rudely and hard,   10
As with hammer or with mace;
That they may render back
Artful thunder, which conveys
Secrets of the solar track,
Sparks of the supersolar blaze.   15
Merlin's blows are strokes of fate,
Chiming with the forest tone,
When boughs buffet boughs in the wood;
Chiming with the gasp and moan
Of the ice-imprisoned flood;   20
With the pulse of manly hearts;
With the voice of orators;
With the din of city arts;
With the cannonade of wars;
With the marches of the brave;   25
And prayers of might from martyrs' cave.

Great is the art,
Great be the manners, of the bard.
He shall not his brain encumber
With the coil of rhythm and number;   30
But, leaving rule and pale forethought,
He shall aye climb
For his rhyme.
"Pass in, pass in," the angels say,
"In to the upper doors,   35
Nor count compartments of the floors,
But mount to paradise
By the stairway of surprise."

Blameless master of the games,
King of sport that never shames,   40
He shall daily joy dispense
Hid in song's sweet influence.

---

2. Merlin, the Welsh bard, is addressing some unnamed poetling, like those
Emerson found around him. Cf. *Journals* (passages 25, 27).

Forms more cheerly live and go,
What time the subtle mind
Sings aloud the tune whereto   45
Their pulses beat,
And march their feet,
And their members are combined.

By Sybarites³ beguiled,
He shall no task decline;   50
Merlin's mighty line
Extremes of nature reconciled,—
Bereaved a tyrant of his will,
And made the lion mild.
Songs can the tempest still,   55
Scattered on the stormy air,
Mold the year to fair increase,
And bring in poetic peace.
He shall not seek to weave,
In weak, unhappy times,   60
Efficacious rhymes;
Wait his returning strength.
Bird that from the nadir's floor
To the zenith's top can soar,—
The soaring orbit of the muse exceeds that journey's length.   65
Nor profane affect to hit
Or compass that, by meddling wit,
Which only the propitious mind
Publishes when 'tis inclined.
There are open hours   70
When the God's will sallies free,
And the dull idiot might see
The flowing fortunes of a thousand years;—
Sudden, at unawares,
Self-moved, fly-to the doors,   75
Nor sword of angels could reveal
What they conceal.

II

The rhyme of the poet
Modulates the king's affairs;
Balance-loving Nature   80
Made all things in pairs.
To every foot its antipode;
Each color with its counter glowed;
To every tone beat answering tones,
Higher or graver;   85
Flavor gladly blends with flavor;
Leaf answers leaf upon the bough;
And match the paired cotyledons.⁴

3. Luxury lovers.   4. Seed leaves.

Hands to hands, and feet to feet,
In one body grooms and brides;   90
Eldest rite, two married sides
In every mortal meet.
Light's far furnace shines,
Smelting balls and bars,
Forging double stars,   95
Glittering twins and trines.
The animals are sick with love,
Lovesick with rhyme;
Each with all propitious Time
Into chorus wove.   100

Like the dancers' ordered band,
Thoughts come also hand in hand;
In equal couples mated,
Or else alternated;
Adding by their mutual gage,   105
One to other, health and age.
Solitary fancies go
Short-lived wandering to and fro,
Most like to bachelors,
Or an ungiven maid,   110
Not ancestors,
With no posterity to make the lie afraid,
Or keep truth undecayed.
Perfect-paired as eagle's wings,
Justice is the rhyme of things;   115
Trade and counting use
The self-same tuneful muse;
And Nemesis,
Who with even matches odd,
Who athwart space redresses   120
The partial wrong,
Fills the just period,
And finishes the song.

Subtle rhymes, with ruin rife,
Murmur in the house of life,   125
Sung by the Sisters[5] as they spin;
In perfect time and measure they
Build and unbuild our echoing clay,
As the two twilights of the day
Fold us music-drunken in.   130
1846   1846

5. The Fates in Greek legend.

Mottoes[6]

Nature

The rounded world is fair to see,
Nine times folded in mystery:
Though baffled seers cannot impart
The secret of its laboring heart,
Throb thine with Nature's throbbing breast,   5
And all is clear from east to west.
Spirit that lurks each form within
Beckons to spirit of its kin;
Self-kindled every atom glows
And hints the future which it owes.   10

1844

Politics

Gold and iron are good
To buy iron and gold;
All earth's fleece and food
For their like are sold.
Boded Merlin wise,   5
Proved Napoleon great,
Nor kind nor coinage buys
Aught above its rate.
Fear, Craft and Avarice
Cannot rear a State.   10
Out of dust to build
What is more than dust,—
Walls Amphion[7] piled
Phoebus stablish must.
When the Muses nine   15
With the Virtues meet,
Find to their design
An Atlantic seat,
By green orchard boughs
Fended from the heat,   20
Where the statesman ploughs
Furrow for the wheat,—
When the Church is social worth,
When the state-house is the hearth,
Then the perfect State is come,   25
The republican at home.

1844

6. Emerson affixed original mottoes to *Essays, Second Series* (1844) and added similar mottoes to most of *Essays, First Series* for the second edition of 1847. He afterward collected a number of them in a volume of his poems, but the text and titles given here are those of the essays. "Nature" is the essay of 1844, not the book of 1836.
7. Amphion, according to Greek legend, built Thebes with the music of his lute; Phoebus Apollo was the god of song.

404 · *Ralph Waldo Emerson*

Nominalist and Realist[8]

In countless upward-striving waves
The moon-drawn tide-wave strives;
In thousand far-transplanted grafts
The parent fruit survives;
So, in the new-born millions,   5
The perfect Adam lives.
Not less are summer mornings dear
To every child they wake,
And each with novel life his sphere
Fills for his proper sake.   10

                                                                  1844

Compensation[9]

The wings of Time are black and white,
Pied with morning and with night.
Mountain tall and ocean deep
Trembling balance duly keep.
In changing moon and tidal wave,   5
Glows the feud of Want and Have.
Gauge of more and less through space,
Electric star or pencil plays.
The lonely Earth amid the balls
That hurry through the eternal halls,   10
A makeweight flying to the void,
Supplemental asteroid,
Or compensatory spark,
Shoots across the neutral Dark.

                                                                  1847

Art

Give to barrows, trays and pans
Grace and glimmer of romance;
Bring the moonlight into noon
Hid in gleaming piles of stone;
On the city's pavéd street   5
Plant gardens lined with lilac sweet;
Let spouting fountains cool the air,
Singing in the sun-baked square;
Let statue, picture, park and hall,
Ballad, flag and festival,   10
The past restore, the day adorn
And make tomorrow a new morn.

8. The realists, in medieval philosophy, taught that general ideas were substantive and "real"; nominalists, that they were names only. The essay to which this poem was motto dealt with the similar "amphibiousness" in man between the world of experience ("new-born millions") and the world of ideas ("perfect Adam") on which much of Emerson's work of the 1840's, like the paired essays "Experience" and "The Poet," was built. Edward Emerson retitled the poem "Promise."
9. Though sometimes printed as the first half of a two-part poem, this was originally a separate motto.

So shall the drudge in dusty frock
Spy behind the city clock
Retinues of airy kings,   15
Skirts of angels, starry wings,
His fathers shining in bright fables,
His children fed at heavenly tables.
'Tis the privilege of Art
Thus to play its cheerful part,   20
Man on Earth to acclimate
And bend the exile to his fate,
And, molded of one element
With the days and firmament,
Teach him on these as stairs to climb   25
And live on even terms with Time;
Whilst upper life the slender rill
Of human sense doth overfill.

1847

Days[1]

Daughters of Time, the hypocritic Days,
Muffled and dumb like barefoot dervishes,
And marching single in an endless file,
Bring diadems and fagots in their hands.
To each they offer gifts after his will,   5
Bread, kingdoms, stars, and sky that holds them all.
I, in my pleached[2] garden, watched the pomp,
Forgot my morning wishes, hastily
Took a few herbs and apples, and the Day
Turned and departed silent. I, too late,   10
Under her solemn fillet saw the scorn.

1851   1857

Brahma[3]

If the red slayer think he slays,
    Or if the slain think he is slain,
They know not well the subtle ways
    I keep, and pass, and turn again.

Far or forgot to me is near;   5
    Shadow and sunlight are the same;

---

1. One influence on this poem is that of the Persian poet Hafiz, whom Emerson had been reading in German translation. Though Emerson wrote in his *Journals* for 1852 that he did not remember when or how he wrote this, the theme recurs frequently in the *Journals* and is the subject of at least one essay ("Works and Days"). See, for instance, *Journals* (passages 108–9).
2. Overarched with boughs.
3. The supreme soul of the universe (Hindu). The poem versifies no one source, but distills one of the central principles of Hindu Scripture, the absolute unity of all in Brahma.

The vanished gods to me appear;
   And one to me are shame and fame.

They reckon ill who leave me out;
   When me they fly, I am the wings;   10
I am the doubter and the doubt,
   And I the hymn the Brahmin sings.

The strong gods pine for my abode,
   And pine in vain the sacred Seven,[4]
But thou, meek lover of the good!   15
   Find me, and turn thy back on heaven.[5]

1856   1857

Two Rivers

Thy summer voice, Musketaquit,[6]
Repeats the music of the rain;
But sweeter rivers pulsing flit
Through thee, as thou through Concord Plain.

Thou in thy narrow banks art pent: 5
The stream I love unbounded goes
Through flood and sea and firmament;
Through light, through life, it forward flows.

I see the inundation sweet,
I hear the spending of the stream   10
Through years, through men, through Nature fleet,
Through love and thought, through power and dream.

Musketaquit, a goblin strong,
Of shard and flint makes jewels gay;
They lose their grief who hear his song,   15
And where he winds is the day of day.

So forth and brighter fares my stream,—
Who drink it shall not thirst again;
No darkness stains its equal gleam,
And ages drop in it like rain.   20

1856   1858

Waldeinsamkeit[7]

I do not count the hours I spend
In wandering by the sea;

4. The "strong gods" and the "sacred Seven" are subordinate Hindu gods and saints.
5. Here the conventional paradise of personal immortality.
6. The Concord River.
7. "Forest solitude."

The forest is my loyal friend,
Like God it useth me.

In plains that room for shadows make   5
Of skirting hills to lie,
Bound in by streams which give and take
Their colors from the sky;

Or on the mountain-crest sublime,
Or down the oaken glade,   10
O what have I to do with time?
For this the day was made.

Cities of mortals woe-begone
Fantastic care derides,
But in the serious landscape lone   15
Stern benefit abides.

Sheen will tarnish, honey cloy,
And merry is only a mask of sad,
But, sober on a fund of joy,
The woods at heart are glad.   20

There the great Planter plants
Of fruitful worlds the grain,
And with a million spells enchants
The souls that walk in pain.

Still on the seeds of all he made   25
The rose of beauty burns;
Through times that wear and forms that fade,
Immortal youth returns.

The black ducks mounting from the lake,
The pigeon in the pines,   30
The bittern's boom, a desert make
Which no false art refines.

Down in yon watery nook,
Where bearded mists divide,
The gray old gods whom Chaos knew,   35
The sires of Nature, hide.

Aloft, in secret veins of air,
Blows the sweet breath of song,
O, few to scale those uplands dare,
Though they to all belong!   40

See thou bring not to field or stone
The fancies found in books;
Leave authors' eyes, and fetch your own,
To brave the landscape's looks.

Oblivion here thy wisdom is, 45
Thy thrift, the sleep of cares;
For a proud idleness like this
Crowns all thy mean affairs.

1857 1858

Terminus[8]

It is time to be old,
To take in sail:—
The god of bounds,
Who sets to seas a shore,
Came to me in his fatal rounds, 5
And said: "No more!
No farther shoot
Thy broad ambitious branches, and thy root.
Fancy departs: no more invent;
Contract thy firmament 10
To compass of a tent.
There's not enough for this and that,
Make thy option which of two;
Economize the failing river,
Not the less revere the Giver, 15
Leave the many and hold the few.
Timely wise accept the terms,
Soften the fall with wary foot;
A little while
Still plan and smile, 20
And,—fault of novel germs,—
Mature the unfallen fruit.
Curse, if thou wilt, thy sires,
Bad husbands of their fires,
Who, when they gave their breath, 25
Failed to bequeath
The needful sinew stark as once,
The Baresark[9] marrow to thy bones,
But left a legacy of ebbing veins,
Inconstant heat and nerveless reins,— 30
Amid the Muses, left thee deaf and dumb,
Amid the gladiators, halt and numb."

As the bird trims her to the gale,
I trim myself to the storm of time,
I man the rudder, reef the sail, 35
Obey the voice at eve obeyed at prime:
"Lowly faithful, banish fear,
Right onward drive unharmed;
The port, well worth the cruise, is near,
And every wave is charmed." 40

1867

---

8. The Roman god of boundaries. 9. Berserk, or savage Viking.

Henry David Thoreau

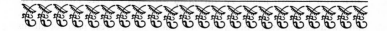

Thoreau (the name is accented *Tho'ro*) was about fourteen years younger than Emerson. Born July 12, 1817, he was the only one of the Concord group—Emerson, Thoreau, Hawthorne, Alcott, and others—who was a native of the village. Unlike most New England writers of his time, he had an undistinguished ancestry. His father, a maker of lead pencils, was of French extraction; his mother, of English and Scotch. At considerable sacrifice on the family's part, Henry was educated at the Concord Academy and at Harvard College, from which he graduated in 1837, the year of Emerson's "American Scholar" address.

Thoreau was immediately engaged to teach in the public schools of his native town, but resigned after only two weeks rather than practice the corporal punishment of students that the school committee insisted upon. After several unsuccessful attempts to find another teaching position (the country was in the midst of a severe depression and jobs were scarce), Thoreau opened a private school of his own in Concord. Although it was avowedly experimental and conducted on principles that we think of as "progressive" in the 20th century, it immediately prospered and soon had a waiting list of students. The school was abandoned, however, in 1841, when Thoreau's brother John, who had assisted him in the teaching, fell ill. Thoreau did not care to continue the task alone.

In 1835 Ralph Waldo Emerson purchased a house in Concord and shortly thereafter became acquainted with Thoreau. Emerson took an immediate liking to his young neighbor, recommended him for scholarships at Harvard, and after Thoreau's graduation and return to Concord in 1837, conversed frequently with him. In 1841 he invited Thoreau to join his household, offering him room and board in exchange for occasional manual labor about the house and garden, with the hope that, through close association, he might assist his younger friend in a writing career. In 1837, at Emerson's instance, Thoreau had started keeping a daily journal and in the early 1840's he began contributing occasional articles and poems culled from his journal to the transcendental periodical *Dial* and other magazines.

Emerson was so convinced of Thoreau's promise that in 1843 he arranged for his protégé to move to Staten Island to be nearer the major publishing houses and editorial offices. Emerson's brother William was a lawyer there and Thoreau was to tutor his sons. The experiment, however, was a failure. Thoreau became desperately homesick and in six months returned to his native Concord, to remain there, except for brief excursions, for the rest of his life.

In the fall of 1844 Emerson purchased a woodlot on the shores of Walden Pond, a small glacial lake two miles from his home in Concord, to protect it from the woodcutter's ax. For several years Thoreau had been looking for a place to retire and devote himself more fully to writing. In the spring of 1845, after having worked out a satisfactory arrangement with Emerson, he went out to the Walden woodlot and built a small cabin with his own hands. At the pond his expenses were minimal. The cabin cost him only $28.12½; his average weekly expenditure for food was only twenty-seven cents. Six weeks of manual labor a year paid for all his needs, and enabled him to devote himself almost entirely to writing rather than to breadwinning. He spent only two years, two months, and two days at the pond, but in that time he not only wrote his first book, *A Week on the Concord and Merrimack Rivers*, but numerous essays, and a goodly portion of his masterpiece, *Walden, or Life in the Woods*. He left Walden Pond in September of 1847 when Emerson, who was about to start on a lecture tour of England, asked him to look after the Emerson family and household while he was gone. Upon Emerson's return from England the next year, Thoreau went back to live with his parents, with whom he resided for the rest of his days.

Concord had for many years been a center of antislavery activities, and Thoreau had been brought up in an abolitionist environment. By the mid-1840's so strongly had his convictions against slavery developed that he refused to pay taxes to a government that not only condoned but even supported slavery. In July 1846, while he was still at Walden, he was arrested for tax delinquency and placed in the Concord jail. Someone, under cover of darkness—it is now generally believed to have been his maiden aunt Maria Thoreau, who was shocked to discover her nephew in jail—paid the tax, and he was released the next morning. Thus deprived of the opportunity of challenging the constitutionality of slavery in the courts, Thoreau turned to the lecture platform and in 1848 read a lecture entitled "The Relation of the Individual to the State," defending his position before his fellow townsmen. This essay was published in 1849 in the short-lived transcendental periodical *Aesthetic Papers* as "Resistance to Civil Government," and later came to be known as "On the Duty of Civil Disobedience," or more simply as "Civil Disobedience."

In 1849 Thoreau published his first book. After circulating it unsuccessfully among the publishers for two years he finally, with Emerson's encouragement, published it at his own expense. *A Week* is ostensibly an account of a rowboat excursion he had taken with his brother John in 1839. However, the narrative is interspersed with essays and poems culled from his contributions to the *Dial* and from his journal. Its publication was an utter failure: of the thousand copies printed, 75 had been given away and only two hundred sold. Four years later his publisher turned over the remainder to the author. That night Thoreau wrote in his journal, "I have now a library of nearly nine hundred volumes, over seven hundred of which I wrote myself."

Walden, Thoreau's second book, was nearly enough ready for publication in 1849 to be announced as "forthcoming" in the advertisements for *A Week*. But the failure of the first book frightened away any potential publishers, and it was five years later, in 1854, before the book was brought out. Thoreau however spent the intervening years in rewriting, revising, and polishing the manuscript, producing at least eight different complete drafts, so that the final published version was a considerably different and vastly improved book.

Walden, or Life in the Woods is basically an account of the two years Thoreau spent in the cabin at Walden Pond, although for artistic reasons he has condensed the narrative of the two years into one. It was begun in reply to the "very particular inquiries * * * made by my townsmen concerning my mode of life." In comparison to *A Week*, its sale was encouraging. It received several favorable reviews and in five years managed to exhaust the edition of two thousand copies.

At the pond Thoreau had adopted the pattern of life which he followed thereafter. His mornings were devoted to writing, his afternoons to sauntering through the Concord countryside, studying the flora and fauna, his evenings to conversation with his friends. As at Walden, he devoted approximately six weeks in the year to earning a living. Surveying, his major source of income, he found a happy profession because the work was out of doors. Occasionally he assisted his father in the family pencil business. A little income came from his writing and lecturing. But he was not above doing any form of manual labor—from mowing lawns to shoveling manure—if the need and opportunity arose. "There is no reason," he wrote to his friend Horace Greeley, "why the scholar who professes to be a little wiser than the mass of men, should not do his work in the ditch occasionally, and by means of his superior wisdom make much less suffice for him."

Occasionally Thoreau varied the pattern of his life with short excursions across the countryside with some friendly companion such as Ellery Channing, the poet, or his Worcester friend, Harrison G. O. Blake. He made three trips to the woods of northern Maine, four the length of Cape Cod, several to the White Mountains of New Hampshire, and one to Quebec. These excursions, while in part vacations, were primarily undertaken to gather material for his writing, and each excursion was carefully written up as a lecture, which eventually became a published essay.

In the 1850's Thoreau took a renewed interest in antislavery activities. He aided more than one escaped slave on his way to freedom in Canada. He was greatly disturbed by the return of Simms and Anthony Burns to slavery under the Fugitive Slave Act and spoke out against his state's part in their capture in a fiery address on "Slavery in Massachusetts" delivered at an abolitionist convention in 1854. He took particular interest in John Brown's activities in Kansas after he had met Brown on a fund-raising campaign in Concord. When Brown struck at Harpers Ferry in the autumn of 1859, Thoreau was one of the first to come vocally to his defense.

Throughout his life Thoreau had suffered from tuberculosis. An early attack forced him to leave college for a while. Several times later he was invalided for several months. In the winter of 1860–61 he caught a bad cold which settled in his lungs. His condition rapidly became worse, and the doctors despaired for his life. Since they recommended a trip to another climate, in May, 1861, he set out for Minnesota with Horace Mann, Jr., the son of the famed educator. But the trip was not successful and in July Thoreau returned to Concord with the realization that he had not many months to live.

The winter of 1861–62 he devoted to revising and polishing his un-published lectures and essays, dictating to his sister Sophia when he was too weak to hold a pencil in his hands. When his Calvinist Aunt Louisa asked him if he had made his peace with God, he replied, "I have never quarreled with him." When Thoreau died in May, 1862, he was only forty-four years of age.

II

Fame eluded Thoreau in his lifetime. His literary contemporaries paid little attention to him, and the rare times when they did notice him, it was usually only to dismiss him as a mere imitator of his neighbor Ralph Waldo Emerson. To many of his fellow townsmen he was just another local eccentric—of which the town already had an ample supply. To many of his friends he was a failure; even Emerson condemned him for being but "the captain of a huckleberry party" when he should have been "engineering for all America."

Just after his death there was a flurry of interest in his works. Both *Walden* and *A Week* were reissued, and in the succeeding four years five new books—*Excursions, The Maine Woods, Cape Cod, Letters to Various Persons,* and *A Yankee in Canada*—were culled from his magazine articles and unpublished manuscripts by his sister Sophia with the aid of his friends Emerson and Ellery Channing. But the growing interest in his work was nipped in the bud in 1865 by the severe critical attack of James Russell Lowell. In a lengthy essay that had wide influence because of Lowell's prestige as a critic, he charged Thoreau with lacking humor, not having a healthy mind, and wanting in ability to observe accurately. A second blow was dealt to Thoreau's fame in 1880 when Robert Louis Stevenson published an essay in the *Cornhill Magazine* in England denounc-ing him as a "skulker."

Nonetheless the tide slowly turned in Thoreau's favor. In the 1880's his Worcester friend H. G. O. Blake edited four volumes of selections from the nature passages in his journal, entitled *Early Spring in Massachusetts, Summer, Autumn,* and *Winter,* and a new interest in Thoreau as a nature-writer was aroused. Then in 1906 a twenty-volume edition of his works, including nearly his complete journal in fourteen volumes, was published, and for the first time critics became aware of the breadth of his interests and the depth of his appeal.

As with both Melville and Whitman, it was in England that Thoreau first received marked critical appreciation. In 1890 Henry S. Salt, one of the "discoverers" of Melville, wrote the first critical biography of Thoreau worthy of the name. Near the turn of the century the nascent British Labour Party not only distributed paperback editions of Thoreau's works, but also named their local party units "Walden Clubs."

But in this, his native country, Thoreau did not receive really wide-spread attention until the depression of the 1930's. Then large masses of people were forced by economic necessity to live the simple life that Thoreau advocated, and the reading of his works, particularly *Walden,* became almost a vogue. "He is the only author you can read without a nickel in your pocket and not feel insulted" was a typical comment of the time. And many there were who predicted that Thoreau's popularity would disappear with the coming of prosperity. Instead his works have been reprinted and increasingly read. More and more he has become a prophet of our times. There are now more editions of *Walden* in print than ever before. Not a year goes by without further studies, analyses, and elucidations of his works. The novelist Theodore Dreiser spoke for our times when just before his death he compiled an anthology of quotations from Thoreau and prefaced it: "Of all my philosophic and scientific reading of recent years from Democritus to Einstein, these scattered notes of Thoreau impress me as being more illuminative, not of the practical results or profits of science * * * but of the implications of scientific results or cosmology."

III

What is the basis of Thoreau's appeal today? The question cannot be answered easily, for one of his greatest strengths lies in the fact that his attraction is so many-faceted. A mere list of names of some of our contemporaries who have acknowledged the influence of Thoreau may indicate his many-sided appeal. It would include such diverse personalities and minds as Mahatma Gandhi, Sinclair Lewis, Frank Lloyd Wright, Charles Ives, Ernest Hemingway, Gene Tunney, C. P. Snow, Robert Frost, Upton Sinclair, Willa Cather, and Henry Miller, among many others.

Thoreau's most widespread fame is perhaps as a nature writer and as such he stands pre-eminent. It was he who in *Walden* and such shorter papers as "Walking" and "Wild Apples" perfected and popularized the nature essay. He was the first to make it a definite and separate literary type distinct from the "letters" of Crèvecœur, the "episodes" of Audubon, the "travels" of Bartram, or the "journals" of various early writers. By cross-breeding the familiar essay of such authors as Lamb and Irving with the more pedestrian reports of the early naturalists, he established the form that most nature-writers since his day have followed and none has surpassed.

Thoreau has the marked ability of making his nature-writing come alive. The reader finds himself rowing on Walden Pond, playing that three-dimensional checker game with the loon, or sitting on the steps of the cabin, witness to a bloody battle between a black and a red ant. Without stooping to the childish anthropomorphizing of the Peter Rabbit school of nature-writers or the "nature-faking" so heartily denounced by President Theodore Roosevelt, he nonetheless succeeds in instilling individuality and character into his animals and birds. Yet Thoreau differs from many nature-writers in that his interest centers on man's place in nature, rather than in nature for itself. He studied nature because he wanted to understand better the environment in which man lived, and because it was his firm conviction that man, like Antaeus of Greek legend, derived his strength from his contact with the soil. Thoreau felt no day worthwhile unless he had spent at least four or five hours of it out of doors sauntering through the woods and fields of his native Concord.

Thoreau's emphasis on individualism also has a strong attraction, especially in an age of conformity and status-seeking. We admire those who have the courage to break with convention and live their own lives. Thoreau is a supreme example of "a man who did what he wanted." After one short experiment in conformity—teaching school—and proving to himself and to his neighbors that he could do it successfully, Thoreau broke with tradition and struck out on his own to live the life that he— and not his neighbors—found good. Thoreau's move to Walden Pond had been greeted with shocked astonishment by many of his friends. They could not understand a college graduate renouncing a professional career and going to live in a cabin in the woods. But Thoreau continued on his own way and, in his own words, met "with a success unexpected in common hours"—not a material success, it is true, but the success of living the life he wanted. He had not only "built castles in the air," but had "put foundations under them."

In this connection it is important to remember that, like Emerson, Thoreau was not attempting to set a pattern of life for his fellow man. "I would not have any one adopt *my* mode of living on any account," he tells us in W*alden;* "for, beside that before he has fairly learned it I may have found out another for myself, I desire that there may be as many different persons in the world as possible; but I would have each one be very careful to find out and pursue *his own* way, and not his father's or his mother's or his neighbor's instead." The true follower of Thoreau does not pattern his life on a cabin in the woods, but instead fashions it to fit his personal dream.

Because of its emphasis on individualism, to some Thoreau's philosophy seems unblushingly egotistic. It is important to remember, however, that Thoreau was a New England transcendentalist—perhaps the most dedicated among them all—and that he firmly believed he was following not his own will but the will of God within him. Like Emerson he affirmed, challengingly, that it was far more difficult—and far more rewarding spiritually—to follow one's conscience than to follow one's neighbors' opinions. "If any one imagines that this law is lax," said Emerson—and Thoreau would have heartily agreed—"let him keep its commandments one day."

Thoreau's own contribution to the cause of individualism and self-reliance is that he offers a practical solution to the economic problems often blocking the attaining of one's dreams—the life of simplicity. "Simplicity, simplicity, simplicity!" he urges. "I say, let your affairs be as two or three, and not a hundred or a thousand; instead of a million count half a dozen, and keep your accounts on your thumb nail." Cut down your needs and you will find the time and freedom to do what you want, "for a man is rich in proportion to the number of things which he can afford to let alone."

Thoreau is sometimes charged with an espousal of primitivism, a Rousseauistic return to savagery. It is true that he is often critical of modern civilization, but he is critical of the one-sided nature of our progress rather than of progress itself. We have concentrated on producing what he terms "improved means to unimproved ends." We invent railroads to save time and then proceed to waste the time we have saved. We lay a cable across the Atlantic and then use it to transmit the trivial information that Princess Adelaide has the whooping cough. He was not critical of our inventions but of the use we made of them; he felt that we needed to develop the inner life as much as we have already developed the material instruments of living.

It would have surprised Thoreau to have heard himself pointed out as a misanthrope (as some critics have done), for he was basically an optimist who had the highest of hopes for mankind. He believed that he was "born into the most estimable place in all the world, and in the very nick of time, too." It is true that he was often disappointed in the behavior of his fellow man (and, significantly, of his own), but he was convinced that would man but try, he could raise himself as far above the level of today as today's man has raised himself above the cave man. Note that every one of Thoreau's major works—*Walden, A Week*, "Civil Disobedience," and "Life without Principle"—ends on a primarily optimistic note, looking forward to that day when so great would be our progress that the light of the sun, in comparison, would seem but that of a morning star. And note throughout his works the constantly recurring images of rebirth and reawakening. Symbolically he opens *Walden* with the epigraph (unfortunately omitted in many modern editions), "I do not propose to write an ode to dejection, but to brag as lustily as chanticleer in the morning, standing on his roost, if only to wake my neighbors up." And he ends the book with the reawakening of spring.

IV

It is important for the reader to recognize the fact that Thoreau in his writings is often crowing loudly to wake his neighbors up. As he once wrote to his friend Blake, "I trust you realize what a great exaggerator I am." He quite consciously makes bold overstatements to shock us into energy of thought. We must not always take what he says literally. When he states that he "could spit a Mexican" or "could live on board nails," he is being ironic, using attention-getting statements to force us to think through our own ideas on slavery or on diet.

Thoreau's writing is vivid with wit and satire. James Russell Lowell's charge that Thoreau had no humor reflects on Lowell rather than Thoreau. With the possible exception of some of his political essays, there is hardly a page that is not lighted up with a variety of humorous touches. Sometimes they are puns (such as his description of the unsuccessful fishermen as members of the ancient sect of Coenobites—that is, "See, no bites"), sometimes slapstick as in the passage in *Cape Cod* where he describes the efforts of the driver to close the door of the overloaded stagecoach while the passengers "timed our inspirations and expirations so as to assist him," but most frequently his is a critical humor akin to that of Jonathan Swift in *Gulliver's Travels*: satire to help us see the foibles of our age and civilization. The difficulty is, of course, that Thoreau's standards of value are so different from those of the man in the street that they seem topsy-turvy and the whole point of his humor is sometimes missed. Instead of poking fun at the town drunkard or idiot, he laughs at the successful merchant or the hardworking farmer. Instead of congratulating the man of means, he offers him condolence. He laughs at the man of fashion and praises the worker in rough clothing. But he is not being perverse. Rather he is seriously questioning popular standards and suggesting by implication (and often explicit statement) that there are higher, more valid standards to follow. His humor is, in other words, not an end in itself, but a means of social criticism. It is an effective element in his style of writing.

As a literary artist, Thoreau is as interested in how he says something as in what he says—although not for any "art for art's sake" reason, but for the purely practical reason that to communicate effectively one must write well. His way of writing well was very different from that of his great contemporaries. The result of his conscientious discipline was perhaps the first really modern prose. One has only to compare his writing with that of most of his contemporaries to see how much their writing has dated, how modern is his.

Concreteness is a basic characteristic of Thoreau's prose. Although many of the other transcendentalists, whatever their felicities, were commonly vague, diffuse, and abstract, Thoreau is down to earth and practical. Even when discussing abstract ideas (as, for example, in the famous "Time is but the stream I go a-fishing in" passage in Walden), he conveys his meaning concretely. While his language is often highly figurative, his images are familiar to the general reader (as, for example, the cock-crowing simile mentioned above).

Thoreau's vocabulary is large. He will send a conscientious reader to the dictionary frequently. His unusual words emerge naturally from his search for the precise word to suit his needs. On those rare occasions when it may appear that he has misused a word, a check with the dictionary will usually reveal that he is using the word in its basic sense. In Walden, for example, when he speaks of his "withdrawing room," he is not coining a phrase but returning to the original form of "drawing room" for the sake of a pun.

Thoreau had a warm interest in form. Although many of his early critics belabored him for what they termed the "formlessness" of his writings, a careful examination of his works should have convinced them that each sentence, each paragraph, each chapter stands in its particular niche for a particular reason and that any attempt to remove it will do damage to the structure as a whole. Thoreau's feeling for form is most obvious in the structure of the two books he had completed before his early death—A Week on the Concord and Merrimack Rivers and Walden. The former is based on the pattern of the week with one chapter for each of the seven days. Walden condenses the experiences of two years into one, as we have already remarked, in order to emphasize the seasonal pattern of life. Beginning with the building of his cabin in the spring, it follows through with an account of his gardening in the summer, his housewarming in the fall, winter life at the pond, and in the end returns once more to spring with its promise of rebirth and revival, giving the book a unity and at the same time enabling Thoreau to symbolize his constant optimistic hope for a spiritual rebirth and revival in mankind.

Thoreau carries this interest in form down into the smaller units of his works. The chapter on "Sounds" in Walden, for example, carries out the pattern of the day, just as the whole book does the year. It begins with the sounds of the morning, moves on into the afternoon, then evening, then night, and ends with the revival of life with the dawn. Similarly he is concerned to make each individual paragraph and sentence interdependent with the preceding and following paragraph and sentence. It causes little surprise, then, to discover Thoreau's interest in architecture, frequently shown in Walden and his other works, for he was well aware of the relationship in structure of both buildings and books. If one need further evidence of Thoreau's interest in form and style, he need only turn to his *Journal* and there he will find the art of writing one of Thoreau's favorite topics. Indeed, one student has culled from the *Journal* more than two hundred pages of quotations devoted to the craft of writing.

v

Of all Thoreau's works, *Walden, or Life in the Woods* is unquestionably the masterpiece. Ostensibly it is the account of the period of two years he spent at Walden Pond. As such the book has its own special appeal. Thoreau is almost a Massachusetts Robinson Crusoe or backyard Daniel Boone who shows us how to satisfy our pioneering instincts without hitting the trail west. He enables us to discover the adventurous life right at home. So appealing does he make the simple life and the charms of nature that the countryside ever since has been dotted with the cabins of aspiring disciples of Thoreau—despite his specific admonition in *Walden* that he wanted no imitators.

But *Walden* is more than another *Adventures of Robinson Crusoe*. It is a devastating commentary on the values of our contemporary civilization—even more pertinent today than when it was written a century ago. In it he dares to ask the questions that most people prefer to leave unexamined. Is what we call success really success? Is what we call happiness really happiness? Are the goals we have set up in life the goals we really want to attain? Why then do "the mass of men lead lives of quiet desperation"? Why then do so many "when they come to die, discover that they have not lived"? Thoreau has a way of asking disconcerting questions, questions aimed at making us think fundamentally. But because *Walden* does challenge us to think, many a man has dated a new era in his life from the reading of the book.

Read on its highest level, however, *Walden* becomes still another book —a *Pilgrim's Progress*—an account of one man's successful search for spiritual values. And here the chapter entitled "Higher Laws" is central. Here one discovers that if he "listens to the faintest but constant suggestions of his genius, which are certainly true, he sees not to what extremes, or even insanity, it may lead him; and yet that way, as he grows more resolute and faithful, his road lies. * * * If the day and the night are such that you greet them with joy, and life emits a fragrance like flowers and sweet-scented herbs, is more elastic, more starry, more immortal,—that is your success." Thoreau found his way to that success, and *Walden* is a guidebook for fellowseekers.

Second to *Walden* in fame is "Civil Disobedience," and indeed in many quarters of the globe Thoreau is better known for the essay than for the book. Written as a protest against the American government's support of slavery, Thoreau's essay caused little stir in his own lifetime or for many years thereafter. Shortly after the turn of the century, however, it was discovered by the young Hindu lawyer Gandhi, who immediately recognized the value of its principles and first applied its techniques in South Africa in a highly successful endeavor to win greater political and economic freedom there for his fellow countrymen. Gandhi then carried the idea back to his native India, once again applying the techniques of civil disobedience, this time in an equally successful campaign for freedom from

British dominion and for the repeal of discriminatory caste laws against the Hindu untouchables. Civil disobedience was used by the resistance movements against the Nazi invaders of Occupied Europe during World War II. It has been used by minority groups the world over in their fights for political and economic freedom. Significantly, Thoreau's works are now banned in some of the countries behind the Iron Curtain.

The basic principle of civil disobedience is that it is as much the duty of the good citizen to break the bad law as to obey the good. The basic technique is passive, that is, nonviolent, resistance. When any government has to choose between repealing an evil law and filling all its jails with the good citizens who refuse to obey that evil law, it must inevitably repeal the law or bring about its own destruction. Purely idealistic in its concept, it has proven extremely workable in practice. Its effectiveness has won Thoreau the everlasting enmity of all dictatorships and all tyrannical governments and has made him the hero of the downtrodden all over the world.

"A Plea for Captain John Brown" was the first and most important of three papers Thoreau wrote in defense of Brown. It was written at white heat fanned by the intense emotions aroused in Thoreau by Brown's attack on Harpers Ferry and first delivered at a meeting Thoreau himself called in the Town Hall in Concord. Brown had brought almost universal condemnation down upon his head by his attack. Even most of the abolitionists thought that he had committed at least a tactical error and feared that he was insane. When they advised Thoreau not to speak in Brown's defense, he replied, "I am not asking for advice; I am announcing a meeting." Thoreau saw Brown's attack as the logical outcome of abolitionist and even transcendentalist principles and delivered his impassioned plea before a crowded hall in Concord. Emerson tells us, "The hall was filled at an early hour by people of all parties, and his earnest eulogy of the hero was heard by all respectfully, by many with a sympathy that surprised themselves." He later repeated the lecture to capacity crowds in Boston and Worcester. It should be noted that Thoreau devotes his praise not so much to the attack on Harpers Ferry as to the fact that John Brown had the courage to live up to his principles and to act rather than merely talk—quite in contrast to many of Thoreau's contemporaries.

"Life without Principle" is in many ways the best brief exposition of Thoreau's total philosophy, although it is perhaps too highly concentrated to make the best introduction. While it was not published until after his death, Thoreau had delivered it many times over a period of years as a lecture entitled "Getting a Living." Its present title was assigned by its first editor, James T. Fields. The general purpose of the essay is indicated by the scriptural text which Thoreau announced for the lecture, "What shall it profit a man if he gain the whole world but lose his own soul?"

Thoreau made almost daily entries in his *Journal* from 1837, just after he graduated from Harvard College, until the fall of 1861, just a few months before his death, when he became too ill to hold a pen. The full *Journal* totals more than two million words and fills fourteen printed volumes. It is one of the most complete records in existence of a man's thoughts and observations over an extended period of years. Thoreau began the *Journal* primarily as a seed-bed of ideas for his essays and books. *Walden* and *A Week*, for example, were in a large part culled from the *Journal*. But by 1850 it had become an end in itself—a multi-faceted portrait of the universe as seen by Henry David Thoreau. He recorded the natural history of Concord, the life of the townspeople, accounts of his reading, and above all his thoughts on the moral, scientific, and spiritual issues of his day and of all time. Brief selections from the *Journal* can give only the faintest suggestion of the power and scope of the complete work. We have chosen, quite arbitrarily, to represent it with some selections from his comments on the art of writing, several of his natural-history sketches, portraits of some of his Concord neighbors, and a brief account of a visit to Cape Cod.

In the early days of his writing career Thoreau thought of himself primarily as a poet. And indeed there are extant more than two hundred of his poems. But only a handful of them are ever anthologized and these primarily for their content rather than their form. Thoreau was primarily a poet of ideas. In Emersonian terms, he was concerned to write not meter, but meter-making arguments. And he was even more concerned to live a poetical life than to write poetry. The best comment on Thoreau as a poet was made by Thoreau himself:

> My life has been the poem I would have writ,
> But I could not both live and utter it.

VI

It has taken Thoreau a full century to achieve his present rank among America's greatest writers. Now that he has achieved it, his position seems secure. His reputation is growing rather than diminishing. But even now he has not achieved a mass appeal. He can hardly be called a "household author," and it is doubtful if he ever will. No postage stamps have been issued in his honor, no statues erected in public parks. His alma mater, Harvard, has endowed no professorial chair in his name nor erected a Thoreau Hall. Thoreau's appeal is to the individual, not to the masses. But among thinking men, men who are concerned with the basic values of life, Thoreau has won a firm place. As Emerson said of him, "His soul was made for the noblest society; he had in a short life exhausted the capabilities of this world; wherever there is knowledge, wherever there is virtue, wherever there is beauty, he will find a home."

From Walden[1]
From *Economy*

When I wrote the following pages, or rather the bulk of them, I lived alone, in the woods, a mile from any neighbor, in a house which I had built myself, on the shore of Walden Pond, in Concord, Massachusetts, and earned my living by the labor of my hands only. I lived there two years and two months. At present I am a sojourner in civilized life again.

1. The text of Walden has been slightly modernized, in conformance with current practice.

I should not obtrude my affairs so much on the notice of my readers if very particular inquiries had not been made by my townsmen concerning my mode of life, which some would call impertinent, though they do not appear to me at all impertinent, but, considering the circumstances, very natural and pertinent. Some have asked what I got to eat; if I did not feel lonesome; if I was not afraid; and the like. Others have been curious to learn what portion of my income I devoted to charitable purposes; and some, who have large families, how many poor children I maintained. I will therefore ask those of my readers who feel no particular interest in me to pardon me if I undertake to answer some of these questions in this book. In most books, the *I*, or first person, is omitted; in this it will be retained; that, in respect to egotism, is the main difference. We commonly do not remember that it is, after all, always the first person that is speaking. I should not talk so much about myself if there were anybody else whom I knew as well. Unfortunately, I am confined to this theme by the narrowness of my experience. Moreover, I, on my side, require of every writer, first or last, a simple and sincere account of his own life, and not merely what he has heard of other men's lives; some such account as he would send to his kindred from a distant land; for if he has lived sincerely, it must have been in a distant land to me. Perhaps these pages are more particularly addressed to poor students. As for the rest of my readers, they will accept such portions as apply to them. I trust that none will stretch the seams in putting on the coat, for it may do good service to him whom it fits.

I would fain say something, not so much concerning the Chinese and Sandwich Islanders[2] as you who read these pages, who are said to live in New England; something about your condition, especially your outward condition or circumstances in this world, in this town, what it is, whether it is necessary that it be as bad as it is, whether it cannot be improved as well as not. I have traveled a good deal in Concord; and everywhere, in shops, and offices, and fields, the inhabitants have appeared to me to be doing penance in a thousand remarkable ways. What I have heard of Bramins sitting exposed to four fires and looking in the face of the sun; or hanging suspended, with their heads downward, over flames; or looking at the heavens over their shoulders "until it becomes impossible for them to resume their natural position, while from the twist of the neck nothing but liquids can pass into the stomach"; or dwelling, chained for life, at the foot of a tree; or measuring with their bodies, like caterpillars, the breadth of vast empires; or standing on one leg on the tops of pillars—even these forms of conscious penance are hardly more incredible and astonishing than the

2. The Sandwich Islands, now the Hawaiian Islands.

scenes which I daily witness. The twelve labors of Hercules were trifling in comparison with those which my neighbors have undertaken; for they were only twelve, and had an end; but I could never see that these men slew or captured any monster or finished any labor. They have no friend Iolas³ to burn with a hot iron the root of the hydra's head, but as soon as one head is crushed, two spring up.

I see young men, my townsmen, whose misfortune it is to have inherited farms, houses, barns, cattle, and farming tools; for these are more easily acquired than got rid of. Better if they had been born in the open pasture and suckled by a wolf, that they might have seen with clearer eyes what field they were called to labor in. Who made them serfs of the soil? Why should they eat their sixty acres, when man is condemned to eat only his peck of dirt? Why should they begin digging their graves as soon as they are born? They have got to live a man's life, pushing all these things before them, and get on as well as they can. How many a poor immortal soul have I met well nigh crushed and smothered under its load, creeping down the road of life, pushing before it a barn seventy-five feet by forty, its Augean stables⁴ never cleansed, and one hundred acres of land, tillage, mowing, pasture, and wood-lot! The portionless, who struggle with no such unnecessary inherited encumbrances, find it labor enough to subdue and cultivate a few cubic feet of flesh.

But men labor under a mistake. The better part of the man is soon ploughed into the soil for compost. By a seeming fate, commonly called necessity, they are employed, as it says in an old book, laying up treasures which moth and rust will corrupt and thieves break through and steal.⁵ It is a fool's life, as they will find when they get to the end of it, if not before. It is said that Deucalion and Pyrrha created men by throwing stones over their heads behind them:⁶

> Inde genus durum sumus, experiensque laborum,
> Et documenta damus quâ simus origine nati.⁷

Or, as Raleigh rhymes it in his sonorous way,

> "From thence our kind hard-hearted is, enduring pain and care,
> Approving that our bodies of a stony nature are."⁸

3. Hercules' servant, who aided him in killing the nine-headed monster, the Lernaean Hydra—one of the twelve labors which Hercules, according to Greek mythology, had to perform in order to win his freedom from slavery.
4. Another of Hercules' labors was to cleanse the stables where King Augeas had kept three thousand oxen for thirty years.

5. Matthew vi.19.
6. According to Greek legend, Deucalion and Pyrrha repeopled the world after Zeus had annihilated all but them, by tossing stones over their shoulders, whereupon the stones turned into men.
7. Ovid, *Metamorphoses* I.414–15.
8. Sir Walter Ralegh, *History of the World* I.i.2, 5.

So much for a blind obedience to a blundering oracle, throwing the stones over their heads behind them, and not seeing where they fell.

Most men, even in this comparatively free country, through mere ignorance and mistake, are so occupied with the factitious cares and superfluously coarse labors of life that its finer fruits cannot be plucked by them. Their fingers, from excessive toil, are too clumsy and tremble too much for that. Actually, the laboring man has not leisure for a true integrity day by day; he cannot afford to sustain the manliest relations to men; his labor would be depreciated in the market. He has no time to be anything but a machine. How can he remember well his ignorance—which his growth requires— who has so often to use his knowledge? We should feed and clothe him gratuitously sometimes, and recruit him with our cordials, before we judge of him. The finest qualities of our nature, like the bloom on fruits, can be preserved only by the most delicate handling. Yet we do not treat ourselves nor one another thus tenderly.

Some of you, we all know, are poor, find it hard to live, are sometimes, as it were, gasping for breath. I have no doubt that some of you who read this book are unable to pay for all the dinners which you have actually eaten, or for the coats and shoes which are fast wearing or are already worn out, and have come to this page to spend borrowed or stolen time, robbing your creditors of an hour. It is very evident what mean and sneaking lives many of you live, for my sight has been whetted by experience; always on the limits, trying to get into business and trying to get out of debt, a very ancient slough, called by the Latins *æs alienum*, another's brass, for some of their coins were made of brass; still living, and dying, and buried by this other's brass; always promising to pay, promising to pay, tomorrow, and dying today, insolvent; seeking to curry favor, to get custom, by how many modes, only not state-prison offenses; lying, flattering, voting, contracting yourselves into a nutshell[9] of civility, or dilating into an atmosphere of thin and vaporous generosity, that you may persuade your neighbor to let you make his shoes, or his hat, or his coat, or his carriage, or import his groceries for him; making yourselves sick, that you may lay up something against a sick day, something to be tucked away in an old chest, or in a stocking behind the plastering, or, more safely, in the brick bank; no matter where, no matter how much or how little.

I sometimes wonder that we can be so frivolous, I may almost say, as to attend to the gross but somewhat foreign form of servitude called Negro Slavery, there are so many keen and subtle masters that enslave both North and South. It is hard to have a South-

9. Cf. *Hamlet* II.ii.260.

ern overseer; it is worse to have a Northern one; but worst of all when you are the slave-driver of yourself. Talk of a divinity in man! Look at the teamster on the highway, wending to market by day or night; does any divinity stir within him?[1] His highest duty to fodder and water his horses! What is his destiny to him compared with the shipping interests? Does not he drive for Squire Make-a-stir? How godlike, how immortal, is he? See how he cowers and sneaks, how vaguely all the day he fears, not being immortal nor divine, but the slave and prisoner of his own opinion of himself, a fame won by his own deeds. Public opinion is a weak tyrant compared with our own private opinion. What a man thinks of himself, that it is which determines, or rather indicates, his fate. Self-emancipation even in the West Indian provinces of the fancy and imagination—what Wilberforce[2] is there to bring that about? Think, also, of the ladies of the land weaving toilet cushions against the last day, not to betray too green an interest in their fates! As if you could kill time without injuring eternity.

The mass of men lead lives of quiet desperation. What is called resignation is confirmed desperation. From the desperate city you go into the desperate country, and have to console yourself with the bravery of minks and muskrats. A stereotyped but unconscious despair is concealed even under what are called the games and amusements of mankind. There is no play in them, for this comes after work. But it is a characteristic of wisdom not to do desperate things.

When we consider what, to use the words of the catechism, is the chief end of man,[3] and what are the true necessaries and means of life, it appears as if men had deliberately chosen the common mode of living because they preferred it to any other. Yet they honestly think there is no choice left. But alert and healthy natures remember that the sun rose clear. It is never too late to give up our prejudices. No way of thinking or doing, however ancient, can be trusted without proof. What everybody echoes or in silence passes by as true today may turn out to be falsehood tomorrow, mere smoke of opinion, which some had trusted for a cloud that would sprinkle fertilizing rain on their fields. What old people say you cannot do you try and find that you can. Old deeds for old people, and new deeds for new. Old people did not know enough once, perchance, to fetch fresh fuel to keep the fire a-going; new people put a little dry wood under a pot,[4] and are whirled round the globe with the speed of birds, in a way to kill old people, as the phrase is. Age is no better, hardly so well, qualified for

1. Joseph Addison, *Cato* V.i.
2. English abolitionist who led the fight in the House of Commons against slavery in the West Indies.
3. The Response in *The Westminster Shorter Catechism* is: "To glorify God, and to enjoy Him forever."
4. Steam locomotive.

an instructor as youth, for it has not profited so much as it has lost. One may almost doubt if the wisest man has learned anything of absolute value by living. Practically, the old have no very important advice to give the young, their own experience has been so partial, and their lives have been such miserable failures, for private reasons, as they must believe; and it may be that they have some faith left which belies that experience, and they are only less young than they were. I have lived some thirty years on this planet, and I have yet to hear the first syllable of valuable or even earnest advice from my seniors. They have told me nothing, and probably cannot tell me anything to the purpose. Here is life, an experiment to a great extent untried by me; but it does not avail me that they have tried it. If I have any experience which I think valuable, I am sure to reflect that this my Mentors said nothing about.

One farmer says to me, "You cannot live on vegetable food solely, for it furnishes nothing to make bones with"; and so he religiously devotes a part of his day to supplying his system with the raw material of bones; walking all the while he talks behind his oxen, which, with vegetable-made bones, jerk him and his lumbering plough along in spite of every obstacle. Some things are really necessaries of life in some circles, the most helpless and diseased, which in others are luxuries merely, and in others still are entirely unknown.

The whole ground of human life seems to some to have been gone over by their predecessors, both the heights and the valleys, and all things to have been cared for. According to Evelyn, "the wise Solomon prescribed ordinances for the very distances of trees; and the Roman prætors have decided how often you may go into your neighbor's land to gather the acorns which fall on it without trespass, and what share belongs to that neighbor."[5] Hippocrates has even left directions how we should cut our nails; that is, even with the ends of the fingers, neither shorter nor longer. Undoubtedly the very tedium and ennui which presume to have exhausted the variety and the joys of life are as old as Adam. But man's capacities have never been measured; nor are we to judge of what he can do by any precedents, so little has been tried. Whatever have been thy failures hitherto, "be not afflicted, my child, for who shall assign to thee what thou hast left undone?"[6]

We might try our lives by a thousand simple tests; as, for instance, that the same sun which ripens my beans illumines at once a system of earths like ours. If I had remembered this it would have prevented some mistakes. This was not the light in which I hoed them. The stars are the apexes of what wonderful triangles!

5. John Evelyn, English government official and diarist, also wrote a treatise on arboriculture—*Sylva* (1664).

6. *Vishnu Purana*, a Hindu classic (Wilson translation, p. 87).

What distant and different beings in the various mansions of the universe are contemplating the same one at the same moment! Nature and human life are as various as our several constitutions. Who shall say what prospect life offers to another? Could a greater miracle take place than for us to look through each other's eyes for an instant? We should live in all the ages of the world in an hour; ay, in all the worlds of the ages. History, Poetry, Mythology! —I know of no reading of another's experience so startling and informing as this would be.

The greater part of what my neighbors call good I believe in my soul to be bad, and if I repent of anything, it is very likely to be my good behavior. What demon possessed me that I behaved so well? You may say the wisest thing you can, old man—you who have lived seventy years,[7] not without honor of a kind—I hear an irresistible voice which invites me away from all that. One generation abandons the enterprises of another like stranded vessels.

I think that we may safely trust a good deal more than we do. We may waive just so much care of ourselves as we honestly bestow elsewhere. Nature is as well adapted to our weakness as to our strength. The incessant anxiety and strain of some is a well-nigh incurable form of disease. We are made to exaggerate the importance of what work we do; and yet how much is not done by us! or, what if we had been taken sick? How vigilant we are! determined not to live by faith if we can avoid it; all the day long on the alert, at night we unwillingly say our prayers and commit ourselves to uncertainties. So thoroughly and sincerely are we compelled to live, reverencing our life, and denying the possibility of change. This is the only way, we say; but there are as many ways as there can be drawn radii from one center. All change is a miracle to contemplate; but it is a miracle which is taking place every instant. Confucius said, "To know that we know what we know, and that we do not know what we do not know, that is true knowledge."[8] When one man has reduced a fact of the imagination to be a fact to his understanding, I foresee that all men will at length establish their lives on that basis.

Let us consider for a moment what most of the trouble and anxiety which I have referred to is about, and how much it is necessary that we be troubled, or at least careful. It would be some advantage to live a primitive and frontier life, though in the midst of an outward civilization, if only to learn what are the gross necessaries of life and what methods have been taken to obtain them; or even to look over the old daybooks of the merchants, to see what it was that men most commonly bought at the stores, what they stored, that is, what are the grossest groceries. For the im-

7. Psalms xc.10.   8. *Confucian Analects* II.17.

provements of ages have had but little influence on the essential laws of man's existence: as our skeletons, probably, are not to be distinguished from those of our ancestors.

By the words, *necessary of life*, I mean whatever, of all that man obtains by his own exertions, has been from the first, or from long use has become, so important to human life that few, if any, whether from savageness, or poverty, or philosophy, ever attempt to do without it. To many creatures there is in this sense but one necessary of life, Food. To the bison of the prairie it is a few inches of palatable grass, with water to drink; unless he seeks the Shelter of the forest or the mountain's shadow. None of the brute creation requires more than Food and Shelter. The necessaries of life for man in this climate may, accurately enough, be distributed under the several heads of Food, Shelter, Clothing, and Fuel; for not till we have secured these are we prepared to entertain the true problems of life with freedom and a prospect of success. Man has invented not only houses but clothes and cooked food; and possibly from the accidental discovery of the warmth of fire, and the consequent use of it, at first a luxury, arose the present necessity to sit by it. We observe cats and dogs acquiring the same second nature. By proper Shelter and Clothing we legitimately retain our own internal heat; but with an excess of these, or of Fuel, that is, with an external heat greater than our own internal, may not cookery properly be said to begin? Darwin, the naturalist, says of the inhabitants of Tierra del Fuego, that while his own party, who were well clothed and sitting close to a fire, were far from too warm, these naked savages, who were farther off, were observed, to his great surprise, "to be streaming with perspiration at undergoing such a roasting."[9] So, we are told, the New Hollander goes naked with impunity, while the European shivers in his clothes. Is it impossible to combine the hardiness of these savages with the intellectualness of the civilized man? According to Liebig,[1] man's body is a stove, and food the fuel which keeps up the internal combustion in the lungs. In cold weather we eat more, in warm less. The animal heat is the result of a slow combustion, and disease and death take place when this is too rapid; or for want of fuel, or from some defect in the draught, the fire goes out. Of course the vital heat is not to be confounded with fire; but so much for analogy. It appears, therefore, from the above list, that the expression, *animal life*, is nearly synonymous with the expression, *animal heat*; for while Food may be regarded as the Fuel which keeps up the fire within us—and Fuel serves only to prepare that Food or to increase the warmth of our bodies by addition from without—Shelter and Clothing also serve

9. *Voyage of the H. M. S. Beagle,* i.284.

1. Justus Liebig (1803–73), a German chemist.

only to retain the *heat* thus generated and absorbed.

The grand necessity, then, for our bodies, is to keep warm, to keep the vital heat in us. What pains we accordingly take, not only with our Food, and Clothing, and Shelter, but with our beds, which are our nightclothes, robbing the nests and breasts of birds to prepare this shelter within a shelter, as the mole has its bed of grass and leaves at the end of its burrow! The poor man is wont to complain that this is a cold world; and to cold, no less physical than social, we refer directly a great part of our ails. The summer, in some climates, makes possible to man a sort of Elysian life.[2] Fuel, except to cook his Food, is then unnecessary; the sun is his fire, and many of the fruits are sufficiently cooked by its rays; while Food generally is more various, and more easily obtained, and Clothing and Shelter are wholly or half unnecessary. At the present day, and in this country, as I find by my own experience, a few implements, a knife, an axe, a spade, a wheelbarrow, etc., and for the studious, lamplight, stationery, and access to a few books, rank next to necessaries, and can all be obtained at a trifling cost. Yet some, not wise, go to the other side of the globe, to barbarous and unhealthy regions, and devote themselves to trade for ten or twenty years, in order that they may live—that is, keep comfortably warm—and die in New England at last. The luxuriously rich are not simply kept comfortably warm, but unnaturally hot; as I implied before, they are cooked, of course à la mode.

Most of the luxuries, and many of the so-called comforts of life, are not only not indispensable, but positive hindrances to the elevation of mankind. With respect to luxuries and comforts, the wisest have ever lived a more simple and meager life than the poor. The ancient philosophers, Chinese, Hindu, Persian, and Greek, were a class than which none has been poorer in outward riches, none so rich in inward. We know not much about them. It is remarkable that *we* know so much of them as we do. The same is true of the more modern reformers and benefactors of their race. None can be an impartial or wise observer of human life but from the vantage ground of what *we* should call voluntary poverty. Of a life of luxury the fruit is luxury, whether in agriculture, or commerce, or literature, or art. There are nowadays professors of philosophy, but not philosophers. Yet it is admirable to profess because it was once admirable to live. To be a philosopher is not merely to have subtle thoughts, nor even to found a school, but so to love wisdom as to live according to its dictates, a life of simplicity, independence, magnanimity, and trust. It is to solve some of the problems of life, not only theoretically, but practically. The success of great scholars and

2. In Greek mythology the Elysian fields were the home of the virtuous, in the afterlife.

thinkers is commonly a courtier-like success, not kingly, not manly. They make shift to live merely by conformity, practically as their fathers did, and are in no sense the progenitors of a nobler race of men. But why do men degenerate ever? What makes families run out? What is the nature of the luxury which enervates and destroys nations? Are we sure that there is none of it in our own lives? The philosopher is in advance of his age even in the outward form of his life. He is not fed, sheltered, clothed, warmed, like his contemporaries. How can a man be a philosopher and not maintain his vital heat by better methods than other men?

When a man is warmed by the several modes which I have described, what does he want next? Surely not more warmth of the same kind, as more and richer food, larger and more splendid houses, finer and more abundant clothing, more numerous incessant and hotter fires, and the like. When he has obtained those things which are necessary to life, there is another alternative than to obtain the superfluities; and that is, to adventure on life now, his vacation from humbler toil having commenced. The soil, it appears, is suited to the seed, for it has sent its radicle downward, and it may now send its shoot upward also with confidence. Why has man rooted himself thus firmly in the earth, but that he may rise in the same proportion into the heavens above?—for the nobler plants are valued for the fruit they bear at last in the air and light, far from the ground, and are not treated like the humbler esculents, which, though they may be biennials, are cultivated only till they have perfected their root, and often cut down at top for this purpose, so that most would not know them in their flowering season.

I do not mean to prescribe rules to strong and valiant natures, who will mind their own affairs whether in heaven or hell, and perchance build more magnificently and spend more lavishly than the richest, without ever impoverishing themselves, not knowing how they live—if, indeed, there are any such, as has been dreamed; nor to those who find their encouragement and inspiration in precisely the present condition of things, and cherish it with the fondness and enthusiasm of lovers—and, to some extent, I reckon myself in this number; I do not speak to those who are well employed, in whatever circumstances, and they know whether they are well employed or not; but mainly to the mass of men who are discontented, and idly complaining of the hardness of their lot or of the times, when they might improve them. There are some who complain most energetically and inconsolably of any, because they are, as they say, doing their duty. I also have in my mind that seemingly wealthy, but most terribly impoverished class of all, who have accumulated dross, but know not how to use it, or get rid of it, and thus have forged their own golden or silver fetters. * * *

Near the end of March, 1845, I borrowed an axe and went down
to the woods by Walden Pond, nearest to where I intended to build
my house, and began to cut down some tall arrowy white pines,
still in their youth, for timber. It is difficult to begin without bor-
rowing, but perhaps it is the most generous course thus to permit
your fellow-men to have an interest in your enterprise. The owner
of the axe, as he released his hold on it, said that it was the apple
of his eye; but I returned it sharper than I received it. It was a
pleasant hillside where I worked, covered with pine woods, through
which I looked out on the pond, and a small open field in the
woods where pines and hickories were springing up. The ice in the
pond was not yet dissolved, though there were some open spaces,
and it was all dark colored and saturated with water. There were
some slight flurries of snow during the days that I worked there;
but for the most part when I came out onto the railroad, on my
way home, its yellow sand heap stretched away gleaming in the
hazy atmosphere, and the rails shone in the spring sun, and I heard
the lark and pewee[3] and other birds already come to commence
another year with us. They were pleasant spring days, in which the
winter of man's discontent[4] was thawing as well as the earth, and
the life that had lain torpid began to stretch itself. One day, when
my axe had come off and I had cut a green hickory for a wedge,
driving it with a stone, and had placed the whole to soak in a pond
hole in order to swell the wood, I saw a striped snake run into the
water, and he lay on the bottom, apparently without inconvenience,
as long as I stayed there, or more than a quarter of an hour; perhaps
because he had not yet fairly come out of the torpid state. It appeared to me that for a like reason men remain in their present low
and primitive condition; but if they should feel the influence of
the spring of springs arousing them, they would of necessity rise to
a higher and more ethereal life. I had previously seen the snakes in
frosty mornings in my path with portions of their bodies still numb
and inflexible, waiting for the sun to thaw them. On the 1st of
April it rained and melted the ice, and in the early part of the day,
which was very foggy, I heard a stray goose groping about over the
pond and cackling as if lost, or like the spirit of the fog.

So I went on for some days cutting and hewing timber, and also
studs and rafters, all with my narrow axe, not having many com-
municable or scholar-like thoughts, singing to myself,

> Men say they know many things;
> But lo! they have taken wings—
> The arts and sciences,
> And a thousand appliances;

3. That is, the meadowlark and the   4. *Richard III* I.i.1.
phoebe.

The wind that blows
Is all that anybody knows.

I hewed the main timbers six inches square, most of the studs on two sides only, and the rafters and floor timbers on one side, leaving the rest of the bark on, so that they were just as straight and much stronger than sawed ones. Each stick was carefully mortised or tenoned by its stump, for I had borrowed other tools by this time. My days in the woods were not very long ones; yet I usually carried my dinner of bread and butter, and read the newspaper in which it was wrapped, at noon, sitting amid the green pine boughs which I had cut off, and to my bread was imparted some of their fragrance, for my hands were covered with a thick coat of pitch. Before I had done I was more the friend than the foe of the pine tree, though I had cut down some of them, having become better acquainted with it. Sometimes a rambler in the wood was attracted by the sound of my axe, and we chatted pleasantly over the chips which I had made.

By the middle of April, for I made no haste in my work, but rather made the most of it, my house was framed and ready for the raising. I had already bought the shanty of James Collins, an Irishman who worked on the Fitchburg Railroad, for boards. James Collins' shanty was considered an uncommonly fine one. When I called to see it he was not at home. I walked about the outside, at first unobserved from within, the window was so deep and high. It was of small dimensions, with a peaked cottage roof, and not much else to be seen, the dirt being raised five feet all around as if it were a compost heap. The roof was the soundest part, though a good deal warped and made brittle by the sun. Doorsill there was none, but a perennial passage for the hens under the door board. Mrs. C. came to the door and asked me to view it from the inside. The hens were driven in by my approach. It was dark, and had a dirt floor for the most part, dank, clammy, and aguish, only here a board and there a board which would not bear removal. She lighted a lamp to show me the inside of the roof and the walls, and also that the board floor extended under the bed, warning me not to step into the cellar, a sort of dust hole two feet deep. In her own words, they were "good boards overhead, good boards all around, and a good window"—of two whole squares originally, only the cat had passed out that way lately. There was a stove, a bed, and a place to sit, an infant in the house where it was born, a silk parasol, gilt-framed looking-glass, and a patent new coffee-mill nailed to an oak sapling, all told. The bargain was soon concluded, for James had in the meanwhile returned. I to pay four dollars and twenty-five cents tonight, he to vacate at five tomorrow morning, selling to nobody else meanwhile: I to take possession at six. It were well, he said, to be there early, and anticipate certain indistinct but wholly unjust claims on the score of ground rent and fuel. This he assured me was the only encumbrance. At six I passed him and his family on the road. One large bundle held their all—bed, coffee-mill, looking-glass, hens—all but the cat; she took to the woods and became a wild cat and, as I learned afterward, trod in a trap set for woodchucks, and so became a dead cat at last.

I took down this dwelling the same morning, drawing the nails, and removed it to the pond side by small cartloads, spreading the boards on the grass there to bleach and warp back again in the sun. One early thrush gave me a note or two as I drove along the wood-land path. I was informed treacherously by a young Patrick that neighbor Seeley, an Irishman, in the intervals of the carting, trans-ferred the still tolerable, straight, and drivable nails, staples, and spikes to his pocket, and then stood when I came back to pass the time of day, and look freshly up, unconcerned, with spring thoughts, at the devastation; there being a dearth of work, as he said. He was there to represent spectatordom, and help make this seemingly in-significant event one with the removal of the gods of Troy.[5]

I dug my cellar in the side of a hill sloping to the south, where a woodchuck had formerly dug his burrow, down through sumach and blackberry roots, and the lowest stain of vegetation, six feet square by seven deep, to a fine sand where potatoes would not freeze in any winter. The sides were left shelving, and not stoned; but the sun having never shone on them, the sand still keeps it place. It was but two hours' work. I took particular pleasure in this breaking of ground, for in almost all latitudes men dig into the earth for an equable temperature. Under the most splendid house in the city is still to be found the cellar where they store their roots as of old, and long after the superstructure has disappeared posterity remark its dent in the earth. The house is still but a sort of porch at the entrance of a burrow.

At length, in the beginning of May, with the help of some of my acquaintances,[6] rather to improve so good an occasion for neighbor-liness than from any necessity, I set up the frame of my house. No man was ever more honored in the character of his raisers than I. They are destined, I trust, to assist at the raising of loftier struc-tures one day. I began to occupy my house on the 4th of July, as soon as it was boarded and roofed, for the boards were carefully feather-edged and lapped, so that it was perfectly impervious to rain, but before boarding I laid the foundation of a chimney at one end, bringing two cartloads of stones up the hill from the pond in

5. Virgil, *Aeneid* II.351.
6. Emerson, Alcott, Ellery Channing, Burrill, and George William Curtis (later editor of *Harper's Weekly*), and the Concord farmer Edmund Hosmer and his sons John, Andrew, and Edmund Jr.

my arms. I built the chimney after my hoeing in the fall, before a fire became necessary for warmth, doing my cooking in the meanwhile out of doors on the ground, early in the morning: which mode I still think is in some respects more convenient and agreeable than the usual one. When it stormed before my bread was baked, I fixed a few boards over the fire, and sat under them to watch my loaf, and passed some pleasant hours in that way. In those days, when my hands were much employed, I read but little, but the least scraps of paper which lay on the ground, my holder, or tablecloth, afforded me as much entertainment, in fact answered the same purpose as the Iliad.

It would be worth the while to build still more deliberately than I did, considering, for instance, what foundation a door, a window, a cellar, a garret, have in the nature of man, and perchance never raising any superstructure until we found a better reason for it than our temporal necessities even. There is some of the same fitness in a man's building his own house that there is in a bird's building its own nest. Who knows but if men constructed their dwellings with their own hands, and provided food for themselves and families simply and honestly enough, the poetic faculty would be universally developed, as birds universally sing when they are so engaged? But alas! we do like cowbirds and cuckoos, which lay their eggs in nests which other birds have built, and cheer no traveler with their chattering and unmusical notes. Shall we forever resign the pleasure of construction to the carpenter? What does architecture amount to in the experience of the mass of men? I never in all my walks came across a man engaged in so simple and natural an occupation as building his house. We belong to the community. It is not the tailor alone who is the ninth part of a man; it is as much the preacher, and the merchant, and the farmer. Where is this division of labor to end? and what object does it finally serve? No doubt another *may* also think for me; but it is not therefore desirable that he should do so to the exclusion of my thinking for myself.

True, there are architects so called in this country, and I have heard of one[7] at least possessed with the idea of making architectural ornaments have a core of truth, a necessity, and hence a beauty, as if it were a revelation to him. All very well perhaps from his point of view, but only a little better than the common dilettantism. A sentimental reformer in architecture, he began at the cornice, not at the foundation. It was only how to put a core of truth within the ornaments, that every sugar plum in fact might have an almond or caraway seed in it—though I hold that almonds

7. Horatio Greenough (1805–52), a sculptor.

are most wholesome without the sugar—and not how the inhabitant, the indweller, might build truly within and without, and let
the ornaments take care of themselves. What reasonable man ever
supposed that ornaments were something outward and in the skin
merely, that the tortoise got his spotted shell, or the shellfish its
mother-o'-pearl tints, by such a contract as the inhabitants of Broadway their Trinity Church? But a man has no more to do with the
style of architecture of his house than a tortoise with that of its
shell: nor need the soldier be so idle as to try to paint the precise
color of his virtue on his standard. The enemy will find it out. He
may turn pale when the trial comes. This man seemed to me to
lean over the cornice, and timidly whisper his half truth to the
rude occupants who really knew it better than he. What of architectural beauty I now see, I know has gradually grown from within
outward, out of the necessities and character of the indweller, who
is the only builder—out of some unconscious truthfulness, and
nobleness, without ever a thought for the appearance; and whatever
additional beauty of this kind is destined to be produced will be
preceded by a like unconscious beauty of life. The most interesting
dwellings in this country, as the painter knows, are the most un-
pretending, humble log huts and cottages of the poor commonly; it
is the life of the inhabitants whose shells they are, and not any
peculiarity in their surfaces merely, which makes them *picturesque*;
and equally interesting will be the citizen's suburban box, when his
life shall be as simple and as agreeable to the imagination, and
there is as little straining after effect in the style of his dwelling. A
great proportion of architectural ornaments are literally hollow,
and a September gale would strip them off, like borrowed plumes,
without injury to the substantials. They can do without *architecture* who have no olives nor wines in the cellar. What if an equal
ado were made about the ornaments of style in literature, and the
architects of our bibles spent as much time about their cornices as
the architects of our churches do? So are made the belles-lettres
and the beaux-arts and their professors. Much it concerns a man,
forsooth, how a few sticks are slanted over him or under him, and
what colors are daubed upon his box. It would signify somewhat, if,
in any earnest sense, *he* slanted them and daubed it; but the spirit
having departed out of the tenant, it is of a piece with constructing
his own coffin—the architecture of the grave, and "carpenter," is
but another name for "coffin-maker." One man says, in his despair
or indifference to life, take up a handful of the earth at your feet,
and paint your house that color. Is he thinking of his last and narrow house?[8] Toss up a copper for it as well. What an abundance
of leisure he must have! Why do you take up a handful of dirt?

8. The grave.

Better paint your house your own complexion; let it turn pale or blush for you. An enterprise to improve the style of cottage architecture! When you have got my ornaments ready I will wear them.

Before winter I built a chimney, and shingled the sides of my house, which were already impervious to rain, with imperfect and sappy shingles made of the first slice of the log, whose edges I was obliged to straighten with a plane.

I have thus a tight shingled and plastered house, ten feet wide by fifteen long, and eight-feet posts, with a garret and a closet, a large window on each side, two trap doors, one door at the end, and a brick fireplace opposite. The exact cost of my house, paying the usual price for such materials as I used, but not counting the work, all of which was done by myself, was as follows; and I give the details because very few are able to tell exactly what their houses cost, and fewer still, if any, the separate cost of the various materials which compose them:

Boards	$8 03½,	mostly shanty boards.
Refuse shingles for roof and sides	4 00	
Laths	1 25	
Two second-hand windows with glass	2 43	
One thousand old brick	4 00	
Two casks of lime	2 40	That was high.
Hair	0 31	More than I needed.
Mantle-tree iron	0 15	
Nails	3 90	
Hinges and screws	0 14	
Latch	0 10	
Chalk	0 01	
Transportation	1 40	{ I carried a good part on my back.
In all	$28 12½	

These are all the materials excepting the timber, stones, and sand, which I claimed by squatter's right. I have also a small woodshed adjoining, made chiefly of the stuff which was left after building the house.

I intend to build me a house which will surpass any on the main street in Concord in grandeur and luxury, as soon as it pleases me as much and will cost me no more than my present one.

I thus found that the student who wishes for a shelter can obtain one for a lifetime at an expense not greater than the rent which he now pays annually. If I seem to boast more than is becoming, my excuse is that I brag for humanity rather than for myself; and my shortcomings and inconsistencies do not affect the truth of my statement. Notwithstanding much cant and hypocrisy—chaff which I find it difficult to separate from my wheat,[9] but for which I am as sorry as any man—I will breathe freely and stretch myself in this respect, it is such a relief to both the moral and physical system; and I am resolved that I will not through humility become the devil's attorney.[1] I will endeavor to speak a good word for the truth. At Cambridge College[2] the mere rent of a student's room, which is only a little larger than my own, is thirty dollars each year, though the corporation had the advantage of building thirty-two side by side and under one roof, and the occupant suffers the inconvenience of many and noisy neighbors, and perhaps a residence in the fourth story. I cannot but think that if we had more true wisdom in these respects, not only less education would be needed, because, forsooth, more would already have been acquired, but the pecuniary expense of getting an education would in a great measure vanish. Those conveniences which the student requires at Cambridge or elsewhere cost him or somebody else ten times as great a sacrifice of life as they would with proper management on both sides. Those things for which the most money is demanded are never the things which the student most wants. Tuition, for instance, is an important item in the term bill, while for the far more valuable education which he gets by associating with the most cultivated of his contemporaries no charge is made. The mode of founding a college is, commonly, to get up a subscription of dollars and cents, and then following blindly the principles of a division of labor to its extreme, a principle which should never be followed but with circumspection, to call in a contractor who makes this a subject of speculation, and he employs Irishmen or other operatives actually to lay the foundations, while the students that are to be are said to be fitting themselves for it; and for these oversights successive generations have to pay. I think that it would be *better than this*, for the students, or those who desire to be benefited by it, even to lay the foundation themselves. The student who secures his coveted leisure and retirement by systematically shirking any labor necessary to man obtains but an ignoble and unprofitable leisure, defrauding himself of the experience which alone can make leisure fruitful. "But," says one, "you do not mean that the students should go to work with their hands instead of their heads?" I do not mean that exactly, but I mean something which he might think a good deal like that; I mean that they should not *play* life, or *study* it merely, while

9. Cf. Jeremiah xxiii.28.
1. In the Roman Catholic Church it is customary for a cardinal to be selected to raise all possible objections to conferring sainthood on an individual. He is called the devil's advocate or attorney.
2. That is, Thoreau's alma mater, Harvard College. Thoreau lived on the fourth floor of Hollis Hall for one year.

the community supports them at this expensive game, but earnestly *live* it from beginning to end. How could youths better learn to live than by at once trying the experiment of living? Methinks this would exercise their minds as much as mathematics. If I wished a boy to know something about the arts and sciences, for instance, I would not pursue the common course, which is merely to send him into the neighborhood of some professor, where anything is professed and practiced but the art of life; to survey the world through a telescope or a microscope, and never with his natural eye; to study chemistry, and not learn how his bread is made, or mechanics, and not learn how it is earned; to discover new satellites to Neptune, and not detect the motes in his eyes,[3] or to what vagabond he is a satellite himself; or to be devoured by the monsters that swarm all around him, while contemplating the monsters in a drop of vinegar. Which would have advanced the most at the end of a month—the boy who had made his own jackknife from the ore which he had dug and smelted, reading as much as would be necessary for this—or the boy who had attended the lectures on metallurgy at the Institute in the meanwhile, and had received a Rogers'[4] penknife from his father? Which would be most likely to cut his fingers? . . . To my astonishment I was informed on leaving college that I had studied navigation!—why, if I had taken one turn down the harbor I should have known more about it. Even the *poor* student studies and is taught only *political* economy, while that economy of living which is synonymous with philosophy is not even sincerely professed in our colleges. The consequence is, that while he is reading Adam Smith, Ricardo, and Say,[5] he runs his father in debt irretrievably.

As with our colleges, so with a hundred "modern improvements"; there is an illusion about them; there is not always a positive advance. The devil goes on exacting compound interest to the last for his early share and numerous succeeding investments in them. Our inventions are wont to be pretty toys, which distract our attention from serious things. They are but improved means to an unimproved end, an end which it was already but too easy to arrive at; as railroads lead to Boston or New York. We are in great haste to construct a magnetic telegraph from Maine to Texas; but Maine and Texas, it may be, have nothing important to communicate. Either is in such a predicament as the man who was earnest to be introduced to a distinguished deaf woman,[6] but when he was presented, and one end of her ear trumpet was put into his hand, had nothing to say. As if the main object were to talk fast and not to talk sensibly. We are eager to tunnel under the Atlantic and

3. Luke vi.41. A satellite to the planet Neptune was discovered by William Lassell in 1846.
4. An English cutlery manufacturer.
5. Prominent 18th-century economists.
6. Harriet Martineau, who toured America from 1834 to 1836.

bring the old world some weeks nearer to the new; but perchance the first news that will leak through into the broad, flapping American ear will be that the Princess Adelaide⁷ has the whooping cough. After all, the man whose horse trots a mile in a minute does not carry the most important messages; he is not an evangelist, nor does he come round eating locusts and wild honey.⁸ I doubt if Flying Childers ever carried a peck of corn to mill.

One says to me, "I wonder that you do not lay up money; you love to travel; you might take the cars and go to Fitchburg⁹ today and see the country." But I am wiser than that. I have learned that the swiftest traveler is he that goes afoot. I say to my friend, Suppose we try who will get there first. The distance is thirty miles; the fare ninety cents. That is almost a day's wages. I remember when wages were sixty cents a day for laborers on this very road. Well, I start now on foot, and get there before night; I have traveled at that rate by the week together. You will in the meanwhile have earned your fare, and arrive there some time tomorrow, or possibly this evening, if you are lucky enough to get a job in season. Instead of going to Fitchburg, you will be working here the greater part of the day. And so, if the railroad reached round the world, I think that I should keep ahead of you; and as for seeing the country and getting experience of that kind, I should have to cut your acquaintance altogether.

Such is the universal law, which no man can ever outwit, and with regard to the railroad even we may say it is as broad as it is long. To make a railroad round the world available to all mankind is equivalent to grading the whole surface of the planet. Men have an indistinct notion that if they keep up this activity of joint stocks and spades long enough all will at length ride somewhere, in next to no time, and for nothing; but though a crowd rushes to the depot, and the conductor shouts "All aboard!" when the smoke is blown away and the vapor condensed, it will be perceived that a few are riding, but the rest are run over—and it will be called, and will be, "A melancholy accident." No doubt they can ride at last who shall have earned their fare, that is, if they survive so long, but they will probably have lost their elasticity and desire to travel by that time. This spending of the best part of one's life earning money in order to enjoy a questionable liberty during the least valuable part of it, reminds me of the Englishman¹ who went to India to make a fortune first, in order that he might return to England and live the life of a poet. He should have gone up garret at once. "What!" exclaim a million Irishmen starting up from all

7. Wife of William IV, Queen Victoria's predecessor.
8. Matthew iii.4. "Flying Childers" was a famous 18th-century English race horse.
9. A small city west of Concord.
1. Probably Robert Clive.

the shanties in the land, "is not this railroad which we have built a good thing?" Yes, I answer, *comparatively* good, that is, you might have done worse; but I wish, as you are brothers of mine, that you could have spent your time better than digging in this dirt.

Before I finished my house, wishing to earn ten or twelve dollars by some honest and agreeable method, in order to meet my unusual expenses, I planted about two acres and a half of light and sandy soil near it chiefly with beans, but also a small part with potatoes, corn, peas, and turnips. The whole lot contains eleven acres, mostly growing up to pines and hickories, and was sold the preceding season for eight dollars and eight cents an acre. One farmer said that it was "good for nothing but to raise cheeping squirrels on." I put no manure whatever on this land, not being the owner, but merely a squatter, and not expecting to cultivate so much again, and I did not quite hoe it all once. I got out several cords of stumps in ploughing, which supplied me with fuel for a long time, and left small circles of virgin mould, easily distinguishable through the summer by the greater luxuriance of the beans there. The dead and for the most part unmerchantable wood behind my house, and the driftwood from the pond, have supplied the remainder of my fuel. I was obliged to hire a team and a man for the ploughing, though I held the plough myself. My farm outgoes for the first season were, for implements, seed, work, etc., $14.72½. The seed corn was given me. This never costs anything to speak of, unless you plant more than enough. I got twelve bushels of beans, and eighteen bushels of potatoes, besides some peas and sweet corn. The yellow corn and turnips were too late to come to anything. My whole income from the farm was

	$23	44
Deducting the outgoes	14	72½
There are left	$8	71½,

beside produce consumed and on hand at the time this estimate was made of the value of $4.50—the amount on hand much more than balancing a little grass which I did not raise. All things considered, that is, considering the importance of a man's soul and of today, notwithstanding the short time occupied by my experiment, nay, partly even because of its transient character, I believe that that was doing better than any farmer in Concord did that year.

The next year I did better still, for I spaded up all the land which I required, about a third of an acre, and I learned from the experience of both years, not being in the least awed by many celebrated works on husbandry, Arthur Young[2] among the rest, that if one would live simply and eat only the crop which he raised, and raise no more than he ate, and not exchange it for an insufficient quantity of more luxurious and expensive things, he would need to cultivate only a few rods of ground, and that it would be cheaper to spade up that than to use oxen to plough it, and to select a fresh spot from time to time than to manure the old, and he could do all his necessary farm work as it were with his left hand at odd hours in the summer; and thus he would not be tied to an ox, or horse, or cow, or pig, as at present. I desire to speak impartially on this point, and as one not interested in the success or failure of the present economical and social arrangements. I was more independent than any farmer in Concord, for I was not anchored to a house or farm, but could follow the bent of my genius, which is a very crooked one, every moment. Besides being better off than they already, if my house had been burned or my crops had failed, I should have been nearly as well off as before.

I am wont to think that men are not so much the keepers of herds as herds are the keepers of men, the former are so much the freer. Men and oxen exchange work; but if we consider necessary work only, the oxen will be seen to have greatly the advantage, their farm is so much the larger. Man does some of his part of the exchange work in his six weeks of haying, and it is no boy's play. Certainly no nation that lived simply in all respects, that is, no nation of philosophers, would commit so great a blunder as to use the labor of animals. True, there never was and is not likely soon to be a nation of philosophers, nor am I certain it is desirable that there should be. However, *I* should never have broken a horse or bull and taken him to board for any work he might do for me, for fear I should become a horse-man or a herds-man merely; and if society seems to be the gainer by so doing, are we certain that what is one man's gain is not another's loss, and that the stableboy has equal cause with his master to be satisfied? Granted that some public works would not have been constructed without this aid, and let man share the glory of such with the ox and horse; does it follow that he could not have accomplished works yet more worthy of himself in that case? When men begin to do, not merely unnecessary or artistic, but luxurious and idle work, with their assistance, it is inevitable that a few do all the exchange work with the oxen, or, in other words, become the slaves of the strongest. Man thus not only works for the animal within him but, for a symbol of this, he works for the animal without him. Though we have many substantial houses of brick or stone, the prosperity of the farmer is still measured by the degree to which the barn over-

2. Author of *Rural Oeconomy* (1773).

shadows the house. This town is said to have the largest houses for oxen, cows, and horses hereabouts, and it is not behindhand in its public buildings; but there are very few halls for free worship or free speech in this county. It should not be by their architecture, but why not even by their power of abstract thought, that nations should seek to commemorate themselves? How much more admirable the Bhagvat-Geeta[3] than all the ruins of the East! Towers and temples are the luxury of princes. A simple and independent mind does not toil at the bidding of any prince. Genius is not a retainer to any emperor, nor is its material silver, or gold, or marble, except to a trifling extent. To what end, pray, is so much stone hammered? In Arcadia,[4] when I was there, I did not see any hammering stone. Nations are possessed with an insane ambition to perpetuate the memory of themselves by the amount of hammered stone they leave. What if equal pains were taken to smooth and polish their manners? One piece of good sense would be more memorable than a monument as high as the moon. I love better to see stones in place. The grandeur of Thebes was a vulgar grandeur. More sensible is a rod of stone wall that bounds an honest man's field than a hundred-gated Thebes[5] that has wandered farther from the true end of life. The religion and civilization which are barbaric and heathenish build splendid temples; but what you might call Christianity does not. Most of the stone a nation hammers goes toward its tomb only. It buries itself alive. As for the Pyramids, there is nothing to wonder at in them so much as the fact that so many men could be found degraded enough to spend their lives constructing a tomb for some ambitious booby, whom it would have been wiser and manlier to have drowned in the Nile, and then given his body to the dogs. I might possibly invent some excuse for them and him, but I have no time for it. As for the religion and love of art of the builders, it is much the same all the world over, whether the building be an Egyptian temple or the United States Bank. It costs more than it comes to. The mainspring is vanity, assisted by the love of garlic and bread and butter. Mr. Balcom, a promising young architect, designs it on the back of his Vitruvius,[6] with hard pencil and ruler, and the job is let out to Dobson & Sons, stonecutters. When the thirty centuries begin to look down on it,[7] mankind begin to look up at it. As for your high towers and monuments, there was a crazy fellow once in this town who undertook to dig through to China, and he got so far that, as he said, he heard the Chinese pots and kettles rattle; but I think that I shall not go

3. A Hindu bible, often called *The Song Celestial*, a portion of the *Mahabarata*.
4. An ideal land.
5. An ancient Egyptian city noted for its hundred-gated wall.
6. An early Roman architect, for many centuries regarded as the final authority on architecture.
7. Napoleon once said of the Pyramids, "From the summit of these monuments forty [*sic*] centuries look down upon you."

out of my way to admire the hole which he made. Many are concerned about the monuments of the West and the East, to know who built them. For my part, I should like to know who in those days did not build them, who were above such trifling. But to proceed with my statistics.

By surveying, carpentry, and day-labor of various other kinds in the village in the meanwhile, for I have as many trades as fingers, I had earned $13.34. The expense of food for eight months, namely, from July 4th to March 1st, the time when these estimates were made—though I lived there more than two years—not counting potatoes, a little green corn, and some peas, which I had raised, nor considering the value of what was on hand at the last date, was

Rice	$1 73½	
Molasses	1 73	Cheapest form of the saccharine.
Rye meal	1 04¾	
Indian meal	0 99¾	Cheaper than rye.
Pork	0 22	
Flour	0 88	Costs more than Indian meal, both money and trouble.
Sugar	0 80	
Lard	0 65	
Apples	0 25	
Dried apple	0 22	
Sweet potatoes	0 10	
One pumpkin	0 06	
One watermelon	0 02	
Salt	0 03	

All experiments which failed.

Yes, I did eat $8.74, all told; but I should not thus unblushingly publish my guilt, if I did not know that most of my readers were equally guilty with myself, and that their deeds would look no better in print. The next year I sometimes caught a mess of fish for my dinner, and once I went so far as to slaughter a woodchuck which ravaged my beanfield—effect his transmigration, as a Tartar[8] would say—and devour him, partly for experiment's sake; but though it afforded me a momentary enjoyment, notwithstanding a musky flavor, I saw that the longest use would not make that a good practice, however it might seem to have your woodchucks ready dressed by the village butcher.

Clothing and some incidental expenses within the same dates, though little can be inferred from this item, amounted to

$8 40¾

Oil and some household utensils   2 00

8. Resident of central Asia.

So that all the pecuniary outgoes, excepting for washing and mending, which for the most part were done out of the house, and their bills[9] have not yet been received—and these are all and more than all the ways by which money necessarily goes out in this part of the world—were

House	$28 12½
Farm one year	14 72½
Food eight months	8 74
Clothing, etc., eight months	8 40¾
Oil, etc., eight months	2 00
In all	$61 99¾

I address myself now to those of my readers who have a living to get. And to meet this I have for farm produce sold

	$23 44
Earned by day-labor	13 34
In all	$36 78

which subtracted from the sum of the outgoes leaves a balance of $25.21¾ on the one side—this being very nearly the means with which I started, and the measure of expenses to be incurred—and on the other, besides the leisure and independence and health thus secured, a comfortable house for me as long as I choose to occupy it.

These statistics, however accidental and therefore uninstructive they may appear, as they have a certain completeness, have a certain value also. Nothing was given me of which I have not rendered some account. It appears from the above estimate, that my food alone cost me in money about twenty-seven cents a week. It was, for nearly two years after this, rye and Indian meal without yeast, potatoes, rice, a very little salt pork, molasses, and salt; and my drink, water. It was fit that I should live on rice, mainly, who loved so well the philosophy of India. To meet the objections of some inveterate cavilers, I may as well state, that if I dined out occasionally,[1] as I always had done, and I trust shall have opportunities to do again, it was frequently to the detriment of my domestic arrangements. But the dining out, being, as I have stated, a constant element, does not in the least affect a comparative statement like this.

I learned from my two years' experience that it would cost incredibly little trouble to obtain one's necessary food, even in this latitude; that a man may use as simple a diet as the animals, and yet retain health and strength. I have made a satisfactory dinner,

9. From his mother and sister.   1. At the home of his parents and with the Emerson family.

satisfactory on several accounts, simply off a dish of purslane
(*Portulaca oleracea*) which I gathered in my cornfield, boiled and
salted. I give the Latin on account of the savoriness of the trivial
name. And pray what more can a reasonable man desire, in peaceful times, in ordinary noons, than a sufficient number of ears of
green sweet-corn boiled, with the addition of salt? Even the little
variety which I used was a yielding to the demands of appetite, and
not of health. Yet men have come to such a pass that they frequently starve, not for want of necessaries, but for want of luxuries;
and I know a good woman who thinks that her son lost his life
because he took to drinking water only.

The reader will perceive that I am treating the subject rather
from an economic than a dietetic point of view, and he will not
venture to put my abstemiousness to the test unless he has a well-
stocked larder.

Bread I at first made of pure Indian meal and salt, genuine hoe-
cakes, which I baked before my fire out of doors on a shingle on
the end of a stick of timber sawed off in building my house; but it
was wont to get smoked and to have a piny flavor. I tried flour
also; but have at last found a mixture of rye and Indian meal most
convenient and agreeable. In cold weather it was no little amusement to bake several small loaves of this in succession, tending and
turning them as carefully as an Egyptian his hatching eggs. They
were a real cereal fruit which I ripened, and they had to my senses
a fragrance like that of other noble fruits, which I kept in as long
as possible by wrapping them in cloths. I made a study of the ancient and indispensable art of breadmaking, consulting such authorities as offered, going back to the primitive days and first invention of the unleavened kind, when from the wildness of nuts
and meats men first reached the mildness and refinement of this
diet, and traveling gradually down in my studies through that accidental souring of the dough which, it is supposed, taught the leaven-
ing process, and through the various fermentations thereafter, till
I came to "good, sweet, wholesome bread," the staff of life. Leaven,
which some deem the soul of bread, the *spiritus* which fills its cellu-
lar tissue, which is religiously preserved like the vestal fire—some
precious bottleful, I suppose, first brought over in the Mayflower,
did the business for America, and its influence is still rising, swelling, spreading, in cerealian billows over the land—this seed I regularly and faithfully procured from the village, till at length one
morning I forgot the rules, and scalded my yeast; by which accident
I discovered that even this was not indispensable—for my discoveries were not by the synthetic but analytic process—and I have gladly
omitted it since, though most housewives earnestly assured me that
safe and wholesome bread without yeast might not be, and elderly

people prophesied a speedy decay of the vital forces. Yet I find it not to be an essential ingredient, and after going without it for a year am still in the land of the living; and I am glad to escape the trivialness of carrying a bottleful in my pocket, which would sometimes pop and discharge its contents to my discomfiture. It is simpler and more respectable to omit it. Man is an animal who more than any other can adapt himself to all climates and circumstances. Neither did I put any sal-soda, or other acid or alkali, into my bread. It would seem that I made it according to the recipe which Marcus Porcius Cato gave about two centuries before Christ. "Panem depsticium sic facito. Manus mortariumque bene lavato. Farinam in mortarium indito, aquae paulatim addito, subigitoque pulchre. Ubi bene subegeris, defingito, coquitoque sub testu."[2] Which I take to mean, "Make kneaded bread thus. Wash your hands and trough well. Put the meal into the trough, add water gradually, and knead it thoroughly. When you have kneaded it well, mould it, and bake it under a cover," that is, in a baking-kettle. Not a word about leaven. But I did not always use this staff of life. At one time, owing to the emptiness of my purse, I saw none of it for more than a month.

Every New Englander might easily raise all his own breadstuffs in this land of rye and Indian corn, and not depend on distant and fluctuating markets for them. Yet so far are we from simplicity and independence that, in Concord, fresh and sweet meal is rarely sold in the shops, and hominy and corn in a still coarser form are hardly used by any. For the most part the farmer gives to his cattle and hogs the grain of his own producing, and buys flour, which is at least no more wholesome, at a greater cost, at the store. I saw that I could easily raise my bushel or two of rye and Indian corn, for the former will grow on the poorest land, and the latter does not require the best, and grind them in a hand-mill, and so do without rice and pork; and if I must have some concentrated sweet, I found by experiment that I could make a very good molasses either of pumpkins or beets, and I knew that I needed only to set out a few maples to obtain it more easily still, and while these were growing I could use various substitutes beside those which I have named. "For," as the Forefathers sang,

> "we can make liquor to sweeten our lips
> Of pumpkins and parsnips and walnut-tree chips."[3]

Finally, as for salt, that grossest of groceries, to obtain this might be a fit occasion for a visit to the seashore, or, if I did without it altogether, I should probably drink the less water. I do not learn

2. *De Agricultura* LXXIV.
3. From an early American ballad to be found in John Barber, *Historical Collections of Massachusetts* (1839).

that the Indians ever troubled themselves to go after it.

Thus I could avoid all trade and barter, so far as my food was concerned, and having a shelter already, it would only remain to get clothing and fuel. The pantaloons which I now wear were woven in a farmer's family—thank Heaven there is so much virtue still in man; for I think the fall from the farmer to the operative as great and memorable as that from the man to the farmer—and in a new country, fuel is an encumbrance. As for a habitat, if I were not permitted still to squat, I might purchase one acre at the same price for which the land I cultivated was sold—namely, eight dollars and eight cents. But as it was, I considered that I enhanced the value of the land by squatting on it.

There is a certain class of unbelievers who sometimes ask me such questions as, if I think that I can live on vegetable food alone; and to strike at the root of the matter at once—for the root is faith—I am accustomed to answer such, that I can live on board nails. If they cannot understand that, they cannot understand much that I have to say. For my part, I am glad to hear of experiments of this kind being tried; as that a young man tried for a fortnight to live on hard, raw corn on the ear, using his teeth for all mortar. The squirrel tribe tried the same and succeeded. The human race is interested in these experiments, though a few old women who are incapacitated for them, or who own their thirds[4] in mills, may be alarmed.

My furniture,[5] part of which I made myself, and the rest cost me nothing of which I have not rendered an account, consisted of a bed, a table, a desk, three chairs, a looking-glass three inches in diameter, a pair of tongs and andirons, a kettle, a skillet, and a frying-pan, a dipper, a wash-bowl, two knives and forks, three plates, one cup, one spoon, a jug for oil, a jug for molasses, and a japanned lamp. None is so poor that he need sit on a pumpkin. That is shiftlessness. There is a plenty of such chairs as I like best in the village garrets to be had for taking them away. Furniture! Thank God, I can sit and I can stand without the aid of a furniture warehouse. What man but a philosopher would not be ashamed to see his furniture packed in a cart and going up country exposed to the light of heaven and the eyes of men, a beggarly account of empty boxes? That is Spaulding's[6] furniture. I could never tell from inspecting such a load whether it belonged to a so-called rich man or a poor one; the owner always seemed poverty-stricken. Indeed, the more you have of such things the poorer you are. Each

4. A widow's share of an estate according to the laws of inheritance.
5. Most of this furniture is now on display in the museum of the Concord Antiquarian Society.
6. A common family name in the Concord area.

load looks as if it contained the contents of a dozen shanties; and if one shanty is poor, this is a dozen times as poor. Pray, for what do we *move* ever but to get rid of our furniture, our *exuviae*;[7] at last to go from this world to another newly furnished, and leave this to be burned? It is the same as if all these traps were buckled to a man's belt, and he could not move over the rough country where our lines are cast without dragging them—dragging his trap. He was a lucky fox that left his tail in the trap.[8] The muskrat will gnaw his third leg off to be free. No wonder man has lost his elasticity. How often he is at a dead set![9] "Sir, if I may be so bold, what do you mean by a dead set?" If you are a seer, whenever you meet a man you will see all that he owns, ay, and much that he pretends to disown, behind him, even to his kitchen furniture and all the trumpery which he saves and will not burn, and he will appear to be harnessed to it and making what headway he can. I think that the man is at a dead set who has got through a knot hole or gateway where his sledge load of furniture cannot follow him. I cannot but feel compassion when I hear some trig, compact-looking man, seemingly free, all girded and ready, speak of his "furniture," as whether it is insured or not. "But what shall I do with my furniture?" My gay butterfly is entangled in a spider's web then. Even those who seem for a long while not to have any, if you inquire more narrowly you will find have some stored in somebody's barn. I look upon England today as an old gentleman who is traveling with a great deal of baggage, trumpery which has accumulated from long housekeeping, which he has not the courage to burn; great trunk, little trunk, bandbox, and bundle. Throw away the first three at least. It would surpass the powers of a well man nowadays to take up his bed and walk, and I should certainly advise a sick one to lay down his bed and run. When I have met an immigrant tottering under a bundle which contained his all—looking like an enormous wen which had grown out of the nape of his neck—I have pitied him, not because that was his all, but because he had all *that* to carry. If I have got to drag my trap, I will take care that it be a light one and do not nip me in a vital part. But perchance it would be wisest never to put one's paw into it.

I would observe, by the way, that it costs me nothing for curtains, for I have no gazers to shut out but the sun and moon, and I am willing that they should look in. The moon will not sour milk nor taint meat of mine, nor will the sun injure my furniture or fade my carpet; and if he is sometimes too warm a friend, I find it still better economy to retreat behind some curtain which nature has provided, than to add a single item to the details of housekeeping.

7. Cast-offs (Latin).
8. See Aesop's fable of "The Fox With-out a Tail."
9. Complete failure.

A lady once offered me a mat, but as I had no room to spare within the house, nor time to spare within or without to shake it, I declined it, preferring to wipe my feet on the sod before my door. It is best to avoid the beginnings of evil.

Not long since I was present at the auction of a deacon's effects, for his life had not been ineffectual:

"The evil that men do lives after them."[1]

As usual, a great proportion was trumpery which had begun to accumulate in his father's day. Among the rest was a dried tapeworm. And now, after lying half a century in his garret and other dust holes, these things were not burned; instead of a *bonfire*, or purifying destruction of them, there was an *auction*,[2] or increasing of them. The neighbors eagerly collected to view them, bought them all, and carefully transported them to their garrets and dust holes, to lie there till their estates are settled, when they will start again. When a man dies he kicks the dust.[3]

The customs of some savage nations might, perchance, be profitably imitated by us, for they at least go through the semblance of casting their slough annually; they have the idea of the thing, whether they have the reality or not. Would it not be well if we were to celebrate such a "busk," or "feast of first fruits," as Bartram[4] describes to have been the custom of the Mucclasse Indians? "When a town celebrates the busk," says he, "having previously provided themselves with new clothes, new pots, pans, and other household utensils and furniture, they collect all their worn-out clothes and other despicable things, sweep and cleanse their houses, squares, and the whole town, of their filth, which with all the remaining grain and other old provisions they cast together into one common heap, and consume it with fire. After having taken medicine, and fasted for three days, all the fire in the town is extinguished. During this fast they abstain from the gratification of every appetite and passion whatever. A general amnesty is proclaimed; all malefactors may return to their town."

"On the fourth morning, the high priest, by rubbing dry wood together, produces new fire in the public square, from whence every habitation in the town is supplied with the new and pure flame."

They then feast on the new corn and fruits, and dance and sing for three days, "and the four following days they receive visits and rejoice with their friends from neighboring towns who have in like manner purified and prepared themselves."

The Mexicans also practiced a similar purification at the end

1. *Julius Caesar* III.ii.81.
2. *Auctio*, in Latin, meant an increase —that is, by bidding.
3. *Iliad* XXII.330.

4. William Bartram, *Travels through North and South Carolina* (1791), IV.iii.

of every fifty-two years, in the belief that it was time for the world to come to an end.

I have scarcely heard of a truer sacrament, that is, as the dictionary defines it, "outward and visible sign of an inward and spiritual grace," than this, and I have no doubt that they were originally inspired directly from Heaven to do thus, though they have no biblical record of the revelation.

For more than five years I maintained myself thus solely by the labor of my hands, and I found, that by working about six weeks in a year, I could meet all the expenses of living. The whole of my winters, as well as most of my summers, I had free and clear for study. I have thoroughly tried school-keeping, and found that my expenses were in proportion, or rather out of proportion, to my income, for I was obliged to dress and train, not to say think and believe, accordingly, and I lost my time into the bargain. As I did not teach for the good of my fellow-men, but simply for a livelihood, this was a failure. I have tried trade; but I found that it would take ten years to get under way in that, and that then I should probably be on my way to the devil. I was actually afraid that I might by that time be doing what is called a good business. When formerly I was looking about to see what I could do for a living, some sad experience in conforming to the wishes of friends being fresh in my mind to tax my ingenuity, I thought often and seriously of picking huckleberries; that surely I could do, and its small profits might suffice—for my greatest skill has been to want but little—so little capital it required, so little distraction from my wonted moods, I foolishly thought. While my acquaintances went unhesitatingly into trade or the professions, I contemplated this occupation as most like theirs; ranging the hills all summer to pick the berries which came in my way, and thereafter carelessly dispose of them; so, to keep the flocks of Admetus.[5] I also dreamed that I might gather the wild herbs, or carry evergreens to such villagers as loved to be reminded of the woods, even to the city, by hay-cart loads. But I have since learned that trade curses everything it handles; and though you trade in messages from heaven, the whole curse of trade attaches to the business.

As I preferred some things to others, and especially valued my freedom, as I could fare hard and yet succeed well, I did not wish to spend my time in earning rich carpets or other fine furniture, or delicate cookery, or a house in the Grecian or the Gothic style just yet. If there are any to whom it is no interruption to acquire these things, and who know how to use them when acquired, I

5. In Greek mythology, Apollo was forced to tend the flocks of Admetus for nine years while he was banished from Olympus.

relinquish to them the pursuit. Some are "industrious," and appear to love labor for its own sake, or perhaps because it keeps them out of worse mischief; to such I have at present nothing to say. Those who would not know what to do with more leisure than they now enjoy, I might advise to work twice as hard as they do—work till they pay for themselves, and get their free papers.[6] For myself I found that the occupation of a day-laborer was the most independent of any, especially as it required only thirty or forty days in a year to support one. The laborer's day ends with the going down of the sun, and he is then free to devote himself to his chosen pursuit, independent of his labor; but his employer, who speculates from month to month, has no respite from one end of the year to the other.

In short, I am convinced, both by faith and experience, that to maintain one's self on this earth is not a hardship but a pastime, if we will live simply and wisely; as the pursuits of the simpler nations are still the sports of the more artificial. It is not necessary that a man should earn his living by the sweat of his brow, unless he sweats easier than I do.

One young man of my acquaintance, who has inherited some acres, told me that he thought he should live as I did, *if he had the means*. I would not have anyone adopt *my* mode of living on any account; for, besides that before he has fairly learned it I may have found out another for myself, I desire that there may be as many different persons in the world as possible; but I would have each one be very careful to find out and pursue *his own* way, and not his father's or his mother's or his neighbor's instead. The youth may build or plant or sail, only let him not be hindered from doing that which he tells me he would like to do. It is by a mathematical point only that we are wise, as the sailor or the fugitive slave keeps the polestar in his eye;[7] but that is sufficient guidance for all our life. We may not arrive at our port within a calculable period, but we would preserve the true course.

Undoubtedly, in this case, what is true for one is truer still for a thousand, as a large house is not proportionally more expensive than a small one, since one roof may cover, one cellar underlie, and one wall separate several apartments. But for my part, I preferred the solitary dwelling. Moreover, it will commonly be cheaper to build the whole yourself than to convince another of the advantage of the common wall; and when you have done this, the common partition, to be much cheaper, must be a thin one, and that other may prove a bad neighbor, and also not keep his side in repair. The

6. In colonial times immigrants often indentured themselves to pay for their passage across the Atlantic.

7. To guide himself north to Canada and freedom.

only co-operation which is commonly possible is exceedingly partial and superficial; and what little true co-operation there is, is as if it were not, being a harmony inaudible to men. If a man has faith, he will co-operate with equal faith everywhere; if he has not faith, he will continue to live like the rest of the world, whatever company he is joined to. To co-operate in the highest as well as the lowest sense, means *to get our living together*. I heard it proposed lately that two young men should travel together over the world, the one without money, earning his means as he went, before the mast and behind the plough, the other carrying a bill of exchange in his pocket. It was easy to see that they could not long be companions or co-operate, since one would not *operate* at all. They would part at the first interesting crisis in their adventures. Above all, as I have implied, the man who goes alone can start today; but he who travels with another must wait till that other is ready, and it may be a long time before they get off. * * *

Where I Lived, and What I Lived For

At a certain season of our life we are accustomed to consider every spot as the possible site of a house. I have thus surveyed the country on every side within a dozen miles of where I live. In imagination I have bought all the farms in succession, for all were to be bought, and I knew their price. I walked over each farmer's premises, tasted his wild apples, discoursed on husbandry with him, took his farm at his price, at any price, mortgaging it to him in my mind; even put a higher price on it—took everything but a deed of it—took his word for his deed, for I dearly loved to talk—cultivated it, and him too to some extent, I trust, and withdrew when I had enjoyed it long enough, leaving him to carry it on. This experience entitled me to be regarded as a sort of real-estate broker by my friends. Wherever I sat, there I might live, and the landscape radiated from me accordingly. What is a house but a *sedes*, a seat?—better if a country seat. I discovered many a site for a house not likely to be soon improved, which some might have thought too far from the village, but to my eyes the village was too far from it. Well, there I might live, I said; and there I did live, for an hour, a summer and a winter life; saw how I could let the years run off, buffet the winter through, and see the spring come in. The future inhabitants of this region, wherever they may place their houses, may be sure that they have been anticipated. An afternoon sufficed to lay out the land into orchard, woodlot, and pasture, and to decide what fine oaks or pines should be left to stand before the door, and whence each blasted tree could be seen to the best advantage; and then I let it lie, fallow perchance, for a man is rich in proportion to the number of things which he can afford to let alone.

My imagination carried me so far that I even had the refusal of several farms—the refusal was all I wanted—but I never got my fingers burned by actual possession. The nearest that I came to actual possession was when I bought the Hollowell place,[8] and had begun to sort my seeds, and collected materials with which to make a wheelbarrow to carry it on or off with; but before the owner gave me a deed of it, his wife—every man has such a wife—changed her mind and wished to keep it, and he offered me ten dollars to release him. Now, to speak the truth, I had but ten cents in the world, and it surpassed my arithmetic to tell, if I was that man who had ten cents, or who had a farm, or ten dollars, or all together. However, I let him keep the ten dollars and the farm too, for I had carried it far enough; or rather, to be generous, I sold him the farm for just what I gave for it, and, as he was not a rich man, made him a present of ten dollars, and still had my ten cents, and seeds, and materials for a wheelbarrow left. I found thus that I had been a rich man without any damage to my poverty. But I retained the landscape, and I have since annually carried off what it yielded without a wheelbarrow. With respect to landscapes,

> "I am monarch of all I *survey*,
>   My right there is none to dispute."[9]

I have frequently seen a poet withdraw, having enjoyed the most valuable part of a farm, while the crusty farmer supposed that he had got a few wild apples only. Why, the owner does not know it for many years when a poet has put his farm in rhyme, the most admirable kind of invisible fence, has fairly impounded it, milked it, skimmed it, and got all the cream, and left the farmer only the skimmed milk.

The real attractions of the Hollowell farm, to me, were: its complete retirement, being about two miles from the village, half a mile from the nearest neighbor, and separated from the highway by a broad field; its bounding on the river, which the owner said protected it by its fogs from frosts in the spring, though that was nothing to me; the gray color and ruinous state of the house and barn, and the dilapidated fences, which put such an interval between me and the last occupant; the hollow and lichen-covered apple trees, gnawed by rabbits, showing what kind of neighbors I should have; but above all, the recollection I had of it from my earliest voyages up the river, when the house was concealed behind a dense grove of red maples, through which I heard the house-dog bark. I was in haste to buy it, before the proprietor finished get-

8. An old farm on the Sudbury River in Concord.
9. William Cowper, "Verses Supposed to be Written by Alexander Selkirk." Thoreau italicizes *survey* to pun on his own profession as a surveyor.

ting out some rocks, cutting down the hollow apple trees, and grubbing up some young birches which had sprung up in the pasture, or, in short, had made any more of his improvements. To enjoy these advantages I was ready to carry it on; like Atlas,[1] to take the world on my shoulders—I never heard what compensation he received for that—and do all those things which had no other motive or excuse but that I might pay for it and be unmolested in my possession of it; for I knew all the while that it would yield the most abundant crop of the kind I wanted if I could only afford to let it alone. But it turned out as I have said.

All that I could say, then, with respect to farming on a large scale (I have always cultivated a garden), was, that I had had my seeds ready. Many think that seeds improve with age. I have no doubt that time discriminates between the good and the bad; and when at last I shall plant, I shall be less likely to be disappointed. But I would say to my fellows, once for all, As long as possible live free and uncommitted. It makes but little difference whether you are committed to a farm or the county jail.

Old Cato, whose *De Re Rustica* is my "Cultivator," says, and the only translation I have seen makes sheer nonsense of the passage, "When you think of getting a farm turn it thus in your mind, not to buy greedily; nor spare your pains to look at it, and do not think it enough to go round it once. The oftener you go there the more it will please you, if it is good."[2] I think I shall not buy greedily, but go round and round it as long as I live, and be buried in it first, that it may please me the more at last.

The present was my next experiment of this kind, which I purpose to describe more at length, for convenience, putting the experience of two years into one. As I have said,[3] I do not propose to write an ode to dejection, but to brag as lustily as chanticleer in the morning, standing on his roost, if only to wake my neighbors up.

When first I took up my abode in the woods, that is, began to spend my nights as well as days there, which, by accident, was on Independence Day, or the Fourth of July, 1845, my house was not finished for winter, but was merely a defense against the rain, without plastering or chimney, the walls being of rough weather-stained boards, with wide chinks, which made it cool at night. The upright white hewn studs and freshly planed door and window casings gave it a clean and airy look, especially in the morning, when its timbers

1. In Greek mythology, Atlas held the world on his shoulders.
2. Chapter I. Marcus Porcius Cato (234–149 B.C.) was a Roman statesman and author.
3. Cf. Coleridge's "Dejection: An Ode." The following sentence was originally printed on the title page of *Walden* as its epigraph.

were saturated with dew, so that I fancied that by noon some sweet gum would exude from them. To my imagination it retained throughout the day more or less of this auroral character, reminding me of a certain house on a mountain which I had visited a year before. This was an airy and unplastered cabin, fit to entertain a traveling god, and where a goddess might trail her garments. The winds which passed over my dwelling were such as sweep over the ridges of mountains, bearing the broken strains, or celestial parts only, of terrestrial music. The morning wind forever blows, the poem of creation is uninterrupted; but few are the ears that hear it. Olympus[4] is but the outside of the earth everywhere.

The only house I had been the owner of before, if I except a boat, was a tent, which I used occasionally when making excursions in the summer, and this is still rolled up in my garret; but the boat, after passing from hand to hand, has gone down the stream of time. With this more substantial shelter about me, I had made some progress toward settling in the world. This frame, so slightly clad, was a sort of crystallization around me, and reacted on the builder. It was suggestive somewhat as a picture in outlines. I did not need to go outdoors to take the air, for the atmosphere within had lost none of its freshness. It was not so much within doors as behind a door where I sat, even in the rainiest weather. The Harivansa says, "An abode without birds is like a meat without seasoning."[5] Such was not my abode, for I found myself suddenly neighbor to the birds; not by having imprisoned one, but having caged myself near them. I was not only nearer to some of those which commonly frequent the garden and the orchard, but to those wilder and more thrilling songsters of the forest which never, or rarely, serenade a villager—the wood-thrush, the veery, the scarlet tanager, the field-sparrow, the whippoorwill, and many others.

I was seated by the shore of a small pond, about a mile and a half south of the village of Concord and somewhat higher than it, in the midst of an extensive wood between that town and Lincoln, and about two miles south of that our only field known to fame, Concord Battle Ground;[6] but I was so low in the woods that the opposite shore, half a mile off, like the rest, covered with wood, was my most distant horizon. For the first week, whenever I looked out on the pond it impressed me like a tarn high up on the side of a mountain, its bottom far above the surface of other lakes, and, as the sun arose, I saw it throwing off its nightly clothing of mist, and here and there, by degrees, its soft ripples or its smooth reflecting surface was revealed, while the mists, like ghosts, were

4. Home of the Greek gods.
5. I.282 (a Hindu religious work). Thoreau is quoting from the Langois

French translation of 1832–35.
6. Site of the Revolutionary War battle of April 19, 1775.

stealthily withdrawing in every direction into the woods, as at the breaking up of some nocturnal conventicle. The very dew seemed to hang upon the trees later into the day than usual, as on the sides of mountains.

This small lake was of most value as a neighbor in the intervals of a gentle rainstorm in August, when, both air and water being perfectly still, but the sky overcast, mid-afternoon had all the serenity of evening, and the wood-thrush sang around, and was heard from shore to shore. A lake like this is never smoother than at such a time; and the clear portion of the air above it being shallow and darkened by clouds, the water, full of light and reflections, becomes a lower heaven itself so much the more important. From a hilltop near by, where the wood had been recently cut off, there was a pleasing vista southward across the pond, through a wide indentation in the hills which form the shore there, where their opposite sides sloping toward each other suggested a stream flowing out in that direction through a wooded valley, but stream there was none. That way I looked between and over the near green hills to some distant and higher ones in the horizon, tinged with blue. Indeed, by standing on tiptoe I could catch a glimpse of some of the peaks of the still bluer and more distant mountain ranges in the northwest, those true-blue coins from heaven's own mint, and also of some portion of the village. But in other directions, even from this point, I could not see over or beyond the woods which surrounded me. It is well to have some water in your neighborhood, to give buoyancy to and float the earth. One value even of the smallest well is, that when you look into it you see that earth is not continent but insular. This is as important as that it keeps butter cool. When I looked across the pond from this peak toward the Sudbury meadows, which in time of flood I distinguished elevated perhaps by a mirage in their seething valley, like a coin in a basin, all the earth beyond the pond appeared like a thin crust insulated and floated even by this small sheet of intervening water, and I was reminded that this on which I dwelt was but *dry land.*

Though the view from my door was still more contracted, I did not feel crowded or confined in the least. There was pasture enough for my imagination. The low shrub-oak plateau to which the opposite shore arose, stretched away toward the prairies of the West and the steppes of Tartary,[7] affording ample room for all the roving families of men. "There are none happy in the world but beings who enjoy freely a vast horizon," said Damodara, when his herds required new and larger pastures.[8]

Both place and time were changed, and I dwelt nearer to those

7. Asiatic Russia.   8. *Harivansa* I.283.

parts of the universe and to those eras in history which had most attracted me. Where I lived was as far off as many a region viewed nightly by astronomers. We are wont to imagine rare and delectable places in some remote and more celestial corner of the system, behind the constellation of Cassiopeia's Chair, far from noise and disturbance. I discovered that my house actually had its site in such a withdrawn, but forever new and unprofaned, part of the universe. If it were worth the while to settle in those parts near to the Pleiades or the Hyades, to Aldebaran or Altair,[9] then I was really there, or at an equal remoteness from the life which I had left behind, dwindled and twinkling with as fine a ray to my nearest neighbor, and to be seen only in moonless nights by him. Such was that part of creation where I had squatted;

> "There was a shepherd that did live,
>   And held his thoughts as high
>   As were the mounts whereon his flocks
>   Did hourly feed him by."[1]

What should we think of the shepherd's life if his flocks always wandered to higher pastures than his thoughts?

Every morning was a cheerful invitation to make my life of equal simplicity, and I may say innocence, with Nature herself. I have been as sincere a worshiper of Aurora[2] as the Greeks. I got up early and bathed in the pond; that was a religious exercise, and one of the best things which I did. They say that characters were engraven on the bathing tub of King Tching-thang to this effect: "Renew thyself completely each day; do it again, and again, and forever again."[3] I can understand that. Morning brings back the heroic ages. I was as much affected by the faint hum of a mosquito making its invisible and unimaginable tour through my apartment at earliest dawn, when I was sitting with door and windows open, as I could be by any trumpet that ever sang of fame. It was Homer's requiem; itself an Iliad and Odyssey in the air, singing its own wrath and wanderings.[4] There was something cosmical about it; a standing advertisement, till forbidden, of the everlasting vigor and fertility of the world. The morning, which is the most memorable season of the day, is the awakening hour. Then there is least somnolence in us; and for an hour, at least, some part of us awakes which slumbers all the rest of the day and night. Little is to be expected of that day, if it can be called a day, to which we are not awakened by our Genius,[5] but by the mechanical nudgings of some servitor, are not awakened by our own newly acquired force and as-

9. Various stars and constellations.
1. An early Jacobean song, author unknown.
2. Greek goddess of the dawn.
3. Confucius, *The Great Learning* I.i.

4. The opening lines of the *Iliad* and the *Odyssey* speak of the "wrath" and the "wanderings" of the Greeks.
5. In classical mythology, the guardian spirit of an individual.

pirations from within, accompanied by the undulations of celestial music, instead of factory bells, and a fragrance filling the air—to a higher life than we fell asleep from; and thus the darkness bear its fruit, and prove itself to be good, no less than the light. That man who does not believe that each day contains an earlier, more sacred and auroral hour than he has yet profaned, has despaired of life, and is pursuing a descending and darkening way. After a partial cessation of his sensuous life, the soul of man, or its organs rather, are reinvigorated each day, and his Genius tries again what noble life it can make. All memorable events, I should say, transpire in morning time and in a morning atmosphere. The Vedas[6] say, "All intelligences awake with the morning." Poetry and art, and the fairest and most memorable of the actions of men, date from such an hour. All poets and heroes, like Memnon,[7] are the children of Aurora, and emit their music at sunrise. To him whose elastic and vigorous thought keeps pace with the sun, the day is a perpetual morning. It matters not what the clocks say or the attitudes and labors of men. Morning is when I am awake and there is a dawn in me. Moral reform is the effort to throw off sleep. Why is it that men give so poor an account of their day if they have not been slumbering? They are not such poor calculators. If they had not been overcome with drowsiness they would have performed something. The millions are awake enough for physical labor; but only one in a million is awake enough for effective intellectual exertion, only one in a hundred millions to a poetic or divine life. To be awake is to be alive. I have never yet met a man who was quite awake. How could I have looked him in the face?

We must learn to reawaken and keep ourselves awake, not by mechanical aids, but by an infinite expectation of the dawn, which does not forsake us in our soundest sleep. I know of no more encouraging fact than the unquestionable ability of man to elevate his life by a conscious endeavor. It is something to be able to paint a particular picture, or to carve a statue, and so to make a few objects beautiful; but it is far more glorious to carve and paint the very atmosphere and medium through which we look, which morally we can do. To affect the quality of the day, that is the highest of arts. Every man is tasked to make his life, even in its details, worthy of the contemplation of his most elevated and critical hour. If we refused, or rather used up, such paltry information as we get, the oracles would distinctly inform us how this might be done.

I went to the woods because I wished to live deliberately, to front only the essential facts of life, and see if I could not learn what it had to teach, and not, when I came to die, discover that I had not

6. Hindu religious books.
7. According to legend, the statue of Memnon, king of Ethiopia, made music when the sun's rays struck it each morning.

lived. I did not wish to live what was not life, living is so dear; nor did I wish to practice resignation, unless it was quite necessary. I wanted to live deep and suck out all the marrow of life, to live so sturdily and Spartan-like[8] as to put to rout all that was not life, to cut a broad swath and shave close, to drive life into a corner, and reduce it to its lowest terms, and, if it proved to be mean, why then to get the whole and genuine meanness of it, and publish its meanness to the world; or if it were sublime, to know it by experience, and be able to give a true account of it in my next excursion. For most men, it appears to me, are in a strange uncertainty about it, whether it is of the devil or of God, and have *somewhat hastily* concluded that it is the chief end of man here to "glorify God and enjoy him forever."[9]

Still we live meanly, like ants; though the fable tells us that we were long ago changed into men;[1] like pygmies we fight with cranes; it is error upon error, and clout upon clout, and our best virtue has for its occasion a superfluous and evitable wretchedness. Our life is frittered away by detail. An honest man has hardly need to count more than his ten fingers, or in extreme cases he may add his ten toes, and lump the rest. Simplicity, simplicity, simplicity! I say, let your affairs be as two or three, and not a hundred or a thousand; instead of a million count half a dozen, and keep your accounts on your thumb nail. In the midst of this chopping sea of civilized life, such are the clouds and storms and quicksands and thousand-and-one items to be allowed for, that a man has to live, if he would not founder and go to the bottom and not make his port at all, by dead reckoning, and he must be a great calculator indeed who succeeds. Simplify, simplify. Instead of three meals a day, if it be necessary eat but one; instead of a hundred dishes, five; and reduce other things in proportion. Our life is like a German Confederacy,[2] made up of petty states, with its boundary forever fluctuating, so that even a German cannot tell you how it is bounded at any moment. The nation itself, with all its so-called internal improvements, which, by the way are all external and superficial, is just such an unwieldy and overgrown establishment, cluttered with furniture and tripped up by its own traps, ruined by luxury and heedless expense, by want of calculation and a worthy aim, as the million households in the land; and the only cure for it as for them is in a rigid economy, a stern and more than Spartan simplicity of life and elevation of purpose. It lives too fast. Men think that it is essential that the *Nation* have commerce, and export ice, and talk

8. The ancient Spartans were noted for their asceticism.
9. From the *Shorter Catechism*.
1. According to Greek mythology, Zeus repeopled the kingdom of Oenopia by

changing the ants into men. The reference to "pygmies" comes from *Iliad* III.
2. Until it was unified by Bismarck, the German Confederacy was constantly changing its borders.

through a telegraph, and ride thirty miles an hour, without a doubt, whether *they* do or not; but whether we should live like baboons or like men, is a little uncertain. If we do not get out sleepers,[3] and forge rails, and devote days and nights to the work, but go to tinkering upon our *lives* to improve *them*, who will build railroads? And if railroads are not built, how shall we get to heaven in season?[4] But if we stay at home and mind our business, who will want railroads? We do not ride on the railroad; it rides upon us. Did you ever think what those sleepers are that underlie the railroad? Each one is a man, an Irishman, or a Yankee man. The rails are laid on them, and they are covered with sand, and the cars run smoothly over them. They are sound sleepers, I assure you. And every few years a new lot is laid down and run over; so that, if some have the pleasure of riding on a rail, others have the misfortune to be ridden upon. And when they run over a man that is walking in his sleep, a supernumerary sleeper in the wrong position, and wake him up, they suddenly stop the cars, and make a hue and cry about it, as if this were an exception. I am glad to know that it takes a gang of men for every five miles to keep the sleepers down and level in their beds as it is, for this is a sign that they may sometime get up again.

Why should we live with such hurry and waste of life? We are determined to be starved before we are hungry. Men say that a stitch in time saves nine, and so they take a thousand stitches to-day to save nine tomorrow. As for *work*, we haven't any of any consequence. We have the Saint Vitus' dance,[5] and cannot possibly keep our heads still. If I should only give a few pulls at the parish bell-rope, as for a fire, that is, without setting the bell, there is hardly a man on his farm in the outskirts of Concord, notwithstanding that press of engagements which was his excuse so many times this morning, nor a boy, nor a woman, I might almost say, but would forsake all and follow that sound, not mainly to save property from the flames, but, if we will confess the truth, much more to see it burn, since burn it must, and we, be it known, did not set it on fire—or to see it put out, and have a hand in it, if that is done as handsomely; yes, even if it were the parish church itself. Hardly a man takes a half hour's nap after dinner, but when he wakes he holds up his head and asks, "What's the news?" as if the rest of mankind had stood his sentinels. Some give directions to be waked every half hour, doubtless for no other purpose; and then, to pay for it, they tell what they have dreamed. After a night's sleep the news is as indispensable as the breakfast. "Pray tell me

---

3. Railroad ties.
4. Cf. Nathaniel Hawthorne, "The Celestial Railroad."

5. A nervous disease characterized by marked trembling.

anything new that has happened to a man anywhere on this globe" —and he reads it over his coffee and rolls, that a man has had his eyes gouged out this morning on the Wachito River;[6] never dreaming the while that he lives in the dark unfathomed mammoth cave of this world, and has but the rudiment of an eye himself.

For my part, I could easily do without the post-office. I think that there are very few important communications made through it. To speak critically, I never received more than one or two letters in my life—I wrote this some years ago—that were worth the postage. The penny-post is, commonly, an institution through which you seriously offer a man that penny for his thoughts which is so often safely offered in jest. And I am sure that I never read any memorable news in a newspaper. If we read of one man robbed, or murdered, or killed by accident, or one house burned, or one vessel wrecked, or one steamboat blown up, or one cow run over on the Western Railroad,[7] or one mad dog killed, or one lot of grasshoppers in the winter—we never need read of another. One is enough. If you are acquainted with the principle, what do you care for a myriad instances and applications? To a philosopher all *news*, as it is called, is gossip, and they who edit and read it are old women over their tea. Yet not a few are greedy after this gossip. There was such a rush, as I hear, the other day at one of the offices to learn the foreign news by the last arrival, that several large squares of plate glass belonging to the establishment were broken by the pressure—news which I seriously think a ready wit might write a twelvemonth or twelve years beforehand with sufficient accuracy. As for Spain, for instance, if you know how to throw in Don Carlos and the Infanta, and Don Pedro[8] and Seville and Granada, from time to time in the right proportions—they may have changed the names a little since I saw the papers—and serve up a bull-fight when other entertainments fail, it will be true to the letter, and give us as good an idea of the exact state or ruin of things in Spain as the most succinct and lucid reports under this head in the newspapers: and as for England, almost the last significant scrap of news from that quarter was the revolution of 1649;[9] and if you have learned the history of her crops for an average year, you never need attend to that thing again, unless your speculations are of a merely pecuniary character. If one may judge who rarely looks into the newspapers, nothing new does ever happen in foreign parts, a French revolution not excepted.

What news! how much more important to know what that is which was never old! "Kieou-he-yu (great dignitary of the state of

6. Now the Ouachita River, in Arkansas.

7. A railroad formerly connecting Worcester, Mass. and Albany, N.Y.

8. Spanish nobility of the mid-19th century.

9. When the Commonwealth was established under Cromwell.

Wei) sent a man to Khoung-tseu to know his news. Khoung-tseu caused the messenger to be seated near him, and questioned him in these terms: What is your master doing? The messenger answered with respect: My master desires to diminish the number of his faults, but he cannot come to the end of them. The messenger being gone, the philosopher remarked: What a worthy messenger! What a worthy messenger!"[1] The preacher, instead of vexing the ears of drowsy farmers on their day of rest at the end of the week—for Sunday is the fit conclusion of an ill-spent week, and not the fresh and brave beginning of a new one—with this one other draggle-tail of a sermon, should shout with thundering voice—"Pause! Avast! Why so seeming fast, but deadly slow?"

Shams and delusions are esteemed for soundest truths, while reality is fabulous. If men would steadily observe realities only, and not allow themselves to be deluded, life, to compare it with such things as we know, would be like a fairy tale and the Arabian Nights' Entertainments. If we respected only what is inevitable and has a right to be, music and poetry would resound along the streets. When we are unhurried and wise, we perceive that only great and worthy things have any permanent and absolute existence—that petty fears and petty pleasures are but the shadow of the reality. This is always exhilarating and sublime. By closing the eyes and slumbering, and consenting to be deceived by shows, men establish and confirm their daily life of routine and habit everywhere, which still is built on purely illusory foundations. Children, who play life, discern its true law and relations more clearly than men, who fail to live it worthily, but who think that they are wiser by experience, that is, by failure. I have read in a Hindu book that "there was a king's son, who, being expelled in infancy from his native city, was brought up by a forester, and, growing up to maturity in that state, imagined himself to belong to the barbarous race with which he lived. One of his father's ministers, having discovered him, revealed to him what he was, and the misconception of his character was removed, and he knew himself to be a prince. So soul," continues the Hindu philosopher, "from the circumstances in which it is placed, mistakes its own character, until the truth is revealed to it by some holy teacher, and then it knows itself to be *Brahme*." I perceive that we inhabitants of New England live this mean life that we do because our vision does not penetrate the surface of things. We think that that *is* which *appears* to be. If a man should walk through this town and see only the reality, where, think you, would the "Mill-dam"[2] go to? If he should give us an account of the realities he beheld there, we should not recognize the place in his description. Look at a meeting-house, or a courthouse, or a jail, or a shop,

1. *Confucian Analects* XIV.xxvi.2.   2. The shopping center of Concord.

or a dwelling-house, and say what that thing really is before a true gaze, and they would all go to pieces in your account of them. Men esteem truth remote, in the outskirts of the system, behind the farthest star, before Adam and after the last man. In eternity there is indeed something true and sublime. But all these times and places and occasions are now and here. God himself culminates in the present moment, and will never be more divine in the lapse of all the ages. And we are enabled to apprehend at all what is sublime and noble only by the perpetual instilling and drenching of the reality that surrounds us. The universe constantly and obediently answers to our conceptions; whether we travel fast or slow, the track is laid for us. Let us spend our lives in conceiving then. The poet or the artist never yet had so fair and noble a design but some of his posterity at least could accomplish it.

Let us spend one day as deliberately as Nature, and not be thrown off the track by every nutshell and mosquito's wing that falls on the rails. Let us rise early and fast, or break fast, gently and without perturbation; let company come and let company go, let the bells ring and the children cry—determined to make a day of it. Why should we knock under and go with the stream? Let us not be upset and overwhelmed in that terrible rapid and whirlpool called a dinner, situated in the meridian shallows. Weather this danger and you are safe, for the rest of the way is down hill. With unrelaxed nerves, with morning vigor, sail by it, looking another way, tied to the mast like Ulysses.[3] If the engine whistles, let it whistle till it is hoarse for its pains. If the bell rings, why should we run? We will consider what kind of music they are like. Let us settle ourselves, and work and wedge our feet downward through the mud and slush of opinion, and prejudice, and tradition, and delusion, and appearance, that alluvion which covers the globe, through Paris and London, through New York and Boston and Concord, through church and state, through poetry and philosophy and religion, till we come to a hard bottom and rocks in place, which we can call *reality*, and say, This is, and no mistake; and then begin, having a *point d'appui*,[4] below freshet and frost and fire, a place where you might found a wall or a state, or set a lamp-post safely, or perhaps a gauge, not a Nilometer,[5] but a Realometer, that future ages might know how deep a freshet of shams and appearances had gathered from time to time. If you stand right fronting and face to face to a fact, you will see the sun glimmer on both its surfaces, as if it were a cimeter, and feel its sweet edge dividing you through the heart and marrow, and so you will happily

3. Ulysses had himself tied to his mast so that he could hear the song of the Sirens and yet not yield to their fatal entreaties.

4. Point of support.

5. A gauge established by the ancient Egyptians to measure the flood stages of the Nile River.

462 · Henry David Thoreau

conclude your mortal career. Be it life or death, we crave only reality. If we are really dying, let us hear the rattle in our throats and reel cold in the extremities; if we are alive, let us go about our business.

Time is but the stream I go a-fishing in. I drink at it; but while I drink I see the sandy bottom and detect how shallow it is. Its thin current slides away, but eternity remains. I would drink deeper; fish in the sky, whose bottom is pebbly with stars. I cannot count one. I know not the first letter of the alphabet. I have always been regretting that I was not as wise as the day I was born. The intellect is a cleaver; it discerns and rifts its way into the secret of things. I do not wish to be any more busy with my hands than is necessary. My head is hands and feet. I feel all my best faculties concentrated in it. My instinct tells me that my head is an organ for burrowing, as some creatures use their snout and forepaws, and with it I would mine and burrow my way through these hills. I think that the richest vein is somewhere hereabouts; so by the divining rod and thin rising vapors I judge; and here I will begin to mine.

Sounds

But while we are confined to books,[6] though the most select and classic, and read only particular written languages, which are themselves but dialects and provincial, we are in danger of forgetting the language which all things and events speak without metaphor, which alone is copious and standard. Much is published, but little printed. The rays which stream through the shutter will be no longer remembered when the shutter is wholly removed. No method nor discipline can supersede the necessity of being forever on the alert. What is a course of history or philosophy, or poetry, no matter how well selected, or the best society, or the most admirable routine of life, compared with the discipline of looking always at what is to be seen? Will you be a reader, a student merely, or a seer? Read your fate, see what is before you, and walk on into futurity.

I did not read books the first summer; I hoed beans. Nay, I often did better than this. There were times when I could not afford to sacrifice the bloom of the present moment to any work, whether of the head or hands. I love a broad margin to my life. Sometimes, in a summer morning, having taken my accustomed bath, I sat in my sunny doorway from sunrise till noon, rapt in a revery, amidst the pines and hickories and sumachs, in undisturbed solitude and stillness, while the birds sang around or flitted noiseless through the house, until by the sun falling in at my west window, or the

6. The preceding chapter had been titled "Reading."

noise of some traveler's wagon on the distant highway, I was reminded of the lapse of time. I grew in those seasons like corn in
the night,[7] and they were far better than any work of the hands
would have been. They were not time subtracted from my life,
but so much over and above my usual allowance. I realized what
the Orientals mean by contemplation and the forsaking of works.
For the most part, I minded not how the hours went. The day advanced as if to light some work of mine; it was morning, and lo,
now it is evening, and nothing memorable is accomplished. Instead
of singing like the birds, I silently smiled at my incessant good
fortune. As the sparrow had its trill, sitting on the hickory before
my door, so had I my chuckle or suppressed warble which he might
hear out of my nest. My days were not days of the week, bearing
the stamp of any heathen deity,[8] nor were they minced into hours
and fretted by the ticking of a clock; for I lived like the Puri Indians, of whom it is said that "for yesterday, today, and tomorrow
they have only one word, and they express the variety of meaning
by pointing backward for yesterday, forward for tomorrow, and
overhead for the passing day."[9] This was sheer idleness to my fel-
low-townsmen, no doubt; but if the birds and flowers had tried
me by their standard, I should not have been found wanting. A
man must find his occasions in himself, it is true. The natural day
is very calm, and will hardly reprove his indolence.

I had this advantage, at least, in my mode of life, over those
who were obliged to look abroad for amusement, to society and
the theater, that my life itself was become my amusement and
never ceased to be novel. It was a drama of many scenes and without an end. If we were always indeed getting our living, and regulating our lives according to the last and best mode we had learned,
we should never be troubled with ennui. Follow your genius closely
enough, and it will not fail to show you a fresh prospect every hour.
Housework was a pleasant pastime. When my floor was dirty, I rose
early, and, setting all my furniture out of doors on the grass, bed
and bedstead making but one budget, dashed water on the floor,
and sprinkled white sand from the pond on it, and then with a
broom scrubbed it clean and white; and by the time the villagers
had broken their fast the morning sun had dried my house sufficiently to allow me to move in again, and my meditations were
almost uninterrupted. It was pleasant to see my whole household
effects out on the grass, making a little pile like a gypsy's pack, and
my three-legged table, from which I did not remove the books and
pen and ink, standing amid the pines and hickories. They seemed

7. Corn is one of the most rapid-grow-
ing of the common garden vegetables.
8. The days of our week derive their
names from such heathen gods as Thor
(Thursday) and Saturn (Saturday).
9. Ida Pfeiffer, *A Lady's Voyage Round
the World* (1852), p. 36.

glad to get out themselves, and as if unwilling to be brought in. I was sometimes tempted to stretch an awning over them and take my seat there. It was worth the while to see the sun shine on these things, and hear the free wind blow on them; so much more interesting most familiar objects look out of doors than in the house. A bird sits on the next bough, life-everlasting grows under the table, and blackberry vines run round its legs; pine cones, chestnut burs, and strawberry leaves are strewn about. It looked as if this was the way these forms came to be transferred to our furniture, to tables, chairs, and bedsteads—because they once stood in their midst.

My house was on the side of a hill, immediately on the edge of the larger wood, in the midst of a young forest of pitch pines and hickories, and half a dozen rods from the pond, to which a narrow footpath led down the hill. In my front yard grew the strawberry, blackberry, and life-everlasting, johnswort and goldenrod, shrub-oaks and sand cherry, blueberry and groundnut. Near the end of May, the sand cherry (*cerasus pumila*) adorned the sides of the path with its delicate flowers arranged in umbels cylindrically about its short stems, which last, in the fall, weighed down with good-sized and handsome cherries, fell over in wreaths like rays on every side. I tasted them out of compliment to Nature, though they were scarcely palatable. The sumach (*rhus glabra*) grew luxuriantly about the house, pushing up through the embankment which I had made, and growing five or six feet the first season. Its broad pinnate tropical leaf was pleasant though strange to look on. The large buds, suddenly pushing out late in the spring from dry sticks which had seemed to be dead, developed themselves as by magic into graceful green and tender boughs, an inch in diameter; and sometimes, as I sat at my window, so heedlessly did they grow and tax their weak joints, I heard a fresh and tender bough suddenly fall like a fan to the ground, when there was not a breath of air stirring, broken off by its own weight. In August, the large masses of berries, which, when in flower, had attracted many wild bees, gradually assumed their bright velvety crimson hue, and by their weight again bent down and broke the tender limbs.

As I sit at my window this summer afternoon, hawks are circling about my clearing; the tantivy of wild pigeons, flying by twos and threes athwart my view, or perching restless on the white-pine boughs behind my house, gives a voice to the air; a fish hawk dimples the glassy surface of the pond and brings up a fish; a mink steals out of the marsh before my door and seizes a frog by the shore; the sedge is bending under the weight of the reed-birds[1] flitting hither and thither; and for the last half hour I have heard the rattle of railroad cars, now dying away and then reviving like the beat of a partridge, conveying travelers from Boston to the country. For I did not live so out of the world as that boy, who, as I hear, was put out to a farmer in the east part of the town, but ere long ran away and came home again, quite down at the heel and homesick. He had never seen such a dull and out-of-the-way place; the folks were all gone off; why, you couldn't even hear the whistle! I doubt if there is such a place in Massachusetts now:

> "In truth, our village has become a butt
> For one of those fleet railroad shafts, and o'er
> Our peaceful plain its soothing sound is—Concord."[2]

The Fitchburg Railroad touches the pond about a hundred rods south of where I dwell. I usually go to the village along its causeway, and am, as it were, related to society by this link. The men on the freight trains, who go over the whole length of the road, bow to me as to an old acquaintance, they pass me so often, and apparently they take me for an employee; and so I am. I too would fain be a track-repairer somewhere in the orbit of the earth.

The whistle of the locomotive penetrates my woods summer and winter, sounding like the scream of a hawk sailing over some farmer's yard, informing me that many restless city merchants are arriving within the circle of the town, or adventurous country traders from the other side. As they come under one horizon, they shout their warning to get off the track to the other, heard sometimes through the circles of two towns. Here come your groceries, country; your rations, countrymen! Nor is there any man so independent on his farm that he can say them nay. And here's your pay for them! screams the countryman's whistle; timber like long battering rams going twenty miles an hour against the city's walls, and chairs enough to seat all the weary and heavy laden that dwell within them. With such huge and lumbering civility the country hands a chair to the city. All the Indian huckleberry hills are stripped, all the cranberry meadows are raked into the city. Up comes the cotton, down goes the woven cloth; up comes the silk, down goes the woolen; up come the books, but down goes the wit than writes them.

When I meet the engine with its train of cars moving off with planetary motion—or, rather, like a comet, for the beholder knows not if with that velocity and with that direction it will ever revisit

1. Now known as bobolinks.
2. Ellery Channing, "Walden Spring."

Channing was Thoreau's closest friend of his adult years.

this system, since its orbit does not look like a returning curve—
with its steam cloud like a banner streaming behind in golden and
silver wreaths, like many a downy cloud which I have seen, high
in the heavens, unfolding its masses to the light—as if this traveling
demigod, this cloud-compeller,[3] would ere long take the sunset sky
for the livery of his train; when I hear the iron horse make the hills
echo[4] with his snort like thunder, shaking the earth with his feet,
and breathing fire and smoke from his nostrils (what kind of winged
horse or fiery dragon they will put into the new Mythology I don't
know), it seems as if the earth had got a race now worthy to inhabit
it. If all were as it seems, and men made the elements their servants
for noble ends! If the cloud that hangs over the engine were the
perspiration of heroic deeds, or as beneficent as that which floats
over the farmer's fields, then the elements and Nature herself would
cheerfully accompany men on their errands and be their escort.

I watch the passage of the morning cars with the same feeling
that I do the rising of the sun, which is hardly more regular. Their
train of clouds stretching far behind and rising higher and higher,
going to heaven while the cars are going to Boston, conceals the
sun for a minute and casts my distant field into the shade, a celestial
train[5] beside which the petty train of cars which hugs the earth
is but the barb of the spear. The stabler of the iron horse was up
early this winter morning by the light of the stars amid the mountains, to fodder and harness his steed. Fire, too, was awakened thus
early to put the vital heat in him and get him off. If the enterprise
were as innocent as it is early! If the snow lies deep, they strap
on his snowshoes, and with the giant plough plough a furrow from
the mountains to the seaboard, in which the cars, like a following
drill-barrow,[6] sprinkle all the restless men and floating merchandise
in the country for seed. All day the fire-steed flies over the country,
stopping only that his master may rest, and I am awakened by his
tramp and defiant snort at midnight, when in some remote glen
in the woods he fronts the elements incased in ice and snow; and
he will reach his stall only with the morning star, to start once
more on his travels without rest or slumber. Or perchance, at evening, I hear him in his stable blowing off the superfluous energy
of the day, that he may calm his nerves and cool his liver and brain
for a few hours of iron slumber. If the enterprise were as heroic and
commanding as it is protracted and unwearied!

Far through unfrequented woods on the confines of towns, where
once only the hunter penetrated by day, in the darkest night dart
these bright saloons without the knowledge of their inhabitants;

3. Zeus, in Greek mythology, since he
supposedly controlled the weather, was
often called "cloud-compeller."
4. Cf. Job xxxix.19–25.

5. Another reference to Hawthorne's
"Celestial Railroad."
6. A device for planting seeds.

this moment stopping at some brilliant station-house in town or city, where a social crowd is gathered, the next in the Dismal Swamp,[7] scaring the owl and fox. The startings and arrivals of the cars are now the epochs in the village day. They go and come with such regularity and precision, and their whistle can be heard so far, that the farmers set their clocks by them, and thus one well conducted institution regulates a whole country. Have not men improved somewhat in punctuality since the railroad was invented? Do they not talk and think faster in the depot than they did in the stage-office? There is something electrifying in the atmosphere of the former place. I have been astonished at the miracles it has wrought; that some of my neighbors, who, I should have prophesied, once for all, would never get to Boston by so prompt a conveyance, are on hand when the bell rings. To do things "railroad fashion" is now the byword; and it is worth the while to be warned so often and so sincerely by any power to get off its track. There is no stopping to read the riot act, no firing over the heads of the mob, in this case. We have constructed a fate, an *Atropos*,[8] that never turns aside. (Let that be the name of your engine.) Men are advertised that at a certain hour and minute these bolts will be shot toward particular points of the compass; yet it interferes with no man's business, and the children go to school on the other track. We live the steadier for it. We are all educated thus to be sons of Tell. The air is full of invisible bolts. Every path but your own is the path of fate. Keep on your own track, then.

What recommends commerce to me is its enterprise and bravery. It does not clasp its hands and pray to Jupiter. I see these men every day go about their business with more or less courage and content, doing more even than they suspect, and perchance better employed than they could have consciously devised. I am less affected by their heroism who stood up for half an hour in the front line at Buena Vista,[9] than by the steady and cheerful valor of the men who inhabit the snowplough for their winter quarters; who have not merely the three-o'-clock in the morning courage, which Bonaparte thought was the rarest,[1] but whose courage does not go to rest so early, who go to sleep only when the storm sleeps or the sinews of their iron steed are frozen. On this morning of the Great Snow, perchance, which is still raging and chilling men's blood, I hear the muffled tone of their engine bell from out the fog bank of their chilled breath, which announces that the cars *are coming*,

7. On the border between Virginia and North Carolina.
8. One of the Greek Fates who supposedly controlled the length of human life.
9. A battle in the War with Mexico in 1847.
1. Napoleon is said to have praised "two [*sic*] o'clock in the morning courage," that is, courage to meet unforeseen difficulties.

without long delay, notwithstanding the veto of a New England northeast snowstorm, and I behold the ploughmen covered with snow and rime, their heads peering above the mould-board which is turning down other than daisies and the nests of field mice,[2] like boulders of the Sierra Nevada, that occupy an outside place in the universe.

Commerce is unexpectedly confident and serene, alert, adventurous, and unwearied. It is very natural in its methods withal, far more so than many fantastic enterprises and sentimental experiments, and hence its singular success. I am refreshed and expanded when the freight train rattles past me, and I smell the stores which go dispensing their odors all the way from Long Wharf[3] to Lake Champlain, reminding me of foreign parts, of coral reefs, and Indian oceans, and tropical climes, and the extent of the globe. I feel more like a citizen of the world at the sight of the palm-leaf[4] which will cover so many flaxen New England heads the next summer, the Manila hemp and coconut husks, the old junk, gunny bags, scrap iron, and rusty nails. This carload of torn sails is more legible and interesting now than if they should be wrought into paper and printed books. Who can write so graphically the history of the storms they have weathered as these rents have done? They are proofsheets which need no correction. Here goes lumber from the Maine woods, which did not go out to sea in the last freshet, risen four dollars on the thousand because of what did go out or was split up; pine, spruce, cedar—first, second, third and fourth qualities, so lately all of one quality, to wave over the bear, and moose, and caribou. Next rolls Thomaston lime,[5] a prime lot, which will get far among the hills before it gets slacked. These rags in bales, of all hues and qualities, the lowest condition to which cotton and linen descend, the final result of dress—of patterns which are now no longer cried up, unless it be in Milwaukee, as those splendid articles, English, French, or American prints, ginghams, muslins, etc., gathered from all quarters both of fashion and poverty, going to become paper of one color or a few shades only, on which forsooth will be written tales of real life, high and low, and founded on fact! This closed car smells of salt fish, the strong New England and commercial scent, reminding me of the Grand Banks and the fisheries. Who has not seen a salt fish, thoroughly cured for this world, so that nothing can spoil it, and putting the perseverance of the saints to the blush? with which you may sweep or pave the streets, and split your kindlings, and the teamster shelter himself and his lading against sun, wind, and rain behind it—and the

2. Robert Burns' poems "To a Mountain Daisy" and "To a Mouse."
3. One of the major wharves in Boston.
4. Summer hats popular in Thoreau's time were made of palm leaves.
5. Thomaston, Maine, was a major source of lime.

trader, as a Concord trader once did, hang it up by his door for
a sign when he commences business, until at last his oldest customer cannot tell surely whether it be animal, vegetable, or mineral, and yet it shall be as pure as a snowflake, and if it be put into
a pot and boiled, will come out an excellent dun fish[6] for a Saturday's dinner. Next Spanish hides, with the tails still preserving
their twist and the angle of elevation they had when the oxen that
wore them were careering over the pampas of the Spanish main—
a type of all obstinacy, and evincing how almost hopeless and incurable are all constitutional vices. I confess, that practically speaking, when I have learned a man's real disposition, I have no hopes
of changing it for the better or worse in this state of existence. As
the Orientals say, "A cur's tail may be warmed, and pressed, and
bound round with ligatures, and after a twelve years' labor bestowed
upon it, still it will retain its natural form."[7] The only effectual cure
for such inveteracies as these tails exhibit is to make glue of them,
which I believe is what is usually done with them, and then they
will stay put and stick. Here is a hogshead of molasses or of brandy
directed to John Smith, Cuttingsville, Vermont, some trader among
the Green Mountains, who imports for the farmers near his clearing, and now perchance stands over his bulkhead and thinks of the
last arrivals on the coast, how they may affect the price for him,
telling his customers this moment, as he has told them twenty
times before this morning, that he expects some by the next train
of prime quality. It is advertised in the Cuttingsville Times.

While these things go up, other things come down. Warned by
the whizzing sound, I look up from my book and see some tall
pine, hewn on far northern hills, which has winged its way over
the Green Mountains and the Connecticut, shot like an arrow
through the township within ten minutes, and scarce another eye
beholds it; going

> "to be the mast
> Of some great ammiral."[8]

And hark! here comes the cattle-train bearing the cattle of a thousand hills,[9] sheepcots, stables, and cowyards in the air, drovers with
their sticks, and shepherd boys in the midst of their flocks, all but
the mountain pastures, whirled along like leaves blown from the
mountains by the September gales. The air is filled with the bleat-
ing of calves and sheep, and the hustling of oxen, as if a pastoral
valley were going by. When the old bellwether at the head rattles
his bell, the mountains do indeed skip like rams and the little hills

6. Dried codfish.
7. *The Hitopadesa* (Charles Wilkins
translation) II.ix. An Indian collection
of animal fables.
8. *Paradise Lost* I.293–94.
9. Psalms i.10.

like lambs.[1] A carload of drovers, too, in the midst, on a level with their droves now, their vocation gone, but still clinging to their useless sticks as their badge of office. But their dogs, where are they? It is a stampede to them; they are quite thrown out; they have lost the scent. Methinks I hear them barking behind the Peterboro' Hills,[2] or panting up the western slope of the Green Mountains. They will not be in at the death. Their vocation, too, is gone. Their fidelity and sagacity are below par now. They will slink back to their kennels in disgrace, or perchance run wild and strike a league with the wolf and the fox. So is your pastoral life whirled past and away. But the bell rings, and I must get off the track and let the cars go by—

> What's the railroad to me?
> I never go to see
> Where it ends.
> It fills a few hollows,
> And makes banks for the swallows,
> It sets the sand a-blowing,
> And the blackberries a-growing,

but I cross it like a cart-path in the woods. I will not have my eyes put out and my ears spoiled by its smoke and steam and hissing.

Now that the cars are gone by and all the restless world with them, and the fishes in the pond no longer feel their rumbling, I am more alone than ever. For the rest of the long afternoon, perhaps, my meditations are interrupted only by the faint rattle of a carriage or team along the distant highway.

Sometimes, on Sundays, I heard the bells, the Lincoln, Acton, Bedford, or Concord bell, when the wind was favorable, a faint, sweet, and, as it were, natural melody, worth importing into the wilderness. At a sufficient distance over the woods this sound acquires a certain vibratory hum, as if the pine needles in the horizon were the strings of a harp which it swept. All sound heard at the greatest possible distance produces one and the same effect, a vibration of the universal lyre, just as the intervening atmosphere makes a distant ridge of earth interesting to our eyes by the azure tint it imparts to it. There came to me in this case a melody which the air had strained, and which had conversed with every leaf and needle of the wood, that portion of the sound which the elements had taken up and modulated and echoed from vale to vale. The echo is, to some extent, an original sound, and therein is the magic and charm of it. It is not merely a repetition of what was worth repeating in the bell, but partly the voice of the wood, the same trivial words and notes sung by a wood-nymph.

---

1. Psalms cxiv.4. 2. A range of mountains in southwestern New Hampshire.

At evening, the distant lowing of some cow in the horizon beyond the woods sounded sweet and melodious, and at first I would mistake it for the voices of certain minstrels by whom I was sometimes serenaded, who might be straying over hill and dale; but soon I was not unpleasantly disappointed when it was prolonged into the cheap and natural music of the cow. I do not mean to be satirical, but to express my appreciation of those youths' singing, when I state that I perceived clearly that it was akin to the music of the cow, and they were at length one articulation of Nature.

Regularly at half past seven, in one part of the summer, after the evening train had gone by, the whippoorwills chanted their vespers for half an hour, sitting on a stump by my door, or upon the ridgepole of the house. They would begin to sing almost with as much precision as a clock, within five minutes of a particular time, referred to the setting of the sun, every evening. I had a rare opportunity to become acquainted with their habits. Sometimes I heard four or five at once in different parts of the wood, by accident one a bar behind another, and so near me that I distinguished not only the cluck after each note, but often that singular buzzing sound like a fly in a spider's web, only proportionally louder. Sometimes one would circle round and round me in the woods a few feet distant as if tethered by a string, when probably I was near its eggs. They sang at intervals throughout the night, and were again as musical as ever just before and about dawn.

When other birds are still the screech owls take up the strain, like mourning women their ancient u-lu-lu. Their dismal scream is truly Ben Jonsonian. Wise midnight hags! It is no honest and blunt tu-whit tu-who of the poets, but, without jesting, a most solemn graveyard ditty, the mutual consolations of suicide lovers remembering the pangs and the delights of supernal love in the infernal groves. Yet I love to hear their wailing, their doleful responses, trilled along the woodside; reminding me sometimes of music and singing birds; as if it were the dark and tearful side of music, the regrets and sighs that would fain be sung. They are the spirits, the low spirits and melancholy forebodings, of fallen souls that once in human shape night-walked the earth and did the deeds of darkness, now expiating their sins with their wailing hymns or threnodies in the scenery of their transgressions. They give me a new sense of the variety and capacity of that nature which is our common dwelling. *Oh-o-o-o-o that I never had been bor-r-r-r-n!* sighs one on this side of the pond, and circles with the restlessness of despair to some new perch on the gray oaks. Then—*that I never had been bor-r-r-r-n!* echoes another on the farther side with tremulous sincerity, and—*bor-r-r-r-n!* comes faintly from far in the Lincoln woods.

I was also serenaded by a hooting owl. Near at hand you could fancy it the most melancholy sound in Nature, as if she meant by this to stereotype and make permanent in her choir the dying moans of a human being, some poor weak relic of mortality who has left hope behind,[3] and howls like an animal, yet with human sobs, on entering the dark valley, made more awful by a certain gurgling melodiousness—I find myself beginning with the letters gl when I try to imitate it—expressive of a mind which has reached the gelatinous mildewy stage in the mortification of all healthy and courageous thought. It reminded me of ghouls and idiots and insane howlings. But now one answers from far woods in a strain made really melodious by distance, *Hoo hoo hoo, hoorer hoo*; and indeed for the most part it suggested only pleasing associations, whether heard by day or night, summer or winter.

I rejoice that there are owls. Let them do the idiotic and maniacal hooting for men. It is a sound admirably suited to swamps and twilight woods which no day illustrates, suggesting a vast and undeveloped nature which men have not recognized. They represent the stark twilight and unsatisfied thoughts which all have. All day the sun has shone on the surface of some savage swamp, where the single spruce stands hung with usnea lichens, and small hawks circulate above, and the chickadee lisps amid the evergreens, and the partridge and rabbit skulk beneath; but now a more dismal and fitting day dawns, and a different race of creatures awakes to express the meaning of Nature there.

Late in the evening I heard the distant rumbling of wagons over bridges, a sound heard farther than almost any other at night, the baying of dogs, and sometimes again the lowing of some disconsolate cow in a distant barnyard. In the meanwhile all the shore rang with the trump of bullfrogs, the sturdy spirits of ancient winebibbers and wassailers, still unrepentant, trying to sing a catch in their Stygian lake[4]—if the Walden nymphs will pardon the comparison, for though there are almost no weeds, there are frogs there —who would fain keep up the hilarious rules of their old festal tables, though their voices have waxed hoarse and solemnly grave, mocking at mirth, and the wine has lost its flavor, and become only liquor to distend their paunches, and sweet intoxication never comes to drown the memory of the past, but mere saturation and waterloggedness and distention. The most aldermanic, with his chin upon a heartleaf, which serves for a napkin to his drooling chaps, under this northern shore quaffs a deep draught of the once scorned water, and passes round the cup with the ejaculation *tr-r-r-oonk, tr-r-r-oonk, tr-r-r-oonk!* and straightway comes over the water from

3. Dante, *Inferno* III.i.9.

4. Like the river Styx, main river of the lower world in Greek mythology.

some distant cove the same password repeated, where the next in seniority and girth has gulped down to his mark;[5] and when this observance has made the circuit of the shores, then ejaculates the master of ceremonies, with satisfaction, *tr-r-r-oonk!* and each in his turn repeats the same down to the least distended, leakiest, and flabbiest paunched, that there be no mistake; and then the bowl goes round again and again, until the sun disperses the morning mist, and only the patriarch is not under the pond,[6] but vainly bellowing *troonk* from time to time, and pausing for a reply.

I am not sure that I ever heard the sound of cock-crowing from my clearing, and I thought that it might be worth the while to keep a cockerel for his music merely, as a singing bird. The note of this once wild Indian pheasant is certainly the most remarkable of any bird's, and if they could be naturalized without being domesticated, it would soon become the most famous sound in our woods, surpassing the clangor of the goose and the hooting of the owl; and then imagine the cackling of the hens to fill the pauses when their lords' clarions rested! No wonder that man added this bird to his tame stock—to say nothing of the eggs and drumsticks. To walk in a winter morning in a wood where these birds abounded, their native woods, and hear the wild cockerels crow on the trees, clear and shrill for miles over the resounding earth, drowning the feebler notes of other birds—think of it! It would put nations on the alert. Who would not be early to rise, and rise earlier and earlier every successive day of his life, till he became unspeakably healthy, wealthy, and wise? This foreign bird's note is celebrated by the poets of all countries along with the notes of their native songsters. All climates agree with brave Chanticleer. He is more indigenous even than the natives. His health is ever good, his lungs are sound, his spirits never flag. Even the sailor on the Atlantic and Pacific is awakened by his voice;[7] but its shrill sound never roused me from my slumbers. I kept neither dog, cat, cow, pig, nor hens, so that you would have said there was a deficiency of domestic sounds; neither the churn, nor the spinningwheel, nor even the singing of the kettle, nor the hissing of the urn, nor children crying, to comfort one. An old-fashioned man would have lost his senses or died of ennui before this. Not even rats in the wall, for they were starved out, or rather were never baited in—only squirrels on the roof and under the floor, a whippoorwill on the ridgepole, a bluejay screaming beneath the window, a hare or woodchuck under the house, a screech-owl or a cat-owl behind it, a flock of wild geese or a laughing loon on the pond, and a fox to bark in the night. Not

5. In ancient drinking bouts, the glasses were marked to indicate how much each man was expected to drink.
6. I.e., under the table.

7. New England sea captains often took a flock of hens and cocks on board ship to furnish a supply of eggs and fresh meat.

even a lark or an oriole, those mild plantation birds, ever visited
my clearing. No cockerels to crow nor hens to cackle in the yard.
No yard! but unfenced Nature reaching up to your very sills. A
young forest growing up under your windows, and wild sumachs
and blackberry vines breaking through into your cellar; sturdy pitch-
pines rubbing and creaking against the shingles for want of room,
their roots reaching quite under the house. Instead of a scuttle or
a blind blown off in the gale, a pine tree snapped off or torn up
by the roots behind your house for fuel. Instead of no path to the
front-yard gate in the Great Snow, no gate—no front yard—and
no path to the civilized world.

Higher Laws

As I came home through the woods with my string of fish, trailing my pole, it being now quite dark, I caught a glimpse of a woodchuck stealing across my path, and felt a strange thrill of savage
delight, and was strongly tempted to seize and devour him raw; not
that I was hungry then, except for that wildness which he represented. Once or twice, however, while I lived at the pond, I found
myself ranging the woods, like a half-starved hound, with a strange
abandonment, seeking some kind of venison which I might devour, and no morsel could have been too savage for me. The wildest scenes had become unaccountably familiar. I found in myself,
and still find, an instinct toward a higher, or, as it is named, spiritual
life, as do most men, and another toward a primitive rank and
savage one, and I reverence them both. I love the wild not less
than the good. The wildness and adventure that are in fishing still
recommended it to me. I like sometimes to take rank hold on life
and spend my day more as the animals do. Perhaps I have owed
to this employment and to hunting, when quite young, my closest
acquaintance with Nature. They early introduce us to and detain
us in scenery with which otherwise, at that age, we should have
little acquaintance. Fishermen, hunters, woodchoppers, and others,
spending their lives in the fields and woods, in a peculiar sense a
part of Nature themselves, are often in a more favorable mood for
observing her, in the intervals of their pursuits, than philosophers
or poets even, who approach her with expectation. She is not afraid
to exhibit herself to them. The traveler on the prairie is naturally a
hunter, on the headwaters of the Missouri and Columbia a trapper,
and at the Falls of St. Mary[8] a fisherman. He who is only a traveler
learns things at second-hand and by the halves, and is poor authority. We are most interested when science reports what those men
already know practically or instinctively, for that alone is a true
humanity, or account of human experience.

8. Probably the falls of the St. Mary's River (between U.S. and Canada).

They mistake who assert that the Yankee has few amusements, because he has not so many public holidays, and men and boys do not play so many games as they do in England, for here the more primitive but solitary amusements of hunting, fishing, and the like have not yet given place to the former. Almost every New England boy among my contemporaries shouldered a fowling piece between the ages of ten and fourteen; and his hunting and fishing grounds were not limited, like the preserves of an English nobleman, but were more boundless even than those of a savage. No wonder, then, that he did not oftener stay to play on the common. But already a change is taking place, owing not to an increased humanity but to an increased scarcity of game, for perhaps the hunter is the greatest friend of the animals hunted, not excepting the Humane Society.

Moreover, when at the pond, I wished sometimes to add fish to my fare for variety. I have actually fished from the same kind of necessity that the first fishers did. Whatever humanity I might conjure up against it was all factitious, and concerned my philosophy more than my feelings. I speak of fishing only now, for I had long felt differently about fowling, and sold my gun before I went to the woods. Not that I am less humane than others, but I did not perceive that my feelings were much affected. I did not pity the fishes nor the worms. This was habit. As for fowling, during the last years that I carried a gun my excuse was that I was studying ornithology, and sought only new or rare birds. But I confess that I am now inclined to think that there is a finer way of studying ornithology than this. It requires so much closer attention to the habits of the birds, that, if for that reason only, I have been willing to omit the gun. Yet notwithstanding the objection on the score of humanity, I am compelled to doubt if equally valuable sports are ever substituted for these; and when some of my friends have asked me anxiously about their boys, whether they should let them hunt, I have answered, yes—remembering that it was one of the best parts of my education—*make* them hunters, though sportsmen only at first, if possible, mighty hunters at last, so that they shall not find game large enough for them in this or any vegetable wilderness—hunters as well as fishers of men.[9] Thus far I am of the opinion of Chaucer's nun, who

> "yave not of the text a pulled hen
> That saith that hunters ben not holy men."[1]

There is a period in the history of the individual, as of the race, when the hunters are the "best men," as the Algonquins called them. We cannot but pity the boy who has never fired a gun; he

9. Mark i.17.
1. Chaucer, General Prologue to the
Canterbury Tales; but the lines are said of the monk rather than of the nun.

is no more humane, while his education has been sadly neglected. This was my answer with respect to those youths who were bent on this pursuit, trusting that they would soon outgrow it. No humane being, past the thoughtless age of boyhood, will wantonly murder any creature, which holds its life by the same tenure that he does. The hare in its extremity cries like a child. I warn you, mothers, that my sympathies do not always make the usual phil-*anthropic* distinctions.

Such is oftenest the young man's introduction to the forest, and the most original part of himself. He goes thither at first as a hunter and fisher, until at last, if he has the seeds of a better life in him, he distinguishes his proper objects, as a poet or naturalist it may be, and leaves the gun and fish-pole behind. The mass of men are still and always young in this respect. In some countries a hunting parson is no uncommon sight. Such a one might make a good shepherd's dog, but is far from being the Good Shepherd. I have been surprised to consider that the only obvious employment, except wood-chopping, ice-cutting, or the like business, which ever to my knowledge detained at Walden Pond for a whole half day any of my fellow citizens, whether fathers or children of the town, with just one exception, was fishing. Commonly they did not think that they were lucky, or well paid for their time, unless they got a long string of fish, though they had the opportunity of seeing the pond all the while. They might go there a thousand times before the sediment of fishing would sink to the bottom and leave their purpose pure; but no doubt such a clarifying process would be going on all the while. The governor and his council[2] faintly remember the pond, for they went a-fishing there when they were boys; but now they are too old and dignified to go a-fishing, and so they know it no more forever. Yet even they expect to go to heaven at last. If the legislature regards it, it is chiefly to regulate the number of hooks to be used there; but they know nothing about the hook of hooks with which to angle for the pond itself, impaling the legislature for a bait. Thus, even in civilized communities, the embryo man passes through the hunter stage of development.

I have found repeatedly, of late years, that I cannot fish without falling a little in self-respect. I have tried it again and again. I have skill at it, and, like many of my fellows, a certain instinct for it, which revives from time to time, but always when I have done I feel that it would have been better if I had not fished. I think that I do not mistake. It is a faint intimation, yet so are the first streaks of morning. There is unquestionably this instinct in me which belongs to the lower orders of creation; yet with every year I am less a fisherman, though without more humanity or even

2. In Massachusetts a council is elected to advise the governor on affairs of state.

wisdom; at present I am no fisherman at all. But I see that if I were to live in a wilderness I should again be tempted to become a fisher and hunter in earnest. Beside, there is something essentially unclean about this diet and all flesh, and I began to see where housework commences, and whence the endeavor, which costs so much, to wear a tidy and respectable appearance each day, to keep the house sweet and free from all ill odors and sights. Having been my own butcher and scullion and cook, as well as the gentleman for whom the dishes were served up, I can speak from an unusually complete experience. The practical objection to animal food in my case was its uncleanness; and besides, when I had caught and cleaned and cooked and eaten my fish, they seemed not to have fed me essentially. It was insignificant and unnecessary, and cost more than it came to. A little bread or a few potatoes would have done as well, with less trouble and filth. Like many of my contemporaries, I had rarely for many years used animal food, or tea, or coffee, etc.; not so much because of any ill effects which I had traced to them, as because they were not agreeable to my imagination. The repugnance to animal food is not the effect of experience, but is an instinct. It appeared more beautiful to live low and fare hard in many respects; and though I never did so, I went far enough to please my imagination. I believe that every man who has ever been earnest to preserve his higher or poetic faculties in the best condition has been particularly inclined to abstain from animal food, and from much food of any kind. It is a significant fact, stated by entomologists, I find it in Kirby and Spence, that "some insects in their perfect state, though furnished with organs of feeding, make no use of them"; and they lay it down as "a general rule, that almost all insects in this state eat much less than in that of larvae. The voracious caterpillar when transformed into a butterfly . . . and the gluttonous maggot when become a fly,"[3] content themselves with a drop or two of honey or some other sweet liquid. The abdomen under the wings of the butterfly still represents the larva. This is the tidbit which tempts his insectivorous fate. The gross feeder is a man in the larva state; and there are whole nations in that condition, nations without fancy or imagination, whose vast abdomens betray them.

It is hard to provide and cook so simple and clean a diet as will not offend the imagination; but this, I think, is to be fed when we feed the body; they should both sit down at the same table. Yet perhaps this may be done. The fruits eaten temperately need not make us ashamed of our appetites, nor interrupt the worthiest pursuits. But put an extra condiment into your dish, and it will poison you. It is not worth the while to live by rich cookery. Most men

3. William Kirby and William Spence, *An Introduction to Entomology* (1846), p. 258.

would feel shame if caught preparing with their own hands precisely such a dinner, whether of animal or vegetable food, as is every day prepared for them by others. Yet till this is otherwise we are not civilized, and, if gentlemen and ladies, are not true men and women. This certainly suggests what change is to be made. It may be vain to ask why the imagination will not be reconciled to flesh and fat. I am satisfied that it is not. Is it not a reproach that man is a carnivorous animal? True, he can and does live, in a great measure, by preying on other animals; but this is a miserable way—as anyone who will go to snaring rabbits, or slaughtering lambs, may learn—and he will be regarded as a benefactor of his race who shall teach man to confine himself to a more innocent and wholesome diet. Whatever my own practice may be, I have no doubt that it is a part of the destiny of the human race, in its gradual improvement, to leave off eating animals, as surely as the savage tribes have left off eating each other when they came in contact with the more civilized.

If one listens to the faintest but constant suggestions of his genius, which are certainly true, he sees not to what extremes, or even insanity, it may lead him; and yet that way, as he grows more resolute and faithful, his road lies. The faintest assured objection which one healthy man feels will at length prevail over the arguments and customs of mankind. No man ever followed his genius till it misled him. Though the result were bodily weakness, yet perhaps no one can say that the consequences were to be regretted, for these were a life in conformity to higher principles. If the day and the night are such that you greet them with joy, and life emits a fragrance like flowers and sweet-scented herbs, is more elastic, more starry, more immortal—that is your success. All nature is your congratulation, and you have cause momentarily to bless yourself. The greatest gains and values are farthest from being appreciated. We easily come to doubt if they exist. We soon forget them. They are the highest reality. Perhaps the facts most astounding and most real are never communicated by man to man. The true harvest of my daily life is somewhat as intangible and indescribable as the tints of morning or evening. It is a little stardust caught, a segment of the rainbow which I have clutched.

Yet, for my part, I was never unusually squeamish; I could sometimes eat a fried rat with a good relish, if it were necessary. I am glad to have drunk water so long, for the same reason that I prefer the natural sky to an opium-eater's heaven. I would fain keep sober always; and there are infinite degrees of drunkenness. I believe that water is the only drink for a wise man; wine is not so noble a liquor; and think of dashing the hopes of a morning with a cup of warm coffee, or of an evening with a dish of tea! Ah, how low I fall when

I am tempted by them! Even music may be intoxicating. Such apparently slight causes destroyed Greece and Rome, and will destroy England and America. Of all ebriosity, who does not prefer to be intoxicated by the air he breathes? I have found it to be the most serious objection to coarse labors long continued, that they compelled me to eat and drink coarsely also. But to tell the truth, I find myself at present somewhat less particular in these respects. I carry less religion to the table, ask no blessing; not because I am wiser than I was, but, I am obliged to confess, because, however much it is to be regretted, with years I have grown more coarse and indifferent. Perhaps these questions are entertained only in youth, as most believe of poetry. My practice is "nowhere," my opinion is here. Nevertheless I am far from regarding myself as one of those privileged ones to whom the Ved refers when it says, that "he who has true faith in the Omnipresent Supreme Being may eat all that exists,"[4] that is, is not bound to inquire what is his food, or who prepares it; and even in their case it is to be observed, as a Hindu commentator has remarked, that the Vedant limits this privilege to "the time of distress."

Who has not sometimes derived an inexpressible satisfaction from his food in which appetite had no share? I have been thrilled to think that I owed a mental perception to the commonly gross sense of taste, that I have been inspired through the palate, that some berries which I had eaten on a hillside had fed my genius. "The soul not being mistress of herself," says Thseng-tseu, "one looks, and one does not see; one listens, and one does not hear; one eats, and one does not know the savor of food."[5] He who distinguishes the true savor of his food can never be a glutton; he who does not cannot be otherwise. A puritan may go to his brown-bread crust with as gross an appetite as ever an alderman to his turtle. Not that food which entereth into the mouth defileth a man,[6] but the appetite with which it is eaten. It is neither the quality nor the quantity, but the devotion to sensual savors; when that which is eaten is not a viand to sustain our animal, or inspire our spiritual life, but food for the worms that possess us. If the hunter has a taste for mud-turtles, muskrats, and other such savage tidbits, the fine lady indulges a taste for jelly made of a calf's foot, or for sardines from over the sea, and they are even. He goes to the mill-pond, she to her preserve-pot. The wonder is how they, how you and I, can live this slimy beastly life, eating and drinking.

Our whole life is startlingly moral. There is never an instant's truce between virtue and vice. Goodness is the only investment that

4. Rajah Roy's *Translation of Several of the Veds* (1832), p. 21. The Veds (or Vedas) were Hindu religious books.

5. Confucius, *The Great Learning* VII.10.
6. Matthew xv.18.

never fails. In the music of the harp which trembles round the world it is the insisting on this which thrills us. The harp is the traveling patterer for the Universe's Insurance Company, recommending its laws, and our little goodness is all the assessment that we pay. Though the youth at last grows indifferent, the laws of the universe are not indifferent, but are forever on the side of the most sensitive. Listen to every zephyr for some reproof, for it is surely there, and he is unfortunate who does not hear it. We cannot touch a string or move a stop but the charming moral transfixes us. Many an irksome noise, go a long way off, is heard as music, a proud sweet satire on the meanness of our lives.

We are conscious of an animal in us, which awakens in proportion as our higher nature slumbers. It is reptile[7] and sensual, and perhaps cannot be wholly expelled; like the worms which, even in life and health, occupy our bodies. Possibly we may withdraw from it, but never change its nature. I fear that it may enjoy a certain health of its own; that we may be well, yet not pure. The other day I picked up the lower jaw of a hog, with white and sound teeth and tusks, which suggested that there was an animal health and vigor distinct from the spiritual. This creature succeeded by other means than temperance and purity. "That in which men differ from brute beasts," says Mencius, "is a thing very inconsiderable; the common herd lose it very soon; superior men preserve it carefully."[8] Who knows what sort of life would result if we had attained to purity? If I knew so wise a man as could teach me purity I would go to seek him forthwith. "A command over our passions, and over the external senses of the body, and good acts, are declared by the Ved to be indispensable in the mind's approximation to God."[9] Yet the spirit can for the time pervade and control every member and function of the body, and transmute what in form is the grossest sensuality into purity and devotion. The generative energy, which, when we are loose, dissipates and makes us unclean, when we are continent invigorates and inspires us. Chastity is the flowering of man; and what are called Genius, Heroism, Holiness, and the like, are but various fruits which succeed it. Man flows at once to God when the channel of purity is open. By turns our purity inspires and our impurity casts us down. He is blessed who is assured that the animal is dying out in him day by day, and the divine being established. Perhaps there is none but has cause for shame on account of the inferior and brutish nature to which he is allied. I fear that we are such gods or demigods

7. Cf. Nathaniel Hawthorne's short story, "Egotism, or the Bosom Serpent."
8. *Works of Mencius* IV.ii.10. Mencius (Meng-Tse) was a Chinese philosopher of the 3rd century B.C.
9. *Translation of Several of the Veds,* p. 19.

only as fauns and satyrs, the divine allied to beasts, the creatures of appetite, and that, to some extent, our very life is our disgrace.—

> "How happy 's he who hath due place assigned
> To his beasts and disafforested his mind!
> .   .   .   .
> Can use his horse, goat, wolf, and ev'ry beast,
> And is not ass himself to all the rest!
> Else man not only is the herd of swine,
> But he's those devils too which did incline
> Them to a headlong rage, and made them worse."[1]

All sensuality is one, though it takes many forms; all purity is one. It is the same whether a man eat, or drink, or cohabit, or sleep sensually. They are but one appetite, and we only need to see a person do any one of these things to know how great a sensualist he is. The impure can neither stand nor sit with purity. When the reptile is attacked at one mouth of his burrow, he shows himself at another. If you would be chaste, you must be temperate. What is chastity? How shall a man know if he is chaste? He shall not know it. We have heard of this virtue, but we know not what it is. We speak conformably to the rumor which we have heard. From exertion come wisdom and purity; from sloth ignorance and sensuality. In the student sensuality is a sluggish habit of mind. An unclean person is universally a slothful one, one who sits by a stove, whom the sun shines on prostrate, who reposes without being fatigued. If you would avoid uncleanness, and all the sins, work earnestly, though it be at cleaning a stable. Nature is hard to be overcome, but she must be overcome. What avails it that you are Christian, if you are not purer than the heathen, if you deny yourself no more, if you are not more religious? I know of many systems of religion esteemed heathenish whose precepts fill the reader with shame, and provoke him to new endeavors, though it be to the performance of rites merely.

I hesitate to say these things, but it is not because of the subject —I care not how obscene my *words* are—but because I cannot speak of them without betraying my impurity. We discourse freely without shame of one form of sensuality, and are silent about another. We are so degraded that we cannot speak simply of the necessary functions of human nature. In earlier ages, in some countries, every function was reverently spoken of and regulated by law. Nothing was too trivial for the Hindu lawgiver, however offensive it may be to modern taste. He teaches how to eat, drink, cohabit, void excrement and urine, and the like, elevating what is

1. John Donne, "To Sr Edward Herbert at Iulyers."

mean, and does not falsely excuse himself by calling these things trifles.

Every man is the builder of a temple,[2] called his body, to the god he worships, after a style purely his own, nor can he get off by hammering marble instead. We are all sculptors and painters, and our material is our own flesh and blood and bones. Any nobleness begins at once to refine a man's features, any meanness or sensuality to imbrute them.

John Farmer sat at his door one September evening, after a hard day's work, his mind still running on his labor more or less. Having bathed he sat down to re-create his intellectual man. It was a rather cool evening, and some of his neighbors were apprehending a frost. He had not attended to the train of his thoughts long when he heard someone playing on a flute, and that sound harmonized with his mood. Still he thought of his work; but the burden of his thought was, that though this kept running in his head, and he found himself planning and contriving it against his will, yet it concerned him very little. It was no more than the scurf of his skin, which was constantly shuffled off. But the notes of the flute came home to his ears out of a different sphere from that he worked in, and suggested work for certain faculties which slumbered in him. They gently did away with the street, and the village, and the state in which he lived. A voice said to him, Why do you stay here and live this mean moiling life, when a glorious existence is possible for you? Those same stars twinkle over other fields than these. But how to come out of this condition and actually migrate thither? All that he could think of was to practice some new austerity, to let his mind descend into his body and redeem it, and treat himself with ever increasing respect.

From *Brute Neighbors*

* * * Why do precisely these objects which we behold make a world? Why has man just these species of animals for his neighbors; as if nothing but a mouse could have filled this crevice? I suspect that Pilpay & Co.[3] have put animals to their best use, for they are all beasts of burden, in a sense, made to carry some portion of our thoughts.

The mice which haunted my house were not the common ones, which are said to have been introduced into the country, but a wild native kind not found in the village. I sent one to a distinguished naturalist,[4] and it interested him much. When I was building, one of these had its nest underneath the house, and before I had laid the second floor, and swept out the shavings, would

2. I Corinthians iii.16.
3. Pilpay was the author of a collection of East Indian fables.
4. Thoreau often collected specimens for Louis Agassiz.

come out regularly at lunch time and pick up the crumbs at my feet. It probably had never seen a man before; and it soon became quite familiar, and would run over my shoes and up my clothes. It could readily ascend the sides of the room by short impulses, like a squirrel, which it resembled in its motions. At length, as I leaned with my elbow on the bench one day, it ran up my clothes, and along my sleeve, and round and round the paper which held my dinner, while I kept the latter close, and dodged and played at bo-peep with it; and when at last I held still a piece of cheese between my thumb and finger, it came and nibbled it, sitting in my hand, and afterward cleaned its face and paws, like a fly, and walked away.

A phoebe soon built in my shed, and a robin for protection in a pine which grew against the house. In June the partridge (*Tetrao umbellus*) which is so shy a bird, led her brood past my windows, from the woods in the rear to the front of my house, clucking and calling to them like a hen, and in all her behavior proving herself the hen of the woods. The young suddenly disperse on your approach, at a signal from the mother, as if a whirlwind had swept them away, and they so exactly resemble the dried leaves and twigs that many a traveler has placed his foot in the midst of a brood, and heard the whir of the old bird as she flew off, and her anxious calls and mewing, or seen her trail her wings to attract his attention, without suspecting their neighborhood. The parent will sometimes roll and spin round before you in such a dishabille, that you cannot for a few moments detect what kind of creature it is. The young squat still and flat, often running their heads under a leaf, and mind only their mother's directions given from a distance, nor will your approach make them run again and betray themselves. You may even tread on them, or have your eyes on them for a minute, without discovering them. I have held them in my open hand at such a time, and still their only care, obedient to their mother and their instinct, was to squat there without fear or trembling. So perfect is this instinct, that once, when I had laid them on the leaves again, and one accidentally fell on its side, it was found with the rest in exactly the same position ten minutes afterward. They are not callow like the young of most birds, but more perfectly developed and precocious even than chickens. The remarkably adult yet innocent expression of their open and serene eyes is very memorable. All intelligence seems reflected in them. They suggest not merely the purity of infancy, but a wisdom clarified by experience. Such an eye was not born when the bird was, but is coeval with the sky it reflects. The woods do not yield another such a gem. The traveler does not often look into such a limpid well. The ignorant or reckless sportsman often shoots the parent at such a time, and leaves these innocents to fall a prey to some prowling beast or bird, or

484 · Henry David Thoreau

gradually mingle with the decaying leaves which they so much resemble. It is said that when hatched by a hen they will directly disperse on some alarm, and so are lost, for they never hear the mother's call which gathers them again. These were my hens and chickens.

It is remarkable how many creatures live wild and free though secret in the woods, and still sustain themselves in the neighborhood of towns, suspected by hunters only. How retired the otter manages to live here! He grows to be four feet long, as big as a small boy, perhaps without any human being getting a glimpse of him. I formerly saw the raccoon in the woods behind where my house is built, and probably still heard their whinnering at night. Commonly I rested an hour or two in the shade at noon, after planting, and ate my lunch, and read a little by a spring which was the source of a swamp and of a brook, oozing from under Brister's Hill, half a mile from my field. The approach to this was through a succession of descending grassy hollows, full of young pitch pines, into a larger wood about the swamp. There, in a very secluded and shaded spot, under a spreading white pine, there was yet a clean firm sward to sit on. I had dug out the spring and made a well of clear gray water, where I could dip up a pailful without roiling it, and thither I went for this purpose almost every day in mid-summer, when the pond was warmest. Thither too the woodcock led her brood, to probe the mud for worms, flying but a foot above them down the bank, while they ran in a troop beneath; but at last, spying me, she would leave her young and circle round and round me, nearer and nearer till within four or five feet, pretending broken wings and legs, to attract my attention, and get off her young, who would already have taken up their march, with faint wiry peep, single file through the swamp, as she directed. Or I heard the peep of the young when I could not see the parent bird. There too the turtle-doves[5] sat over the spring, or fluttered from bough to bough of the soft white pines over my head; or the red squirrel, coursing down the nearest bough, was particularly familiar and inquisitive. You only need sit still long enough in some attractive spot in the woods that all its inhabitants may exhibit themselves to you by turns.

I was witness to events of a less peaceful character. One day when I went out to my wood pile, or rather my pile of stumps, I observed two large ants, the one red, the other much larger, nearly half an inch long, and black, fiercely contending with one another. Having once got hold they never let go, but struggled and wrestled and rolled on the chips incessantly. Looking farther, I was surprised to find that the chips were covered with such combatants, that it

5. Now more commonly called mourning doves.

was not a *duellum*, but a *bellum*, a war between two races of ants, the red always pitted against the black, and frequently two red ones to one black. The legions of these Myrmidons[6] covered all the hills and vales in my wood-yard, and the ground was already strewn with the dead and dying, both red and black. It was the only battle which I have ever witnessed, the only battlefield I ever trod while the battle was raging; internecine war; the red republicans on the one hand, and the black imperialists on the other. On every side they were engaged in deadly combat, yet without any noise that I could hear, and human soldiers never fought so resolutely. I watched a couple that were fast locked in each other's embraces, in a little sunny valley amid the chips, now at noonday prepared to fight till the sun went down, or life went out. The smaller red champion had fastened himself like a vice to his adversary's front, and through all the tumblings on that field never for an instant ceased to gnaw at one of his feelers near the root, having already caused the other to go by the board; while the stronger black one dashed him from side to side, and, as I saw on looking nearer, had already divested him of several of his members. They fought with more pertinacity than bulldogs. Neither manifested the least disposition to retreat. It was evident that their battle-cry was Conquer or die.[7] In the meanwhile there came along a single red ant on the hillside of this valley, evidently full of excitement, who either had despatched his foe, or had not yet taken part in the battle; probably the latter, for he had lost none of his limbs; whose mother had charged him to return with his shield or upon it.[8] Or perchance he was some Achilles, who had nourished his wrath apart, and had now come to avenge or rescue his Patroclus.[9] He saw this unequal combat from afar—for the blacks were nearly twice the size of the red—he drew near with rapid pace till he stood on his guard within half an inch of the combatants; then, watching his opportunity, he sprang upon the black warrior, and commenced his operations near the root of his right foreleg, leaving the foe to select among his own members; and so there were three united for life, as if a new kind of attraction had been invented which put all other locks and cements to shame. I should not have wondered by this time to find that they had their respective musical bands stationed on some eminent chip, and playing their national airs the while, to excite the slow and cheer the dying combatants. I was myself excited somewhat even as if they had been men. The more you think of it, the less the difference. And certainly there is not the fight recorded in Concord history, at least, if in the history of America, that will

6. Warriors from ancient Thessaly who aided Achilles in the Trojan War.
7. The motto of the Duke of Kent.
8. From the "Sayings of the Spartan Women" as recorded by Plutarch.
9. Achilles refused to participate in the Trojan War until angered by the death of his friend Patroclus.

bear a moment's comparison with this, whether for the numbers engaged in it, or for the patriotism and heroism displayed. For numbers and for carnage it was an Austerlitz or Dresden.[1] Concord Fight! Two killed on the patriots' side, and Luther Blanchard wounded! Why here every ant was a Buttrick—"Fire! for God's sake fire!"—and thousands shared the fate of Davis and Hosmer.[2] There was not one hireling there. I have no doubt that it was a principle they fought for, as much as our ancestors, and not to avoid a three-penny tax on their tea; and the results of this battle will be as important and memorable to those whom it concerns as those of the battle of Bunker Hill, at least.

I took up the chip on which the three I have particularly described were struggling, carried it into my house, and placed it under a tumbler on my window sill, in order to see the issue. Holding a microscope to the first-mentioned red ant, I saw that, though he was assiduously gnawing at the near foreleg of his enemy, having severed his remaining feeler, his own breast was all torn away, exposing what vitals he had there to the jaws of the black warrior, whose breastplate was apparently too thick for him to pierce; and the dark carbuncles of the sufferer's eyes shone with ferocity such as war only could excite. They struggled half an hour longer under the tumbler, and when I looked again the black soldier had severed the heads of his foes from their bodies, and the still living heads were hanging on either side of him like ghastly trophies at his saddle-bow, still apparently as firmly fastened as ever, and he was endeavoring with feeble struggles, being without feelers and with only the remnant of a leg, and I know not how many other wounds, to divest himself of them; which at length, after half an hour more, he accomplished. I raised the glass, and he went off over the window sill in that crippled state. Whether he finally survived that combat, and spent the remainder of his days in some Hotel des Invalides,[3] I do not know; but I thought that his industry would not be worth much thereafter. I never learned which party was victorious, nor the cause of the war; but I felt for the rest of that day as if I had had my feelings excited and harrowed by witnessing the struggle, the ferocity and carnage, of a human battle before my door.

Kirby and Spence[4] tell us that the battles of ants have long been celebrated and the date of them recorded, though they say that Huber is the only modern author who appears to have witnessed them. "Aeneas Sylvius,"[5] say they, "after giving a very circum-

---

1. Two of Napoleon's bloodiest battles.
2. Soldiers killed in the Battle of Concord of April 19, 1775.
3. A hospital for invalided veterans in Paris, now the site of Napoleon's tomb.

4. *An Introduction to Entomology* (1846), pp. 361–62. François Huber (1750–1831), a French entomologist.
5. Better known as Pope Pius II (1405–64).

stantial account of one contested with great obstinacy by a great and small species on the trunk of a pear tree," adds that " 'This action was fought in the pontificate of Eugenius the Fourth,[6] in the presence of Nicholas Pistoriensis, an eminent lawyer, who related the whole history of the battle with the greatest fidelity.' A similar engagement between great and small ants is recorded by Olaus Magnus,[7] in which the small ones, being victorious, are said to have buried the bodies of their own soldiers, but left those of their giant enemies a prey to the birds. This event happened previous to the expulsion of the tyrant Christiern the Second[8] from Sweden." The battle which I witnessed took place in the Presidency of Polk, five years before the passage of Webster's Fugitive-Slave Bill.[9]

Many a village Bose,[1] fit only to course a mud-turtle in a victualing cellar, sported his heavy quarters in the woods, without the knowledge of his master, and ineffectually smelled at old fox burrows and woodchucks' holes; led perchance by some slight cur which nimbly threaded the wood, and might still inspire a natural terror in its denizens; now far behind his guide, barking like a canine bull toward some small squirrel which had treed itself for scrutiny, then, cantering off, bending the bushes with his weight, imagining that he is on the track of some stray member of the jerbilla family.[2] Once I was surprised to see a cat walking along the stony shore of the pond, for they rarely wander so far from home. The surprise was mutual. Nevertheless the most domestic cat, which has lain on a rug all her days, appears quite at home in the woods, and, by her sly and stealthy behavior, proves herself more native there than the regular inhabitants. Once, when berrying, I met with a cat with young kittens in the woods, quite wild, and they all, like their mother had their backs up and were fiercely spitting at me. A few years before I lived in the woods there was what was called a "winged cat" in one of the farmhouses in Lincoln nearest the pond, Mr. Gilian Baker's. When I called to see her in June, 1842, she was gone a-hunting in the woods, as was her wont (I am not sure whether it was a male or female, and so use the more common pronoun), but her mistress told me that she came into the neighborhood a little more than a year before, in April, and was finally taken into their house; that she was of a dark brownish-gray color, with a white spot on her throat, and white feet, and had a large bushy tail like a fox; that in the winter the fur grew thick and flatted out along her sides, forming strips ten or twelve inches long by two and a half wide, and under her chin like a muff, the

6. Pope from 1431 to 1447.
7. Archbishop of Upsala (1490–1558).
8. 16th-century ruler of Denmark and Sweden.
9. Daniel Webster was not the author of the Fugitive Slave Bill, but he was

roundly condemned by the abolitionists for its passage.
1. Popular 19th-century name for dogs.
2. Or Gerbillus; i.e., member of the mouse family.

upper side loose, the under matted like felt, and in the spring these appendages dropped off. They gave me a pair of her "wings," which I keep still. There is no appearance of a membrane about them. Some thought it was part flying-squirrel or some other wild animal, which is not impossible, for, according to naturalists, prolific hybrids have been produced by the union of the marten and domestic cat. This would have been the right kind of cat for me to keep, if I had kept any; for why should not a poet's cat be winged as well as his horse?[3]

In the fall the loon (*Colymbus glacialis*) came, as usual, to moult and bathe in the pond, making the woods ring with his wild laughter before I had risen. At rumor of his arrival all the Mill-dam sportsmen are on the alert, in gigs and on foot, two by two and three by three, with patent rifles and conical balls and spy-glasses. They come rustling through the woods like autumn leaves, at least ten men to one loon. Some station themselves on this side of the pond, some on that, for the poor bird cannot be omnipresent; if he dive here he must come up there. But now the kind October wind rises, rustling the leaves and rippling the surface of the water, so that no loon can be heard or seen, though his foes sweep the pond with spyglasses, and make the woods resound with their discharges. The waves generously rise and dash angrily, taking sides with all waterfowl, and our sportsmen must beat a retreat to town and shop and unfinished jobs. But they were too often successful. When I went to get a pail of water early in the morning I frequently saw this stately bird sailing out of my cove within a few rods. If I endeavored to overtake him in a boat, in order to see how he would maneuver, he would dive and be completely lost, so that I did not discover him again, sometimes, till the latter part of the day. But I was more than a match for him on the surface. He commonly went off in a rain.

As I was paddling along the north shore one very calm October afternoon, for such days especially they settle onto the lakes, like the milkweed down, having looked in vain over the pond for a loon, suddenly one, sailing out from the shore toward the middle a few rods in front of me, set up his wild laugh and betrayed himself. I pursued with a paddle and he dived, but when he came up I was nearer than before. He dived again, but I miscalculated the direction he would take, and we were fifty rods apart when he came to the surface this time, for I had helped to widen the interval; and again he laughed long and loud, and with more reason than before. He maneuvered so cunningly that I could not get within half a dozen rods of him. Each time, when he came to the surface, turning his head this way and that, he coolly surveyed the water

3. Pegasus, the winged horse of Greek mythology, is traditionally the steed of poets.

and the land, and apparently chose his course so that he might come up where there was the widest expanse of water and at the greatest distance from the boat. It was surprising how quickly he made up his mind and put his resolve into execution. He led me at once to the widest part of the pond, and could not be driven from it. While he was thinking one thing in his brain, I was endeavoring to divine his thought in mine. It was a pretty game, played on the smooth surface of the pond, a man against a loon. Suddenly your adversary's checker disappears beneath the board, and the problem is to place yours nearest to where his will appear again. Sometimes he would come up unexpectedly on the opposite side of me, having apparently passed directly under the boat. So long-winded was he and so unweariable, that when he had swum farthest he would immediately plunge again, nevertheless; and then no wit could divine where in the deep pond, beneath the smooth surface, he might be speeding his way like a fish, for he had time and ability to visit the bottom of the pond in its deepest part. It is said that loons have been caught in the New York lakes eighty feet beneath the surface, with hooks set for trout[4]—though Walden is deeper than that. How surprised must the fishes be to see this ungainly visitor from another sphere speeding his way amid their schools! Yet he appeared to know his course as surely under water as on the surface, and swam much faster there. Once or twice I saw a ripple where he approached the surface, just put his head out to reconnoiter, and instantly dived again. I found that it was as well for me to rest on my oars and wait his reappearing as to endeavor to calculate where he would rise; for again and again, when I was straining my eyes over the surface one way, I would suddenly be startled by his unearthly laugh behind me. But why, after displaying so much cunning, did he invariably betray himself the moment he came up by that loud laugh? Did not his white breast enough betray him? He was indeed a silly loon, I thought. I could commonly hear the plash of the water when he came up, and so also detected him. But after an hour he seemed as fresh as ever, dived as willingly, and swam yet farther than at first. It was surprising to see how serenely he sailed off with unruffled breast when he came to the surface, doing all the work with his webbed feet beneath. His usual note was this demoniac laughter, yet somewhat like that of a waterfowl; but occasionally, when he had balked me most successfully and come up a long way off, he uttered a long-drawn unearthly howl, probably more like that of a wolf than any bird; as when a beast puts his muzzle to the ground and deliberately howls. This was his looning, perhaps

4. Susan Fenimore Cooper, *Rural Hours* (1850), p. 10. Miss Cooper was the daughter of the novelist James Fenimore Cooper.

the wildest sound that is ever heard here, making the woods ring far and wide. I concluded that he laughed in derision of my efforts, confident of his own resources. Though the sky was by this time overcast, the pond was so smooth that I could see where he broke the surface when I did not hear him. His white breast, the stillness of the air, and the smoothness of the water were all against him. At length, having come up fifty rods off, he uttered one of those prolonged howls, as if calling on the god of loons to aid him, and immediately there came a wind from the east and rippled the surface, and filled the whole air with misty rain, and I was impressed as if it were the prayer of the loon answered, and his god was angry with me; and so I left him disappearing far away on the tumultuous surface.

For hours, in fall days, I watched the ducks cunningly tack and veer and hold the middle of the pond, far from the sportsman; tricks which they will have less need to practice in Louisiana bayous. When compelled to rise they would sometimes circle round and round and over the pond at a considerable height, from which they could easily see to other ponds and the river, like black motes in the sky; and, when I thought they had gone off thither long since, they would settle down by a slanting flight of a quarter of a mile onto a distant part which was left free; but what beside safety they got by sailing in the middle of Walden I do not know, unless they love its water for the same reason that I do.

Conclusion

To the sick the doctors wisely recommend a change of air and scenery. Thank Heaven, here is not all the world. The buckeye does not grow in New England, and the mocking-bird is rarely heard here. The wild goose is more of a cosmopolite than we; he breaks his fast in Canada, takes a luncheon in the Ohio, and plumes himself for the night in a southern bayou. Even the bison, to some extent, keeps pace with the seasons, cropping the pastures of the Colorado only till a greener and sweeter grass awaits him by the Yellowstone. Yet we think that if rail fences are pulled down, and stone walls piled up on our farms, bounds are henceforth set to our lives and our fates decided. If you are chosen town clerk, forsooth, you cannot go to Tierra del Fuego[5] this summer: but you may go to the land of infernal fire nevertheless. The universe is wider than our views of it.

Yet we should oftener look over the tafferel of our craft, like curious passengers, and not make the voyage like stupid sailors

5. A group of islands at the southern tip of South America; Tierra del Fuego is literally translated as "land of fire."

picking oakum.[6] The other side of the globe is but the home of our correspondent. Our voyaging is only great-circle sailing,[7] and the doctors prescribe for diseases of the skin merely. One hastens to Southern Africa to chase the giraffe; but surely that is not the game he would be after. How long, pray, would a man hunt giraffes if he could? Snipes and woodcocks also may afford rare sport; but I trust it would be nobler game to shoot one's self.

> "Direct your eye right inward, and you'll find
> A thousand regions in your mind
> Yet undiscovered. Travel them, and be
> Expert in home-cosmography."[8]

What does Africa, what does the West, stand for? Is not our own interior white on the chart?[9] black though it may prove, like the coast, when discovered. Is it the source of the Nile, or the Niger, or the Mississippi, or a Northwest Passage around this continent, that we would find? Are these the problems which most concern mankind? Is Franklin the only man who is lost, that his wife should be so earnest to find him? Does Mr. Grinnell[1] know where he himself is? Be rather the Mungo Park, the Lewis and Clark and Frobisher,[2] of your own streams and oceans; explore your own higher latitudes—with shiploads of preserved meats to support you, if they be necessary; and pile the empty cans sky-high for a sign.[3] Were preserved meats invented to preserve meat merely? Nay, be a Columbus to whole new continents and worlds within you, opening new channels, not of trade, but of thought. Every man is the lord of a realm beside which the earthly empire of the Czar[4] is but a petty state, a hummock left by the ice. Yet some can be patriotic who have no *self*-respect, and sacrifice the greater to the less. They love the soil which makes their graves, but have no sympathy with the spirit which may still animate their clay. Patriotism is a maggot in their heads. What was the meaning of that South-Sea Exploring Expedition,[5] with all its parade and expense, but an indirect recog-

6. On sailing vessels a good part of the sailor's time was spent in preparing calking material (oakum) from old rope.
7. The shortest distance between two points on a globe is the arc cut by a plane passed through the center of the sphere.
8. William Habington, "To My Honoured Friend Sir. Ed. P. Knight." Thoreau misquotes the third word, which should read "eye-sight."
9. Unexplored areas are left blank on maps.
1. Henry Grinnell was the patron of an expedition sent out unsuccessfully to find the British explorer Sir John Franklin, lost in the Arctic in 1847.
2. Famous explorers: Park in Africa, Lewis and Clark in our Northwest, and Frobisher in many quarters of the globe.
3. One of the few clues found to the fate of Sir John Franklin was a pile of meat cans discovered by Elisha Kent Kane.
4. The largest body of land under one dominion in Thoreau's time.
5. An exploration of the Antarctic islands led by Charles Wilkes for the United States government from 1838 to 1842.

nition of the fact, that there are continents and seas in the moral world, to which every man is an isthmus or an inlet, yet unexplored by him, but that it is easier to sail many thousand miles through cold and storm and cannibals, in a government ship, with five hundred men and boys to assist one, than it is to explore the private sea, the Atlantic and Pacific Ocean of one's being alone.

"Erret, et extremos alter scrutetur Iberos.
Plus habet hic vitae, plus habet ille viae."[6]

Let them wander and scrutinize the outlandish Australians.
I have more of God, they more of the road.

It is not worth the while to go round the world to count the cats in Zanzibar. Yet do this even till you can do better, and you may perhaps find some "Symmes' Hole"[7] by which to get at the inside at last. England and France, Spain and Portugal, Gold Coast and Slave Coast, all front on this private sea; but no bark from them has ventured out of sight of land, though it is without doubt the direct way to India. If you would learn to speak all tongues and conform to the customs of all nations, if you would travel farther than all travelers, be naturalized in all climes, and cause the Sphinx to dash her head against a stone,[8] even obey the precept of the old philosopher, and Explore thyself. Herein are demanded the eye and the nerve. Only the defeated and deserters go to the wars, cowards that run away and enlist. Start now on the farthest western way, which does not pause at the Mississippi or the Pacific, nor conduct toward a worn-out China or Japan, but leads on direct a tangent to this sphere, summer and winter, day and night, sundown, moondown, and at last earth down too.

It is said that Mirabeau[9] took to highway robbery "to ascertain what degree of resolution was necessary in order to place one's self in formal opposition to the most sacred laws of society." He declared that "a soldier who fights in the ranks does not require half so much courage as a foot-pad"—"that honor and religion have never stood in the way of a well-considered and a firm resolve." This was manly, as the world goes; and yet it was idle, if not desperate. A saner man would have found himself often enough "in formal opposition" to what are deemed "the most sacred laws of society," through obedience to yet more sacred laws, and to have tested his resolution without going out of his way. It is not for a

6. Claudian, "Old Man of Verona." Thoreau has mistranslated "Iberos" ("Spaniards") as "Australians" to make the poem more appropriate to his time, and "vitae" ("of life") as "of God."
7. Capt. J. C. Symmes in 1818 advanced a theory that the world was hollow and open at both poles.
8. When Oedipus, in Greek mythology, solved the riddle of the Sphinx, she dashed her head against a rock and killed herself.
9. A statesman in the French Revolution. Thoreau is quoting from Harper's Monthly, I, 648.

man to put himself in such an attitude to society, but to maintain himself in whatever attitude he finds himself through obedience to the laws of his being which will never be one of opposition to a just government, if he should chance to meet with such.

I left the woods for as good a reason as I went there. Perhaps it seemed to me that I had several more lives to live, and could not spare any more time for that one. It is remarkable how easily and insensibly we fall into a particular route, and make a beaten track for ourselves. I had not lived there a week before my feet wore a path from my door to the pond-side; and though it is five or six years since I trod it, it is still quite distinct. It is true, I fear that others may have fallen into it, and so helped to keep it open. The surface of the earth is soft and impressible by the feet of men; and so with the paths which the mind travels. How worn and dusty, then, must be the highways of the world, how deep the ruts of tradition and conformity! I did not wish to take a cabin passage, but rather to go before the mast[1] and on the deck of the world, for there I could best see the moonlight amid the mountains. I do not wish to go below now.

I learned this, at least, by my experiment; that if one advances confidently in the direction of his dreams, and endeavors to live the life which he has imagined, he will meet with a success unexpected in common hours. He will put some things behind, will pass an invisible boundary; new, universal, and more liberal laws will begin to establish themselves around and within him; or the old laws be expanded, and interpreted in his favor in a more liberal sense, and he will live with the license of a higher order of beings. In proportion as he simplifies his life, the laws of the universe will appear less complex, and solitude will not be solitude, nor poverty poverty, nor weakness weakness. If you have built castles in the air, your work need not be lost; that is where they should be. Now put the foundations under them.

It is a ridiculous demand which England and America make, that you shall speak so that they can understand you. Neither men nor toadstools grow so. As if that were important, and there were not enough to understand you without them. As if Nature could support but one order of understandings, could not sustain birds as well as quadrupeds, flying as well as creeping things, and *hush* and *who*,[2] which Bright can understand, were the best English. As if there were safety in stupidity alone. I fear chiefly lest my expression may not be *extra-vagant* enough, may not wander far enough beyond the narrow limits of my daily experience, so as to be ade-

1. That is, to be a sailor rather than a passenger. Sailors' quarters are in front of the mast in sailing vessels.

2. Terms used in directing oxen. "Bright" was a common name for an ox.

quate to the truth of which I have been convinced. *Extra vagance!* it depends on how you are yarded. The migrating buffalo, which seeks new pastures in another latitude, is not extravagant like the cow which kicks over the pail, leaps the cowyard fence, and runs after her calf, in milking time. I desire to speak somewhere *without* bounds; like a man in a waking moment, to men in their waking moments; for I am convinced that I cannot exaggerate enough even to lay the foundation of a true expression. Who that has heard a strain of music feared then lest he should speak extravagantly any more forever? In view of the future or possible, we should live quite laxly and undefined in front, our outlines dim and misty on that side; as our shadows reveal an insensible perspiration toward the sun. The volatile truth of our words should continually betray the inadequacy of the residual statement. Their truth is instantly *translated*; its literal monument alone remains. The words which express our faith and piety are not definite; yet they are significant and fragrant like frankincense to superior natures.

Why level downward to our dullest perception always, and praise that as common sense? The commonest sense is the sense of men asleep, which they express by snoring. Sometimes we are inclined to class those who are once-and-a-half witted with the half-witted, because we appreciate only a third part of their wit. Some would find fault with the morning-red, if they ever got up early enough. "They pretend," as I hear, "that the verses of Kabir have four different senses; illusion, spirit, intellect, and the exoteric doctrine of the Vedas";[3] but in this part of the world it is considered a ground for complaint if a man's writings admit of more than one interpretation. While England endeavors to cure the potato-rot,[4] will not any endeavor to cure the brain-rot, which prevails so much more widely and fatally?

I do not suppose that I have attained to obscurity, but I should be proud if no more fatal fault were found with my pages on this score than was found with the Walden ice. Southern customers objected to its blue color, which is the evidence of its purity, as if it were muddy, and preferred the Cambridge ice, which is white, but tastes of weeds. The purity men love is like the mists which envelop the earth, and not like the azure ether beyond.

Some are dinning in our ears that we Americans, and moderns generally, are intellectual dwarfs compared with the ancients, or even the Elizabethan men. But what is that to the purpose? A living dog is better than a dead lion.[5] Shall a man go and hang himself because he belongs to the race of pygmies, and not be the biggest

3. M. Garcin de Tassy, *Histoire de la Littérature Hindoui* (1839), p. 279.
4. A severe blight struck the potato crop in the British Isles in 1846.
5. Ecclesiastes ix.4.

pygmy that he can? Let everyone mind his own business, and endeavor to be what he was made.

Why should we be in such desperate haste to succeed and in such desperate enterprises? If a man does not keep pace with his companions, perhaps it is because he hears a different drummer. Let him step to the music which he hears, however measured or far away. It is not important that he should mature as soon as an apple tree or an oak. Shall he turn his spring into summer? If the condition of things which we were made for is not yet, what were any reality which we can substitute? We will not be shipwrecked on a vain reality. Shall we with pains erect a heaven of blue glass over ourselves, though when it is done we shall be sure to gaze still at the true ethereal heaven far above, as if the former were not?

There was an artist in the city of Kouroo who was disposed to strive after perfection. One day it came into his mind to make a staff. Having considered that in an imperfect work time is an ingredient, but into a perfect work time does not enter, he said to himself, It shall be perfect in all respects, though I should do nothing else in my life. He proceeded instantly to the forest for wood, being resolved that it should not be made of unsuitable material; and as he searched for and rejected stick after stick, his friends gradually deserted him, for they grew old in their works and died, but he grew not older by a moment. His singleness of purpose and resolution, and his elevated piety, endowed him, without his knowledge, with perennial youth. As he made no compromise with Time, Time kept out of his way, and only sighed at a distance because he could not overcome him. Before he had found a stock in all respects suitable the city of Kouroo was a hoary ruin, and he sat on one of its mounds to peel the stick. Before he had given it the proper shape the dynasty of the Candahars was at an end, and with the point of the stick he wrote the name of the last of that race in the sand, and then resumed his work. By the time he had smoothed and polished the staff Kalpa[6] was no longer the pole-star; and ere he had put on the ferule and the head adorned with precious stones, Brahma had awoke and slumbered many times.[7] But why do I stay to mention these things? When the finishing stroke was put to his work, it suddenly expanded before the eyes of the astonished artist into the fairest of all the creations of Brahma. He had made a new system in making a staff, a world with full and fair proportions; in which, though the old cities and dynasties had passed away, fairer and more glorious ones had taken their places. And now he saw by the heap of shavings still fresh at his feet, that,

---

6. In Hindu literature, Kalpa is not a star but a period of approximately four billion years.

7. A day of Brahma was supposedly approximately two billion years.

for him and his work, the former lapse of time had been an illusion, and that no more time had elapsed than is required for a single scintillation from the brain of Brahma to fall on and inflame the tinder of a mortal brain. The material was pure, and his art was pure; how could the result be other than wonderful?

No face which we can give to a matter will stead us so well at last as the truth. This alone wears well. For the most part, we are not where we are, but in a false position. Through an infirmity of our natures, we suppose a case, and put ourselves into it, and hence are in two cases at the same time, and it is doubly difficult to get out. In sane moments we regard only the facts, the case that is. Say what you have to say, not what you ought. Any truth is better than make-believe. Tom Hyde, the tinker, standing on the gallows, was asked if he had anything to say. "Tell the tailors," said he, "to remember to make a knot in their thread before they take the first stitch." His companion's prayer is forgotten.

However mean your life is, meet it and live it; do not shun it and call it hard names. It is not so bad as you are. It looks poorest when you are richest. The faultfinder will find faults even in paradise. Love your life, poor as it is. You may perhaps have some pleasant, thrilling, glorious hours, even in a poorhouse. The setting sun is reflected from the windows of the almshouse as brightly as from the rich man's abode; the snow melts before its door as early in the spring. I do not see but a quiet mind may live as contentedly there, and have as cheering thoughts, as in a palace. The town's poor seem to me often to live the most independent lives of any. Maybe they are simply great enough to receive without misgiving. Most think that they are above being supported by the town; but it oftener happens that they are not above supporting themselves by dishonest means, which should be more disreputable. Cultivate poverty like a garden herb, like sage. Do not trouble yourself much to get new things, whether clothes or friends. Turn the old; return to them. Things do not change; we change. Sell your clothes and keep your thoughts. God will see that you do not want society. If I were confined to a corner of a garret all my days, like a spider, the world would be just as large to me while I had my thoughts about me. The philosopher said: "From an army of three divisions one can take away its general, and put it in disorder; from the man the most abject and vulgar one cannot take away his thought." [8] Do not seek so anxiously to be developed, to subject yourself to many influences to be played on; it is all dissipation. Humility like darkness reveals the heavenly lights. The shadows of poverty and meanness gather around us, "and lo! creation widens

8. *Confucian Analects* IX.25.

to our view."[9] We are often reminded that if there were bestowed on us the wealth of Croesus,[1] our aims must still be the same, and our means essentially the same. Moreover, if you are restricted in your range by poverty, if you cannot buy books and newspapers, for instance, you are but confined to the most significant and vital experiences; you are compelled to deal with the material which yields the most sugar and the most starch. It is life near the bone where it is sweetest. You are defended from being a trifler. No man loses ever on a lower level by magnanimity on a higher. Superfluous wealth can buy superfluities only. Money is not required to buy one necessary of the soul.

I live in the angle of a leaden wall, into whose composition was poured a little alloy of bell metal. Often, in the repose of my mid-day, there reaches my ears a confused *tintinnabulum* from without. It is the noise of my contemporaries. My neighbors tell me of their adventures with famous gentlemen and ladies, what notabilities they met at the dinner-table; but I am no more interested in such things than in the contents of the Daily Times. The interest and the conversation are about costume and manners chiefly; but a goose is a goose still, dress it as you will. They tell me of California and Texas, of England and the Indies, of the Hon. Mr. ———— of Georgia or of Massachusetts, all transient and fleeting phenomena, till I am ready to leap from their courtyard like the Mameluke bey.[2] I delight to come to my bearings—not walk in procession with pomp and parade, in a conspicuous place, but to walk even with the Builder of the universe, if I may—not to live in this restless, nerv-ous, bustling, trivial nineteenth century, but stand or sit thought-fully while it goes by. What are men celebrating? They are all on a committee of arrangements, and hourly expect a speech from somebody. God is only the president of the day, and Webster[3] is his orator. I love to weigh, to settle, to gravitate toward that which most strongly and rightfully attracts me; not hang by the beam of the scale and try to weigh less, not suppose a case, but take the case that is; to travel the only path I can, and that on which no power can resist me. It affords me no satisfaction to commence to spring an arch before I have got a solid foundation. Let us not play at kittlybenders.[4] There is a solid bottom everywhere. We read that the traveler asked the boy if the swamp before him had a hard bottom. The boy replied that it had. But presently the

9. Joseph Blanco White, "Sonnet: To Night."
1. A ruler of ancient Lydia, supposedly the wealthiest man of all time.
2. In 1811, the Pasha of Egypt or-dered the massacre of all the Mamelukes, but one escaped by leap-ing the ramparts and fleeing to Syria.
3. Daniel Webster (1782–1852) was the most famous orator of Thoreau's day.
4. A child's game wherein one tries to run out on thin ice without breaking through.

traveler's horse sank in up to the girths, and he observed to the boy, "I thought you said that this bog had a hard bottom." "So it has," answered the latter, "but you have not got half way to it yet." So it is with the bogs and quicksands of society; but he is an old boy that knows it. Only what is thought, said, or done at a certain rare coincidence is good. I would not be one of those who will foolishly drive a nail into mere lath and plastering; such a deed would keep me awake nights. Give me a hammer, and let me feel for the furrowing. Do not depend on the putty. Drive a nail home and clinch it so faithfully that you can wake up in the night and think of your work with satisfaction—a work at which you would not be ashamed to invoke the Muse.[5] So will help you God, and so only. Every nail driven should be as another rivet in the machine of the universe, you carrying on the work.

Rather than love, than money, than fame, give me truth. I sat at a table where were rich food and wine in abundance, and obsequious attendance, but sincerity and truth were not; and I went away hungry from the inhospitable board. The hospitality was as cold as the ices. I thought that there was no need of ice to freeze them. They talked to me of the age of the wine and the fame of the vintage; but I thought of an older, a newer, and purer wine, of a more glorious vintage, which they had not got, and could not buy. The style, the house and grounds and "entertainment" pass for nothing with me. I called on the king, but he made me wait in his hall, and conducted like a man incapacitated for hospitality. There was a man in my neighborhood who lived in a hollow tree. His manners were truly regal. I should have done better had I called on him.

How long shall we sit in our porticoes practicing idle and musty virtues, which any work would make impertinent? As if one were to begin the day with long-suffering, and hire a man to hoe his potatoes, and in the afternoon go forth to practice Christian meekness and charity with goodness aforethought! Consider the China pride and stagnant self-complacency of mankind. This generation inclines a little to congratulate itself on being the last of an illustrious line; and in Boston and London and Paris and Rome, thinking of its long descent, it speaks of its progress in art and science and literature with satisfaction. There are the Records of the Philosophical Societies, and the public Eulogies of *Great Men!* It is the good Adam contemplating his own virtue. "Yes, we have done great deeds, and sung divine songs, which shall never die"— that is, as long as *we* can remember them. The learned societies and great men of Assyria—where are they? What youthful phi-

5. Authors traditionally invoke the aid of the Muse when they embark upon a new work.

losophers and experimentalists we are! There is not one of my readers who has yet lived a whole human life. These may be but the spring months in the life of the race. If we have had the seven-years' itch, we have not seen the seventeen-year locust[6] yet in Concord. We are acquainted with a mere pellicle of the globe on which we live. Most have not delved six feet beneath the surface, nor leaped as many above it. We know not where we are. Besides, we are sound asleep nearly half our time. Yet we esteem ourselves wise, and have an established order on the surface. Truly, we are deep thinkers, we are ambitious spirits! As I stand over the insect crawling amid the pine needles on the forest floor, and endeavoring to conceal itself from my sight, and ask myself why it will cherish those humble thoughts, and hide its head from me who might, perhaps, be its benefactor, and impart to its race some cheering information, I am reminded of the greater Benefactor and Intelligence that stands over me the human insect.

There is an incessant influx of novelty into the world, and yet we tolerate incredible dullness. I need only suggest what kind of sermons are still listened to in the most enlightened countries. There are such words as joy and sorrow, but they are only the burden of a psalm, sung with a nasal twang, while we believe in the ordinary and mean. We think that we can change our clothes only. It is said that the British Empire is very large and respectable, and that the United States are a first-rate power. We do not believe that a tide rises and falls behind every man which can float the British Empire like a chip, if he should ever harbor it in his mind. Who knows what sort of seventeen-year locust will next come out of the ground? The government of the world I live in was not framed, like that of Britain, in after-dinner conversations over the wine.

The life in us is like the water in the river. It may rise this year higher than man has ever known it, and flood the parched uplands; even this may be the eventful year, which will drown out all our muskrats.[7] It was not always dry land where we dwell. I see far inland the banks which the stream anciently washed, before science began to record its freshets. Every one has heard the story[8] which has gone the rounds of New England, of a strong and beautiful bug which came out of the dry leaf of an old table of apple-tree wood, which had stood in a farmer's kitchen for sixty years, first in Connecticut, and afterward in Massachusetts—from an egg deposited in the living tree many years earlier still, as appeared by counting the annual layers beyond it; which was heard gnawing

6. A species of cicada emerges as an adult only after having been seventeen years in the larval stage.
7. Muskrats are occasionally caught in their houses by floods and drowned.
8. This story, as Thoreau implies, has been recorded in numerous places, among them Timothy Dwight, *Travels in New England and New York* (1821), II, 398. Melville also used the story as the basis for his "The Apple-Tree Table."

out for several weeks, hatched perchance by the heat of an urn. Who does not feel his faith in a resurrection and immortality strengthened by hearing of this? Who knows what beautiful and winged life, whose egg has been buried for ages under many concentric layers of woodenness in the dead dry life of society, deposited at first in the alburnum of the green and living tree, which has been gradually converted into the semblance of its well-seasoned tomb—heard perchance gnawing out now for years by the astonished family of man, as they sat round the festive board—may unexpectedly come forth from amidst society's most trivial and handselled furniture, to enjoy its perfect summer life at last!

I do not say that John or Jonathan[9] will realize all this; but such is the character of that morrow which mere lapse of time can never make to dawn. The light which puts out our eyes is darkness to us. Only that day dawns to which we are awake. There is more day to dawn. The sun is but a morning-star.

1854

Civil Disobedience

I heartily accept the motto,[1] "That government is best which governs least"; and I should like to see it acted up to more rapidly and systematically. Carried out, it finally amounts to this, which also I believe—"That government is best which governs not at all"; and when men are prepared for it, that will be the kind of government which they will have. Government is at best but an expedient; but most governments are usually, and all governments are sometimes, inexpedient. The objections which have been brought against a standing army, and they are many and weighty, and deserve to prevail, may also at last be brought against a standing government. The standing army is only an arm of the standing government. The government itself, which is only the mode which the people have chosen to execute their will, is equally liable to be abused and perverted before the people can act through it. Witness the present Mexican war,[2] the work of comparatively a few individuals using the standing government as their tool; for, in the outset, the people would not have consented to this measure.

This American government—what is it but a tradition, though a recent one, endeavoring to transmit itself unimpaired to posterity, but each instant losing some of its integrity? It has not the vitality

9. John (Bull), traditional name for the Britisher, and Jonathan for the American, derived from James Kirke Paulding's *The Diverting History of John Bull and Brother Jonathan* (1812).
1. From the masthead of the *Demo-cratic Review*, a literary-political journal to which Thoreau occasionally contributed.
2. The war of 1846–48, which Thoreau, like many other Northerners, opposed because he believed its purpose to be the extension of slave territory.

and force of a single living man; for a single man can bend it to his will. It is a sort of wooden gun to the people themselves. But it is not the less necessary for this; for the people must have some complicated machinery or other, and hear its din, to satisfy that idea of government which they have. Governments show thus how successfully men can be imposed on, even impose on themselves, for their own advantage. It is excellent, we must all allow. Yet this government never of itself furthered any enterprise, but by the alacrity with which it got out of its way. *It* does not keep the country free. *It* does not settle the West. *It* does not educate. The character inherent in the American people has done all that has been accomplished; and it would have done somewhat more, if the government had not sometimes got in its way. For government is an expedient by which men would fain succeed in letting one another alone; and, as has been said, when it is most expedient, the governed are most let alone by it. Trade and commerce, if they were not made of india-rubber, would never manage to bounce over the obstacles which legislators are continually putting in their way; and, if one were to judge these men wholly by the effects of their actions and not partly by their intentions, they would deserve to be classed and punished with those mischievous persons who put obstructions on the railroads.

But, to speak practically and as a citizen, unlike those who call themselves no-government men, I ask for, not at once no government, but *at once* a better government. Let every man make known what kind of government would command his respect, and that will be one step toward obtaining it.

After all, the practical reason why, when the power is once in the hands of the people, a majority are permitted, and for a long period continue, to rule is not because they are most likely to be in the right, nor because this seems fairest to the minority, but because they are physically the strongest. But a government in which the majority rule in all cases cannot be based on justice, even as far as men understand it. Can there not be a government in which majorities do not virtually decide right and wrong, but conscience? —in which majorities decide only those questions to which the rule of expediency is applicable? Must the citizen ever for a moment, or in the least degree, resign his conscience to the legislator? Why has every man a conscience, then? I think that we should be men first, and subjects afterward. It is not desirable to cultivate a respect for the law, so much as for the right. The only obligation which I have a right to assume is to do at any time what I think right. It is truly enough said that a corporation has no conscience; but a corporation of conscientious men is a corporation *with* a conscience. Law never made men a whit more just; and, by means of their respect for it, even the well-disposed are daily made the agents of injustice. A common and natural result of an undue respect for law is, that you may see a file of soldiers, colonel, captain, corporal, privates, powder-monkeys,[3] and all, marching in admirable order over hill and dale to the wars, against their wills, ay, against their common sense and consciences, which makes it very steep marching indeed, and produces a palpitation of the heart. They have no doubt that it is a damnable business in which they are concerned; they are all peaceably inclined. Now, what are they? Men at all? or small movable forts and magazines, at the service of some unscrupulous man in power? Visit the Navy Yard, and behold a marine, such a man as an American government can make, or such as it can make a man with its black arts—a mere shadow and reminiscence of humanity, a man laid out alive and standing, and already, as one may say, buried under arms with funeral accompaniments, though it may be,

> "Not a drum was heard, not a funeral note,
>   As his corse to the rampart we hurried;
> Not a soldier discharged his farewell shot
>   O'er the grave where our hero we buried."[4]

The mass of men serve the state thus, not as men mainly, but as machines, with their bodies. They are the standing army, and the militia, jailers, constables, *posse comitatus*,[5] etc. In most cases there is no free exercise whatever of the judgment or of the moral sense; but they put themselves on a level with wood and earth and stones; and wooden men can perhaps be manufactured that will serve the purpose as well. Such command no more respect than men of straw or a lump of dirt. They have the same sort of worth only as horses and dogs. Yet such as these even are commonly esteemed good citizens. Others—as most legislators, politicians, lawyers, ministers, and office-holders—serve the state chiefly with their heads; and, as they rarely make any moral distinctions, they are as likely to serve the devil, without *intending* it, as God. A very few—as heroes, patriots, martyrs, reformers in the great sense, and *men*—serve the state with their consciences also, and so necessarily resist it for the most part; and they are commonly treated as enemies by it. A wise man will only be useful as a man, and will not submit to be "clay," and "stop a hole to keep the wind away,"[6] but leave that office to his dust at least:

> "I am too high-born to be propertied,
>   To be a secondary at control,

---

3. Underlings who carry the gunpowder for military operations.
4. Charles Wolfe (1791–1823), "Burial of Sir John Moore at Corunna."

5. The entire body of inhabitants of an area who may be summoned by a sheriff to assist in preserving peace.
6. *Hamlet* V.i.236–37.

Or useful serving-man and instrument
To any sovereign state throughout the world."[7]

He who gives himself entirely to his fellow men appears to them useless and selfish; but he who gives himself partially to them is pronounced a benefactor and philanthropist.

How does it become a man to behave toward this American government today? I answer, that he cannot without disgrace be associated with it. I cannot for an instant recognize that political organization as *my* government which is the *slave's* government also.

All men recognize the right of revolution; that is, the right to refuse allegiance to, and to resist, the government, when its tyranny or its inefficiency are great and unendurable. But almost all say that such is not the case now. But such was the case, they think, in the Revolution of '75. If one were to tell me that this was a bad government because it taxed certain foreign commodities brought to its ports, it is most probable that I should not make an ado about it, for I can do without them. All machines have their friction; and possibly this does enough good to counterbalance the evil. At any rate, it is a great evil to make a stir about it. But when the friction comes to have its machine, and oppression and robbery are organized, I say, let us not have such a machine any longer. In other words, when a sixth of the population of a nation which has undertaken to be the refuge of liberty are slaves, and a whole country is unjustly overrun and conquered by a foreign army, and subjected to military law, I think that it is not too soon for honest men to rebel and revolutionize. What makes this duty the more urgent is the fact that the country so overrun is not our own, but ours is the invading army.

Paley, a common authority with many on moral questions, in his chapter on the "Duty of Submission to Civil Government," resolves all civil obligation into expediency; and he proceeds to say that "so long as the interest of the whole society requires it, that is, so long as the established government cannot be resisted or changed without public inconveniency, it is the will of God . . . that the established government be obeyed—and no longer. This principle being admitted, the justice of every particular case of resistance is reduced to a computation of the quantity of the danger and grievance on the one side, and of the probability and expense of redressing it on the other."[8] Of this, he says, every man shall judge for himself. But Paley appears never to have contemplated those cases to which the rule of expediency does not apply, in which a people, as well as an individual, must do justice, cost what

7. *King John* V.ii.79–82.   8. William Paley (1743–1805), *Moral and Political Philosophy* VI.ii.

it may. If I have unjustly wrested a plank from a drowning man,[9] I must restore it to him though I drown myself. This, according to Paley, would be inconvenient. But he that would save his life, in such a case, shall lose it. This people must cease to hold slaves, and to make war on Mexico, though it cost them their existence as a people.

In their practice, nations agree with Paley; but does anyone think that Massachusetts does exactly what is right at the present crisis?

"A drab of state, a cloth-o'-silver slut,
To have her train borne up, and her soul trail in the dirt."[1]

Practically speaking, the opponents to a reform in Massachusetts are not a hundred thousand politicians at the South, but a hundred thousand merchants and farmers here, who are more interested in commerce and agriculture than they are in humanity, and are not prepared to do justice to the slave and to Mexico, *cost what it may.* I quarrel not with far-off foes, but with those who, near at home, co-operate with, and do the bidding of, those far away, and without whom the latter would be harmless. We are accustomed to say, that the mass of men are unprepared; but improvement is slow, because the few are not materially wiser or better than the many. It is not so important that many should be as good as you, as that there be some absolute goodness somewhere; for that will leaven the whole lump.[2] There are thousands who are *in opinion* opposed to slavery and to the war, who yet in effect do nothing to put an end to them; who, esteeming themselves children of Washington and Franklin, sit down with their hands in their pockets, and say that they know not what to do, and do nothing; who even postpone the question of freedom to the question of free trade, and quietly read the prices-current along with the latest advices from Mexico, after dinner, and, it may be, fall asleep over them both. What is the price-current of an honest man and patriot today? They hesitate, and they regret, and sometimes they petition; but they do nothing in earnest and with effect. They will wait, well disposed, for others to remedy the evil, that they may no longer have it to regret. At most, they give only a cheap vote, and a feeble countenance and Godspeed, to the right, as it goes by them. There are nine hundred and ninety-nine patrons of virtue to one virtuous man. But it is easier to deal with the real possessor of a thing than with the temporary guardian of it.

All voting is a sort of gaming, like checkers or backgammon, with a slight moral tinge to it, a playing with right and wrong, with

9. See Cicero, *De Officiis* III.   *Tragaedie* (1608) IV.iv.
1. Cyril   Tourneur,   *The   Revengers*   2. I Corinthians v.6.

moral questions; and betting naturally accompanies it. The character of the voters is not staked. I cast my vote, perchance, as I think right; but I am not vitally concerned that that right should prevail. I am willing to leave it to the majority. Its obligation, therefore, never exceeds that of expediency. Even voting *for the right* is *doing* nothing for it. It is only expressing to men feebly your desire that it should prevail. A wise man will not leave the right to the mercy of chance, nor wish it to prevail through the power of the majority. There is but little virtue in the action of masses of men. When the majority shall at length vote for the abolition of slavery, it will be because they are indifferent to slavery, or because there is but little slavery left to be abolished by their vote. *They* will then be the only slaves. Only *his* vote can hasten the abolition of slavery who asserts his own freedom by his vote.

I hear of a convention[3] to be held at Baltimore, or elsewhere, for the selection of a candidate for the Presidency, made up chiefly of editors, and men who are politicians by profession; but I think, what is it to any independent, intelligent, and respectable man what decision they may come to? Shall we not have the advantage of his wisdom and honesty, nevertheless? Can we not count upon some independent votes? Are there not many individuals in the country who do not attend conventions? But no: I find that the respectable man, so called, has immediately drifted from his position, and despairs of his country, when his country has more reason to despair of him. He forthwith adopts one of the candidates thus selected as the only *available* one, thus proving that he is himself *available* for any purposes of the demagogue. His vote is of no more worth than that of any unprincipled foreigner or hireling native, who may have been bought. O for a man who is a *man*, and, as my neighbor says, has a bone in his back which you cannot pass your hand through! Our statistics are at fault: the population has been returned too large. How many *men* are there to a square thousand miles in this country? Hardly one. Does not America offer any inducement for men to settle here? The American has dwindled into an Odd Fellow[4]—one who may be known by the development of his organ of gregariousness, and a manifest lack of intellect and cheerful self-reliance; whose first and chief concern, on coming into the world, is to see that the almshouses are in good repair; and, before yet he has lawfully donned the virile garb,[5] to collect a fund for the support of the widows and orphans

3. The Democratic Party held its 1848 convention in Baltimore, nominated Lewis Cass for President, and scrupulously ignored the issue of slavery.
4. The Independent Order of Odd Fellows is a secret fraternal society still popular in the rural United States.
5. A Roman boy was permitted to wear the *toga virilis* when he attained the age of fourteen.

that may be; who, in short, ventures to live only by the aid of the Mutual Insurance company, which has promised to bury him decently.

It is not a man's duty, as a matter of course, to devote himself to the eradication of any, even the most enormous, wrong; he may still properly have other concerns to engage him; but it is his duty, at least, to wash his hands of it, and, if he gives it no thought longer, not to give it practically his support. If I devote myself to other pursuits and contemplations, I must first see, at least, that I do not pursue them sitting upon another man's shoulders. I must get off him first, that he may pursue his contemplations too. See what gross inconsistency is tolerated. I have heard some of my townsmen say, "I should like to have them order me out to help put down an insurrection of the slaves, or to march to Mexico—see if I would go"; and yet these very men have each, directly by their allegiance, and so indirectly, at least, by their money, furnished a substitute. The soldier is applauded who refuses to serve in an unjust war by those who do not refuse to sustain the unjust government which makes the war; is applauded by those whose own act and authority he disregards and sets at naught; as if the state were penitent to that degree that it hired one to scourge it while it sinned, but not to that degree that it left off sinning for a moment. Thus, under the name of Order and Civil Government, we are all made at last to pay homage to and support our own meanness. After the first blush of sin comes its indifference; and from immoral it becomes, as it were, *un*moral, and not quite unnecessary to that life which we have made.

The broadest and most prevalent error requires the most disinterested virtue to sustain it. The slight reproach to which the virtue of patriotism is commonly liable, the noble are most likely to incur. Those who, while they disapprove of the character and measures of a government, yield to it their allegiance and support are undoubtedly its most conscientious supporters, and so frequently the most serious obstacles to reform. Some are petitioning the State to dissolve the Union, to disregard the requisitions of the President. Why do they not dissolve it themselves—the union between themselves and the State—and refuse to pay their quota into its treasury? Do not they stand in the same relation to the State that the State does to the Union? And have not the same reasons prevented the State from resisting the Union which have prevented them from resisting the State?

How can a man be satisfied to entertain an opinion merely, and enjoy *it*? Is there any enjoyment in it, if his opinion is that he is aggrieved? If you are cheated out of a single dollar by your neighbor, you do not rest satisfied with knowing that you are cheated, or with saying that you are cheated, or even with petitioning him to pay you your due; but you take effectual steps at once to obtain the full amount, and see that you are never cheated again. Action from principle, the perception and the performance of right, changes things and relations; it is essentially revolutionary, and does not consist wholly with anything which was. It not only divides States and churches, it divides families; ay, it divides the *individual*, separating the diabolical in him from the divine.

Unjust laws exist: shall we be content to obey them, or shall we endeavor to amend them, and obey them until we have succeeded, or shall we transgress them at once? Men generally, under such a government as this, think that they ought to wait until they have persuaded the majority to alter them. They think that, if they should resist, the remedy would be worse than the evil. But it is the fault of the government itself that the remedy *is* worse than the evil. *It* makes it worse. Why is it not more apt to anticipate and provide for reform? Why does it not cherish its wise minority? Why does it cry and resist before it is hurt? Why does it not encourage its citizens to be on the alert to point out its faults, and *do* better than it would have them? Why does it always crucify Christ, and excommunicate Copernicus and Luther,[6] and pronounce Washington and Franklin rebels?

One would think, that a deliberate and practical denial of its authority was the only offence never contemplated by government; else, why has it not assigned its definite, its suitable and proportionate, penalty? If a man who has no property refuses but once to earn nine shillings for the State, he is put in prison for a period unlimited by any law that I know, and determined only by the discretion of those who placed him there; but if he should steal ninety times nine shillings from the State, he is soon permitted to go at large again.

If the injustice is part of the necessary friction of the machine of government, let it go, let it go: perchance it will wear smooth—certainly the machine will wear out. If the injustice has a spring, or a pulley, or a rope, or a crank, exclusively for itself, then perhaps you may consider whether the remedy will not be worse than the evil; but if it is of such a nature that it requires you to be the agent of injustice to another, then, I say, break the law. Let your life be a counter-friction to stop the machine. What I have to do is to see, at any rate, that I do not lend myself to the wrong which I condemn.

As for adopting the ways which the State has provided for

6. Nicolaus Copernicus (1473–1543) was not excommunicated, probably because he was on his deathbed when his dissertation on the solar system was published, but the dissertation itself was banned by the church. Martin Luther was excommunicated in 1521.

remedying the evil, I know not of such ways. They take too much time, and a man's life will be gone. I have other affairs to attend to. I came into this world, not chiefly to make this a good place to live in, but to live in it, be it good or bad. A man has not everything to do, but something; and because he cannot do *everything*, it is not necessary that he should do *something* wrong. It is not my business to be petitioning the Governor or the Legislature any more than it is theirs to petition me; and if they should not hear my petition, what should I do then? But in this case the State has provided no way: its very Constitution is the evil. This may seem to be harsh and stubborn and unconciliatory; but it is to treat with the utmost kindness and consideration the only spirit that can appreciate or deserves it. So is all change for the better, like birth and death, which convulse the body.

I do not hesitate to say, that those who call themselves Abolitionists should at once effectually withdraw their support, both in person and property, from the government of Massachusetts, and not wait till they constitute a majority of one, before they suffer the right to prevail through them. I think that it is enough if they have God on their side, without waiting for that other one.[7] Moreover, any man more right than his neighbors constitutes a majority of one already.

I meet this American government, or its representative, the State government, directly, and face to face, once a year—no more—in the person of its tax-gatherer; this is the only mode in which a man situated as I am necessarily meets it; and it then says distinctly, Recognize me; and the simplest, the most effectual, and, in the present posture of affairs, the indispensablest mode of treating with it on this head, of expressing your little satisfaction with and love for it, is to deny it then. My civil neighbor, the tax-gatherer, is the very man I have to deal with—for it is, after all, with men and not with parchment that I quarrel—and he has voluntarily chosen to be an agent of the government. How shall he ever know well what he is and does as an officer of the government, or as a man, until he is obliged to consider whether he shall treat me, his neighbor, for whom he has respect, as a neighbor and well-disposed man, or as a maniac and disturber of the peace, and see if he can get over this obstruction to his neighborliness without a ruder and more impetuous thought or speech corresponding with his action. I know this well, that if one thousand, if one hundred, if ten men whom I could name—if ten *honest* men only—ay, if *one* HONEST man, in this State of Massachusetts, *ceasing to hold slaves*, were actually to withdraw from this copartnership, and be locked up in the county jail therefor, it would be the abolition of slavery in

7. Cf. the proverb, "One on God's side is a majority."

America. For it matters not how small the beginning may seem to be: what is once well done is done forever. But we love better to talk about it: that we say is our mission. Reform keeps many scores of newspapers in its service, but not one man. If my esteemed neighbor, the State's ambassador,[8] who will devote his days to the settlement of the question of human rights in the Council Chamber, instead of being threatened with the prisons of Carolina, were to sit down the prisoner of Massachusetts, that State which is so anxious to foist the sin of slavery upon her sister—though at present she can discover only an act of inhospitality to be the ground of a quarrel with her—the Legislature would not wholly waive the subject the following winter.

Under a government which imprisons any unjustly, the true place for a just man is also a prison. The proper place today, the only place which Massachusetts has provided for her freer and less desponding spirits, is in her prisons, to be put out and locked out of the State by her own act, as they have already put themselves out by their principles. It is there that the fugitive slave, and the Mexican prisoner on parole, and the Indian come to plead the wrongs of his race should find them; on that separate, but more free and honorable, ground, where the State places those who are not *with* her, but *against* her—the only house in a slave State in which a free man can abide with honor. If any think that their influence would be lost there, and their voices no longer afflict the ear of the State, that they would not be as an enemy within its walls, they do not know by how much truth is stronger than error, nor how much more eloquently and effectively he can combat injustice who has experienced a little in his own person. Cast your whole vote, not a strip of paper merely, but your whole influence. A minority is powerless while it conforms to the majority; it is not even a minority then; but it is irresistible when it clogs by its whole weight. If the alternative is to keep all just men in prison, or give up war and slavery, the State will not hesitate which to choose. If a thousand men were not to pay their tax-bills this year, that would not be a violent and bloody measure, as it would be to pay them, and enable the State to commit violence and shed innocent blood. This is, in fact, the definition of a peaceable revolution, if any such is possible. If the tax-gatherer, or any other public officer, asks me, as one has done, "But what shall I do?" my answer is, "If you really wish to do anything, resign your office." When the subject has refused allegiance, and the officer has resigned his office, then the revolution is accomplished. But even

8. Samuel Hoar (1778–1856), Massachusetts senator and Concord neighbor of Thoreau, was sent to South Carolina by his native state to protest treatment of Negro seamen on Massachusetts ships in South Carolina harbors. He was forcibly evicted from South Carolina by act of its legislature.

suppose blood should flow. Is there not a sort of blood shed when the conscience is wounded? Through this wound a man's real manhood and immortality flow out, and he bleeds to an everlasting death. I see this blood flowing now.

I have contemplated the imprisonment of the offender, rather than the seizure of his goods—though both will serve the same purpose—because they who assert the purest right, and consequently are most dangerous to a corrupt State, commonly have not spent much time in accumulating property. To such the State renders comparatively small service, and a slight tax is wont to appear exorbitant, particularly if they are obliged to earn it by special labor with their hands. If there were one who lived wholly without the use of money, the State itself would hesitate to demand it of him. But the rich man—not to make any invidious comparison —is always sold to the institution which makes him rich. Absolutely speaking, the more money, the less virtue; for money comes between a man and his objects, and obtains them for him; and it was certainly no great virtue to obtain it. It puts to rest many questions which he would otherwise be taxed to answer; while the only new question which it puts is the hard but superfluous one, how to spend it. Thus his moral ground is taken from under his feet. The opportunities of living are diminished in proportion as what are called the "means" are increased. The best thing a man can do for his culture when he is rich is to endeavor to carry out those schemes which he entertained when he was poor. Christ answered the Herodians according to their condition. "Show me the tribute-money," said he—and one took a penny out of his pocket—if you use money which has the image of Caesar on it, and which he has made current and valuable, that is, *if you are men of the State*, and gladly enjoy the advantages of Caesar's government, then pay him back some of his own when he demands it. "Render therefore to Caesar that which is Caesar's, and to God those things which are God's"[9]—leaving them no wiser than before as to which was which; for they did not wish to know.

When I converse with the freest of my neighbors, I perceive that, whatever they may say about the magnitude and seriousness of the question, and their regard for the public tranquillity, the long and the short of the matter is, that they cannot spare the protection of the existing government, and they dread the consequences to their property and families of disobedience to it. For my own part, I should not like to think that I ever rely on the protection of the State. But, if I deny the authority of the State when it presents its tax bill, it will soon take and waste all my property, and so harass me and my children without end. This is

9. Matthew xxii.19–21.

hard. This makes it impossible for a man to live honestly, and at the same time comfortably, in outward respects. It will not be worth the while to accumulate property; that would be sure to go again. You must hire or squat somewhere, and raise but a small crop, and eat that soon. You must live within yourself, and depend upon yourself always tucked up and ready for a start, and not have many affairs. A man may grow rich in Turkey even, if he will be in all respects a good subject of the Turkish government. Confucius said: "If a state is governed by the principles of reason, poverty and misery are subjects of shame; if a state is not governed by the principles of reason, riches and honors are the subjects of shame."[1] No: until I want the protection of Massachusetts to be extended to me in some distant Southern port, where my liberty is endangered, or until I am bent solely on building up an estate at home by peaceful enterprise, I can afford to refuse allegiance to Massachusetts, and her right to my property and life. It costs me less in every sense to incur the penalty of disobedience to the State than it would to obey. I should feel as if I were worth less in that case.

Some years ago, the State met me in behalf of the Church,[2] and commanded me to pay a certain sum toward the support of a clergyman whose preaching my father attended, but never I myself. "Pay," it said, "or be locked up in the jail." I declined to pay. But, unfortunately, another man saw fit to pay it. I did not see why the schoolmaster should be taxed to support the priest, and not the priest the schoolmaster; for I was not the State's schoolmaster, but I supported myself by voluntary subscription. I did not see why the lyceum[3] should not present its tax bill, and have the State to back its demand, as well as the Church. However, at the request of the selectmen, I condescended to make some such statement as this in writing: "Know all men by these presents, that I, Henry Thoreau, do not wish to be regarded as a member of any incorporated society which I have not joined." This I gave to the town clerk; and he has it. The State, having thus learned that I did not wish to be regarded as a member of that church, has never made a like demand on me since; though it said that it must adhere to its original presumption that time. If I had known how to name them, I should then have signed off in detail from all the societies which I never signed on to; but I did not know where to find a complete list.

I have paid no poll-tax for six years. I was put into a jail once

1. *The Analects* VIII.xiii.
2. Until the mid-19th century it was the custom in Massachusetts for the town authorities to send out tax bills for the various churches.
3. Thoreau was an officer of and a fre-
quent speaker before the Concord Lyceum, which annually sponsored a series of lectures. "Civil Disobedience" was first delivered before the Concord Lyceum.

on this account, for one night;[4] and, as I stood considering the
walls of solid stone, two or three feet thick, the door of wood and
iron, a foot thick, and the iron grating which strained the light,
I could not help being struck with the foolishness of that institution which treated me as if I were mere flesh and blood and bones,
to be locked up. I wondered that it should have concluded at length
that this was the best use it could put me to, and had never thought
to avail itself of my services in some way. I saw that, if there was
a wall of stone between me and my townsmen, there was a still
more difficult one to climb or break through before they could
get to be as free as I was. I did not for a moment feel confined,
and the walls seemed a great waste of stone and mortar. I felt as
if I alone of all my townsmen had paid my tax. They plainly did
not know how to treat me, but behaved like persons who are un-
derbred. In every threat and in every compliment there was a
blunder; for they thought that my chief desire was to stand the
other side of that stone wall. I could not but smile to see how in-
dustriously they locked the door on my meditations, which followed them out again without let or hindrance, and *they* were
really all that was dangerous. As they could not reach me, they
had resolved to punish my body; just as boys, if they cannot come
at some person against whom they have a spite, will abuse his dog.
I saw that the State was half-witted, that it was timid as a lone
woman with her silver spoons, and that it did not know its friends
from its foes, and I lost all my remaining respect for it, and pitied it.

Thus the State never intentionally confronts a man's sense, intellectual or moral, but only his body, his senses. It is not armed
with superior wit or honesty, but with superior physical strength.
I was not born to be forced. I will breathe after my own fashion.
Let us see who is the strongest. What force has a multitude? They
only can force me who obey a higher law than I. They force me to
become like themselves. I do not hear of *men* being *forced* to live
this way or that by masses of men. What sort of life were that to
live? When I meet a government which says to me, "Your money
or your life," why should I be in haste to give it my money? It may
be in a great strait, and not know what to do: I cannot help that.
It must help itself; do as I do. It is not worth the while to snivel
about it. I am not responsible for the successful working of the
machinery of society. I am not the son of the engineer. I perceive
that, when an acorn and a chestnut fall side by side, the one does
not remain inert to make way for the other, but both obey their
own laws, and spring and grow and flourish as best they can, till
one, perchance, overshadows and destroys the other. If a plant

4. Probably the night of July 23 or 24,
1846. The implication in *Walden*
("The Village," not included in our
text) that the arrest occurred in 1845
is incorrect.

cannot live according to its nature, it dies; and so a man.

The night in prison was novel and interesting enough. The prisoners in their shirtsleeves were enjoying a chat and the evening air in the doorway, when I entered. But the jailer said, "Come, boys, it is time to lock up"; and so they dispersed, and I heard the sound of their steps returning into the hollow apartments. My roommate was introduced to me by the jailer as "a first-rate fellow and a clever man." When the door was locked, he showed me where to hang my hat, and how he managed matters there. The rooms were whitewashed once a month; and this one, at least, was the whitest, most simply furnished, and probably the neatest apartment in the town. He naturally wanted to know where I came from, and what brought me there; and, when I had told him, I asked him in my turn how he came there, presuming him to be an honest man, of course; and, as the world goes, I believe he was. "Why," said he, "they accuse me of burning a barn; but I never did it." As near as I could discover, he had probably gone to bed in a barn when drunk, and smoked his pipe there; and so a barn was burnt. He had the reputation of being a clever man, had been there some three months waiting for his trial to come on, and would have to wait as much longer; but he was quite domesticated and contented, since he got his board for nothing, and thought that he was well treated.

He occupied one window, and I the other; and I saw that if one stayed there long, his principal business would be to look out the window. I had soon read all the tracts that were left there, and examined where former prisoners had broken out, and where a grate had been sawed off, and heard the history of the various occupants of that room; for I found that even here there was a history and a gossip which never circulated beyond the walls of the jail. Probably this is the only house in the town where verses are composed, which are afterward printed in a circular form, but not published. I was shown quite a long list of verses which were composed by some young men who had been detected in an attempt to escape, who avenged themselves by singing them.

I pumped my fellow-prisoner as dry as I could, for fear I should never see him again; but at length he showed me which was my bed, and left me to blow out the lamp.

It was like traveling into a far country, such as I had never expected to behold, to lie there for one night. It seemed to me that I never had heard the town clock strike before, nor the evening sounds of the village; for we slept with the windows open, which were inside the grating. It was to see my native village in the light of the Middle Ages, and our Concord was turned into a Rhine stream, and visions of knights and castles passed before me. They were the voices of old burghers that I heard in the streets. I was an involuntary spectator and auditor of whatever was done and said in the kitchen of the adjacent village inn—a wholly new and rare experience to me. It was a closer view of my native town. I was fairly inside of it. I never had seen its institutions before. This is one of its peculiar institutions; for it is a shire town.[5] I began to comprehend what its inhabitants were about.

In the morning, our breakfasts were put through the hole in the door, in small oblong-square tin pans, made to fit, and holding a pint of chocolate, with brown bread, and an iron spoon. When they called for the vessels again, I was green enough to return what bread I had left; but my comrade seized it, and said that I should lay that up for lunch or dinner. Soon after he was let out to work at haying in a neighboring field, whither he went every day, and would not be back till noon; so he bade me good-day, saying that he doubted if he should see me again.

When I came out of prison—for some one[6] interfered, and paid that tax—I did not perceive that great changes had taken place on the common, such as he observed who went in a youth and emerged a tottering and gray-headed man; and yet a change had to my eyes come over the scene—the town, and State, and country—greater than any that mere time could effect. I saw yet more distinctly the State in which I lived. I saw to what extent the people among whom I lived could be trusted as good neighbors and friends; that their friendship was for summer weather only; that they did not greatly propose to do right; that they were a distinct race from me by their prejudices and superstitions, as the Chinamen and Malays are; that in their sacrifices to humanity they ran no risks, not even to their property; that after all they were not so noble but they treated the thief as he had treated them, and hoped, by a certain outward observance and a few prayers, and by walking in a particular straight though useless path from time to time, to save their souls. This may be to judge my neighbors harshly; for I believe that many of them are not aware that they have such an institution as the jail in their village.

It was formerly the custom in our village, when a poor debtor came out of jail, for his acquaintances to salute him, looking through their fingers, which were crossed to represent the grating of a jail window, "How do ye do?" My neighbors did not thus salute me, but first looked at me, and then at one another, as if I had returned from a long journey. I was put into jail as I was going to the shoemaker's to get a shoe which was mended. When I was let out the next morning, I proceeded to finish my errand,

5. Concord was then the county seat of Middlesex County (or "shire").
6. It is now generally believed to have been his aunt Maria Thoreau, who was appalled at the thought of a nephew in jail.

and, having put on my mended shoe, joined a huckleberry party, who were impatient to put themselves under my conduct; and in half an hour—for the horse was soon tackled—was in the midst of a huckleberry field, on one of our highest hills, two miles off, and then the State was nowhere to be seen.

This is the whole history of "My Prisons."[7]

I have never declined paying the highway tax, because I am as desirous of being a good neighbor as I am of being a bad subject; and as for supporting schools, I am doing my part to educate my fellow-countrymen now. It is for no particular item in the tax bill that I refuse to pay it. I simply wish to refuse allegiance to the State, to withdraw and stand aloof from it effectually. I do not care to trace the course of my dollar, if I could, till it buys a man or a musket to shoot one with—the dollar is innocent—but I am concerned to trace the effects of my allegiance. In fact, I quietly declare war with the State, after my fashion, though I will still make what use and get what advantage of her I can, as is usual in such cases.

If others pay the tax which is demanded of me, from a sympathy with the State, they do but what they have already done in their own case, or rather they abet injustice to a greater extent than the State requires. If they pay the tax from a mistaken interest in the individual taxed, to save his property, or prevent his going to jail, it is because they have not considered wisely how far they let their private feelings interfere with the public good.

This, then, is my position at present. But one cannot be too much on his guard in such a case, lest his action be biased by obstinacy or an undue regard for the opinions of men. Let him see that he does only what belongs to himself and to the hour.

I think sometimes, Why, this people mean well, they are only ignorant; they would do better if they knew how: why give your neighbors this pain to treat you as they are not inclined to? But I think again, This is no reason why I should do as they do, or permit others to suffer much greater pain of a different kind. Again, I sometimes say to myself, When many millions of men, without heat, without ill will, without personal feeling of any kind, demand of you a few shillings only, without the possibility, such is their constitution, of retracting or altering their present demand, and without the possibility, on your side, of appeal to any other millions, why expose yourself to this overwhelming brute force? You do not resist cold and hunger, the winds and the waves, thus obstinately; you quietly submit to a thousand similar necessities. You

7. The title of a volume of memoirs by the Italian patriot Silvio Pellico (1789–1854), then popular in this country.

do not put your head into the fire. But just in proportion as I regard this as not wholly a brute force, but partly a human force, and consider that I have relations to those millions as to so many millions of men, and not of mere brute or inanimate things, I see that appeal is possible, first and instantaneously, from them to the Maker of them, and, secondly, from them to themselves. But if I put my head deliberately into the fire, there is no appeal to fire or to the Maker of fire, and I have only myself to blame. If I could convince myself that I have any right to be satisfied with men as they are, and to treat them accordingly, and not according, in some respects, to my requisitions and expectations of what they and I ought to be, then, like a good Mussulman[8] and fatalist, I should endeavor to be satisfied with things as they are, and say it is the will of God. And, above all, there is this difference between resisting this and a purely brute or natural force, that I can resist this with some effect; but I cannot expect, like Orpheus, to change the nature of the rocks and trees and beasts.[9]

I do not wish to quarrel with any man or nation. I do not wish to split hairs, to make fine distinctions, or set myself up as better than my neighbors. I seek rather, I may say, even an excuse for conforming to the laws of the land. I am but too ready to conform to them. Indeed, I have reason to suspect myself on this head; and each year, as the tax-gatherer comes round, I find myself disposed to review the acts and position of the general and State governments, and the spirit of the people, to discover a pretext for conformity.

> "We must affect our country as our parents,
> And if at any time we alienate
> Our love or industry from doing it honor,
> We must respect effects and teach the soul
> Matter of conscience and religion,
> And not desire of rule or benefit."

I believe that the State will soon be able to take all my work of this sort out of my hands, and then I shall be no better a patriot than my fellow-countrymen. Seen from a lower point of view, the Constitution, with all its faults, is very good; the law and the courts are very respectable; even this State and this American government are, in many respects, very admirable, and rare things, to be thankful for, such as a great many have described them; but seen from a point of view a little higher, they are what I have described them; seen from a higher still, and the highest, who shall say what they are, or that they are worth looking at or thinking of

8. A Moslem.
9. In Greek mythology, Orpheus was the son of the Muse Calliope and great- est of all musicians. So great was his skill that he could enchant even the trees and stones.

at all?

However, the government does not concern me much, and I shall bestow the fewest possible thoughts on it. It is not many moments that I live under a government, even in this world. If a man is thought-free, fancy-free, imagination-free, that which *is not* never for a long time appearing *to be* to him, unwise rulers or reformers cannot fatally interrupt him.

I know that most men think differently from myself; but those whose lives are by profession devoted to the study of these or kindred subjects content me as little as any. Statesmen and legislators, standing so completely within the institution, never distinctly and nakedly behold it. They speak of moving society, but have no resting-place without it. They may be men of a certain experience and discrimination, and have no doubt invented ingenious and even useful systems, for which we sincerely thank them; but all their wit and usefulness lie within certain not very wide limits. They are wont to forget that the world is not governed by policy and expediency. Webster[1] never goes behind government, and so cannot speak with authority about it. His words are wisdom to those legislators who contemplate no essential reform in the existing government; but for thinkers, and those who legislate for all time, he never once glances at the subject. I know of those whose serene and wise speculations on this theme would soon reveal the limits of his mind's range and hospitality. Yet, compared with the cheap professions of most reformers, and the still cheaper wisdom and eloquence of politicians in general, his are almost the only sensible and valuable words, and we thank Heaven for him. Comparatively, he is always strong, original, and, above all, practical. Still, his quality is not wisdom, but prudence. The lawyer's truth is not Truth, but consistency or a consistent expediency. Truth is always in harmony with herself, and is not concerned chiefly to reveal the justice that may consist with wrong-doing. He well deserves to be called, as he has been called, the Defender of the Constitution. There are really no blows to be given by him but defensive ones. He is not a leader, but a follower. His leaders are the men of '87.[2] "I have never made an effort," he says, "and never propose to make an effort; I have never countenanced an effort, and never mean to countenance an effort, to disturb the arrangement as originally made, by which the various States came into the Union."[3] Still thinking of the sanction which the Constitution gives to slavery, he says, "Because it was a part of the original compact—let it stand." Notwithstanding his special acuteness and ability, he is unable to

1. Daniel Webster (1782–1852), Massachusetts senator and noted orator.
2. The framers of the American Constitution.

3. From Webster's speech on the Texas question, delivered on December 22, 1845.

take a fact out of its merely political relations, and behold it as it
lies absolutely to be disposed of by the intellect—what, for instance,
it behooves a man to do here in America today with regard to slavery
—but ventures, or is driven, to make some such desperate answer
as the following, while professing to speak absolutely, and as a
private man—from which what new and singular code of social
duties might be inferred? "The manner," says he, "in which the
governments of those States where slavery exists are to regulate it
is for their own consideration, under their reponsibility to their
constituents, to the general laws of propriety, humanity, and justice,
and to God. Associations formed elsewhere, springing from a feeling of humanity, or any other cause, have nothing whatever to do
with it. They have never received any encouragement from me, and
they never will."[4]

They who know of no purer sources of truth, who have traced
up its stream no higher, stand, and wisely stand, by the Bible and
the Constitution, and drink at it there with reverence and humility;
but they who behold where it comes trickling into this lake or that
pool, gird up their loins[5] once more, and continue their pilgrimage
toward its fountainhead.

No man with a genius for legislation has appeared in America.
They are rare in the history of the world. There are orators, politicians, and eloquent men, by the thousand; but the speaker has
not yet opened his mouth to speak who is capable of settling the
much-vexed questions of the day. We love eloquence for its own
sake, and not for any truth which it may utter, or any heroism it
may inspire. Our legislators have not yet learned the comparative
value of free trade and of freedom, of union, and of rectitude, to a
nation. They have no genius or talent for comparatively humble
questions of taxation and finance, commerce and manufactures
and agriculture. If we were left solely to the wordy wit of legislators in Congress for our guidance, uncorrected by the seasonable
experience and the effectual complaints of the people, America
would not long retain her rank among the nations. For eighteen
hundred years, though perchance I have no right to say it, the
New Testament has been written; yet where is the legislator who
has wisdom and practical talent enough to avail himself of the light
which it sheds on the science of legislation?

The authority of government, even such as I am willing to submit to—for I will cheerfully obey those who know and can do better than I, and in many things even those who neither know nor
can do so well—is still an impure one: to be strictly just, it must

4. From Webster's speech on the bill to
exclude slavery from the territories, delivered August 12, 1848. Thoreau here
adds the footnote: "These extracts have
been inserted since the lecture was
read."
5. Luke xii.35.

have the sanction and consent of the governed. It can have no pure right over my person and property but what I concede to it. The progress from an absolute to a limited monarchy, from a limited monarchy to a democracy, is a progress toward a true respect for the individual. Even the Chinese philosopher[6] was wise enough to regard the individual as the basis of the empire. Is a democracy, such as we know it, the last improvement possible in government? Is it not possible to take a step further towards recognizing and organizing the rights of man? There will never be a really free and enlightened State until the State comes to recognize the individual as a higher and independent power, from which all its own power and authority are derived, and treats him accordingly. I please myself with imagining a State at last which can afford to be just to all men, and to treat the individual with respect as a neighbor; which even would not think it inconsistent with its own repose if a few were to live aloof from it, not meddling with it, nor embraced by it, who fulfilled all the duties of neighbors and fellow men. A State which bore this kind of fruit, and suffered it to drop off as fast as it ripened, would prepare the way for a still more perfect and glorious State, which also I have imagined, but not yet anywhere seen.

1849, 1866

A Plea for Captain John Brown[7]

I trust that you will pardon me for being here. I do not wish to force my thoughts upon you, but I feel forced myself. Little as I know of Captain Brown,[8] I would fain do my part to correct the tone and the statements of the newspapers, and of my countrymen generally, respecting his character and actions. It costs us nothing to be just. We can at least express our sympathy with, and admiration of, him and his companions, and that is what I now propose to do.

First, as to his history. I will endeavor to omit, as much as possible, what you have already read. I need not describe his person to you, for probably most of you have seen and will not soon forget him. I am told that his grandfather, John Brown, was an officer in the Revolution; that he himself was born in Connecticut about the beginning of this century, but early went with his father to Ohio. I heard him say that his father was a contractor who fur-

6. Confucius.
7. Delivered as a lecture on October 30, 1859, in Concord Town Hall, in defense of John Brown and his attack on Harpers Ferry. Thoreau had called the meeting against the advice of many of the local abolitionists who feared violent reaction to any defense of Brown at this time.
8. Thoreau had met Brown twice in Concord, but only briefly each time, and he had known nothing in advance of Brown's Harpers Ferry plans.

nished beef to the army there, in the war of 1812; that he accompanied him to the camp, and assisted him in that employment, seeing a good deal of military life,—more, perhaps, than if he had been a soldier; for he was often present at the councils of the officers. Especially, he learned by experience how armies are supplied and maintained in the field,—a work which, he observed, requires at least as much experience and skill as to lead them in battle. He said that few persons had any conception of the cost, even the pecuniary cost, of firing a single bullet in war. He saw enough, at any rate, to disgust him with a military life; indeed, to excite in him a great abhorrence of it; so much so, that though he was tempted by the offer of some petty office in the army, when he was about eighteen, he not only declined that, but he also refused to train when warned, and was fined for it. He then resolved that he would never have anything to do with any war, unless it were a war for liberty.

When the troubles in Kansas[9] began, he sent several of his sons thither to strengthen the party of the Free State men, fitting them out with such weapons as he had; telling them that if the troubles should increase, and there should be need of him, he would follow, to assist them with his hand and counsel. This, as you all know, he soon after did; and it was through his agency, far more than any other's, that Kansas was made free.

For a part of his life he was a surveyor, and at one time he was engaged in wool-growing, and he went to Europe as an agent about that business. There, as everywhere, he had his eyes about him, and made many original observations. He said, for instance, that he saw why the soil of England was so rich, and that of Germany (I think it was) so poor, and he thought of writing to some of the crowned heads about it. It was because in England the peasantry live on the soil which they cultivate, but in Germany they are gathered into villages at night. It is a pity that he did not make a book of his observations.

I should say that he was an old-fashioned man in his respect for the Constitution, and his faith in the permanence of this Union. Slavery he deemed to be wholly opposed to these, and he was its determined foe.

He was by descent and birth a New England farmer, a man of great common sense, deliberate and practical as that class is, and tenfold more so. He was like the best of those who stood at Concord Bridge once, on Lexington Common, and on Bunker Hill, only he was firmer and higher principled than any that I have chanced to hear of as there. It was no abolition lecturer that con-

9. When it was decided by Congress that Kansas should vote to determine whether or not to legalize slavery, Brown had been one of the leaders of the fight to keep Kansas a free state.

verted him. Ethan Allen and Stark,[1] with whom he may in some respects be compared, were rangers in a lower and less important field. They could bravely face their country's foes, but he had the courage to face his country herself when she was in the wrong. A Western writer says, to account for his escape from so many perils, that he was concealed under a "rural exterior;" as if, in that prairie land, a hero should, by good rights, wear a citizen's dress only.

He did not go to the college called Harvard, good old Alma Mater as she is. He was not fed on the pap that is there furnished. As he phrased it, "I know no more of grammar than one of your calves." But he went to the great university of the West, where he sedulously pursued the study of Liberty, for which he had early betrayed a fondness, and having taken many degrees, he finally commenced the public practice of Humanity in Kansas, as you all know. Such were *his humanities*, and not any study of grammar. He would have left a Greek accent slanting the wrong way, and righted up a falling man.

He was one of that class of whom we hear a great deal, but, for the most part, see nothing at all,—the Puritans. It would be in vain to kill him. He died lately in the time of Cromwell, but he reappeared here. Why should he not? Some of the Puritan stock are said to have come over and settled in New England. They were a class that did something else than celebrate their forefathers' day, and eat parched corn in remembrance of that time. They were neither Democrats nor Republicans, but men of simple habits, straightforward, prayerful; not thinking much of rulers who did not fear God, not making many compromises, nor seeking after available candidates.

"In his camp," as one has recently written, and as I have myself heard him state, "he permitted no profanity; no man of loose morals was suffered to remain there, unless, indeed, as a prisoner of war. 'I would rather,' said he, 'have the small-pox, yellow fever, and cholera, all together in my camp, than a man without principle. . . . It is a mistake, sir, that our people make, when they think that bullies are the best fighters, or that they are the fit men to oppose these Southerners. Give me men of good principles,—God-fearing men,—men who respect themselves, and with a dozen of them I will oppose any hundred such men as these Buford ruffians.' "[2] He said that if one offered himself to be a soldier under him, who was forward to tell what he could or would do if he could only get sight of the enemy, he had but little confidence in

1. Revolutionary War heroes—Allen from Vermont, and John Stark from New Hampshire.
2. John Buford commanded the U.S. Army forces in Kansas during the strife there. The abolitionists felt he served only to support the slave owners.

him.

He was never able to find more than a score or so of recruits whom he would accept, and only about a dozen, among them his sons, in whom he had perfect faith. When he was here, some years ago, he showed to a few a little manuscript book,—his "orderly book" I think he called it,—containing the names of his company in Kansas, and the rules by which they bound themselves; and he stated that several of them had already sealed the contract with their blood. When some one remarked that, with the addition of a chaplain, it would have been a perfect Cromwellian troop, he observed that he would have been glad to add a chaplain to the list, if he could have found one who could fill that office worthily. It is easy enough to find one for the United States army. I believe that he had prayers in his camp morning and evening, nevertheless.

He was a man of Spartan habits, and at sixty was scrupulous about his diet at your table, excusing himself by saying that he must eat sparingly and fare hard, as became a soldier, or one who was fitting himself for difficult enterprises, a life of exposure.

A man of rare common sense and directness of speech, as of action; a transcendentalist above all, a man of ideas and principles, —that was what distinguished him. Not yielding to a whim or transient impulse, but carrying out the purpose of a life. I noticed that he did not overstate anything, but spoke within bounds. I remember, particularly, how, in his speech here, he referred to what his family had suffered in Kansas, without ever giving the least vent to his pent-up fire. It was a volcano with an ordinary chimney-flue. Also referring to the deeds of certain Border Ruffians,[3] he said, rapidly paring away his speech, like an experienced soldier, keeping a reserve of force and meaning, "They had a perfect right to be hung." He was not in the least a rhetorician, was not talking to Buncombe[4] or his constituents anywhere, had no need to invent anything but to tell the simple truth, and communicate his own resolution; therefore he appeared incomparably strong, and eloquence in Congress and elsewhere seemed to me at a discount. It was like the speeches of Cromwell compared with those of an ordinary king.

As for his tact and prudence, I will merely say, that at a time when scarcely a man from the Free States was able to reach Kansas by any direct route, at least without having his arms taken from him, he, carrying what imperfect guns and other weapons he could collect, openly and slowly drove an ox-cart through Missouri, ap-

3. The supporters of slavery who crossed from Missouri into Kansas to harass the free-state supporters.
4. Felix Walker, representative to Congress from Buncombe County, N.C., 1819–21, defended his filibustering in Congress by saying he was "speaking for Buncombe"—thus any insincere speaker.

parently in the capacity of a surveyor, with his surveying compass exposed in it, and so passed unsuspected, and had ample opportunity to learn the designs of the enemy. For some time after his arrival he still followed the same profession. When, for instance, he saw a knot of the ruffians on the prairie, discussing, of course, the single topic which then occupied their minds, he would, perhaps, take his compass and one of his sons, and proceed to run an imaginary line right through the very spot on which that conclave had assembled, and when he came up to them, he would naturally pause and have some talk with them, learning their news, and, at last, all their plans perfectly; and having thus completed his real survey he would resume his imaginary one, and run on his line till he was out of sight.

When I expressed surprise that he could live in Kansas at all, with a price set upon his head, and so large a number, including the authorities, exasperated against him, he accounted for it by saying, "It is perfectly well understood that I will not be taken." Much of the time for some years he has had to skulk in swamps, suffering from poverty and from sickness, which was the consequence of exposure, befriended only by Indians and a few whites. But though it might be known that he was lurking in a particular swamp, his foes commonly did not care to go in after him. He could even come out into a town where there were more Border Ruffians than Free State men, and transact some business, without delaying long, and yet not be molested; for, said he, "no little handful of men were willing to undertake it, and a large body could not be got together in season."

As for his recent failure, we do not know the facts about it. It was evidently far from being a wild and desperate attempt. His enemy, Mr. Vallandigham,[5] is compelled to say that "it was among the best planned and executed conspiracies that ever failed."

Not to mention his other successes, was it a failure, or did it show a want of good management, to deliver from bondage a dozen human beings, and walk off with them by broad daylight, for weeks if not months, at a leisurely pace, through one State after another, for half the length of the North, conspicuous to all parties, with a price set upon his head, going into a court-room on his way and telling what he had done, thus convincing Missouri that it was not profitable to try to hold slaves in his neighborhood?—and this, not because the government menials were lenient, but because they were afraid of him.

Yet he did not attribute his success, foolishly, to "his star," or to any magic. He said, truly, that the reason why such greatly superior

5. Clement Laird Vallandigham, representative from Ohio and anti-abolition-ist, who interviewed Brown at Harpers Ferry after he was wounded.

numbers quailed before him was, as one of his prisoners confessed, because they *lacked a cause,*—a kind of armor which he and his party never lacked. When the time came, few men were found willing to lay down their lives in defense of what they knew to be wrong; they did not like that this should be their last act in this world.

But to make haste to *his* last act, and its effects.

The newspapers seem to ignore, or perhaps are really ignorant, of the fact that there are at least as many as two or three individuals to a town throughout the North who think much as the present speaker does about him and his enterprise. I do not hesitate to say that they are an important and growing party. We aspire to be something more than stupid and timid chattels, pretending to read history and our Bibles, but desecrating every house and every day we breathe in. Perhaps anxious politicians may prove that only seventeen white men and five negroes were concerned in the late enterprise; but their very anxiety to prove this might suggest to themselves that all is not told. Why do they still dodge the truth? They are so anxious because of a dim consciousness of the fact, which they do not distinctly face, that at least a million of the free inhabitants of the United States would have rejoiced if it had succeeded. They at most only criticise the tactics. Though we wear no crape, the thought of that man's position and probable fate is spoiling many a man's day here at the North for other thinking. If any one who has seen him here can pursue successfully any other train of thought, I do not know what he is made of. If there is any such who gets his usual allowance of sleep, I will warrant him to fatten easily under any circumstances which do not touch his body or purse. I put a piece of paper and a pencil under my pillow, and when I could not sleep I wrote in the dark.

On the whole, my respect for my fellow-men, except as one may outweigh a million, is not being increased these days. I have noticed the cold-blooded way in which newspaper writers and men generally speak of this event, as if an ordinary malefactor, though one of unusual "pluck,"—as the Governor of Virginia is reported to have said, using the language of the cock-pit, "the gamest man he ever saw,"—had been caught, and were about to be hung. He was not dreaming of his foes when the governor thought he looked so brave. It turns what sweetness I have to gall, to hear, or hear of, the remarks of some of my neighbors. When we heard at first that he was dead, one of my townsmen observed that "he died as the fool dieth;" which, pardon me, for an instant suggested a likeness in him dying to my neighbor living. Others, craven-hearted, said disparagingly, that "he threw his life away," because he resisted the government. Which way have they thrown *their* lives, pray?—such as would praise a man for attacking singly an ordinary band of thieves or murderers. I hear another ask, Yankee-like, "What will he gain by it?" as if he expected to fill his pockets by this enterprise. Such a one has no idea of gain but in this worldly sense. If it does not lead to a "surprise" party, if he does not get a new pair of boots, or a vote of thanks, it must be a failure. "But he won't gain anything by it." Well, no, I don't suppose he could get four-and-sixpence a day for being hung, take the year round; but then he stands a chance to save a considerable part of his soul,—and *such* a soul!—when *you* do not. No doubt you can get more in your market for a quart of milk than for a quart of blood, but that is not the market that heroes carry their blood to.

Such do not know that like the seed is the fruit, and that, in the moral world, when good seed is planted, good fruit is inevitable, and does not depend on our watering and cultivating; that when you plant, or bury, a hero in his field, a crop of heroes is sure to spring up. This is a seed of such force and vitality, that it does not ask our leave to germinate.

The momentary charge at Balaklava,[6] in obedience to a blundering command, proving what a perfect machine the soldier is, has, properly enough, been celebrated by a poet laureate; but the steady, and for the most part successful, charge of this man, for some years, against the legions of Slavery, in obedience to an infinitely higher command, is as much more memorable than that as an intelligent and conscientious man is superior to a machine. Do you think that that will go unsung?

"Served him right,"—"A dangerous man,"—"He is undoubtedly insane." So they proceed to live their sane, and wise, and altogether admirable lives, reading their Plutarch a little, but chiefly pausing at that feat of Putnam,[7] who was let down into a wolf's den; and in this wise they nourish themselves for brave and patriotic deeds some time or other. The Tract Society could afford to print that story of Putnam. You might open the district schools with the reading of it, for there is nothing about Slavery or the Church in it; unless it occurs to the reader that some pastors are *wolves* in sheep's clothing. "The American Board of Commissioners for Foreign Missions," even, might dare to protest against *that* wolf. I have heard of boards, and of American boards, but it chances that I never heard of this particular lumber till lately. And yet I hear of Northern men, and women, and children, by families, buying a "life-membership" in such societies as these. A life-membership in the grave! You can get buried cheaper than that.

6. The Crimean War attack commemorated in the poet laureate Tennyson's poem, "The Charge of the Light Brigade."

7. According to tradition, Israel Putnam, Revolutionary War hero, crept into a wolf's lair and killed the beast at close quarters.

Our foes are in our midst and all about us. There is hardly a house but is divided against itself, for our foe is the all but universal woodenness of both head and heart, the want of vitality in man, which is the effect of our vice; and hence are begotten fear, superstition, bigotry, persecution, and slavery of all kinds. We are mere figure-heads upon a hulk, with livers in the place of hearts. The curse is the worship of idols, which at length changes the worshiper into a stone image himself; and the New Englander is just as much an idolator as the Hindoo. This man was an exception, for he did not set up even a political graven image between him and his God.[8]

A church that can never have done with excommunicating Christ while it exists! Away with your broad and flat churches, and your narrow and tall churches! Take a step forward, and invent a new style of out-houses. Invent a salt that will save you, and defend our nostrils.

The modern Christian is a man who has consented to say all the prayers in the liturgy, provided you will let him go straight to bed and sleep quietly afterward. All his prayers begin with "Now I lay me down to sleep," and he is forever looking forward to the time when he shall go to his "*long* rest." He has consented to perform certain old-established charities, too, after a fashion, but he does not wish to hear of any new-fangled ones; he doesn't wish to have any supplementary articles added to the contract, to fit it to the present time. He shows the whites of his eyes on the Sabbath, and the blacks all the rest of the week. The evil is not merely a stagnation of blood, but a stagnation of spirit. Many, no doubt, are well disposed, but sluggish by constitution and by habit, and they cannot conceive of a man who is actuated by higher motives than they are. Accordingly they pronounce this man insane, for they know that *they* could never act as he does, as long as they are themselves.

We dream of foreign countries, of other times and races of men, placing them at a distance in history or space; but let some significant event like the present occur in our midst, and we discover, often, this distance and this strangeness between us and our nearest neighbors. *They* are our Austrias, and Chinas, and South Sea Islands. Our crowded society becomes well spaced all at once, clean and handsome to the eye,—a city of magnificent distances.[9] We discover why it was that we never got beyond compliments and surfaces with them before; we become aware of as many versts[1] between us and them as there are between a wandering Tartar and a Chinese town. The thoughtful man becomes a hermit in the

8. Exodus xx.4.
9. Pierre Charles L'Enfant's description of his original plan for Washington,

D.C.
1. A Russian measure equivalent to two-thirds of a mile.

thoroughfares of the market-place. Impassable seas suddenly find their level between us, or dumb steppes stretch themselves out there. It is the difference of constitution, of intelligence, and faith, and not streams and mountains, that make the true and impassable boundaries between individuals and between states. None but the like-minded can come plenipotentiary to our court.

I read all the newspapers I could get within a week after this event, and I do not remember in them a single expression of sympathy for these men. I have since seen one noble statement, in a Boston paper, not editorial. Some voluminous sheets decided not to print the full report of Brown's words to the exclusion of other matter. It was as if a publisher should reject the manuscript of the New Testament, and print Wilson's[2] last speech. The same journal which contained this pregnant news was chiefly filled, in parallel columns, with the reports of the political conventions that were being held. But the descent to them was too steep. They should have been spared this contrast,—been printed in an extra, at least. To turn from the voices and deeds of earnest men to the *cackling* of political conventions! Office-seekers and speech-makers, who do not so much as lay an honest egg, but wear their breasts bare upon an egg of chalk! Their great game is the game of straws, or rather that universal aboriginal game of the platter, at which the Indians cried *hub, bub!*[3] Exclude the reports of religious and political conventions, and publish the words of a living man.

But I object not so much to what they have omitted as to what they have inserted. Even the *Liberator*[4] called it "a misguided, wild, and apparently insane—effort." As for the herd of newspapers and magazines, I do not chance to know an editor in the country who will deliberately print anything which he knows will ultimately and permanently reduce the number of his subscribers. They do not believe that it would be expedient. How then can they print truth? If we do not say pleasant things, they argue, nobody will attend to us. And so they do like some traveling auctioneers, who sing an obscene song, in order to draw a crowd around them. Republican editors, obliged to get their sentences ready for the morning edition, and accustomed to look at everything by the twilight of politics, express no admiration, nor true sorrow even, but call these men "deluded fanatics,"—"mistaken men,"—"insane," or "crazed." It suggests what a *sane* set of editors we are blessed with, *not* "mistaken men;" who know very well on which side their bread is buttered, at least.

A man does a brave and humane deed, and at once, on all

2. Henry Wilson, United States senator from Massachusetts, who spoke out frequently against slavery.
3. The word *hubbub* originated from an Indian game which was accompanied by a continual shouting of "Hub-bub."
4. The antislavery periodical edited by William Lloyd Garrison.

sides, we hear people and parties declaring, "I didn't do it, nor countenance *him* to do it, in any conceivable way. It can't be fairly inferred from my past career." I, for one, am not interested to hear you define your position. I don't know that I ever was or ever shall be. I think it is mere egotism, or impertinent at this time. Ye needn't take so much pains to wash your skirts of him. No intelligent man will ever be convinced that he was any creature of yours. He went and came, as he himself informs us, "under the auspices of John Brown and nobody else." The Republican party does not perceive how many his *failure* will make to vote more correctly than they would have them. They have counted the votes of Pennsylvania & Co., but they have not correctly counted Captain Brown's vote. He has taken the wind out of their sails,—the little wind they had,—and they may as well lie to and repair.

What though he did not belong to your clique! Though you may not approve of his method or his principles, recognize his magnanimity. Would you not like to claim kindredship with him in that, though in no other thing he is like, or likely, to you? Do you think that you would lose your reputation so? What you lost at the spile, you would gain at the bung.[5]

If they do not mean all this, then they do not speak the truth, and say what they mean. They are simply at their old tricks still.

"It was always conceded to him," *says one who calls him crazy,* "that he was a conscientious man, very modest in his demeanor, apparently inoffensive, until the subject of Slavery was introduced, when he would exhibit a feeling of indignation unparalleled."

The slave-ship is on her way, crowded with its dying victims; new cargoes are being added in mid-ocean; a small crew of slave-holders, countenanced by a large body of passengers, is smothering four millions under the hatches, and yet the politician asserts that the only proper way by which deliverance is to be obtained is by "the quiet diffusion of the sentiments of humanity," without any "outbreak." As if the sentiments of humanity were ever found unaccompanied by its deeds, and you could disperse them, all finished to order, the pure article, as easily as water with a watering-pot, and so lay the dust. What is that that I hear cast overboard? The bodies of the dead that have found deliverance. That is the way we are "diffusing" humanity, and its sentiments with it.

Prominent and influential editors, accustomed to deal with politicians, men of an infinitely lower grade, say, in their ignorance, that he acted "on the principle of revenge." They do not know the man. They must enlarge themselves to conceive of him. I have no doubt that the time will come when they will begin to

5. What you lose in one place, you may gain in another. What beer a tavern-keeper loses in opening a barrel he may regain by shortchanging his customers.

see him as he was. They have got to conceive of a man of faith and of religious principle, and not a politician or an Indian; of a man who did not wait till he was personally interfered with or thwarted in some harmless business before he gave his life to the cause of the oppressed.

If Walker[6] may be considered the representative of the South, I wish I could say that Brown was the representative of the North. He was a superior man. He did not value his bodily life in comparison with ideal things. He did not recognize unjust human laws, but resisted them as he was bid. For once we are lifted out of the trivialness and dust of politics into the region of truth and manhood. No man in America has ever stood up so persistently and effectively for the dignity of human nature, knowing himself for a man, and the equal of any and all governments. In that sense he was the most American of us all. He needed no babbling lawyer, making false issues, to defend him. He was more than a match for all the judges that American voters, or office-holders of whatever grade, can create. He could not have been tried by a jury of his peers, because his peers did not exist. When a man stands up serenely against the condemnation and vengeance of mankind, rising above them literally *by a whole body*,—even though he were of late the vilest murderer, who has settled that matter with himself,—the spectacle is a sublime one,—didn't ye know it, ye *Liberators*, ye *Tribunes*, ye *Republicans*?[7]—and we become criminal in comparison. Do yourselves the honor to recognize him. He needs none of your respect.

As for the Democratic journals, they are not human enough to affect me at all. I do not feel indignation at anything they may say.

I am aware that I anticipate a little,—that he was still, at the last accounts, alive in the hands of his foes; but that being the case, I have all along found myself thinking and speaking of him as physically dead.

I do not believe in erecting statues to those who still live in our hearts, whose bones have not yet crumbled in the earth around us, but I would rather see the statue of Captain Brown in the Massachusetts State-House yard[8] than that of any other man whom I know. I rejoice that I live in this age, that I am his contemporary.

What a contrast, when we turn to that political party which is so anxiously shuffling him and his plot out of its way, and looking

6. Robert J. Walker of Mississippi, who had been appointed governor of Kansas Territory in 1856 during Brown's strife there.
7. Thoreau believed that Garrison's *Liberator*, Greeley's *Tribune*, and the Springfield *Republican*, all ostensibly abolitionist papers, had hedged at defending Brown in their pages.

8. Shortly after the death of Horace Mann, the educator, in 1859, a statue to him was erected in the yard of the Massachusetts State House. Thoreau declined to contribute to the fund for the statue, saying, "A man ought not any more to take up room in the world after he was dead."

around for some available slaveholder, perhaps, to be its candidate, at least for one who will execute the Fugitive Slave Law, and all those other unjust laws which he took up arms to annul!

Insane! A father and six sons, and one son-in-law, and several more men besides,—as many at least as twelve disciples,—all struck with insanity at once; while the sane tyrant holds with a firmer grip than ever his four millions of slaves, and a thousand sane editors, his abettors, are saving their country and their bacon! Just as insane were his efforts in Kansas. Ask the tyrant who is his most dangerous foe, the sane man or the insane? Do the thousands who know him best, who have rejoiced at his deeds in Kansas, and have afforded him material aid there, think him insane? Such a use of this word is a mere trope with most who persist in using it, and I have no doubt that many of the rest have already in silence retracted their words.

Read his admirable answers to Mason[9] and others. How they are dwarfed and defeated by the contrast! On the one side, half-brutish, half-timid questioning; on the other, truth, clear as lightning, crashing into their obscene temples. They are made to stand with Pilate, and Gessler,[1] and the Inquisition. How ineffectual their speech and action! and what a void their silence! They are but helpless tools in this great work. It was no human power that gathered them about this preacher.

What have Massachusetts and the North sent a few *sane* representatives to Congress for, of late years?—to declare with effect what kind of sentiments? All their speeches put together and boiled down—and probably they themselves will confess it—do not match for manly directness and force, and for simple truth, the few casual remarks of crazy John Brown on the floor of the Harper's Ferry engine-house,[2]—that man whom you are about to hang, to send to the other world, though not to represent *you* there. No, he was not our representative in any sense. He was too fair a specimen of a man to represent the like of us. Who, then, *were* his constituents? If you read his words understandingly you will find out. In his case there is no idle eloquence, no made, nor maiden speech, no compliments to the oppressor. Truth is his inspirer, and earnestness the polisher of his sentences. He could afford to lose his Sharps rifles,[3] while he retained his faculty of speech,—a Sharps rifle of infinitely surer and longer range.

And the New York *Herald* reports the conversation *verbatim!* It

9. James Murray Mason, senator from Virginia, who later conducted the Senate hearings on the Harpers Ferry incident.
1. Tyrannical Austrian bailiff of a Swiss canton, whom the legendary William Tell supposedly killed.

2. Brown was finally captured in the engine house of the Harpers Ferry arsenal by Col. Robert E. Lee's forces.
3. The efficient rifles used by the abolitionists in Kansas gave them an advantage over the proslavery men.

does not know of what undying words it is made the vehicle.

I have no respect for the penetration of any man who can read the report of that conversation and still call the principal in it insane. It has the ring of a saner sanity than an ordinary discipline and habits of life, than an ordinary organization, secure. Take any sentence of it,—"Any questions that I can honorably answer, I will; not otherwise. So far as I am myself concerned, I have told everything truthfully. I value my word, sir." The few who talk about his vindictive spirit, while they really admire his heroism, have no test by which to detect a noble man, no amalgam to combine with his pure gold. They mix their own dross with it.

It is a relief to turn from these slanders to the testimony of his more truthful, but frightened jailers and hangmen. Governor Wise[4] speaks far more justly and appreciatingly of him than any Northern editor, or politician, or public personage, that I chance to have heard from. I know that you can afford to hear him again on this subject. He says: "They are themselves mistaken who take him to be a madman. . . . He is cool, collected, and indomitable, and it is but just to him to say that he was humane to his prisoners. . . . And he inspired me with great trust in his integrity as a man of truth. He is a fanatic, vain and garrulous" (I leave that part to Mr. Wise), "but firm, truthful, and intelligent. His men, too, who survive, are like him. . . . Colonel Washington[5] says that he was the coolest and firmest man he ever saw in defying danger and death. With one son dead by his side, and another shot through, he felt the pulse of his dying son with one hand, and held his rifle with the other, and commanded his men with the utmost composure, encouraging them to be firm, and to sell their lives as dear as they could. Of the three white prisoners, Brown, Stevens, and Coppoc,[6] it was hard to say which was most firm."

Almost the first Northern men whom the slaveholder has learned to respect!

The testimony of Mr. Vallandigham, though less valuable, is of the same purport, that "it is vain to underrate either the man or his conspiracy. . . . He is the farthest possible removed from the ordinary ruffian, fanatic, or madman."

"All is quiet at Harper's Ferry," say the journals. What is the character of that calm which follows when the law and the slaveholder prevail? I regard this event as a touchstone designed to bring out, with glaring distinctness, the character of this government. We needed to be thus assisted to see it by the light of history. It needed to see itself. When a government puts forth its strength

4. Henry Alexander Wise, governor of Virginia at the time of the Harpers Ferry incident.
5. Lewis Washington, a farmer on the outskirts of Harpers Ferry, who was taken hostage by Brown's forces.
6. Aaron D. Stevens, Edwin Coppoc, and Brown himself.

532 · *Henry David Thoreau*

on the side of injustice, as ours to maintain slavery and kill the
liberators of the slave, it reveals itself a merely brute force, or
worse, a demoniacal force. It is the head of the Plug-Uglies.[7] It
is more manifest than ever that tyranny rules. I see this government to be effectually allied with France and Austria in oppressing
mankind. There sits a tyrant holding fettered four millions of
slaves; here comes their heroic liberator. This most hypocritical
and diabolical government looks up from its seat on the gasping
four millions, and inquires with an assumption of innocence:
"What do you assault me for? Am I not an honest man? Cease agitation on this subject, or I will make a slave of you, too, or else
hang you."

We talk about a *representative* government; but what a monster
of a government is that where the noblest faculties of the mind, and
the *whole* heart, are not *represented*. A semi-human tiger or ox,
stalking over the earth, with its heart taken out and the top of its
brain shot away. Heroes have fought well on their stumps when
their legs were shot off, but I never heard of any good done by
such a government as that.

The only government that I recognize—and it matters not how
few are at the head of it, or how small its army—is that power that
establishes justice in the land, never that which establishes injustice. What shall we think of a government to which all the
truly brave and just men in the land are enemies, standing between
it and those whom it oppresses? A government that pretends to be
Christian and crucifies a million Christs every day!

Treason! Where does such treason take its rise? I cannot help
thinking of you as you deserve, ye governments. Can you dry up
the fountains of thought? High treason, when it is resistance to
tyranny here below, has its origin in, and is first committed by, the
power that makes and forever recreates man. When you have
caught and hung all these human rebels, you have accomplished
nothing but your own guilt, for you have not struck at the fountainhead. You presume to contend with a foe against whom West
Point cadets and rifled cannon *point* not. Can all the art of the
cannon-founder tempt matter to turn against its maker? Is the
form in which the founder thinks he casts it more essential than
the constitution of it and of himself?

The United States have a coffle[8] of four millions of slaves. They
are determined to keep them in this condition; and Massachusetts
is one of the confederated overseers to prevent their escape. Such
are not all the inhabitants of Massachusetts, but such are they
who rule and are obeyed here. It was Massachusetts, as well as

7. Ardent proslavery advocates in the
Kansas struggle.

8. A train of men fastened together
by chains.

Virginia, that put down this insurrection at Harper's Ferry. She sent the marines there, and she will have *to pay the penalty of her sin.*

Suppose that there is a society in this State that out of its own purse and magnanimity saves all the fugitive slaves that run to us, and protects our colored fellow-citizens, and leaves the other work to the government, so called. Is not that government fast losing its occupation, and becoming contemptible to mankind? If private men are obliged to perform the offices of government, to protect the weak and dispense justice, then the government becomes only a hired man, or clerk, to perform menial or indifferent services. Of course, that is but the shadow of a government whose existence necessitates a Vigilant Committee. What should we think of the Oriental Cadi even, behind whom worked in secret a Vigilant Committee? But such is the character of our Northern States generally; each has its Vigilant Committee. And, to a certain extent, these crazy governments recognize and accept this relation. They say, virtually, "We'll be glad to work for you on these terms, only don't make a noise about it." And thus the government, its salary being insured, withdraws into the back shop, taking the Constitution with it, and bestows most of its labor on repairing that. When I hear it at work sometimes, as I go by, it reminds me, at best, of those farmers who in winter contrive to turn a penny by following the cooperating business. And what kind of spirit is their barrel made to hold? They speculate in stocks, and bore holes in mountains, but they are not competent to lay out even a decent highway. The only *free* road, the Underground Railroad, is owned and managed by the Vigilant Committee. *They* have tunneled under the whole breadth of the land. Such a government is losing its power and respectability as surely as water runs out of a leaky vessel, and is held by one that can contain it.

I hear many condemn these men because they were so few. When were the good and the brave ever in a majority? Would you have had him wait till that time came?—till you and I came over to him? The very fact that he had no rabble or troop of hirelings about him would alone distinguish him from ordinary heroes. His company was small indeed, because few could be found worthy to pass muster. Each one who there laid down his life for the poor and oppressed was a picked man, culled out of many thousands, if not millions; apparently a man of principle, of rare courage, and devoted humanity; ready to sacrifice his life at any moment for the benefit of his fellow-man. It may be doubted if there were as many more their equals in these respects in all the country,—I speak of his followers only,—for their leader, no doubt, scoured the land far and wide, seeking to swell his troop. These alone were ready to step between the oppressor and the oppressed. Surely they were the very best men you could select to be hung. That was the greatest compliment which this country could pay them. They were ripe for her gallows. She has tried a long time, she has hung a good many, but never found the right one before.

When I think of him, and his six sons, and his son-in-law, not to enumerate the others, enlisted for this fight, proceeding coolly, reverently, humanely to work, for months if not years, sleeping and waking upon it, summering and wintering the thought, without expecting any reward but a good conscience, while almost all America stood ranked on the other side,—I say again that it affects me as a sublime spectacle. If he had had any journal advocating "*his cause*," any organ, as the phrase is, monotonously and wearisomely playing the same old tune, and then passing round the hat, it would have been fatal to his efficiency. If he had acted in any way so as to be let alone by the government, he might have been suspected. It was the fact that the tyrant must give place to him, or he to the tyrant, that distinguished him from all the reformers of the day that I know.

It was his peculiar doctrine that a man has a perfect right to interfere by force with the slave-holder, in order to rescue the slave. I agree with him. They who are continually shocked by slavery have some right to be shocked by the violent death of the slave-holder, but no others. Such will be more shocked by his life than by his death. I shall not be forward to think him mistaken in his method who quickest succeeds to liberate the slave. I speak for the slave when I say that I prefer the philanthropy of Captain Brown to that philanthropy which neither shoots me nor liberates me. At any rate, I do not think it is quite sane for one to spend his whole life in talking or writing about this matter, unless he is continuously inspired, and I have not done so. A man may have other affairs to attend to. I do not wish to kill nor to be killed, but I can foresee circumstances in which both these things would be by me unavoidable. We preserve the so-called peace of our community by deeds of petty violence every day. Look at the policeman's billy and handcuffs! Look at the jail! Look at the gallows! Look at the chaplain of the regiment! We are hoping only to live safely on the outskirts of *this* provisional army. So we defend ourselves and our hen-roosts, and maintain slavery. I know that the mass of my countrymen think that the only righteous use that can be made of Sharps rifles and revolvers is to fight duels with them, when we are insulted by other nations, or to hunt Indians, or shoot fugitive slaves with them, or the like. I think that for once the Sharps rifles and the revolvers were employed in a righteous cause. The tools were in the hands of one who could use them.

The same indignation that is said to have cleared the temple once will clear it again. The question is not about the weapon, but the spirit in which you use it. No man has appeared in America, as yet, who loved his fellow-man so well, and treated him so tenderly. He lived for him. He took up his life and he laid it down for him. What sort of violence is that which is encouraged, not by soldiers, but by peaceable citizens, not so much by laymen as by ministers of the Gospel, not so much by the fighting sects as by the Quakers, and not so much by Quaker men as by Quaker women?

This event advertises me that there is such a fact as death,—the possibility of a man's dying. It seems as if no man had ever died in America before; for in order to die you must first have lived. I don't believe in the hearses, and palls, and funerals that they have had. There was no death in the case, because there had been no life; they merely rotted or sloughed off, pretty much as they had rotted or sloughed along. No temple's veil was rent,[9] only a hole dug somewhere. Let the dead bury their dead. The best of them fairly ran down like a clock. Franklin,—Washington,—they were let off without dying; they were merely missing one day. I hear a good many pretend that they are going to die; or that they have died, for aught that I know. Nonsense! I'll defy them to do it. They haven't got life enough in them. They'll deliquesce like fungi, and keep a hundred eulogists mopping the spot where they left off. Only half a dozen or so have died since the world began. Do you think that you are going to die, sir? No, there's no hope of you. You haven't got your lesson yet. You've got to stay after school. We make a needless ado about capital punishment,—taking lives, when there is no life to take. *Memento mori!*[1] We don't understand that sublime sentence which some worthy got sculptured on his gravestone once. We've interpreted it in a groveling and sniveling sense; we've wholly forgotton how to die.

But be sure you do die nevertheless. Do your work, and finish it. If you know how to begin, you will know when to end.

These men, in teaching us how to die, have at the same time taught us how to live. If this man's acts and words do not create a revival, it will be the severest possible satire on the acts and words that do. It is the best news that America has ever heard. It has already quickened the feeble pulse of the North, and infused more and more generous blood into her veins and heart than any number of years of what is called commercial and political prosperity could. How many a man who was lately contemplating suicide has now something to live for!

9. Mark xv.38.   1. Literally, remember to die—i.e., be prepared for death.

One writer says that Brown's peculiar monomania made him to be "dreaded by the Missourians as a supernatural being." Sure enough, a hero in the midst of us cowards is always so dreaded. He is just that thing. He shows himself superior to nature. He has a spark of divinity in him.

> "Unless above himself he can
> Erect himself, how poor a thing is man!"[2]

Newspaper editors argue also that it is a proof of his *insanity* that he thought he was appointed to do this work which he did,— that he did not suspect himself for a moment! They talk as if it were impossible that a man could be "divinely appointed" in these days to do any work whatever; as if vows and religion were out of date as connected with any man's daily work; as if the agent to abolish slavery could only be somebody appointed by the President, or by some political party. They talk as if a man's death were a failure, and his continued life, be it of whatever character, were a success.

When I reflect to what a cause this man devoted himself, and how religiously, and then reflect to what cause his judges and all who condemn him so angrily and fluently devote themselves, I see that they are as far apart as the heavens and earth are asunder.

The amount of it is, our *"leading men"* are a harmless kind of folk, and they know *well enough* that *they* were not divinely appointed, but elected by the votes of their party.

Who is it whose safety requires that Captain Brown be hung? Is it indispensable to any Northern man? Is there no resource but to cast this man also to the Minotaur?[3] If you do not wish it, say so distinctly. While these things are being done, beauty stands veiled and music is a screeching lie. Think of him,—of his rare qualities!—such a man as it takes ages to make, and ages to understand; no mock hero, nor the representative of any party. A man such as the sun may not rise upon again in this benighted land. To whose making went the costliest material, the finest adamant; sent to be the redeemer of those in captivity; and the only use to which you can put him is to hang him at the end of a rope! You who pretend to care for Christ crucified, consider what you are about to do to him who offered himself to be the saviour of four millions of men.

Any man knows when he is justified, and all the wits in the world cannot enlighten him on that point. The murderer always knows that he is justly punished; but when a government takes the

2. Samuel Daniel (1562–1619), "To the Countess of Cumberland."
3. In Greek mythology, a celebrated monster, half man and half bull. When Minos defeated Athens, he demanded an annual tribute of fourteen youths and maidens to be fed to the monster.

life of a man without the consent of his conscience, it is an audacious government, and is taking a step toward its own dissolution. Is it not possible that an individual may be right and a government wrong? Are laws to be enforced simply because they were made? or declared by any number of men to be good, if they are *not* good? Is there any necessity for a man's being a tool to perform a deed of which his better nature disapproves? Is it the intention of law-makers that *good* men shall be hung ever? Are judges to interpret the law according to the letter, and not the spirit? What right have *you* to enter into a compact with yourself that you *will* do thus or so, against the light within you? Is it for *you* to *make up* your mind,—to form any resolution whatever,— and not accept the convictions that are forced upon you, and which ever pass your understanding? I do not believe in lawyers, in that mode of attacking or defending a man, because you descend to meet the judge on his own ground, and, in cases of the highest importance, it is of no consequence whether a man breaks a human law or not. Let lawyers decide trivial cases. Business men may arrange that among themselves. If they were the interpreters of the everlasting laws which rightfully bind man, that would be another thing. A counterfeiting law-factory, standing half in a slave land and half in a free! What kind of laws for free men can you expect from that?

I am here to plead his cause with you. I plead not for his life, but for his character,—his immortal life; and so it becomes your cause wholly, and is not his in the least. Some eighteen hundred years ago Christ was crucified; this morning, perchance, Captain Brown was hung. These are the two ends of a chain which is not without its links. He is not Old Brown any longer; he is an angel of light.

I see now that it was necessary that the bravest and humanest man in all the country should be hung. Perhaps he saw it himself. I *almost fear* that I may yet hear of his deliverance, doubting if a prolonged life, if *any* life, can do as much good as his death.

"Misguided!" "Garrulous!" "Insane!" "Vindictive!" So ye write in your easy-chairs, and thus he wounded responds from the floor of the Armory, clear as a cloudless sky, true as the voice of nature is: "No man sent me here; it was my own prompting and that of my Maker. I acknowledge no master in human form."

And in what a sweet and noble strain he proceeds, addressing his captors, who stand over him: "I think, my friends, you are guilty of a great wrong against God and humanity, and it would be perfectly right for any one to interfere with you so far as to free those you willfully and wickedly hold in bondage."

And, referring to his movement: "It is, in my opinion, the greatest service a man can render to God."

"I pity the poor in bondage that have none to help them; that is why I am here; not to gratify any personal animosity, revenge, or vindictive spirit. It is my sympathy with the oppressed and the wronged, that are as good as you, and as precious in the sight of God."

You don't know your testament when you see it.

"I want you to understand that I respect the rights of the poorest and weakest of colored people, oppressed by the slave power, just as much as I do those of the most wealthy and powerful."

"I wish to say, furthermore, that you had better, all you people at the South, prepare yourselves for a settlement of that question, that must come up for settlement sooner than you are prepared for it. The sooner you are prepared the better. You may dispose of me very easily. I am nearly disposed of now; but this question is still to be settled,—this negro question, I mean; the end of that is not yet."

I foresee the time when the painter will paint that scene, no longer going to Rome for a subject;[4] the poet will sing it; the historian record it; and, with the Landing of the Pilgrims and the Declaration of Independence,[5] it will be the ornament of some future national gallery, when at least the present form of slavery shall be no more here. We shall then be at liberty to weep for Captain Brown. Then, and not till then, we will take our revenge.

1859   1860, 1866

Life Without Principle

At a lyceum, not long since, I felt that the lecturer had chosen a theme too foreign to himself, and so failed to interest me as much as he might have done. He described things not in or near to his heart, but toward his extremities and superficies. There was, in this sense, no truly central or centralizing thought in the lecture. I would have had him deal with his privatest experience, as the poet does. The greatest compliment that was ever paid me was when one asked me what I *thought*, and attended to my answer. I am surprised, as well as delighted, when this happens, it is such a rare use he would make of me, as if he were acquainted with the tool. Commonly, if men want anything of me, it is only to know how many acres I make of their land—since I am a surveyor—or,

---

4. Thoreau's prophecies have been fulfilled with a heroic painting of John Brown by John Curry in the Kansas State House and the Civil War marching song, "John Brown's Body."

5. John Trumbull's "Declaration of Independence" hangs in the Capitol in Washington; Henry Sargent's "Landing of the Pilgrims," at Pilgrim Hall in Plymouth, Mass.

at most, what trivial news I have burdened myself with. They never will go to law for my meat; they prefer the shell. A man once came a considerable distance to ask me to lecture on Slavery; but on conversing with him, I found that he and his clique expected seven eighths of the lecture to be theirs, and only one eighth mine; so I declined. I take it for granted, when I am invited to lecture anywhere—for I have had a little experience in that business—that there is a desire to hear what I *think* on some subject, though I may be the greatest fool in the country, and not that I should say pleasant things merely, or such as the audience will assent to; and I resolve, accordingly, that I will give them a strong dose of myself. They have sent for me, and engaged to pay for me, and I am determined that they shall have me, though I bore them beyond all precedent.

So now I would say something similar to you, my readers. Since *you* are my readers, and I have not been much of a traveler, I will not talk about people a thousand miles off, but come as near home as I can. As the time is short, I will leave out all the flattery, and retain all the criticism.

Let us consider the way in which we spend our lives.

This world is a place of business. What an infinite bustle! I am awaked almost every night by the panting of the locomotive. It interrupts my dreams. There is no sabbath. It would be glorious to see mankind at leisure for once. It is nothing but work, work, work. I cannot easily buy a blankbook to write thoughts in; they are commonly ruled for dollars and cents. An Irishman, seeing me making a minute in the fields, took it for granted that I was calculating my wages. If a man was tossed out of a window when an infant, and so made a cripple for life, or scared out of his wits by the Indians, it is regretted chiefly because he was thus incapacitated for—business! I think that there is nothing, not even crime, more opposed to poetry, to philosophy, ay, to life itself, than this incessant business.

There is a coarse and boisterous money-making fellow in the outskirts of our town, who is going to build a bank-wall under the hill along the edge of his meadow. The powers have put this into his head to keep him out of mischief, and he wishes me to spend three weeks digging there with him. The result will be that he will perhaps get some more money to hoard, and leave for his heirs to spend foolishly. If I do this, most will commend me as an industrious and hard-working man; but if I choose to devote myself to certain labors which yield more real profit, though but little money, they may be inclined to look on me as an idler. Nevertheless, as I do not need the police of meaningless labor to regulate me, and do not see anything absolutely praiseworthy in this fellow's undertaking any more than in many an enterprise of our own or foreign governments, however amusing it may be to him or them, I prefer to finish my education at a different school.

If a man walk in the woods for love of them half of each day, he is in danger of being regarded as a loafer; but if he spends his whole day as a speculator, shearing off those woods and making earth bald before her time, he is esteemed an industrious and enterprising citizen. As if a town had no interest in its forests but to cut them down!

Most men would feel insulted if it were proposed to employ them in throwing stones over a wall, and then in throwing them back, merely that they might earn their wages. But many are no more worthily employed now. For instance: just after sunrise, one summer morning, I noticed one of my neighbors walking beside his team, which was slowly drawing a heavy hewn stone swung under the axle, surrounded by an atmosphere of industry—his day's work begun, his brow commenced to sweat—a reproach to all sluggards and idlers—pausing abreast the shoulders of his oxen, and half turning round with a flourish of his merciful whip, while they gained their length on him. And I thought, Such is the labor which the American Congress exists to protect—honest, manly toil —honest as the day is long—that makes his bread taste sweet, and keeps society sweet—which all men respect and have consecrated; one of the sacred band, doing the needful but irksome drudgery. Indeed, I felt a slight reproach, because I observed this from a window, and was not abroad and stirring about a similar business. The day went by, and at evening I passed the yard of another neighbor, who keeps many servants, and spends much money foolishly, while he adds nothing to the common stock, and there I saw the stone of the morning lying beside a whimsical structure intended to adorn this Lord Timothy Dexter's[6] premises, and the dignity forthwith departed from the teamster's labor, in my eyes. In my opinion, the sun was made to light worthier toil than this. I may add that his employer has since run off, in debt to a good part of the town, and, after passing through Chancery, has settled somewhere else, there to become once more a patron of the arts.

The ways by which you may get money almost without exception lead downward. To have done anything by which you earned money *merely* is to have been truly idle or worse. If the laborer gets no more than the wages which his employer pays him, he is cheated, he cheats himself. If you would get money as a writer or lecturer, you must be popular, which is to go down perpendicularly. Those services which the community will most readily pay for, it is

6. 1747–1806. An eccentric who ornamented his gardens in Newburyport, Mass., with statues of the great, his own statue being included among them.

most disagreeable to render. You are paid for being something less than a man. The state does not commonly reward a genius any more wisely. Even the poet laureate would rather not have to celebrate the accidents of royalty. He must be bribed with a pipe of wine;[7] and perhaps another poet is called away from his muse to gauge that very pipe. As for my own business, even that kind of surveying which I could do with most satisfaction my employers do not want. They would prefer that I should do my work coarsely and not too well, ay, not well enough. When I observe that there are different ways of surveying, my employer commonly asks which will give him the most land, not which is most correct. I once invented a rule for measuring cordwood, and tried to introduce it in Boston; but the measurer there told me that the sellers did not wish to have their wood measured correctly—that he was already too accurate for them, and therefore they commonly got their wood measured in Charlestown before crossing the bridge.

The aim of the laborer should be, not to get his living, to get "a good job," but to perform well a certain work; and, even in a pecuniary sense, it would be economy for a town to pay its laborers so well that they would not feel that they were working for low ends, as for a livelihood merely, but for scientific, or even moral ends. Do not hire a man who does your work for money, but him who does it for love of it.

It is remarkable that there are few men so well employed, so much to their minds, but that a little money or fame would commonly buy them off from their present pursuit. I see advertisements for *active* young men, as if activity were the whole of a young man's capital. Yet I have been surprised when one has with confidence proposed to me, a grown man, to embark in some enterprise of his, as if I had absolutely nothing to do, my life having been a complete failure hitherto. What a doubtful compliment this to pay me! As if he had met me halfway across the ocean beating up against the wind, but bound nowhere, and proposed to me to go along with him! If I did, what do you think the underwriters would say? No, no! I am not without employment at this stage of the voyage. To tell the truth, I saw an advertisement for able-bodied seamen, when I was a boy, sauntering in my native port, and as soon as I came of age I embarked.

The community has no bribe that will tempt a wise man. You may raise money enough to tunnel a mountain, but you cannot raise money enough to hire a man who is minding *his own* business. An efficient and valuable man does what he can, whether the community pay him for it or not. The inefficient offer their inefficiency to the highest bidder, and are forever expecting to be put into office.

7. The poet laureate's salary in England is traditionally paid in casks of wine.

One would suppose that they were rarely disappointed.

Perhaps I am more than usually jealous with respect to my freedom. I feel that my connection with and obligation to society are still very slight and transient. Those slight labors which afford me a livelihood, and by which it is allowed that I am to some extent serviceable to my contemporaries, are as yet commonly a pleasure to me, and I am not often reminded that they are a necessity. So far I am successful. But I foresee that if my wants should be much increased, the labor required to supply them would become a drudgery. If I should sell both my forenoons and afternoons to society, as most appear to do, I am sure that for me there would be nothing left worth living for. I trust that I shall never thus sell my birthright for a mess of pottage.[8] I wish to suggest that a man may be very industrious, and yet not spend his time well. There is no more fatal blunderer than he who consumes the greater part of his life getting his living. All great enterprises are self-supporting. The poet, for instance, must sustain his body by his poetry, as a steam planing-mill feeds its boilers with the shavings it makes. You must get your living by loving. But as it is said of the merchants that ninety-seven in a hundred fail, so the life of men generally, tried by this standard, is a failure, and bankruptcy may be surely prophesied.

Merely to come into the world the heir of a fortune is not to be born, but to be stillborn, rather. To be supported by the charity of friends, or a government pension—provided you continue to breathe—by whatever fine synonyms you describe these relations, is to go into the almshouse. On Sundays the poor debtor goes to church to take an account of stock, and finds, of course, that his outgoes have been greater than his income. In the Catholic Church, especially, they go into chancery, make a clean confession, give up all, and think to start again. Thus men will lie on their backs, talking about the fall of man, and never make an effort to get up.

As for the comparative demand which men make on life, it is an important difference between two, that the one is satisfied with a level success, that his marks can all be hit by point-blank shots, but the other, however low and unsuccessful his life may be, constantly elevates his aim, though at a very slight angle to the horizon. I should much rather be the last man, though, as the Orientals say, "Greatness doth not approach him who is forever looking down; and all those who are looking high are growing poor."

It is remarkable that there is little or nothing to be remembered written on the subject of getting a living; how to make getting a living not merely honest and honorable, but altogether inviting and

8. Esau sold his inheritance to Jacob for a bowl of food (Genesis xxv.33).

glorious; for if *getting* a living is not so, then living is not. One would think, from looking at literature, that this question had never disturbed a solitary individual's musings. Is it that men are too much disgusted with their experience to speak of it? The lesson of value which money teaches, which the Author of the Universe has taken so much pains to teach us, we are inclined to skip altogether. As for the means of living, it is wonderful how indifferent men of all classes are about it, even reformers, so called— whether they inherit, or earn, or steal it. I think that Society has done nothing for us in this respect, or at least has undone what she has done. Cold and hunger seem more friendly to my nature than those methods which men have adopted and advise to ward them off.

The title *wise* is, for the most part, falsely applied. How can one be a wise man, if he does not know any better how to live than other men?—if he is only more cunning and intellectually subtle? Does Wisdom work in a treadmill? or does she teach how to succeed *by her example?* Is there any such thing as wisdom not applied to life? Is she merely the miller who grinds the finest logic? It is pertinent to ask if Plato got his *living* in a better way or more successfully than his contemporaries—or did he succumb to the difficulties of life like other men? Did he seem to prevail over some of them merely by indifference, or by assuming grand airs? or find it easier to live, because his aunt remembered him in her will? The ways in which most men get their living, that is, live, are mere makeshifts, and a shirking of the real business of life—chiefly because they do not know, but partly because they do not mean, any better.

The rush to California, for instance, and the attitude, not merely of merchants, but of philosophers and prophets, so called, in relation to it, reflect the greatest disgrace on mankind. That so many are ready to live by luck, and so get the means of commanding the labor of others less lucky, without contributing any value to society! And that is called enterprise! I know of no more startling development of the immorality of trade, and all the common modes of getting a living. The philosophy and poetry and religion of such a mankind are not worth the dust of a puffball. The hog that gets his living by rooting, stirring up the soil so, would be ashamed of such company. If I could command the wealth of all the worlds by lifting my finger, I would not pay *such* a price for it. Even Mahomet knew that God did not make this world in jest. It makes God to be a moneyed gentleman who scatters a handful of pennies in order to see mankind scramble for them. The world's raffle! A subsistence in the domains of Nature a thing to be raffled for! What a comment, what a satire, on our institutions! The conclusion will be, that mankind will hang itself upon a tree. And have all the precepts in all the Bibles taught men only this? and is the last and most admirable invention of the human race only on improved muck-rate? Is this the ground on which Orientals and Occidentals meet? Did God direct us so to get our living, digging where we never planted—and He would, perchance, reward us with lumps of gold?

God gave the righteous man a certificate entitling him to food and raiment, but the unrighteous man found a facsimile of the same in God's coffers, and appropriated it, and obtained food and raiment like the former. It is one of the most extensive systems of counterfeiting that the world has seen. I did not know that mankind was suffering for want of gold. I have seen a little of it. I know that it is very malleable, but not so malleable as wit. A grain of gold will gild a great surface, but not so much as a grain of wisdom.

The gold digger in the ravines of the mountains is as much a gambler as his fellow in the saloons of San Francisco. What difference does it make whether you shake dirt or shake dice? If you win, society is the loser. The gold digger is the enemy of the honest laborer, whatever checks and compensations there may be. It is not enough to tell me that you worked hard to get your gold. So does the Devil work hard. The way of transgressors may be hard[9] in many respects. The humblest observer who goes to the mines sees and says that gold digging is of the character of a lottery; the gold thus obtained is not the same thing with the wages of honest toil. But, practically, he forgets what he has seen, for he has seen only the fact, not the principle, and goes into trade there, that is, buys a ticket in what commonly proves another lottery, where the fact is not so obvious.

After reading Howitt's account[1] of the Australian gold diggings one evening, I had in my mind's eye, all night, the numerous valleys, with their streams, all cut up with foul pits, from ten to one hundred feet deep, and half a dozen feet across, as close as they can be dug, and partly filled with water—the locality to which men furiously rush to probe for their fortunes—uncertain where they shall break ground—not knowing but the gold is under their camp itself—sometimes digging one hundred and sixty feet before they strike the vein, or then missing it by a foot—turned into demons, and regardless of each others' rights, in their thirst for riches— whole valleys, for thirty miles, suddenly honeycombed by the pits of the miners, so that even hundreds are drowned in them—standing in water, and covered with mud and clay, they work night and

9. Proverbs xiii.15.
1. Richard Howitt, *Impressions of Aus-* tralia Felix during Four Years' Residence in that Colony (1845).

day, dying of exposure and disease. Having read this, and partly forgotten it, I was thinking, accidentally, of my own unsatisfactory
life, doing as others do; and with that vision of the diggings still
before me, I asked myself why I might not be washing some gold
daily, though it were only the finest particles—why I might not
sink a shaft down to the gold within me, and work that mine.
There is a Ballarat, a Bendigo[2] for you—what though it were a
sulky-gully? At any rate, I might pursue some path, however solitary
and narrow and crooked, in which I could walk with love and
reverence. Wherever a man separates from the multitude, and goes
his own way in this mood, there indeed is a fork in the road, though
ordinary travelers may see only a gap in the paling. His solitary path
across lots will turn out the *higher way* of the two.

Men rush to California and Australia as if the true gold were to
be found in that direction; but that is to go to the very opposite
extreme to where it lies. They go prospecting farther and farther
away from the true lead, and are most unfortunate when they
think themselves most successful. Is not our *native* soil auriferous?
Does not a stream from the golden mountains flow through our
native valley? and has not this for more than geologic ages been
bringing down the shining particles and forming the nuggets for
us? Yet, strange to tell, if a digger steal away, prospecting for this
true gold, into the unexplored solitudes around us, there is no
danger that any will dog his steps, and endeavor to supplant him.
He may claim and undermine the whole valley even, both the
cultivated and the uncultivated portions, his whole life long in
peace, for no one will ever dispute his claim. They will not mind
his cradles or his toms. He is not confined to a claim twelve feet
square, as at Ballarat, but may mine anywhere, and wash the
whole wide world in his tom.

Howitt says of the man who found the great nugget which
weighed twenty-eight pounds, at the Bendigo diggings in Australia:
"He soon began to drink; got a horse, and rode all about, generally at full gallop, and, when he met people, called out to inquire if they knew who he was, and then kindly informed them
that he was 'the bloody wretch that had found the nugget.' At last
he rode full speed against a tree, and nearly knocked his brains
out." I think, however, there was no danger of that, for he had
already knocked his brains out against the nugget. Howitt adds,
"He is a hopelessly ruined man." But he is a type of the class. They
are all fast men. Hear some of the names of the places where they
dig: "Jackass Flat"—"Sheep's-Head Gully"—"Murderer's Bar,"
etc. Is there no satire in these names? Let them carry their ill-
gotten wealth where they will, I am thinking it will still be "Jack-

2. Two cities in the Australian gold-mining area.

ass Flat," if not "Murderer's Bar," where they live.

The last resource of our energy has been the robbing of grave-yards on the Isthmus of Darien,[3] an enterprise which appears to be but in its infancy; for, according to late accounts, an act has passed its second reading in the legislature of New Granada, regulating this kind of mining; and a correspondent of the *Tribune* writes: "In the dry season, when the weather will permit of the country being properly prospected, no doubt other rich *guacas* [that is, graveyards] will be found." To emigrants he says: "Do not come before December; take the Isthmus route in preference to the Boca del Toro one; bring no useless baggage, and do not cumber youself with a tent; but a good pair of blankets will be necessary; a pick, shovel, and axe of good material will be almost all that is required": advice which might have been taken from the "Burker's Guide."[4] And he concludes with this line in italics and small capitals: "*If you are doing well at home,* STAY THERE," which may fairly be interpreted to mean, "If you are getting a good living by robbing graveyards at home, stay there."

But why go to California for a text? She is the child of New England, bred at her own school and church.

It is remarkable that among all the preachers there are so few moral teachers. The prophets are employed in excusing the ways of men. Most reverend seniors, the *illuminati* of the age, tell me, with a gracious, reminiscent smile, betwixt an aspiration and a shudder, not to be too tender about these things—to lump all that, that is, make a lump of gold of it. The highest advice I have heard on these subjects was groveling. The burden of it was—It is not worth your while to undertake to reform the world in this particular. Do not ask how your bread is buttered; it will make you sick, if you do—and the like. A man had better starve at once than lose his innocence in the process of getting his bread. If within the sophisticated man there is not an unsophisticated one, then he is but one of the devil's angels. As we grow old, we live more coarsely, we relax a little in our disciplines, and, to some extent, cease to obey our finest instincts. But we should be fastidious to the extreme of sanity, disregarding the gibes of those who are more unfortunate than ourselves.

In our science and philosophy, even, there is commonly no true and absolute account of things. The spirit of sect and bigotry has planted its hoof amid the stars. You have only to discuss the problem, whether the stars are inhabited or not, in order to dis-

3. Now Isthmus of Panama. Many Forty-niners on their way west crossed the Isthmus of Panama to avoid the long voyage around Cape Horn. New Granada was the then current name for Columbia. Boca Del Toro is a city in Panama.
4. Burke, a notorious Scotch criminal executed in 1829, had murdered to get bodies for doctors because graverobbing was becoming too difficult. Thus, a murderer's handbook.

cover it. Why must we daub the heavens as well as the earth? It was an unfortunate discovery that Dr. Kane[5] was a Mason, and that Sir John Franklin was another. But it was a more cruel suggestion that possibly that was the reason why the former went in search of the latter. There is not a popular magazine in this country that would dare to print a child's thought on important subjects without comment. It must be submitted to the D.D.'s I would it were the chickadee-dees.

You come from attending the funeral of mankind to attend to a natural phenomenon. A little thought is sexton to all the world.

I hardly know an *intellectual* man, even, who is so broad and truly liberal that you can think aloud in his society. Most with whom you endeavor to talk soon come to a stand against some institution in which they appear to hold stock, that is, some particular, not universal, way of viewing things. They will continually thrust their own low roof, with its narrow skylight, between you and the sky, when it is the unobstructed heavens you would view. Get out of the way with your cobwebs; wash your windows, I say! In some lyceums they tell me that they have voted to exclude the subject of religion. But how do I know what their religion is, and when I am near to or far from it? I have walked into such an arena and done my best to make a clean breast of what religion I have experienced, and the audience never suspected what I was about. The lecture was as harmless as moonshine to them. Whereas, if I had read to them the biography of the greatest scamps in history, they might have thought that I had written the lives of the deacons of their church. Ordinarily, the inquiry is, Where did you come from? or, Where are you going? That was a more pertinent question which I overheard one of my auditors put to another once —"What does he lecture for?" It made me quake in my shoes.

To speak impartially, the best men that I know are not serene, a world in themselves. For the most part, they dwell in forms, and flatter and study effect only more finely than the rest. We select granite for the underpinning of our houses and barns; we build fences of stone; but we do not ourselves rest on an underpinning of granitic truth, the lowest primitive rock. Our sills are rotten. What stuff is the man made of who is not coexistent in our thought with the purest and subtilest truth? I often accuse my finest acquaintances of an immense frivolity; for, while there are manners and compliments we do not meet, we do not teach one another the lessons of honesty and sincerity that the brutes do, or of steadiness and solidity that the rocks do. The fault is commonly mutual, however; for we do not habitually demand any

5. Elisha Kent Kane participated in two unsuccessful searches for Franklin, an explorer lost in the Arctic regions in 1847.

more of each other.

That excitement about Kossuth, consider how characteristic, but superficial, it was!—only another kind of politics or dancing. Men were making speeches to him all over the country, but each expressed only the thought, or the want of thought, of the multitude. No man stood on truth. They were merely banded together, as usual one leaning on another, and all together on nothing; as the Hindus made the world rest on an elephant, the elephant on a tortoise, and the tortoise on a serpent, and had nothing to put under the serpent. For all fruit of that stir we have the Kossuth hat.[6]

Just so hollow and ineffectual, for the most part, is our ordinary conversation. Surface meets surface. When our life ceases to be inward and private, conversation degenerates into mere gossip. We rarely meet a man who can tell us any news which he has not read in a newspaper, or been told by his neighbor; and, for the most part, the only difference between us and our fellow is that he has seen the newspaper, or been out to tea, and we have not. In proportion as our inward life fails, we go more constantly and desperately to the post office. You may depend on it, that the poor fellow who walks away with the greatest number of letters, proud of his extensive correspondence, has not heard from himself this long while.

I do not know but it is too much to read one newspaper a week. I have tried it recently, and for so long it seems to me that I have not dwelt in my native region. The sun, the clouds, the snow, the trees say not so much to me. You cannot serve two masters. It requires more than a day's devotion to know and to possess the wealth of a day.

We may well be ashamed to tell what things we have read or heard in our day. I do not know why my news should be so trivial —considering what one's dreams and expectations are, why the developments should be so paltry. The news we hear, for the most part, is not news to our genius. It is the stalest repetition. You are often tempted to ask why such stress is laid on a particular experience which you have had—that, after twenty-five years, you should meet Hobbins, Registrar of Deeds, again on the sidewalk. Have you not budged an inch, then? Such is the daily news. Its facts appear to float in the atmosphere, insignificant as the sporules of fungi, and impinge on some neglected *thallus*, or surface of our minds, which affords a basis for them, and hence a parasitic growth. We should wash ourselves clean of such news. Of what consequence, though our planet explode, if there is no character involved

6. Louis Kossuth, Hungarian patriot, popularized the wearing of a slouch felt hat on his visits to America in 1852 and 1853.

in the explosion? In health we have not the least curiosity about such events. We do not live for idle amusement. I would not run round a corner to see the world blow up.

All summer, and far into the autumn, perchance, you unconsciously went by the newspapers and the news, and now you find it was because the morning and the evening were full of news to you. Your walks were full of incidents. You attended, not to the affairs of Europe, but to your own affairs in Massachusetts fields. If you chance to live and move and have your being in that thin stratum in which the events that make the news transpire—thinner than the paper on which it is printed—then these things will fill the world for you; but if you soar above or dive below that plane, you cannot remember nor be reminded of them. Really to see the sun rise or go down every day, so to relate ourselves to a universal fact, would preserve us sane forever. Nations! What are nations? Tartars, and Huns, and Chinamen! Like insects, they swarm. The historian strives in vain to make them memorable. It is for want of a man that there are so many men. It is individuals that populate the world. Any man thinking may say with the Spirit of Lodin,

> "I look down from my height on nations,
> And they become ashes before me;—
> Calm is my dwelling in the clouds;
> Pleasant are the great fields of my rest."[7]

Pray, let us live without being drawn by dogs, Esquimaux-fashion, tearing over hill and dale, and biting each other's ears.

Not without a slight shudder at the danger, I often perceive how near I had come to admitting into my mind the details of some trivial affair—the news of the street; and I am astonished to observe how willing men are to lumber their minds with such rubbish—to permit idle rumors and incidents of the most insignificant kind to intrude on ground which should be sacred to thought. Shall the mind be a public arena, where the affairs of the street and the gossip of the tea-table chiefly are discussed? Or shall it be a quarter of heaven itself—an hypethral[8] temple, consecrated to the service of the gods? I find it so difficult to dispose of the few facts which to me are significant, that I hesitate to burden my attention with those which are insignificant, which only a divine mind could illustrate. Such is, for the most part, the news in newspapers and conversation. It is important to preserve the mind's chastity in this respect. Think of admitting the details of a single case of the criminal court into our thoughts, to stalk profanely through their very *sanctum sanctorum* for an hour, ay, for many

7. From a speech by the Spirit of Loda [*sic*] in James Macpherson's *Carric-* *thura* (1761).
8. Open to the sky.

hours! to make a very barroom of the mind's inmost apartment, as if for so long the dust of the street had occupied us—the very street itself, with all its travel, its bustle, and filth, had passed through our thoughts' shrine! Would it not be an intellectual and moral suicide? When I have been compelled to sit spectator and auditor in a courtroom for some hours, and have seen my neighbors, who were not compelled, stealing in from time to time, and tiptoeing about with washed hands and faces, it has appeared to my mind's eye, that, when they took off their hats, their ears suddenly expanded into vast hoppers for sound, between which even their narrow heads were crowded. Like the vanes of windmills, they caught the broad but shallow stream of sound, which, after a few titillating gyrations in their coggy brains, passed out the other side. I wondered if, when they got home, they were as careful to wash their ears as before their hands and faces. It has seemed to me, at such a time, that the auditors and the witnesses, the jury and the counsel, the judge and the criminal at the bar—if I may presume him guilty before he is convicted—were all equally criminal, and a thunderbolt might be expected to descend and consume them all together.

By all kinds of traps and signboards, threatening the extreme penalty of the divine law, exclude such trespassers from the only ground which can be sacred to you. It is so hard to forget what it is worse than useless to remember! If I am to be a thoroughfare, I prefer that it be of the mountain brooks, the Parnassian streams, and not the town sewers. There is inspiration, that gossip which comes to the ear of the attentive mind from the courts of heaven. There is the profane and stale revelation of the barroom and the police court. The same ear is fitted to receive both communications. Only the character of the hearer determines to which it shall be open, and to which closed. I believe that the mind can be permanently profaned by the habit of attending to trivial things, so that all our thoughts shall be tinged with triviality. Our very intellect shall be macadamized, as it were, its foundation broken into fragments for the wheels of travel to roll over; and if you would know what will make the most durable pavement, surpassing rolled stones, spruce blocks, and asphaltum, you have only to look into some of our minds which have been subjected to this treatment so long.

If we have thus desecrated ourselves—as who has not?—the remedy will be by wariness and devotion to reconsecrate ourselves, and make once more a fane of the mind. We should treat our minds, that is, ourselves, as innocent and ingenuous children, whose guardians we are, and be careful what objects and what subjects we thrust on their attention. Read not the Times. Read the

Eternities. Conventionalities are at length as bad as impurities. Even the facts of science may dust the mind by their dryness, unless they are in a sense effaced each morning, or rather rendered fertile by the dews of fresh and living truth. Knowledge does not come to us by details, but in flashes of light from heaven. Yes, every thought that passes through the mind helps to wear and tear it, and to deepen the ruts, which, as in the streets of Pompeii, evince how much it has been used. How many things there are concerning which we might well deliberate whether we had better know them—had better let their peddling-carts be driven, even at the slowest trot or walk, over that bridge of glorious span by which we trust to pass at last from the farthest brink of time to the nearest shore of eternity! Have we no culture, no refinement—but skill only to live coarsely and serve the Devil?—to acquire a little worldly wealth, or fame, or liberty, and make a false show with it, as if we were all husk and shell, with no tender and living kernel to us? Shall our institutions be like those chestnut burs which contain abortive nuts, perfect only to prick the fingers?

America is said to be the arena on which the battle of freedom is to be fought; but surely it cannot be freedom in a merely political sense that is meant. Even if we grant that the American has freed himself from a political tyrant, he is still the slave of an economical and moral tyrant. Now that the republic—the *res-publica*—has been settled, it is time to look after the *res-privata* —the private state—to see, as the Roman senate charged its consuls, *"ne quid res-*PRIVATA *detrimenti caperet,"* that the *private* state receive no detriment.

Do we call this the land of the free? What is it to be free from King George and continue the slaves of King Prejudice? What is it to be born free and not to live free? What is the value of any political freedom, but as a means to moral freedom? Is it a freedom to be slaves, or a freedom to be free, of which we boast? We are a nation of politicians, concerned about the outmost defenses only of freedom. It is our children's children who may perchance be really free. We tax ourselves unjustly. There is a part of us which is not represented. It is taxation without representation. We quarter troops, we quarter fools and cattle of all sorts upon ourselves. We quarter our gross bodies on our poor souls, till the former eat up all the latter's substance.

With respect to a true culture and manhood, we are essentially provincial still, not metropolitan—mere Jonathans.[9] We are provincial, because we do not find at home our standards; because we do not worship truth, but the reflection of truth; because we are warped and narrowed by an exclusive devotion to trade and com-

9. Type name for a Yankee. See *Walden,* "Conclusion."

merce and manufactures and agriculture and the like, which are but means, and not the end.

So is the English Parliament provincial. Mere country bumpkins, they betray themselves, when any more important question arises for them to settle, the Irish question, for instance—the English question why did I not say? Their natures are subdued to what they work in. Their "good breeding" respects only secondary objects. The finest manners in the world are awkwardness and fatuity when contrasted with a finer intelligence. They appear but as the fashions of past days—mere courtliness, knee-buckles and small-clothes, out of date. It is the vice, but not the excellence of manners, that they are continually being deserted by the character; they are cast-off clothes or shells, claiming the respect which belonged to the living creature. You are presented with the shells instead of the meat, and it is no excuse generally, that, in the case of some fishes, the shells are of more worth than the meat. The man who thrusts his manners upon me does as if he were to insist on introducing me to his cabinet of curiosities, when I wished to see himself. It was not in this sense that the poet Decker called Christ "the first true gentleman that ever breathed."[1] I repeat that in this sense the most splendid court in Christendom is provincial, having authority to consult about Transalpine interests only, and not the affairs of Rome. A praetor or proconsul would suffice to settle the questions which absorb the attention of the English Parliament and the American Congress.

Government and legislation! these I thought were respectable professions. We have heard of heaven-born Numas, Lycurguses, and Solons,[2] in the history of the world, whose *names* at least may stand for ideal legislators; but think of legislating to *regulate* the breeding of slaves, or the exportation of tobacco! What have divine legislators to do with the exportation or the importation of tobacco? what humane ones with the breeding of slaves? Suppose you were to submit the question to any son of God—and has He no children in the Nineteenth Century? is it a family which is extinct?—in what condition would you get it again? What shall a State like Virginia say for itself at the last day, in which these have been the principal, the staple productions? What ground is there for patriotism in such a State? I derive my facts from statistical tables which the States themselves have published.

A commerce that whitens every sea in quest of nuts and raisins, and makes slaves of its sailors for this purpose! I saw, the other day, a vessel which had been wrecked, and many lives lost, and her cargo of rags, juniper berries, and bitter almonds were strewn

1. Thomas Decker (or Dekker), *1 The Honest Whore* I.xii.

2. Three ancient lawgivers, respectively Roman, Spartan, and Athenian.

along the shore.[3] It seemed hardly worth the while to tempt the
dangers of the sea between Leghorn and New York for the sake
of a cargo of juniper berries and bitter almonds. America sending
to the Old World for her bitters! Is not the sea-brine, is not shipwreck, bitter enough to make the cup of life go down here? Yet
such, to a great extent, is our boasted commerce; and there are
those who style themselves statesmen and philosophers who are
so blind as to think that progress and civilization depend on precisely this kind of interchange and activity—the activity of flies
about a molasses-hogshead. Very well, observes one, if men were
oysters. And very well, answer I, if men were mosquitoes.

Lieutenant Herndon,[4] whom our government sent to explore
the Amazon, and, it is said, to extend the area of slavery, observed
that there was wanting there "an industrious and active population, who know what the comforts of life are, and who have artificial wants to draw out the great resources of the country." But
what are the "artificial wants" to be encouraged? Not the love of
luxuries, like the tobacco and slaves of, I believe, his native Virginia, nor the ice and granite and other material wealth of our
native New England; nor are "the great resources of a country"
that fertility or barrenness of soil which produces these. The chief
want, in every State that I have been into, was a high and earnest
purpose in its inhabitants. This alone draws out "the great resources" of Nature, and at last taxes her beyond her resources; for
man naturally dies out of her. When we want culture more than
potatoes, and illumination more than sugar-plums, then the great
resources of a world are taxed and drawn out, and the result, or
staple production, is, not slaves, nor operatives, but men—those
rare fruits called heroes, saints, poets, philosophers, and redeemers.

In short, as a snowdrift is formed where there is a lull in the
wind, so, one would say, where there is a lull of truth, an institution
springs up. But the truth blows right on over it, nevertheless, and
at length blows it down.

What is called politics is comparatively something so superficial
and inhuman, that practically I have never fairly recognized that
it concerns me at all. The newspapers, I perceive, devote some of
their columns specially to politics or government without charge;
and this, one would stay, is all that saves it; but as I love literature
and to some extent the truth also, I never read those columns at
any rate. I do not wish to blunt my sense of right so much. I have
not got to answer for having read a single President's Message. A
strange age of this world this, when empires, kingdoms, and repub-

3. Probably the *Elizabeth*, in which
Margaret Fuller was drowned, wrecked
off Long Island in 1850.

4. William Lewis Herndon in 1851 explored the Amazon River for the United
States Navy.

lics come a-begging to a private man's door, and utter their complaints at his elbow! I cannot take up a newspaper but I find that some wretched government or other, hard pushed and on its last legs, is interceding with me, the reader, to vote for it—more importunate than an Italian beggar; and if I have a mind to look at its certificate, made, perchance, by some benevolent merchant's clerk, or the skipper that brought it over, for it cannot speak a word of English itself, I shall probably read of the eruption of some Vesuvius, or the overflowing of some Po, true or forged, which brought it into this condition. I do not hesitate, in such a case, to suggest work, or the almshouse; or why not keep its castle in silence, as I do commonly? The poor President,[5] what with preserving his popularity and doing his duty, is completely bewildered. The newspapers are the ruling power. Any other government is reduced to a few marines at Fort Independence.[6] If a man neglects to read the Daily Times, government will go down on its knees to him, for this is the only treason in these days.

Those things which now most engage the attention of men, as politics and the daily routine, are, it is true, vital functions of human society, but should be unconsciously performed, like the corresponding functions of the physical body. They are *infra*-human, a kind of vegetation. I sometimes awake to a half-consciousness of them going on about me, as a man may become conscious of some of the processes of digestion in a morbid state, and so have the dyspepsia, as it is called. It is as if a thinker submitted himself to be rasped by the great gizzard of creation. Politics is, as it were, the gizzard of society, full of grit and gravel, and the two political parties are its two opposite halves—sometimes split into quarters, it may be, which grind on each other. Not only individuals, but states, have thus a confirmed dyspepsia, which expresses itself, you can imagine by what sort of eloquence. Thus our life is not altogether a forgetting,[7] but also, alas! to a great extent, a remembering, of that which we should never have been conscious of, certainly not in our waking hours. Why should we not meet, not always as dyspeptics, to tell our bad dreams, but sometimes as *eu*peptics, to congratulate each other on the ever-glorious morning? I do not make an exorbitant demand, surely.

1863, 1866

5. Thoreau's *Journal* version of this passage makes it clear he was referring to Franklin Pierce.
6. An island fortification in Boston Harbor.
7. "Our birth is but a sleep and a forgetting." Wordsworth, "Ode: Intimations of Immortality."

From Journal[8]

[On Writing—I]

[1851] *Sept.* 2. * * * We cannot write well or truly but what we write with gusto. The body, the senses, must conspire with the mind. Expression is the act of the whole man, that our speech may be vascular. The intellect is powerless to express thought without the aid of the heart and liver and of every member. Often I feel that my head stands out too dry, when it should be immersed. A writer, a man writing, is the scribe of all nature; he is the corn and the grass and the atmosphere writing. It is always essential that we love to do what we are doing, do it with a heart. The maturity of the mind, however, may perchance consist with a certain dryness. * * *

Sept. 4. * * * It is wise to write on many subjects, to try many themes, that so you may find the right and inspiring one. Be greedy of occasions to express your thought. Improve the opportunity to draw analogies. There are innumerable avenues to a perception of the truth. Improve the suggestion of each object however humble, however slight and transient the provocation. What else is there to be improved? Who knows what opportunities he may neglect? It is not in vain that the mind turns aside this way or that: follow its leading; apply it whither it inclines to go. Probe the universe in a myriad points. Be avaricious of these impulses. You must try a thousand themes before you find the right one, as nature makes a thousand acorns to get one oak. He is a wise man and experienced who has taken many views; to whom stones and plants and animals and a myriad objects have each suggested something, contributed something. * * *

Sept. 8. * * * Shall I not have words as fresh as my thoughts? Shall I use any other man's word? A genuine thought or feeling can find expression for itself, if it have to invent hieroglyphics. It has the universe for type-metal. It is for want of original thought that one man's style is like another's. * * *

Dec. 20. * * * Say the thing with which you labor. It is a waste of time for the writer to use his talents merely. Be faithful to your genius. Write in the strain that interests you most. Consult not the popular taste. * * *

[1852] *Jan.* 26. * * * Whatever wit has been produced on the spur of the moment will bear to be reconsidered and reformed with phlegm. The arrow had best not be loosely shot. The most transient and passing remark must be reconsidered by the writer, made sure and warranted, as if the earth had rested on its axle

---

8. The *Journal* was first published in 1906, in fourteen volumes. The extracts here reprinted have been selected and titled by the present editor.

to back it, and all the natural forces lay behind it. The writer must direct his sentences as carefully and leisurely as the marksman his rifle, who shoots sitting and with a rest, with patent sights and conical balls beside. He must not merely seem to speak the truth. He must really speak it. If you foresee that a part of your essay will topple down after the lapse of time, throw it down now yourself. * * *

Feb. 10. * * * Write while the heat is in you. When the farmer burns a hole in his yoke, he carries the hot iron quickly from the fire to the wood, for every moment it is less effectual to penetrate (pierce) it. It must be used instantly, or it is useless. The writer who postpones the recording of his thoughts uses an iron which has cooled to burn a hole with. He cannot inflame the minds of his audience. * * *

[A *Meeting with a Woodchuck*]

April 16. * * * As I turned round the corner of Hubbard's Grove, saw a woodchuck, the first of the season, in the middle of the field, six or seven rods from the fence which bounds the wood, and twenty rods distant. I ran along the fence and cut him off, or rather overtook him, though he started at the same time. When I was only a rod and a half off, he stopped, and I did the same; then he ran again, and I ran up within three feet of him, when he stopped again, the fence being between us. I squatted down and surveyed him at my leisure. His eyes were dull black and rather inobvious, with a faint chestnut (?) iris, with but little expression and that more of resignation than of anger. The general aspect was a coarse grayish brown, a sort of grisel (?). A lighter brown next the skin, then black or very dark brown and tipped with whitish rather loosely. The head between a squirrel and a bear, flat on the top and dark brown, and darker still or black on the tip of the nose. The whiskers black, two inches long. The ears very small and roundish, set far back and nearly buried in the fur. Black feet, with long and slender claws for digging. It appeared to tremble, or perchance shivered with cold. When I moved, it gritted its teeth quite loud, sometimes striking the under jaw against the other chatteringly, sometimes grinding one jaw on the other, yet as if more from instinct than anger. Whichever way I turned, that way it headed. I took a twig a foot long and touched its snout, at which it started forward and bit the stick, lessening the distance between us to two feet, and still it held all the ground it gained. I played with it tenderly awhile with the stick, trying to open its gritting jaws. Ever its long incisors, two above and two below, were presented. But I thought it would go to sleep if I stayed long enough. It did not sit upright as sometimes, but *stand-*

ing on its fore feet with its head down, *i.e.* half sitting, half standing. We sat looking at one another about half an hour, till we began to feel mesmeric influences. When I was tired, I moved away, wishing to see him run, but I could not start him. He would not stir as long as I was looking at him or could see him. I walked round him; he turned as fast and fronted me still. I sat down by his side within a foot. I talked to him *quasi* forest lingo, baby-talk, at any rate in a conciliatory tone, and thought that I had some influence on him. He gritted his teeth less. I chewed checkerberry leaves and presented them to his nose at last without a grit; though I saw that by so much gritting of the teeth he had worn them rapidly and they were covered with a fine white powder, which, if you measured it thus, would have made his anger terrible. He did not mind any noise I might make. With a little stick I lifted one of his paws to examine it, and held it up at pleasure. I turned him over to see what color he was beneath (darker or more purely brown), though he turned himself back again sooner than I could have wished. His tail was also all brown, though not very dark, rat-tail like, with loose hairs standing out on all sides like a caterpillar brush. He had a rather mild look. I spoke kindly to him. I reached checkerberry leaves to his mouth. I stretched my hands over him, though he turned up his head and still gritted a little. I laid my hand on him, but immediately took it off again, instinct not being wholly overcome. If I had had a few fresh bean leaves, thus in advance of the season, I am sure I should have tamed him completely. It was a frizzly tail. His is a humble, terrestrial color like the partridge's, well concealed where dead wiry grass rises above darker brown or chestnut dead leaves,—a modest color. If I had had some food, I should have ended with stroking him at my leisure. Could easily have wrapped him in my handkerchief. He was not fat nor particularly lean. I finally had to leave him without seeing him move from the place. A large, clumsy, burrowing squirrel. *Arctomys*, bear-mouse. I respect him as one of the natives. He lies there, by his color and habits so naturalized amid the dry leaves, the withered grass, and the bushes. A sound nap, too, he has enjoyed in his native fields, the past winter. I think I might learn some wisdom of him. His ancestors have lived here longer than mine. He is more thoroughly acclimated and naturalized than I. Bean leaves the red man raised for him, but he can do without them. * * *

[Three Ultra-Reformers]

[1853] *June* 17. * * * Here have been three ultra-reformers, lecturers on Slavery, Temperance, the Church, etc., in and about our house and Mrs. Brooks's the last three or four days,—A. D.

Foss, once a Baptist minister in Hopkinton, N. H.; Loring Moody, a sort of travelling pattern-working chaplain; and H. C. Wright, who shocks all the old women with his infidel writings. Though Foss was a stranger to the others, you would have thought them old and familiar cronies. (They happened here together by accident.) They addressed each other constantly by their Christian names, and rubbed you continually with the greasy cheeks of their kindness. They would not keep their distance, but cuddle up and lie spoon-fashion with you, no matter how hot the weather nor how narrow the bed,—chiefly ————. I was awfully pestered with his benignity; feared I should get greased all over with it past restoration; tried to keep some starch in my clothes. He wrote a book called "A Kiss for a Blow," and he behaved as if there were no alternative between these, or as if I had given him a blow. I would have preferred the blow, but he was bent on giving me the kiss, when there was neither quarrel nor agreement between us. I wanted that he should straighten his back, smooth out those ogling wrinkles of benignity about his eyes, and, with a healthy reserve, pronounce something in a downright manner. It was difficult to keep clear of his slimy benignity, with which he sought to cover you before he swallowed you and took you fairly into his bowels. It would have been far worse than the fate of Jonah. I do not wish to get any nearer to a man's bowels than usual. They lick you as a cow her calf. They would fain wrap you about with their bowels.

———— addressed me as "Henry" within one minute from the time I first laid eyes on him, and when I spoke, he said with drawling, sultry sympathy, "Henry, I know all you would say; I understand you perfectly; you need not explain anything to me;" and to another, "I am going to dive into Henry's inmost depths." I said, "I trust you will not strike your head against the bottom." He could tell in a dark room, with his eyes blinded and in perfect stillness, if there was one there whom he loved. One of the most attractive things about the flowers is their beautiful reserve. The truly beautiful and noble puts its lover, as it were, at an infinite distance, while it attracts him more strongly than ever. I do not like the men who come so near me with their bowels. It is the most disagreeable kind of snare to be caught in. Men's bowels are far more slimy than their brains. They must be ascetics indeed who approach you by this side. What a relief to have heard the ring of one healthy reserved tone! With such a forgiving disposition, as if he were all the while forgiving you for existing. Considering our condition or *habit* of soul,—maybe corpulent and asthmatic,— maybe dying of atrophy, with all our bones sticking out,—is it kindness to embrace a man? They lay their sweaty hand on your shoulder, or your knee, to magnetize you. * * *

[On Writing—II]

[1854] March 1.* * * In correcting my manuscripts, which I do with sufficient phlegm, I find that I invariably turn out much that is good along with the bad, which it is then impossible for me to distinguish—so much for keeping bad company; but after the lapse of time, having purified the main body and thus created a distinct standard for comparison, I can review the rejected sentences and easily detect those which deserve to be readmitted.

April 8. * * * I find that I can criticise my composition best when I stand at a little distance from it,—when I do not see it, for instance. I make a little chapter of contents which enables me to recall it page by page to my mind, and judge it more impartially when my manuscript is out of the way. The distraction of surveying enables me rapidly to take new points of view. A day or two surveying is equal to a journey. * * *

[A Flying Squirrel]

[1855] March 22. * * * Going [along] the steep side-hill on the south of the pond about 4 P. M., on the edge of the little patch of wood which the choppers have not yet levelled,—though they have felled many an acre around it this winter,—I observed a rotten and hollow hemlock stump about two feet high and six inches in diameter, and instinctively approached with my right hand ready to cover it. I found a flying squirrel in it, which, as my left hand had covered a small hole at the bottom, ran directly into my right hand. It struggled and bit not a little, but my cotton glove protected me, and I felt its teeth only once or twice. It also uttered three or four dry shrieks at first, something like *cr-r-rack cr-r-r-ack cr-r-r-ack*. I rolled it up in my handkerchief and, holding the ends tight, carried it home in my hand, some three miles. It struggled more or less all the way, especially when my feet made any unusual or louder noise going through leaves or bushes. I could count its claws as they appeared through the handkerchief, and once it got its head out a hole. It even bit through the handkerchief.

Color, as I remember, above a chestnut ash, inclining to fawn or cream color (?), slightly browned; beneath white, the under edge of its wings (?) tinged yellow, the upper dark, perhaps black, making a dark stripe. Audubon and Bachman[9] do not speak of any such stripe! It was a very cunning little animal, reminding me of a mouse in the room. Its very large and prominent black eyes gave it an interesting innocent look. Its very neat flat, fawn-colored, distichous tail was a great ornament. Its "sails" were not very ob-

9. John James Audubon and John Bachman, *The Quadrupeds of North America* (1851).

vious when it was at rest, merely giving it a flat appearance beneath. It would leap off and upward into the air two or three feet from a table, spreading its "sails," and fall to the floor in vain; perhaps strike the side of the room in its upward spring and endeavor to cling to it. It would run up the window by the sash, but evidently found the furniture and walls and floor too hard and smooth for it and after some falls became quiet. In a few moments it allowed me to stroke it, though far from confident.

I put it in a barrel and covered it for the night. It was quite busy all the evening gnawing out, clinging for this purpose and gnawing at the upper edge of a sound oak barrel, and then dropping to rest from time to time. It had defaced the barrel considerably by morning, and would probably have escaped if I had not placed a piece of iron against the gnawed part. I had left in the barrel some bread, apple, shagbarks, and cheese. It ate some of the apple and one shagbark, cutting it quite in two transversely.

In the morning it was quiet, and *squatted* somewhat curled up amid the straw, with its tail passing under it and the end curled over its head very prettily, as if to shield it from the light and keep it warm. I always found it in this position by day when I raised the lid.

March 23. P. M.—To Fair Haven Pond.[1]

Carried my flying squirrel back to the woods in my handkerchief. I placed it, about 3.30 P. M., on the very stump I had taken it from. It immediately ran about a rod over the leaves and up a slender maple sapling about ten feet, then after a moment's pause sprang off and skimmed downward toward a large maple nine feet distant, whose trunk it struck three or four feet from the ground. This it rapidly ascended, on the opposite side from me, nearly thirty feet, and there clung to the main stem with its head downward, eying me. After two or three minutes' pause I saw that it was preparing for another spring by raising its head and looking off, and away it went in admirable style, more like a bird than any quadruped I had dreamed of and far surpassing the impression I had received from naturalists' accounts. I marked the spot it started from and the place where it struck, and measured the height and distance carefully. It sprang off from the maple at the height of twenty-eight and a half feet, and struck the ground at the foot of a tree fifty and a half feet distant, measured horizontally. Its flight was not a *regular* descent; it varied from a direct line both horizontally and vertically. Indeed it skimmed much like a hawk and part of its flight was nearly horizontal, and it diverged from a right line eight or ten feet to the right, making a curve in that direction. There were six trees from six inches to a foot in diameter, one a

1. A large bay in the Sudbury River, a mile south of Walden Pond.

hemlock, in a direct line between the two termini, and these it skimmed partly round, and passed through their thinner limbs; did not as I could perceive touch a twig. It skimmed its way like a hawk between and around the trees. Though it was a windy day, this was on a steep hillside away from the wind and covered with wood, so it was not aided by that. As the ground rose about two feet, the distance was to the absolute height as fifty and a half to twenty-six and a half, or it advanced about two feet for every one foot of descent. After its vain attempts in the house, I was not prepared for this exhibition. It did not fall heavily as in the house, but struck the ground gently enough, and I cannot believe that the mere extension of the skin enabled it to skim so far. It must be still further aided by its organization. Perhaps it fills itself with air first. Perhaps I had a fairer view than common of its flight, now at 3.30 P. M. Audubon and Bachman say *he* saw it skim "about fifty yards," curving upwards at the end and alighting on the trunk of a tree. This in a meadow in which were scattered oaks and beeches. This near Philadelphia. Wesson [?] says he has seen them fly five or six rods.

Kicking over the hemlock stump, which was a mere shell with holes below, and a poor refuge, I was surprised to find a little nest at the bottom, open above just like a bird's nest, a mere bed. It was composed of leaves, shreds of bark, and dead pine-needles. As I remember, it was not more than an inch and a half broad when at rest, but when skimming through the air I should say it was four inches broad. This is the impression I now have. Captain John Smith says it is said to fly thirty or forty yards. Audubon and Bachman quote one Gideon B. Smith, M. D., of Baltimore, who has had much to do with these squirrels and speaks of their curving upward at the end of their flight to alight on a tree-trunk and of their "flying" into his windows. In order to perform all these flights,—to strike a tree at such a distance, etc., etc.,—it is evident it must be able to steer. I should say that mine steered as a hawk that moves without flapping its wings, never being able, however, to get a new impetus after the first spring.

[A *Happy Neighbor*]

Nov. 17 * * * It is interesting to me to talk with Rice,[2] he lives so thoroughly and satisfactorily to himself. He has learned that rare art of living, the very elements of which most professors do not know. His life has been not a failure but a success. Seeing me going to sharpen some plane-irons, and hearing me complain of the want of tools, he said that I ought to have a chest of tools. But I said it was not worth the while. I should not use them enough

2. A Concord neighbor.

to pay for them. "You would use them more, if you had them,"
said he. "When I came to do a piece of work I used to find commonly that I wanted a certain tool, and I made it a rule first
always to make that tool. I have spent as much as $3000 thus on
my tools." Comparatively speaking, his life is a success; not such
a failure as most men's. He gets more out of any enterprise than
his neighbors, for he helps himself more and hires less. Whatever
pleasure there is in it he enjoys. By good sense and calculation he
has become rich and has invested his property well, yet practices
a fair and neat economy, dwells not in untidy luxury. It costs him
less to live, and he gets more out of life, than others. To get his
living, or keep it, is not a hasty or disagreeable toil. He works
slowly but surely, enjoying the sweet of it. He buys a piece of
meadow at a profitable rate, works at it in pleasant weather, he
and his son, when they are inclined, goes a-fishing or a-bee-hunting
or a-rifle-shooting quite as often, and thus the meadow gets redeemed, and potatoes get planted, perchance, and he is very sure
to have a good crop stored in his cellar in the fall, and some to
sell. He always has the best of potatoes there. In the same spirit
in which he and his son tackle up their Dobbin (he never keeps
a fast horse) and go a-spearing or a-fishing through the ice, they
also tackle up and go to their Sudbury farm to hoe or harvest a
little, and when they return they bring home a load of stumps in
their hay-rigging, which impeded their labors, but, perchance,
supply them with their winter wood. All the woodchucks they
shoot or trap in the bean-field are brought home also. And thus
their life is a long sport and they know not what hard times
are. * * *

[A Pig's Tale]

[1856] *Aug.* 8. * * * 3.30 P. M.—When I came forth, thinking
to empty my boat and go a-meditating along the river,—for the
full ditches and drenched grass forbade other routes, except the
highway,—and this is one advantage of a boat,—I learned to my
chagrin that Father's pig was gone. He had leaped out of the pen
some time since his breakfast, but his dinner was untouched. Here
was an ugly duty not to be shirked,—a wild shoat that weighed
but ninety to be tracked, caught, and penned,—an afternoon's work,
at least (if I were lucky enough to accomplish it so soon), prepared for me, quite different from what I had anticipated. I felt
chagrined, it is true, but I could not ignore the fact nor shirk the
duty that lay so near to me. Do the duty that lies nearest to thee.
I proposed to Father to sell the pig as he was running (somewhere)
to a neighbor who had talked of buying him, making a considerable
reduction. But my suggestion was not acted on, and the responsi-

bilities of the case all devolved on me, for I could run faster than Father. Father looked to me, and I ceased to look to the river. Well, let us see if we can track him. Yes, this is the corner where he got out, making a step of his trough. Thanks to the rain, his tracks are quite distinct. Here he went along the edge of the garden over the water and muskmelons, then through the beans and potatoes, and even along the front-yard walk I detect the print of his divided hoof, his two sharp toes (*ungulæ*). It's a wonder we did not see him. And here he passed out under the gate, across the road,—how naked he must have felt!—into a grassy ditch, and whither next? Is it of any use to go hunting him up unless you have devised some mode of catching him when you have found? Of what avail to know where he has been, even where he is? He was so shy the little while we had him, of course he will never come back; he cannot be tempted by a swill-pail. Who knows how many miles off he is! Perhaps he has taken the back track and gone to Brighton,[3] or Ohio! At most, probably we shall only have the satisfaction of glimpsing the nimble beast at a distance, from time to time, as he trots swiftly through the green meadows and corn-fields. But, now I speak, what is that I see pacing deliberately up the middle of the street forty rods off? It is *he*. As if to tantalize, to tempt us to waste our afternoon without further hesitation, he thus offers himself. He roots a foot or two and then lies down on his belly in the middle of the street. But think not to catch him a-napping. He has his eyes about, and his ears too. He has already been chased. He gives that wagon a wide berth, and now, seeing me, he turns and trots back down the street. He turns into a front yard. Now if I can only close that gate upon him ninety-nine hundredths of the work is done, but ah! he hears me coming afar off, he foresees the danger, and, with swinish cunning and speed, he scampers out. My neighbor in the street tries to head him; he jumps to this side the road, then to that, before him; but the third time the pig was there first and went by. "Whose is it?" he shouts. "It's ours." He bolts into that neighbor's yard and so across his premises. He has been twice there before, it seems; he knows the road; see what work he has made in his flower-garden! He must be fond of bulbs. Our neighbor picks up one tall flower with its bulb attached, holds it out at arm's length. He is excited about the pig; it is a subject he is interested in. But where is [he] gone now? The last glimpse I had of him was as he went through the cow-yard; here are his tracks again in this corn-field, but they are lost in the grass. We lose him; we beat the bushes in vain; he may be far away. But hark! I heard a grunt. Nevertheless for half an hour I do not see him that grunted. At last I find fresh tracks

3. Suburb of Boston then noted for its slaughterhouses.

564 · Henry David Thoreau

along the river, and again lose them. Each neighbor whose garden
I traverse tells me some anecdote of losing pigs, or the attempt to
drive them, by which I am not encouraged. Once more he crosses
our first neighbor's garden and is said to be in the road. But I am
not there yet; it is a good way off. At length my eyes rest on him
again, after three quarters of an hour's separation. There he trots
with the whole road to himself, and now again drops on his belly
in a puddle. Now he starts again, seeing me twenty rods [off],
deliberates, considers which way I want him to go, and goes the
other. There was some chance of driving him along the sidewalk,
or letting him go rather, till he slipped under our gate again, but
of what avail would that be? How corner and catch him who keeps
twenty rods off? He never lets the open side of the triangle be less
than half a dozen rods wide. There was one place where a narrower
street turned off at right angles with the main one, just this side
our yard, but I could not drive him past that. Twice he ran up the
narrow street, for he knew I did not wish it, but though the main
street was broad and open and no traveller in sight, when I tried
to drive him past this opening he invariably turned his piggish
head toward me, dodged from side to side, and finally ran up the
narrow street or down the main one as if there were a high barrier
erected before him. But really he is no more obstinate than I.
I cannot but respect his tactics and his independence. He will be
he, and I may be I. He is not unreasonable because he thwarts
me, but only the more reasonable. He has a strong will. He stands
upon his idea. There is a wall across the path not where a man
bars the way, but where he is resolved not to travel. Is he not
superior to man therein? Once more he glides down the narrow
street, deliberates at a corner, chooses wisely for him, and disappears
through an openwork fence eastward. He has gone to fresh gardens and pastures new. Other neighbors stand in the doorways
but half sympathizing, only observing, "Ugly thing to catch." "You
have a job on your hands." I lose sight of him, but hear that he is
far ahead in a large field. And there we try to let him alone a while,
giving him a wide berth.

At this stage an Irishman was engaged to assist. "I can catch
him," says he, with Buonapartean confidence. He thinks him a
family Irish pig. His wife is with him, bareheaded, and his little
flibbertigibbet of a boy, seven years old. "Here, Johnny, do you
run right off there" (at the broadest possible angle with his own
course). "Oh, but he can't do anything." "Oh, but I only want
him to tell me where he is,—to keep sight of him." Michael soon
discovers that he is not an Irish pig, and his wife and Johnny's
occupation are soon gone. Ten minutes afterward I am patiently
tracking him step by step through a corn-field, a near-sighted man

helping me, and then into garden after garden far eastward, and finally into the highway, at the graveyard; but hear and see nothing. One suggests a dog to track him. Father is meanwhile selling him to the blacksmith, who also is trying to get sight of him. After fifteen minutes since he disappeared eastward, I hear that he has been to the river twice far on [?] the north, through the first neighbor's premises. I wend that way. He crosses the street far ahead, Michael behind; he dodges up an avenue. I stand in the gap there, Michael at the other end, and now he tries to corner him. But it is a vain hope to corner him in a yard. I see a carriage-manufactory door open. "Let him go in there, Flannery." For once the pig and I are of one mind; he bolts in, and the door is closed. Now for a rope. It is a large barn, crowded with carriages. The rope is at length obtained; the windows are barred with carriages lest he bolt through. He is resting quietly on his belly in the further corner, thinking unutterable things.

Now the course recommences within narrower limits. Bump, bump, bump he goes, against wheels and shafts. We get no hold yet. He is all ear and eye. Small boys are sent under the carriages to drive him out. He froths at the mouth and deters them. At length he is stuck for an instant between the spokes of a wheel, and I am securely attached to his hind leg. He squeals deafeningly, and is silent. The rope is attached to a hind leg, The door is opened, and the *driving* commences. Roll an egg as well. You may drag him, but you cannot drive him. But he is in the road, and now another thunder-shower greets us. I leave Michael with the rope in one hand and a switch in the other and go home. He seems to be gaining a little westward. But, after long delay, I look out and find that he makes but doubtful progress. A boy is made to face him with a stick, and it is only when the pig springs at him savagely that progress is made homeward. He will be killed before he is driven home. I get a wheelbarrow and go to the rescue. Michael is alarmed. The pig is rabid, snaps at him. We drag him across the barrow, hold him down, and so, at last, get him home.

If a wild shoat like this gets loose, first track him if you can, or otherwise discover where he is. Do not scare him more than you can help. Think of some yard or building or other inclosure that will hold him and, by showing your forces—yet as if uninterested parties—fifteen or twenty rods off, let him of his own accord enter it. Then slightly shut the gate. Now corner and tie him and put him into a cart or barrow.

All progress in driving at last was made by facing and endeavoring to switch him from home. He rushed upon you and made a few feet in the desired direction. When I approached with the barrow he advanced to meet it with determination.

So I get home at dark, wet through and supperless, covered with mud and wheel-grease, without any rare flowers.

[On Writing—III]

Oct. 8. * * * Men commonly exaggerate the theme. Some themes they think are significant and others insignificant. I feel that my life is very homely, my pleasures very cheap. Joy and sorrow, success and failure, grandeur and meanness, and indeed most words in the English language do not mean for me what they do for my neighbors. I see that my neighbors look with compassion on me, that they think it is a mean and unfortunate destiny which makes me to walk in these fields and woods so much and sail on this river alone. But so long as I find here the only real elysium, I cannot hesitate in my choice. My work is writing, and I do not hesitate, though I know that no subject is too trivial for me, tried by ordinary standards; for, ye fools, the theme is nothing, the life is everything. All that interests the reader is the depth and intensity of the life excited. We touch our subject but by a point which has no breadth, but the pyramid of our experience, or our interest in it, rests on us by a broader or narrower base. That is, man is all in all, Nature nothing, but as she draws him out and reflects him. Give me simple, cheap, and homely themes.

Dec. 23. * * * If the writer would interest readers, he must report so much life, using a certain satisfaction always as a *point d'appui*.[4] However mean and limited, it must be a genuine and contented life that he speaks out of. They must have the essence or oil of himself, tried out of the fat of his experience and joy. * * *

[1857] *Mar.* 24. * * * If you are describing any occurrence, or a man, make two or more distinct reports at different times. Though you may think you have said all, you will to-morrow remember a whole new class of facts which perhaps interested most of all at the time, but did not present themselves to be reported. If we have recently met and talked with a man, and would report our experience, we commonly make a very partial report at first, failing to seize the most significant, picturesque, and dramatic points; we describe only what we have had time to digest and dispose of in our minds, without being conscious that there were other things really more novel and interesting to us, which will not fail to recur to us and impress us suitably at last. How little that occurs to us in any way are we prepared at once to appreciate! We discriminate at first only a few features, and we need to reconsider our experience from many points of view and in various moods, to preserve the whole fruit of it. * * *

---

4. Point of support.

Mar. 28. * * * Often I can give the truest and most interesting account of any adventure I have had after years have elapsed, for then I am not confused, only the most significant facts surviving in my memory. Indeed, all that continues to interest me after such a lapse of time is sure to be pertinent, and I may safely record all that I remember. * * *

[A Visit to Cape Cod]

June 21. *Sunday.* About noon it cleared up, and after dinner I set out for Provincetown, straight across the country to the Bay[5] where the new road strikes it, directly through the pine plantation about one mile from the lighthouse. The pines have apparently not done so well here as in some other places on the Cape. I observed a tuft of crow-berry, together with poverty-grass, about one mile west of the light. This part of Truro[6] affords singularly interesting and cheering walks for me, with regular hollows or dimples shutting out the sea as completely as if in the midst of the continent, though when you stand on the plain you commonly see the sails of vessels standing up or down the coast on each side of you, though you may not see the water. At first you may take them for the roofs of barns or houses. It is plain for miles without a tree, where the new telegraph-wires are a godsend to the birds, affording them something to perch upon. That solitude was sweet to me as a flower. I sat down on the boundless level and enjoyed the solitude, drank it in, the medicine for which I had pined, worth more than the bear-berry so common on the Cape. As I was approaching the Bay through a sandy hollow a mile east of High Head, I found two or three arrow-points and a rude axe or hammer, a flattish stone from the beach with a deep groove chipped around it.

The beach on the Bay Side was completely strewn with seaweed (the grassy kind), which does not grow on the Atlantic side, as if the Bay were a meadow compared with the Atlantic. The beach was harder than the Back Side, the hardest part being on the weed at high-water line. The skulls and backbones of blackfish, their vertebræ and spinal processes, and disk-shaped bones, five inches in diameter, from the spine were strewn all along. These looked like rough crackers.

Also the ribs of whale (probably humpbacked),—they get humpback and finback and right whales, I heard,—six feet long, lay under the bank, hardly to be distinguished from their gray rails. Some of those whale ribs, ten inches wide, were from time to time set up in the sand, like mile stones (or bones); they seemed to answer that purpose along the new road. They had taken a whale in Provincetown Harbor on the previous 17th, and stripped off the blubber at one of the wharves. I saw many dogfish whose livers had been extracted.

At East Harbor River, as I sat on the Truro end of the bridge, I saw a great flock of mackerel gulls, one hundred at least, on a sandy point, whitening the shore there like so many white stones on the shore and in the water, uttering all together their vibrating shrill note. They had black heads, light bluish-slate wings, and light rump and tail and beneath. From time to time all or most would rise and circle about with a clamor, then settle again on the same spot close together.

Soon after crossing the bridge, I turned off and ascended Mt. Ararat.[7] It exhibited a remarkable landscape: on the one side the desert, of smooth and spotless palest fawn-colored sand, slightly undulating, and beyond, the Atlantic; on the other, the west, side, a few valleys and hills, *densely* clothed with a short, almost moss-like (to look down at) growth of huckleberry, blueberry, bear-berry, Josh-pear (which is so abundant in Provincetown), bayberry, rose, checkerberry, and other bushes, and beyond, the Bay. All these bushes formed an even and dense covering to the sand-hills, much as bear-berry alone might. It was a very strange scenery. You would think you might be in Labrador, or some other place you have imagined. The shrubbery at the very summit was swarming with mosquitoes, which troubled me when I sat down, but they did not rise above the level of the bushes.

At the Pilgrim House,[8] though it was not crowded, they put me into a small attic chamber which had two double beds in it, and only one window, high in a corner, twenty and a half inches by twenty-five and a half, in the alcove when it was swung open, and it required a chair to look out conveniently. Fortunately it was not a cold night and the window could be kept open, though at the risk of being visited by the cats, which appear to swarm on the roofs of Provincetown like the mosquitoes on the summits of its hills. I have spent four memorable nights there in as many different years, and have added considerable thereby to my knowledge of the natural history of the cat and the bedbug. Sleep was out of the question. A night in one of the attics of Provincetown! to say nothing of what is to be learned in entomology. It would be worth the while to send a professor there, one who was also skilled in entomology. Such is your *Pilgerruhe* or Pilgrims'-Rest. Every now and then one of these animals on its travels leaped from a neighboring roof on to mine, with such a noise as if a six-pounder had fallen within two feet of my head,—the discharge of a catapult,—a

7. A high sand dune just over the line   8. A Provincetown hotel.
into Provincetown.

twelve-pounder discharged by a catapult,—and then followed such a scrambling as banished sleep for a long season, while I watched lest they came in at the open window. A kind of foretaste, methought, of the infernal regions. I didn't wonder they gave quit-claim deeds of their land here. My experience is that you fare best at private houses. The barroom may be defined a place to spit.

> "Soon as the evening shades prevail,
> The *cats take* up the wondrous tale."[9]

At still midnight, when, half awake, half asleep, you seem to be weltering in your own blood on a battlefield, you hear the stealthy tread of padded feet belonging to some animal of the cat tribe, perambulating the roof within a few inches of your head.

I had already this evening called on Mr. Atwood, the Representative of the town and one of the commissioners appointed by the legislature to superintend the experiments in the artificial breeding of fishes. He said that he knew (I think) eighty-two kinds of fishes there.

When Mr. Pool, the Doorkeeper of the House of Representatives, —if that is his name and title,—who makes out a list of the Representatives and their professions, asked him his business, he answered, "Fisherman." At which Pool was disturbed and said that no representative had ever called himself a fisherman before. It would not do to print it so. And so Atwood is put down as "Master Mariner"!! So much for American democracy. I reminded him that Fisherman had been a title of honor with a large party ever since the Christian Era at least. When next we have occasion to speak of the apostles I suppose we should call them "Master Mariners"!

Atwood said that his brother here took the bone shark recently which I read was thirty feet long. Fog again at night.

[Brooks Clark]

Oct. 20. * * * I had gone but little way on the old Carlisle road when I saw Brooks Clark, who is now about eighty and bent like a bow, hastening along the road, barefooted, as usual, with an axe in his hand; was in haste perhaps on account of the cold wind on his bare feet. It is he who took the *Centinel* so long. When he got up to me, I saw that besides the axe in one hand, he had his shoes in the other, filled with knurly apples and a dead robin. He stopped and talked with me a few moments; said that we had had a noble autumn and might now expect some cold weather. I asked if he had found the robin dead. No, he said, he found it with its wing broken and killed it. He also added that he had found some

9. A parody of two lines in Joseph Addison's famous hymn, "The Spacious Firmament on High." The second line of the original reads, "The moon takes up the wondrous tale."

apples in the woods, and as he hadn't anything to carry them in, he put 'em in his shoes. They were queer-looking trays to carry fruit in. How many he got in along toward the toes, I don't know. I noticed, too, that his pockets were stuffed with them. His old tattered frock coat was hanging in strips about the skirts, as were his pantaloons about his naked feet. He appeared to have been out on a scout this gusty afternoon, to see what he could find, as the youngest boy might. It pleased me to see this cheery old man, with such a feeble hold on life, bent almost double, thus enjoying the evening of his days. Far be it from me to call it avarice or penury, this childlike delight in finding something in the woods or fields and carrying it home in the October evening, as a trophy to be added to his winter's store. Oh, no: he was happy to be Nature's pensioner still, and birdlike to pick up his living. Better his robin than your turkey, his shoes full of apples than your barrels full; they will be sweeter and suggest a better tale. He can afford to tell how he got them, and we to listen. There is an old wife, too, at home, to share them and hear how they were obtained. Like an old squirrel shuffling to his hole with a nut. Far less pleasing to me the loaded wain, more suggestive of avarice and of spiritual penury.

This old man's cheeriness was worth a thousand of the church's sacraments and *memento mori*'s. It was better than a prayerful mood. It proves to me old age as tolerable, as happy, as infancy. I was glad of an occasion to suspect that this afternoon he had not been at "work" but living somewhat after my own fashion (though he did not explain the axe),—had been out to see what nature had for him, and now was hastening home to a burrow he knew, where he could warm his old feet. If he had been a young man, he would probably have thrown away his apples and put on his shoes when he saw me coming, for shame. But old age is manlier; it has learned to live, makes fewer apologies, like infancy. This seems a very manly man. I have known him within a few years building stone wall by himself, barefooted. * * *

[The Study of Frogs]

[1858] *April* 18. * * * Examined the pools and ditches in that neighborhood, *i.e.* of Skull-Cap Ditch, for frogs. All that I saw distinctly, except two *R. fontinalis*, were what I have considered young bullfrogs, middling-sized frogs with a greenish-brown back and a throat commonly white or whitish. I saw in a deep and cold pool some spawn placed just like that of the *R. sylvatica* and the *R. halecina*,—it was in the open field,—and the only frog I could distinguish near it was a middling sized one, or larger, with a yellow throat, not distinctly green, but brown or greenish-brown above, but green along each upper jaw. A small portion of bright-golden ring about the eye was to be seen in front.

In the spring near by, I see two unquestionable R. *fontinalis*, one much the largest and with brighter mottlings, probably on account of the season. The upper and forward part of their bodies distinct green, but their throats, white or whitish, not yellow. There were also two small and dark-colored frogs, yet with a little green tinge about the snouts, in the same spring.

I suspect that all these frogs may be the R. *fontinalis*, and none of them bullfrogs. Certainly those two unquestionable R. *fontinalis* had no yellow to throats, and probably they vary very much in the greenness of the back. Those two were not so much barred on the legs as mottled, and in one the mottlings had quite bright halos. They had the yellow segment in front part of eye, as also had the two smallest. Have the bullfrogs this? I doubt if I have seen a bullfrog yet.

I should say, with regard to that spawn, that I heard in the neighboring pool the stertorous *tut tut tut* like the R. *halecina*, and also one dump sound.

Frogs are strange creatures. One would describe them as peculiarly wary and timid, another as equally bold and imperturbable. All that is required in studying them is patience. You will sometimes walk a long way along a ditch and hear twenty or more leap in one after another before you, and see where they rippled the water, without getting sight of one of them. Sometimes, as this afternoon the two R. *fontinalis*, when you approach a pool or spring a frog hops in and buries itself at the bottom. You sit down on the brink and wait patiently for his reappearance. After a quarter of an hour or more he is sure to rise to the surface and put out his nose quietly without making a ripple, eying you steadily. At length he becomes so curious about you as you can be about him. He suddenly hops straight toward [you], pausing within a foot, and takes a near and leisurely view of you. Perchance you may now scratch its nose with your finger and examine it to your heart's content, for it is become as imperturbable as it was shy before. You conquer them by superior patience and immovableness; not by quickness, but by slowness; not by heat, but by coldness. You see only a pair of heels disappearing in the weedy bottom, and, saving a few insects, the pool becomes as smooth as a mirror and apparently as uninhabited. At length, after half an hour, you detect a frog's snout and a pair of eyes above the green slime, turned toward you,—etc. * * *

[A *Pout on Her Nest*]

June 7. * * * As I was wading in this Wyman meadow, looking for bullfrog-spawn, I saw a hole at the bottom, where it was six or eight inches deep, by the side of a mass of mud and weeds which rose just to the surface three or four feet from the shore. It was about five inches in diameter, with some sand at the mouth, just like a musquash's hole. As I stood there within two feet, a pout put her head out, as if to see who was there, and directly came forth and disappeared under the target-weed; but as I stood perfectly still, waiting for the water which I had disturbed to settle about the hole, she circled round and round several times between me and the hole, cautiously, stealthily approaching the entrance but as often withdrawing, and at last mustered courage to enter it. I then noticed another similar hole in the same mass, two or three feet from this. I thrust my arm into the first, running it in and downward about fifteen inches. It was a little more than a foot long and enlarged somewhat at the end, the bottom, also, being about a foot beneath the surface,—for it slanted downward,— but I felt nothing within; I only felt a pretty regular and rounded apartment with firm walls of weedy or fibrous mud. I then thrust my arm into the other hole, which was longer and deeper, but at first discovered nothing; but, trying again, I found that I had not reached the end, for it turned a little and descended more than I supposed. Here I felt a similar apartment or enlargement, some six inches in diameter horizontally but not quite so high nor nearly so wide at its throat. Here, to my surprise, I felt something soft, like a gelatinous mass of spawn, but, feeling a little further, felt the horns of a pout. I deliberately took hold of her by the head and lifted her out of the hole and the water, having run my arm in two thirds its length. She offered not the slightest resistance from first to last, even when I held her out of water before my face, and only darted away suddenly when I dropped her in the water. The entrance to her apartment was so narrow that she could hardly have escaped if I had tried to prevent her. Putting in my arm again, I felt, under where she had been, a flattish mass of ova, several inches in diameter, resting on the mud, and took out some. Feeling again in the first hole, I found as much more there. Though I had been stepping round and over the second nest for several minutes, I had not scared the pout. The ova of the first nest already contained white wiggling young. I saw no motion in the others. The ova in each case were dull-yellowish and the size of small buckshot. These nests did not communicate with each other and had no other outlet.

Pouts, then, make their nests in shallow mud-holes or bays, in masses of weedy mud, or probably in the muddy bank; and the old pout hovers over the spawn or keeps guard at the entrance. Where do the Walden pouts breed when they have not access to this meadow? The first pout, whose eggs were most developed, was the largest and had some slight wounds on the back. The other may have been the male in the act of fertilizing the ova.

[On Writing—IV]

[1859] *Jan.* 2. * * * When I hear the hypercritical quarrelling about grammar and style, the position of the particles, etc., etc., stretching or contracting every speaker to certain rules of theirs,— Mr. Webster, perhaps, not having spoken according to Mr. Kirkham's rule,[1]—I see that they forget that the first requisite and rule is that expression shall be vital and natural, as much as the voice of a brute or an interjection: first of all, mother tongue; and last of all, artificial or father tongue. Essentially your truest poetic sentence is as free and lawless as a lamb's bleat. The grammarian is often one who can neither cry nor laugh, yet thinks that he can express human emotions. So the posture-masters tell you how you shall walk,—turning your toes out, perhaps, excessively,—but so the beautiful walkers are not made. * * *

Feb. 3. * * * The writer must to some extent inspire himself. Most of his sentences may at first lie dead in his essay, but when all are arranged, some life and color will be reflected on them from the mature and successful lines; they will appear to pulsate with fresh life, and he will be enabled to eke out their slumbering sense, and make them worthy of their neighborhood. In his first essay on a given theme, he produces scarcely more than a frame and groundwork for his sentiment and poetry. Each clear thought that he attains to draws in its train many divided thoughts or perceptions. The writer has much to do even to create a theme for himself. Most that is first written on any subject is a mere groping after it, mere rubble-stone and foundation. It is only when many observations of different periods have been brought together that he begins to grasp his subject and can make one pertinent and just observation.

Feb. 13. * * * A transient acquaintance with any phenomenon is not sufficient to make it completely the subject of your muse. You must be so conversant with it as to *remember* it and be reminded of it long afterward, while it lies remotely fair and elysian in the horizon, approachable only by the imagination.

Feb. 20. * * * In the composition it is the greatest art to find out as quickly as possible which are the best passages you have written, and tear the rest away to come at them. Even the poorest parts will be most effective when they serve these, as pediments to the column. * * *

March 11. * * * Find out as soon as possible what are the

---

1. Daniel Webster was the most noted orator of Thoreau's day; Samuel Kirk-ham was author of *A Compendium of English Grammar* (1823).

best things in your composition, and then shape the rest to fit them.
The former will be the midrib and veins of the leaf.

There is always some accident in the best things, whether
thoughts or expressions or deeds. The memorable thought, the
happy expression, the admirable deed are only partly ours. The
thought came to us because we were in a fit mood; also we were
unconscious and did not know that we had said or done a good
thing. We must walk consciously only part way toward our goal,
and then leap in the dark to our success. What we do best or
most perfectly is what we have most thoroughly learned by the longest practice, and at length it falls from us without our notice, as a
leaf from a tree. It is the *last* time we shall do it,—our unconscious
leavings.

[Tracks in the Snow]

[1860] *Jan.* 4. * * * In Hosmer's pitch pine wood just north of
the bridge, I find myself on the track of a fox—as I take it—that has
run about a great deal. Next I come to the tracks of rabbits, see
where they have travelled back and forth, making a well-trodden
path in the snow; and soon after I see where one has been killed
and apparently devoured. There are to be seen only the tracks of
what I take to be the fox. The snow is much trampled, or rather
flattened by the body of the rabbit. It is somewhat bloody and is
covered with flocks of slate-colored and brown fur, but only the
rabbit's tail, a little ball of fur, an inch and a half long and about
as wide, white beneath, and the contents of its paunch or of its en-
trails are left,—nothing more. Half a dozen rods further, I see
where the rabbit has been dropped on the snow again, and some
fur is left, and there are the tracks of the fox to the spot and about
it. There, or within a rod or two, I notice a considerable furrow
in the snow, three or four inches wide and some two rods long, as
if one had drawn a stick along, but there is no other mark or
track whatever; so I conclude that a partridge, perhaps scared by the
fox, had dashed swiftly along so low as to plow the snow. But two
or three rods further on one side I see more sign, and lo! there is
the remainder of the rabbit,—the whole, indeed, but the tail and
the inward or soft parts,—all frozen stiff; but here there is no
distinct track of any creature, only a few scratches and marks where
some great bird of prey—a hawk or owl—has struck the snow with
its primaries on each side, and one or two holes where it has stood.
Now I understand how that long furrow was made, the bird with
the rabbit in its talons flying low there, and now I remember that
at the first bloody spot I saw some of these quill-marks; and therefore it is certain that the bird had it there, and probably he killed
it, and he, perhaps disturbed by the fox, carried it to the second

place, and it is certain that he (probably disturbed by the fox again) carried it to the last place, making a furrow on the way.

If it had not been for the snow on the ground I probably should not have noticed any signs that a rabbit had been killed. Or, if I had chanced to see the scattered fur, I should not have known what creature did it, or how recently. But now it is partly certain, partly probable,—or, supposing that the bird could not have taken it from the fox, it is almost all certain,—that an owl or hawk killed a rabbit here last night (the fox-tracks are so fresh), and, when eating it on the snow, was disturbed by a fox, and so flew off with it half a dozen rods, but, being disturbed again by the fox, it flew with it again about as much further, trailing it in the snow for a couple of rods as it flew, and there it finished its meal without being approached. A fox would probably have torn and eaten some of the skin.

When I turned off from the road my expectation was to see some tracks of wild animals in the snow, and, before going a dozen rods, I crossed the track of what I had no doubt was a fox, made apparently the last night,—which had travelled extensively in this pitch pine wood, searching for game. Then I came to rabbit-tracks, and saw where they had travelled back and forth in the snow in the woods, making a perfectly trodden path, and within a rod of that was a hollow in the snow a foot and a half across, where a rabbit had been killed. There were many tracks of the fox about that place, and I had no doubt then that he had killed that rabbit, and I supposed that some scratches which I saw might have been made by his frisking some part of the rabbit back and forth, shaking it in his mouth. I thought, Perhaps he has carried off to his young, or buried, the rest. But as it turned out, though the circumstantial evidence against the fox was very strong, I was mistaken. I had made him kill the rabbit, and shake and tear the carcass, and eat it all up but the tail (almost); but it seems that he didn't do it at [all], and apparently never got a mouthful of the rabbit. Something, surely, must have disturbed the bird, else why did it twice fly along with the heavy carcass?

The tracks of the bird at the last place were two little round holes side by side, the dry snow having fallen in and concealed the track of its feet.

It was most likely an owl, because it was most likely that the fox would be abroad by night. * * *

Again see what the snow reveals. Opposite Dodge's Brook I see on the snow and ice some fragments of frozen-thawed apples under an oak. How came they there? There are apple trees thirty rods off by the road. On the snow under the oak I see two or three tracks of a crow, and the droppings of several that were perched on the tree, and here and there is a perfectly round hole in the snow under the tree. I put down my hand and draw up an apple [out] of each, from beneath the snow. (There are no tracks of squirrels about the oak.) Crows carried these frozen-thawed apples from the apple trees to the oak, and there ate them,—what they did not let fall into the snow or on to the ice.

See that long meandering track where a deer mouse hopped over the soft snow last night, scarcely making any impression. What if you could witness with owls' eyes the revelry of the wood mice some night, frisking about the wood like so many little kangaroos? Here is a palpable evidence that the woods are nightly thronged with little creatures which most have never seen,—such populousness as commonly only the imagination dreams of.

The circumstantial evidence against that fox was very strong, for the deed was done since the snow fell and I saw no other tracks but his at the first places. Any jury would have convicted him, and he would have been hung, if he could have been caught.

1906

[Sic Vita][2]

I am a parcel of vain strivings tied
    By a chance bond together,
Dangling this way and that, their links
    Were made so loose and wide,
        Methinks,   5
      For milder weather.

A bunch of violets without their roots,
    And sorrel intermixed,[3]
Encircled by a wisp of straw
    Once coiled about their shoots,   10
        The law
    By which I'm fixed.

A nosegay which Time clutched from out
    Those fair Elysian fields,
With weeds and broken stems, in haste,   15
    Doth make the rabble rout
        That waste
      The day he yields.

2. "Thus Life." This poem was written on a sheet of paper wrapped around a bunch of violets, tied loosely with a straw, and thrown into the window of Thoreau's friend Mrs. Lucy Jackson Brown, sister of Mrs. Ralph Waldo Emerson, as a romantic gesture whose exact meaning is impossible to determine from evidence now available. The stanza form is reminiscent of the "shape" poems of the metaphysical poets, the odd line-lengths representing the dangling flower stems.

3. According to the "language of flowers" popular in Thoreau's day, the violet represented modesty. The sorrel represented "wit ill-timed": this is not surprising when one considers to whom the poem was addressed.

And here I bloom for a short hour unseen,
    Drinking my juices up,   20
  With no root in the land
    To keep my branches green,
      But stand
      In a bare cup.

Some tender buds were left upon my stem   25
    In mimicry of life,
  But ah! the children will not know,
    Till time has withered them,
      The woe
      With which they're rife.   30

But now I see I was not plucked for naught,
    And after in life's vase
  Of glass set while I might survive,
    But by a kind hand brought
      Alive   35
      To a strange place.

That stock thus thinned will soon redeem its hours,
    And by another year,
  Such as God knows, with freer air,
    More fruits and fairer flowers   40
      Will bear,
      While I droop here.

                  1841, 1849

My Prayer

Great God, I ask thee for no meaner pelf
Than that I may not disappoint myself;
That in my action I may soar as high
As I can now discern with this clear eye.

And next in value, which thy kindness lends,   5
That I may greatly disappoint my friends,
Howe'er they think or hope that it may be,
They may not dream how thou'st distinguished me;

That my weak hand may equal my firm faith,
And my life practice more than my tongue saith;   10
  That my low conduct may not show,
    Nor my relenting lines,
  That I thy purpose did not know,
    Or overrated thy designs.

                  1842, 1866

Smoke[4]

Light-winged Smoke, Icarian bird,[5]
Melting thy pinions in thy upward flight;
Lark without song, and messenger of dawn,
Circling above the hamlets as thy nest;
Or else, departing dream, and shadowy form   5
Of midnight vision, gathering up thy skirts;
By night star-veiling, and by day
Darkening the light and blotting out the sun;
Go thou my incense upward from this hearth,
And ask the gods to pardon this clear flame.   10

1843, 1854

Haze

Woof of the sun, ethereal gauze,
Woven of Nature's richest stuffs,
Visible heat, air-water, and dry sea,
Last conquest of the eye;
Toil of the day displayed, sun-dust,   5
Aerial surf upon the shores of earth,
Ethereal estuary, frith[6] of light,
Breakers of air, billows of heat,
Fine summer spray on inland seas;
Bird of the sun, transparent-winged   10
Owlet of noon, soft-pinioned,
From heath or stubble rising without song,—
Establish thy serenity o'er the fields.

1843, 1849

Inspiration[7]

Whate'er we leave to God, God does,
    And blesses us;
The work we choose should be our own,
    God leaves alone.

If with light head erect I sing,   5
    Though all the Muses lend their force,
From my poor love of anything,
    The verse is weak and shallow as its source.

4. Originally published in the transcendentalist periodical *The Dial*, this poem was later incorporated into the text of *Walden*, in the chapter "House-Warming" (not included in our text).
5. Icarus, according to Greek mythology, made wings of feathers and wax, but when he flew too near the sun, the wax melted and he plunged to his death.
6. That is, a firth, the opening of a river into a sea.
7. This poem is one of the best brief expositions of the transcendentalist theory of divine inspiration that we have. Stanzas six, seven, and eight are a particularly succinct description of the "transcending of the senses."

But if with bended neck I grope
   Listening behind me for my wit,   10
With faith superior to hope,
   More anxious to keep back than forward it;

Making my soul accomplice there
   Unto the flame my heart hath lit,
Then will the verse forever wear—   15
   Time cannot bend the line which God hath writ.

Always the general show of things
   Floats in review before my mind,
And such true love and reverence brings,
   That sometimes I forget that I am blind.   20

But now there comes unsought, unseen,
   Some clear divine electuary,[8]
And I, who had but sensual been,
   Grow sensible, and as God is, am wary.

I hearing get, who had but ears,   25
   And sight, who had but eyes before,
I moments live, who lived but years,
   And truth discern, who knew but learning's lore.

I hear beyond the range of sound,
   I see beyond the range of sight,   30
New earths and skies and seas around,
   And in my day the sun doth pale his light.

A clear and ancient harmony
   Pierces my soul through all its din,
As through its utmost melody,—   35
   Farther behind than they, farther within.

More swift its bolt than lightning is,
   Its voice than thunder is more loud,
It doth expand my privacies
   To all, and leave me single in the crowd.   40

It speaks with such authority,
   With so serene and lofty tone,
That idle Time runs gadding by,
   And leaves me with Eternity alone.

Now chiefly is my natal hour,   45
   And only now my prime of life,
Of manhood's strength it is the flower,
   'Tis peace's end and war's beginning strife.

It comes in summer's broadest noon,
   By a grey wall or some chance place,   50

8. Medicine.

Unseasoning Time, insulting June,
  And vexing day with its presuming face.

Such fragrance round my couch it makes,
  More rich than are Arabian drugs,
That my soul scents its life and wakes   55
  The body up beneath its perfumed rugs.

Such is the Muse, the heavenly maid,
  The star that guides our mortal course,
Which shows where life's true kernel's laid,
  Its wheat's fine flour, and its undying force.   60

She with one breath attunes the spheres,
  And also my poor human heart,
With one impulse propels the years
  Around, and gives my throbbing pulse its start.

I will not doubt for evermore,   65
  Nor falter from a steadfast faith,
For though the system be turned o'er,
  God takes not back the word which once He saith.

I will not doubt the love untold
  Which not my worth nor want has bought,   70
Which wooed me young, and wooes me old,
  And to this evening hath me brought.

My memory I'll educate
  To know the one historic truth,
Remembering to the latest date   75
  The only true and sole immortal youth.

Be but thy inspiration given,
  No matter through what danger sought,
I'll fathom hell or climb to heaven,
  And yet esteem that cheap which love has bought.   80

Fame cannot tempt the bard
  Who's famous with his God,
Nor laurel him reward
  Who has his Maker's nod.

1848   1849, 1895

Fog

Dull water spirit—and Protean[9] god
Descended cloud fast anchored to the earth
That drawest too much air for shallow coasts
Thou ocean branch that flowest to the sun

9. Proteus was a Greek sea god who possessed the power constantly to change his shape.

Incense of earth, perfumed with flowers—   5
Spirit of lakes and rivers, seas and rills
Come to revisit now thy native scenes
Night thoughts of earth—dream drapery
Dew cloth and fairy napkin
Thou wind-blown meadow of the air.   10

1905

Nathaniel Hawthorne

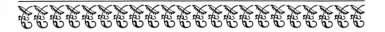

It has been remarked that despite the relative uneventfulness of his life, there are more biographies of Hawthorne than of any other American literary man. The most striking external happening in his life was probably his term as American consul at Liverpool (1853–57), together with subsequent visits to Rome and to Florence: matters of moment, certainly, to Hawthorne and his family, but not of vital consequence to the great world and ourselves.

There are, however, a number of reasons for finding Hawthorne's life interesting. For one thing, we naturally expect a literary man's career to be centered on his writing, and find our profit in considering the relations of his life to his art. Again, Hawthorne's character, like his writing, presents suggestive and stimulating complications. He has been portrayed, and with good evidence, alike as a proud recluse and as a normal man of society: as a haunted misanthrope and as a cheerful and devoted husband and father; as a cold and withdrawn spectator and also as a lover of the warm domestic hearth. Herman Melville, with whom he enjoyed one of the great American literary friendships and who dedicated *Moby Dick* to Hawthorne, always regarded him as a man with a tragic secret: a verdict which on the other hand aroused amused astonishment in his son Julian, to whom he was an affectionate and companionable father. It is not strange, then, that Hawthorne has tempted the biographer to elucidate his mystery.

Yet a further reason for special attention to Hawthorne's life might be found in its representative qualities, what might more pretentiously be called its potentialities for symbol. The problems of his career as a writer are those of other early 19th-century American authors, in his case enhanced in significance by his genius. His solitary struggle during young manhood against a chill and unfriendly literary environment; his gradual rise from anonymity in the journals and annuals of the 1830's to some reputation with the collected *Twice-Told Tales* of 1837; his participation in the Brook Farm experiment, in a mood at once sympathetic and withdrawn; his emergence from shadow into sunlight with his engagement and marriage to Sophia Peabody; his financial difficulties and consequent alternation between literature and business to keep his family going; his first decisive success in *The Scarlet Letter* (1850), which was written because he lost his job at the Salem Custom House: these circumstances and events have a pattern, they are balanced and symmetrical. It might be said that they move constantly between poles of (to use the Toynbean formula) "withdrawal and return," in a design formed partly from within by the nature of the man. The pattern was to be continued throughout Hawthorne's life, as he widened his horizons with an important political job and foreign travel but returned to New England and lonely authorship once more. His death itself, peaceful yet mysterious, on an outward journey and yet not unaccompanied, is consistent with the design of Hawthorne's life.

I

Nathaniel Hawthorne was born in 1804 in Salem, Massachusetts, in the sixth generation of his family to live in New England. His ancestors included statesmen, judges, and sea captains. One of them, John Hathorne, was a magistrate at the Salem witchcraft trials of 1692, a fact deeply engraved on Hawthorne's imagination. For several generations his forebears were seamen, while the family gradually declined; the death of his father, Captain Nathaniel Hathorne (the son added the *w* to the name), in Dutch Guiana in 1808 left his widow and children dependent at least in part upon relatives for support. Nathaniel, the only son, was brought up in Salem and in Raymond, Maine. A leg injury in childhood immobilized the boy for several years, during which he developed a taste for reading and contemplative habits exceptional for his age.

By virtue of help from his uncles the Mannings, Nathaniel attended Bowdoin College in Brunswick, Maine, from which he was graduated in 1825 in the same class with Longfellow; Franklin Pierce, a future President of the United States; and Horatio Bridge, who was to subsidize the first publication of *Twice-Told Tales*. Hawthorne's career at Bowdoin was harmonious and unremarkable: he read widely on his own, did very well in English composition and Latin, on one occasion was fined fifty cents for playing cards for money, and persistently declined to engage in the public speaking that was part of Bowdoin's curriculum. In general he followed his own bent without any marked clashes with authority, made good friends, and came out of college determined to be a writer.

Hawthorne looked back upon the years from 1825 to 1837 in his life as a period of dreamlike isolation and solitude, spent in a "haunted chamber," where he sat still while the world moved on. These twelve years were his term of apprenticeship to writing. His view of it is significant of a tension in him, a pull in two directions at once. He was later, in the Preface to the 1851 edition of *Twice-Told Tales*, to speak of "the apparently opposite peculiarities" of his stories of this era of his life. Despite the seclusion in which they were produced, "they are not," he said, "the talk of a secluded man with his own mind and heart * * * but his attempts, and very imperfectly successful ones, to open an intercourse with the world." He published anonymously and with small financial return in magazines and Christmas annual collections, and resorted to hack work for a little more money. In 1837 Horatio Bridge, his old college friend, engineered the publication of the *Twice-Told Tales* by guaranteeing the costs of the volume, and Hawthorne, in his own words "for a good many years, the obscurest man of letters in America," began to achieve some public recognition.

The growth of Hawthorne's reputation was steady, but modest and slow. At no time of his life were his literary sales enough to support the family he was shortly to acquire. Falling in love with Sophia Peabody, a

Salem neighbor, in 1838, he went to work for two years in the Boston Custom House and then spent part of a year at the famous Brook Farm community in 1841, actuated chiefly by the hope of supporting a wife by his membership in the group, in the stock of which he invested from his scanty savings. His mingled sympathy with and skepticism of the Brook Farm experiment is expressed in *The Blithedale Romance*. Marriage with Miss Peabody in 1842 was followed by several years of idyllic happiness in semi-retirement at the Old Manse in Concord, where he came in contact with Emerson, Thoreau, and Ellery Channing. Faced once again with the problem of making a living, he succeeded in getting a political job in 1846 as Surveyor in the Salem Custom House, from which, as a Democrat, he was evicted by the Whigs under the spoils system in 1849.

Hawthorne left his place in the customs only after a determined struggle to hold it, and with considerable bitterness, as evidenced in the "Custom House" sketch that precedes *The Scarlet Letter*. He was later to pillory his chief enemy among the Whigs, the Reverend Charles W. Upham, as Judge Pyncheon in *The House of the Seven Gables*. His dismissal, however, turned out to be a blessing in disguise. Turning directly to literature, he wrote his first (if we except his early *Fanshawe*, which he suppressed shortly after its publication) and finest novel, *The Scarlet Letter* (1850). The book was well received, and he was stimulated by its success to publish two other novels, or as he preferred to say, "romances," *The House of the Seven Gables* and *The Blithedale Romance*, in the next two years, along with *A Wonder Book* (1852), exquisite tales of Greek myth for children, which he subsequently followed with *Tanglewood Tales* (1853). Residing during 1850 in Lenox in the Berkshires, he had met Herman Melville, who was living nearby at his farm of Arrowhead. A friendship between them followed, although they were only for a short time in close contact and Melville, fifteen years younger and a more impressionable man, was by far the more deeply influenced of the two.

The election to the Presidency in 1852 of his friend Franklin Pierce led to Hawthorne's acceptance of the United States consulship in Liverpool, which he held for over four years from 1853 to 1857. The Hawthornes then traveled in Italy, where they settled especially in Rome and for a period in Florence. They returned to England while Hawthorne finished and prepared for the press his Roman romance, *The Marble Faun* (1860), and came back to the United States on June 28, 1860, after an absence of seven years, to take up residence in their first permanent home, the Wayside at Concord.

Hawthorne was to live only four more years. He had been an exceptionally strong and vigorous man, but by 1863 his health had markedly and inexplicably declined—"inexplicably" especially since he refused to have a physician examine him. During this last period he struggled with no fewer than four romances, *The Ancestral Footstep*, *Dr. Grimshawe's Secret*, *Septimius Felton*, and *The Dolliver Romance*, but could bring none to satisfactory completion. The circumstances of Hawthorne's death are at once natural and strange, and are characteristic of the man. In search of change he set off on a carriage expedition into the New Hampshire hills with his old friend Franklin Pierce; he had been fond of such excursions from his youth on, and looked to this one for a tonic. The second night of the carriage journey Hawthorne died, probably in his sleep, on May 19, 1864. He was just short of sixty.

II

. The oppositions and complications of Hawthorne's career have been mentioned. Some of them might be explained quite simply in terms of the difficulties of the writer in early 19th-century America: an unsympathetic environment, the matter-of-fact materialism of a physically expanding nation, and inadequate remuneration. At his most successful Hawthorne could not live well and support his family comfortably on the proceeds of his fiction. There were other problems, however, that came from within. Hawthorne's Puritan heritage both fostered and fought with his genius. Puritan seriousness and its tradition of self-searching led to moral and psychological profundity, and the Puritan habit of looking to natural events for spiritual meaning provided Hawthorne with a method and a way of seeing. On the other hand, the Puritan creed was not friendly to fiction, which as make-believe was vanity and as imitation of the creations of God was impious and idolatrous. Correspondingly, for a sixth-generation New Englander the conflict of claims between present and past was an important matter, as *The House of the Seven Gables* shows in the history of the Pyncheons.

Hawthorne also inherited the 18th-century Augustan culture, overlaying the 17th-century Puritan in him. He thus exhibited a certain coolness and classic balance, a strong respect for moderation and reason that was at odds with other instincts in him. He desired to live fully, to make good use of his sensibilities—and the desire might be called romantic. Yet as a rational and cautious person he was content to exist in different compartments, and not try to be everything at once. He did not push himself. He usually refused to write in the summer, for example, and his utmost heat of effort, the composition of *The Scarlet Letter*, is considerably below the temperature of Melville in the later stages of *Moby Dick*. Hawthorne could not write successfully while otherwise employed, and he soon recognized the fact.

He could be a competent and hard-headed man of affairs, as he proved at the Boston and Salem Custom Houses and later as American consul at Liverpool, but could not combine business with creative thought. He knew himself extremely well, so that he was able to move harmoniously from his rather solitary youth into an ideally successful career as husband and as father. There was within him an iron vein of stern strength, an indomitable self-command that manifested itself in his life and in his fiction alike. He was so strong that he could well afford to be gentle; he could expend much and hold much in reserve. A serious and conscientious artist, he was nevertheless not committed to literature as was, say, Balzac or Henry James. He enjoyed experience, though with characteristic moderation, for its own sake; he held if anything too pessimistic a view of his talent. He wished to fulfill himself in his life as well as in his art, and was therefore not minded to sacrifice either himself or those who depended upon him for their happiness. The amount of his writing is substantial but not great, and the scope of his work is in some respects limited.

Hawthorne's Puritan skepticism of the value of human effort is also to be considered in assessing him. His strong sense of Necessity and of Providence tended to make man's achievement in itself mere vanity. This fatalism may have hindered him at times: on the other hand it is part of his strength. He stood out against the optimism of his time, he resisted the intoxicating attractions of transcendental individualism, and in doing so was able to contribute something uniquely his own. With Melville he was one of the great no-sayers of 19th-century America, who have been sadly vindicated by the experience of the 20th. He was a believer, imaginatively if not literally, in the doctrine of the Fall of Man, with its consequence—the radical imperfection of natural man and his world. His vision of life possessed, as Melville said, "the power of blackness."

Examination of Hawthorne's tales and romances will show as much light as darkness. Characteristically, the two are quite evenly distributed in his work. Yet the dark is in some respects the more dramatic hue, and it is Hawthorne's special gift to look steadily upon the face of evil, unafraid though not unimpressed. "The great thing about Nathaniel Hawthorne," said Melville in a letter about *The House of the Seven Gables*, "is that he can say No! in thunder."

This attitude runs counter to America's characteristic optimism. Our material good fortune, our national origin in the period of the Enlightenment, along with other causes, gave rise to belief in endless progress and in the concept of man as essentially good and perfectible, as though a human being was a machine improvable, like an automobile or airplane, by scientific experiment and technology. Latterly we have found that nuclear weapons are more immediately susceptible of improvement, but perhaps we have not entirely taken in this fact. For the most part the evil our literature has dealt with has been social or economic, the result of bad judgment, easily corrected when once pointed out. In a word, not evil at all, since evil is not eradicable by science or the intellect. And most of those American writers who have possessed the vision of evil, it has been remarked, have been in a sense unmanned by it. Unprepared, they have found its face unbearable. This is true of Melville, our most sensitive and most instinctively religious writer, who in *Moby Dick* and the dismaying *Pierre* is almost blasted by the horror of his imaginative apprehension of "the mysteries of iniquity." The more self-possessed Hawthorne, perhaps because of a Calvinist heritage in part also Melville's, is like him somewhat Manichaean, somewhat heretical in dividing the world equally between light and darkness. Perhaps in his emphasis he still concedes the greater power to the Prince of Darkness; and he is thus characteristic of the paradox of American literature. Yet Hawthorne's imaginative genius was an instrument for probing the American mind as well as the problem of evil.

Imaginative literature is always Janus-faced and ambiguous. It looks outward at reality and inward at itself. It is at once a commentary upon its world and an autonomous activity. Literarily speaking, evil is an aesthetic principle, the dark as contrast to the light. It is an indispensable element of structure, necessary for full imaginative realization. One notes when one thinks of the matter that a "happy ending" is not interesting or exciting unless it is significant, unless the happiness it portrays has been really seriously threatened. Every plot, every action, is to some degree about something that has gone wrong, in all shades of darkness from the contretemps and mistaken identities of farce (Shakespeare's *Comedy of Errors*) to the fundamental dislocation of values that sets off the tragic action of *Hamlet.*

This aesthetic principle is not opposed, except as a necessary logical distinction, to any principle of reality or morality. An artist like Hawthorne may be fascinated by the problem of evil as a matter of aesthetics and at the same time treat it with the utmost seriousness. Tragedy is traditionally the most highly respected literary form, the most artistically complex, while it is also treasured as a storehouse of imaginative knowledge in which the human spirit is tested to the limit and thus broadened and deepened as the result of its struggle with the utmost imaginable adversity.

III

To keep our discussion as concrete as possible, we might give special attention to "Young Goodman Brown," a short story which Melville pronounced "as deep as Dante." An allegorical journey of the soul amid difficulties and dangers, it is a kind of miniature *Pilgrim's Progress.* How deeply Bunyan's masterpiece impressed Hawthorne is amply evident in his writings, very obviously in "The Celestial Railroad." Here the pilgrims travel comfortably by rail and check to the baggage car the burden of sin that Bunyan's Christian bore painfully on his back—a satirical adaptation of the *Progress* to 19th-century America. "Young Goodman Brown" owes something as well to another favorite allegory of Hawthorne's, Edmund Spenser's *Faerie Queene,* in its theme of disguise and the dark wood of its scene, which resembles Spenser's Forest of Errour. More immediately, however, the background of the tale is legendary New England history, drawn from Cotton Mather and accounts of the Salem witchcraft trials in which Hawthorne's ancestor had played a tragic part. Thus the time is the 1690's, and the place is Salem.

The story can well be interpreted as a parable of American extremism on the problem of evil. The Devil himself is an American devil, who is perhaps taken in by his own propaganda. Young Goodman Brown, being impressed with the fact that all men are sinful and subject to moral evil, jumps to the conclusion that sin and evil are the only realities, dismissing the appearance of good as illusion and deception. Since he rebels against this conclusion and has no mind to join the brotherhood of sin, his predicament is singularly painful, for he lives isolated as the only righteous man in a world given over completely to unrighteousness. He has lost his Faith, even though she stands always at his side. Hawthorne does not map out the territories of good and evil, but he makes clear that both exist. In "The Minister's Black Veil" he presents a similar distortion of moral view: the veil darkens the unhappy minister's vision.

"Young Goodman Brown" is not only American but Puritan as well, for the rigorous Puritan standards force men to appear more virtuous than human nature will allow of, shut them off from sympathy, and thus render them liable to hypocrisy, perversion, and self-despair. Hawthorne is said to have furnished us with our stereotype of the New England Puritan, the disagreeable figure of our blue-law cartoons. Actually, his view of his ancestors was complex, but there is no doubt that he invested them with the iron hardness of the mailclad Endicott of "The Maypole of Merry Mount," the sternness of the Puritan crowd of *The Scarlet Let-*

ter, who on a festival day "appeared scarcely more grave than most other communities at a period of general affliction."

As a fine story thoroughly representative of Hawthorne's tales, "Young Goodman Brown" is a good base for further discussion of his art and his ideas. In the first place, it is an allegory, in that it universalizes. It means more than it seems to be saying; its characters represent moral qualities and states of mind; its scenes, images, and objects stand for something beyond their literal significations. It employs the dream convention of medieval allegory and of *The Pilgrim's Progress* ("Now I saw in my dream * * *"). "Had Goodman Brown," asks Hawthorne, "fallen asleep in the forest and only dreamed a wild dream of a witch-meeting?" The question suggests that the story's action has been invented to serve an ulterior purpose, and can be discarded from thought when the purpose has been fulfilled. This, as we shall find, is not so, but the problem of allegory remains.

Allegory has a certain taint of thinness, of sterility, of threadbare moralizings. We are irritated, too, to find ourselves cheated into accepting something we did not bargain on or want, when we find that the author is more interested in making a point than in telling a story. This, indeed, is the crucial test for literary value. If the interest inheres within the work itself the work is literature; if not, we must at least partially reject it. Hawthorne's imagination was happy with the allegorical vision and method, and his very infrequent failures are failures not of method but of imagination. He differs from contemporary writers in his willingness to state his meanings directly and in general terms, but his "morals" are integral elements of his art, not substitutes for it nor prescribed interpretations of it; his stories present themselves as imaginative wholes, their life diffused throughout. Hawthorne himself speaks to this point in his Preface to *The House of the Seven Gables.* The moral of the book, he says, is "the truth, namely, that the wrong-doing of one generation lives into the successive ones, and, divesting itself of every temporary advantage, becomes a pure and uncontrollable mischief." But the moral is not the book. "When romances do really teach anything, or produce any effective operation, it is usually through a far more subtle process than the ostensible one. * * * A high truth, indeed, fairly, finely, and skilfully wrought out, brightening at every step, and crowning the final development of a work of fiction, may add an artistic glory, but it is never any truer, and seldom any more evident, at the last page than at the first."

The method of allegory is, then, an aesthetic virtue in "Young Goodman Brown"; it furnishes its foundations without obtruding upon other virtues. Since allegory is systematic and sustained, the story gets clarity and design from it, in the opposition of Salem village and the wild forest, the stylized entrapment of Goodman Brown as the Devil leads him step by step down the winding forest path, and the sudden hush that succeeds the crescendo of the witch meeting as the scene vanishes and Brown finds himself alone. The allegory, on the other hand, does not limit suggestion. Faith, for example, is of course a quality of Brown's mind, but she is also a young woman, and the stress between these different aspects of her is an added interest.

IV

Hawthorne's tales are notably unified and clean of outline. A case can be made for honoring him as the first practitioner of the modern short story. Poe, as we know, formulated his famous theory of the short story as a result of contemplating the *Twice-Told Tales*. One might remark that Poe's formula calls for a tighter unity, a greater attention to effect, a closer observance of limitation of time, scene, and action, as also of length, than is to be found in Hawthorne, while as an "effect" critic primarily interested in psychological response, Poe reduces meaning to mere illusion. Some of Hawthorne's tales, such as "Roger Malvin's Burial" and "Wakefield," cover a span of years. Generally speaking he focuses strongly upon scene and the dramatic action that goes with it—"Young Goodman Brown" presents six definite scenes—but he alternates these freely with fluid narrative. And he takes more liberties with comment than Poe quite approved, following the tradition of the English novel from Fielding on, which places upon the author the social obligation of performing as a graceful and witty master of ceremonies, as well as following in his "morals" the tradition of Puritan allegory. Poe was later to speak out harshly against the allegorical vein in Hawthorne, which he wrongly attributed to the influence of the New England transcendentalists. These two masters of the tale were of course only partly in sympathy, as is evidenced by Poe's interesting misinterpretation of "The Minister's Black Veil," which he praises highly for quite the wrong reasons: "The *moral* put into the mouth of the dying minister will be supposed to convey the *true* import of the narrative; and that a crime of dark dye (having reference to the 'young lady') has been committed, is a point which only minds congenial with that of the author will perceive." Actually, Poe has seized upon a possibility that Hawthorne deliberately (one guesses) held out to the reader, but only on full consideration to be rejected.

As regards unity of tone and effect, Hawthorne fulfills the spirit but not the letter of Poe's requirements. His prose is always lucid, uncomplicated, and elegant. "It is, in fact," he said in the Preface to *Twice-Told Tales*, "the style of a man of society. Every sentence, so far as it embodies thought or sensibility, may be understood and felt by anybody who will give himself the trouble to read it, and will take up the book in a proper mood." The effects of this limpid discourse of Hawthorne's are varied and complicated by his unfailing command of prose rhythms and cadences. One notes the deeper strains as Goodman Brown rushes wildly through the forest, or in the strangely elegiac melancholy of Satan's address to his young neophytes: Miltonic organ tones, one might say, as opposed to the Restoration-like elegancies of Brown's temptation.

These effects are quiet, as is the steady play of irony and humor in Hawthorne's writing. He never insists. He is both less and more objective than Poe, in that on the one hand he permits himself to comment but on the other neither surrenders himself wholly nor calls upon the reader to surrender to the chief effect he is seeking. "Young Goodman Brown" is a gloomy story, but it is rich in delightful ironies both of situation and tone, so disinterested that they lighten into humor. Thus the hero's mixture of mischief and compunction at the outset, remorseful at deceiving his wife: " 'Well, she's a blessed angel on earth; and after this one night

I'll cling to her skirts and follow her to heaven.'" To which Hawthorne adds coolly, "With this excellent resolve for the future, Goodman Brown felt himself justified in making more haste on his present evil purpose." If one considers the events of the night in question there is still a further touch of irony. Brown comes to doubt very seriously that his wife is an "angel on earth," and rather than clinging to her skirts he finds himself under the necessity of bidding her to " 'look up to heaven, and resist the wicked one.' " Hawthorne's foreshadowings, or (as one critic calls them) his prefigurations, are extremely artful. Again, the reversal of values in the forest makes for an irony that sometimes rises into comedy. Goody Cloyse, Brown's catechist, finds herself unhappily without her broomstick. But she will foot it to the witch meeting if necessary, for " 'they tell me there is a nice young man to be taken into communion to-night.' " She is balanced by Deacon Gookin and the minister, who "had rather miss an ordination dinner than to-night's meeting," and who are much enlivened by the news that "there is a goodly young woman to be taken into communion."

v

Ambiguity, an opposite quality, supplements and enriches Hawthorne's characteristic clarity of design and diction. In the case of "Young Goodman Brown" the ambiguity is tragic and organically related to the central theme, for the possibility that Brown has dreamed the entire action is never withdrawn. At no point are we permitted to be entirely certain that what seems to be happening is real. The Devil carries a staff "which bore the likeness of a great black snake, so curiously wrought that it might almost be seen to twist and wriggle itself like a living serpent." If it is alive, the Devil's supernatural quality is definitely established, and we drop double meanings—but "this, of course, must have been an ocular deception, assisted by the uncertain light." Thus Brown hears but does not see the Deacon and the minister. "These mingled sounds appeared to pass along the road, within a few yards of the young man's hiding-place; but, owing doubtless to the depth of the gloom at that particular spot, neither the travellers nor their steeds were visible." The figures at the witch meeting are ambiguously lighted by a fitfully blazing fire: "As the red light arose and fell, a numerous congregation alternately shone forth, then disappeared in shadow." His wife herself appears to Brown as "the slender form of a veiled female," although here it must be added that a little later "by the blaze of the hell-kindled torches the wretched man beheld his Faith." Finally there is the culminating ambiguity, "Had Goodman Brown fallen asleep in the forest and only dreamed a wild dream of a witch-meeting?" to which Hawthorne answers only, "Be it so if you will; but, alas! it was a dream of evil omen for young Goodman Brown." This means presumably that the question should not be pressed, lest the writer be stripped of the advantages he sought in the first place. Hawthorne spoke quite explicitly on this point a good deal later, in his Epilogue to *The Marble Faun*. For those who ask the question whether Donatello the faun actually had furry ears, he declared, "the book is a failure." The action of "Young Goodman Brown" is essentially true and meaningful. To ask if it is also literally true is to destroy a delicate and vital metaphorical relationship. Of course Hawthorne tempts us to ask; the suspension is part of the effect.

Hawthorne's ambiguity is in part the protective device of the "Romancer" who defends his imaginative illusion against the attack of irrelevant or unsympathetic matter-of-fact. This protection he found peculiarly necessary in his America. "No author," he said in the Preface to *The Marble Faun*, "without a trial, can conceive of the difficulty of writing a romance about a country where there is no shadow, no antiquity, no mystery, no picturesque and gloomy wrong, nor anything but a commonplace prosperity in broad and simple daylight, as is happily the case with my dear native land." And the Romance is obligated only to essential truth, "the truth of the human heart." The writer "may so manage his medium as to bring out or mellow the lights and deepen and enrich the shadows of the picture." Ambiguity, then, is a device of art for significant emphasis, with a certain Platonic and also Christian distinction between appearance and reality underlying it. It can at times be a fundamental ambiguity of moral meaning, as it nearly is in "Young Goodman Brown" and in "Rappaccini's Daughter," where Giovanni Guasconti persistently doubts the truth of what he sees and is in fact in the end deceived as to its deepest meaning. As a device of "alternative possibilities" or of "multiple choice" Hawthorne's use of ambiguities is also a means of securing density and objectivity. Dealing as he does with moral themes, he is faced with the necessity of moral interpretation and judgment, but he wishes to respect the individualities and complexities of this concrete world and of human character. He makes his judgments, but he permits the reader a choice: no less than four interpretations of Dimmesdale's death are proposed in *The Scarlet Letter*, although it is pretty clear which one is Hawthorne's preference. Alternatively, his ambiguities express a basic caution and skepticism in Hawthorne: skepticism even of his own judgment. His caution, however, seldom leads him into indecision.

"Young Goodman Brown" and the problems of ambiguity are connected with one of Hawthorne's chief preoccupations, the relation between reality and dream or unreality. The vision of the real is essential to the soul's survival, and one loses this vision by distorting what one sees or by ignoring a part of it. The truth lies in wholeness. Goodman Brown's vision of evil is a dream of evil omen because it represents a half-truth. What Giovanni sees in Dr. Rappaccini's garden is true on one level but profoundly false on another, and the poison he absorbs from Beatrice comes most deeply from himself. " 'Oh, was there not, from the first, more poison in thy nature than in mine?' " asks the unhappy girl.

This poison has the effect of isolating Giovanni from society. He is lost. So Wakefield condemns himself to limbo by his strange freak of cutting his ties with the world. "He had contrived, or rather he had happened, to dissever himself from the world—to vanish—to give up his place and privileges with living men, without being admitted among the dead." Wakefield has lost his hold on reality through lack of imagination, and falls into a cold, dull egotism. Ethan Brand is more positively damned by an overmastering preoccupation which first isolates him from mankind, then causes an enormous imbalance, a kind of hypertrophy of the intellect, and finally drives him to the symbolic act of suicide by fire in a supreme gesture of self-isolation.

The loss of reality most characteristically results in Hawthorne's fiction from an imbalance of head or the intellect and heart, a term that includes the emotions, intuition, the passions, the unconscious mind. It is the heart that contains man's deepest potentialities for good and evil, that constitutes man's vital connection to reality. Emphasis upon the head leads always to intellectual and spiritual pride or distortion of reality. Since Hawthorne most feared this sin or calamity, he gave the heart a little too much the best of the argument, as Melville implied in his comment upon "Ethan Brand": "It is a frightful poetic creed that the cultivation of the brain eats out the heart. But it's my *prose* opinion that in most cases, in those men who have fine brains and work them well, the heart extends down to hams. And though you smoke them with the fire of tribulation, yet, like veritable hams, the head only gives the richer and the better flavor." It does sometimes seem that for Hawthorne any unusual ability or aspiration leads to disaster. The scientist, such as Dr. Rappaccini or Aylmer in "The Birthmark," sacrifices men to his cold intellectual curiosity, or trifles presumptuously with God's creations. The artist, as in the portrait-painter of "The Prophetic Pictures," runs grave dangers, since his art leads him to violate the privacy of his subjects' souls.

What Hawthorne undoubtedly intended, however, was to advocate the full, undistorted vision, the perfect balance of head and heart. In "The Artist of the Beautiful," perhaps his most affirmative story, Owen Warland aspires to and achieves the creation of ideal beauty without sacrificing his humanity. He sacrifices a good many human relationships to achieve his end, but not his sense of their existence. He is able, indeed, to envision the ideal without losing his grasp upon the real.

It has earlier been remarked that while Hawthorne sought and succeeded in leading a full life, he found he could not combine occupations and interests. He did things in turns, not all at once. The same observation can be made of the vision of life he presents in his fiction. His solution to life's problems lies in balance, wise moderation, unflinching acceptance of difficulties, contradictions, and evils; it does not lie in the kind of synthesis that Melville had in mind in his comment on "Ethan Brand." Hawthorne gives us a very large measure, but he gives it to us in parts, distributed among his stories and romances. In "The Maypole of Merry Mount," for instance, young Edgar and Edith find their way amid the conflicting values of the Maypole and the Puritans. They presumably bring something, too, to the stern society in which they must live. Yet the story gives us little imaginative sense of a reconciliation of opposites; they adopt the Puritan way, which is imperfect but workable, and sacrifice much in the adoption. The Puritan vision is incomplete, though it is the closer to reality in its perception of "earth's doom of care and sorrow, and troubled joy." Only in "The Artist of the Beautiful" do we encounter true fulfillment, and in the flash of insight that concludes "The Birthmark": "Yet, had Aylmer reached a profounder wisdom, he need not thus have flung away the happiness which would have woven his mortal life of the selfsame texture with the celestial. The momentary circumstance was too strong for him; he failed to look beyond the shadowy scope of time, and, living once for all in eternity, to find the perfect future in the present."

This very insight, however, suggests a word of caution. It is not necessarily a flaw in Hawthorne that he shows us incomplete felicities, since his theme is the limitations, not the sufficiency of the human condition. Aylmer's mistake was in wanting everything at once, in trying to mix the imperfections of time with the ideal of eternity. Hawthorne's sense of ideal perfection is very strong, and the impact of "The Maypole of Merry Mount" considerably depends upon the attractions of the misplaced Golden Age the Merry Mounters have tried to achieve. But in his fiction the ideal of fulfillment depends upon as it also supports the actuality, which is the radical imperfection of human nature and of human life.

Preface to the 1851 Edition of *Twice-Told Tales*

The Author of "TWICE-TOLD TALES" has a claim to one distinction, which, as none of his literary brethren will care about disputing it with him, he need not be afraid to mention. He was, for a good many years, the obscurest man of letters in America.

These stories were published in magazines and annuals, extending over a period of ten or twelve years, and comprising the whole of the writer's young manhood, without making (so far as he has ever been aware) the slightest impression on the public. One or two among them, the "Rill from the Town Pump," in perhaps a greater degree than any other, had a pretty wide newspaper circulation; as for the rest, he had no grounds for supposing that, on their first appearance, they met with the good or evil fortune to be read by anybody. Throughout the time above specified, he had no incitement to literary effort in a reasonable prospect of reputation or profit, nothing but the pleasure itself of composition —an enjoyment not at all amiss in its way, and perhaps essential to the merit of the work in hand, but which, in the long run, will hardly keep the chill out of a writer's heart, or the numbness out of his fingers. To this total lack of sympathy, at the age when his mind would naturally have been most effervescent, the public owe it (and it is certainly an effect not to be regretted on either part) that the Author can show nothing for the thought and industry of that portion of his life, save the forty sketches, or thereabouts, included in these volumes.

Much more, indeed, he wrote; and some very small part of it might yet be rummaged out (but it would not be worth the trouble) among the dingy pages of fifteen-or-twenty-year-old periodicals, or within the shabby morocco covers of faded souvenirs. The remainder of the works alluded to had a very brief existence, but, on the score of brilliancy, enjoyed a fate vastly superior to that of their brotherhood, which succeeded in getting through the press. In a word, the Author burned them without mercy or remorse, and, moreover, without any subsequent regret, and had more than one occasion to marvel that such very dull stuff, as he knew his condemned manuscripts to be, should yet have possessed inflammability enough to set the chimney on fire!

After a long while the first collected volume of the "Tales" was published. By this time, if the Author had ever been greatly tormented by literary ambition (which he does not remember or believe to have been the case), it must have perished, beyond resuscitation, in the dearth of nutriment. This was fortunate; for the success of the volume was not such as would have gratified a craving desire for notoriety. A moderate edition was "got rid of" (to use the publisher's very significant phrase) within a reasonable time, but apparently without rendering the writer or his productions much more generally known than before. The great bulk of the reading public probably ignored the book altogether. A few persons read it, and liked it better than it deserved. At an interval of three or four years, the second volume was published, and encountered much the same sort of kindly, but calm, and very limited reception. The circulation of the two volumes was chiefly confined to New England; nor was it until long after this period, if it even yet be the case, that the Author could regard himself as addressing the American public, or, indeed, any public at all. He was merely writing to his known or unknown friends.

As he glances over these long-forgotten pages, and considers his way of life while composing them, the Author can very clearly discern why all this was so. After so many sober years, he would have reason to be ashamed if he could not criticise his own work as fairly as another man's; and, though it is little his business, and perhaps still less his interest, he can hardly resist a temptation to achieve something of the sort. If writers were allowed to do so, and would perform the task with perfect sincerity and unreserve, their opinions of their own productions would often be more valuable and instructive than the works themselves.

At all events, there can be no harm in the Author's remarking that he rather wonders how the "Twice-Told Tales" should have gained what vogue they did than that it was so little and so gradual. They have the pale tint of flowers that blossomed in too retired a shade,—the coolness of a meditative habit, which diffuses itself through the feeling and observation of every sketch. Instead of passion there is sentiment; and, even in what purport to be pictures of actual life, we have allegory, not always so warmly dressed in its habiliments of flesh and blood as to be taken into the reader's mind without a shiver. Whether from lack of power, or an unconquerable reserve, the Author's touches have often an effect of tameness; the merriest man can hardly contrive to laugh at his broadest humor; the tenderest woman, one would suppose, will hardly shed warm tears at his deepest pathos. The book, if you would see anything in it, requires to be read in the clear, brown, twilight atmosphere in which it was written; if opened in the sunshine, it is apt to look exceedingly like a volume of blank pages.

With the foregoing characteristics, proper to the production of a person in retirement (which happened to be the Author's category at the time), the book is devoid of others that we should quite as naturally look for. The sketches are not, it is hardly necessary to say, profound; but it is rather more remarkable that they so seldom, if ever, show any design on the writer's part to make them so. They have none of the abstruseness of idea, or obscurity of expression, which mark the written communications of a solitary mind with itself. They never need translation. It is, in fact, the style of a man of society. Every sentence, so far as it embodies thought or sensibility, may be understood and felt by anybody who will give himself the trouble to read it, and will take up the book in a proper mood.

This statement of apparently opposite peculiarities leads us to a perception of what the sketches truly are. They are not the talk of a secluded man with his own mind and heart (had it been so, they could hardly have failed to be more deeply and permanently valuable), but his attempts, and very imperfectly successful ones, to open an intercourse with the world.

The Author would regret to be understood as speaking sourly or querulously of the slight mark made by his earlier literary efforts on the Public at large. It is so far the contrary, that he has been moved to write this Preface chiefly as affording him an opportunity to express how much enjoyment he has owed to these volumes, both before and since their publication. They are the memorials of very tranquil and not unhappy years. They failed, it is true,—nor could it have been otherwise,—in winning an extensive popularity. Occasionally, however, when he deemed them entirely forgotten, a paragraph or an article, from a native or foreign critic, would gratify his instincts of authorship with unexpected praise,—too generous praise, indeed, and too little alloyed with censure, which, therefore, he learned the better to inflict upon himself. And, by the by, it is a very suspicious symptom of a deficiency of the popular element in a book when it calls forth no harsh criticism. This has been particularly the fortune of the "TWICE-TOLD TALES." They made no enemies, and were so little known and talked about that those who read, and chanced to like them, were apt to conceive the sort of kindness for the book which a person naturally feels for a discovery of his own.

This kindly feeling (in some cases, at least) extended to the Au-

thor, who, on the internal evidence of his sketches, came to be
regarded as a mild, shy, gentle, melancholic, exceedingly sensitive,
and not very forcible man, hiding his blushes under an assumed
name, the quaintness of which was supposed, somehow or other,
to symbolize his personal and literary traits. He is by no means
certain that some of his subsequent productions have not been
influenced and modified by a natural desire to fill up so amiable an
outline, and to act in consonance with the character assigned to
him; nor, even now, could he forfeit it without a few tears of
tender sensibility. To conclude, however: these volumes have
opened the way to most agreeable associations, and to the formation of imperishable friendships; and there are many golden
threads interwoven with his present happiness, which he can follow up more or less directly, until he finds their commencement
here; so that his pleasant pathway among realities seems to proceed out of the Dreamland of his youth, and to be bordered with
just enough of its shadowy foliage to shelter him from the heat of
the day. He is therefore satisfied with what the "TWICE-TOLD
TALES" have done for him, and feels it to be far better than fame.

1851

The Maypole of Merry Mount[1]

*There is an admirable foundation for a philosophic romance in
the curious history of the early settlement of Mount Wollaston, or
Merry Mount. In the slight sketch here attempted, the facts, recorded on the grave pages of our New England annalists, have
wrought themselves, almost spontaneously, into a sort of allegory.
The masques, mummeries, and festive customs, described in the
text, are in accordance with the manners of the age. Authority on
these points may be found in Strutt's Book of English Sports and
Pastimes.*

Bright were the days at Merry Mount, when the Maypole was
the banner staff of that gay colony! They who reared it, should
their banner be triumphant, were to pour sunshine over New England's rugged hills, and scatter flower seeds throughout the soil.

1. Contemporary historians of this
Cavalier community were Thomas Morton, second director of Merry Mount,
New English Canaan (1637), and William Bradford, Governor of the Plymouth Plantation, *History of Plymouth
Plantation*. Perhaps their opposing accounts suggested the polar oppositions
of Hawthorne's tale, in which Blackstone is set off against Endicott, the
maypole against the whipping post,
sunshine against shadow, festival
against fast day, drinking song against
psalm, and silk against iron. Hawthorne portrays Endicott as the archetypal Puritan in another tale, "Endicott and the Red Cross," in which he
also as here indulges himself in a
symbolic act of pious destruction at a
crucial moment of early American history. "The Maypole of Merry Mount"
was first published in *The Token* in
1836 and reprinted in 1837 in *Twice-
Told Tales*.

Jollity and gloom were contending for an empire. Midsummer eve had come, bringing deep verdure to the forest, and roses in her lap, of a more vivid hue than the tender buds of Spring. But May, or her mirthful spirit, dwelt all the year round at Merry Mount, sporting with the Summer months, and revelling with Autumn, and basking in the glow of Winter's fireside. Through a world of toil and care she flitted with a dreamlike smile, and came hither to find a home among the lightsome hearts of Merry Mount.

Never had the Maypole been so gayly decked as at sunset on midsummer eve. This venerated emblem was a pine-tree, which had preserved the slender grace of youth, while it equalled the loftiest height of the old wood monarchs. From its top streamed a silken banner, colored like the rainbow. Down nearly to the ground the pole was dressed with birchen boughs, and others of the liveliest green, and some with silvery leaves, fastened by ribbons that fluttered in fantastic knots of twenty different colors, but no sad ones. Garden flowers, and blossoms of the wilderness, laughed gladly forth amid the verdure, so fresh and dewy that they must have grown by magic on that happy pine-tree. Where this green and flowery splendor terminated, the shaft of the Maypole was stained with the seven brilliant hues of the banner at its top. On the lowest green bough hung an abundant wreath of roses, some that had been gathered in the sunniest spots of the forest, and others, of still richer blush, which the colonists had reared from English seed. O, people of the Golden Age, the chief of your husbandry was to raise flowers!

But what was the wild throng that stood hand in hand about the Maypole? It could not be that the fauns and nymphs, when driven from their classic groves and homes of ancient fable, had sought refuge, as all the persecuted did, in the fresh woods of the West. These were Gothic monsters, though perhaps of Grecian ancestry. On the shoulders of a comely youth uprose the head and branching antlers of a stag; a second, human in all other points, had the grim visage of a wolf; a third, still with the trunk and limbs of a mortal man, showed the beard and horns of a venerable he-goat. There was the likeness of a bear erect, brute in all but his hind legs, which were adorned with pink silk stockings. And here again, almost as wondrous, stood a real bear of the dark forest, lending each of his fore paws to the grasp of a human hand, and as ready for the dance as any in that circle. His inferior nature rose half way, to meet his companions as they stooped. Other faces wore the similitude of man or woman, but distorted or extravagant, with red noses pendulous before their mouths, which seemed of awful depth, and stretched from ear to ear in an eternal fit of laughter. Here might be seen the Salvage Man, well known in heraldry, hairy as a baboon, and girdled with green leaves. By his side, a noble figure, but still a counterfeit, appeared an Indian hunter, with feathery crest and wampum belt. Many of this strange company wore foolscaps, and had little bells appended to their garments, tinkling with a silvery sound, responsive to the inaudible music of their gleesome spirits. Some youths and maidens were of soberer garb, yet well maintained their places in the irregular throng by the expression of wild revelry upon their features. Such were the colonists of Merry Mount, as they stood in the broad smile of sunset round their venerated Maypole.

Had a wanderer, bewildered in the melancholy forest, heard their mirth, and stolen a half-affrighted glance, he might have fancied them the crew of Comus, some already transformed to brutes, some midway between man and beast, and the others rioting in the flow of tipsy jollity that foreran the change. But a band of Puritans, who watched the scene, invisible themselves, compared the masques to those devils and ruined souls with whom their superstition peopled the black wilderness.

Within the ring of monsters appeared the two airiest forms that had ever trodden on any more solid footing than a purple and golden cloud. One was a youth in glistening apparel, with a scarf of the rainbow pattern crosswise on his breast. His right hand held a gilded staff, the ensign of high dignity among the revellers, and his left grasped the slender fingers of a fair maiden, not less gayly decorated than himself. Bright roses glowed in contrast with the dark and glossy curls of each, and were scattered round their feet, or had sprung up spontaneously there. Behind this lightsome couple, so close to the Maypole that its boughs shaded his jovial face, stood the figure of an English priest, canonically dressed, yet decked with flowers, in heathen fashion, and wearing a chaplet of the native vine leaves. By the riot of his rolling eye, and the pagan decorations of his holy garb, he seemed the wildest monster there, and the very Comus of the crew.

"Votaries of the Maypole," cried the flower-decked priest, "merrily, all day long, have the woods echoed to your mirth. But be this your merriest hour, my hearts! Lo, here stands the Lord and Lady of the May, whom I, a clerk of Oxford, and high priest of Merry Mount, am presently to join in holy matrimony. Up with your nimble spirits, ye morris-dancers, green men, and glee maidens, bears and wolves, and horned gentlemen! Come; a chorus now, rich with the old mirth of Merry England, and the wilder glee of this fresh forest; and then a dance, to show the youthful pair what life is made of, and how airily they should go through it! All ye that love the Maypole, lend your voices to the nuptial song of the Lord and Lady of the May!"

This wedlock was more serious than most affairs of Merry Mount, where jest and delusion, trick and fantasy, kept up a continual carnival. The Lord and Lady of the May, though their titles must be laid down at sunset, were really and truly to be partners for the dance of life, beginning the measure that same bright eve. The wreath of roses, that hung from the lowest green bough of the Maypole, had been twined for them, and would be thrown over both their heads, in symbol of their flowery union. When the priest had spoken, therefore, a riotous uproar burst from the rout of monstrous figures.

"Begin you the stave, reverend Sir," cried they all; "and never did the woods ring to such a merry peal as we of the Maypole shall send up!"

Immediately a prelude of pipe, cithern, and viol, touched with practised minstrelsy, began to play from a neighboring thicket, in such a mirthful cadence that the boughs of the Maypole quivered to the sound. But the May Lord, he of the gilded staff, chancing to look into his Lady's eyes, was wonder struck at the almost pensive glance that met his own.

"Edith, sweet Lady of the May," whispered he reproachfully, "is yon wreath of roses a garland to hang above our graves, that you look so sad? O, Edith, this is our golden time! Tarnish it not by any pensive shadow of the mind; for it may be that nothing of futurity will be brighter than the mere remembrance of what is now passing."

"That was the very thought that saddened me! How came it in your mind too?" said Edith, in a still lower tone than he, for it was high treason to be sad at Merry Mount. "Therefore do I sigh amid the festive music. And besides, dear Edgar, I struggle as with a dream, and fancy that these shapes of our jovial friends are visionary, and their mirth unreal, and that we are no true Lord and Lady of the May. What is the mystery in my heart?"

Just then, as if a spell had loosened them, down came a little shower of withering rose leaves from the Maypole. Alas, for the young lovers! No sooner had their hearts glowed with real passion than they were sensible of something vague and unsubstantial in their former pleasures, and felt a dreary presentiment of inevitable change. From the moment that they truly loved, they had subjected themselves to earth's doom of care and sorrow, and troubled joy, and had no more a home at Merry Mount. That was Edith's mystery. Now leave we the priest to marry them, and the masquers to sport round the Maypole, till the last sunbeam be withdrawn from its summit, and the shadows of the forest mingle gloomily in the dance. Meanwhile, we may discover who these gay people were.

Two hundred years ago, and more, the old world and its inhabitants became mutually weary of each other. Men voyaged by thousands to the West: some to barter glass beads, and such like jewels, for the furs of the Indian hunter; some to conquer virgin empires; and one stern band to pray. But none of these motives had much weight with the colonists of Merry Mount. Their leaders were men who had sported so long with life, that when Thought and Wisdom came, even these unwelcome guests were led astray by the crowd of vanities which they should have put to flight. Erring Thought and perverted Wisdom were made to put on masques, and play the fool. The men of whom we speak, after losing the heart's fresh gayety, imagined a wild philosophy of pleasure, and came hither to act out their latest day-dream. They gathered followers from all that giddy tribe whose whole life is like the festal days of soberer men. In their train were minstrels, not unknown in London streets; wandering players, whose theatres had been the halls of noblemen; mummers, rope-dancers, and mountebanks, who would long be missed at wakes, church ales, and fairs; in a word, mirth makers of every sort, such as abounded in that age, but now began to be discountenanced by the rapid growth of Puritanism. Light had their footsteps been on land, and as lightly they came across the sea. Many had been maddened by their previous troubles into a gay despair; others were as madly gay in the flush of youth, like the May Lord and his Lady; but whatever might be the quality of their mirth, old and young were gay at Merry Mount. The young deemed themselves happy. The elder spirits, if they knew that mirth was but the counterfeit of happiness, yet followed the false shadow wilfully, because at least her garments glittered brightest. Sworn triflers of a lifetime, they would not venture among the sober truths of life not even to be truly blest.

All the hereditary pastimes of Old England were transplanted hither. The King of Christmas was duly crowned, and the Lord of Misrule bore potent sway. On the Eve of St. John, they felled whole acres of the forest to make bonfires, and danced by the blaze all night, crowned with garlands, and throwing flowers into the flame. At harvest time, though their crop was of the smallest, they made an image with the sheaves of Indian corn, and wreathed it with autumnal garlands, and bore it home triumphantly. But what chiefly characterized the colonists of Merry Mount was their veneration for the Maypole. It has made their true history a poet's tale. Spring decked the hallowed emblem with young blossoms and fresh green boughs; Summer brought roses of the deepest blush, and the perfected foliage of the forest; Autumn enriched it with that red and yellow gorgeousness which converts each wildwood leaf into a painted flower; and Winter silvered it with sleet, and hung it round with icicles, till it flashed in the cold sunshine, itself a frozen sunbeam. Thus each alternate season did homage to the Maypole, and paid it a tribute of its own richest splendor. Its votaries danced round it, once, at least, in every month; sometimes they called it their religion, or their altar; but always, it was the banner staff of Merry Mount.

Unfortunately, there were men in the new world of a sterner faith than those Maypole worshippers. Not far from Merry Mount was a settlement of Puritans, most dismal wretches, who said their prayers before daylight, and then wrought in the forest or the cornfield till evening made it prayer time again. Their weapons were always at hand to shoot down the straggling savage. When they met in conclave, it was never to keep up the old English mirth, but to hear sermons three hours long, or to proclaim bounties on the heads of wolves and the scalps of Indians. Their festivals were fast days, and their chief pastime the singing of psalms. Woe to the youth or maiden who did but dream of a dance! The selectman nodded to the constable; and there sat the light-heeled reprobate in the stocks; or if he danced, it was round the whipping-post, which might be termed the Puritan Maypole.[2]

A party of these grim Puritans, toiling through the difficult woods, each with a horseload of iron armor to burden his footsteps, would sometimes draw near the sunny precincts of Merry Mount. There were the silken colonists, sporting round their Maypole; perhaps teaching a bear to dance, or striving to communicate their mirth to the grave Indian; or masquerading in the skins of deer and wolves, which they had hunted for that especial purpose. Often, the whole colony were playing at blindman's buff, magistrates and all, with their eyes bandaged, except a single scapegoat, whom the blinded sinners pursued by the tinkling of the bells at his garments. Once, it is said, they were seen following a flower-decked corpse, with merriment and festive music, to his grave. But did the dead man laugh? In their quietest times, they sang ballads and told tales, for the edification of their pious visitors; or perplexed them with juggling tricks; or grinned at them through horse collars; and when sport itself grew wearisome, they made game of their own stupidity, and began a yawning match. At the very least of these enormities, the men of iron shook their heads and frowned so darkly that the revellers looked up imagin-

2. For other somber pictures of the Puritans see "The Gentle Boy," "The Gray Champion," *The Scarlet Letter*, and *The House of the Seven Gables*. In "Young Goodman Brown" the Devil claims that "I have been as well acquainted with your [Brown's] family as with ever a one among the Puritans; and that's no trifle to say. I helped your grandfather, the constable, when he lashed the Quaker woman so smartly through the streets of Salem; and it was I that brought your father a pitch-pine knot, kindled at my own hearth, to set fire to an Indian village, in King Philip's war."

ing that a momentary cloud had overcast the sunshine, which was to be perpetual there. On the other hand, the Puritans affirmed that, when a psalm was pealing from their place of worship, the echo which the forest sent them back seemed often like the chorus of a jolly catch, closing with a roar of laughter. Who but the fiend, and his bond slaves, the crew of Merry Mount, had thus disturbed them? In due time, a feud arose, stern and bitter on one side, and as serious on the other as anything could be among such light spirits as had sworn allegiance to the Maypole. The future complexion of New England was involved in this important quarrel. Should the grizzly saints establish their jurisdiction over the gay sinners, then would their spirits darken all the clime, and make it a land of clouded visages, of hard toil, of sermon and psalm forever. But should the banner staff of Merry Mount be fortunate, sunshine would break upon the hills, and flowers would beautify the forests, and late posterity do homage to the Maypole.

After these authentic passages from history, we return to the nuptials of the Lord and Lady of the May. Alas! we have delayed too long, and must darken our tale too suddenly. As we glance again at the Maypole, a solitary sunbeam is fading from the summit, and leaves only a faint, golden tinge blended with the hues of the rainbow banner. Even that dim light is now withdrawn, relinquishing the whole domain of Merry Mount to the evening gloom, which has rushed so instantaneously from the black surrounding woods. But some of these black shadows have rushed forth in human shape.

Yes, with the setting sun, the last day of mirth had passed from Merry Mount. The ring of gay masquers was disordered and broken; the stag lowered his antlers in dismay; the wolf grew weaker than a lamb; the bells of the morris-dancers tinkled with tremulous affright. The Puritans had played a characteristic part in the Maypole mummeries. Their darksome figures were intermixed with the wild shapes of their foes, and made the scene a picture of the moment, when waking thoughts start up amid the scattered fantasies of a dream. The leader of the hostile party stood in the centre of the circle, while the route of monsters cowered around him, like evil spirits in the presence of a dread magician. No fantastic foolery could look him in the face. So stern was the energy of his aspect, that the whole man, visage, frame, and soul, seemed wrought of iron, gifted with life and thought, yet all of one substance with his headpiece and breastplate. It was the Puritan of Puritans; it was Endicott himself!

"Stand off, priest of Baal!" said he, with a grim frown, and laying no reverent hand upon the surplice. "I know thee, Blackstone![3] Thou art the man who couldst not abide the rule even of thine own corrupted church, and hast come hither to preach iniquity, and to give example of it in thy life. But now shall it be seen that the Lord hath sanctified this wilderness for his peculiar people. Woe unto them that would defile it! And first, for this flower-decked abomination, the altar of thy worship!"

And with his keen sword Endicott assaulted the hallowed Maypole. Nor long did it resist his arm. It groaned with a dismal sound; it showered leaves and rosebuds upon the remorseless enthusiast; and finally, with all its green boughs and ribbons and flowers, symbolic of departed pleasures, down fell the banner staff of Merry Mount. As it sank, tradition says, the evening sky grew darker, and the woods threw forth a more sombre shadow.

"There," cried Endicott, looking triumphantly on his work, "there lies the only Maypole in New England! The thought is strong within me that, by its fall, is shadowed forth the fate of light and idle mirth makers, amongst us and our posterity. Amen, saith John Endicott."

"Amen!" echoed his followers.

But the votaries of the Maypole gave one groan for their idol. At the sound, the Puritan leader glanced at the crew of Comus, each a figure of broad mirth, yet, at this moment, strangely expressive of sorrow and dismay.

"Valiant captain," quoth Peter Palfrey, the Ancient of the band, "what order shall be taken with the prisoners?"

"I thought not to repent me of cutting down a Maypole," replied Endicott, "yet now I could find in my heart to plant it again, and give each of these bestial pagans one other dance round their idol. It would have served rarely for a whipping-post!"

"But there are pine-trees enow," suggested the lieutenant.

"True, good Ancient," said the leader. "Wherefore, bind the heathen crew, and bestow on them a small matter of stripes apiece, as earnest of our future justice. Set some of the rogues in the stocks to rest themselves, so soon as Providence shall bring us to one of our own well-ordered settlements where such accommodations may be found. Further penalties, such as branding and cropping of ears, shall be thought of hereafter."

"How many stripes for the priest?" inquired Ancient Palfrey.

"None as yet," answered Endicott, bending his iron frown upon the culprit. "It must be for the Great and General Court to determine, whether stripes and long imprisonment, and other grievous

3. "Did Governor Endicott speak less positively, we should suspect a mistake here. The Rev. Mr. Blackstone, though an eccentric, is not known to have been an immoral man. We rather doubt his identity with the priest of Merry Mount" [Hawthorne's note].

penalty, may atone for his transgressions. Let him look to himself! For such as violate our civil order, it may be permitted us to show mercy. But woe to the wretch that troubleth our religion."

"And this dancing bear," resumed the officer. "Must he share the stripes of his fellows?"

"Shoot him through the head!" said the energetic Puritan. "I suspect witchcraft in the beast."

"Here be a couple of shining ones," continued Peter Palfrey, pointing his weapon at the Lord and Lady of the May. "They seem to be of high station among these misdoers. Methinks their dignity will not be fitted with less than a double share of stripes."

Endicott rested on his sword, and closely surveyed the dress and aspect of the hapless pair. There they stood, pale, downcast, and apprehensive. Yet there was an air of mutual support and of pure affection, seeking aid and giving it, that showed them to be man and wife, with the sanction of a priest upon their love. The youth, in the peril of the moment, had dropped his gilded staff, and thrown his arm about the Lady of the May, who leaned against his breast, too lightly to burden him, but with weight enough to express that their destinies were linked together, for good or evil. They looked first at each other, and then into the grim captain's face. There they stood, in the first hour of wedlock, while the idle pleasures, of which their companions were the emblems, had given place to the sternest cares of life, personified by the dark Puritans. But never had their youthful beauty seemed so pure and high as when its glow was chastened by adversity.

"Youth," said Endicott, "ye stand in an evil case, thou and thy maiden wife. Make ready presently, for I am minded that ye shall both have a token to remember your wedding day!"

"Stern man," cried the May Lord, "how can I move thee? Were the means at hand, I would resist to the death. Being powerless, I entreat! Do with me as thou wilt, but let Edith go untouched!"

"Not so," replied the immitigable zealot. "We are not wont to show an idle courtesy to that sex, which requireth the stricter discipline. What sayest thou, maid? Shall thy silken bridegroom suffer thy share of the penalty, besides his own?"

"Be it death," said Edith, "and lay it all on me!"

Truly, as Endicott had said, the poor lovers stood in a woful case. Their foes were triumphant, their friends captive and abased, their home desolate, the benighted wilderness around them, and a rigorous destiny, in the shape of the Puritan leader, their only guide. Yet the deepening twilight could not altogether conceal that the iron man was softened; he smiled at the fair spectacle of early love; he almost sighed for the inevitable blight of early hopes.

"The troubles of life have come hastily on this young couple," observed Endicott. "We will see how they comport themselves under their present trials ere we burden them with greater. If, among the spoil, there be any garments of a more decent fashion, let them be put upon this May Lord and his Lady, instead of their glistening vanities. Look to it, some of you."

"And shall not the youth's hair be cut?" asked Peter Palfrey, looking with abhorrence at the lovelock and long glossy curls of the young man.

"Crop it forthwith, and that in the true pumpkin-shell fashion," answered the captain. "Then bring them along with us, but more gently than their fellows. There be qualities in the youth, which may make him valiant to fight, and sober to toil, and pious to pray; and in the maiden, that may fit her to become a mother in our Israel, bringing up babes in better nurture than her own hath been. Nor think ye, young ones, that they are the happiest, even in our lifetime of a moment, who misspend it in dancing round a Maypole!"

And Endicott, the severest Puritan of all who laid the rock foundation of New England, lifted the wreath of roses from the ruin of the Maypole, and threw it, with his own gauntleted hand, over the heads of the Lord and Lady of the May. It was a deed of prophecy. As the moral gloom of the world overpowers all systematic gayety, even so was their home of wild mirth made desolate amid the sad forest. They returned to it no more. But as their flowery garland was wreathed of the brightest roses that had grown there, so, in the tie that united them, were intertwined all the purest and best of their early joys. They went heavenward, supporting each other along the difficult path which it was their lot to tread, and never wasted one regretful thought on the vanities of Merry Mount.

1836, 1837

The Gray Champion[4]

There was once a time when New England groaned under the actual pressure of heavier wrongs than those threatened ones

4. It has been persuasively suggested that Sir Walter Scott provided the model for this tale. "The Angel of Hadley," the legend behind "The Gray Champion," was actually used in Scott's *Peveril of the Peak* (1822).

The enemies are Indians, and the time King Philip's War (1675), while the place is the town of Hadley, Massachusetts. The story is told by President Stiles of Yale in *A History of Three of the Judges of King Charles I* (1794): "Suddenly, and in the midst of the people there appeared a man of very venerable aspect, and different from the inhabitants in his apparel, who took the command, arranged, and ordered them in the best military manner, and under his direction they repelled and routed the Indians, and the town was saved. He immediately vanished, and the inhabitants could not account for the phenomenon, but by considering that person as an Angel sent of God upon that special occasion for their deliverance." He was later identi-

which brought on the Revolution. James II., the bigoted successor of Charles the Voluptuous, had annulled the charters of all the colonies, and sent a harsh and unprincipled soldier to take away our liberties and endanger our religion. The administration of Sir Edmund Andros lacked scarcely a single characteristic of tyranny: a Governor and Council, holding office from the King, and wholly independent of the country, laws made and taxes levied without concurrence of the people, immediate or by their representatives; the rights of private citizens violated, and the titles of all landed property declared void; the voice of complaint stifled by restrictions on the press; and, finally, disaffection overawed by the first band of mercenary troops that ever marched on our free soil. For two years our ancestors were kept in sullen submission by that filial love which had invariably secured their allegiance to the mother country, whether its head chanced to be a Parliament, Protector, or Popish Monarch. Till these evil times, however, such allegiance had been merely nominal, and the colonists had ruled themselves, enjoying far more freedom than is even yet the privilege of the native subjects of Great Britain.

At length a rumor reached our shores that the Prince of Orange had ventured on an enterprise, the success of which would be the triumph of civil and religious rights and the salvation of New England. It was but a doubtful whisper; it might be false, or the attempt might fail; and, in either case, the man that stirred against King James would lose his head. Still the intelligence produced a marked effect. The people smiled mysteriously in the streets, and threw bold glances at their oppressors; while far and wide there was a subdued and silent agitation, as if the slightest signal would rouse the whole land from its sluggish despondency. Aware of their danger, the rulers resolved to avert it by an imposing display of strength, and perhaps to confirm their despotism by yet harsher measures. One afternoon in April, 1689, Sir Edmund Andros and his favorite councillors, being warm with wine, assembled the redcoats of the Governor's Guard, and made their appearance in the streets of Boston. The sun was near setting when the march commenced.

The roll of the drum at that unquiet crisis seemed to go through the streets, less as the martial music of the soldiers, than as a muster-call to the inhabitants themselves. A multitude, by various avenues, assembled in King Street, which was destined to be the scene, nearly a century afterwards, of another encounter between the troops of Britain and a people struggling against her tyranny.

fied as an actual person, William Goffe, one of the regicide judges of Charles I, who fled to America for refuge at the Restoration. "The Gray Champion" first appeared in the *New-England Magazine* for January, 1835, and was included in the 1837 *Twice-Told Tales*.

Though more than sixty years had elapsed since the pilgrims came, this crowd of their descendants still showed the strong and sombre features of their character perhaps more strikingly in such a stern emergency than on happier occasions. There were the sober garb, the general severity of mien, the gloomy but undismayed expression, the scriptural forms of speech, and the confidence in Heaven's blessing on a righteous cause, which would have marked a band of the original Puritans, when threatened by some peril of the wilderness. Indeed, it was not yet time for the old spirit to be extinct; since there were men in the street that day who had worshipped there beneath the trees, before a house was reared to the God for whom they had become exiles. Old soldiers of the Parliament were here, too, smiling grimly at the thought that their aged arms might strike another blow against the house of Stuart. Here, also, were the veterans of King Philip's war, who had burned villages and slaughtered young and old, with pious fierceness, while the godly souls throughout the land were helping them with prayer. Several ministers were scattered among the crowd, which, unlike all other mobs, regarded them with such reverence, as if there were sanctity in their very garments. These holy men exerted their influence to quiet the people, but not to disperse them. Meantime, the purpose of the Governor, in disturbing the peace of the town at a period when the slightest commotion might throw the country into a ferment, was almost the universal subject of inquiry, and variously explained.

"Satan will strike his master-stroke presently," cried some, "because he knoweth that his time is short. All our godly pastors are to be dragged to prison! We shall see them at a Smithfield fire in King Street!"

Hereupon the people of each parish gathered closer round their minister, who looked calmly upwards and assumed a more apostolic dignity, as well befitted a candidate for the highest honor of his profession, the crown of martyrdom. It was actually fancied, at that period, that New England might have a John Rogers of her own to take the place of that worthy in the Primer.

"The Pope of Rome has given orders for a new St. Bartholomew!" cried others. "We are to be massacred, man and male child!"

Neither was this rumor wholly discredited, although the wiser class believed the Governor's object somewhat less atrocious. His predecessor under the old charter, Bradstreet, a venerable companion of the first settlers, was known to be in town. There were grounds for conjecturing, that Sir Edmund Andros intended at once to strike terror by a parade of military force, and to confound the opposite faction by possessing himself of their chief.

"Stand firm for the old charter Governor!" shouted the crowd, seizing upon the idea. "The good old Governor Bradstreet!"

While this cry was at the loudest, the people were surprised by the well-known figure of Governor Bradstreet himself, a patriarch of nearly ninety, who appeared on the elevated steps of a door, and, with characteristic mildness, besought them to submit to the constituted authorities.

"My children," concluded this venerable person, "do nothing rashly. Cry not aloud, but pray for the welfare of New England, and expect patiently what the Lord will do in this matter!"

The event was soon to be decided. All this time, the roll of the drum had been approaching through Cornhill, louder and deeper, till with reverberations from house to house, and the regular tramp of martial footsteps, it burst into the street. A double rank of soldiers made their appearance, occupying the whole breadth of the passage, with shouldered matchlocks, and matches burning, so as to present a row of fires in the dusk. Their steady march was like the progress of a machine, that would roll irresistibly over everything in its way. Next, moving slowly, with a confused clatter of hoofs on the pavement, rode a party of mounted gentlemen, the central figure being Sir Edmund Andros, elderly, but erect and soldier-like. Those around him were his favorite councillors, and the bitterest foes of New England. At his right hand rode Edward Randolph, our arch-enemy, that "blasted wretch," as Cotton Mather calls him, who achieved the downfall of our ancient government, and was followed with a sensible curse, through life and to his grave. On the other side was Bullivant, scattering jests and mockery as he rode along. Dudley came behind, with a downcast look, dreading, as well he might, to meet the indignant gaze of the people, who beheld him, their only countryman by birth, among the oppressors of his native land. The captain of a frigate in the harbor, and two or three civil officers under the Crown, were also there. But the figure which most attracted the public eye, and stirred up the deepest feeling, was the Episcopal clergyman of King's Chapel, riding haughtily among the magistrates in his priestly vestments, the fitting representative of prelacy and persecution, the union of church and state, and all those abominations which had driven the Puritans to the wilderness. Another guard of soldiers, in double rank, brought up the rear.

The whole scene was a picture of the condition of New England, and its moral, the deformity of any government that does not grow out of the nature of things and the character of the people. On one side the religious multitude, with their sad visages and dark attire, and on the other, the group of despotic rulers, with the high churchman in the midst, and here and there a crucifix at their bosoms, all magnificently clad, flushed with wine, proud of unjust authority, and scoffing at the universal groan. And the mercenary soldiers, waiting but the word to deluge the street with blood, showed the only means by which obedience could be secured.

"O Lord of Hosts," cried a voice among the crowd, "provide a Champion for thy people!"

This ejaculation was loudly uttered, and served as a herald's cry, to introduce a remarkable personage. The crowd had rolled back, and were now huddled together nearly at the extremity of the street, while the soldiers had advanced no more than a third of its length. The intervening space was empty—a paved solitude, between lofty edifices, which threw almost a twilight shadow over it. Suddenly, there was seen the figure of an ancient man, who seemed to have emerged from among the people, and was walking by himself along the centre of the street, to confront the armed band. He wore the old Puritan dress, a dark cloak and a steeple-crowned hat, in the fashion of at least fifty years before, with a heavy sword upon his thigh, but a staff in his hand to assist the tremulous gait of age.[5]

When at some distance from the multitude, the old man turned slowly round, displaying a face of antique majesty, rendered doubly venerable by the hoary beard that descended on his breast. He made a gesture at once of encouragement and warning, then turned again, and resumed his way.

"Who is this gray patriarch?" asked the young men of their sires.

"Who is this venerable brother?" asked the old men among themselves.

But none could make reply. The fathers of the people, those of fourscore years and upwards, were disturbed, deeming it strange that they should forget one of such evident authority, whom they must have known in their early days, the associate of Winthrop, and all the old councillors, giving laws, and making prayers, and leading them against the savage. The elderly men ought to have remembered him, too, with locks as gray in their youth, as their own were now. And the young! How could he have passed so utterly from their memories—that hoary sire, the relic of long-departed times, whose awful benediction had surely been bestowed on their uncovered heads, in childhood?

"Whence did he come? What is his purpose? Who can this old man be?" whispered the wondering crowd.

Meanwhile, the venerable stranger, staff in hand, was pursuing his solitary walk along the centre of the street. As he drew near the

5. Note (as in "The Maypole of Merry Mount") the precise oppositions between Cavalier and Puritan. The champion is a "dark old man."

advancing soldiers, and as the roll of their drum came full upon his ear, the old man raised himself to a loftier mien, while the decrepitude of age seemed to fall from his shoulders, leaving him in gray but unbroken dignity. Now, he marched onward with a warrior's step, keeping time to the military music. Thus the aged form advanced on one side, and the whole parade of soldiers and magistrates on the other, till, when scarcely twenty yards remained between, the old man grasped his staff by the middle, and held it before him like a leader's truncheon.

"Stand!" cried he.

The eye, the face, and attitude of command; the solemn, yet warlike peal of that voice, fit either to rule a host in the battle-field or be raised to God in prayer, were irresistible. At the old man's word and outstretched arm, the roll of the drum was hushed at once, and the advancing line stood still. A tremulous enthusiasm seized upon the multitude. That stately form, combining the leader and the saint, so gray, so dimly seen, in such an ancient garb, could only belong to some old champion of the righteous cause, whom the oppressor's drum had summoned from his grave. They raised a shout of awe and exultation, and looked for the deliverance of New England.

The Governor, and the gentlemen of his party, perceiving themselves brought to an unexpected stand, rode hastily forward, as if they would have pressed their snorting and affrighted horses right against the hoary apparition. He, however, blenched not a step, but glancing his severe eye round the group, which half encompassed him, at last bent it sternly on Sir Edmund Andros. One would have thought that the dark old man was chief ruler there, and that the Governor and Council, with soldiers at their back, representing the whole power and authority of the Crown, had no alternative but obedience.

"What does this old fellow here?" cried Edward Randolph, fiercely. "On, Sir Edmund! Bid the soldiers forward, and give the dotard the same choice that you give all his countrymen—to stand aside or be trampled on!"

"Nay, nay, let us show respect to the good grandsire," said Bullivant, laughing. "See you not, he is some old roundheaded dignitary, who hath lain asleep these thirty years, and knows nothing of the change of time? Doubtless, he thinks to put us down with a proclamation in Old Noll's name!"

"Are you mad, old man?" demanded Sir Edmund Andros, in loud and harsh tones. "How dare you stay the march of King James's Governor?"

"I have stayed the march of a King himself, ere now," replied the gray figure, with stern composure. "I am here, Sir Governor, because the cry of an oppressed people hath disturbed me in my secret place; and beseeching this favor earnestly of the Lord, it was vouchsafed me to appear once again on earth, in the good old cause of his saints. And what speak ye of James? There is no longer a Popish tyrant on the throne of England, and by to-morrow noon, his name shall be a byword in this very street, where ye would make it a word of terror. Back, thou that wast a Governor, back! With this night thy power is ended—to-morrow, the prison!—back, lest I foretell the scaffold!"

The people had been drawing nearer and nearer, and drinking in the words of their champion, who spoke in accents long disused, like one unaccustomed to converse, except with the dead of many years ago. But his voice stirred their souls. They confronted the soldiers, not wholly without arms, and ready to convert the very stones of the street into deadly weapons. Sir Edmund Andros looked at the old man; then he cast his hard and cruel eye over the multitude, and beheld them burning with that lurid wrath, so difficult to kindle or to quench; and again he fixed his gaze on the aged form, which stood obscurely in an open space, where neither friend nor foe had thrust himself. What were his thoughts, he uttered no word which might discover. But whether the oppressor were overawed by the Gray Champion's look, or perceived his peril in the threatening attitude of the people, it is certain that he gave back, and ordered his soldiers to commence a slow and guarded retreat. Before another sunset, the Governor, and all that rode so proudly with him, were prisoners, and long ere it was known that James had abdicated, King William was proclaimed throughout New England.

But where was the Gray Champion? Some reported that, when the troops had gone from King Street, and the people were thronging tumultuously in their rear, Bradstreet, the aged Governor, was seen to embrace a form more aged than his own. Others soberly affirmed, that while they marvelled at the venerable grandeur of his aspect, the old man had faded from their eyes, melting slowly into the hues of twilight, till, where he stood, there was an empty space. But all agreed that the hoary shape was gone. The men of that generation watched for his reappearance, in sunshine and in twilight, but never saw him more, nor knew when his funeral passed, nor where his gravestone was.

And who was the Gray Champion? Perhaps his name might be found in the records of that stern Court of Justice, which passed a sentence, too mighty for the age, but glorious in all aftertimes, for its humbling lesson to the monarch and its high example to the subject. I have heard, that whenever the descendants of the Puritans are to show the spirit of their sires, the old man appears again. When eighty years had passed, he walked once more in King Street. Five years later, in the twilight of an April morning, he stood on the green, beside the meeting-house, at Lexington, where now the obelisk of granite, with a slab of slate inlaid, commemorates the first fallen of the Revolution. And when our fathers were toiling at the breastwork on Bunker's Hill, all through that night the old warrior walked his rounds. Long, long may it be, ere he comes again! His hour is one of darkness, and adversity, and peril. But should domestic tyranny oppress us, or the invader's step pollute our soil, still may the Gray Champion come, for he is the type of New England's hereditary spirit; and his shadowy march, on the eve of danger, must ever be the pledge, that New England's sons will vindicate their ancestry.

1835, 1837

Young Goodman Brown[6]

Young Goodman Brown came forth at sunset into the street at Salem village; but put his head back, after crossing the threshold, to exchange a parting kiss with his young wife. And Faith, as the wife was aptly named, thrust her own pretty head into the street, letting the wind play with the pink ribbons of her cap while she called to Goodman Brown.[7]

"Dearest heart," whispered she, softly and rather sadly, when her lips were close to his ear, "prithee put off your journey until sunrise and sleep in your own bed to-night. A lone woman is troubled with such dreams and such thoughts that she's afeared of herself sometimes. Pray tarry with me this night, dear husband, of all nights in the year."

"My love and my Faith," replied young Goodman Brown, "of all nights in the year, this one night must I tarry away from thee. My journey, as thou callest it, forth and back again, must needs be done

6. The chief "source" for "Young Goodman Brown" is doubtless Cotton Mather's *Wonders of the Invisible World* (1693). Mather speaks of "Diabolic Sacraments, imitating the *Baptism* and the *Supper* of our Lord." Of particular interest is his statement "that the Devils have obtain'd the power, to take on them the likeness of harmless people." "Spectral evidence" was an important issue at the Salem witchcraft trials, and has a bearing on the interpretation of Hawthorne's story. David Levin has remarked that "readers familiar with the seventeenth-century documents will recognize not only the specific setting of Salem Village and actual names and charges, but also the care with which Hawthorne's devil amasses spectral evidence for the credu-lous goodman" (*What Happened in Salem?*, 1960). Literal acceptance of this implication would of course short-circuit the meaning of "Young Goodman Brown": it is one possibility to be considered among others. This story appeared in the *New-England Magazine* for April, 1835, and was collected in *Mosses from an Old Manse* (1846). It is curious that Hawthorne considered it unworthy of inclusion in the 1837 *Twice-Told Tales*. An analogue is Washington Irving's "The Devil and Tom Walker," *Tales of a Traveller* (1824).
7. The several appearances of Faith's pink ribbons have attracted critical interest. One might note the interplay of their color with the red of the witch meeting.

'twixt now and sunrise. What, my sweet, pretty wife, dost thou doubt me already, and we but three months married?"

"Then God bless you!" said Faith, with the pink ribbons; "and may you find all well when you come back."

"Amen!" cried Goodman Brown. "Say thy prayers, dear Faith, and go to bed at dusk, and no harm will come to thee."

So they parted; and the young man pursued his way until, being about to turn the corner by the meeting-house, he looked back and saw the head of Faith still peeping after him with a melancholy air, in spite of her pink ribbons.

"Poor little Faith!" thought he, for his heart smote him. "What a wretch am I to leave her on such an errand! She talks of dreams, too. Methought as she spoke there was trouble in her face, as if a dream had warned her what work is to be done to-night. But no, no; 't would kill her to think it. Well, she's a blessed angel on earth; and after this one night I'll cling to her skirts and follow her to heaven."

With this excellent resolve for the future, Goodman Brown felt himself justified in making more haste on his present evil purpose. He had taken a dreary road, darkened by all the gloomiest trees of the forest, which barely stood aside to let the narrow path creep through, and closed immediately behind. It was all as lonely as could be; and there is this peculiarity in such a solitude, that the traveller knows not who may be concealed by the innumerable trunks and the thick boughs overhead; so that with lonely footsteps he may yet be passing through an unseen multitude.

"There may be a devilish Indian behind every tree," said Goodman Brown to himself; and he glanced fearfully behind him as he added, "What if the devil himself should be at my very elbow!"

His head being turned back, he passed a crook of the road, and, looking forward again, beheld the figure of a man, in grave and decent attire, seated at the foot of an old tree. He arose at Goodman Brown's approach and walked onward side by side with him.

"You are late, Goodman Brown," said he. "The clock of the Old South was striking as I came through Boston, and that is full fifteen minutes agone."

"Faith kept me back a while," replied the young man, with a tremor in his voice, caused by the sudden appearance of his companion, though not wholly unexpected.

It was now deep dusk in the forest, and deepest in that part of it where these two were journeying. As nearly as could be discerned, the second traveller was about fifty years old, apparently in the same rank of life as Goodman Brown, and bearing a considerable resemblance to him, though perhaps more in expression than features. Still they might have been taken for father and son. And yet, though the elder person was as simply clad as the younger, and as simple in manner too, he had an indescribable air of one who knew the world, and who would not have felt abashed at the governor's dinner table or in King William's court, were it possible that his affairs should call him thither. But the only thing about him that could be fixed upon as remarkable was his staff, which bore the likeness of a great black snake, so curiously wrought that it might almost be seen to twist and wriggle itself like a living serpent.[8] This, of course, must have been an ocular deception, assisted by the uncertain light.

"Come, Goodman Brown," cried his fellow-traveller, "this is a dull pace for the beginning of a journey. Take my staff, if you are so soon weary."

"Friend," said the other, exchanging his slow pace for a full stop, "having kept covenant by meeting thee here, it is my purpose now to return whence I came. I have scruples touching the matter thou wot'st of."

"Sayest thou so?" replied he of the serpent, smiling apart. "Let us walk on, nevertheless, reasoning as we go; and if I convince thee not thou shalt turn back. We are but a little way in the forest yet."

"Too far! too far!" exclaimed the goodman, unconsciously resuming his walk. "My father never went into the woods on such an errand, nor his father before him. We have been a race of honest men and good Christians since the days of the martyrs; and shall I be the first of the name of Brown that ever took this path and kept"—

"Such company, thou wouldst say," observed the elder person, interpreting his pause. "Well said, Goodman Brown! I have been as well acquainted with your family as with ever a one among the Puritans; and that's no trifle to say. I helped your grandfather, the constable, when he lashed the Quaker woman so smartly through the streets of Salem; and it was I that brought your father a pitch-pine knot, kindled at my own heart, to set fire to an Indian village, in King Philip's war. They were my good friends, both; and many a pleasant walk have we had along this path, and returned merrily after midnight. I would fain be friends with you for their sake."

"If it be as thou sayest," replied Goodman Brown, "I marvel they never spoke of these matters; or, verily, I marvel not, seeing that the least rumor of the sort would have driven them from New England. We are a people of prayer, and good works to boot, and abide no such wickedness."

"Wickedness or not," said the traveller with the twisted staff, "I have a very general acquaintance here in New England. The dea-

8. Compare the serpent-staff of Mercury in "The Miraculous Pitcher," *A Wonder Book* (1852) and the stick carried by Westervelt, the villain of *The Blithedale Romance* (1852).

cons of many a church have drunk the communion wine with me; the selectmen of divers towns make me their chairman; and a majority of the Great and General Court are firm supporters of my interest. The governor and I, too— But these are state secrets."

"Can this be so?" cried Goodman Brown, with a stare of amazement at his undisturbed companion. "Howbeit, I have nothing to do with the governor and council; they have their own ways, and are no rule for a simple husbandman like me. But, were I to go on with thee, how should I meet the eye of that good old man, our minister, at Salem village? Oh, his voice would make me tremble both Sabbath day and lecture day."

Thus far the elder traveller had listened with due gravity; but now burst into a fit of irrepressible mirth, shaking himself so violently that his snake-like staff actually seemed to wriggle in sympathy.

"Ha! ha! ha!" shouted he again and again; then composing himself, "Well, go on, Goodman Brown, go on; but, prithee, don't kill me with laughing."

"Well, then, to end the matter at once," said Goodman Brown, considerably nettled, "there is my wife, Faith. It would break her dear little heart; and I'd rather break my own."

"Nay, if that be the case," answered the other, "e'en go thy ways, Goodman Brown. I would not for twenty old women like the one hobbling before us that Faith should come to any harm."

As he spoke he pointed his staff at a female figure on the path, in whom Goodman Brown recognized a very pious and exemplary dame, who had taught him his catechism in youth, and was still his moral and spiritual adviser, jointly with the minister and Deacon Gookin.

"A marvel, truly, that Goody Cloyse[9] should be so far in the wilderness at nightfall," said he. "But with your leave, friend, I shall take a cut through the woods until we have left this Christian woman behind. Being a stranger to you, she might ask whom I was consorting with and whither I was going."

"Be it so," said his fellow-traveller. "Betake you to the woods, and let me keep the path."

Accordingly the young man turned aside, but took care to watch his companion, who advanced softly along the road until he had come within a staff's length of the old dame. She, meanwhile, was making the best of her way, with singular speed for so aged a woman, and mumbling some indistinct words—a prayer, doubtless

9. Goody Cloyse, Goody Cory, and Martha Carrier were among the "witches" condemned at the Salem trials of 1692. Goody Cory's husband Giles suffered the ghastly punishment of the *peine forte et dure* for standing mute to avoid the confiscation of his property. He was crushed to death under a heavy slab of stone.

—as she went. The traveller put forth his staff and touched her withered neck with what seemed the serpent's tail.

"The devil!" screamed the pious old lady.

"Then Goody Cloyse knows her old friend?" observed the traveller, confronting her and leaning on his writhing stick.

"Ah, forsooth, and is it your worship indeed?" cried the good dame. "Yea, truly is it, and in the very image of my old gossip, Goodman Brown, the grandfather of the silly fellow that now is. But—would your worship believe it?—my broomstick hath strangely disappeared, stolen, as I suspect, by that unhanged witch, Goody Cory, and that, too, when I was all anointed with the juice of small-age, and cinquefoil, and wolf's bane"—

"Mingled with fine wheat and the fat of a new-born babe," said the shape of old Goodman Brown.

"Ah, your worship knows the recipe," cried the old lady, cackling aloud. "So, as I was saying, being all ready for the meeting, and no horse to ride on, I made up my mind to foot it; for they tell me there is a nice young man to be taken into communion to-night. But now your good worship will lend me your arm, and we shall be there in a twinkling."

"That can hardly be," answered her friend. "I may not spare you my arm, Goody Cloyse; but here is my staff, if you will."

So saying, he threw it down at her feet, where, perhaps, it assumed life, being one of the rods which its owner had formerly lent to the Egyptian magi. Of this fact, however, Goodman Brown could not take cognizance. He had cast up his eyes in astonishment, and, looking down again, beheld neither Goody Cloyse nor the serpentine staff, but his fellow-traveller alone, who waited for him as calmly as if nothing had happened.

"That old woman taught me my catechism," said the young man; and there was a world of meaning in this simple comment.

They continued to walk onward, while the elder traveller exhorted his companion to make good speed and persevere in the path, discoursing so aptly that his arguments seemed rather to spring up in the bosom of his auditor than to be suggested by himself. As they went, he plucked a branch of maple to serve for a walking stick, and began to strip it of the twigs and little boughs, which were wet with evening dew. The moment his fingers touched them they became strangely withered and dried up as with a week's sunshine. Thus the pair proceeded, at a good free pace, until suddenly, in a gloomy hollow of the road, Goodman Brown sat himself down on the stump of a tree and refused to go any farther.

"Friend," said he, stubbornly, "my mind is made up. Not another step will I budge on this errand. What if a wretched old woman do choose to go to the devil when I thought she was going to heaven: is that any reason why I should quit my dear Faith and go after her?"

"You will think better of this by and by," said his acquaintance, composedly. "Sit here and rest yourself a while; and when you feel like moving again, there is my staff to help you along."

Without more words, he threw his companion the maple stick, and was as speedily out of sight as if he had vanished into the deepening gloom. The young man sat a few moments by the roadside, applauding himself greatly, and thinking with how clear a conscience he should meet the minister in his morning walk, nor shrink from the eye of good old Deacon Gookin. And what calm sleep would be his that very night, which was to have been spent so wickedly, but so purely and sweetly now, in the arms of Faith! Amidst these pleasant and praiseworthy meditations, Goodman Brown heard the tramp of horses along the road, and deemed it advisable to conceal himself within the verge of the forest, conscious of the guilty purpose that had brought him thither, though now so happily turned from it.

On came the hoof tramps and the voices of the riders, two grave old voices, conversing soberly as they drew near. These mingled sounds appeared to pass along the road, within a few yards of the young man's hiding-place; but, owing doubtless to the depth of the gloom at that particular spot, neither the travellers nor their steeds were visible. Though their figures brushed the small boughs by the wayside, it could not be seen that they intercepted, even for a moment, the faint gleam from the strip of bright sky athwart which they must have passed. Goodman Brown alternately crouched and stood on tiptoe, pulling aside the branches and thrusting forth his head as far as he durst without discerning so much as a shadow. It vexed him the more, because he could have sworn, were such a thing possible, that he recognized the voices of the minister and Deacon Gookin, jogging along quietly, as they were wont to do, when bound to some ordination or ecclesiastical council. While yet within hearing, one of the riders stopped to pluck a switch.

"Of the two, reverend sir," said the voice like the deacon's, "I had rather miss an ordination dinner than to-night's meeting. They tell me that some of our community are to be here from Falmouth and beyond, and others from Connecticut and Rhode Island, besides several of the Indian powwows, who, after their fashion, know almost as much deviltry as the best of us. Moreover, there is a goodly young woman to be taken into communion."

"Mighty well, Deacon Gookin!" replied the solemn old tones of the minister. "Spur up, or we shall be late. Nothing can be done, you know, until I get on the ground."

The hoofs clattered again; and the voices, talking so strangely in

618 · *Nathaniel Hawthorne*

the empty air, passed on through the forest, where no church had ever been gathered or solitary Christian prayed. Whither, then, could these holy men be journeying so deep into the heathen wilderness? Young Goodman Brown caught hold of a tree for support, being ready to sink down on the ground, faint and overburdened with the heavy sickness of his heart. He looked up to the sky, doubting whether there really was a heaven above him. Yet there was the blue arch, and the stars brightening in it.

"With heaven above and Faith below, I will yet stand firm against the devil!" cried Goodman Brown.

While he still gazed upward into the deep arch of the firmament and had lifted his hands to pray, a cloud, though no wind was stirring, hurried across the zenith and hid the brightening stars. The blue sky was still visible, except directly overhead, where this black mass of cloud was sweeping swiftly northward. Aloft in the air, as if from the depths of the cloud, came a confused and doubtful sound of voices. Once the listener fancied that he could distinguish the accents of towns-people of his own, men and women, both pious and ungodly, many of whom he had met at the communion table, and had seen others rioting at the tavern. The next moment, so indistinct were the sounds, he doubted whether he had heard aught but the murmur of the old forest, whispering without a wind. Then came a stronger swell of those familiar tones, heard daily in the sunshine at Salem village, but never until now from a cloud of night. There was one voice, of a young woman, uttering lamentations, yet with an uncertain sorrow, and entreating for some favor, which, perhaps, it would grieve her to obtain; and all the unseen multitude, both saints and sinners, seemed to encourage her onward.

"Faith!" shouted Goodman Brown, in a voice of agony and desperation; and the echoes of the forest mocked him, crying, "Faith! Faith!" as if bewildered wretches were seeking her all through the wilderness.

The cry of grief, rage, and terror was yet piercing the night, when the unhappy husband held his breath for a response. There was a scream, drowned immediately in a louder murmur of voices, fading into far-off laughter, as the dark cloud swept away, leaving the clear and silent sky above Goodman Brown. But something fluttered lightly down through the air and caught on the branch of a tree. The young man seized it, and beheld a pink ribbon.

"My Faith is gone!" cried he, after one stupefied moment. "There is no good on earth; and sin is but a name. Come, devil; for to thee is this world given."

And, maddened with despair, so that he laughed loud and long, did Goodman Brown grasp his staff and set forth again, at such a rate that he seemed to fly along the forest path rather than to walk or run. The road grew wilder and drearier and more faintly traced, and vanished at length, leaving him in the heart of the dark wilderness, still rushing onward with the instinct that guides mortal man to evil. The whole forest was peopled with frightful sounds—the creaking of the trees, the howling of wild beasts, and the yell of Indians; while sometimes the wind tolled like a distant church bell, and sometimes gave a broad roar around the traveller, as if all Nature were laughing him to scorn. But he was himself the chief horror of the scene, and shrank not from its other horrors.

"Ha! ha! ha!" roared Goodman Brown when the wind laughed at him. "Let us hear which will laugh loudest. Think not to frighten me with your deviltry. Come witch, come wizard, come Indian powwow, come devil himself, and here comes Goodman Brown. You may as well fear him as he fear you."

In truth, all through the haunted forest there could be nothing more frightful than the figure of Goodman Brown. On he flew among the black pines, brandishing his staff with frenzied gestures, now giving vent to an inspiration of horrid blasphemy, and now shouting forth such laughter as set all the echoes of the forest laughing like demons around him. The fiend in his own shape is less hideous than when he rages in the breast of man. Thus sped the demoniac on his course, until, quivering among the trees, he saw a red light before him, as when the felled trunks and branches of a clearing have been set on fire, and throw up their lurid blaze against the sky, at the hour of midnight. He paused, in a lull of the tempest that had driven him onward, and heard the swell of what seemed a hymn, rolling solemnly from a distance with the weight of many voices. He knew the tune; it was a familiar one in the choir of the village meeting-house. The verse died heavily away, and was lengthened by a chorus, not of human voices, but of all the sounds of the benighted wilderness pealing in awful harmony together. Goodman Brown cried out, and his cry was lost to his own ear by its unison with the cry of the desert.

In the interval of silence he stole forward until the light glared full upon his eyes. At one extremity of an open space, hemmed in by the dark wall of the forest, arose a rock, bearing some rude, natural resemblance either to an altar or a pulpit, and surrounded by four blazing pines, their tops aflame, their stems untouched, like candles at an evening meeting. The mass of foliage that had overgrown the summit of the rock was all on fire, blazing high into the night and fitfully illuminating the whole field. Each pendent twig and leafy festoon was in a blaze. As the red light arose and fell, a numerous congregation alternately shone forth, then disappeared in shadow, and again grew, as it were, out of the darkness, peopling the heart of the solitary woods at once.

"A grave and dark-clad company," quoth Goodman Brown.

In truth they were such. Among them, quivering to and fro between gloom and splendor, appeared faces that would be seen next day at the council board of the province, and others which, Sabbath after Sabbath, looked devoutly heavenward, and benignantly over the crowded pews, from the holiest pulpits in the land. Some affirm that the lady of the governor was there. At least there were high dames well known to her, and wives of honored husbands, and widows, a great multitude, and ancient maidens, all of excellent repute, and fair young girls, who trembled lest their mothers should espy them. Either the sudden gleams of light flashing over the obscure field bedazzled Goodman Brown, or he recognized a score of the church members of Salem village famous for their especial sanctity. Good old Deacon Gookin had arrived, and waited at the skirts of that venerable saint, his revered pastor. But, irreverently consorting with these grave, reputable, and pious people, these elders of the church, these chaste dames and dewy virgins, there were men of dissolute lives and women of spotted fame, wretches given over to all mean and filthy vice, and suspected even of horrid crimes. It was strange to see that the good shrank not from the wicked, nor were the sinners abashed by the saints.[1] Scattered also among their pale-faced enemies were the Indian priests, or powwows, who had often scared their native forest with more hideous incantations than any known to English witchcraft.

"But where is Faith?" thought Goodman Brown; and, as hope came into his heart, he trembled.

Another verse of the hymn arose, a slow and mournful strain, such as the pious love, but joined to words which expressed all that our nature can conceive of sin, and darkly hinted at far more. Unfathomable to mere mortals is the lore of fiends. Verse after verse was sung; and still the chorus of the desert swelled between like the deepest tone of a mighty organ; and with the final peal of that dreadful anthem there came a sound, as if the roaring wind, the rushing streams, the howling beasts, and every other voice of the unconcerted wilderness were mingling and according with the voice of guilty man in homage to the prince of all. The four blazing pines threw up a loftier flame, and obscurely discovered shapes and visages of horror on the smoke wreaths above the impious assembly. At the same moment the fire on the rock shot redly forth and formed a glowing arch above its base, where now appeared a figure. With reverence be it spoken, the figure bore no slight simili-

---

1. This theme of "the brotherhood of sin" recurs in "The Minister's Black Veil" and in *The Scarlet Letter*, Chapter V. Hester Prynne "shuddered to believe, yet could not help believing, that it [the scarlet letter] gave her a sympathetic knowledge of the hidden sin in other hearts."

tude, both in garb and manner, to some grave divine of the New England churches.

"Bring forth the converts!" cried a voice that echoed through the field and rolled into the forest.

At the word, Goodman Brown stepped forth from the shadow of the trees and approached the congregation, with whom he felt a loathful brotherhood by the sympathy of all that was wicked in his heart. He could have well-nigh sworn that the shape of his own dead father beckoned him to advance, looking downward from a smoke wreath, while a woman, with dim features of despair, threw out her hand to warn him back. Was it his mother? But he had no power to retreat one step, nor to resist, even in thought, when the minister and good old Deacon Gookin seized his arms and led him to the blazing rock. Thither came also the slender form of a veiled female, led between Goody Cloyse, that pious teacher of the catechism, and Martha Carrier, who had received the devil's promise to be queen of hell. A rampant hag was she. And there stood the proselytes beneath the canopy of fire.

"Welcome, my children," said the dark figure, "to the communion of your race. Ye have found thus young your nature and your destiny. My children, look behind you!"

They turned; and flashing forth, as it were, in a sheet of flame, the fiend worshippers were seen; the smile of welcome gleamed darkly on every visage.

"There," resumed the sable form, "are all whom ye have reverenced from youth. Ye deemed them holier than yourselves and shrank from your own sin, contrasting it with their lives of righteousness and prayerful aspirations heavenward. Yet here are they all in my worshipping assembly. This night it shall be granted you to know their secret deeds: how hoary-bearded elders of the church have whispered wanton words to the young maids of their households; how many a woman, eager for widows' weeds, has given her husband a drink at bedtime and let him sleep his last sleep in her bosom; how beardless youths have made haste to inherit their fathers' wealth; and how fair damsels—blush not, sweet ones— have dug little graves in the garden, and bidden me, the sole guest, to an infant's funeral. By the sympathy of your human hearts for sin ye shall scent out all the places—whether in church, bedchamber, street, field, or forest—where crime has been committed, and shall exult to behold the whole earth one stain of guilt, one mighty blood spot. Far more than this. It shall be yours to penetrate, in every bosom, the deep mystery of sin, the fountain of all wicked arts, and which inexhaustibly supplies more evil impulses than human power—than my power at its utmost—can make manifest in deeds. And now, my children, look upon each other."

They did so; and, by the blaze of the hell-kindled torches, the wretched man beheld his Faith, and the wife her husband, trembling before that unhallowed altar.

"Lo, there ye stand, my children," said the figure, in a deep and solemn tone, almost sad with its despairing awfulness, as if his once angelic nature could yet mourn for our miserable race. "Depending upon one another's hearts, ye had still hoped that virtue were not all a dream. Now are ye undeceived. Evil is the nature of mankind. Evil must be your only happiness. Welcome again, my children, to the communion of your race."

"Welcome," repeated the fiend worshippers, in one cry of despair and triumph.

And there they stood, the only pair, as it seemed, who were yet hesitating on the verge of wickedness in this dark world. A basin was hollowed, naturally, in the rock. Did it contain water, reddened by the lurid light? or was it blood? or, perchance, a liquid flame? Herein did the shape of evil dip his hand and prepare to lay the mark of baptism upon their foreheads, that they might be partakers of the mystery of sin, more conscious of the secret guilt of others, both in deed and thought, than they could now be of their own. The husband cast one look at his pale wife, and Faith at him. What polluted wretches would the next glance show them to each other, shuddering alike at what they disclosed and what they saw!

"Faith! Faith!" cried the husband, "look up to heaven, and resist the wicked one."

Whether Faith obeyed he knew not. Hardly had he spoken when he found himself amid calm night and solitude, listening to a roar of the wind which died heavily away through the forest. He staggered against the rock, and felt it chill and damp; while a hanging twig, that had been all on fire, besprinkled his cheek with the coldest dew.

The next morning young Goodman Brown came slowly into the street of Salem village, staring around him like a bewildered man. The good old minister was taking a walk along the graveyard to get an appetite for breakfast and meditate his sermon, and bestowed a blessing, as he passed, on Goodman Brown. He shrank from the venerable saint as if to avoid an anathema. Old Deacon Gookin was at domestic worship, and the holy words of his prayer were heard through the open window. "What God doth the wizard pray to?" quoth Goodman Brown. Goody Cloyse, that excellent old Christian, stood in the early sunshine at her own lattice, catechizing a little girl who had brought her a pint of morning's milk. Goodman Brown snatched away the child as from the grasp of the fiend himself. Turning the corner by the meeting-house, he spied the head of Faith, with the pink ribbons, gazing anxiously forth, and bursting into such joy at sight of him that she skipped along the street and almost kissed her husband before the whole village. But Goodman Brown looked sternly and sadly into her face, and passed on without a greeting.

Had Goodman Brown fallen asleep in the forest and only dreamed a wild dream of a witch-meeting?

Be it so if you will; but, alas! it was a dream of evil omen for young Goodman Brown. A stern, a sad, a darkly meditative, a distrustful, if not a desperate man did he become from the night of that fearful dream. On the Sabbath day, when the congregation were singing a holy psalm, he could not listen because an anthem of sin rushed loudly upon his ear and drowned all the blessed strain. When the minister spoke from the pulpit with power and fervid eloquence, and, with his hand on the open Bible, of the sacred truths of our religion, and of saint-like lives and triumphant deaths, and of future bliss or misery unutterable, then did Goodman Brown turn pale, dreading lest the roof should thunder down upon the gray blasphemer and his hearers. Often, awaking suddenly at midnight, he shrank from the bosom of Faith; and at morning or eventide, when the family knelt down at prayer, he scowled and muttered to himself, and gazed sternly at his wife, and turned away. And when he had lived long, and was borne to his grave a hoary corpse, followed by Faith, an aged woman, and children and grandchildren, a goodly procession, besides neighbors not a few, they carved no hopeful verse upon his tombstone, for his dying hour was gloom.

1835, 1846

The Minister's Black Veil[2]

A Parable

The sexton stood in the porch of Milford meeting-house, pulling busily at the bell-rope. The old people of the village came stooping along the street. Children, with bright faces, tripped merrily beside their parents, or mimicked a graver gait, in the conscious dignity of their Sunday clothes. Spruce bachelors looked sidelong at the

2. "Another clergyman in New England, Mr. Joseph Moody, of York, Maine, who died about eighty years since, made himself remarkable by the same eccentricity that is here related of the Reverend Mr. Hooper. In his case, however, the symbol had a different import. In early life he had accidentally killed a beloved friend; and from that day till the hour of his own death, he hid his face from men" [Hawthorne's note]. Austin Warren remarks that the story is told with some notable differences from the version in Hawthorne's note in William Sprague, *Annals of the American Pulpit*, I, 248–49. The central symbol or emblem of the veil resembles the scarlet letter, or the less impressive snake of Roderick Elliston in the tale of "Egotism; or the Bosom Serpent." It might have some relationship to the veil symbol prominent in Shelley's poetry, insofar as it interposes between the minister and the truth of things. Printed in *The Token* (1836) and *Twice-Told Tales* (1837).

624 · Nathaniel Hawthorne

pretty maidens, and fancied that the Sabbath sunshine made them prettier than on week days. When the throng had mostly streamed into the porch, the sexton began to toll the bell, keeping his eye on the Reverend Mr. Hooper's door. The first glimpse of the clergyman's figure was the signal for the bell to cease its summons.

"But what has good Parson Hooper got upon his face?" cried the sexton in astonishment.

All within hearing immediately turned about, and beheld the semblance of Mr. Hooper, pacing slowly his meditative way towards the meeting-house. With one accord they started, expressing more wonder than if some strange minister were coming to dust the cushions of Mr. Hooper's pulpit.

"Are you sure it is our parson?" inquired Goodman Gray of the sexton.

"Of a certainty it is good Mr. Hooper," replied the sexton. "He was to have exchanged pulpits with Parson Shute, of Westbury; but Parson Shute sent to excuse himself yesterday, being to preach a funeral sermon."

The cause of so much amazement may appear sufficiently slight. Mr. Hooper, a gentlemanly person, of about thirty, though still a bachelor, was dressed with due clerical neatness, as if a careful wife had starched his band, and brushed the weekly dust from his Sunday's garb. There was but one thing remarkable in his appearance. Swathed about his forehead, and hanging down over his face, so low as to be shaken by his breath, Mr. Hooper had on a black veil. On a nearer view it seemed to consist of two folds of crape, which entirely concealed his features, except the mouth and chin, but probably did not intercept his sight, further than to give a darkened aspect to all living and inanimate things. With this gloomy shade before him, good Mr. Hooper walked onward, at a slow and quiet pace, stooping somewhat, and looking on the ground, as is customary with abstracted men, yet nodding kindly to those of his parishioners who still waited on the meeting-house steps. But so wonder-struck were they that his greeting hardly met with a return.

"I can't really feel as if good Mr. Hooper's face was behind that piece of crape," said the sexton.

"I don't like it," muttered an old woman, as she hobbled into the meeting-house. "He has changed himself into something awful, only by hiding his face."

"Our parson has gone mad!" cried Goodman Gray, following him across the threshold.

A rumor of some unaccountable phenomenon had preceded Mr. Hooper into the meeting-house, and set all the congregation astir. Few could refrain from twisting their heads towards the door; many stood upright, and turned directly about; while several little boys clambered upon the seats, and came down again with a terrible racket. There was a general bustle, a rustling of the women's gowns and shuffling of the men's feet, greatly at variance with that hushed repose which should attend the entrance of the minister. But Mr. Hooper appeared not to notice the perturbation of his people. He entered with an almost noiseless step, bent his head mildly to the pews on each side, and bowed as he passed his oldest parishioner, a white-haired great-grandsire, who occupied an arm-chair in the centre of the aisle. It was strange to observe how slowly this venerable man became conscious of something singular in the appearance of his pastor. He seemed not fully to partake of the prevailing wonder, till Mr. Hooper had ascended the stairs, and showed himself in the pulpit, face to face with his congregation, except for the black veil. That mysterious emblem was never once withdrawn. It shook with his measured breath, as he gave out the psalm; it threw its obscurity between him and the holy page, as he read the Scriptures; and while he prayed, the veil lay heavily on his uplifted countenance. Did he seek to hide it from the dread Being whom he was addressing?

Such was the effect of this simple piece of crape, that more than one woman of delicate nerves was forced to leave the meeting-house. Yet perhaps the pale-faced congregation was almost as fearful a sight to the minister, as his black veil to them.

Mr. Hooper had the reputation of a good preacher, but not an energetic one: he strove to win his people heavenward by mild, persuasive influences, rather than to drive them thither by the thunders of the Word. The sermon which he now delivered was marked by the same characteristics of style and manner as the general series of his pulpit oratory. But there was something, either in the sentiment of the discourse itself, or in the imagination of the auditors, which made it greatly the most powerful effort that they had ever heard from their pastor's lips. It was tinged, rather more darkly than usual, with the gentle gloom of Mr. Hooper's temperament. The subject had reference to secret sin, and those sad mysteries which we hide from our nearest and dearest, and would fain conceal from our own consciousness, even forgetting that the Omniscient can detect them. A subtle power was breathed into his words. Each member of the congregation, the most innocent girl, and the man of hardened breast, felt as if the preacher had crept upon them, behind his awful veil, and discovered their hoarded iniquity of deed or thought.[3] Many spread their clasped hands on their bosoms. There was noth-

3. Concerning the effect of Mr. Hooper's preaching one might compare the situation in *The Scarlet Letter,* Chapter XI, in which Dimmesdale exercises a like power over his congregation: "his heart vibrated in unison with theirs, and received their pain into itself, and sent its own throb of pain through a thousand other hearts, in gushes of sad, persuasive eloquence." But whereas Mr. Hooper is displaying the emblem of secret sin openly Dimmesdale, a "remorseful hypocrite," is concealing a scarlet letter under his clerical garments, the emblem of a sin that he has actually and individually committed.

ing terrible in what Mr. Hooper said, at least, no violence; and yet, with every tremor of his melancholy voice, the hearers quaked. An unsought pathos came hand in hand with awe. So sensible were the audience of some unwanted attribute in their minister, that they longed for a breath of wind to blow aside the veil, almost believing that a stranger's visage would be discovered, though the form, gesture, and voice were those of Mr. Hooper.

At the close of the services, the people hurried out with indecorous confusion, eager to communicate their pent-up amazement, and conscious of lighter spirits the moment they lost sight of the black veil. Some gathered in little circles, huddled closely together, with their mouths all whispering in the centre; some went homeward alone, wrapt in silent meditation; some talked loudly, and profaned the Sabbath day with ostentatious laughter. A few shook their sagacious heads, intimating that they could penetrate the mystery; while one or two affirmed that there was no mystery at all, but only that Mr. Hooper's eyes were so weakened by the midnight lamp, as to require a shade. After a brief interval, forth came good Mr. Hooper also, in the rear of his flock. Turning his veiled face from one group to another, he paid due reverence to the hoary heads, saluted the middle aged with kind dignity as their friend and spiritual guide, greeted the young with mingled authority and love, and laid his hands on the little children's heads to bless them. Such was always his custom on the Sabbath day. Strange and bewildered looks repaid him for his courtesy. None, as on former occasions, aspired to the honor of walking by their pastor's side. Old Squire Saunders, doubtless by an accidental lapse of memory, neglected to invite Mr. Hooper to his table, where the good clergyman had been wont to bless the food, almost every Sunday since his settlement. He returned, therefore, to the parsonage, and, at the moment of closing the door, was observed to look back upon the people, all of whom had their eyes fixed upon the minister. A sad smile gleamed faintly from beneath the black veil, and flickered about his mouth, glimmering as he disappeared.

"How strange," said a lady, "that a simple black veil, such as any woman might wear on her bonnet, should become such a terrible thing on Mr. Hooper's face!"

"Something must surely be amiss with Mr. Hooper's intellects," observed her husband, the physician of the village. "But the strangest part of the affair is the effect of this vagary, even on a soberminded man like myself. The black veil, though it covers only our pastor's face, throws its influence over his whole person, and makes him ghostlike from head to foot. Do you not feel it so?"

"Truly do I," replied the lady; "and I would not be alone with him for the world. I wonder he is not afraid to be alone with himself!"

"Men sometimes are so," said her husband.

The afternoon service was attended with similar circumstances. At its conclusion, the bell tolled for the funeral of a young lady. The relatives and friends were assembled in the house, and the more distant acquaintances stood about the door, speaking of the good qualities of the deceased, when their talk was interrupted by the appearance of Mr. Hooper, still covered with his black veil. It was now an appropriate emblem. The clergyman stepped into the room where the corpse was laid, and bent over the coffin, to take a last farewell of his deceased parishioner. As he stooped, the veil hung straight down from his forehead, so that, if her eyelids had not been closed forever, the dead maiden might have seen his face. Could Mr. Hooper be fearful of her glance, that he so hastily caught back the black veil? A person who watched the interview between the dead and living, scrupled not to affirm, that, at the instant when the clergyman's features were disclosed, the corpse had slightly shuddered, rustling the shroud and muslin cap, though the countenance retained the composure of death. A superstitious old woman was the only witness of this prodigy. From the coffin Mr. Hooper passed into the chamber of the mourners, and thence to the head of the staircase, to make the funeral prayer. It was a tender and heart-dissolving prayer, full of sorrow, yet so imbued with celestial hopes, that the music of a heavenly harp, swept by the fingers of the dead, seemed faintly to be heard among the saddest accents of the minister. The people trembled, though they but darkly understood him when he prayed that they, and himself, and all of mortal race, might be ready, as he trusted this young maiden had been, for the dreadful hour that should snatch the veil from their faces. The bearers went heavily forth, and the mourners followed, saddening all the street, with the dead before them, and Mr. Hooper in his black veil behind.

"Why do you look back?" said one in the procession to his partner.

"I had a fancy," replied she, "that the minister and the maiden's spirit were walking hand in hand."

"And so had I, at the same moment," said the other.

That night, the handsomest couple in Milford village were to be joined in wedlock.[4] Though reckoned a melancholy man, Mr. Hooper had a placid cheerfulness for such occasions, which often excited a sympathetic smile where livelier merriment would have been thrown away. There was no quality of his disposition which

4. In connection with Poe's interpretation (mentioned in the introduction), the representative quality of the occasions presided over by the minister might be observed: a funeral and a wedding.

made him more beloved than this. The company at the wedding awaited his arrival with impatience, trusting that the strange awe, which had gathered over him throughout the day, would now be dispelled. But such was not the result. When Mr. Hooper came, the first thing that their eyes rested on was the same horrible black veil, which had added deeper gloom to the funeral, and could portend nothing but evil to the wedding. Such was its immediate effect on the guests that a cloud seemed to have rolled duskily from beneath the black crape, and dimmed the light of the candles. The bridal pair stood up before the minister. But the bride's cold fingers quivered in the tremulous hand of the bridegroom, and her death-like paleness caused a whisper that the maiden who had been buried a few hours before was come from her grave to be married. If ever another wedding were so dismal, it was that famous one where they tolled the wedding knell. After performing the ceremony, Mr. Hooper raised a glass of wine to his lips, wishing happiness to the new-married couple in a strain of mild pleasantry that ought to have brightened the features of the guests, like a cheerful gleam from the hearth. At that instant, catching a glimpse of his figure in the looking-glass, the black veil involved his own spirit in the horror with which it overwhelmed all others. His frame shuddered, his lips grew white, he spilt the untasted wine upon the carpet, and rushed forth into the darkness. For the Earth, too, had on her Black Veil.

The next day, the whole village of Milford talked of little else than Parson Hooper's black veil. That, and the mystery concealed behind it, supplied a topic for discussion between acquaintances meeting in the street, and good women gossiping at their open windows. It was the first item of news that the tavern-keeper told to his guests. The children babbled of it on their way to school. One imitative little imp covered his face with an old black handkerchief, thereby so affrighting his playmates that the panic seized himself, and he well-nigh lost his wits by his own waggery.

It was remarkable that of all the busy bodies and impertinent people in the parish, not one ventured to put the plain question to Mr. Hooper, wherefore he did this thing. Hitherto, whenever there appeared the slightest call for such interference, he had never lacked advisers, nor shown himself averse to be guided by their judgment. If he erred at all, it was by so painful a degree of self-distrust, that even the mildest censure would lead him to consider an indifferent action as a crime. Yet, though so well acquainted with this amiable weakness, no individual among his parishioners chose to make the black veil a subject of friendly remonstrance. There was a feeling of dread, neither plainly confessed nor carefully concealed, which caused each to shift the responsibility upon another, till at length it was found expedient to send a deputation of the church, in order to deal with Mr. Hooper about the mystery, before it should grow into a scandal. Never did an embassy so ill discharge its duties. The minister received them with friendly courtesy, but became silent, after they were seated, leaving to his visitors the whole burden of introducing their important business. The topic, it might be supposed, was obvious enough. There was the black veil swathed round Mr. Hooper's forehead, and concealing every feature above his placid mouth, on which, at times, they could perceive the glimmering of a melancholy smile. But that piece of crape, to their imagination, seemed to hang down before his heart, the symbol of a fearful secret between him and them. Were the veil but cast aside, they might speak freely of it, but not till then. Thus they sat a considerable time, speechless, confused, and shrinking uneasily from Mr. Hooper's eye, which they felt to be fixed upon them with an invisible glance. Finally, the deputies returned abashed to their constituents, pronouncing the matter too weighty to be handled, except by a council of the churches, if, indeed, it might not require a general synod.

But there was one person in the village unappalled by the awe with which the black veil had impressed all beside herself. When the deputies returned without an explanation, or even venturing to demand one, she, with the calm energy of her character, determined to chase away the strange cloud that appeared to be settling round Mr. Hooper, every moment more darkly than before. As his plighted wife, it should be her privilege to know what the black veil concealed. At the minister's first visit, therefore, she entered upon the subject with a direct simplicity, which made the task easier both for him and her. After he had seated himself, she fixed her eyes steadfastly upon the veil, but could discern nothing of the dreadful gloom that had so overawed the multitude: it was but a double fold of crape, hanging down from his forehead to his mouth, and slightly stirring with his breath.

"No," said she aloud, and smiling, "there is nothing terrible in this piece of crape, except that it hides a face which I am always glad to look upon. Come, good sir, let the sun shine from behind the cloud. First lay aside your black veil: then tell me why you put it on."

Mr. Hooper's smile glimmered faintly.

"There is an hour to come," said he, "when all of us shall cast aside our veils. Take it not amiss, beloved friend, if I wear this piece of crape till then."

"Your words are a mystery, too," returned the young lady. "Take away the veil from them, at least."

"Elizabeth, I will," said he, "so far as my vow may suffer me.

Know, then, this veil is a type and a symbol, and I am bound to wear it ever, both in light and darkness, in solitude and before the gaze of multitudes, and as with strangers, so with my familiar friends. No mortal eye will see it withdrawn. This dismal shade must separate me from the world: even you, Elizabeth, can never come behind it!"

"What grievous affliction hath befallen you," she earnestly inquired, "that you should thus darken your eyes forever?"

"If it be a sign of mourning," replied Mr. Hooper, "I, perhaps, like most other mortals, have sorrows dark enough to be typified by a black veil."

"But what if the world will not believe that it is the type of an innocent sorrow?" urged Elizabeth. "Beloved and respected as you are, there may be whispers that you hide your face under the consciousness of secret sin. For the sake of your holy office, do away this scandal!"

The color rose into her cheeks as she intimated the nature of the rumors that were already abroad in the village. But Mr. Hooper's mildness did not forsake him. He even smiled again—that same sad smile, which always appeared like a faint glimmering of light, proceeding from the obscurity beneath the veil.

"If I hide my face for sorrow, there is cause enough," he merely replied; "and if I cover it for secret sin, what mortal might not do the same?"

And with this gentle, but unconquerable obstinacy did he resist all her entreaties. At length Elizabeth sat silent. For a few moments she appeared lost in thought, considering, probably, what new methods might be tried to withdraw her lover from so dark a fantasy, which, if it had no other meaning, was perhaps a symptom of mental disease. Though of a firmer character than his own, the tears rolled down her cheeks. But, in an instant, as it were, a new feeling took the place of sorrow: her eyes were fixed insensibly on the black veil, when, like a sudden twilight in the air, its terrors fell around her. She arose, and stood trembling before him.

"And do you feel it then, at last?" said he mournfully.

She made no reply, but covered her eyes with her hand, and turned to leave the room. He rushed forward and caught her arm.

"Have patience with me, Elizabeth!" cried he, passionately. "Do not desert me, though this veil must be between us here on earth. Be mine, and hereafter there shall be no veil over my face, no darkness between our souls! It is but a mortal veil—it is not for eternity! O! you know not how lonely I am, and how frightened, to be alone behind my black veil. Do not leave me in this miserable obscurity forever!"

"Lift the veil but once, and look me in the face," said she.

"Never! It cannot be!" replied Mr. Hooper.

"Then farewell!" said Elizabeth.

She withdrew her arm from his grasp, and slowly departed, pausing at the door, to give one long shuddering gaze, that seemed almost to penetrate the mystery of the black veil. But, even amid his grief, Mr. Hooper smiled to think that only a material emblem had separated him from happiness, though the horrors, which it shadowed forth, must be drawn darkly between the fondest of lovers.

From that time no attempts were made to remove Mr. Hooper's black veil, or, by a direct appeal, to discover the secret which it was supposed to hide. By persons who claimed a superiority to popular prejudice, it was reckoned merely an eccentric whim, such as often mingles with the sober actions of men otherwise rational, and tinges them all with its own semblance of insanity. But with the multitude, good Mr. Hooper was irreparably a bugbear. He could not walk the street with any peace of mind, so conscious was he that the gentle and timid would turn aside to avoid him, and that others would make it a point of hardihood to throw themselves in his way. The impertinence of the latter class compelled him to give up his customary walk at sunset to the burial ground; for when he leaned pensively over the gate, there would always be faces behind the gravestones, peeping at his black veil. A fable went the rounds that the stare of the dead people drove him thence. It grieved him, to the very depth of his kind heart, to observe how the children fled from his approach, breaking up their merriest sports, while his melancholy figure was yet afar off. Their instinctive dread caused him to feel more strongly than aught else, that a preternatural horror was interwoven with the threads of the black crape. In truth, his own antipathy to the veil was known to be so great, that he never willingly passed before a mirror, nor stooped to drink at a still fountain, lest, in its peaceful bosom, he should be affrighted by himself. This was what gave plausibility to the whispers, that Mr. Hooper's conscience tortured him for some great crime too horrible to be entirely concealed, or otherwise than so obscurely intimated. Thus, from beneath the black veil, there rolled a cloud into the sunshine, an ambiguity of sin or sorrow, which enveloped the poor minister, so that love or sympathy could never reach him. It was said that ghost and fiend consorted with him there. With self-shudderings and outward terrors, he walked continually in its shadow, groping darkly within his own soul, or gazing through a medium that saddened the whole world. Even the lawless wind, it was believed, respected his dreadful secret, and never blew aside the veil. But still good Mr. Hooper sadly smiled at the pale visages of the worldly throng as he passed by.

Among all its bad influences, the black veil had the one desirable effect, of making its wearer a very efficient clergyman. By the aid of his mysterious emblem—for there was no other apparent cause—he became a man of awful power over souls that were in agony for sin. His converts always regarded him with a dread peculiar to themselves, affirming, though but figuratively, that, before he brought them to celestial light, they had been with him behind the black veil. Its gloom, indeed, enabled him to sympathize with all dark affections. Dying sinners cried aloud for Mr. Hooper, and would not yield their breath till he appeared; though ever, as he stooped to whisper consolation, they shuddered at the veiled face so near their own. Such were the terrors of the black veil, even when Death had bared his visage! Strangers came long distances to attend service at his church, with the mere idle purpose of gazing at his figure, because it was forbidden them to behold his face. But many were made to quake ere they departed! Once, during Governor Belcher's administration, Mr. Hooper was appointed to preach the election sermon. Covered with his black veil, he stood before the chief magistrate, the council, and the representatives, and wrought so deep an impression, that the legislative measures of that year were characterized by all the gloom and piety of our earliest ancestral sway.

In this manner Mr. Hooper spent a long life, irreproachable in outward act, yet shrouded in dismal suspicions; kind and loving, though unloved, and dimly feared; a man apart from men, shunned in their health and joy, but ever summoned to their aid in mortal anguish. As years wore on, shedding their snows above his sable veil, he acquired a name throughout the New England churches, and they called him Father Hooper. Nearly all his parishioners, who were of mature age when he was settled, had been borne away by many a funeral: he had one congregation in the church, and a more crowded one in the churchyard; and having wrought so late into the evening, and done his work so well, it was now good Father Hooper's turn to rest.

Several persons were visible by the shaded candle-light, in the death chamber of the old clergyman. Natural connections he had none. But there was the decorously grave, though unmoved physician, seeking only to mitigate the last pangs of the patient whom he could not save. There were the deacons, and other eminently pious members of his church. There, also, was the Reverend Mr. Clark, of Westbury, a young and zealous divine, who had ridden in haste to pray by the bedside of the expiring minister. There was the nurse, no hired hand-maiden of death, but one whose calm affection had endured thus long in secrecy, in solitude, amid the chill of age, and would not perish, even at the dying hour. Who, but Elizabeth! And there lay the hoary head of good Father Hooper upon the death pillow, with the black veil still swathed about his brow, and reaching down over his face, so that each more difficult gasp of his faint breath caused it to stir. All through life that piece of crape had hung between him and the world: it had separated him from cheerful brotherhood and woman's love, and kept him in that saddest of all prisons, his own heart; and still it lay upon his face, as if to deepen the gloom of his darksome chamber, and shade him from the sunshine of eternity.

For some time previous, his mind had been confused, wavering doubtfully between the past and the present, and hovering forward, as it were, at intervals, into the indistinctness of the world to come. There had been feverish turns, which tossed him from side to side, and wore away what little strength he had. But in his most convulsive struggles, and in the wildest vagaries of his intellect, when no other thought retained its sober influence, he still showed an awful solicitude lest the black veil should slip aside. Even if his bewildered soul could have forgotten, there was a faithful woman at his pillow, who, with averted eyes, would have covered that aged face, which she had last beheld in the comeliness of manhood. At length the death-stricken old man lay quietly in the torpor of mental and bodily exhaustion, with an imperceptible pulse, and breath that grew fainter and fainter, except when a long, deep, and irregular inspiration seemed to prelude the flight of his spirit.

The minister of Westbury approached the bedside.

"Venerable Father Hooper," said he, "the moment of your release is at hand. Are you ready for the lifting of the veil that shuts in time from eternity?"

Father Hooper at first replied merely by a feeble motion of his head; then, apprehensive, perhaps, that his meaning might be doubtful, he exerted himself to speak.

"Yea," said he, in faint accents, "my soul hath a patient weariness until that veil be lifted."

"And is it fitting," resumed the Reverend Mr. Clark, "that a man so given to prayer, of such a blameless example, holy in deed and thought, so far as mortal judgment may pronounce; is it fitting that a father in the church should leave a shadow on his memory, that may seem to blacken a life so pure? I pray you, my venerable brother, let not this thing be! Suffer us to be gladdened by your triumphant aspect as you go to your reward. Before the veil of eternity be lifted, let me cast aside this black veil from your face!"

And thus speaking, the Reverend Mr. Clark bent forward to reveal the mystery of so many years. But, exerting a sudden energy, that made all the beholders stand aghast, Father Hooper snatched both his hands from beneath the bedclothes, and pressed them strongly on the black veil, resolute to struggle, if the minister of Westbury would contend with a dying man.

"Never!" cried the veiled clergyman. "On earth, never!"

"Dark old man!" exclaimed the affrighted minister, "with what horrible crime upon your soul are you now passing to the judgment?"

Father Hooper's breath heaved; it rattled in his throat; but, with a mighty effort, grasping forward with his hands, he caught hold of life, and held it back till he should speak. He even raised himself in bed; and there he sat, shivering with the arms of death around him, while the black veil hung down, awful, at that last moment, in the gathered terrors of a lifetime. And yet the faint, sad smile, so often there, now seemed to glimmer from its obscurity, and linger on Father Hooper's lips.

"Why do you tremble at me alone?" cried he, turning his veiled face round the circle of pale spectators. "Tremble also at each other! Have men avoided me, and women shown no pity, and children screamed and fled, only for my black veil? What, but the mystery which it obscurely typifies, has made this piece of crape so awful? When the friend shows his inmost heart to his friend; the lover to his best beloved; when man does not vainly shrink from the eye of his Creator, loathsomely treasuring up the secret of his sin; then deem me a monster, for the symbol beneath which I have lived, and die! I look around me, and lo! on every visage a Black Veil!"

While his auditors shrank from one another, in mutual affright, Father Hooper fell back upon his pillow, a veiled corpse, with a faint smile lingering on the lips. Still veiled, they laid him in his coffin, and a veiled corpse they bore him to the grave. The grass of many years has sprung up and withered on that grave, the burial stone is moss-grown, and good Mr. Hooper's face is dust; but awful is still the thought that it mouldered beneath the Black Veil!

1836, 1837

The Birthmark[5]

In the latter part of the last century there lived a man of science, an eminent proficient in every branch of natural philosophy, who

5. The germ of this story appears in a note of 1837 and more concretely in a passage of 1839: "A person to be in the possession of something as perfect as mortal man has a right to demand; he tries to make it better, and ruins it entirely" (*Passages from the American Notebooks*, 1883, p. 106); and "a person to be the death of his beloved in trying to raise her to more than mortal perfection; yet this should be a comfort to him for having aimed so highly and holily" (*ibid.*, p. 210). In 1842 Hawthorne cited "the case quoted in Combe's Physiology [Andrew Combe, *The Principles of Physiology*, 1836], from Pinel, of a young man of great talents and profound knowledge of chemistry, who had in view some new discovery of importance. In order to put

not long before our story opens had made experience of a spiritual affinity more attractive than any chemical one. He had left his laboratory to the care of an assistant, cleared his fine countenance from the furnace smoke, washed the stain of acids from his fingers, and persuaded a beautiful woman to become his wife. In those days when the comparatively recent discovery of electricity and other kindred mysteries of Nature seemed to open paths into the region of miracle, it was not unusual for the love of science to rival the love of woman in its depth and absorbing energy. The higher intellect, the imagination, the spirit, and even the heart might all find their congenial aliment in pursuits which, as some of their ardent votaries believed, would ascend from one step of powerful intelligence to another, until the philosopher should lay his hand on the secret of creative force and perhaps make new worlds for himself. We know not whether Aylmer possessed this degree of faith in man's ultimate control over Nature. He had devoted himself, however, too unreservedly to scientific studies ever to be weaned from them by any second passion. His love for his young wife might prove the stronger of the two; but it could only be by intertwining itself with his love of science, and uniting the strength of the latter to his own.

Such a union accordingly took place, and was attended with truly remarkable consequences and a deeply impressive moral. One day, very soon after their marriage. Aylmer sat gazing at his wife with a trouble in his countenance that grew stronger until he spoke.

"Georgiana," said he, "has it never occurred to you that the mark upon your cheek might be removed?"

"No, indeed," said she, smiling; but perceiving the seriousness of his manner, she blushed deeply. "To tell you the truth it has been so often called a charm that I was simple enough to imagine it might be so."

"Ah, upon another face perhaps it might," replied her husband; "but never on yours. No, dearest Georgiana, you came so nearly perfect from the hand of Nature that this slightest possible defect, which we hesitate whether to term a defect or a beauty, shocks me, as being the visible mark of earthly imperfection."

"Shocks you, my husband!" cried Georgiana, deeply hurt; at first

his mind into the highest possible activity, he shut himself up, for several successive days, and used various methods of excitement; he had a singing girl with him; he drank spirits; smelled penetrating odors, sprinkled cologne-water round the room &c &c. Eight days thus passed, when he was seized with a fit of frenzy, which terminated in mania" (*The American Notebooks by Nathaniel Hawthorne*, ed. Randall Stewart, 1932, p. 97). This anecdote evidently suggested the outlines of Aylmer's experiment, but the intended stimulus shifts from the experimenter to the subject in Hawthorne's tale. Stewart discusses the relations between Hawthorne's notes and his fiction in his Introduction to the *Notebooks*, pp. xxiv–vii. "The Birthmark" appeared in *The Pioneer* for March, 1843, and was collected in *Mosses from an Old Manse* (1846).

reddening with momentary anger, but then bursting into tears. "Then why did you take me from my mother's side? You cannot love what shocks you!"

To explain this conversation it must be mentioned that in the centre of Georgiana's left cheek there was a singular mark, deeply interwoven, as it were, with the texture and substance of her face. In the usual state of her complexion—a healthy though delicate bloom—the mark wore a tint of deeper crimson, which imperfectly defined its shape amid the surrounding rosiness. When she blushed it gradually became more indistinct, and finally vanished amid the triumphant rush of blood that bathed the whole cheek with its brilliant glow. But if any shifting motion caused her to turn pale there was the mark again, a crimson stain upon the snow, in what Aylmer sometimes deemed an almost fearful distinctness. Its shape bore not a little similarity to the human hand, though of the smallest pygmy size. Georgiana's lovers were wont to say that some fairy at her birth hour had laid her tiny hand upon the infant's cheek, and left this impress there in token of the magic endowments that were to give her such sway over all hearts. Many a desperate swain would have risked life for the privilege of pressing his lips to the mysterious hand. It must not be concealed, however, that the impression wrought by this fairy sign manual varied exceedingly, according to the difference of temperament in the beholders. Some fastidious persons—but they were exclusively of her own sex—affirmed that the bloody hand, as they chose to call it, quite destroyed the effect of Georgiana's beauty, and rendered her countenance even hideous. But it would be as reasonable to say that one of those small blue stains which sometimes occur in the purest statuary marble would convert the Eve of Powers[6] to a monster. Masculine observers, if the birthmark did not heighten their admiration, contented themselves with wishing it away, that the world might possess one living specimen of ideal loveliness without the semblance of a flaw. After his marriage,—for he thought little or nothing about the matter before,—Aylmer discovered that this was the case with himself.

Had she been less beautiful,—if Envy's self could have found aught else to sneer at,—he might have felt his affection heightened by the prettiness of this mimic hand, now vaguely portrayed, now lost, now stealing forth again and glimmering to and fro with every pulse of emotion that throbbed within her heart; but seeing her otherwise so perfect, he found this one defect grow more and more intolerable with every moment of their united lives. It was the fatal flaw of humanity which Nature, in one shape or another,

6. "Eve Before the Fall," a statue by the 19th-century American sculptor Hiram Powers.

stamps ineffaceably on all her productions, either to imply that they are temporary and finite, or that their perfection must be wrought by toil and pain. The crimson hand expressed the ineludible gripe in which mortality clutches the highest and purest of earthly mold, degrading them into kindred with the lowest, and even with the very brutes, like whom their visible frames return to dust. In this manner, selecting it as the symbol of his wife's liability to sin, sorrow, decay, and death, Aylmer's sombre imagination was not long in rendering the birthmark a frightful object, causing him more trouble and horror than ever Georgiana's beauty, whether of soul or sense, had given him delight.

At all the seasons which should have been their happiest, he invariably and without intending it, nay, in spite of a purpose to the contrary, reverted to this one disastrous topic. Trifling as it at first appeared, it so connected itself with innumerable trains of thought and modes of feeling that it became the central point of all. With the morning twilight Aylmer opened his eyes upon his wife's face and recognized the symbol of imperfection; and when they sat together at the evening hearth his eyes wandered stealthily to her cheek, and beheld, flickering with the blaze of the wood fire, the spectral hand that wrote mortality where he would fain have worshipped. Georgiana soon learned to shudder at his gaze. It needed but a glance with the peculiar expression that his face often wore to change the roses of her cheek into a deathlike paleness, amid which the crimson hand was brought strongly out, like a bas-relief of ruby on the whitest marble.

Late one night when the lights were growing dim, so as hardly to betray the stain on the poor wife's cheek, she herself, for the first time, voluntarily took up the subject.

"Do you remember, my dear Aylmer," said she, with a feeble attempt at a smile, "have you any recollection of a dream last night about this odious hand?"

"None! none whatever!" replied Aylmer, starting; but then he added, in a dry, cold tone, affected for the sake of concealing the real depth of his emotion, "I might well dream of it; for before I fell asleep it had taken a pretty firm hold of my fancy."

"And you did dream of it?" continued Georgiana, hastily; for she dreaded lest a gush of tears should interrupt what she had to say. "A terrible dream! I wonder that you can forget it. Is it possible to forget this one expression?—'It is in her heart now; we must have it out!' Reflect, my husband; for by all means I would have you recall that dream."

The mind is in a sad state when Sleep, the all-involving, cannot confine her spectres within the dim region of her sway, but suffers them to break forth, affrighting this actual life with secrets that perchance belong to a deeper one. Aylmer now remembered his dream. He had fancied himself with his servant Aminadab, attempting an operation for the removal of the birthmark; but the deeper went the knife, the deeper sank the hand, until at length its tiny grasp appeared to have caught hold of Georgiana's heart; whence, however, her husband was inexorably resolved to cut or wrench it away.

When the dream had shaped itself perfectly in his memory, Aylmer sat in his wife's presence with a guilty feeling. Truth often finds its way to the mind close muffled in robes of sleep, and then speaks with uncompromising directness of matters in regard to which we practise an unconscious self-deception during our waking moments. Until now he had not been aware of the tyrannizing influence acquired by one idea over his mind, and of the lengths which he might find in his heart to go for the sake of giving himself peace.

"Aylmer," resumed Georgiana, solemnly, "I know not what may be the cost to both of us to rid me of this fatal birthmark. Perhaps its removal may cause cureless deformity; or it may be the stain goes as deep as life itself. Again: do we know that there is a possibility, on any terms, of unclasping the firm gripe of this little hand which was laid upon me before I came into the world?"[7]

"Dearest Georgiana, I have spent much thought upon the subject," hastily interrupted Aylmer. "I am convinced of the perfect practicability of its removal."

"If there be the remotest possibility of it," continued Georgiana, "let the attempt be made at whatever risk. Danger is nothing to me; for life, while this hateful mark makes me the object of your horror and disgust,—life is a burden which I would fling down with joy. Either remove this dreadful hand, or take my wretched life! You have deep science. All the world bears witness of it. You have achieved great wonders. Cannot you remove this little, little mark, which I cover with the tips of two small fingers? Is this beyond your power, for the sake of your own peace, and to save your poor wife from madness?"

"Noblest, dearest, tenderest wife," cried Aylmer, rapturously, "doubt not my power. I have already given this matter the deepest thought—thought which might almost have enlightened me to create a being less perfect than yourself. Georgiana, you have led me deeper than ever into the heart of science. I feel myself fully competent to render this dear cheek as faultless as its fellow; and

---

7. Melville remembered Georgiana's birthmark and transformed it into Billy Budd's stutter: "though our Handsome Sailor had as much of masculine beauty as one can expect anywhere to see; nevertheless, like the beautiful woman in one of Hawthorne's minor tales, there was just one thing amiss in him. * * * In this particular Billy was a striking instance that the arch interferer, the envious marplot of Eden, still has more or less to do with every human consignment to this planet of earth. In every case, one way or another he is sure to slip in his little card, as much as to remind us—I too have a hand here."

then, most beloved, what will be my triumph when I shall have corrected what Nature left imperfect in her fairest work! Even Pygmalion, when his sculptured woman assumed life, felt not greater ecstasy than mine will be."

"It is resolved, then," said Georgiana, faintly smiling. "And, Aylmer, spare me not, though you should find the birthmark take refuge in my heart at last."

Her husband tenderly kissed her cheek—her right cheek—not that which bore the impress of the crimson hand.

The next day Aylmer apprised his wife of a plan that he had formed whereby he might have opportunity for the intense thought and constant watchfulness which the proposed operation would require; while Georgiana, likewise, would enjoy the perfect repose essential to its success. They were to seclude themselves in the extensive apartments occupied by Aylmer as a laboratory, and where, during his toilsome youth, he had made discoveries in the elemental powers of Nature that had roused the admiration of all the learned societies in Europe. Seated calmly in this laboratory, the pale philosopher had investigated the secrets of the highest cloud region and of the profoundest mines; he had satisfied himself of the causes that kindled and kept alive the fires of the volcano; and had explained the mystery of fountains, and how it is that they gush forth, some so bright and pure, and others with such rich medicinal virtues, from the dark bosom of the earth. Here, too, at an earlier period, he had studied the wonders of the human frame, and attempted to fathom the very process by which Nature assimilates all her precious influences from earth and air, and from the spiritual world, to create and foster man, her masterpiece. The latter pursuit, however, Aylmer had long laid aside in unwilling recognition of the truth—against which all seekers sooner or later stumble —that our great creative Mother, while she amuses us with apparently working in the broadest sunshine, is yet severely careful to keep her own secrets, and, in spite of her pretended openness, shows us nothing but results. She permits us, indeed, to mar, but seldom to mend, and, like a jealous patentee, on no account to make. Now, however, Aylmer resumed these half-forgotten investigations; not, of course, with such hopes or wishes as first suggested them; but because they involved much physiological truth and lay in the path of his proposed scheme for the treatment of Georgiana.

As he led her over the threshold of the laboratory, Georgiana was cold and tremulous. Aylmer looked cheerfully into her face, with intent to reassure her, but was so startled with the intense glow of the birthmark upon the whiteness of her cheek that he could not restrain a strong convulsive shudder. His wife fainted.

"Aminadab! Aminadab!" shouted Aylmer, stamping violently on

the floor.

Forthwith there issued from an inner apartment a man of low stature, but bulky frame, with shaggy hair hanging about his visage, which was grimed with the vapors of the furnace. This personage had been Aylmer's underworker during his whole scientific career, and was admirably fitted for that office by his great mechanical readiness, and the skill with which, while incapable of comprehending a single principle, he executed all the details of his master's experiments. With his vast strength, his shaggy hair, his smoky aspect, and the indescribable earthiness that incrusted him, he seemed to represent man's physical nature; while Aylmer's slender figure, and pale, intellectual face, were no less apt a type of the spiritual element.[8]

"Throw open the door of the boudoir, Aminadab," said Aylmer, "and burn a pastil."

"Yes, master," answered Aminadab, looking intently at the lifeless form of Georgiana; and then he muttered to himself, "If she were my wife, I'd never part with that birthmark."

When Georgiana recovered consciousness she found herself breathing an atmosphere of penetrating fragrance, the gentle potency of which had recalled her from her deathlike faintness. The scene around her looked like enchantment. Aylmer had converted those smoky, dingy, sombre rooms, where he had spent his brightest years in recondite pursuits, into a series of beautiful apartments not unfit to be the secluded abode of a lovely woman. The walls were hung with gorgeous curtains, which imparted the combination of grandeur and grace that no other species of adornment can achieve; and as they fell from the ceiling to the floor, their rich and ponderous folds, concealing all angles and straight lines, appeared to shut in the scene from infinite space. For aught Georgiana knew, it might be a pavilion among the clouds. And Aylmer, excluding the sunshine, which would have interfered with his chemical processes, had supplied its place with perfumed lamps, emitting flames of various hue, but all uniting in a soft, impurpled radiance. He now knelt by his wife's side, watching her earnestly, but without alarm; for he was confident in his science, and felt that he could draw a magic circle round her within which no evil might intrude.

"Where am I? Ah, I remember," said Georgiana, faintly; and she placed her hand over her cheek to hide the terrible mark from her

8. Compare Aminadab with Danforth of "The Artist of the Beautiful," Bartram the limeburner in "Ethan Brand," and Dr. Baglioni in "Rappaccini's Daughter." Aylmer is too spiritual, Aminadab too earthy. There is an interesting parallel in S. T. Coleridge's treatment of *Don Quixote* as an allegory of the divided soul, in which the hero is reason without common sense and Sancho Panza is common sense without reason (*Miscellaneous Criticism*, ed. T. M. Raysor, 1936, p. 102). Perhaps Aminadab has some relation to Shakespeare's Caliban.

husband's eyes.

"Fear not, dearest!" exclaimed he. "Do not shrink from me! Believe me, Georgiana, I even rejoice in this single imperfection, since it will be such a rapture to remove it."

"Oh, spare me!" sadly replied his wife. "Pray do not look at it again. I never can forget that convulsive shudder."

In order to soothe Georgiana, and, as it were, to release her mind from the burden of actual things, Aylmer now put in practice some of the light and playful secrets which science had taught him among its profounder lore. Airy figures, absolutely bodiless ideas, and forms of unsubstantial beauty came and danced before her, imprinting their momentary footsteps on beams of light. Though she had some indistinct idea of the method of these optical phenomena, still the illusion was almost perfect enough to warrant the belief that her husband possessed sway over the spiritual world. Then again, when she felt a wish to look forth from her seclusion, immediately, as if her thoughts were answered, the procession of external existence flitted across a screen. The scenery and the figures of actual life were perfectly represented, but with that bewitching, yet indescribable difference which always makes a picture, an image, or a shadow so much more attractive than the original. When wearied of this, Aylmer bade her cast her eyes upon a vessel containing a quantity of earth. She did so, with little interest at first; but was soon startled to perceive the germ of a plant shooting upward from the soil. Then came the slender stalk; the leaves gradually unfolded themselves; and amid them was a perfect and lovely flower.

"It is magical!" cried Georgiana. "I dare not touch it."

"Nay, pluck it," answered Aylmer,—"pluck it, and inhale its brief perfume while you may. The flower will wither in a few moments and leave nothing save its brown seed vessels; but thence may be perpetuated a race as ephemeral as itself."

But Georgiana had no sooner touched the flower than the whole plant suffered a blight, its leaves turning coal-black as if by the agency of fire.

"There was too powerful a stimulus," said Aylmer, thoughtfully.

To make up for this abortive experiment, he proposed to take her portrait by a scientific process of his own invention. It was to be effected by rays of light striking upon a polished plate of metal. Georgiana assented; but, on looking at the result, was affrighted to find the features of the portrait blurred and indefinable; while the minute figure of a hand appeared where the cheek should have been. Aylmer snatched the metallic plate and threw it into a jar of corrosive acid.

Soon, however, he forgot these mortifying failures. In the intervals of study and chemical experiment he came to her flushed and exhausted, but seemed invigorated by her presence, and spoke in glowing language of the resources of his art. He gave a history of the long dynasty of the alchemists, who spent so many ages in quest of the universal solvent by which the golden principle might be elicited from all things vile and base. Aylmer appeared to believe that, by the plainest scientific logic, it was altogether within the limits of possibility to discover this long-sought medium; "but," he added, "a philosopher who should go deep enough to acquire the power would attain too lofty a wisdom to stoop to the exercise of it." Not less singular were his opinions in regard to the elixir vitæ.[9] He more than intimated that it was at his option to concoct a liquid that should prolong life for years, perhaps interminably; but that it would produce a discord in Nature which all the world, and chiefly the quaffer of the immortal nostrum, would find cause to curse.

"Aylmer, are you in earnest?" asked Georgiana, looking at him with amazement and fear. "It is terrible to possess such power, or even to dream of possessing it."

"Oh, do not tremble, my love," said her husband. "I would not wrong either you or myself by working such inharmonious effects upon our lives; but I would have you consider how trifling, in comparison, is the skill requisite to remove this little hand."

At the mention of the birthmark, Georgiana, as usual, shrank as if a redhot iron had touched her cheek.

Again Aylmer applied himself to his labors. She could hear his voice in the distant furnace room giving directions to Aminadab, whose harsh, uncouth, misshapen tones were audible in response, more like the grunt or growl of a brute than human speech. After hours of absence, Aylmer reappeared and proposed that she should now examine his cabinet of chemical products and natural treasures of the earth. Among the former he showed her a small vial, in which, he remarked, was contained a gentle yet most powerful fragrance, capable of impregnating all the breezes that blow across the kingdom. They were of inestimable value, the contents of that little vial; and, as he said so, he threw some of the perfume into the air and filled the room with piercing and invigorating delight.

"And what is this?" asked Georgiana, pointing to a small crystal globe containing a gold-colored liquid. "It is so beautiful to the eye that I could imagine it the elixir of life."

"In one sense it is," replied Aylmer; "or, rather, the elixir of immortality. It is the most precious poison that ever was concocted in this world. By its aid I could apportion the lifetime of any mortal at whom you might point your finger. The strength of the dose would

9. The elixir of life attracted Hawthorne's imagination. He treats the theme more fully in "Dr. Heidegger's experiment" and the posthumous *Septimius Felton* and *The Dolliver Romance*.

determine whether he were to linger out years, or drop dead in the midst of a breath. No king on his guarded throne could keep his life if I, in my private station, should deem that the welfare of millions justified me in depriving him of it."

"Why do you keep such a terrific drug?" inquired Georgiana in horror.

"Do not mistrust me, dearest," said her husband, smiling; "its virtuous potency is yet greater than its harmful one. But see! here is a powerful cosmetic. With a few drops of this in a vase of water, freckles may be washed away as easily as the hands are cleansed. A stronger infusion would take the blood out of the cheek, and leave the rosiest beauty a pale ghost."

"Is it with this lotion that you intend to bathe my cheek?" asked Georgiana, anxiously.

"Oh, no," hastily replied her husband; "this is merely superficial. Your case demands a remedy that shall go deeper."

In his interviews with Georgiana, Aylmer generally made minute inquiries as to her sensations and whether the confinement of the rooms and the temperature of the atmosphere agreed with her. These questions had such a particular drift that Georgiana began to conjecture that she was already subjected to certain physical influences, either breathed in with the fragrant air or taken with her food. She fancied likewise, but it might be altogether fancy, that there was a stirring up of her system—a strange, indefinite sensation creeping through her veins, and tingling, half painfully, half pleasurably, at her heart. Still, whenever she dared to look into the mirror, there she beheld herself pale as a white rose and with the crimson birthmark stamped upon her cheek. Not even Aylmer now hated it so much as she.

To dispel the tedium of the hours which her husband found it necessary to devote to the processes of combination and analysis, Georgiana turned over the volumes of his scientific library. In many dark old tomes she met with chapters full of romance and poetry. They were the works of the philosophers of the middle ages, such as Albertus Magnus, Cornelius Agrippa, Paracelsus, and the famous friar who created the prophetic Brazen Head. All these antique naturalists stood in advance of their centuries, yet were imbued with some of their credulity, and therefore were believed, and perhaps imagined themselves to have acquired from the investigation of Nature a power above Nature, and from physics a sway over the spiritual world. Hardly less curious and imaginative were the early volumes of the Transactions of the Royal Society, in which the members, knowing little of the limits of natural possibility, were continually recording wonders or proposing methods whereby wonders might be wrought.

But to Georgiana the most engrossing volume was a large folio from her husband's own hand, in which he had recorded every experiment of his scientific career, its original aim, the methods adopted for its development, and its final success or failure, with the circumstances to which either event was attributable. The book, in truth, was both the history and emblem of his ardent, ambitious, imaginative, yet practical and laborious life. He handled physical details as if there were nothing beyond them; yet spiritualized them all, and redeemed himself from materialism by his strong and eager aspiration towards the infinite. In his grasp the veriest clod of earth assumed a soul. Georgiana, as she read, reverenced Aylmer and loved him more profoundly than ever, but with a less entire dependence on his judgment than heretofore. Much as he had accomplished, she could not but observe that most splendid successes were almost invariably failures, if compared with the ideal at which he aimed. His brightest diamonds were the merest pebbles, and felt to be so by himself, in comparison with the inestimable gems which lay hidden beyond his reach. The volume, rich with achievements that had won renown for its author, was yet as melancholy a record as ever mortal hand had penned. It was the sad confession and continual exemplification of the shortcomings of the composite man, the spirit burdened with clay and working in matter, and of the despair that assails the higher nature at finding itself so miserably thwarted by the earthly part. Perhaps every man of genius in whatever sphere might recognize the image of his own experience in Aylmer's journal.

So deeply did these reflections affect Georgiana that she laid her face upon the open volume and burst into tears. In this situation she was found by her husband.

"It is dangerous to read in a sorcerer's books," said he with a smile, though his countenance was uneasy and displeased. "Georgiana, there are pages in that volume which I can scarcely glance over and keep my senses. Take heed lest it prove as detrimental to you."

"It has made me worship you more than ever," said she.

"Ah, wait for this one success," rejoined he, "then worship me if you will. I shall deem myself hardly unworthy of it. But come, I have sought you for the luxury of your voice. Sing to me, dearest."

So she poured out the liquid music of her voice to quench the thirst of his spirit. He then took his leave with a boyish exuberance of gaiety, assuring her that her seclusion would endure but a little longer, and that the result was already certain. Scarcely had he departed when Georgiana felt irresistibly impelled to follow him. She had forgotten to inform Aylmer of a symptom which for two or three hours past had begun to excite her attention. It was a sensation in the fatal birthmark, not painful, but which induced a restlessness throughout her system. Hastening after her husband, she intruded for the first time into the laboratory.

The first thing that struck her eye was the furnace, that hot and feverish worker, with the intense glow of its fire, which by the quantities of soot clustered above it seemed to have been burning for ages. There was a distilling apparatus in full operation. Around the room were retorts, tubes, cylinders, crucibles, and other apparatus of chemical research. An electrical machine stood ready for immediate use. The atmosphere felt oppressively close; and was tainted with gaseous odors which had been tormented forth by the processes of science. The severe and homely simplicity of the apartment with its naked walls and brick pavement, looked strange, accustomed as Georgiana had become to the fantastic elegance of her boudoir. But what chiefly, indeed almost solely, drew her attention, was the aspect of Aylmer himself.

He was pale as death, anxious and absorbed, and hung over the furnace as if it depended upon his utmost watchfulness whether the liquid which it was distilling should be the draught of immortal happiness or misery. How different from the sanguine and joyous mien that he had assumed for Georgiana's encouragement!

"Carefully now, Aminadab; carefully, thou human machine; carefully, thou man of clay!" muttered Aylmer, more to himself than his assistant. "Now, if there be a thought too much or too little, it is all over."

"Ho! ho!" mumbled Aminadab. "Look, master! look!"

Aylmer raised his eyes hastily, and at first reddened, then grew paler than ever, on beholding Georgiana. He rushed towards her and seized her arm with a gripe that left the print of his fingers upon it.

"Why do you come hither? Have you no trust in your husband?" cried he, impetuously. "Would you throw the blight of that fatal birthmark over my labors? It is not well done. Go, prying woman, go!"

"Nay, Aylmer," said Georgiana with the firmness of which she possessed no stinted endowment, "it is not you that have a right to complain. You mistrust your wife; you have concealed the anxiety with which you watch the development of this experiment. Think not so unworthily of me, my husband. Tell me all the risk we run, and fear not that I shall shrink; for my share in it is far less than your own."

"No, no, Georgiana!" said Aylmer, impatiently; "it must not be."

"I submit," replied she calmly. "And, Aylmer, I shall quaff whatever draught you bring me; but it will be on the same principle that would induce me to take a dose of poison if offered by your hand."

"My noble wife," said Aylmer, deeply moved; "I knew not the

height and depth of your nature until now. Nothing shall be concealed. Know, then, that this crimson hand, superficial as it seems, has clutched its grasp into your being with a strength of which I had no previous conception. I have already administered agents powerful enough to do aught except to change your entire physical system. Only one thing remains to be tried. If that fails us we are ruined."

"Why did you hesitate to tell me this?" asked she.

"Because, Georgiana," said Aylmer, in a low voice, "there is danger."

"Danger? There is but one danger—that this horrible stigma shall be left upon my cheek!" cried Georgiana. "Remove it, remove it, whatever be the cost, or we shall both go mad!"

"Heaven knows your words are too true," said Aylmer, sadly. "And now, dearest, return to your boudoir. In a little while all will be tested."

He conducted her back and took leave of her with a solemn tenderness which spoke far more than his words how much was now at stake. After his departure Georgiana became rapt in musings. She considered the character of Aylmer, and did it completer justice than at any previous moment. Her heart exulted, while it trembled, at his honorable love—so pure and lofty that it would accept nothing less than perfection nor miserably make itself contented with an earthlier nature than he had dreamed of. She felt how much more precious was such a sentiment than that meaner kind which would have borne with the imperfection for her sake, and have been guilty of treason to holy love by degrading its perfect idea to the level of the actual; and with her whole spirit she prayed that, for a single moment, she might satisfy his highest and deepest conception. Longer than one moment she well knew it could not be; for his spirit was ever on the march, ever ascending, and each instant required something that was beyond the scope of the instant before.

The sound of her husband's footsteps aroused her. He bore a crystal goblet containing a liquor colorless as water, but bright enough to be the draught of immortality. Aylmer was pale; but it seemed rather the consequence of a highly-wrought state of mind and tension of spirit than of fear or doubt.

"The concoction of the draught has been perfect," said he, in answer to Georgiana's look. "Unless my science have deceived me, it cannot fail."

"Save on your account, my dearest Aylmer," observed his wife, "I might wish to put off this birthmark of mortality by relinquishing mortality itself in preference to any other mode. Life is but a sad possession to those who have attained precisely the degree of moral advancement at which I stand. Were I weaker and blinder it might be happiness. Were I stronger, it might be endured hopefully. But, being what I find myself, me thinks I am of all mortals the most fit to die."

"You are fit for heaven without tasting death!" replied her husband. "But why do we speak of dying? The draught cannot fail. Behold its effect upon this plant."

On the window seat there stood a geranium diseased with yellow blotches, which had overspread all its leaves. Aylmer poured a small quantity of the liquid upon the soil in which it grew. In a little time, when the roots of the plant had taken up the moisture, the unsightly blotches began to be extinguished in a living verdure.

"There needed no proof," said Georgiana, quietly. "Give me the goblet. I joyfully stake all upon your word."

"Drink, then, thou lofty creature!" exclaimed Aylmer, with fervid admiration. "There is no taint of imperfection on thy spirit. Thy sensible frame, too, shall soon be all perfect."

She quaffed the liquid and returned the goblet to his hand.

"It is grateful," said she with a placid smile. "Methinks it is like water from a heavenly fountain; for it contains I know not what of unobtrusive fragrance and deliciousness. It allays a feverish thirst that had parched me for many days. Now, dearest, let me sleep. My earthly senses are closing over my spirit like the leaves around the heart of a rose at sunset."

She spoke the last words with a gentle reluctance, as if it required almost more energy than she could command to pronounce the faint and lingering syllables. Scarcely had they loitered through her lips ere she was lost in slumber. Aylmer sat by her side, watching her aspect with the emotions proper to a man the whole value of whose existence was involved in the process now to be tested. Mingled with this mood, however, was the philosophic investigation characteristic of the man of science. Not the minutest symptom escaped him. A heightened flush of the cheek, a slight irregularity of breath, a quiver of the eyelid, a hardly perceptible tremor through the frame,—such were the details which, as the moments passed, he wrote down in his folio volume. Intense thought had set its stamp upon every previous page of that volume, but the thoughts of years were all concentrated upon the last.

While thus employed, he failed not to gaze often at the fatal hand, and not without a shudder. Yet once, by a strange and unaccountable impulse, he pressed it with his lips. His spirit recoiled, however, in the very act; and Georgiana, out of the midst of her deep sleep, moved uneasily and murmured as if in remonstrance. Again Aylmer resumed his watch. Nor was it without avail. The crimson hand, which at first had been strongly visible upon the marble paleness of Georgiana's cheek, now grew more faintly outlined. She remained not less pale than ever; but the birthmark, with every breath that came and went, lost somewhat of its former distinctness. Its presence had been awful; its departure was more awful still. Watch the stain of the rainbow fading out of the sky, and you will know how that mysterious symbol passed away.

"By Heaven! it is well-nigh gone!" said Aylmer to himself, in almost irrepressible ecstasy. "I can scarcely trace it now. Success! success! And now it is like the faintest rose color. The lightest flush of blood across her cheek would overcome it. But she is so pale!"

He drew aside the window curtain and suffered the light of natural day to fall into the room and rest upon her cheek. At the same time he heard a gross, hoarse chuckle, which he had long known as his servant Aminadab's expression of delight.

"Ah, clod! ah, earthly mass!" cried Aylmer, laughing a sort of frenzy, "you have served me well! Matter and spirit—earth and heaven—have both done their part in this! Laugh, thing of the senses! You have earned the right to laugh."

These exclamations broke Georgiana's sleep. She slowly unclosed her eyes and gazed into the mirror which her husband had arranged for that purpose. A faint smile flitted over her lips when she recognized how barely perceptible was now that crimson hand which had once blazed forth with such disastrous brilliancy as to scare away all their happiness. But then her eyes sought Aylmer's face with a trouble and anxiety that he could by no means account for.

"My poor Aylmer!" murmured she.

"Poor? Nay, richest, happiest, most favored!" exclaimed he. "My peerless bride, it is successful! You are perfect!"

"My poor Aylmer," she repeated, with a more than human tenderness, "you have aimed loftily; you have done nobly. Do not repent that with so high and pure a feeling, you have rejected the best the earth could offer. Aylmer, dearest Aylmer, I am dying!"

Alas! it was too true! The fatal hand had grappled with the mystery of life, and was the bond by which an angelic spirit kept itself in union with a mortal frame. As the last crimson tint of the birthmark—that sole token of human imperfection—faded from her cheek, the parting breath of the now perfect woman passed into the atmosphere, and her soul, lingering a moment near her husband, took its heavenward flight. Then a hoarse, chuckling laugh was heard again! Thus ever does the gross fatality of earth exult in its invariable triumph over the immortal essence which, in this dim sphere of half development, demands the completeness of a higher state. Yet, had Aylmer reached a profounder wisdom, he need not thus have flung away the happiness which would have woven his mortal life of the selfsame texture with the celestial. The momentary circumstance was too strong for him; he failed to look beyond the shadowy scope of time, and living once for all in eternity, to find the perfect future in the present.

1843, 1846

The Artist of the Beautiful[1]

An elderly man, with his pretty daughter on his arm, was passing along the street, and emerged from the gloom of the cloudy evening into the light that fell across the pavement from the window of a small shop. It was a projecting window; and on the inside were suspended a variety of watches, pinchbeck, silver, and one or two of gold, all with their faces turned from the streets, as if churlishly disinclined to inform the wayfarers what o'clock it was. Seated within the shop, sidelong to the window, with his pale face bent earnestly over some delicate piece of mechanism on which was thrown the concentrated lustre of a shade lamp, appeared a young man.

"What can Owen Warland be about?" muttered old Peter Hovenden, himself a retired watchmaker, and the former master of this same young man whose occupation he was now wondering at. "What can the fellow be about? These six months past I have never come by his shop without seeing him just as steadily at work as now. It would be a flight beyond his usual foolery to seek for the perpetual motion; and yet I know enough of my old business to be certain that what he is now so busy with is no part of the machinery of a watch."

"Perhaps, father," said Annie, without showing much interest in the question, "Owen is inventing a new kind of timekeeper. I am sure he has ingenuity enough."

"Poh, child! He has not the sort of ingenuity to invent anything better than a Dutch toy," answered her father, who had formerly been put to much vexation by Owen Warland's irregular genius. "A plague on such ingenuity! All the effect that ever I knew of it was to spoil the accuracy of some of the best watches in my shop. He would turn the sun out of its orbit and derange the whole course of time, if, as I said before, his ingenuity could grasp anything bigger than a child's toy!"

"Hush, father! He hears you!" whispered Annie, pressing the

1. In 1840 Hawthorne wrote a memorandum "to represent a man as spending life and the intensest labor in the accomplishment of some mechanical trifle,—as in making a miniature coach to be drawn by fleas, or a dinner-service to be put into a cherry-stone" (*Passages*, p. 211). His note is interesting as much for what it leaves out of the subsequent "Artist of the Beautiful" as for what it includes. It emphasizes the problems raised by Owen Warland's physical smallness, his devotion to miniature-work, and the mechanical basis of his art. The story appeared in the *Democratic Review* (June, 1844), and was included in *Mosses from an Old Manse*.

old man's arm. "His ears are as delicate as his feelings; and you know how easily disturbed they are. Do let us move on."

So Peter Hovenden and his daughter Annie plodded on without further conversation, until in a by-street of the town they found themselves passing the open door of a blacksmith's shop. Within was seen the forge, now blazing up and illuminating the high and dusky roof, and now confining its lustre to a narrow precinct of the coal-strewn floor, according as the breath of the bellows was puffed forth or again inhaled into its vast leathern lungs. In the intervals of brightness it was easy to distinguish objects in remote corners of the shop and the horseshoes that hung upon the wall; in the momentary gloom the fire seemed to be glimmering amidst the vagueness of unenclosed space. Moving about in this red glare and alternate dusk was the figure of the blacksmith, well worthy to be viewed in so picturesque an aspect of light and shade, where the bright blaze struggled with the black night, as if each would have snatched his comely strength from the other. Anon he drew a white-hot bar of iron from the coals, laid it on the anvil, uplifted his arm of might, and was soon enveloped in the myriads of sparks which the strokes of his hammer scattered into the surrounding gloom.

"Now, that is a pleasant sight," said the old watchmaker. "I know what it is to work in gold; but give me the worker in iron after all is said and done. He spends his labor upon a reality. What say you, daughter Annie?"

"Pray don't speak so loud, father," whispered Annie, "Robert Danforth will hear you."

"And what if he should hear me?" said Peter Hovenden. "I say again, it is a good and a wholesome thing to depend upon main strength and reality, and to earn one's bread with the bare and brawny arm of a blacksmith. A watchmaker gets his brain puzzled by his wheels within a wheel, or loses his health or the nicety of his eyesight, as was my case, and finds himself at middle age, or a little after, past labor at his own trade and fit for nothing else, yet too poor to live at his ease. So I say once again, give me main strength for my money. And then, how it takes the nonsense out of a man! Did you ever hear of a blacksmith being such a fool as Owen Warland yonder?"

"Well said, uncle Hovenden!" shouted Robert Danforth from the forge, in a full, deep, merry voice, that made the roof reëcho. "And what says Miss Annie to that doctrine? She, I suppose, will think it a genteeler business to tinker up a lady's watch than to forge a horseshoe or make a gridiron."

Annie drew her father onward without giving him time for reply. But we must return to Owen Warland's shop, and spend more meditation upon his history and character than either Peter Hovenden, or probably his daughter Annie, or Owen's old schoolfellow, Robert Danforth, would have thought due to so slight a subject. From the time that his little fingers could grasp a penknife, Owen had been remarkable for a delicate ingenuity, which sometimes produced pretty shapes in wood, principally figures of flowers and birds, and sometimes seemed to aim at the hidden mysteries of mechanism. But it was always for purposes of grace, and never with any mockery of the useful. He did not, like the crowd of school-boy artisans, construct little windmills on the angle of a barn or watermills across the neighboring brook. Those who discovered such peculiarity in the boy as to think it worth their while to observe him closely, sometimes saw reason to suppose that he was attempting to imitate the beautiful movements of Nature as exemplified in the flight of birds or the activity of little animals. It seemed, in fact, a new development of the love of the beautiful, such as might have made him a poet, a painter, or a sculptor, and which was as completely refined from all utilitarian coarseness as it could have been in either of the fine arts. He looked with singular distaste at the stiff and regular processes of ordinary machinery. Being once carried to see a steam-engine, in the expectation that his intuitive comprehension of mechanical principles would be gratified, he turned pale and grew sick, as if something monstrous and unnatural had been presented to him. This horror was partly owing to the size and terrible energy of the iron laborer; for the character of Owen's mind was microscopic, and tended naturally to the minute, in accordance with his diminutive frame and the marvellous smallness and delicate power of his fingers. Not that his sense of beauty was thereby diminished into a sense of prettiness. The beautiful idea has no relation to size, and may be as perfectly developed in a space too minute for any but microscopic investigation as within the ample verge that is measured by the arc of the rainbow. But, at all events, this characteristic minuteness in his objects and accomplishments made the world even more incapable than it might otherwise have been of appreciating Owen Warland's genius. The boy's relatives saw nothing better to be done—as perhaps there was not—than to bind him apprentice to a watchmaker, hoping that his strange ingenuity might thus be regulated and put to utilitarian purposes.

Peter Hovenden's opinion of his apprentice has already been expressed. He could make nothing of the lad. Owen's apprehension of the professional mysteries, it is true, was inconceivably quick; but he altogether forgot or despised the grand object of a watchmaker's business, and cared no more for the measurement of time than if it had been merged into eternity. So long, however, as he remained under his old master's care, Owen's lack of sturdiness made it possible, by strict injunctions and sharp oversight, to restrain his creative eccentricity within bounds; but when his apprenticeship was served out, and he had taken the little shop which Peter Hovenden's failing eyesight compelled him to relinquish, then did people recognize how unfit a person was Owen Warland to lead old blind Father Time along his daily course. One of his most rational projects was to connect a musical operation with the machinery of his watches, so that all the harsh dissonances of life might be rendered tuneful, and each flitting moment fall into the abyss of the past in golden drops of harmony. If a family clock was intrusted to him for repair,—one of those tall, ancient clocks that have grown nearly allied to human nature by measuring out the lifetime of many generations,—he would take upon himself to arrange a dance or funeral procession of figures across its venerable face, representing twelve mirthful or melancholy hours. Several freaks of this kind quite destroyed the young watchmaker's credit with that steady and matter-of-fact class of people who hold the opinion that time is not to be trifled with, whether considered as the medium of advancement and prosperity in this world or preparation for the next. His custom rapidly diminished—a misfortune, however, that was probably reckoned among his better accidents by Owen Warland, who was becoming more and more absorbed in a secret occupation which drew all his science and manual dexterity into itself, and likewise gave full employment to the characteristic tendencies of his genius. This pursuit had already consumed many months.

After the old watchmaker and his pretty daughter had gazed at him out of the obscurity of the street, Owen Warland was seized with a fluttering of the nerves, which made his hand tremble too violently to proceed with such delicate labor as he was now engaged upon.

"It was Annie herself!" murmured he. "I should have known it, by this throbbing of my heart, before I heard her father's voice. Ah, how it throbs! I shall scarcely be able to work again on this exquisite mechanism to-night. Annie! dearest Annie! thou shouldst give firmness to my heart and hand, and not shake them thus; for if I strive to put the very spirit of beauty into form and give it motion, it is for thy sake alone. O throbbing heart, be quiet! If my labor be thus thwarted, there will come vague and unsatisfied dreams which will leave me spiritless to-morrow."

As he was endeavoring to settle himself again to his task, the shop door opened and gave admittance to no other than the stalwart figure which Peter Hovenden had paused to admire, as seen amid the light and shadow of the blacksmith's shop. Robert Danforth had brought a little anvil of his own manufacture, and peculiarly constructed, which the young artist had recently bespoken. Owen examined the article and pronounced it fashioned according to his wish.

"Why, yes," said Robert Danforth, his strong voice filling the shop as with the sound of a bass viol, "I consider myself equal to anything in the way of my own trade; though I should have made but a poor figure at yours with such a fist as this," added he, laughing, as he laid his vast hand beside the delicate one of Owen. "But what then? I put more main strength into one blow of my sledge hammer than all that you have expended since you were a 'prentice. Is not that the truth?"

"Very probably," answered the low and slender voice of Owen. "Strength is an earthly monster. I make no pretensions to it. My force, whatever there may be of it, is altogether spiritual."

"Well, but, Owen, what are you about?" asked his old schoolfellow, still in such a hearty volume of tone that it made the artist shrink, especially as the question related to a subject so sacred as the absorbing dreams of his imagination. "Folks do say that you are trying to discover the perpetual motion."

"The perpetual motion? Nonsense!" replied Owen Warland, with a movement of disgust; for he was full of little petulances. "It can never be discovered. It is a dream that may delude men whose brains are mystified with matter, but not me. Besides, if such a discovery were possible, it would not be worth my while to make it only to have the secret turned to such purposes as are now effected by steam and water power. I am not ambitious to be honored with the paternity of a new kind of cotton machine."

"That would be droll enough!" cried the blacksmith, breaking out into such an uproar of laughter that Owen himself and the bell glasses on his work-board quivered in unison. "No, no, Owen! No child of yours will have iron joints and sinews. Well, I won't hinder you any more. Good night, Owen, and success, and if you need any assistance, so far as a downright blow of hammer upon anvil will answer the purpose, I'm your man."

And with another laugh the man of main strength left the shop.

"How strange it is," whispered Owen Warland to himself, leaning his head upon his hand, "that all my musings, my purposes, my passion for the beautiful, my consciousness of power to create it,—a finer, more ethereal power, of which this earthly giant can have no conception,—all, all, look so vain and idle whenever my path is crossed by Robert Danforth! He would drive me mad were I to meet him often. His hard, brute force darkens and confuses the spiritual element within me; but I, too, will be strong in my own way. I will not yield to him."

He took from beneath a glass a piece of minute machinery, which he set in the condensed light of his lamp, and, looking intently at it through a magnifying glass, proceeded to operate with a delicate instrument of steel. In an instant, however, he fell back in his chair and clasped his hands, with a look of horror on his face that made its small features as impressive as those of a giant would have been.

"Heaven! What have I done?" exclaimed he. "The vapor, the influence of that brute force,—it has bewildered me and obscured my perception. I have made the very stroke—the fatal stroke—that I have dreaded from the first. It is all over—the toil of months, the object of my life. I am ruined!"

And there he sat, in strange despair, until his lamp flickered in the socket and left the Artist of the Beautiful in darkness.

Thus it is that ideas, which grow up within the imagination and appear so lovely to it and of a value beyond whatever men call valuable, are exposed to be shattered and annihilated by contact with the practical. It is requisite for the ideal artist to possess a force of character that seems hardly compatible with its delicacy; he must keep his faith in himself while the incredulous world assails him with its utter disbelief; he must stand up against mankind and be his own sole disciple, both as respects his genius and the objects to which it is directed.

For a time Owen Warland succumbed to this severe but inevitable test. He spent a few sluggish weeks with his head so continually resting in his hands that the towns-people had scarcely an opportunity to see his countenance. When at last it was again uplifted to the light of day, a cold, dull, nameless change was perceptible upon it. In the opinion of Peter Hovenden, however, and that order of sagacious understandings who think that life should be regulated, like clockwork, with leaden weights, the alteration was entirely for the better. Owen now, indeed, applied himself to business with dogged industry. It was marvellous to witness the obtuse gravity with which he would inspect the wheels of a great old silver watch; thereby delighting the owner, in whose fob it had been worn till he deemed it a portion of his own life, and was accordingly jealous of its treatment. In consequence of the good report thus acquired, Owen Warland was invited by the proper authorities to regulate the clock in the church steeple. He succeeded so admirably in this matter of public interest that the merchants gruffly acknowledged his merits on 'Change; the nurse whispered his praises as she gave the potion in the sick-chamber; the lover blessed him at the hour of appointed interview; and the town in general thanked Owen for the punctuality of dinner time. In a word, the heavy weight upon his spirits kept everything in order, not merely within his own system, but wheresoever the iron accents of the church clock were audible. It was a circumstance, though minute, yet characteristic of his present state, that, when employed to engrave names or initials on silver spoons, he now wrote the requisite letters in the plainest possible style, omitting a variety of fanciful flourishes that had heretofore distinguished his work in this kind.

One day, during the era of this happy transformation, old Peter Hovenden came to visit his former apprentice.

"Well, Owen," said he, "I am glad to hear such good accounts of you from all quarters, and especially from the town clock yonder, which speaks in your commendation every hour of the twenty-four. Only get rid altogether of your nonsensical trash about the beautiful, which I nor nobody else, nor yourself to boot, could ever understand,—only free yourself of that, and your success in life is as sure as daylight. Why, if you go on in this way, I should even venture to let you doctor this precious old watch of mine; though, except my daughter Annie, I have nothing else so valuable in the world."

"I should hardly dare touch it, sir," replied Owen, in a depressed tone; for he was weighed down by his old master's presence.

"In time," said the latter,—"in time, you will be capable of it."

The old watchmaker, with the freedom naturally consequent on his former authority, went on inspecting the work which Owen had in hand at the moment, together with other matters that were in progress. The artist, meanwhile, could scarcely lift his head. There was nothing so antipodal to his nature as this man's cold, unimaginative sagacity, by contact with which everything was converted into a dream except the densest matter of the physical world. Owen groaned in spirit and prayed fervently to be delivered from him.

"But what is this?" cried Peter Hovenden abruptly, taking up a dusty bell glass, beneath which appeared a mechanical something, as delicate and minute as the system of a butterfly's anatomy. "What have we here? Owen! Owen! there is witchcraft in these little chains, and wheels, and paddles. See! with one pinch of my finger and thumb I am going to deliver you from all future peril."

"For Heaven's sake," screamed Owen Warland, springing up with wonderful energy, "as you would not drive me mad, do not touch it! The slightest pressure of your finger would ruin me forever."

"Aha, young man! And is it so?" said the old watchmaker, looking at him with just enough penetration to torture Owen's soul with the bitterness of worldly criticism. "Well, take your own course; but I warn you again that in this small piece of mechanism lives your evil spirit. Shall I exorcise him?"

"You are my evil spirit," answered Owen, much excited,— "you and the hard, coarse world! The leaden thoughts and the despondency that you fling upon me are my clogs, else I should long ago have achieved the task that I was created for."

Peter Hovenden shook his head, with the mixture of contempt and indignation which mankind, of whom he was partly a representative, deem themselves entitled to feel towards all simpletons who seek other prizes than the dusty one along the highway. He then took his leave, with an uplifted finger and a sneer upon his face that haunted the artist's dreams for many a night afterwards. At the time of his old master's visit, Owen was probably on the point of taking up the relinquished task; but, by this sinister event, he was thrown back into the state whence he had been slowly emerging.

But the innate tendency of his soul had only been accumulating fresh vigor during its apparent sluggishness. As the summer advanced he almost totally relinquished his business and permitted Father Time, so far as the old gentleman was represented by the clocks and watches under his control, to stray at random through human life, making infinite confusion among the train of bewildered hours. He wasted the sunshine, as people said, in wandering through the woods and fields and along the banks of streams. There, like a child, he found amusement in chasing butterflies or watching the motions of water insects. There was something truly mysterious in the intentness with which he contemplated these living playthings as they sported on the breeze or examined the structure of an imperial insect whom he had imprisoned. The chase of butterflies was an apt emblem of the ideal pursuit in which he had spent so many golden hours; but would the beautiful idea ever be yielded to his hand like the butterfly that symbolized it? Sweet, doubtless, were these days, and congenial to the artist's soul. They were full of bright conceptions, which gleamed through his intellectual world as the butterflies gleamed through the outward atmosphere, and were real to him, for the instant, without the toil, and perplexity, and many disappointments of attempting to make them visible to the sensual eye. Alas that the artist, whether in poetry, or whatever other material, may not content himself with the inward enjoyment of the beautiful, but must chase the flitting mystery beyond the verge of his ethereal domain, and crush its frail being in seizing it with a material grasp. Owen Warland felt the impulse to give external reality to his ideas as irresistibly as any of the poets or painters who have arrayed the world in a dimmer and fainter beauty, imperfectly copied from the richness of their visions.

The night was now his time for the slow progress of re-creating the one idea to which all his intellectual activity referred itself. Always at the approach of dusk he stole into the town, locked himself within his shop, and wrought with patient delicacy of touch for many hours. Sometimes he was startled by the rap of the watchman, who, when all the world should be asleep, had caught the gleam of lamplight through the crevices of Owen Warland's shutters. Daylight, to the morbid sensibility of his mind, seemed to have an intrusiveness that interfered with his pursuits. On cloudy and inclement days, therefore, he sat with his head upon his hands, muffling, as it were, his sensitive brain in a mist of indefinite musings; for it was a relief to escape from the sharp distinctness with which he was compelled to shape out his thoughts during his nightly toil.

From one of these fits of torpor he was aroused by the entrance of Annie Hovenden, who came into the shop with the freedom of a customer, and also with something of the familiarity of a childish friend. She had worn a hole through her silver thimble, and wanted Owen to repair it.

"But I don't know whether you will condescend to such a task," said she, laughing, "now that you are so taken up with the notion of putting spirit into machinery."

"Where did you get that idea, Annie?" said Owen, starting in surprise.

"Oh, out of my own head," answered she, "and from something that I heard you say, long ago, when you were but a boy and I a little child. But come; will you mend this poor thimble of mine?"

"Anything for your sake, Annie," said Owen Warland,—"anything, even were it to work at Robert Danforth's forge."

"And that would be a pretty sight!" retorted Annie, glancing with imperceptible slightness at the artist's small and slender frame. "Well; here is the thimble."

"But that is a strange idea of yours," said Owen, "about the spiritualization of matter."

And then the thought stole into his mind that this young girl possessed the gift to comprehend him better than all the world besides. And what a help and strength would it be to him in his lonely toil if he could gain the sympathy of the only being whom he loved! To persons whose pursuits are insulated from the common business of life—who are either in advance of mankind or apart from it—there often comes a sensation of moral cold that makes the spirit shiver as if it had reached the frozen solitudes around the pole. What the prophet, the poet, the reformer, the criminal, or any other man with human yearnings, but separated from the multitude by a peculiar lot, might feel, poor Owen felt.

"Annie," cried he, growing pale as death at the thought, "how gladly would I tell you the secret of my pursuit! You, methinks, would estimate it rightly. You, I know, would hear it with a reverence that I must not expect from the harsh, material world."

"Would I not? to be sure I would!" replied Annie Hovenden, lightly laughing. "Come; explain to me quickly what is the meaning of this little whirligig, so delicately wrought that it might be a plaything for Queen Mab. See! I will put it in motion."

"Hold!" exclaimed Owen, "hold!"

Annie had but given the slightest possible touch, with the point of a needle, to the same minute portion of complicated machinery which has been more than once mentioned, when the artist seized her by the wrist with a force that made her scream aloud. She was affrighted at the convulsion of intense rage and anguish that writhed across his features. The next instant he let his head sink upon his hands.

"Go, Annie," murmured he; "I have deceived myself, and must suffer for it. I yearned for sympathy, and thought, and fancied, and dreamed that you might give it to me; but you lack the talisman, Annie, that should admit you into my secrets. That touch has undone the toil of months and the thought of a lifetime! It was not your fault, Annie; but you have ruined me!"

Poor Owen Warland! He had indeed erred, yet pardonably; for if any human spirit could have sufficiently reverenced the processes so sacred in his eyes, it must have been a woman's. Even Annie Hovenden, possibly, might not have disappointed him had she been enlightened by the deep intelligence of love.

The artist spent the ensuing winter in a way that satisfied any persons who had hitherto retained a hopeful opinion of him that he was, in truth, irrevocably doomed to unutility as regarded the world, and to an evil destiny on his own part. The decease of a relative had put him in possession of a small inheritance. Thus freed from the necessity of toil, and having lost the steadfast influence of a great purpose,—great, at least, to him,—he abandoned himself to habits from which it might have been supposed the mere delicacy of his organization would have availed to secure him. But when the ethereal portion of a man of genius is obscured, the earthly part assumes an influence the more uncontrollable, because the character is now thrown off the balance to which Providence had so nicely adjusted it, and which, in coarser natures, is adjusted by some other method. Owen Warland made proof of whatever show of bliss may be found in riot. He looked at the world through the golden medium of wine, and contemplated the visions that bubble up so gayly around the brim of the glass, and that people the air with shapes of pleasant madness, which so soon grow ghostly and forlorn. Even when this dismal and inevitable change had taken place, the young man might still have continued to quaff the cup of enchantments, though its vapor did but shroud life in gloom and fill the gloom with spectres that mocked at him. There was a certain irksomeness of spirit, which, being real, and the deepest sensation of which the artist was now conscious, was more intolerable than any fantastic miseries and horrors that the abuse of wine could summon up. In the latter case he could remember, even out of the midst of his trouble, that all was but a delusion; in the former, the heavy anguish was his actual life.

From this perilous state he was redeemed by an incident which more than one person witnessed, but of which the shrewdest could not explain or conjecture the operation on Owen Warland's mind. It was very simple. On a warm afternoon of spring, as the artist sat among his riotous companions with a glass of wine before him, a splendid butterfly flew in at the open window and fluttered about his head.

"Ah," exclaimed Owen, who had drank freely, "are you alive again, child of the sun and playmate of the summer breeze, after your dismal winter's nap? Then it is time for me to be at work!"

And, leaving his unemptied glass upon the table, he departed and was never known to sip another drop of wine.

And now, again, he resumed his wanderings in the woods and fields. It might be fancied that the bright butterfly, which had come so spirit-like into the window as Owen sat with the rude revellers, was indeed a spirit commissioned to recall him to the pure, ideal life that had so etherealized him among men. It might be fancied that he went forth to seek this spirit in its sunny haunts; for still, as in the summer time gone by, he was seen to steal gently up wherever a butterfly had alighted, and lose himself in contemplation of it. When it took flight his eyes followed the winged vision, as if its airy track would show the path to heaven. But what could be the purpose of the unseasonable toil, which was again resumed, as the watchman knew by the lines of lamplight through the crevices of Owen Warland's shutters? The towns-people had one comprehensive explanation of all these singularities. Owen Warland had gone mad! How universally efficacious—how satisfactory, too, and soothing to the injured sensibility of narrowness and dulness—is this easy method of accounting for whatever lies beyond the world's most ordinary scope! From St. Paul's days down to our poor little Artist of the Beautiful, the same talisman had been applied to the elucidation of all mysteries in the words or deeds of men who spoke or acted too wisely or too well. In Owen Warland's case the judgment of his towns-people may have been correct. Perhaps he was mad. The lack of sympathy—that contrast between himself and his neighbors which took away the restraint of example—was enough to make him so. Or possibly he had caught just so much of ethereal radiance as served to bewilder him, in an earthly sense, by its intermixture with the common daylight.

One evening, when the artist had returned from a customary ramble and had just thrown the lustre of his lamp on the delicate piece of work so often interrupted, but still taken up again, as if his fate were embodied in its mechanism, he was surprised by the entrance of old Peter Hovenden. Owen never met this man without a shrinking of the heart. Of all the world he was most terrible, by reason of a keen understanding which saw so distinctly what it did see, and disbelieved so uncompromisingly in what it could not see. On this occasion the old watchmaker had merely a gracious word or two to say.

"Owen, my lad," said he, "we must see you at my house tomorrow night."

The artist began to mutter some excuse.

"Oh, but it must be so," quoth Peter Hovenden, "for the sake of the days when you were one of the household. What, my boy! don't you know that my daughter Annie is engaged to Robert Danforth? We are making an entertainment, in our humble way, to celebrate the event."

"Ah!" said Owen.

That little monosyllable was all he uttered; its tone seemed cold and unconcerned to an ear like Peter Hovenden's; and yet there was in it the stifled outcry of the poor artist's heart, which he compressed within him like a man holding down an evil spirit. One slight outbreak, however, imperceptible to the old watchmaker, he allowed himself. Raising the instrument with which he was about to begin his work, he let it fall upon the little system of machinery that had, anew, cost him months of thought and toil. It was shattered by the stroke!

Owen Warland's story would have been no tolerable representation of the troubled life of those who strive to create the beautiful, if, amid all other thwarting influences, love had not interposed to steal the cunning from his hand. Outwardly he had been no ardent or enterprising lover; the career of his passion had confined its tumults and vicissitudes so entirely within the artist's imagination that Annie herself had scarcely more than a woman's intuitive perception of it; but, in Owen's view, it covered the whole field of his life. Forgetful of the time when she had shown herself incapable of any deep response, he had persisted in connecting all his dreams of artistical success with Annie's image; she was the visible shape in which the spiritual power that he worshipped, and on whose altar he hoped to lay a not unworthy offering, was made manifest to him. Of course he had deceived himself; there were no such attributes in Annie Hovenden as his imagination had endowed her with. She, in the aspect which she wore to his inward vision, was as much a creature of his own as the mysterious piece of mechanism would be were it ever realized. Had he become convinced of his mistake through the medium of successful love,—had he won Annie to his bosom, and there beheld her fade from angel into ordinary woman,—the disappointment might have driven him back, with concentrated energy, upon his sole remaining object. On the other hand, had he found Annie what he fancied, his lot would have been so rich in beauty that out of its mere redundancy he might have wrought the beautiful into many a worthier type than he had toiled for; but the guise in which his sorrow came to him, the sense that the angel of his life had been snatched away and given to a rude man of earth and iron, who could neither need nor appreciate her ministrations,— this was the very perversity of fate that makes human existence appear too absurd and contradictory to be the scene of one other hope or one other fear. There was nothing left for Owen Warland but to sit down like a man that had been stunned.

He went through a fit of illness. After his recovery his small and slender frame assumed an obtuser garniture of flesh than it had ever before worn. His thin cheeks became round; his delicate little hand, so spiritually fashioned to achieve fairy task-work, grew plumper than the hand of a thriving infant. His aspect had a childishness such as might have induced a stranger to pat him on the head—pausing, however, in the act, to wonder what manner of child was here. It was as if the spirit had gone out of him, leaving the body to flourish in a sort of vegetable existence. Not that Owen Warland was idiotic. He could talk, and not irrationally. Somewhat of a babbler, indeed, did people begin to think him; for he was apt to discourse at wearisome length of marvels of mechanism that he had read about in books, but which he had learned to consider as absolutely fabulous. Among them he enumerated the Man of Brass, constructed by Albertus Magnus, and the Brazen Head of Friar Bacon; and, coming down to later times, the automata of a little coach and horses, which it was pretended had been manufactured for the Dauphin of France; together with an insect that buzzed about the ear like a living fly, and yet was but a contrivance of minute steel springs. There was a story, too, of a duck that waddled, and quacked, and ate; though, had any honest citizen purchased it for dinner, he would have found himself cheated with the mere mechanical apparition of a duck.

"But all these accounts," said Owen Warland, "I am now satisfied are mere impositions."

Then, in a mysterious way, he would confess that he once thought differently. In his idle and dreamy days he had considered it possible, in a certain sense, to spiritualize machinery, and to combine with the new species of life and motion thus produced a beauty that should attain to the ideal which Nature has proposed to herself in all her creatures, but has never taken pains to realize. He seemed, however, to retain no very distinct perception either of the process of achieving this object or of the design itself.

"I have thrown it all aside now," he would say. "It was a dream such as young men are always mystifying themselves with. Now that I have acquired a little common sense, it makes me laugh to think of it."

Poor, poor and fallen Owen Warland! These were the symptoms that he had ceased to be an inhabitant of the better sphere that lies unseen around us. He had lost his faith in the invisible, and now prided himself, as such unfortunates invariably do, in the wisdom which rejected much that even his eye could see, and trusted confidently in nothing but what his hand could touch. This is the calamity of men whose spiritual part dies out of them and leaves the grosser understanding to assimilate them more and more to the things of which alone it can take cognizance; but in Owen Warland the spirit was not dead nor passed away; it only slept.

How it awoke again is not recorded. Perhaps the torpid slumber was broken by a convulsive pain. Perhaps, as in a former instance, the butterfly came and hovered about his head and reinspired him, —as indeed this creature of the sunshine had always a mysterious mission for the artist,—reinspired him with the former purpose of his life. Whether it were pain or happiness that thrilled through his veins, his first impulse was to thank Heaven for rendering him again the being of thought, imagination, and keenest sensibility that he had long ceased to be.

"Now for my task," said he. "Never did I feel such strength for it as now."

Yet, strong as he felt himself, he was incited to toil the more diligently by an anxiety lest death should surprise him in the midst of his labors. This anxiety, perhaps, is common to all men who set their hearts upon anything so high, in their own view of it, that life becomes of importance only as conditional to its accomplishment. So long as we love life for itself, we seldom dread the losing it. When we desire life for the attainment of an object, we recognize the frailty of its texture. But, side by side with this sense of insecurity, there is a vital faith in our invulnerability to the shaft of death while engaged in any task that seems assigned by Providence as our proper thing to do, and which the world would have cause to mourn for should we leave it unaccomplished. Can the philosopher, big with the inspiration of an idea that is to reform mankind, believe that he is to be beckoned from this sensible existence at the very instant when he is mustering his breath to speak the word of light? Should he perish so, the weary ages may pass away—the world's, whose life sand may fall, drop by drop— before another intellect is prepared to develop the truth that might have been uttered then. But history affords many an example where the most precious spirit, at any particular epoch manifested in human shape, has gone hence untimely, without space allowed him, so far as mortal judgment could discern, to perform his mission on the earth. The prophet dies, and the man of torpid heart and sluggish brain lives on. The poet leaves his song half sung, or finishes it, beyond the scope of mortal ears, in a celestial choir. The painter—as Allston[2] did—leaves half his conception on the canvas to sadden us with its imperfect beauty, and goes to picture forth the whole, if it be no irreverence to say so, in the hues of heaven. But rather such incomplete designs of this life will be perfected nowhere. This so frequent abortion of man's dearest projects must be taken as a proof that the deeds of earth, however etherealized by piety or genius, are without value, except as exercises and manifestations of the spirit. In heaven, all ordinary thought is higher and more melodious than Milton's song. Then, would he add another verse to any strain that he had left unfinished here?

But to return to Owen Warland. It was his fortune, good or ill, to achieve the purpose of his life. Pass we over a long space of intense thought, yearning effort, minute toil, and wasting anxiety, succeeded by an instant of solitary triumph: let all this be imagined; and then behold the artist, on a winter evening, seeking admittance to Robert Danforth's fireside circle. There he found the man of iron, with his massive substance thoroughly warmed and attempered by domestic influences. And there was Annie, too, now transformed into a matron, with much of her husband's plain and sturdy nature, but imbued, as Owen Warland still believed, with a finer grace, that might enable her to be the interpreter between strength and beauty. It happened, likewise, that old Peter Hovenden was a guest this evening at his daughter's fireside, and it was his well-remembered expression of keen, cold criticism that first encountered the artist's glance.

"My old friend Owen!" cried Robert Danforth, starting up,

---

2. Washington Allston (1779–1843), the leading American painter of his time, who achieved international reputation.

and compressing the artist's delicate fingers within a hand that was accustomed to gripe bars of iron. "This is kind and neighborly to come to us at last. I was afraid your perpetual motion had bewitched you out of the remembrance of old times."

"We are glad to see you," said Annie, while a blush reddened her matronly cheek. "It was not like a friend to stay from us so long."

"Well, Owen," inquired the old watchmaker, as his first greeting, "how comes on the beautiful? Have you created it at last?"

The artist did not immediately reply, being startled by the apparition of a young child of strength that was tumbling about on the carpet,—a little personage who had come mysteriously out of the infinite, but with something so sturdy and real in his composition that he seemed moulded out of the densest substance which earth could supply. This hopeful infant crawled towards the new-comer, and setting himself on end, as Robert Danforth expressed the posture, stared at Owen with a look of such sagacious observation that the mother could not help exchanging a proud glance with her husband. But the artist was disturbed by the child's look, as imaging a resemblance between it and Peter Hovenden's habitual expression. He could have fancied that the old watchmaker was compressed into this baby shape, and looking out of those baby eyes, and repeating, as he now did, the malicious question:—

"The beautiful, Owen! How comes on the beautiful? Have you succeeded in creating the beautiful?'

"I have succeeded," replied the artist, with a momentary light of triumph in his eyes and a smile of sunshine, yet steeped in such depth of thought that it was almost sadness. "Yes, my friends, it is the truth. I have succeeded."

"Indeed!" cried Annie, a look of maiden mirthfulness peeping out of her face again. "And is it lawful, now, to inquire what the secret is?"

"Surely; it is to disclose it that I have come," answered Owen Warland. "You shall know, and see, and touch, and possess the secret! For, Annie,—if by that name I may still address the friend of my boyish years,—Annie, it is for your bridal gift that I have wrought this spiritualized mechanism, this harmony of motion, this mystery of beauty. It comes late, indeed; but it is as we go onward in life, when objects begin to lose their freshness of hue and our souls their delicacy of perception, that the spirit of beauty is most needed. If,—forgive me, Annie,—if you know how to value this gift, it can never come too late."

He produced, as he spoke, what seemed a jewel box. It was carved richly out of ebony by his own hand, and inlaid with a fanciful tracery of pearl, representing a boy in pursuit of a butterfly, which, elsewhere, had become a winged spirit, and was flying heavenward; while the boy, or youth, had found such efficacy in his strong desire that he ascended from earth to cloud, and from cloud to celestial atmosphere, to win the beautiful.[3] This case of ebony the artist opened, and bade Annie place her fingers on its edge. She did so, but almost screamed as a butterfly fluttered forth, and, alighting on her finger's tip, sat waving the ample magnificence of its purple and gold-speckled wings, as if in prelude to a flight. It is impossible to express by words the glory, the splendor, the delicate gorgeousness which were softened into the beauty of this object. Nature's ideal butterfly was here realized in all its perfection; not in the pattern of such faded insects as flit among earthly flowers, but of those which hover across the meads of paradise for child-angels and the spirits of departed infants to disport themselves with. The rich down was visible upon its wings; the lustre of its eyes seemed instinct with spirit. The firelight glimmered around this wonder—the candles gleamed upon it; but it glistened apparently by its own radiance, and illuminated the finger and outstretched hand on which it rested with a white gleam like that of precious stones. In its perfect beauty, the consideration of size was entirely lost. Had its wings overreached the firmament, the mind could not have been more filled or satisfied.

"Beautiful! beautiful!" exclaimed Annie. "Is it alive? Is it alive?"

"Alive? To be sure it is," answered her husband. "Do you suppose any mortal has skill enough to make a butterfly, or would put himself to the trouble of making one, when any child may catch a score of them in a summer's afternoon? Alive? Certainly! But this pretty box is undoubtedly of our friend Owen's manufacture; and really it does him credit."

At this moment the butterfly waved its wings anew, with a motion so absolutely lifelike that Annie was startled, and even awe-stricken; for, in spite of her husband's opinion, she could not satisfy herself whether it was indeed a living creature or a piece of wondrous mechanism.

"Is it alive?" she repeated, more earnestly than before.

"Judge for yourself," said Owen Warland, who stood gazing in her face with fixed attention.

The butterfly now flung itself upon the air, fluttered round Annie's head, and soared into a distant region of the parlor, still making itself perceptible to sight by the starry gleam in which the motion of its wings enveloped it. The infant on the floor followed its course with his sagacious little eyes. After flying about the room, it returned in a spiral curve and settled again on Annie's finger.

3. The butterfly is a common symbol for the psyche or soul.

"But is it alive?" exclaimed she again; and the finger on which the gorgeous mystery had alighted was so tremulous that the butterfly was forced to balance himself with his wings. "Tell me if it be alive, or whether you created it."

"Wherefore ask who created it, so it be beautiful?" replied Owen Warland. "Alive? Yes, Annie; it may well be said to possess life, for it has absorbed my own being into itself; and in the secret of that butterfly, and in its beauty,—which is not merely outward, but deep as its whole system,—is represented the intellect, the imagination, the sensibility, the soul of an Artist of the Beautiful! Yes; I created it. But"—and here his countenance somewhat changed—"this butterfly is not now to me what it was when I beheld it afar off in the daydreams of my youth."

"Be it what it may, it is a pretty plaything," said the blacksmith, grinning with childlike delight. "I wonder whether it would condescend to alight on such a great clumsy finger as mine? Hold it hither, Annie."

By the artist's direction, Annie touched her finger's tip to that of her husband; and, after a momentary delay, the butterfly fluttered from one to the other. It preluded a second flight by a similar, yet not precisely the same, waving of wings as in the first experiment; then, ascending from the blacksmith's stalwart finger, it rose in a gradually enlarging curve to the ceiling, made one wide sweep around the room, and returned with an undulating movement to the point whence it had started.

"Well, that does beat all nature!" cried Robert Danforth, bestowing the heartiest praise that he could find expression for; and, indeed, had he paused there, a man of finer words and nicer perception could not easily have said more. "That goes beyond me, I confess. But what then? There is more real use in one downright blow of my sledge hammer than in the whole five years' labor that our friend Owen has wasted on this butterfly."

Here the child clapped his hands and made a great babble of indistinct utterance, apparently demanding that the butterfly should be given him for a plaything.

Owen Warland, meanwhile, glanced sidelong at Annie, to discover whether she sympathized in her husband's estimate of the comparative value of the beautiful and the practical. There was, amid all her kindness towards himself, amid all the wonder and admiration with which she contemplated the marvellous work of his hands and incarnation of his idea, a secret scorn—too secret, perhaps, for her own consciousness, and perceptible only to such intuitive discernment as that of the artist. But Owen, in the latter stages of his pursuit, had risen out of the region in which such a discovery might have been torture. He knew that the world, and

Annie as the representative of the world, whatever praise might be bestowed, could never say the fitting word nor feel the fitting sentiment which should be the perfect recompense of an artist who, symbolizing a lofty moral by a material trifle,—converting what was earthly to spiritual gold,—had won the beautiful into his handiwork. Not at this latest moment was he to learn that the reward of all high performance must be sought within itself, or sought in vain. There was, however, a view of the matter which Annie and her husband, and even Peter Hovenden, might fully have understood, and which would have satisfied them that the toil of years had here been worthily bestowed. Owen Warland might have told them that this butterfly, this plaything, this bridal gift of a poor watchmaker to a blacksmith's wife, was, in truth, a gem of art that a monarch would have purchased with honors and abundant wealth, and have treasured it among the jewels of his kingdom as the most unique and wondrous of them all. But the artist smiled and kept the secret to himself.

"Father," said Annie, thinking that a word of praise from the old watchmaker might gratify his former apprentice, "do come and admire this pretty butterfly."

"Let us see," said Peter Hovenden, rising from his chair, with a sneer upon his face that always made people doubt, as he himself did, in everything but a material existence. "Here is my finger for it to alight upon. I shall understand it better when once I have touched it."

But, to the increased astonishment of Annie, when the tip of her father's finger was pressed against that of her husband, on which the butterfly still rested, the insect drooped its wings and seemed on the point of falling to the floor. Even the bright spots of gold upon its wings and body, unless her eyes deceived her, grew dim, and the glowing purple took a dusky hue, and the starry lustre that gleamed around the blacksmith's hand became faint and vanished.

"It is dying! it is dying!" cried Annie, in alarm.

"It has been delicately wrought," said the artist, calmly. "As I told you, it has imbibed a spiritual essence—call it magnetism, or what you will. In an atmosphere of doubt and mockery its exquisite susceptibility suffers torture, as does the soul of him who instilled his own life into it. It has already lost its beauty; in a few moments more its mechanism would be irreparably injured."

"Take away your hand, father!" entreated Annie turning pale. "Here is my child; let it rest on his innocent hand. There, perhaps, its life will revive and its colors grow brighter than ever."

Her father, with an acrid smile, withdrew his finger. The butterfly then appeared to recover the power of voluntary motion, while its hues assumed much of their original lustre, and the gleam of starlight, which was its most ethereal attribute, again formed a halo round about it. At first, when transferred from Robert Danforth's hand to the small finger of the child, this radiance grew so powerful that it positively threw the little fellow's shadow back against the wall. He, meanwhile, extended his plump hand as he had seen his father and mother do, and watched the waving of the insect's wings with infantine delight. Nevertheless, there was a certain odd expression of sagacity that made Owen Warland feel as if here were old Peter Hovenden, partially, and but partially, redeemed from his hard scepticism into childish faith.

"How wise the little monkey looks!" whispered Robert Danforth to his wife.

"I never saw such a look on a child's face," answered Annie, admiring her own infant, and with good reason, far more than the artistic butterfly. "The darling knows more of the mystery than we do."

As if the butterfly, like the artist, were conscious of something not entirely congenial in the child's nature, it alternately sparkled and grew dim. At length it arose from the small hand of the infant with an airy motion that seemed to bear it upward without an effort, as if the ethereal instincts with which its master's spirit had endowed it impelled this fair vision involuntarily to a higher sphere. Had there been no obstruction, it might have soared into the sky and grown immortal. But its lustre gleamed upon the ceiling; the exquisite texture of its wings brushed against that earthly medium; and a sparkle or two, as of stardust, floated downward and lay glimmering on the carpet. Then the butterfly came fluttering down, and, instead of returning to the infant, was apparently attracted towards the artist's hand.

"Not so! not so!" murmured Owen Warland, as if his handiwork could have understood him. "Thou hast gone forth out of thy master's heart. There is no return for thee."

With a wavering movement, and emitting a tremulous radiance, the butterfly struggled, as it were, towards the infant, and was about to alight upon his finger; but while it still hovered in the air, the little child of strength, with his grandsire's sharp and shrewd expression in his face, made a snatch at the marvellous insect and compressed it in his hand. Annie screamed. Old Peter Hovenden burst into a cold and scornful laugh. The blacksmith, by main force, unclosed the infant's hand, and found within the palm a small heap of glittering fragments, whence the mystery of beauty had fled forever. And as for Owen Warland, he looked placidly at what seemed the ruin of his life's labor, and which was yet no ruin. He had caught a far other butterfly than this. When the artist rose high enough to achieve the beautiful, the symbol by which he made it perceptible to mortal senses became of little value in his eyes while his spirit possessed itself in the enjoyment of the reality.

1844, 1846

The Prophetic Pictures[4]

"But this painter!" cried Walter Ludlow, with animation. "He not only excels in his peculiar art, but possesses vast acquirements in all other learning and science. He talks Hebrew with Dr. Mather, and gives lectures in anatomy to Dr. Boylston. In a word, he will meet the best instructed man among us on his own ground. Moreover, he is a polished gentleman—a citizen of the world—yes, a true cosmopolite; for he will speak like a native of each clime and country of the globe, except our own forests, whither he is now going. Nor is all this what I most admire in him."

"Indeed!" said Elinor, who had listened with a woman's interest to the description of such a man. "Yet this is admirable enough."

"Surely it is," replied her lover, "but far less so than his natural gift of adapting himself to every variety of character, insomuch that all men—and all women too, Elinor—shall find a mirror of themselves in this wonderful painter. But the greatest wonder is yet to be told."

"Nay, if he have more wonderful attributes than these," said Elinor, laughing, "Boston is a perilous abode for the poor gentleman. Are you telling me of a painter, or a wizard?"

"In truth," answered he, "that question might be asked much more seriously than you suppose. They say that he paints not merely a man's features, but his mind and heart. He catches the secret sentiments and passions, and throws them upon the canvas, like sunshine—or perhaps, in the portraits of dark-souled men, like a gleam of infernal fire. It is an awful gift," added Walter, lowering his voice from its tone of enthusiasm. "I shall be almost afraid to sit to him."

4. "This story was suggested by an anecdote of Stuart, related in Dunlap's *History of the Arts of Design,*—a most entertaining book to the general reader, and a deeply interesting one, we should think, to the artist" [Hawthorne's note]. Gilbert Stuart (1755–1828), the portrayer of George Washington, is the painter referred to. The anecdote runs as follows: "Lord Mulgrave employed Stuart to paint the portrait of his brother, General Phipps, previous to his going abroad. On seeing the picture, which he did not do until it was finished, Mulgrave exclaimed, 'What is this?—this is very strange!' and stood gazing at the portrait. 'I have painted your brother as I saw him,' said the artist. 'I see insanity in that face,' was the brother's reply. The General went to India, and the first account his brother had of him was that of suicide from insanity. He went mad and cut his throat. It is thus that the real portrait-painter dives into the recesses of his sitters' minds." "The Prophetic Pictures" was first published in *The Token* in 1837, and was included in the *Twice-Told Tales* of that year.

"Walter, are you in earnest?" exclaimed Elinor.

"For Heaven's sake, dearest Elinor, do not let him paint the look which you now wear," said her lover, smiling, though rather perplexed. "There: it is passing away now, but when you spoke you seemed frightened to death, and very sad besides. What were you thinking of?"

"Nothing, nothing," answered Elinor hastily. "You paint my face with your own fantasies. Well, come for me to-morrow, and we will visit this wonderful artist."

But when the young man had departed, it cannot be denied that a remarkable expression was again visible on the fair and youthful face of his mistress. It was a sad and anxious look, little in accordance with what should have been the feelings of a maiden on the eve of wedlock. Yet Walter Ludlow was the chosen of her heart.

"A look!" said Elinor to herself. "No wonder that it startled him, if it expressed what I sometimes feel. I know, by my own experience, how frightful a look may be. But it was all fancy. I thought nothing of it at the time—I have seen nothing of it since—I did but dream it."

And she busied herself about the embroidery of a ruff, in which she meant that her portrait should be taken.

The painter, of whom they had been speaking, was not one of those native artists who, at a later period than this, borrowed their colors from the Indians, and manufactured their pencils of the furs of wild beasts. Perhaps, if he could have revoked his life and prearranged his destiny, he might have chosen to belong to that school without a master, in the hope of being at least original, since there were no works of art to imitate nor rules to follow. But he had been born and educated in Europe. People said that he had studied the grandeur or beauty of conception, and every touch of the master hand, in all the most famous pictures, in cabinets and galleries, and on the walls of churches, till there was nothing more for his powerful mind to learn. Art could add nothing to its lessons, but Nature might. He had therefore visited a world whither none of his professional brethren had preceded him, to feast his eyes on visible images that were noble and picturesque, yet had never been transferred to canvas. America was too poor to afford other temptations to an artist of eminence, though many of the colonial gentry, on the painter's arrival, had expressed a wish to transmit their lineaments to posterity by means of his skill. Whenever such proposals were made, he fixed his piercing eyes on the applicant, and seemed to look him through and through. If he beheld only a sleek and comfortable visage, though there were a gold-laced coat to adorn the picture and golden guineas to pay for it, he civilly rejected the task and the reward. But if the face were the index of any thing uncommon, in thought, sentiment, or experience, or if he met a beggar in the street, with a white beard and a furrowed brow; or if sometimes a child happened to look up and smile, he would exhaust all the art on them that he denied to wealth.

Pictorial skill being so rare in the colonies, the painter became an object of general curiosity. If few or none could appreciate the technical merit of his productions, yet there were points, in regard to which the opinion of the crowd was as valuable as the refined judgment of the amateur. He watched the effect that each picture produced on such untutored beholders, and derived profit from their remarks, while they would as soon have thought of instructing Nature herself as him who seemed to rival her. Their admiration, it must be owned, was tinctured with the prejudices of the age and country. Some deemed it an offence against the Mosaic law, and even a presumptuous mockery of the Creator, to bring into existence such lively images of his creatures. Others, frightened at the art which could raise phantoms at will, and keep the form of the dead among the living, were inclined to consider the painter as a magician, or perhaps the famous Black Man, of old witch times, plotting mischief in a new guise. These foolish fancies were more than half believed among the mob. Even in superior circles his character was invested with a vague awe, partly rising like smoke wreaths from the popular superstitions, but chiefly caused by the varied knowledge and talents which he made subservient to his profession.

Being on the eve of marriage, Walter Ludlow and Elinor were eager to obtain their portraits, as the first of what, they doubtless hoped, would be a long series of family pictures. The day after the conversation above recorded they visited the painter's rooms. A servant ushered them into an apartment, where, though the artist himself was not visible, there were personages whom they could hardly forbear greeting with reverence. They knew, indeed, that the whole assembly were but pictures, yet felt it impossible to separate the idea of life and intellect from such striking counterfeits. Several of the portraits were known to them, either as distinguished characters of the day or their private acquaintances. There was Governor Burnet, looking as if he had just received an undutiful communication from the House of Representatives, and were inditing a most sharp response. Mr. Cooke hung beside the ruler whom he opposed, sturdy, and somewhat puritanical, as befitted a popular leader. The ancient lady of Sir William Phipps eyed them from the wall, in ruff and farthingale,—an imperious old dame, not unsuspected of witchcraft. John Winslow, then a very young man, wore the expression of warlike enterprise, which long afterwards made him a distinguished general. Their personal friends were recognized at a glance. In most of the pictures, the whole mind and character were brought out on the countenance, and concentrated into a single look, so that, to speak paradoxically, the originals hardly resembled themselves so strikingly as the portraits did.

Among these modern worthies there were two old bearded Saints, who had almost vanished into the darkening canvas. There was also a pale, but unfaded Madonna, who had perhaps been worshipped in Rome, and now regarded the lovers with such a mild and holy look that they longed to worship too.

"How singular a thought," observed Walter Ludlow, "that this beautiful face has been beautiful for above two hundred years! Oh, if all beauty would endure so well! Do you not envy her, Elinor?"

"If earth were heaven, I might," she replied. "But where all things fade, how miserable to be the one that could not fade!"

"This dark old St. Peter has a fierce and ugly scowl, saint though he be," continued Walter. "He troubles me. But the Virgin looks kindly at us."

"Yes; but very sorrowfully, methinks," said Elinor.

The easel stood beneath these three old pictures, sustaining one that had been recently commenced. After a little inspection, they began to recognize the features of their own minister, the Rev. Dr. Colman, growing into shape and life, as it were, out of a cloud.

"Kind old man!" exclaimed Elinor. "He gazes at me as if he were about to utter a word of paternal advice."

"And at me," said Walter, "as if he were about to shake his head and rebuke me for some suspected iniquity. But so does the original. I shall never feel quite comfortable under his eye till we stand before him to be married."

They now heard a footstep on the floor, and turning, beheld the painter, who had been some moments in the room, and had listened to a few of their remarks. He was a middle-aged man, with a countenance well worthy of his own pencil. Indeed, by the picturesque, though careless arrangement of his rich dress, and, perhaps, because his soul dwelt always among painted shapes, he looked somewhat like a portrait himself. His visitors were sensible of a kindred between the artist and his works, and felt as if one of the pictures had stepped from the canvas to salute them.

Walter Ludlow, who was slightly known to the painter, explained the object of their visit. While he spoke, a sunbeam was falling athwart his figure and Elinor's, with so happy an effect that they also seemed living pictures of youth and beauty, gladdened by bright fortune. The artist was evidently struck.

"My easel is occupied for several ensuing days, and my stay in Boston must be brief," said he, thoughtfully; then, after an observant glance, he added: "but your wishes shall be gratified, though I disappoint the Chief Justice and Madam Oliver. I must not lose this opportunity, for the sake of painting a few ells of broadcloth and brocade."

The painter expressed a desire to introduce both their portraits into one picture, and represent them engaged in some appropriate action. This plan would have delighted the lovers, but was necessarily rejected, because so large a space of canvas would have been unfit for the room which it was intended to decorate. Two half-length portraits were therefore fixed upon. After they had taken leave, Walter Ludlow asked Elinor, with a smile, whether she knew what an influence over their fates the painter was about to acquire.

"The old women of Boston affirm," continued he, "that after he has once got possession of a person's face and figure, he may paint him in any act or situation whatever—and the picture will be prophetic. Do you believe it?"

"Not quite," said Elinor, smiling. "Yet if he has such magic, there is something so gentle in his manner that I am sure he will use it well."

It was the painter's choice to proceed with both the portraits at the same time, assigning as a reason, in the mystical language which he sometimes used, that the faces threw light upon each other. Accordingly he gave now a touch to Walter, and now to Elinor, and the features of one and the other began to start forth so vividly that it appeared as if his triumphant art would actually disengage them from the canvas. Amid the rich light and deep shade, they beheld their phantom selves. But, though the likeness promised to be perfect, they were not quite satisfied with the expression; it seemed more vague than in most of the painter's works. He, however, was satisfied with the prospect of success, and being much interested in the lovers, employed his leisure moments, unknown to them, in making a crayon sketch of their two figures. During their sittings, he engaged them in conversation, and kindled up their faces with characteristic traits, which, though continually varying, it was his purpose to combine and fix. At length he announced that at their next visit both the portraits would be ready for delivery.

"If my pencil will but be true to my conception, in the few last touches which I meditate," observed he, "these two pictures will be my very best performances. Seldom, indeed, has an artist such subjects."

While speaking, he still bent his penetrative eye upon them, nor withdrew it till they had reached the bottom of the stairs.

Nothing, in the whole circle of human vanities, takes stronger hold of the imagination than this affair of having a portrait painted. Yet why should it be so? The looking-glass, the polished globes of the andirons, the mirror-like water, and all other reflecting surfaces, continually present us with portraits, or rather ghosts of ourselves, which we glance at, and straightway forget them. But we forget them only because they vanish. It is the idea of duration—of earthy immortality—that gives such a mysterious interest to our own portraits. Walter and Elinor were not insensible to this feeling, and hastened to the painter's room, punctually at the appointed hour, to meet those pictured shapes which were to be their representatives with posterity. The sunshine flashed after them into the apartment, but left it somewhat gloomy as they closed the door.

Their eyes were immediately attracted to their portraits, which rested against the farthest wall of the room. At the first glance, through the dim light and the distance, seeing themselves in precisely their natural attitudes, and with all the air that they recognized so well, they uttered a simultaneous exclamation of delight.

"There we stand," cried Walter, enthusiastically, "fixed in sunshine forever! No dark passions can gather on our faces!"

"No," said Elinor, more calmly; "no dreary change can sadden us."

This was said while they were approaching, and had yet gained only an imperfect view of the pictures. The painter, after saluting them, busied himself at a table in completing a crayon sketch, leaving his visitors to form their own judgment as to his perfected labors. At intervals, he sent a glance from beneath his deep eyebrows, watching their countenances in profile, with his pencil suspended over the sketch. They had now stood some moments, each in front of the other's picture, contemplating it with entranced attention, but without uttering a word. At length, Walter stepped forward—then back—viewing Elinor's portrait in various lights, and finally spoke.

"Is there not a change?" said he, in a doubtful and meditative tone. "Yes; the perception of it grows more vivid the longer I look. It is certainly the same picture that I saw yesterday; the dress— the features—all are the same; and yet something is altered."

"Is then the picture less like than it was yesterday?" inquired the painter, now drawing near, with irrepressible interest.

"The features are perfect, Elinor," answered Walter, "and, at the first glance, the expression seemed also hers. But, I could fancy that the portrait has changed countenance, while I have been looking at it. The eyes are fixed on mine with a strangely sad and anxious expression. Nay, it is grief and terror! Is this like Elinor?"

"Compare the living face with the pictured one," said the

painter.

Walter glanced sidelong at his mistress, and started. Motionless and absorbed—fascinated, as it were—in contemplation of Walter's portrait, Elinor's face had assumed precisely the expression of which he had just been complaining. Had she practised for whole hours before a mirror, she could not have caught the look so successfully. Had the picture itself been a mirror, it could not have thrown back her present aspect with stronger and more melancholy truth. She appeared quite unconscious of the dialogue between the artist and her lover.

"Elinor," exclaimed Walter, in amazement, "what change has come over you?"

She did not hear him, nor desist from her fixed gaze, till he seized her hand, and thus attracted her notice; then, with a sudden tremor, she looked from the picture to the face of the original.

"Do you see no change in your portrait?" asked she.

"In mine?—None!" replied Walter, examining it. "But let me see! Yes; there is a slight change—an improvement, I think, in the picture, though none in the likeness. It has a livelier expression than yesterday, as if some bright thought were flashing from the eyes, and about to be uttered from the lips. Now that I have caught the look, it becomes very decided."

While he was intent on these obeservations, Elinor turned to the painter. She regarded him with grief and awe, and felt that he repaid her with sympathy and commiseration, though wherefore, she could but vaguely guess.

"That look!" whispered she, and shuddered. "How came it there?"

"Madam," said the painter, sadly, taking her hand, and leading her apart, "in both these pictures, I have painted what I saw. The artist—the true artist—must look beneath the exterior. It is his gift—his proudest, but often a melancholy one—to see the inmost soul, and, by a power indefinable even to himself, to make it glow or darken upon the canvas, in glances that express the thought and sentiment of years. Would that I might convince myself of error in the present instance!"

They had now approached the table, on which were heads in chalk, hands almost as expressive as ordinary faces, ivied church towers, thatched cottages, old thunder-stricken trees, Oriental and antique costume, and all such picturesque vagaries of an artist's idle moments. Turning them over, with seeming carelessness, a crayon sketch of two figures was disclosed.

"If I have failed," continued he—"if your heart does not see itself reflected in your own portrait—if you have no secret cause to trust my delineation of the other—it is not yet too late to alter them. I might change the action of these figures too. But would it influence the event?"

He directed her notice to the sketch. A thrill ran through Elinor's frame; a shriek was upon her lips; but she stifled it, with the self-command that becomes habitual to all who hide thoughts of fear and anguish within their bosoms. Turning from the table, she perceived that Walter had advanced near enough to have seen the sketch, though she could not determine whether it had caught his eye.

"We will not have the pictures altered," said she, hastily. "If mine is sad, I shall but look the gayer for the contrast."

"Be it so," answered the painter, bowing. "May your griefs be such fanciful ones that only your picture may mourn for them! For your joys—may they be true and deep, and paint themselves upon this lovely face till it quite belie my art!"

After the marriage of Walter and Elinor, the pictures formed the two most splendid ornaments of their abode. They hung side by side, separated by a narrow panel, appearing to eye each other constantly, yet always returning the gaze of the spectator. Travelled gentlemen, who professed a knowledge of such subjects, reckoned these among the most admirable specimens of modern portraiture; while common observers compared them with the originals, feature by feature, and were rapturous in praise of the likeness. But it was on a third class—neither travelled connoisseurs nor common observers, but people of natural sensibility—that the pictures wrought their strongest effect. Such persons might gaze carelessly at first, but, becoming interested, would return day after day, and study these painted faces like the pages of a mystic volume. Walter Ludlow's portrait attracted their earliest notice. In the absence of himself and his bride, they sometimes disputed as to the expression which the painter had intended to throw upon the features; all agreeing that there was a look of earnest import, though no two explained it alike. There was less diversity of opinion in regard to Elinor's picture. They differed, indeed, in their attempts to estimate the nature and depth of the gloom that dwelt upon her face, but agreed that it was gloom, and alien from the natural temperament of their youthful friend. A certain fanciful person announced, as the result of much scrutiny, that both these pictures were parts of one design, and that the melancholy strength of feeling, in Elinor's countenance, bore reference to the more vivid emotion, or, as he termed it, the wild passion, in that of Walter. Though unskilled in the art, he even began a sketch, in which the action of the two figures was to correspond with their mutual expression.

It was whispered among friends that, day by day, Elinor's face was assuming a deeper shade of pensiveness, which threatened

soon to render her too true a counterpart of her melancholy picture. Walter, on the other hand, instead of acquiring the vivid
look which the painter had given him on the canvas, became reserved and downcast, with no outward flashes of emotion, however it might be smouldering within. In course of time, Elinor
hung a gorgeous curtain of purple silk, wrought with flowers and
fringed with heavy golden tassels, before the pictures, under pretence that the dust would tarnish their hues, or the light dim
them. It was enough. Her visitors felt, that the massive folds of the
silk must never be withdrawn, nor the portraits mentioned in her
presence.

Time wore on; and the painter came again. He had been far
enough to the north to see the silver cascade of the Crystal Hills,
and to look over the vast round of cloud and forest from the summit of New England's loftiest mountain. But he did not profane
that scene by the mockery of his art. He had also lain in a canoe
on the bosom of Lake George, making his soul the mirror of its
loveliness and grandeur, till not a picture in the Vatican was more
vivid than his recollection. He had gone with the Indian hunters to
Niagara, and there, again, had flung his hopeless pencil down the
precipice, feeling that he could as soon paint the roar, as aught else
that goes to make up the wondrous cataract. In truth, it was seldom
his impulse to copy natural scenery, except as a framework for the
delineations of the human form and face, instinct with thought,
passion, or suffering. With store of such his adventurous ramble
had enriched him: the stern dignity of Indian chiefs; the dusky
loveliness of Indian girls; the domestic life of wigwams; the stealthy
march; the battle beneath gloomy pine-trees; the frontier fortress
with its garrison; the anomaly of the old French partisan, bred in
courts, but grown gray in shaggy deserts; such were the scenes and
portraits that he had sketched. The glow of perilous moments;
flashes of wild feeling; struggles of fierce power,—love, hate, grief,
frenzy; in a word, all the worn-out heart of the old earth had been
revealed to him under a new form. His portfolio was filled with
graphic illustrations of the volume of his memory, which genius
would transmute into its own substance, and imbue with immortality. He felt that the deep wisdom in his art, which he had sought
so far, was found.

But amid stern or lovely nature, in the perils of the forest or its
overwhelming peacefulness, still there had been two phantoms, the
companions of his way. Like all other men around whom an engrossing purpose wreathes itself, he was insulated from the mass of
human kind. He had no aim—no pleasure—no sympathies—but
what were ultimately connected with his art. Though gentle in
manner and upright in intent and action, he did not possess kindly

feelings; his heart was cold; no living creature could be brought near enough to keep him warm.[5] For these two beings, however, he had felt, in its greatest intensity, the sort of interest which always allied him to the subjects of his pencil. He had pried into their souls with his keenest insight, and pictured the result upon their features with his utmost skill, so as barely to fall short of that standard which no genius ever reached, his own severe conception. He had caught from the duskiness of the future—at least, so he fancied—a fearful secret, and had obscurely revealed it on the portraits. So much of himself—of his imagination and all other powers—had been lavished on the study of Walter and Elinor, that he almost regarded them as creations of his own, like the thousands with which he had peopled the realms of Picture. Therefore did they flit through the twilight of the woods, hover on the mist of waterfalls, look forth from the mirror of the lake, nor melt away in the noontide sun. They haunted his pictorial fancy, not as mockeries of life, nor pale goblins of the dead, but in the guise of portraits, each with the unalterable expression which his magic had evoked from the caverns of the soul. He could not recross the Atlantic till he had again beheld the originals of those airy pictures.

"O glorious Art!" thus mused the enthusiastic painter as he trod the street, "thou art the image of the Creator's own. The innumerable forms, that wander in nothingness, start into being at thy beck. The dead live again. Thou recallest them to their old scenes, and givest their gray shadows the lustre of a better life, at once earthly and immortal. Thou snatchest back the fleeting moments of History. With thee there is no Past, for, at thy touch, all that is great becomes forever present; and illustrious men live through long ages, in the visible performance of the very deeds which made them what they are. O potent Art! as thou bringest the faintly revealed Past to stand in that narrow strip of sunlight, which we call Now, canst thou summon the shrouded Future to meet her there? Have I not achieved it? Am I not thy Prophet?"

Thus, with a proud, yet melancholy fervor, did he almost cry aloud, as he passed through the toilsome street, among people that knew not of his reveries, nor could understand nor care for them. It is not good for man to cherish a solitary ambition. Unless there be those around him by whose example he may regulate himself, his thoughts, desires, and hopes will become extravagant, and he the semblance, perhaps the reality, of a madman. Reading other bosoms with an acuteness almost preternatural, the painter failed to see the disorder of his own.

5. It has been suggested that this passage represents Hawthorne's view of his own situation as an artist. Owen Warland, "the artist of the beautiful," has a less difficult spiritual problem because he does not deal with human character in his art.

"And this should be the house," said he, looking up and down the front, before he knocked. "Heaven help my brains! That picture! Methinks it will never vanish. Whether I look at the windows or the door, there it is framed within them, painted strongly, and glowing in the richest tints—the faces of the portraits—the figures and action of the sketch!"

He knocked.

"The Portraits! Are they within?" inquired he of the domestic; then recollecting himself—"your master and mistress! Are they at home?"

"They are, sir," said the servant, adding, as he noticed that picturesque aspect of which the painter could never divest himself, "and the Portraits too!"

The guest was admitted into a parlor, communicating by a central door with an interior room of the same size. As the first apartment was empty, he passed to the entrance of the second, within which his eyes were greeted by those living personages, as well as their pictured representatives, who had long been the objects of so singular an interest. He involuntarily paused on the threshold.

They had not perceived his approach. Walter and Elinor were standing before the portraits, whence the former had just flung back the rich and voluminous folds of the silken curtain, holding its golden tassel with one hand, while the other grasped that of his bride. The pictures, concealed for months, gleamed forth again in undiminished splendor, appearing to throw a sombre light across the room, rather than to be disclosed by a borrowed radiance. That of Elinor had been almost prophetic. A pensiveness, and next a gentle sorrow, had successively dwelt upon her countenance, deepening, with the lapse of time, into a quiet anguish. A mixture of affright would now have made it the very expression of the portrait. Walter's face was moody and dull, or animated only by fitful flashes, which left a heavier darkness for their momentary illumination. He looked from Elinor to her portrait, and thence to his own, in the contemplation of which he finally stood absorbed.

The painter seemed to hear the step of Destiny approaching behind him, on its progress towards its victims. A strange thought darted into his mind. Was not his own the form in which that destiny had embodied itself, and he a chief agent of the coming evil which he had foreshadowed?[6]

6. This speculation resembles another question that interested Hawthorne: whether sin meditated were not essentially the same as sin realized in action. After a considerable discussion of the problem in "Fancy's Show Box," he concludes, "Let us hope, therefore, that all the dreadful consequences of sin will not be incurred, unless the act have set its seal upon the thought." Nevertheless, "man must not disclaim his brotherhood, even with the guiltiest, since, though his hand be clean, his heart has surely been polluted by the flitting phantoms of iniquity." One may think here of the conclusion of *The Scarlet Letter:* "Among many morals which press upon us from the poor

Still, Walter remained silent before the picture, communing with it as with his own heart, and abandoning himself to the spell of evil influence that the painter had cast upon the features. Gradually his eyes kindled; while as Elinor watched the increasing wildness of his face, her own assumed a look of terror; and when at last he turned upon her, the resemblance of both to their portraits was complete.

"Our fate is upon us!" howled Walter. "Die!"

Drawing a knife, he sustained her, as she was sinking to the ground, and aimed it at her bosom. In the action, and in the look and attitude of each, the painter beheld the figures of his sketch. The picture, with all its tremendous coloring, was finished.

"Hold, madman!" cried he, sternly.

He had advanced from the door, and interposed himself between the wretched beings, with the same sense of power to regulate their destiny as to alter a scene upon the canvas. He stood like a magician, controlling the phantoms which he had evoked.

"What!" muttered Walter Ludlow, as he relapsed from fierce excitement into silent gloom. "Does Fate impede its own decree?"

"Wretched lady!" said the painter, "did I not warn you?"

"You did," replied Elinor, calmly, as her terror gave place to the quiet grief which it had disturbed. "But—I love him!"

Is there not a deep moral in the tale? Could the result of one, or all our deeds, be shadowed forth and set before us, some would call it Fate, and hurry onward, others be swept along by their passionate desires, and none be turned aside by the PROPHETIC PICTURES.

1837

Roger Malvin's Burial[7]

One of the few incidents of Indian warfare naturally susceptible of the moonlight of romance was that expedition undertaken for the defence of the frontiers in the year 1725, which resulted in

minister's miserable experience, we put only this into a sentence:—'Be true! Be true! Be true! Show freely to the world, if not your worst, yet some trait whereby the worst may be inferred!' " The artist, as in "The Prophetic Pictures," runs the moral danger of penetrating the guilty human heart without sympathy, himself untouched and unparticipating. The problem is most fully canvassed in Miles Coverdale, the narrator of *The Blithedale Romance.*
7. This early story of Hawthorne, like the following "My Kinsman, Major Molineux," has aroused much recent critical interest after a long period of relative neglect. It was written by 1829, and intended as one of a collection to be called *Provincial Tales,* which did not materialize. It was first printed in *The Token* for 1832, and not reprinted by Hawthorne until 1846 in *Mosses from an Old Manse.* Randall Stewart places its hero Reuben Bourne in a sequence of characters—Bourne, Mr. Hooper of "The Minister's Black Veil," and Roderick Elliston in "Egotism; or, The Bosom Serpent"—who lead to Dimmesdale in *The Scarlet Letter* as men "tortured by a secret guilt" (*American Notebooks,* p. xlvii).

the well-remembered "Lovell's Fight."[8] Imagination, by casting certain circumstances judicially into the shade, may see much to admire in the heroism of a little band who gave battle to twice their number in the heart of the enemy's country. The open bravery displayed by both parties was in accordance with civilized ideas of valor; and chivalry itself might not blush to record the deeds of one or two individuals. The battle, though so fatal to those who fought, was not unfortunate in its consequences to the country; for it broke the strength of a tribe and conduced to the peace which subsisted during several ensuing years. History and tradition are unusually minute in their memorials of their affair; and the captain of a scouting party of frontier men has acquired as actual a military renown as many a victorious leader of thousands. Some of the incidents contained in the following pages will be recognized, notwithstanding the substitution of fictitious names, by such as have heard, from old men's lips, the fate of the few combatants who were in a condition to retreat after "Lovell's Fight."

. . . . . .

The early sunbeams hovered cheerfully upon the tree-tops, beneath which two weary and wounded men had stretched their limbs the night before. Their bed of withered oak leaves was strewn upon the small level space, at the foot of a rock, situated near the summit of one of the gentle swells by which the face of the country is there diversified. The mass of granite, rearing its smooth, flat surface fifteen or twenty feet above their heads, was not unlike a gigantic gravestone, upon which the veins seemed to form an inscription in forgotten characters. On a tract of several acres around this rock, oaks and other hard-wood trees had supplied the place of the pines, which were the usual growth of the land; and a young and vigorous sapling stood close beside the travellers.

The severe wound of the elder man had probably deprived him of sleep; for, so soon as the first ray of sunshine rested on the top of the highest tree, he reared himself painfully from his recumbent posture and sat erect. The deep lines of his countenance and the scattered gray of his hair marked him as past the middle age; but his muscular frame would, but for the effect of his wound, have been as capable of sustaining fatigue as in the early vigor of life. Languor and exhaustion now sat upon his haggard features; and the despairing glance which he sent forward through the depths of the forest proved his own conviction that his pilgrimage was at an end. He next turned his eyes to the companion who reclined by his side. The youth—for he had scarcely attained the years of man-

8. Against the Penobscot Indians. For discussion of Hawthorne's sources see G. Harrison Orians, "The Source of Hawthorne's 'Roger Malvin's Burial,' " *American Literature,* X (November, 1938), 313–18.

hood—lay, with his head upon his arm, in the embrace of an unquiet sleep, which a thrill of pain from his wounds seemed each moment on the point of breaking. His right hand grasped a musket; and, to judge from the violent action of his features, his slumbers were bringing back a vision of the conflict of which he was one of the few survivors. A shout—deep and loud in his dreaming fancy—found its way in an imperfect murmur to his lips; and, starting even at the slight sound of his own voice, he suddenly awoke. The first act of reviving recollection was to make anxious inquiries respecting the condition of his wounded fellow-traveller. The latter shook his head.

"Reuben, my boy," said he, "this rock beneath which we sit will serve for an old hunter's gravestone. There is many and many a long mile of howling wilderness before us yet; nor would it avail me anything if the smoke of my own chimney were but on the other side of that swell of land. The Indian bullet was deadlier than I thought."

"You are weary with our three days' travel," replied the youth, "and a little longer rest will recruit you. Sit you here while I search the woods for the herbs and roots that must be our sustenance; and, having eaten, you shall lean on me, and we will turn our faces homeward. I doubt not that, with my help, you can attain to some one of the frontier garrisons."

"There is not two days' life in me, Reuben," said the other, calmly, "and I will no longer burden you with my useless body, when you can scarcely support your own. Your wounds are deep and your strength is failing fast; yet, if you hasten onward alone, you may be preserved. For me there is no hope, and I will await death here."

"If it must be so, I will remain and watch by you," said Reuben, resolutely.

"No, my son, no," rejoined his companion. "Let the wish of a dying man have weight with you; give me one grasp of your hand and get you hence. Think you that my last moments will be eased by the thought that I leave you to die a more lingering death? I have loved you like a father, Reuben; and at a time like this I should have something of a father's authority. I charge you to be gone that I may die in peace."

"And because you have been a father to me, should I therefore leave you to perish and to lie unburied in the wilderness?" exclaimed the youth. "No; if your end be in truth approaching, I will watch by you and receive your parting words. I will dig a grave here by the rock, in which, if my weakness overcome me, we will rest together; or, if Heaven gives me strength, I will seek my way home."

"In the cities and wherever men dwell," replied the other, "they bury their dead in the earth; they hide them from the sight of the living; but here, where no step may pass perhaps for a hundred years, wherefore should I not rest beneath the open sky, covered only by the oak leaves when the autumn winds shall strew them? And for a monument, here is this gray rock, on which my dying hand shall carve the name of Roger Malvin; and the traveller in days to come will know that here sleeps a hunter and a warrior. Tarry not, then, for a folly like this, but hasten away, if not for your own sake, for hers who will else be desolate."

Malvin spoke the last few words in a faltering voice, and their effect upon his companion was strongly visible. They reminded him that there were other and less questionable duties than that of sharing the fate of a man whom his death could not benefit. Nor can it be affirmed that no selfish feeling strove to enter Reuben's heart, though the consciousness made him more earnestly resist his companion's entreaties.

"How terrible to wait the slow approach of death in this solitude!" exclaimed he. "A brave man does not shrink in the battle; and, when friends stand round the bed, even women may die composedly; but here"—

"I shall not shrink even here, Reuben Bourne," interrupted Malvin. "I am a man of no weak heart, and, if I were, there is a surer support than that of earthly friends. You are young, and life is dear to you. Your last moments will need comfort far more than mine; and when you have laid me in the earth, and are alone, and night is settling on the forest, you will feel all the bitterness of the death that may now be escaped. But I will urge no selfish motive to your generous nature. Leave me for my sake, that, having said a prayer for your safety, I may have space to settle my account undisturbed by worldly sorrows."

"And your daughter,—how shall I dare to meet her eye?" exclaimed Reuben. "She will ask the fate of her father, whose life I vowed to defend with my own. Must I tell her that he travelled three days' march with me from the field of battle and that then I left him to perish in the wilderness? Were it not better to lie down and die by your side than to return safe and say this to Dorcas?"

"Tell my daughter," said Roger Malvin, "that, though yourself sore wounded, and weak, and weary, you led my tottering footsteps many a mile, and left me only at my earnest entreaty, because I would not have your blood upon my soul. Tell her that through pain and danger you were faithful, and that, if your lifeblood could have saved me, it would have flowed to its last drop; and tell her that you will be something dearer than a father, and that my blessing is with you both, and that my dying eyes can see a long and pleasant path in which you will journey together."

As Melvin spoke he almost raised himself from the ground, and the energy of his concluding words seemed to fill the wild and lonely forest with a vision of happiness; but, when he sank exhausted upon his bed of oak leaves, the light which had kindled in Reuben's eye was quenched. He felt as if it were both sin and folly to think of happiness at such a moment. His companion watched his changing countenance, and sought with generous art to wile him to his own good.

"Perhaps I deceive myself in regard to the time I have to live," he resumed. "It may be that, with speedy assistance, I might recover of my wound. The foremost fugitives must, ere this, have carried tidings of our fatal battle to the frontiers, and parties will be out to succor those in like condition with ourselves. Should you meet one of these and guide them hither, who can tell but that I may sit by my own fireside again?"

A mournful smile strayed across the features of the dying man as he insinuated that unfounded hope,—which, however, was not without its effect on Reuben. No merely selfish motive, nor even the desolate condition of Dorcas, could have induced him to desert his companion at such a moment—but his wishes seized on the thought that Malvin's life might be preserved, and his sanguine nature heightened almost to certainty the remote possibility of procuring human aid.

"Surely there is reason, weighty reason, to hope that friends are not far distant," he said, half aloud. "There fled one coward, unwounded, in the beginning of the fight, and most probably he made good speed. Every true man on the frontier would shoulder his musket at the news; and, though no party may range so far into the woods as this, I shall perhaps encounter them in one day's march. Counsel me faithfully," he added, turning to Malvin, in distrust of his own motives. "Were your situation mine, would you desert me while life remained?"

"It is now twenty years," replied Roger Malvin,—sighing, however, as he secretly acknowledged the wide dissimilarity between the two cases,—"it is now twenty years since I escaped with one dear friend from Indian captivity near Montreal. We journeyed many days through the woods, till at length overcome with hunger and weariness, my friend lay down and besought me to leave him; for he knew that, if I remained, we both must perish; and, with but little hope of obtaining succor, I heaped a pillow of dry leaves beneath his head and hastened on."

"And did you return in time to save him?" asked Reuben, hanging on Malvin's words as if they were to be prophetic of his own success.

"I did," answered the other. "I came upon the camp of a hunting party before sunset of the same day. I guided them to the spot where my comrade was expecting death; and he is now a hale and hearty man upon his own farm, far within the frontiers, while I lie wounded here in the depths of the wilderness."

This example, powerful in affecting Reuben's decision, was aided, unconsciously to himself, by the hidden strength of many another motive. Roger Malvin perceived that the victory was nearly won.

"Now, go, my son, and Heaven prosper you!" he said. "Turn not back with your friends when you meet them, lest your wounds and weariness overcome you; but send hitherward two or three, that may be spared, to search for me; and believe me, Reuben, my heart will be lighter with every step you take towards home." Yet there was, perhaps, a change both in his countenance and voice as he spoke thus; for, after all, it was a ghastly fate to be left expiring in the wilderness.

Reuben Bourne, but half convinced that he was acting rightly, at length raised himself from the ground and prepared himself for his departure. And first, though contrary to Malvin's wishes, he collected a stock of roots and herbs, which had been their only food during the last two days. This useless supply he placed within reach of the dying man, for whom, also, he swept together a bed of dry oak leaves. Then climbing to the summit of the rock, which on one side was rough and broken, he bent the oak sapling downward, and bound his handkerchief to the topmost branch. This precaution was not unnecessary to direct any who might come in search of Malvin; for every part of the rock, except its broad, smooth front, was concealed at a little distance by the dense undergrowth of the forest. The handkerchief had been the bandage of a wound upon Reuben's arm; and, as he bound it to the tree, he vowed by the blood that stained it that he would return, either to save his companion's life or to lay his body in the grave. He then descended, and stood, with downcast eyes, to receive Roger Malvin's parting words.

The experience of the latter suggested much and minute advice respecting the youth's journey through the trackless forest. Upon this subject he spoke with calm earnestness, as if he were sending Reuben to the battle or the chase while he himself remained secure at home, and not as if the human countenance that was about to leave him were the last he would ever behold. But his firmness was shaken before he concluded.

"Carry my blessing to Dorcas, and say that my last prayer shall be for her and you. Bid her to have no hard thoughts because you left me here,"—Reuben's heart smote him,—"for that your life would not have weighed with you if its sacrifice could have done me good. She will marry you after she has mourned a little while for her father; and Heaven grant you long and happy days, and may your children's children stand round your death bed! And, Reuben," added he, as the weakness of mortality made its way at last, "return, when your wounds are healed and your weariness refreshed,—return to this wild rock, and lay my bones in the grave, and say a prayer over them."

An almost superstitious regard, arising perhaps from the customs of the Indians, whose war was with the dead as well as the living, was paid by the frontier inhabitants to the rites of sepulture; and there are many instances of the sacrifice of life in the attempt to bury those who had fallen by the "sword of the wilderness." Reuben, therefore, felt the full importance of the promise which he most solemnly made to return and perform Roger Malvin's obsequies. It was remarkable that the latter, speaking his whole heart in his parting words, no longer endeavored to persuade the youth that even the speediest succor might avail to the preservation of his life. Reuben was internally convinced that he should see Malvin's living face no more. His generous nature would fain have delayed him, at whatever risk, till the dying scene were past; but the desire of existence and the hope of happiness had strengthened in his heart, and he was unable to resist them.

"It is enough," said Roger Malvin, having listened to Reuben's promise. "Go, and God speed you!"

The youth pressed his hand in silence, turned, and was departing. His slow and faltering steps, however, had borne him but a little way before Malvin's voice recalled him.

"Reuben, Reuben," said he, faintly; and Reuben returned and knelt down by the dying man.

"Raise me, and let me lean against the rock," was his last request. "My face will be turned towards home, and I shall see you a moment longer as you pass among the trees."

Reuben, having made the desired alteration in his companion's posture, again began his solitary pilgrimage. He walked more hastily at first than was consistent with his strength; for a sort of guilty feeling, which sometimes torments men in their most justifiable acts, caused him to seek concealment from Malvin's eyes; but after he had trodden far upon the rustling forest leaves he crept back, impelled by a wild and painful curiosity, and, sheltered by the earthy roots of an uptorn tree, gazed earnestly at the desolate man. The morning sun was unclouded, and the trees and shrubs imbibed the sweet air of the month of May; yet there seemed a gloom on Nature's face, as if she sympathized with mortal pain and sorrow. Roger Malvin's hands were uplifted in a fervent prayer, some of the words of which stole through the stillness of the woods and entered Reuben's heart, torturing it with an unutterable pang. They were the broken accents of a petition for his own happiness and that of Dorcas; and, as the youth listened, conscience, or something in its similitude, pleaded strongly with him to return and lie down again by the rock. He felt how hard was the doom of the kind and generous being whom he had deserted in his extremity. Death would come like the slow approach of a corpse, stealing gradually towards him through the forest, and showing its ghastly and motionless features from behind a nearer and yet a nearer tree. But such must have been Reuben's own fate had he tarried another sunset; and who shall impute blame to him if he shrink from so useless a sacrifice? As he gave a parting look, a breeze waved the little banner upon the sapling oak and reminded Reuben of his vow.

. . . . . .

Many circumstances combined to retard the wounded traveller in his way to the frontiers. On the second day the clouds, gathering densely over the sky, precluded the possibility of regulating his course by the position of the sun; and he knew not but that every effort of his almost exhausted strength was removing him farther from the home he sought. His scanty sustenance was supplied by the berries and other spontaneous products of the forest. Herds of deer, it is true, sometimes bounded past him, and partridges frequently whirred up before his footsteps; but his ammunition had been expended in the fight, and he had no means of slaying them. His wounds, irritated by the constant exertion in which lay the only hope of life, wore away his strength and at intervals confused his reason. But, even in the wanderings of intellect, Reuben's young heart clung strongly to existence; and it was only through absolute incapacity of motion that he at last sank down beneath a tree, compelled there to await death.

In this situation he was discovered by a party who, upon the first intelligence of the fight, had been despatched to the relief of the survivors. They conveyed him to the nearest settlement, which chanced to be that of his own residence.

Dorcas, in the simplicity of the olden time, watched by the bedside of her wounded lover, and administered all those comforts that are in the sole gift of woman's heart and hand. During several days Reuben's recollection strayed drowsily among the perils and hardships through which he had passed, and he was incapable of returning definite answers to the inquiries with which many were eager to harass him. No authentic particulars of the battle had yet been circulated; nor could mothers, wives, and children tell whether their loved ones were detained by captivity or by the stronger chain of death. Dorcas nourished her apprehensions in silence till one afternoon when Reuben awoke from an unquiet sleep, and seemed to recognize her more perfectly than at any previous time. She saw that his intellect had become composed, and she could no longer restrain her filial anxiety.

"My father, Reuben?" she began; but the change in her lover's countenance made her pause.

The youth shrank as if with a bitter pain, and the blood gushed vividly into his wan and hollow cheeks. His first impulse was to cover his face; but, apparently with a desperate effort, he half raised himself and spoke vehemently, defending himself against an imaginary accusation.

"Your father was sore wounded in the battle, Dorcas; and he bade me not burden myself with him, but only to lead him to the lakeside, that he might quench his thirst and die. But I would not desert the old man in his extremity, and, though bleeding myself, I supported him; I gave him half my strength, and led him away with me. For three days we journeyed on together, and your father was sustained beyond my hopes, but, awaking at sunrise on the fourth day, I found him faint and exhausted; he was unable to proceed; his life had ebbed away fast; and"—

"He died!" exclaimed Dorcas, faintly.

Reuben felt it impossible to acknowledge that his selfish love of life had hurried him away before her father's fate was decided. He spoke not; he only bowed his head; and between shame and exhaustion, sank back and hid his face in the pillow. Dorcas wept when her fears were thus confirmed; but the shock, as it had been long anticipated, was on that account the less violent.

"You dug a grave for my poor father in the wilderness, Reuben?" was the question by which her filial piety manifested itself.

"My hands were weak; but I did what I could," replied the youth in a smothered tone. "There stands a noble tombstone above his head; and I would to Heaven I slept as soundly as he!"

Dorcas, perceiving the wildness of his latter words, inquired no further at the time; but her heart found ease in the thought that Roger Malvin had not lacked such funeral rites as it was possible to bestow. The tale of Reuben's courage and fidelity lost nothing when she communicated it to her friends; and the poor youth, tottering from his sick chamber to breathe the sunny air, experienced from every tongue the miserable and humiliating torture of unmerited praise. All acknowledged that he might worthily demand the hand of the fair maiden to whose father he had been "faithful unto death;" and, as my tale is not of love, it shall suffice to say that in the space of a few months Reuben became the husband of Dorcas Malvin. During the marriage ceremony the bride was covered with blushes, but the bridegroom's face was pale.

There was now in the breast of Reuben Bourne an incommunicable thought—something which he was to conceal most heedfully from her whom he most loved and trusted. He regretted, deeply and bitterly, the moral cowardice that had restrained his words when he was about to disclose the truth to Dorcas; but pride, the fear of losing her affection, the dread of universal scorn, forbade him to rectify this falsehood. He felt that for leaving Roger Malvin he deserved no censure. His presence, the gratuitous sacrifice of his own life, would have added only another and a needless agony to the last moments of the dying man; but concealment had imparted to a justifiable act much of the secret effect of guilt; and Reuben, while reason told him that he had done right, experienced in no small degree the mental horrors which punish the perpetrator of undiscovered crime. By a certain association of ideas, he at times almost imagined himself a murderer. For years, also, a thought would occasionally recur, which, though he perceived all its folly and extravagance, he had not power to banish from his mind. It was a haunting and torturing fancy that his father-in-law was yet sitting at the foot of the rock, on the withered forest leaves, alive, and awaiting his pledged assistance. These mental deceptions, however, came and went, nor did he ever mistake them for realities, but in the calmest and clearest moods of his mind he was conscious that he had a deep vow unredeemed, and that an unburied corpse was calling to him out of the wilderness. Yet such was the consequence of his prevarication that he could not obey the call. It was now too late to require the assistance of Roger Malvin's friends in performing his long-deferred sepulture; and superstitious fears, of which none were more susceptible than the people of the outward settlements, forbade Reuben to go alone. Neither did he know where in the pathless and illimitable forest to seek that smooth and lettered rock at the base of which the body lay: his remembrance of every portion of his travel thence was indistinct, and the latter part had left no impression upon his mind. There was, however, a continual impulse, a voice audible only to himself, commanding him to go forth and redeem his vow; and he had a strange impression that, were he to make the trial, he would be led straight to Malvin's bones. But year after year that summons, unheard but felt, was disobeyed. His one secret thought became like a chain binding down his spirit and like a serpent gnawing into his heart; and he was transformed into a sad and downcast yet irritable man.

In the course of a few years after their marriage changes began to be visible in the external prosperity of Reuben and Dorcas. The only riches of the former had been his stout heart and strong arm; but the latter, her father's sole heiress, had made her husband master of a farm, under older cultivation, larger, and better stocked than most of the frontier establishments. Reuben Bourne, however, was a neglectful husbandman; and, while the lands of the other settlers became annually more fruitful, his deteriorated in the same proportion. The discouragements to agriculture were greatly lessened by the cessation of Indian war, during which men held the plough in one hand and the musket in the other, and were fortunate if the products of their dangerous labor were not destroyed, either in the field or in the barn, by the savage enemy. But Reuben did not profit by the altered condition of the country; nor can it be denied that his intervals of industrious attention to his affairs were but scantily rewarded with success. The irritability by which he had recently become distinguished was another cause of his declining prosperity, as it occasioned frequent quarrels in his unavoidable intercourse with the neighboring settlers. The results of these were innumerable lawsuits; for the people of New England, in the earliest stages and wildest circumstances of the country, adopted, whenever attainable, the legal mode of deciding their differences. To be brief, the world did not go well with Reuben Bourne; and, though not till many years after his marriage, he was finally a ruined man, with but one remaining expedient against the evil fate that had pursued him. He was to throw sunlight into some deep recess of the forest, and seek subsistence from the virgin bosom of the wilderness.

The only child of Reuben and Dorcas was a son, now arrived at the age of fifteen years, beautiful in youth, and giving promise of a glorious manhood. He was peculiarly qualified for, and already began to excel in, the wild accomplishments of frontier life. His foot was fleet, his aim true, his apprehension quick, his heart glad and high; and all who anticipated the return of Indian war spoke of Cyrus Bourne as a future leader in the land. The boy was loved by his father with a deep and silent strength, as if whatever was good and happy in his own nature had been transferred to his child, carrying his affections with it. Even Dorcas, though loving and beloved, was far less dear to him; for Reuben's secret thoughts and insulated emotions had gradually made him a selfish man, and he could no longer love deeply except where he saw or imagined some reflection or likeness of his own mind. In Cyrus he recognized what he had himself been in other days; and at intervals he seemed to partake of the boy's spirit, and to be revived with a fresh and happy life. Reuben was accompanied by his son in the expedition, for the purpose of selecting a tract of land and felling and burning the timber, which necessarily preceded the removal of the household gods. Two months of autumn were thus occupied, after which Reuben Bourne and his young hunter returned to spend their last winter in the settlements.

. . . . . .

It was early in the month of May that the little family snapped assunder whatever tendrils of affections had clung to inanimate objects, and bade farewell to the few who, in the blight of fortune, called themselves their friends. The sadness of the parting moment had, to each of the pilgrims, its peculiar alleviations. Reuben, a moody man, and misanthropic because unhappy, strode onward with his usual stern brown and downcast eye, feeling few regrets and disdaining to acknowledge any. Dorcas, while she wept abundantly over the broken ties by which her simple and affectionate nature had bound itself to everything, felt that the inhabitants of her inmost heart moved on with her, and that all else would be supplied wherever she might go. And the boy dashed one teardrop from his eye, and thought of the adventurous pleasures of the untrodden forest.

Oh, who, in the enthusiasm of a daydream, has not wished that he were a wanderer in a world of summer wilderness, with one fair and gentle being hanging lightly on his arm? In youth his free and exulting step would know no barrier but the rolling ocean or the snow-topped mountains; calmer manhood would choose a home where Nature had strewn a double wealth in the vale of some transparent stream; and when hoary age, after long, long years of that pure life, stole on and found him there, it would find him the father of a race, the patriarch of a people, the founder of a mighty nation yet to be. When death, like the sweet sleep which we welcome after a day of happiness, came over him, his far descendants would mourn over the venerated dust. Enveloped by tradition in mysterious attributes, the men of future generations would call him godlike; and remote posterity would see him standing, dimly glorious, far up the valley of a hundred centuries.

The tangled and gloomy forest through which the personages of my tale were wandering differed widely from the dreamer's land of fantasy; yet there was something in their way of life that Nature asserted as her own, and the gnawing cares which went with them from the world were all that now obstructed their happiness. One stout and shaggy steed, the bearer of all their wealth, did not shrink from the added weight of Dorcas; although her hardy breeding sustained her, during the latter part of each day's journey, by her husband's side. Reuben and his son, their muskets on their shoulders and their axes slung behind them, kept an unwearied pace, each watching with a hunter's eye for the game that supplied their food. When hunger bade, they halted and prepared their meal on the bank of some unpolluted forest brook, which, as they knelt down with thirsty lips to drink, murmured a sweet unwillingness, like a maiden at love's first kiss. They slept beneath a hut of branches, and awoke at peep of light refreshed for the toils of another day. Dorcas and the boy went on joyously, and even Reuben's spirit shone at intervals with an outward gladness; but inwardly there was a cold, cold sorrow, which he compared to the snowdrifts lying deep in the glens and hollows of the rivulets while the leaves were brightly green above.

Cyrus Bourne was sufficiently skilled in the travel of the woods to observe that his father did not adhere to the course they had pursued in their expedition of the preceding autumn. They were now keeping farther to the north, striking out more directly from the settlements, and into a region of which savage beasts and savage men were as yet the sole possessors. The boy sometimes hinted his opinions upon the subject, and Reuben listened attentively, and once or twice altered the direction of their march in accordance with his son's counsel; but, having so done, he seemed ill at ease. His quick and wandering glances were sent forward, apparently in search of enemies lurking behind the tree trunks; and, seeing nothing there, he would cast his eyes backwards as if in fear of some pursuer. Cyrus, perceiving that his father gradually resumed the old direction, forbore to interfere; nor, though something began to weigh upon his heart, did his adventurous nature permit him to regret the increased length and the mystery of their way.

On the afternoon of the fifth day they halted, and made their simple encampment nearly an hour before sunset. The face of the country, for the last few miles, had been diversified by swells of land resembling huge waves of a petrified sea; and in one of the corresponding hollows, a wild and romantic spot, had the family reared their hut and kindled their fire. There is something chilling, and yet heart-warming, in the thought of these three, united by strong bands of love and insulated from all that breathe beside. The dark and gloomy pines looked down upon them, and, as the wind swept through their tops, a pitying sound was heard in the forest; or did those old trees groan in fear that men were come to lay the axe to their roots at last? Reuben and his son, while Dorcas made ready their meal, proposed to wander out in search of game, of which that day's march had afforded no supply. The boy, promising not to quit the vicinity of the encampment, bounded off with a step as light and elastic as that of the deer he hoped to slay; while his father, feeling a transient happiness as he gazed after him, was about to pursue an opposite direction. Dorcas, in the meanwhile, had seated herself near their fire of fallen branches, upon the mossgrown and mouldering trunk of a tree uprooted years before. Her employment, diversified by an occasional glance at the pot, now beginning to simmer over the blaze, was the perusal of the current year's Massachusetts Almanac, which, with the exception of an old black-letter Bible, comprised all the literary wealth of the family. None pay a greater regard to arbitrary divisions of time than those who are excluded from society; and Dorcas mentioned, as if the information were of importance, that it was now the twelfth of May. Her husband started.

"The twelfth of May! I should remember it well," muttered he, while many thoughts occasioned a momentary confusion in his mind. "Where am I? Whither am I wandering? Where did I leave him?"

Dorcas, too well accustomed to her husband's wayward moods to note any peculiarity of demeanor, now laid aside the almanac and addressed him in that mournful tone which the tender hearted appropriate to griefs long cold and dead.

"It was near this time of the month, eighteen years ago, that my poor father left this world for a better. He had a kind arm to hold his head and a kind voice to cheer him, Reuben, in his last moments; and the thought of the faithful care you took of him has comforted me many a time since. Oh, death would have been awful to a solitary man in a wild place like this!"

"Pray Heaven, Dorcas," said Reuben, in a broken voice,— "pray Heaven that neither of us three dies solitary and lies unburied in this howling wilderness!" And he hastened away, leaving her to watch the fire beneath the gloomy pines.

Reuben Bourne's rapid pace gradually slackened as the pang, unintentionally inflicted by the words of Dorcas, became less acute. Many strange reflections, however, thronged upon him; and, straying onward rather like a sleep walker than a hunter, it was attributable to no care of his own that his devious course kept him in the vicinity of the encampment. His steps were imperceptibly led almost in a circle; nor did he observe that he was on the verge of a tract of land heavily timbered, but not with pine-trees. The place of the latter was here supplied by oaks and other of the harder woods; and around their roots clustered a dense and bushy under-growth, leaving, however, barren spaces between the trees, thick strewn with withered leaves. Whenever the rustling of the branches or the creaking of the trunks made a sound, as if the forest were waking from slumber, Reuben instinctively raised the musket that rested on his arm, and cast a quick, sharp glance on every side; but, convinced by a partial observation that no animal was near, he would again give himself up to his thoughts. He was musing on the strange influence that had led him away from his premeditated course, and so far into the depths of the wilderness. Unable to penetrate to the secret place of his soul where his motives lay hidden, he believed that a supernatural voice had called him onward, and that a supernatural power had obstructed his retreat. He trusted that it was Heaven's intent to afford him an opportunity of expiating his sin; he hoped that he might find the bones so long unburied; and that, having laid the earth over them, peace would throw its sunlight into the sepulchre of his heart. From these thoughts he was aroused by a rustling in the forest at some distance from the spot to which he had wandered. Perceiving the motion of some object behind a thick veil of undergrowth, he fired, with the instinct of a hunter and the aim of a practised marksman. A low moan, which told his success, and by which even animals can express their dying agony, was unheeded by Reuben Bourne. What were the recollections now breaking upon him?

The thicket into which Reuben had fired was near the summit of a swell of land, and was clustered around the base of a rock, which, in the shape and smoothness of one of its surfaces, was not unlike a gigantic gravestone. As if reflected in a mirror, its likeness was in Reuben's memory. He even recognized the veins which seemed to form an inscription in forgotten characters: everything remained the same, except that a thick covert of bushes shrouded the lower part of the rock, and would have hidden Roger Malvin had he still been sitting there. Yet in the next moment Reuben's eye was caught by another change that time had effected since he last stood where he was now standing again behind the earthy roots of the uptorn tree. The sapling to which he had bound the bloodstained symbol of his vow had increased and strengthened into an oak, far indeed from its maturity, but with no mean spread of shadowy branches. There was one singularity observable in this tree which made Reuben tremble. The middle and lower branches were in luxuriant life, and an excess of vegetation had fringed the trunk almost to the ground; but a blight had apparently stricken the upper part of the oak, and the very topmost bough was withered, sapless, and utterly dead. Reuben remembered how the little banner had fluttered on that topmost bough, when it was green and lovely, eighteen years before. Whose guilt had blasted it?

· · · · · ·

Dorcas, after the departure of the two hunters, continued her preparations for their evening repast. Her sylvan table was the moss-covered trunk of a large fallen tree, on the broadest part of which she had spread a snow-white cloth and arranged what were left of the bright pewter vessels that had been her pride in the settlements. It had a strange aspect, that one little spot of homely comfort in the desolate heart of Nature. The sunshine yet lingered upon the higher branches of the trees that grew on rising ground; but the shadows of evening had deepened into the hollow where the encampment was made, and the firelight began to redden as it gleamed up the tall trunks of the pines or hovered on the dense and obscure mass of foliage that circled round the spot. The heart of Dorcas was not sad; for she felt that it was better to journey in the wilderness with two whom she loved than to be a lonely woman in a crowd that cared not for her. As she busied herself in arranging seats of mouldering wood, covered with leaves, for Reuben and her son, her voice danced through the gloomy forest in the measure of a song that she had learned in youth. The rude melody, the production of a bard who won no name, was descriptive of a winter evening in a frontier cottage, when, secured from savage inroad by the high-piled snow-drifts, the family rejoiced by their own fireside. The whole song possessed the nameless charm peculiar to unborrowed thought, but four continually-recurring lines shone out from the rest like the blaze of the hearth whose joys they celebrated. Into them, working magic with a few simple words, the poet had instilled the very essence of domestic love and household happiness, and they were poetry and picture joined in one. As Dorcas sang, the walls of her forsaken home seemed to encircle her; she no longer saw the gloomy pines, nor heard the wind which still, as he began each verse, sent a heavy breath through the branches, and died away in a hollow moan from the burden of the song. She was aroused by the report of a gun in the vicinity of the encampment; and either the sudden sound, or her loneliness by the glowing fire, caused her to tremble violently. The next moment she laughed in the pride of a mother's heart.

"My beautiful young hunter! My boy has slain a deer!" she exclaimed, recollecting that in the direction whence the shot proceeded Cyrus had gone to the chase.

She waited a reasonable time to hear her son's light step bounding over the rustling leaves to tell of his success. But he did not immediately appear; and she sent her cheerful voice among the trees in search of him.

"Cyrus! Cyrus!"

His coming was still delayed; and she determined, as the report had apparently been very near, to seek for him in person. Her assistance, also, might be necessary in bringing home the venison which she flattered herself he had obtained. She therefore set forward, directing her steps by the long-past sound, and singing as she went, in order that the boy might be aware of her approach and run to meet her. From behind the trunk of every tree, and from every hiding-place in the thick foliage of the undergrowth, she hoped to discover the countenance of her son, laughing with the sportive mischief that is born of affection. The sun was now beneath the horizon, and the light that came down among the leaves was sufficiently dim to create many illusions in her expecting fancy. Several times she seemed indistinctly to see his face gazing out from among the leaves; and once she imagined that he stood beckoning to her at the base of a craggy rock. Keeping her eyes on this object, however, it proved to be no more than the trunk of an oak fringed to the very ground with little branches, one of which, thrust out farther than the rest, was shaken by the breeze. Making her way round the foot of the rock, she suddenly found herself close to her husband, who had approached in another direction. Leaning upon the butt of his gun, the muzzle of which rested upon the withered leaves, he was apparently absorbed in the contemplation of some object at his feet.

"How is this, Reuben? Have you slain the deer and fallen asleep over him?" exclaimed Dorcas, laughing cheerfully, on her first slight observation of his posture and appearance.

He stirred not, neither did he turn his eyes towards her; and a cold, shuddering fear, indefinite in its source and object, began to creep into her blood. She now perceived that her husband's face was ghastly pale, and his features were rigid, as if incapable of assuming any other expression than the strong despair which had hardened upon them. He gave not the slightest evidence that he was aware of her approach.

"For the love of Heaven, Reuben, speak to me!" cried Dorcas; and the strange sound of her own voice affrighted her even more than the dead silence.

Her husband started, stared into her face, drew her to the front of the rock, and pointed with his finger.

Oh, there lay the boy, asleep, but dreamless, upon the fallen forest leaves! His cheek rested upon his arm—his curled locks were thrown back from his brow—his limbs were slightly relaxed. Had a sudden weariness overcome the youthful hunter? Would his mother's voice arouse him? She knew that it was death.

"This broad rock is the gravestone of your near kindred, Dorcas," said her husband. "Your tears will fall at once over your father and your son."

She heard him not. With one wild shriek, that seemed to force its way from the sufferer's inmost soul, she sank insensibly by the side of her dead boy. At that moment the withered topmost bough of the oak loosened itself in the stilly air, and fell in soft, light fragments upon the rock, upon the leaves, upon Reuben, upon his wife and child, and upon Roger Malvin's bones. Then Reuben's heart was stricken, and the tears gushed out like water from a rock. The vow that the wounded youth had made the blighted man had come to redeem. His sin was expiated,—the curse was gone from him; and in the hour when he had shed blood dearer to him than his own, a prayer, the first for years, went up to Heaven from the lips of Reuben Bourne.

1829? 1832, 1846

My Kinsman, Major Molineux[9]

After the kings of Great Britain had assumed the right of appointing the colonial governors, the measures of the latter seldom met with the ready and generous approbation which had been paid to those of their predecessors, under the original charters. The people looked with most jealous scrutiny to the exercise of power which did not emanate from themselves, and they usually rewarded their rulers with slender gratitude for the compliances by which, in softening their instructions from beyond the sea, they had incurred the reprehension of those who gave them. The annals of Massachusetts Bay will inform us, that of six governors in the space of about forty years from the surrender of the old charter, under James II., two were imprisoned by a popular insurrection; a third, as Hutchinson[1] inclines to believe, was driven from the province by the whizzing of a musket-ball; a fourth, in the opinion of the same historian, was hastened to his grave by continual bickerings with the House of Representatives; and the remaining two, as well as their successors, till the revolution, were favored with few and brief intervals of peaceful sway. The inferior members of the court party, in times of high political excitement, led scarcely a more desirable life. These remarks may serve as a preface to the following adventures, which chanced upon a summer night, not far from a hundred years ago. The reader, in order to avoid a long and dry detail of colonial affairs, is requested to dispense with an account of the train of circumstances that had caused much temporary inflammation of the popu-

9. Published in *The Token* (1832); collected in *The Snow Image* (1851). A note, which is later (1836) than the story, suggests the red and black face of the "party-colored" character: "Our body to be possessed by two different spirits; so that half of the visage shall express one mood, and the other half another" (*Passages*, p. 42). Like "Young Goodman Brown," "My Kinsman, Major Molineux" examines the problem of growth and maturity, catching its hero at a crucial point of his development. Interest in it has therefore been stimulated by the increased interest of critics in depth psychology and in anthropological studies of "initiation" ceremonies.
1. Thomas Hutchinson, last royal governor of Massachusetts and the author of *History of Massachusetts Bay* (1764).

lar mind.

It was near nine o'clock of a moonlight evening, when a boat crossed the ferry with a single passenger, who had obtained his conveyance at that unusual hour by the promise of an extra fare. While he stood on the landing-place, searching in either pocket for the means of fulfilling his agreement, the ferryman lifted a lantern, by the aid of which, and the newly risen moon, he took a very accurate survey of the stranger's figure. He was a youth of barely eighteen years, evidently country-bred, and now, as it should seem, upon his first visit to town. He was clad in a coarse gray coat, well worn, but in excellent repair; his under garments were durably constructed of leather, and fitted tight to a pair of serviceable and well-shaped limbs; his stockings of blue yarn were the incontrovertible work of a mother or a sister; and on his head was a three-cornered hat, which in its better days had perhaps sheltered the graver brow of the lad's father. Under his left arm was a heavy cudgel formed of an oak sapling, and retaining a part of the hardened root; and his equipment was completed by a wallet, not so abundantly stocked as to incommode the vigorous shoulders on which it hung. Brown, curly hair, well-shaped features, and bright, cheerful eyes were nature's gifts, and worth all that art could have done for his adornment.

The youth, one of whose names was Robin, finally drew from his pocket the half of a little province bill of five shillings, which, in the depreciation in that sort of currency, did but satisfy the ferryman's demand, with the surplus of a sexangular piece of parchment, valued at three pence. He then walked forward into the town, with as light a step as if his day's journey had not already exceeded thirty miles, and with as eager an eye as if he were entering London city, instead of the little metropolis of a New England colony. Before Robin had proceeded far, however, it occurred to him that he knew not whither to direct his steps; so he paused, and looked up and down the narrow street, scrutinizing the small and mean wooden buildings that were scattered on either side.

"This low hovel cannot be my kinsman's dwelling," thought he, "nor yonder old house, where the moonlight enters at the broken casement; and truly I see none hereabouts that might be worthy of him. It would have been wise to inquire my way of the ferryman, and doubtless he would have gone with me, and earned a shilling from the Major for his pains. But the next man I meet will do as well."

He resumed his walk, and was glad to perceive that the street now became wider, and the houses more respectable in their appearance. He soon discerned a figure moving on moderately in advance, and hastened his steps to overtake it. As Robin drew nigh, he saw that the passenger was a man in years, with a full periwig of gray hair, a wide-skirted coat of dark cloth, and silk stockings rolled above his knees. He carried a long and polished cane, which he struck down perpendicularly before him at every step; and at regular intervals he uttered two successive hems, of a peculiarly solemn and sepulchral intonation. Having made these observations, Robin laid hold of the skirt of the old man's coat, just when the light from the open door and windows of a barber's shop fell upon both their figures.

"Good evening to you, honored sir," said he, making a low bow, and still retaining his hold of the skirt. "I pray you tell me whereabouts is the dwelling of my kinsman, Major Molineux."

The youth's question was uttered very loudly; and one of the barbers, whose razor was descending on a well-soaped chin, and another who was dressing a Ramillies wig, left their occupations, and came to the door. The citizen, in the mean time, turned a long-favored countenance upon Robin, and answered him in a tone of excessive anger and annoyance. His two sepulchral hems, however, broke into the very centre of his rebuke, with most singular effect, like a thought of the cold grave obtruding among wrathful passions.

"Let go my garment, fellow! I tell you, I know not the man you speak of. What! I have authority, I have—hem, hem—authority; and if this be the respect you show for your betters, your feet shall be brought acquainted with the stocks by daylight, tomorrow morning!"

Robin released the old man's skirt, and hastened away, pursued by an ill-mannered roar of laughter from the barber's shop. He was at first considerably surprised by the result of his question, but, being a shrewd youth, soon thought himself able to account for the mystery.

"This is some country representative," was his conclusion, "who has never seen the inside of my kinsman's door, and lacks the breeding to answer a stranger civilly. The man is old, or verily— I might be tempted to turn back and smite him on the nose. Ah, Robin, Robin! even the barber's boys laugh at you for choosing such a guide! You will be wiser in time, friend Robin."

He now became entangled in a succession of crooked and narrow streets, which crossed each other, and meandered at no great distance from the water-side. The smell of tar was obvious to his nostrils, the masts of vessels pierced the moonlight above the tops of the buildings, and the numerous signs, which Robin paused to read, informed him that he was near the centre of business. But the streets were empty, the shops were closed, and lights were visible only in the second stories of a few dwelling-houses. At length, on the corner of a narrow lane, through which he was passing, he beheld the broad countenance of a British hero swinging before the door of an inn, whence proceeded the voices of many guests. The casement of one of the lower windows was thrown back, and a very thin curtain permitted Robin to distinguish a party at supper, round a well-furnished table. The fragrance of the good cheer steamed forth into the outer air, and the youth could not fail to recollect that the last remnant of his travelling stock of provision had yielded to his morning appetite, and that noon had found and left him dinnerless.

"Oh, that a parchment three-penny might give me a right to sit down at yonder table!" said Robin, with a sigh. "But the Major will make me welcome to the best of his victuals; so I will even step boldly in, and inquire my way to his dwelling."

He entered the tavern, and was guided by the murmur of voices and the fumes of tobacco to the public-room. It was a long and low apartment, with oaken walls, grown dark in the continual smoke, and a floor which was thickly sanded, but of no immaculate purity. A number of persons—the larger part of whom appeared to be mariners, or in some way connected with the sea—occupied the wooden benches, or leather-bottomed chairs, conversing on various matters, and occasionally lending their attention to some topic of general interest. Three or four little groups were draining as many bowls of punch, which the West India trade had long since made a familiar drink in the colony. Others, who had the appearance of men who lived by regular and laborious handicraft, preferred the insulated bliss of an unshared potation, and became more taciturn under its influence. Nearly all, in short, evinced a predilection for the Good Creature in some of its various shapes, for this is a vice to which, as Fast Day sermons of a hundred years ago will testify, we have a long hereditary claim. The only guests to whom Robin's sympathies inclined him were two or three sheepish countrymen, who were using the inn somewhat after the fashion of a Turkish caravansary; they had gotten themselves into the darkest corner of the room, and heedless of the Nicotian[2] atmosphere, were supping on the bread of their own ovens, and the bacon cured in their own chimney-smoke. But though Robin felt a sort of brotherhood with these strangers, his eyes were attracted from them to a person who stood near the door, holding whispered conversation with a group of ill-dressed associates. His features were separately striking almost to grotesqueness, and the whole face left a deep impression on the memory.

2. Equivalent to nicotine, and the original form of the word, although it is here used as an adjective. From Jean Nicot, who introduced tobacco into France in 1560.

The forehead bulged out into a double prominence, with a vale between; the nose came boldly forth in an irregular curve, and its bridge was of more than a finger's breadth; the eyebrows were deep and shaggy, and the eyes glowed beneath them like fire in a cave.

While Robin deliberated of whom to inquire respecting his kinsman's dwelling, he was accosted by the innkeeper, a little man in a stained white apron, who had come to pay his professional welcome to the stranger. Being in the second generation from a French Protestant, he seemed to have inherited the courtesy of his parent nation; but no variety of circumstances was ever known to change his voice from the one shrill note in which he now addressed Robin.

"From the country, I presume, sir?" said he, with a profound bow. "Beg leave to congratulate you on your arrival, and trust you intend a long stay with us. Fine town here, sir, beautiful buildings, and much that may interest a stranger. May I hope for the honor of your commands in respect to supper?"

"The man sees a family likeness! the rogue has guessed that I am related to the Major!" thought Robin, who had hitherto experienced little superfluous civility.

All eyes were now turned on the country lad, standing at the door, in his worn three-cornered hat, gray coat, leather breeches, and blue yarn stockings, leaning on an oaken cudgel, and bearing a wallet on his back.

Robin replied to the courteous innkeeper, with such an assumption of confidence as befitted the Major's relative. "My honest friend," he said, "I shall make it a point to patronize your house on some occasion, when"—here he could not help lowering his voice —"when I may have more than a parchment three-pence in my pocket. My present business," continued he, speaking with lofty confidence, "is merely to inquire my way to the dwelling of my kinsman, Major Molineux."

There was a sudden and general movement in the room, which Robin interpreted as expressing the eagerness of each individual to become his guide. But the innkeeper turned his eyes to a written paper on the wall, which he read, or seemed to read, with occasional recurrences to the young man's figure.

"What have we here?" said he, breaking his speech into little dry fragments. "'Left the house of the subscriber, bounden servant, Hezekiah Mudge,—had on, when he went away, gray coat, leather breeches, master's third-best hat. One pound currency reward to whosoever shall lodge him in any jail of the providence.' Better trudge, boy; better trudge!"

Robin had begun to draw his hand towards the lighter end of the oak cudgel, but a strange hostility in every countenance induced him to relinquish his purpose of breaking the courteous innkeeper's head. As he turned to leave the room, he encountered a sneering glance from the bold-featured personage whom he had before noticed; and no sooner was he beyond the door, than he heard a general laugh, in which the innkeeper's voice might be distinguished, like the dropping of small stones into a kettle.

"Now, is it not strange," thought Robin, with his usual shrewdness,—"is it not strange that the confession of an empty pocket should outweigh the name of my kinsman, Major Molineux? Oh, if I had one of those grinning rascals in the woods, where I and my oak sapling grew up together, I would teach him that my arm is heavy though my purse be light!"

On turning the corner of the narrow lane, Robin found himself in a spacious street, with an unbroken line of lofty houses on each side, and a steepled building at the upper end, whence the ringing of a bell announced the hour of nine. The light of the moon, and the lamps from the numerous shop-windows, discovered people promenading on the pavement, and amongst them Robin had hoped to recognize his hitherto inscrutable relative. The result of his former inquiries made him unwilling to hazard another, in a scene of such publicity, and he determined to walk slowly and silently up the street, thrusting his face close to that of every elderly gentleman, in search of the Major's lineaments. In his progress, Robin encountered many gay and gallant figures. Embroidered garments of showy colors, enormous periwigs, gold-laced hats, and silver-hilted swords glided past him and dazzled his optics. Travelled youths, imitators of the European fine gentlemen of the period, trod jauntily along, half dancing to the fashionable tunes which they hummed, and making poor Robin ashamed of his quiet and natural gait. At length, after many pauses to examine the gorgeous display of goods in the shop-windows, and after suffering some rebukes for the impertinence of his scrutiny into people's faces, the Major's kinsman found himself near the steepled building, still unsuccessful in his search. As yet, however, he had seen only one side of the thronged street; so Robin crossed, and continued the same sort of inquisition down the opposite pavement, with stronger hopes than the philosopher seeking an honest man, but with no better fortune. He had arrived about midway towards the lower end, from which his course began, when he overheard the approach of some one who struck down a cane on the flag-stones at every step, uttering at regular intervals, two sepulchral hems.

"Mercy on us!" quoth Robin, recognizing the sound.

Turning a corner, which chanced to be close at his right hand, he hastened to pursue his researches in some other part of the town. His patience now was wearing low, and he seemed to feel more fatigue from his rambles since he crossed the ferry, than from his journey of several days on the other side. Hunger also pleaded loudly within him, and Robin began to balance the propriety of demanding, violently, and with lifted cudgel, the necessary guidance from the first solitary passenger whom he should meet. While a resolution to this effect was gaining strength, he entered a street of mean appearance, on either side of which a row of ill-built houses was straggling towards the harbor. The moonlight fell upon no passenger along the whole extent, but in the third domicile which Robin passed there was a half-opened door, and his keen glance detected a woman's garment within.

"My luck may be better here," said he to himself.

Accordingly, he approached the door, and beheld it shut closer as he did so; yet an open space remained, sufficing for the fair occupant to observe the stranger, without a corresponding display on her part. All that Robin could discern was a strip of scarlet petticoat, and the occasional sparkle of an eye, as if the moonbeams were trembling on some bright thing.

"Pretty mistress," for I may call her so with a good conscience, thought the shrewd youth, since I know nothing to the contrary, —"my sweet pretty mistress, will you be kind enough to tell me whereabouts I must seek the dwelling of my kinsman, Major Molineux?"

Robin's voice was plaintive and winning, and the female, seeing nothing to be shunned in the handsome country youth, thrust open the door, and came forth into the moonlight. She was a dainty little figure, with a white neck, round arms, and a slender waist, at the extremity of which her scarlet petticoat jutted out over a hoop, as if she were standing in a balloon. Moreover, her face was oval and pretty, her hair dark beneath the little cap, and her bright eyes possessed a sly freedom, which triumphed over those of Robin.

"Major Molineux dwells here," said this fair woman.

Now, her voice was the sweetest Robin had heard that night, yet he could not help doubting whether that sweet voice spoke Gospel truth. He looked up and down the mean street, and then surveyed the house before which they stood. It was a small, dark edifice of two stories, the second of which projected over the lower floor, and the front apartment had the aspect of a shop for petty commodities.

"Now, truly, I am in luck," replied Robin, cunningly, "and so indeed is my kinsman, the Major, in having so pretty a housekeeper. But I prithee trouble him to step to the door; I will deliver him a message from his friends in the country, and then go back to my lodgings at the inn."

"Nay, the Major has been abed this hour or more," said the lady
of the scarlet petticoat; "and it would be to little purpose to disturb
him to-night, seeing his evening draught was of the strongest. But
he is a kind-hearted man, and it would be as much as my life's
worth to let a kinsman of his turn away from the door. You are the
good old gentleman's very picture, and I could swear that was his
rainy-weather hat. Also he has garments very much resembling
those leather small-clothes. But come in, I pray, for I bid you
hearty welcome in his name."

So saying, the fair and hospitable dame took our hero by the
hand; and the touch was light, and the force was gentleness, and
though Robin read in her eyes what he did not hear in her words,
yet the slender-waisted woman in the scarlet petticoat proved
stronger than the athletic country youth. She had drawn his half-
willing footsteps nearly to the threshold, when the opening of a
door in the neighborhood startled the Major's housekeeper, and,
leaving the Major's kinsman, she vanished speedily into her own
domicile. A heavy yawn preceded the appearance of a man, who,
like the Moonshine of Pyramus and Thisbe,[3] carried a lantern,
needlessly aiding his sister luminary in the heavens. As he walked
sleepily up the street, he turned his broad, dull face on Robin, and
displayed a long staff, spiked at the end.

"Home, vagabond, home!" said the watchman, in accents that
seemed to fall asleep as soon as they were uttered. "Home, or we'll
set you in the stocks by peep of day!"

"This is the second hint of the kind," thought Robin. "I wish
they would end my difficulties, by setting me there to-night."

Nevertheless, the youth felt an instinctive antipathy towards the
guardian of midnight order, which at first prevented him from asking his usual question. But just when the man was about to vanish
behind the corner, Robin resolved not to lose the opportunity, and
shouted lustily after him,—

"I say, friend! will you guide me to the house of my kinsman,
Major Molineux?"

The watchman made no reply, but turned the corner and was
gone; yet Robin seemed to hear the sound of drowsy laughter
stealing along the solitary street. At that moment, also, a pleasant
titter saluted him from the open window above his head; he looked
up, and caught the sparkle of a saucy eye; a round arm beckoned
to him, and next he heard light footsteps descending the staircase
within. But Robin, being of the household of a New England
clergyman, was a good youth, as well as a shrewd one; so he resisted
temptation, and fled away.

3. See Shakespeare, *A Midsummer Night's Dream* III.1.

He now roamed desperately, and at random, through the town, almost ready to believe that a spell was on him, like that by which a wizard of his country had once kept three pursuers wandering, a whole winter night, within twenty paces of the cottage which they sought. The streets lay before him, strange and desolate, and the lights were extinguished in almost every house. Twice, however, little parties of men, among whom Robin distinguished individuals in outlandish attire, came hurrying along; but, though on both occasions, they paused to address him, such intercourse did not at all enlighten his perplexity. They did but utter a few words in some language of which Robin knew nothing, and perceiving his inability to answer, bestowed a curse upon him in plain English and hastened away. Finally, the lad determined to knock at the door of every mansion that might appear worthy to be occupied by his kinsman, trusting that perseverance would overcome the fatality that had hitherto thwarted him. Firm in this resolve, he was passing beneath the walls of a church, which formed the corner of two streets, when, as he turned into the shade of its steeple, he encountered a bulky stranger, muffled in a cloak. The man was proceeding with the speed of earnest business, but Robin planted himself full before him, holding the oak cudgel with both hands across his body as a bar to further passage.

"Halt, honest man, and answer me a question," said he, very resolutely. "Tell me, this instant, whereabouts is the dwelling of my kinsman, Major Molineux!"

"Keep your tongue between your teeth, fool, and let me pass!" said a deep, gruff voice, which Robin partly remembered. "Let me pass, or I'll strike you to the earth!"

"No, no, neighbor!" cried Robin, flourishing his cudgel, and then thrusting its larger end close to the man's muffled face. "No, no, I'm not the fool you take me for, nor do you pass till I have an answer to my question. Whereabouts is the dwelling of my kinsman, Major Molineux?"

The stranger, instead of attempting to force his passage, stepped back into the moonlight, unmuffled his face, and stared full into that of Robin.

"Watch here an hour, and Major Molineux will pass by," said he.

Robin gazed with dismay and astonishment on the unprecedented physiognomy of the speaker. The forehead with its double prominence, the broad hooked nose, the shaggy eyebrows, and fiery eyes were those which he had noticed at the inn, but the man's complexion had undergone a singular, or, more properly, a twofold change. One side of the face blazed an intense red, while the other was black as midnight, the division line being in the broad bridge of the nose; and a mouth which seemed to extend from ear to ear was black or red, in contrast to the color of the cheek. The effect was as if two individual devils, a fiend of fire and a fiend of darkness, had united themselves to form this infernal visage. The stranger grinned in Robin's face, muffled his party-colored features, and was out of sight in a moment.

"Strange things we travellers see!" ejaculated Robin.

He seated himself, however, upon the steps of the church-door, resolving to wait the appointed time for his kinsman. A few moments were consumed in philosophical speculations upon the species of man who had just left him; but having settled this point shrewdly, rationally, and satisfactorily, he was compelled to look elsewhere for his amusement. And first he threw his eyes along the street. It was of more respectable appearance than most of those into which he had wandered; and the moon, creating, like the imaginative power, a beautiful strangeness in familiar objects, gave something of romance to a scene that might not have possessed it in the light of day. The irregular and often quaint architecture of the houses, some of whose roofs were broken into numerous little peaks, while others ascended, steep and narrow, into a single point, and others again were square; the pure snow-white of some of their complexions, the aged darkness of others, and the thousand sparklings, reflected from bright substances in the walls of many; these matters engaged Robin's attention for a while, and then began to grow wearisome. Next he endeavored to define the forms of distant objects, starting away, with almost ghostly indistinctness, just as his eye appeared to grasp them; and finally he took a minute survey of an edifice which stood on the opposite side of the street, directly in front of the church-door, where he was stationed. It was a large, square mansion, distinguished from its neighbors by a balcony, which rested on tall pillars, and by an elaborate Gothic window, communicating therewith.

"Perhaps this is the very house I have been seeking," thought Robin.

Then he strove to speed away the time, by listening to a murmur which swept continually along the street, yet was scarcely audible, except to an unaccustomed ear like his; it was a low, dull, dreamy sound, compounded of many noises, each of which was at too great a distance to be separately heard. Robin marvelled at this snore of a sleeping town, and marvelled more whenever its continuity was broken by now and then a distant shout, apparently loud where it originated. But altogether it was a sleep-inspiring sound, and, to shake off its drowsy influence, Robin arose, and climbed a window-frame, that he might view the interior of the church. There the moonbeams came trembling in, and fell down upon the deserted pews, and extended along the quiet aisles. A fainter yet more awful radiance was hovering around the pulpit, and one solitary ray had dared to rest upon the open page of the great Bible. Had nature, in that deep hour, become a worshipper in the house which man had builded? Or was that heavenly light the visible sanctity of the place,—visible because no earthly and impure feet were within the walls? The scene made Robin's heart shiver with a sensation of loneliness stronger than he had ever felt in the remotest depths of his native woods; so he turned away and sat down again before the door. There were graves around the church, and now an uneasy thought obtruded into Robin's breast. What if the object of his search, which had been so often and so strangely thwarted, were all the time mouldering in his shroud? What if his kinsman should glide through yonder gate, and nod and smile to him in dimly passing by?

"Oh that any breathing thing were here with me!" said Robin.

Recalling his thoughts from this uncomfortable track, he sent them over forest, hill, and stream, and attempted to imagine how that evening of ambiguity and weariness had been spent by his father's household. He pictured them assembled at the door, beneath the tree, the great old tree, which had been spared for its huge twisted trunk and venerable shade, when a thousand leafy brethren fell. There, at the going down of the summer sun, it was his father's custom to perform domestic worship, that the neighbors might come and join with him like brothers of the family, and that the wayfaring man might pause to drink at that fountain, and keep his heart pure by freshening the memory of home. Robin distinguished the seat of every individual of the little audience; he saw the good man in the midst, holding the Scriptures in the golden light that fell from the western clouds; he beheld him close the book and all rise up to pray. He heard the old thanksgivings for daily mercies, the old supplications for their continuance, to which he had so often listened in weariness, but which were now among his dear remembrances. He perceived the slight inequality of his father's voice when he came to speak of the absent one; he noted how his mother turned her face to the broad and knotted trunk; how his elder brother scorned, because the beard was rough upon his upper lip, to permit his features to be moved; how the younger sister drew down a low hanging branch before her eyes; and how the little one of all, whose sports had hitherto broken the decorum of the scene, understood the prayer for her playmate, and burst into clamorous grief. Then he saw them go in at the door; and when Robin would have entered also, the latch tinkled into its place, and he was excluded from his home.

"Am I here, or there?" cried Robin, starting; for all at once, when his thoughts had become visible and audible in a dream, the long, wide, solitary street shone out before him.

He aroused himself, and endeavored to fix his attention steadily upon the large edifice which he had surveyed before. But still his mind kept vibrating between fancy and reality; by turns, the pillars of the balcony lengthened into the tall, bare stems of pines, dwindled down to human figures, settled again into their true shape and size, and then commenced a new succession of changes. For a single moment, when he deemed himself awake, he could have sworn that a visage—one which he seemed to remember, yet could not absolutely name as his kinsman's—was looking towards him from the Gothic window. A deeper sleep wrestled with and nearly overcame him, but fled at the sound of footsteps along the opposite pavement. Robin rubbed his eyes, discerned a man passing at the foot of the balcony, and addressed him in a loud, peevish, and lamentable cry.

"Hallo, friend! must I wait here all night for my kinsman, Major Molineux?"

The sleeping echoes awoke, and answered the voice; and the passenger, barely able to discern a figure sitting in the oblique shade of the steeple, traversed the street to obtain a nearer view. He was himself a gentleman in his prime, of open, intelligent, cheerful, and altogether prepossessing countenance. Perceiving a country youth, apparently homeless and without friends, he accosted him in a tone of real kindness, which had become strange to Robin's ears.

"Well, my good lad, why are you sitting here?" inquired he. "Can I be of service to you in any way?"

"I am afraid not, sir," replied Robin, despondingly; "yet I shall take it kindly, if you'll answer me a single question. I've been searching, half the night, for one Major Molineux; now, sir, is there really such a person in these parts, or am I dreaming?"

"Major Molineux! The name is not altogether strange to me," said the gentleman, smiling. "Have you any objection to telling me the nature of your business with him?"

Then Robin briefly related that his father was a clergyman, settled on a small salary, at a long distance back in the country, and that he and Major Molineux were brothers' children. The Major, having inherited riches, and acquired civil and military rank, had visited his cousin, in great pomp, a year or two before; had manifested much interest in Robin and an elder brother, and, being childless himself, had thrown out hints respecting the future establishment of one of them in life. The elder brother was destined to succeed to the farm which his father cultivated in the interval of sacred duties; it was therefore determined that Robin should profit by his kinsman's generous intentions, especially as he seemed to be rather the favorite, and was thought to possess other necessary endowments.

"For I have the name of being a shrewd youth," observed Robin, in this part of his story.

"I doubt not you deserve it," replied his new friend, good-naturedly; "but pray proceed."

"Well, sir, being nearly eighteen years old, and well grown, as you see," continued Robin, drawing himself up to his full height, "I thought it high time to begin in the world. So my mother and sister put me in handsome trim, and my father gave me half the remnant of his last year's salary, and five days ago I started for this place, to pay the Major a visit. But, would you believe it, sir! I crossed the ferry a little after dark, and have yet found nobody that would show me the way to his dwelling; only, an hour or two since, I was told to wait here, and Major Molineux would pass by."

"Can you describe the man who told you this?" inquired the gentleman.

"Oh, he was a very ill-favored fellow, sir," replied Robin, "with two great bumps on his forehead, a hook nose, fiery eyes; and, what struck me as the strangest, his face was of two different colors. Do you happen to know such a man, sir?"

"Not intimately," answered the stranger, "but I chanced to meet him a little time previous to your stopping me. I believe you may trust his word, and that the Major will very shortly pass through this street. In the mean time, as I have a singular curiosity to witness your meeting, I will sit down here upon the steps and bear you company."

He seated himself accordingly, and soon engaged his companion in animated discourse. It was but of brief continuance, however, for a noise of shouting, which had long been remotely audible, drew so much nearer that Robin inquired its cause.

"What may be the meaning of this uproar?" asked he. "Truly, if your town be always as noisy, I shall find little sleep while I am an inhabitant."

"Why, indeed, friend Robin, there do appear to be three or four riotous fellows abroad to-night," replied the gentleman. "You must not expect all the stillness of your native woods here in our streets. But the watch will shortly be at the heels of these lads and"—

"Ay, and set them in the stocks by peep of day," interrupted Robin, recollecting his own encounter with the drowsy lantern-bearer. "But, dear sir, if I may trust my ears, an army of watchmen would never make head against such a multitude of rioters. There were at least a thousand voices went up to make that one shout."

"May not a man have several voices, Robin, as well as two complexions?" said his friend.

"Perhaps a man may; but Heaven forbid that a woman should!" responded the shrewd youth, thinking of the seductive tones of the Major's housekeeper.

The sounds of a trumpet in some neighboring street now became so evident and continual, that Robin's curiosity was strongly excited. In addition to the shouts, he heard frequent bursts from many instruments of discord, and a wild and confused laughter filled up the intervals. Robin rose from the steps, and looked wistfully towards a point whither people seemed to be hastening.

"Surely some prodigious merry-making is going on," exclaimed he. "I have laughed very little since I left home, sir, and should be sorry to lose an opportunity. Shall we step round the corner by that darkish house, and take our share of the fun?"

"Sit down again, sit down, good Robin," replied the gentleman, laying his hand on the skirt of the gray coat. "You forget that we must wait here for your kinsman; and there is reason to believe that he will pass by, in the course of a very few moments."

The near approach of the uproar had now disturbed the neighborhood; windows flew open on all sides; and many heads, in the attire of the pillow, and confused by sleep suddenly broken, were protruded to the gaze of whoever had leisure to observe them. Eager voices hailed each other from house to house, all demanding the explanation, which not a soul could give. Half-dressed men hurried towards the unknown commotion, stumbling as they went over the stone steps that thrust themselves into the narrow footwalk. The shouts, the laughter, and the tuneless bray, the antipodes of music, came onwards with increasing din, till scattered individuals, and then denser bodies, began to appear round a corner at the distance of a hundred yards.

"Will you recognize your kinsman, if he passes in this crowd?" inquired the gentleman.

"Indeed, I can't warrant it, sir; but I'll take my stand here, and keep a bright lookout," answered Robin, descending to the outer edge of the pavement.

A mighty stream of people now emptied into the street, and came rolling slowly towards the church. A single horseman wheeled the corner in the midst of them, and close behind him came a band of fearful wind-instruments, sending forth a fresher discord now that no intervening buildings kept it from the ear. Then a redder light disturbed the moonbeams, and a dense multitude of torches shone along the street, concealing, by their glare, whatever object they illuminated. The single horseman, clad in a military dress, and bearing a drawn sword, rode onward as the leader, and,

by his fierce and variegated countenance, appeared like war personified; the red of one cheek was an emblem of fire and sword;
the blackness of the other betokened the mourning that attends
them. In his train were wild figures in the Indian dress, and many
fantastic shapes without a model, giving the whole march a visionary air, as if a dream had broken forth from some feverish brain,
and were sweeping visibly through the midnight streets. A mass of
people, inactive, except as applauding spectators, hemmed the
procession in; and several women ran along the sidewalk, piercing
the confusion of heavier sounds with their shrill voices of mirth or
terror.

"The double-faced fellow has his eye upon me," muttered Robin,
with an indefinite but an uncomfortable idea that he was himself
to bear a part in the pageantry.

The leader turned himself in the saddle, and fixed his glance
full upon the country youth, as the steed went slowly by. When
Robin had freed his eyes from those fiery ones, the musicians were
passing before him, and the torches were close at hand; but the unsteady brightness of the latter formed a veil which he could not
penetrate. The rattling of wheels over the stones sometimes found
its way to his ear, and confused traces of a human form appeared
at intervals, and then melted into the vivid light. A moment more,
and the leader thundered a command to halt: the trumpets vom-
ited a horrid breath, and then held their peace; the shouts and
laughter of the people died away, and their remained only a universal hum, allied to silence. Right before Robin's eyes was an uncovered cart. There the torches blazed the brightest, there the
moon shone out like day, and there, in tar-and-feathery dignity,
sat his kinsman, Major Molineux!

He was an elderly man, of large and majestic person, and strong,
square features, betokening a steady soul; but steady as it was, his
enemies had found means to shake it. His face was pale as death,
and far more ghastly; the broad forehead was contracted in his
agony, so that his eyebrows formed one grizzled line; his eyes
were red and wild, and the foam hung white upon his quivering
lip. His whole frame was agitated by a quick and continual tremor,
which his pride strove to quell, even in those circumstances of
overwhelming humiliation. But perhaps the bitterest pang of all
was when his eyes met those of Robin; for he evidently knew him
on the instant, as the youth stood witnessing the foul disgrace of a
head grown gray in honor. They stared at each other in silence,
and Robin's knees shook, and his hair bristled, with a mixture of
pity and terror. Soon, however, a bewildering excitement began to
seize upon his mind; the preceding adventures of the night, the
unexpected appearance of the crowd, the torches, the confused din

and the hush that followed, the spectre of his kinsman reviled by that great multitude,—all this, and, more than all, a perception of tremendous ridicule in the whole scene, affected him with a sort of mental inebriety. At that moment a voice of sluggish merriment saluted Robin's ears; he turned instinctively, and just behind the corner of the church stood the lantern-bearer, rubbing his eyes, and drowsily enjoying the lad's amazement. Then he heard a peal of laughter like the ringing of silvery bells; a woman twitched his arm, a saucy eye met his, and he saw the lady of the scarlet petti-coat. A sharp, dry cachinnation appealed to his memory, and stand-ing on tiptoe in the crowd, with his white apron over his head, he beheld the courteous little innkeeper. And lastly, there sailed over the heads of the multitude a great, broad laugh, broken in the midst by two sepulchral hems; thus, "Haw, haw, haw,—hem, hem, —haw, haw, haw, haw!"

The sound proceeded from the balcony of the opposite edifice, and thither Robin turned his eyes. In front of the Gothic window stood the old citizen, wrapped in a wide gown, his gray periwig exchanged for a nightcap, which was thrust back from his fore-head, and his silk stockings hanging about his legs. He supported himself on his polished cane in a fit of convulsive merriment, which manifested itself on his solemn old features like a funny in-scription on a tombstone. Then Robin seemed to hear the voices of the barbers, of the guests of the inn, and of all who had made sport of him that night. The contagion was spreading among the multitude, when all at once, it seized upon Robin, and he sent forth a shout of laughter that echoed through the street,—every man shook his sides, every man emptied his lungs, but Robin's shout was the loudest there. The cloud-spirits peeped from their silvery islands, as the congregated mirth went roaring up the sky! The Man in the Moon heard the far bellow. "Oho," quoth he, "the old earth is frolicsome to-night!"

When there was a momentary calm in that tempestuous sea of sound, the leader gave the sign, the procession resumed its march. On they went, like fiends that throng in mockery around some dead potentate, mighty no more, but majestic still in his agony. On they went, in counterfeited pomp, in senseless uproar, in frenzied merriment, trampling all on an old man's heart. On swept the tu-mult, and left a silent street behind.

. . . . . .

"Well, Robin, are you dreaming?" inquired the gentleman, lay-ing his hand on the youth's shoulder.

Robin started, and withdrew his arm from the stone post to which he had instinctively clung, as the living stream rolled by him. His cheek was somewhat pale, and his eye not quite as lively as in the earlier part of the evening.

"Will you be kind enough to show me the way to the ferry?" said he, after a moment's pause.

"You have, then, adopted a new subject of inquiry?" observed his companion, with a smile.

"Why, yes, sir," replied Robin, rather dryly. "Thanks to you, and to my other friends, I have at last met my kinsman, and he will scarce desire to see my face again. I begin to grow weary of a town life, sir. Will you show me the way to the ferry?"

"No, my good friend Robin,—not to-night, at least," said the gentleman. "Some few days hence, if you wish it, I will speed you on your journey. Or, if you prefer to remain with us, perhaps, as you are a shrewd youth, you may rise in the world without the help of your kinsman, Major Molineux."

1832, 1851

The Canterbury Pilgrims[4]

The summer moon, which shines in so many a tale, was beaming over a broad extent of uneven country. Some of its brightest rays were flung into a spring of water, where no traveller, toiling, as the writer has, up the hilly road beside which it gushes, ever failed to quench his thirst. The work of neat hands and considerate art was visible about this blessed fountain. An open cistern, hewn and hollowed out of solid stone, was placed above the waters, which filled it to the brim, but by some invisible outlet were conveyed away without dripping down its sides. Though the basin had not room for another drop, and the continual gush of water made a tremor on the surface, there was a secret charm that forbade it to overflow. I remember, that when I had slaked my summer thirst, and sat panting by the cistern, it was my fanciful theory that Nature could not afford to lavish so pure a liquid, as she does the waters of all meaner fountains.

While the moon was hanging almost perpendicularly over this

4. In 1831 Hawthorne visited a large Shaker community in Canterbury, N. H. On this occasion, on which his story is based, he said of the Shakers, "On the whole, they lead a good and comfortable life, and, if it were not for their ridiculous ceremonies, a man could not do a wiser thing than to join them. Those whom I conversed with were intelligent, and appeared happy." Later he made two visits to Shaker villages, once to Harvard, Mass., with Emerson in 1842, and again to Hancock. His last impression was decidedly less favorable than the first. "They are certainly the most singular and bedevilled set of people that ever existed in a civilized land; and one of these days, when their sect and system shall have passed away, a History of the Shakers will be a very curious book" (*American Notebooks*, p. 230). He wrote another tale upon this sect, "The Shaker Bridal" (1833). The present story appeared in *The Token* in 1833 and was collected in *The Snow Image*.

spot, two figures appeared on the summit of the hill, and came with noiseless footsteps down towards the spring. They were then in the first freshness of youth; nor is there a wrinkle now on either of their brows, and yet they wore a strange, old-fashioned garb. One, a young man with ruddy cheeks, walked beneath the canopy of a broad-brimmed gray hat; he seemed to have inherited his great-grandsire's square-skirted coat, and a waistcoat that extended its immense flaps to his knees; his brown locks, also, hung down behind, in a mode unknown to our times. By his side was a sweet young damsel, her fair features sheltered by a prim little bonnet, within which appeared the vestal muslin of a cap; her close, long-waisted gown, and indeed her whole attire, might have been worn by some rustic beauty who had faded half a century before. But that there was something too warm and life-like in them, I would here have compared this couple to the ghosts of two young lovers who had died long since in the glow of passion, and now were straying out of their graves, to renew the old vows, and shadow forth the unforgotten kiss of their earthly lips, beside the moonlit spring.

"Thee and I will rest here a moment, Miriam," said the young man, as they drew near the stone cistern, "for there is no fear that the elders know what we have done; and this may be the last time we shall ever taste this water."

Thus speaking, with a little sadness in his face, which was also visible in that of his companion, he made her sit down on a stone, and was about to place himself very close to her side; she, however, repelled him, though not unkindly.

"Nay, Josiah," said she, giving him a timid push with her maiden hand, "thee must sit farther off, on that other stone, with the spring between us. What would the sisters say, if thee were to sit so close to me?"

"But we are of the world's people now, Miriam," answered Josiah.

The girl persisted in her prudery, nor did the youth, in fact, seem altogether free from a similar sort of shyness; so they sat apart from each other, gazing up the hill, where the moonlight discovered the tops of a group of buildings. While their attention was thus occupied, a party of travellers, who had come wearily up the long ascent, made a halt to refresh themselves at the spring. There were three men, a woman, and a little girl and boy. Their attire was mean, covered with the dust of the summer's day, and damp with the night-dew; they all looked woebegone, as if the cares and sorrows of the world had made their steps heavier as they climbed the hill; even the two little children appeared older in evil days than the young man and maiden who had first approached the spring.

"Good evening to you, young folks," was the salutation of the travellers; and "Good evening, friends," replied the youth and damsel.

"Is that white building the Shaker meeting-house?" asked one of the strangers. "And are those the red roofs of the Shaker village?"

"Friend, it is the Shaker village," answered Josiah, after some hesitation.

The travellers, who, from the first, had looked suspiciously at the garb of these young people, now taxed them with an intention which all the circumstances, indeed, rendered too obvious to be mistaken.

"It is true, friends," replied the young man, summoning up his courage. "Miriam and I have a gift to love each other, and we are going among the world's people, to live after their fashion. And ye know that we do not transgress the law of the land; and neither ye, nor the elders themselves, have a right to hinder us."

"Yet you think it expedient to depart without leave-taking," remarked one of the travellers.

"Yea, ye-a," said Josiah, reluctantly, "because father Job is a very awful man to speak with; and being aged himself, he has but little charity for what he calls the iniquities of the flesh."

"Well," said the stranger, "we will neither use force to bring you back to the village, nor will we betray you to the elders. But sit you here awhile, and when you have heard what we shall tell you of the world which we have left, and into which you are going, perhaps you will turn back with us of your own accord. What say you?" added he, turning to his companions. "We have travelled thus far without becoming known to each other. Shall we tell our stories, here by this pleasant spring, for our own pastime, and the benefit of these misguided young lovers?"

In accordance with this proposal, the whole party stationed themselves round the stone cistern; the two children, being very weary, fell asleep upon the damp earth, and the pretty Shaker girl, whose feelings were those of a nun or a Turkish lady, crept as close as possible to the female traveller, and as far as she well could from the unknown men. The same person who had hitherto been the chief spokesman now stood up, waving his hat in his hand, and suffered the moonlight to fall full upon his front.

"In me," said he, with a certain majesty of utterance,—"in me, you behold a poet."

Though a lithographic print of this gentleman is extant, it may be well to notice that he was now nearly forty, a thin and stooping figure, in a black coat, out at elbows; notwithstanding the ill condition of his attire, there were about him several tokens of a peculiar sort of foppery, unworthy of a mature man, particularly in the arrangement of his hair, which was so disposed as to give all possible loftiness and breadth to his forehead. However, he had an intelligent eye, and, on the whole, a marked countenance.

"A poet!" repeated the young Shaker, a little puzzled how to understand such a designation, seldom heard in the utilitarian community where he had spent his life. "Oh, ay, Miriam, he means a varse-maker, thee must know."

This remark jarred upon the susceptible nerves of the poet; nor could he help wondering what strange fatality had put into this young man's mouth an epithet, which ill-natured people had affirmed to be more proper to his merit than the one assumed by himself.

"True, I am a verse-maker," he resumed, "but my verse is no more than the material body into which I breathe the celestial soul of thought. Alas! how many a pang has it cost me, this same insensibility to the ethereal essence of poetry, with which you have here tortured me again, at the moment when I am to relinquish my profession forever! O Fate! why hast thou warred with Nature, turning all her higher and more perfect gifts to the ruin of me, their possessor? What is the voice of song, when the world lacks the ear of taste? How can I rejoice in my strength and delicacy of feeling, when they have but made great sorrows out of little ones? Have I dreaded scorn like death, and yearned for fame as others pant for vital air, only to find myself in a middle state between obscurity and infamy? But I have my revenge! I could have given existence to a thousand bright creations. I crush them into my heart, and there let them putrefy! I shake off the dust of my feet against my countrymen! But posterity, tracing my footsteps up this weary hill, will cry shame upon the unworthy age that drove one of the fathers of American song to end his days in a Shaker village!"

During this harangue, the speaker gesticulated with great energy, and, as poetry is the natural language of passion, there appeared reason to apprehend his final explosion into an ode extempore. The reader must understand that, for all these bitter words, he was a kind, gentle, harmless, poor fellow enough, whom Nature, tossing her ingredients together without looking at her recipe, had sent into the world with too much of one sort of brain, and hardly any of another.

"Friend," said the young Shaker, in some perplexity, "thee seemest to have met with great troubles; and, doubtless, I should pity them, if—if I could but understand what they were."

"Happy in your ignorance!" replied the poet, with an air of sublime superiority. "To your coarser mind, perhaps, I may seem to speak of more important griefs when I add, what I had wellnigh forgotten, that I am out at elbows, and almost starved to death. At any rate, you have the advice and example of one individual to warn you back; for I am come hither, a disappointed man, flinging aside the fragments of my hopes, and seeking shelter in the calm retreat which you are so anxious to leave."

"I thank thee, friend," rejoined the youth, "but I do not mean to be a poet, nor, Heaven be praised! do I think Miriam ever made a varse in her life. So we need not fear thy disappointments. But, Miriam," he added, with real concern, "thee knowest that the elders admit nobody that has not a gift to be useful. Now, what under the sun can they do with this poor varse-maker?"

"Nay, Josiah, do not thee discourage the poor man," said the girl, in all simplicity and kindness. "Our hymns are very rough, and perhaps they may trust him to smooth them."

Without noticing this hint of professional employment, the poet turned away, and gave himself up to a sort of vague reverie, which he called thought. Sometimes he watched the moon, pouring a silvery liquid on the clouds, through which it slowly melted till they became all bright; then he saw the same sweet radiance dancing on the leafy trees which rustled as if to shake it off, or sleeping on the high tops of hills, or hovering down in distant valleys, like the material of unshaped dreams; lastly, he looked into the spring, and there the light was mingling with the water. In its crystal bosom, too, beholding all heaven reflected there, he found an emblem of a pure and tranquil breast. He listened to that most ethereal of all sounds, the song of crickets, coming in full choir upon the wind, and fancied that, if moonlight could be heard, it would sound just like that. Finally, he took a draught at the Shaker spring, and, as if it were the true Castalia, was forthwith moved to compose a lyric, a Farewell to his Harp, which he swore should be its closing strain, the last verse that an ungrateful world should have from him. This effusion, with two or three other little pieces, subsequently written, he took the first opportunity to send, by one of the Shaker brethren, to Concord, where they were published in the New Hampshire Patriot.

Meantime, another of the Canterbury pilgrims, one so different from the poet that the delicate fancy of the latter could hardly have conceived of him, began to relate his sad experience. He was a small man, of quick and unquiet gestures, about fifty years old, with a narrow forehead, all wrinkled and drawn together. He held in his hand a pencil, and a card of some commission-merchant in foreign parts, on the back of which, for there was light enough to read or write by, he seemed ready to figure out a calculation.

"Young man," said he, abruptly, "what quantity of land do the Shakers own here, in Canterbury?"

"That is more than I can tell thee, friend," answered Josiah, "but it is a very rich establishment, and for a long way by the roadside thee may guess the land to be ours, by the neatness of the fences."

"And what may be the value of the whole," continued the stranger, "with all the buildings and improvements, pretty nearly, in round numbers?"

"Oh, a monstrous sum,—more than I can reckon," replied the young Shaker.

"Well, sir," said the pilgrim, "there was a day, and not very long ago, neither, when I stood at my counting-room window, and watched the signal flags of three of my own ships entering the harbor, from the East Indies, from Liverpool, and from up the Straits, and I would not have given the invoice of the least of them for the title-deeds of this whole Shaker settlement. You stare. Perhaps, now, you won't believe that I could have put more value on a little piece of paper, no bigger than the palm of your hand, than all these solid acres of grain, grass, and pasture-land would sell for?"

"I won't dispute it, friend," answered Josiah, "but I know I had rather have fifty acres of this good land than a whole sheet of thy paper."

"You may say so now," said the ruined merchant, bitterly, "for my name would not be worth the paper I should write it on. Of course, you must have heard of my failure?"

And the stranger mentioned his name, which, however mighty it might have been in the commercial world, the young Shaker had never heard of among the Canterbury hills.

"Not heard of my failure!" exclaimed the merchant, considerably piqued. "Why, it was spoken of on 'Change in London, and from Boston to New Orleans men trembled in their shoes. At all events, I did fail, and you see me here on my road to the Shaker village, where, doubtless (for the Shakers are a shrewd sect), they will have a due respect for my experience, and give me the management of the trading part of the concern, in which case I think I can pledge myself to double their capital in four or five years. Turn back with me, young man; for though you will never meet with my good luck, you can hardly escape my bad."

"I will not turn back for this," replied Josiah, calmly, "any more than for the advice of the varse-maker, between whom and thee, friend, I see a sort of likeness, though I can't justly say where it lies. But Miriam and I can earn our daily bread among the world's people as well as in the Shaker village. And do we want anything more, Miriam?"

"Nothing more, Josiah," said the girl, quietly.

"Yea, Miriam, and daily bread for some other little mouths, if

God send them," observed the simple Shaker lad.

Miriam did not reply, but looked down into the spring, where she encountered the image of her own pretty face, blushing within the prim little bonnet. The third pilgrim now took up the conversation. He was a sunburnt countryman, of tall frame and bony strength, on whose rude and manly face there appeared a darker, more sullen and obstinate despondency, than on those of either the poet or the merchant.

"Well, now, youngster," he began, "these folks have had their say, so I'll take my turn. My story will cut but a poor figure by the side of theirs; for I never supposed that I could have a right to meat and drink, and great praise besides, only for tagging rhymes together, as it seems this man does; nor ever tried to get the substance of hundreds into my own hands, like the trader there. When I was about of your years, I married me a wife,—just such a neat and pretty young woman as Miriam, if that's her name,—and all I asked of Providence was an ordinary blessing on the sweat of my brow, so that we might be decent and comfortable, and have daily bread for ourselves, and for some other little mouths that we soon had to feed. We had no very great prospects before us; but I never wanted to be idle; and I thought it a matter of course that the Lord would help me, because I was willing to help myself."

"And didn't He help thee, friend?" demanded Josiah, with some eagerness.

"No," said the yeoman, sullenly; "for then you would not have seen me here. I have labored hard for years; and my means have been growing narrower, and my living poorer, and my heart colder and heavier, all the time; till at last I could bear it no longer. I set myself down to calculate whether I had best go on the Oregon expedition, or come here to the Shaker village; but I had not hope enough left in me to begin the world over again; and, to make my story short, here I am. And now, youngster, take my advice, and turn back; or else, some few years hence, you'll have to climb this hill, with as heavy a heart as mine."

This simple story had a strong effect on the young fugitives. The misfortunes of the poet and merchant had won little sympathy from their plain good sense and unworldly feelings, qualities which made them such unprejudiced and inflexible judges, that few men would have chosen to take the opinion of this youth and maiden as to the wisdom or folly of their pursuits. But here was one whose simple wishes had resembled their own, and who, after efforts which almost gave him a right to claim success from fate, had failed in accomplishing them.

"But thy wife, friend?" exclaimed the younger man. "What became of the pretty girl, like Miriam? Oh, I am afraid she is dead!"

"Yea, poor man, she must be dead,—she and the children, too," sobbed Miriam.

The female pilgrim had been leaning over the spring, wherein latterly a tear or two might have been seen to fall, and form its little circle on the surface of the water. She now looked up, disclosing features still comely, but which had acquired an expression of fretfulness, in the same long course of evil fortune that had thrown a sullen gloom over the temper of the unprosperous yeoman.

"I am his wife," said she, a shade of irritability just perceptible in the sadness of her tone. "These poor little things, asleep on the ground, are two of our children. We had two more, but God has provided better for them than we could, by taking them to Himself."

"And what would thee advise Josiah and me to do?" asked Miriam, this being the first question which she had put to either of the strangers.

"'Tis a thing almost against nature for a woman to try to part true lovers," answered the yeoman's wife, after a pause; "but I'll speak as truly to you as if these were my dying words. Though my husband told you some of our troubles, he didn't mention the greatest, and that which makes all the rest so hard to bear. If you and your sweetheart marry, you'll be kind and pleasant to each other for a year or two, and while that's the case, you never will repent; but, by and by, he'll grow gloomy, rough, and hard to please, and you'll be peevish, and full of little angry fits, and apt to be complaining by the fireside, when he comes to rest himself from his troubles out of doors; so your love will wear away by little and little, and leave you miserable at last. It has been so with us; and yet my husband and I were true lovers once, if ever two young folks were."

As she ceased, the yeoman and his wife exchanged a glance, in which there was more and warmer affection than they had supposed to have escaped the frost of a wintry fate, in either of their breasts. At that moment, when they stood on the utmost verge of married life, one word fitly spoken, or perhaps one peculiar look, had they had mutual confidence enough to reciprocate it, might have renewed all their old feelings, and sent them back, resolved to sustain each other amid the struggles of the world. But the crisis passed and never came again. Just then, also, the children, roused by their mother's voice, looked up, and added their wailing accents to the testimony borne by all the Canterbury pilgrims against the world from which they fled.

"We are tired and hungry!" cried they. "Is it far to the Shaker village?"

The Shaker youth and maiden looked mournfully into each other's eyes. They had but stepped across the threshold of their homes, when lo! the dark array of cares and sorrows that rose up to warn them back. The varied narratives of the strangers had arranged themselves into a parable; they seemed not merely instances of woful fate that had befallen others, but shadowy omens of disappointed hope and unavailing toil, domestic grief and estranged affection, that would cloud the onward path of these poor fugitives. But after one instant's hesitation, they opened their arms, and sealed their resolve with as pure and fond an embrace as ever youthful love had hallowed.

"We will not go back," said they. "The world never can be dark to us, for we will always love one another."

Then the Canterbury pilgrims went up the hill, while the poet chanted a drear and desperate stanza of the Farewell to his Harp, fitting music for that melancholy band. They sought a home where all former ties of nature or society would be sundered, and all old distinctions levelled, and a cold and passionless security be substituted for mortal hope and fear, as in that other refuge of the world's weary outcasts, the grave. The lovers drank at the Shaker spring, and then, with chastened hopes, but more confiding affections, went on to mingle in an untried life.

1833, 1851

Ethan Brand[5]

A Chapter from an Abortive Romance

Bartram the lime-burner, a rough, heavy-looking man, begrimed with charcoal, sat watching his kiln, at nightfall, while his little son played at building houses with the scattered fragments of marble,

5. The germ of this story is in two notebook entries of 1844: "The search of an investigator for the Unpardonable Sin;—he at last finds it in his own heart and practice"; and "the Unpardonable Sin might consist in a want of love and reverence for the Human Soul; in consequence of which, the investigator pried into its dark depths, not with a hope or purpose of making it better, but from a cold philosophical curiosity,—content that it should be wicked in what ever kind or degree, and only desiring to study it out. Would not this, in other words, be the separation of the intellect from the heart?" (*American Notebooks*, p. 106). Ethan Brand is akin to the artist of "The Prophetic Pictures," to Dr. Rappaccini, and to Roger Chillingworth in *The Scarlet Letter*. The story was presumably written largely between autumn, 1848, and autumn, 1849, shortly before

Hawthorne began *The Scarlet Letter* (Randall Stewart, *Nathaniel Hawthorne*, 1948, pp. 92–93). Its subtitle and its references to antecedent action as material already familiar to the reader indicate that it is a fragment of a large-scale enterprise presumably superseded by *The Scarlet Letter*. Hawthorne wrote of it to C. W. Webber that "at last, by main strength, I have wrenched and torn an idea out of my miserable brain; or rather, the fragment of an idea, like a tooth ill-drawn, and leaving the roots to torture me." These "roots" or loose ends undoubtedly mar "Ethan Brand," but it is one of Hawthorne's major tales in spite of them. It appeared in the Boston *Museum* for January 5, 1850, and again in the *Dollar Magazine* for May of the same year. It was included in *The Snow Image*.

when, on the hillside below them, they heard a roar of laughter, not mirthful, but slow, and even solemn, like a wind shaking the boughs of the forest.

"Father, what is that?" asked the little boy, leaving his play, and pressing betwixt his father's knees.

"Oh, some drunken man, I suppose," answered the lime-burner; "some merry fellow from the bar-room in the village, who dared not laugh loud enough within doors lest he should blow the roof of the house off. So here he is, shaking his jolly sides at the foot of Graylock."[6]

"But, father," said the child, more sensitive than the obtuse, middle-aged clown, "he does not laugh like a man that is glad. So the noise frightens me!"

"Don't be a fool, child!" cried his father, gruffly. "You will never make a man, I do believe; there is too much of your mother in you. I have known the rustling of a leaf startle you. Hark! Here comes the merry fellow now. You shall see that there is no harm in him."

Bartram and his little son, while they were talking thus, sat watching the same lime-kiln that had been the scene of Ethan Brand's solitary and meditative life, before he began his search for the Unpardonable Sin. Many years, as we have seen, had now elapsed, since that portentous night when the IDEA was first developed. The kiln, however, on the mountain-side, stood unimpaired, and was in nothing changed since he had thrown his dark thoughts into the intense glow of its furnace, and melted them, as it were, into the one thought that took possession of his life. It was a rude, round, tower-like structure about twenty feet high, heavily built of rough stones, and with a hillock of earth heaped about the larger part of its circumference; so that the blocks and fragments of marble might be drawn by cart-loads, and thrown in at the top. There was an opening at the bottom of the tower, like an oven-mouth, but large enough to admit a man in a stooping posture, and provided with a massive iron door. With the smoke and jets of flame issuing from the chinks and crevices of this door, which seemed to give admittance into the hillside, it resembled nothing so much as the private entrance to the infernal regions, which the shepherds of the Delectable Mountains[7] were accustomed to show to pilgrims.

There are many such lime-kilns in that tract of country, for the purpose of burning the white marble which composes a large part

6. Mount Greylock in the Berkshires, the highest elevation in Massachusetts. "Ethan Brand" is unique among Hawthorne's tales in that its setting and many of its characters and incidents are drawn directly from observation. Hawthorne spent a holiday in and near North Adams, Mass., in the summer of 1838, recorded what he saw there very fully, and used it later in fiction. The stage-agent, the doctor, the soapmaker, little Joe, the dog who chases his tail, the traveling showman, and others are from life; see *American Notebooks*, pp. 33–67.
7. An allusion to Bunyan's *Pilgrim's Progress*.

of the substance of the hills. Some of them, built years ago, and long deserted, with weeds growing in the vacant round of the interior, which is open to the sky, and grass and wild-flowers rooting themselves into the chinks of the stones, look already like relics of antiquity, and may yet be overspread with the lichens of centuries to come. Others, where the lime-burner still feeds his daily and nightlong fire, afford points of interest to the wanderer among the hills, who seats himself on a log of wood or a fragment of marble, to hold a chat with the solitary man. It is a lonesome, and, when the character is inclined to thought, may be an intensely thoughtful occupation; as it proved in the case of Ethan Brand, who had mused to such strange purpose, in days gone by, while the fire in this very kiln was burning.

The man who now watched the fire was of a different order, and troubled himself with no thoughts save the very few that were requisite to his business. At frequent intervals, he flung back the clashing weight of the iron door, and, turning his face from the insufferable glare, thrust in huge logs of oak, or stirred the immense brands with a long pole. Within the furnace were seen the curling and riotous flames, and the burning marble, almost molten with the intensity of heat; while without, the reflection of the fire quivered on the dark intricacy of the surrounding forest, and showed in the foreground a bright and ruddy little picture of the hut, the spring beside its door, the athletic and coal-begrimed figure of the lime-burner, and the half-frightened child, shrinking into the protection of his father's shadow.[8] And when again the iron door was closed, then reappeared the tender light of the half-full moon, which vainly strove to trace out the indistinct shapes of the neighboring mountains; and, in the upper sky, there was a flitting congregation of clouds, still faintly tinged with the rosy sunset, though thus far down into the valley the sunshine had vanished long and long ago.

The little boy now crept still closer to his father, as footsteps were heard ascending the hillside, and a human form thrust aside the bushes that clustered beneath the trees.

"Halloo! who is it?" cried the lime-burner, vexed at his son's timidity, yet half infected by it. "Come forward, and show yourself, like a man, or I'll fling this chunk of marble at your head!"

"You offer me a rough welcome," said a gloomy voice, as the unknown man drew nigh. "Yet I neither claim nor desire a kinder one, even at my own fireside."

To obtain a distincter view, Bartram threw open the iron door of the kiln, whence immediately issued a gush of fierce light, that

8. The opening and closing of the kiln door causes the light to rise and sink as does the fire at the witch meeting in "Young Goodman Brown." The "tender light of the half-full moon," however, adds an element not present in the earlier story—unless the pink ribbons of Faith are an equivalent.

smote full upon the stranger's face and figure. To a careless eye there appeared nothing very remarkable in his aspect, which was that of a man in a coarse, brown, country-made suit of clothes, tall and thin, with the staff and heavy shoes of a wayfarer. As he advanced, he fixed his eyes—which were very bright—intently upon the brightness of the furnace, as if he beheld, or expected to behold, some object worthy of note within it.

"Good evening, stranger," said the lime-burner; "whence come you, so late in the day?"

"I come from my search," answered the wayfarer; "for, at last, it is finished."

"Drunk!—or crazy!" muttered Bartram to himself. "I shall have trouble with the fellow. The sooner I drive him away, the better."

The little boy, all in a tremble, whispered to his father, and begged him to shut the door of the kiln, so that there might not be so much light; for that there was something in the man's face which he was afraid to look at, yet could not look away from. And, indeed, even the lime-burner's dull and torpid sense began to be impressed by an indescribable something in that thin, rugged, thoughtful visage, with the grizzled hair hanging wildly about it, and those deeply sunken eyes, which gleamed like fires within the entrance of a mysterious cavern. But, as he closed the door, the stranger turned towards him, and spoke in a quiet, familiar way, that made Bartram feel as if he were a sane and sensible man, after all.

"Your task draws to an end, I see," said he. "This marble has already been burning three days. A few hours more will convert the stone to lime."

"Why, who are you?" exclaimed the lime-burner. "You seem as well acquainted with my business as I am myself."

"And well I may be," said the stranger; "for I followed the same craft many a long year, and here, too, on this very spot. But you are a new-comer in these parts. Did you never hear of Ethan Brand?"

"The man that went in search of the Unpardonable Sin?" asked Bartram, with a laugh.

"The same," answered the stranger. "He has found what he sought, and therefore he comes back again."

"What! then you are Ethan Brand himself?" cried the lime-burner, in amazement. "I am a new-comer here, as you say, and they call it eighteen years since you left the foot of Graylock. But, I can tell you, the good folks still talk about Ethan Brand, in the village yonder, and what a strange errand took him away from his lime-kiln. Well, and so you have found the Unpardonable Sin?"

"Even so!" said the stranger, calmly.

"If the question is a fair one," proceeded Bartram, "where might it be?"

Ethan Brand laid his finger on his own heart.

"Here!" replied he.

And then, without mirth in his countenance, but as if moved by an involuntary recognition of the infinite absurdity of seeking throughout the world for what was the closest of all things to himself, and looking into every heart, save his own, for what was hidden in no other breast, he broke into a laugh of scorn. It was the same slow, heavy laugh, that had almost appalled the lime-burner when it heralded the wayfarer's approach.

The solitary mountain-side was made dismal by it. Laughter, when out of place, mistimed, or bursting forth from a disordered state of feeling, may be the most terrible modulation of the human voice. The laughter of one asleep, even if it be a little child,—the madman's laugh,—the wild, screaming laugh of a born idiot,—are sounds that we sometimes tremble to hear, and would always willingly forget. Poets have imagined no utterance of fiends or hobgoblins so fearfully appropriate as a laugh. And even the obtuse lime-burner felt his nerves shaken, as this strange man looked inward at his own heart, and burst into laughter that rolled away into the night, and was indistinctly reverberated among the hills.

"Joe," said he to his little son, "scamper down to the tavern in the village, and tell the jolly fellows there that Ethan Brand has come back, and that he has found the Unpardonable Sin!"

The boy darted away on his errand, to which Ethan Brand made no objection, nor seemed hardly to notice it. He sat on a log of wood, looking steadfastly at the iron door of the kiln. When the child was out of sight, and his swift and light footsteps ceased to be heard treading first on the fallen leaves and then on the rocky mountain-path, the lime-burner began to regret his departure. He felt that the little fellow's presence had been a barrier between his guest and himself, and that he must now deal, heart to heart, with a man who, on his own confession, had committed the one only crime for which Heaven could afford no mercy. That crime, in its indistinct blackness, seemed to overshadow him. The lime-burner's own sins rose up within him, and made his memory riotous with a throng of evil shapes that asserted their kindred with the Master Sin, whatever it might be, which it was within the scope of man's corrupted nature to conceive and cherish. They were all of one family; they went to and fro between his breast and Ethan Brand's, and carried dark greetings from one to the other.

Then Bartram remembered the stories which had grown traditionary in reference to this strange man, who had come upon him like a shadow of the night, and was making himself at home in his old place, after so long absence that the dead people, dead and buried for years, would have had more right to be at home, in any familiar spot, than he. Ethan Brand, it was said, had conversed with Satan himself in the lurid blaze of this very kiln. The legend had been matter of mirth heretofore, but looked grisly now. According to this tale, before Ethan Brand departed on his search, he had been accustomed to evoke a fiend from the hot furnace of the lime-kiln, night after night, in order to confer with him about the Unpardonable Sin; the man and the fiend each laboring to frame the image of some mode of guilt which could neither be atoned for nor forgiven. And, with the first gleam of light upon the mountaintop, the fiend crept in at the iron door, there to abide the intensest element of fire, until again summoned forth to share in the dreadful task of extending man's possible guilt beyond the scope of Heaven's else infinite mercy.

While the lime-burner was struggling with the horror of these thoughts, Ethan Brand rose from the log, and flung open the door of the kiln. The action was in such accordance with the idea in Bartram's mind, that he almost expected to see the Evil One issue forth, red-hot, from the raging furnace.

"Hold! hold!" cried he, with a tremulous attempt to laugh; for he was ashamed of his fears, although they overmastered him. "Don't, for mercy's sake, bring out your Devil now!"

"Man!" sternly replied Ethan Brand, "what need have I of the Devil? I have left him behind me, on my track. It is with such half-way sinners as you that he busies himself. Fear not, because I open the door. I do but act by old custom, and am going to trim your fire, like a lime-burner, as I was once."

He stirred the vast coals, thrust in more wood, and bent forward to gaze into the hollow prison-house of the fire, regardless of the fierce glow that reddened upon his face. The lime-burner sat watching him, and half suspected this strange guest of a purpose, if not to evoke a fiend, at least to plunge bodily into the flames, and thus vanish from the sight of man. Ethan Brand, however, drew quietly back, and closed the door of the kiln.

"I have looked," said he, "into many a human heart that was seven times hotter with sinful passions than yonder furnace is with fire. But I found not there what I sought. No, not the Unpardonable Sin!"

"What is the Unpardonable Sin?" asked the lime-burner; and then he shrank farther from his companion, trembling lest his question should be answered.

"It is a sin that grew within my own breast," replied Ethan Brand, standing erect, with a pride that distinguishes all enthusiasts of his stamp. "A sin that grew nowhere else! The sin of an intellect that triumphed over the sense of brotherhood with man and reverence for God, and sacrificed everything to its own mighty claims! The only sin that deserves a recompense of immortal agony! Freely, were it to do again, would I incur the guilt. Unshrinkingly I accept the retribution!"

"The man's head is turned," muttered the lime-burner to himself. "He may be a sinner like the rest of us,—nothing more likely, —but, I'll be sworn, he is a madman too."

Nevertheless, he felt uncomfortable at his situation, alone with Ethan Brand on the wild mountain-side, and was right glad to hear the rough murmur of tongues, and the footsteps of what seemed a pretty numerous party, stumbling over the stones and rustling through the underbrush. Soon appeared the whole lazy regiment that was wont to infest the village tavern, comprehending three or four individuals who had drunk flip beside the bar-room fire through all the winters, and smoked their pipes beneath the stoop through all the summers, since Ethan Brand's departure. Laughing boisterously, and mingling all their voices together in unceremonious talk, they now burst into the moonshine and narrow streaks of firelight that illuminated the open space before the lime-kiln. Bartram set the door ajar again, flooding the spot with light, that the whole company might get a fair view of Ethan Brand, and he of them.

There, among other old acquaintances, was a once ubiquitous man, now almost extinct, but whom we were formerly sure to encounter at the hotel of every thriving village throughout the country. It was the stage-agent. The present specimen of the genus was a wilted and smoke-dried man, wrinkled and red-nosed, in a smartly cut, brown, bob-tailed coat, with brass buttons, who, for a length of time unknown, had kept his desk and corner in the bar-room, and was still puffing what seemed to be the same cigar that he had lighted twenty years before. He had great fame as a dry joker, though, perhaps, less on account of any intrinsic humor than from a certain flavor of brandy-toddy and tobacco-smoke, which impregnated all his ideas and expressions, as well as his person. Another well-remembered, though strangely altered, face was that of Lawyer Giles, as people still called him in courtesy; an elderly ragamuffin, in his soiled shirt-sleeves and tow-cloth trousers. This poor fellow had been an attorney, in what he called his better days, a sharp practitioner, and in great vogue among the village litigants; but flip, and sling, and toddy, and cocktails, imbibed at all hours, morning, noon, and night, had caused him to slide from intellectual to various kinds and degrees of bodily labor, till at last, to adopt his own phrase, he slid into a soap-vat. In other words, Giles was now a soap-boiler, in a small way. He had come to be but the fragment of a human being, a part of one foot having been chopped off by an axe, and an entire hand torn away by the devilish grip of a steam-engine. Yet, though the corporeal hand was gone, a spiritual member remained; for, stretching forth the stump, Giles steadfastly averred that he felt an invisible thumb and fingers with as vivid a sensation as before the real ones were amputated. A maimed and miserable wretch he was; but one, nevertheless, whom the world could not trample on, and had no right to scorn, either in this or any previous stage of his misfortunes, since he had still kept up the courage and spirit of a man, asked nothing in charity, and with his one hand—and that the left one—fought a stern battle against want and hostile circumstances.

Among the throng, too, came another personage, who, with certain points of similarity to Lawyer Giles, had many more of difference. It was the village doctor; a man of some fifty years, whom, at an earlier period of his life, we introduced as paying a professional visit to Ethan Brand during the latter's supposed insanity. He was now a purple-visaged, rude, and brutal, yet half-gentlemanly figure, with something wild, ruined, and desperate in his talk, and in all the details of his gesture and manners. Brandy possessed this man like an evil spirit, and made him as surly and savage as a wild beast, and as miserable as a lost soul; but there was supposed to be in him such wonderful skill, such native gifts of healing, beyond any which medical science could impart, that society caught hold of him, and would not let him sink out of its reach. So, swaying to and fro upon his horse, and grumbling thick accents at the bedside, he visited all the sick-chambers for miles about among the mountain towns, and sometimes raised a dying man, as it were, by miracle, or quite as often, no doubt, sent his patient to a grave that was dug many a year too soon. The doctor had an everlasting pipe in his mouth, and, as somebody said, in allusion to his habit of swearing, it was always alight with hell-fire.

These three worthies pressed forward, and greeted Ethan Brand each after his own fashion, earnestly inviting him to partake of the contents of a certain black bottle, in which, as they averred, he would find something far better worth seeking for than the Unpardonable Sin. No mind, which has wrought itself by intense and solitary meditation into a high state of enthusiasm, can endure the kind of contact with low and vulgar modes of thought and feeling to which Ethan Brand was now subjected. It made him doubt—and, strange to say, it was a painful doubt—whether he had indeed found the Unpardonable Sin, and found it within himself. The whole question on which he had exhausted life, and more than life, looked like a delusion.

"Leave me," he said bitterly, "ye brute beasts, that have made yourselves so, shrivelling up your souls with fiery liquors! I have done with you. Years and years ago, I groped into your hearts, and found nothing there for my purpose. Get ye gone!"

"Why, you uncivil scoundrel," cried the fierce doctor, "is that the way you respond to the kindness of your best friends? Then let me tell you the truth. You have no more found the Unpardonable Sin than yonder boy Joe has. You are but a crazy fellow,—I told you so twenty years ago,—neither better nor worse than a crazy fellow, and the fit companion of old Humphrey, here!"

He pointed to an old man, shabbily dressed, with long white hair, thin visage, and unsteady eyes. For some years past this aged person had been wandering about among the hills, inquiring of all travellers whom he met for his daughter. The girl, it seemed, had gone off with a company of circus-performers; and occasionally tidings of her came to the village, and fine stories were told of her glittering appearance as she rode on horseback in the ring, or performed marvellous feats on the tight-rope.

The white-haired father now approached Ethan Brand, and gazed unsteadily into his face.

"They tell me you have been all over the earth," said he, wringing his hands with earnestness. "You must have seen my daughter, for she makes a grand figure in the world, and everybody goes to see her. Did she send any word to her old father, or say when she was coming back?"

Ethan Brand's eye quailed beneath the old man's. That daughter, from whom he so earnestly desired a word of greeting, was the Esther of our tale, the very girl whom, with such cold and remorseless purpose, Ethan Brand had made the subject of a psychological experiment, and wasted, absorbed, and perhaps annihilated her soul, in the process.

"Yes," murmured he, turning away from the hoary wanderer; "it is no delusion. There is an Unpardonable Sin!"

While these things were passing, a merry scene was going forward in the area of cheerful light, beside the spring and before the door of the hut. A number of the youth of the village, young men and girls, had hurried up the hillside, impelled by curiosity to see Ethan Brand, the hero of so many a legend familiar to their childhood. Finding nothing, however, very remarkable in his aspect,—nothing but a sunburnt wayfarer, in plain garb and dusty shoes, who sat looking into the fire as if he fancied pictures among the coals,—these young people speedily grew tired of observing him. As it happened, there was other amusement at hand. An old German Jew, travelling with a diorama on his back, was passing down the mountain-road towards the village just as the party turned aside from it, and, in hopes of eking out the profits of the day, the showman had kept them company to the lime-kiln.

"Come, old Dutchman," cried one of the young men, "let us see your pictures, if you can swear they are worth looking at!"

"Oh, yes, Captain," answered the Jew,—whether as a matter of courtesy or craft, he styled everybody Captain,—"I shall show you, indeed, some very superb pictures!"

So, placing his box in a proper position, he invited the young men and girls to look through the glass orifices of the machine, and proceeded to exhibit a series of the most outrageous scratchings and daubings, as specimens of the fine arts, that ever an itinerant showman had the face to impose upon his circle of spectators. The pictures were worn out, moreover, tattered, full of cracks and wrinkles, dingy with tobacco-smoke, and otherwise in a most pitiable condition. Some purported to be cities, public edifices, and ruined castles in Europe; others represented Napoleon's battles and Nelson's sea-fights; and in the midst of these would be seen a gigantic, brown, hairy hand,—which might have been mistaken for the Hand of Destiny, though, in truth, it was only the showman's,—pointing its forefinger to various scenes of the conflict, while its owner gave historical illustrations. When, with much merriment at its abominable deficiency of merit, the exhibition was concluded, the German bade little Joe put his head into the box. Viewed through the magnifying-glasses, the boy's round, rosy visage assumed the strangest imaginable aspect of an immense Titanic child, the mouth grinning broadly, and the eyes and every other feature overflowing with fun at the joke. Suddenly, however, that merry face turned pale, and its expression changed to horror, for this easily impressed and excitable child had become sensible that the eye of Ethan Brand was fixed upon him through the glass.

"You make the little man to be afraid, Captain," said the German Jew, turning up the dark and strong outline of his visage, from his stooping posture. "But look again, and, by chance, I shall cause you to see somewhat that is very fine, upon my word!"

Ethan Brand gazed into the box for an instant, and then starting back, looked fixedly at the German. What had he seen? Nothing, apparently; for a curious youth, who had peeped in almost at the same moment, beheld only a vacant space of canvas.

"I remember you now," muttered Ethan Brand to the showman.

"Ah, Captain," whispered the Jew of Nuremberg, with a dark smile, "I find it to be a heavy matter in my show-box,—this Unpardonable Sin! By my faith, Captain, it has wearied my shoulders, this long day, to carry it over the mountain."

"Peace," answered Ethan Brand, sternly, "or get thee into the furnace yonder!"

The Jew's exhibition had scarcely concluded, when a great, elderly dog—who seemed to be his own master, as no person in the company laid claim to him—saw fit to render himself the object of public notice. Hitherto, he had shown himself a very quiet, well-disposed old dog, going round from one to another, and, by way of being sociable, offering his rough head to be patted by any kindly hand that would take so much trouble. But now, all of a sudden, this grave and venerable quadruped, of his own mere motion, and without the slightest suggestion from anybody else, began to run round after his tail, which, to heighten the absurdity of the proceeding, was a great deal shorter than it should have been. Never was seen such headlong eagerness in pursuit of an object that could not possibly be attained; never was heard such a tremendous outbreak of growling, snarling, barking, and snapping,—as if one end of the ridiculous brute's body were at deadly and most unforgivable enmity with the other. Faster and faster, round about went the cur; and faster and still faster fled the unapproachable brevity of his tail; and louder and fiercer grew his yells of rage and animosity; until, utterly exhausted, and as far from the goal as ever, the foolish old dog ceased his performance as suddenly as he had begun it. The next moment he was as mild, quiet, sensible, and respectable in his deportment, as when he first scraped acquaintance with the company.

As may be supposed, the exhibition was greeted with universal laughter, clapping of hands, and shouts of encore, to which the canine performer responded by wagging all that there was to wag of his tail, but appeared totally unable to repeat his very successful effort to amuse the spectators.

Meanwhile, Ethan Brand had resumed his seat upon the log, and moved, it might be, by a perception of some remote analogy between his own case and that of this self-pursuing cur, he broke into the awful laugh, which, more than any other token, expressed the condition of his inward being. From that moment, the merriment of the party was at an end; they stood aghast, dreading lest the inauspicious sound should be reverberated around the horizon, and that mountain would thunder it to mountain, and so the horror be prolonged upon their ears. Then, whispering one to another that it was late,—that the moon was almost down,—that the August night was growing chill,—they hurried homewards, leaving the limeburner and little Joe to deal as they might with their unwelcome guest. Save for these three human beings, the open space on the hillside was a solitude, set in a vast gloom of forest. Beyond that darksome verge, the firelight glimmered on the stately trunks and almost black foliage of pines, intermixed with the lighter verdure of sapling oaks, maples, and poplars, while here and there lay the gigantic corpses of dead trees, decaying on the leaf-strewn soil. And it seemed to little Joe—a timorous and imaginative child—that the silent forest was holding its breath until some fearful thing should happen.

Ethan Brand thrust more wood into the fire, and closed the door of the kiln; then looking over his shoulder at the lime-burner and his son, he bade, rather than advised, them to retire to rest.

"For myself, I cannot sleep," said he. "I have matters that it concerns me to meditate upon. I will watch the fire, as I used to do in the old time."

"And call the Devil out of the furnace to keep you company, I suppose," muttered Bartram, who had been making intimate acquaintance with the black bottle above mentioned. "But watch, if you like, and call as many devils as you like! For my part, I shall be all the better for a snooze. Come, Joe!"

As the boy followed his father into the hut, he looked back at the wayfarer, and the tears came into his eyes, for his tender spirit had an intuition of the bleak and terrible loneliness in which this man had enveloped himself.

When they had gone, Ethan Brand sat listening to the crackling of the kindled wood, and looking at the little spirts of fire that issued through the chinks of the door. These trifles, however, once so familiar, had but the slightest hold of his attention, while deep within his mind he was reviewing the gradual but marvellous change that had been wrought upon him by the search to which he had devoted himself. He remembered how the night dew had fallen upon him,—how the dark forest had whispered to him,—how the stars had gleamed upon him,—a simple and loving man, watching his fire in the years gone by, and ever musing as it burned. He remembered with what tenderness, with what love and sympathy for mankind, and what pity for human guilt and woe, he had first begun to contemplate those ideas which afterwards became the inspiration of his life; with what reverence he had then looked into the heart of man, viewing it as a temple originally divine, and, however desecrated, still to be held sacred by a brother; with what awful fear he had deprecated the success of his pursuit, and prayed that the Unpardonable Sin might never be revealed to him. Then ensued that vast intellectual development, which, in its progress, disturbed the counterpoise between his mind and heart. The Idea that possessed his life had operated as a means of education; it had gone on cultivating his powers to the highest point of which they were susceptible; it had raised him from the level of an unlettered laborer to stand on a starlit eminence, whither the philosophers of the earth, laden with the lore of universities, might vainly strive to clamber after him. So much for the intellect! But where was the heart? That, indeed, had withered,—had contracted,—had hardened,—had perished! It had ceased to partake of the universal throb. He had lost his hold of the magnetic chain of humanity. He was no longer a brother-man, opening the chambers or the dungeons of our common nature by the key of holy sympathy, which gave him a right to share in all its secrets; he was now a cold observer, looking on mankind as the subject of his experiment, and, at length, converting man and woman to be his puppets, and pulling the wires that moved them to such degrees of crime as were demanded for his study.

Thus Ethan Brand became a fiend. He began to be so from the moment that his moral nature had ceased to keep the pace of improvement with his intellect. And now, as his highest effort and inevitable development,—as the bright and gorgeous flower, and rich, delicious fruit of his life's labor,—he had produced the Unpardonable Sin!

"What more have I to seek? What more to achieve?" said Ethan Brand to himself. "My task is done, and well done!"

Starting from the log with a certain alacrity in his gait and ascending the hillock of earth that was raised against the stone circumference of the lime-kiln, he thus reached the top of the structure. It was a space of perhaps ten feet across, from edge to edge, presenting a view of the upper surface of the immense mass of broken marble with which the kiln was heaped. All these innumerable blocks and fragments of marble were red-hot and vividly on fire, sending up great spouts of blue flame, which quivered aloft and danced madly, as within a magic circle, and sank and rose again, with continual and multitudinous activity. As the lonely man bent forward over this terrible body of fire, the blasting heat smote up against his person with a breath that, it might be supposed, would have scorched and shrivelled him up in a moment.

Ethen Brand stood erect, and raised his arms on high. The blue flames played upon his face, and imparted the wild and ghastly light which alone could have suited its expression; it was that of a fiend on the verge of plunging into his gulf of intensest torment.

"O Mother Earth," cried he, "who art no more my Mother, and into whose bosom this frame shall never be resolved! O mankind, whose brotherhood I have cast off, and trampled thy great heart beneath my feet! O stars of heaven, that shone on me of old, as if to light me onward and upward!—farewell all, and forever. Come, deadly element of Fire,—henceforth my familiar frame! Embrace me, as I do thee!"

That night the sound of a fearful peal of laughter rolled heavily through the sleep of the lime-burner and his little son; dim shapes of horror and anguish haunted their dreams, and seemed still present in the rude hovel, when they opened their eyes to the daylight.

"Up, boy, up!" cried the lime-burner, staring about him. "Thank Heaven, the night is gone, at last; and rather than pass such another, I would watch my lime-kiln, wide awake, for a twelvemonth. This Ethan Brand, with his humbug of an Unpardonable Sin, has done me no such mighty favor, in taking my place!"

He issued from the hut, followed by little Joe, who kept fast hold of his father's hand. The early sunshine was already pouring its gold upon the mountain-tops, and though the valleys were still in shadow, they smiled cheerfully in the promise of the bright day that was hastening onward. The village, completely shut in by hills, which swelled away gently about it, looked as if it had rested peacefully in the hollow of the great hand of Providence. Every dwelling was distinctly visible; the little spires of the two churches pointed upwards, and caught a foreglimmering of brightness from the sun-gilt skies upon their gilded weathercocks. The tavern was astir, and the figure of the old, smoke-dried stage-agent, cigar in mouth, was seen beneath the stoop. Old Graylock was glorified with a golden cloud upon his head. Scattered likewise over the breasts of the surrounding mountains, there were heaps of hoary mist, in fantastic shapes, some of them far down into the valley, others high up towards the summits, and still others, of the same family of mist or cloud, hovering in the gold radiance of the upper atmosphere. Stepping from one to another of the clouds that rested on the hills, and thence to the loftier brotherhood that sailed in air, it seemed almost as if a mortal man might thus ascend into the heavenly regions. Earth was so mingled with sky that it was a day-dream to look at it.

To supply that charm of the familiar and homely, which Nature so readily adopts into a scene like this, the stage coach was rattling down the mountain-road, and the driver sounded his horn, while Echo caught up the notes, and intertwined them into a rich and varied and elaborate harmony, of which the original performer could lay claim to little share. The great hills played a concert among themselves, each contributing a strain of airy sweetness.

Little Joe's face brightened at once.

"Dear father," cried he, skipping cheerily to and fro, "that strange man is gone, and the sky and the mountains all seem glad of it!"

"Yes," growled the lime-burner, with an oath, "but he has let the fire go down, and no thanks to him if five hundred bushels of lime are not spoiled. If I catch the fellow hereabouts again, I shall feel like tossing him into the furnace!"

With his long pole in his hand, he ascended to the top of the kiln. After a moment's pause, he called to his son.

"Come up here, Joe!" said he.

So little Joe ran up the hillock, and stood by his father's side. The marble was all burnt into perfect, snow-white lime. But on its surface, in the midst of the circle,—snow-white too, and thoroughly converted into lime,—lay a human skeleton, in the attitude of a person who, after long toil, lies down to long repose. Within the ribs—strange to say—was the shape of a human heart.

"Was the fellow's heart made of marble?" cried Bartram, in some perplexity at this phenomenon. "At any rate, it is burnt into what looks like special good lime; and, taking all the bones together, my kiln is half a bushel the richer for him."

So saying, the rude lime-burner lifted his pole, and, letting it fall upon the skeleton, the relics of Ethan Brand were crumbled into fragments.

1850, 1851

Rappaccini's Daughter[9]

A young man, named Giovanni Guasconti, came, very long ago, from the more southern region of Italy, to pursue his studies at the University of Padua. Giovanni, who had but a scanty supply of gold ducats in his pocket, took lodgings in a high and gloomy chamber of an old edifice which looked not unworthy to have been the palace of a Paduan noble, and which, in fact, exhibited over its entrance the armorial bearings of a family long since extinct. The young stranger, who was not unstudied in the great poem of his country, recollected that one of the ancestors of this family, and perhaps an occupant of this very mansion, had been pictured by Dante as a partaker of the immortal agonies of his Inferno.[1] These reminiscences and associations, together with the tendency to heartbreak natural to a young man for the first time out of his native

9. On January 4, 1839, Hawthorne copied a sentence from Sir Thomas Browne's *Vulgar Errors* (1646): "A story there passeth of an Indian king that sent unto Alexander a fair woman, fed with aconite and other poisons, with this intent complexionally to destroy him!" (*Passages*, p. 209. Browne's phrase "either by converse or copulation," between "intent" and "complexionally," was omitted in Mrs. Hawthorne's version of Hawthorne's notebook.) A later passage presents another parallel: "Madame Calderon de la B (in Life in Mexico) speaks of persons who have been inoculated with the venom of rattlesnakes, by pricking them in various places with the tooth. These persons are thus secured forever after against the bite of any venomous reptile. They have the power of calling snakes, and feel great pleasure in playing with and handling them. Their own bite becomes poisonous to people not inoculated in the same manner. Thus a part of the serpent's nature appears to be transfused into them" (*American Notebooks*, p. 98). The idea of the fair woman baneful through no fault of her own is in Keats's poem *Lamia* (1820). It might be noted as well that in the

setting of the palace and the wizard (Rappaccini) the story has connections with the Gothic tale of the supernatural, and further that it is an ironic variation upon fairy tales like "The Sleeping Beauty," in which a handsome prince (Giovanni) comes to set a lady (Beatrice) free from enchantment. Again, Rappaccini's garden is a poisonous Garden of Eden, Giovanni and Beatrice are Adam and Eve, and Rappaccini is both God and Satan. "Rappaccini's Daughter" is perhaps Hawthorne's most complex story, and its possible relationships are many. It was published in the *Democratic Review* for December, 1844, and collected in *Mosses from an Old Manse*.
1. "Hawthorne, like Giovanni, was 'not unstudied' in the great poem of Italy, and the allusion to 'reminiscences and associations' from *The Divine Comedy* * * * is highly suggestive. We need not expect rigid correspondence with Dante's work, but it is clear that Giovanni, like Dante, is being instructed and tested, that he too has a chance of winning a high and holy faith through Beatrice" (Roy R. Male, *Hawthorne's Tragic Vision*, 1957, p. 61).

sphere, caused Giovanni to sigh heavily as he looked around the desolate and ill-furnished apartment.

"Holy Virgin, signor!" cried old Dame Lisabetta, who, won by the youth's remarkable beauty of person, was kindly endeavoring to give the chamber a habitable air, "what a sigh was that to come out of a young man's heart! Do you find this old mansion gloomy? For the love of Heaven, then, put your head out of the window, and you will see as bright sunshine as you have left in Naples."

Guasconti mechanically did as the old woman advised, but could not quite agree with her that the Paduan sunshine was as cheerful as that of southern Italy. Such as it was, however, it fell upon a garden beneath the window and expended its fostering influences on a variety of plants, which seemed to have been cultivated with exceeding care.

"Does this garden belong to the house?" asked Giovanni.

"Heaven forbid, signor, unless it were fruitful of better pot herbs than any that grow there now," answered old Lisabetta. "No; that garden is cultivated by the own hands of Signor Giacomo Rappaccini, the famous doctor, who, I warrant him, has been heard of as far as Naples. It is said that he distils these plants into medicines that are as potent as a charm. Oftentimes you may see the signor doctor at work, and perchance the signora, his daughter, too, gathering the strange flowers that grow in the garden."

The old woman had now done what she could for the aspect of the chamber; and, commending the young man to the protection of the saints, took her departure.

Giovanni still found no better occupation than to look down into the garden beneath his window. From its appearance, he judged it to be one of those botanic gardens which were of earlier date in Padua than elsewhere in Italy or in the world. Or, not improbably, it might once have been the pleasure-place of an opulent family; for there was the ruin of a marble fountain, in the centre, sculptured with rare art, but so wofully shattered that it was impossible to trace the original design from the chaos of remaining fragments. The water, however, continued to gush and sparkle into the sunbeams as cheerfully as ever. A little gurgling sound ascended to the young man's window, and made him feel as if the fountain were an immortal spirit that sung its song unceasingly and without heeding the vicissitudes around it, while one century imbodied it in marble and another scattered the perishable garniture on the soil. All about the pool into which the water subsided grew various plants, that seemed to require a plentiful supply of moisture for the nourishment of gigantic leaves, and, in some instances, flowers gorgeously magnificent. There was one shrub in particular, set in a marble vase in the midst of the pool, that bore a profusion of purple blossoms, each of which had the lustre and richness of a gem; and the whole together made a show so resplendent that it seemed enough to illuminate the garden, even had there been no sunshine.[2] Every portion of the soil was peopled with plants and herbs, which, if less beautiful, still bore tokens of assiduous care, as if all had their individual virtues, known to the scientific mind that fostered them. Some were placed in urns, rich with old carving, and others in common garden pots; some crept serpent-like along the ground or climbed on high, using whatever means of ascent was offered them. One plant had wreathed itself round a statue of Vertumnus, which was thus quite veiled and shrouded in a drapery of hanging foliage, so happily arranged that it might have served a sculptor for a study.

While Giovanni stood at the window he heard a rustling behind a screen of leaves, and became aware that a person was at work in the garden. His figure soon emerged into view, and showed itself to be that of no common laborer, but a tall, emaciated, sallow, and sickly-looking man, dressed in a scholar's garb of black. He was beyond the middle term of life, with gray hair, a thin, gray beard, and a face singularly marked with intellect and cultivation, but which could never, even in his more youthful days, have expressed much warmth of heart.

Nothing could exceed the intentness with which this scientific gardener examined every shrub which grew in his path: it seemed as if he was looking into their inmost nature, making observations in regard to their creative essence, and discovering why one leaf grew in this shape and another in that, and wherefore such and such flowers differed among themselves in hue and perfume. Nevertheless, in spite of this deep intelligence on his part, there was no approach to intimacy between himself and these vegetable existences.[3] On the contrary, he avoided their actual touch or the direct inhaling of their odors with a caution that impressed Giovanni most disagreeably; for the man's demeanor was that of one walking among malignant influences, such as savage beasts, or deadly snakes, or evil spirits, which, should he allow them one moment of license, would wreak upon him some terrible fatality. It was strangely frightful to the young man's imagination to see this air of insecurity in a person cultivating a garden, that most simple and innocent of human toils, and which had been alike the joy and labor of the unfallen parents of the race. Was this garden, then, the Eden of the present world? And this man, with such a perception of harm in what his own hands caused to grow,—was he the Adam?

2. This fountain and shrub are the central symbols of the story, if we make Beatrice its central character. They are different aspects of her for Giovanni to perceive, but only the fountain with its shattered marble is the true Beatrice.
3. Rappaccini the scientist is like the artist in "The Prophetic Pictures" in possessing power without sympathy.

The distrustful gardener, while plucking away the dead leaves or pruning the too luxuriant growth of the shrubs, defended his hands with a pair of thick gloves. Nor were these his only armor. When, in his walk through the garden, he came to the magnificent plant that hung its purple gems beside the marble fountain, he placed a kind of mask over his mouth and nostrils, as if all this beauty did but conceal a deadlier malice; but, finding his task still too dangerous, he drew back, removed the mask, and called loudly, but in the infirm voice of a person affected with inward disease,—

"Beatrice! Beatrice!"

"Here am I, my father. What would you?" cried a rich and youthful voice from the window of the opposite house—a voice as rich as a tropical sunset, and which made Giovanni, though he knew not why, think of deep hues of purple or crimson and of perfumes heavily delectable. "Are you in the garden?"

"Yes, Beatrice," answered the gardener, "and I need your help."

Soon there emerged from under a sculptured portal the figure of a young girl, arrayed with as much richness of taste as the most splendid of the flowers, beautiful as the day, and with a bloom so deep and vivid that one shade more would have been too much. She looked redundant with life, health, and energy; all of which attributes were bound down and compressed, as it were, and girdled tensely, in their luxuriance, by her virgin zone.[4] Yet Giovanni's fancy must have grown morbid while he looked down into the garden; for the impression which the fair stranger made upon him was as if here were another flower, the human sister of those vegetable ones, as beautiful as they, more beautiful than the richest of them, but still to be touched only with a glove, nor to be approached without a mask. As Beatrice came down the garden path, it was observable that she handled and inhaled the odor of several of the plants which her father had most sedulously avoided.

"Here, Beatrice," said the latter, "see how many needful offices require to be done to our chief treasure. Yet, shattered as I am, my life might pay the penalty of approaching it so closely as circumstances demand. Henceforth, I fear, this plant must be consigned to your sole charge."

"And gladly will I undertake it," cried again the rich tones of the young lady, as she bent towards the magnificent plant and opened her arms as if to embrace it. "Yes, my sister, my splendor, it shall be Beatrice's task to nurse and serve thee; and thou shalt reward her with thy kisses and perfumed breath, which to her is as the breath of life."

Then, with all the tenderness in her manner that was so strikingly expressed in her words, she busied herself with such atten-

4. A belt or girdle worn by unmarried women.

tions as the plant seemed to require; and Giovanni, at his lofty window, rubbed his eyes and almost doubted whether it were a girl tending her favorite flower, or one sister performing the duties of affection to another. The scene soon terminated. Whether Dr. Rappaccini had finished his labors in the garden, or that his watchful eye had caught the stranger's face, he now took his daughter's arm and retired. Night was already closing in; oppressive exhalations seemed to proceed from the plants and steal upward past the open window; and Giovanni, closing the lattice, went to his couch and dreamed of a rich flower and beautiful girl. Flower and maiden were different, and yet the same, and fraught with some strange peril in either shape.

But there is an influence in the light of morning that tends to rectify whatever errors of fancy, or even of judgment, we may have incurred during the sun's decline, or among the shadows of the night, or in the less wholesome glow of moonshine. Giovanni's first movement, on starting from sleep, was to throw open the window and gaze down into the garden which his dreams had made so fertile of mysteries. He was surprised and a little ashamed to find how real and matter-of-fact an affair it proved to be, in the first rays of the sun which gilded the dew-drops that hung upon leaf and blossom, and, while giving a brighter beauty to each rare flower, brought everything within the limits of ordinary experience. The young man rejoiced that, in the heart of the barren city, he had the privilege of overlooking this spot of lovely and luxuriant vegetation. It would serve, he said to himself, as a symbolic language to keep him in communion with Nature. Neither the sickly and thoughtworn Dr. Giacomo Rappaccini, it is true, nor his brilliant daughter, were now visible; so that Giovanni could not determine how much of the singularity which he attributed to both was due to their own qualities and how much to his wonder-working fancy; but he was inclined to take a most rational view of the whole matter.

In the course of the day he paid his respects to Signor Pietro Baglioni, professor of medicine in the university, a physician of eminent repute, to whom Giovanni had brought a letter of introduction. The professor was an elderly personage, apparently of genial nature, and habits that might almost be called jovial. He kept the young man to dinner, and made himself very agreeable by the freedom and liveliness of his conversation, especially when warmed by a flask or two of Tuscan wine. Giovanni, conceiving that men of science, inhabitants of the same city, must needs be on familiar terms with one another, took an opportunity to mention the name of Dr. Rappaccini. But the professor did not respond with so much cordiality as he had anticipated.

"Ill would it become a teacher of the divine art of medicine," said

Professor Pietro Baglioni, in answer to a question of Giovanni, "to withhold due and well-considered praise of a physician so eminently skilled as Rappaccini; but, on the other hand, I should answer it but scantily to my conscience were I to permit a worthy youth like yourself, Signor Giovanni, the son of an ancient friend, to imbibe erroneous ideas respecting a man who might hereafter chance to hold your life and death in his hands. The truth is, our worshipful Dr. Rappaccini has as much science as any member of the faculty—with perhaps one single exception—in Padua, or all Italy; but there are certain grave objections to his professional character."

"And what are they?" asked the young man.

"Has my friend Giovanni any disease of body or heart, that he is so inquisitive about physicians?" said the professor, with a smile. "But as for Rappaccini, it is said of him—and I, who know the man well, can answer for its truth—that he cares infinitely more for science than for mankind. His patients are interesting to him only as subjects for some new experiment. He would sacrifice human life, his own among the rest, or whatever else was dearest to him, for the sake of adding so much as a grain of mustard seed to the great heap of his accumulated knowledge."

"Methinks he is an awful man indeed," remarked Guasconti, mentally recalling the cold and purely intellectual aspect of Rappaccini. "And yet, worshipful professor, is it not a noble spirit? Are there many men capable of so spiritual a love of science?"

"God forbid," answered the professor, somewhat testily; "at least, unless they take sounder views of the healing art than those adopted by Rappaccini. It is his theory that all medicinal virtues are comprised within those substances which we term vegetable poisons. These he cultivates with his own hands, and is said even to have produced new varieties of poison, more horribly deleterious than Nature, without the assistance of this learned person, would ever have plagued the world withal. That the signor doctor does less mischief than might be expected with such dangerous substances is undeniable. Now and then, it must be owned, he has effected, or seemed to effect, a marvellous cure; but, to tell you my private mind, Signor Giovanni, he should receive little credit for such instances of success,—they being probably the work of chance,—but should be held strictly accountable for his failures, which may justly be considered his own work."

The youth might have taken Baglioni's opinions with many grains of allowance had he known that there was a professional warfare of long continuance between him and Dr. Rappaccini, in which the latter was generally thought to have gained the advantage. If the reader be inclined to judge for himself, we refer him to certain black-letter tracts on both sides, preserved in the medical department of the University of Padua.

"I know not, most learned professor," returned Giovanni, after musing on what had been said of Rappaccini's exclusive zeal for science,—"I know not how dearly this physician may love his art; but surely there is one object more dear to him. He has a daughter."

"Aha!" cried the professor, with a laugh. "So now our friend Giovanni's secret is out. You have heard of this daughter, whom all the young men in Padua are wild about, though not half a dozen have ever had the good hap to see her face. I know little of the Signora Beatrice save that Rappaccini is said to have instructed her deeply in his science, and that, young and beautiful as fame reports her, she is already qualified to fill a professor's chair. Perchance her father destines her for mine! Other absurd rumors there be, not worth talking about or listening to. So now, Signor Giovanni, drink off your glass of lachryma."[5]

Guasconti returned to his lodgings somewhat heated with the wine he had quaffed, and which caused his brain to swim with strange fantasies in reference to Dr. Rappaccini and the beautiful Beatrice. On his way, happening to pass by a florist's, he bought a fresh bouquet of flowers.

Ascending to his chamber, he seated himself near the window, but within the shadow thrown by the depth of the wall, so that he could look down into the garden with little risk of being discovered. All beneath his eye was a solitude. The strange plants were basking in the sunshine, and now and then nodding gently to one another, as if in acknowledgment of sympathy and kindred. In the midst, by the shattered fountain, grew the magnificent shrub, with its purple gems clustering all over it; they glowed in the air, and gleamed back again out of the depths of the pool, which thus seemed to overflow with colored radiance from the rich reflection that was steeped in it. At first, as we have said, the garden was a solitude. Soon, however,—as Giovanni had half hoped, half feared, would be the case, —a figure appeared beneath the antique sculptured portal, and came down between the rows of plants, inhaling their various perfumes as if she were one of those beings of old classic fable that lived upon sweet odors. On again beholding Beatrice, the young man was even startled to perceive how much her beauty exceeded his recollection of it; so brilliant, so vivid, was its character, that she glowed amid the sunlight, and, as Giovanni whispered to himself, positively illuminated the more shadowy intervals of the garden path. Her face being now more revealed than on the former occasion, he was struck by its expression of simplicity and sweetness,— qualities that had not entered into his idea of her character, and which made him ask anew what manner of mortal she might be.

5. Lachryma Christi ("tear of Christ"), a rich, sweet Neapolitan wine.

Nor did he fail again to observe, or imagine, an analogy between the beautiful girl and the gorgeous shrub that hung its gemlike flowers over the fountain,—a resemblance which Beatrice seemed to have indulged a fantastic humor in heightening, both by the arrangement of her dress and the selection of its hues.

Approaching the shrub, she threw open her arms, as with a passionate ardor, and drew its branches into an intimate embrace—so intimate that her features were hidden in its leafy bosom and her glistening ringlets all intermingled with the flowers.

"Give me thy breath, my sister," exclaimed Beatrice; "for I am faint with common air. And give me this flower of thine, which I separate with gentlest fingers from the stem and place it close beside my heart."

With these words the beautiful daughter of Rappaccini plucked one of the richest blossoms of the shrub, and was about to fasten it in her bosom. But now, unless Giovanni's draughts of wine had bewildered his senses, a singular incident occurred. A small orange-colored reptile, of the lizard or chameleon species, chanced to be creeping along the path, just at the feet of Beatrice. It appeared to Giovanni,—but, at the distance from which he gazed, he could scarcely have seen anything so minute,—it appeared to him, however, that a drop or two of moisture from the broken stem of the flower descended upon the lizard's head. For an instant the reptile contorted itself violently, and then lay motionless in the sunshine. Beatrice observed this remarkable phenomenon, and crossed herself, sadly, but without surprise; nor did she therefore hesitate to arrange the fatal flower in her bosom. There it blushed, and almost glimmered with the dazzling effect of a precious stone, adding to her dress and aspect the one appropriate charm which nothing else in the world could have supplied. But Giovanni, out of the shadow of his window, bent forward and shrank back, and murmured and trembled.

"Am I awake? Have I my senses?" said he to himself. "What is this being? Beautiful shall I call her, or inexpressibly terrible?"

Beatrice now strayed carelessly through the garden, approaching closer beneath Giovanni's window, so that he was compelled to thrust his head quite out of its concealment in order to gratify the intense and painful curiosity which she excited. At this moment there came a beautiful insect over the garden wall; it had, perhaps, wandered through the city, and found no flowers or verdure among those antique haunts of men until the heavy perfumes of Dr. Rappaccini's shrubs had lured it from afar. Without alighting on the flowers, this winged brightness seemed to be attracted by Beatrice, and lingered in the air and fluttered about her head. Now, here it could not be but that Giovanni Guasconti's eyes deceived him. Be that as it might, he fancied that, while Beatrice was gazing at the insect with childish delight, it grew faint and fell at her feet; its bright wings shivered; it was dead—from no cause that he could discern, unless it were the atmosphere of her breath. Again Beatrice crossed herself and sighed heavily as she bent over the dead insect.

An impulsive movement of Giovanni drew her eyes to the window. There she beheld the beautiful head of the young man—rather a Grecian than an Italian head, with fair, regular features, and a glistening of gold among his ringlets—gazing down upon her like a being that hovered in mid air. Scarcely knowing what he did, Giovanni threw down the bouquet which he had hitherto held in his hand.

"Signora," said he, "there are pure and healthful flowers. Wear them for the sake of Giovanni Guasconti."

"Thanks, signor," replied Beatrice, with her rich voice, that came forth as it were like a gush of music, and with a mirthful expression half childish and half woman-like. "I accept your gift, and would fain recompense it with this precious purple flower; but if I toss it into the air it will not reach you. So Signor Guasconti must even content himself with my thanks."

She lifted the bouquet from the ground, and then, as if inwardly ashamed at having stepped aside from her maidenly reserve to respond to a stranger's greeting, passed swiftly homeward through the garden. But few as the moments were, it seemed to Giovanni, when she was on the point of vanishing beneath the sculptured portal, that his beautiful bouquet was already beginning to wither in her grasp. It was an idle thought; there could be no possibility of distinguishing a faded flower from a fresh one at so great a distance.

For many days after this incident the young man avoided the window that looked into Dr. Rappaccini's garden, as if something ugly and monstrous would have blasted his eyesight had he been betrayed into a glance. He felt conscious of having put himself, to a certain extent, within the influence of an unintelligible power by the communication which he had opened with Beatrice. The wisest course would have been, if his heart were in any real danger, to quit his lodgings and Padua itself at once; the next wiser, to have accustomed himself, as far as possible, to the familiar and daylight view of Beatrice—thus bringing her rigidly and systematically within the limits of ordinary experience. Least of all, while avoiding her sight, ought Giovanni to have remained so near this extraordinary being that the proximity and possibility even of intercourse should give a kind of substance and reality to the wild vagaries which his imagination ran riot continually in producing. Guasconti had not a deep heart—or, at all events, its depths were not sounded now; but he had a quick fancy, and an ardent southern temperament, which rose every instant to a higher fever pitch. Whether or no Beatrice possessed those terrible attributes, that fatal breath, the affinity with those so beautiful and deadly flowers which were indicated by what Giovanni had witnessed, she had at least instilled a fierce and subtle poison into his system. It was not love, although her rich beauty was a madness to him; nor horror, even while he fancied her spirit to be imbued with the same baneful essence that seemed to pervade her physical frame; but a wild offspring of both love and horror that had each parent in it, and burned like one and shivered like the other. Giovanni knew not what to dread; still less did he know what to hope; yet hope and dread kept a continual warfare in his breast, alternately vanquishing one another and starting up afresh to renew the contest. Blessed are all simple emotions, be they dark or bright! It is the lurid intermixture of the two that produces the illuminating blaze of the infernal regions.

Sometimes he endeavored to assuage the fever of his spirit by a rapid walk through the streets of Padua or beyond its gates: his footsteps kept time with the throbbings of his brain, so that the walk was apt to accelerate itself to a race. One day he found himself arrested; his arm was seized by a portly personage, who had turned back on recognizing the young man and expended much breath in overtaking him.

"Signor Giovanni! Stay, my young friend!" cried he. "Have you forgotten me? That might well be the case if I were as much altered as yourself."

It was Baglioni, whom Giovanni had avoided ever since their first meeting, from a doubt that the professor's sagacity would look too deeply into his secrets. Endeavoring to recover himself, he stared forth wildly from his inner world into the outer one and spoke like a man in a dream.

"Yes; I am Giovanni Guasconti. You are Professor Pietro Baglioni. Now let me pass!"

"Not yet, not yet, Signor Giovanni Guasconti," said the professor, smiling, but at the same time scrutinizing the youth with an earnest glance. "What! did I grow up side by side with your father? and shall his son pass me like a stranger in these old streets of Padua? Stand still, Signor Giovanni; for we must have a word or two before we part."

"Speedily, then, most worshipful professor, speedily," said Giovanni, with feverish impatience. "Does not your worship see that I am in haste?"

Now, while he was speaking there came a man in black along the street, stooping and moving feebly like a person in inferior health. His face was all overspread with a most sickly and sallow hue, but yet so pervaded with an expression of piercing and active intellect that an observer might easily have overlooked the merely physical attributes and have seen only this wonderful energy. As he passed, this person exchanged a cold and distant salutation with Baglioni, but fixed his eyes upon Giovanni with an intentness that seemed to bring out whatever was within him worthy of notice. Nevertheless, there was a peculiar quietness in the look, as if taking merely a speculative, not a human, interest in the young man.

"It is Dr. Rappaccini!" whispered the professor when the stranger had passed. "Has he ever seen your face before?"

"Not that I know," answered Giovanni, starting at the name.

"He *has* seen you! he must have seen you!" said Baglioni, hastily. "For some purpose or other, this man of science is making a study of you. I know that look of his! It is the same that coldly illuminates his face as he bends over a bird, a mouse, or a butterfly, which, in pursuance of some experiment, he has killed by the perfume of a flower; a look as deep as Nature itself, but without Nature's warmth of love. Signor Giovanni, I will stake my life upon it, you are the subject of one of Rappaccini's experiments!"

"Will you make a fool of me?" cried Giovanni, passionately. "*That*, signor professor, were an untoward experiment."

"Patience! patience!" replied the imperturbable professor. "I tell thee, my poor Giovanni, that Rappaccini has a scientific interest in thee. Thou hast fallen into fearful hands! And the Signora Beatrice,—what part does she act in this mystery?"

But Guasconti, finding Baglioni's pertinacity intolerable, here broke away, and was gone before the professor could again seize his arm. He looked after the young man intently and shook his head.

"This must not be," said Baglioni to himself. "The youth is the son of my old friend, and shall not come to any harm from which the arcana of medical science can preserve him. Besides, it is too insufferable an impertinence in Rappaccini, thus to snatch the lad out of my own hands, as I may say, and make use of him for his infernal experiments. This daughter of his! It shall be looked to. Perchance, most learned Rappaccini, I may foil you where you little dream of it!"

Meanwhile Giovanni had pursued a circuitous route, and at length found himself at the door of his lodgings. As he crossed the threshold he was met by old Lisabetta, who smirked and smiled, and was evidently desirous to attract his attention; vainly, however, as the ebullition of his feelings had momentarily subsided into a cold and dull vacuity. He turned his eyes full upon the withered face that was puckering itself into a smile, but seemed to behold it not. The old dame, therefore, laid her grasp upon his cloak.

"Signor! signor!" whispered she, still with a smile over the whole breadth of her visage, so that it looked not unlike a grotesque carving in wood, darkened by centuries. "Listen, signor! There is a private entrance into the garden!"

"What do you say?" exclaimed Giovanni, turning quickly about, as if an inanimate thing should start into feverish life. "A private entrance into Dr. Rappaccini's garden?"

"Hush! hush! not so loud!" whispered Lisabetta, putting her hand over his mouth. "Yes; into the worshipful doctor's garden, where you may see all his fine shrubbery. Many a young man in Padua would give gold to be admitted among those flowers."

Giovanni put a piece of gold into her hand.

"Show me the way," said he.

A surmise, probably excited by his conversation with Baglioni, crossed his mind, that this interposition of old Lisabetta might perchance be connected with the intrigue, whatever were its nature, in which the professor seemed to suppose that Dr. Rappaccini was involving him. But such a suspicion, though it disturbed Giovanni was inadequate to restrain him. The instant that he was aware of the possibility of approaching Beatrice, it seemed an absolute necessity of his existence to do so. It mattered not whether she were angel or demon; he was irrevocably within her sphere, and must obey the law that whirled him onward, in ever-lessening circles, towards a result which he did not attempt to foreshadow; and yet, strange to say, there came across him a sudden doubt whether this intense interest on his part were not delusory; whether it were really of so deep and positive a nature as to justify him in now thrusting himself into an incalculable position; whether it were not merely the fantasy of a young man's brain, only slightly or not at all connected with his heart.

He paused, hesitated, turned half about, but again went on. His withered guide led him along several obscure passages, and finally undid a door, through which, as it was opened, there came the sight and sound of rustling leaves, with the broken sunshine glimmering among them. Giovanni stepped forth, and, forcing himself through the entanglement of a shrub that wreathed its tendrils over the hidden entrance, stood beneath his own window in the open area of Dr. Rappaccini's garden.

How often is it the case that, when impossibilities have come to pass and dreams have condensed their misty substance into tangible realities, we find ourselves calm, and even coldly self-possessed, amid circumstances which it would have been a delirium of joy or agony to anticipate! Fate delights to thwart us thus. Passion will choose his own time to rush upon the scene, and lingers sluggishly behind when an appropriate adjustment of events would seem to summon his appearance. So was it now with Giovanni. Day after day his pulses had throbbed with feverish blood at the improbable idea of an interview with Beatrice, and of standing with her, face to face, in this very garden, basking in the Oriental sunshine of her beauty, and snatching from her full gaze the mystery which he deemed the riddle of his own existence. But now there was a singular and untimely equanimity within his breast. He threw a glance around the garden to discover if Beatrice or her father were present, and, perceiving that he was alone, began a critical observation of the plants.

The aspect of one and all of them dissatisfied him; their gorgeousness seemed fierce, passionate, and even unnatural. There was hardly an individual shrub which a wanderer, straying by himself through a forest, would not have been startled to find growing wild, as if an unearthly face had glared at him out of the thicket. Several also would have shocked a delicate instinct by an appearance of artificialness indicating that there had been such commixture, and, as it were, adultery, of various vegetable species, that the production was no longer of God's making, but the monstrous offspring of man's depraved fancy, glowing with only an evil mockery of beauty. They were probably the result of experiment, which in one or two cases had succeeded in mingling plants individually lovely into a compound possessing the questionable and ominous character that distinguished the whole growth of the garden. In fine, Giovanni recognized but two or three plants in the collection, and those of a kind that he well knew to be poisonous. While busy with these contemplations he heard the rustling of a silken garment, and, turning, beheld Beatrice emerging from beneath the sculptured portal.

Giovanni had not considered with himself what should be his deportment; whether he should apologize for his intrusion into the garden, or assume that he was there with the privity at least, if not by the desire, of Dr. Rappaccini or his daughter; but Beatrice's manner placed him at his ease, though leaving him still in doubt by what agency he had gained admittance. She came lightly along the path and met him near the broken fountain. There was surprise in her face, but brightened by a simple and kind expression of pleasure.

"You are a connoisseur in flowers, signor," said Beatrice, with a smile, alluding to the bouquet which he had flung her from the window. "It is no marvel, therefore, if the sight of my father's rare collection has tempted you to take a nearer view. If he were here, he could tell you many strange and interesting facts as to the nature and habits of these shrubs; for he has spent a lifetime in such studies, and this garden is his world."

"And yourself, lady," observed Giovanni, "if fame says true,—you likewise are deeply skilled in the virtues indicated by these rich

blossoms and these spicy perfumes. Would you deign to be my in-
structress, I should prove an apter scholar than if taught by Signor
Rappaccini himself."

"Are there such idle rumors?" asked Beatrice, with the music of
a pleasant laugh. "Do people say that I am skilled in my father's
science of plants? What a jest is there! No; though I have grown
up among these flowers, I know no more of them than their hues
and perfume; and sometimes methinks I would fain rid myself of
even that small knowledge. There are many flowers here, and those
not the least brilliant, that shock and offend me when they meet
my eye. But pray, signor, do not believe these stories about my
science. Believe nothing of me save what you see with your own
eyes."

"And must I believe all that I have seen with my own eyes?"
asked Giovanni, pointedly, while the recollection of former scenes
made him shrink. "No, signora; you demand too little of me. Bid
me believe nothing save what comes from your own lips."

It would appear that Beatrice understood him. There came a deep
flush to her cheek; but she looked full into Giovanni's eyes, and
responded to his gaze of uneasy suspicion with a queenlike haughtiness.

"I do so bid you, signor," she replied. "Forget whatever you may
have fancied in regard to me. If true to the outward senses, still it
may be false in its essence; but the words of Beatrice Rappaccini's
lips are true from the depths of the heart outward. Those you may
believe."

A fervor glowed in her whole aspect and beamed upon Giovanni's
consciousness like the light of truth itself; but while she spoke there
was a fragrance in the atmosphere around her, rich and delightful,
though evanescent, yet which the young man, from an indefinable
reluctance, scarcely dared to draw into his lungs. It might be the
odor of the flowers. Could it be Beatrice's breath which thus embalmed her words with a strange richness, as if by steeping them
in her heart? A faintness passed like a shadow over Giovanni and
flitted away; he seemed to gaze through the beautiful girl's eyes into
her transparent soul, and felt no more doubt or fear.

The tinge of passion that had colored Beatrice's manner vanished; she became gay, and appeared to derive a pure delight from
her communion with the youth not unlike what the maiden of a
lonely island might have felt conversing with a voyager from the
civilized world.[6] Evidently her experience of life had been confined
within the limits of that garden. She talked now about matters as
simple as the daylight or summer clouds, and now asked questions

6. Perhaps a reminiscence of the situation of Miranda and Ferdinand in Shakespeare's *Tempest*.

in reference to the city, or Giovanni's distant home, his friends, his mother, and his sisters—questions indicating such seclusion, and such lack of familiarity with modes and forms, that Giovanni responded as if to an infant. Her spirit gushed out before him like a fresh rill that was just catching its first glimpse of the sunlight and wandering at the reflections of earth and sky which were flung into its bosom. There came thoughts, too, from a deep source, and fantasies of a gemlike brilliancy, as if diamonds and rubies sparkled upward among the bubbles of the fountain. Ever and anon there gleamed across the young man's mind a sense of wonder that he should be walking side by side with the being who had so wrought upon his imagination, whom he had idealized in such hues of terror, in whom he had positively witnessed such manifestations of dreadful attributes,—that he should be conversing with Beatrice like a brother, and should find her so human and so maidenlike. But such reflections were only momentary; the effect of her character was too real not to make itself familiar at once.

In this free intercourse they had strayed through the garden, and now, after many turns among its avenues, were come to the shattered fountain, beside which grew the magnificent shrub, with its treasury of glowing blossoms. A fragrance was diffused from it which Giovanni recognized as identical with that which he had attributed to Beatrice's breath, but incomparably more powerful. As her eyes fell upon it, Giovanni beheld her press her hand to her bosom as if her heart were throbbing suddenly and painfully.

"For the first time in my life," murmured she, addressing the shrub, "I had forgotten thee."

"I remember, signora," said Giovanni, "that you once promised to reward me with one of these living gems for the bouquet which I had the happy boldness to fling to your feet. Permit me now to pluck it as a memorial of this interview."

He made a step towards the shrub with extended hand; but Beatrice darted forward, uttering a shriek that went through his heart like a dagger. She caught his hand and drew it back with the whole force of her slender figure. Giovanni felt her touch thrilling through his fibres.

"Touch it not!" exclaimed she, in a voice of agony. "Not for thy life! It is fatal!"

Then, hiding her face, she fled from him and vanished beneath the sculptured portal. As Giovanni followed her with his eyes, he beheld the emaciated figure and pale intelligence of Dr. Rappaccini, who had been watching the scene, he knew not how long, within the shadow of the entrance.

No sooner was Guasconti alone in his chamber than the image of Beatrice came back to his passionate musings, invested with all the witchery that had been gathering around it ever since his first glimpse of her, and now likewise imbued with a tender warmth of girlish womanhood. She was human; her nature was endowed with all gentle and feminine qualities; she was worthiest to be worshipped; she was capable, surely, on her part, of the height and heroism of love. Those tokens which he had hitherto considered as proofs of a frightful peculiarity in her physical and moral system were now either forgotten, or, by the subtle sophistry of passion transmitted into a golden crown of enchantment, rendering Beatrice the more admirable by so much as she was the more unique. Whatever had looked ugly was now beautiful; or, if incapable of such a change, it stole away and hid itself among those shapeless half ideas which throng the dim region beyond the daylight of our perfect consciousness. Thus did he spend the night, nor fell asleep until the dawn had begun to awake the slumbering flowers in Dr. Rappaccini's garden, whither Giovanni's dreams doubtless led him. Up rose the sun in his due season, and, flinging his beams upon the young man's eyelids, awoke him to a sense of pain. When thoroughly aroused, he became sensible of a burning and tingling agony in his hand—in his right hand—the very hand which Beatrice had grasped in her own when he was on the point of plucking one of the gemlike flowers. On the back of that hand there was now a purple print like that of four small fingers, and the likeness of a slender thumb upon his wrist.

Oh, how stubbornly does love,—or even that cunning semblance of love which flourishes in the imagination, but strikes no depth of root into the heart,—how stubbornly does it hold its faith until the moment comes when it is doomed to vanish into thin mist! Giovanni wrapped a handkerchief about his hand and wondered what evil thing had stung him, and soon forgot his pain in a reverie of Beatrice.

After the first interview, a second was in the inevitable course of what we call fate. A third; a fourth; and a meeting with Beatrice in the garden was no longer an incident in Giovanni's daily life, but the whole space in which he might be said to live; for the anticipation and memory of that ecstatic hour made up the remainder. Nor was it otherwise with the daughter of Rappaccini. She watched for the youth's appearance, and flew to his side with confidence as unreserved as if they had been playmates from early infancy—as if they were such playmates still. If, by any unwonted chance, he failed to come at the appointed moment, she stood beneath the window and sent up the rich sweetness of her tones to float around him in his chamber and echo and reverberate throughout his heart: "Giovanni! Giovanni! Why tarriest thou? Come down!" And down he hastened into that Eden of poisonous flowers.

But, with all this intimate familiarity, there was still a reserve in Beatrice's demeanor, so rigidly and invariably sustained that the idea of infringing it scarcely occurred to his imagination. By all appreciable signs, they loved; they had looked love with eyes that conveyed the holy secret from the depths of one soul into the depths of the other, as if it were too sacred to be whispered by the way; they had even spoken love in those gushes of passion when their spirits darted forth in articulated breath like tongues of long-hidden flame; and yet there had been no seal of lips, no clasp of hands, nor any slightest caress such as love claims and hallows. He had never touched one of the gleaming ringlets of her hair; her garment—so marked was the physical barrier between them—had never been waved against him by a breeze. On the few occasions when Giovanni had seemed tempted to overstep the limit, Beatrice grew so sad, so stern, and withal wore such a look of desolate separation, shuddering at itself, that not a spoken word was requisite to repel him. At such times he was startled at the horrible suspicions that rose, monster-like, out of the caverns of his heart and stared him in the face; his love grew thin and faint as the morning mist, his doubts alone had substance. But, when Beatrice's face brightened again after the momentary shadow, she was transformed at once from the mysterious, questionable being whom he had watched with so much awe and horror; she was now the beautiful and unsophisticated girl whom he felt his spirit knew with a certainty beyond all other knowledge.

A considerable time had now passed since Giovanni's last meeting with Baglioni. One morning, however, he was disagreeably surprised by a visit from the professor, whom he had scarcely thought of for whole weeks, and would willingly have forgotten still longer. Given up as he had long been to a pervading excitement, he could tolerate no companions except upon condition of their perfect sympathy with his present state of feeling. Such sympathy was not to be expected from Professor Baglioni.

The visitor chatted carelessly for a few moments about the gossip of the city and the university, and then took up another topic.

"I have been reading an old classic author lately," said he, "and met with a story that strangely interested me. Possibly you may remember it. It is of an Indian prince, who sent a beautiful woman as a present to Alexander the Great. She was as lovely as the dawn and gorgeous as the sunset; but what especially distinguished her was a certain rich perfume in her breath—richer than a garden of Persian roses. Alexander, as was natural to a youthful conqueror, fell in love at first sight with this magnificent stranger; but a certain sage physician, happening to be present, discovered a terrible secret in regard to her."

"And what was that?" asked Giovanni, turning his eyes downward to avoid those of the professor.

"That this lovely woman," continued Baglioni, with emphasis, "had been nourished with poison from her birth upward, until her whole nature was so imbued with them that she herself had become the deadliest poison in existence. Poison was her element of life. With that rich perfume of her breath she blasted the very air. Her love would have been poison—her embrace death. Is not this a marvellous tale?"

"A childish fable," answered Giovanni, nervously starting from his chair. "I marvel how your worship finds time to read such nonsense among your graver studies."

"By the by," said the professor, looking uneasily about him, "what singular fragrance is this in your apartment? Is it the perfume of your gloves? It is faint, but delicious; and yet, after all, by no means agreeable. Were I to breathe it long, methinks it would make me ill. It is like the breath of a flower; but I see no flowers in the chamber."

"Nor are there any," replied Giovanni, who had turned pale as the professor spoke; "nor, I think, is there any fragrance except in your worship's imagination. Odors, being a sort of element combined of the sensual and the spiritual, are apt to deceive us in this manner. The recollection of a perfume, the bare idea of it, may easily be mistaken for a present reality."

"Ay; but my sober imagination does not often play such tricks," said Baglioni; "and, were I to fancy any kind of odor, it would be that of some vile apothecary drug, wherewith my fingers are likely enough to be imbued. Our worshipful friend Rappaccini, as I have heard, tinctures his medicaments with odors richer than those of Araby. Doubtless, likewise, the fair and learned Signora Beatrice would minister to her patients with draughts as sweet as a maiden's breath; but woe to him that sips them!"

Giovanni's face evinced many contending emotions. The tone in which the professor alluded to the pure and lovely daughter of Rappaccini was a torture to his soul; and yet the intimation of a view of her character, opposite to his own, gave instantaneous distinctness to a thousand dim suspicions, which now grinned at him like so many demons. But he strove hard to quell them and to respond to Baglioni with a true lover's perfect faith.

"Signor professor," said he, "you were my father's friend; perchance, too, it is your purpose to act a friendly part towards his son. I would fain feel nothing towards you save respect and deference; but I pray you to observe, signor, that there is one subject on which we must not speak. You know not the Signora Beatrice. You cannot, therefore, estimate the wrong—the blasphemy, I may even say—that is offered to her character by a light or injurious word."

"Giovanni! my poor Giovanni!" answered the professor, with a calm expression of pity, "I know this wretched girl far better than yourself. You shall hear the truth in respect to the poisoner Rappaccini and his poisonous daughter; yes, poisonous as she is beautiful. Listen; for, even should you do violence to my gray hairs, it shall not silence me. That old fable of the Indian woman has become a truth by the deep and deadly science of Rappaccini and in the person of the lovely Beatrice."

Giovanni groaned and hid his face.

"Her father," continued Baglioni, "was not restrained by natural affection from offering up his child in this horrible manner as the victim of his insane zeal for science; for, let us do him justice, he is as true a man of science as ever distilled his own heart in an alembic. What, then, will be your fate? Beyond a doubt you are selected as the material of some new experiment. Perhaps the result is to be death; perhaps a fate more awful still. Rappaccini, with what he calls the interest of science before his eyes, will hesitate at nothing."

"It is a dream," muttered Giovanni to himself; "surely it is a dream."

"But," resumed the professor, "be of good cheer, son of my friend. It is not yet too late for the rescue. Possibly we may even succeed in bringing back this miserable child within the limits of ordinary nature, from which her father's madness has estranged her. Behold this little silver vase! It was wrought by the hands of the renowned Benvenuto Cellini, and is well worthy to be a love gift to the fairest dame in Italy. But its contents are invaluable. One little sip of this antidote would have rendered the most virulent poisons of the Borgias innocuous. Doubt not that it will be as efficacious against those of Rappaccini. Bestow the vase, and the precious liquid within it, on your Beatrice, and hopefully await the result."

Baglioni laid a small, exquisitely wrought silver vial on the table and withdrew, leaving what he had said to produce its effect upon the young man's mind.

"We will thwart Rappaccini yet," thought he, chuckling to himself, as he descended the stairs; "but, let us confess the truth of him, he is a wonderful man—a wonderful man indeed; a vile empiric, however, in his practice, and therefore not to be tolerated by those who respect the good old rules of the medical profession."

Throughout Giovanni's whole acquaintance with Beatrice, he had occasionally, as we have said, been haunted by dark surmises as to her character; yet so thoroughly had she made herself felt by him as a simple, natural, most affectionate, and guileless creature, that the image now held up by Professor Baglioni looked as strange and incredible as if it were not in accordance with his own original conception. True, there were ugly recollections connected with his first glimpses of the beautiful girl; he could not quite forget the bouquet that withered in her grasp, and the insect that perished amid the sunny air, by no ostensible agency save the fragrance of her breath. These incidents, however, dissolving in the pure light of her character, had no longer the efficacy of facts, but were acknowledged as mistaken fantasies, by whatever testimony of the senses they might appear to be substantiated. There is something truer and more real than what we can see with the eyes and touch with the finger. On such better evidence had Giovanni founded his confidence in Beatrice, though rather by the necessary force of her high attributes than by any deep and generous faith on his part. But now his spirit was incapable of sustaining itself at the height to which the early enthusiasm of passion had exalted it; he fell down, grovelling among earthly doubts, and defiled therewith the pure whiteness of Beatrice's image. Not that he gave her up; he did but distrust. He resolved to institute some decisive test that should satisfy him, once for all, whether there were those dreadful peculiarities in her physical nature which could not be supposed to exist without some corresponding monstrosity of soul. His eyes, gazing down afar, might have deceived him as to the lizard, the insect, and the flowers; but if he could witness, at the distance of a few paces, the sudden blight of one fresh and healthful flower in Beatrice's hand, there would be room for no further question. With this idea he hastened to the florist's and purchased a bouquet that was still gemmed with the morning dew-drops.

It was now the customary hour of his daily interview with Beatrice. Before descending into the garden, Giovanni failed not to look at his figure in the mirror,—a vanity to be expected in a beautiful young man, yet, as displaying itself at that troubled and feverish moment, the token of a certain shallowness of feeling and insincerity of character. He did gaze, however, and said to himself that his features had never before possessed so rich a grace, nor his eyes such vivacity, nor his cheeks so warm a hue of superabundant life.

"At least," thought he, "her poison has not yet insinuated itself into my system. I am no flower to perish in her grasp."

With that thought he turned his eyes on the bouquet, which he had never once laid aside from his hand. A thrill of indefinable horror shot through his frame on perceiving that those dewy flowers were already beginning to droop; they wore the aspect of things that had been fresh and lovely yesterday. Giovanni grew white as marble, and stood motionless before the mirror, staring at his own reflection there as at the likeness of something frightful. He remembered Baglioni's remark about the fragrance that seemed to pervade the chamber. It must have been the poison in his breath! Then he shuddered—shuddered at himself. Recovering from his stupor, he began to watch with curious eye a spider that was busily at work hanging its web from the antique cornice of the apartment, crossing and recrossing the artful system of interwoven lines—as vigorous and active a spider as ever dangled from an old ceiling. Giovanni bent towards the insect, and emitted a deep, long breath. The spider suddenly ceased its toil; the web vibrated with a tremor originating in the body of the small artisan. Again Giovanni sent forth a breath, deeper, longer, and imbued with a venomous feeling out of his heart: he knew not whether he were wicked or only desperate. The spider made a convulsive gripe with his limbs and hung dead across the window.

"Accursed! accursed!" muttered Giovanni, addressing himself. "Hast thou grown so poisonous that this deadly insect perishes by thy breath?"

At that moment a rich, sweet voice came floating up from the garden.

"Giovanni! Giovanni! It is past the hour! Why tarriest thou? Come down!"

"Yes," muttered Giovanni again. "She is the only being whom my breath may not slay! Would that it might!"

He rushed down, and in an instant was standing before the bright and loving eyes of Beatrice. A moment ago his wrath and despair had been so fierce that he could have desired nothing so much as to wither her by a glance; but with her actual presence there came influences which had too real an existence to be at once shaken off: recollections of the delicate and benign power of her feminine nature, which had so often enveloped him in a religious calm; recollections of many a holy and passionate outgush of her heart, when the pure fountain had been unsealed from its depths and made visible in its transparency to his mental eye; recollections which, had Giovanni known how to estimate them, would have assured him that all this ugly mystery was but an earthly illusion, and that, whatever mist of evil might seem to have gathered over her, the real Beatrice was a heavenly angel. Incapable as he was of such high faith, still her presence had not utterly lost its magic. Giovanni's rage was quelled into an aspect of sullen insensibility. Beatrice, with a quick spiritual sense, immediately felt that there was a gulf of blackness between them which neither he nor she could pass. They walked on together, sad and silent, and came thus to the marble fountain and to its pool of water on the ground, in the midst of which grew the shrub that bore gem-like blossoms. Giovanni was affrighted at the eager enjoyment—the appetite, as it were—with which he found himself inhaling the fragrance of the flowers.

"Beatrice," asked he, abruptly, "whence came this shrub?"

"My father created it," answered she, with simplicity.

"Created it! created it!" repeated Giovanni. "What mean you, Beatrice?"

"He is a man fearfully acquainted with the secrets of Nature," replied Beatrice; "and, at the hour when I first drew breath, this plant sprang from the soil, the offspring of his science, of his intellect, while I was but his earthly child. Approach it not!" continued she, observing with terror that Giovanni was drawing nearer to the shrub. "It has qualities that you little dream of. But I, dearest Giovanni,—I grew up and blossomed with the plant and was nourished with its breath. It was my sister, and I loved it with a human affection; for, alas!—hast thou not suspected it?—there was an awful doom."

Here Giovanni frowned so darkly upon her that Beatrice paused and trembled. But her faith in his tenderness reassured her, and made her blush that she had doubted for an instant.

"There was an awful doom," she continued, "the effect of my father's fatal love of science, which estranged me from all society of my kind. Until Heaven sent thee, dearest Giovanni, oh, how lonely was thy poor Beatrice!"

"Was it a hard doom?" asked Giovanni, fixing his eyes upon her.

"Only of late have I known how hard it was," answered she, tenderly. "Oh, yes; but my heart was torpid, and therefore quiet."

Giovanni's rage broke forth from his sullen gloom like a lightning flash out of a dark cloud.

"Accursed one!" cried he, with venomous scorn and anger. "And, finding thy solitude wearisome, thou hast severed me likewise from all the warmth of life and enticed me into thy region of unspeakable horror!"

"Giovanni!" exclaimed Beatrice, turning her large bright eyes upon his face. The force of his words had not found its way into her mind; she was merely thunderstruck.

"Yes, poisonous thing!" repeated Giovanni, beside himself with passion. "Thou hast done it! Thou hast blasted me! Thou hast filled my veins with poison! Thou hast made me as hateful, as ugly, as loathsome and deadly a creature as thyself—a world's wonder of hideous monstrosity! Now, if our breath be happily as fatal to ourselves as to all others, let us join our lips in one kiss of unutterable hatred, and so die!"

"What has befallen me?" murmured Beatrice, with a low moan out of her heart. "Holy Virgin, pity me, a poor heartbroken child!"

"Thou,—dost thou pray?" cried Giovanni, still with the same fiendish scorn. "Thy very prayers, as they come from thy lips, taint the atmosphere with death. Yes, yes; let us pray! Let us to church

and dip our fingers in the holy water at the portal! They that come
after us will perish as by a pestilence! Let us sign crosses in the air!
It will be scattering curses abroad in the likeness of holy symbols!"

"Giovanni," said Beatrice, calmly, for her grief was beyond passion, "why dost thou join thyself with me thus in those terrible
words? I, it is true, am the horrible thing thou namest me. But thou,
—what hast thou to do, save with one other shudder at my hideous
misery to go forth out of the garden and mingle with thy race, and
forget that there ever crawled on earth such a monster as poor
Beatrice?"

"Dost thou pretend ignorance?" asked Giovanni, scowling upon
her. "Behold! this power have I gained from the pure daughter of
Rappaccini."

There was a swarm of summer insects flitting through the air in
search of the food promised by the flower odors of the fatal garden.
They circled round Giovanni's head, and were evidently attracted
towards him by the same influence which had drawn them for an
instant within the sphere of several of the shrubs. He sent forth a
breath among them, and smiled bitterly at Beatrice as at least a
score of the insects fell dead upon the ground.

"I see it! I see it!" shrieked Beatrice. "It is my father's fatal science! No, no, Giovanni; it was not I! Never! never! I dreamed only
to love thee and be with thee a little time, and so to let thee pass
away, leaving but thine image in mine heart; for, Giovanni, believe
it, though my body be nourished with poison, my spirit is God's creature, and craves love as its daily food. But my father,—he has united
us in this fearful sympathy. Yes; spurn me, tread upon me, kill me!
Oh, what is death after such words as thine? But it was not I. Not
for a world of bliss would I have done it."

Giovanni's passion had exhausted itself in its outburst from his
lips. There now came across him a sense, mournful, and not without
tenderness, of the intimate and peculiar relationship between Beatrice and himself. They stood, as it were, in an utter solitude, which
would be made none the less solitary by the densest throng of human life. Ought not, then, the desert of humanity around them to
press this insulated pair closer together? If they should be cruel to
one another, who was there to be kind to them? Besides, thought
Giovanni, might there not still be a hope of his returning within the
limits of ordinary nature, and leading Beatrice, the redeemed Beatrice, by the hand? O, weak, and selfish, and unworthy spirit, that
could dream of an earthly union and earthly happiness as possible,
after such deep love had been so bitterly wronged as was Beatrice's
love by Giovanni's blighting words! No, no; there could be no such
hope. She must pass heavily, with that broken heart, across the
borders of Time—she must bathe her hurts in some fount of para-

dise, and forget her grief in the light of immortality, and *there* be
well.

But Giovanni did not know it.

"Dear Beatrice," said he, approaching her, while she shrank away
as always at his approach, but now with a different impulse, "dearest Beatrice, our fate is not yet so desperate. Behold! there is a
medicine, potent, as a wise physician has assured me, and almost
divine in its efficacy. It is composed of ingredients the most opposite
to those by which thy awful father has brought this calamity upon
thee and me. It is distilled of blessed herbs. Shall we not quaff it
together, and thus be purified from evil?"

"Give it me!" said Beatrice, extending her hand to receive the
little silver vial which Giovanni took from his bosom. She added,
with a peculiar emphasis, "I will drink; but do thou await the result."

She put Baglioni's antidote to her lips; and, at the same moment,
the figure of Rappaccini emerged from the portal and came slowly
towards the marble fountain. As he drew near, the pale man of
science seemed to gaze with a triumphant expression at the beautiful youth and maiden, as might an artist who should spend his life
in achieving a picture or a group of statuary and finally be satisfied
with his success. He paused; his bent form grew erect with conscious
power; he spread out his hands over them in the attitude of a father
imploring a blessing upon his children; but those were the same
hands that had thrown poison into the stream of their lives. Giovanni trembled. Beatrice shuddered nervously, and pressed her hand
upon her heart.

"My daughter," said Rappaccini, "thou art no longer lonely in
the world. Pluck one of those precious gems from thy sister shrub
and bid thy bridegroom wear it in his bosom. It will not harm him
now. My science and the sympathy between thee and him have so
wrought within his system that he now stands from common men,
as thou dost, daughter of my pride and triumph, from ordinary
women. Pass on, then, through the world, most dear to one another
and dreadful to all besides!"

"My father," said Beatrice, feebly,—and still as she spoke she
kept her hand upon her heart,—"wherefore didst thou inflict this
miserable doom upon thy child?"

"Miserable!" exclaimed Rappaccini. "What mean you, foolish
girl? Dost thou deem it misery to be endowed with marvellous gifts
against which no power nor strength could avail an enemy—misery,
to be able to quell the mightiest with a breath—misery, to be as
terrible as thou art beautiful? Wouldst thou, then, have preferred
the condition of a weak woman, exposed to all evil and capable of
none?"

"I would fain have been loved, not feared," murmured Beatrice, sinking down upon the ground. "But now it matters not. I am going, father, where the evil which thou hast striven to mingle with my being will pass away like a dream—like the fragrance of these poisonous flowers, which will no longer taint my breath among the flowers of Eden. Farewell, Giovanni! Thy words of hatred are like lead within my heart; but they, too, will fall away as I ascend. Oh, was there not, from the first, more poison in thy nature than in mine?"

To Beatrice,—so radically had her earthly part been wrought upon by Rappaccini's skill,—as poison had been life, so the powerful antidote was death;[7] and thus the poor victim of man's ingenuity and of thwarted nature, and of the fatality that attends all such efforts of perverted wisdom, perished there, at the feet of her father and Giovanni. Just at that moment Professor Pietro Baglioni looked forth from the window, and called loudly, in a tone of triumph mixed with horror, to the thunderstricken man of science,—

"Rappaccini! Rappaccini! and is *this* the upshot of your experiment!"[8]

1844, 1846

Wakefield[9]

In some old magazine or newspaper, I recollect a story, told as truth, of a man—let us call him Wakefield—who absented himself for a long time from his wife. The fact thus abstractedly stated is not very uncommon, nor—without a proper distinction of circumstances—to be condemned either as naughty or nonsensical. Howbeit, this, though far from the most aggravated, is perhaps the

7. The death of Georgiana in "The Birthmark" is comparable to Beatrice's fate.
8. Compare the malignant laughter of Aminadab, the "gross fatality of earth," at the conclusion of "The Birthmark."
9. The anecdote that suggested "Wakefield" was told in Dr. William King, *Anecdotes of His Own Times* (1818), pp. 236–45: an acquaintance of King's named Howe absented himself from his wife for seventeen years. "After he returned home, he would never confess, even to his most intimate friends, what was the real cause of such a singular conduct; apparently there was none." Wakefield's dreamlike isolation recalls Hawthorne's account of his own state in the twelve years after he was graduated from Bowdoin College, and during which he wrote "Wakefield." He said in a letter to his classmate Longfellow in 1837 that "by some witchcraft or other—for I really cannot assign any reasonable why and wherefore—I have been carried apart from the main current of life, and find it impossible to get back again. Since we last met * * * I have secluded myself from society; and yet I never meant any such thing, nor dreamed what sort of life I was going to lead. I have made a captive of myself and put me into a dungeon; and now I cannot find the key to let myself out—and if the door were open, I should be almost afraid to come out * * * there is no fate in this world so horrible as to have no share in either its joys or sorrows. For the last ten years, I have not lived, but only dreamed about living" (quoted from *American Notebooks*, p. lxviii). "Wakefield" was first published in the *New-England Magazine* for May, 1835, and was included in the 1837 *Twice-Told Tales*.

strangest instance on record of marital delinquency; and, moreover, as remarkable a freak as may be found in the whole list of human oddities. The wedded couple lived in London. The man, under pretence of going a journey, took lodgings in the next street to his own house, and there, unheard of by his wife or friends, and without the shadow of a reason for such self-banishment, dwelt upwards of twenty years. During that period, he beheld his home every day, and frequently the forlorn Mrs. Wakefield. And after so great a gap in his matrimonial felicity—when his death was reckoned certain, his estate settled, his name dismissed from memory, and his wife, long, long ago, resigned to her autumnal widowhood—he entered the door one evening, quietly, as from a day's absence, and became a loving spouse till death.

This outline is all that I remember. But the incident, though of the purest originality, unexampled, and probably never to be repeated, is one, I think, which appeals to the generous sympathies of mankind. We know, each for himself, that none of us would perpetrate such a folly, yet feel as if some other might. To my own contemplations, at least, it has often recurred, always exciting wonder, but with a sense that the story must be true and a conception of its hero's character. Whenever any subject so forcibly affects the mind, time is well spent in thinking of it. If the reader choose, let him do his own meditation; or if he prefer to ramble with me through the twenty years of Wakefield's vagary, I bid him welcome; trusting that there will be a pervading spirit and a moral, even should we fail to find them, done up neatly, and condensed into the final sentence. Thought has always its efficacy, and every striking incident its moral.[1]

What sort of a man was Wakefield? We are free to shape out our own idea, and call it by his name. He was now in the meridian of life; his matrimonial affections, never violent, were sobered into a calm, habitual sentiment; of all husbands, he was likely to be the most constant, because a certain sluggishness would keep his heart at rest, wherever it might be placed. He was intellectual, but not actively so; his mind occupied itself in long and lazy musings, that tended to no purpose, or had not vigour to attain it; his thoughts were seldom so energetic as to seize hold of words. Imagination, in the proper meaning of the term, made no part of Wakefield's gifts. With a cold but not depraved nor wandering heart, and a mind never feverish with riotous thoughts, nor perplexed with originality, who could have anticipated that our friend would entitle himself to a foremost place among the doers of eccentric deeds? Had his acquaintances been asked, who was the man in London, the surest to perform

1. "Wakefield" is perhaps a sketch rather than a story proper, since Hawthorne frankly abjures dramatic immediacy and illusion in it.

nothing to-day which should be remembered on the morrow, they would have thought of Wakefield. Only the wife of his bosom might have hesitated. She, without having analysed his character, was partly aware of a quiet selfishness, that had rusted into his inactive mind,—of a peculiar sort of vanity, the most uneasy attribute about him,—of a disposition to craft, which had seldom produced more positive effects than the keeping of petty secrets, hardly worth revealing,—and, lastly, of what she called a little strangeness, sometimes, in the good man. This latter quality is indefinable, and perhaps nonexistent.

Let us now imagine Wakefield bidding adieu to his wife. It is the dusk of an October evening. His equipment is a drab great-coat, a hat covered with an oil-cloth, top-boots, an umbrella in one hand and a small portmanteau in the other. He has informed Mrs. Wakefield that he is to take the night coach into the country. She would fain inquire the length of his journey, its object, and the probable time of his return; but, indulgent to his harmless love of mystery, interrogates him only by a look. He tells her not to expect him positively by the return coach, not to be alarmed should he tarry three or four days; but, at all events, to look for him at supper on Friday evening. Wakefield himself, be it considered, has no suspicion of what is before him. He holds out his hand; she gives her own, and meets his parting kiss, in the matter-of-course way of a ten years' matrimony; and forth goes the middle-aged Mr. Wakefield, almost resolved to perplex his good lady by a whole week's absence. After the door has closed behind him, she perceives it thrust partly open, and a vision of her husband's face, through the aperture, smiling on her, and gone in a moment. For the time, this little incident is dismissed without a thought. But, long afterwards, when she has been more years a widow than a wife, that smile recurs, and flickers across all her reminiscences of Wakefield's visage. In her many musings, she surrounds the original smile with a multitude of fantasies, which make it strange and awful; as, for instance, if she imagines him in a coffin, that parting look is frozen on his pale features; or, if she dreams of him in heaven, still his blessed spirit wears a quiet and crafty smile. Yet, for its sake, when all others have given him up for dead, she sometimes doubts whether she is a widow.

But our business is with the husband. We must hurry after him, along the street, ere he lose his individuality, and melt into the great mass of London life. It would be vain searching for him there. Let us follow close at his heels, therefore, until, after several superfluous turns and doublings, we find him comfortably established by the fireside of a small apartment, previously bespoken. He is in the next street to his own, and at his journey's end. He can scarcely trust his good fortune in having got thither unperceived,—recollecting that, at one time, he was delayed by the throng, in the very focus of a lighted lantern; and, again, there were footsteps, that seemed to tread behind his own, distinct from the multitudinous tramp around him; and, anon, he heard a voice shouting afar, and fancied that it called his name. Doubtless, a dozen busybodies had been watching him, and told his wife the whole affair. Poor Wakefield! Little knowest thou thine own insignificance in this great world! No mortal eye but mine has traced thee. Go quietly to thy bed, foolish man; and, on the morrow, if thou wilt be wise, get thee home to good Mrs. Wakefield, and tell her the truth. Remove not thyself, even for a little week, from thy place in her chaste bosom. Were she, for a single moment, to deem thee dead, or lost, or lastingly divided from her, thou wouldst be woefully conscious of a change in thy true wife, forever after. It is perilous to make a chasm in human affections; not that they gape so long and wide, but so quickly close again!

Almost repenting of his frolic, or whatever it may be termed, Wakefield lies down betimes, and starting from his first nap, spreads forth his arms into the wide and solitary waste of the unaccustomed bed. "No,"—thinks he, gathering the bedclothes about him,—"I will not sleep alone another night."

In the morning, he rises earlier than usual, and sets himself to consider what he really means to do. Such are his loose and rambling modes of thought that he has taken this very singular step, with the consciousness of a purpose, indeed, but without being able to define it sufficiently for his own contemplation. The vagueness of the project, and the convulsive effort with which he plunges into the execution of it, are equally characteristic of a feeble-minded man. Wakefield sifts his ideas, however, as minutely as he may, and finds himself curious to know the progress of matters at home,—how his exemplary wife will endure her widowhood of a week; and, briefly, how the little sphere of creatures and circumstances, in which he was a central object, will be affected by his removal. A morbid vanity, therefore, lies nearest the bottom of the affair. But, how is he to attain his ends? Not, certainly, by keeping close in this comfortable lodging, where, though he slept and awoke in the next street to his home, he is as effectually abroad, as if the stage-coach had been whirling him away all night. Yet, should he reappear, the whole project is knocked on the head. His poor brains being hopelessly puzzled with this dilemma, he at length ventures out, partly resolving to cross the head of the street, and send one hasty glance towards his forsaken domicile. Habit—for he is a man of habits—takes him by the hand, and guides him, wholly unaware to his own door, where, just at the critical moment, he is aroused by the scraping of his foot upon the step. Wakefield! whither are you going?

At that instant, his fate was turning on the pivot. Little dreaming of the doom to which his first backward step devotes him, he hurries away, breathless with agitation hitherto unfelt, and hardly dares turn his head, at the distant corner. Can it be that nobody caught sight of him? Will not the whole household—the decent Mrs. Wakefield, the smart maid-servant, and the dirty little footboy—raise a hue and cry, through London streets, in pursuit of their fugitive lord and master? Wonderful escape! He gathers courage to pause and look homeward, but is perplexed with a sense of change about the familiar edifice, such as affects us all, when, after a separation of months or years, we again see some hill or lake, or work of art, with which we were friends of old. In ordinary cases, this indescribable impression is caused by the comparison and contrast between our imperfect reminiscences and the reality. In Wakefield, the magic of a single night has wrought a similar transformation, because, in that brief period, a great moral change has been affected. But this is a secret from himself. Before leaving the spot, he catches a far and momentary glimpse of his wife, passing athwart the front window, with her face turned towards the head of the street. The crafty nincompoop takes to his heels, scared with the idea, that, among a thousand such atoms of mortality, her eye must have detected him. Right glad is his heart, though his brain be somewhat dizzy, when he finds himself by the coalfire of his lodgings.

So much for the commencement of this long whim-wham. After the initial conception, and the stirring up of the man's sluggish temperament to put it in practice, the whole matter evolves itself in a natural train. We may suppose him, as the result of deep deliberation, buying a new wig, of reddish hair, and selecting sundry garments, in a fashion unlike his customary suit of brown, from a Jew's old-clothes bag. It is accomplished. Wakefield is another man. The new system being now established, a retrograde movement to the old would be almost as difficult as the step that placed him in his unparalleled position. Furthermore, he is rendered obstinate by a sulkiness, occasionally incident to his temper, and brought on, at present, by the inadequate sensation which he conceives to have been produced in the bosom of Mrs. Wakefield. He will not go back until she be frightened half to death. Well, twice or thrice has she passed before his sight, each time with a heavier step, a paler cheek, and more anxious brow; and in the third week of his non-appearance, he detects a portent of evil entering the house, in the guise of an apothecary. Next day, the knocker is muffled. Towards nightfall comes the chariot of a physician, and deposits its big-wigged and solemn burden at Wakefield's door, whence, after a quarter of an hour's visit, he emerges, perchance the herald of a funeral. Dear woman! Will she die? By this time, Wakefield is excited to something like energy of feeling, but still lingers away from his wife's bedside, pleading with his conscience, that she must not be disturbed at such a juncture. If aught else restrains him, he does not know it. In the course of a few weeks, she gradually recovers; the crisis is over; her heart is sad, perhaps, but quiet; and, let him return soon or late, it will never be feverish for him again. Such ideas glimmer through the mist of Wakefield's mind, and render him indistinctly conscious that an almost impassable gulf divides his hired apartment from his former home. "It is but in the next street!" he sometimes says. Fool! it is in another world. Hitherto, he has put off his return from one particular day to another; henceforward, he leaves the precise time undetermined. Not to-morrow,—probably next week,—pretty soon. Poor man! The dead have nearly as much chance of revisiting their earthly homes, as the self-banished Wakefield.

Would that I had a folio to write, instead of an article of a dozen pages! Then might I exemplify how an influence, beyond our control, lays its strong hand on every deed which we do, and weaves its consequences into an iron tissue of necessity. Wakefield is spellbound. We must leave him, for ten years or so, to haunt around his house, without once crossing the threshold, and to be faithful to his wife, with all the affection of which his heart is capable, while he is slowly fading out of hers. Long since, it must be remarked, he has lost the perception of singularity in his conduct.

Now for a scene! Amid the throng of a London street, we distinguish a man, now waxing elderly, with few characteristics to attract careless observers, yet bearing, in his whole aspect, the handwriting of no common fate, for such as have the skill to read it. He is meagre; his low and narrow forehead is deeply wrinkled; his eyes, small and lustreless, sometimes wander apprehensively about him, but oftener seem to look inward. He bends his head, and moves with an indescribable obliquity of gait, as if unwilling to display his full front to the world. Watch him, long enough to see what we have described, and you will allow, that circumstances—which often produce remarkable men from nature's ordinary handiwork—have produced one such here. Next, leaving him to sidle along the footwalk, cast your eyes in the opposite direction, where a portly female, considerably in the wane of life, with a prayer-book in her hand, is proceeding to yonder church. She has the placid mien of settled widowhood. Her regrets have either dried away, or have become so essential to her heart, that they would be poorly exchanged for joy. Just as the lean man and well-conditioned woman are passing, a slight obstruction occurs, and brings these two figures directly in contact. Their hands touch; the pressure of the crowd forces her bosom against his shoulder; they stand, face to face, staring into each other's eyes. After a ten years' separation, thus Wakefield meets his wife!

The throng eddies away, and carries them asunder. The sober widow, resuming her former pace, proceeds to church, but pauses in the portal, and throws a perplexed glance along the street. She passes in, however, opening her prayer-book as she goes. And the man! with so wild a face, that busy and selfish London stands to gaze after him, he hurries to his lodgings, bolts the door, and throws himself upon the bed. The latent feelings of years break out; his feeble mind acquires a brief energy from their strength; all the miserable strangeness of his life is revealed to him at a glance: and he cries out, passionately, "Wakefield! Wakefield! You are mad!"

Perhaps he was so. The singularity of his situation must have so moulded him to himself, that, considered in regard to his fellow-creatures and the business of life, he could not be said to possess his right mind. He had contrived, or rather he had happened, to dissever himself from the world,—to vanish,—to give up his place and privileges with living men, without being admitted among the dead. The life of a hermit is nowise parallel to his. He was in the bustle of the city, as of old; but the crowd swept by, and saw him not; he was, we may figuratively say, always beside his wife, and at his hearth, yet must never feel the warmth of the one, nor the affection of the other. It was Wakefield's unprecedented fate, to retain his original share of human sympathies, and to be still involved in human interests, while he had lost his reciprocal influence on them. It would be a cost curious speculation, to trace out the effect of such circumstances on his heart and intellect, separately, and in unison. Yet, changed as he was, he would seldom be conscious of it, but deem himself the same man as ever; glimpses of the truth, indeed, would come, but only for the moment; and still he would keep saying, "I shall soon go back!" nor reflect that he had been saying so for twenty years.

I conceive, also, that these twenty years would appear, in the retrospect, scarcely longer than the week to which Wakefield had at first limited his absence. He would look on the affair as no more than an interlude in the main business of his life. When, after a little while more, he should deem it time to re-enter his parlour, his wife would clap her hands for joy, on beholding the middle-aged Mr. Wakefield. Alas, what a mistake! Would Time but await the close of our favourite follies, we should be young men, all of us, and till Doomsday.

One evening, in the twentieth year since he vanished, Wakefield is taking his customary walk towards the dwelling which he still calls his own. It is a gusty night of autumn, with frequent showers, that patter down upon the pavement, and are gone, before a man can put up his umbrella. Pausing near the house, Wakefield discerns, through the parlour windows of the second floor, the red glow, and the glimmer and fitful flash of a comfortable fire.[2] On the ceiling appears a grotesque shadow of good Mrs. Wakefield. The cap, the nose and chin, and the broad waist form an admirable caricature, which dances, moreover, with the up-flickering and down-sinking blaze, almost too merrily for the shade of an elderly widow. At this instant, a shower chances to fall, and is driven, by the unmannerly gust, full into Wakefield's face and bosom. He is quite penetrated with its autumnal chill. Shall he stand, wet and shivering here, when his own hearth has a good fire to warm him, and his own wife will run to fetch the gray coat and small clothes, which doubtless she has kept carefully in the closet of their bedchamber? No! Wakefield is no such fool. He ascends the steps,—heavily!—for twenty years have stiffened his legs, since he came down,—but he knows it not. Stay, Wakefield! Would you go to the sole home that is left you? Then step into your grave! The door opens. As he passes in, we have a parting glimpse of his visage, and recognize the crafty smile, which was the precursor of the little joke that he has ever since been playing off at his wife's expense. How unmercifully has he quizzed the poor woman! Well, a good night's rest to Wakefield!

This happy event—supposing it to be such—could only have occurred at an unpremeditated moment. We will not follow our friend across the threshold. He has left us much food for thought, a portion of which shall lend its wisdom to a moral, and be shaped into a figure. Amid the seeming confusion of our mysterious world, individuals are so nicely adjusted to a system, and systems to one another, and to a whole, that, by stepping aside for a moment, a man exposes himself to a fearful risk of losing his place for ever. Like Wakefield, he may become, as it were, the Outcast of the Universe.

1835, 1837

The Celestial Railroad[3]

Not a great while ago, passing through the gate of dreams,[4] I visited that region of the earth in which lies the famous City of De-

2. The hearth fire is often a heart-symbol of tranquil social relationship in Hawthorne, just as the kiln fire of "Ethan Brand" and the bonfire of "Young Goodman Brown" are emblems of hellish evil, which also resides in the human heart. The fire in Robert Danforth's smithy ("The Artist of the Beautiful") is ambiguous, with possibilities for both good and evil.
3. Hawthorne noted as a theme "An Auction (perhaps in Vanity Fair) of offices, honors, and all sorts of things considered desirable by mankind; together with things eternally valuable, which shall be considered by most people as worthless lumber" (*American Notebooks*, p. 98). This accents the appearance-reality, delusion-truth opposition that pervades "The Celestial Railroad." It is a sustained satirical allegory, aimed at "modernism" in religion in general, and more specifically at the transcendentalism and Unitarianism of Hawthorne's contemporary New England. The piece was composed at the Old Manse in Concord, the very seat of transcendentalism, home of Emerson and Thoreau. It is of course inspired by Bunyan's *Pilgrim's Progress*. "The Celestial Railroad" was published in May, 1843, in the *Democratic Review*, and included in *Mosses from an Old Manse*.
4. The dream-vision convention of traditional allegory, more organically employed in "Young Goodman Brown."

struction. It interested me much to learn that by the public spirit of some of the inhabitants a railroad has recently been established between this populous and flourishing town and the Celestial City. Having a little time upon my hands, I resolved to gratify a liberal curiosity by making a trip thither. Accordingly, one fine morning after paying my bill at the hotel, and directing the porter to stow my luggage behind a coach, I took my seat in the vehicle and set out for the station-house. It was my good fortune to enjoy the company of a gentleman—one Mr. Smooth-it-away—who, though he had never actually visited the Celestial City, yet seemed as well acquainted with its laws, customs, policy, and statistics, as with those of the City of Destruction, of which he was a native townsman. Being, moreover, a director of the railroad corporation and one of its largest stockholders, he had it in his power to give me all desirable information respecting that praiseworthy enterprise.

Our coach rattled out of the city, and at a short distance from its outskirts passed over a bridge of elegant construction, but some-what too slight, as I imagined, to sustain any considerable weight. On both sides lay an extensive quagmire, which could not have been more disagreeable, either to sight or smell, had all the kennels of the earth emptied their pollution there.

"This," remarked Mr. Smooth-it-away, "is the famous Slough of Despond—a disgrace to all the neighborhood; and the greater that it might so easily be converted into firm ground."

"I have understood," said I, "that efforts have been made for that purpose from time immemorial. Bunyan mentions that above twenty thousand cartloads of wholesome instructions had been thrown in here without effect."

"Very probably! And what effect could be anticipated from such unsubstantial stuff?" cried Mr. Smooth-it-away. "You observe this convenient bridge. We obtained a sufficient foundation for it by throwing into the slough some editions of books of morality; volumes of French philosophy and German rationalism; tracts, sermons, and essays of modern clergymen; extracts from Plato, Confucius, and various Hindoo sages, together with a few ingenious commentaries upon texts of Scripture,—all of which by some scientific process, have been converted into a mass like granite. The whole bog might be filled up with similar matter."

It really seemed to me, however, that the bridge vibrated and heaved up and down in a very formidable manner; and, spite of Mr. Smooth-it-away's testimony to the solidity of its foundation, I should be loath to cross it in a crowded omnibus, especially if each passenger were encumbered with as heavy luggage as that gentleman and myself. Nevertheless we got over without accident, and soon found ourselves at the station-house. This very neat and spacious edifice is erected on the site of the little wicket gate, which formerly, as all old pilgrims will recollect, stood directly across the highway, and, by its inconvenient narrowness, was a great obstruction to the traveller of liberal mind and expansive stomach. The reader of John Bunyan will be glad to know that Christian's old friend Evangelist, who was accustomed to supply each pilgrim with a mystic roll, now presides at the ticket office. Some malicious persons it is true deny the identity of this reputable character with the Evangelist of old times, and even pretend to bring competent evidence of an imposture. Without involving myself in a dispute I shall merely observe that, so far as my experience goes, the square pieces of pasteboard now delivered to passengers are much more convenient and useful along the road than the antique roll of parchment. Whether they will be as readily received at the gate of the Celestial City I decline giving an opinion.

A large number of passengers were already at the station-house awaiting the departure of the cars. By the aspect and demeanor of these persons it was easy to judge that the feelings of the community had undergone a very favorable change in reference to the celestial pilgrimage. It would have done Bunyan's heart good to see it. Instead of a lonely and ragged man with a huge burden on his back, plodding along sorrowfully on foot while the whole city hooted after him, here were parties of the first gentry and most respectable people in the neighborhood setting forth towards the Celestial City as cheerfully as if the pilgrimage were merely a summer tour. Among the gentlemen were characters of deserved eminence—magistrates, politicians, and men of wealth, by whose example religion could not but be greatly recommended to their meaner brethren. In the ladies' apartment, too, I rejoiced to distinguish some of those flowers of fashionable society who are so well fitted to adorn the most elevated circles of the Celestial City. There was much pleasant conversation about the news of the day, topics of business and politics, or the lighter matters of amusement; while religion, though indubitably the main thing at heart, was thrown tastefully into the background. Even an infidel would have heard little or nothing to shock his sensibility.

One great convenience of the new method of going on pilgrimage I must not forget to mention. Our enormous burdens, instead of being carried on our shoulders as had been the custom of old, were all snugly deposited in the baggage car, and, as I was assured, would be delivered to their respective owners at the journey's end. Another thing, likewise, the benevolent reader will be delighted to understand. It may be remembered that there was an ancient feud between Prince Beelzebub and the keeper of the wicket gate, and that the adherents of the former distinguished personage were accustomed to shoot deadly arrows at honest pilgrims while knocking at the door. This dispute, much to the credit as well of the illustrious potentate above mentioned as of the worthy and enlightened directors of the railroad, has been pacifically arranged on the principle of mutual compromise. The prince's subjects are now pretty numerously employed about the station-house, some in taking care of the baggage, others in collecting fuel, feeding the engines, and such congenial occupations; and I can conscientiously affirm that persons more attentive to their business, more willing to accommodate, or more generally agreeable to the passengers, are not to be found on any railroad. Every good heart must surely exult at so satisfactory an arrangement of an immemorial difficulty.

"Where is Mr. Greatheart?" inquired I. "Beyond a doubt the directors have engaged that famous old champion to be chief conductor on the railroad?"

"Why, no," said Mr. Smooth-it-away, with a dry cough. "He was offered the situation of brakeman; but, to tell you the truth, our friend Greatheart has grown preposterously stiff and narrow in his old age. He has so often guided pilgrims over the road on foot that he considers it a sin to travel in any other fashion. Besides, the old fellow had entered so heartily into the ancient feud with Prince Beelzebub that he would have been perpetually at blows or ill language with some of the prince's subjects, and thus have embroiled us anew. So, on the whole, we were not sorry when honest Greatheart went off to the Celestial City in a huff and left us at liberty to choose a more suitable and accommodating man. Yonder comes the engineer of the train. You will probably recognize him at once."

The engine at this moment took its station in advance of the cars, looking, I must confess, much more like a sort of mechanical demon that would hurry us to the infernal regions than a laudable contrivance for smoothing our way to the Celestial City. On its top sat a personage almost enveloped in smoke and flame, which, not to startle the reader, appeared to gush from his own mouth and stomach as well as from the engine's brazen abdomen.

"Do my eyes deceive me?" cried I. "What on earth is this! A living creature? If so, he is own brother to the engine he rides upon!"

"Poh, poh, you are obtuse!" said Mr. Smooth-it-away, with a hearty laugh. "Don't you know Apollyon, Christian's old enemy, with whom he fought so fierce a battle in the Valley of Humiliation? He was the very fellow to manage the engine; and so we have reconciled him to the custom of going on pilgrimage, and engaged him as chief engineer."

"Bravo, bravo!" exclaimed I, with irrepressible enthusiasm; "this shows the liberality of the age; this proves, if anything can, that all musty prejudices are in a fair way to be obliterated. And how will Christian rejoice to hear of this happy transformation of his old antagonist! I promise myself great pleasure in informing him of it when we reach the Celestial City."

The passengers being all comfortably seated, we now rattled away merrily, accomplishing a greater distance in ten minutes than Christian probably trudged over in a day. It was laughable, while we glanced along, as it were, at the tail of a thunderbolt, to observe two dusty foot travellers in the old pilgrim guise, with cockle shell and staff, their mystic rolls of parchment in their hands and their intolerable burdens on their backs. The preposterous obstinacy of these honest people in persisting to groan and stumble along the difficult pathway rather than take advantage of modern improvements, excited great mirth among our wiser brotherhood. We greeted the two pilgrims with many pleasant gibes and a roar of laughter; whereupon they gazed at us with such woful and absurdly compassionate visages that our merriment grew tenfold more obstreperous. Apollyon also entered heartily into the fun, and contrived to flirt the smoke and flame of the engine, or of his own breath, into their faces, and envelop them in an atmosphere of scalding steam. These little practical jokes amused us mightily, and doubtless afforded the pilgrims the gratification of considering themselves martyrs.

At some distance from the railroad Mr. Smooth-it-away pointed to a large, antique edifice, which, he observed, was a tavern of long standing, and had formerly been a noted stopping-place for pilgrims. In Bunyan's road-book it is mentioned as the Interpreter's House.

"I have long had a curiosity to visit that old mansion," remarked I.

"It is not one of our stations, as you perceive," said my companion. "The keeper was violently opposed to the railroad; and well he might be, as the track left his house of entertainment on one side, and thus was pretty certain to deprive him of all his reputable customers. But the footpath still passes his door, and the old gentleman now and then receives a call from some simple traveller, and entertains him with fare as old-fashioned as himself."

Before our talk on this subject came to a conclusion we were rushing by the place where Christian's burden fell from his shoulders at the sight of the Cross. This served as a theme for Mr. Smooth-it-away, Mr. Live-for-the-world, Mr. Hide-sin-in-the-heart, Mr. Scaly-conscience, and a knot of gentlemen from the town of Shun-repentance, to descant upon the inestimable advantages resulting from the safety of our baggage. Myself, and all the passengers indeed, joined with great unanimity in this view of the matter; for our burdens were rich in many things esteemed precious throughout the world; and, especially, we each of us possessed a great variety of favorite Habits, which we trusted would not be out of fashion even in the polite circles of the Celestial City. It would have been a sad spectacle to see such an assortment of valuable articles tumbling into the sepulchre. Thus pleasantly conversing on the favorable circumstances of our position as compared with those of past pilgrims and of narrow-minded ones at the present day, we soon found ourselves at the foot of the Hill Difficulty. Through the very heart of this rocky mountain a tunnel has been constructed of most admirable architecture, with a lofty arch and a spacious double track; so that, unless the earth and rocks should chance to crumble down, it will remain an eternal monument of the builder's skill and enterprise. It is a great though incidental advantage that the materials from the heart of the Hill Difficulty have been employed in filling up the Valley of Humiliation, thus obviating the necessity of descending into that disagreeable and unwholesome hollow.

"This is a wonderful improvement, indeed," said I. "Yet I should have been glad of an opportunity to visit the Palace Beautiful and be introduced to the charming young ladies—Miss Prudence, Miss Piety, Miss Charity, and the rest—who have the kindness to entertain pilgrims there."

"Young ladies!" cried Mr. Smooth-it-away, as soon as he could speak for laughing. "And charming young ladies! Why, my dear fellow, they are old maids, every soul of them—prim, starched, dry, and angular; and not one of them, I will venture to say, has altered so much as the fashion of her gown since the days of Christian's pilgrimage."

"Ah, well," said I, much comforted, "then I can very readily dispense with their acquaintance."

The respectable Apollyon was now putting on the steam at a prodigious rate, anxious, perhaps, to get rid of the unpleasant reminiscences connected with the spot where he had so disastrously encountered Christian. Consulting Mr. Bunyan's road-book, I perceived that we must now be within a few miles of the Valley of the Shadow of Death, into which doleful region, at our present speed, we should plunge much sooner than seemed at all desirable. In truth, I expected nothing better than to find myself in the ditch on one side or the quag on the other; but on communicating my apprehensions to Mr. Smooth-it-away, he assured me that the difficulties of this passage, even in its worst condition, had been vastly exaggerated, and that, in its present state of improvement, I might consider myself as safe as on any railroad in Christendom.

Even while we were speaking the train shot into the entrance of this dreaded Valley. Though I plead guilty to some foolish palpitations of the heart during our headlong rush over the causeway here constructed, yet it were unjust to withhold the highest encomiums on the boldness of its original conception and the ingenuity of those who executed it. It was gratifying, likewise, to observe how much care had been taken to dispel the everlasting gloom and supply the defect of cheerful sunshine, not a ray of which has ever penetrated among these awful shadows. For this purpose, the inflammable gas which exudes plentifully from the soil is collected by means of pipes, and thence communicated to a quadruple row of lamps along the whole extent of the passage. Thus a radiance has been created even out of the fiery and sulphurous curse that rests forever upon the valley—a radiance hurtful, however, to the eyes, and somewhat bewildering, as I discovered by the changes which it wrought in the visages of my companions. In this respect, as compared with natural daylight, there is the same difference as between truth and falsehood; but if the reader have ever travelled through the dark Valley, he will have learned to be thankful for any light that he could get—if not from the sky above, then from the blasted soil beneath. Such was the red brilliancy of these lamps that they appeared to build walls of fire on both sides of the track, between which we held our course at lightning speed, while a reverberating thunder filled the Valley with its echoes. Had the engine run off the track,—a catastrophe, it is whispered, by no means unprecedented,—the bottomless pit, if there be any such place, would undoubtedly have received us. Just as some dismal fooleries of this nature had made my heart quake there came a tremendous shriek, careering along the valley as if a thousand devils had burst their lungs to utter it, but which proved to be merely the whistle of the engine on arriving at a stopping-place.

The spot where we had now paused is the same that our friend Bunyan—a truthful man, but infected with many fantastic notions —has designated, in terms plainer than I like to repeat, as the mouth of the infernal region. This, however, must be a mistake, inasmuch as Mr. Smooth-it-away, while we remained in the smoky and lurid cavern, took occasion to prove that Tophet has not even a metaphorical existence. The place, he assured us, is no other than the crater of a half-extinct volcano, in which the directors had caused forges to be set up for the manufacture of railroad iron. Hence, also, is obtained a plentiful supply of fuel for the use of the engines. Whoever had gazed into the dismal obscurity of the broad cavern mouth, whence ever and anon darted huge tongues of dusky flame, and had seen the strange, half-shaped monsters, and visions of faces horribly grotesque, into which the smoke seemed to wreathe itself, and had heard the awful murmurs, and shrieks, and deep shuddering whispers of the blast, sometimes forming themselves into words almost articulate, would have seized upon Mr. Smooth-it-away's comfortable explanation as greedily as we did. The inhabitants of the cavern, moreover, were unlovely personages, dark, smoke-begrimed, generally deformed, with misshapen feet, and a glow of dusky redness in their eyes as if their hearts had caught fire and were blazing out of the upper windows. It struck me as a peculiarity that the laborers at the forge and those who brought fuel to the engine, when they began to draw short breath, positively emitted smoke from their mouth and nostrils.

Among the idlers about the train, most of whom were puffing cigars which they had lighted at the flame of the crater, I was perplexed to notice several who, to my certain knowledge, had heretofore set forth by railroad for the Celestial City. They looked dark, wild, and smoky, with a singular resemblance, indeed, to the native inhabitants, like whom, also, they had a disagreeable propensity to ill-natured gibes and sneers, the habit of which had wrought a settled contortion of their visages. Having been on speaking terms with one of these persons,—an indolent, good-for-nothing fellow, who went by the name of Take-it-easy,—I called him, and inquired what was his business there.

"Did you not start," said I, "for the Celestial City?"

"That's a fact," said Mr. Take-it-easy, carelessly puffing some smoke into my eyes. "But I heard such bad accounts that I never took pains to climb the hill on which the city stands. No business doing, no fun going on, nothing to drink, and no smoking allowed, and a thrumming of church music from morning till night. I would not stay in such a place if they offered me house room and living free."

"But, my good Mr. Take-it-easy," cried I, "why take up your residence here, of all places in the world?"

"Oh," said the loafer, with a grin, "it is very warm hereabouts, and I meet with plenty of old acquaintances, and altogether the place suits me. I hope to see you back again some day soon. A pleasant journey to you."

While he was speaking the bell of the engine rang, and we dashed away after dropping a few passengers, but receiving no new ones. Rattling onward through the Valley, we were dazzled with the fiercely gleaming gas lamps, as before. But sometimes, in the dark of intense brightness, grim faces, that bore the aspect and expression of individual sins, or evil passions, seemed to thrust themselves through the veil of light, glaring upon us, and stretching forth a great, dusky hand, as if to impede our progress. I almost thought that they were my own sins that appalled me there. These were freaks of imagination—nothing more, certainly—mere delusions, which I ought to be heartily ashamed of; but all through the Dark Valley I was tormented, and pestered, and dolefully bewildered with the same kind of waking dreams. The mephitic gases of that region intoxicate the brain. As the light of natural day, however, began to struggle with the glow of the lanterns, these vain imaginations lost their vividness, and finally vanished with the first ray of sunshine that greeted our escape from the Valley of the Shadow of Death. Ere we had gone a mile beyond it I could well-nigh have taken my oath that this whole gloomy passage was a dream.

At the end of the valley, as John Bunyan mentions, is a cavern, where, in his days, dwelt two cruel giants, Pope and Pagan, who had strown the ground about their residence with the bones of slaughtered pilgrims. These vile old troglodytes are no longer there; but into their deserted cave another terrible giant has thrust himself, and makes it his business to seize upon honest travellers and fatten them for his table with plentiful meals of smoke, mist, moonshine, raw potatoes, and sawdust. He is a German by birth, and is called Giant Transcendentalist; but as to his form, his features, his substance, and his nature generally, it is the chief peculiarity of this huge miscreant that neither he for himself, nor anybody for him, has ever been able to describe them. As we rushed by the cavern's mouth we caught a hasty glimpse of him, looking somewhat like an ill-proportioned figure, but considerably more like a heap of fog and duskiness. He shouted after us, but in so strange a phraseology that we knew not what he meant, nor whether to be encouraged or affrighted.

It was late in the day when the train thundered into the ancient city of Vanity, where Vanity Fair is still at the height of prosperity, and exhibits an epitome of whatever is brilliant, gay, and fascinating beneath the sun. As I purposed to make a considerable stay here, it gratified me to learn that there is no longer the want of harmony between the town's-people and pilgrims, which impelled the former to such lamentably mistaken measures as the persecution of Christian and the fiery martyrdom of Faithful. On the contrary, as the new railroad brings with it great trade and a constant influx of strangers, the lord of Vanity Fair is its chief patron, and the capitalists of the city are among the largest stockholders. Many passengers stop to take their pleasure or make their profit in the Fair, instead of going onward to the Celestial City. Indeed, such are the charms of the place that people often affirm it to be the true and only heaven; stoutly contending that there is no other, that those who seek further are mere dreamers, and that, if the fabled brightness of the Celestial City lay but a bare mile beyond the gates of Vanity, they would not be fools enough to go thither. Without subscribing to these perhaps exaggerated encomiums, I can truly say that my abode in the city was mainly agreeable, and my intercourse with the inhabitants productive of much amusement and instruction.

Being naturally of a serious turn, my attention was directed to the solid advantages derivable from a residence here, rather than to the effervescent pleasures which are the grand object with too many visitants. The Christian reader, if he have had no accounts of the city later than Bunyan's time, will be surprised to hear that almost every street has its church, and that the reverend clergy are nowhere held in higher respect than at Vanity Fair. And well do they deserve such honorable estimation; for the maxims of wisdom and virtue which fall from their lips come from as deep a spiritual source, and tend to as lofty a religious aim, as those of the sagest philosophers of old. In justification of this high praise I need only mention the names of the Rev. Mr. Shallow-deep, the Rev. Mr. Stumble-at-truth, that fine old clerical character the Rev. Mr. This-to-day, who expects shortly to resign his pulpit to the Rev. Mr. That-to-morrow; together with the Rev. Mr. Bewilderment, the Rev. Mr. Clog-the-spirit, and, last and greatest, the Rev. Dr. Wind-of-doctrine. The labors of these eminent divines are aided by those of innumerable lecturers, who diffuse such a various profundity, in all subjects of human or celestial science, that any man may acquire an omnigenous erudition without the trouble of even learning to read. Thus literature is etherealized by assuming for its medium the human voice; and knowledge, depositing all its heavier particles, except, doubtless, its gold, becomes exhaled into a sound, which forthwith steals into the ever-open ear of the community. These ingenious methods constitute a sort of machinery, by which thought and study are done to every person's hand without his putting himself to the slightest inconvenience in the matter. There is another species of machine for the wholesale manufacture of individual morality. This excellent result is effected by societies for all manner of virtuous purposes, with which a man has merely to connect himself, throwing, as it were, his quota of virtue into the common stock, and the president and directors will take care that the aggregate amount be well applied. All these, and other wonderful improvements in ethics, religion, and literature, being made plain to my comprehension by the ingenious Mr. Smooth-it-away, inspired me with a vast admiration of Vanity Fair.

It would fill a volume, in an age of pamphlets, were I to record all my observations in this great capital of human business and pleasure. There was an unlimited range of society—the powerful, the wise, the witty, and the famous in every walk of life; princes, presidents, poets, generals, artists, actors, and philanthropists,— all making their own market at the fair, and deeming no price too exorbitant for such commodities as hit their fancy. It was well worth one's while, even if he had no idea of buying or selling, to loiter through the bazaars and observe the various sorts of traffic that were going forward.

Some of the purchasers, I thought, made very foolish bargains. For instance, a young man having inherited a splendid fortune, laid out a considerable portion of it in the purchase of diseases, and finally spent all the rest for a heavy lot of repentance and a suit of rags. A very pretty girl bartered a heart as clear as crystal, and which seemed her most valuable possession, for another jewel of the same kind, but so worn and defaced as to be utterly worthless. In one shop there were a great many crowns of laurel and myrtle, which soldiers, authors, statesmen, and various other people pressed eagerly to buy; some purchased these paltry wreaths with their lives, others by a toilsome servitude of years, and many sacrificed whatever was most valuable, yet finally slunk away without the crown. There was a sort of stock or scrip, called Conscience, which seemed to be in great demand, and would purchase almost anything. Indeed, few rich commodities were to be obtained without paying a heavy sum in this particular stock, and a man's business was seldom very lucrative unless he knew precisely when and how to throw his hoard of conscience into the market. Yet as this stock was the only thing of permanent value, whoever parted with it was sure to find himself a loser in the long run. Several of the speculations were of a questionable character. Occasionally a member of Congress recruited his pocket by the sale of his constituents; and I was assured that public officers have often sold their country at very moderate prices. Thousands sold their happiness for a whim. Gilded chains were in great demand, and purchased with almost any sacrifice. In truth, those who desired, according to the old adage, to sell anything valuable for a song, might find customers all over the Fair; and there were innumerable messes of pottage, piping hot, for such as chose to buy them with their birthrights. A few articles, however, could not be found genuine at Vanity Fair. If a customer wished to renew his stock of youth the dealers offered him a set of false teeth and an auburn wig; if he demanded peace of mind, they recommended opium or a brandy bottle.

Tracts of land and golden mansions, situate in the Celestial

City, were often exchanged, at very disadvantageous rates, for a few years' lease of small, dismal, inconvenient tenements in Vanity Fair. Prince Beelzebub himself took great interest in this sort of traffic, and sometimes condescended to meddle with smaller matters. I once had the pleasure to see him bargaining with a miser for his soul, which, after much ingenious skirmishing on both sides, his highness succeeded in obtaining at about the value of sixpence. The prince remarked with a smile, that he was a loser by the transaction.

Day after day, as I walked the streets of Vanity, my manners and deportment became more and more like those of the inhabitants. The place began to seem like home; the idea of pursuing my travels to the Celestial City was almost obliterated from my mind. I was reminded of it, however, by the sight of the same pair of simple pilgrims at whom we had laughed so heartily when Apollyon puffed smoke and steam into their faces at the commencement of our journey. There they stood amidst the densest bustle of Vanity; the dealers offering them their purple and fine linen and jewels, the men of wit and humor gibing at them, a pair of buxom ladies ogling them askance, while the benevolent Mr. Smooth-it-away whispered some of his wisdom ot their elbows, and pointed to a newly-erected temple; but there were these worthy simpletons, making the scene look wild and monstrous, merely by their sturdy repudiation of all part in its business or pleasures.

One of them—his name was Stick-to-the-right—perceived in my face, I suppose, a species of sympathy and almost admiration, which, to my own great surprise, I could not help feeling for this pragmatic couple. It prompted him to address me.

"Sir," inquired he, with a sad, yet mild and kindly voice, "do you call yourself a pilgrim?"

"Yes," I replied, "my right to that appellation is indubitable. I am merely a sojourner here in Vanity Fair, being bound to the Celestial City by the new railroad."

"Alas, friend," rejoined Mr. Stick-to-the-right, "I do assure you, and beseech you to receive the truth of my words, that that whole concern is a bubble. You may travel on it all your lifetime, were you to live thousands of years, and yet never get beyond the limits of Vanity Fair. Yea, though you should deem yourself entering the gates of the blessed city, it will be nothing but a miserable delusion."

"The Lord of the Celestial City," began the other pilgrim, whose name was Mr. Foot-it-to-heaven, "has refused, and will ever refuse, to grant an act of incorporation for this railroad; and unless that be obtained, no passenger can ever hope to enter his dominions. Wherefore every man who buys a ticket must lay his account with losing the purchase money, which is the value of his own soul."

"Poh, nonsense!" said Mr. Smooth-it-away, taking my arm and leading me off, "these fellows ought to be indicted for a libel. If the law stood as it once did in Vanity Fair we should see them grinning through the iron bars of the prison window."

This incident made a considerable impression on my mind, and contributed with other circumstances to indispose me to a permanent residence in the city of Vanity; although, of course, I was not simple enough to give up my original plan of gliding along easily and commodiously by railroad. Still, I grew anxious to be gone. There was one strange thing that troubled me. Amid the occupations or amusements of the Fair, nothing was more common than for a person—whether at feast, theatre, or church, or trafficking for wealth and honors, or whatever he might be doing, and however unseasonable the interruption—suddenly to vanish like a soap bubble, and be never more seen of his fellows; and so accustomed were the latter to such little accidents that they went on with their business as quietly as if nothing had happened. But it was otherwise with me.

Finally, after a pretty long residence at the Fair, I resumed my journey towards the Celestial City, still with Mr. Smooth-it-away at my side. At a short distance beyond the suburbs of Vanity we passed the ancient silver mine, of which Demas was the first discoverer, and which is now wrought to great advantage, supplying nearly all the coined currency of the world. A little further onward was the spot where Lot's wife had stood forever under the semblance of a pillar of salt. Curious travellers have long since carried it away piecemeal. Had all regrets been punished as rigorously as this poor dame's were, my yearning for the relinquished delights of Vanity Fair might have produced a similar change in my own corporeal substance, and left me a warning to future pilgrims.

The next remarkable object was a large edifice, constructed of mossgrown stone, but in a modern and airy style of architecture. The engine came to a pause in its vicinity, with the usual tremendous shriek.

"This was formerly the castle of the redoubted giant Despair," observed Mr. Smooth-it-away; "but since his death Mr. Flimsyfaith has repaired it, and keeps an excellent house of entertainment here. It is one of our stopping-places."

"It seems but slightly put together," remarked I, looking at the frail yet ponderous walls. "I do not envy Mr. Flimsy-faith his habitation. Some day it will thunder down upon the heads of the occupants."

"We shall escape at all events," said Mr. Smooth-it-away, "for Apollyon is putting on the steam again."

The road now plunged into a gorge of the Delectable Mountains, and traversed the field where in former ages the blind men wandered and stumbled among the tombs. One of these ancient tombstones had been thrust across the track by some malicious person, and gave the train of cars a terrible jolt. Far up the rugged side of a mountain I perceived a rusty iron door, half overgrown with bushes and creeping plants, but with smoke issuing from its crevices.

"Is that," inquired I, "the very door in the hill-side which the shepherds assured Christian was a by-way to hell?"

"That was a joke on the part of the shepherds," said Mr. Smooth-it-away, with a smile. "It is neither more nor less than the door of a cavern which they use as a smoke-house for the preparation of mutton hams."

My recollections of the journey are now, for a little space, dim and confused, inasmuch as a singular drowsiness here overcame me, owing to the fact that we were passing over the enchanted ground, the air of which encourages a disposition to sleep. I awoke, however, as soon as we crossed the borders of the pleasant land of Beulah. All the passengers were rubbing their eyes, comparing watches, and congratulating one another on the prospect of arriving so seasonably at the journey's end. The sweet breezes of this happy clime came refreshingly to our nostrils; we beheld the glimmering gush of silver fountains, overhung by trees of beautiful foliage and delicious fruit, which were propagated by grafts from the celestial gardens. Once, as we dashed onward like a hurricane, there was a flutter of wings and the bright appearance of an angel in the air, speeding forth on some heavenly mission. The engine now announced the close vicinity of the final station-house by one last and horrible scream, in which there seemed to be distinguishable every kind of wailing and woe, and bitter fierceness of wrath, all mixed up with the wild laughter of a devil or a madman. Throughout our journey, at every stopping-place, Apollyon had exercised his ingenuity in screwing the most abominable sounds out of the whistle of the steam-engine; but in this closing effort he outdid himself and created an infernal uproar, which, besides disturbing the peaceful inhabitants of Beulah, must have sent its discord even through the celestial gates.

While the horrid clamor was still ringing in our ears we heard an exulting strain, as if a thousand instruments of music, with height and depth and sweetness in their tones, at once tender and triumphant, were struck in unison, to greet the approach of some illustrious hero, who had fought the good fight and won a

glorious victory, and was come to lay aside his battered arms forever. Looking to ascertain what might be the occasion of this glad
harmony, I perceived, on alighting from the cars, that a multitude
of shining ones had assembled on the other side of the river, to
welcome two poor pilgrims, who were just emerging from its
depths. They were the same whom Apollyon and ourselves had
persecuted with taunts, and gibes, and scalding steam, at the commencement of our journey—the same whose unworldly aspect and
impressive words had stirred my conscience amid the wild revellers
of Vanity Fair.

"How amazingly well those men have got on," cried I to Mr.
Smooth-it-away. "I wish we were secure of as good a reception."

"Never fear, never fear!" answered my friend. "Come, make
haste; the ferry boat will be off directly, and in three minutes you
will be on the other side of the river. No doubt you will find
coaches to carry you up to the city gates."

A steam ferry boat, the last improvement on this important
route, lay at the river side, puffing, snorting, and emitting all those
other disagreeable utterances which betoken the departure to be
immediate. I hurried on board with the rest of the passengers, most
of whom were in great perturbation: some bawling out for their
baggage; some tearing their hair and exclaiming that the boat
would explode or sink; some already pale with the heaving of the
stream; some gazing affrighted at the ugly aspect of the steersman;
and some still dizzy with the slumberous influences of the Enchanted Ground. Looking back to the shore, I was amazed to
discern Mr. Smooth-it-away waving his hand in token of farewell.

"Don't you go over to the Celestial City?" exclaimed I.

"Oh, no!" answered he with a queer smile, and that same disagreeable contortion of visage which I had remarked in the inhabitants of the Dark Valley. "Oh, no! I have come thus far only for
the sake of your pleasant company. Good-by! We shall meet again."

And then did my excellent friend Mr. Smooth-it-away laugh outright, in the midst of which cachinnation a smoke-wreath issued
from his mouth and nostrils, while a twinkle of lurid flame darted
out of either eye, proving indubitably that his heart was all of a
red blaze. The impudent fiend! To deny the existence of Tophet,
when he felt its fiery tortures raging within his breast. I rushed
to the side of the boat, intending to fling myself on shore; but the
wheels, as they began their revolutions, threw a dash of spray over
me so cold—so deadly cold, with the chill that will never leave
those waters until Death be drowned in his own river—that with
a shiver and a heartquake I awoke. Thank Heaven it was a Dream!

1843, 1846

Herman Melville

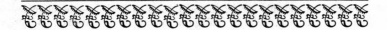

Herman Melville was born in New York City on August 1, 1819, and died there on September 28, 1891; and his literary life can be conveniently divided into three distinct periods. The first was that of his autobiographical romances and major novels, from the end of his wandering in 1844 to the autumn of 1852. The second was devoted to magazine writing, with a particular interest in short stories, from 1853 through 1856. And the third, from the end of an unsuccessful attempt at lecturing in 1859 to the conclusion of his life, produced mostly poetry, although he successfully returned to prose fiction in his last years. During most of the first period he was well known, both at home and abroad, as one of the most promising of young American authors; during the second he was one of the best paid, if not one of the most highly appreciated, contributors to the popular literary magazines; and during the third he became so completely forgotten that his last two volumes of verse were printed at his own expense in editions limited to twenty-five copies for exclusive distribution among his few close friends. His disappearance from public view was so complete, in fact, that he was only briefly mentioned in histories of American literature before the hundredth anniversary of his birth in 1919; his growth to the stature of one of America's—and the world's—greatest authors is almost entirely a phenomenon of recent history and criticism.

The Melville revival brought to life one of the most interesting persons as well as one of the most exciting authors in the history of American literature. At the time of Herman's birth his father, Alan, was on the verge of failing in the import business and retreating to Albany where his wife's family were people of position and influence. There he died in 1832, leaving his widow with a pitifully small income and eight children—four boys and four girls, of whom Herman was the fourth child and second son. At the age of thirteen Herman was put to work as a messenger boy in a bank, and his formal education afterward consisted only of a year's course in the Albany Classical School in preparation for teaching or clerking and an equally brief engineering course at the Lansingburg Academy in the vain anticipation of a job on the project for enlarging the Erie Canal. He was interested in self-improvement, however, and became an active member of the Albany Young Men's Association; and a few fragmentary contributions to the newspaper in the small town of Lansingburg (to which his mother moved, for economy's sake, in 1838) show that he had some early literary ambitions.

But a serious economic depression overshadowed his approach to maturity as an earlier one had overshadowed his birth, and the only employment he could find was that of a poorly paid schoolteacher. During the summer of 1839 he escaped by going to sea, on merchant ship to Liverpool, and in the following summer he visited the Great Lakes and the Mississippi River on a trip to Galena, Illinois. Returning to New York and vainly seeking employment as a lawyer's clerk for several months, he desperately decided that instead of going home for Christmas he would go to New Bedford and ship out for the South Seas on a whaler—the ultimate refuge of criminals, outcasts, and green country boys who knew of no better way to see the world. He sailed on the *Acushnet* on January 3, 1841, not to return until October 14, 1844.

The adventures of his three and a half years in the Pacific formed the basis for his earliest and most popular romances. Made rebellious by ill treatment and bad luck on the *Acushnet*, Melville and a companion jumped ship in the Marquesas on July 9, 1842, and took refuge with the cannibal Typees, from whom Melville was rescued by an Australian whaler, the *Lucy Ann*, four weeks later. When he found conditions there far worse than those on the *Acushnet* he refused duty after the ship had put into harbor at Papeete, Tahiti, and in late September he was arrested and held prisoner in the local open-air *calabooza*. From this he was conveniently allowed to escape to the neighboring island of Moorea, where he and an Australian shipmate wandered as beachcombers for a couple of weeks before Melville shipped as a harpooner on a Nantucket whaler, the *Charles and Henry*, whose captain agreed to take him "for the voyage" and discharge him when they touched the Hawaiian Islands. Reaching Honolulu in May, 1843, Melville settled down as a clerk in a drygoods store with the intention of remaining for a year or more. But he became homesick when the frigate *United States* dropped anchor in the harbor and the word was passed around that it was bound for Boston, so short of hands that it was accepting enlistments exclusively for the voyage home. The temptation was too great, and on August 17 Melville joined the Navy.

It was a mistake. The *United States* lay or cruised off the coasts of South and Central America for nearly a year before making the long voyage home; and Melville, who had endured the brutality of merchant and whaling vessels and had observed the obtuse inhumanity of missionaries in Tahiti and the Sandwich Isles, found himself almost overcome by the miniature world of a man-of-war. The crowded conditions, the strict discipline, and the constant threat of hard punishment under the articles of war (for the Navy, at that time, was alert to attack by England) permanently affected him and made him glad enough to get home and settle down in Lansingburg, where he entertained his family and friends with tales of adventures until he was persuaded to write them out for publication.

His first attempt became *Typee: A Peep at Polynesian Life*, which was published in England and then in America in 1846. It was a charming romance, based upon his real experience in the Marquesas, of a bold sailor and a dusky maiden and a tribe of sociable cannibals who seemed equally likely to adopt or eat him; and it was given an air of authenticity both by his memories and by research into other travel books. It was also an immediate popular success, and although he had to expurgate it for his second American edition, he was so encouraged that he began an immediate sequel dealing with his Tahitian adventures. *Omoo,* which appeared in the following years, resembled *Typee* in that it represented an exaggeration of the time Melville spent in acquiring the experiences on which the book was based and in the introduction of new material derived from his researches; but it was more humorous in tone and perhaps more convincing as a narrative of actual fact—which was what the English publisher, John Murray, wanted. But in it Melville used up his most novel experiences, and when he undertook to go on with a sequel to it he was compelled to draw upon his imagination and try to invent a story that would be as interesting as that of his own life.

By the time Melville was firmly committed to his third book he was successful enough to contemplate settling into matrimony and a career as a professional writer. So, in the late summer of 1847, he married Elizabeth Shaw (a friend of his sisters, and the daughter of the Chief Justice of Massachusetts) and moved to New York, taking with him his mother and entire family with the exception of an older brother who had recently died in England. There he found a stimulating intellectual environment in the company of Evert and George Duyckinck and other writers associated with the *Literary World,* but little stimulation for the narrative invention on which a professional writer would have to depend. Consequently his new book (which was to be called *Mardi, and a Voyage Thither* when it was published in 1849) took on a new character. Instead of remaining an adventure story, it became a collection of incidents and discussions related to a group of distinctive characters engaged on a quest; and the quest itself became an allegory of man's search for happiness into which was introduced, shortly before publication, a survey of the politics of the whole civilized world as it was affected by the revolutionary and social movements of 1848. The result was a strange, rambling, and sometimes chaotic book, but one which provides fascinating evidence of Melville's extraordinarily rapid growth toward intellectual and stylistic maturity.

His greatest imaginative development, however, was to come later, and it occurred under intense pressure. For *Mardi* was a commercial failure, and Melville (whose first son, Malcolm, had just been born) was under many obligations. Accordingly he fell back on his earliest adventuring and rapidly wrote *Redburn: His First Voyage* in the spring of 1849 and followed it with *White Jacket* (1850), which was based on his Navy experiences and written even more rapidly during the summer. Melville spoke contemptuously of the first book and with no great enthusiasm of the second, yet he managed to get into both of them those qualities of the living, vitalizing imagination which were essential to his literary growth. In *Redburn* it was the imagined experience, vitalized and made profound by an immediate emotion, which added a new quality to his work. The outward voyage of Redburn to Liverpool was perhaps as close to Melville's own experience as *Typee* and *Omoo* had been. The return was almost wholly imaginary: the immigrant ship, the plague, and the dying sailor with his strange sick grip on the crew were not a part of Melville's life. Yet the plague, traced to its origin in an immigrant ship, was raging in New York when Melville wrote; and he was acutely, even fearfully, aware of humanity's sick grip on humanity. This he got into his book, realizing the general in the particular, and this he was to do again in other books. *White Jacket* contained material of the same sort—particularly the scene in which the narrator was brought to the gratings for flogging, and perhaps the brutal surgical scenes and the fall from the yardarm as well. But there was more remembered emotion in this book, which Melville broadened into general significance with such suggestive implications that the microcosm of the ship almost becomes an allegory of the world.

The completion of *White Jacket* gave Melville the literary experience and the intellectual and imaginative growth which prepared him to write his masterpiece. But he had no thought of doing so at the time. His major concern, at the end of 1849, was to obtain a more favorable contract with his English publisher; and he went abroad for that purpose, keeping a notebook for material to be used in a historical novel about an American Revolutionary patriot in exile. The voyage stirred him deeply—intellectually by throwing him into contact with two young transcendental philosophers and emotionally by reviving his feeling for the sea. On his return he abandoned his historical novel in favor of another project which for some time had been in the back of his mind—a romantic and fanciful book concerning the whale fishery, about which he knew so much and about which other writers had written with so little imagination. This became *Moby Dick* (1851). He had almost completed a draft of the book when he took his summer vacation in the hills of western Massachusetts and invited some of his New York literary friends up for a weekend.

The visit of the New Yorkers provided the occasion for a gathering of all the literary people in the Berkshire region, an animated discussion of the potential greatness of American literature, and Melville's first meeting with Nathaniel Hawthorne. Melville was impressed with his new acquaintance and summer neighbor, both by Hawthorne's person and by *Mosses from an Old Manse*, which he read immediately after the meeting. Out of his enthusiasm for the man, the book, and the potentialities of American literature, he composed the extravagant essay on "Hawthorne and His Mosses" which appeared in the *Literary World* a few weeks later. If a 19th-century American Shakespeare should arise, he felt, he would appear as a novelist somewhat like Hawthorne, who in one respect at least —his willingness to reveal the "blackness" of "vital truth"—excelled the "divine William." In such a frame of mind as this Melville sat down to put the finishing touches to his whaling story and add to it, as was his custom, those factual details he was too hurried or too uninformed to put in the original draft.

The story required fifteen months (during which Melville moved his family to western Massachusetts, and settled on a farm in Pittsfield) for its "finishing touches" and must have substantially changed its character under the influence of Melville's new literary and intellectual excitement. The black truth of Hawthorne, it would seem from the stories Melville admired, was quite different from the truth revealed by the transcendental intuitions of such authors as Coleridge, Carlyle, and Emerson, who saw the physical world as some mask or emblem for a spiritual reality which was both divine and good. Hawthorne looked behind the mask of appearances and saw that the heart of man created its own evil. Under a new stimulus Melville experienced a second intellectual growth, in which he discovered within himself the basic philosophical conflict of the 19th-century—that of faith and doubt, transcendentalism and empiricism, or (as it later became symbolized) religion and scientific skepticism. Could one accept the philosophical belief that beyond the physical universe there existed some spiritual reality? Or was this belief a psychological delusion, born of man's refusal to face the fact that his own heart was the creator of good and evil? These were the questions of vital truth which beset Melville—as they beset so many other thoughtful men of his century—when he sat down to revise his book.

As the book—vitalized by remembered emotions and by the impelling new emotions of its composition—grew in revision, these questions were dramatized in a hero of the sort that might have appeared in one of Shakespeare's tragedies—Captain Ahab, whose impassioned search throughout the South Seas for one particular White Whale provided the action of the story. Ahab looked at the Whale from the point of view of the hero in Carlyle's transcendental novel, *Sartor Resartus*, seeing him as the visible emblem of universal evil, and hurling an "Everlasting No" of defiance against him. At the same time Melville looked at Ahab from the point of view newly inspired by Hawthorne, seeing him as a madman whose "heart" generated its own evil. Yet his emotions were with Ahab. Whether it was the experience of writing *White Jacket* or something else, he apparently felt cooped up or walled in; and his impulse toward a rebellious outburst provided the emotional energy in the book, pervaded its imagery, and made him seek (in such a chapter as that on "The Whiteness of the Whale") loopholes in Hawthorne's empirical attitude. As a result, the book *Moby Dick* acquired philosophical implications and an ambiguous imaginative intensity which was too great for the contemporary readers who had admired Melville's autobiographical romances but which makes some modern readers regard it as the greatest of American novels.

Some of this imaginative intensity carried over into Melville's next novel, *Pierre* (1852), to which he gave the subtitle "The Ambiguities," although he began it with the intention of creating a pleasant romance to recapture his popular audience. The story of another rebel—but a younger and more sophomoric one—it became a melodrama through which Melville explored "the cavern of man" in an effort to determine whether an impractical devotion to transcendental morality represented an admirable idealism or a human reaction against psychological truths too "black" to face. He seems never to have reached a firm conclusion, but his exploration of the question produced the most profound as well as one of the most fantastic psychological novels of the 19th century.

Commercially, however, *Pierre* was a complete failure; and after its publication in the summer of 1852 Melville's wise father-in-law took him on a trip to Nantucket in an effort to renew his interest in the sea which he handled so well. There, perhaps worn out by the futility of his own rebellion against public taste, Melville discovered the virtue of patience as exemplified by the women of the island; and he revealed his fascinated interest in the new theme in a letter of August 13 (reprinted in this anthology), urging the "Agatha" story upon Hawthorne. He was reluctant to undertake it himself, but when he made an effort to regain his public, through the magazine as a publishing medium and the short story as a

literary form, he did so in an emotional frame of mind considerably removed from the rebelliousness of *Moby Dick* and *Pierre*.

II

Although Melville's short stories lack the power of *Moby Dick* and the
psychological depth of *Pierre*, they are perhaps more clearly representative
of the full range of his art. He had shown his interest in stating the general in terms of the particular in the allegorical parts of *Mardi*, and he had
displayed his capacity for realizing this relationship in a more vital and convincing way through the narrative of *Redburn*. *White Jacket*, like *Moby
Dick* and *Pierre*, shows him crossing the symbolic bridge between general
ideas and particular facts and figures so freely in either direction that it is
often difficult to tell whether he is indulging in old-fashioned allegory or
the more suggestive art which is "symbolic" in the manner of the French
poets and in the terminology of much modern criticism—that based on
materials which were themselves "instinct with significance," as he had
put it in his "Agatha" letter to Hawthorne. Consequently it might be
well to look carefully at his first published short story in order to see the
variety of considerations that should enter into any critical interpretation
of his work.

The story was called "Bartleby, the Scrivener. A Story of Wall Street"
and was published in *Putnam's Monthly Magazine* in November and December, 1853. It was a fantasy related to real life—to Melville's own attempt to find employment as a lawyer's copyist; to the life of a Western
traveling companion who had found such employment, had become a confirmed invalid, and had recently retreated to Vermont to die; and to one
of his transcendental fellow voyagers to Europe who had just developed
such a severe case of agoraphobia that he was confined in an asylum in
October. Melville must also have known from his brother Alan (who had
a lawyer's office in Wall Street) something of the eccentricities of clerical
help, and he knew and made allusion in "Bartleby" to the story of the
well-known lawyer who had been murdered by a deranged clerk some
twelve years before. On the most superficial level of critical interpretation
we might assume that Melville spun a whimsical story, suitable for a popular magazine, out of such materials as these and concluded it with another
bit of whimsey and a teasing exclamation.

Yet few experienced readers of Melville would accept such an interpretation. Some who have looked beneath its surface have been disposed to
see it as some sort of personal allegory. They have reasoned that Melville
had come up against the blank wall of public indifference to what he had
to say and that, rather than adapt himself to the customary ways of the
contemporary literary world, he would "prefer not to" write any more;
and they conclude that this story is a veiled announcement of his decision.
At least one critical reader has gone so far as to generalize this sort of interpretation to the point of making "Bartleby" a fable expressing Melville's
opinion of the frustrated position of the creative writer as a member of
modern society. To do so he had to make a great deal of the fact that a
"scrivener" is a "writer" and then somehow confuse the writer as a copyist
with the creative writer; but such logical fallacies are common in Melville criticism, and the wise student will learn more from contemplating
the text than from trying to find an easy secondhand explanation of what

the text might mean.

The contemplation of "Bartleby" is especially productive because it reveals how coherent a great writer's imagination may remain while its expression is being affected by a variety of interests and emotions. For Bartleby is intimately connected, imaginatively, with Captain Ahab of *Moby Dick*. Both are heroes who refuse to accept, and set their wills against, the realities of sane everyday life. Their difference is that Ahab is active and aggressive; Bartleby, passive and patient. In the language of Carlyle's *Sartor Resartus*, Ahab is in the stage of "The Everlasting No," vigorously denying the power of evil to crush him with its physical symbols; Bartleby has sunk into "The Centre of Indifference." Ahab is a tragic hero, whose force provides the action for a mighty drama; Bartleby is a pathetic figure, around whom revolves the action of a slight comedy. But however different they may appear in character and in their literary context, they are two of a kind in the way they set themselves up against the sanities of the everyday world.

Their differences may be explained in terms of Melville's interests and probable emotions while creating them. Ahab was the product of Melville's imagination when he was interested in writing a dramatic novel which would be Shakespearean in its tragic power. Bartleby was created while he was interested in writing an entertaining story for a popular magazine. But his interests were not wholly determined by the literary forms he chose to use. During the year immediately preceding the composition of "Bartleby" he had become fascinated by the patient endurance of the women of Nantucket and challenged by the notion of writing a story on such a theme. "Bartleby" was to be merely the first of such attempts. For somehow since writing *Pierre*, or perhaps while composing that curious book, Melville's sympathies had evidently shifted. He seems to have been no longer so intense in his identification of himself with the active rebels. He had become willing to explore, with his sympathetic imagination at least, the possibilities of passive resistance to the circumstances of fate.

The possible reasons for this shift in emotional interests offer a problem for Melville's biographer rather than for the literary critic. But the fact that it seems to occur invites critical attention to an imaginative union between *Moby Dick* and "Bartleby" which is deeper and more absolute than that found in resemblances of characters or comparisons of plot. It is to be found in certain pervading and even formative imagery which welled up from the deepest depths of the author's creative mind, perhaps without any awareness on his own part of its full significance. Readers of *Moby Dick* will recall that Ahab spoke of himself as a prisoner and of the White Whale as a wall through which he had to thrust in order to escape; and the image of the frustrating wall, sometimes engraved with hieroglyphics and often relieved by a slight but hopeful bit of green or light, pervades the novel up to the last great scenes when Ahab drives his boat directly against the high wrinkled forehead of the Whale. The same image dominates "Bartleby" to such an extent that one suspects a deliberate pun in the subtitle calling it "A Story of Wall Street." As one of the most acute of Melville scholars has demonstrated, this image came constantly to the surface of Melville's mind—from *White Jacket* to the end of his life—whenever his imagination was deeply stirred. What it signifies with reference to the author's personality we do not know, and even a psychiatrist's guess, at the present time, might be entirely too superficial. What it signifies with reference to "Bartleby" is that the story is by no means a casual magazine piece but a work of literature which has its origins in the most mysterious depths of the creative imagination.

The theme of patient resistance dominated another story of the same time, "Cock-a-doodle-Doo!" which appeared in *Harper's Magazine* for December, 1853, and was also in Melville's mind when he contemplated his next novel. The Harpers had given him an advance for a tale about hunting the giant tortoises of the Galápagos Islands, and he composed a number of background sketches (later to be called "The Encantadas; or Enchanted Islands") for the book. He lacked a story suitable for his subject and his scene, however, and the poetic epigraphs he eventually attached to his sketches suggest that he tried to stimulate his creative imagination by rereading his favorite allegorical poet, Edmund Spenser, in an effort to cross the bridge from his general theme of patience to some particular narrative which would illustrate it. The best story he could find or imagine was the one he told briefly in the eighth sketch, "Norfolk Isle and the Chola Widow." The Chola Widow was adaptable to the fascinating theme outlined in the Agatha letter, but he could not penetrate the mystery of her personality. She was his frustrating wall. She but showed him "her soul's lid, and the strange ciphers thereon engraved; all within, with pride's timidity, was withheld." Yet he told the circumstantial part of her story effectively and reserved even the most delicate hint of its symbolic implications until the end; the concluding figure of the cross "brought tears into the eyes" of James Russell Lowell and made him say that "he thought it the finest touch of genius he had seen in prose."

Whether Melville, by a determined effort of the imagination, could have lifted the lid of the Chola Widow's soul and found within the substance of a full-length novel is uncertain. In actuality he did not try. The Harpers' publishing plant was destroyed by fire in December, 1853, and he sold the Galápagos sketches to *Putnam's* for publication during the following spring. He should not have done so, for the Harpers complained, and there was probably an estrangement between the author and his publishers for some years thereafter. And, whether it was for this reason or for some other, the emotional undercurrents of Melville's writings came closer to the surface. He was still deeply concerned with frustration; but instead of trying to understand its effect upon character, he began to express resentment against a society which walled out the lonely individual with economic barriers. He sent to *Putnam's* in May, 1854, sketches of "The Two Temples," but the editor recognized the satire upon the new Grace Church in New York and was unwilling to offend the congregation by printing it. A more innocuous satire of the same sort, dealing with the Lord Mayor's annual feast in London, "Poor Man's Pudding and Rich Man's Crumbs," had already gone to *Harper's* for publication in June. "The Two Temples" has more emotional force than the other satire, perhaps because the irony of an exclusive church is greater than that of an exclusive banquet, but in each the emotion seems closer to petulance than to real bitterness; and the same quality appears in his satiric portrait of Benjamin Franklin in *Israel Potter* when he at last finished his story of his Revolutionary exile and published it serially in *Putnam's* in 1854–55.

Melville seems to have been at loose ends, imaginatively, at this time, for he ranged from a forced acceptance of the world in "The Happy Failure" for *Harper's* in July, 1854, to anger at its deceits in "The Lightning-Rod Man" for *Putnam's* in August. He was obviously not at his best when he was seeking a story to express an attitude of mind. He needed "a skeleton of actual reality to build about with fulness and veins and beauty"—a story which was "instinct" with the sort of "significance" that called from the conscious and unconscious depths of his being those thoughts and feelings, perceptions and sensibilities, of which the whole artist rather than the occasional magazine-writer was made. He found such a story in the forgotten, privately printed autobiography of Captain Amasa Delano, whose *Narrative of Voyages and Travels* told of his extraordinary experience in boarding the Spanish ship *Tryal* near the Pacific island of Santa Maria in February, 1805. From Captain Delano's stark and matter-of-fact account of his adventure, and the documents supporting it, Melville created "Benito Cereno" (1855), one of the most vividly imaginative of all his narratives.

He did so by adopting a narrative method he had never before used in his fiction but one which Henry James was to perfect a generation later —that of entering into the mind of an objectively conceived character to whom the significance of a situation was gradually unfolded through a series of events which were not particularly exciting until they reached a dramatic denouement. He "lifted the lid" of Captain Delano's soul and revealed his expanding consciousness as he never could for that of the Chola Widow. He showed the Captain as interested, puzzled, speculative, inquisitive, and alternately suspicious and sympathetic until his hard-headed New England attitude was transformed into a state of "dreamy inquietude" which made him feel—"though upon the wide sea"—like a "prisoner in some deserted château, left to stare at empty grounds, and peer out at vague roads, where never wagon or wayfarer passed." Recovering, the Captain became more aware of his own moods in relation to his perceptions. But this awareness, in itself, increased the tension as the story approached its climax. By dramatizing a situation from within the consciousness of a central character, Melville the story-teller achieved a narrative which is unique in the canon of his literary works.

But Melville the artist wove his own peculiar magic around the storyteller's achievement. The reader is always ahead of Captain Delano in his approach to inquietude and in his awareness of ominous overtones which make him sense the validity of the Captain's suspicions and feel the irony of his New England "Duxbury" mood. Part of this feeling is created by such obvious devices as those of the stage setting—the oakum pickers, the hatchet polishers, and the mysteriously shrouded figurehead of the ship. Part of it is achieved by the handling of characters, the black frustration of white privacy, whether by convergence of the mob or by the excessive attentions of the servant or the silent watchfulness of the giant in chains; and part is achieved by many hints of many mysteries. To accomplish all this Melville had to sacrifice self-indulgence in such emotions as the petulant bitterness of "The Two Temples" and yield himself to the demands of imaginative creation. But he could not escape that mysterious emotion which existed somewhere in his creative depths, formed so much of his imagery, and kept so much of his work coherent: Don Benito's situation is that of Ahab and Bartleby, that of a man who is walled in by something he does not fully understand and whose desolation is relieved by only a single symbol (in the person of Captain Delano) of hope. He differs from his predecessors only in that he is beyond either active or passive resistance. He can make only a last, desperate effort to escape. Yet, even though he escapes physically, the symbol of his frustration and defeat hangs over him like a shadow with a destructiveness more complete for him than for the heroic Ahab or the pathetic Bartleby.

The editorial reader for *Putnam's*, George W. Curtis, complained at the "dreary" documentation at the end of "Benito Cereno" and announced that Melville "does everything too hurriedly now." But he may have been himself at fault. Melville had recently proposed a new novel for the magazine, and Curtis had advised the new owner to decline it unless it was "extremely good." There is persuasive evidence in the changes Melville made in his source—especially in the documentation—that he had planned a much longer tale than the one actually published in *Putnam's* in the last three months of 1855; and it may be that he was discouraged by lack of encouragement and by a severe attack of rheumatism in his back, which left him physically helpless shortly before he made his proposal, and therefore simply revised the fragment of a novel into a long short story. But in any event the story is sufficient in itself. Such continuation as he may have planned would have had to be in the form of further explanation of the events leading up to the central experience and of those following it: the imaginative core of the work is complete, and the summary of what went before and came afterward may be enough.

The attack of rheumatism in February and the rejection of his proposed novel in March seem to have brought about another emotional change in Melville, which is reflected in what was to be his last phase as a short-story writer. He became more introspective and more consciously inclined to parade his troubles under a thin veil of allegory. He had already begun to experiment with a somewhat mischievous allegory in "The Paradise of Bachelors and The Tartarus of Maids" (for *Harper's* in April, 1855) in which, describing a New England paper mill, he gave a symbolic account of the process of gestation his wife was going through at the time. In "The Bell-Tower" for *Putnam's* in August, however, Melville was more directly concerned with himself. Its style was more artificial than that of any of his stories based on a skeleton of reality, and its general allegorical implications were clearly summarized in a moralizing conclusion. But he did not say what he doubtless thought, in his discouraged state of mind during the spring and early summer—that his own popular reputation as a novelist had been destroyed by such of his creatures as Captain Ahab and Pierre, that his books were too heavy for public support, that their commercial weakness was the life's blood he had put in them, that his own pride was going before the fall. His only attempt at what may now be called science fiction was actually a melancholy reflection on his own literary career.

It was followed by another melancholy story of pride going before a fall—"Jimmy Rose," in *Harper's* for November—but before Melville undertook another personal allegory his spirits had improved. His rheumatic back had become worse in June, 1855, and Oliver Wendell Holmes, Professor of Anatomy and Dean of the Harvard Medical School, had been called in for consultation by his worried family. It was probably this examination and consultation that Melville had reference to in the sketch "I and My Chimney" in *Putnam's* for March, 1855; for, although many critics have referred it to some mysterious and undocumented mental breakdown, the actual circumstances of his life suggest that the "chimney" was his spinal column and that the tone of the story is humorous rather than tragic. At any rate the three other sketches he published that spring —"The 'Gees" in *Harper's* for March, "The Apple-Tree Table" in *Putnam's* for May, and "The Piazza," which served as the introduction to the collection of *Putnam's* stories published as *Piazza Tales* (1856)— showed few if any traces of the melancholia which had beset him during the preceding year. He closed his career as a short story writer on a more cheerful, if more superficial, note than that with which he began.

What these stories reveal is the great variety of ways in which Melville's imagination worked and the close relation between his imaginative and his emotional life. This variety and this relationship may cast some light on the puzzle of a final novel, written during the year of his change from melancholia to comparative cheerfulness and published in 1856—*The Confidence Man*, which deals with a Mississippi River steamer and appears to begin as an allegorical satire on gullibility and end as a suggestive illustration of the evils of distrust. Another commercial failure, it was to be his last published work of fiction during his lifetime, although he was to leave in manuscript one of the finest and most interesting of his novels, *Billy Budd*. But before he wrote this in his last years he was to turn poet and to acquire other qualities which made another prose masterpiece possible.

III

Melville's activities as a poet are difficult to follow because he did not devote to his verse the prolonged periods of concentrated intensity which were required by his novels—and, as a result, his poems quite often lack the imaginative depth of his best prose. He probably began writing serious verse during his trip through the Mediterranean countries and the Holy Land, which he made during the winter of 1856–57, and continued while engaged in lecturing during the three following winters. In any event, when he started on a round-the-world trip with his younger brother Tom (master of the sailing ship *Meteor*) in 1860 he had accumulated a volume of verses which he left behind for publication. Neither the trip nor the publication was accomplished, however, and when the author returned home after leaving the ship in San Francisco he probably destroyed the manuscript, although some of his early poems were undoubtedly saved for later revision and publication.

The Civil War (for which he vainly volunteered his services to the Navy) provided him with a new inspiration, and in 1866 he brought out a unified volume entitled *Battle-Pieces and Other Aspects of the War*. Some of the poems in it were artificially composed in order to make the book a comprehensive survey of the war, but others show that certain events stirred him deeply. A perfect naval action such as "Dupont's Round Fight" impressed him both by the neatness of its tactics and by its aptness as a symbol, and the victory of the *Monitor* over the *Merrimac* struck his imagination as a significant foreshadowing of an era of technology which would bring to an end the sort of seamanship he knew from his own experience. In retrospect, he could see the hanging of John Brown as a darkly ominous "Portent" of the bloodshed to come, and the assassination of Lincoln five days after Lee's surrender made him question his confidence in the ultimate victory of law: Lincoln's murderer was as "grimy" a slur on man's belief in his own nobility as was the mob Melville imagined having seen from "The House-Top" during the draft riots of two years before. These were among the poems marked by a genuine excitement of imaginative feeling.

But soon after the publication of *Battle-Pieces* Melville (who had moved his family from the Berkshires to New York City near the end of the war) obtained a job in the Custom House and to all appearances abandoned literature. Secretly, though, he continued composing verse related to his travels and to the conflicts of philosophy revealed in *Moby Dick* and now symbolized (for Melville and for most of the English-speaking world after the publication of Darwin's *The Origin of Species* in 1859) as a conflict between religious faith and scientific doubt. The background for his new interest in traditional Christianity was provided by his own tour of the Holy Land, and his unifying character was a young theological student named Clarel, who was seeking the restoration of his own faith by exposing himself to the associations of holy places and the conversation of the many men of many religions that he met there. When a whisper went through the family circle that Melville was writing again, his uncle Peter Gansevoort offered to subsidize the publication of the book, and Melville once more and for the last time went through the strain of completing and preparing for publication an ambitious work of literature. *Clarel: A Poem and Pilgrimage in the Holy Land* was published in two volumes in 1876. Some twenty thousand lines in length and filled with a great variety of characters and subtly conflicting ideas, it was one of the most ambitious poetic works of the 19th century.

Curiously, though, it seems to represent the development of Melville the novelist rather than Melville the poet. The plot deals with the inner and outer experiences of Clarel, who comes to Jerusalem, meets and falls in love with Ruth (the daughter of a Puritan agnostic turned Jew and Zionist), and goes on a pilgrimage through the Holy Land when the death of Ruth's father forces her into a period of seclusion and mourning. His travels take him through the strange places that Melville himself had visited on his trip and about which he had read extensively after his return, and they culminate in the emotional shock of Clarel's return to Jerusalem and the death of Ruth, which leaves him as desolate emotionally as the country is physically. Throughout the narrative also runs the theme of spiritual desolation, represented by Clarel's doubts and questionings and by the attitudes expressed by such a variety of characters as the smooth and superficial Derwent, the buoyant and optimistic Rolfe, the mysteriously reserved Vine, the embittered Ungar and the bleak Mortmain, and the saintly but weak-minded Nehemiah. The narrative was designed to be one of ideas— dealing with speculations on such questions as those raised in a section called "The High Desert"—but they led to no conclusion for Clarel, and Melville's own conclusions could find no dramatic place in the poem but had to be stated in an admonitory "Epilogue."

One reason why the poem did not achieve emotional and imaginative coherence, perhaps, was that Melville himself was no longer deeply concerned with the conflicts of belief which lifted *Moby Dick* to heights of poetic intensity. He was less interested in beliefs than in the sort of people who could hold them—more like the novelist, concerned with characters, than the poet, concerned with the vital image. In the light of what he had done in *Moby Dick* and *Pierre* and in "Bartleby" and other short stories, the traditional Jewish "Wailing Wall" should have been for him a stirring symbol for the frustrations of a race, but he made it only a picturesque meeting place for Clarel and Ruth and other characters who were to figure in the narrative. A clue to his own state of mind while writing the poem might possibly be found in "A Sketch" he gave of Nehemiah, whose life history was much like that of Captain Ahab but who had reached the third stage of Carlyle's transcendental hero—that of "The Everlasting Yea." Nehemiah did not defy the universe as Ahab did, nor did he rest in Bartleby's center of indifference. He accepted the physical world as a symbol and the spiritual reality behind it as good. He was, to Melville's mind, a saint but no hero. And Clarel, searching for the power of acceptance, had none of the potentialities of a hero with whom Melville could identify himself in a way that would give power and coherence to his poem.

Some of the best sections of *Clarel*, in fact, are not direct outgrowths of its plot and purpose but are digressions, like a casual character's account of "The Island" which Melville had seen on his youthful visits to the Galápagos and about which he had meditated more recently in "The Encantadas." Brought to mind by thoughts of the comparable desolation of the scenery around Bethlehem, the Pacific scene was infused with new emotions and made productive of new speculations concerning the ability of man to solve the mystery of the universe by translating the reality into "verbiage." And it was this retrospective imagination, infused with new emotions and new ideas, which was responsible for the best of Melville's later work in verse and prose. Among the minor sea-pieces in the privately printed *John Marr and Other Sailors* (1888), "The Maldive Shark" was a grim recollection from his youth made grimmer by his later broodings upon the ironies of life. The more varied contents of *Timoleon*, published shortly before his death in 1891, were drawn from many memories, thoughtfully meditated. Although the scene in a poem called "After the Pleasure Party" is the Mediterranean coast, its dramatization of a star-gazer on a "terrace chill in Northern air" suggests that it may have been inspired by one of the patient women of Nantucket who had dedicated her life to science and became a famous astronomer, but who remained a fascinating puzzle to Melville because he found in her spirit and fate something closely akin to his own.

In any event, reflections on art and artists, his own struggles, and his kinship with others who had struggled formed a strong theme in this last volume. "Lone Founts" and "Art" are expressions of his own aspirations and efforts, whereas "Monody" is almost certainly a belated elegy on his old friend Hawthorne and "Shelley's Vision" is an attribution to another poet of what was probably Melville's own reaction (as he saw it in retrospect) to literary disappointment. The reason why art was so much in Melville's consciousness at the reflective end of his life may be suggested by his memory of "The Apparition" of the Parthenon as he had seen it apparently hanging in the sky as he approached Athens from the sea: art was his last faith, the nearest thing to religion he could give his heart to at a time when he was wondering whether his own wholehearted struggles with the world had been worthwhile.

Melville was to leave behind him manuscripts enough for two other small volumes of verse (from which "The New Rosicrucians" and "Immolated" are taken), but the most important of his manuscripts was that of the short novel *Billy Budd*, which was begun after he left the Custom House in 1888 and finished just before his last illness. It was another retrospective work, infused with new emotions and new ideas and, like *Clarel*, less concerned with the truth of particular ideas than with the true understanding of the human beings who could hold or represent them. For the story of a young sailor, hanged for an alleged mutiny, who died with a blessing on his lips had been a part of Melville's family history: his cousin, Guert Gansevoort, had presided at the court-martial, and the later investigation of the case had been a great public scandal in 1843. Melville had revived his memories of Guert by making him a character in the poem "Bridegroom Dick" for *John Marr and Other Sailors*, and he may have planned to revive the young sailor for the poem "Billy in the Darbies" for the same volume. But Billy interested him too much as a type of innocence for the short treatment he could give him in the prose introduction to a casual poem, and he undertook a fuller telling of his story and a more complete treatment of his character. In opposition to him he placed the master-of-arms Claggert as a type of evil drawn from his memories of the petty officer under whom he had suffered in the U.S. Frigate *United States*. Claggert also fascinated him, and in a revision of the manuscript he developed him as almost as fine a figure of human malignancy as was Shakespeare's Iago. And, finally, he became carried away by the problem of Captain Vere, who had controlled the court-martial and been the sympathetic author of Billy's doom, and in the last revisions and additions to the manuscript he made him the central character of the tale.

The result was a novel which has fascinated modern readers almost as much as has *Moby Dick* and *Pierre*. It was a story of innocent goodness and dark malevolence and of the efforts of a wise and good man to deal justly with a problem they presented. For Billy, made speechless by a false accusation from Claggert, had struck out in unpremeditated protest and by accident had killed his accuser. Everyone knew that he was morally innocent. But Melville had set the scene in the British navy during the Napoleonic wars, when discipline was imperative for the safety of the country, and discipline demanded Billy's death. Justice became a matter of choosing between the absolute and the expedient, between the individual and society, between the dictates of the impulsive and the reasoning conscience. Melville was sensitive to the intellectual trend of the times— to the growing belief that the individual was of relatively small importance in comparison to the compulsions of social necessity—and he allowed Captain Vere to sacrifice Billy to the demands of national security. Billy accepted the judgment and died with a "God bless Captain Vere" on his lips—not because he understood the necessity but because he had a simple-minded faith in the goodness which lay back of the stern decision.

But in his last great book Melville himself finally looked behind the wall which every man, in one way or another, faces as a symbol of fate or frustration. Billy's "Everlasting Yea" had in it a strong element of irony. Captain Vere, who determined his fate, may have been wise in mind and good in heart, but his heart was not in his wisdom. He remained forever haunted by his decision. Was there wisdom in his heart? Would he have been wiser and happier if his decision had been governed by his spontaneous impulse toward individual justice rather than by his reasoned considerations of the good of society? Melville was not prepared to say so. But he knew more at the age of 71 than he had known forty years before when he composed *Moby Dick*. He knew that behind the wall which Ahab defied, which Bartleby faced with indifference, and which Billy accepted, there was no absolute spiritual reality, either good or evil. Men might die in various attitudes toward fate, but those who survived—Melville and Captain Vere among them—knew that behind the pasteboard mask of justice itself lay only uncertainty. What they might (in the language of the "Epilogue" to *Clarel*) "be astounded into" knowing later was a mystery that even the power of art could not penetrate.

From Hawthorne and His Mosses[1]

* * * Where Hawthorne is known, he seems to be deemed a pleasant writer, with a pleasant style—a sequestered, harmless man, from whom any deep and weighty thing would hardly be anticipated: a man who means no meanings. But there is no man, in whom humor and love, like mountain peaks, soar to such a rapt height, as to receive the irradiations of the upper skies; there is no man in whom humor and love are developed in that high form called genius—no such man can exist without also possessing, as the indispensable complement of these, a great, deep intellect, which drops down into the universe like a plummet. Or, love and humor are only the eyes, through which such an intellect views this world. The great beauty in such a mind is but the product of its strength. What, to all readers, can be more charming than the piece entitled "Monsieur du Miroir"; and to a reader at all capable of fully fathoming it, what, at the same time, can possess more mystical depth of meaning?—Yes, there he sits, and looks at me—this "shape of mystery," this "identical Monsieur du Miroir."—"Methinks I should tremble now, were his wizard power, of glid-

---

1. Melville was given a copy of Hawthorne's *Mosses from an Old Manse* by his aunt on July 18, 1850, but did not read it until after he met the author for the first time (on August 5). The impression Hawthorne made upon him, at a crucial period in the composition of *Moby Dick,* is evident from this review; it was published in the *Literary World* as "by a Virginian Spending July in Vermont" and was marked by references to a "Carolinian cousin" and other attempts to disguise its authorship.

ing through all impediments in search of me, to place him suddenly before my eyes."

How profound, nay, appalling, is the moral evolved by the "Earth's Holocaust," where—beginning with the hollow follies and affectations of the world—all vanities and empty theories and forms are, one after another, and by an admirably graduated, growing comprehensiveness, thrown into the allegorical fire, till, at length, nothing is left but the all-engendering heart of man; which remaining still unconsumed, the great conflagration is naught.

Of a piece with this is "The Intelligence Office," a wondrous symbolizing of the secret workings in men's souls. There are other sketches, still more charged with ponderous import.

"The Christmas Banquet" and "The Bosom Serpent" would be fine subjects for a curious and elaborate analysis, touching the conjectural parts of the mind that produced them. For spite of all the Indian-summer sunlight on the hither side of Hawthorne's soul, the other side—like the dark half of the physical sphere—is shrouded in a blackness, ten times black. But this darkness but gives more effect to the ever-moving dawn, that forever advances through it, and circumnavigates his world. Whether Hawthorne has simply availed himself of this mystical blackness as a means to the wondrous effects he makes it to produce in his lights and shades; or whether there really lurks in him, perhaps unknown to himself, a touch of Puritanic gloom—this, I cannot altogether tell. Certain it is, however, that this great power of blackness in him derives its force from its appeals to that Calvinistic sense of Innate Depravity and Original Sin, from whose visitations, in some shape or other, no deeply thinking mind is always and wholly free. For, in certain moods, no man can weigh this world, without throwing in something, somehow like Original Sin, to strike the uneven balance. At all events, perhaps no writer has ever wielded this terrific thought with greater terror than this same harmless Hawthorne. Still more: this black conceit pervades him, through and through. You may be witched by his sunlight, transported by the bright gildings in the skies he builds over you, but there is the blackness of darkness beyond; and even his bright gildings but fringe and play upon the edges of thunder-clouds.—In one word, the world is mistaken in this Nathaniel Hawthorne. He himself must often have smiled at its absurd misconception of him. He is immeasurably deeper than the plummet of the mere critic. For it is not the brain that can test such a man; it is only the heart. You cannot come to know greatness by inspecting it; there is no glimpse to be caught of it, except by intuition; you need not ring it, you but touch it, and you find it is gold.

Now it is that blackness in Hawthorne, of which I have spoken,

that so fixes and fascinates me. It may be, nevertheless, that it is
too largely developed in him. Perhaps he does not give us a ray of
his light for every shade of his dark. But however this may be,
this blackness it is that furnishes the infinite obscure of his background—that background, against which Shakespeare plays his
grandest conceits, the things that have made for Shakespeare his
loftiest but most circumscribed renown, as the profoundest of
thinkers. For by philosophers Shakespeare is not adorned as the
great man of tragedy and comedy.—"Off with his head! so much
for Buckingham!" This sort of rant, interlined by another hand,
brings down the house—those mistaken souls, who dream of Shakespeare as a mere man of Richard-the-Third humps, and Macbeth
daggers. But it is those deep far-away things in him; those occasional flashings-forth of the intuitive Truth in him; those short,
quick probings at the very axis of reality;—these are the things
that make Shakespeare Shakespeare. Through the mouths of the
dark characters of Hamlet, Timon, Lear, and Iago, he craftily says,
or sometimes insinuates, the things which we feel to be so terrifically true that it were all but madness for any good man, in his
own proper character, to utter, or even hint of them. Tormented
into desperation, Lear the frantic king tears off the mask, and speaks
the sane madness of vital truth. But, as I before said, it is the
least part of genius that attracts admiration. And so, much of the
blind, unbridled admiration that has been heaped upon Shakespeare has been lavished upon the least part of him. And few of
his endless commentators and critics seem to have remembered, or
even perceived, that the immediate products of a great mind are
not so great as that undeveloped, and sometimes undevelopable
yet dimly discernible greatness, to which these immediate products are but the infallible indices. In Shakespeare's tomb lies infinitely more than Shakespeare ever wrote. And if I magnify Shakespeare, it is not so much for what he did do, as for what he did
not do, or refrained from doing. For in this world of lies, Truth is
forced to fly like a scared white doe in the woodlands; and only
by cunning glimpses will she reveal herself, as in Shakespeare and
other masters of the great Art of Telling the Truth—even though
it be covertly, and by snatches.

But if this view of the all-popular Shakespeare be seldom taken
by his readers, and if very few who extol him have ever read him
deeply, or, perhaps, only have seen him on the tricky stage (which
alone made, and is still making, him his mere mob renown)—if
few men have time, or patience, or palate, for the spiritual truth
as it is in that great genius—it is, then, no matter of surprise that
in a contemporaneous age, Nathaniel Hawthorne is a man as yet
almost utterly mistaken among men. Here and there, in some quiet

armchair in the noisy town, or some deep nook among the noiseless mountains, he may be appreciated for something of what he is. But unlike Shakespeare, who was forced to the contrary course by circumstances, Hawthorne (either from simple disinclination, or else from inaptitude) refrains from all the popularizing noise and show of broad farce, and blood-besmeared tragedy; content with the still, rich utterances of a great intellect in repose, and which sends few thoughts into circulation, except they be arterialized at his large warm lungs, and expanded in his honest heart.

Nor need you fix upon that blackness in him, if it suit you not. Nor, indeed, will all readers discern it, for it is, mostly, insinuated to those who may best understand it, and account for it; it is not obtruded upon every one alike.

Some may start to read of Shakespeare and Hawthorne on the same page. They may say, that if an illustration were needed, a lesser light might have sufficed to elucidate this Hawthorne, this small man of yesterday. But I am not, willingly, one of those who, as touching Shakespeare at least, exemplify the maxim of Roche-foucauld,[2] that "we exalt the reputation of some, in order to de-press that of others"; who, to teach all noble-souled aspirants that there is no hope for them, pronounce Shakespeare absolutely un-approachable. But Shakespeare has been approached. There are minds that have gone as far as Shakespeare into the universe. And hardly a mortal man, who, at some time or other, has not felt as great thoughts in him as any you will find in *Hamlet*. We must not inferentially malign mankind for the sake of any one man, whoever he may be. This is too cheap a purchase of contentment for conscious mediocrity to make. Besides, this absolute and un-conditional adoration of Shakespeare has grown to be a part of our Anglo-Saxon superstitions. The Thirty-Nine Articles[3] are now Forty. Intolerance has come to exist in this matter. You must be-lieve in Shakespeare's unapproachability, or quit the country. But what sort of a belief is this for an American, a man who is bound to carry republican progressiveness into Literature, as well as into Life? Believe me, my friends, that men not very much inferior to Shakespeare are this day being born on the banks of the Ohio. And the day will come when you shall say; who reads a book by an Englishman that is a modern? The great mistake seems to be that even with those Americans who look forward to the coming of a great literary genius among us, they somehow fancy he will come in the costume of Queen Elizabeth's day, be a writer of dramas founded upon old English history, or the tales of Boccaccio.[4]

2. François, Duc de La Rochefoucauld (1613–80), was a French writer of moralistic maxims.
3. The Anglican Church's "Articles of Faith."
4. Italian author (1313–75) of the Decameron.

Whereas great geniuses are parts of the times; they themselves are the times, and possess a correspondent coloring. It is of a piece with the Jews, who, while their Shiloh[5] was meekly walking in their streets, were still praying for his magnificent coming; looking for him in a chariot, who was already among them on an ass. Nor must we forget that, in his own lifetime, Shakespeare was not Shakespeare, but only Master William Shakespeare of the shrewd, thriving business firm of Condell, Shakespeare & Co., proprietors of the Globe Theatre in London, and by a courtly author, of the name of Chettle, was looked at as an "upstart crow" beautified "with other birds' feathers."[6] For, mark it well, imitation is often the first charge brought against real originality. Why this is so, there is not space to set forth here. You must have plenty of sea-room to tell the Truth in; especially when it seems to have an aspect of newness, as America did in 1492, though it was then just as old, and perhaps older than Asia, only those sagacious philosophers, the common sailors, had never seen it before, swearing it was all water and moonshine there.

Now, I do not say that Nathaniel of Salem is a greater than William of Avon, or as great. But the difference between the two men is by no means immeasurable. Not a very great deal more, and Nathaniel were verily William.

This, too, I mean—that if Shakespeare has not been equaled, give the world time, and he is sure to be surpassed, in one hemisphere or the other. Nor will it at all do to say that the world is getting gray and grizzled now, and has lost that fresh charm which she wore of old, and by virtue of which the great poets of past times made themselves what we esteem them to be. Not so. The world is as young today as when it was created and this Vermont morning dew is as wet to my feet as Eden's dew to Adam's. Nor has Nature been all over ransacked by our progenitors, so that no new charms and mysteries remain for this latter generation to find. Far from it. The trillionth part has not yet been said, and all that has been said but multiplies the avenues to what remains to be said. It is not so much paucity as superabundance of material that seems to incapacitate modern authors.

Let America then prize and cherish her writers; yea, let her glorify them. They are not so many in number as to exhaust her good will. And while she has good kith and kin of her own, to take to her bosom, let her not lavish her embraces upon the household

5. Savior.
6. The allusions are to Henry Condell, Shakespeare's friend and fellow actor (one of the editors of the First Folio of Shakespeare's works), and to Henry Chettle, who edited Robert Greene's *Groatsworth of Wit* (1592), in which Shakespeare was actually alluded to as an "upstart Crow."

of an alien. For believe it or not, England, after all, is, in many things, an alien to us. China has more bowels of real love for us than she. But even were there no strong literary individualities among us,[7] as there are some dozen at least, nevertheless, let America first praise mediocrity even, in her own children, before she praises (for everywhere, merit demands acknowledgment from every one) the best excellence in the children of any other land. Let her own authors, I say, have the priority of appreciation. I was much pleased with a hot-headed Carolina cousin of mine, who once said, "If there were no other American to stand by, in Literature —why, then, I would stand by Pop Emmons[8] and his *Fredoniad*, and till a better epic came along, swear it was not very far behind the *Iliad*." Take away the words, and in spirit he was sound.

Not that American genius needs patronage in order to expand. For that explosive sort of stuff will expand though screwed up in a vise, and burst it, though it were triple steel. It is for the nation's sake, and not for her authors' sake, that I would have America be heedful of the increasing greatness among her writers. For how great the shame, if other nations should be before her, in crowning her heroes of the pen! But this is almost the case now. American authors have received more just and discriminating praise (however loftily and ridiculously given, in certain cases) even from some Englishmen, than from their own countrymen. There are hardly five critics in America; and several of them are asleep. As for patronage, it is the American author who now patronizes his country, and not his country him. And if at times some among them appeal to the people for more recognition, it is not always with selfish motives, but patriotic ones.

It is true that but few of them as yet have evinced that decided originality which merits great praise. But that graceful writer, who perhaps of all Americans has received the most plaudits from his own country for his productions—that very popular and amiable writer,[9] however good, and self-reliant in many things, perhaps owes his chief reputation to the self-acknowledged imitation of a foreign model, and to the studied avoidance of all topics but smooth ones. But it is better to fail in originality than to succeed in imitation. He who has never failed somewhere, that man can not be great. Failure is the true test of greatness. And if it be said that continual success is a proof that a man wisely knows his powers, it is only to be added that, in that case, he knows them to be small. Let us believe it, then, once for all, that there is no hope

7. The manuscript originally identified these "individualities" as Hawthorne, Emerson, Whittier, Irving, Bryant, Dana, Cooper, and Willis.
8. Richard Emmons (1788–1840); his

Fredoniad was perhaps the poorest and most notorious of the inflated patriotic epics in early American literature.
9. Washington Irving (1783–1859).

for us in these smooth, pleasing writers that know their powers. Without malice, but to speak the plain fact, they but furnish an appendix to Goldsmith, and other English authors. And we want no American Goldsmiths; nay, we want no American Miltons. It were the vilest thing you could say of a true American author, that he were an American Tompkins. Call him an American, and have done; for you cannot say a nobler thing of him.—But it is not meant that all American writers should studiously cleave to nationality in their writings; only this, no American writer should write like an Englishman, or a Frenchman; let him write like a man, for then he will be sure to write like an American. Let us away with this leaven[1] of literary flunkyism towards England. If either must play the flunky in this thing, let England do it, not us.[2] While we are rapidly preparing for that political supremacy among the nations, which prophetically awaits us at the close of the present century, in a literary point of view we are deplorably unprepared for it, and we seem studious to remain so. Hitherto, reasons might have existed why this should be; but no good reason exists now. And all that is requisite to amendment in this matter is simply this: that, while freely acknowledging all excellence, everywhere, we should refrain from unduly lauding foreign writers and, at the same time, duly recognize the meritorious writers that are our own; those writers who breathe that unshackled, democratic spirit of Christianity in all things, which now takes the practical lead in this world, though at the same time led by ourselves—us Americans. Let us boldly contemn all imitation, though it comes to us graceful and fragrant as the morning, and foster all originality, though, at first, it be crabbed and ugly as our own pine knots. And if any of our authors fail, or seem to fail, then, in the words of my enthusiastic Carolina cousin, let us clap him on the shoulder, and back him against all Europe for his second round. The truth is that, in our point of view, this matter of a national literature has come to such a pass with us that in some sense we must turn bullies, else the day is lost, or superiority so far beyond us, that we can hardly say it will ever be ours. * * *

But with whatever motive, playful or profound, Nathaniel Hawthorne has chosen to entitle his pieces in the manner he has, it is certain that some of them are directly calculated to deceive—egregiously deceive—the superficial skimmer of pages. To be downright and candid once more, let me cheerfully say that two of these titles did dolefully dupe no less an eagle-eyed reader than myself; and that, too, after I had been impressed with a sense of the

---

1. The manuscript reads, "this Bostonian leaven."
2. In the manuscript this was followed by the sentence "And the time is not far off when circumstances may force her to it."

great depth and breadth of this American man. "Who in the name of thunder" (as the country people say in this neighborhood), "who in the name of thunder," would anticipate any marvel in a piece entitled "Young Goodman Brown"? You would of course suppose that it was a simple little tale, intended as a supplement to "Goody Two-Shoes." Whereas it is deep as Dante; nor can you finish it, without addressing the author in his own words: "It is yours to penetrate, in every bosom, the deep mystery of sin." And with Young Goodman, too, in allegorical pursuit of his Puritan wife, you cry out in your anguish:

> "Faith!" shouted Goodman Brown, in a voice of agony and desperation; and the echoes of the forest mocked him, crying— "Faith! Faith!" as if bewildered wretches were seeking her, all through the wilderness.

Now this same piece, entitled "Young Goodman Brown," is one of the two that I had not at all read yesterday; and I allude to it now, because it is, in itself, such a strong positive illustration of that blackness in Hawthorne which I had assumed from the mere occasional shadows of it, as revealed in several of the other sketches. But had I previously perused "Young Goodman Brown," I should have been at no pains to draw the conclusion which I came to at a time when I was ignorant that the book contained one such direct and unqualified manifestation of it.

The other piece of the two referred to is entitled "A Select Party," which, in my first simplicity upon originally taking hold of the book, I fancied must treat of some pumpkin-pie party in Old Salem, or some chowder party on Cape Cod. Whereas, by all the gods of Peedee! it is the sweetest and sublimest thing that has been written since Spenser wrote. Nay, there is nothing in Spenser that surpasses it, perhaps, nothing that equals it. And the test is this: read any canto in *The Faery Queen*, and then read "A Select Party," and decide which pleases you the most—that is, if you are qualified to judge. Do not be frightened at this; for when Spenser was alive, he was thought of very much as Hawthorne is now, was generally accounted just such a "gentle" harmless man. It may be that, to common eyes, the sublimity of Hawthorne seems lost in his sweetness—as perhaps in this same "Select Party" of his, for whom he has builded so august a dome of sunset clouds, and served them on richer plate than Belshazzar's when he banqueted his lords in Babylon.[3]

But my chief business now is to point out a particular page in this piece, having reference to an honored guest, who, under the name of "The Master Genius" but in the guise "of a young

3. See Daniel V.

man of poor attire, with no insignia of rank or acknowledged eminence," is introduced to the Man of Fancy, who is the giver of the feast. Now the page having reference to this "Master Genius" so happily expresses much of what I yesterday wrote, touching the coming of the literary Shiloh of America, that I cannot but be charmed by the coincidence; especially, when it shows such a parity of ideas, at least in this one point, between a man like Hawthorne and a man like me.

And here, let me throw out another conceit of mine touching this American Shiloh, or "Master Genius," as Hawthorne calls him. May it not be, that this commanding mind has not been, is not, and never will be, individually developed in any one man? And would it, indeed, appear so unreasonable to suppose that this great fullness and overflowing may be, or may be destined to be, shared by a plurality of men of genius? Surely, to take the very greatest example on record, Shakespeare cannot be regarded as in himself the concretion of all the genius of his time, nor as so immeasurably beyond Marlowe, Webster, Ford, Beaumont, Jonson, that those great men can be said to share none of his power? For one, I conceive that there were dramatists in Elizabeth's day, between whom and Shakespeare the distance was by no means great. Let anyone, hitherto little acquainted with those neglected old authors, for the first time read them thoroughly, or even read Charles Lamb's *Specimens*[4] of them, and he will be amazed at the wondrous ability of those Anaks[5] of men, and shocked at this renewed example of the fact that Fortune has more to do with fame than merit—though, without merit, lasting fame there can be none.

Nevertheless, it would argue too illy of my country were this maxim to hold good concerning Nathaniel Hawthorne, a man, who already, in some few minds, has shed "such a light as never illuminates the earth, save when a great heart burns as the household fire of a grand intellect."

The words are his—in "A Select Party"; and they are a magnificent setting to a coincident sentiment of my own, but ramblingly expressed yesterday, in reference to himself. Gainsay it who will, as I now write, I am Posterity speaking by proxy—and after times will make it more than good, when I declare that the American, who up to the present day, has evinced, in Literature, the largest brain with the largest heart—that man is Nathaniel Hawthorne. Moreover, that whatever Nathaniel Hawthorne may hereafter write, the *Mosses from an Old Manse* will be ultimately accounted his masterpiece. For there is a sure though a secret sign in some works

4. *Specimens of English Dramatic*   (1808).
Poets Contemporary with Shakespeare   5. Giants; see Numbers xiii.33.

which proves the culmination of the powers (only the developable ones, however) that produced them. But I am by no means desirous of the glory of a prophet. I pray Heaven that Hawthorne may *yet* prove me an impostor in this prediction. Especially, as I somehow cling to the strange fancy that, in all men, hiddenly reside certain wondrous, occult properties—as in some plants and minerals—which by some happy but very rare accident (as bronze was discovered by the melting of the iron and brass in the burning of Corinth) may chance to be called forth here on earth, not entirely waiting for their better discovery in the more congenial, blessed atmosphere of heaven.

Once more—for it is had to be finite upon an infinite subject, and all subjects are infinite. By some people, this entire scrawl of mine may be esteemed altogether unnecessary, inasmuch, "as years ago" (they may say) "we found out the rich and rare stuff in this Hawthorne, whom you now parade forth as if only *yourself* were the discoverer of this Portuguese diamond in our Literature." —But even granting all this—and adding to it, the assumption that the books of Hawthorne have sold by the five thousand—what does that signify? They should be sold by the hundred thousand, and read by the million, and admired by every one who is capable of admiration.

1850

The "Agatha" Letter to Hawthorne

Pittsfield Aug 13ᵗʰ 1852

[*Salutation missing*]
—While visiting Nantucket some four weeks ago, I made the acquaintance of a gentleman from New Bedford, a lawyer,[6] who gave me considerable information upon several matters concerning which I was curious.—One night we were talking, I think, of the great patience, & endurance, & resignedness of the women of the island in submitting so uncomplainingly to the long, long absences of their sailor husbands, when, by way of anecdote, this lawyer gave me a leaf from his professional experience. Altho' his memory was a little confused with regard to some of the items of the story, yet he told me enough to awaken the most lively interest in me; and I begged him to be sure and send me a more full account so soon as he arrived home—he having previously told me that at the time of the affair he had made a record in his books.—— I heard nothing more, till a few days after arriving here at Pitts-

6. The lawyer was John H. Clifford, whose own account of Agatha Hatch was enclosed with the letter.

field I received thro' the Post Office the enclosed document.——
You will perceive by the gentleman's note to me that he assumed
that I had purposed making literary use of the story; but I had
not hinted anything of the kind to him, & my first spontaneous
interest in it arose from very different considerations. I confess,
however, that since then I have a little turned the subject over
in my mind with a view to a regular story to be founded on these
striking incidents. But, thinking again, it has occurred to me that
this thing lies very much in a vein, with which you are peculiarly
familiar. To be plump, I think that in this matter you would
make a better hand at it than I would.——Besides the thing seems
naturally to gravitate towards you (to speak [*half a line missing*]
should of right belong to you. I could [*half a line missing*] the
Steward to deliver it to you.——

The very great interest I felt in this story while narrating to
me, was heightened by the emotion of the gentleman who told
it, who evinced the most unaffected sympathy in it, tho' now a
matter of his past.——But perhaps this great interest of mine
may have been largely helped by some accidental circumstance or
other; so that, possibly, to you the story may not seem to possess
so much of pathos, & so much of depth. But you will see how it
is.——

In estimating the character of Robinson[7] Charity should be
allowed a liberal play. I take exception to that passage from the
Diary which says that *"he must have received a portion of his
punishment in this life"*—thus hinting of a future supplemental
castigation.——I do not at all suppose that his desertion of his
wife was a premeditated thing. If it had been so, he would have
changed his name, probably, after quitting her.——No: he was
a weak man, & his temptations (tho' we know little of them) were
strong. The whole sin stole upon him insensibly—so that it would
perhaps have been hard for him to settle upon the exact *day* when
he could say to himself, *"Now I have deserted my wife;"* unless,
indeed upon the day he wedded the Alexandria lady.——And
here I am reminded of your *London husband:*[8] tho' the cases so
widely contrast.——Many more things might be mentioned; but
I forbear; you will find out the suggestiveness for yourself; & all
the better perhaps, for my not intermeddling.——

If you should be sufficiently interested, to engage upon a regular
story founded on this narration; then I consider you but fairly
entitled to the following tributary items, collected by me, by
chance, during my strolls thro the islands; & which—as you will
perceive—seem legitimately to belong to the story, in its rounded

7. He was called "Robertson" in Clif-   8. In Hawthorne's story "Wakefield."
ford's account.

& beautified & thoroughly developed state;—but of all this you must
of course be your own judge—I but submit matter to you—I dont
decide.

Supposing the story to open with the wreck—then there must
be a storm; & it were well if some faint shadow of the preceding
calm were thrown forth to lead the whole.——Now imagine a
high cliff overhanging the sea & crowned with a pasture for sheep; a
little way off—higher up,—a light-house, where resides the father
of the future Mrs Robinson the First. The afternoon is mild &
warm. The sea with an air of solemn deliberation, with an elaborate
deliberation, ceremoniously rolls upon the beach. The air is sup-
pressedly charged with the sound of long lines of surf. There is
no land over against this cliff short of Europe & the West Indies.
Young Agatha (but you must give her some other name) comes
wandering along the cliff. She marks how the continual assaults of
the sea have undermined it; so that the fences fall over, & have
need of many shiftings inland. The sea has encroached also upon
that part where their dwelling-house stands near the light-house.
——Filled with meditations, she reclines along the edge of the
cliff & gazes out seaward. She marks a handful of cloud on the
horizon, presaging a storm thro' all this quietude. (Of a maritime
family & always dwelling on the coast, she is learned in these matters) This again gives food for thought. Suddenly she catches the
long shadow of the cliff cast upon the beach 100 feet beneath
her; and now she notes a shadow moving along the shadow. It is
cast by a sheep from the pasture. It has advanced to the very edge
of the water. There, in strange & beautiful contrast, we have the
innocence of the lamb placidly eyeing the malignity of the sea,
(All this having poetic reference to Agatha & her sea-lover, who is
coming in the storm: the storm carries her lover to her; she catches
a dim distant glimpse of his ship ere quitting the cliff)——P.S. It
were well, if from her knowledge of the deep miseries produced to
wives by marrying seafaring men, Agatha should have formed a
young determination never to marry a sailor; which resolve in her,
however, is afterwards overborne by the omnipotence of love.——
P.S. No 2. Agatha should be active during the wreck, and should,
in some way, be made the saviour of young Robinson. He should
be the only survivor. He should be ministered to by Agatha at
the house during the illness ensuing upon his injuries from the
wreck.——Now this wrecked ship has driven over the shoals, &
driven upon the beach where she goes to pieces, all but her stem-
part. This in course of time becomes embedded in the sand—after
the lapse of some years showing nothing but the sturdy stem (or,
prow-bone) projecting some two feet at low water. All the rest is
filled & packed down with the sand.——So that after her husband

has disappeared the sad Agatha every day sees this melancholy monument, with all its remindings.——

After a sufficient lapse of time—when Agatha has become alarmed about the protracted absence of her young husband & is feverishly expecting a letter from—then we must introduce the mail-post—no, that phrase wont do, but here is the *thing*.—— Owing to the remoteness of the lighthouse from any settled place no regular mail reaches it. But some mile or so distant there is a road leading between two post-towns. And at the junction of what we shall call the Light-House road with this Post Road, there stands a post surmounted with a little rude wood box with a lid to it & a leather hinge. Into this box the Post boy drops all letters for the people of the light house & that vicinity of fishermen. To this post they must come for their letters. And, of course, young Agatha goes—for seventeen years she goes thither daily. As her hopes gradually decay in her, so does the post itself, & the little box decay. The post rots in the ground at last. Owing to its being little used—hardly used at all—grass grows rankly about it. At last a little bird nests in it. At last the post falls.

The father of Agatha must be an old widower—a man of the sea, but early driven away from it by repeated disasters. Hence, is he subdued & quiet & wise in his life. And now he tends a light house, to warn people from those very perils, from which he himself has suffered.

Some few other items occur to me—but nothing material—and I fear to weary you, if not, make you smile at my strange impertinent officiousness.——And it would be so, were it not that these things do, in my mind, seem legitimately to belong to the story; for they were visibly suggested to me by scenes I actually beheld while on the very coast where the story of Agatha occurred.——I do not therefore, My Dear Hawthorne, at all imagine that you will think that I am so silly as to flatter myself I am giving you anything of my own. I am but restoring to you your own property—which you would quickly enough have identified for yourself—had you but been on the spot as I happened to be.

Let me conclude by saying that it seems to me that with your great power in these things, you can construct a story of remarkable interest out of this material furnished by the New Bedford lawyer.——You have a skeleton of actual reality to build about with fulness & veins & beauty. And if I thought I could do it as well as you, why, I should not let you have it.——The narrative from the Diary is instinct with significance.——Consider the mention of the *shawls*—& the inference derived from it. Ponder the conduct of this Robinson throughout.——Mark his trepidation & suspicion when anyone called upon him.——But why prate so—you will mark it all & mark it deeper than I would, perhaps.

I have written all this in a great hurry; so you must spell it out the best way you may.[9] * * *

Bartleby the Scrivener

A STORY OF WALL STREET

I am a rather elderly man. The nature of my avocations, for the last thirty years, has brought me into more than ordinary contact with what would seem an interesting and somewhat singular set of men, of whom, as yet, nothing, that I know of, has ever been written—I mean the law-copyists, or scriveners. I have known very many of them, professionally and privately, and, if I pleased, could relate divers histories, at which good-natured gentlemen might smile, and sentimental souls might weep. But I waive the biographies of all other scriveners, for a few passages in the life of Bartleby, who was a scrivener, the strangest I ever saw, or heard of. While, of other law-copyists, I might write the complete life, of Bartleby nothing of that sort can be done. I believe that no materials exist for a full and satisfactory biography of this man. It is an irreparable loss to literature. Bartleby was one of those beings of whom nothing is ascertainable, except from the original sources, and, in his case, those are very small. What my own astonished eyes saw of Bartleby, that is all I know of him, except, indeed, one vague report, which will appear in the sequel.

Ere introducing the scrivener, as he first appeared to me, it is fit I make some mention of myself, my employees, my business, my chambers, and general surroundings, because some such description is indispensable to an adequate understanding of the chief character about to be presented. Imprimis: I am a man who, from his youth upward, has been filled with a profound conviction that the easiest way of life is the best. Hence, though I belong to a profession proverbially energetic and nervous, even to turbulence, at times, yet nothing of that sort have I ever suffered to invade my peace. I am one of those unambitious lawyers who never address a jury, or in any way draw down public applause; but, in the cool tranquillity of a snug retreat, do a snug business among rich men's bonds, and mortgages, and title-deeds. All who know me consider me an eminently safe man. The late John Jacob Astor,[1] a personage little given to poetic enthusiasm, had no hesitation in pronouncing my first grand point to be prudence; my next, method. I do not speak it in vanity, but simply record the fact, that I was

9. Hawthorne never undertook to write the story, and in the later part of the year Melville wrote as though he himself might do so. There is no indication, however, that he actually did.

1. By the time of his death (in 1848, at the age of 85) Astor had become a symbol of great wealth, and the allusion helps to characterize the narrator.

not unemployed in my profession by the late John Jacob Astor; a name which, I admit, I love to repeat; for it hath a rounded and orbicular sound to it, and rings like unto bullion. I will freely add that I was not insensible to the late John Jacob Astor's good opinion.

Some time prior to the period at which this little history begins, my avocations had been largely increased. The good old office, now extinct in the State of New York, of a Master in Chancery had been conferred upon me. It was not a very arduous office, but very pleasantly remunerative. I seldom lose my temper; much more seldom indulge in dangerous indignation at wrongs and outrages; but I must be permitted to be rash here and declare that I consider the sudden and violent abrogation of the office of Master in Chancery, by the new Constitution,[2] as a——premature act; inasmuch as I had counted upon a life-lease of the profits, whereas I only received those of a few short years. But this is by the way.

My chambers were up stairs, at No. — Wall Street. At one end, they looked upon the white wall of the interior of a spacious skylight shaft, penetrating the building from top to bottom.

This view might have been considered rather tame than otherwise, deficient in what landscape painters call "life." But, if so, the view from the other end of my chambers offered, at least, a contrast, if nothing more. In that direction, my windows commanded an unobstructed view of a lofty brick wall, black by age and everlasting shade; which wall required no spy-glass to bring out its lurking beauties, but, for the benefit of all near-sighted spectators, was pushed up to within ten feet of my window-panes. Owing to the great height of the surrounding buildings, and my chambers being on the second floor, the interval between this wall and mine not a little resembled a huge square cistern.

At the period just preceding the advent of Bartleby, I had two persons as copyists in my employment, and a promising lad as an office-boy. First, Turkey; second, Nippers; third, Ginger Nut. These may seem names the like of which are not usually found in the Directory. In truth, they were nicknames, mutually conferred upon each other by my three clerks, and were deemed expressive of their respective persons or characters. Turkey was a short, pursy Englishman, of about my own age—that is, somewhere not far from sixty. In the morning, one might say, his face was of a fine florid hue, but after twelve o'clock, meridian—his dinner hour—it blazed like a grate full of Christmas coals, and continued blazing—but, as it were, with a gradual wane—till six o'clock, P.M., or therea-

2. Another characterizing allusion: the New York Constitutional Convention of 1846 was the result of a reform movement dedicated to the abolition of many well-established privileges of the wealthy classes.

bouts; after which, I saw no more of the proprietor of the face, which, gaining its meridian with the sun, seemed to set with it, to rise, culminate, and decline the following day, with the like regularity and undiminished glory. There are many singular coincidences I have known in the course of my life, not the least among which was the fact, that, exactly when Turkey displayed his fullest beams from his red and radiant countenance, just then, too, at that critical moment, began the daily period when I considered his business capacities as seriously disturbed for the remainder of the twenty-four hours. Not that he was absolutely idle, or averse to business then; far from it. The difficulty was, he was apt to be altogether too energetic. There was a strange, inflamed, flurried, flighty recklessness of activity about him. He would be incautious in dipping his pen into his inkstand. All his blots upon my documents were dropped there after twelve o'clock, meridian. Indeed, not only would he be reckless and sadly given to making blots in the afternoon, but, some days, he went further, and was rather noisy. At such times, too, his face flamed with augmented blazonry, as if cannel coal had been heaped on anthracite. He made an unpleasant racket with his chair, spilled his sand-box; in mending his pens, impatiently split them all to pieces, and threw them on the floor in a sudden passion; stood up, and leaned over his table, boxing his papers about in a most indecorous manner, very sad to behold in an elderly man like him. Nevertheless, as he was in many ways a most valuable person to me, and all the time before twelve o'clock, meridian, was the quickest, steadiest creature, too, accomplishing a great deal of work in a style not easily to be matched —for these reasons, I was willing to overlook his eccentricities, though, indeed, occasionally, I remonstrated with him. I did this very gently, however, because, though the civilest, nay, the blandest and most reverential of men in the morning, yet, in the afternoon, he was disposed, upon provocation, to be slightly rash with his tongue—in fact, insolent. Now, valuing his morning services as I did, and resolved not to lose them—yet, at the same time, made uncomfortable by his inflamed ways after twelve o'clock—and being a man of peace, unwilling by my admonitions to call forth unseemly retorts from him, I took upon me, one Saturday noon (he was always worse on Saturdays) to hint to him, very kindly, that, perhaps, now that he was growing old, it might be well to abridge his labors; in short, he need not come to my chambers after twelve o'clock, but, dinner over, had best go home to his lodgings, and rest himself till tea-time. But no; he insisted upon his afternoon devotions. His countenance became intolerably fervid, as he oratorically assured me—gesticulating with a long ruler at the other end of the room—that if his services in the morning were useful, how indispensable, then, in the afternoon?

"With submission, sir," said Turkey, on this occasion, "I consider myself your right-hand man. In the morning I but marshal and deploy my columns; but in the afternoon I put myself at their head, and gallantly charge the foe"—and he made a violent thrust with the ruler.

"But the blots, Turkey," intimated I.

"True; but, with submission, sir, behold these hairs! I am getting old. Surely, sir, a blot or two of a warm afternoon is not to be severely urged against gray hairs. Old age—even if it blot the page—is honorable. With submission, sir, we both are getting old."

This appeal to my fellow-feeling was hardly to be resisted. At all events, I saw that go he would not. So I made up my mind to let him stay, resolving, nevertheless, to see to it that, during the afternoon, he had to do with my less important papers.

Nippers, the second on my list, was a whiskered, sallow, and, upon the whole, rather piratical-looking young man, of about five-and-twenty. I always deemed him the victim of two evil powers—ambition and indigestion. The ambition was evinced by a certain impatience of the duties of a mere copyist, an unwarrantable usurpation of strictly professional affairs, such as the original drawing up of legal documents. The indigestion seemed betokened in an occasional nervous testiness and grinning irritability, causing the teeth to audibly grind together over mistakes committed in copying; unnecessary maledictions, hissed, rather than spoken, in the heat of business; and especially by a continual discontent with the height of the table where he worked. Though of a very ingenious mechanical turn, Nippers could never get this table to suit him. He put chips under it, blocks of various sorts, bits of pasteboard, and at last went so far as to attempt an exquisite adjustment, by final pieces of folded blotting-paper. But no invention would answer. If, for the sake of easing his back, he brought the table-lid at a sharp angle well up toward his chin, and wrote there like a man using the steep roof of a Dutch house for his desk, then he declared that it stopped the circulation in his arms. If now he lowered the table to his waistbands, and stooped over it in writing, then there was a sore aching in his back. In short, the truth of the matter was, Nippers knew not what he wanted. Or, if he wanted anything, it was to be rid of a scrivener's table altogether. Among the manifestations of his diseased ambition was a fondness he had for receiving visits from certain ambiguous-looking fellows in seedy coats, whom he called his clients. Indeed, I was aware that not only was he, at times, considerable of a ward-politician, but he occasionally did a little business at the Justices' courts, and was not unknown on the steps of the Tombs.[3] I have good reason to believe, however, that one individual who called upon him at my chambers, and who, with a grand air, he insisted was his client, was no other than a dun, and the alleged title-deed, a bill. But, with all his failings, and the annoyances he caused me, Nippers, like his compatriot Turkey, was a very useful man to me; wrote a neat, swift hand; and, when he chose, was not deficient in a gentlemanly sort of deportment. Added to this, he always dressed in a gentlemanly sort of way; and so, incidentally, reflected credit upon my chambers. Whereas, with respect to Turkey, I had much ado to keep him from being a reproach to me. His clothes were apt to look oily, and smell of eating-houses. He wore his pantaloons very loose and baggy in summer. His coats were execrable; his hat not to be handled. But while the hat was a thing of indifference to me, inasmuch as his natural civility and deference, as a dependent Englishman, always led him to doff it the moment he entered the room, yet his coat was another matter. Concerning his coats, I reasoned with him, but with no effect. The truth was, I suppose, that a man with so small an income could not afford to sport such a lustrous face and a lustrous coat at one and the same time. As Nippers once observed, Turkey's money went chiefly for red ink. One winter day, I presented Turkey with a highly respectable-looking coat of my own—a padded gray coat, of a most comfortable warmth, and which buttoned straight up from the knee to the neck. I thought Turkey would appreciate the favor, and abate his rashness and obstreperousness of afternoons. But no; I verily believe that buttoning himself up in so downy and blanket-like a coat had a pernicious effect upon him—upon the same principle that too much oats are bad for horses. In fact, precisely as a rash, restive horse is said to feel his oats, so Turkey felt his coat. It made him insolent. He was a man whom prosperity harmed.

Though, concerning the self-indulgent habits of Turkey, I had my own private surmises, yet, touching Nippers, I was well persuaded that, whatever might be his faults in other respects, he was, at least, a temperate young man. But, indeed, Nature herself seemed to have been his vintner, and, at his birth, charged him so thoroughly with an irritable, brandy-like disposition, that all subsequent potations were needless. When I consider how, amid the stillness of my chambers, Nippers would sometimes impatiently rise from his seat, and stooping over his table, spread his arms wide apart, seize the whole desk, and move it, and jerk it, with a grim, grinding motion on the floor, as if the table were a perverse voluntary agent, intent on thwarting and vexing him, I plainly

3. The massive New York City prison, adjoining the criminal court.

perceive that, for Nippers, brandy-and-water were altogether superfluous.

It was fortunate for me that, owing to its peculiar cause—indigestion—the irritability and consequent nervousness of Nippers were mainly observable in the morning, while in the afternoon he was comparatively mild. So that, Turkey's paroxysms only coming on about twelve o'clock, I never had to do with their eccentricities at one time. Their fits relieved each other, like guards. When Nippers's was on, Turkey's was off; and vice versa. This was a good natural arrangement, under the circumstances.

Ginger Nut, the third on my list, was a lad, some twelve years old. His father was a car-man, ambitious of seeing his son on the bench instead of a cart, before he died. So he sent him to my office, as student at law, errand-boy, cleaner, and sweeper, at the rate of one dollar a week. He had a little desk to himself, but he did not use it much. Upon inspection, the drawer exhibited a great array of the shells of various sorts of nuts. Indeed, to this quick-witted youth, the whole noble science of the law was contained in a nutshell. Not the least among the employments of Ginger Nut, as well as one which he discharged with the most alacrity, was his duty as cake and apple purveyor for Turkey and Nippers. Copying law papers being proverbially a dry, husky sort of business, my two scriveners were fain to moisten their mouths very often with Spitzenbergs, to be had at the numerous stalls nigh the Custom House and Post Office. Also, they sent Ginger Nut very frequently for that peculiar cake—small, flat, round, and very spicy—after which he had been named by them. Of a cold morning, when business was but dull, Turkey would gobble up scores of these cakes, as if they were mere wafers—indeed, they sell them at the rate of six or eight for a penny—the scrape of his pen blending with the crunching of the crisp particles in his mouth. Of all the fiery afternoon blunders and flurried rashnesses of Turkey, was his once moistening a ginger-cake between his lips, and clapping it on to a mortgage, for a seal. I came within an ace of dismissing him then. But he mollified me by making an Oriental bow, and saying—

"With submission, sir, it was generous of me to find you in stationery on my own account."

Now my original business—that of a conveyancer and title hunter, and drawer-up of recondite documents of all sorts—was considerably increased by receiving the Master's office. There was now great work for scriveners. Not only must I push the clerks already with me, but I must have additional help.

In answer to my advertisement, a motionless young man one morning stood upon my office threshold, the door being open, for it was summer. I can see that figure now—pallidly neat, pitiably respectable, incurably forlorn! It was Bartleby.

After a few words touching his qualifications, I engaged him, glad to have among my corps of copyists a man of so singularly sedate an aspect, which I thought might operate beneficially upon the flighty temper of Turkey and the fiery one of Nippers.

I should have stated before that ground glass folding-doors divided my premises into two parts, one of which was occupied by my scriveners, the other by myself. According to my humor, I threw open these doors, or closed them. I resolved to assign Bartleby a corner by the folding-doors, but on my side of them, so as to have this quiet man within easy call, in case any trifling thing was to be done. I placed his desk close up to a small side window in that part of the room, a window which originally had afforded a lateral view of certain grimy backyards and bricks, but which owing to subsequent erections commanded at present no view at all, though it gave some light. Within three feet of the panes was a wall, and the light came down from far above, between two lofty buildings, as from a very small opening in a dome. Still further to a satisfactory arrangement, I procured a high green folding screen, which might entirely isolate Bartleby from my sight, though not remove him from my voice. And thus, in a manner, privacy and society were conjoined.

At first, Bartleby did an extraordinary quantity of writing. As if long famishing for something to copy, he seemed to gorge himself on my documents. There was no pause for digestion. He ran a day and night line, copying by sun-light and by candle-light. I should have been quite delighted with his application, had he been cheerfully industrious. But he wrote on silently, palely, mechanically.

It is, of course, an indispensable part of a scrivener's business to verify the accuracy of his copy, word by word. Where there are two or more scriveners in an office, they assist each other in this examination, one reading from the copy, the other holding the original. It is a very dull, wearisome, and lethargic affair. I can readily imagine that, to some sanguine temperaments, it would be altogether intolerable. For example, I cannot credit that the mettlesome poet, Byron, would have contentedly sat down with Bartleby to examine a law document of, say, five hundred pages, closely written in a crimpy hand.

Now and then, in the haste of business, it had been my habit to assist in comparing some brief document myself, calling Turkey or Nippers for this purpose. One object I had, in placing Bartleby so handy to me behind the screen, was to avail myself of his services on such trivial occasions. It was on the third day, I think, of his being with me, and before any necessity had arisen for having his own writing examined, that, being much hurried to complete a small affair I had in hand, I abruptly called to Bartleby. In my haste and natural expectancy of instant compliance, I sat with my head bent over the original on my desk, and my right hand sideways, and somewhat nervously extended with the copy, so that, immediately upon emerging from his retreat, Bartleby might snatch it and proceed to business without the least delay.

In this very attitude did I sit when I called to him, rapidly stating what it was I wanted him to do—namely, to examine a small paper with me. Imagine my surprise, nay, my consternation, when, without moving from his privacy, Bartleby, in a singularly mild, firm voice, replied, "I would prefer not to."

I sat awhile in perfect silence rallying my stunned faculties. Immediately it occurred to me that my ears had deceived me, or Bartleby had entirely misunderstood my meaning. I repeated my request in the clearest tone I could assume; but in quite as clear a one came the previous reply, "I would prefer not to."

"Prefer not to," echoed I, rising in high excitement, and crossing the room with a stride. "What do you mean? Are you moonstruck? I want you to help me compare this sheet here—take it," and I thrust it towards him.

"I would prefer not to," said he.

I looked at him steadfastly. His face was leanly composed; his gray eye dimly calm. Not a wrinkle of agitation rippled him. Had there been the least uneasiness, anger, impatience or impertinence in his manner; in other words, had there been anything ordinarily human about him, doubtless I should have violently dismissed him from the premises. But as it was, I should have as soon thought of turning my pale plaster-of-Paris bust of Cicero out of doors. I stood gazing at him awhile, as he went on with his own writing, and then reseated myself at my desk. This is very strange, thought I. What had one best do? But my business hurried me. I concluded to forget the matter for the present, reserving it for my future leisure. So, calling Nippers from the other room, the paper was speedily examined.

A few days after this, Bartleby concluded four lengthy documents, being quadruplicates of a week's testimony taken before me in my High Court of Chancery. It became necessary to examine them. It was an important suit, and great accuracy was imperative. Having all things arranged, I called Turkey, Nippers, and Ginger Nut from the next room, meaning to place the four copies in the hands of my four clerks, while I should read from the original. Accordingly, Turkey, Nippers, and Ginger Nut had taken their seats in a row, each with his document in his hand, when I called to Bartleby to join this interesting group.

"Bartleby! quick, I am waiting."

I heard a slow scrape of his chair legs on the uncarpeted floor, and soon he appeared standing at the entrance of his hermitage.

"What is wanted?" said he, mildly.

"The copies, the copies," said I, hurriedly. "We are going to examine them. There"—and I held toward him the fourth quadruplicate.

"I would prefer not to," he said, and gently disappeared behind the screen.

For a few moments I was turned into a pillar of salt, standing at the head of my seated column of clerks. Recovering myself, I advanced toward the screen, and demanded the reason for such extraordinary conduct.

"Why do you refuse?"

"I would prefer not to."

With any other man I should have flown outright into a dreadful passion, scorned all further words, and thrust him ignominiously from my presence. But there was something about Bartleby that not only strangely disarmed me, but, in a wonderful manner, touched and disconcerted me. I began to reason with him.

"These are your own copies we are about to examine. It is labor saving to you, because one examination will answer for your four papers. It is common usage. Every copyist is bound to help examine his copy. Is it not so? Will you not speak? Answer!"

"I prefer not to," he replied in a flute-like tone. It seemed to me that, while I had been addressing him, he carefully revolved every statement that I made; fully comprehended the meaning; could not gainsay the irresistible conclusion; but, at the same time, some paramount consideration prevailed with him to reply as he did.

"You are decided, then, not to comply with my request—a request made according to common usage and common sense?"

He briefly gave me to understand that on that point my judgment was sound. Yes: his decision was irreversible.

It is not seldom the case that, when a man is browbeaten in some unprecedented and violently unreasonable way, he begins to stagger in his own plainest faith. He begins, as it were, vaguely to surmise that, wonderful as it may be, all the justice and all the reason is on the other side. Accordingly, if any disinterested persons are present, he turns to them for some reinforcement for his own faltering mind.

"Turkey," said I, "what do you think of this? Am I not right?"

"With submission, sir," said Turkey, in his blandest tone, "I think that you are."

"Nippers," said I, "what do you think of it?"

"I think I should kick him out of the office."

(The reader of nice perceptions will here perceive that, it being morning, Turkey's answer is couched in polite and tranquil terms, but Nippers replies in ill-tempered ones. Or, to repeat a previous sentence, Nippers's ugly mood was on duty, and Turkey's off.)

"Ginger Nut," said I, willing to enlist the smallest suffrage in my behalf, "what do *you* think of it?"

"I think, sir, he's a little *luny*," replied Ginger Nut, with a grin.

"You hear what they say," said I, turning towards the screen. "Come forth and do your duty."

But he vouchsafed no reply. I pondered a moment in sore perplexity. But once more business hurried me. I determined again to postpone the consideration of this dilemma to my future leisure. With a little trouble we made out to examine the papers without Bartleby, though at every page or two Turkey deferentially dropped his opinion, that this proceeding was quite out of the common; while Nippers, twitching in his chair with a dyspeptic nervousness, ground out, between his set teeth, occasional hissing maledictions against the stubborn oaf behind the screen. And for his (Nippers's) part, this was the first and the last time he would do another man's business without pay.

Meanwhile Bartleby sat in his hermitage, oblivious to everything but his own peculiar business there.

Some days passed, the scrivener being employed upon another lengthy work. His late remarkable conduct led me to regard his ways narrowly. I observed that he never went to dinner; indeed, that he never went anywhere. As yet I had never, of my personal knowledge, known him to be outside of my office. He was a perpetual sentry in the corner. At about eleven o'clock though, in the morning, I noticed that Ginger Nut would advance toward the opening in Bartleby's screen, as if silently beckoned thither by a gesture invisible to me where I sat. The boy would then leave the office, jingling a few pence, and reappear with a handful of ginger-nuts, which he delivered in the hermitage, receiving two of the cakes for his trouble.

He lives, then, on ginger-nuts, thought I; never eats a dinner, properly speaking; he must be a vegetarian, then; but no; he never eats even vegetables, he eats nothing but ginger-nuts. My mind then ran on in reveries concerning the probable effects upon the human constitution of living entirely on ginger-nuts. Ginger-nuts are so called, because they contain ginger as one of their peculiar constituents, and the final flavoring one. Now, what was ginger? A hot, spicy thing. Was Bartleby hot and spicy? Not at all. Ginger, then, had no effect upon Bartleby. Probably he preferred it should have none.

Nothing so aggravates an earnest person as a passive resistance.

If the individual so resisted be of a not inhumane temper, and the resisting one perfectly harmless in his passivity, then, in the better moods of the former, he will endeavor charitably to construe to his imagination what proves impossible to be solved by his judgment. Even so, for the most part, I regarded Bartleby and his ways. Poor fellow! thought I, he means no mischief; it is plain he intends no insolence; his aspect sufficiently evinces that his eccentricities are involuntary. He is useful to me. I can get along with him. If I turn him away, the chances are he will fall in with some less indulgent employer, and then he will be rudely treated, and perhaps driven forth miserably to starve. Yes. Here I can cheaply purchase a delicious self-approval. To befriend Bartleby; to humor him in his strange willfulness, will cost me little or nothing, while I lay up in my soul what will eventually prove a sweet morsel for my conscience. But this mood was not invariable with me. The passiveness of Bartleby sometimes irritated me. I felt strangely goaded on to encounter him in new opposition—to elicit some angry spark from him answerable to my own. But, indeed, I might as well have essayed to strike fire with my knuckles against a bit of Windsor soap. But one afternoon the evil impulse in me mastered me, and the following little scene ensued:

"Bartleby," said I, "when those papers are all copied, I will compare them with you."

"I would prefer not to."

"How? Surely you do not mean to persist in that mulish vagary?" No answer.

I threw open the folding-doors near by, and, turning upon Turkey and Nippers, exclaimed: "Bartleby a second time says he won't examine his papers. What do you think of it, Turkey?"

It was afternoon, be it remembered. Turkey sat glowing like a brass boiler, his bald head steaming, his hands reeling among his blotted papers.

"Think of it?" roared Turkey. "I think I'll just step behind his screen, and black his eyes for him!"

So saying, Turkey rose to his feet and threw his arms into a pugilistic position. He was hurrying away to make good his promise, when I detained him, alarmed at the effect of incautiously rousing Turkey's combativeness after dinner.

"Sit down, Turkey," said I, "and hear what Nippers has to say. What do you think of it, Nippers? Would I not be justified in immediately dismissing Bartleby?"

"Excuse me, that is for you to decide, sir. I think his conduct quite unusual, and, indeed, unjust, as regards Turkey and myself. But it may only be a passing whim."

"Ah," exclaimed I, "you have strangely changed your mind, then

—you speak very gently of him now."

"All beer," cried Turkey; "gentleness is effects of beer—Nippers and I dined together to-day. You see how gentle *I* am, sir. Shall I go and black his eyes?"

"You refer to Bartleby, I suppose. No, not to-day, Turkey," I replied. "Pray, put up your fists."

I closed the doors, and again advanced toward Bartleby. I felt additional incentives tempting me to my fate. I burned to be rebelled against again. I remembered that Bartleby never left the office.

"Bartleby," said I, "Ginger Nut is away; just step around to the postoffice, won't you? (it was but a three minutes' walk) and see if there is anything for me."

"I would prefer not to."

"You *will* not?"

"I *prefer* not."

I staggered to my desk and sat there in a deep study. My blind inveteracy returned. Was there any other thing in which I could procure myself to be ignominiously repulsed by this lean, penniless wight?—my hired clerk? What added thing is there, perfectly reasonable, that he will be sure to refuse to do?

"Bartleby!"

No answer.

"Bartleby," in a louder tone.

No answer.

"Bartleby," I roared.

Like a very ghost, agreeably to the laws of magical invocation, at the third summons, he appeared at the entrance of his hermitage.

"Go to the next room, and tell Nippers to come to me."

"I prefer not to," he respectfully and slowly said, and mildly disappeared.

"Very good, Bartleby," said I, in a quiet sort of serenely severe self-possessed tone, intimating the unalterable purpose of some terrible retribution very close at hand. At the moment I half intended something of the kind. But upon the whole, as it was drawing towards my dinner hour, I thought it best to put on my hat and walk home for the day, suffering much from perplexity and distress of mind.

Shall I acknowledge it? The conclusion of this whole business was that it soon became a fixed fact of my chambers, that a pale young scrivener, by the name of Bartleby, had a desk there; that he copied for me at the usual rate of four cents a folio (one hundred words); but he was permanently exempt from examining the work done by him, the duty being transferred to Turkey and Nippers, out of compliment, doubtless, to their superior acuteness; moreover, said Bartleby was never, on any account, to be dispatched on the most trivial errand of any sort; and that, even if entreated to take upon him such a matter, it was generally understood that he would "prefer not to"—in other words, that he would refuse point-blank.

As days passed on, I became considerably reconciled to Bartleby. His steadiness, his freedom from all dissipation, his incessant industry (except when he chose to throw himself into a standing reverie behind his screen), his great stillness, his unalterableness of demeanor under all circumstances, made him a valuable acquisition. One prime thing was this—he was always there—first in the morning, continually through the day, and the last at night. I had a singular confidence in his honesty. I felt my most precious papers perfectly safe in his hands. Sometimes, to be sure, I could not, for the very soul of me, avoid falling into sudden spasmodic passions with him. For it was exceeding difficult to bear in mind all the time those strange peculiarities, privileges, and unheard-of exemptions, forming the tacit stipulations on Bartleby's part under which he remained in my office. Now and then, in the eagerness of dispatching pressing business, I would inadvertently summon Bartleby, in a short, rapid tone, to put his finger, say, on the incipient tie of a bit of red tape with which I was about compressing some papers. Of course, from behind the screen the usual answer, "I prefer not to," was sure to come; and then how could a human creature, with the common infirmities of our nature, refrain from bitterly exclaiming upon such perverseness—such unreasonableness? However, every added repulse of this sort which I received only tended to lessen the probability of my repeating the inadvertence.

Here it must be said that, according to the custom of most legal gentlemen occupying chambers in densely populated law buildings, there were several keys to my door. One was kept by a woman residing in the attic, which person weekly scrubbed and daily swept and dusted my apartments. Another was kept by Turkey for convenience' sake. The third I sometimes carried in my own pocket. The fourth I knew not who had.

Now, one Sunday morning I happened to go to Trinity Church,[4] to hear a celebrated preacher, and finding myself rather early on the ground I thought I would walk round to my chambers for a while. Luckily I had my key with me; but upon applying it to the lock, I found it resisted by something inserted from the inside. Quite surprised, I called out; when to my consternation a key was turned from within; and thrusting his lean visage at me, and holding the

---

4. A third characterizing allusion: Trinity Church, completed in 1844 at the top of Wall Street on Broadway, was a fashionable and wealthy Protestant Episcopal institution, with massive bronze doors cast as a memorial to John Jacob Astor.

door ajar, the apparition of Bartleby appeared, in his shirt-sleeves, and otherwise in a strangely tattered deshabille, saying quietly that he was sorry, but he was deeply engaged just then, and—preferred not admitting me at present. In a brief word or two, he moreover added, that perhaps I had better walk round the block two or three times, and by that time he would probably have concluded his affairs.

Now, the utterly unsurmised appearance of Bartleby, tenanting my law-chambers of a Sunday morning, with his cadaverously gentlemanly *nonchalance*, yet withal firm and self-possesssed, had such a strange effect upon me, that incontinently I slunk away from my own door, and did as desired. But not without sundry twinges of impotent rebellion against the mild effrontery of this unaccountable scrivener. Indeed, it was his wonderful mildness chiefly which not only disarmed me, but unmanned me, as it were. For I consider that one, for the time, is a sort of unmanned when he tranquilly permits his hired clerk to dictate to him, and order him away from his own premises. Furthermore, I was full of uneasiness as to what Bartleby could possibly be doing in my office in his shirt-sleeves, and in an otherwise dismantled condition, of a Sunday morning. Was anything amiss going on? Nay, that was out of the question. It was not to be thought of for a moment that Bartleby was an immoral person. But what could he be doing there?—copying? Nay again, whatever might be his eccentricities, Bartleby was an eminently decorous person. He would be the last man to sit down to his desk in any state approaching to nudity. Besides, it was Sunday; and there was something about Bartleby that forbade the supposition that he would by any secular occupation violate the proprieties of the day.

Nevertheless, my mind was not pacified; and full of a restless curiosity, at last I returned to the door. Without hindrance I inserted my key, opened it, and entered. Bartleby was not to be seen. I looked round anxiously, peeped behind his screen; but it was very plain that he was gone. Upon more closely examining the place, I surmised that for an indefinite period Bartleby must have ate, dressed, and slept in my office, and that too without plate, mirror, or bed. The cushioned seat of a rickety old sofa in one corner bore the faint impress of a lean, reclining form. Rolled away under his desk, I found a blanket; under the empty grate, a blacking box and brush; on a chair, a tin basin, with soap and a ragged towel; in a newspaper a few crumbs of ginger-nuts and a morsel of cheese. Yes, thought I, it is evident enough that Bartleby has been making his home here, keeping Bachelor's Hall all by himself. Immediately then the thought came sweeping across me, what miserable friendlessness and loneliness are here revealed! His poverty is great; but his solitude, how horrible! Think of it. Of a Sunday, Wall Street is deserted as Petra;[5] and every night of every day it is an emptiness. This building, too, which of week-days hums with industry and life, at nightfall echoes with sheer vacancy, and all through Sunday is forlorn. And here Bartleby makes his home; sole spectator of a solitude which he has seen all populous—a sort of innocent and transformed Marius[6] brooding among the ruins of Carthage!

For the first time in my life a feeling of overpowering stinging melancholy seized me. Before, I had never experienced aught but a not unpleasing sadness. The bond of a common humanity now drew me irresistibly to gloom. A fraternal melancholy! For both I and Bartleby were sons of Adam. I remembered the bright silks and sparkling faces I had seen that day, in gala trim, swan-like sailing down the Mississippi of Broadway; and I contrasted them with the pallid copyist, and thought to myself, Ah, happiness courts the light, so we deem the world is gay; but misery hides aloof, so we deem that misery there is none. These sad fancyings—chimeras, doubtless, of a sick and silly brain—led on to other and more special thoughts, concerning the eccentricities of Bartleby. Presentiments of strange discoveries hovered round me. The scrivener's pale form appeared to me laid out, among uncaring strangers, in its shivering winding-sheet.

Suddenly I was attracted by Bartleby's closed desk, the key in open sight left in the lock.

I mean no mischief, seek the gratification of no heartless curiosity, thought I; besides, the desk is mine, and its contents, too, so I will make bold to look within. Everything was methodically arranged, the papers smoothly placed. The pigeon-holes were deep, and removing the files of documents, I groped into their recesses. Presently I felt something there, and dragged it out. It was an old bandanna handkerchief, heavy and knotted. I opened it, and saw it was a savings bank.

I now recalled all the quiet mysteries which I had noted in the man. I remembered that he never spoke but to answer; that, though at intervals he had considerable time to himself, yet I had never seen him reading—no, not even a newspaper; that for long periods he would stand looking out, at his pale window behind the screen,

5. Literally, the "rock." A ruined city between the Dead Sea and the Gulf of Akabar which was once a natural fortress walled in by towering rocks and dominating the ancient caravan routes. The association with Wall Street has both physical and economic references.
6. Gaius Marius (155?–86 B.C.) was a consul of the Roman Republic who quarreled with a rival general, was defeated in a civil war, and fled to Carthage, where he was forbidden to land. He told the messenger to report to the Carthaginian governor that he had "seen Marius sitting as a fugitive among the ruins of Carthage." The allusion seems to have reference to Bartleby's defiance. Like Marius (who returned to Rome and started a reign of terror), Bartleby is a threatening figure but not a vicious or violent one.

upon the dead brick wall; I was quite sure he never visited any refectory or eating-house; while his pale face clearly indicated that he never drank beer like Turkey, or tea and coffee even, like other men; that he never went anywhere in particular that I could learn; never went out for a walk, unless, indeed, that was the case at present; that he had declined telling who he was, or whence he came, or whether he had any relatives in the world; that though so thin and pale, he never complained of ill-health. And more than all, I remembered a certain unconscious air of pallid—how shall I call it?—of pallid haughtiness, say, or rather an austere reserve about him, which had positively awed me into my tame compliance with his eccentricities, when I had feared to ask him to do the slightest incidental thing for me, even though I might know, from his long-continued motionlessness, that behind his screen he must be standing in one of those dead-wall reveries of his.

Revolving all these things, and coupling them with the recently discovered fact that he made my office his constant abiding place and home, and not forgetful of his morbid moodiness; revolving all these things, a prudential feeling began to steal over me. My first emotions had been those of pure melancholy and sincerest pity; but just in proportion as the forlornness of Bartleby grew and grew to my imagination, did that same melancholy merge into fear, that pity into repulsion. So true it is, and so terrible, too, that up to a certain point the thought or sight of misery enlists our best affections; but, in certain special cases, beyond that point it does not. They err who would assert that invariably this is owing to the inherent selfishness of the human heart. It rather proceeds from a certain hopelessness of remedying excessive and organic ill. To a sensitive being, pity is not seldom pain. And when at last it is perceived that such pity cannot lead to effectual succor, common sense bids the soul be rid of it. What I saw that morning persuaded me that the scrivener was the victim of innate and incurable disorder. I might give alms to his body; but his body did not pain him; it was his soul that suffered, and his soul I could not reach.

I did not accomplish the purpose of going to Trinity Church that morning. Somehow, the things I had seen disqualified me for the time from church-going. I walked homeward, thinking what I would do with Bartleby. Finally, I resolved upon this—I would put certain calm questions to him the next morning, touching his history, etc., and if he declined to answer them openly and unreservedly (and I supposed he would prefer not), then to give him a twenty dollar bill over and above whatever I might owe him, and tell him his services were no longer required; but that if in any other way I could assist him, I would be happy to do so, especially if he desired to return to his native place, wherever that might be, I would willingly help to defray the expenses. Moreover, if, after reaching home, he found himself at any time in want of aid, a letter from him would be sure of a reply.

The next morning came.

"Bartleby," said I, gently calling to him behind his screen.

No reply.

"Bartleby," said I, in a still gentler tone, "come here; I am not going to ask you to do anything you would prefer not to do—I simply wish to speak to you."

Upon this he noiselessly slid into view.

"Will you tell me, Bartleby, where you were born?"

"I would prefer not to."

"Will you tell me *anything* about yourself?"

"I would prefer not to."

"But what reasonable objection can you have to speak to me? I feel friendly towards you."

He did not look at me while I spoke, but kept his glance fixed upon my bust of Cicero, which, as I then sat, was directly behind me, some six inches above my head.

"What is your answer, Bartleby?" said I, after waiting a considerable time for a reply, during which his countenance remained immovable, only there was the faintest conceivable tremor of the white attenuated mouth.

"At present I prefer to give no answer," he said, and retired into his hermitage.

It was rather weak in me, I confess, but his manner, on this occasion, nettled me. Not only did there seem to lurk in it a certain calm disdain, but his perverseness seemed ungrateful, considering the undeniable good usage and indulgence he had received from me.

Again I sat ruminating what I should do. Mortified as I was at his behavior, and resolved as I had been to dismiss him when I entered my office, nevertheless I strangely felt something superstitious knocking at my heart, and forbidding me to carry out my purpose, and denouncing me for a villain if I dared to breathe one bitter word against this forlornest of mankind. At last, familiarly drawing my chair behind his screen, I sat down and said: "Bartleby, never mind, then, about revealing your history; but let me entreat you, as a friend, to comply as far as may be with the usages of this office. Say now, you will help to examine papers to-morrow or next day: in short, say now, that in a day or two you will begin to be a little reasonable:—say so, Bartleby."

"At present I would prefer not to be a little reasonable," was his mildly cadaverous reply.

Just then the folding-doors opened, and Nippers approached. He seemed suffering from an unusually bad night's rest, induced by severer indigestion than common. He overheard those final words of Bartleby.

"*Prefer not*, eh?" gritted Nippers—"I'd *prefer* him, if I were you, sir," addressing me—"I'd *prefer* him; I'd give him preferences, the stubborn mule! What is it, sir, pray, that he *prefers* not to do now?"

Bartleby moved not a limb.

"Mr. Nippers," said I, "I'd prefer that you would withdraw for the present."

Somehow, of late, I had got into the way of involuntarily using this word "prefer" upon all sorts of not exactly suitable occasions. And I trembled to think that my contact with the scrivener had already and seriously affected me in a mental way. And what further and deeper aberration might it not yet produce? This apprehension had not been without efficacy in determining me to summary measures.

As Nippers, looking very sour and sulky, was departing, Turkey blandly and deferentially approached.

"With submission, sir," said he, "yesterday I was thinking about Bartleby here, and I think that if he would but prefer to take a quart of good ale every day, it would do much towards mending him, and enabling him to assist in examining his papers."

"So you have got the word, too," said I, slightly excited.

"With submission, what word, sir?" asked Turkey, respectfully crowding himself into the contracted space behind the screen, and by so doing, making me jostle the scrivener. "What word, sir?"

"I would prefer to be left alone here," said Bartleby, as if offended at being mobbed in his privacy.

"*That's* the word, Turkey," said I, "*that's* it."

"Oh, *prefer?* oh yes—queer word. I never use it myself. But, sir, as I was saying, if he would but prefer—"

"Turkey," interrupted I, "you will please withdraw."

"Oh certainly, sir, if you prefer that I should."

As he opened the folding-door to retire, Nippers at his desk caught a glimpse of me, and asked whether I would prefer to have a certain paper copied on blue paper or white. He did not in the least roguishly accent the word "prefer." It was plain that it involuntarily rolled from his tongue. I thought to myself, surely I must get rid of a demented man, who already has in some degree turned the tongues, if not the heads, of myself and clerks. But I thought it prudent not to break the dismission at once.

The next day I noticed that Bartleby did nothing but stand at his window in his dead-wall reverie. Upon asking him why he did not write, he said that he had decided upon doing no more writing.

"Why, how now? what next?" exclaimed I, "do no more writing?"

"No more."

"And what is the reason?"

"Do you not see the reason for yourself?" he indifferently replied.

I looked steadfastly at him, and perceived that his eyes looked dull and glazed. Instantly it occurred to me, that his unexampled diligence in copying by his dim window for the first few weeks of his stay with me might have temporarily impaired his vision.

I was touched. I said something in condolence with him. I hinted that of course he did wisely in abstaining from writing for a while, and urged him to embrace that opportunity of taking wholesome exercise in the open air. This, however, he did not do. A few days after this, my other clerks being absent, and being in a great hurry to dispatch certain letters by the mail, I thought that, having nothing else earthly to do, Bartleby would surely be less inflexible than usual, and carry these letters to the postoffice. But he blankly declined. So, much to my inconvenience, I went myself.

Still added days went by. Whether Bartleby's eyes improved or not, I could not say. To all appearance, I thought they did. But when I asked him if they did, he vouchsafed no answer. At all events, he would do no copying. At last, in reply to my urgings, he informed me that he had permanently given up copying.

"What!" exclaimed I; "suppose your eyes should get entirely well —better than ever before—would you not copy then?"

"I have given up copying," he answered, and slid aside.

He remained as ever, a fixture in my chamber. Nay—if that were possible—he became still more of a fixture than before. What was to be done? He would do nothing in the office; why should he stay there? In plain fact, he had now become a millstone to me, not only useless as a necklace, but afflictive to bear. Yet I was sorry for him. I speak less than truth when I say that, on his own account, he occasioned me uneasiness. If he would but have named a single relative or friend, I would instantly have written, and urged their taking the poor fellow away to some convenient retreat. But he seemed alone, absolutely alone in the universe. A bit of wreck in the mid-Atlantic. At length, necessities connected with my business tyrannized over all other considerations. Decently as I could, I told Bartleby that in six days' time he must unconditionally leave the office. I warned him to take measures, in the interval, for procuring some other abode. I offered to assist him in this endeavor, if he himself would but take the first step towards a removal. "And when you finally quit me, Bartleby," added I, "I shall see that you go not away entirely unprovided. Six days from this hour, remember."

At the expiration of that period, I peeped behind the screen, and lo! Bartleby was there.

I buttoned up my coat, balanced myself, advanced slowly towards him, touched his shoulder, and said, "The time has come; you must quit this place; I am sorry for you; here is money; but you must go."

"I would prefer not," he replied, with his back still towards me.

"You *must*."

He remained silent.

Now I had an unbounded confidence in this man's common honesty. He had frequently restored to me sixpences and shillings carelessly dropped upon the floor, for I am apt to be very reckless in such shirt-button affairs. The proceeding, then, which followed will not be deemed extraordinary.

"Bartleby," said I, "I owe you twelve dollars on account; here are thirty-two; the odd twenty are yours—Will you take it?" and I handed the bills towards him.

But he made no motion.

"I will leave them here, then," putting them under a weight on the table. Then taking my hat and cane and going to the door, I tranquilly turned and added, "After you have removed your things from these offices, Bartleby, you will of course lock the door—since every one is now gone for the day but you—and if you please, slip your key underneath the mat, so that I may have it in the morning. I shall not see you again; so good-by to you. If, hereafter, in your new place of abode, I can be of any service to you, do not fail to advise me by letter. Good-by, Bartleby, and fare you well."

But he answered not a word; like the last column of some ruined temple, he remained standing mute and solitary in the middle of the otherwise deserted room.

As I walked home in a pensive mood, my vanity got the better of my pity. I could not but highly plume myself on my masterly management in getting rid of Bartleby. Masterly I call it, and such it must appear to any dispassionate thinker. The beauty of my procedure seemed to consist in its perfect quietness. There was no vulgar bullying, no bravado of any sort, no choleric hectoring, and striding to and fro across the apartment, jerking out vehement commands for Bartleby to bundle himself off with his beggarly traps. Nothing of the kind. Without loudly bidding Bartleby depart— as an inferior genius might have done—I *assumed* the ground that depart he must; and upon that assumption built all I had to say. The more I thought over my procedure, the more I was charmed with it. Nevertheless, next morning, upon awakening, I had my doubts—I had somehow slept off the fumes of vanity. One of the coolest and wisest hours a man has is just after he awakes in the

morning. My procedure seemed as sagacious as ever—but only in
theory. How it would prove in practice—there was the rub. It was
truly a beautiful thought to have assumed Bartleby's departure;
but, after all, that assumption was simply my own, and none of
Bartleby's. The great point was, not whether I had assumed that
he would quit me, but whether he would prefer so to do. He was
more a man of preferences than assumptions.

After breakfast, I walked down town, arguing the probabilities
pro and *con.* One moment I thought it would prove a miserable failure, and Bartleby would be found all alive at my office as usual; the
next moment it seemed certain that I should find his chair empty.
And so I kept veering about. At the corner of Broadway and Canal
Street, I saw quite an excited group of people standing in earnest
conversation.

"I'll take odds he doesn't," said a voice as I passed.

"Doesn't go?—done!" said I, "put up your money."

I was instinctively putting my hand in my pocket to produce my
own, when I remembered that this was an election day. The words
I had overheard bore no reference to Bartleby, but to the success
or non-success of some candidate for the mayoralty. In my intent
frame of mind, I had, as it were, imagined that all Broadway
shared in my excitement, and were debating the same question
with me. I passed on, very thankful that the uproar of the street
screened my momentary absent-mindedness.

As I had intended, I was earlier than usual at my office door. I
stood listening for a moment. All was still. He must be gone. I
tried the knob. The door was locked. Yes, my procedure had worked
to a charm; he indeed must be vanished. Yet a certain melancholy
mixed with this: I was almost sorry for my brilliant success. I was
fumbling under the door mat for the key, which Bartleby was to
have left there for me, when accidentally my knee knocked against
a panel, producing a summoning sound, and in response a voice
came to me from within—"Not yet; I am occupied."

It was Bartleby.

I was thunderstruck. For an instant I stood like the man who,
pipe in mouth, was killed one cloudless afternoon long ago in
Virginia, by summer lightning; at his own warm open window he
was killed, and remained leaning out there upon the dreamy afternoon, till some one touched him, when he fell.

"Not gone!" I murmured at last. But again obeying that wondrous ascendancy which the inscrutable scrivener had over me, and
from which ascendancy, for all my chafing, I could not completely
escape, I slowly went down stairs and out into the street, and
while walking round the block, considered what I should next do
in this unheard-of perplexity. Turn the man out by an actual

thrusting I could not; to drive him away by calling him hard names would not do; calling in the police was an unpleasant idea; and yet, permit him to enjoy his cadaverous triumph over me—this, too, I could not think of. What was to be done? or, if nothing could be done, was there anything further that I could *assume* in the matter? Yes, as before I had prospectively assumed that Bartleby would depart, so now I might retrospectively assume that departed he was. In the legitimate carrying out of this assumption, I might enter my office in a great hurry, and pretending not to see Bartleby at all, walk straight against him as if he were air. Such a proceeding would in a singular degree have the appearance of a home-thrust. It was hardly possible that Bartleby could withstand such an application of the doctrine of assumptions. But upon second thoughts the success of the plan seemed rather dubious. I resolved to argue the matter over with him again.

"Bartleby," said I, entering the office, with a quietly severe expression, "I am seriously displeased. I am pained, Bartleby. I had thought better of you. I had imagined you of such a gentlemanly organization that in any delicate dilemma a slight hint would suffice—in short, an assumption. But it appears I am deceived. Why," I added, unaffectedly starting, "you have not even touched that money yet," pointing to it, just where I had left it the evening previous.

He answered nothing.

"Will you, or will you not, quit me?" I now demanded in a sudden passion, advancing close to him.

"I would prefer *not* to quit you," he replied, gently emphasizing the *not*.

"What earthly right have you to stay here? Do you pay any rent? Do you pay my taxes? Or is this property yours?"

He answered nothing.

"Are you ready to go on and write now? Are your eyes recovered? Could you copy a small paper for me this morning? or help examine a few lines? or step round to the postoffice? In a word, will you do anything at all, to give a coloring to your refusal to depart the premises?"

He silently retired into his hermitage.

I was now in such a state of nervous resentment that I thought it but prudent to check myself at present from further demonstrations. Bartleby and I were alone. I remembered the tragedy of the unfortunate Adams and the still more unfortunate Colt[7] in the solitary office of the latter; and how poor Colt, being dreadfully incensed by Adams, and imprudently permitting himself to get

7. The actual murder of Samuel Adams by John C. Colt occurred on September 17, 1841, while Melville was on his first whaling voyage.

wildly excited, was at unawares hurried into his fatal act—an act which certainly no man could possibly deplore more than the actor himself. Often it had occurred to me in my ponderings upon the subject that had altercation taken place in the public street, or at a private residence, it would not have terminated as it did. It was the circumstance of being alone in a solitary office, up stairs, of a building entirely unhallowed by humanizing domestic associations —an uncarpeted office, doubtless, of a dusty, haggard sort of appearance—this it must have been, which greatly helped to enhance the irritable desperation of the hapless Colt.

But when this old Adam of resentment rose in me and tempted me concerning Bartleby, I grappled him and threw him. How? Why, simply by recalling the divine injunction: "A new commandment give I unto you, that ye love one another." Yes, this it was that saved me. Aside from higher considerations, charity often operates as a vastly wise and prudent principle—a great safeguard to its possessor. Men have committed murder for jealousy's sake, and anger's sake, and hatred's sake, and selfishness' sake, and spiritual pride's sake; but no man that ever I heard of ever committed a diabolical murder for sweet charity's sake. Mere self-interest, then, if no better motive can be enlisted should, especially with high-tempered men, prompt all beings to charity and philanthropy. At any rate, upon the occasion in question, I strove to drown my exasperated feelings towards the scrivener by benevolently construing his conduct. Poor fellow, poor fellow! thought I, he don't mean anything; and besides, he has seen hard times, and ought to be indulged.

I endeavored, also, immediately to occupy myself, and at the same time to comfort my despondency. I tried to fancy, that in the course of the morning, at such time as might prove agreeable to him, Bartleby, of his own free accord, would emerge from his hermitage and take up some decided line of march in the direction of the door. But no. Half-past twelve o'clock came; Turkey began to glow in the face, overturn his inkstand, and become generally obstreperous; Nippers abated down into quietude and courtesy; Ginger Nut munched his noon apple; and Bartleby remained standing at his window in one of his profoundest dead-wall reveries. Will it be credited? Ought I to acknowledge it? That afternoon I left the office without saying one further word to him.

Some days now passed, during which, at leisure intervals I looked a little into *Edwards on the Will*, and *Priestley on Necessity*.[8]

8. Jonathan Edwards' *A Careful and Strict Enquiry into the Modern prevailing Notions of that Freedom of the Will which is supposed to be essential to Moral Agency, Vertue and Vice,* *Reward and Punishment, Praise and Blame* (1754) and Joseph Priestley's *The Doctrine of Philosophical Necessity illustrated* (1777) both taught that any given event was the inevitable

Under the circumstances, those books induced a salutary feeling. Gradually I slid into the persuasion that these troubles of mine, touching the scrivener, had been all predestinated from eternity, and Bartleby was billeted upon me for some mysterious purpose of an all-wise Providence, which it was not for a mere mortal like me to fathom. Yes, Bartleby, stay there behind your screen, thought I; I shall persecute you no more; you are harmless and noiseless as any of these old chairs; in short, I never feel so private as when I know you are here. At last I see it, I feel it; I penetrate to the predestinated purpose of my life. I am content. Others may have loftier parts to enact; but my mission in this world, Bartleby, is to furnish you with office room for such period as you may see fit to remain.

I believe that this wise and blessed frame of mind would have continued with me, had it not been for the unsolicited and uncharitable remarks obtruded upon me by my professional friends who visited the rooms. But thus it often is, that the constant friction of illiberal minds wears out at last the best resolves of the more generous. Though to be sure, when I reflected upon it, it was not strange that people entering my office should be struck by the peculiar aspect of the unaccountable Bartleby, and so be tempted to throw out some sinister observations concerning him. Sometimes an attorney, having business with me, and calling at my office, and finding no one but the scrivener there, would undertake to obtain some sort of precise information from him touching my whereabouts; but without heeding his idle talk, Bartleby would remain standing immovable in the middle of the room. So after contemplating him in that position for a time, the attorney would depart, no wiser than he came.

Also, when a reference was going on, and the room full of lawyers and witnesses, and business driving fast, some deeply occupied legal gentleman present, seeing Bartleby wholly unemployed, would request him to run round to his (the legal gentleman's) office and fetch some papers for him. Thereupon, Bartleby would tranquilly decline, and yet remain idle as before. Then the lawyer would give a great stare, and turn to me. And what could I say? At last I was made aware that all through the circle of my professional acquaintance, a whisper of wonder was running round, having reference to the strange creature I kept at my office. This worried me very much. And as the idea came upon me of his possibly turning out a long-lived man, and keep occupying my chambers, and denying my authority, and perplexing my visitors, and scandal-

result of a long chain of cause and effect. The juxtaposition of the two, however, is ironic, for Edwards was a reactionary defender of Calvinistic predestination against the religious rationalism which Priestley preached.

832 · *Herman Melville*

izing my professional reputation, and casting a general gloom over
the premises; keeping soul and body together to the last upon his
savings (for doubtless he spent but half a dime a day), and in the
end perhaps outlive me, and claim possession of my office by right
of his perpetual occupancy: as all these dark anticipations crowded
upon me more and more, and my friends continually intruded their
relentless remarks upon the apparition in my room, a great change
was wrought in me. I resolved to gather all my faculties together,
and forever rid me of this intolerable incubus.

Ere revolving any complicated project, however, adapted to this
end, I first simply suggested to Bartleby the propriety of his permanent departure. In a calm and serious tone, I commended the idea
to his careful and mature consideration. But, having taken three
days to meditate upon it, he apprised me that his original determination remained the same; in short, that he still preferred to
abide with me.

What shall I do? I now said to myself, buttoning up my coat to
the last button. What shall I do? what ought I to do? what does
conscience say I *should* do with this man, or, rather, ghost. Rid
myself of him, I must; go, he shall. But how? You will not thrust
him, the poor, pale, passive mortal—you will not thrust such a
helpless creature out of your door? you will not dishonor yourself
by such cruelty? No, I will not, I cannot do that. Rather would I
let him live and die here, and then mason up his remains in the
wall. What, then, will you do? For all your coaxing, he will not
budge. Bribes he leaves under your own paper-weight on your table;
in short, it is quite plain that he prefers to cling to you.

Then something severe, something unusual must be done. What!
surely you will not have him collared by a constable, and commit his
innocent pallor to the common jail? And upon what ground could
you procure such a thing to be done?—a vagrant, is he? What! he
a vagrant, a wanderer, who refuses to budge? It is because he will
not be a vagrant, then, that you seek to count him *as* a vagrant.
That is too absurd. No visible means of support: there I have him.
Wrong again: for indubitably he *does* support himself, and that is
the only unanswerable proof that any man can show of his possessing the means so to do. No more, then. Since he will not quit me,
I must quit him. I will change my offices; I will move elsewhere,
and give him fair notice that if I find him on my new premises I
will then proceed against him as a common trespasser.

Acting accordingly, next day I thus addressed him: "I find these
chambers too far from the City Hall; the air is unwholesome. In a
word, I propose to remove my offices next week, and shall no longer
require your services. I tell you this now, in order that you may
seek another place."

He made no reply, and nothing more was said.

On the appointed day I engaged carts and men, proceeded to my chambers, and, having but little furniture, everything was removed in a few hours. Throughout, the scrivener remained standing behind the screen, which I directed to be removed the last thing. It was withdrawn, and, being folded up like a huge folio, left him the motionless occupant of a naked room. I stood in the entry watching him a moment, while something from within me upbraided me.

I re-entered, with my hand in my pocket—and—and my heart in my mouth.

"Good-by, Bartleby; I am going—good-by, and God some way bless you; and take that," slipping something in his hand. But it dropped upon the floor, and then—strange to say—I tore myself from him whom I had so longed to be rid of.

Established in my new quarters, for a day or two I kept the door locked, and started at every footfall in the passages. When I returned to my rooms, after any little absence, I would pause at the threshold for an instant, and attentively listen, ere applying my key. But these fears were needless. Bartleby never came nigh me.

I thought all was going well, when a perturbed-looking stranger visited me, inquiring whether I was the person who had recently occupied rooms at No. — Wall Street.

Full of forebodings, I replied that I was.

"Then, sir," said the stranger, who proved a lawyer, "you are responsible for the man you left there. He refuses to do any copying; he refuses to do anything; he says he prefers not to; and he refuses to quit the premises."

"I am very sorry, sir," said I, with assumed tranquillity, but an inward tremor, "but, really, the man you allude to is nothing to me —he is no relation or apprentice of mine, that you should hold me responsible for him."

"In mercy's name, who is he?"

"I certainly cannot inform you. I know nothing about him. Formerly I employed him as a copyist; but he has done nothing for me now for some time past."

"I shall settle him, then—good morning, sir."

Several days passed, and I heard nothing more; and, though I often felt a charitable prompting to call at the place and see poor Bartleby, yet a certain squeamishness, of I know not what, withheld me.

All is over with him, by this time, thought I, at last, when, through another week, no further intelligence reached me. But, coming to my room the day after, I found several persons waiting at my door in a high state of nervous excitement.

"That's the man—here he comes," cried the foremost one, whom

I recognized as the lawyer who had previously called upon me alone.

"You must take him away, sir, at once," cried a portly person among them, advancing upon me, and whom I knew to be the landlord of No. — Wall Street. "These gentlemen, my tenants, cannot stand it any longer; Mr. B——," pointing to the lawyer, "has turned him out of his room, and he now persists in haunting the building generally, sitting upon the banisters of the stairs by day, and sleeping in the entry by night. Everybody is concerned; clients are leaving the offices; some fears are entertained of a mob; something you must do, and that without delay."

Aghast at this torrent, I fell back before it, and would fain have locked myself in my new quarters. In vain I persisted that Bartleby was nothing to me—no more than to any one else. In vain— I was the last person known to have anything to do with him, and they held me to the terrible account. Fearful, then, of being exposed in the papers (as one person present obscurely threatened), I considered the matter, and, at length, said, that if the lawyer would give me a confidential interview with the scrivener, in his (the lawyer's) own room, I would, that afternoon, strive my best to rid them of the nuisance they complained of.

Going up stairs to my old haunt, there was Bartleby silently sitting upon the banister at the landing.

"What are you doing here, Bartleby?" said I.

"Sitting upon the banister," he mildly replied.

I motioned him into the lawyer's room, who then left us.

"Bartleby," said I, "are you aware that you are the cause of great tribulation to me, by persisting in occupying the entry after being dismissed from the office?"

No answer.

"Now one of two things must take place. Either you must do something, or something must be done to you. Now what sort of business would you like to engage in? Would you like to re-engage in copying for someone?"

"No; I would prefer not to make any change."

"Would you like a clerkship in a dry-goods store?"

"There is too much confinement about that. No, I would not like a clerkship; but I am not particular."

"Too much confinement," I cried, "why, you keep yourself confined all the time!"

"I would prefer not to take a clerkship," he rejoined, as if to settle that little item at once.

"How would a bar-tender's business suit you? There is no trying of the eyesight in that."

"I would not like it at all; though, as I said before, I am not particular."

His unwonted wordiness inspirited me. I returned to the charge.

"Well, then, would you like to travel through the country collecting bills for the merchants? That would improve your health."

"No, I would prefer to be doing something else."

"How, then, would going as a companion to Europe, to entertain some young gentleman with your conversation—how would that suit you?"

"Not at all. It does not strike me that there is anything definite about that. I like to be stationary. But I am not particular."

"Stationary you shall be, then," I cried, now losing all patience, and, for the first time in all my exasperating connection with him, fairly flying into a passion. "If you do not go away from these premises before night, I shall feel bound—indeed, I *am* bound —to—to—to quit the premises myself!" I rather absurdly concluded, knowing not with what possible threat to try to frighten his immobility into compliance. Despairing of all further efforts, I was precipitately leaving him, when a final thought occurred to me—one which had not been wholly unindulged before.

"Bartleby," said I, in the kindest tone I could assume under such exciting circumstances, "will you go home with me now—not to my office, but my dwelling—and remain there till we can conclude upon some convenient arrangement for you at our leisure? Come, let us start now, right away."

"No, at present I would prefer not to make any change at all."

I answered nothing; but, effectually dodging every one by the suddenness and rapidity of my flight, rushed from the building, ran up Wall Street towards Broadway, and, jumping into the first omnibus, was soon removed from pursuit. As soon as tranquillity returned, I distinctly perceived that I had now done all that I possibly could, both in respect to the demands of the landlord and his tenants, and with regard to my own desire and sense of duty, to benefit Bartleby, and shield him from rude persecution. I now strove to be entirely carefree and quiescent; and my conscience justified me in attempt; though, indeed, it was not so successful as I could have wished. So fearful was I of being again hunted out by the incensed landlord and his exasperated tenants, that, surrendering my business to Nippers for a few days, I drove about the upper part of the town and through the suburbs, in my rockaway, crossed over to Jersey City and Hoboken, and paid fugitive visits to Manhattanville and Astoria. In fact, I almost lived in my rockaway[9] for the time.

When again I entered my office, lo, a note from the landlord lay upon the desk. I opened it with trembling hands. It informed me

9. A light, four-wheeled carriage made in Rockaway, N.J. The towns mentioned were then all on the outskirts of New York.

that the writer had sent to the police, and had Bartleby removed to the Tombs as a vagrant. Moreover, since I knew more about him than any one else, he wished me to appear at that place, and make a suitable statement of the facts. These tidings had a conflicting effect upon me. At first I was indignant, but, at last, almost approved. The landlord's energetic, summary disposition had led him to adopt a procedure which I do not think I would have decided upon myself; and yet, as a last resort, under such peculiar circumstances, it seemed the only plan.

As I afterwards learned, the poor scrivener, when told that he must be conducted to the Tombs, offered not the slightest obstacle, but, in his pale, unmoving way, silently acquiesced.

Some of the compassionate and curious bystanders joined the party; and headed by one of the constables arm-in-arm with Bartleby, the silent procession filed its way through all the noise, and heat, and joy of the roaring thoroughfares at noon.

The same day I received the note, I went to the Tombs, or, to speak more properly, the Halls of Justice. Seeking the right officer, I stated the purpose of my call, and was informed that the individual I described was, indeed, within. I then assured the functionary that Bartleby was a perfectly honest man, and greatly to be compassionated, however unaccountably eccentric. I narrated all I knew, and closed by suggesting the idea of letting him remain in as indulgent confinement as possible, till something less harsh might be done—though, indeed, I hardly knew what. At all events, if nothing else could be decided upon, the almshouse must receive him. I then begged to have an interview.

Being under no disgraceful charge, and quite serene and harmless in all his ways, they had permitted him freely to wander about the prison, and, especially, in the inclosed grass-platted yards thereof. And so I found him there, standing all alone in the quietest of the yards, his face towards a high wall, while all around, from the narrow slits of the jail windows, I thought I saw peering out upon him the eyes of murderers and thieves.

"Bartleby!"

"I know you," he said, without looking round, "and I want nothing to say to you."

"It was not I that brought you here, Bartleby," said I, keenly pained at his implied suspicion. "And to you, this should not be so vile a place. Nothing reproachful attaches to you by being here. And see, it is not so sad a place as one might think. Look, there is the sky, and here is the grass."

"I know where I am," he replied, but would say nothing more, and so I left him.

As I entered the corridor again, a broad meat-like man, in an apron, accosted me, and, jerking his thumb over his shoulder, said, "Is that your friend?"

"Yes."

"Does he want to starve? If he does, let him live on the prison fare, that's all."

"Who are you?" asked I, not knowing what to make of such an unofficially speaking person in such a place.

"I am the grub-man. Such gentlemen as have friends here hire me to provide them with something good to eat."

"Is this so?" said I, turning to the turnkey.

He said it was.

"Well, then," said I, slipping some silver into the grub-man's hands (for so they called him), "I want you to give particular attention to my friend there; let him have the best dinner you can get. And you must be as polite to him as possible."

"Introduce me, will you?" said the grub-man, looking at me with an expression which seemed to say he was all impatience for an opportunity to give a specimen of his breeding.

Thinking it would prove of benefit to the scrivener, I acquiesced, and, asking the grub-man his name, went up with him to Bartleby.

"Bartleby, this is a friend; you will find him very useful to you."

"Your sarvant, sir, your sarvant," said the grub-man, making a low salutation behind his apron. "Hope you find it pleasant here, sir; nice grounds—cool apartments—hope you'll stay with us some time—try to make it agreeable. What will you have for dinner to-day?"

"I prefer not to dine to-day," said Bartleby, turning away. "It would disagree with me; I am unused to dinners." So saying, he slowly moved to the other side of the inclosure, and took up a position fronting the dead-wall.

"How's this?" said the grub-man, addressing me with a stare of astonishment. "He's odd, ain't he?"

"I think he is a little deranged," said I, sadly.

"Deranged? deranged is it? Well, now, upon my word, I thought that friend of yourn was a gentleman forger; they are always pale and genteel-like, them forgers. I can't help pity 'em—can't help it, sir. Did you know Monroe Edwards?" he added, touchingly, and paused, then, laying his hand piteously on my shoulder, sighed, "He died of consumption at Sing-Sing. So you weren't acquainted with Monroe?"

"No, I was never socially acquainted with any forgers. But I cannot stop longer. Look to my friend yonder. You will not lose by it. I will see you again."

Some few days after this, I again obtained admission to the Tombs, and went through the corridors in quest of Bartleby, but without finding him.

"I saw him coming from his cell not long ago," said a turnkey, "may be he's gone to loiter in the yards."

So I went in that direction.

"Are you looking for the silent man?" said another turnkey, passing me. "Yonder he lies—sleeping in the yard there. 'Tis not twenty minutes since I saw him lie down."

The yard was entirely quiet. It was not accessible to the common prisoners. The surrounding walls, of amazing thickness, kept off all sounds behind them. The Egyptian character of the masonry weighed upon me with its gloom. But a soft imprisoned turf grew under foot. The heart of the eternal pyramids, it seemed, wherein, by some strange magic, through the clefts, grass seed, dropped by birds, had sprung.

Strangely huddled at the base of the wall, his knees drawn up, and lying on his side, his head touching the cold stones, I saw the wasted Bartleby. But nothing stirred. I paused; then went close up to him; stooped over, and saw that his dim eyes were open; otherwise he seemed profoundly sleeping. Something prompted me to touch him. I felt his hand, when a tingling shiver ran up my arm and down my spine to my feet.

The round face of the grub-man peered upon me now. "His dinner is ready. Won't he dine today, either? Or does he live without dining?"

"Lives without dining," said I, and closed the eyes.

"Eh!—He's asleep, ain't he?"

"With kings and counselors,"[1] murmured I.

There would seem little need for proceeding further in this history. Imagination will readily supply the meager recital of poor Bartleby's interment. But, ere parting with the reader, let me say that if this little narrative has sufficiently interested him to awaken curiosity as to who Bartleby was, and what manner of life he led prior to the present narrator's making his acquaintance, I can only reply that in such curiosity I fully share, but am wholly unable to gratify it. Yet here I hardly know whether I should divulge one little item of rumor, which came to my ear a few months after the scrivener's decease. Upon what basis it rested, I could never ascertain, and hence how true it is I cannot tell. But, inasmuch as this vague report has not been without a certain suggestive interest to me, however sad, it may prove the same with some others; and so I will briefly mention it. The report was this: that Bartleby had been a subordinate clerk in the Dead Letter Office at Washing-

1. To be "at rest, with kings and counsellors," as a synonym for death, occurs in Job iii. 13–14.

ton, from which he had been suddenly removed by a change in the administration. When I think over this rumor, hardly can I express the emotions which seize me. Dead letters! does it not sound like dead men? Conceive a man by nature and misfortune prone to a pallid hopelessness, can any business seem more fitted to heighten it than that of continually handling these dead letters, and assorting them for the flames? For by the cart-load they are annually burned. Sometimes from out the folded paper the pale clerk takes a ring—the finger it was meant for, perhaps, moulders in the grave; a bank-note sent in swiftest charity—he whom it would relieve nor eats nor hungers any more; pardon for those who died despairing; hope for those who died unhoping; good tidings for those who died stifled by unrelieved calamities. On errands of life, these letters speed to death.

Ah, Bartleby! Ah, humanity!

1853, 1856

From The Encantadas

Sketch Eighth: Norfolk Isle and the Chola Widow

"At last they in an island did espy
A seemly woman sitting by the shore,
That with great sorrow and sad agony
Seemed some great misfortune to deplore,
And loud to them for succor called evermore."

. . . . .

"Black his eye as the midnight sky,
White his neck as the driven snow,
Red his cheek as the morning light;—
Cold he lies in the ground below.
    My love is dead,
    Gone to his death-bed,
All under the cactus tree."

. . . . .

"Each lonely scene shall thee restore,
For thee the tear be duly shed;
Belov'd till life can charm no more,
And mourned till Pity's self be dead."[2]

Far to the northeast of Charles's Isle, sequestered from the rest, lies Norfolk Isle; and, however insignificant to most voyagers, to me, through sympathy, that lone island has become a spot made sacred by the strangest trials of humanity.

It was my first visit to the Encantadas.[3] Two days had been spent ashore in hunting tortoises. There was not time to capture many; so on the third afternoon we loosed our sails. We were

2. The epigraphs are from Spenser's *The Faerie Queene* (II.xii.27), Chatterton's *The Mynstrelles Songe*, and William Collins' "Dirge in [Shakespeare's] *Cymbeline*." The first two are slightly changed from the originals, and the last was added for publication in the *Piazza Tales*.
3. Melville visited the Galápagos or "Enchanted" Islands in November, 1841.

just in the act of getting under way, the uprooted anchor yet suspended and invisibly swaying beneath the wave, as the good ship gradually turned her heel to leave the isle behind, when the seaman who heaved with me at the windlass paused suddenly, and directed my attention to something moving on the land, not along the beach, but somewhat back, fluttering from a height.

In view of the sequel of this little story, be it here narrated how it came to pass, that an object which partly from its being so small was quite lost to every other man on board, still caught the eye of my handspike companion. The rest of the crew, myself included, merely stood up to our spikes in heaving, whereas, unwontedly exhilarated, at every turn of the ponderous windlass, my belted comrade leaped atop of it, with might and main giving a downward, thewey, perpendicular heave, his raised eye bent in cheery animation upon the slowly receding shore. Being high lifted above all others was the reason he perceived the object, otherwise unperceivable; and this elevation of his eye was owing to the elevation of his spirits; and this again—for truth must out—to a dram of Peruvian pisco,[4] in guerdon for some kindness done, secretly administered to him that morning by our mulatto steward. Now, certainly, pisco does a deal of mischief in the world; yet seeing that, in the present case, it was the means, though indirect, of rescuing a human being from the most dreadful fate, must we not also needs admit that sometimes pisco does a deal of good?

Glancing across the water in the direction pointed out, I saw some white thing hanging from an inland rock, perhaps half a mile from the sea.

"It is a bird; a white-winged bird; perhaps a——no; it is——it is a handkerchief!"

"Ay, a handkerchief!" echoed my comrade, and with a louder shout apprised the captain.

Quickly now—like the running out and training of a great gun —the long cabin spy-glass was thrust through the mizzen rigging from the high platform of the poop; whereupon a human figure was plainly seen upon the inland rock, eagerly waving towards us what seemed to be the handkerchief.

Our captain was a prompt, good fellow. Dropping the glass, he lustily ran forward, ordering the anchor to be dropped again; hands to stand by a boat, and lower away.

In a half-hour's time the swift boat returned. It went with six and came with seven; and the seventh was a woman.

It is not artistic heartlessness, but I wish I could but draw in crayons; for this woman was a most touching sight; and crayons, tracing softly melancholy lines, would best depict the mournful

4. A South American brandy made at Pisco, Peru.

image of the dark-damasked Chola widow.

Her story was soon told, and though given in her own strange language was as quickly understood; for our captain, from long trading on the Chilian coast, was well versed in the Spanish. A Cholo, or half-breed Indian woman of Payta in Peru, three years gone by, with her young new-wedded husband Felipe, of pure Castilian blood, and her one only Indian brother, Truxill, Hunilla had taken passage on the main in a French whaler, commanded by a joyous man; which vessel, bound to the cruising grounds beyond the Enchanted Isles, proposed passing close by their vicinity. The object of the little party was to procure tortoise oil, a fluid which for its great purity and delicacy is held in high estimation wherever known; and it is well known all along this part of the Pacific coast. With a chest of clothes, tools, cooking utensils, a rude apparatus for trying out the oil, some casks of biscuit, and other things, not omitting two favorite dogs, of which faithful animal all the Cholos are very fond, Hunilla and her companions were safely landed at their chosen place; the Frenchman, according to the contract made ere sailing, engaged to take them off upon returning from a four months' cruise in the westward seas; which interval the three adventurers deemed quite sufficient for their purposes.

On the isle's lone beach they paid him in silver for their passage out, the stranger having declined to carry them at all except upon that condition; though willing to take every means to insure the due fulfillment of his promise. Felipe had striven hard to have this payment put off to the period of the ship's return. But in vain. Still they thought they had, in another way, ample pledge of the good faith of the Frenchman. It was arranged that the expenses of the passage home should not be payable in silver, but in tortoises; one hundred tortoises ready captured to the returning captain's hand. These the Cholos meant to secure after their own work was done, against the probable time of the Frenchman's coming back; and no doubt in prospect already felt, that in those hundred tortoises—now somewhere ranging the isle's interior—they possessed one hundred hostages. Enough: the vessel sailed; the gazing three on shore answered the loud glee of the singing crew; and ere evening, the French craft was hull down in the distant sea, its masts three faintest lines which quickly faded from Hunilla's eye.

The stranger had given a blithesome promise, and anchored it with oaths; but oaths and anchors equally will drag; naught else abides on fickle earth but unkept promises of joy. Contrary winds from out unstable skies, or contrary moods of his more varying mind, or shipwreck and sudden death in solitary waves; whatever

was the cause, the blithe stranger never was seen again.

Yet, however dire a calamity was here in store, misgivings of it ere due time never disturbed the Cholos' busy mind, now all intent upon the toilsome matter which had brought them hither. Nay, by swift doom coming like the thief at night, ere seven weeks went by, two of the little party were removed from all anxieties of land or sea. No more they sought to gaze with feverish fear, or still more feverish hope, beyond the present's horizon line; but into the furthest future their own silent spirits sailed. By persevering labor beneath that burning sun, Felipe and Truxill had brought down to their hut many scores of tortoises, and tried out the oil, when, elated with their good success, and to reward themselves for such hard work, they, too hastily, made a catamaran, or Indian raft, much used on the Spanish main, and merrily started on a fishing trip, just without a long reef with many jagged gaps, running parallel with the shore, about half a mile from it. By some bad tide or hap, or natural negligence of joyfulness (for though they could not be heard, yet by their gestures they seemed singing at the time) forced in deep water against that iron bar, the ill-made catamaran was overset, and came all to pieces; when dashed by broad-chested swells between their broken logs and the sharp teeth of the reef, both adventurers perished before Hunilla's eyes.

Before Hunilla's eyes they sank. The real woe of this event passed before her sight as some sham tragedy on the stage. She was seated on a rude bower among the withered thickets, crowning a lofty cliff, a little back from the beach. The thickets were so disposed, that in looking upon the sea at large she peered out from among the branches as from the lattice of a high balcony. But upon the day we speak of here, the better to watch the adventure of those two hearts she loved, Hunilla had withdrawn the branches to one side, and held them so. They formed an oval frame, through which the bluely boundless sea rolled like a painted one. And there, the invisible painter painted to her view the wave-tossed and disjointed raft, its once level logs slantingly upheaved, as raking masts, and the four struggling arms undistinguishable among them; and then all subsided into smooth-flowing creamy waters, slowly drifting the splintered wreck; while first and last, no sound of any sort was heard. Death in a silent picture; a dream of the eye; such vanishing shapes as the mirage shows.

So instant was the scene, so trance-like its mild pictorial effect, so distant from her blasted bower and her common sense of things, that Hunilla gazed and gazed, nor raised a finger or a wail. But as good to sit thus dumb, in stupor staring on that dumb show, for all that otherwise might be done. With half a mile of sea between, how could her two enchanted arms aid those four fated ones? The distance long, the time one sand. After the lightning is beheld, what fool shall stay the thunderbolt? Felipe's body was washed ashore, but Truxill's never came; only his gay, braided hat of golden straw—that same sunflower thing he waved to her, pushing from the strand—and now, to the last gallant, it still saluted her. But Felipe's body floated to the marge, with one arm encirclingly outstretched. Lockjawed in grim death, the lover-husband softly clasped his bride, true to her even in death's dream. Ah, heaven, when man thus keeps his faith, wilt thou be faithless who created the faithful one? But they cannot break faith who never plighted it.

It needs not to be said what nameless misery now wrapped the lonely widow. In telling her own story she passed this almost entirely over, simply recounting the event. Construe the comment of her features as you might, from her mere words little would you have weened that Hunilla was herself the heroine of her tale. But not thus did she defraud us of our tears. All hearts bled that grief could be so brave.

She but showed us her soul's lid, and the strange ciphers thereon engraved; all within, with pride's timidity, was withheld. Yet was there one exception. Holding out her small olive hand before her captain, she said in mild and slowest Spanish, "Señor, I buried him;" then paused, struggled as against the writhed coilings of a snake, and cringing suddenly, leaped up, repeating in impassioned pain, "I buried him, my life, my soul!"

Doubtless, it was by half-unconscious, automatic motions of her hands, that this heavy-hearted one performed the final office for Felipe, and planted a rude cross of withered sticks—no green ones might be had—at the head of that lonely grave, where rested now in lasting uncomplaint and quiet haven he whom untranquil seas had overthrown.

But some dull sense of another body that should be interred, of another cross that should hallow another grave—unmade as yet—some dull anxiety and pain touching her undiscovered brother, now haunted the oppressed Hunilla. Her hands fresh from the burial earth, she slowly went back to the beach, with unshaped purposes wandering there, her spell-bound eye bent upon the incessant waves. But they bore nothing to her but a dirge, which maddened her to think that murderers should mourn. As time went by, and these things came less dreamingly to her mind, the strong persuasions of her Romish faith, which sets peculiar store by consecrated urns, prompted her to resume in waking earnest that pious search which had but been begun as in somnambulism. Day after day, week after week, she trod the cindery beach, till at length a double motive edged every eager glance. With equal

longing she now looked for the living and the dead; the brother
and the captain; alike vanished, never to return. Little accurate
note of time had Hunilla taken under such emotions as were hers,
and little, outside herself, served for calendar or dial. As to poor
Crusoe in the self-same sea,[5] no saint's bell pealed forth the lapse
of week or month; each day went by unchallenged; no chanticleer
announced those sultry dawns, no lowing herds those poisonous
nights. All wonted and steadily recurring sounds, human, or hu-
manized by sweet fellowship with man, but one stirred that torrid
trance—the cry of dogs; save which naught but the rolling sea
invaded it, an all-pervading monotone; and to the widow that was
the least loved voice she could have heard.

No wonder, that as her thoughts now wandered to the unre-
turning ship, and were beaten back again, the hope against hope
so struggled in her soul, that at length she desperately said, "Not
yet, not yet; my foolish heart runs on too fast." So she forced
patience for some further weeks. But to those whom earth's sure
indraft draws, patience or impatience is still the same.

Hunilla now sought to settle precisely in her mind, to an hour,
how long it was since the ship had sailed; and then, with the same
precision, how long a space remained to pass. But this proved impossible. What present day or month it was she could not say.
Time was her labyrinth, in which Hunilla was entirely lost.

And now follows——

Against my own purposes a pause descends upon me here. One
knows not whether nature doth not impose some secrecy upon him
who has been privy to certain things. At least, it is to be doubted
whether it be good to blazon such. If some books are deemed most
baneful and their sale forbid, how, then, with deadlier facts, not
dreams of doting men? Those whom books will hurt will not be
proof against events. Events, not books, should be forbid. But in all
things man sows upon the wind, which bloweth just there whither
it listeth; for ill or good, man cannot know. Often ill comes from
the good, as good from ill.

When Hunilla——

Dire sight it is to see some silken beast long dally with a golden
lizard ere she devour. More terrible, to see how feline Fate will
sometimes dally with a human soul, and by a nameless magic make
it repulse a sane despair with a hope which is but mad. Unwittingly
I imp this cat-like thing, sporting with the heart of him who reads;
for if he feel not he reads in vain.

—"The ship sails this day, to-day," at last said Hunilla to herself; "this gives me certain time to stand on; without certainty

5. The island most often associated with Robinson Crusoe was San Juan Fernan-
dez, south of the Galápagos.

I go mad. In loose ignorance I have hoped and hoped; now in firm knowledge I will but wait. Now I live and no longer perish in bewilderings. Holy Virgin, aid me! Thou wilt waft back the ship. Oh, past length of weary weeks—all to be dragged over—to buy the certainty of to-day, I freely give ye, though I tear ye from me!"

As mariners, tost in tempest on some desolate ledge, patch them a boat out of the remnants of their vessel's wreck, and launch it in the self-same waves, see here Hunilla, this lone shipwrecked soul, out of treachery invoking trust. Humanity, thou strong thing, I worship thee, not in the laureled victor, but in this vanquished one.

Truly Hunilla leaned upon a reed, a real one; no metaphor; a real Eastern reed. A piece of hollow cane, drifted from unknown isles, and found upon the beach, it once jagged ends rubbed smoothly even as by sand-paper; its golden glazing gone. Long ground between the sea and land, upper and nether stone, the unvarnished substance was filed bare, and wore another polish now, one with itself, the polish of its agony. Circular lines at intervals cut all round this surface, divided it into six panels of unequal length. In the first were scored the days, each tenth one marked by a longer and deeper notch; the second was scored for the number of sea-fowl eggs for sustenance, picked out from the rocky nests; the third, how many fish had been caught from the shore; the fourth, how many small tortoises found inland; the fifth, how many days of sun; the sixth, of clouds; which last, of the two, was the greater one. Long night of busy numbering, misery's mathematics, to weary her too-wakeful soul to sleep; yet sleep for that was none.

The panel of the days was deeply worn—the long tenth notches half effaced, as alphabets of the blind. Ten thousand times the longing widow had traced her finger over the bamboo—dull flute, which played on, gave no sound—as if counting birds flown by in air would hasten tortoises creeping through the woods.

After the one hundred and eightieth day no further mark was seen; that last one was the faintest, as the first the deepest.

"There were more days," said our Captain; "many, many more; why did you not go on and notch them, too, Hunilla?"

"Señor, ask me not."

"And meantime, did no other vessel pass the isle?"

"Nay, Señor;—but——"

"You do not speak; but *what*, Hunilla?"

"Ask me not, Señor."

"You saw ships pass, far away; you waved to them; they passed on;—was that it, Hunilla?"

"Señor, be it as you say."

Braced against her woe, Hunilla would not, durst not trust the weakness of her tongue. Then when our Captain asked whether any whale-boats had——

But no, I will not file this thing complete for scoffing souls to quote, and call it firm proof upon their side. The half shall here remain untold. Those two unnamed events which befell Hunilla on this isle, let them abide between her and her God. In nature, as in law, it may be libelous to speak some truths.

Still, how it was that, although our vessel had lain three days anchored nigh the isle, its one human tenant should not have discovered us till just upon the point of sailing, never to revisit so lone and far a spot, this needs explaining ere the sequel come.

The place where the French captain had landed the little party was on the further and opposite end of the isle. There, too, it was that they had afterwards built their hut. Nor did the widow in her solitude desert the spot where her loved ones had dwelt with her, and where the dearest of the twain now slept his last long sleep, and all her plaints awaked him not, and he of husbands the most faithful during life.

Now, high broken land rises between the opposite extremities of the isle. A ship anchored at one side is invisible from the other. Neither is the isle so small, but a considerable company might wander for days through the wilderness of one side, and never be seen, or their halloos heard, by any stranger holding aloof on the other. Hence Hunilla, who naturally associated the possible coming of ships with her own part of the isle, might to the end have remained quite ignorant of the presence of our vessel, were it not for a mysterious presentiment, borne to her, so our mariners averred, by this isle's enchanted air. Nor did the widow's answer undo the thought.

"How did you come to cross the isle this morning, then, Hunilla?" said our Captain.

"Señor, something came flitting by me. It touched my cheek, my heart, Señor."

"What do you say, Hunilla?"

"I have said, Señor, something came through the air."

It was a narrow chance. For when in crossing the isle Hunilla gained the high land in the centre, she must then for the first have perceived our masts, and also marked that their sails were being loosed, perhaps even heard the echoing chorus of the windlass song. The strange ship was about to sail, and she behind. With all haste she now descends the height on the hither side, but soon loses sight of the ship among the sunken jungles at the mountain's base. She struggles on through the withered branches, which seek at every step to bar her path, till she comes to the isolated rock, still some way from the water. This she climbs, to reassure herself. The ship is still in plainest sight. But now, worn out with over tension, Hunilla all but faints; she fears to step down from her giddy perch; she is fain to pause, there where she is, and as a last resort catches the turban from her head, unfurls and waves it over the jungles towards us.

During the telling of her story the mariners formed a voiceless circle round Hunilla and the Captain; and when at length the word was given to man the fastest boat, and pull round to the isle's thither side, to bring away Hunilla's chest and the tortoise-oil, such alacrity of both cheery and sad obedience seldom before was seen. Little ado was made. Already the anchor had been re-committed to the bottom, and the ship swung calmly to it.

But Hunilla insisted upon accompanying the boat as indis-pensable pilot to her hidden hut. So being refreshed with the best the steward could supply, she started with us. Nor did ever any wife of the most famous admiral, in her husband's barge, receive more silent reverence of respect than poor Hunilla from this boat's crew.

Rounding many a vitreous cape and bluff, in two hours' time we shot inside the fatal reef; wound into a secret cove, looked up along a green many-gabled lava wall, and saw the island's solitary dwelling.

It hung upon an impending cliff, sheltered on two sides by tangled thickets, and half-screened from view in front by juttings of the rude stairway, which climbed the precipice from the sea. Built of canes, it was thatched with long, mildewed grass. It seemed an abandoned hay-rick, whose haymakers were now no more. The roof inclined but one way; the eaves coming to within two feet of the ground. And here was a simple apparatus to collect the dews, or rather doubly-distilled and finest winnowed rains, which, in mercy or in mockery, the night-skies sometimes drop upon these blighted Encantadas. All along beneath the eaves, a spotted sheet, quite weather-stained, was spread, pinned to short, upright stakes, set in the shallow sand. A small clinker, thrown into the cloth, weighed its middle down, thereby straining all moisture into a calabash placed below. This vessel supplied each drop of water ever drunk upon the isle by the Cholos. Hunilla told us the calabash would sometimes, but not often, be half filled overnight. It held six quarts, perhaps. "But," said she, "we were used to thirst. At sandy Payta, where I live, no shower from heaven ever fell; all the water there is brought on mules from the inland vales."

Tied among the thickets were some twenty moaning tortoises, supplying Hunilla's lonely larder; while hundreds of vast tableted black bucklers, like displaced, shattered tombstones of dark slate,

848 · Herman Melville

were also scattered round. These were the skeleton backs of those
great tortoises from which Felipe and Truxill had made their precious oil. Several large calabashes and two goodly kegs were filled
with it. In a pot near by were the caked crusts of a quantity which
had been permitted to evaporate. "They meant to have strained
it off next day," said Hunilla, as she turned aside.

I forgot to mention the most singular sight of all, though the
first that greeted us after landing.

Some ten small, soft-haired, ringleted dogs, of a beautiful breed,
peculiar to Peru, set up a concert of glad welcomings when we
gained the beach, which was responded to by Hunilla. Some of
these dogs had, since her widowhood, been born upon the isle,
the progeny of the two brought from Payta. Owing to the jagged
steeps and pitfalls, tortuous thickets, sunken clefts and perilous
intricacies of all sorts in the interior, Hunilla, admonished by the
loss of one favorite among them, never allowed these delicate
creatures to follow her in her occasional birds'-nests climbs and
other wanderings; so that, through long habituation, they offered
not to follow, when that morning she crossed the land, and her
own soul was then too full of other things to heed their lingering
behind. Yet, all along she had so clung to them, that, besides what
moisture they lapped up at early daybreak from the small scoop-
holes among the adjacent rocks, she had shared the dew of her calabash among them; never laying by any considerable store against
those prolonged and utter droughts which, in some disastrous seasons, warp these isles.

Having pointed out, at our desire, what few things she would
like transported to the ship—her chest, the oil, not omitting the
live tortoises which she intended for a grateful present to our
Captain—we immediately set to work, carrying them to the boat
down the long, sloping stair of deeply-shadowed rock. While my
comrades were thus employed, I looked and Hunilla had disappeared.

It was not curiosity alone, but, it seems to me, something different mingled with it, which prompted me to drop my tortoise,
and once more gaze slowly around. I remembered the husband
buried by Hunilla's hands. A narrow pathway led into a dense
part of the thickets. Following it through many mazes, I came out
upon a small, round, open space, deeply chambered there.

The mound rose in the middle; a bare heap of finest sand, like
that unverdured heap found at the bottom of an hourglass run
out. At its head stood the cross of withered sticks; the dry, peeled
bark still fraying from it; its transverse limb tied up with rope,
and forlornly adroop in the silent air.

Hunilla was partly prostrate upon the grave; her dark head

bowed, and lost in her long, loosened Indian hair; her hands extended to the cross-foot, with a little brass crucifix clasped between; a crucifix worn featureless, like an ancient graven knocker long plied in vain. She did not see me, and I made no noise, but slid aside, and left the spot.

A few moments ere all was ready for our going, she reappeared among us. I looked into her eyes, but saw no tear. There was something which seemed strangely haughty in her air, and yet it was the air of woe. A Spanish and an Indian grief, which would not visibly lament. Pride's height in vain abased to proneness on the rack; nature's pride subduing nature's torture.

Like pages the small and silken dogs surrounded her, as she slowly descended towards the beach. She caught the two most eager creatures in her arms:—"Mia Teeta! Mia Tomoteeta!" and fondling them, inquired how many could we take on board.

The mate commanded the boat's crew; not a hard-hearted man, but his way of life had been such that in most things, even in the smallest, simple utility was his leading motive.

"We cannot take them all, Hunilla; our supplies are short; the winds are unreliable; we may be a good many days going to Tombez. So take those you have, Hunilla; but no more."

She was in the boat; the oarsmen, too, were seated; all save one, who stood ready to push off and then spring himself. With the sagacity of their race, the dogs now seemed aware that they were in the very instant of being deserted upon a barren strand. The gunwales of the boat were high; its prow—presented inland—was lifted; so owing to the water, which they seem instinctively to shun, the dogs could not well leap into the little craft. But their busy paws hard scraped the prow, as it had been some farmer's door shutting them out from shelter in a winter storm. A clamorous agony of alarm. They did not howl, or whine; they all but spoke.

"Push off! Give way!" cried the mate. The boat gave one heavy drag and lurch, and next moment shot swiftly from the beach, turned on her heel, and sped. The dogs ran howling along the water's marge; now pausing to gaze at the flying boat, then motioning as if to leap in chase, but mysteriously withheld themselves; and again ran howling along the beach. Had they been human beings, hardly would they have more vividly inspired the sense of desolation. The oars were plied as confederate feathers of two wings. No one spoke. I looked back upon the beach, and then upon Hunilla, but her face was set in a stern dusky calm. The dogs crouching in her lap vainly licked her rigid hands. She never looked behind her; but sat motionless, till we turned a promontory of the coast and lost all sights and sounds astern. She seemed as one who, having experienced the sharpest of mortal pangs, was henceforth content to have all lesser heartstrings riven, one by one. To Hunilla, pain seemed so necessary, that pain in other beings, though by love and sympathy made her own, was unrepiningly to be borne. A heart of yearning in a frame of steel. A heart of earthly yearning, frozen by the frost which falleth from the sky.

The sequel is soon told. After a long passage, vexed by calms and baffling winds, we made the little port of Tombez in Peru, there to recruit the ship. Payta was not very distant. Our captain sold the tortoise oil to a Tombez merchant; and adding to the silver a contribution from all hands, gave it to our silent passenger, who knew not what the mariners had done.

The last seen of lone Hunilla she was passing into Payta town, riding upon a small gray ass; and before her on the ass's shoulders, she eyed the jointed workings of the beast's armorial cross.[6]

1854, 1856

Benito Cereno

In the year 1799, Captain Amasa Delano,[7] of Duxbury, in Massachusetts, commanding a large sealer and general trader, lay at anchor with a valuable cargo, in the harbor of St. Maria—a small, desert, uninhabited island toward the southern extremity of the long coast of Chili. There he had touched for water.

On the second day, not long after dawn, while lying in his berth, his mate came below, informing him that a strange sail was coming into the bay. Ships were then not so plenty in those waters as now. He rose, dressed, and went on deck.

The morning was one peculiar to that coast. Everything was mute and calm; everything gray. The sea, though undulated into long roods of swells, seemed fixed, and was sleeked at the surface like waved lead that has cooled and set in the smelter's mould. The sky seemed a gray surtout. Flights of troubled gray fowl, kith and kin with flights of troubled gray vapors among which they were mixed, skimmed low and fitfully over the waters, as

6. The allusion to the cross was probably more explicitly suggestive in Melville's manuscript, for it was modified, with apologies, by the editor of *Putnam's Magazine*, who quoted James Russell Lowell as saying "that the figure of the cross in the ass's neck, brought tears into his eyes, and he thought it the finest touch of genius he had seen in prose."
7. A real person whose *Narrative of Voyages and Travels* (1817) provided the substance for this story. Melville, however, made many departures from the original. He changed the date from 1805 to 1799, moved the island of St. Maria southward, transformed the ships from the *Perseverance* and the *Tryal* to the *Bachelor's Delight* and the *San Dominick*, and made Babo rather than Muri the servant of Don Benito. He also revised the document at the end in a way which suggests that he planned a longer narrative than he actually composed. The dramatic atmosphere provided by the oakum pickers, the hatchet polishers, and the description of the Spanish ship is Melville's invention.

swallows over meadows before storms. Shadows present, fore-shadowing deeper shadows to come.

To Captain Delano's surprise, the stranger, viewed through the glass, showed no colors; though to do so upon entering a haven, however uninhabited in its shores, where but a single other ship might be lying, was the custom among peaceful seamen of all nations. Considering the lawlessness and loneliness of the spot, and the sort of stories, at that day, associated with those seas, Captain Delano's surprise might have deepened into some uneasiness had he not been a person of a singularly undistrustful good nature, not liable, except on extraordinary and repeated incentives, and hardly then, to indulge in personal alarms, any way involving the imputation of malign evil in man. Whether, in view of what humanity is capable, such a trait implies, along with a benevolent heart, more than ordinary quickness and accuracy of intellectual perception, may be left to the wise to determine.

But whatever misgivings might have obtruded on first seeing the stranger, would almost, in any seaman's mind, have been dissipated by observing that, the ship, in navigating into the harbor, was drawing too near the land; a sunken reef making out off her bow. This seemed to prove her a stranger, indeed, not only to the sealer, but the island; consequently, she could be no wonted freebooter on that ocean. With no small interest, Captain Delano continued to watch her—a proceeding not much facilitated by the vapors partly mantling the hull, through which the far matin light from her cabin streamed equivocally enough; much like the sun—by this time hemisphered on the rim of the horizon, and, apparently, in company with the strange ship entering the harbor—which, wimpled by the same low, creeping clouds, showed not unlike a Lima *intriguante's* one sinister eye peering across the Plaza from the Indian loop-hole of her dusk *saya-y-manta*.[8]

It might have been but a deception of the vapors, but, the longer the stranger was watched the more singular appeared her manœuvres. Ere long it seemed hard to decide whether she meant to come in or no—what she wanted, or what she was about. The wind, which had breezed up a little during the night, was now extremely light and baffling, which the more increased the apparent uncertainty of her movements.

Surmising, at last, that it might be a ship in distress, Captain Delano order his whale-boat to be dropped, and, much to the wary opposition of his mate, prepared to board her, and, at the least, pilot her in. On the night previous, a fishing-party of the seamen had gone a long distance to some detached rocks out of sight from the sealer, and, an hour or two before daybreak, had

8. Skirt and shawl. An *"intriguante"* is a feminine intriguer or flirt.

returned, having met with no small success. Presuming that the stranger might have been long off soundings, the good captain put several baskets of the fish, for presents, into his boat, and so pulled away. From her continuing too near the sunken reef, deeming her in danger, calling to his men, he made all haste to apprise those on board of their situation. But, some time ere the boat came up, the wind, light though it was, having shifted, had headed the vessel off, as well as partly broken the vapors from about her.

Upon gaining a less remote view, the ship, when made signally visible on the verge of the leaden-hued swells, with the shreds of fog here and there raggedly furring her, appeared like a white-washed monastery after a thunder-storm, seen perched upon some dun cliff among the Pyrenees. But it was no purely fanciful resemblance which now, for a moment, almost led Captain Delano to think that nothing less than a shipload of monks was before him. Peering over the bulwarks were what really seemed, in the hazy distance, throngs of dark cowls; while, fitfully revealed through the open port-holes, other dark moving figures were dimly described, as of Black Friars[9] pacing the cloisters.

Upon a still nigher approach, this appearance was modified, and the true character of the vessel was plain—a Spanish merchant-man of the first class, carrying negro slaves, amongst other valuable freight, from one colonial port to another. A very large, and, in its time, a very fine vessel, such as in those days were at intervals encountered along that main; sometimes superseded Acapulco[1] treasure-ships, or retired frigates of the Spanish king's navy, which, like superannuated Italian palaces, still, under a decline of masters, preserved signs of former state.

As the whale-boat drew more and more nigh, the cause of the peculiar pipe-clayed aspect of the stranger was seen in the slovenly neglect pervading her. The spars, ropes, and great part of the bulwarks, looked woolly, from long unacquaintance with the scraper, tar, and the brush. Her keel seemed laid, her ribs put together, and she launched, from Ezekiel's Valley of Dry Bones.[2]

In the present business in which she was engaged, the ship's general model and rig appeared to have undergone no material change from their original warlike and Froissart[3] pattern. However, no guns were seen.

The tops were large, and were railed about with what had once been octagonal net-work, all now in sad disrepair. These tops hung

9. Members of the Dominican order. The reference anticipates the name of the ship.
1. A port on the Pacific coast of Mexico.
2. See Ezekiel xxxvii.1–10.

3. Jean Froissart (1337–1410) was the author of the famous medieval *Chronicles;* Melville apparently uses his name here to suggest that the Spanish ship was of old-fashioned design.

overhead like three ruinous aviaries, in one of which was seen perched, on a ratlin, a white noddy, a strange fowl, so called from its lethargic, somnambulistic character, being frequently caught by hand at sea. Battered and mouldy, the castellated forecastle seemed some ancient turret, long ago taken by assault, and then left to decay. Toward the stern, two high-raised quarter galleries— the balustrades here and there covered with dry, tindery sea-moss —opening out from the unoccupied state-cabin, whose dead-lights, for all the mild weather, were hermetically closed and calked— these tenantless balconies hung over the sea as if it were the grand Venetian canal. But the principal relic of faded grandeur was the ample oval of the shield-like stern-piece, intricately carved with the arms of Castile and Leon,[4] medallioned about by groups of mythological or symbolical devices; uppermost and central of which was a dark satyr in a mask, holding his foot on the prostrate neck of a writhing figure, likewise masked.

Whether the ship had a figure-head, or only a plain beak, was not quite certain, owing to canvas wrapped about that part, either to protect it while undergoing a re-furbishing, or else decently to hide its decay. Rudely painted or chalked, as in a sailor freak, along the forward side of a sort of pedestal below the canvas, was the sentence, "*Seguid vuestro jefe,*" (follow your leader); while upon the tarnished headboards, near by, appeared, in stately capitals, once gilt, the ship's name, "SAN DOMINICK," each letter streakingly corroded with tricklings of copper-spike rust; while, like mourning weeds, dark festoons of sea-grass slimily swept to and fro over the name, with every hearse-like roll of the hull.

As, at last, the boat was hooked from the bow along toward the gangway amidship, its keel, while yet some inches separated from the hull, harshly grated as on a sunken coral reef. It proved a huge bunch of conglobated barnacles adhering below the water to the side like a wen—a token of baffling airs and long calms passed somewhere in those seas.

Climbing the side, the visitor was at once surrounded by a clamorous throng of whites and blacks, but the latter outnumbering the former more than could have been expected, negro transportation-ship at the stranger in port was. But, in one language, and as with one voice, all poured out a common tale of suffering; in which the negresses, of whom there were not a few, exceeded the others in their dolorous vehemence. The scurvy, together with the fever, had swept off a great part of their number, more especially the Spaniards. Off Cape Horn they had narrowly escaped shipwreck; then, for days together, they had lain tranced without wind; their provisions were low; their water next to none; their lips that mo-

4. Spanish kingdoms.

ment were baked.

While Captain Delano was thus made the mark of all eager tongues, his one eager glance took in all faces, with every other object about him.

Always upon first boarding a large and populous ship at sea, especially a foreign one, with a nondescript crew such as Lascars or Manilla men, the impression varies in a peculiar way from that produced by first entering a strange house with strange inmates in a strange land. Both house and ship—the one by its walls and blinds, the other by its high bulwarks like ramparts—hoard from view their interiors till the last moment: but in the case of the ship there is this addition; that the living spectacle it contains, upon its sudden and complete disclosure, has, in contrast with the blank ocean which zones it, something of the effect of enchantment. The ship seems unreal; these strange costumes, gestures, and faces, but a shadowy tableau just emerged from the deep, which directly must receive back what it gave.

Perhaps it was some such influence, as above is attempted to be described, which, in Captain Delano's mind, heightened whatever, upon a staid scrutiny, might have seemed unusual; especially the conspicuous figures of four elderly grizzled negroes, their heads like black, doddered willow tops, who, in venerable contrast to the tumult below them, were couched, sphynx-like, one on the starboard cat-head, another on the larboard, and the remaining pair face to face on the opposite bulwarks above the main-chains. They each had bits of unstranded old junk in their hands, and, with a sort of stoical self-content, were picking the junk into oakum, a small heap of which lay by their sides. They accompanied the task with a continuous, low, monotonous chant; droning and druling away like so many gray-headed bag-pipers playing a funeral march.

The quarter-deck rose into an ample elevated poop, upon the forward verge of which, lifted, like the oakum-pickers, some eight feet above the general throng, sat along in a row, separated by regular spaces, the cross-legged figures of six other blacks; each with a rusty hatchet in his hand, which, with a bit of brick and a rag, he was engaged like a scullion in scouring; while between each two was a small stack of hatchets, their rusted edges turned forward awaiting a like operation. Though occasionally the four oakum-pickers would briefly address some person or persons in the crowd below, yet the six hatchet-polishers neither spoke to others, nor breathed a whisper among themselves, but sat intent upon their task, except at intervals, when, with the peculiar love in negroes of uniting industry with pastime, two and two they sideways clashed their hatchets together, like cymbals, with a barbarous din. All six, unlike the generality, had the raw aspect of unsophisticated

Africans.

But that first comprehensive glance which took in those ten figures, with scores less conspicuous, rested but an instant upon them, as, impatient of the hubbub of voices, the visitor turned in quest of whosoever it might be that commanded the ship.

But as if not unwilling to let nature make known her own case among his suffering charge, or else in despair of restraining it for the time, the Spanish captain, a gentlemanly, reserved-looking, and rather young man to a stranger's eye, dressed with singular richness, but bearing plain traces of recent sleepless cares and disquietudes, stood passively by, leaning against the main-mast, at one moment casting a dreary, spiritless look upon his excited people, at the next an unhappy glance toward his visitor. By his side stood a black of small stature, in whose rude face, as occasionally, like a shepherd's dog, he mutely turned it up into the Spaniard's, sorrow and affection were equally blended.

Struggling through the throng, the American advanced to the Spaniard, assuring him of his sympathies, and offering to render whatever assistance might be in his power. To which the Spaniard returned for the present but grave and ceremonious acknowledgments, his national formality dusked by the saturnine mood of ill-health.

But losing no time in mere compliments, Captain Delano, returning to the gangway, had his basket of fish brought up; and as the wind still continued light, so that some hours at least must elapse ere the ship could be brought to the anchorage, he bade his men return to the sealer, and fetch back as much water as the whale-boat could carry, with whatever soft bread the steward might have, all the remaining pumpkins on board, with a box of sugar, and a dozen of his private bottles of cider.

Not many minutes after the boat's pushing off, to the vexation of all, the wind entirely died away, and the tide turning, began drifting back the ship helplessly seaward. But trusting this would not long last, Captain Delano sought, with good hopes, to cheer up the strangers, feeling no small satisfaction that, with persons in their condition, he could—thanks to his frequent voyages along the Spanish main—converse with some freedom in their native tongue.

While left alone with them, he was not long in observing some things tending to heighten his first impressions; but surprise was lost in pity, both for the Spaniards and blacks, alike evidently reduced from scarcity of water and provisions; while long-continued suffering seemed to have brought out the less good-natured qualities of the negroes, besides, at the same time, impairing the Spaniard's authority over them. But, under the circumstances, precisely this condition of things was to have been anticipated. In armies, navies, cities, or families, in nature herself, nothing more relaxes good order than misery. Still, Captain Delano was not without the idea, that had Benito Cereno been a man of greater energy, misrule would hardly have come to the present pass. But the debility, constitutional or induced by hardships, bodily and mental, of the Spanish captain, was too obvious to be overlooked. A prey to settled dejection, as if long mocked with hope he would not now indulge it, even when it had ceased to be a mock, the prospect of that day, or evening at furthest, lying at anchor, with plenty of water for his people, and a brother captain to counsel and befriend, seemed in no perceptible degree to encourage him. His mind appeared unstrung, if not still more seriously affected. Shut up in these oaken walls, chained to one dull round of command, whose unconditionality cloyed him, like some hypochondriac abbot he moved slowly about, at times suddenly pausing, starting, or staring, biting his lip, biting his fingernail, flushing, paling, twitching his beard, with other symptoms of an absent or moody mind. This distempered spirit was lodged, as before hinted, in as distempered a frame. He was rather tall, but seemed never to have been robust, and now with nervous suffering was almost worn to a skeleton. A tendency to some pulmonary complaint appeared to have been lately confirmed. His voice was like that of one with lungs half gone—hoarsely suppressed, a husky whisper. No wonder that, as in this state he tottered about, his private servant apprehensively followed him. Sometimes the negro gave his master his arm, or took his handkerchief out of his pocket for him; performing these and similar offices with that affectionate zeal which transmutes into something filial or fraternal acts in themselves but menial; and which has gained for the negro the repute of making the most pleasing body-servant in the world; one, too, whom a master need be on no stiffly superior terms with, but may treat with familiar trust; less a servant than a devoted companion.

Marking the noisy indocility of the blacks in general, as well as what seemed the sullen inefficiency of the whites it was not without humane satisfaction that Captain Delano witnessed the steady good conduct of Babo.

But the good conduct of Babo, hardly more than the ill-behavior of others, seemed to withdraw the half-lunatic Don Benito from his cloudy languor. Not that such precisely was the impression made by the Spaniard on the mind of his visitor. The Spaniard's individual unrest was, for the present, but noted as a conspicuous feature in the ship's general affliction. Still, Captain Delano was not a little concerned at what he could not help taking for the time to be Don Benito's unfriendly indifference towards himself. The

Spaniard's manner, too, conveyed a sort of sour and gloomy disdain, which he seemed at no pains to disguise. But this the American in charity ascribed to the harassing effects of sickness, since, in former instances, he had noted that there are peculiar natures on whom prolonged physical suffering seems to cancel every social instinct of kindness; as if, forced to black bread themselves, they deemed it but equity that each person coming nigh them should, indirectly, by some slight or affront, be made to partake of their fare.

But ere long Captain Delano bethought him that, indulgent as he was at the first, in judging the Spaniard, he might not, after all, have exercised charity enough. At bottom it was Don Benito's reserve which displeased him; but the same reserve was shown towards all but his faithful personal attendant. Even the formal reports which, according to sea-usage, were, at stated times, made to him by some petty underling, either a white, mulatto or black, he hardly had patience enough to listen to, without betraying contemptuous aversion. His manner upon such occasions was, in its degree, not unlike that which might be supposed to have been his imperial countryman's, Charles V., just previous to the anchoritish retirement of that monarch from the throne.[5]

This splenetic disrelish of his place was evinced in almost every function pertaining to it. Proud as he was moody, he condescended to no personal mandate. Whatever special orders were necessary, their delivery was delegated to his body-servant, who in turn transferred them to their ultimate destination, through runners, alert Spanish boys or slave boys, like pages or pilot-fish within easy call continually hovering round Don Benito. So that to have beheld this undemonstrative invalid gliding about, apathetic and mute, no landsman could have dreamed that in him was lodged a dictatorship beyond which, while at sea, there was no earthly appeal.

Thus, the Spaniard, regarded in his reserve, seemed the involuntary victim of mental disorder. But, in fact, his reserve might, in some degree, have proceeded from design. If so, then here was evinced the unhealthy climax of that icy though conscientious policy, more or less adopted by all commanders of large ships, which, except in signal emergencies, obliterates alike the manifestation of sway with every trace of sociality; transforming the man into a block, or rather into a loaded canon, which, until there is call for thunder, has nothing to say.

Viewing him in this light, it seemed but a natural token of the perverse habit induced by a long course of such hard self-

5. Charles V (1500–1558), Holy Roman Emperor and King of Spain (as Charles I); prior to his retirement to a small house attached to a monastery in 1556, he described himself as "old and feeble" and resigned his kingdoms.

restraint, that, notwithstanding the present condition of his ship, the Spaniard should still persist in a demeanor, which, however harmless, or, it may be, appropriate, in a well-appointed vessel, such as the San Dominick might have been at the outset of the voyage, was anything but judicious now. But the Spaniard, perhaps, thought that it was with captains as with gods: reserve, under all events, must still be their cue. But probably this appearance of slumbering dominion might have been but an attempted disguise to conscious imbecility—not deep policy, but shallow device. But be all this as it might, whether Don Benito's manner was designed or not, the more Captain Delano noted its pervading reserve, the less he felt uneasiness at any particular manifestation of that reserve towards himself.

Neither were his thoughts taken up by the captain alone. Wonted to the quiet orderliness of the sealer's comfortable family of a crew, the noisy confusion of the San Dominick's suffering host repeatedly challenged his eye. Some prominent breaches, not only of discipline but of decency, were observed. These Captain Delano could not but ascribe, in the main, to the absence of those subordinate deck-officers to whom, along with higher duties, is intrusted what may be styled the police department of a populous ship. True, the old oakum-pickers appeared at times to act the part of monitorial constables to their countrymen, the blacks; but though occasionally succeeding in allaying trifling outbreaks now and then between man and man, they could do little or nothing toward establishing general quiet. The San Dominick was in the condition of a transatlantic emigrant ship, among whose multitude of living freight are some individuals, doubtless, as little troublesome as crates and bales; but the friendly remonstrances of such with their ruder companions are of not so much avail as the unfriendly arm of the mate. What the San Dominick wanted was, what the emigrant ship has, stern superior officers. But on these decks not so much as a fourth-mate was to be seen.

The visitor's curiosity was roused to learn the particulars of those mishaps which had brought about such absenteeism, with its consequences; because, though deriving some inkling of the voyage from the wails which at the first moment had greeted him, yet of the details no clear understanding had been had. The best account would, doubtless, be given by the captain. Yet at first the visitor was both to ask it, unwilling to provoke some distant rebuff. But plucking up courage, he at last accosted Don Benito, renewing the expression of his benevolent interest, adding, that did he (Captain Delano) but know the particulars of the ship's misfortunes, he would, perhaps, be better able in the end to relieve them. Would Don Benito favor him with the whole story.

Don Benito faltered; then, like some somnambulist suddenly interfered with, vacantly stared at his visitor, and ended by looking down on the deck. He maintained this posture so long, that Captain Delano, almost equally disconcerted, and involuntarily almost as rude, turned suddenly from him, walking forward to accost one of the Spanish seamen for the desired information. But he had hardly gone five paces, when, with a sort of eagerness, Don Benito invited him back, regretting his momentary absence of mind, and professing readiness to gratify him.

While most part of the story was being given, the two captains stood on the after part of the main-deck, a privileged spot, no one being near but the servant.

"It is now a hundred and ninety days," began the Spaniard, in his husky whisper, "that this ship, well officered and well manned, with several cabin passengers—some fifty Spaniards in all—sailed from Buenos Ayres bound to Lima, with a general cargo, hardware, Paraguay tea and the like—and," pointing forward, "that parcel of negroes, now not more than a hundred and fifty, as you see, but then numbering over three hundred souls. Off Cape Horn we had heavy gales. In one moment, by night, three of my best officers, with fifteen sailors, were lost, with the main-yard; the spar snapping under them in the slings, as they sought, with heavers, to beat down the icy sail. To lighten the hull, the heavier sacks of mata[6] were thrown into the sea, with most of the water-pipes lashed on deck at the time. And this last necessity it was, combined with the prolonged detentions afterwards experienced, which eventually brought about our chief causes of suffering. When——"

Here there was a sudden fainting attack of his cough, brought on, no doubt, by his mental distress. His servant sustained him, and drawing a cordial from his pocket placed it to his lips. He a little revived. But unwilling to leave him unsupported while yet imperfectly restored, the black with one arm still encircled his master, at the same time keeping his eye fixed on his face, as if to watch for the first sign of complete restoration, or relapse, as the event might prove.

The Spaniard proceeded, but brokenly and obscurely, as one in a dream.

—"Oh, my God! rather than pass through what I have, with joy I would have hailed the most terrible gales; but——"

His cough returned and with increased violence; this subsiding, with reddened lips and closed eyes he fell heavily against his supporter.

"His mind wanders. He was thinking of the plague that followed the gales," plaintively sighed the servant; "my poor, poor

6. Maté or Paraguay tea. "Water-pipes": casks of water.

master!" wringing one hand, and with the other wiping the mouth. "But be patient, Señor," again turning to Captain Delano, "these fits do not last long; master will soon be himself."

Don Benito reviving, went on; but as this portion of the story was very brokenly delivered, the substance only will here be set down.

It appeared that after the ship had been many days tossed in storms off the Cape, the scurvy broke out, carrying off numbers of the whites and blacks. When at last they had worked round into the Pacific, their spars and sails were so damaged, and so inadequately handled by the surviving mariners, most of whom were become invalids, that, unable to lay her northerly course by the wind, which was powerful, the unmanageable ship, for successive days and nights, was blown northwestward, where the breeze suddenly deserted her, in unknown waters, to sultry calms. The absence of the water-pipes now proved as fatal to life as before their presence had menaced it. Induced, or at least aggravated, by the more than scanty allowance of water, a malignant fever followed the scurvy; with the excessive heat of the lengthened calm, making such short work of it as to sweep away, as by billows, whole families of the Africans, and a yet larger number, proportionably, of the Spaniards, including, by a luckless fatality, every remaining officer on board. Consequently, in the smart west winds eventually following the calm, the already rent sails, having to be simply dropped, not furled, at need, had been gradually reduced to the beggars' rags they were now. To procure substitutes for his lost sailors, as well as supplies of water and sails, the captain, at the earliest opportunity, had made for Baldivia, the southernmost civilized port of Chili and South America; but upon nearing the coast the thick weather had prevented him from so much as sighting that harbor. Since which period, almost without a crew, and almost without canvas and almost without water, and, at intervals, giving its added dead to the sea, the San Dominick had been battle-dored about by contrary winds, inveigled by currents, or grown weedy in calms. Like a man lost in woods, more than once she had doubled upon her own track.

"But throughout these calamities," huskily continued Don Benito, painfully turning in the half embrace of his servant, "I have to thank those negroes you see, who, though to your inexperienced eyes appearing unruly, have, indeed, conducted themselves with less of restlessness than even their owner could have thought possible under such circumstances."

Here he again fell faintly back. Again his mind wandered; but he rallied, and less obscurely proceeded.

"Yes, their owner was quite right in assuring me that no fetters would be needed with his blacks; so that while, as is wont in this transportation, those negroes have always remained upon deck—not thrust below, as in the Guineamen[7]—they have, also, from the beginning, been freely permitted to range within given bounds at their pleasure."

Once more the faintness returned—his mind roved—but, recovering, he resumed:

"But it is Babo here to whom, under God, I owe not only my own preservation, but likewise to him, chiefly, the merit is due, of pacifying his more ignorant brethren, when at intervals tempted to murmurings."

"Ah, master," sighed the black, bowing his face, "don't speak of me; Babo is nothing; what Babo has done was but duty."

"Faithful fellow!" cried Captain Delano. "Don Benito, I envy you such a friend; slave I cannot call him."

As master and man stood before him, the black upholding the white, Captain Delano could not but bethink him of the beauty of that relationship which could present such a spectacle of fidelity on the one hand and confidence on the other. The scene was heightened by the contrast in dress, denoting their relative positions. The Spaniard wore a loose Chili jacket of dark velvet; white small-clothes and stockings, with silver buckles at the knee and instep; a high-crowned sombrero, of fine grass; a slender sword, silver mounted, hung from a knot in his sash—the last being an almost invariable adjunct, more for utility than ornament, of a South American gentleman's dress to this hour. Excepting when his occasional nervous contortions brought about disarray, there was a certain precision in his attire curiously at variance with the unsightly disorder around; especially in the belittered Ghetto, forward of the mainmast, wholly occupied by the blacks.

The servant wore nothing but wide trowsers, apparently, from their coarseness and patches, made out of some old topsail; they were clean, and confined at the waist by a bit of unstranded rope, which, with his composed, deprecatory air at times, made him look something like a begging friar of St. Francis.

However unsuitable for the time and place, at least in the blunt-thinking American's eyes, and however strangely surviving in the midst of all his afflictions, the toilette of Don Benito might not, in fashion at least, have gone beyond the style of the day among South Americans of his class. Though on the present voyage sailing from Buenos Ayres, he had avowed himself a native and resident of Chili, whose inhabitants had not so generally adopted the plain coat and once plebeian pantaloons; but, with a becoming modification, adhered to their provincial costume, picturesque as

7. Slave ships, so called because of their trade with the west African coast of Guinea.

any in the world. Still, relatively to the pale history of the voyage, and his own pale face, there seemed something so incongruous in the Spaniard's apparel, as almost to suggest the image of an invalid courtier tottering about London streets in the time of the plague.

The portion of the narrative which, perhaps, most excited interest, as well as some surprise, considering the latitudes in question, was the long calms spoken of, and more particularly the ship's so long drifting about. Without communicating the opinion, of course, the American could not but impute at least part of the detentions both to clumsy seamanship and faulty navigation. Eyeing Don Benito's small, yellow hands, he easily inferred that the young captain had not got into command at the hawse-hole, but the cabin-window; and if so, why wonder at incompetence, in youth, sickness, and gentility united?

But drowning criticism in compassion, after a fresh repetition of his sympathies, Captain Delano, having heard out his story, not only engaged, as in the first place, to see Don Benito and his people supplied in their immediate bodily needs, but, also, now further promised to assist him in procuring a large permanent supply of water, as well as some sails and rigging; and, though it would involve no small embarrassment to himself, yet he would spare three of his best seamen for temporary deck officers; so that without delay the ship might proceed to Conception, there fully to refit for Lima, her destined port.

Such generosity was not without its effect, even upon the invalid. His face lighted up; eager and hectic, he met the honest glance of his visitor. With gratitude he seemed overcome.

"This excitement is bad for master," whispered the servant, taking his arm, and with soothing words gently drawing him aside.

When Don Benito returned, the American was pained to observe that his hopefulness, like the sudden kindling in his cheek, was but febrile and transient.

Ere long, with a joyless mien, looking up towards the poop, the host invited his guest to accompany him there, for the benefit of what little breath of wind might be stirring.

As, during the telling of the story, Captain Delano had once or twice started at the occasional cymballing of the hatchet-polishers, wondering why such an interruption should be allowed, especially in that part of the ship, and in the ears of an invalid; and moreover, as the hatchets had anything but an attractive look, and the handlers of them still less so, it was, therefore, to tell the truth, not without some lurking reluctance, or even shrinking, it may be, that Captain Delano, with apparent complaisance, acquiesced in his host's invitation. The more so, since, with an untimely caprice of punctilio, rendered distressing by his cadaverous aspect, Don

Benito, with Castilian bows, solemnly insisted upon his guest's preceding him up the ladder leading to the elevation; where, one on each side of the last step, sat for armorial supporters and sentries two of the ominous file. Gingerly enough stepped good Captain Delano between them, and in the instant of leaving them behind, like one running the gauntlet, he felt an apprehensive twitch in the calves of his legs.

But when, facing about, he saw the whole file, like so many organ-grinders, still stupidly intent on their work, unmindful of everything beside, he could not but smile at his late fidgety panic.

Presently, while standing with his host, looking forward upon the decks below, he was struck by one of those instances of insubordination previously alluded to. Three black boys, with two Spanish boys, were sitting together on the hatches, scraping a rude wooden platter, in which some scanty mess had recently been cooked. Suddenly, one of the black boys, enraged at a word dropped by one of his white companions, seized a knife, and, though called to forbear by one of the oakum-pickers, struck the lad over the head, inflicting a gash from which blood flowed.

In amazement, Captain Delano inquired what this meant. To which the pale Don Benito dully muttered, that it was merely the sport of the lad.

"Pretty serious sport, truly," rejoined Captain Delano. "Had such a thing happened on board the Bachelor's Delight, instant punishment would have followed."

At these words the Spaniard turned upon the American one of his sudden, staring, half-lunatic looks; then, relapsing into his torpor, answered, "Doubtless, doubtless, Señor."

Is it, thought Captain Delano, that this hapless man is one of those paper captains I've known, who by policy wink at what by power they cannot put down? I know no sadder sight than a commander who has little of command but the name.

"I should think, Don Benito," he now said, glancing towards the oakum-picker who had sought to interfere with the boys, "that you would find it advantageous to keep all your blacks employed, especially the younger ones, no matter at what useless task, and no matter what happens to the ship. Why, even with my little band, I find such a course indispensable. I once kept a crew on my quarterdeck thrumming mats for my cabin, when, for three days I had given up my ship—mats, men, and all—for a speedy loss, owing to the violence of a gale, in which we could do nothing but helplessly drive before it."

"Doubtless, doubtless," muttered Don Benito.

"But," continued Captain Delano, again glancing upon the oakum-pickers and then at the hatchet-polishers, near by, "I see you keep some, at least, of your host employed."

"Yes," was again the vacant response.

"Those old men there, shaking their pows from their pulpits," continued Captain Delano, pointing to the oakum-pickers, "seem to act the part of old dominies to the rest, little heeded as their admonitions are at times. Is this voluntary on their part, Don Benito, or have you appointed them shepherds to your flock of black sheep?"

"What posts they fill, I appointed them," rejoined the Spaniard, in an acrid tone, as if resenting some supposed satiric reflection.

"And these others, these Ashantee conjurors here," continued Captain Delano, rather uneasily eyeing the brandished steel of the hatchet-polishers, where, in spots, it had been brought to a shine, "this seems a curious business they are at, Don Benito?"

"In the gales we met," answered the Spaniard, "what of our general cargo was not thrown overboard was much damaged by the brine. Since coming into calm weather, I have had several cases of knives and hatchets daily brought up for overhauling and cleaning."

"A prudent idea, Don Benito. You are part owner of ship and cargo, I presume; but none of the slaves, perhaps?"

"I am owner of all you see," impatiently returned Don Benito, "except the main company of blacks, who belonged to my late friend, Alexandro Aranda."

As he mentioned this name, his air was heart-broken; his knees shook; his servant supported him.

Thinking he divined the cause of such unusual emotion, to confirm his surmise, Captain Delano, after a pause, said: "And may I ask, Don Benito, whether—since awhile ago you spoke of some cabin passengers—the friend, whose loss so afflicts you, at the outset of the voyage accompanied his blacks?"

"Yes."

"But died of the fever?"

"Died of the fever. Oh, could I but——"

Again quivering, the Spaniard paused.

"Pardon me," said Captain Delano, lowly, "but I think that, by a sympathetic experience, I conjecture, Don Benito, what it is that gives the keener edge to your grief. It was once my hard fortune to lose, at sea, a dear friend, my own brother, then supercargo. Assured of the welfare of his spirit, its departure I could have borne like a man; but that honest eye, that honest hand—both of which had so often met mine—and that warm heart; all, all—like scraps to the dogs—to throw all to the sharks! It was then I vowed never to have for fellow-voyager a man I loved, unless, unbeknown to him, I had provided every requisite, in case of a fatality, for embalming his mortal part for interment on shore. Were your friend's remains now on board this ship, Don Benito, not thus strangely would the mention of his name affect you."

"On board this ship?" echoed the Spaniard. Then, with horrified gestures, as directed against some spectre, he unconsciously fell into the ready arms of his attendant, who, with a silent appeal toward Captain Delano, seemed beseeching him not again to broach a theme so unspeakably distressing to his master.

This poor fellow now, thought the pained American, is the victim of that sad superstition which associates goblins with the deserted body of man, as ghosts with an abandoned house. How unlike are we made! What to me, in like case, would have been a solemn satisfaction, the bare suggestion, even, terrifies the Spaniard into this trance. Poor Alexandro Aranda! what would you say could you here see your friend—who, on former voyages, when you, for months, were left behind, has, I dare say, often longed, and longed, for one peep at you—now transported with terror at the least thought of having you anyway nigh him.

At this moment, with a dreary grave-yard toll, betokening a flaw, the ship's forecastle bell, smote by one of the grizzled oakum-pickers, proclaimed ten o'clock, through the leaden calm; when Captain Delano's attention was caught by the moving figure of a gigantic black, emerging from the general crowd below, and slowly advancing towards the elevated poop. An iron collar was about his neck, from which depended a chain, thrice wound round his body; the terminating links padlocked together at a broad band of iron, his girdle.

"How like a mute Atufal moves," murmured the servant.

The black mounted the steps of the poop, and, like a brave prisoner, brought up to receive sentence, stood in unquailing muteness before Don Benito, now recovered from his attack.

At the first glimpse of his approach, Don Benito had started, a resentful shadow swept over his face; and, as with the sudden memory of bootless rage, his white lips glued together.

This is some mulish mutineer, thought Captain Delano, surveying, not without a mixture of admiration, the colossal form of the negro.

"See, he waits your question, master," said the servant.

Thus reminded, Don Benito, nervously averting his glance, as if shunning, by anticipation, some rebellious response, in a disconcerted voice, thus spoke:—

"Atufal, will you ask my pardon, now?"

The black was silent.

"Again, master," murmured the servant, with bitter upbraiding eyeing his countryman, "Again, master; he will bend to master yet."

"Answer," said Don Benito, still averting his glance, "say but the one word, *pardon*, and your chains shall be off."

Upon this, the black, slowly raising both arms, let them lifelessly fall, his links clanking, his head bowed; as much as to say, "no, I am content."

"Go," said Don Benito, with inkept and unknown emotion.

Deliberately as he had come, the black obeyed.

"Excuse me, Don Benito," said Captain Delano, "but this scene surprises me; what means it, pray?"

"It means that that negro alone, of all the band, has given me peculiar cause of offense. I have put him in chains; I——"

Here he paused; his hand to his head, as if there were a swimming there, or a sudden bewilderment of memory had come over him; but meeting his servant's kindly glance seemed reassured, and proceeded:—

"I could not scourge such a form. But I told him he must ask my pardon. As yet he has not. At my command, every two hours he stands before me."

"And how long has this been?"

"Some sixty days."

"And obedient in all else? And respectful?"

"Yes."

"Upon my conscience, then," exclaimed Captain Delano, impulsively, "he has a royal spirit in him, this fellow."

"He may have some right to it," bitterly returned Don Benito, "he says he was king in his own land."

"Yes," said the servant, entering a word, "those slits in Atufal's ears once held wedges of gold; but poor Babo here, in his own land, was only a poor slave; a black man's slave was Babo, who now is the white's."

Somewhat annoyed by these conversational familiarities, Captain Delano turned curiously upon the attendant, then glanced inquiringly at his master; but, as if long wonted to these little informalities, neither master nor man seemed to understand him.

"What, pray, was Atufal's offense, Don Benito?" asked Captain Delano; "if it was not something very serious, take a fool's advice, and, in view of his general docility, as well as in some natural respect for his spirit, remit him his penalty."

"No, no, master never will do that," here murmured the servant to himself, "proud Atufal must first ask master's pardon. The slave there carries the padlock, but master here carries the key."

His attention thus directed, Captain Delano now noticed for the first, that, suspended by a slender silken cord, from Don Benito's neck, hung a key. At once, from the servant's muttered syllables, divining the key's purpose, he smiled and said:—"So, Don Benito—padlock and key—significant symbols, truly."

Biting his lip, Don Benito faltered.

Though the remark of Captain Delano, a man of such native simplicity as to be incapable of satire or irony, had been dropped in playful allusion to the Spaniard's singularly evidenced lordship over the black; yet the hypochondriac seemed some way to have taken it as a malicious reflection upon his confessed inability thus far to break down, at least, on a verbal summons, the entrenched will of the slave. Deploring this supposed misconception, yet despairing of correcting it, Captain Delano shifted the subject; but finding his companion more than ever withdrawn, as if still sourly digesting the lees of the presumed affront above-mentioned, by-and-by Captain Delano likewise became less talkative, oppressed, against his own will, by what seemed the secret vindictiveness of the morbidly sensitive Spaniard. But the good sailor, himself of a quite contrary disposition, refrained, on his part, alike from the appearance as from the feeling of resentment, and if silent, was only so from contagion.

Presently the Spaniard, assisted by his servant, somewhat discourteously crossed over from his guest; a procedure which, sensibly enough, might have been allowed to pass for idle caprice of ill-humor, had not master and man, lingering round the corner of the elevated skylight, began whispering together in low voices. This was unpleasing. And more; the moody air of the Spaniard, which at times had not been without a sort of valetudinarian stateliness, now seemed anything but dignified; while the menial familiarity of the servant lost its original charm of simple-hearted attachment.

In his embarrassment, the visitor turned his face to the other side of the ship. By so doing, his glance accidentally fell on a young Spanish sailor, a coil of rope in his hand, just stepped from the deck to the first round of the mizzen-rigging. Perhaps the man would not have been particularly noticed, were it not that, during his ascent to one of the yards, he, with a sort of covert intentness, kept his eye fixed on Captain Delano, from whom, presently, it passed, as if by a natural sequence, to the two whisperers.

His own attention thus redirected to that quarter, Captain Delano gave a slight start. From something in Don Benito's manner just then, it seemed as if the visitor had, at least partly, been the subject of the withdrawn consultation going on—a conjecture as little agreeable to the guest as it was little flattering to the host.

The singular alternations of courtesy and ill-breeding in the Spanish captain were unaccountable, except on one of two suppositions—innocent lunacy, or wicked imposture.

But the first idea, though it might naturally have occurred to an indifferent observer, and, in some respect, had not hitherto been wholly a stranger to Captain Delano's mind, yet, now that, in an incipient way, he began to regard the stranger's conduct something in the light of an intentional affront, of course the idea of lunacy was virtually vacated. But if not a lunatic, what then? Under the circumstances, would a gentleman, nay, any honest boor, act the part now acted by his host? The man was an imposter. Some low-born adventurer, masquerading as an oceanic grandee; yet so ignorant of the first requisites of mere gentlemanhood as to be betrayed into the present remarkable indecorum. That strange ceremoniousness, too, at other times evinced, seemed not uncharacteristic of one playing a part above his real level. Benito Cereno—Don Benito Cereno—a sounding name. One, too, at that period, not unknown, in the surname, to supercargoes and sea captains trading along the Spanish Main, as belonging to one of the most enterprising and extensive mercantile families in all those provinces; several members of it having titles; a sort of Castilian Rothschild,[8] with a noble brother, or cousin, in every great trading town of South America. The alleged Don Benito was in early manhood, about twenty-nine or thirty. To assume a sort of roving cadetship in the maritime affairs of such a house, what more likely scheme for a young knave of talent and spirit? But the Spaniard was a pale invalid. Never mind. For even to the degree of simulating mortal disease, the craft of some tricksters had been known to attain. To think that, under the aspect of infantile weakness, the most savage energies might be couched—those velvets of the Spaniard but the silky paw of his fangs.

From no train of thought did these fancies come; not from within, but from without; suddenly, too, and in one throng, like hoar frost; yet as soon to vanish as the mild sun of Captain Delano's good-nature regained its meridian.

Glancing over once more towards his host—whose side-face, revealed above the skylight, was now turned towards him—he was struck by the profile, whose clearness of cut was refined by the thinness, incident to ill-health, as well as ennobled about the chin by the beard. Away with suspicion. He was a true off-shoot of a true hidalgo Cereno.

Relieved by these and other better thoughts, the visitor, lightly humming a tune, now began indifferently pacing the poop, so as not to betray to Don Benito that he had at all mistrusted incivility, much less duplicity; for such mistrust would yet be proved illusory, and by the event; though, for the present, the circumstance which had provoked that distrust remained unexplained. But when that

8. A wealthy and widespread banking family.

little mystery should have been cleared up, Captain Delano thought he might extremely regret it, did he allow Don Benito to become aware that he had indulged in ungenerous surmises. In short, to the Spaniard's black-letter text, it was best, for awhile, to leave open margin.

Presently, his pale face twitching and overcast, the Spaniard, still supported by his attendant, moved over towards his guest, when, with even more than his usual embarrassment, and a strange sort of intriguing intonation in his husky whisper, the following conversation began:—

"Señor, may I ask how long you have lain at this isle?"

"Oh, but a day or two, Don Benito."

"And from what port are you last?"

"Canton."

"And there, Señor, you exchanged your sealskins for teas and silks, I think you said?"

"Yes. Silks, mostly."

"And the balance you took in specie, perhaps?"

Captain Delano, fidgeting a little, answered—

"Yes; some silver; not a very great deal, though."

"Ah—well. May I ask how many men have you, Señor?"

Captain Delano slightly started, but answered—

"About five-and-twenty, all told."

"And at present, Señor, all on board, I suppose?"

"All on board, Don Benito," replied the Captain, now with satisfaction.

"And will be to-night, Señor?"

At this last question, following so many pertinacious ones, for the soul of him Captain Delano could not but look very earnestly at the questioner, who, instead of meeting the glance, with every token of craven discomposure dropped his eyes to the deck; presenting an unworthy contrast to his servant, who, just then, was kneeling at his feet, adjusting a loose shoe-buckle; his disengaged face meantime, with humble curiosity, turned openly up into his master's downcast one.

The Spaniard, still with a guilty shuffle, repeated his question:

"And—and will be to-night, Señor?"

"Yes, for aught I know," returned Captain Delano—"but nay," rallying himself into fearless truth, "some of them talked of going off on another fishing party about midnight."

"Your ships generally go—go more or less armed, I believe, Señor?"

"Oh, a six-pounder or two, in case of emergency," was the intrepidly indifferent reply, "with a small stock of muskets, sealing-spears, and cutlasses, you know."

As he thus responded, Captain Delano again glanced at Don Benito, but the latter's eyes were averted; while abruptly and awkwardly shifting the subject, he made some peevish allusion to the calm, and then, without apology, once more, with his attendant, withdrew to the opposite bulwarks, where the whispering was resumed.

At this moment, and ere Captain Delano could cast a cool thought upon what had just passed, the young Spanish sailor, before mentioned, was seen descending from the rigging. In act of stooping over to spring inboard to the deck, his voluminous, unconfined frock, or shirt, of coarse woolen, much spotted with tar, opened out far down the chest, revealing a soiled under garment of what seemed the finest linen, edged, about the neck, with a narrow blue ribbon, sadly faded and worn. At this moment the young sailor's eye was again fixed on the whispers, and Captain Delano thought he observed a lurking significance in it, as if silent signs, of some Freemason sort, had that instant been interchanged.

This once more impelled his own glance in the direction of Don Benito, and, as before, he could not but infer that himself formed the subject of the conference. He paused. The sound of the hatchet-polishing fell on his ears. He cast another swift side-look at the two. They had the air of conspirators. In connection with the late questionings, and the incident of the young sailor, these things now begat such return of involuntary suspicion, that the singular guilelessness of the American could not endure it. Plucking up a gay and humorous expression, he crossed over to the two rapidly, saying:—"Ha, Don Benito, your black here seems high in your trust; a sort of privy-counselor, in fact."

Upon this, the servant looked up with a good-natured grin, but the master started as from a venomous bite. It was a moment or two before the Spaniard sufficiently recovered himself to reply; which he did, at last, with cold constraint:—"Yes, Señor, I have trust in Babo."

Here Babo, changing his previous grin of mere animal humor into an intelligent smile, not ungratefully eyed his master.

Finding that the Spaniard now stood silent and reserved, as if involuntarily, or purposely giving hint that his guest's proximity was inconvenient just then, Captain Delano, unwilling to appear uncivil even to incivility itself, made some trivial remark and moved off; again and again turning over in his mind the mysterious demeanor of Don Benito Cereno.

He had descended from the poop, and, wrapped in thought, was passing near a dark hatchway, leading down into the steerage, when, perceiving motion there, he looked to see what moved. The same instant there was a sparkle in the shadowy hatchway, and he saw one of the Spanish sailors, prowling there, hurriedly placing his hand in the bosom of his frock, as if hiding something. Before the man could have been certain who it was that was passing, he slunk below out of sight. But enough was seen of him to make it sure that he was the same young sailor before noticed in the rigging.

What was that which so sparkled? thought Captain Delano. It was no lamp—no match—no live coal. Could it have been a jewel? But how come sailors with jewels?—or with silk-trimmed under-shirts either? Has he been robbing the trunks of the dead cabin-passengers? But if so, he would hardly wear one of the stolen articles on board ship here. Ah, ah—if, now, that was, indeed, a secret sign I saw passing between this suspicious fellow and his captain awhile since; if I could only be certain that, in my uneasiness, my senses did not deceive me, then——

Here, passing from one suspicious thing to another, his mind revolved the strange questions put to him concerning his ship.

By a curious coincidence, as each point was recalled, the black wizards of Ashantee would strike up with their hatchets, as in ominous comment on the white stranger's thoughts. Pressed by such enigmas and portents, it would have been almost against nature, had not, even into the least distrustful heart, some ugly misgivings obtruded.

Observing the ship, now helplessly fallen into a current, with enchanted sails, drifting with increased rapidity seaward; and noting that, from a lately intercepted projection of the land, the sealer was hidden, the stout mariner began to quake at thoughts which he barely durst confess to himself. Above all, he began to feel a ghostly dread of Don Benito. And yet, when he roused himself, dilated his chest, felt himself strong on his legs, and coolly considered it —what did all these phantoms amount to?

Had the Spaniard any sinister scheme, it must have reference not so much to him (Captain Delano) as to his ship (the Bachelor's Delight). Hence the present drifting away of the one ship from the other, instead of favoring any such possible scheme, was, for the time, at least, opposed to it. Clearly any suspicion, combining such contradictions, must need be delusive. Beside, was it not absurd to think of a vessel in distress—a vessel by sickness almost dismanned of her crew—a vessel whose inmates were parched for water—was it not a thousand times absurd that such a craft should, at present, be of a piratical character; or her commander, either for himself or those under him, cherish any desire but for speedy relief and refreshment? But then, might not general distress, and thirst in particular, be affected? And might not that same undiminished Spanish crew, alleged to have perished off to a remnant, be at that very moment lurking in the hold? On heart-broken pretense of entreating a cup of cold water, fiends in human form had got into lonely dwellings, nor retired until a dark deed had been done. And among the Malay pirates, it was no unusual thing to lure ships after them into their treacherous harbors, or entice boarders from a declared enemy at sea, by the spectacle of thinly manned or vacant decks, beneath which prowled a hundred spears with yellow arms ready to upthrust them through the mats. Not that Captain Delano had entirely credited such things. He had heard of them—and now, as stories, they recurred. The present destination of the ship was the anchorage. There she would be near his own vessel. Upon gaining that vicinity, might not the San Dominick, like a slumbering volcano, suddenly let loose energies now hid?

He recalled the Spaniard's manner while telling his story. There was a gloomy hesitancy and subterfuge about it. It was just the manner of one making up his tale for evil purposes, as he goes. But if that story was not true, what was the truth? That the ship had unlawfully come into the Spaniard's possession? But in many of its details, especially in reference to the more calamitous parts, such as the fatalities among the seamen, the consequent prolonged beating about, the past sufferings from obstinate calms, and still continued suffering from thirst; in all these points, as well as others, Don Benito's story had corroborated not only the wailing ejaculations of the indiscriminate multitude, white and black, but likewise—what seemed impossible to be counterfeit—by the very expression and play of every human feature, which Captain Delano saw. If Don Benito's story was, throughout, an invention, then every soul on board, down to the youngest negress, was his carefully drilled recruit in the plot: an incredible inference. And yet, if there was ground for mistrusting his veracity, that inference was a legitimate one.

But those questions of the Spaniard. There, indeed, one might pause. Did they not seem put with much the same object with which the burglar or assassin, by day-time, reconnoitres the walls of a house? But, with ill purposes, to solicit such information openly of the chief person endangered, and so, in effect, setting him on his guard; how unlikely a procedure was that? Absurd, then, to suppose that those questions had been prompted by evil designs. Thus, the same conduct, which, in this instance, had raised the alarm, served to dispel it.[9] In short, scarce any suspicion or uneasiness, however apparently reasonable at the time, which was not now, with equal apparent reason, dismissed.

At last he began to laugh at his former forebodings; and laugh

9. The preceding six sentences ("But those questions * * * dispel it"), emphasizing Captain Delano's uneasiness, were introduced when Melville revised the original *Putnam's* version of the story for publication in the *Piazza Tales*.

at the strange ship for, in its aspect, someway siding with them, as it were; and laugh, too, at the odd-looking blacks, particularly those old scissors-grinders, the Ashantees; and those bed-ridden old knitting women, the oakum-pickers; and almost at the dark Spaniard himself, the central hobgoblin of all.

For the rest, whatever in a serious way seemed enigmatical, was now good-naturedly explained away by the thought that, for the most part, the poor invalid scarcely knew what he was about; either sulking in black vapors, or putting idle questions without sense or object. Evidently, for the present, the man was not fit to be in- trusted with the ship. On some benevolent plea withdrawing the command from him, Captain Delano would yet have to send her to Conception, in charge of his second mate, a worthy person and good navigator—a plan not more convenient for the San Dominick than for Don Benito; for, relieved from all anxiety, keeping wholly to his cabin, the sick man, under the good nursing of his servant, would, probably, by the end of the passage, be in a measure re- stored to health, and with that he should also be restored to au- thority.

Such were the American's thoughts. They were tranquilizing. There was a difference between the idea of Don Benito's darkly pre-ordaining Captain Delano's fate, and Captain Delano's lightly arranging Don Benito's. Nevertheless, it was not without some- thing of relief that the good seaman presently perceived his whale- boat in the distance. Its absence had been prolonged by unexpected detention at the sealer's side, as well as its returning trip length- ened by the continual recession of the goal.

The advancing speck was observed by the blacks. Their shouts attracted the attention of Don Benito, who, with a return of courtesy, approaching Captain Delano, expressed satisfaction at the coming of some supplies, slight and temporary as they must neces- sarily prove.

Captain Delano responded; but while doing so, his attention was drawn to something passing on the deck below: among the crowd climbing the landward bulwarks, anxiously watching the coming boat, two blacks, to all appearances accidentally incommoded by one of the sailors, violently pushed him aside, which the sailor some- way resenting, they dashed him to the deck, despite the earnest cries of the oakum-pickers.

"Don Benito," said Captain Delano quickly, "do you see what is going on there? Look!"

But, seized by his cough, the Spaniard staggered, with both hands to his face, on the point of falling. Captain Delano would have supported him, but the servant was more alert, who, with one hand sustaining his master, with the other applied the cordial. Don

Benito restored, the black withdrew his support, slipping aside a little, but dutifully remaining within call of a whisper. Such discretion was here evinced as quite wiped away, in the visitor's eyes, any blemish of impropriety which might have attached to the attendant, from the indecorous conferences before mentioned; showing, too, that if the servant were to blame, it might be more the master's fault than his own, since, when left to himself, he could conduct thus well.

His glance called away from the spectacle of disorder to the more pleasing one before him, Captain Delano could not avoid again congratulating his host upon possessing such a servant, who, though perhaps a little too forward now and then, must upon the whole be invaluable to one in the invalid's situation.

"Tell me, Don Benito," he added, with a smile—"I should like to have your man here, myself—what will you take for him? Would fifty doubloons be any object?"

"Master wouldn't part with Babo for a thousand doubloons," murmured the black, overhearing the offer, and taking it in earnest, and, with the strange vanity of a faithful slave, appreciated by his master, scorning to hear so paltry a valuation put upon him by a stranger. But Don Benito, apparently hardly yet completely restored, and again interrupted by his cough, made but some broken reply.

Soon his physical distress became so great, affecting his mind, too, apparently, that, as if to screen the sad spectacle, the servant gently conducted his master below.

Left to himself, the American, to while away the time till his boat should arrive, would have pleasantly accosted some one of the few Spanish seamen he saw; but recalling something that Don Benito had said touching their ill conduct, he refrained; as a shipmaster indisposed to countenance cowardice or unfaithfulness in seamen.

While, with these thoughts, standing with eye directed forward towards that handful of sailors, suddenly he thought that one or two of them returned the glance and with a sort of meaning. He rubbed his eyes, and looked again; but again seemed to see the same thing. Under a new form, but more obscure than any previous one, the old suspicions recurred, but, in the absence of Don Benito, with less of panic than before. Despite the bad account given of the sailors, Captain Delano resolved forthwith to accost one of them. Descending the poop, he made his way through the blacks, his movement drawing a queer cry from the oakum-pickers, prompted by whom, the negroes, twitching each other aside, divided before him; but, as if curious to see what was the object of this deliberate visit to their ghetto, closing in behind, in tolerable order, followed the white stranger up. His progress thus proclaimed as by mounted kings-at-arms, and escorted as by a Caffre[1] guard of honor, Captain Delano, assuming a good-humored, off-handed air, continued to advance; now and then saying a blithe word to the negroes, and his eye curiously surveying the white faces, here and there sparsely mixed in with the blacks, like stray white pawns venturously involved in the ranks of the chess-men opposed.

While thinking which of them to select for his purpose, he chanced to observe a sailor seated on the deck engaged in tarring the strap of a large block, a circle of blacks squatted round him inquisitively eyeing the process.

The mean employment of the man was in contrast with something superior in his figure. His hand, black with continually thrusting it into the tar-pot held for him by a negro, seemed not naturally allied to his face, a face which would have been a very fine one but for its haggardness. Whether this haggardness had aught to do with criminality, could not be determined; since, as intense heat and cold, though unlike, produce like sensations, so innocence and guilt, when, through casual association with mental pain, stamping any visible impress, use one seal—a hacked one.

Not again that this reflection occurred to Captain Delano at the time, charitable man as he was. Rather another idea. Because observing so singular a haggardness combined with a dark eye, averted as in trouble and shame, and then again recalling Don Benito's confessed ill opinion of his crew, insensibly he was operated upon by certain general notions which, while disconnecting pain and abashment from virtue, invariably link them with vice.

If, indeed, there be any wickedness on board this ship, thought Captain Delano, be sure that man there has fouled his hand in it, even as now he fouls it in the pitch. I don't like to accost him. I will speak to this other, this old Jack here on the windlass.

He advanced to an old Barcelona tar, in ragged red breeches and dirty night-cap, cheeks trenched and bronzed, whiskers dense as thorn hedges. Seated between two sleepy-looking Africans, this mariner, like his younger shipmate, was employed upon some rigging—splicing a cable—the sleepy-looking blacks performing the inferior function of holding the outer parts of the ropes for him.

Upon Captain Delano's approach, the man at once hung his head below its previous level; the one necessary for business. It appeared as if he desired to be thought absorbed, with more than common fidelity, in his task. Being addressed, he glanced up, but with what seemed a furtive, diffident air, which sat strangely enough on his weather-beaten visage, much as if a grizzly bear, instead of

---

1. Kaffir (Bantu race of South Africa). The "king-at-arms" is the chief heraldic officer of a country.

876 · *Herman Melville*

growling and biting, should simper and cast sheep's eyes. He was asked several questions concerning the voyage—questions purposely referring to several particulars in Don Benito's narrative, not previously corroborated by those impulsive cries greeting the visitor on first coming on board. The questions were briefly answered, confirming all that remained to be confirmed of the story. The negroes about the windlass joined in with the old sailor; but, as they became talkative, he by degrees became mute, and at length quite glum, seemed morosely unwilling to answer more questions, and yet, all the while, this ursine air was somehow mixed with his sheepish one.

Despairing of getting into unembarrassed talk with such a centaur, Captain Delano, after glancing round for a more promising countenance, but seeing none, spoke pleasantly to the blacks to make way for him; and so, amid various grins and grimaces, returned to the poop, feeling a little strange at first, he could hardly tell why, but upon the whole with regained confidence in Benito Cereno.

How plainly, thought he, did that old whiskerando yonder betray a consciousness of ill desert. No doubt, when he saw me coming, he dreaded lest I, apprised by his Captain of the crew's general misbehavior, came with sharp words for him, and so down with his head. And yet—and yet, now that I think of it, that very old fellow, if I err not, was one of those who seemed so earnestly eyeing me here awhile since. Ah, these currents spin one's head round almost as much as they do the ship. Ha, there now's a pleasant sort of sunny sight; quite sociable, too.

His attention had been drawn to a slumbering negress, partly disclosed through the lace-work of some rigging, lying, with youthful limbs carelessly disposed, under the lee of the bulwarks, like a doe in the shade of a woodland rock. Sprawling at her lapped breasts, was her wide-awake fawn, stark naked, its black little body half lifted from the deck, crosswise with its dam's; its hands, like two paws, clambering upon her; its mouth and nose ineffectually rooting to get at the mark; and meantime giving a vexatious half-grunt, blending with the composed snore of the negress.

The uncommon vigor of the child at length roused the mother. She started up, at a distance facing Captain Delano. But as if not at all concerned at the attitude in which she had been caught, delightedly she caught the child up, with maternal transports, covering it with kisses.

There's naked nature, now; pure tenderness and love, thought Captain Delano, well pleased.

This incident prompted him to remark the other negresses more particularly than before. He was gratified with their manners: like most uncivilized women, they seemed at once tender of heart and tough of constitution; equally ready to die for their infants or fight for them. Unsophisticated as leopardesses; loving as doves. Ah! thought Captain Delano, these, perhaps, are some of the very women whom Ledyard[2] saw in Africa, and gave such a noble account of.

These natural sights somehow insensibly deepened his confidence and ease. At last he looked to see how his boat was getting on; but it was still pretty remote. He turned to see if Don Benito had returned; but he had not.

To change the scene, as well as to please himself with a leisurely observation of the coming boat, stepping over into the mizzen-chains, he clambered his way into the starboard quarter-gallery—one of those abandoned Venetian-looking water-balconies previously mentioned—retreats cut off from the deck. As his foot pressed the half-damp, half-dry sea-mosses matting the place, and a chance phantom cats-paw—an islet of breeze, unheralded, unfollowed—as this ghostly cats-paw came fanning his cheek; as his glance fell upon the row of small, round dead-lights—all closed like coppered eyes of the coffined—and the state-cabin door, once connecting with the gallery, even as the dead-lights had once looked out upon it, but now calked fast like a sarcophagus lid; and to a purple-black tarred-over, panel, threshold, and post; and he bethought him of the time when that state-cabin and this state-balcony had heard the voices of the Spanish king's officers, and the forms of the Lima viceroy's daughters had perhaps leaned where he stood—as these and other images flitted through his mind, as the cats-paw through the calm, gradually he felt rising a dreamy inquietude, like that of one who alone on the prairie feels unrest from the repose of the moon.

He leaned against the carved balustrade, again looking off toward his boat; but found his eye falling upon the ribbon grass, trailing along the ship's water-line, straight as a border of green box; and parterres of sea-weed, broad ovals and crescents, floating nigh and far, with what seemed long formal alleys between, crossing the terraces of swells, and sweeping round as if leading to the grottoes below. And overhanging all was the balustrade by his arm, which, partly stained with pitch and partly embossed with moss, seemed the charred ruin of some summer-house in a grand garden long running to waste.

Trying to break one charm, he was but becharmed anew. Though upon the wide sea, he seemed in some far inland country; prisoner in some deserted château, left to stare at empty grounds, and peer out at vague roads, where never wagon or wayfarer passed.

2. John Ledyard (1751–88) was a well-known American traveler. Melville originally used the name of the Scottish explorer Mungo Park (1771– 1805) in the *Putnam's* version, and probably made the change because Park quoted Ledyard in the passage to which he referred.

But these enchantments were a little disenchanted as his eye fell on the corroded main-chains. Of an ancient style, massy and rusty in link, shackle and bolt, they seemed even more fit for the ship's present business than the one for which she had been built.

Presently he thought something moved nigh the chains. He rubbed his eyes, and looked hard. Groves of rigging were about the chains; and there, peering from behind a great stay, like an Indian from behind a hemlock, a Spanish sailor, a marlingspike in his hand, was seen, who made what seemed an imperfect gesture towards the balcony, but immediately, as if alarmed by some advancing step along the deck within, vanished into the recesses of the hempen forest, like a poacher.

What meant this? Something the man had sought to communicate, unbeknown to any one, even to his captain. Did the secret involve aught unfavorable to his captain? Were those previous misgivings of Captain Delano's about to be verified? Or, in his haunted mood at the moment, had some random, unintentional motion of the man, while busy with the stay, as if repairing it, been mistaken for a significant beckoning?

Not unbewildered, again he gazed off for his boat. But it was temporarily hidden by a rocky spur of the isle. As with some eagerness he bent forward, watching for the first shooting view of its beak, the balustrade gave way before him like charcoal. Had he not clutched an outreaching rope he would have fallen into the sea. The crash, though feeble, and the fall, though hollow, of the rotten fragments, must have been overheard. He glanced up. With sober curiosity peering down upon him was one of the old oakum-pickers, slipped from his perch to an outside boom; while below the old negro and, invisible to him, reconnoitering from a port-hole like a fox from the mouth of its den, crouched the Spanish sailor again. From something suddenly suggested by the man's air, the mad idea now darted into Captain Delano's mind, that Don Benito's plea of indisposition, in withdrawing below, was but a pretense: that he was engaged there maturing his plot, of which the sailor, by some means gaining an inkling, had a mind to warn the stranger against; incited, it may be, by gratitude for a kind word on first boarding the ship. Was it from foreseeing some possible interference like this, that Don Benito had, beforehand, given such a bad character of his sailors, while praising the negroes; though, indeed, the former seemed as docile as the latter the contrary? The whites, too, by nature, were the shrewder race. A man with some evil design, would he not be likely to speak well of that stupidity which was blind to his depravity, and malign that intelligence from which it might be hidden? Not unlikely, perhaps. But if the whites had dark secrets concerning Don Benito, could then Don Benito be any way in complicity with the blacks? But they were too stupid. Besides, who ever heard of a white so far a renegade as to apostatize from his very species almost, by leaguing in against it with negroes? These diffculties recalled former ones. Lost in their mazes, Captain Delano, who had now regained the deck, was uneasily advancing along it, when he observed a new face; an aged sailor seated cross-legged near the main hatchway. His skin was shrunk up with wrinkles like a pelican's empty pouch; his hair frosted; his countenance grave and composed. His hands were full of ropes, which he was working into a large knot. Some blacks were about him obligingly dipping the strands for him, here and there, as the exigencies of the operation demanded.

Captain Delano crossed over to him, and stood in silence surveying the knot; his mind, by a not uncongenial transition, passing from its own entanglements to those of the hemp. For intricacy, such a knot he had never seen in an American ship, nor indeed any other. The old man looked liked an Egyptian priest, making Gordian knots for the temple of Ammon.[3] The knot seemed a combination of double-bowline-knot, treble-crown-knot, back-handed-well-knot, knot-in-and-out-knot, and jamming-knot.

At last, puzzled to comprehend the meaning of such a knot, Captain Delano addressed the knotter:—

"What are you knotting there, my man?"

"The knot," was the brief reply, without looking up.

"So it seems; but what is it for?"

"For some one else to undo," muttered back the old man, plying his fingers harder than ever, the knot being now nearly completed.

While Captain Delano stood watching him, suddenly the old man threw the knot towards him, saying in broken English—the first heard in the ship—something to this effect: "Undo it, cut it, quick." It was said lowly, but with such condensation of rapidity, that the long, slow words in Spanish, which had preceded and followed, almost operated as covers to the brief English between.

For a moment, knot in hand, and knot in head, Captain Delano stood mute; while, without further heeding him, the old man was now intent upon other ropes. Presently there was a slight stir behind Captain Delano. Turning, he saw the chained negro, Atufal, standing quietly there. The next moment the old sailor rose, muttering, and, followed by his subordinate negroes, removed to the forward part of the ship, where in the crowd he disappeared.

An elderly negro, in a clout like an infant's, and with a pepper and salt head, and a kind of attorney air, now approached Captain

3. An oracle declared that anyone who could untie the knot made by King Gordius would be master of Asia; Alexander the Great solved the difficulty by cutting it with his sword. Melville's association of it with Egyptian priests is a visual image.

Delano. In tolerable Spanish, and with a good-natured, knowing wink, he informed him that the old knotter was simple-witted, but harmless; often playing his odd tricks. The negro concluded by begging the knot, for of course the stranger would not care to be troubled with it. Unconsciously, it was handed to him. With a sort of congé, the negro received it, and, turning his back, ferreted into it like a detective custom-house office after smuggled laces. Soon, with some African word, equivalent to pshaw, he tossed the knot overboard.

All this is very queer now, thought Captain Delano, with a qualmish sort of emotion; but, as one feeling incipient sea-sickness, he strove, by ignoring the symptoms, to get rid of the malady. Once more he looked off for his boat. To his delight, it was now again in view, leaving the rocky spur astern.

The sensation here experienced, after at first relieving his un-easiness, with unforeseen efficacy soon began to remove it. The less distant sight of that well-known boat—showing it, not as before, half blended with the haze, but with outline defined, so that its in-dividuality, like a man's, was manifest; that boat, Rover by name, which, though now in strange seas, had often pressed the beach of Captain Delano's home, and, brought to its threshold for repairs, had familiarly lain there, as a Newfoundland dog; the sight of that household boat evoked a thousand trustful associations, which, contrasted with previous suspicions, filled him not only with light-some confidence, but somehow with half humorous self-reproaches at his former lack of it.

"What, I, Amasa Delano—Jack of the Beach, as they called me when a lad—I, Amasa; the same that, duck-satchel in hand, used to paddle along the water-side to the schoolhouse made from the old hulk—I, little Jack of the Beach, that used to go berrying with cousin Nat and the rest; I to be murdered here at the ends of the earth, on board a haunted pirate-ship by a horrible Spaniard? Too nonsensical to think of! Who would murder Amasa Delano? His conscience is clean. There is some one above. Fie, fie, Jack of the Beach! you are a child indeed; a child of the second childhood, old boy; you are beginning to dote and drule, I'm afraid."

Light of heart and foot, he stepped aft, and there was met by Don Benito's servant, who, with a pleasing expression, responsive to his own present feelings, informed him that his master had re-covered from the effects of his coughing fit, and had just ordered him to go present his compliments to his good guest, Don Amasa, and say that he (Don Benito) would soon have the happiness to rejoin him.

There now, do you mark that? again thought Captain Delano, walking the poop. What a donkey I was. This kind gentleman who here sends me his kind compliments, he, but ten minutes ago, dark-lantern in hand, was dodging round some old grind-stone in the hold, sharpening a hatchet for me, I thought. Well, well; these long calms have a morbid effect on the mind, I've often heard, though I never believed it before. Ha! glancing towards the boat; there's Rover; good dog; a white bone in her mouth. A pretty big bone though, seems to me.—What? Yes, she has fallen afoul of the bubbling tide-rip there. It sets her the other way, too, for the time. Patience.

It was now about noon, though, from the grayness of every-thing, it seemed to be getting towards dusk.

The calm was confirmed. In the far distance, away from the influence of land, the leaden ocean seemed laid out and leaded up, its course finished, soul gone, defunct. But the current from land-ward, where the ship was, increased; silently sweeping her further and further towards the tranced waters beyond.

Still, from his knowledge of those latitudes, cherishing hopes of a breeze, and a fair and fresh one, at any moment, Captain Delano, despite present prospects, buoyantly counted upon bringing the San Dominick safely to anchor ere night. The distance swept over was nothing; since, with a good wind, ten minutes' sailing would retrace more than sixty minutes, drifting. Meantime, one moment turning to mark "Rover" fighting the tide-rip, and the next to see Don Benito approaching, continued walking the poop.

Gradually he felt a vexation arising from the delay of his boat; this soon merged into uneasiness; and at last—his eye falling con-tinually, as from a stage-box into the pit, upon the strange crowd before and below him, and, by-and-by, recognizing there the face—now composed to indifference—of the Spanish sailor who had seemed to beckon from the main-chains—something of his old trepidations returned.

Ah, thought he—gravely enough—this is like the ague: because it went off, it follows not that it won't come back.

Though ashamed of the relapse, he could not altogether subdue it; and so, exerting his good-nature to the utmost, insensibly he came to a compromise.

Yes, this is a strange craft; a strange history, too, and strange folks on board. But—nothing more.

By way of keeping his mind out of mischief till the boat should arrive, he tried to occupy it with turning over and over, in a purely speculative sort of way, some lesser peculiarities of the captain and crew. Among others, four curious points recurred:

First, the affair of the Spanish lad assailed with a knife by the slave boy; an act winked at by Don Benito. Second, the tyranny in Don Benito's treatment of Atufal, the black; as if a child should

lead a bull of the Nile by the ring in his nose. Third, the trampling
of the sailor by the two negroes; a piece of insolence passed over
without so much as a reprimand. Fourth, the cringing submission
to their master, of all the ship's underlings, mostly blacks; as if by
the least inadvertence they feared to draw down his despotic displeasure.

Coupling these points, they seemed somewhat contradictory.
But what then, thought Captain Delano, glancing towards his
now nearing boat—what then? Why, Don Benito is a very capricious commander. But he is not the first of the sort I have seen;
though it's true he rather exceeds any other. But as a nation—continued he in his reveries—these Spaniards are all an odd set; the
very word Spaniard has a curious, conspirator, Guy-Fawkish[4] twang
to it. And yet, I dare say, Spaniards in the main are as good folks
as any in Duxbury, Massachusetts. Ah good! At last "Rover" has
come.

As, with its welcome freight, the boat touched the side, the
oakum-pickers, with venerable gestures, sought to restrain the blacks,
who, at the sight of three gurried[5] water-casks in its bottom, and a
pile of wilted pumpkins in its bow, hung over the bulwarks in
disorderly raptures.

Don Benito, with his servant, now appeared; his coming, perhaps, hastened by hearing the noise. Of him Captain Delano sought
permission to serve out the water, so that all might share alike, and
none injure themselves by unfair excess. But sensible, and, on Don
Benito's account, kind as this offer was, it was received with what
seemed impatience; as if aware that he lacked energy as a commander, Don Benito, with the true jealousy of weakness, resented
as an affront any interference. So, at least, Captain Delano inferred.

In another moment the casks were being hoisted in, when some
of the eager negroes accidentally jostled Captain Delano, where he
stood by the gangway; so that, unmindful of Don Benito, yielding
to the impulse of the moment, with good-natured authority he
bade the blacks stand back; to enforce his words making use of a
half-mirthful, half-menacing gesture. Instantly the blacks paused,
just where they were, each negro and negress suspended in his or
her posture, exactly as the word had found them—for a few seconds continuing so—while, as between the responsive posts of a
telegraph, an unknown syllable ran from man to man among the
perched oakum-pickers. While the visitor's attention was fixed by
this scene, suddenly the hatchet-polishers half rose, and a rapid
cry came from Don Benito.

4. The conspirator Guy Fawkes (1570–
1606) attempted to blow up the British House of Lords in the Gunpowder
Plot of November 5, 1605.
5. Filthy.

Thinking that at the signal of the Spaniard he was about to be massacred, Captain Delano would have sprung for his boat, but paused, as the oakum-pickers, dropping down into the crowd with earnest exclamations, forced every white and every negro back, at the same moment, with gestures friendly and familiar, almost jocose, bidding him, in substance, not be a fool. Simultaneously the hatchet-polishers resumed their seats, quietly as so many tailors, and at once, as if nothing had happened, the work of hoisting in the casks was resumed, whites and blacks singing at the tackle.

Captain Delano glanced towards Don Benito. As he saw his meagre form in the act of recovering itself from reclining in the servant's arms, into which the agitated invalid had fallen, he could not but marvel at the panic by which himself had been surprised, on the darting supposition that such a commander, who, upon a legitimate occasion, so trivial, too, as it now appeared, could lose all self-command, was, with energetic iniquity, going to bring about his murder.

The casks being on deck, Captain Delano was handed a number of jars and cups by one of the steward's aids, who, in the name of his captain, entreated him to do as he had proposed—dole out the water. He complied, with republican impartiality as to this republican element, which always seeks one level, serving the oldest white no better than the youngest black; excepting, indeed, poor Don Benito, whose condition, if not rank, demanded an extra allowance. To him, in the first place, Captain Delano presented a fair pitcher of the fluid; but, thirsting as he was for it, the Spaniard quaffed not a drop until after several grave bows and salutes. A reciprocation of courtesies which the sight-loving Africans hailed with clapping of hands.

Two of the less wilted pumpkins being reserved for the cabin table, the residue were minced up on the spot for the general regalement. But the soft bread, sugar, and bottled cider, Captain Delano would have given the whites alone, and in chief Don Benito; but the latter objected; which disinterestedness not a little pleased the American; and so mouthfuls all around were given alike to whites and blacks; excepting one bottle of cider, which Babo insisted upon setting aside for his master.

Here it may be observed that as, on the first visit of the boat, the American had not permitted his men to board the ship, neither did he now; being unwilling to add to the confusion of the decks.

Not influenced by the peculiar good-humor at present prevailing, and for the time oblivious of any but benevolent thoughts, Captain Delano, who, from recent indications, counted upon a breeze within an hour or two at furthest, dispatched the boat back to the sealer, with orders for all the hands that could be spared immediately to set about rafting casks to the watering-place and filling them. Likewise he bade word be carried to his chief officer, that if, against present expectation, the ship was not brought to anchor by sunset, he need be under no concern; for as there was to be a full moon that night, he (Captain Delano) would remain on board ready to play the pilot, come the wind soon or late.

As the two captains stood together, observing the departing boat —the servant, as it happened, having just spied a spot on his master's velvet sleeve, and silently engaged rubbing it out—the American expressed his regrets that the San Dominick had no boats; none, at least, but the unseaworthy old hulk of the long-boat, which, warped as a camel's skeleton in the desert, and almost as bleached, lay pot-wise inverted amidships, one side a little tipped, furnishing a subterraneous sort of den for family groups of the blacks, mostly women and small children; who, squatting on old mats below, or perched above in the dark dome, on the elevated seats, were described, some distance within, like a social circle of bats, sheltering in some friendly cave; at intervals, ebon flights of naked boys and girls, three or four years old, darting in and out of the den's mouth.

"Had you three or four boats now, Don Benito," said Captain Delano, "I think that, by tugging at the oars, your negroes here might help along matters some. Did you sail from port without boats, Don Benito?"

"They were stove in the gales, Señor."

"That was bad. Many men, too, you lost then. Boats and men. Those must have been hard gales, Don Benito."

"Past all speech," cringed the Spaniard.

"Tell me, Don Benito," continued his companion with increased interest, "tell me, were these gales immediately off the pitch of Cape Horn?"

"Cape Horn?—who spoke of Cape Horn?"

"Yourself did, when giving me an account of your voyage," answered Captain Delano, with almost equal astonishment at this eating of his own words, even as he ever seemed eating his own heart, on the part of the Spaniard. "You yourself, Don Benito, spoke of Cape Horn," he emphatically repeated.

The Spaniard turned, in a sort of stooping posture, pausing an instant, as one about to make a plunging exchange of elements, as from air to water.

At this moment a messenger-boy, a white, hurried by, in the regular performance of his function carrying the last expired half hour forward to the forecastle, from the cabin time-piece, to have it struck at the ship's large bell.

"Master," said the servant, discontinuing his work on the coat sleeve, and addressing the rapt Spaniard with a sort of timid apprehensiveness, as one charged with a duty, the discharge of which, it was foreseen, would prove irksome to the very person who had imposed it, and for whose benefit it was intended, "master told me never mind where he was, or how engaged, always to remind him, to a minute, when shaving-time comes. Miguel has gone to strike the half-hour afternoon. It is *now*, master. Will master go into the cuddy?"

"Ah—yes," answered the Spaniard, starting, as from dreams into realities; then turning upon Captain Delano, he said that ere long he would resume the conversation.

"Then if master means to talk more to Don Amasa," said the servant, "why not let Don Amasa sit by master in the cuddy, and master can talk, and Don Amasa can listen, while Babo here lathers and strops."

"Yes," said Captain Delano, not unpleased with this sociable plan, "yes, Don Benito, unless you had rather not, I will go with you."

"Be it so, Señor."

As the three passed aft, the American could not but think it another strange instance of his host's capriciousness, this being shaved with such uncommon punctuality in the middle of the day. But he deemed it more than likely that the servant's anxious fidelity had something to do with the matter; inasmuch as the timely interruption served to rally his master from the mood which had evidently been coming upon him.

The place called the cuddy was a light deck-cabin formed by the poop, a sort of attic to the large cabin below. Part of it had formerly been the quarters of the officers; but since their death all the partitionings had been thrown down, and the whole interior converted into one spacious and airy marine hall; for absence of fine furniture and picturesque disarray of odd appurtenances, somewhat answering to the wide, cluttered hall of some eccentric bachelor-squire in the country, who hangs his shooting-jacket and tobacco-pouch on deer antlers, and keeps his fishing-rod, tongs, and walking-stick in the same corner.

The similitude was heightened, if not originally suggested, by glimpses of the surrounding sea; since, in one aspect, the country and the ocean seem cousins-german.

The floor of the cuddy was matted. Overhead, four or five old muskets were stuck into horizontal holes along the beams. On one side was a claw-footed old table lashed to the deck; a thumbed missal on it, and over it a small, meagre crucifix attached to the bulk-head. Under the table lay a dented cutlass or two, with a hacked harpoon, among some melancholy old rigging, like a heap of poor friars' girdles. There were also two long, sharp-ribbed settees of Malacca cane, black with age, and uncomfortable to look at as inquisitors' racks,[6] with a large, misshapen arm-chair, which, furnished with a rude barber's crotch at the back, working with a screw, seemed some grotesque engine of torment. A flag locker was in one corner, open, exposing various colored bunting, some rolled up, others half unrolled, still others tumbled. Opposite was a cumbrous washstand, of black mahogany, all of one block, with a pedestal, like a font, and over it a railed shelf, containing combs, brushes, and other implements of the toilet. A torn hammock of stained grass swung near; the sheets tossed, and the pillow wrinkled up like a brow, as if whoever slept here slept but illy, with alternate visitations of sad thoughts and bad dreams.

The further extremity of the cuddy, overhanging the ship's stern, was pierced with three openings, windows or port-holes, according as men or cannon might peer, socially or unsocially, out of them. At present neither men nor cannon were seen, though huge ring-bolts and other rusty iron fixtures of the wood-work hinted of twenty-four-pounders.

Glancing towards the hammock as he entered, Captain Delano said, "You sleep here, Don Benito?"

"Yes, Señor, since we got into mild weather."

"This seems a sort of dormitory, sitting-room, sail-loft, chapel, armory, and private closet all together, Don Benito," added Captain Delano, looking round.

"Yes, Señor; events have not been favorable to much order in my arrangements."

Here the servant, napkin on arm, made a motion as if waiting his master's good pleasure. Don Benito signified his readiness, when, seating him in the Malacca arm-chair, and for the guest's convenience drawing opposite one of the settees, the servant commenced operations by throwing back his master's collar and loosening his cravat.

There is something in the negro which, in a peculiar way, fits him for avocations about one's person. Most negroes are natural valets and hair-dressers; taking to the comb and brush congenially as to the castanets, and flourishing them apparently with almost equal satisfaction. There is, too, a smooth tact about them in this employment, with a marvelous, noiseless, gliding briskness, not ungraceful in its way, singularly pleasing to behold, and still more so to be the manipulated subject of. And above all is the great gift of good-humor. Not the mere grin or laugh is here meant. Those were unsuitable. But a certain easy cheerfulness, harmonious in every glance and gesture; as though God had set the whole negro

6. Many of the incidents of the shaving scene suggest the Spanish Inquisition, in which the Dominicans played an active part.

to some pleasant tune.

When to this is added the docility arising from the unaspiring contentment of a limited mind, and that susceptibility of bland attachment sometimes inhering in indisputable inferiors, one readily perceives why those hypochondriacs, Johnson and Byron—it may be, something like the hypochondriac Benito Cereno—took to their hearts, almost to the exclusion of the entire white race, their serving men, the negroes, Barber and Fletcher. But if there be that in the negro which exempts him from the inflicted sourness of the morbid or cynical mind, how, in his most prepossessing aspects, must he appear to a benevolent one? When at ease with respect to exterior things, Captain Delano's nature was not only benign, but familiarly and humorously so. At home, he had often taken rare satisfaction in sitting in his door, watching some free man of color at his work or play. If on a voyage he chanced to have a black sailor, invariably he was on chatty and half-gamesome terms with him. In fact, like most men of a good, blithe heart, Captain Delano took to negroes, not philanthropically, but genially, just as other men to Newfoundland dogs.

Hitherto, the circumstances in which he found the San Dominick had repressed the tendency. But in the cuddy, relieved from his his former uneasiness, and, for various reasons, more sociably inclined than at any previous period of the day, and seeing the colored servant, napkin on arm, so debonair about his master, in a business so familiar as that of shaving, too, all his old weakness for negroes returned.

Among other things, he was amused with an odd instance of the African love of bright colors and fine shows, in the black's informally taking from the flag-locker a great piece of bunting of all hues, and lavishly tucking it under his master's chin for an apron.

The mode of shaving among the Spaniards is a little different from what it is with other nations. They have a basin, specifically called a barber's basin, which on one side is scooped out, so as accurately to receive the chin, against which it is closely held in lathering; which is done, not with a brush, but with soap dipped in the water of the basin and rubbed on the face.

In the present instance salt-water was used for lack of better; and the parts lathered were only the upper lip, and low down under the throat, all the rest being cultivated beard.

The preliminaries being somewhat novel to Captain Delano, he sat curiously eyeing them, so that no conversation took place, nor, for the present, did Don Benito appear disposed to renew any.

Setting down his basin, the negro searched among the razors, as for the sharpest, and having found it, gave it an additional edge by expertly strapping it on the firm, smooth, oily skin of his open palm; he then made a gesture as if to begin, but midway stood suspended for an instant, one hand elevating the razor, the other professionally dabbling among the bubbling suds on the Spaniard's lank neck. Not unaffected by the close sight of the gleaming steel, Don Benito nervously shuddered; his usual ghastliness was heightened by the lather, which lather, again, was intensified in its hue by the contrasting sootiness of the negro's body. Altogether the scene was somewhat peculiar, at least to Captain Delano, nor, as he saw the two thus postured, could he resist the vagary, that in the black he saw a headsman, and in the white a man at the block. But this was one of those antic conceits, appearing and vanishing in a breath, from which, perhaps, the best regulated mind is not always free.

Meantime the agitation of the Spaniard had a little loosened the bunting from around him, so that one broad fold swept curtain-like over the chair-arm to the floor, revealing, amid a profusion of armorial bars and ground-colors—black, blue, and yellow—a closed castle in a blood-red field diagonal with a lion rampant in a white.[7]

"The castle and the lion," exclaimed Captain Delano—"why, Don Benito, this is the flag of Spain you use here. It's well it's only I, and not the King, that sees this," he added, with a smile, "but"—turning towards the black—"it's all one, I suppose, so the colors be gay;" which playful remark did not fail somewhat to tickle the negro.

"Now, master," he said, readjusting the flag, and pressing the head gently further back into the crotch of the chair; "now, master," and the steel glanced nigh the throat.

Again Don Benito faintly shuddered.

"You must not shake so, master. See, Don Amasa, master always shakes when I shave him. And yet master knows I never yet have drawn blood, though it's true, if master will shake so, I may some of these times. Now master," he continued. "And now, Don Amasa, please go on with your talk about the gale, and all that; master can hear, and, between times, master can answer."

"Ah yes, these gales," said Captain Delano; "but the more I think of your voyage, Don Benito, the more I wonder, not at the gales, terrible as they must have been, but at the disastrous interval following them. For here, by your account, have you been these two months and more getting from Cape Horn to St. Maria, a distance which I myself, with a good wind, have sailed in a few days. True, you had calms, and long ones, but to be becalmed for two months, that is, at least, unusual. Why, Don Benito, had

7. The arms of Castile and León, which also appeared on the stern of the ship.

almost any other gentleman told me such a story, I should have been half disposed to a little incredulity."

Here an involuntary expression came over the Spaniard, similar to that just before on the deck, and whether it was the start he gave, or a sudden gawky roll of the hull in the calm, or a momentary unsteadiness of the servant's hand, however it was, just then the razor drew blood, spots of which stained the creamy lather under the throat: immediately the black barber drew back his steel, and, remaining in his professional attitude, back to Captain Delano, and face to Don Benito, held up the trickling razor, saying, with a sort of half humorous sorrow, "See, master—you shook so—here's Babo's first blood."

No sword drawn before James the First of England, no assassination in that timid King's presence, could have produced a more terrified aspect than was now presented by Don Benito.

Poor fellow, thought Captain Delano, so nervous he can't even bear the sight of barber's blood; and this unstrung, sick man, is it credible that I should have imagined he meant to spill all my blood, who can't endure the sight of one little drop of his own? Surely, Amasa Delano, you have been beside yourself this day. Tell it not when you get home, sappy Amasa. Well, well, he looks like a murderer, doesn't he? More like as if himself were to be done for. Well, well, this day's experience shall be a good lesson.

Meantime, while these things were running through the honest seaman's mind, the servant had taken the napkin from his arm, and to Don Benito had said—"But answer Don Amasa, please, master, while I wipe this ugly stuff off the razor, and strop it again."

As he said the words, his face was turned half round, so as to be alike visible to the Spaniard and the American, and seemed, by its expression, to hint, that he was desirous, by getting his master to go on with the conversation, considerately to withdraw his attention from the recent annoying accident. As if glad to snatch the offered relief, Don Benito resumed, rehearsing to Captain Delano, that not only were the calms of unusual duration, but the ship had fallen in with obstinate currents; and other things he added, some of which were but repetitions of former statements, to explain how it came to pass that the passage from Cape Horn to St. Maria had been so exceedingly long; now and then mingling with his words, incidental praises, less qualified than before, to the blacks, for their general good conduct. These particulars were not given consecutively, the servant, at convenient times, using his razor, and so, between the intervals of shaving, the story and panegyric went on with more than usual huskiness.

To Captain Delano's imagination, now again not wholly at rest, there was something so hollow in the Spaniard's manner, with apparently some reciprocal hollowness in the servant's dusky comment of silence, that the idea flashed across him, that possibly master and man, for some unknown purpose, were acting out, both in word and deed, nay, to the very tremor of Don Benito's limbs, some juggling play before him. Neither did the suspicion of collusion lack apparent support, from the fact of those whispered conferences before mentioned. But then, what could be the object of enacting this play of the barber before him? At last, regarding the notion as a whimsy, insensibly suggested, perhaps, by the theatrical aspect of Don Benito in his harlequin ensign, Captain Delano speedily banished it.

The shaving over, the servant bestirred himself with a small bottle of scented waters, pouring a few drops on the head, and then diligently rubbing; the vehemence of the exercise causing the muscles of his face to twitch rather strangely.

His next operation was with comb, scissors, and brush; going round and round, smoothing a curl here, clipping an unruly whisker-hair there, giving a graceful sweep to the temple-lock, with other impromptu touches evincing the hand of a master; while, like any resigned gentleman in barber's hands, Don Benito bore all, much less uneasily, at least, than he had done the razoring; indeed, he sat so pale and rigid now, that the negro seemed a Nubian sculptor finishing off a white statue-head.

All being over at last, the standard of Spain removed, tumbled up, and tossed back into the flag-locker, the negro's warm breath blowing away any stray hair which might have lodged down his master's neck; collar and cravat readjusted; a speck of lint whisked off the velvet lapel; all this being done; backing off a little space, and pausing with an expression of subdued self-complacency, the servant for a moment surveyed his master, as, in toilet at least, the creature of his own tasteful hands.

Captain Delano playfully complimented him upon his achievement; at the same time congratulating Don Benito.

But neither sweet waters, nor shampooing, nor fidelity, nor sociality, delighted the Spaniard. Seeing him relapsing into forbidding gloom, and still remaining seated, Captain Delano, thinking that his presence was undesired just then, withdrew, on pretense of seeing whether, as he had prophesied, any signs of a breeze were visible.

Walking forward to the main-mast, he stood awhile thinking over the scene, and not without some undefined misgivings, when he heard a noise near the cuddy, and turning, saw the negro, his hand to his cheek. Advancing, Captain Delano perceived that the cheek was bleeding. He was about to ask the cause, when the negro's wailing soliloquy enlightened him.

"Ah, when will master get better from his sickness; only the sour heart that sour sickness breeds made him serve Babo so; cutting Babo with the razor, because, only by accident, Babo had given master one little scratch; and for the first time in so many a day, too. Ah, ah, ah," holding his hand to his face.

Is it possible, thought Captain Delano; was it to wreak in private his Spanish spite against this poor friend of his, that Don Benito, by his sullen manner, impelled me to withdraw? Ah, this slavery breeds ugly passions in man.—Poor fellow!

He was about to speak in sympathy to the negro, but with a timid reluctance he now re-entered the cuddy.

Presently master and man came forth; Don Benito leaning on his servant as if nothing had happened.

But a sort of love-quarrel, after all, thought Captain Delano.

He accosted Don Benito, and they slowly walked together. They had gone but a few paces, when the steward—a tall, rajah-looking mulatto, orientally set off with a pagoda turban formed by three or four Madras handkerchiefs wound about his head, tier on tier —approaching with a salam, announced lunch in the cabin.

On their way thither, the two captains were preceded by the mulatto, who, turning round as he advanced, with continual smiles and bows, ushered them on, a display of elegance which quite completed the insignificance of the small bareheaded Babo, who, as if not unconscious of inferiority, eyed askance the graceful steward. But in part, Captain Delano imputed his jealous watchfulness to that peculiar feeling which the full-blooded African entertains for the adulterated one. As for the steward, his manner, if not bespeaking much dignity or self-respect, yet evidenced his extreme desire to please; which is doubly meritorious, as at once Christian and Chesterfieldian.[8]

Captain Delano observed with interest that while the complexion of the mulatto was hybrid, his physiognomy was European—classically so.

"Don Benito," whispered he, "I am glad to see this usher-of-the-golden-rod of yours; the sight refutes an ugly remark once made to me by a Barbadoes planter; that when a mulatto has a regular European face, look out for him; he is a devil. But see, your steward here has features more regular than King George's of England; and yet there he nods, and bows, and smiles; a king, indeed —the king of kind hearts and polite fellows. What a pleasant voice he has, too?"

"He has, Señor."

"But tell me, has he not, so far as you have known him, always

8. Urbane, an adjective derived from Lord Chesterfield (1694–1773) whose *Letters* to his son gave instruction in polite worldliness.

proved a good, worthy fellow?" said Captain Delano, pausing, while with a final genuflexion the steward disappeared into the cabin; "come, for the reason just mentioned, I am curious to know."

"Francesco is a good man," somewhat sluggishly responded Don Benito, like a phlegmatic appreciator, who would neither find fault nor flatter.

"Ah, I thought so. For it were strange, indeed, and not very creditable to us white-skins, if a little of our blood mixed with the African's, should, far from improving the latter's quality, have the sad effect of pouring vitriolic acid into black broth; improving the hue, perhaps, but not the wholesomeness."

"Doubtless, doubtless, Señor, but"—glancing at Babo—"not to speak of negroes, your planter's remark I have heard applied to the Spanish and Indian intermixtures in our provinces. But I know nothing about the matter," he listlessly added.

And here they entered the cabin.

The lunch was a frugal one. Some of Captain Delano's fresh fish and pumpkins, biscuit and salt beef, the reserved bottle of cider, and the San Dominick's last bottle of Canary.

As they entered, Francesco, with two or three colored aids, was hovering over the table giving the last adjustments. Upon perceiving their master they withdrew, Francesco making a smiling congé, and the Spaniard, without condescending to notice it, fastidiously remarking to his companion that he relished not superfluous attendance.

Without companions, host and guest sat down, like a childless married couple, at opposite ends of the table, Don Benito waving Captain Delano to his place, and, weak as he was, insisting upon that gentleman being seated before himself.

The negro placed a rug under Don Benito's feet, and a cushion behind his back, and then stood behind, not his master's chair, but Captain Delano's. At first, this a little surprised the latter. But it was soon evident that, in taking his position, the black was still true to his master; since by facing him he could the more readily anticipate his slightest want.

"This is an uncommonly intelligent fellow of yours, Don Benito," whispered Captain Delano across the table.

"You say true, Señor."

During the repast, the guest again reverted to parts of Don Benito's story, begging further particulars here and there. He inquired how it was that the scurvy and fever should have committed such wholesale havoc upon the whites, while destroying less than half of the blacks. As if this question reproduced the whole scene of plague before the Spaniard's eyes, miserably reminding him of his solitude in a cabin where before he had had so many friends and officers round him, his hand shook, his face became hueless, broken words escaped; but directly the sane memory of the past seemed replaced by insane terrors of the present. With starting eyes he stared before him at vacancy. For nothing was to be seen but the hand of his servant pushing the Canary over towards him. At length a few sips served partially to restore him. He made random reference to the different constitution of races, enabling one to offer more resistance to certain maladies than another. The thought was new to his companion.

Presently Captain Delano, intending to say something to his host concerning the pecuniary part of the business he had undertaken for him, especially—since he was strictly accountable to his owners—with reference to the new suit of sails, and other things of that sort; and naturally preferring to conduct such affairs in private, was desirous that the servant should withdraw; imagining that Don Benito for a few minutes could dispense with his attendance. He, however, waited awhile; thinking that, as the conversation proceeded, Don Benito, without being prompted, would perceive the propriety of the step.

But it was otherwise. At last catching his host's eye, Captain Delano, with a slight backward gesture of his thumb, whispered, "Don Benito, pardon me, but there is an interference with the full expression of what I have to say to you."

Upon this the Spaniard changed countenance; which was imputed to his resenting the hint, as in some way a reflection upon his servant. After a moment's pause, he assured his guest that the black's remaining with them could be of no disservice; because since losing his officers he had made Babo (whose original office, it now appeared, had been captain of the slaves) not only his constant attendant and companion, but in all things his confidant.

After this, nothing more could be said; though, indeed, Captain Delano could hardly avoid some little tinge of irritation upon being left ungratified in so inconsiderable a wish, by one, too, for whom he intended such solid services. But it is only his querulousness, thought he; and so filling his glass he proceeded to business.

The price of the sails and other matters was fixed upon. But while this was being done, the American observed that, though his original offer of assistance had been hailed with hectic animation, yet now when it was reduced to a business transaction, indifference and apathy were betrayed. Don Benito, in fact, appeared to submit to hearing the details more out of regard to common propriety, than from any impression that weighty benefit to himself and his voyage was involved.

Soon, his manner became still more reserved. The effort was vain to seek to draw him into social talk. Gnawed by his splenetic mood, he sat twitching his beard, while to little purpose the hand of his servant, mute as that on the wall, slowly pushed over the Canary.

Lunch being over, they sat down on the cushioned transom; the servant placing a pillow behind his master. The long continuance of the calm had now affected the atmosphere. Don Benito sighed heavily, as if for breath.

"Why not adjourn to the cuddy," said Captain Delano; "there is more air there." But the host sat silent and motionless.

Meantime his servant knelt before him, with a large fan of feathers. And Francesco coming in on tiptoes, handed the negro a little cup of aromatic waters, with which at intervals he chafed his master's brow; smoothing the hair along the temples as a nurse does a child's. He spoke no word. He only rested his eye on his master's, as if, amid all Don Benito's distress, a little to refresh his spirit by the silent sight of fidelity.

Presently the ship's bell sounded two o'clock; and through the cabin windows a slight rippling of the sea was discerned; and from the desired direction.

"There," exclaimed Captain Delano, "I told you so, Don Benito, look!"

He had risen to his feet, speaking in a very animated tone, with a view the more to rouse his companion. But though the crimson curtain of the stern-window near him that moment fluttered against his pale cheek, Don Benito seemed to have even less welcome for the breeze than the calm.

Poor fellow, thought Captain Delano, bitter experience has taught him that one ripple does not make a wind, any more than one swallow a summer. But he is mistaken for once. I will get his ship in for him, and prove it.

Briefly alluding to his weak condition, he urged his host to remain quietly where he was, since he (Captain Delano) would with pleasure take upon himself the responsibility of making the best use of the wind.

Upon gaining the deck, Captain Delano started at the unexpected figure of Atufal, monumentally fixed at the threshold, like one of those sculptured porters of black marble guarding the porches of Egyptian tombs.

But this time the start was, perhaps, purely physical. Atufal's presence, singularly attesting docility even in sullenness, was contrasted with that of the hatchet-polishers, who in patience evinced their industry; while both spectacles showed, that lax as Don Benito's general authority might be, still, whenever he chose to exert it, no man so savage or colossal but must, more or less, bow.

Snatching a trumpet which hung from the bulwarks, with a free step Captain Delano advanced to the forward edge of the poop, issuing his orders in his best Spanish. The few sailors and many negroes, all equally pleased, obediently set about heading the ship towards the harbor.

While giving some directions about setting a lower stu'n'-sail, suddenly Captain Delano heard a voice faithfully repeating his orders. Turning, he saw Babo, now for the time acting, under the pilot, his original part of captain of the slaves. This assistance proved valuable. Tattered sails and warped yards were soon brought into some trim. And no brace or halyard was pulled but to the blithe songs of the inspirited negroes.

Good fellows, thought Captain Delano, a little training would make fine sailors of them. Why see, the very women pull and sing too. These must be some of those Ashantee negresses that make such capital soldiers, I've heard. But who's at the helm. I must have a good hand there.

He went to see.

The San Dominick steered with a cumbrous tiller, with large horizontal pullies attached. At each pulley-end stood a subordinate black, and between them, at the tiller-head, the responsible post, a Spanish seaman, whose countenance evinced his due share in the general hopefulness and confidence at the coming of the breeze.

He proved the same man who had behaved with so shamefaced an air on the windlass.

"Ah,—it is you, my man," exclaimed Captain Delano—"well, no more sheep's-eyes now;—look straight forward and keep the ship so. Good hand, I trust? And want to get into the harbor, don't you?"

The man assented with an inward chuckle, grasping the tiller-head firmly. Upon this, unperceived by the American, the two blacks eyed the sailor intently.

Finding all right at the helm, the pilot went forward to the forecastle, to see how matters stood there.

The ship now had way enough to breast the current. With the approach of evening, the breeze would be sure to freshen.

Having done all that was needed for the present, Captain Delano, giving his last orders to the sailors, turned aft to report affairs to Don Benito in the cabin; perhaps additionally incited to rejoin him by the hope of snatching a moment's private chat while the servant was engaged upon deck.

From opposite sides, there were, beneath the poop, two approaches to the cabin; one further forward than the other, and consequently communicating with a longer passage. Marking the servant still above, Captain Delano, taking the nighest entrance— the one last named, and at whose porch Atufal still stood—hurried on his way, till, arrived at the cabin threshold, he paused an instant, a little to recover from his eagerness. Then, with the words of his intended business upon his lips, he entered. As he advanced toward the seated Spaniard, he heard another footstep, keeping time with his. From the opposite door, a salver in hand, the servant was likewise advancing.

"Confound the faithful fellow," thought Captain Delano; "what a vexatious coincidence."

Possibly, the vexation might have been something different, were it not for the brisk confidence inspired by the breeze. But even as it was, he felt a slight twinge, from a sudden indefinite association in his mind of Babo with Atufal.

"Don Benito," said he, "I give you joy; the breeze will hold, and will increase. By the way, your tall man and time-piece, Atufal, stands without. By your order, of course?"

Don Benito recoiled, as if at some bland satirical touch, delivered with such adroit garnish of apparent good breeding as to present no handle for retort.

He is like one flayed alive, thought Captain Delano; where may one touch him without causing a shrink?

The servant moved before his master, adjusting a cushion; recalled to civility, the Spaniard stiffly replied: "You are right. The slave appears where you saw him, according to my command; which is, that if at the given hour I am below, he must take his stand and abide my coming."

"Ah now, pardon me, but that is treating the poor fellow like an ex-king indeed. Ah, Don Benito," smiling, "for all the license you permit in some things, I fear lest, at bottom, you are a bitter hard master."

Again Don Benito shrank; and this time, as the good sailor thought, from a genuine twinge of his conscience.

Again conversation became constrained. In vain Captain Delano called attention to the now perceptible motion of the keel gently cleaving the sea; with lack-lustre eye, Don Benito returned words few and reserved.

By-and-by, the wind having steadily risen, and still blowing right into the harbor, bore the San Dominick swiftly on. Rounding a point of land, the sealer at distance came into open view.

Meantime Captain Delano had again repaired to the deck, remaining there sometime. Having at last altered the ship's course, so as to give the reef a wide berth, he returned for a few moments below.

I will cheer up my poor friend, this time, thought he.

"Better and better, Don Benito," he cried as he blithely re-entered: "there will soon be an end to your cares, at least for awhile.

For when, after a long, sad voyage, you know, the anchor drops into the haven, all its vast weight seems lifted from the captain's heart. We are getting on famously, Don Benito. My ship is in sight. Look through this side-light here; there she is; all a-taunt-o! The Bachelor's Delight, my good friend. Ah, how this wind braces one up. Come, you must take a cup of coffee with me this evening. My old steward will give you as fine a cup as ever any sultan tasted. What say you, Don Benito, will you?"

At first, the Spaniard glanced feverishly up, casting a longing look towards the sealer, while with mute concern his servant gazed into his face. Suddenly the old ague of coldness returned, and dropping back to his cushions he was silent.

"You do not answer. Come, all day you have been my host; would you have hospitality all on one side?"

"I cannot go," was the response.

"What? it will not fatigue you. The ships will lie together as near as they can, without swinging foul. It will be little more than stepping from deck to deck; which is but as from room to room. Come, come, you must not refuse me."

"I cannot go," decisively and repulsively repeated Don Benito.

Renouncing all but the last appearance of courtesy, with a sort of cadaverous sullenness, and biting his thin nails to the quick, he glanced, almost glared, at his guest, as if impatient that a stranger's presence should interfere with the full indulgence of his morbid hour. Meantime the sound of the parted waters came more and more gurglingly and merrily in at the windows; as reproaching him for his dark spleen; as telling him that, sulk as he might, and go mad with it, nature cared not a jot; since, whose fault was it, pray?

But the foul mood was now at its depth, as the fair wind at its height.

There was something in the man so far beyond any mere unsociality or sourness previously evinced, that even the forbearing good-nature of his guest could no longer endure it. Wholly at a loss to account for such demeanor, and deeming sickness with eccentricity, however extreme, no adequate excuse, well satisfied, too, that nothing in his own conduct could justify it, Captain Delano's pride began to be roused. Himself became reserved. But all seemed one to the Spaniard. Quitting him, therefore, Captain Delano once more went to the deck.

The ship was now within less than two miles of the sealer. The whale-boat was seen darting over the interval.

To be brief, the two vessels, thanks to the pilot's skill, ere long in neighborly style lay anchored together.

Before returning to his own vessel, Captain Delano had intended communicating to Don Benito the smaller details of the proposed services to be rendered. But, as it was, unwilling anew to subject himself to rebuffs, he resolved, now that he had seen the San Dominick safely moored, immediately to quit her, without further allusion to hospitality or business. Indefinitely postponing his ulterior plans, he would regulate his future actions according to future circumstances. His boat was ready to receive him; but his host still tarried below. Well, thought Captain Delano, if he has little breeding, the more need to show mine. He descended to the cabin to bid a ceremonious, and, it may be, tacitly rebukeful adieu. But to his great satisfaction, Don Benito, as if he began to feel the weight of that treatment with which his slighted guest had, not indecorously, retaliated upon him, now supported by his servant, rose to his feet, and grasping Captain Delano's hand, stood tremulous; too much agitated to speak. But the good augury hence drawn was suddenly dashed, by his resuming all his previous reserve, with augmented gloom, as, with half-averted eyes, he silently reseated himself on his cushions. With a corresponding return of his own chilled feelings, Captain Delano bowed and withdrew.

He was hardly midway in the narrow corridor, dim as a tunnel, leading from the cabin to the stairs, when a sound, as of the tolling for execution in some jail-yard, fell on his ears. It was the echo of the ship's flawed bell, striking the hour, drearily reverberated in this subterranean vault. Instantly, by a fatality not to be withstood, his mind, responsive to the portent, swarmed with superstitious suspicions. He paused. In images far swifter than these sentences, the minutest details of all his former distrusts swept through him.

Hitherto, credulous good-nature had been too ready to furnish excuses for reasonable fears. Why was the Spaniard, so superfluously punctilious at times, now heedless of common propriety in not accompanying to the side his departing guest? Did indisposition forbid? Indisposition had not forbidden more irksome exertion that day. His last equivocal demeanor recurred. He had risen to his feet, grasped his guest's hand, motioned toward his hat; then, in an instant, all was eclipsed in sinister muteness and gloom. Did this imply one brief, repentant relenting at the final moment, from some iniquitous plot, followed by remorseless return to it? His last glance seemed to express a calamitous, yet acquiescent farewell to Captain Delano forever. Why decline the invitation to visit the sealer that evening? Or was the Spaniard less hardened than the Jew,[9] who refrained not from supping at the board of him whom the same night he meant to betray? What

9. I.e., Judas Iscariot, who betrayed Jesus (Matthew xxvi).

imported all those day-long enigmas and contradictions, except they were intended to mystify, preliminary to some stealthy blow? Atufal, the pretended rebel, but punctual shadow, that moment lurked by the threshold without. He seemed a sentry, and more. Who, by his own confession, had stationed him there? Was the negro now lying in wait?

The Spaniard behind—his creature before: to rush from darkness to light was the involuntary choice.

The next moment, with clenched jaw and hand, he passed Atufal, and stood unharmed in the light. As he saw his trim ship lying peacefully at anchor, and almost within ordinary call; as he saw his household boat, with familiar faces in it, patiently rising and falling on the short waves by the San Dominick's side; and then, glancing about the decks where he stood, saw the oakum-pickers still gravely plying their fingers; and heard the low, buzzing whistle and industrious hum of the hatchet-polishers, still bestirring themselves over their endless occupation; and more than all, as he saw the benign aspect of nature, taking her innocent repose in the evening; the screened sun in the quiet camp of the west shining out like the mild light from Abraham's tent; as charmed eye and ear took in all these, with the chained figure of the black, clenched jaw and hand relaxed. Once again he smiled at the phantoms which had mocked him, and felt something like a tinge of remorse, that, by harboring them even for a moment, he should, by implication, have betrayed an atheist doubt of the ever-watchful Providence above.

There was a few minutes' delay, while, in obedience to his orders, the boat was being hooked along to the gangway. During this interval, a sort of saddened satisfaction stole over Captain Delano, at thinking of the kindly offices he had that day discharged for a stranger. Ah, thought he, after good actions one's conscience is never ungrateful, however much so the benefited party may be.

Presently, his foot, in the first act of descent into the boat, pressed the first round of the side-ladder, his face presented inward upon the deck. In the same moment, he heard his name courteously sounded; and, to his pleased surprise, saw Don Benito advancing —an unwonted energy in his air, as if, at the last moment, intent upon making amends for his recent discourtesy. With instinctive good feeling, Captain Delano, withdrawing his foot, turned and reciprocally advanced. As he did so, the Spaniard's nervous eagerness increased, but his vital energy failed; so that, the better to support him, the servant, placing his master's hand on his naked shoulder, and gently holding it there, formed himself into a sort of crutch.

When the two captains met, the Spaniard again fervently took the hand of the American, at the same time casting an earnest glance into his eyes, but, as before, too much overcome to speak. *I have done him wrong,* self-reproachfully thought Captain Delano; *his apparent coldness has deceived me; in no instance has he meant to offend.*

Meantime, as if fearful that the continuance of the scene might too much unstring his master, the servant seemed anxious to terminate it. And so, still presenting himself as a crutch, and walking between the two captains, he advanced with them towards the gangway; while still, as if full of kindly contrition, Don Benito would not let go the hand of Captain Delano, but retained it in his, across the black's body.

Soon they were standing by the side, looking over into the boat, whose crew turned up their curious eyes. Waiting a moment for the Spaniard to relinquish his hold, the now embarrassed Captain Delano lifted his foot, to overstep the threshold of the open gangway; but still Don Benito would not let go his hand. And yet, with an agitated tone, he said, "I can go no further; here I must bid you adieu. Adieu, my dear, dear Don Amasa. Go—go!" suddenly tearing his hand loose, "go, and God guard you better than me, my best friend."

Not unaffected, Captain Delano would now have lingered; but catching the meekly admonitory eye of the servant, with a hasty farewell he descended into his boat, followed by the continual adieus of Don Benito, standing rooted in the gangway.

Seating himself in the stern, Captain Delano, making a last salute, ordered the boat shoved off. The crew had their oars on end. The bowsmen pushed the boat a sufficient distance for the oars to be lengthwise dropped. The instant that was done, Don Benito sprang over the bulwarks, falling at the feet of Captain Delano; at the same time calling towards his ship, but in tones so frenzied, that none in the boat could understand him. But, as if not equally obtuse, three sailors, from three different and distant parts of the ship, splashed into the sea, swimming after their captain, as if intent upon his rescue.

The dismayed officer of the boat eagerly asked what this meant. To which, Captain Delano, turning a disdainful smile upon the unaccountable Spaniard, answered that, for his part, he neither knew nor cared; but it seemed as if Don Benito had taken it into his head to produce the impression among his people that the boat wanted to kidnap him. "Or else—give way for your lives," he wildly added, starting at a clattering hubbub in the ship, above which rang the tocsin of the hatchet-polishers; and seizing Don Benito by the throat he added, "this plotting pirate means murder!" Here, in apparent verification of the words, the servant, a dagger in

his hand, was seen on the rail overhead, poised, in the act of leaping, as if with desperate fidelity to befriend his master to the last;
while, seemingly to aid the black, the three white sailors were trying to clamber into the hampered bow. Meantime, the whole host
of negroes, as if inflamed at the sight of their jeopardized captain,
impended in one sooty avalanche over the bulwarks.

All this, with what preceded, and what followed, occurred with
such involutions of rapidity, that past, present, and future seemed
one.

Seeing the negro coming, Captain Delano had flung the Spaniard
aside, almost in the very act of clutching him, and, by the unconscious recoil, shifting his place, with arms thrown up, so promptly
grappled the servant in his descent, that with dagger presented at
Captain Delano's heart, the black seemed of purpose to have
leaped there as to his mark. But the weapon was wrenched away,
and the assailant dashed down into the bottom of the boat, which
now, with disentangled oars, began to speed through the sea.

At this juncture, the left hand of Captain Delano, on one side,
again clutched the half-reclined Don Benito, heedless that he was
in a speechless faint, while his right foot, on the other side, ground
the prostrate negro; and his right arm pressed for added speed on
the after oar, his eye bent forward, encouraging his men to their
utmost.

But here, the officer of the boat, who had at last succeeded in
beating off the towing sailors, and was now, with face turned aft,
assisting the bowsman at his oar, suddenly called to Captain Delano, to see what the black was about; while a Portuguese oarsman
shouted to him to give heed to what the Spaniard was saying.

Glancing down at his feet, Captain Delano saw the freed hand
of the servant aiming with a second dagger—a small one, before
concealed in his wool—with this he was snakishly writhing up
from the boat's bottom, at the heart of his master, his countenance
lividly vindictive, expressing the centred purpose of his soul; while
the Spaniard, half-choked, was vainly shrinking way, with husky
words, incoherent to all but the Portuguese.

That moment, across the long-benighted mind of Captain Delano, a flash of revelation swept, illuminating, in unanticipated
clearness, his host's whole mysterious demeanor, with every enigmatic event of the day, as well as the entire past voyage of the San
Dominick. He smote Babo's hand down, but his own heart smote
him harder. With infinite pity he withdrew his hold from Don
Benito. Not Captain Delano, but Don Benito, the black, in leaping into the boat, had intended to stab.

Both the black's hands were held, as, glancing up towards the
San Dominick, Captain Delano, now with scales dropped from his

eyes, saw the negroes, not in misrule, not in tumult, not as if frantically concerned for Don Benito, but with mask torn away, flourishing hatchets and knives, in ferocious piratical revolt. Like delirious black dervishes, the six Ashantees danced on the poop. Prevented by their foes from springing into the water, the Spanish boys were hurrying up to the topmost spars, while such of the few Spanish sailors, not already in the sea, less alert, were described, helplessly mixed in, on deck, with the blacks.

Meantime Captain Delano hailed his own vessel, ordering the ports up, and the guns run out. But by this time the cable of the San Dominick had been cut; and the fag-end, in lashing out, whipped away the canvas shroud about the beak, suddenly revealing, as the bleached hull swung round towards the open ocean, death for the figure-head, in a human skeleton; chalky comment on the chalked words below, *"Follow your leader."*

At the sight, Don Benito, covering his face, wailed out: " 'Tis he, Aranda! my murdered, unburied friend!"

Upon reaching the sealer, calling for ropes, Captain Delano bound the negro, who made no resistance, and had him hoisted to the deck. He would then have assisted the now almost helpless Don Benito up the side; but Don Benito, wan as he was, refused to move, or be moved, until the negro should have been first put below out of view. When, presently assured that it was done, he no more shrank from the ascent.

The boat was immediately dispatched back to pick up the three swimming sailors. Meantime, the guns were in readiness, though, owing to the San Dominick having glided somewhat astern of the sealer, only the aftermost one could be brought to bear. With this, they fired six times; thinking to cripple the fugitive ship by bringing down her spars. But only a few inconsiderable ropes were shot away. Soon the ship was beyond the gun's range, steering broad out of the bay; the blacks thickly clustering round the bowsprit, one moment with taunting cries towards the whites, the next with upthrown gestures hailing the now dusky moors of ocean— cawing crows escaped from the hand of the fowler.

The first impulse was to slip the cables and give chase. But, upon second thoughts, to pursue with whale-boat and yawl seemed more promising.

Upon inquiring of Don Benito what fire-arms they had on board the San Dominick, Captain Delano was answered that they had none that could be used; because, in the earlier stages of the mutiny, a cabin-passenger, since dead, had secretly put out of order the locks of what few muskets there were. But with all his remaining strength, Don Benito entreated the American not to give chase, either with ship or boat; for the negroes had already proved themselves such desperadoes, that, in case of a present assault, nothing but a total massacre of the whites could be looked for. But, regarding this warning as coming from one whose spirit had been crushed by misery the American did not give up his design.

The boats were got ready and armed. Captain Delano ordered his men into them. He was going himself when Don Benito grasped his arm.

"What! have you saved my life, Señor, and are you now going to throw away your own?"

The officers also, for reasons connected with their interests and those of the voyage, and a duty owing to the owners, strongly objected against their commander's going. Weighing their remonstrances a moment, Captain Delano felt bound to remain; appointing his chief mate—an athletic and resolute man, who had been a privateer's-man—to head the party. The more to encourage the sailors, they were told, that the Spanish captain considered his ship good as lost; that she and her cargo, including some gold and silver, were worth more than a thousand dubloons. Take her, and no small part should be theirs. The sailors replied with a shout.

The fugitives had now almost gained an offing. It was nearly night; but the moon was rising. After hard, prolonged pulling, the boats came up on the ship's quarters, at a suitable distance laying upon their oars to discharge their muskets. Having no bullets to return, the negroes sent their yells. But, upon the second volley, Indian-like, they hurtled their hatchets. One took off a sailor's fingers. Another struck the whale-boat's bow, cutting off the rope there, and remaining stuck in the gunwale like a woodman's axe. Snatching it, quivering from its lodgment, the mate hurled it back. The returned gauntlet now stuck in the ship's broken quarter-gallery, and so remained.

The negroes giving too hot a reception, the whites kept a more respectful distance. Hovering now just out of reach of the hurtling hatchets, they, with a view to the close encounter which must soon come, sought to decoy the blacks into entirely disarming themselves of their most murderous weapons in a hand-to-hand fight, by foolishly flinging them, as missiles, short of the mark, into the sea. But, ere long, perceiving the stratagem, the negroes desisted, though not before many of them had to replace their lost hatchets with handspikes; an exchange which, as counted upon, proved, in the end, favorable to the assailants.

Meantime, with a strong wind, the ship still clove the water; the boats alternately falling behind, and pulling up, to discharge fresh volleys.

The fire was mostly directed towards the stern, since there, chiefly, the negroes, at present, were clustering. But to kill or maim the negroes was not the object. To take them, with the ship, was the object. To do it, the ship must be boarded; which could not be done by boats while she was sailing so fast.

A thought now struck the mate. Observing the Spanish boys still aloft, high as they could get, he called to them to descend to the yards, and cut adrift the sails. It was done. About this time, owing to causes hereafter to be shown, two Spaniards, in the dress of sailors, and conspicuously showing themselves, were killed; not by volleys, but by deliberate marksman's shots; while, as it afterwards appeared, by one of the general discharges, Atufal, the black, and the Spaniard at the helm likewise were killed. What now, with the loss of the sails, and loss of leaders, the ship became unmanageable to the negroes.

With creaking masts, she came heavily round to the wind; the prow slowly swinging into view of the boats, its skeleton gleaming in the horizontal moonlight, and casting a gigantic ribbed shadow upon the water. One extended arm of the ghost seemed beckoning the whites to avenge it.

"Follow your leader!" cried the mate; and, one on each bow, the boats boarded. Sealing-spears and cutlasses crossed hatchets and hand-spikes. Huddled upon the long-boat amidships, the negresses raised a wailing chant, whose chorus was the clash of the steel.

For a time, the attack wavered; the negroes wedging themselves to beat it back; the half-repelled sailors, as yet unable to gain a footing, fighting as troopers in the saddle, one leg sideways flung over the bulwarks, and one without, plying their cutlasses like carters' whips. But in vain. They were almost overborne, when, rallying themselves into a squad as one man, with a huzza, they sprang inboard, where, entangled, they involuntarily separated again. For a few breaths' space, there was a vague, muffled, inner sound, as of submerged sword-fish rushing hither and thither through shoals of black-fish. Soon, in a reunited band, and joined by the Spanish seamen, the whites came to the surface, irresistibly driving the negroes toward the stern. But a barricade of casks and sacks, from side to side, had been thrown up by the mainmast. Here the negroes faced about, and though scorning peace or truce, yet fain would have had respite. But, without pause, overleaping the barrier, the unflagging sailors again closed. Exhausted, the blacks now fought in despair. Their red tongues lolled, wolf-like, from their black mouths. But the pale sailors' teeth were set; not a word was spoken; and, in five minutes more, the ship was won.

Nearly a score of the negroes were killed. Exclusive of those by the balls, many were mangled; their wounds—mostly inflicted by the long-edged sealing-spears, resembling those shaven ones of the

English at Preston Pans,[1] made by the poled scythes of the High-landers. On the other side, none were killed, though several were wounded; some severely, including the mate. The surviving negroes were temporarily secured, and the ship, towed back into the harbor at midnight, once more lay anchored.

Omitting the incidents and arrangements ensuing, suffice it that, after two days spent in refitting, the ships sailed in company for Conception, in Chili, and thence for Lima, in Peru; where, before the vice-regal courts, the whole affair, from the beginning, under-went investigation.

Though, midway on the passage, the ill-fated Spaniard, relaxed from constraint, showed some signs of regaining health with free-will; yet, agreeably to his own foreboding, shortly before arriving at Lima, he relapsed, finally becoming so reduced as to be carried ashore in arms. Hearing of his story and plight, one of the many religious institutions of the City of Kings opened an hospitable refuge to him, where both physician and priest were his nurses, and a member of the order volunteered to be his one special guardian and consoler, by night and by day.

The following extracts, translated from one of the official Span-ish documents, will, it is hoped, shed light on the preceding narra-tive, as well as, in the first place, reveal the true port of departure and true history of the San Dominick's voyage, down to the time of her touching at the island of St. Maria.

But, ere the extracts come, it may be well to preface them with a remark.

The document selected, from among many others, for partial translation, contains the deposition of Benito Cereno; the first taken in the case. Some disclosures therein were, at the time, held dubious for both learned and natural reasons. The tribunal in-clined to the opinion that the deponent, not undisturbed in his mind by recent events, raved of some things which could never have happened. But subsequent depositions of the surviving sailors, bearing out the revelations of their captain in several of the strang-est particulars, gave credence to the rest. So that the tribunal, in its final decision, rested its capital sentences upon statements which, had they lacked confirmation, it would have deemed it but duty to reject.

———————

I, Don Jose de Abos and Padilla, His Majesty's Notary for the Royal Revenue, and Register of this Province, and Notary Public of the Holy Crusade of this Bishopric, etc.

Do certify and declare, as much as is requisite in law, that, in the criminal cause commenced the twenty-fourth of the month of

———

1. The battle of Prestonpans was fought in 1745.

September, in the year seventeen hundred and ninety-nine, against the negroes of the ship San Dominick, the following declaration before me was made:

Declaration of the first witness, DON BENITO CERENO.

The same day, and month, and year, His Honor, Doctor Juan Martinez de Rozas, Councilor of the Royal Audience of this Kingdom, and learned in the law of this Intendency, ordered the captain of the ship San Dominick, Don Benito Cereno, to appear; which he did in his litter, attended by the monk Infelez; of whom he received the oath, which he took by God, our Lord, and a sign of the Cross; under which he promised to tell the truth of whatever he should know and should be asked;—and being interrogated agreeably to the tenor of the act commencing the process, he said, that on the twentieth of May last, he set sail with his ship from the port of Valparaiso, bound to that of Callao; loaded with the produce of the country beside thirty cases of hardware and one hundred and sixty blacks, of both sexes, mostly belonging to Don Alexandro Aranda, gentleman, of the city of Mendoza; that the crew of the ship consisted of thirty-six men, beside the persons who went as passengers; that the negroes were in part as follows:

[Here, in the original, follows a list of some fifty names, descriptions, and ages, compiled from certain recovered documents of Aranda's, and also from recollections of the deponent, from which portions only are extracted.]

—One, from about eighteen to nineteen years, named José, and this was the man that waited upon his master, Don Alexandro, and who speaks well the Spanish, having served him four or five years; . . . a mulatto, named Francesco, the cabin steward, of a good person and voice, having sung in the Valparaiso churches, native of the province of Buenos Ayres, aged about thirty-five years. . . . A smart negro, named Dago, who had been for many years a grave-digger among the Spaniards, aged forty-six years. . . . Four old negroes, born in Africa, from sixty to seventy, but sound, calkers by trade, whose names are as follows:—the first was named Muri, and he was killed (as was also his son named Diamelo); the second, Nacta; the third, Yola, likewise killed; the fourth, Ghofan; and six full-grown negroes, aged from thirty to forty-five, all raw, and born among the Ashantees—Matiluqui, Yan, Lecbe, Mapenda, Yambaio, Akim; four of whom were killed; . . . a powerful negro named Atufal, who being supposed to have been a chief in Africa, his owner set great store by him. . . . And a small negro of Senegal, but some years among the Spaniards, aged about thirty, which negro's name was Babo; . . . that he does not remember the names of the others, but that still expecting the residue of Don Alexandro's papers will be found, will then take due account of them all, and remit to the court; . . . and thirty-nine women and children of all ages.

[*The catalogue over, the deposition goes on.*]

. . . That all the negroes slept upon deck, as is customary in this navigation, and none wore fetters, because the owner, his friend Aranda, told him that they were all tractable; . . . that on the seventh day after leaving port, at three o'clock in the morning, all the Spaniards being asleep except the two officers on the watch, who were the boatswain, Juan Robles, and the carpenter, Juan Bautista Gayete, and the helmsman and his boy, the negroes revolted suddenly, wounded dangerously the boatswain and the carpenter, and successively killed eighteen men of those who were sleeping upon deck, some with handspikes and hatchets, and others by throwing them alive overboard, after tying them; that of the Spaniards upon deck, they left about seven, as he thinks, alive and tied, to manoeuvre the ship, and three or four more, who hid themselves, remained also alive. Although in the act of revolt the negroes made themselves masters of the hatchway, six or seven wounded went through it to the cockpit, without any hindrance on their part; that during the act of revolt, the mate and another person, whose name he does not recollect, attempted to come up through the hatchway, but being quickly wounded, were obliged to return to the cabin; that the deponent resolved at break of day to come up the companion-way, where the negro Babo was, being the ringleader, and Atufal, who assisted him, and having spoken to them, exhorted them to cease committing such atrocities, asking them, at the same time, what they wanted and intended to do, offering, himself, to obey their commands; that notwithstanding this, they threw, in his presence, three men, alive and tied, overboard; that they told the deponent to come up, and that they would not kill him; which having done, the negro Babo asked him whether there were in those seas any negro countries where they might be carried, and he answered them, No; that the negro Babo afterwards told him to carry them to Senegal, or to the neighboring islands of St. Nicholas; and he answered, that this was impossible, on account of the great distance, the necessity involved of rounding Cape Horn, the bad condition of the vessel, the want of provisions, sails, and water; but that the negro Babo replied to him he must carry them in any way; that they would do and conform themselves to everything the deponent should require as to eating and drinking; that after a long conference, being absolutely compelled to please them, for they threatened to kill all the whites if they were not, at all events, carried to Senegal, he told them that what was most wanting for the voyage was water; that they would go near the coast to take it, and thence they would proceed on their course; that the negro Babo agreed to it; and the deponent steered towards the intermediate ports, hoping to meet some Spanish or foreign vessel that would save them; that within ten or eleven days they saw the land, and continued their course by it in the vicinity of Nasca; that the deponent observed that the negroes were now restless and mutinous, because he did not effect the taking in of water, the negro Babo having required, with threats, that it should be done, without fail, the following day; he told him he saw plainly that the coast was steep, and the rivers designated in the maps were not to be found, with other reasons suitable to the circumstances; that the best way would be to go to the island of Santa Maria, where they might water easily, it being a solitary island, as the foreigners did; that the deponent did not go to Pisco, that was near, nor make any other port of the coast, because the negro Babo had intimated to him several times, that he would kill all the whites the very moment he should perceive any city, town, or settlement of any kind on the shores to which they should be carried: that having determined to go to the island of Santa Maria, as the deponent had planned, for the purpose of trying whether, on the passage or near the island itself, they could find any vessel that should favor them, or whether he could escape from it in a boat to the neighboring coast of Arruco, to adopt the necessary means he immediately changed his course, steering for the island; that the negroes Babo and Atufal held daily conferences, in which they discussed what was necessary for their design of returning to Senegal, whether they were to kill all the Spaniards, and particularly the deponent; that eight days after parting from the coast of Nasca, the deponent being on the watch a little after daybreak, and soon after the negroes had their meeting, the negro Babo came to the place where the depondent was, and told him that he had determined to kill his master, Don Alexandro Aranda, both because he and his companions could not otherwise be sure of their liberty, and that to keep the seamen in subjection, he wanted to prepare a warning of what road they should be made to take did they or any of them oppose him; and that, by means of the death of Don Alexandro, that warning would best be given; but, that what this last meant, the deponent did not at the time comprehend, nor could not, further than that the death of Don Alexandro was intended; and moreover the negro Babo proposed to the deponent to call the mate Raneds, who was sleeping in the cabin, before the thing was done, for fear, as the deponent understood it, that the mate, who was a good navigator, should be killed with Don Alexandro and the rest; that the deponent, who was the friend, from youth, of Don Alexandro, prayed and conjured, but all was useless; for the negro Babo answered him that the thing could not be prevented, and that all the Spaniards risked their death if they could attempt to frustrate his will in this matter, or any other; that, in this conflict, the deponent called the mate, Raneds, who was forced to go apart, and immediately the negro Babo commanded the Ashantee Martinqui and the Ashantee Lecbe to go and commit the murder; that those two went down with hatchets to the berth of Don Alexandro; that, yet half alive and mangled, they dragged him on deck; that they were going to throw him overboard in that state, but the negro Babo stopped them, bidding the murder be completed on the deck before him, which was done, when, by his orders, the body was carried below, forward; that nothing more was seen of it by the deponent for three days; . . . that Don Alonzo Sidonia, an old man, long resident at Valparaiso, and lately appointed to a civil office in Peru, whither he had taken passage, was at the time sleeping in the berth opposite Don Alexandro's; that awakening at his cries, surprised by them, and at the sight of the negroes with their bloody hatchets in their hands, he threw himself into the sea through a window which was near him, and was drowned, without it being in the power of the deponent to assist or take him up; . . . that a short time after killing Aranda, they brought upon deck his german-cousin, of middle-age, Don Francisco Masa, of Mendoza, and the young Don Joaquin, Marques de Aramboalaza, then lately from Spain, with his Spanish servant Ponce, and the three young clerks of Aranda, José Mozairi, Lorenzo Bargas, and Hermenegildo Gandix, all of Cadiz; that Don Joaquin and Hermenegildo Gandix, the negro Babo, for purposes hereafter to appear, preserved alive; but Don Francisco Masa, José Mozairi, and Lorenzo Bargas, with Ponce the servant, beside the boatswain, Juan Robles, the boatswain's mates, Manual Viscaya and Roderigo Hurta, and four of the sailors, the negro Babo ordered to be thrown alive into the sea, although they made no resistance, nor begged for anything else but mercy; that the boatswain, Juan Robles, who knew how to swim, kept the longest above water, making acts of contrition, and, in the last words he uttered, charged this deponent to cause mass to be said for his soul to our Lady of Succor: . . . that, during the three days which followed, the deponent, uncertain what fate had befallen the remains of Don Alexandro, frequently asked the negro Babo where they were, and, if still on board, whether they were to be preserved for interment ashore, entreating him so to order it; that the negro Babo answered nothing till the fourth day, when at sunrise, the deponent coming on deck, the negro

Babo showed him a skeleton, which had been substituted for the ship's proper figure-head—the image of Christopher Colon, the discoverer of the New World; that the negro Babo asked him whose skeleton that was, and whether, from its whiteness, he should not think it a white's; that, upon discovering his face, the negro Babo, coming close, said words to this effect: "Keep faith with the blacks from here to Senegal, or you shall in spirit, as now in body, follow your leader," pointing to the prow; . . . that the same morning the negro Babo took by succession each Spaniard forward, and asked him whose skeleton that was, and whether, from its whiteness, he should not think it a white's; that each Spaniard covered his face; that then to each the negro Babo repeated the words in the first place said to the deponent; . . . that they (the Spaniards), being then assembled aft, the negro Babo harangued them, saying that he had now done all; that the deponent (as navigator for the negroes) might pursue his course, warning him and all of them that they should, soul and body, go the way of Don Alexandro, if he saw them (the Spaniards) speak or plot anything against them (the negroes)—a threat which was repeated every day; that, before the events last mentioned, they had tied the cook to throw him overboard, for it is not known what thing they heard him speak, but finally the negro Babo spared his life, at the request of the deponent; that a few days after, the deponent, endeavoring not to admit any means to preserve the lives of the remaining whites, spoke to the negroes of peace and tranquillity, and agreed to draw up a paper, signed by the deponent and the sailors who could write, as also by the negro Babo, for himself and all the blacks, in which the deponent obliged himself to carry them to Senegal, and they not to kill any more, and he formally to make over to them the ship, with the cargo, with which they were for that time satisfied and quieted. . . . But the next day, the more surely to guard against the sailors' escape, the negro Babo commanded all the boats to be destroyed but the long-boat, which was unseaworthy, and another, a cutter in good condition, which knowing it would yet be wanted for towing the water casks, he had it lowered down into the hold.

. . . . .

[*Various particulars of the prolonged and perplexed navigation ensuing here follow, with incidents of a calamitous calm, from which portion one passage is extracted, to wit:*]
—That on the fifth day of the calm, all on board suffering much from the heat, and want of water, and five having died in fits, and mad, the negroes became irritable, and for a chance gesture, which they deemed suspicious—though it was harmless—made by

the mate, Raneds, to the deponent in the act of handing a quadrant, they killed him; but that for this they afterwards were sorry, the mate being the only remaining navigator on board, except the deponent.

· · · · ·

—That omitting other events, which daily happened, and which can only serve uselessly to recall past misfortunes and conflicts, after seventy-three days' navigation, reckoned from the time they sailed from Nasca, during which they navigated under a scanty allowance of water, and were afflicted with the calms before mentioned, they at last arrived at the island of Santa Maria, on the seventeenth of the month of August, at about six o'clock in the afternoon, at which hour they cast anchor very near the American ship, Bachelor's Delight, which lay in the same bay, commanded by the generous Captain Amasa Delano; but at six o'clock in the morning, they had already described the port, and the negroes became uneasy, as soon as at distance they saw the ship, not having expected to see one there; that the negro Babo pacified them, assuring them that no fear need be had; that straightway he ordered the figure on the bow to be covered with canvas, as for repairs, and had the decks a little set in order; that for a time the negro Babo and the negro Atufal conferred; that the negro Atufal was for sailing away, but the negro Babo would not, and, by himself, cast about what to do; that at last he came to the deponent, proposing to him to say and do all that the deponent declares to have said and done to the American captain;

· · · · ·

that the negro Babo warned him that if he varied in the least, or uttered any word, or gave any look that should give the least intimation of the past events or present state, he would instantly kill him, with all his companions, showing a dagger, which he carried hid, saying something which, as he understood it, meant that that dagger would be alert as his eye; that the negro Babo then announced the plan to all his companions, which pleased them; that he then, the better to disguise the truth, devised many expedients, in some of them uniting deceit and defense; that of this sort was the device of the six Ashantees before named, who were his bravoes; that them he stationed on the break of the poop, as if to clean certain hatchets (in cases, which were part of the cargo), but in reality to use them, and distribute them at need, and at a given word he told them; that, among other devices, was the device of presenting Atufal, his right hand man, as chained, though in a moment the chains could be dropped; that in every particular he informed the deponent what part he was expected to

enact in every device, and what story he was to tell on every occasion, always threatening him with instant death if he varied in the
least: that, conscious that many of the negroes would be turbulent,
the negro Babo appointed the four aged negroes, who were calkers,
to keep what domestic order they could on the decks; that again
and again he harangued the Spaniards and his companions, informing them of his intent, and of his devices, and of the invented
story that this deponent was to tell; charging them lest any of them
varied from that story; that these arrangements were made and
matured during the interval of two or three hours, between their
first sighting the ship and the arrival on board of Captain Amasa
Delano; that this happened about half-past seven o'clock in the
morning, Captain Amasa Delano coming in his boat, and all gladly
receiving him; that the deponent, as well as he could force himself,
acting then the part of principal owner, and a free captain of the
ship, told Captain Amasa Delano, when called upon, that he
came from Buenos Ayres, bound to Lima, with three hundred
negroes; that off Cape Horn, and in a subsequent fever, many
negroes had died; that also, by similar casualties, all the sea officers
and the greatest part of the crew had died.

· · · · ·

[*And so the deposition goes on, circumstantially recounting the
fictitious story dictated to the deponent by Babo, and through
the deponent imposed upon Captain Delano; and also recounting
the friendly offers of Captain Delano, with other things, but all of
which is here omitted. After the fictitious story, etc. the deposition
proceeds:*]

· · · · ·

—that the generous Captain Amasa Delano remained on board
all the day, till he left the ship anchored at six o'clock in the
evening, deponent speaking to him always of his pretended
misfortunes, under the fore-mentioned principles, without having had it in his power to tell a single word, or give him the
least hint, that he might know the truth and state of things; because the negro Babo, performing the office of an officious
servant with all the appearance of submission of the humble
slave, did not leave the deponent one moment; that this was in
order to observe the deponent's actions and words, for the
negro Babo understands well the Spanish; and besides, there
were thereabout some others who were constantly on the
watch, and likewise understood the Spanish; . . . that upon
one occasion, while deponent was standing on the deck conversing with Amasa Delano, by a secret sign the negro Babo
drew him (the deponent) aside, the act appearing as if origi-

nating with the deponent; that then, he being drawn aside, the negro Babo purposed to him to gain from Amasa Delano full particulars about his ship, and crew, and arms; that the deponent asked "For what?" that the negro Babo answered he might conceive; that, grieved at the prospect of what might overtake the generous Captain Amasa Delano, the deponent at first refused to ask the desired questions, and used every argument to induce the negro Babo to give up this new design; that the negro Babo showed the point of his dagger; that, after the information had been obtained the negro Babo again drew him aside, telling him that that very night he (the deponent) would be captain of two ships, instead of one, for that, great part of the American's ship's crew being to be absent fishing, the six Ashantees, without any one else, would easily take it; that at this time he said other things to the same purpose; that no entreaties availed; that before Amasa Delano's coming on board, no hint had been given touching the capture of the American ship: that to prevent this project the deponent was powerless; . . . —that in some things his memory is confused, he cannot distinctly recall every event; . . . —that as soon as they had cast anchor at six of the clock in the evening, as has before been stated, the American Captain took leave, to return to his vessel; that upon a sudden impulse, which the deponent believes to have come from God and his angels, he, after the farewell had been said, followed the generous Captain Amasa Delano as far as the gunwale, where he stayed, under pretense of taking leave, until Amasa Delano should have been seated in his boat; that on shoving off, the deponent sprang from the gunwale into the boat, and fell into it, he knows not how, God guarding him; that—

. . . . .

[Here, in the original, follows the account of what further happened at the escape, and how the San Dominick was retaken. and of the passage to the coast; including in the recital many expressions of "eternal gratitude" to the "generous Captain Amasa Delano." The deposition then proceeds with recapitulatory remarks, and a partial renumeration of the negroes, making record of their individual part in the past events, with a view to furnishing, according to command of the court, the data whereon to found the criminal sentences to be pronounced. From this portion is the following;]

—That he believes that all the negroes, though not in the first place knowing to the design of revolt, when it was accomplished, approved it. . . . That the negro, José, eighteen years old, and in the personal service of Don Alexandro, was the one who communicated the information to the negro Babo, about the state of things in the cabin, before the revolt; that this is known, because, in the preceding midnight, he used to come from his berth, which was under his master's, in the cabin, to the deck where the ringleader and his associates were, and had secret conversations with the negro Babo, in which he was several times seen by the mate; that, one night, the mate drove him away twice; . . . that this same negro José was the one who, without being commanded to do so by the negro Babo, as Lecbe and Martinqui were, stabbed his master, Don Alexandro, after he had been dragged half-lifeless to the deck; . . . that the mulatto steward, Francesco, was of the first band of revolters, that he was, in all things, the creature and tool of the negro Babo; that, to make his court, he, just before a repast in the cabin, proposed, to the negro Babo, poisoning a dish for the generous Captain Amasa Delano; that is known and believed, because the negroes have said it; but that the negro Babo, having another design, forbade Francesco; . . . that the Ashantee Lecbe was one of the worst of them; for that, on the day the ship was retaken, he assisted in the defense of her, with a hatchet in each hand, with one of which he wounded, in the breast, the chief mate of Amasa Delano, in the first act of boarding; this all knew; that, in sight of the deponent, Lecbe struck, with a hatchet, Don Francisco Masa, when, by the negro Babo's orders, he was carrying him to throw him overboard, alive, beside participating in the murder, before mentioned, of Don Alexandro Aranda, and others of the cabin-passengers; that, owing to the fury with which the Ashantees fought in the engagement with the boats, but this Lecbe and Yan survived; that Yan was as bad as Lecbe; that Yan was the man who, by Babo's command, willingly prepared the skeleton of Don Alexandro, in a way the negroes afterwards told the deponent, but which he, so long as reason is left him, can never divulge; that Yan and Lecbe were the two who, in a calm by night, riveted the skeleton to the bow; this also the negroes told him; that the negro Babo was he who traced the inscription below it; that the negro Babo was the plotter from first to last; he ordered every murder, and was the helm and keel of the revolt; that Atufal was his lieutenant in all; but Atufal, with his own hand, committed no murder; nor did the negro Babo; . . . that Atufal was shot, being killed in the fight with the boats, ere boarding; . . . that the negresses, of age, were knowing to the revolt, and testified themselves satisfied at the death of their master, Don Alexandro; that, had the negroes not restrained them, they would have tortured to death, instead of simply killing, the Spaniards slain by command of the negro Babo; that the negresses used their utmost influence to have the deponent made away with; that, in the various acts of murder, they sang songs and danced—not gaily, but solemnly; and before the engagement with the boats, as well as during the action, they sang melancholy songs to the negroes, and that this melancholy tone was more inflaming than a different one would have been, and was so intended; that all this is believed, because the negroes have said it.

—that of the thirty-six men of the crew, exclusive of the passengers (all of whom are now dead), which the deponent had knowledge of, six only remained alive, with four cabin-boys and ship-boys, not included with the crew; . . . —that the negroes broke an arm of one of the cabin-boys and gave him strokes with hatchets.

[*Then follow various random disclosures referring to various periods of time. The following are extracted;*]

—That during the presence of Captain Amasa Delano on board, some attempts were made by the sailors, and one by Hermenegildo Gandix, to convey hints to him of the true state of affairs; but that these attempts were ineffectual, owing to fear of incurring death, and, furthermore, owing to the devices which offered contradictions to the true state of affairs, as well as owing to the generosity and piety of Amasa Delano incapable of sounding such wickedness; . . . that Luys Galgo, a sailor about sixty years of age, and formerly of the king's navy, was one of those who sought to convey tokens to Captain Amasa Delano; but his intent, though undiscovered, being suspected, he was, on a pretense, made to retire out of sight, and at last into the hold, and there was made away with. This the negroes have since said; . . . that one of the ship-boys feeling, from Captain Amasa Delano's presence, some hopes of release, and not having enough prudence, dropped some chance-word respecting his expectations, which being overheard and understood by a slave-boy with whom he was eating at the time, the latter struck him on the head with a knife, inflicting a bad wound, but of which the boy is now healing; that likewise, not long before the ship was brought to anchor, one of the seamen, steering at the time, endangered himself by letting the blacks remark some expression in his countenance, arising from a cause similar to the above; but this sailor, by his heedful after conduct, escaped; . . . that these statements are made to show the court that from the beginning to the end of the revolt, it was impossible for the deponent and his men to act otherwise than they did; . . . —that the third clerk, Hermenegildo Gandix, who before had been forced to live among the seamen, wearing a seaman's habit, and in all respects appearing to be one for the time; he, Gandix, was killed by a musket ball fired through mistake from the boats before boarding; having in his fright run up the mizzen-rigging, calling to the boats—"don't board," lest upon their boarding the negroes should kill him; that this inducing the Americans to believe he some way favored the cause of the negroes, they fired two balls at him, so that he fell wounded from the rigging, and was drowned in the sea; . . . —that the young Don Joaquin, Marques de Aramboalaza, like Hermenegildo Gandix, the third clerk, was degraded to the office and appearance of a common seaman; that upon one occasion when Don Joaquin shrank, the negro Babo commanded the Ashantee Lecbe to take tar and heat it, and pour it upon Don Joaquin's hands; . . . —that Don Joaquin was killed owing to another mistake of the Americans, but one impossible to be avoided, as upon the approach of the boats, Don Joaquin, with a hatchet tied edge out, and upright to his hand, was made by the negroes to appear on the bulwarks; whereupon, seen with arms in his hands and in a questionable attitude, he was shot for a renegade seaman; . . . —that on the person of Don Joaquin was found secreted a jewel, which, by papers that were discovered, proved to have been meant for the shrine of our Lady of Mercy in Lima; a votive offering, beforehand prepared and guarded, to attest his gratitude, when he should have landed in Peru, his last destination, for the safe conclusion of his entire voyage from Spain; . . . —that the jewel, with the other effects of the late Don Joaquin, is in the custody of the brethren of the Hospital ed Sacerdotes, awaiting the disposition of the honorable court; . . . —that, owing to the condition of the deponent, as well as the haste in which the boats departed for the attack, the Americans were not forewarned that there were, among the apparent crew, a passenger and one of the clerks disguised by the negro Babo; . . . —that, beside the negroes killed in the action, some were killed after the capture and re-anchoring at night, when shackled to the ring-bolts on deck; that these deaths were committed by the sailors, ere they could be prevented. That so soon as informed of it, Captain Amasa Delano used all his authority, and, in particular with his own hand, struck down Martinez Gola, who, having found a razor in the pocket of an old jacket of his, which one of the shackled negroes had on, was aiming it at the negro's throat; that the noble Captain Amasa Delano also wrenched from the hand of Bartholomew Barlo a dagger, secreted at the time of the massacre of the whites, with which he was in the act of stabbing a shackled negro, who, the same day, with another negro, had thrown him down and jumped upon him; . . . —that, for all the events, befalling through so long a time, during which the ship was in the hands of the negro Babo, he cannot here give account; but that, what he has said is the most substantial of what occurs to him at present, and is the truth under the oath which he has taken; which declaration he affirmed and ratified, after hearing it read to him.

He said that he is twenty-nine years of age, and broken in body and mind; that when finally dismissed by the court, he shall not return home to Chili, but betake himself to the monastery on Mount Agonia without; and signed with his honor, and crossed himself, and, for the time, departed as he came, in his litter, with the monk Infelez, to the Hospital de Sacerdotes.

BENITO CERENO

DOCTOR ROZAS

———————

If the Deposition have served as the key to fit into the lock of the complications which precede it, then, as a vault whose door has been flung back, the San Dominick's hull lies open to-day.

Hitherto the nature of this narrative, besides rendering the intricacies in the beginning unavoidable, has more or less required that many things, instead of being set down in the order of occurrence, should be retrospectively, or irregularly given; this last is the case with the following passages, which will conclude the account:

During the long, mild voyage to Lima, there was, as before hinted, a period during which the sufferer a little recovered his health, or, at least in some degree, his tranquillity. Ere the decided relapse which came, the two captains had many cordial conversations—their fraternal unreserve in singular contrast with former withdrawments.

Again and again it was repeated, how hard it had been to enact the part forced on the Spaniard by Babo.

"Ah, my dear friend," Don Benito once said, "at those very times when you thought me so morose and ungrateful, nay, when, as you now admit, you half thought me plotting your murder, at those very times my heart was frozen; I could not look at you, thinking of what, both on board this ship and your own, hung, from other hands, over my kind benefactor. And as God lives, Don Amasa, I know not whether desire for my own safety alone could have nerved me to that leap into your boat, had it not been for the thought that, did you, unenlightened, return to your ship, you, my best friend, with all who might be with you, stolen upon, that night, in your hammocks, would never in this world have wakened again. Do but think how you walked this deck, how you sat in this cabin, every inch of ground mined into honey-combs under you. Had I dropped the least hint, made the least advance towards an understanding between us, death, explosive death—yours as mine —would have ended the scene."

"True, true," cried Captain Delano, starting, "you have saved my life, Don Benito, more than I yours; saved it, too, against my knowledge and will."

"Nay, my friend," rejoined the Spaniard, courteous even to the point of religion, "God charmed your life, but you saved mine. To think of some things you did—those smilings and chattings, rash pointings and gesturings. For less than these, they slew my mate, Raneds; but you had the Prince of Heaven's safe-conduct through all ambuscades."

"Yes, all is owing to Providence, I know: but the temper of my mind that morning was more than commonly pleasant, while the sight of so much suffering, more apparent than real, added to my good-nature, compassion, and charity, happily interweaving the three. Had it been otherwise, doubtless, as you hint, some of my interferences might have ended unhappily enough. Besides, those feelings I spoke of enabled me to get the better of momentary distrust, at times when acuteness might have cost me my life, without saving another's. Only at the end did my suspicions get the better of me, and you know how wide of the mark they then proved."

"Wide, indeed," said Don Benito, sadly; "you were with me all day; stood with me, sat with me, talked with me, looked at me, ate with me, drank with me; and yet, your last act was to clutch for a monster, not only an innocent man, but the most pitiable of all men. To such degree may malign machinations and deceptions impose. So far may even the best man err, in judging the conduct of one with the recesses of whose condition he is not acquainted. But you were forced to it; and you were in time undeceived. Would that, in both respects, it was so ever, and with all men."

"You generalize, Don Benito; and mournfully enough. But the past is passed; why moralize upon it? Forget it. See, yon bright sun has forgotten it all, and the blue sea, and the blue sky; these have turned over new leaves."

"Because they have no memory," he dejectedly replied; "because they are not human."

"But these mild trades that now fan your cheek, do they not come with a human-like healing to you? Warm friends, steadfast friends are the trades."

"With their steadfastness they but waft me to my tomb, Señor," was the foreboding response.

"You are saved," cried Captain Delano, more and more astonished and pained; "you are saved: what has cast such a shadow upon you?"

"The negro."

There was silence, while the moody man sat, slowly and unconsciously gathering his mantle about him, as if it were a pall.

There was no more conversation that day.

But if the Spaniard's melancholy sometimes ended in muteness upon topics like the above, there were others upon which he never spoke at all; on which, indeed, all his old reserves were piled. Pass over the worst, and, only to elucidate, let an item or two of these be cited. The dress, so precise and costly, worn by him on the day whose events have been narrated, had not willingly been put on. And that silver-mounted sword, apparent symbol of despotic command, was not, indeed, a sword, but the ghost of one. The scabbard, artificially stiffened, was empty.

As for the black—whose brain, not body, had schemed and led the revolt, with the plot—his slight frame, inadequate to that which it held, had at once yielded to the superior muscular strength of his captor, in the boat. Seeing all was over, he uttered no sound, and could not be forced to. His aspect seemed to say, since I cannot do deeds, I will not speak words. Put in irons in the hold, with the rest, he was carried to Lima. During the passage, Don Benito did not visit him. Nor then, nor at any time after, would he look at him. Before the tribunal he refused. When pressed by the judges he fainted. On the testimony of the sailors alone rested the legal identity of Babo.

Some months after, dragged to the gibbet at the tail of a mule, the black met his voiceless end. The body was burned to ashes; but for many days, the head, that hive of subtlety, fixed on a pole in the Plaza, met, unabashed, the gaze of the whites; and across the Plaza looked towards St. Bartholomew's church, in whose vaults slept then, as now, the recovered bones of Aranda: and across the Rimac bridge looked towards the monastery, on Mount Agonia without; where, three months after being dismissed by the court, Benito Cereno, borne on the bier, did, indeed, follow his leader.

1855, 1856

The Bell-Tower

Like negroes, these powers own man sullenly; mindful of their higher master; while serving, plot revenge.

The world is apoplectic with high-living of ambition; and apoplexy has its fall.

Seeking to conquer a larger liberty, man but extends the empire of necessity.

from a private MS.[2]

In the south of Europe, nigh a once frescoed capital, now with dank mould cankering its bloom, central in a plain, stands what, at distance, seems the black mossed stump of some immeasurable pine, fallen, in forgotten days, with Anak and the Titan.[3]

As all along where the pine tree falls, its dissolution leaves a mossy mound—last-flung shadow of the perished trunk; never lengthening, never lessening; unsubject to the fleet falsities of the sun; shade immutable, and true gauge which cometh by prostration—so westward from what seems the stump, one steadfast spear of lichened ruin veins the plain.

From that tree-top, what birded chimes of silver throats had rung. A stone pine; a metallic aviary in its crown: the Bell-Tower, built by the great mechanician, the unblest foundling, Bannadonna.

Like Babel's, its base was laid in a high hour of renovated earth, following the second deluge, when the waters of the Dark Ages had dried up, and once more the green appeared. No wonder that, after so long and deep submersion, the jubilant expectation of the race should, as with Noah's sons, soar into Shinar aspiration.[4]

In firm resolve, no man in Europe at that period went beyond Bannadonna. Enriched through commerce with the Levant, the state in which he lived voted to have the noblest Bell-Tower in Italy. His repute assigned him to be architect.

Stone by stone, month by month, the tower rose. Higher, higher; snail-like in pace, but torch or rocket in its pride.

After the masons would depart, the builder, standing alone upon its ever-ascending summit, at close of every day, saw that he overtopped still higher walls and trees. He would tarry till a late hour there, wrapped in schemes of other and still loftier piles. Those who of saints' days thronged the spot—hanging to the rude poles of scaffolding, like sailors on yards, or bees on boughs, unmindful of lime and dust, and falling chips of stone—their homage not the less inspirited him to self-esteem.

At length the holiday of the Tower came. To the sound of

2. Presumably Melville's own. The first epigraph suggests a connection between this story and "Benito Cereno."
3. Giants; the sons of Anak from the Old Testament (Numbers xiii.33), the Titans from Greek mythology.
4. See Genesis xi.1–9. The building of

towers, however, was a subject of active debate in Melville's own day. Bunker Hill Monument was finished in 1843, and the capital city's Washington Monument was still a highly controversial proposal.

viols, the climax-tone slowly rose in air, and, amid the firing of ordnance, was laid by Bannadonna's hands upon the final course. Then mounting it, he stood erect, alone, with folded arms, gazing upon the white summits of blue inland Alps, and whiter crests of bluer Alps off-shore—sights invisible from the plain. Invisible, too, from thence was that eye he turned below, when, like the cannon booms, came up to him the people's combustions of applause.

That which stirred them so was, seeing with what serenity the builder stood three hundred feet in air, upon an unrailed perch. This none but he durst do. But his periodic standing upon the pile, in each stage of its growth—such discipline had its last result.

Little remained now but the bells. These, in all respects, must correspond with their receptacle.

The minor ones were prosperously cast. A highly enriched one followed, of a singular make, intended for suspension in a manner before unknown. The purpose of this bell, its rotary motion, and connection with the clock-work, also executed at the time, will, in the sequel, receive mention.

In the one erection, bell-tower and clock-tower were united, though, before that period, such structures had commonly been built distinct; as the Campanile and Torre del 'Orologio of St. Mark to this day attest.

But it was upon the great state-bell that the founder lavished his more daring skill. In vain did some of the less elated magistrates here caution him; saying that though truly the tower was Titanic, yet limit should be set to the dependent weight of its swaying masses. But undeterred, he prepared his mammoth mould, dented with mythological devices; kindled his fires of balsamic firs; melted his tin and copper, and, throwing in much plate, contributed by the public spirit of the nobles, let loose the tide.

The unleashed metals bayed like hounds. The workmen shrunk. Through their fright, fatal harm to the bell was dreaded. Fearless as Shadrach,[5] Bannadonna, rushing through the glow, smote the chief culprit with his ponderous ladle. From the smitten part, a splinter was dashed into the seething mass, and at once was melted in.

Next day a portion of the work was heedfully uncovered. All seemed right. Upon the third morning, with equal satisfaction, it was bared still lower. At length, like some old Theban king, the whole cooled casting was disinterred. All was fair except in one strange spot. But as he suffered no one to attend him in these inspections, he concealed the blemish by some preparation which none knew better to devise.

The casting of such a mass was deemed no small triumph for

5. One of the three youths thrown into the fiery furnace (Daniel iii.12–30).

the caster; one, too, in which the state might not scorn to share. The homicide was overlooked. By the charitable that deed was but imputed to sudden transports of esthetic passion, not to any flagitious quality. A kick from an Arabian charger; not sign of vice, but blood.

His felony remitted by the judge, absolution given him by the priest, what more could even a sickly conscience have desired.

Honoring the tower and its builder with another holiday, the republic witnessed the hoisting of the bells and clockwork amid shows and pomps superior to the former.

Some months of more than usual solitude on Bannadonna's part ensued. It was not unknown that he was engaged upon something for the belfry, intended to complete it, and surpass all that had gone before. Most people imagined that the design would involve a casting like the bells. But those who thought they had some further insight, would shake their heads, with hints, that not for nothing did the mechanician keep so secret. Meantime, his seclusion failed not to invest his work with more or less of that sort of mystery pertaining to the forbidden.

Ere long he had a heavy object hoisted to the belfry, wrapped in a dark sack or cloak—a procedure sometimes had in the case of an elaborate piece of sculpture, or statue, which, being intended to grace the front of a new edifice, the architect does not desire exposed to critical eyes, till set up, finished, in its appointed place. Such was the impression now. But, as the object rose, a statuary present observed, or thought he did, that it was not entirely rigid, but was, in a manner, pliant. At last, when the hidden thing had attained its final height, and, obscurely seen from below, seemed almost of itself to step into the belfry, as if with little assistance from the crane, a shrewd old blacksmith present ventured the suspicion that it was but a living man. This surmise was thought a foolish one, while the general interest failed not to augment.

Not without demur from Bannadonna, the chief-magistrate of the town, with an associate—both elderly men—followed what seemed the image up the tower. But, arrived at the belfry, they had little recompense. Plausibly entrenching himself behind the conceded mysteries of his art, the mechanician withheld present explanation. The magistrates glanced toward the cloaked object, which, to their surprise, seemed now to have changed its attitude, or else had before been more perplexingly concealed by the violent muffling action of the wind without. It seemed now seated upon some sort of frame, or chair, contained within the domino. They observed that nigh the top, in a sort of square, the web of the cloth, either from accident or design, had its warp partly withdrawn, and the cross threads plucked out here and there, so as to form a sort of woven grating. Whether it were the low wind or no, stealing through the stone lattice-work, or only their own perturbed imaginations, is uncertain, but they thought they discerned a slight sort of fitful, spring-like motion, in the domino. Nothing, however incidental or insignificant, escaped their uneasy eyes. Among other things, they pried out, in a corner, an earthen cup, partly corroded and partly encrusted, and one whispered to the other, that this cup was just such a one as might, in mockery, be offered to the lips of some brazen statue, or, perhaps, still worse.

But, being questioned, the mechanician said, that the cup was simply used in his founder's business, and described the purpose; in short, a cup to test the condition of metals in fusion. He added, that it had got into the belfry by the merest chance.

Again, and again, they gazed at the domino, as at some suspicious incognito at a Venetian mask. All sorts of vague apprehensions stirred them. They even dreaded lest, when they should descend, the mechanician, though without a flesh and blood companion, for all that, would not be left alone.

Affecting some merriment at their disquietude, he begged to relieve them, by extending a coarse sheet of workman's canvas between them and the object.

Meantime he sought to interest them in his other work; nor, now that the domino was out of sight, did they long remain insensible to the artistic wonders lying round them; wonders hitherto beheld but in their unfinished state; because, since hoisting the bells, none but the caster had entered within the belfry. It was one trait of his, that, even in details, he would not let another do what he could, without too great loss of time, accomplish for himself. So, for several preceding weeks, whatever hours were unemployed in his secret design, had been devoted to elaborating the figures on the bells.

The clock-bell, in particular, now drew attention. Under a patient chisel, the latent beauty of its enrichments, before obscured by the cloudings incident to casting, that beauty in its shyest grace, was now revealed. Round and round the bell, twelve figures of gay girls, garlanded, hand-in-hand, danced in a choral ring—the embodied hours.

"Bannadonna," said the chief, "this bell excels all else. No added touch could here improve. Hark!" hearing a sound, "was that the wind?"

"The wind, Excellenza," was the light response. "But the figures, they are not yet without their faults. They need some touches yet. When those are given, and the——block yonder," pointing towards the canvas screen, "when Haman[6] there, as I merrily call him,—him? *it*, I mean——when Haman is fixed on this, his lofty tree, then, gentlemen, will I be most happy to receive you here again."

The equivocal reference to the object caused some return of restlessness. However, on their part, the visitors forbore further allusion to it, unwilling, perhaps, to let the foundling see how easily it lay within his plebeian art to stir the placid dignity of nobles.

"Well, Bannadonna," said the chief, "how long ere you are ready to set the clock going, so that the hour shall be sounded? Our interest in you, not less than in the work itself, makes us anxious to be assured of your success. The people, too,—why, they are shouting now. Say the exact hour when you will be ready."

"To-morrow, Excellenza, if you listen for it,—or should you not, all the same—strange music will be heard. The stroke of one shall be the first from yonder bell," pointing to the bell adorned with girls and garlands, "that stroke shall fall there, where the hand of Una clasps Dua's. The stroke of one shall sever that loved clasp. To-morrow, then, at one o'clock, as struck here, precisely here," advancing and placing his finger upon the clasp, "the poor mechanic will be most happy once more to give you liege audience, in this his littered shop. Farewell till then, illustrious magnificoes, and hark ye for your vassal's stroke."

His still, Vulcanic face hiding its burning brightness like a forge, he moved with ostentatious deference towards the scuttle, as if so far to escort their exit. But the junior magistrate, a kind-hearted man, troubled at what seemed to him a certain sardonical disdain, lurking beneath the foundling's humble mien, and in Christian sympathy more distressed at it on his account than on his own, dimly surmising what might be the final fate of such a cynic solitaire, nor perhaps uninfluenced by the general strangeness of surrounding things, this good magistrate had glanced sadly, sideways from the speaker, and thereupon his foreboding eye had started at the expression of the unchanging face of the Hour Una.

"How is this, Bannadonna?" he lowly asked, "Una looks unlike her sisters."

"In Christ's name, Bannadonna," impulsively broke in the chief, his attention, for the first attracted to the figure, by his associate's remark, "Una's face looks just like that of Deborah,[7] the prophetess, as painted by the Florentine, Del Fonca."

"Surely, Bannadonna," lowly resumed the milder magistrate, "you

6. Haman ordered a gallows fifty cubits (approximately 75 feet) high prepared for Mordecai but was hanged on it himself (Esther v.14, vii.10).

7. Deborah prophesied the destruction of Sisera, who died of a nail driven into his temple (Judges iv.4–22). The Florentine painter is fictitious.

meant the twelve should wear the same jocundly abandoned air. But see, the smile of Una seems but a fatal one. 'Tis different."

While his mild associate was speaking, the chief glanced, inquiringly, from him to the caster, as if anxious to mark how the discrepancy would be accounted for. As the chief stood, his advanced foot was on the scuttle's curb.

Bannadonna spoke:

"Excellenza, now that, following your keener eye, I glance upon the face of Una, I do, indeed, perceive some little variance. But look all round the bell, and you will find no two faces entirely correspond. Because there is a law in art——but the cold wind is rising more; these lattices are but a poor defense. Suffer me, magnificoes, to conduct you, at least, partly on your way. Those in whose well-being there is a public stake, should be heedfully attended."

"Touching the look of Una, you were saying, Bannadonna, that there was a certain law in art," observed the chief, as the three now descended the stone shaft, "pray, tell me, then——."

"Pardon; another time, Excellenza;—the tower is damp."

"Nay, I must rest, and hear it now. Here,—here is a wide landing, and through this leeward slit, no wind, but ample light. Tell us of your law; and at large."

"Since, Excellenza, you insist, know that there is a law in art, which bars the possibility of duplicates. Some years ago, you may remember, I graved a small seal for your republic, bearing, for its chief device, the head of your own ancestor, its illustrious founder. It becoming necessary, for the customs' use, to have innumerable impressions for bales and boxes, I graved an entire plate, containing one hundred of the seals. Now, though, indeed, my object was to have those hundred heads identical, and though, I dare say, people think them so, yet, upon closely scanning an uncut impression from the plate, no two of those five-score faces, side by side, will be found alike. Gravity is the air of all; but, diversified in all. In some, benevolent; in some, ambiguous; in two or three, to a close scrutiny, all but incipiently malign, the variation of less than a hair's breadth in the linear shadings round the mouth sufficing to all this. Now, Excellenza, transmute that general gravity into joyousness, and subject it to twelve of those variations I have described, and tell me, will you not have my hours here, and Una one of them? But I like——."

"Hark! is that——a footfall above?"

"Mortar, Excellenza; sometimes it drops to the belfry-floor from the arch where the stone-work was left undressed. I must have it seen to. As I was about to say: for one, I like this law forbidding duplicates. It evokes fine personalities. Yes, Excellenza, that strange, and—to you—uncertain smile, and those fore-looking eyes of Una, suit Bannadonna very well."

"Hark!—sure we left no soul above?"

"No soul, Excellenza; rest assured, no *soul*.—Again the mortar."

"It fell not while we were there."

"Ah, in your presence, it better knew its place, Excellenza," blandly bowed Bannadonna.

"But, Una," said the milder magistrate, "she seemed intently gazing on you; one would have almost sworn that she picked you out from among us three."

"If she did, possibly, it might have been her finer apprehension, Excellenza."

"How, Bannadonna? I do not understand you."

"No consequence, no consequence, Excellenza—but the shifted wind is blowing through the slit. Suffer me to escort you on; and then, pardon, but the toiler must to his tools."

"It may be foolish, Signor," said the milder magistrate, as, from the third landing, the two now went down unescorted, "but, somehow, our great mechanician moves me strangely. Why, just now, when he so superciliously replied, his walk seemed Sisera's, God's vain foe, in Del Fonca's painting. And that young, sculptured Deborah, too. Ay, and that——."

"Tush, tush, Signor!" returned the chief. "A passing whim. Deborah?—Where's Jael, pray?"

"Ah," said the other, as they now stepped upon the sod, "Ah, Signor, I see you leave your fears behind you with the chill and gloom; but mine, even in this sunny air, remain. Hark!"

It was a sound from just within the tower door, whence they had emerged. Turning, they saw it closed.

"He has slipped down and barred us out," smiled the chief; "but it is his custom."

Proclamation was now made, that the next day, at one hour after meridian, the clock would strike, and—thanks to the mechanician's powerful art—with unusual accompaniments. But what those should be, none as yet could say. The announcement was received with cheers.

By the looser sort, who encamped about the tower all night, lights were seen gleaming through the topmost blindwork, only disappearing with the morning sun. Strange sounds, too, were heard, or were thought to be, by those whom anxious watching might not have left mentally undisturbed—sounds, not only of some ringing implement, but also—so they said—half-suppressed screams and plainings, such as might have issued from some ghostly engine, overplied.

Slowly the day drew on; part of the concourse chasing the weary time with songs and games, till, at last, the great blurred sun rolled, like a football, against the plain.

At noon, the nobility and principal citizens came from the town in cavalcade, a guard of soldiers, also, with music, the more to honor the occasion.

Only one hour more. Impatience grew. Watches were held in hands of feverish men, who stood, now scrutinizing their small dial-plates, and then, with neck thrown back, gazing toward the belfry, as if the eye might foretell that which could only be made sensible to the ear; for, as yet, there was no dial to the tower-clock.

The hour hands of a thousand watches now verged within a hair's breadth of the figure 1. A silence, as of the expectation of some Shiloh,[8] pervaded the swarming plain. Suddenly a dull, mangled sound—naught ringing in it; scarcely audible, indeed, to the outer circles of the people—that dull sound dropped heavily from the belfry. At the same moment, each man stared at his neighbor blankly. All watches were upheld. All hour-hands were at—had passed—the figure 1. No bell-stroke from the tower. The multitude became tumultuous.

Waiting a few moments, the chief magistrate, commanding silence, hailed the belfry, to know what thing unforeseen had happened there.

No response.

He hailed again and yet again.

All continued hushed.

By his order, the soldiers burst in the tower-door; when, stationing guards to defend it from the now surging mob, the chief, accompanied by his former associate, climbed the winding stairs. Halfway up, they stopped to listen. No sound. Mounting faster, they reached the belfry; but, at the threshold, started at the spectacle disclosed. A spaniel, which, unbeknown to them, had followed them thus far, stood shivering as before some unknown monster in a brake: or, rather, as if it snuffed footsteps leading to some other world. Bannadonna lay, prostrate and bleeding, at the base of the bell which was adorned with girls and garlands. He lay at the feet of the hour Una; his head coinciding, in a vertical line, with her left hand, clasped by the hour Dua. With downcast face impending over him, like Jael over nailed Sisera in the tent, was the domino; now no more becloaked.

It had limbs, and seemed clad in a scaly mail, lustrous as a dragon-beetle's. It was manacled, and its clubbed arms were uplifted, as if, with its manacles, once more to smite its already smitten victim. One advanced foot of it was inserted beneath the dead body, as if

8. Revelation. Although the word *Shiloh* has various connotations, the reference here is probably to I Samuel iii.21, where "the Lord appeared again in Shiloh" and revealed himself to Samuel.

in the act of spurning it.

Uncertainty falls on what now followed.

It were but natural to suppose that the magistrates would, at first, shrink from immediate personal contact with what they saw. At the least, for a time, they would stand in involuntary doubt; it may be, in more or less of horrified alarm. Certain it is, that an arquebuss was called for from below. And some add, that its report, followed by a fierce whiz, as of the sudden snapping of a main-spring, with a steely din, as if a stack of sword-blades should be dashed upon a pavement, these blended sounds came ringing to the plain, attracting every eye far upward to the belfry, whence, through the lattice-work, thin wreaths of smoke were curling.

Some averred that it was the spaniel, gone mad by fear, which was shot. This, others denied. True it was, the spaniel never more was seen; and, probably, for some unknown reason, it shared the burial now to be related of the domino. For, whatever the preceding circumstances may have been, the first instinctive panic over, or else all ground of reasonable fear removed, the two magistrates, by themselves, quickly rehooded the figure in the dropped cloak wherein it had been hoisted. The same night, it was secretly lowered to the ground, smuggled to the beach, pulled far out to sea, and sunk. Nor to any after urgency, even in free convivial hours, would the twain ever disclose the full secrets of the belfry.

From the mystery unavoidably investing it, the popular solution of the foundling's fate involved more or less of supernatural agency. But some few less unscientific minds pretended to find little difficulty in otherwise accounting for it. In the chain of circumstantial inferences drawn, there may, or may not, have been some absent or defective links. But, as the explanation in question is the only one which tradition has explicitly preserved, in dearth of better, it will here be given. But, in the first place, it is requisite to present the supposition entertained as to the entire motive and mode, with their origin, of the secret design of Bannadonna; the minds above-mentioned assuming to penetrate as well into his soul as into the event. The disclosure will indirectly involve reference to peculiar matters, none of the clearest, beyond the immediate subject.

At that period, no large bell was made to sound otherwise than as at present, by agitation of a tongue within, by means of ropes, or percussion from without, either from cumbrous machinery, or stalwart watchmen, armed with heavy hammers, stationed in the belfry, or in sentry-boxes on the open roof, according as the bell was sheltered or exposed.

It was from observing these exposed bells, with their watchmen, that the foundling, as was opined, derived the first suggestion of his scheme. Perched on a great mast or spire, the human figure, viewed from below, undergoes such a reduction in its apparent size, as to obliterate its intelligent features. It evinces no personality. Instead of bespeaking volition, its gestures rather resemble the automatic ones of the arms of a telegraph.

Musing, therefore, upon the purely Punchinello aspect of the human figure thus beheld, it had indirectly occurred to Bannadonna to devise some metallic agent, which should strike the hour with its mechanic hand, with even greater precision than the vital one. And, moreover, as the vital watchman on the roof, sallying from his retreat at the given periods, walked to the bell with uplifted mace, to smite it, Bannadonna had resolved that his invention should likewise possess the power of locomotion, and, along with that, the appearance, at least, of intelligence and will.

If the conjectures of those who claimed acquaintance with the intent of Bannadonna be thus far correct, no unenterprising spirit could have been his. But they stopped not here; intimating that though, indeed, his design had, in the first place, been prompted by the sight of the watchman, and confined to the devising of a subtle substitute for him: yet, as is not seldom the case with projectors, by insensible gradations, proceeding from comparatively pigmy aims to Titanic ones, the original scheme had, in its anticipated eventualities, at last, attained to an unheard of degree of daring. He still bent his efforts upon the locomotive figure for the belfry, but only as a partial type of an ulterior creature, a sort of elephantine helot, adapted to further, in a degree scarcely to be imagined, the universal conveniences and glories of humanity; supplying nothing less than a supplement to the Six Days' Work;[9] stocking the earth with a new serf, more useful than the ox, swifter than the dolphin, stronger than the lion, more cunning than the ape, for industry an ant, more fiery than serpents, and yet, in patience, another ass. All excellences of all God-made creatures, which served man, were here to receive advancement, and then to be combined in one. Talus[1] was to have been the all-accomplished helot's name. Talus, iron slave to Bannadonna, and, through him, to man.

Here, it might well be thought that, were these last conjectures as to the foundling's secrets not erroneous, then must he have been hopelessly infected with the craziest chimeras of his age; far outgoing Albert Magus[2] and Cornelius Agrippa. But the contrary was averred. However marvelous his design, however apparently transcending not alone the bounds of human invention, but those of

9. Genesis i. The culmination of the "Six Days' Work" was the creation of man.
1. A mythological robot or giant man of brass who guarded the island of Crete. In Spenser's *Faerie Queene* he was an iron man (V.i.12).

2. Probably Albertus Magnus (1193?–1280), teacher of Thomas Aquinas, who was described as *"magnus in magia."* Both he and Cornelius Agrippa (1486–1535) were popularly associated with alchemy and magic.

divine creation, yet the proposed means to be employed were alleged to have been confined within the sober forms of sober reason. It was affirmed that, to a degree of more than skeptic scorn, Banna-donna had been without sympathy for any of the vain-glorious ir-rationalities of his time. For example, he had not concluded, with the visionaries among the metaphysicians, that between the finer mechanic forces and the ruder animal vitality some germ of corre-spondence might prove discoverable. As little did his scheme par-take of the enthusiasm of some natural philosophers, who hoped, by physiological and chemical inductions, to arrive at a knowledge of the source of life, and so qualify themselves to manufacture and improve upon it. Much less had he aught in common with the tribe of alchemists, who sought, by a species of incantations, to evoke some surprising vitality from the laboratory. Neither had he im-agined, with certain sanguine theosophists, that, by faithful adora-tion of the Highest, unheard-of powers would be vouchsafed to man. A practical materialist, what Bannadonna had aimed at was to have been reached, not by logic, not by crucible, not by conjura-tion, not by altars; but by plain vice-bench and hammer. In short, to solve nature, to steal into her, to intrigue beyond her, to procure some one else to bind her to his hand;—these, one and all, had not been his objects; but, asking no favors from any element or any being, of himself, to rival her, outstrip her, and rule her. He stooped to conquer. With him, common sense was theurgy;[3] machinery, miracle; Prometheus, the heroic name for machinist; man, the true God.

Nevertheless, in his initial step, so far as the experimental autom-aton for the belfry was concerned, he allowed fancy some little play; or, perhaps, what seemed his fancifulness was but his utilitarian ambition collaterally extended. In figure, the creature for the belfry should not be likened after the human pattern, nor any animal one, nor after the ideas, however wild, of ancient fable, but equally in aspect as in organism be an original production; the more terrible to behold, the better.

Such, then, were the suppositions as to the present scheme, and the reserved intent. How, at the very threshold, so unlooked for a catastrophe overturned all, or rather, what was the conjecture here, is now to be set forth.

It was thought that on the day preceding the fatality, his visitors having left him, Bannadonna had unpacked the belfry image, ad-justed it, and placed it in the retreat provided—a sort of sentry-box in one corner of the belfry; in short, throughout the night, and for

3. The power of compelling supernat-ural beings to do something. Prome-theus, in classical mythology, was the creator of man, who stole fire from heaven for his benefit.

some part of the ensuing morning, he had been engaged in arranging everything connected with the domino; the issuing from the
sentry-box each sixty minutes; sliding along a grooved way, like a
railway; advancing to the clock-bell, with uplifted manacles; striking it at one of the twelve junctions of the four-and-twenty hands;
then wheeling, circling the bell, and retiring to its post, there to
bide for another sixty minutes, when the same process was to be
repeated; the bell, by a cunning mechanism, meantime turning on
its vertical axis, so as to present, to the descending mace, the clasped
hands of the next two figures, when it would strike two, three, and
so on, to the end. The musical metal in this time-bell being so
managed in the fusion, by some art, perishing with its originator,
that each of the clasps of the four-and-twenty hands should give
forth its own peculiar resonance when parted.

But on the magic metal, the magic and metallic stranger never
struck but that one stroke, drove but that one nail, severed but that
one clasp, by which Bannadonna clung to his ambitious life. For,
after winding up the creature in the sentry-box, so that, for the present, skipping the intervening hours, it should not emerge till the
hour of one, but should then infallibly emerge, and, after deftly
oiling the grooves whereon it was to slide, it was surmised that the
mechanician must then have hurried to the bell, to give his final
touches to its sculpture. True artist, he here became absorbed; and
absorption still further intensified, it may be, by his striving to abate
that strange look of Una; which, though, before others, he had
treated with such unconcern, might not, in secret, have been without its thorn.

And so, for the interval, he was oblivious of his creature; which,
not oblivious of him, and true to its creation, and true to its heedful winding up, left its post precisely at the given moment; along
its well-oiled route, slid noiselessly towards its mark; and, aiming
at the hand of Una, to ring one clangorous note, dully smote the
intervening brain of Bannadonna, turned backwards to it; the manacled arms then instantly up-springing to their hovering poise. The
falling body clogged the thing's return; so there it stood, still impending over Bannadonna, as if whispering some post-mortem
terror. The chisel lay dropped from the hand, but beside the hand;
the oil-flask spilled across the iron track.

In his unhappy end, not unmindful of the rare genius of the
mechanician, the republic decreed him a stately funeral. It was
resolved that the great bell—the one whose casting had been jeopardized through the timidity of the ill-starred workman—should be
rung upon the entrance of the bier into the cathedral. The most
robust man of the country round was assigned the office of bell-
ringer.

But as the pall-bearers entered the cathedral porch, naught but a broken and disastrous sound, like that of some lone Alpine landslide, fell from the tower upon their ears. And then, all was hushed.

Glancing backwards, they saw the groined belfry crashed sideways in. It afterwards appeared that the powerful peasant, who had the bell-rope in charge, wishing to test at once the full glory of the bell, had swayed down upon the rope with one concentrate jerk. The mass of quaking metal, too ponderous for its frame, and strangely feeble somewhere at its top, loosed from its fastening, tore sideways down, and tumbling in one sheer fall, three hundred feet to the soft sward below, buried itself inverted and half out of sight.

Upon its disinterment, the main fracture was found to have started from a small spot in the ear; which, being scraped, revealed a defect, deceptively minute, in the casting; which defect must subsequently have been pasted over with some unknown compound.

The remolten metal soon reassumed its place in the tower's repaired superstructure. For one year the metallic choir of birds sang musically in its belfry-bough-work of sculptured blinds and traceries. But on the first anniversary of the tower's completion—at early dawn, before the concourse had surrounded it—an earthquake came; one loud crash was heard. The stone-pine, with all its bower of songsters, lay overthrown upon the plain.

So the blind slave obeyed its blinder lord; but, in obedience, slew him. So the creator was killed by the creature. So the bell was too heavy for the tower. So the bell's main weakness was where man's blood had flawed it. And so pride went before the fall.

1855

I and My Chimney

I and my chimney, two gray-headed old smokers, reside in the country. We are, I may say, old settlers here; particularly my old chimney, which settles more and more every day.

Though I always say, *I and my chimney*, as Cardinal Wolsey used to say, *I and my King*,[4] yet this egotistic way of speaking, wherein I take precedence of my chimney, is hardly borne out by the facts; in everything, except the above phrase, my chimney taking precedence of me.

4. The king to whom the powerful Cardinal Wolsey (1475–1530) referred was Henry VIII of England (to whom Melville compares his chimney a few lines below), and the allusion is probably to Shakespeare's *Henry VIII* III.ii.313–16, where the Duke of Nor- folk charges Wolsey with making the king his "servant" by using the phrase *Ego et Rex meus* (scholars like to point out, however, that the first personal pronoun must come first in proper Latin word order).

Within thirty feet of the turf-sided road, my chimney—a huge, corpulent old Harry VIII of a chimney—rises full in front of me and all my possessions. Standing well up a hill-side, my chimney, like Lord Rosse's monster telescope,[5] swung vertical to hit the meridian moon, is the first object to greet the approaching traveler's eye; nor is it the last which the sun salutes. My chimney, too, is before me in receiving the first-fruits of the seasons. The snow is on its head ere on my hat; and every spring, as in a hollow beech tree, the first swallows build their nests in it.

But it is within doors that the pre-eminence of my chimney is most manifest. When in the rear room, set apart for that object, I stand to receive my guests (who, by the way, call more, I suspect, to see my chimney than me), I then stand, not so much before, as, strictly speaking, behind my chimney, which is, indeed, the true host. Not that I demur. In the presence of my betters, I hope I know my place.

From this habitual precedence of my chimney over me, some even think that I have got into a sad rearward way altogether; in short, from standing behind my old-fashioned chimney so much, I have got to be quite behind the age too, as well as running be-hindhand in everything else. But to tell the truth, I never was a very forward old fellow, nor what my farming neighbors call a fore-handed one. Indeed, those rumors about my behindhandedness are so far correct, that I have an odd sauntering way with me some-times of going about with my hands behind my back. As for my belonging to the rear-guard in general, certain it is, I bring up the rear of my chimney—which, by the way, is this moment before me—and that, too, both in fancy and fact. In brief, my chimney is my superior; my superior by I know not how many heads and shoulders; my superior, too, in that humbly bowing over with shovel and tongs, I much minister to it; yet never does it minister, or in-cline over to me; but, if anything, in its settlings, rather leans the other way.

My chimney is grand seignior here—the one great domineering object, not more of the landscape, than of the house; all the rest of which house, in each architectural arrangement, as may shortly appear, is, in the most marked manner, accommodated, not to my wants, but to my chimney's, which, among other things, has the centre of the house to himself, leaving but the odd holes and corners to me.

But I and my chimney must explain; and, as we are both rather obese, we may have to expatiate.

5. The six-foot reflecting telescope con-structed by William Parsons, 3rd Earl of Rosse, was a marvel of the scientific world when it was put into use in 1848. It had a focal length of 57 feet.

In those houses which are strictly double houses—that is, where the hall is in the middle—the fireplaces usually are on opposite sides; so that while one member of the household is warming himself at a fire built into a recess of the north wall, say another member, the former's own brother, perhaps, may be holding his feet to the blaze before a hearth in the south wall—the two thus fairly sitting back to back. Is this well? Be it put to any man who has a proper fraternal feeling. Has it not a sort of sulky appearance? But very probably this style of chimney building originated with some architect afflicted with a quarrelsome family.

Then again, almost every modern fireplace has its separate flue—separate throughout, from hearth to chimney-top. At least such an arrangement is deemed desirable. Does not this look egotistical, selfish? But still more, all these separate flues, instead of having independent masonry establishments of their own, or instead of being grouped together in one federal stock in the middle of the house—instead of this, I say, each flue is surreptitiously honeycombed into the walls; so that these last are here and there, or indeed almost anywhere, treacherously hollow, and, in consequence, more or less weak. Of course, the main reason of this style of chimney building is to economize room. In cities, where lots are sold by the inch, small space is to spare for a chimney constructed on magnanimous principles; and, as with most thin men, who are generally tall, so with such houses, what is lacking in breadth must be made up in height. This remark holds true even with regard to many very stylish abodes, built by the most stylish of gentlemen. And yet, when that stylish gentleman, Louis le Grand of France,[6] would build a palace for his lady friend, Madame de Maintenon, he built it but one story high—in fact, in the cottage style. But then, how uncommonly quadrangular, spacious, and broad—horizontal acres, not vertical ones. Such is the palace, which, in all its one-storied magnificence of Languedoc marble, in the garden of Versailles, still remains to this day. Any man can buy a square foot of land and plant a liberty-pole on it; but it takes a king to set apart whole acres for a Grand Trianon.

But nowadays it is different; and furthermore, what originated in a necessity has been mounted into a vaunt. In towns there is large rivalry in building tall houses. If one gentleman builds his house four stories high, and another gentleman comes next door and builds five stories high, then the former, not to be looked down upon that way, immediately sends for his architect and claps a fifth

6. The Grand Monarch, Louis XIV (1638–1715), actually built the Grand Trianon at Versailles in 1670, before Françoise d'Aubigné joined the court (as the governess of his children) and became Mme. de Maintenon. The new palace, which Melville describes, was constructed in 1687, after she had been privately married to the king.

and a sixth story on top of his previous four. And, not till the gentleman has achieved his aspiration, not till he has stolen over the way by twilight and observed how his sixth story soars beyond his neighbor's fifth—not till then does he retire to his rest with satisfaction.

Such folks, it seems to me, need mountains for neighbors, to take this emulous conceit of soaring out of them.

If, considering that mine is a very wide house, and by no means lofty, aught in the above may appear like interested pleading, as if I did but fold myself about in the cloak of a general proposition, cunningly to tickle my individual vanity beneath it, such misconception must vanish upon my frankly conceding that land adjoining my alder swamp was sold last month for ten dollars an acre, and thought a rash purchase at that; so that for wide houses hereabouts there is plenty of room, and cheap. Indeed, so cheap—dirt cheap—is the soil, that our elms thrust out their roots in it, and hang their great boughs over it, in the most lavish and reckless way. Almost all our crops, too, are sown broadcast, even peas and turnips. A farmer among us, who should go about his twenty-acre field, poking his finger into it here and there, and dropping down a mustard seed, would be thought a penurious, narrow-minded husbandman. The dandelions in the river-meadows, and the forget-me-nots along the mountain roads, you see at once they are put to no economy in space. Some seasons, too, our rye comes up, here and there a spear sole and single like a church-spire. It doesn't care to crowd itself where it knows there is such a deal of room. The world is wide, the world is all before us, says the rye. Weeds, too, it is amazing how they spread. No such thing as arresting them—some of our pastures being a sort of Alsatia[7] for the weeds. As for the grass, every spring it is like Kossuth's rising of what he calls the peoples.[8] Mountains, too, a regular camp-meeting of them. For the same reason, the same all-sufficiency of room, our shadows march and countermarch, going through their various drills and masterly evolutions, like the old imperial guard on the Champs de Mars. As for the hills, especially where the roads cross them, the supervisors of our various towns have given notice to all concerned, that they can come and dig them down and cart them off and never a cent to pay, no more than for the privilege of picking blackberries. The stranger who is buried here, what liberal-hearted landed proprietor among us grudges

7. The district of Whitefriars in London, once a sanctuary for debtors and lawbreakers.
8. Lajos (or Louis) Kossuth (1802–94) was the leader of the Hungarians and the inspirer of other European "peoples" in the revolutionary movement which began in France in 1848.

The tone of Melville's allusion may be the result of the controversy Kossuth aroused in 1852 after his first enthusiastic reception in the United States. But he left his impression upon the American scene by popularizing the full beard which can be seen in every extant portrait of Melville himself.

him his six feet of rocky pasture?

Nevertheless, cheap, after all, as our land is, and much as it is trodden under foot, I, for one, am proud of it for what it bears; and chiefly for its three great lions—the Greak Oak, Ogg Mountain, and my chimney.

Most houses here are but one and a half stories high; few exceed two. That in which I and my chimney dwell, is in width nearly twice its height, from sill to eaves—which accounts for the magnitude of its main content—besides showing that in this house, as in this country at large, there is abundance of space, and to spare, for both of us.

The frame of the old house is of wood—which but the more sets forth the solidity of the chimney, which is of brick. And as the great wrought nails, binding the clapboards, are unknown in these degenerate days, so are the huge bricks in the chimney walls. The architect of the chimney must have had the pyramid of Cheops before him; for after that famous structure it seems modeled, only its rate of decrease towards the summit is considerably less, and it is truncated. From the exact middle of the mansion it soars from the cellar, right up through each successive floor, till, four feet square, it breaks water from the ridge-pole of the roof, like an anvil-headed whale, through the crest of a billow. Most people, though, liken it, in that part, to a razeed[9] observatory, masoned up.

The reason for its peculiar appearance above the roof touches upon rather delicate ground. How shall I reveal that, forasmuch as many years ago the original gable roof of the old house had become very leaky, a temporary proprietor hired a band of woodmen, with their huge, crosscut saws, and went to sawing the old gable roof clean off. Off it went, with all its birds' nests, and dormer windows. It was replaced with a modern roof, more fit for a railway wood-house than an old country gentleman's abode. This operation—razeeing the structure some fifteen feet—was, in effect upon the chimney, something like the falling of the great spring tides. It left uncommon low water all about the chimney—to abate which appearance, the same person now proceeds to slice fifteen feet off the chimney itself, actually beheading my royal old chimney—a regicidal act which, were it not for the palliating fact that he was a poulterer by trade, and, therefore, hardened to such neck-wringings, should send that former proprietor down to posterity in the same cart with Cromwell.[1]

Owing to its pyramidal shape, the reduction of the chimney inordinately widened its razeed summit. Inordinately, I say, but only

9. Cut down to a less number of decks (used of ships).
1. Oliver Cromwell (1599–1658) was the leader of the English Puritan revolution during which King Charles I was beheaded.

in the estimation of such as have no eye to the picturesque. What care I, if, unaware that my chimney, as a free citizen of this free land, stands upon an independent basis of its own, people passing it wonder how such a brick-kiln, as they call it, is supported upon mere joists and rafters? What care I? I will give a traveler a cup of switchel,[2] if he want it; but am I bound to supply him with a sweet taste? Men of cultivated minds see, in my old house and chimney, a goodly old elephant-and-castle.[3]

All feeling hearts will sympathize with me in what I am now about to add. The surgical operation, above referred to, necessarily brought into the open air a part of the chimney previously under cover, and intended to remain so and, therefore, not built of what are called weather-bricks. In consequence, the chimney, though of a vigorous constitution, suffered not a little from so naked an exposure; and, unable to acclimate itself, ere long began to fail— showing blotchy symptoms akin to those in measles. Whereupon travelers, passing my way, would wag their heads, laughing: "See that wax nose—how it melts off!" But what cared I? The same travelers would travel across the sea to view Kenilworth[4] peeling away, and for a very good reason: that of all artists of the picturesque, decay wears the palm—I would say, the ivy. In fact, I've often thought that the proper place for my old chimney is ivied old England.

In vain my wife—with what probable ulterior intent will, ere long, appear—solemnly warned me, that unless something were done, and speedily, we should be burnt to the ground, owing to the holes crumbling through the aforesaid blotchy parts, where the chimney joined the roof. "Wife," said I, "far better that my house should burn down, than that my chimney should be pulled down, though but a few feet. They call it a wax nose; very good; not for me to tweak the nose of my superior." But at last the man who has a mortgage on the house dropped me a note, reminding me that, if my chimney was allowed to stand in that invalid condition, my policy of insurance would be void. This was a sort of hint not to be neglected. All the world over, the picturesque yields to the pocketesque. The mortgagor cared not, but the mortgagee did.

So another operation was performed. The wax nose was taken off, and a new one fitted on. Unfortunately for the expression— being put up by a squint-eyed mason who, at the time, had a bad stitch in the same side—the new nose stands a little awry, in the same direction.

Of one thing, however, I am proud. The horizontal dimensions

2. A drink of water, ginger, and molasses, sometimes laced with rum.
3. Name of a famous London tavern.
4. The ruins of a famous castle (built in the 12th century) where the Earl of Leicester gave a lavish entertainment for Queen Elizabeth in 1575.

of the new part are unreduced.

Large as the chimney appears upon the roof, that is nothing to its spaciousness below. At its base in the cellar, it is precisely twelve feet square; and hence covers precisely one hundred and forty-four superficial feet. What an appropriation of terra firma for a chimney, and what a huge load for this earth! In fact, it was only because I and my chimney formed no part of his ancient burden, that that stout peddler, Atlas of old, was enabled to stand up so bravely under his pack. The dimensions given may, perhaps, seem fabulous. But, like those stones at Gilgal,[5] which Joshua set up for a memorial of having passed over Jordan, does not my chimney remain, even unto this day?

Very often I go down into my cellar, and attentively survey that vast square of masonry. I stand long, and ponder over, and wonder at it. It has a druidical[6] look, away down in the umbrageous cellar there, whose numerous vaulted passages, and far glens of gloom, resemble the dark, damp depths of primeval woods. So strongly did this conceit steal over me, so deeply was I penetrated with wonder at the chimney, that one day—when I was a little out of my mind, I now think—getting a spade from the garden, I set to work, digging round the foundation, especially at the corners thereof, obscurely prompted by dreams of striking upon some old, earthen-worn memorial of that bygone day when, into all this gloom, the light of heaven entered, as the masons laid the foundation-stones, peradventure sweltering under an August sun, or pelted by a March storm. Plying my blunted spade, how vexed was I by that ungracious interruption of a neighbor, who, calling to see me upon some business, and being informed that I was below, said I need not be troubled to come up, but he would go down to me; and so, without ceremony, and without my having been forewarned, suddenly discovered me, digging in my cellar.

"Gold-digging, sir?"

"Nay, sir," answered I, starting, "I was merely—ahem! merely —I say I was merely digging—round my chimney."

"Ah, loosening the soil, to make it grow. Your chimney, sir, you regard as too small, I suppose; needing further development, especially at the top?"

"Sir!" said I, throwing down the spade, "do not be personal. I and my chimney—"

"Personal?"

"Sir, I look upon this chimney less as a pile of masonry than as a personage. It is the king of the house. I am but a suffered

5. See Joshua iv.8–9.
6. The Druids were priests in ancient Gaul, Britain, and Ireland; they were associated with the mysteries of nature worship and such examples of masonry as the great stone circles at Stonehenge.

and inferior subject."

In fact, I would permit no gibes to be cast at either myself or my chimney; and never again did my visitor refer to it in my hearing, without coupling some compliment with the mention. It well deserves a respectful consideration. There it stands, solitary and alone —not a council-of-ten[7] flues, but, like his sacred majesty of Russia, a unit of an autocrat.

Even to me, its dimensions, at times, seem incredible. It does not look so big—no, not even in the cellar. By the mere eye, its magnitude can be but imperfectly comprehended, because only one side can be received at one time; and said side can only present twelve feet, linear measure. But then, each other side also is twelve feet long; and the whole obviously forms a square; and twelve times twelve is one hundred and forty-four. And so, an adequate conception of the magnitude of this chimney is only to be got at by a sort of process in the higher mathematics, by a method somewhat akin to those whereby the surprising distances of fixed stars are computed.

It need hardly be said that the walls of my house are entirely free from fireplaces. These all congregate in the middle—in the one grand central chimney, upon all four sides of which are hearths— two tiers of hearths—so that when, in the various chambers, my family and guests are warming themselves of a cold winter's night, just before retiring, then, though at the time they may not be thinking so, all their faces mutually look towards each other, yea, all their feet point to one centre; and, when they go to sleep in their beds, they all sleep round one warm chimney, like so many Iroquois Indians, in the woods, round their one heap of embers. And just as the Indians' fire serves, not only to keep them comfortable, but also to keep off wolves, and other savage monsters, so my chimney, by its obvious smoke at top, keeps off prowling burglars from the towns —for what burglar or murderer would dare break into an abode from whose chimney issues such a continual smoke—betokening that if the inmates are not stirring, at least fires are, and in case of an alarm, candles may readily be lighted, to say nothing of muskets.

But stately as is the chimney—yea, grand high altar as it is, right worthy for the celebration of High Mass before the Pope of Rome, and all his cardinals—yet what is there perfect in this world? Caius Julius Caesar, had he not been so inordinately great, they say that Brutus, Cassius, Antony, and the rest, had been greater. My chimney, were it not so mighty in its magnitude, my chambers had been larger. How often has my wife ruefully told me, that my chimney, like the English aristocracy, casts a contracting shade all round it. She avers that endless domestic inconveniences arise—more particularly from the chimney's stubborn central locality. The grand

7. The members of the Council of Ten were the autocratic rulers of medieval Venice.

objection with her is that it stands midway in the place where a fine entrance-hall ought to be. In truth, there is no hall whatever to the house—nothing but a sort of square landing-place, as you enter from the wide front door. A roomy enough landing-place, I admit, but not attaining to the dignity of a hall. Now, as the front door is precisely in the middle of the front of the house, inwards it faces the chimney. In fact, the opposite wall of the landing-place is formed solely by the chimney; and hence—owing to the gradual tapering of the chimney—is a little less than twelve feet in width. Climbing the chimney in this part, is the principal stair-case— which, by three abrupt turns, and three minor landing-places, mounts to the second floor, where, over the front door, runs a sort of narrow gallery, something less than twelve feet long, leading to chambers on either hand. This gallery, of course, is railed; and so, looking down upon the stairs, and all those landing-places together, with the main one at bottom, resembles not a little a balcony for musicians, in some jolly old abode, in times Elizabethan. Shall I tell a weakness? I cherish the cobwebs there, and many a time arrest Biddy in the act of brushing them with her broom, and have many a quarrel with my wife and daughters about it.

Now the ceiling, so to speak, of the place where you enter the house, that ceiling is, in fact, the ceiling of the second floor, not the first. The two floors are made one here; so that ascending this turning stairs, you seem going up into a kind of soaring tower, or light-house. At the second landing, midway up the chimney, is a mysterious door, entering to a mysterious closet; and here I keep mysterious cordials, of a choice, mysterious flavor, made so by the constant nurturing and subtle ripening of the chimney's gentle heat, distilled through that warm mass of masonry. Better for wines is it than voyages to the Indies; my chimney itself a tropic. A chair by my chimney in a November day is as good for an invalid as a long season spent in Cuba. Often I think how grapes might ripen against my chimney. How my wife's geraniums bud there! Bud in December. Her eggs, too—can't keep them near the chimney, on account of hatching. Ah, a warm heart has my chimney.

How often my wife was at me about that projected grand entrance-hall of hers, which was to be knocked clean through the chimney, from one end of the house to the other, and astonish all guests by its generous amplitude. "But, wife," said I, "the chimney —consider the chimney: if you demolish the foundation, what is to support the superstructure?" "Oh, that will rest on the second floor." The truth is, women know next to nothing about the realities of architecture. However, my wife still talked of running her entries and partitions. She spent many long nights elaborating her plans; in imagination building her boasted hall through the chimney, as though its high mightiness were a mere spear of sorrel-top. At last, I gently reminded her that, little as she might fancy it, the chimney was a fact—a sober, substantial fact, which, in all her plannings, it would be well to take into full consideration. But this was not of much avail.

And here, respectfully craving her permission, I must say a few words about this enterprising wife of mine. Though in years nearly old as myself, in spirit she is young as my little sorrel mare, Trigger, that threw me last fall. What is extraordinary, though she comes of a rheumatic family, she is straight as a pine, never has any aches; while for me with the sciatica, I am sometimes as crippled up as any old apple tree.[8] But she has not so much as a toothache. As for her hearing—let me enter the house in my dusty boots, and she away up in the attic. And for her sight—Biddy, the housemaid, tells other people's housemaids, that her mistress will spy a spot on the dresser straight through the pewter platter, put up on purpose to hide it. Her faculties are alert as her limbs and her senses. No danger of my spouse dying of torpor. The longest night in the year I've known her lie awake, planning her campaign for the morrow. She is a natural projector. The maxim, "Whatever is, is right," is not hers. Her maxim is, Whatever is, is wrong; and what is more, must be altered; and what is still more, must be altered right away. Dreadful maxim for the wife of a dozy old dreamer like me, who dotes on seventh days as days of rest, and, out of a sabbatical horror of industry, will, on a week-day, go out of my road a quarter of a mile, to avoid the sight of a man at work.

That matches are made in heaven, may be, but my wife would have been just the wife for Peter the Great, or Peter the Piper. How she would have set in order that huge littered empire of the one, and with indefatigable painstaking picked the peck of pickled peppers for the other.

But the most wonderful thing is, my wife never thinks of her end. Her youthful incredulity, as to the plain theory, and still plainer fact of death, hardly seems Christian. Advanced in years, as she knows she must be, my wife seems to think that she is to teem on, and be inexhaustible forever. She doesn't believe in old age. At that strange promise in the plain of Mamre, my old wife, unlike old Abraham's, would not have jeeringly laughed within herself.[9]

Judge how to me, who, sitting in the comfortable shadow of my

8. Melville's first attack of rheumatism in the back occurred in February, 1855, and his severe attack of sciatica in June (less than three months before he completed this story). Personal allusions in the story are ambiguous, but Elizabeth Melville, in her memoir of her husband, recognized their existence and said that the activities attributed to the author's wife were those of his mother.
9. See Genesis xviii.10–12. The "strange promise" was that Sarah should bear a son after "it ceased to be with Sarah after the manner of women."

chimney, smoking my comfortable pipe, with ashes not unwelcome at my feet, and ashes not unwelcome all but in my mouth; and who am thus in a comfortable sort of not unwelcome, though, indeed, ashy enough way, reminded of the ultimate exhaustion even of the most fiery life; judge how to me this unwarrantable vitality in my wife must come, sometimes, it is true, with a moral and a calm, but oftener with a breeze and a ruffle.

If the doctrine be true, that in wedlock contraries attract, by how cogent a fatality must I have been drawn to my wife! While spicily impatient of present and past, like a glass of ginger-beer she overflows with her schemes; and, with like energy as she puts down her foot, puts down her preserves and her pickles, and lives with them in a continual future; or ever full of expectations both from time and space, is ever restless for newspapers, and ravenous for letters. Content with the years that are gone, taking no thought for the morrow, and looking for no new thing from any person or quarter whatever, I have not a single scheme or expectation on earth, save in unequal resistance of the undue encroachment of hers.

Old myself, I take to oldness in things; for that cause mainly loving old Montaigne,[1] and old cheese, and old wine; and eschewing young people, hot rolls, new books, and early potatoes, and very fond of my old claw-footed chair, and old club-footed Deacon White, my neighbor, and that still nigher old neighbor, my betwisted old grape-vine, that of a summer evening leans in his elbow for cosy company at my window-sill, while I, within doors, lean over mine to meet his; and above all, high above all, am fond of my highmanteled old chimney. But she, out of that infatuate juvenility of hers, takes to nothing but newness; for that cause mainly, loving new cider in autumn, and in spring, as if she were own daughter of Nebuchadnezzar, fairly raving after all sorts of salads and spinaches, and more particularly green cucumbers (though all the time nature rebukes such unsuitable young hankerings in so elderly a person, by never permitting such things to agree with her), and has an itch after recently-discovered fine prospects (so no grave-yard be in the background), and also after Swedenborgianism, and the Spirit Rapping philosophy,[2] with other new views, alike in things natural and unnatural; and immortally hopeful, is forever making new flower-beds even on the north side of the house, where the bleak mountain wind would scarce allow the wiry weed called hard-hack to gain a thorough footing; and on the road-side sets out mere

1. The *Essays* of Michel de Montaigne (1533–92) were among Melville's favorite books.
2. The mystical doctrines of Emanuel Swedenborg (1688–1772) had a strong influence upon Emerson and his fellow transcendentalists and upon such individual eccentrics as the elder Henry James. The table rappings of the Fox Sisters of Rochester, N.Y., in 1850 started the vogue for Spiritualism.

pipestems of young elms; though there is no hope of any shade from them, except over the ruins of her great granddaughters' gravestones; and won't wear caps, but plaits her gray hair; and takes the Ladies' Magazine for the fashions; and always buys her new almanac a month before the new year; and rises at dawn; and to the warmest sunset turns a cold shoulder; and still goes on at odd hours with her new course of history, and her French, and her music; and likes young company; and offers to ride young colts; and sets out young suckers in the orchard; and has a spite against my elbowed old grape-vine, and my club-footed old neighbor, and my claw-footed old chair, and above all, high above all, would fain persecute, unto death, my high-manteled old chimney. By what perverse magic, I a thousand times think, does such a very autumnal old lady have such a very vernal young soul? When I would remonstrate at times, she spins round on me with, "Oh, don't you grumble, old man (she always called me old man), it's I, young I, that keep you from stagnating." Well, I suppose it is so. Yea, after all, these things are well ordered. My wife, as one of her poor relations, good soul, intimates, is the salt of the earth, and none the less the salt of my sea, which otherwise were unwholesome. She is its monsoon, too blowing a brisk gale over it, in the one steady direction of my chimney.

Not insensible of her superior energies, my wife has frequently made me propositions to take upon herself all the responsibilities of my affairs. She is desirous that, domestically, I should abdicate; that, renouncing further rule, like the venerable Charles V, I should retire into some sort of monastery.[3] But indeed, the chimney excepted, I have little authority to lay down. By my wife's ingenious application of the principle that certain things belong of right to female jurisdiction, I find myself, through my easy compliances, insensibly stripped by degrees of one masculine prerogative after another. In a dream I go about my fields, a sort of lazy, happy-go-lucky, good-for-nothing, loafing old Lear.[4] Only by some sudden revelation am I reminded who is over me; as year before last, one day seeing in one corner of the premises fresh deposits of mysterious boards and timbers, the oddity of the incident at length begat serious meditation. "Wife," said I, "whose boards and timbers are those I see near the orchard there? Do you know anything about them, wife? Who put them there? You know I do not like the neighbors to use my land that way; they should ask permission first."

3. Charles V (1500–1558) of the Holy Roman Empire and King of Spain (as Charles I) described himself as "old and feeble" in 1555, when he began to resign his kingdoms in preparation for his retirement to a small house attached to a monastery the following year.

4. Shakespeare's King Lear, of course, was a tragic figure—"a poor, infirm, weak, and despis'd old man" whose wits were beginning to crack—when he roamed the open country near Gloucester's castle.

She regarded me with a pitying smile.

"Why, old man, don't you know I am building a new barn? Didn't you know that, old man?"

This is the poor old lady that was accusing me of tyrannizing over her.

To return now to the chimney. Upon being assured of the futility of her proposed hall, so long as the obstacle remained, for a time my wife was for a modified project. But I could never exactly comprehend it. As far as I could see through it, it seemed to involve the general idea of a sort of irregular archway, or elbowed tunnel, which was to penetrate the chimney at some convenient point under the stair-case, and carefully avoiding dangerous contact with the fireplaces, and particularly steering clear of the great interior flue, was to conduct the enterprising traveler from the front door all the way into the dining-room in the remote rear of the mansion. Doubtless it was a bold stroke of genius, that plan of hers, and so was Nero's when he schemed his grand canal through the Isthmus of Corinth.[5] Nor will I take oath, that, had her project been accomplished, then, by help of lights hung at judicious intervals through the tunnel, some Belzoni[6] or other might have succeeded in future ages in penetrating through the masonry, and actually emerging into the dining-room, and once there, it would have been inhospitable treatment of such a traveler to have denied him a recruiting meal.

But my bustling wife did not restrict her objections, nor in the end confine her proposed alterations to the first floor. Her ambition was of the mounting order. She ascended with her schemes to the second floor, and so to the attic. Perhaps there was some small ground for her discontent with things as they were. The truth is, there was no regular passage-way up stairs or down, unless we again except that little orchestra-gallery before mentioned. And all this was owing to the chimney, which my gamesome spouse seemed despitefully to regard as the bully of the house. On all its four sides, nearly all the chambers sidled up to the chimney for the benefit of a fireplace. The chimney would not go to them; they must needs go to it. The consequence was, almost every room, like a philosophical system, was in itself an entry, or passage-way to other rooms, and systems of rooms—a whole suite of entries, in fact. Going through the house, you seem to be forever going somewhere, and getting nowhere. It is like losing one's self in the woods; round and round the chimney you go, and if you arrive at all, it is just where you

---

5. The Roman Emperor Nero began cutting such a canal in A.D. 67 but abandoned it.
6. Giovanni Battista Belzoni (1778–1832) was an Italian explorer of Egyptian antiquities whose achievements included the penetration of the second pyramid of Giza and the opening of the tomb of Seti I (which became known as "Belzoni's tomb").

started, and so you begin again, and again get nowhere. Indeed—
though I say it not in the way of fault-finding at all—never was
there so labyrinthine an abode. Guests will tarry with me several
weeks and every now and then, be anew astonished at some unforeseen apartment.

The puzzling nature of the mansion, resulting from the chimney,
is peculiarly noticeable in the dining-room, which has no less than
nine doors, opening in all directions, and into all sorts of places. A
stranger for the first time entering this dining-room, and naturally
taking no special heed at what door he entered, will, upon rising to
depart, commit the strangest blunders. Such, for instance, as opening the first door that comes handy, and finding himself stealing up
stairs by the back passage. Shutting that door, he will proceed to
another, and be aghast at the cellar yawning at his feet. Trying a
third, he surprises the housemaid at her work. In the end, no more
relying on his own unaided efforts, he procures a trusty guide in
some passing person, and in good time successfully emerges. Perhaps as curious a blunder as any, was that of a certain stylish young
gentleman, a great exquisite, in whose judicious eyes my daughter
Anna had found especial favor. He called upon the young lady one
evening, and found her alone in the dining-room at her needle-work.
He stayed rather late; and after abundance of superfine discourse,
all the while retaining his hat and cane, made his profuse adieus,
and with repeated graceful bows proceeded to depart, after the
fashion of courtiers from the Queen, and by so doing, opening a
door at random, with one hand placed behind, very effectively succeeded in backing himself into a dark pantry, where he carefully
shut himself up, wondering there was no light in the entry. After
several strange noises as of a cat among the crockery, he reappeared
through the same door, looking uncommonly crestfallen, and, with
a deeply embarrassed air, requested my daughter to designate at
which of the nine he should find exit. When the mischievous Anna
told me the story, she said it was surprising how unaffected and
matter-of-fact the young gentleman's manner was after his reappearance. He was more candid than ever, to be sure; having inadvertently
thrust his white kids into an open drawer of Havana sugar, under the
impression, probably, that being what they call "a sweet fellow," his
route might possibly lie in that direction.

Another inconvenience resulting from the chimney is the bewilderment of a guest in gaining his chamber, many strange doors
lying between him and it. To direct him by finger-posts would look
rather queer; and just as queer in him to be knocking at every door
on his route, like London's city guest, the King, at Temple Bar.[7]

---

7. Temple Bar was once a barred entrance to the City of London at what is
now the juncture of Fleet Street and
the Strand. An old custom required that

Now, of all these things and many, many more, my family continually complained. At last my wife came out with her sweeping proposition—*in toto* to abolish the chimney.

"What!" said I, "abolish the chimney? To take out the backbone of anything, wife, is a hazardous affair. Spines out of backs, and chimneys out of houses, are not to be taken like frosted lead-pipes from the ground. Besides," added I, "the chimney is the one grand permanence of this abode. If undisturbed by innovators, then in future ages, when all the house shall have crumbled from it, this chimney will still survive—a Bunker Hill monument.[8] No, no, wife, I can't abolish my backbone."

So said I then. But who is sure of himself, especially an old man, with both wife and daughters ever at his elbow and ear? In time, I was persuaded to think a little better of it; in short, to take the matter into preliminary consideration. At length it came to pass that a master-mason—a rough sort of architect—one Mr. Scribe,[9] was summoned to a conference. I formally introduced him to my chimney. A previous introduction from my wife had introduced him to myself. He had been not a little employed by that lady, in preparing plans and estimates for some of her extensive operations in drainage. Having, with much ado, extorted from my spouse the promise that she would leave us to an unmolested survey, I began by leading Mr. Scribe down to the root of the matter, in the cellar. Lamp in hand, I descended; for though upstairs it was noon, below it was night.

We seemed in the pyramids; and I, with one hand holding my lamp overhead, and with the other pointing out, in the obscurity, the hoar mass of the chimney, seemed some Arab guide, showing the cob-webbed mausoleum of the great god Apis.[1]

"This is a most remarkable structure, sir," said the master-mason, after long contemplating it in silence, "a most remarkable structure, sir."

"Yes," said I, complacently, "every one says so."

"But large as it appears above the roof, I would not have inferred the magnitude of this foundation, sir," eyeing it critically.

Then taking out his rule, he measured it.

"Twelve feet square; one hundred and forty-four square feet!

when the king entered the City in state the entrance should be barred until the Lord Mayor presented him with the sword of the city.
8. The 221-foot monument to the Revolutionary battle of Bunker Hill was completed in 1843, and Melville had dedicated his novel *Israel Potter* to it—perhaps because the opening chapters of the book were accepted for publication on Bunker Hill Day, June 17, 1854.
9. This may be a personal allusion. The poet Oliver Wendell Holmes, Professor of Anatomy in the Harvard Medical School and a summer resident of Pittsfield, examined Melville after his attack of sciatica in June, 1855.
1. The name for a succession of sacred bulls worshiped by the Egyptians and embalmed and buried in the necropolis at Memphis.

Sir, this house would appear to have been built simply for the accommodation of your chimney."

"Yes, my chimney and me. Tell me candidly, now," I added, "would you have such a famous chimney abolished?"

"I wouldn't have it in a house of mine, sir, for a gift," was the reply. "It's a losing affair altogether, sir. Do you know, sir, that in retaining this chimney, you are losing, not only one hundred and forty-four square feet of good ground, but likewise a considerable interest upon a considerable principal?"

"How?"

"Look, sir," said he, taking a bit of red chalk from his pocket, and figuring against a whitewashed wall, "twenty times eight is so and so; then forty-two times thirty-nine is so and so—ain't it, sir? Well, add those together, and subtract this here, then that makes so and so," still chalking away.

To be brief, after no small ciphering, Mr. Scribe informed me that my chimney contained, I am ashamed to say how many thousand and odd valuable bricks.

"No more," said I, fidgeting. "Pray now, let us have a look above."

In that upper zone we made two more circumnavigations for the first and second floors. That done, we stood together at the foot of the stairway by the front door; my hand upon the knob, and Mr. Scribe hat in hand.

"Well, sir," said he, a sort of feeling his way, and, to help himself, fumbling with his hat, "well, sir, I think it can be done."

"What, pray, Mr. Scribe; *what* can be done?"

"Your chimney, sir; it can without rashness be removed, I think."

"I will think of it, too, Mr. Scribe," said I, turning the knob, and bowing him towards the open space without, "I will *think* of it, sir; it demands consideration; much obliged to ye; good morning, Mr. Scribe."

"It is all arranged, then," cried my wife with great glee, bursting from the nighest room.

"When will they begin?" demanded my daughter Julia.

"To-morrow?" asked Anna.

"Patience, patience, my dears," said I, "such a big chimney is not to be abolished in a minute."

Next morning it began again.

"You remember the chimney," said my wife.

"Wife," said I, "it is never out of my house, and never out of my mind."

"But when is Mr. Scribe to begin to pull it down?" asked Anna.

"Not to-day, Anna," said I.

"*When*, then?" demanded Julia in alarm.

Now, if this chimney of mine was, for size, a sort of belfry, for ding-donging at me about it, my wife and daughters were a sort of bells, always chiming together, or taking up each other's melodies at every pause, my wife the key-clapper of all. A very sweet ringing, and pealing, and chiming, I confess; but then, the most silvery of bells may, sometimes, dismally toll, as well as merrily play. And as touching the subject in question, it became so now. Perceiving a strange relapse of opposition in me, wife and daughters began a soft and dirge-like, melancholy tolling over it.

At length my wife, getting much excited, declared to me, with pointed finger, that so long as that chimney stood, she should regard it as the monument of what she called my broken pledge. But finding this did not answer, the next day she gave me to understand that either she or the chimney must quit the house.

Finding matters coming to such a pass, I and my pipe philosophized over them awhile, and finally concluded between us, that little as our hearts went with the plan, yet for peace's sake, I might write out the chimney's death-warrant, and, while my hand was in, scratch a note to Mr. Scribe.

Considering that I, and my chimney, and my pipe, from having been so much together, were three great cronies, the facility with which my pipe consented to a project so fatal to the goodliest of our trio; or rather, the way in which I and my pipe, in secret, conspired together, as it were, against our unsuspicious old comrade—this may seem rather strange, if not suggestive of sad reflections upon us two. But, indeed, we sons of clay,[2] that is my pipe and I, are no whit better than the rest. Far from us, indeed, to have volunteered the betrayal of our crony. We are of a peaceable nature, too. But that love of peace it was which made us false to a mutual friend, as soon as his cause demanded a vigorous vindication. But I rejoice to add, that better and braver thoughts soon returned, as will now briefly be set forth.

To my note, Mr. Scribe replied in person.

Once more we made a survey, mainly now with a view to a pecuniary estimate.

"I will do it for five hundred dollars," said Mr. Scribe at last, again hat in hand.

"Very well, Mr. Scribe, I will think of it," replied I, again bowing him to the door.

Not unvexed by this, for the second time, unexpected response, again he withdrew, and from my wife and daughters again burst the old exclamations.

The truth is, resolve how I would, at the last pinch I and my chimney could not be parted.

2. See Genesis ii.7.

"So Holofernes³ will have his way, never mind whose heart breaks for it," said my wife next morning, at breakfast, in that half-didactic, half-reproachful way of hers, which is harder to bear than her most energetic assault. Holofernes, too, is with her a pet name for any fell domestic despot. So, whenever, against her most ambitious innovations, those which saw me quite across the grain, I, as in the present instance, stand with however little steadfastness on the defence, she is sure to call me Holofernes, and ten to one takes the first opportunity to read aloud, with a suppressed emphasis, of an evening, the first newspaper paragraph about some tyrannic day-laborer who, after being for many years the Caligula⁴ of his family, ends by beating his long-suffering spouse to death, with a garret door wrenched off its hinges, and then, pitching his little innocents out of the window, suicidally turns inward towards the broken wall scored with the butcher's and baker's bills, and so rushes headlong to his dreadful account.

Nevertheless, for a few days, not a little to my surprise, I heard no further reproaches. An intense calm pervaded my wife, but beneath which, as in the sea, there was no knowing what portentous movements might be going on. She frequently went abroad, and in a direction which I thought not unsuspicious; namely, in the direction of New Petra,⁵ a griffin-like house of wood and stucco, in the highest style of ornamental art, graced with four chimneys in the form of erect dragons spouting smoke from their nostrils; the elegant modern residence of Mr. Scribe, which he had built for the purpose of a standing advertisement, not more of his taste as an architect, than his solidity as a master-mason.

At last, smoking my pipe one morning, I heard a rap at the door, and my wife, with an air unusually quiet for her, brought me a note. As I have no correspondents except Solomon, with whom, in his sentiments, at least, I entirely correspond,⁶ the note occasioned me some little surprise, which was not diminished upon reading the following:

"New Petra, April 1.

"Sir:—During my last examination of your chimney, possibly you may have noted that I frequently applied my rule to it in a manner apparently unnecessary. Possibly also, at the same time,

<hr/>

3. General of the armies of the Assyrian king Nebuchadnezzar whose power and cruelty was so great that "the fear and dread of him fell upon all the inhabitants." The Israelite heroine Judith eventually cut off his head as he lay in a drunken stupor. See the apocryphal book of Judith ii–xiii.
4. Roman emperor (12–41) whose brief reign was noted for its tyrannical cruelty.

5. Petra (literally, "the rock") was a ruined city between the Dead Sea and the Gulf of Akbar, once a natural fortress walled in by towering rocks and dominating the ancient caravan routes. "New Petra" is, of course, Melville's invention.
6. Solomon's "sentiments" are probably those expressed in Ecclesiastes, especially the statements that all is vanity and vexation of spirit.

you might have observed in me more or less of perplexity, to which, however, I refrained from giving any verbal expression.

"I now feel it obligatory upon me to inform you of what was then but a dim suspicion, and as such would have been unwise to give utterance to, but which now, from various subsequent calculations assuming no little probability, it may be important that you should not remain in further ignorance of.

"It is my solemn duty to warn you, sir, that there is architectural cause to conjecture that somewhere concealed in your chimney is a reserved space, hermetically closed, in short, a secret chamber, or rather closet. How long it has been there, it is for me impossible to say. What it contains is hid, with itself, in darkness. But probably a secret closet would not have been contrived except for some extraordinary object, whether for the concealment of treasure, or what other purpose, may be left to those better acquainted with the history of the house to guess.

"But enough; in making this disclosure, sir, my conscience is eased. Whatever step you choose to take upon it is, of course, a matter of indifference to me; though, I confess, as respects the character of the closet, I cannot but share in a natural curiosity.

"Trusting that you may be guided aright, in determining whether it is Christian-like knowingly to reside in a house, hidden in which is a secret closet; I remain, with much respect, yours very humbly,

"HIRAM SCRIBE."

My first thought upon reading this note was, not of the alleged mystery of manner to which, at the outset, it alluded—for none such had I at all observed in the master-mason during his surveys—but of my late kinsman, Captain Julian Dacres, long a ship-master and merchant in the Indian trade, who, about thirty years ago, and at the ripe age of ninety, died a bachelor, and in this very house, which he had built. He was supposed to have retired into this country with a large fortune. But to the general surprise, after being at great cost in building himself this mansion, he settled down into a sedate, reserved, and inexpensive old age, which by the neighbors was thought all the better for his heirs; but lo! upon opening the will, his property was found to consist but of the house and grounds, and some ten thousand dollars in stocks; but the place, being found heavily mortgaged, was in consequence sold. Gossip had its day, and left the grass quietly to creep over the captain's grave, where he still slumbers in a privacy as unmolested as if the billows of the Indian Ocean, instead of the billows of inland verdure, rolled over him. Still, I remembered long ago hearing strange solutions whispered by the country people for the mystery involving his will, and, by reflex, himself; and that, too, as well in conscience as purse. But people who could circulate the report (which they did), that Captain Julian Dacres had, in his day, been a Borneo pirate, surely were not worthy of credence in their collateral notions. It is queer what wild whimsies of rumors will, like toadstools, spring up about any accentric stranger who, settling down among a rustic population, keeps quietly to himself. With some, inoffensiveness would seem a prime cause of offense. But what chiefly had led me to scout at these rumors, particularly as referring to concealed treasure, was the circumstance, that the stranger (the same who razeed the roof and the chimney) into whose hands the estate had passed on my kinsman's death, was of that sort of character, that had there been the least ground for those reports, he would speedily have tested them, by tearing down and rummaging the walls.

Nevertheless, the note of Mr. Scribe, so strangely recalling the memory of my kinsman, very naturally chimed in with what had been mysterious, or at least unexplained, about him; vague flashings of ingots united in my mind with vague gleamings of skulls. But the first cool thought soon dismissed such chimeras; and, with a calm smile, I turned towards my wife, who, meantime, had been sitting near by, impatient enough, I dare say, to know who could have taken it into his head to write me a letter.

"Well, old man," said she, "who is it from, and what is it about?"

"Read it, wife," said I, handing it.

Read it she did, and then—such an explosion! I will not pretend to describe her emotions, or repeat her expressions. Enough that my daughters were quickly called in to share the excitement. Although they had never before dreamed of such a revelation as Mr. Scribe's, yet upon the first suggestion they instinctively saw the extreme likelihood of it. In corroboration, they cited first my kinsman, and second, my chimney; alleging that the profound mystery involving the former, and the equally profound masonry involving the latter, though both acknowledged facts, were alike preposterous on any other supposition than the secret closet.

But all this time I was quietly thinking to myself: Could it be hidden from me that my credulity in this instance would operate very favorably to a certain plan of theirs? How to get to the secret closet, or how to have any certainty about it at all, without making such fell work with the chimney as to render its set destruction superfluous? That my wife wished to get rid of the chimney, it needed no reflection to show; and that Mr. Scribe, for all his pretended disinterestedness, was not opposed to pocketing five hundred dollars by the operation, seemed equally evident. That my wife had, in secret, laid heads together with Mr. Scribe, I at present refrain from affirming. But when I consider her enmity against my chimney, and the steadiness with which at the last she is wont to carry out her schemes, if by hook or by crook she can, especially after having been once baffled, why, I scarcely knew at what step of hers to be surprised.

Of one thing only was I resolved, that I and my chimney should not budge.

In vain all protests. Next morning I went out into the road, where I had noticed a diabolical-looking old gander that, for its doughty exploits in the way of scratching into forbidden inclosures, had been rewarded by its master with a portentous, four-pronged, wooden decoration, in the shape of a collar of the Order of the Garotte.[7] This gander I cornered, and rummaging out its stiffest quill, plucked it, took it home, and making a stiff pen, inscribed the following stiff note:

"Chimney Side, April 2.

"Mr. Scribe.

"Sir:—For your conjecture, we return you our joint thanks and compliments, and beg leave to assure you, that we shall remain, very faithfully, the same,

"I AND MY CHIMNEY."

Of course, for this epistle we had to endure some pretty sharp raps. But having at last explicitly understood from me that Mr. Scribe's note had altered my mind one jot, my wife, to move me, among other things said, that if she remembered aright, there was a statute placing the keeping in private houses of secret closets on the same unlawful footing with the keeping of gunpowder. But it had no effect.

A few days after, my spouse changed her key.

It was nearly midnight, and all were in bed but ourselves, who sat up, one in each chimney-corner; she, needles in hand, indefatigably knitting a sock; I, pipe in mouth, indolently weaving my vapors.

It was one of the first of the chill nights in autumn. There was a fire on the hearth, burning low. The air without was torpid and heavy; the wood, by an oversight, of the sort called soggy.

"Do look at the chimney," she began; "can't you see that something must be in it?"

"Yes, wife. Truly there is smoke in the chimney, as in Mr. Scribe's note."

"Smoke? Yes, indeed, and in my eyes, too. How you two wicked old sinners do smoke!—this wicked old chimney and you."

"Wife," said I, "I and my chimney like to have a quiet smoke

7. A garotte was an iron collar, attached to a post and tightened by a screw, used as a means of execution in Spain. The allusion puns on the elaborate collar which was one of the decorations of the British Order of the Garter.

together, it is true, but we don't like to be called names."

"Now, dear old man," said she, softening down, and a little shifting the subject, "when you think of that old kinsman of yours, you *know* there must be a secret closet in this chimney."

"Secret ash-hole, wife, why don't you have it? Yes, I dare say there is a secret ash-hole in the chimney; for where do all the ashes go to that we drop down the queer hole yonder?"

"I know where they go to; I've been there almost as many times as the cat."

"What devil, wife, prompted you to crawl into the ash-hole! Don't you know that St. Dunstan's devil[8] emerged from the ash-hole? You will get your death one of these days, exploring all about as you do. But, supposing there be a secret closet, what then?"

"What then? why what should be in a secret closet but—"

"Dry bones, wife," broke in I with a puff, while the sociable old chimney broke in with another.

"There again! Oh, how this wretched old chimney smokes," wiping her eyes with her handkerchief. "I've no doubt the reason it smokes so is, because that secret closet interferes with the flue. Do see, too, how the jambs here keep settling; and it's down hill all the way from the door to this hearth. This horrid old chimney will fall on our heads yet; depend upon it, old man."

"Yes, wife, I do depend on it; yes, indeed, I place every dependence on my chimney. As for its settling, I like it. I, too, am settling, you know, in my gait. I and my chimney are settling together, and shall keep settling, too, till, as in a great feather-bed, we shall both have settled away clean out of sight. But this secret oven; I mean, secret closet of yours, wife; where exactly do you suppose that secret closet is?"

"That is for Mr. Scribe to say."

"But suppose he cannot say exactly; what then?"

"Well then, he can prove, I am sure, that it must be somewhere or other in this horrid old chimney."

"And if he can't prove that; what then?"

"Why then, old man," with a stately air, "I shall say little more about it."

"Agreed, wife," returned I, knocking my pipe-bowl against the jamb; "and now, to-morrow, I will a third time send for Mr. Scribe. Wife, the sciatica takes me; be so good as to put this pipe on the mantel."

"If you get the step-ladder for me, I will. This shocking old chimney, this abominable old-fashioned old chimney's mantels are so

8. St. Dunstan was a 10th-century Abbot of Glastonbury and Archbishop of Canterbury; he was also a metal-worker. The Devil was said to have tempted him in the form of a woman but was seized by the nose with red-hot tongs.

high, I can't reach them."

No opportunity, however trivial, was overlooked for a subordinate fling at the pile.

Here, by way of introduction, it should be mentioned, that besides the fireplaces all round it, the chimney was, in the most haphazard way, excavated on each floor for certain curious out-of-the-way cupboards and closets, of all sorts and sizes, clinging here and there, like nests in the crotches of some old oak. On the second floor these closets were by far the most irregular and numerous. And yet this should hardly have been so, since the theory of the chimney was, that it pyramidically diminished as it ascended. The abridgment of its square on the roof was obvious enough; and it was supposed that the reduction must be methodically graduated from bottom to top.

"Mr. Scribe," said I when, the next day, with an eager aspect, that individual again came, "my object in sending for you this morning is, not to arrange for the demolition of my chimney, nor to have any particular conversation about it, but simply to allow you every reasonable facility for verifying, if you can, the conjecture communicated in your note."

Though in secret not a little crestfallen, it may be, by my phlegmatic reception, so different from what he had looked for; with much apparent alacrity he commenced the survey; throwing open the cupboards on the first floor, and peering into the closets on the second; measuring one within, and then comparing that measurement with the measurement without. Removing the fire-boards, he would gaze up the flues. But no sign of the hidden work yet.

Now, on the second floor the rooms were the most rambling conceivable. They, as it were, dovetailed into each other. They were of all shapes; not one mathematically square room among them all— a peculiarity which by the master-mason had not been unobserved. With a significant, not to say portentous expression, he took a circuit of the chimney, measuring the area of each room around it; then going down stairs, and out of doors, he measured the entire ground area; then compared the sum-total of all the areas of all the rooms on the second floor with the ground area; then, returning to me in no small excitement, announced that there was a difference of no less than two hundred and odd square feet—room enough, in all conscience, for a secret closet.

"But, Mr. Scribe," said I, stroking my chin, "have you allowed for the walls, both main and sectional? They take up some space, you know."

"Ah, I had forgotten that," tapping his forehead; "but," still ciphering on his paper, "that will not make up the deficiency."

"But, Mr. Scribe, have you allowed for the recesses of so many fireplaces on a floor, and for the firewalls, and the flues; in short, Mr. Scribe, have you allowed for the legitimate chimney itself—some one hundred and forty-four square feet or thereabouts, Mr. Scribe?"

"How unaccountable. That slipped my mind, too."

"Did it, indeed, Mr. Scribe?"

He faltered a little, and burst forth with, "But we must not allow one hundred and forty-four square feet for the legitimate chimney. My position is, that within those undue limits the secret closet is contained."

I eyed him in silence a moment; then spoke:

"Your survey is concluded, Mr. Scribe; be so good now as to lay your finger upon the exact part of the chimney wall where you believe this secret closet to be; or would a witch-hazel wand[9] assist you, Mr. Scribe?"

"No, sir, but a crow-bar would," he, with temper, rejoined.

Here, now, thought I to myself, the cat leaps out of the bag. I looked at him with a calm glance, under which he seemed somewhat uneasy. More than ever now I suspected a plot. I remembered what my wife had said about abiding by the decision of Mr. Scribe. In a bland way, I resolved to buy up the decision of Mr. Scribe.

"Sir," said I, "really I am much obliged to you for this survey. It has quite set my mind at rest. And no doubt you, too, Mr. Scribe, must feel much relieved. Sir," I added, "you have made three visits to the chimney. With a business man, time is money. Here are fifty dollars, Mr. Scribe. Nay, take it. You have earned it. Your opinion is worth it. And by the way—" as he modestly received the money— "have you any objections to give me a—a—little certificate— something, say, like a steam-boat certificate, certifying that you, a competent surveyor, have surveyed my chimney, and found no reason to believe any unsoundness; in short, any—any secret closet in it. Would you be so kind, Mr. Scribe?"

"But, but, sir," stammered he with honest hesitation.

"Here, here are pen and paper," said I, with entire assurance.

Enough.

That evening I had the certificate framed and hung over the dining-room fireplace, trusting that the continual sight of it would forever put at rest at once the dreams and stratagems of my household.

But, no. Inveterately bent upon the extirpation of that noble old chimney, still to this day my wife goes about it, with my daughter Anna's geological hammer, tapping the wall all over, and then holding her ear against it, as I have seen the physicians of life insurance companies tap a man's chest, and then incline over for the

9. Witch-hazel wands were frequently used as divining rods in rural districts for the purpose of discovering underground water or treasure.

echo. Sometimes of nights she almost frightens one, going about on this phantom errand, and still following the sepulchral response of the chimney, round and round, as if it were leading her to the threshold of the secret closet.

"How hollow it sounds," she will hollowly cry. "Yes, I declare," with an emphatic tap, "there is a secret here. Here, in this very spot. Hark! How hollow!"

"Pshaw! wife, of course it is hollow. Who ever heard of a solid chimney?"

But nothing avails. And my daughters take after, not me, but their mother.

Sometimes all three abandon the theory of the secret closet, and return to the genuine ground of attack—the unsightliness of so cumbrous a pile, with comments upon the great addition of room to be gained by its demolition, and the fine effect of the projected grand hall, and the convenience resulting from the collateral running in one direction and another of their various partitions. Not more ruthlessly did the Three Powers partition away poor Poland,[1] than my wife and daughters would fain partition away my chimney.

But seeing that, despite all, I and my chimney still smoke our pipes, my wife reoccupies the ground of the secret closet, enlarging upon what wonders are there, and what a shame it is, not to seek it out and explore it.

"Wife," said I, upon one of these occasions, "why speak more of that secret closet, when there before you hangs contrary testimony of a master-mason, elected by yourself to decide. Besides, even if there were a secret closet, secret it should remain, and secret it shall. Yes, wife, here, for once, I must say my say. Infinite sad mischief has resulted from the profane bursting open of secret recesses. Though standing in the heart of this house, though hitherto we have all nestled about it, unsuspicious of aught hidden within, this chimney may or may not have a secret closet. But if it have, it is my kinsman's. To break into that wall would be to break into his breast. And that wallbreaking wish of Momus I account the wish of a church-robbing gossip and knave. Yes, wife, a vile eavesdropping varlet was Momus."[2]

"Moses?—Mumps? Stuff with your mumps and your Moses!"

The truth is, my wife, like all the rest of the world, cares not a fig for my philosophical jabber. In dearth of other philosophical companionship, I and my chimney have to smoke and philosophize together. And sitting up so late as we do at it, a mighty smoke it is that we two smoky old philosophers make.

But my spouse, who likes the smoke of my tobacco as little as she does that of the soot, carries on her war against both. I live in continual dread lest, like the golden bowl, the pipes of me and my chimney shall yet be broken.[3] To stay that mad project of my wife's, naught answers. Or, rather, she herself is incessantly answering, incessantly besetting me with her terrible alacrity for improvement, which is a softer name for destruction. Scarce a day I do not find her with her tape-measure, measuring for her grand hall, while Anna holds a yard-stick on one side, and Julia looks approvingly on from the other. Mysterious intimations appear in the nearest village paper, signed "Claude," to the effect that a certain structure, standing on a certain hill, is a sad blemish to an otherwise lovely landscape. Anonymous letters arrive, threatening me with I know not what, unless I remove my chimney. Is it my wife, too, or who, that sets up the neighbors to badgering me on the same subject, and hinting to me that my chimney, like a huge elm, absorbs all moisture from my garden? At night, also, my wife will start as from sleep, professing to hear ghostly noises from the secret closet. Assailed on all sides, and in all ways, small peace have I and my chimney.

Were it not for the baggage, we would together pack up, and remove from the country.

What narrow escapes have been ours! Once I found in a drawer a whole portfolio of plans and estimates. Another time, upon returning after a day's absence, I discovered my wife standing before the chimney in earnest conversation with a person whom I at once recognized as a meddlesome architectural reformer, who, because he had no gift for putting up anything, was ever intent upon pulling down; in various parts of the country having prevailed upon half-witted old folks to destroy their old-fashioned houses, particularly the chimneys.

But worst of all was that time I unexpectedly returned at early morning from a visit to the city, and upon approaching the house, narrowly escaped three brickbats which fell, from high aloft, at my feet. Glancing up, what was my horror to see three savages, in blue jean overalls, in the very act of commencing the long-threatened attack. Aye, indeed, thinking of those three brickbats, I and my chimney have had narrow escapes.

It is now some seven years since I have stirred from home. My city friends all wonder why I don't come to see them, as in former times. They think I am getting sour and unsocial. Some say that I have become a sort of mossy old misanthrope, while all the time the fact is, I am simply standing guard over my mossy old chimney; for it is resolved between me and my chimney, that I and my chimney will never surrender.

1855

---

3. See Ecclesiastes xii.6.

The Portent
(1859)

Hanging from the beam,
  Slowly swaying (such the law),
Gaunt the shadow on your green,
  Shenandoah![4]
The cut is on the crown   5
  (Lo, John Brown),
And the stabs shall heal no more.

Hidden in the cap
  Is the anguish none can draw;
So your future veils its face,   10
  Shenandoah!
But the streaming beard is shown
  (Weird John Brown),
The meteor of the war.

1866

Dupont's Round Fight[5]
(November, 1861)

In time and measure perfect moves
  All Art whose aim is sure;
Evolving rhyme and stars divine
  Have rules, and they endure.

Nor less the Fleet that warred for Right,   5
  And, warring so, prevailed,
In geometric beauty curved,
  And in an orbit sailed.

The rebel at Port Royal felt
  The Unity overawe,   10
And rued the spell. A type was here,
  And victory of LAW.

1866

A Utilitarian View of the Monitor's Fight[6]

Plain be the phrase, yet apt the verse,
  More ponderous than nimble;

4. Harpers Ferry, where John Brown was hanged for inciting a slave rebellion, is in the Shenandoah Valley.
5. During the battle of Port Royal, South Carolina, Rear Admiral Samuel Francis Dupont (1803–65), of the Federal blockading fleet, performed a classic circular maneuver in order to attack the Confederate Forts Walker and Beauregard in one continuous action.
6. The defeat of the Confederate ironclad *Merrimac* by the first armored turret ship, the *Monitor*, on March 9, 1862, marked the beginning of a new era in warfare and the replacement of sailing ships by steam-powered iron vessels.

For since grimed War here laid aside
His Orient pomp, 'twould ill befit
      Overmuch to ply 5
The rhyme's barbaric cymbal.

Hail to victory without the gaud
  Of glory; zeal that needs no fans
Of banners; plain mechanic power
Plied cogently in War now placed— 10
     Where War belongs—
Among the trades and artisans.

Yet this was battle, and intense—
  Beyond the strife of fleets heroic;
Deadlier, closer, calm 'mid storm; 15
No passion; all went on by crank,
     Pivot, and screw,
And calculations of caloric.[7]

Needless to dwell; the story's known.
  The ringing of those plates on plates 20
Still ringeth round the world—
The clangor of that blacksmiths' fray.
     The anvil-din
Resounds this message from the Fates:

War shall yet be, and to the end; 25
  But war-paint shows the streaks of weather;
War yet shall be, but warriors
Are now but operatives; War's made
     Less grand than Peace,
And a singe runs through lace and feather. 30

1866

The House-Top

A NIGHT PIECE

(JULY, 1863)

No sleep. The sultriness pervades the air
And binds the brain—a dense oppression, such
As tawny tigers feel in matted shades,
Vexing their blood and making apt for ravage.
Beneath the stars the roofy desert spreads 5
Vacant as Libya. All is hushed near by.
Yet fitfully from far breaks a mixed surf
Of muffled sound, the Atheist roar of riot.[8]

7. Heat.
8. The New York Draft Riots, July 11–13, were in protest against the Conscription Act which permitted an individual to purchase exemption for $300. They were suppressed by militia brought into the city. Melville's own note on the poem read: " 'I dare not write the horrible and inconceivable atrocities committed,' says Froissart,

Yonder, where parching Sirius set in drought,
Balefully glares red Arson—there—and there.   10
The Town is taken by its rats—ship-rats
And rats of the wharves. All civil charms
And priestly speels which late held hearts in awe—
Fear-bound, subjected to a better sway
Than sway of self; these like a dream dissolve,   15
And man rebounds whole aeons back in nature.
Hail to the low dull rumble, dull and dead,
And ponderous drag that shakes the wall.
Wise Draco⁹ comes, deep in the midnight roll
Of black artillery; he comes, though late;   20
In code corroborating Calvin's creed
And cynic tyrannies of honest kings;
He comes, nor parlies; and the Town, redeemed,
Gives thanks devout; nor, being thankful, heeds
The grimy slur on the Republic's faith implied,   25
Which holds that Man is naturally good,
And—more—is Nature's Roman, never to be scourged.

1866

From Clarel

Part I, Section xxxvii: A Sketch

Not knowing them in very heart
Nor why to join him they were loth,
He,¹ disappointed, moved apart,
With sad pace creeping, dull, as doth
Along the bough the nerveless sloth.   5

    For ease upon the ground they sit;
And Rolfe, with eye still following
Where Nehemiah slow footed it,
Asked Clarel: "Know you anything
Of this man's prior life at all?"   10
"Nothing," said Clarel.—"I recall,"
Said Rolfe, "a mariner like him."
"A mariner?"—"Yes; one who grim
Disaster made as meek as he
There plodding." Vine here showed the zest   15

in alluding to the remarkable sedition in France during his time. The like may be hinted at some proceedings of the draft-rioters."
9. The name of a constellation (the Dragon) as well as that of the Greek law-giver who became a symbol of severity. Hence the flames suggested by the bright Dog Star, Sirius, are followed by retribution with the inevitability of celestial motion or Calvinistic predestination.

1. Nehemiah, an old man with a gentle and saintlike character, has invited Clarel and his two companions, Rolfe and Vine, to stroll with him to Bethany. But they are in no mood to do so, and Rolfe dismisses him with a "Some other day." The relationship between the mariner of Rolfe's "sketch" and Captain Ahab of *Moby Dick* is significant.

Of a deep human interest:
"We crave of you his history":
    And Rolfe began: "Scarce would I tell
Of what this mariner befell—
So much is it with cloud o'ercast—   20
Were he not now gone home at last
Into the green land of the dead,
Where he encamps and peace is shed.
Hardy he was, sanguine and bold,
The master of a ship. His mind   25
In night-watch frequent he unrolled—
As seamen sometimes are inclined—
On serious topics, to his mate,
A man to creed austere resigned.
The master ever spurned at fate,   30
Calvin's or Zeno's.[2] Always still
Man-like he stood by man's free will
And power to effect each thing he would,
Did reason but pronounce it good.
The subaltern held in humble way   35
That still Heaven's overrulings sway
Will and event.
             "On waters far,
Where map-man never made survey,
Gliding along in easy plight,
The strong one brake the lull of night   40
Emphatic in his wilful war—
But staggered, for there came a jar
With fell arrest to keel and speech:
A hidden rock. The pound—the grind—
Collapsing sails o'er deck declined—   45
Sleek billows curling in the breach,
And nature with her neutral mind.
A wreck. 'Twas in the former days,
Those waters then obscure; a maze;
The isles were dreaded—every chain;   50
Better to brave the immense of sea,
And venture for the Spanish Main,
Beating and rowing against the trades,
Than to float to valleys 'neath the lee,
Nor far removed, and palmy shades.   55
So deemed he, strongly erring there.
To boats they take; the weather fair—
Never the sky a cloudlet knew;
A temperate wind unvarying blew
Week after week; yet came despair;   60

2. The Stoic school of philosophy founded by Zeno (ca. 308 B.C.) taught a submission to fate and natural law comparable to the doctrines of predestination and submission to divine will of John Calvin (1509–64).

The bread tho' doled, and water stored
Ran low and lower—ceased. They burn—
They agonise til crime abhorred
Lawful might be. O trade-wind, turn!
    "Well may some items sleep unrolled— 65
Never by the one survivor told.
Him they picked up, where, cuddled down,
They saw the jacketed skeleton,
Lone in the only boat that lived—
His signal frittered to a shred. 70
    " 'Strong need'st thou be,' the rescuers said,
'Who hast such trial sole survived.'
'I *willed* it,' gasped he. And the man,
Renewed ashore, pushed off again.
How bravely sailed the pennoned ship 75
Bound outward on her sealing trip
Antarctic. Yes; but who returns
Too soon, regaining port by land
Who left it by the bay? What spurns
Were his that so could countermand? 80
Nor mutineer, nor rock, nor gale
Nor leak had foiled him. No; a whale
Of purpose aiming, stove the bow:
They foundered. To the master now
Owners and neighbours all impute 85
An inauspiciousness. His wife—
Gentle, but unheroic—she,
Poor thing, at heart knew bitter strife
Between her love and her simplicity:
A Jonah[3] is he?—and men bruit 90
The story. None will give him place
In a third venture. Came the day
Dire need constrained the man to pace
A night patrolman on the quay
Watching the bales till morning hour 95
Through fair and foul. Never he smiled;
Call him, and he would come; not sour
In spirit, but meek and reconciled;
Patient he was, he none withstood;
Oft on some secret thing would brood. 100
He ate what came, though but a crust;
In Calvin's creed he put his trust;
Praised heaven, and said that God was good,
And his calamity but just.
So Sylvio Pellico[4] from his cell-door 105
Forth tottering, after dungeoned years,

3. The Old Testament Jonah became the type of a bringer of ill-luck.
4. Italian dramatist (1788–1854) who was imprisoned in the dungeon of Spielberg for membership in the secret revolutionary society of Carbonari.

Crippled and bleached, and dead his peers:
'Grateful, I thank the Emperor.' "

There ceasing, after pause Rolfe drew
Regard to Nehemiah in view: 110
"Look, the changed master, roams he there?
I mean, is such the guise, the air?"
The speaker sat between mute Vine
And Clarel. From the mystic sea
Laocoön's serpent,[5] sleek and fine,   115
In loop on loop seemed here to twine
His clammy coils about the three.
Then unto them the wannish man
Draws nigh; but absently they scan;
A phantom seems he, and from zone   120
Where naught is real tho' the winds aye moan.

From *Part III, Section v: The High Desert*[6]

* * *

Science and Faith, can these unite?
Or is that priestly instinct right
(Right as regards conserving still
The Church's reign) whose strenuous will
Made Galileo[7] pale recite   5
The Penitential Psalms in vest
Of sackcloth; which to-day would blight
Those potent solvents late expressed
In laboratories of the West?
But in her Protestant repose   10
Snores faith toward her mortal close?
Nay, like a sachem petrified,
Encaved found in the mountain-side,
Perfect in feature, true in limb,
Life's full similitude in him,   15
Yet all mere stone—is faith dead *now*,
A petrifaction? Grant it so,
Then what's in store? what shapeless birth?
Reveal the doom reserved for earth?
How far may seas retiring go?   20
But, to redeem us, shall we say

5. Laocoön and his two sons were strangled by a serpent after he had warned the Trojans of the wooden horse left behind by the Greeks when they pretended to have abandoned the siege of Troy. The implication here seems to be that Rolfe actually had identified Nehemiah.
6. As the pilgrims in Clarel's party rest on the elevated plain overlooking Judea, Derwent, the easy-going Anglican priest, moves away, and the others meditate the authenticity of the Scriptures (i.e., whether they are works of history or of revelation) until they approach what seems to be Melville's own statement of the central problem with which he was concerned while writing *Clarel*. Our extract begins with line 64 of Section v.
7. The Italian astronomer (1564–1642) who demonstrated the fact of the earth's movement around the sun but was forced to recant.

That faith, undying, does but range,
Casting the skin—the creed. In change
Dead always does some creed delay—
Dead, not interred, though hard upon   25
Interment's brink? At Saint Denis,[8]
Where slept the Capets, sire and son,
Eight centuries of lineal clay,
On steps that led down into vault
The prince inurned last made a halt,   30
The coffin left they there, 'tis said,
Till the inheritor was dead;
Then, not till then 'twas laid away.
But if no more the creeds be linked,
If the long line's at last extinct,   35
If time both creed and faith betray,
Vesture and vested—yet again
What interregnum or what reign
Ensues? Or does a period come?
The Sibyls' books[9] lodged in the tomb?   40
Shall endless time no more unfold
Of truth at core? Some things discerned
By the far Noahs[1] of India old—
Earth's first spectators, the clear-eyed,
Unvitiated, unfalsified   45
Seers at first hand—shall these be learned,
Though late, even by the New World, say,
Which now contemns?
                          But what shall stay
The fever of advance? London immense
Still wax for aye? A check: but whence?   50
How of the teeming Prairie-Land?
There shall the plenitude expand
Unthinned, unawed? Or does it need
Only that men should breed and breed
To enrich those forces into play   55
Which in past times could oversway
Pride at his proudest? Do they come,
The locusts, only to the bloom?
Prosperity sire them?
                          Thus they swept,
Nor sequence held, consistent tone—   60
Imagination wandering on
Through vacant halls which faith once kept
With ushers good.
                          Themselves thus lost,

8. A church famous for being the burial place of the French kings, who were, from 987 to Melville's own day, members of the Capet family.
9. A collection of oracles or prophetic books.
1. The story of the deluge (Genesis vi-viii) appears in many mythologies, of which the Indian is one of the oldest.

At settled hearts they wonder most.
For those (they asked) who still adhere   65
In homely habit's dull delay,
To dreams dreamed out or passed away;
Do these, our pagans, all appear
Much like each poor and busy one
Who when the Tartar took Pekin   70
(If credence hearsay old may win),
Knew not the fact—so vast the town,
The multitude, the maze, the din?
    Still laggeth in deferred adieu
The A. D. (Anno Domini)   75
Overlapping into era new
Even as the Roman A. U. C.[2]
Yet ran for time, regardless all
That Christ was born, and after fall
Of Rome itself?
               But now our age,   80
So infidel in equipage,
While carrying still the Christian name—
For all its self-asserted claim,
How fares it, tell? Can the age stem
Its own conclusions? is't a king   85
Awed by his conquests which enring
With menaces his diadem?
Bright visions of the times to be—
Must these recoil, ere long be cowed
Before the march in league avowed   90
Of Mammon[3] and Democracy?
    In one result whereto we tend
Shall Science disappoint the hope,
Yea, to confound us in the end,
New doors to superstition ope?   95
    As years, as years and annals grow,
And action and reaction vie,
And never men attain, but know
How waves on waves forever die;
Does all more enigmatic show?   100

Part IV, Section xxxi: Dirge[4]

Stay, Death. Not mine the Christus-wand
Wherewith to charge thee and command:
I plead. Most gently hold the hand
Of her thou leadest far away;

---

2. *Anno Urbis Conditae:* in the year of the founded city (i.e., Rome, 753 B.C.).
3. The symbol of wealth or cupidity.
4. At the end of his pilgrimage Clarel returns to Jerusalem and finds that his sweetheart, Ruth, has just died. The "Dirge" suggests the emotional situation which complicates the intellectual problem of faith set forth on the High Desert.

966 · *Herman Melville*

Fear thou to let her naked feet   5
Tread ashes—but let mosses sweet
Her footing tempt, where'er ye stray.
Shun Orcus;[5] win the moonlit land
Belulled—the silent meadows lone,
Where never any leaf is blown   10
From lily-stem in Azrael's[6] hand.
There, till her love rejoin her lowly
(Pensive, a shade, but all her own),
On honey feed her, wild and holy;
Or trance her with thy choicest charm.   15
And if, ere yet the lover's free,
Some added dusk thy rule decree—
That shadow only let it be
Thrown in the moon-glade by the palm.[7]

Part IV, Section xxxv: Epilogue[8]

If Luther's day expand to Darwin's year,[9]
Shall that exclude the hope—foreclose the fear?

Unmoved by all the claims our times avow,
The Ancient Sphinx[1] still keeps the porch of shade;
And comes Despair, whom not her calm may cow,   5
And coldly on that adamantine brow
Scrawls undeterred his bitter pasquinade.
But Faith (who from the scrawl indignant turns)
With blood warm oozing from her wounded trust,
Inscribes even on her shards of broken urns   10
The sign o' the cross—*the spirit above the dust!*

Yea, ape and angel, strife and old debate—
The harps of heaven and dreary gongs of hell;
Science the feud can only aggravate—
No umpire she betwixt the chimes and knell;   15
The running battle of the star and clod
Shall run forever—if there be no God.

Degrees we know, unknown in days before;
The light is greater, hence the shadow more;

5. The primitive Roman god of the dead, and also the land of the dead.
6. The Jewish and Mohammedan angel of death.
7. The palm was a complex symbol for Melville. He was aware of it as an emblem of triumph and rejoicing and of its association with Christ's entry into Jerusalem; he was also fascinated by the solitary date palm which he had seen half-way up a precipice on the barren way from Jerusalem to Bethlehem and which he made into the focal point for various meditations in *Clarel*, apparently absorbing it into the wall image which played so important a part in his work.
8. The problem of faith and doubt is unresolved within the poem *Clarel*, and the Epilogue is Melville's own solution, addressed to the hero of the poem.
9. Martin Luther (1483–1546) appears here as a representative of religious faith; Charles Darwin (1809–82), of scientific doubt. The ape in line 12 has reference, of course, to Darwin's theory of human origins.
1. The Sphinx is the mythological—and proverbial—asker of riddles.

And tantalized and apprehensive Man   20
Appealing—Wherefore ripen us to pain?
Seems there the spokesman of dumb Nature's train.

   But through such strange illusions have they passed
Who in life's pilgrimage have baffled striven—
Even death may prove unreal at the last,   25
And stoics be astounded into heaven.

   Then keep thy heart, though yet but ill resigned—
Clarel, thy heart, the issues there but mind;
That like the crocus budding through the snow—
That like a swimmer rising from the deep—   30
That like a burning secret which doth go
Even from the bosom that would hoard and keep;
Emerge thou mayst from the last whelming sea,
And prove that death but routs life into victory.

1876

The Maldive Shark

About the Shark, phlegmatical one,
Pale sot of the Maldive sea,[2]
The sleek little pilot-fish, azure and slim,
How alert in attendance be.
From his saw-pit of mouth, from his charnel of maw   5
They have nothing of harm to dread,
But liquidly glide on his ghastly flank
Or before his Gorgonian[3] head;
Or lurk in the port of serrated teeth
In white triple tiers of glittering gates,   10
And there find a haven when peril's abroad,
An asylum in jaws of the Fates!
They are friends; and friendly they guide him to prey,
Yet never partake of the treat—
Eyes and brains to the dotard lethargic and dull,   15
Pale ravener of horrible meat.

1888

Monody

To have known him,[4] to have loved him
After loneness long;

2. The Indian Ocean, in which the Maldive Archipelago is located. The shovel-nosed shark, with his companion pilot fish, is described in *Mardi*, Chapter XVIII.
3. Petrifying. The face of a mythical Gorgon turned its beholder to stone.
4. Presumably Nathaniel Hawthorne. Cf. the essay "Hawthorne and his Mosses" and perhaps the character Vine in *Clarel*. Melville saw very little of Hawthorne after his first year of enthusiastic friendship.

And then to be estranged in life,
  And neither in the wrong;
And now for death to set his seal—   5
  Ease me, a little ease, my song!

By wintry hills his hermit-mound
  The sheeted snow-drifts drape,
And houseless there the snow-bird flits
  Beneath the fir-trees' crape: 10
Glazed now with ice the cloistral vine
  That hid the shyest grape.

1891

Lone Founts

Though fast youth's glorious fable flies,
View not the world with worldling's eyes;
Nor turn with weather of the time.
Foreclose the coming of surprise:
Stand where Posterity shall stand;   5
Stand where the Ancients stood before,
And, dipping in lone founts thy hand,
Drink of the never-varying lore:
Wise once, and wise thence evermore.

1891

Art

In placid hours well pleased we dream
Of many a brave unbodied scheme.
But form to lend, pulsed life create,
What unlike things must meet and mate:
A flame to melt—a wind to freeze;   5
Sad patience—joyous energies;
Humility—yet pride and scorn;
Instinct and study; love and hate;
Audacity—reverence. These must mate,
And fuse with Jacob's[5] mystic heart,   10
To wrestle with the angel—Art.

1891

Shelley's Vision

Wandering late by morning seas
  When my heart with pain was low—

5. Jacob wrestled with an angel in Genesis xxxii. 24–30.

Hate the censor pelted me—
  Deject I saw my shadow go.

In elf-caprice of bitter tone   5
I too would pelt the pelted one:
At my shadow I cast a stone.

When lo, upon that sun lit ground
  I saw the quivering phantom take
The likeness of St. Stephen[6] crowned: 10
  Then did self-reverence awake.

                                                    1891

The Apparition

(THE PARTHENON UPLIFTED ON ITS ROCK FIRST CHALLENGING
THE VIEW ON THE APPROACH TO ATHENS)

Abrupt the supernatural Cross,
  Vivid in startled air,
Smote the Emperor Constantine[7]
And turned his soul's allegiance there.

With other power appealing down,   5
  Trophy of Adam's best!
If cynic minds you scarce convert,
You try them, shake them, or molest.

Diogenes,[8] that honest heart,
  Lived ere your date began;   10
Thee had he seen, he might have swerved
In mood nor barked so much at Man.

                                                    1891

The New Rosicrucians

To us, disciples of the Order
Whose Rose-Vine twines the Cross,
Who have drained the rose's chalice
Never heeding gain or loss;
For all the preacher's din   5
There is no mortal sin—
No, none to us but Malice!

6. St. Stephen was martyred by being stoned to death. Shelley was persecuted in England and wrote his best poetry after settling on the Continent.
7. Constantine the Great (280?–337), Emperor of Rome, saw a vision of a cross in the sky and made it the official symbol of Christianity.
8. Greek Cynic philosopher (412?–323 B.C.) who became notorious for going around with a lantern, in daylight, searching for "an honest man."

Exempt from that, in blest recline
We let life's billows toss;
If sorrow come, anew we twine   10
The Rose-Vine round the Cross.

1924

Immolated

Children of my happier prime,
When One yet lived with me, and threw
Her rainbow over life and time,
Even Hope, my bride, and mother to you!
O, nurtured in sweet pastoral air,   5
And fed on flowers and light and dew
Of morning meadows—spare, ah, spare
Reproach; spare, and upbraid me not
That, yielding scarce to reckless mood
But jealous of your future lot,   10
I sealed you in a fate subdued.
Have I not saved you from the drear
Theft and ignoring which need be
The triumph of the insincere
Unanimous Mediocrity?   15
Rest therefore, free from all despite,
Snugged in the arms of comfortable night.

1924

Walt Whitman

In 1855, when Walt Whitman was 36 years old, he published the first edition of *Leaves of Grass*. Tradition gives the date as July 4. With his keen sense of the dramatic, Whitman would have planned it that way.

1855 is a signal date in literary history, even though that original edition was a slender volume of only twelve poems and ran to only a thousand copies, of which most were sent out free by the author. For many years America had been seeking her intellectual independence. Emerson, according to Oliver Wendell Holmes, had declared it in his 1837 Phi Beta Kappa address on "The American Scholar"; and he had later called for an American bard in "The Poet" (1844). The intensity of the national search for literary independence is suggested by Whittier's 1847 review of Longfellow's *Evangeline*, opening: "EUREKA! Here, then, we have it at last, —an American poem."

It happened that Longfellow published one of his major works in the birth-year of Whitman's masterpiece. While *Leaves of Grass* seemed to enter quietly into its modest existence, *Hiawatha* rose like a new American meteor in 1855. To judge the contemporary obstacles to prolonged life which the infant *Leaves* faced, we need but compare the receptions of these two 1855 poems: *Hiawatha* was gathered to the bosoms of the American people and also of the entrenched Boston literati of the time; *Leaves of Grass* went largely ignored. Whitman himself wrote three energetic and favorable reviews of his *Leaves*, one of them opening: "An American bard at last!"

Of the copies the New Yorker Whitman sent to his fellow poets, mostly the genteel Bostonians and their satellites, the Quaker poet Whittier is said to have thrown his into the fire. Perhaps many others consigned the unabashed, offensive, disturbing book to a similar violent fate. Only that intellectual Dean of America then at the height of his fame as essayist, poet, lecturer—only Ralph Waldo Emerson responded with a refreshing honesty that is a measure of his greatness. In a brief letter of remarkable praise to the unknown Brooklyn poet, the Concord oracle proclaimed *Leaves of Grass* the "most extraordinary piece of wit and wisdom that America has yet contributed."

It is impossible for us to see *Leaves of Grass* the same way that staid, literary Boston viewed it. But we can guess at the shock and the shudder that went down delicate spines when the book was read. By midcentury the vigor of the romantic movement had thinned to a polite, drawing-room gentility that made poetry more the amusing province of young ladies in the academies than the vital interest of young men on the open road. Poetry had lost touch with its primitive, bardic origins and had become burdened with excess convention, cliché, and sentimentality. Moralistic flower-poems were fashionable: witness William Cullen Bryant's "To a Fringed Gentian" (1832) or James Russell Lowell's "To the Dandelion" (1845). Poetry became dedicated to a debased patriotism (as in Whittier's "Barbara Frietchie," 1863), or to a pretentious philosophy (as in Longfellow's "Psalm of Life," 1839), or to a private sentimentality (as in Oliver Wendell Holmes's "The Boys," 1859).

It is no wonder that, reading American poetry chronologically, we breathe a sigh of relief when we reach Whitman. His *Leaves* come as a fresh breeze that shatters and dispels the stagnant air of the closed drawing room. We recognize in his "wild, barbaric yawp" the accents of both a finisher and a beginner. Whitman is the climax of the American romantic movement; but he is also the originator of modern American poetry. He is one of the great transitional literary figures: he represents the vigorous culmination of an important tradition but at the same time contains the seeds of the radical innovations of the future.

Although Whitman openly embraced and poetically embodied his own time, he did not cut himself off from either the past or the future. There are strong links connecting his 1855 Preface, limning the vagabond cosmic poet, with Wordsworth's Preface to the second edition of *Lyrical Ballads* (1800), launching the romantic revolution. But there are links, likewise strong, connecting his mid-19th-century mystic affirmations (upon contemplation of a spear of summer grass) with Dylan Thomas's mid-20th-century ebullient acceptances (upon discovering in his own green age the force that through the green fuse drives the flower).

Whitman looked to the poets of the past when he affirmed his intention of permitting Nature to speak "without check with original energy"; and he looked to poets of the future when he listened to the sounds of cities, with their "blab of the pave, tires of carts, sluff of boot-soles." Whitman looked back when he affirmed his faith in a poet's world of the imagination; he looked forward when he shouted, "Hurrah for positive science!" He looked to the past when he identified himself as "poet of the Soul"; and he looked to the future when he declared himself equally "poet of the Body." He did not deny the reality of the feudal systems of the past; but he stressed the validity of democracy as an ideal filling the future.

Whitman was not temperamentally suited to accept a role that drew its sole significance from the currents of the past. He said of history:

Regarding it all intently a long while, then dismissing it,
I stand in my place with my own day here.

But neither was Whitman psychologically adjusted to a static present. He always had his eye on the "long brown path" of the open road, his heart set on discovery of a *real* sea-passage to India. True son and heir of the past, he was also a Beginner, ready to pay the "inexorable price" for the "great purchase."

I

When Whitman was born in 1819, America was a fledgling nation of some nine million souls, just forty years or so away from dependence on a mother country. When he died in 1892, the population had risen to some 63 million—and the United States had survived a fratricidal war and experienced an industrial revolution. Both the war and the revolution thrust *democracy* and *science* forward as the central issues of a civilization and a century, spreading them broadcast into the folklore of the people, raising them in the imaginative realization of their possibilities to the level of myth. In embodying his time and nation, his century and his culture, in becoming the American epic poet, Whitman inevitably became the poet of science and democracy, simultaneously assimilating and creating a national myth.

Although he was born in rural Long Island, close to both the soil and the sea, Whitman and his family could not for long withstand the strong gravitational pull of the city of Brooklyn, with its richer possibilities for employment and pleasure. From his birth in 1819 until the birth of his masterpiece in 1855, Whitman's life seemed constantly on the verge of shattering into a myriad of irrelevant details—at least, as we look back on it now. His formal schooling in Brooklyn was brief, though not so scanty as to prevent him from becoming a schoolmaster on Long Island for a short time. But Whitman was not destined for teaching. He early served an apprenticeship as a printer and soon moved through the various jobs offered by a series of newspapers, reaching the fairly exalted editorship of the Brooklyn *Daily Eagle* during 1846–47, a position which he lost only after a dispute over his support of the free-soil against the slavery Democrats.

In spite of his righteous political position, we cannot dispel the feeling, after glancing over the long list of Whitman's early jobs which followed one another in quick succession, that he was a drifter, perhaps a restless dreamer, probably a loafer with occasional furious enthusiasms. The job which Whitman accepted with a New Orleans newspaper in 1848 is unusual only in that it offered the Brooklynite his one chance to see the America he was later to sing with such robust assurance. Whitman was in New Orleans for about four months (not several years, as he once implied) and he followed the prescribed routes, traveling on the Ohio and Mississippi on his way down, returning up the Mississippi and by way of the Great Lakes and Canada. Although it is not likely that the New Orleans episode contained the secret inspiration of Whitman's poetry (some early biographers imaginatively supplied a Creole romance), the travels no doubt contributed a large measure to the poet's expanding vision of his country's physical and spiritual horizons.

Upon returning to Brooklyn, Whitman did a little editing, printing, carpentry, continuing the old pattern of restless shifting from job to job, until in 1855, already 36 years old, he suddenly discovered his life's work in the publication of the first edition of *Leaves of Grass*. Emerson wrote: "I greet you at the beginning of a great career, which yet must have had a long foreground somewhere." Whitman exploited the "greeting" by using it on the spine of the second edition of his book, without bothering to get Emerson's permission—and thereby precluding Emerson's public praise forever after. Biographers have searched exhaustively for that "foreground" which Emerson so casually assumed, but generally to no avail. Whitman's journalistic writings, and especially the occasional poems, are disappointingly mediocre, offering no hint of the genius of *Leaves*.

If the long foreground is to be discovered, we must search not the external but the internal biography, the shaping of the secret imagination by the unrecorded experiences of the soul. What did the boy Whitman absorb from his walks along the seashore as he listened to the measured rhythms of the waves? Or from the itinerant folk orators and evangelists as he listened to them roar and rant of politics and religion? What did the languorous young man absorb from his early reading of the balanced phrases of the Bible, or the beach-stroller from his declamation of Shakespeare to the rolling ocean? What did the dandyish young journalist absorb from his intense passion for the music and drama of opera? Whitman's long foreground must have been an extended emotional and imaginative preparation largely submerged beneath the main currents of his life.

After 1855, Whitman's life seemed largely to disappear into his book, as edition after edition, nine in all, occupied his time and absorbed the various "poses" he assumed, among them the carpenter-Christ and the vagabond poet. Before the Civil War, however, Whitman seemed to have become a Bohemian, frequenting the arty New York German beer cellars, where casually dressed young men intensely discussed poetry, music, and art. But when news reached the Whitman family that Walt's brother George was wounded in the fighting in Virginia, it was Walt (by then in his forties, beyond draft age) who undertook the journey to find and help his brother. The trip was to alter radically the life of the poet. He was deeply moved by the sight of the haphazardly cared-for wounded who overflowed the hospital facilities of Washington, D.C., and after tending to his only slightly wounded brother, he settled down to the semi-volunteer task of caring for the wounded. Whitman quickly transformed himself from Bohemian into Wound-Dresser, and probably found greater purpose and more satisfying fulfillment than ever before in his life. His affections were captured by the masses of men under arms, his sympathies were engaged by the suffering of both Union and Confederate soldiers, and his imagination was stirred by the occasional street glimpses he had of the great western leader, Abraham Lincoln—a new kind of American. The poems of *Drum-Taps* grew out of the varied Civil War experiences, and, later, the Lincoln elegy "When Lilacs Last in the Dooryard Bloom'd" out of profound personal grief at the national loss.

After the war Whitman remained in Washington with a government job, from which he was released by superiors when they discovered that he had written an "immoral" book—the *Leaves*. But with the aid of his friends, among them the novelist W. D. O'Connor (who wrote a fiery defense called *The Good Gray Poet*) and the naturalist John Burroughs, Whitman left one office to take up a desk in another. More important, however, than the notoriety gained from this incident was the publication in England, in 1868, of a selection of *Leaves* introduced by the Pre-Raphaelite author William Michael Rossetti, attracting a foreign audience for the American poet. But now that his reputation was on the rise, Whitman's creative productivity was waning. There were important works yet to appear—principally *Democratic Vistas* and "Passage to India" in 1871. But Whitman himself must have sensed his approaching collapse, which came in 1873 in the form of a crippling paralytic stroke. Later the same year, his mother, to whom he was closely attached, died. Whitman endured these personal blows, removed from Washington to Camden, New Jersey, and lived out his life in the role of the grand old bearded sage of the grade-school photographs.

These last years were not by any means barren of achievement. Whitman obviously had fun playing the amateur naturalist in days spent at Timber Creek, Stafford Farm (New Jersey)—experiences he recorded in *Specimen Days and Collect* (1882). In 1888 he published some autumn leaves in *November Boughs*, together with "A Backward Glance o'er Travel'd Roads," a reminiscence of early dreams seen in the "early candle-light of old age." But more important than any other activity throughout these years was Whitman's constant revision and regrouping of his poems through a series of editions of *Leaves of Grass*, an intuitive reshaping of his masterpiece to achieve the ideal form he sought. This long task was not finally finished to the poet's satisfaction until he reached the end of his life. He was able to see the ninth edition, the so-called "deathbed" edition of 1891–92, through the press before his last "So Long" and "Finalè to the Shore" in March, 1892.

II

Poets are mortal, but their books, if they have the vital juices of life in them, endure. From its very birth in 1855, *Leaves of Grass* seemed to throb with the pulse of life. More than with most books, it seems appropriate with *Leaves of Grass* to speak of its growth. Whitman saw his book evolve through nine editions over a period of some thirty years. He guided its growth through a period of wild adolescence, then of meditative maturity, and finally wise serenity. The miracle of this growth is that one stage followed another without doing violence to either. Whitman never tried to cut away old passages simply because they revealed feelings no longer central to his emotional being. He wanted his book to be honest to life in its fullest range, not selective or partial in its vision.

Reading the first edition (1855) of *Leaves of Grass* is like gazing down into a man's soul, far below the levels of consciousness, into the primordial spirit-stuff of being, where heaven and hell intermingle and become one, where a thousand obscure impulses spring to life and die in joy or agony all in a moment—where the teeming mystery of life lies vibrant and hidden. Seldom has so much primitive power and energy been so quietly released to the world as in the slender volume of twelve untitled poems. Their lines flowed across their wide pages in a cocky, free, and self-assured way that fitted the posture of the vagabond whose picture replaced the author's name in the opening pages of the book.

Emerson's extraordinary letter may well have given the obscure Brooklyn poet just the reassurance he needed to set him off in a burst of creative energy. The second edition of *Leaves of Grass* appeared in 1856, as small and fat as the first was large and slim. Although the poems seemed cramped in this little volume, its corpulence suggested its imaginative abundance—some twenty new poems added to the original twelve. To the distinguished poems of the first edition (including "Song of Myself" and "The Sleepers") were added such important pieces as "Song of the Open Road" and "Crossing Brooklyn Ferry." In addition to spreading Emerson's greeting along the spine, Whitman reprinted the entire letter in the back of the book together with an effusive reply to the "master," in which he lied about the extensive sales of the first edition and boasted of the number of poems he intended to write.

These exaggerations seem all the more quaint in the face of the four-year period of silence before the appearance of the third edition in 1860. For the first time Whitman did not himself have to publish the book but found a publisher in Boston, capital of literary gentility. There while the book was at press, Emerson pleaded with Whitman to eliminate the sex poems from his work, but Whitman did not heed the master except to follow his doctrine of self-reliance. The 1860 edition represents the culmination in the first stage of the growth of the *Leaves*, and, at the same time, shadows forth in its structure the shape of *Leaves* to come. In this third edition Whitman hit upon the successfully executed idea of rearranging and grouping his poems thematically so as to give his book less the look of a miscellany and more the look of a totality, with a beginning, middle, and end as naturally in sequence as the stages of a journey. The volume opened with "Proto-Leaf" (later called "Starting from Paumanok") and closed with "So Long!" In between there appeared such programmatic and provocative clusters as the procreative poems, "Children of Adam," and the comradeship poems, "Calamus," together with such apparently personal outcries of mystic anguish and joy as "Out of the Cradle Endlessly Rocking."

Before Whitman could expand the scope of his *Leaves*, he needed the impact of some major experience on a level beyond the personal. The second stage of the growth of *Leaves*, lasting through the three editions of 1867, 1871–72, and 1876, reflects in the main an infusion into the book of the experiences and insights, enthusiasms and anxieties of the national experience of civil war. Whitman published *Drum-Taps* separately in 1865 and almost immediately after added a *Sequel* containing the Lincoln poems, including "When Lilacs Last in the Dooryard Bloom'd" and "O Captain! My Captain!" Both the cluster of war poems and the *Sequel* Whitman looked upon at first as entities quite distinct from his finished work, *Leaves of Grass*. But gradually his attitude changed, and by 1876 "Drum-Taps" and the Lincoln elegies had found their niche in the master edifice. This 1876 edition was called the Centennial Edition, in honor of the hundredth anniversary of the signing of the Declaration of Independence, and it was issued in two handsome volumes. One volume was the old *Leaves of Grass* reshaped to incorporate the war poems. The other volume, entitled "Two Rivulets," was a miscellaneous collection of prose and poetry, and included a cluster of poems under the title "Passage to India." Whitman once again looked upon his *Leaves* as finished and the "India" poems, "chants of Death and Immortality," as constituting a separate but allied volume.

The final form of *Leaves* was achieved in the third stage of its growth, a stage that, like the previous two, evolved through three editions—1881–82, 1889, and 1891–92—the "deathbed" edition. But in this stage the first edition represented the final maturing in the long life of the *Leaves*. For in the 1881–82 version of his masterpiece, Whitman reshaped his book to include the "Passage to India" poems which had been gathered into a separate volume in previous editions. *Leaves of Grass* at last incorporated the total vision of the poet, embodying his three major themes and weaving them powerfully together in a finished and intricate structure. It is ironic that this edition should have been chosen by fate to be banned in Boston, and that Philadelphia (city of brotherly love) took as its own what Boston cast out. The remaining editions of *Leaves* did not alter the basic form. The 1889 edition added some old-age poems ("First Annex: Sands at Seventy") and the prose piece, "A Backward Glance o'er Travel'd Roads," which at the end of the book looked back over the same years the 1855 Preface had once excitedly surveyed from the beginning. The deathbed edition of 1891–92, which the ailing poet lived to see through the press, added only the "Second Annex: Good-Bye My Fancy," a last and final farewell.

In tracing the evolution of *Leaves of Grass*, we may become so fascinated by the interplay of the life of the poet and the life of his *Leaves* as to leap to the conclusion that the poetry is "mere" autobiography. *Leaves of Grass* is autobiographical inasmuch as any work of the spirit must derive its character from the inner life of the artist. But it is also autonomous and independent and complete in itself, as all great works of art must be. It is most rewarding to read *Leaves of Grass* not as a transcription of an individual life but as the *dramatization* of a composite Modern Man. Whitman once described the intent of his *Leaves*: "to express by sharp-cut self assertion, One's self & also, or may be still more, to map out, to throw together for American use, a gigantic embryo or skeleton of Personality,—fit for the West, for native models." We shall avoid confusion if we read the "I" in *Leaves* not as the historical Whitman but as a central character created for the heroic role in a modern epic. This central character ("gigantic embryo") is first portrayed as achieving self- and other-consciousness in the early poems such as "Song of Myself," "Children of Adam," and "Calamus." The "skeleton of Personality" is next fleshed out in the context of a specific place and time in the "middle" poems, such as those on the Civil War and Lincoln. And finally, this epic hero of the West is dramatized primarily on the intuitive level of cosmic consciousness in the poems of death and immortality, found in the latter part of *Leaves* around "Passage to India." The three stages of growth of *Leaves*, through some nine editions, resulted not in an arbitrary gathering together of disparate poems but in an integrated drama of cosmic, national—and always human—significance.

III

Every genuinely great writer stamps his work with the unmistakable signature of his individual genius—those qualities which distinguish his art from all that has appeared before or after, qualities on whose ready recognition the parodist must depend when he twists them to his own comic purpose. In searching for these qualities in Whitman we may well glance briefly at his free verse, his polyglot language, his sexual imagery, and his "physical" mysticism.

Although Whitman did not invent free verse, he was the first to demonstrate the full range of its possibilities; and he remains one of the best examples of its use. Whitman helped to free modern poetry from the bonds of conventional meter, line length, and rhyme—restrictions which had brought verse, through the unquestioning acceptance of mediocre poets, to a low ebb of tinkling prettiness. In the midst of the dainty decoration which had debased poetry, Whitman's free, sweeping line seemed to have all the freshness of a wholesome outdoor life which he invited the reader to share:

> Loafe with me on the grass, loose the stop from your throat,
> Not words, not music or rhyme I want, not custom or lecture, not even the best,
> Only the lull I like, the hum of your valvèd voice.

In bursting the bonds of an imposed form, Whitman proclaimed the higher discipline of an organic form. *Leaves of Grass* is filled with music of many kinds, both in repeated sound and recurring beat—the music has, however, not the simplicity of a short melody, but the complexity of a symphony. The music of *Leaves* reinforces one of its principal themes— democracy: it asserts the freedom of the individual from external repressions, but it assumes the imposition of an internal discipline. One of the secrets of the success of Whitman's free verse is that it subtly complements his free themes, his chants of democracy and freedom.

Although they are not so well known, Whitman's innovations in poetic language are as revolutionary as those in verse forms. The language of poetry, like its form, had become in Whitman's day convention-ridden and genteel, dull and predictable. Whitman broke away from this deadening tradition and introduced into his poetry the language of all levels of usage. He once remarked that he thought that his *Leaves* was primarily a "language experiment." He wrote in a brief but brilliant essay, "Slang in America": "Considering Language then as some mighty potentate, into the majestic audience-hall of the monarch ever enters a personage like one of Shakespeare's clowns, and takes position there, and plays a part even in the stateliest ceremonies." It was certainly no violation of the serious epic intent of *Leaves of Grass* to permit in its "majestic audience-hall" some of the language-clowns of slang. When Whitman declared, "I wear my hat as I please indoors or out," or "I find no sweeter fat than sticks to my own bones," or "I dote on myself, there is that lot of me and all so luscious," he was fulfilling the prophecy of his "Song of the Exposition"—that is, he was removing the old-world epic muse from her remote grandeur and installing her "by drain-pipe, gasometers, artificial fertilizers," and "amid the kitchen ware!" Whitman ranged far and wide in his language, assimilating and adapting the vocabularies of trades (such as building and carpentry), the vocabularies of sciences (including that pseudo-psychology, phrenology, which analyzes the personality by studying the bumps on the head), and the vocabularies of a variety of foreign tongues ("Accouche! Accouchez!" "No dainty dolce affetuoso I"). At a pinch, Whitman was not averse to making up a word to fill a gap. Indeed, in language as in all else, Whitman was a great democratic mixer, ever ready to place side by side high and low, foreign and native, familiar and obscure, common and learned—and, with surprising frequency, to good effect.

Of the sex imagery in the *Leaves*, Whitman once wrote: "At last analogy the lines I allude to and the spirit in which they are spoken, permeate all 'Leaves of Grass,' and the work must stand or fall with them, as the human body and soul must remain as an entirety." In deliberately setting out to be the poet of procreation, Whitman was attacking what he took to be the prevailing belief in the "inherent nastiness of sex." He explained in "Song of Myself," "voices indecent by me clarified and transfigur'd." Sexual imagery runs through, frequently dominating, "Song of Myself," "Children of Adam," and "Calamus," the three initial poetic assertions in *Leaves of Grass*. The progression from emphasis on the isolate self to concern for man-woman relationships and finally to exploration of man-man relationships in these three sections has been reduced by some hasty readers to mere sexual impulse—auto-, hetero-, or homo-eroticism. The trouble with this easy interpretation is that it reduces Whitman's complex imagination to an absurd simplicity, useful only for the pseudo-psychoanalyst who wants to prove something perverse about Whitman's sexuality. Although we may indulge our morbid interest in Whitman's sexual nature, there is little chance that we shall ever learn very much about it, and what little we do learn should not affect our interpretation of the *Leaves*. Perhaps one day when the *Leaves* are more deeply understood, we shall acknowledge Whitman as one of the great innovators who glimpsed far below the levels of consciousness into the turbulent heart of sexual feeling in all its complex variety and conflicting tendencies—becoming, in his embracement of all, not auto- or homo- or hetero-sexual but omni-sexual in his understanding and sympathies. Whitman's was indeed a lone voice, and surely a brave one, especially in an era of propriety and prudery. And it is highly relevant that to the last, in "A Backward Glance o'er Travel'd Roads," Whitman affirmed the centrality to his book of the sex theme: "I shall only say the espousing principle of those lines so gives breath of life to my whole scheme that the bulk of the pieces might as well have been left unwritten were those lines omitted." Whitman was right: *Leaves of Grass* would have been mortally wounded by the sexual mutilation, by the castration urged on him by the ultra-refined.

One of the great paradoxes of *Leaves of Grass* is that its author asserts simultaneously his claims to be poet of the body *and* poet of the soul, poet of sexuality and poet of spirituality. Whitman asserted in the 1855 Preface, "The poets of the kosmos advance through all interpositions and coverings and turmoils and stratagems to first principles." As a cosmic poet, he seemed to his readers to have done just that. To readers accustomed to New England transcendentalism, with its philosophy compounded of Christian mysticism, German and Platonic idealism, and Oriental spiritualism, Whitman's cosmic mysticism probably seemed not only natural but inevitable. One of his closest friends and admirers, Dr. R. M. Bucke, wrote a book, *Cosmic Consciousness*, to show that Whitman, like the Buddha and Christ, was one of those rare individuals who pass beyond the animal level of consciousness of *other* and the human level of consciousness of *self* to a superhuman level of consciousness of the *cosmos*. Whatever the validity of this claim, subsequent critics have acknowledged the necessity of defining or dismissing Whitman's mysticism. Some of his critics have identified his mysticism (clearly related to the romantic mysticism of Wordsworth, Shelley, and others) as Christian—Protestant or Catholic—while others have asserted that his mystical tendencies are Oriental—Hindu, Taoist, or Zen Buddhist. Obviously Whitman shares much with both Christian and Oriental, but it is true that ultimately his mysticism seems alien to the extreme passivity of the Oriental and the extreme selflessness of the Christian. It should not perhaps seem strange that America would demand its own brand of mysticism that would sacrifice neither individuality nor vitality in its achievement of union with the Transcendent. Characteristically Whitman referred to the Deity as the great "Camerado," a term he invented for his most intimate companions. As in all of his innovations, in his mysticism Whitman was the great leveler. He did not relegate the body to the lower regions nor did he elevate God to the ethereal heights. In insisting on accepting the body and fraternizing with God, Whitman delineated a democratic and physical mysticism that differed markedly and intentionally from both Eastern and Western, Oriental and Christian.

IV

More perhaps than with most poets there are currently many gross misconceptions of Whitman's major themes. Some critics have charged that he was a superpatriot, an unreasoning lover of America in all its crudeness and rawness, a chauvinist who delighted in screaming his country's name and size. Others have claimed that he did not write poems but made inventories of man's and the world's warehouses. Still others have asserted that he was an indiscriminate accepter and merger, and blurred the differences, both gross and subtle, that give men and their lives moral significance.

All of these charges are distortions, but to deny them at length would give them attention beyond their due. At the risk of another kind of distortion, it is perhaps better (and surely more Whitman-like) to attempt some definitions of the recurring themes of *Leaves of Grass*. Whitman himself both assists and hinders such an attempt when he writes near the beginning of his book some lines that simultaneously tantalize with their suggestions and dismay with their vagueness:

> My comrade!
> For you to share with me two greatnesses, and a third one rising inclu-
> sive and more resplendent,
> The greatness of Love and Democracy, and the greatness of Religion.

In such sweeping statements the vagueness is perhaps inevitable, but we should be thankful for the clues.

Love, Democracy, and Religion may be identified as the major themes of *Leaves of Grass* only after they have been given the definitions Whitman gave them throughout his writing: Love is more than sex, Democracy transcends America, Religion escapes all institutions. In Whitman's view, Love, Democracy, and Religion are comprehensive: Love embodies all personal relationships, Democracy embraces the relationships of man and organized society (*this* world), and Religion envisions the relationships of man and spirituality (the transcendent reality that lies beyond this world).

These major themes thread their way through the whole of *Leaves of Grass*, intermingling, shifting, never long absent from any page. In the final version of the book, these themes dominate in the precise order in which Whitman lists them in the lines above. In the first segment of *Leaves*, emphasis falls on the personal consciousness of the individual. Such poems and clusters as "Song of Myself," "Children of Adam," and "Calamus" may be read as a drama of the creation, first of the self, then of woman, and then of fellow man and the world. But this creation is a self-creation, a self-awakening to consciousness of the physical world and its wondrous contents and creatures. Throughout this section of *Leaves* there runs an ebullient note of joy in love that begins with the self but extends ever outward to, finally, a universal embrace.

At the center of *Leaves*, giving it solidity and ballast, are the Civil War and Abraham Lincoln poems. The poetry gathered in and around "Drum-Taps" and "When Lilacs Last in the Dooryard Bloom'd" represents a shift in emphasis from a *personal* to a *social* consciousness. No longer does the poetry deal with abstractions or ideals, but it plants itself firmly in a specific country at a specific time—19th-century America in its crucial test of survival. There has been much said, but with little understanding, about Whitman as the poet of democracy. The clue to his central meaning stands at the very opening of *Leaves of Grass*, in the initial lines:

> One's-self I sing, a simple separate person,
> Yet utter the word Democratic, the word En-Masse.

This simple idea involves a complex balance between the individual and the group, the self and the mass, individuality and equality. The concept is elaborated on the personal level specifically in "Song of Myself" and "Calamus." But the idea receives its major dramatization in "Drum-Taps" and the Lincoln elegy. Whitman believed that in the Civil War he saw his idea of democracy, primarily an ideal, fleshed forth in reality —in the rise of innumerable young men to form the armies and in the rise of the man Lincoln to give moral guidance through the crisis. But even so, Whitman looked upon the Civil War as only the proof of a possibility; he made emphatically clear in *Democratic Vistas* (1871) that *his* democracy was basically a dream for the future, a far cry from the materialistic, corrupt America he saw about him.

It may seem odd that such an intensely physical poet as Whitman, who was repeatedly charged with obscenity, should have considered himself fundamentally a religious poet. In the 1855 Preface, he warned himself —"folks expect of the poet to indicate more than the beauty and dignity which always attach to dumb real objects * * * they expect him to indicate the path between reality and their souls." In his 1888 "Backward Glance," he affirmed once again: "While I cannot understand it or argue it out, I fully believe in a clue and purpose in Nature, entire and several; and that invisible spiritual results, just as real and definite as the visible, eventuate all concrete life and all materialism, through Time." Whenever Whitman used the word "religion," he meant not the theology of some man-made institution but, rather, the spirituality lurking within or lying beyond the entire physical world. This concept, related variously to Platonic and German idealism, to Oriental and Christian mysticism, to British and New England transcendentalism, runs all through the *Leaves*, even those like "Children of Adam" celebrating man's physical life, but it comes to the fore in the poems surrounding "Passage to India," which itself is perhaps Whitman's most purely religious poem.

Love, democracy, religion—these themes, properly defined, provide the key to the understanding of Whitman and his *Leaves*. But when extracted from the book and generalized, they are likely to fade and disappear, to lose all of the vital significance with which Whitman endowed them in his poetry. To know them on his terms, we must venture firsthand far into the *Leaves*, demanding little, accepting much. Only after we have explored far beyond the beaten paths, the familiar seas, are we likely to comprehend Whitman's farthest flights and deepest diving.

V

Whitman wrote in the 1855 Preface, "The proof of a poet is that his country absorbs him as affectionately as he has absorbed it." He must at times have wondered about the truth of the statement, for at no time did America en masse reciprocate Whitman's affections. And even today, when Whitman is generally acknowledged as America's greatest poet, he is not popular in the sense that Longfellow was or even as Robert Frost currently is. *Leaves of Grass* has won its way to the pinnacle it now occupies only haltingly and slowly, and over the powerful objections of any number of detractors. There are some even today who challenge Whitman's stature as a major American poet.

Though the book's battle for recognition seems now largely won, there were times when oblivion seemed not only possible but likely. Emerson's prolonged public silence after the first warm private response must have been cuttingly disappointing. And the episodes involving the charge of obscenity must have had (in spite of their usual happy endings) adverse effects on the steady, solid growth of the reputation of the *Leaves*. Whitman could not count on the support of any of the respectable American poets of his day, and indeed he was lucky that they did not openly display their hostilities. Abroad, he did have the good fortune of getting William Michael Rossetti as his first editor and promoter, and he attracted some slavish imitators such as the poet Edward Carpenter, but even in England his reputation suffered strange setbacks, such as the sudden transformation of Swinburne's early and lavish admiration into a snarling attack.

By the time that Whitman had won full academic respectability, during the 1920's, he was being most sophisticatedly denounced by the leading poets of the 20th century. Ezra Pound claimed he was unable to find one good line in all of *Leaves of Grass*, but he did grudgingly acknowledge Whitman as a "pig-headed father." T. S. Eliot said of Whitman that he "had to conquer an aversion to his form, as well as to much of his matter" in order to read him. These judgments may not seem so severe in isolation, but it must be remembered that they were taken as gospel by generations of critics. It is only recently that poets have argued with Eliot's pronouncement, principally Randall Jarrell and Karl Shapiro; and among the Beat Generation, both the literary and nonliterary variety, Whitman—especially in his rebel-vagabond pose—has developed into a culture hero. Although it was once thought that the Whitman tradition had run its course in such poets as Edgar Lee Masters, Vachel Lindsay, and Carl Sandburg, it has recently been asserted that the real vigor of the Whitman tradition lies in another series of first-rate talents—Hart Crane, D. H. Lawrence, and Dylan Thomas. These poets are true heirs of Whitman's bardic themes of individuality and vitality, of acceptance and aliveness, and these are the poets most likely to form the nucleus for the gathering revolt against the severely intellectualized, world-weary, and negative tradition of Pound and Eliot.

It does not seem possible that *Leaves of Grass* will, like so many classics, remain on the shelf monumental and unread. A book so full of the excitements of the cities and the joys of the open road cannot easily be contained within a library's walls. And moreover, it seems probable that the *Leaves* will serve as a training manual for poetic revolutions to come. For the young poet uneasy in the company of secondhand certainties, restless in his search for his own identity, what better assertion of individual self-hood than Whitman's: "All forces have been steadily employ'd to complete and delight me, / Now on this spot I stand with my robust soul!" Whatever the role of *Leaves of Grass* in the literary insurrections and rebellions of the future, it must be acknowledged now as one of America's founding spiritual documents and archetypal poems.

NOTE ON THE TEXT

The text of the deathbed edition of *Leaves of Grass* (1891–92) has been used for the selections in this volume. Dates after the poems indicate the first appearance in an edition of *Leaves of Grass*; additional dates are given when the poems first appeared in *Drum-Taps* (1865) and *November Boughs* (1888); these dates are followed by the notation "(*DT*)" or "(*NB*)." Whitman's sometimes eccentric spelling has been preserved throughout; for example, he frequently substitutes "k" for "c" ("kosmos") and omits the "e" in past participles ("bloom'd").

Preface to the 1855 Edition of *Leaves of Grass*[1]

America does not repel the past or what it has produced under its forms or amid other politics or the idea of castes or the old religions . . . accepts the lesson with calmness . . . is not so impatient as has been supposed that the slough still sticks to opinions and manners and literature while the life which served its requirements has passed into the new life of the new forms . . . perceives that the corpse is slowly borne from the eating and sleeping

1. The 1855 Preface appeared as a kind of manifesto in the opening pages of the 1st edition of *Leaves of Grass*, comparable in intent to Wordsworth's historic Preface to *Lyrical Ballads* (2nd edition, 1800). Many of the ideas have an Emersonian ring—"The United States themselves are essentially the greatest poem"; "the poetic quality is not marshalled in rhyme or uniformity or abstract addresses to things * * * " Although Whitman begins by describing the American poet, he ends by calling for "poets of the kosmos," who will exhibit the highest attributes of original genius. The 1855 Preface may be profitably read as both a declaration of poetic independence for America and a thinly disguised commentary by Whitman on his ambitious plans for his own newly born *Leaves*. The 1855 Preface did not reappear in subsequent editions of *Leaves*, but parts of it were turned into verse ("By Blue Ontario's Shore").

rooms of the house . . . perceives that it waits a little while in the door . . . that it was fittest for its days . . . that its action has descended to the stalwart and wellshaped heir who approaches . . . and that he shall be fittest for his days.

The Americans of all nations at any time upon the earth have probably the fullest poetical nature. The United States themselves are essentially the greatest poem. In the history of the earth hitherto the largest and most stirring appear tame and orderly to their ampler largeness and stir. Here at last is something in the doings of man that corresponds with the broadcast doings of the day and night. Here is not merely a nation but a teeming nation of nations. Here is action untied from strings necessarily blind to particulars and details magnificently moving in vast masses. Here is the hospitality which forever indicates heroes. . . . Here are the roughs and beards and space and ruggedness and nonchalance that the soul loves. Here the performance disdaining the trivial unapproached in the tremendous audacity of its crowds and groupings and the push of its perspective spreads with crampless and flowing breath and showers its prolific and splendid extravagance. One sees it must indeed own the riches of the summer and winter, and need never be bankrupt while corn grows from the ground or the orchards drop apples or the bays contain fish or men beget children upon women.

Other states indicate themselves in their deputies . . . but the genius of the United States is not best or most in its executives or legislatures, nor in its ambassadors or authors or colleges or churches or parlors, nor even in its newspapers or inventors . . . but always most in the common people. Their manners speech dress friendships—the freshness and candor of their physiognomy—the picturesque looseness of their carriage . . . their deathless attachment to freedom—their aversion to anything indecorous or soft or mean—the practical acknowledgment of the citizens of one state by the citizens of all other states—the fierceness of their roused resentment—their curiosity and welcome of novelty—their selfesteem and wonderful sympathy—their susceptibility to a slight—the air they have of persons who never knew how it felt to stand in the presence of superiors—the fluency of their speech—their delight in music, the sure symptom of manly tenderness and native elegance of soul . . . their good temper and openhandedness—the terrible significance of their elections—the President's taking off his hat to them not they to him—these too are unrhymed poetry. It awaits the gigantic and generous treatment worthy of it.

The largeness of nature or the nation were monstrous without a corresponding largeness and generosity of the spirit of the citizen.

Not nature nor swarming states nor streets and steamships nor prosperous business nor farms nor capital nor learning may suffice for the ideal of man . . . nor suffice the poet. No reminiscences may suffice either. A live nation can always cut a deep mark and can have the best authority the cheapest . . . namely from its own soul. This is the sum of the profitable uses of individuals or states and of present action and grandeur and of the subjects of poets.—As if it were necessary to trot back generation after generation to the eastern records! As if the beauty and sacredness of the demonstrable must fall behind that of the mythical! As if men do not make their mark out of any times! As if the opening of the western continent by discovery and what has transpired since in North and South America were less than the small theatre of the antique or the aimless sleepwalking of the middle ages! The pride of the United States leaves the wealth and finesse of the cities and all returns of commerce and agriculture and all the magnitude of geography or shows of exterior victory to enjoy the breed of full sized men or one full sized man unconquerable and simple.

The American poets are to enclose old and new for America is the race of races. Of them a bard is to be commensurate with a people. To him the other continents arrive as contributions . . . he gives them reception for their sake and his own sake. His spirit responds to his country's spirit . . . he incarnates its geography and natural life and rivers and lakes. Mississippi with annual freshets and changing chutes, Missouri and Columbia and Ohio and Saint Lawrence with the falls and beautiful masculine Hudson, do not embouchure[2] where they spend themselves more than they embouchure into him. The blue breadth over the inland sea of Virginia and Maryland and the sea off Massachusetts and Maine and over Manhattan bay and over Champlain and Erie and over Ontario and Huron and Michigan and Superior, and over the Texan and Mexican and Floridian and Cuban seas and over the seas off California and Oregon, is not tallied by the blue breadth of the waters below more than the breadth of above and below is tallied by him. When the long Atlantic coast stretches longer and the Pacific coast stretches longer he easily stretches with them north or south. He spans between them also from east to west and reflects what is between them. On him rise solid growths that offset the growths of pine and cedar and hemlock and liveoak and locust and chestnut and cypress and hickory and limetree and cottonwood and tuliptree and cactus and wildvine and tamarind and persimmon . . . and tangles as tangled as any canebreak or swamp . . . and forests coated with transparent ice and icicles hanging

2. Pour out from a mouth.

from the boughs and crackling in the wind . . . and sides and peaks of mountains . . . and pasturage sweet and free as savannah or upland or prairie . . . with flights and songs and screams that answer those of the wildpigeon and highhold and orchard-oriole and coot and surf-duck and redshouldered-hawk and fish-hawk and white-ibis and indian-hen and cat-owl and water-pheasant and qua-bird and pied-sheldrake and blackbird and mockingbird and buzzard and condor and night-heron and eagle. To him the hereditary countenance descends both mother's and father's. To him enter the essences of the real things and past and present events—of the enormous diversity of temperature and agriculture and mines —the tribes of red aborigines—the weather-beaten vessels entering new ports or making landings on rocky coasts—the first settlements north or south—the rapid stature and muscle—the haughty defiance of '76,[3] and the war and peace and formation of the constitution . . . the union always surrounded by blatherers and always calm and impregnable—the perpetual coming of immigrants—the wharf-hemm'd cities and superior marine—the unsurveyed interior —the loghouses and clearings and wild animals and hunters and trappers . . . the free commerce—the fisheries and whaling and gold-digging—the endless gestation of new states—the convening of Congress every December, the members duly coming up from all climates and the uttermost parts . . . the noble character of the young mechanics and of all free American workmen and workwomen . . . the general ardor and friendliness and enterprise— the perfect equality of the female with the male . . . the large amativeness[4]—the fluid movement of the population—the factories and mercantile life and labor-saving machinery—the Yankee swap —the New-York firemen and the target excursion—the southern plantation life—the character of the northeast and of the northwest and southwest—slavery and the tremulous spreading of hands to protect it, and the stern opposition to it which shall never cease till it ceases or the speaking of tongues and the moving of lips cease. For such the expression of the American poet is to be transcendant and new. It is to be indirect and not direct or descriptive or epic. Its quality goes through these to much more. Let the age and wars of other nations be chanted and their eras and characters be illustrated and that finish the verse. Not so the great psalm of the republic. Here the theme is creative and has vista. Here comes one among the wellbeloved stonecutters and plans with decision and science and sees the solid and beautiful forms of the future where there are now no solid forms.

3. The American Revolution.
4. Term from phrenology: propensity to love, sexual passion. (Phrenology was the pseudoscience of measuring the bumps on the head to determine certain personality traits.)

Of all nations the United States with veins full of poetical stuff most need poets and will doubtless have the greatest and use them the greatest. Their Presidents shall not be their common referee so much as their poets shall. Of all mankind the great poet is the equable man. Not in him but off from him things are grotesque or eccentric or fail of their sanity. Nothing out of its place is good and nothing in its place is bad. He bestows on every object or quality its fit proportions neither more nor less. He is the arbiter of the diverse and he is the key. He is the equalizer of his age and land . . . he supplies what wants supplying and checks what wants checking. If peace is the routine out of him speaks the spirit of peace, large, rich, thrifty, building vast and populous cities, encouraging agriculture and the arts and commerce—lighting the study of man, the soul, immortality—federal, state or municipal government, marriage, health, free trade, intertravel by land and sea . . . nothing too close, nothing too far off . . . the stars not too far off. In war he is the most deadly force of the war. Who recruits him recruits horse and foot . . . he fetches parks of artillery the best that engineer ever knew. If the time becomes slothful and heavy he knows how to arouse it . . . he can make every word he speaks draw blood. Whatever stagnates in the flat[5] of custom or obedience or legislation he never stagnates. Obedience does not master him, he masters it. High up out of reach he stands turning a concentrated light . . . he turns the pivot with his finger . . . he baffles the swiftest runners as he stands and easily overtakes and envelops them. The time straying toward infidelity and confections and persiflage he withholds by his steady faith . . . he spreads out his dishes . . . he offers the sweet firmfibred meat that grows men and women. His brain is the ultimate brain. He is no arguer . . . he is judgment. He judges not as the judge judges but as the sun falling around a helpless thing. As he sees the farthest he has the most faith. His thoughts are the hymns of the praise of things. In the talk on the soul and eternity and God off of his equal plane he is silent. He sees eternity less like a play with a prologue and denouement . . . he sees eternity in men and women . . . he does not see men and women as dreams or dots. Faith is the antiseptic of the soul . . . it pervades the common people and preserves them . . . they never give up believing and expecting and trusting. There is that indescribable freshness and unconsciousness about an illiterate person that humbles and mocks the power of the noblest expressive genius. The poet sees for a certainty how one not a great artist may be just as sacred as the greatest artist. . . . The power to destroy or remould is freely used by him but never the power of attack. What is past is past. If he does not expose superior models and prove him-

5. Marsh.

self by every step he takes he is not what is wanted. The presence of the greatest poet conquers . . . not parleying or struggling or any prepared attempts. Now he has passed that way see after him! there is not left any vestige of despair or misanthropy or cunning or exclusiveness or the ignominy of a nativity or color or delusion of hell or the necessity of hell . . . and no man thenceforward shall be degraded for ignorance or weakness or sin.

The greatest poet hardly knows pettiness or triviality. If he breathes into any thing that was before thought small it dilates with the grandeur and life of the universe. He is a seer . . . he is individual . . . he is complete in himself . . . the others are as good as he, only he sees it and they do not. He is not one of the chorus . . . he does not stop for any regulations . . . he is the president of regulation. What the eyesight does to the rest he does to the rest. Who knows the curious mystery of the eyesight? The other senses corroborate themselves, but this is removed from any proof but its own and foreruns the identities of the spiritual world. A single glance of it mocks all the investigations of man and all the instruments and books of the earth and all reasoning. What is marvelous? what is unlikely? what is impossible or baseless or vague? after you have once just opened the space of a peachpit and given audience to far and near and to the sunset and had all things enter with electric swiftness softly and duly without confusion or jostling or jam.

The land and sea, the animals fishes and birds, the sky of heaven and the orbs, the forests mountains and rivers, are not small themes . . . but folks expect of the poet to indicate more than the beauty and dignity which always attach to dumb real objects . . . they expect him to indicate the path between reality and their souls. Men and women perceive the beauty well enough . . . probably as well as he. The passionate tenacity of hunters, woodmen, early risers, cultivators of gardens and orchards and fields, the love of healthy women for the manly form, seafaring persons, drivers of horses, the passion for light and the open air, all is an old varied sign of the unfailing perception of beauty and of a residence of the poetic in outdoor people. They can never be assisted by poets to perceive . . . some may but they never can. The poetic quality is not marshalled in rhyme or uniformity or abstract addresses to things nor in melancholy complaints or good precepts, but is the life of these and much else and is in the soul. The profit of rhyme is that it drops seeds of a sweeter and more luxuriant rhyme, and of uniformity that it conveys itself into its own roots in the ground out of sight. The rhyme and uniformity of perfect poems show the free growth of metrical laws and bud from them as unerringly and loosely as lilacs or roses on a bush, and take shapes as compact as the shapes of chestnuts

and oranges and melons and pears, and shed the perfume impalpable
to form. The fluency and ornaments of the finest poems or music
or orations or recitations are not independent but dependent. All
beauty comes from beautiful blood and a beautiful brain. If the
greatnesses are in conjunction in a man or woman it is enough . . .
the fact will prevail through the universe . . . but the gaggery and
gilt of a million years will not prevail. Who troubles himself about
his ornaments or fluency is lost. This is what you shall do: Love
the earth and sun and the animals, despise riches, give alms to
every one that asks, stand up for the stupid and crazy, devote your
income and labor to others, hate tyrants, argue not concerning God,
have patience and indulgence toward the people, take off your hat
to nothing known or unknown or to any man or number of men,
go freely with powerful uneducated persons and with the young
and with the mothers of families, read these leaves in the open air
every season of every year of your life, re-examine all you have been
told at school or church or in any book, dismiss whatever insults
your own soul, and your very flesh shall be a great poem and have
the richest fluency not only in its words but in the silent lines of
its lips and face and between the lashes of your eyes and in every
motion and joint of your body. . . . The poet shall not spend his
time in unneeded work. He shall know that the ground is always
ready plowed and manured . . . others may not know it but he
shall. He shall go directly to the creation. His trust shall master
the trust of everything he touches . . . and shall master all attachment.

The known universe has one complete lover and that is the greatest poet. He consumes an eternal passion and is indifferent which
chance happens and which possible contingency of fortune or misfortune and persuades daily and hourly his delicious pay. What
balks or breaks others is fuel for his burning progress to contact
and amorous joy. Other proportions of the reception of pleasure
dwindle to nothing to his proportions. All expected from heaven
or from the highest he is rapport with in the sight of the daybreak
or a scene of the winterwoods or the presence of children playing
or with his arm round the neck of a man or woman. His love above
all love has leisure and expanse . . . he leaves room ahead of himself. He is no irresolute or suspicious lover . . . he is sure . . . he
scorns intervals. His experience and the showers and thrills are not
for nothing. Nothing can jar him . . . suffering and darkness cannot—death and fear cannot. To him complaint and jealousy and
envy are corpses buried and rotten in the earth . . . he saw them
buried. The sea is not surer of the shore or the shore of the sea
than he is of the fruition of his love and of all perfection and beauty.

The fruition of beauty is no chance of hit or miss . . . it is inevitable as life . . . it is exact and plum as gravitation. From the eyesight proceeds another eyesight and from the hearing proceeds another hearing and from the voice proceeds another voice eternally curious of the harmony of things with man. To these respond perfections not only in the committees that were supposed to stand for the rest but in the rest themselves just the same. These understand the law of perfection in masses and floods . . . that its finish is to each for itself and onward from itself . . . that it is profuse and impartial . . . that there is not a minute of the light or dark nor an acre of the earth or sea without it—nor any direction of the sky nor any trade or employment nor any turn of events. This is the reason that about the proper expression of beauty there is precision and balance . . . one part does not need to be thrust above another. The best singer is not the one who has the most lithe and powerful organ . . . the pleasure of poems is not in them that take the handsomest measure and similes and sound.

Without effort and without exposing in the least how it is done the greatest poet brings the spirit of any or all events and passions and scenes and persons some more and some less to bear on your individual character as you hear or read. To do this well is to compete with the laws that pursue and follow time. What is the purpose must surely be there and the clue of it must be there . . . and the faintest indication is the indication of the best and then becomes the clearest indication. Past and present and future are not disjoined but joined. The greatest poet forms the consistence of what is to be from what has been and is. He drags the dead out of their coffins and stands them again on their feet . . . he says to the past, Rise and walk before me that I may realize you. He learns the lesson . . . he places himself where the future becomes present. The greatest poet does not only dazzle his rays over character and scenes and passions . . . he finally ascends and finishes all . . . he exhibits the pinnacles that no man can tell what they are for or what is beyond . . . he glows a moment on the extremest verge. He is most wonderful in his last half-hidden smile or frown . . . by that flash of the moment of parting the one that sees it shall be encouraged or terrified afterwards for many years. The greatest poet does not moralize or make applications of morals . . . he knows the soul. The soul has that measureless pride which consists in never acknowledging any lessons but its own. But it has sympathy as measureless as its pride and the one balances the other and neither can stretch too far while it stretches in company with the other. The inmost secrets of art sleep with the twain. The greatest poet has lain close betwixt both and they are vital in his style and thoughts.

The art of art, the glory of expression and the sunshine of the light of letters is simplicity. Nothing is better than simplicity . . . nothing can make up for excess or for the lack of definiteness. To carry on the heave of impulse and pierce intellectual depths and give all subjects their articulations are powers neither common nor very uncommon. But to speak in literature with the perfect rectitude and insousiance[6] of the movements of animals and the unimpeachableness of the sentiment of trees in the woods and grass by the roadside is the flawless triumph of art. If you have looked on him who has achieved it you have looked on one of the masters of the artists of all nations and times. You shall not contemplate the flight of the graygull over the bay or the mettlesome action of the blood horse or the tall leaning of sunflowers on their stalk or the appearance of the sun journeying through heaven or the appearance of the moon afterward with any more satisfaction than you shall contemplate him. The greatest poet has less a marked style and is more the channel of thoughts and things without increase or diminution, and is the free channel of himself. He swears to his art, I will not be meddlesome, I will not have in my writing any elegance or effect or originality to hang in the way between me and the rest like curtains. I will have nothing hang in the way, not the richest curtains. What I tell I tell for precisely what it is. Let who may exalt or startle or fascinate or sooth I will have purposes as health or heat or snow has and be as regardless of observation. What I experience or portray shall go from my composition without a shred of my composition. You shall stand by my side and look in the mirror with me.

The old red blood and stainless gentility of great poets will be proved by their unconstraint. A heroic person walks at his ease through and out of that custom or precedent or authority that suits him not. Of the traits of the brotherhood of writers savans musicians inventors and artists nothing is finer than silent defiance advancing from new free forms. In the need of poems philosophy politics mechanism science behaviour, the craft of art, an appropriate native grand-opera, shipcraft, or any craft, he is greatest forever and forever who contributes the greatest original practical example. The cleanest expression is that which finds no sphere worthy of itself and makes one.

The messages of great poets to each man and woman are, Come to us on equal terms, Only then can you understand us, We are no better than you, What we enclose you enclose, What we enjoy you may enjoy. Did you suppose there could be only one Supreme? We affirm there can be unnumbered Supremes, and that one does not countervail another any more than one eyesight countervails another . . . and that men can be good or grand only of the consciousness

---

6. Freedom from concern (correctly, *insouciance*).

of their supremacy within them. What do you think is the grandeur of storms and dismemberments and the deadliest battles and wrecks and the wildest fury of the elements and the power of the sea and the motion of nature and of the throes of human desires and dignity and hate and love? It is that something in the soul which says, Rage on, Whirl on, I tread master here and everywhere, Master of the spasms of the sky and of the shatter of the sea, Master of nature and passion and death, And of all terror and all pain.

The American bards shall be marked for generosity and affection and for encouraging competitors. . . . They shall be kosmos . . . without monopoly or secresy . . . glad to pass any thing to any one . . . hungry for equals night and day. They shall not be careful of riches and privilege they shall be riches and privilege . . . they shall perceive who the most affluent man is. The most affluent man is he that confronts all the shows he sees by equivalents out of the stronger wealth of himself. The American bard shall delineate no class of persons nor one or two out of the strata of interests nor love most nor truth most nor the soul most nor the body most . . . and not be for the eastern states more than the western or the northern states more than the southern.

Exact science and its practical movements are no checks on the greatest poet but always his encouragement and support. The outset and remembrance are there . . . there are the arms that lifted him first and brace him best . . . there he returns after all his goings and comings. The sailor and traveler . . . the atomist chemist astronomer geologist phrenologist spiritualist mathematician historian and lexicographer are not poets, but they are the lawgivers of poets and their construction underlies the structure of every perfect poem. No matter what rises or is uttered they sent the seed of the conception of it . . . of them and by them stand the visible proofs of souls . . . always of their fatherstuff must be begotten the sinewy races of bards. If there shall be love and content between the father and the son and if the greatness of the son is the exuding of the greatness of the father there shall be love between the poet and the man of demonstrable science. In the beauty of poems are the tuft and final applause of science.

Great is the faith of the flush of knowledge and of the investigation of the depths of qualities and things. Cleaving and circling here swells the soul of the poet yet is president of itself always. The depths are fathomless and therefore calm. The innocence and nakedness are resumed . . . they are neither modest nor immodest. The whole theory of the special and supernatural and all that was twined with it or educed out of it departs as a dream. What has ever happened . . . what happens and whatever may or shall happen, the vital laws enclose all . . . they are sufficient for any case

and for all cases . . . none to be hurried or retarded . . . any
miracle of affairs or persons inadmissible in the vast clear scheme
where every motion and every spear of grass and the frames and
spirits of men and women and all that concerns them are unspeakably perfect miracles all referring to all and each distinct and in its
place. It is also not consistent with the reality of the soul to admit
that there is anything in the known universe more divine than men
and women.

Men and women and the earth and all upon it are simply to be
taken as they are, and the investigation of their past and present
and future shall be unintermitted and shall be done with perfect
candor. Upon this basis philosophy speculates ever looking toward
the poet, ever regarding the eternal tendencies of all toward happiness never inconsistent with what is clear to the senses and to the
soul. For the eternal tendencies of all toward happiness make the
only point of sane philosophy. Whatever comprehends less than
that . . . whatever is less than the laws of light and of astronomical
motion . . . or less than the laws that follow the thief the liar the
glutton and the drunkard through this life and doubtless afterward
. . . or less than vast stretches of time or the slow formation of
density or the patient upheaving of strata—is of no account. Whatever would put God in a poem or system of philosophy as contending against some being or influence, is also of no account. Sanity
and ensemble characterise the great master . . . spoilt in one principle all is spoilt. The great master has nothing to do with miracles.
He sees health for himself in being one of the mass . . . he sees
the hiatus in singular eminence. To the perfect shape comes common ground. To be under the general law is great for that is to
correspond with it. The master knows that he is unspeakably great
and that all are unspeakably great . . . that nothing for instance
is greater than to conceive children and bring them up well . . .
that to be is just as great as to perceive or tell.

In the make of the great masters the idea of political liberty is indispensable. Liberty takes the adherence of heroes wherever men
and women exist . . . but never takes any adherence or welcome
from the rest more than from poets. They are the voice and exposition of liberty. They out of ages are worthy the grand idea . . .
to them it is confided and they must sustain it. Nothing has precedence of it and nothing can warp or degrade it. The attitude of
great poets is to cheer up slaves and horrify despots. The turn of
their necks, the sound of their feet, the motions of their wrists,
are full of hazard to the one and hope to the other. Come nigh
them awhile and though they neither speak or advise you shall
learn the faithful American lesson. Liberty is poorly served by men
whose good intent is quelled from one failure or two failures or

any number of failures, or from the casual indifference or ingratitude of the people, or from the sharp show of the tushes[7] of power, or the bringing to bear soldiers and cannon or any penal statutes. Liberty relies upon itself, invites no one, promises nothing, sits in calmness and light, is positive and composed, and knows no discouragement. The battle rages with many a loud alarm and frequent advance and retreat . . . the enemy triumphs . . . the prison, the handcuffs, the iron necklace and anklet, the scaffold, garrote and leadballs do their work . . . the cause is asleep . . . the strong throats are choked with their own blood . . . the young men drop their eyelashes toward the ground when they pass each other . . . and is liberty gone out of that place? No never. When liberty goes it is not the first to go nor the second nor third to go . . . it waits for all the rest to go . . . it is the last. . . . When the memories of the old martyrs are faded utterly away . . . when the large names of patriots are laughed at in the public halls from the lips of the orators . . . when the boys are no more christened after the same but christened after tyrants and traitors instead . . . when the laws of the free are grudgingly permitted and laws for informers and blood-money are sweet to the taste of the people . . . when I and you walk abroad upon the earth stung with compassion at the sight of numberless brothers answering our equal friendship and calling no man master—and when we are elated with noble joy at the sight of slaves . . . when the soul retires in the cool communion of the night and surveys its experience and has much extasy over the word and deed that put back a helpless innocent person into the gripe of the gripers or into any cruel inferiority . . . when those in all parts of these states who could easier realize the true American character but do not yet—when the swarms of cringers, suckers, doughfaces, lice of politics, planners of sly involutions for their own preferment to city offices or state legislatures or the judiciary or congress or the presidency, obtain a response of love and natural deference from the people whether they get the offices or no . . . when it is better to be a bound booby and rogue in office at a high salary than the poorest free mechanic or farmer with his hat removed from his head and firm eyes, and a candid and generous heart . . . and when servility by town or state or the federal government or any oppression on a large scale or small scale can be tried on without its own punishment following duly after in exact proportion against the smallest chance of escape . . . or rather when all life and all the souls of men and women are discharged from any part of the earth—then only shall the instinct of liberty be discharged from that part of the earth.

As the attributes of the poets of the kosmos concentre in the real

7. Exclamations of impatience or contempt.

body and soul and in the pleasure of things they possess the superiority of genuineness over all fiction and romance. As they emit themselves facts are showered over with light . . . the daylight is lit with more volatile light . . . also the deep between the setting and rising sun goes deeper many fold. Each precise object or condition or combination or process exhibits a beauty . . . the multiplication table its—old age its—the carpenter's trade its—the grandopera its . . . the hugehulled cleanshaped New-York clipper at sea under steam or full sail gleams with unmatched beauty . . . the American circles and large harmonies of government gleam with theirs . . . and the commonest definite intentions and actions with theirs. The poets of the kosmos advance through all interpositions and coverings and turmoils and stratagems to first principles. They are of use . . . they dissolve poverty from its need and riches from its conceit. You large proprietor they say shall not realize or perceive more than any one else. The owner of the library is not he who holds a legal title to it having bought and paid for it. Any one and every one is owner of the library who can read the same through all the varieties of tongues and subjects and styles, and in whom they enter with ease and take residence and force toward paternity and maternity, and make supple and powerful and rich and large. . . . These American states strong and healthy and accomplished shall receive no pleasure from violations of natural models and must not permit them. In paintings or mouldings or carvings in mineral or wood, or in the illustrations of books or newspapers, or in any comic or tragic prints, or in the patterns of woven stuffs or anything to beautify rooms or furniture or costumes, or to put upon cornices or monuments or on the prows or sterns of ships, or to put anywhere before the human eye indoors or out, that which distorts honest shapes or which creates unearthly beings or places or contingencies is a nuisance and revolt. Of the human form especially it is so great it must never be made ridiculous. Of ornaments to a work nothing outre can be allowed . . . but those ornaments can be allowed that conform to the perfect facts of the open air and that flow out of the nature of the work and come irrepressibly from it and are necessary to the completion of the work. Most works are most beautiful without ornament. . . . Exaggerations will be revenged in human physiology. Clean and vigorous children are jetted and conceived only in those communities where the models of natural forms are public every day. . . . Great genius and the people of these states must never be demeaned to romances. As soon as histories are properly told there is no more need of romances.

The great poets are also to be known by the absence in them of tricks and by the justification of perfect personal candor. Then folks echo a new cheap joy and a divine voice leaping from their brains: How beautiful is candor! All faults may be forgiven of him who has perfect candor. Henceforth let no man of us lie, for we have seen that openness wins the inner and outer world and that there is no single exception, and that never since our earth gathered itself in a mass have deceit or subterfuge or prevarication attracted its smallest particle or the faintest tinge of a shade—and that through the enveloping wealth and rank of a state or the whole republic of states a sneak or sly person shall be discovered and despised . . . and that the soul has never been once fooled and never can be fooled . . . and thrift without the loving nod of the soul is only a fœtid puff . . . and there never grew up in any of the continents of the globe nor upon any planet or satellite or star, nor upon the asteroids, nor in any part of ethereal space, nor in the midst of density, nor under the fluid wet of the sea, nor in the condition which precedes the birth of babes, nor at any time during the changes of life, nor in that condition that follows what we term death, nor in any stretch of abeyance or action afterward of vitality, nor in any process of formation or reformation anywhere, a being whose instinct hated the truth.

Extreme caution or prudence, the soundest organic health, large hope and comparison and fondness for women and children, large alimentiveness and destructiveness and causality,[8] with a perfect sense of the oneness of nature and the propriety of the same spirit applied to human affairs . . . these are called up of the float of the brain of the world to be parts of the greatest poet from his birth out of his mother's womb and from her birth out of her mother's. Caution seldom goes far enough. It has been thought that the prudent citizen was the citizen who applied himself to solid gains and did well for himself and his family and completed a lawful life without debt or crime. The greatest poet sees and admits these economies as he sees the economies of food and sleep, but has higher notions of prudence than to think he gives much when he gives a few slight attentions at the latch of the gate. The premises of the prudence of life are not the hospitality of it or the ripeness and harvest of it. Beyond the independence of a little sum laid aside for burial-money, and of a few clapboards around and shingles overhead on a lot of American soil owned, and the easy dollars that supply the year's plain clothing and meals, the melancholy prudence of the abandonment of such a great being as a man is to the toss and pallor of years of moneymaking with all their scorching days and icy nights and all their stifling deceits and underhanded dodgings, or infinitessimals of parlors, or shameless stuffing while others

8. Most of these terms ("caution," "alimentiveness") were used in phre- nology to designate elements of the personality.

starve . . . and all the loss of the bloom and odor of the earth and of the flowers and atmosphere and of the sea and of the true taste of the women and men you pass or have to do with in youth or middle age, and the issuing sickness and desperate revolt at the close of a life without elevation or naivete, and the ghastly chatter of a death without serenity or majesty, is the great fraud upon modern civilization and forethought, blotching the surface and system which civilization undeniably drafts, and moistening with tears the immense features it spreads and spreads with such velocity before the reached kisses of the soul. . . . Still the right explanation remains to be made about prudence. The prudence of the mere wealth and respectability of the most esteemed life appears too faint for the eye to observe at all when little and large alike drop quietly aside at the thought of the prudence suitable for immortality. What is wisdom that fills the thinness of a year or seventy or eighty years to wisdom spaced out by ages and coming back at a certain time with strong reinforcements and rich presents and the clear faces of wedding-guests as far as you can look in every direction running gaily toward you? Only the soul is of itself . . . all else has reference to what ensues. All that a person does or thinks is of consequence. Not a move can a man or woman make that affects him or her in a day or a month or any part of the direct lifetime or the hour of death but the same affects him or her onward afterward through the indirect lifetime. The indirect is always as great and real as the direct. The spirit receives from the body just as much as it gives to the body. Not one name of word or deed . . . not of venereal sores or discolorations . . . not the privacy of the onanist . . . not of the putrid veins of gluttons or rum-drinkers . . . not peculation or cunning or betrayal or murder . . . no serpentine poison of those that seduce women . . . not the foolish yielding of women . . . not prostitution . . . not of any depravity of young men . . . not of the attainment of gain by discreditable means . . . not any nastiness of appetite . . . not any harshness of officers to men or judges to prisoners or fathers to sons or sons to fathers or husbands to wives or bosses to their boys . . . not of greedy looks or malignant wishes . . . nor any of the wiles practised by people upon themselves . . . ever is or ever can be stamped on the programme but it is duly realized and returned, and that returned in further performances . . . and they returned again. Nor can the push of charity or personal force ever be any thing else than the profoundest reason, whether it brings arguments to hand or no. No specification is necessary . . . to add or subtract or divide is in vain. Little or big, learned or unlearned, white or black, legal or illegal, sick or well, from the first inspiration down the windpipe to the last expiration out of it, all that a

male or female does that is vigorous and benevolent and clean is
so much sure profit to him or her in the unshakable order of the
universe and through the whole scope of it forever. If the savage
or felon is wise it is well . . . if the greatest poet or savan is wise
it is simply the same . . . if the President or chief justice is wise
it is the same . . . if the young mechanic or farmer is wise it is
no more or less . . . if the prostitute is wise it is no more nor less.
The interest will come round . . . all will come round. All the
best actions of war and peace . . . all help given to relatives and
strangers and the poor and old and sorrowful and young children
and widows and the sick, and to all shunned persons . . . all furtherance of fugitives and of the escape of slaves . . . all the self-
denial that stood steady and aloof on wrecks and saw others take
the seats of the boats . . . all offering of substance or life for the
good old cause, or for a friend's sake or opinion's sake . . . all
pains of enthusiasts scoffed at by their neighbors . . . all the vast
sweet love and precious suffering of mothers . . . all honest men
baffled in strifes recorded or unrecorded . . . all the grandeur and
good of the few ancient nations whose fragments of annals we inherit . . . and all the good of the hundreds of far mightier and
more ancient nations unknown to us by name or date or location
. . . all that was ever manfully begun, whether it succeeded or
not . . . all that has at any time been well suggested out of the
divine heart of man or by the divinity of his mouth or by the shaping of his great hands . . . and all that is well thought or done
this day on any part of the surface of the globe . . . or on any
of the wandering stars or fixed stars by those there as we are here
. . . or that is henceforth to be well thought or done by you whoever you are, or by any one—these singly and wholly inured at their
time and inure now and will inure always to the identities from
which they sprung or shall spring. . . . Did you guess any of them
lived only its moment? The world does not so exist . . . no parts
palpable or impalpable so exist . . . no result exists now without
being from its long antecedent result, and that from its antecedent,
and so backward without the farthest mentionable spot coming a
bit nearer to the beginning than any other spot. . . . What ever
satisfies the soul is truth. The prudence of the greatest poet answers
at last the craving and glut of the soul, is not contemptuous of less
ways of prudence if they conform to its ways, puts off nothing, permits no let-up for its own case or any case, has no particular sabbath
or judgment-day, divides not the living from the dead or the righteous from the unrighteous, is satisfied with the present, matches
every thought or act by its correlative, knows no possible forgiveness or deputed atonement . . . knows that the young man who
composedly periled his life and lost it has done exceeding well for

himself, while the man who has not periled his life and retains it
to old age in riches and ease has perhaps achieved nothing for himself worth mentioning . . . and that only that person has no great
prudence to learn who has learnt to prefer real longlived things,
and favors body and soul the same, and perceives the indirect assuredly following the direct, and what evil or good he does leaping
onward and waiting to meet him again—and who in his spirit in
any emergency whatever neither hurries or avoids death.

The direct trial of him who would be the greatest poet is today.
If he does not flood himself with the immediate age as with vast
oceanic tides . . . and if he does not attract his own land body
and soul to himself and hang on its neck with incomparable love
and plunge his semitic muscle into its merits and demerits . . .
and if he be not himself the age transfigured . . . and if to him
is not opened the eternity which gives similitude to all periods and
locations and processes and animate and inanimate forms, and
which is the bond of time, and rises up from its inconceivable
vagueness and infiniteness in the swimming shape of today, and
is held by the ductile anchors of life, and makes the present spot
the passage from what was to what shall be, and commits itself
to the representation of this wave of an hour and this one of the
sixty beautiful children of the wave—let him merge in the general
run and wait his development. . . . Still the final test of poems
or any character or work remains. The prescient poet projects himself centuries ahead and judges performer or performance after the
changes of time. Does it live through them? Does it still hold on
untired? Will the same style and the direction of genius to similar
points be satisfactory now? Has no new discovery in science or arrival at superior planes of thought and judgment and behaviour
fixed him or his so that either can be looked down upon? Have the
marches of tens and hundreds and thousands of years made willing
detours to the right hand and the left hand for his sake? Is he beloved long and long after he is buried? Does the young man think
often of him? and the young woman think often of him? and do
the middle-aged and the old think of him?

A great poem is for ages and ages in common and for all degrees
and complexions and all departments and sects and for a woman
as much as a man and a man as much as a woman. A great poem
is no finish to a man or woman but rather a beginning. Has any
one fancied he could sit at last under some due authority and rest
satisfied with explanations and realize and be content and full? To
no such terminus does the greatest poet bring . . . he brings
neither cessation or sheltered fatness and ease. The touch of him
tells in action. Whom he takes he takes with firm sure grasp into
live regions previously unattained . . . thenceforward is no rest

. . . they see the space and ineffable sheen that turn the old spots and lights into dead vacuums. The companion of him beholds the birth and progress of stars and learns one of the meanings. Now there shall be a man cohered out of tumult and chaos . . . the elder encourages the younger and shows him how . . . they two shall launch off fearlessly together till the new world fits an orbit for itself and looks unabashed on the lesser orbits of the stars and sweeps through the ceaseless rings and shall never be quiet again.

There will soon be no more priests. Their work is done. They may wait awhile . . . perhaps a generation or two . . . dropping off by degrees. A superior breed shall take their place . . . the gangs of kosmos and prophets en masse shall take their place. A new order shall arise and they shall be the priests of man, and every man shall be his own priest. The churches built under their umbrage shall be the churches of men and women. Through the divinity of themselves shall the kosmos and the new breed of poets be interpreters of men and women and of all events and things. They shall find their inspiration in real objects today, symptoms of the past and future . . . They shall not deign to defend immortality or God or the perfection of things or liberty or the exquisite beauty and reality of the soul. They shall arise in America and be responded to from the remainder of the earth.

The English language befriends the grand American expression . . . it is brawny enough and limber and full enough. On the tough stock of a race who through all change of circumstances was never without the idea of political liberty, which is the animus of all liberty, it has attracted the terms of daintier and gayer and subtler and more elegant tongues. It is the powerful language of resistance . . . it is the dialect of common sense. It is the speech of the proud and melancholy races and of all who aspire. It is the chosen tongue to express growth faith self-esteem freedom justice equality friendliness amplitude prudence decision and courage. It is the medium that shall well nigh express the inexpressible.

No great literature nor any like style of behaviour or oratory or social intercourse or household arrangements or public institutions or the treatment by bosses of employed people, nor executive detail or detail of the army or navy, nor spirit of legislation or courts or police or tuition or architecture or songs or amusements or the costumes of young men, can long elude the jealous and passionate instinct of American standards. Whether or no the sign appears from the mouths of the people, it throbs a live interrogation in every freeman's and freewoman's heart after that which passes by or this built to remain. Is it uniform with my country? Are its disposals without ignominious distinctions? Is it for the evergrowing communes of brothers and lovers, large, well-united, proud beyond the

old models, generous beyond all models? Is it something grown
fresh out of the fields or drawn from the sea for use to me today
here? I know that what answers for me an American must answer
for any individual or nation that serves for a part of my materials.
Does this answer? or is it without reference to universal needs? or
sprung of the needs of the less developed society of special ranks?
or old needs of pleasure overlaid by modern science and forms?
Does this acknowledge liberty with audible and absolute acknowledgment, and set slavery at naught for life and death? Will it help
breed one goodshaped and wellhung man, and a woman to be his
perfect and independent mate? Does it improve manners? Is it for
the nursing of the young of the republic? Does it solve readily with
the sweet milk of the nipples of the breasts of the mother of many
children? Has it too the old ever-fresh forbearance and impartiality?
Does it look with the same love on the last born and those hard-
ening toward stature, and on the errant, and on those who disdain
all strength of assault outside of their own?

The poems distilled from other poems will probably pass away.
The coward will surely pass away. The expectation of the vital and
great can only be satisfied by the demeanor of the vital and great.
The swarms of the polished deprecating and reflectors and the polite
float off and leave no remembrance. America prepares with composure and goodwill for the visitors that have sent word. It is not
intellect that is to be their warrant and welcome. The talented, the
artist, the ingenious, the editor, the statesman, the erudite . . .
they are not unappreciated . . . they fall in their place and do
their work. The soul of the nation also does its work. No disguise
can pass on it . . . no disguise can conceal from it. It rejects none,
it permits all. Only toward as good as itself and toward the like of
itself will it advance half-way. An individual is as superb as a nation
when he has the qualities which make a superb nation. The soul of
the largest and wealthiest and proudest nation may well go half-way
to meet that of its poets. The signs are effectual. There is no fear
of mistake. If the one is true the other is true. The proof of a poet
is that his country absorbs him as affectionately as he has absorbed
it.

1855

From INSCRIPTIONS[9]
One's-Self I Sing

One's-self I sing, a simple separate person,
Yet utter the word Democratic, the word En-Masse.[1]

Of physiology from top to toe I sing,
Not physiognomy alone nor brain alone is worthy for the Muse, I
    say the Form complete is worthier far,
The Female equally with the Male I sing.   5

Of Life immense in passion, pulse, and power,
Cheerful, for freest action form'd under the laws divine,
The Modern Man I sing.

                                                          1867

As I Ponder'd in Silence

As I ponder'd in silence,
Returning upon my poems, considering, lingering long,
A phantom arose before me with distrustful aspect,
Terrible in beauty, age, and power,
The genius of poets of old lands,   5
As to me directing like flame its eyes,
With finger pointing to many immortal songs,
And menacing voice, *What singest thou?* it said,
Know'st thou not there is but one theme for ever-enduring bards?
And that is the theme of War, the fortune of battles,   10
The making of perfect soldiers.

Be it so, then I answer'd,
I too haughty Shade also sing war, and a longer and greater one than
    any,
Waged in my book with varying fortune, with flight, advance and
    retreat, victory deferr'd and wavering,
(Yet methinks certain, or as good as certain, at the last,) the field
    the world,   15
For life and death, for the Body and for the eternal Soul,
Lo, I too am come, chanting the chant of battles,
I above all promote brave soldiers.

                                                          1871–72

9. The idea of beginning his *Leaves* with a cluster of poems—"Inscriptions"—evolved gradually with Whitman. "Inscription" (later "One's-Self I Sing") opened the 4th (1867) edition. In the next edition (1871–72), Whitman gathered together a number of other introductory poems to accompany the lone "Inscription," and all subsequent editions were introduced by the group (although Whitman continued to add and shift poems). The "Inscriptions" constitute an invitation and a welcome to the *Leaves;* they serve to introduce the major themes, to reveal the intentions and purposes, and to display the dominant imagery and techniques of the entire volume.
1. French, "all together."

When I Read the Book

When I read the book, the biography famous,
And is this then (said I) what the author calls a man's life?
And so will some one when I am dead and gone write my life?
(As if any man really knew aught of my life,
Why even I myself I often think know little or nothing of my real
 life,   5
Only a few hints, a few diffused faint clews and indirections
I seek for my own use to trace out here.)

                                                              1867

Beginning My Studies

Beginning my studies the first step pleas'd me so much,
The mere fact consciousness, these forms, the power of motion,
The least insect or animal, the senses, eyesight, love,
The first step I say awed me and pleas'd me so much,
I have hardly gone and hardly wish'd to go any farther,   5
But stop and loiter all the time to sing it in ecstatic songs.

                                                              1867

Beginners

How they are provided for upon the earth, (appearing at intervals,)
How dear and dreadful they are to the earth,
How they inure to[2] themselves as much as to any—what a paradox
 appears their age,
How people respond to them, yet know them not,
How there is something relentless in their fate all times,   5
How all times mischoose the objects of their adulation and reward,
And how the same inexorable price must still be paid for the same
 great purchase.

                                                              1860

Me Imperturbe

Me imperturbe,[3] standing at ease in Nature,
Master of all or mistress of all, aplomb in the midst of irrational
 things,
Imbued as they, passive, receptive, silent as they,
Finding my occupation, poverty, notoriety, foibles, crimes, less im-
 portant than I thought,
Me toward the Mexican sea, or in the Mannahatta[4] or the Tennes-
 see, or far north or inland,   5

2. Toughen or harden by exercise or
use.

3. Imperturbable; undisturbed, calm.
4. Indian name for Manhattan.

A river man, or a man of the woods or of any farm-life of these
  States or of the coast, or the lakes or Kanada,
Me wherever my life is lived, O to be self-balanced for contingencies,
To confront night, storms, hunger, ridicule, accidents, rebuffs, as
  the trees and animals do.

1860

I Hear America Singing

I hear America singing, the varied carols I hear,
Those of mechanics, each one singing his as it should be blithe and
  strong,
The carpenter singing his as he measures his plank or beam,
The mason singing his as he makes ready for work, or leaves off
  work,
The boatman singing what belongs to him in his boat, the deck-
  hand singing on the steamboat deck,   5
The shoemaker singing as he sits on his bench, the hatter singing as
  he stands,
The wood-cutter's song, the ploughboy's on his way in the morning,
  or at noon intermission or at sundown,
The delicious singing of the mother, or of the young wife at work,
  or of the girl sewing or washing,
Each singing what belongs to him or her and to none else,
The day what belongs to the day—at night the party of young fel-
  lows, robust, friendly,   10
Singing with open mouths their strong melodious songs.

1860

Shut Not Your Doors

Shut not your doors to me proud libraries,
For that which was lacking on all your well-fill'd shelves, yet needed
  most, I bring,
Forth from the war emerging, a book I have made,
The words of my book nothing, the drift of it every thing,
A book separate, not link'd with the rest nor felt by the intellect,   5
But you ye untold latencies will thrill to every page.

1865(DT), 1867

Poets To Come

Poets to come! orators, singers, musicians to come!
Not to-day is to justify me and answer what I am for,
But you, a new brood, native, athletic, continental, greater than
  before known,
Arouse! for you must justify me.

I myself but write one or two indicative words for the future,   5
I but advance a moment only to wheel and hurry back in the dark-
      ness.

I am a man who, sauntering along without fully stopping, turns a
      casual look upon you and then averts his face,
Leaving it to you to prove and define it,
Expecting the main things from you.

                                                            1860

To You

Stranger, if you passing meet me and desire to speak to me, why
      should you not speak to me?
And why should I not speak to you?

                                                            1860

Thou Reader

Thou reader throbbest life and pride and love the same as I,
Therefore for thee the following chants.

                                                            1881–82

Song of Myself⁵

1

I celebrate myself, and sing myself,
And what I assume you shall assume,
For every atom belonging to me as good belongs to you.

5. "Song of Myself" has been the foundation poem of *Leaves of Grass* ever
since its appearance in the first edition
of 1855. The poem, Whitman's longest,
underwent many revisions in the various editions of *Leaves,* and at one point
was divided into the numbered sections.
Although for a long time "Song of
Myself" was looked upon as a kind
of chaotic compendium of Whitman's
ideas and themes, recent criticism has
attempted to discover a structure in the
poem. Carl F. Strauch ("The Structure
of Walt Whitman's 'Song of Myself,'"
English Journal, XXVII, September,
1938, 597–607) asserted that "Whitman was in command of his materials"
and worked out the following organization—*1.* Paragraphs 1–18, the Self;
mystical interpenetration of the Self
with all life and experience. *2.* Paragraphs 19–25, definition of the Self;
identification with the degraded, and
transfiguration of it; final merit of
Self withheld; silence; end of the first

half. *3.* Paragraphs 26–38, life flowing
in upon Self, then evolutionary interpenetration of life. *4.* Paragraphs 39–41,
the Superman. *5.* Paragraphs 42–52,
larger questions of life—religion, faith,
God, death; immortality and happiness
mystically affirmed.

   James E. Miller, Jr. (*A Critical
Guide to Leaves of Grass,* 1957, pp.
6–35) analyzed "Song of Myself" as
the dramatic representation of an "inverted mystical experience." According
to this interpretation, the experience
dramatized in the poem conforms remarkably well to the traditional mystical experience, with the major exception of Whitman's inversion of the
mystic's attitude toward the senses:
whereas the traditional mystic mortifies
the senses, Whitman accepts and celebrates them. Miller defined the various
stages of the inverted mystical experience in "Song of Myself" as follows—
I. Sections 1–5: entry into the mystical
state. *II.* Sections 6–16: awakening of

I loafe and invite my soul,
I lean and loafe at my ease observing a spear of summer grass.   5

My tongue, every atom of my blood, form'd from this soil, this air,
Born here of parents born here from parents the same, and their
  parents the same,
I, now thirty-seven years old in perfect health begin,
Hoping to cease not till death.

Creeds and schools in abeyance,   10
Retiring back a while sufficed at what they are, but never forgotten,
I harbor for good or bad, I permit to speak at every hazard,
Nature without check with original energy.

2

Houses and rooms are full of perfumes, the shelves are crowded with
  perfumes,
I breathe the fragrance myself and know it and like it,   15
The distillation would intoxicate me also, but I shall not let it.

The atmosphere is not a perfume, it has no taste of the distillation,
  it is odorless,
It is for my mouth forever, I am in love with it,
I will go to the bank by the wood and become undisguised and
  naked,
I am mad for it to be in contact with me.   20

The smoke of my own breath,
Echoes, ripples, buzz'd whispers, love-root, silk-thread, crotch and
  vine,
My respiration and inspiration, the beating of my heart, the passing
  of blood and air through my lungs,
The sniff of green leaves and dry leaves, and of the shore and dark-
  color'd sea-rocks, and of hay in the barn,
The sound of the belch'd words of my voice loos'd to the eddies of
  the wind,   25
A few light kisses, a few embraces, a reaching around of arms,
The play of shine and shade on the trees as the supply boughs
  wag,

Self. *III*. Sections 17–32: purification of Self. *IV*. Sections 33–37: illumination and the dark night of the soul. *V*. Sections 38–43: union (faith and love). *VI*. Sections 44–49: union (perception). *VII*. Sections 50–52: emergence from the mystical state.

Malcolm Cowley (*Walt Whitman's Leaves of Grass: The First* [*1855*] *Edition*, 1959, pp. xiv–xx) based his analysis of "Song of Myself" on the 1st edition, which he believed superior. The subject, according to Cowley, "is a state of illumination induced by two (or three) separate moments of ecstasy." The mysticism of "Song of My-

self" seems to him more Oriental than Christian; his analysis of the "narrative structure" of the poem runs thus—*1st sequence* (chants 1–4): the poet or hero introduced to his audience. *2nd sequence* (chant 5): the ecstasy. *3rd sequence* (chants 6–19): the grass. *4th sequence* (chants 20–25): the poet in person. *5th sequence* (chants 26–29): ecstasy through the senses. *6th sequence* (chants 30–38): the power of identification. *7th sequence* (chants 39–41): the superman. *8th sequence* (chants 42–50): the sermon. *9th sequence* (chants 51–52): the poet's farewell.

The delight alone or in the rush of the streets, or along the fields
    and hill-sides,
The feeling of health, the full-noon trill, the song of me rising from
    bed and meeting the sun.

Have you reckon'd a thousand acres much? have you reckon'd the
    earth much?   30
Have you practis'd so long to learn to read?
Have you felt so proud to get at the meaning of poems?

Stop this day and night with me and you shall possess the origin of
    all poems,
You shall possess the good of the earth and sun, (there are millions
    of suns left,)
You shall no longer take things at second or third hand, nor look
    through the eyes of the dead, nor feed on the spectres in
    books,   35
You shall not look through my eyes either, nor take things from me,
You shall listen to all sides and filter them from your self.

3

I have heard what the talkers were talking, the talk of the beginning
    and the end,
But I do not talk of the beginning or the end.

There was never any more inception than there is now,   40
Nor any more youth or age than there is now,
And will never be any more perfection than there is now,
Nor any more heaven or hell than there is now.

Urge and urge and urge,
Always the procreant urge of the world.   45

Out of the dimness opposite equals advance, always substance and
    increase, always sex,
Always a knit of identity, always distinction, always a breed of life.

To elaborate is no avail, learn'd and unlearn'd feel that it is so.

Sure as the most certain sure, plumb in the uprights, well entretied,
    braced in the beams,
Stout as a horse, affectionate, haughty, electrical,   50
I and this mystery here we stand.

Clear and sweet is my soul, and clear and sweet is all that is not my
    soul.

Lack one lacks both, and the unseen is proved by the seen,
Till that becomes unseen and receives proof in its turn.

Showing the best and dividing it from the worst age vexes age,   55
Knowing the perfect fitness and equanimity of things, while they
    discuss I am silent, and go bathe and admire myself.

Welcome is every organ and attribute of me, and of any man hearty
    and clean,

Not an inch nor a particle of an inch is vile, and none shall be less
    familiar than the rest.

I am satisfied—I see, dance, laugh, sing;
As the hugging and loving bed-fellow sleeps at my side through the
    night, and withdraws at the peep of the day with stealthy
    tread,   60
Leaving me baskets cover'd with white towels swelling the house
    with their plenty,
Shall I postpone my acceptation and realization and scream at my
    eyes,
That they turn from gazing after and down the road,
And forthwith cipher and show me to a cent,
Exactly the value of one and exactly the value of two, and which is
    ahead?   65

4

Trippers and askers surround me,
People I meet, the effect upon me of my early life or the ward and
    city I live in, or the nation,
The latest dates, discoveries, inventions, societies, authors old and
    new,
My dinner, dress, associates, looks, compliments, dues,
The real or fancied indifference of some man or woman I love,   70
The sickness of one of my folks or of myself, or ill-doing or loss or
    lack of money, or depressions or exaltations,
Battles, the horrors of fratricidal war, the fever of doubtful news, the
    fitful events;
These come to me days and nights and go from me again,
But they are not the Me myself.

Apart from the pulling and hauling stands what I am,   75
Stands amused, complacent, compassionating, idle, unitary,
Looks down, is erect, or bends an arm on an impalpable certain rest,
Looking with side-curved head curious what will come next,
Both in and out of the game and watching and wondering at it.

Backward I see in my own days where I sweated through fog with
    linguists and contenders,   80
I have no mockings or arguments, I witness and wait.

5

I believe in you my soul, the other I am must not abase itself to you,
And you must not be abased to the other.

Loafe with me on the grass, loose the stop from your throat,
Not words, not music or rhyme I want, not custom or lecture, not
    even the best,   85
Only the lull I like, the hum of your valvèd voice.

I mind how once we lay such a transparent summer morning,
How you settled your head athwart my hips and gently turn'd over
    upon me,

And parted the shirt from my bosom-bone, and plunged your tongue
    to my bare-stript heart,
And reach'd till you felt my beard, and reach'd till you held my
    feet.   90
Swiftly arose and spread around me the peace and knowledge that
    pass all the argument of the earth,
And I know that the hand of God is the promise of my own,
And I know that the spirit of God is the brother of my own,
And that all the men ever born are also my brothers, and the women
    my sisters and lovers,
And that a kelson[6] of the creation is love,   95
And limitless are leaves stiff or drooping in the fields,
And brown ants in the little wells beneath them,
And mossy scabs of the worm fence, heap'd stones, elder, mullein
    and poke-weed.

6

A child said *What is the grass?* fetching it to me with full hands,
How could I answer the child? I do not know what it is any more
    than he.   100

I guess it must be the flag of my disposition, out of hopeful green
    stuff woven.

Or I guess it is the handkerchief of the Lord,
A scented gift and remembrancer designedly dropt,
Bearing the owner's name someway in the corners, that we may see
    and remark, and say *Whose?*

Or I guess the grass is itself a child, the produced babe of the vege-
    tation.   105

Or I guess it is a uniform hieroglyphic,
And it means, Sprouting alike in broad zones and narrow zones,
Growing among black folks as among white,
Kanuck, Tuckahoe, Congressman, Cuff,[7] I give them the same, I
    receive them the same.

And now it seems to me the beautiful uncut hair of graves.   110

Tenderly will I use you curling grass,
It may be you transpire from the breasts of young men,
It may be if I had known them I would have loved them,
It may be you are from old people, or from offspring taken soon out
    of their mothers' laps,
And here you are the mothers' laps.   115

This grass is very dark to be from the white heads of old mothers,
Darker than the colorless beards of old men,
Dark to come from under the faint red roofs of mouths.

6. A strengthening line of timbers or
iron plates in a ship, laid above and
parallel with the keel.

7. "Kanuck" is a French-Canadian;
"Tuckahoe" is a Tidewater Virginian;
"Cuff" is a Negro.

O I perceive after all so many uttering tongues,
And I perceive they do not come from the roofs of mouths for
  nothing.   120

I wish I could translate the hints about the dead young men and
  women,
And the hints about old men and mothers, and the offspring taken
  soon out of their laps.

What do you think has become of the young and old men?
And what do you think has become of the women and children?

They are alive and well somewhere,   125
The smallest sprout shows there is really no death,
And if ever there was it led forward life, and does not wait at the
  end to arrest it,
And ceas'd the moment life appear'd.

All goes onward and outward, nothing collapses,
And to die is different from what any one supposed, and luckier. 130

7

Has any one supposed it lucky to be born?
I hasten to inform him or her it is just as lucky to die, and I know it.

I pass death with the dying and birth with the new-wash'd babe, and
  am not contain'd between my hat and boots,
And peruse manifold objects, no two alike and every one good,
The earth good and the stars good, and their adjuncts all good. 135

I am not an earth nor an adjunct of an earth,
I am the mate and companion of people, all just as immortal and
  fathomless as myself,
(They do not know how immortal, but I know.)

Every kind for itself and its own, for me mine male and female,
For me those that have been boys and that love women,   140
For me the man that is proud and feels how it stings to be slighted,
For me the sweet-heart and the old maid, for me mothers and the
  mothers of mothers,
For me lips that have smiled, eyes that have shed tears,
For me children and the begetters of children.

Undrape! you are not guilty to me, nor stale nor discarded,   145
I see through the broadcloth and gingham whether or no,
And am around, tenacious, acquisitive, tireless, and cannot be
  shaken away.

8

The little one sleeps in its cradle,
I lift the gauze and look a long time, and silently brush away flies
  with my hand.

The youngster and the red-faced girl turn aside up the bushy
  hill,   150
I peeringly view them from the top.

The suicide sprawls on the bloody floor of the bedroom,
I witness the corpse with its dabbled hair, I note where the pistol
　　has fallen.

The blab of the pave,[8] tires of carts, sluff of boot-soles, talk of the
　　promenaders,
The heavy omnibus, the driver with his interrogating thumb, the
　　clank of the shod horses on the granite floor,　　　155
The snow-sleighs, clinking, shouted jokes, pelts of snow-balls,
The hurrahs for popular favorites, the fury of rous'd mobs,
The flap of the curtain'd litter, a sick man inside borne to the
　　hospital,
The meeting of enemies, the sudden oath, the blows and fall,
The excited crowd, the policeman with his star quickly working his
　　passage to the centre of the crowd,　　　160
The impassive stones that receive and return so many echoes,
What groans of over-fed or half-starv'd who fall sunstruck or in
　　fits,
What exclamations of women taken suddenly who hurry home and
　　give birth to babes,
What living and buried speech is always vibrating here, what howls
　　restrain'd by decorum,
Arrests of criminals, slights, adulterous offers made, acceptances, re-
　　jections with convex lips,　　　165
I mind them or the show or resonance of them—I come and I de-
　　part.

9

The big doors of the country barn stand open and ready,
The dried grass of the harvest-time loads the slow-drawn wagon,
The clear light plays on the brown gray and green intertinged,
The armfuls are pack'd to the sagging mow.　　　170

I am there, I help, I came stretch'd atop of the load,
I felt its soft jolts, one leg reclined on the other,
I jump from the cross-beams and seize the clover and timothy,
And roll head over heels and tangle my hair full of wisps.

10

Alone far in the wilds and mountains I hunt,　　　175
Wandering amazed at my own lightness and glee,
In the late afternoon choosing a safe spot to pass the night,
Kindling a fire and broiling the fresh-kill'd game,
Falling asleep on the gather'd leaves with my dog and gun by my
　　side.

The Yankee clipper is under her sky-sails, she cuts the sparkle and
　　scud,[9]　　　180
My eyes settle the land, I bend at her prow or shout joyously from
　　the deck.

---

8. Idle talk of the street.　　　9. Ocean foam driven by the wind.

The boatmen and clam-diggers arose early and stopt for me,
I tuck'd my trouser-ends in my boots and went and had a good time;
You should have been with us that day round the chowder-kettle.

I saw the marriage of the trapper in the open air in the far west, the
    bride was a red girl,   185
Her father and his friends sat near cross-legged and dumbly smoking,
    they had moccasins to their feet and large thick blankets hang-
    ing from their shoulders,
On a bank lounged the trapper, he was drest mostly in skins, his
    luxuriant beard and curls protected his neck, he held his bride
    by the hand,
She had long eyelashes, her head was bare, her coarse straight locks
    descended upon her voluptuous limbs and reach'd to her feet.

The runaway slave came to my house and stopt outside,
I heard his motions crackling the twigs of the woodpile,   190
Through the swung half-door of the kitchen I saw him, limpsy[1] and
    weak,
And went where he sat on a log and led him in and assured him,
And brought water and fill'd a tub for his sweated body and bruis'd
    feet,
And gave him a room that enter'd from my own, and gave him some
    coarse clean clothes,
And remember perfectly well his revolving eyes and his awkward-
    ness,   195
And remember putting plasters on the galls of his neck and ankles;
He staid with me a week before he was recuperated and pass'd
    north,
I had him sit next me at table, my fire-lock lean'd in the corner.

11

Twenty-eight young men bathe by the shore,
Twenty-eight young men and all so friendly;   200
Twenty-eight years of womanly life and all so lonesome.

She owns the fine house by the rise of the bank,
She hides handsome and richly drest aft the blinds of the window.

Which of the young men does she like the best?
Ah the homeliest of them is beautiful to her.   205

Where are you off to, lady? for I see you,
You splash in the water there, yet stay stock still in your room.

Dancing and laughing along the beach came the twenty-ninth
    bather,
The rest did not see her, but she saw them and loved them.

The beards of the young men glisten'd with wet, it ran from their
    long hair,   210
Little streams pass'd all over their bodies.

1. Limp, wanting in stiffness.

An unseen hand also pass'd over their bodies,
It descended tremblingly from their temples and ribs.

The young men float on their backs, their white bellies bulge to the
    sun, they do not ask who seizes fast to them,
They do not know who puffs and declines with pendant and bend-
    ing arch,
They do not think whom they souse with spray.   215

12
The butcher-boy puts off his killing-clothes, or sharpens his knife
    at the stall in the market,
I loiter enjoying his repartee and his shuffle and break-down.

Blacksmiths with grimed and hairy chests environ the anvil,
Each has main-sledge, they are all out, there is a great heat in the
    fire.   220

From the cinder-strew'd threshold I follow their movements,
The lithe sheer of their waists plays even with their massive arms,
Overhand the hammers swing, overhand so slow, overhand so sure,
They do not hasten, each man hits in his place.

13
The negro holds firmly the reins of his four horses, the block swags
    underneath on its tied-over chain,   225
The negro that drives the long dray of the stone-yard, steady and
    tall he stands pois'd on one leg on the string-piece,
His blue shirt exposes his ample neck and breast and loosens over
    his hip-band,
His glance is calm and commanding, he tosses the slouch of his hat
    away from his forehead,
The sun falls on his crispy hair and mustache, falls on the black of
    his polish'd and perfect limbs.

I behold the picturesque giant and love him, and I do not stop
    there,   230
I go with the team also.

In me the caresser of life wherever moving, backward as well as for-
    ward sluing,
To niches aside and junior bending, not a person or object missing,
Absorbing all to myself and for this song.

Oxen that rattle the yoke and chain or halt in the leafy shade, what
    is that you express in your eyes?   235
It seems to me more than all the print I have read in my life.

My tread scares the wood-drake and wood-duck on my distant and
    day-long ramble,
They rise together, they slowly circle around.

I believe in those wing'd purposes,
And acknowledge red, yellow, white, playing within me,   240
And consider green and violet and the tufted crown intentional,

And do not call the tortoise unworthy because she is not something
    else,
And the jay in the woods never studied the gamut,[2] yet trills pretty
    well to me,
And the look of the bay mare shames silliness out of me.

14

The wild gander leads his flock through the cool night,   245
Ya-honk he says, and sounds it down to me like an invitation,
The pert may suppose it meaningless, but I listening close,
Find its purpose and place up there toward the wintry sky.

The sharp-hoof'd moose of the north, the cat on the house-sill, the
    chickadee, the prairie-dog,
The litter of the grunting sow as they tug at her teats,   250
The brood of the turkey-hen and she with her half-spread wings,
I see in them and myself the same old law.

The press of my foot to the earth springs a hundred affections,
They scorn the best I can do to relate them.

I am enamour'd of growing out-doors,   255
Of men that live among cattle or taste of the ocean or woods,
Of the builders and steerers of ships and the wielders of axes and
    mauls, and the drivers of horses,
I can eat and sleep with them week in and week out.

What is commonest, cheapest, nearest, easiest, is Me,
Me going in for my chances, spending for vast returns,   260
Adorning myself to bestow myself on the first that will take me,
Not asking the sky to come down to my good will,
Scattering it freely forever.

15

The pure contralto sings in the organ loft,
The carpenter dresses his plank, the tongue of his foreplane whistles
    its wild ascending lisp,   265
The married and unmarried children ride home to their Thanksgiv-
    ing dinner,
The pilot seizes the king-pin, he heaves down with a strong arm,
The mate stands braced in the whale-boat, lance and harpoon are
    ready,
The duck-shooter walks by silent and cautious stretches,
The deacons are ordain'd with cross'd hands at the altar,   270
The spinning-girl retreats and advances to the hum of the big wheel,
The farmer stops by the bars as he walks on a First-day[3] loafe and
    looks at the oats and rye,
The lunatic is carried at last to the asylum a confirm'd case,
(He will never sleep any more as he did in the cot in his mother's
    bedroom;)

2. The musical scale.
3. Sunday. Quakers used such names for days of the week and also months of the year (see later, "Seventh-Month" for July) to avoid the "pagan" (Norse and Roman) names more commonly used.

The jour printer[4] with gray head and gaunt jaws works at his
case,   275
He turns his quid of tobacco while his eyes blurr with the manu-
script;
The malform'd limbs are tied to the surgeon's table,
What is removed drops horribly in a pail;
The quadroon girl is sold at the auction-stand, the drunkard nods
by the bar-room stove,
The machinist rolls up his sleeves, the policeman travels his beat,
the gate-keeper marks who pass,   280
The young fellow drives the express-wagon, (I love him, though I
do not know him;)
The half-breed straps on his light boots to compete in the race,
The western turkey-shooting draws old and young, some lean on
their rifles, some sit on logs,
Out from the crowd steps the marksman, takes his position, levels
his piece;
The groups of newly-come immigrants cover the wharf or levee, 285
As the woolly-pates hoe in the sugar-field, the overseer views them
from his saddle,
The bugle calls in the ball-room, the gentlemen run for their part-
ners, the dancers bow to each other,
The youth lies awake in the cedar-roof'd garret and harks to the
musical rain,
The Wolverine sets traps on the creek that helps fill the Huron,
The squaw wrapt in her yellow-hemm'd cloth is offering moccasins
and bead-bags for sale,   290
The connoisseur peers along the exhibition-gallery with half-shut
eyes bent sideways,
As the deck-hands make fast the steamboat the plank is thrown for
the shore-going passengers,
The young sister holds out the skein while the elder sister winds it
off in a ball, and stops now and then for the knots,
The one-year wife is recovering and happy having a week ago borne
her first child,
The clean-hair'd Yankee girl works with her sewing-machine or in
the factory or mill,   295
The paving-man leans on his two-handed rammer, the reporter's
lead flies swiftly over the note-book, the sign-painter is lettering
with blue and gold,
The canal boy trots on the tow-path, the book-keeper counts at his
desk, the shoemaker waxes his thread,
The conductor beats time for the band and all the performers follow him,
The child is baptized, the convert is making his first professions,
The regatta is spread on the bay, the race is begun, (how the white
sails sparkle!)   300

---

4. I.e., a journeyman printer, one who works for wages rather than on his own
account.

The drover watching his drove sings out to them that would stray,
The pedler sweats with his pack on his back, (the purchaser hig-
    gling[5] about the odd cent;)
The bride unrumples her white dress, the minute-hand of the clock
    moves slowly,
The opium-eater reclines with rigid head and just-open'd lips,
The prostitute draggles her shawl, her bonnet bobs on her tipsy
    and pimpled neck,   305
The crowd laugh at her blackguard oaths, the men jeer and wink to
    each other,
(Miserable! I do not laugh at your oaths nor jeer you;)
The President holding a cabinet council is surrounded by the great
    Secretaries,
On the piazza walk three matrons stately and friendly with twined
    arms,
The crew of the fish-smack pack repeated layers of halibut in the
    hold,   310
The Missourian crosses the plains toting his wares and his cattle,
As the fare-collector goes through the train he gives notice by the
    jingling of loose change,
The floor-men are laying the floor, the tinners are tinning the roof,
    the masons are calling for mortar,
In single file each shouldering his hod pass onward the laborers;
Seasons pursuing each other the indescribable crowd in gather'd, it
    is the fourth of Seventh-month,[6] (what salutes of cannon and
    small arms!)   315
Seasons pursuing each other the plougher ploughs, the mower mows,
    and the winter-grain falls in the ground;
Off on the lakes the pike-fisher watches and waits by the hole in the
    frozen surface,
The stumps stand thick round the clearing, the squatter strikes deep
    with his axe,
Flatboatmen make fast towards dusk near the cotton-wood or pecan-
    trees,
Coon-seekers go through the regions of the Red river or through
    those drain'd by the Tennessee, or through those of the Arkan-
    sas,   320
Torches shine in the dark that hangs on the Chattahooche or Alta-
    mahaw,
Patriarchs sit at supper with sons and grandsons and great grandsons
    around them,
In walls of adobie, in canvas tents, rest hunters and trappers after
    their day's sport,
The city sleeps and the country sleeps,
The living sleep for their time, the dead sleep for their time,   325
The old husband sleeps by his wife and the young husband sleeps by
    his wife;
And these tend inward to me, and I tend outward to them,

5. Bargaining for a small gain.   6. July 4.

And such as it is to be of these more or less I am,
And of these one and all I weave the song of myself.

16

I am of old and young, of the foolish as much as the wise,   330
Regardless of others, ever regardful of others,
Maternal as well as paternal, a child as well as a man,
Stuff'd with the stuff that is coarse and stuff'd with the stuff that is
    fine,
One of the Nation of many nations, the smallest the same and the
    largest the same,
A Southerner soon as a Northerner, a planter nonchalant and hos-
    pitable down by the Oconee I live,   335
A Yankee bound my own way ready for trade, my joints the limber-
    est joints on earth and the sternest joints on earth,
A Kentuckian walking the vale of the Elkhorn in my deer-skin leg-
    gings, a Louisianian or Georgian,
A boatman over lakes or bays or along coasts, a Hoosier, Badger,
    Buckeye;
At home on Kanadian snow-shoes or up in the bush, or with fisher-
    men off Newfoundland,
At home in the fleet of ice-boats, sailing with the rest and tack-
    ing,   340
At home on the hills of Vermont or in the woods of Maine, or the
    Texan ranch,
Comrade of Californians, comrade of free North-Westerners, (lov-
    ing their big proportions,)
Comrade of raftsmen and coalmen, comrade of all who shake hands
    and welcome to drink and meat,
A learner with the simplest, a teacher of the thoughtfullest,
A novice beginning yet experient of myriads of seasons,   345
Of every hue and caste am I, of every rank and religion,
A farmer, mechanic, artist, gentleman, sailor, quaker,
Prisoner, fancy-man, rowdy, lawyer, physician, priest.

I resist any thing better than my own diversity,
Breathe the air but leave plenty after me,   350
And am not stuck up, and am in my place.

(The moth and the fish-eggs are in their place,
The bright suns I see and the dark suns I cannot see are in their
    place,
The palpable is in its place and the impalpable is in its place.)

17

These are really the thoughts of all men in all ages and lands, they
    are not original with me,   355
If they are not yours as much as mine they are nothing, or next to
    nothing.
If they are not the riddle and the untying of the riddle they are
    nothing,
If they are not just as close as they are distant they are nothing.

This is the grass that grows wherever the land is and the water is,
This the common air that bathes the globe.   360

18

With music strong I come, with my cornets and my drums,
I play not marches for accepted victors only, I play marches for con-
    quer'd and slain persons.

Have you heard that it was good to gain the day?
I also say it is good to fall, battles are lost in the same spirit in
    which they are won.

I beat and pound for the dead,   365
I blow through my embouchures[7] my loudest and gayest for them.

Vivas to those who have fail'd!
And to those whose war-vessels sank in the sea!
And to those themselves who sank in the sea!
And to all generals that lost engagements, and all overcome he-
    roes!   370
And the numberless unknown heroes equal to the greatest heroes
    known!

19

This is the meal equally set, this the meat for natural hunger,
It is for the wicked just the same as the righteous, I make appoint-
    ments with all,
I will not have a single person slighted or left away,
The kept-woman, sponger, thief, are hereby invited,   375
The heavy-lipp'd slave is invited, the venerealee is invited;
There shall be no difference between them and the rest.

This is the press of a bashful hand, this the float and odor of hair,
This the touch of my lips to yours, this the murmur of yearning,
This the far-off depth and height reflecting my own face,   380
This the thoughtful merge of myself, and the outlet again.

Do you guess I have some intricate purpose?
Well I have, for the Fourth-month showers have, and the mica on
    the side of a rock has.

Do you take it I would astonish?
Does the daylight astonish? does the early redstart twittering through
    the woods?   385
Do I astonish more than they?

This hour I tell things in confidence,
I might not tell everybody, but I will tell you.

20

Who goes there? hankering, gross, mystical, nude;
How is it I extract strength from the beef I eat?   390

What is a man anyhow? what am I? what are you?

---

7. Mouthpieces of wind instruments.

All I mark as my own you shall offset it with your own,
Else it were time lost listening to me.

I do not snivel that snivel the world over,
That months are vacuums and the ground but wallow and filth.   395

Whimpering and truckling fold with powders for invalids, conform-
    ity goes to the fourth-remov'd,
I wear my hat as I please indoors or out.

Why should I pray? why should I venerate and be ceremonious?

Having pried through the strata, analyzed to a hair, counsel'd with
    doctors and calculated close,
I find no sweeter fat than sticks to my own bones.   400

In all people I see myself; none more and not one a barley-corn less,
And the good or bad I say of myself I say of them.

I know I am solid and sound,
To me the converging objects of the universe perpetually flow,
All are written to me, and I must get what the writing means.   405

I know I am deathless,
I know this orbit of mine cannot be swept by a carpenter's compass,
I know I shall not pass like a child's carlacue[8] cut with a burnt
    stick at night.

I know I am august,
I do not trouble my spirit to vindicate itself or be understood,   410
I see that the elementary laws never apologize,
(I reckon I behave no prouder than the level I plant my house by,
    after all.)

I exist as I am, that is enough,
If no other in the world be aware I sit content,
And if each and all be aware I sit content.   415

One world is aware and by far the largest to me, and that is myself,
And whether I come to my own to-day or in ten thousand or ten
    million years,
I can cheerfully take it now, or with equal cheerfulness I can wait.

My foothold is tenon'd and mortis'd[9] in granite,
I laugh at what you call dissolution,   420
And I know the amplitude of time.

                21
I am the poet of the Body and I am the poet of the Soul,
The pleasures of heaven are with me and the pains of hell are with
    me,
The first I graft and increase upon myself, the latter I translate into
    a new tongue.

8. Curlicue, a fancy curve or flourish.   9. Tightly jointed.

I am the poet of the woman the same as the man,   425
And I say it is as great to be a woman as to be a man,
And I say there is nothing greater than the mother of men.

I chant the chant of dilation or pride,
We have had ducking and deprecating about enough,
I show that size is only development.   430

Have you outstript the rest? are you the President?
It is a trifle, they will more than arrive there every one, and still
      pass on.

I am he that walks with the tender and growing night,
I call to the earth and sea half-held by the night.

Press close bare-bosom'd night—press close magnetic nourishing
      night!   435
Night of south winds—night of the large few stars!
Still nodding night—mad naked summer night.

Smile O voluptuous cool-breath'd earth!
Earth of the slumbering and liquid trees!
Earth of departed sunset—earth of the mountains misty-topt!   440
Earth of the vitreous pour of the full moon just tinged with blue!
Earth of shine and dark mottling the tide of the river!
Earth of the limpid gray of clouds brighter and clearer for my sake!
Far-swooping elbow'd earth—rich apple-blossom'd earth!
Smile, for your lover comes.   445

Prodigal, you have given me love—therefore I to you give love!
O unspeakable passionate love.

                                      22
You sea! I resign myself to you also—I guess what you mean,
I behold from the beach your crooked inviting fingers,
I believe you refuse to go back without feeling of me,   450
We must have a turn together, I undress, hurry me out of sight of
      the land,
Cushion me soft, rock me in billowy drowse,
Dash me with amorous wet, I can repay you.

Sea of stretch'd ground-swells,
Sea breathing broad and convulsive breaths,   455
Sea of the brine of life and of unshovell'd yet always-ready graves,
Howler and scooper of storms, capricious and dainty sea,
I am integral with you, I too am of one phase and of all phases.

Partaker of influx and efflux, I, extoller of hate and conciliation,
Extoller of amies[1] and those that sleep in each others' arms,   460
I am he attesting sympathy,
(Shall I make my list of things in the house and skip the house that
      supports them?)

---

1. French, "lovers."

I am not the poet of goodness only, I do not decline to be the poet
of wickedness also.

What blurt is this about virtue and about vice?
Evil propels me and reform of evil propels me, I stand indiffer-
ent,   465
My gait is no fault-finder's or rejecter's gait,
I moisten the roots of all that has grown.

Did you fear some scrofula out of the unflagging pregnancy?
Did you guess the celestial laws are yet to be work'd over and recti-
fied?

I find one side a balance and the antipodal side a balance,   470
Soft doctrine as steady help as stable doctrine,
Thoughts and deeds of the present our rouse and early start.

This minute that comes to me over the past decillions,
There is no better than it and now.

What behaved well in the past or behaves well to-day is not such a
wonder,   475
The wonder is always and always how there can be a mean man or
an infidel.

23

Endless unfolding of words of ages!
And mine a word of the modern, the word En-Masse.[2]

A word of the faith that never balks,
Here or henceforward it is all the same to me, I accept Time absolutely.   480

It alone is without flaw, it alone rounds and completes all,
That mystic baffling wonder alone completes all.

I accept Reality and dare not question it,
Materialism first and last imbuing.

Hurrah for positive science! long live exact demonstration!   485
Fetch stonecrop[3] mixt with cedar and branches of lilac,
This is the lexicographer, this the chemist, this made a grammar of
the old cartouches,[4]
These mariners put the ship through dangerous unknown seas,
This is the geologist, this works with the scalpel, and this is a mathe-
matician.

Gentlemen, to you the first honors always!   490
Your facts are useful, and yet they are not my dwelling,
I but enter by them to an area of my dwelling.

2. French, "all together."   4. Oval or oblong figures in Egyptian
3. Sedum, an herb which grows on   hieroglyphics.
rocks and stones.

Less the reminders of properties told my words,
And more the reminders they of life untold, and of freedom and ex-
    trication,
And make short account of neuters and geldings, and favor men and
    women fully equipt,
And beat the gong of revolt, and stop with fugitives and them that   495
    plot and conspire.

24

Walt Whitman, a kosmos, of Manhattan the son,
Turbulent, fleshy, sensual, eating, drinking and breeding,
No sentimentalist, no stander above men and women or apart from
    them,
No more modest than immodest.   500

Unscrew the locks from the doors!
Unscrew the doors themselves from their jambs!

Whoever degrades another degrades me,
And whatever is done or said returns at last to me.

Through me the afflatus[5] surging and surging, through me the cur-
    rent and index.   505

I speak the pass-word primeval, I give the sign of democracy,
By God! I will accept nothing which all cannot have their counter-
    part of on the same terms.

Through me many long dumb voices,
Voices of the interminable generations of prisoners and slaves,
Voices of the diseas'd and despairing and of thieves and dwarfs,   510
Voices of cycles of preparation and accretion,
And of the threads that connect the stars, and of wombs and of the
    father-stuff,
And of the rights of them the others are down upon,
Of the deform'd, trivial, flat, foolish, despised,
Fog in the air, beetles rolling balls of dung.   515

Through me forbidden voices,
Voices of sexes and lusts, voices veil'd and I remove the veil,
Voices indecent by me clarified and transfigur'd.

I do not press my fingers across my mouth,
I keep as delicate around the bowels as around the head and
    heart,   520
Copulation is no more rank to me than death is.

I believe in the flesh and the appetites,
Seeing, hearing, feeling, are miracles, and each part and tag of me is
    a miracle.

Divine am I inside and out, and I make holy whatever I touch or am
    touch'd from,

5. Poetic inspiration.

The scent of these arm-pits aroma finer than prayer,   525
This head more than churches, bibles, and all the creeds.

If I worship one thing more than another it shall be the spread of
  my own body, or any part of it,
Translucent mould of me it shall be you!
Shaded ledges and rests it shall be you!
Firm masculine colter[6] it shall be you!   530
Whatever goes to the tilth of me it shall be you!
You my rich blood! your milky stream pale strippings of my life!
Breast that presses against other breasts it shall be you!
My brain it shall be your occult convolutions!
Root of wash'd sweet-flag! timorous pond-snipe! nest of guarded du-
  plicate eggs! it shall be you!   535
Mix'd tussled hay of head, beard, brawn, it shall be you!
Trickling sap of maple, fibre of manly wheat, it shall be you!
Sun so generous it shall be you!
Vapors lighting and shading my face it shall be you!
You sweaty brooks and dews it shall be you!   540
Winds whose soft-tickling genitals rub against me it shall be you!
Broad muscular fields, branches of live oak, loving lounger in my
  winding paths, it shall be you!
Hands I have taken, face I have kiss'd, mortal I have ever touch'd,
  it shall be you.

I dote on myself, there is that lot of me and all so luscious,
Each moment and whatever happens thrills me with joy,   545
I cannot tell how my ankles bend, nor whence the cause of my faint-
  est wish,
Nor the cause of the friendship I emit, nor the cause of the friend-
  ship I take again.

That I walk up my stoop, I pause to consider if it really be,
A morning-glory at my window satisfies me more than the metaphysics of books.

To behold the day-break!   550
The little light fades the immense and diaphanous shadows,
The air tastes good to my palate.

Hefts[7] of the moving world at innocent gambols silently rising,
  freshly exuding,
Scooting obliquely high and low.

Something I cannot see puts upward libidinous prongs,   555
Seas of bright juice suffuse heaven.

The earth by the sky staid with, the daily close of their junction,
The heav'd challenge from the east that moment over my head,
The mocking taunt, See then whether you shall be master!

6. An iron blade attached to the front   7. Mass, bulk, main part.
of a plowshare. "Tilth": cultivation.

2 5

Dazzling and tremendous how quick the sun-rise would kill me, 560
If I could not now and always send sun-rise out of me.

We also ascend dazzling and tremendous as the sun,
We found our own O my soul in the calm and cool of the daybreak.

My voice goes after what my eyes cannot reach,
With the twirl of my tongue I encompass worlds and volumes of
worlds. 565

Speech is the twin of my vision, it is unequal to measure itself,
It provokes me forever, it says sarcastically,
Walt you contain enough, why don't you let it out then?

Come now I will not be tantalized, you conceive too much of articu-
lation,
Do you not know O speech how the buds beneath you are
folded? 570
Waiting in gloom, protected by frost,
The dirt receding before my prophetical screams,
I underlying causes to balance them at last,
My knowledge my live parts, it keeping tally with the meaning of all
things,
Happiness, (which whoever hears me let him or her set out in search
of this day.) 575

My final merit I refuse you, I refuse putting from me what I really
am,
Encompass worlds, but never try to encompass me,
I crowd your sleekest and best by simply looking toward you.
Writing and talk do not prove me,
I carry the plenum[8] of proof and every thing else in my face, 580
With the hush of my lips I wholly confound the skeptic.

26

Now I will do nothing but listen,
To accrue what I hear into this song, to let sounds contribute toward it.

I hear bravuras of birds, bustle of growing wheat, gossip of flames,
clack of sticks cooking my meals,
I hear the sound I love, the sound of the human voice, 585
I hear all sounds running together, combined, fused or following,
Sounds of the city and sounds out of the city, sounds of the day and
night,
Talkative young ones to those that like them, the loud laugh of
work-people at their meals,
The angry base of disjointed friendship, the faint tones of the sick,
The judge with hands tight to the desk, his pallid lips pronouncing
a death-sentence, 590

8. Fullness.

The heave'e'yo of stevedores unlading ships by the wharves, the refrain of the anchor-lifters,
The ring of alarm-bells, the cry of fire, the whirr of swift-streaking
  engines and hose-carts with premonitory tinkles and color'd
  lights,
The steam-whistle, the solid roll of the train of approaching cars,
The slow march play'd at the head of the association marching two
  and two,
(They go to guard some corpse, the flag-tops are draped with black
  muslin.)   595

I hear the violoncello, ('tis the young man's heart's complaint,)
I hear the key'd cornet, it glides quickly in through my ears,
It shakes mad-sweet pangs through my belly and breast.

I hear the chorus, it is a grand opera,
Ah this indeed is music—this suits me.   600

A tenor large and fresh as the creation fills me,
The orbic flex of his mouth is pouring and filling me full.

I hear the train'd soprano (what work with hers is this?)
The orchestra whirls me wider than Uranus flies,
It wrenches such ardors from me I did not know I possess'd
  them,   605
It sails me, I dab with bare feet, they are lick'd by the indolent
  waves,
I am cut by bitter and angry hail, I lose my breath,
Steep'd amid honey'd morphine, my windpipe throttled in fakes[9]
  of death,
At length let up again to feel the puzzle of puzzles,
And that we call Being.   610

27

To be in any form, what is that?
(Round and round we go, all of us, and ever come back thither,)
If nothing lay more develop'd the quahaug[1] in its callous shell were
  enough.

Mine is no callous shell,
I have instant conductors all over me whether I pass or stop,   615
They seize every object and lead it harmlessly through me.

I merely stir, press, feel with my fingers, and am happy,
To touch my person to some one else's is about as much as I can
  stand.

28

Is this then a touch? quivering me to a new identity,
Flames and ether making a rush for my veins,   620
Treacherous tip of me reaching and crowding to help them,
My flesh and blood playing out lightning to strike what is hardly
  different from myself,

9. Loops of a coil of rope (nautical).   1. An edible clam.

On all sides prurient provokers stiffening my limbs,
Straining the udder of my heart for its withheld drip,
Behaving licentious toward me, taking no denial,   625
Depriving me of my best as for a purpose,
Unbuttoning my clothes, holding me by the bare waist,
Deluding my confusion with the calm of the sunlight and pasture-
     fields,
Immodestly sliding the fellow-senses away,
They bribed to swap off with touch and go and graze at the edges
     of me,   630
No consideration, no regard for my draining strength or my anger,
Fetching the rest of the herd around to enjoy them a while,
Then all uniting to stand on a headland and worry me.

The sentries desert every other part of me,
They have left me helpless to a red marauder,   635
They all come to the headland to witness and assist against me.

I am given up by traitors,
I talk wildly, I have lost my wits, I and nobody else am the greatest
     traitor,
I went myself first to the headland, my own hands carried me there.

You villain touch! what are you doing? my breath is tight in its
     throat,
Unclench your floodgates, you are too much for me.   640

                          29
Blind loving wrestling touch, sheath'd hooded sharp-tooth'd touch!
Did it make you ache so, leaving me?

Parting track'd by arriving, perpetual payment of perpetual loan,
Rich showering rain, and recompense richer afterward.   645

Sprouts take and accumulate, stand by the curb prolific and vital,
Landscapes projected masculine, full-sized and golden.
                          30
All truths wait in all things,
They neither hasten their own delivery nor resist it,
They do not need the obstetric forceps of the surgeon,   650
The insignificant is as big to me as any,
(What is less or more than a touch?)

Logic and sermons never convince,
The damp of the night drives deeper into my soul.

(Only what proves itself to every man and woman is so,   655
Only what nobody denies is so.)

A minute and a drop of me settle my brain,
I believe the soggy clods shall become lovers and lamps,
And a compend[2] of compends is the meat of a man or woman,

2. Compendium, epitome.

And a summit and flower there is the feeling they have for each
    other,   660
And they are to branch boundlessly out of that lesson until it be-
    comes omnific,[3]
And until one and all shall delight us, and we them.

31
I believe a leaf of grass is no less than the journey-work of the stars,
And the pismire[4] is equally perfect, and a grain of sand, and the egg
    of the wren,
And the tree-toad is a chef-d'œuvre[5] for the highest,   665
And the running blackberry would adorn the parlors of heaven,
And the narrowest hinge in my hand puts to scorn all machinery,
And the cow crunching with depress'd head surpasses any statue,
And a mouse is miracle enough to stagger sextillions of infidels.

I find I incorporate gneiss, coal, long-threaded moss, fruits, grains,
    esculent roots,   670
And am stucco'd with quadrupeds and birds all over,
And have distanced what is behind me for good reasons,
But call any thing back again when I desire it.

In vain the speeding or shyness,
In vain the plutonic rocks send their old heat against my ap-
    proach,   675
In vain the mastodon retreats beneath its own powder'd bones,
In vain objects stand leagues off and assume manifold shapes,
In vain the ocean settling in hollows and the great monsters lying
    low,
In vain the buzzard houses herself with the sky,
In vain the snake slides through the creepers and logs,   680
In vain the elk takes to the inner passes of the woods,
In vain the razor-bill'd auk sails far north to Labrador,
I follow quickly, I ascend to the nest in the fissure of the cliff.

32
I think I could turn and live with animals, they're so placid and self-
    contain'd,
I stand and look at them long and long.   685

They do not sweat and whine about their condition,
They do not lie awake in the dark and weep for their sins,
They do not make me sick discussing their duty to God,
Not one is dissatisfied, not one is demented with the mania of own-
    ing things,
Not one kneels to another, nor to his kind that lived thousands of
    years ago,   690
Not one is respectable or unhappy over the whole earth.

So they show their relations to me and I accept them,
They bring me tokens of myself, they evince them plainly in their
    possession.

3. Making all things.   5. Masterpiece.
4. Ant.

I wonder where they get those tokens,
Did I pass that way huge times ago and negligently drop them? 695

Myself moving forward then and now and forever,
Gathering and showing more always and with velocity,
Infinite and omnigenous,[6] and the like of these among them,
Not too exclusive toward the reachers of my remembrancers,
Picking out here one that I love, and now go with him on brotherly
    terms. 700

A gigantic beauty of a stallion, fresh and responsive to my caresses,
Head high in the forehead, wide between the ears,
Limbs glossy and supple, tail dusting the ground,
Eyes full of sparkling wickedness, ears finely cut, flexibly moving.

His nostrils dilate as my heels embrace him, 705
His well-built limbs tremble with pleasure as we race around and
    return,
I but use you a minute, then I resign you, stallion,
Why do I need your paces when I myself out-gallop them?
Even as I stand or sit passing faster than you.

33

Space and Time! now I see it is true, what I guess'd at, 710
What I guess'd when I loaf'd on the grass,
What I guess'd while I lay alone in my bed,
And again as I walk'd the beach under the paling stars of the morn-
    ing.

My ties and ballasts leave me, my elbows rest in sea-gaps,
I skirt sierras, my palms cover continents, 715
I am afoot with my vision.

By the city's quadrangular houses—in log huts, camping with lum-
    bermen,
Along the ruts of the turnpike, along the dry gulch and rivulet bed,
Weeding my onion-patch or hoeing rows of carrots and parsnips,
    crossing savannas, trailing in forests,
Prospecting, gold-digging, girdling the trees of a new purchase, 720
Scorch'd ankle-deep by the hot sand, hauling my boat down the
    shallow river,
Where the panther walks to and fro on a limb overhead, where the
    buck turns furiously at the hunter,
Where the rattlesnake suns his flabby length on a rock, where the
    otter is feeding on fish,
Where the alligator in his tough pimples sleeps by the bayou,
Where the black bear is searching for roots or honey, where the
    beaver pats the mud with his paddle-shaped tail; 725
Over the growing sugar, over the yellow-flower'd cotton plant, over
    the rice in its low moist field,

6. Of all kinds.

Over the sharp-peak'd farm house, with its scallop'd scum[7] and
    slender shoots from the gutters,
Over the western persimmon, over the long-leav'd corn, over the
    delicate blue-flower flax,
Over the white and brown buckwheat, a hummer and buzzer there
    with the rest,
Over the dusky green of the rye as it ripples and shades in the
    breeze;   730
Scaling mountains, pulling myself cautiously up, holding on by low
    scragged[8] limbs,
Walking the path worn in the grass and beat through the leaves of
    the brush,
Where the quail is whistling betwixt the woods and the wheat-lot,
Where the bat flies in the Seventh-month eve, where the great gold-
    bug drops through the dark,
Where the brook puts out of the roots of the old tree and flows to
    the meadow,   735
Where cattle stand and shake away flies with the tremulous shudder-
    ing of their hides,
Where the cheese-cloth hangs in the kitchen, where andirons strad-
    dle the hearth-slab, where cobwebs fall in festoons from the
    rafters;
Where trip-hammers crash, where the press is whirling its cylinders,
Where the human heart beats with terrible throes under its ribs,
Where the pear-shaped balloon is floating aloft, (floating in it my-
    self and looking composedly down,)   740
Where the life-car[9] is drawn on the slip-noose, where the heat
    hatches pale-green eggs in the dented sand,
Where the she-whale swims with her calf and never forsakes it,
Where the steam-ship trails hind-ways its long pennant of smoke,
Where the fin of the shark cuts like a black chip out of the water,
Where the half-burn'd brig is riding on unknown currents,   745
Where shells grow to her slimy deck, where the dead are corrupting
    below;
Where the dense-starr'd flag is borne at the head of the regiments,
Approaching Manhattan up by the long-stretching island,
Under Niagara, the cataract falling like a veil over my countenance,
Upon a door-step, upon the horse-block of hard wood outside,   750
Upon the race-course, or enjoying picnics or jigs or a good game of
    base-ball,
At he-festivals, with blackguard jibes, ironical license, bull-dances,
    drinking, laughter,
At the cider-mill tasting the sweets of the brown mash, sucking the
    juice through a straw,
At apple-peelings wanting kisses for all the red fruit I find,
At musters, beach-parties, friendly bees, huskings, house-raisings;   755

7. Froth; figuratively, unnecessary
trimming.
8. Scraggy, ragged.

9. A watertight vessel moved by ropes
and used to bring shipwrecked persons
ashore through heavy seas.

Where the mocking-bird sounds his delicious gurgles, cackles, screams, weeps,

Where the hay-rick stands in the barn-yard, where the dry-stalks are scatter'd, where the brood-cow waits in the hovel,

Where the bull advances to do his masculine work, where the stud to the mare, where the cock is treading the hen,

Where the heifers browse, where geese nip their food with short jerks,

Where sun-down shadows lengthen over the limitless and lonesome prairie,   760

Where herds of buffalo make a crawling spread of the square miles far and near,

Where the humming-bird shimmers, where the neck of the long-lived swan is curving and winding,

Where the laughing-gull scoots by the shore, where she laughs her near-human laugh,

Where bee-hives range on a gray bench in the garden half hid by the high weeds,

Where band-neck'd partridges roost in a ring on the ground with their heads out,   765

Where burial coaches enter the arch'd gates of a cemetery,

Where winter wolves bark amid wastes of snow and icicled trees,

Where the yellow-crown'd heron comes to the edge of the marsh at night and feeds upon small crabs,

Where the splash of swimmers and divers cools the warm noon,

Where the katy-did works her chromatic reed on the walnut-tree over the well,   770

Through patches of citrons and cucumbers with silver-wired leaves,

Through the salt-lick or orange glade, or under conical firs,

Through the gymnasium, through the curtain'd saloon, through the office or public hall;

Pleas'd with the native and pleas'd with the foreign, pleas'd with the new and old,

Pleas'd with the homely woman as well as the handsome,   775

Pleas'd with the quakeress as she puts off her bonnet and talks melodiously,

Pleas'd with the tune of the choir of the whitewash'd church,

Pleas'd with the earnest words of the sweating Methodist preacher, impress'd seriously at the camp-meeting;

Looking in at the shop-windows of Broadway the whole forenoon, flatting the flesh of my nose on the thick plate glass,

Wandering the same afternoon with my face turn'd up to the clouds, or down a lane or along the beach,   780

My right and left arms round the sides of two friends, and I in the middle;

Coming home with the silent and dark-cheek'd bush-boy, (behind me he rides at the drape of the day,)

Far from the settlements studying the print of animals' feet, or the moccasin print,

By the cot in the hospital reaching lemonade to a feverish patient,
Nigh the coffin'd corpse when all is still, examining with a candle;   785
Voyaging to every port to dicker and adventure,
Hurrying with the modern crowd as eager and fickle as any,
Hot toward one I hate, ready in my madness to knife him,
Solitary at midnight in my back yard, my thoughts gone from me a
 long while,
Walking the old hills of Judæa with the beautiful gentle God by my
 side,   790
Speeding through space, speeding through heaven and the stars,
Speeding amid the seven satellites and the broad ring, and the
 diameter of eighty thousand miles,
Speeding with tail'd meteors, throwing fire-balls like the rest,
Carrying the crescent child that carries its own full mother in its
 belly,
Storming, enjoying, planning, loving, cautioning,   795
Backing and filling, appearing and disappearing,
I tread day and night such roads.

I visit the orchards of spheres and look at the product,
And look at quintillions ripen'd and look at quintillions green.

I fly those flights of a fluid and swallowing soul,   800
My course runs below the sounding of plummets.

I help myself to material and immaterial,
No guard can shut me off, no law prevent me.

I anchor my ship for a little while only,
My messengers continually cruise away or bring their returns to
 me.   805

I go hunting polar furs and the seal, leaping chasms with a pike-
 pointed staff, clinging to topples of brittle and blue.

I ascend to the foretruck,[1]
I take my place late at night in the crow's-nest,
We sail the arctic sea, it is plenty light enough,
Through the clear atmosphere I stretch around on the wonderful
 beauty,   810
The enormous masses of ice pass me and I pass them, the scenery
 is plain in all directions,
The white-topt mountains show in the distance, I fling out my
 fancies toward them,
We are approaching some great battle-field in which we are soon to
 be engaged,
We pass the colossal outposts of the encampment, we pass with still
 feet and caution,
Or we are entering by the suburbs some vast and ruin'd city,   815

1. A platform on the head of a foremast.

The blocks and fallen architecture more than all the living cities of
    the globe.

I am a free companion, I bivouac by invading watchfires,
I turn the bridegroom out of bed and stay with the bride myself,
I tighten her all night to my thighs and lips.

My voice is the wife's voice, the screech by the rail of the stairs,   ₈₂₀
They fetch my man's body up dripping and drown'd.

I understand the large hearts of heroes,
The courage of present times and all times,
How the skipper saw the crowded and rudderless wreck of the steam-
    ship, and Death chasing it up and down the storm,
How he knuckled tight and gave not back an inch, and was faithful
    of days and faithful of nights,   825
And chalk'd in large letters on a board, *Be of good cheer, we will not
    desert you;*
How he follow'd with them and tack'd with them three days and
    would not give it up,
How he saved the drifting company at last,
How the lank loose-gown'd women look'd when boated from the
    side of their prepared graves,
How the silent old-faced infants and the lifted sick, and the sharp-
    lipp'd unshaved men;   830
All this I swallow, it tastes good, I like it well, it becomes mine,
I am the man, I suffer'd, I was there.

The disdain and calmness of martyrs,
The mother of old, condemn'd for a witch, burnt with dry wood,
    her children gazing on,
The hounded slave that flags in the race, leans by the fence, blowing,
    cover'd with sweat,   835
The twinges that sting like needles his legs and neck, the murderous
    buckshot and the bullets,
All these I feel or am.

I am the hounded slave, I wince at the bite of the dogs,
Hell and despair are upon me, crack and again crack the marksmen,
I clutch the rails of the fence, my gore dribs, thinn'd with the ooze
    of my skin,   840
I fall on the weeds and stones,
The riders spur their unwilling horses, haul close,
Taunt my dizzy ears and beat me violently over the head with whip-
    stocks.

Agonies are one of my changes of garments,
I do not ask the wounded person how he feels, I myself become the
    wounded person,   845
My hurts turn livid upon me as I lean on a cane and observe.

I am the mash'd fireman with breast-bone broken,
Tumbling walls buried me in their debris,
Heat and smoke I inspired,[2] I heard the yelling shouts of my com-
rades,
I heard the distant click of their picks and shovels,   850
They have clear'd the beams away, they tenderly lift me forth.

I lie in the night air in my red shirt, the pervading hush is for my
sake,
Painless after all I lie exhausted but not so unhappy,
White and beautiful are the faces around me, the heads are bared
of their fire-caps,
The kneeling crowd fades with the light of the torches.   855

Distant and dead resuscitate,
They show me as the dial or move as the hands of me, I am the
clock myself.

I am an old artillerist, I tell of my fort's bombardment,
I am there again.

Again the long roll of the drummers,   860
Again the attacking cannon, mortars,
Again to my listening ears the cannon responsive.

I take part, I see and hear the whole,
The cries, curses, roar, the plaudits for well-aim'd shots,
The ambulanza[3] slowly passing trailing its red drip,   865
Workmen searching after damages, making indispensable repairs,
The fall of grenades through the rent roof, the fan-shaped explosion,
The whizz of limbs, heads, stone, wood, iron, high in the air.

Again gurgles the mouth of my dying general, he furiously waves
with his hand,
He gasps through the clot *Mind not me—mind—the entrench-
ments*.   870

34

Now I tell what I knew in Texas in my early youth,
(I tell not the fall of Alamo,
Not one escaped to tell the fall of Alamo,
The hundred and fifty are dumb yet at Alamo,)
'Tis the tale of the murder in cold blood of four hundred and twelve
young men.[4]   875

Retreating they had form'd in a hollow square with their baggage for
breastworks,
Nine hundred lives out of the surrounding enemy's, nine times their
number, was the price they took in advance,

2. Inhaled.
3. Army ambulance.

4. The Mexican massacre of Texas
troops at Goliad, March 27, 1836.

Their colonel was wounded and their ammunition gone,
They treated for an honorable capitulation, receiv'd writing and
    seal, gave up their arms and march'd back prisoners of war.

They were the glory of the race of rangers, 880
Matchless with horse, rifle, song, supper, courtship,
Large, turbulent, generous, handsome, proud, and affectionate,
Bearded, sunburnt, drest in the free costume of hunters,
Not a single one over thirty years of age.

The second First-day morning they were brought out in squads and
    massacred, it was beautiful early summer, 885
The work commenced about five o'clock and was over by eight.

None obey'd the command to kneel,
Some made a mad and helpless rush, some stood stark and straight,
A few fell at once, shot in the temple or heart, the living and dead
    lay together,
The maim'd and mangled dug in the dirt, the new-comers saw
    them there, 890
Some half-kill'd attempted to crawl away,
These were despatch'd with bayonets or batter'd with the blunts of
    muskets,
A youth not seventeen years old seiz'd his assassin till two more
    came to release him,
The three were all torn and cover'd with the boy's blood.

At eleven o'clock began the burning of the bodies; 895
That is the tale of the murder of the four hundred and twelve young
    men.

35

Would you hear of an old-time sea-fight?[5]
Would you learn who won by the light of the moon and stars?
List to the yarn, as my grandmother's father the sailor told it to me.

Our foe was no skulk in his ship I tell you, (said he,) 900
His was the surly English pluck, and there is no tougher or truer,
    and never was, and never will be;
Along the lower'd eve he came horribly raking us.

We closed with him, the yards entangled, the cannon touch'd,
My captain lash'd fast with his own hands.

We had receiv'd some eighteen pound shots under the water, 905
On our lower-gun-deck two large pieces had burst at the first fire,
    killing all around and blowing up overhead.

Fighting at sun-down, fighting at dark,
Ten o'clock at night, the full moon well up, our leaks on the gain,
    and five feet of water reported,

---

5. The battle of the American *Bon-homme Richard*, commanded by John Paul Jones, and the British *Serapis* during the American Revolution.

The master-at-arms loosing the prisoners confined in the after-hold
    to give them a chance for themselves.

The transit to and from the magazine is now stopt by the sen-
    tinels,   910
They see so many strange faces they do not know whom to trust.

Our frigate takes fire,
The other asks if we demand quarter?
If our colors are struck and the fighting done?

Now I laugh content, for I hear the voice of my little captain,   915
We have not struck, he composedly cries, *we have just begun our
    part of the fighting.*

Only three guns are in use,
One is directed by the captain himself against the enemy's main-
    mast,
Two well serv'd with grape and canister[6] silence his musketry and
    clear his decks.

The tops alone second the fire of this little battery, especially the
    main-top,   920
They hold out bravely during the whole of the action.

Not a moment's cease,
The leaks gain fast on the pumps, the fire eats toward the powder-
    magazine.

One of the pumps has been shot away, it is generally thought we are
    sinking.

Serene stands the little captain,   925
He is not hurried, his voice is neither high nor low,
His eyes give more light to us than our battle-lanterns.

Toward twelve there in the beams of the moon they surrender to us.

36

Stretch'd and still lies the midnight,
Two great hulls motionless on the breast of the darkness,   930
Our vessel riddled and slowly sinking, preparations to pass to the
    one we have conquer'd,
The captain on the quarter-deck coldly giving his orders through a
    countenance white as a sheet,
Near by the corpse of the child that serv'd in the cabin,
The dead face of an old salt with long white hair and carefully
    curl'd whiskers,
The flames spite of all that can be done flickering aloft and be-
    low,   935
The husky voices of the two or three officers yet fit for duty,
Formless stacks of bodies and bodies by themselves, dabs of flesh
    upon the masts and spars,

6. Grape shot and canister shot; projectiles fired from a cannon.

Cut of cordage, dangle of rigging, slight shock of the soothe of
    waves,
Black and impassive guns, litter of powder-parcels, strong scent,
A few large stars overhead, silent and mournful shining,   940
Delicate sniffs of sea-breeze, smells of sedgy grass and fields by the
    shore, death-messages given in charge to survivors,
The hiss of the surgeon's knife, the gnawing teeth of his saw,
Wheeze, cluck, swash[7] of falling blood, short wild scream, and long,
    dull, tapering groan,
These so, these irretrievable.

37

You laggards there on guard! look to your arms!   945
In at the conquer'd doors they crowd! I am possess'd!
Embody all presences outlaw'd or suffering,
See myself in prison shaped like another man,
And feel the dull unintermitted pain.

For me the keepers of convicts shoulder their carbines and keep
    watch,
It is I let out in the morning and barr'd at night.   950

Not a mutineer walks handcuff'd to jail but I am handcuff'd to him
    and walk by his side,
(I am less the jolly one there, and more the silent one with sweat
    on my twitching lips.)

Not a youngster is taken for larceny but I go up too, and am tried
    and sentenced.

Not a cholera patient lies at the last gasp but I also lie at the last
    gasp,   955
My face is ash-color'd, my sinews gnarl, away from me people re-
    treat.

Askers embody themselves in me and I am embodied in them,
I project my hat, sit shame-faced, and beg.

38

Enough! enough! enough!
Somehow I have been stunn'd. Stand back!   960
Give me a little time beyond my cuff'd head, slumbers, dreams,
    gaping,
I discover myself on the verge of a usual mistake.

That I could forget the mockers and insults!
That I could forget the trickling tears and the blows of the bludg-
    eons and hammers!
That I could look with a separate look on my own crucifixion and
    bloody crowning.   965

I remember now,
I resume the overstaid fraction,

7. Wet refuse (or the splashing sound of it).

The grave of rock multiplies what has been confided to it, or to any
    graves,
Corpses rise, gashes heal, fastenings roll from me.

I troop forth replenish'd with supreme power, one of an average
    unending procession,   970
Inland and sea-coast we go, and pass all boundary lines,
Our swift ordinances on their way over the whole earth,
The blossoms we wear in our hats the growth of thousands of years.

Eleves,[8] I salute you! come forward!
Continue your annotations, continue your questionings.   975

39

The friendly and flowing savage, who is he?
Is he waiting for civilization, or past it and mastering it?

Is he some Southwesterner rais'd out-doors? is he Kanadian?
Is he from the Mississippi country? Iowa, Oregon, California?
The mountains? prairie-life, bush-life? or sailor from the sea?   980

Wherever he goes men and women accept and desire him,
They desire he should like them, touch them, speak to them, stay
    with them.

Behavior lawless as snow-flakes, words simple as grass, uncomb'd
    head, laughter, and naivetè,
Slow-stepping feet, common features, common modes and emana-
    tions,
They descend in new forms from the tips of his fingers,   985
They are wafted with the odor of his body or breath, they fly out of
    the glance of his eyes.

40

Flaunt of the sunshine I need not your bask—lie over!
You light surfaces only, I force surfaces and depths also.

Earth! you seem to look for something at my hands,
Say, old top-knot, what do you want?   990

Man or woman, I might tell how I like you, but cannot,
And might tell what it is in me and what it is in you, but cannot,
And might tell that pining I have, that pulse of my nights and days.

Behold, I do not give lectures or a little charity,
When I give I give myself.   995

You there, impotent, loose in the knees,
Open your scarf'd chops[9] till I blow grit within you,
Spread your palms and lift the flaps of your pockets,
I am not to be denied, I compel, I have stores plenty and to spare,
And any thing I have I bestow.   1000

8. French, "pupils."
9. "Scarf'd chops" are jaws bound up
with a scarf; reference is to a person so
wrapped or bandaged.

I do not ask who you are, that is not important to me,
You can do nothing and be nothing but what I will infold you.

To cotton-field drudge or cleaner of privies I lean,
On his right cheek I put the family kiss,
And in my soul I swear I never will deny him.   1005

On women fit for conception I start bigger and nimbler babes,
(This day I am jetting the stuff of far more arrogant republics.)

To any one dying, thither I speed and twist the knob of the door,
Turn the bed-clothes toward the foot of the bed,
Let the physician and the priest go home.   1010

I seize the descending man and raise him with resistless will,
O despairer, here is my neck,
By God, you shall not go down! hang your whole weight upon me.

I dilate you with tremendous breath, I buoy you up,
Every room of the house do I fill with an arm'd force,   1015
Lovers of me, bafflers of graves.

Sleep—I and they keep guard all night,
Not doubt, not disease shall dare to lay finger upon you,
I have embraced you, and henceforth possess you to myself,
And when you rise in the morning you will find what I tell you is
     so.   1020

41

I am he bringing help for the sick as they pant on their backs,
And for strong upright men I bring yet more needed help.

I heard what was said of the universe,
Heard it and heard it of several thousand years;
It is middling well as far as it goes—but is that all?   1025

Magnifying and applying come I,
Outbidding at the start the old cautious hucksters,
Taking myself the exact dimensions of Jehovah,
Lithographing Kronos, Zeus his son, and Hercules his grandson,
Buying drafts of Osiris, Isis, Belus, Brahma, Buddha,   1030
In my portfolio placing Manito loose, Allah on a leaf, the crucifix
     engraved,
With Odin and the hideous-faced Mexitli and every idol and image,
Taking them all for what they are worth and not a cent more,
Admitting they were alive and did the work of their days,
(They bore mites as for unfledg'd birds who have now to rise and
     fly and sing for themselves,)   1035
Accepting the rough deific sketches to fill out better in myself, be-
     stowing them freely on each man and woman I see,
Discovering as much or more in a framer framing a house,
Putting higher claims for him there with his roll'd-up sleeves driving
     the mallet and chisel,

Not objecting to special revelations, considering a curl of smoke or a
    hair on the back of my hand just as curious as any revelation,
Lads ahold of fire-engines and hook-and-ladder ropes no less to me
    than the gods of the antique wars,   1040
Minding their voices peal through the crash of destruction,
Their brawny limbs passing safe over charr'd laths, their white fore-
    heads whole and unhurt out of the flames;
By the mechanic's wife with her babe at her nipple interceding for
    every person born,
Three scythes at harvest whizzing in a row from three lusty angels
    with shirts bagg'd out at their waists,
The snag-tooth'd hostler with red hair redeeming sins past and to
    come,   1045
Selling all he possesses, traveling on foot to fee lawyers for his
    brother and sit by him while he is tried for forgery;
What was strewn in the amplest strewing the square rod about me,
    and not filling the square rod then,
The bull and the bug never worshipp'd half enough,
Dung and dirt more admirable than was dream'd,
The supernatural of no account, myself waiting my time to be one
    of the supremes,   1050
The day getting ready for me when I shall do as much good as the
    best, and be as prodigious;
By my life-lumps! becoming already a creator,
Putting myself here and now to the ambush'd womb of the shadows.

42

A call in the midst of the crowd,
My own voice, orotund sweeping and final.   1055

Come my children,
Come my boys and girls, my women, household and intimates,
Now the performer launches his nerve, he has pass'd his prelude on
    the reeds within.

Easily written loose-finger'd chords—I feel the thrum of your climax
    and close.

My head slues round on my neck,   1060
Music rolls, but not from the organ,
Folks are around me, but they are no household of mine.

Ever the hard unsunk ground,
Ever the eaters and drinkers, ever the upward and downward sun,
    ever the air and the ceaseless tides,
Ever myself and my neighbors, refreshing, wicked, real,   1065
Ever the old inexplicable query, ever that thorn'd thumb, that
    breath of itches and thirsts,
Ever the vexer's *hoot! hoot!* till we find where the sly one hides and
    bring him forth,
Ever love, ever the sobbing liquid of life,

Ever the bandage under the chin, ever the trestles of death.

Here and there with dimes on the eyes walking, 1070
To feed the greed of the belly the brains liberally spooning,
Tickets buying, taking, selling, but in to the feast never once going,
Many sweating, ploughing, thrashing, and then the chaff for pay-
ment receiving,
A few idly owning, and they the wheat continually claiming.

This is the city and I am one of the citizens, 1075
Whatever interests the rest interests me, politics, wars, markets,
newspapers, schools,
The mayor and councils, banks, tariffs, steamships, factories, stocks,
stores, real estate and personal estate.

The little plentiful manikins skipping around in collars and tail'd
coats,
I am aware who they are, (they are positively not worms or fleas,)
I acknowledge the duplicates of myself, the weakest and shallowest
is deathless with me, 1080
What I do and say the same waits for them,
Every thought that flounders in me the same flounders in them.

I know perfectly well my own egotism,
Know my omnivorous lines and must not write any less,
And would fetch you whoever you are flush with myself. 1085

Not words of routine this song of mine,
But abruptly to question, to leap beyond yet nearer bring;
This printed and bound book—but the printer and the printing-
office boy?
The well-taken photograph—but your wife or friend close and solid
in your arms?
The black ship mail'd with iron, her mighty guns in her turrets—
but the pluck of the captain and engineers? 1090
In the houses the dishes and fare and furniture—but the host and
hostess, and the look out of their eyes?
The sky up there—yet here or next door, or across the way?
The saints and sages in history—but you yourself?
Sermons, creeds, theology—but the fathomless human brain,
And what is reason? and what is love? and what is life? 1095

43
I do not despise you priests, all time, the world over,
My faith is the greatest of faiths and the least of faiths,
Enclosing worship ancient and modern and all between ancient and
modern,
Believing I shall come again upon the earth after five thousand
years,
Waiting responses from oracles, honoring the gods, saluting the
sun, 1100

Making a fetich[1] of the first rock or stump, powowing with sticks in
    the circle of obis,
Helping the llama or brahmin as he trims the lamps of the idols,
Dancing yet through the streets in a phallic procession, rapt and
    austere in the woods a gymnosophist,[2]
Drinking mead from the skull-cup, to Shastas and Vedas admirant,[3]
    minding the Koran,
Walking the teokallis,[4] spotted with gore from the stone and knife,
    beating the serpent-skin drum,   1105
Accepting the Gospels, accepting him that was crucified, knowing
    assuredly that he is divine,
To the mass kneeling or the puritan's prayer rising, or sitting pa-
    tiently in a pew,
Ranting and frothing in my insane crisis, or waiting dead-like till my
    spirit arouses me,
Looking forth on pavement and land, or outside of pavement and
    land,
Belonging to the winders of the circuit of circuits.   1110

One of that centripetal and centrifugal gang I turn and talk like a
    man leaving charges before a journey.

Down-hearted doubters, dull and excluded,
Frivolous, sullen, moping, angry, affected, dishearten'd, atheistical,
I know every one of you, I know the sea of torment, doubt, despair
    and unbelief.

How the flukes[5] splash!   1115
How they contort rapid as lightning, with spasms and spouts of
    blood!

Be at peace bloody flukes of doubters and sullen mopers,
I take my place among you as much as among any,
The past is the push of you, me, all, precisely the same,
And what is yet untried and afterward is for you, me, all, precisely
    the same.   1120

I do not know what is untried and afterward,
But I know it will in its turn prove sufficient, and cannot fail.

Each who passes is consider'd, each who stops is consider'd, not a
    single one can it fail.

It cannot fail the young man who died and was buried,
Nor the young woman who died, and was put by his side,   1125
Nor the little child that peep'd in at the door, and then drew back
    and was never seen again,
Nor the old man who has lived without purpose, and feels it with
    bitterness worse than gall,

1. Fetish, a worshipped inanimate object. "Obis" are charms.
2. Ancient Hindu philosopher of ascetic
habits.
3. Regarding with wonder. "Shastas"
(or Shastras) and "Vedas" are sacred
books and scriptures of Hindu religion.
4. Ancient Mexican temples built on a
truncated pyramid.
5. Tail of a whale.

Nor him in the poor house tubercled by rum and the bad disorder,
Nor the numberless slaughter'd and wreck'd, nor the brutish koboo[6]
    call'd the ordure of humanity,
Nor the sacs merely floating with open mouths for food to slip
    in,   1130
Nor any thing in the earth, or down in the oldest graves of the earth,
Nor any thing in the myriads of spheres, nor the myriads of myriads
    that inhabit them,
Nor the present, nor the least wisp that is known.

44

It is time to explain myself—let us stand up.

What is known I strip away,   1135
I launch all men and women forward with me into the Unknown.

The clock indicates the moment—but what does eternity indicate?

We have thus far exhausted trillions of winters and summers,
There are trillions ahead, and trillions ahead of them.

Births have brought us richness and variety,   1140
And other births will bring us richness and variety.

I do not call one greater and one smaller,
That which fills its period and place is equal to any.

Were mankind murderous or jealous upon you, my brother, my sister?
I am sorry for you, they are not murderous or jealous upon me,   1145
All has been gentle with me, I keep no account with lamentation,
(What have I to do with lamentation?)

I am an acme of things accomplish'd, and I an encloser of things to
    be.

My feet strike an apex[7] of the apices of the stairs,
On every step bunches of ages, and larger bunches between the
    steps,   1150
All below duly travel'd, and still I mount and mount.

Rise after rise bow the phantoms behind me,
Afar down I see the huge first Nothing, I know I was even there,
I waited unseen and always, and slept through the lethargic mist,
And took my time, and took no hurt from the fetid carbon.   1155

Long I was hugg'd close—long and long.

Immense have been the preparations for me,
Faithful and friendly the arms that have help'd me.

---

6. A low form of humanity. Whitman writes: "Brutish human beings, wild men, the 'Koboo.' * * * A very low kind of human beings * * * in one of the Ladrone islands, they were quite hairy, had a few rags for clothing and lived in earthen shelters, something like ovens, into which they crawled." "Ordure" is filth, excrement.
7. The tip; in botany, the tip of a young plant shoot.

Cycles ferried my cradle, rowing and rowing like cheerful boatmen,
For room to me stars kept aside in their own rings,   1160
They sent influences to look after what was to hold me.

Before I was born out of my mother generations guided me,
My embryo has never been torpid, nothing could overlay it.

For it the nebula cohered to an orb,
The long slow strata piled to rest it on,   1165
Vast vegetables gave it sustenance,
Monstrous sauroids[8] transported it in their mouths and deposited it
    with care.

All forces have been steadily employ'd to complete and delight me,
Now on this spot I stand with my robust soul!

                            45
O span of youth! ever-push'd elasticity!   1170
O manhood, balanced, florid and full.

My lovers suffocate me,
Crowding my lips, thick in the pores of my skin,
Jostling me through streets and public halls, coming naked to me at
    night,
Crying by day *Ahoy!* from the rocks of the river, swinging and chirp-
    ing over my head,   1175
Calling my name from flower-beds, vines, tangled underbrush,
Lighting on every moment of my life,
Bussing my body with soft balsamic busses,
Noiselessly passing handfuls out of their hearts and giving them to
    be mine.

Old age superbly rising! O welcome, ineffable grace of dying
    days!   1180
Every condition promulges[9] not only itself, it promulges what grows
    after and out of itself,
And the dark hush promulges as much as any.

I open my scuttle[1] at night and see the far-sprinkled systems,
And all I see multiplied as high as I can cipher edge but the rim of
    the farther systems.

Wider and wider they spread, expanding, always expanding,   1185
Outward and outward and forever outward.

My sun has his sun and around him obediently wheels,
He joins with his partners a group of superior circuit,
And greater sets follow, making specks of the greatest inside them.

8. Large extinct lizardlike animals.   1. An opening in a building's roof or
9. Exposes to public view; sets forth or   wall closed with a shutter or lid.
declares publicly.

There is no stoppage and never can be stoppage,   1190
If I, you, and the worlds, and all beneath or upon their surfaces,
 were this moment reduced back to a pallid float,[2] it would not
 avail in the long run,
We should surely bring up again where we now stand,
And surely go as much farther, and then farther and farther.

A few quadrillions of eras, a few octillions of cubic leagues, do not
 hazard the span or make it impatient,
They are but parts, any thing is but a part.   1195

See ever so far, there is limitless space outside of that,
Count ever so much, there is limitless time around that.

My rendezvous is appointed, it is certain,
The Lord will be there and wait till I come on perfect terms,
The great Camerado,[3] the lover true for whom I pine will be
 there.   1200

46

I know I have the best of time and space, and was never measured
 and never will be measured.

I tramp a perpetual journey, (come listen all!)
My signs are a rain-proof coat, good shoes, and a staff cut from the
 woods,
No friend of mine takes his ease in my chair,
I have no chair, no church, no philosophy,   1205
I lead no man to a dinner-table, library, exchange,
But each man and each woman of you I lead upon a knoll,
My left hand hooking you round the waist,
My right hand pointing to landscapes of continents and the public
 road.

Not I, not any one else can travel that road for you,   1210
You must travel it for yourself.

It is not far, it is within reach,
Perhaps you have been on it since you were born and did not know,
Perhaps it is everywhere on water and on land.

Shoulder your duds dear son, and I will mine, and let us hasten
 forth,   1215
Wonderful cities and free nations we shall fetch[4] as we go.

If you tire, give me both burdens, and rest the chuff[5] of your hand
 on my hip,
And in due time you shall repay the same service to me,
For after we start we never lie by again.

---

2. Suspension in water of the infinitesimal particles from which, in Whitman's view, all life derives. Compare
with the use of "float" in "Song of the
Open Road" (line 82 and note) and
"Crossing Brooklyn Ferry" (line 62
and note).

3. Whitman's word for the ideal of the
close companion.
4. Arrive at, reach.
5. Literally, a cheek swollen or puffed
with fat; as used here, probably the
fleshy part, or cheek, of the hand.

This day before dawn I ascended a hill and look'd at the crowded
    heaven, 1220
And I said to my spirit *When we become the enfolders of those*
    orbs, and the pleasure and knowledge of every thing in them,
    shall we be fill'd and satisfied then?
And my spirit said *No, we are but level that lift to pass and con-*
    tinue beyond.

You are also asking me questions and I hear you,
I answer that I cannot answer, you must find out for yourself.

Sit a while dear son, 1225
Here are biscuits to eat and here is milk to drink,
But as soon as you sleep and renew yourself in sweet clothes, I kiss
    you with a good-by kiss and open the gate for your egress hence.

Long enough have you dream'd contemptible dreams,
Now I wash the gum from your eyes,
You must habit yourself to the dazzle of the light and of every
    moment of your life. 1230

Long have you timidly waded holding a plank by the shore,
Now I will you to be a bold swimmer,
To jump off in the midst of the sea, rise again, nod to me, shout,
    and laughingly dash with your hair.

47

I am the teacher of athletes,
He that by me spreads a wider breast than my own proves the width
    of my own, 1235
He most honors my style who learns under it to destroy the teacher.

The boy I love, the same becomes a man not through derived
    power, but in his own right,
Wicked rather than virtuous out of conformity or fear,
Fond of his sweetheart, relishing well his steak,
Unrequited love or a slight cutting him worse than sharp steel
    cuts, 1240
First-rate to ride, to fight, to hit the bull's eye, to sail a skiff, to sing
    a song or play on the banjo,
Preferring scars and the beard and faces pitted with small-pox over
    all latherers,
And those well-tann'd to those that keep out of the sun.

I teach straying from me, yet who can stray from me?
I follow you whoever you are from the present hour, 1245
My words itch at your ears till you understand them.

I do not say these things for a dollar or to fill up the time while I
    wait for a boat,
(It is you talking just as much as myself, I act as the tongue of you,
Tied in your mouth, in mine it begins to be loosen'd.)

I swear I will never again mention love or death inside a house,   1250
And I swear I will never translate myself at all, only to him or her
   who privately stays with me in the open air.

If you would understand me go to the heights or water-shore,
The nearest gnat is an explanation, and a drop or motion of waves a
   key,
The maul, the oar, the hand-saw, second my words.

No shutter'd room or school can commune with me,   1255
But roughs and little children better than they.

The young mechanic is closest to me, he knows me well,
The woodman that takes his axe and jug with him shall take me
   with him all day,
The farm-boy ploughing in the field feels good at the sound of my
   voice,
In vessels that sail my words sail, I go with fishermen and seamen
   and love them.   1260

The soldier camp'd or upon the march is mine,
On the night ere the pending battle many seek me, and I do not
   fail them,
On that solemn night (it may be their last) those that know me
   seek me.

My face rubs to the hunter's face when he lies down alone in his
   blanket,
The driver thinking of me does not mind the jolt of his wagon,   1265
The young mother and old mother comprehend me,
The girl and the wife rest the needle a moment and forget where
   they are,
They and all would resume what I have told them.

48

I have said that the soul is not more than the body,
And I have said that the body is not more than the soul,   1270
And nothing, not God, is greater to one than one's self is,
And whoever walks a furlong without sympathy walks to his own
   funeral drest in his shroud,
And I or you pocketless of a dime may purchase the pick of the
   earth,
And to glance with an eye or show a bean in its pod confounds the
   learning of all times,
And there is no trade or employment but the young man following
   it may become a hero,   1275
And there is no object so soft but it makes a hub for the wheel'd
   universe,
And I say to any man or woman, Let your soul stand cool and composed before a million universes.

And I say to mankind, Be not curious about God,
For I who am curious about each am not curious about God,

(No array of terms can say how much I am at peace about God and
    about death.)   1280

I hear and behold God in every object, yet understand God not in
    the least,
Nor do I understand who there can be more wonderful than myself.

Why should I wish to see God better than this day?
I see something of God each hour of the twenty-four, and each
    moment then,
In the faces of men and women I see God, and in my own face in
    the glass,   1285
I find letters from God dropt in the street, and every one is sign'd
    by God's name,
And I leave them where they are, for I know that wheresoe'er I go
Others will punctually come for ever and ever.

49

And as to you Death, and you bitter hug of mortality, it is idle to
    try to alarm me.

To his work without flinching the accoucheur[6] comes,   1290
I see the elder-hand pressing receiving supporting,
I recline by the sills of the exquisite flexible doors,
And mark the outlet, and mark the relief and escape.

And as to you Corpse I think you are good manure, but that does
    not offend me,
I smell the white roses sweet-scented and growing,   1295
I reach to the leafy lips, I reach to the polish'd breasts of melons.

And as to you Life I reckon you are the leavings of many deaths,
(No doubt I have died myself ten thousand times before.)

I hear you whispering there O stars of heaven,
O suns—O grass of graves—O perpetual transfers and promo-
    tions,   1300
If you do not say any thing how can I say any thing?

Of the turbid pool that lies in the autumn forest,
Of the moon that descends the steeps of the soughing twilight,
Toss, sparkles of day and dusk—toss on the black stems that decay
    in the muck,
Toss to the moaning gibberish of the dry limbs.   1305

I ascend from the moon, I ascend from the night,
I perceive that the ghastly glimmer is noonday sunbeams reflected,
And debouch[7] to the steady and central from the offspring great or
    small.

50

There is that in me—I do not know what it is—but I know it is in
    me.

6. Obstetrician.   7. Pour out.

Wrench'd and sweaty—calm and cool then my body becomes,   1310
I sleep—I sleep long.

I do not know it—it is without name—it is a word unsaid,
It is not in any dictionary, utterance, symbol.

Something it swings on more than the earth I swing on,
To it the creation is the friend whose embracing awakes me.   1315

Perhaps I might tell more. Outlines! I plead for my brothers and
  sisters.

Do you see O my brothers and sisters?
It is not chaos or death—it is form, union, plan—it is eternal life—
  it is Happiness.

51

The past and present wilt—I have fill'd them, emptied them,
And proceed to fill my next fold of the future.   1320

Listener up there! what have you to confide to me?
Look in my face while I snuff the sidle[8] of evening,
(Talk honestly, no one else hears you, and I stay only a minute
  longer.)

Do I contradict myself?
Very well then I contradict myself,   1325
(I am large, I contain multitudes.)

I concentrate toward them that are nigh, I wait on the door-slab.

Who has done his day's work? who will soonest be through with his
  supper?
Who wishes to walk with me?

Will you speak before I am gone? will you prove already too
  late?   1330

52

The spotted hawk swoops by and accuses me, he complains of my
  gab and my loitering.

I too am not a bit tamed, I too am untranslatable,
I sound my barbaric yawp[9] over the roofs of the world.

The last scud[1] of day holds back for me,
It flings my likeness after the rest and true as any on the shadow'd
  wilds,   1335
It coaxes me to the vapor and the dusk.

I depart as air, I shake my white locks at the runaway sun,
I effuse[2] my flesh in eddies, and drift it in lacy jags.

8. Moving sideward in an unobtrusive
manner.
9. A loud cry or yell.

1. Light wind-driven clouds.
2. Pour out, flow.

I bequeath myself to the dirt to grow from the grass I love,
If you want me again look for me under your boot-soles. 1340

You will hardly know who I am or what I mean,
But I shall be good health to you nevertheless,
And filter and fibre your blood.

Failing to fetch me at first keep encouraged,
Missing me one place search another, 1345
I stop somewhere waiting for you.

                                                    1855

From CHILDREN OF ADAM[3]
To the Garden the World

To the garden the world anew ascending,
Potent mates, daughters, sons, preluding,
The love, the life of their bodies, meaning and being,
Curious here behold my resurrection after slumber,
The revolving cycles in their wide sweep having brought me
    again, 5
Amorous, mature, all beautiful to me, all wondrous,
My limbs and the quivering fire that ever plays through them, for
    reasons, most wondrous,
Existing I peer and penetrate still,
Content with the present, content with the past,
By my side or back of me Eve following, 10
Or in front, and I following her just the same.

                                                    1860

From Pent-up Aching Rivers

From pent-up aching rivers,
From that of myself without which I were nothing,
From what I am determin'd to make illustrious, even if I stand sole
    among men,

<hr>

3. The poems of this section were originally brought together under the title *Enfans d'Adam* in the 3rd (1860) edition of *Leaves of Grass* and remained essentially unchanged through subsequent editions—in spite of Emerson's personal attempt in 1860 to dissuade Whitman from publishing the sex poems; in spite of Whitman's loss of his government job in 1865 as the author of indecent poems (he moved to another bureau); and in spite of his Boston publishers' cancellation of the 7th (1881) edition after the poet rejected the request to expurgate the sex passages. Whitman felt, and said repeatedly, that the procreation theme, sounded most loudly in "Children of Adam," was too close to the heart of his book's meaning to be excised. The origin for the idea of the "Children of Adam" poems may be found in Whitman's notebooks: "Theory of a Cluster of Poems the same *to the passion of Woman-love* as the *Calamus-Leaves* are to adhesiveness, manly love. Full of animal-fire, tender, burning,—the tremulous ache, delicious, yet such a torment. The swelling elate and vehement, that will not be denied. Adam, as a central figure and type" (*The Complete Writings of Walt Whitman* IX.150).

From my own voice resonant, singing the phallus,
Singing the song of procreation, 5
Singing the need of superb children and therein superb grown peo-
ple,
Singing the muscular urge and the blending,
Singing the bedfellow's song, (O resistless yearning!
O for any and each the body correlative attracting!
O for you whoever you are your correlative body! O it, more than all
else, you delighting!) 10
From the hungry gnaw that eats me night and day,
From native moments, from bashful pains, singing them,
Seeking something yet unfound though I have diligently sought it
many a long year,
Singing the true song of the soul fitful at random,
Renascent with grossest Nature or among animals, 15
Of that, of them and what goes with them my poems informing,
Of the smell of apples and lemons, of the pairing of birds,
Of the wet of woods, of the lapping of waves,
Of the mad pushes of waves upon the land, I them chanting,
The overture lightly sounding, the strain anticipating, 20
The welcome nearness, the sight of the perfect body,
The swimmer swimming naked in the bath, or motionless on his
back lying and floating,
The female form approaching, I pensive, love-flesh tremulous ach-
ing,
The divine list for myself or you or for any one making,
The face, the limbs, the index from head to foot, and what it
arouses, 25
The mystic deliria, the madness amorous, the utter abandonment,
(Hark close and still what I now whisper to you,
I love you, O you entirely possess me,
O that you and I escape from the rest and go utterly off, free and
lawless,
Two hawks in the air, two fishes swimming in the sea not more law-
less than we;) 30
The furious storm through me careering, I passionately trembling,
The oath of the inseparableness of two together, of the woman that
loves me and whom I love more than my life, that oath swear-
ing,
(O I willingly stake all for you,
O let me be lost if it must be so!
O you and I! what is it to us what the rest do or think? 35
What is all else to us? only that we enjoy each other and exhaust
each other if it must be so;)
From the master, the pilot I yield the vessel to,
The general commanding me, commanding all, from him permis-
sion taking,
From time the programme hastening, (I have loiter'd too long as it
is,)

From sex, from the warp and from the woof,   40
From privacy, from frequent repinings alone,
From plenty of persons near and yet the right person not near,
From the soft sliding of hands over me and thrusting of fingers
    through my hair and beard,
From the long sustain'd kiss upon the mouth or bosom,
From the close pressure that makes me or any man drunk, fainting
    with excess,   45
From what the divine husband knows, from the work of fatherhood,
From exultation, victory and relief from the bedfellow's embrace in
    the night,
From the act-poems of eyes, hands, hips and bosoms,
From the cling of the trembling arm,
From the bending curve and the clinch,   50
From side by side the pliant coverlet off-throwing,
From the one so unwilling to have me leave, and me just as unwill-
    ing to leave,
(Yet a moment O tender waiter, and I return,)
From the hour of shining stars and dropping dews,
From the night a moment I emerging flitting out,   55
Celebrate you act divine and you children prepared for,
And you stalwart loins.

                                                                      1860

Spontaneous Me

Spontaneous me, Nature,
The loving day, the mounting sun, the friend I am happy with,
The arm of my friend hanging idly over my shoulder,
The hillside whiten'd with blossoms of the mountain ash,
The same late in autumn, the hues of red, yellow, drab, purple, and
    light and dark green,   5
The rich coverlet of the grass, animals and birds, the private un-
    trimm'd bank, the primitive apples, the pebble-stones,
Beautiful dripping fragments, the negligent list of one after another
    as I happen to call them to me or think of them,
The real poems, (what we call poems being merely pictures,)
The poems of the privacy of the night, and of men like me,
This poem drooping shy and unseen that I always carry, and that
    all men carry,   10
(Know once for all, avow'd on purpose, wherever are men like me,
    are our lusty lurking masculine poems,)
Love-thoughts, love-juice, love-odor, love-yielding, love-climbers, and
    the climbing sap,
Arms and hands of love, lips of love, phallic thumb of love, breasts
    of love, bellies press'd and glued together with love,
Earth of chaste love, life that is only life after love,
The body of my love, the body of the woman I love, the body of the
    man, the body of the earth,   15
Soft forenoon airs that blow from the south-west,

The hairy wild-bee that murmurs and hankers up and down, that
    gripes the full-grown lady-flower, curves upon her with amorous
    firm legs, takes his will of her, and holds himself tremulous and
    tight till he is satisfied;
The wet of woods through the early hours,
Two sleepers at night lying close together as they sleep, one with an
    arm slanting down across and below the waist of the other,
The smell of apples, aromas from crush'd sage-plant, mint, birch-
    bark,   20
The boy's longings, the glow and pressure as he confides to me what
    he was dreaming,
The dead leaf whirling its spiral whirl and falling still and content to
    the ground,
The no-form'd stings that sights, people, objects, sting me with,
The hubb'd sting of myself, stinging me as much as it ever can any
    one,
The sensitive, orbic, underlapp'd brothers, that only privileged feel-
    ers may be intimate where they are,   25
The curious roamer the hand roaming all over the body, the bashful
    withdrawing of flesh where the fingers soothingly pause and
    edge themselves,
The limpid liquid within the young man,
The vex'd corrosion so pensive and so painful,
The torment, the irritable tide that will not be at rest,
The like of the same I feel, the like of the same in others,   30
The young man that flushes and flushes, and the young woman that
    flushes and flushes,
The young man that wakes deep at night, the hot hand seeking to
    repress what would master him,
The mystic amorous night, the strange half-welcome pangs, visions,
    sweats,
The pulse pounding through palms and trembling encircling fingers,
    the young man all color'd, red, ashamed, angry;
The souse upon me of my lover the sea, as I lie willing and naked, 35
The merriment of the twin babies that crawl over the grass in the
    sun, the mother never turning her vigilant eyes from them,
The walnut-trunk, the walnut-husks, and the ripening or ripen'd
    long-round walnuts,
The continence of vegetables, birds, animals,
The consequent meanness of me should I skulk or find myself inde-
    cent, while birds and animals never once skulk or find them-
    selves indecent,
The great chastity of paternity, to match the great chastity of mater-
    nity,   40
The oath of procreation I have sworn, my Adamic and fresh daugh-
    ters,
The greed that eats me day and night with hungry gnaw, till I satu-
    rate what shall produce boys to fill my place when I am
    through,

The wholesome relief, repose, content,
And this bunch pluck'd at random from myself,
It has done its work—I toss it carelessly to fall where it may.   45
                                                                        1856

We Two, How Long We Were Fool'd

We two, how long we were fool'd,
Now transmuted, we swiftly escape as Nature escapes,
We are Nature, long have we been absent, but now we return,
We become plants, trunks, foliage, roots, bark,
We are bedded in the ground, we are rocks,   5
We are oaks, we grow in the openings side by side,
We browse, we are two among the wild herds spontaneous as any,
We are two fishes swimming in the sea together,
We are what locust blossoms are, we drop scent around lanes morn-
    ings and evenings,
We are also the coarse smut of beasts, vegetables, minerals,   10
We are two predatory hawks, we soar above and look down,
We are two resplendent suns, we it is who balance ourselves orbic
    and stellar, we are as two comets,
We prowl fang'd and four-footed in the woods, we spring on prey,
We are two clouds forenoons and afternoons driving overhead,
We are seas mingling, we are two of those cheerful waves rolling
    over each other and interwetting each other,   15
We are what the atmosphere is, transparent, receptive, pervious, im-
    pervious,
We are snow, rain, cold, darkness, we are each product and influ-
    ence of the globe,
We have circled and circled till we have arrived home again, we
    two,
We have voided all but freedom and all but our own joy.
                                                                        1860

Native Moments

Native moments—when you come upon me—ah you are here now,
Give me now libidinous joys only,
Give me the drench of my passions, give me life coarse and rank,
To-day I go consort with Nature's darlings, to-night too,
I am for those who believe in loose delights, I share the midnight
    orgies of young men,   5
I dance with the dancers and drink with the drinkers,
The echoes ring with our indecent calls, I pick out some low person
    for my dearest friend,
He shall be lawless, rude, illiterate, he shall be one condemned by
    others for deeds done,

I will play a part no longer, why should I exile myself from my companions?
O you shunn'd persons, I at least do not shun you,   10
I come forthwith in your midst, I will be your poet,
I will be more to you than to any of the rest.

1860

From CALAMUS[4]
In Paths Untrodden

In paths untrodden,
In the growth by margins of pond-waters,
Escaped from the life that exhibits itself,
From all the standards hitherto publish'd, from the pleasures, profits, conformities,
Which too long I was offering to feed my soul,   5
Clear to me now standards not yet publish'd, clear to me that my soul,
That the soul of the man I speak for rejoices in comrades,
Here by myself away from the clank of the world,
Tallying and talk'd to here by tongues aromatic,
No longer abash'd, (for in this secluded spot I can respond as I would not dare elsewhere,)   10
Strong upon me the life that does not exhibit itself, yet contains all the rest,
Resolv'd to sing no songs to-day but those of manly attachment,
Projecting them along that substantial life,
Bequeathing hence types of athletic love,
Afternoon this delicious Ninth-month in my forty-first year,[5]   15
I proceed for all who are or have been young men,
To tell the secret of my nights and days,
To celebrate the need of comrades.

1860

4. The "Calamus" poems were brought together in the 1860 edition and remained without radical change through subsequent editions. Light has been thrown on the origins of these and other poems in the edition with the publication of Fredson Bowers' *Whitman's Manuscripts: Leaves of Grass (1860)* (1955). Whitman himself has written about his use of Calamus as a symbol (William Sloane Kennedy, *The Fight of a Book for the World*, 1926, p. 177): "Calamus is the very large and aromatic grass, or rush, growing about water ponds in the valley—spears about three feet high; often called Sweet Flag; grows all over the Northern and Middle States. The recherchè or ethereal sense of the term, as used in my book, arises probably from the actual Calamus presenting the biggest and hardiest kind of spears of grass, and their fresh, aquatic, pungent bouquet." For the post-Freudian reader, the suggestion of phallic symbolism in the plant cannot be escaped. Indeed, as Whitman's sex poems were most objectionable to the 19th century, the "friendship" poems have proved the most suspicious in the 20th. For the argument that the "Calamus" poems represent an abnormal love, see Mark Van Doren's "Walt Whitman, Stranger," *The Private Reader* (1942); for the contention that "Calamus" represents intentional poetic ambiguity but not abnormality, see James E. Miller, Jr., " 'Calamus': The Leaf and the Root," *A Critical Guide to Leaves of Grass* (1957).
5. September, 1860.

Scented Herbage of My Breast

Scented herbage of my breast,
Leaves from you I glean, I write, to be perused best afterwards,
Tomb-leaves, body-leaves growing up above me above death,
Perennial roots, tall leaves, O the winter shall not freeze you delicate leaves,
Every year shall you bloom again, out from where you retired you shall emerge again;   5
O I do not know whether many passing by will discover you or inhale your faint odor, but I believe a few will;
O slender leaves! O blossoms of my blood! I permit you to tell in your own way of the heart that is under you,
O I do not know what you mean there underneath yourselves, you are not happiness,
You are often more bitter than I can bear, you burn and sting me,
Yet you are beautiful to me you faint-tinged roots, you make me think of death,   10
Death is beautiful from you, (what indeed is finally beautiful except death and love?)
O I think it is not for life I am chanting here my chant of lovers, I think it must be for death,
For how calm, how solemn it grows to ascend to the atmosphere of lovers,
Death or life I am then indifferent, my soul declines to prefer,
(I am not sure but the high soul of lovers welcomes death most,)   15
Indeed O death, I think now these leaves mean precisely the same as you mean,
Grow up taller sweet leaves that I may see! grow up out of my breast!
Spring away from the conceal'd heart there!
Do not fold yourself so in your pink-tinged roots timid leaves!
Do not remain down there so ashamed, herbage of my breast!   20
Come I am determin'd to unbare this broad breast of mine, I have long enough stifled and choked;
Emblematic and capricious blades I leave you, now you serve me not,
I will say what I have to say by itself,
I will sound myself and comrades only, I will never again utter a call only their call,
I will raise with it immortal reverberations through the States,   25
I will give an example to lovers to take permanent shape and will through the States,
Through me shall the words be said to make death exhilarating,
Give me your tone therefore O death, that I may accord with it,
Give me yourself, for I see that you belong to me now above all, and are folded inseparably together, you love and death are,
Nor will I allow you to balk me any more with what I was calling life,   30
For now it is convey'd to me that you are the purports essential,

That you hide in these shifting forms of life, for reasons, and that
    they are mainly for you,
That you beyond them come forth to remain, the real reality,
That behind the mask of materials you patiently wait, no matter
    how long,
That you will one day perhaps take control of all,   35
That you will perhaps dissipate this entire show of appearance,
That may-be you are what it is all for, but it does not last so very
    long,
But you will last very long.

                                         1860

For You O Democracy

Come, I will make the continent indissoluble,
I will make the most splendid race the sun ever shone upon,
I will make divine magnetic lands,
        With the love of comrades,
            With the life-long love of comrades.   5

I will plant companionship thick as trees along all the rivers of
    America, and along the shores of the great lakes, and all over
    the prairies,
I will make inseparable cities with their arms about each other's
    necks,
        By the love of comrades,
        By the manly love of comrades,

For you these from me, O Democracy, to serve you ma femme![6] 10
For you, for you I am trilling these songs.

                                         1860

These I Singing in Spring

These I singing in spring collect for lovers,
(For who but I should understand lovers and all their sorrow and
    joy?
And who but I should be the poet of comrades?)
Collecting I traverse the garden the world, but soon I pass the gates,
Now along the pond-side, now wading in a little, fearing not the
    wet,   5
Now by the post-and-rail fences where the old stones thrown there,
    pick'd from the fields, have accumulated,
(Wild-flowers and vines and weeds come up through the stones and
    partly cover them, beyond these I pass,)

---

6. French, "my woman," "my wife." Whitman uses this phrase as a personification of democracy.

Far, far in the forest, or sauntering later in summer, before I think
　　where I go,
Solitary, smelling the earthy smell, stopping now and then in the
　　silence,
Alone I had thought, yet soon a troop gathers around me,　　10
Some walk by my side and some behind, and some embrace my arms
　　or neck,
They the spirits of dear friends dead or alive, thicker they come, a
　　great crowd, and I in the middle,
Collecting, dispensing, singing, there I wander with them,
Plucking something for tokens, tossing toward whoever is near
　　me,
Here, lilac, with a branch of pine,　　15
Here, out of my pocket, some moss which I pull'd off a live-oak in
　　Florida as it hung trailing down,
Here, some pinks and laurel leaves, and a handful of sage,
And here what I now draw from the water, wading in the pond-side,
(O here I last saw him that tenderly loves me, and returns again
　　never to separate from me,
And this, O this shall henceforth be the token of comrades, this
　　calamus-root shall,　　20
Interchange it youths with each other! let none render it back!)
And twigs of maple and a bunch of wild orange and chestnut,
And stems of currants and plum-blows, and the aromatic cedar,
These I compass'd around by a thick cloud of spirits,
Wandering, point to or touch as I pass, or throw them loosely from
　　me,　　25
Indicating to each one what he shall have, giving something to each;
But what I drew from the water by the pond-side, that I reserve,
I will give of it, but only to them that love as I myself am capable
　　of loving.

　　　　　　　　　　　　　　　　　　　　1860

Recorders Ages Hence

Recorders ages hence,
Come, I will take you down underneath this impassive exterior, I
　　will tell you what to say of me,
Publish my name and hang up my picture as that of the tenderest
　　lover,
The friend the lover's portrait, of whom his friend his lover was
　　fondest,
Who was not proud of his songs, but of the measureless ocean of
　　love within him, and freely pour'd it forth,　　5
Who often walk'd lonesome walks thinking of his dear friends, his
　　lovers,
Who pensive away from one he lov'd often lay sleepless and dis-
　　satisfied at night,

Who knew too well the sick, sick dread lest the one he lov'd might
    secretly be indifferent to him,
Whose happiest days were far away through fields, in woods, on
    hills, he and another wandering hand in hand, they twain apart
    from other men,
Who oft as he saunter'd the streets curv'd with his arm the shoulder
    of his friend, while the arm of his friend rested upon him
    also.   10
                                      1860

When I Heard at the Close of the Day

When I heard at the close of the day how my name had been re-
    ceiv'd with plaudits in the capitol, still it was not a happy night
    for me that follow'd,
And else when I carous'd, or when my plans were accomplish'd, still
    I was not happy,
But the day when I rose at dawn from the bed of perfect health, re-
    fresh'd, singing, inhaling the ripe breath of autumn,
When I saw the full moon in the west grow pale and disappear in
    the morning light,
When I wander'd alone over the beach, and undressing bathed,
    laughing with the cool waters, and saw the sun rise,   5
And when I thought how my dear friend my lover was on his way
    coming, O then I was happy,
O then each breath tasted sweeter, and all that day my food nour-
    ish'd me more, and the beautiful day pass'd well,
And the next came with equal joy, and with the next at evening
    came my friend,
And that night while all was still I heard the waters roll slowly con-
    tinually up the shores,
I heard the hissing rustle of the liquid and sands as directed to me
    whispering to congratulate me,   10
For the one I love most lay sleeping by me under the same cover in
    the cool night,
In the stillness in the autumn moonbeams his face was inclined to-
    ward me,
And his arm lay lightly around my breast—and that night I was
    happy.
                                        1860

City of Orgies

City of orgies, walks and joys,
City whom that I have lived and sung in your midst will one day
    make you illustrious,
Not the pageants of you, not your shifting tableaus, your spectacles,
    repay me,

Not the interminable rows of your houses, nor the ships at the
  wharves,
Nor the processions in the streets, nor the bright windows with
  goods in them,   5
Nor to converse with learn'd persons, or bear my share in the soiree
  or feast;
Not those, but as I pass O Manhattan, your frequent and swift flash
  of eyes offering me love,
Offering response to my own—these repay me,
Lovers, continual lovers, only repay me.

1860

I Saw in Louisiana a Live-Oak Growing

I saw in Louisiana a live-oak growing,
All alone stood it and the moss hung down from the branches,
Without any companion it grew there uttering joyous leaves of dark
  green,
And its look, rude, unbending, lusty, made me think of myself,
But I wonder'd how it could utter joyous leaves standing alone there
  without its friend near, for I knew I could not,   5
And I broke off a twig with a certain number of leaves upon it, and
  twined around it a little moss,
And brought it away, and I have placed it in sight in my room,
It is not needed to remind me as of my own dear friends,
(For I believe lately I think of little else than of them,)
Yet it remains to me a curious token, it makes me think of manly
  love;   10
For all that, and though the live-oak glistens there in Louisiana soli-
  tary in a wide flat space,
Uttering joyous leaves all its life without a friend a lover near,
I know very well I could not.

1860

I Hear It Was Charged Against Me

I hear it was charged against me that I sought to destroy institutions,
But really I am neither for nor against institutions,
(What indeed have I in common with them? or what with the de-
  struction of them?)
Only I will establish in the Mannahatta[7] and in every city of these
  States inland and seaboard,
And in the fields and woods, and above every keel little or large that
  dents the water,   5
Without edifices or rules or trustees or any argument,
The institution of the dear love of comrades.

1860

7. Indian name for Manhattan; New York City.

Here the Frailest Leaves of Me

Here the frailest leaves of me and yet my strongest lasting,
Here I shade and hide my thoughts, I myself do not expose them,
And yet they expose me more than all my other poems.

1860

Earth, My Likeness

Earth, my likeness,
Though you look so impassive, ample and spheric there,
I now suspect that is not all;
I now suspect there is something fierce in you eligible to burst forth,
For an athlete is enamour'd of me, and I of him,   5
But toward him there is something fierce and terrible in me eligible
    to burst forth,
I dare not tell it in words, not even in these songs.

1860

Sometimes with One I Love

Sometimes with one I love I fill myself with rage for fear I effuse un-
    return'd love,
But now I think there is no unreturn'd love, the pay is certain one
    way or another,
(I loved a certain person ardently and my love was not return'd,
Yet out of that I have written these songs.)

1860

Fast-anchor'd Eternal O Love!

Fast-anchor'd eternal O love! O woman I love!
O bride! O wife! more resistless than I can tell, the thought of you!
Then separate, as disembodied or another born,
Ethereal, the last athletic reality, my consolation,
I ascend, I float in the regions of your love O man,   5
O sharer of my roving life.

1860

Full of Life Now

Full of life now, compact, visible,
I, forty years old the eighty-third year of the States,
To one a century hence or any number of centuries hence,
To you yet unborn these, seeking you.

When you read these I that was visible am become invisible, 5
Now it is you, compact, visible, realizing my poems, seeking me,
Fancying how happy you were if I could be with you and become
    your comrade;
Be it as if I were with you. (Be not too certain but I am now with
    you.)

        1860

Song of the Open Road

1

Afoot and light-hearted I take to the open road,
Healthy, free, the world before me,
The long brown path before me leading wherever I choose.

Henceforth I ask not good-fortune, I myself am good-fortune,
Henceforth I whimper no more, postpone no more, need nothing, 5
Done with indoor complaints, libraries, querulous criticisms,
Strong and content I travel the open road.

The earth, that is sufficient,
I do not want the constellations any nearer,
I know they are very well where they are, 10
I know they suffice for those who belong to them.

(Still here I carry my old delicious burdens,
I carry them, men and women, I carry them with me wherever I go,
I swear it is impossible for me to get rid of them,
I am fill'd with them, and I will fill them in return.) 15

2

You road I enter upon and look around, I believe you are not all
    that is here,
I believe that much unseen is also here.

Here the profound lesson of reception, nor preference nor denial,
The black with his woolly head, the felon, the diseas'd, the illiterate
    person, are not denied;
The birth, the hasting after the physician, the beggar's tramp, the
    drunkard's stagger, the laughing party of mechanics, 20
The escaped youth, the rich persons' carriage, the fop, the eloping
    couple,
The early market-man, the hearse, the moving of furniture into the
    town, the return back from the town,
They pass, I also pass, any thing passes, none can be interdicted,
None but are accepted, none but shall be dear to me.

3

You air that serves me with breath to speak! 25
You objects that call from diffusion my meanings and give them
    shape!

You light that wraps me and all things in delicate equable showers!
You paths worn in the irregular hollows by the roadsides!
I believe you are latent with unseen existences, you are so dear to
    me.

You flagg'd walks of the cities! you strong curbs at the edges!   30
You ferries! you planks and posts of wharves! you timber-lined sides!
    you distant ships!
You rows of houses! you window-pierc'd façades! you roofs!
You porches and entrances! you copings and iron guards!
You windows whose transparent shells might expose so much!
You doors and ascending steps! you arches!   35
You gray stones of interminable pavements! you trodden crossings!
From all that has touch'd you I believe you have imparted to your-
    selves, and now would impart the same secretly to me,
From the living and the dead you have peopled your impassive sur-
    faces, and the spirits thereof would be evident and amicable
    with me.

4

The earth expanding right hand and left hand,
The picture alive, every part in its best light,   40
The music falling in where it is wanted, and stopping where it is
    not wanted,
The cheerful voice of the public road, the gay fresh sentiment of the
    road.

O highway I travel, do you say to me *Do not leave me?*
Do you say *Venture not—if you leave me you are lost?*
Do you say *I am already prepared, I am well-beaten and undenied,*
    adhere to me?   45

O public road, I say back I am not afraid to leave you, yet I love you,
You express me better than I can express myself,
You shall be more to me than my poem.

I think heroic deeds were all conceiv'd in the open air, and all free
    poems also,
I think I could stop here myself and do miracles,   50
I think whatever I shall meet on the road I shall like, and whoever
    beholds me shall like me,
I think whoever I see must be happy.

5

From this hour I ordain myself loos'd of limits and imaginary lines,
Going where I list, my own master total and absolute,
Listening to others, considering well what they say,   55
Pausing, searching, receiving, contemplating,
Gently, but with undeniable will, divesting myself of the holds that
    would hold me.

I inhale great draughts of space,
The east and the west are mine, and the north and the south are
    mine.

I am larger, better than I thought,   60
I did not know I held so much goodness.

All seems beautiful to me,
I can repeat over to men and women You have done such good to
    me I would do the same to you,
I will recruit for myself and you as I go,
I will scatter myself among men and women as I go,   65
I will toss a new gladness and roughness among them,
Whoever denies me it shall not trouble me,
Whoever accepts me he or she shall be blessed and shall bless me.

6

Now if a thousand perfect men were to appear it would not amaze
    me,
Now if a thousand beautiful forms of women appear'd it would not
    astonish me.   70

Now I see the secret of the making of the best persons,
It is to grow in the open air and to eat and sleep with the earth.

Here a great personal deed has room,
(Such a deed seizes upon the hearts of the whole race of men,
Its effusion of strength and will overwhelms law and mocks all au-
    thority and all argument against it.)   75

Here is the test of wisdom,
Wisdom is not finally tested in schools,
Wisdom cannot be pass'd from one having it to another not having
    it,
Wisdom is of the soul, is not susceptible of proof, is its own proof,
Applies to all stages and objects and qualities and is content,   80
Is the certainty of the reality and immortality of things, and the
    excellence of things;
Something there is in the float[8] of the sight of things that provokes
    it out of the soul.

Now I re-examine philosophies and religions,
They may prove well in lecture-rooms, yet not prove at all under the
    spacious clouds and along the landscape and flowing currents.

Here is realization,   85
Here is a man tallied—he realizes here what he has in him,

8. Here Whitman seems to mean the spiritual element ("float") of objects which is somehow revealed in the act of perception. See "Crossing Brooklyn Ferry," line 62.

The past, the future, majesty, love—if they are vacant of you, you are vacant of them.

Only the kernel of every object nourishes;
Where is he who tears off the husks for you and me?
Where is he that undoes stratagems and envelopes for you and me?   90

Here is adhesiveness,[9] it is not previously fashion'd, it is apropos;
Do you know what it is as you pass to be loved by strangers?
Do you know the talk of those turning eye-balls?

7

Here is the efflux of the soul,
The efflux of the soul comes from within through embower'd gates, ever provoking questions,   95
These yearnings why are they? these thoughts in the darkness why are they?
Why are there men and women that while they are nigh me the sunlight expands my blood?
Why when they leave me do my pennants of joy sink flat and lank?
Why are there trees I never walk under but large and melodious thoughts descend upon me?
(I think they hang there winter and summer on those trees and always drop fruit as I pass;)   100
What is it I interchange so suddenly with strangers?
What with some driver as I ride on the seat by his side?
What with some fisherman drawing his seine by the shore as I walk by and pause?
What gives me to be free to a woman's and man's good-will? what gives them to be free to mine?

8

The efflux of the soul is happiness, here is happiness,   105
I think it pervades the open air, waiting at all times,
Now it flows unto us, we are rightly charged.

Here rises the fluid and attaching character,
The fluid and attaching character is the freshness and sweetness of man and woman,
(The herbs of the morning sprout no fresher and sweeter every day out of the roots of themselves, than it sprouts fresh and sweet continually out of itself.)   110

Toward the fluid and attaching character exudes the sweat of the love of young and old,
From it falls distill'd the charm that mocks beauty and attainments,
Toward it heaves the shuddering longing ache of contact.

9. From phrenology: a mental faculty manifested in lasting friendship, fraternity, companionship.

9

Allons![1] whoever you are come travel with me!
Traveling with me you find what never tires.   115

The earth never tires,
The earth is rude, silent, incomprehensible at first, Nature is rude
     and incomprehensible at first,
Be not discouraged, keep on, there are divine things well envelop'd,
I swear to you there are divine things more beautiful than words
     can tell.

Allons! we must not stop here,   120
However sweet these laid-up stores, however convenient this dwell-
     ing we cannot remain here,
However shelter'd this port and however calm these waters we must
     not anchor here,
However welcome the hospitality that surrounds us we are permitted
     to receive it but a little while.

10

Allons! the inducements shall be greater,
We will sail pathless and wild seas,   125
We will go where winds blow, waves dash, and the Yankee clipper
     speeds by under full sail.

Allons! with power, liberty, the earth, the elements,
Health, defiance, gayety, self-esteem, curiosity;
Allons! from all formules![2]
From your formules, O bat-eyed and materialistic priests.   130

The stale cadaver blocks up the passage—the burial waits no longer.

Allons! yet take warning!
He traveling with me needs the best blood, thews,[3] endurance,
None may come to the trial till he or she bring courage and health,
Come not here if you have already spent the best of yourself,   135
Only those may come who come in sweet and determin'd bodies,
No diseas'd person, no rum-drinker or venereal taint is permitted
     here.

(I and mine do not convince by arguments, similes, rhymes,
We convince by our presence.)

11

Listen! I will be honest with you,   140
I do not offer the old smooth prizes, but offer rough new prizes,
These are the days that must happen to you:

1. French, "let us go."
2. French, "set form of words," "formulas."

3. The bodily powers of a man; muscles
or tendons.

You shall not heap up what is call'd riches,

You shall scatter with lavish hand all that you earn or achieve,

You but arrive at the city to which you were destin'd, you hardly
settle yourself to satisfaction, before you are call'd by an irresistible call to depart,

You shall be treated to the ironical smiles and mockings of those ₁₄₅
who remain behind you,

What beckonings of love you receive you shall only answer with passionate kisses of parting,

You shall not allow the hold of those who spread their reach'd
hands toward you.

12

Allons! after the great Companions, and to belong to them!

They too are on the road—they are the swift and majestic men—
they are the greatest women, ₁₅₀

Enjoyers of calms of seas and storms of seas,

Sailors of many a ship, walkers of many a mile of land,

Habituès of many distant countries, habituès of far-distant dwellings,

Trusters of men and women, observers of cities, solitary toilers,

Pausers and contemplators of tufts, blossoms, shells of the shore, ₁₅₅

Dancers at wedding-dances, kissers of brides, tender helpers of children, bearers of children,

Soldiers of revolts, standers by gaping graves, lowerers-down of coffins,

Journeyers over consecutive seasons, over the years, the curious years
each emerging from that which preceded it,

Journeyers as with companions, namely their own diverse phases,

Forth-steppers from the latent unrealized baby-days, ₁₆₀

Journeyers gayly with their own youth, journeyers with their bearded
and well-grain'd manhood,

Journeyers with their womanhood, ample, unsurpass'd, content,

Journeyers with their own sublime old age of manhood or womanhood,

Old age, calm, expanded, broad with the haughty breadth of the
universe,

Old age, flowing free with the delicious near-by freedom of
death. ₁₆₅

13

Allons! to that which is endless as it was beginningless,

To undergo much, tramps of days, rests of nights,

To merge all in the travel they tend to, and the days and nights they
tend to,

Again to merge them in the start of superior journeys,

To see nothing anywhere but what you may reach it and pass it, ₁₇₀

To conceive no time, however distant, but what you may reach it
and pass it,

To look up or down no road but it stretches and waits for you, however long but it stretches and waits for you,

To see no being, not God's or any, but you also go thither,
To see no possession but you may possess it, enjoying all without
    labor or purchase, abstracting the feast yet not abstracting one
    particle of it,
To take the best of the farmer's farm and the rich man's elegant
    villa, and the chaste blessings of the well-married couple, and
    the fruits of orchards and flowers of gardens,   175
To take to your use out of the compact cities as you pass through,
To carry buildings and streets with you afterward wherever you go,
To gather the minds of men out of their brains as you encounter
    them, to gather the love out of their hearts,
To take your lovers on the road with you, for all that you leave
    them behind you,
To know the universe itself as a road, as many roads, as roads for
    traveling souls.   180

All parts away for the progress of souls,
All religion, all solid things, arts, governments—all that was or is
    apparent upon this globe or any globe, falls into niches and
    corners before the procession of souls along the grand roads
    of the universe.

Of the progress of the souls of men and women along the grand
    roads of the universe, all other progress is the needed emblem
    and sustenance.

Forever alive, forever forward,
Stately, solemn, sad, withdrawn, baffled, mad, turbulent, feeble, dis-
    satisfied,   185
Desperate, proud, fond, sick, accepted by men, rejected by men,
They go! they go! I know that they go, but I know not where they
    go,
But I know that they go toward the best—toward something great.

Whoever you are, come forth! or man or woman come forth!
You must not stay sleeping and dallying there in the house, though
    you built it, or though it has been built for you.   190

Out of the dark confinement! out from behind the screen!
It is useless to protest. I know all and expose it.

Behold through you as bad as the rest,
Through the laughter, dancing, dining, supping, of people,
Inside of dresses and ornaments, inside of those wash'd and trimm'd
    faces,   195
Behold a secret silent loathing and despair.

No husband, no wife, no friend, trusted to hear the confession,
Another self, a duplicate of every one, skulking and hiding it goes,

Formless and wordless through the streets of the cities, polite and
    bland in the parlors,
In the cars of railroads, in steamboats, in the public assembly,   200
Home to the houses of men and women, at the table, in the bed-
    room, everywhere,
Smartly attired, countenance smiling, form upright, death under the
    breast-bones, hell under the skull-bones,
Under the broadcloth and gloves, under the ribbons and artificial
    flowers,
Keeping fair with the customs, speaking not a syllable of itself,
Speaking of any thing else but never of itself.   205

14

Allons! through struggles and wars!
The goal that was named cannot be countermanded.

Have the past struggles succeeded?
What has succeeded? yourself? your nation? Nature?
Now understand me well—it is provided in the essence of things
    that from any fruition of success, no matter what, shall come
    forth something to make a greater struggle necessary.   210

My call is the call of battle, I nourish active rebellion,
He going with me must go well arm'd,
He going with me goes often with spare diet, poverty, angry ene-
    mies, desertions.

15

Allons! the road is before us!
It is safe—I have tried it—my own feet have tried it well—be not
    detain'd!   215
Let the paper remain on the desk unwritten, and the book on the
    shelf unopen'd!
Let the tools remain in the workshop! let the money remain un-
    earn'd!
Let the school stand! mind not the cry of the teacher!
Let the preacher preach in his pulpit! let the lawyer plead in the
    court, and the judge expound the law.

Camerado,[4] I give you my hand!   220
I give you my love more precious than money,
I give you myself before preaching or law;
Will you give me yourself? will you come travel with me?
Shall we stick by each other as long as we live?

    1856

4. Close companion, one who shares all.

Crossing Brooklyn Ferry[5]

1

Flood-tide below me! I see you face to face!
Clouds of the west—sun there half an hour high—I see you also
    face to face.

Crowds of men and women attired in the usual costumes, how curi-
    ous you are to me!
On the ferry-boats the hundreds and hundreds that cross, returning
    home, are more curious to me than you suppose,
And you that shall cross from shore to shore years hence are more
    to me, and more in my meditations, than you might suppose. 5

2

The impalpable sustenance of me from all things at all hours of the
    day,
The simple, compact, well-join'd scheme, myself disintegrated, every
    one disintegrated yet part of the scheme,
The similitudes[6] of the past and those of the future,
The glories strung like beads on my smallest sights and hearings, on
    the walk in the street and the passage over the river,
The current rushing so swiftly and swimming with me far away, 10
The others that are to follow me, the ties between me and them,
The certainty of others, the life, love, sight, hearing of others.

Others will enter the gates of the ferry and cross from shore to shore,
Others will watch the run of the flood-tide,
Others will see the shipping of Manhattan north and west, and the
    heights of Brooklyn to the south and east, 15
Others will see the islands large and small;
Fifty years hence, others will see them as they cross, the sun half an
    hour high,
A hundred years hence, or ever so many hundred years hence, others
    will see them,
Will enjoy the sunset, the pouring-in of the flood-tide, the falling-
    back to the sea of the ebb-tide.

3

It avails not, time nor place—distance avails not, 20

---

5. First published in the 2nd (1856) edition, "Crossing Brooklyn Ferry" turns up on every critic's list of the five or six best poems of *Leaves of Grass.* Originally titled "Sun Down Poem," it was one of Henry David Thoreau's two favorites (the other was "Song of Myself"). Upon reading the 1856 edition, Thoreau wrote: "To be sure I sometimes feel a little imposed on. By his heartiness & broad generalities he puts me into a liberal frame of mind prepared to see wonders—as it were sets me upon a hill or in the midst of a plain—stirs me well up, and then —throws in a thousand of brick. Though rude & sometimes ineffectual, it is a great primitive poem,—an alarum or trumpet-note ringing through the American camp. Wonderfully like the Orientals, too, considering that when I asked him if he had read them, he answered, 'No: tell me about them' " (*The Correspondence of Henry David Thoreau,* ed. Walter Harding and Carl Bode, 1958, p. 445). In reading "Crossing Brooklyn Ferry" the modern reader might accept Thoreau's clue and keep in mind relevant elements of Oriental philosophy and mysticism (as in Emerson's "Brahma").

6. Counterparts, resemblances.

I am with you, you men and women of a generation, or ever so many
    generations hence,
Just as you feel when you look on the river and sky, so I felt,
Just as any of you is one of a living crowd, I was one of a crowd,
Just as you are refresh'd by the gladness of the river and the bright
    flow, I was refresh'd,
Just as you stand and lean on the rail, yet hurry with the swift cur-
    rent, I stood yet was hurried,   25
Just as you look on the numberless masts of ships and the thick-
    stemm'd pipes of steamboats, I look'd.

I too many and many a time cross'd the river of old,
Watched the Twelfth-month[7] sea-gulls, saw them high in the air
    floating with motionless wings, oscillating their bodies,
Saw how the glistening yellow lit up parts of their bodies and left
    the rest in strong shadow,
Saw the slow-wheeling circles and the gradual edging toward the
    south,   30
Saw the reflection of the summer sky in the water,
Had my eyes dazzled by the shimmering track of beams,
Look'd at the fine centrifugal spokes of light round the shape of my
    head in the sunlit water,
Look'd on the haze on the hills southward and south-westward,
Look'd on the vapor as it flew in fleeces tinged with violet,   35
Look'd toward the lower bay to notice the vessels arriving,
Saw their approach, saw aboard those that were near me,
Saw the white sails of schooners and sloops, saw the ships at anchor,
The sailors at work in the rigging or out astride the spars,
The round masts, the swinging motion of the hulls, the slender
    serpentine pennants,   40
The large and small steamers in motion, the pilots in their pilot-
    houses,
The white wake left by the passage, the quick tremulous whirl of
    the wheels,
The flags of all nations, the falling of them at sunset,
The scallop-edged waves in the twilight, the ladled cups, the frolic-
    some crests and glistening,
The stretch afar growing dimmer and dimmer, the gray walls of the
    granite storehouses by the docks,   45
On the river the shadowy group, the big steam-tug closely flank'd on
    each side by the barges, the hay-boat, the belated lighter,
On the neighboring shore the fires from the foundry chimneys burn-
    ing high and glaringly into the night,
Casting their flicker of black contrasted with wild red and yellow
    light over the tops of houses, and down into the clefts of streets.

4

These and all else were to me the same as they are to you,
I loved well those cities, loved well the stately and rapid river,   50

7. December.

The men and women I saw were all near to me,
Others the same—others who look back on me because I look'd forward to them,
(The time will come, though I stop here to-day and to-night.)

5

What is it then between us?
What is the count of the scores or hundreds of years between us? 55

Whatever it is, it avails not—distance avails not, and place avails not,
I too lived, Brooklyn of ample hills was mine,
I too walk'd the streets of Manhattan island, and bathed in the waters around it,
I too felt the curious abrupt questionings stir within me,
In the day among crowds of people sometimes they came upon me, 60
In my walks home late at night or as I lay in my bed they came upon me,
I too had been struck from the float[8] forever held in solution,
I too had receiv'd identity by my body,
That I was I knew was of my body, and what I should be I knew I should be of my body.

6

It is not upon you alone the dark patches fall, 65
The dark threw its patches down upon me also,
The best I had done seem'd to me blank and suspicious,
My great thoughts as I supposed them, were they not in reality meagre?
Nor is it you alone who know what it is to be evil,
I am he who knew what it was to be evil, 70
I too knitted the old knot of contrariety,[9]
Blabb'd, blush'd, resented, lied, stole, grudg'd,
Had guile, anger, lust, hot wishes I dared not speak,
Was wayward, vain, greedy, shallow, sly, cowardly, malignant,
The wolf, the snake, the hog, not wanting in me, 75
The cheating look, the frivolous word, the adulterous wish, not wanting,
Refusals, hates, postponements, meanness, laziness, none of these wanting,
Was one with the rest, the days and haps[1] of the rest,
Was call'd by my nighest name by clear loud voices of young men as they saw me approaching or passing,
Felt their arms on my neck as I stood, or the negligent leaning of their flesh against me as I sat, 80

8. The image seems to be primarily chemical, with the suggestion that the individual is precipitated from (and returns to) the oversoul ("float" or spiritual source) much as a dissolved solid may be precipitated from and returned to the solution. See "Song of the Open Road," line 82.
9. Roughly synonymous with evil, derived from "contrary" in the sense of willful.
1. Happenings.

Saw many I loved in the street or ferry-boat or public assembly, yet
never told them a word,
Lived the same life with the rest, the same old laughing, gnawing,
sleeping,
Play'd the part that still looks back on the actor or actress,
The same old role, the role that is what we make it, as great as we
like,
Or as small as we like, or both great and small.   85

7
Closer yet I approach you,
What thought you have of me now, I had as much of you—I laid
in my stores in advance,
I consider'd long and seriously of you before you were born.

Who was to know what should come home to me?
Who knows but I am enjoying this?   90
Who knows, for all the distance, but I am as good as looking at you
now, for all you cannot see me?

8
Ah, what can ever be more stately and admirable to me than mast-
hemm'd Manhattan?
River and sunset and scallop-edg'd waves of flood-tide?
The sea-gulls oscillating their bodies, the hay-boat in the twilight,
and the belated lighter?

What gods can exceed these that clasp me by the hand, and with
voices I love call me promptly and loudly by my nighest name
as I approach?   95
What is more subtle than this which ties me to the woman or man
that looks in my face?
Which fuses me into you now, and pours my meaning into you?

We understand then do we not?
What I promis'd without mentioning it, have you not accepted?
What the study could not teach—what the preaching could not
accomplish is accomplish'd, is it not?   100

9
Flow on, river! flow with the flood-tide, and ebb with the ebb-tide!
Frolic on, crested and scallop-edg'd waves!
Gorgeous clouds of the sunset! drench with your splendor me, or
the men and women generations after me!
Cross from shore to shore, countless crowds of passengers!
Stand up, tall masts of Mannahatta! stand up, beautiful hills of
Brooklyn!   105
Throb, baffled and curious brain! throw out questions and answers!
Suspend here and everywhere, eternal float of solution!
Gaze, loving and thirsting eyes, in the house or street or public as-
sembly!
Sound out, voices of young men! loudly and musically call me by
my nighest name!

Live, old life! play the part that looks back on the actor or ac-
    tress!   110
Play the old role, the role that is great or small according as one
    makes it!
Consider, you who peruse me, whether I may not in unknown ways
    be looking upon you;
Be firm, rail over the river, to support those who lean idly, yet haste
    with the hasting current;
Fly on, sea-birds! fly sideways, or wheel in large circles high in the
    air;
Receive the summer sky, you water, and faithfully hold it till all
    downcast eyes have time to take it from you!   115
Diverge, fine spokes of light, from the shape of my head, or any
    one's head, in the sunlit water!
Come on, ships from the lower bay! pass up or down, white-sail'd
    schooners, sloops, lighters!
Flaunt away, flags of all nations! be duly lower'd at sunset!
Burn high your fires, foundry chimneys! cast black shadows at night-
    fall! cast red and yellow light over the tops of the houses!
Appearances, now or henceforth, indicate what you are,   120
You necessary film, continue to envelop the soul,
About my body for me, and your body for you, be hung our di-
    vinest aromas,
Thrive, cities—bring your freight, bring your shows, ample and
    sufficient rivers,
Expand, being than which none else is perhaps more spiritual,
Keep your places, objects than which none else is more lasting.   125

You have waited, you always wait, you dumb, beautiful ministers,
We receive you with free sense at last, and are insatiate hencefor-
    ward,
Not you any more shall be able to foil us, or withhold yourselves
    from us,
We use you, and do not cast you aside—we plant you permanently
    within us,
We fathom you not—we love you—there is perfection in you
    also,   130
You furnish your parts toward eternity,
Great or small, you furnish your parts toward the soul.

        1856

From BIRDS OF PASSAGE
Song of the Universal

1

Come said the Muse,
Sing me a song no poet yet has chanted,
Sing me the universal.

In this broad earth of ours,

Amid the measureless grossness and the slag,   5
Enclosed and safe within its central heart,
Nestles the seed perfection.

By every life a share or more or less,
None born but it is born, conceal'd or unconceal'd the seed is wait-
    ing.

2

Lo! keen-eyed towering science,   10
As from tall peaks the modern overlooking,
Successive absolute fiats issuing.

Yet again, lo! the soul, above all science,
For it has history gather'd like husks around the globe,
For it the entire star-myriads roll through the sky.   15

In spiral routes by long detours,
(As a much-tacking ship upon the sea,)
For it the partial to the permanent flowing,
For it the real to the ideal tends.

For it the mystic evolution,   20
Not the right only justified, what we call evil also justified.

Forth from their masks, no matter what,
From the huge festering trunk, from craft and guile and tears,
Health to emerge and joy, joy universal.

Out of the bulk, the morbid and the shallow,   25
Out of the bad majority, the varied countless frauds of men and
    states,
Electric, antiseptic yet, cleaving, suffusing all,
Only the good is universal.

3

Over the mountain-growths disease and sorrow,
An uncaught bird is ever hovering, hovering,   30
High in the purer, happier air.

From imperfection's murkiest cloud,
Darts always forth one ray of perfect light,
One flash of heaven's glory.

To fashion's, custom's discord,   35
To the mad Babel-din, the deafening orgies,
Soothing each lull a strain is heard, just heard,
From some far shore the final chorus sounding.
O the blest eyes, the happy hearts,
That see, that know the guiding thread so fine,   40
Along the mighty labyrinth.

4

And thou America,
For the scheme's culmination, its thought and its reality,

For these (not for thyself) thou hast arrived.

Thou too surroundest all, 45
Embracing carrying welcoming all, thou too by pathways broad and
      new,
To the ideal tendest.

The measur'd faiths of other lands, the grandeurs of the past,
Are not for thee, but grandeurs of thine own,
Deific faiths and amplitudes, absorbing, comprehending all, 50
All eligible to all.

All, all for immortality,
Love like the light silently wrapping all,
Nature's amelioration blessing all,
The blossoms, fruits of ages, orchards divine and certain, 55
Forms, objects, growths, humanities, to spiritual images ripening.

Give me O God to sing that thought,
Give me, give him or her I love this quenchless faith,
In Thy ensemble, whatever else withheld withhold not from us,
Belief in plan of Thee enclosed in Time and Space, 60
Health, peace, salvation universal.

Is it a dream?
Nay but the lack of it the dream,
And failing it life's lore and wealth a dream,
And all the world a dream. 65

1876

Pioneers! O Pioneers!

Come my tan-faced children,
Follow well in order, get your weapons ready,
Have you your pistols? have you your sharp-edged axes?
      Pioneers! O pioneers!

For we cannot tarry here, 5
We must march my darlings, we must bear the brunt of danger,
We the youthful sinewy races, all the rest on us depend,
      Pioneers! O pioneers!

O you youths, Western youths,
So impatient, full of action, full of manly pride and friendship, 10
Plain I see you Western youths, see you tramping with the fore-
      most,
      Pioneers! O pioneers!

Have the elder races halted?
Do they droop and end their lesson, wearied over there beyond the
      seas?
We take up the task eternal, and the burden and the lesson, 15

Pioneers! O pioneers!

All the past we leave behind,
We debouch[2] upon a newer mightier world, varied world,
Fresh and strong the world we seize, world of labor and the march,
Pioneers! O pioneers!   20

We detachments steady throwing,
Down the edges, through the passes, up the mountains steep,
Conquering, holding, daring, venturing as we go the unknown
ways,
Pioneers! O pioneers!

We primeval forests felling,   25
We the rivers stemming, vexing we and piercing deep the mines
within,
We the surface broad surveying, we the virgin soil upheaving,
Pioneers! O pioneers!

Colorado men are we,
From the peaks gigantic, from the great sierras and the high pla-
teaus,   30
From the mine and from the gully, from the hunting trail we come,
Pioneers! O pioneers!

From Nebraska, from Arkansas,
Central inland race are we, from Missouri, with the continental
blood intervein'd,
All the hands of comrades clasping, all the Southern, all the North-
ern,   35
Pioneers! O pioneers!

O resistless restless race!
O beloved race in all! O my breast aches with tender love for all!
O I mourn and yet exult, I am rapt with love for all,
Pioneers! O pioneers!   40

Raise the mighty mother mistress,
Waving high the delicate mistress, over all the starry mistress, (bend
your heads all,)
Raise the fang'd and warlike mistress, stern, impassive, weapon'd
mistress,
Pioneers! O pioneers!

See my children, resolute children,   45
By those swarms upon our rear we must never yield or falter,
Ages back in ghostly millions frowning there behind us urging,
Pioneers ! O pioneers!

On and on the compact ranks,

2. Emerge from a narrow place into a wider place.

With accessions ever waiting, with the places of the dead quickly
fill'd,   50
Through the battle, through defeat, moving yet and never stopping,
   Pioneers! O pioneers!

   O to die advancing on!
Are there some of us to droop and die? has the hour come?
Then upon the march we fittest die, soon and sure the gap is fill'd, 55
   Pioneers! O pioneers!

   All the pulses of the world,
Falling in they beat for us, with the Western movement beat,
Holding single or together, steady moving to the front, all for us,
   Pioneers! O pioneers!   60

   Life's involv'd and varied pageants,
All the forms and shows, all the workmen at their work,
All the seamen and the landsmen, all the masters with their slaves,
   Pioneers! O pioneers!

   All the hapless silent lovers,   65
All the prisoners in the prisons, all the righteous and the wicked,
All the joyous, all the sorrowing, all the living, all the dying,
   Pioneers! O pioneers!

   I too with my soul and body,
We, a curious trio, picking, wandering on our way,   70
Through these shores amid the shadows, with the apparitions press-
ing,
   Pioneers! O pioneers!

   Lo, the darting bowling orb!
Lo, the brother orbs around, all the clustering suns and planets,
All the dazzling days, all the mystic nights with dreams,   75
   Pioneers! O pioneers!

   These are of us, they are with us,
All for primal needed work, while the followers there in embryo wait
behind,
We to-day's procession heading, we the route for travel clearing,
   Pioneers! O pioneers!   80

   O you daughters of the West!
O you young and elder daughters! O you mothers and you wives!
Never must you be divided, in our ranks you move united,
   Pioneers! O pioneers!

   Minstrels latent on the prairies!   85
(Shrouded bards of other lands, you may rest, you have done your
work,)
Soon I hear you coming warbling, soon you rise and tramp amid us,
   Pioneers! O pioneers!

Not for delectations sweet,
Not the cushion and the slipper, not the peaceful and the studi-
ous,   90
Not the riches safe and palling, not for us the tame enjoyment,
                    Pioneers! O pioneers!

Do the feasters gluttonous feast?
Do the corpulent sleepers sleep? have they lock'd and bolted doors?
Still be ours the diet hard, and the blanket on the ground,   95
                    Pioneers! O pioneers!

Has the night descended?
Was the road of late so toilsome? did we stop discouraged nodding
    on our way?
Yet a passing hour I yield you in your tracks to pause oblivious,
                    Pioneers! O pioneers!   100

Till with sound of trumpet,
Far, far off the daybreak call—hark! how loud and clear I hear it
    wind,
Swift! to the head of the army!—swift! spring to your places,
                    Pioneers! O pioneers!
                                              1865 (*DT*), 1867

From SEA-DRIFT
Out of the Cradle Endlessly Rocking[3]

Out of the cradle endlessly rocking,
Out of the mocking-bird's throat, the musical shuttle,
Out of the Ninth-month[4] midnight,
Over the sterile sands and the fields beyond, where the child leav-
    ing his bed wander'd alone, bareheaded, barefoot,
Down from the shower'd halo,   5
Up from the mystic play of shadows twining and twisting as if they
    were alive,
Out from the patches of briers and blackberries,
From the memories of the bird that chanted to me,

3. This poem, undoubtedly one of Whitman's greatest, first appeared in the
Saturday Press in 1859 under the title,
"A Child's Reminiscence." This first
version of the poem together with a
criticism of the poem and a reply (probably Whitman's) have been gathered
into *A Child's Reminiscence*, ed. Thomas O. Mabbott and Rollo G. Silver
(1930). In the magazine version, the
poem was introduced by a brief note
which read in part: " * * * the purport of this wild and plaintive song,
well-enveloped, and eluding definition, is
positive and unquestionable, like the
effect of music. The piece will bear
reading many times—perhaps, indeed,
only comes forth, as from recesses, by

many repetitions." Whitman's reply to
the attack on his poetry contains a
number of important suggestions about
reading it. Challenged as to his meaning, Whitman asserted that the "mystic
leaves" appealed not to the intellect
but to the soul, and, further—"Walt
Whitman's method in the construction
of his songs is strictly the method of
the Italian opera." Of all Whitman's
poems, "Out of the Cradle Endlessly
Rocking" most readily exhibits a structure which may be analyzed in musical
and specifically in operatic terms—with
aria and recitative. See Robert D.
Faner, *Walt Whitman and Opera*
(1951).
4. September.

From your memories sad brother, from the fitful risings and fall-
    ings I heard,
From under that yellow half-moon late-risen and swollen as if with
    tears,   10
From those beginning notes of yearning and love there in the mist,
From the thousand responses of my heart never to cease,
From the myriad thence-arous'd words,
From the word stronger and more delicious than any,
From such as now they start the scene revisiting,   15
As a flock, twittering, rising, or overhead passing,
Borne hither, ere all eludes me, hurriedly,
A man, yet by these tears a little boy again,
Throwing myself on the sand, confronting the waves,
I, chanter of pains and joys, uniter of here and hereafter,   20
Taking all hints to use them, but swiftly leaping beyond them,
A reminiscence sing.

Once Paumanok,[5]
When the lilac-scent was in the air and Fifth-month[6] grass was
    growing,
Up this seashore in some briers,   25
Two feather'd guests from Alabama, two together,
And their nest, and four light-green eggs spotted with brown,
And every day the he-bird to and fro near at hand,
And every day the she-bird crouch'd on her nest, silent, with bright
    eyes,
And every day I, a curious boy, never too close, never disturbing
    them,   30
Cautiously peering, absorbing, translating.

Shine! shine! shine!
Pour down your warmth, great sun!
While we bask, we two together.

Two together!   35
Winds blow south, or winds blow north,
Day come white, or night come black,
Home, or rivers and mountains from home,
Singing all time, minding no time,
While we two keep together.   40

Till of a sudden,
May-be kill'd, unknown to her mate,
One forenoon the she-bird crouch'd not on the nest,
Nor return'd that afternoon, nor the next,
Nor ever appear'd again.   45

And thenceforward all summer in the sound of the sea,
And at night under the full of the moon in calmer weather,
Over the hoarse surging of the sea,

---

5. Indian name for Long Island.   6. May.

Or flitting from brier to brier by day,
I saw, I heard at intervals the remaining one, the he-bird,   50
The solitary guest from Alabama.

Blow! blow! blow!
Blow up sea-winds along Paumanok's shore;
I wait and I wait till you blow my mate to me.

Yes, when the stars glisten'd,   55
All night long on the prong of a moss-scallop'd stake,
Down almost amid the slapping waves,
Sat the lone singer wonderful causing tears.

He call'd on his mate,
He pour'd forth the meanings which I of all men know.   60

Yes my brother I know,
The rest might not, but I have treasur'd every note,
For more than once dimly down to the beach gliding,
Silent, avoiding the moonbeams, blending myself with the shadows,
Recalling now the obscure shapes, the echoes, the sounds and sights
          after their sorts,   65
The white arms out in the breakers tirelessly tossing,
I, with bare feet, a child, the wind wafting my hair,
Listen'd long and long.

Listen'd to keep, to sing, now translating the notes,
Following you my brother.   70

Soothe! soothe! soothe!
Close on its wave soothes the wave behind,
And again another behind embracing and lapping, every one close,
But my love soothes not me, not me.

Low hangs the moon, it rose late,   75
It is lagging—O I think it is heavy with love, with love.

O madly the sea pushes upon the land,
With love, with love.

O night! do I not see my love fluttering out among the breakers?
What is that little black thing I see there in the white?   80

Loud! loud! loud!
Loud I call to you, my love!
High and clear I shoot my voice over the waves,
Surely you must know who is here, is here,
You must know who I am, my love.   85

Low-hanging moon!
What is that dusky spot in your brown yellow?
O it is the shape, the shape of my mate!
O moon do not keep her from me any longer.

Land! land! O land!
Whichever way I turn, O I think you could give me my mate back
    again if you only would,
For I am almost sure I see her dimly whichever way I look.   90

O rising stars!
Perhaps the one I want so much will rise, will rise with some of you.

O throat! O trembling throat!   95
Sound clearer through the atmosphere!
Pierce the woods, the earth,
Somewhere listening to catch you must be the one I want.

Shake out carols!
Solitary here, the night's carols!   100
Carols of lonesome love! death's carols!
Carols under that lagging, yellow, waning moon!
O under that moon where she droops almost down into the sea!
O reckless despairing carols.

But soft! sink low!   105
Soft! let me just murmur,
And do you wait a moment you husky-nois'd sea,
For somewhere I believe I heard my mate responding to me,
So faint, I must be still, be still to listen,
But not altogether still, for then she might not come immediately
    to me.   110

Hither my love!
Here I am! here!
With this just-sustain'd note I announce myself to you,
This gentle call is for you my love, for you.

Do not be decoy'd elsewhere,   115
That is the whistle of the wind, it is not my voice,
That is the fluttering, the fluttering of the spray,
Those are the shadows of leaves.

O darkness! O in vain!
O I am very sick and sorrowful.   120

O brown halo in the sky near the moon, drooping upon the sea!
O troubled reflection in the sea!
O throat! O throbbing heart!
And I singing uselessly, uselessly all the night.

O past! O happy life! O songs of joy!   125
In the air, in the woods, over fields,
Loved! loved! loved! loved! loved!
But my mate no more, no more with me!
We two together no more.

The aria sinking,   130
All else continuing, the stars shining,

The winds blowing, the notes of the bird continuous echoing,
With angry moans the fierce old mother incessantly moaning,
On the sands of Paumanok's shore gray and rustling,
The yellow half-moon enlarged, sagging down, drooping, the face
    of the sea almost touching,   135
The boy ecstatic, with his bare feet the waves, with his hair the
    atmosphere dallying,
The love in the heart long pent, now loose, now at last tumultuously
    bursting,
The aria's meaning, the ears, the soul, swiftly depositing,
The strange tears down the cheeks coursing,
The colloquy there, the trio, each uttering,   140
The undertone, the savage old mother incessantly crying,
To the boy's soul's questions sullenly timing, some drown'd secret
    hissing,
To the outsetting bard.

Demon or bird! (said the boy's soul,)
Is it indeed toward your mate you sing? or is it really to me?   145
For I, that was a child, my tongue's use sleeping, now I have heard
    you,
Now in a moment I know what I am for, I awake,
And already a thousand singers, a thousand songs, clearer, louder
    and more sorrowful than yours,
A thousand warbling echoes have started to life within me, never
    to die.

O you singer solitary, singing by yourself, projecting me,   150
O solitary me listening, never more shall I cease perpetuating you,
Never more shall I escape, never more the reverberations,
Never more the cries of unsatisfied love be absent from me,
Never again leave me to be the peaceful child I was before what
    there in the night,
By the sea under the yellow and sagging moon,   155
The messenger there arous'd, the fire, the sweet hell within,
The unknown want, the destiny of me.

O give me the clew! (it lurks in the night here somewhere,)
O if I am to have so much, let me have more!

A word then, (for I will conquer it,)   160
The word final, superior to all,
Subtle, sent up—what is it?—I listen;
Are you whispering it, and have been all the time, you sea-waves?
Is that it from your liquid rims and wet sands?

Whereto answering, the sea,   165
Delaying not, hurrying not,
Whisper'd me through the night, and very plainly before daybreak,
Lisp'd to me the low and delicious word death,
And again death, death, death, death,

Hissing melodious, neither like the bird nor like my arous'd child's
    heart,   170
But edging near as privately for me rustling at my feet,
Creeping thence steadily up to my ears and laving me softly all over,
Death, death, death, death, death.

Which I do not forget,
But fuse the song of my dusky demon and brother,   175
That he sang to me in the moonlight on Paumanok's gray beach,
With the thousand responsive songs at random,
My own songs awaked from that hour,
And with them the key, the word up from the waves,
The word of the sweetest song and all songs,   180
That strong and delicious word which, creeping to my feet,
(Or like some old crone rocking the cradle, swathed in sweet gar-
    ments, bending aside,)
The sea whisper'd me.

                    1860

As I Ebb'd with the Ocean of Life

1

As I ebb'd with the ocean of life,
As I wended the shores I know,
As I walk'd where the ripples continually wash you Paumanok,[7]
Where they rustle up hoarse and sibilant,
Where the fierce old mother endlessly cries for her castaways,   5
I musing late in the autumn day, gazing off southward,
Held by this electric self out of the pride of which I utter poems,
Was seiz'd by the spirit that trails in the lines underfoot,
The rim, the sediment that stands for all the water and all the land
    of the globe.

Fascinated, my eyes reverting from the south, dropt, to follow those
    slender windrows,   10
Chaff, straw, splinters of wood, weeds, and the sea-gluten,
Scum, scales from shining rocks, leaves of salt-lettuce, left by the
    tide,
Miles walking, the sound of breaking waves the other side of me,
Paumanok there and then as I thought the old thought of likenesses,
These you presented to me you fish-shaped island,   15
As I wended the shores I know,
As I walk'd with that electric self seeking types.

2

As I wend to the shores I know not,
As I list to the dirge, the voices of men and women wreck'd,
As I inhale the impalpable breezes that set in upon me,   20
As the ocean so mysterious rolls toward me closer and closer,

---

7. Indian name for Long Island.

I too but signify at the utmost a little wash'd-up drift,
A few sands and dead leaves to gather,
Gather, and merge myself as part of the sands and drift.

O baffled, balk'd, bent to the very earth,   25
Oppress'd with myself that I have dared to open my mouth,
Aware now that amid all that blab whose echoes recoil upon me I
    have not once had the least idea who or what I am,
But that before all my arrogant poems the real Me stands yet un-
    touch'd, untold, altogether unreach'd,
Withdrawn far, mocking me with mock-congratulatory signs and
    bows,
With peals of distant ironical laughter at every word I have writ-
    ten,   30
Pointing in silence to these songs, and then to the sand beneath.

I perceive I have not really understood any thing, not a single ob-
    ject, and that no man ever can,
Nature here in sight of the sea taking advantage of me to dart
    upon me and sting me,
Because I have dared to open my mouth to sing at all.

3

You oceans both, I close with you,   35
We murmur alike reproachfully rolling sands and drift, knowing not
    why,
These little shreds indeed standing for you and me and all.

You friable shore with trails of debris,
You fish-shaped island, I take what is underfoot,
What is yours is mine my father.   40

I too Paumanok,
I too have bubbled up, floated the measureless float,[8] and been
    wash'd on your shores,
I too am but a trail of drift and debris,
I too leave little wrecks upon you, you fish-shaped island.

I throw myself upon your breast my father,   45
I cling to you so that you cannot unloose me,
I hold you so firm till you answer me something.

Kiss me my father,
Touch me with your lips as I touch those I love,
Breathe to me while I hold you close the secret of the murmuring
    I envy.   50

4

Ebb, ocean of life, (the flow will return,)
Cease not your moaning you fierce old mother,
Endlessly cry for your castaways, but fear not, deny not me,

---

8. The flux or flood of the tide. Cf. "float" in "Crossing Brooklyn Ferry," line 62.

Rustle not up so hoarse and angry against my feet as I touch you
    or gather from you.

I mean tenderly by you and all,   55
I gather for myself and for this phantom looking down where we
    lead, and following me and mine.

Me and mine, loose windrows, little corpses,
Froth, snowy white, and bubbles,
(See, from my dead lips the ooze exuding at last,
See, the prismatic colors glistening and rolling,   60
Tufts of straw, sands, fragments,
Buoy'd hither from many moods, one contradicting another,
From the storm, the long calm, the darkness, the swell,
Musing, pondering, a breath, a briny tear, a dab of liquid or soil,
Up just as much out of fathomless workings fermented and thrown,
A limp blossom or two, torn, just as much over waves floating,
    drifted at random,   66
Just as much for us that sobbing dirge of Nature,
Just as much whence we come that blare of the cloud-trumpets,
We, capricious, brought hither we know not whence, spread out be-
    fore you,
You up there walking or sitting,   70
Whoever you are, we too lie in drifts at your feet.

                                     1860

Tears

Tears! tears! tears!
In the night, in solitude, tears,
On the white shore dripping, dripping, suck'd in by the sand,
Tears, not a star shining, all dark and desolate,
Moist tears from the eyes of a muffled head;   5
O who is that ghost? that form in the dark, with tears?
What shapeless lump is that, bent, crouch'd there on the sand?
Steaming tears, sobbing tears, throes, choked with wild cries;
O storm, embodied, rising, careering with swift steps along the
    beach!
O wild and dismal night storm, with wind—O belching and des-
    perate!   10
O shade so sedate and decorous by day, with calm countenance and
    regulated pace,
But away at night as you fly, none looking—O then the unloosen'd
    ocean,
Of tears! tears! tears!

                                     1867

The World Below the Brine

The world below the brine,
Forests at the bottom of the sea, the branches and leaves,
Sea-lettuce, vast lichens, strange flowers and seeds, the thick tangle,
    openings, and pink turf,
Different colors, pale gray and green, purple, white, and gold, the
    play of light through the water,
Dumb swimmers there among the rocks, coral, gluten, grass, rushes,
    and the aliment[9] of the swimmers,   5
Sluggish existences grazing there suspended, or slowly crawling close
    to the bottom,
The sperm-whale at the surface blowing air and spray, or disporting
    with his flukes,
The leaden-eyed shark, the walrus, the turtle, the hairy sea-leopard,
    and the sting-ray,
Passions there, wars, pursuits, tribes, sight in those ocean-depths,
    breathing that thick-breathing air, as so many do,
The change thence to the sight here, and to the subtle air breathed
    by beings like us who walk this sphere,   10
The change onward from ours to that of beings who walk other
    spheres.

1860

From By the Roadside
A Hand-Mirror

Hold it up sternly—see this it sends back, (who is it? is it you?)
Outside fair costume, within ashes and filth,
No more a flashing eye, no more a sonorous voice or springy step,
Now some slave's eye, voice, hands, step,
A drunkard's breath, unwholesome eater's face, venerealee's flesh, 5
Lungs rotting away piecemeal, stomach sour and cankerous,
Joints rheumatic, bowels clogged with abomination,
Blood circulating dark and poisonous streams,
Words babble, hearing and touch callous,
No brain, no heart left, no magnetism of sex;   10
Such from one look in this looking-glass ere you go hence,
Such a result so soon—and from such a beginning!

1860

When I Heard the Learn'd Astronomer

When I heard the learn'd astronomer,
When the proofs, the figures, were ranged in columns before me,

9. Food, nourishment.

When I was shown the charts and diagrams, to add, divide, and
    measure them,
When I sitting heard the astronomer where he lectured with much
    applause in the lecture-room,
How soon unaccountable I became tired and sick,   5
Till rising and gliding out I wander'd off by myself,
In the mystical moist night air, and from time to time,
Look'd up in perfect silence at the stars.

1865 (DT), 1867

I Sit and Look Out

I sit and look out upon all the sorrows of the world, and upon all
    oppression and shame,
I hear secret convulsive sobs from young men at anguish with them-
    selves, remorseful after deeds done,
I see in low life the mother misused by her children, dying, neg-
    lected, gaunt, desperate,
I see the wife misused by her husband, I see the treacherous seducer
    of young women,
I mark the ranklings of jealousy and unrequited love attempted to
    be hid, I see these sights on the earth,   5
I see the workings of battle, pestilence, tyranny, I see martyrs and
    prisoners,
I observe a famine at sea, I observe the sailors casting lots who shall
    be kill'd to preserve the lives of the rest,
I observe the slights and degradations cast by arrogant persons upon
    laborers, the poor, and upon negroes, and the like;
All these—all the meanness and agony without end I sitting look
    out upon,
See, hear, and am silent.   10

1860

The Dalliance of the Eagles

Skirting the river road, (my forenoon walk, my rest,)
Skyward in air a sudden muffled sound, the dalliance of the eagles,
The rushing amorous contact high in space together,
The clinching interlocking claws, a living, fierce, gyrating wheel,
Four beating wings, two beaks, a swirling mass tight grappling,   5
In tumbling turning clustering loops, straight downward falling,
Till o'er the river pois'd, the twain yet one, a moment's lull,
A motionless still balance in the air, then parting, talons loosing,
Upward again on slow-firm pinions slanting, their separate diverse
    flight,
She hers, he his, pursuing.   10

1881–82

From Drum-Taps[1]
First O Songs for a Prelude

First O songs for a prelude,
Lightly strike on the stretch'd tympanum[2] pride and joy in my city,
How she led the rest to arms, how she gave the cue,
How at once with lithe limbs unwaiting a moment she sprang,
(O superb! O Manhattan, my own, my peerless!   5
O strongest you in the hour of danger, in crisis! O truer than steel!)
How you sprang—how you threw off the costumes of peace with
    indifferent hand,
How your soft opera-music changed, and the drum and fife were
    heard in their stead,
How you led to the war, (that shall serve for our prelude, songs of
    soldiers,)
How Manhattan drum-taps led.   10

Forty years had I in my city seen soldiers parading,
Forty years as a pageant, till unawares the lady of this teeming and
    turbulent city,
Sleepless amid her ships, her houses, her incalculable wealth,
With her million children around her, suddenly,
At dead of night, at news from the south,   15
Incens'd struck with clinch'd hand the pavement.

A shock electric, the night sustain'd it,
Till with ominous hum our hive at daybreak pour'd out its myriads.

From the houses then and the workshops, and through all the door-
    ways,
Leapt they tumultuous, and lo! Manhattan arming.   20

To the drum-taps prompt,
The young men falling in and arming,

1. *Drum-Taps* first appeared as a separate volume in 1865, with many more
poems than the section finally contained
when the cluster was later integrated
in the master volume of *Leaves.* The
emotions represented in the poems range
widely from exhilaration to dumb grief.
It should be recalled that Whitman first
viewed the war as a civilian on the side-
lines in New York, that he later saw
the battlefields close at hand when he
sought for his wounded brother in Virginia, and that, finally, he witnessed
the multitude of sick and injured, the
suffering and dying, of both sides in
the Washington hospitals when he became a "wound-dresser." Whitman realized that each of his various attitudes
toward the war had its own emotional
validity. At one time, *Drum-Taps* was
significantly introduced by the lines:
"Aroused and angry, / I thought to
beat the alarum, and urge relentless
war; / But soon my fingers fail'd me,
my face droop'd, and I resign'd myself, / To sit by the wounded and
soothe them, or silently watch the
dead." These lines were later included
in "The Wound-Dresser." The reader
should note that a number of these
poems, particularly "Vigil Strange I
Kept on the Field One Night" and "The
Artilleryman's Vision," are "narrated"
by fictional characters created by Whitman; these examples should serve as
warning against concluding too quickly
that the "I" in any Whitman poem is
simply nothing more nor less than the
poet.
2. Eardrum.

The mechanics arming, (the trowel, the jack-plane, the blacksmith's
    hammer, tost aside with precipitation,)
The lawyer leaving his office and arming, the judge leaving the
    court,
The driver deserting his wagon in the street, jumping down, throw-
    ing the reins abruptly down on the horses' backs,   25
The salesman leaving the store, the boss, book-keeper, porter, all
    leaving;
Squads gather everywhere by common consent and arm,
The new recruits, even boys, the old men show them how to wear
    their accoutrements, they buckle the straps carefully,
Outdoors arming, indoors arming, the flash of the musket-barrels,
The white tents cluster in camps, the arm'd sentries around, the
    sunrise cannon and again at sunset,   30
Arm'd regiments arrive every day, pass through the city, and em-
    bark from the wharves,
(How good they look as they tramp down to the river, sweaty,
    with their guns on their shoulders!
How I love them! how I could hug them, with their brown faces
    and their clothes and knapsacks cover'd with dust!)
The blood of the city up—arm'd! arm'd! the cry everywhere,
The flags flung out from the steeples of churches and from all the
    public buildings and stores,   35
The tearful parting, the mother kisses her son, the son kisses his
    mother,
(Loth is the mother to part, yet not a word does she speak to detain
    him,)
The tumultuous escort, the ranks of policemen preceding, clearing
    the way,
The unpent enthusiasm, the wild cheers of the crowd for their
    favorites,
The artillery, the silent cannons bright as gold, drawn along, rumble
    lightly over the stones,   40
(Silent cannons, soon to cease your silence,
Soon unlimber'd to begin the red business;)
All the mutter of preparation, all the determin'd arming,
The hospital service, the lint, bandages and medicines,
The women volunteering for nurses, the work begun for in earnest,
    no mere parade now;   45
War! an arm'd race is advancing! the welcome for battle, no turn-
    ing away;
War! be it weeks, months, or years, an arm'd race is advancing to
    welcome it.

Mannahatta a-march—and it's O to sing it well!
It's O for a manly life in the camp.

And the sturdy artillery,   50
The guns bright as gold, the work for giants, to serve well the guns,

Unlimber them! (no more as the past forty years for salute for courtesies merely,
Put in something now besides powder and wadding.)

And you lady of ships, you Mannahatta,
Old matron of this proud, friendly, turbulent city,   55
Often in peace and wealth you were pensive or covertly frown'd
amid all your children,
But now you smile with joy exulting old Mannahatta.

                                                  1865 (*DT*), 1867

Beat! Beat! Drums!

Beat! beat! drums!—blow! bugles! blow!
Through the windows—through doors—burst like a ruthless force,
Into the solemn church, and scatter the congregation,
Into the school where the scholar is studying;
Leave not the bridegroom quiet—no happiness must he have now
with his bride,   5
Nor the peaceful farmer any peace, ploughing his field or gathering
his grain,
So fierce you whirr and pound you drums—so shrill you bugles
blow.

Beat! beat! drums!—blow! bugles! blow!
Over the traffic of cities—over the rumble of wheels in the streets;
Are beds prepared for sleepers at night in the houses? no sleepers
must sleep in those beds,   10
No bargainers' bargains by day—no brokers or speculators—would
they continue?
Would the talkers be talking? would the singer attempt to sing?
Would the lawyer rise in the court to state his case before the
judge?
Then rattle quicker, heavier drums—you bugles wilder blow.

Beat! beat! drums!—blow! bugles! blow!   15
Make no parley—stop for no expostulation,
Mind not the timid—mind not the weeper or prayer,
Mind not the old man beseeching the young man,
Let not the child's voice be heard, nor the mother's entreaties,
Make even the trestles to shake the dead where they lie awaiting the
hearses,   20
So strong you thump O terrible drums—so loud you bugles blow.

                                                  1865 (*DT*), 1867

Cavalry Crossing a Ford

A line in long array where they wind betwixt green islands,
They take a serpentine course, their arms flash in the sun—hark
    to the musical clank,
Behold the silvery river, in it the splashing horses loitering stop to
    drink,
Behold the brown-faced men, each group, each person a picture,
    the negligent rest on the saddles,
Some emerge on the opposite bank, others are just entering the
    ford—while,   5
Scarlet and blue and snowy white,
The guidon flags flutter gayly in the wind.

                                        1865 (*DT*), 1867

Bivouac on a Mountain Side

I see before me now a traveling army halting,
Below a fertile valley spread, with barns and the orchards of sum-
    mer,
Behind, the terraced sides of a mountain, abrupt, in places rising
    high,
Broken, with rocks, with clinging cedars, with tall shapes dingily
    seen,
The numerous camp-fires scatter'd near and far, some away up on
    the mountain,   5
The shadowy forms of men and horses, looming, large-sized, flicker-
    ing,
And over all the sky—the sky! far, far out of reach, studded, break-
    ing out, the eternal stars.

                                          1865 (*DT*), 1867

An Army Corps on the March

With its cloud of skirmishers in advance,
With now the sound of a single shot snapping like a whip, and
    now an irregular volley,
The swarming ranks press on and on, the dense brigades press on,
Glittering dimly, toiling under the sun—the dust-cover'd men,
In columns rise and fall to the undulations of the ground,   5
With artillery interspers'd—the wheels rumble, the horses sweat,
As the army corps advances.

                                          1865 (*DT*), 1867

By the Bivouac's Fitful Flame

By the bivouac's fitful flame,
A procession winding around me, solemn and sweet and slow—but
    first I note,
The tents of the sleeping army, the fields' and woods' dim outline,
The darkness lit by spots of kindled fire, the silence,
Like a phantom far or near an occasional figure moving,   5
The shrubs and trees, (as I lift my eyes they seem to be stealthily
    watching me,)
While wind in procession thoughts, O tender and wondrous
    thoughts,
Of life and death, of home and the past and loved, and of those
    that are far away;
A solemn and slow procession there as I sit on the ground,
By the bivouac's fitful flame.   10

                          1865 (DT), 1867

Come up from the Fields Father

Come up from the fields father, here's a letter from our Pete,
And come to the front door mother, here's a letter from thy dear
    son.

Lo, 'tis autumn,
Lo, where the trees, deeper green, yellower and redder,
Cool and sweeten Ohio's villages with leaves fluttering in the mod-
    erate wind,
Where apples ripe in the orchards hang and grapes on the trellis'd
    vines,   5
(Smell you the smell of the grapes on the vines?
Smell you the buckwheat where the bees were lately buzzing?)
Above all, lo, the sky so calm, so transparent after the rain, and
    with wondrous clouds,
Below too, all calm, all vital and beautiful, and the farm prospers
    well.   10

Down in the fields all prospers well,
But now from the fields come father, come at the daughter's call,
And come to the entry mother, to the front door come right away.

Fast as she can she hurries, something ominous, her steps trem-
    bling,
She does not tarry to smooth her hair nor adjust her cap.   15

Open the envelope quickly,
O this is not our son's writing, yet his name is sign'd,
O a strange hand writes for our dear son, O stricken mother's soul!

All swims before her eyes, flashes with black, she catches the main
 words only,
Sentences broken, *gunshot wound in the breast, cavalry skirmish,
 taken to hospital,* 20
At present low, but will soon be better.

Ah now the single figure to me,
Amid all teeming and wealthy Ohio with all its cities and farms,
Sickly white in the face and dull in the head, very faint,
By the jamb of a door leans. 25

Grieve not so, dear mother, (the just-grown daughter speaks through
 her sobs,
The little sisters huddle around speechless and dismay'd,)
See, dearest mother, the letter says Pete will soon be better.

Alas poor boy, he will never be better, (nor may-be needs to be
 better, that brave and simple soul,)
While they stand at home at the door he is dead already, 30
The only son is dead.

But the mother needs to be better,
She with thin form presently drest in black,
By day her meals untouch'd, then at night fitfully sleeping, often
 waking,
In the midnight waking, weeping, longing with one deep longing, 35
O that she might withdraw unnoticed, silent from life escape and
 withdraw,
To follow, to seek, to be with her dear dead son.
                                                    1865 (*DT*), 1867

Vigil Strange I Kept on the Field One Night

Vigil strange I kept on the field one night;
When you my son and my comrade dropt at my side that day,
One look I but gave which your dear eyes return'd with a look I
 shall never forget,
One touch of your hand to mine O boy, reach'd up as you lay on
 the ground,
Then onward I sped in the battle, the even-contested battle, 5
Till late in the night reliev'd to the place at last again I made my
 way,
Found you in death so cold dear comrade, found your body son of
 responding kisses, (never again on earth responding,)
Bared your face in the starlight, curious the scene, cool blew the
 moderate night-wind,
Long there and then in vigil I stood, dimly around me the battle-
 field spreading,
Vigil wondrous and vigil sweet there in the fragrant silent night, 10

But not a tear fell, not even a long-drawn sigh, long, long I gazed,
Then on the earth partially reclining sat by your side leaning my
    chin in my hands,
Passing sweet hours, immortal and mystic hours with you dearest
    comrade—not a tear, not a word,
Vigil of silence, love and death, vigil for you my son and my soldier,
As onward silently stars aloft, eastward new ones upward stole,   15
Vigil final for you brave boy, (I could not save you, swift was your
    death,
I faithfully loved you and cared for you living, I think we shall
    surely meet again,)
Till at latest lingering of the night, indeed just as the dawn appear'd,
My comrade I wrapt in his blanket, envelop'd well his form,
Folded the blanket well, tucking it carefully over head and care-
    fully under feet,   20
And there and then and bathed by the rising sun, my son in his
    grave, in his rude-dug grave I deposited,
Ending my vigil strange with that, vigil of night and battle-field
    dim,
Vigil for boy of responding kisses, (never again on earth respond-
    ing,)
Vigil for comrade swiftly slain, vigil I never forget, how as day
    brighten'd,
I rose from the chill ground and folded my soldier well in his
    blanket,   25
And buried him where he fell.

                      1865 (*DT*), 1867

A March in the Ranks Hard-prest,
and the Road Unknown

A march in the ranks hard-prest, and the road unknown,
A route through a heavy wood with muffled steps in the darkness,
Our army foil'd with loss severe, and the sullen remnant retreating,
Till after midnight glimmer upon us the lights of a dim-lighted
    building,
We come to an open space in the woods, and halt by the dim-
    lighted building,   5
'Tis a large old church at the crossing roads, now an impromptu
    hospital,
Entering but for a minute I see a sight beyond all the pictures and
    poems ever made,
Shadows of deepest, deepest black, just lit by moving candles and
    lamps,
And by one great pitchy torch stationary with wild red flame and
    clouds of smoke,
By these, crowds, groups of forms vaguely I see on the floor, some
    in the pews laid down,   10

At my feet more distinctly a soldier, a mere lad, in danger of bleed-
    ing to death, (he is shot in the abdomen,)
I stanch the blood temporarily, (the youngster's face is white as a
    lily,)
Then before I depart I sweep my eyes o'er the scene fain to absorb
    it all,
Faces, varieties, postures beyond description, most in obscurity,
    some of them dead,
Surgeons operating, attendants holding lights, the smell of ether,
    the odor of blood,   15
The crowd, O the crowd of the bloody forms, the yard outside also
    fill'd,
Some on the bare ground, some on planks or stretchers, some in
    the death-spasm sweating,
An occasional scream or cry, the doctor's shouted orders or calls,
The glisten of the little steel instruments catching the glint of the
    torches,
These I resume as I chant, I see again the forms, I smell the odor,
Then hear outside the orders given, *Fall in, my men, fall in;*   21
But first I bend to the dying lad, his eyes open, a half-smile gives
    he me,
Then the eyes close, calmly close, and I speed forth to the dark-
    ness,
Resuming, marching, ever in darkness marching, on in the ranks,
The unknown road still marching.   25

                                    1865 (*DT*), 1867

A Sight in Camp in the Daybreak Gray and Dim

A sight in camp in the daybreak gray and dim,
As from my tent I emerge so early sleepless,
As slow I walk in the cool fresh air the path near by the hospital
    tent,
Three forms I see on stretchers lying, brought out there untended
    lying,
Over each the blanket spread, ample brownish woolen blanket,   5
Gray and heavy blanket, folding, covering all.

Curious I halt and silent stand,
Then with light fingers I from the face of the nearest the first just
    lift the blanket;
Who are you elderly man so gaunt and grim, with well-gray'd hair,
    and flesh all sunken about the eyes?
Who are you my dear comrade?   10

Then to the second I step—and who are you my child and darling?
Who are you sweet boy with cheeks yet blooming?

Then to the third—a face nor child nor old, very calm, as of beautiful yellow-white ivory;
Young man I think I know you—I think this face is the face of
  the Christ himself,
Dead and divine and brother of all, and here again he lies.   15

                                          1865 (*DT*), 1867

As Toilsome I Wander'd Virginia's Woods

As toilsome I wander'd Virginia's woods,
To the music of rustling leaves kick'd by my feet, (for 'twas au-
  tumn,)
I mark'd at the foot of a tree the grave of a soldier;
Mortally wounded he and buried on the retreat, (easily all could I
  understand,)
The halt of a mid-day hour, when up! no time to lose—yet this
  sign left,   5
On a tablet scrawl'd and nail'd on the tree by the grave,
Bold, cautious, true, and my loving comrade.

Long, long I muse, then on my way go wandering,
Many a changeful season to follow, and many a scene of life,
Yet at times through changeful season and scene, abrupt, alone, or
  in the crowded street,   10
Comes before me the unknown soldier's grave, comes the inscrip-
  tion rude in Virginia's woods,
Bold, cautious, true, and my loving comrade.

                                          1865 (*DT*), 1867

The Wound-Dresser

1

An old man bending I come among new faces,
Years looking backward resuming in answer to children,
Come tell us old man, as from young men and maidens that love
  me,
(Arous'd and angry, I'd thought to beat the alarum, and urge re-
  lentless war,
But soon my fingers fail'd me, my face droop'd and I resign'd my-
  self,   5
To sit by the wounded and soothe them, or silently watch the
  dead;)
Years hence of these scenes, of these furious passions, these chances,
Of unsurpass'd heroes, (was one side so brave? the other was equally
  brave;)
Now be witness again, paint the mightiest armies of earth,
Of those armies so rapid so wondrous what saw you to tell us?   10

What stays with you latest and deepest? of curious panics,
Of hard-fought engagements or sieges tremendous what deepest
  remains?

2

O maidens and young men I love and that love me,
What you ask of my days those the strangest and sudden your
  talking recalls,
Soldier alert I arrive after a long march cover'd with sweat and
  dust,   15
In the nick of time I come, plunge in the fight, loudly shout in the
  rush of successful charge,
Enter the captur'd works—yet lo, like a swift-running river they
  fade,
Pass and are gone they fade—I dwell not on soldiers' perils or
  soldiers' joys,
(Both I remember well—many of the hardships, few the joys, yet I
  was content.)

But in silence, in dreams' projections,   20
While the world of gain and appearance and mirth goes on,
So soon what is over forgotten, and waves wash the imprints off the
  sand,
With hinged knees returning I enter the doors, (while for you up
  there,
Whoever you are, follow without noise and be of strong heart.)

Bearing the bandages, water and sponge,   25
Straight and swift to my wounded I go,
Where they lie on the ground after the battle brought in,
Where their priceless blood reddens the grass the ground,
Or to the rows of the hospital tent, or under the roof'd hospital,
To the long rows of cots up and down each side I return,   30
To each and all one after another I draw near, not one do I miss,
An attendant follows holding a tray, he carries a refuse pail,
Soon to be fill'd with clotted rags and blood, emptied, and fill'd
  again.

I onward go, I stop,
With hinged knees and steady hand to dress wounds,   35
I am firm with each, the pangs are sharp yet unavoidable,
One turns to me his appealing eyes—poor boy! I never knew you,
Yet I think I could not refuse this moment to die for you, if that
  would save you.

3

On, on I go, (open doors of time! open hospital doors!)
The crush'd head I dress, (poor crazed hand tear not the bandage
  away,)   40
The neck of the cavalry-man with the bullet through and through I
  examine,

Hard the breathing rattles, quite glazed already the eye, yet life
     struggles hard,
(Come sweet death! be persuaded O beautiful death!
In mercy come quickly.)

From the stump of the arm, the amputated hand,   45
I undo the clotted lint, remove the slough, wash off the matter and
     blood,
Back on his pillow the soldier bends with curv'd neck and side
     falling head,
His eyes are closed, his face is pale, he dares not look on the bloody
     stump,
And has not yet look'd on it.

I dress a wound in the side, deep, deep,   50
But a day or two more, for see the frame all wasted and sinking,
And the yellow-blue countenance see.

I dress the perforated shoulder, the foot with the bullet-wound,
Cleanse the one with a gnawing and putrid gangrene, so sickening,
     so offensive,
While the attendant stands behind aside me holding the tray and
     pail.   55

I am faithful, I do not give out,
The fractur'd thigh, the knee, the wound in the abdomen,
These and more I dress with impassive hand, (yet deep in my breast
     a fire, a burning flame.)

4

Thus in silence in dreams' projections,
Returning, resuming, I thread my way through the hospitals, 60
The hurt and wounded I pacify with soothing hand,
I sit by the restless all the dark night, some are so young,
Some suffer so much, I recall the experience sweet and sad,
(Many a soldier's loving arms about this neck have cross'd and
     rested,
Many a soldier's kiss dwells on these bearded lips.) 65
     1865 (DT), 1867

Give Me the Splendid Silent Sun

1

Give me the splendid silent sun with all his beams full-dazzling,
Give me juicy autumnal fruit ripe and red from the orchard,
Give me a field where the unmow'd grass grows,
Give me an arbor, give me the trellis'd grape,
Give me fresh corn and wheat, give me serene-moving animals
     teaching content, 5

Give me nights perfectly quiet as on high plateaus west of the
    Mississippi, and I looking up at the stars,
Give me odorous at sunrise a garden of beautiful flowers where I
    can walk undisturb'd,
Give me for marriage a sweet-breath'd woman of whom I should
    never tire,
Give me a perfect child, give me away aside from the noise of the
    world a rural domestic life,
Give me to warble spontaneous songs recluse by myself, for my
    own ears only,   10
Give me solitude, give me Nature, give me again O Nature your
    primal sanities!

These demanding to have them, (tired with ceaseless excitement,
    and rack'd by the war-strife,)
These to procure incessantly asking, rising in cries from my heart,
While yet incessantly asking still I adhere to my city,
Day upon day and year upon year O city, walking your streets,   15
Where you hold me enchain'd a certain time refusing to give me up,
Yet giving to make me glutted, enrich'd of soul, you give me for-
    ever faces;
(O I see what I sought to escape, confronting, reversing my cries,
I see my own soul trampling down what it ask'd for.)

2

Keep your splendid silent sun,   20
Keep your woods O Nature, and the quiet places by the woods,
Keep your fields of clover and timothy, and your corn-fields and
    orchards,
Keep the blossoming buckwheat fields where the Ninth-month bees
    hum;
Give me faces and streets—give me these phantoms incessant and
    endless along the trottoirs![3]
Give me interminable eyes—give me women—give me comrades
    and lovers by the thousand!   25
Let me see new ones every day—let me hold new ones by the hand
    every day!
Give me such shows—give me the streets of Manhattan!
Give me Broadway, with the soldiers marching—give me the sound
    of the trumpets and drums!
(The soldiers in companies or regiments—some starting away,
    flush'd and reckless,
Some, their time up, returning with thinn'd ranks, young, yet very
    old, worn, marching, noticing nothing;)   30
Give me the shores and wharves heavy-fringed with black ships!
O such for me! O an intense life, full to repletion and varied!
The life of the theatre, bar-room, huge hotel, for me!
The saloon of the steamer! the crowded excursion for me! the torch-
    light procession!

---

3. Sidewalks.

The dense brigade bound for the war, with high piled military
    wagons following;   35
People, endless, streaming, with strong voices, passions, pageants,
Manhattan streets with their powerful throbs, with beating drums
    as now,
The endless and noisy chorus, the rustle and clank of muskets,
    (even the sight of the wounded,)
Manhattan crowds, with their turbulent musical chorus!
Manhattan faces and eyes forever for me.   40

                1865 (DT), 1867

Dirge for Two Veterans

        The last sunbeam
  Lightly falls from the finish'd Sabbath,
On the pavement here, and there beyond it is looking,
    Down a new-made double grave.

        Lo, the moon ascending,   5
Up from the east the silvery round moon,
Beautiful over the house-tops, ghastly, phantom moon,
    Immense and silent moon.

        I see a sad procession,
And I hear the sound of coming full-key'd bugles,   10
All the channels of the city streets they're flooding,
    As with voices and with tears.

        I hear the great drums pounding,
And the small drums steady whirring,
And every blow of the great convulsive drums,   15
    Strikes me through and through.

        For the son is brought with the father,
(In the foremost ranks of the fierce assault they fell,
Two veterans son and father dropt together,
    And the double grave awaits them.)   20

        Now nearer blow the bugles,
And the drums strike more convulsive,
And the daylight o'er the pavement quite has faded,
    And the strong dead-march enwraps me.

        In the eastern sky up-buoying,   25
The sorrowful vast phantom moves illumin'd,
('Tis some mother's large transparent face,
    In heaven brighter growing.)

O strong dead-march you please me!
O moon immense with your silvery face you soothe me! 30
O my soldiers twain! O my veterans passing to burial!
What I have I also give you.

The moon gives you light,
And the bugles and the drums give you music,
And my heart, O my soldiers, my veterans, 35
My heart gives you love.

1865 (*DT*), 1867

The Artilleryman's Vision

While my wife at my side lies slumbering, and the wars are over
long,
And my head on the pillow rests at home, and the vacant midnight
passes,
And through the stillness, through the dark, I hear, just hear, the
breath of my infant,
There in the room as I wake from sleep this vision presses upon me;
The engagement opens there and then in fantasy unreal, 5
The skirmishers begin, they crawl cautiously ahead, I hear the ir-
regular snap! snap!
I hear the sounds of the different missiles, the short *t-h-t! t-h-t!* of
the rifle-balls,
I see the shells exploding leaving small white clouds, I hear the
great shells shrieking as they pass,
The grape[4] like the hum and whirr of wind through the trees,
(tumultuous now the contest rages,)
All the scenes at the batteries rise in detail before me again, 10
The crashing and smoking, the pride of the men in their pieces,
The chief-gunner ranges and sights his piece and selects a fuse of
the right time,
After firing I see him lean aside and look eagerly off to note the
effect;
Elsewhere I hear the cry of a regiment charging, (the young colo-
nel leads himself this time with brandish'd sword,)
I see the gaps cut by the enemy's volleys, (quickly fill'd up, no de-
lay,)
15
I breathe the suffocating smoke, then the flat clouds hover low
concealing all;
Now a strange lull for a few seconds, not a shot fired on either side,
Then resumed the chaos louder than ever, with eager calls and
orders of officers,
While from some distant part of the field the wind wafts to my
ears a shout of applause, (some special success,)

4. Grapeshot; a cluster of small cast-iron balls used as a charge for a cannon.

And ever the sound of the cannon far or near, (rousing even in
    dreams a devilish exultation and all the old mad joy in the
    depths of my soul,)   20
And ever the hastening of infantry shifting positions, batteries,
    cavalry, moving hither and thither,
(The falling, dying, I heed not, the wounded dripping and red I
    heed not, some to the rear are hobbling,)
Grime, heat, rush, aides-de-camp galloping by or on a full run,
With the patter of small arms, the warning *s-s-t* of the rifles, (these
    in my vision I hear or see,)
And bombs bursting in air, and at night the vari-color'd rockets. 25

                          1865 (*DT*), 1867

MEMORIES OF PRESIDENT LINCOLN[5]
When Lilacs Last in the Dooryard Bloom'd[6]

1

When lilacs last in the dooryard bloom'd,
And the great star early droop'd in the western sky in the night,
I mourn'd, and yet shall mourn with ever-returning spring.

Ever-returning spring, trinity sure to me you bring,
Lilac blooming perennial and drooping star in the west,   5
And thought of him I love.

2

O powerful western fallen star!
O shades of night—O moody, tearful night!
O great star disappear'd—O the black murk that hides the star!
O cruel hands that hold me powerless—O helpless soul of me!   10
O harsh surrounding cloud that will not free my soul.

5. Reprinted here are all the poems that Whitman wrote in memory of the Civil War president, Abraham Lincoln. These include "When Lilacs Last in the Dooryard Bloom'd," a masterpiece expressing personal grief and reconciliation; "O Captain! My Captain!" a public piece expressing popular sentiment; and two shorter lesser-known lyrics, expressing still different points of view. Although Lincoln represented for Whitman the symbolic fulfillment of the poet's prophecy that democracy would produce great persons from the mass, the two never met. Whitman has recorded, however, that during the Civil War they bowed to each other in the streets of Washington when the president's barouche passed the poet-pedestrian.
6. Lincoln was assassinated in April, 1865, when Whitman was in Brooklyn in lilac-time. Later in the month, a train carrying Lincoln's body passed through the large eastern cities on its way to Springfield, Illinois. Soon after these events, Whitman wrote most of his Lincoln poems and published them, with other poems, in a *Sequel to Drum-Taps*. "When Lilacs Last in the Dooryard Bloom'd" (like Milton's "Lycidas") takes the classic form of the elegy, opening with an expression of uncontrollable grief over a death and working gradually toward reconciliation through insight and understanding. Although Whitman's major symbols may be identified—the star as Lincoln, the lilac as love, the cloud as grief, the hermit-thrush as spiritual insight—they seem throughout to suggest a more complex or deeper meaning. The curious reader might turn to "Chanting the Square Deific" and attempt to relate the star to Jehovah, the lilac to Consolator, the cloud to Satan, and the hermit-thrush to Santa Spirita.

3

In the dooryard fronting an old farm-house near the white-wash'd
palings,
Stands the lilac-bush tall-growing with heart-shaped leaves of rich
green,
With many a pointed blossom rising delicate, with the perfume
strong I love,
With every leaf a miracle—and from this bush in the dooryard,   15
With delicate-color'd blossoms and heart-shaped leaves of rich
green,
A sprig with its flower I break.

4

In the swamp in secluded recesses,
A shy and hidden bird is warbling a song.

Solitary the thrush,   20
The hermit withdrawn to himself, avoiding the settlements,
Sings by himself a song.

Song of the bleeding throat,
Death's outlet song of life, (for well dear brother I know,
If thou wast not granted to sing thou would'st surely die.)   25

5

Over the breast of the spring, the land, amid cities,
Amid lanes and through old woods, where lately the violets peep'd
from the ground, spotting the gray debris,
Amid the grass in the fields each side of the lanes, passing the end-
less grass,
Passing the yellow-spear'd wheat, every grain from its shroud in the
dark-brown fields uprisen,
Passing the apple-tree blows of white and pink in the orchards,   30
Carrying a corpse to where it shall rest in the grave,
Night and day journeys a coffin.

6

Coffin that passes through lanes and streets,
Through day and night with the great cloud darkening the land,
With the pomp of the inloop'd flags with the cities draped in
black,   35
With the show of the States themselves as of crape-veil'd women
standing,
With processions long and winding and the flambeaus of the night,
With the countless torches lit, with the silent sea of faces and the
unbared heads,
With the waiting depot, the arriving coffin, and the sombre faces,
With dirges through the night, with the thousand voices rising
strong and solemn,   40
With all the mournful voices of the dirges pour'd around the coffin,
The dim-lit churches and the shuddering organs—where amid these
you journey,

With the tolling tolling bells' perpetual clang,
Here, coffin that slowly passes,
I give you my sprig of lilac.   45

7

(Nor for you, for one alone,
Blossoms and branches green to coffins all I bring,
For fresh as the morning, thus would I chant a song for you O
    sane and sacred death.

All over bouquets of roses,
O death, I cover you over with roses and early lilies,   50
But mostly and now the lilac that blooms the first,
Copious I break, I break the sprigs from the bushes,
With loaded arms I come, pouring for you,
For you and the coffins all of you O death.)

8

O western orb sailing the heaven,   55
Now I know what you must have meant as a month since I walk'd,
As I walk'd in silence the transparent shadowy night,
As I saw you had something to tell as you bent to me night after
    night,
As you droop'd from the sky low down as if to my side, (while the
    other stars all look'd on,)
As we wander'd together the solemn night, (for something I know
    not what kept me from sleep,)   60
As the night advanced, and I saw on the rim of the west how full
    you were of woe,
As I stood on the rising ground in the breeze in the cool trans-
    parent night,
As I watch'd where you pass'd and was lost in the netherward black
    of the night,
As my soul in its trouble dissatisfied sank, as where you sad orb,
Concluded, dropt in the night, and was gone.   65

9

Sing on there in the swamp,
O singer bashful and tender, I hear your notes, I hear your call,
I hear, I come presently, I understand you,
But a moment I linger, for the lustrous star has detain'd me,
The star my departing comrade holds and detains me.   70

10

O how shall I warble myself for the dead one there I loved?
And how shall I deck my song for the large sweet soul that has
    gone?
And what shall my perfume be for the grave of him I love?

Sea-winds blown from east and west,
Blown from the Eastern sea and blown from the Western sea, till
    there on the prairies meeting,   75

These and with these and the breath of my chant,
I'll perfume the grave of him I love.

11

O what shall I hang on the chamber walls?
And what shall the pictures be that I hang on the walls,
To adorn the burial-house of him I love?   80

Pictures of growing spring and farms and homes,
With the Fourth-month eve at sundown, and the gray smoke lucid
    and bright,
With floods of the yellow gold of the gorgeous, indolent, sinking
    sun, burning, expanding the air,
With the fresh sweet herbage under foot, and the pale green leaves
    of the trees prolific,
In the distance the flowing glaze, the breast of the river, with a
    wind-dapple here and there,   85
With ranging hills on the banks, with many a line against the sky,
    and shadows,
And the city at hand with dwellings so dense, and stacks of chim-
    neys,
And all the scenes of life and the workshops, and the workmen
    homeward returning.

12

Lo, body and soul—this land,
My own Manhattan with spires, and the sparkling and hurrying
    tides, and the ships,   90
The varied and ample land, the South and the North in the light,
    Ohio's shores and flashing Missouri,
And ever the far-spreading prairies cover'd with grass and corn.

Lo, the most excellent sun so calm and haughty,
The violet and purple morn with just-felt breezes,
The gentle soft-born measureless light,   95
The miracle spreading bathing all, the fulfill'd noon,
The coming eve delicious, the welcome night and the stars,
Over my cities shining all, enveloping man and land.

13

Sing on, sing on you gray-brown bird,
Sing from the swamps, the recesses, pour your chant from the
    bushes,   100
Limitless out of the dusk, out of the cedars and pines.

Sing on dearest brother, warble your reedy song,
Loud human song, with voice of uttermost woe.

O liquid and free and tender!
O wild and loose to my soul—O wondrous singer,   105
You only I hear—yet the star holds me, (but will soon depart,)
Yet the lilac with mastering odor holds me.

14

Now while I sat in the day and look'd forth,
In the close of the day with its light and the fields of spring, and the
farmers preparing their crops,
In the large unconscious scenery of my land with its lakes and for-
ests,
In the heavenly aerial beauty, (after the perturb'd winds and the
storms,)
Under the arching heavens of the afternoon swift passing, and the
voices of children and women,
The many-moving sea-tides, and I saw the ships how they sail'd,
And the summer approaching with richness, and the fields all busy
with labor,
And the infinite separate houses, how they all went on, each with
its meals and minutia of daily usages,
And the streets how their throbbings throbb'd, and the cities pent—
lo, then and there,
Falling upon them all and among them all, enveloping me with the
rest,
Appear'd the cloud, appear'd the long black trail,
And I knew death, its thought, and the sacred knowledge of death.

Then with the knowledge of death as walking one side of me,
And the thought of death close-walking the other side of me,
And I in the middle as with companions, and as holding the hands
of companions,
I fled forth to the hiding receiving night that talks not,
Down to the shores of the water, the path by the swamp in the
dimness,
To the solemn shadowy cedars and ghostly pines so still.

And the singer so shy to the rest receiv'd me,
The gray-brown bird I know receiv'd us comrades three,
And he sang the carol of death, and a verse for him I love.

From deep secluded recesses,
From the fragrant cedars and the ghostly pines so still,
Came the carol of the bird.

And the charm of the carol rapt me,
As I held as if by their hands my comrades in the night,
And the voice of my spirit tallied the song of the bird.

Come lovely and soothing death,
Undulate round the world, serenely arriving, arriving,
In the day, in the night, to all, to each,
Sooner or later delicate death.

Prais'd be the fathomless universe,
For life and joy, and for objects and knowledge curious,   140
And for love, sweet love—but praise! praise! praise!
For the sure-enwinding arms of cool-enfolding death.

Dark mother always gliding near with soft feet,
Have none chanted for thee a chant of fullest welcome?
Then I chant it for thee, I glorify thee above all,   145
I bring thee a song that when thou must indeed come, come un-
*   falteringly.*

Approach strong deliveress,
When it is so, when thou hast taken them I joyously sing the dead,
Lost in the loving floating ocean of thee,
Laved in the flood of thy bliss O death.   150

From me to thee glad serenades,
Dances for thee I propose saluting thee, adornments and feastings
*   for thee,*
And the sights of the open landscape and the high-spread sky are
*   fitting,*
And life and the fields, and the huge and thoughtful night.

The night in silence under many a star,   155
The ocean shore and the husky whispering wave whose voice I know,
And the soul turning to thee O vast and well-veil'd death,
And the body gratefully nestling close to thee.

Over the tree-tops I float thee a song,
Over the rising and sinking waves, over the myriad fields and the
*   prairies wide,*   160
Over the dense-pack'd cities all and the teeming wharves and ways,
I float this carol with joy, with joy to thee O death.

15

To the tally of my soul,
Loud and strong kept up the gray-brown bird,
With pure deliberate notes spreading filling the night.   165

Loud in the pines and cedars dim,
Clear in the freshness moist and the swamp-perfume,
And I with my comrades there in the night.

While my sight that was bound in my eyes unclosed,
As to long panoramas of visions.   170

And I saw askant[7] the armies,
I saw as in noiseless dreams hundreds of battle-flags,

7. Askance, with mistrust.

Borne through the smoke of the battles and pierc'd with missiles I
    saw them,
And carried hither and yon through the smoke, and torn and bloody,
And at last but a few shreds left on the staffs, (and all in si-
    lence,)   175
And the staffs all splinter'd and broken.

I saw battle-corpses, myriads of them,
And the white skeletons of young men, I saw them,
I saw the debris and debris of all the slain soldiers of the war,
But I saw they were not as was thought,   180
They themselves were fully at rest, they suffer'd not,
The living remain'd and suffer'd, the mother suffer'd,
And the wife and the child and the musing comrade suffer'd,
And the armies that remain'd suffer'd.

16

Passing the visions, passing the night,   185
Passing, unloosing the hold of my comrade's hands,
Passing the song of the hermit bird and the tallying song of my soul,
Victorious song, death's outlet song, yet varying ever-altering song,
As low and wailing, yet clear the notes, rising and falling, flooding
    the night,
Sadly sinking and fainting, as warning and warning, and yet again
    bursting with joy,   190
Covering the earth and filling the spread of the heaven,
As that powerful psalm in the night I heard from recesses,
Passing, I leave thee lilac with heart-shaped leaves,
I leave thee there in the door-yard, blooming, returning with spring.

I cease from my song for thee,   195
From my gaze on thee in the west, fronting the west, communing
    with thee,
O comrade lustrous with silver face in the night.

Yet each to keep and all, retrievements out of the night,
The song, the wondrous chant of the gray-brown bird,
And the tallying chant, the echo arous'd in my soul,   200
With the lustrous and drooping star with the countenance full of
    woe,
With the holders holding my hand nearing the call of the bird,
Comrades mine and I in the midst, and their memory ever to keep,
    for the dead I loved so well,
For the sweetest, wisest soul of all my days and lands—and this for
    his dear sake,
Lilac and star and bird twined with the chant of my soul,   205
There in the fragrant pines and the cedars dusk and dim.

                           1865 (DT), 1867

O Captain! My Captain!

O Captain! my Captain! our fearful trip is done,
The ship has weather'd every rack, the prize we sought is won,
The port is near, the bells I hear, the people all exulting,
While follow eyes the steady keel, the vessel grim and daring;
          But O heart! heart! heart!   5
           O the bleeding drops of red,
              Where on the deck my Captain lies,
              Fallen cold and dead.

O Captain! my Captain! rise up and hear the bells;
Rise up—for you the flag is flung—for you the bugle trills,   10
For you bouquets and ribbon'd wreaths—for you the shores a-crowd-
    ing,
For you they call, the swaying mass, their eager faces turning;
          Here Captain! dear father!
            This arm beneath your head!
              It is some dream that on the deck,   15
              You've fallen cold and dead.

My Captain does not answer, his lips are pale and still,
My father does not feel my arm, he has no pulse nor will,
The ship is anchor'd safe and sound, its voyage closed and done,
From fearful trip the victor ship comes in with object won;   20
          Exult O shores, and ring O bells!
            But I with mournful tread,
              Walk the deck my Captain lies,
              Fallen cold and dead.

                         1865 (*DT*), 1867

Hush'd Be the Camps To-Day
(MAY 4, 1865)[8]

Hush'd be the camps to-day,
And soldiers let us drape our war-worn weapons,
And each with musing soul retire to celebrate,
Our dear commander's death.

No more for him life's stormy conflicts,   5
Nor victory, nor defeat—no more time's dark events,
Charging like ceaseless clouds across the sky.

But sing poet in our name,
Sing of the love we bore him—because you, dweller in camps, know
    it truly.

---

8. The day Lincoln's body was entombed in Springfield.

As they invault the coffin there,   10
Sing—as they close the doors of earth upon him—one verse,
For the heavy hearts of soldiers.

1865 (DT), 1867

This Dust Was Once the Man

This dust was once the man,
Gentle; plain, just and resolute, under whose cautious hand,
Against the foulest crime in history known in any land or age,
Was saved the Union of these States.

1871–72

From AUTUMN RIVULETS
As Consequent, Etc.

As consequent from store of summer rains,
Or wayward rivulets in autumn flowing,
Or many a herb-lined brook's reticulations,[9]
Or subterranean sea-rills making for the sea,
Songs of continued years I sing.   5

Life's ever-modern rapids first, (soon, soon to blend,
With the old streams of death.)

Some threading Ohio's farm-fields or the woods,
Some down Colorado's cañons from sources of perpetual snow,
Some half-hid in Oregon, or away southward in Texas,   10
Some in the north finding their way to Erie, Niagara, Ottawa,
Some to Atlantica's bays, and so to the great salt brine.

In you whoe'er you are my book perusing,
In I myself, in all the world, these currents flowing,
All, all toward the mystic ocean tending.   15

Currents for starting a continent new,
Overtures sent to the solid out of the liquid,
Fusion of ocean and land, tender and pensive waves,
(Not safe and peaceful only, waves rous'd and ominous too,
Out of the depths the storm's abysmic waves, who knows whence? 20
Raging over the vast, with many a broken spar and tatter'd sail.)

Or from the sea of Time, collecting vasting[1] all, I bring,
A windrow-drift of weeds and shells.

O little shells, so curious-convolute, so limpid-cold and voiceless,
Will you not little shells to the tympans of temples held,   25

9. Networks.   1. Laying waste, destroying.

Murmurs and echoes still call up, eternity's music faint and far,
Wafted inland, sent from Atlantica's rim, strains for the soul of the
   prairies,
Whisper'd reverberations, chords for the ear of the West joyously
   sounding,
Your tidings old, yet ever new and untranslatable,
Infinitesimals out of my life, and many a life,   30
(For not my life and years alone I give—all, all I give,)
These waifs from the deep, cast high and dry,
Wash'd on America's shores?

                                                    1876

There Was a Child Went Forth

There was a child went forth every day,
And the first object he look'd upon, that object he became,
And that object became part of him for the day or a certain part of
   the day,
Or for many years or stretching cycles of years.

The early lilacs became part of this child,   5
And grass and white and red morning-glories, and white and red
   clover, and the song of the phœbe-bird,
And the Third-month lambs and the sow's pink-faint litter, and the
   mare's foal and the cow's calf,
And the noisy brood of the barnyard or by the mire of the pond-
   side,
And the fish suspending themselves so curiously below there, and
   the beautiful curious liquid,
And the water-plants with their graceful flat heads, all became part
   of him.   10

The field-sprouts of Fourth-month and Fifth-month became part of
   him,
Winter-grain sprouts and those of the light-yellow corn, and the
   esculent roots of the garden,
And the apple-trees cover'd with blossoms and the fruit afterward,
   and wood-berries, and the commonest weeds by the road,
And the old drunkard staggering home from the outhouse of the
   tavern whence he had lately risen,
And the schoolmistress that pass'd on her way to the school,   15
And the friendly boys that pass'd, and the quarrelsome boys,
And the tidy and fresh-cheek'd girls, and the barefoot negro boy and
   girl,
And all the changes of city and country wherever he went.

His own parents, he that had father'd him and she that had conceiv'd him in her womb and birth'd him,

They gave this child more of themselves than that,   20
They gave him afterward every day, they became part of him.

The mother at home quietly placing the dishes on the supper-table,
The mother with mild words, clean her cap and gown, a wholesome
    odor falling off her person and clothes as she walks by,
The father, strong, self-sufficient, manly, mean, anger'd, unjust,
The blow, the quick loud word, the tight bargain, the crafty lure,   25
The family usages, the language, the company, the furniture, the
    yearning and swelling heart,
Affection that will not be gainsay'd, the sense of what is real, the
    thought if after all it should prove unreal,
The doubts of day-time and the doubts of night-time, the curious
    whether and how,
Whether that which appears so is so, or is it all flashes and specks?
Men and women crowding fast in the streets, if they are not flashes
    and specks what are they?   30
The streets themselves and the façades of houses, and goods in the
    windows,
Vehicles, teams, the heavy-plank'd wharves, the huge crossing at the
    ferries,
The village on the highland seen from afar at sunset, the river be-
    tween,
Shadows, aureola and mist, the light falling on roofs and gables
    of white or brown two miles off,
The schooner near by sleepily dropping down the tide, the little
    boat slack-tow'd astern,   35
The hurrying tumbling waves, quick-broken crests, slapping,
The strata of color'd clouds, the long bar of maroon-tint away soli-
    tary by itself, the spread of purity it lies motionless in,
The horizon's edge, the flying sea-crow, the fragrance of salt marsh
    and shore mud,
These became part of that child who went forth every day, and who
    now goes, and will always go forth every day.

                                                    1855

Out from Behind This Mask

(TO CONFRONT A PORTRAIT)

1

Out from behind this bending rough-cut mask,
These lights and shades, this drama of the whole,
This common curtain of the face contain'd in me for me, in you
    for you, in each for each,
(Tragedies, sorrows, laughter, tears—O heaven!
The passionate teeming plays this curtain hid!)   5
This glaze of God's serenest purest sky,
This film of Satan's seething pit,

This heart's geography's map, this limitless small continent, this
    soundless sea;
Out from the convolutions of this globe,
This subtler astronomic orb than sun or moon, than Jupiter, Venus,
    Mars,   10
This condensation of the universe, (nay here the only universe,
Here the idea, all in this mystic handful wrapt;)
These burin'd[2] eyes, flashing to you to pass to future time,
To launch and spin through space revolving sideling, from these to
    emanate,
To you whoe'er you are—a look.   15

2

A traveler of thoughts and years, of peace and war,
Of youth long sped and middle age declining,
(As the first volume of a tale perused and laid away, and this the
    second,
Songs, ventures, speculations, presently to close,)
Lingering a moment here and now, to you I opposite turn,   20
As on the road or at some crevice door by chance, or open'd window,
Pausing, inclining, baring my head, you specially I greet,
To draw and clinch your soul for once inseparably with mine,
Then travel travel on.

                                          1876

To a Common Prostitute

Be composed—be at ease with me—I am Walt Whitman, liberal
    and lusty as Nature,
Not till the sun excludes you do I exclude you,
Not till the waters refuse to glisten for you and the leaves to rustle
    for you, do my words refuse to glisten and rustle for you.

My girl I appoint with you an appointment, and I charge you that
    you make preparation to be worthy to meet me,
And I charge you that you be patient and perfect till I come.   5

Till then I salute you with a significant look that you do not forget
    me.

                                          1860

Sparkles from the Wheel

Where the city's ceaseless crowd moves on the livelong day,
Withdrawn I join a group of children watching, I pause aside with
    them.

2. Engraved on a copper plate.

By the curb toward the edge of the flagging,
A knife-grinder works at his wheel sharpening a great knife,
Bending over he carefully holds it to the stone, by foot and knee,   5
With measur'd tread he turns rapidly, as he presses with light but
    firm hand,
Forth issue then in copious golden jets,
Sparkles from the wheel.

The scene and all its belongings, how they seize and affect me,
The sad sharp-chinn'd old man with worn clothes and broad shoul-
    der-band of leather,   10
Myself effusing and fluid, a phantom curiously floating, now here
    absorb'd and arrested,
The group, (an unminded point set in a vast surrounding,)
The attentive, quiet children, the loud, proud, restive base of the
    streets,
The low hoarse purr of the whirling stone, the light-press'd blade,
Diffusing, dropping, sideways-darting, in tiny showers of gold,   15
Sparkles from the wheel.

1871–72

Unfolded out of the Folds

Unfolded out of the folds of the woman man comes unfolded, and
    is always to come unfolded,
Unfolded only out of the superbest woman of the earth is to come
    the superbest man of the earth,
Unfolded out of the friendliest woman is to come the friendliest
    man,
Unfolded only out of the perfect body of a woman can a man be
    form'd of perfect body,
Unfolded only out of the inimitable poems of woman can come the
    poems of man, (only thence have my poems come;)   5
Unfolded out of the strong and arrogant woman I love, only thence
    can appear the strong and arrogant man I love,
Unfolded by brawny embraces from the well-muscled woman I love,
    only thence come the brawny embraces of the man,
Unfolded out of the folds of the woman's brain come all the folds of
    the man's brain, duly obedient,
Unfolded out of the justice of the woman all justice is unfolded,
Unfolded out of the sympathy of the woman is all sympathy;   10
A man is a great thing upon the earth and through eternity, but
    every jot of the greatness of man is unfolded out of woman;
First the man is shaped in the woman, he can then be shaped in
    himself.

1856

Kosmos

Who includes diversity and is Nature,
Who is the amplitude of the earth, and the coarseness and sexual-
　　ity of the earth, and the great charity of the earth, and the
　　equilibrium also,
Who has not look'd forth from the windows the eyes for nothing,
　　or whose brain held audience with messengers for nothing,
Who contains believers and disbelievers, who is the most majestic
　　lover,
Who holds duly his or her triune proportion of realism, spiritualism,
　　and of the æsthetic or intellectual,　　　　　　　　　　5
Who having consider'd the body finds all its organs and parts good,
Who, out of the theory of the earth and of his or her body under-
　　stands by subtle analogies all other theories,
The theory of a city, a poem, and of the large politics of these States;
Who believes not only in our globe with its sun and moon, but in
　　other globes with their suns and moons,
Who, constructing the house of himself or herself, not for a day but
　　for all time, sees races, eras, dates, generations,　　　　10
The past, the future, dwelling there, like space, inseparable together.
　　　　　　　　　　　　　　　　　　　　　　　　1860

My Picture-Gallery

In a little house[3] keep I pictures suspended, it is not a fix'd house,
It is round, it is only a few inches from one side to the other;
Yet behold, it has room for all the shows of the world, all memories!
Here the tableaus of life, and here the groupings of death;
Here, do you know this? this is cicerone[4] himself,　　　　5
With finger rais'd he points to the prodigal pictures.
　　　　　　　　　　　　　　　　　　　　1881–82

The Prairie States

A newer garden of creation, no primal solitude,
Dense, joyous, modern, populous millions, cities and farms,
With iron interlaced, composite, tied, many in one,
By all the world contributed—freedom's and law's and thrift's so-
　　ciety,
The crown and teeming paradise, so far, of time's accumulations,　5
To justify the past.
　　　　　　　　　　　　　　　　　　　　1881–82

3. I.e., the brain.　　　　　　　4. A guide who shows the curiosities of
　　　　　　　　　　　　　　　a place to strangers.

Passage to India[5]

1

Singing my days,
Singing the great achievements of the present,
Singing the strong light works of engineers,
Our modern wonders, (the antique ponderous Seven outvied,)
In the Old World the east the Suez canal,   5
The New by its mighty railroad spann'd,
The seas inlaid with eloquent gentle wires;
Yet first to sound, and ever sound, the cry with thee O soul,
The Past! the Past! the Past!

The Past—the dark unfathom'd retrospect!   10
The teeming gulf—the sleepers and the shadows!
The past—the infinite greatness of the past!
For what is the present after all but a growth out of the past?
(As a projectile form'd, impell'd, passing a certain line, still keeps
    on,
So the present, utterly form'd, impell'd by the past.)   15

2

Passage O soul to India!
Eclaircise[6] the myths Asiatic, the primitive fables.

Not you alone proud truths of the world,
Nor you alone ye facts of modern science,
But myths and fables of eld,[7] Asia's, Africa's fables,   20
The far-darting beams of the spirit, the unloos'd dreams,
The deep diving bibles and legends,
The daring plots of the poets, the elder religions;
O you temples fairer than lilies pour'd over by the rising sun!
O you fables spurning the known, eluding the hold of the known,
    mounting to heaven!   25
You lofty and dazzling towers, pinnacled, red as roses, burnish'd
    with gold!
Towers of fables immortal fashion'd from mortal dreams!
You too I welcome and fully the same as the rest!
You too with joy I sing.

5. In this poem, the major production of the latter part of his life, Whitman celebrates the completion of three engineering feats: the completion of the Suez Canal in 1869; the joining of the Union Pacific and the Central Pacific railroads at Promontory Point, Utah, on May 10, 1869; and the laying of the Atlantic cable in 1866. These events, symbolizing the conclusion of the long search (beginning with Columbus) for a passage to India, fired Whitman's poetic imagination to its greatest heights, and he calls for a spiritual achievement to match the material. The poem is carefully constructed. The first three sections are devoted primarily to man's spanning the earth (space); the next three sections are glimpses down the slopes of history, both mythic and actual (time); and the final three sections describe the circumnavigation of the soul, the possibility of transcending both space and time, in mystic union with "light of the light" or the "Elder Brother," God.
6. Clear up or enlighten.
7. Antiquity.

Passage to India!   30
Lo, soul, seest thou not God's purpose from the first?
The earth to be spann'd, connected by network,
The races, neighbors, to marry and be given in marriage,
The oceans to be cross'd, the distant brought near,
The lands to be welded together.   35

A worship new I sing,
You captains, voyagers, explorers, yours,
You engineers, you architects, machinists, yours,
You, not for trade or transportation only,
But in God's name, and for thy sake O soul.   40

3

Passage to India!
Lo soul for thee of tableaus twain,
I see in one the Suez canal initiated, open'd,
I see the procession of steamships, the Empress Eugenie's leading
    the van,
I mark from on deck the strange landscape, the pure sky, the level
    sand in the distance,   45
I pass swiftly the picturesque groups, the workmen gather'd,
The gigantic dredging machines.

In one again, different, (yet thine, all thine, O soul, the same,)
I see over my own continent the Pacific railroad surmounting every
    barrier,
I see continual trains of cars winding along the Platte carrying
    freight and passengers,   50
I hear the locomotives rushing and roaring, and the shrill steam-
    whistle,
I hear the echoes reverberate through the grandest scenery in the
    world,
I cross the Laramie plains, I note the rocks in grotesque shapes, the
    buttes,
I see the plentiful larkspur and wild onions, the barren, colorless,
    sage-deserts,
I see in glimpses afar or towering immediately above me the great
    mountains, I see the Wind river and the Wahsatch moun-
    tains,   55
I see the Monument mountain and the Eagle's Nest, I pass the
    Promontory, I ascend the Nevadas,
I scan the noble Elk mountain and wind around its base,
I see the Humboldt range, I thread the valley and cross the river,
I see the clear waters of lake Tahoe, I see forests of majestic
    pines,
Or crossing the great desert, the alkaline plains, I behold enchant-
    ing mirages of waters and meadows,   60
Marking through these and after all, in duplicate slender lines,
Bridging the three or four thousand miles of land travel,

Tying the Eastern to the Western sea,
The road between Europe and Asia.

(Ah Genoese[8] thy dream! thy dream!   65
Centuries after thou art laid in thy grave,
The shore thou foundest verifies thy dream.)

4

Passage to India!
Struggles of many a captain, tales of many a sailor dead,
Over my mood stealing and spreading they come,   70
Like clouds and cloudlets in the unreach'd sky.

Along all history, down the slopes,
As a rivulet running, sinking now, and now again to the surface ris-
    ing,
A ceaseless thought, a varied train—lo, soul, to thee, thy sight, they
    rise,
The plans, the voyages again, the expeditions,   75
Again Vasco de Gama[9] sails forth,
Again the knowledge gain'd, the mariner's compass,
Lands found and nations born, thou born America,
For purpose vast, man's long probation fill'd,
Thou rondure of the world at last accomplish'd.   80

5

O vast Rondure, swimming in space,
Cover'd all over with visible power and beauty,
Alternate light and day and the teeming spiritual darkness,
Unspeakable high processions of sun and moon and countless stars
    above,
Below, the manifold grass and waters, animals, mountains, trees,   85
With inscrutable purpose, some hidden prophetic intention,
Now first it seems my thought begins to span thee.

Down from the gardens of Asia descending radiating,
Adam and Eve appear, then their myriad progeny after them,
Wandering, yearning, curious, with restless explorations,   90
With questionings, baffled, formless, feverish, with never-happy
    hearts,
With that sad incessant refrain, *Wherefore unsatisfied soul?* and
    Whither O mocking life?
Ah who shall soothe these feverish children?
Who justify these restless explorations?
Who speak the secret of impassive earth?   95
Who bind it to us? what is this separate Nature so unnatural?
What is this earth to our affections? (unloving earth, without a
    throb to answer ours,
Cold earth, the place of graves.)

8. I.e., Christopher Columbus.   9. Whitman's spelling for "da Gama."

Yet soul be sure the first intent remains, and shall be carried out,
Perhaps even now the time has arrived.   100

After the seas are all cross'd, (as they seem already cross'd,)
After the great captains and engineers have accomplish'd their work,
After the noble inventors, after the scientists, the chemist, the geolo-
    gist, ethnologist,
Finally shall come the poet worthy that name,
The true son of God shall come singing his songs.   105

Then not your deeds only O voyagers, O scientists and inventors,
    shall be justified,
All these hearts as of fretted children shall be sooth'd,
All affection shall be fully responded to, the secret shall be told,
All these separations and gaps shall be taken up and hook'd and
    link'd together,
The whole earth, this cold, impassive, voiceless earth, shall be com-
    pletely justified,   110
Trinitas divine shall be gloriously accomplish'd and compacted by
    the true son of God, the poet,
(He shall indeed pass the straits and conquer the mountains,
He shall double the cape of Good Hope to some purpose,)
Nature and Man shall be disjoin'd and diffused no more,
The true son of God shall absolutely fuse them.   115

6

Year at whose wide-flung door I sing!
Year of the purpose accomplish'd!
Year of the marriage of continents, climates and oceans!
(No mere doge of Venice now wedding the Adriatic,)
I see O year in you the vast terraqueous globe given and giving
    all,   120
Europe to Asia, Africa join'd, and they to the New World,
The lands, geographies, dancing before you, holding a festival gar-
    land,
As brides and bridegrooms hand in hand.

Passage to India!
Cooling airs from Caucasus far, soothing cradle of man,   125
The river Euphrates flowing, the past lit up again.

Lo soul, the retrospect brought forward,
The old, most populous, wealthiest of earth's lands,
The streams of the Indus and the Ganges and their many afflu-
    ents,
(I my shores of America walking to-day behold, resuming all,)   130
The tale of Alexander on his warlike marches suddenly dying,
On one side China and on the other side Persia and Arabia,
To the south the great seas and the bay of Bengal,
The flowing literatures, tremendous epics, religions, castes,

Old occult Brahma interminably far back, the tender and junior
    Buddha,   135
Central and southern empires and all their belongings, possessors,
The wars of Tamerlane, the reign of Aurungzebe,
The traders, rulers, explorers, Moslems, Venetians, Byzantium, the
    Arabs, Portuguese,
The first travelers famous yet, Marco Polo, Batouta the Moor,
Doubts to be solv'd, the map incognita, blanks to be fill'd,   140
The foot of man unstay'd, the hands never at rest,
Thyself O soul that will not brook a challenge.

The mediæval navigators rise before me,
The world of 1492, with its awaken'd enterprise,
Something swelling in humanity now like the sap of the earth in
    spring,   145
The sunset splendor of chivalry declining.

And who art thou sad shade?
Gigantic, visionary, thyself a visionary,
With majestic limbs and pious beaming eyes,
Spreading around with every look of thine a golden world,   150
Enhuing it with gorgeous hues.

As the chief histrion,[1]
Down to the footlights walks in some great scena,
Dominating the rest I see the Admiral[2] himself,
(History's type of courage, action, faith,)   155
Behold him sail from Palos leading his little fleet,
His voyage behold, his return, his great fame,
His misfortunes, calumniators, behold him a prisoner, chain'd,
Behold his dejection, poverty, death.

(Curious in time I stand, noting the efforts of heroes,   160
Is the deferment long? bitter the slander, poverty, death?
Lies the seed unreck'd for centuries in the ground? lo, to God's due
    occasion,
Uprising in the night, it sprouts, blooms,
And fills the earth with use and beauty.)

7

Passage indeed O soul to primal thought,   165
Not lands and seas alone, thy own clear freshness,
The young maturity of brood and bloom,
To realms of budding bibles.

O soul, repressless, I with thee and thou with me,
Thy circumnavigation of the world begin,   170
Of man, the voyage of his mind's return,
To reason's early paradise,

1. Actor.   2. Columbus.

Back, back to wisdom's birth, to innocent intuitions,
Again with fair creation.

8

O we can wait no longer,   175
We too take ship O soul,
Joyous we too launch out on trackless seas,
Fearless for unknown shores on waves of ecstasy to sail,
Amid the wafting winds, (thou pressing me to thee, I thee to me,
    O soul,)
Caroling free, singing our song of God,   180
Chanting our chant of pleasant exploration.

With laugh and many a kiss,
(Let others deprecate, let others weep for sin, remorse, humiliation,)
O soul, thou pleasest me, I thee.

Ah more than any priest O soul we too believe in God,   185
But with the mystery of God we dare not dally.

O soul thou pleasest me, I thee,
Sailing these seas or on the hills, or waking in the night,
Thoughts, silent thoughts, of Time and Space and Death, like wa-
    ters flowing,
Bear me indeed as through the regions infinite,   190
Whose air I breathe, whose ripples hear, lave me all over,
Bathe me O God in thee, mounting to thee,
I and my soul to range in range of thee.

O Thou transcendent,
Nameless, the fibre and the breath,   195
Light of the light, shedding forth universes, thou centre of them,
Thou mightier centre of the true, the good, the loving,
Thou moral, spiritual fountain—affection's source—thou reservoir,
(O pensive soul of me—O thirst unsatisfied—waitest not there?
Waitest not haply for us somewhere there the Comrade perfect?)   200
Thou pulse—thou motive of the stars, suns, systems,
That, circling, move in order, safe, harmonious,
Athwart the shapeless vastnesses of space,
How should I think, how breathe a single breath, how speak, if, out
    of myself,
I could not launch, to those, superior universes?   205

Swiftly I shrivel at the thought of God,
At Nature and its wonders, Time and Space and Death,
But that I, turning, call to thee O soul, thou actual Me,
And lo, thou gently masterest the orbs,
Thou matest Time, smilest content at Death,   210
And fillest, swellest full the vastnesses of Space.

Greater than stars or suns,
Bounding O soul thou journeyest forth;
What love than thine and ours could wider amplify?
What aspirations, wishes, outvie thine and ours O soul? 215
What dreams of the ideal? what plans of purity, perfection, strength,
What cheerful willingness for others' sake to give up all?
For others' sake to suffer all?

Reckoning ahead O soul, when thou, the time achiev'd,
The seas all cross'd, weather'd the capes, the voyage done, 220
Surrounded, copest, frontest God, yieldest, the aim attain'd,
As fill'd with friendship, love complete, the Elder Brother found,
The Younger melts in fondness in his arms.

9

Passage to more than India!
Are thy wings plumed indeed for such far flights? 225
O soul, voyagest thou indeed on voyages like those?
Disportest thou on waters such as those?
Soundest below the Sanscrit[3] and the Vedas?
Then have thy bent[4] unleash'd.

Passage to you, your shores, ye aged fierce enigmas! 230
Passage to you, to mastership of you, ye strangling problems!
You, strew'd with the wrecks of skeletons, that, living, never reach'd
    you.

Passage to more than India!
O secret of the earth and sky!
Of you O waters of the sea! O winding creeks and rivers! 235
Of you O woods and fields! of you strong mountains of my land!
Of you O prairies! of you gray rocks!
O morning red! O clouds! O rain and snows!
O day and night, passage to you!

O sun and moon and all you stars! Sirius and Jupiter! 240
Passage to you!

Passage, immediate passage! the blood burns in my veins!
Away O soul! hoist instantly the anchor!
Cut the hawsers—haul out—shake out every sail!
Have we not stood here like trees in the ground long enough? 245
Have we not grovel'd here long enough, eating and drinking like
    mere brutes?
Have we not darken'd and dazed ourselves with books long enough?

Sail forth—steer for the deep waters only,
Reckless O soul, exploring, I with thee, and thou with me,

3. Sanskrit (ancient classical language   of Hinduism.
of India). "Vedas": sacred scriptures   4. Impetus, concentrated energy.

For we are bound where mariner has not yet dared to go, 250
And we will risk the ship, ourselves and all.

O my brave soul!
O farther farther sail!
O daring joy, but safe! are they not all the seas of God?
O farther, farther, farther sail! 255

1871–72

Prayer of Columbus[5]

A batter'd, wreck'd old man,
Thrown on this savage shore, far, far from home,
Pent by the sea and dark rebellious brows, twelve dreary months,
Sore, stiff with many toils, sicken'd and nigh to death,
I take my way along the island's edge, 5
Venting a heavy heart.

I am too full of woe!
Haply I may not live another day;
I cannot rest O God, I cannot eat or drink or sleep,
Till I put forth myself, my prayer, once more to Thee, 10
Breathe, bathe myself once more in Thee, commune with Thee,
Report myself once more to Thee.

Thou knowest my years entire, my life,
My long and crowded life of active work, not adoration merely;
Thou knowest the prayers and vigils of my youth, 15
Thou knowest my manhood's solemn and visionary meditations,
Thou knowest how before I commenced I devoted all to come to
    Thee,
Thou knowest I have an age ratified all those vows and strictly kept
    them,
Thou knowest I have not once lost nor faith nor ecstasy in Thee,
In shackles, prison'd, in disgrace, repining not, 20
Accepting all from Thee, as duly come from Thee.

5. In 1876, the poem was introduced by the following note: "It was near the close of his indomitable and pious life—on his last voyage when nearly 70 years of age—that Columbus, to save his two remaining ships from foundering in the Caribbean Sea in a terrible storm, had to run them ashore on the Island of Jamaica where, laid up for a long and miserable year—1503 —he was taken very sick, had several relapses, his men revolted, and death seem'd daily imminent; though he was eventually rescued, and sent home to Spain to die, unrecognized, neglected and in want. * * * It is only ask'd, as preparation and atmosphere for the following lines, that the bare authentic facts be recall'd and realized, and nothing contributed by the fancy. See, the Antillean Island, with its florid skies and rich foliage and scenery, the waves beating the solitary sands, and the hulls of the ships in the distance. See, the figure of the great Admiral, walking the beach, as a stage, in this sublimest tragedy—for what tragedy, what poem, so piteous and majestic as the real scene?—and hear him uttering—as his mystical and religious soul surely utter'd, the ideas following—perhaps, in their equivalents, the very words."

All my emprises[6] have been fill'd with Thee,
My speculations, plans, begun and carried on in thoughts of Thee,
Sailing the deep or journeying the land for Thee;
Intentions, purports, aspirations mine, leaving results to Thee.   25

O I am sure they really came from Thee,
The urge, the ardor, the unconquerable will,
The potent, felt, interior command, stronger than words,
A message from the Heavens whispering to me even in sleep,
These sped me on.   30

By me and these the work so far accomplish'd,
By me earth's elder cloy'd and stifled lands uncloy'd, unloos'd,
By me the hemispheres rounded and tied, the unknown to the
     known.

The end I know not, it is all in Thee,
Or small or great I know not—haply what broad fields, what lands,
Haply the brutish measureless human undergrowth I know,   36
Transplanted there may rise to stature, knowledge worthy Thee,
Haply the swords I know may there indeed be turn'd to reaping-
     tools,
Haply the lifeless cross I know, Europe's dead cross, may bud and
     blossom there.

One effort more, my altar this bleak sand;   40
That Thou O God my life hast lighted,
With ray of light, steady, ineffable, vouchsafed of Thee,
Light rare untellable, lighting the very light,
Beyond all signs, descriptions, languages;
For that O God, be it my latest word, here on my knees,   45
Old, poor, and paralyzed, I thank Thee.

My terminus near,
The clouds already closing in upon me,
The voyage balk'd, the course disputed, lost,
I yield my ships to Thee.   50

My hands, my limbs grow nerveless,
My brain feels rack'd, bewilder'd,
Let the old timbers part, I will not part,
I will cling fast to Thee, O God, though the waves buffet me,
Thee, Thee at least I know.   55

Is it the prophet's thought I speak, or am I raving?
What do I know of life? what of myself?
I know not even my own work past or present,
Dim ever-shifting guesses of it spread before me,
Of newer better worlds, their mighty parturition,   60
Mocking, perplexing me.

6. Undertakings of an adventurous nature.

And these things I see suddenly, what mean they?
As if some miracle, some hand divine unseal'd my eyes,
Shadowy vast shapes smile through the air and sky,
And on the distant waves sail countless ships,   65
And anthems in new tongues I hear saluting me.

                                                                  1876

The Sleepers[7]

1

I wander all night in my vision,
Stepping with light feet, swiftly and noiselessly stepping and stop-
    ping,
Bending with open eyes over the shut eyes of sleepers,
Wandering and confused, lost to myself, ill-assorted, contradictory,
Pausing, gazing, bending, and stopping.   5

How solemn they look there, stretch'd and still,
How quiet they breathe, the little children in their cradles.

The wretched features of ennuyés,[8] the white features of corpses,
    the livid faces of drunkards, the sick-gray faces of onanists,
The gash'd bodies on battle-fields, the insane in their strong-door'd
    rooms, the sacred idiots, the new-born emerging from gates,
    and the dying emerging from gates,
The night pervades them and infolds them.   10

The married couple sleep calmly in their bed, he with his palm on
    the hip of the wife, and she with her palm on the hip of the
    husband,
The sisters sleep lovingly side by side in their bed,
The men sleep lovingly side by side in theirs,
And the mother sleeps with her little child carefully wrapt.

The blind sleep, and the deaf and dumb sleep,   15
The prisoner sleeps well in the prison, the runaway son sleeps,
The murderer that is to be hung next day, how does he sleep?
And the murder'd person, how does he sleep?

7. This is one of the most remarkable poems in *Leaves of Grass*, especially in its technique, which resembles in a startling way the stream-of-consciousness technique popular in the modern novel. Whitman's previous titles are illuminating as to his intention— "Night Poem" (1856) and "Sleep-Chasings" (1860). The device of the dream is used in such a way as to suggest Whitman's anticipation of the theories of dreams of the new psychologies of the 20th century. The flow or movement of the poem first suggests the restlessness and confusion of dream in early sleep, develops gradually into the lucidity of dream of profound sleep, and then changes again to the miscellaneous and fragmentary character of light dream in the emergence from sleep. The symbolism of the poem is complex, and is only hinted at in relating night to the world of spirituality and sleep to death, or release of the soul.
8. Bored and dissatisfied people.

The female that loves unrequited sleeps,
And the male that loves unrequited sleeps,   20
The head of the money-maker that plotted all day sleeps,
And the enraged and treacherous dispositions, all, all sleep.

I stand in the dark with drooping eyes by the worst-suffering and
    the most restless,
I pass my hands soothingly to and fro a few inches from them,
The restless sink in their beds, they fitfully sleep.   25

Now I pierce the darkness, new beings appear,
The earth recedes from me into the night,
I saw that it was beautiful, and I see that what is not the earth is
    beautiful.

I go from bedside to bedside, I sleep close with the other sleepers
    each in turn,
I dream in my dream all the dreams of the other dreamers,   30
And I become the other dreamers.

I am a dance—play up there! the fit is whirling me fast!

I am the ever-laughing—it is new moon and twilight,
I see the hiding of douceurs,[9] I see nimble ghosts whichever way I
    look,
Cache and cache again deep in the ground and sea, and where it is
    neither ground nor sea.   35

Well do they do their jobs those journeymen divine,
Only from me can they hide nothing, and would not if they could,
I reckon I am their boss and they make me a pet besides,
And surround me and lead me and run ahead when I walk,
To lift their cunning covers to signify me with stretch'd arms, and
    resume the way;   40
Onward we move, a gay gang of blackguards! with mirth-shouting
    music and wild-flapping pennants of joy!

I am the actor, the actress, the voter, the politician,
The emigrant and the exile, the criminal that stood in the box,
He who has been famous and he who shall be famous after to-day,
The stammerer, the well-formed person, the wasted or feeble per-
    son.   45

I am she who adorn'd herself and folded her hair expectantly,
My truant lover has come, and it is dark.

Double yourself and receive me darkness,
Receive me and my lover too, he will not let me go without him.

9. Bribes.

I roll myself upon you as upon a bed, I resign myself to the dusk. 50

He whom I call answers me and takes the place of my lover,
He rises with me silently from the bed.

Darkness, you are gentler than my lover, his flesh was sweaty and
    panting,
I feel the hot moisture yet that he left me.

My hands are spread forth, I pass them in all directions, 55
I would sound up the shadowy shore to which you are journeying.

Be careful darkness! already what was it touch'd me?
I thought my lover had gone, else darkness and he are one,
I hear the heart-beat, I follow, I fade away.

2

I descend my western course, my sinews are flaccid, 60
Perfume and youth course through me and I am their wake.

It is my face yellow and wrinkled instead of the old woman's,
I sit low in a straw-bottom chair and carefully darn my grandson's
    stockings.

It is I too, the sleepless widow looking out on the winter midnight,
I see the sparkles of starshine on the icy and pallid earth. 65

A shroud I see and I am the shroud, I wrap a body and lie in the
    coffin,
It is dark here under ground, it is not evil or pain here, it is blank
    here, for reasons.

(It seems to me that every thing in the light and air ought to be
    happy,
Whoever is not in his coffin and the dark grave let him know he
    has enough.)

3

I see a beautiful gigantic swimmer swimming naked through the
    eddies of the sea, 70
His brown hair lies close and even to his head, he strikes out with
    courageous arms, he urges himself with his legs,
I see his white body, I see his undaunted eyes,
I hate the swift-running eddies that would dash him head-foremost
    on the rocks.

What are you doing you ruffianly red-trickled waves?
Will you kill the courageous giant? will you kill him in the prime
    of his middle age? 75

Steady and long he struggles,
He is baffled, bang'd, bruis'd, he holds out while his strength holds
out,
The slapping eddies are spotted with his blood, they bear him away,
they roll him, swing him, turn him,
His beautiful body is borne in the circling eddies, it is continually
bruis'd on rocks,
Swiftly and out of sight is borne the brave corpse.   80

4

I turn but do not extricate myself,
Confused, a past-reading, another, but with darkness yet.

The beach is cut by the razory ice-wind, the wreck-guns sound,
The tempest lulls, the moon comes floundering through the drifts.

I look where the ship helplessly heads end on, I hear the burst as
she strikes, I hear the howls of dismay, they grow fainter and
fainter.   85

I cannot aid with my wringing fingers,
I can but rush to the surf and let it drench me and freeze upon me.

I search with the crowd, not one of the company is wash'd to us
alive,
In the morning I help pick up the dead and lay them in rows in a
barn.

5

Now of the older war-days, the defeat at Brooklyn,   90
Washington stands inside the lines, he stands on the intrench'd
hills amid a crowd of officers,
His face is cold and damp, he cannot repress the weeping drops,
He lifts the glass perpetually to his eyes, the color is blanch'd from
his cheeks,
He sees the slaughter of the southern braves confided to him by
their parents.

The same at last and at last when peace is declared,   95
He stands in the room of the old tavern, the well-belov'd soldiers
all pass through,
The officers speechless and slow draw near in their turns,
The chief encircles their necks with his arm and kisses them on the
cheek,
He kisses lightly the wet cheeks one after another, he shakes hands
and bids good-by to the army.

6

Now what my mother told me one day as we sat at dinner together,   100
Of when she was a nearly grown girl living home with her parents
on the old homestead.

A red squaw came one breakfast-time to the old homestead,
On her back she carried a bundle of rushes for rush-bottoming
    chairs,
Her hair, straight, shiny, coarse, black, profuse, half-envelop'd her
    face,
Her step was free and elastic, and her voice sounded exquisitely as
    she spoke.   105

My mother look'd in delight and amazement at the stranger,
She look'd at the freshness of her tall-borne face and full and pliant
    limbs,
The more she look'd upon her she loved her,
Never before had she seen such wonderful beauty and purity,
She made her sit on a bench by the jamb of the fireplace, she cook'd
    food for her,   110
She had no work to give her, but she gave her remembrance and
    fondness.

The red squaw staid all the forenoon, and toward the middle of the
    afternoon she went away,
O my mother was loth[1] to have her go away,
All the week she thought of her, she watch'd for her many a month,
She remember'd her many a winter and many a summer,   115
But the red squaw never came nor was heard of there again.

7

A show of the summer softness—a contact of something unseen—
    an amour of the light and air,
I am jealous and overwhelm'd with friendliness,
And will go gallivant with the light and air myself.

O love and summer, you are in the dreams and in me,   120
Autumn and winter are in the dreams, the farmer goes with his
    thrift,
The droves and crops increase, the barns are well-fill'd.

Elements merge in the night, ships make tacks in the dreams,
The sailor sails, the exile returns home,
The fugitive returns unharm'd, the immigrant is back beyond
    months and years,   125
The poor Irishman lives in the simple house of his childhood with
    the well-known neighbors and faces,
They warmly welcome him, he is barefoot again, he forgets he is
    well off,
The Dutchman voyages home, and the Scotchman and Welshman
    voyage home, and the native of the Mediterranean voyages
    home,
To every port of England, France, Spain, enter well-fill'd ships,

1. Loath, reluctant.

The Swiss foots it toward his hills, the Prussian goes his way, the
    Hungarian his way, and the Pole his way,   130
The Swede returns, and the Dane and Norwegian return.

The homeward bound and the outward bound,
The beautiful lost swimmer, the ennuyé, the onanist, the female
    that loves unrequited, the money-maker,
The actor and actress, those through with their parts and those wait-
    ing to commence,
The affectionate boy, the husband and wife, the voter, the nominee
    that is chosen and the nominee that has fail'd,   135
The great already known and the great any time after to-day,
The stammerer, the sick, the perfect-form'd, the homely,
The criminal that stood in the box, the judge that sat and sentenced
    him, the fluent lawyers, the jury, the audience,
The laugher and weeper, the dancer, the midnight widow, the red
    squaw,
The consumptive, the erysipalite, the idiot, he that is wrong'd,   140
The antipodes, and every one between this and them in the dark,
I swear they are averaged now—one is no better than the other,
The night and sleep have liken'd them and restored them.

I swear they are all beautiful,
Every one that sleeps is beautiful, every thing in the dim light is
    beautiful,   145
The wildest and bloodiest is over, and all is peace.

Peace is always beautiful,
The myth of heaven indicates peace and night.

The myth of heaven indicates the soul,
The soul is always beautiful, it appears more or it appears less, it
    comes or it lags behind,   150
It comes from its embower'd garden and looks pleasantly on itself
    and encloses the world,
Perfect and clean the genitals previously jetting,[2] and perfect and
    clean the womb cohering,
The head well-grown proportion'd and plumb, and the bowels
    and joints proportion'd and plumb.

The soul is always beautiful,
The universe is duly in order, every thing is in its place,   155
What has arrived is in its place and what waits shall be in its place,
The twisted skull waits, the watery or rotten blood waits,
The child of the glutton or venerealee waits long, and the child of
    the drunkard waits long, and the drunkard himself waits long,
The sleepers that lived and died wait, the far advanced are to go on
    in their turns, and the far behind are to come on in their turns,

2. Spurting forth of sperm.

The diverse shall be no less diverse, but they shall flow and unite—
    they unite now.   160

8

The sleepers are very beautiful as they lie unclothed,
They flow hand in hand over the whole earth from east to west as
    they lie unclothed,
The Asiatic and African are hand in hand, the European and Ameri-
    can are hand in hand,
Learn'd and unlearn'd are hand in hand, and male and female are
    hand in hand,
The bare arm of the girl crosses the bare breast of her lover, they
    press close without lust, his lips press her neck,   165
The father holds his grown or ungrown son in his arms with meas-
    ureless love, and the son holds the father in his arms with
    measureless love,
The white hair of the mother shines on the white wrist of the
    daughter,
The breath of the boy goes with the breath of the man, friend is
    inarm'd by friend,
The scholar kisses the teacher and the teacher kisses the scholar, the
    wrong'd is made right,
The call of the slave is one with the master's call, and the master
    salutes the slave,   170
The felon steps forth from the prison, the insane becomes sane, the
    suffering of sick persons is reliev'd,
The sweatings and fevers stop, the throat that was unsound is
    sound, the lungs of the consumptive are resumed, the poor
    distress'd head is free,
The joints of the rheumatic move as smoothly as ever, and smoother
    than ever,
Stiflings and passages open, the paralyzed become supple,
The swell'd and convuls'd and congested awake to themselves in
    condition,   175
They pass the invigoration of the night and the chemistry of the
    night, and awake.

I too pass from the night,
I stay a while away O night, but I return to you again and love you.

Why should I be afraid to trust myself to you?
I am not afraid, I have been well brought forward by you,   180
I love the rich running day, but I do not desert her in whom I lay
    so long,
I know not how I came of you and I know not where I go with
    you, but I know I came well and shall go well.

I will stop only a time with the night, and rise betimes,
I will duly pass the day O my mother, and duly return to you.

1855

From WHISPERS OF HEAVENLY DEATH
Whispers of Heavenly Death

Whispers of heavenly death murmur'd I hear,
Labial gossip of night, sibilant chorals,
Footsteps gently ascending, mystical breezes wafted soft and low,
Ripples of unseen rivers, tides of a current flowing, forever flowing,
(Or is it the plashing of tears? the measureless waters of human
    tears?)   5

I see, just see skyward, great cloud-masses,
Mournfully slowly they roll, silently swelling and mixing,
With at times a half-dimm'd sadden'd far-off star,
Appearing and disappearing.

(Some parturition rather, some solemn immortal birth;   10
On the frontiers to eyes impenetrable,
Some soul is passing over.)

                          1871–72

Chanting the Square Deific

1

Chanting the square deific, out of the One advancing, out of the
    sides,
Out of the old and new, out of the square entirely divine,
Solid, four-sided, (all the sides needed,) from this side Jehovah am
    I,
Old Brahm I, and I Saturnius am;[3]
Not Time affects me—I am Time, old, modern as any,   5
Unpersuadable, relentless, executing righteous judgments,
As the Earth, the Father, the brown old Kronos, with laws,
Aged beyond computation, yet ever new, ever with those mighty
    laws rolling,
Relentless I forgive no man—whoever sins dies—I will have that
    man's life;
Therefore let none expect mercy—have the seasons, gravitation, the
    appointed days, mercy? no more have I,   10
But as the seasons and gravitation, and as all the appointed days
    that forgive not,
I dispense from this side judgments inexorable without the least re-
    morse.

2

Consolator most mild, the promis'd one advancing,
With gentle hand extended, the mightier God am I,

3. "Brahm": Brahma, the Supreme Being in Hinduism. "Saturnius": Saturn,
in classical times identified with the
Greek Kronos, the father of Zeus
(Jupiter).

Foretold by prophets and poets in their most rapt prophecies and
  poems,   15
From this side, lo! the Lord Christ gazes—lo! Hermes I—lo! mine is
  Hercules' face,
All sorrow, labor, suffering, I, tallying it, absorb in myself,
Many times have I been rejected, taunted, put in prison, and cruci-
  fied, and many times shall be again,
All the world have I given up for my dear brothers' and sisters' sake,
  for the soul's sake,
Wending my way through the homes of men, rich or poor, with the
  kiss of affection,   20
For I am affection, I am the cheer-bringing God, with hope and all-
  enclosing charity,
With indulgent words as to children, with fresh and sane words,
  mine only,
Young and strong I pass knowing well I am destin'd myself to an
  early death;
But my charity has no death—my wisdom dies not, neither early
  nor late,
And my sweet love bequeath'd here and elsewhere never dies.   25

3

Aloof, dissatisfied, plotting revolt,
Comrade of criminals, brother of slaves,
Crafty, despised, a drudge, ignorant,
With sudra[4] face and worn brow, black, but in the depths of my
  heart, proud as any,
Lifted now and always against whoever scorning assumes to rule
  me,   30
Morose, full of guile, full of reminiscences, brooding, with many
  wiles,
(Though it was thought I was baffled and dispel'd, and my wiles
  done, but that will never be,)
Defiant, I, Satan, still live, still utter words, in new lands duly ap-
  pearing, (and old ones also,)
Permanent here from my side, warlike, equal with any, real as
  any,
Nor time nor change shall ever change me or my words.   35

4

Santa Spirita, breather, life,
Beyond the light, lighter than light,
Beyond the flames of hell, joyous, leaping easily above hell,
Beyond Paradise, perfumed solely with mine own perfume,
Including all life on earth, touching, including God, including Sav-
  iour and Satan,   40
Ethereal, pervading all, (for without me what were all? what were
  God?)
Essence of forms, life of the real identities, permanent, positive,
  (namely the unseen,)

4. Pertaining to a Sudra, a member of the lowest of the four great Hindu castes.

Life of the great round world, the sun and stars, and of man, I, the
general soul,
Here the square finishing, the solid, I the most solid,
Breathe my breath also through these songs.   45

1865 (DT), 1867

Quicksand Years

Quicksand years that whirl me I know not whither,
Your schemes, politics, fail, lines give way, substances mock and
elude me,
Only the theme I sing, the great and strong-possess'd soul, eludes
not,
One's-self must never give way—that is the final substance—that
out of all is sure,
Out of politics, triumphs, battles, life, what at last finally remains? 5
When shows break up what but One's-Self is sure?

1865 (DT), 1867

That Music Always Round Me

That music always round me, unceasing, unbeginning, yet long un-
taught I did not hear,
But now the chorus I hear and am elated,
A tenor, strong, ascending with power and health, with glad notes
of daybreak I hear,
A soprano at intervals sailing buoyantly over the tops of immense
waves,
A transparent base shuddering lusciously under and through the universe,   5
The triumphant tutti, the funeral wailings with sweet flutes and vio-
lins, all these I fill myself with,
I hear not the volumes of sound merely, I am moved by the exquisite
meanings,
I listen to the different voices winding in and out, striving, contending with fiery vehemence to excel each other in emotion;
I do not think the performers know themselves—but now I think I
begin to know them.

1860

A Noiseless Patient Spider

A noiseless patient spider,
I mark'd where on a little promontory it stood isolated,
Mark'd how to explore the vacant vast surrounding,
It launch'd forth filament, filament, filament, out of itself,
Ever unreeling them, ever tirelessly speeding them.   5

And you O my soul where you stand,
Surrounded, detached, in measureless oceans of space,
Ceaselessly musing, venturing, throwing, seeking the spheres to con-
    nect them,
Till the bridge you will need be form'd, till the ductile anchor hold,
Till the gossamer thread you fling catch somewhere, O my soul. 10

1871–72

From FROM NOON TO STARRY NIGHT
To a Locomotive in Winter

Thee for my recitative,
Thee in the driving storm even as now, the snow, the winter-day
    declining,
Thee in thy panoply, thy measur'd dual throbbing and thy beat
    convulsive,
Thy black cylindric body, golden brass and silvery steel,
Thy ponderous side-bars, parallel and connecting rods, gyrating,
    shuttling at thy sides,   5
Thy metrical, now swelling pant and roar, now tapering in the dis-
    tance,
Thy great protruding head-light fix'd in front,
Thy long, pale, floating vapor-pennants, tinged with delicate pur-
    ple,
The dense and murky clouds out-belching from thy smoke-stack,
Thy knitted frame, thy springs and valves, the tremulous twinkle of
    thy wheels,   10
Thy train of cars behind, obedient, merrily following,
Through gale or calm, now swift, now slack, yet steadily careering;
Type of the modern—emblem of motion and power—pulse of the
    continent,
For once come serve the Muse and merge in verse, even as here I
    see thee,
With storm and buffeting gusts of wind and falling snow,   15
By day thy warning ringing bell to sound its notes,
By night thy silent signal lamps to swing.

Fierce-throated beauty!
Roll through my chant with all thy lawless music, thy swinging
    lamps at night,
Thy madly-whistled laughter, echoing, rumbling like an earthquake,
    rousing all,   20
Law of thyself complete, thine own track firmly holding,
(No sweetness debonair of tearful harp or glib piano thine,)
Thy trills of shrieks by rocks and hills return'd,
Launch'd o'er the prairies wide, across the lakes,
To the free skies unpent and glad and strong.   25

1876

From Songs of Parting
Joy, Shipmate, Joy!

Joy, shipmate, joy!
(Pleas'd to my soul at death I cry,)
Our life is closed, our life begins,
The long, long anchorage we leave,
The ship is clear at last, she leaps!   5
She swiftly courses from the shore,
Joy, shipmate, joy!

                                                1871–72

Now Finalè to the Shore

Now finalè to the shore,
Now land and life finalè and farewell,
Now Voyager depart, (much, much for thee is yet in store,)
Often enough hast thou adventur'd o'er the seas,
Cautiously cruising, studying the charts,   5
Duly again to port and hawser's tie returning;
But now obey thy cherish'd secret wish,
Embrace thy friends, leave all in order,
To port and hawser's tie no more returning,
Depart upon thy endless cruise old Sailor.   10

                                                1871–72

So Long![5]

To conclude, I announce what comes after me.

I remember I said before my leaves sprang at all,
I would raise my voice jocund and strong with reference to consum-
      mations.

When America does what was promis'd,
When through these States walk a hundred millions of superb per-
      sons,   5
When the rest part away for superb persons and contribute to them,
When breeds of the most perfect mothers denote America,
Then to me and mine our due fruition.

I have press'd through in my own right,
I have sung the body and the soul, war and peace have I sung, and
      the songs of life and death,   10
And the songs of birth, and shown that there are many births.

I have offer'd my style to every one, I have journey'd with confident
      step;

5. Whitman's comment: "A delicious American-New York-idiomatic phrase at parting—equivalent to 'good bye' 'adieu' etc."

While my pleasure is yet at the full I whisper *So long!*
And take the young woman's hand and the young man's hand for
the last time.

I announce natural persons to arise,   15
I announce justice triumphant,
I announce uncompromising liberty and equality,
I announce the justification of candor and the justification of pride.

I announce that the identity of these States is a single identity only,
I announce the Union more and more compact, indissoluble,   20
I announce splendors and majesties to make all the previous politics
of the earth insignificant.

I announce adhesiveness,[6] I say it shall be limitless, unloosen'd,
I say you shall yet find the friend you were looking for.

I announce a man or woman coming, perhaps you are the one, (*So
long!*)
I announce the great individual, fluid as Nature, chaste, affectionate,
compassionate, fully arm'd.   25

I announce a life that shall be copious, vehement, spiritual, bold,
I announce an end that shall lightly and joyfully meet its translation.

I announce myriads of youths, beautiful, gigantic, sweet-blooded,
I announce a race of splendid and savage old men.

O thicker and faster—(*So long!*)   30
O crowding too close upon me,
I foresee too much, it means more than I thought,
It appears to me I am dying.

Hasten throat and sound your last,
Salute me—salute the days once more. Peal the old cry once
more.   35

Screaming electric, the atmosphere using,
At random glancing, each as I notice absorbing,
Swiftly on, but a little while alighting,
Curious envelop'd messages delivering,
Sparkles hot, seed ethereal down in the dirt dropping,   40
Myself unknowing, my commission obeying, to question it never
daring,
To ages and ages yet the growth of the seed leaving,
To troops out of the war arising, they the tasks I have set promulging,
To women certain whispers of myself bequeathing, their affection
me more clearly explaining,
To young men my problems offering—no dallier I—I the muscle of
their brains trying,
So I pass, a little time vocal, visible, contrary,   45

---

6. Term from phrenology: a mental faculty manifested in lasting friendship, fraternity, companionship.

Afterward a melodious echo, passionately bent for, (death making
    me really undying,)
The best of me then when no longer visible, for toward that I have
    been incessantly preparing.

What is there more, that I lag and pause and crouch extended with
    unshut mouth?
Is there a single final farewell?   50

My songs cease, I abandon them,
From behind the screen where I hid I advance personally solely to
    you.

Camerado, this is no book,
Who touches this touches a man,
(Is it night? are we here together alone?)   55
It is I you hold and who holds you,
I spring from the pages into your arms—decease calls me forth.

O how your fingers drowse me,
Your breath falls around me like dew, your pulse lulls the tympans
    of my ears,
I feel immerged from head to foot,   60
Delicious, enough.

Enough O deed impromptu and secret,
Enough O gliding present—enough O summ'd-up past.

Dear friend whoever you are take this kiss,
I give it especially to you, do not forget me,   65
I feel like one who has done work for the day to retire awhile,
I receive now again of my many translations, from my avataras[7]
    ascending, while others doubtless await me,
An unknown sphere more real than I dream'd, more direct, darts
    awakening rays about me, *So long!*
Remember my words, I may again return,
I love you, I depart from materials,   70
I am as one disembodied, triumphant, dead.

                                   1860

From FIRST ANNEX: SANDS AT SEVENTY
As I Sit Writing Here

As I sit writing here, sick and grown old,
Not my least burden is that dulness of the years, querilities,
Ungracious glooms, aches, lethargy, constipation, whimpering *ennui*,
May filter in my daily songs.
                       1888 (*NB*), 1889

7. Sanskrit for *avatars,* incarnations.

With Husky-Haughty Lips, O Sea!

With husky-haughty lips, O sea!
Where day and night I wend thy surf-beat shore,
Imaging to my sense thy varied strange suggestions,
(I see and plainly list thy talk and conference here,)
Thy troops of white-maned racers racing to the goal, 5
Thy ample, smiling face, dash'd with the sparkling dimples of the
 sun,
Thy brooding scowl and murk—thy unlos'd hurricanes,
Thy unsubduedness, caprices, wilfulness;
Great as thou art above the rest, thy many tears—a lack from all
 eternity in thy content,
(Naught but the greatest struggles, wrongs, defeats, could make thee
 greatest—no less could make thee,) 10
Thy lonely state—something thou ever seek'st and seek'st, yet never
 gain'st,
Surely some right withheld—some voice, in huge monotonous rage,
 of freedom-lover pent,
Some vast heart, like a planet's, chain'd and chafing in those break-
 ers,
By lengthen'd swell, and spasm, and panting breath,
And rhythmic rasping of thy sands and waves, 15
And serpent hiss, and savage peals of laughter,
And undertones of distant lion roar,
(Sounding, appealing to the sky's deaf ear—but now, rapport for
 once,
A phantom in the night thy confidant for once,)
The first and last confession of the globe, 20
Outsurging, muttering from thy soul's abysms,
The tale of cosmic elemental passion,
Thou tellest to a kindred soul.

 1888 (NB), 1889

After the Supper and Talk

After the supper and talk—after the day is done,
As a friend from friends his final withdrawal prolonging,
Good-bye and Good-bye with emotional lips repeating,
(So hard for his hand to release those hands—no more will they
 meet,
No more for communion of sorrow and joy, of old and young, 5
A far-stretching journey awaits him, to return no more,)
Shunning, postponing severance—seeking to ward off the last word
 ever so little,
E'en at the exit-door turning—charges superfluous calling back—
 e'en as he descends the steps,

Something to eke out a minute additional—shadows of nightfall
    deepening,
Farewells, messages lessening—dimmer the forthgoer's visage and
    form,   10
Soon to be lost for aye in the darkness—loth, O so loth to depart!
Garrulous to the very last.

1888 (NB), 1889

From SECOND ANNEX: GOOD-BYE MY FANCY
L. of G.'s Purport

Not to exclude or demarcate, or pick out evils from their formidable
    masses (even to expose them,)
But add, fuse, complete, extend—and celebrate the immortal and
    the good.

Haughty this song, its words and scope,
To span vast realms of space and time,
Evolution—the cumulative—growths and generations.   5

Begun in ripen'd youth and steadily pursued,
Wandering, peering, dallying with all—war, peace, day and night
    absorbing,
Never even for one brief hour abandoning my task,
I end it here in sickness, poverty, and old age.

I sing of life, yet mind me well of death: 10
To-day shadowy Death dogs my steps, my seated shape, and has for
    years—
Draws sometimes close to me, as face to face.

1891–92

Unseen Buds

Unseen buds, infinite, hidden well,
Under the snow and ice, under the darkness, in every square or cubic
    inch,
Germinal, exquisite, in delicate lace, microscopic, unborn,
Like babes in wombs, latent, folded, compact, sleeping;
Billions of billions, and trillions of trillions of them waiting,   5
(On earth and in the sea—the universe—the stars there in the
    heavens,)
Urging slowly, surely forward, forming endless,
And waiting ever more, forever more behind.

1891–92

Good-Bye My Fancy!

Good-bye my Fancy!
Farewell dear mate, dear love!
I'm going away, I know not where,
Or to what fortune, or whether I may ever see you again,
So Good-bye my Fancy.   5

Now for my last—let me look back a moment;
The slower fainter ticking of the clock is in me,
Exit, nightfall, and soon the heart-thud stopping.

Long have we lived, joy'd, caress'd together;
Delightful!—now separation—Good-bye my Fancy.   10

Yet let me not be too hasty,
Long indeed have we lived, slept, filter'd, become really blended
    into one;
Then if we die we die together, (yes, we'll remain one,)
If we go anywhere we'll go together to meet what happens,
May-be we'll be better off and blither, and learn something,   15
May-be it is yourself now really ushering me to the true songs, (who
    knows?)
May-be it is you the mortal knob really undoing, turning—so now
    finally,
Good-bye—and hail! my Fancy.

1891–92

A Backward Glance o'er Travel'd Roads[8]
[*Preface to* November Boughs, *1888*]

Perhaps the best of songs heard, or of any and all true love, or
life's fairest episodes, or sailors', soldiers' trying scenes on land or
sea, is the *résumé* of them, or any of them, long afterwards, looking
at the actualities away back past, with all their practical excitations
gone. How the soul loves to float amid such reminiscences!

So here I sit gossiping in the early candle-light of old age—I and
my book—casting backward glances over our travel'd road. After
completing, as it were, the journey—(a varied jaunt of years, with
many halts and gaps of intervals—or some lengthen'd ship-voyage,

8. As the 1855 Preface was an expression of ambition and vision, "Backward Glance" (first published in *November Boughs*, 1888) is an assessment
of achievement. In many ways, this is
Whitman's most satisfactory prose
piece, as it somewhat systematically
defines the various themes of *Leaves*
and measures their actual realization.
Whitman included "A Backward
Glance" in both the 8th (1889) edition
and the 9th edition of *Leaves;* it therefore has immense importance as his final
statement (the one he wanted preserved
and known) on his work.

wherein more than once the last hour had apparently arrived, and we seem'd certainly going down—yet reaching port in a sufficient way through all discomfitures at last)—After completing my poems, I am curious to review them in the light of their own (at the time unconscious, or mostly unconscious) intentions, with certain unfoldings of the thirty years they seek to embody. These lines, therefore, will probably blend the weft of first purposes and speculations, with the warp[9] of that experience afterwards, always bringing strange developments.

Result of seven or eight stages and struggles extending through nearly thirty years, (as I nigh my three-score-and-ten I live largely on memory,) I look upon "Leaves of Grass," now finish'd to the end of its opportunities and powers, as my definitive *carte visite* to the coming generations of the New World,[1] if I may assume to say so. That I have not gain'd the acceptance of my own time, but have fallen back on fond dreams of the future—anticipations—("still lives the song, though Regnar dies")—That from a worldly and business point of view "Leaves of Grass" has been worse than a failure—that public criticism on the book and myself as author of it yet shows mark'd anger and contempt more than anything else —("I find a solid line of enemies to you everywhere,"—letter from W. S. K., Boston, May 28, 1884)—And that solely for publishing it I have been the object of two or three pretty serious special official buffetings—is all probably no more than I ought to have expected. I had my choice when I commenc'd. I bid neither for soft eulogies, big money returns, nor the approbation of existing schools and conventions. As fulfill'd or partially fulfill'd, the best comfort of the whole business (after a small band of the dearest friends and upholders ever vouchsafed to man or cause—doubtless all the more faithful and uncompromising—this little phalanx!—for being so few) is that, unstopp'd and unwarp'd by any influence outside the soul within me, I have had my say entirely my own way, and put it unerringly on record—the value thereof to be decided by time.

In calculating that decision, William O'Connor and Dr. Bucke[2] are far more peremptory than I am. Behind all else that can be said, I consider "Leaves of Grass" and its theory experimental—as, in the deepest sense, I consider our American republic itself to be, with its theory. (I think I have at least enough philosophy not to be too absolutely certain of anything, or any results.) In the second place, the volume is a *sortie*—whether to prove triumphant, and conquer its field of aim and escape and construction, nothing less than a

9. "Weft" is the filling yarn; "warp" is the yarn placed lengthwise in a loom.
1. "When Champollion [French Egyptologist, 1790–1832], on his death-bed, handed to the printer the revised proof of his 'Egyptian Grammar,' he said gayly, 'Be careful of this—it is my *carte de visite* to posterity' " [Whitman's note].
2. Friends and admirers of Whitman.

hundred years from now can fully answer. I consider the point that I have positively gain'd a hearing, to far more than make up for any and all other lacks and withholdings. Essentially, *that* was from the first, and has remain'd throughout, the main object. Now it seems to be achiev'd, I am certainly contented to waive any otherwise momentous drawbacks, as of little account. Candidly and dispassionately reviewing all my intentions, I feel that they were creditable—and I accept the result, whatever it may be.

After continued personal ambition and effort, as a young fellow, to enter with the rest into competition for the usual rewards, business, political, literary, &c.—to take part in the great *mêlée*, both for victory's prize itself and to do some good—After years of those aims and pursuits, I found myself remaining possess'd, at the age of thirty-one to thirty-three, with a special desire and conviction. Or rather, to be quite exact, a desire that had been flitting through my previous life, or hovering on the flanks, mostly indefinite hitherto, had steadily advanced to the front, defined itself, and finally dominated everything else. This was a feeling or ambition to articulate and faithfully express in literary or poetic form, and uncompromisingly, my own physical, emotional, moral, intellectual, and æsthetic Personality, in the midst of, and tallying, the momentous spirit and facts of its immediate days, and of current America—and to exploit that Personality, identified with place and date, in a far more candid and comprehensive sense than any hitherto poem or book.

Perhaps this is in brief, or suggests, all I have sought to do. Given the Nineteenth Century, with the United States, and what they furnish as area and points of view, "Leaves of Grass" is, or seeks to be, simply a faithful and doubtless self-will'd record. In the midst of all, it gives one man's—the author's—identity, ardors, observations, faiths, and thoughts, color'd hardly at all with any decided coloring from other faiths or other identities. Plenty of songs had been sung—beautiful, matchless songs—adjusted to other lands than these—another spirit and stage of evolution; but I would sing, and leave out or put in, quite solely with reference to America and to-day. Modern science and democracy seem'd to be throwing out their challenge to poetry to put them in its statements in contradistinction to the songs and myths of the past. As I see it now (perhaps too late,) I have unwittingly taken up that challenge and made an attempt at such statements—which I certainly would not assume to do now, knowing more clearly what it means.

For grounds for "Leaves of Grass" as a poem, I abandon'd the conventional themes, which do not appear in it: none of the stock ornamentation, or choice plots of love or war, or high, exceptional personages of Old-World song; nothing, as I may say, for beauty's sake—no legend, or myth, or romance, nor euphemism, nor rhyme. But the broadest average of humanity and its identities in the now ripening Nineteenth Century, and especially in each of their countless examples and practical occupations in the United States to-day.

One main contrast of the ideas behind every page of my verses, compared with establish'd poems, is their different relative attitude towards God, towards the objective universe, and still more (by reflection, confession, assumption, &c.) the quite changed attitude of the ego, the one chanting or talking, towards himself and towards his fellow-humanity. It is certainly time for America, above all, to begin this readjustment in the scope and basic point of view of verse; for everything else has changed. As I write, I see in an article on Wordsworth, in one of the current English magazines, the lines, "A few weeks ago an eminent French critic said that, owing to the special tendency to science and to its all-devouring force, poetry would cease to be read in fifty years." But I anticipate the very contrary. Only a firmer, vastly broader, new area begins to exist— nay, is already form'd—to which the poetic genius must emigrate. Whatever may have been the case in years gone by, the true use for the imaginative faculty of modern times is to give ultimate vivification to facts, to science, and to common lives, endowing them with the glows and glories and final illustriousness which belong to every real thing, and to real things only. Without that ultimate vivification—which the poet or other artist alone can give— reality would seem incomplete, and science, democracy, and life itself, finally in vain.

Few appreciate the moral revolutions, our age, which have been profounder far than the material or inventive or war-produced ones. The Nineteenth Century, now well towards its close (and ripening into fruit the seeds of the two preceding centuries[3])—the uprisings of national masses and shiftings of boundary-lines—the historical and other prominent facts of the United States—the war of attempted Secession—the stormy rush and haste of nebulous forces— never can future years witness more excitement and din of action— never completer change of army front along the whole line, the whole civilized world. For all these new and evolutionary facts, meanings, purposes, new poetic messages, new forms and expressions, are inevitable.

My Book and I—what a period we have presumed to span! those thirty years from 1850 to '80—and America in them! Proud, proud

3. "The ferment and germination even of the United States to-day, dating back to and in my opinion mainly founded on, the Elizabethan age in English history, the age of Francis Bacon and Shakspere. Indeed, when we pursue it, what growth or advent is there that does not date back, back, until lost— perhaps its most tantalizing clues lost —in the receded horizons of the past?" [Whitman's note].

indeed may we be, if we have cull'd enough of that period in its own spirit to worthily waft a few live breaths of it to the future!

Let me not dare, here or anywhere, for my own purposes, or any purposes, to attempt the definition of Poetry, nor answer the question what it is. Like Religion, Love, Nature, while those terms are indispensable, and we all give a sufficiently accurate meaning to them, in my opinion no definition that has ever been made sufficiently encloses the name Poetry; nor can any rule or convention ever so absolutely obtain but some great exception may arise and disregard and overturn it.

Also it must be carefully remember'd that first-class literature does not shine by any luminosity of its own; nor do its poems. They grow of circumstances, and are evolutionary. The actual living light is always curiously from elsewhere—follows unaccountable sources, and is lunar and relative at the best. There are, I know, certain controlling themes that seem endlessly appropriated to the poets—as war, in the past—in the Bible, religious rapture and adoration— always love, beauty, some fine plot, or pensive or other emotion. But, strange as it may sound at first, I will say there is something striking far deeper and towering far higher than those themes for the best elements of modern song.

Just as all the old imaginative works rest, after their kind, on long trains of presuppositions, often entirely unmention'd by themselves, yet supplying the most important bases of them, and without which they could have had no reason for being, so "Leaves of Grass," before a line was written, presupposed something different from any other, and, as it stands, is the result of such presupposition. I should say, indeed, it were useless to attempt reading the book without first carefully tallying that preparatory background and quality in the mind. Think of the United States to-day—the facts of these thirty-eight or forty empires solder'd in one—sixty or seventy millions of equals, with their lives, their passions, their future—these incalculable, modern, American, seething multitudes around us, of which we are inseparable parts! Think, in comparison, of the petty environage and limited area of the poets of past or present Europe, no matter how great their genius. Think of the absence and ignorance in all cases hitherto, of the multitudinousness, vitality, and the unprecedented stimulants of to-day and here. It almost seems as if a poetry with cosmic and dynamic features of magnitude and limitlessness suitable to the human soul, were never possible before. It is certain that a poetry of absolute faith and equality for the use of the democratic masses never was.

In estimating first-class song, a sufficient Nationality, or, on the other hand, what may be call'd the negative and lack of it (as in Goethe's case, it sometimes seems to me,) is often, if not always, the first element. One needs only a little penetration to see, at more or less removes, the material facts of their country and radius, with the coloring of the moods of humanity at the time, and its gloomy or hopeful prospects, behind all poets and each poet, and forming their birthmarks. I know very well that my "Leaves" could not possibly have emerged or been fashion'd or completed, from any other era than the latter half of the Nineteenth Century, nor any other land than democratic America, and from the absolute triumph of the National Union arms.

And whether my friends claim it for me or not, I know well enough, too, that in respect to pictorial talent, dramatic situations, and especially in verbal melody and all the conventional technique of poetry, not only the divine works that to-day stand ahead in the world's reading, but dozens more, transcend (some of them immeasurably transcend) all I have done, or could do. But it seem'd to me, as the objects in Nature, the themes of æstheticism, and all special exploitations of the mind and soul, involve not only their own inherent quality, but the quality, just as inherent and important, of *their point of view*,[4] the time had come to reflect all themes and things, old and new, in the lights thrown on them by the advent of America and democracy—to chant those themes through the utterance of one, not only the grateful and reverent legatee of the past, but the born child of the New World—to illustrate all through the genesis and ensemble of to-day; and that such illustration and ensemble are the chief demands of America's prospective imaginative literature. Not to carry out, in the approved style, some choice plot of fortune or misfortune, or fancy, or fine thoughts, or incidents, or courtesies—all of which has been done overwhelmingly and well, probably never to be excell'd—but that while in such æsthetic presentation of objects, passions, plots, thoughts, &c., our lands and days do not want, and probably will never have, anything better than they already possess from the bequests of the past, it still remains to be said that there is even towards all those a subjective and contemporary point of view appropriate to ourselves alone, and to our new genius and environments, different from anything hitherto; and that such conception of current or gone-by life and art is for us the only means of their assimilation consistent with the Western world.

Indeed, and anyhow, to put it specifically, has not the time arrived when, (if it must be plainly said, for democratic America's sake, if for no other) there must imperatively come a readjustment of the whole theory and nature of Poetry? The question is im-

4. "According to Immanuel Kant, the last essential reality, giving shape and significance to all the rest" [Whitman's note].

portant, and I may turn the argument over and repeat it: Does not the best thought of our day and Republic conceive of a birth and spirit of song superior to anything past or present? To the effectual and moral consolidation of our lands (already, as materially establish'd, the greatest factors in known history, and far, far greater through what they prelude and necessitate, and are to be in future)—to conform with and build on the concrete realities and theories of the universe furnish'd by science, and henceforth the only irrefragable[5] basis for anything, verse included—to root both influences in the emotional and imaginative action of the modern time, and dominate all that precedes or opposes them—is not either a radical advance and step forward, or a new verteber of the best song indispensable?

The New World receives with joy the poems of the antique, with European feudalism's rich fund of epics, plays, ballads—seeks not in the least to deaden or displace those voices from our ear and area—holds them indeed as indispensable studies, influences, records, comparisons. But though the dawn-dazzle of the sun of literature is in those poems for us of to-day—though perhaps the best parts of current character in nations, social groups, or any man's or woman's individuality, Old World or New, are from them—and though if I were ask'd to name the most precious bequest to current American civilization from all the hitherto ages, I am not sure but I would name those old and less old songs ferried hither from east and west—some serious words and debits remain; some acrid considerations demand a hearing. Of the great poems receiv'd from abroad and from the ages, and to-day enveloping and penetrating America, is there one that is consistent with these United States, or essentially applicable to them as they are and are to be? Is there one whose underlying basis is not a denial and insult to democracy? What a comment it forms, anyhow, on this era of literary fulfillment, with the splendid day-rise of science and resuscitation of history, that our chief religious and poetical works are not our own, nor adapted to our light, but have been furnish'd by far-back ages out of their arriere and darkness, or, at most, twilight dimness! What is there in those works that so imperiously and scornfully dominates all our advanced civilization, and culture?

Even Shakspere, who so suffuses current letters and art (which indeed have in most degrees grown out of him,) belongs essentially to the buried past. Only he holds the proud distinction for certain important phases of that past, of being the loftiest of the singers life has yet given voice to. All, however, relate to and rest upon

5. Undeniable.

conditions, standards, politics, sociologies, ranges of belief, that
have been quite eliminated from the Eastern hemisphere, and
never existed at all in the Western. As authoritative types of song
they belong in America just about as much as the persons and in-
stitutes they depict. True, it may be said, the emotional, moral,
and æsthetic natures of humanity have not radically changed—
that in these the old poems apply to our times and all times, ir-
respective of date; and that they are of incalculable value as pictures of the past. I willingly make those admissions, and to their
fullest extent; then advance the points herewith as of serious, even
paramount importance.

I have indeed put on record elsewhere my reverence and eulogy
for those never-to-be-excell'd poetic bequests and their indescribable
preciousness as heirlooms for America. Another and separate point
must now be candidly stated. If I had not stood before those poems
with uncover'd head, fully aware of their colossal grandeur and
beauty of form and spirit, I could not have written "Leaves of
Grass." My verdict and conclusions as illustrated in its pages are
arrived at through the temper and inculcation of the old works as
much as through anything else—perhaps more than through anything else. As America fully and fairly construed is the legitimate
result and evolutionary outcome of the past, so I would dare to
claim for my verse. Without stopping to qualify the averment, the
Old World has had the poems of myths, fictions, feudalism, conquest, caste, dynastic wars, and splendid exceptional characters and
affairs, which have been great; but the New World needs the poems
of realities and science and of the democratic average and basic
equality, which shall be greater. In the centre of all, and object of
all, stands the Human Being, towards whose heroic and spiritual
evolution poems and everything directly or indirectly tend, Old
World or New.

Continuing the subject, my friends have more than once suggested—or may be the garrulity of advancing age is possessing me—
some further embryonic facts of "Leaves of Grass," and especially
how I enter'd upon them. Dr. Bucke has, in his volume, already
fully and fairly described the preparation of my poetic field, with
the particular and general plowing, planting, seeding, and occupation of the ground, till everything was fertilized, rooted, and ready
to start its own way for good or bad. Not till after this, did I attempt
any serious acquaintance with poetic literature. Along in my six-
teenth year I had become possessor of a stout, well-cramm'd one
thousand page octavo volume (I have it yet,) containing Walter
Scott's poetry entire—an inexhaustible mine and treasury of poetic
forage (especially the endless forests and jungles of notes)—has

been so to me for fifty years, and remains so to this day.[6]

Later, at intervals, summers and falls, I used to go off, sometimes for a week at a stretch, down in the country, or to Long Island's seashores—there, in the presence of outdoor influences, I went over thoroughly the Old and New Testaments, and absorb'd (probably to better advantage for me than in any library or indoor room —it makes such difference *where* you read,) Shakspere, Ossian, the best translated versions I could get of Homer, Eschylus, Sophocles, the old German Nibelungen, the ancient Hindoo poems, and one or two other masterpieces, Dante's among them. As it happen'd, I read the latter mostly in an old wood. The *Iliad* (Buckley's prose version) I read first thoroughly on the peninsula of Orient, northeast end of Long Island, in a shelter'd hollow of rocks and sand, with the sea on each side. (I have wonder'd since why I was not overwhelm'd by those mighty masters. Likely because I read them, as described, in the full presence of Nature, under the sun, with the far-spreading landscape and vistas, or the sea rolling in.)

Toward the last I had among much else look'd over Edgar Poe's poems—of which I was not an admirer, tho' I always saw that beyond their limited range of melody (like perpetual chimes of music bells, ringing from lower *b* flat up to *g*) they were melodious expressions, and perhaps never excell'd ones, of certain pronounc'd phases of human morbidity. (The Poetic area is very spacious— has room for all—has so many mansions!) But I was repaid in Poe's prose by the idea that (at any rate for our occasions, our day) there can be no such thing as a long poem. The same thought had been haunting my mind before, but Poe's argument, though short, work'd the sum and proved it to me.

Another point had an early settlement, clearing the ground greatly. I saw, from the time my enterprise and questionings positively shaped themselves (how best can I express my own distinctive era and surroundings, America, Democracy?) that the trunk and centre whence the answer was to radiate, and to which all should return from straying however far a distance, must be an identical body and soul, a personality—which personality, after many considerations and ponderings I deliberately settled should be myself—indeed could not be any other. I also felt strongly (whether I have shown it or not) that to the true and full estimate

6. "Sir Walter Scott's *COMPLETE POEMS;* especially including BORDER MINSTRELSY; then Sir Tristrem; Lay of the Last Minstrel; Ballads from the German; Marmion; Lady of the Lake; Vision of Don Roderick; Lord of the Isles; Rokeby; Bridal of Triermain; Field of Waterloo; Harold the Dauntless; all the Dramas; various Introductions, endless interesting Notes, and Essays on Poetry, Romance, Etc.

"Lockhart's 1833 (or '34) edition with Scott's latest and copious revisions and annotations. (All the poems were thoroughly read by me, but the ballads of the Border Minstrelsy over and over again.)" [Whitman's note]

of the Present both the Past and the Future are main considerations.

These, however, and much more might have gone on and come to naught (almost positively would have come to naught,) if a sudden, vast, terrible, direct and indirect stimulus for new and national declamatory expression had not been given to me. It is certain, I say, that, although I had made a start before, only from the occurrence of the Secession War, and what it show'd me as by flashes of lightning, with emotional depths it sounded and arous'd (of course, I don't mean in my own heart only, I saw it just as plainly in others, in millions)—that only from the strong flare and provocation of that war's sights and scenes the final reasons-for-being of an autochthonic⁷ and passionate song definitely came forth.

I went down to the war fields in Virginia (end of 1862,) lived thenceforward in camp—saw great battles and the days and nights afterward—partook of all the fluctuations, gloom, despair, hopes again arous'd, courage evoked—death readily risk'd—*the cause*, too —along and filling those agonistic and lurid following years, 1863–'64-'65—the real parturition years (more than 1776-'83) of this henceforth homogeneous Union. Without those three or four years and the experiences they gave, "Leaves of Grass" would not now be existing.

But I set out with the intention also of indicating or hinting some point-characteristics which I since see (though I did not then, at least not definitely) were bases and object-urgings toward those "Leaves" from the first. The word I myself put primarily for the description of them as they stand at last, is the word Suggestiveness. I round and finish little, if anything; and could not, consistently with my scheme. The reader will always have his or her part to do, just as much as I have had mine. I seek less to state or display any theme or thought, and more to bring you, reader, into the atmosphere of the theme or thought—there to pursue your own flight. Another impetus-word is Comradeship as for all lands, and in a more commanding and acknowledg'd sense than hitherto. Other word signs would be Good Cheer, Content, and Hope.

The chief trait of any given poet is always the spirit he brings to the observation of Humanity and Nature—the mood out of which he contemplates his subjects. What kind of temper and what amount of faith report these things? Up to how recent a date is the song carried? What the equipment, and special raciness of the singer—what his tinge of coloring? The last value of artistic expressers, past and present—Greek æsthetes, Shakspere— or in our own day Tennyson, Victor Hugo, Carlyle, Emerson—is

7. Indigenous, native to the land.

certainly involv'd in such questions. I say the profoundest service that poems or any other writings can do for their reader is not merely to satisfy the intellect, or supply something polish'd and interesting, nor even to depict great passions, or persons or events, but to fill him with vigorous and clean manliness, religiousness, and give him *good heart* as a radical possession and habit. The educated world seems to have been growing more and more ennuyed[8] for ages, leaving to our time the inheritance of it all. Fortunately there is the original inexhaustible fund of buoyancy, normally resident in the race, forever eligible to be appeal'd to and relied on.

As for native American individuality, though certain to come, and on a large scale, the distinctive and ideal type of Western character (as consistent with the operative political and even money-making features of the United States' humanity in the Nineteenth Century as chosen knights, gentlemen and warriors were the ideals of the centuries of European feudalism) it has not yet appear'd. I have allow'd the stress of my poems from beginning to end to bear upon American individuality and assist it—not only because that is a great lesson in Nature, amid all her generalizing laws, but as counterpoise to the leveling tendencies of Democracy— and for other reasons. Defiant of ostensible literary and other conventions, I avowedly chant "the great pride of man in himself," and permit it to be more or less a *motif* of nearly all my verse. I think this pride indispensable to an American. I think it not inconsistent with obedience, humility, deference, and self-questioning.

Democracy has been so retarded and jeopardized by powerful personalities, that its first instincts are fain[9] to clip, conform, bring in stragglers, and reduce everything to a dead level. While the ambitious thought of my song is to help the forming of a great aggregate Nation, it is, perhaps, altogether through the forming of myriads of fully develop'd and enclosing individuals. Welcome as are equality's and fraternity's doctrines and popular education, a certain liability accompanies them all, as we see. That primal and interior something in man, in his soul's abysms, coloring all, and, by exceptional fruitions, giving the last majesty to him—something continually touch'd upon and attain'd by the old poems and ballads of feudalism, and often the principal foundation of them—modern science and democracy appear to be endangering, perhaps eliminating. But that forms an appearance only; the reality is quite different. The new influences, upon the whole, are surely preparing the way for grander individualities than ever. To-day and here personal force is behind everything, just the same. The times and depictions from the Iliad to Shakspere inclusive can happily never again be realized—but the elements of courageous and lofty man-

8. Weary, bored.   9. Content, willing.

hood are unchanged.

Without yielding an inch the working-man and working-woman were to be in my pages from first to last. The ranges of heroism and loftiness with which Greek and feudal poets endow'd their god-like or lordly born characters—indeed prouder and better based and with fuller ranges than those—I was to endow the democratic averages of America. I was to show that we, here and to-day, are eligible to the grandest and the best—more eligible now than any times of old were. I will also want my utterances (I said to myself before beginning) to be in spirit the poems of the morning. (They have been founded and mainly written in the sunny forenoon and early midday of my life.) I will want them to be the poems of women entirely as much as men. I have wish'd to put the complete Union of the States in my songs without any preference or partiality whatever. Henceforth, if they live and are read, it must be just as much South as North—just as much along the Pacific as Atlantic—in the valley of the Mississippi, in Canada, up in Maine, down in Texas, and on the shores of Puget Sound.

From another point of view "Leaves of Grass" is avowedly the song of Sex and Amativeness,[1] and even Animality—though meanings that do not usually go along with those words are behind all, and will duly emerge; and all are sought to be lifted into a different light and atmosphere. Of this feature, intentionally palpable in a few lines, I shall only say the espousing principle of those lines so gives breath of life to my whole scheme that the bulk of the pieces might as well have been left unwritten were those lines omitted. Difficult as it will be, it has become, in my opinion, imperative to achieve a shifted attitude from superior men and women towards the thought and fact of sexuality, as an element in character, personality, the emotions, and a theme in literature. I am not going to argue the question by itself; it does not stand by itself. The vitality of it is altogether in its relations, bearings, significance—like the clef of a symphony. At last analogy the lines I allude to, and the spirit in which they are spoken, permeate all "Leaves of Grass," and the work must stand or fall with them, as the human body and soul must remain as an entirety.

Universal as are certain facts and symptoms of communities or individuals all times, there is nothing so rare in modern conventions and poetry as their normal recognizance. Literature is always calling in the doctor for consultation and confession, and always giving evasions and swathing suppressions in place of that "heroic nudity"[2] on which only a genuine diagnosis of serious cases can be built. And in respect to editions of "Leaves of Grass" in time to

1. Term from phrenology: propensity to love, sexual passion.

2. " 'Nineteenth Century,' July, 1883" [Whitman's note].

come (if there should be such) I take occasion now to confirm those lines with the settled convictions and deliberate renewals of thirty years, and to hereby prohibit, as far as word of mine can do so, any elision of them.

Then still a purpose enclosing all, and over and beneath all. Ever since what might be call'd thought, or the budding of thought, fairly began in my youthful mind, I had had a desire to attempt some worthy record of that entire faith and acceptance ("to justify the ways of God to man" is Milton's well-known and ambitious phrase) which is the foundation of moral America. I felt it all as positively then in my young days as I do now in my old ones; to formulate a poem whose every thought or fact should directly or indirectly be or connive at an implicit belief in the wisdom, health, mystery, beauty of every process, every concrete object, every human or other existence, not only consider'd from the point of view of all, but of each.

While I cannot understand it or argue it out, I fully believe in a clue and purpose in Nature, entire and several; and that invisible spiritual results, just as real and definite as the visible, eventuate all concrete life and all materialism, through Time. My book ought to emanate buoyancy and gladness legitimately enough, for it was grown out of those elements, and has been the comfort of my life since it was originally commenced.

One main genesis-motive of the "Leaves" was my conviction (just as strong to-day as ever) that the crowning growth of the United States is to be spiritual and heroic. To help start and favor that growth—or even to call attention to it, or the need of it—is the beginning, middle and final purpose of the poems. (In fact, when really cipher'd out and summ'd to the last, plowing up in earnest the interminable average fallows of humanity—not "good government" merely, in the common sense—is the justification and main purpose of these United States.)

Isolated advantages in any rank or grace or fortune—the direct or indirect threads of all the poetry of the past—are in my opinion distasteful to the republican genius, and offer no foundation for its fitting verse. Establish'd poems, I know, have the very great advantage of chanting the already perform'd, so full of glories, reminiscences dear to the minds of men. But my volume is a candidate for the future. "All original art," says Taine, anyhow, "is self-regulated, and no original art can be regulated from without; it carries its own counterpoise, and does not receive it from elsewhere—lives on its own blood"—a solace to my frequent bruises and sulky vanity.

As the present is perhaps mainly an attempt at personal statement or illustration, I will allow myself as further help to extract the following anecdote from a book, "Annals of Old Painters," conn'd by me in youth. Rubens, the Flemish painter, in one of his wanderings through the galleries of old convents, came across a singular work. After looking at it thoughtfully for a good while, and listening to the criticisms of his suite of students, he said to the latter, in answer to their questions, (as to what school the work implied or belong'd,) "I do not believe the artist, unknown and perhaps no longer living, who has given the world this legacy, ever belong'd to any school, or ever painted anything but this one picture, which is a personal affair—a piece out of a man's life."

"Leaves of Grass" indeed (I cannot too often reiterate) has mainly been the outcropping of my own emotional and other personal nature—an attempt, from first to last, to put *a Person*, a human being (myself, in the latter half of the Nineteenth Century, in America,) freely, fully and truly on record. I could not find any similar personal record in current literature that satisfied me. But it is not on "Leaves of Grass" distinctively as *literature*, or a specimen thereof, that I feel to dwell, or advance claims. No one will get at my verses who insists upon viewing them as a literary performance, or attempt at such performance, or as aiming mainly toward art or æstheticism.

I say no land or people or circumstances ever existed so needing a race of singers and poems differing from all others, and rigidly their own, as the land and people and circumstances of our United States need such singers and poems to-day, and for the future. Still further, as long as the States continue to absorb and be dominated by the poetry of the Old World, and remain unsupplied with autochthonous song, to express, vitalize and give color to and define their material and political success, and minister to them distinctively, so long will they stop short of first-class Nationality and remain defective.

In the free evening of my day I give to you, reader, the foregoing garrulous talk, thoughts, reminiscences,

> As idly drifting down the ebb,
> Such ripples, half-caught voices, echo from the shore.

Concluding with two items for the imaginative genius of the West, when it worthily rises—First, what Herder taught to the young Goethe, that really great poetry is always (like the Homeric or Biblical canticles) the result of a national spirit, and not the privilege of a polish'd and select few; Second, that the strongest and sweetest songs yet remain to be sung.

1888

From Democratic Vistas[3]

[*The Keynote*]

But preluding no longer, let me strike the keynote of the following strain. First premising that, though the passages of it have been written at widely different times (it is, in fact, a collection of memoranda, perhaps for future designers, comprehenders), and though it may be open to the charge of one part contradicting another—for there are opposite sides to the great question of democracy, as to every great question—I feel the parts harmoniously blended in my own realization and convictions, and present them to be read only in such oneness, each page and each claim and assertion modified and temper'd by the others. Bear in mind, too, that they are not the result of studying up in political economy, but of the ordinary sense, observing, wandering among men, these States, these stirring years of war and peace. I will not gloss over the appaling dangers of universal suffrage in the United States. In fact, it is to admit and face these dangers I am writing. To him or her within whose thought rages the battle, advancing, retreating, between democracy's convictions, aspirations, and the people's crudeness, vice, caprices, I mainly write this essay. I shall use the words America and democracy as convertible terms. Not an ordinary one is the issue. The United States are destined either to surmount the gorgeous history of feudalism, or else prove the most tremendous failure of time. Not the least doubtful am I on any prospects of their material success. The triumphant future of their business, geographic and productive departments, on larger scales and in more varieties than ever, is certain. In those respects the republic must soon (if she does not already) outstrip all examples hitherto afforded, and dominate the world.

Admitting all this, with the priceless value of our political institutions, general suffrage (and fully acknowledging the latest, widest opening of the doors), I say that, far deeper than these, what

---

3. *Democratic Vistas* appeared first as a separate volume in 1871, but some passages had appeared earlier in periodicals. This long work constitutes Whitman's most serious claim to fame in prose. Five passages have been printed here (the bracketed subtitles are in Whitman's language, but were not devised as titles by him). The first, "[The Keynote]," suggests the basic organization, while the second, "[Alarm and Caution]," is a sample of Whitman's strong condemnation of the materialism of his own time and country, a passage that those who brush Whitman aside as a chauvinist sometimes forget. The last three passages have been chosen from the main body of the essay to indicate the three main themes. At the beginning of *Leaves of Grass* stand the lines: "One's-self I sing, a simple separate person, / Yet utter the word Democratic, the word En-Masse." *Democratic Vistas* is a profound exploration of this paradox. In "[Political Democracy]," Whitman explores the "En-Masse" side of democracy, while in "[Personalism]" he probes the complexities of the "simple separate person," or a vital individuality. And in "[Archetypal Literature for America]" he asserts democracy's need for a great literature if it is to avoid both mediocrity and anarchy and to produce both great masses and great individuals.

finally and only is to make of our Western world a nationality superior to any hitherto known, and outtopping the past, must be vigorous, yet unsuspected Literatures, perfect personalities and sociologies, original, transcendental, and expressing (what, in highest sense, are not yet express'd at all) democracy and the modern. With these, and out of these, I promulge new races of Teachers, and of perfect Women, indispensable to endow the birth-stock of a New World. For feudalism, caste, the ecclesiastic traditions, though palpably retreating from political institutions, still hold essentially, by their spirit, even in this country, entire possession of the more important fields, indeed the very subsoil, of education, and of social standards and literature.

I say that democracy can never prove itself beyond cavil, until it founds and luxuriantly grows its own forms of art, poems, schools, theology, displacing all that exists, or that has been produced anywhere in the past, under opposite influences. It is curious to me that while so many voices, pens, minds, in the press, lecture-rooms, in our Congress, etc., are discussing intellectual topics, pecuniary dangers, legislative problems, the suffrage, tariff and labor questions, and the various business and benevolent needs of America, with propositions, remedies, often worth deep attention, there is one need, a hiatus the profoundest, that no eye seems to perceive, no voice to state. Our fundamental want today in the United States, with closest, amplest reference to present conditions, and to the future, is of a class, and the clear idea of a class, of native authors, literatuses, far different, far higher in grade, than any yet known, sacerdotal, modern, fit to cope with our occasions, lands, permeating the whole mass of American mentality, taste, belief, breathing into it a new breath of life, giving it decision, affecting politics far more than the popular superficial suffrage, with results inside and underneath the elections of Presidents or Congresses—radiating, begetting appropriate teachers, schools, manners, and, as its grandest result, accomplishing (what neither the schools nor the churches and their clergy have hitherto accomplish'd, and without which this nation will no more stand, permanently, soundly, than a house will stand without a substratum,) a religious and moral character beneath the political and productive and intellectual bases of the States. For know you not, dear, earnest reader, that the people of our land may all read and write, and may all possess the right to vote—and yet the main things may be entirely lacking?—(and this to suggest them).

[*Alarm and Caution*]

For my part, I would alarm and caution even the political and business reader, and to the utmost extent, against the prevailing delusion that the establishment of free political institutions, and plentiful intellectual smartness, with general good order, physical plenty, industry, etc. (desirable and precious advantages as they all are), do, of themselves, determine and yield to our experiment of democracy the fruitage of success. With such advantages at present fully, or almost fully, possess'd—the Union just issued, victorious, from the struggle with the only foes it need ever fear (namely, those within itself, the interior ones), and with unprecedented materialistic advancement—society, in these States, is canker'd, crude, superstitious, and rotten. Political, or law-made society is, and private, or voluntary society, is also. In any vigor, the element of the moral conscience, the most important, the verteber to State or man, seems to me either entirely lacking, or seriously enfeebled or ungrown.

I say we had best look our times and lands searchingly in the face, like a physician diagnosing some deep disease. Never was there, perhaps, more hollowness at heart than at present, and here in the United States. Genuine belief seems to have left us. The underlying principles of the States are not honestly believ'd in (for all this hectic glow, and these melodramatic screamings), nor is humanity itself believ'd in. What penetrating eye does not everywhere see through the mask? The spectacle is appalling. We live in an atmosphere of hypocrisy throughout. The men believe not in the women, nor the women in the men. A scornful superciliousness rules in literature. The aim of all the *littérateurs* is to find something to make fun of. A lot of churches, sects, etc., the most dismal phantasms I know, usurp the name of religion. Conversation is a mass of badinage. From deceit in the spirit, the mother of all false deeds, the offspring is already incalcuble. An acute and candid person, in the revenue department in Washington, who is led by the course of his employment to regularly visit the cities, north, south, and west, to investigate frauds, has talked much with me about his discoveries. The depravity of the business classes of our country is not less than has been supposed, but infinitely greater. The official services of America, national, state, and municipal, in all their branches and departments, except the judiciary, are saturated in corruption, bribery, falsehood, maladministration; and the judiciary is tainted. The great cities reek with respectable as much as non-respectable robbery and scoundrelism. In fashionable life, flippancy, tepid amours, weak infidelism, small aims, or no aims at all, only to kill time. In business (this all-devouring modern word, business), the one sole object is, by any means, pecuniary gain. The magician's serpent in the fable ate up all the other serpents; and money-making is our magician's serpent, remaining to-day sole master of the field. The best class we show, is but a mob of fashionably dress'd speculators and vulgarians. True, indeed, behind this fantastic farce, enacted on the visible stage of society, solid things and stupendous labors are to be discover'd, existing crudely and going on in the background, to advance and tell themselves in time. Yet the truths are none the less terrible. I say that our New World democracy, however great a success in uplifting the masses out of their sloughs, in materialistic development, products, and in a certain highly deceptive superficial popular intellectuality, is, so far, an almost complete failure in its social aspects, and in really grand religious, moral, literary, and æsthetic results. In vain do we march with unprecedented strides to empire so colossal, outvying the antique, beyond Alexander's, beyond the proudest sway of Rome. In vain have we annex'd Texas, California, Alaska, and reach north for Canada and south for Cuba. It is as if we were somehow being endow'd with a vast and more and more thoroughly-appointed body, and then left with little or no soul.

Let me illustrate further, as I write, with current observations, localities, etc. The subject is important, and will bear repetition. After an absence, I am now again (September, 1870) in New York City and Brooklyn, on a few weeks' vacation. The splendor, picturesqueness, and oceanic amplitude and rush of these great cities, the unsurpassed situation, rivers and bay, sparkling sea-tides, costly and lofty new buildings, façades of marble and iron, of original grandeur and elegance of design, with the masses of gay color, the preponderance of white and blue, the flags flying, the endless ships, the tumultuous streets, Broadway, the heavy, low, musical roar, hardly ever intermitted, even at night; the jobbers' houses, the rich shops, the wharves, the great Central Park, and the Brooklyn Park of hills (as I wander among them this beautiful fall weather, musing, watching, absorbing)—the assemblages of the citizens in their groups, conversations, trades, evening amusements, or along the by-quarters—these, I say, and the like of these, completely satisfy my senses of power, fullness, motion, etc., and give me, through such senses and appetites, and through my æsthetic conscience, a continued exaltation and absolute fulfillment. Always and more and more, as I cross the East and North rivers, the ferries, or with the pilots in their pilot-houses, or pass an hour in Wall Street, or the Gold Exchange, I realize (if we must admit such partialisms) that not Nature alone is great in her fields of freedom and the open air, in her storms, the shows of night and day, the mountains, forests, sea—but in the artificial, the work of man too is equally great—in this profusion of teeming humanity—in these ingenuities, streets, goods, houses, ships—these hurrying, feverish, electric crowds of men, their complicated business genius (not least among the geniuses), and all this mighty, many-threaded wealth and industry concentrated here.

But sternly discarding, shutting our eyes to the glow and grandeur of the general superficial effect, coming down to what is of the only real importance, Personalities, and examining minutely, we question we ask, Are there, indeed, *men* here worthy the name? Are there athletes? Are there perfect women, to match the generous material luxuriance? Is there a pervading atmosphere of beautiful manners? Are there crops of fine youths, and majestic old persons? Are there arts worthy freedom and a rich people? Is there a great moral and religious civilization—the only justification of a great material one? Confess that to severe eyes, using the moral microscope upon humanity, a sort of dry and flat Sahara appears, these cities, crowded with petty grotesques, malformations, phantoms, playing meaningless antics. Confess that everywhere, in shop, street, church, theatre, barroom, official chair, are pervading flippancy and vulgarity, low cunning, infidelity—everywhere the youth puny, impudent, foppish, prematurely ripe—everywhere an abnormal libidinousness, unhealthy forms, male, female, painted, padded, dyed, chignon'd, muddy complexions, bad blood, the capacity for good motherhood deceasing or deceas'd, shallow notions of beauty, with a range of manners, or rather lack of manners (considering the advantages enjoy'd), probably the meanest to be seen in the world.

[Political Democracy]

First, let us see what we can make out of a brief, general, sentimental consideration of political democracy, and whence it has arisen, with regard to some of its current features, as an aggregate, and as the basic structure of our future literature and authorship. We shall, it is true, quickly and continually find the origin-idea of the singleness of man, individualism, asserting itself, and cropping forth, even from the opposite ideas. But the mass, or lump character, for imperative reasons, is to be ever carefully weigh'd, borne in mind, and provided for. Only from it, and from its proper regulation and potency, comes the other, comes the chance of individualism. The two are contradictory, but our task is to reconcile them.

The political history of the past may be summ'd up as having grown out of what underlies the words, order, safety, caste, and especially out of the need of some prompt deciding authority, and of cohesion at all cost. Leaping time, we come to the period within the memory of people now living, when, as from some lair where they had slumber'd long, accumulating wrath, sprang up and are yet active (1790, and on even to the present, 1870) those noisy eructations,[4] destructive iconoclasms, a fierce sense of wrongs,

4. Violent belchings forth.

amid which moves the form, well known in modern history, in the Old World, stain'd with much blood, and mark'd by savage reactionary clamors and demands. These bear, mostly, as on one inclosing point of need.

For after the rest is said—after the many time-honor'd and really true things for subordination, experience, rights of property, etc., have been listen'd to and acquiesced in—after the valuable and well-settled statement of our duties and relations in society is thoroughly conn'd over and exhausted—it remains to bring forward and modify everything else with the idea of that Something a man is (last precious consolation of the drudging poor), standing apart from all else, divine in his own right, and a woman in hers, sole and untouchable by any canons of authority, or any rule derived from precedent, state-safety, the acts of legislatures, or even from what is called religion, modesty, or art. The radiation of this truth is the key of the most significant doings of our immediately preceding three centuries, and has been the political genesis and life of America. Advancing visibly, it still more advances invisibly. Underneath the fluctuations of the expressions of society, as well as the movements of the politics of the leading nations of the world, we see steadily pressing ahead and strengthening itself, even in the midst of immense tendencies toward aggregation, this image of completeness in separatism, of individual personal dignity, of a single person, either male or female, characterized in the main, not from extrinsic acquirements or position, but in the pride of himself or herself alone; and, as an eventual conclusion and summing up (or else the entire scheme of things is aimless, a cheat, a crash), the simple idea that the last, best dependence is to be upon humanity itself, and its own inherent, normal, full-grown qualities without any superstitious support whatever. This idea of perfect individualism it is indeed that deepest tinges and gives character to the idea of the aggregate. For it is mainly or altogether to serve independent separatism that we favor a strong generalization, consolidation. As it is to give the best vitality and freedom to the rights of the States (every bit as important as the right of nationality, the union), that we insist on the identity of the Union at all hazards.

The purpose of democracy—supplanting old belief in the necessary absoluteness of establish'd dynastic rulership, temporal, ecclesiastical, and scholastic, as furnishing the only security against chaos, crime, and ignorance—is, through many transmigrations and amid endless ridicules, arguments, and ostensible failures, to illustrate, at all hazards, this doctrine or theory that man, properly train'd in sanest, highest freedom, may and must become a law, and series of laws, unto himself, surrounding and providing for, not only his own personal control, but all his relations to other individuals, and to the State; and that, while other theories, as in the past histories of nations, have proved wise enough, and indispensable perhaps for their conditions, *this*, as matters now stand in our civilized world, is the only scheme worth working from, as warranting results like those of Nature's laws, reliable, when once establish'd, to carry on themselves.

The argument of the matter is extensive, and, we admit, by no means all on one side. What we shall offer will be far, far from sufficient. But while leaving unsaid much that should properly even prepare the way for the treatment of this many-sided question of political liberty, equality, or republicanism—leaving the whole history and consideration of the feudal plan and its products, embodying humanity, its politics and civilization, through the retrospect of past time (which plan and products, indeed, make up all of the past, and a large part of the present)—leaving unanswer'd, at least by any specific and local answer, many a well-wrought argument and instance, and many a conscientious declamatory cry and warning—as, very lately, from an eminent and venerable person abroad—things, problems, full of doubt, dread, suspense (not new to me, but old occupiers of many an anxious hour in city's din, or night's silence), we still may give a page or so, whose drift is opportune. Time alone can finally answer these things. But as a substitute in passing, let us, even if fragmentarily, throw forth a short direct or indirect suggestion of the premises of that other plan, in the new spirit, under the new forms, started here in our America.

As to the political section of Democracy, which introduces and breaks ground for further and vaster sections, few probably are the minds, even in these republican States, that fully comprehend the aptness of that phrase, "the government of the people, by the people, for the people," which we inherit from the lips of Abraham Lincoln; a formula whose verbal shape is homely wit, but whose scope includes both the totality and all minutiæ of the lesson.

The People! Like our huge earth itself, which, to ordinary scansion, is full of vulgar contradictions and offence, man, viewed in the lump, displeases, and is a constant puzzle and affront to the merely educated classes. The rare, cosmical, artist-mind, lit with the Infinite, alone confronts his manifold and oceanic qualities—but taste, intelligence and culture (so-called), have been against the masses, and remain so. There is plenty of glamour about the most damnable crimes and hoggish meannesses, special and general, of the feudal and dynastic world over there, with its *personnel* of lords and queens and courts, so well-dress'd and so handsome. But the People are ungrammatical, untidy, and their sins gaunt and ill-bred.

Literature, strictly consider'd, has never recognized the People, and, whatever may be said, does not today. Speaking generally, the tendencies of literature, as hitherto pursued, have been to make mostly critical and querulous men. It seems as if, so far, there were some natural repugnance between a literary and professional life, and the rude rank spirit of the democracies. There is, in later literature, a treatment of benevolence, a charity business, rife enough it is true; but I know nothing more rare, even in this country, than a fit scientific estimate and reverent appreciation of the People—of their measureless wealth of latent power and capacity, their vast, artistic contrasts of lights and shades—with, in America, their entire reliability in emergencies, and a certain breadth of historic grandeur, of peace or war, far surpassing all the vaunted samples of book-heroes, or any *haut ton* coteries, in all the records of the world.

[Personalism]

So much contributed, to be conn'd well, to help prepare and brace our edifice, our plann'd Idea—we still proceed to give it in another of its aspects—perhaps the main, the high façade of all. For to democracy, the leveler, the unyielding principle of the average, is surely join'd another principle, equally unyielding, closely tracking the first, indispensable to it, opposite (as the sexes are opposite), and whose existence, confronting and ever modifying the other, often clashing, paradoxical, yet neither of highest avail without the other, plainly supplies to these grand cosmic politics of ours, and to the launch'd forth mortal dangers of republicanism, today, or any day, the counterpart and offset whereby Nature restrains the deadly original relentlessness of all her first-class laws. This second principle is individuality, the pride and centripetal isolation of a human being in himself—identity—personalism. Whatever the name, its acceptance and thorough infusions through the organizations of political commonalty now shooting Aurora-like about the world, are of utmost importance, as the principle itself is needed for very life's sake. It forms, in a sort, or is to form, the compensating balance-wheel of the successful working machinery of aggregate America.

And, if we think of it, what does civilization itself rest upon—and what object has it, with its religions, arts, schools, etc., but rich, luxuriant, varied personalism? To that, all bends; and it is because toward such result democracy alone, on anything like Nature's scale, breaks up the limitless fallows of humankind, and plants the seed, and gives fair play, that its claims now precede the rest. The literature, songs, æsthetics, etc., of a country are of importance principally because they furnish the materials and suggestions of personality for the women and men of that country, and enforce them in a thousand effective ways. As the topmost claim of a strong consolidating of the nationality of these States, is, that only by such powerful compaction can the separate States secure that full and free swing within their spheres, which is becoming to them, each after its kind, so will individuality, with unimpeded branchings, flourish best under imperial republican forms.

Assuming Democracy to be at present in its embryo condition, and that the only large and satisfactory justification of it resides in the future, mainly through the copious production of perfect characters among the people, and through the advent of a sane and pervading religiousness, it is with regard to the atmosphere and spaciousness fit for such characters, and of certain nutriment and cartoon-draftings proper for them, and indicating them for New World purposes, that I continue the present statement—an exploration, as of new ground, wherein, like other primitive surveyors, I must do the best I can, leaving it to those who come after me to do much better. (The service, in fact, if any, must be to break a sort of first path or track, no matter how rude and ungeometrical.)

We have frequently printed the word Democracy. Yet I cannot too often repeat that it is a word the real gist of which still sleeps, quite unawaken'd, notwithstanding the resonance and the many angry tempests out of which its syllables have come, from pen or tongue. It is a great word, whose history, I suppose, remains unwritten, because that history has yet to be enacted. It is, in some sort, younger brother of another great and often-used word, Nature, whose history also waits unwritten. As I perceive, the tendencies of our day, in the States (and I entirely respect them), are toward those vast and sweeping movements, influences, moral and physical, of humanity, now and always current over the planet, on the scale of the impulses of the elements. Then it is also good to reduce the whole matter to the consideration of a single self, a man, a woman, on permanent grounds. Even for the treatment of the universal, in politics, metaphysics, or anything, sooner or later we come down to one single, solitary soul.

There is, in sanest hours, a consciousness, a thought that rises, independent, lifted out from all else, calm, like the stars, shining eternal. This is the thought of identity—yours for you, whoever you are, as mine for me. Miracle of miracles, beyond statement, most spiritual and vaguest of earth's dreams, yet hardest basic fact, and only entrance to all facts. In such devout hours, in the midst of the significant wonders of heaven and earth (significant only because of the Me in the centre), creeds, conventions, fall away and become of no account before this simple idea. Under the luminousness of real vision, it alone takes possession, takes value. Like the shadowy dwarf in the fable, once liberated and look'd upon, it expands over the whole earth, and spreads to the roof of heaven.

The quality of BEING, in the object's self, according to its own central idea and purpose, and of growing therefrom and thereto—not criticism by other standards, and adjustments thereto—is the lesson of Nature. True, the full man wisely gathers, culls, absorbs; but if, engaged disproportionately in that, he slights or overlays the precious idiocrasy and special nativity and intention that he is, the man's self, the main thing, is a failure, however wide his general cultivation. Thus, in our times, refinement and delicatesse are not only attended to sufficiently, but threaten to eat us up, like a cancer. Already, the democratic genius watches, ill-pleased, these tendencies. Provision for a little healthy rudeness, savage virtue, justification of what one has in one's self, whatever it is, is demanded. Negative qualities, even deficiencies, would be a relief. Singleness and normal simplicity and separation, amid this more and more complex, more and more artificialized state of society—how pensively we yearn for them! how we would welcome their return!

[*Archetypal Literature for America*]

Much is there, yet, demanding line and outline in our Vistas, not only on these topics, but others quite unwritten. Indeed, we could talk the matter, and expand it, through lifetime. But it is necessary to return to our original premises. In view of them, we have again pointedly to confess that all the objective grandeurs of the world, for highest purposes, yield themselves up, and depend on mentality alone. Here, and here only, all balances, all rests. For the mind, which alone builds the permanent edifice, haughtily builds it to itself. By it, with what follows it, are convey'd to mortal sense the culminations of the materialistic, the known, and a prophecy of the unknown. To take expression, to incarnate, to endow a literature with grand and archetypal models—to fill with pride and love the utmost capacity, and to achieve spiritual meanings, and suggest the future—these, and these only, satisfy the soul. We must not say one word against real materials; but the wise know that they do not become real till touched by emotions, the mind. Did we call the latter imponderable? Ah, let us rather proclaim that the slightest song-tune, the countless ephemera of passions aroused by orators and tale-tellers, are more dense, more weighty than the engines there in the great factories, or the granite blocks in their foundations.

Approaching thus the momentous spaces, and considering with

reference to a new and greater personalism, the needs and possibilities of American imaginative literature, through the medium-
light of what we have already broach'd, it will at once be appreciated that a vast gulf of difference separates the present accepted
condition of these spaces, inclusive of what is floating in them,
from any condition adjusted to, or fit for, the world, the America,
there sought to be indicated, and the copious races of complete
men and women, along these Vistas crudely outlined. It is, in some
sort, no less a difference than lies between that long-continued
nebular state and vagueness of the astronomical worlds, compared
with the subsequent state, the definitely-form'd worlds themselves,
duly compacted, clustering in systems, hung up there, chandeliers
of the universe, beholding and mutually lit by each other's lights,
serving for ground of all substantial foothold, all vulgar uses—yet
serving still more as an undying chain and echelon of spiritual
proofs and shows. A boundless field to fill! A new creation, with
needed orbic works launch'd forth, to revolve in free and lawful
circuits—to move, self-poised, through the ether, and shine like
heaven's own suns! With such, and nothing less, we suggest that
New World literature, fit to rise upon, cohere, and signalize in
time, these States.

What, however, do we more definitely mean by New World literature? Are we not doing well enough here already? Are not the
United States this day busily using, working, more printer's type,
more presses, than any other country? uttering and absorbing more
publications than any other? Do not our publishers fatten quicker
and deeper? (helping themselves, under shelter of a delusive and
sneaking law, or rather absence of law, to most of their forage,
poetical, pictorial, historical, romantic, even comic, without money
and without price—and fiercely resisting the timidest proposal to
pay for it). Many will come under this delusion—but my purpose
is to dispel it. I say that a nation may hold and circulate rivers and
oceans of very readable print, journals, magazines, novels, library
books, "poetry," etc.—such as the States today possess and circulate
—of unquestionable aid and value—hundreds of new volumes
annually composed and brought out here, respectable enough, indeed unsurpass'd in smartness and erudition—with further hundreds, or rather millions (as by free forage or theft aforementioned),
also thrown into the market—and yet, all the while, the said nation, land, strictly speaking, may possess no literature at all.

Repeating our inquiry, what, then, do we mean by real literature? especially the democratic literature of the future? Hard questions to meet. The clues are inferential, and turn us to the past.
At best, we can only offer suggestions, comparisons, circuits.

It must still be reiterated, as, for the purpose of these memoranda,

the deep lesson of history and time, that all else in the contributions
of a nation or age, through its politics, materials, heroic personalities, military *éclat*, etc., remains crude, and defers, in any close
and thorough-going estimate, until vitalized by national, original
archetypes in literature. They only put the nation in form, finally
tell anything—prove, complete anything—perpetuate anything.
Without doubt, some of the richest and most powerful and populous communities of the antique world, and some of the grandest
personalities and events, have, to after and present times, left themselves entirely unbequeath'd. Doubtless, greater than any that have
come down to us, were among those lands, heroisms, persons, that
have not come down to us at all, even by name, date, or location.
Others have arrived safely, as from voyages over wide, century-
stretching seas. The little ship, the miracles that have buoy'd them,
and by incredible chances safely convey'd them (or the best of
them, their meaning and essence) over long wastes, darkness, lethargy, ignorance, etc., have been a few inscriptions—a few immortal
compositions, small in size, yet compassing what measureless values
of reminiscence, contemporary portraitures, manners, idioms and beliefs, with deepest inference, hint and thought, to tie and touch forever the old, new body, and the old, new soul! These! and still
these! bearing the freight so dear—dearer than pride—dearer than
love. All the best experience of humanity, folded, saved, freighted
to us here. Some of these tiny ships we call Old and New Testament, Homer, Eschylus, Plato, Juvenal, etc. Precious minims![5] I
think, if we were forced to choose, rather than have you, and the
likes of you, and what belongs to, and has grown of you, blotted
out and gone, we could better afford, appalling as that would be,
to lose all actual ships, this day fasten'd by wharf, or floating on
wave, and see them, with all their cargoes, scuttled and sent to the
bottom.

Gathered by geniuses of city, race or age, and put by them in
highest of art's forms, namely, the literary form, the peculiar combinations and the outshows of that city, age, or race, its particular
modes of the universal attributes and passions, its faiths, heroes,
lovers and gods, wars, traditions, struggles, crimes, emotions, joys
(or the subtle spirit of these), having been pass'd on to us to illumine our own selfhood, and its experiences—what they supply,
indispensable and highest, if taken away, nothing else in all the
world's boundless storehouses could make up to us, or ever again
return.

For us, along the great highways of time, those monuments stand
—those forms of majesty and beauty. For us those beacons burn
through all the nights. Unknown Egyptians, graving hieroglyphs;

5. Things very small or insignificant.

Hindus, with hymn and apothegm[6] and endless epic; Hebrew prophet, with spirituality, as in flashes of lightning, conscience like red-hot iron, plaintive songs and screams of vengeance for tyrannies and enslavement; Christ, with bent head, brooding love and peace, like a dove; Greek, creating eternal shapes of physical and æsthetic proportion; Roman, lord of satire, the sword, and the codex;—of the figures, some far off and veil'd, others nearer and visible; Dante, stalking with lean form, nothing but fibre, not a grain of superfluous flesh; Angelo,[7] and the great painters, architects, musicians; rich Shakspere, luxuriant as the sun, artist and singer of feudalism in its sunset, with all the gorgeous colors, owner thereof, and using them at will; and so to such as German Kant and Hegel, where they, though near us, leaping over the ages, sit again, impassive, imperturbable, like the Egyptian gods. Of these, and the like of these, is it too much, indeed, to return to our favorite figure, and view them as orbs and systems of orbs, moving in free paths in the spaces of that other heaven, the kosmic intellect, the soul?

Ye powerful and resplendent ones! ye were, in your atmospheres, grown not for America, but rather for her foes, the feudal and the old—while our genius is democratic and modern. Yet could ye, indeed, but breathe your breath of life into our New World's nostrils —not to enslave us, as now, but, for our needs, to breed a spirit like your own—perhaps (dare we to say it?) to dominate, even destroy, what you yourselves have left! On your plane, and no less, but even higher and wider, must we mete and measure for today and here. I demand races of orbic bards, with unconditional, uncompromising sway. Come forth, sweet democratic despots of the west! * * *

In the future of these States must arise poets immenser far, and make great poems of death. The poems of life are great, but there must be the poems of the purports of life, not only in itself, but beyond itself. I have eulogized Homer, the sacred bards of Jewry, Eschylus, Juvenal, Shakspere, etc., and acknowledged their inestimable value. But (with perhaps the exception, in some, not all respects, of the second mention'd) I say there must, for future and democratic purposes, appear poets (dare I to say so?) of higher class even than any of those—poets not only possess'd of the religious fire and abandon of Isaiah, luxuriant in the epic talent of Homer, or for proud characters as in Shakspere, but consistent with the Hegelian formulas, and consistent with modern science. America needs, and the world needs, a class of bards who will, now and ever, so link and tally the rational physical being of man, with the ensembles of time and space, and with this vast and multiform

---

6. Short, instructive saying; maxim.   7. Michelangelo, Italian sculptor, painter, architect, and poet.

show, Nature, surrounding him, ever tantalizing him, equally a part, and yet not a part of him, as to essentially harmonize, satisfy, and put at rest. Faith, very old, now scared away by science, must be restored, brought back by the same power that caused her departure—restored with new sway, deeper, wider, higher than ever. Surely, this universal ennui, this coward fear, this shuddering at death, these low, degrading views, are not always to rule the spirit pervading future society, as it has the past, and does the present. What the Roman Lucretius sought most nobly, yet all too blindly, negatively to do for his age and its successors, must be done positively by some great coming literatus, especially poet, who, while remaining fully poet, will absorb whatever science indicates, with spiritualism, and out of them, and out of his own genius, will compose the great poem of death. Then will man indeed confront Nature, and confront time and space, both with science, and *con amore*,[8] and take his right place, prepared for life, master of fortune and misfortune. And then that which was long wanted will be supplied, and the ship that had it not before in all her voyages, will have an anchor.

There are still other standards, suggestions, for products of high literatuses. That which really balances and conserves the social and political world is not so much legislation, police, treaties, and dread of punishment, as the latent eternal intuitional sense, in humanity, of fairness, manliness, decorum, etc. Indeed, this perennial regulation, control, and oversight, by self-suppliance, is *sine qua non* to democracy; and a highest, widest aim of democratic literature may well be to bring forth, cultivate, brace, and strengthen this sense, in individuals and society. A strong mastership of the general inferior self by the superior self, is to be aided, secured, indirectly, but surely, by the literatus, in his works, shaping, for individual or aggregate democracy, a great passionate body, in and along with which goes a great masterful spirit.

1871

8. With love.

Samuel L. Clemens

The international status now accorded Mark Twain (Samuel Langhorne Clemens) rests firmly on his writings. But in his own time and his own country his dazzling popularity lay largely in the idea that he was a picturesque embodiment of the American character and a symbol of the "American Dream." Carrying out the Horatio Alger success theme that he himself caustically derided, he made the Dream come true in his own life. From a lowly beginning he rose to a towering fame.

His personality strongly moved people who did not even know who he was. He was occasionally spectacular and always good copy. Everything that he touched went off like a rocket. One of his maxims states, "Truth is more of a stranger than fiction"; perhaps, but not in his case. Life was always singling him out for moments of high dramatic effect. He was pleased that he had been born when Halley's comet hung in the night sky; he boasted that he had "come in with it," and he confidently expected to "go out with it." And he did, although he did not know as he lay on his deathbed that it was again shining in the heavens.

I

Clemens was born in Florida, Missouri, on November 30, 1835—an impetuous, imaginative child, who loved the companionship of the slaves on the farm of his uncle John Quarles and visited the Negro quarters as a place of enchantment. After his family moved, when he was four years old, to Hannibal on the "left bank" of the Mississippi, he was constantly running away in the direction of the river and, as he later wrote, was "drowned nine times in Bear Creek and was suspected of being a cat in disguise." He was a child who loved all downtrodden things; a child who would retain through life that "exquisite sensibility" of which so many have spoken.

In his perceptive boyhood, spent in a village more Southern than Western in mores, he suddenly "grew up" at nine and became the leader of his boy companions. His slow, measured way of speaking—"Sammy's long talk," his mother called it—had an arresting quality even then.

When Sam was twelve, his father died, with his last words urging his family to hold on to "the Tennessee land," a large tract which he expected to make them rich. But family finances were so low that Sam became a printer's apprentice at twelve; later, as printer for his older brother Orion on the Hannibal *Journal*, he sometimes set into type literary efforts of his own. One of these was a poem addressed "To Miss Katie of H——l"; perhaps the name "Hannibal" had proved too wide for the newspaper column.

A youthful satirist, as "W. Epaminondas Adrastus Blabb" he hit at the state legislature in a sketch, "Blabbing Government Secrets," in the *Journal* for September 16, 1852. An earlier sketch, "The Dandy Frightening the Squatter," had appeared May 1, 1852, in *The Carpet-Bag*, a humorous weekly published in Boston. A river story about Hannibal, signed "S. L. C.," it has been authenticated as Samuel Langhorne Clemens' first published story. He was then sixteen years old. For a time Orion permitted him an outlet in "Our Assistant's Column," but in May, 1853, Sam left for St. Louis where he found work on the *Evening News*. By August he was in New York working in a printing house and sending back letters, travel letters in embryo, to the hometown paper. Readers who think of Mark Twain as a gifted but careless writer who simply "wrote as he talked" and thus became famous without any trouble, would be surprised to learn of the strict training to which he subjected himself at various intervals in his life. From the New York printing house he wrote to his mother that all the typesetters there must "put exactly the same space between every two words and *every line must be spaced alike.*" But Sam had expected these rules and had worked accordingly from the beginning. He confided to his mother that out of all proofs he saw, "mine was by far the cleanest. In St. Louis, Mr. Baird said my proofs were the cleanest that were ever set in his office." Thus he acquired mastery over troublesome details long before his ordeal of "learning the river." He left New York for printing work in Philadelphia but finally returned to the St. Louis *Evening News*. In 1855 he rejoined Orion in a job-printing shop in Keokuk, Iowa, and worked there until November, 1856. Then fate and a strong wind blew a fifty-dollar bill into Sam's path.

With this windfall, he decided to seek his fortune along the Amazon; but first he needed to earn more money. He worked as a printer in Cincinnati that winter, sending back to the Keokuk *Evening Post* three humorous letters under the pseudonym "Thomas Jefferson Snodgrass"; he received five dollars each for these letters, his first literary earnings. When spring came, he thought he was ready for the Amazon. In April, 1857, he took passage to New Orleans on the *Paul Jones*, steered by Horace Bixby, a famous pilot. By the time the boat reached New Orleans, Bixby had agreed to teach Sam the river. Some unusual quality of mind and heart was making itself felt: when Bixby took Sam on to "learn the river," the last thing he wanted was a "cub pilot"; but he yielded to something in young Sam Clemens, then 21, slender, with keen gray eyes and a great tangle of auburn hair.

Sam now set himself to memorize twelve hundred miles of the Mississippi so that he could follow it as easily as a man follows the hallway in his own home. Bixby told him he must learn the river "with such absolute certainty that you can always steer by the shape that's *in your head*, and never mind the one that's before your eyes."

His pilot license was granted in April, 1859, and afterwards Bixby recalled that "Sam was always scribbling when not at the wheel." He published in May, 1859, in the New Orleans *True Delta* a sketch entitled "Sergeant Fathom," burlesquing Isaiah Sellers, an old pilot who wrote paragraphs of river information beginning "My opinion for the benefit of the citizens." Before Sam left the river, the New Orleans *Daily Crescent* had published his ten letters signed "Quintus Curtius Snodgrass," satirizing the martial glory of war, the mechanical-doll effect of military life, and the irony of the concern for a slain man's uniforms and military supplies rather than for his life.

At 23, making a good salary as pilot on the *City of Memphis*, "the largest boat in the trade," he dressed as a dandy in blue serge, white duck, and patent leather shoes. From New Orleans he wrote to Orion about dissipating on a ten-dollar dinner at a French restaurant—"breathe it not unto Ma!" But in April, 1861, the guns of Fort Sumter ended his piloting glory forever.

Afterwards he spent a few weeks in a loosely organized adjunct of the Confederate Army, a sort of home-talent militia whose exploits he recorded in "The Private History of a Campaign That Failed." Since he hated this brief acquaintance with army regimentation and, even more, the thought of killing, under the label of war, men "who had never done me any harm," he accompanied Orion Clemens west when Orion was appointed by President Abraham Lincoln as Territorial Secretary of Nevada. By tradition and environment Sam belonged with the Confederacy; but, if his consistent condemnation of slavery means anything, his sympathies must have been partially with the Union. Thus he forecast in his own life the conflict between tradition and conscience later fought out by Huckleberry Finn. Life and Lincoln and the trip west provided him with an escape from an intolerable situation.

He had soldiered unofficially with his Confederate friends; now he became, again unofficially, the "Assistant Secretary of the Territory of Nevada." This title, carrying no salary, was perhaps his price for the money he lent the Secretary, his brother Orion, to make the trip. Upon the arrival of the two brothers in Carson City in August, 1861, Sam immediately became fashionable in the Western mode: clad in old slouch hat, flannel shirt, rough trousers, and cowhide boots, he stood about the streets studying the chaotic drama of the new West. And at night Carson residents gathered about the stove in Orion's office to hear Sam tell river yarns in his inimitable drawl.

He succumbed to the mining mania, working as quartz-miller, pocket miner, prospector, stamp-mill operator, silver miner; but he never made a lucky strike. In July, 1862, he wrote to Orion, "If I can't move the bowels of those hills this fall, I will come up and clerk for you." From the Esmeralda mines he had sent to the *Territorial Enterprise* of Virginia City, Nevada, several burlesque letters signed "Josh." These letters amused Joseph Goodman, editor of the *Enterprise*, then one of the most famous newspapers west of the Mississippi. Accepting Goodman's offer of a job, Sam arrived at the *Enterprise* office in August, 1862, after walking most of the way. He announced as he dropped into a chair: "My starboard leg seems to be unshipped," and added, "My name is Clemens and I've come to write for the paper."

Critics have noted that up to this time Sam Clemens had served three "abortive apprenticeships"—as printer, pilot, and miner—and that his life work was still undetermined. Today it seems clear that during these three apprenticeships there was a fourth that he had never abandoned, that of the writing craft. This apprenticeship lasted from 1852 to 1862;

from this point on, he was a journalist, sometimes a superlative journalist, who finally matured into a great writer.

Early in 1863 Joe Goodman sent him to Carson City to report the proceedings of the legislature; and to a dispatch that appeared in the *Enterprise* of February 3, 1863, he signed for the first time the pseudonym "Mark Twain," a river term meaning two fathoms, or twelve feet, of water—a phrase he had liked to hear the leadsman call out on dark nights, for it meant "safe water for any boat on the river." This name soon replaced his real name even among his personal friends; with its fitness to the writer and his work, "Mark Twain" is the most famous pen name ever worn by an American.

In May, 1864, he came to San Francisco to work as a reporter on the *Morning Call*, routine work that he found "fearful drudgery"; but after the barren Nevada country, which had reminded him of "a singed cat," San Francisco at first seemed to him "heaven on the half shell." From March to July, 1866, he was in the Sandwich (Hawaiian) Islands, paying for his trip by letters published in the Sacramento *Union*. Returning to the mainland, with the encouragement of his friend Artemus Ward he launched himself in a new profession: in October, 1866, he delivered in San Francisco his first public lecture, "The Sandwich Islands," and found that he possessed the rare ability to entertain an audience. In May, 1867, he first lectured in New York City.

In June, 1867, he sailed on the *Quaker City* excursion which resulted in the book *The Innocents Abroad*. He was to write travel letters for publication in the *Alta California* and the New York *Tribune*. Upon his return he served briefly as secretary to a pompous senator in Washington, D.C., amidst the corruption and chicanery of the period that he himself later christened "The Gilded Age." When *The Innocents Abroad* was published, William Dean Howells, then the leading American critic, wrote a favorable review and Mark Twain called at the offices of the *Atlantic Monthly* to thank Howells characteristically in these words: "When I read that review of yours, I felt like the woman who was so glad that her baby had come white." The friendship begun on that day lasted for more than forty years.

On the *Quaker City* voyage Clemens had fallen romantically in love with the pictured face of Olivia Langdon, first seen in a miniature in the stateroom of her brother Charley. In 1870, after a persistent courtship, he married Olivia, a "correct" Eastern woman from a wealthy family, and they settled first in Buffalo and later in Hartford, where Mark Twain remained as a Connecticut Yankee for seventeen years. Four children were born to them, a son who died in infancy and three talented daughters. Much has been written on the damage Mrs. Clemens is supposed to have done to Twain's writings with her prudish editing; the record shows, however, that although he yielded to her in little things—"I would quit wearing socks if she thought them immoral"—in larger matters his influence was the dominant one.

Mark Twain once described himself as being in his young manhood "strangely handsome," so handsome that even inanimate things, "like locomotives and district messenger boys," stopped to look: "In San Francisco, in the rainy season, I was often mistaken for fair weather." Nearing fifty, he was amused by the description of him written by his little daughter Susy, aged thirteen: "He is the loveliest man I ever saw or ever hope to see, and oh so absent minded!" Susy continued her analysis: "The difference between papa and mama is, that mama loves morals and papa loves cats." He had many interests: lecturer on the public platform for the Redpath circuit, he was also inventor, publisher, business man of the Gilded Age; and once, summing up all his wide experience of living, he added the characteristic Twainian touch: "And I have been an author for 20 years and an ass for 55."

He never grew too old for clowning. In 1877 came his greatest fiasco—the speech at a birthday dinner honoring Whittier, in which he burlesqued Longfellow, Emerson, and Holmes to the cringing horror of all reverent Bostonians. Afterwards he wrote to Howells: "How could I ever— Ah, well, I am a great and sublime fool. But then I am God's fool, and all his works must be contemplated with respect."

He roamed restlessly about the world, maintaining his residence in Europe continuously for nine years, from June, 1891, to October, 1900. At various times he resided in London, Vienna, Paris, Berlin, Munich, and Florence, with summers in Switzerland and Sweden. He had invested in the Paige typesetting machine, which seemed to him a "cunning devil" of steel that could all but think. But this forerunner of the Mergenthaler proved impractical, and he lost the fortune of $190,000 that he had sunk in it. When his publishing company, managed by a nephew, was forced into bankruptcy, he wrote that the law "recognizes no mortgage on a man's brain," and a merchant may take advantage of the laws of insolvency and start again for himself: "But I am not a business man, and honor is a harder master than the law. It cannot compromise for less than 100 cents on the dollar, and its debts never outlaw." Almost sixty, he set off with his wife and his daughter Clara to "go platforming around the world" in order to pay his debts, a lecture tour recorded in the book *Following the Equator*. By 1898 all the debts were paid; but while the parents were away, the eldest daughter Susy, who had seemed to inherit her father's literary genius, died of meningitis. Feeling that if her parents had been there Susy might somehow have been saved, the grief-stricken Mark Twain bitterly denounced the trip they had taken because "it was packed with a sense of honor—honor—honor."

In 1904 the death of his wife Olivia in Italy left him, as he put it, "washing about on a forlorn sea of banquets." But when Oxford University desired to make him an honorary Doctor of Literature, he accepted: "Although I wouldn't cross the ocean again for the price of the ship that carried me, I am glad to do it for an Oxford degree." The rich scarlet of his Oxford gown enhanced the value of the degree in his eyes; he declared: "I like the degree well enough, but I'm crazy about the clothes!" Near his seventy-first birthday he began to wear white clothes for summer and winter alike, a striking complement to his white hair. In his famous white flannels he made an impressive figure striding up and down the stage of the world.

The elderly Mark Twain liked to lie in his huge carved bed in a red-walled room; he had acquired the habit of working in bed long before he grew old. There he read, he wrote, he smoked, and he frequently gave dictations to his official biographer, Albert Bigelow Paine. Sometimes in the dictations he went back to his earlier habit of a slow, circular walk, "the ceaseless, slippered, shuffling walk" described by Paine, with its rolling movement acquired long ago within the confines of the pilothouse. With that great mane of white hair, walking a regular measured beat, he must have resembled an aged lion, pacing the length of his cage.

But he retained his faculty of living in the present moment. His family, his friends, his pipe, his cats, his billiards, his books—all were sources of intense enjoyment. Of his immediate family only his daughter Clara remained alive during his last months. He died at his home in Redding, Connecticut, April 21, 1910, in his seventy-fifth year.

II

A study of Mark Twain's mind is a necessary accompaniment to a study of his work; but how can any mind, particularly a mind like Mark Twain's, be explained? Two years before he died, he wrote: "There are times—thousands of times—when I can expose the half of my mind and conceal the other half." Such mental legerdemain does not lessen the difficulty; neither does the dream quality which threaded his life. He wrote in his *Autobiography*: "What a wee little part of a person's life are his acts and his words. His real life is led in his head, and is known to none but himself; and his thoughts, not those other things, are his history." His "double personality" affected his entire life. In a book presenting Mark Twain as a business man, his great-nephew Samuel C. Webster comments that Twain's natural gifts were not those best suited for business success and that his own book could have been called *Mark Twain vs. Mark Twain*, a title applying not only to Twain's business life but also to the struggle that went on between his conscious and his unconscious: "What came to him from the inside was as real as what came from the outside." Mark Twain claimed to live a dream life independent of the life lived in his body. In our dreams, he maintained, "we do see the things we seem to see," the people, the horses, the cats, the dogs; these creatures are "immortal and indestructible," and they go "whither they will."

But most of the flowerings of his creativity were rooted in realism, and the soil that nourished those widely branching roots was American. Mark Twain, too, was American, perhaps to a degree no other writer before him, or since, has equalled. His father was a Virginian, his mother a Kentuckian. Florida, his birthplace, was in the "Pike" country of Missouri. And Hannibal was on the Mississippi, the Main Street of middle America, the Giant Midway for what must have seemed then a continuous world's fair. This fact added a tang of cosmopolitanism to the pre-industrial, rural flavor of the little river town. Mark Twain *lived* in the South; he *lived* in the Midwest, in Iowa; he *lived* in the Far West, in Nevada and San Francisco; he *lived* in Connecticut; he *lived* in New York. By the time he was thirty, he knew the behavior patterns of his nation and its authentic idioms as few have ever known them, and of three of its great folk experiences he had been a part: the settlement of the Southwestern frontier; the steamboat era on the Mississippi; and the bonanza fever in the Far West. He had a bone-deep sense of the South, its ingrown sense of honor, its rigid tradition; yet Howells called him in later years "the most de-southernized Southerner I have ever known."

His moods were myriad; his intensity was remarkable. Capable of a savage vindictiveness, he was ordinarily the kindest of men. Orion early wrote that "Sam's organization is such as to feel the utmost extreme of every feeling." His sensitivity was recorded by Helen Keller: "He knew with keen and sure intuition many things about me; how it felt to be blind and not to be able to keep up with the swift ones," things that others "learned slowly or not at all." This imaginative fellow-feeling with the lives of others was, surely, his greatest artistic asset. And he might have said with Whitman, "I am the man, I suffered, I was there," with the difference—as Dixon Wecter noted—that Whitman's immediacy was imaginative, Mark Twain's actual.

Howells realized that Twain's casual acquaintances might know him "from his fierce intensity, his wild pleasure in shocking people with his ribaldries and profanities, as anything but exquisite, and yet that was what in the last analysis he was."

Critical controversy began in 1920 with *The Ordeal of Mark Twain* by Van Wyck Brooks, who felt that Twain exhibited the signs of an endowment "more extraordinary than that of any other American writer"; and yet his boyhood on the raw Missouri frontier had stunted his artistic development, while the Far West had further thwarted it. To Brooks, Hannibal was a barren place, devoid of aesthetic experiences, where the child Sam Clemens had only, on the one hand, the narrowness of his mother's iron-clad Calvinism and, on the other, the nerve-shattering voodoo tales of the Negro slaves. The imagination of a fanciful child, however, is seldom a literal copy of his surroundings; and actually much of Sam's environment was rich in imaginative quality. By his village flowed the Mississippi, in his words, "the majestic, the magnificent Mississippi, rolling its mile-wide tide along, shining in the sun"; and his literary treatment of the river evidences the power which its beauty and its grandeur exerted over his imagination. The fact that he grew up among Negroes, too, is important for the artist; for, as Bernard DeVoto noticed, much in his art springs from "the melancholy, the music, the laughter, the terror, and the magic of the slaves." In 1932 DeVoto published *Mark Twain's America*, in part an answer to the assertion of Brooks that Mark Twain's Western frontier was "the barrenest spot in all Christendom, surely, for the seed of genius to fall in." DeVoto believed that the West, far from stultifying Twain's artistic growth, had actually developed his latent capacities. Denying Brooks's charge that by becoming a humorist Twain "was arrested in his moral and aesthetic development," DeVoto held that he had abundantly fulfilled himself through the writing of humor.

Mark Twain's formal schooling was brief, although he enrolled early in what Lincoln called the poor boy's college—the printing shop. Speaking of his own assets as a novelist, he once wrote: "I surely have the equipment, a wide culture and all of it real, none of it artificial, for I don't know anything about books." Yet the compilations of his reading, made by various critics and biographers, are impressive. He has been described as "unacademic, but not unliterary," and his light-handed attitude towards his own literary work must always be discounted. In 1909, looking backward over a long life packed with fame, fortune, and misfortune, he said, "To me, the most important feature of my life is its literary feature." And when his daughter Clara seemed completely absorbed in her music, he said, "It is as I used to be with the pen long ago, and it is life, *life*, LIFE— there is no life comparable to it for a moment."

He once remarked, "I like history, biography, travels, curious facts and strange happenings, and science. And I detest novels, poetry, and the- ology." But the novels he detested were those of sentimental "lady au- thoresses" and "jejune romanticism." In 1874, in "What Paul Bourget Thinks of Us," he gave the novel an importance only recently accorded it in our own time, placing the novelist above the statistician and the sociolo- gist. He insisted that only one expert "is qualified to examine the soul and the life of a people and make a valuable report—the native novelist." Each novelist writes of his own place, and when a thousand novels are written, they give "the soul of the people, the life of the people, the speech of the people; and not anywhere else can these be had."

Humor is a complex genre. It is usually premeditated, not spontaneous, and arises from a background of such gloom that emergent flashes of humor only seem spontaneous by contrast. The genuine humorist is an intense individualist who feels his own great powers and yet recognizes the hopelessness of trying to change the world; baffled, he "laughs it off." A Law of Humor might demand as its components an intensely sensitive person surrounded by a soul-searing misery; critics have applied such terms to Dickens.

Unlike Dickens, Sam Clemens seems to have had a delightful child- hood; yet part of his work is marked by a humor blended with sadness, a humor different from his earlier Western brand of exaggeration, antiro- manticism, and broad irony. Reviewing Mark Twain's work, Howells spoke of "the instinct of right and wrong which keeps him clear as to the con- ditions that formed him, and their injustice." What unjust conditions formed Mark Twain? Apparently Howells had in mind the conditions of slavery. In the Preface to *The Marble Faun*, Hawthorne had complained of the difficulty of writing about America, "a country where there is no shadow" and "no picturesque and gloomy wrong." For Mark Twain, slavery furnished these requisites.

For in that childhood of Sam Clemens, mainly so delightful, some ter- rible moments sank deep into the mind of a sensitive child. He saw a white man kill his slave with a lump of iron for some slight offense. He remembered seeing black men and women chained together, lying on the pavement, awaiting shipment down the river: "They had the saddest faces I ever saw." His knowledge of slavery was present in his buried conscious- ness, as revealed by an incident in India in 1896. There he saw a brutal innkeeper strike a native servant across the face; and instantly, back through three-score years, for just one moment "All that goes to make the *me* in me was in a Missourian village, on the other side of the globe." The memories of slavery which life had hung up in the back of his mind, tapes- tried with other elements of fear and dread woven into the fiber of his frontier village, furnished the somber curtain over which the flashes of his humor played. The ill-treatment of Chinese laborers in San Francisco; the exploitation by whites of the brown-skinned natives in the Hawaiian Islands and the Philippines; the plight of the Maoris; the prolonged dis- crimination in some quarters against the Jews—always the spectacle of the weak being oppressed by the strong aroused him to write. He was not only a "born humorist"; he was also a born reformer.

Politically, he cherished a "no-party independence," blasting the "tyranny of party" that turns voters into "chattels, slaves, rabbits." He urged Joe Twichell to get out of "that sewer"—party politics—and fumigate himself. Philosophically, he was not profound. His reaction to life was intuitive rather than analytical, emotional rather than intellectual; and his criticism of life followed the same pattern.

In Dixon Wecter's phrase, Mark Twain's was "not a single-track mind, but a whole switchyard." A Puritan-Presbyterian by the early training of his mother, he was by temperament inclined to the "free thinking" of his father. An inheritor of various Southern traditions, he was in spirit akin to the Western freedom from tradition, even hatred of it. His experience placed him in the current conflict between realism and romanticism: the adventures of settling the West invited a romantic coloring, while the hardships of frontier life enforced a realistic point of view. And there was still another conflict, more influential than these in its effect on his art.

Abnormally sensitive, Mark Twain looked upon the woes of the world and suffered, at the same time contemplating with absorbed fascination the depravity of Man. A rabid reformer, eager to uplift, instruct, and purify mankind, he was also a dogmatic determinist, preaching as his "Gospel" that the innate disposition of mankind is "as permanent as rock, and never undergoes any actual change between cradle and grave"—a doctrine which renders futile all attempts to uplift, instruct, or purify mankind. This clash of ideas sometimes made for a lack of unity in his writing; but in his greatest works the skill of the artist fused literary elements in such a way as to overcome the logical dilemma of a mind divided against itself.

He tried to uplift "the mighty mass" of mankind; but when human nature refused to change, then he remembered that mankind is only "the damned human race." Perhaps Twain's sense of sharing in the baseness of the human race, coupled with his extreme sensitivity, explains his compulsive urge toward reform as well as the self-accusations, the feelings of guilt with which he punished himself.

There was marked difference between his opinion of humanity in the abstract and his opinion of individuals whom he knew and loved. Like Swift, he hated Man, but loved men. Clara Clemens says that he always "took for granted that anyone he met must be a nice person." Yet when he contemplated humanity-at-large, he longed for a pen "warmed up in hell." Because he carried in his soul the intolerable burden of pity, he was pulled in two directions at once. Rage and pity constantly fought within him: rage at the blundering human pack with its crassness, stupidity, and meanness; pity for the helpless victims of man's inhumanity to man.

III

Mark Twain's work, covering many levels of significance, does not lend itself readily to classification; but most of it is pervaded by his humor, which varies in aims and importance. Seeming effortless when well done, humor demands such a discipline to the exacting regulations of the craft that the mortality rate among humorists is extremely high. In his boyish

Thomas Jefferson Snodgrass letters, Mark Twain exploited cacography as used by Artemus Ward and Josh Billings; later he learned from John Phoenix that humor need not be illiterate. In its infinite variety, humor is often, as he himself wrote, "merely an odd trick of speech." He used numerous examples of this type, such as the opening of his "biography" of Washington: "This day, many years ago precisely, George Washington was born"; or his claim that he had been all through the newspaper business "from Alpha to Omaha."

Amid the patterns of the world's humor, through the techniques of the professional humorist, he wandered at will, selecting now one device, now another. For reasons of his own he favored burlesque, which entails a double vision: the thing itself is seen and judged; then it is viewed at a different angle so that it is thrown out of perspective, with a caricature as the result. Upon examination, most of Mark Twain's Western sketches, though deeply sheathed in buffoonery and burlesque, will be found to contain elements of social, political, and moral satire. His own early intention toward satire embodied in burlesque he stated in the *Galaxy* in 1870: "One can deliver a satire with telling force through the insidious medium of a travesty, if he is careful not to overwhelm the satire with the extraneous interest of the travesty, and so bury it from the reader's sight and leave him a joked and defrauded victim, when the honest intent was to add to either his knowledge or his wisdom."

In the West, Mark Twain concerned himself, not with the degenerates pictured by Bret Harte, but with the primitives. Nor did he select the "heroic personalities" that Whitman associated with the West, but rather the stolid, steadfast creatures of the frontier, concentrating on their minute characteristics of appearance, speech, behavior, and thought. Later he asserted: "One isn't a printer ten years without setting up acres of good and bad literature, and learning—unconsciously at first, consciously later—to discriminate between the two." From boyhood on, he had been familiar with a group of Southern and Southwestern humorists, including Augustus B. Longstreet, W. T. Thompson, J. J. Hooper, J. G. Baldwin, G. W. Harris, and T. B. Thorpe. These men, skilled local-colorists and raconteurs, were America's first realists. Their studies of pioneer characters crossed the country in newspaper columns, always at hand for use as fillers in the exchanges. Sam Clemens knew their humor well, but had perhaps forgotten it in his interest in the burlesque-bearing-a-moral.

Then in 1864 he visited Jim Gillis on Jackass Hill, near Angel's Camp in the Tuolumne region of California. Gillis was a finished artist in the genre of the tall tale, and some of his yarns were recognized by Mark Twain as masterpieces. Twain's immediate resources were his quick eye, his sensitive ear (he had long delighted in transferring to print a dialect, a vernacular, or any oddity of speech), and his keen insight into human nature. But until his three-month visit with Gillis, he had used these assets mainly for his satiric burlesques written as social criticism; now he began to draw frontier personalities for their own sakes.

His notebook recorded a tale of a jumping frog, told by Ben Coon in the barroom at Angel's Camp. By the time he wrote out the frog anecdote, he had already arrived at most of the knowledge that he set forth in 1896 in "How to Tell a Story." When Artemus Ward invited him to contribute to a volume of sketches, Twain sent him "Jim Smiley and His Jumping Frog." Reaching New York too late for publication in the book, it appeared in the *Saturday Press* of November 18, 1865; from the *Press* it was copied all over the country, and Mark Twain was a celebrity. His familiarity with the Southwestern humor led, in his work, to the American tall tale produced on the level of genius. The Far West, too, aided in his literary growth by sharpening his natural satiric gift.

In the *Autobiography*, speaking of a group of American humorists then forgotten but famous thirty years before, he said they had failed because they "were merely humorists. Humorists of the 'mere' sort cannot survive." He insisted, "Humor must not professedly teach and it must not professedly preach, but it must do both if it would live forever. By forever, I mean thirty years." And he added, "I have always preached." In many humorous sketches his satire is delivered "through the insidious medium" of burlesque; but in the novels his "preaching" lies mainly in selection and presentation. Let one example suffice, a brief and nonchalant, but reader-chilling, conversation in *Huckleberry Finn* in which Huck reports to kindly Aunt Sally Phelps that a steamboat has just "blowed out a cylinder-head" and Aunt Sally exclaims:

"Good gracious! anybody hurt?"
"No'm. Killed a nigger."
"Well, it's lucky; because sometimes people do get hurt."

His gifts were particularly suited to travel-writing: acute observation, sharp sensuous impression, and a detached point of view are requisites. In this type, his first success was *The Innocents Abroad* (1869), often called the American literary declaration of independence from Europe; and so it was. Written by one who, in his formative years, looked inward to the Mississippi, not outward to the Atlantic and to Europe beyond, the book exhibits sometimes a disdain of European culture, sometimes a sheer indifference to it. But Twain frequently turns his attention to his countrymen, as when he derides the aura of self-satisfaction that hangs about the typical American tourist or contrasts the European leisurely pace of living with the American frantic rush and restlessness and worry.

Roughing It (1871) is imbued with the very spirit of the West, grotesque, violent, ironic. It contains passages tinged with nostalgia for the vanishing West, as *Life on the Mississippi* catches the sunset color of the flush times on the river. Personalized narrative, laced with description and anecdote, is the vehicle of *The Innocents Abroad*, *Roughing It*, *A Tramp Abroad* (1880), and *Life on the Mississippi*; after the first two, gusto gradually diminishes until *Following the Equator* (1897), in which flippancy also dies under the spell which India laid upon him, India which seemed "to ache with age and penury" and a haunting sense of "the myriads of human lives that have blossomed, and withered, and perished here."

In 1873 he began *The Gilded Age*, his first novel, in collaboration with his Hartford neighbor, Charles Dudley Warner. Twain said that he himself "wrote the first eleven chapters, every word and every line." In them he portrayed the village in its filth, apathy, and repression of personal ambition—the literary treatment hailed by Carl Van Doren as something new when Edgar Lee Masters presented it in 1915, closely followed by

Sherwood Anderson and Sinclair Lewis. Twain here introduces the fabulous Colonel Sellers, synthesis of all the get-rich-quick speculators produced by the era that still wears the name Mark Twain gave it. Yet Sellers personally is warmhearted, generous, likable, and pathetic, sincerely convinced that his schemes are for the public good as well as for his own.

In *The Adventures of Tom Sawyer* (1876), Tom's village, St. Petersburg, of all Mark Twain's villages most nearly resembles Hannibal. Softened by nostalgia, various scenes exhibit the cowardice, instability, and greed of this village. The theme presented here becomes the core of his later fiction: a boy led through initiatory experiences into the beginnings of manhood: "So endeth this chronicle. It being strictly the history of a *boy*, it must stop here; the story could not go much further without becoming the history of a *man*." *Tom Sawyer*, perhaps the supreme idyl of boyhood in American literature, contains the proof that Hannibal held for the boy Sam Clemens anxiety, fear of violence, horror of the supernatural, and an all-enveloping dread. In Hannibal Mark Twain apparently recognized the ambiguity of life: murder, robbery, stupidity on one hand; on the other, the slow, golden peace of Tom Sawyer's long summer; and thus the forces of good and evil are held in the tension that art demands. In the book the two boys go beyond natural innocence to the knowledge of evil, even to indirect participation in evil.

The *Prince and the Pauper* (1880) was Twain's first full-length study of the power of determining environment and circumstance; here, changing prince into beggar and beggar into prince, he ridicules superstition, meaningless ritual, and laws that force men into thievery. And here, as in *Huckleberry Finn*, boys journey about, learning much of the way of the world through their travels.

In July, 1876, Mark Twain had begun a new book, *Adventures of Huckleberry Finn*. The evocative power of his memories of boyhood, the village, and the river produced the three books generally accounted his best: *Tom Sawyer, Life on the Mississippi,* and *Huckleberry Finn.* The last named is his masterpiece, now viewed as one of the great American novels—some will have it the greatest American novel—and one of the classics of world literature. Its episodic form is held together only by the character of Huck, the narrator, and by the river, to Nigger Jim the symbol of freedom.

Huck's book falls naturally into three thematic units. The first centers around St. Petersburg; Huck, Tom, Pap, and Nigger Jim are all important. The second includes the most satiric, the most powerful part, bringing Huck and Jim into contact with every level of the South. Huck witnesses scenes etched into the reader's memory: the Grangerford-Shepherdson feud, ending in the murder of boys; the killing of old Boggs—a pitiful figure, drunken, red-faced, gray-haired, egged on by street loafers for their entertainment on a dull afternoon; the swift gathering of the mob to lynch Colonel Sherburn; and the Colonel's efficient wilting of the mob. The third thematic unit is short, covering the period in which Tom re-enters the story, ready to free Jim by tried-and-trite devices, thus repeating the romanticized motif of the first part, to come full circle.

The characters and their interrelationships determine the arrangement and structure of the book. The three thematic units subdivide into little units notable for the contrast they offer each other. The first three chapters, continuing the vein of *Tom Sawyer*, are colored by the excitement of Tom's romantic adventures. In the next four the story veers sharply from the mood of *Tom Sawyer*; a note of dark foreboding is struck, and Pap Finn, drunken and disreputable, becomes dominant. This unit ends when Huck flees because he fears his father will kill him in a fit of delirium tremens. After so much violence, Jackson's Island gives him a feeling of peace; then he discovers Jim, a runaway Negro, and the two share the island and their loneliness. This small unit of four chapters, the interlude on Jackson's Island, ends once more in the threat of violence and fear. Men are approaching the island to search for Jim.

The three figures, Tom, Huck, and Jim, aid Mark Twain in presenting a satire on institutionalism. Tom, though the most "civilized," represents a mawkish, artificial civilization; he is in bondage to his romantic books, which he consults and follows. Nigger Jim is in bondage to his voodoo fears and taboos and charms. Only Huck is free of institutions (Mark Twain seems to view the village as an "institution"). With Tom, Huck is willing to join in following the books; with Jim, after some heretical arguments, he accepts the taboos and tries not to break them. But when he is alone, he "studies things out" and is guided by the voice inside him, what we call his soul.

The use of Huck as narrator was a boon to Mark Twain. In 1878 he had written Howells that "a man can't write successful satire except he be in a calm, judicial good humour," confessing that "I don't ever seem to be in a good enough humour with anything to satirize it. No, I want to stand up before it and curse it and foam at the mouth." But here, all the meannesses of "the damned human race" are seen through the eyes and reported through the lips of Huck Finn. And thus Twain was able to attain the detachment that satire demands.

A *Connecticut Yankee in King Arthur's Court* (1889) brings Hank, the Yankee, "loaded" with 19th-century technical efficiency, into head-on collision with the feudal society of 528. The book points up not only the injustices of Arthur's England, but also those of Victoria's England and Mark Twain's America. The Yankee felt that what most of the enslaved English needed was "a new deal." The phrase "New Deal" became a United States government slogan some years ago; but in Twain's book, so-called "Progress" loses out to entrenched Superstition. Electrically charged fences indirectly kill the Yankee's eager students of technology, left to die "in a trap of our own making"; the pestilence, fatal for everyone except Hank, comes of using the invention that destroys its creators by diseases bred of the decaying human flesh stacked up against the electric fence. Not a pretty thought, but neither is the death-dealing power of the atom bomb in our own century.

Pudd'nhead Wilson (1894) presents Twain's most detailed study of determinism; he had discovered that the old idea of babies swapped in their cradles—master for slave, slave for master—was a "natural" for his deterministic theme. The locale is Dawson's Landing, and again the narrow confines of village life enable the writer to bring the inhabitants under a microscopic scrutiny. Obedstown, Murpheysburg, Hawkeye, St. Petersburg, Pokeville, Bricksville, the little town "below the P'int," Dawson's Landing—

all these are included in Twain's fictional itinerary. Near the end of the line stands Hadleyburg. At the very end stands Eseldorf—translation, "Assville." And the book coming out of Eseldorf is *The Mysterious Stranger*.

When Twain read *The Mysterious Stranger* to his wife Livy, her reaction was that it was "Perfectly horrible—and perfectly beautiful!" A strange mingling of the beautiful and the horrible permeates the book. When young Satan (the unfallen nephew of a better-known Satan) decides to "help" the village, his remedies are fortunate death and merciful insanity; at the book's close, he adds a third: one must cling to the idea that life is only a dream. When Mark Twain at last arrives at the bitter nihilism of *The Mysterious Stranger*, he arrives by a path on which his feet have been set since the Sandwich Island letters of 1866, with their siren song of escape from an active life to an isle of dreams—of peace, of emptiness. Satan's name on earth is Philip Traum, and *traum* means "dream." The Mark Twain of *The Mysterious Stranger* affirms, too, the creed of that Mark Twain of Western journalism who had insisted that "one can deliver a satire with telling force through the insidious medium of a travesty"; for Satan explains to young Theodor that "your race, in its poverty, has unquestionably one really effective weapon—laughter."

Horror impinges on beauty in every scene in which young Satan figures. Satan's last conclusion is that "there is no God, no universe, no human race, no earthly life, no heaven, no hell. It is all a dream—a grotesque and foolish dream." In this dreamlike hopelessness, the despair is greater than in the anger that rages and foams. But the art is greater, too. Through forty years as a professional writer, Mark Twain developed certain devices to enable himself to write satire without "foaming at the mouth": by speaking through the lips of Huck Finn or through the childlike mind of Nigger Jim or Captain Stormfield; by setting satiric scenes far off in time and space—the 6th-century England of King Arthur, the 15th-century France of Joan of Arc, the 16th-century England of Edward VI, the 16th-century Austria of Eseldorf, the far-off Heaven of Captain Stormfield; by diminishing to microscopic proportions scenes in which human beings are involved in terrible sufferings, as when viewed from a balloon in *Tom Sawyer Abroad*, or glimpsed through the wrong end of a telescope in "The Great Dark," or seen through the Olympian eye of a god in *The Mysterious Stranger*; finally, by reducing life to a dream, as in both "The Great Dark" and *The Mysterious Stranger*, where the greatest wrongs become bearable simply because they are not real. The effect of all these devices is the same—to lend perspective, aesthetic distance, serenity, the qualities Mark Twain needed most as a writer.

IV

Opinions expressed on Mark Twain and his work make an interesting study in themselves. In spite of his prolonged youthful attempts at writing, his widest fame came first from the lecture platform, where he demonstrated what Paine called "the purest exemplification of the platform entertainer's art which this country has ever seen." He memorized his speeches and then tried by every artifice to make them sound unmemorized and spontaneous. Howells declared: "He was the most consummate public performer I ever saw."

Off the platform, he threw out comment and anecdote that amazed and dazzled his friends. Little by little, the American East—following the lead of England—succumbed to the charm of his personality. But, unlike English readers, Americans were slow to see anything in his books except his humor, beneath which lay the hard core of his truth.

Those who met him were frequently struck by his masklike expression. Howells said that "he was apt to smile into your face with a subtle but amiable perception, and yet with a sort of remote absence; you were all there for him, but he was not all there for you." Hamlin Garland, too, found in Twain a curious aloofness, as though he spoke through a mask. Lewis Leary recently wrote that "Mark Twain is a mask, a controlled, drawling, and whimsical voice, a posturing and flamboyant figure, behind which exists the man, Samuel Langhorne Clemens," who created him. As early as 1870 Bret Harte, reviewing *The Innocents Abroad*, warned readers they should remember "that the irascible pilgrim, 'Mark Twain,' is a very eccentric creation of Mr. Clemens."

Critics have hailed his style as one of the great styles of American literature, possessing remarkable simplicity, clarity, and flexibility. DeVoto called it "so lucid that it seems effortless," maintaining that Mark Twain "had a greater effect than any other writer on the evolution of American prose."

Truly, the liberating effect on American writing of such innovations as Twain's use of the vernacular and his early "revolt from the village" can hardly be overstated. The chief vehicle of his influence has been *Adventures of Huckleberry Finn*, which had confused and bewildered many contemporary critics by its unorthodoxy; but there were perceptive critics as early as 1900, when Barrett Wendell of Harvard spoke of it as "the most admirable work of literary art as yet produced on this continent." Later, John Erskine pointed out that the way Twain blends realism, romanticism, and satire here has produced a thing that is art—a book "so close to the life of the people that it can hold any reader, and yet so subtle in its art that the craftsman tries to find out how it was done."

Sometimes the overwhelming effect of *Huck Finn* has been feared. In the first decade of this century it was banned by libraries in Concord, Denver, and Omaha, and also, as Twain said, was "flung out of Brooklyn." Although for fifty years *Huck* and young readers existed amicably together, in 1957, according to Walter Blair, the Board of Education of New York City excluded the book from some reading lists.

But acclaim has been tremendous. Even Van Wyck Brooks, who held that Mark Twain had not fulfilled himself as a writer, spoke of "the beauty, the eternal freshness" of *Huckleberry Finn*: "it flies like a gay, bright, shining arrow through the tepid atmosphere of American literature." In 1935 Ernest Hemingway wrote: "All modern American literature comes from one book by Mark Twain called *Huckleberry Finn*"; he called it "the best book we've had. All American writing comes from that. There was nothing before. There has been nothing as good since." In Nagano, Japan, early in 1956, William Faulkner said, "Mark Twain was the first truly American writer, and all of us since are his heirs, we descended from him." Among Mark Twain's American "heirs," critics have listed Jack London, O. Henry, Ring Lardner, Theodore Dreiser, Booth Tarkington, Sherwood Anderson, Sinclair Lewis, and J. D. Salinger, as well as Hemingway and Faulkner. Recently the assertion has been made that Mark Twain's colloquial style has even "spilled over into world literature."

His old friend Howells, although a professional writer, admitted his failure at catching in words the essence of Mark Twain: "It is in vain that I try to give a notion of the intensity with which he pierced to the heart of life." And Howells, who had known Emerson, Longfellow, Lowell, Holmes—"I knew them all and all the rest of our sages, poets, seers, critics, humorists; they were like one another and like other literary men"— Howells pronounced Mark Twain's nature "rich and fertile beyond any I have known." In Howells' final judgment, "Clemens was sole, incomparable."

From The Innocents Abroad[1]
Chapter XIII. [Paris Guides and Paris Sights]

The next morning we were up and dressed at ten o'clock.[2] We went to the *commissionaire* of the hotel—I don't know what a *commissionaire* is, but that is the man we went to—and told him we wanted a guide. He said the great International Exposition had drawn such multitudes of Englishmen and Americans to Paris that it would be next to impossible to find a good guide unemployed. He said he usually kept a dozen or two on hand, but he only had three now. He called them. One looked so like a very pirate that we let him go at once. The next one spoke with a simpering precision of pronunciation that was irritating, and said:

"If ze zhentlemans will to me make ze grande honneur to me rattain in hees serveece, I shall show to him everysing zat is magnifique to look upon in ze beautiful Parree. I speaky ze Angleesh pairfaitemaw."

He would have done well to have stopped there, because he had that much by heart and said it right off without making a mistake. But his self-complacency seduced him into attempting a flight into regions of unexplored English, and the reckless experiment was his ruin. Within ten seconds he was so tangled up in a maze of mutilated verbs and torn and bleeding forms of speech that no human ingenuity could ever have gotten him out of it with credit. It was plain that he could not "speaky" the English quite as "pairfaitemaw" as he had pretended he could.

The third man captured us. He was plainly dressed, but he had a noticeable air of neatness about him. He wore a high silk hat which was a little old, but had been carefully brushed. He wore second-hand kid gloves, in good repair, and carried a small rattan cane with a curved handle—a female leg, of ivory. He stepped as

1. *The Innocents Abroad, or The New Pilgrim's Progress*, appeared in 1869, recording Mark Twain's five months of travel in Europe, the Holy Land, and Egypt. The present text is from the Author's Uniform Edition (1899).
2. This chapter begins the travelers' second day in Paris, in early July, 1867.

gently and as daintily as a cat crossing a muddy street; and oh, he
was urbanity; he was quiet, unobtrusive self-possession; he was deference itself! He spoke softly and guardedly; and was about to
make a statement on his sole responsibility, or offer a suggestion,
he weighed it by drachms and scruples first,[3] with the crook of his
little stick placed meditatively to his teeth. His opening speech was
perfect. It was perfect in construction, in phraseology, in grammar,
in emphasis, in pronunciation—everything. He spoke little and
guardedly, after that. We were charmed. We were more than
charmed—we were overjoyed. We hired him at once. We never
even asked him his price. This man—our lackey, our servant, our
unquestioning slave though he was, was still a gentleman—we
could see that—while of the other two one was coarse and awkward,
and the other was a born pirate. We asked our man Friday's name.
He drew from his pocketbook a snowy little card, and passed it to
us with a profound bow:

A. BILLFINGER,
Guide to Paris, France, Germany,
Spain, &c., &c.,
Grande Hotel du Louvre.

"Billfinger! Oh, carry me home to die!"

That was an "aside" from Dan. The atrocious name grated
harshly on my ear, too. The most of us can learn to forgive, and
even to like, a countenance that strikes us unpleasantly at first, but
few of us, I fancy, become reconciled to a jarring name so easily.
I was almost sorry we had hired this man, his name was so unbearable. However, no matter. We were impatient to start. Billfinger stepped to the door to call a carriage, and then the doctor[4]
said:

"Well, the guide goes with the barber-shop, with the billiard
table, with the gasless room, and maybe with many another pretty
romance of Paris. I expected to have a guide named Henri de
Montmorency, or Armand de la Chartreuse, or something that
would sound grand in letters to the villagers at home; but to think
of a Frenchman by the name of Billfinger! Oh! this is absurd, you
know. This will never do. We can't say Billfinger; it is nauseating.
Name him over again; what had we better call him? Alexis du
Caulaincourt?"

"Alphonse Henri Gustave de Hauteville," I suggested.

"Call him Ferguson," said Dan.

This was practical, unromantic good sense. Without debate, we

---

3. The "drachm," or drachma, was in
ancient Greece a small weight of various values; the "scruple" was the smallest unit of weight in Roman antiquity.

4. Dr. A. Reeves Jackson, a Pennsyl-
vania physician; "Dan" was Dan Slote,
Mark Twain's roommate on the *Quaker
City* voyage.

expunged Billfinger *as* Billfinger, and called him Ferguson.

The carriage—an open barouche—was ready. Ferguson mounted beside the driver, and we whirled away to breakfast. As was proper, Mr. Ferguson stood by to transmit our orders and answer questions. By and by, he mentioned casually—the artful adventurer— that he would go and get his breakfast as soon as we had finished ours. He knew we could not get along without him, and that we would not want to loiter about and wait for him. We asked him to sit down and eat with us. He begged, with many a bow, to be excused. It was not proper, he said; he would sit at another table. We ordered him peremptorily to sit down with us.

Here endeth the first lesson. It was a mistake.

As long as we had the fellow after that, he was always hungry; he was always thirsty. He came early; he stayed late; he could not pass a restaurant; he looked with a lecherous eye upon every wine-shop. Suggestions to stop, excuses to eat and to drink were forever on his lips. We tried all we could to fill him so full that he would have no room to spare for a fortnight; but it was a failure. He did not hold enough to smother the cravings of his superhuman appetite.

He had another "discrepancy" about him. He was always wanting us to buy things. On the shallowest pretenses, he would inveigle us into shirt-stores, boot-stores, tailor-shops, glove-shops—anywhere under the broad sweep of the heavens that there seemed a chance of our buying anything. Any one could have guessed that the shopkeepers paid him a percentage on the sales; but in our blessed innocence we didn't, until this feature of his conduct grew unbearably prominent. One day, Dan happened to mention that he thought of buying three or four silk dress-patterns for presents. Ferguson's hungry eye was upon him in an instant. In the course of twenty minutes, the carriage stopped.

"What's this?"

"Zis is ze finest silk magazin in Paris—ze most celebrate."

"What did you come here for? We told you to take us to the palace of the Louvre."

"I suppose ze gentleman say he wish to buy some silk."

"You are not required to 'suppose' things for the party, Ferguson. We do not wish to tax your energies too much. We will bear some of the burden and heat of the day ourselves. We will endeavor to do such 'supposing' as is really necessary to be done. Drive on." So spake the doctor.

Within fifteen minutes the carriage halted again, and before another silk-store. The doctor said:

"Ah, the palace of the Louvre; beautiful, beautiful edifice! Does the Emperor Napoleon live here now, Ferguson?"

"Ah, doctor! you do jest; zis is not ze palace; we come there directly. But since we pass right by zis store, where is such beautiful silk——"

"Ah! I see, I see. I meant to have told you that we did not wish to purchase any silks to-day; but in my absentmindedness I forgot it. I also meant to tell you we wished to go directly to the Louvre; but I forgot that also. However, we will go there now. Pardon my seeming carelessness, Ferguson. Drive on."

Within the half-hour, we stopped again—in front of another silk-store. We were angry; but the doctor was always serene, always smooth-voiced. He said,

"At last! How imposing the Louvre is, and yet how small! how exquisitely fashioned! how charmingly situated! Venerable, venerable pile——"

"Pairdon, doctor, zis is not ze Louvre—it is——"

"*What* is it?"

"I have ze idea—it come to me in a moment—zat ze silk in zis magazin——"

"Ferguson, how heedless I am! I fully intended to tell you that we did not wish to buy any silks to-day, and I also intended to tell you that we yearned to go immediately to the palace of the Louvre, but enjoying the happiness of seeing you devour four breakfasts this morning has so filled me with pleasurable emotions that I neglect the commonest interests of the time. However, we will proceed now to the Louvre, Ferguson."

"But, doctor" (excitedly), "it will take not a minute—not but one small minute! Ze gentleman need not to buy if he not wish to—but only *look* at ze silk—*look* at ze beautiful fabric." [Then pleadingly.] "*Sair*—just only one *leetle* moment!"

Dan said, "Confound the idiot! I don't want to see any silks to-day, and I *won't* look at them. Drive on."

And the doctor: "We need no silks now, Ferguson. Our hearts yearn for the Louvre. Let us journey on—let us journey on."

"But, *doctor!* it is only one moment—one leetle moment. And ze time will be save—entirely save! Because zere is nothing to see, now—it is too late. It want ten minute to four and ze Louvre close at four—*only* one leetle moment, doctor!"

The treacherous miscreant! After four breakfasts and a gallon of champagne, to serve us such a scurvy trick. We got no sight of the countless treasures of art in the Louvre galleries that day, and our only poor little satisfaction was in the reflection that Ferguson sold not a solitary silk dress-pattern.

I am writing this chapter partly for the satisfaction of abusing that accomplished knave, Billfinger, and partly to show whosoever shall read this how Americans fare at the hands of the Paris guides, and what sort of people Paris guides are. It need not be

supposed that we were a stupider or an easier prey than our countrymen generally are, for we were not. The guides deceive and
defraud every American who goes to Paris for the first time and
sees its sights alone or in company with others as little experienced
as himself. I shall visit Paris again some day, and then let the
guides beware! I shall go in my war-paint—I shall carry my toma-
hawk along.

I think we have lost but little time in Paris. We have gone to
bed every night tired out. Of course, we visited the renowned
International Exposition. All the world did that. We went there
on our third day in Paris—and we stayed there *nearly two hours.*
That was our first and last visit. To tell the truth, we saw at a
glance that one would have to spend weeks—yea, even months—in
that monstrous establishment, to get an intelligible idea of it. It
was a wonderful show, but the moving masses of people of all
nations we saw there were a still more wonderful show. I discovered that if I were to stay there a month, I should still find
myself looking at the people instead of the inanimate objects on
exhibition. I got a little interested in some curious old tapestries
of the thirteenth century, but a party of Arabs came by, and their
dusky faces and quaint costumes called my attention away at once.[5]
I watched a silver swan, which had a living grace about his movements, and a living intelligence in his eyes—watched him swimming about as comfortably and as unconcernedly as if he had
been born in a morass instead of a jeweler's shop—watched him
seize a silver fish from under the water and hold up his head and
go through all the customary and elaborate motions of swallowing
it—but the moment it disappeared down his throat some tattooed
South Sea Islanders approached and I yielded to their attractions.
Presently I found a revolving pistol several hundred years old
which looked strangely like a modern Colt, but just then I heard
that the Empress of the French[6] was in another part of the building, and hastened away to see what she might look like. We heard
martial music—we saw an unusual number of soldiers walking
hurriedly about—there was a general movement among the people.
We inquired what it was all about, and learned that the Emperor
of the French and the Sultan of Turkey were about to review
twenty-five thousand troops at the *Arc de l'Étoile.* We immediately
departed. I had a greater anxiety to see these men than I could
have had to see twenty expositions.

We drove away and took up a position in an open space op-

5. In *Following the Equator,* his final
piece of sustained travel writing, Mark
Twain said that his interests when
traveling were "first, the people; next,
the novelties; and finally, the history
of the places and countries visited."

He could have said the same at this
early date.
6. The Spanish countess Eugénie de
Montijo, whom Louis Napoleon had
married in 1853.

posite the American minister's house. A speculator bridged a couple of barrels with a board and we hired standing places on it. Presently there was a sound of distant music; in another minute a pillar of dust came moving slowly toward us; a moment more, and then, with colors flying and a grand crash of military music, a gallant array of cavalrymen emerged from the dust and came down the street on a gentle trot. After them came a long line of artillery; then more cavalry, in splendid uniforms; and then their Imperial Majesties, Napoleon III and Abdul Aziz.[7] The vast concourse of people swung their hats and shouted—the windows and housetops in the wide vicinity burst into a snow-storm of waving handkerchiefs, and the wavers of the same mingled their cheers with those of the masses below. It was a stirring spectacle.

But the two central figures claimed all my attention. Was ever such a contrast set up before a multitude till then? Napoleon, in military uniform—a long-bodied, short-legged man, fiercely mustached, old, wrinkled, with eyes half closed, and *such* a deep, crafty, scheming expression about them! Napoleon, bowing ever so gently to the loud plaudits, and watching everything and everybody with his cat-eyes from under his depressed hatbrim, as if to discover any sign that those cheers were not heartfelt and cordial.

Abdul Aziz, absolute lord of the Ottoman Empire,—clad in dark green European clothes, almost without ornament or insignia of rank; a red Turkish fez on his head—a short, stout, dark man, black-bearded, black-eyed, stupid, unprepossessing—a man whose whole appearance somehow suggested that if he only had a cleaver in his hand and a white apron on, one would not be at all surprised to hear him say: "A mutton roast to-day, or will you have a nice porterhouse steak?"

Napoleon III, the representative of the highest modern civilization, progress, and refinement; Abdul Aziz, the representative of a people by nature and training filthy, brutish, ignorant, unprogressive, superstitious—and a government whose Three Graces are Tyranny, Rapacity, Blood. Here in brilliant Paris, under this majestic Arch of Triumph, the First Century greets the Nineteenth!

NAPOLEON III, Emperor of France! Surrounded by shouting thousands, by military pomp, by the splendors of his capital city, and companioned by kings and princes—this is the man who was sneered at, and reviled, and called Bastard—yet who was dreaming of a crown and an empire all the while; who was driven into exile —but carried his dreams with him; who associated with the common herd in America, and ran foot-races for a wager—but still

7. Sultan of Turkey (1861–76). Louis Napoleon, nephew of Napoleon I, was Emperor of the French as Napoleon III (1852–70).

sat upon a throne, in fancy; who braved every danger to go to his dying mother—and grieved that she could not be spared to see him cast aside his plebeian vestments for the purple of royalty; who kept his faithful watch and walked his weary beat a common policeman of London—but dreamed the while of a coming night when he should tread the long-drawn corridors of the Tuileries; who made the miserable *fiasco* of Strasbourg;[8] saw his poor, shabby eagle, forgetful of its lesson, refuse to perch upon his shoulder; delivered his carefully prepared, sententious burst of eloquence upon unsympathetic ears; found himself a prisoner, the butt of small wits, a mark for the pitiless ridicule of all the world—yet went on dreaming of coronations and splendid pageants as before; who lay a forgotten captive in the dungeons of Ham—and still schemed and planned and pondered over future glory and future power; President of France at last! a *coup d'état* and surrounded by applauding armies, welcomed by the thunders of cannon, he mounts a throne and waves before an astounded world the scepter of a mighty empire! Who talks of the marvels of fiction? Who speaks of the wonders of romance? Who prates of the tame achievements of Aladdin and the Magi of Arabia?

ABDUL AZIZ, Sultan of Turkey, Lord of the Ottoman Empire! Born to a throne; weak, stupid, ignorant, almost, as his meanest slave; chief of a vast royalty, yet the puppet of his premier and the obedient child of a tyrannical mother; a man who sits upon a throne—the beck of whose finger moves navies and armies—who holds in his hands the power of life and death over millions—yet who sleeps, sleeps, eats, eats, idles with his eight hundred concubines, and when he is surfeited with eating and sleeping and idling, and would rouse up and take the reins of government and threaten to *be* a Sultan, is charmed from his purpose by wary Fuad Pacha with a pretty plan for a new palace or a new ship—charmed away with a new toy, like any other restless child; a man who sees his people robbed and oppressed by soulless tax-gatherers, but speaks no word to save them; who believes in gnomes and genii and the wild fables of the Arabian Nights, but has small regard for the mighty magicians of to-day, and is nervous in the presence of their mysterious railroads and steamboats and telegraphs; who would see undone in Egypt all that great Mehemet Ali achieved, and would prefer rather to forget than emulate him; a man who found his great empire a blot upon the earth—a degraded, poverty-stricken, miserable, infamous agglomeration of ignorance, crime, and brutality, and will idle away the allotted days of his trivial life, and then pass to the dust and the worms and leave it so!

Napoleon has augmented the commercial prosperity of France,

8. Alluding to an unsuccessful revolt plotted by Louis Napoleon in 1836.

in ten years, to such a degree that figures can hardly compute it. He has rebuilt Paris, and has partly rebuilt every city in the state. He condemns a whole street at a time, assesses the damages, pays them, and rebuilds superbly. Then speculators buy up the ground and sell, but the original owner is given the first choice by the government at a stated price before the speculator is permitted to purchase. But above all things, he has taken the sole control of the empire of France into his hands, and made it a tolerably free land—for people who will not attempt to go too far in meddling with government affairs. No country offers greater security to life and property than France, and one has all the freedom he wants, but no license—no license to interfere with anybody, or make any one uncomfortable.

As for the Sultan, one could set a trap anywhere and catch a dozen abler men in a night.

The bands struck up, and the brilliant adventurer, Napoleon III, the genius of Energy, Persistence, Enterprise; and the feeble Abdul Aziz, the genius of Ignorance, Bigotry, and Indolence, prepared for the Forward—March!

We saw the splendid review, we saw the white-moustached old Crimean soldier, Canrobert, Marshal of France, we saw—well, we saw everything, and then we went home satisfied.

From *Chapter XXVII*. [*The* Genus *Ferguson*]

So far, good. If any man has a right to feel proud of himself, and satisfied, surely it is I. For I have written about the Coliseum and the gladiators, the martyrs and the lions, and yet have never once used the phrase "butchered to make a Roman holiday." I am the only free white man of mature age who has accomplished this since Byron originated the expression.

Butchered to make a Roman holiday sounds well for the first seventeen hundred thousand times one sees it in print, but after that it begins to grow tiresome. I find it in all the books concerning Rome—and here latterly it reminds me of Judge Oliver.[9] Oliver was a young lawyer, fresh from the schools, who had gone out to the deserts of Nevada to begin life. He found that country, and our ways of life there, in those early days, different from life in New England or Paris. But he put on a woolen shirt and strapped a navy revolver to his person, took to the bacon and beans of the country, and determined to do in Nevada as Nevada did. Oliver accepted the situation so completely that, although he must have sorrowed over many of his trials, he never complained —that is, he never complained but once. He, two others, and myself, started to the new silver mines in the Humboldt mountains—

9. A. W. "Gus" Oliver, twice elected Probate Judge of Humboldt County, Nevada.

he to be Probate Judge of Humboldt county, and we to mine. The distance was two hundred miles. It was dead of winter. We bought a two-horse wagon and put eighteen hundred pounds of bacon, flour, beans, blasting powder, picks, and shovels in it; we bought two sorry-looking Mexican "plugs," with the hair turned the wrong way and more corners on their bodies than there are on the mosque of Omar; we hitched up and started. It was a dreadful trip. But Oliver did not complain. The horses dragged the wagon two miles from town and then gave out. Then we three pushed the wagon seven miles, and Oliver moved ahead and pulled the horses after him by the bits. We complained, but Oliver did not. The ground was frozen, and it froze our backs while we slept; the wind swept across our faces and froze our noses. Oliver did not complain. Five days of pushing the wagon by day and freezing by night brought us to the bad part of the journey—the Forty Mile Desert, or the Great American Desert, if you please. Still, this mildest-mannered man that ever was had not complained. We started across at eight in the morning, pushing through sand that had no bottom; toiling all day long by the wrecks of a thousand wagons, the skeletons of ten thousand oxen; by wagon-tires enough to hoop the Washington Monument to the top, and ox-chains enough to girdle Long Island; by human graves; with our throats parched always with thirst; lips bleeding from the alkali dust; hungry, perspiring, and very, very weary—so weary that when we dropped in the sand every fifty yards to rest the horses, we could hardly keep from going to sleep—no complaints from Oliver; none the next morning at three o'clock, when we got across, tired to death. Awakened two or three nights afterward at midnight, in a narrow cañon, by the snow falling on our faces, and appalled at the imminent danger of being "snowed in," we harnessed up and pushed on till eight in the morning, passed the "Divide" and knew we were saved. No complaints. Fifteen days of hardship and fatigue brought us to the end of the two hundred miles, and the judge had not complained. We wondered if anything *could* exasperate him. We built a Humboldt house. It is done in this way. You dig a square in the steep base of the mountain, and set up two uprights and top them with two joists. Then you stretch a great sheet of "cotton domestic" from the point where the joists join the hillside down over the joists to the ground; this makes the roof and the front of the mansion; the sides and back are the dirt walls your digging has left. A chimney is easily made by turning up one corner of the roof. Oliver was sitting alone in this dismal den, one night, by a sagebrush fire, writing poetry; he was very fond of digging poetry out of himself—or blasting it out when it came hard. He heard an animal's footsteps close to the roof; a stone or two and some dirt came through and fell by him. He grew uneasy and said: "Hi!—clear out from there, can't you!"—from time to time. But by and by he fell asleep where he sat, and pretty soon a mule fell down the chimney! The fire flew in every direction, and Oliver went over backwards. About ten nights after that he recovered confidence enough to go to writing poetry again. Again he dozed off to sleep, and again a mule fell down the chimney. This time, about half of that side of the house came in with the mule. Struggling to get up, the mule kicked the candle out and smashed most of the kitchen furniture, and raised considerable dust. These violent awakenings must have been annoying to Oliver, but he never complained. He moved to a mansion on the opposite side of the cañon, because he had noticed the mules did not go there. One night about eight o'clock he was endeavoring to finish his poem, when a stone rolled in—then a hoof appeared below the canvas—then part of a cow—the after part. He leaned back in dread, and shouted "Hooy! hooy! get out of this!" and the cow struggled manfully—lost ground steadily—dirt and dust streamed down, and before Oliver could get well away, the entire cow crashed through on to the table and made a shapeless wreck of everything!

Then, for the first time in his life, I think, Oliver complained. He said:

"This thing is growing monotonous!"

Then he resigned his judgeship and left Humboldt county. "Butchered to make a Roman holiday" has grown monotonous to me.

In this connection I wish to say one word about Michael Angelo Buonarotti. I used to worship the mighty genius of Michael Angelo—that man who was great in poetry, painting, sculpture, architecture—great in everything he undertook. But I do not want Michael Angelo for breakfast—for luncheon—for dinner—for tea—for supper—for between meals. I like a change, occasionally. In Genoa, he designed everything; in Milan he or his pupils designed everything; he designed the Lake of Como; in Padua, Verona, Venice, Bologna, who did we ever hear of, from guides, but Michael Angelo? In Florence, he painted everything, designed everything, nearly, and what he did not design he used to sit on a favorite stone and look at, and they showed us the stone. In Pisa he designed everything but the old shot-tower, and they would have attributed that to him if it had not been so awfully out of the perpendicular. He designed the piers of Leghorn and the custom-house regulations of Civita Vecchia. But, here—here it is frightful. He designed St. Peter's; he designed the Pope; he designed the Pantheon, the uniform of the Pope's soldiers, the

Tiber, the Vatican, the Coliseum, the Capitol, the Tarpeian Rock, the Barberini Palace, St. John Lateran, the Campagna, the Appian Way, the Seven Hills, the Baths of Caracalla, the Claudian Aqueduct, the Cloaca Maxima—the eternal bore designed the Eternal City, and unless all men and books do lie, he painted everything in it! Dan said the other day to the guide, "Enough, enough, enough! Say no more! Lump the whole thing! say that the Creator made Italy from designs by Michael Angelo!"

I never felt so fervently thankful, so soothed, so tranquil, so filled with a blessed peace, as I did yesterday when I learned that Michael Angelo was dead.

But we have taken it out of this guide. He has marched us through miles of pictures and sculpture in the vast corridors of the Vatican; and through miles of pictures and sculpture in twenty other palaces; he has shown us the great picture in the Sistine Chapel,[1] and frescoes enough to fresco the heavens—pretty much all done by Michael Angelo. So with him we have played that game which has vanquished so many guides for us—imbecility and idiotic questions. These creatures never suspect—they have no idea of a sarcasm.

He shows us a figure and says: "Statoo brunzo." (Bronze statue.)

We look at it indifferently and the doctor asks: "By Michael Angelo?"

"No—not know who."

Then he shows us the ancient Roman Forum. The doctor asks: "Michael Angelo?"

A stare from the guide. "No—a thousan' year before he is born."

Then an Egyptian obelisk. Again: "Michael Angelo?"

"Oh, *mon dieu*, genteelmen! Zis is *two* thousan' year before he is born!"

He grows so tired of that unceasing question sometimes, that he dreads to show us anything at all. The wretch has tried all the ways he can think of to make us comprehend that Michael Angelo is only responsible for the creation of a *part* of the world, but somehow he has not succeeded yet. Relief for overtasked eyes and brain from study and sightseeing is necessary, or we shall become idiotic sure enough. Therefore this guide must continue to suffer. If he does not enjoy it, so much the worse for him. We do.

In this place I may as well jot down a chapter concerning those necessary nuisances, European guides. Many a man has wished in his heart he could do without his guide; but knowing he could not, has wished he could get some amusement out of him as a remuneration for the affliction of his society. We accomplished

---

1. "The Last Judgment," on which Michelangelo worked for seven years (1534–41).

this latter matter, and if our experience can be made useful to others they are welcome to it.

Guides know about enough English to tangle everything up so that a man can make neither head nor tail of it. They know their story by heart—the history of every statue, painting, cathedral, or other wonder they show you. They know it and tell it as a parrot would—and if you interrupt, and throw them off the track, they have to go back and begin over again. All their lives long, they are employed in showing strange things to foreigners and listening to their bursts of admiration. It is human nature to take delight in exciting admiration. It is what prompts children to say "smart" things, and do absurd ones, and in other ways "show off" when company is present. It is what makes gossips turn out in rain and storm to go and be the first to tell a startling bit of news. Think, then, what a passion it becomes with a guide, whose privilege it is, every day, to show to strangers wonders that throw them into perfect ecstasies of admiration! He gets so that he could not by any possibility live in a soberer atmosphere. After we discovered this, we *never* went into ecstasies any more—we never admired anything—we never showed any but impassible faces and stupid indifference in the presence of the sublimest wonders a guide had to display. We had found their weak point. We have made good use of it ever since. We have made some of those people savage, at times, but we have never lost our own serenity.

The doctor asks the questions, generally, because he can keep his countenance, and look more like an inspired idiot, and throw more imbecility into the tone of his voice than any man that lives. It comes natural to him.

The guides in Genoa are delighted to secure an American party, because Americans so much wonder, and deal so much in sentiment and emotion before any relic of Columbus. Our guide there fidgeted about as if he had swallowed a spring mattress. He was full of animation—full of impatience. He said:

"Come wis me, genteelmen!—come! I show you ze letterwriting by Christopher Colombo!—write it himself!—write it wis his own hand!—come!"

He took us to the municipal palace. After much impressive fumbling of keys and opening of locks, the stained and aged document was spread before us. The guide's eyes sparkled. He danced about us and tapped the parchment with his finger:

"What I tell you, genteelmen! Is it not so? See! handwriting Christopher Colombo!—write it himself!"

We looked indifferent—unconcerned. The doctor examined the document very deliberately, during a painful pause. Then he said, without any show of interest:

"Ah—Ferguson[2]—what—what did you say was the name of the party who wrote this?"

"Christopher Colombo! ze great Christopher Colombo!"

Another deliberate examination.

"Ah—did he write it himself, or—or how?"

"He write it himself!—Christopher Colombo! he's own handwriting, write by himself!"

Then the doctor laid the document down and said:

"Why, I have seen boys in America only fourteen years old that could write better than that."

"But zis is ze great Christo——"

"I don't care who it is! It's the worst writing I ever saw. Now you mustn't think you can impose on us because we are strangers. We are not fools, by a good deal. If you have got any specimens of penmanship of real merit, trot them out!—and if you haven't, drive on!"

We drove on. The guide was considerably shaken up, but he made one more venture. He had something which he thought would overcome us. He said:

"Ah, genteelmen, you come wis me! I show you beautiful, oh, magnificent bust Christopher Colombo!—splendid, grand, magnificent!"

He brought us before the beautiful bust—for it *was* beautiful —and sprang back and struck an attitude:

"Ah, look, genteelmen!—beautiful, grand,—bust Christopher Colombo!—beautiful bust, beautiful pedestal!"

The doctor put up his eyeglass—procured for such occasions:

"Ah—what did you say this gentleman's name was?"

"Christopher Colombo!—ze great Christopher Colombo!"

"Christopher Colombo—the great Christopher Colombo. Well, what did *he* do?"

"Discover America!—discover America, oh, ze devil!"

"Discover America. No—that statement will hardly wash. We are just from America ourselves. We heard nothing about it. Christopher Colombo—pleasant name—is—is he dead?"

"Oh, corpo di Baccho!—three hundred year!"

"What did he die of?"

"I do not know!—I cannot tell."

"Small-pox, think?"

"I do not know, genteelmen!—I do not know *what* he die of!"

"Measles, likely?"

"May be—may be—I do *not* know—I think he die of some-

---

2. After their Paris experience with the guide Billfinger, they called all guides "Ferguson."

things."

"Parents living?"

"Im-posseeble!"

"Ah—which is the bust and which is the pedestal?"

"Santa Maria!—*zis* ze bust!—*zis* ze pedestal!"

"Ah, I see, I see—happy combination—very happy combination, indeed. Is—is this the first time this gentleman was ever on a bust?"

That joke was lost on the foreigner—guides cannot master the subtleties of the American joke.

We have made it interesting for this Roman guide. Yesterday we spent three or four hours in the Vatican again, that wonderful world of curiosities. We came very near expressing interest, sometimes—even admiration—it was very hard to keep from it. We succeeded though. Nobody else ever did, in the Vatican museums. The guide was bewildered—nonplussed. He walked his legs off, nearly, hunting up extraordinary things, and exhausted all his ingenuity on us, but it was a failure; we never showed any interest in anything. He had reserved what he considered to be his greatest wonder till the last—a royal Egyptian mummy, the best-preserved in the world, perhaps. He took us there. He felt so sure, this time, that some of his old enthusiasm came back to him:

"See, genteelmen!—Mummy! Mummy!"

The eyeglass came up as calmly, as deliberately as ever.

"Ah,—Ferguson—what did I understand you to say the gentleman's name was?"

"Name?—he got no name!—Mummy!—'Gyptian mummy!"

"Yes, yes. Born here?"

"No! *'Gyptian* mummy!"

"Ah, just so. Frenchman, I presume?"

"No!—*not* Frenchman, not Roman!—born in Egypta!"

"Born in Egypta. Never heard of Egypta before. Foreign locality, likely. Mummy—mummy. How calm he is—how self-possessed. Is, ah—is he dead?"

"Oh, *sacré bleu*, been dead three thousan' year!"

The doctor turned on him savagely:

"Here, now, what do you mean by such conduct as this! Playing us for Chinamen because we are strangers and trying to learn! Trying to impose your vile second-hand carcasses on *us!*—thunder and lightning, I've a notion to—to—if you've got a nice *fresh* corpse, fetch him out!—or, by George, we'll brain you!"

We make it exceedingly interesting for this Frenchman. However, he has paid us back, partly, without knowing it. He came to the hotel this morning to ask if we were up, and he endeavored as well as he could to describe us, so that the landlord would know

which persons he meant. He finished with the casual remark that
we were lunatics. The observation was so innocent and so honest
that it amounted to a very good thing for a guide to say.

There is one remark (already mentioned) which never yet has
failed to disgust these guides. We use it always, when we can think
of nothing else to say. After they have exhausted their enthusiasm
pointing out to us and praising the beauties of some ancient bronze
image or broken-legged statue, we look at it stupidly and in silence
for five, ten, fifteen minutes—as long as we can hold out, in fact
—and then ask:

"Is—is he dead?"

That conquers the serenest of them. It is not what they are
looking for—especially a new guide. Our Roman Ferguson is the
most patient, unsuspecting, long-suffering subject we have had yet.
We shall be sorry to part with him. We have enjoyed his society
very much. We trust he has enjoyed ours, but we are harassed with
doubts. * * *

From A *Newspaper Valedictory:*
[*We Were Americans—Americans!*][3]

* * * Wherever we went, in Europe, Asia, or Africa, we made
a sensation, and, I suppose I may add, created a famine. None of
us had ever been any where before; we all hailed from the interior;
travel was a wild novelty to us, and we conducted ourselves in accordance with the natural instincts that were in us, and trammeled
ourselves with no ceremonies, no conventionalities. We always
took care to make it understood that we were Americans—Americans! When we found that a good many foreigners had hardly ever
heard of America, and that a good many more knew it only as a
barbarous province away off somewhere, that had lately been at
war with somebody, we pitied the ignorance of the Old World,
but abated no jot of our importance. Many and many a simple
community in the Eastern hemisphere will remember for years the
incursion of the strange horde in the year of our Lord 1867, that
called themselves Americans, and seemed to imagine in some unaccountable way that they had a right to be proud of it. We generally created a famine, partly because the coffee on the *Quaker
City* was unendurable, and sometimes the more substantial fare
was not strictly first-class; and partly because one naturally tires of
sitting long at the same board and eating from the same dishes.

The people of those foreign countries are very, very ignorant.
They looked curiously at the costumes we had brought from the

3. On the night on which the *Quaker City* returned to port in New York City, Mark Twain wrote this article for the New York *Herald.* He spoke of it ironically as "fulsomely complimentary."

wilds of America. They observed that we talked loudly at table sometimes. They noticed that we looked out for expenses, and got what we conveniently could out of a franc, and wondered where in the mischief we came from. In Paris they just simply opened their eyes and stared when we spoke to them in French! We never did succeed in making those idiots understand their own language. One of our passengers said to a shopkeeper, in reference to a proposed return to buy a pair of gloves, "*Allong restay trankeel —may be ve coom Moonday;*" and would you believe it, that shopkeeper, a born Frenchman, had to ask what it was that had been said. Sometimes it seems to me, somehow, that there must be a difference between Parisian French and *Quaker City* French.

The people stared at us everywhere, and we stared at them. We generally made them feel rather small, too, before we got done with them, because we bore down on them with America's greatness until we crushed them. And yet we took kindly to the manners and customs, and especially to the fashions of the various people we visited. When we left the Azores, we wore awful capotes[4] and used fine tooth combs—successfully. When we came back from Tangier, in Africa, we were topped with fezzes of the bloodiest hue, hung with tassels like an Indian's scalp-lock. In France and Spain we attracted some attention in these costumes. In Italy they naturally took us for distempered Garibaldians,[5] and set a gunboat to look for anything significant in our changes of uniform. We made Rome howl. We could have made any place howl when we had all our clothes on. We got no fresh raiment in Greece—they had but little there of any kind. But at Constantinople, how we turned out! Turbans, scimitars, fezzes, horse-pistols, tunics, sashes, baggy trousers, yellow slippers— Oh, we were gorgeous! The illustrious dogs of Constantinople barked their under jaws off, and even then failed to do us justice. They are all dead by this time. They could not go through such a run of business as we gave them and survive.

And then we went to see the Emperor of Russia. We just called on him as comfortably as if we had known him a century or so, and when we had finished our visit we variegated ourselves with selections from Russian costumes and sailed away again more picturesque than ever. In Smyrna we picked up camel's hair shawls and other dressy things from Persia; but in Palestine—ah, in Palestine—our splendid career ended. They didn't wear any clothes there to speak of. We were satisfied, and stopped. We made no experiments. We did not try their costume. But we astonished the natives of that country. We astonished them with such eccen-

4. Long hooded cloaks.
5. A reference to Giuseppe Garibaldi

(1807–82), Italian patriot, one of the greatest masters of revolutionary war.

tricities of dress as we could muster. We prowled through the Holy Land, from Cesarea Philippi to Jerusalem and the Dead Sea, a weird procession of pilgrims, gotten up regardless of expense, solemn, gorgeous, green-spectacled, drowsing under blue umbrellas, and astride of a sorrier lot of horses, camels, and asses than those that came out of Noah's ark, after eleven months of seasickness and short rations. If ever those children of Israel in Palestine forget when Gideon's Band went through there from America, they ought to be cursed once more and finished. It was the rarest spectacle that ever astounded mortal eyes, perhaps.

Well, we were at home in Palestine. It was easy to see that that was the grand feature of the expedition. We had cared nothing much about Europe. We galloped through the Louvre, the Pitti, the Uffizzi, the Vatican—all the galleries—and through the pictured and frescoed churches of Venice, Naples, and the cathedrals of Spain; some of us said that certain of the great works of the old masters were glorious creations of genius (we found it out in the guide-book, though we got hold of the wrong picture sometimes), and the others said they were disgraceful old daubs. We examined modern and ancient statuary with a critical eye in Florence, Rome, or anywhere we found it, and praised it if we saw fit, and if we didn't we said we preferred the wooden Indians in front of the cigar stores of America. But the Holy Land brought out all our enthusiasm. We fell into raptures by the barren shores of Galilee; we pondered at Tabor and at Nazareth; we exploded into poetry over the questionable loveliness of Esdraelon; we meditated at Jezreel and Samaria over the missionary zeal of Jehu; we rioted—fairly rioted among the holy places of Jerusalem; we bathed in Jordan and the Dead Sea, reckless whether our accident-insurance policies were extra-hazardous or not, and brought away so many jugs of precious water from both places that all the country from Jericho to the mountains of Moab will suffer from drouth this year, I think. Yes, the pilgrimage part of the excursion was its pet feature—there is no question about that. After dismal, smileless Palestine, beautiful Egypt had few charms for us. We merely glanced at it and were ready for home.

They wouldn't let us land at Malta—quarantine; they would not let us land in Sardinia; nor at Algiers, Africa; nor at Malaga, Spain, nor Cadiz, nor at the Madeira Islands. So we got offended at all foreigners and turned our backs upon them and came home. I suppose we only stopped at the Bermudas because they were in the programme. We did not care anything about any place at all. We wanted to go home. Homesickness was abroad in the ship—it was epidemic. If the authorities of New York had known how badly we had it, they would have quarantined us here.

The grand pilgrimage is over. Good-bye to it, and a pleasant memory to it, I am able to say in all kindness. I bear no malice, no ill-will toward any individual that was connected with it, either as passenger or officer. Things I did not like at all yesterday I like very well to-day, now that I am at home, and always hereafter I shall be able to poke fun at the whole gang if the spirit so moves me to do, without ever saying a malicious word. The expedition accomplished all that its programme promised that it should accomplish, and we ought all to be satisfied with the management of the matter, certainly. Bye-bye!

MARK TWAIN.

1867, 1869

From Roughing It[6]

From *Vol. I, Chapter VII.*

[*The Buffalo That Climbed a Tree*]

* * * Next morning just before dawn, when about five hundred and fifty miles from St. Joseph, our mud-wagon[7] broke down. We were to be delayed five or six hours, and therefore we took horses, by invitation, and joined a party who were just starting on a buffalo hunt. It was noble sport galloping over the plain in the dewy freshness of the morning, but our part of the hunt ended in disaster and disgrace, for a wounded buffalo bull chased the passenger Bemis nearly two miles, and then he forsook his horse and took to a lone tree. He was very sullen about the matter for some twenty-four hours, but at last he began to soften little by little, and finally he said:

"Well, it was not funny, and there was no sense in those gawks making themselves so facetious over it. I tell you I was angry in earnest for awhile. I should have shot that long gangly lubber they called Hank, if I could have done it without crippling six or seven other people—but of course I couldn't, the old 'Allen' 's[8] so confounded comprehensive. I wish those loafers had been up in the tree; they wouldn't have wanted to laugh so. If I had had a horse worth a cent—but no, the minute he saw that buffalo bull wheel on him and give a bellow, he raised straight up in the air

6. *Roughing It,* published in 1872, exists in embryo in Chapter XII of *The Innocents Abroad,* in a passage where Twain contrasts the unpleasantness of railway travel in France with the delights of "stage-coaching" in the American West. The book begins with an account of his trip by stage coach to Carson, Nevada, in 1861, in company with his older brother, Orion Clemens. The present text is from the Author's Uniform Edition (1899). In the present selection, they are six days out from St. Joseph, Missouri, the starting point for most of the westbound travel of the day.
7. A coach with open sides (hence the mud sometimes bespattered the passengers).
8. A revolver with six barrels, named for its inventor.

and stood on his heels. The saddle began to slip, and I took him round the neck and laid close to him, and began to pray. Then he came down and stood up on the other end awhile, and the bull actually stopped pawing sand and bellowing to contemplate the inhuman spectacle. Then the bull made a pass at him and uttered a bellow that sounded perfectly frightful, it was so close to me, and that seemed to literally prostrate my horse's reason, and make a raving distracted maniac of him, and I wish I may die if he didn't stand on his head for a quarter of a minute and shed tears. He was absolutely out of his mind—he was, as sure as truth itself, and he really didn't know what he was doing. Then the bull came charging at us, and my horse dropped down on all fours and took a fresh start—and then for the next ten minutes he would actually throw one handspring after another so fast that the bull began to get unsettled, too, and didn't know where to start in—and so he stood there sneezing, and shoveling dust over his back, and bellowing every now and then, and thinking he had got a fifteen-hundred dollar circus horse for breakfast, certain. Well, I was first out on his neck—the horse's, not the bull's—and then underneath, and next on his rump, and sometimes head up, and sometimes heels—but I tell you it seemed solemn and awful to be ripping and tearing and carrying on so in the presence of death, as you might say. Pretty soon the bull made a snatch for us and brought away some of my horse's tail (I suppose, but do not know, being pretty busy at the time), but *something* made him hungry for solitude and suggested to him to get up and hunt for it. And then you ought to have seen that spider-legged old skeleton go! and you ought to have seen the bull cut out after him, too —head down, tongue out, tail up, bellowing like everything, and actually mowing down the weeds, and tearing up the earth, and boosting up the sand like a whirlwind! By George, it was a hot race! I and the saddle were back on the rump, and I had the bridle in my teeth and holding on to the pommel with both hands. First we left the dogs behind; then we passed a jackass rabbit; then we overtook a cayote,[9] and were gaining on an antelope when the rotten girths let go and threw me about thirty yards off to the left, and as the saddle went down over the horse's rump he gave it a lift with his heels that sent it more than four hundred yards up in the air, I wish I may die in a minute if he didn't. I fell at the foot of the only solitary tree there was in nine counties adjacent (as any creature could see with the naked eye), and the next second I had hold of the bark with four sets of nails and my teeth, and the next second after that I was astraddle of the main limb and blaspheming my luck in a way that made my breath

9. Mark Twain's spelling of *coyote,* a prairie wolf.

smell of brimstone. I *had* the bull, now, if he did not think of *one* thing. But that one thing I dreaded. I dreaded it very seriously. There was a possibility that the bull might not think of it, but there were greater chances that he would. I made up my mind what I would do in case he did. It was a little over forty feet to the ground from where I sat. I cautiously unwound the lariat from the pommel of my saddle—"

"Your *saddle?* Did you take your saddle up in the tree with you?"

"Take it up in the tree with me? Why, how you talk. Of course I didn't. No man could do that. It *fell* in the tree when it came down."

"Oh—exactly."

Certainly. I unwound the lariat, and fastened one end of it to the limb. It was the very best green raw-hide, and capable of sustaining tons. I made a slip-noose in the other end, and then hung it down to see the length. It reached down twenty-two feet—half way to the ground. I then loaded every barrel of the Allen with a double charge. I felt satisfied. I said to myself, if he never thinks of that one thing that I dread, all right—but if he does, all right anyhow—I am fixed for him. But don't you know that the very thing a man dreads is the thing that always happens? Indeed it is so. I watched the bull, now, with anxiety—anxiety which no one can conceive of who has not been in such a situation and felt that at any moment death might come. Presently a thought came into the bull's eye. I knew it! said I—if my nerve fails now, I am lost. Sure enough, it was just as I had dreaded, he started in to climb the tree—"

"What, the bull?"

"Of course—who else?"

"But a bull can't climb a tree."

"He can't, can't he? Since you know so much about it, did you ever see a bull try?"

"No! I never dreamt of such a thing."

"Well, then, what is the use of your talking that way, then? Because you never saw a thing done, is that any reason why it can't be done?"

"Well, all right—go on. What did you do?"

"The bull started up, and got along well for about ten feet, then slipped and slid back. I breathed easier. He tried it again—got up a little higher—slipped again. But he came at it once more, and this time he was careful. He got gradually higher and higher, and my spirits went down more and more. Up he came—an inch at a time—with his eyes hot, and his tongue hanging out. Higher and higher—hitched his foot over the stump of a limb, and looked up, as much as to say, 'You are my meat, friend.' Up again—higher and higher, and getting more excited the closer he got. He was within ten feet of me! I took a long breath,—and then said I, 'It is now or never.' I had the coil of the lariat all ready; I paid it out slowly, till it hung right over his head; all of a sudden I let go of the slack, and the slipnoose fell fairly round his neck! Quicker than lightning I out with the Allen and let him have it in the face. It was an awful roar, and must have scared the bull out of his senses. When the smoke cleared away, there he was, dangling in the air, twenty foot from the ground, and going out of one convulsion into another faster than you could count! I didn't stop to count, anyhow—I shinned down the tree and shot for home."

"Bemis, is all that true, just as you have stated it?"

"I wish I may rot in my tracks and die the death of a dog if it isn't."

"Well, we can't refuse to believe it, and we don't. But if there were some proofs—"

"Proofs! Did I bring back my lariat?"

"No."

"Did I bring back my horse?"

"No."

"Did you ever see the bull again?"

"No."

"Well, then, what more do you want? I never saw anybody as particular as you are about a little thing like that."

I made up my mind that if this man was not a liar he only missed it by the skin of his teeth. * * *

Vol. II, Chapter VI. [*Buck Fanshaw's Funeral*]

Somebody has said that in order to know a community, one must observe the style of its funerals and know what manner of men they bury with most ceremony. I cannot say which class we buried with most éclat in our "flush times," the distinguished public benefactor or the distinguished rough—possibly the two chief grades or grand divisions of society honored their illustrious dead about equally; and hence, no doubt, the philosopher I have quoted from would have needed to see two representative funerals in Virginia[1] before forming his estimate of the people.

There was a grand time over Buck Fanshaw when he died. He was a representative citizen. He had "killed his man"—not in his own quarrel, it is true, but in defence of a stranger unfairly beset by numbers. He had kept a sumptuous saloon.[2] He had been the

---

1. Virginia City, Nevada, so christened by "Ole Virginny," James Fennimore, in honor of his native state. The town was built up the steep slope of Sun Mountain, later called Mount Davidson.
2. The Sazerac, famous saloon on C Street, Virginia City, owned by Tom Peaseley, the original of "Buck Fan-

proprietor of a dashing helpmeet whom he could have discarded without the formality of a divorce. He had held a high position in the fire department and been a very Warwick[3] in politics. When he died there was great lamentation throughout the town, but especially in the vast bottom-stratum of society.

On the inquest it was shown that Buck Fanshaw, in the delirium of a wasting typhoid fever, had taken arsenic, shot himself through the body, cut his throat, and jumped out of a four-story window and broken his neck—and after due deliberation, the jury, sad and tearful, but with intelligence unblinded by its sorrow, brought in a verdict of death "by the visitation of God." What could the world do without juries?

Prodigious preparations were made for the funeral. All the vehicles in town were hired, all the saloons put in mourning, all the municipal and fire-company flags hung at half-mast, and all the firemen ordered to muster in uniform and bring their machines duly draped in black. Now—let us remark in parenthesis—as all the peoples of the earth had representative adventurers in the Silverland,[4] and as each adventurer had brought the slang of his nation or his locality with him, the combination made the slang of Nevada the richest and the most infinitely varied and copious that had ever existed anywhere in the world, perhaps, except in the mines of California in the "early days." Slang was the language of Nevada. It was hard to preach a sermon without it, and be understood. Such phrases as "You bet!" "Oh, no, I reckon not!" "No Irish need apply," and a hundred others, became so common as to fall from the lips of a speaker unconsciously—and very often when they did not touch the subject under discussion and consequently failed to mean anything.

After Buck Fanshaw's inquest, a meeting of the short-haired brotherhood was held,[5] for nothing can be done on the Pacific coast without a public meeting and an expression of sentiment. Regretful resolutions were passed and various committees appointed; among others, a committee of one was deputed to call on

shaw." Peaseley, fire chief, political boss, and one-time sheriff of Storey County, impressed Mark Twain so much that he used him (shortly after writing *Roughing It*) as the prototype of Oliver Higgins in *The Gilded Age*.

3. Richard Neville (1428–71), called Warwick the King-Maker because of his activities during the Wars of the Roses. The Sazerac saloon of Tom Peaseley was one of the two places in Nevada Territory where almost everything of political importance was settled; the other was the Magnolia saloon in Carson City.

4. The famous Comstock Lode was the center of the Washoe silver district,

and Virginia City was the center of the Lode. As Mark Twain said, the Comstock Lode "stretched its opulent length straight through the town from north to south." The plank sidewalks on C Street were laid over ledges of silver ore.

5. Perhaps an extension of Twain's division of funeral-holders into two chief grades of society; in England (ca. 1641) some of the Puritans wore their hair closely cropped (the "Roundheads") in marked contrast to the long, curled ringlets of the Cavaliers. Here, the "short-haired brotherhood" are the roughs.

the minister,[6] a fragile, gentle spiritual new fledgling from an Eastern theological seminary, and as yet unacquainted with the ways of the mines. The committeeman, "Scotty" Briggs, made his visit; and in after days it was worth something to hear the minister tell about it. Scotty was a stalwart rough, whose customary suit, when on weighty official business, like committee work, was a fire helmet, flaming red flannel shirt, patent leather belt with spanner and revolver attached, coat hung over arm, and pants stuffed into boot tops. He formed something of a contrast to the pale theological student. It is fair to say of Scotty, however, in passing, that he had a warm heart, and a strong love for his friends, and never entered into a quarrel when he could reasonably keep out of it. Indeed, it was commonly said that whenever one of Scotty's fights was investigated, it always turned out that it had originally been no affair of his, but that out of native goodheartedness he had dropped in of his own accord to help the man who was getting the worst of it. He and Buck Fanshaw were bosom friends, for years, and had often taken adventurous "potluck" together. On one occasion, they had thrown off their coats and taken the weaker side in a fight among strangers, and after gaining a hard-earned victory, turned and found that the men they were helping had deserted early, and not only that, but had stolen their coats and made off with them! But to return to Scotty's visit to the minister. He was on a sorrowful mission, now, and his face was the picture of woe. Being admitted to the presence he sat down before the clergyman, placed his fire-hat on an unfinished manuscript sermon under the minister's nose, took from it a red silk handkerchief, wiped his brow and heaved a sigh of dismal impressiveness, explanatory of his business. He choked, and even shed tears; but with an effort he mastered his voice and said in lugubrious tones:

"Are you the duck that runs the gospel-mill next door?"

"Am I the—pardon me, I believe I do not understand?"

With another sigh and a half-sob, Scotty rejoined:

"Why you see we are in a bit of trouble, and the boys thought maybe you would give us a lift, if we'd tackle you—that is, if I've got the rights of it and you are the head clerk of the doxology-works next door."

"I am the shepherd in charge of the flock whose fold is next door."

"The which?"

"The spiritual adviser of the little company of believers whose

<hr />

6. The Rev. Franklin S. Rising, a young Episcopal rector; later, Rising was living in the Sandwich (Hawaiian) Islands when Mark Twain arrived there in 1866.

sanctuary adjoins these premises."

Scotty scratched his head, reflected a moment, and then said:

"You ruther hold over me, pard. I reckon I can't call that hand. Ante and pass the buck."

"How? I beg pardon. What did I understand you to say?"

"Well, you've ruther got the bulge on me. Or maybe we've both got the bulge, somehow. You don't smoke me and I don't smoke you. You see, one of the boys has passed in his checks, and we want to give him a good send-off, and so the thing I'm on now is to roust out somebody to jerk a little chin-music for us and waltz him through handsome."

"My friend, I seem to grow more and more bewildered. Your observations are wholly incomprehensible to me. Cannot you simplify them in some way? At first I thought perhaps I understood you, but I grope now. Would it not expedite matters if you restricted yourself to categorical statements of fact unencumbered with obstructing accumulations of metaphor and allegory?"

Another pause, and more reflection. Then, said Scotty:

"I'll have to pass, I judge."

"How?"

"You've raised me out, pard."

"I still fail to catch your meaning."

"Why, that last lead of yourn is too many for me—that's the idea. I can't neither trump nor follow suit."

The clergyman sank back in his chair perplexed. Scotty leaned his head on his hand and gave himself up to thought. Presently his face came up, sorrowful but confident.

"I've got it now, so's you can savvy," he said. "What we want is a gospel-sharp. See?"

"A what?"

"Gospel-sharp. Parson."

"Oh! Why did you not say so before? I am a clergyman—a parson."

"Now you talk! You see my blind and straddle it like a man. Put it there!"—extending a brawny paw, which closed over the minister's small hand and gave it a shake indicative of fraternal sympathy and fervent gratification.

"Now we're all right, pard. Let's start fresh. Don't you mind my snuffling a little—becuz we're in a power of trouble. You see, one of the boys has gone up the flume—"

"Gone where?"

"Up the flume—throwed up the sponge, you understand."

"Thrown up the sponge?"

"Yes—kicked the bucket—"

"Ah—has departed to that mysterious country from whose

bourne no traveler returns.''

"Return! I reckon not. Why, pard, he's *dead!*"

"Yes, I understand."

"Oh, you do? Well I thought maybe you might be getting tangled some more. Yes, you see he's dead again—"

"*Again!* Why, has he ever been dead before?"

"Dead before? No! Do you reckon a man has got as many lives as a cat? But you bet you he's awful dead now, poor old boy, and I wish I'd never seen this day. I don't want no better friend than Buck Fanshaw. I knowed him by the back;[7] and when I know a man and like him, I freeze to him—you hear *me*. Take him all round, pard, there never was a bullier man in the mines. No man ever knowed Buck Fanshaw to go back on a friend. But it's all up, you know, it's all up. It ain't no use. They've scooped him."

"Scooped him?"

"Yes—death has. Well, well, well, we've got to give him up. Yes, indeed. It's a kind of a hard world, after all, *ain't* it? But pard, he was a rustler! You ought to seen him get started once. He was a bully boy with a glass eye! Just spit in his face and give him room according to his strength, and it was just beautiful to see him peel and go in. He was the worst son of a thief that ever drawed breath. Pard, he was *on* it! He was on it bigger than an Injun!"

"On it? On what?"

"On the shoot. On the shoulder. On the fight, you understand. *He* didn't give a continental for *any*body. *Beg* your pardon, friend, for coming so near saying a cuss-word—but you see I'm on an awful strain, in this palaver, on account of having to cramp down and draw everything so mild. But we've got to give him up. There ain't any getting around that, I don't reckon. Now if we can get you to help plant him—"

"Preach the funeral discourse? Assist at the obsequies?"

"Obs'quies is good. Yes. That's it—that's our little game. We are going to get the thing up regardless, you know. He was always nifty himself, and so you bet you his funeral ain't going to be no slouch—solid silver door-plate on his coffin, six plumes on the hearse, and a nigger on the box in a biled shirt and a plug hat—how's that for high? And we'll take care of *you*, pard. We'll fix you all right. There'll be a kerridge for you; and whatever you want, you just 'scape out and we'll 'tend to it. We've got a shebang fixed up for you to stand behind, in No. 1's house, and don't you be afraid. Just go in and toot your horn, if you don't sell a clam. Put Buck through as bully as you can, pard, for anybody that knowed him will tell you that he was one of the whitest men that was

7. Apparently a corruption of the expression "to know something by the book" —i.e., by heart.

ever in the mines. You can't draw it too strong. He never could
stand it to see things going wrong. He's done more to make this
town quiet and peaceable than any man in it. I've seen him lick
four Greasers in eleven minutes, myself. If a thing wanted regulating, *he* warn't a man to go browsing around after somebody to
do it, but he would prance in and regulate it himself. He warn't a
Catholic. Scasely. He was down on 'em. His word was, 'No Irish
need apply!' But it didn't make no difference about that when it
came down to what a man's rights was—and so, when some roughs
jumped the Catholic boneyard and started in to stake out town-
lots in it he *went* for 'em! And he *cleaned* 'em, too! I was there,
pard, and I seen it myself."

"That was very well indeed—at least the impulse was—whether
the act was strictly defensible or not. Had deceased any religious
convictions? That is to say, did he feel a dependence upon, or
acknowledge allegiance to a higher power?"

More reflection.

"I reckon you've stumped me again, pard. Could you say it
over once more, and say it slow?"

"Well, to simplify it somewhat, was he, or rather had he ever
been connected with any organization sequestered from secular
concerns and devoted to self-sacrifice in the interests of morality?"

"All down but nine—set 'em up on the other alley, pard."

"What did I understand you to say?"

"Why, you're most too many for me, you know. When you get
in with your left I hunt grass every time. Every time you draw,
you fill; but I don't seem to have any luck. Let's have a new deal."

"How? Begin again?"

"That's it."

"Very well. Was he a good man, and—"

"There—I see that; don't put up another chip till I look at my
hand. A good man, says you? Pard, it ain't no name for it. He was
the best man that ever—pard, you would have doted on that man.
He could lam any galoot of his inches in America. It was him that
put down the riot last election before it got a start; and everybody
said he was the only man that could have done it. He waltzed in
with a spanner in one hand and a trumpet in the other, and sent
fourteen men home on a shutter in less than three minutes. He had
that riot all broke up and prevented nice before anybody ever got
a chance to strike a blow. He was always for peace, and he would
have peace—he could not stand disturbances. Pard, he was a great
loss to this town. It would please the boys if you could chip in
something like that and do him justice. Here once when the Micks
got to throwing stones through the Methodis' Sunday-school windows, Buck Fanshaw, all of his own notion, shut up his saloon

and took a couple of six-shooters and mounted guard over the Sunday-school. Says he, 'No Irish need apply!' And they didn't. He was the bulliest man in the mountains, pard! He could run faster, jump higher, hit harder, and hold more tanglefoot whisky without spilling it than any man in seventeen counties.[8] Put that in, pard —it'll please the boys more than anything you could say. And you can say, pard, that he never shook his mother."

"Never shook his mother?"

"That's it—any of the boys will tell you so."

"Well, but why *should* he shake her?"

"That what *I* say—but some people does."

"Not people of any repute?"

"Well, some that averages pretty so-so."

"In my opinion the man that would offer personal violence to his own mother, ought to—"

"Cheese it, pard; you've banked your ball clean outside the string. What I was a drivin' at, was, that he never *throwed off* on his mother—don't you see? No indeedy. He give her a house to live in, and town lots, and plenty of money; and he looked after her and took care of her all the time; and when she was down with the smallpox I'm d—d if he didn't set up nights and nuss her himself! *Beg* your pardon for saying it, but it hopped out too quick for yours truly. You've treated me like a gentleman, pard, and I ain't the man to hurt your feelings intentional. I think you're white. I think you're a square man, pard. I like you, and I'll lick any man that don't. I'll lick him till he can't tell himself from a last year's corpse! Put it *there!*" [Another fraternal hand-shake— and exit.]

The obsequies were all that "the boys" could desire. Such a marvel of funeral pomp had never been seen in Virginia. The plumed hearse, the dirge-breathing brass bands, the closed marts of business, the flags drooping at half mast, the long, plodding procession of uniformed secret societies, military battalions and fire companies, draped engines, carriages of officials, and citizens in vehicles and on foot, attracted multitudes of spectators to the sidewalks, roofs, and windows; and for years afterward, the degree of grandeur attained by any civic display in Virginia was determined by comparison with Buck Fanshaw's funeral.

Scotty Briggs, as a pall-bearer and a mourner, occupied a prominent place at the funeral, and when the sermon was finished and the last sentence of the prayer for the dead man's soul ascended, he responded, in a low voice, but with feeling.

"AMEN. No Irish need apply."

8. A foretaste of the kind of bragging done by the skilled braggarts of "Fres- cos from the Past" in Chapter III of *Life on the Mississippi.*

As the bulk of the response was without apparent relevancy, it was probably nothing more than a humble tribute to the memory of the friend that was gone; for, as Scotty had once said, it was "his word."

Scotty Briggs, in after days, achieved the distinction of becoming the only convert to religion that was ever gathered from the Virginia roughs; and it transpired that the man who had it in him to espouse the quarrel of the weak out of inborn nobility of spirit was no mean timber whereof to construct a Christian. The making him one did not warp his generosity or diminish his courage; on the contrary it gave intelligent direction to the one and a broader field to the other. If his Sunday-school class progressed faster than the other classes, was it matter for wonder? I think not. He talked to his pioneer small-fry in a language they understood! It was my large privilege, a month before he died, to hear him tell the beautiful story of Joseph and his brethren to his class "without looking at the book." I leave it to the reader to fancy what it was like, as it fell, riddled with slang, from the lips of that grave, earnest teacher, and was listened to by his little learners with a consuming interest that showed that they were as unconscious as he was that any violence was being done to the sacred proprieties!

From *Vol. II, Chapter XX.* [*Tom Quartz*]

One of my comrades there—another of those victims of eighteen years of unrequited toil and blighted hopes—was one of the gentlest spirits that ever bore its patient cross in a weary exile: grave and simple Dick Baker,[9] pocket-miner of Dead-Horse Gulch. He was forty-six, gray as a rat, earnest, thoughtful, slenderly educated, slouchily dressed, and clay-soiled, but his heart was finer metal than any gold his shovel ever brought to light—than any, indeed, that ever was mined or minted.

Whenever he was out of luck and a little downhearted, he would fall to mourning over the loss of a wonderful cat he used to own (for where women and children are not, men of kindly impulses take up with pets, for they must love something). And he always spoke of the strange sagacity of that cat with the air of a man who believed in his secret heart that there was something human about it—maybe even supernatural.

I heard him talking about this animal once. He said:

"Gentlemen, I used to have a cat here, by the name of Tom Quartz, which you'd a took an interest in I reckon—most anybody

9. Dick Baker was really Dick Stoker, the mining partner of Jim Gillis, whom Mark Twain had visited on Jackass Hill, near Angel's Camp, California. In *Mark Twain in Eruption* (part of the *Autobi-* *ography*, ed. Bernard DeVoto, 1940), Twain says that the yarn of Tom Quartz was actually related to him by Jim Gillis and was an "invention" of Gillis's, with Dick Stoker as its hero.

would. I had him here eight year—and he was the remarkablest cat I ever see. He was a large gray one of the Tom specie, an' he had more hard, natchral sense than any man in this camp—'n' a *power* of dignity—he wouldn't let the Gov'ner of Californy be familiar with him. He never ketched a rat in his life—'peared to be above it. He never cared for nothing but mining. He knowed more about mining, that cat did, than any man I ever, ever see. You couldn't tell *him* noth'n' 'bout placer diggin's—'n' as for pocket-mining, why he was just born for it. He would dig out after me an' Jim when we went over the hills prospect'n', and he would trot along behind us for as much as five mile, if we went so fur. An' he had the best judgment about mining ground—why you never see anything like it. When we went to work, he'd scatter a glance around, 'n' if he didn't think much of the indications, he would give a look as much as to say, 'Well, I'll have to get you to excuse *me*,' 'n' without another word he'd hyste his nose into the air 'n' shove for home. But if the ground suited him, he would lay low 'n' keep dark till the first pan was washed, 'n' then he would sidle up 'n' take a look, an' if there was about six or seven grains of gold *he* was satisfied—he didn't want no better prospect 'n' that—'n' then he would lay down on our coats and snore like a steamboat till we'd struck the pocket, an' then get up 'n' superintend. He was nearly lightnin' on superintending.

"Well, by an' by, up comes this yer quartz excitement. Everybody was into it—everybody was pick'n' 'n' blast'n' instead of shovelin' dirt on the hillside—everybody was put'n' down a shaft instead of scrapin' the surface. Noth'n' would do Jim, but *we* must tackle the ledges, too, 'n' so we did. We commenced put'n' down a shaft, 'n' Tom Quartz he begin to wonder what in the Dickens it was all about. *He* hadn't ever seen any mining like that before, 'n' he was all upset, as you may say—he couldn't come to a right understanding of it no way—it was too many for *him*. He was down on it, too, you bet you—he was down on it powerful —'n' always appeared to consider it the cussedest foolishness out. But that cat, you know, was *always* agin new-fangled arrangements—somehow he never could abide 'em. *You* know how it is with old habits. But by an' by Tom Quartz begin to git sort of reconciled a little, though he never *could* altogether understand that eternal sinkin' of a shaft an' never pannin' out anything. At last he got to comin' down in the shaft, hisself, to try to cipher it out. An' when he'd git the blues, 'n' feel kind o' scruffy, 'n' aggravated 'n' disgusted—knowin' as he did, that the bills was runnin' up all the time an' we warn't makin' a cent—he would curl up on a gunny sack in the corner an' go to sleep. Well, one day when the shaft was down about eight foot, the rock got so hard that we had to put in a blast—the first blast 'n' we'd ever done since Tom Quartz was born. An' then we lit the fuse 'n' clumb out 'n' got off 'bout fifty yards—'n' forgot 'n' left Tom Quartz sound asleep on the gunny sack. In 'bout a minute we seen a puff of smoke bust up out of the hole, 'n' then everything let go with an awful crash, 'n' about four million ton of rocks 'n' dirt 'n' smoke 'n' splinters shot up 'bout a mile an' a half into the air, an' by George, right in the dead center of it was old Tom Quartz a goin' end over end, an' a snortin' an' a sneez'n', an' a clawin' an' a reachin' for things like all possessed. But it warn't no use, you know, it warn't no use. An' that was the last we see of *him* for about two minutes 'n' a half, an' then all of a sudden it begin to rain rocks and rubbage, an' directly he come down ker-whop about ten foot off f'm where we stood. Well, I reckon he was p'raps the orneriest lookin' beast you ever see. One ear was sot back on his neck, 'n' his tail was stove up, 'n' his eye-winkers was swinged off, 'n' he was all blacked up with powder an' smoke, an' all sloppy with mud 'n' slush f'm one end to the other. Well, sir, it warn't no use to try to apologize—we couldn't say a word. He took a sort of a disgusted look at hisself, 'n' then he looked at us—an' it was just exactly the same as if he had said—'Gents, may be *you* think it's smart to take advantage of a cat that 'ain't had no experience of quartz minin', but *I* think *different*'—an' then he turned on his heel 'n' marched off home without ever saying another word.

"That was jest his style. An' may be you won't believe it, but after that you never see a cat so prejudiced agin quartz mining as what he was. An' by an' by when he *did* get to goin' down in the shaft agin, you'd 'a been astonished at his sagacity. The minute we'd tetch off a blast 'n' the fuse'd begin to sizzle, he'd give a look as much as to say: 'Well, I'll have to git you to excuse *me*,' an' it was surpris'n' the way he'd shin out of that hole 'n' go f'r a tree. Sagacity? It ain't no name for it. 'Twas *inspiration!*"

I said, "Well, Mr. Baker, his prejudice against quartz-mining *was* remarkable, considering how he came by it. Couldn't you ever cure him of it?"

"*Cure him!* No! When Tom Quartz was sot once, he was *always* sot—and you might a blowed him up as much as three million times 'n' you'd never broken him of his cussed prejudice agin quartz mining."

The affection and the pride that lit up Baker's face when he delivered this tribute to the firmness of his humble friend of other days, will always be a vivid memory with me. * * *

From *Vol. II, Chapter XXXVII.*
[*The Trouble Will Begin at* 8]

I was home again,[1] in San Francisco, without means and without employment. I tortured my brain for a saving scheme of some kind, and at last a public lecture occurred to me![2] I sat down and wrote one, in a fever of hopeful anticipation. I showed it to several friends, but they all shook their heads. They said nobody would come to hear me, and I would make a humiliating failure of it. They said that as I had never spoken in public, I would break down in the delivery, anyhow. I was disconsolate now. But at last an editor slapped me on the back and told me to "go ahead." He said, "Take the largest house in town, and charge a dollar a ticket." The audacity of the proposition was charming; it seemed fraught with practical worldly wisdom, however. The proprietor of the several theaters endorsed the advice, and said I might have his handsome new opera house[3] at half price—fifty dollars. In sheer desperation I took it—on credit, for sufficient reasons. In three days I did a hundred and fifty dollars' worth of printing and advertising, and was the most distressed and frightened creature on the Pacific coast. I could not sleep—who could, under such circumstances? For other people there was facetiousness in the last line of my posters, but to me it was plaintive with a pang when I wrote it:

"Doors open at 7½. The trouble will begin at 8."

That line has done good service since. Showmen have borrowed it frequently. I have even seen it appended to a newspaper advertisement reminding school pupils in vacation what time next term would begin. As those three days of suspense dragged by, I grew more and more unhappy. I had sold two hundred tickets among my personal friends, but I feared they might not come. My lecture, which had seemed "humorous" to me, at first, grew steadily more and more dreary, till not a vestige of fun seemed left, and I grieved that I could not bring a coffin on the stage and turn the thing into a funeral. I was so panic-stricken, at last, that I went to three old friends, giants in stature, cordial by nature, and stormy-voiced, and said:

"This thing is going to be a failure; the jokes in it are so dim that nobody will ever see them; I would like to have you sit in the parquette,[4] and help me through."

1. From March to July, 1866, he had been in Hawaii, then called the Sandwich Islands.
2. He had studied the technique of Artemus Ward (Charles Farrar Browne) when Ward lectured on the Comstock in December, 1863.
3. Tom Maguire, proprietor of opera houses in both San Francisco and Virginia City.
4. Mark Twain's spelling of *parquet*, the forward part of the main floor of the theater, now included in the orchestra.

They said they would. Then I went to the wife of a popular citizen, and said that if she was willing to do me a very great kindness, I would be glad if she and her husband would sit prominently in the left-hand stage-box, where the whole house could see them. I explained that I should need help, and would turn toward her and smile, as a signal, when I had been delivered of an obscure joke—"and then," I added, "don't wait to investigate, but *respond!*"

She promised. Down the street I met a man I never had seen before. He had been drinking, and was beaming with smiles and good nature. He said:

"My name's Sawyer. You don't know me, but that don't matter. I haven't got a cent, but if you knew how bad I wanted to laugh, you'd give me a ticket. Come, now, what do you say?"

"Is your laugh hung on a hair-trigger?—that is, is it critical, or can you get it off *easy?*"

My drawling infirmity of speech so affected him that he laughed a specimen or two that struck me as being about the article I wanted, and I gave him a ticket, and appointed him to sit in the second circle, in the center, and be responsible for that division of the house. I gave him minute instructions about how to detect indistinct jokes, and then went away, and left him chuckling placidly over the novelty of the idea.

I ate nothing on the last of the three eventful days—I only suffered. I had advertised that on this third day the box-office would be opened for the sale of reserved seats. I crept down to the theater at four in the afternoon to see if any sales had been made. The ticket-seller was gone, the box-office was locked up. I had to swallow suddenly, or my heart would have got out. "No sales," I said to myself; "I might have known it." I thought of suicide, pretended illness, flight. I thought of these things in earnest, for I was very miserable and scared. But of course I had to drive them away, and prepare to meet my fate. I could not wait for half-past seven—I wanted to face the horror, and end it— the feeling of many a man doomed to hang, no doubt. I went down back streets at six o'clock, and entered the theater by the back door. I stumbled my way in the dark among the ranks of canvas scenery, and stood on the stage. The house was gloomy and silent, and its emptiness depressing. I went into the dark among the scenes again, and for an hour and a half gave myself up to the horrors, wholly unconscious of everything else. Then I heard a murmur; it rose higher and higher, and ended in a crash, mingled with cheers. It made my hair raise, it was so close to me, and so loud. There was a pause, and then another; presently came a third, and before I well knew what I was about, I was in the middle of the stage, staring at a sea of faces, bewildered by the fierce glare of the lights, and quaking in every limb with a terror that seemed like to take my life away. The house was full, aisles and all.

The tumult in my heart and brain and legs continued a full minute before I could gain any command over myself. Then I recognized the charity and the friendliness in the faces before me, and little by little my fright melted away, and I began to talk. Within three or four minutes I was comfortable, and even content. My three chief allies, with three auxiliaries, were on hand, in the parquette, all sitting together, all armed with bludgeons, and all ready to make an onslaught upon the feeblest joke that might show its head. And whenever a joke did fall, their bludgeons came down and their faces seemed to split from ear to ear; Sawyer, whose hearty countenance was seen looming redly in the center of the second circle, took it up, and the house was carried handsomely. Inferior jokes never fared so royally before. Presently, I delivered a bit of serious matter with impressive unction (it was my pet), and the audience listened with an absorbed hush that gratified me more than any appaluse; and as I dropped the last word of the clause, I happened to turn and catch Mrs. ———'s intent and waiting eye; my conversation with her flashed upon me, and in spite of all I could do I smiled. She took it for the signal, and promptly delivered a mellow laugh that touched off the whole audience; and the explosion that followed was the triumph of the evening. I thought that that honest man Sawyer would choke himself; and as for the bludgeons, they performed like pile-drivers. But my poor little morsel of pathos was ruined. It was taken in good faith as an intentional joke, and the prize one of the entertainment, and I wisely let it go at that.

All the papers were kind in the morning; my appetite returned; I had abundance of money. All's well that ends well.

1872

From The Gilded Age[5]

Chapter VII. [*Col. Sellers' Schemes*]

Bearing Washington Hawkins and his fortunes, the stage-coach tore out of Swansea at a fearful gait, with horn tooting gayly and half the town admiring from doors and windows. But it did not tear any more after it got to the outskirts; it dragged along stupidly enough, then—till it came in sight of the next hamlet; and then the bugle tooted gayly again, and again the vehicle went tearing by the houses. This sort of conduct marked every entry to a station

5. Published 1873; the present text is from the edition of 1899. Although Mark Twain and his neighbor Charles Dudley Warner collaborated on this novel, the chapters given here are by Twain.

and every exit from it; and so in those days children grew up with the idea that stage-coaches always tore and always tooted; but they also grew up with the idea that pirates went into action in their Sunday clothes, carrying the black flag in one hand and pistoling people with the other, merely because they were so represented in the pictures: but these illusions vanished when later years brought their disenchanting wisdom. They learned then that the stage-coach is but a poor, plodding, vulgar thing in the solitudes of the highway; and that the pirate is only a seedy, unfantastic "rough," when he is out of the pictures.

Toward evening, the stage-coach came thundering into Hawkeye with a perfectly triumphant ostentation—which was natural and proper, for Hawkeye was a pretty large town for interior Missouri. Washington, very stiff and tired and hungry, climbed out, and wondered how he was to proceed now. But his difficulty was quickly solved. Col. Sellers came down the street on a run and arrived panting for breath. He said:

"Lord bless you—I'm glad to see you, Washington—perfectly delighted to see you, my boy! I got your message. Been on the lookout for you. Heard the stage horn, but had a party I couldn't shake off—man that's got an enormous thing on hand—wants me to put some capital into it—and I tell you, my boy, I could do worse, I could do a deal worse. No, now, let that luggage alone; I'll fix that. Here, Jerry, got anything to do? All right—shoulder this plunder and follow me. Come along, Washington. Lord, I'm glad to see you! Wife and the children are just perishing to look at you. Bless you, they won't know you, you've grown so. Folks all well, I suppose? That's good—glad to hear that. We're always going to run down and see them, but I'm into so many operations, and they're not things a man feels like trusting to other people, and so somehow we keep putting it off. Fortunes in them! Good gracious, it's the country to pile up wealth in! Here we are—here's where the Sellers dynasty hangs out. Dump it on the doorstep, Jerry—the blackest niggro in the state, Washington, but got a good heart—mighty likely boy, is Jerry. And now I suppose you've got to have ten cents, Jerry. That's all right—when a man works for me—when a man—in the other pocket, I reckon—when a man—why, where the mischief *is* that portmonnaie!—when a— well now that's odd— Oh, now I remember, must have left it at the bank; and b'George I've left my checkbook, too—Polly says I ought to have a nurse—well, no matter. Let me have a dime, Washington, if you've got—ah, thanks. Now clear out, Jerry, your complexion has brought on the twilight half an hour ahead of time. Pretty fair joke—pretty fair. Here he is, Polly! Washington's come, children!—come now, don't eat him up—finish him in the house. Welcome, my boy, to a mansion that is proud to shelter the son of the best man that walks on the ground. Si Hawkins[6] has been a good friend to me, and I believe I can say that whenever I've had a chance to put him into a good thing I've done it, and done it pretty cheerfully, too. I put him into that sugar speculation—what a grand thing that was, if we hadn't held on too long!"

True enough; but holding on too long had utterly ruined both of them; and the saddest part of it was, that they never had had so much money to lose before, for Sellers' sale of their mule crop that year in New Orleans had been a great financial success. If he had kept out of sugar and gone back home content to stick to mules it would have been a happy wisdom. As it was, he managed to kill two birds with one stone—that is to say, he killed the sugar speculation by holding for high rates till he had to sell at the bottom figure, and that calamity killed the mule that laid the golden egg—which is but a figurative expression and will be so understood. Sellers had returned home cheerful but empty-handed, and the mule business lapsed into other hands. The sale of the Hawkins property by the sheriff had followed, and the Hawkins hearts been torn to see Uncle Dan'l and his wife pass from the auction-block into the hands of a negro trader and depart for the remote South to be seen no more by the family. It had seemed like seeing their own flesh and blood sold into banishment.

Washington was greatly pleased with the Sellers mansion. It was a two-story-and-a-half brick, and much more stylish than any of its neighbors. He was borne to the family sitting-room in triumph by the swarm of little Sellerses, the parents following with their arms about each other's waists.

The whole family were poorly and cheaply dressed; and the clothing, although neat and clean, showed many evidences of having seen long service. The Colonel's "stovepipe" hat was napless and shiny with much polishing, but nevertheless it had an almost convincing expression about it of having been just purchased new. The rest of his clothing was napless and shiny, too, but it had the air of being entirely satisfied with itself and blandly sorry for other people's clothes. It was growing rather dark in the house, and the evening air was chilly, too. Sellers said:

"Lay off your overcoat, Washington, and draw up to the stove and make yourself at home—just consider yourself under your own shingles, my boy—I'll have a fire going, in a jiffy. Light the lamp, Polly, dear, and let's have things cheerful—just as glad to see you,

6. Silas Hawkins, called Squire Hawkins, is a portrait of John Marshall Clemens, father of Mark Twain. The impractical, visionary Washington Hawkins is based on Twain's older brother, Orion Clemens. Mark Twain always said that James Lampton, a cousin of his mother's, was the original of Colonel Sellers.

Washington, as if you'd been lost a century and we'd found you again!"

By this time the Colonel was conveying a lighted match into a poor little stove. Then he propped the stove-door to its place by leaning the poker against it, for the hinges had retired from business. This door framed a small square of isinglass, which now warmed up with a faint glow. Mr. Sellers lit a cheap, showy lamp, which dissipated a good deal of the gloom, and then everybody gathered into the light and took the stove into close companionship.

The children climbed all over Sellers, fondled him, petted him, and were lavishly petted in return. Out from this tugging, laughing, chattering disguise of legs and arms and little faces, the Colonel's voice worked its way and his tireless tongue ran blithely on without interruption; and the purring little wife, diligent with her knitting, sat near at hand and looked happy and proud and grateful; and she listened as one who listens to oracles and gospels and whose grateful soul is being refreshed with the bread of life. By and by the children quieted down to listen; clustered about their father, and resting their elbows on his legs, they hung upon his words as if he were uttering the music of the spheres.

A dreary old haircloth sofa against the wall; a few damaged chairs; the small table the lamp stood on; the crippled stove—these things constituted the furniture of the room. There was no carpet on the floor; on the wall were occasional square-shaped interruptions of the general tint of the plaster which betrayed that there used to be pictures in the house—but there were none now. There were no mantel ornaments, unless one might bring himself to regard as an ornament a clock which never came within fifteen strokes of striking the right time, and whose hands always hitched together at twenty-two minutes past anything and traveled in company the rest of the way home.

"Remarkable clock!" said Sellers, and got up and wound it. "I've been offered—well, I wouldn't expect you to believe what I've been offered for that clock. Old Gov. Hager never sees me but he says, 'Come, now, Colonel, name your price—I *must* have that clock!' But my goodness I'd as soon think of selling my wife. As I was saying to —— silence in the court, now, she's begun to strike! You can't talk against her—you have to just be patient and hold up till she's said her say. Ah—well, as I was saying, when—she's beginning again! Nineteen, twenty, twenty-one, twenty-two, twen——ah, that's all. Yes, as I was saying to old Judge —— go, it old girl, don't mind me. Now how is that? Isn't that a good, spirited tone? She can wake the dead! Sleep? Why you might as well try to sleep in a thunder-factory. Now just listen at that. She'll strike a hundred and fifty, now, without stopping,—you'll see. There ain't another clock like that in Christendom."

Washington hoped that this might be true, for the din was distracting—though the family, one and all, seemed filled with joy; and the more the clock "buckled down to her work" as the Colonel expressed it, and the more insupportable the clatter became, the more enchanted they all appeared to be. When there was silence, Mrs. Sellers lifted upon Washington a face that beamed with a childlike pride, and said:

"It belonged to his grandmother."

The look and the tone were a plain call for admiring surprise, and therefore Washington said—(it was the only thing that offered itself at the moment):

"Indeed!"

"Yes, it did, didn't it, father!" exclaimed one of the twins. "She was my great-grandmother—and George's too; wasn't she, father! *You* never saw her, but Sis has seen her, when Sis was a baby—didn't you, Sis! Sis has seen her most a hundred times. She was awful deef—she's dead, now. Ain't she, father!"

All the children chimed in, now, with one general Babel of information about deceased—nobody offering to read the riot act or seeming to discountenance the insurrection or disapprove of it in any way—but the head twin drowned all the turmoil and held his own against the field:

"It's our clock, now—and it's got wheels inside of it, and a thing that flutters every time she strikes—don't it, father! Great-grandmother died before hardly any of us was born—she was an Old-School Baptist and had warts all over her—you ask father if she didn't. She had an uncle once that was bald-headed and used to have fits; he wasn't *our* uncle, I don't know what he was to us —some kin or another I reckon—father's seen him a thousand times—hain't you, father! We used to have a calf that et apples and just chawed up dishrags like nothing, and if you stay here you'll see lots of funerals—won't he, Sis! Did you ever see a house afire? I have! Once me and Jim Terry——"

But Sellers began to speak now, and the storm ceased. He began to tell about an enormous speculation he was thinking of embarking some capital in—a speculation which some London bankers had been over to consult with him about—and soon he was building glittering pyramids of coin, and Washington was presently growing opulent under the magic of his eloquence. But at the same time Washington was not able to ignore the cold entirely. He was nearly as close to the stove as he could get, and yet he could not persuade himself that he felt the slightest heat, notwithstanding the isinglass door was still gently and serenely glowing.

He tried to get a trifle closer to the stove, and the consequence was, he tripped the supporting poker and the stove-door tumbled to the floor. And then there was a revelation—there was nothing in the stove but a lighted tallow-candle!

The poor youth blushed and felt as if he must die with shame. But the Colonel was only disconcerted for a moment—he straight-way found his voice again:

"A little idea of my own, Washington—one of the greatest things in the world! You must write and tell your father about it —don't forget that, now. I have been reading up some European scientific reports—friend of mine, Count Fugier, sent them to me—sends me all sorts of things from Paris—he thinks the world of me, Fugier does. Well, I saw that the Academy of France had been testing the properties of heat, and they came to the con-clusion that it was a non-conductor or something like that, and of course its influence must necessarily be deadly in nervous organi-zations with excitable temperaments, especially where there is any tendency toward rheumatic affections. Bless you I saw in a mo-ment what was the matter with us, and says I, out goes your fires!—no more slow torture and certain death for me, sir. What you want is the *appearance* of heat, not the heat itself—that's the idea. Well how to do it was the next thing. I just put my head to work, pegged away a couple of days, and here you are! Rheuma-tism? Why a man can't any more start a case of rheumatism in this house than he can shake an opinion out of a mummy! Stove with a candle in it and a transparent door—that's it—it has been the salvation of this family. Don't you fail to write your father about it, Washington. And tell him the idea is mine—I'm no more conceited than most people, I reckon, but you know it is human nature for a man to want credit for a thing like that."

Washington said with his blue lips that he would, but he said in his secret heart that he would promote no such iniquity. He tried to believe in the healthfulness of the invention, and suc-ceeded tolerably well; but after all he could not feel that good health in a frozen body was any real improvement on the rheuma-tism.

Chapter VIII. Col. Sellers Entertains Washington Hawkins

The supper at Col. Sellers's was not sumptuous, in the begin-ning, but it improved on acquaintance. That is to say, that what Washington regarded at first sight as mere lowly potatoes, presently became awe-inspiring agricultural productions that had been reared in some ducal garden beyond the sea, under the sacred eye of the duke himself, who had sent them to Sellers; the bread was from corn which could be grown in only one favored locality in the earth and only a favored few could get it; the Rio coffee, which at first seemed execrable to the taste, took to itself an improved flavor when Washington was told to drink it slowly and not hurry what should be a lingering luxury in order to be fully appreciated—it was from the private stores of a Brazilian noble-man with an unrememberable name. The Colonel's tongue was a magician's wand that turned dried apples into figs and water into wine as easily as it could change a hovel into a palace and present poverty into imminent future riches.

Washington slept in a cold bed in a carpetless room and woke up in a palace in the morning; at least the palace lingered during the moment that he was rubbing his eyes and getting his bear-ings—and then it disappeared and he recognized that the Colonel's inspiring talk had been influencing his dreams. Fatigue had made him sleep late; when he entered the sitting-room he noticed that the old haircloth sofa was absent; when he sat down to breakfast the Colonel tossed six or seven dollars in bills on the table, counted them over, said he was a little short and must call upon his banker; then returned the bills to his wallet with the indifferent air of a man who is used to money. The breakfast was not an im-provement upon the supper, but the Colonel talked it up and transformed it into an oriental feast. By and by, he said:

"I intend to look out for you, Washington, my boy. I hunted up a place for you yesterday, but I am not referring to that, now —that is a mere livelihood—mere bread and butter; but when I say I mean to look out for you I mean something very different. I mean to put things in your way that will make a mere livelihood a trifling thing. I'll put you in a way to make more money than you'll ever know what to do with. You'll be right here where I can put my hand on you when anything turns up. I've got some prodigious operations on foot; but I'm keeping quiet; mum's the word; your old hand don't go around pow-wowing and letting everybody see his k'yards and find out his little game. But all in good time, Washington, all in good time. You'll see. Now, there's an operation in corn that looks well. Some New York men are trying to get me to go into it—buy up all the growing crops and just boss the market when they mature—ah, I tell you it's a great thing. And it only costs a trifle; two million or two and a half will do it. I haven't exactly promised yet—there's no hurry— the more indifferent I seem, you know, the more anxious those fellows will get. And then there is the hog speculation—that's big-ger still. We've got quiet men at work," [he was very impressive here,] "mousing around, to get propositions out of all the farmers in the whole West and Northwest for the hog crop, and other agents quietly getting propositions and terms out of all the manufactories—and don't you see, if we can get all the hogs and all the slaughter-houses into our hands on the dead quiet—whew! it would take three ships to carry the money. I've looked into the thing—calculated all the chances for and all the chances against, and though I shake my head and hesitate and keep on thinking, apparently, I've got my mind made up that if the thing can be done on a capital of six millions, that's the horse to put up money on! Why, Washington—but what's the use of talking about it—any man can see that there's whole Atlantic oceans of cash in it, gulfs and bays thrown in. But there's a bigger thing than that, yet—a bigger——"

"Why, Colonel, you can't want anything bigger!" said Washington, his eyes blazing. "Oh, I wish I could go into either of those speculations—I only wish I had money—I wish I wasn't cramped and kept down and fettered with poverty, and such prodigious chances lying right here in sight! Oh, it is a fearful thing to be poor. But don't throw away those things—they are so splendid and I can see how sure they are. Don't throw them away for something still better and maybe fail in it! I wouldn't, Colonel. I would stick to these. I wish father were here and were his old self again. Oh, he never in his life had such chances as these are. Colonel, you *can't* improve on these—no man can improve on them!"

A sweet, compassionate smile played about the Colonel's features, and he leaned over the table with the air of a man who is "going to show you" and do it without the least trouble:

"Why Washington, my boy, these things are nothing. They *look* large—of course they look large to a novice, but to a man who has been all his life accustomed to large operations—shaw! They're well enough to while away an idle hour with, or furnish a bit of employment that will give a trifle of idle capital a chance to earn its bread while it is waiting for something to *do*, but—now just listen a moment—just let me give you an idea of what we old veterans of commerce call 'business.' Here's the Rothschilds'[7] proposition—this is between you and me, you understand——"

Washington nodded three or four times impatiently, and his glowing eyes said, "Yes, yes—hurry—I understand——"

"——for I wouldn't have it get out for a fortune. They want me to go in with them on the sly—agent was here two weeks ago about it—go in on the sly" [voice down to an impressive whisper, now] "and buy up a hundred and thirteen wildcat banks in Ohio, Indiana, Kentucky, Illinois, and Missouri—notes of these banks are at all sorts of discount now—average discount of the hundred and thirteen is forty-four per cent.—buy them all up, you

7. Prominent London bankers.

see, and then all of a sudden let the cat out of the bag! Whiz! the stock of every one of those wildcats would spin up to a tremendous premium before you could turn a handspring—profit on the speculation not a dollar less than forty millions!" [An eloquent pause, while the marvelous vision settled into W.'s focus.] "Where's your hogs now! Why, my dear innocent boy, we would just sit down on the front doorsteps and peddle banks like lucifer matches!"

Washington finally got his breath and said:

"Oh, it is perfectly wonderful! Why couldn't these things have happened in father's day? And I—it's of no use—they simply lie before my face and mock me. There is nothing for me but to stand helpless and see other people reap the astonishing harvest."

"Never mind, Washington, don't you worry. I'll fix you. There's plenty of chances. How much money have you got?"

In the presence of so many millions, Washington could not keep from blushing when he had to confess that he had but eighteen dollars in the world.

"Well, all right—don't despair. Other people have been obliged to begin with less. I have a small idea that may develop into something for us both, all in good time. Keep your money close and add to it. I'll make it breed. I've been experimenting (to pass away the time) on a little preparation for curing sore eyes —a kind of decoction nine-tenths water and the other tenth drugs that don't cost more than a dollar a barrel; I'm still experimenting; there's one ingredient wanted yet to perfect the thing, and somehow I can't just manage to hit upon the thing that's necessary, and I don't dare talk with a chemist, of course. But I'm progressing, and before many weeks I wager the country will ring with the fame of Beriah Sellers' Infallible Imperial Oriental Optic Liniment and Salvation for Sore Eyes—the Medical Wonder of the Age! Small bottles fifty cents, large ones a dollar. Average cost, five and seven cents for the two sizes. The first year sell, say, ten thousand bottles in Missouri, seven thousand in Iowa, three thousand in Arkansas, four thousand in Kentucky, six thousand in Illinois, and say twenty-five thousand in the rest of the country. Total, fifty-five thousand bottles; profit clear of all expenses, twenty thousand dollars at the very lowest calculation. All the capital needed is to manufacture the first two thousand bottles—say a hundred and fifty dollars—then the money would begin to flow in. The second year, sales would reach 200,000 bottles—clear profit, say, $75,000—and in the meantime the great factory would be building in St. Louis, to cost, say, $100,000. The third year we could easily sell 1,000,000 bottles in the United States and——"

"O, splendid!" said Washington. "Let's commence right away —let's——"

"——1,000,000 bottles in the United States—profit at least $350,000—and *then* it would begin to be time to turn our attention toward the *real* idea of the business."

"The *real* idea of it! Ain't $350,000 year a pretty real"——

"Stuff! Why, what an infant you are, Washington—what a guileless, short-sighted, easily-contented innocent you are, my poor little country-bred know-nothing! Would I go to all that trouble and bother for the poor crumbs a body might pick up in *this* country? Now do I look like a man who—does my history suggest that I am a man who deals in trifles, contents himself with the narrow horizon that hems in the common herd, sees no further than the end of his nose? Now, *you* know that that is not me— couldn't *be* me. *You* ought to know that if I throw my time and abilities into a patent medicine, it's a patent medicine whose field of operations is the solid earth! its clients the swarming nations that inhabit it! Why what is the republic of America for an eye-water country? Lord bless you, it is nothing but a barren highway that you've got to cross to get *to* the true eye-water market! Why, Washington, in the Oriental countries people swarm like the sands of the desert; every square mile of ground upholds its thousands upon thousands of struggling human creatures—and every separate and individual devil of them's got the ophthalmia! It's as natural to them as noses are—and sin. It's born with them, it stays with them, it's all that some of them have left when they die. Three years of introductory trade in the Orient and what will be the result? Why, our headquarters would be in Constantinople and our hindquarters in Further India! Factories and warehouses in Cairo, Ispahan, Bagdad, Damascus, Jerusalem, Yedo, Peking, Bangkok, Delhi, Bombay, and Calcutta! Annual income—well, God only knows how many millions and millions apiece!"

Washington was so dazed, so bewildered—his heart and his eyes had wandered so far away among the strange lands beyond the seas, and such avalanches of coin and currency had fluttered and jingled confusedly down before him, that he was now as one who has been whirling round and round for a time, and, stopping all at once, finds his surroundings still whirling and all objects a dancing chaos. However, little by little the Sellers family cooled down and crystallized into shape, and the poor room lost its glitter and resumed its poverty. Then the youth found his voice and begged Sellers to drop everything and hurry up the eye-water; and he got his eighteen dollars and tried to force it upon the Colonel —pleaded with him to take it—implored him to do it. But the Colonel would not; said he would not need the capital (in his native magnificent way he called that eighteen dollars capital) till the eye-water was an accomplished fact. He made Washington easy in his mind, though, by promising that he would call for it just as soon as the invention was finished, and he added the glad tidings that nobody but just they two should be admitted to a share in the speculation.

When Washington left the breakfast table he could have worshiped that man. Washington was one of that kind of people whose hopes are in the very clouds one day, and in the gutter the next. He walked on air, now. The Colonel was ready to take him around and introduce him to the employment he had found for him, but Washington begged for a few moments in which to write home; with his kind of people, to ride to-day's new interest to death and put off yesterday's until another time, is nature itself. He ran upstairs and wrote glowingly, enthusiastically, to his mother about the hogs and the corn, the banks and the eye-water—and added a few inconsequential millions to each project. And he said that people little dreamed what a man Col. Sellers was, and that the world would open its eyes when it found out. And he closed his letter thus:

> "So make yourself perfectly easy, mother—in a little while you shall have everything you want, and more. I am not likely to stint *you* in anything, I fancy. This money will not be for me, alone, but for all of us. I want all to share alike; and there is going to be far more for each than one person can spend. Break it to father cautiously—you understand the need of that— break it to him cautiously, for he has had such cruel hard fortune, and is so stricken by it that great good news might prostrate him more surely than even bad, for he is used to the bad but is grown sadly unaccustomed to the other. Tell Laura—tell all the children. And write to Clay about it if he is not with you yet. You may tell Clay that whatever I get he can freely share in—freely. He knows that that is true—there will be no need that I should swear to that to make him believe it. Good-bye— and mind what I say: Rest perfectly easy, one and all of you, for our troubles are nearly at an end."

Poor lad, he could not know that his mother would cry some loving, compassionate tears over his letter and put off the family with a synopsis of its contents which conveyed a deal of love to them but not much idea of his prospects or projects. And he never dreamed that such a joyful letter could sadden her and fill her night with sighs, and troubled thoughts, and bodings of the future, instead of filling it with peace and blessing it with restful sleep.

When the letter was done, Washington and the Colonel sallied forth, and as they walked along Washington learned what he was to be. He was to be a clerk in a real estate office. Instantly the fickle youth's dreams forsook the magic eye-water and flew back to the Tennessee Land.[8] And the gorgeous possibilities of that great domain straightway began to occupy his imagination to such a degree that he could scarcely manage to keep even enough of his attention upon the Colonel's talk to retain the general run of what he was saying. He was glad it was a real estate office—he was a made man now, sure.

The Colonel said that General Boswell was a rich man and had a good and growing business; and that Washington's work would be light and he would get forty dollars a month and be boarded and lodged in the General's family—which was as good as ten dollars more; and even better, for he could not live as well even at the "City Hotel" as he would there, and yet the hotel charged fifteen dollars a month where a man had a good room.

General Boswell was in his office; a comfortable looking place, with plenty of outline maps hanging about the walls and in the windows, and a spectacled man was marking out another one on a long table. The office was in the principal street. The General received Washington with a kindly but reserved politeness. Washington rather liked his looks. He was about fifty years old, dignified, well preserved, and well dressed. After the Colonel took his leave, the General talked a while with Washington—his talk consisting chiefly of instructions about the clerical duties of the place. He seemed satisfied as to Washington's ability to take care of the books, he was evidently a pretty fair theoretical bookkeeper, and experience would soon harden theory into practice. By and by dinner-time came, and the two walked to the General's house; and now Washington noticed an instinct in himself that moved him to keep not in the General's rear, exactly, but yet not at his side—somehow the old gentleman's dignity and reserve did not inspire familiarity.

From *Chapter XI*. [*A Dinner Party*]

Two months had gone by[9] and the Hawkins family were domiciled in Hawkeye. Washington was at work in the real estate office again, and was alternately in paradise or the other place just as it happened that Louise[1] was gracious to him or seemingly indifferent—because indifference or preoccupation could mean nothing else than that she was thinking of some other young per-

---

8. Actually called by this title in Sam Clemens' own family; a huge tract of land, close to 100,000 acres, which John Marshall Clemens had bought in Tennessee, expecting it to make the family rich.

9. In the chapters omitted here, Squire Hawkins has died, urging his family,

"Never lose sight of the Tennessee land," because it would mean "wealth that is boundless!" John Clemens, at his death, had also urged his family to "cling to the Tennessee land."

1. The daughter of General Boswell, Washington Hawkins' employer in the real estate office.

son. Col. Sellers had asked him several times to dine with him, when he first returned to Hawkeye, but Washington, for no particular reason, had not accepted. No particular reason except one which he preferred to keep to himself—viz., that he could not bear to be away from Louise. It occurred to him, now, that the Colonel had not invited him lately—could he be offended? He resolved to go that very day, and give the Colonel a pleasant surprise. It was a good idea; especially as Louise had absented herself from breakfast that morning, and torn his heart; he would tear hers, now, and let her see how it felt.

The Sellers family were just starting to dinner when Washington burst upon them with his surprise. For an instant the Colonel looked nonplussed, and just a bit uncomfortable; and Mrs. Sellers looked actually distressed: but the next moment the head of the house was himself again, and exclaimed:

"All right, my boy, all right—always glad to see you—always glad to hear your voice and take you by the hand. Don't wait for special invitations—that's all nonsense among friends. Just come whenever you can, and come as often as you can—the oftener the better. You can't please us any better than that, Washington; the little woman will tell you so herself. We don't pretend to style. Plain folks, you know—plain folks. Just a plain family dinner, but such as it is, our friends are *always* welcome, I reckon you know that yourself, Washington. Run along, children, run along; Lafayette,[2] stand off the cat's tail, child, can't you see what you're doing? Come, come, come, Roderick Dhu,[3] it isn't nice for little boys to hang on to young gentlemen's coat-tails— but never mind him, Washington, he's full of spirits and don't mean any harm. Children will be children, you know. Take the chair next to Mrs. Sellers, Washington—tut, tut, Marie Antoinette, let your brother have the fork if he wants it, you are bigger than he is."

Washington contemplated the banquet, and wondered if he were in his right mind. Was this the plain family dinner? And was it all present? It was soon apparent that this was indeed the dinner: it was all on the table: it consisted of abundance of clear, fresh water, and a basin of raw turnips—nothing more.

Washington stole a glance at Mrs. Sellers's face, and would have given the world, the next moment, if he could have spared

2. "In those old days the average man called his children after his most revered literary and historical idols; consequently there was hardly a family, at least in the West, but had a Washington in it—and also a Lafayette, a Franklin, and six or eight sounding names from Byron, Scott, and the Bible, if the offspring held out. To visit such a family was to find one's self confronted by a congress made up of representatives of the imperial myths and the majestic dead of all the ages. There was something thrilling about it, to a stranger, not to say awe-inspiring" [Mark Twain's note].
3. A rebel Highland chief in Scott's *Lady of the Lake*.

her that. The poor woman's face was crimson, and the tears stood in her eyes. Washington did not know what to do. He wished he had never come there and spied out this cruel poverty and brought pain to that poor little lady's heart and shame to her cheek; but he was there, and there was no escape. Col. Sellers hitched back his coat sleeves airily from his wrists as who should say *"Now* for solid enjoyment!" seized a fork, flourished it and began to harpoon turnips and deposit them in the plates before him:

"Let me help you, Washington—Lafayette, pass this plate to Washington—ah, well, well, my boy, things are looking pretty bright, now, I tell you. Speculation—my! the whole atmosphere's full of money. I wouldn't take three fortunes for one little operation I've got on hand now—have anything from the casters? No? Well, you're right, you're right. Some people like mustard with turnips, but—now there was Baron Poniatowski[4]—Lord, but that man did know how to live!—true Russian you know, Russian to the backbone; I say to my wife, give me a Russian every time, for a table comrade. The Baron used to say, 'Take mustard, Sellers, try the mustard,—a man *can't* know what turnips are in perfection without mustard,' but I always said, 'No, Baron, I'm a plain man, and I want my food plain—none of your embellishments for Beriah Sellers—no made dishes for me!' And it's the best way— high living kills more than it cures in this world, you can rest assured of that. Yes, indeed, Washington, I've got one little operation on hand that—take some more water—help yourself, won't you? help yourself, there's plenty of it. You'll find it pretty good, I guess. How does that fruit strike you?"

Washington said he did not know that he had ever tasted better. He did not add that he detested turnips even when they were cooked—loathed them in their natural state. No, he kept this to himself, and praised the turnips to the peril of his soul.

"I thought you'd like them. Examine them—examine them— they'll bear it. See how perfectly firm and juicy they are—they can't start any like them in this part of the country, I can tell you. These are from New Jersey—I imported them myself. They cost like sin, too; but, Lord bless me, I go in for having the best of a thing, even if it does cost a little more—it's the best economy, in the long run. These are the Early Malcolm—it's a turnip that can't be produced except in just one orchard, and the supply never is up to the demand. Take some more water, Washington—you

4. This name may have sounded "true Russian" to Colonel Sellers, but actually it belonged to a Polish princely family of Italian origin; the most famous of the name fought with Napoleon I against Russia and became marshal of France; the young Poniatowski of Mark Twain's time was equerry to Napoleon III.

can't drink too much water with fruit—all the doctors say that. The plague can't come where this article is, my boy!"

"Plague? What plague?"

"What plague, indeed? Why the Asiatic plague that nearly depopulated London a couple of centuries ago."

"But how does that concern us? There is no plague here, I reckon."

"Sh! I've let it out! Well, never mind—just keep it to yourself. Perhaps I oughtn't said anything, but it's *bound* to come out sooner or later, so what is the odds? Old McDowells wouldn't like me to—to—bother it all, I'll just tell the whole thing and let it go. You see, I've been down to St. Louis, and I happened to run across old Dr. McDowells—thinks the world of me, does the doctor. He's a man that keeps himself to himself, and well he may, for he knows that he's got a reputation that covers the whole earth— he won't condescend to open himself out to many people, but, Lord bless you, he and I are just like brothers; he won't let me go to a hotel when I'm in the city—says I'm the only man that's company to him, and I don't know but there's some truth in it, too, because although I never like to glorify myself and make a great to-do over what I am or what I can do or what I know, I don't mind saying here among friends that I *am* better read up in most sciences, maybe, than the general run of professional men in these days. Well, the other day he let me into a little secret, strictly on the quiet, about this matter of the plague.

"You see it's booming right along in our direction—follows the Gulf Stream, you know, just as all those epidemics do,—and within three months it will be just waltzing through this land like a whirlwind! And whoever it touches can make his will and contract for the funeral. Well, you can't *cure* it, you know, but you can prevent it. How? Turnips! that's it! Turnips and water! Nothing like it in the world, old McDowells says, just fill yourself up two or three times a day, and you can snap your fingers at the plague. Sh! keep mum, but just you confine yourself to that diet and you're all right. I wouldn't have old McDowells know that I told about it for anything—he never would speak to me again. Take some more water, Washington—the more water you drink, the better. Here, let me give you some more of the turnips. No, no, no, now, I insist. There, now. Absorb those. They're mighty sustaining—brimful of nutriment—all the medical books say so. Just eat from four to seven goodsized turnips at a meal, and drink from a pint and a half to a quart of water, and then just sit around a couple of hours and let them ferment. You'll feel like a fighting cock next day."

Fifteen or twenty minutes later the Colonel's tongue was still chattering away—he had piled up several future fortunes out of several incipient "operations" which he had blundered into within the past week, and was now soaring along through some brilliant expectations born of late promising experiments upon the lacking ingredient of the eye-water. And at such a time Washington ought to have been a rapt and enthusiastic listener, but he was not, for two matters disturbed his mind and distracted his attention. One was, that he discovered, to his confusion and shame, that in allowing himself to be helped a second time to the turnips, he had robbed those hungry children. He had not needed the dreadful "fruit," and had not wanted it; and when he saw the pathetic sorrow in their faces when they asked for more and there was no more to give them, he hated himself for his stupidity and pitied the famishing young things with all his heart. The other matter that disturbed him was the dire inflation that had begun in his stomach. It grew and grew, it became more and more insupportable. Evidently the turnips were "fermenting." He forced himself to sit still as long as he could, but his anguish conquered him at last.

He rose in the midst of the Colonel's talk and excused himself on the plea of a previous engagement. The Colonel followed him to the door, promising over and over again that he would use his influence to get some of the Early Malcolms for him, and insisting that he should not be such a stranger but come and take pot-luck with him every chance he got. Washington was glad enough to get away and feel free again. He immediately bent his steps toward home.

In bed he passed an hour that threatened to turn his hair gray, and then a blessed calm settled down upon him that filled his heart with gratitude. Weak and languid, he made shift to turn himself about and seek rest and sleep; and as his soul hovered upon the brink of unconsciousness, he heaved a long, deep sigh, and said to himself that in his heart he had cursed the Colonel's preventive of rheumatism, before, and now *let* the plague come if it must—he was done with preventives; if ever any man beguiled him with turnips and water again, let him die the death. * * *

From *Chapter XXIV. The City of Washington*

* * * Washington is an interesting city to any of us. It seems to become more and more interesting the oftener we visit it. Perhaps the reader has never been there? Very well.[5] You arrive

5. The day after the *Quaker City* docked in New York, returning from the *Innocents Abroad* excursion, Twain departed for Washington, D.C., to become private secretary to William M. Stewart, first United States Senator elected from the new state of Nevada. Although this secretarial experience lasted only two and a half months, perhaps it made Twain feel qualified to conduct the reader through a tour of the nation's capital.

either at night, rather too late to do anything or see anything until morning, or you arrive so early in the morning that you consider it best to go to your hotel and sleep an hour or two while the sun bothers along over the Atlantic. You cannot well arrive at a pleasant intermediate hour because the railway corporation that keeps the keys of the only door that leads into the town or out of it take care of that. You arrive in tolerably good spirits, because it is only thirty-eight miles from Baltimore to the capital, and so you have only been insulted three times (provided you are not in a sleeping car—the average is higher, there): once when you renewed your ticket after stopping over in Baltimore, once when you were about to enter the "ladies' car" without knowing it *was* a lady's car, and once when you asked the conductor at what hour you would reach Washington.

You are assailed by a long rank of hackmen who shake their whips in your face as you step out upon the sidewalk; you enter what they regard as a "carriage," in the capital, and you wonder why they do not take it out of service and put it in the museum: we have few enough antiquities, and it is little to our credit that we make scarcely any effort to preserve the few we have. You reach your hotel, presently—and here let us draw the curtain of charity —because of course you have gone to the wrong one. You being a stranger, how could you do otherwise? There are a hundred and eighteen bad hotels, and only one good one. The most renowned and popular hotel of them all is perhaps the worst one known to history.

It is winter, and night. When you arrived, it was snowing. When you reached the hotel, it was sleeting. When you went to bed, it was raining. During the night it froze hard, and the wind blew some chimneys down. When you got up in the morning, it was foggy. When you finished your breakfast at ten o'clock and went out, the sunshine was brilliant, the weather balmy and delicious, and the mud and slush deep and all-pervading. You will like the climate—when you get used to it.

You naturally wish to view the city; so you take an umbrella, an overcoat, and a fan, and go forth. The prominent features you soon locate and get familiar with; first you glimpse the ornamental upper works of a long, snowy palace projecting above a grove of trees, and a tall, graceful white dome with a statue on it surmounting the palace and pleasantly contrasting with the background of blue sky. That building is the Capitol; gossips will tell you that by the original estimates it was to cost $12,000,000, and that the government did come within $27,200,000 of building it for that sum.

You stand at the back of the Capitol to treat yourself to a view, and it is a very noble one. You understand, the Capitol stands upon the verge of a high piece of table land, a fine commanding position, and its front looks out over this noble situation for a city—but it don't see it, for the reason that when the Capitol extension was decided upon, the property owners at once advanced their prices to such inhuman figures that the people went down and built the city in the muddy low marsh *behind* the temple of liberty; so now the lordly front of the building, with its imposing colonnades, its projecting, graceful wings, its picturesque groups of statuary, and its long terraced ranges of steps, flowing down in white marble waves to the ground, merely looks out upon a sorrowful little desert of cheap boarding houses.

So you observe, that you take your view from the back of the Capitol. And not yet from the airy outlooks of the dome, by the way, because to get there you must pass through the great rotunda: and to do that, you would have to see the marvelous Historical Paintings that hang there, and the bas-reliefs—and what have you done that you should suffer thus? And besides, you might have to pass through the old part of the building, and you could not help seeing Mr. Lincoln, as petrified by a young lady artist for $10,000—and you might take his marble emancipation proclamation, which he holds out in his hand and contemplates, for a folded napkin; and you might conceive from his expression and his attitude, that he is finding fault with the washing. Which is not the case. Nobody knows what *is* the matter with him; but everybody feels for him. Well, you ought not to go into the dome anyhow, because it would be utterly impossible to go up there without seeing the frescoes in it—and why should you be interested in the delirium tremens of art?

The Capitol is a very noble and a very beautiful building, both within and without, but you need not examine it now. Still, if you greatly prefer going into the dome, go. Now your general glance gives you picturesque stretches of gleaming water, on your left, with a sail here and there and a lunatic asylum on shore; over beyond the water, on a distant elevation, you see a squat yellow temple which your eye dwells upon lovingly through a blur of unmanly moisture, for it recalls your lost boyhood and the Parthenons done in molasses candy which made it blest and beautiful. Still in the distance, but on this side of the water and close to its edge, the Monument to the Father of his Country towers out of the mud—sacred soil is the customary term. It has the aspect of a factory chimney with the top broken off. The skeleton of a decaying scaffolding lingers about its summit, and tradition says that the spirit of Washington often comes down and sits on those rafters to enjoy this tribute of respect which the nation has reared as the symbol of its unappeasable gratitude. The Monument is to be finished, some day, and at that time our Washington will have risen still higher in the nation's veneration, and will be known as the Great-Great-Grandfather of his Country. The memorial Chimney stands in a quiet pastoral locality that is full of reposeful expression. With a glass you can see the cow-sheds about its base, and the contented sheep nibbling pebbles in the desert solitudes that surround it, and the tired pigs dozing in the holy calm of its protecting shadow.

Now you wrench your gaze loose and you look down in front of you and see the broad Pennsylvania Avenue stretching straight ahead for a mile or more till it brings up against the iron fence in front of a pillared granite pile, the Treasury building—an edifice that would command respect in any capital. The stores and hotels that wall in this broad avenue are mean, and cheap, and dingy, and are better left without comment. Beyond the Treasury is a fine large white barn, with wide unhandsome grounds about it. The President lives there. It is ugly enough outside, but that is nothing to what it is inside. Dreariness, flimsiness, bad taste reduced to mathematical completeness is what the inside offers to the eye, if it remains yet what it always has been.

The front and right hand views give you the city at large. It is a wide stretch of cheap little brick houses, with here and there a noble architectural pile lifting itself out of the midst—government buildings, these. If the thaw is still going on when you come down and go about town, you will wonder at the short-sightedness of the city fathers, when you come to inspect the streets, in that they do not dilute the mud a little more and use them for canals.

If you inquire around a little, you will find that there are more boarding houses to the square acre in Washington than there are in any other city in the land, perhaps. If you apply for a home in one of them, it will seem odd to you to have the landlady inspect you with a severe eye and then ask you if you are a member of Congress. Perhaps, just as a pleasantry, you will say yes. And then she will tell you that she is "full." Then you show her her advertisement in the morning paper, and there she stands, convicted and ashamed. She will try to blush, and it will be only polite in you to take the effort for the deed. She shows you her rooms, now, and lets you take one—but she makes you pay in advance for it. That is what you will get for pretending to be a member of Congress. If you had been content to be merely a private citizen, your trunk would have been sufficient security for your board. If you are curious and inquire into this thing, the chances are that your landlady will be ill-natured enough to say that the person and property of a Congressman are exempt from arrest or detention, and that with the tears in her eyes she has seen several of the people's representatives walk off to their several States and Territories carrying her unreceipted board bills in their pockets for keepsakes. And before you have been in Washington many weeks you will be mean enough to believe her, too.

Of course you contrive to see everything and find out everything. And one of the first and most startling things you find out is, that every individual you encounter in the city of Washington almost—and certainly every separate and distinct individual in the public employment, from the highest bureau chief, clear down to the maid who scrubs Department halls, the night watchmen of the public buildings, and the darkey boy who purifies the Department spittoons—represents Political Influence. Unless you can get the ear of a Senator, or a Congressman, or a Chief of a Bureau or Department, and persuade him to use his "influence" in your behalf, you cannot get an employment of the most trivial nature in Washington. Mere merit, fitness, and capability, are useless baggage to you without "influence." The population of Washington consists pretty much entirely of government employés and the people who board them. There are thousands of these employés, and they have gathered there from every corner of the Union and got their berths through the intercession (command is nearer the word) of the Senators and Representatives of their respective States.[6] It would be an odd circumstance to see a girl get employment at three or four dollars a week in one of the great public cribs without any political grandee to back her, but merely because she was worthy, and competent, and a good citizen of a free country that "treats all persons alike." Washington would be mildly thunderstruck at such a thing as that. If you are a member of Congress (no offense), and one of your constituents who doesn't know anything, and does not want to go into the bother of learning something, and has no money, and no employment, and can't earn a living, comes besieging you for help, do you say, "Come, my friend, if your services were valuable you could get employment elsewhere—don't want you here"? Oh, no. You take him to a Department and say, "Here, give this person something to pass away the time at—and a salary"—and the thing is done. You throw him on his country. He is his country's child, let his country support him. There is something good and motherly about

6. A part of Twain's secretarial duties consisted in meeting numerous job-seekers; he had also to cover the sessions of Congress every day and answer letters from Stewart's Nevada constituents. At the same time he was being besieged by social invitations to dinners and receptions and was writing his book *The Innocents Abroad* at night.

Tradition says that Mark Twain was fired, to his own great relief. Products of his Washington association are such sketches as "My Late Senatorial Secretaryship," "Facts Concerning the Recent Resignation," "Facts in the Case of the Great Beef Contract," and "The Case of George Fisher," all humorous but keenly satiric writings.

Washington, the grand old benevolent National Asylum for the Helpless.

The wages received by this great hive of employés are placed at the liberal figure meet and just for skilled and competent labor. Such of them as are immediately employed about the two Houses of Congress are not only liberally paid also, but are remembered in the customary Extra Compensation bill which slides neatly through, annually, with the general grab that signalizes the last night of a session, and thus twenty per cent. is added to their wages, for—for fun, no doubt. * * *

1873

From A Tramp Abroad[7]

From Vol. I, Chapter II. [*Baker's Bluejay Yarn: Prologue*]

Animals talk to each other, of course. There can be no question about that; but I suppose there are very few people who can understand them. I never knew but one man who could. I knew he could, however, because he told me so himself. He was a middle-aged, simple-hearted miner who had lived in a lonely corner of California, among the woods and mountains, a good many years, and had studied the ways of his only neighbors, the beasts and the birds, until he believed he could accurately translate any remark which they made. This was Jim Baker.[8] According to Jim Baker, some animals have only a limited education, and use only very simple words, and scarcely ever a comparison or a flowery figure; whereas, certain other animals have a large vocabulary, a fine command of language and a ready and fluent delivery; consequently these latter talk a great deal; they like it; they are conscious of their talent, and they enjoy "showing off." Baker said, that after long and careful observation, he had come to the conclusion that the bluejays were the best talkers he had found among birds and beasts. Said he:

"There's more *to* a bluejay than any other creature. He has got more moods, and more different kinds of feelings than other creatures; and, mind you, whatever a bluejay feels, he can put into

7. An account of Mark Twain's second trip to Europe; this time he was accompanied by his Hartford neighbor, the Rev. Joseph Twichell. The present text is from the Author's Uniform Edition. In our selection, Twain is staying at the Schloss Hotel in Heidelberg and has taken a mile walk, alone, into the woods. In the solitude of the forest, he falls "into a train of dreamy thought about animals which talk, and kobolds, and enchanted folk"; meanwhile, three impertinent ravens have gathered on a limb, looking him over and making fun of his vest. Chagrined, he walks away; but he has been reminded of a yarn about talking blue jays; thus he makes the skillful transition which appears here.

8. Actually Jim Gillis, whom Mark Twain had visited in 1864 in the Tuolumne region. Gillis was the original of Bret Harte's "Truthful James," as well as of Twain's yarn spinner. Another Gillis tale used by Mark Twain was "The Burning Shame," which furnished a chapter in *Huckleberry Finn*.

language. And no mere commonplace language, either, but rattling, out-and-out book-talk—and bristling with metaphor, too—just bristling! And as for command of language—why *you* never see a bluejay get stuck for a word. No man ever did. They just boil out of him! And another thing: I've noticed a good deal, and there's no bird, or cow, or anything that uses as good grammar as a blue-jay. You may say a cat uses good grammar. Well, a cat does—but you let a cat get excited once; you let a cat get to pulling fur with another cat on a shed, nights, and you'll hear grammar that will give you the lockjaw. Ignorant people think it's the *noise* which fighting cats make that is so aggravating, but it ain't so; it's the sickening grammar they use. Now I've never heard a jay use bad grammar but very seldom; and when they do, they are as ashamed as a human; they shut right down and leave.

"You may call a jay a bird. Well, so he is, in a measure—be-cause he's got feathers on him, and don't belong to no church, perhaps; but otherwise he is just as much a human as you be. And I'll tell you for why. A jay's gifts, and instincts, and feelings, and interests, cover the whole ground. A jay hasn't got any more principle than a Congressman. A jay will lie, a jay will steal, a jay will deceive, a jay will betray; and four times out of five, a jay will go back on his solemnest promise. The sacredness of an obligation is a thing which you can't cram into no bluejay's head. Now, on top of all this, there's another thing; a jay can outswear any gentle-man in the mines. You think a cat can swear. Well, a cat can; but you give a bluejay a subject that calls for his reserve-powers, and where is your cat? Don't talk to *me*—I know too much about this thing. And there's yet another thing; in the one little particular of scolding—just good, clean, out-and-out scolding—a bluejay can lay over anything, human or divine. Yes, sir, a jay is everything that a man is. A jay can cry, a jay can laugh, a jay can feel shame, a jay can reason and plan and discuss, a jay likes gossip and scandal, a jay has got a sense of humor, a jay knows when he is an ass just as well as you do—maybe better. If a jay ain't human, he bet-ter take in his sign, that's all. Now I'm going to tell you a perfectly true fact about some bluejays."

Vol. I, Chapter III. Baker's Bluejay Yarn

"When I first begun to understand jay language correctly, there was a little incident happened here. Seven years ago, the last man in this region but me moved away. There stands his house,—been empty ever since; a log house, with a plank roof—just one big room, and no more; no ceiling—nothing between the rafters and the floor. Well, one Sunday morning I was sitting out here in front of my cabin, with my cat, taking the sun, and looking at the blue hills, and listening to the leaves rustling so lonely in the trees, and thinking of the home away yonder in the states, that I hadn't heard from in thirteen years,[9] when a bluejay lit on that house, with an acorn in his mouth, and says, 'Hello, I reckon I've struck something.' When he spoke, the acorn dropped out of his mouth and rolled down the roof, of course, but he didn't care; his mind was all on the thing he had struck. It was a knot-hole in the roof. He cocked his head to one side, shut one eye and put the other one to the hole, like a 'possum looking down a jug; then he glanced up with his bright eyes, gave a wink or two with his wings—which signifies gratification, you understand,—and says, 'It looks like a hole, it's located like a hole,—blamed if I don't believe it *is* a hole!'

"Then he cocked his head down and took another look; he glances up perfectly joyful, this time; winks his wings and his tail both, and says, 'Oh, no, this ain't no fat thing, I reckon! If I ain't in luck!—why it's a perfectly elegant hole!' So he flew down and got that acorn, and fetched it up and dropped it in, and was just tilting his head back, with the heavenliest smile on his face, when all of a sudden he was paralyzed into a listening attitude and that smile faded gradually out of his countenance like breath off'n a razor, and the queerest look of surprise took its place. Then he says, 'Why, I didn't hear it fall!' He cocked his eye at the hole again, and took a long look; raised up and shook his head; stepped around to the other side of the hole and took another look from that side; shook his head again. He studied a while, then he just went into the *details*—walked round and round the hole and spied into it from every point of the compass. No use. Now he took a thinking attitude on the comb of the roof and scratched the back of his head with his right foot a minute, and finally says, 'Well, it's too many for *me*, that's certain; must be a mighty long hole; however, I ain't got no time to fool around here, I got to 'tend to business; I reckon it's all right—chance it, anyway.'

"So he flew off and fetched another acorn and dropped it in, and tried to flirt his eye to the hole quick enough to see what become of it, but he was too late. He held his eye there as much as a minute; then he raised up and sighed, and says, 'Confound it, I don't seem to understand this thing, no way; however, I'll tackle her again.' He fetched another acorn, and done his level best to see what become of it, but he couldn't. He says, 'Well, *I* never struck no such a hole as this before; I'm of the opinion it's a totally new kind of a hole.' Then he begun to get mad. He held in for a spell, walking up and down the comb of the roof and shak-

9. This sketch is famous as a mingling of fantasy and realism: fantasy in its subject matter and realism in the manner of its presentation by the old miner.

ing his head and muttering to himself; but his feelings got the upper hand of him, presently, and he broke loose and cussed himself black in the face. I never see a bird take on so about a little thing. When he got through he walks to the hole and looks in again for half a minute; then he says, 'Well, you're a long hole, and a deep hole, and a mighty singular hole altogether—but I've started in to fill you, and I'm d—d if I *don't* fill you, if it takes a hundred years!'

"And with that, away he went. You never see a bird work so since you was born. He laid into his work like a nigger, and the way he hove acorns into that hole for about two hours and a half was one of the most exciting and astonishing spectacles I ever struck. He never stopped to take a look any more—he just hove 'em in and went for more. Well, at last he could hardly flop his wings, he was so tuckered out. He comes a-drooping down, once more, sweating like an ice-pitcher, drops his acorn in and says, 'Now I guess I've got the bulge on you by this time!' So he bent down for a look. If you'll believe me, when his head come up again he was just pale with rage. He says, 'I've shoveled acorns enough in there to keep the family thirty years, and if I can see a sign of one of 'em I wish I may land in a museum with a belly full of sawdust in two minutes!'

"He just had strength enough to crawl up on to the comb and lean his back again the chimbly, and then he collected his impressions and begun to free his mind. I see in a second that what I had mistook for profanity in the mines was only just the rudiments, as you may say.

"Another jay was going by, and heard him doing his devotions, and stops to inquire what was up. The sufferer told him the whole circumstance, and says, 'Now yonder's the hole, and if you don't believe me, go and look for yourself.' So this fellow went and looked, and comes back and says, 'How many did you say you put in there?' 'Not any less than two tons,' says the sufferer. The other jay went and looked again. He couldn't seem to make it out, so he raised a yell, and three more jays come. They all examined the hole, they all made the sufferer tell it over again, then they all discussed it, and got off as many leather-headed opinions about it as an average crowd of humans could have done.

"They called in more jays; then more and more, till pretty soon this whole region 'peared to have a blue flush about it. There must have been five thousand of them; and such another jawing and disputing and ripping and cussing, you never heard. Every jay in the whole lot put his eye to the hole and delivered a more chuckle-headed opinion about the mystery than the jay that went there before him. They examined the house all over, too. The door was standing half open, and at last one old jay happened to go and light on it and look in. Of course, that knocked the mystery galley-west in a second. There lay the acorns, scattered all over the floor. He flopped his wings and raised a whoop. 'Come here!' he says, 'Come here, everybody; hang'd if this fool hasn't been trying to fill up a house with acorns!' They all came a-swooping down like a blue cloud, and as each fellow lit on the door and took a glance, the whole absurdity of the contract that that first jay had tackled hit him home and he fell over backwards suffocating with laughter, and the next jay took his place and done the same.

"Well, sir, they roosted around here on the housetop and the trees for an hour, and guffawed over that thing like human beings. It ain't any use to tell me a bluejay hasn't got a sense of humor, because I know better. And memory, too. They brought jays here from all over the United States to look down that hole, every summer for three years. Other birds, too. And they could all see the point, except an owl that come from Nova Scotia to visit the Yo Semite, and he took this thing in on his way back. He said he couldn't see anything funny in it. But then he was a good deal disappointed about Yo Semite, too."

1879

From Life on the Mississippi[1]
Chapter III. Frescos from the Past[2]

Apparently the river was ready for business, now. But no; the distribution of a population along its banks was as calm and deliberate and time-devouring a process as the discovery and exploration had been.

Seventy years elapsed after the exploration before the river's borders had a white population worth considering; and nearly fifty more before the river had a commerce. Between La Salle's opening of the river[3] and the time when it may be said to have become the vehicle of anything like a regular and active commerce, seven sovereigns had occupied the throne of England, America had become an independent nation, Louis XIV. and Louis XV. had rotted and died, the French monarchy had gone

1. On a walk with Joseph Twichell, Mark Twain told him about "old Mississippi days of steamboating glory and grandeur" as seen from the pilot house, and Twichell exclaimed: "What a virgin subject to hurl into a magazine!" As a result, fourteen glowing chapters (Chapters IV–XVII) of what is now *Life on the Mississippi* appeared in the *Atlantic Monthly* under the title "Old Times on the Mississippi," running from

January through August, 1875 (omitting July). The book was published in 1883; the present text is from the Author's Uniform Edition.
2. This section, not a part of the *Atlantic Monthly* series, appeared for the first time in the book.
3. The French explorer La Salle descended the river to its mouth and named the region Louisiana in honor of the French king on April 9, 1682.

down in the red tempest of the Revolution, and Napoleon was a name that was beginning to be talked about. Truly, there were snails in those days.[4]

The river's earliest commerce was in great barges—keelboats, broadhorns.[5] They floated and sailed from the upper rivers to New Orleans, changed cargoes there, and were tediously warped and poled back by hand. A voyage down and back sometimes occupied nine months. In time this commerce increased until it gave employment to hordes of rough and hardy men; rude, uneducated, brave, suffering terrific hardships with sailor-like stoicism; heavy drinkers, coarse frolickers in moral sties like the Natchez-under-the-hill[6] of that day, heavy fighters, reckless fellows, every one, elephantinely jolly, foul-witted, profane, prodigal of their money, bankrupt at the end of the trip, fond of barbaric finery, prodigious braggarts; yet, in the main, honest, trustworthy, faithful to promises and duty, and often picturesquely magnanimous.[7]

By and by the steamboat intruded. Then, for fifteen or twenty years, these men continued to run their keelboats down-stream, and the steamers did all of the up-stream business, the keelboat-men selling their boats in New Orleans, and returning home as deck passengers in the steamers.

But after a while the steamboats so increased in number and in speed that they were able to absorb the entire commerce; and then keelboating died a permanent death. The keelboatman became a deck-hand, or a mate, or a pilot on the steamer; and when steamer-berths were not open to him, he took a berth on a Pittsburg coal-flat, or on a pine raft constructed in the forests up toward the sources of the Mississippi.

In the heyday of the steamboating prosperity, the river from end to end was flaked with coal-fleets and timber-rafts, all managed by hand, and employing hosts of the rough characters whom I have been trying to describe. I remember the annual processions of mighty rafts that used to glide by Hannibal when I was a boy, —an acre or so of white, sweet-smelling boards in each raft, a crew of two dozen men or more, three or four wigwams scattered

---

4. A recasting of the oft-quoted Biblical statement, "There were giants in the earth in those days" (Genesis vi.4).
5. A "keelboat" was a long, narrow, pointed, flat-bottomed boat, with a "keel" projecting below the plating to give it stability. A "broadhorn" was a flatboat covered by an arched roof; a long oar projecting from each side gave the craft its name.
6. Situated at the base of the bluff below Natchez, Mississippi, this was a spot frequented by "toughs"—prostitutes, gunmen, gamblers.

7. The river was by no means limited to these rough specimens. In Chapter XVIII, speaking of his years as a pilot, Twain remarks that "in that brief, sharp schooling" he got familiarly acquainted with "about all the different types of humanity that are to be found in fiction, biography, or history": "When I find a well-drawn character in fiction or biography, I generally take a warm personal interest in him, for the reason that I have known him before— met him on the river."

about the raft's vast level space for storm-quarters,—and I remember the rude ways and the tremendous talk of their big crews, the ex-keelboatmen and their admiringly patterning successors; for we used to swim out a quarter or a third of a mile and get on these rafts and have a ride.

By way of illustrating keelboat talk and manners, and that now departed and hardly-remembered raft-life, I will throw in, in this place, a chapter from a book[8] which I have been working at, by fits and starts, during the past five or six years, and may possibly finish in the course of five or six more. The book is a story which details some passages in the life of an ignorant village boy, Huck Finn, son of the town drunkard of my time out West, there. He has run away from his persecuting father, and from a persecuting good widow who wishes to make a nice, truth-telling, respectable boy of him; and with him a slave of the widow's has also escaped. They have found a fragment of a lumber raft (it is high water and dead summer time), and are floating down the river by night, and hiding in the willows by day—bound for Cairo,[9] whence the negro will seek freedom in the heart of the free States. But, in a fog, they pass Cairo without knowing it. By and by they begin to suspect the truth, and Huck Finn is persuaded to end the dismal suspense by swimming down to a huge raft which they have seen in the distance ahead of them, creeping aboard under cover of the darkness, and gathering the needed information by eavesdropping:

> But you know a young person can't wait very well when he is impatient to find a thing out. We talked it over, and by and by Jim said it was such a black night, now, that it wouldn't be no risk to swim down to the big raft and crawl aboard and listen—they would talk about Cairo, because they would be calculating to go ashore there for a spree, maybe; or anyway they would send boats ashore to buy whisky or fresh meat or something. Jim had a wonderful level head, for a nigger: he could most always start a good plan when you wanted one.
>
> I stood up and shook my rags off and jumped into the river, and struck out for the raft's light. By and by, when I got down nearly to her, I eased up and went slow and cautious. But everything was all right—nobody at the sweeps. So I swum down

8. *Adventures of Huckleberry Finn*, published in England and Canada in 1884; in the United States in 1885. Mark Twain had begun the book in 1876, but after the incident in which the raft was smashed by a steamboat, he apparently came to a stalemate. But when he went down the Mississippi in 1882 at the request of his publishers, to gather materials for expanding the magazine series into a full-length book, the contact with the river apparently freshened *Huckleberry Finn* in his mind and made Huck more vivid than ever. The result was that he not only produced forty additional chapters of travel writing to complete the Mississippi book, but also completed *Huckleberry Finn*, now accounted his masterpiece.
9. Pronounced "Kay-ro"; situated in Illinois at the juncture of the Mississippi and the Ohio.

along the raft till I was most abreast the camp fire in the middle, then I crawled aboard and inched along and got in among some bundles of shingles on the weather side of the fire. There was thirteen men there—they was the watch on deck of course. And a mighty rough-looking lot, too. They had a jug, and tin cups, and they kept the jug moving. One man was singing—roaring, you may say; and it wasn't a nice song—for a parlor, anyway. He roared through his nose, and strung out the last word of every line very long. When he was done they all fetched a kind of Injun war-whoop, and then another was sung. It begun:

"There was a woman in our towdn,
    In our towdn did dwed'l [dwell],
She loved her husband dear-i-lee,
    But another man twyste as wed'l.

"Singing too, riloo, riloo, riloo,
    Ri-too, riloo, rilay - - - e,
She loved her husband dear-i-lee,
    But another man twyste as wed'l."[1]

And so on—fourteen verses. It was kind of poor, and when he was going to start on the next verse one of them said it was the tune the old cow died on; and another one said: "Oh, give us a rest!" And another one told him to take a walk. They made fun of him till he got mad and jumped up and begun to cuss the crowd, and said he could lam any thief in the lot.

They was all about to make a break for him, but the biggest man there jumped up and says:

"Set whar you are, gentlemen. Leave him to me; he's my meat."

Then he jumped up in the air three times, and cracked his heels together every time. He flung off a buckskin coat that was all hung with fringes, and says, "You lay thar tell the chawin-up's done;" and flung his hat down, which was all over ribbons, and says, "You lay thar tell his sufferin's is over."

Then he jumped up in the air and cracked his heels together again, and shouted out:

"Whoo-oop! I'm the old original iron-jawed, brass-mounted, copper-bellied corpse-maker from the wilds of Arkansaw! Look at me! I'm the man they call Sudden Death and General Desolation! Sired by a hurricane, dam'd by an earthquake, half-brother to the cholera, nearly related to the small-pox on the mother's side! Look at me! I take nineteen alligators and a bar'l of whiskey for breakfast when I'm in robust health, and a bushel of rattlesnakes and a dead body when I'm ailing.[2] I split the everlasting rocks with my glance, and I squench the thunder

---

1. See *Ballads and Songs Collected by the Missouri Folk-Lore Society*, ed. H. M. Belden (1940), for a version of this song still sung today.

2. Reminiscent of the "half-horse, half-alligator" school of braggarts in the frontier tradition of such folk heroes as Davy Crockett and Mike Fink.

when I speak! Whoo-oop! Stand back and give me room according to my strength! Blood's my natural drink, and the wails of the dying is music to my ear! Cast your eye on me, gentlemen! and lay low and hold your breath, for I'm 'bout to turn myself loose!"

All the time he was getting this off, he was shaking his head and looking fierce, and kind of swelling around in a little circle, tucking up his wristbands, and now and then straightening up and beating his breast with his fist, saying, "Look at me, gentlemen!" When he got through, he jumped up and cracked his heels together three times, and let off a roaring "Whoo-oop! I'm the bloodiest son of a wildcat that lives!"

Then the man that had started the row tilted his old slouch hat down over his right eye; then he bent stooping forward, with his back sagged and his south end sticking out far, and his fists a-shoving out and drawing in in front of him, and so went around in a little circle about three times, swelling himself up and breathing hard. Then he straightened, and jumped up and cracked his heels together three times before he lit again (that made them cheer), and he began to shout like this:

"Whoo-oop! bow your neck and spread, for the kingdom of sorrow's a-coming! Hold me down to the earth, for I feel my powers a-working! whoo-oop! I'm a child of sin, *don't* let me get a start! Smoked glass, here, for all! Don't attempt to look at me with the naked eye, gentlemen! When I'm playful I use the meridians of longitude and parallels of latitude for a seine, and drag the Atlantic Ocean for whales! I scratch my head with the lightning and purr myself to sleep with the thunder![3] When I'm cold, I bile the Gulf of Mexico and bathe in it; when I'm hot I fan myself with an equinoctial storm; when I'm thirsty I reach up and suck a cloud dry like a sponge; when I range the earth hungry, famine follows in my tracks! Whoo-oop! Bow your neck and spread! I put my hand on the sun's face and make it night in the earth; I bite a piece out of the moon and hurry the seasons; I shake myself and crumble the mountains! Contemplate me through leather—*don't* use the naked eye! I'm the man with a petrified heart and biler-iron bowels! The massacre of isolated communities is the pastime of my idle moments, the destruction of nationalities the serious business of my life! The boundless vastness of the great American desert is my enclosed property, and I bury my dead on my own premises!" He jumped up and cracked his heels together three times before he lit (they cheered him again), and as he come down he shouted out: "Whoo-oop! bow your neck and spread, for the Pet Child of Calamity's a-coming!"

Then the other one went to swelling around and blowing again—the first one—the one they called Bob; next, the Child of Calamity chipped in again, bigger than ever; then they both

3. Many of these speeches have the mythic flavor of the utterances of primitive gods; this is America's mythology, truly a folk mythology.

got at it at the same time, swelling round and round each other and punching their fists most into each other's faces, and whooping and jawing like Injuns; then Bob called the Child names, and the Child called him names back again; next, Bob called him a heap rougher names, and the Child come back at him with the very worst kind of language; next, Bob knocked the Child's hat off, and the Child picked it up and kicked Bob's ribbony hat about six foot; Bob went and got it and said never mind, this warn't going to be the last of this thing, because he was a man that never forgot and never forgive, and so the Child better look out, for there was a time a-coming, just as sure as he was a living man, that he would have to answer to him with the best blood in his body. The Child said no man was willinger than he for that time to come, and he would give Bob fair warning, *now*, never to cross his path again, for he could never rest till he had waded in his blood, for such was his nature, though he was sparing him now on account of his family, if he had one.

Both of them was edging away in different directions, growling and shaking their heads and going on about what they was going to do; but a little black-whiskered chap skipped up and says:

"Come back here, you couple of chicken-livered cowards, and I'll thrash the two of ye!"

And he done it, too. He snatched them, he jerked them this way and that, he booted them around, he knocked them sprawling faster than they could get up. Why, it warn't two minutes till they begged like dogs—and how the other lot did yell and laugh and clap their hands all the way through, and shout, "Sail in, Corpse-Maker!" "Hi! at him again, Child of Calamity!" "Bully for you, little Davy!" Well, it was a perfect pow-wow for a while. Bob and the Child had red noses and black eyes when they got through. Little Davy made them own up that they was sneaks and cowards and not fit to eat with a dog or drink with a nigger; then Bob and the Child shook hands with each other, very solemn, and said they had always respected each other and was willing to let bygones be bygones. So then they washed their faces in the river; and just then there was a loud order to stand by for a crossing, and some of them went forward to man the sweeps there, and the rest went aft to handle the after sweeps.

I lay still and waited for fifteen minutes, and had a smoke out of a pipe that one of them left in reach; then the crossing was finished, and they stumped back and had a drink around and went to talking and singing again. Next they got out an old fiddle, and one played, and another patted juba, and the rest turned themselves loose on a regular old-fashioned keelboat breakdown. They couldn't keep that up very long without getting winded, so by and by they settled around the jug again.

They sung "Jolly, Jolly Raftsman's the Life for Me," with a rousing chorus, and then they got to talking about differences betwixt hogs, and their different kind of habits; and next about women and their different ways; and next about the best ways to put out houses that was afire; and next about what ought to be done with the Injuns; and next about what a king had to do, and how much he got; and next about how to make cats fight; and next about what to do when a man has fits; and next about differences betwixt clear-water rivers and muddy-water ones. The man they called Ed said the muddy Mississippi water was wholesomer to drink than the clear water of the Ohio; he said if you let a pint of this yaller Mississippi water settle, you would have about a half to three-quarters of an inch of mud in the bottom, according to the stage of the river, and then it warn't no better than Ohio water—what you wanted to do was to keep it stirred up—and when the river was low, keep mud on hand to put in and thicken the water up the way it ought to be.

The Child of Calamity said that was so; he said there was nutritiousness in the mud, and a man that drank Mississippi water could grow corn in his stomach if he wanted to. He says:

"You look at the graveyards; that tells the tale. Trees won't grow worth shucks in a Cincinnati graveyard, but in a Sent Louis graveyard they grow upwards of eight hundred foot high. It's all on account of the water the people drunk before they laid up. A Cincinnati corpse don't richen a soil any."

And they talked about how Ohio water didn't like to mix with Mississippi water. Ed said if you take the Mississippi on a rise when the Ohio is low, you'll find a wide band of clear water all the way down the east side of the Mississippi for a hundred mile or more, and the minute you get out a quarter of a mile from shore and pass the line, it is all thick and yaller the rest of the way across. Then they talked about how to keep tobacco from getting mouldy, and from that they went into ghosts and told about a lot that other folks had seen; but Ed says:

"Why don't you tell something that you've seen yourselves? Now let me have a say. Five years ago I was on a raft as big as this, and right along here it was a bright moonshiny night, and I was on watch and boss of the stabboard oar forrard, and one of my pards was a man named Dick Allbright, and he come along to where I was sitting, forrard—gaping and stretching, he was—and stooped down on the edge of the raft and washed his face in the river, and come and set down by me and got out his pipe, and had just got it filled, when he looks up and says:

" 'Why looky-here,' he says, 'ain't that Buck Miller's place, over yander in the bend?'

" 'Yes,' says I, 'it is—why?' He laid his pipe down and leant his head on his hands, and says:

" 'I thought we'd be furder down.' I says:

" 'I thought it, too, when I went off watch'—we was standing six hours on and six off—'but the boys told me,' I says, 'that the raft didn't seem to hardly move, for the last hour,' says I, 'though she's a-slipping along all right now,' says I. He gave a kind of a groan, and says:

" 'I've seed a raft act so before, along here,' he says, ' 'pears to me the current has most quit above the head of this bend durin' the last two years,' he says.

"Well, he raised up two or three times, and looked away off and around on the water. That started me at it, too. A body is always doing what he sees somebody else doing, though there mayn't be no sense in it. Pretty soon I see a black something floating on the water away off to stabboard and quartering behind us. I see he was looking at it, too. I says:

" 'What's that?' He says, sort of pettish:

" 'Tain't nothing but an old empty bar'l.'

" 'An empty bar'l!' says I, 'why,' says I, 'a spy-glass is a fool to *your* eyes. How can you tell it's an empty bar'l?' He says:

" 'I don't know; I reckon it ain't a bar'l, but I thought it might be,' says he.

" 'Yes,' I says, 'so it might be, and it might be anything else, too; a body can't tell nothing about it, such a distance as that,' I says.

"We hadn't nothing else to do, so we kept on watching it. By and by I says:

" 'Why looky-here, Dick Allbright, that thing's a-gaining on us, I believe.'

"He never said nothing. The thing gained and gained, and I judged it must be a dog that was about tired out. Well, we swung down into the crossing, and the thing floated across the bright streak of the moonshine, and, by George, it *was* a bar'l. Says I:

" 'Dick Allbright, what made you think that thing was a bar'l, when it was half a mile off?' says I. Says he:

" 'I don't know.' Says I:

" 'You tell me, Dick Allbright.' Says he:

" 'Well, I knowed it was a bar'l; I've seen it before; lots has seen it; they says it's a ha'nted bar'l.'

"I called the rest of the watch, and they come and stood there, and I told them what Dick said. It floated right along abreast, now, and didn't gain any more. It was about twenty foot off. Some was for having it aboard, but the rest didn't want to. Dick Allbright said rafts that had fooled with it had got bad luck by it. The captain of the watch said he didn't believe in it. He said he reckoned the bar'l gained on us because it was in a little better current than what we was. He said it would leave by and by.

"So then we went to talking about other things, and we had a song, and then a breakdown; and after that the captain of the watch called for another song; but it was clouding up now, and the bar'l stuck right thar in the same place, and the song didn't seem to have much warm-up to it, somehow, and so they didn't finish it, and there warn't any cheers, but it sort of dropped flat, and nobody said anything for a minute. Then everybody

tried to talk at once, and one chap got off a joke, but it warn't
no use, they didn't laugh, and even the chap that made the
joke didn't laugh at it, which ain't usual. We all just settled
down glum, and watched the bar'l, and was oneasy and oncom-
fortable. Well, sir, it shut down black and still, and then the
wind began to moan around, and next the lightning began to
play and the thunder to grumble. And pretty soon there was a
regular storm, and in the middle of it a man that was running aft
stumbled and fell and sprained his ankle so that he had to lay
up. This made the boys shake their heads. And every time the
lightning come, there was that bar'l with the blue lights wink-
ing around it. We was always on the lookout for it. But by and
by, toward dawn, she was gone. When the day come we couldn't
see her anywhere, and we warn't sorry, either.

"But next night about half-past nine, when there was songs
and high jinks going on, here she comes again, and took her old
roost on the stabboard side. There warn't no more high jinks.
Everybody got solemn; nobody talked; you couldn't get anybody
to do anything but set around moody and look at the bar'l. It
began to cloud up again. When the watch changed, the off
watch stayed up, 'stead of turning in. The storm ripped and
roared around all night, and in the middle of it another man
tripped and sprained his ankle, and had to knock off. The bar'l
left toward day, and nobody see it go.

"Everybody was sober and down in the mouth all day. I don't
mean the kind of sober that comes of leaving liquor alone—not
that. They was quiet, but they all drunk more than usual—not
together, but each man sidled off and took it private, by himself.

"After dark the off watch didn't turn in; nobody sung, nobody
talked; the boys didn't scatter around, neither; they sort of
huddled together, forrard; and for two hours they set there, perfectly still, looking steady in the one direction, and heaving a
sigh once in a while. And then, here comes the bar'l again. She
took up her old place. She stayed there all night; nobody turned
in. The storm come on again, after midnight. It got awful
dark; the rain poured down; hail, too; the thunder boomed and
roared and bellowed; the wind blowed a hurricane; and the
lightning spread over everything in big sheets of glare, and
showed the whole raft as plain as day; and the river lashed up
white as milk as far as you could see for miles, and there was
that bar'l jiggering along, same as ever. The captain ordered the
watch to man the after sweeps for a crossing, and nobody would
go—no more sprained ankles for them, they said. They wouldn't
even *walk* aft. Well, then, just then the sky split wide open, with
a crash, and the lightning killed two men of the after watch,
and crippled two more. Crippled them how, say you? Why,
sprained their ankles!

"The bar'l left in the dark betwixt lightnings, toward dawn.
Well, not a body eat a bite at breakfast that morning. After
that the men loafed around, in twos and threes, and talked low

together. But none of them herded with Dick Allbright. They all give him the cold shake. If he come around where any of the men was, they split up and sidled away. They wouldn't man the sweeps with him. The captain had all the skiffs hauled up on the raft, alongside of his wigwam, and wouldn't let the dead men be took ashore to be planted; he didn't believe a man that got ashore would come back; and he was right.

"After night come, you could see pretty plain that there was going to be trouble if that bar'l come again; there was such a muttering going on. A good many wanted to kill Dick Allbright, because he'd seen the bar'l on other trips, and that had an ugly look. Some wanted to put him ashore. Some said: 'Let's all go ashore in a pile, if the bar'l comes again.'

"This kind of whispers was still going on, the men being bunched together forrard watching for the bar'l, when lo and behold you! here she comes again. Down she comes, slow and steady, and settles into her old tracks. You could 'a' heard a pin drop. Then up comes the captain, and says:

" 'Boys, don't be a pack of children and fools; I don't want this bar'l to be dogging us all the way to Orleans, and *you* don't: Well, then, how's the best way to stop it? Burn it up—that's the way. I'm going to fetch it aboard,' he says. And before anybody could say a word, in he went.

"He swum to it, and as he come pushing it to the raft, the men spread to one side. But the old man got it aboard and busted in the head, and there was a baby in it! Yes, sir; a stark-naked baby. It was Dick Allbright's baby; he owned up and said so.

" 'Yes,' he says, a-leaning over it, 'yes, it is my own lamented darling, my poor lost Charles William Allbright deceased,' says he—for he could curl his tongue around the bulliest words in the language when he was a mind to, and lay them before you without a jint started anywheres. Yes, he said, he used to live up at the head of this bend, and one night he choked his child, which was crying, not intending to kill it,—which was prob'ly a lie,—and then he was scared, and buried it in a bar'l, before his wife got home, and off he went, and struck the northern trail and went to rafting; and this was the third year that the bar'l had chased him. He said the bad luck always begun light, and lasted till four men was killed, and then the bar'l didn't come any more after that. He said if the men would stand it one more night,—and was a-going on like that,—but the men had got enough. They started to get out a boat to take him ashore and lynch him, but he grabbed the little child all of a sudden and jumped overboard with it hugged up to his breast and shedding tears, and we never see him again in this life, poor old suffering soul, nor Charles William neither."

"*Who* was shedding tears?" says Bob; "was it Allbright or the baby?"

"Why, Allbright, of course; didn't I tell you the baby was

dead? Been dead three years—how could it cry?"

"Well, never mind how it could cry—how could it *keep* all that time?" says Davy. "You answer me that."

"I don't know how it done it," says Ed. "It done it, though—that's all I know about it."

"Say—what did they do with the bar'l?" says the Child of Calamity.

"Why, they hove it overboard, and it sunk like a chunk of lead."

"Edward, did the child look like it was choked?" says one.

"Did it have its hair parted?" says another.

"What was the brand on that bar'l, Eddy?" says a fellow they called Bill.

"Have you got the papers for them statistics, Edmund?" says Jimmy.

"Say, Edwin, was you one of the men that was killed by the lightning?" says Davy.

"Him? Oh, no! he was both of 'em," says Bob. Then they all haw-hawed.

"Say, Edward, don't you reckon you'd better take a pill? You look bad—don't you feel pale?" says the Child of Calamity.

"Oh, come, now, Eddy," says Jimmy, "show up; you must 'a' kept part of that bar'l to prove the thing by. Show us the bung-hole—*do*—and we'll all believe you."

"Say, boys," says Bill, "less divide it up. Thar's thirteen of us. I can swaller a thirteenth of the yarn, if you can worry down the rest."

Ed got up mad and said they could all go to some place which he ripped out pretty savage, and then walked off aft, cussing to himself, and they yelling and jeering at him, and roaring and laughing so you could hear them a mile.

"Boys, we'll split a watermelon on that," says the Child of Calamity; and he came rummaging around in the dark amongst the shingle bundles where I was, and put his hand on me. I was warm and soft and naked; so he says "Ouch!" and jumped back.

"Fetch a lantern or a chunk of fire here, boys—there's a snake here as big as a cow!"

So they run there with a lantern, and crowded up and looked in on me.

"Come out of that, you beggar!" says one.

"Who are you?" says another.

"What are you after here? Speak up prompt, or overboard you go."

"Snake him out, boys. Snatch him out by the heels."

I began to beg, and crept out amongst them trembling. They looked me over, wondering, and the Child of Calamity says:

"A cussed thief! Lend a hand and less heave him overboard!"

"No," says Big Bob, "less get out the paint-pot and paint him a sky-blue all over from head to heel, and *then* heave him over."

"Good! that's it. Go for the paint, Jimmy."

When the paint come, and Bob took the brush and was just going to begin, the others laughing and rubbing their hands, I begun to cry, and that sort of worked on Davy, and he says:

" 'Vast there. He's nothing but a cub. I'll paint the man that teches him!"

So I looked around on them, and some of them grumbled and growled, and Bob put down the paint, and the others didn't take it up.

"Come here to the fire, and less see what you're up to here," says Davy. "Now set down there and give an account of yourself. How long have you been aboard here?"

"Not over a quarter of a minute, sir," says I.

"How did you get dry so quick?"

"I don't know, sir. I'm always that way, mostly."

"Oh, you are, are you? What's your name?"

I warn't going to tell my name. I didn't know what to say, so I just says:

"Charles William Allbright, sir."

Then they roared—the whole crowd; and I was mighty glad I said that, because, maybe, laughing would get them in a better humor.

When they got done laughing, Davy says:

"It won't hardly do, Charles William. You couldn't have growed this much in five year, and you was a baby when you come out of the bar'l, you know, and dead at that. Come, now, tell a straight story, and nobody 'll hurt you, if you ain't up to anything wrong. What *is* your name?"

"Aleck Hopkins, sir. Aleck James Hopkins."

"Well, Aleck, where did you come from, here?"

"From a trading scow. She lays up the bend yonder. I was born on her. Pap has traded up and down here all his life; and he told me to swim off here, because when you went by he said he would like to get some of you to speak to a Mr. Jonas Turner, in Cairo, and tell him——"

"Oh, come!"

"Yes, sir, it's as true as the world. Pap he says——"

"Oh, your grandmother!"

They all laughed, and I tried again to talk, but they broke in on me and stopped me.

"Now, looky-here," says Davy; "you're scared, and so you talk wild. Honest, now, do you live in a scow, or is it a lie?"

"Yes, sir, in a trading scow. She lays up at the head of the bend. But I warn't born in her. It's our first trip."

"Now you're talking! What did you come aboard here for? To steal?"

"No, sir, I didn't. It was only to get a ride on the raft. All boys does that."

"Well, I know that. But what did you hide for?"

"Sometimes they drive the boys off."

"So they do. They might steal. Looky-here; if we let you off this time, will you keep out of these kind of scrapes hereafter?"

" 'Deed I will, boss. You try me."

"All right, then. You ain't but little ways from shore. Overboard with you, and don't make a fool of yourself another time this way. Blast it, boy, some raftsmen would rawhide you till you were black and blue!"

I didn't wait to kiss good-by, but went overboard and broke for shore. When Jim come along by and by, the big raft was away out of sight around the point. I swum out and got aboard, and was mighty glad to see home again.

The boy did not get the information he was after, but his adventure has furnished the glimpse of the departed raftsman and keelboatman which I desire to offer in this place.[4]

I now come to a phase of the Mississippi River life of the flush times of steamboating, which seems to me to warrant full examination—the marvelous science of piloting, as displayed there. I believe there has been nothing like it elsewhere in the world.

Chapter IV. The Boys' Ambition

When I was a boy, there was but one permanent ambition among my comrades in our village[5] on the west bank of the Mississippi River. That was, to be a steamboatman. We had transient ambitions of other sorts, but they were only transient. When a circus came and went, it left us all burning to become clowns; the first negro minstrel show that ever came to our section left us all suffering to try that kind of life; now and then we had a hope that, if we lived and were good, God would permit us to be pirates. These ambitions faded out, each in its turn; but the ambition to be a steamboatman always remained.

Once a day a cheap, gaudy packet arrived upward from St. Louis, and another downward from Keokuk. Before these events, the day was glorious with expectancy; after them, the day was a dead and empty thing. Not only the boys, but the whole village, felt this. After all these years I can picture that old time to myself now, just as it was then: the white town drowsing in the sunshine of a summer's morning; the streets empty, or pretty nearly so; one or two clerks sitting in front of the Water street stores,

4. Mark Twain intended to restore this section to *Huckleberry Finn* when that book was ready for publication, but the publishers felt the book would then be too long; consequently, this chapter remains in *Life on the Mississippi*. As Mark Twain was working on the two books at the same time, several interesting parallels exist between them, which the reader may explore for himself. In an interview given to a Canadian newspaper in 1895 (discovered by Fred W. Lorch), Twain said to the reporter: "By a series of events—accidents—I was the only one who wrote about old times on the Mississippi. Wherever else I have been, some better have been there before and will come after, but the Mississippi was a virgin field. No one could write that life but a pilot, because no one else but a pilot entered into the spirit of it. But the pilots were the last men in the world to write its history."

5. "Hannibal, Missouri" [Mark Twain's note].

with their splint-bottomed chairs tilted back against the walls, chins on breasts, hats slouched over their faces, asleep—with shingle-shavings enough around to show what broke them down; a sow and a litter of pigs loafing along the sidewalk, doing a good business in watermelon rinds and seeds; two or three lonely little freight piles scattered about the "levee"; a pile of "skids" [6] on the slope of the stone-paved wharf, and the fragrant town drunkard asleep in the shadow of them; two or three wood flats at the head of the wharf, but nobody to listen to the peaceful lapping of the wavelets against them; the great Mississippi, the majestic, the magnificent Mississippi, rolling its mile-wide tide along, shining in the sun; the dense forest away on the other side; the "point" above the town, and the "point" below, bounding the river-glimpse and turning it into a sort of sea, and withal a very still and brilliant and lonely one. Presently a film of dark smoke appears above one of those remote "points"; instantly a negro drayman, famous for his quick eye and prodigious voice, lifts up the cry, "S-t-e-a-m-boat a-comin'!" and the scene changes! The town drunkard stirs, the clerks wake up, a furious clatter of drays follows, every house and store pours out a human contribution, and all in a twinkling the dead town is alive and moving. Drays, carts, men, boys, all go hurrying from many quarters to a common center, the wharf. Assembled there, the people fasten their eyes upon the coming boat as upon a wonder they are seeing for the first time. And the boat *is* rather a handsome sight, too. She is long and sharp and trim and pretty; she has two tall, fancy-topped chimneys, with a gilded device of some kind swung between them; a fanciful pilot-house, all glass and "gingerbread," perched on top of the "texas" deck[7] behind them; the paddle-boxes are gorgeous with a picture or with gilded rays above the boat's name; the boiler deck, the hurricane deck, and the texas deck are fenced and ornamented with clean white railings; there is a flag gallantly flying from the jack-staff; the furnace doors are open and the fires glaring bravely; the upper decks are black with passengers; the captain stands by the big bell, calm, imposing, the envy of all; great volumes of the blackest smoke are rolling and tumbling out of the chimneys— a husbanded grandeur created with a bit of pitch pine just before arriving at a town; the crew are grouped on the forecastle; the broad stage is run far out over the port bow, and an envied deck-hand stands picturesquely on the end of it with a coil of rope in his hand; the pent steam is screaming through the gauge-cocks; the captain lifts his hand, a bell rings, the wheels stop; then they

6. Wooden fenders that were hung over the side of a vessel to protect it while handling cargo.

7. As the officers' quarters were the largest on the boat, the deck above these quarters was the "texas deck."

turn back, churning the water to foam, and the steamer is at rest. Then such a scramble as there is to get aboard, and to get ashore, and to take in freight and to discharge freight, all at one and the same time; and such a yelling and cursing as the mates facilitate it all with! Ten minutes later the steamer is under way again, with no flag on the jack-staff and no black smoke issuing from the chimneys. After ten more minutes the town is dead again, and the town drunkard asleep by the skids once more.

My father was a justice of the peace, and I supposed he possessed the power of life and death over all men, and could hang anybody that offended him. This was distinction enough for me as a general thing; but the desire to be a steamboatman kept intruding, nevertheless. I first wanted to be a cabin-boy, so that I could come out with a white apron on and shake a table-cloth over the side, where all my old comrades could see me; later I thought I would rather be the deck-hand who stood on the end of the stage-plank with the coil of rope in his hand, because he was particularly conspicuous. But these were only day-dreams—they were too heavenly to be contemplated as real possibilities. By and by one of our boys went away. He was not heard of for a long time. At last he turned up as apprentice engineer or "striker" on a steamboat. This thing shook the bottom out of all my Sunday-school teachings. That boy had been notoriously worldly, and I just the reverse; yet he was exalted to this eminence, and I left in obscurity and misery. There was nothing generous about this fellow in his greatness. He would always manage to have a rusty bolt to scrub while his boat tarried at our town, and he would sit on the inside guard and scrub it, where we all could see him and envy him and loathe him. And whenever his boat was laid up he would come home and swell around the town in his blackest and greasiest clothes, so that nobody could help remembering that he was a steamboatman; and he used all sorts of steamboat technicalities in his talk, as if he were so used to them that he forgot common people could not understand them. He would speak of the "labboard" side of a horse in an easy, natural way that would make one wish he was dead. And he was always talking about "St. Looy" like an old citizen; he would refer casually to occasions when he was "coming down Fourth street," or when he was "passing by the Planter's House," or when there was a fire and he took a turn on the brakes of "the old Big Missouri"; and then he would go on and lie about how many towns the size of ours were burned down there that day. Two or three of the boys had long been persons of consideration among us because they had been to St. Louis once and had a vague general knowledge of its wonders, but the day of their glory was over now. They lapsed into a humble silence, and learned to disappear when the ruthless "cub"-engineer approached. This fellow had money, too, and hair-oil. Also an ignorant silver watch and a showy brass watch-chain. He wore a leather belt and used no suspenders. If ever a youth was cordially admired and hated by his comrades, this one was. No girl could withstand his charms. He "cut out" every boy in the village. When his boat blew up at last, it diffused a tranquil contentment among us such as we had not known for months. But when he came home the next week, alive, renowned, and appeared in church all battered up and bandaged, a shining hero, stared at and wondered over by everybody, it seemed to us that the partiality of Providence for an undeserving reptile had reached a point where it was open to criticism.

This creature's career could produce but one result, and it speedily followed. Boy after boy managed to get on the river. The minister's son became an engineer. The doctor's and the postmaster's sons became "mud clerks"; the wholesale liquor dealer's son became a barkeeper on a boat; four sons of the chief merchant, and two sons of the county judge, became pilots. Pilot was the grandest position of all. The pilot, even in those days of trivial wages, had a princely salary—from a hundred and fifty to two hundred and fifty dollars a month, and no board to pay. Two months of his wages would pay a preacher's salary for a year. Now some of us were left disconsolate. We could not get on the river —at least our parents would not let us.

So, by and by, I ran away. I said I would never come home again till I was a pilot and could come in glory. But somehow I could not manage it. I went meekly aboard a few of the boats that lay packed together like sardines at the long St. Louis wharf, and humbly inquired for the pilots, but got only a cold shoulder and short words from mates and clerks. I had to make the best of this sort of treatment for the time being, but I had comforting daydreams of a future when I should be a great and honored pilot, with plenty of money, and could kill some of these mates and clerks and pay for them.

From *Chapter V. I Want To Be a Cub-Pilot*

Months afterward the hope within me struggled to a reluctant death, and I found myself without an ambition. But I was ashamed to go home. I was in Cincinnati, and I set to work to map out a new career. I had been reading about the recent exploration of the river Amazon by an expedition sent out by our government. It was said that the expedition, owing to difficulties, had not thoroughly explored a part of the country lying about the headwaters, some four thousand miles from the mouth of the river. It was only about fifteen hundred miles from Cincinnati to New Orleans, where I could doubtless get a ship. I had thirty dollars left; I would go and complete the exploration of the Amazon. This was all the thought I gave to the subject. I never was great in matters of detail. I packed my valise, and took passage on an ancient tub called the *Paul Jones*, for New Orleans. For the sum of sixteen dollars I had the scarred and tarnished splendors of "her" main saloon principally to myself, for she was not a creature to attract the eye of wiser travelers.

When we presently got under way and went poking down the broad Ohio, I became a new being, and the subject of my own admiration. I was a traveler! A word never had tasted so good in my mouth before. I had an exultant sense of being bound for mysterious lands and distant climes which I never have felt in so uplifting a degree since. I was in such a glorified condition that all ignoble feelings departed out of me, and I was able to look down and pity the untraveled with a compassion that had hardly a trace of contempt in it. Still, when we stopped at villages and wood-yards, I could not help lolling carelessly upon the railings of the boiler-deck to enjoy the envy of the country boys on the bank. If they did not seem to discover me, I presently sneezed to attract their attention, or moved to a position where they could not help seeing me. And as soon as I knew they saw me I gaped and stretched, and gave other signs of being mightily bored with traveling.

I kept my hat off all the time, and stayed where the wind and the sun could strike me, because I wanted to get the bronzed and weather-beaten look of an old traveler. Before the second day was half gone I experienced a joy which filled me with the purest gratitude; for I saw that the skin had begun to blister and peel off my face and neck. I wished that the boys and girls at home could see me now.

We reached Louisville in time—at least the neighborhood of it. We stuck hard and fast on the rocks in the middle of the river, and lay there four days. I was now beginning to feel a strong sense of being a part of the boat's family, a sort of infant son to the captain and younger brother to the officers. There is no estimating the pride I took in this grandeur, or the affection that began to swell and grow in me for those people. I could not know how the lordly steamboatman scorns that sort of presumption in a mere landsman. I particularly longed to acquire the least trifle of notice from the big stormy mate, and I was on the alert for an opportunity to do him a service to that end. It came at last. The riotous powwow of setting a spar was going on down on the forecastle, and I went down there and stood around in the way—or mostly skipping out of it—till the mate suddenly roared a general order for somebody to bring him a capstan bar. I sprang to his side and said: "Tell me where it is—I'll fetch it!"

If a rag-picker had offered to do a diplomatic service for the Emperor of Russia, the monarch could not have been more astounded than the mate was. He even stopped swearing. He stood and stared down at me. It took him ten seconds to scrape his disjointed remains together again. Then he said impressively: "Well, if this don't beat h——l!" and turned to his work with the air of a man who had been confronted with a problem too abstruse for solution.

I crept away, and courted solitude for the rest of the day. I did not go to dinner; I stayed away from supper until everybody else had finished. I did not feel so much like a member of the boat's family now as before. However, my spirits returned, in installments, as we pursued our way down the river. I was sorry I hated the mate so, because it was not in (young) human nature not to admire him. He was huge and muscular, his face was bearded and whiskered all over; he had a red woman and a blue woman tattooed on his right arm—one on each side of a blue anchor with a red rope to it; and in the matter of profanity he was sublime. When he was getting out cargo at a landing, I was always where I could see and hear. He felt all the majesty of his great position, and made the world feel it, too. When he gave even the simplest order, he discharged it like a blast of lightning, and sent a long, reverberating peal of profanity thundering after it. I could not help contrasting the way in which the average landsman would give an order with the mate's way of doing it. If the landsman should wish the gang-plank moved a foot farther forward, he would probably say: "James, or William, one of you push that plank forward, please;" but put the mate in his place, and he would roar out: "Here, now, start that gang-plank for'ard! Lively, now! What're you about! Snatch it! *snatch* it! There! there! Aft again! aft again! Don't you hear me? Dash it to dash! are you going to *sleep* over it! 'V*ast* heaving. 'Vast heaving, I tell you! Going to heave it clear astern? WHERE're you going with that barrel! for'ard with it 'fore I make you swallow it, you dash-dash-dash-*dashed* split between a tired mud-turtle and a crippled hearse-horse!"

I wished I could talk like that. * * *

From *Chapter* VI. *A Cub-Pilot's Experience*

What with lying on the rock four days at Louisville, and some other delays, the poor old *Paul Jones* fooled away about two weeks in making the voyage from Cincinnati to New Orleans. This gave me a chance to get acquainted with one of the pilots, and he

taught me how to steer the boat, and thus made the fascination of
river life more potent than ever for me.

It also gave me a chance to get acquainted with a youth who
had taken deck passage—more's the pity; for he easily borrowed six
dollars of me on a promise to return to the boat and pay it back
to me the day after we should arrive. But he probably died or
forgot, for he never came. It was doubtless the former, since he
had said his parents were wealthy, and he only traveled deck passage because it was cooler.[8]

I soon discovered two things. One was that a vessel would not
be likely to sail for the mouth of the Amazon under ten or twelve
years; and the other was that the nine or ten dollars still left in
my pocket would not suffice for so impossible an exploration as I
had planned, even if I could afford to wait for a ship. Therefore
it followed that I must contrive a new career. The *Paul Jones* was
now bound for St. Louis. I planned a siege against my pilot, and
at the end of three hard days he surrendered. He agreed to teach
me the Mississippi River from New Orleans to St. Louis for five
hundred dollars, payable out of the first wages I should receive
after graduating. I entered upon the small enterprise of "learning" twelve or thirteen hundred miles of the great Mississippi
River with the easy confidence of my time of life. If I had really
known what I was about to require of my faculties, I should not
have had the courage to begin. I supposed that all a pilot had to
do was to keep his boat in the river, and I did not consider that
that could be much of a trick, since it was so wide.

The boat backed out from New Orleans at four in the afternoon, and it was "our watch" until eight. Mr. Bixby, my chief,
"straightened her up," ploughed her along past the sterns of the
other boats that lay at the Levee, and then said, "Here, take her;
shave those steamships as close as you'd peel an apple." I took the
wheel, and my heart-beat fluttered up into the hundreds; for it
seemed to me that we were about to scrape the side off every ship
in the line, we were so close. I held my breath and began to claw
the boat away from the danger; and I had my own opinion of
the pilot who had known no better than to get us into such peril,
but I was too wise to express it. In half a minute I had a wide
margin of safety intervening between the *Paul Jones* and the ships;
and within ten seconds more I was set aside in disgrace, and Mr.
Bixby was going into danger again and flaying me alive with abuse
of my cowardice. I was stung, but I was obliged to admire the
easy confidence with which my chief loafed from side to side of
his wheel, and trimmed the ships so closely that disaster seemed
ceaselessly imminent. When he had cooled a little he told me that

8. " 'Deck' passage—i.e., steerage passage" [Mark Twain's note].

the easy water was close ashore and the current outside, and therefore we must hug the bank, up-stream, to get the benefit of the former, and stay well out, down-stream, to take advantage of the latter. In my own mind I resolved to be a down-stream pilot and leave the up-streaming to people dead to prudence.

Now and then Mr. Bixby called my attention to certain things. Said he, "This is Six-Mile Point." I assented. It was pleasant enough information, but I could not see the bearing of it. I was not conscious that it was a matter of any interest to me. Another time he said, "This is Nine-Mile Point." Later he said, "This is Twelve-Mile Point." They were all about level with the water's edge; they all looked about alike to me; they were monotonously unpicturesque. I hoped Mr. Bixby would change the subject. But no; he would crowd up around a point, hugging the shore with affection, and then say: "The slack water ends here, abreast this bunch of China-trees; now we cross over." So he crossed over. He gave me the wheel once or twice, but I had no luck. I either came near chipping off the edge of a sugar plantation, or I yawed too far from shore, and so dropped back into disgrace again and got abused.

The watch was ended at last, and we took supper and went to bed. At midnight the glare of a lantern shone in my eyes, and the night watchman said:

"Come, turn out!"

And then he left. I could not understand this extraordinary procedure; so I presently gave up trying to, and dozed off to sleep. Pretty soon the watchman was back again, and this time he was gruff. I was annoyed. I said:

"What do you want to come bothering around here in the middle of the night for? Now, as like as not, I'll not get to sleep again to-night."

The watchman said:

"Well, if this ain't good, I'm blessed."

The "off-watch" was just turning in, and I heard some brutal laughter from them, and such remarks as "Hello, watchman! ain't the new cub turned out yet? He's delicate, likely. Give him some sugar in a rag, and send for the chambermaid to sing 'Rock-a-by Baby,' to him."

About this time Mr. Bixby appeared on the scene. Something like a minute later I was climbing the pilothouse steps with some of my clothes on and the rest in my arms. Mr. Bixby was close behind, commenting. Here was something fresh—this thing of getting up in the middle of the night to go to work. It was a detail in piloting that had never occurred to me at all. I knew that boats ran all night, but somehow I had never happened to reflect that somebody had to get up out of a warm bed to run them. I began to fear that piloting was not quite so romantic as I had imagined it was; there was something very real and worklike about this new phase of it.

It was a rather dingy night, although a fair number of stars were out. The big mate was at the wheel, and he had the old tub pointed at a star and was holding her straight up the middle of the river. The shores on either hand were not much more than half a mile apart, but they seemed wonderfully far away and ever so vague and indistinct. The mate said:

"We've got to land at Jones' plantation, sir."

The vengeful spirit in me exulted. I said to myself, "I wish you joy of your job, Mr. Bixby; you'll have a good time finding Mr. Jones' plantation such a night as this; and I hope you never *will* find it as long as you live."

Mr. Bixby said to the mate:

"Upper end of the plantation, or the lower?"

"Upper."

"I can't do it. The stumps there are out of water at this stage. It's no great distance to the lower, and you'll have to get along with that."

"All right, sir. If Jones don't like it, he'll have to lump it, I reckon."

And then the mate left. My exultation began to cool and my wonder to come up. Here was a man who not only proposed to find this plantation on such a night, but to find either end of it you preferred. I dreadfully wanted to ask a question, but I was carrying about as many short answers as my cargo-room would admit of, so I held my peace. All I desired to ask Mr. Bixby was the simple question whether he was ass enough to really imagine he was going to find that plantation on a night when all plantations were exactly alike and all of the same color. But I held in. I used to have fine inspirations of prudence in those days.

Mr. Bixby made for the shore and soon was scraping it, just the same as if it had been daylight. And not only that, but singing:

"Father in heaven, the day is declining," etc.

It seemed to me that I had put my life in the keeping of a peculiarly reckless outcast. Presently he turned on me and said:

"What's the name of the first point above New Orleans?"

I was gratified to be able to answer promptly, and I did. I said I didn't know.

"Don't *know?*"

This manner jolted me. I was down at the foot again, in a moment. But I had to say just what I had said before.

"Well, you're a smart one!" said Mr. Bixby. "What's the name of the *next* point?"

Once more I didn't know.

"Well, this beats anything. Tell me the name of *any* point or place I told you."

I studied a while and decided that I couldn't.

"Look here! What do you start out from, above Twelve-Mile Point, to cross over?"

"I—I—don't know."

"You—you—don't know?" mimicking my drawling manner of speech. "What *do* you know?"

"I—I—nothing, for certain."

"By the great Cæsar's ghost, I believe you! You're the stupidest dunderhead I ever saw or ever heard of, so help me Moses! The idea of *you* being a pilot—*you!* Why, you don't know enough to pilot a cow down a lane."

Oh, but his wrath was up! He was a nervous man, and he shuffled from one side of his wheel to the other as if the floor was hot. He would boil a while to himself, and then overflow and scald me again.

"Look here! What do you suppose I told you the names of those points for?"

I tremblingly considered a moment, and then the devil of temptation provoked me to say:

"Well—to—to—be entertaining, I thought."

This was a red rag to the bull. He raged and stormed so (he was crossing the river at the time) that I judge it made him blind, because he ran over the steering-oar of a trading-scow. Of course the traders sent up a volley of red-hot profanity. Never was a man so grateful as Mr. Bixby was; because he was brimful, and here were subjects who could *talk back*. He threw open a window, thrust his head out, and such an irruption followed as I never had heard before. The fainter and farther away the scowmen's curses drifted, the higher Mr. Bixby lifted his voice and the weightier his adjectives grew. When he closed the window he was empty. You could have drawn a seine through his system and not caught curses enough to disturb your mother with. Presently he said to me in the gentlest way:

"My boy, you must get a little memorandum-book; and every time I tell you a thing, put it down right away. There's only one way to be a pilot, and that is to get this entire river by heart. You have to know it just like A B C."

That was a dismal revelation to me; for my memory was never loaded with anything but blank cartridges. However, I did not feel discouraged long. I judged that it was best to make some allowances, for doubtless Mr. Bixby was "stretching." Presently he pulled a rope and struck a few strokes on the big bell. The stars were all gone now, and the night was as black as ink. I could hear the wheels churn along the bank, but I was not entirely certain that I could see the shore. The voice of the invisible watchman called up from the hurricane deck:

"What's this, sir?"

"Jones' plantation."

I said to myself, "I wish I might venture to offer a small bet that it isn't." But I did not chirp. I only waited to see. Mr. Bixby handled the engine-bells, and in due time the boat's nose came to the land, a torch glowed from the forecastle, a man skipped ashore, a darkey's voice on the bank said, "Gimme de k'yarpet-bag, Mass' Jones," and the next moment we were standing up the river again, all serene. I reflected deeply a while, and then said—but not aloud—"Well, the finding of that plantation was the luckiest accident that ever happened; but it couldn't happen again in a hundred years." And I fully believed it *was* an accident, too.[9]

* * *

From *Chapter VII. A Daring Deed*[1]

* * * Meantime, the thing that was running in my mind was, "Now, if my ears hear aright, I have not only to get the names of all the towns and islands and bends, and so on, by heart, but I must even get up a warm personal acquaintanceship with every old snag and one-limbed cottonwood and obscure wood-pile that ornaments the banks of this river for twelve hundred miles; and more than that, I must actually know where these things are in the dark, unless these guests are gifted with eyes that can pierce through two miles of solid blackness. I wish the piloting business was in Jericho and I had never thought of it."

At dusk Mr. Bixby tapped the big bell three times (the signal to land), and the captain emerged from his drawing-room in the forward end of the "texas," and looked up inquiringly. Mr. Bixby said:

"We will lay up here all night, captain."

"Very well, sir."

That was all. The boat came to shore and was tied up for the

---

9. In the omitted portion of this chapter, the cub pilot has some experience over seven hundred miles of navigation upstream. At St. Louis, Mr. Bixby leaves the *Paul Jones* for a "big New Orleans boat," a "grand affair," and takes his apprentice Sam Clemens with him.

1. In the omitted part of Chapter VII, Mark Twain explains that the boat is heading downstream in "low water." Several unemployed pilots are aboard "looking at the river," a pastime which has two benefits: with a fresh look at the river they will be better able to carry out their next piloting assignments; and while on the boat for this reason, they get free room and board. This chapter appeared first in "Old Times."

night. It seemed to me a fine thing that the pilot could do as he pleased, without asking so grand a captain's permission. I took my supper and went immediately to bed, discouraged by my day's observations and experiences. My late voyage's notebooking was but a confusion of meaningless names. It had tangled me all up in a knot every time I had looked at it in the daytime. I now hoped for respite in sleep; but no, it reveled all through my head till sunrise again, a frantic and tireless nightmare.

Next morning I felt pretty rusty and low-spirited. We went booming along, taking a good many chances, for we were anxious to "get out of the river" (as getting out to Cairo was called) before night should overtake us. But Mr. Bixby's partner, the other pilot, presently grounded the boat, and we lost so much time getting her off that it was plain the darkness would overtake us a good long way above the mouth. This was a great misfortune, especially to certain of our visiting pilots, whose boats would have to wait for their return, no matter how long that might be. It sobered the pilot-house talk a good deal. Coming up-stream, pilots did not mind low water or any kind of darkness; nothing stopped them but fog. But down-stream work was different; a boat was too nearly helpless, with a stiff current pushing behind her; so it was not customary to run down-stream at night in low water.

There seemed to be one small hope, however: if we could get through the intricate and dangerous Hat Island crossing before night, we could venture the rest, for we would have plainer sailing and better water. But it would be insanity to attempt Hat Island at night. So there was a deal of looking at watches all the rest of the day, and a constant ciphering upon the speed we were making; Hat Island was the eternal subject; sometimes hope was high and sometimes we were delayed in a bad crossing, and down it went again. For hours all hands lay under the burden of this suppressed excitement; it was even communicated to me, and I got to feeling so solicitous about Hat Island, and under such an awful pressure of responsibility, that I wished I might have five minutes on shore to draw a good, full, relieving breath, and start over again. We were standing no regular watches. Each of our pilots ran such portions of the river as he had run when coming up-stream, because of his greater familiarity with it; but both remained in the pilot-house constantly.

An hour before sunset Mr. Bixby took the wheel, and Mr. W. stepped aside. For the next thirty minutes every man held his watch in his hand and was restless, silent, and uneasy. At last somebody said, with a doomful sigh:

"Well, yonder's Hat Island—and we can't make it."

All the watches closed with a snap, everybody sighed and mut-

tered something about its being "too bad, too bad—ah, if we
could *only* have got here half an hour sooner!" and the place was
thick with the atmosphere of disappointment. Some started to go
out, but loitered, hearing no bell-tap to land. The sun dipped behind the horizon, the boat went on. Inquiring looks passed from
one guest to another; and one who had his hand on the door-knob
and had turned it, waited, then presently took away his hand and
let the knob turn back again. We bore steadily down the bend.
More looks were exchanged, and nods of surprised admiration—
but no words. Insensibly the men drew together behind Mr. Bixby,
as the sky darkened and one or two dim stars came out. The dead
silence and sense of waiting became oppressive. Mr. Bixby pulled
the cord, and two deep, mellow notes from the big bell floated
off on the night. Then a pause, and one more note was struck. The
watchman's voice followed, from the hurricane deck:

"Labboard lead, there! Stabboard lead!"

The cries of the leadsmen began to rise out of the distance,
and were gruffly repeated by the word-passers on the hurricane
deck.

"M-a-r-k three! M-a-r-k three! Quarter-less-three! Half twain!
Quarter twain! M-a-r-k twain! Quarter-less [2]——"

Mr. Bixby pulled two bell-ropes, and was answered by faint
jinglings far below in the engine-room, and our speed slackened.
The steam began to whistle through the gauge-cocks. The cries
of the leadsmen went on—and it is a weird sound, always, in the
night. Every pilot in the lot was watching now, with fixed eyes, and
talking under his breath. Nobody was calm and easy but Mr.
Bixby. He would put his wheel down and stand on a spoke, and as
the steamer swung into her (to me) utterly invisible marks—for
we seemed to be in the midst of a wide and gloomy sea—he would
meet and fasten her there. Out of the murmur of half-audible
talk, one caught a coherent sentence now and then—such as:

"There; she's over the first reef all right!"

After a pause, another subdued voice:

"Her stern's coming down just *exactly* right, by *George!*"

"Now she's in the marks; over she goes!"

Somebody else muttered:

"Oh, it was done beautiful—*beautiful!*"

Now the engines were stopped altogether, and we drifted with
the current. Not that I could see the boat drift, for I could not,
the stars being all gone by this time. This drifting was the dis-
malest work; it held one's heart still. Presently I discovered a

2. A fathom is six feet. "Mark three" is three fathoms (18 feet) on the leadsman's sounding line; "quarter-less-three" is 16½ feet; "half twain" is two fathoms and a half, or 15 feet; "quarter twain" is 13½ feet; "mark twain" is two fathoms, or 12 feet; "quarter-less-twain" is 10½ feet.

blacker gloom than that which surrounded us. It was the head of the island. We were closing right down upon it. We entered its deeper shadow, and so imminent seemed the peril that I was likely to suffocate; and I had the strongest impulse to do *something*, anything, to save the vessel. But still Mr. Bixby stood by his wheel, silent, intent as a cat, and all the pilots stood shoulder to shoulder at his back.

"She'll not make it!" somebody whispered.

The water grew shoaler and shoaler, by the leadsman's cries, till it was down to:

"Eight-and-a-half! E-i-g-h-t feet! E-i-g-h-t feet! Seven-and——"

Mr. Bixby said warningly through his speaking tube to the engineer:

"Stand by, now!"

"Ay, ay, sir!"

"Seven-and-a-half! Seven feet! *Six*-and——"

We touched bottom! Instantly Mr. Bixby set a lot of bells ringing, shouted through the tube, "*Now*, let her have it—every ounce you've got!" then to his partner, "Put her hard down! snatch her! snatch her!" The boat rasped and ground her way through the sand, hung upon the apex of disaster a single tremendous instant, and then over she went! And such a shout as went up at Mr. Bixby's back never loosened the roof of a pilot-house before!

There was no more trouble after that. Mr. Bixby was a hero that night; and it was some little time, too, before his exploit ceased to be talked about by river men.

Fully to realize the marvelous precision required in laying the great steamer in her marks in that murky waste of water, one should know that not only must she pick her intricate way through snags and blind reefs, and then shave the head of the island so closely as to brush the overhanging foliage with her stern, but at one place she must pass almost within arm's reach of a sunken and invisible wreck that would snatch the hull timbers from under her if she should strike it, and destroy a quarter of a million dollars' worth of steamboat and cargo in five minutes, and maybe a hundred and fifty human lives into the bargain.

The last remark I heard that night was a compliment to Mr. Bixby, uttered in soliloquy and with unction by one of our guests. He said:

"By the Shadow of Death, but he's a lightning pilot!"

From *Chapter XXXVIII. The House Beautiful*

We took passage in a Cincinnati boat for New Orleans; or on a Cincinnati boat—either is correct; the former is the Eastern form of putting it, the latter the Western.

Mr. Dickens declined to agree[3] that the Mississippi steamboats were "magnificent," or that they were "floating palaces,"—terms which had always been applied to them; terms which did not over-express the admiration with which the people viewed them.

Mr. Dickens' position was unassailable, possibly; the people's position was certainly unassailable. If Mr. Dickens was comparing these boats with the crown jewels; or with the Taj, or with the Matterhorn; or with some other priceless or wonderful thing which he had seen, they were not magnificent—he was right. The people compared them with what *they* had seen; and, thus measured, thus judged, the boats were magnificent—the term was the correct one, it was not at all too strong. The people were as right as was Mr. Dickens. The steamboats were finer than anything on shore. Compared with superior dwelling-houses and first-class hotels in the Valley, they were indubitably magnificent, they were "palaces." To a few people living in New Orleans and St. Louis they were not magnificent, perhaps; not palaces; but to the great majority of those populations, and to the entire populations spread over both banks between Baton Rouge and St. Louis, they were palaces; they tallied with the citizen's dream of what magnificence was, and satisfied it.

Every town and village along that vast stretch of double river-frontage had a best dwelling, finest dwelling, mansion—the home of its wealthiest and most conspicuous citizen. It is easy to describe it: large grassy yard, with paling fence painted white—in fair repair; brick walk from gate to door; big, square, two-story "frame" house, painted white and porticoed like a Grecian temple—with this difference, that the imposing fluted columns and Corinthian capitals were a pathetic sham, being made of white pine, and painted; iron knocker; brass door knob—discolored, for lack of polishing. Within, an uncarpeted hall, of planed boards; opening out of it, a parlor, fifteen feet by fifteen—in some instances five or ten feet larger; ingrain carpet; mahogany center-table; lamp on it, with green-paper shade—standing on a gridiron, so to speak, made of high-colored yarns, by the young ladies of the house, and called a lamp-mat; several books, piled and disposed, with cast-iron exactness, according to an inherited and unchangeable plan; among them, Tupper, much penciled; also, "Friendship's Offering," and "Affection's Wreath," with their sappy inanities illustrated in die-away mezzotints; also, Ossian; "Alonzo and Melissa"; maybe "Ivanhoe"; also "Album," full of original "poetry" of the Thou-hast-wounded-the-spirit-that-loved-thee breed; two or three goody-goody works—"Shepherd of Salisbury Plain," etc.; current number

3. Charles Dickens wrote in *American Notes* (1842) some unflattering com- ments on his steamboat travel on the Ohio and the Mississippi.

of the chaste and innocuous "Godey's Lady's Book," with painted fashion-plate of wax-figure women with mouths all alike—lips and eyelids the same size—each five-foot woman with a two-inch wedge sticking from under her dress and letting-on to be half of her foot.[4] Polished air-tight stove (new and deadly invention), with pipe passing through a board which closes up the discarded good old fireplace. On each end of the wooden mantel, over the fireplace, a large basket of peaches and other fruits, natural size, all done in plaster, rudely, or in wax, and painted to resemble the originals—which they don't. Over middle of mantel, engraving— Washington Crossing the Delaware; on the wall by the door, copy of it done in thunder-and-lightning crewels[5] by one of the young ladies—work of art which would have made Washington hesitate about crossing, if he could have foreseen what advantage was going to be taken of it. Piano—kettle in disguise—with music, bound and unbound, piled on it, and on a stand near by: Battle of Prague; Bird Waltz; Arkansas Traveler; Rosin the Bow; Marseillaise Hymn; On a Lone Barren Isle (St. Helena); The Last Link Is Broken; She Wore a Wreath of Roses the Night When Last We Met; Go, Forget Me, Why Should Sorrow o'er That Brow a Shadow Fling; Hours There Were to Memory Dearer; Long, Long Ago; Days of Absence; A Life on the Ocean Wave, a Home on the Rolling Deep; Bird at Sea; and spread open on the rack, where the plaintive singer has left it, *Ro*-holl on, silver *moo*-hoon, guide the *trav*-el-err on his *way*, etc.[6] Tilted pensively against the piano, a guitar—guitar capable of playing the Spanish fandango by itself, if you give it a start. Frantic work of art on the wall—pious motto, done on the premises, sometimes in colored yarns, sometimes in faded grasses: progenitor of the "God Bless Our Home" of modern commerce. Framed in black mouldings on the wall, other works of art, conceived and committed on the premises, by the young ladies; being grim black-and-white crayons; landscapes, mostly: lake, solitary sailboat, petrified clouds, pre-geological trees on shore, anthracite precipice; name of criminal conspicuous in the corner. Litho-

4. Some of the references in Twain's list may be identified as follows: "Tupper" alludes probably to Martin Tupper's *Proverbial Philosophy* (1838–42), a popular collection of poetical maxims. *The Poems of Ossian* were supposed to have been written by an Irish hero of the 3rd century and translated by James Macpherson (1760, 1762); actually, they were largely Macpherson's own work. *The Asylum, or Alonzo and Melissa* (1811), was a Gothic novel by Isaac Mitchell. "The Shepherd of Salisbury Plain" was one of Hannah More's *Cheap Repository Tracts* (1795–98); *Godey's Lady's Book* (1830–98) was the leading magazine for women for much of the 19th century.
5. Crewelwork, or embroidery done with crewel (a slackly twisted worsted yarn).
6. "She Wore a Wreath" was by Thomas Haynes Bayley (1797–1839); "Go, Forget Me," by Charles Wolfe (1791–1823), author of "The Burial of Sir John Moore," which Twain claimed for years as his favorite poem; "Long, Long Ago," also by Bayley; "A Life on the Ocean Wave," by Epes Sargent (1813–81); "Ro-holl on, silver moo-hoon" was composed by Joseph W. Turner (later music editor of *The Waverly Magazine*), but the author of the words is unknown.

graph, Napoleon Crossing the Alps. Lithograph, The Grave at St. Helena. Steel-plates, Trumbull's Battle of Bunker Hill, and the Sally from Gibraltar. Copper-plates, Moses Smiting the Rock, and Return of the Prodigal Son. In big gilt frame, slander of the family in oil: papa holding a book ("Constitution of the United States"); guitar leaning against mamma, blue ribbons fluttering from its neck; the young ladies, as children, in slippers and scalloped pantalettes, one embracing toy horse, the other beguiling kitten with ball of yarn, and both simpering up at mamma, who simpers back. These persons all fresh, raw, and red—apparently skinned. Opposite, in gilt frame, grandpa and grandma, at thirty and twenty-two, stiff, old-fashioned, high-collared, puff-sleeved, glaring pallidly out from a background of solid Egyptian night. Under a glass French clock dome, large bouquet of stiff flowers done in corpsy white wax. Pyramidal what-not in the corner, the shelves occupied chiefly with bric-a-brac of the period, disposed with an eye to best effect: shell, with the Lord's Prayer carved on it; another shell—of the long-oval sort, narrow, straight orifice, three inches long, running from end to end—portrait of Washington carved on it; not well done; the shell had Washington's mouth, originally—artist should have built to that. These two are memorials of the long-ago bridal trip to New Orleans and the French Market. Other bric-a-brac: Californian "specimens"—quartz, with gold wart adhering; old Guinea-gold locket, with circlet of ancestral hair in it; Indian arrow-heads, of flint; pair of bead moccasins, from uncle who crossed the Plains; three "alum" baskets of various colors—being skeleton-frame of wire, clothed-on with cubes of crystallized alum in the rock-candy style—works of art which were achieved by the young ladies; their doubles and duplicates to be found upon all what-nots in the land; convention of desiccated bugs and butterflies pinned to a card; painted toy-dog, seated upon bellows-attachment—drops its under jaw and squeaks when pressed upon; sugar-candy rabbit—limbs and features merged together, not strongly defined; pewter presidential-campaign medal; miniature cardboard wood-sawyer, to be attached to the stovepipe and operated by the heat; small Napoleon, done in wax; spread-open daguerreotypes of dim children, parents, cousins, aunts, and friends, in all attitudes but customary ones; no templed portico at back, and manufactured landscape stretching away in the distance—that came in later, with the photograph; all these vague figures lavishly chained and ringed—metal indicated and secured from doubt by stripes and splashes of vivid gold bronze; all of them too much combed, too much fixed up; and all of them uncomfortable in inflexible Sunday clothes of a pattern which the spectator cannot realize could ever have been in fashion;

husband and wife generally grouped together—husband sitting, wife standing, with hand on his shoulder—and both preserving, all these fading years, some traceable effect of the daguerreotypist's brisk "Now smile, if you please!" Bracketed over what-not—place of special sacredness—an outrage in water-color, done by the young niece that came on a visit long ago, and died. Pity, too; for she might have repented of this in time. Horsehair chairs, horsehair sofa which keeps sliding from under you. Window-shades, of oil stuff, with milkmaids and ruined castles stenciled on them in fierce colors. Lambrequins dependent from gaudy boxings of beaten tin, gilded. Bedrooms with rag carpets; bedsteads of the "corded" sort, with a sag in the middle, the cords needing tightening; snuffy feather-bed—not aired often enough; cane-seat chairs, splint-bottomed rocker; looking-glass on wall, school-slate size, veneered frame; inherited bureau; wash-bowl and pitcher, possibly—but not certainly; brass candlestick, tallow candle, snuffers. Nothing else in the room. Not a bathroom in the house; and no visitor likely to come along who has ever seen one.

That was the residence of the principal citizen, all the way from the suburbs of New Orleans to the edge of St. Louis. * * *

1883

How to Tell a Story[7]

I do not claim that I can tell a story as it ought to be told. I only claim to know how a story ought to be told, for I have been almost daily in the company of the most expert story-tellers for many years.

There are several kinds of stories, but only one difficult kind—the humorous. I will talk mainly about that one. The humorous story is American, the comic story is English, the witty story is French. The humorous story depends for its effect upon the *manner* of the telling; the comic story and the witty story upon the *matter*.

The humorous story may be spun out to great length, and may wander around as much as it pleases, and arrive nowhere in particular; but the comic and witty stories must be brief and end with a point. The humorous story bubbles gently along, the others burst.

The humorous story is strictly a work of art—high and delicate art—and only an artist can tell it; but no art is necessary in telling the comic and the witty story; anybody can do it. The art of telling a humorous story—understand, I mean by word of mouth, not

7. The present text is from *How to Tell a Story and Other Essays*, 1897; this piece originally appeared in *The Youth's Companion* in 1895.

print—was created in America, and has remained at home.

The humorous story is told gravely; the teller does his best to conceal the fact that he even dimly suspects that there is anything funny about it; but the teller of the comic story tells you before-hand that it is one of the funniest things he has ever heard, then tells it with eager delight, and is the first person to laugh when he gets through. And sometimes, if he has had good success, he is so glad and happy that he will repeat the "nub" of it and glance around from face to face, collecting applause, and then repeat it again. It is a pathetic thing to see.

Very often, of course, the rambling and disjointed humorous story finishes with a nub, point, snapper, or whatever you like to call it. Then the listener must be alert, for in many cases the teller will divert attention from that nub by dropping it in a carefully casual and indifferent way, with the pretence that he does not know it is a nub.

Artemus Ward[8] used that trick a good deal; then when the be-lated audience presently caught the joke he would look up with innocent surprise, as if wondering what they had found to laugh at. Dan Setchell used it before him, Nye and Riley and others use it to-day.[9]

But the teller of the comic story does not slur the nub; he shouts it at you—every time. And when he prints it, in England, France, Germany, and Italy, he italicizes it, puts some whooping exclama-tion-points after it, and sometimes explains it in a parenthesis. All of which is very depressing, and makes one want to renounce joking and lead a better life.

Let me set down an instance of the comic method, using an anecdote which has been popular all over the world for twelve or fifteen hundred years. The teller tells it in this way:

THE WOUNDED SOLDIER

In the course of a certain battle a soldier whose leg had been shot off appealed to another soldier who was hurrying by to carry him to the rear, informing him at the same time of the loss which he had sustained; whereupon the generous son of Mars, shouldering the unfortunate, proceeded to carry out his desire. The bullets and cannon-balls were flying in all directions, and presently one of the latter took the wounded man's head off—without, how-ever, his deliverer being aware of it. In no long time he was hailed by an officer, who said:

8. Artemus Ward (Charles Farrar Browne, 1834–67), the humorist who first, by his brilliant example, caused Mark Twain to attempt public lecturing.
9. Bill Nye, a humorous lecturer, author of a comic *History of the United States* (1894); James Whitcomb Riley (1849–1916), Indiana folk poet and humorous lecturer.

"Where are you going with that carcass?"

"To the rear, sir—he's lost his leg!"

"His leg, forsooth?" responded the astonished officer; "you mean his head, you booby."

Whereupon the soldier dispossessed himself of his burden, and stood looking down upon it in great perplexity. At length he said:

"It is true, sir, just as you have said." Then after a pause he added, *"But he* TOLD *me* IT WAS HIS LEG! ! ! ! !"

Here the narrator bursts into explosion after explosion of thunderous horse-laughter, repeating that nub from time to time through his gaspings and shriekings and suffocatings.

It takes only a minute and a half to tell that in its comic-story form; and isn't worth the telling, after all. Put into the humorous-story form it takes ten minutes, and is about the funniest thing I have ever listened to—as James Whitcomb Riley tells it.

He tells it in the character of a dull-witted old farmer who has just heard it for the first time, thinks it is unspeakably funny, and is trying to repeat it to a neighbor. But he can't remember it; so he gets all mixed up and wanders helplessly round and round, putting in tedious details that don't belong in the tale and only retard it; taking them out conscientiously and putting in others that are just as useless; making minor mistakes now and then and stopping to correct them and explain how he came to make them; remembering things which he forgot to put in in their proper place and going back to put them in there; stopping his narrative a good while in order to try to recall the name of the soldier that was hurt, and finally remembering that the soldier's name was not mentioned, and remarking placidly that the name is of no real importance, anyway—better, of course, if one knew it, but not essential, after all—and so on, and so on, and so on.

The teller is innocent and happy and pleased with himself, and has to stop every little while to hold himself in and keep from laughing outright; and does hold in, but his body quakes in a jelly-like way with interior chuckles; and at the end of the ten minutes the audience have laughed until they are exhausted, and the tears are running down their faces.

The simplicity and innocence and sincerity and unconsciousness of the old farmer are perfectly simulated, and the result is a performance which is thoroughly charming and delicious. This is art —and fine and beautiful, and only a master can compass it; but a machine could tell the other story.

To string incongruities and absurdities together in a wandering and sometimes purposeless way, and seem innocently unaware that they are absurdities, is the basis of the American art, if my position is correct. Another feature is the slurring of the point. A

third is the dropping of a studied remark apparently without knowing it, as if one were thinking aloud. The fourth and last is the
pause.

Artemus Ward dealt in numbers three and four a good deal. He
would begin to tell with great animation something which he
seemed to think was wonderful; then lose confidence, and after an
apparently absent-minded pause add an incongruous remark in a
soliloquizing way; and that was the remark intended to explode
the mine—and it did.

For instance, he would say eagerly, excitedly, "I once knew a
man in New Zealand who hadn't a tooth in his head"—here his
animation would die out; a silent, reflective pause would follow,
then he would say dreamily, and as if to himself, "and yet that
man could beat a drum better than any man I ever saw."

The pause is an exceedingly important feature in any kind of
story, and a frequently recurring feature, too. It is a dainty thing,
and a delicate, and also uncertain and treacherous; for it must be
exactly the right length—no more and no less—or it fails of its
purpose and makes trouble. If the pause is too short the impressive point is passed, and the audience have had time to divine
that a surprise is intended—and then you can't surprise them, of
course.

On the platform I used to tell a negro ghost story that had a
pause in front of the snapper on the end, and that pause was the
most important thing in the whole story. If I got it the right
length precisely, I could spring the finishing ejaculation with effect enough to make some impressible girl deliver a startled little
yelp and jump out of her seat—and that was what I was after.
This story was called "The Golden Arm,"[1] and was told in this
fashion. You can practise with it yourself—and mind you look out
for the pause and get it right.

THE GOLDEN ARM

Once 'pon a time dey wuz a monsus mean man, en he live 'way
out in de prairie all 'lone by hisself, 'cep'n he had a wife. En
bimeby she died, en he tuck en toted her way out dah in de
prairie en buried her. Well, she had a golden arm—all solid gold,
fum de shoulder down. He wuz pow'ful mean—pow'ful; en dat
night he couldn't sleep, caze he want dat golden arm so bad.

When it come midnight he couldn't stan' it no mo'; so he git
up, he did, en tuck his lantern en shoved out thoo de storm en
dug her up en got de golden arm; en he bent his head down 'gin
de win', en plowed en plowed en plowed thoo de snow. Den all

1. First told to Mark Twain, when he
was the small scared child Sam Clemens, by "Uncle Dan'l," a slave owned
by Sam's uncle, John Quarles.

on a sudden he stop (make a considerable pause here, and look startled, and take a listening attitude) en say: "My *lan*', what's dat!"

En he listen—en listen—en de win' say (set your teeth together and imitate the wailing and wheezing singsong of the wind), "Bzzz-z-zzz"—en den, way back yonder whah de grave is, he hear a *voice!*—he hear a voice all mix' up in de win'—can't hardly tell 'em 'part—"Bzzz-zzz—W-h-o—g-o-t—m-y—g-o-l-d-e-n *arm?*—zzz —zzz—W-h-o g-o-t m-y g-o-l-d-e-n *arm?*" (You must begin to shiver violently now.)

En he begin to shiver en shake, en say, "Oh, my! *Oh*, my lan'!" en de win' blow de lantern out, en de snow en sleet blow in his face en mos' choke him, en he start a-plowin' knee-deep towards home mos' dead, he so sk'yerd—en pooty soon he hear de voice agin, en (pause) it 'us comin' *after* him! "Bzzz—zzz—zzz—W-h-o —g-o-t—m-y—g-o-l-d-e-n—*arm?*"

When he git to de pasture he hear it agin—closter now, en a-*comin'!*—a-comin' back dah in de dark en de storm—(repeat the wind and the voice). When he git to de house he rush upstairs en jump in de bed en kiver up, head and years, en lay dah shiverin' en shakin'—en den way out dah he hear it *agin!*—en a-*comin'!* En bimeby he hear (pause—awed, listening attitude)— pat—pat—pat—*hit's a-comin' up-stairs!* Den he hear de latch, en he *know* it's in de room!

Den pooty soon he know it's a-*stannin' by de bed!* (Pause.) Den—he know it's a-*bendin' down over him*—en he cain't skasely git his breath! Den—den—he seem to feel someth'n *c-o-l-d*, right down 'most agin his head! (Pause.)

Den de voice say, *right at his year*—"W-h-o—g-o-t—m-y —g-o-l-d-e-n *arm?*" (You must wail it out very plaintively and accusingly; then you stare steadily and impressively into the face of the farthest-gone auditor—a girl, preferably—and let that awe-inspiring pause begin to build itself in the deep hush. When it has reached exactly the right length, jump suddenly at that girl and yell, "*You've* got it!"

If you've got the *pause* right, she'll fetch a dear little yelp and spring right out of her shoes. But you *must* get the pause right; and you will find it the most troublesome and aggravating and uncertain thing you ever undertook.)

1897

From Following the Equator[2]
From Vol. II, Chapter II. [Bombay]

Prosperity is the best protector of principle.
—*Pudd'nhead Wilson's New Calendar.*

* * * *January 20.* Bombay! A bewitching place, a bewildering place, an enchanting place—the Arabian Nights come again! It is a vast city; contains about a million inhabitants. Natives, they are, with a slight sprinkling of white people—not enough to have the slightest modifying effect upon the massed dark complexion of the public.[3] It is winter here, yet the weather is the divine weather of June, and the foliage is the fresh and heavenly foliage of June. There is a rank of noble great shade trees across the way from the hotel, and under them sit groups of picturesque natives of both sexes; and the juggler in his turban is there with his snakes and his magic; and all day long the cabs and the multitudinous varieties of costumes flock by. It does not seem as if one could ever get tired of watching this moving show, this shining and shifting spectacle. * * *

Tramp, tramp, tramping along the road, in singles, couples, groups, and gangs, you have the workingman and the working-woman—but not clothed like ours. Usually the man is a nobly-built great athlete, with not a rag on but his loin-handkerchief; his color a deep dark brown, his skin satin, his rounded muscles knobbing it as if it had eggs under it. Usually the woman is a slender and shapely creature, as erect as a lightning-rod, and she has but one thing on—a bright-colored piece of stuff which is wound about her head and her body down nearly half-way to her knees, and which clings like her own skin. Her legs and feet are bare, and so are her arms, except for her fanciful bunches of loose silver rings on her ankles and on her arms. She has jewelry bunched on the side of her nose also, and showy cluster-rings on her toes. When she undresses for bed she takes off her jewelry, I suppose. If she took off anything more she would catch cold. As a rule, she has a large shiny brass water-jar of graceful shape on her head, and one of her naked arms curves up and the hand holds it there. She is so straight, so erect, and steps with such style, and such easy grace and dignity; and her curved arm and her brazen jar are such a help to the picture—indeed, our workingwomen cannot begin with her as a road decoration. * * *

2. Published 1897; the present text is from the Author's Uniform Edition (1899), called by the publisher the National Edition.
3. Mark Twain preferred brown—even black—complexions to the pale faces of Caucasians. He argued to his daughter Jean that God himself must prefer the dark-skinned people since he made so many of them—"two-thirds, you see, of the human race."

From Vol. II, Chapter XXIII. [*The Taj Mahal*]

* * * I mean to speak of only one of these many world-renowned buildings, the Taj Mahal, the most celebrated construction in the earth. I had read a great deal too much about it. I saw it in the daytime, I saw it in the moonlight, I saw it near at hand, I saw it from a distance; and I knew all the time, that of its kind it was *the* wonder of the world, with no competitor now and no possible future competitor; and yet, it was not *my* Taj. My Taj had been built by excitable literary people; it was solidly lodged in my head, and I could not blast it out. * * *

I had to visit Niagara fifteen times before I succeeded in getting my imaginary Falls gauged to the actuality and could begin to sanely and wholesomely wonder at them for what they were, not what I had expected them to be. When I first approached them it was with my face lifted toward the sky, for I thought I was going to see an Atlantic ocean pouring down thence, over cloud-vexed Himalayan heights, a sea-green wall of water sixty miles front and six miles high, and so, when the toy reality came suddenly into view—that beruffled little wet apron hanging out to dry—the shock was too much for me, and I fell with a dull thud.

Yet slowly, surely, steadily, in the course of my fifteen visits, the proportions adjusted themselves to the facts, and I came at last to realize that a waterfall a hundred and sixty-five feet high and a quarter of a mile wide was an impressive thing. It was not a dipperful to my vanished great vision, but it would answer.

I know that I ought to do with the Taj as I was obliged to do with Niagara—see it fifteen times, and let my mind gradually get rid of the Taj built in it by its describers, by help of my imagination, and substitute for it the Taj of fact. It would be noble and fine, then, and a marvel; not the marvel which it replaced, but still a marvel, and fine enough. I am a careless reader, I suppose—an *impressionist* reader; an impressionist reader of what is *not* an impressionist picture; a reader who overlooks the informing details or masses their sum improperly, and gets only a large, splashy, general effect—an effect which is not correct, and which is not warranted by the particulars placed before me—particulars which I did not examine, and whose meanings I did not cautiously and carefully estimate. It is an effect which is some thirty-five or forty times finer than the reality, and is therefore a great deal better and more valuable than the reality; and so, I ought never to hunt up the reality, but stay miles away from it, and thus preserve undamaged my own private mighty Niagara tumbling out of the vault of heaven, and my own ineffable Taj, built of tinted mists upon jeweled arches of rainbows supported by colonnades of moonlight. It is a mistake for a person with an unregulated imagination to go and look at an illustrious world's wonder. * * *

From Vol. II, Chapter XXIV. [At Jeypore]

* * * We were pleasantly situated in a small two-storied inn, in an empty large compound which was surrounded by a mud wall as high as a man's head. The inn was kept by nine Hindoo brothers, its owners. They lived, with their families, in a one-storied building within the compound, but off to one side, and there was always a long pile of their little comely brown children loosely stacked in its veranda, and a detachment of the parents wedged among them, smoking the hookah or the howdah, or whatever they call it. By the veranda stood a palm, and a monkey lived in it, and led a lonesome life, and always looked sad and weary, and the crows bothered him a good deal.

The inn cow poked about the compound and emphasized the secluded and country air of the place, and there was a dog of no particular breed, who was always present in the compound, and always asleep, always stretched out baking in the sun and adding to the deep tranquillity and reposefulness of the place, when the crows were away on business. White-draperied servants were coming and going all the time, but they seemed only spirits, for their feet were bare and made no sound. Down the lane a piece lived an elephant in the shade of a noble tree, and rocked and rocked, and reached about with his trunk, begging of his brown mistress or fumbling the children playing at his feet. And there were camels about, but they go on velvet feet, and were proper to the silence and serenity of the surroundings.[4] * * *

As we passed through the great public pleasure garden on our way to the city we found it crowded with natives. That was one sight. Then there was another. In the midst of the spacious lawns stands the palace which contains the museum—a beautiful construction of stone which shows arched colonnades, one above another, and receding, terrace-fashion, toward the sky. Every one of these terraces, all the way to the top one, was packed and jammed with natives. One must try to imagine those solid masses of splendid color, one above another, up and up, against the blue sky, and the Indian sun turning them all to beds of fire and flame.

Later, when we reached the city, and glanced down the chief avenue, smouldering in its crushed-strawberry tint, those splendid effects were repeated; for every balcony, and every fanciful bird-cage of a snuggery countersunk in the house-fronts, and all the long lines of roofs, were crowded with people, and each crowd

4. The passage describing the compound at Jeypore is an excellent example of the style of Mark Twain at its ripe maturity. The dominant note of serenity is emphasized by the absence of sound.

was an explosion of brilliant color.

Then the wide street itself, away down and down and down into the distance, was alive with gorgeously-clothed people—not still, but moving, swaying, drifting, eddying, a delirious display of all colors and all shades of color, delicate, lovely, pale, soft, strong, stunning, vivid, brilliant, a sort of storm of sweet-pea blossoms passing on the wings of a hurricane; and presently, through this storm of color, came swaying and swinging the majestic elephants, clothed in their Sunday best of gaudinesses, and the long procession of fanciful trucks freighted with their groups of curious and costly images, and then the long rear-guard of stately camels, with their picturesque riders.

For color, and picturesqueness, and novelty, and outlandishness, and sustained interest and fascination, it was the most satisfying show I had ever seen, and I suppose I shall not have the privilege of looking upon its like again.

1897

From Mark Twain's Autobiography[5]
[Early Days]

* * * My father left a fine estate behind him in the region roundabout Jamestown—75,000 acres.[6] When he died in 1847 he had owned it about twenty years. The taxes were almost nothing (five dollars a year for the whole), and he had always paid them regularly and kept his title perfect. He had always said that the land would not become valuable in his time, but that it would be a commodious provision for his children some day. It contained coal, copper, iron, and timber, and he said that in the course of time railways would pierce to that region and then the property would be property in fact as well as in name. It also produced a wild grape of a promising sort. He had sent some samples to Nicholas Longworth of Cincinnati to get his judgment upon them, and Mr. Longworth had said that they would make as good wine as his Catawbas. The land contained all these riches; and also oil, but my father did not know that, and of course in those early days he would have cared nothing about it if he had known it. The oil was not discovered until about 1895. I wish I owned a couple of acres of the land now, in which case I would not be writing autobiographies for a living. My father's dying charge was, "Cling to the land and wait; let nothing beguile it away from you." My mother's favorite cousin, James Lampton,

5. The present extract is from Volume I of the two-volume book edited by Albert Bigelow Paine, published in 1924.

6. "Correction (1906)—it was above 100,000, it appears" [Mark Twain's note].

who figures in the *Gilded Age* as Colonel Sellers, always said of that land—and said it with blazing enthusiasm, too—"There's millions in it—millions!" It is true that he always said that about everything—and was always mistaken, too, but this time he was right; which shows that a man who goes around with a prophecy-gun ought never to get discouraged. If he will keep up his heart and fire at everything he sees, he is bound to hit something by and by.

Many persons regarded Colonel Sellers as a fiction, an invention, an extravagant impossibility, and did me the honor to call him a "creation"; but they were mistaken. I merely put him on paper as he was; he was not a person who could be exaggerated. The incidents which looked most extravagant, both in the book and on the stage, were not inventions of mine, but were facts of his life; and I was present when they were developed. John T. Raymond's[7] audiences used to come near to dying with laughter over the turnip-eating scene; but, extravagant as the scene was, it was faithful to the facts, in all its absurd details. The thing happened in Lampton's own house, and I was present. In fact, I was myself the guest who ate the turnips. In the hands of a great actor that piteous scene would have dimmed any manly spectator's eyes with tears, and racked his ribs apart with laughter at the same time. But Raymond was great in humorous portrayal only. In that he was superb, he was wonderful—in a word, great; in all things else he was a pygmy of pygmies. The real Colonel Sellers, as I knew him in James Lampton, was a pathetic and beautiful spirit, a manly man, a straight and honorable man, a man with a big, foolish, unselfish heart in his bosom, a man born to be loved; and he was loved by all his friends, and by his family worshiped. It is the right word. To them he was but little less than a god. The real Colonel Sellers was never on the stage. Only half of him was there. Raymond could not play the other half of him; it was above his level. There was only one man who could have played the whole of Colonel Sellers, and that was Frank Mayo.[8]

It is a world of surprises. They fall, too, where one is least expecting them. When I introduced Sellers into the book, Charles Dudley Warner, who was writing the story with me, proposed a change of Sellers's Christian name. Ten years before, in a remote corner of the West, he had come across a man named Eschol Sellers, and he thought that Eschol was just the right and fitting name for our Sellers, since it was odd and quaint and all that. I

7. John T. Raymond acted the title role in the play *Colonel Sellers*, written by Twain in collaboration with a California dramatist, Gilbert S. Densmore.
8. "Raymond was playing Colonel Sellers in 1876 and along there. About twenty years later Mayo dramatized *Pudd'nhead Wilson* and played the title role delightfully" [Mark Twain's note].

liked the idea, but I said that the man might turn up and object. But Warner said it couldn't happen; that he was doubtless dead by this time and, be he dead or alive, we must have the name; it was exactly the right one and we couldn't do without it. So the change was made. Warner's man was a farmer in a cheap and humble way. When the book had been out a week, a college-bred gentleman of courtly manners and ducal upholstery arrived in Hartford in a sultry state of mind and with a libel suit in his eye, and *his* name was Eschol Sellers! He had never heard of the other one and had never been within a thousand miles of him. This damaged aristocrat's program was quite definite and business-like: the American Publishing Company must suppress the edition as far as printed and change the name in the plates, or stand a suit for $10,000. He carried away the company's promise and many apologies, and we changed the name back to Colonel Mulberry Sellers in the plates. Apparently there is nothing that cannot happen. Even the existence of two unrelated men wearing the impossible name of Eschol Sellers is a possible thing.

James Lampton floated, all his days, in a tinted mist of magnificent dreams, and died at last without seeing one of them realized. I saw him last in 1884, when it had been twenty-six years since I ate the basin of raw turnips and washed them down with a bucket of water in his house. He was become old and white-headed, but he entered to me in the same old breezy way of his earlier life, and he was all there yet—not a detail wanting; the happy light in his eye, the abounding hope in his heart, the persuasive tongue, the miracle-breeding imagination—they were all there; and before I could turn around he was polishing up his Aladdin's lamp and flashing the secret riches of the world before me. I said to myself: "I did not overdraw him by a shade, I set him down as he was; and he is the same man to-day. Cable[9] will recognize him." I asked him to excuse me a moment and ran into the next room, which was Cable's. Cable and I were stumping the Union on a reading tour. I said:

"I am going to leave your door open so that you can listen. There is a man in there who is interesting."

I went back and asked Lampton what he was doing now. He began to tell me of a "small venture" he had begun in New Mexico through his son; "only a little thing—a mere trifle—partly to amuse my leisure, partly to keep my capital from lying idle, but mainly to develop the boy—develop the boy. Fortune's wheel is ever revolving; he may have to work for his living some day—as strange things have happened in this world. But it's only a little

9. George Washington Cable (1844– 1925), American novelist who special- ized in the "local color" of the French quarter of New Orleans.

thing—a mere trifle, as I said."

And so it was—as he began it. But under his deft hands it grew and blossomed and spread—oh, beyond imagination. At the end of half an hour he finished; finished with the remark, uttered in an adorably languid manner:

"Yes, it is but a trifle, as things go nowadays—a bagatelle—but amusing. It passes the time. The boy thinks great things of it, but he is young, you know, and imaginative; lacks the experience which comes of handling large affairs, and which tempers the fancy and perfects the judgment. I suppose there's a couple of millions in it, possibly three, but not more, I think; still, for a boy, you know, just starting in life, it is not bad. I should not want him to make a fortune—let that come later. It could turn his head, at his time of life, and in many ways be a damage to him."

Then he said something about his having left his pocketbook lying on the table in the main drawing-room at home, and about its being after banking hours, now, and——

I stopped him there and begged him to honor Cable and me by being our guest at the lecture—with as many friends as might be willing to do us the honor. He accepted. And he thanked me as a prince might who had granted us a grace. The reason I stopped his speech about the tickets was because I saw that he was going to ask me to furnish them to him and let him pay next day; and I knew that if he made the debt he would pay it if he had to pawn his clothes. After a little further chat he shook hands heartily and affectionately and took his leave. Cable put his head in at the door and said:

"That was Colonel Sellers."

· · · · · · · · ·

As I have said, that vast plot of Tennessee land was held by my father twenty years—intact. When he died in 1847 we began to manage it ourselves. Forty years afterward we had managed it all away except 10,000 acres, and gotten nothing to remember the sales by. About 1887—possibly it was earlier—the 10,000 went. My brother[1] found a chance to trade it for a house and lot in the town of Corry, in the oil regions of Pennsylvania. About 1894 he sold this property for $250. That ended the Tennessee land.

If any penny of cash ever came out of my father's wise investment but that, I have no recollection of it. No, I am overlooking a detail. It furnished me a field for Sellers and a book. Out of my half of the book I got $20,000, perhaps something more; out of the play I got $75,000—just about a dollar an acre. It is curious; I was not alive when my father made the investment, therefore he

---

1. Orion Clemens.

was not intending any partiality; yet I was the only member of the family that ever profited by it. I shall have occasion to mention this land again now and then, as I go along, for it influenced our life in one way or another during more than a generation. Whenever things grew dark it rose and put out its hopeful Sellers hand and cheered us up, and said, "Do not be afraid—trust in me—wait." It kept us hoping and hoping during forty years, and forsook us at last. It put our energies to sleep and made visionaries of us— dreamers and indolent. We were always going to be rich next year —no occasion to work. It is good to begin life poor; it is good to begin life rich—these are wholesome; but to begin it poor and *prospectively* rich! The man who has not experienced it cannot imagine the curse of it.

My parents removed to Missouri in the early 'thirties; I do not remember just when, for I was not born then and cared nothing for such things. It was a long journey in those days, and must have been a rough and tiresome one. The home was made in the wee village of Florida, in Monroe County, and I was born there in 1835. The village contained a hundred people and I increased the population by 1 per cent. It is more than many of the best men in history could have done for a town. It may not be modest in me to refer to this, but it is true. There is no record of a person doing as much—not even Shakespeare. But I did it for Florida, and it shows that I could have done it for any place—even London, I suppose.

Recently some one in Missouri has sent me a picture of the house I was born in. Heretofore I have always stated that it was a palace, but I shall be more guarded now.

I used to remember my brother Henry walking into a fire outdoors when he was a week old. It was remarkable in me to remember a thing like that, and it was still more remarkable that I should cling to the delusion, for thirty years, that I *did* remember it—for of course it never happened; he would not have been able to walk at that age. If I had stopped to reflect, I should not have burdened my memory with that impossible rubbish so long. It is believed by many people that an impression deposited in a child's memory within the first two years of its life cannot remain there five years, but that is an error. The incident of Benvenuto Cellini and the salamander must be accepted as authentic and trustworthy; and then that remarkable and indisputable instance in the experience of Helen Keller— However, I will speak of that at another time. For many years I believed that I remembered helping my grandfather drink his whisky toddy when I was six weeks old, but I do not tell about that any more, now; I am grown old and my memory is not as active as it used to be. When I was younger I could remember anything, whether it had happened or not; but my faculties are decaying now, and soon I shall be so I cannot remember any but the things that never happened. It is sad to go to pieces like this, but we all have to do it.

My uncle, John A. Quarles, was a farmer, and his place was in the country four miles from Florida. He had eight children and fifteen or twenty negroes, and was also fortunate in other ways, particularly in his character. I have not come across a better man than he was. I was his guest for two or three months every year, from the fourth year after we removed to Hannibal till I was eleven or twelve years old. I have never consciously used him or his wife in a book, but his farm has come very handy to me in literature once or twice. In *Huck Finn* and in *Tom Sawyer, Detective* I moved it down to Arkansas. It was all of six hundred miles, but it was no trouble; it was not a very large farm—five hundred acres, perhaps—but I could have done it if it had been twice as large. And as for the morality of it, I cared nothing for that; I would move a state if the exigencies of literature required it.

It was a heavenly place for a boy, that farm of my uncle John's. The house was a double log one, with a spacious floor (roofed in) connecting it with the kitchen. In the summer the table was set in the middle of that shady and breezy floor, and the sumptuous meals—well, it makes me cry to think of them. Fried chicken, roast pig; wild and tame turkeys, ducks, and geese; venison just killed; squirrels, rabbits, pheasants, partridges, prairie-chickens; biscuits, hot batter cakes, hot buckwheat cakes, hot "wheat bread," hot rolls, hot corn pone; fresh corn boiled on the ear, succotash, butter-beans, string-beans, tomatoes, peas, Irish potatoes, sweet potatoes; buttermilk, sweet milk, "clabber"; watermelons, muskmelons, cantaloupes—all fresh from the garden; apple pie, peach pie, pumpkin pie, apple dumplings, peach cobbler—I can't remember the rest. The way that the things were cooked was perhaps the main splendor—particularly a certain few of the dishes. For instance, the corn bread, the hot biscuits and wheat bread, and the fried chicken. These things have never been properly cooked in the North—in fact, no one there is able to learn the art, so far as my experience goes. The North thinks it knows how to make corn bread, but this is mere superstition. Perhaps no bread in the world is quite so good as Southern corn bread, and perhaps no bread in the world is quite so bad as the Northern imitation of it. The North seldom tries to fry chicken, and this is well; the art cannot be learned north of the line of Mason and Dixon, nor anywhere in Europe. This is not hearsay; it is experience that is speaking. In Europe it is imagined that the custom of serving various kinds of bread blazing hot is "American," but that is too broad a spread; it is custom in the South, but is much less than that in the North. In the North and in Europe hot bread is considered unhealthy. This is probably another fussy superstition, like the European superstition that ice-water is unhealthy. Europe does not need ice-water and does not drink it; and yet, notwithstanding this, its word for it is better than ours, because it describes it, whereas ours doesn't. Europe calls it "iced" water. Our word describes water made from melted ice—a drink which has a characterless taste and which we have but little acquaintance with.

It seems a pity that the world should throw away so many good things merely because they are unwholesome. I doubt if God has given us any refreshment which, taken in moderation, is unwholesome, except microbes. Yet there are people who strictly deprive themselves of each and every eatable, drinkable, and smokable which has in any way acquired a shady reputation. They pay this price for health. And health is all they get for it. How strange it is! It is like paying out your whole fortune for a cow that has gone dry.

The farmhouse stood in the middle of a very large yard, and the yard was fenced on three sides with rails and on the rear side with high palings; against these stood the smoke-house; beyond the palings was the orchard; beyond the orchard were the negro quarters and the tobacco fields. The front yard was entered over a stile made of sawed-off logs of graduated heights; I do not remember any gate. In a corner of the front yard were a dozen lofty hickory trees and a dozen black walnuts, and in the nutting season riches were to be gathered there.

Down a piece, abreast the house, stood a little log cabin against the rail fence; and there the woody hill fell sharply away, past the barns, the corn-crib, the stables, and the tobacco-curing house, to a limpid brook which sang along over its gravelly bed and curved and frisked in and out and here and there and yonder in the deep shade of overhanging foliage and vines—a divine place for wading, and it had swimming pools, too, which were forbidden to us and therefore much frequented by us. For we were little Christian children and had early been taught the value of forbidden fruit.

In the little log cabin lived a bedridden white-headed slave woman whom we visited daily and looked upon with awe, for we believed she was upward of a thousand years old and had talked with Moses. The younger negroes credited these statistics and had furnished them to us in good faith. We accommodated all the details which came to us about her; and so we believed that she had lost her health in the long desert trip coming out of Egypt, and had never been able to get it back again. She had a round bald place on the crown of her head, and we used to creep around and gaze at it in reverent silence, and reflect that it was caused by fright through seeing Pharaoh drowned. We called her "Aunt" Hannah, Southern fashion. She was superstitious, like the other negroes; also, like them, she was deeply religious. Like them, she had great faith in prayer and employed it in all ordinary exigencies, but not in cases where a dead certainty of result was urgent. Whenever witches were around she tied up the remnant of her wool in little tufts, with white thread, and this promptly made the witches impotent.

All the negroes were friends of ours, and with those of our own age we were in effect comrades. I say in effect, using the phrase as a modification. We were comrades, and yet not comrades; color and condition interposed a subtle line which both parties were conscious of and which rendered complete fusion impossible. We had a faithful and affectionate good friend, ally, and adviser in "Uncle Dan'l," a middle-aged slave whose head was the best one in the negro quarter, whose sympathies were wide and warm, and whose heart was honest and simple and knew no guile. He has served me well these many, many years. I have not seen him for more than half a century, and yet spiritually I have had his welcome company a good part of that time, and have staged him in books under his own name[2] and as "Jim," and carted him all around—to Hannibal, down the Mississippi on a raft, and even across the Desert of Sahara in a balloon—and he has endured it all with the patience and friendliness and loyalty which were his birthright. It was on the farm that I got my strong liking for his race and my appreciation of certain of its fine qualities. This feeling and this estimate have stood the test of sixty years and more, and have suffered no impairment. The black face is as welcome to me now as it was then.

In my schoolboy days I had no aversion to slavery. I was not aware that there was anything wrong about it. No one arraigned it in my hearing; the local papers said nothing against it; the local pulpit taught us that God approved it, that it was a holy thing, and that the doubter need only look in the Bible if he wished to settle his mind—and then the texts were read aloud to us to make the matter sure; if the slaves themselves had an aversion to slavery, they were wise and said nothing. In Hannibal we seldom saw a slave misused; on the farm, never.

There was, however, one small incident of my boyhood days which touched this matter, and it must have meant a good deal to me or it would not have stayed in my memory, clear and sharp, vivid and shadowless, all these slow-drifting years. We had a little slave boy whom we had hired from some one, there in Hannibal.

2. He appears under his own name in *The Gilded Age*.

He was from the eastern shore of Maryland, and had been brought away from his family and his friends, halfway across the American continent, and sold. He was a cheery spirit, innocent and gentle, and the noisiest creature that ever was, perhaps. All day long he was singing, whistling, yelling, whooping, laughing—it was maddening, devastating, unendurable. At last, one day, I lost all my temper, and went raging to my mother and said Sandy had been singing for an hour without a single break, and I couldn't stand it, and *wouldn't* she please shut him up. The tears came into her eyes and her lip trembled, and she said something like this:

"Poor thing, when he sings it shows that he is not remembering, and that comforts me; but when he is still I am afraid he is thinking, and I cannot bear it. He will never see his mother again; if he can sing, I must not hinder it, but be thankful for it. If you were older, you would understand me; then that friendless child's noise would make you glad."

It was a simple speech and made up of small words, but it went home, and Sandy's noise was not a trouble to me any more. She never used large words, but she had a natural gift for making small ones do effective work. She lived to reach the neighborhood of ninety years and was capable with her tongue to the last—especially when a meanness or an injustice roused her spirit. She has come handy to me several times in my books, where she figures as Tom Sawyer's Aunt Polly. I fitted her out with a dialect and tried to think up other improvements for her, but did not find any. I used Sandy once, also; it was in *Tom Sawyer*. I tried to get him to whitewash the fence, but it did not work. I do not remember what name I called him by in the book.[3]

I can see the farm yet, with perfect clearness. I can see all its belongings, all its details; the family room of the house, with a "trundle" bed in one corner and a spinning-wheel in another—a wheel whose rising and falling wail, heard from a distance, was the mournfulest of all sounds to me, and made me homesick and low spirited, and filled my atmosphere with the wandering spirits of the dead; the vast fireplace, piled high, on winter nights, with flaming hickory logs from whose ends a sugary sap bubbled out, but did not go to waste, for we scraped it off and ate it; the lazy cat spread out on the rough hearthstones; the drowsy dogs braced against the jambs and blinking; my aunt in one chimney corner, knitting; my uncle in the other, smoking his corn-cob pipe; the slick and carpetless oak floor faintly mirroring the dancing flame tongues and freckled with black indentations where fire coals had popped out and died a leisurely death; half a dozen children romping in the background twilight; "split"-bottomed chairs here

3. The young Negro boy in the whitewashing scene is called Jim.

and there, some with rockers; a cradle—out of service, but waiting, with confidence; in the early cold mornings a snuggle of children, in shirts and chemises, occupying the hearthstone and procrastinating—they could not bear to leave that comfortable place and go out on the wind-swept floor space between the house and kitchen where the general tin basin stood, and wash.

Along outside of the front fence ran the country road, dusty in the summertime, and a good place for snakes—they liked to lie in it and sun themselves; when they were rattlesnakes or puff adders, we killed them; when they were black snakes, or racers, or belonged to the fabled "hoop" breed, we fled, without shame; when they were "house snakes," or "garters," we carried them home and put them in Aunt Patsy's work basket for a surprise; for she was prejudiced against snakes, and always when she took the basket in her lap and they began to climb out of it it disordered her mind. She never could seem to get used to them; her opportunities went for nothing. And she was always cold toward bats, too, and could not bear them; and yet I think a bat is as friendly a bird as there is. My mother was Aunt Patsy's sister and had the same wild superstitions. A bat is beautifully soft and silky; I do not know any creature that is pleasanter to the touch or is more grateful for caressings, if offered in the right spirit. I know all about these coleoptera, because our great cave, three miles below Hannibal, was multitudinously stocked with them, and often I brought them home to amuse my mother with. It was easy to manage if it was a school day, because then I had ostensibly been to school and hadn't any bats. She was not a suspicious person, but full of trust and confidence; and when I said, "There's something in my coat pocket for you," she would put her hand in. But she always took it out again, herself; I didn't have to tell her. It was remarkable, the way she couldn't learn to like private bats. The more experience she had, the more she could not change her views.

I think she was never in the cave in her life; but everybody else went there. Many excursion parties came from considerable distances up and down the river to visit the cave. It was miles in extent and was a tangled wilderness of narrow and lofty clefts and passages. It was an easy place to get lost in; anybody could do it— including the bats. I got lost in it myself, along with a lady, and our last candle burned down to almost nothing before we glimpsed the search party's lights winding about in the distance.

"Injun Joe," the half-breed, got lost in there once, and would have starved to death if the bats had run short. But there was no chance of that; there were myriads of them. He told me all his story. In the book called *Tom Sawyer* I starved him entirely to death in the cave, but that was in the interest of art; it never happened. "General" Gaines, who was our first town drunkard before Jimmy Finn got the place, was lost in there for the space of a week, and finally pushed his handkerchief out of a hole in a hilltop near Saverton, several miles down the river from the cave's mouth, and somebody saw it and dug him out. There is nothing the matter with his statistics except the handkerchief. I knew him for years and he hadn't any. But it could have been his nose. That would attract attention.

The cave was an uncanny place, for it contained a corpse—the corpse of a young girl of fourteen. It was in a glass cylinder inclosed in a copper one which was suspended from a rail which bridged a narrow passage. The body was preserved in alcohol, and it was said that loafers and rowdies used to drag it up by the hair and look at the dead face. The girl was the daughter of a St. Louis surgeon of extraordinary ability and wide celebrity. He was an eccentric man and did many strange things. He put the poor thing in that forlorn place himself.

· · · · · · ·

Beyond the road where the snakes sunned themselves was a dense young thicket, and through it a dim-lighted path led a quarter of a mile; then out of the dimness one emerged abruptly upon a level great prairie which was covered with wild strawberry plants, vividly starred with prairie pinks, and walled in on all sides by forests. The strawberries were fragrant and fine, and in the season we were generally there in the crisp freshness of the early morning, while the dew beads still sparkled upon the grass and the woods were ringing with the first songs of the birds.

Down the forest slopes to the left were the swings. They were made of bark stripped from hickory saplings. When they became dry they were dangerous. They usually broke when a child was forty feet in the air, and this was why so many bones had to be mended every year. I had no ill luck myself, but none of my cousins escaped. There were eight of them, and at one time and another they broke fourteen arms among them. But it cost next to nothing, for the doctor worked by the year—twenty-five dollars for the whole family. I remember two of the Florida doctors, Chowning and Meredith. They not only tended an entire family for twenty-five dollars a year, but furnished the medicines themselves. Good measure, too. Only the largest persons could hold a whole dose. Castor oil was the principal beverage. The dose was half a dipperful, with half a dipperful of New Orleans molasses added to help it down and make it taste good, which it never did. The next standby was calomel; the next, rhubarb; and the next, jalap. Then they bled the patient, and put mustard plasters on him. It was a dreadful system, and yet the death rate was not heavy. The calomel was nearly sure to salivate the patient and cost him some of his teeth. There were no dentists. When teeth became touched with decay or were otherwise ailing, the doctor knew of but one thing to do—he fetched his tongs and dragged them out. If the jaw remained, it was not his fault. Doctors were not called in cases of ordinary illness; the family grandmother attended to those. Every old woman was a doctor, and gathered her own medicines in the woods, and knew how to compound doses that would stir the vitals of a cast-iron dog. And then there was the "Indian doctor"; a grave savage, remnant of his tribe, deeply read in the mysteries of nature and the secret properties of herbs; and most backswoodsmen had high faith in his powers and could tell of wonderful cures achieved by him. In Mauritius, away off yonder in the solitudes of the Indian Ocean, there is a person who answers to our Indian doctor of the old times. He is a negro, and has had no teaching as a doctor, yet there is one disease which he is master of and can cure and the doctors can't. They send for him when they have a case. It is a child's disease of a strange and deadly sort, and the negro cures it with a herb medicine which he makes, himself, from a prescription which has come down to him from his father and grandfather. He will not let anyone see it. He keeps the secret of its components to himself, and it is feared that he will die without divulging it; then there will be consternation in Mauritius. I was told these things by the people there, in 1896.

We had the "faith doctor," too, in those early days—a woman. Her specialty was toothache. She was a farmer's old wife and lived five miles from Hannibal. She would lay her hand on the patient's jaw and say, "Believe!" and the cure was prompt. Mrs. Utterback. I remember her very well. Twice I rode out there behind my mother, horseback, and saw the cure performed. My mother was the patient.

Doctor Meredith removed to Hannibal, by and by, and was our family physician there, and saved my life several times. Still, he was a good man and meant well. Let it go.

I was always told that I was a sickly and precarious and tiresome and uncertain child, and lived mainly on allopathic medicines during the first seven years of my life. I asked my mother about this, in her old age—she was in her eighty-eighth year—and said:

"I suppose that during all that time you were uneasy about me?"

"Yes, the whole time."

"Afraid I wouldn't live?"

After a reflective pause—ostensibly to think out the facts—"No —afraid you would."

The country schoolhouse was three miles from my uncle's farm. It stood in a clearing in the woods and would hold about twenty-five boys and girls. We attended the school with more or less regularity once or twice a week, in summer, walking to it in the cool of the morning by the forest paths, and back in the gloaming at the end of the day. All the pupils brought their dinners in baskets—corn dodger, buttermilk, and other good things—and sat in the shade of the trees at noon and ate them. It is the part of my education which I look back upon with the most satisfaction. My first visit to the school was when I was seven. A strapping girl of fifteen, in the customary sunbonnet and calico dress, asked me if I "used tobacco"—meaning did I chew it. I said no. It roused her scorn. She reported me to all the crowd, and said:

"Here is a boy seven years old who can't chew tobacco."

By the looks and comments which this produced I realized that I was a degraded object, and was cruelly ashamed of myself. I determined to reform. But I only made myself sick; I was not able to learn to chew tobacco. I learned to smoke fairly well, but that did not conciliate anybody and I remained a poor thing, and characterless. I longed to be respected, but I never was able to rise. Children have but little charity for one another's defects.

As I have said, I spent some part of every year at the farm until I was twelve or thirteen years old. The life which I led there with my cousins was full of charm, and so is the memory of it yet. I can call back the solemn twilight and mystery of the deep woods, the earthy smells, the faint odors of the wild flowers, the sheen of rain-washed foliage, the rattling clatter of drops when the wind shook the trees, the far-off hammering of woodpeckers and the muffled drumming of wood pheasants in the remoteness of the forest, the snapshot glimpses of disturbed wild creatures scurrying through the grass—I can call it all back and make it as real as it ever was, and as blessed. I can call back the prairie, and its loneliness and peace, and a vast hawk hanging motionless in the sky, with his wings spread wide and the blue of the vault showing through the fringe of their end feathers. I can see the woods in their autumn dress, the oaks purple, the hickories washed with gold, the maples and the sumachs luminous with crimson fires, and I can hear the rustle made by the fallen leaves as we plowed through them. I can see the blue clusters of wild grapes hanging among the foliage of the saplings, and I remember the taste of them and the smell. I know how the wild blackberries looked, and how they tasted, and the same with the pawpaws, the hazelnuts, and the persimmons; and I can feel the thumping rain, upon my head, of hickory nuts and walnuts when we were out in the frosty dawn to scramble for them with the pigs, and the gusts of wind loosed them and sent them down. I know the stain of blackberries, and how pretty it is, and I know the stain of walnut hulls, and how little it minds soap and water, also what grudged experience it had of either of them. I know the taste of maple sap, and when to gather it, and how to arrange the troughs and the delivery tubes, and how to boil down the juice, and how to hook the sugar after it is made, also how much better hooked sugar tastes than any that is honestly come by, let bigots say what they will. I know how a prize watermelon looks when it is sunning its fat rotundity among pumpkin vines and "simblins"; I know how to tell when it is ripe without "plugging" it; I know how inviting it looks when it is cooling itself in a tub of water under the bed, waiting; I know how it looks when it lies on the table in the sheltered great floor space between house and kitchen, and the heart standing up, a luxury fit for the elect; I know how a boy looks behind a yard-long slice of that melon, and I know how he feels; for I have been there. I know the taste of the watermelon which has been honestly come by, and I know the taste of the watermelon which has been acquired by art. Both taste good, but the experienced know which tastes best. I know the look of green apples and peaches and pears on the trees, and I know how entertaining they are when they are inside of a person. I know how ripe ones look when they are piled in pyramids under the trees, and how pretty they are and how vivid their colors. I know how a frozen apple looks, in a barrel down cellar in the wintertime, and how hard it is to bite, and how the frost makes the teeth ache, and yet how good it is, notwithstanding. I know the disposition of elderly people to select the specked apples for the children, and I once knew ways to beat the game. I know the look of an apple that is roasting and sizzling on a hearth on a winter's evening, and I know the comfort that comes of eating it hot, along with some sugar and a drench of cream. I know the delicate art and mystery of so cracking hickory nuts and walnuts on a flatiron with a hammer that the kernels will be delivered whole, and I know how the nuts, taken in conjunction with winter apples, cider, and doughnuts, make old people's old tales and old jokes sound fresh and crisp and enchanting, and juggle an evening away before you know what went with the time. I know the look of Uncle Dan'l's kitchen as it was on the privileged nights, when I was a child, and I can see the white and black children grouped on the hearth, with the firelight playing on their faces and the shadows flickering upon the walls, clear back toward the cavernous gloom of the rear, and I can hear Uncle Dan'l telling the immortal tales which Uncle Remus Harris was to gather into his book and charm the world with, by and by; and I can feel again the creepy joy which quivered through me when the time for the ghost story was reached—and the sense of regret, too, which came over me, for it was always the last story of the evening and there was nothing between it and the unwelcome bed.

I can remember the bare wooden stairway in my uncle's house, and the turn to the left above the landing, and the rafters and the slanting roof over my bed, and the squares of moonlight on the floor, and the white cold world of snow outside, seen through the curtainless window. I can remember the howling of the wind and the quaking of the house on stormy nights, and how snug and cozy one felt, under the blankets, listening; and how the powdery snow used to sift in, around the sashes, and lie in little ridges on the floor and make the place look chilly in the morning and curb the wild desire to get up—in case there was any. I can remember how very dark that room was, in the dark of the moon, and how packed it was with ghostly stillness when one woke up by accident away in the night, and forgotten sins came flocking out of the secret chambers of the memory and wanted a hearing; and how ill chosen the time seemed for this kind of business; and how dismal was the hoo-hooing of the owl and the wailing of the wolf, sent mourning by on the night wind.

I remember the raging of the rain on that roof, summer nights, and how pleasant it was to lie and listen to it, and enjoy the white splendor of the lightning and the majestic booming and crashing of the thunder. It was a very satisfactory room, and there was a lightning rod which was reachable from the window, an adorable and skittish thing to climb up and down, summer nights, when there were duties on hand of a sort to make privacy desirable.

I remember the 'coon and 'possum hunts, nights, with the negroes, and the long marches through the black gloom of the woods, and the excitement which fired everybody when the distant bay of an experienced dog announced that the game was treed; then the wild scramblings and stumblings through briers and bushes and over roots to get to the spot; then the lighting of a fire and the felling of the tree, the joyful frenzy of the dogs and the negroes, and the weird picture it all made in the red glare —I remember it all well, and the delight that everyone got out of it, except the 'coon.

I remember the pigeon seasons, when the birds would come in millions and cover the trees and by their weight break down the branches. They were clubbed to death with sticks; guns were not necessary and were not used. I remember the squirrel hunts, and prairie-chicken hunts, and wild-turkey hunts, and all that; and how we turned out, mornings, while it was still dark, to go on these expeditions, and how chilly and dismal it was, and how often I regretted that I was well enough to go. A toot on a tin horn brought twice as many dogs as were needed, and in their happiness they raced and scampered about, and knocked small people down, and made no end of unnecessary noise. At the word, they vanished away toward the woods, and we drifted silently after them in the melancholy gloom. But presently the gray dawn stole over the world, the birds piped up, then the sun rose and poured light and comfort all around, everything was fresh and dewy and fragrant, and life was a boon again. After three hours of tramping we arrived back wholesomely tired, overladen with game, very hungry, and just in time for breakfast.

1870, 1897, 1906   1924

From MARK TWAIN'S LETTERS [4]
To Orion Clemens [5]
[A *Young Pilot Off Duty*]

"ALONZO CHILD," N. ORLEANS, *Sep. 28th 1860.*

DEAR BROTHER,—I just received yours and Mollie's letter yesterday—they had been here two weeks—forwarded from St. Louis. We got here yesterday—will leave at noon to-day. Of course I have had no time, in 24 hours, to do anything. Therefore I'll answer after we are under way again. Yesterday, I had many things to do, but Bixby and I got with the pilots of two other boats and went off dissipating on a ten dollar dinner at a French restaurant —breathe it not unto Ma!—where we ate sheep-head, fish with mushrooms, shrimps and oysters—birds—coffee with brandy burnt in it, &c &c,—ate, drank and smoked, from 1 p.m. until 5 o'clock, and then—then the day was too far gone to do any thing.

Please find enclosed and acknowledge receipt of—$20.00

In haste

SAM L. CLEMENS

To Mrs. Jane Clemens [6]
[A *Country "Fabulously Rich"*]

(Date not given, but *Sept.* or *Oct.*, *1861.*)

MY DEAR MOTHER,— * * *

"Tell everything as it is—no better, and no worse." Well, "Gold Hill" sells at $5,000 per foot, cash down; "Wild cat" isn't worth ten cents. The country is fabulously rich in gold, silver, copper, lead, coal, iron, quicksilver, marble, granite, chalk, plaster of Paris,

4. Edited by Albert Bigelow Paine, in two volumes, 1917.
5. Orion was at this time in Keokuk, Iowa.

6. She was then in St. Louis. The letter was written not long after Clemens' arrival in Carson, Nevada, in August, 1861 (the dateline is Paine's).

(gypsum,) thieves, murderers, desperadoes, ladies, children, lawyers, Christians, Indians, Chinamen, Spaniards, gamblers, sharpers,
coyotes (pronounced Ki-yo-ties,) poets, preachers, and jackass rabbits. I overheard a gentleman say, the other day, that it was
"the d—dest country under the sun."—and that comprehensive
conception I fully subscribe to. It never rains here, and the dew
never falls. No flowers grow here, and no green thing gladdens
the eye. The birds that fly over the land carry their provisions with
them. Only the crow and the raven tarry with us. Our city lies in
the midst of a desert of the purest—most unadulterated, and compromising *sand*—in which infernal soil nothing but that fag-end
of vegetable creation, "sage-brush," ventures to grow. If you will
take a lilliputian cedar tree for a model, and build a dozen imitations of it with the stiffest article of telegraph wire—set them
one foot apart and then try to walk through them, you'll understand (provided the floor is covered 12 inches deep with sand,)
what it is to wander through a sage-brush desert. When crushed,
sage brush emits an odor which isn't exactly magnolia and equally
isn't exactly polecat—but is a sort of compromise between the two.
It looks a good deal like grease-wood, and is the ugliest plant that
was ever conceived of. It is gray in color. On the plains, sage-
brush and grease-wood grow about twice as large as the common
geranium—and in my opinion they are a very good substitute for
that useless vegetable. Grease-wood is a perfect—*most* perfect
imitation in miniature of a live oak tree—barring the color of it.
As to the *other* fruits and flowers of the country, there ain't any,
except "Pulu" or "Tuler," or whatever they call it,—a species of
unpoetical willow that grows on the banks of the Carson—a *river*,
20 yards wide, kneedeep, and so villainously rapid and crooked,
that it looks like it had wandered into the country without intending it, and had run about in a bewildered way and got lost, in its
hurry to get out again before some thirsty man came along and
drank it up. I said we are situated in a flat, sandy desert—true. And
surrounded on all sides by such prodigious mountains, that when
you gaze at them awhile,—and begin to conceive of their grandeur
—and next to feel their vastness expanding your soul—and ultimately find yourself growing and swelling and spreading into a
giant—I say when this point is reached, you look disdainfully
down upon the insignificant village of Carson, and in that instant
you are seized with a burning desire to stretch forth your hand,
put the city in your pocket, and walk off with it.

As to churches, I believe they *have* got a Catholic one here, but
like that one the New York fireman spoke of, I believe "they don't
run her now." * * *

The houses are mostly frame, unplastered, but "papered" inside with flour-sacks sewed together,—and the handsomer the "brand" upon the sacks is, the neater the house looks. Occasionally, you stumble on a stone house. On account of the dryness of the country, the shingles on the houses warp till they look like short joints of stove pipe split lengthwise.[7]

To the New York Society of California Pioneers[8]
[Talking "Pioneer"]

ELMIRA, October 11, 1869.

GENTLEMEN,—Circumstances render it out of my power to take advantage of the invitation extended to me through Mr. Simonton, and be present at your dinner at New York. I regret this very much, for there are several among you whom I would have a right to join hands with on the score of old friendship, and I suppose I would have a sublime general right to shake hands with the rest of you on the score of kinship in California ups and downs in search of fortune.

If I were to tell some of my experience, you would recognize California blood in me; I fancy the old, old story would sound familiar, no doubt. I have the usual stock of reminiscences. For instance: I went to Esmeralda early. I purchased largely in the "Wide West," "Winnemucca," and other fine claims, and was very wealthy. I fared sumptuously on bread when flour was $200 a barrel and had beans for dinner every Sunday, when none but bloated aristocrats could afford such grandeur. But I finished by feeding batteries in a quartz mill at $15 a week, and wishing I was a battery myself and had somebody to feed me. My claims in Esmeralda are there yet. I suppose I could be persuaded to sell.

I went to Humboldt District when it was new; I became largely interested in the "Alba Nueva" and other claims with gorgeous names, and was rich again—in prospect. I owned a vast mining property there. I would not have sold out for less than $400,000 at that time. But I will now. Finally I walked home—200 miles—partly for exercise, and partly because stage fare was expensive. Next I entered upon an affluent career in Virginia City, and by a judicious investment of labor and the capital of friends, became the owner of about all the worthless wild cat mines there were in that part of the country. Assessments did the business for me there. There were a hundred and seventeen assessments to one dividend, and the proportion of income to outlay was a little against me. My financial barometer went down to 32 Fahrenheit, and the sub-

7. Paine notes that the remainder is missing.
8. Response to an invitation to attend a banquet in New York on October 13, 1869; the letter was read to the assembled diners.

scriber was frozen out.

I took up extensions on the main lead—extensions that reached to British America in one direction, and to the Isthmus of Panama in the other—and I verily believe I would have been a rich man if I had ever found those infernal extensions. But I didn't. I ran tunnels till I tapped the Arctic Ocean, and I sunk shafts till I broke through the roof of perdition; but those extensions turned up missing every time. I am willing to sell all that property and throw in the improvements.

Perhaps you remember that celebrated "North Ophir?" I bought that mine. It was very rich in pure silver. You could take it out in lumps as large as a filbert. But when it was discovered that those lumps were melted half dollars, and hardly melted at that, a painful case of "salting" was apparent, and the undersigned adjourned to the poorhouse again.

I paid assessments on "Hale and Norcross" until they sold me out, and I had to take in washing for a living—and the next month that infamous stock went up to $7,000 a foot.

I own millions and millions of feet of affluent silver leads in Nevada—in fact the entire undercrust of that country nearly, and if Congress would move that State off my property so that I could get at it, I would be wealthy yet. But no, there she squats—and here am I. Failing health persuades me to sell. If you know of any one desiring a permanent investment, I can furnish one that will have the virtue of being eternal.

I have been through the California mill, with all its "dips, spurs and angles, variations and sinuosities." I have worked there at all the different trades and professions known to the catalogues. I have been everything, from a newspaper editor down to a cow-catcher on a locomotive, and I am encouraged to believe that if there had been a few more occupations to experiment on, I might have made a dazzling success at last, and found out what mysterious designs Providence had in creating me.

But you perceive that although I am not a Pioneer, I have had a sufficiently variegated time of it to enable me to talk Pioneer like a native, and feel like a Forty-Niner. Therefore, I cordially welcome you to your old-remembered homes and your long deserted firesides, and close this screed with the sincere hope that your visit here will be a happy one, and not embittered by the sorrowful surprises that absence and lapse of years are wont to prepare for wanderers; surprises which come in the form of old friends missed from their places; silence where familiar voices should be; the young grown old; change and decay everywhere; home a delusion and a disappointment; strangers at hearthstone; sorrow where gladness was; tears for laughter; the melancholy pomp of death where the grace of life has been!

With all good wishes for the Returned Prodigals, and regrets that I cannot partake of a small piece of the fatted calf (rare and no gravy,)

I am yours, cordially,

MARK TWAIN.

To James Redpath[9]
[*Different from Other Women*]

HARTFORD, *Tuesday Aug. 8, 1871.*

DEAR RED,—I am different from other women; my mind changes oftener. People who have no mind can easily be steadfast and firm, but when a man is loaded down to the guards with it, as I am, every heavy sea of foreboding or inclination, maybe of indolence, shifts the cargo. See? Therefore, if you will notice, one week I am likely to give rigid instructions to confine me to New England; next week, send me to Arizona; the next week withdraw my name; the next week give you full untrammelled swing; and the week following modify it. You must try to keep the run of my mind, Redpath, it is your business being the agent, and it always was too many for me. It appears to me to be one of the finest pieces of mechanism I have ever met with. Now about the West, this week, I am willing that you shall retain all the Western engagements. But what I shall want *next* week is still with God.

Let us not profane the mysteries with soiled hands and prying eyes of sin.

Yours,

MARK.

P. S.   Shall be here 2 weeks, will run up there when Nasby comes.[1]

To William Dean Howells[2]
[*Difficult Negro Talk*]

FARMINGTON AVENUE, HARTFORD, *Sept. 20, 1874.*

MY DEAR HOWELLS,—All right, my boy, send proof sheets *here*. I amend dialect stuff by talking and talking and *talking* it

9. In Boston; Redpath was head of the Redpath Lyceum Bureau, founded in 1868.
1. "Petroleum Vesuvius Nasby" (David Ross Locke), a humorist whose writing President Lincoln greatly enjoyed.
2. Howells (1837–1920) was a novelist, critic, man of letters; his favorable review of *Innocents Abroad* began a friendship with Twain that lasted forty years. The "proof sheets" referred to are those of "A True Story," Twain's first publication in the *Atlantic Monthly*. Written in the summer of 1872, while he was working on *Tom Sawyer*, this Negro story was told to him by Auntie Cord, cook in the household of Sue Crane, Mrs. Clemens' sister; Howells praised the dialect as "the realest kind of black talk."

till it sounds right—and I had difficulty with this negro talk because a negro sometimes (rarely) says "goin' " and sometimes "gwyne," and they make just such discrepancies in other words—and when you come to reproduce them on paper they look as if the variation resulted from the writer's carelessness. But I want to work at the proofs and get the dialect as nearly right as possible.

We are in part of the new house. Goodness knows when we'll get in the rest of it—full of workmen yet.

I worked a month at my play, and launched it in New York last Wednesday. I believe it will go. The newspapers have been complimentary. It is simply a *setting* for the one character, Col. Sellers—as a *play* I guess it will not bear a critical assault in force.[3] * * *

Yrs ever
MARK.

To William Dean Howells

["*As to the Adjective—*"]

HARTFORD, Nov. 23, '75.

MY DEAR HOWELLS,—Herewith is the proof. In spite of myself, how awkwardly I do jumble words together; and how often I do use three words where one would answer—a thing I am always trying to guard against. I shall become as slovenly a writer as Charles Francis Adams, if I don't look out. (That is said in jest; because of course I do not seriously fear getting so bad as that. I never shall drop so far toward his and Bret Harte's level as to catch myself saying "It must have been wiser to have believed that he might have accomplished it if he could have felt that he would have been supported by those who should have &c. &c. &c.)[4] * * *

Yrs Ever   MARK.

To William Dean Howells

[A "*Delicious*" *Presidential Campaign*]

ELMIRA, Aug. 21, '84.

MY DEAR HOWELLS,—This presidential campaign[5] is too delicious for anything. *Isn't* human nature the most consummate

---

3. See *Autobiography*, note 7. Theatergoers delighted in the character of "Colonel Sellers," as played by John T. Raymond.
4. Mark Twain was violently antagonistic to what the modern writer terms "jargon." He admired the "pemmican sentences" of Thomas Fuller (1608-61) and praised the prose style of Susy Clemens, his daughter, as "good style—no barnacles on it in the way of un-necessary, retarding words." And a Pudd'nhead Wilson maxim warns, "As to the Adjective, when in doubt, strike it out."
5. The hard-fought Blaine-Cleveland campaign of 1884. Mark Twain began his political life, apparently, as a Democrat, then became what he spoke of as a "good Republican," and finally "graduated" to a "no-party independence."

sham and lie that was ever invented? Isn't man a creature to be
ashamed of in pretty much all his aspects? Man, "know thyself"
—and then thou wilt despise thyself, to a dead moral certainty.
Take three quite good specimens—Hawley, Warner, and Charley
Clark. Even *I* do not loathe Blaine more than they do; Yet Hawley
is howling for Blaine, Warner and Clark are eating their daily crow
in the paper for him, and all three will vote for him. O Stultifica-
tion, where is thy sting, O slave where is thy hickory!⁶ * * *

Yrs Ever   Mark.

To William Dean Howells
[*Conscience or Party?*]

Elmira, *Sept. 17, '84.*

My dear Howells,—Somehow I can't seem to rest quiet under
the idea of your voting for Blaine. I believe you said something
about the country and the party. Certainly allegiance to these is
well; but as certainly a man's *first* duty is to his own conscience
and honor—the party or the country come second to that, and
never first. * * *

It is not *parties* that make or save countries or that build them
to greatness—it is clean men, clean ordinary citizens, rank and
file, the masses. Clean masses are not made by individuals standing back till the rest become clean.

As I said before, I think a man's first duty is to his own honor;
not to his country and not to his party. Don't be offended; I mean
no offence. I am not so concerned about the *rest* of the nation,
but—well, good-bye.

Ys Ever   Mark.

[An Unmailed Letter]⁷

Hartford, *Sept. 8, '87.*

Dear Sir,—And so it has got around to you, at last; and you
also have "taken the liberty." You are No. 1365. When 1364
sweeter and better people, including the author, have "tried" to
dramatize Tom Sawyer and did not arrive, what sort of show do
you suppose you stand? That is a book, dear sir, which cannot be
dramatized. One might as well try to dramatize any other hymn.
Tom Sawyer is simply a hymn, put into prose form to give it a

6. Cf. the Biblical passage, "O death, where is thy sting? O grave, where is thy victory?" (I Corinthians xvi.55).
7. His hot temper flared at the drop of a word, and he sometimes sent out scorching letters that he later regretted; he hit upon the "unmailed letter" as a safety valve for letting off steam. One of the most famous of his unmailed letters is the one he wrote to a local utility company, a classic of exaspera-tion and vituperation; the letter printed here appears because of its connection with *Tom Sawyer.*

worldly air.

Why the pale doubt that flitteth dim and nebulous athwart the forecastle of your third sentence? Have no fears. Your piece will be a Go. It will go out the back door on the first night. They've all done it—the 1364. So will—1365. Not one of us ever thought of the simple device of half-soling himself with a stove-lid. Ah, what suffering a little hindsight would have saved us. Treasure this hint.

How kind of you to invite me to the funeral. Go to; I have attended a thousand of them. I have seen Tom Sawyer's remains in all the different kinds of dramatic shrouds there are. You cannot start anything fresh. Are you serious when you propose to pay my expence—if that is the Susquehannian way of spelling it? And can you be aware that I charge a hundred dollars a mile when I travel for pleasure? Do you realize that it is 432 miles to Susquehanna? Would it be handy for you to send me the $43,200 first, so I could be counting it as I come along; because railroading is pretty dreary to a sensitive nature when there's nothing sordid to buck at for Zeitvertreib.[8]

Now as I understand it, dear and magnanimous 1365, you are going to re-create Tom Sawyer dramatically, and then do me the compliment to put me in the bills as father of this shady offspring. Sir, do you know that this kind of a compliment has destroyed people before now? Listen.

Twenty-four years ago, I was strangely handsome. The remains of it are still visible through the rifts of time. I was so handsome that human activities ceased as if spellbound when I came in view, and even inanimate things stopped to look—like locomotives, and district messenger boys and so-on. In San Francisco, in the rainy season I was often mistaken for fair weather. Upon one occasion I was traveling in the Sonora region, and stopped for an hour's nooning, to rest my horse and myself. All the town came out to look. The tribes of Indians gathered to look. A Piute squaw named her baby for me,—a voluntary compliment which pleased me greatly. Other attentions were paid me. Last of all arrived the president and faculty of Sonora University and offered me the post of Professor of Moral Culture and the Dogmatic Humanities; which I accepted gratefully, and entered at once upon my duties. But my name had pleased the Indians, and in the deadly kindness of their hearts they went on naming their babies after me. I tried to stop it, but the Indians could not understand why I should object to so manifest a compliment. The thing grew and grew and spread and spread and became exceedingly embarrassing. The University stood it a couple of years; but then for the sake of the

8. For pastime.

college they felt obliged to call a halt, although I had the sympathy of the whole faculty. The president himself said to me, "I am as sorry as I can be for you, and would still hold out if there were any hope ahead; but you see how it is: there are a hundred and thirty-two of them already, and fourteen precincts to hear from. The circumstance has brought your name into most wide and unfortunate renown. It causes much comment—I believe that that is not an over-statement. Some of this comment is palliative, but some of it—by patrons at a distance, who only know the statistics without the explanation,—is offensive, and in some cases even violent. Nine students have been called home. The trustees of the college have been growing more and more uneasy all these last months—steadily along with the implacable increase in your census—and I will not conceal from you that more than once they have touched upon the expediency of a change in the Professorship of Moral Culture. The coarsely sarcastic editorial in yesterday's *Alta*,—headed Give the Moral Acrobat a Rest—has brought things to a crisis, and I am charged with the unpleasant duty of receiving your resignation."

I know you only mean me a kindness, dear 1365, but it is a most deadly mistake. Please do not name your Injun for me. Truly Yours.

[The Mailed Letter]

NEW YORK, *Sept. 8. 1887.*

DEAR SIR,—Necessarily I cannot assent to so strange a proposition. And I think it but fair to warn you that if you put the piece on the stage, you must take the legal consequences.

Yours respectfully,

S. L. CLEMENS.

To ———[9]

[*None of It Artificial*]

* * * I confine myself to life with which I am familiar when pretending to portray life. But I confined myself to the *boy*-life out on the Mississippi because that had a peculiar charm for me, and not because I was not familiar with other phases of life. I was a *soldier* two weeks once[1] in the beginning of the war, and was hunted like a rat the whole time. Familiar? My splendid Kipling himself[2] hasn't a more burnt-in, hard-baked, and unforgetable

9. Fragment of a letter to a person unknown (1891).
1. Reference to Sam Clemens' brief military experience just before his leaving for the West with Orion in 1861.
2. Rudyard Kipling (1865–1936) had called on Mark Twain two years before.

On a round-the-world tour, Kipling insisted that he had come fourteen thousand miles to meet Mark Twain. Twain liked Kipling's stirring *Barrack-Room Ballads* and read them from the platform.

familiarity with that death-on-the-pale-horse-with-hell-following-after, which is a raw soldier's first fortnight in the field—and which, without any doubt, is the most tremendous fortnight and the vividest he is ever going to see.

Yes, and I have shoveled silver tailings in a quartz-mill a couple of weeks, and acquired the last possibilities of culture in *that* direction. And I've done "pocket-mining" during three months in the one little patch of ground in the whole globe where Nature conceals gold in pockets—or *did* before we robbed all of those pockets and exhausted, obliterated, annihilated the most curious freak Nature ever indulged in. There are not thirty men left alive who, being told there was a pocket hidden on the broad slope of a mountain, would know how to go and find it, or have even the faintest idea of how to set about it; but I am one of the possible 20 or 30 who possess the secret, and I could go and put my hand on that hidden treasure with a most deadly precision.

And I've been a prospector, and know pay rock from poor when I find it—just with a touch of the tongue. And I've been a *silver* miner and know how to dig and shovel and drill and put in a blast. And so I know the mines and the miners interiorly as well as Bret Harte knows them exteriorly.

And I was a newspaper reporter four years in cities, and so saw the inside of many things; and was reporter in a legislature two sessions and the same in Congress one session, and thus learned to know personally three sample bodies of the smallest minds and the selfishest souls and the cowardliest hearts that God makes.

And I was some years a Mississippi pilot, and familiarly knew all the different kinds of steamboatmen—a race apart, and not like other folk.

And I was for some years a traveling "jour" printer, and wandered from city to city—and so I know *that* sect familiarly.

And I was a lecturer on the public platform a number of seasons and was a responder to toasts at all the different kinds of banquets—and so I know a great many secrets about audiences—secrets not to be got out of books, but only acquirable by experience.

And I watched over one dear project[3] of mine for years, spent a fortune on it, and failed to make it go—and the history of that would make a large book in which a million men would see themselves as in a mirror; and they would testify and say, Verily, this is not imagination; this fellow has been there—and after would cast dust upon their heads, cursing and blaspheming.

And I am a publisher, and did pay to one author's widow (General Grant's) the largest copyright checks this world has seen —aggregating more than £80,000 in the first year.

3. The Paige typesetting machine, which was a failure.

And I have been an author for 20 years and an ass for 55.

Now then; as the most valuable capital or culture or education usable in the building of novels is personal experience I ought to be well equipped for that trade.

I surely have the equipment, a wide culture, and all of it real, none of it artificial, for I don't know anything about books.[4]

To Rev. J. H. Twichell[5]

[*The Jubilee Singers*]

LUCERNE, Aug. 22, '97.

DEAR JOE,— * * *

The other night we had a detachment of the Jubilee Singers—6. I had known one of them in London 24 years ago. Three of the 6 were born in slavery, the others were children of slaves. How charming they were—in spirit, manner, language, pronunciation, enunciation, grammar, phrasing, matter, carriage, clothes—in every detail that goes to make the real lady and gentleman, and welcome guest. We went down to the village hotel and bought our tickets and entered the beer-hall, where a crowd of German and Swiss men and women sat grouped at round tables with their beer mugs in front of them—self contained and unimpressionable looking people, an indifferent and unposted and disheartened audience— and up at the far end of the room sat the Jubilees in a row. The Singers got up and stood—the talking and glass jingling went on. Then rose and swelled out above those common earthly sounds one of those rich chords the secret of whose make only the Jubilees possess, and a spell fell upon that house. It was fine to see the faces light up with the pleased wonder and surprise of it. No one was indifferent any more; and when the singers finished, the camp was theirs. It was a triumph. It reminded me of Launcelot riding in Sir Kay's armor and astonishing complacent Knights who thought they had struck a soft thing.[6] The Jubilees sang a lot of pieces. Arduous and painstaking cultivation has not diminished or arti-ficialized their music, but on the contrary—to my surprise—has mightily reinforced its eloquence and beauty. Away back in the beginning—to my mind—their music made all other vocal music cheap; and that early notion is emphasized now. It is utterly beau-tiful, to me; and it moves me infinitely more than any other music can. I think that in the Jubilees and their songs America has pro-duced the perfectest flower of the ages; and I wish it were a

4. "No signature" [Paine's note].
5. Twain's Hartford neighbor, who had accompanied him on the European trip described in *A Tramp Abroad*. After the death of Susy Clemens in the Hartford house in 1896, the Clemens family lived abroad for several years.
6. *Morte D'Arthur* VI.xii, by Sir Thom-as Malory, published 1485. "Old Mal-ory" was a great favorite of Mark Twain's.

foreign product, so that she would worship it and lavish money on it and go properly crazy over it.

Now, these countries are different: they would do all that, if it were *native*. It is true they praise God, but that is merely a formality, and nothing in it; they open out their whole hearts to no foreigner. * * *

With love from us all. MARK.

To William Dean Howells
[*Privately Speaking—*]

WELLINGTON COURT, KNIGHTSBRIDGE, *Jan.* 25, 1900.

* * * Privately speaking, this is a sordid and criminal war,[7] and in every way shameful and excuseless. Every day I write (in my head) bitter magazine articles about it, but I have to stop with that. For England must not fall; it would mean an inundation of Russian and German political degradations which would envelop the globe and steep it in a sort of Middle-Age night and slavery which would last till Christ comes again. Even wrong—and she is wrong—England must be upheld. He is an enemy of the human race who shall speak against her now. Why *was* the human race created? Or at least why wasn't something creditable created in place of it. God had his opportunity. He could have made a reputation. But no, He must commit this grotesque folly—a lark which must have cost him a regret or two when He came to think it over and observe effects. For a giddy and unbecoming caprice there has been nothing like it till this war. I talk the war with both sides—always waiting until the other man introduces the topic. Then I say "My head is with the Briton, but my heart and such rags of morals as I have are with the Boer—now we will talk, unembarrassed and without prejudice." And so we discuss, and have no trouble.[8]

To Brander Matthews[9]
[*On Sir Walter Scott*]

NEW YORK CITY, *May* 4, '03.

DEAR BRANDER,—I haven't been out of my bed for four weeks, but—well, I have been reading, a good deal * * *

Brander, I lie here dying, slowly dying, under the blight of Sir Walter.[1] I have read the first volume of Rob Roy, and as far as

7. The Boer War, fought between the English and the Dutch in South Africa (1899–1902).
8. No signature.
9. Matthews was Professor of Literature in Columbia University.
1. Mark Twain abhorred what he called "the Sir Walter disease" that

chapter XIX of Guy Mannering, and I can no longer hold my head up nor take my nourishment. Lord, it's all so juvenile! so artificial, so shoddy; and such wax figures and skeletons and spectres. Interest? Why, it is impossible to feel an interest in these bloodless shams, these milk-and-water humbugs. And oh, the poverty of the invention! Not poverty in inventing situations, but poverty in furnishing reasons for them. Sir Walter usually gives himself away when he arranges for a situation—elaborates, and elaborates, and elaborates, till if you live to get to it you don't believe in it when it happens.

I can't find the rest of Rob Roy, I can't stand any more Mannering—I do not know just what to do, but I will reflect, and not quit this great study rashly. * * *

Sincerely Yours

S. L. CLEMENS.

To Brander Matthews
[*On* Quentin Durward]

RIVERDALE, *May* 8, '03 (Mailed *June*, 1910).

DEAR BRANDER,—I'm still in bed, but the days have lost their dulness since I broke into Sir Walter and lost my temper. I finished Guy Mannering—that curious, curious book, with its mob of squalid shadows jabbering around a single flesh-and-blood being—Dinmont; a book crazily put together out of the very refuse of the romance-artist's stage properties—finished it and took up Quentin Durward, and finished that.

It was like leaving the dead to mingle with the living: it was like withdrawing from the infant class in the College of Journalism to sit under the lectures in English literature in Columbia University.

I wonder who wrote Quentin Durward?

Yrs ever   MARK.

To Rev. J. H. Twichell
[*Progress from Age to Age*]

March 14, '05.

DEAR JOE,—I have a Puddn'head maxim:[2]

"When a man is a pessimist before 48 he knows too much; if he is an optimist after it, he knows too little." * * *

---

had "debilitated the South"; in *Life on the Mississippi* he charged that the South derived her "jejune romanticism" and "medieval chivalry silliness" from Scott, and he wound up holding Scott responsible for the Civil War.

2. In his book *Pudd'nhead Wilson*, Mark Twain had headed each chapter with a carefully coined "maxim."

Yes, oh, yes, I am not overlooking the "steady progress from age to age of the coming of the kingdom of God and righteousness." "From age to age"—yes, it describes that giddy gait. I (and the rocks) will not live to see it arrive, but that is all right—it will arrive, it surely will. * * * The source of "righteousness"—is in the heart? Yes. And engineered and directed by the brain? Yes. Well, history and tradition testify that the heart is just about what it was in the beginning; it has undergone no shade of change. Its good and evil impulses and their consequences are the same to-day that they were in Old Bible times, in Egyptian times, in Greek times, in Middle Age times, in Twentieth Century times. There has been no change.

Meantime, the brain has undergone no change. It is what it always was. There are a few good brains and a multitude of poor ones. It was so in Old Bible times and in all other times—Greek, Roman, Middle Ages and Twentieth Century. Among the savages —all the savages—the average brain is as competent as the average brain here or elsewhere. I will prove it to you, some time, if you like. And there are great brains among them, too. I will prove that also, if you like.

Well, the 19th century made progress—the first progress after "ages and ages"—colossal progress. In what? Materialities. Prodigious acquisitions were made in things which add to the comfort of many and make life harder for as many more. But the addition to righteousness? Is that discoverable? I think not. The materialities were not invented in the interest of righteousness; that there is more righteousness in the world because of them than there was before, is hardly demonstrable, I think. In Europe and America there is a vast change (due to them) in ideals—do you admire it? All Europe and all America are feverishly scrambling for money. Money is the supreme ideal—all others take tenth place with the great bulk of the nations named. Money-lust has always existed, but not in the history of the world was it ever a craze, a madness, until your time and mine. This lust has rotted these nations; it has made them hard, sordid, ungentle, dishonest, oppressive.[3] * * *

N. B. No charge for these informations. Do come down soon, Joe.

With love,

MARK.

3. Signs of the times were bringing bitterness to Mark Twain. "Has the Kingdom of God advanced in Russia since the beginning of time?" he asked Twichell. Earlier, he had compared England's imperialism with that which he considered America was exhibiting in the Philippines; when he introduced young Winston Churchill at a New York dinner in 1900, he remarked that their two countries were "kin in sin." At the outbreak of the Spanish-American War, he had been aflame with interest: "It is a worthy thing to fight for one's freedom; it is another sight finer to fight for another man's. And I think this is the first time it has been done." But he was writing from Vi-

The Mysterious Stranger[4]
Chapter I

It was in 1590—winter. Austria was far away from the world, and asleep; it was still the Middle Ages in Austria, and promised to remain so forever. Some even set it away back centuries upon centuries and said that by the mental and spiritual clock it was still the Age of Belief in Austria. But they meant it as a compliment, not a slur, and it was so taken, and we were all proud of it. I remember it well, although I was only a boy; and I remember, too, the pleasure it gave me.

Yes, Austria was far from the world, and asleep, and our village was in the middle of that sleep, being in the middle of Austria. It drowsed in peace in the deep privacy of a hilly and woodsy solitude where news from the world hardly ever came to disturb its dreams, and was infinitely content. At its front flowed the tranquil river, its surface painted with cloud-forms and the reflections of drifting arks and stone-boats; behind it rose the woody steeps to the base of the lofty precipice; from the top of the precipice frowned a vast castle, its long stretch of towers and bastions mailed in vines; beyond the river, a league to the left, was a tumbled expanse of forest-clothed hills cloven by winding gorges where the sun never penetrated; and to the right a precipice overlooked the river, and between it and the hills just spoken of lay a far-reaching plain dotted with little homesteads nested among orchards and shade trees.

The whole region for leagues around was the hereditary property of a prince, whose servants kept the castle always in perfect condition for occupancy, but neither he nor his family came there oftener than once in five years. When they came it was as if the lord of the world had arrived, and had brought all the glories

enna, and when he heard belatedly that we had "seized the Philippines," he felt that our boys were dying "under a polluted flag." He suggested that we needed a new flag, one more in keeping with our aspirations: "the white stripes painted black and the stars replaced by the skull and crossbones." Boers, Boxers, Filipinos, the blacks in the Belgian Congo—all were being oppressed. In the United States murders, lynchings, crimes were crowding each other in the newspapers; he suggested to Twichell in 1901 that all of these wrongs might be ended quite simply: "by extinguishing God's most elegant invention, the Human Race."

4. Entries pertaining to *The Mysterious Stranger* appeared in Mark Twain's *Notebook* in 1897, even earlier; the story was mainly written in 1898, but awaited posthumous publication until 1916. It was later collected in *The Mysterious Stranger and Other Stories*, 1922. The present text is from the 1916 edition, which retained Twain's own punctuation; two obvious misprints have been corrected. The long story "The Man That Corrupted Hadleyburg" (1899), the philosophic nihilism called *What Is Man?* (1917), and this book represent Mark Twain's final creative period. As he always expressed himself more effectively through imaginative fiction than through formal prose, both the fictional pieces are better than the Socratic dialectics of *What Is Man?*, although similar ideas connect all three. *The Mysterious Stranger* contains Mark Twain's final expression of the village and its inhabitants, a crystallization of his despair.

of its kingdoms along; and when they went they left a calm behind which was like the deep sleep which follows an orgy.

Eseldorf was a paradise for us boys.[5] We were not overmuch pestered with schooling. Mainly we were trained to be good Christians; to revere the Virgin, the Church, and the saints above everything. Beyond these matters we were not required to know much; and, in fact, not allowed to. Knowledge was not good for the common people, and could make them discontented with the lot which God had appointed for them, and God would not endure discontentment with His plans. We had two priests. One of them, Father Adolf, was a very zealous and strenuous priest, much considered.

There may have been better priests, in some ways, than Father Adolf, but there was never one in our commune who was held in more solemn and awful respect. This was because he had absolutely no fear of the Devil. He was the only Christian I have ever known of whom that could be truly said. People stood in deep dread of him on that account; for they thought that there must be something supernatural about him, else he could not be so bold and so confident. All men speak in bitter disapproval of the Devil, but they do it reverently, not flippantly; but Father Adolf's way was very different; he called him by every name he could lay his tongue to, and it made everyone shudder that heard him; and often he would even speak of him scornfully and scoffingly; then the people crossed themselves and went quickly out of his presence, fearing that something fearful might happen.

Father Adolf had actually met Satan face to face more than once, and defied him. This was known to be so. Father Adolf said it himself. He never made any secret of it, but spoke it right out. And that he was speaking true there was proof in at least one instance, for on that occasion he quarreled with the enemy, and intrepidly threw his bottle at him; and there, upon the wall of his study, was the ruddy splotch where it struck and broke.

But it was Father Peter, the other priest, that we all loved best and were sorriest for. Some people charged him with talking around in conversation that God was all goodness and would find a way to save all his poor human children. It was a horrible thing to say, but there was never any absolute proof that Father Peter said it; and it was out of character for him to say it, too, for he was al-

5. A *Notebook* entry of 1898 reads: "Story of little Satan Jr., who came to Hannibal, went to school, was popular and greatly liked by those who knew his secret. The others were jealous and the girls didn't like him because he smelled of brimstone. He was always doing miracles." The note shows that he first intended to use Tom and Huck as the companions of young Satan; but by changing Hannibal to Eseldorf, Austria, and the Missouri boy-time to 1590, he gave the story perspective, placing it far away in both time and space. "Eseldorf" is translated "Assville" or "Donkeytown."

ways good and gentle and truthful. He wasn't charged with saying it in the pulpit, where all the congregation could hear and testify, but only outside, in talk; and it is easy for enemies to manufacture *that*. Father Peter had an enemy and a very powerful one, the astrologer who lived in a tumbled old tower up the valley, and put in his nights studying the stars. Every one knew he could foretell wars and famines, though that was not so hard, for there was always a war and generally a famine somewhere. But he could also read any man's life through the stars in a big book he had, and find lost property, and every one in the village except Father Peter stood in awe of him. Even Father Adolf, who had defied the Devil, had a wholesome respect for the astrologer when he came through our village wearing his tall, pointed hat and his long, flowing robe with stars on it, carrying his big book, and a staff which was known to have magic power. The bishop himself sometimes listened to the astrologer, it was said, for, besides studying the stars and prophesying, the astrologer made a great show of piety, which would impress the bishop, of course.

But Father Peter took no stock in the astrologer. He denounced him openly as a charlatan—a fraud with no valuable knowledge of any kind, or powers beyond those of an ordinary and rather inferior human being, which naturally made the astrologer hate Father Peter and wish to ruin him. It was the astrologer, as we all believed, who originated the story about Father Peter's shocking remark and carried it to the bishop. It was said that Father Peter had made the remark to his niece, Marget, though Marget denied it and implored the bishop to believe her and spare her old uncle from poverty and disgrace. But the bishop wouldn't listen. He suspended Father Peter indefinitely, though he wouldn't go so far as to excommunicate him on the evidence of only one witness; and now Father Peter had been out a couple of years, and our other priest, Father Adolf, had his flock.

Those had been hard years for the old priest and Marget. They had been favorites, but of course that changed when they came under the shadow of the bishop's frown. Many of their friends fell away entirely, and the rest became cool and distant. Marget was a lovely girl of eighteen when the trouble came, and she had the best head in the village, and the most in it. She taught the harp, and earned all her clothes and pocket money by her own industry. But her scholars fell off one by one now; she was forgotten when there were dances and parties among the youth of the village; the young fellows stopped coming to the house, all except Wilhelm Meidling—and he could have been spared; she and her uncle were sad and forlorn in their neglect and disgrace, and the sunshine was gone out of their lives. Matters went worse and worse, all through the two years. Clothes were wearing out, bread was harder and harder to get. And now, at last, the very end was come. Solomon Isaacs had lent all the money he was willing to put on the house, and gave notice that to-morrow he would fore-close.

Chapter II

Three of us boys were always together, and had been so from the cradle, being fond of one another from the beginning, and this affection deepened as the years went on—Nikolaus Bauman, son of the principal judge of the local court; Seppi Wohlmeyer, son of the keeper of the principal inn, the "Golden Stag," which had a nice garden, with shade trees reaching down to the riverside, and pleasure boats for hire; and I was the third—Theodor Fischer, son of the church organist, who was also leader of the village musicians, teacher of the violin, composer, tax-collector of the commune, sexton, and in other ways a useful citizen, and respected by all. We knew the hills and the woods as well as the birds knew them; for we were always roaming them when we had leisure—at least, when we were not swimming or boating or fishing, or play-ing on the ice or sliding down hill.

And we had the run of the castle park, and very few had that. It was because we were pets of the oldest servingman in the castle —Felix Brandt; and often we went there, nights, to hear him talk about old times and strange things, and to smoke with him (he taught us that) and to drink coffee; for he had served in the wars, and was at the siege of Vienna;[6] and there, when the Turks were defeated and driven away, among the captured things were bags of coffee, and the Turkish prisoners explained the character of it and how to make a pleasant drink out of it, and now he al-ways kept coffee by him, to drink himself and also to astonish the ignorant with. When it stormed he kept us all night; and while it thundered and lightened outside he told us about ghosts and horrors of every kind, and of battles and murders and mutilations, and such things, and made it pleasant and cozy in-side; and he told these things from his own experience largely. He had seen many ghosts in his time, and witches and enchanters, and once he was lost in a fierce storm at midnight in the moun-tains, and by the glare of the lightning had seen the Wild Hunts-man[7] rage on the blast with his specter dogs chasing after him through the driving cloud-rack. Also he had seen an incubus[8]

---

6. In 1529 a Turkish army attempted unsuccessfully to take Vienna.
7. Condemned to ride his horse forever because he had refused to permit Jesus to drink from a horse-trough; he is usu-ally seen in stormy weather.
8. An evil spirit, supposed to lie upon persons as they sleep; the next line refers to the vampire bat.

once, and several times he had seen the great bat that sucks the blood from the necks of people while they are asleep, fanning them softly with its wings and so keeping them drowsy till they die.

He encouraged us not to fear supernatural things, such as ghosts, and said they did no harm, but only wandered about because they were lonely and distressed and wanted kindly notice and compassion; and in time we learned not to be afraid, and even went down with him in the night to the haunted chamber in the dungeons of the castle. The ghost appeared only once, and it went by very dim to the sight and floated noiseless through the air, and then disappeared; and we scarcely trembled, he had taught us so well. He said it came up sometimes in the night and woke him by passing its clammy hand over his face, but it did him no hurt; it only wanted sympathy and notice. But the strangest thing was that he had seen angels—actual angels out of heaven—and had talked with them. They had no wings, and wore clothes, and talked and looked and acted just like any natural person, and you would never know them for angels except for the wonderful things they did which a mortal could not do, and the way they suddenly disappeared while you were talking with them, which was also a thing which no mortal could do. And he said they were pleasant and cheerful, not gloomy and melancholy, like ghosts.

It was after that kind of a talk one May night that we got up next morning and had a good breakfast with him and then went down and crossed the bridge and went away up into the hills on the left to a woody hill-top which was a favorite place of ours,[9] and there we stretched out on the grass in the shade to rest and smoke and talk over these strange things, for they were in our minds yet, and impressing us. But we couldn't smoke, because we had been heedless and left our flint and steel behind.

Soon there came a youth strolling toward us through the trees, and he sat down and began to talk in a friendly way, just as if he knew us. But we did not answer him, for he was a stranger and we were not used to strangers and were shy of them. He had new and good clothes on, and was handsome and had a winning face and a pleasant voice, and was easy and graceful and unembarrassed, not slouchy and awkward and diffident, like other boys. We wanted to be friendly with him, but didn't know how to begin. Then I thought of the pipe, and wondered if it would be taken as kindly meant if I offered it to him. But I remembered that we had no fire, so I was sorry and disappointed. But he looked up bright and pleased, and said:

9. Reminiscent of Holliday's Hill near Hannibal, known to Tom and Huck as Cardiff Hill.

"Fire? Oh, that is easy; I will furnish it."

I was so astonished I couldn't speak; for I had not said any-thing. He took the pipe and blew his breath on it, and the tobacco glowed red, and spirals of blue smoke rose up. We jumped up and were going to run, for that was natural; and we did run a few steps, although he was yearningly pleading for us to stay, and giving us his word that he would not do us any harm, but only wanted to be friends with us and have company. So we stopped and stood, and wanted to go back, being full of curiosity and wonder, but afraid to venture. He went on coaxing, in his soft, persuasive way; and when we saw that the pipe did not blow up and nothing happened, our confidence returned by little and little, and presently our curiosity got to be stronger than our fear, and we ventured back—but slowly, and ready to fly at any alarm.

He was bent on putting us at ease, and he had the right art; one could not remain doubtful and timorous where a person was so earnest and simple and gentle, and talked so alluringly as he did; no, he won us over, and it was not long before we were con-tent and comfortable and chatty, and glad we had found this new friend. When the feeling of constraint was all gone we asked him how he had learned to do that strange thing, and he said he hadn't learned it at all; it came natural to him—like other things—other curious things.

"What ones?"

"Oh, a number; I don't know how many."

"Will you let us see you do them?"

"Do—please!" the others said.

"You won't run away again?"

"No—indeed we won't. Please do. Won't you?"

"Yes, with pleasure; but you mustn't forget your promise, you know."

We said we wouldn't, and he went to a puddle and came back with water in a cup which he had made out of a leaf, and blew upon it and threw it out, and it was a lump of ice the shape of the cup. We were astonished and charmed, but not afraid any more; we were very glad to be there, and asked him to go on and do some more things. And he did. He said he would give us any kind of fruit we liked, whether it was in season or not. We all spoke at once:

"Orange!"

"Apple!"

"Grapes!"

"They are in your pockets," he said, and it was true. And they were of the best, too, and we ate them and wished we had more, though none of us said so.

"You will find them where those came from," he said, "and everything else your appetites call for; and you need not name the thing you wish; as long as I am with you, you have only to wish and find."

And he said true. There was never anything so wonderful and so interesting. Bread, cakes, sweets, nuts—whatever one wanted, it was there. He ate nothing himself, but sat and chatted, and did one curious thing after another to amuse us. He made a tiny toy squirrel out of clay, and it ran up a tree and sat on a limb overhead and barked down at us. Then he made a dog that was not much larger than a mouse, and it treed the squirrel and danced about the tree, excited and barking, and was as alive as any dog could be. It frightened the squirrel from tree to tree and followed it up until both were out of sight in the forest. He made birds out of clay and set them free, and they flew away, singing.

At last I made bold to ask him to tell us who he was.

"An angel," he said, quite simply, and set another bird free and clapped his hands and made it fly away.

A kind of awe fell upon us when we heard him say that, and we were afraid again; but he said we need not be troubled, there was no occasion for us to be afraid of an angel, and he liked us, anyway. He went on chatting as simply and unaffectedly as ever; and while he talked he made a crowd of little men and women the size of your finger, and they went diligently to work and cleared and leveled off a space a couple of yards square in the grass and began to build a cunning little castle in it, the women mixing the mortar and carrying it up the scaffoldings in pails on their heads, just as our work-women have always done, and the men laying the courses of masonry—five hundred of these toy people swarming briskly about and working diligently and wiping the sweat off their faces as natural as life. In the absorbing interest of watching those five hundred little people make the castle grow step by step and course by course, and take shape and symmetry, that feeling and awe soon passed away and we were quite comfortable and at home again. We asked if we might make some people, and he said yes, and told Seppi to make some cannon for the walls, and told Nikolaus to make some halberdiers,[1] with breastplates and greaves and helmets, and I was to make some cavalry, with horses, and in allotting these tasks he called us by our names, but did not say how he knew them. Then Seppi asked him what his own name was, and he said, tranquilly, "Satan," and held out a chip and caught a little woman on it who was falling

---

1. Soldiers bearing halberds or halberts, long-handled weapons combining spear and battle-ax. "Greaves": leg armor, worn below the knee.

from the scaffolding and put her back where she belonged, and said, "She is an idiot to step backward like that and not notice what she is about."

It caught us suddenly, that name did, and our work dropped out of our hands and broke to pieces—a cannon, a halberdier, and a horse. Satan laughed, and asked what was the matter. I said, "Nothing, only it seemed a strange name for an angel." He asked why.

"Because it's—it's—well, it's his name, you know."

"Yes—he is my uncle."

He said it placidly, but it took our breath for a moment and made our hearts beat. He did not seem to notice that, but mended our halberdiers and things with a touch, handing them to us finished, and said, "Don't you remember?—he was an angel himself, once."

"Yes—it's true," said Seppi; "I didn't think of that."

"Before the Fall[2] he was blameless."

"Yes," said Nikolaus, "he was without sin."

"It is a good family—ours," said Satan; "there is not a better. He is the only member of it that has ever sinned."

I should not be able to make any one understand how exciting it all was. You know that kind of quiver that trembles around through you when you are seeing something so strange and enchanting and wonderful that it is just a fearful joy to be alive and look at it; and you know how you gaze, and your lips turn dry and your breath comes short, but you wouldn't be anywhere but there, not for the world. I was bursting to ask one question— I had it on my tongue's end and could hardly hold it back—but I was ashamed to ask it; it might be a rudeness. Satan set an ox down that he had been making, and smiled up at me and said:

"It wouldn't be a rudeness, and I should forgive it if it was. Have I seen him? Millions of times. From the time that I was a little child a thousand years old I was his second favorite among the nursery angels of our blood and lineage—to use a human phrase —yes, from that time until the Fall, eight thousand years, measured as you count time."

"Eight—thousand!"

"Yes." He turned to Seppi, and went on as if answering something that was in Seppi's mind: "Why, naturally I look like a boy, for that is what I am. With us what you call time is a spacious thing; it takes a long stretch of it to grow an angel to full age." There was a question in my mind, and he turned to me and answered it, "I am sixteen thousand years old—counting as you count." Then he turned to Nikolaus and said: "No, the Fall

2. The fall of Lucifer, not the Fall of Man. See Isaiah xiv.12–15.

did not affect me nor the rest of the relationship. It was only he that I was named for who ate of the fruit of the tree and then beguiled the man and the woman with it. We others are still ignorant of sin; we are not able to commit it; we are without blemish, and shall abide in that estate always. We—" Two of the little workmen were quarreling, and in buzzing little bumblebee voices they were cursing and swearing at each other; now came blows and blood; then they locked themselves together in a life-and-death struggle. Satan reached out his hand and crushed the life out of them with his fingers, threw them away, wiped the red from his fingers on his handkerchief, and went on talking where he had left off: "We cannot do wrong; neither have we any disposition to do it, for we do not know what it is."

It seemed a strange speech, in the circumstances, but we barely noticed that, we were so shocked and grieved at the wanton murder he had committed—for murder it was, that was its true name, and it was without palliation or excuse, for the men had not wronged him in any way. It made us miserable, for we loved him, and had thought him so noble and so beautiful and gracious, and had honestly believed he was an angel; and to have him do this cruel thing—ah, it lowered him so, and we had had such pride in him. He went right on talking, just as if nothing had happened, telling about his travels, and the interesting things he had seen in the big worlds of our solar systems and of other solar systems far away in the remotenesses of space, and about the customs of the immortals that inhabit them, somehow fascinating us, enchanting us, charming us in spite of the pitiful scene that was now under our eyes, for the wives of the little dead men had found the crushed and shapeless bodies and were crying over them, and sobbing and lamenting, and a priest was kneeling there with his hands crossed upon his breast, praying; and crowds and crowds of pitying friends were massed about them, reverently uncovered, with their bare heads bowed, and many with the tears running down—a scene which Satan paid no attention to until a small noise of the weeping and praying began to annoy him, then he reached out and took the heavy board seat out of our swing and brought it down and mashed all those people into the earth just as if they had been flies, and went on talking just the same.

An angel, and kill a priest! An angel who did not know how to do wrong, and yet destroys in cold blood hundreds of helpless poor men and women who had never done him any harm! It made us sick to see that awful deed, and to think that none of those poor creatures was prepared except the priest, for none of them had ever heard a mass or seen a church. And we were witnesses; we had seen these murders done and it was our duty to tell, and let the law take its course.

But he went on talking right along, and worked his enchantments upon us again with that fatal music of his voice. He made us forget everything; we could only listen to him, and love him, and be his slaves, to do with us as he would. He made us drunk with the joy of being with him, and of looking into the heaven of his eyes, and of feeling the ecstasy that thrilled along our veins from the touch of his hand.

Chapter III

The Stranger had seen everything, he had been everywhere, he knew everything, and he forgot nothing. What another must study, he learned at a glance; there were no difficulties for him. And he made things live before you when he told about them. He saw the world made; he saw Adam created; he saw Samson surge against the pillars and bring the temple down in ruins about him; he saw Cæsar's death; he told of the daily life in heaven; he had seen the damned writhing in the red waves of hell; and he made us see all these things, and it was as if we were on the spot and looking at them with our own eyes. And we felt them, too, but there was no sign that they were anything to him beyond mere entertainments. Those visions of hell, those poor babes and women and girls and lads and men shrieking and supplicating in anguish —why, we could hardly bear it, but he was as bland about it as if it had been so many imitation rats in an artificial fire.

And always when he was talking about men and women here on the earth and their doings—even their grandest and sublimest —we were secretly ashamed, for his manner showed that to him they and their doings were of paltry poor consequence; often you would think he was talking about flies, if you didn't know. Once he even said, in so many words, that our people down here were quite interesting to him, notwithstanding they were so dull and ignorant and trivial and conceited, and so diseased and rickety, and such a shabby, poor, worthless lot all around. He said it in a quite matter-of-course way and without bitterness, just as a person might talk about bricks or manure or any other thing that was of no consequence and hadn't feelings. I could see he meant no offense, but in my thoughts I set it down as not very good manners.

"Manners!" he said. "Why, it is merely the truth, and truth is good manners; manners are a fiction. The castle is done. Do you like it?"

Any one would have been obliged to like it. It was lovely to look at, it was so shapely and fine, and so cunningly perfect in all its particulars, even to the little flags waving from the turrets. Satan said we must put the artillery in place now, and station the halberdiers and display the cavalry. Our men and horses were a spectacle to see, they were so little like what they were intended for; for, of course, we had no art in making such things. Satan said they were the worst he had seen; and when he touched them and made them alive, it was just ridiculous the way they acted, on account of their legs not being of uniform lengths. They reeled and sprawled around as if they were drunk, and endangered everybody's lives around them, and finally fell over and lay helpless and kicking. It made us all laugh, though it was a shameful thing to see. The guns were charged with dirt, to fire a salute, but they were so crooked and so badly made that they all burst when they went off, and killed some of the gunners and crippled the others. Satan said we would have a storm now, and an earthquake, if we liked, but we must stand off a piece, out of danger. We wanted to call the people away, too, but he said never mind them; they were of no consequence, and we could make more, some time or other, if we needed them.

A small storm-cloud began to settle down black over the castle, and the miniature lightning and thunder began to play, and the ground to quiver, and the wind to pipe and wheeze, and the rain to fall, and all the people flocked into the castle for shelter. The cloud settled down blacker and blacker, and one could see the castle only dimly through it; the lightning blazed out flash upon flash and pierced the castle and set it on fire, and the flames shone out red and fierce through the cloud, and the people came flying out, shrieking, but Satan brushed them back, paying no attention to our begging and crying and imploring; and in the midst of the howling of the wind and volleying of the thunder the magazine blew up, the earthquake rent the ground wide, and the castle's wreck and ruin tumbled into the chasm, which swallowed it from sight, and closed upon it, with all that innocent life, not one of the five hundred poor creatures escaping. Our hearts were broken; we could not keep from crying.

"Don't cry," Satan said; "they were of no value."

"But they are gone to hell!"

"Oh, it is no matter; we can make plenty more."

It was of no use to try to move him; evidently he was wholly without feeling, and could not understand. He was full of bubbling spirits, and as gay as if this were a wedding instead of a fiendish massacre. And he was bent on making us feel as he did, and of course his magic accomplished his desire. It was no trouble to him; he did whatever he pleased with us. In a little while we were dancing on that grave, and he was playing to us on a strange, sweet instrument which he took out of his pocket; and the music—but there is no music like that, unless perhaps in heaven, and that was where he brought it from, he said. It made one mad, for pleasure; and we could not take our eyes from him, and the looks that went out of our eyes came from our hearts, and their dumb speech was worship. He brought the dance from heaven, too, and the bliss of paradise was in it.

Presently he said he must go away on an errand. But we could not bear the thought of it, and clung to him, and pleaded with him to stay; and that pleased him, and he said so, and said he would not go yet, but would wait a little while and we would sit down and talk a few minutes longer; and he told us Satan was only his real name, and he was to be known by it to us alone, but he had chosen another one to be called by in the presence of others; just a common one, such as people have—Philip Traum.

It sounded so odd and mean for such a being! But it was his decision, and we said nothing; his decision was sufficient.

We had seen wonders this day; and my thoughts began to run on the pleasure it would be to tell them when I got home, but he noticed those thoughts, and said:

"No, all these matters are a secret among us four. I do not mind your trying to tell them, if you like, but I will protect your tongues, and nothing of the secret will escape from them."

It was a disappointment, but it couldn't be helped, and it cost us a sigh or two. We talked pleasantly along, and he was always reading our thoughts and responding to them, and it seemed to me that this was the most wonderful of all the things he did, but he interrupted my musings and said:

"No, it would be wonderful for you, but it is not wonderful for me. I am not limited like you. I am not subject to human conditions. I can measure and understand your human weaknesses, for I have studied them; but I have none of them. My flesh is not real, although it would seem firm to your touch; my clothes are not real; I am a spirit. Father Peter is coming." We looked around, but did not see any one. "He is not in sight yet, but you will see him presently."

"Do you know him, Satan?"

"No."

"Won't you talk with him when he comes? He is not ignorant and dull, like us, and he would so like to talk with you. Will you?"

"Another time, yes, but not now. I must go on my errand after a little. There he is now; you can see him. Sit still, and don't say anything."

We looked up and saw Father Peter approaching through the chestnuts. We three were sitting together in the grass, and Satan sat in front of us in the path. Father Peter came slowly along with his head down, thinking, and stopped within a couple of yards of us and took off his hat and got out his silk handkerchief, and stood there mopping his face and looking as if he were going to speak to us, but he didn't. Presently he muttered, "I can't think what brought me here; it seems as if I were in my study a minute ago—but I suppose I have been dreaming along for an hour and have come all this stretch without noticing; for I am not myself in these troubled days." Then he went mumbling along to himself and walked straight through Satan, just as if nothing were there. It made us catch our breath to see it. We had the impulse to cry out, the way you nearly always do when a startling thing happens, but something mysteriously restrained us and we remained quiet, only breathing fast. Then the trees hid Father Peter after a little, and Satan said:

"It is as I told you—I am only a spirit."

"Yes, one perceives it now," said Nikolaus, "but we are not spirits. It is plain he did not see you, but were we invisible, too? He looked at us, but he didn't seem to see us."

"No, none of us was visible to him, for I wished it so."

It seemed almost too good to be true, that we were actually seeing these romantic and wonderful things, and that it was not a dream. And there he sat, looking just like anybody—so natural and simple and charming, and chatting along again the same as ever, and—well, words cannot make you understand what we felt. It was an ecstasy; and an ecstasy is a thing that will not go into words; it feels like music, and one cannot tell about music so that another person can get the feeling of it. He was back in the old ages once more now, and making them live before us. He had seen so much, so much! It was just a wonder to look at him and try to think how it must seem to have such experience behind one.

But it made you seem sorrowfully trivial, and the creature of a day, and such a short and paltry day, too. And he didn't say anything to raise up your drooping pride—no, not a word. He always spoke of men in the same old indifferent way—just as one speaks of bricks and manure-piles and such things; you could see that they were of no consequence to him, one way or the other. He didn't mean to hurt us, you could see that; just as we don't mean to insult a brick when we disparage it; a brick's emotions are nothing to us; it never occurs to us to think whether it has any or not.

Once when he was bunching the most illustrious kings and conquerors and poets and prophets and pirates and beggars together—just a brick-pile—I was shamed into putting in a word for man, and asked him why he made so much difference between men and himself. He had to struggle with that a moment; he didn't seem to understand how I could ask such a strange question. Then he said:

"The difference between man and me? The difference between a mortal and an immortal? between a cloud and a spirit?" He picked up a wood-louse that was creeping along a piece of bark: "What is the difference between Cæsar and this?"

I said, "One cannot compare things which by their nature and by the interval between them are not comparable."

"You have answered your own question," he said. "I will expand it. Man is made of dirt—I saw him made. I am not made of dirt. Man is a museum of diseases, a home of impurities; he comes to-day and is gone to-morrow; he begins as dirt and departs as stench; I am of the aristocracy of the Imperishables. And man has the *Moral Sense*. You understand? He has the *Moral Sense*. That would seem to be difference enough between us, all by itself."

He stopped there, as if that settled the matter. I was sorry, for at that time I had but a dim idea of what the Moral Sense was. I merely knew that we were proud of having it, and when he talked like that about it, it wounded me, and I felt as a girl feels who thinks her dearest finery is being admired and then overhears strangers making fun of it. For a while we were all silent, and I, for one, was depressed. Then Satan began to chat again, and soon he was sparkling along in such a cheerful and vivacious vein that my spirits rose once more. He told some very cunning things that put us in a gale of laughter; and when he was telling about the time that Samson tied the torches to the foxes' tails and set them loose in the Philistines' corn,[3] and Samson sitting on the fence slapping his thighs and laughing, with the tears running down his cheeks, and lost his balance and fell off the fence, the memory of that picture got him to laughing, too, and we did have a most lovely and jolly time. By and by he said:

"I am going on my errand now."

"Don't!" we all said. "Don't go; stay with us. You won't come back."

"Yes, I will; I give you my word."

"When? To-night? Say when."

"It won't be long. You will see."

"We like you."

"And I you. And as a proof of it I will show you something fine to see. Usually when I go I merely vanish; but now I will dissolve myself and let you see me do it."

He stood up, and it was quickly finished. He thinned away and thinned away until he was a soap-bubble, except that he kept his

3. Samson was angered because his wife's father had given her to Samson's companion. See Judges xv.4–8.

shape. You could see the bushes through him as clearly as you see things through a soap-bubble, and all over him played and flashed the delicate iridescent colors of the bubble, and along with them was that thing shaped like a window-sash which you always see on the globe of the bubble. You have seen a bubble strike the carpet and lightly bound along two or three times before it bursts. He did that. He sprang—touched the grass—bounded—floated along—touched again—and so on, and presently exploded —puff! and in his place was vacancy.

It was a strange and beautiful thing to see. We did not say anything, but sat wondering and dreaming and blinking; and finally Seppi roused up and said, mournfully sighing:

"I suppose none of it has happened."

Nikolaus sighed and said about the same.

I was miserable to hear them say it, for it was the same cold fear that was in my own mind. Then we saw poor old Father Peter wandering along back, with his head bent down, searching the ground. When he was pretty close to us he looked up and saw us, and said, "How long have you been here, boys?"

"A little while, Father."

"Then it is since I came by, and maybe you can help me. Did you come up by the path?"

"Yes, Father."

"That is good. I came the same way. I have lost my wallet. There wasn't much in it, but a very little is much to me, for it was all I had. I suppose you haven't seen anything of it?"

"No, Father, but we will help you hunt."

"It is what I was going to ask you. Why, here it is!"

We hadn't noticed it; yet there it lay, right where Satan stood when he began to melt—if he did melt and it wasn't a delusion. Father Peter picked it up and looked very much surprised.

"It is mine," he said, "but not the contents. This is fat; mine was flat; mine was light; this is heavy." He opened it; it was stuffed as full as it could hold with gold coins. He let us gaze our fill; and of course we did gaze, for we had never seen so much money at one time before. All our mouths came open to say "Satan did it!" but nothing came out. There it was, you see—we couldn't tell what Satan didn't want told; he had said so himself.

"Boys, did you do this?"

It made us laugh. And it made him laugh, too, as soon as he thought what a foolish question it was.

"Who has been here?"

Our mouths came open to answer, but stood so for a moment, because we couldn't say "Nobody," for it wouldn't be true, and the right word didn't seem to come; then I thought of the right one, and said it:

"Not a human being."

"That is so," said the others, and let their mouths go shut.

"It is not so," said Father Peter, and looked at us very severely. "I came by here a while ago, and there was no one here, but that is nothing; some one has been here since. I don't mean to say that the person didn't pass here before you came, and I don't mean to say you saw him, but some one did pass, that I know. On your honor—you saw no one?"

"Not a human being."

"That is sufficient; I know you are telling me the truth."

He began to count the money on the path, we on our knees eagerly helping to stack it in little piles.

"It's eleven hundred ducats odd!" he said. "Oh dear! if it were only mine—and I need it so!" and his voice broke and his lips quivered.

"It is yours, sir!" we all cried out at once, "every heller!"[4]

"No—it isn't mine. Only four ducats are mine; the rest . . . !" He fell to dreaming, poor old soul, and caressing some of the coins in his hands, and forgot where he was, sitting there on his heels with his old gray head bare; it was pitiful to see. "No," he said, waking up, "it isn't mine. I can't account for it. I think some enemy . . . it must be a trap."

Nikolaus said: "Father Peter, with the exception of the astrologer you haven't a real enemy in the village—nor Marget, either. And not even a half-enemy that's rich enough to chance eleven hundred ducats to do you a mean turn. I'll ask you if that's so or not?"

He couldn't get around that argument, and it cheered him up. "But it isn't mine, you see—it isn't mine, in any case."

He said it in a wistful way, like a person that wouldn't be sorry, but glad, if anybody would contradict him.

"It is yours, Father Peter, and we are witness to it. Aren't we, boys?"

"Yes, we are—and we'll stand by it, too."

"Bless your hearts, you do almost persuade me; you do, indeed. If I had only a hundred-odd ducats of it! The house is mortgaged for it, and we've no home for our heads if we don't pay to-morrow. And that four ducats is all we've got in the—"

"It's yours, every bit of it, and you've got to take it—we are bail that it's all right. Aren't we, Theodor? Aren't we, Seppi?"

We two said yes, and Nikolaus stuffed the money back into the shabby old wallet and made the owner take it. So he said he would use two hundred of it, for his house was good enough security for that, and would put the rest at interest till the rightful owner

4. A small copper coin of Austria.

came for it; and on our side we must sign a paper showing how he got the money—a paper to show to the villagers as proof that he had not got out of his troubles dishonestly.

Chapter IV

It made immense talk next day, when Father Peter paid Solomon Isaacs in gold and left the rest of the money with him at interest. Also, there was a pleasant change; many people called at the house to congratulate him, and a number of cool old friends became kind and friendly again; and, to top all, Marget was invited to a party.

And there was no mystery; Father Peter told the whole circumstance just as it happened, and said he could not account for it, only it was the plain hand of Providence, so far as he could see.

One or two shook their heads and said privately it looked more like the hand of Satan; and really that seemed a surprisingly good guess for ignorant people like that. Some came slyly buzzing around and tried to coax us boys to come out and "tell the truth;" and promised they wouldn't ever tell, but only wanted to know for their own satisfaction, because the whole thing was so curious. They even wanted to buy the secret, and pay money for it; and if we could have invented something that would answer—but we couldn't; we hadn't the ingenuity, so we had to let the chance go by, and it was a pity.

We carried that secret around without any trouble, but the other one, the big one, the splendid one, burned the very vitals of us, it was so hot to get out and we so hot to let it out and astonish people with it. But we had to keep it in; in fact, it kept itself in. Satan said it would, and it did. We went off every day and got to ourselves in the woods so that we could talk about Satan, and really that was the only subject we thought of or cared anything about; and day and night we watched for him and hoped he would come, and we got more and more impatient all the time. We hadn't any interest in the other boys any more, and wouldn't take part in their games and enterprises. They seemed so tame, after Satan; and their doings so trifling and commonplace after his adventures in antiquity and the constellations, and his miracles and meltings and explosions, and all that.

During the first day we were in a state of anxiety on account of one thing, and we kept going to Father Peter's house on one pretext or another to keep track of it. That was the gold coin; we were afraid it would crumble and turn to dust, like fairy money. If it did— But it didn't. At the end of the day no complaint had been made about it, so after that we were satisfied that it was real gold, and dropped the anxiety out of our minds.

There was a question which we wanted to ask Father Peter, and finally we went there the second evening, a little diffidently, after drawing straws, and I asked it as casually as I could, though it did not sound as casual as I wanted, because I didn't know how:

"What is the Moral Sense, sir?"

He looked down, surprised, over his great spectacles, and said, "Why, it is the faculty which enables us to distinguish good from evil."

It threw some light, but not a glare, and I was a little disappointed, also to some degree embarrassed. He was waiting for me to go on, so, in default of anything else to say, I asked, "Is it valuable?"

"Valuable? Heavens! lad, it is the one thing that lifts man above the beasts and makes him heir to immortality!"

This did not remind me of anything further to say, so I got out, with the other boys, and we went away with that indefinite sense you have often had of being filled but not fatted. They wanted me to explain, but I was tired.

We passed out through the parlor, and there was Marget at the spinet teaching Marie Lueger.[5] So one of the deserting pupils was back; and an influential one, too; the others would follow. Marget jumped up and ran and thanked us again, with tears in her eyes—this was the third time—for saving her and her uncle from being turned into the street, and we told her again we hadn't done it; but that was her way, she never could be grateful enough for anything a person did for her; so we let her have her say. And as we passed through the garden, there was Wilhelm Meidling sitting there waiting, for it was getting toward the edge of the evening, and he would be asking Marget to take a walk along the river with him when she was done with the lesson. He was a young lawyer, and succeeding fairly well and working his way along, little by little. He was very fond of Marget, and she of him. He had not deserted along with the others, but had stood his ground all through. His faithfulness was not lost on Marget and her uncle. He hadn't so very much talent, but he was handsome and good, and these are a kind of talents themselves and help along. He asked us how the lesson was getting along, and we told him it was about done. And maybe it was so; we didn't know anything about it, but we judged it would please him, and it did, and didn't cost us anything.

5. An autobiographical note; Sam Clemens' older sister Pamela added to the family income by giving piano and guitar lessons; the guitar perhaps suggested the harp for Marget; cf. above, Chapter I.

Chapter V

On the fourth day comes the astrologer from his crumbling old tower up the valley, where he had heard the news, I reckon. He had a private talk with us, and we told him what we could, for we were mightily in dread of him. He sat there studying and studying awhile to himself; then he asked:

"How many ducats did you say?"

"Eleven hundred and seven, sir."

Then he said, as if he were talking to himself: "It is ver-y singular. Yes . . . very strange. A curious coincidence." Then he began to ask questions, and went over the whole ground from the beginning, we answering. By and by he said: "Eleven hundred and six ducats. It is a large sum."

"Seven," said Seppi, correcting him.

"Oh, seven, was it? Of course a ducat more or less isn't of consequence, but you said eleven hundred and six before."

It would not have been safe for us to say he was mistaken, but we knew he was. Nikolaus said, "We ask pardon for the mistake, but we meant to say seven."

"Oh, it is no matter, lad; it was merely that I noticed the discrepancy. It is several days, and you cannot be expected to remember precisely. One is apt to be inexact when there is no particular circumstance to impress the count upon the memory."

"But there was one, sir," said Seppi, eagerly.

"What was it, my son?" asked the astrologer, indifferently.

"First, we all counted the piles of coin, each in turn, and all made it the same—eleven hundred and six. But I had slipped one out, for fun, when the count began, and now I slipped it back and said, 'I think there is a mistake—there are eleven hundred and seven; let us count again.' We did, and of course I was right. They were astonished; then I told how it came about."

The astrologer asked us if this was so, and we said it was.

"That settles it," he said. "I know the thief now. Lads, the money was stolen."

Then he went away, leaving us very much troubled, and wondering what he could mean. In about an hour we found out; for by that time it was all over the village that Father Peter had been arrested for stealing a great sum of money from the astrologer. Everybody's tongue was loose and going. Many said it was not in Father Peter's character and must be a mistake; but the others shook their heads and said misery and want could drive a suffering man to almost anything. About one detail there were no differences; all agreed that Father Peter's account of how the money came into his hands was just about unbelievable—it had such an impossible look. They said it might have come into the astrologer's hands in some such way, but into Father Peter's, never! Our characters began to suffer now. We were Father Peter's only witnesses; how much did he probably pay us to back up his fantastic tale? People talked that kind of talk to us pretty freely and frankly, and were full of scoffings when we begged them to believe really we had told only the truth. Our parents were harder on us than any one else. Our fathers said we were disgracing our families, and they commanded us to purge ourselves of our lie, and there was no limit to their anger when we continued to say we had spoken true. Our mothers cried over us and begged us to give back our bribe and get back our honest names and save our families from shame, and come out and honorably confess. And at last we were so worried and harassed that we tried to tell the whole thing, Satan and all—but no, it wouldn't come out. We were hoping and longing all the time that Satan would come and help us out of our trouble, but there was no sign of him.

Within an hour after the astrologer's talk with us, Father Peter was in prison and the money sealed up and in the hands of the officers of the law. The money was in a bag, and Solomon Isaacs said he had not touched it since he had counted it; his oath was taken that it was the same money, and that the amount was eleven hundred and seven ducats. Father Peter claimed trial by the ecclesiastical court, but our other priest, Father Adolf, said an ecclesiastical court hadn't jurisdiction over a suspended priest. The bishop upheld him. That settled it; the case would go to trial in the civil court. The court would not sit for some time to come. Wilhelm Meidling would be Father Peter's lawyer and do the best he could, of course, but he told us privately that a weak case on his side and all the power and prejudice on the other made the outlook bad.

So Marget's new happiness died a quick death. No friends came to condole with her, and none were expected; an unsigned note withdrew her invitation to the party. There would be no scholars to take lessons. How could she support herself? She could remain in the house, for the mortgage was paid off, though the government and not poor Solomon Isaacs had the mortgage-money in its grip for the present. Old Ursula, who was cook, chambermaid, housekeeper, laundress, and everything else for Father Peter, and had been Marget's nurse in earlier years, said God would provide. But she said that from habit, for she was a good Christian. She meant to help in the providing, to make sure, if she could find a way.

We boys wanted to go and see Marget and show friendliness for her, but our parents were afraid of offending the community and wouldn't let us. The astrologer was going around inflaming everybody against Father Peter, and saying he was an abandoned thief and had stolen eleven hundred and seven gold ducats from him. He said he knew he was a thief from that fact, for it was exactly the sum he had lost and which Father Peter pretended he had "found."

In the afternoon of the fourth day after the catastrophe old Ursula appeared at our house and asked for some washing to do, and begged my mother to keep this secret, to save Marget's pride, who would stop this project if she found it out, yet Marget had not enough to eat and was growing weak. Ursula was growing weak herself, and showed it; and she ate of the food that was offered her like a starving person, but could not be persuaded to carry any home, for Marget would not eat charity food. She took some clothes down to the stream to wash them, but we saw from the window that handling the bat[6] was too much for her strength; so she was called back and a trifle of money offered her, which she was afraid to take lest Marget should suspect; then she took it, saying she would explain that she found it in the road. To keep it from being a lie and damning her soul, she got me to drop it while she watched; then she went along by there and found it, and exclaimed with surprise and joy, and picked it up and went her way. Like the rest of the village, she could tell everyday lies fast enough and without taking any precautions against fire and brimstone on their account; but this was a new kind of lie, and it had a dangerous look because she hadn't had any practice in it. After a week's practice it wouldn't have given her any trouble. It is the way we are made.

I was in trouble, for how would Marget live? Ursula could not find a coin in the road every day—perhaps not even a second one. And I was ashamed, too, for not having been near Marget, and she so in need of friends; but that was my parents' fault, not mine, and I couldn't help it.

I was walking along the path, feeling very downhearted, when a most cheery and tingling freshening-up sensation went rippling through me, and I was too glad for any words, for I knew by that sign that Satan was by. I had noticed it before. Next moment he was alongside of me and I was telling him all my trouble and what had been happening to Marget and her uncle. While we were talking we turned a curve and saw old Ursula resting in the shade of a tree, and she had a lean stray kitten in her lap and was petting it. I asked her where she got it, and she said it came out of the woods and followed her; and she said it probably hadn't any mother or any friends and she was going to take it home and

6. A piece of wood shaped for pounding clothes in a stream.

take care of it. Satan said:

"I understand you are very poor. Why do you want to add another mouth to feed? Why don't you give it to some rich person?"

Ursula bridled at this and said: "Perhaps you would like to have it. You must be rich, with your fine clothes and quality airs." Then she sniffed and said: "Give it to the rich—the idea! The rich don't care for anybody but themselves; it's only the poor that have feeling for the poor, and help them. The poor and God. God will provide for this kitten."

"What makes you think so?"

Ursula's eyes snapped with anger. "Because I know it!" she said. "Not a sparrow falls to the ground without His seeing it."

"But it falls, just the same. What good is seeing it fall?"

Old Ursula's jaws worked, but she could not get any word out for the moment, she was so horrified. When she got her tongue she stormed out, "Go about your business, you puppy, or I will take a stick to you!"

I could not speak, I was so scared. I knew that with his notions about the human race Satan would consider it a matter of no consequence to strike her dead, there being "plenty more;" but my tongue stood still, I could give her no warning. But nothing happened; Satan remained tranquil—tranquil and indifferent. I suppose he could not be insulted by Ursula any more than the king could be insulted by a tumble-bug. The old woman jumped to her feet when she made her remark, and did it as briskly as a young girl. It had been many years since she had done the like of that. That was Satan's influence; he was a fresh breeze to the weak and the sick, wherever he came. His presence affected even the lean kitten, and it skipped to the ground and began to chase a leaf. This surprised Ursula, and she stood looking at the creature and nodding her head wonderingly, her anger quite forgotten.

"What's come over it?" she said. "Awhile ago it could hardly walk."

"You have not seen a kitten of that breed before," said Satan.

Ursula was not proposing to be friendly with the mocking stranger, and she gave him an ungentle look and retorted: "Who asked you to come here and pester me, I'd like to know? And what do you know about what I've seen and what I haven't seen?"

"You haven't seen a kitten with the hair-spines on its tongue pointing to the front, have you?"

"No—nor you, either."

"Well, examine this one and see."

Ursula was become pretty spry, but the kitten was spryer, and she could not catch it, and had to give it up. Then Satan said:

"Give it a name, and maybe it will come."

Ursula tried several names, but the kitten was not interested.

"Call it Agnes. Try that."

The creature answered to the name and came. Ursula examined its tongue. "Upon my word, it's true!" she said. "I have not seen this kind of a cat before. Is it yours?"

"No."

"Then how did you know its name so pat?"

"Because all cats of that breed are named Agnes; they will not answer to any other."

Ursula was impressed. "It is the most wonderful thing!" Then a shadow of trouble came into her face, for her superstitions were aroused, and she reluctantly put the creature down, saying: "I suppose I must let it go; I am not afraid—no, not exactly that, though the priest—well, I've heard people—indeed, many people . . . And, besides, it is quite well now and can take care of itself." She sighed, and turned to go, murmuring: "It is such a pretty one, too, and would be such company—and the house is so sad and lonesome these troubled days . . . Miss Marget so mournful and just a shadow, and the old master shut up in jail."

"It seems a pity not to keep it," said Satan.

Ursula turned quickly—just as if she were hoping some one would encourage her.

"Why?" she asked, wistfully.

"Because this breed brings luck."

"Does it? Is it true? Young man, do you know it to be true? How does it bring luck?"

"Well, it brings money, anyway."

Ursula looked disappointed. "Money? A cat bring money? The idea! You could never sell it here; people do not buy cats here; one can't even give them away." She turned to go.

"I don't mean sell it. I mean have an income from it. This kind is called the Lucky Cat. Its owner finds four silver groschen[7] in his pocket every morning."

I saw the indignation rising in the old woman's face. She was insulted. This boy was making fun of her. That was her thought. She thrust her hands into her pockets and straightened up to give him a piece of her mind. Her temper was all up, and hot. Her mouth came open and let out three words of a bitter sentence, . . . then it fell silent, and the anger in her face turned to surprise or wonder or fear, or something, and she slowly brought out her hands from her pockets and opened them and held them so. In one was my piece of money, in the other lay four silver groschen. She gazed a little while, perhaps to see if the groschen

7. A silver coin (varying in value).

would vanish away; then she said, fervently:

"It's true—it's true—and I'm ashamed and beg forgiveness, O dear master and benefactor!" And she ran to Satan and kissed his hand, over and over again, according to the Austrian custom.

In her heart she probably believed it was a witch-cat and an agent of the Devil; but no matter, it was all the more certain to be able to keep its contract and furnish a daily good living for the family, for in matters of finance even the piousest of our peasants would have more confidence in an arrangement with the Devil than with an archangel. Ursula started homeward, with Agnes in her arms, and I said I wished I had her privilege of seeing Marget.

Then I caught my breath, for we were there. There in the parlor, and Marget standing looking at us, astonished. She was feeble and pale, but I knew that those conditions would not last in Satan's atmosphere, and it turned out so. I introduced Satan— that is, Philip Traum—and we sat down and talked. There was no constraint. We were simple folk, in our village, and when a stranger was a pleasant person we were soon friends. Marget wondered how we got in without her hearing us. Traum said the door was open, and we walked in and waited until she should turn around and greet us. This was not true; no door was open; we entered through the walls or the roof or down the chimney, or somehow; but no matter, what Satan wished a person to believe, the person was sure to believe, and so Marget was quite satisfied with that explanation. And then the main part of her mind was on Traum, anyway; she couldn't keep her eyes off him, he was so beautiful. That gratified me, and made me proud. I hoped he would show off some, but he didn't. He seemed only interested in being friendly and telling lies. He said he was an orphan. That made Marget pity him. The water came into her eyes. He said he had never known his mamma; she passed away while he was a young thing; and said his papa was in shattered health, and had no property to speak of—in fact, none of any earthly value—but he had an uncle in business down in the tropics, and he was very well off and had a monopoly, and it was from this uncle that he drew his support. The very mention of a kind uncle was enough to remind Marget of her own, and her eyes filled again. She said she hoped their two uncles would meet, some day. It made me shudder. Philip said he hoped so, too; and that made me shudder again.

"Maybe they will," said Marget. "Does your uncle travel much?"

"Oh yes, he goes all about; he has business everywhere."

And so they went on chatting, and poor Marget forgot her sorrow for one little while, anyway. It was probably the only really bright and cheery hour she had known lately. I saw she liked

Philip, and I knew she would. And when he told her he was studying for the ministry I could see that she liked him better than ever. And then, when he promised to get her admitted to the jail so that she could see her uncle, that was the capstone. He said he would give the guards a little present, and she must always go in the evening after dark, and say nothing, "but just show this paper and pass in, and show it again when you come out"—and he scribbled some queer marks on the paper and gave it to her, and she was ever so thankful, and right away was in a fever for the sun to go down; for in that old, cruel time prisoners were not allowed to see their friends, and sometimes they spent years in the jails without ever seeing a friendly face. I judged that the marks on the paper were an enchantment, and that the guards would not know what they were doing, nor have any memory of it afterward; and that was indeed the way of it. Ursula put her head in at the door now and said:

"Supper's ready, miss." Then she saw us and looked frightened, and motioned me to come to her, which I did, and she asked if we had told about the cat. I said no, and she was relieved, and said please don't; for if Miss Marget knew, she would think it was an unholy cat and would send for a priest and have its gifts all purified out of it, and then there wouldn't be any more dividends. So I said we wouldn't tell, and she was satisfied. Then I was beginning to say good-by to Marget, but Satan interrupted and said, ever so politely—well, I don't remember just the words, but anyway he as good as invited himself to supper, and me, too. Of course Marget was miserably embarrassed, for she had no reason to suppose there would be half enough for a sick bird. Ursula heard him, and she came straight into the room, not a bit pleased. At first she was astonished to see Marget looking so fresh and rosy, and said so; then she spoke up in her native tongue, which was Bohemian, and said—as I learned afterward—"Send him away, Miss Marget; there's not victuals enough."

Before Marget could speak, Satan had the word, and was talking back to Ursula in her own language—which was a surprise to her, and for her mistress, too. He said, "Didn't I see you down the road awhile ago?"

"Yes, sir."

"Ah, that pleases me; I see you remember me." He stepped to her and whispered: "I told you it is a Lucky Cat. Don't be troubled; it will provide."

That sponged the slate of Ursula's feelings clean of its anxieties, and a deep, financial joy shone in her eyes. The cat's value was augmenting. It was getting full time for Marget to take some sort of notice of Satan's invitation, and she did it in the best way, the honest way that was natural to her. She said she had little to offer, but that we were welcome if we would share it with her.

We had supper in the kitchen, and Ursula waited at table. A small fish was in the frying-pan, crisp and brown and tempting, and one could see that Marget was not expecting such respectable food as this. Ursula brought it, and Marget divided it between Satan and me, declining to take any of it herself; and was beginning to say she did not care for fish to-day, but she did not finish the remark. It was because she noticed that another fish had appeared in the pan. She looked surprised, but did not say anything. She probably meant to inquire of Ursula about this later. There were other surprises: flesh and game and wines and fruits—things which had been strangers in that house lately; but Marget made no exclamations, and now even looked unsurprised, which was Satan's influence, of course. Satan talked right along, and was entertaining, and made the time pass pleasantly and cheerfully; and although he told a good many lies, it was no harm in him, for he was only an angel and did not know any better. They do not know right from wrong; I knew this, because I remembered what he had said about it. He got on the good side of Ursula. He praised her to Marget, confidentially, but speaking just loud enough for Ursula to hear. He said she was a fine woman, and he hoped some day to bring her and his uncle together. Very soon Ursula was mincing and simpering around in a ridiculous girly way, and smoothing out her gown and prinking at herself like a foolish old hen, and all the time pretending she was not hearing what Satan was saying. I was ashamed, for it showed us to be what Satan considered us, a silly race and trivial. Satan said his uncle entertained a great deal, and to have a clever woman presiding over the festivities would double the attractions of the place.

"But your uncle is a gentleman, isn't he?" asked Marget.

"Yes," said Satan indifferently; "some even call him a Prince, out of compliment, but he is not bigoted; to him personal merit is everything, rank nothing."

My hand was hanging down by my chair; Agnes came along and licked it; by this act a secret was revealed. I started to say, "It is all a mistake; this is just a common, ordinary cat; the hair-needles on her tongue point inward, not outward." But the words did not come, because they couldn't. Satan smiled upon me, and I understood.

When it was dark Marget took food and wine and fruit, in a basket, and hurried away to the jail, and Satan and I walked toward my home. I was thinking to myself that I should like to see what the inside of the jail was like; Satan overheard the thought, and the next moment we were in the jail. We were in the torture-chamber, Satan said. The rack was there, and the other instruments, and there was a smoky lantern or two hanging on the walls and helping to make the place look dim and dreadful. There were people there—and executioners—but as they took no notice of us, it meant that we were invisible. A young man lay bound, and Satan said he was suspected of being a heretic, and the executioners were about to inquire into it. They asked the man to confess to the charge, and he said he could not, for it was not true. Then they drove splinter after splinter under his nails, and he shrieked with the pain. Satan was not disturbed, but I could not endure it, and had to be whisked out of there. I was faint and sick, but the fresh air revived me, and we walked toward my home. I said it was a brutal thing.

"No, it was a human thing. You should not insult the brutes by such a misuse of that word; they have not deserved it," and he went on talking like that. "It is like your paltry race—always lying, always claiming virtues which it hasn't got, always denying them to the higher animals, which alone possess them. No brute ever does a cruel thing—that is the monopoly of those with the Moral Sense. When a brute inflicts pain he does it innocently; it is not wrong; for him there is no such thing as wrong. And he does not inflict pain for the pleasure of inflicting it—only man does that. Inspired by that mongrel Moral Sense of his! A sense whose function is to distinguish between right and wrong, with liberty to chose which of them he will do. Now what advantage can he get out of that? He is always choosing, and in nine cases out of ten he prefers the wrong. There shouldn't be any wrong; and without the Moral Sense there couldn't be any. And yet he is such an unreasoning creature that he is not able to perceive that the Moral Sense degrades him to the bottom layer of animated beings and is a shameful possession. Are you feeling better? Let me show you something."

Chapter VI

In a moment we were in a French village. We walked through a great factory of some sort, where men and women and little children were toiling in heat and dirt and a fog of dust; and they were clothed in rags, and drooped at their work, for they were worn and half starved, and weak and drowsy. Satan said:

"It is some more Moral Sense. The proprietors are rich, and very holy; but the wage they pay to these poor brothers and sisters of theirs is only enough to keep them from dropping dead with hunger. The work-hours are fourteen per day, winter and summer —from six in the morning till eight at night—little children and all. And they walk to and from the pigsties which they inhabit—four miles each way, through mud and slush, rain, snow, sleet, and storm, daily, year in and year out. They get four hours of sleep. They kennel together, three families in a room, in unimaginable filth and stench; and disease comes, and they die off like flies. Have they committed a crime, these mangy things? No. What have they done, that they are punished so? Nothing at all, except getting themselves born into your foolish race. You have seen how they treat a misdoer there in the jail; now you see how they treat the innocent and the worthy. Is your race logical? Are these ill-smelling innocents better off than that heretic? Indeed, no; his punishment is trivial compared with theirs. They broke him on the wheel and smashed him to rags and pulp after we left, and he is dead now, and free of your precious race; but these poor slaves here—why, they have been dying for years, and some of them will not escape from life for years to come. It is the Moral Sense which teaches the factory proprietors the difference between right and wrong—you perceive the result. They think themselves better than dogs. Ah, you are such an illogical, unreasoning race! And paltry—oh, unspeakably!"

Then he dropped all seriousness and just over-strained himself making fun of us, and deriding our pride in our warlike deeds, our great heroes, our imperishable fames, our mighty kings, our ancient aristocracies, our venerable history—and laughed and laughed till it was enough to make a person sick to hear him; and finally he sobered a little and said, "But, after all, it is not all ridiculous; there is a sort of pathos about it when one remembers how few are your days, how childish your pomps, and what shadows you are!"

Presently all things vanished suddenly from my sight, and I knew what it meant. The next moment we were walking along in our village; and down toward the river I saw the twinkling lights of the Golden Stag. Then in the dark I heard a joyful cry:

"He's come again!"

It was Seppi Wohlmeyer. He had felt his blood leap and his spirits rise in a way that could mean only one thing, and he knew Satan was near, although it was too dark to see him. He came to us, and we walked along together, and Seppi poured out his gladness like water. It was as if he were a lover and had found his sweetheart who had been lost. Seppi was a smart and animated boy, and had enthusiasm and expression, and was a contrast to Nikolaus and me. He was full of the last new mystery, now—the disappearance of Hans Oppert, the village loafer. People were beginning to be curious about it, he said. He did not say anxious —curious was the right word, and strong enough. No one had seen Hans for a couple of days.

"Not since he did that brutal thing, you know," he said.

"What brutal thing?" It was Satan that asked.

"Well, he is always clubbing his dog, which is a good dog, and his only friend, and is faithful, and loves him, and does no one any harm; and two days ago he was at it again, just for nothing —just for pleasure—and the dog was howling and begging, and Theodor and I begged, too, but he threatened us, and struck the dog again with all his might and knocked one of his eyes out, and he said to us, 'There, I hope you are satisfied now; that's what you have got for him by your damned meddling'—and he laughed, the heartless brute." Seppi's voice trembled with pity and anger. I guessed what Satan would say, and he said it.

"There is that misused word again—that shabby slander. Brutes do not act like that, but only men."

"Well, it was inhuman, anyway."

"No, it wasn't, Seppi; it was human—quite distinctly human. It is not pleasant to hear you libel the higher animals by attributing to them dispositions which they are free from, and which are found nowhere but in the human heart. None of the higher animals is tainted with the disease called the Moral Sense. Purify your language, Seppi; drop those lying phrases out of it."

He spoke pretty sternly—for him—and I was sorry I hadn't warned Seppi to be more particular about the word he used. I knew how he was feeling. He would not want to offend Satan; he would rather offend all his kin. There was an uncomfortable silence, but relief soon came, for that poor dog came along now, with his eye hanging down, and went straight to Satan, and began to moan and mutter brokenly, and Satan began to answer in the same way, and it was plain that they were talking together in the dog language. We all sat down in the grass, in the moonlight, for the clouds were breaking away now, and Satan took the dog's head in his lap and put the eye back in its place, and the dog was comfortable, and he wagged his tail and licked Satan's hand, and looked thankful and said the same; I knew he was saying it, though I did not understand the words. Then the two talked together a bit, and Satan said:

"He says his master was drunk."

"Yes, he was," said we.

"And an hour later he fell over the precipice there beyond the Cliff Pasture."

"We know the place; it is three miles from here."

"And the dog has been often to the village, begging people to go there, but he was only driven away and not listened to."

We remembered it, but hadn't understood what he wanted.

"He only wanted help for the man who had misused him, and

he thought only of that, and has had no food nor sought any. He has watched by his master two nights. What do you think of your race? Is heaven reserved for it, and this dog ruled out, as your teachers tell you? Can your race add anything to this dog's stock of morals and magnanimities?" He spoke to the creature, who jumped up, eager and happy, and apparently ready for orders and impatient to execute them. "Get some men; go with the dog —he will show you that carrion; and take a priest along to arrange about insurance, for death is near."

With the last word he vanished, to our sorrow and disappointment. We got the men and Father Adolf, and we saw the man die. Nobody cared but the dog; he mourned and grieved, and licked the dead face, and could not be comforted. We buried him where he was, and without a coffin, for he had no money, and no friend but the dog. If we had been an hour earlier the priest would have been in time to send that poor creature to heaven, but now he was gone down into the awful fires, to burn forever. It seemed such a pity that in a world where so many people have difficulty to put in their time, one little hour could not have been spared for this poor creature who needed it so much, and to whom it would have made the difference between eternal joy and eternal pain. It gave an appalling idea of the value of an hour, and I thought I could never waste one again without remorse and terror. Seppi was depressed and grieved, and said it must be so much better to be a dog and not run such awful risks. We took this one home with us and kept him for our own. Seppi had a very good thought as we were walking along, and it cheered us up and made us feel much better. He said the dog had forgiven the man that had wronged him so, and maybe God would accept that absolution.

There was a very dull week, now, for Satan did not come, nothing much was going on, and we boys could not venture to go and see Marget, because the nights were moonlit and our parents might find us out if we tried. But we came across Ursula a couple of times taking a walk in the meadows beyond the river to air the cat, and we learned from her that things were going well. She had natty new clothes on and bore a prosperous look. The four groschen a day were arriving without a break, but were not being spent for food and wine and such things—the cat attended to all that.

Marget was enduring her forsakenness and isolation fairly well, all things considered, and was cheerful, by help of Wilhelm Meidling. She spent an hour or two every night in the jail with her uncle, and had fattened him up with the cat's contributions. But she was curious to know more about Philip Traum, and hoped

I would bring him again. Ursula was curious about him herself, and asked a good many questions about his uncle. It made the boys laugh, for I had told them the nonsense Satan had been stuffing her with. She got no satisfaction out of us, our tongues being tied.

Ursula gave us a small item of information: money being plenty now, she had taken on a servant to help about the house and run errands. She tried to tell it in a commonplace, matter-of-course way, but she was so set up by it and so vain of it that her pride in it leaked out pretty plainly. It was beautiful to see her veiled delight in this grandeur, poor old thing, but when he heard the name of the servant we wondered if she had been altogether wise; for although we were young, and often thoughtless, we had fairly good perception on some matters. This boy was Gottfried Narr,[8] a dull, good creature, with no harm in him and nothing against him personally; still, he was under a cloud, and properly so, for it had not been six months since a social blight had mildewed the family—his grandmother had been burned as a witch. When that kind of a malady is in the blood it does not always come out with just one burning. Just now was not a good time for Ursula and Marget to be having dealings with a member of such a family, for the witch-terror had risen higher during the past year than it had ever reached in the memory of the oldest villagers. The mere mention of a witch was almost enough to frighten us out of our wits. This was natural enough, because of late years there were more kinds of witches than there used to be; in old times it had been only old women, but of late years they were of all ages— even children of eight and nine; it was getting so that anybody might turn out to be a familiar of the Devil—age and sex hadn't anything to do with it. In our little region we had tried to extirpate the witches, but the more of them we burned the more of the breed rose up in their places.

Once, in a school for girls only ten miles away, the teachers found that the back of one of the girls was all red and inflamed, and they were greatly frightened, believing it to be the Devil's marks. The girl was scared, and begged them not to denounce her, and said it was only fleas; but of course it would not do to let the matter rest there. All the girls were examined, and eleven out of the fifty were badly marked, the rest less so. A commission was appointed, but the eleven only cried for their mothers and would not confess. Then they were shut up, each by herself, in the dark, and put on black bread and water for ten days and nights; and by that time they were haggard and wild, and their eyes were dry and they did not cry any more, but only sat and mumbled, and

8. *Narr* means "fool."

would not take the food. Then one of them confessed, and said they had often ridden through the air on broomsticks to the witches' Sabbath,[9] and in a bleak place high up in the mountains had danced and drunk and caroused with several hundred other witches and the Evil One, and all had conducted themselves in a scandalous way and had reviled the priests and blasphemed God. That is what she said—not in narrative form, for she was not able to remember any of the details without having them called to her mind one after the other; but the commission did that, for they knew just what questions to ask, they being all written down for the use of witch-commissioners two centuries before. They asked, "Did you do so and so?" and she always said yes, and looked weary and tired, and took no interest in it. And so when the other ten heard that this one confessed, they confessed, too, and answered yes to the questions. Then they were burned at the stake all together, which was just and right; and everybody went from all the countryside to see it. I went, too; but when I saw that one of them was a bonny, sweet girl I used to play with, and looked so pitiful there chained to the stake, and her mother crying over her and devouring her with kisses and clinging around her neck, and saying, "Oh, my God! oh, my God!" it was too dreadful, and I went away.

It was bitter cold weather when Gottfried's grandmother was burned. It was charged that she had cured bad headaches by kneading the person's head and neck with her fingers—as she said—but really by the Devil's help, as everybody knew. They were going to examine her, but she stopped them, and confessed straight off that her power was from the Devil. So they appointed to burn her next morning, early, in our market-square. The officer who was to prepare the fire was there first, and prepared it. She was there next—brought by the constables, who left her and went to fetch another witch. Her family did not come with her. They might be reviled, maybe stoned, if the people were excited. I came, and gave her an apple. She was squatting at the fire, warming herself and waiting; and her old lips and hands were blue with the cold. A stranger came next. He was a traveler, passing through; and he spoke to her gently, and, seeing nobody but me there to hear, said he was sorry for her. And he asked if what she confessed was true, and she said no. He looked surprised and still more sorry then, and asked her:

"Then why did you confess?"

"I am old and very poor," she said, "and I work for my living.

<hr>

9. A meeting of witches and warlocks, usually deep in a forest or high on a mountain, at which blasphemous traves-ties of religious ceremonies are held, often with the Devil as high priest.

There was no way but to confess. If I hadn't they might have set
me free. That would ruin me, for no one would forget that I had
been suspected of being a witch, and so I would get no more work,
and wherever I went they would set the dogs on me. In a little
while I would starve. The fire is best; it is soon over. You have
been good to me, you two, and I thank you."

She snuggled closer to the fire, and put out her hands to warm
them, the snow-flakes descending soft and still on her old gray
head and making it white and whiter. The crowd was gathering
now, and an egg came flying and struck her in the eye, and broke
and ran down her face. There was a laugh at that.

I told Satan all about the eleven girls and the old woman, once,
but it did not affect him. He only said it was the human race, and
what the human race did was of no consequence. And he said he
had seen it made; and it was not made of clay; it was made of
mud—part of it was, anyway. I knew what he meant by that—
the Moral Sense. He saw the thought in my head, and it tickled
him and made him laugh. Then he called a bullock out of a
pasture and petted it and talked with it, and said:

"There—he wouldn't drive children mad with hunger and
fright and loneliness, and then burn them for confessing to things
invented for them which had never happened. And neither would
he break the hearts of innocent, poor old women and make them
afraid to trust themselves among their own race; and he would
not insult them in their death-agony. For he is not besmirched
with the Moral Sense, but is as the angels are, and knows no
wrong, and never does it."

Lovely as he was, Satan could be cruelly offensive when he
chose; and he always chose when the human race was brought to
his attention. He always turned up his nose at it, and never had a
kind word for it.

Well, as I was saying, we boys doubted if it was a good time for
Ursula to be hiring a member of the Narr family. We were right.
When the people found it out they were naturally indignant. And,
moreover, since Marget and Ursula hadn't enough to eat themselves, where was the money coming from to feed another mouth?
That is what they wanted to know; and in order to find out they
stopped avoiding Gottfried and began to seek his society and have
sociable conversations with him. He was pleased—not thinking
any harm and not seeing the trap—and so he talked innocently
along, and was no discreeter than a cow.

"Money!" he said; "they've got plenty of it. They pay me two
groschen a week, besides my keep. And they live on the fat of the
land, I can tell you; the prince himself can't beat their table."

This astonishing statement was conveyed by the astrologer to

Father Adolf on a Sunday morning when he was returning from mass. He was deeply moved, and said:

"This must be looked into."

He said there must be witchcraft at the bottom of it, and told the villagers to resume relations with Marget and Ursula in a private and unostentatious way, and keep both eyes open. They were told to keep their own counsel, and not rouse the suspicions of the household. The villagers were at first a bit reluctant to enter such a dreadful place, but the priest said they would be under his protection while there, and no harm could come to them, particularly if they carried a trifle of holy water along and kept their beads and crosses handy. This satisfied them and made them willing to go; envy and malice made the baser sort even eager to go.

And so poor Marget began to have company again, and was as pleased as a cat. She was like 'most anybody else—just human, and happy in her prosperities and not averse from showing them off a little; and she was humanly grateful to have the warm shoulder turned to her and be smiled upon by her friends and the village again; for of all the hard things to bear, to be cut by your neighbors and left in contemptuous solitude is maybe the hardest.

The bars were down, and we could all go there now, and we did—our parents and all—day after day. The cat began to strain herself. She provided the top of everything for those companies, and in abundance—among them many a dish and many a wine which they had not tasted before and which they had not even heard of except at second-hand from the prince's servants. And the tableware was much above ordinary, too.

Marget was troubled at times, and pursued Ursula with questions to an uncomfortable degree; but Ursula stood her ground and stuck to it that it was Providence, and said no word about the cat. Marget knew that nothing was impossible to Providence, but she could not help having doubts that this effort was from there, though she was afraid to say so, lest disaster come of it. Witchcraft occurred to her, but she put the thought aside, for this was before Gottfried joined the household, and she knew Ursula was pious and a bitter hater of witches. By the time Gottfried arrived Providence was established, unshakably intrenched, and getting all the gratitude. The cat made no murmur, but went on composedly improving in style and prodigality by experience.

In any community, big or little, there is always a fair proportion of people who are not malicious or unkind by nature, and who never do unkind things except when they are overmastered by fear, or when their self-interest is greatly in danger, or some such matter as that. Eseldorf had its proportion of such people, and ordinarily their good and gentle influence was felt, but these were not ordinary times—on account of the witch-dread—and so we did not seem to have any gentle and compassionate hearts left, to speak of. Every person was frightened at the unaccountable state of things at Marget's house, not doubting that witchcraft was at the bottom of it, and fright frenzied their reason. Naturally there were some who pitied Marget and Ursula for the danger that was gathering about them, but naturally they did not say so; it would not have been safe. So the others had it all their own way, and there was none to advise the ignorant girl and the foolish woman and warn them to modify their doings. We boys wanted to warn them, but we backed down when it came to the pinch, being afraid. We found that we were not manly enough nor brave enough to do a generous action when there was a chance that it could get us into trouble. Neither of us confessed this poor spirit to the others, but did as other people would have done—dropped the subject and talked about something else. And I knew we all felt mean, eating and drinking Marget's fine things along with those companies of spies, and petting her and complimenting her with the rest, and seeing with self-reproach how foolishly happy she was, and never saying a word to put her on her guard. And, indeed, she was happy, and as proud as a princess, and so grateful to have friends again. And all the time these people were watching with all their eyes and reporting all they saw to Father Adolf.

But he couldn't make head or tail of the situation. There must be an enchanter somewhere on the premises, but who was it? Marget was not seen to do any jugglery, nor was Ursula, nor yet Gottfried; and still the wines and dainties never ran short, and a guest could not call for a thing and not get it. To produce these effects was usual enough with witches and enchanters—that part of it was not new; but to do it without any incantations, or even any rumblings or earthquakes or lightnings or apparitions—that was new, novel, wholly irregular. There was nothing in the books like this. Enchanted things were always unreal. Gold turned to dirt in an unenchanted atmosphere, food withered away and vanished. But this test failed in the present case. The spies brought samples: Father Adolf prayed over them, exorcised them, but it did no good; they remained sound and real, they yielded to natural decay only, and took the usual time to do it.

Father Adolf was not merely puzzled, he was also exasperated; for these evidences very nearly convinced him—privately—that there was no witchcraft in the matter. It did not wholly convince him, for this could be a new kind of witchcraft. There was a way to find out as to this: if this prodigal abundance of provender was not brought in from the outside, but produced on the premises, there was witchcraft, sure.

Chapter VII

Marget announced a party, and invited forty people; the date for it was seven days away. This was a fine opportunity. Marget's house stood by itself, and it could be easily watched. All the week it was watched night and day. Marget's household went out and in as usual, but they carried nothing in their hands, and neither they nor others brought anything to the house. This was ascertained. Evidently rations for forty people were not being fetched. If they were furnished any sustenance it would have to be made on the premises. It was true that Marget went out with a basket every evening, but the spies ascertained that she always brought it back empty.

The guests arrived at noon and filled the place. Father Adolf followed; also, after a little, the astrologer, without invitation. The spies had informed him that neither at the back nor the front had any parcels been brought in. He entered, and found the eating and drinking going on finely, and everything progressing in a lively and festive way. He glanced around and perceived that many of the cooked delicacies and all of the native and foreign fruits were of a perishable character, and he also recognized that these were fresh and perfect. No apparitions, no incantations, no thunder. That settled it. This was witchcraft. And not only that, but of a new kind—a kind never dreamed of before. It was a prodigious power, an illustrious power; he resolved to discover its secret. The anouncement of it would resound throughout the world, penetrate to the remotest lands, paralyze all the nations with amazement—and carry his name with it, and make him renowned forever. It was a wonderful piece of luck, a splendid piece of luck; the glory of it made him dizzy.

All the house made room for him; Marget politely seated him; Ursula ordered Gottfried to bring a special table for him. Then she decked it and furnished it, and asked for his orders.

"Bring me what you will," he said.

The two servants brought supplies from the pantry, together with white wine and red—a bottle of each. The astrologer, who very likely had never seen such delicacies before, poured out a beaker of red wine, drank it off, poured another, then began to eat with a grand appetite.

I was not expecting Satan, for it was more than a week since I had seen or heard of him, but now he came in—I knew it by the feel, though people were in the way and I could not see him.

I heard him apologizing for intruding; and he was going away, but Marget urged him to stay, and he thanked her and stayed. She brought him along, introducing him to the girls, and to Meidling, and to some of the elders; and there was quite a rustle of whispers: "It's the young stranger we hear so much about and can't get sight of, he is away so much." "Dear, dear, but he is beautiful—what is his name?" "Philip Traum." "Ah, it fits him!" (You see, "Traum" is German for "Dream.") "What does he do?" "Studying for the ministry, they say." "His face is his fortune—he'll be a cardinal some day." "Where is his home?" "Away down somewhere in the tropics, they say—has a rich uncle down there." And so on. He made his way at once; everybody was anxious to know him and talk with him. Everybody noticed how cool and fresh it was, all of a sudden, and wondered at it, for they could see that the sun was beating down the same as before, outside, and the sky was clear of clouds, but no one guessed the reason, of course.

The astrologer had drunk his second beaker; he poured out a third. He set the bottle down, and by accident overturned it. He seized it before much was spilled, and held it up to the light, saying, "What a pity—it is royal wine." Then his face lighted with joy or triumph, or something, and he said, "Quick! Bring a bowl."

It was brought—a four-quart one. He took up that two-pint bottle and began to pour; went on pouring, the red liquor gurgling and gushing into the white bowl and rising higher and higher up its sides, everybody staring and holding their breath—and presently the bowl was full to the brim.

"Look at the bottle," he said, holding it up; "it is full yet!" I glanced at Satan, and in that moment he vanished. Then Father Adolf rose up, flushed and excited, crossed himself, and began to thunder in his great voice, "This house is bewitched and accursed!" People began to cry and shriek and crowd toward the door. "I summon this detected household to—"

His words were cut off short. His face became red, then purple, but he could not utter another sound. Then I saw Satan, a transparent film, melt into the astrologer's body; then the astrologer put up his hand, and apparently in his own voice said, "Wait—remain where you are." All stopped where they stood. "Bring a funnel!" Ursula brought it, trembling and scared, and he stuck it in the bottle and took up the great bowl and began to pour the wine back, the people gazing and dazed with astonishment, for they knew the bottle was already full before he began. He emptied the whole of the bowl into the bottle, then smiled out over the room, chuckled, and said, indifferently: "It is nothing—anybody can do it! With my powers I can even do much more."

A frightened cry burst out everywhere. "Oh, my God, he is possessed!" and there was a tumultuous rush for the door which swiftly emptied the house of all who did not belong in it except us boys and Meidling. We boys knew the secret, and would have told it if we could, but we couldn't. We were very thankful to Satan for furnishing that good help at the needful time.

Marget was pale, and crying; Meidling looked kind of petrified; Ursula the same; but Gottfried was the worst—he couldn't stand, he was so weak and scared. For he was of a witch family, you know, and it would be bad for him to be suspected. Agnes came loafing in, looking pious and unaware, and wanted to rub up against Ursula and be petted, but Ursula was afraid of her and shrank away from her, but pretending she was not meaning any incivility, for she knew very well it wouldn't answer to have strained relations with that kind of a cat. But we boys took Agnes and petted her, for Satan would not have befriended her if he had not had a good opinion of her, and that was indorsement enough for us. He seemed to trust anything that hadn't the Moral Sense.

Outside the guests, panic-stricken, scattered in every direction and fled in a pitiable state of terror; and such a tumult as they made with their running and sobbing and shrieking and shouting that soon all the village came flocking from their houses to see what had happened, and they thronged the street and shouldered and jostled one another in excitement and fright; and then Father Adolf appeared, and they fell apart in two walls like the cloven Red Sea,[1] and presently down this lane the astrologer came striding and mumbling, and where he passed the lanes surged back in packed masses, and fell silent with awe, and their eyes stared and their breasts heaved, and several women fainted; and when he was gone by the crowd swarmed together and followed him at a distance, talking excitedly and asking questions and finding out the facts. Finding out the facts and passing them on to others, with improvements—improvements which soon enlarged the bowl of wine to a barrel, and made the one bottle hold it all and yet remain empty to the last.

When the astrologer reached the market-square he went straight to a juggler, fantastically dressed, who was keeping three brass balls in the air, and took them from him and faced around upon the approaching crowd and said: "This poor clown is ignorant of his art. Come forward and see an expert perform."

So saying, he tossed the balls up one after another and set

---

1. The Lord divided the Red Sea before Moses and the children of Israel, fleeing from the Egyptians, so that they went through on dry land (Exodus xiv.21–23).

them whirling in a slender bright oval in the air, and added another, then another and another, and soon—no one seeing whence he got them—adding, adding, adding, the oval lengthening all the time, his hands moving so swiftly that they were just a web or a blur and not distinguishable as hands; and such as counted said there were now a hundred balls in the air. The spinning great oval reached up twenty feet in the air and was a shining and glinting and wonderful sight. Then he folded his arms and told the balls to go on spinning without his help—and they did it. After a couple of minutes he said, "There, that will do," and the oval broke and came crashing down, and the balls scattered abroad and rolled every whither. And wherever one of them came the people fell back in dread, and no one would touch it. It made him laugh, and he scoffed at the people and called them cowards and old women. Then he turned and saw the tight-rope, and said foolish people were daily wasting their money to see a clumsy and ignorant varlet degrade that beautiful art; now they should see the work of a master. With that he made a spring into the air and lit firm on his feet on the rope. Then he hopped the whole length of it back and forth on one foot, with his hands clasped over his eyes; and next he began to throw somersaults, both backward and forward, and threw twenty-seven.

The people murmured, for the astrologer was old, and always before had been halting of movement and at times even lame, but he was nimble enough now and went on with his antics in the liveliest manner. Finally he sprang lightly down and walked away, and passed up the road and around the corner and disappeared. Then that great, pale, silent, solid crowd drew a deep breath and looked into one another's faces as if they said: "Was it real? Did you see it, or was it only I—and I was dreaming?" Then they broke into a low murmur of talking, and fell apart in couples, and moved toward their homes, still talking in that awed way, with faces close together and laying a hand on an arm and making other such gestures as people make when they have been deeply impressed by something.

We boys followed behind our fathers, and listened, catching all we could of what they said; and when they sat down in our house and continued their talk they still had us for company. They were in a sad mood, for it was certain, they said, that disaster for the village must follow this awful visitation of witches and devils. Then my father remembered that Father Adolf had been struck dumb at the moment of his denunciation.

"They have not ventured to lay their hands upon an anointed servant of God before," he said; "and how they could have dared it this time I cannot make out, for he wore his crucifix. Isn't it so?"

"Yes," said the others, "we saw it."

"It is serious, friends, it is very serious. Always before, we had a protection. It has failed."

The others shook, as with a sort of chill, and muttered those words over—"It has failed." "God has forsaken us."

"It is true," said Seppi Wohlmeyer's father; "there is nowhere to look for help."

"The people will realize this," said Nikolaus's father, the judge, "and despair will take away their courage and their energies. We have indeed fallen upon evil times."

He sighed, and Wohlmeyer said, in a troubled voice: "The report of it all will go about the country, and our village will be shunned as being under the displeasure of God. The Golden Stag will know hard times."

"True, neighbor," said my father; "all of us will suffer—all in repute, many in estate. And, good God!—"

"What is it?"

"That can come—to finish us!"

"Name it—um Gottes Willen!"[2]

"The Interdict!"

It smote like a thunderclap, and they were like to swoon with the terror of it. Then the dread of this calamity roused their energies, and they stopped brooding and began to consider ways to avert it. They discussed this, that, and the other way, and talked till the afternoon was far spent, then confessed that at present they could arrive at no decision. So they parted sorrowfully, with oppressed hearts which were filled with bodings.

While they were saying their parting words I slipped out and set my course for Marget's house to see what was happening there. I met many people, but none of them greeted me. It ought to have been surprising, but it was not, for they were so distraught with fear and dread that they were not in their right minds, I think; they were white and haggard, and walked like persons in a dream, their eyes open but seeing nothing, their lips moving but uttering nothing, and worriedly clasping and unclasping their hands without knowing it.

At Marget's it was like a funeral. She and Wilhelm sat together on the sofa, but said nothing, and not even holding hands. Both were steeped in gloom, and Marget's eyes were red from the crying she had been doing. She said:

2. "For God's sake!" The "Interdict" is a formal ecclesiastical censure, pro- hibiting the sacraments or other privi- leges to certain people or places.

"I have been begging him to go, and come no more, and so save himself alive. I cannot bear to be his murderer. This house is bewitched, and no inmate will escape the fire. But he will not go, and he will be lost with the rest."

Wilhelm said he would not go; if there was danger for her, his place was by her, and there he would remain. Then she began to cry again, and it was all so mournful that I wished I had stayed away. There was a knock, now, and Satan came in, fresh and cheery and beautiful, and brought that winy atmosphere of his and changed the whole thing. He never said a word about what had been happening, nor about the awful fears which were freezing the blood in the hearts of the community, but began to talk and rattle on about all manner of gay and pleasant things: and next about music—an artful stroke which cleared away the remnant of Marget's depression and brought her spirits and her interests broad awake. She had not heard any one talk so well and so knowingly on that subject before, and she was so uplifted by it and so charmed that what she was feeling lit up her face and came out in her words; and Wilhelm noticed it and did not look as pleased as he ought to have done. And next Satan branched off into poetry, and recited some, and did it well, and Marget was charmed again; and again Wilhelm was not as pleased as he ought to have been, and this time Marget noticed it and was remorseful.

I fell asleep to pleasant music that night—the patter of rain upon the panes and the dull growling of distant thunder. Away in the night Satan came and roused me and said: "Come with me. Where shall we go?"

"Anywhere—so it is with you."

Then there was a fierce glare of sunlight, and he said, "This is China."

That was a grand surprise, and made me sort of drunk with vanity and gladness to think I had come so far—so much, much farther than anybody else in our village, including Bartel Sperling, who had such a great opinion of his travels. We buzzed around over that empire for more than half an hour, and saw the whole of it. It was wonderful, the spectacles we saw; and some were beautiful, others too horrible to think. For instance— However, I may go into that by and by, and also why Satan chose China for this excursion instead of another place; it would interrupt my tale to do it now. Finally we stopped flitting and lit.

We sat upon a mountain commanding a vast landscape of mountain-range and gorge and valley and plain and river, with cities and villages slumbering in the sunlight, and a glimpse of blue sea on the farther verge. It was a tranquil and dreamy picture, beautiful to the eye and restful to the spirit. If we could only make a change like that whenever we wanted to, the world would be easier to live in than it is, for change of scene shifts the mind's burdens to the other shoulder and banishes old, shop-worn weariness from mind and body both.

We talked together, and I had the idea of trying to reform Satan and persuade him to lead a better life. I told him about all those things he had been doing, and begged him to be more considerate and stop making people unhappy. I said I knew he did not mean any harm, but that he ought to stop and consider the possible consequences of a thing before launching it in that impulsive and random way of his; then he would not make so much trouble. He was not hurt by this plain speech; he only looked amused and surprised, and said:

"What? I do random things? Indeed, I never do. I stop and consider possible consequences? Where is the need? I know what the consequences are going to be—always."

"Oh, Satan, then how could you do these things?"

"Well, I will tell you, and you must understand if you can. You belong to a singular race. Every man is a suffering-machine and a happiness-machine combined. The two functions work together harmoniously, with a fine and delicate precision, on the give-and-take principle. For every happiness turned out in the one department the other stands ready to modify it with a sorrow or a pain—maybe a dozen. In most cases the man's life is about equally divided between happiness and unhappiness. When this is not the case the unhappiness predominates—always; never the other. Sometimes a man's make and disposition are such that his misery-machine is able to do nearly all the business. Such a man goes through life almost ignorant of what happiness is. Everything he touches, everything he does, brings a misfortune upon him. You have seen such people? To that kind of a person life is not an advantage, is it? It is only a disaster. Sometimes for an hour's happiness a man's machinery makes him pay years of misery. Don't you know that? It happens every now and then. I will give you a case or two presently. Now the people of your village are nothing to me—you know that, don't you?"

I did not like to speak out too flatly, so I said I had suspected it.

"Well, it is true that they are nothing to me. It is not possible that they should be. The difference between them and me is abysmal, immeasurable. They have no intellect."

"No intellect?"

"Nothing that resembles it. At a future time I will examine what man calls his mind and give you the details of that chaos, then you will see and understand. Men have nothing in common with me—there is no point of contact; they have foolish little feelings and foolish little vanities and impertinences and ambitions; their foolish little life is but a laugh, a sigh, and extinction; and they have no sense.[3] Only the Moral Sense. I will show you what I mean. Here is a red spider, not so big as a pin's head. Can you imagine an elephant being interested in him—caring whether he is happy or isn't, or whether he is wealthy or poor, or whether his sweetheart returns his love or not, or whether his mother is sick or well, or whether he is looked up to in society or not, or whether his enemies will smite him or his friends desert him, or whether his hopes will suffer blight or his political ambitions fail, or whether he shall die in the bosom of his family or neglected and despised in a foreign land? These things can never be important to the elephant; they are nothing to him; he cannot shrink his sympathies to the microscopic size of them. Man is to me as the red spider is to the elephant. The elephant has nothing against the spider—he cannot get down to that remote level; I have nothing against man. The elephant is indifferent; I am indifferent. The elephant would not take the trouble to do the spider an ill turn; if he took the notion he might do him a good turn, if it came in his way and cost nothing. I have done men good service, but no ill turns.

"The elephant lives a century, the red spider a day; in power, intellect, and dignity the one creature is separated from the other by a distance which is simply astronomical. Yet in these, as in all qualities, man is immeasurably further below me than is the wee spider below the elephant.

"Man's mind clumsily and tediously and laboriously patches little trivialities together and gets a result—such as it is. My mind creates! Do you get the force of that? Creates anything it desires —and in a moment. Creates without material. Creates fluids, solids, colors—anything, everything—out of the airy nothing which is called Thought. A man imagines a silk thread, imagines a machine to make it, imagines a picture, then by weeks of labor embroiders it on canvas with the thread. I think the whole thing, and in a moment it is before you—created.

"I think a poem, music, the record of a game of chess—anything—and it is there. This is the immortal mind—nothing is beyond its reach. Nothing can obstruct my vision; the rocks are transparent to me, and darkness is daylight. I do not need to open a book; I take the whole of its contents into my mind at a single glance, through the cover; and in a million years I could not forget

3. In 1899 Mark Twain wrote to Howells that he had "put the potboiler pen away" to allow himself the luxury of saying his say in a book without limitations of any sort: "I believe I can make it tell what I think of Man, and how he is constructed, and what a shabby poor ridiculous thing he is." This book, of course, was *The Mysterious Stranger*.

a single word of it, or its place in the volume. Nothing goes on in the skull of man, bird, fish, insect, or other creature which can be hidden from me. I pierce the learned man's brain with a single glance, and the treasures which cost him threescore years to accumulate are mine; he can forget, and he does forget, but I retain.

"Now, then, I perceive by your thoughts that you are understanding me fairly well. Let us proceed. Circumstances might so fall out that the elephant could like the spider—supposing he can see it—but he could not love it. His love is for his own kind—for his equals. An angel's love is sublime, adorable, divine, beyond the imagination of man—infinitely beyond it! But it is limited to his own august order. If it fell upon one of your race for only an instant, it would consume its object to ashes. No, we cannot love men, but we can be harmlessly indifferent to them; we can also like them, sometimes. I like you and the boys, I like Father Peter, and for your sakes I am doing all these things for the villagers."

He saw that I was thinking a sarcasm, and he explained his position.

"I have wrought well for the villagers, though it does not look like it on the surface. Your race never know good fortune from ill. They are always mistaking the one for the other. It is because they cannot see into the future. What I am doing for the villagers will bear good fruit some day; in some cases to themselves; in others, to unborn generations of men. No one will ever know that I was the cause, but it will be none the less true, for all that. Among you boys you have a game: you stand a row of bricks on end a few inches apart; you push a brick, it knocks its neighbor over, the neighbor knocks over the next brick—and so on till all the row is prostrate. That is human life. A child's first act knocks over the initial brick, and the rest will follow inexorably. If you could see into the future, as I can, you would see everything that was going to happen to that creature; for nothing can change the order of its life after the first event has determined it. That is, nothing will change it, because each act unfailingly begets an act, that act begets another, and so on to the end,[4] and the seer can look forward down the line and see just when each act is to have birth, from cradle to grave."

"Does God order the career?"

"Foreordain it? No. The man's circumstances and environment order it. His first act determines the second and all that follow after. But suppose, for argument's sake, that the man should skip one of these acts; an apparently trifling one, for instance; suppose

4. Mark Twain once told Paine, his biographer, that "the first act of the first atom has led inevitably to the act of my standing here in my dressing gown at this instant talking to you."

that it had been appointed that on a certain day, at a certain hour and minute and second and fraction of a second he should go to the well, and he didn't go. That man's career would change utterly, from that moment;[5] thence to the grave it would be wholly different from the career which his first act as a child had arranged for him. Indeed, it might be that if he had gone to the well he would have ended his career on a throne, and that omitting to do it would set him upon a career that would lead to beggary and a pauper's grave. For instance: if at any time—say in boyhood— Columbus had skipped the triflingest little link in the chain of acts projected and made inevitable by his first childish act, it would have changed his whole subsequent life, and he would have become a priest and died obscure in an Italian village, and America would not have been discovered for two centuries afterward. I know this. To skip any one of the billion acts in Columbus's chain would have wholly changed his life. I have examined his billion of possible careers, and in only one of them occurs the discovery of America. You people do not suspect that all of your acts are of one size and importance, but it is true; to snatch at an appointed fly is as big with fate for you as in any other appointed act—"

"As the conquering of a continent, for instance?"

"Yes. Now, then, no man ever does drop a link—the thing has never happened! Even when he is trying to make up his mind as to whether he will do a thing or not, that itself is a link, an act, and has its proper place in his chain; and when he finally decides an act, that also was the thing which he was absolutely certain to do. You see, now, that a man will never drop a link in his chain. He cannot. If he made up his mind to try, that project would itself be an unavoidable link—a thought bound to occur to him at that precise moment, and made certain by the first act of his babyhood."

It seemed so dismal!

"He is a prisoner for life," I said sorrowfully, "and cannot get free."

"No, of himself he cannot get away from the consequences of his first childish act. But I can free him."

I looked up wistfully.

"I have changed the careers of a number of your villagers."

I tried to thank him, but found it difficult, and let it drop.

"I shall make some other changes. You know that little Lisa Brandt?"

"Oh yes, everybody does. My mother says she is so sweet and so

5. He once remarked to Kipling: "Suppose we took the next four-and-twenty years of Tom Sawyer's life, and gave a little joggle to the circumstances that controlled him. He would, logically and according to the joggle, turn out a rip or an angel."

lovely that she is not like any other child. She says she will be the pride of the village when she grows up; and its idol, too, just as she is now."

"I shall change her future."

"Make it better?" I asked.

"Yes. And I will change the future of Nikolaus."

I was glad, this time, and said, "I don't need to ask about his case; you will be sure to do generously by him."

"It is my intention."

Straight off I was building that great future of Nicky's in my imagination, and had already made a renowned general of him and hofmeister[6] at the court, when I noticed that Satan was waiting for me to get ready to listen again. I was ashamed of having exposed my cheap imaginings to him, and was expecting some sarcasms, but it did not happen. He proceeded with his subject:

"Nicky's appointed life is sixty-two years."

"That's grand!" I said.

"Lisa's, thirty-six. But, as I told you, I shall change their lives and those ages. Two minutes and a quarter from now Nikolaus will wake out of his sleep and find the rain blowing in. It was appointed that he should turn over and go to sleep again. But I have appointed that he shall get up and close the window first. That trifle will change his career entirely. He will rise in the morning two minutes later than the chain of his life had appointed him to rise. By consequence, thenceforth nothing will ever happen to him in accordance with the details of the old chain." He took out his watch and sat looking at it a few moments, then said: "Nikolaus has risen to close the window. His life is changed, his new career has begun. There will be consequences."

It made me feel creepy; it was uncanny.

"But for this change certain things would happen twelve days from now. For instance, Nikolaus would save Lisa from drowning. He would arrive on the scene at exactly the right moment—four minutes past ten, the long-ago appointed instant of time—and the water would be shoal, the achievement easy and certain. But he will arrive some seconds too late, now; Lisa will have struggled into deeper water. He will do his best, but both will drown."

"Oh, Satan! oh, dear Satan!" I cried, with the tears rising in my eyes, "save them! Don't let it happen. I can't bear to lose Nikolaus, he is my loving playmate and friend; and think of Lisa's poor mother!"

I clung to him and begged and pleaded, but he was not moved. He made me sit down again, and told me I must hear him out.

"I have changed Nikolaus's life, and this has changed Lisa's. If I

6. Court-master; a post of honor.

had not done this, Nikolaus would save Lisa, then he would catch cold from his drenching; one of your race's fantastic and desolating scarlet fevers would follow, with pathetic after-effects; for forty-six years he would lie in his bed a paralytic log, deaf, dumb, blind, and praying night and day for the blessed relief of death. Shall I change his life back?"

"Oh no! Oh, not for the world! In charity and pity leave it as it is."

"It is best so. I could not have changed any other link in his life and done him so good a service. He had a billion possible careers, but not one of them was worth living; they were charged full with miseries and disasters. But for my intervention he would do his brave deed twelve days from now—a deed begun and ended in six minutes—and get for all reward those forty-six years of sorrow and suffering I told you of. It is one of the cases I was thinking of awhile ago when I said that sometimes an act which brings the actor an hour's happiness and self-satisfaction is paid for—or punished—by years of suffering."

I wondered what poor little Lisa's early death would save her from. He answered the thought:

"From ten years of pain and slow recovery from an accident, and then from nineteen years' pollution, shame, depravity, crime, ending with death at the hands of the executioner. Twelve days hence she will die; her mother would save her life if she could. Am I not kinder than her mother?"

"Yes—oh, indeed yes; and wiser."

"Father Peter's case is coming on presently. He will be acquitted, through unassailable proofs of his innocence."

"Why, Satan, how can that be? Do you really think it?"

"Indeed, I know it. His good name will be restored, and the rest of his life will be happy."

"I can believe it. To restore his good name will have that effect."

"His happiness will not proceed from that cause. I shall change his life that day, for his good. He will never know his good name has been restored."

In my mind—and modestly—I asked for particulars, but Satan paid no attention to my thought. Next, my mind wandered to the astrologer, and I wondered where he might be.

"In the moon," said Satan, with a fleeting sound which I believed was a chuckle. "I've got him on the cold side of it, too. He doesn't know where he is, and is not having a pleasant time; still, it is good enough for him, a good place for his star studies. I shall need him presently; then I shall bring him back and possess him again. He has a long and cruel and odious life before him, but I will change that, for I have no feeling against him and am quite willing to do him a kindness. I think I shall get him burned."

He had such strange notions of kindness! But angels are made so, and do not know any better. Their ways are not like our ways; and, besides, human beings are nothing to them; they think they are only freaks. It seemed to me odd that he should put the astrologer so far away; he could have dumped him in Germany just as well, where he would be handy.

"Far away?" said Satan. "To me no place is far away; distance does not exist for me. The sun is less than a hundred million miles from here, and the light that is falling upon us has taken eight minutes to come; but I can make that flight, or any other, in a fraction of time so minute that it cannot be measured by a watch. I have but to think the journey, and it is accomplished."

I held out my hand and said, "The light lies upon it; think it into a glass of wine, Satan."

He did it. I drank the wine.

"Break the glass," he said.

I broke it.

"There—you see it is real. The villagers thought the brass balls were magic stuff and as perishable as smoke. They were afraid to touch them. You are a curious lot—your race. But come along; I have business. I will put you to bed." Said and done. Then he was gone; but his voice came back to me through the rain and darkness saying, "Yes, tell Seppi, but no other."

It was the answer to my thought.

Chapter VIII

Sleep would not come. It was not because I was proud of my travels and excited about having been around the big world to China, and feeling contemptuous of Bartel Sperling, "the traveler," as he called himself, and looked down upon us others because he had been to Vienna once and was the only Eseldorf boy who had made such a journey and seen the world's wonders. At another time that would have kept me awake, but it did not affect me now. No, my mind was filled with Nikolaus, my thoughts ran upon him only, and the good days we had seen together at romps and frolics in the woods and the fields and the river in the long summer days, and skating and sliding in the winter when our parents thought we were in school. And now he was going out of this young life, and the summers and winters would come and go, and we others would rove and play as before, but his place would be vacant; we should see him no more. To-morrow he would not suspect, but would be as he had always been, and it would shock me to hear him laugh, and see him do lightsome and frivolous things, for to me he would be a corpse, with waxen hands and dull eyes, and I should see the shroud around his face; and the next day he would not suspect, nor the next, and all the time his handful of days would be wasting swiftly away and that awful thing coming nearer and nearer, his fate closing steadily around him and no one knowing it but Seppi and me. Twelve days—only twelve days. It was awful to think of. I noticed that in my thoughts I was not calling him by his familiar names, Nick and Nicky, but was speaking of him by his full name, and reverently, as one speaks of the dead. Also, as incident after incident of our comradeship came thronging into my mind out of the past, I noticed that they were mainly cases where I had wronged him or hurt him, and they rebuked me and reproached me, and my heart was wrung with remorse, just as it is when we remember our unkindnesses to friends who have passed beyond the veil, and we wish we could have them back again, if only for a moment, so that we could go on our knees to them and say, "Have pity, and forgive."

Once when we were nine years old he went a long errand of nearly two miles for the fruiterer, who gave him a splendid big apple for reward, and he was flying home with it, almost beside himself with astonishment and delight, and I met him, and he let me look at the apple, not thinking of treachery, and I ran off with it, eating it as I ran, he following me and begging; and when he overtook me I offered him the core, which was all that was left; and I laughed. Then he turned away, crying, and said he had meant to give it to his little sister. That smote me, for she was slowly getting well of a sickness, and it would have been a proud moment for him, to see her joy and surprise and have her caresses. But I was ashamed to say I was ashamed, and only said something rude and mean, to pretend I did not care, and he made no reply in words, but there was a wounded look in his face as he turned away toward his home which rose before me many times in after years, in the night, and reproached me and made me ashamed again. It had grown dim in my mind, by and by, then it disappeared; but it was back now, and not dim.

Once at school, when we were eleven, I upset my ink and spoiled four copy-books, and was in danger of severe punishment; but I put it upon him, and he got the whipping.

And only last year I had cheated him in a trade, giving him a large fish-hook which was partly broken through for three small sound ones. The first fish he caught broke the hook, but he did not know I was blamable, and he refused to take back one of the small hooks which my conscience forced me to offer him, but he said, "A trade is a trade; the hook was bad, but that was not your fault."

No, I could not sleep. These little, shabby wrongs upbraided me and tortured me, and with a pain much sharper than one feels when the wrongs have been done to the living. Nikolaus was living, but no matter; he was to me as one already dead. The wind was still moaning about the eaves, the rain still pattering upon the panes.

In the morning I sought out Seppi and told him. It was down by the river. His lips moved, but he did not say anything, he only looked dazed and stunned, and his face turned very white. He stood like that a few moments, the tears welling into his eyes, then he turned away and I locked my arm in his and we walked along thinking, but not speaking. We crossed the bridge and wandered through the meadows and up among the hills and the woods, and at last the talk came and flowed freely, and it was all about Nikolaus and was a recalling of the life we had lived with him. And every now and then Seppi said, as if to himself:

"Twelve days!—less than twelve days."

We said we must be with him all the time; we must have all of him we could; the days were precious now. Yet we did not go to seek him. It would be like meeting the dead, and we were afraid. We did not say it, but that was what we were feeling. And so it gave us a shock when we turned a curve and came upon Nikolaus face to face. He shouted, gaily:

"Hi-hi! What is the matter? Have you seen a ghost?"

We couldn't speak, but there was no occasion; he was willing to talk for us all, for he had just seen Satan and was in high spirits about it. Satan had told him about our trip to China, and he had begged Satan to take him a journey, and Satan had promised. It was to be a far journey, and wonderful and beautiful; and Nikolaus had begged him to take us, too, but he said no, he would take us some day, maybe, but not now. Satan would come for him on the 13th, and Nikolaus was already counting the hours, he was so impatient.

That was the fatal day. We were already counting the hours, too.

We wandered many a mile, always following paths which had been our favorites from the days when we were little, and always we talked about the old times. All the blitheness was with Nikolaus; we others could not shake off our depression. Our tone toward Nikolaus was so strangely gentle and tender and yearning that he noticed it, and was pleased; and we were constantly doing him deferential little offices of courtesy, and saying, "Wait, let me do that for you," and that pleased him, too. I gave him seven fish-hooks—all I had—and made him take them; and Seppi gave him his new knife and a humming-top painted red and yellow—atone-ments for swindles practised upon him formerly, as I learned later, and probably no longer remembered by Nikolaus now. These things touched him, and he could not have believed that we loved him so; and his pride in it and gratefulness for it cut us to the heart, we were so undeserving of them. When we parted at last, he was radiant, and said he had never had such a happy day.

As we walked along homeward, Seppi said, "We always prized him, but never so much as now, when we are going to lose him."

Next day and every day we spent all of our spare time with Nikolaus; and also added to it time which we (and he) stole from work and other duties, and this cost the three of us some sharp scoldings, and some threats of punishment. Every morning two of us woke with a start and a shudder, saying, as the days flew along, "Only ten days left;" "only nine days left;" "only eight;" "only seven." Always it was narrowing. Always Nikolaus was gay and happy, and always puzzled because we were not. He wore his invention to the bone trying to invent ways to cheer us up, but it was only a hollow success; he could see that our jollity had no heart in it, and that the laughs we broke into came up against some obstruction or other and suffered damage and decayed into a sigh. He tried to find out what the matter was, so that he could help us out of our trouble or make it lighter by sharing it with us; so we had to tell many lies to deceive him and appease him.

But the most distressing thing of all was that he was always making plans, and often they went beyond the 13th! Whenever that happened it made us groan in spirit. All his mind was fixed upon finding some way to conquer our depression and cheer us up; and at last, when he had but three days to live, he fell upon the right idea and was jubilant over it—a boys-and-girls' frolic and dance in the woods, up there where we first met Satan, and this was to occur on the 14th. It was ghastly, for that was his funeral day. We couldn't venture to protest; it would only have brought a "Why?" which we could not answer. He wanted us to help him invite his guests, and we did it—one can refuse nothing to a dying friend. But it was dreadful, for really we were inviting them to his funeral.

It was an awful eleven days; and yet, with a lifetime stretching back between to-day and then, they are still a grateful memory to me, and beautiful. In effect they were days of companionship with one's sacred dead, and I have known no comradeship that was so close or so precious. We clung to the hours and the minutes, counting them as they wasted away, and parting with them with that pain and bereavement which a miser feels who sees his hoard filched from him coin by coin by robbers and is helpless to prevent it.

When the evening of the last day came we stayed out too long; Seppi and I were in fault for that; we could not bear to part with

Nikolaus; so it was very late when we left him at his door. We lingered near awhile, listening; and that happened which we were fearing. His father gave him the promised punishment, and we heard his shrieks. But we listened only a moment, then hurried away, remorseful for this thing which we had caused. And sorry for the father, too; our thought being, "If he only knew—if he only knew!"

In the morning Nikolaus did not meet us at the appointed place, so we went to his home to see what the matter was. His mother said:

"His father is out of all patience with these goings-on, and will not have any more of it. Half the time when Nick is needed he is not to be found; then it turns out that he has been gadding around with you two. His father gave him a flogging last night. It always grieved me before, and many's the time I have begged him off and saved him, but this time he appealed to me in vain, for I was out of patience myself."

"I wish you had saved him just this one time," I said, my voice trembling a little; "it would ease a pain in your heart to remember it some day."

She was ironing at the time, and her back was partly toward me. She turned about with a startled or wondering look in her face and said, "What do you mean by that?"

I was not prepared, and didn't know anything to say; so it was awkward, for she kept looking at me; but Seppi was alert and spoke up:

"Why, of course it would be pleasant to remember, for the very reason we were out so late was that Nikolaus got to telling how good you are to him, and how he never got whipped when you were by to save him; and he was so full of it, and we were so full of the interest of it, that none of us noticed how late it was getting."

"Did he say that? Did he?" and she put her apron to her eyes.

"You can ask Theodor—he will tell you the same."

"It is a dear, good lad, my Nick," she said. "I am sorry I let him get whipped; I will never do it again. To think—all the time I was sitting here last night, fretting and angry at him, he was loving me and praising me! Dear, dear, if we could only know! Then we shouldn't ever go wrong; but we are only poor, dumb beasts groping around and making mistakes. I sha'n't ever think of last night without a pang."

She was like all the rest; it seemed as if nobody could open a mouth, in these wretched days, without saying something that made us shiver. They were "groping around," and did not know what true, sorrowfully true things they were saying by accident.

Seppi asked if Nikolaus might go out with us.

"I am sorry," she answered, "but he can't. To punish him further, his father doesn't allow him to go out of the house to-day."

We had a great hope! I saw it in Seppi's eyes. We thought, "If he cannot leave the house, he cannot be drowned." Seppi asked, to make sure:

"Must he stay in all day, or only the morning?"

"All day. It's such a pity, too; it's a beautiful day, and he is so unused to being shut up. But he is busy planning his party, and maybe that is company for him. I do hope he isn't too lonesome."

Seppi saw that in her eye which emboldened him to ask if we might go up and help him pass his time.

"And welcome!" she said, right heartily. "Now I call that real friendship, when you might be abroad in the fields and the woods, having a happy time. You are good boys, I'll allow that, though you don't always find satisfactory ways of improving it. Take these cakes—for yourselves—and give him this one, from his mother."

The first thing we noticed when we entered Nikolaus's room was the time—a quarter to 10. Could that be correct? Only such a few minutes to live! I felt a contraction at my heart. Nikolaus jumped up and gave us a glad welcome. He was in good spirits over his plannings for his party and had not been lonesome.

"Sit down," he said, "and look at what I've been doing. And I've finished a kite that you will say is a beauty. It's drying, in the kitchen; I'll fetch it."

He had been spending his penny savings in fanciful trifles of various kinds, to go as prizes in the games, and they were marshaled with fine and showy effect upon the table. He said:

"Examine them at your leisure while I get mother to touch up the kite with her iron if it isn't dry enough yet."

Then he tripped out and went clattering downstairs, whistling.

We did not look at the things; we couldn't take any interest in anything but the clock. We sat staring at it in silence, listening to the ticking, and every time the minute-hand jumped we nodded recognition—one minute fewer to cover in the race for life or for death. Finally Seppi drew a deep breath and said:

"Two minutes to ten. Seven minutes more and he will pass the death-point. Theodor, he is going to be saved! He's going to—"

"Hush! I'm on needles. Watch the clock and keep still."

Five minutes more. We were panting with the strain and the excitement. Another three minutes, and there was a footstep on the stair.

"Saved!" And we jumped up and faced the door.

The old mother entered, bringing the kite. "Isn't it a beauty?" she said. "And, dear me, how he has slaved over it—ever since

daylight, I think, and only finished it awhile before you came."
She stood it against the wall, and stepped back to take a view of
it. "He drew the pictures his own self, and I think they are very
good. The church isn't so very good, I'll have to admit, but look
at the bridge—any one can recognize the bridge in a minute. He
asked me to bring it up. . . . Dear me! it's seven minutes past
ten, and I—"

"But where is he?"

"He? Oh, he'll be here soon; he's gone out a minute."

"Gone out?"

"Yes. Just as he came down-stairs little Lisa's mother came in
and said the child had wandered off somewhere, and as she was a
little uneasy I told Nikolaus to never mind about his father's orders—go and look her up. . . . Why, how white you two do look!
I do believe you are sick. Sit down; I'll fetch something. That cake
has disagreed with you. It is a little heavy, but I thought—"

She disappeared without finishing her sentence, and we hurried at once to the back window and looked toward the river.
There was a great crowd at the other end of the bridge, and people were flying toward that point from every direction.

"Oh, it is all over—poor Nikolaus! Why, oh, why did she let
him get out of the house!"

"Come away," said Seppi, half sobbing, "come quick—we can't
bear to meet her; in five minutes she will know."

But we were not to escape. She came upon us at the foot of the
stairs, with her cordials in her hands, and made us come in and
sit down and take the medicine. Then she watched the effect, and
it did not satisfy her; so she made us wait longer, and kept upbraiding herself for giving us the unwholesome cake.

Presently the thing happened which we were dreading. There
was a sound of tramping and scraping outside, and a crowd came
solemnly in, with heads uncovered, and laid the two drowned
bodies on the bed.

"Oh, my God!" that poor mother cried out, and fell on her
knees, and put her arms about her dead boy and began to cover
the wet face with kisses. "Oh, it was I that sent him, and I have
been his death. If I had obeyed, and kept him in the house, this
would not have happened. And I am rightly punished; I was cruel
to him last night, and him begging me, his own mother, to be his
friend."

And so she went on and on, and all the women cried, and pitied
her, and tried to comfort her, but she could not forgive herself
and could not be comforted, and kept on saying if she had not sent
him out he would be alive and well now, and she was the cause of
his death.

It shows how foolish people are when they blame themselves for anything they have done. Satan knows, and he said nothing happens that your first act hasn't arranged to happen and made inevitable; and so, of your own motion you can't ever alter the scheme or do a thing that will break a link. Next we heard screams, and Frau Brandt came wildly plowing and plunging through the crowd with her dress in disorder and hair flying loose, and flung herself upon her dead child with moans and kisses and pleadings and endearments; and by and by she rose up almost exhausted with her outpourings of passionate emotion, and clenched her fist and lifted it toward the sky, and her tear-drenched face grew hard and resentful, and she said:

"For nearly two weeks I have had dreams and presentiments and warnings that death was going to strike what was most precious to me, and day and night and night and day I have groveled in the dirt before Him praying Him to have pity on my innocent child and save it from harm—and here is His answer!"

Why, He had saved it from harm—but she did not know.

She wiped the tears from her eyes and cheeks, and stood awhile gazing down at the child and caressing its face and its hair with her hands; then she spoke again in that bitter tone: "But in His hard heart is no compassion. I will never pray again."

She gathered her dead child to her bosom and strode away, the crowd falling back to let her pass, and smitten dumb by the awful words they had heard. Ah, that poor woman! It is as Satan said, we do not know good fortune from bad, and are always mistaking the one for the other. Many a time since I have heard people pray to God to spare the life of sick persons, but I have never done it.

Both funerals took place at the same time in our little church next day. Everybody was there, including the party guests. Satan was there, too; which was proper, for it was on account of his efforts that the funerals had happened. Nikolaus had departed this life without absolution, and a collection was taken up for masses, to get him out of purgatory. Only two-thirds of the required money was gathered, and the parents were going to try to borrow the rest, but Satan furnished it. He told us privately that there was no purgatory, but he had contributed in order that Nikolaus's parents and their friends might be saved from worry and distress. We thought it very good of him, but he said money did not cost him anything.

At the graveyard the body of little Lisa was seized for debt by a carpenter to whom the mother owed fifty groschen for work done the year before. She had never been able to pay this, and was not able now. The carpenter took the corpse home and kept it four days in his cellar, the mother weeping and imploring about his house all the time; then he buried it in his brother's cattle-yard, without religious ceremonies. It drove the mother wild with grief and shame, and she forsook her work and went daily about the town, cursing the carpenter and blaspheming the laws of the emperor and the church, and it was pitiful to see. Seppi asked Satan to interfere, but he said the carpenter and the rest were members of the human race and were acting quite neatly for that species of animal. He would interfere if he found a horse acting in such a way, and we must inform him when we came across that kind of horse doing that kind of a human thing, so that he could stop it. We believed this was sarcasm, for of course there wasn't any such horse.

But after a few days we found that we could not abide that poor woman's distress, so we begged Satan to examine her several possible careers, and see if he could not change her, to her profit, to a new one. He said the longest of her careers as they now stood gave her forty-two years to live, and her shortest one twenty-nine, and that both were charged with grief and hunger and cold and pain. The only improvement he could make would be to enable her to skip a certain three minutes from now; and he asked us if he should do it. This was such a short time to decide in that we went to pieces with nervous excitement, and before we could pull ourselves together and ask for particulars he said the time would be up in a few more seconds; so then we gasped out, "Do it!"

"It is done," he said; "she was going around a corner; I have turned her back; it has changed her career."

"Then what will happen, Satan?"

"It is happening now. She is having words with Fischer, the weaver. In his anger Fischer will straightway do what he would not have done but for this accident. He was present when she stood over her child's body and uttered those blasphemies."

"What will he do?"

"He is doing it now—betraying her. In three days she will go to the stake."

We could not speak; we were frozen with horror, for if we had not meddled with her career she would have been spared this awful fate. Satan noticed these thoughts, and said:

"What you are thinking is strictly human-like—that is to say, foolish. The woman is advantaged. Die when she might, she would go to heaven. By this prompt death she gets twenty-nine years more of heaven than she is entitled to, and escapes twenty-nine years of misery here."

A moment before we were bitterly making up our minds that we would ask no more favors of Satan for friends of ours, for he did not seem to know any way to do a person a kindness but by killing him; but the whole aspect of the case was changed now, and we were glad of what we had done and full of happiness in the thought of it.

After a little I began to feel troubled about Fischer, and asked, timidly, "Does this episode change Fischer's life-scheme, Satan?"

"Change it? Why, certainly. And radically. If he had not met Frau Brandt awhile ago he would die next year, thirty-four years of age. Now he will live to be ninety, and have a pretty prosperous and comfortable life of it, as human lives go."

We felt a great joy and pride in what we had done for Fischer, and were expecting Satan to sympathize with this feeling; but he showed no sign and this made us uneasy. We waited for him to speak, but he didn't; so, to assuage our solicitude we had to ask him if there was any defect in Fischer's good luck. Satan considered the question a moment, then said, with some hesitation:

"Well, the fact is, it is a delicate point. Under his several former possible life-careers he was going to heaven."

We were aghast. "Oh, Satan! and under this one—"

"There, don't be so distressed. You were sincerely trying to do him a kindness; let that comfort you."

"Oh, dear, dear, that cannot comfort us. You ought to have told us what we were doing, then we wouldn't have acted so."

But it made no impression on him. He had never felt a pain or a sorrow, and did not know what they were, in any really informing way. He had no knowledge of them except theoretically —that is to say, intellectually. And of course that is no good. One can never get any but a loose and ignorant notion of such things except by experience. We tried our best to make him comprehend the awful thing that had been done and how we were compromised by it, but he couldn't seem to get hold of it. He said he did not think it important where Fischer went to; in heaven he would not be missed, there were "plenty there." We tried to make him see that he was missing the point entirely; that Fischer, and not other people, was the proper one to decide about the importance of it; but it all went for nothing; he said he did not care for Fischer—there were plenty more Fischers.

The next minute Fischer went by on the other side of the way, and it made us sick and faint to see him, remembering the doom that was upon him, and we the cause of it. And how unconscious he was that anything had happened to him! You could see by his elastic step and his alert manner that he was well satisfied with himself for doing that hard turn for poor Frau Brandt. He kept glancing back over his shoulder expectantly. And, sure enough, pretty soon Frau Brandt followed after, in charge of the officers and wearing jingling chains. A mob was in her wake, jeering and shouting, "Blasphemer and heretic!" and some among them were neighbors and friends of her happier days. Some were trying to strike her, and the officers were not taking as much trouble as they might to keep them from it.

"Oh, stop them, Satan!" It was out before we remembered that he could not interrupt them for a moment without changing their whole after-lives. He puffed a little puff toward them with his lips and they began to reel and stagger and grab at the empty air; then they broke apart and fled in every direction, shrieking, as if in intolerable pain. He had crushed a rib of each of them with that little puff. We could not help asking if their life-chart was changed.

"Yes, entirely. Some have gained years, some have lost them. Some few will profit in various ways by the change, but only that few."

We did not ask if we had brought poor Fischer's luck to any of them. We did not wish to know. We fully believed in Satan's desire to do us kindnesses, but we were losing confidence in his judgment. It was at this time that our growing anxiety to have him look over our life-charts and suggest improvements began to fade out and give place to other interests.

For a day or two the whole village was a chattering turmoil over Frau Brandt's case and over the mysterious calamity that had overtaken the mob, and at her trial the place was crowded. She was easily convicted of her blasphemies, for she uttered those terrible words again and said she would not take them back. When warned that she was imperiling her life, she said they could take it in welcome, she did not want it, she would rather live with the professional devils in perdition than with these imitators in the village. They accused her of breaking all those ribs by witchcraft, and asked her if she was not a witch. She answered scornfully:

"No. If I had that power would any of you holy hypocrites be alive five minutes? No; I would strike you all dead. Pronounce your sentence and let me go; I am tired of your society."

So they found her guilty, and she was excommunicated and cut off from the joys of heaven and doomed to the fires of hell; then she was clothed in a coarse robe and delivered to the secular arm,[7] and conducted to the market-place, the bell solemnly tolling the while. We saw her chained to the stake, and saw the first film of blue smoke rise on the still air. Then her hard face softened, and she looked upon the packed crowd in front of her and said, with gentleness:

"We played together once, in long-agone days when we were innocent little creatures. For the sake of that, I forgive you."

7. Secular officers of the village; church officials do not execute a death sentence.

We went away then, and did not see the fires consume her, but we heard the shrieks, although we put our fingers in our ears. When they ceased we knew she was in heaven, notwithstanding the excommunication; and we were glad of her death and not sorry that we had brought it about.

One day, a little while after this, Satan appeared again. We were always watching out for him, for life was never very stagnant when he was by. He came upon us at that place in the woods where we had first met him. Being boys, we wanted to be entertained; we asked him to do a show for us.

"Very well," he said; "would you like to see a history of the progress of the human race?—its development of that product which it calls civilization?"

We said we should.

So, with a thought, he turned the place into the Garden of Eden, and we saw Abel praying by his altar; then Cain came walking toward him with his club, and did not seem to see us, and would have stepped on my foot if I had not drawn it in. He spoke to his brother in a language which we did not understand; then he grew violent and threatening, and we knew what was going to happen, and turned away our heads for the moment; but we heard the crash of the blows and heard the shrieks and the groans; then there was silence, and we saw Abel lying in his blood and gasping out his life, and Cain standing over him and looking down at him, vengeful and unrepentant.

Then the vision vanished, and was followed by a long series of unknown wars, murders, and massacres. Next we had the Flood, and the Ark tossing around in the stormy waters, with lofty mountains in the distance showing veiled and dim through the rain. Satan said:

"The progress of your race was not satisfactory. It is to have another chance now."

The scene changed, and we saw Noah overcome with wine.

Next, we had Sodom and Gomorrah, and "the attempt to discover two or three respectable persons there," as Satan described it. Next, Lot and his daughters in the cave.[8]

Next came the Hebraic wars, and we saw the victims[9] massacre the survivors and their cattle, and save the young girls alive and distribute them around.

Next we had Jael; and saw her slip into the tent and drive the nail into the temple of her sleeping guest;[1] and we were so close that when the blood gushed out it trickled in a little, red stream

---

8. Cf. Genesis xix.30–36.
9. Misprint for "victors"?
1. Sisera, whom she killed in his sleep as an enemy of Israel. See Judges iv.17–22.

to our feet, and we could have stained our hands in it if we had wanted to.

Next we had Egyptian wars, Greek wars, Roman wars, hideous drenchings of the earth with blood; and we saw the treacheries of the Romans toward the Carthaginians, and the sickening spectacle of the massacre of those brave people. Also we saw Cæsar invade Britain—"not that those barbarians had done him any harm, but because he wanted their land, and desired to confer the blessings of civilization upon their widows and orphans," as Satan explained.

Next, Christianity was born. Then ages of Europe passed in review before us, and we saw Christianity and Civilization march hand in hand through those ages, "leaving famine and death and desolation in their wake, and other signs of the progress of the human race," as Satan observed.

And always we had wars, and more wars, and still other wars—all over Europe, all over the world. "Sometimes in the private interest of royal families," Satan said, "sometimes to crush a weak nation; but never a war started by the aggressor for any clean purpose—there is no such war in the history of the race."

"Now," said Satan, "you have seen your progress down to the present, and you must confess that it is wonderful—in its way. We must now exhibit the future."

He showed us slaughters more terrible in their destruction of life, more devastating in their engines of war, than any we had seen.

"You perceive," he said, "that you have made continual progress. Cain did his murder with a club; the Hebrews did their murders with javelins and swords; the Greeks and Romans added protective armor and the fine arts of military organization and generalship; the Christian has added guns and gunpowder; a few centuries from now he will have so greatly improved the deadly effectiveness of his weapons of slaughter that all men will confess that without Christian civilization war must have remained a poor and trifling thing to the end of time."

Then he began to laugh in the most unfeeling way, and make fun of the human race, although he knew that what he had been saying shamed us and wounded us. No one but an angel could have acted so; but suffering is nothing to them; they do not know what it is, except by hearsay.

More than once Seppi and I had tried in a humble and diffident way to convert him, and as he had remained silent we had taken his silence as a sort of encouragement; necessarily, then, this talk of his was a disappointment to us, for it showed that we had made no deep impression upon him. The thought made us sad,

and we knew then how the missionary must feel when he has
been cherishing a glad hope and has seen it blighted. We kept our
grief to ourselves, knowing that this was not the time to continue our work.

Satan laughed his unkind laugh to a finish; then he said: "It is
a remarkable progress. In five or six thousand years five or six high
civilizations have risen, flourished, commanded the wonder of the
world, then faded out and disappeared; and not one of them
except the latest ever invented any sweeping and adequate way
to kill people. They all did their best—to kill being the chiefest
ambition of the human race and the earliest incident in its history
—but only the Christian civilization has scored a triumph to be
proud of. Two or three centuries from now it will be recognized
that all the competent killers are Christians; then the pagan
world will go to school to the Christian—not to acquire his religion, but his guns. The Turk and the Chinaman will buy those
to kill missionaries and converts with."

By this time his theater was at work again, and before our eyes
nation after nation drifted by, during two or three centuries, a
mighty procession, an endless procession, raging, struggling, wal-
lowing through seas of blood, smothered in battle-smoke through
which the flags glinted and the red jets from the cannon darted;
and always we heard the thunder of the guns and the cries of the
dying.

"And what does it amount to?" said Satan, with his evil chuckle.
"Nothing at all. You gain nothing; you always come out where
you went in. For a million years the race has gone on monotonously propagating itself and monotonously reperforming this dull
nonsense—to what end? No wisdom can guess! Who gets a profit
out of it? Nobody but a parcel of usurping little monarchs and
nobilities who despise you; would feel defiled if you touched them;
would shut the door in your face if you proposed to call; whom
you slave for, fight for, die for, and are not ashamed of it, but
proud; whose existence is a perpetual insult to you and you are
afraid to resent it; who are mendicants supported by your alms,
yet assume toward you the airs of benefactor toward beggar; who
address you in the language of master to slave, and are answered
in the language of slave to master; who are worshiped by you
with your mouth, while in your heart—if you have one—you
despise yourselves for it. The first man was a hypocrite and a
coward, qualities which have not yet failed in his line; it is the
foundation upon which all civilizations have been built. Drink
to their perpetuation! Drink to their augmentation! Drink to—"
Then he saw by our faces how much we were hurt, and he cut
his sentence short and stopped chuckling, and his manner

changed. He said, gently: "No, we will drink one another's health, and let civilization go. The wine which has flown to our hands out of space by desire is earthly, and good enough for that other toast; but throw away the glasses; we will drink this one in wine which has not visited this world before."

We obeyed, and reached up and received the new cups as they descended. They were shapely and beautiful goblets, but they were not made of any material that we were acquainted with. They seemed to be in motion, they seemed to be alive; and certainly the colors in them were in motion. They were very brilliant and sparkling, and of every tint, and they were never still, but flowed to and fro in rich tides which met and broke and flashed out dainty explosions of enchanting color. I think it was most like opals washing about in waves and flashing out their splendid fires. But there is nothing to compare the wine with. We drank it, and felt a strange and witching ecstasy as of heaven go stealing through us, and Seppi's eyes filled and he said worshipingly:

"We shall be there some day, and then—"

He glanced furtively at Satan, and I think he hoped Satan would say, "Yes, you will be there some day," but Satan seemed to be thinking about something else, and said nothing. This made me feel ghastly, for I knew he had heard; nothing, spoken or unspoken, ever escaped him. Poor Seppi looked distressed, and did not finish his remark. The goblets rose and clove their way into the sky, a triplet of radiant sundogs, and disappeared. Why didn't they stay? It seemed a bad sign, and depressed me. Should I ever see mine again? Would Seppi ever see his?

Chapter IX

It was wonderful, the mastery Satan had over time and distance. For him they did not exist. He called them human inventions, and said they were artificialities. We often went to the most distant parts of the globe with him, and stayed weeks and months, and yet were gone only a fraction of a second, as a rule. You could prove it by the clock. One day when our people were in such awful distress because the witch commission were afraid to proceed against the astrologer and Father Peter's household, or against any, indeed, but the poor and the friendless, they lost patience and took to witch-hunting on their own score, and began to chase a born lady who was known to have the habit of curing people by devilish arts, such as bathing them, washing them, and nourishing them instead of bleeding them and purging them through the ministrations of a barber-surgeon[2] in the proper way.

2. For centuries the two professions were united, as symbolized in the red and white of the barber's pole.

She came flying down, with the howling and cursing mob after her, and tried to take refuge in houses, but the doors were shut in her face. They chased her more than half an hour, we following to see it, and at last she was exhausted and fell, and they caught her. They dragged her to a tree and threw a rope over the limb, and began to make a noose in it, some holding her, meantime, and she crying and begging, and her young daughter looking on and weeping, but afraid to say or do anything.

They hanged the lady, and I threw a stone at her, although in my heart I was sorry for her; but all were throwing stones and each was watching his neighbor, and if I had not done as the others did it would have been noticed and spoken of. Satan burst out laughing.

All that were near by turned upon him, astonished and not pleased. It was an ill time to laugh, for his free and scoffing ways and his supernatural music had brought him under suspicion all over the town and turned many privately against him. The big blacksmith called attention to him now, raising his voice so that all should hear, and said:

"What are you laughing at? Answer! Moreover, please explain to the company why you threw no stone."

"Are you sure I did not throw a stone?"

"Yes. You needn't try to get out of it; I had my eye on you."

"And I—I noticed you!" shouted two others.

"Three witnesses," said Satan: "Mueller, the blacksmith; Klein, the butcher's man; Pfeiffer, the weaver's journeyman. Three very ordinary liars. Are there any more?"

"Never mind whether there are others or not, and never mind about what you consider us—three's enough to settle your matter for you. You'll prove that you threw a stone, or it shall go hard with you."

"That's so!" shouted the crowd, and surged up as closely as they could to the center of interest.

"And first you will answer that other question," cried the blacksmith, pleased with himself for being mouthpiece to the public and hero of the occasion. "What are you laughing at?"

Satan smiled and answered, pleasantly: "To see three cowards stoning a dying lady when they were so near death themselves."

You could see the superstitious crowd shrink and catch their breath, under the sudden shock. The blacksmith, with a show of bravado, said:

"Pooh! What do you know about it?"

"I? Everything. By profession I am a fortune-teller, and I read the hands of you three—and some others—when you lifted them to stone the woman. One of you will die to-morrow week; another of you will die to-night; the third has but five minutes to live—and yonder is the clock!"

It made a sensation. The faces of the crowd blanched, and turned mechanically toward the clock. The butcher and the weaver seemed smitten with an illness, but the blacksmith braced up and said, with spirit:

"It is not long to wait for prediction number one. If it fails, young master, you will not live a whole minute after, I promise you that."

No one said anything; all watched the clock in a deep stillness which was impressive. When four and a half minutes were gone the blacksmith gave a sudden gasp and clapped his hands upon his heart, saying, "Give me breath! Give me room!" and began to sink down. The crowd surged back, no one offering to support him, and he fell lumbering to the ground and was dead. The people stared at him, then at Satan, then at one another; and their lips moved, but no words came. Then Satan said:

"Three saw that I threw no stone. Perhaps there are others; let them speak."

It struck a kind of panic into them, and, although no one answered him, many began to violently accuse one another, saying, "You said he didn't throw," and getting for reply, "It is a lie, and I will make you eat it!" And so in a moment they were in a raging and noisy turmoil, and beating and banging one another; and in the midst was the only indifferent one—the dead lady hanging from her rope, her troubles forgotten, her spirit at peace.

So we walked away, and I was not at ease, but was saying to myself, "He told them he was laughing at them, but it was a lie—he was laughing at me."

That made him laugh again, and he said, "Yes, I was laughing at you, because, in fear of what others might report about you, you stoned the woman when your heart revolted at the act—but I was laughing at the others, too."

"Why?"

"Because their case was yours."

"How is that?"

"Well, there were sixty-eight people there, and sixty-two of them had no more desire to throw a stone than you had."

"Satan!"

"Oh, it's true. I know your race. It is made up of sheep. It **is** governed by minorities, seldom or never by majorities. It suppresses its feelings and its beliefs and follows the handful that makes the most noise. Sometimes the noisy handful is right, sometimes wrong; but no matter, the crowd follows it. The vast majority of the race, whether savage or civilized, are secretly kind-hearted and shrink from inflicting pain, but in the presence of the aggressive and pitiless minority they don't dare to assert themselves. Think of it! One kind-hearted creature spies upon another, and sees to it that he loyally helps in iniquities which revolt both of them. Speaking as an expert, I know that ninety-nine out of a hundred of your race were strongly against the killing of witches when that foolishness was first agitated by a handful of pious lunatics in the long ago. And I know that even to-day, after ages of transmitted prejudice and silly teaching, only one person in twenty puts any real heart into the harrying of a witch. And yet apparently everybody hates witches and wants them killed. Some day a handful will rise up on the other side and make the most noise—perhaps even a single daring man with a big voice and a determined front will do it—and in a week all the sheep will wheel and follow him, and witch-hunting will come to a sudden end.

"Monarchies, aristocracies, and religions are all based upon that large defect in your race—the individual's distrust of his neighbor, and his desire, for safety's or comfort's sake, to stand well in his neighbor's eye. These institutions will always remain, and always flourish, and always oppress you, affront you, and degrade you, because you will always be and remain slaves of minorities. There was never a country where the majority of the people were in their secret hearts loyal to any of these institutions."

I did not like to hear our race called sheep, and said I did not think they were.

"Still, it is true, lamb," said Satan. "Look at you in war—what mutton you are, and how ridiculous!"

"In war? How?"

"There has never been a just one, never an honorable one—on the part of the instigator of the war. I can see a million years ahead, and this rule will never change in so many as half a dozen instances. The loud little handful—as usual—will shout for the war. The pulpit will—warily and cautiously—object—at first; the great, big, dull bulk of the nation will rub its sleepy eyes and try to make out why there should be a war, and will say, earnestly and indignantly, 'It is unjust and dishonorable, and there is no necessity for it.' Then the handful will shout louder. A few fair men on the other side will argue and reason against the war with speech and pen, and at first will have a hearing and be applauded; but it will not last long; those others will outshout them, and presently the anti-war audiences will thin out and lose popularity. Before long you will see this curious thing: the speakers stoned from the platform, and free speech strangled by hordes of furious men who in their secret hearts are still at one with those stoned speakers—as earlier—but do not dare to say so. And now the whole nation

—pulpit and all—will take up the war-cry, and shout itself hoarse, and mob any honest man who ventures to open his mouth; and presently such mouths will cease to open. Next the statesmen will invent cheap lies, putting the blame upon the nation that is attacked, and every man will be glad of those conscience-soothing falsities, and will diligently study them, and refuse to examine any refutations of them; and thus he will by and by convince himself that the war is just, and will thank God for the better sleep he enjoys after this process of grotesque self-deception."

Chapter X

Days and days went by now, and no Satan. It was dull without him. But the astrologer, who had returned from his excursion to the moon, went about the village, braving public opinion, and getting a stone in the middle of his back now and then when some witch-hater got a safe chance to throw it and dodge out of sight. Meantime two influences had been working well for Marget. That Satan, who was quite indifferent to her, had stopped going to her house after a visit or two had hurt her pride, and she had set herself the task of banishing him from her heart. Reports of Wilhelm Meidling's dissipation brought to her from time to time by old Ursula had touched her with remorse, jealousy of Satan being the cause of it; and so now, these two matters working upon her together, she was getting a good profit out of the combination—her interest in Satan was steadily cooling, her interest in Wilhelm as steadily warming. All that was needed to complete her conversion was that Wilhelm should brace up and do something that should cause favorable talk and incline the public toward him again.

The opportunity came now. Marget sent and asked him to defend her uncle in the approaching trial, and he was greatly pleased, and stopped drinking and began his preparations with diligence. With more diligence than hope, in fact, for it was not a promising case. He had many interviews in his office with Seppi and me, and threshed out our testimony pretty thoroughly, thinking to find some valuable grains among the chaff, but the harvest was poor, of course.

If Satan would only come! That was my constant thought. He could invent some way to win the case; for he had said it would be won, so he necessarily knew how it could be done. But the days dragged on, and still he did not come. Of course I did not doubt that it would win, and that Father Peter would be happy for the rest of his life, since Satan had said so; yet I knew I should be much more comfortable if he would come and tell us how to manage it. It was getting high time for Father Peter to have a saving change toward happiness, for by general report he was worn out with his imprisonment and the ignominy that was burdening him, and was like to die of his miseries unless he got relief soon.

At last the trial came on, and the people gathered from all around to witness it; among them many strangers from considerable distances. Yes, everybody was there except the accused. He was too feeble in body for the strain. But Marget was present, and keeping up her hope and her spirit the best she could. The money was present, too. It was emptied on the table, and was handled and caressed and examined by such as were privileged.

The astrologer was put in the witness-box. He had on his best hat and robe for the occasion.

Question. You claim that this money is yours?

Answer. I do.

Q. How did you come by it?

A. I found the bag in the road when I was returning from a journey.

Q. When?

A. More than two years ago.

Q. What did you do with it?

A. I brought it home and hid it in a secret place in my observatory, intending to find the owner if I could.

Q. You endeavored to find him?

A. I made diligent inquiry during several months, but nothing came of it.

Q. And then?

A. I thought it not worth while to look further, and was minded to use the money in finishing the wing of the foundling-asylum connected with the priory and nunnery. So I took it out of its hiding-place and counted it to see if any of it was missing. And then—

Q. Why do you stop? Proceed.

A. I am sorry to have to say this, but just as I had finished and was restoring the bag to its place, I looked up and there stood Father Peter behind me.

Several murmured, "That looks bad," but others answered, "Ah, but he is such a liar!"

Q. That made you uneasy?

A. No; I thought nothing of it at the time, for Father Peter often came to me unannounced to ask for a little help in his need.

Marget blushed crimson at hearing her uncle falsely and impudently charged with begging, especially from one he had always denounced as a fraud, and was going to speak, but remembered herself in time and held her peace.

Q. Proceed.

A. In the end I was afraid to contribute the money to the foundling-asylum, but elected to wait yet another year and continue my inquiries. When I heard of Father Peter's find I was glad, and no suspicion entered my mind; when I came home a day or two later and discovered that my own money was gone I still did not suspect until three circumstances connected with Father Peter's good fortune struck me as being singular coincidences.

Q. Pray name them.

A. Father Peter had found his money in a path—I had found mine in a road. Father Peter's find consisted exclusively of gold ducats—mine also. Father Peter found eleven hundred and seven ducats—I exactly the same.

This closed his evidence, and certainly it made a strong impression on the house; one could see that.

Wilhelm Meidling asked him some questions, then called us boys, and we told our tale. It made the people laugh, and we were ashamed. We were feeling pretty badly, anyhow, because Wilhelm was hopeless, and showed it. He was doing as well as he could, poor young fellow, but nothing was in his favor, and such sympathy as there was was now plainly not with his client. It might be difficult for court and people to believe the astrologer's story, considering his character, but it was almost impossible to believe Father Peter's. We were already feeling badly enough, but when the astrologer's lawyer said he believed he would not ask us any questions—for our story was a little delicate and it would be cruel for him to put any strain upon it—everybody tittered, and it was almost more than we could bear. Then he made a sarcastic little speech, and got so much fun out of our tale, and it seemed so ridiculous and childish and every way impossible and foolish, that it made everybody laugh till the tears came; and at last Marget could not keep up her courage any longer, but broke down and cried, and I was so sorry for her.

Now I noticed something that braced me up. It was Satan standing alongside of Wilhelm! And there was such a contrast! —Satan looked so confident, had such a spirit in his eyes and face, and Wilhelm looked so depressed and despondent. We two were comfortable now, and judged that he would testify and persuade the bench and the people that black was white and white black, or any other color he wanted it. We glanced around to see what the strangers in the house thought of him, for he was beautiful, you know—stunning, in fact—but no one was noticing him; so we knew by that that he was invisible.

The lawyer was saying his last words; and while he was saying them Satan began to melt into Wilhelm. He melted into him and disappeared; and then there was a change, when his spirit began to look out of Wilhelm's eyes.

That lawyer finished quite seriously, and with dignity. He pointed to the money, and said:

"The love of it is the root of all evil.[3] There it lies, the ancient tempter, newly red with the shame of its latest victory—the dishonor of a priest of God and his two poor juvenile helpers in crime. If it could but speak, let us hope that it would be constrained to confess that of all its conquests this was the basest and the most pathetic."

He sat down. Wilhelm rose and said:

"From the testimony of the accuser I gather that he found this money in a road more than two years ago. Correct me, sir, if I misunderstood you."

The astrologer said his understanding of it was correct.

"And the money so found was never out of his hands thenceforth up to a certain definite date—the last day of last year. Correct me, sir, if I am wrong."

The astrologer nodded his head. Wilhelm turned to the bench and said:

"If I prove that this money here was not that money, then it is not his?"

"Certainly not; but this is irregular. If you had such a witness it was your duty to give proper notice of it and have him here to—" He broke off and began to consult with the other judges. Meantime that other lawyer got up excited and began to protest against allowing new witnesses to be brought into the case at this late stage.

The judges decided that his contention was just and must be allowed.

"But this is not a new witness," said Wilhelm. "It has already been partly examined. I speak of the coin."

"The coin? What can the coin say?"

"It can say it is not the coin that the astrologer once possessed. It can say it was not in existence last December. By its date it can say this."

And it was so! There was the greatest excitement in the court

3. Cf. I Timothy vi.10. Among other Mark Twain stories which hinge on money and its importance to the human race are "The £1,000,000 Bank Note" (1893), "The $30,000 Bequest" (1904), and much of *Roughing It* (1872). Money is the central focus of most of *The Gilded Age*, particularly for Colonel Sellers and his enthusiastic comment, "There's millions in it—millions!" And in "The Man That Corrupted Hadleyburg" the sack of "coins," the cynosure of all eyes and the desire of all hearts, becomes the baleful agent of corruption. In the *Autobiography*, Twain denounces "the Tennessee land" because the dreams of wealth it fostered in members of his own family robbed them of initiative and industry.

while that lawyer and the judges were reaching for coins and examining them and exclaiming. And everybody was full of admiration of Wilhelm's brightness in happening to think of that neat idea. At last order was called and the court said:

"All of the coins but four are of the date of the present year. The court tenders its sincere sympathy to the accused, and its deep regret that he, an innocent man, through an unfortunate mistake, has suffered the undeserved humiliation of imprisonment and trial. The case is dismissed."

So the money could speak, after all, though that lawyer thought it couldn't. The court rose, and almost everybody came forward to shake hands with Marget and congratulate her, and then to shake with Wilhelm and praise him; and Satan had stepped out of Wilhelm and was standing around looking on full of interest, and people walking through him every which way, not knowing he was there. And Wilhelm could not explain why he only thought of the date on the coins at the last moment, instead of earlier; he said it just occurred to him, all of a sudden, like an inspiration, and he brought it right out without any hesitation, for, although he didn't examine the coins, he seemed, somehow, to know it was true. That was honest of him, and like him; another would have pretended he had thought of it earlier, and was keeping it back for a surprise.

He had dulled down a little now; not much, but still you could notice that he hadn't that luminous look in his eyes that he had while Satan was in him. He nearly got it back, though, for a moment when Marget came and praised him and thanked him and couldn't keep him from seeing how proud she was of him. The astrologer went off dissatisfied and cursing, and Solomon Isaacs gathered up the money and carried it away. It was Father Peter's for good and all, now.

Satan was gone. I judged that he had spirited himself away to the jail to tell the prisoner the news; and in this I was right. Marget and the rest of us hurried thither at our best speed, in a great state of rejoicing.

Well, what Satan had done was this: he had appeared before that poor prisoner, exclaiming, "The trial is over, and you stand forever disgraced as a thief—by verdict of the court!"

The shock unseated the old man's reason. When we arrived, ten minutes later, he was parading pompously up and down and delivering commands to this and that and the other constable or jailer, and calling them Grand Chamberlain, and Prince This and Prince That, and Admiral of the Fleet, Field Marshal in Command, and all such fustian, and was as happy as a bird. He thought he was Emperor!

Marget flung herself on his breast and cried, and indeed everybody was moved almost to heartbreak. He recognized Marget, but
could not understand why she should cry. He patted her on the
shoulder and said:

"Don't do it, dear; remember, there are witnesses, and it is not
becoming in the Crown Princess. Tell me your trouble—it shall
be mended; there is nothing the Emperor cannot do." Then he
looked around and saw old Ursula with her apron to her eyes. He
was puzzled at that, and said, "And what is the matter with you?"

Through her sobs she got out words explaining that she was
distressed to see him—"so." He reflected over that a moment,
then muttered, as if to himself: "A singular old thing, the Dowa-
ger Duchess—means well, but is always snuffling and never able
to tell what it is about. It is because she doesn't know."
His eyes fell on Wilhelm. "Prince of India," he said, "I divine
that it is you that the Crown Princess is concerned about. Her
tears shall be dried; I will no longer stand between you; she shall
share your throne; and between you you shall inherit mine. There,
little lady, have I done well? You can smile now—isn't it so?"

He petted Marget and kissed her, and was so contented with
himself and with everybody that he could not do enough for us
all, but began to give away kingdoms and such things right and
left, and the least that any of us got was a principality. And so
at last, being persuaded to go home, he marched in imposing
state; and when the crowds along the way saw how it gratified him
to be hurrahed at, they humored him to the top of his desire, and
he responded with condescending bows and gracious smiles, and
often stretched out a hand and said, "Bless you, my people!"

As pitiful a sight as ever I saw. And Marget, and old Ursula
crying all the way.

On my road home I came upon Satan, and reproached him with
deceiving me with that lie. He was not embarrassed, but said,
quite simply and composedly:

"Ah, you mistake; it was the truth. I said he would be happy
the rest of his days, and he will, for he will always think he is
the Emperor, and his pride in it and his joy in it will endure to
the end. He is now, and will remain, the one utterly happy person in this empire."

"But the method of it, Satan, the method! Couldn't you have
done it without depriving him of his reason?"

It was difficult to irritate Satan, but that accomplished it.

"What an ass you are!" he said. "Are you so unobservant as
not to have found out that sanity and happiness are an impossible
combination? No sane man can be happy, for to him life is real,
and he sees what a fearful thing it is. Only the mad can be happy,

and not many of those. The few that imagine themselves kings or gods are happy, the rest are no happier than the sane. Of course, no man is entirely in his right mind at any time, but I have been referring to the extreme cases. I have taken from this man that trumpery thing which the race regards as a Mind; I have replaced his tin life with a silver-gilt fiction; you see the result—and you criticize! I said I would make him permanently happy, and I have done it. I have made him happy by the only means possible to his race—and you are not satisfied!" He heaved a discouraged sigh, and said, "It seems to me that this race is hard to please."

There it was, you see. He didn't seem to know any way to do a person a favor except by killing him or making a lunatic out of him. I apologized, as well as I could; but privately I did not think much of his processes—at that time.

Satan was accustomed to say that our race lived a life of continuous and uninterrupted self-deception. It duped itself from cradle to grave with shams and delusions which it mistook for realities, and this made its entire life a sham. Of the score of fine qualities which it imagined it had and was vain of, it really possessed hardly one. It regarded itself as gold, and was only brass. One day when he was in this vein he mentioned a detail—the sense of humor. I cheered up then, and took issue. I said we possessed it.

"There spoke the race!" he said; "always ready to claim what it hasn't got, and mistake its ounce of brass filings for a ton of gold-dust. You have a mongrel perception of humor, nothing more; a multitude of you possess that. This multitude see the comic side of a thousand low-grade and trivial things—broad incongruities, mainly; grotesqueries, absurdities, evokers of the horse-laugh. The ten thousand high-grade comicalities which exist in the world are sealed from their dull vision. Will a day come when the race will detect the funniness of these juvenilities and laugh at them—and by laughing at them destroy them? For your race, in its poverty, has unquestionably one really effective weapon—laughter. Power, money, persuasion, supplication, persecution—these can lift at a colossal humbug—push it a little—weaken it a little, century by century; but only laughter can blow it to rags and atoms at a blast. Against the assault of laughter nothing can stand. You are always fussing and fighting with your other weapons. Do you ever use that one? No; you leave it lying rusting. As a race, do you ever use it at all? No; you lack sense and the courage."

We were traveling at the time and stopped at a little city in India and looked on while a juggler did his tricks before a group of natives. They were wonderful, but I knew Satan could beat that game, and I begged him to show off a little, and he said he would. He changed himself into a native in turban and breech-cloth, and very considerately conferred on me a temporary knowl-edge of the language.

The juggler exhibited a seed, covered it with earth in a small flower-pot, then put a rag over the pot; after a minute the rag began to rise; in ten minutes it had risen a foot; then the rag was removed and a little tree was exposed, with leaves upon it and ripe fruit. We ate the fruit, and it was good. But Satan said:

"Why do you cover the pot? Can't you grow the tree in the sunlight?"

"No," said the juggler; "no one can do that."

"You are only an apprentice; you don't know your trade. Give me the seed. I will show you." He took the seed and said, "What shall I raise from it?"

"It is a cherry seed; of course you will raise a cherry."

"Oh no; that is a trifle; any novice can do that. Shall I raise an orange-tree from it?"

"Oh yes!" and the juggler laughed.

"And shall I make it bear other fruits as well as oranges?"

"If God wills!" and they all laughed.

Satan put the seed in the ground, put a handful of dust on it, and said, "Rise!"

A tiny stem shot up and began to grow, and grew so fast that in five minutes it was a great tree, and we were sitting in the shade of it. There was a murmur of wonder, then all looked up and saw a strange and pretty sight, for the branches were heavy with fruits of many kinds and colors—oranges, grapes, bananas, peaches, cherries, apricots, and so on. Baskets were brought, and the un-lading of the tree began; and the people crowded around Satan and kissed his hand, and praised him, calling him the prince of jugglers. The news went about the town, and everybody came run-ning to see the wonder—and they remembered to bring baskets, too. But the tree was equal to the occasion; it put out new fruits as fast as any were removed; baskets were filled by the score and by the hundred, but always the supply remained undiminished. At last a foreigner in white linen and sun-helmet arrived, and ex-claimed, angrily:

"Away from here! Clear out, you dogs; the tree is on my lands and is my property."

The natives put down their baskets and made humble obeisance. Satan made humble obeisance, too, with his fingers to his fore-head, in the native way, and said:

"Please let them have their pleasure for an hour, sir—only that, and no longer. Afterward you may forbid them; and you will still have more fruit than you and the state together can consume in a year."

This made the foreigner very angry, and he cried out, "Who are you, you vagabond, to tell your betters what they may do and what they mayn't!" and he struck Satan with his cane and followed this error with a kick.

The fruits rotted on the branches, and the leaves withered and fell. The foreigner gazed at the bare limbs with the look of one who is surprised, and not gratified. Satan said:

"Take good care of the tree, for its health and yours are bound together. It will never bear again, but if you tend it well it will live long. Water its roots once in each hour every night—and do it yourself; it must not be done by proxy, and to do it in daylight will not answer. If you fail only once in any night, the tree will die, and you likewise. Do not go home to your own country any more—you would not reach there; make no business or pleasure engagements which require you to go outside your gate at night—you cannot afford the risk; do not rent or sell this place—it would be injudicious."

The foreigner was proud and wouldn't beg, but I thought he looked as if he would like to. While he stood gazing at Satan we vanished away and landed in Ceylon.

I was sorry for that man; sorry Satan hadn't been his customary self and killed him or made him a lunatic. It would have been a mercy. Satan overheard the thought, and said:

"I would have done it but for his wife, who has not offended me. She is coming to him presently from their native land, Portugal. She is well, but has not long to live, and has been yearning to see him and persuade him to go back with her next year. She will die without knowing he can't leave that place."

"He won't tell her?"

"He? He will not trust that secret with any one; he will reflect that it could be revealed in sleep, in the hearing of some Portuguese guest's servant some time or other."

"Did none of those natives understand what you said to him?"

"None of them understood, but he will always be afraid that some of them did. That fear will be torture to him, for he has been a harsh master to them. In his dreams he will imagine them chopping his tree down. That will make his days uncomfortable —I have already arranged for his nights."

It grieved me, though not sharply, to see him take such a malicious satisfaction in his plans for this foreigner.

"Does he believe what you told him, Satan?"

"He thought he didn't, but our vanishing helped. The tree, where there had been no tree before—that helped. The insane and uncanny variety of fruits—the sudden withering—all these things are helps. Let him think as he may, reason as he may, one thing is certain, he will water the tree. But between this and night he will begin his changed career with a very natural precaution— for him."

"What is that?"

"He will fetch a priest to cast out the tree's devil. You are such a humorous race—and don't suspect it."

"Will he tell the priest?"

"No. He will say a juggler from Bombay created it, and that he wants the juggler's devil driven out of it, so that it will thrive and be fruitful again. The priest's incantations will fail; then the Portuguese will give up that scheme and get his watering-pot ready."

"But the priest will burn the tree. I know it; he will not allow it to remain."

"Yes, and anywhere in Europe he would burn the man, too. But in India the people are civilized, and these things will not happen. The man will drive the priest away and take care of the tree."

I reflected a little, then said, "Satan, you have given him a hard life, I think."

"Comparatively. It must not be mistaken for a holiday."

We flitted from place to place around the world as we had done before, Satan showing me a hundred wonders, most of them reflecting in some way the weakness and triviality of our race. He did this now every few days—not out of malice—I am sure of that—it only seemed to amuse and interest him, just as a naturalist might be amused and interested by a collection of ants.

Chapter XI

For as much as a year Satan continued these visits, but at last he came less often, and then for a long time he did not come at all. This always made me lonely and melancholy. I felt that he was losing interest in our tiny world and might at any time abandon his visits entirely. When one day he finally came to me I was overjoyed, but only for a little while. He had come to say good-by, he told me, and for the last time. He had investigations and undertakings in other corners of the universe, he said, that would keep him busy for a longer period than I could wait for his return.

"And you are going away, and will not come back any more?"

"Yes," he said. "We have comraded long together, and it has been pleasant—pleasant for both; but I must go now, and we shall not see each other any more."

"In this life, Satan, but in another? We shall meet in another, surely?"

Then, all tranquilly and soberly, he made the strange answer, "*There is no other*."

A subtle influence blew upon my spirit from his, bringing with it a vague, dim, but blessed and hopeful feeling that the incredible words might be true—even *must* be true.

"Have you never suspected this, Theodor?"

"No. How could I? But if it can only be true—"

"It is true."

A gust of thankfulness rose in my breast, but a doubt checked it before it could issue in words, and I said, "But—but—we have seen that future life—seen it in its actuality, and so—"

"It was a vision—it had no existence."

I could hardly breathe for the great hope that was struggling in me. "A vision?—a vi—"

"*Life itself is only a vision, a dream.*"

It was electrical. By God! I had had that very thought a thousand times in my musings!

"*Nothing* exists; all is a dream. God—man—the world—the sun, the moon, the wilderness of stars—a dream, all a dream; they have no existence. *Nothing exists save empty space—and you!*"

"I!"

"And you are not you—you have no body, no blood, no bones, you are but a *thought*. I myself have no existence; I am but a dream—your dream, creature of your imagination. In a moment you will have realized this, then you will banish me from your visions and I shall dissolve into the nothingness out of which you made me. . . .

"I am perishing already—I am failing—I am passing away. In a little while you will be alone in shoreless space, to wander its limitless solitudes without friend or comrade forever—for you will remain a *thought*, the only existent thought, and by your nature inextinguishable, indestructible. But I, your poor servant, have revealed you to yourself and set you free. Dream other dreams, and better!

"Strange! that you should not have suspected years ago—centuries, ages, eons, ago!—for you have existed, companionless, through all the eternities. Strange, indeed, that you should not have suspected that your universe and its contents were only dreams, visions, fiction! Strange, because they are so frankly and hysterically insane—like all dreams: a God who could make good children as easily as bad, yet preferred to make bad ones; who could have made every one of them happy, yet never made a single happy one; who made them prize their bitter life, yet stingily cut it short; who gave his angels eternal happiness unearned, yet required his other children to earn it; who gave his angels painless lives, yet cursed his other children with biting miseries and maladies of mind and body; who mouths justice and invented hell —mouths mercy and invented hell—mouths Golden Rules, and forgiveness multiplied by seventy times seven, and invented hell; who mouths morals to other people and has none himself; who frowns upon crimes, yet commits them all; who created man without invitation, then tries to shuffle the responsibility for man's acts upon man, instead of honorably placing it where it belongs, upon himself; and finally, with altogether divine obtuseness, invites this poor, abused slave to worship him! . . .

"You perceive, *now*, that these things are all impossible except in a dream. You perceive that they are pure and puerile insanities, the silly creations of an imagination that is not conscious of its freaks—in a word, that they are a dream, and you the maker of it. The dream-marks are all present; you should have recognized them earlier.

"It is true, that which I have revealed to you; there is no God, no universe, no human race, no earthly life, no heaven, no hell. It is all a dream—a grotesque and foolish dream. Nothing exists but you. And you are but a *thought*—a vagrant thought, a useless thought, a homeless thought, wandering forlorn among the empty eternities!"

He vanished, and left me appalled; for I knew, and realized, that all he had said was true.

1898   1916

Henry James

Henry James, Jr., was born in New York City, near Washington Square, on April 15, 1843, the second son of a gifted Irish-American family whose immigrant founder had amassed a large fortune in land rental and other businesses in Albany, N.Y. The novelist's father, a friend of Emerson and Carlyle, was a spiritual reformer given to Swedenborgian visions and reformist theories who gave his sons the kind of education designed to cultivate genius. He exposed them to books, literary people, private tutors, and above all, European travel. At six months of age, Henry James and his brother William were taken to England and France, where they almost literally opened their eyes upon the European scene. James's emotional discovery of the old world became for him a "passionate pilgrimage" which lasted a lifetime and provided the underlying theme of most of his later writing. The James family contained at least four members exceptionally endowed for the life of the mind—the father, a "domestic Socrates"; William, the oldest son, who became a professor of psychology at Harvard and a world-renowned philosopher; Henry, Jr., who won equal fame as a psychological novelist; and Alice, the talented invalid sister. It was one of the father's "ideas" to surround his children with an "atmosphere of freedom" and to avoid dictating the direction which their instincts should take them. Henry, Jr., was the first to make up his mind: he dedicated his life to the art of fiction.

He never married. During his fifty years of celibate writing and traveling, mostly in the capitals of European culture—London, Rome, Paris, Florence, Venice—he produced over 65 volumes, including twenty book-length novels, over a hundred shorter tales and *nouvelles*, and eight volumes of criticism. He also wrote plays, travel sketches, and volumes of letters, kept a journal, edited his own works, and produced one long biography and several books of autobiography. He was one of the great Victorian novelists and the most cosmopolitan of them all. He knew and talked with Turgenev, Flaubert, Zola, Daudet, and Maupassant. His correspondence included such names as Howells, Stevenson, Shaw, H. G. Wells, Edmund Gosse, Lowell, Henry Adams, Walpole, Conrad, and Galsworthy. Fame was his from the start, but only once, with the appearance of *Daisy Miller* in 1879, did he achieve anything like popular success, and that was mostly a success of notoriety.

James has often been treated not as if he were a man living through the trials to which the flesh is heir, but a pure and disembodied artist or a "cerebrating genius." It is true that his outward life was relatively uneventful, without emotional upheavals or severe social challenge, and apparently without any strong physical attachments. His energies were channeled into his work, yet in his 72 years of life one can distinguish a variety of personal roles which help to humanize for later generations the lonely, wayfaring artist figure he presented to the world. He once called himself "that queer monster, the artist, an obstinate finality, and inexhaustible sensibility."

As a small boy, James was shy and sensitive, with a feeling of estrangement from others and inferiority toward his older, bright, and more favored brother. He felt, he says, as if William were always somehow ahead of him "around the corner and out of sight." His father described Henry at fourteen as an immense reader, a "devourer of libraries." This period of receptivity and meditation was marked by spells of withdrawal and ill health. He suffered an "obscure" injury to his back while fighting a fire, an accident which prevented him from joining his younger brothers in action during the Civil War. The quest for a profession took him to Harvard Law School, but he quickly abandoned legal studies in favor of literature and art. Both William and Henry served an apprenticeship to portrait-painting in the studio of William Morris Hunt, a Boston painter, and under John La Farge, a disciple of Hunt—an experience which linked together in Henry's mind the two disciplines of portrait-painting and character delineation in fiction.

His literary career began tentatively with book reviews, stories, and articles in the *North American Review* and the *Atlantic Monthly* in 1864–65. The late 60's were years of experiment and transition. The elder James's theory of unlimited opportunity and a minimum of indoctrination left the sons free to choose their profession, but without conventional training or direction. Henry somewhat desperately sought for a decision. A portrait of him at the age of eighteen by La Farge reveals a handsome, poetic, exotic youth with an inward look of questing idealism. Outwardly sedate and tranquil of temper, "Harry" was content to hover in the background of the admirers around his unfortunate cousin, Minny Temple, who died in 1871 and who later became for him a symbol of a girl loved and lost and a source of two of his later portraits of women.

His first adult trip to Europe took place in 1869. He was beginning to "inhale" the old world. His enthusiasms were breathless, but alternating with them were moods of depression and strangely prophetic visions. One such was the nightmarish episode described in *A Small Boy and Others* where he recalled a childhood dream-adventure of a threatening nature experienced in the Galerie d'Apollon of the Louvre. It was "the most appalling yet most admirable nightmare of my life," he wrote, and it was compounded of a memory of thunder, lightning, and the Napoleonic splendor of the First Empire in which, as a child, he emerged victorious over a ghostly figure of hostility. From such fluctuations of doubt and confidence and the publication during the 1870's of a series of brilliant stories, a masterly interpretation of Hawthorne, and two major novels, James became by 1880 an internationally known author and critic. In appearance, at the age of 37, he was a striking figure, heavy set and formidable. His full, silky beard and olive complexion produced the almost Semitic look of a Renaissance trader or an Anglicized merchant of Venice.

His manner was grave, formal, extremely courteous. Later he grew bald and portly, impressing observers with his keen penetrating eyes. He dressed formally, carrying a stick and gloves and wearing a top hat. Gradually this Victorian profile became that of the heavy-set, smooth-shaven "lion of Lamb House" in Rye, referred to by admirers as "Master." Women especially noted the strange power of his glance. His secretary described James at the age of sixty as resembling an artistic sea captain with a sensitive, mobile mouth, and Edith Wharton referred to the "noble Roman mask" of his face.

This was the final impression of him during the 1908–12 period when he was revising his collected works for the New York Edition and when he received honorary degrees from Harvard and Oxford. In 1915 James became a naturalized British citizen as a gesture of loyalty to his adopted country in the midst of war with Germany. This same year he suffered a series of strokes prior to his final illness. Conscious of impending death, he could still remain the imaginative artist, for during one of these attacks, James recalled hearing a voice distinctly not his own, saying: "So here it is at last, the distinguished thing!"

I

Genuine originality is seldom appreciated on first appearance. In James's case, it took nearly 75 years for criticism fully to recognize the nature of his genius. Reviewers of his early books spoke of them as anti-romantic, analytical, disappointedly lacking in the expected happy endings and wedding bells. His international novels offended the national pride. *Daisy Miller* was called "an outrage on American womanhood," and when James published his *Hawthorne* in 1879, the stigma of "expatriatism" began to be attached to his name because he had placed emphasis on the want of depth and cultural shadow in the American environment. Serious criticism in our time has rejected these opinions as provincial, but serious criticism was rare in 1880, and only a few perceptive writers attempted to interpret James's work in a larger context. By the mid-80's, he wrote sadly to Howells after the negligible reception of *The Bostonians* and *The Princess Casamassima*: "I have entered upon evil days. * * * They [the two novels] have reduced the desire, and the demand, for my productions to zero. * * * I remain irremediably unpublished." Thereafter, he never wholly emerged from this cloud of indifference despite a remarkable achievement, during the 90's and after 1900, of brilliant, ironic tales of the creative life, masterly ghost stories and dramatic *nouvelles*, and three "major" novels now regarded as among his finest work. His misguided effort to restore his reputation and put money in his purse by plunging into the theatrical world of London ended in 1895 when, after a performance of his drama, *Guy Domville*, a call for the author brought him all unsuspecting to the stage where he was roundly jeered and catcalled. Stung by this episode, he returned to fiction, but the late novels and his collected edition fell largely unread from the press. He referred to the New York Edition as "a sort of miniature Ozymandias of Egypt—look on my works, ye mighty, and despair!"

After his death criticism in America continued to disparage James as an expatriate, an aristocratic snob uninterested in social problems, or a gossipy and interminable purveyor of the psychic nuances of decadent aesthetes or fortune hunters. V. L. Parrington and Van Wyck Brooks por-

trayed James as an alienated artist whose talent was frustrated and attenuated by his suspension between the American and the European worlds.
Vitalist and naturalist critics continued to ring the changes on this theme
until a groundswell of reaction began to be felt during the late 30's. By
1943, the centenary of James's birth, it became correct to speak of a "revival" of critical interest in his work, and from then to the present time
he has come into his own as one of the acknowledged masters of world fiction. In the years from 1956 to 1961 he has been the subject of more
scholarly dissertations and research than any other American, including
Hawthorne, Melville, and Mark Twain. Recent criticism has investigated
many different aspects of his work, especially his techniques and philosophy of fiction. This body of opinion has helped to define the nature of
James's reputation as an early forerunner of the modern psychological
novel, a prophetic figure of late Victorian realism, and a critic of fine perceptions who provided the succeeding age with a revitalized language for
the serious discussion of the art of fiction.

It has been said that James was the one really fine American writer of
the 19th century whose career demonstrated the principle of growth.
That is, one can perceive successive periods in his development showing
increasing mastery of form and deepening of tone. For convenience, these
periods may be described as follows: (1) the years of experiment and gradual control of the international theme, from about 1870–1880, in which
he wrote tales of American adventurers in Europe, culminating with *The
Portrait of a Lady*; (2) the middle period, extending to about 1895, in
which he produced two impressive social novels, a series of plays, a sequence of tales of the supernatural, and a number of cleverly satiric stories
of writers and artists; and (3) the final complex phase which includes his
mature ghostly stories, his tales of threatened children and troubled adolescents, and the long psychological novels in the famous "late manner."
These periods, however, coincide and overlap in thematic matter, for the
subject of the innocent American in Europe which began with *The Passionate Pilgrim* (1871) is essentially the same as that of *The Ambassadors*
(1903) and *The Golden Bowl* (1904). Similarly, the portraits of artists
in the early "The Madonna of the Future" (1873) and *Roderick Hudson* (1876) reappear in *The Tragic Muse* (1890). Throughout the 90's
James continued to explore his own developing philosophy of art. A prevailing motif in his later work reveals the "dark side" of human nature—
psychological cross-currents between husbands and wives or parents and
children, and complex love triangles or quadrangles. Frequently, he recurs
to the subject of the baleful influence of the corrupt and sophisticated over
the innocent and young. This theme may be seen in a fine early story,
"Madame de Mauves" (1875), and it figures prominently in many later
ones, but perhaps with greatest effect in such ghostly tales as "The Turn
of the Screw," "The Beast in the Jungle," "The Jolly Corner," and in the
long novel, *The Wings of the Dove*—all late works.

The critical interest in James today may be explained in part by the
reaction against the naturalistic novel. Social reform and broad pictures of
conditions have lost some of their force and, though James admired the
scientific methods of the French school, he could not entirely share Bal-

zac's historical irony or Zola's pessimism. His interest was in psychology and character ("What is incident but the illustration of character?") and his artistic orientation drew him toward the art of the portrait-painter and the novelist of manners. By "character" James did not mean the allegorical personages of Hawthorne or George Eliot. Neither did he admire the sharply drawn English class-types of Dickens. His characters were essentially generic, formed from his sense of the contrast between the New World and the Old. As he developed, this underlying contrast receded into the background, and he concentrated on the subtle interplay of mind among a few highly sensitive individuals. Furthermore, James's strong sense of form in the novel brought him into conflict with what he once disparagingly called "the loose and baggy monsters" of Victorian fiction. He cultivated dramatic dialogue, the use of symbols, indirect methods of revelation, and reflected experience to carry the weight of meaning. His effort to refine upon the Victorian novel led him in a direction opposite from that of Dickens or Thackeray or Hardy. He is now regarded not so much as a late Victorian, but as a precursor of such conscious artists as Joyce, Conrad, Edith Wharton, and Virginia Woolf.

The evidence of change and growth in James's writing shows less in his basic plots or themes than in technical experimentation. He placed much emphasis, for instance, upon the "center of consciousness" or point-of-view character. The reader of *The Ambassadors* discovers the story largely through the mind of Lambert Strether who, in turn, discovers *himself* through such "reflectors" as Maria Gostrey, Waymarsh, and Mamie Pocock. Episodes in the late novels are conceived as "scenes of revelation," each contributing to the further elucidation of the protagonist and his fate. There are climactic scenes of sudden illumination—an unguarded moment discloses the true hypocrisy of a designing character, a half-spoken word or a sudden glimpse of a retreating figure become moments of insight in the developing situation. The story is often two or three stories in one—the outward narrative, the reflected consciousness of the observer, the story within the story.

As his techniques grew more complex, so did his language. The prose is increasingly crowded and condensed with subtleties of expression, refinements and shaded meanings, tortured sentences, psychological undercurrents and suggestions. All these things marked the famous "late manner," a style influenced in part by the fact that James began to dictate his stories. In his final period he stripped away all the furniture of the documentary novel, substituting for its surface action much psychological and verbal fencing among a few characters. Some of the stories are told almost entirely in piled metaphors; states of mind are analyzed to a hair's breadth. This much-discussed "difficult" style became the bane of vigorous minds like H. G. Wells and the meat of parodists, but it was in part the expression of James's personal shyness and in part a skillful and deliberate method of circumventing the Victorian proprieties and editorial taboos of the genteel tradition. Later, more perceptive readers began to discover behind the veil of James's mannered and decorous prose (as Thomas Beer phrased it) "a sunny garden where poisons blew as perfumes" and where crimes like shadows "swept across his shaved and watered turf."

II

"I have not the least hesitation in saying," James wrote in 1888, "that I aspire to write in such a way that it would be impossible to an outsider to say whether at a given moment I am an American writing about England or an Englishman writing about America." He felt it his "complex fate" to be an American in exile, a writer who could never feel truly at home until he was in Europe. This complexity came gradually, however. At first, there was mainly the ecstasy of discovery. Clement Searle in *The Passionate Pilgrim* (1871) and Theobald, the exiled American artist of "The Madonna of the Future" (1873), are mouthpieces for their author's worship of European antiquities and his disparagement of American cultural barrenness, "our crude and garish climate, our silent past, our deafening present." This latter, successful story combined two of James's favorite themes, America versus Europe and the struggle of the artist for some mediation between his idealized vision of beauty and his need for realistic techniques. It may be read as a parable of James's own search for a synthesis between his inherited Emersonian transcendentalism (with its inadequate sense of an embodying form) and his admiration for the French mastery of method. The central incident of the blank canvas was derived from Balzac's *Le Chef d'œuvre inconnu*, but the harmonizing force in the tale came from James's own fear of the two extremes which could silence or stultify the writer. He might, like Theobald, allow his work to wither and die while dreaming of an ideal, or even worse, like the vulgar artist of the cats and the monkeys, stoop to a low and cynical view of life and art.

Late in life James was asked to suggest a list of his novels to a young man anxious to be guided in reading his work. Two of his early books which appeared on the lists (one labeled the more "advanced" group) were *Roderick Hudson* and *The American*, both written in the 70's. The former was a full-dress portrait of the artist as American which James handled as an international problem—the innocent abroad. Behind the story of a young American sculptor corrupted by the Old-World atmosphere of Rome and by his fatal passion for the exotic *femme du monde*, Christina Light, lay the author's questioning of his own departure from America, his search for values in the aesthetic wealth of the Old World— in short, his weighing of the alternatives in his own case. *Roderick Hudson* is a distinguished first novel with a breadth of canvas worthy of Balzac, a vivid account of expatriate artists in Rome, and an Italian atmosphere reminiscent, in its mingling of beauty and moral decadence, of Hawthorne's *The Marble Faun*. It is a romantic novel with a complicated subject and a tragic ending, and, although James later felt that he had failed to master the technical difficulties of the plot, it remains a mature and sustained treatment of a significant theme.

Balzac had provided James with the necessary ballast of social reality and sense of milieu to counteract the strong influence upon him of Hawthorne's moral allegory and symbolism. In these early novels, he was trying to work out a proper synthesis of opposites, a mediation between the Anglo-Saxon morality of Hawthorne and George Eliot, and the French naturalism he saw in Honoré de Balzac and Gustave Flaubert. He found the right mixture in the Russian Ivan Turgenev, with whom he had had long con-

versations in Paris in 1875–76. In Turgénev James seemed to find a "realist" who was nevertheless far from the determining "liability to sordid
accidents" and who possessed an "ideal of delicacy" and an "ideal of
joy." Turgenev also taught James to limit the number of his characters
and to allow them to reveal themselves dramatically as actors on a stage
without authorial intrusions. Some of these considerations account for the
differences between *Roderick Hudson* and its immediate successors in James's
fiction, *The American* (1877), *Daisy Miller* and *The Europeans* (1879),
and the novel which most nearly achieved the balance he sought, *The Portrait of a Lady* (1882).

  The American was a novel of manners skillfully blended of several thematic threads—the American innocent discovering the moral corruption of
the Old World, the assessment of the American "type" one hundred years
after the Declaration of Independence, a romantic plot of intrigue, and a
sympathetic portrait of the American business-millionaire. The style is
James at his youthful best. The dialogue sparkles. The story of Christopher Newman's rejection of revenge against his French persecutors who
have denied him their daughter in marriage is more impressive when read
as a work of art than when seen as a document in behalf of aesthetic idealism or Puritan renunciation—as it has sometimes been interpreted. "I had
been plotting arch-romance without knowing it," James later thought when
he scrutinized the novel for weaknesses. But he had aimed at romantic
tragedy. When critics complained of the tragic conclusion, James quickly
defended himself against "cheerful endings." "It is the tragedies in life
that arrest my attention," he wrote to Howells.

  Daisy Miller was another tragedy, though on a lesser scale, a story of a
young American woman in Europe. This character type became suddenly
emergent in the 70's as "the heiress of all the ages." James reviewed one
of William Dean Howells' early novels, *A Foregone Conclusion*, and was
especially struck by its heroine, whom he described as "possessed of a
lovely face and an irritable moral consciousness." He had observed such
American girls in Europe and, following Howells' lead, began to place
their innocence in juxtaposition with the complexities of Old World society and objectively to describe the results. This formula brought James
his moment of greatest literary "fame." He chose a Europeanized American like himself as the observer of Daisy's brief adventure, one who was
half in love with her, but unprepared to go beyond a sympathetic impartiality in judging her conduct. To Winterbourne she was an intriguing but
puzzling mixture of audacity and innocence. To shocked nativist readers of
the novel she was a defamation of American womanhood in her flouting of
continental mores and genteel proprieties. Some critics saw in the story a
concealed intrigue of a fake Italian nobleman seeking to marry an American
heiress for her money. James himself obscured the controversy over Daisy's
character by insisting that his portrait was solely a "poetic" (i.e., sympathetic) one, but it is now easier to perceive the satiric implications, the
melodramatic plot, and the undertone of "French" license in this story,
somewhat ambiguously subtitled "A Study."

  The Portrait of a Lady (1882) was the culmination of James's early international phase. It was his most ambitious psychological portrait and his
greatest effort thus far to write a "big" novel. The lady was Isabel Archer,

an American "madonna" whom James sought to paint in the center of his canvas, surrounded by figures in varying attitudes of love, adoration, friendly counsel, or hostile intent. The conception was in part derived from Turgenev, "the beautiful genius," who along with George Eliot contended for mastery of James's artistic conscience in this novel. Freedom and fate were deftly balanced in the portrait of Isabel, though it is circumstance which determines and eventually subdues her romantic illusions. A Victorian plot—of a betrayed heiress schemed against by enemies pretending to be friends—is deeply embedded in the tissue of the story, woven out of the psychological materials and verbal subtleties which were to become James's trademarks in fiction. The intellectual and literary influences upon *The Portrait of a Lady* were complex, but at the heart of the story was James's poignant memory of his youthful cousin, Minny Temple.

III

The death of James's father and mother severed his closest tie with America, and in 1883 he returned to England to spend twenty years away from his native land. During the middle years of his career to about 1895 he wrote many of his finest tales, as well as the two "social" novels, *The Bostonians* and *The Princess Casamassima* (1886). This was also the period of James's unsuccessful and misguided effort to take the theatrical world by storm. With the publication of *The Portrait of a Lady* his early literary phase was over. He had succeeded admirably in "doing" the international theme on a large and serious scale, and he was now ready to respond to the new realism, which Howells predicted was taking the place of romance in fiction. He had already begun with a study of "place" in *Washington Square*, in which he sought to sketch an American locale as a background for the story of a plain American girl, another heiress, this time pursued by an *American* fortune hunter. The book was long underrated, perhaps because James himself considered it a light *jeu d'esprit*, but its recent dramatization (on the stage and in a Hollywood version) as *The Heiress* has sent readers back to the book with a sense of its masterly balance of romantic and satiric elements, its mirror-clear prose, and a psychological interpretation of a father-daughter relationship which looks ahead to a much later period of Freudian fiction.

James began about 1880 to keep a notebook in which he jotted down ideas for stories, outlined plans, gazed into a crystal ball for ideas, and pleaded with his coy mistress, the muse of fiction. Together with the famous late Prefaces which he wrote for the collected edition of his novels and tales, the *Notebooks* provide a remarkable insight into a writer's workshop and into his mind. They reveal the extent of James's dedication to his art, and they contain the germinal ideas for almost all the fiction he wrote after 1880. Often they illustrate step by step the growth of his stories from a chance conversation or overheard remark at dinner to the point where they become fully developed *données*, or plots. They have become indispensable to the student and serious reader of his later work. The Prefaces show the author in his declining years reliving the experiences of his novels, commenting upon them, analyzing their strong and weak points, and judging them in terms of the changed standards which marked his late style. James was unrelenting in his quest for "form." Seldom did he satisfy this torment, and he was constantly rewriting in his mind novels which we now acknowledge as masterpieces.

During the 1880's he traveled extensively in Italy, France, and Switzerland, keeping his residence mainly, however, in London where his sister, Alice, now came to live. *A Little Tour of France* (1885) was a record of his travels, and a visit to Paris renewed his associations with Zola and Daudet and perhaps motivated the two long documentary novels of the mid-80's. In London, "the great gray Babylon," he settled into a steady routine of writing in the morning hours and socializing at dinner parties or on weekend visits to the country. He knew Stevenson, Edmund Gosse, and the artist George Du Maurier and himself became one of the literary lions of Victorian society. It was a busy period. Besides his long works, he produced two shorter novels, *The Reverberator* and *The Aspern Papers* (1888), the latter a superbly dramatic mystery about an old lady, dying in Venice, the former mistress of a famous poet. She seeks to prevent a collector, "a publishing scoundrel," from appropriating her youthful love-letters from the poet. James published a skillful volume of critical essays, *Partial Portraits*, four collections of tales and the long novel *The Tragic Muse*—all before 1890. Also, he acted as his own secretary, conducting a busy publishing correspondence, negotiating with editors and publishers, bargaining for terms, administering his literary capital.

The poor reception of the long novels, *The Bostonians* and *The Princess Casamassima*, disappointed him. These were James's attempts to write Dickensian social fiction or naturalistic problem-novels of the Zola school. In both cases, however, the problem itself remained in the background—the first dealing with Boston suffragettes, the second with the restive, anarchist underground in London. Sharp satire pervaded his handling of the feminists, and James may have been influenced to omit *The Bostonians* from his collected edition by the cries of protest which reached him from the bluestocking world. He was taken to task by his brother William for the pointed parallel between his characterization of Miss Birdseye, whose spectacles were always in the wrong place, and the aging Elizabeth Peabody of Boston. His portrayal of the relationship between the prim and mannish Olive Chancellor and her protégé, an attractive young girl with a gift for public speaking, went deep into companionate-psychology and has been interpreted by some as an early instance in fiction of an unnatural, Lesbian attraction. Both *The Bostonians* and *The Princess* were far more important than James himself, or his contemporaries, would allow, and though they have marked defects as social documents, they belong in the best tradition of Victorian fiction. "I don't despair," James wrote, lamenting the contemporary indifference to these books. "Very likely, some day, all my buried prose will kick off its various tombstones at once."

The appearance of *The Tragic Muse* in 1890 marked a turn in James's interests toward the theater which was to occupy him for the next five years and bring to a close his middle period with the bitter incident of *Guy Domville*. The story of Miriam Rooth was a backstage study of an actress in which James sought once again to capture the essence of the artist temperament. But the effort to broaden the plot by a complementary political theme complicated it beyond successful handling, and despite bright elements, the book was structurally a failure. He recognized this weakness by directing his work into the more compact and confining form of the drama and the shorter tale.

He dedicated himself once more to writing "a large number of perfect short things, *nouvelles* and tales," and he found his theme again in the problems of the artist. A quality quite different from the romanticism of *Roderick Hudson*, however, entered these ironic studies, a bitter humor provoked by James's own frustrations over public apathy toward his work. In a series of sharply edged barbs at the literary life of the Yellow Nineties, he now explored its every facet—critics, readers, editors, publishers, lion hunters, and the host of parasites who hovered over the writer's desk and danced upon his inkstand. Beginning with "the Lesson of the Master" (1888), these satiric tales reveal a new maturity in James. Their crisp, part-burlesque, part-tragic tone distinguishes them as a group. They satisfied his innermost feelings about art and at the same time challenged his concern for "foreshortening" ("I delight in a deep-breathing economy and an organic form"). It would be wrong to read these tales as literal autobiography, but unquestionably they all gain an added dimension from James's sublimation of his own dilemma of the unappreciated artist.

"The Real Thing" (1892) posed the question of source material for the artist. Was literal reality an adequate substitute for the shaping and selecting mind? The intellectual framework of the story, however, is so gracefully and impressionistically shaded by the surface action concerning a shabby-genteel couple looking for employment as artist's models that its point comes through only by indirection—though no doubt all the more forcefully for that. James holds in balance the narrator's aesthetic distrust of the Monarchs as "real" models for his illustrations with his sympathy for their poverty and their pride. "The Lesson of the Master" examined the theme of the disastrous effect of marriage on the dedicated man of letters, a subject James had previously treated in "The Author of Beltraffio" (1884). In "Greville Fane" (1892) he distilled into a satiric masterpiece of seven thousand words a tale of filial ingratitude and maternal blindness that makes one think of King Lear and his daughters. Intricately counterpointed with this theme is the ironic attitude of the narrator toward Greville Fane, a dowdy, tireless composer of popular trash, who "could invent stories by the yard, but couldn't write a page of English." One side of this deft parable derived from James's unfailing human sympathy for the woman-writer as a mother unable to realize the appalling hypocrisy and selfishness of her impossible offspring. The other stemmed from his contempt for the success of the "pastrycook" writer, dealing in tarts and puddings for her customers. The taut string of this situation holds the reader in perfect sympathy with the narrator-critic whose view of Greville Fane is balanced: "That's why I liked her—she rested me so from literature."

Hugh Dencombe ("The Middle Years"), Neil Paraday ("The Death of the Lion"), Hugh Vereker ("The Figure in the Carpet"), Ray Limbert ("The Next Time")—each confronts his different destiny as artist. Together their stories from James's portrait of his profession, touching every note in the scale from the grimly realistic through pathos and irony, to burlesque and the ludicrous, usually several of these combined. Yet each has its own theme, limited in range, but various and memorable in the development. An aging and ill writer, conscious of the nearness of death, hopes for another chance to recapture his art. A young and gifted one in dire need of money tries again and again to write a best-seller to support his growing family, but each novel he writes is acclaimed by the critics as a profound work and remains unsold—for Ray Limbert there is never a "next time." A famous author lies ill upstairs in the country house of Mrs. Weeks Wimbush, a devouring patron of the arts, while her guests lionize his manuscript and finally lose it without ever bothering to read it. A young critic interviews a great novelist about his work and is told to search for the hidden meaning behind the books. Hugh Vereker sends his young protégé on a frantic quest for "the exquisite scheme," "the buried treasure," "the complex figure in a Persian carpet" which underlies everything he has written. This fascinating tale is treated by James in seriocomic tones and with a mystery-story technique. The weird chase after Vereker's secret provides a near-burlesque movement to a story with a serious aesthetic principle at its core. The title phrase has remained to influence a new school of analytical criticism and has sent many a latter-day critic on a similar search for the "general intention," the "little trick" or secret which formed the texture of James's own work.

IV

In 1896 James was living in London at De Vere Gardens (Kensington). That summer he leased Lamb House in Rye, Sussex, later purchasing the ivy-covered, gardened residence where, during the years just before and after the turn of the century, he entertained his family and many visiting admirers. Edmund Gosse, A. C. Benson, Edith Wharton, the William Jameses, and many others visited him there and described him as resembling "a successful lawyer or banker of the old school" or a member of the house of Rothschild with age-old eyes like those of cultured Jews. His hospitality was unfailingly generous, and he impressed his guests with the studied, tantalizing charm of his talk, its elaborateness and precision—a rich species of intellectual performance, as one writer described it. In the summer months he lived the life of a village squire, chatting with neighbors on his daily walks. In winter he returned to London where he kept rooms at the Reform Club.

Gradually James struggled to distill his failures and self-doubts of the dramatic years into the permanence of imaginative literature, and his outward serenity was a reverse measure of the inner disquiet and tension revealed in his writing during this complex phase of his career. His mood was phrased in the notebooks: "I take up my old pen again—the pen of all my old unforgettable efforts and sacred struggles. * * * Large and full and high the future still opens." This new complexity of mind derived in part from a determination to withdraw from the competition of the stage and to return to his earlier literary form, fiction. It was at the same time a withdrawal into himself. No longer impelled to be a crowd-pleaser of entertainment-hungry audiences, he could once again fall back upon the old art of reflection. He could also return to his strongest weapon, his prose style, now with an added prolixity. The renewed determination to succeed in fiction and to search his mind in the quiet of Lamb House gave him the needed leisure to meditate old themes. Memories of the past, dream visions, and psychic experiences were allowed to well up to the level of consciousness and to take literary form with the aid of the lessons he had learned in the theater. The scenic art of the stage had not been his real form, he now realized, but it provided a key to certain dramatic disciplines and angles of observation he now contemplated in his narrative plans.

Two themes which preoccupied James at this time were those of psychic and supernatural experience and of threatened and troubled childhood. In his meditations he now recalled some of the dream adventures of his own youthful years, such as that in the Galerie d'Apollon, giving them a new coloring which came from the *fin de siècle* vogue for psychic phenomena, apparitions of returned dead, séances, and hypnotic delusions. His early reading of the romantic fantasies of Poe and Hawthorne now blended in his mind with such psychological investigations as his brother William was making into the varieties of religious experience. In the air, too, were the early studies of the nature of hysteria in the work of Pierre Janet, Freud, and the French physician, J. M. Charcot. James had discussed such matters with George Du Maurier who had employed the device of hypnotism with great popular success in the novel *Trilby* (1894). James himself had already written a series of psychic ghost stories such as "Sir Edmund Orme," "The Private Life," and "Owen Wingrave." In 1898 he wrote his most successful tale of the supernatural, combining it with the theme of children threatened by evil forces, "The Turn of the Screw." This story of a governess in a haunted English mansion who sees the ghosts of two former servants of the house, now dead, and tries to prevent them from gaining an occult influence over the children of her employer has provoked more critical comment in recent years than any other of James's ghostly tales. It has also been successful as a stage and cinema production. The haunted house at Bly, the crenellated tower, and the lake where the shapes of Peter Quint and Miss Jessel appear to the frightened governess-narrator of the story have been given a "Freudian" and an "anti-Freudian" interpretation by two different schools of opinion. Edna Kenton and Edmund Wilson have read the tale as one of sex repression on the part of the deluded governess: the ghosts are merely hallucinations of her mind, stimulated by the weird circumstances at Bly and her unconfessed and frustrated sexual impulses toward her master, the uncle of Miles and Flora. James himself, on the other hand, characterized the story in a later preface as "a fairly-tale pure and simple" and added that it was designed as "a cold, artistic calculation" to catch those not easily caught. Those who have disagreed with the Freudians cite James's preface as evidence that "The Turn of the Screw" was primarily a tale intended to produce in the reader a sense of horror and evil and to preserve the ambiguity so as to allow the reader's imagination to do much of the work. James mentioned folk elements like the Bluebeard theme as part of the background of the governess's search for the secret of Bly and her strict instructions not to communicate with her employer in any way. Witchcraft, too, was an influence, as were such books as *Jane Eyre* and *The Mysteries of Udolpho*, but the final word about "The Turn of the Screw" must be the reader's own. James's mastery here has derived from many sources: literary echoes, personal experiences, fairly tales, and his own distracted state of mind during the late years of the century.

A series of psychological tales of occult experience followed and were collected in two volumes, *The Soft Side* (1900) and *The Better Sort* (1903). "Maud-Evelyn," one of the best of these, treated the whole machinery of spirit mediums, séances, and fixations in a part comic, part fantastic way

—the story of a young man adopted by a couple whose daughter has died in childhood. It becomes their strange delusion that she had in fact grown up, married the young man, and *then* died, leaving him a widower. The bizarre tale rests on the margin of madness, but is complicated by the ambiguity of Marmaduke's motives. He is cunning enough to see the advantages of accepting the delusion of the Dedricks, and he jilts his own fiancé to follow his slightly deranged adoptive parents.

One group of these late stories of psychic phenomena explores the theme of a shared experience between a man, usually one of James's "poor sensitive gentlemen" (James once said he was embarrassed by his predilection for poor sensitive gentlemen), and a mature woman whose relation to him is that of a mother-image and second consciousness. John Marcher in "The Beast in the Jungle" confides to May Bartram his haunting sense that something rare and strange was destined to happen to him. They grow intimate over this shared secret, but Marcher never suspects that she is in love with him. His premonition of something about to spring at him from the jungle passes into a fear that he will be the one man to whom *nothing* is to happen, and he finally becomes aware, at May's death, of his real "beast." John Marcher had never perceived her love until at her grave he senses the spring of the tiger. This motif of lost experience is given a reverse twist in "The Jolly Corner" where Spencer Brydon, like Henry James, returns to his ancestral home in New York in his late age and wonders what he would have become had he stayed in America instead of living his artist life in Europe. The story grew from Howells' suggestion that James write a story of an "international ghost." Again there is the almost oedipal relationship to a woman who shares the psychic world of Brydon. When he encounters on his midnight rambles through the old house an apparition of horror, a kind of alter ego of himself, at a closed doorway, he faints from fright and wakes in the arms of Alice Staverton. The American Spencer Brydon, the figure he might have been, is a black stranger, somehow associated with the hard commercialism James saw in his native country after 1900 when he returned to write *The American Scene*. Alice Staverton becomes the symbol, for Brydon, of both his remembered life at home and his aesthetic life in Europe. In their communion of spirit, Brydon approaches, as nearly as James himself was to approach, a final reconciliation of his expatriate and his American lives.

The stories of childhood and adolescence reveal James rethinking the theme of innocence and experience which he had treated in the romantic 70's. But the Daisy Millers and Isabel Archers were now converted into children, puzzled, disturbed, and tormented by their glimpses into an adult world of shoddy sophistication and moral decadence. *What Maisie Knew* (1897), *In the Cage* (1898), and *The Awkward Age* (1899) all found their center in the idea of discovery and curiosity, on the part of innocent, yet precocious children and female adolescents, about the world of adult manners and sex habits which lay just beyond their understanding. In these books, along with *The Spoils of Poynton* (1896), James was preparing himself for his longer and perhaps most completely realized novels of the final decade. The latter, a short novel of a family quarrel over a houseful of antiques, develops as an extended metaphor in which the "spoils" function as a central symbol around which Mrs. Gereth, her son, and the two rival young women revolve like satellites and display a galaxy of human foibles and conflicting tastes. James conceived the story in three acts to correspond to three periodical installments, but failed in the effort at dramatic conciseness and finally produced a novelette of much greater length. The technical problem of combining stage discipline with a restricted point of view by which the action is revealed through the eyes of a single observer continued to preoccupy him in these years.

What Maisie Knew, for example, forced its readers to discover through a young girl's oblique and clouded angle of vision the marital and extramarital carryings-on of bejeweled divorcées and leering gentlemen in the upper class of London's West End society. Similarly experimental was The Awkward Age, a kind of late Victorian "restoration comedy of manners" written largely in dialogue and arranged in developing scenes with much use of stage mechanics.

Virtuosity seemed the keynote of these puzzling social novels of the late 90's, but the balance was amply restored as between moral content and technical skill in the three long books which followed, regarded by many critics as the ultimate fruition of James's art of the novel. The Ambassadors, The Wings of the Dove, and The Golden Bowl, all written between 1900 and 1904, have in common a subdued but nonetheless recognizable tone of affirmation not present in James's writing during the 90's. The two poles of James's intellectual life, American innocence with its strain of Protestant idealism and Old World experience, came together in the larger perspective and the high style of the late manner. The three novels were reworkings of the early international theme of Daisy Miller and The Portrait of a Lady in James's mature style, but with an added dimension: they probed more deeply into the moral and psychological ambiguities of the theme, and they rendered a final decision which preserved something of the values of both Europe and America. Biblical imagery is at the heart of two of these novels, and the central symbol of The Wings of the Dove is one of moral triumph and Christian forgiveness.

Milly Theale, the "dove" whose wings spread widely enough to cover even her enemies, was the one example of James's character portraits admittedly taken from his own life. He explained in the final chapter of his Notes of a Son and Brother (1914) that the fatally ill heroine of that novel of temptation and renunciation was modeled on Minny Temple. The bare plot of The Wings of the Dove is that of a betrayed heiress tragically dying whose fate is momentarily stayed by the prospect of marriage with Merton Densher. She accidentally discovers, however, that the proposal is the result of an intrigue to acquire her fortune. In her death Milly forgives her betrayers and bequeaths them her estate, but Densher, brushed by "the wings of the dove," refuses to marry Kate Croy and fulfill their agreement. Such a summary barely hints at the full, metaphorical meaning of the novel, however, or the struggle of conscience in Merton Densher which occupies the final parts of the book. It is essentially a tragedy on the theme of the unlived life, the pathos of missed experience which affected James so intensely in his memories of Minny Temple.

The Ambassadors had its origin in a remark attributed to James's lifelong friend, Howells. On a visit to Paris late in his life Howells felt that he had devoted himself to duty and effort but had somehow failed to "live."

James again explores the theme of lost experience, but this time in a mood of high comedy with a satisfying resolution, thus complementing the tragic denouement of *The Wings of the Dove*. Lambert Strether is the hero of this masterfully proportioned and skillfully wrought novel, the one which James himself thought to be "quite the best, all round, of my compositions." Strether comes to his realization at the mature age of 55 when he goes to Paris as the designated ambassador of the wealthy Mrs. Newsome of Woollett, Massachusetts, with the mission of rescuing her son from the influences of a French *femme du monde*. His gradual awareness of the aesthetic richness and imaginative "life" of Paris is subtly interwoven with his discovery that Mme. de Vionnet, instead of being a *femme fatale* exerting an evil influence upon Chad, is a woman of great charm and high lineage. In a key scene of revelation, one of idyllic beauty weighted with suggestions of the Garden of Eden and framed artistically as in a landscape, Strether learns that her relationship with Chad is one of intimacy. The shock of this recognition, however, only intensifies within him a feeling of the superior density of life which Paris holds over the barren atmosphere of Woollett and Mrs. Newsome's relatives. Strether fails as the ambassador and prospective husband of the wealthy widow, but as a true Jamesian aesthetic hero he has learned the lesson of Old World beauty and provocative "life."

Maggie Verver in *The Golden Bowl*, James's last major novel, is a later Isabel Archer who finds herself in an equivocal relationship to her husband, an Italian prince, and her best friend, Charlotte Stant, formerly her husband's consort. Maggie is another of James's innocent heroines whose marriage is threatened, but by maintaining her independence and seeing her situation through she manages successfully to solve her problems and restore her relationship to Prince Amerigo. The golden bowl with its ominous crack is a controlling image in this novel, a symbol of the possibilities of evil and menace in Maggie's life. The international marriage, productive of so much heartbreak in the earlier novels, now became a test of character in which Maggie's success in winning back her husband proves the measure of her achieved maturity. In its tone this novel belongs to a middle zone of tragicomedy, somewhere between *The Wings of the Dove* and *The Ambassadors*. Image and symbol carry much of its larger meaning, and the famous "late manner" functions both as a barrier to inattentive readers and a challenge to perceptive ones.

James returned to America in 1904 after twenty years, and for the first time he traveled throughout his home country, writing a book of his impressions, *The American Scene*. The prevailing note he struck was the unhappy alteration from his memories of old New York, Boston, or Newport to the materialistic nation he now observed. In 1905 James returned to England to begin the extensive revision of his works for the collected edition. Two autobiographical volumes were yet to come, but the "passionate pilgrimage" of this American-born master of Victorian fiction was approaching an end.

For James the art of fiction encompassed every province of life. In his now famous essay "The Art of Fiction" (1884) he defined the novel as "all life, all feeling, all observation, all vision." Art, by which he meant the art of the novel, had for him no limitations. "It is," he wrote in an impressive sentence, "an immense sensibility, a kind of huge spider web of the finest silken threads suspended in the chamber of consciousness and catching every air-borne particle in its tissue." For this reason, and because the human mind and the English language do not easily apprehend such infinite possibilities, James's work, especially in its mature phase, will remain a partially understood monument to a dedicated artist. If, as he said, "the deepest quality of a work of art will always be the quality of mind of the producer," it follows that the reader, too, must cultivate an intelligence nearly as fine in order to follow the artist into so rarefied an atmosphere. To be a reader of James's most advanced work, one must be (to apply another phrase from this essay) "one of the people on whom nothing is lost!"

The Madonna of the Future[1]

We had been talking about the masters who had achieved but a single masterpiece,—the artists and poets who but once in their lives had known the divine afflatus, and touched the high level of the best. Our host had been showing us a charming little cabinet picture by a painter whose name we had never heard, and who, after this one spasmodic bid for fame, had apparently relapsed into fatal mediocrity. There was some discussion as to the frequency of this phenomenon; during which, I observed, H—— sat silent, finishing his cigar with a meditative air, and looking at the picture, which was being handed round the table. "I don't know how a common a case it is," he said at last, "but I've seen it. I've known a poor fellow who painted his one masterpiece, and"— he added with a smile—"he didn't even paint that. He made his bid for fame, and missed it." We all knew H—— for a clever man who had seen much of men and manners, and had a great stock of reminiscences. Some one immediately questioned him further, and, while I was engrossed with the raptures of my neighbor over the little picture,[2] he was induced to tell his tale. If I were to doubt whether it would bear repeating, I should only have to remember how that charming woman, our hostess, who had left the table, ventured back in rustling rose-color, to pronounce our lingering a want of gallantry, and, finding us a listening circle, had sunk into her chair in spite of our cigars, and heard the story out so graciously, that when the catastrophe was

1. First published in the *Atlantic Monthly* for March, 1873. It was reprinted in *A Passionate Pilgrim, and Other Tales* (1875) and again in *The Madonna of the Future, and Other Tales* (2 vols., 1879). James revised the text extensively for all later editions, especially for the collected edition of his work (1907–9). The original text of 1873 is used here as an example of James's early style, though he later felt it was too "romantic" in tone and diction. His changes were mostly in the direction of what he regarded as greater precision of statement. See examples of his changes in the notes.
2. In the latest edition James changed "the little picture" to "the precious object in circulation."

reached she glanced across at me, and showed me a tender tear in each of her beautiful eyes.

It relates to my youth, and to Italy: two fine things! (H——— began.) I had arrived late in the evening at Florence, and while I finished my bottle of wine at supper, had fancied that, tired traveller though I was, I might pay the city a finer compliment than by going vulgarly to bed. A narrow passage wandered darkly away out of the little square before my hotel, and looked as if it bored into the heart of Florence. I followed it, and at the end of ten minutes emerged upon a great piazza, filled only with the mild autumn moonlight. Opposite rose the Palazzo Vecchio[3] like some huge civic fortress, with the great bell-tower springing from its embattled verge like a mountain-pine from the edge of a cliff. At its base, in its projected shadow, gleamed certain dim sculptures which I wonderingly approached. One of the images, on the left of the palace door, was a magnificent colossus shining through the dusky air like some young god of Defiance. In a moment I recognized him as Michael Angelo's David.[4] I turned with a certain relief from his sinister strength to a slender figure in bronze, stationed beneath the high, light *loggia*, which opposes the free and elegant span of its arches to the dead masonry of the palace; a figure supremely shapely and graceful; gentle, almost, in spite of his holding out with his light nervous arm the snaky head of the slaughtered Gorgon. His name is Perseus, and you may read his story, not in the Greek mythology, but in the memoirs of Benvenuto Cellini.[5] Glancing from one of these fine fellows to the other, I probably uttered some irrepressible commonplace of praise, for, as if provoked by my voice, a man rose from the steps of the Loggia, where he had been sitting in the shadow, and addressed me in good English,—a small, slim personage, clad in a sort of black velvet tunic (as it seemed), and with a mass of auburn hair, which gleamed in the moonlight escaping from a little mediæval *berretta*. In a tone of the most insinuating deference, he asked me for my "impressions." He seemed picturesque, fantastic, slightly unreal. Hovering there in this consecrated neighborhood, he might have passed for the genius of æsthetic hospitality,—if the

3. Great civic building of the Florentine Renaissance, completed about 1314, containing a huge tower. Once the official residence of the Medici, it now contains a gallery of art. It is located on a central square, the Piazza della Signoria.

4. Heroic-sized, white marble statue of the young King David, completed by Michelangelo about 1500. It was placed in the courtyard of the Palazzo Vecchio. James describes the original work, though present visitors to Florence see only a copy, the original having been placed under cover in the Galleria dell' Accademia.

5. In the Loggia dei Lanzi, another building adjacent to the palace, is a famous group of sculptures including the intricate bronze "Perseus," holding the head of Medusa, completed by Benvenuto Cellini, famous Florentine engraver and goldsmith, in 1554.

genius of æsthetic hospitality were not commonly some shabby little *custode*, flourishing a calico pocket-handkerchief, and openly resentful of the divided franc. This fantasy was made none the less plausible by the fine tirade with which he greeted my embarrassed silence.

"I've known Florence long, sir, but I've never known her so lovely as to-night. It's as if the ghosts of her past were abroad in the empty streets. The present is sleeping; the past hovers about us like a dream made visible. Fancy the old Florentines strolling up in couples to pass judgment on the last performance of Michael, of Benvenuto! We should come in for a precious lesson if we might overhear what they say. The plainest burgher of them, in his cap and gown, had a taste in the matter! That was the prime of art, sir. The sun stood high in heaven, and his broad and equal blaze made the darkest places bright and the dullest eyes clear. We live in the evening of time! We grope in the gray dusk, carrying each our poor little taper of selfish and painful wisdom, holding it up to the great models and to the dim ideal, and seeing nothing but overwhelming greatness and dimness. The days of illumination are gone! But do you know I fancy—I fancy,"—and he grew suddenly almost familiar in this visionary fervor,—"I fancy the light of that time rests upon us here for an hour! I have never seen the David so grand, the Perseus so fair! Even the inferior productions of John of Bologna and of Baccio Bandinelli[6] seem to realize the artist's dream. I feel as if the moonlit air were charged with the secrets of the masters, and as if, standing here in religious contemplation, we might—we might witness a revelation!" Perceiving at this moment, I suppose, my halting comprehension reflected in my puzzled face, this interesting rhapsodist paused and blushed. Then with a melancholy smile, "You think me a moonstruck charlatan, I suppose. It's not my habit to hang about the piazza and pounce upon innocent tourists. But to-night, I confess, I'm under the charm. And then, somehow, I fancied you, too, were an artist!"

"I'm not an artist, I'm sorry to say, as you must understand the term. But pray make no apologies. I am also under the charm; your eloquent reflections have only deepened it."

"If you're not an artist, you're worthy to be one!" he rejoined, with a bow. "A young man who arrives at Florence late in the evening, and, instead of going prosaically to bed, or hanging over the travellers' book at his hotel, walks forth without loss of time to pay his *devoirs* to the Beautiful, is a young man after my own

6. Giovanni da Bologna (sometimes written "Giambologna"), Flemish sculptor (1529?–1608), whose "Rape of the Sabines" is one of the group of statues in the Loggia dei Lanzi. Baccio Bandinelli, Italian sculptor (1493–1560).

heart!"

The mystery was suddenly solved; my friend was an American! He must have been, to take the picturesque so prodigiously to heart. "None the less so, I trust," I answered, "if the young man is a sordid New-Yorker."

"New-Yorkers," he solemnly proclaimed, "have been munificent patrons of art!"

For a moment I was alarmed. Was this midnight revery mere Yankee enterprise, and was he simply a desperate brother of the brush who had posted himself here to extort an "order" from a sauntering tourist? But I was not called to defend myself. A great brazen note broke suddenly from the far-off summit of the bell-tower above us and sounded the first stroke of midnight. My companion started, apologized for detaining me, and prepared to retire. But he seemed to offer so lively a promise of further entertainment, that I was indisposed to part with him, and suggested that we should stroll homeward together. He cordially assented, so we turned out of the Piazza, passed down before the statued arcade of the Uffizi,[7] and came out upon the Arno. What course we took I hardly remember, but we roamed slowly about for an hour, my companion delivering by snatches a sort of moon-touched æsthetic lecture. I listened in puzzled fascination, and wondered who the deuce he was. He confessed with a melancholy but all-respectful head-shake to his American origin. "We are the disinherited of Art!" he cried. "We are condemned to be superficial! We are excluded from the magic circle. The soil of American perception is a poor little barren, artificial deposit. Yes! we are wedded to imperfection. An American, to excel, has just ten times as much to learn as a European. We lack the deeper sense. We have neither taste nor tact nor force. How should we have them? Our crude and garish climate, our silent past, our deafening present, the constant pressure about us of unlovely circumstance, are as void of all that nourishes and prompts and inspires the artist, as my sad heart is void of bitterness in saying so! We poor aspirants must live in perpetual exile."

"You seem fairly at home in exile," I answered, "and Florence seems to me a very pretty Siberia. But do you know my own thought? Nothing is so idle as to talk about our want of a nutritive soil, of opportunity, of inspiration, and all the rest of it. The worthy part is to do something fine! There's no law in our glorious Constitution against that. Invent, create, achieve! No matter if you've to study fifty times as much as one of these! What else

7. The Uffizi ("Gallery of Offices") was built by the Medici family in 1560–80. The upper corridor has become one of the four or five most important art galleries of the world.

are you an artist for? Be you our Moses," I added, laughing and
laying my hand on his shoulder, "and lead us out of the house of
bondage!"

"Golden words,—golden words, young man!" he cried, with a
tender smile. " 'Invent, create, achieve!' Yes, that's our business:
I know it well. Don't take me, in Heaven's name, for one of your
barren complainers,—querulous cynics who have neither talent
nor faith. I'm at work!"—and he glanced about him and lowered
his voice as if this were a quite peculiar secret,—"I'm at work
night and day. I've undertaken a *creation!* I'm no Moses; I'm only
a poor, patient artist; but it would be a fine thing if I were to
cause some slender stream of beauty to flow in our thirsty land!
Don't think me a monster of conceit," he went on, as he saw me
smile at the avidity with which he adopted my fantasy; "I confess
that I'm in one of those moods when great things seem possible!
This is one of my nervous nights,—I dream waking! When the
south-wind blows over Florence at midnight, it seems to coax the
soul from all the fair things locked away in her churches and galleries; it comes into my own little studio with the moonlight, and
sets my heart beating too deeply for rest. You see I am always
adding a thought to my conception! This evening I felt that I
couldn't sleep unless I had communed with the genius of Michael!"[8]

He seemed deeply versed in local history and tradition, and he
expatiated *con amore* on the charms of Florence. I gathered that
he was an old resident, and that he had taken the lovely city into
his heart. "I owe her everything," he declared. "It's only since I
came here that I have really lived, intellectually. One by one, all
profane desires, all mere worldly aims, have dropped away from me,
and left me nothing but my pencil, my little note-book" (and he
tapped his breast-pocket), "and the worship of the pure masters,
—those who were pure because they were innocent and those who
were pure because they were strong!"

"And have you been very productive all this time?" I asked,
with amenity.

He was silent awhile before replying. "Not in the vulgar sense!"
he said, at last. "I have chosen never to manifest myself by imperfection. The good in every performance I have reabsorbed into
the generative force of new creations; the bad—there's always
plenty of that—I have religiously destroyed. I may say, with some
satisfaction, that I have not added a mite to the rubbish of the
world. As a proof of my conscientiousness,"—and he stopped short,
and eyed me with extraordinary candor, as if the proof were to be
overwhelming,—"I've never sold a picture! 'At least no merchant

8. Michelangelo Buonarotti (1475–1564).

traffics in my heart!' Do you remember the line in Browning? My little studio has never been profaned by superficial, feverish, mercenary work. It's a temple of labor, but of leisure! Art is long. If we work for ourselves, of course we must hurry. If we work for her, we must often pause. She can wait!"

This had brought us to my hotel door, somewhat to my relief, I confess, for I had begun to feel unequal to the society of a genius of this heroic strain. I left him, however, not without expressing a friendly hope that we should meet again. The next morning my curiosity had not abated; I was anxious to see him by common daylight. I counted upon meeting him in one of the many æsthetic haunts of Florence, and I was gratified without delay. I found him in the course of the morning in the Tribune of the Uffizi,—that little treasure-chamber of perfect works. He had turned his back on the Venus di Medici, and with his two arms resting on the railing which protects the pictures, and his head buried in his hands, he was lost in the contemplation of that superb triptych of Andrea Mantegna,[9]—a work which has neither the material splendor nor the commanding force of some of its neighbors, but which, glowing there with the loveliness of patient labor, suits possibly a more constant need of the soul. I looked at the picture for some time over his shoulder; at last, with a heavy sigh, he turned away and our eyes met. As he recognized me a deep blush rose to his face; he fancied, perhaps, that he had made a fool of himself overnight. But I offered him my hand with a frankness which assured him I was not a scoffer. I knew him by his ardent *chevelure*; otherwise he was much altered. His midnight mood was over, and he looked as haggard as an actor by daylight. He was far older than I had supposed, and he had less bravery of costume and gesture. He seemed the quite poor, patient artist he had proclaimed himself, and the fact that he had never sold a picture was more obvious than glorious. His velvet coat was threadbare, and his short slouched hat, of an antique pattern, revealed a rustiness which marked it an "original," and not one of the picturesque reproductions which brethren of his craft affect. His eye was mild and heavy, and his expression singularly gentle and acquiescent; the more so for a certain pallid leanness of visage which I hardly knew whether to refer to the consuming fire of genius or to a meagre diet. A very little talk, however, cleared his brow and brought back his eloquence.

"And this is your first visit to these enchanted halls?" he cried. "Happy, thrice happy youth!" And taking me by the arm, he prepared to lead me to each of the pre-eminent works in turn and show me the cream of the gallery. But before we left the Mantegna,

9. Mantuan painter (1431–1506), several of whose pictures adorn the Uffizi galleries.

he pressed my arm and gave it a loving look. "*He* was not in a hurry," he murmured. "He knew nothing of 'raw Haste, half-sister to Delay'!" How sound a critic my friend was I am unable to say, but he was an extremely amusing one;[1] overflowing with opinions, theories, and sympathies, with disquisition and gossip and anecdote. He was a shade too sentimental for my own sympathies, and I fancied he was rather too fond of superfine discriminations and of discovering subtle intentions in the shallow felicities of chance. At moments, too, he plunged into the sea of metaphysics and floundered awhile in waters too deep for intellectual security. But his abounding knowledge and happy judgment told a touching story of long attentive hours in this worshipful company; there was a reproach to my wasteful saunterings in so devoted a culture of opportunity. "There are two moods," I remember his saying, "in which we may walk through galleries, the critical and the ideal. They seize us at their pleasure, and we can never tell which is to take its turn. The critical mood, oddly, is the genial one; the friendly, the condescending. It relishes the pretty trivialities of art, its vulgar clevernesses, its conscious graces. It has a kindly greeting for anything which looks as if, according to his light, the painter had enjoyed doing it,—for the little Dutch cabbages and kettles, for the taper fingers and breezy mantles of late-coming Madonnas, for the little blue-hilled pastoral, sceptical Italian landscapes. Then there are the days of fierce, fastidious longing,—solemn church-feasts of the intellect,—when all vulgar effort and all petty success is a weariness, and everything but the best—the best of the best—disgusts. In these hours we are relentless aristocrats of taste. We'll not take Michael for granted, we'll not swallow Raphael whole!"

The gallery of the Uffizi is not only rich in its possessions, but peculiarly fortunate in that fine architectural accident, as one may call it, which unites it—with the breadth of river and city between them—to those princely chambers of the Pitti Palace.[2] The Louvre and the Vatican hardly give you such a sense of sustained enclosure as those long passages projected over street and stream to establish a sort of inviolate transition between the two palaces of art. We passed along the gallery in which those precious drawings by eminent hands hang chaste and gray above the swirl and murmur of the yellow Arno, and reached the ducal saloons of the

1. The beginning of this sentence was altered in the latest edition to, "How sound a critic he might have been didn't seem to concern me even then to concern me—it so served that he was an amusing one."
2. The Pitti Palace, begun about 1450, became a residence of the Medici family after Cosimo I. It is now mainly an art museum containing many masterpieces. As James describes, it is connected by a covered passage to the Uffizi. The passage rests upon the old bridge, Ponte Vecchio, the only one of several bridges across the Arno left intact in World War II.

Pitti. Ducal as they are, it must be confessed that they are imperfect as show-rooms, and that, with their deep-set windows and their massive mouldings, it is rather a broken light that reaches the pictured walls. But here the masterpieces hang thick, and you seem to see them in a luminous atmosphere of their own. And the great saloons, with their superb dim ceilings, their outer wall in splendid shadow, and the sombre opposite glow of mellow canvas and dusky gilding, make, themselves, almost as fine a picture as the Titians and Raphaels they imperfectly reveal. We lingered briefly before many a Raphael and Titian; but I saw my friend was impatient, and I suffered him at last to lead me directly to the goal of our journey,—the most tenderly fair of Raphael's Virgins, the Madonna in the Chair.[3] Of all the fine pictures of the world, it seemed to me this is the one with which criticism has least to do. None betrays less effort, less of the mechanism of effect and of the irrepressible discord between conception and result, which shows dimly in so many consummate works. Graceful, human, near to our sympathies as it is, it has nothing of manner, of method, nothing, almost, of style; it blooms there in rounded softness, as instinct with harmony as if it were an immediate exhalation of genius. The figure melts away the spectator's mind into a sort of passionate tenderness which he knows not whether he has given to heavenly purity or to earthly charm. He is intoxicated with the fragrance of the tenderest blossom of maternity that ever bloomed on earth.

"That's what I call a fine picture," said my companion, after we had gazed awhile in silence. "I have a right to say so, for I've copied it so often and so carefully that I could repeat it now with my eyes shut. Other works are of Raphael: this *is* Raphael himself. Others you can praise, you can qualify, you can measure, explain, account for: this you can only love and admire. I don't know in what seeming he walked among men, while this divine mood was upon him; but after it, surely, he could do nothing but die; this world had nothing more to teach him. Think of it awhile, my friend, and you'll admit that I'm not raving. Think of his seeing that spotless image, not for a moment, for a day, in a happy dream, as a restless fever-fit, not as a poet in a five minutes' time to snatch his phrase and scribble his immortal stanza, but for days together, while the slow labor of the brush went on, while the foul vapors of life interposed, and the fancy ached with tension, fixed, radiant, distinct, as we see it now! What a master, certainly! But ah, what a seer!"

"Don't you imagine," I answered, "that he had a model, and

---

3. One of Raphael's most popular paintings, a round canvas showing the Madonna seated in a chair, holding the Child, in an adoring pose.

that some pretty young woman?"

"As pretty a young woman as you please! It doesn't diminish the miracle! He took his hint, of course, and the young woman, possibly, sat smiling before his canvas. But, meanwhile, the painter's idea had taken wings. No lovely human outline could charm it to vulgar fact. He saw the fair form made perfect; he rose to the vision without tremor, without effort of wing; he communed with it face to face, and resolved into finer and lovelier truth the purity which completes it as the perfume completes the rose. That's what they call idealism; the word's vastly abused, but the thing is good. It's my own creed, at any rate. Lovely Madonna, model at once and muse, I call you to witness that I too am an idealist!"

"An idealist, then," I said, half-jocosely, wishing to provoke him to further utterance, "is a gentleman who says to Nature in the person of a beautiful girl, 'Go to, you're all wrong! Your fine is coarse, your bright is dim, your grace is *gaucherie*. This is the way you should have done it!' Isn't the chance against him?"

He turned upon me almost angrily, but perceiving the genial flavor of my sarcasm, he smiled gravely. "Look at that picture," he said, "cease your irreverent mockery! Idealism is *that*! There's no explaining it; one must feel the flame! It says nothing to Nature, or to any beautiful girl, that they'll not both forgive! It says to the fair woman, 'Accept me as your artist-friend, lend me your beautiful face, trust me, help me, and your eyes shall be half my masterpiece!' No one so loves and respects the rich realities of nature as the artist whose imagination caresses and flatters them. He knows what a fact may hold; (whether Raphael knew, you may judge by his portrait behind us there, of Tommaso Inghirami;) but his fancy hovers above it, as Ariel above the sleeping prince. There is only one Raphael, but an artist may still be an artist. As I said last night, the days of illumination are gone; visions are rare; we have to look long to see them. But in meditation we may still woo the ideal; round it, smooth it, perfect it. The result —the result" (here his voice faltered suddenly, and he fixed his eyes for a moment on the picture; when they met my own again they were full of tears)—"the result may be less than this; but still it may be good, it may be *great!*" he cried with vehemence. "It may hang somewhere, in after years, in goodly company, and keep the artist's memory warm. Think of being known to mankind after some such fashion as this! of hanging here through the slow centuries in the gaze of an altered world, living on and on in the cunning of an eye and hand that are part of the dust of ages, a delight and a law to remote generations; making beauty a force and purity an example!"

"Heaven forbid," I said, smiling, "that I should take the wind out of your sails; but doesn't it occur to you that beside being strong in his genius, Raphael was happy in a certain good faith of which we have lost the trick? There are people, I know, who deny that his spotless Madonnas are anything more than pretty blondes of that period, enhanced by the Raphaelesque touch, which they declare is a profane touch. Be that as it may, people's religious and æsthetic needs went hand in hand, and there was, as I may say, a demand for the Blessed Virgin, visible and adorable, which must have given firmness to the artist's hand. I'm afraid there is no demand now."

My companion seemed painfully puzzled; he shivered, as it were, in this chilling blast of scepticism. Then shaking his head with sublime confidence: "There is always a demand!" he cried; "that ineffable type is one of the eternal needs of man's heart; but pious souls long for it in silence, almost in shame; let it appear, and this faith grows brave. How *should* it appear in this corrupt generation? It can't be made to order. It could, indeed, when the order came, trumpet-toned, from the lips of the Church herself, and was addressed to genius panting with inspiration. But it can spring now only from the soil of passionate labor and culture. Do you really fancy that while, from time to time, a man of complete artistic vision is born into the world, that image can perish? The man who paints it has painted everything. The subject admits of every perfection,—form, color, expression, composition. It can be as simple as you please, and yet as rich, as broad and pure, and yet as full of delicate detail. Think of the chance for flesh in the little naked, nestling child, irradiating divinity; of the chance for drapery in the chaste and ample garment of the mother! Think of the great story you compress into that simple theme! Think, above all, of the mother's face and its ineffable suggestiveness, of the mingled burden of joy and trouble, the tenderness turned to worship, and the worship turned to far-seeing pity! Then look at it all in perfect line and lovely color, breathing truth and beauty and mastery!"

"*Anch' io son pittore!*"[4] I cried. "Unless I'm mistaken, you've a masterpiece on the stocks. If you put all that in, you'll do more than Raphael himself did. Let me know when your picture is finished, and wherever in the wide world I may be, I'll post back to Florence and salute—the *Madonna of the future!*"

He blushed vividly and gave a heavy sigh, half of protest, half of resignation. "I don't often mention my picture, in so many words. I detest this modern custom of premature publicity. A great work needs silence, privacy, mystery even. And then, do you know, people are so cruel, so frivolous, so unable to imagine a man's

4. "Even I am an artist!"

wishing to paint a Madonna at this time of day, that I've been
laughed at,—laughed at, sir!" And his blush deepened to crimson.
"I don't know what has prompted me to be so frank and trustful
with you. You look as if you wouldn't laugh at me. My dear young
man,"—and he laid his hand on my arm,—"I'm worthy of respect. Whatever my talents may be, I'm honest. There's nothing
grotesque in a pure ambition, or in a life devoted to it!"

There was something so sternly sincere in his look and tone,
that further questions seemed impertinent. I had repeated opportunity to ask them, however; for after this we spent much time
together. Daily, for a fortnight, we met by appointment, to see the
sights. He knew the city so well, he had strolled and lounged so
often through its streets and churches and galleries, he was so
deeply versed in its greater and lesser memories, so imbued with
the local genius, that he was an altogether ideal *valet de place*,
and I was glad enough to leave my Murray at home, and gather
facts and opinions alike from his gossiping commentary. He talked
of Florence like a lover, and admitted that it was a very old affair;[5]
he had lost his heart to her at first sight. "It's the fashion to talk
of all cities as feminine," he said, "but, as a rule, it's a monstrous
mistake. Is Florence of the same sex as New York, as Chicago?
She's the sole true woman of them all; one feels towards her as
a lad in his teens feels to some beautiful older woman with a
'history.' It's a sort of aspiring gallantry she creates." This disinterested passion seemed to stand my friend in stead of the common social ties; he led a lonely life, apparently, and cared for
nothing but his work. I was duly flattered by his having taken my
frivolous self into his favor, and by his generous sacrifice of precious hours, as they must have been, to my society. We spent
many of these hours among those early paintings in which Florence
is so rich, returning ever and anon with restless sympathies to
wonder whether these tender blossoms of art had not a vital
fragrance and savor more precious than the full-fruited knowledge
of the later works. We lingered often in the sepulchral chapel of
San Lorenzo, and watched Michael Angelo's dim-visaged warrior
sitting there like some awful Genius of Doubt and brooding behind
his eternal mask upon the mysteries of life.[6] We stood more than
once in the little convent chambers where Fra Angelico[7] wrought,

5. In the later edition this sentence
read: "He talked of Florence as a devoted old lover might still speak of an
old incomparable mistress who remained proof against time."
6. San Lorenzo, known as the church
of the Medici, was designed by Bru-
neschelli and built between 1425 and
1446. Completed by Michelangelo, it
contains several chapels with carved
tombs. James refers to one of the most
unique of these chapels, the New Sac-
risty, with Michelangelo's sculptured
figure of Lorenzo II, seated in a meditative pose.
7. The common name of Fra Giovanni
da Fiesole (1387–1455), a Dominican
friar and one of the Renaissance painters celebrated for his devotional portraits and religious scenes.

as if an angel indeed had held his hand, and gathered that sense of scattered dews and early bird-notes which makes an hour among his relics seem like a morning stroll in some monkish garden. We did all this and much more, wandered into dark chapels, damp courts, and dusty palace-rooms, in quest of lingering hints of fresco and lurking treasures of carving. I was more and more impressed with my companion's prodigious singleness of purpose. Everything was a pretext for some wild æsthetic rhapsody or revery. Nothing could be seen or said that didn't end sooner or later in a glowing discourse on the true, the beautiful, and the good. If my friend was not a genius, he was certainly a monomaniac; and I found as great a fascination in watching the odd lights and shades of his character as if he had been a creature from another planet. He seemed, indeed, to know very little of this one, and lived and moved altogether in his own little province of art. A creature more unsullied by the world it is impossible to conceive, and I often thought it a flaw in his artistic character that he hadn't a harmless vice or two. It amused me vastly at times to think that he was of our shrewd Yankee race; but, after all, there could be no better token of his American origin than this same fantastic fever. The very heat of his devotion was a sign of conversion; those born to European opportunity manage better to reconcile enthusiasm with comfort. He had, moreover, all our native mistrust for intellectual discretion and our native relish for sonorous superlatives. As a critic he was vastly more generous than just, and his mildest terms of approbation were "glorious," "superb," and "magnificent." The small change of admiration seemed to him no coin for a gentleman to handle; and yet, frank as he was intellectually, he was, personally, altogether a mystery. His professions, somehow, were all half-professions, and his allusions to his work and circumstances left something dimly ambiguous in the background. He was modest and proud, and never spoke of his domestic matters. He was evidently poor; yet he must have had some slender independence, since he could afford to make so merry over the fact that his culture of ideal of beauty had never brought him a penny. His poverty, I supposed, was his motive for never inviting me to his lodging nor mentioning its whereabouts. We met either in some public place or at my hotel, where I entertained him as freely as I might without appearing to be moved by charity. He seemed always hungry, which was his nearest approach to a "redeeming vice." I made a point of asking no impertinent questions, but, each time we met, I ventured to make some respectful allusion to the *magnum opus*, to inquire, as it were, as to its health and progress. "We're getting on, with the Lord's help," he would say with a grave smile. "We're doing well. You

see I have the grand advantage that I lose no time. These hours I
spend with you are pure profit. They're *suggestive*! Just as the truly
religious soul is always at worship, the genuine artist is always in
labor. He takes his property wherever he finds it, and learns some
precious secret from every object that stands up in the light. If
you but knew the rapture of observation! I gather with every glance
some hint for light, for color or relief! When I get home, I pour
out my treasures into the lap of my Madonna. O, I'm not idle!
Nulla dies sine linea."[8]

I was introduced in Florence to an American lady whose drawing-room had long formed an attractive place of reunion for the
foreign residents. She lived on the fourth floor, and she was not
rich; but she offered her visitors very good tea, little cakes at
option, and conversation not quite to match. Her conversation
had mainly an æsthetic flavor, for Mrs. Coventry was famously
"artistic." Her apartment was a sort of Pitti Palace *au petit pied*.
She possessed "early masters" by the dozen,—a cluster of
Peruginos in her dining-room, a Giotto in her boudoir, an Andrea
del Sarto over her parlor chimney-piece.[9] Backed by these treasures,
and by innumerable bronzes, mosaics, majolica dishes, and little
worm-eaten diptychs showing angular saints on gilded panels, our
hostess enjoyed the dignity of a sort of high-priestess of the arts.
She always wore on her bosom a huge miniature copy of the
Madonna della Seggiola.[1] Gaining her ear quietly one evening, I
asked her whether she knew that remarkable man, Mr. Theobald.

"Know him!" she exclaimed; "know poor Theobald! All Florence knows him, his flame-colored locks, his black velvet coat, his
interminable harangues on the beautiful, and his wondrous Madonna that mortal eye has never seen, and that mortal patience has
quite given up expecting."

"Really," I cried, "you don't believe in his Madonna?"

"My dear ingenuous youth," rejoined my shrewd friend, "has
he made a convert of you? Well, we all believed in him once; he
came down upon Florence and took us by storm. Another Raphael,
at the very least, had been born among men, and poor, dear America was to have the credit of him. Hadn't he the very hair of
Raphael flowing down on his shoulders? The hair, alas, but not
the head! We swallowed him whole, however; we hung upon his
lips and proclaimed his genius on the house-tops. The women
were all dying to sit to him for their portraits and be made im-

8. "No day [passes] without a line."
9. Giotto (1276?–1337), whose work
marked a shift from the Byzantine to
the Renaissance style of painting; Peru-
gino (1446–1523?), Umbrian School,
and teacher of Raphael; Andrea del
Sarto (1486–1531), known as the
"faultless" painter, whose style typified
the late, "high Renaissance" period (see
Browning's poem, "Andrea del Sarto").
1. The "Madonna of the Chair."

mortal, like Leonardo's Jocande.[2] We decided that his manner was a good deal like Leonardo's,—mysterious and inscrutable and fascinating. Mysterious it certainly was; mystery was the beginning and the end of it. The months passed by, and the miracle hung fire; our master never produced his masterpiece. He passed hours in the galleries and churches, posturing, musing, and gazing; he talked more than ever about the beautiful, but he never put brush to canvas. We had all subscribed, as it were, to the great performance; but as it never came off, people began to ask for their money again. I was one of the last of the faithful; I carried devotion so far as to sit to him for my head. If you could have seen the horrible creature he made of me, you would admit that even a woman with no more vanity than will tie her bonnet straight must have cooled off then. The man didn't know the very alphabet of drawing! His strong point, he intimated, was his sentiment; but is it a consolation, when one has been painted a fright, to know it has been done with peculiar gusto? One by one, I confess, we fell away from the faith, and Mr. Theobald didn't lift his little finger to preserve us. At the first hint that we were tired of waiting and that we should like the show to begin, he was off in a huff. 'Great work requires time, contemplation, privacy, mystery! O ye of little faith!' We answered that we didn't insist on a great work; that the fine-art tragedy might come at his convenience; that we merely asked for something to keep us from yawning, some inexpensive little *lever de rideau*.[3] Hereupon the poor man took his stand as a genius misconceived and persecuted, an *âme méconnue*,[4] and washed his hands of us from that hour! No, I believe he does me the honor to consider me the head and front of the conspiracy formed to nip his glory in the bud,—a bud that has taken twenty years to blossom. Ask him if he knows me, and he'd tell you I'm a horribly ugly old woman who has vowed his destruction because he wouldn't paint her portrait as a *pendant* to Titian's Flora.[5] I fancy that since then he has had none but chance followers, innocent strangers like yourself, who have taken him at his word. The mountain's still in labor; I've not heard that the mouse has been born. I pass him once in a while in the galleries, and he fixes his great dark eyes on me with a sublimity of indifference, as if I were a bad copy of a Sassoferrato.[6] It is a long time ago now that I heard that he

2. Model for Leonardo da Vinci's famous "Mona Lisa" (correctly, "Monna [Lady] Lisa"). She was the wife of Francesco del Gioconda. James later corrected his spelling to "Gioconda."
3. Raising of the curtain.
4. An unrecognized spirit.
5. Tiziano Vecellio (Titian) (1477–1576), noted for his sumptuous nude figures and flesh colors, painted "Flora," a romantic figure of a girl, in 1515.
6. Giovanni Battista Salvi (Il Sassoferato) (1605–85) painted mainly portraits of the Madonna and Child.

was making studies for a Madonna who was to be a *résumé* of all the other Madonnas of the Italian school, like that antique Venus who borrowed a nose from one great image and an ankle from another. It's certainly a masterly idea. The parts may be fine, but when I think of my unhappy portrait I tremble for the whole. He has communicated this fine idea under the pledge of solemn secrecy to fifty chosen spirits, to every one he has ever been able to button-hole for five minutes. I suppose he wants to get an order for it, and he's not to blame; for heaven knows how he lives. I see by your blush," my hostess frankly continued, "that you have been honored with his confidence. You needn't be ashamed, my dear young man; a man of your age is none the worse for a certain generous credulity, only allow me to give you a word of advice: keep your credulity out of your pockets. Don't pay for the picture till it's delivered. You've not been treated to a peep at it, I imagine. No more have your fifty predecessors in the faith. There are people who doubt whether there is any picture to be seen. I fancy, myself, that if one were to get into his studio, one would find something very like the picture in that tale of Balzac's,—a mere mass of incoherent scratches and daubs, a jumble of dead paint!"[7]

I listened to this pungent recital in silent wonder. It had a pain-fully plausible sound, and was not inconsistent with certain shy suspicions of my own. My hostess was a clever woman, and presumably a generous one. I determined to let my judgment wait upon events. Possibly she was right; but if she was wrong, she was cruelly wrong! Her version of my friend's eccentricities made me impatient to see him again and examine him in the light of public opinion. On our next meeting, I immediately asked him if he knew Mrs. Coventry. He laid his hand on my arm and gave me a sad smile. "Has she taxed *your* gallantry at last?" he asked. "She's a foolish woman. She's frivolous and heartless, and she pretends to be serious and kind. She prattles about Giotto's second manner and Vittoria Colonna's *liaison* with 'Michael,'[8]—one would think that Michael lived across the way and was expected in to take a hand at whist,—but she knows as little about art, and about the conditions of production, as I know about Buddhism. She profanes sacred words," he added more vehemently, after a pause. "She cares for you only as some one to hand tea-cups in that horrible mendacious little parlor of hers, with its trumpery Peruginos! If you can't dash off a new picture every three days, to

---

7. Honoré de Balzac's "The Unknown Masterpiece" (*Le Chef d'œuvre in-connu*) told of a painter who deluded himself with dreams of a portrait so true to life as to be indistinguishable from a living girl, but could produce only an unrecognizable jumble of color and line.

8. Vittoria Colonna was an Italian poetess. There was gossip about her relation with Michelangelo, who addressed verses to her.

show to her guests, she tells them in plain English you're an impostor!"

This attempt of mine to test Mrs. Coventry's accuracy was made in the course of a late afternoon walk to the quiet old church of San Miniato, on one of the hill-tops which directly overlook the city, from whose gate you are guided to it by a stony and cypress-bordered walk, which seems a most fitting avenue to a shrine. No spot is more propitious to lingering repose than the broad terrace in front of the church, where, lounging against the parapet, you may glance in slow alternation from the black and yellow marbles of the church façade, seamed and cracked with time and wind-sown with a tender flora of its own, down to the full domes and slender towers of Florence and over to the blue sweep of the wide-mouthed cup of mountains into whose hollow the little treasure-city has been dropped. I had proposed, as a diversion from the painful memories evoked by Mrs. Coventry's name, that Theobald should go with me the next evening to the opera, where some rarely played work was to be given. He declined, as I had half expected, for I had observed that he regularly kept his evenings in reserve, and never alluded to his manner of passing them. "You have reminded me before," I said, smiling, "of that charming speech of the Florentine painter in Alfred de Musset's Lorenzaccio:[9] '*I do no harm to any one. I pass my days in my studio. On Sunday, I go to the Annunziata or to Santa Maria; the monks think I have a voice; they dress me in a white gown and a red cap, and I take a share in the choruses, sometimes I do a little solo: these are the only times I go into public. In the evening, I visit my sweetheart; when the night is fine, we pass it on her balcony.*' I don't know whether you have a sweetheart, or whether she has a balcony. But if you're so happy, it's certainly better than trying to find a charm in a third-rate *prima donna*."

He made no immediate response, but at last he turned to me solemnly. "Can you look upon a beautiful woman with reverent eyes?"

"Really," I said, "I don't pretend to be sheepish, but I should be sorry to think I was impudent." And I asked him what in the world he meant. When at last I had assured him that I could undertake to temper admiration with respect, he informed me, with an air of religious mystery, that it was in his power to introduce me to the most beautiful woman in Italy. "A beauty with a soul!"

9. French historical drama with setting and theme of the Medici in Florence. James had translated it, and a minor character named Theobald may have suggested the name of his character.

"Upon my word," I cried, "you're extremely fortunate. And I shall rejoice to witness the conjunction."

"This woman's beauty," he answered, "is a lesson, a morality, a poem! It's my daily study."

Of course, after this, I lost no time in reminding him of what, before we parted, had taken the shape of a promise. "I feel somehow," he had said, "as if it were a sort of violation of that privacy in which I have always contemplated her beauty. This is friendship, my friend. No hint of her existence has ever fallen from my lips. But with too great a familiarity, we are apt to lose a sense of the real value of things, and you perhaps will throw some new light upon it and offer a fresher interpretation." We went accordingly by appointment to a certain ancient house in the heart of Florence,—the precinct of the Mercato Vecchio,[1]—and climbed a dark, steep staircase to the very summit of the edifice. Theobald's beauty seemed as jealously exalted above the line of common vision as the Belle aux Cheveux d'Or in her tower-top. He passed without knocking into the dark vestibule of a small apartment and, flinging open an inner door, ushered me into a small saloon. The room seemed mean and sombre, though I caught a glimpse of white curtains swaying gently at an open window. At a table, near a lamp, sat a woman dressed in black, working at a piece of embroidery. As Theobald entered, she looked up calmly, with a smile; but seeing me, she made a movement of surprise, and rose with a kind of stately grace. Theobald stepped forward, took her hand and kissed it, with an indescribable air of immemorial usage. As he bent his head, she looked at me askance, and I thought she blushed.

"*Ecco la Serafina!*" said Theobald, frankly, waving me forward. "This is a friend, and a lover of the arts," he added, introducing me. I received a smile, a courtesy, and a request to be seated.

The most beautiful woman in Italy was a person of a generous Italian type and of great simplicity of demeanor. Seated again at her lamp with her embroidery, she seemed to have nothing whatever to say. Theobald, bending towards her in a sort of Platonic ecstasy, asked her a dozen paternally tender questions as to her health, her state of mind, her occupations, and the progress of her embroidery, which he examined minutely and summoned me to admire. It was some portion of an ecclesiastical vestment,— yellow satin wrought with an elaborate design of silver and gold. She made answer in a full, rich voice, but with a brevity which I hesitated whether to attribute to native reserve or to the profane constraint of my presence. She had been that morning to confession; she had also been to market, and had bought a chicken

1. Market or shopping center near the Palazzo Vecchio.

for dinner. She felt very happy; she had nothing to complain of, except that the people for whom she was making her vestment, and who furnished her materials, should be willing to put such rotten silver thread into the garment, as one might say, of the Lord. From time to time, as she took her slow stitches, she raised her eyes and covered me with a glance which seemed at first to denote a placid curiosity, but in which, as I saw it repeated, I thought I perceived the dim glimmer of an attempt to establish an understanding with me at the expense of our companion. Meanwhile, as mindful as possible of Theobald's injunction of reverence, I considered the lady's personal claims to the fine compliment he had paid her.

That she was indeed a beautiful woman I perceived, after recovering from the surprise of finding her without the freshness of youth. Her beauty was of a sort which, in losing youth, loses little of its essential charm, expressed for the most part as it was in form and structure, and, as Theobald would have said, in "composition." She was broad and ample, low-browed and large-eyed, dark and pale. Her thick brown hair hung low beside her cheek and ear, and seemed to drape her head with a covering as chaste and formal as the veil of a nun. The poise and carriage of her head was admirably free and noble, and the more effective that their freedom was at moments discreetly corrected by a little sanctimonious droop, which harmonized admirably with the level gaze of her dark and quiet eye. A strong, serene physical nature and the placid temper which comes of no nerves and no troubles seemed this lady's comfortable portion. She was dressed in plain dull black, save for a sort of dark blue kerchief which was folded across her bosom and exposed a glimpse of her massive throat. Over this kerchief was suspended a little silver cross. I admired her greatly, and yet with a large reserve. A certain mild intellectual apathy belonged properly to her type of beauty, and had always seemed to round and enrich it; but this *bourgeoise* Egeria,[2] if I viewed her right, betrayed a rather vulgar stagnation of mind. There might have been once a dim, spiritual light in her face; but it had long since begun to wane. And furthermore, in plain prose, she was growing stout. My disappointment amounted very nearly to complete disenchantment when Theobald, as if to facilitate my covert inspection, declaring that the lamp was very dim and that she would ruin her eyes without more light, rose and fetched a couple of candles from the mantel-piece, which he placed, lighted, on the table. In this brighter illumination I

2. A nymph or goddess of the legendary period of Roman history who was supposed to have provided the ruler, Numa, with guidance for establishing the code of laws for the city, known as the Numaean Code.

perceived that our hostess was decidedly an elderly woman. She was neither haggard nor worn nor gray: she was simply coarse. The "soul" which Theobald had promised seemed scarcely worth making such a point of; it was no deeper mystery than a sort of matronly mildness of lip and brow. I would have been ready even to declare that that sanctified bend of the head was nothing more than the trick of a person constantly working at embroidery. It occurred to me even that it was a trick of a less innocent sort; for, in spite of the mellow quietude of her wits, this stately needle-woman dropped a hint that she took the situation rather less *au sérieux* than her friend. When he rose to light the candles, she looked across at me with a quick, intelligent smile and tapped her forehead with her forefinger; then, as, from a sudden feeling of compassionate loyalty to poor Theobald, I preserved a blank face, she gave a little shrug and resumed her work.

What was the relation of this singular couple? Was he the most ardent of friends or the most respectful of lovers? Did she regard him as an eccentric youth whose benevolent admiration of her beauty she was not ill-pleased to humor at this small cost of having him climb into her little parlor and gossip of summer nights? With her decent and sombre dress, her simple gravity, and that fine piece of priestly needlework, she looked like some pious lay-member of a sisterhood, living by special permission outside her convent walls. Or was she maintained here aloft by her friend in comfortable leisure, so that he might have before him the perfect, eternal type, uncorrupted and untarnished by the struggle for existence? Her shapely hands, I observed, were very fair and white; they lacked the traces of what is called "honest toil."

"And the pictures, how do they come on?" she asked of Theobald, after a long pause.

"Finely, finely! I have here a friend whose sympathy and encouragement give me new faith and ardor."

Our hostess turned to me, gazed at me a moment rather inscrutably, and then tapping her forehead with the gesture she had used a minute before, "He has a magnificent genius!" she said, with perfect gravity.

"I'm inclined to think so," I answered, with a smile.

"Eh, why do you smile?" she cried. "If you doubt it, you must see the *bambino!*" And she took the lamp and conducted me to the other side of the room, where on the wall, in a plain black frame, hung a large drawing in red chalk. Beneath it was festooned a little bowl for holy-water. The drawing represented a very young child, entirely naked, half nestling back against his mother's gown, but with his two little arms outstretched, as if in the act of benediction. It was executed with singular freedom and power, and yet seemed vivid with the sacred bloom of infancy. A sort of dimpled elegance and grace, in the midst of its boldness, recalled the touch of Correggio.[3] "That's what he can do!" said my hostess. "It's the blessed little boy whom I lost. It's his very image, and the Signor Teobaldo gave it me as a gift. He has given me many things beside!"

I looked at the picture for some time and admired it vastly. Turning back to Theobald, I assured him that if it were hung among the drawings in the Uffizi and labelled with a glorious name, it would hold its own. My praise seemed to give him extreme pleasure; he pressed my hands, and his eyes filled with tears. It moved him apparently with the desire to expatiate on the history of the drawing, for he rose and made his adieux to our companion, kissing her hand with the same mild ardor as before. It occurred to me that the offer of a similar piece of gallantry on my own part might help me to know what manner of woman she was. When she perceived my intention, she withdrew her hand, dropped her eyes solemnly, and made me a severe courtesy. Theobald took my arm and led me rapidly into the street.

"And what do you think of the divine Serafina?" he cried with fervor.

"It's certainly good solid beauty!"

He eyed me an instant askance, and then seemed hurried along by the current of remembrance. "You should have seen the mother and the child together, seen them as I first saw them,—the mother with her head draped in a shawl, a divine trouble in her face, and the bambino pressed to her bosom. You would have said, I think, that Raphael had found his match in common chance. I was coming in, one summer night, from a long walk in the country, when I met this apparition at the city gate. The woman held out her hand. I hardly knew whether to say, 'What do you want?' or to fall down and worship. She asked for a little money. I saw that she was beautiful and pale. She might have stepped out of the stable of Bethlehem! I gave her money and helped her on her way into the town. I had guessed her story. She, too, was a maiden mother, and she had been turned out into the world in her shame. I felt in all my pulses that here was my subject marvellously realized. I felt like one of the old convent artists who had had a vision. I rescued them, cherished them, watched them as I would have done some precious work of art, some lovely fragment of fresco discovered in a mouldering cloister. In a month, —as if to deepen and consecrate the pathos of it all,—the poor little child died. When she felt that he was going, she held him

3. Antonio Correggio (1494–1534) painted appealingly human and sentimentalized figures of the Holy Family.

up to me for ten minutes, and I made that sketch. You saw a feverish haste in it, I suppose; I wanted to spare the poor little mortal the pain of his position. After that, I doubly valued the mother. She is the simplest, sweetest, most natural creature that ever bloomed in this brave old land of Italy. She lives in the memory of her child, in her gratitude for the scanty kindness I have been able to show her, and in her simple religion! She's not even conscious of her beauty; my admiration has never made her vain. Heaven knows I've made no secret of it. You must have observed the singular transparency of her expression, the lovely modesty of her glance. And was there ever such a true virginal brow, such a natural classic elegance in the wave of the hair and the arch of the forehead? I've studied her; I may say I know her. I've absorbed her little by little; my mind is stamped and imbued, and I have determined now to clinch the impression; I shall at last invite her to sit for me!"

" 'At last,—at last'?" I repeated, in much amazement. "Do you mean that she has never done so yet?"

"I've not really had—a—a sitting," said Theobald, speaking very slowly. "I've taken notes, you know; I've got my grand fundamental impression. That's the great thing! But I've not actually had her as a model, posed and draped and lighted, before my easel."

What had become for the moment of my perception and my tact I am at a loss to say; in their absence, I was unable to repress a piece of *brusquerie* which I was destined to regret. We had stopped at a turning, beneath a lamp. "My poor friend," I exclaimed, laying my hand on his shoulder, "you've *dawdled!* She's an old, old woman—for a Madonna!"

It was as if I had brutally struck him; I shall never forget the long, slow, almost ghastly look of pain with which he answered me. "Dawdled—old, old!" he stammered. "Are you joking?"

"Why, my dear fellow, I suppose you don't take the woman for twenty?"

He drew a long breath and leaned against a house, looking at me with questioning, protesting, reproachful eyes. At last, starting forward, and grasping my arm: "Answer me solemnly: does she seem to you truly old? Is she wrinkled, is she faded, am I blind?"

Then at last I understood the immensity of his illusion; how, one by one, the noiseless years had ebbed away, and left him brooding in charmed inaction, forever preparing for a work forever deferred. It seemed to me almost a kindness now to tell him the plain truth. "I should be sorry to say you're blind," I answered, "but I think you're deceived. You've lost time in effortless contemplation. Your friend was once young and fresh and virginal;

but, I protest, that was some years ago. Still, she has *beaux restes*.[4] By all means make her sit for you!" I broke down; his face was too horribly reproachful.

He took off his hat and stood passing his handkerchief mechanically over his forehead. "*De beaux restes?* I thank you for sparing me the plain English. I must make up my Madonna out of *beaux restes!* What a masterpiece she'll be! Old—old! Old—old!" he murmured.

"Never mind her age," I cried, revolted at what I had done, "never mind my impression of her! You have your memory, your notes, your genius. Finish your picture in a month. I proclaim it beforehand a masterpiece, and I hereby offer you for it any sum you may choose to ask."

He stared, but he seemed scarcely to understand me. "Old— old!" he kept stupidly repeating. "If she is old, what am I? If her beauty has faded, where—where is my strength? Has life been a dream? Have I worshipped too long,—have I loved too well?" The charm, in truth, was broken. That the chord of illusion should have snapped at my light, accidental touch showed how it had been weakened by excessive tension. The poor fellow's sense of wasted time, of vanished opportunity, seemed to roll in upon his soul in waves of darkness. He suddenly dropped his head and burst into tears.

I led him homeward with all possible tenderness, but I attempted neither to check his grief, to restore his equanimity, nor to unsay the hard truth. When we reached my hotel I tried to induce him to come in. "We'll drink a glass of wine," I said, smiling, "to the completion of the Madonna!"

With a violent effort he held up his head, mused for a moment with a formidably sombre frown, and then giving me his hand, "I'll finish it," he cried, "in a month! No, in a fortnight! After all, I have it *here!*" and he tapped his forehead. "Of course she's old! She can afford to have it said of her,—a woman who has made twenty years pass like a twelvemonth! Old—old! Why, sir, she shall be eternal!"

I wished to see him safely to his own door, but he waved me back and walked away with an air of resolution, whistling, and swinging his cane. I waited a moment, and then followed him at a distance and saw him proceed to cross the Santa Trinità Bridge. When he reached the middle, he suddenly paused, as if his strength had deserted him, and leaned upon the parapet gazing over into the river. I was careful to keep him in sight; I confess that I passed ten very nervous minutes. He recovered himself at last, and went his way, slowly and with hanging head.

4. "The vestiges of beauty."

That I should really have startled poor Theobald into a bolder use of his long-garnered stores of knowledge and taste, into the vulgar effort and hazard of production, seemed at first reason enough for his continued silence and absence; but as day followed day without his either calling or sending me a line, and without my meeting him in his customary haunts, in the galleries, in the chapel at San Lorenzo, or strolling between the Arno-side and the great hedge-screen of verdure which, along the drive of the Cascine,[5] throws the fair occupants of barouche and phaeton into such becoming relief,—as for more than a week I got neither tidings nor sight of him, I began to fear that I had fatally offended him, and that, instead of giving a wholesome impetus to his talent, I had brutally paralyzed it. I had a wretched suspicion that I had made him ill. My stay at Florence was drawing to a close, and it was important that, before resuming my journey, I should assure myself of the truth. Theobald to the last had kept his lodging a mystery, and I was altogether at a loss where to look for him. The simplest course was to make inquiry of the beauty of the Mercato Vecchio, and I confess that unsatisfied curiosity as to the lady herself counselled it as well. Perhaps I had done her injustice, and she was as immortally fresh and fair as he conceived her. I was, at any rate, anxious to behold once more the ripe enchantress who had made twenty years pass for a twelve-month. I repaired accordingly, one morning, to her abode, climbed the interminable staircase, and reached her door. It stood ajar, and as I hesitated whether to enter, a little serving-maid came clattering out with an empty kettle, as if she had just performed some savory errand. The inner door, too, was open; so I crossed the little vestibule and entered the room in which I had formerly been received. It had not its evening aspect. The table, or one end of it, was spread for a late breakfast, and before it sat a gentleman,—an individual, at least, of the male sex,—dealing justice upon a beefsteak and onions and a bottle of wine. At his elbow, in friendly proximity, was placed the lady of the house. Her attitude, as I entered, was not that of an enchantress. With one hand she held in her lap a plate of smoking maccaroni; with the other she had lifted high in air one of the pendulous filaments of this succulent compound, and was in the act of slipping it gently down her throat. On the uncovered end of the table, facing her companion, were ranged half a dozen small statuettes, of some snuff-colored substance resembling terra-cotta. He, brandishing his knife with ardor, was apparently descanting on their merits.

Evidently, I darkened the door. My hostess dropped her

5. The Cascine Park drives, in the northwest end of the city, are lined with trees along the Arno River.

maccaroni—into her mouth, and rose hastily with a harsh exclamation and a flushed face. I immediately perceived that the Signora
Serafina's secret was even better worth knowing than I had supposed, and that the way to learn it was to take it for granted. I
summoned my best Italian, I smiled and bowed and apologized
for my intrusion; and in a moment, whether or no I had dispelled the lady's irritation, I had, at least, recalled her prudence.
I was welcome, she said; I must take a seat; this was another
friend of hers, also an artist, she declared with a smile which was
almost amiable. Her companion wiped his mustache and bowed
with great civility. I saw at a glance that he was equal to the
situation. He was presumably the author of the statuettes on the
table, and he knew a money-spending *forestiere*[6] when he saw one.
He was a small, wiry man, with a clever, impudent, *retroussé*
nose, a sharp little black eye, and waxed ends to his mustache. On
the side of his head he wore jauntily a little crimson velvet
smoking-cap, and I observed that his feet were encased in brilliant
slippers. On Serafina's remarking with dignity that I was the friend
of Mr. Theobald, he broke out into that fantastic French in which
Italians so freely indulge, and declared with fervor that Mr. Theobald was a magnificent genius.

"I'm sure I don't know," I answered with a shrug. "If you're in
a position to affirm it, you have the advantage of me. I've seen
nothing from his hand but the bambino yonder, which certainly
is fine."

He declared that the bambino was a masterpiece, a pure
Correggio. It was only a pity, he added with a knowing smile, that
the sketch had not been made on some good bit of genuine old
panel. The Signora Serafina hereupon protested that Mr. Theobald
was the soul of honor, and that he would never lend himself to
a deceit. "I'm not a judge of genius," she said, "and I know nothing of pictures. I'm but a poor simple widow; but I know that
the Signor Teobaldo has the heart of an angel and the virtue of
a saint. He's my benefactor," she added sententiously. The
after-glow of the somewhat sinister flush with which she had
greeted me still lingered in her cheek, and perhaps did not favor
her beauty; I could not but fancy it a wise custom of Theobald's
to visit her only by candlelight. She was coarse, and her poor
adorer was a poet.

"I have the greatest esteem for him," I said; "it is for this
reason that I have been uneasy at not seeing him for ten days.
Have you seen him? Is he perhaps ill?"

"Ill! Heaven forbid!" cried Serafina, with genuine vehemence.
Her companion uttered a rapid expletive, and reproached her

6. A foreigner.

with not having been to see him. She hesitated a moment; then she simpered the least bit and bridled. "He comes to see me— without reproach! But it would not be the same for me to go to him, though, indeed, you may almost call him a man of holy life."

"He has the greatest admiration for you," I said. "He would have been honored by your visit."

She looked at me a moment sharply. "More admiration than you. Admit that!" Of course I protested with all the eloquence at my command, and the Signora Serafina then confessed that she had taken no fancy to me on my former visit, and that, Theobald not having returned, she believed I had poisoned his mind against her. "It would be no kindness to the poor gentleman, I can tell you that," she said. "He has come to see me every evening for years. It's a long friendship! No one knows him as well as I."

"I don't pretend to know him, or to understand him," I said. "He's a mystery! Nevertheless he seems to me a little—" And I touched my forehead and waved my hand in the air.

Serafina glanced at her companion a moment, as if for inspiration. He contented himself with shrugging his shoulders, as he filled his glass again. The Signora hereupon gave me a more softly insinuating smile than would have seemed likely to bloom on so candid a brow. "It's for that that I love him!" she said. "The world has so little kindness for such persons. It laughs at them, and despises them, and cheats them. He is too good for this wicked life! It's his fancy that he finds a little Paradise up here in my poor apartment. If he thinks so, how can I help it? He has a strange belief—really, I ought to be ashamed to tell you—that I resemble the Blessed Virgin: Heaven forgive me! I let him think what he pleases, so long as it makes him happy. He was very kind to me once, and I am not one that forgets a favor. So I receive him every evening civilly, and ask after his health, and let him look at me on this side and that! For that matter, I may say it without vanity, I was worth looking at once! And he's not always amusing, poor man! He sits sometimes for an hour without speaking a word, or else he talks away without stopping on art and nature, and beauty and duty, and fifty fine things that are all so much Latin to me. I beg you to understand that he has never said a word to me that I mightn't decently listen to. He may be a little cracked, but he's one of the saints."

"Eh!" cried the man, "the saints were all a little cracked!"

Serafina, I fancied, left part of her story untold; but she told enough of it to make poor Theobald's own statement seem intensely pathetic in its exalted simplicity. "It's a strange fortune, certainly," she went on, "to have such a friend as this dear man, —a friend who's less than a lover and more than a friend." I glanced at her companion, who preserved an impenetrable smile, twisted the end of his mustache, and disposed of a copious mouthful. Was *he* less than a lover? "But what will you have?" Serafina pursued. "In this hard world one mustn't ask too many questions; one must take what comes and keep what one gets. I've kept my good friend for twenty years, and I do hope that, at this time of day, Signore, you've not come to turn him against me!"

I assured her that I had no such design, and that I should vastly regret disturbing Mr. Theobald's habits or convictions. On the contrary, I was alarmed about him, and I should immediately go in search of him. She gave me his address and a florid account of her sufferings at his non-appearance. She had not been to him, for various reasons; chiefly because she was afraid of displeasing him, as he had always made such a mystery of his home. "You might have sent this gentleman!" I ventured to suggest.

"Ah!" cried the gentleman, "he admires the Signora Serafina, but he wouldn't admire me." And then, confidentially, with his finger on his nose, "He's a purist!"

I was about to withdraw, on the promise that I would inform the Signora Serafina of my friend's condition, when her companion, who had risen from table and girded his loins apparently for the onset, grasped me gently by the arm, and led me before the row of statuettes. "I perceive by your conversation, signore, that you are a patron of the arts. Allow me to request your honorable attention for these modest products of my own ingenuity. They are brand-new, fresh from my *atelier*, and have never been exhibited in public. I have brought them here to receive the verdict of the Signora Serafina, who is a good critic, for all she may pretend to the contrary. I am the inventor of this peculiar style of statuette,—of subject, manner, material, everything. Touch them, I pray you; handle them; you needn't fear. Delicate as they look, it is impossible they should break! My various creations have met with great success. They are especially admired by Americans. I have sent them all over Europe,—to London, Paris, Vienna! You may have observed some little specimens in Paris, on the Boulevard, in a shop of which they constitute the specialty. There is always a crowd about the window. They form a very pleasing ornament for the mantel-shelf of a *jeune homme élégant*, for the boudoir of a *jolie femme*. You couldn't make a prettier present to a person with whom you wished to exchange a harmless joke. It is not classic art, signore, of course; but, between ourselves, isn't classic art sometimes rather a bore? Caricature, burlesque, *la charge*, as the French say, has hitherto been confined to paper, to the pen and pencil. Now, it has been my inspiration to introduce it into statuary. For this purpose I have invented a peculiar plastic compound which you will permit me not to divulge. That's my secret, signore! It's as light, you perceive, as cork, and yet as firm as alabaster! I frankly confess that I really pride myself as much on this little stroke of chemical ingenuity as upon the other element of novelty in my creations,—my types. What do you say to my types, signore? The idea is bold; does it strike you as happy? Cats and monkeys,—monkeys and cats,—all human life is there! Human life, of course, I mean, viewed with the eye of the satirist! To combine sculpture and satire, signore, has been my unprecedented ambition. I flatter myself that I have not egregiously failed."

As this jaunty Juvenal[7] of the chimney-piece delivered himself of his seductive allocution, he took up his little groups successively from the table, held them aloft, turned them about, rapped them with his knuckles, and gazed at them lovingly with his head on one side. They consisted each of a cat and a monkey, fantastically draped, in some preposterously sentimental conjunction. They exhibited a certain sameness of motive, and illustrated chiefly the different phases of what, in delicate terms, may be called gallantry and coquetry; but they were strikingly clever and expressive, and were at once very perfect cats and monkeys and very natural men and women. I confess, however, that they failed to amuse me. I was doubtless not in a mood to enjoy them, for they seemed to me peculiarly cynical and vulgar. Their imitative felicity was revolting. As I looked askance at the complacent little artist, brandishing them between finger and thumb, and caressing them with an amorous eye, he seemed to me himself little more than an exceptionally intelligent ape. I mustered an admiring grin, however, and he blew another blast. "My figures are studied from life! I have a little menagerie of monkeys whose frolics I contemplate by the hour. As for the cats, one has only to look out of one's back window! Since I have begun to examine these expressive little brutes, I have made many profound observations. Speaking, signore, to a man of imagination, I may say that my little designs are not without a philosophy of their own. Truly, I don't know whether the cats and monkeys imitate us, or whether it's we who imitate them." I congratulated him on his philosophy, and he resumed: "You will do me the honor to admit that I have handled my subjects with delicacy. Eh, it was needed, signore! I have been free, but not licentious. Just a hint, you know! You may see as much or as little as you please. These little groups, however, are no measure of my invention. If you will favor me with a call at my studio, I think that you will

7. Famous Roman satirist of the 1st century A.D. noted for the sharpness of his attacks upon human vice and folly.

admit that my combinations are really infinite. I likewise execute figures to command. You have perhaps some little motive,—the fruit of your own philosophy of life, signore,—which you would like to have interpreted. I can promise to work it up to your satisfaction; it shall be as malicious as you please. Allow me to present you with my card, and to remind you that my prices are moderate. Only sixty francs for a little group like that. My statuettes are as durable as bronze,—*ære perennius*, signore,—and, between ourselves, I think they are more amusing."

As I pocketed his card, I glanced at the worthy Serafina, wondering whether she had an eye for contrasts. She had picked up one of the little couples and was tenderly dusting it with a feather broom.

What I had just seen and heard had so deepened my compassionate interest in my deluded friend, that I took a summary leave, and made my way directly to the house designated by the Signora Serafina. It was in an obscure corner of the opposite side of the town, and presented a sombre and squalid appearance. An old woman in the doorway, on my inquiring for Theobald, ushered me in with a mumbled blessing and an expression of relief that the poor gentleman had a friend. His lodging seemed to consist of a single room at the top of the house. On getting no answer to my knock, I opened the door, supposing that he was absent; so that it gave me a certain shock to find him sitting there helpless and dumb. He was seated near the single window, facing an easel which supported a large canvas. On my entering, he looked up at me blankly, without changing his position, which was that of absolute lassitude and dejection, his arms loosely folded, his legs stretched before him, his head hanging on his breast. Advancing into the room, I perceived that his face vividly corresponded with his attitude. He was pale, haggard, and unshaven, and his dull and sunken eye gazed at me without a spark of recognition. I had been afraid that he would greet me with fierce reproaches, as the cruelly officious friend who had turned his peace to bitterness, and I was relieved to find that my appearance awakened no visible resentment. "Don't you know me?" I asked, as I put out my hand. "Have you already forgotten me?"

He made no response, kept his position stupidly, and left me staring about the room. It spoke most plaintively for itself. Shabby, sordid, naked, it contained, beyond the wretched bed, but the scantiest provision for personal comfort. It was bedroom at once and studio,—a grim ghost of a studio. A few dusty casts and prints on the walls, three or four old canvases turned face inward, and a rusty-looking color-box formed, with the easel at the window, the sum of its appurtenances. The place savored horribly of poverty. Its only wealth was the picture on the easel, presumably the famous Madonna. Averted as this was from the door, I was unable to see its face; but at last, sickened by the vacant misery of the spot, I passed behind Theobald, eagerly and tenderly, and yet I can hardly say that I was surprised at what I found,—a canvas that was a mere dead blank, cracked and discolored by time. This was his immortal work! But though not surprised, I confess I was powerfully moved, and I think that for five minutes I could not have trusted myself to speak. At last, my silence affected him; he stirred and turned, and then rose and looked at me with a slowly kindling eye. I murmured some kind, ineffective nothings about his being ill and needing advice and care, but he seemed absorbed in the effort to recall distinctly what had last passed between us. "You were right," he said with a pitiful smile, "I'm a dawdler! I'm a failure! I shall do nothing more in this world. You opened my eyes; and, though the truth is bitter, I bear you no grudge. Amen! I've been sitting here for a week face to face with the truth, with the past, with my weakness and poverty and nullity. I shall never touch a brush! I believe I've neither eaten nor slept. Look at that canvas!" he went on, as I relieved my emotion in the urgent request that he would come home with me and dine. "That was to have contained my masterpiece! Isn't it a promising foundation? The elements of it are all *here*." And he tapped his forehead with that mystic confidence which had marked the gesture before. "If I could only transpose them into some brain that had the hand, the will! Since I've been sitting here taking stock of my intellects, I've come to believe that I have the material for a hundred masterpieces. But my hand is paralyzed now, and they'll never be painted. I never began! I waited and waited to be worthier to begin, and wasted my life in preparation. While I fancied my creation was growing, it was dying. I've taken it all too hard! Michael Angelo didn't, when he went at the Lorenzo! He did his best at a venture, and his venture is immortal. *That's* mine!" And he pointed with a gesture I shall never forget at the empty canvas. "I suppose we're a genus by ourselves in the providential scheme,—we talents that can't act, that can't do or dare! We take it out in talk, in plans and promises, in study, in visions! But our visions, let me tell you," he cried, with a toss of his head, "have a way of being brilliant, and a man hasn't lived in vain who has seen the things I have! Of course you'll not believe in them when that bit of worm-eaten cloth is all I have to show for them; but to convince you, to enchant and astound the world, I need only the hand of Raphael. I have his brain. A pity, you'll say, I haven't his modesty. Ah, let me babble now; it's all I have left! I'm the half of a genius! Where in the wide world is my other half? Lodged perhaps in the vulgar soul, the cunning, ready fingers of some dull copyist or some trivial artisan who turns out by the dozen his easy prodigies of touch! But it's not for me to sneer at him; he at least does something. He's not a dawdler! Well for me if I had been vulgar and clever and reckless, if I could have shut my eyes and dealt my stroke!"

What to say to the poor fellow, what to do for him, seemed hard to determine; I chiefly felt that I must break the spell of his present inaction, and remove him from the haunted atmosphere of the little room it seemed such cruel irony to call a studio. I cannot say I persuaded him to come out with me; he simply suffered himself to be led, and when we began to walk in the open air I was able to measure his pitifully weakened condition. Nevertheless, he seemed in a certain way to revive, and murmured at last that he would like to go to the Pitti Gallery. I shall never forget our melancholy stroll through those gorgeous halls, every picture on whose walls seemed, even to my own sympathetic vision, to glow with a sort of insolent renewal of strength and lustre. The eyes and lips of the great portraits seemed to smile in ineffable scorn of the dejected pretender who had dreamed of competing with their glorious authors; the celestial candor, even, of the Madonna in the Chair, as we paused in perfect silence before her, was tinged with the sinister irony of the women of Leonardo. Perfect silence indeed marked our whole progress,—the silence of a deep farewell; for I felt in all my pulses, as Theobald, leaning on my arm, dragged one heavy foot after the other, that he was looking his last. When we came out, he was so exhausted that, instead of taking him to my hotel to dine, I called a carriage and drove him straight to his own poor lodging. He had sunk into an extraordinary lethargy; he lay back in the carriage, with his eyes closed, as pale as death, his faint breathing interrupted at intervals by a sudden gasp, like a smothered sob or a vain attempt to speak. With the help of the old woman who had admitted me before, and who emerged from a dark back court, I contrived to lead him up the long steep staircase and lay him on his wretched bed. To her I gave him in charge, while I prepared in all haste to seek a physician. But she followed me out of the room with a pitiful clasping of her hands.

"Poor, dear, blessed gentleman," she murmured; "is he dying?"

"Possibly. How long has he been thus?"

"Since a night he passed ten days ago. I came up in the morning to make his poor bed, and found him sitting up in his clothes before that great canvas he keeps there, and, poor, dear, strange man, says his prayers to! He had not been to bed, nor since then, properly! What has happened to him? Has he found out about the Serafina?" she whispered with a glittering eye and a toothless grin.

"Prove at least that one old woman can be faithful," I said, "and watch him well till I come back." My return was delayed, through the absence of the English physician on a round of visits, and my vainly pursuing him from house to house before I overtook him. I brought him to Theobald's bedside none too soon. A violent fever had seized our patient, and the case was evidently grave. A couple of hours later I knew that he had brain-fever. From this moment I was with him constantly, but I am far from wishing to describe his illness. Excessively painful to witness, it was happily brief. Life burned out in delirium. A certain night that I passed at his pillow, listening to his wild snatches of regret, of aspiration, of rapture and awe at the phantasmal pictures with which his brain seemed to swarm, recurs to my memory now like some stray page from a lost masterpiece of tragedy. Before a week was over we had buried him in the little Protestant cemetery on the way to Fiesole. The Signora Serafina, whom I had caused to be informed of his illness, had come in person, I was told, to inquire about its progress; but she was absent from his funeral, which was attended by but a scanty concourse of mourners. Half a dozen old Florentine sojourners, in spite of the prolonged estrangement which had preceded his death, had felt the kindly impulse to honor his grave. Among them was my friend Mrs. Coventry, whom I found, on my departure, waiting at her carriage door at the gate of the cemetery.

"Well," she said, relieving at last with a significant smile the solemnity of our immediate greeting, "and the great Madonna? Have you seen her, after all?"

"I've seen her," I said; "she's mine,—by bequest. But I shall never show her to you."

"And why not, pray?"

"My dear Mrs. Coventry, you'd not understand her!"

"Upon my word, you're polite."

"Excuse me; I'm sad and vexed and bitter." And with reprehensible rudeness, I marched away. I was excessively impatient to leave Florence; my friend's dark spirit seemed diffused through all things. I had packed my trunk to start for Rome that night, and meanwhile, to beguile my unrest, I aimlessly paced the streets. Chance led me at last to the church of San Lorenzo. Remembering poor Theobald's phrase about Michael Angelo,—"He did his best at a venture,"—I went in and turned my steps to the chapel of the tombs. Viewing in sadness the sadness of its immortal treasures, I fancied, while I stood there, that the scene demanded no ampler commentary. As I passed through the church again to depart, a woman, turning away from one of the side-altars, met me face to face. The black shawl depending from her head draped picturesquely the handsome visage of the Signora Serafina. She stopped as she recognized me, and I saw that she wished to speak. Her eye was bright and her ample bosom heaved in a way that seemed to portend a certain sharpness of reproach. But the expression of my own face, apparently, drew the sting from her resentment, and she addressed me in a tone in which bitterness was tempered by a sort of dogged resignation.[8] "I know it was you, now, that separated us," she said. "It was a pity he ever brought you to see me! Of course, you couldn't think of me as he did. Well, the Lord gave him, the Lord has taken him. I've just paid for a nine days' mass for his soul. And I can tell you this, signore, I never deceived him. Who put it into his head that I was made to live on holy thoughts and fine phrases? It was his own fancy, and it pleased him to think so. Did he suffer much?" she added more softly, after a pause.

"His sufferings were great, but they were short."

"And did he speak of me?" she had hesitated and dropped her eyes; she raised them with her question, and revealed in their sombre stillness a gleam of feminine confidence which, for the moment, revived and illumined her beauty. Poor Theobald! Whatever name he had given his passion, it was still her fine eyes that had charmed him.

"Be contented, madam," I answered, gravely.

She dropped her eyes again and was silent. Then exhaling a full, rich sigh, as she gathered her shawl together: "He was a magnificent genius!"

I bowed, and we separated.

Passing through a narrow side-street on my way back to my hotel, I perceived above a doorway a sign which it seemed to me I had read before. I suddenly remembered that it was identical with the superscription of a card that I had carried for an hour in my waistcoat-pocket. On the threshold stood the ingenious artist whose claims to public favor were thus distinctly signalized, smoking a pipe in the evening air, and giving the finishing polish with a bit of rag to one of his inimitable "combinations." I caught the expressive curl of a couple of tails. He recognized me, removed his little red cap with a most obsequious bow, and motioned me to enter his studio. I returned his bow and passed on, vexed with the apparition. For a week afterwards, whenever I was seized

8. James later changed the last part of this sentence to read: " * * * was tempered by an acceptance of anticlimax that had been after all so long and so wondrously postponed."

among the ruins of Roman greatness with some peculiarly poignant memory of Theobald's transcendent illusions and deplorable
failure, I seemed to hear a fantastic, impertinent murmur, "Cats
and monkeys, monkeys and cats; all human life is there!"

1873, 1875

The Real Thing[9]

When the porter's wife (she used to answer the house-bell), announced "A gentleman and a lady, sir," I had, as I often had in
those days—the wish being father to the thought—an immediate
vision of sitters. Sitters my visitors in this case proved to be; but not
in the sense I should have preferred. There was nothing at first
however to indicate that they mightn't have come for a portrait.
The gentleman, a man of fifty, very high and very straight, with a
moustache slightly grizzled and a dark grey walking-coat admirably
fitted, both of which I noted professionally—I don't mean as a barber or yet as a tailor—would have struck me as a celebrity if celebri-
ties often were striking. It was a truth of which I had for some time
been conscious that a figure with a good deal of frontage was, as
one might say, almost never a public institution. A glance at the
lady helped to remind me of this paradoxical law: she also looked
too distinguished to be a "personality." Moreover one would scarcely
come across two variations together.

Neither of the pair spoke immediately—they only prolonged the
preliminary gaze suggesting that each wished to give the other a
chance. They were visibly shy; they stood there letting me take them
in—which, as I afterwards perceived, was the most practical thing
they could have done. In this way their embarrassment served their
cause. I had seen people painfully reluctant to mention that they desired anything so gross as to be represented on canvas; but the scruples of my new friends appeared almost insurmountable. Yet the
gentleman might have said "I should like a portrait of my wife,"
and the lady might have said "I should like a portrait of my husband." Perhaps they weren't husband and wife—this naturally

---

9. The first appearance of this story
was in *Black and White*, April 16,
1892; the first book publication was in
The Real Thing, and Other Tales
(1893). The latter text is used here.
James revised it later for the New York
Edition. For the source idea of the story
James was indebted to the writer and
artist, George Du Maurier, who (as
James writes in his later Preface)
"had spoken to me of a call from a
strange and striking couple desirous to
propose themselves as artist's models
for his weekly 'social' illustrations to
Punch." This couple, whom James
named the Monarchs, had been "overtaken by reverses even while conforming impeccably to the standard of
superficial 'smartness.' " The question
which interested James was the rival
claims of the Monarchs as "the real
thing" and of Miss Churm and Oronte,
his two professional models, "who had
had, for dear life, to *know how* to do
something." This question struck him
as "exquisite," he wrote, "and out of
a momentary fond consideration of it
The Real Thing sprang at a bound."

would make the matter more delicate. Perhaps they wished to be done together—in which case they ought to have brought a third person to break the news.

"We come from Mr. Rivet," the lady finally said with a dim smile that had the effect of a moist sponge passed over a "sunk" piece of painting, as well as of a vague allusion to vanished beauty. She was as tall and straight, in her degree, as her companion, and with ten years less to carry. She looked as sad as a woman could look whose face was not charged with expression; that is her tinted oval mask showed friction as an exposed surface shows it. The hand of time had played over her freely, but only to simplify. She was slim and stiff, and so well-dressed, in dark blue cloth, with lappets and pockets and buttons, that it was clear she employed the same tailor as her husband. The couple had an indefinable air of prosperous thrift—they evidently got a good deal of luxury for their money. If I was to be one of their luxuries, it would behoove me to consider my terms.

"Ah, Claude Rivet recommended me?" I echoed; and I added that it was very kind of him, though I could reflect that, as he only painted landscape, this was not a sacrifice.

The lady looked very hard at the gentleman, and the gentleman looked round the room. Then, staring at the door a moment and stroking his moustache, he rested his pleasant eyes on me with the remark: "He said you were the right one."

"I try to be, when people want to sit."

"Yes, we should like to," said the lady anxiously.

"Do you mean together?"

My visitors exchanged a glance. "If you could do anything with *me* I suppose it would be double," the gentleman stammered.

"Oh, yes, there's naturally a higher charge for two figures than for one."

"We should like to make it pay," the husband confessed.

"That's very good of you," I returned, appreciating so unwonted a sympathy—for I supposed he meant pay the artist.

A sense of strangeness seemed to dawn on the lady. "We mean for the illustrations—Mr. Rivet said you might put one in."

"Put one in—an illustration?" I was equally confused.

"Sketch her off, you know," said the gentleman, colouring.

It was only then that I understood the service Claude Rivet had rendered me; he had told them how I worked in black and white, for magazines, for storybooks, for sketches of contemporary life, and consequently had copious employment for models. These things were true, but it was not less true—I may confess it now; whether because the aspiration was to lead to everything or to nothing I leave the reader to guess—that I couldn't get the honours, to say nothing of the emoluments, of a great painter of portraits out of my head. My "illustrations" were my pot-boilers; I looked to a different branch of art—far and away the most interesting it had always seemed to me—to perpetuate my fame. There was no shame in looking to it also to make my fortune; but that fortune was by so much further from being made from the moment my visitors wished to be "done" for nothing. I was disappointed; for in the pictorial sense I had immediately *seen* them. I had seized their type—I had already settled what I would do with it. Something that wouldn't absolutely have pleased them, I afterwards reflected.

"Ah, you're—you're—a—?" I began as soon as I had mastered my surprise. I couldn't bring out the dingy word "models": it seemed to fit the case so little.

"We haven't had much practice," said the lady.

"We've got to *do* something, and we've thought that an artist in your line might perhaps make something for us," her husband threw off. He further mentioned that they didn't know many artists and that they had gone first, on the off chance—he painted views of course, but sometimes put in figures; perhaps I remembered—to Mr. Rivet, whom they had met a few years before at a place in Norfolk where he was sketching.

"We used to sketch a little ourselves," the lady hinted.

"It's very awkward, but we absolutely *must* do something," her husband went on.

"Of course we're not so *very* young," she admitted with a wan smile.

With the remark that I might as well know something more about them the husband had handed me a card extracted from a neat new pocket-book—their appurtenances were all of the freshest—and inscribed with the words "Major Monarch." Impressive as these words were they didn't carry my knowledge much further; but my visitor presently added: "I've left the army and we've had the misfortune to lose our money. In fact our means are dreadfully small."

"It's an awful bore," said Mrs. Monarch.

They evidently wished to be discreet—to take care not to swagger because they were gentlefolk. I perceived they would have been willing to recognise this as something of a drawback, at the same time that I guessed at an underlying sense—their consolation in adversity—that they *had* their points. They certainly had; but these advantages struck me as preponderantly social; such, for instance, as would help to make a drawing-room look well. However, a drawing-room was always, or ought to be, a picture.

In consequence of his wife's allusion to their age Major Monarch observed: "Naturally it's more for the figure that we thought of going in. We can still hold ourselves up." On the instant I saw that the figure was indeed their strong point. His "naturally" didn't sound vain, but it lighted up the question. "*She* has got the best," he continued, nodding at his wife with a pleasant after-dinner absence of circumlocution. I could only reply, as if we were in fact sitting over our wine, that this didn't prevent his own from being very good; which led him in turn to rejoin: "We thought that if you ever have to do people like us we might be something like it. *She* particularly—for a lady in a book, you know."

I was so amused by them that, to get more of it, I did my best to take their point of view; and though it was an embarrassment to find myself appraising physically, as if they were animals on hire or useful blacks, a pair whom I should have expected to meet only in one of the relations in which criticism is tacit, I looked at Mrs. Monarch judicially enough to be able to exclaim after a moment with conviction: "Oh, yes, a lady in a book!" She was singularly like a bad illustration.

"We'll stand up, if you like," said the Major; and he raised himself before me with a really grand air.

I could take his measure at a glance—he was six feet two and a perfect gentleman. It would have paid any club in process of formation and in want of a stamp to engage him at a salary to stand in the principal window. What struck me at once was that in coming to me they had rather missed their vocation; they could surely have been turned to better account for advertising purposes. I couldn't of course see the thing in detail, but I could see them make somebody's fortune—I don't mean their own. There was something in them for a waistcoat-maker, an hotel-keeper or a soap-vendor. I could imagine "We always use it" pinned on their bosoms with the greatest effect; I had a vision of the promptitude with which they would launch a table d'hôte.

Mrs. Monarch sat still, not from pride but from shyness, and presently her husband said to her: "Get up, my dear, and show how smart you are." She obeyed, but she had no need to get up to show it. She walked to the end of the studio and then came back blushing, with her fluttered eyes on her husband. I was reminded of an incident I had accidentally had a glimpse of in Paris—being with a friend there, a dramatist about to produce a play, when an actress came to him to ask to be entrusted with a part. She went through her paces before him, walked up and down as Mrs. Monarch was doing. Mrs. Monarch did it quite as well, but I abstained from applauding. It was very odd to see such people apply for such poor pay. She looked as if she had ten thousand a year. Her husband had used the word that described her: she was in the London current jargon essentially and typically "smart." Her figure was, in the same order of ideas, conspicuously and irreproachably "good." For a

woman of her age her waist was surprisingly small; her elbow moreover had the orthodox crook. She held her head at the conventional
angle, but why did she come to *me?* She ought to have tried on
jackets at a big shop. I feared my visitors were not only destitute but
"artistic"—which would be a great complication. When she sat
down again I thanked her, observing that what a draughtsman most
valued in his model was the faculty of keeping quiet.

"Oh, *she* can keep quiet," said Major Monarch. Then he added
jocosely: "I've always kept her quiet."

"I'm not a nasty fidget, am I?" Mrs. Monarch appealed to her
husband.

He addressed his answer to me. "Perhaps it isn't out of place to
mention—because we ought to be quite businesslike, oughtn't we?
—that when I married her she was known as the Beautiful Statue."

"Oh dear!" said Mrs. Monarch ruefully.

"Of course I should want a certain amount of expression," I rejoined.

"Of *course!*" they both exclaimed.

"And then I suppose you know that you'll get awfully tired."

"Oh, we *never* get tired!" they eagerly cried.

"Have you had any kind of practice?"

They hesitated—they looked at each other. "We've been photographed—*immensely*," said Mrs. Monarch.

"She means the fellows have asked us themselves," added the
Major.

"I see—because you're so good-looking."

"I don't know what they thought, but they were always after us."

"We always got our photographs for nothing," smiled Mrs. Monarch.

"We might have brought some, my dear," her husband remarked.

"I'm not sure we have any left. We've given quantities away," she
explained to me.

"With our autographs and that sort of thing," said the Major.

"Are they to be got in the shops?" I inquired as a harmless pleasantry.

"Oh, yes, *hers*—they used to be."

"Not now," said Mrs. Monarch with her eyes on the floor.

II

I could fancy the "sort of thing" they put on the presentation
copies of their photographs, and I was sure they wrote a beautiful
hand. It was odd how quickly I was sure of everything that concerned them. If they were now so poor as to have to earn shillings
and pence they could never have had much of a margin. Their good
looks had been their capital, and they had good-naturedly made the
most of the career that this resource marked out for them. It was in

their faces, the blankness, the deep intellectual repose of the twenty years of country-house visiting that had given them pleasant intonations. I could see the sunny drawing-rooms, sprinkled with periodicals she didn't read, in which Mrs. Monarch had continuously sat; I could see the wet shrubberies in which she had walked, equipped to admiration for either exercise. I could see the rich covers the Major had helped to shoot and the wonderful garments in which, late at night, he repaired to the smoking-room to talk about them. I could imagine their leggings and waterproofs, their knowing tweeds and rugs, their rolls of sticks and cases of tackle and neat umbrellas; and I could evoke the exact appearance of their servants and the compact variety of their luggage on platforms of country stations.

They gave small tips, but they were liked; they didn't do anything themselves, but they were welcome. They looked so well everywhere; they gratified the general relish for stature, complexion and "form." They knew it without fatuity or vulgarity, and they respected themselves in consequence. They weren't superficial; they were thorough and kept themselves up—it had been their line. People with such a taste for activity had to have some line. I could feel how even in a dull house they could have been counted on for cheerfulness. At present something had happened—it didn't matter what, their little income had grown less, it had grown least—and they had to do something for pocket-money. Their friends could like them, but didn't like to support them. There was something about them that represented credit—their clothes, their manners, their type; but if credit is a large empty pocket in which an occasional chink reverberates, the chink at least must be audible. What they wanted of me was help to make it so. Fortunately they had no children—I soon divined that. They would also perhaps wish our relations to be kept secret: this was why it was "for the figure"—the reproduction of the face would betray them.

I liked them—they were so simple; and I had no objection to them if they would suit. But somehow with all their perfections I didn't easily believe in them. After all they were amateurs, and the ruling passion of my life was the detestation of the amateur. Combined with this was another perversity—an innate preference for the represented subject over the real one: the defect of the real one was so apt to be a lack of representation. I liked things that appeared; then one was sure. Whether they *were* or not was a subordinate and almost always a profitless question. There were other considerations, the first of which was that I already had two or three people in use, notably a young person with big feet, in alpaca, from Kilburn, who for a couple of years had come to me regularly for my illustrations and with whom I was still—perhaps ignobly—satisfied. I frankly explained to my visitors how the case stood, but they had

taken more precautions than I supposed. They had reasoned out
their opportunity, for Claude Rivet had told them of the projected
édition de luxe of one of the writers of our day—the rarest of the
novelists—who, long neglected by the multitudinous vulgar and
dearly prized by the attentive (need I mention Philip Vincent?),
had had the happy fortune of seeing, late in life, the dawn and then
the full light of a higher criticism; an estimate in which on the part
of the public there was something really of expiation. The edition
in question, planned by a publisher of taste, was practically an act
of high reparation; the woodcuts with which it was to be enriched
were the homage of English art to one of the most independent
representatives of English letters. Major and Mrs. Monarch confessed to me they had hoped I might be able to work *them* into my
share of the enterprise. They knew I was to do the first of the books,
Rutland Ramsay, but I had to make clear to them that my participation in the rest of the affair—this first book was to be a test—must
depend on the satisfaction I should give. If this should be limited
my employers would drop me without a scruple.[1] It was therefore a
crisis for me, and naturally I was making special preparations, looking about for new people, should they be necessary, and securing
the best types. I admitted however that I should like to settle down
to two or three good models who would do for everything.

"Should we have often to—a—put on special clothes?" Mrs. Monarch timidly demanded.

"Dear, yes—that's half the business."

"And should we be expected to supply our own costumes?"

"Oh, no; I've got a lot of things. A painter's models put on—or
put off—anything he likes."

"And you mean—a—the same?"

"The same?"

Mrs. Monarch looked at her husband again.

"Oh, she was just wondering," he explained, "if the costumes are
in *general* use." I had to confess that they were, and I mentioned
further that some of them—I had a lot of genuine greasy last-century
things—had served their time, a hundred years ago, on living world-
stained men and women. "We'll put on anything that *fits*," said the
Major.

"Oh, I arrange that—they fit in the pictures."

"I'm afraid I should do better for the modern books. I'd come as
you like," said Mrs. Monarch.

"She has got a lot of clothes at home: they might do for contemporary life," her husband continued.

"Oh, I can fancy scenes in which you'd be quite natural." And in-

---

1. The final three words of this sentence were changed in the last version of
the story to: "with scarce common
forms."

deed I could see the slipshod rearrangements of stale properties—
the stories I tried to produce pictures for without the exasperation
of reading them—whose sandy tracts the good lady might help to
people. But I had to return to the fact that for this sort of work—
the daily mechanical grind—I was already equipped: the people I
was working with were fully adequate.

"We only thought we might be more like *some* characters," said
Mrs. Monarch mildly, getting up.

Her husband also rose; he stood looking at me with a dim wistful-
ness that was touching in so fine a man. "Wouldn't it be rather a
pull sometimes to have—a—to have—?" He hung fire; he wanted
me to help him by phrasing what he meant. But I couldn't—I didn't
know. So he brought it out awkwardly: "The *real* thing; a gentleman, you know, or a lady." I was quite ready to give a general assent
—I admitted that there was a great deal in that. This encouraged
Major Monarch to say, following up his appeal with an unacted
gulp: "It's awfully hard—we've tried everything." The gulp was com-
municative; it proved too much for his wife. Before I knew it Mrs.
Monarch had dropped again upon a divan and burst into tears. Her
husband sat down beside her, holding one of her hands; whereupon
she quickly dried her eyes with the other, while I felt embarrassed
as she looked up at me. "There isn't a confounded job I haven't applied for—waited for—prayed for. You can fancy we'd be pretty
bad first. Secretaryships and that sort of thing? You might as well
ask for a peerage. I'd be *anything*—I'm strong; a messenger or a coal-
heaver. I'd put on a gold-laced cap and open carriage-doors in front
of the haberdasher's; I'd hang about a station to carry portmanteaus;
I'd be a postman. But they won't *look* at you; there are thousands as
good as yourself already on the ground. *Gentlemen*, poor beggars,
who've drunk their wine, who've kept their hunters!"

I was as reassuring as I knew how to be, and my visitors were presently on their feet again while, for the experiment, we agreed on an
hour. We were discussing it when the door opened and Miss Churm
came in with a wet umbrella. Miss Churm had to take the omnibus
to Maida Vale and then walk half a mile. She looked a trifle blowsy
and slightly splashed. I scarcely ever saw her come in without thinking afresh how odd it was that, being so little in herself, she should
yet be so much in others. She was a meagre little Miss Churm, but
was an ample heroine of romance. She was only a freckled cockney, but she could represent everything, from a fine lady to a shep-
herdess; she had the faculty as she might have had a fine voice or
long hair. She couldn't spell and she loved beer, but she had two or
three "points," and practice, and a knack, and mother-wit, and a
whimsical sensibility, and a love of the theatre, and seven sisters,
and not an ounce of respect, especially for the *h*. The first thing my

visitors saw was that her umbrella was wet, and in their spotless perfection they visibly winced at it. The rain had come on since their arrival.

"I'm all in a soak; there *was* a mess of people in the 'bus. I wish you lived near a styton," said Miss Churm. I requested her to get ready as quickly as possible, and she passed into the room in which she always changed her dress. But before going out she asked me what she was to get into this time.

"It's the Russian princess, don't you know?" I answered; "the one with the 'golden eyes,' in black velvet, for the long thing in the *Cheapside*."

"Golden eyes? I *say!*" cried Miss Churm, while my companions watched her with intensity as she withdrew. She always arranged herself, when she was late, before I could turn round; and I kept my visitors a little on purpose, so that they might get an idea, from seeing her, what would be expected of themselves. I mentioned that she was quite my notion of an excellent model—she was really very clever.

"Do you think she looks like a Russian princess?" Major Monarch asked with lurking alarm.

"When I make her, yes."

"Oh, if you have to *make* her—!" he reasoned, acutely.

"That's the most you can ask. There are so many who are not makeable."

"Well, now, *here's* a lady"—and with a persuasive smile he passed his arm into his wife's—"who's already made!"

"Oh, I'm not a Russian princess," Mrs. Monarch protested a little coldly. I could see she had known some and didn't like them. There, immediately, was a complication of a kind I never had to fear with Miss Churm.

This young lady came back in black velvet—the gown was rather rusty and very low on her lean shoulders—and with a Japanese fan in her red hands. I reminded her that in the scene I was doing she had to look over someone's head. "I forget whose it is; but it doesn't matter. Just look over a head."

"I'd rather look over a stove," said Miss Churm; and she took her station near the fire. She fell into position, settled herself into a tall attitude, gave a certain backward inclination to her head and a certain forward droop to her fan, and looked, at least to my prejudiced sense, distinguished and charming, foreign and dangerous. We left her looking so while I went downstairs with Major and Mrs. Monarch.

"I think I could come about as near it as that," said Mrs. Monarch.

"Oh, you think she's shabby, but you must allow for the alchemy of art."

However, they went off with an evident increase of comfort founded on their demonstrable advantage in being the real thing. I could fancy them shuddering over Miss Churm. She was very droll about them when I went back, for I told her what they wanted.

"Well, if *she* can sit I'll tyke to bookkeeping," said my model.

"She's very ladylike," I replied as an innocent form of aggravation.

"So much the worse for *you*. That means she can't turn round."

"She'll do for the fashionable novels."

"Oh, yes, she'll *do* for them!" my model humorously declared. "Ain't they bad enough without her?" I had often sociably denounced them to Miss Churm.

III

It was for the elucidation of a mystery in one of these works that I first tried Mrs. Monarch. Her husband came with her, to be useful if necessary—it was sufficiently clear that as a general thing he would prefer to come with her. At first I wondered if this were for "propriety's" sake—if he were going to be jealous and meddling. The idea was too tiresome, and if it had been confirmed it would speedily have brought our acquaintance to a close. But I soon saw there was nothing in it and that if he accompanied Mrs. Monarch it was—in addition to the chance of being wanted—simply because he had nothing else to do. When she was away from him his occupation was gone —she never *had* been away from him. I judged rightly that in their awkward situation their close union was their main comfort and that this union had no weak spot. It was a real marriage, an encouragement to the hesitating, a nut for pessimists to crack. Their address was humble—I remember afterwards thinking it had been the only thing about them that was really professional—and I could fancy the lamentable lodgings in which the Major would have been left alone. He could bear them with his wife—he couldn't bear them without her.

He had too much tact to try and make himself agreeable when he couldn't be useful; so when I was too absorbed in my work to talk he simply sat and waited. But I liked to hear him talk—it made my work, when not interrupting it, less sordid, less special. To listen to him was to combine the excitement of going out with the economy of staying at home. There was only one hindrance—that I seemed not to know any of the people he and his wife had known. I think he wondered extremely, during the term of our intercourse, whom the deuce I *did* know. He hadn't a stray sixpence of an idea to fumble for, so we didn't spin it very fine; we confined ourselves to questions of leather and even of liquor—saddlers and breeches-makers and how to get excellent claret cheap—and matters like "good trains" and the habits of small game. His lore on these last subjects was astonishing—he managed to interweave the station-master with the ornithologist. When he couldn't talk about greater things he could talk cheerfully about small, and since I couldn't accompany him into reminiscences of the fashionable world he could lower the conversation without a visible effort to my level.

So earnest a desire to please was touching in a man who could so easily have knocked one down. He looked after the fire and had an opinion on the draught of the stove without my asking him, and I could see that he thought many of my arrangements not half clever enough. I remember telling him that if I were only rich I'd offer him a salary to come and teach me how to live. Sometimes he gave a random sigh of which the essence was: "Give me even such a bare old barrack as *this*, and I'd do something with it!" When I wanted to use him he came alone; which was an illustration of the superior courage of women. His wife could bear her solitary second floor, and she was in general more discreet; showing by various small reserves that she was alive to the propriety of keeping our relations markedly professional—not letting them slide into sociability. She wished it to remain clear that she and the Major were employed, not cultivated, and if she approved of me as a superior, who could be kept in his place, she never thought me quite good enough for an equal.

She sat with great intensity, giving the whole of her mind to it, and was capable of remaining for an hour almost as motionless as if she were before a photographer's lens. I could see she had been photographed often, but somehow the very habit that made her good for that purpose unfitted her for mine. At first I was extremely pleased with her ladylike air, and it was a satisfaction, on coming to follow her lines, to see how good they were and how far they could lead the pencil. But after a few times I began to find her too insurmountably stiff; do what I would with it my drawing looked like a photograph or a copy of a photograph. Her figure had no variety of expression—she herself had no sense of variety. You may say that this was my business and was only a question of placing her. I placed her in every conceivable position but she managed to obliterate their differences. She was always a lady certainly, and into the bargain was always the same lady. She was the real thing, but always the same thing. There were moments when I was oppressed by the serenity of her confidence that she *was* the real thing. All her dealings with me and all her husband's were an implication that this was lucky for *me*. Meanwhile I found myself trying to invent types that approached her own, instead of making her own transform itself—in the clever way that was not impossible for instance to poor Miss Churm. Arrange as I would and take the precautions I would, she always came out, in my pictures, too tall—landing me in the dilemma of having represented a fascinating woman as seven feet high, which (out of respect perhaps to my own very much scantier inches) was far from my idea of such a personage.

The case was worse with the Major—nothing I could do would keep *him* down, so that he became useful only for representation of brawny giants. I adored variety and range, I cherished human accidents, the illustrative note; I wanted to characterise closely, and the thing in the world I most hated was the danger of being ridden by a type. I had quarrelled with some of my friends about it; I had parted company with them for maintaining that one *had* to be, and that if the type was beautiful—witness Raphael and Leonardo—the servitude was only a gain. I was neither Leonardo nor Raphael; I might only be a presumptuous young modern searcher, but I held that everything was to be sacrificed sooner than character. When they averred that the haunting type in question could easily *be* character I retorted, perhaps superficially, "Whose?" It couldn't be everybody's—it might end in being nobody's.

After I had drawn Mrs. Monarch a dozen times I perceived more clearly than before that the value of such a model as Miss Churm resided precisely in the fact that she had no positive stamp, combined of course with the other fact that what she did have was a curious and inexplicable talent for imitation. Her usual appearance was like a curtain which she could draw up at request for a capital performance. This performance was simply suggestive; but it was a word to the wise—it was vivid and pretty. Sometimes, even, I thought it, though she was plain herself, too insipidly pretty; I made it a reproach to her that the figures drawn from her were monotonously (*bêtement*,[2] as we used to say) graceful. Nothing made her more angry: it was so much her pride to feel she could sit for characters that had nothing in common with each other. She would accuse me at such moments of taking away her "reputytion."

It suffered a certain shrinkage, this queer quantity, from the repeated visits of my new friends. Miss Churm was greatly in demand, never in want of employment, so I had no scruple in putting her off occasionally, to try them more at my ease. It was certainly amusing at first to do the real thing—it was amusing to do Major Monarch's trousers. They *were* the real thing, even if he did come out colossal. It was amusing to do his wife's back hair—it was so mathematically neat—and the particular "smart" tension of her tight stays. She lent herself especially to positions in which the face was somewhat averted or blurred; she abounded in ladylike back views and *profils perdus*.[3] When she stood erect she took naturally one of the attitudes in which court painters represent queens and princesses;

2. Foolishly.   3. Lost (disappearing) profiles.

so that I found myself wondering whether, to draw out this accomplishment, I couldn't get the editor of the *Cheapside* to publish a really royal romance, "A Tale of Buckingham Palace." Sometimes, however, the real thing and the make-believe came into contact; by which I mean that Miss Churm, keeping an appointment or coming to make one on days when I had much work in hand, encountered her invidious rivals. The encounter was not on their part, for they noticed her no more than if she had been the housemaid; not from intentional loftiness, but simply because as yet, professionally, they didn't know how to fraternise, as I could imagine they would have liked—or at least that the Major would. They couldn't talk about the omnibus—they always walked; and they didn't know what else to try—she wasn't interested in good trains or cheap claret. Besides, they must have felt—in the air—that she was amused at them, secretly derisive of their ever knowing how. She was not a person to conceal the limits of her faith if she had had a chance to show it. On the other hand Mrs. Monarch didn't think her tidy; for why else did she take pains to say to me—it was going out of the way, for Mrs. Monarch—that she didn't like dirty women?

One day when my young lady happened to be present with my other sitters—she even dropped in, when it was convenient, for a chat—I asked her to be so good as to lend a hand in getting tea, a service with which she was familiar and which was one of a class that, living as I did in a small way, with slender domestic resources, I often appealed to my models to render. They liked to lay hands on my property, to break the sitting, and sometimes the china—it made them feel Bohemian. The next time I saw Miss Churm after this incident she surprised me greatly by making a scene about it—she accused me of having wished to humiliate her. She hadn't resented the outrage at the time, but had seemed obliging and amused, enjoying the comedy of asking Mrs. Monarch, who sat vague and silent, whether she would have cream and sugar, and putting an exaggerated simper into the question. She had tried intonations—as if she too wished to pass for the real thing—till I was afraid my other visitors would take offence.

Oh, they were determined not to do this, and their touching patience was the measure of their great need. They would sit by the hour, uncomplaining, till I was ready to use them; they would come back on the chance of being wanted and would walk away cheerfully if they were not. I used to go to the door with them to see in what magnificent order they retreated. I tried to find other employment for them—I introduced them to several artists. But they didn't "take," for reasons I could appreciate, and I became rather anxiously aware that after such disappointments they fell back upon me with a heavier weight. They did me the honour to think that it was I who was most *their* form. They were not picturesque enough for the painters, and in those days there were few serious workers in black-and-white. Besides, they had an eye to the great job I had mentioned to them—they had secretly set their hearts on supplying the right essence for my pictorial vindication of our fine novelist. They knew that for this undertaking I should want no costume effects, none of the frippery of past ages—that it was a case in which everything would be contemporary and satirical and presumably genteel. If I could work them into it their future would be assured, for the labour would of course be long and the occupation steady.

One day Mrs. Monarch came without her husband—she explained his absence by his having had to go to the City. While she sat there in her usual anxious stiffness there came at the door a knock which I immediately recognised as the subdued appeal of a model out of work. It was followed by the entrance of a young man whom I easily perceived to be a foreigner and who proved in fact an Italian acquainted with no English word but my name, which he uttered in a way that made it seem to include all others. I hadn't then visited his country, nor was I proficient in his tongue; but as he was not so meanly constituted—what Italian is?—as to depend only on that member for expression he conveyed to me, in familiar but graceful mimicry, that he was in search of exactly the employment in which the lady before me was engaged. I was not struck with him at first, and while I continued to draw I emitted rough sounds of discouragement and dismissal. He stood his ground, however—not importunately, but with a dumb dog-like fidelity in his eyes that amounted to innocent impudence, the manner of a devoted servant—he might have been in the house for years—unjustly suspected. Suddenly I saw that this very attitude and expression made a picture, whereupon I told him to sit down and wait till I should be free. There was another picture in the way he obeyed me, and I observed as I worked that there were others still in the way he looked wonderingly, with his head thrown back, about the high studio. He might have been crossing himself in Saint Peter's. Before I finished I said to myself, "The fellow's a bankrupt orange-monger, but a treasure."

When Mrs. Monarch withdrew he passed across the room like a flash to open the door for her, standing there with the rapt, pure gaze of the young Dante spellbound by the young Beatrice. As I never insisted, in such situations, on the blankness of the British domestic, I reflected that he had the making of a servant—and I needed one, but couldn't pay him to be only that—as well as of a model; in short I resolved to adopt my bright adventurer if he would agree to officiate in the double capacity. He jumped at my offer, and in the event my rashness—for I had really known nothing about him—wasn't brought home to me. He proved a sympathetic though a desultory ministrant, and had in a wonderful degree the *sentiment de la pose*.[4] It was uncultivated, instinctive, a part of the happy instinct that had guided him to my door and helped him to spell out my name on the card nailed to it. He had had no other introduction to me than a guess, from the shape of my high north window, seen outside, that my place was a studio and that as a studio it would contain an artist. He had wandered to England in search of fortune, like other itinerants, and had embarked, with a partner and a small green handcart, on the sale of penny ices. The ices had melted away and the partner had dissolved in their train. My young man wore tight yellow trousers with reddish stripes and his name was Oronte. He was sallow but fair, and when I put him into some old clothes of my own he looked like an Englishman. He was as good as Miss Churm, who could look, when requested, like an Italian.

IV

I thought Mrs. Monarch's face slightly convulsed when, on her coming back with her husband, she found Oronte installed. It was strange to have to recognise in a scrap of a lazzarone[5] a competitor to her magnificent Major. It was she who scented danger first, for the Major was anecdotically unconscious. But Oronte gave us tea, with a hundred eager confusions—he had never been concerned in so queer a process—and I think she thought better of me for having at last an "establishment." They saw a couple of drawings that I had made of the establishment, and Mrs. Monarch hinted that it never would have struck her he had sat for them. "Now the drawings you make from *us*, they look exactly like us," she reminded me, smiling in triumph; and I recognised that this was indeed just their defect. When I drew the Monarchs I couldn't somehow get away from them—get into the character I wanted to represent; and I hadn't the least desire my model should be discoverable in my picture. Miss Churm never was, and Mrs. Monarch thought I hid her, very properly, because she was vulgar; whereas if she was lost it was only as the dead who go to heaven are lost—in the gain of an angel the more.

By this time I had got a certain start with "Rutland Ramsay," the first novel in the great projected series; that is, I had produced a dozen drawings, several with the help of the Major and his wife, and I had sent them in for approval. My understanding with the publishers, as I have already hinted, had been that I was to be left to do my work, in this particular case, as I liked, with the whole book committed to me; but my connexion with the rest of the series was only contingent. There were moments when, frankly, it *was* a comfort to have the real thing under one's hand; for there were

4. Instinct for posing.   5. A vagabond (thief).

characters in "Rutland Ramsay" that were very much like it. There were people presumably as erect as the Major and women of as good a fashion as Mrs. Monarch. There was a great deal of country-house life—treated, it is true, in a fine fanciful ironical generalised way —and there was a considerable implication of knickerbockers and kilts. There were certain things I had to settle at the outset; such things for instance as the exact appearance of the hero and the particular bloom of the heroine. The author of course gave me a lead, but there was a margin for interpretation. I took the Monarchs into my confidence, I told them frankly what I was about, I mentioned my embarrassments and alternatives. "Oh, take *him!*" Mrs. Monarch murmured sweetly, looking at her husband; and "What could you want better than my life?" the Major inquired with the comfortable candour that now prevailed between us.

I wasn't obliged to answer these remarks—I was only obliged to place my sitters. I wasn't easy in mind, and I postponed a little timidly perhaps the solution of the question. The book was a large canvas, the other figures were numerous, and I worked off at first some of the episodes in which the hero and the heroine were not concerned. When once I had set *them* up I should have to stick to them—I couldn't make my young man seven feet high in one place and five feet nine in another. I inclined on the whole to the latter measurement, though the Major more than once reminded me that *he* looked about as young as any one. It was indeed quite possible to arrange him, for the figure, so that it would have been difficult to detect his age. After the spontaneous Oronte had been with me a month, and after I had given him to understand several times over that his native exuberance would presently constitute an insurmountable barrier to our further intercourse, I waked to a sense of his heroic capacity. He was only five feet seven, but the remaining inches were latent. I tried him almost secretly at first, for I was really rather afraid of the judgement my other models would pass on such a choice. If they regarded Miss Churm as little better than a snare what would they think of the representation of a person so little the real thing as an Italian street-vendor of a protagonist formed by a public school?

If I went a little in fear of them it wasn't because they bullied me, because they had got an oppressive foothold, but because in their really pathetic decorum and mysteriously permanent newness they counted on me so intensely. I was therefore very glad when Jack Hawley came home: he was always of such good counsel. He painted badly himself, but there was no one like him for putting his finger on the place. He had been absent from England for a year; he had been somewhere—I don't remember where—to get a fresh eye. I was in a good deal of dread of any such organ, but we were old friends; he had been away for months and a sense of emptiness was creeping into my life. I hadn't dodged a missile for a year.

He came back with a fresh eye, but with the same old black velvet blouse, and the first evening he spent in my studio we smoked cigarettes till the small hours. He had done no work himself, he had only got the eye; so the field was clear for the production of my little things. He wanted to see what I had done for the *Cheapside*, but he was disappointed in the exhibition. That at least seemed the meaning of two or three comprehensive groans which, as he lounged on my big divan, on a folded leg, looking at my latest drawings, issued from his lips with the smoke of the cigarette.

"What's the matter with you?" I asked.

"What's the matter with *you?*"

"Nothing save that I'm mystified."

"You are indeed. You're quite off the hinge. What's the meaning of this new fad?" And he tossed me, with visible irreverence, a drawing in which I happened to have depicted both my majestic models. I asked if he didn't think it good, and he replied that it struck him as execrable, given the sort of thing I had always represented myself to him as wishing to arrive at; but I let that pass—I was so anxious to see exactly what he meant. The two figures in the picture looked colossal, but I supposed this was *not* what he meant, inasmuch as, for aught he knew to the contrary, I might have been trying for that. I maintained that I was working exactly in the same way as when he last had done me the honour to tell me I might do something some day. "Well, there's a big hole somewhere," he answered; "wait a bit and I'll discover it." I depended upon him to do so: where else was the fresh eye? But he produced at last nothing more luminous than "I don't know—I don't like your types." This was lame for a critic who had never consented to discuss with me anything but the question of execution, the direction of strokes and the mystery of values.

"In the drawings you've been looking at I think my types are very handsome."

"Oh, they won't do!"

"I've been working with new models."

"I see you have. *They* won't do."

"Are you very sure of that?"

"Absolutely—they're stupid."

"You mean I am—for I ought to get round that."

"You *can't*—with such people. Who are they?"

I told him, so far as was necessary, and he concluded heartlessly: "*Ce sont des gens qu'il faut mettre à la porte.*"[6]

"You've never seen them; they're awfully good," I compassion-

6. "They are the kind who should be shown the door."

ately objected.

"Not seen them? Why all this recent work of yours drops to pieces with them. It's all I want to see of them."

"No one else has said anything against it—the *Cheapside* people are pleased."

"Every one else is an ass, and the *Cheapside* people the biggest asses of all. Come, don't pretend at this time of day to have pretty illusions about the public, especially about publishers and editors. It's not for *such* animals you work—it's for those who know, *coloro che sanno;*[7] so keep straight for *me* if you can't keep straight for yourself. There's a certain sort of thing you tried for from the first —and a very good thing it is. But this twaddle isn't *in* it." When I talked with Hawley later about "Rutland Ramsay" and its possible successors he declared that I must get back into my boat again or I would go to the bottom. His voice in short was the voice of warning.

I noted the warning, but I didn't turn my friends out of doors. They bored me a good deal; but the very fact that they bored me admonished me not to sacrifice them—if there was anything to be done with them—simply to irritation. As I look back at this phase they seem to me to have pervaded my life not a little. I have a vision of them as most of the time in my studio, seated against the wall on an old velvet bench to be out of the way, and resembling the while a pair of patient courtiers in a royal ante-chamber. I'm convinced that during the coldest weeks of the winter they held their ground because it saved them fire. Their newness was losing its gloss, and it was impossible not to feel them objects of charity. Whenever Miss Churm arrived they went away, and after I was fairly launched in "Rutland Ramsay" Miss Churm arrived pretty often. They managed to express to me tacitly that they supposed I wanted her for the low life of the book, and I let them suppose it, since they had attempted to study the work—it was lying about the studio—without discovering that it dealt only with the highest circles. They had dipped into the most brilliant of our novelists without deciphering many passages. I still took an hour from them, now and again, in spite of Jack Hawley's warning: it would be time enough to dismiss them, if dismissal should be necessary, when the rigour of the season was over. Hawley had made their acquaintance—he had met them at my fireside—and thought them a ridiculous pair. Learning that he was a painter they tried to approach him, to show him too that they were the real thing; but he looked at them, across the big room, as if they were miles away: they were a compendium of everything he most objected to in the social system of his country. Such people as that, all convention and patent-leather, with ejaculations that

7. In *Inferno* IV.131, Dante meets the spirit of Aristotle, "the master of those who know" (*"il Maestro di color che sanno"*).

stopped conversation, had no business in a studio. A studio was a place to learn to see, and how could you see through a pair of feather-beds?

The main inconvenience I suffered at their hands was that at first I was shy of letting them discover that my artful little servant had begun to sit to me for "Rutland Ramsay." They knew I had been odd enough—they were prepared by this time to allow oddity to artists—to pick a foreign vagabond out of the streets when I might have had a person with whiskers and credentials; but it was some time before they learned how high I rated his accomplishments. They found him in an attitude more than once, but they never doubted I was doing him as an organ-grinder. There were several things they never guessed, and one of them was that for a striking scene in the novel, in which a footman briefly figured, it occurred to me to make use of Major Monarch as the menial. I kept putting this off, I didn't like to ask him to don the livery—besides the difficulty of finding a livery to fit him. At last, one day late in the winter, when I was at work on the despised Oronte, who caught one's idea on the wing, and was in the glow of feeling that I was going very straight, they came in, the Major and his wife, with their society laugh about nothing (there was less and less to laugh at); came in like country-callers—they always reminded me of that—who have walked across the park after church and are presently persuaded to stay to luncheon. Luncheon was over, but they could stay to tea—I knew they wanted it. The fit was on me, however, and I couldn't let my ardour cool and my work wait, with the fading daylight, while my model prepared it. So I asked Mrs. Monarch if she would mind laying it out—a request which for an instant brought all the blood to her face. Her eyes were on her husband's for a second, and some mute telegraphy passed between them. Their folly was over the next instant; his cheerful shrewdness put an end to it. So far from pitying their wounded pride, I must add, I was moved to give it as complete a lesson as I could. They bustled about together and got out the cups and saucers and made the kettle boil. I know they felt as if they were waiting on my servant, and when the tea was prepared I said: "He'll have a cup, please—he's tired." Mrs. Monarch brought him one where he stood, and he took it from her as if he had been a gentleman at a party squeezing a crush-hat with an elbow.

Then it came over me that she had made a great effort for me—made it with a kind of nobleness—and that I owed her a compensation. Each time I saw her after this I wondered what the compensation could be. I couldn't go on doing the wrong thing to oblige them. Oh, it *was* the wrong thing, the stamp of the work for which they sat—Hawley was not the only person to say it now. I sent in a large number of the drawings I had made for "Rutland Ramsay," and I received a warning that was more to the point than Hawley's. The artistic adviser of the house for which I was working was of opinion than many of my illustrations were not what had been looked for. Most of these illustrations were the subjects in which the Monarchs had figured. Without going into the question of what *had* been looked for, I had to face the fact that at this rate I shouldn't get the other books to do. I hurled myself in despair on Miss Churm— I put her through all her paces. I not only adopted Oronte publicly as my hero, but one morning when the Major looked in to see if I didn't require him to finish a *Cheapside* figure for which he had begun to sit the week before, I told him I had changed my mind—I'd do the drawing from my man. At this my visitor turned pale and stood looking at me. "Is *he* your idea of an English gentleman?" he asked.

I was disappointed, I was nervous, I wanted to get on with my work; so I replied with irritation: "Oh my dear Major—I can't be ruined for *you!*"

It was a horrid speech, but he stood another moment—then, without a word, he quitted the studio. I drew a long breath, for I said to myself that I shouldn't see him again. I hadn't told him definitely that I was in danger of having my work rejected, but I was vexed at his not having felt the catastrophe in the air, read with me the moral of our fruitless collaboration, the lesson that in the deceptive atmosphere of art even the highest respectability may fail of being plastic.

I didn't owe my friends money, but I did see them again. They reappeared together three days later, and, given all the other facts, there was something tragic in the fact. It was a clear proof they could find nothing else in life to do. They had threshed the matter out in a dismal conference—they had digested the bad news that they were not in for the series. If they weren't useful to me even for the *Cheapside*, their function seemed difficult to determine, and I could only judge at first that they had come, forgivingly, decorously, to take a last leave. This made me rejoice in secret that I had little leisure for a scene; for I had placed both my other models in position together and I was pegging away at a drawing from which I hoped to derive glory. It had been suggested by the passage in which Rutland Ramsay, drawing up a chair to Artemisia's piano-stool, says extraordinary things to her while she ostensibly fingers out a difficult piece of music. I had done Miss Churm at the piano before—it was an attitude in which she knew how to take on an absolutely poetic grace. I wished the two figures to "compose" together, intensely, and my little Italian had entered perfectly into my conception. The pair were vividly before me, the piano had been pulled out; it was a charming picture of blended youth and murmured love, which I had only to catch and keep. My visitors stood and looked at it, and I was friendly to them over my shoulder.

They made no response, but I was used to silent company and went on with my work, only a little disconcerted—even though exhilarated by the sense that *this* was at least the ideal thing—at not having got rid of them after all. Presently I heard Mrs. Monarch's sweet voice beside or rather above me: "I wish her hair were a little better done." I looked up and she was staring with a strange fixedness at Miss Churm, whose back was turned to her. "Do you mind my just touching it?" she went on—a question which made me spring up for an instant as with the instinctive fear that she might do the young lady a harm. But she quieted me with a glance I shall never forget—I confess I should like to have been able to paint *that* —and went for a moment to my model. She spoke to her softly, laying a hand on her shoulder and bending over her; and as the girl, understanding, gratefully assented, she disposed her rough curls, with a few quick passes, in such a way as to make Miss Churm's head twice as charming. It was one of the most heroic personal services I've ever seen rendered. Then Mrs. Monarch turned away with a low sigh and, looking about her as if for something to do, stooped to the floor with a noble humility and picked up a dirty rag that had dropped out of my paint-box.

The Major meanwhile had also been looking for something to do, and, wandering to the other end of the studio, saw before him my breakfast-things neglected, unremoved. "I say, can't I be useful *here?*" he called out to me with an irrepressible quaver. I assented with a laugh that I fear was awkward, and for the next ten minutes, while I worked, I heard the light clatter of china and the tinkle of spoons and glass. Mrs. Monarch assisted her husband—they washed up my crockery, they put it away. They wandered off into my little scullery, and I afterwards found that they had cleaned my knives and that my slender stock of plate had an unprecedented surface. When it came over me, the latent eloquence of what they were doing, I confess that my drawing was blurred for a moment—the picture swam. They had accepted their failure, but they couldn't accept their fate. They had bowed their heads in bewilderment to the perverse and cruel law in virtue of which the real thing could be so much less precious than the unreal; but they didn't want to starve. If my servants were my models, then my models might be my servants. They would reverse the parts—the others would sit for the ladies and gentlemen and *they* would do the work. They would still be in the studio—it was an intense dumb appeal to me not to turn them out. "Take us on," they wanted to say—"we'll do *anything*."

My pencil dropped from my hand; my sitting was spoiled and I got rid of my sitters, who were also evidently rather mystified and awestruck. Then, alone with the Major and his wife I had a most uncomfortable moment. He put their prayer into a single sentence: "I say, you know—just let *us* do for you, can't you?" I couldn't— it was dreadful to see them emptying my slops; but I pretended I could, to oblige them, for about a week. Then I gave them a sum of money to go away, and I never saw them again. I obtained the remaining books, but my friend Hawley repeats that Major and Mrs. Monarch did me a permanent harm, got me into a second-rate trick. If it be true I'm content to have paid the price—for the memory.

1892, 1893

Greville Fane[8]

Coming in to dress for dinner I found a telegram: "Mrs. Stormer dying; can you give us half a column for to-morrow evening? Let her down easily, but not too easily." I was late; I was in a hurry; I had very little time to think; but at a venture I despatched a reply: "Will do what I can." It was not till I had dressed and was rolling away to dinner that, in the hansom, I bethought myself of the diffi- culty of the condition attached. The difficulty was not of course in letting her down easily but in qualifying that indulgence. "So I simply won't qualify it," I said. I didn't admire but liked her, and had known her so long that I almost felt heartless in sitting down at such an hour to a feast of indifference. I must have seemed ab- stracted, for the early years of my acquaintance with her came back to me. I spoke of her to the lady I had taken down, but the lady I had taken down had never heard of Greville Fane. I tried my other neighbour, who pronounced her books "too vile." I had never thought them very good, but I should let her down more easily than that.

I came away early, for the express purpose of driving to ask about her. The journey took time, for she lived in the northwest district,. in the neighbourhood of Primrose Hill.[9] My apprehension that I should be too late was justified in a fuller sense than I had attached to it—I had only feared that the house would be shut up. There were lights in the windows, and the temperate tinkle of my bell brought

---

8. The story first appeared in the *Illus- trated London News*, a weekly journal, in September, 1892. It was reprinted in *The Real Thing, and Other Tales* (1893). James revised it slightly for the collected New York Edition of his works, which is the text followed here. For an account of the origin of the story, see the selection from the *Notebooks*. In his later Preface he could recall little about its composition except the great effort he made to get the tale into a limited space. He called it "a minor miracle of foreshortening."
9. Hilly area on the north side of Re- gent's Park, London. A respectable, upper-class neighborhood and residence section.

a servant immediately to the door; but poor Mrs. Stormer had passed into a state in which the resonance of no earthly knocker was to be feared. A lady hovering behind the servant came forward into the hall when she heard my voice. I recognised Lady Luard, but she had mistaken me for the doctor.

"Pardon my appearing at such an hour," I said; "it was the first possible moment after I heard."

"It's all over," Lady Luard replied. "Dearest mamma!"

She stood there under the lamp with her eyes on me; she was very tall, very stiff, very cold, and always looked as if these things, and some others beside, in her dress, in her manner and even in her name, were an implication that she was very admirable. I had never been able to follow the argument, but that's a detail. I expressed briefly and frankly what I felt, while the little mottled maidservant flattened herself against the wall of the narrow passage and tried to look detached without looking indifferent. It was not a moment to make a visit, and I was on the point of retreating when Lady Luard arrested me with a queer casual drawling "Would you—a—would you perhaps be *writing* something?" I felt for the instant like an infamous interviewer, which I wasn't. But I pleaded guilty to this intention, on which she returned: "I'm so very glad—but I think my brother would like to see you." I detested her brother, but it wasn't an occasion to act this out; so I suffered myself to be inducted, to my surprise, into a small back room which I immediately recognised as the scene, during the later years, of Mrs. Stormer's imperturbable industry. Her table was there, the battered and blotted accessory to innumerable literary lapses, with its contracted space for the arms (she wrote only from the elbow down) and the confusion of scrappy scribbled sheets which had already become literary remains. Leolin was also there, smoking a cigarette before the fire and looking impudent even in his grief, sincere as it well might have been.

To meet him, to greet him, I had to make a sharp effort; for the air he wore to me as he stood before me was quite that of his mother's murderer. She lay silent for ever upstairs—as dead as an unsuccessful book, and his swaggering erectness was a kind of symbol of his having killed her. I wondered if he had already, with his sister, been calculating what they could get for the poor papers on the table; but I hadn't long to wait to learn, since in reply to the few words of sympathy I addressed him he puffed out: "It's miserable, miserable, yes; but she has left three books complete." His words had the oddest effect; they converted the cramped little room into a seat of trade and made the "book" wonderfully feasible. He would certainly get all that could be got for the three. Lady Luard explained to me that her husband had been with them, but had had to go down to the House. To her brother she mentioned that I was going to write something, and to me again made it clear that she hoped I would "do mamma justice." She added that she didn't think this had ever been done. She said to her brother: "Don't you think there are some things he ought thoroughly to understand?" and on his instantly exclaiming "Oh thoroughly, thoroughly!" went on rather austerely: "I mean about mamma's birth."

"Yes and her connexions," Leolin added.

I professed every willingness, and for five minutes I listened; but it would be too much to say I clearly understood. I don't even now, but it's not important. My vision was of other matters than those they put before me, and while they desired there should be no mistake about their ancestors I became keener and keener about themselves. I got away as soon as possible and walked home through the great dusky empty London—the best of all conditions for thought. By the time I reached my door my little article was practically composed—ready to be transferred on the morrow from the polished plate of fancy. I believe it attracted some notice, was thought "graceful" and was said to be by some one else. I had to be pointed without being lively, and it took some doing. But what I said was much less interesting than what I thought—especially during the half-hour I spent in my armchair by the fire, smoking the cigar I always light before going to bed. I went to sleep there, I believe; but I continued to moralise about Greville Fane. I'm reluctant to lose that retrospect altogether, and this is a dim little memory of it, a document not to "serve." The dear woman had written a hundred stories, but none so curious as her own.

When first I knew her she had published half a dozen fictions, and I believe I had also perpetrated a novel. She was more than a dozen years my elder, but a person who always acknowledged her comparative state. It wasn't so very long ago, but in London, amid the big waves of the present, even a near horizon gets hidden. I met her at some dinner and took her down, rather flattered at offering my arm to a celebrity. She didn't look like one, with her matronly mild inanimate face, but I supposed her greatness would come out in her conversation. I gave it all the opportunities I could, but was nevertheless not disappointed when I found her only a dull kind woman. This was why I liked her—she rested me so from literature. To myself literature was an irritation, a torment; but Greville Fane slumbered in the intellectual part of it even as a cat on a hearthrug or a Creole in a hammock. She wasn't a woman of genius, but her faculty was so special, so much a gift out of hand, that I've often wondered why she fell below that distinction. This was doubtless because the transaction, in her case, had remained incomplete; genius always pays for the gift, feels the debt, and she was placidly unconscious of a call. She could invent stories by the yard, but couldn't write a page of English. She went down to her grave without suspecting that though she had contributed volumes to the diversion of her contemporaries she hadn't contributed a sentence to the language. This hadn't prevented bushels of criticism from being heaped on her head; she was worth a couple of columns any day to the weekly papers, in which it was shown that her pictures of life were dreadful but her style superior. She asked me to come and see her and I complied. She lived then in Montpelier Square; which helped me to see how dissociated her imagination was from her character.[1]

An industrious widow, devoted to her daily stint, to meeting the butcher and baker and making a home for her son and daughter, from the moment she took her pen in her hand she became a creature of passion. She thought the English novel deplorably wanting in that element, and the task she had cut out for herself was to supply the deficiency. Passion in high life was the general formula of this work, for her imagination was at home only in the most exalted circles. She adored in truth the aristocracy, and they constituted for her the romance of the world or, what is more to the point, the prime material of fiction. Their beauty and luxury, their loves and revenges, their temptations and surrenders, their immoralities and diamonds were as familiar to her as the blots on her writing-table. She was not a belated producer of the old fashionable novel, but, with a cleverness and a modernness of her own, had freshened up the fly-blown tinsel. She turned off plots by the hundred and—so far as her flying quill could convey her—was perpetually going abroad. Her types, her illustrations, her tone were nothing if not cosmopolitan. She recognised nothing less provincial than European society, and her fine folk knew each other and made love to each other from Doncaster to Bucharest. She had an idea that she resembled Balzac, and her favourite historical characters were Lucien de Rubempré and the Vidame de Pamiers.[2] I must add that when I once asked her who the latter personage was she was unable to tell me. She was very brave and healthy and cheerful, very abundant and innocent and wicked. She was expert and vulgar and snobbish, and never so intensely British as when she was particularly foreign.

This combination of qualities had brought her early success, and I remember having heard with wonder and envy of what she "got," in those days, for a novel. The revelation gave me a pang: it was such a proof that, practising a totally different style, I should never

1. James was living in De Vere Gardens, Kensington, west of central London, while writing this story, and the place names reflect the status of certain neighborhoods in the vicinity of Kensington Gardens. Montpelier Square was a laboring-class and business district near Knightsbridge.

2. Lucien de Rubempré was a young journalist of the French Republic in the first half of the 19th century. Vidame de Pamiers was a military and political figure of the Fauborg Saint-Germain under the Restoration. Both were treated in Balzac's fictionalized history of the Republic, La Comédie Humaine.

make my fortune. And yet when, as I knew her better she told me her real tariff and I saw how rumour had quadrupled it, I liked her enough to be sorry. After a while I discovered too that if she got less it was not that *I* was to get any more. My failure never had what Mrs. Stormer would have called the banality of being relative—it was always admirably absolute. She lived at ease however in those days—ease is exactly the word, though she produced three novels a year. She scorned me when I spoke of difficulty—it was the only thing that made her angry. If I hinted at the grand licking into shape that a work of art required she thought it a pretension and a *pose*. She never recognised the "torment of form"; the furthest she went was to introduce into one of her books (in satire her hand was heavy) a young poet who was always talking about it. I couldn't quite understand her irritation on this score, for she had nothing at stake in the matter. She had a shrewd perception that form, in prose at least, never recommended any one to the public we were condemned to address; according to which she lost nothing (her private humiliation not counted) by having none to show. She made no pretence of producing works of art, but had comfortable tea-drinking hours in which she freely confessed herself a common pastrycook, dealing in such tarts and puddings as would bring customers to the shop. She put in plenty of sugar and of cochineal, or whatever it is that gives these articles a rich and attractive colour. She had a calm independence of observation and opportunity which constituted an inexpugnable strength and would enable her to go on indefinitely. It's only real success that wanes, it's only solid things that melt. Greville Fane's ignorance of life was a resource still more unfailing than the most approved receipt. On her saying once that the day would come when she should have written herself out I answered: "Ah, you open straight into fairyland, and the fairies love you and *they* never change. Fairyland's always there; it always was from the beginning of time and always will be to the end. They've given you the key and you can always open the door. With me it's different; I try, in my clumsy way, to be in some direct relation to life." "Oh bother your direct relation to life!" she used to reply, for she was always annoyed by the phrase—which wouldn't in the least prevent her using it as a note of elegance. With no more prejudices than an old sausage-mill, she would give forth again with patient punctuality any poor verbal scrap that had been dropped into her. I cheered her with saying that the dark day, at the end, would be for the 'likes' of *me*; since, proceeding in our small way by experience and study —priggish we!—we depended not on a revelation but on a little tiresome process. Attention depended on occasion, and where should we be when occasion failed?

One day she told me that as the novelist's life was so delightful and, during the good years at least, such a comfortable support—she had these staggering optimisms—she meant to train up her boy to follow it. She took the ingenious view that it was a profession like another and that therefore everything was to be gained by beginning young and serving an apprenticeship. Moreover the education would be less expensive than any other special course, inasmuch as she could herself administer it. She didn't profess to keep a school, but she could at least teach her own child. It wasn't that she had such a gift, but—she confessed to me as if she were afraid I should laugh at her—that *he* had. I didn't laugh at her for that, because I thought the boy sharp—I had seen him sundry times. He was well-grown and good-looking and unabashed, and both he and his sister made me wonder about their defunct papa, concerning whom the little I knew was that he had been a country vicar and brother to a small squire. I explained them to myself by suppositions and imputations possibly unjust to the departed; so little were they—superficially at least—the children of their mother. There used to be on an easel in her drawing-room an enlarged photograph of her husband, done by some horrible posthumous "process" and draped, as to its florid frame, with a silken scarf which testified to the candour of Greville Fane's bad taste. It made him look like an unsuccessful tragedian, but it wasn't a thing to trust. He may have been a successful comedian. Of the two children the girl was the elder, and struck me in all her younger years as singularly colourless. She was only long, very long, like an undecipherable letter. It wasn't till Mrs. Stormer came back from a protracted residence abroad that Ethel (which was this young lady's name) began to produce the effect, large and stiff and afterwards eminent in her, of a certain kind of resolution, something as public and important as if a meeting and a chairman had passed it. She gave one to understand she meant to do all she could for herself. She was long-necked and near-sighted and striking, and I thought I had never seen sweet seventeen in a form so hard and high and dry. She was cold and affected and ambitious, and she carried an eyeglass with a long handle, which she put up whenever she wanted not to see. She had come out, as the phrase is, immensely; and yet I felt as if she were surrounded with a spiked iron railing. What she meant to do for herself was to marry, and it was the only thing, I think, that she meant to do for any one else; yet who would be inspired to clamber over that bristling barrier? What flower of tenderness or of intimacy would such an adventurer conceive as his reward?

This was for Sir Baldwin Luard to say; but he naturally never confided me the secret. He was a joyless jokeless young man, with the air of having other secrets as well, and a determination to get on politically that was indicated by his never having been known to commit himself—as regards any proposition whatever—beyond an unchallengeable "Oh!" His wife and he must have conversed mainly in prim ejaculations, but they understood sufficiently that they were kindred spirits. I remember being angry with Greville Fane when she announced these nuptials to me as magnificent; I remember asking her what splendour there was in the union of the daughter of a woman of genius with an irredeemable mediocrity. "Oh he has immense ability," she said; but she blushed for the maternal fib. What she meant was that though Sir Baldwin's estates were not vast—he had a dreary house in South Kensington and a still drearier "Hall" somewhere in Essex, which was let—the connexion was a "smarter" one than a child of hers could have aspired to form. In spite of the social bravery of her novels she took a very humble and dingy view of herself, so that of all her productions "my daughter Lady Luard" was quite the one she was proudest of. That personage thought our authoress vulgar and was distressed and perplexed by the frequent freedoms of her pen, but had a complicated attitude for this indirect connexion with literature. So far as it was lucrative her ladyship approved of it and could compound with the inferiority of the pursuit by practical justice to some of its advantages. I had reason to know—my reason was simply that poor Mrs. Stormer told me—how she suffered the inky fingers to press an occasional banknote into her palm. On the other hand she deplored the "peculiar style" to which Greville Fane had devoted herself, and wondered where a spectator with the advantage of so ladylike a daughter could have picked up such views about the best society. "She might know better, with Leolin and me," Lady Luard had been heard to remark; but it appeared that some of Greville Fane's superstitions were incurable. She didn't live in Lady Luard's society, and the best wasn't good enough for her—she must improve on it so prodigiously.

I could see this necessity increase in her during the years she spent abroad, when I had glimpses of her in the shifting sojourns that lay in the path of my annual ramble. She betook herself from Germany to Switzerland and from Switzerland to Italy; she favoured cheap places and set up her desk in the smaller capitals. I took a look at her whenever I could, and I always asked how Leolin was getting on. She gave me beautiful accounts of him, and, occasion favouring, the boy was produced for my advantage. I had entered from the first into the joke of his career—I pretended to regard him as a consecrated child. It had been a joke for Mrs. Stormer at first, but the youth himself had been shrewd enough to make the matter serious. If his parent accepted the principle that the intending novelist can't begin too early to see life, Leolin wasn't interested in hanging back from the application of it. He was eager to qualify himself and took to cigarettes at ten on the highest literary grounds. His fond mother gazed at him with extravagant envy and, like Desdemona, wished heaven had made *her* such a man. She explained to me more than once that in her profession she had found her sex a dreadful drawback. She loved the story of Madame George Sand's early rebellion against this hindrance, and believed that if she had worn trousers she could have written as well as that lady.[3] Leolin had for the career at least the qualification of trousers, and as he grew older he recognised its importance by laying in ever so many pair. He grew up thus in gorgeous apparel, which was his way of interpreting his mother's system. Whenever I met her, accordingly, I found her still under the impression that she was carrying this system out and that the sacrifices made him were bearing heavy fruit. She was giving him experience, she was giving him impressions, she was putting a *gagne-pain*[4] into his hand. It was another name for spoiling him with the best conscience in the world. The queerest pictures come back to me of this period of the good lady's life and of the extraordinarily virtuous muddled bewildering tenor of it. She had an idea she was seeing foreign manners as well as her petticoats would allow; but in reality she wasn't seeing anything, least of all, fortunately, how much she was laughed at. She drove her whimsical pen at Dresden and at Florence—she produced in all places and at all times the same romantic and ridiculous fictions. She carried about her box of properties, tumbling out promptly the familiar tarnished old puppets. She believed in them when others couldn't, and as they were like nothing that was to be seen under the sun it was impossible to prove by comparison that they were wrong. You can't compare birds and fishes; you could only feel that, as Greville Fane's characters had the fine plumage of the former species, human beings must be of the latter.

It would have been droll if it hadn't been so exemplary to see her tracing the loves of the duchesses beside the innocent cribs of her children. The immoral and the maternal lived together, in her diligent days, on the most comfortable terms, and she stopped curling the moustaches of her Guardsmen to pat the heads of her babes. She was haunted by solemn spinsters who came to tea from Continental pensions, and by unsophisticated Americans who told her she was just loved in *their* country. "I had rather be just paid there," she usually replied; for this tribute of transatlantic opinion was the only thing that galled her. The Americans went away thinking her coarse; though as the author of so many beautiful love-stories she was disappointing to most of these pilgrims, who hadn't expected to find a shy stout ruddy lady in a cap like a crumbled pyramid. She wrote

3. Amandine Aurore Lucie Dupin, French novelist (1803–76), wrote under the name "George Sand." She often wore masculine clothes during her Bohemian days in Paris, and rebelled against marriage and restraints upon women.
4. "Breadwinner," or "experience-of-breadwinning."

about the affections and the impossibility of controlling them, but she talked of the price of pension and the convenience of an English chemist. She devoted much thought and many thousands of francs to the education of her daughter, who spent three years at a very superior school at Dresden, receiving wonderful instruction in sciences, arts and tongues, and who, taking a different line from Leolin, was to be brought up wholly as a *femme du monde*. The girl was musical and philological; she went in for several languages and learned enough about them to be inspired with a great contempt for her mother's artless accents. Greville Fane's French and Italian were droll; the imitative faculty had been denied her, and she had an unequalled gift, especially pen in hand, of squeezing big mistakes into small opportunities. She knew it but didn't care; correctness was the virtue in the world that, like her heroes and heroines, she valued least. Ethel, who had noted in her pages some remarkable lapses, undertook at one time to revise her proofs; but I remember her telling me a year after the girl had left school that this function had been very briefly exercised. "She can't read me," said Mrs. Stormer; "I offend her taste. She tells me that at Dresden—at school—I was never allowed." The good lady seemed surprised at this, having the best conscience in the world about her lucubrations. She had never meant to fly in the face of anything, and considered that she grovelled before the Rhadamanthus of the English literary tribunal, the celebrated and awful Young Person.[5] I assured her, as a joke, that she was frightfully indecent—she had in fact that element of truth as little as any other—my purpose being solely to prevent her guessing that her daughter had dropped her not because she was immoral but because she was vulgar. I used to figure her children closeted together and putting it to each other with a gaze of dismay: "Why should she *be* so—and so *fearfully* so—when she has the advantage of our society? Shouldn't *we* have taught her better?" Then I imagined their recognising with a blush and a shrug that she was unteachable, irreformable. Indeed she was, poor lady, but it's never fair to read by the light of taste things essentially not written in it. Greville Fane kept through all her riot of absurdity a witless confidence that should have been as safe from criticism as a stutter or a squint.

She didn't make her son ashamed of the profession to which he was destined, however; she only made him ashamed of the way she herself exercised it. But he bore his humiliation much better than his sister, being ready to assume he should one day restore the balance. A canny and far-seeing youth, with appetites and aspirations,

---

5. In Greek legend, Rhadamanthus was a lawgiver. The reference is to restraints imposed upon novelists (in 1890) by the necessity to "write down" to young readers, especially young women.

he hadn't a scruple in his composition. His mother's theory of the happy knack he could pick up deprived him of the wholesome discipline required to prevent young idlers from becoming cads. He enjoyed on foreign soil a casual tutor and the common snatch or two of a Swiss school, but addressed himself to no consecutive study nor to any prospect of a university or a degree. It may be imagined with what zeal, as the years went on, he entered into the pleasantry of there being no manual so important to him as the massive book of life. It was an expensive volume to peruse, but Mrs. Stormer was willing to lay out a sum in what she would have called her *premier frais*.[6] Ethel disapproved—she found this education irregular for an English gentleman. Her voice was for Eton and Oxford or for any public school—she would have resigned herself to one of the scrubbier—with the army to follow. But Leolin never was afraid of his sister, and they visibly disliked, though they sometimes agreed to assist, each other. They could combine to work the oracle—to keep their mother at her desk.

When she reappeared in England, telling me she had "secured" all the Continent could give her, Leolin was a broad-shouldered red-faced young man with an immense wardrobe and an extraordinary assurance of manner. She was fondly, quite aggressively certain she had taken the right course with him, and addicted to boasting of all he knew and had seen. He was now quite ready to embark on the family profession, to commence author, as they used to say, and a little while later she told me he had started. He had written something tremendously clever which was coming out in the "Cheapside." I believe it came out; I had no time to look for it; I never heard anything about it. I took for granted that if this contribution had passed through his mother's hands it would virtually rather illustrate *her* fine facility, and it was interesting to consider the poor lady's future in the light of her having to write her son's novels as well as her own. This wasn't the way she looked at it herself— she took the charming ground that he'd help her to write hers. She used to assure me he supplied passages of the greatest value to these last—all sorts of telling technical things, happy touches about hunting and yachting and cigars and wine, about City slang and the way men talk at clubs—that she couldn't be expected to get very straight. It was all so much practice for him and so much alleviation for herself. I was unable to identify such pages, for I had long since ceased to "keep up" with Greville Fane; but I could quite believe at least that the wine-question had been put by Leolin's good offices on a better footing, for the dear woman used to mix her drinks—she was perpetually serving the most splendid suppers—in the queerest fashion. I could see him quite ripe to embrace regu-

6. First expenses.

larly that care. It occurred to me indeed, when she settled in England again, that she might by a shrewd use of both her children be able to rejuvenate her style. Ethel had come back to wreak her native, her social yearning, and if she couldn't take her mother into company would at least go into it herself. Silently, stiffly, almost grimly, this young lady reared her head, clenched her long teeth, squared her lean elbows and found her way up the staircases she had marked. The only communication she ever made, the only effusion of confidence with which she ever honoured me, was when she said "I don't want to know the people mamma knows, I mean to know others." I took due note of the remark, for I wasn't one of the "others." I couldn't trace therefore the steps and stages of her climb; I could only admire it at a distance and congratulate her mother in due course on the results. The results, the gradual, the final, the wonderful, were that Ethel went to "big" parties and got people to take her. Some of them were people she had met abroad, and others people the people she had met abroad had met. They ministered alike to Miss Ethel's convenience, and I wondered how she extracted so many favours without the expenditure of a smile. Her smile was the dimmest thing in nature, diluted, unsweetened, inexpensive lemonade, and she had arrived precociously at social wisdom, recognising that if she was neither pretty enough nor rich enough nor clever enough, she could at least, in her muscular youth, be rude enough. Therefore, so placed to give her parent tips, to let her know what really occurred in the mansions of the great, to supply her with local colour, with *data* to work from, she promoted the driving of the well-worn quill, over the brave old battered blotting book, to a still lustier measure and precisely at the moment when most was to depend on this labour. But if she became a great critic it appeared that the labourer herself was constitutionally inapt for the lesson. It was late in the day for Greville Fane to learn, and I heard nothing of her having developed a new manner. She was to have had only one manner, as Leolin would have said, from start to finish.

She was weary and spent at last, but confided to me that she couldn't afford to pause. She continued to speak of her son's work as the great hope of their future—she had saved no money—though the young man wore to my sense an air more and more professional if you like, but less and less literary. There was at the end of a couple of years something rare in the impudence of his playing of his part in the comedy. When I wondered how she could play hers it was to feel afresh the fatuity of her fondness, which was proof, I believed— I indeed saw to the end—against any interference of reason. She loved the young impostor with a simple blind benighted love, and of all the heroes of romance who had passed before her eyes he was by far the brightest. He was at any rate the most real—she could touch him, pay for him, suffer for him, worship him. He made her think of her princes and dukes, and when she wished to fix these figures in her mind's eyes she thought of her boy. She had often told me she was herself carried away by her creations, and she was certainly carried away by Leolin. He vivified—by what romantically might have been at least—the whole question of youth and passion. She held, not unjustly, that the sincere novelist should feel the whole flood of life; she acknowledged with regret that she hadn't had time to feel it herself, and the lapse in her history was in a manner made up by the sight of its rush through this magnificent young man. She exhorted him, I suppose, to encourage the rush; she wrung her own flaccid little sponge into the torrent. What passed between them in her pedagogic hours was naturally a blank to me, but I gathered that she mainly impressed on him that the great thing was to live, because that gave you material. He asked nothing better; he collected material, and the recipe served as a universal pretext. You had only to look at him to see that, with his rings and breastpins, his cross-barred jackets, his early *embonpoint*,[7] his eyes that looked like imitation jewels, his various indications of a dense full-blown temperament, his idea of life was singularly vulgar; but he was so far auspicious as that his response to his mother's expectations was in a high degree practical. If she had imposed a profession on him from his tenderest years it was exactly a profession that he followed. The two were not quite the same, inasmuch as the one he had adopted was simply to live at her expense; but at least she couldn't say he hadn't taken a line. If she insisted on believing in him he offered himself to the sacrifice. My impression is that her secret dream was that he should have a *liaison* with a countess, and he persuaded her without difficulty that he had one. I don't know what countesses are capable of, but I've a clear notion of what Leolin was.

He didn't persuade his sister, who despised him—she wished to work her mother in her own way; so that I asked myself why the girl's judgement of him didn't make me like her better. It was because it didn't save her after all from the mute agreement with him to go halves. There were moments when I couldn't help looking hard into his atrocious young eyes, challenging him to confess his fantastic fraud and give it up. Not a little tacit conversation passed between us in this way, but he had always the best of the business. If I said: "Oh come now, with *me* you needn't keep it up; plead guilty and I'll let you off," he wore the most ingenuous, the most candid expression, in the depths of which I could read: "Ah yes, I know it exasperates you—that's just why I do it." He took the

7. Stoutness.

line of earnest inquiry, talked about Balzac and Flaubert, asked me if I thought Dickens *did* exaggerate and Thackeray *ought* to be called a pessimist. Once he came to see me, at his mother's suggestion he declared, on purpose to ask me how far, in my opinion, in the English novel, one really might venture to "go." He wasn't resigned to the usual pruderies, the worship of childish twaddle; he suffered already from too much bread and butter. He struck out the brilliant idea that nobody knew how far we might go, since nobody had ever tried. Did I think *he* might safely try—would it injure his mother if he did? He would rather disgrace himself by his timidities than injure his mother, but certainly some one ought to try. Wouldn't *I* try—couldn't I be prevailed upon to look at it as a duty? Surely the ultimate point ought to be fixed—he was worried, haunted by the question. He patronised me unblushingly, made me feel a foolish amateur, a helpless novice, inquired into my habits of work and conveyed to me that I was utterly *vieux jeu*[8] and hadn't had the advantage of an early training. I hadn't been brought up from the egg, I knew nothing of life—didn't go at it on *his* system. He had dipped into French feuilletons[9] and picked up plenty of phrases, and he made a much better show in talk than his poor mother, who never had time to read anything and could only be showy with her pen. If I didn't kick him downstairs it was because he would have landed on her at the bottom.

When she went to live at Primrose Hill I called there and found her wasted and wan. It had visibly dropped, the elation caused the year before by Ethel's marriage; the foam on the cup had subsided and there was bitterness in the draught. She had had to take a cheaper house—and now had to work still harder to pay even for that. Sir Baldwin was obliged to be close; his charges were fearful, and the dream of her living with her daughter—a vision she had never mentioned to me—must be renounced. "I'd have helped them with things, and could have lived perfectly in one room," she said; "I'd have paid for everything, and—after all—I'm some one, ain't I? But I don't fit in, and Ethel tells me there are tiresome people she *must* receive. I can help them from here, no doubt, better than from there. She told me once, you know, what she thinks of my picture of life. 'Mamma, your picture of life's preposterous!' No doubt it is, but she's vexed with me for letting my prices go down; and I had to write three novels to pay for all her marriage cost me. I did it very well—I mean the outfit and the wedding; but that's why I'm here. At any rate she doesn't want a dingy old woman at Blicket. I should give the place an atmosphere of literary prestige, but literary prestige is only the eminence of nobodies. Besides, she knows what

8. Old hat, out-of-date.　　　　　　　9. Newspapers.

to think of my glory—she knows I'm glorious only at Peckham and Hackney.[1] She doesn't want her friends to ask if I've never known nice people. She can't tell them I've never been in society. She tried to teach me better once, but I couldn't catch on. It would seem too as if Peckham and Hackney had had enough of me; for (don't tell any one) I've had to take less for my last than I ever took for anything." I asked her how little this had been, not from curiosity, but in order to upbraid her, more disinterestedly than Lady Luard had done, for such concessions. She answered "I'm ashamed to tell you" and then began to cry.

I had never seen her break down and I was proportionately moved; she sobbed like a frightened child over the extinction of her vogue and the exhaustion of her vein. Her little workroom seemed indeed a barren place to grow flowers for the market, and I wondered in the after years (for she continued to produce and publish) by what desperate and heroic process she dragged them out of the soil. I remember asking her on that occasion what had become of Leolin and how much longer she intended to allow him to amuse himself at her cost. She retorted with spirit, wiping her eyes, that he was down at Brighton hard at work—he was in the midst of a novel— and that he *felt* life so, in all its misery and mystery, that it was cruel to speak of such experiences as a pleasure. "He goes beneath the surface," she said, "and he *forces* himself to look at things from which he'd rather turn away. Do you call that amusing yourself? You should see his face sometimes! And he does it for me as much as for himself. He tells me everything—he comes home to me with his *trouvailles*. We're artists together, and to the artist all things are pure. I've often heard you say so yourself." The novel Leolin was engaged in at Brighton never saw the light, but a friend of mine and of Mrs. Stormer's who was staying there happened to mention to me later that he had seen the young apprentice to fiction driving, in a dog-cart, a young lady with a very pink face. When I suggested that she was perhaps a woman of title with whom he was conscientiously flirting my informant replied: "She is indeed, but do you know what her title is?" He pronounced it—it was familiar and descriptive—but I won't reproduce it here. I don't know whether Leolin mentioned it to his mother: she would have needed all the purity of the artist to forgive him. I hated so to come across him that in the very last years I went rarely to see her, though I knew she had come pretty well to the end of her rope. I didn't want her to tell me she had fairly to give her books away; I didn't want to see her old and abandoned and derided; I didn't want, in a word, to see her terribly cry. She still, however, kept it up amazingly, and every few months, at my club, I saw three new volumes, in green,

1. Sections of London in which there are blocks of flats, mainly for working people.

in crimson, in blue, on the book-table that groaned with light literature. Once I met her at the Academy soirée, where you meet people
you thought were dead, and she vouchsafed the information, as if
she owed it to me in candour, that Leolin had been obliged to recognise the insuperable difficulties of the question of *form*—he was so
fastidious; but that she had now arrived at a definite understanding
with him (it was such a comfort!) that *she* would do the form if
he would bring home the substance. That was now his employ—he
foraged for her in the great world at a salary. "He's my 'devil,' don't
you see? as if I were a great lawyer: he gets up the case and I argue
it." She mentioned further that in addition to his salary he was paid
by the piece: he got so much for a striking character, so much for a
pretty name, so much for a plot, so much for an incident, and had so
much promised him if he would invent a new crime.

"He *has* invented one," I said, "and he's paid every day of his
life."

"What is it?" she asked, looking hard at the picture of the year,
"Baby's Tub," near which we happened to be standing.

I hesitated a moment. "I myself will write a little story about it,
and then you'll see."

But she never saw; she had never seen anything, and she passed
away with her fine blindness unimpaired. Her son published every
scrap of scribbled paper that could be extracted from her table-
drawers, and his sister quarrelled with him mortally about the proceeds, which showed her only to have wanted a pretext, for they
can't have been great. I don't know what Leolin lives on unless on
a queer lady many years older than himself, whom he lately married. The last time I met him he said to me with his infuriating
smile: "Don't you think we can go a little further still—just a
little?" *He* really—with me at least—goes too far.

1892, 1893

The Figure in the Carpet[2]

I had done a few things and earned a few pence—I had perhaps
even had time to begin to think I was finer than was perceived by
the patronising; but when I take the little measure of my course

2. This tale first appeared in *Cosmopolis*, an English journal, for January–February, 1896. It was reprinted
in the volume, *Embarrassments* (1896)
and in the New York Edition (1907–9).
The latter text is used here. See the
selections from the *Notebooks* for
James's account of the growth of the
idea for the story. In the later Preface
to Volume XV of the New York Edition he wrote that his starting point

was a sense of the "marked collective
mistrust," in the English-speaking
world, "of anything like close or analytic appreciation" of fiction. Such appreciation, he felt, was the gate to enjoyment of literature. This "odd numbness of the general sensibility" led him,
he said, to the case of Hugh Vereker
and his undiscovered secret. "What I
most remember of my proper process
is the lively impulse, at the root of it,

(a fidgety habit, for it's none of the longest yet) I count my real start from the evening George Corvick, breathless and worried, came in to ask me a service. He had done more things than I, and earned more pence, though there were chances for cleverness I thought he sometimes missed. I could only, however, that evening declare to him that he never missed one for kindness. There was almost rapture in hearing it proposed to me to prepare for *The Middle*, the organ of our lucubrations, so called from the position in the week of its day of appearance, an article for which he had made himself responsible and of which, tied up with a stout string, he laid on my table the subject. I pounced upon my opportunity—that is on the first volume of it—and paid scant attention to my friend's explanation of his appeal. What explanation could be more to the point than my obvious fitness for the task? I had written on Hugh Vereker, but never a word in *The Middle*, where my dealings were mainly with the ladies and the minor poets. This was his new novel, an advance copy, and whatever much or little it should do for his reputation I was clear on the spot as to what it should do for mine. Moreover if I always read him as soon as I could get hold of him I had a particular reason for wishing to read him now: I had accepted an invitation to Bridges for the following Sunday, and it had been mentioned in Lady Jane's note that Mr. Vereker was to be there. I was young enough for a flutter at meeting a man of his renown, and innocent enough to believe the occasion would demand the display of an acquaintance with his "last."

Corvick, who had promised a review of it, had not even had time to read it; he had gone to pieces in consequence of news requiring —as on precipitate reflexion he judged—that he should catch the night-mail to Paris. He had had a telegram from Gwendolen Erme in answer to his letter offering to fly to her aid. I knew already about Gwendolen Erme; I had never seen her, but I had my ideas, which were mainly to the effect that Corvick would marry her if her mother would only die. That lady seemed now in a fair way to oblige him; after some dreadful mistake about a climate or a "cure" she had suddenly collapsed on the return from abroad. Her daughter, unsup-

to reinstate analytic appreciation, by some ironic or fantastic stroke, so far as possible, in its virtually forfeited rights and dignities. * * * I came to Hugh Vereker, in fine, by this travelled road of a generalization; the habit of having noted for many years how strangely and helplessly, among us all, what we call criticism—its curiosity never emerging from the limp state—is apt to stand off from the intended sense of things, from such finely attested matters, on the artist's part, as a spirit and a form, a bias and a logic, of his own. * * * Vereker's drama, indeed—

or I should perhaps rather say that of the aspiring young analyst whose report we read and to whom, I ruefully grant, I have ventured to impute a developed wit—is that at a given moment the limpness begins to throb and heave, to become conscious of a comparative tension." The question which comes to the front, James said, was "whether the very secret of perception hasn't been lost." The story thus becomes an examination into the state of criticism. The reader is left to form his own conclusion.

ported and alarmed, desiring to make a rush for home but hesitating at the risk, had accepted our friend's assistance, and it was my secret belief that at sight of him Mrs. Erme would pull round. His own belief was scarcely to be called secret; it discernibly at any rate differed from mine. He had showed me Gwendolen's photograph with the remark that she wasn't pretty but was awfully interesting; she had published at the age of nineteen a novel in three volumes, "Deep Down," about which, in *The Middle*, he had been really splendid. He appreciated my present eagerness and undertook that the periodical in question should do no less; then at the last, with his hand on the door, he said to me: "Of course you'll be all right, you know." Seeing I was a trifle vague he added: "I mean you won't be silly."

"Silly—about Vereker! Why what do I ever find him but awfully clever?"

"Well, what's that but silly? What on earth does 'awfully clever' mean? For God's sake try to get *at* him. Don't let him suffer by our arrangement. Speak of him, you know, if you can, as *I* should have spoken of him."

I wondered an instant. "You mean as far and away the biggest of the lot—that sort of thing?"

Corvick almost groaned. "Oh you know, I don't put them back to back that way; it's the infancy of art! But he gives me a pleasure so rare; the sense of"—he mused a little—"something or other."

I wondered again. "The sense, pray, of what?"

"My dear man, that's just what I want *you* to say!"

Even before he had banged the door I had begun, book in hand, to prepare myself to say it. I sat up with Vereker half the night; Corvick couldn't have done more than that. He was awfully clever—I stuck to that, but he wasn't a bit the biggest of the lot. I didn't allude to the lot, however; I flattered myself that I emerged on this occasion from the infancy of art. "It's all right," they declared vividly at the office; and when the number appeared I felt there was a basis on which I could meet the great man. It gave me confidence for a day or two—then that confidence dropped. I had fancied him reading it with relish, but if Corvick wasn't satisfied how could Vereker himself be? I reflected indeed that the heat of the admirer was sometimes grosser even than the appetite of the scribe. Corvick at all events wrote me from Paris a little ill-humouredly. Mrs. Erme was pulling round, and I hadn't at all said what Vereker gave him the sense of.

II

The effect of my visit to Bridges was to turn me out for more profundity. Hugh Vereker, as I saw him there, was of a contact so void of angles that I blushed for the poverty of imagination involved in my small precautions. If he was in spirits it wasn't because he had read my review; in fact on the Sunday morning I felt sure he hadn't read it, though *The Middle* had been out three days and bloomed, I assured myself, in the stiff garden of periodicals which gave one of the ormolu tables the air of a stand at a station. The impression he made on me personally was such that I wished him to read it, and I corrected to this end with a surreptitious hand what might be wanting in the careless conspicuity of the sheet. I'm afraid I even watched the result of my manœuvre, but up to luncheon I watched in vain.

When afterwards, in the course of our gregarious walk, I found myself for half an hour, not perhaps without another manœuvre, at the great man's side, the result of his affability was a still livelier desire that he shouldn't remain in ignorance of the peculiar justice I had done him. It wasn't that he seemed to thirst for justice; on the contrary I hadn't yet caught in his talk the faintest grunt of a grudge —a note for which my young experience had already given me an ear. Of late he had had more recognition, and it was pleasant, as we used to say in *The Middle*, to see how it drew him out. He wasn't of course popular, but I judged one of the sources of his good humour to be precisely that his success was independent of that. He had none the less become in a manner the fashion; the critics at least had put on a spurt and caught up with him. We had found out at last how clever he was, and he had had to make the best of the loss of his mystery. I was strongly tempted, as I walked beside him, to let him know how much of that unveiling was my act; and there was a moment when I probably should have done so had not one of the ladies of our party, snatching a place at his other elbow, just then appealed to him in a spirit comparatively selfish. It was very discouraging: I almost felt the liberty had been taken with myself.

I had had on my tongue's end, for my own part, a phrase or two about the right word at the right time; but later on I was glad not to have spoken, for when on our return we clustered at tea I perceived Lady Jane, who had not been out with us, brandishing *The Middle* with her longest arm. She had taken it up at her leisure; she was delighted with what she had found, and I saw that, as a mistake in a man may often be a felicity in a woman, she would practically do for me what I hadn't been able to do for myself. "Some sweet little truths that needed to be spoken," I heard her declare, thrusting the paper at rather a bewildered couple by the fireplace. She grabbed it away from them again on the reappearance of Hugh Vereker, who after our walk had been upstairs to change something. "I know you don't in general look at this kind of thing, but it's an occasion really for doing so. You *haven't* seen it? Then you must. The man has actually got *at* you, at what *I* always feel, you know."

Lady Jane threw into her eyes a look evidently intended to give an idea of what she always felt; but she added that she couldn't have expressed it. The man in the paper expressed it in a striking manner. "Just see there, and there, where I've dashed it, how he brings it out." She had literally marked for him the brightest patches of my prose, and if I was a little amused Vereker himself may well have been. He showed how much he was when before us all Lady Jane wanted to read something aloud. I liked at any rate the way he defeated her purpose by jerking the paper affectionately out of her clutch. He'd take it upstairs with him and look at it on going to dress. He did this half an hour later—I saw it in his hand when he repaired to his room. That was the moment at which, thinking to give her pleasure, I mentioned to Lady Jane that I was the author of the review. I did give her pleasure, I judged, but perhaps not quite so much as I had expected. If the author was "only me" the thing didn't seem quite so remarkable. Hadn't I had the effect rather of diminishing the lustre of the article than of adding to my own? Her ladyship was subject to the most extraordinary drops. It didn't matter; the only effect I cared about was the one it would have on Vereker up there by his bedroom fire.

At dinner I watched for the signs of this impression, tried to fancy some happier light in his eyes; but to my disappointment Lady Jane gave me no chance to make sure. I had hoped she'd call triumphantly down the table, publicly demand if she hadn't been right. The party was large—there were people from outside as well, but I had never seen a table long enough to deprive Lady Jane of a triumph. I was just reflecting in truth that this interminable board would deprive *me* of one when the guest next me, dear woman—she was Miss Poyle, the vicar's sister, a robust unmodulated person—had the happy inspiration and the unusual courage to address herself across it to Vereker, who was opposite, but not directly, so that when he replied they were both leaning forward. She inquired, artless body, what he thought of Lady Jane's "panegyric," which she had read—not connecting it however with her right-hand neighbour; and while I strained my ear for his reply I heard him, to my stupefaction, call back gaily, his mouth full of bread: "Oh it's all right—the usual twaddle!"

I had caught Vereker's glance as he spoke, but Miss Poyle's surprise was a fortunate cover for my own. "You mean he doesn't do you justice?" said the excellent woman.

Vereker laughed out, and I was happy to be able to do the same. "It's a charming article," he tossed us.

Miss Poyle thrust her chin half across the cloth. "Oh you're so deep!" she drove home.

"As deep as the ocean! All I pretend is that the author doesn't see—" But a dish was at this point passed over his shoulder, and we had to wait while he helped himself.

"Doesn't see what?" my neighbour continued.

"Doesn't see anything."

"Dear me—how very stupid!"

"Not a bit," Vereker laughed again. "Nobody does."

The lady on his further side appealed to him and Miss Poyle sank back to myself. "Nobody sees anything!" she cheerfully announced; to which I replied that I had often thought so too, but had somehow taken the thought for a proof on my own part of a tremendous eye. I didn't tell her the article was mine; and I observed that Lady Jane, occupied at the end of the table, had not caught Vereker's words.

I rather avoided him after dinner, for I confess he struck me as cruelly conceited, and the revelation was a pain. "The usual twaddle"—my acute little study! That one's admiration should have had a reserve or two could gall him to that point? I had thought him placid, and he was placid enough; such a surface was the hard polished glass that encased the bauble of his vanity. I was really ruffled, and the only comfort was that if nobody saw anything George Corvick was quite as much out of it as I. This comfort however was not sufficient, after the ladies had dispersed, to carry me in the proper manner—I mean in a spotted jacket and humming an air—into the smoking-room. I took my way in some dejection to bed; but in the passage I encountered Mr. Vereker, who had been up once more to change, coming out of his room. *He* was humming an air and had on a spotted jacket, and as soon as he saw me his gaiety gave a start.

"My dear young man," he exclaimed, "I'm so glad to lay hands on you! I'm afraid I most unwittingly wounded you by those words of mine at dinner to Miss Poyle. I learned but half an hour ago from Lady Jane that you're the author of the little notice in *The Middle*."

I protested that no bones were broken; but he moved with me to my own door, his hand, on my shoulder, kindly feeling for a fracture; and on hearing that I had come up to bed he asked leave to cross my threshold and just tell me in three words what his qualification of my remarks had represented. It was plain he really feared I was hurt, and the sense of his solicitude suddenly made all the difference to me. My cheap review fluttered off into space, and the best things I had said in it became flat enough beside the brilliancy of his being there. I can see him there still, on my rug, in the firelight and his spotted jacket, his fine clear face all bright with the desire to be tender to my youth. I don't know what he had at first meant to say, but I think the sight of my relief touched him, excited him, brought up words to his lips from far within. It was so these words presently conveyed to me something that, as I afterwards knew, he had never uttered to any one. I've always done justice to the generous impulse that made him speak; it was simply compunction for a snub unconsciously administered to a man of letters in a position inferior to his own, a man of letters moreover in the very act of praising him. To make the thing right he talked to me exactly as an equal and on the ground of what we both loved best. The hour, the place, the unexpectedness deepened the impression: he couldn't have done anything more intensely effective.

III

"I don't quite know how to explain it to you," he said, "but it was the very fact that your notice of my book had a spice of intelligence, it was just your exceptional sharpness, that produced the feeling—a very old story with me, I beg you to believe—under the momentary influence of which I used in speaking to that good lady the words you so naturally resent. I don't read the things in the newspapers unless they're thrust upon me as that one was—it's always one's best friend who does it! But I used to read them sometimes—ten years ago. I dare say they were in general rather stupider then; at any rate it always struck me they missed my little point with a perfection exactly as admirable when they patted me on the back as when they kicked me in the shins. Whenever since I've happened to have a glimpse of them they were still blazing away—still missing it, I mean, deliciously. *You* miss it, my dear fellow, with inimitable assurance; the fact of your being awfully clever and your article's being awfully nice doesn't make a hair's breadth of difference. It's quite with you rising young men," Vereker laughed, "that I feel most what a failure I am!"

I listened with keen interest; it grew keener as he talked. "*You* a failure—heavens! What then may your 'little point' happen to be?"

"Have I got to *tell* you, after all these years and labours?" There was something in the friendly reproach of this—jocosely exaggerated—that made me, as an ardent young seeker for truth, blush to the roots of my hair. I'm as much in the dark as ever, though I've grown used in a sense to my obtuseness; at that moment, however, Vereker's happy accent made me appear to myself, and probably to him, a rare dunce. I was on the point of exclaiming "Ah yes, don't tell me: for my honour, for that of the craft, don't!" when he went on in a manner that showed he had read my thought and had his own idea of the probability of our some day redeeming ourselves. "By my little point I mean—what shall I call it?—the particular thing I've written my books most *for*. Isn't there for every writer a particular thing of that sort, the thing that most makes him apply himself, the thing without the effort to achieve which he wouldn't write at all, the very passion of his passion, the part of the business in which, for him, the flame of art burns most intensely? Well, it's *that*!"

I considered a moment—that is I followed at a respectful distance, rather gasping. I was fascinated—easily, you'll say; but I wasn't going after all to be put off my guard. "Your description's certainly beautiful, but it doesn't make what you describe very distinct."

"I promise you it would be distinct if it should dawn on you at all." I saw that the charm of our topic overflowed for my companion into an emotion as lively as my own. "At any rate," he went on, "I can speak for myself: there's an idea in my work without which I wouldn't have given a straw for the whole job. It's the finest fullest intention of the lot, and the application of it has been, I think, a triumph of patience, of ingenuity. I ought to leave that to somebody else to say; but that nobody does say it is precisely what we're talking about. It stretches, this little trick of mine, from book to book, and everything else, comparatively, plays over the surface of it. The order, the form, the texture of my books will perhaps someday constitute for the initiated a complete representation of it. So it's naturally the thing for the critic to look for. It strikes me," my visitor added, smiling, "even as the thing for the critic to find."

This seemed a responsibility indeed. "You call it a little trick?"

"That's only my little modesty. It's really an exquisite scheme."

"And you hold that you've carried the scheme out?"

"The way I've carried it out is the thing in life I think a bit well of myself for."

I had a pause. "Don't you think you ought—just a trifle—to assist the critic?"

"Assist him? What else have I done with every stroke of my pen? I've shouted my intention in his great blank face!" At this, laughing out again, Vereker laid his hand on my shoulder to show the allusion wasn't to my personal appearance.

"But you talk about the initiated. There must therefore, you see, *be* initiation."

"What else in heaven's name is criticism supposed to be?" I'm afraid I coloured at this too; but I took refuge in repeating that his account of his silver lining was poor in something or other that a plain man knows things by. "That's only because you've never had a glimpse of it," he returned. "If you had had one the element in question would soon have become practically all you'd see. To me it's exactly as palpable as the marble of this chimney. Besides, the critic just *isn't* a plain man: if he were, pray, what would he be doing in his neighbour's garden? You're anything but a plain man yourself, and the very *raison d'être* of you all is that you're little demons of subtlety. If my great affair's a secret, that's only because it's a secret in spite of itself—the amazing event has made it one. I not only never took the smallest precaution to keep it so, but never dreamed of any such accident. If I had I shouldn't in advance have had the heart to go on. As it was, I only became aware little by little, and meanwhile I had done my work."

"And now you quite like it?" I risked.

"My work?"

"Your secret. It's the same thing."

"Your guessing that," Vereker replied, "is a proof that you're as clever as I say!" I was encouraged by this to remark that he would clearly be pained to part with it, and he confessed that it was indeed with him now the great amusement of life. "I live almost to see if it will ever be detected." He looked at me for a jesting challenge; something far within his eyes seemed to peep out. "But I needn't worry—it won't!"

"You fire me as I've never been fired," I declared; "you make me determined to do or die." Then I asked: "Is it a kind of esoteric message?"

His countenance fell at this—he put out his hand as if to bid me good-night. "Ah my dear fellow, it can't be described in cheap journalese!"

I knew of course he'd be awfully fastidious, but our talk had made me feel how much his nerves were exposed. I was unsatisfied—I kept hold of his hand. "I won't make use of the expression then," I said, "in the article in which I shall eventually announce my discovery, though I dare say I shall have hard work to do without it. But meanwhile, just to hasten that difficult birth, can't you give a fellow a clue?" I felt much more at my ease.

"My whole lucid effort gives him the clue—every page and line and letter. The thing's as concrete there as a bird in a cage, a bait on a hook, a piece of cheese in a mouse-trap. It's stuck into every volume as your foot is stuck into your shoe. It governs every line, it chooses every word, it dots every i, it places every comma."

I scratched my head. "Is it something in the style or something in the thought? An element of form or an element of feeling?"

He indulgently shook my hand again, and I felt my questions to be crude and my distinctions pitiful. "Good-night, my dear boy—don't bother about it. After all, you do like a fellow."

"And a little intelligence might spoil it?" I still detained him.

He hesitated. "Well, you've got a heart in your body. Is that an element of form or an element of feeling? What I contend that nobody has ever mentioned in my work is the organ of life."

"I see—it's some idea *about* life, some sort of philosophy. Unless it be," I added with the eagerness of a thought perhaps still happier, "some kind of game you're up to with your style, something you're after in the language. Perhaps it's a preference for the letter P!" I ventured profanely to break out. "Papa, potatoes, prunes—that sort of thing?" He was suitably indulgent: he only said I hadn't got the right letter. But his amusement was over; I could see he was bored. There was nevertheless something else I had absolutely to learn. "Should you be able, pen in hand, to state it clearly yourself —to name it, phrase it, formulate it?"

"Oh," he almost passionately sighed, "if I were only, pen in hand, one of *you* chaps!"

"That would be a great chance for you of course. But why should you despise us chaps for not doing what you can't do yourself?"

"Can't do?" He opened his eyes. "Haven't I done it in twenty volumes? I do it in my way," he continued. "Go *you* and do it in yours."

"Ours is so devilish difficult," I weakly observed.

"So's mine! We each choose our own. There's no compulsion. You won't come down and smoke?"

"No. I want to think this thing out."

"You'll tell me then in the morning that you've laid me bare?"

"I'll see what I can do; I'll sleep on it. But just one word more," I added. We had left the room—I walked again with him a few steps along the passage. "This extraordinary 'general intention,' as you call it—for that's the most vivid description I can induce you to make of it—is then, generally, a sort of buried treasure?"

His face lighted. "Yes, call it that, though it's perhaps not for me to do so."

"Nonsense!" I laughed. "You know you're hugely proud of it."

"Well, I didn't propose to tell you so; but it *is* the joy of my soul!"

"You mean it's a beauty so rare, so great?"

He waited a little again. "The loveliest thing in the world!" We had stopped, and on these words he left me; but at the end of the corridor, while I looked after him rather yearningly, he turned and caught sight of my puzzled face. It made him earnestly, indeed I thought quite anxiously, shake his head and wave his finger. "Give it up—give it up!"

This wasn't a challenge—it was fatherly advice. If I had had one of his books at hand I'd have repeated my recent act of faith—I'd have spent half the night with him. At three o'clock in the morning, not sleeping, remembering moreover how indispensable he was to Lady Jane, I stole down to the library with a candle. There wasn't, so far as I could discover, a line of his writing in the house.

IV

Returning to town I feverishly collected them all; I picked out each in its order and held it up to the light. This gave me a maddening month, in the course of which several things took place. One of these, the last, I may as well immediately mention, was that I acted on Vereker's advice: I renounced my ridiculous attempt. I could really make nothing of the business; it proved a dead loss.

After all I had always, as he had himself noted, liked him; and what now occurred was simply that my new intelligence and vain pre-occupation damaged my liking. I not only failed to run a general intention to earth, I found myself missing the subordinate intentions I had formerly enjoyed. His books didn't even remain the charming things they had been for me; the exasperation of my search put me out of conceit of them. Instead of being a pleasure the more they became a resource the less; for from the moment I was unable to follow up the author's hint I of course felt it a point of honour not to make use professionally of my knowledge of them. I *had* no knowledge—nobody had any. It was humiliating, but I could bear it—they only annoyed me now. At last they even bored me, and I accounted for my confusion—perversely, I allow—by the idea that Vereker had made a fool of me. The buried treasure was a bad joke, the general intention a monstrous *pose*.

The great point of it all is, however, that I told George Corvick what had befallen me and that my information had an immense effect on him. He had at last come back, but so, unfortunately, had Mrs. Erme, and there was as yet, I could see, no question of his nuptials. He was immensely stirred up by the anecdote I had brought from Bridges; it fell in so completely with the sense he had had from the first that there was more in Vereker than met the eye. When I remarked that the eye seemed what the printed page had been expressly invented to meet he immediately accused me of being spiteful because I had been foiled. Our commerce had always that pleasant latitude. The thing Vereker had mentioned to me was exactly the thing he, Corvick, had wanted me to speak of in my review. On my suggesting at last that with the assistance I had now given him he would doubtless be prepared to speak of it himself he admitted freely that before doing this there was more he must understand. What he would have said, had he reviewed the new book, was that there was evidently in the writer's inmost art something to *be* understood. I hadn't so much as hinted at that: no wonder the writer hadn't been flattered! I asked Corvick what he really considered he meant by his own supersubtlety, and, unmistakably kindled, he replied: "It isn't for the vulgar—it isn't for the vulgar!" He had hold of the tail of something: he would pull hard, pull it right out. He pumped me dry on Vereker's strange confidence and, pronouncing me the luckiest of mortals, mentioned half-a-dozen questions he wished to goodness I had had the gumption to put. Yet on the other hand he didn't want to be told too much—it would spoil the fun of seeing what would come. The failure of *my* fun was at the moment of our meeting not complete, but I saw it ahead, and Corvick saw that I saw it. I, on my side, saw likewise that one of the first things he would do would be to rush off with my story to Gwendolen.

On the very day after my talk with him I was surprised by the receipt of a note from Hugh Vereker, to whom our encounter at Bridges had been recalled, as he mentioned, by his falling, in a magazine, on some article to which my signature was attached. "I read it with great pleasure," he wrote, "and remembered under its influence our lively conversation by your bedroom fire. The consequence of this has been that I begin to measure the temerity of my having saddled you with a knowledge that you may find something of a burden. Now that the fit's over I can't imagine how I came to be moved so much beyond my wont. I had never before mentioned, no matter in what state of expansion, the fact of my little secret, and I shall never speak of that mystery again. I was accidentally so much more explicit with you than it had ever entered into my game to be, that I find this game—I mean the pleasure of playing it—suffers considerably. In short, if you can understand it, I've rather spoiled my sport. I really don't want to give anybody what I believe you clever young men call the tip. That's of course a selfish solicitude, and I name it to you for what it may be worth to you. If you're disposed to humour me don't repeat my revelation. Think me demented—it's your right; but don't tell anybody why."

The sequel to this communication was that as early on the morrow as I dared I drove straight to Mr. Vereker's door. He occupied in those years one of the honest old houses in Kensington Square. He received me immediately, and as soon as I came in I saw I hadn't lost my power to minister to his mirth. He laughed out at sight of my face, which doubtless expressed my perturbation. I had been indiscreet—my compunction was great. "I *have* told somebody," I panted, "and I'm sure that person will by this time have told somebody else! It's a woman, into the bargain."

"The person you've told?"

"No, the other person. I'm quite sure he must have told her."

"For all the good it will do her—or do *me!* A woman will never find out."

"No, but she'll talk all over the place: she'll do just what you don't want."

Vereker thought a moment, but wasn't so disconcerted as I had feared: he felt that if the harm was done it only served him right. "It doesn't matter—don't worry."

"I'll do my best, I promise you, that your talk with me shall go no further."

"Very good; do what you can."

"In the meantime," I pursued, "George Corvick's possession of the tip may, on his part, really lead to something."

"That will be a brave day."

I told him about Corvick's cleverness, his admiration, the intensity of his interest in my anecdote; and without making too much of the divergence of our respective estimates mentioned that my friend was already of opinion that he saw much further into a certain affair than most people. He was quite as fired as I had been at Bridges. He was moreover in love with the young lady: perhaps the two together would puzzle something out.

Vereker seemed struck with this. "Do you mean they're to be married?"

"I dare say that's what it will come to."

"That may help them," he conceded, "but we must give them time!"

I spoke of my own renewed assault and confessed my difficulties; whereupon he repeated his former advice: "Give it up, give it up!" He evidently didn't think me intellectually equipped for the adventure. I stayed half an hour, and he was most good-natured, but I couldn't help pronouncing him a man of unstable moods. He had been free with me in a mood, he had repented in a mood, and now in a mood he had turned indifferent. This general levity helped me to believe that, so far as the subject of the tip went, there wasn't much in it. I contrived however to make him answer a few more questions about it, though he did so with visible impatience. For himself, beyond doubt, the thing we were all so blank about was vividly there. It was something, I guessed, in the primal plan; something like a complex figure in a Persian carpet. He highly approved of this image when I used it, and he used another himself. "It's the very string," he said, "that my pearls are strung on!" The reason of his note to me had been that he really didn't want to give us a grain of succour—our density was a thing too perfect in its way to touch. He had formed the habit of depending on it, and if the spell was to break it must break by some force of its own. He comes back to me from that last occasion—for I was never to speak to him again—as a man with some safe preserve for sport. I wondered as I walked away where he had got *his* tip.

V

When I spoke to George Corvick of the caution I had received he made me feel that any doubt of his delicacy would be almost an insult. He had instantly told Gwendolen, but Gwendolen's ardent response was in itself a pledge of discretion. The question would now absorb them and would offer them a pastime too precious to be shared with the crowd. They appeared to have caught instinctively at Vereker's high idea of enjoyment. Their intellectual pride, however, was not such as to make them indifferent to any further light I might throw on the affair they had in hand. They were indeed of the "artistic temperament," and I was freshly struck with my colleague's power to excite himself over a question of art. He'd call it letters, he'd call it life, but it was all one thing. In what he said I now seemed to understand that he spoke equally for Gwendolen, to whom, as soon as Mrs. Erme was sufficiently better to allow her a little leisure, he made a point of introducing me. I remember our going together one Sunday in August to a huddled house in Chelsea, and my renewed envy of Corvick's possession of a friend who had some light to mingle with his own. He could say things to her that I could never say to him. She had indeed no sense of humour and, with her pretty way of holding her head on one side, was one of those persons whom you want, as the phrase is, to shake, but who have learnt Hungarian by themselves. She conversed perhaps in Hungarian with Corvick; she had remarkably little English for his friend. Corvick afterwards told me that I had chilled her by my apparent indisposition to oblige them with the detail of what Vereker had said to me. I allowed that I felt I had given thought enough to that indication: hadn't I even made up my mind that it was vain and would lead nowhere? The importance they attached to it was irritating and quite envenomed my doubts.

That statement looks unamiable, and what probably happened was that I felt humiliated at seeing other persons deeply beguiled by an experiment that had brought me only chagrin. I was out in the cold while, by the evening fire, under the lamp, they followed the chase for which I myself had sounded the horn. They did as I had done, only more deliberately and sociably—they went over their author from the beginning. There was no hurry, Corvick said—the future was before them and the fascination could only grow; they would take him page by page, as they would take one of the classics, inhale him in slow draughts and let him sink all the way in. They would scarce have got so wound up, I think, if they hadn't been in love: poor Vereker's inner meaning gave them endless occasion to put and to keep their young heads together. None the less it represented the kind of problem for which Corvick had a special aptitude, drew out the particular pointed patience of which, had he lived, he would have given more striking and, it is to be hoped, more fruitful examples. He at least was, in Vereker's words, a little demon of subtlety. We had begun by disputing, but I soon saw that without my stirring a finger his infatuation would have its bad hours. He would bound off on false scents as I had done—he would clap his hands over new lights and see them blown out by the wind of the turned page. He was like nothing, I told him, but the maniacs who embrace some bedlamitical theory of the cryptic character of Shakespeare. To this he replied that if we had had Shakespeare's own word for his being cryptic he would at once have accepted it. The case there was altogether different—we had nothing but the word of

Mr. Snooks. I returned that I was stupefied to see him attach such importance even to the word of Mr. Vereker. He wanted thereupon to know if I treated Mr. Vereker's word as a lie. I wasn't perhaps prepared, in my unhappy rebound, to go so far as that, but I insisted that till the contrary was proved I should view it as too fond an imagination. I didn't, I confess, say—I didn't at that time quite know—all I felt. Deep down, as Miss Erme would have said, I was uneasy, I was expectant. At the core of my disconcerted state—for my wonted curiosity lived in its ashes—was the sharpness of a sense that Corvick would at last probably come out somewhere. He made, in defence of his credulity, a great point of the fact that from of old, in his study of this genius, he had caught whiffs and hints of he didn't know what, faint wandering notes of a hidden music. That was just the rarity, that was the charm: it fitted so perfectly into what I reported.

If I returned on several occasions to the little house in Chelsea I dare say it was as much for news of Vereker as for news of Miss Erme's ailing parent. The hours spent there by Corvick were present to my fancy as those of a chessplayer bent with a silent scowl, all the lamplit winter, over his board and his moves. As my imagination filled it out the picture held me fast. On the other side of the table was a ghostlier form, the faint figure of an antagonist good-humouredly but a little wearily secure—an antagonist who leaned back in his chair with his hands in his pockets and a smile on his fine clear face. Close to Corvick, behind him, was a girl who had begun to strike me as pale and wasted and even, on more familiar view, as rather handsome, and who rested on his shoulder and hung on his moves. He would take up a chessman and hold it poised a while over one of the little squares, and then would put it back in its place with a long sigh of disappointment. The young lady, at this, would slightly but uneasily shift her position and look across, very hard, very long, very strangely, at their dim participant. I had asked them at an early stage of the business if it mightn't contribute to their success to have some closer communication with him. The special circumstances would surely be held to have given me a right to introduce them. Corvick immediately replied that he had no wish to approach the altar before he had prepared the sacrifice. He quite agreed with our friend both as to the delight and as to the honour of the chase—he would bring down the animal with his own rifle. When I asked him if Miss Erme were as keen a shot he said after thinking: "No, I'm ashamed to say she wants to set a trap. She'd give anything to see him; she says she requires another tip. She's really quite morbid about it. But she must play fair—she *shan't* see him!" he emphatically added. I wondered if they hadn't even quarrelled a little on the subject—a suspicion not corrected by the way he more than once exclaimed to me: "She's quite incredibly literary, you know—quite fantastically!" I remember his saying of her that she felt in italics and thought in capitals. "Oh when I've run him to earth," he also said, "then, you know, I shall knock at his door. Rather—I beg you to believe. I'll have it from his own lips: 'Right you are, my boy; you've done it this time!' He shall crown me victor —with the critical laurel."

Meanwhile he really avoided the chances London life might have given him of meeting the distinguished novelist; a danger, however, that disappeared with Vereker's leaving England for an indefinite absence, as the newspapers announced—going to the south for motives connected with the health of his wife, which had long kept her in retirement. A year—more than a year—had elapsed since the incident at Bridges, but I had had no further sight of him. I think I was at bottom rather ashamed—I hated to remind him that, though I had irremediably missed his point, a reputation for acuteness was rapidly overtaking me. This scruple led me a dance; kept me out of Lady Jane's house, made me even decline, when in spite of my bad manners she was a second time so good as to make me a sign, an invitation to her beautiful seat. I once became aware of her under Vereker's escort at a concert, and was sure I was seen by them, but I slipped out without being caught. I felt, as on that occasion I splashed along in the rain, that I couldn't have done anything else; and yet I remember saying to myself that it was hard, was even cruel. Not only had I lost the books, but I had lost the man himself: they and their author had been alike spoiled for me. I knew too which was the loss I most regretted. I had taken to the man still more than I had ever taken to the books.

VI

Six months after our friend had left England George Corvick, who made his living by his pen, contracted for a piece of work which imposed on him an absence of some length and a journey of some difficulty, and his undertaking of which was much of a surprise to me. His brother-in-law had become editor of a great provincial paper, and the great provincial paper, in a fine flight of fancy, had conceived the idea of sending a "special commissioner" to India. Special commissioners had begun, in the "metropolitan press," to be the fashion, and the journal in question must have felt it had passed too long for a mere country cousin. Corvick had no hand, I knew, for the big brush of the correspondent, but that was his brother-in-law's affair, and the fact that a particular task was not in his line was apt to be with himself exactly a reason for accepting it. He was prepared to out-Herod the metropolitan press; he took solemn precautions against priggishness, he exquisitely outraged taste. Nobody ever knew it—that offended principle was all his own. In addition to his expenses he was to be conveniently paid, and I found myself able to help him, for the usual fat book, to a plausible arrangement with the usual fat publisher. I naturally inferred that his obvious desire to make a little money was not unconnected with the prospect of a union with Gwendolen Erme. I was aware that her mother's opposition was largely addressed to his want of means and of lucrative abilities, but it so happened that, on my saying the last time I saw him something that bore on the question of his separation from our young lady, he brought out with an emphasis that startled me: "Ah I'm not a bit engaged to her, you know!"

"Not overtly," I answered, "because her mother doesn't like you. But I've always taken for granted a private understanding."

"Well, there *was* one. But there isn't now." That was all he said save something about Mrs. Erme's having got on her feet again in the most extraordinary way—a remark pointing, as I supposed, the moral that private understandings were of little use when the doctor didn't share them. What I took the liberty of more closely inferring was that the girl might in some way have estranged him. Well, if he had taken the turn of jealousy, for instance, it could scarcely be jealousy of me. In that case—over and above the absurdity of it—he wouldn't have gone away just to leave us together. For some time before his going we had indulged in no allusion to the buried treasure, and from his silence, which my reserve simply emulated, I had drawn a sharp conclusion. His courage had dropped, his ardour had gone the way of mine—this appearance at least he left me to scan. More than that he couldn't do; he couldn't face the triumph with which I might have greeted an explicit admission. He needn't have been afraid, poor dear, for I had by this time lost all need to triumph. In fact I considered I showed magnanimity in not reproaching him with his collapse, for the sense of his having thrown up the game made me feel more than ever how much I at last depended on him. If Corvick had broken down I should never know; no one would be of any use if *he* wasn't. It wasn't a bit true I had ceased to care for knowledge; little by little my curiosity not only had begun to ache again, but had become the familiar torment of my days and my nights. There are doubtless people to whom torments of such an order appear hardly more natural than the contortions of disease; but I don't after all know why I should in this connexion so much as mention them. For the few persons, at any rate, abnormal or not, with whom my anecdote is concerned, literature was a game of skill, and skill meant courage, and courage meant honour, and honour meant passion, meant life. The stake on the table was a special substance and our roulette the revolving mind, but we sat round the green board as intently as the grim gamblers at Monte Carlo. Gwendolen Erme, for that matter, with her white

1482 · Henry James

face and her fixed eyes, was of the very type of the lean ladies one
had met in the temples of chance. I recognised in Corvick's absence that she made this analogy vivid. It was extravagant, I admit, the way she lived for the art of the pen. Her passion visibly
preyed on her, and in her presence I felt almost tepid. I got hold
of "Deep Down" again: it was a desert in which she had lost herself, but in which too she had dug a wonderful hole in the sand—a
cavity out of which Corvick had still more remarkably pulled her.

Early in March I had a telegram from her, in consequence of
which I repaired immediately to Chelsea, where the first thing she
said to me was: "He has got it, he has got it!"

She was moved, as I could see, to such depths that she must mean
the great thing. "Vereker's idea?"

"His general intention. George has cabled from Bombay."

She had the missive open there; it was emphatic though concise.
"Eureka. Immense." That was all—he had saved the cost of the
signature. I shared her emotion, but I was disappointed. "He
doesn't say what it is."

"How could he—in a telegram? He'll write it."

"But how does he know?"

"Know it's the real thing? Oh I'm sure that when you see it you
do know. _Vera incessu patuit dea!_"[3]

"It's you, Miss Erme, who are a 'dear' for bringing me such news!"
—I went all lengths in my high spirits. "But fancy finding our goddess in the temple of Vishnu! How strange of George to have been
able to go into the thing again in the midst of such different and
such powerful solicitations!"

"He hasn't gone into it, I know; it's the thing itself, let severely
alone for six months, that has simply sprung out at him like a tigress
out of the jungle. He didn't take a book with him—on purpose;
indeed he wouldn't have needed to—he knows every page, as I do,
by heart. They all worked in him together, and some day somewhere, when he wasn't thinking, they fell, in all their superb intricacy, into the one right combination. The figure in the carpet came
out. That's the way he knew it would come and the real reason—you
didn't in the least understand, but I suppose I may tell you now—
why he went and why I consented to his going. We knew the
change would do it—that the difference of thought, of scene, would
give the needed touch, the magic shake. We had perfectly, we had
admirably calculated. The elements were all in his mind, and in
the _secousse_ of a new and intense experience they just struck light."
She positively struck light herself—she was literally, facially luminous. I stammered something about unconscious cerebration, and
she continued: "He'll come right home—this will bring him."

3. Latin, "The approach to the true goddess lies open."

"To see Vereker, you mean?"

"To see Vereker—and to see *me*. Think what he'll have to tell me!"

I hesitated. "About India?"

"About fiddlesticks! About Vereker—about the figure in the carpet."

"But, as you say, we shall surely have that in a letter."

She thought like one inspired, and I remembered how Corvick had told me long before that her face was interesting. "Perhaps it can't be got into a letter if it's 'immense.' "

"Perhaps not if it's immense bosh. If he has hold of something that can't be got into a letter he hasn't hold of *the* thing. Vereker's own statement to me was exactly that the 'figure' *would* fit into a letter."

"Well, I cabled to George an hour ago—two words," said Gwendolen.

"Is it indiscreet of me to ask what they were?"

She hung fire, but at last brought them out. " 'Angel, write.' "

"Good!" I cried. "I'll make it sure—I'll send him the same."

VII

My words however were not absolutely the same—I put something instead of "angel"; and in the sequel my epithet seemed the more apt, for when eventually we heard from our traveller it was merely, it was thoroughly to be tantalised. He was magnificent in his triumph, he described his discovery as stupendous; but his ecstasy only obscured it—there were to be no particulars till he should have submitted his conception to the supreme authority. He had thrown up his commission, he had thrown up his book, he had thrown up everything but the instant need to hurry to Rapallo, on the Genoese shore, where Vereker was making a stay. I wrote him a letter which was to await him at Aden—I besought him to relieve my suspense. That he had found my letter was indicated by a telegram which, reaching me after weary days and in the absence of any answer to my laconic dispatch to him at Bombay, was evidently intended as a reply to both communications. Those few words were in familiar French, the French of the day, which Corvick often made use of to show he wasn't a prig. It had for some persons the opposite effect, but his message may fairly be paraphrased. "Have patience; I want to see, as it breaks on you, the face you'll make!" "*Tellement envie de voir ta tête!*"[4]—that was what I had to sit down with. I can certainly not be said to have sat down, for I seem to remember myself at this time as rattling constantly between the little house in Chelsea and my own. Our impatience, Gwendolen's and mine, was equal, but I kept hoping her light would be greater.

4. "I have a great desire to see your face!"

We all spent during this episode, for people of our means, a great deal of money in telegrams and cabs, and I counted on the receipt of news from Rapallo immediately after the junction of the discoverer with the discovered. The interval seemed an age, but late one day I heard a hansom precipitated to my door with the crash engendered by a hint of liberality. I lived with my heart in my mouth and accordingly bounded to the window—a movement which gave me a view of a young lady erect on the footboard of the vehicle and eagerly looking up at my house. At sight of me she flourished a paper with a movement that brought me straight down, the movement with which, in melodramas, handkerchiefs and reprieves are flourished at the foot of the scaffold.

"Just seen Vereker—not a note wrong. Pressed me to bosom—keeps me a month." So much I read on her paper while the cabby dropped a grin from his perch. In my excitement I paid him profusely and in hers she suffered it; then as he drove away we started to walk about and talk. We had talked, heaven knows, enough before, but this was a wondrous lift. We pictured the whole scene at Rapallo, where he would have written, mentioning my name, for permission to call; that is I pictured it, having more material than my companion, whom I felt hang on my lips as we stopped on purpose before shop-windows we didn't look into. About one thing we were clear: if he was staying on for fuller communication we should at least have a letter from him that would help us through the dregs of delay. We understood his staying on, and yet each of us saw, I think, that the other hated it. The letter we were clear about arrived; it was for Gwendolen, and I called on her in time to save her the trouble of bringing it to me. She didn't read it out, as was natural enough; but she repeated to me what it chiefly embodied. This consisted of the remarkable statement that he'd tell her after they were married exactly what she wanted to know.

"Only *then*, when I'm his wife—not before," she explained. "It's tantamount to saying—isn't it?—that I must marry him straight off!" She smiled at me while I flushed with disappointment, a vision of fresh delay that made me at first unconscious of my surprise. It seemed more than a hint that on me as well he would impose some tiresome condition. Suddenly, while she reported several more things from his letter, I remembered what he had told me before going away. He had found Mr. Vereker deliriously interesting and his own possession of the secret a real intoxication. The buried treasure was all gold and gems. Now that it was there it seemed to grow and grow before him; it would have been, through all time and taking all tongues, one of the most wonderful flowers of literary art. Nothing, in especial, once you were face to face with it, could show for more consummately *done*. When once it came out it came out, was there with a splendour that made you ashamed; and there hadn't been, save in the bottomless vulgarity of the age, with every one tasteless and tainted, every sense stopped, the smallest reason why it should have been overlooked. It was great, yet so simple, was simple, yet so great, and the final knowledge of it was an experience quite apart. He intimated that the charm of such an experience, the desire to drain it, in its freshness, to the last drop, was what kept him there close to the source. Gwendolen, frankly radiant as she tossed me these fragments, showed the elation of a prospect more assured than my own. That brought me back to the question of her marriage, prompted me to ask if what she meant by what she had just surprised me with was that she was under an engagement.

"Of course I am!" she answered. "Didn't you know it?" She seemed astonished, but I was still more so, for Corvick had told me the exact contrary. I didn't mention this, however; I only reminded her how little I had been on that score in her confidence, or even in Corvick's, and that moreover I wasn't in ignorance of her mother's interdict. At bottom I was troubled by the disparity of the two accounts; but after a little I felt Corvick's to be the one I least doubted. This simply reduced me to asking myself if the girl had on the spot improvised an engagement—vamped up an old one or dashed off a new—in order to arrive at the satisfaction she desired. She must have had resources of which I was destitute, but she made her case slightly more intelligible by returning presently: "What the state of things has been is that we felt of course bound to do nothing in mamma's lifetime."

"But now you think you'll just dispense with mamma's consent?"

"Ah it mayn't come to that!" I wondered what it might come to, and she went on: "Poor dear, she may swallow the dose. In fact, you know," she added with a laugh, "she really *must!*"—a proposition of which, on behalf of every one concerned, I fully acknowledged the force.

VIII

Nothing more vexatious had ever happened to me than to become aware before Corvick's arrival in England that I shouldn't be there to put him through. I found myself abruptly called to Germany by the alarming illness of my younger brother, who, against my advice, had gone to Munich to study, at the feet indeed of a great master, the art of portraiture in oils. The near relative who made him an allowance had threatened to withdraw it if he should, under specious pretexts, turn for superior truth to Paris—Paris being somehow, for a Cheltenham aunt, the school of evil, the abyss. I deplored this prejudice at the time, and the deep injury of it was now visible—first in the fact that it hadn't saved the poor boy, who was clever frail and foolish, from congestion of the lungs, and sec-

ond in the greater break with London to which the event condemned me. I'm afraid that what was uppermost in my mind during several anxious weeks was the sense that if we had only been in
Paris I might have run over to see Corvick. This was actually out
of the question from every point of view: my brother, whose recovery gave us both plenty to do, was ill for three months, during
which I never left him and at the end of which we had to face the
absolute prohibition of a return to England. The consideration of
climate imposed itself, and he was in no state to meet it alone. I
took him to Meran and there spent the summer with him, trying
to show him by example how to get back to work and nursing a
rage of another sort that I tried *not* to show him.

The whole business proved the first of a series of phenomena so
strangely interlaced that, taken all together—which was how I had
to take them—they form as good an illustration as I can recall of the
manner in which, for the good of his soul doubtless, fate sometimes
deals with a man's avidity. These incidents certainly had larger bearings than the comparatively meagre consequence we are here concerned with—though I feel that consequence also a thing to speak
of with some respect. It's mainly in such a light, I confess, at any
rate, that the ugly fruit of my exile is at this hour present to me.
Even at first indeed the spirit in which my avidity, as I have called
it, made me regard that term owed no element of ease to the fact
that before coming back from Rapallo George Corvick addressed
me in a way I objected to. His letter had none of the sedative action I must to-day profess myself sure he had wished to give it, and
the march of occurrences was not so ordered as to make up for what
it lacked. He had begun on the spot, for one of the quarterlies, a
great last word on Vereker's writings, and this exhaustive study, the
only one that would have counted, have existed, was to turn on the
new light, to utter—oh so quietly!—the unimagined truth. It was
in other words to trace the figure in the carpet through every con-
volution, to reproduce it in every tint. The result, according to my
friend, would be the greatest literary portrait ever painted, and
what he asked of me was just to be so good as not to trouble him
with questions till he should hang up his masterpiece before me.
He did me the honour to declare that, putting aside the great sitter
himself, all aloft in his indifference, I was individually the connoisseur he was most working for. I was therefore to be a good boy
and not try to peep under the curtain before the show was ready:
I should enjoy it all the more if I sat very still.

I did my best to sit very still, but I couldn't help giving a jump on
seeing in *The Times*, after I had been a week or two in Munich and
before, as I knew, Corvick had reached London, the announcement
of the sudden death of poor Mrs. Erme. I instantly, by letter, ap-

pealed to Gwendolen for particulars, and she wrote me that her mother had yielded to long-threatened failure of the heart. She didn't say, but I took the liberty of reading into her words, that from the point of view of her marriage and also of her eagerness, which was quite a match for mine, this was a solution more prompt than could have been expected and more radical than waiting for the old lady to swallow the dose. I candidly admit indeed that at the time—for I heard from her repeatedly—I read some singular things into Gwendolen's words and some still more extraordinary ones into her silences. Pen in hand, this way, I live the time over, and it brings back the oddest sense of my having been, both for months and in spite of myself, a kind of coerced spectator. All my life had taken refuge in my eyes, which the procession of events appeared to have committed itself to keep astare. There were days when I thought of writing to Hugh Vereker and simply throwing myself on his charity. But I felt more deeply that I hadn't fallen quite so low—besides which, quite properly, he would send me about my business. Mrs. Erme's death brought Corvick straight home, and within the month he was united "very quietly"—as quietly, I seemed to make out, as he meant in his article to bring out his *trouvaille*—to the young lady he had loved and quitted. I use this last term, I may parenthetically say, because I subsequently grew sure that at the time he went to India, at the time of his great news from Bombay, there had been no positive pledge between them whatever. There had been none at the moment she was affirming to me the very opposite. On the other hand he had certainly become engaged the day he returned. The happy pair went down to Torquay for their honeymoon, and there, in a reckless hour, it occurred to poor Corvick to take his young bride a drive. He had no command of that business: this had been brought home to me of old in a little tour we had once made together in a dogcart. In a dogcart he perched his companion for a rattle over Devonshire hills, on one of the likeliest of which he brought his horse, who, it was true, had bolted, down with such violence that the occupants of the cart were hurled forward and that he fell horribly on his head. He was killed on the spot; Gwendolen escaped unhurt.

I pass rapidly over the question of this unmitigated tragedy, of what the loss of my best friend meant for me, and I complete my little history of my patience and my pain by the frank statement of my having, in a postscript to my very first letter to her after the receipt of the hideous news, asked Mrs. Corvick whether her husband mightn't at least have finished the great article on Vereker. Her answer was as prompt as my question: the article, which had been barely begun, was a mere heartbreaking scrap. She explained that our friend, abroad, had just settled down to it when interrupted

by her mother's death, and that then, on his return, he had been
kept from work by the engrossments into which that calamity was
to plunge them. The opening pages were all that existed; they were
striking, they were promising, but they didn't unveil the idol. That
great intellectual feat was obviously to have formed his climax. She
said nothing more, nothing to enlighten me as to the state of her
own knowledge—the knowledge for the acquisition of which I had
fancied her prodigiously acting. This was above all what I wanted
to know: had *she* seen the idol unveiled? Had there been a private
ceremony for a palpitating audience of one? For what else but that
ceremony had the nuptials taken place? I didn't like as yet to press
her, though when I thought of what had passed between us on the
subject in Corvick's absence her reticence surprised me. It was therefore not till much later, from Meran, that I risked another appeal,
risked it in some trepidation, for she continued to tell me nothing.
"Did you hear in those few days of your blighted bliss," I wrote,
"what we desired so to hear?" I said "we" as a little hint; and she
showed me she could take a little hint. "I heard everything," she
replied, "and I mean to keep it to myself!"

IX

It was impossible not to be moved with the strongest sympathy
for her, and on my return to England I showed her every kindness
in my power. Her mother's death had made her means sufficient,
and she had gone to live in a more convenient quarter. But her loss
had been great and her visitation cruel; it never would have occurred to me, moreover, to suppose she could come to feel the possession of a technical tip, of a piece of literary experience, a counterpoise to her grief. Strange to say, none the less, I couldn't help believing after I had seen her a few times that I caught a glimpse of
some such oddity. I hasten to add that there had been other things
I couldn't help believing, or at least imagining; and as I never felt
I was really clear about these, so, as to the point I here touch on,
I give her memory the benefit of the doubt. Stricken and solitary,
highly accomplished and now, in her deep mourning, her maturer
grace and her uncomplaining sorrow, incontestably handsome, she
presented herself as leading a life of singular dignity and beauty. I
had at first found a way to persuade myself that I should soon get
the better of the reserve formulated, the week after the catastrophe,
in her reply to an appeal as to which I was not unconscious that it
might strike her as mistimed. Certainly that reserve was something
of a shock to me—certainly it puzzled me the more I thought of it
and even though I tried to explain it (with moments of success)
by an imputation of exalted sentiments, of superstitious scruples,
of a refinement of loyalty. Certainly it added at the same time
hugely to the price of Vereker's secret, precious as this mystery al-

ready appeared. I may as well confess abjectly that Mrs. Corvick's unexpected attitude was the final tap on the nail that was to fix fast my luckless idea, convert it into the obsession of which I'm for ever conscious.

But this only helped me the more to be artful, to be adroit, to allow time to elapse before renewing my suit. There were plenty of speculations for the interval, and one of them was deeply absorbing. Corvick had kept his information from his young friend till after the removal of the last barrier to their intimacy—then only had he let the cat out of the bag. Was it Gwendolen's idea, taking a hint from him, to liberate this animal only on the basis of the renewal of such a relation? Was the figure in the carpet traceable or describable only for husbands and wives—for lovers supremely united? It came back to me in a mystifying manner that in Kensington Square, when I mentioned that Corvick would have told the girl he loved, some word had dropped from Vereker that gave colour to this possibility. There might be little in it, but there was enough to make me wonder if I should have to marry Mrs. Corvick to get what I wanted. Was I prepared to offer her this price for the blessing of her knowledge? Ah that way madness lay!—so I at least said to myself in bewildered hours. I could see meanwhile the torch she refused to pass on flame away in her chamber of memory—pour through her eyes a light that shone in her lonely house. At the end of six months I was fully sure of what this warm presence made up to her for. We had talked again and again of the man who had brought us together —of his talent, his character, his personal charm, his certain career, his dreadful doom, and even of his clear purpose in that great study which was to have been a supreme literary portrait, a kind of critical Vandyke or Velasquez. She had conveyed to me in abundance that she was tongue-tied by her perversity, by her piety, that she would never break the silence it had not been given to the "right person," as she said, to break. The hour, however, finally arrived. One evening when I had been sitting with her longer than usual I laid my hand firmly on her arm. "Now at last what *is* it?"

She had been expecting me and was ready. She gave a long slow soundless headshake, merciful only in being inarticulate. This mercy didn't prevent its hurling at me the largest finest coldest "Never!" I had yet, in the course of a life that had known denials, had to take full in the face. I took it and was aware that with the hard blow the tears had come into my eyes. So for a while we sat and looked at each other; after which I slowly rose. I was wondering if some day she would accept me; but this was not what I brought out. I said as I smoothed down my hat: "I know what to think then. It's nothing!"

A remote disdainful pity for me gathered in her dim smile; then she spoke in a voice that I hear at this hour. "It's my *life!*" As I stood at the door she added: "You've insulted him!"

"Do you mean Vereker?"

"I mean the Dead!"

I recognised when I reached the street the justice of her charge. Yes, it was her life—I recognised that too; but her life none the less made room with the lapse of time for another interest. A year and a half after Corvick's death she published in a single volume her second novel, "Overmastered," which I pounced on in the hope of finding in it some tell-tale echo or some peeping face. All I found was a much better book than her younger performance, showing I thought the better company she had kept. As a tissue tolerably intricate it was a carpet with a figure of its own; but the figure was not the figure I was looking for. On sending a review of it to *The Middle* I was surprised to learn from the office that a notice was already in type. When the paper came out I had no hesitation in attributing this article, which I thought rather vulgarly overdone, to Drayton Deane, who in the old days had been something of a friend of Corvick's, yet had only within a few weeks made the acquaintance of his widow. I had had an early copy of the book, but Deane had evidently had an earlier. He lacked all the same the light hand with which Corvick had gilded the gingerbread—he laid on the tinsel in splotches.

X

Six months later appeared "The Right of Way," the last chance, though we didn't know it, that we were to have to redeem ourselves. Written wholly during Vereker's sojourn abroad, the book had been heralded, in a hundred paragraphs, by the usual ineptitudes. I carried it, as early a copy as any, I this time flattered myself, straightway to Mrs. Corvick. This was the only use I had for it; I left the inevitable tribute of *The Middle* to some more ingenious mind and some less irritated temper. "But I already have it," Gwendolen said. "Drayton Deane was so good as to bring it to me yesterday, and I've just finished it."

"Yesterday? How did he get it so soon?"

"He gets everything so soon! He's to review it in *The Middle*."

"He—Drayton Deane—review Vereker?" I couldn't believe my ears.

"Why not? One fine ignorance is as good as another."

I winced but I presently said: "You ought to review him yourself!"

"I don't 'review,' " she laughed. "I'm reviewed!"

Just then the door was thrown open. "Ah yes, here's your reviewer!" Drayton Deane was there with his long legs and his tall!

forehead: he had come to see what she thought of "The Right of Way," and to bring news that was singularly relevant. The evening papers were just out with a telegram on the author of that work, who, in Rome, had been ill for some days with an attack of malarial fever. It had at first not been thought grave, but had taken, in consequence of complications, a turn that might give rise to anxiety. Anxiety had indeed at the latest hour begun to be felt.

I was struck in the presence of these tidings with the fundamental detachment that Mrs. Corvick's overt concern quite failed to hide: it gave me the measure of her consummate independence. That independence rested on her knowledge, the knowledge which nothing now could destroy and which nothing could make different. The figure in the carpet might take on another twist or two, but the sentence had virtually been written. The writer might go down to his grave: she was the person in the world to whom—as if she had been his favoured heir—his continued existence was least of a need. This reminded me how I had observed at a particular moment—after Corvick's death—the drop of her desire to see him face to face. She had got what she wanted without that. I had been sure that if she hadn't got it she wouldn't have been restrained from the endeavour to sound him personally by those superior reflexions, more conceivable on a man's part than on a woman's, which in my case had served as a deterrent. It wasn't however, I hasten to add, that my case, in spite of this invidious comparison, wasn't ambiguous enough. At the thought that Vereker was perhaps at that moment dying there rolled over me a wave of anguish—a poignant sense of how inconsistently I still depended on him. A delicacy that it was my one compensation to suffer to rule me had left the Alps and the Apennines between us, but the sense of the waning occasion suggested that I might in my despair at last have gone to him. Of course I should really have done nothing of the sort. I remained five minutes, while my companions talked of the new book, and when Drayton Deane appealed to me for my opinion of it I made answer, getting up, that I detested Hugh Vereker and simply couldn't read him. I departed with the moral certainty that as the door closed behind me Deane would brand me for awfully superficial. His hostess wouldn't contradict *that* at least.

I continue to trace with a briefer touch our intensely odd successions. Three weeks after this came Vereker's death, and before the year was out the death of his wife. That poor lady I had never seen, but I had had a futile theory that, should she survive him long enough to be decorously accessible, I might approach her with the feeble flicker of my plea. Did she know and if she knew would she speak? It was much to be presumed that for more reasons than one

she would have nothing to say; but when she passed out of all reach
I felt renouncement indeed my appointed lot. I was shut up in my
obsession for ever—my gaolers had gone off with the key. I find
myself quite as vague as a captive in a dungeon about the time that
further elapsed before Mrs. Corvick became the wife of Drayton
Deane. I had foreseen, through my bars, this end of the business,
though there was no indecent haste and our friendship had rather
fallen off. They were both so "awfully intellectual" that it struck
people as a suitable match, but I had measured better than any one
the wealth of understanding the bride would contribute to the union. Never, for a marriage in literary circles—so the newspapers described the alliance—had a lady been so bravely dowered. I began
with due promptness to look for the fruit of the affair—that fruit,
I mean, of which the premonitory symptoms would be peculiarly
visible in the husband. Taking for granted the splendour of the
other party's nuptial gift, I expected to see him make a show commensurate with his increase of means. I knew what his means had
been—his article on "The Right of Way" had distinctly given one
the figure. As he was now exactly in the position in which still more
exactly I was not I watched from month to month, in the likely
periodicals, for the heavy message poor Corvick had been unable to
deliver and the responsibility of which would have fallen on his
successor. The widow and wife would have broken by the rekindled
hearth the silence that only a widow and wife might break, and
Deane would be as aflame with the knowledge as Corvick in his own
hour, as Gwendolen in hers, had been. Well, he was aflame doubtless, but the fire was apparently not to become a public blaze. I
scanned the periodicals in vain: Drayton Deane filled them with
exuberant pages, but he withheld the page I most feverishly sought.
He wrote on a thousand subjects, but never on the subject of
Vereker. His special line was to tell truths that other people either
"funked," as he said, or overlooked, but he never told the only truth
that seemed to me in these days to signify. I met the couple in those
literary circles referred to in the papers: I have sufficiently intimated
that it was only in such circles we were all constructed to revolve.
Gwendolen was more than ever committed to them by the publication of her third novel, and I myself definitely classed by holding
the opinion that this work was inferior to its immediate predecessor.
Was it worse because she had been keeping worse company? If her
secret was, as she had told me, her life—a fact discernible in her
increasing bloom, an air of conscious privilege that, cleverly corrected by pretty charities, gave distinction to her appearance—it
had yet not a direct influence on her work. That only made one—
everything only made one—yearn the more for it; only rounded it
off with a mystery finer and subtler.

XI

It was therefore from her husband I could never remove my eyes: I beset him in a manner that might have made him uneasy. I went even so far as to engage him in conversation. *Didn't* he know, hadn't he come into it as a matter of course?—that question hummed in my brain. Of course he knew; otherwise he wouldn't return my stare so queerly. His wife had told him what I wanted and he was amiably amused at my impotence. He didn't laugh—he wasn't a laugher: his system was to present to my irritation, so that I could crudely expose myself, a conversational blank as vast as his big bare brow. It always happened that I turned away with a settled conviction from these unpeopled expanses, which seemed to complete each other geographically and to symbolise together Drayton Deane's want of voice, want of form. He simply hadn't the art to use what he knew; he literally was incompetent to take up the duty where Corvick had left it. I went still further—it was the only glimpse of happiness I had. I made up my mind that the duty didn't appeal to him. He wasn't interested, he didn't care. Yes, it quite comforted me to believe him too stupid to have joy of the thing I lacked. He was as stupid after as he had been before, and that deepened for me the golden glory in which the mystery was wrapped. I had of course none the less to recollect that his wife might have imposed her conditions and exactions. I had above all to remind myself that with Vereker's death the major incentive dropped. He was still there to be honoured by what might be done—he was no longer there to give it his sanction. Who alas but he had the authority?

Two children were born to the pair, but the second cost the mother her life. After this stroke I seemed to see another ghost of a chance. I jumped at it in thought, but I waited a certain time for manners, and at last my opportunity arrived in a remunerative way. His wife had been dead a year when I met Drayton Deane in the smoking-room of a small club of which we both were members, but where for months—perhaps because I rarely entered it—I hadn't seen him. The room was empty and the occasion propitious. I deliberately offered him, to have done with the matter for ever, that advantage for which I felt he had long been looking.

"As an older acquaintance of your late wife's than even you were," I began, "you must let me say to you something I have on my mind. I shall be glad to make any terms with you that you see fit to name for the information she must have had from George Corvick—the information, you know, that had come to *him*, poor chap, in one of the happiest hours of his life, straight from Hugh Vereker."

He looked at me like a dim phrenological bust. "The information—?"

"Vereker's secret, my dear man—the general intention of his books: the string the pearls were strung on, the buried treasure, the figure in the carpet."

He began to flush—the numbers on his bumps to come out. "Vereker's books had a general intention?"

I stared in my turn. "You don't mean to say you don't know it?" I thought for a moment he was playing with me. "Mrs. Deane knew it; she had it, as I say, straight from Corvick, who had, after infinite search and to Vereker's own delight, found the very mouth of the cave. Where *is* the mouth? He told after their marriage—and told alone—the person who, when the circumstances were reproduced, must have told *you*. Have I been wrong in taking for granted that she admitted you, as one of the highest privileges of the relation in which you stood to her, to the knowledge of which she was after Corvick's death the sole depository? All *I* know is that that knowledge is infinitely precious, and what I want you to understand is that if you'll in your turn admit me to it you'll do me a kindness for which I shall be lastingly grateful."

He had turned at last very red; I dare say he had begun by thinking I had lost my wits. Little by little he followed me; on my own side I stared with a livelier surprise. Then he spoke. "I don't know what you're talking about."

He wasn't acting—it was the absurd truth. "She *didn't* tell you—?"

"Nothing about Hugh Vereker."

I was stupefied; the room went round. It had been too good even for that! "Upon your honour?"

"Upon my honour. What the devil's the matter with you?" he growled.

"I'm astounded—I'm disappointed. I wanted to get it out of you."

"It isn't *in* me!" he awkwardly laughed. "And even if it were—"

"If it were you'd let me have it—oh yes, in common humanity. But I believe you. I see—I see!" I went on, conscious, with the full turn of the wheel, of my great delusion, my false view of the poor man's attitude. What I saw, though I couldn't say it, was that his wife hadn't thought him worth enlightening. This struck me as strange for a woman who had thought him worth marrying. At last I explained it by the reflexion that she couldn't possibly have married him for his understanding. She had married him for something else.

He was to some extent enlightened now, but he was even more astonished, more disconcerted: he took a moment to compare my story with his quickened memories. The result of his meditation was his presently saying with a good deal of rather feeble form: "This is the first I hear of what you allude to. I think you must be mistaken as to Mrs. Drayton Deane's having had any unmentioned, and still less any unmentionable, knowledge of Hugh Vereker. She'd certainly have wished it—should it have borne on his literary character —to be used."

"It *was* used. She used it herself. She told me with her own lips that she 'lived' on it."

I had no sooner spoken than I repented of my words; he grew so pale that I felt as if I had struck him. "Ah 'lived'—!" he murmured, turning short away from me.

My compunction was real; I laid my hand on his shoulder. "I beg you to forgive me—I've made a mistake. You *don't* know what I thought you knew. You could, if I had been right, have rendered me a service; and I had my reasons for assuming that you'd be in a position to meet me."

"Your reasons?" he echoed. "What were your reasons?"

I looked at him well; I hesitated; I considered. "Come and sit down with me here and I'll tell you." I drew him to a sofa, I lighted another cigar and, beginning with the anecdote of Vereker's one descent from the clouds, I recited to him the extraordinary chain of accidents that had, in spite of the original gleam, kept me till that hour in the dark. I told him in a word just what I've written out here. He listened with deepening attention, and I became aware, to my surprise, by his ejaculations, by his questions, that he would have been after all not unworthy to be trusted by his wife. So abrupt an experience of her want of trust had now a disturbing effect on him; but I saw the immediate shock throb away little by little and then gather again into waves of wonder and curiosity—waves that promised, I could perfectly judge, to break in the end with the fury of my own highest tides. I may say that to-day as victims of unappeased desire there isn't a pin to choose between us. The poor man's state is almost my consolation; there are really moments when I feel it to be quite my revenge.

1896

Maud-Evelyn[5]

On some allusion to a lady who, though unknown to myself, was known to two or three of the company, it was asked by one of these

5. This bizarre tale first appeared in the *Atlantic Monthly* in April, 1900. It was reprinted the same year in James's volume, *The Soft Side*. He omitted it from the New York Edition of his writings, but it was included by Percy Lubbock in the 35-volume edition published in 1921–23. It has been regarded by recent critics as one of James's best stories of the supernatural, combined with a psychological motivation. In his *Notebooks* James recorded the first hint of the story in 1895. Paul Bourget told him a tale, attributed to the Italian writer, Luigi Gualdo, of a childless couple who asked

if we had heard the odd circumstance of what she had just "come in for"—the piece of luck suddenly overtaking, in the gray afternoon of her career, so obscure and lonely a personage. We were at first, in our ignorance, mainly reduced to crude envy; but old Lady Emma, who for a while had said nothing, scarcely even appearing to listen and letting the chatter, which was indeed plainly beside the mark, subside of itself, came back from a mental absence to observe that if what had happened to Lavinia was wonderful, certainly, what had for years gone before it, led up to it, had likewise not been without some singular features. From this we perceived that Lady Emma had a story—a story moreover out of the ken even of those of her listeners acquainted with the quiet person who was the subject of it. Almost the oddest thing—as came out afterwards—was that such a situation should, for the world, have remained so in the background of this person's life. By "afterwards" I mean simply before we separated; for what came out came on the spot, under encouragement and pressure, our common, eager solicitation. Lady Emma, who always reminded me of a fine old instrument that has first to be tuned, agreed, after a few of our scrapings and fingerings, that, having said so much, she couldn't without wantonly tormenting us, forbear to say all. She had known Lavinia, whom she mentioned throughout only by that name, from far away, and she had also known ———— But what she had known I must give as nearly as possible as she herself gave it. She talked to us from her corner of the sofa, and the flicker of the firelight in her face was like the glow of memory, the play of fancy, from within.

I

"Then why on earth don't you take him?" I asked. I think that was the way that, one day when she was about twenty—before some of you perhaps were born—the affair, for me, must have begun. I put the question because I knew she had had a chance, though I didn't know how great a mistake her failure to embrace it was to prove. I took an interest because I liked them both—you see how I like young people still—and because, as they had originally met at my house, I had in a manner to answer to each for the other. I'm afraid I'm thrown baldly back on the fact that if the girl was

a painter to do a portrait for them of the child they *might* have had. Three years later James returned to this subject and made the following notes: "Imagine old couple, liking young man: 'You must have married our daughter.' 'Your daughter?' 'The one we lost. You were her fiancé, or her *mari*.' Imagine situation for young man (as regards some living girl) who has more or less accepted it. He succumbs to suggestion. He has sworn fidelity to a memory. He ends by believing it. He lives with the parents. They leave him their money. I see him later. *He is a widower.* He dies, to rejoin his wife. He leaves their fortune to the girl he doesn't marry." This is a nearly complete summary of the story James wrote in 1899. It remained only to add, in the writing, the additional complication of Marmaduke's relationship to Lavinia—in short, to give the theme of disappointed parents adopting a strange delusion a further psychological twist.

the daughter of my earliest, almost my only governess, to whom I had remained much attached and who, after leaving me, had married—for a governess—"well," Marmaduke (it isn't *his* real name!) was the son of one of the clever men who had—I was charming then, I assure you I was—wanted, years before, and this one as a widower, to marry me. I hadn't cared, somehow, for widowers, but even after I had taken somebody else I was conscious of a pleasant link with the boy whose stepmother it had been open to me to become and to whom it was perhaps a little a matter of vanity with me to show that I should have been for him one of the kindest. This was what the woman his father eventually did marry was not, and that threw him upon me the more.

Lavinia was one of nine, and her brothers and sisters, who have never done anything for her, help, actually, in different countries and on something, I believe, of that same scale, to people the globe. There were mixed in her then, in a puzzling way, two qualities that mostly exclude each other—an extreme timidity and, as the smallest fault that could qualify a harmless creature for a world of wickedness, a self-complacency hard in tiny, unexpected spots, for which I used sometimes to take her up, but which, I subsequently saw, would have done something for the flatness of her life had they not evaporated with everything else. She was at any rate one of those persons as to whom you don't know whether they might have been attractive if they had been happy, or might have been happy if they had been attractive. If I was a trifle vexed at her not jumping at Marmaduke, it was probably rather less because I expected wonders of him than because I thought she took her own prospect too much for granted. She had made a mistake and, before long, admitted it; yet I remember that when she expressed to me a conviction that he would ask her again, I also thought this highly probable, for in the meantime I had spoken to him. "She does care for you," I declared; and I can see at this moment, long ago though it be, his handsome, empty young face look, on the words, as if, in spite of itself for a little, it really thought. I didn't press the matter, for he had, after all, no great things to offer; yet my conscience was easier, later on, for having not said less. He had three hundred and fifty a year from his mother, and one of his uncles had promised him something—I don't mean an allowance, but a place, if I recollect, in a business. He assured me that he loved as a man loves—a man of twenty-two! —but once. He said it, at all events, as a man says it but once.

"Well, then," I replied, "your course is clear."

"To speak to her again, you mean?"

"Yes—try it."

He seemed to try it a moment in imagination; after which, a little to my surprise, he asked: "Would it be very awful if she should speak to *me?*"

I stared. "Do you mean pursue you—overtake you? Ah, if you're running away——"

"I'm not running away!"—he was positive as to that. "But when a fellow has gone so far——"

"He can't go any further? Perhaps," I replied dryly. "But in that case he shouldn't talk of 'caring.' "

"Oh, but I do, I do."

I shook my head. "Not if you're too proud!" On which I turned away, looking round at him again, however, after he had surprised me by a silence that seemed to accept my judgment. Then I saw he had not accepted it; I perceived it indeed to be essentially absurd. He expressed more, on this, than I had yet seen him do—had the queerest, frankest, and, for a young man of his conditions, saddest smile.

"I'm *not* proud. It isn't *in* me. If you're not, you're not, you know. I don't think I'm proud enough."

It came over me that this was, after all, probable; yet somehow I didn't at the moment like him the less for it, though I spoke with some sharpness. "Then what's the matter with you?"

He took a turn or two about the room, as if what he had just said had made him a little happier. "Well, how can a man say more?" Then, just as I was on the point of assuring him that I didn't know what he had said, he went on: "I swore to her that I would never marry. Oughtn't that to be enough?"

"To make her come after you?"

"No—I suppose scarcely that; but to make her feel sure of me—to make her wait."

"Wait for what?"

"Well, till I come back."

"Back from where?"

"From Switzerland—haven't I told you? I go there next month with my aunt and my cousin."

He was quite right about not being proud—this was an alternative distinctly humble.

II

And yet see what it brought forth—the beginning of which was something that, early in the autumn, I learned from poor Lavinia. He had written to her, they were still such friends; and thus it was that she knew his aunt and his cousin to have come back without him. He had stayed on—stayed much longer and traveled much further: he had been to the Italian lakes and to Venice; he was now in Paris. At this I vaguely wondered, knowing that he was always short of funds and that he must, by his uncle's beneficence, have started on the journey on a basis of expense paid. "Then whom has he picked up?" I asked; but feeling sorry, as soon as I had spoken, to have made Lavinia blush. It was almost as if he had picked up some improper lady, though in this case he wouldn't have told her, and it wouldn't have saved him money.

"Oh, he makes acquaintance so quickly, knows people in two minutes," the girl said. "And everyone always wants to be nice to him."

This was perfectly true, and I saw what she saw in it. "Ah, my dear, he will have an immense circle ready for you!"

"Well," she replied, "if they do run after us I'm not likely to suppose it will ever be for me. It will be for *him*, and they may do to me what they like. My pleasure will be—but you'll see." I already saw—saw at least what she supposed she herself saw: her drawing room crowded with female fashion and her attitude angelic. "Do you know what he said to me again before he went?" she continued.

I wondered; he *had* then spoken to her. "That he will never, never marry——"

"Anyone but *me!*" She ingenuously took me up. "Then you knew?"

It might be. "I guessed."

"And don't you believe it?"

Again I hesitated. "Yes." Yet all this didn't tell me why she had changed color. "Is it a secret—whom he's with?"

"Oh, no, they seem so nice. I was only struck with the way you know him—your seeing immediately that it must be a new friendship that has kept him over. It's the devotion of the Dedricks," Lavinia said. "He's traveling with them."

Once more I wondered. "Do you mean they're taking him about?"

"Yes—they've invited him."

No, indeed, I reflected—he wasn't proud. But what I said was: "Who in the world are the Dedricks?"

"Kind, good people whom, last month, he accidentally met. He was walking some Swiss pass—a long, rather stupid one, I believe, without his aunt and his cousin, who had gone round some other way and were to meet him somewhere. It came on to rain in torrents, and while he was huddling under a shelter he was overtaken by some people in a carriage, who kindly made him get in. They drove him, I gather, for several hours; it began an intimacy, and they've continued to be charming to him."

I thought a moment. "Are they ladies?"

Her own imagination meanwhile had also strayed a little. "I think about forty."

"Forty ladies?"

She quickly came back. "Oh, no; I mean Mrs. Dedrick is."

"About forty? Then Miss Dedrick——"

"There isn't any Miss Dedrick."

"No daughter?"

"Not with them, at any rate. No one but the husband."

I thought again. "And how old is *he?*"

Lavinia followed my example. "Well, about forty, too."

"About forty-two?" We laughed, but "That's all right!" I said; and so, for the time, it seemed.

He continued absent, none the less, and I saw Lavinia repeatedly, and we always talked of him, though this represented a greater concern with his affairs than I had really supposed myself committed to. I had never sought the acquaintance of his father's people, nor seen either his aunt or his cousin, so that the account given by these relatives of the circumstances of their separation reached me at last only through the girl, to whom, also—for she knew them as little—it had circuitously come. They considered, it appeared, the poor ladies he had started with, that he had treated them ill and thrown them over, sacrificing them selfishly to company picked up on the road—a reproach deeply resented by Lavinia, though about the company too I could see she was not much more at her ease. "How can he help it if he's so taking?" she asked; and to be properly indignant in one quarter she had to pretend to be delighted in the other. Marmaduke *was* "taking"; yet it also came out between us at last that the Dedricks must certainly be extraordinary. We had scant added evidence, for his letters stopped, and that naturally was one of our signs. I had meanwhile leisure to reflect—it was a sort of study of the human scene I always liked—on what to be taking consisted of. The upshot of my meditations, which experience has only confirmed, was that it consisted simply of itself. It was a quality implying no others. Marmaduke *had* no others. What indeed was his need of any?

III

He at last, however, turned up; but then it happened that if, on his coming to see me, his immediate picture of his charming new friends quickened even more than I had expected my sense of the variety of the human species, my curiosity about them failed to make me respond when he suggested I should go to see them. It's a difficult thing to explain, and I don't pretend to put it successfully, but doesn't it often happen that one may think well enough of a person without being inflamed with the desire to meet—on the ground of any such sentiment—other persons who think still better? Somehow—little harm as there was in Marmaduke—it was but half a recommendation of the Dedricks that they were crazy about him. I didn't say this—I was careful to say little; which didn't prevent his presently asking if he mightn't then bring them to *me*. "If not, why not?" he laughed. He laughed about everything.

"Why not? Because it strikes me that your surrender doesn't require any backing. Since you've done it you must take care of yourself."

"Oh, but they're as safe," he returned, "as the Bank of England. They're wonderful—for respectability and goodness."

"Those are precisely qualities to which my poor intercourse can contribute nothing." He hadn't, I observed, gone so far as to tell me they would be "fun," and he *had*, on the other hand, promptly mentioned that they lived in Westbourne Terrace. They were not forty—they were forty-five; but Mr. Dedrick had already, on considerable gains, retired from some primitive profession. They were the simplest, kindest, yet most original and unusual people, and nothing could exceed, frankly, the fancy they had taken to him. Marmaduke spoke of it with a placidity of resignation that was almost irritating. I suppose I should have despised him if, after benefits accepted, he had said they bored him; yet their not boring him vexed me even more than it puzzled. "Whom do they know?"

"No one but me. There are people in London like that."

"Who know no one but you?"

"No—I mean no one at all. There are extraordinary people in London, and awfully nice. You haven't an idea. You people don't know everyone. They lead their lives—they go their way. One finds —what do you call it?—refinement, books, cleverness, don't you know, and music, and pictures, and religion, and an excellent table —all sorts of pleasant things. You only come across them by chance; but it's all perpetually going on."

I assented to this: the world was very wonderful, and one must certainly see what one could. In my own quarter too I found wonders enough. "But are you," I asked, "as fond of them—"

"As they are of *me*?" He took me up promptly, and his eyes were quite unclouded. "I'm quite sure I shall become so."

"Then are you taking Lavinia——?"

"Not to see them—no." I saw, myself, the next minute, of course, that I had made a mistake. "On what footing *can* I?"

I bethought myself. "I keep forgetting you're not engaged."

"Well," he said after a moment, "I shall never marry another."

It somehow, repeated again, gave on my nerves. "Ah, but what good will that do her, or me either, if you don't marry *her*?"

He made no answer to this—only turned away to look at something in the room; after which, when he next faced me, he had a heightened color. "She ought to have taken me that day," he said gravely and gently; fixing me also as if he wished to say more.

I remember that his very mildness irritated me; some show of resentment would have been a promise that the case might still be righted. But I dropped it, the silly case, without letting him say more, and, coming back to Mr. and Mrs. Dedrick, asked him how in the world, without either occupation or society, they passed so much of their time. My question appeared for a moment to leave him at a loss, but he presently found light; which, at the same time, I saw on my side, really suited him better than further talk about Lavinia. "Oh, they live for Maud-Evelyn."

"And who's Maud-Evelyn?"

"Why, their daughter."

"Their daughter?" I had supposed them childless.

He partly explained. "Unfortunately they've lost her."

"Lost her?" I required more.

He hesitated again. "I mean that a great many people would take it that way. But *they* don't—they won't."

I speculated. "Do you mean other people would have given her up?"

"Yes—perhaps even tried to forget her. But the Dedricks can't."

I wondered what she had done: had it been anything very bad? However, it was none of my business, and I only said: "They communicate with her?"

"Oh, all the while."

"Then why isn't she with them?"

Marmaduke thought. "She *is*—now."

" 'Now?' Since when?"

"Well, this last year."

"Then why do you say they've lost her?"

"Ah," he said, smiling sadly, "*I* should call it that. I, at any rate," he went on, "don't see her."

Still more I wondered. "They keep her apart?"

He thought again. "No, it's not that. As I say, they live for her."

"But they don't want *you* to—is that it?"

At this he looked at me for the first time, as I thought, a little strangely. "How *can* I?"

He put it to me as if it were bad of him, somehow, that he shouldn't; but I made, to the best of my ability, a quick end of that. "You can't. Why in the world *should* you? Live for *my* girl. Live for Lavinia."

IV

I had unfortunately run the risk of boring him again with that idea, and, though he had not repudiated it at the time, I felt in my having returned to it the reason why he never reappeared for weeks. I saw "my girl," as I had called her, in the interval, but we avoided with much intensity the subject of Marmaduke. It was just this that gave me my perspective for finding her constantly full of him. It determined me, in all the circumstances, not to rectify her mistake about the childlessness of the Dedricks. But whatever I left unsaid, her naming the young man was only a question of time, for at the end of a month she told me he had been twice to her mother's and that she had seen him on each of these occasions.

"Well then?"

"Well then, he's very happy."

"And still taken up——"

"As much as ever, yes, with those people. He didn't tell me so, but I could see it."

I could, too, and her own view of it. "What, in that case, did he tell you?"

"Nothing—but I think there's something he wants to. Only not what *you* think," she added.

I wondered then if it were what I had had from him the last time. "Well, what prevents him?" I asked.

"From bringing it out? I don't know."

It was in the tone of this that she struck, to my ear, the first note of an acceptance so deep and a patience so strange that they gave me, at the end, even more food for wonderment than the rest of the business. "If he can't speak, why does he come?"

She almost smiled. "Well, I think I *shall* know."

I looked at her; I remember that I kissed her. "You're admirable; but it's very ugly."

"Ah," she replied, "he only wants to be kind!"

"To *them*? Then he should let others alone. But what I call ugly is his being content to be so 'beholden'——"

"To Mr. and Mrs. Dedrick?" She considered as if there might be many sides to it. "But mayn't he do them some good?"

The idea failed to appeal to me. "What good can Marmaduke do? There's one thing," I went on, "in case he should want you to know them. Will you promise me to refuse?"

She only looked helpless and blank. "Making their acquaintance?"

"Seeing them, going near them—ever, ever."

Again she brooded. "Do you mean *you* won't?"

"Never, never."

"Well, then, I don't think I want to."

"Ah, but that's not a promise." I kept her up to it. "I want your word."

She demurred a little. "But why?"

"So that at least he shan't make use of you," I said with energy.

My energy overbore her, though I saw how she would really have given herself. "I promise, but it's only because it's something I know he will never ask."

I differed from her at the time, believing the proposal in question

to have been exactly the subject she had supposed him to be wishing to broach; but on our very next meeting I heard from her of
quite another matter, upon which, as soon as she came in, I saw
her to be much excited.

"You know then about the daughter without having told me? He
called again yesterday," she explained as she met my stare at her
unconnected plunge, "and now I know that he *has* wanted to speak
to me. He at last brought it out."

I continued to stare. "Brought what?"

"Why, everything." She looked surprised at my face. "Didn't he
tell you about Maud-Evelyn?"

I perfectly recollected, but I momentarily wondered. "He spoke
of there being a daughter, but only to say that there's something
the matter with her. What is it?"

The girl echoed my words. "What 'is' it?—you dear, strange
thing! The matter with her is simply that she's dead."

"Dead?" I was naturally mystified. "When, then, did she die?"

"Why, years and years ago—fifteen, I believe. As a little girl.
Didn't you understand it so?"

"How *should* I?—when he spoke of her as 'with' them and said
that they lived for her!"

"Well," my young friend explained, "that's just what he meant
—they live for her memory. She *is* with them in the sense that they
think of nothing else."

I found matter for surprise in this correction, but also, at first,
matter for relief. At the same time it left, as I turned it over, a fresh
ambiguity. "If they think of nothing else, how can they think so
much of Marmaduke?"

The difficulty struck her, though she gave me even then a dim
impression of being already, as it were, rather on Marmaduke's side,
or, at any rate—almost as against herself—in sympathy with the
Dedricks. But her answer was prompt: "Why, that's just their reason—that they can talk to him so much about her."

"I see." Yet still I wondered. "But what's *his interest*——?"

"In being drawn into it?" Again Lavinia met her difficulty. "Well,
that she was so interesting! It appears she was lovely."

I doubtless fairly gaped. "A little girl in a pinafore?"

"She was out of pinafores; she was, I believe, when she died, about
fourteen. Unless it was sixteen! She was at all events wonderful for
beauty."

"That's the rule. But what good does it do him if he has never
seen her?"

She thought a moment, but this time she had no answer. "Well,
you must ask him!"

I determined without delay to do so; but I had before me meanwhile other contradictions. "Hadn't I better ask him on the same occasion what he means by their 'communicating'?"

Oh, this was simple. "They go in for 'mediums,' don't you know, and raps, and sittings. They began a year or two ago."

"Ah, the idiots!" I remember, at this, narrow-mindedly exclaiming. "Do they want to drag *him* in——?"

"Not in the least; they don't desire it, and he has nothing to do with it."

"Then where does his fun come in?"

Lavinia turned away; again she seemed at a loss. At last she brought out: "Make him show you her little photograph."

But I remained unenlightened. "Is her little photograph his fun?"

Once more she colored for him. "Well, it represents a young loveliness!"

"That he goes about showing?"

She hesitated. "I think he has only shown it to *me*."

"Ah, you're just the last one!" I permitted myself to observe.

"Why so, if I'm also struck?"

There was something about her that began to escape me, and I must have looked at her hard. "It's very good of you to be struck!"

"I don't only mean by the beauty of the face," she went on; "I mean by the whole thing—by that also of the attitude of the parents, their extraordinary fidelity and the way that, as she says, they have made of her memory a real religion. That was what, above all, he came to tell me about."

I turned away from her now, and she soon afterwards left me; but I couldn't help its dropping from me before we parted that I had never supposed him to be *that* sort of fool.

V

If I were really the perfect cynic you probably think me, I should frankly say that the main interest of the rest of this matter lay for me in fixing the sort of fool I *did* suppose him. But I'm afraid, after all, that my anecdote amounts mainly to a presentation of my own folly. I shouldn't be so in possession of the whole spectacle had I not ended by accepting it, and I shouldn't have accepted it had it not, for my imagination, been saved somehow from grotesqueness. Let me say at once, however, that grotesqueness, and even indeed something worse, did at first appear to me strongly to season it. After that talk with Lavinia I immediately addressed to our friend a request that he would come to see me; when I took the liberty of challenging him outright on everything she had told me. There was one point in particular that I desired to clear up and that seemed to me much more important than the color of Maud-Evelyn's hair or the length of her pinafores: the question, I of course mean, of my young man's good faith. Was he altogether silly or was he only altogether mercenary? I felt my choice restricted for the moment to these alternatives.

After he had said to me "It's as ridiculous as you please, but they've simply adopted me," I had it out with him, on the spot, on the issue of common honesty, the question of what he was conscious, so that his self-respect should be saved, of being able to give such benefactors in return for such bounty. I'm obliged to say that to a person so inclined at the start to quarrel with him his amiability could yet prove persuasive. His contention was that the equivalent he represented was something for his friends alone to measure. He didn't for a moment pretend to sound deeper than the fancy they had taken to him. He had not, from the first, made up to them in any way: it was all their own doing, their own insistence, their own eccentricity, no doubt, and even, if I liked, their own insanity. Wasn't it enough that he was ready to declare to me, looking me straight in the eye, that he was "really and truly" fond of them and that they didn't bore him a mite? I had evidently—didn't I see?—an ideal for him that he wasn't at all, if I didn't mind, the fellow to live up to. It was he himself who put it so, and it drew from me the pronouncement that there *was* something irresistible in the refinement of his impudence. "I don't go near Mrs. Jex," he said—Mrs. Jex was their favorite medium: "I do find *her* ugly and vulgar and tiresome, and I hate that part of the business. Besides," he added in words that I afterwards remembered, "I don't require it: I do beautifully without it. But my friends themselves," he pursued, "though they're of a type you've never come within miles of, are not ugly, are not vulgar, are not in any degree whatever any sort of a 'dose.' They're, on the contrary, in their own unconventional way, the very best company. They're endlessly amusing. They're delightfully queer and quaint and kind—they're like people in some old story of some old time. It's at any rate our own affair—mine and theirs—and I beg you to believe that I should make short work of a remonstrance on the subject from anyone but you."

I remember saying to him three months later: "You've never yet told me what they really want of you"; but I'm afraid this was a form of criticism that occurred to me precisely because I had already begun to guess. By that time indeed I had had great initiations, and poor Lavinia had had them as well—hers in fact throughout went further than mine—and we shared them together, and I had settled down to a tolerably exact sense of what I was to see. It was what Lavinia added to it that really made the picture. The portrait of the little dead girl had evoked something attractive, though one had not lived so long in the world without hearing of plenty of little dead girls; and the day came when I felt as if I had actually sat with Marmaduke in each of the rooms converted by her parents

—with the aid not only of the few small, cherished relics, but that of the fondest figments and fictions, ingenious imaginary mementoes and tokens, the unexposed make-believes of the sorrow that broods and the passion that clings—into a temple of grief and worship. The child, incontestably beautiful, had evidently been passionately loved, and in the absence from their lives—I suppose originally a mere accident—of such other elements, either new pleasures or new pains, as abound for most people, their feeling had drawn to itself their whole consciousness: it had become mildly maniacal. The idea was fixed, and it kept others out. The world, for the most part, allows no leisure for such a ritual, but the world had consistently neglected this plain, shy couple, who were sensitive to the wrong things and whose sincerity and fidelity, as well as their tameness and twaddle, were of a rigid, antique pattern.

I must not represent that either of these objects of interest, or my care for their concerns, took up all my leisure; for I had many claims to meet and many complications to handle, a hundred preoccupations and much deeper anxieties. My young woman, on her side, had other contacts and contingencies—other troubles too, poor girl; and there were stretches of time in which I neither saw Marmaduke nor heard a word of the Dedricks. Once, only once, abroad, in Germany at a railway station, I met him in their company. They were colorless, commonplace, elderly Britons, of the kind you identify by the livery of their footman or the labels of their luggage, and the mere sight of them justified me to my conscience in having avoided, from the first, the stiff problem of conversation with them. Marmaduke saw me on the spot and came over to me. There was no doubt whatever of *his* vivid bloom. He had grown fat—or almost, but not with grossness—and might perfectly have passed for the handsome, happy, full-blown son of doting parents who couldn't let him out of view and to whom he was a model of respect and solicitude. They followed him with placid, pleased eyes when he joined me, but asking nothing at all for themselves and quite fitting into his own manner of saying nothing about them. It had its charm, I confess, the way he could be natural and easy, and yet intensely conscious too, on such a basis. What he was conscious of was that there were things I by this time knew; just as, while we stood there and good-humoredly sounded each other's faces—for, having accepted everything at last, I was only a little curious—I knew that he measured my insight. When he returned again to his doting parents I had to admit that, doting as they were, I felt him not to have been spoiled. It was incongruous in such a career, but he was rather more of a man. There came back to me with a shade of regret after I had got on this occasion into my train, which was not theirs, a memory of some words that, a couple of years before,

I had uttered to poor Lavinia. She had said to me, speaking in reference to what was then our frequent topic and on some fresh evidence that I have forgotten: "He feels now, you know, about Maud-Evelyn quite as the old people themselves do."

"Well," I had replied, "it's only a pity he's paid for it!"

"Paid?" She had looked very blank.

"By all the luxuries and conveniences," I had explained, "that he comes in for through living with them. For that's what he practically does."

At present I saw how wrong I had been. He was paid, but paid differently, and the mastered wonder of that was really what had been between us in the waiting room of the station. Step by step, after this, I followed.

VI

I can see Lavinia, for instance, in her ugly new mourning immediately after her mother's death. There had been long anxieties connected with this event, and she was already faded, already almost old. But Marmaduke, on her bereavement, had been to her, and she came straightway to me.

"Do you know what he thinks now?" she soon began. "He thinks he knew her."

"Knew the child?" It came to me as if I had half expected it.

"He speaks of her now as if she hadn't been a child." My visitor gave me the strangest fixed smile. "It appears that she wasn't so young—it appears she had grown up."

I started. "How can it 'appear'? They *know* at least! There were the facts."

"Yes," said Lavinia, "but they seem to have come to take a different view of them. He talked to me a long time, and all about *her*. He told me things."

"What kind of things? Not trumpery stuff, I hope, about 'communicating'—about his seeing or hearing her?"

"Oh, no, he doesn't go in for that; he leaves it to the old couple, who, I believe, cling to their mediums, keep up their sittings and their rappings and find in it all a comfort, an amusement, that he doesn't grudge them and that he regards as harmless. I mean anecdotes—memories of his own. I mean things she said to him and that they did together—places they went to. His mind is full of them."

I turned it over. "Do you think he's decidedly mad?"

She shook her head with her bleached patience. "Oh, no, it's too beautiful!"

"Then are *you* taking it up? I mean the preposterous theory——"

"It *is* a theory," she broke in, "but it isn't necessarily preposterous. Any theory has to suppose something," she sagely pursued, "and it depends at any rate on what it's a theory *of*. It's wonderful to see this one work."

"Wonderful always to see the growth of a legend!" I laughed. "This is a rare chance to watch one in formation. They're all three in good faith building it up. Isn't that what you made out from him?"

Her tired face fairly lighted. "Yes—you understand it; and you put it better than I. It's the gradual effect of brooding over the past; the past, that way, grows and grows. They make it and make it. They've persuaded each other—the parents—of so many things that they've at last also persuaded *him*. It has been contagious."

"It's you who put it well," I returned. "It's the oddest thing I ever heard of, but it is, in its way, a reality. Only we mustn't speak of it to others."

She quite accepted that precaution. "No—to nobody. *He* doesn't. He keeps it only for me."

"Conferring on you thus," I again laughed, "such a precious privilege!"

She was silent a moment, looking away from me. "Well, he has kept his vow."

"You mean of not marrying? Are you very sure?" I asked. "Didn't he perhaps——?" But I faltered at the boldness of my joke.

The next moment I saw I needn't. "He *was* in love with her," Lavinia brought out.

I broke now into a peal which, however provoked, struck even my own ear at the moment as rude almost to profanity. "He literally tells you outright that he's making believe?"

She met me effectively enough. "I don't think he *knows* he is. He's just completely in the current."

"The current of the old people's twaddle?"

Again my companion hesitated; but she knew what she thought. "Well, whatever we call it, I like it. It isn't so common, as the world goes, for anyone—let alone for two or three—to feel and to care for the dead as much as that. It's self-deception, no doubt, but it comes from something that—well," she faltered again, "is beautiful when one does hear of it. They make her out older, so as to imagine they had her longer; and they make out that certain things really happened to her, so that she shall have had more life. They've invented a whole experience for her, and Marmaduke has become a part of it. There's one thing, above all, they want her to have had." My young friend's face, as she analyzed the mystery, fairly grew bright with her vision. It came to me with a faint dawn of awe that the attitude of the Dedricks *was* contagious. "And she did have it!" Lavinia declared.

I positively admired her, and if I could yet perfectly be rational without being ridiculous, it was really, more than anything else, to draw from her the whole image. "She had the bliss of knowing Marmaduke? Let us agree to it, then, since she's not here to contradict us. But what I don't get over is the scant material for *him!*" It may easily be conceived how little, for the moment, I could get over it. It was the last time my impatience was to be too much for me, but I remember how it broke out. "A man who might have had *you!*"

For an instant I feared I had upset her—thought I saw in her face the tremor of a wild wail. But poor Lavinia was magnificent. "It wasn't that he might have had 'me'—that's nothing: it was, at the most, that I might have had *him.* Well, isn't that just what has happened? He's mine from the moment no one else has him. I give up the past, but don't you see what it does for the rest of life? I'm surer than ever that he won't marry."

"O course, he won't—to quarrel, with those people!"

For a minute she answered nothing; then, "Well, for whatever reason!" she simply said. Now, however, I had gouged out of her a couple of still tears, and I pushed away the whole obscure comedy.

VII

I might push it away, but I couldn't really get rid of it; nor, on the whole, doubtless, did I want to, for to have in one's life, year after year, a particular question or two that one couldn't comfortably and imposingly make up one's mind about was just the sort of thing to keep one from turning stupid. There had been little need of my enjoining reserve upon Lavinia: she obeyed, in respect to impenetrable silence save with myself, an instinct, an interest of her own. We never therefore gave poor Marmaduke, as you call it, "away"; we were much too tender, let alone that she was also too proud; and, for himself, evidently, there was not, to the end, in London, another person in his confidence. No echo of the queer part he played ever came back to us; and I can't tell you how this fact, just by itself, brought home to me little by little a sense of the charm he was under. I met him "out" at long intervals—met him usually at dinner. He had grown like a person with a position and a history. Rosy and rich-looking, fat, moreover, distinctly fat at last, there was almost in him something of the bland—yet not too bland —young head of an hereditary business. If the Dedricks had been bankers he might have constituted the future of the house. There was none the less a long middle stretch during which, though we were all so much in London, he dropped out of my talks with Lavinia. We were conscious, she and I, of his absence from them; but we clearly felt in each quarter that there are things after all unspeakable, and the fact, in any case, had nothing to do with her seeing or not seeing our friend. I was sure, as it happened, that she did see him. But there were moments that for myself still stand out.

One of these was a certain Sunday afternoon when it was so dismally wet that, taking for granted I should have no visitors, I had drawn up to the fire with a book—a successful novel of the day—that I promised myself comfortably to finish. Suddenly, in my absorption, I heard a firm rat-tat-tat; on which I remember giving a groan of inhospitality. But my visitor proved in due course Marmaduke, and Marmaduke proved—in a manner even less, at the point we had reached, to have been counted on—still more attaching than my novel. I think it was only an accident that he became so; it would have been the turn of a hair either way. He hadn't come to speak—he had only come to talk, to show once more that we could continue good old friends without his speaking. But somehow there were the circumstances: the insidious fireside, the things in the room, with their reminders of his younger time; perhaps even too the open face of my book, looking at him from where I had laid it down for him and giving him a chance to feel that he could supersede Wilkie Collins.[6] There was at all events a promise of intimacy, of opportunity for him in the cold lash of the windows by the storm. We should be alone, it was cosy; it was safe.

The action of these impressions was the more marked that what was touched by them, I afterwards saw, was not at all a desire for an effect—was just simply a spirit of happiness that needed to overflow. It had finally become too much for him. His past, rolling up year after year, had grown too interesting. But he was, all the same, directly stupefying. I forget what turn of our preliminary gossip brought it out, but it came, in explanation of something or other, as it had not yet come: "When a man has had for a few months what I had, you know!" The moral appeared to be that nothing in the way of human experience of the exquisite could again particularly matter. He saw, however, that I failed immediately to fit his reflection to a definite case, and he went on with the frankest smile: "You look as bewildered as if you suspected me of alluding to some sort of thing that isn't usually spoken of; but I assure you I mean nothing more reprehensible than our blessed engagement itself."

"Your blessed engagement?" I couldn't help the tone in which I took him up; but the way he disposed of that was something of which I feel to this hour the influence. It was only a look, but it put an end to my tone forever. It made me, on my side, after an instant, look at the fire—look hard and even turn a little red. During this moment I saw my alternatives and I chose; so that when I met his eyes again I was fairly ready. "You still feel," I asked with sympathy, "how much it did for you?"

6. English novelist (1824–89), author of widely read books of the 1860's and 1870's, sometimes called the father of the detective story.

I had no sooner spoken than I saw that that would be from that moment the right way. It instantly made all the difference. The main question would be whether I could keep it up. I remember that only a few minutes later, for instance, this question gave a flare. His reply had been abundant and imperturbable—had included some glance at the way death brings into relief even the faintest things that have preceded it; on which I felt myself suddenly as restless as if I had grown afraid of him. I got up to ring for tea; he went on talking—talking about Maud-Evelyn and what she had been for him; and when the servant had come up I prolonged, nervously, on purpose, the order I had wished to give. It made time, and I could speak to the footman sufficiently without thinking: what I thought of really was the risk of turning right round with a little outbreak. The temptation was strong; the same influences that had worked for my companion just worked, in their way, during that minute or two, for me. *Should* I, taking him unaware, flash at him a plain "I say, just settle it for me once for all. *Are* you the boldest and basest of fortune hunters, or have you only, more innocently and perhaps more pleasantly, suffered your brain slightly to soften?" But I missed the chance—which I didn't in fact afterwards regret. My servant went out, and I faced again to my visitor, who continued to converse. I met his eyes once more, and their effect was repeated. If anything had happened to his brain this effect was perhaps the domination of the madman's stare. Well, he was the easiest and gentlest of madmen. By the time the footman came back with tea I was in for it; I was in for everything. By "everything" I mean my whole subsequent treatment of the case. It *was*—the case was—really beautiful. So, like all the rest, the hour comes back to me: the sound of the wind and the rain; the look of the empty, ugly, cabless square and of the stormy spring light; the way that, uninterrupted and absorbed, we had tea together by my fire. So it was that he found me receptive and that I found myself able to look merely grave and kind when he said, for example: "Her father and mother, you know, really, that first day—the day they picked me up on the Splügen—recognized me as the proper one."

"The proper one?"

"To make their son-in-law. They wanted her so," he went on, "to have had, don't you know, just everything."

"Well, if she did have it"—I tried to be cheerful—"isn't the whole thing then all right?"

"Oh, it's all right *now*," he replied—"now that we've got it all there before us. You see, they couldn't like me so much"—he wished me thoroughly to understand—"without wanting me to have been the man."

"I see—that was natural."

"Well," said Marmaduke, "it prevented the possibility of any-one else."

"Ah, that would never have done!" I laughed.

His own pleasure at it was impenetrable, splendid. "You see, they couldn't do much, the old people—and they can do still less now—with the future; so they had to do what they could with the past."

"And they seem to have done," I concurred, "remarkably much."

"Everything, simply. Everything," he repeated. Then he had an idea, though without insistence or importunity—I noticed it just flicker in his face. "If you *were* to come to Westbourne Ter-race——"

"Oh, don't speak of that!" I broke in. "It wouldn't be decent now. I should have come, if at all, ten years ago."

But he saw, with his good humor, further than this. "I see what you mean. But there's much more in the place now than then."

"I daresay. People get new things. All the same——" I was at bottom but resisting my curiosity.

Marmaduke didn't press me, but he wanted me to know. "There are our rooms—the whole set; and I don't believe you ever saw anything more charming, for *her* taste was extraordinary. I'm afraid too that I myself have had much to say to them." Then as he made out that I was again a little at sea, "I'm talking," he went on, "of the suite prepared for her marriage." He "talked" like a crown prince. "They were ready, to the last touch—there was nothing more to be done. And they're just as they were—not an object moved, not an arrangement altered, not a person but ourselves coming in: they're only exquisitely kept. All our presents are there—I should have liked you to see them."

It had become a torment by this time—I saw that I had made a mistake. But I carried it off. "Oh, I couldn't have borne it!"

"They're not sad," he smiled—"they're too lovely to be sad. They're happy. And the things—!" He seemed, in the excitement of our talk, to have them before him.

"They're so very wonderful?"

"Oh, selected with a patience that makes them almost priceless. It's really a museum. There was nothing they thought too good for her."

I had lost the museum, but I reflected that it could contain no object so rare as my visitor. "Well, you've helped them—you could do *that*."

He quite eagerly assented. "I could do that, thank God—I could do that! I felt it from the first, and it's what I *have* done." Then as if the connection were direct: "All *my* things are there."

I thought a moment. "Your presents?"

"Those I made her. She loved each one, and I remember about each the particular thing she said. Though I do say it," he continued, "none of the others, as a matter of fact, come near mine. I look at them every day, and I assure you I'm not ashamed." Evidently, in short, he had spared nothing, and he talked on and on. He really quite swaggered.

VIII

In relation to times and intervals I can only recall that if this visit of his to me had been in the early spring it was one day in the late autumn—a day, which couldn't have been in the same year, with the difference of hazy, drowsy sunshine and brown and yellow leaves—that, taking a short cut across Kensington Gardens, I came, among the untrodden ways, upon a couple occupying chairs under a tree, who immediately rose at the sight of me. I had been behind them at recognition, the fact that Marmaduke was in deep mourning having perhaps, so far as I had observed it, misled me. In my desire both not to look flustered at meeting them and to spare their own confusion I bade them again be seated and asked leave, as a third chair was at hand, to share a little their rest. Thus it befell that after a minute Lavinia and I had sat down, while our friend, who had looked at his watch, stood before us among the fallen foliage and remarked that he was sorry to have to leave us. Lavinia said nothing, but I expressed regret; I couldn't, however, as it struck me, without a false or a vulgar note speak as if I had interrupted a tender passage or separated a pair of lovers. But I could look him up and down, take in his deep mourning. He had not made, for going off, any other pretext than that his time was up and that he was due at home. "Home," with him now, had but one meaning: I knew him to be completely quartered in Westbourne Terrace. "I hope nothing has happened," I said—"that you've lost no one whom *I* know."

Marmaduke looked at my companion, and she looked at Marmaduke. "He has lost his wife," she then observed.

Oh, this time, I fear, I had a small quaver of brutality; but it was at him I directed it. "Your wife? I didn't know you had *had* a wife!"

"Well," he replied, positively gay in his black suit, his black gloves, his high hatband, "the more we live in the past, the more things we find in it. That's a literal fact. You would see the truth of it if your life had taken such a turn."

"*I* live in the past," Lavinia put in gently and as if to help us both.

"But with the result, my dear," I returned, "of not making, I hope, such extraordinary discoveries!" It seemed absurd to be afraid to be light.

"May none of her discoveries be more fatal than mine!" Marmaduke wasn't uproarious, but his treatment of the matter had the good taste of simplicity. "They've wanted it so for her," he continued to me wonderfully, "that we've at last seen our way to it— I mean to what Lavinia has mentioned." He hesitated but three seconds—he brought it brightly out. "Maud-Evelyn had *all* her young happiness."

I stared, but Lavinia was, in her peculiar manner, as brilliant. "The marriage *did* take place," she quietly, stupendously explained to me.

Well, I was determined not to be left. "So you're a widower," I gravely asked, "and these are the signs?"

"Yes; I shall wear them always now."

"But isn't it late to have begun?"

My question had been stupid, I felt the next instant; but it didn't matter—he was quite equal to the occasion. "Oh, I had to wait, you know, till all the facts about my marriage had given me the right." And he looked at his watch again. "Excuse me—I *am* due. Good-by, good-by." He shook hands with each of us, and as we sat there together watching him walk away I was struck with his admirable manner of looking the character. I felt indeed as our eyes followed him that we were at one on this, and I said nothing till he was out of sight. Then by the same impulse we turned to each other.

"I thought he was never to marry!" I exclaimed to my friend.

Her fine wasted face met me gravely. "He isn't—ever. He'll be still more faithful."

"Faithful this time to whom?"

"Why, to Maud-Evelyn." I said nothing—I only checked an ejaculation; but I put out a hand and took one of hers, and for a minute we kept silence. "Of course it's only an idea," she began again at last, "but it seems to me a beautiful one." Then she continued resignedly and remarkably: "And now *they* can die."

"Mr. and Mrs. Dedrick?" I pricked up my ears. "Are they dying?"

"Not quite, but the old lady, it appears, is failing, steadily weakening; less, as I understand it, from any definite ailment than because she just feels her work done and her little sum of passion, as Marmaduke calls it, spent. Fancy, with her convictions, all her reasons for wanting to die! And if she goes, he says, Mr. Dedrick won't long linger. It will be quite 'John Anderson my jo.'"

"Keeping her company down the hill, to lie beside her at the foot?"

"Yes, having settled all things."

I turned these things over as we walked away, and how they had settled them—for Maud-Evelyn's dignity and Marmaduke's high advantage; and before we parted that afternoon—we had taken a cab in the Bayswater Road and she had come home with me—I remember saying to her: "Well then, when they die won't he be free?"

She seemed scarce to understand. "Free?"

"To do what he likes?"

She wondered. "But he does what he likes now."

"Well then, what *you* like!"

"Oh, you know what I like——!"

Ah, I closed her mouth! "You like to tell horrid fibs—yes, I know it!"

What she had then put before me, however, came in time to pass: I heard in the course of the next year of Mrs. Dedrick's extinction, and some months later, without, during the interval, having seen a sign of Marmaduke, wholly taken up with his bereaved patron, learned that her husband had touchingly followed her. I was out of England at the time; we had had to put into practice great economies and let our little place; so that, spending three winters successively in Italy, I devoted the periods between, at home, altogether to visits among people, mainly relatives, to whom these friends of mine were not known. Lavina of course wrote to me—wrote, among many things, that Marmaduke was ill and had not seemed at all himself since the loss of his "family," and this in spite of the circumstance, which she had already promptly communicated, that they had left him, by will, "almost everything." I knew before I came back to remain that she now saw him often and, to the extent of the change that had overtaken his strength and his spirits, greatly ministered to him. As soon as we at last met I asked for news of him; to which she replied: "He's gradually going." Then on my surprise: "He has had his life."

"You mean that, as he said of Mrs. Dedrick, his sum of passion is spent?"

At this she turned away. "You've never understood."

I *had*, I conceived; and when I went subsequently to see him I was moreover sure. But I only said to Lavinia on this first occasion that I would immediately go; which was precisely what brought out the climax, as I feel it to be, of my story. "He's not now, you know," she turned round to admonish me, "in Westbourne Terrace. He has taken a little old house in Kensington."

"Then he hasn't kept the things?"

"He has kept everything." She looked at me still more as if I had never understood.

"You mean he has moved them?"

She was patient with me. "He has moved nothing. Everything is as it was, and kept with the same perfection."

I wondered. "But if he doesn't live there?"

"It's just what he does."

"Then how can he be in Kensington?"

She hesitated, but she had still more than her old grasp of it. "He's in Kensington—without living."

"You mean that at the other place——?"

"Yes, he spends most of his time. He's driven over there every day—he remains there for hours. He keeps it for that."

"I see—it's still the museum."

"It's still the temple!" Lavinia replied with positive austerity.

"Then why did he move?"

"Because, you see, there"—she faltered again—"I could come to him. And he wants me," she said with admirable simplicity.

Little by little I took it in. "After the death of the parents, even, you never went?"

"Never."

"So you haven't seen anything?"

"Anything of hers? Nothing."

I understood, oh perfectly; but I won't deny that I was disappointed: I had hoped for an account of his wonders and I immediately felt that it wouldn't be for me to take a step that she had declined. When, a short time later, I saw them together in Kensington Square—there were certain hours of the day that she regularly spent with him—I observed that everything about him was new, handsome, and simple. They were, in their strange, final union—if union it could be called—very natural and very touching; but he was visibly stricken—he had his ailment in his eyes. She moved about him like a sister of charity—at all events like a sister. He was neither robust nor rosy now, nor was his attention visibly very present, and I privately and fancifully asked myself where it wandered and waited. But poor Marmaduke was a gentleman to the end—he wasted away with an excellent manner. He died twelve days ago; the will was opened; and last week, having meanwhile heard from her of its contents, I saw Lavinia. He leaves her everything that he himself had inherited. But she spoke of it all in a way that caused me to say in surprise: "You haven't yet been to the house?"

"Not yet. I've only seen the solicitors, who tell me there will be no complications."

There was something in her tone that made me ask more. "Then you're not curious to see what's there?"

She looked at me with a troubled—almost a pleading—sense, which I understood; and presently she said: "Will you go with me?"

"Some day, with pleasure—but not the first time. You must go alone then. The 'relics' that you'll find there," I added—for I had read her look—"you must think of now not as hers—"

"But as his?"

"Isn't that what his death—with his so close relation to them— has made them for you?" Her face lighted—I saw it was a view she could thank me for putting into words. "I see—I see. They *are* his. I'll go."

She went, and three days ago she came to me. They're really marvels, it appears treasures extraordinary, and she has them all. Next week I go with her—I shall see them at last. Tell *you* about them you say? My dear man, everything.

1900

The Jolly Corner⁷

I

"Every one asks me what I 'think' of everything," said Spencer Brydon; "and I make answer as I can—begging or dodging the question, putting them off with any nonsense. It wouldn't matter to any of them really," he went on, "for, even were it possible to meet in that stand-and-deliver way so silly a demand on so big a subject, my 'thoughts' would still be almost altogether about something that concerns only myself." He was talking to Miss Staverton, with whom for a couple of months now he had availed himself of every possible occasion to talk; this disposition and this resource, this comfort and support, as the situation in fact presented itself, having promptly enough taken the first place in the considerable array of rather unattenuated surprises attending his so strangely belated return to America. Everything was somehow a surprise; and that might be natural when one had so long and so consistently neglected everything, taken pains to give surprises so much margin for play. He had given them more than thirty years—thirty-three,

---

7. After rejections from several magazine editors, this story was accepted and published in *The English Review* for December, 1908. James then reprinted it in the New York Edition among a group of stories dealing with ghostly and apparitional experiences of psychic life. The theme of the story is "repatriation," the reverse of the expatriate American in Europe which dominated James's earlier writing. It is also related to his unfinished novel, *The Sense of the Past*, in which a young American finds himself at night in his ancestral home in England suddenly transported to the past, his identity exchanged for that of a forbear whose portrait he has admired. James had returned to America in 1904–5 after twenty years of "exile" in Europe, and in his efforts to recover his past life he wandered through Washington Square where the house in which he was born had been torn down. His thoughts suggested to him a story which would reverse the situation of *The Sense of the Past*—the other side of the coin of the "international theme" of his earlier fiction. The psychological treatment he gave this story has led critics to consider Spencer Brydon's nightmare confrontation of his own alter ego as somehow a reflection of buried elements in James's own psychic life. It has also been pointed out that "The Jolly Corner" should be related to James's account in *A Small Boy and Others* of his encounter with a similar creature or presence in the gallery of the Louvre (see the introduction to James).

to be exact; and they now seemed to him to have organised their performance quite on the scale of that licence. He had been twenty-three on leaving New York—he was fifty-six today: unless indeed he were to reckon as he had sometimes, since his repatriation, found himself feeling; in which case he would have lived longer than is often allotted to man. It would have taken a century, he repeatedly said to himself, and said also to Alice Staverton, it would have taken a longer absence and a more averted mind than those even of which he had been guilty, to pile up the differences, the newnesses, the queernesses, above all the bignesses, for the better or the worse, that at present assaulted his vision wherever he looked.

The great fact all the while however had been the incalculability; since he *had* supposed himself, from decade to decade, to be allowing, and in the most liberal and intelligent manner, for brilliancy of change. He actually saw that he had allowed for nothing; he missed what he would have been sure of finding, he found what he would never have imagined. Proportions and values were upsidedown; the ugly things he had expected, the ugly things of his faraway youth, when he had too promptly waked up to a sense of the ugly—these uncanny phenomena placed him rather, as it happened, under the charm; whereas the "swagger" things, the modern, the monstrous, the famous things, those he had more particularly, like thousands of ingenuous enquirers every year, come over to see, were exactly his sources of dismay. They were as so many set traps for displeasure, above all for reaction, of which his restless tread was constantly pressing the spring. It was interesting, doubtless, the whole show, but it would have been too disconcerting hadn't a certain finer truth saved the situation. He had distinctly not, in this steadier light, come over *all* for the monstrosities; he had come, not only in the last analysis but quite on the face of the act, under an impulse with which they had nothing to do. He had come—putting the thing pompously—to look at his "property," which he had thus for a third of a century not been within four thousand miles of; or, expressing it less sordidly, he had yielded to the humour of seeing again his house on the jolly corner, as he usually, and quite fondly, described it—the one in which he had first seen the light, in which various members of his family had lived and had died, in which the holidays of his overschooled boyhood had been passed and the few social flowers of his chilled adolescence gathered, and which, alienated then for so long a period, had, through the successive deaths of his two brothers and the termination of old arrangements, come wholly into his hands. He was the owner of another, not quite so "good"—the jolly corner having been, from far back, superlatively extended and consecrated; and the value of the pair represented his main capital, with an income consisting, in these later years, of their respective rents which (thanks precisely to their original excellent type) had never been depressingly low. He could live in "Europe," as he had been in the habit of living, on the product of these flourishing New York leases, and all the better since, that of the second structure, the mere number in its long row, having within a twelvemonth fallen in, renovation at a high advance had proved beautifully possible.

These were items of property indeed, but he had found himself since his arrival distinguishing more than ever between them. The house within the street, two bristling blocks westward, was already in course of reconstruction as a tall mass of flats; he had acceded, some time before, to overtures for this conversion—in which, now that it was going forward, it had been not the least of his astonishments to find himself able, on the spot, and though without a previous ounce of such experience, to participate with a certain intelligence, almost with a certain authority. He had lived his life with his back so turned to such concerns and his face addressed to those of so different an order that he scarce knew what to make of this lively stir, in a compartment of his mind never yet penetrated, of a capacity for business and a sense for construction. These virtues, so common all round him now, had been dormant in his own organism—where it might be said of them perhaps that they had slept the sleep of the just. At present, in the splendid autumn weather—the autumn at least was a pure boon in the terrible place— he loafed about his "work" undeterred, secretly agitated; not in the least "minding" that the whole proposition, as they said, was vulgar and sordid, and ready to climb ladders, to walk the plank, to handle materials and look wise about them, to ask questions, in fine, and challenge explanations and really "go into" figures.

It amused, it verily quite charmed him; and, by the same stroke, it amused, and even more, Alice Staverton, though perhaps charming her perceptibly less. She wasn't however going to be better off for it, as *he* was—and so astonishingly much: nothing was now likely, he knew, ever to make her better off than she found herself, in the afternoon of life, as the delicately frugal possessor and tenant of the small house in Irving Place to which she had subtly managed to cling through her almost unbroken New York career. If he knew the way to it now better than to any other address among the dreadful multiplied numberings which seemed to him to reduce the whole place to some vast ledger-page, overgrown, fantastic, of ruled and criss-crossed lines and figures—if he had formed, for his consolation, that habit, it was really not a little because of the charm of his having encountered and recognised, in the vast wilderness of the wholesale, breaking through the mere gross generalisation of wealth and force and success, a small still scene where items and shades, all delicate things, kept the sharpness of the notes of a high voice perfectly trained, and where economy hung about like the scent of a garden. His old friend lived with one maid and herself, dusted her relics and trimmed her lamps and polished her silver; she stood off, in the awful modern crush, when she could, but she sallied forth and did battle when the challenge was really to "spirit," the spirit she after all confessed to, proudly and a little shyly, as to that of the better time, that of *their* common, their quite far-away and antediluvian social period and order. She made use of the street-cars when need be, the terrible things that people scrambled for as the panic-stricken at sea scramble for the boats; she affronted, inscrutably, under stress, all the public concussions and ordeals; and yet, with that slim mystifying grace of her appearance, which defied you to say if she were a fair young woman who looked older through trouble, or a fine smooth older one who looked young through successful indifference; with her precious reference, above all, to memories and histories into which he could enter, she was as exquisite for him as some pale pressed flower (a rarity to begin with), and, failing other sweetnesses, she was a sufficient reward of his effort. They had communities of knowledge, "their" knowledge (this discriminating possessive was always on her lips) of presences of the other age, presences all overlaid, in his case, by the experience of a man and the freedom of a wanderer, overlaid by pleasure, by infidelity, by passages of life that were strange and dim to her, just by "Europe" in short, but still unobscured, still exposed and cherished, under that pious visitation of the spirit from which she had never been diverted.

She had come with him one day to see how his "apartment-house" was rising; he had helped her over gaps and explained to her plans, and while they were there had happened to have, before her, a brief but lively discussion with the man in charge, the representative of the building-firm that had undertaken his work. He had found himself quite "standing-up" to this personage over a failure on the latter's part to observe some detail of one of their noted conditions, and had so lucidly argued his case that, besides ever so prettily flushing, at the time, for sympathy in his triumph, she had afterwards said to him (though to a slightly greater effect of irony) that he had clearly for too many years neglected a real gift. If he had but stayed at home he would have anticipated the inventor of the sky-scraper. If he had but stayed at home he would have discovered his genius in time really to start some new variety of awful architectural hare and run it till it burrowed in a gold-mine. He was to remember these words, while the weeks elapsed, for the small silver ring they had sounded over the queerest and deepest of his own lately most disguised and most muffled vibrations.

It had begun to be present to him after the first fortnight, it had broken out with the oddest abruptness, this particular wanton wonderment: it met him there—and this was the image under which he himself judged the matter, or at least, not a little, thrilled and flushed with it—very much as he might have been met by some strange figure, some unexpected occupant, at a turn of one of the dim passages of an empty house. The quaint analogy quite hauntingly remained with him, when he didn't indeed rather improve it by a still intenser form: that of his opening a door behind which he would have made sure of finding nothing, a door into a room shuttered and void, and yet so coming, with a great suppressed start, on some quite erect confronting presence, something planted in the middle of the place and facing him through the dusk. After that visit to the house in construction he walked with his companion to see the other and always so much the better one, which in the eastward direction formed one of the corners, the "jolly" one precisely, of the street now so generally dishonoured and disfigured in its westward reaches, and of the comparatively conservative Avenue. The Avenue still had pretensions, as Miss Staverton said, to decency; the old people had mostly gone, the old names were unknown, and here and there an old association seemed to stray, all vaguely, like some very aged person, out too late, whom you might meet and feel the impulse to watch or follow, in kindness, for safe restoration to shelter.

They went in together, our friends; he admitted himself with his key, as he kept no one there, he explained, preferring, for his reasons, to leave the place empty, under a simple arrangement with a good woman living in the neighbourhood and who came for a daily hour to open windows and dust and sweep. Spencer Brydon had his reasons and was growingly aware of them; they seemed to him better each time he was there, though he didn't name them all to his companion, any more than he told her as yet how often, how quite absurdly often, he himself came. He only let her see for the present, while they walked through the great blank rooms, that absolute vacancy reigned and that, from top to bottom, there was nothing but Mrs. Muldoon's broomstick, in a corner, to tempt the burglar. Mrs. Muldoon was then on the premises, and she loquaciously attended the visitors, preceding them from room to room and pushing back shutters and throwing up sashes—all to show them, as she remarked, how little there was to see. There was little indeed to see in the great gaunt shell where the main dispositions and the general apportionment of space, the style of an age of ampler allowances, had nevertheless for its master their honest pleading message, affecting him as some good old servant's, some lifelong retainer's appeal for a character, or even for a retiring-pension; yet it was also a remark of Mrs. Muldoon's that, glad as she was to oblige him by her noonday round, there was a request she greatly hoped he would never make of her. If he should wish her for any reason to come in after dark she would just tell him, if he "plased," that he must ask it of somebody else.

The fact that there was nothing to see didn't militate for the worthy woman against what one *might* see, and she put it frankly to Miss Staverton that no lady could be expected to like, could she? "scraping up to thim top storeys in the ayvil hours." The gas and the electric light were off the house, and she fairly evoked a gruesome vision of her march through the great grey rooms—so many of them as there were too!—with her glimmering taper. Miss Staverton met her honest glare with a smile and the profession that she herself certainly would recoil from such an adventure. Spencer Brydon meanwhile held his peace—for the moment; the question of the "evil" hours in his old home had already become too grave for him. He had begun some time since to "crape," and he knew just why a packet of candles addressed to that pursuit had been stowed by his own hand, three weeks before, at the back of a drawer of the fine old sideboard that occupied, as a "fixture," the deep recess in the dining-room. Just now he laughed at his companions— quickly however changing the subject; for the reason that, in the first place, his laugh struck him even at that moment as starting the odd echo, the conscious human resonance (he scarce knew how to qualify it) that sound made while he was there alone sent back to his ear or his fancy; and that, in the second, he imagined Alice Staverton for the instant on the point of asking him, with a divination, if he ever so prowled. There were divinations he was unprepared for, and he had at all events averted enquiry by the time Mrs. Muldoon had left them, passing on to other parts.

There was happily enough to say, on so consecrated a spot, that could be said freely and fairly; so that a whole train of declarations was precipitated by his friend's having herself broken out, after a yearning look round: "But I hope you don't mean they want you to pull *this* to pieces!" His answer came, promptly, with his re-awakened wrath: it was of course exactly what they wanted, and what they were "at" him for, daily, with the iteration of people who couldn't for their life understand a man's liability to decent feelings. He had found the place, just as it stood and beyond what he could express, an interest and a joy. There were values other than the beastly rent-values, and in short, in short—! But it was thus Miss Staverton took him up. "In short you're to make so good a thing of your sky-scraper that, living in luxury on *those* ill-gotten gains, you can afford for a while to be sentimental here!" Her smile had for him, with the words, the particular mild irony with which he found half her talk suffused; an irony without bitterness and that came, exactly, from her having so much imagination—not, like the cheap sarcasms with which one heard most people, about the world of "society," bid for the reputation of cleverness, from nobody's really having any. It was agreeable to him at this very moment to be sure that when he had answered, after a brief demur, "Well yes: so, precisely, you may put it!" her imagination would still do him justice. He explained that even if never a dollar were to come to him from the other house he would nevertheless cherish this one; and he dwelt, further, while they lingered and wandered, on the fact of the stupefaction he was already exciting, the positive mystification he felt himself create.

He spoke of the value of all he read into it, into the mere sight of the walls, mere shapes of the rooms, mere sound of the floors, mere feel, in his hand, of the old silver-plated knobs of the several mahogany doors, which suggested the pressure of the palms of the dead; the seventy years of the past in fine that these things represented, the annals of nearly three generations, counting his grandfather's, the one that had ended there, and the impalpable ashes of his long-extinct youth, afloat in the very air like microscopic motes. She listened to everything; she was a woman who answered intimately but who utterly didn't chatter. She scattered abroad therefore no cloud of words; she could assent, she could agree, above all she could encourage, without doing that. Only at the last she went a little further than he had done himself. "And then how do you know? You may still, after all, want to live here." It rather indeed pulled him up, for it wasn't what he had been thinking, at least in her sense of the words. "You mean I may decide to stay on for the sake of it?"

"Well, *with* such a home—!" But, quite beautifully, she had too much tact to dot so monstrous an *i*, and it was precisely an illustration of the way she didn't rattle. How could any one—of any wit—insist on any one else's "wanting" to live in New York?

"Oh," he said, "I *might* have lived here (since I had my opportunity early in life); I might have put in here all these years. Then everything would have been different enough—and, I dare say, 'funny' enough. But that's another matter. And then the beauty of it—I mean of my perversity, of my refusal to agree to a 'deal'—is just in the total absence of a reason. Don't you see that if I had a reason about the matter at all it would *have* to be the other way, and would then be inevitably a reason of dollars? There are no reasons here *but* of dollars. Let us therefore have none whatever—not the ghost of one."

They were back in the hall then for departure, but from where they stood the vista was large, through an open door, into the great square main saloon, with its almost antique felicity of brave spaces between windows. Her eyes came back from that reach and met his own a moment. "Are you very sure the 'ghost' of one doesn't, much rather, serve—?"

He had a positive sense of turning pale. But it was as near as they were then to come. For he made answer, he believed, between a glare and a grin: "Oh ghosts—of course, the place must swarm with them! I should be ashamed of it if it didn't. Poor Mrs. Muldoon's right, and it's why I haven't asked her to do more than look in."

Miss Staverton's gaze again lost itself, and things she didn't utter, it was clear, came and went in her mind. She might even for the minute, off there in the fine room, have imagined some element dimly gathering. Simplified like the death-mask of a handsome face, it perhaps produced for her just then an effect akin to the stir of an expression in the "set" commemorative plaster. Yet whatever her impression may have been she produced instead a vague platitude. "Well, if it were only furnished and lived in—!"

She appeared to imply that in case of its being still furnished he might have been a little less opposed to the idea of a return. But she passed straight into the vestibule, as if to leave her words behind her, and the next moment he had opened the house-door and was standing with her on the steps. He closed the door and, while he re-pocketed his key, looking up and down, they took in the comparatively harsh actuality of the Avenue, which reminded him of the assault of the outer light of the Desert on the traveller emerging from an Egyptian tomb. But he risked before they stepped into the street his gathered answer to her speech. "For me it *is* lived in. For me it *is* furnished." At which it was easy for her to sigh "Ah yes—!" all vaguely and discreetly; since his parents and his favourite sister, to say nothing of other kin, in numbers, had run their course and met their end there. That represented, within the walls, ineffaceable life.

It was a few days after this that, during an hour passed with her again, he had expressed his impatience of the too flattering curiosity—among the people he met—about his appreciation of New York. He had arrived at none at all that was socially producible, and as for that matter of his "thinking" (thinking the better or the worse of anything there) he was wholly taken up with one subject of thought. It was mere vain egoism, and it was moreover, if she liked, a morbid obsession. He found all things come back to the question of what he personally might have been, how he might have led his life and "turned out," if he had not so, at the outset, given it up. And confessing for the first time to the intensity within him of this absurd speculation—which but proved also, no doubt, the habit of too selfishly thinking—he affirmed the impotence there of any other source of interest, any other native appeal. "What would it have made of me, what would it have made of me? I keep for ever wondering, all idiotically; as if I could possibly know! I see what it has made of dozens of others, those I meet, and it positively aches within me, to the point of exasperation, that it would have made something of me as well. Only I can't make out *what*, and the worry of it, the small rage of curiosity never to be satisfied, brings back what I remember to have felt, once or twice, after judging best, for reasons, to burn some important letter unopened. I've been sorry, I've hated it—I've never known what was in the letter. You may of course say it's a trifle—!"

"I don't say it's a trifle," Miss Staverton gravely interrupted.

She was seated by her fire, and before her, on his feet and restless, he turned to and fro between this intensity of his idea and a fitful and unseeing inspection, through his single eye-glass, of the dear little old objects on her chimney-piece. Her interruption made him for an instant look at her harder. "I shouldn't care if you did!" he laughed, however; "and it's only a figure, at any rate, for the way I now feel. *Not* to have followed my perverse young course—and almost in the teeth of my father's curse, as I may say; not to have kept it up, so, 'over there,' from that day to this, without a doubt or a pang; not, above all, to have liked it, to have loved it, so much, loved it, no doubt, with such an abysmal conceit of my own preference: some variation from *that*, I say, must have produced some different effect for my life and for my 'form.' I should have stuck here—if it had been possible; and I was too young, at twenty-three, to judge, *pour deux sous*,[8] whether it *were* possible. If I had waited I might have seen it was, and then I might have been, by staying here, something nearer to one of these types who have been hammered so hard and made so keen by their conditions. It isn't that I admire them so much—the question of any charm in them, or of any charm, beyond that of the rank money-passion, exerted by their conditions *for* them, has nothing to do with the matter: it's only a question of what fantastic, yet perfectly possible, development of my own nature I mayn't have missed. It comes over me that I had then a strange *alter ego* deep down somewhere within me, as the full-blown flower is in the small tight bud, and that I just took the course, I just transferred him to the climate, that blighted him for once and for ever."

"And you wonder about the flower," Miss Staverton said. "So do I, if you want to know; and so I've been wondering these several weeks. I believe in the flower," she continued, "I feel it would have been quite splendid, quite huge and monstrous."

"Monstrous above all!" her visitor echoed; "and I imagine, by

8. Literally, "for two cents." Here, idiomatically, "even slightly."

the same stroke, quite hideous and offensive."

"You don't believe that," she returned; "if you did you wouldn't wonder. You'd know, and that would be enough for you. What you feel—and what I feel *for* you—is that you'd have had power."

"You'd have liked me that way?" he asked.

She barely hung fire. "How should I not have liked you?"

"I see. You'd have liked me, have preferred me, a billionaire!"

"How should I not have liked you?" she simply again asked.

He stood before her still—her question kept him motionless. He took it in, so much there was of it; and indeed his not otherwise meeting it testified to that. "I know at least what I am," he simply went on; "the other side of the medal's clear enough. I've not been edifying—I believe I'm thought in a hundred quarters to have been barely decent. I've followed strange paths and worshipped strange gods; it must have come to you again and again—in fact you've admitted to me as much—that I was leading, at any time these thirty years, a selfish frivolous scandalous life. And you see what it has made of me."

She just waited, smiling at him. "You see what it has made of *me*."

"Oh you're a person whom nothing can have altered. You were born to be what you are, anywhere, anyway: you've the perfection nothing else could have blighted. And don't you see how, without my exile, I shouldn't have been waiting till now—?" But he pulled up for the strange pang.

"The great thing to see," she presently said, "seems to me to be that it has spoiled nothing. It hasn't spoiled your being here at last. It hasn't spoiled this. It hasn't spoiled your speaking—" She also however faltered.

He wondered at everything her controlled emotion might mean. "Do you believe then—too dreadfully!—that I *am* as good as I might ever have been?"

"Oh no! Far from it!" With which she got up from her chair and was nearer to him. "But I don't care," she smiled.

"You mean I'm good enough?"

She considered a little. "Will you believe it if I say so? I mean will you let that settle your question for you?" And then as if making out in his face that he drew back from this, that he had some idea which, however absurd, he couldn't yet bargain away: "Oh you don't care either—but very differently: you don't care for anything but yourself."

Spencer Brydon recognised it—it was in fact what he had absolutely professed. Yet he importantly qualified. "*He* isn't myself. He's the just so totally other person. But I do want to see him," he added. "And I can. And I shall."

Their eyes met for a minute while he guessed from something in hers that she divined his strange sense. But neither of them otherwise expressed it, and her apparent understanding, with no protesting shock, no easy derision, touched him more deeply than anything yet, constituting for his stifled perversity, on the spot, an element that was like breathable air. What she said however was unexpected. "Well, *I've* seen him."

"You—?"

"I've seen him in a dream."

"Oh a 'dream'—!" It let him down.

"But twice over," she continued. "I saw him as I see you now."

"You've dreamed the same dream—?"

"Twice over," she repeated. "The very same."

This did somehow a little speak to him, as it also gratified him. "You dream about me at that rate?"

"Ah about *him!*" she smiled.

His eyes again sounded her. "Then you know all about him." And as she said nothing more: "What's the wretch like?"

She hesitated, and it was as if he were pressing her so hard that, resisting for reasons of her own, she had to turn away. "I'll tell you some other time!"

II

It was after this that there was most of a virtue for him, most of a cultivated charm, most of a preposterous secret thrill, in the particular form of surrender to his obsession and of address to what he more and more believed to be his privilege. It was what in these weeks he was living for—since he really felt life to begin but after Mrs. Muldoon had retired from the scene and, visiting the ample house from attic to cellar, making sure he was alone, he knew himself in safe possession and, as he tacitly expressed it, let himself go. He sometimes came twice in the twenty-four hours; the moments he liked best were those of gathering dusk, of the short autumn twilight; this was the time of which, again and again, he found himself hoping most. Then he could, as seemed to him, most intimately wander and wait, linger and listen, feel his fine attention, never in his life before so fine, on the pulse of the great vague place: he preferred the lampless hour and only wished he might have prolonged each day the deep crepuscular spell. Later—rarely much before midnight, but then for a considerable vigil—he watched with his glimmering light; moving slowly, holding it high, playing it far, rejoicing above all, as much as he might, in open vistas, reaches of communication between rooms and by passages; the long straight chance or show, as he would have called it, for the revelation he pretended to invite. It was a practice he found he could perfectly "work" without exciting remark; no one was in the least the wiser for it; even Alice Staverton, who was moreover a well of discretion, didn't quite fully imagine.

He let himself in and let himself out with the assurance of calm proprietorship; and accident so far favoured him that, if a fat Avenue "officer" had happened on occasion to see him entering at eleven-thirty, he had never yet, to the best of his belief, been noticed as emerging at two. He walked there on the crisp November nights, arrived regularly at the evening's end; it was as easy to do this after dining out as to take his way to a club or to his hotel. When he left his club, if he hadn't been dining out, it was ostensibly to go to his hotel; and when he left his hotel, if he had spent a part of the evening there, it was ostensibly to go to his club. Everything was easy in fine; everything conspired and promoted: there was truly even in the strain of his experience something that glossed over, something that salved and simplified, all the rest of consciousness. He circulated, talked, renewed, loosely and pleasantly, old relations—met indeed, so far as he could, new expectations and seemed to make out on the whole that in spite of the career, of such different contacts, which he had spoken of to Miss Staverton as ministering so little, for those who might have watched it, to edification, he was positively rather liked than not. He was a dim secondary social success—and all with people who had truly not an idea of him. It was all mere surface sound, this murmur of their welcome, this popping of their corks—just as his gestures of response were the extravagant shadows, emphatic in proportion as they meant little, of some game of *ombres chinoises*.[9] He projected himself all day, in thought, straight over the bristling line of hard unconscious heads and into the other, the real, the waiting life; the life that, as soon as he had heard behind him the click of his great house-door, began for him, on the jolly corner, as beguilingly as the slow opening bars of some rich music follows the tap of the conductor's wand.

He always caught the first effect of the steel point of his stick on the old marble of the hall pavement, large black-and-white squares that he remembered as the admiration of his childhood and that had then made in him, as he now saw, for the growth of an early conception of style. This effect was the dim reverberating tinkle as of some far-off bell hung who should say where?—in the depths of the house, of the past, of that mystical other world that might have flourished for him had he not, for weal or woe, abandoned it. On this impression he did ever the same thing; he put his stick noiselessly away in a corner—feeling the place once more in the likeness of some great glass bowl, all precious concave crystal, set delicately humming by the play of a moist finger round its edge. The concave

9. Chinese cards.

crystal held, as it were, this mystical other world, and the indescrib-
ably fine murmur of its rim was the sigh there, the scarce audible
pathetic wail to his strained ear, of all the old baffled forsworn
possibilities. What he did therefore by this appeal of his hushed
presence was to wake them into such measure of ghostly life as they
might still enjoy. They were shy, all but unappeasably shy, but they
weren't really sinister; at least they weren't as he had hitherto felt
them—before they had taken the Form he so yearned to make
them take, the Form he at moments saw himself in the light of
fairly hunting on tiptoe, the points of his evening-shoes, from room
to room and from storey to storey.

That was the essence of his vision—which was all rank folly, if
one would, while he was out of the house and otherwise occupied,
but which took on the last verisimilitude as soon as he was placed
and posted. He knew what he meant and what he wanted; it was
as clear as the figure on a cheque presented in demand for cash.
His *alter ego* "walked"—that was the note of his image of him,
while his image of his motive for his own odd pastime was the desire to waylay him and meet him. He roamed, slowly, warily, but
all restlessly, he himself did—Mrs. Muldoon had been right, absolutely, with her figure of their "craping"; and the presence he
watched for would roam restlessly too. But it would be as cautious
and as shifty; the conviction of its probable, in fact its already
quite sensible, quite audible evasion of pursuit grew for him from
night to night, laying on him finally a rigour to which nothing in
his life had been comparable. It had been the theory of many super-
ficially-judging persons, he knew, that he was wasting that life in a
surrender to sensations, but he had tasted of no pleasure so fine as
his actual tension, had been introduced to no sport that demanded
at once the patience and the nerve of this stalking of a creature more
subtle, yet at bay perhaps more formidable, than any beast of the
forest. The terms, the comparisons, the very practices of the chase
positively came again into play; there were even moments when
passages of his occasional experience as a sportsman, stirred memories, from his younger time, of moor and mountain and desert,
revived for him—and to the increase of his keenness—by the tremendous force of analogy. He found himself at moments—once he
had placed his single light on some mantel-shelf or in some recess—
stepping back into shelter or shade, effacing himself behind a door
or in an embrasure, as he had sought of old the vantage of rock and
tree; he found himself holding his breath and living in the joy of
the instant, the supreme suspense created by big game alone.

He wasn't afraid (though putting himself the question as he believed gentlemen on Bengal tiger-shoots or in close quarters with the
great bear of the Rockies had been known to confess to having put

it); and this indeed—since here at least he might be frank!—because of the impression, so intimate and so strange, that he himself produced as yet a dread, produced certainly a strain, beyond the
liveliest he was likely to feel. They fell for him into categories, they
fairly became familiar, the signs, for his own perception, of the
alarm his presence and his vigilance created; though leaving him
always to remark, portentously, on his probably having formed a
relation, his probably enjoying a consciousness, unique in the
experience of man. People enough, first and last, had been in terror of apparitions, but who had ever before so turned the tables and
become himself, in the apparitional world, an incalculable terror?
He might have found this sublime had he quite dared to think of
it; but he didn't too much insist, truly, on that side of his privilege.
With habit and repetition he gained to an extraordinary degree the
power to penetrate the dusk of distances and the darkness of corners, to resolve back into their innocence the treacheries of uncertain light, the evil-looking forms taken in the gloom by mere
shadows, by accidents of the air, by shifting effects of perspective;
putting down his dim luminary he could still wander on without
it, pass into other rooms and, only knowing it was there behind
him in case of need, see his way about, visually project for his purpose a comparative clearness. It made him feel, this acquired faculty,
like some monstrous stealthy cat; he wondered if he would have
glared at these moments with large shining yellow eyes, and what
it mightn't verily be, for the poor hard-pressed *alter ego*, to be confronted with such a type.

He liked however the open shutters; he opened everywhere those
Mrs. Muldoon had closed, closing them as carefully afterwards, so
that she shouldn't notice: he liked—oh this he did like, and above
all in the upper rooms!—the sense of the hard silver of the autumn
stars through the window-panes, and scarcely less the flare of the
street-lamps below, the white electric lustre which it would have
taken curtains to keep out. This was human actual social; this was
of the world he had lived in, and he was more at his ease certainly
for the countenance, coldly general and impersonal, that all the
while and in spite of his detachment it seemed to give him. He had
support of course mostly in the rooms at the wide front and the
prolonged side; it failed him considerably in the central shades and
the parts at the back. But if he sometimes, on his rounds, was glad
of his optical reach, so none the less often the rear of the house
affected him as the very jungle of his prey. The place was there more
subdivided; a large "extension" in particular, where small rooms for
servants had been multiplied, abounded in nooks and corners, in
closets and passages, in the ramifications especially of an ample back
staircase over which he leaned, many a time, to look far down—

not deterred from his gravity even while aware that he might, for a spectator, have figured some solemn simpleton playing at hide-and-seek. Outside in fact he might himself make that ironic *rapprochement*; but within the walls, and in spite of the clear windows, his consistency was proof against the cynical light of New York.

It had belonged to that idea of the exasperated consciousness of his victim to become a real test for him; since he had quite put it to himself from the first that, oh distinctly! he could "cultivate" his whole perception. He had felt it as above all open to cultivation —which indeed was but another name for his manner of spending his time. He was bringing it on, bringing it to perfection, by practice; in consequence of which it had grown so fine that he was now aware of impressions, attestations of his general postulate, that couldn't have broken upon him at once. This was the case more specifically with a phenomenon at last quite frequent for him in the upper rooms, the recognition—absolutely unmistakeable, and by a turn dating from a particular hour, his resumption of his campaign after a diplomatic drop, a calculated absence of three nights—of his being definitely followed, tracked at a distance carefully taken and to the express end that he should the less confidently, less arrogantly, appear to himself merely to pursue. It worried, it finally quite broke him up, for it proved, of all the conceivable impressions, the one least suited to his book. He was kept in sight while remaining himself—as regards the essence of his position—sightless, and his only recourse then was in abrupt turns, rapid recoveries of ground. He wheeled about, retracing his steps, as if he might so catch in his face at least the stirred air of some other quick revolution. It was indeed true that his fully dislocalised thought of these manœuvres recalled to him Pantaloon, at the Christmas farce, buffeted and tricked from behind by ubiquitous Harlequin; but it left intact the influence of the conditions themselves each time he was re-exposed to them, so that in fact this association, had he suffered it to become constant, would on a certain side have but ministered to his intenser gravity. He had made, as I have said, to create on the premises the baseless sense of a reprieve, his three absences; and the result of the third was to confirm the after-effect of the second.

On his return, that night—the night succeeding his last intermission—he stood in the hall and looked up the staircase with a certainty more intimate than any he had yet known. "He's *there*, at the top, and waiting—not, as in general, falling back for disappearance. He's holding his ground, and it's the first time—which is a proof, isn't it? that something has happened for him." So Brydon argued with his hand on the banister and his foot on the lowest stair; in which position he felt as never before the air chilled by his logic. He himself turned cold in it, for he seemed of a sudden to know what now was involved. "Harder pressed?—yes, he takes it in, with its thus making clear to him that I've come, as they say, 'to stay.' He finally doesn't like and can't bear it, in the sense, I mean, that his wrath, his menaced interest, now balances with his dread. I've hunted him till he has 'turned': that, up there, is what has happened—he's the fanged or the antlered animal brought at last to bay." There came to him, as I say—but determined by an influence beyond my notation!—the acuteness of this certainty; under which however the next moment he had broken into a sweat that he would as little have consented to attribute to fear as he would have dared immediately to act upon it for enterprise. It marked none the less a prodigious thrill, a thrill that represented sudden dismay, no doubt, but also represented, and with the selfsame throb, the strangest, the most joyous, possibly the next minute almost the proudest, duplication of consciousness.

"He has been dodging, retreating, hiding, but now, worked up to anger, he'll fight!"—this intense impression made a single mouthful, as it were, of terror and applause. But what was wondrous was that the applause, for the felt fact, was so eager, since, if it was his other self he was running to earth, this ineffable identity was thus in the last resort not unworthy of him. It bristled there—somewhere near at hand, however unseen still—as the hunted thing, even as the trodden worm of the adage *must* at last bristle; and Brydon at this instant tasted probably of a sensation more complex than had ever before found itself consistent with sanity. It was as if it would have shamed him that a character so associated with his own should triumphantly succeed in just skulking, should to the end not risk the open, so that the drop of this danger was, on the spot, a great lift of the whole situation. Yet with another rare shift of the same subtlety he was already trying to measure by how much more he himself might now be in peril of fear; so rejoicing that he could, in another form, actively inspire that fear, and simultaneously quaking for the form in which he might passively know it.

The apprehension of knowing it must after a little have grown in him, and the strangest moment of his adventure perhaps, the most memorable or really most interesting, afterwards, of his crisis, was the lapse of certain instants of concentrated conscious *combat*, the sense of a need to hold on to something, even after the manner of a man slipping and slipping on some awful incline; the vivid impulse, above all, to move, to act, to charge, somehow and upon something—to show himself, in a word, that he wasn't afraid. The state of "holding-on" was thus the state to which he was momentarily reduced; if there had been anything, in the great vacancy, to seize, he would presently have been aware of having clutched it as he might under a shock at home have clutched the nearest chair-back. He had been surprised at any rate—of this he *was* aware—into something unprecedented since his original appropriation of the place; he had closed his eyes, held them tight, for a long minute, as with that instinct of dismay and that terror of vision. When he opened them the room, the other contiguous rooms, extraordinarily, seemed lighter—so light, almost, that at first he took the change for day. He stood firm, however that might be, just where he had paused; his resistance had helped him—it was as if there were something he had tided over. He knew after a little what this was—it had been in the imminent danger of flight. He had stiffened his will against going; without this he would have made for the stairs, and it seemed to him that, still with his eyes closed, he would have descended them, would have known how, straight and swiftly, to the bottom.

Well, as he had held out, here he was—still at the top, among the more intricate upper rooms and with the gauntlet of the others, of all the rest of the house, still to run when it should be his time to go. He would go at his time—only at his time: didn't he go every night very much at the same hour? He took out his watch—there was light for that: it was scarcely a quarter past one, and he had never withdrawn so soon. He reached his lodgings for the most part at two—with his walk of a quarter of an hour. He would wait for the last quarter—he wouldn't stir till then; and he kept his watch there with his eyes on it, reflecting while he held it that this deliberate wait, a wait with an effort, which he recognised, would serve perfectly for the attestation he desired to make. It would prove his courage—unless indeed the latter might most be proved by his budging at last from his place. What he mainly felt now was that, since he hadn't originally scuttled, he had his dignities—which had never in his life seemed so many—all to preserve and to carry aloft. This was before him in truth as a physical image, an image almost worthy of an age of greater romance. That remark indeed glimmered for him only to glow the next instant with a finer light; since what age of romance, after all, could have matched either the state of his mind or, "objectively," as they said, the wonder of his situation? The only difference would have been that, brandishing his dignities over his head as in a parchment scroll, he might then—that is in the heroic time—have proceeded downstairs with a drawn sword in his other grasp.

At present, really, the light he had set down on the mantel of the next room would have to figure his sword; which utensil, in the course of a minute, he had taken the requisite number of steps to possess himself of. The door between the rooms was open, and from the second another door opened to a third. These rooms, as he remembered, gave all three upon a common corridor as well, but there was a fourth, beyond them, without issue save through the preceding. To have moved, to have heard his step again, was appreciably a help; though even in recognising this he lingered once more a little by the chimney-piece on which his light had rested. When he next moved, just hesitating where to turn, he found himself considering a circumstance that, after his first and comparatively vague apprehension of it, produced in him the start that often attends some pang of recollection, the violent shock of having ceased happily to forget. He had come into sight of the door in which the brief chain of communication ended and which he now surveyed from the nearer threshold, the one not directly facing it. Placed at some distance to the left of this point, it would have admitted him to the last room of the four, the room without other approach or egress, had it not, to his intimate conviction, been closed *since* his former visitation, the matter probably of a quarter of an hour before. He stared with all his eyes at the wonder of the fact, arrested again where he stood and again holding his breath while he sounded its sense. Surely it had been *subsequently* closed—that is it had been on his previous passage indubitably open!

He took it full in the face that something had happened between —that he couldn't not have noticed before (by which he meant on his original tour of all the rooms that evening) that such a barrier had exceptionally presented itself. He had indeed since that moment undergone an agitation so extraordinary that it might have muddled for him any earlier view; and he tried to convince himself that he might perhaps then have gone into the room and, inadvertently, automatically, on coming out, have drawn the door after him. The difficulty was that this exactly was what he never did; it was against his whole policy, as he might have said, the essence of which was to keep vistas clear. He had them from the first, as he was well aware, quite on the brain: the strange apparition, at the far end of one of them, of his baffled "prey" (which had become by so sharp an irony so little the term now to apply!) was the form of success his imagination had most cherished, projecting into it always a refinement of beauty. He had known fifty times the start of perception that had afterwards dropped; had fifty times gasped to himself "There!" under some fond brief hallucination. The house, as the case stood, admirably lent itself; he might wonder at the taste, the native architecture of the particular time, which could rejoice so in the multiplication of doors—the opposite extreme to the modern, the actual almost complete proscription of them; but it had fairly contributed to provoke this obsession of the presence encountered telescopically, as he might say, focussed and studied in diminishing perspective and as by a rest for the elbow.

It was with these considerations that his present attention was charged—they perfectly availed to make what he saw portentous. He *couldn't,* by any lapse, have blocked that aperture; and if he hadn't, if it was unthinkable, why what else was clear but that there had been another agent? Another agent?—he had been catching, as he felt, a moment back, the very breath of him; but when had he been so close as in this simple, this logical, this completely personal act? It was so logical, that is, that one might have *taken* it for personal; yet for what did Brydon take it, he asked himself, while, softly panting, he felt his eyes almost leave their sockets. Ah this time at last they *were,* the two, the opposed projections of him, in presence; and this time, as much as one would, the question of danger loomed. With it rose, as not before, the question of courage— for what he knew the blank face of the door to say to him was "Show us how much you have!" It stared, it glared back at him with that challenge; it put to him the two alternatives: should he just push it open or not? Oh to have this consciousness was to *think*— and to think, Brydon knew, as he stood there, was, with the lapsing moments, not to have acted! Not to have acted—that was the misery and the pang—was even still not to act; was in fact *all* to feel the thing in another, in a new and terrible way. How long did he pause and how long did he debate? There was presently nothing to measure it; for his vibration had already changed—as just by the effect of its intensity. Shut up there, at bay, defiant, and with the prodigy of the thing palpably proveably *done,* thus giving notice like some stark signboard—under that accession of accent the situation itself had turned; and Brydon at last remarkably made up his mind on what it had turned to.

It had turned altogether to a different admonition; to a supreme hint, for him, of the value of Discretion! This slowly dawned, no doubt—for it could take its time; so perfectly, on his threshold, had he been stayed, so little as yet had he either advanced or retreated. It was the strangest of all things that now when, by his taking ten steps and applying his hand to a latch, or even his shoulder and his knee, if necessary, to a panel, all the hunger of his prime need might have been met, his high curiosity crowned, his unrest assuaged—it was amazing, but it was also exquisite and rare, that insistence should have, at a touch, quite dropped from him. Discretion—he jumped at that; and yet not, verily, at such a pitch, because it saved his nerves or his skin, but because, much more valuably, it saved the situation. When I say he "jumped" at it I feel the consonance of this term with the fact that—at the end indeed of I know not how long—he did move again, he crossed straight to the door. He wouldn't touch it—it seemed now that he might *if* he would: he would only just wait there a little, to show, to prove, that he wouldn't. He had thus another station, close to the thin partition by which revelation was denied him; but with his eyes bent and his hands held off in a mere intensity of stillness. He listened as if there had been something to hear, but this attitude, while it lasted, was his own communication. "If you won't then —good: I spare you and I give up. You affect me as by the appeal positively for pity: you convince me that for reasons rigid and sublime—what do I know?—we both of us should have suffered. I respect them then, and, though moved and privileged as, I believe, it has never been given to man, I retire, I renounce—never, on my honour, to try again. So rest for ever—and let *me!*"

That, for Brydon was the deep sense of this last demonstration —solemn, measured, directed, as he felt it to be. He brought it to a close, he turned away; and now verily he knew how deeply he had been stirred. He retraced his steps, taking up his candle, burnt, he observed, well-nigh to the socket, and marking again, lighten it as he would, the distinctness of his footfall; after which, in a moment, he knew himself at the other side of the house. He did here what he had not yet done at these hours—he opened half a casement, one of those in the front, and let in the air of the night; a thing he would have taken at any time previous for a sharp rupture of his spell. His spell was broken now, and it didn't matter—broken by his concession and his surrender, which made it idle henceforth that he should ever come back. The empty street—its other life so marked even by the great lamplit vacancy—was within call, within touch; he stayed there as to be in it again, high above it though he was still perched; he watched as for some comforting common fact, some vulgar human note, the passage of a scavenger or a thief, some night-bird however base. He would have blessed that sign of life; he would have welcomed positively the slow approach of his friend the policeman, whom he had hitherto only sought to avoid, and was not sure that if the patrol had come into sight he mightn't have felt the impulse to get into relation with it, to hail it, on some pretext, from his fourth floor.

The pretext that wouldn't have been too silly or too compromising, the explanation that would have saved his dignity and kept his name, in such a case, out of the papers, was not definite to him: he was so occupied with the thought of recording his Discretion— as an effect of the vow he had just uttered to his intimate adversary —that the importance of this loomed large and something had overtaken all ironically his sense of proportion. If there had been a ladder applied to the front of the house, even one of the vertiginous perpendiculars employed by painters and roofers and sometimes left standing overnight, he would have managed somehow, astride of the window-sill, to compass by outstretched leg and arm that mode of descent. If there had been some such uncanny thing as he had found in his room at hotels, a workable fire-escape in the form of notched cable or a canvas shoot, he would have availed himself of it as a proof—well, of his present delicacy. He nursed that sentiment, as the question stood, a little in vain, and even—at the end of he scarce knew, once more, how long—found it, as by the action on his mind of the failure of response of the outer world, sinking back to vague anguish. It seemed to him he had waited an age for some stir of the great grim hush; the life of the town was itself under a spell—so unnaturally, up and down the whole prospect of known and rather ugly objects, the blankness and the silence lasted. Had they ever, he asked himself, the hard-faced houses, which had begun to look livid in the dim dawn, had they ever spoken so little to any need of his spirit? Great builded voids, great crowded stillnesses put on, often, in the heart of cities, for the small hours, a sort of sinister mask, and it was of this large collective negation that Brydon presently became conscious—all the more that the break of day was, almost incredibly, now at hand, proving to him what a night he had made of it.

He looked again at his watch, saw what had become of his time-values (he had taken hours for minutes—not, as in other tense situations, minutes for hours) and the strange air of the streets was but the weak, the sullen flush of a dawn in which everything was still locked up. His choked appeal from his own open window had been the sole note of life, and he could but break off at last as for a worse despair. Yet while so deeply demoralised he was capable again of an impulse denoting—at least by his present measure—extraordinary resolution; of retracing his steps to the spot where he had turned cold with the extinction of his last pulse of doubt as to there being in the place another presence than his own. This required an effort strong enough to sicken him; but he had his reason, which overmastered for the moment everything else. There was the whole of the rest of the house to traverse, and how should he screw himself to that if the door he had seen closed were at present open? He could hold to the idea that the closing had practically been for him an act of mercy, a chance offered him to descend, depart, get off the ground and never again profane it. This conception held together, it worked; but what it meant for him depended now clearly on the amount of forbearance his recent action, or rather his recent inaction, had engendered. The image of the "presence," whatever it was, waiting there for him to go—this image had not yet been so concrete for his nerves as when he stopped short of the point at which certainty would have come to him. For, with all his resolution, or more exactly with all his dread, he did stop short—he hung back from really seeing. The risk was too great and his fear too definite: it took at this moment an awful specific form.

He knew—yes, as he had never known anything—that, *should* he see the door open, it would all too abjectly be the end of him. It would mean that the agent of his shame—for his shame was the deep abjection—was once more at large and in general possession; and what glared him thus in the face was the act that this would determine for him. It would send him straight about to the window he had left open, and by that window, be long ladder and dangling rope as absent as they would, he saw himself uncontrollably insanely fatally take his way to the street. The hideous chance of this he at least could avert; but he could only avert it by recoiling in time from assurance. He had the whole house to deal with, this fact was still there; only he now knew that uncertainty alone could start him. He stole back from where he had checked himself—merely to do so was suddenly like safety—and, making blindly for the greater staircase, left gaping rooms and sounding passages behind. Here was the top of the stairs, with a fine large dim descent and three spacious landings to mark off. His instinct was all for mildness, but his feet were harsh on the floors, and, strangely, when he had in a couple of minutes become aware of this, it counted somehow for help. He couldn't have spoken, the tone of his voice would have scared him, and the common conceit or resource of "whistling in the dark" (whether literally or figuratively) have appeared basely vulgar; yet he liked none the less to hear himself go, and when he had reached his first landing—taking it all with no rush, but quite steadily—that stage of success drew from him a gasp of relief.

The house, withal, seemed immense, the scale of space again inordinate; the open rooms, to no one of which his eyes deflected, gloomed in their shuttered state like mouths of caverns; only the high skylight that formed the crown of the deep well created for him a medium in which he could advance, but which might have been, for queerness of colour, some watery under-world. He tried to think of something noble, as that his property was really grand, a splendid possession; but this nobleness took the form too of the clear delight with which he was finally to sacrifice it. They might come in now, the builders, the destroyers—they might come as soon as they would. At the end of two flights he had dropped to another zone, and from the middle of the third, with only one more left, he recognised the influence of the lower windows, of half-drawn blinds, of the occasional gleam of street-lamps, of the glazed spaces of the vestibule. This was the bottom of the sea, which showed an illumination of its own and which he even saw paved—when at a given moment he drew up to sink a long look over the banisters— with the marble squares of his childhood. By that time indubitably he felt, as he might have said in a commoner cause, better; it had allowed him to stop and draw breath, and the ease increased with the sight of the old black-and-white slabs. But what he most felt was that now surely, with the element of impunity pulling him as by hard firm hands, the case was settled for what he might have seen above had he dared that last look. The closed door, blessedly remote now, was still closed—and he had only in short to reach that of the house.

He came down further, he crossed the passage forming the access to the last flight; and if here again he stopped an instant it was almost for the sharpness of the thrill of assured escape. It made him shut his eyes—which opened again to the straight slope of the remainder of the stairs. Here was impunity still, but impunity almost excessive; inasmuch as the side-lights and the high fan-tracery of the entrance were glimmering straight into the hall; an appearance produced, he the next instant saw, by the fact that the vestibule gaped wide, that the hinged halves of the inner door had been thrown far back. Out of that again the *question* sprang at him, making his eyes, as he felt, half-start from his head, as they had done, at the top of the house, before the sign of the other door. If he had left that one open, hadn't he left this one closed, and wasn't he now in *most* immediate presence of some inconceivable occult activity? It was as sharp, the question, as a knife in his side, but the answer hung fire still and seemed to lose itself in the vague darkness to which the thin admitted dawn, glimmering archwise over the whole outer door, made a semicircular margin, a cold silvery nimbus that seemed to play a little as he looked—to shift and expand and contract.

It was as if there had been something within it, protected by indistinctness and corresponding in extent with the opaque surface behind, the painted panels of the last barrier to his escape, of which the key was in his pocket. The indistinctness mocked him even while he stared, affected him as somehow shrouding or challenging certitude, so that after faltering an instant on his step he let himself go with the sense that here *was* at last something to meet, to touch, to take, to know—something all unnatural and dreadful, but to advance upon which was the condition for him either of liberation or of supreme defeat. The penumbra, dense and dark, was the virtual screen of a figure which stood in it as still as some image erect in a niche or as some black-vizored sentinel guarding a treasure. Brydon was to know afterwards, was to recall and make out, the particular thing he had believed during the rest of his descent. He saw, in its great grey glimmering margin, the central vagueness diminish, and he felt it to be taking the very form toward which, for so many days, the passion of his curiosity had yearned. It gloomed, it loomed, it was something, it was somebody, the prodigy of a personal presence.

Rigid and conscious, spectral yet human, a man of his own substance and stature waited there to measure himself with his power to dismay. This only could it be—this only till he recognised, with his advance, that what made the face dim was the pair of raised hands that covered it and in which, so far from being offered in defiance, it was buried as for dark deprecation. So Brydon, before him, took him in; with every fact of him now, in the higher light, hard and acute—his planted stillness, his vivid truth, his grizzled bent head and white masking hands, his queer actuality of evening-dress, of dangling double eye-glass, of gleaming silk lappet and white linen, of pearl button and gold watch-guard and polished shoe. No portrait by a great modern master could have presented him with more intensity, thrust him out of his frame with more art, as if there had been "treatment," of the consummate sort, in his every shade and salience. The revulsion, for our friend, had become, before he knew it, immense—this drop, in the act of apprehension, to the sense of his adversary's inscrutable manœuvre. That meaning at least, while he gaped, it offered him; for he could but gape at his other self in this other anguish, gape as a proof that *he*, standing there for the achieved, the enjoyed, the triumphant life, couldn't be faced in his triumph. Wasn't the proof in the splendid covering hands, strong and completely spread?—so spread and so intentional that, in spite of a special verity that surpassed every other, the fact that one of these hands had lost two fingers, which were reduced to stumps, as if accidentally shot away, the face was effectually guarded and saved.

"Saved," though, *would* it be?—Brydon breathed his wonder till the very impunity of his attitude and the very insistence of his eyes produced, as he felt, a sudden stir which showed the next instant as a deeper portent, while the head raised itself, the betrayal of a braver purpose. The hands, as he looked, began to move, to open; then, as if deciding in a flash, dropped from the face and left it uncovered and presented. Horror, with the sight, had leaped into Brydon's throat, gasping there in a sound he couldn't utter; for the bared identity was too hideous as *his*, and his glare was the passion of his protest. The face, *that* face, Spencer Brydon's?—he searched it still, but looking away from it in dismay and denial, falling straight from his height of sublimity. It was unknown, inconceivable, awful, disconnected from any possibility—! He had been "sold," he inwardly moaned, stalking such game as this: the presence before him was a presence, the horror within him a horror, but the waste of his nights had been only grotesque and the success of his adventure an irony. Such an identity fitted his at *no* point, made its alternative monstrous. A thousand times yes, as it came upon him nearer now—the face was the face of a stranger. It came upon him nearer now, quite as one of those expanding fantastic images projected by the magic lantern of childhood; for the stranger, whoever he might be, evil, odious, blatant, vulgar, had advanced as for aggression, and he knew himself give ground. Then harder pressed still, sick with the force of his shock, and falling back as under the hot breath and the roused passion of a life larger than his own, a rage of personality before which his own collapsed, he felt the whole vision turn to darkness and his very feet give way. His head went round; he was going; he had gone.

III

What had next brought him back, clearly—though after how long?—was Mrs. Muldoon's voice, coming to him from quite near, from so near that he seemed presently to see her as kneeling on the ground before him while he lay looking up at her; himself not wholly on the ground, but half-raised and upheld—conscious, yes, of tenderness of support and, more particularly, of a head pillowed in extraordinary softness and faintly refreshing fragrance. He considered, he wondered, his wit but half at his service; then another face intervened, bending more directly over him, and he finally knew that Alice Staverton had made her lap an ample and perfect cushion to him, and that she had to this end seated herself on the lowest degree of the staircase, the rest of his long person remaining stretched on his old black-and-white slabs. They were cold, these marble squares of his youth; but *he* somehow was not, in this rich return of consciousness—the most wonderful hour, little by little, that he had ever known, leaving him, as it did, so gratefully, so abysmally passive, and yet as with a treasure of intelligence waiting all round him for quiet appropriation; dissolved, he might call it, in the air of the place and producing the golden glow of a late autumn afternoon. He had come back, yes—come back from further away than any man but himself had ever travelled; but it was strange how with this sense what he had come back *to* seemed really the great thing, and as if his prodigious journey had been all for the sake of it. Slowly but surely his consciousness grew, his vision of his state thus completing itself: he had been miraculously *carried* back—lifted and carefully borne as from where he had been picked up, the uttermost end of an interminable grey passage. Even with this he was suffered to rest, and what had now brought him to knowledge was the break in the long mild motion.

It had brought him to knowledge, to knowledge—yes, this was the beauty of his state; which came to resemble more and more that of a man who has gone to sleep on some news of a great inheritance, and then, after dreaming it away, after profaning it with matters strange to it, has waked up again to serenity of certitude and has only to lie and watch it grow. This was the drift of his patience— that he had only to let it shine on him. He must moreover, with intermissions, still have been lifted and borne; since why and how else should he have known himself, later on, with the afternoon glow intenser, no longer at the foot of his stairs—situated as these now seemed at that dark other end of his tunnel—but on a deep window-bench of his high saloon, over which had been spread, couch-fashion, a mantle of soft stuff lined with grey fur that was familiar to his eyes and that one of his hands kept fondly feeling as for its pledge of truth. Mrs. Muldoon's face had gone, but the other, the second he had recognised, hung over him in a way that showed how he was still propped and pillowed. He took it all in, and the more he took it the more it seemed to suffice: he was as much at peace as if he had had food and drink. It was the two women who had found him, on Mrs. Muldoon's having plied, at her usual hour, her latch-key—and on her having above all arrived while Miss Staverton still lingered near the house. She had been turning away, all anxiety, from worrying the vain bell-handle—her calculation having been of the hour of the good woman's visit; but the latter, blessedly, had come up while she was still there, and they had entered together. He had then lain, beyond the vestibule, very much as he was lying now—quite, that is, as he appeared to have fallen, but all so wondrously without bruise or gash; only in a depth of stupor. What he most took in, however, at present, with the steadier clearance, was that Alice Staverton had for a long unspeakable moment not doubted he was dead.

"It must have been that I *was*." He made it out as she held him. "Yes—I can only have died. You brought me literally to life. Only," he wondered, his eyes rising to her, "only, in the name of all the benedictions, how?"

It took her but an instant to bend her face and kiss him, and something in the manner of it, and in the way her hands clasped and locked his head while he felt the cool charity and virtue of her lips, something in all this beatitude somehow answered everything. "And now I keep you," she said.

"Oh keep me, keep me!" he pleaded while her face still hung over him: in response to which it dropped again and stayed close, clingingly close. It was the seal of their situation—of which he tasted the impress for a long blissful moment in silence. But he came back. "Yet how did you know—?"

"I was uneasy. You were to have come, you remember—and you had sent no word."

"Yes, I remember—I was to have gone to you at one today." It caught on to their "old" life and relation—which were so near and so far. "I was still out there in my strange darkness—where was it, what was it? I must have stayed there so long." He could but wonder at the depth and the duration of his swoon.

"Since last night?" she asked with a shade of fear for her possible indiscretion.

"Since this morning—it must have been: the cold dim dawn of today. Where have I been," he vaguely wailed, "where have I been?" He felt her hold him close, and it was as if this helped him now to make in all security his mild moan. "What a long dark day!"

All in her tenderness she had waited a moment. "In the cold dim dawn?" she quavered.

But he had already gone on piecing together the parts of the whole prodigy. "As I didn't turn up you came straight—?"

She barely cast about. "I went first to your hotel—where they told me of your absence. You had dined out last evening and hadn't been back since. But they appeared to know you had been at your club."

"So you had the idea of *this*—?"

"Of what?" she asked in a moment.

"Well—of what has happened."

"I believed at least you'd have been here. I've known, all along," she said, "that you've been coming."

" 'Known' it—?"

"Well, I've believed it. I said nothing to you after that talk we had a month ago—but I felt sure. I knew you *would*," she declared.

"That I'd persist, you mean?"

"That you'd see him."

"Ah but I didn't!" cried Brydon with his long wail. "There's somebody—an awful beast; whom I brought, too horribly, to bay. But it's not me."

At this she bent over him again, and her eyes were in his eyes. "No—it's not you." And it was as if, while her face hovered, he might have made out in it, hadn't it been so near, some particular meaning blurred by a smile. "No, thank heaven," she repeated— "it's not you! Of course it wasn't to have been."

"Ah but it *was*," he gently insisted. And he stared before him now as he had been staring for so many weeks. "I was to have known myself."

"You couldn't!" she returned consolingly. And then reverting, and as if to account further for what she had herself done, "But it wasn't only *that*, that you hadn't been at home," she went on. "I waited till the hour at which we had found Mrs. Muldoon that day of my going with you; and she arrived, as I've told you, while, failing to bring any one to the door, I lingered in my despair on the steps. After a little, if she hadn't come, by such a mercy, I should have found means to hunt her up. But it wasn't," said Alice Staverton, as if once more with her fine intention—"it wasn't only that."

His eyes, as he lay, turned back to her. "What more then?"

She met it, the wonder she had stirred. "In the cold dim dawn, you say? Well, in the cold dim dawn of this morning I too saw you."

"Saw *me*—?"

"Saw *him*," said Alice Staverton. "It must have been at the same moment."

He lay an instant taking it in—as if he wished to be quite reasonable. "At the same moment?"

"Yes—in my dream again, the same one I've named to you. He came back to me. Then I knew it for a sign. He had come to you."

At this Brydon raised himself; he had to see her better. She helped him when she understood his movement, and he sat up, steadying himself beside her there on the window-bench and with his right hand grasping her left. "*He* didn't come to me."

"You came to yourself," she beautifully smiled.

"Ah I've come to myself now—thanks to you, dearest. But this brute, with his awful face—this brute's a black stranger. He's none of *me*, even as I *might* have been," Brydon sturdily declared.

But she kept the clearness that was like the breath of infallibility. "Isn't the whole point that you'd have been different?"

He almost scowled for it. "As different as *that*—?"

Her look again was more beautiful to him than the things of this world. "Haven't you exactly wanted to know *how* different? So this morning," she said, "you appeared to me."

"Like *him*?"

"A black stranger!"

"Then how did you know it was I?"

"Because, as I told you weeks ago, my mind, my imagination, had worked so over what you might, what you mightn't have been —to show you, you see, how I've thought of you. In the midst of that you came to me—that my wonder might be answered. So I knew," she went on; "and believed that, since the question held you too so fast, as you told me that day, you too would see for yourself. And when this morning I again saw I knew it would be because you had—and also then, from the first moment, because you somehow wanted me. *He* seemed to tell me of that. So why," she strangely smiled, "shouldn't I like him?"

It brought Spencer Brydon to his feet. "You 'like' that horror—?"

"I *could* have liked him. And to me," she said, "he was no horror. I had accepted him."

" 'Accepted'—?" Brydon oddly sounded.

"Before, for the interest of his difference—yes. And as *I* didn't disown him, as *I* knew him—which you at last, confronted with him in his difference, so cruelly didn't, my dear—well, he must have been, you see, less dreadful to me. And it may have pleased him that I pitied him."

She was beside him on her feet, but still holding his hand—still with her arm supporting him. But though it all brought for him thus a dim light, "You 'pitied' him?" he grudgingly, resentfully asked.

"He has been unhappy; he has been ravaged," she said.

"And haven't *I* been unhappy? Am not *I*—you've only to look at me!—ravaged?"

"Ah I don't say I like him *better*," she granted after a thought. "But he's grim, he's worn—and things have happened to him. He doesn't make shift, for sight, with your charming monocle."

"No"—it struck Brydon: "I couldn't have sported mine 'downtown.' They'd have guyed me there."

"His great convex pince-nez—I saw it, I recognised the kind —is for his poor ruined sight. And his poor right hand—!"

"Ah!" Brydon winced—whether for his proved identity or for his lost fingers. Then, "He has a million a year," he lucidly added. "But he hasn't *you*."

"And he isn't—no, he isn't—*you!*" she murmured as he drew her to his breast.

1908, 1909

The Art of Fiction[1]

I should not have affixed so comprehensive a title to these few remarks, necessarily wanting in any completeness upon a subject the full consideration of which would carry us far, did I not seem to discover a pretext for my temerity in the interesting pamphlet lately published under this name by Mr. Walter Besant. Mr. Bes-

1. First published in *Longman's Magazine* for September, 1884. It was reprinted without James's authorization in a pamphlet, together with Sir Walter Besant's essay of the same title, in 1885. James reprinted it in his volume of essays, *Partial Portraits* (1888), making minor changes in the text. The latter text is used here. Besant (1836–1901), an English novelist and critic, had first given his ideas in a lecture before a general audience at the Royal Institution, London, in April, 1884. His essay expressed three general propositions: (1) that fiction, like painting or sculpture, is an art; (2) that it is governed by certain rules which can be learned; and (3) that the rules can be applied only by those with natural gifts. In *Longman's Magazine* for December, 1884, Robert Louis Stevenson published an essay, "A Humble Remonstrance," using Besant's and James's views as a starting point to express his belief that the novel is not like life, but different from it and consisting in "romance" or adventure or passion. Stevenson's essay began a correspondence and lifelong friendship with James during which each man expressed great admiration for the other's work. (See *Henry James and Robert Louis Stevenson, A Record of Friendship and Criticism*, ed. J. A. Smith, 1948.)

ant's lecture at the Royal Institution—the original form of his pamphlet—appears to indicate that many persons are interested in the art of fiction, and are not indifferent to such remarks, as those who practise it may attempt to make about it. I am therefore anxious not to lose the benefit of this favourable association, and to edge in a few words under cover of the attention which Mr. Besant is sure to have excited. There is something very encouraging in his having put into form certain of his ideas on the mystery of story-telling.

It is a proof of life and curiosity—curiosity on the part of the brotherhood of novelists as well as on the part of their readers. Only a short time ago it might have been supposed that the English novel was not what the French call *discutable*. It had no air of having a theory, a conviction, a consciousness of itself behind it—of being the expression of an artistic faith, the result of choice and comparison. I do not say it was necessarily the worse for that: it would take much more courage than I possess to intimate that the form of the novel as Dickens and Thackeray (for instance) saw it had any taint of incompleteness. It was, however, *naïf* (if I may help myself out with another French word); and evidently if it be destined to suffer in any way for having lost its *naïveté* it has now an idea of making sure of the corresponding advantages. During the period I have alluded to there was a comfortable, good-humoured feeling abroad that a novel is a novel, as a pudding is a pudding, and that our only business with it could be to swallow it. But within a year or two, for some reason or other, there have been signs of returning animation —the era of discussion would appear to have been to a certain extent opened. Art lives upon discussion, upon experiment, upon variety of attempt, upon the exchange of views and the comparison of standpoints; and there is a presumption that those times when no one has anything particular to say about it, and has no reason to give for practice or preference, though they may be times of honour, are not times of development—are times, possibly even, a little of dulness. The successful application of any art is a delightful spectacle, but the theory too is interesting; and though there is a great deal of the latter without the former I suspect there has never been a genuine success that has not had a latent core of conviction. Discussion, suggestion, formulation, these things are fertilising when they are frank and sincere. Mr. Besant has set an excellent example in saying what he thinks, for his part, about the way in which fiction should be written, as well as about the way in which it should be published; for his view of the "art," carried on into an appendix, covers that too. Other labourers in the same field will doubtless take up the argument, they will give it the light of their experience, and the effect will surely be to make our interest in the novel a little more what it had for some time threatened to fail to be—a serious, active, inquiring interest, under protection of which this delightful study may, in moments of confidence, venture to say a little more what it thinks of itself.

It must take itself seriously for the public to take it so. The old superstition about fiction being "wicked" has doubtless died out in England; but the spirit of it lingers in a certain oblique regard directed toward any story which does not more or less admit that it is only a joke. Even the most jocular novel feels in some degree the weight of the proscription that was formerly directed against literary levity: the jocularity does not always succeed in passing for orthodoxy. It is still expected, though perhaps people are ashamed to say it, that a production which is after all only a "make-believe" (for what else is a "story"?) shall be in some degree apologetic— shall renounce the pretension of attempting really to represent life. This, of course, any sensible, wide-awake story declines to do, for it quickly perceives that the tolerance granted to it on such a condition is only an attempt to stifle it disguised in the form of generosity. The old evangelical hostility to the novel, which was as explicit as it was narrow, and which regarded it as little less favourable to our immortal part than a stage-play, was in reality far less insulting. The only reason for the existence of a novel is that it does attempt to represent life. When it relinquishes this attempt, the same attempt that we see on the canvas of the painter, it will have arrived at a very strange pass. It is not expected of the picture that it will make itself humble in order to be forgiven; and the analogy between the art of the painter and the art of the novelist is, so far as I am able to see, complete. Their inspiration is the same, their process (allowing for the different quality of the vehicle) is the same, their success is the same. They may learn from each other, they may explain and sustain each other. Their cause is the same, and the honour of one is the honour of another. The Mahometans think a picture an unholy thing, but it is a long time since any Christian did, and it is therefore the more odd that in the Christian mind the traces (dissimulated though they may be) of a suspicion of the sister art should linger to this day. The only effectual way to lay it to rest is to emphasise the analogy to which I just alluded —to insist on the fact that as the picture is reality, so the novel is history. That is the only general description (which does it justice) that we may give of the novel. But history also is allowed to represent life; it is not, any more than painting, expected to apologise. The subject-matter of fiction is stored up likewise in documents and records, and if it will not give itself away, as they say in California, it must speak with assurance, with the tone of the historian. Certain accomplished novelists have a habit of giving themselves away which must often bring tears to the eyes of people who take their fiction seriously. I was lately struck, in reading over many pages of Anthony Trollope, with his want of discretion in this particular. In a digression, a parenthesis or an aside, he concedes to the reader that he and this trusting friend are only "making believe." He admits that the events he narrates have not really happened, and that he can give his narrative any turn the reader may like best. Such a betrayal of a sacred office seems to me, I confess, a terrible crime; it is what I mean by the attitude of apology, and it shocks me every whit as much in Trollope as it would have shocked me in Gibbon or Macaulay. It implies that the novelist is less occupied in looking for the truth (the truth, of course I mean, that he assumes, the premises that we must grant him, whatever they may be), than the historian, and in doing so it deprives him at a stroke of all his standing-room. To represent and illustrate the past, the actions of men, is the task of either writer, and the only difference that I can see is, in proportion as he succeeds, to the honour of the novelist, consisting as it does in his having more difficulty in collecting his evidence, which is so far from being purely literary. It seems to me to give him a great character, the fact that he has at once so much in common with the philosopher and the painter; this double analogy is a magnificent heritage.

It is of all this evidently that Mr. Besant is full when he insists upon the fact that fiction is one of the *fine* arts, deserving in its turn of all the honours and emoluments that have hitherto been reserved for the successful profession of music, poetry, painting, architecture. It is impossible to insist too much on so important a truth, and the place that Mr. Besant demands for the work of the novelist may be represented, a trifle less abstractly, by saying that he demands not only that it shall be reputed artistic, but that it shall be reputed very artistic indeed. It is excellent that he should have struck this note, for his doing so indicates that there was need of it, that his proposition may be to many people a novelty. One rubs one's eyes at the thought; but the rest of Mr. Besant's essay confirms the revelation. I suspect in truth that it would be possible to confirm it still further, and that one would not be far wrong in saying that in addition to the people to whom it has never occurred that a novel ought to be artistic, there are a great many others who, if this principle were urged upon them, would be filled with an indefinable mistrust. They would find it difficult to explain their repugnance, but it would operate strongly to put them on their guard. "Art," in our Protestant communities, where so many things have got so strangely twisted about, is supposed in certain circles to have some vaguely injurious effect upon those who make it an important consideration, who let it weigh in the balance. It is assumed to be opposed in some mysterious manner to morality, to amusement, to instruction. When it is embodied in the work of the painter (the sculptor is another affair!) you know what it is: it stands there before you, in the honesty of pink and green and a gilt frame; you can see the worst of it at a glance, and you can be on your guard. But when it is introduced into literature it becomes more insidious—there is danger of its hurting you before you know it. Literature should be either instructive or amusing, and there is in many minds an impression that these artistic preoccupations, the search for form, contribute to neither end, interfere indeed with both. They are too frivolous to be edifying, and too serious to be diverting; and they are moreover priggish and paradoxical and super-fluous. That, I think, represents the manner in which the latent thought of many people who read novels as an exercise in skipping would explain itself if it were to become articulate. They would argue, of course, that a novel ought to be "good," but they would interpret this term in a fashion of their own, which indeed would vary considerably from one critic to another. One would say that being good means representing virtuous and aspiring characters, placed in prominent positions; another would say that it depends on a "happy ending," on a distribution at the last of prizes, pen-sions, husbands, wives, babies, millions, appended paragraphs, and cheerful remarks. Another still would say that it means being full of incident and movement, so that we shall wish to jump ahead, to see who was the mysterious stranger, and if the stolen will was ever found, and shall not be distracted from this pleasure by any tiresome analysis or "description." But they would all agree that the "artistic" idea would spoil some of their fun. One would hold it accountable for all the description, another would see it revealed in the absence of sympathy. Its hostility to a happy ending would be evident, and it might even in some cases render any ending at all impossible. The "ending" of a novel is, for many persons, like that of a good dinner, a course of dessert and ices, and the artist in fiction is regarded as a sort of meddlesome doctor who forbids agreeable aftertastes. It is therefore true that this conception of Mr. Besant's of the novel as a superior form encounters not only a nega-tive but a positive indifference. It matters little that as a work of art it should really be as little or as much of its essence to supply happy endings, sympathetic characters, and an objective tone, as if it were a work of mechanics: the association of ideas, however incongruous, might easily be too much for it if an eloquent voice were not sometimes raised to call attention to the fact that it is at once as free and as serious a branch of literature as any other.

Certainly this might sometimes be doubted in presence of the enormous number of works of fiction that appeal to the credulity of our generation, for it might easily seem that there could be no great character in a commodity so quickly and easily produced. It must be admitted that good novels are much compromised by bad ones, and that the field at large suffers discredit from overcrowding. I think, however, that this injury is only superficial, and that the superabundance of written fiction proves nothing against the principle itself. It has been vulgarised, like all other kinds of literature, like everything else to-day, and it has proved more than some kinds accessible to vulgarisation. But there is as much difference as there ever was between a good novel and a bad one: the bad is swept with all the daubed canvases and spoiled marble into some unvisited limbo, or infinite rubbish-yard beneath the back-windows of the world, and the good subsists and emits its light and stimulates our desire for perfection. As I shall take the liberty of making but a single criticism of Mr. Besant, whose tone is so full of the love of his art, I may as well have done with it at once. He seems to me to mistake in attempting to say so definitely beforehand what sort of an affair the good novel will be. To indicate the danger of such an error as that has been the purpose of these few pages; to suggest that certain traditions on the subject, applied *a priori*, have already had much to answer for, and that the good health of an art which undertakes so immediately to reproduce life must demand that it be perfectly free. It lives upon exercise, and the very meaning of exercise is freedom. The only obligation to which in advance we may hold a novel, without incurring the accusation of being arbitrary, is that it be interesting. That general responsibility rests upon it, but it is the only one I can think of. The ways in which it is at liberty to accomplish this result (of interesting us) strike me as innumerable, and such as can only suffer from being marked out or fenced in by prescription. They are as various as the temperament of man, and they are successful in proportion as they reveal a particular mind, different from others. A novel is in its broadest definition a personal, a direct impression of life: that, to begin with, constitutes its value, which is greater or less according to the intensity of the impression. But there will be no intensity at all, and therefore no value, unless there is freedom to feel and say. The tracing of a line to be followed, of a tone to be taken, of a form to be filled out, is a limitation of that freedom and a suppression of the very thing that we are most curious about. The form, it seems to me, is to be appreciated after the fact; then the author's choice has been made, his standard has been indicated; then we can follow lines and directions and compare tones and resemblances. Then in a word we can enjoy one of the most charming of pleasures, we can estimate quality, we can apply the test of execution. The execution belongs to the author alone; it is what is most personal to him, and we measure him by that. The advantage, the luxury, as well as the torment and responsibility of the novelist, is that there is no limit to what he may attempt as an executant—no limit to his possible experiments, efforts, discoveries, successes. Here it is especially that he works, step by step, like his brother of the brush, of whom we may always say that he has painted his picture in a manner best known to himself. His manner is his secret, not necessarily a jealous one. He cannot disclose it as a general thing if he would; he would be at a loss to teach it to others. I say this with a due recollection of having insisted on the community of method of the artist who paints a picture and the artist who writes a novel. The painter *is* able to teach the rudiments of his practice, and it is possible, from the study of good work (granted the aptitude), both to learn how to paint and to learn how to write. Yet it remains true, without injury to the *rapprochement*,[2] that the literary artist would be obliged to say to his pupil much more than the other, "Ah, well, you must do it as you can!" It is a question of degree, a matter of delicacy. If there are exact sciences, there are also exact arts, and the grammar of painting is so much more definite that it makes the difference.

I ought to add, however, that if Mr. Besant says at the beginning of his essay that the "laws of fiction may be laid down and taught with as much precision and exactness as the laws of harmony, perspective, and proportion," he mitigates what might appear to be an extravagance by applying his remark to "general" laws, and by expressing most of these rules in a manner with which it would certainly be unaccommodating to disagree. That the novelist must write from his experience, that his "characters must be real and such as might be met with in actual life"; that "a young lady brought up in a quiet country village should avoid descriptions of garrison life," and "a writer whose friends and personal experiences belong to the lower middle-class should carefully avoid introducing his characters into society"; that one should enter one's notes in a common-place book; that one's figures should be clear in outline; that making them clear by some trick of speech or of carriage is a bad method, and "describing them at length" is a worse one; that English Fiction should have a "conscious moral purpose"; that "it is almost impossible to estimate too highly the value of careful workmanship— that is, of style"; that "the most important point of all is the story," that "the story is everything": these are principles with most of which it is surely impossible not to sympathise. That remark about the lower middle-class writer and his knowing his place is perhaps rather chilling; but for the rest I should find it difficult to dissent from any one of these recommendations. At the same time, I should find it difficult positively to assent to them, with the exception, per-

2. The "analogy" (i.e., between painting and writing).

haps, of the injunction as to entering one's notes in a common-place book. They scarcely seem to me to have the quality that Mr. Besant attributes to the rules of the novelist—the "precision and exactness" of "the laws of harmony, perspective, and proportion." They are suggestive, they are even inspiring, but they are not exact, though they are doubtless as much so as the case admits of: which is a proof of that liberty of interpretation for which I just contended. For the value of these different injunctions—so beautiful and so vague— is wholly in the meaning one attaches to them. The characters, the situation, which strike one as real will be those that touch and interest one most, but the measure of reality is very difficult to fix. The reality of Don Quixote or of Mr. Micawber is a very delicate shade; it is a reality so coloured by the author's vision that, vivid as it may be, one would hesitate to propose it as a model: one would expose one's self to some very embarrassing questions on the part of a pupil. It goes without saying that you will not write a good novel unless you possess the sense of reality; but it will be difficult to give you a recipe for calling that sense into being. Humanity is immense, and reality has a myriad forms; the most one can affirm is that some of the flowers of fiction have the odour of it, and others have not; as for telling you in advance how your nosegay should be composed, that is another affair. It is equally excellent and inconclusive to say that one must write from experience; to our suppositious aspirant such a declaration might savour of mockery. What kind of experience is intended, and where does it begin and end? Experience is never limited, and it is never complete; it is an immense sensibility, a kind of huge spiderweb of the finest silken threads suspended in the chamber of consciousness, and catching every air-borne particle in its tissue. It is the very atmosphere of the mind; and when the mind is imaginative—much more when it happens to be that of a man of genius—it takes to itself the faintest hints of life, it converts the very pulses of the air into revelations. The young lady living in a village has only to be a damsel upon whom nothing is lost to make it quite unfair (as it seems to me) to declare to her that she shall have nothing to say about the military. Greater miracles have been seen than that, imagination assisting, she should speak the truth about some of these gentlemen. I remember an English novelist,[3] a woman of genius, telling me that she was much commended for the impression she had managed to give in one of her tales of the nature and way of life of the French Protestant youth. She had been asked where she learned so much about this recondite being, she had been congratulated on her peculiar opportunities. These opportunities consisted in her having

---

3. The novelist was Anne Thackeray Ritchie; her novel was *The Story of Elizabeth,* published in *Cornhill* magazine (1862–63).

once, in Paris, as she ascended a staircase, passed an open door where, in the household of a *pasteur*, some of the young Protestants were seated at table round a finished meal. The glimpse made a picture; it lasted only a moment, but that moment was experience. She had got her direct personal impression, and she turned out her type. She knew what youth was, and what Protestantism; she also had the advantage of having seen what it was to be French, so that she converted these ideas into a concrete image and produced a reality. Above all, however, she was blessed with the faculty which when you give it an inch takes an ell, and which for the artist is a much greater source of strength than any accident of residence or of place in the social scale. The power to guess the unseen from the seen, to trace the implication of things, to judge the whole piece by the pattern, the condition of feeling life in general so completely that you are well on your way to knowing any particular corner of it—this cluster of gifts may also be said to constitute experience, and they occur in country and in town, and in the most differing stages of education. If experience consists of impressions, it may be said that impressions *are* experience, just as (have we not seen it?) they are the very air we breathe. Therefore, if I should certainly say to a novice, "Write from experience and experience only," I should feel that this was rather a tantalising monition if I were not careful immediately to add, "Try to be one of the people on whom nothing is lost!"

I am far from intending by this to minimise the importance of exactness—of truth of detail. One can speak best from one's own taste, and I may therefore venture to say that the air of reality (solidity of specification) seems to me to be the supreme virtue of a novel—the merit on which all its other merits (including that conscious moral purpose of which Mr. Besant speaks) helplessly and submissively depend. If it be not there they are all as nothing, and if these be there, they owe their effect to the success with which the author has produced the illusion of life. The cultivation of this success, the study of this exquisite process, form, to my taste, the beginning and the end of the art of the novelist. They are his inspiration, his despair, his reward, his torment, his delight. It is here in very truth that he competes with life; it is here that he competes with his brother the painter in *his* attempt to render the look of things, the look that conveys their meaning, to catch the colour, the relief, the expression, the surface, the substance of the human spectacle. It is in regard to this that Mr. Besant is well inspired when he bids him take notes. He cannot possibly take too many, he cannot possibly take enough. All life solicits him, and to "render" the simplest surface, to produce the most momentary illusion, is a very complicated business. His case would be easier, and the rule would be more exact, if Mr. Besant had been able to tell him what notes to take. But this, I fear, he can never learn in any manual; it is the business of his life. He has to take a great many in order to select a few, he has to work them up as he can, and even the guides and philosophers who might have most to say to him must leave him alone when it comes to the application of precepts, as we leave the painter in communion with his palette. That his characters "must be clear in outline," as Mr. Besant says—he feels that down to his boots; but how he shall make them so is a secret between his good angel and himself. It would be absurdly simple if he could be taught that a great deal of "description" would make them so, or that on the contrary the absence of description and the cultivation of dialogue, or the absence of dialogue and the multiplication of "incident," would rescue him from his difficulties. Nothing, for instance, is more possible than that he be of a turn of mind for which this odd, literal opposition of description and dialogue, incident and description, has little meaning and light. People often talk of these things as if they had a kind of internecine distinctness, instead of melting into each other at every breath, and being intimately associated parts of one general effort of expression. I cannot imagine composition existing in a series of blocks, nor conceive, in any novel worth discussing at all, of a passage of description that is not in its intention narrative, a passage of dialogue that is not in its intention descriptive, a touch of truth of any sort that does not partake of the nature of incident, or an incident that derives its interest from any other source than the general and only source of the success of a work of art—that of being illustrative. A novel is a living thing, all one and continuous, like any other organism, and in proportion as it lives will it be found, I think, that in each of the parts there is something of each of the other parts. The critic who over the close texture of a finished work shall pretend to trace a geography of items will mark some frontiers as artificial, I fear, as any that have been known to history. There is an old-fashioned distinction between the novel of character and the novel of incident which must have cost many a smile to the intending fabulist who was keen about his work. It appears to me as little to the point as the equally celebrated distinction between the novel and the romance—to answer as little to any reality. There are bad novels and good novels, as there are bad pictures and good pictures; but that is the only distinction in which I see any meaning, and I can as little imagine speaking of a novel of character as I can imagine speaking of a picture of character. When one says picture one says of character, when one says novel one says of incident, and the terms may be transposed at will. What is character but the determination of incident? What is incident but the

1556 · *Henry James*

illustration of character? What is either a picture or a novel that is *not* of character? What else do we seek in it and find in it? It is an incident for a woman to stand up with her hand resting on a table and look out at you in a certain way; or if it be not an incident I think it will be hard to say what it is. At the same time it is an expression of character. If you say you don't see it (character in *that—allons donc!*), this is exactly what the artist who has reasons of his own for thinking he *does* see it undertakes to show you. When a young man makes up his mind that he has not faith enough after all to enter the church as he intended, that is an incident, though you may not hurry to the end of the chapter to see whether perhaps he doesn't change once more. I do not say that these are extraordinary or startling incidents. I do not pretend to estimate the degree of interest proceeding from them, for this will depend upon the skill of the painter. It sounds almost puerile to say that some incidents are intrinsically much more important than others, and I need not take this precaution after having professed my sympathy for the major ones in remarking that the only classification of the novel that I can understand is into that which has life and that which has it not.

The novel and the romance, the novel of incident and that of character—these clumsy separations appear to me to have been made by critics and readers for their own convenience, and to help them out of some of their occasional queer predicaments, but to have little reality or interest for the producer, from whose point of view it is of course that we are attempting to consider the art of fiction. The case is the same with another shadowy category which Mr. Besant apparently is disposed to set up—that of the "modern English novel"; unless indeed it be that in this matter he has fallen into an accidental confusion of standpoints. It is not quite clear whether he intends the remarks in which he alludes to it to be didactic or historical. It is as difficult to suppose a person intending to write a modern English as to suppose him writing an ancient English novel: that is a label which begs the question. One writes the novel, one paints the picture, of one's language and of one's time, and calling it modern English will not, alas! make the difficult task any easier. No more, unfortunately, will calling this or that work of one's fellow-artist a romance—unless it be, of course, simply for the pleasantness of the thing, as for instance when Hawthorne gave this heading to his story of *Blithedale*.[4] The French, who have brought the theory of fiction to remarkable completeness, have but one name for the novel, and have not attempted smaller things in it, that I can see, for that. I can think of no obligation to

---

4. Hawthorne entitled his novel about the socialist community of Brook Farm *The Blithedale Romance*.

which the "romancer" would not be held equally with the novelist; the standard of execution is equally high for each. Of course it is of execution that we are talking—that being the only point of a novel that is open to contention. This is perhaps too often lost sight of, only to produce interminable confusions and cross-purposes. We must grant the artist his subject, his idea, his *donnée:* [5] our criticism is applied only to what he makes of it. Naturally I do not mean that we are bound to like it or find it interesting: in case we do not our course is perfectly simple—to let it alone. We may believe that of a certain idea even the most sincere novelist can make nothing at all, and the event may perfectly justify our belief; but the failure will have been a failure to execute, and it is in the execution that the fatal weakness is recorded. If we pretend to respect the artist at all, we must allow him his freedom of choice, in the face, in particular cases, of innumerable presumptions that the choice will not fructify. Art derives a considerable part of its beneficial exercise from flying in the face of presumptions, and some of the most interesting experiments of which it is capable are hidden in the bosom of common things. Gustave Flaubert has written a story about the devotion of a servant-girl to a parrot,[6] and the production, highly finished as it is, cannot on the whole be called a success. We are perfectly free to find it flat, but I think it might have been interesting; and I, for my part, am extremely glad he should have written it; it is a contribution to our knowledge of what can be done—or what cannot. Ivan Turgenev has written a tale about a deaf and dumb serf and a lap-dog,[7] and the thing is touching, loving, a little masterpiece. He struck the note of life where Gustave Flaubert missed it—he flew in the face of a presumption and achieved a victory.

Nothing, of course, will ever take the place of the good old fashion of "liking" a work of art or not liking it: the most improved criticism will not abolish that primitive, that ultimate test. I mention this to guard myself from the accusation of intimating that the idea, the subject, of a novel or a picture, does not matter. It matters, to my sense, in the highest degree, and if I might put up a prayer it would be that artists should select none but the richest. Some, as I have already hastened to admit, are much more remunerative than others, and it would be a world happily arranged in which persons intending to treat them should be exempt from confusions and mistakes. This fortunate condition will arrive only, I fear, on the same day that critics become purged from error. Meanwhile, I repeat, we do not judge the artist with fairness unless we say to

---

5. The original concept or given starting point of an artist.
6. *Un Cœur Simple* ("A Simple Soul"), 1877.

7. The tale was "Mumu" (1852), written during Turgenev's exile to his estate for his liberal opinions. It reflected the lot of the Russian serf.

him, "Oh, I grant you your starting-point, because if I did not I
should seem to prescribe to you, and heaven forbid I should take
that responsibility. If I pretend to tell you what you must not take,
you will call upon me to tell you then what you must take; in which
case I shall be prettily caught. Moreover, it isn't till I have accepted
your data that I can begin to measure you. I have the standard,
the pitch; I have no right to tamper with your flute and then criticise your music. Of course I may not care for your idea at all; I may
think it silly, or stale, or unclean; in which case I wash my hands
of you altogether. I may content myself with believing that you
will not have succeeded in being interesting, but I shall, of course,
not attempt to demonstrate it, and you will be as indifferent to me
as I am to you. I needn't remind you that there are all sorts of
tastes: who can know it better? Some people, for excellent reasons,
don't like to read about carpenters; others, for reasons even better,
don't like to read about courtesans. Many object to Americans.
Others (I believe they are mainly editors and publishers) won't
look at Italians. Some readers don't like quiet subjects; others don't
like bustling ones. Some enjoy a complete illusion, others the consciousness of large concessions. They choose their novels accordingly,
and if they don't care about your idea they won't, *a fortiori*, care
about your treatment."

So that it comes back very quickly, as I have said, to the liking:
in spite of M. Zola, who reasons less powerfully than he represents,
and who will not reconcile himself to this absoluteness of taste,
thinking that there are certain things that people ought to like,
and that they can be made to like.[8] I am quite at a loss to imagine
anything (at any rate in this matter of fiction) that people *ought*
to like or to dislike. Selection will be sure to take care of itself, for
it has a constant motive behind it. That motive is simply experience.
As people feel life, so they will feel the art that is most closely related to it. This closeness of relation is what we should never forget
in talking of the effort of the novel. Many people speak of it as a
factitious, artificial form, a product of ingenuity, the business of
which is to alter and arrange the things that surround us, to translate them into conventional, traditional moulds. This, however, is
a view of the matter which carries us but a very short way, condemns the art to an eternal repetition of a few familiar *clichés*, cuts
short its development, and leads us straight up to a dead wall.
Catching the very note and trick, the strange irregular rhythm of
life, that is the attempt whose strenuous force keeps Fiction upon
her feet. In proportion as in what she offers us we see life *without*
rearrangement do we feel that we are touching the truth; in pro-

8. Zola's *Le roman expérimental* was for naturalism and the scientific method
published in 1880. It was an argument in fiction.

portion as we see it *with* rearrangement do we feel that we are being put off with a substitute, a compromise and convention. It is not uncommon to hear an extraordinary assurance of remark in regard to this matter of rearranging, which is often spoken of as if it were the last word of art. Mr. Besant seems to me in danger of falling into the great error with his rather unguarded talk about "selection." Art is essentially selection, but it is a selection whose main care is to be typical, to be inclusive. For many people art means rose-coloured window-panes, and selection means picking a bouquet for Mrs. Grundy.[9] They will tell you glibly that artistic considerations have nothing to do with the disagreeable, with the ugly; they will rattle off shallow commonplaces about the province of art and the limits of art till you are moved to some wonder in return as to the province and the limits of ignorance. It appears to me that no one can ever have made a seriously artistic attempt without becoming conscious of an immense increase—a kind of revelation—of freedom. One perceives in that case—by the light of a heavenly ray—that the province of art is all life, all feeling, all observation, all vision. As Mr. Besant so justly intimates, it is all experience. That is a sufficient answer to those who maintain that it must not touch the sad things of life, who stick into its divine unconscious bosom little prohibitory inscriptions on the end of sticks, such as we see in public gardens—"It is forbidden to walk on the grass; it is forbidden to touch the flowers; it is not allowed to introduce dogs or to remain after dark; it is requested to keep to the right." The young aspirant in the line of fiction whom we continue to imagine will do nothing without taste, for in that case his freedom would be of little use to him; but the first advantage of his taste will be to reveal to him the absurdity of the little sticks and tickets. If he have taste, I must add, of course he will have ingenuity, and my disrespectful reference to that quality just now was not meant to imply that it is useless in fiction. But it is only a secondary aid; the first is a capacity for receiving straight impressions.

Mr. Besant has some remarks on the question of "the story" which I shall not attempt to criticise, though they seem to me to contain a singular ambiguity, because I do not think I understand them. I cannot see what is meant by talking as if there were a part of a novel which is the story and part of it which for mystical reasons is not—unless indeed the distinction be made in a sense in which it is difficult to suppose that any one should attempt to convey anything. "The story," if it represents anything, represents the subject, the idea, the *donnée* of the novel; and there is surely no "school"—Mr. Besant speaks of a school—which urges that a novel

9. A character in Thomas Morton's comedy, *Speed the Plough* (1798), who became a symbol of middle-class prudishness and propriety.

should be all treatment and no subject. There must assuredly be something to treat; every school is intimately conscious of that. This sense of the story being the idea, the starting-point, of the novel, is the only one that I see in which it can be spoken of as something different from its organic whole; and since in proportion as the work is successful the idea permeates and penetrates it, informs and animates it, so that every word and every punctuation-point contribute directly to the expression, in that proportion do we lose our sense of the story being a blade which may be drawn more or less out of its sheath. The story and the novel, the idea and the form, are the needle and thread, and I never heard of a guild of tailors who recommended the use of the thread without the needle, or the needle without the thread. Mr. Besant is not the only critic who may be observed to have spoken as if there were certain things in life which constitute stories, and certain others which do not. I find the same odd implication in an entertaining article in the *Pall Mall Gazette*, devoted, as it happens, to Mr. Besant's lecture. "The story is the thing!" says this grateful writer, as if with a tone of opposition to some other idea. I should think it was, as every painter who, as the time for "sending in" his picture looms in the distance, finds himself still in quest of a subject— as every belated artist not fixed about his theme will heartily agree. There are some subjects which speak to us and others which do not, but he would be a clever man who should undertake to give a rule—an index expurgatorius[1]—by which the story and the no story should be known apart. It is impossible (to me at least) to imagine any such rule which shall not be altogether arbitrary. The writer in the *Pall Mall* opposes the delightful (as I suppose) novel of *Margot la Balafrée*[2] to certain tales in which "Bostonian nymphs" appear to have "rejected English dukes for psychological reasons." I am not acquainted with the romance just designated, and can scarcely forgive the *Pall Mall* critic for not mentioning the name of the author, but the title appears to refer to a lady who may have received a scar in some heroic adventure. I am inconsolable at not being acquainted with this episode, but am utterly at a loss to see why it is a story when the rejection (or acceptance) of a duke is not, and why a reason, psychological or other, is not a subject when a cicatrix is. They are all particles of the multitudinous life with which the novel deals, and surely no dogma which pretends to make it lawful to touch the one and unlawful to touch the other will stand for a moment on its feet. It is the special picture that must stand or fall, according as it seem to possess truth or to lack it. Mr. Besant does not, to my sense, light up the subject by intimat-

---

1. James refers to the Catholic Index of forbidden books.

2. Fortuné Du Boisgobey, *Margot la Balafrée* ("Lady with a Scar"), 1884.

ing that a story must, under penalty of not being a story, consist of "adventures." Why of adventures more than of green spectacles?[3] He mentions a category of impossible things, and among them he places "fiction without adventure." Why without adventure, more than without matrimony, or celibacy, or parturition, or cholera, or hydropathy, or Jansenism?[4] This seems to me to bring the novel back to the hapless little *rôle* of being an artificial, ingenious thing— bring it down from its large, free character of an immense and exquisite correspondence with life. And what *is* adventure, when it comes to that, and by what sign is the listening pupil to recognise it? It is an adventure—an immense one—for me to write this little article; and for a Bostonian nymph to reject an English duke is an adventure only less stirring, I should say, than for an English duke to be rejected by a Bostonian nymph. I see dramas within dramas in that, and innumerable points of views. A psychological reason is, to my imagination, an object adorably pictorial; to catch the tint of its complexion—I feel as if that idea might inspire one to Titianesque efforts. There are few things more exciting to me, in short, than a psychological reason, and yet, I protest, the novel seems to me the most magnificent form of art. I have just been reading, at the same time, the delightful story of *Treasure Island*, by Mr. Robert Louis Stevenson and, in a manner less consecutive, the last tale from M. Edmond de Goncourt, which is entitled *Chérie*. One of these works treats of murders, mysteries, islands of dreadful renown, hear-breadth escape, miraculous coincidences and buried doubloons. The other treats of a little French girl who lived in a fine house in Paris, and died of wounded sensibility because no one would marry her. I call *Treasure Island* delightful, because it appears to me to have succeeded wonderfully in what it attempts; and I venture to bestow no epithet upon *Chérie*, which strikes me as having failed deplorably in what it attempts—that is in tracing the development of the moral consciousness of a child. But one of these productions strikes me as exactly as much of a novel as the other, and as having a "story" quite as much. The moral consciousness of a child is as much a part of life as the islands of the Spanish Main, and the one sort of geography seems to me to have those "surprises" of which Mr. Besant speaks quite as much as the other. For myself (since it comes back in the last resort, as I say, to the preference of the individual), the picture of the child's experience has the advantage that I can at successive steps (an immense luxury, near to the "sensual pleasure" of which Mr. Besant's critic in the *Pall Mall* speaks) say Yes or No, as it may be, to what the artist puts

3. The reference is to a famous episode in Goldsmith's *The Vicar of Wakefield* (1766).
4. Cornelius Jansenius propounded doctrines of free will and grace which were considered heresy by the Catholic Church. They were published in 1640.

before me. I have been a child in fact, but I have been on a quest
for a buried treasure only in supposition,[5] and it is a simple accident
that with M. de Goncourt I should have for the most part to say
No. With George Eliot, when she painted that country with a far
other intelligence, I always said Yes.

The most interesting part of Mr. Besant's lecture is unfortunately
the briefest passage—his very cursory allusion to the "conscious
moral purpose" of the novel. Here again it is not very clear whether
he be recording a fact or laying down a principle; it is a great pity
that in the latter case he should not have developed his idea. This
branch of the subject is of immense importance, and Mr. Besant's
few words point to considerations of the widest reach, not to be
lightly disposed of. He will have treated the art of fiction superficially who is not prepared to go every inch of the way that these
considerations will carry him. It is for this reason that at the beginning of these remarks I was careful to notify the reader that
my reflections on so large a theme have no pretension to be exhaustive. Like Mr. Besant, I have left the question of the morality of
the novel till the last, and at the last I find I have used up my
space. It is a question surrounded with difficulties, as witness the
very first that meets us, in the form of a definite question, on the
threshold. Vagueness, in such a discussion, is fatal, and what is
the meaning of your morality and your conscious moral purpose?
Will you not define your terms and explain how (a novel being a
picture) a picture can be either moral or immoral? You wish to
paint a moral picture or carve a moral statue: will you not tell us
how you would set about it? We are discussing the Art of Fiction;
questions of art are questions (in the widest sense) of execution;
questions of morality are quite another affair, and will you not let
us see how it is that you find it so easy to mix them up? These
things are so clear to Mr. Besant that he has deduced from them a
law which he sees embodied in English Fiction, and which is "a
truly admirable thing and a great cause for congratulation." It is a
great cause for congratulation indeed when such thorny problems
become as smooth as silk. I may add that in so far as Mr. Besant
perceives that in point of fact English Fiction has addressed itself
preponderantly to these delicate questions he will appear to many
people to have made a vain discovery. They will have been positively struck, on the contrary, with the moral timidity of the usual
English novelist; with his (or with her) aversion to face the difficulties with which on every side the treatment of reality bristles. He

5. In the earliest form of the essay, James wrote: "I have been a child, but I have never been on a quest for buried treasure." Stevenson took exception to the statement in his "A Humble Remonstrance" by arguing that pirates, buried treasure, and similar experiences are part of the imagination of all young persons. In his revision for book publication, James rewrote the phrase as above.

is apt to be extremely shy (whereas the picture that Mr. Besant draws is a picture of boldness), and the sign of his work, for the most part, is a cautious silence on certain subjects. In the English novel (by which of course I mean the American as well), more than in any other, there is a traditional difference between that which people know and that which they agree to admit that they know, that which they see and that which they speak of, that which they feel to be a part of life and that which they allow to enter into literature. There is the great difference, in short, between what they talk of in conversation and what they talk of in print. The essence of moral energy is to survey the whole field, and I should directly reverse Mr. Besant's remark and say not that the English novel has a purpose, but that it has a diffidence. To what degree a purpose in a work of art is a source of corruption I shall not attempt to inquire; the one that seems to me least dangerous is the purpose of making a perfect work. As for our novel, I may say lastly on this score that as we find it in England to-day it strikes me as addressed in a large degree to "young people," and that this in itself constitutes a presumption that it will be rather shy. There are certain things which it is generally agreed not to discuss, not even to mention, before young people. That is very well, but the absence of discussion is not a symptom of the moral passion. The purpose of the English novel—"a truly admirable thing, and a great cause for congratulation"—strikes me therefore as rather negative.

There is one point at which the moral sense and the artistic sense lie very near together; that is in the light of the very obvious truth that the deepest quality of a work of art will always be the quality of the mind of the producer. In proportion as that intelligence is fine will the novel, the picture, the statue partake of the substance of beauty and truth. To be constituted of such elements is, to my vision, to have purpose enough. No good novel will ever proceed from a superficial mind; that seems to me an axiom which, for the artist in fiction, will cover all needful moral ground: if the youthful aspirant take it to heart it will illuminate for him many of the mysteries of "purpose." There are many other useful things that might be said to him, but I have come to the end of my article, and can only touch them as I pass. The critic in the *Pall Mall Gazette*, whom I have already quoted, draws attention to the danger, in speaking of the art of fiction, of generalising. The danger that he has in mind is rather, I imagine, that of particularising, for there are some comprehensive remarks which, in addition to those embodied in Mr. Besant's suggestive lecture, might without fear of misleading him be addressed to the ingenuous student. I should remind him first of the magnificence of the form that is open to him, which offers to sight so few restrictions and such innumerable opportunities. The other arts, in comparison, appear confined and hampered; the various conditions under which they are exercised are so rigid and definite. But the only condition that I can think of attaching to the composition of the novel is, as I have already said, that it be sincere. This freedom is a splendid privilege, and the first lesson of the young novelist is to learn to be worthy of it. "Enjoy it as it deserves," I should say to him; "take possession of it, explore it to its utmost extent, publish it, rejoice in it. All life belongs to you, and do not listen either to those who would shut you up into corners of it and tell you that it is only here and there that art inhabits, or to those who would persuade you that this heavenly messenger wings her way outside of life altogether, breathing a superfine air, and turning away her head from the truth of things. There is no impression of life, no manner of seeing it and feeling it, to which the plan of the novelist may not offer a place; you have only to remember that talents so dissimilar as those of Alexandre Dumas and Jane Austen, Charles Dickens and Gustave Flaubert have worked in this field with equal glory. Do not think too much about optimism and pessimism; try and catch the colour of life itself. In France to-day we see a prodigious effort (that of Emile Zola, to whose solid and serious work no explorer of the capacity of the novel can allude without respect), we see an extraordinary effort, vitiated by a spirit of pessimism on a narrow basis. M. Zola is magnificent, but he strikes an English reader as ignorant; he has an air of working in the dark; if he had as much light as energy, his results would be of the highest value. As for the aberrations of a shallow optimism, the ground (of English fiction especially) is strewn with their brittle particles as with broken glass. If you must indulge in conclusions, let them have the taste of a wide knowledge. Remember that your first duty is to be as complete as possible—to make as perfect a work. Be generous and delicate and pursue the prize."

1884, 1888

From Notebooks[6]
[Greville Fane]

February 27th, 1889. * * *

There comes back to me with a certain vividness of solicitation, an idea that I noted a long time ago, suggested by something that Jennie Thackeray once said or repeated to me. That is, her story of Trollope's having had the plan of bringing up his son to write

---

6. The excerpts are from *The Notebooks of Henry James*, edited by F. O. Matthiessen and K. B. Murdock (New York, 1947). The angle brackets (for editorial interpolations) and the *x*'s (used to separate entries, divide sections, or mark unfinished sentences) are Matthiessen's and Murdock's.

novels, as a lucrative trade. She added (as Mrs. R. Ritchie) that she and her husband had the same idea with regard to her little girl. They would train her up to it as to a regular profession. This suggested to me the figure of a weary battered labourer in the field of fiction attempting to carry out this project with a child and meeting, by the irony of fate, the strangest discomfiture. All sorts of possibilities vaguely occur to one as latent in it. The child is given a chance to 'see life,' etc., that it may have material, and sees life to such a tune that he (or she) is swamped and destroyed. That is one element. Then the mother (this especially if it be a 'lady-novelist') tries to enable the son to go out into the world for *her own* purposes—to see society, hear things, etc. The poor mother describes fashionable life and the upper classes—and wants data and material. She is frowsy and dingy herself—she can't go—and she is too busy. The stupidity of the children, who bring home nothing—have no observation, etc. But there must be an *action*, of some little sort—and this occurs to me. There is a daughter and she has appeared pretty and clever—she is the one (there is a son beside), whom there has been this attempt to *form*, to train. In the early years there must be the dim vision of a handsome, idle father, living upon his wife. The expense of the girl's education, etc.—and also the boy's, who is good-looking and unaddicted to any literary pursuit. The particular drama to be that the girl proves quite use-less as a novelist, but grows up, marries a snob on the edge of good society, is worldly and hard and would be smart, and is ashamed of her mother. Thinks her novels are vulgar rubbish—keeps her at a distance—almost ignores her—makes her very unhappy. The poor lady is obliged to go on writing, meanwhile, to meet the demands of her son—whom she has thrown into the world to pick up in-formation for her, and who has simply become idle, selfish, extrava-gant and vicious. She has all sorts of ⟨lurking?⟩ romanticisms and *naïvetés*—make a very vivid amusing pathetic picture of her mix-ture of queer qualities, etc.—her immorality, her natural penchant to license *à la Ouida*, of which her priggish daughter is ashamed. Her love of splendour, of the aristocracy, of high society—the wealth and beauty which she attributes to her people, etc.—contrasted with the small shabby facts of her own life. She dies at the end, worn out, disappointed, poor. The thing had much best be told by a witness of her life—a friend—a critic, a journalist, etc.: in the 1st person: rapid notes. I speak of the telegram from the editor of one of the big papers when she dies, asking for ½ a column about her. I saw and wrote the ½ column and made it kinder. Then for my-self I wrote these other notes—kinder still.—The thing to be called by the *nom de plume* of the poor lady—some rather smart *man's* name.

This little sketch of which I think very well on the whole (Feb. 28th) would gain in effect by the supposititious narrator being himself a novelist but of the younger generation and of the modern psychological type. There would be touches there which might throw the poor woman's funny old art into contrast with his point of view—touches of bewilderment at his work on *her* side and of indulgence and humour on his.

[*The Real Thing*]

Paris, Hotel Westminster, February 22d, 1891.

In pursuance of my plan of writing some very short tales—things of from 7000 to 10,000 words, the easiest length to 'place,' I began yesterday the little story that was suggested to me some time ago by an incident related to me by George du Maurier—the lady and gentleman who called upon him with a word from Frith, an oldish, faded, ruined pair—he an officer in the army—who unable to turn a penny in any other way, were trying to find employment as models. I was struck with the pathos, the oddity and typicalness of the situation—the little tragedy of good-looking gentlefolk, who had been all their life stupid and well-dressed, living, on a fixed income, at country-houses, watering places and clubs, like so many others of their class in England, and were now utterly unable to *do* anything, had no cleverness, no art nor craft to make use of as a *gagne-pain*[7]—could only *show* themselves, clumsily, for the fine, clean, well-groomed animals that they were, only hope to make a little money by—in this manner—just simply *being*. I thought I saw a subject for very brief treatment in this *donnée*—and I think I do still; but to do anything worth while with it I must (as always, great Heavens!) be very clear as to what is in it and what I wish to get out of it. I tried a beginning yesterday, but I instantly became conscious that I must straighten out the little idea. It must be an idea—it can't be a 'story' in the vulgar sense of the word. It must be a picture; it must illustrate something. God knows that's enough—if the thing *does* illustrate. To make little anecdotes of this kind real *morceaux de vie*[8] is a plan quite inspiring enough. V*oyons un peu,*[9] therefore, what one can put into this one—I mean how much of life. One must put a little action—not a stupid, mechanical, arbitrary action, but something that is of the real essence of the subject. I thought of representing the husband as jealous of the wife—that is, jealous of the artist employing her, from the moment that, in point of fact, she begins to sit. But this is vulgar and obvious—worth nothing. What I wish to represent is the baffled, ineffectual, in-

7. "Means of earning bread."
8. Slice of life.
9. "Let us consider a little." James often talks to himself in this way in his *Notebooks.*

competent character of their attempt, and how it illustrates once again the everlasting English amateurishness—the way superficial, untrained, unprofessional effort goes to the wall when confronted with trained, competitive, intelligent, *qualified* art—in whatever line it may be a question of. It is out of *that* element that my little action and movement must come; and now I begin to see just how—as one always *does*—Glory be to the Highest—when one begins to look at a thing hard and straight and seriously—to fix it— as I am so sadly lax and desultory about doing. What subjects I should find—for *everything*—if I could only achieve this more as a habit! Let my contrast and complication here come from the op- position—to my melancholy Major and his wife—of a couple of little vulgar professional people *who know*, with the consequent be- wilderment, vagueness, depression of the former—their failure to understand how such people can be better than *they*—their fail- ure, disappointment, disappearance—going forth into the vague again. *Il y a bien quelque chose à tirer de ça.*[1] They have no pic- torial sense. They are only clean and stiff and stupid. The others are dirty, even—the melancholy Major and his wife remark on it, won- dering. The artist is beginning a big illustrated book, a new edition of a famous novel—say *Tom Jones*: and he is willing to try to work them in—for he takes an interest in their predicament, and feels— sceptically, but, with his flexible artistic sympathy—the appeal of their type. He is willing to give them a trial. Make it out that *he* himself is on trial—he is young and 'rising,' but he has still his golden spurs to win. He can't afford, *en somme*, to make many mistakes. He has regular work in drawing every week for a serial novel in an illustrated paper; but the great project—that of a big house—of issuing an illustrated Fielding promises him a big lift. He has been intrusted with (say) *Joseph Andrews*, experimentally; he will have to do this brilliantly in order to have the engagement for the rest confirmed. He has already 2 models in his service—the 'complication' must come from *them*. One is a common, clever, London girl, of the smallest origin and without conventional beauty, but of aptitude, of perceptions—knowing thoroughly *how*. She says 'lydy' and 'plice,' but she has the pictorial sense; and can look like anything he wants her to look like. She poses, in short, in perfection. So does her colleague, a professional Italian, a little fel- low—ill dressed, smelling of garlic, but admirably serviceable, quite universal. They must be contrasted, confronted, *juxtaposed* with the others; whom they take for people who *pay*, themselves, till they learn the truth when they are overwhelmed with derisive amaze- ment. The denouement simply that the melancholy Major and his wife won't do—they're not 'in it.' Their surprise—their helpless,

---

1. "There is something good to be drawn from this."

proud assent—without other prospects: yet at the same time *their* degree of more silent amazement at the success of the two inferior people—who are so much less nice-looking than themselves. Frankly, however, is this contrast enough of a *story*, by itself? It seems to me Yes—for it's an IDEA—and how the deuce should I get *more* into 7000 words? It must be simply 50 pp. of my manuscript. The little tale of *The Servant* (*Brooksmith*) which I did the other day for *Black and White* and which I thought of at the same time as this, proved a very tight squeeze into the same tiny number of words, and I probably shall find that there is much more to be done with this than the compass will admit of. Make it tremendously succinct—with a very short pulse or rhythm—and the closest selection of detail—in other words *summarize* intensely and keep down the lateral development. It *should* be a little gem of bright, quick, vivid form. I shall get every grain of 'action' that the space admits of if I make something, for the artist, hang in the balance—depend on the way he does this particular work. It's when he finds that he shall lose his great opportunity if he keeps on with them, that he has to tell the gentlemanly couple, that, frankly, they won't serve his turn—and make them wander forth into the cold world again. I must keep them the age I've made them—50 and 40—because it's more touching; but I must bring up the age of the 2 real models to almost the same thing. That increases the incomprehensibility (to the amateurs) of their usefulness. Picture the immanence, in the latter, of the idle, provided-for, country-house habit—the blankness of their *manière d'être*.[2] But in how tremendously few words I must do it. This is a lesson—a *magnificent* lesson—if I'm to do a good many. Something as admirably compact and *selected* as Maupassant.

[The Figure in the Carpet]

Torquay, October 24th, 1895.

I seem to see a little subject in this idea: that of the author of certain books who is known to hold—and to declare as much, *au besoin*,[3] to the few with whom he communicates—that his writings contain a very beautiful and valuable, very interesting and remunerative *secret*, or latent intention, for those who read them with a right intelligence—who see *into* them, as it were—bring to the perusal of them a certain perceptive sense. There's a general idea *qui s'en dégage*:[4] he doesn't tell what it is—it's for the reader to find out. 'It's there—it's *there*,' he says; 'I can't—or I won't—tell you what it is; but my books constitute the expression of it.' I

2. "Manner of being," or "way of life."
3. "In a pinch."
4. "Which is to be disengaged from it."

should premise that I think I see these books necessarily to be NOVELS; it is in fact essentially as a novelist that the personage *se présente à ma pensée*.[5] He has such qualities of art and style and skill as may be fine and honourable ones presumably—but he himself holds that they don't *know* his work who don't know, who haven't felt, or guessed, or perceived, this interior thought—this special *beauty* (that is mainly the just word) that pervades and controls and animates them. No reviewer, no 'critic,' as dreamed of it: lovely chance for fine irony on the subject of that fraternity. *Mettons*[6] that he mentions, after all, the fact of the thing to only one person—to *me*, say, who narrate, in my proper identity, the little episode. Say *I'm* a 'critic,' another little writer, a newspaper man. I am in relation with him, somehow—relation, admiring, inquisitive, sympathetic, mystified, sceptical—whatever it may be. *I* haven't, in the books, seen anything, but just certain pleasant and charming things—or whatever these things, merits, features, may superficially and obviously be. No, *I* haven't discovered anything. But he tells *me*: say (yes), I'm the only person he tells. (I can't go into the stages and details here—this is the barest of summaries.) That is, he tells me the fact: the *existence* of the latent beauty: oh, what it *is*, what it consists of, he doesn't tell me or tell anybody, at all. This he confides to no one, and is serenely, happily content not to confide to any one. There it is, there it is: there let it stay! His great amusement in life is really to see if any one will ever see it—if the great race of critics, above all, will ever be sufficiently perceptive for it some day to flash upon them. '*Does* it flash—is that the way it comes—in a sudden revelation?,' I ask him. My worriment, my wonderment—my little torment about what the devil it can be. My questions, my readings-over—and his answers, his indifference, his serenity, his amusement at all our densities and imbecilities: but without a shadow of *real* information. His answers only play with my curiosity—and he doesn't care. It isn't the 'esoteric meaning,' as the newspapers say: 'it's the *only* meaning, it's the very soul and core of the work.' I wonder if he's only joking—or if he's mad. I somehow don't believe he's joking (circumstances contradict it), and if he's mad, how can he have made his work so *perfect?* How can it be, in form and substance, so sane and sound? Decidedly, it must be distinguished, the work, must have the qualities of charm that are patent. That is needed to preclude the idea of madness. *Voyons*, then: after he makes his communication to me (tells me the thing is there), I, immediately, in turn, make it to another friend of mine, a young man of letters, say. He is interested in our author—he is much interested in the fact, in the revelation, imperfect as it is. Just after this the author tells me that I had better not mention or repeat what he has told me—it was for *me*: it wasn't for the vulgar world. I tell him that I *have* already repeated it to my young friend, etc.; but that I will tell him not to tell others. The Author says, 'Oh, it doesn't matter!'—he doesn't seem really to care, after all. I do tell my young friend what he has said to me—his caution about diffusing his statement; and my young friend says: 'I'm very sorry—I've already told So-and-So!' So-and-So is a young lady in whom he is much interested. 'Well, tell her to keep it to herself,' I say. He does so—he tells me afterward that she will. But he tells me also that she is much interested— she is an 'admirer,' and she wants to find out—if she can—what the reference bears upon. The young man, the 2d young man (my friend), does too—and it is *his* torment, *his* worry, *his* study of the pretty books, that I perhaps mainly represent. *I* have given them up—the game isn't worth the candle. It's all a bad joke and a mystification: *that's* the ground I take. But I know that he talks the matter over with his young lady, goes into it with her, wonders, worries, seeks, renounces, with her. Say *I* take the ground of our hero's madness, or mere persistent pleasantry amounting almost to madness— and that it's he who take⟨s⟩ the side of the outright beauty and sanity of the work. He too is a critic—only he's the shamed one, the one sensitive to the reproach. I'm not, I don't care, I cling to my vulgar explanation: I've not been a particular admirer of the novels. My friend has always seen more in them than I do. He has his theories—he has his explanations, his clues and glimpses—he puts forward one, then another, then a third—which he successively renounces—they won't hold. The young lady has hers—which he tells me about and which break down, too. They quarrel about them—they are quite possessed with their search. Does the young man, my friend, know the author, meet him, talk with him? A point to be settled, but I think not: he *wants* to, but he wants to wait till he can really say, 'Eureka!,' and then go and submit his solution to him and get a reply: say 'Isn't *that* it?'—and have perhaps at last the great assent. Well, before this, the Author dies— and that test, that light, that disclosure, become forever inaccessible. No one knows, now—he carries the secret away with him. But (to make a long story—it's really—it must be really—of the briefest— short) my young man continues to be haunted by it. At last he lets me know—from a distance—that he has discovered it. He has, he *has*, this time—it's a revelation—it's wonderful. Or I must learn, perhaps from the young woman, that this has occurred. Yes, that's the way I'll have it! He's at a distance and *she* has heard from him. She doesn't at all know what it is—but he's to tell her. I am then devoured with curiosity and suspense. 'When is he to tell you?' 'Well, after we're married,' she replies with some embarrassment. 'You're to be married?' I have thought they had quarrelled—but it appears they have made it up. She tells me *when*—he is coming on to London (he's abroad, or in the East, or in Scotland) and it will then take place. I write to him, however, before that—I ask him to appease my curiosity. He replies that he is coming on to his wedding and will do so then. I write that I shall not be in London, alas, for it, and that he had better make me the revelation by letter. He rejoins that he can do it much better *viva voce*, and would rather so do it; and I have to rest content with that. He has specified some near time at which we *shall* be likely to meet. But we don't meet—we never meet. I leave town before he comes—and he is married in my absence. Three months later, before I get back, he is killed—by an accident. He carries away his discovery with him—save in so far as he *has*, after marriage, told it to his wife. I must KNOW that he *has* so told it. But somehow I feel it to be a thing I can't ask her and she can't tell me. There is evidently, about it, a strange mystifying uncomfortable delicacy. She never offers to satisfy me—though I meet her and she has a chance and knows how curious I am. So I have to go unsatisfied. I do so for a long time. The strange thing is that now, somehow, I feel the mystery to be a reality. I feel that the deceased wasn't mad. I almost want to marry the widow—to learn from her *de quoi*, in the name of wonder, *il s'agit*.[7] I feel as if she might tell me if we should be married—but that she'll never tell me otherwise. But I don't marry her—I *can't*, simply for that! At last she marries some one else. I feel sure she tells *him*. I want to ask him—I hover about him—I come very near it. But I don't—I don't think it, when I come to the point, quite delicate or fair. I don't—I forbear. In the course of time—in childbirth—*she* dies. Then, after an interval, I get my chance. She is the 3d person who has carried the mystery to the grave; but she, at last will have left, in the person of her husband, a depositary. I am able to approach him, and I do so. I put the question to him, ask him if his wife didn't tell him. He stares—he's blank—he doesn't know what I'm talking about. 'So-and-So? The secret of his books—?' He looks at me as if *I* am mad. She has never told him anything: she has carried the mystery uncommunicated to the grave. x x x x x

Two little things, in relation to this, occur to me. One is the importance of my being *sure* the disclosure has been made to the wife by her 1st husband. The other is the importance of *his* having been sure he had got hold of the right thing. The only way for this would be to have made him submit his idea to the Author himself. To this end the Author's death would have *not* to precede his discovery. Say I make him get *at* the Author, with his 'discovery,' and the latter's

7. "What he was agitated about."

death occurs, away from London, therefore, between that event and my ascertainment of the intended marriage. The form in which I hear of it from the girl is that her fiancé HAS submitted it to the Author. *Then* the Author dies—abroad, ill, in a climate. It's *there* my young man has gone to him—is with him. All this mere suggestion—to be figured out. The thing to be REALLY brief. x x x x x

34 De Vere Gardens, November 4th, 1895.

I am thinking of trying the little *sujet de nouvelle*[8] I noted the other day at Torquay—the one on the Author's Secret—for the 1st no. of the new review, *Cosmopolis,* to which the editor has asked me to contribute; but I must make it fit neatly into 11,000 words or, in other words, into a hundred (*close*) pages of my MS. V*oyons, voyons.* x x x x x I must take 10 little chapters of 10 pages of my MS. each. So! x x x x x

I. The visit from my friend who, owing to his *empêchement*[9] (specify) asks me to do—to oblige him—a review of the Author's new novel, which he has made himself responsible for. He has to go off—to meet the girl who subsequently figures—meet her and her mother—returning from abroad: strike—yes—the note of the appearance of the girl here. He hasn't time—I must do it; and besides, it's a chance for me. I recognize the chance—I introduce the incident, in the very 1st words of my narration—as my FIRST real or good chance: the beginning of my little success or little career. I accept; we speak a moment or two of the Author—during which our note of divergence appears—and I mention, as a coincidence, that I have accepted an invitation to go from the following Saturday to Monday down to a place in the country where it has been mentioned to me that I may meet him. 'Oh, then, you'll write handsomely—if you are going to look him in the face.—You must tell me all about him.' 'Yes, I'll tell you: I *will* look him in the face!' He goes off—I write my notice—I go down to the place. But I needn't detail here, so much, the points—only broadly indicate them.

II. I report to Corvick—I communicate: I set, in a word, the ball in motion. I see Vereker again and he warns me. I repeat this to Corvick and he tells me he has told the girl. x x x x x

I have brought the little subject treated of in the foregoing to p. 68 of my MS. (Nov. 22d), and must be sharply definite as to the skeleton of the rest. I have at the most 40 pages more. But they are, thank God, enough. *These,* at the point I've reached, are the

8. "Subject of a story."   9. "Opposition."

facts still to be handled:—

    Corvick has gone to the East on a commission from a newspaper. Mrs. Erme is still alive and he is not yet engaged to Gwendolen. She tells me that he writes to her from (Bombay?) that he has 'found it.'

    What is it?

    She doesn't know—he hasn't told her. (He says he'll tell her 'when we're married.') (She marries to find out [?]) He's to stop and see Vereker at Mentone and submit his idea to him. THEN he'll tell—if it's *right*—if it proves so. I hasten to Gwendolen to learn. Yes—it's right. Vereker says so. He's *with* Vereker. 'Then what is it?' 'He says he'll tell me when we're married.' 'You're engaged?' 'We've become so—but we can't marry in my mother's lifetime.' I don't ask after her mother's health, but I wonder—just wonder—! Corvick has told me before leaving England that they're *not* engaged. I write to him—he replies, telling me to wait. I am called away before his return: so I haven't the chance to see him face to face. I go to America—Vereker dies. Corvick dies 4 months after his marriage. The foregoing in 2 sections—leaving the last one for all that follows. Each to be of 12 pp. MS.

Preface to *The Ambassadors*[1]

    Nothing is more easy than to state the subject of "The Ambassadors," which first appeared in twelve numbers of "The North American Review" (1903) and was published as a whole the same year. The situation involved is gathered up betimes, that is in the second chapter of Book Fifth, for the reader's benefit, into as few words as possible—planted or "sunk," stiffly and saliently, in the centre of the current, almost perhaps to the obstruction of traffic. Never can a composition of this sort have sprung straighter from a dropped grain of suggestion, and never can that grain, developed, overgrown and smothered, have yet lurked more in the mass as an independent particle. The whole case, in fine, is in Lambert Strether's irrepressible outbreak to little Bilham on the Sunday afternoon in Gloriani's garden, the candour with which he yields, for his young friend's enlightenment, to the charming admonition of that crisis. The idea of the tale resides indeed in the very fact that an hour of such unprecedented ease should have been felt by him *as* a crisis, and he is at pains to express it for us as neatly as we could desire. The remarks to which he thus gives utterance contain the essence of "The Ambassadors," his fingers close, before he has done, round the stem of the full-blown flower; which, after that fashion, he continues officiously to present to us. "Live all you can;

1. From *The Novels and Tales of Henry James* (New York, 1909), Vol. XXI.

it's a mistake not to. It doesn't so much matter what you do in particular so long as you have your life. If you haven't had that what *have* you had? I'm too old—too old at any rate for what I see. What one loses one loses; make no mistake about that. Still, we have the illusion of freedom; therefore don't, like me to-day, be without the memory of that illusion. I was either, at the right time, too stupid or too intelligent to have it, and now I'm a case of reaction against the mistake. Do what you like so long as you don't make it. For it *was* a mistake. Live, live!" Such is the gist of Strether's appeal to the impressed youth, whom he likes and whom he desires to befriend; the word "mistake" occurs several times, it will be seen, in the course of his remarks—which gives the measure of the signal warning he feels attached to his case. He has accordingly missed too much, though perhaps after all constitutionally qualified for a better part, and he wakes up to it in conditions that press the spring of a terrible question. *Would* there yet perhaps be time for reparation?—reparation, that is, for the injury done his character; for the affront, he is quite ready to say, so stupidly put upon it and in which he has even himself had so clumsy a hand? The answer to which is that he now at all events *sees*; so that the business of my tale and the march of my action, not to say the precious moral of everything, is just my demonstration of this process of vision.

Nothing can exceed the closeness with which the whole fits again into its germ. That had been given me bodily, as usual, by the spoken word, for I was to take the image over exactly as I happened to have met it. A friend[2] had repeated to me, with great ap-

2. James's friend was Jonathan Sturges, a Princeton graduate who, despite chronic invalidism, wrote essays and did French translations. He was admired by James, Whistler, and others for his personal charm and conversation. The "man of distinction," his senior, was William Dean Howells. James wrote in his *Notebooks* in October, 1895: "I was struck last evening with something that Jonathan Sturges * * * mentioned to me: it was only ten words, but I seemed, as usual, to catch a glimpse of a *sujet de nouvelle* in it. We were talking of W.D.H. and of his having seen him during a short and interrupted stay H. had made eighteen months ago in Paris —called away—back to America, when he had just come—at the end of ten days by the news of the death—or illness, of his father. He had scarcely been in Paris, ever, in former days. * * * Virtually in the evening of life, as it were, it was all new to him: all, all, all. Sturges said he seemed sad— rather brooding; and I asked him what gave him (Sturges) that impression." James then relates that Howells placed his hand on Sturges' shoulder and spoke the few words about living life fully, which became the germinal idea of *The Ambassadors*. James's *Notebook* entry then goes on to develop the first conception in his mind of the plot of the novel. The anecdote about Howells gave him the idea, he said, "of an elderly man who hasn't 'lived,' hasn't at all. * * * He has never really enjoyed—he has lived only for duty and conscience." Thus, Howells was the unwitting original of Lambert Strether in the novel, and the theme was that of missed experience— a theme which preoccupied James in his later work.

When James finished the novel in 1901 he wrote Howells that it had been on his conscience to tell him of this incident and that Howells' words had started the novel in his mind. But he hastened to add that in writing the novel, Strether was in no way modeled upon Howells, but had become an independent character of the author's mind.

The details of the story formed in James's mind after hearing the anec-

preciation, a thing or two said to him by a man of distinction, much his senior, and to which a sense akin to that of Strether's melancholy eloquence might be imputed—said as chance would have, and so easily might, in Paris, and in a charming old garden attached to a house of art,[3] and on a Sunday afternoon of summer, many persons of great interest being present. The observation there listened to and gathered up had contained part of the "note" that I was to recognise on the spot as to my purpose—had contained in fact the greater part; the rest was in the place and the time and the scene they sketched: these constituents clustered and combined to give me further support, to give me what I may call the note absolute. There it stands, accordingly, full in the tide-way; driven in, with hard taps, like some strong stake for the noose of a cable, the swirl of the current roundabout it. What amplified the hint to more than the bulk of hints in general was the gift with it of the old Paris garden, for in that token were sealed up values infinitely precious. There was of course the seal to break and each item of the packet to count over and handle and estimate; but somehow, in the light of the hint, all the elements of a situation of the sort most to my taste were there. I could even remember no occasion on which, so confronted, I had found it of a livelier interest to take stock, in this fashion, of suggested wealth. For I think, verily, that there are degrees of merit in subjects—in spite of the fact that to treat even one of the most ambiguous with due decency we must for the time, for the feverish and prejudiced hour, at least figure its merit and its dignity as *possibly* absolute. What it comes to, doubtless, is that even among the supremely good—since with such alone is it one's theory of one's honour to be concerned—there is an ideal *beauty* of goodness the invoked action of which is to raise the ar-

---

dote from Sturges. His hero was to have come to Paris from New England and to undergo some new revelation about life at a late age. "Say he 'goes out,' " James wrote, "to look after, to bring home, some young man whom his family are anxious about, who won't come home etc. * * * Say our friend is a widower, and that the *jeune homme* is the son of a widow to whom he is engaged to be married. She is of the strenuous pattern—she is the reflection of his old self. She has money—she admires and approves him. * * * He is 55. He married at 20! Displeasing the strenuous widow is a sacrifice—an injury to him. To marry her means rest and security *pour ses vieux jours.* The 'revolution' endangers immensely his situation with her. But of course my denouement is that it takes place—that he makes the sacrifice, does the thing I have, vaguely, represented him, *supra,* as doing, and loses the woman he was

to marry and all the advantages attaching to her. It is too late, too late *now,* for HIM to live—but what stirs in him with a dumb passion of desire, of I don't know what, is the sense that he may have a little supersensual hour in the vicarious freedom of another. His little drama is the administration of the touch that contributes to—that prolongs—that freedom."
3. The reference here is to the garden belonging to James MacNeill Whistler in the Faubourg Saint Germaine section of Paris, an old, picturesque area long familiar to James since the 1870's when he visited with Turgenev and Flaubert. In Book Five of *The Ambassadors* he described this scene of old, noble houses far back from the streets, containing quiet courts and an atmosphere of antiquity and strong social tradition. These memories became deeply interwoven with the main theme of the novel.

tistic faith to its maximum. Then truly, I hold, one's theme may be said to shine, and that of "The Ambassadors," I confess, wore this glow for me from beginning to end. Fortunately thus I am able to estimate this as, frankly, quite the best, "all round," of my productions; any failure of that justification would have made such an extreme of complacency publicly fatuous.

I recall then in this connexion no moment of subjective intermittence, never one of those alarms as for a suspected hollow beneath one's feet, a felt ingratitude in the scheme adopted, under which confidence fails and opportunity seems but to mock. If the motive of "The Wings of the Dove," as I have noted, was to worry me at moments by a sealing-up of its face—though without prejudice to its again, of a sudden, fairly grimacing with expression—so in this other business I had absolute conviction and constant clearness to deal with; it had been a frank proposition, the whole bunch of data, installed on my premises like a monotony of fine weather. (The order of composition, in these things, I may mention, was reversed by the order of publication; the earlier written of the two books having appeared as the later.) Even under the weight of my hero's years I could feel my postulate firm; even under the strain of the difference between those of Madame de Vionnet and those of Chad Newsome, a difference liable to be denounced as shocking, I could still feel it serene. Nothing resisted, nothing betrayed, I seem to make out, in this full and sound sense of the matter; it shed from any side I could turn it to the same golden glow. I rejoiced in the promise of a hero so mature, who would give me thereby the more to bite into—since it's only into thickened motive and accumulated character, I think, that the painter of life bites more than a little. My poor friend should have accumulated character, certainly; or rather would be quite naturally and handsomely possessed of it, in the sense that he would have, and would always have felt he had, imagination galore, and that this yet wouldn't have wrecked him. It was immeasurable, the opportunity to "do" a man of imagination, for if *there* mightn't be a chance to "bite," where in the world might it be? This personage of course, so enriched, wouldn't give me, for his type, imagination in *predominance* or as his prime faculty, nor should I, in view of other matters, have found that convenient. So particular a luxury—some occasion, that is, for study of the high gift in *supreme* command of a case or of a career—would still doubtless come on the day I should be ready to pay for it; and till then might, as from far back, remain hung up well in view and just out of reach. The comparative case meanwhile would serve—it was only on the minor scale that I had treated myself even to comparative cases.

I was to hasten to add however that, happy stopgaps as the minor scale had thus yielded, the instance in hand should enjoy the advantage of the full range of the major; since most immediately to the point was the question of that *supplement* of situation logically involved in our gentleman's impulse to deliver himself in the Paris garden on the Sunday afternoon—or if not involved by strict logic then all ideally and enchantingly implied in it. (I say "ideally," because I need scarce mention that for development, for expression of its maximum, my glimmering story was, at the earliest stage, to have nipped the thread of connexion with the possibilities of the actual reported speaker.[4] *He* remains but the happiest of accidents; his actualities, all too definite, precluded any range of possibilities; it had only been his charming office to project upon that wide field of the artist's vision—which hangs there ever in place like the white sheet suspended for the figures of a child's magic-lantern—a more fantastic and more moveable shadow.) No privilege of the teller of tales and the handler of puppets is more delightful, or has more of the suspense and the thrill of a game of difficulty breathlessly played, than just this business of looking for the unseen and the occult, in a scheme half-grasped, by the light or, so to speak, by the clinging scent, of the gage already in hand. No dreadful old pursuit of the hidden slave with bloodhounds and the rag of association can ever, for "excitement," I judge, have bettered it at its best. For the dramatist always, by the very law of his genius, believes not only in a possible right issue from the rightly-conceived tight place; he does much more than this—he believes, irresistibly, in the necessary, the precious "tightness" of the place (whatever the issue) on the strength of any respectable hint. It being thus the respectable hint that I had with such avidity picked up, what would be the story to which it would most inevitably form the centre? It is part of the charm attendant on such questions that the "story," with the omens true, as I say, puts on from this stage the authenticity of concrete existence. It then *is*, essentially—it begins to be, though it may more or less obscurely lurk; so that the point is not in the least what to make of it, but only, very delightfully and very damnably, where to put one's hand on it.

In which truth resides surely much of the interest of that admirable mixture for salutary application which we know as art. Art deals with what we see, it must first contribute full-handed that ingredient; it plucks its material, otherwise expressed, in the garden of life—which material elsewhere grown is stale and uneatable. But it has no sooner done this than it has to take account of a *process* —from which only when it's the basest of the servants of man, incurring ignominious dismissal with no "character," does it, and whether under some muddled pretext of morality or on any other,

4. That is, Howells. See note 2 above.

pusillanimously edge away. The process, that of the expression, the
literal squeezing-out, of value is another affair—with which the
happy luck of mere finding has little to do. The joys of finding, at
this stage, are pretty well over; that quest of the subject as a whole
by "matching," as the ladies say at the shops, the big piece with
the snippet, having ended, we assume, with a capture. The subject
is found, and if the problem is then transferred to the ground of
what to do with it the field opens out for any amount of doing. This
is precisely the infusion that, as I submit, completes the strong mixture. It is on the other hand the part of the business that can least
be likened to the chase with horn and hound. It's all a sedentary
part—involves as much ciphering, of sorts, as would merit the highest salary paid to a chief accountant. Not, however, that the chief
accountant hasn't *his* gleams of bliss; for the felicity, or at least the
equilibrium, of the artist's state dwells less, surely, in the further
delightful complications he can smuggle in than in those he succeeds in keeping out. He sows his seed at the risk of too thick a
crop; wherefore yet again, like the gentlemen who audit ledgers,
he must keep his head at any price. In consequence of all which,
for the interest of the matter, I might seem here to have my choice
of narrating my "hunt" for Lambert Strether, of describing the capture of the shadow projected by my friend's anecdote, or of reporting on the occurrences subsequent to that triumph. But I had probably best attempt a little to glance in each direction; since it comes
to me again and again, over this licentious record, that one's bag
of adventures, conceived or conceivable, has been only half-emptied
by the mere telling of one's story. It depends so on what one means
by that equivocal quantity. There is the story of one's hero, and
then, thanks to the intimate connexion of things, the story of one's
story itself. I blush to confess it, but if one's a dramatist one's a
dramatist, and the latter imbroglio is liable on occasion to strike me
as really the more objective of the two.

The philosophy imputed to him in that beautiful outbreak, the
hour there, amid such happy provision, striking for him, would have
been then, on behalf of my man of imagination, to be logically and,
as the artless craft of comedy has it, "led up" to; the probable course
to such a goal, the goal of so conscious a predicament, would have
in short to be finely calculated. Where has he come from and why
has he come, what is he doing (as we Anglo-Saxons, and we only,
say, in our foredoomed clutch of exotic aids to expression) in that
galère?[5] To answer these questions plausibly, to answer them as
under cross-examination in the witness-box by counsel for the prosecution, in other words satisfactorily to account for Strether and for
his "peculiar tone," was to possess myself of the entire fabric. At

5. Predicament, scrape.

the same time the clue to its whereabouts would lie in a certain *principle* of probability: he wouldn't have indulged in his peculiar tone without a reason; it would take a felt predicament or a false position to give him so ironic an accent. One hadn't been noting "tones" all one's life without recognising when one heard it the voice of the false position. The dear man in the Paris garden was then admirably and unmistakeably *in* one—which was no small point gained; what next accordingly concerned us was the determination of *this* identity. One could only go by probabilities, but there was the advantage that the most general of the probabilities were virtual certainties. Possessed of our friend's nationality, to start with, there was a general probability in his narrower localism; which, for that matter, one had really but to keep under the lens for an hour to see it give up its secrets. He would have issued, our rueful worthy, from the very heart of New England—at the heels of which matter of course a perfect train of secrets tumbled for me into the light. They had to be sifted and sorted, and I shall not reproduce the detail of that process; but unmistakeably they were all there, and it was but a question, auspiciously, of picking among them. What the "position" would infallibly be, and why, on his hands, it had turned "false"—these inductive steps could only be as rapid as they were distinct. I accounted for everything—and "everything" had by this time become the most promising quantity—by the view that he had come to Paris in some state of mind which was literally undergoing, as a result of new and unexpected assaults and infusions, a change almost from hour to hour. He had come with a view that might have been figured by a clear green liquid, say, in a neat glass phial; and the liquid, once poured into the open cup of *application*, once exposed to the action of another air, had begun to turn from green to red, or whatever, and might, for all he knew, be on its way to purple, to black, to yellow. At the still wilder extremes represented perhaps, for all he could say to the contrary, by a variability so violent, he would at first, naturally, but have gazed in surprise and alarm; whereby the *situation* clearly would spring from the play of wildness and the development of extremes. I saw in a moment that, should this development proceed both with force and logic, my "story" would leave nothing to be desired. There is always, of course, for the story-teller, the irresistible determinant and the incalculable advantage of his interest in the story *as such*; it is ever, obviously, overwhelmingly, the prime and precious thing (as other than this I have never been able to see it); as to which what makes for it, with whatever headlong energy, may be said to pale before the energy with which it simply makes for itself. It rejoices, none the less, at its best, to seem to offer itself in a light, to seem to know, and with the very last knowledge, what it's about

—liable as it yet is at moments to be caught by us with its tongue in its cheek and absolutely no warrant but its splendid impudence. Let us grant then that the impudence is always there—there, so to speak, for grace and effect and *allure;* there, above all, because the Story is just the spoiled child of art, and because, as we are always disappointed when the pampered don't "play up," we like it, to that extent, to look all its character. It probably does so, in truth, even when we most flatter ourselves that we negotiate with it by treaty.

All of which, again, is but to say that the *steps,* for my fable, placed themselves with a prompt and, as it were, functional assurance—an air quite as of readiness to have dispensed with logic had I been in fact too stupid for my clue. Never, positively, none the less, as the links multiplied, had I felt less stupid than for the determination of poor Strether's errand and for the apprehension of his issue. These things continued to fall together, as by the neat action of their own weight and form, even while their commentator scratched his head about them; he easily sees now that they were always well in advance of him. As the case completed itself he had in fact, from a good way behind, to catch up with them, breathless and a little flurried, as he best could. *The* false position, for our belated man of the world—belated because he had endeavoured so long to escape being one, and now at last had really to face his doom—the false position for him, I say, was obviously to have presented himself at the gate of that boundless menagerie primed with a moral scheme of the most approved pattern which was yet framed to break down on any approach to vivid facts; that is to any at all liberal appreciation of them. There would have been of course the case of the Strether prepared, wherever presenting himself, only to judge and to feel meanly; but *he* would have moved for me, I confess, enveloped in no legend whatever. The actual man's note, from the first of our seeing it struck, is the note of discrimination, just as his drama is to become, under stress, the drama of discrimination. It would have been his blest imagination, we have seen, that had already helped him to discriminate; the element that was for so much of the pleasure of my cutting thick, as I have intimated, into his intellectual, into his moral substance. Yet here it was, at the same time, just here, that a shade for a moment fell across the scene.

There was the dreadful little old tradition, one of the platitudes of the human comedy, that people's moral scheme *does* break down in Paris; that nothing is more frequently observed; that hundreds of thousands of more or less hypocritical or more or less cynical persons annually visit the place for the sake of the probable catastrophe, and that I came late in the day to work myself up about it.

There was in fine the *trivial* association, one of the vulgarest in the world; but which gave me pause no longer, I think, simply because its vulgarity is so advertised. The revolution performed by Strether under the influence of the most interesting of great cities was to have nothing to do with any *bêtise* of the imputably "tempted" state; he was to be thrown forward, rather, thrown quite with violence, upon his lifelong trick of intense reflexion: which friendly test indeed was to bring him out, through winding passages, through alternations of darkness and light, very much *in* Paris, but with the surrounding scene itself a minor matter, a mere symbol for more things than had been dreamt of in the philosophy of Woollett. Another surrounding scene would have done as well for our show could it have represented a place in which Strether's errand was likely to lie and his crisis to await him. The *likely* place had the great merit of sparing me preparations; there would have been too many involved—not at all impossibilities, only rather worrying and delaying difficulties—in positing elsewhere Chad Newsome's interesting relation, his so interesting complexity of relations. Strether's appointed stage, in fine, could be but Chad's most luckily selected one. The young man had gone in, as they say, for circumjacent charm; and where he would have found it, by the turn of his mind, most "authentic," was where his earnest friend's analysis would most find *him*; as well as where, for that matter, the former's whole analytic faculty would be led such a wonderful dance.

"The Ambassadors" had been, all conveniently, "arranged for"; its first appearance was from month to month, in "The North American Review" during 1903, and I had been open from far back to any pleasant provocation for ingenuity that might reside in one's actively adopting—so as to make it, in its way, a small compositional law—recurrent breaks and resumptions. I had made up my mind here regularly to exploit and enjoy these often rather rude jolts—having found, as I believed, an admirable way to it; yet every question of form and pressure, I easily remember, paled in the light of the major propriety, recognised as soon as really weighed; that of employing but one centre and keeping it all within my hero's compass.[6] The thing was to be so much this worthy's intimate adventure that even the projection of his consciousness upon it from beginning to end without intermission or deviation would probably still leave a part of its value for him, and *a fortiori* for ourselves, unexpressed. I might, however, express every grain of it that there would be room for—on condition of contriving a splendid particular economy. Other persons in no small number were to people the

6. The concept of a central intelligence, or commanding center, around which everything in a novel could be unified is a constant theme with James in his Prefaces. It was closely bound up with his theory of the novel as an organic form in which a fine intelligence becomes the agent of the action.

scene, and each with his or her axe to grind, his or her situation to treat, his or her coherency not to fail of, his or her relation to my leading motive, in a word, to establish and carry on. But Strether's sense of these things, and Strether's only, should avail me for showing them; I should know them but through his more or less groping knowledge of them, since his very gropings would figure among his most interesting motions, and a full observance of the rich rigour I speak of would give me more of the effect I should be most "after" than all other possible observances together. It would give me a large unity, and that in turn would crown me with the grace to which the enlightened story-teller will at any time, for his interest, sacrifice if need be all other graces whatever. I refer of course to the grace of intensity, which there are ways of signally achieving and ways of signally missing—as we see it, all round us, helplessly and woefully missed. Not that it isn't, on the other hand, a virtue eminently subject to appreciation—there being no strict, no absolute measure of it; so that one may hear it acclaimed where it has quite escaped one's perception, and see it unnoticed where one has gratefully hailed it. After all of which I am not sure, either, that the immense amusement of the whole cluster of difficulties so arrayed may not operate, for the fond fabulist, when judicious not less than fond, as his best of determinants. That charming principle is always there, at all events, to keep interest fresh: it is a principle, we remember, essentially ravenous, without scruple and without mercy, appeased with no cheap nor easy nourishment. It enjoys the costly sacrifice and rejoices thereby in the very odour of difficulty—even as ogres, with their "Fee-faw-fum!" rejoice in the smell of the blood of Englishmen.

Thus it was, at all events, that the ultimate, though after all so speedy, definition of my gentleman's job—his coming out, all solemnly appointed and deputed, to "save" Chad, and his then finding the young man so disobligingly and, at first, so bewilderingly not lost that a new issue altogether, in the connexion, prodigiously faces them, which has to be dealt with in a new light—promised as many calls on ingenuity and on the higher branches of the compositional art as one could possibly desire. Again and yet again, as, from book to book, I proceed with my survey, I find no source of interest equal to this verification after the fact, as I may call it, and the more in detail the better, of the scheme of consistency "gone in" for. As always—since the charm never fails—the retracing of the process from point to point brings back the old illusion. The old intentions bloom again and flower—in spite of all the blossoms they were to have dropped by the way. This is the charm, as I say, of adventure *transposed*—the thrilling ups and downs, the intricate ins and outs of the compositional problem,

made after such a fashion admirably objective, becoming the question at issue and keeping the author's heart in his mouth. Such an
element, for instance, as his intention that Mrs. Newsome, away
off with her finger on the pulse of Massachusetts, should yet be
no less intensely than circuitously present through the whole thing,
should be no less felt as to be reckoned with than the most direct
exhibition, the finest portrayal at first hand could make her, such
a sign of artistic good faith, I say, once it's unmistakeably there,
takes on again an actuality not too much impaired by the comparative dimness of the particular success. Cherished intention too inevitably acts and operates, in the book, about fifty times as little
as I had fondly dreamt it might; but that scarce spoils for me the
pleasure of recognising the fifty ways in which I had sought to provide for it. The mere charm of seeing such an idea constituent, in
its degree; the fineness of the measures taken—a real extension, if
successful, of the very terms and possibilities of representation and
figuration—such things alone were, after this fashion, inspiring,
such things alone were a gage of the probable success of that dissimulated calculation with which the whole effort was to square.
But oh the cares begotten, none the less, of that same "judicious"
sacrifice to a particular form of interest! One's work should have
composition, because composition alone is positive beauty; but all
the while—apart from one's inevitable consciousness too of the dire
paucity of readers ever recognising or ever missing positive beauty—
how, as to the cheap and easy, at every turn, how, as to immediacy
and facility, and even as to the commoner vivacity, positive beauty
might have to be sweated for and paid for! Once achieved and installed it may always be trusted to make the poor seeker feel he
would have blushed to the roots of his hair for failing of it; yet,
how, as its virtue can be essentially but the virtue of the whole, the
wayside traps set in the interest of muddlement and pleading but
the cause of the moment, of the particular bit in itself, have to be
kicked out of the path! All the sophistications in life, for example,
might have appeared to muster on behalf of the menace—the menace to a bright variety—involved in Strether's having all the subjective "say," as it were, to himself.

Had I meanwhile, made him at once hero and historian, endowed
him with the romantic privilege of the "first person"—the darkest
abyss of romance this, inveterately, when enjoyed on the grand
scale—variety, and many other queer matters as well, might have
been smuggled in by a back door. Suffice it, to be brief, that the
first person, in the long piece, is a form foredoomed to looseness,[7]

7. Frequently in the Prefaces James
states his disapproval of the "first person narrator method" of telling a story.
The reader of *The Ambassadors* should
consider the distinction James draws
between the "center of consciousness"
and the "first person narrative method."
It is connected with James's preference
for the novel as "drama" rather than
the novel as autobiography.

1584 · *Henry James*

and that looseness, never much my affair, had never been so little
so as on this particular occasion. All of which reflexions flocked to
the standard from the moment—a very early one—the question of
how to keep my form amusing while sticking so close to my central
figure and constantly taking its pattern from him had to be faced.
He arrives (arrives at Chester) as for the dreadful purpose of giving his creator "no end" to tell about him—before which rigorous
mission the serenest of creators might well have quailed. I was far
from the serenest; I was more than agitated enough to reflect that,
grimly deprived of one alternative or one substitute for "telling,"
I must address myself tooth and nail to another. I couldn't, save
by implication, make other persons tell *each other* about him—
blest resource, blest necessity, of the drama, which reaches its effects of unity, all remarkably, by paths absolutely opposite to the
paths of the novel: with other persons, save as they were primarily
his persons (not he primarily but one of theirs), I had simply nothing to do. I had relations for him none the less, by the mercy of
Providence, quite as much as if my exhibition *was* to be a muddle;
if I could only by implication and a show of consequence make
other persons tell each other about him, I could at least make him
tell *them* whatever in the world he must; and could so, by the same
token—which was a further luxury thrown in—see straight into
the deep differences between what that could do for me, or at all
events for *him,* and the large ease of "autobiography." It may be
asked why, if one so keeps to one's hero, one shouldn't make a
single mouthful of "method," shouldn't throw the reins on his
neck and, letting them flap there as free as in "Gil Blas" or in
"David Copperfield," equip him with the double privilege of subject and object—a course that has at least the merit of brushing
away questions at a sweep. The answer to which is, I think, that
one makes that surrender only if one is prepared *not* to make certain precious discriminations.

The "first person" then, so employed, is addressed by the author
directly to ourselves, his possible readers, whom he has to reckon
with, at the best, by our English tradition, so loosely and vaguely
after all, so little respectfully, on so scant a presumption of exposure
to criticism. Strether, on the other hand, encaged and provided for
as "The Ambassadors" encages and provides, has to keep in view
proprieties much stiffer and more salutary than any our straight
and credulous gape are likely to bring home to him, has exhibitional
conditions to meet, in a word, that forbid the terrible *fluidity* of self-
revelation. I may seem not to better the case for my discrimination
if I say that, for my first care, I had thus inevitably to set him up
a confidant or two, to wave away with energy the custom of the
seated mass of explanation after the fact, the inserted block of

merely referential narrative, which flourishes so, to the shame of the modern impatience, on the serried page of Balzac, but which seems simply to appal our actual, our general weaker, digestion. "Harking back to make up" took at any rate more doing, as the phrase is, not only than the reader of to-day demands, but than he will tolerate at any price any call upon him either to understand or remotely to measure; and for the beauty of the thing when done the current editorial mind in particular appears wholly without sense. It is not, however, primarily for either of these reasons, whatever their weight, that Strether's friend Waymarsh is so keenly clutched at, on the threshold of the book, or that no less a pounce is made on Maria Gostrey—without even the pretext, either, of *her* being, in essence, Strether's friend. She is the reader's friend much rather—in consequence of dispositions that make him so eminently require one; and she acts in that capacity, and *really* in that capacity alone, with exemplary devotion, from beginning to end of the book. She is an enrolled, a direct, aid to lucidity; she is in fine, to tear off her mask, the most unmitigated and abandoned of *ficelles*.[8] Half the dramatist's art, as we well know—since if we don't it's not the fault of the proofs that lie scattered about us—is in the use of *ficelles*; by which I mean in a deep dissimulation of his dependence on them. Waymarsh only to a slighter degree belongs, in the whole business, less to my subject than to my treatment of it; the interesting proof, in these connexions, being that one has but to take one's subject for the stuff of drama to interweave with enthusiasm as many Gostreys as need be.

The material of "The Ambassadors," conforming in this respect exactly to that of "The Wings of the Dove," published just before it, is taken absolutely for the stuff of drama; so that, availing myself of the opportunity given me by this edition for some prefatory remarks on the latter work, I had mainly to make on its behalf the point of its scenic consistency. It disguises that virtue, in the oddest way in the world, by just *looking*, as we turn its pages, as little scenic as possible; but it sharply divides itself, just as the composition before us does, into the parts that prepare, that tend in fact to over-prepare, for scenes, and the parts, or otherwise into the scenes, that justify and crown the preparation. It may definitely be said, I think, that everything in it that is not scene (not, I of course mean, complete and functional scene, treating *all* the submitted matter, as by logical start, logical turn, and logical finish) is discriminated preparation, is the fusion and synthesis of picture. These alternations propose themselves all recogniseably, I think,

---

8. French theatrical term: literally, "string"; by extension, the string used to dangle a puppet. James's meaning is that of a character used to bring out the protagonist—that is, a confidante.

from an early stage, as the very form and figure of "The Ambassadors"; so that, to repeat, such an agent as Miss Gostrey, pre-engaged at a high salary, but waits in the draughty wing with her shawl and her smelling-salts. Her function speaks at once for itself, and by the time she has dined with Strether in London and gone to a play with him her intervention as a *ficelle* is, I hold, expertly justified. Thanks to it we have treated scenically, and scenically alone, the whole lumpish question of Strether's "past," which has seen us more happily on the way than anything else could have done; we have strained to a high lucidity and vivacity (or at least we hope we have) certain indispensable facts; we have seen our two or three immediate friends all conveniently and profitably in "action"; to say nothing of our beginning to descry others, of a remoter intensity, getting into motion, even if a bit vaguely as yet, for our further enrichment. Let my first point be here that the scene in question, that in which the whole situation at Woollett and the complex forces that have propelled my hero to where this lively extractor of his value and distiller of his essence awaits him, is normal and entire, is really an excellent *standard* scene; copious, comprehensive, and accordingly never short, but with its office as definite as that of the hammer on the gong of the clock, the office of expressing *all that is in* the hour.

The *"ficelle"* character of the subordinate party is as artfully dissimulated, throughout, as may be, and to that extent that, with the seams or joints of Maria Gostrey's ostensible connectedness taken particular care of, duly smoothed over, that is, and anxiously kept from showing as "pieced on," this figure doubtless achieves, after a fashion, something of the dignity of a prime idea: which circumstance but shows us afresh how many quite incalculable but none the less clear sources of enjoyment for the infatuated artist, how may copious springs of our never-to-be-slighted "fun" for the reader and critic susceptible of contagion, may sound their incidental plash as soon as an artistic process begins to enjoy free development. Exquisite—in illustration of this—the mere interest and amusement of such at once "creative" and critical questions as how and where and why to make Miss Gostrey's false connexion carry itself, under a due high polish, as a real one. Nowhere is it more of an artful expedient for mere consistency of form, to mention a case, than in the last "scene" of the book, where its function is to give or to add nothing whatever, but only to express as vividly as possible certain things quite other than itself and that are of the already fixed and appointed measure. Since, however, all art is *expression*, and is thereby vividness, one was to find the door open here to any amount of delightful dissimulation. These verily are the refinements and ecstasies of method—amid which, or certainly under the influence of any exhilarated demonstration of which, one must keep one's head and not lose one's way. To cultivate an adequate intelligence for them and to make that sense operative is positively to find a charm in any produced ambiguity of appearance that is not by the same stroke, and all helplessly, an ambiguity of sense. To project imaginatively, for my hero, a relation that has nothing to do with the matter (the matter of my subject) but has everything to do with the manner (the manner of my presentation of the same) and yet to treat it, at close quarters and for fully economic expression's possible sake, as if it were important and essential—to do that sort of thing and yet muddle nothing may easily become, as one goes, a signally attaching proposition; even though it all remains but part and parcel, I hasten to recognise, of the merely general and related question of expressional curiosity and expressional decency.

I am moved to add after so much insistence on the scenic[9] side of my labour that I have found the steps of re-perusal almost as much waylaid here by quite another style of effort in the same signal interest—or have in other words not failed to note how, even so associated and so discriminated, the finest proprieties and charms of the non-scenic may, under the right hand for them, still keep their intelligibility and assert their office. Infinitely suggestive such an observation as this last on the whole delightful head, where representation is concerned, of possible variety, of effective expressional change and contrast. One would like, at such an hour as this, for critical license, to go into the matter of the noted inevitable deviation (from too fond an original vision) that the exquisite treachery even of the straightest execution may ever be trusted to inflict even on the most mature plan—the case being that, though one's last reconsidered production always seems to bristle with that particular evidence, "The Ambassadors," would place a flood of such light at my service. I must attach to my final remark here a different import; noting in the other connexion I just glanced at that such passages as that of my hero's first encounter with Chad Newsome, absolute attestations of the non-scenic form though they be, yet lay the firmest hand too—so far at least as intention goes—on representational effect. To report at all closely and completely of what "passes" on a given occasion is inevitably to become more or less scenic; and yet in the instance I allude to, *with* the conveyance, expressional curiosity and expressional decency are sought and arrived at under quite another law. The true inwardness of this may be at bottom

---

9. The difficulty of James's technical discussion here and throughout the Preface of "scenic" art may best be resolved by comparing his words with specific scenes in the novel. The broad distinction he draws in this passage is that between presenting his material dramatically (that is, scenically) and presenting it through the consciousness of a single character like Mamie Pocock in the chapter describing her meditations on the balcony overlooking the Tuileries gardens.

but that one of the suffered treacheries has consisted precisely, for Chad's whole figure and presence, of a direct presentability diminished and compromised—despoiled, that is, of its *proportional* advantage; so that, in a word, the whole economy of his author's relation to him has at important points to be redetermined. The book, however, critically viewed, is touchingly full of these disguised and repaired losses, these insidious recoveries, these intensely redemptive consistencies. The pages in which Mamie Pocock gives her appointed and, I can't but think, duly felt lift to the whole action by the so inscrutably-applied side-stroke or short-cut of our just watching, and as quite at an angle of vision as yet untried, her single hour of suspense in the hotel salon, in our partaking of her concentrated study of the sense of matters bearing on her own case, all the bright warm Paris afternoon, from the balcony that overlooks the Tuileries garden—these are as marked an example of the representational virtue that insists here and there on being, for the charm of opposition and renewal, other than the scenic. It wouldn't take much to make me further argue that from an equal play of such oppositions the book gathers an intensity that fairly adds to the dramatic—though the latter is supposed to be the sum of all intensities; or that has at any rate nothing to fear from juxtaposition with it. I consciously fail to shrink in fact from that extravagance —I risk it, rather, for the sake of the moral involved; which is not that the particular production before us exhausts the interesting questions it raises, but that the Novel remains still, under the right persuasion, the most independent, most elastic, most prodigious of literary forms.

1909

Selected Bibliographies

Eight American Authors, edited by Floyd Stovall for the American Literature Group of the MLA, 1956, is a series of descriptive-critical bibliographies in essay form. It surveys scholarship on the same authors as those represented in the present volume. It has been reissued in paperback, 1963, with a Bibliographical Supplement (1955–1962) especially prepared by J. Chesley Mathews. *Literary History of the United States*, Vol. III, edited by Robert E. Spiller, Willard Thorp, Thomas H. Johnson, and Henry Seidel Canby, 1948, and a *Supplementary Bibliography* by Richard Ludwig, 1959, provide extensive descriptive and critical lists. *Articles on American Literature, 1900–1950*, 1954, edited by Lewis Leary, is based on the periodicals of the half-century. For references to current books and articles see the bibliographies published annually in *PMLA* and those published quarterly in *American Literature*.

EDGAR ALLAN POE

The best and most nearly complete edition of Poe's writings is the Virginia Edition, edited by J. A. Harrison, *The Complete Works of Edgar Allan Poe*, 17 vols., 1902, now out of print. Scholarly and dependable, *The Complete Poems and Stories of Edgar Allan Poe with Selections from His Critical Writings*, 2 vols., 1946, edited by A. H. Quinn and E. H. O'Neill, is useful and still in print. The poems and stories are available in numerous cheap editions, but the best scholarly editions, all now out of print, are Killis Campbell's editions of *The Poems of Edgar Allan Poe*, 1917, and *Poe's Short Stories*, 1927, and J. S. Wilson's *Tales of Edgar Allan Poe*, 1927. J. W. Ostrom's edition of *The Letters of Edgar Allan Poe*, 2 vols., 1948, is as nearly complete as such collections can be expected to be, and is indispensable to the student of Poe's life and work.

Of the many biographies, several may be named here. George E. Woodberry's *The Life of Edgar Allan Poe, Personal and Literary, with his Chief Correspondence with Men of Letters*, 2 vols., 1909, an expansion of the original *Edgar Allan Poe*, 1885, is still worth consulting for its critical judgments; Hervey Allen's *Israfel: The Life and Times of Edgar Allan Poe*, 2 vols., 1926, revised and reprinted in one volume (1934), is very readable but not always dependable as to facts; Vincent Burenelli's *Edgar Allan Poe*, 1961, is a useful recent biography, brief but well-balanced and generally accurate; A. H. Quinn's *Edgar Allan Poe: A Critical Biography*, 1941, though not distinguished as criticism, is factually authoritative and still in print.

No thorough and comprehensive single critical study of Poe's entire literary work has yet been published. The French poets and critics were the first to recognize his genius, and following the lead of Charles Baudelaire they have contributed much to the establishment of his fame in America as well as abroad. Baudelaire's influential essays, written within a decade after Poe's death, are available in English in *Baudelaire on Poe*, 1952, edited by Lois and Francis E. Hyslop, Jr. French criticism of Poe, including that of Baudelaire, Mallarmé, and Valéry, is effectively summarized by P. F. Quinn, along with his own comments, in *The French Face of Edgar Poe*, 1957. The most comprehensive study to date is E. H. Davidson's *Poe: A Critical Study*, 1957, which supplements Quinn's book and is especially helpful in understanding "Eureka" and the tales of ratiocination. Other extended studies are the introduction to the American Writers Series *Poe*, 1935, edited by Margaret Alterton and Hardin Craig; N. B. Fagin's *The Histrionic Mr. Poe*, 1949, which emphasizes the dramatic character of Poe's tales and poems; Joseph Chiari's *Symbolisme from Poe to Mallarmé*, 1956, which develops T. S. Eliot's ideas on Poe; and D. M. Rein's *Edgar A. Poe: the Inner Pattern*, 1959, which leans heavily on psychoanalytical techniques.

Among general estimates in shorter form, two of the best were the work of American critics in the nineteenth century. James Russell Lowell's essay "Edgar Allan Poe," as originally published in *Graham's Magazine* for February, 1845, and reprinted in Edmund Wilson's *The Shock of Recognition*, 1943, proves that Poe was not unappreciated by his American contemporaries. E. C. Stedman's essay, first published in *Scribner's Monthly* for May, 1880, and reprinted in his *Poets of America*, 1885, is well balanced, intelligent, and sympathetic. Less sympathetic but perhaps more acute is W. C. Brownell's essay in *American Prose Masters*, 1909. Among scholars of the present century Poe has fared moderately well. One of the most devoted and sympathetic of them was Killis Campbell, some of whose meticulous studies are preserved in his volume *The Mind of Poe and Other Studies*, 1933. The most careful and judicious analysis of Poe's literary criticism is that of Norman Foerster in *American Criticism*, 1928. Among the nonacademic critics he has not fared so well. T. S. Eliot, though acknowledging Poe's genius in "From Poe to Valéry," *Hudson Review* (August, 1949), concludes that he was defective as an artist and intellectually immature. Allen Tate, in *The Forlorn Demon*, 1953, is more sympathetic than Eliot and he feels in some ways akin to Poe, but in the end dismisses him as a man of letters whose interest for modern students is primarily historical. Yvor Winters, in *Maule's Curse*, 1938, is more severe yet, undertaking to prove that Poe is a third-rate poet, a critic ignorant of his trade, and a bad writer generally. Writers more habitually imaginative have also had their say about Poe. Of these it will suffice to mention D. H. Lawrence, whose essay in *Studies in Classic American Literature*, 1923, is stimulating but not very informative, and William Carlos Williams, who says in his *In the American Grain*, 1925, that Poe was rejected by his contemporaries because of his originality—yet calls "To One in Paradise" his best poem.

Innumerable essays and articles have been published on special aspects of Poe's life and work. Among the more important of these a few only can be mentioned here. Floyd Stovall's "Poet's Debt to Coleridge," University of Texas *Studies in English*, X (1930), 70–127; Walter Blair's "Poe's Conception of Incident and Tone in the Tale," *Modern Philology*, XLI (1944), 228–40; Marvin Laser's "The Growth and Structure of Poe's Concept of Beauty," *Journal of English Literary History*, XV (1948), 69–84; A. J. Lubell's "Poe and A. W. Schlegel," *Journal of English and Germanic Philology*, LII (1953), 1–12; George Kelly's "Poe's Theory of Beauty," *American Literature*, XXVII (1956), 521–36; Laura Hofrichter's "From Poe to Kafka," *University of Toronto Quarterly*, XXIX (1960), 405–19; E. R. Marks' "Poe as a Literary Theorist: A Reappraisal," *American Literature*, XXXIII (1961), 296–306, will all be found helpful in the understanding of Poe's theory and practice of literary criticism. Roy Basler's "The Interpretation of 'Ligeia,' " *College English*, V (1944), 363–72, reprinted in *Sex, Symbolism and Psychology*, 1948; J. W. Gargano's "Poe's 'Ligeia': Dream and Destruction," *College English*, XXIII (1962), 337–42; Darrel Abel's "A Key to the House of Usher," *University of Toronto Quarterly*, XVIII (1949), 176–85; and Maurice Beebe's "The Universe of Roderick Usher," *The Personalist*, XXXVII (1956), 147–60, are examples of the interpretation of difficult stories. Essays of biographical and historical interest are Edward Hungerford's "Poe and Phrenology," *American Literature*, II (1930), 209–31; J. S. Wilson's "The Personality of Poe," *Virginia Magazine of History and Biography*, LXVII (1959); and J. B. Hubbell's "Poe and the Southern Literary Tradition," *Texas Studies in Literature and Language*, II (1960), 151–71.

RALPH WALDO EMERSON

No definitive edition of Emerson's *Works* exists. The text generally accepted is the Centenary Edition, 1904, edited in twelve volumes and annotated by his son, Edward Emerson. Edward also, with Waldo Emerson Forbes, edited a ten-volume selection from the *Journals*, 1909–14. A more complete and accurate, if less readable, edition is now being brought out under the editorship of William Gilman. Emerson's *Early Lectures*, 1833–47, Vol. I, is edited by Stephen E. Whicher and Robert E. Spiller. Six volumes of *Letters* not previously published have been impeccably edited by Ralph L. Rusk, 1939. Another volume is planned, and the correspondence with Carlyle has been re-edited by Joseph Slater.

Bibliographical aids to the study of Emerson are many and good. The best is *Emerson Handbook*, 1953, by F. I. Carpenter, which no student of Emerson can be without. The standard *Life*, a full, accurate, and most readable one, is by R. L. Rusk, 1949. Still valuable is the *Memoir*, 1887, by James Elliot Cabot. G. E. Woodberry's *Emerson*, 1907, is the most perceptive if least sympathetic of the three. A pleasantly unpretentious introduction is Bliss Perry, *Emerson Today*, 1931; the chapter on Emerson in *LHUS*, by Robert E. Spiller, is also excellent. The most brilliant general essay on Emerson is by John Jay Chapman, 1898.

Basic studies of his thought include O. W. Firkins, *Emerson*, 1915, a somewhat mannered but shrewd performance; H. D. Gray, *Emerson:*

A Statement of New England Transcendentalism As Expressed in the Philosophy of Its Chief Exponent, 1917, a formal exposition that is still indispensable; Paul Sakmann, *Emersons Geisteswelt* (Stuttgart, 1927), the best of the foreign studies; and S. E. Whicher, *Freedom and Fate,* 1953. The most important study of Emerson in our generation is Sherman Paul, *Emerson's Angle of Vision,* 1952, which has yet to find its proper place as the foundation of all future attempts to demonstrate Emerson's continuing relevance. A sign of its emerging influence is Harry Modean Campbell, "Emerson and Whitehead," *PMLA,* LXXV (1960), 577–82. Something similar to Paul forms part of a major study of classic American literature, Charles Feidelson, Jr., *Symbolism and American Literature,* 1952, but Feidelson's very specialized "angle of vision" prevents him, as he himself points out, from adequately treating Emerson. The general reader should be warned that both books are difficult.

A mark of Emerson's greatness is his power to attract the interest of the best minds. Among those essays that are distinguished by the distinction of their authors should be mentioned Matthew Arnold, "Emerson," in *Discourses in America,* 1885; John Dewey, "Ralph Waldo Emerson," *Character and Events,* 1929; Henry James, Jr., "Emerson," *Partial Portraits,* 1888; William James, "Address at the Emerson Centenary," *Memories and Studies,* 1911; and George Santayana, "Emerson," *Interpretations of Poetry and Religion,* 1900, reprinted in *Essays in Literary Criticism of George Santayana* (1956). Though he apparently wrote little about it, Nietzsche is reputed to have felt the influence of Emerson.

Important special studies relating to Emerson are numerous. The matter of Emerson's relation to New England tradition is illuminated in Perry Miller, "From Edwards to Emerson," *Errand into the Wilderness,* 1956, and *The Transcendentalists: An Anthology,* 1950; to aristocratic tradition, in Edwin Cady, *The Gentleman in America,* 1949. See also Alfred J. Kloeckner, "Intellect and Moral Sentiment in Emerson's Opinions of 'The Meaner Kinds' of Men," *American Literature,* XXX (1958), 322–38. On Emerson's relation to public affairs, the bibliographies must suffice; we cannot omit mention, however, of the chapter on Emerson in V. L. Parrington, *Main Currents of American Thought,* Vol. II. Interest is reviving in Emerson's art and aesthetics. F. O. Matthiessen, *American Renaissance,* 1941, though unsympathetic, is fundamental here. In connection with Matthiessen's influential stress on Emerson's deficient awareness of evil, see S. E. Whicher, "Emerson's Tragic Sense," *American Scholar,* XXII, 1953, 285–92, reprinted in *Interpretations of American Literature,* 1959, and Newton Arvin, "The House of Pain: Emerson and the Tragic Sense," *Hudson Review,* XII (1959), 37–53. The most comprehensive study of Emerson's aesthetics is Vivian Hopkins, *Spires of Form,* 1951. The most recent is René Wellek, "Emerson's Literary Theory and Criticism," a chapter from Vol. III of his *History of Modern Criticism* which has been printed in *Worte und Werte: Bruno Markwardt zum 60. Geburtstag* (Berlin, 1961), pp. 444–56. Still valuable, also, is Norman Foerster, "Emerson," *American Criticism,* 1928. A much-cited study of "Emerson's Literary Method" is by Walter Blair and Clarence Faust, *Modern Philology,* XLII (1944), 79–95; see, however, the corrective discussion in R. P.

Adams, "Emerson and the Organic Metaphor," *PMLA*, LXIX (1954), 117–30 (also in *Interpretations of American Literature*). An illuminating approach to Emerson's theory of communication is Roland F. Lee, "Emerson through Kierkegaard: Toward a Definition of Emerson's Theory of Communication," *ELH*, XXIV (1957), 229–48. A start toward a close semantic analysis of his prose is Paul Lauter, "Truth and Nature: Emerson's Use of Two Complex Words," *ELH*, XXVII (1960), 66–85. Two suggestive treatments of the poetry are Roy Harvey Pearce, "On the Continuity of American Poetry," *Hudson Review*, X (1957), 518–39, and Andrew Schiller, "Gnomic Structure in Emerson's Poetry," *Papers of the Michigan Academy of Science, Arts, and Letters*, XL (1955), 313–20.

Between the two World Wars a reaction to Emerson's till-then imposing reputation set in which contributed some keen if excessively acidulous comment. For leading examples, see James T. Adams, "Emerson Reread," *Atlantic Monthly*, CXLVI (1930), 484–92; H. B. Parkes, *The Pragmatic Test*, 1941, and *The American Experience*, 1947; and Yvor Winters, *Maule's Curse*, 1938.

Even a short bibliography must include mention of two outstanding students of Emerson. One is Carl F. Strauch, who, while engaged upon a definitive edition of the poems, has produced much fresh and authoritative work. An example is his article "Emerson's Sacred Science," *PMLA*, LXXIII (1958), 237–50. The other is Kenneth Walter Cameron, whose many publications, beginning with *Ralph Waldo Emerson's Reading*, 1941, and *Emerson the Essayist*, 1945, along with his editorship of the *Emerson Society Quarterly*, have contributed importantly to Emerson scholarship.

HENRY DAVID THOREAU

The standard edition of Thoreau's works is the Manuscript Edition of *The Writings of Thoreau*, 20 vols., 1906. The Walden Edition, 1906, was printed from the same plates. The last fourteen volumes of this set were reprinted as *The Journal of Thoreau*, 1949. Carl Bode edited the *Collected Poems of Henry Thoreau*, 1943, the definitive edition of his poetry. Walter Harding and Carl Bode, ed., *The Correspondence of Henry David Thoreau*, 1958, prints many letters not in earlier editions. The only fully annotated edition of *Walden* is Walter Harding's edition of *The Variorum Walden*, 1961. Perry Miller edited *Consciousness in Concord*, 1958, which prints an early journal not included in the standard editions. There are many one-volume collections of Thoreau's works: among the best are H. S. Canby, ed., *The Works of Thoreau*, 1937; Brooks Atkinson, ed., *Walden and Other Writings of Henry David Thoreau*, 1937; and Carl Bode, ed., *The Portable Thoreau*, 1947.

A recent full-length biography is Henry Seidel Canby, *Thoreau*, 1939. It contains more factual data than earlier biographies, but unfortunately it has many errors of fact and interpretation. Even though it is more than seventy years old, Henry Salt, *The Life of Henry D. Thoreau*, 1890, is more satisfactory. The various biographies of Thoreau by F. B. Sanborn benefit from Sanborn's first-hand contact with his subject but are so erratically written that only the Thoreau specialist will want to read them through. Milton Meltzer and Walter Harding, *A Thoreau Profile*, 1962, is a pictorial biography, with most of its text taken from Thoreau's own autobiographical writings.

The best critical study of Thoreau's ideas is Sherman Paul, *The Shores of America*, 1958, though strangely it ignores his political essays. The beginning student of Thoreau may find it at times rather heavy going. A more easily read general critical study is Joseph Wood Krutch, *Henry David Thoreau*, 1948. Walter Harding, ed., *Thoreau: A Century of Criticism*, 1954, collects twenty-four of the major critical articles on Thoreau, including the well-known Emerson, Lowell, and Stevenson essays. Sherman Paul, ed., *Thoreau: A Collection of Critical Essays*, 1962, includes 17 twentieth-century essays on Thoreau. Lauriat Lane, Jr., ed., *Approaches to Walden*, 1961, includes various background materials for a study of Thoreau's masterpiece. Walter Harding, *A Study Guide to Walden*, 1962, analyzes the book paragraph by paragraph. Other more specialized studies include Reginald L. Cook, *Passage to Walden*, 1949, particularly good on Thoreau as a nature writer; J. Lyndon Shanley, *The Making of Walden*, 1957, a fascinating study of the early drafts of *Walden*; and Leo Stoller, *After Walden*, 1957, a study of Thoreau's ideas on economics.

Useful articles published in periodicals since the 1930's are: Raymond Adams, "Thoreau's Literary Apprenticeship," *Studies in Philology*, XXIX (1932), 617–29; and his "Thoreau's Science," *Scientific Monthly*, LX (1945), 379–82; James Paul Brawner, "Thoreau as Wit and Humorist," *South Atlantic Quarterly*, XLIV (1945), 170–76; John Broderick, "Imagery in *Walden*," *University of Texas Studies in English*, XXXIII (1954), 80–89; Frank Davidson, "Thoreau's Hound, Bay Horse, and Turtle Dove," *New England Quarterly*, XXVII (1954), 521–24; Edward Deevey, "A Reexamination of Thoreau's 'Walden,'" *Quarterly Review of Biology*, XVII (1942), 1–11; N. A. Ford, "Henry David Thoreau, Abolitionist," *New England Quarterly*, XIX (1946), 359–71; Stanley Edgar Hyman, "Henry Thoreau in Our Time," *Atlantic Monthly*, CLXXVIII (1946), 137–46; Joseph Kwiat, "Thoreau's Philosophical Apprenticeship," *New England Quarterly*, XVIII (1945), 51–69; Frederick W. Lorch, "Thoreau and the Organic Principle in Poetry," *PMLA*, LIII (1938), 286–302; Louis B. Salomon, "The Practical Thoreau," *College English*, XVII (1956), 229–32; Andrew Schiller, "Thoreau and Whitman," *New England Quarterly*, XXVIII (1955), 186–97; Randall Stewart, "The Growth of Thoreau's Reputation," *College English*, VII (1946), 208–14; Henry Wells, "An Evaluation of Thoreau's Poetry," *American Literature*, XVI (1944), 99–109; Kathryn Whitford, "Thoreau and the Woodlots of Concord," *New England Quarterly*, XXIII (1950), 291–306.

Thoreau scholarship prior to 1959 is summarized and evaluated in Walter Harding, *A Thoreau Handbook*, 1959.

NATHANIEL HAWTHORNE

The standard "complete" edition is *The Complete Works of Nathaniel Hawthorne*, edited by G. P. Lathrop, 13 vols., 1882–83. Randall Stewart has provided authoritative texts of Hawthorne's *American Notebooks*, 1932, and of his *English Notebooks*, 1941. The *American Notebooks* need to be supplemented by Mrs. Hawthorne's less reliable *Passages from the*

American Notebooks (included in the complete edition) for important material for which no manuscript exists.

Julian Hawthorne's *Nathaniel Hawthorne and His Wife*, 1884, is the fundamental sourcebook for Hawthorne's life. Randall Stewart's *Nathaniel Hawthorne*, 1948, is the most reliable and authoritative biography. Among other critical biographies G. E. Woodberry's *Nathaniel Hawthorne*, 1902, is still notable for its critiques, especially of the novels; Newton Arvin's *Hawthorne*, 1929, contains original and suggestive criticism and psychological analysis; and Mark Van Doren's *Nathaniel Hawthorne*, 1949, is balanced and judicious on the life and the principal works.

Full-length critiques are G. P. Lathrop, A *Study of Hawthorne*, 1876, still valuable and especially penetrating on Hawthorne's symbols; Henry James, *Hawthorne*, 1879, entertainingly snobbish but extremely perceptive; Leland Schubert, *Hawthorne the Artist*, 1944, which treats of both Hawthorne's reactions to art and the aesthetic patterns of his work; R. H. Fogle, *Hawthorne's Fiction: The Light and the Dark*, 1952, an account of six stories and the four major novels with emphasis upon light-dark oppositions; William Bysshe Stein, *Hawthorne's Faust: A Study of the Devil Archetype*, 1953, which distorts but illuminates; Rudolph Von Abele, *The Death of the Artist: A Study of Hawthorne's Disintegration*, 1955, judicial criticism with some detailed explications; Hyatt H. Waggoner, *Hawthorne: A Critical Study*, 1955, an excellent critique with notable essays on "The Canterbury Pilgrims" and "My Kinsman, Major Molineux" among others; and Roy R. Male, *Hawthorne's Tragic Vision*, 1957, which combines intensive analysis of individual works with a firmly maintained central thesis. Fogle, Von Abele, Waggoner, and Male present a new departure in Hawthorne criticism by close examination of the form-and-content relationships of his fiction.

Other treatments of Hawthorne's art appear in Yvor Winters, *Maule's Curse*, 1938; F. O. Matthiessen's epoch-making *American Renaissance*, 1941, in which Hawthorne is compared with and contrasted to Melville, as he is also in Charles Feidelson, Jr., *Symbolism and American Literature*, 1953, which extends the implications of Matthiessen as far as they will stretch; Austin Warren, *Rage for Order*, 1948, which emphasizes Hawthorne's debt to the technique of Gothic romance; Marius Bewley, *The Complex Fate*, 1952, an austere comparison of Hawthorne and James; R. W. B. Lewis, *The American Adam*, 1955, a book very influential upon subsequent critics; and Richard Chase, *The American Novel and Its Tradition*, 1957, illuminating on Hawthorne in the American tradition of "Romance." Edward Wagenknecht's *Nathaniel Hawthorne: Man and Writer*, 1961, interestingly returns Hawthorne to his 19th-century relationships, as does Hubert H. Hoeltje in *Inward Sky: The Mind and Art of Nathaniel Hawthorne*, 1962. Millicent Bell's *Hawthorne's View of the Artist*, 1962, is a well-focused and helpful treatment of an important topic, which Hoeltje deals with more broadly.

Hawthorne scholarship and criticism has been very rich, and it would be impossible here to give an adequate representation of the essays on Hawthorne in collections and journals. A few of the most notable are E. P. Whipple, "Hawthorne," *Character and Characteristic Men*, 1860, by a critic for whom Hawthorne himself had the greatest respect; L. E. Gates, "Hawthorne," *Studies and Appreciations*, 1900, enlightened impressionism; P. E. More, "The Origins of Hawthorne and Poe" and "The Solitude of Hawthorne," *Shelburne Essays*, First Series, 1904, which anticipate many later insights; W. C. Brownell, "Hawthorne," *American Prose Masters*, 1909, a famous though unfavorable estimate; Walter Blair, "Color, Light and Shadow in Hawthorne's Fiction," *New England Quarterly*, XV, (1942), 74–94; Malcolm Cowley, "Hawthorne in the Looking Glass," *Sewanee Review*, LVI (1948), 545–63, a psychological study of Hawthorne's mirror images; Donald A. Ringe, "Hawthorne's Psychology of the Head and the Heart," *PMLA*, LXV (1950), 106–19; John W. Shroeder, " 'That Inward Sphere': Notes on Hawthorne's Heart Imagery and Symbolism," *PMLA*, LXV (1950), 106–19; Darrel Abel, "The Theme of Isolation in Hawthorne," *The Personalist*, XXXII (1951), 42–59, 182–90; and Richard P. Adams, "Hawthorne's *Provincial Tales*," *New England Quarterly*, XXX (1957), 39–57.

HERMAN MELVILLE

The Standard Edition of *The Works of Herman Melville*, edited by R. M. Weaver, 16 vols., 1922–24, is the only comprehensive collection of Melville's writings that has been made, and it includes the works printed during his lifetime, a considerable number of poems published from manuscripts, and the first printing of *Billy Budd and Other Prose Pieces*. A projected American edition of the *Complete Works* has so far produced only the *Collected Poems* (ed. H. P. Vincent, 1947), *Piazza Tales* (ed. E. S. Oliver, 1948), *Pierre* (ed. H. A. Murray, 1949), *Moby-Dick* (ed. L. S. Mansfield and H. P. Vincent, 1952), and *The Confidence Man* (ed. Elizabeth Foster, 1954); of these, the last three are the most valuable for their introductions and notes. All were published in two forms: a numbered set with textual notes, and a trade edition without them. Among the many editions designed for the general reader there is little choice except for *Typee* (which circulates in both an expurgated and unexpurgated edition) and *Billy Budd* (for which no satisfactory text is available, although that in Jay Leyda's *Portable Melville* is the best). The most interesting popular edition of *Moby-Dick* is the accurately annotated and illustrated one by Willard Thorp (1947).

Melville kept three journals which have survived and been printed as follows: "Journal of Melville's Voyage on a Clipper Ship," *New England Quarterly*, June, 1929; *Journal of a Visit to London and the Continent by Herman Melville, 1849–50*, ed. Eleanor Melville Metcalf, 1948; and *Journal of a Visit to Europe and the Levant*, ed. H. C. Horsford, 1955. His public lectures have been reconstructed from newspaper accounts by M. M. Sealts in *Melville as Lecturer*, 1957, and the complete *Letters of Herman Melville* have been published by M. R. Davis and W. H. Gilman, 1960.

R. M. Weaver's *Herman Melville, Mariner and Mystic*, 1921, was the pioneer study which formed the basis for John Freeman's slight but readable *Herman Melville*, 1926, and the advance in knowledge made by three decades of Melville scholarship can be observed by comparing the factual material contained in these with that in Leon Howard's *Herman Melville: A Biography*, 1951, Jay Leyda's documentary *Melville Log*, 2 vols., 1951, and E. M. Metcalf's *Herman Melville, Cycle and Epicycle*, 1953. Full-length studies which are particularly valuable for more restricted periods of Melville's life are Charles Anderson's *Melville in the South Seas*, 1939, and W. H. Gilman's *Melville's Early Life and Redburn*, 1951.

Of the biographical studies primarily concerned with an interpretation of Melville's life and thought Lewis Mumford's *Herman Melville*, 1929, was the earliest and most stimulating, and Newton Arvin's *Herman Melville*, 1950, is the most sensitive and readable. Related to these, but more directly focused on Melville's writings, are W. E. Sedgwick's *Herman Melville, The Tragedy of Mind*, 1945; Richard Chase's *Herman Melville, A Critical Study*, 1949; and Ronald Mason's *The Spirit Above the Dust*, 1951.

The best of the comprehensive critical studies which do not follow a biographical pattern is Merlin Bowen's *The Long Encounter*, 1960, which deals with the conflict between Melville's search for personal identity and the demands of the external world. C. L. R. James's *Mariners, Renegades and Castaways*, 1953, is a sensitive examination of Melville's sympathy for the lower classes. A substantial portion of J. R. Baird's *Ishmael*, 1956, is devoted to a study of Melville from the point of view of anthropology and Jungian psychology. M. R. Stern's *The Fine Hammered Steel of Herman Melville*, 1957, deals with what its author calls the romantic expression of Melville's naturalistic thought. Charles Olson's *Call Me Ishmael*, 1947, although based on a mistranscription of Melville marginalia, has proved to be a stimulating illustration of a poet's response to an older author. Other specialized critical approaches may be found in more general studies of American literature: D. H. Lawrence's *Studies in Classic American Literature*, 1923, is Freudian; F. O. Matthiessen's *American Renaissance*, 1941, is eclectic; Yvor Winters' *Maule's Curse*, 1938, is moral; R. P. Blackmur's *The Expense of Greatness*, 1940, is technical; and C. N. Feidelson's *Symbolism and American Literature*, 1953, is epistemological and New-Critical.

Studies on more specialized topics are William Braswell's *Melville's Religious Thought*, 1943; Lawrance Thompson's *Melville's Quarrel with God*, 1952; E. H. Rosenberry's *Melville and the Comic Spirit*, 1955; Nathalia Wright's *Melville's Use of the Bible*, 1949; and H. E. Pommer's *Milton and Melville*, 1950.

Among the special studies of individual books the most interesting and informative are M. R. Davis's *Melville's Mardi: A Chartless Voyage*, 1952, a comprehensive "biography of a book," and H. P. Vincent's *The Trying Out of Moby Dick*, 1949, an exhaustive study of Melville's sources and the way he used them. Gilman's study of *Redburn* (mentioned above) is valuable for the book as for Melville's life, and M. O. Percival's *A Reading of Moby-Dick*, 1950, provides an interesting illustration of the changes in critical attitudes since W. S. Gleim's *The Meaning of Moby Dick*, 1938.

For selections included in this anthology the most comprehensive commentary is R. H. Fogle's *Melville's Shorter Fiction*, 1960, although others are to be found in the biographical and critical studies mentioned above.

"Benito Cereno" has attracted the most attention from contributors to the learned journals. H. H. Scudder, "Melville's *Benito Cereno* and Captain Delano's Voyages," *PMLA*, XLIII (1928), 502–32, printed the source material on which it was based, and the most useful critical discussions of it are S. T. Williams' " 'Follow Your Leader': Melville's *Benito Cereno*" in the *Virginia Quarterly Review*, XXIII (1947), 61–76, and Rosalie Feltenstein's "Melville's *Benito Cereno*," *American Literature*, XIX (1947), 245–55. M. M. Sealts presents a quite different interpretation of "I and My Chimney" from that given in the present volume in "Herman Melville's 'I and My Chimney,' " *American Literature*, XIII (1941), 142–54; and C. A. Fenton has commented on " 'The Bell-Tower': Melville and Technology," *American Literature*, XXIII (1951), 219–32. Leo Marx has discussed "Melville's Parable of the Walls" in the *Sewanee Review*, LXI (1953), 602–27. But the comment in the present volume is most indebted to an unpublished study of Melville's wall imagery by Harrison G. Hayford which goes more deeply and coherently into the author's imagination than anything that has yet appeared in print.

WALT WHITMAN

There were some nine editions of *Leaves of Grass* during Whitman's lifetime: 1855, 1856, 1860, 1867, 1871, 1876 (two volumes, *Leaves of Grass* and *Two Rivulets*), 1881, 1889, 1891–92 (for description of these editions see the introduction on Whitman in the present volume). Other important lifetime publications were: *Drum-Taps*, 1865; *Democratic Vistas*, 1871; *Specimen Days and Collect*, 1882–83; *November Boughs*, 1888.

The *Complete Writings of Walt Whitman*, under the editorship of the three literary executors, Richard M. Bucke, Thomas B. Harned, and Horace L. Traubel, appeared in ten volumes in 1902. This edition contained variorum readings of *Leaves*, rejected poems, and much of the prose, including letters. Emory Holloway edited a one-volume "inclusive edition" in 1926 which reprinted the 1902 text of *Leaves* together with the variorum readings, rejected poems, and prefaces. The first two volumes of *The Collected Writings of Walt Whitman*, edited by Gay Wilson Allen and Sculley Bradley, have been edited by Edwin Haviland Miller: *The Correspondence of Walt Whitman, Volume I: 1842–1867, Volume II: 1868–1875*, 1961. Malcolm Cowley has edited *Walt Whitman's Leaves of Grass: The First (1855) Edition*, 1959; and Roy Harvey Pearce has edited *Leaves of Grass by Walt Whitman: Facsimile Edition of the 1860 Text*, 1961.

After Whitman's death, many volumes of unpublished material began to appear, of which the most important are collections of letters: *Calamus* (letters to Peter Doyle), 1897; *The Wound Dresser* (letters during the Civil War), 1898; *Letters Written by Walt Whitman to His Mother from 1866 to 1872*, 1902; and *The Letters of Anne Gilchrist and Walt Whitman*, 1918.

There are three important lifetime biographies which are primary sources: William Douglas O'Connor, *The Good Gray Poet, A Vindication*, 1866; John Burroughs, *Notes on Walt Whitman as Poet and Person*, 1867, later revised as *Whitman, A Study*, 1896; and Richard Maurice Bucke,

M.D., *Walt Whitman* (important because of Whitman's assistance in the writing), 1883. The most copious source material for Whitman's biography is in Horace Traubel's multi-volume *With Walt Whitman in Camden*. Some four volumes appeared between 1906 and 1953.

Of the many biographies, six might be selected as representative and important. They are listed here in chronological order, reflecting advances in Whitman scholarship. Bliss Perry, *Walt Whitman: His Life and Work*, 1906, the first scholarly biography, remains useful and readable. Emory Holloway, *Whitman: An Interpretation in Narrative*, 1926, mixes narrative with criticism in a still interesting biography. Edgar Lee Masters, *Whitman*, 1937, is a pedestrian but important commentary by a sympathetic poet. Newton Arvin, *Whitman*, 1938, is most valuable in tracing Whitman's political, economic, and social views. Henry Seidel Canby, *Walt Whitman, An American*, 1943, treats Whitman primarily as the poet of democracy. Gay Wilson Allen, *The Solitary Singer*, 1955, is the fullest and most reliable biography yet to appear.

Most useful for an introduction to Whitman is Gay Wilson Allen's *Walt Whitman Handbook*, 1946. It contains omnibus accounts of all aspects of Whitman scholarship, criticism, and selective bibliographies. Bringing it up to date is the same author's *Walt Whitman: As Man, Poet, and Legend*, 1962.

Certain books, all of a general critical nature, have something rewarding to offer. Arthur E. Briggs, *Walt Whitman: Thinker and Artist*, 1952, emphasizes mainly Whitman's philosophy. Richard Chase, *Walt Whitman Reconsidered*, 1955, is a provocative and unusual "mythic" interpretation. Milton Hindus, ed., *Leaves of Grass One Hundred Years After*, 1955, contains important essays by the editor, William Carlos Williams, Richard Chase, Leslie Fiedler, Kenneth Burke, David Daiches, and J. Middleton Murry. James E. Miller, Jr., *A Critical Guide to Leaves of Grass*, 1957, is primarily a series of critical analyses of poems and an analysis of the structure of *Leaves*. A recent critical study is the same author's *Walt Whitman*, 1962. R. W. B. Lewis is the editor of *The Presence of Walt Whitman*, 1962. Frederik Schyberg, *Walt Whitman*, 1933, 1951, is especially valuable in its discussion of the evolution of *Leaves*. John Addington Symonds, *Walt Whitman: A Study*, 1893, is an early psychological study of the poems of sex.

Books treating limited aspects of Whitman are all of value: Joseph Beaver, *Walt Whitman—Poet of Science*, 1951; Robert D. Faner, *Walt Whitman and Opera*, 1951; Maurice O. Johnson, *Walt Whitman as a Critic of Literature*, 1938; Esther Shephard, *Walt Whitman's Pose*, 1938; Clara Barrus, *Whitman and Burroughs, Comrades*, 1931; William E. Barton, *Abraham Lincoln and Walt Whitman*, 1928; and S. Musgrove, *T. S. Eliot and Walt Whitman*, 1952. Reputation studies are: Gay Wilson Allen, ed., *Walt Whitman Abroad*, 1955; Harold Blodgett, *Walt Whitman in England*, 1934; Charles B. Willard, *Whitman's American Fame*, 1950.

Among many shorter treatments of Whitman, the following may be mentioned. Malcolm Cowley's introduction in *Walt Whitman's Leaves of Grass: The First* (1855) *Edition* is of particular importance in relating

Whitman to Oriental mysticism and in showing many superior qualities in the first edition of *Leaves*. Norman Foerster's treatment of Whitman in *American Criticism*, 1928, emphasizes a neglected aspect of the poet. Randall Jarrell's "Some Lines from Whitman" in *Poetry and the Age*, 1953, is a close and convincing examination by a sensitive poet. D. H. Lawrence's chapter in *Studies in Classic American Literature*, 1923, is both unusual and provocative. F. O. Matthiessen's detailed work on Whitman in *American Renaissance*, 1941, remains important and illuminating. James E. Miller, Jr., Bernice Slote, and Karl Shapiro demonstrate, in *Start With the Sun*, that the Whitman tradition of cosmic poetry continues most persuasively through D. H. Lawrence, Hart Crane, and Dylan Thomas. Floyd Stovall treats Whitman as a key figure in his *American Idealism*, 1943; and his "Introduction" to *Walt Whitman: Representative Selections* (American Writers Series, 1934) is an excellent short general treatment.

Recent collections of criticism in paperbound editions are John C. Broderick, ed., *Whitman the Poet*, 1962; William Coyle, ed., *The Poet and the President: Whitman's Lincoln Poems*, 1962; Roy Harvey Pearce, ed., *Whitman: A Collection of Critical Essays*, 1962.

SAMUEL L. CLEMENS

The definitive edition of Mark Twain's works is *The Writings of Mark Twain*, 37 vols., edited by Albert Bigelow Paine, 1922–25. Less inclusive is The Author's National Edition, 25 vols., 1907–18. Much of Mark Twain's writing is found outside these collections.

Basic to any study are three publications edited by Paine: *Mark Twain's Autobiography*, 2 vols., 1924; *Mark Twain's Letters*, 2 vols., 1917; and *Mark Twain's Notebook*, 1935. Paine also edited *Mark Twain's Speeches*, 1910 and 1923. DeLancey Ferguson, "The Uncollected Portions of Mark Twain's Autobiography," *American Literature*, March, 1936, is important. DeVoto's *Mark Twain in Eruption*, 1940, is in effect a third volume of the *Autobiography*. Charles Neider edited the *Autobiography* in 1959, for the first time arranged chronologically. Collections of Twain's personal correspondence and of his Western, Hawaiian, and early New York work may be found in bibliographies.

The present custodian of the largest body of unpublished manuscripts owned by the Mark Twain Estate is Henry Nash Smith, University of California; Bernard DeVoto, a former custodian, described these as "The Mark Twain Papers," *Saturday Review of Literature*, December 10, 1938.

The authorized biography is *Mark Twain, A Biography*, 3 vols., 1912, 1935; written by Twain's literary executor, A. B. Paine, it is colorful and entertaining but contains minor errors now corrected by other writers. William Dean Howells' *My Mark Twain*, 1910, contains "reminiscences and criticisms." Scenes of family life appear in *My Father, Mark Twain*, by Clara Clemens, 1931.

Van Wyck Brooks's *The Ordeal of Mark Twain*, 1920, rev. 1933, shows Twain as a "thwarted artist," frustrated by the commercialism and prudishness of America and the barrenness of the Western frontier. In *Mark Twain's America*, 1932, Bernard DeVoto defends the West and holds that

Twain's "literary intelligence was shaped" by the frontier, which "completed" him. Edward Wagenknecht's *Mark Twain, The Man and His Work*, 1935, is valuable as an introduction to Twain, as it cites the chief problems although it does not attempt to solve them; in general, Wagenknecht follows DeVoto's thesis of the frontier. Ivan Benson's *Mark Twain's Western Years*, 1938; Effie M. Mack's *Mark Twain in Nevada*, 1947; and Franklin Walker's *San Francisco's Literary Frontier*, 1939, all deal with the pre-*Innocents Abroad* period.

In *Mark Twain, Son of Missouri*, 1934, Minnie M. Brashear maintains that Hannibal was not the cultural desert pictured by Brooks; succeeding DeVoto as custodian of the Mark Twain Papers, Dixon Wecter drew on them for his *Sam Clemens of Hannibal*, 1952, which emphasizes the importance of the matrix. Kenneth Andrews' *Nook Farm*, 1950, shows the Eastern influence exerted through the "Hartford circle" of C. D. Warner, Harriet Beecher Stowe, and the Reverend Joseph Twichell.

Perhaps the best biography is DeLancey Ferguson's *Mark Twain, Man and Legend*, 1943, which displays Twain's career as a writing man. F. W. Lorch's "Mark Twain and the 'Campaign That Failed,' " in *American Literature* for January, 1941, covers Clemens' brief experience as a Confederate soldier. Samuel C. Webster, Clemens' great-nephew, uses biographical materials in *Mark Twain, Business Man*, 1946.

Of the books listed above, those by Andrews, Brashear, Brooks, Ferguson, Howells, Wagenknecht, and Wecter offer criticism as well as biography. Items appearing below are alphabetized according to author.

Gladys C. Bellamy, in *Mark Twain as a Literary Artist*, 1950, presents Twain as a conscious craftsman, shows the conflict between his moralism and his determinism, and studies the structure of *Huck Finn*. Walter Blair, in *Native American Humor*, 1937, finds in Twain the culmination of a long indigenous tradition; Blair's "On the Structure of *Tom Sawyer*," in *Modern Philology* for August, 1939, accents Twain's careful craftsmanship; in *Horse Sense in American Humor*, 1942, Blair finds in *A Connecticut Yankee* much satire on Twain's times; his comprehensive *Mark Twain and Huck Finn*, 1960, is a rewarding study of a masterpiece. Edgar M. Branch's *The Literary Apprenticeship of Mark Twain*, 1950, offers the most detailed analysis of Twain's work up to 1867 and analyzes the thematic structure of *Huckleberry Finn*.

H. S. Canby's *Turn West, Turn East*, 1951, compares and contrasts Mark Twain and Henry James. In *The Rise of the American Novel*, 1948, Alexander Cowie summarizes Twain's political-social, religious-ethical, and literary opinions. In *Mark Twain at Work*, 1942, DeVoto traces the making of *Huck Finn* and *The Mysterious Stranger*; his Introduction, in both *Mark Twain in Eruption*, 1940, and *The Portable Mark Twain*, 1946, should be read. L. T. Dickinson's "Mark Twain's Revisions in Writing *The Innocents Abroad*," in *American Literature* for May, 1947, shows how Twain used the *Alta California* letters. T. S. Eliot's "Introduction," *Huckleberry Finn*, New York, 1950, defends the ending of the book. DeLancey Ferguson, "Huck Finn Aborning," *Colophon*, III (Spring, 1938), shows over 900 changes in the manuscript, testifying to Twain's conscious craftsmanship. In "The Structural Problem of *The Mysterious*

Stranger," *Studies in Philology* for January, 1952, E. S. Fussell shows a progressive preparation for Twain's final philosophical position. A. E. Jones's "Mark Twain and Sexuality," *PMLA*, LXXI (Summer, 1956), explores a subject baffling to many critics of Twain. Lauriat Lane, in "Why Huckleberry Finn Is a Great World Novel," *College English*, XVII (October, 1955), stresses its "total dramatic and moral irony." Lewis Leary's "Tom, Huck: Innocence on Trial," *Virginia Quarterly Review*, Summer, 1954, analyzes the intricate time-scheme and structure of the two boys' books; his *Mark Twain*, 1960, No. 5 in *Pamphlets on American Writers*, Univ. of Minnesota, serves admirably as an introduction to Twain. Kenneth S. Lynn's *Mark Twain and Southwestern Humor*, 1960, is excellent.

John Macy, *The Spirit of American Literature*, 1913, offers an early appreciation of Mark Twain as an artist. Barry A. Marks edited *Mark Twain's "Huckleberry Finn": Readings Selected by the Department of American Studies*, Amherst College, 1959. Leo Marx, in "Mr. Eliot, Mr. Trilling, *and Huckleberry Finn*," *American Scholar*, XXII (Autumn, 1953), argues that the ending of the book fails; in "The Pilot and the Passenger," *American Literature*, May, 1956, Marx studies the change in Huck's landscape descriptions as compared with Twain's style in earlier books. Olin H. Moore, in "Mark Twain and Don Quixote," *PMLA*, XXXVII (June, 1922), was among the first to trace a European influence. William Van O'Connor, in "Why Huckleberry Finn Is Not the Great American Novel," *College English*, XVII (October, 1955), summarizes the weaknesses of the book. V. L. Parrington, *Main Currents of American Thought*, 1930, sees *Huck Finn* as "a drama of the struggle between the individual and the village *mores*." Constance Rourke, *American Humor*, 1931, displays Mark Twain as a synthesis of many native strains.

Friedrich Schönemann, *Mark Twain als literarische Persönlichkeit*, Jena, 1925, traces Twain's various literary debts, counterbalancing the frontier. A. L. Scott edited *Mark Twain: Selected Criticism*, 1955. S. P. Sherman's "Mark Twain," *CHAL*, Vol. III, 1921, reflects opinions of the time but sees Twain as "an influence because he is an innovator." W. F. Taylor's *The Economic Novel in America*, 1942, treats *The Gilded Age* as exposing business and political corruption. Lionel Trilling, in *The Liberal Imagination*, 1950, analyzes the "intense and even complex moral quality" of *Huck Finn*. Edward Wagenknecht's *Cavalcade of the American Novel*, 1952, cites recent scholarship and, as in his earlier biography, mainly follows DeVoto: Twain "was that [Midwestern] frontier in literature." Victor R. West's monograph *Folklore in the Works of Mark Twain*, 1930, was an important early study.

HENRY JAMES

The most complete uniform edition is *The Novels and Stories of Henry James*, 35 vols., 1921–23. James's own revised edition containing the famous critical prefaces is *The Novels and Tales of Henry James: New York Edition*, 26 vols., 1907–17. The Prefaces have been edited separately by R. P. Blackmur, with introduction, in *The Art of the Novel*, 1934, 1959. These, together with *The Notebooks of Henry James*, ed. F. O. Matthiessen and K. Murdock, 1947, 1955, are indispensable for a knowledge of

James's working methods. Good reading editions with critical introductions, notes, and/or bibliographies are *The American Novels and Stories of Henry James*, ed. Matthiessen, 1947; *Henry James: Stories of Writers and Artists*, ed. Matthiessen, 1944; *The Ghostly Tales of Henry James*, ed. Leon Edel, 1948; and *The Portable Henry James*, ed. M. D. Zabel, 1951. James's literary criticism may be found at its best in his *Hawthorne*, 1879, reprinted recently in Edmund Wilson, ed., *The Shock of Recognition*, 1943. *The Future of the Novel* and *Henry James: The American Essays*, ed. Edel, 1956, are recent collections of his criticism. *The Complete Plays of Henry James*, ed. Edel, 1949, is the only available collection of his dramatic writing. His writings on the drama, theater, and acting have been edited by Allan Wade, *The Scenic Art*, 1948, and his travel sketches have been selected in Zabel, ed., *The Art of Travel, Scenes from the Travel Writing of Henry James*, 1958.

The best sources for James's life are his own autobiographical writings, *A Small Boy and Others*, 1913; *Notes of a Son and Brother*, 1914; and *The Middle Years*, 1917. Next in importance are his letters: *The Letters of Henry James*, ed. Percy Lubbock, 2 vols., 1920, and *Selected Letters of Henry James*, ed. Edel, 1955, 1960. Both provide biographical information. Further materials may be found in F. O. Matthiessen, ed., *The James Family*, 1947; A. R. Burr, ed., *Alice James: Her Brothers and Her Journal*, 1934; H. James, Jr., ed., *The Letters of William James*, 2 vols., 1920; and C. H. Grattan, *The Three Jameses: A Family of Minds*, 1932. Partial portraits and personal legends of James are interestingly arranged by S. Nowell-Smith, *The Legend of the Master*, 1948. The only one-volume biography (including criticism) is F. W. Dupee, *Henry James*, 1951. Leon Edel has planned a 3-volume biography of which the first, *The Untried Years*, 1953, is published covering his life to 1870. R. C. LeClair's *The Young Henry James*, 1955, is a detailed account of the same period, factual and less interpretive than Edel. F. W. Dupee edited James's personal memoirs in *Henry James's Autobiography*, 1956. Glimpses of the later James are to be found in Edith Wharton's *A Backward Glance*, 1934; Theodora Bosanquet, his secretary, described *Henry James at Work*, 1924.

Pure biography, in the case of James's rather uneventful life, has been subordinated to cultural or psychological discussion of his work. Beginning in 1916 critics including Rebecca West (*Henry James*, 1916), Van Wyck Brooks (*The Pilgrimage of Henry James*, 1925), Matthew Josephson (*Portrait of the Artist as American*, 1930) concentrated on the expatriate theme. Brooks especially attributed faults in his later writing to his international life. Pelham Edgar, *Henry James, Man and Author*, 1927, replied to Brooks by viewing Europe as favorable to James's art. Other volumes with a national emphasis are H. S. Canby, *Turn East, Turn West: Mark Twain and Henry James*, 1951; F. Nuhn, *The Wind Blew from the East: A Study in the Orientation of American Culture*, 1942; and Q. Anderson, *The American Henry James: The Novelist as Moralist*, 1956—the latter dealing with the intellectual influence of the elder James on his son. Books treating more exclusively literary methods and influences include J. W. Beach, *The Method of Henry James*, 1918, 1954 (authoritative on James's style); C. P. Kelley, *The Early Development of Henry James*, University of Illinois Studies, XV, 1930 (sound on his literary roots); F. O. Matthiessen, *Henry James: The Major Phase*, 1944 (detailed analysis of the late novels); and E. Stevenson, *The Crooked Corridor: A Study of Henry James*, 1949. A penetrating study of the early novels in terms of James's use of "free" and "fixed" characters is Richard Poirier's *The Comic Sense of Henry James*, 1960. Recent and useful are Leon Edel, *Henry James*, Univ. of Minnesota Pamphlets on American Writers, 1960, and Holder-Barrell's *Development of Imagery and Its Functional Significance in Henry James's Novels*, Cooper Monographs, Vol. III (Bern, 1959).

In addition to various chapters in the volumes listed above, the student will find special studies of individual novels and stories in the following books and articles: R. P. Blackmur, "Henry James," in Spiller *et al.*, eds., *The Literary History of the United States*, Vol. II, 1948; E. T. Bowden, *The Themes of Henry James*, 1956 (on James's use of the visual arts); M. Bewley, *The Complex Fate*, 1952; A. Cowie, *The Rise of the American Novel*, 1948; C. Fadiman, *The Short Stories of Henry James*, 1948; F. R. Leavis, *The Great Tradition*, 1949. On James as critic see M. Roberts, *Henry James's Criticism*, 1929 and R. Falk, "The Literary Criticism of the Genteel Decades," in F. Stovall, ed., *The Development of American Criticism*, 1955. A good symposium of critical essays about James's work is F. W. Dupee, ed., *The Question of Henry James*, 1945. *The Hound and Horn*, VII (April–June, 1934), devoted its pages to "Homage to Henry James." Also, *The Kenyon Review*, V (Autumn, 1943) was a Henry James number. The following essays and articles may be consulted for special discussion of separate works: Q. Anderson, "Henry James and the New Jerusalem," *Kenyon Review*, VIII (1946), 515–66 (on the late novels); M. Allott, "Symbol and Image in the Later Work of Henry James," *Essays in Criticism*, III (1953), 321–36; O. Cargill, "*The Portrait of a Lady*: A Critical Reappraisal," *Modern Fiction Studies*, III (1957), 11–32; R. Falk, "Henry James and The Age of Innocence," *Nineteenth Century Fiction* (1952), 171–88 (on *Daisy Miller* and *The American*); W. M. Gibson, "Metaphor in the Plot of *The Ambassadors*," *New England Quarterly*, XXIV (1951), 291–305; R. B. Heilman, "The Freudian Reading of 'The Turn of the Screw,'" *Modern Language Notes*, LXII (1947), 433–45 (see E. Wilson, below, for opposing view); W. D. Howells, "James's *Passionate Pilgrim*," *Atlantic Monthly*, XXXV (1875), 490–95 (on "The Madonna of the Future"); D. Krook, "The Golden Bowl," *Cambridge Journal*, VII (1954), 716–37; G. Munson, "The Real Thing: A Parable for Writers of Fiction," *University of Kansas City Review*, XVI (1950), 261–64; S. Rosenzweig, "The Ghost of Henry James: A Study in Thematic Apperception," *Partisan Review*, XI (1944), 436–55 (a psychological inquiry, analysis of "The Jolly Corner"); E. Wilson, "The Ambiguity of Henry James," in *The Triple Thinkers*, 1948 (contains much cited Freudian reading of "The Turn of the Screw"); V. Woolf, "Henry James's Ghost Stories," in *Granite and Rainbow*, 1958.

Recent articles of importance include: Hopkins, Viola, "Visual Art Devices and Parallels in the Fiction of Henry James," *PMLA*, LXXVI, 561–574 (Dec., 1961); Fussell, Edwin, "Hawthorne, James, and 'The Common Doom,'" *American Quarterly*, X, 438–453 (Winter, 1958); Roper, A. H.,

"The Moral and Metaphorical Meaning of *The Spoils of Poynton*," *American Literature*, XXXII, 182–196 (May, 1960); and Wellek, René, "Henry James's Literary Theory and Criticism," *American Literature*, XXX, 293–321 (Nov., 1958).

Index